THE SPORTS ILLUSTRATED

1997 Sports Almanac

By the Editors of Sports Illustrated

1837

LITTLE, BROWN AND COMPANY

Boston   New York   Toronto   London

Sports Illustrated

1997

Sports Almanac

First Edition
ISBN 0-316-80882-2

Sports Illustrated 1997 Sports Almanac was produced by
Bishop Books of New York City.

Sports Illustrated Editorial Director for Books: Joe Marshall
Sports Illustrated Manager, Printed Products: Stanley Weil

Front cover photography credits:
Tiger Woods (right): John Biever
Dennis Rodman (center): John W. McDonough
Brett Favre (bottom left): John W. McDonough
Ken Griffey Jr. (left): Chuck Solomon
Back cover photography credits:
Frank Thomas (left):Tom Lynn
Bobby Clarke (right): Mel Digiacomo
Magic Johnson (bottom right): Walter Iooss Jr.
Title page photography credit: Al Tielemans

10 9 8 7 6 5 4 3 2

COM

Published simultaneously in Canada by
Little, Brown & Company (Canada) Limited

PRINTED IN THE UNITED STATES OF AMERICA

CONTENTS

Expanded Contents

Expanded Contents (Cont.)

Expanded Contents (Cont.)

Expanded Contents (Cont.)

Expanded Contents *(Cont.)*

Expanded Contents *(Cont.)*

SOURCES

In compiling the *Sports Illustrated 1997 Sports Almanac*, the editors would again like to thank Natasha Simon and Linda Wachtel of the *Sports Illustrated* library for their invaluable assistance. They would also like to extend their gratitude to the media relations offices of the following organizations for their help in providing information and materials relating to their sports: Major League Baseball; the Canadian Football League; the National Football League; the National Collegiate Athletic Association; the National Basketball Association; the National Hockey League; the Association of Tennis Professionals; the World Tennis Association; the U.S. Tennis Association; the U.S. Golf Association; the Ladies Professional Golf Association; the Professional Golfers Association; Thoroughbred Racing Communications, Inc.; the U.S. Trotting Association; the Breeders' Cup; Churchill Downs; the New York Racing Association, Inc.; the Maryland Jockey Club; Championship Auto Racing Teams; the National Hot Rod Association; the International Motor Sports Association; the National Association for Stock Car Auto Racing; the Professional Bowlers Association; the Ladies Professional Bowlers Tour; the American Professional Soccer League; the National Professional Soccer League; the *Fédération Internationale de Football* Association; the U.S. Soccer Federation; the U.S. Olympic Committee; USA Track & Field; U.S. Swimming; U.S. Diving; U.S. Skiing; U.S. Skating; the U.S. Chess Federation; U.S. Curling; the Iditarod Trail Committee; the International Game Fish Association; the U.S. Gymnastics Federation; U.S. Handball Association; the Lacrosse Foundation; the American Power Boat Association; the Hydroplane Racing Association; the Professional Rodeo Cowboys Association; U.S. Rowing; the American Softball Association; the U.S. Speed Skating Association; U.S. Rugby Football Union; the Triathlon Federation USA; the National Archery Association; USA Wrestling; the U.S. Squash Racquets Association; the U.S. Polo Association; ABC Sports and the U.S. Volleyball Association.

The following sources were consulted in gathering information:

Baseball   *The Baseball Encyclopedia*, Macmillan Publishing Co., 1990; *Total Baseball*, Warner Books, 1995; *Baseballistics*, St. Martin's Press, 1990; *The Book of Baseball Records*, Seymour Siwoff, publisher, 1991; *The Complete Baseball Record Book*, The Sporting News Publishing Co., 1992; *The Sporting News Baseball Guide*, The Sporting News Publishing Co., 1993; *The Sporting News Official Baseball Register*, The Sporting News Publishing Co., 1996; *National League Green Book—1994*, The Sporting News Publishing Co., 1993; *American League Red Book—1994*, The Sporting News Publishing Co., 1993; *The Scouting Report: 1996,* Harper Perennial, 1996.

Pro Football   *The Official 1995 National Football League Record & Fact Book*, The National Football League, 1995; *The Official National Football League Encyclopedia*, New American Library, 1990; *The Sporting News Football Guide*, The Sporting News Publishing Co., 1993; *The Sporting News Football Register*, The Sporting News Publishing Co., 1993; *The 1993 National Football League Record & Fact Book,* Workman Publishing, 1993; *The Football Encyclopedia,* David Neft and Richard Cohen, St. Martin's Press, 1991.

College Football   *1994 NCAA Football*, The National Collegiate Athletic Association, 1993.

Pro Basketball   *The Official NBA Basketball Encyclopedia*, Villard Books, 1994; *The Sporting News Official NBA Guide*, The Sporting News Publishing Co., 1995; *The Sporting News Official NBA Register*, The Sporting News Publishing Co., 1995.

College Basketball   *1996 NCAA Basketball*, The National Collegiate Athletic Association, 1995.

Hockey *The National Hockey League Official Guide & Record Book 1995-96*, The National Hockey League, 1995; *The Sporting News Complete Hockey Book,* The Sporting News Publishing Co., 1993; *The Complete Encyclopedia of Hockey,* Visible Ink Press, 1993.

Tennis *1993 Official USTA Tennis Yearbook*, H. O. Zimman, Inc., 1993; *IBM/ATP Tour 1995 Player Guide*, Association of Tennis Professionals, 1995; *1996 Corel WTA Tour Media Guide*, Corel WTA Tour, 1996.

Golf *PGA Tour Book 1994*, PGA Tour Creative Services, 1994; *LPGA 1994 Player Guide*, LPGA Communications Department, 1994; *Senior PGA Tour Book 1994*, PGA Tour Creative Services, 1994; *USGA Yearbook 1994*, U.S. Golf Association, 1994.

Boxing *The Ring 1986–87 Record Book and Boxing Encyclopedia*, The Ring Publishing Corp., 1987. (To subscribe to *The Ring* magazine, write to P.O. Box 768, Rockville Centre, New York 11571-9905; or call (516) 678-7464); *Computer Boxing Update*, Ralph Citro, Inc., 1992; Bob Yalen, boxing statistician at ESPN.

Horse Racing *The American Racing Manual 1994*, Daily Racing Form, Inc., 1994; *1994 Directory and Record Book*, The Thoroughbred Racing Association, 1994; *The Trotting and Pacing Guide 1994*, United States Trotting Association, 1994; *Breeders' Cup 1993 Statistics*, Breeders' Cup Limited, 1993; *NYRA Media Guide 1993*, The New York Racing Association, 1994; *The 120th Kentucky Derby Media Guide, 1994*, Churchill Downs Public Relations Dept., 1994; *The 120th Preakness Press Guide, 1994*, Maryland Jockey Club, 1994; *Harness Racing News,* Harness Racing Communications.

Motor Sports *The Official NASCAR Yearbook and Press Guide 1994*, UMI Publications, Inc., 1994; *1994 Indianapolis 500 Media Fact Book*, Indy 500 Publications, 1994; *IMSA Yearbook 1995 Season Review*, International Motor Sports Association, 1995; *1994 Winston Drag Racing Series Media Guide*, Sports Marketing Enterprises, 1994.

Bowling *1994 Professional Bowlers Association Press, Radio and Television Guide*, Professional Bowlers Association, Inc., 1994; *The Ladies Pro Bowlers Tour 1994 Souvenir Tour Guide*, Ladies Pro Bowlers Tour, 1994.

Soccer *Major Soccer League Official Guide 1991–92*, Major Soccer League, Inc., 1991; *Rothmans Football Yearbook 1993–94*, Headline Book Publishing, 1993; *American Professional Soccer League 1992 Media Guide*, APSL Media Relations Department, 1992; *The European Football Yearbook*, Facer Publications Limited, 1988; *Soccer America,* Burling Communications.

NCAA Sports *1993–94 National Collegiate Championships*, The National Collegiate Athletic Association, 1994; *1993-94 National Directory of College Athletics,* Collegiate Directories Inc., 1993.

Olympics *The Complete Book of the Olympics*, Little, Brown and Co., 1991.

Track and Field *American Athletics Annual 1993*, The Athletics Congress/USA, 1993.

Swimming *6th World Swimming Championships Media Guide*, The World Swimming Championships Organizing Committee, 1991.

Skiing *U.S. Ski Team 1994 Media Guide / USSA Directory*, U.S. Ski Association, 1993; *Ski Racing Annual Competition Guide 1993–94*, Ski Racing International, 1993; *Ski Magazine's Encyclopedia of Skiing*, Harper & Row, 1974; *Caffä Lavazza Ski World Cup Press Kit*, Biorama, 1991.

Scorecard

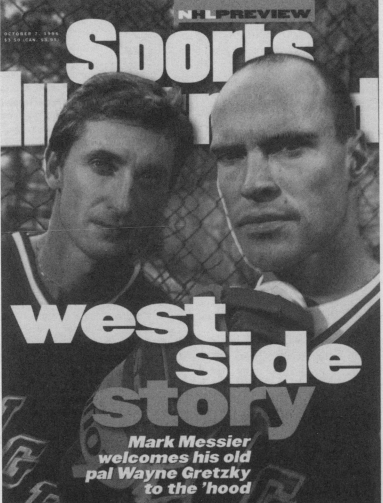

NHL PREVIEW

OCTOBER 7, 1996
$3.50 (CAN. $3.95)

Sports Illustrated

west. side story

Mark Messier welcomes his old pal Wayne Gretzky to the 'hood

A summary of Fall 1996 events

CLIVE MASON/ALLSPORT

Like father, like son: Damon Hill won his family's third Formula One title.

AUTO RACING

Illustrious families have always been one of the more intriguing features of the sport of auto racing. Damon Hill followed in his dad's tire tracks by clinching his first Formula One season championship with a win at the season-ending Japanese Grand Prix at Suzuka on October 13. His father, Graham, won F1 titles in 1962 and '68. The championship was decided on the 37th lap when Hill's teammate, Jacques Villeneuve, spun off the track. The Canadian rookie could have won the championship if he'd won the race and Hill had finished seventh or lower.

Jimmy Vasser, 30, clinched the IndyCar championship on September 8, when he finished fourth in the Toyota Grand Prix of Monterey (Calif.). Needing to finish fifth or better, Vasser started fifth and never fell below sixth, while the only two drivers with a chance to catch him, Michael Andretti and Al Unser Jr., never threatened him. "I was basically on a Sunday drive, cruising around the first half of the race just being nice to my car," said the remarkably consistent Vasser, who finished all 16 races in the series, scoring points in all but one. "Then, when I found out that Al and Michael were having some problems we stepped it up. They needed to be up front and they weren't. So I decided to stop cruising and I went for it."

On October 20 defending NASCAR series champion Jeff Gordon started the AC Delco 400 at the North Carolina Motor Speedway in Rockingham, N.C., with a one-point lead over his Hendrick Motorsports teammate Terry Labonte. But when Gordon finished 12th and Labonte third (behind winner Ricky Rudd), the lead changed hands. Labonte led Gordon, 4,327 points to 4,295. Also in the hunt with two races remaining in the 31-race series was Dale Jarrett, who had 4,251 points.

PRO BASKETBALL

The American Basketball League, a women's pro league made up of the Atlanta Glory, the Richmond (Va.) Rage, the Columbus (Ohio) Quest, the Colorado Xplosion, the San Jose Lasers, the Portland Power, the New England Blizzard and the Seattle Reign, commenced play on October 18, with New England beating Richmond 100–73; Colorado topping Seattle 82–75; and San Jose beating Atlanta 78–70.

BOXING

Fight fans are beginning to feel like those hunted humans in *Night of the Living Dead*, looking on in horror as one fighter after another deemed safely retired totters back into the ring for "one last fight." George Foreman, 48, was scheduled to meet Crawford Grimsley in Tokyo on November 2. Larry Holmes, a grandfather of 47, was planning to meet Brian Nielsen of Denmark in Copenhagen on January 24 for the IBO title. ("It's a chance to help that organization become legitimate," explained Holmes.) And Sugar Ray Leonard, a callow youth of 40, announced on October 15 that he would end a five-year retirement and return to the ring to face Hector (Macho) Camacho in February of 1997.

Tommy Morrison, who announced last February that he was retiring from the ring after testing positive for the virus that causes AIDS, changed his mind in late September and announced that he would fight one more time to raise money for Knockout AIDS, a foundation for children with HIV and AIDS. The bout, originally scheduled for the Foreman–Grimsley undercard, was later thrown into doubt by Morrison's manager, Tony Holden, who called the fight "highly unlikely."

That left the Mike Tyson–Evander Holyfield bout, scheduled for November 9 in Las Vegas, as the only meaningful heavyweight fight in sight. And it too lost a bit of its luster when, heaping confusion on top of the usual mountain of shenanigans, Tyson informed the World Boxing Council in September that he would relinquish his WBC heavyweight title rather than fight No. 1 contender Lennox Lewis. "We are disappointed and surprised that Tyson decided to give up the title instead of fighting Lennox," huffed Dino Duva, who co-promotes Lewis along with Panos Eliades. "For Tyson to just throw it away like this is incredible. I thought he was a warrior. I was wrong."

But how much of a surprise can Tyson's decision really have been? One of the terms of the binding contract Tyson signed with Bruce Seldon stipulated that he would yield the WBC crown if he beat Seldon, which he did earlier in the month.

CYCLING

U.S. cycling received a serious blow on October 8, when Lance Armstrong, the U.S.'s top athlete in a sport still dominated by Europeans, announced that he has testicular cancer and that it had spread to his abdomen and lungs. Two months earlier Armstrong, who is the two-time defending champion in the Tour DuPont and was the 1993 world road race champion, finished 12th in the road race at the Atlanta Olympics.

Armstrong, 25, had the testicle removed on October 3 and four days later began a 12-week chemotherapy program. Armstrong's doctors, who rate his chances of survival at 65% to 85%, gave him permission to cycle up to 50 miles a day "to stay in some sort of shape," said Armstrong, vowing to beat his

Armstrong is determined to triumph over testicular cancer.

illness and race again. "As soon as the wounds heal, I want to be back on the bike. I might have a bald head and might not be as fast, but I'll be out there."

COLLEGE FOOTBALL

College football did not have to wait long this season for some major shakeups to occur. On September 21—technically still the summer—top-ranked Nebraska, poised, it seemed, on the brink of an unprecedented third straight national championship, traveled to Sun Devil Stadium in Tempe for what most expected would be a routine win over Arizona State. After all, the Cornhusker steamroller had 14 starters back from a team that had trounced Arizona State 77–28 last year. But what a difference a year makes! The Sun Devils scored only one touchdown, but nailed the stunned Huskers for three safeties while outgaining them 401–226 in total yards. The final score was 19–0, and the season suddenly looked a lot different.

"Now everything is up for grabs," said Ohio State cornerback Shawn Springs, whose Buckeyes were one of several teams whose hopes for a national title had unexpectedly skyrocketed.

Indeed, though no one knew it at the time, the identity of Nebraska's successor as No. 1 had been decided earlier in the day, in Knoxville, where Florida blew out Tennessee 35–29 before an NCAA-record crowd of 107,608. If that score doesn't *sound* like a blowout, consider the fact that in the game's first 20 minutes Gator quarterback Danny Wuerffel threw four touchdown passes to four different receivers, the Vols committed three turnovers, and Florida took a 35–0 lead that basically ended the game. Florida moved to No. 1 in the polls, a position the Gators would hold onto more tightly in the following weeks while winning their first seven games by an average score of 52–13. Gator coach Steve Spurrier signed a five-year contract

Wuerffel put himself into contention for the Heisman with an impressive start.

that will pay him more than $1 million a year.

Other undefeated teams midway through the season were Florida State (5–0); Ohio State (7–0), which beat Notre Dame 29–16 in South Bend and then trounced Penn State 38–7 in Columbus; Alabama (7–0); surprising Arizona State, No. 26 in SI's preseason poll but winner of its first seven games, several thanks to breathtaking comebacks; West Virginia (7–0); Army (6–0); and Columbia (5–0 for the first time since 1945).

The Florida–Tennessee game was also a showdown between two leading Heisman candidates, Wuerffel and Tennessee quarterback Peyton Manning. Against Tennessee Wuerffel had one of his least impressive games statistically, completing just 11 of 22 passes for 155 yards. Still, he threw no interceptions, and that gave him a clear edge over Manning, who amassed 492 yards and four touchdowns but also threw two interceptions. As quarterback for the No. 1 team in the nation, Wuerffel was guaranteed the spotlight, and he made the most of it. Through seven games, he had a 62.3% completion rate and had thrown 20 touchdown against just four interceptions. He also had a passing efficiency rating of 181.04, more than two points higher than his NCAA-record rating of a year ago.

Another intriguing candidate, especially if fourth quarter heroics count for anything, was Jake (the Snake) Plummer of Arizona State. On October 12, with the Sun Devils trailing UCLA 34–21 midway through the fourth quarter, Plummer put on a virtuoso display of all-around quarterbacking skills. Not only did he throw for a touchdown, he ran for a second score and then caught a pass for a third on a halfback option. The following week Plummer rallied the Sun Devils to a 48–35 overtime defeat of Southern Cal, throwing for 277 yards, two touchdowns and three interceptions.

Much less conspicuous because they played for teams outside the Top 10 were several strong Heisman candidates. Among them were Iowa State's Troy Davis, who rushed for 378 yards—the third-highest game in college history—against Missouri and was averaging a nation-leading 215.5 yards per game through seven games; Texas Tech running back Byron

DAVID STROHMEYER

532 yards in the Cowboys' first seven games, a total that placed him 11th in the league.

The Cowboys' slow start can be traced in part to that vague complaint, "distractions"—not least of them Michael Irvin's offseason legal problems and the five-game suspension the league gave him as punishment. Irvin returned to the team on October 13, catching five passes for 51 yards in the Cowboys' 17–3 win over the Arizona Cardinals.

Meanwhile, the Broncos, paced by John Elway's bionic arm and Terrell Davis's league-leading 817 rushing yards, ran their record to 6–1. In that sixth win, a come-from-behind defeat of the Baltimore Ravens, Davis rushed 28 times for a franchise record 194 yards while Elway threw three touchdown passes, all to Ed McCaffrey, and ran for another. The surprising Redskins, who lost 10 games last season, lost their opener, then won six straight, powered by running back Terry Allen, who rushed for 679 yards in those seven games.

On October 21, one day after the New Orleans Saints were beaten 19–7 by the Carolina Panthers, Saints coach Jim Mora resigned as coach of the 2–6 Saints. On the same day, Dave Shula was fired as coach of the Cincinnati Bengals, who were 1–6. Two days later the New Orleans front office named Rick Venturi, the team's linebacker coach, as Mora's replacement.

More woeful than either the Saints or the Bengals were both the Atlanta Falcons and the New York Jets, who were winless in seven and eight games, respectively. The lone bright spot for the Jets was the kicking of veteran Nick Lowery, who passed Jan Stenerud as the NFL's alltime leading field goal kicker. Lowery's 20-yarder in the fourth quarter of the Jets' 21–17 loss to the Jacksonville Jaguars was the 374th of his career.

Hanspard, who was averaging 201.9 yards per game; and BYU quarterback Steve Sarkisian, who had completed 68.1% of his passes for an average of 343.4 yards per game and a total of 23 touchdowns.

Just about everyone seemed to agree that the best player in college football was Ohio State's gargantuan (6' 6", 330-pound) offensive lineman Orlando Pace. But no one gave Pace much chance of reversing 60 years of Heisman history, during which no purely defensive player has ever won the trophy.

PRO FOOTBALL

The biggest surprise in the first two months of the 1996 NFL season was not so much the teams that were doing well—Washington, Green Bay and Denver, all at 6–1—but the team that wasn't, the Super Bowl-champion Dallas Cowboys. Midway through the season the Cowboys had clawed their way back over the .500 mark, by sneaking past winless Atlanta 32–28 to go 4–3. Even Emmitt Smith, the league rushing leader four of the past five years, got off to a slow start, accumulating just

GOLF

Though it was less than two months old, Tiger Woods's pro career acquired yet another astonishing chapter on October 20, when he won his second tournament in three weeks, shooting a six-under-par 66 to beat Payne Stewart by one stroke in the Disney Golf Classic in Orlando. The win was anything but routine. The 20-year-old rookie had to overcome a terrible cold, three three-putt greens and the charge of fellow rookie Taylor Smith. In the end, Smith's final round of 67 was disallowed after his playing partner, Lennie Clements, turned him in for using a putter whose flat grips made it illegal under rule 4-1c of the Rules of Golf. Though Clements notified PGA Tour officials at the ninth hole, Smith finished the round and then filed an appeal, which was turned down.

O'Meara burned up the Old Course with a 63.

"This is very gratifying, very satisfying, but I have mixed emotions," said Woods. "I feel like I should have been in a playoff with Taylor. It's unfortunate, what happened to him, because he played his heart out."

For the record, Woods's scoring average for his first seven professional tournaments was 67.89, he was 95 under par for his 27 rounds and he had won $734,794, a sum that placed him 23rd on this year's money list. "It may be surprising to some guys, but it's not surprising to people who know me, but I haven't really played my best yet," said Woods. "I've hit the ball pretty good, but not the greatest. I haven't yet had the greatest putting round."

Woods was not the only story in the wide world of golf, though it certainly felt that way at times. Two noteworthy events were held in Great Britain. First, on October 10–13, at the Old Course in St. Andrews, the U.S. team of Mark O'Meara, Phil Mickelson and Steve Stricker won the 16-nation Dunhill Cup, beating Sweden 2–1 in the semifinals and New Zealand 2–1 in the final.

Especially impressive for the U.S. in the first round was O'Meara, who shot a 10-under-par 63—one shot off Curtis Strange's record for the Old Course—while beating Costantino Rocca of Italy. After a par on the first hole, O'Meara ran off eight straight birdies—something no one had ever done at the Old Course—to card a 28 for the front nine. Sadly for O'Meara, the 17th, the notorious Road Hole, wreaked its usual havoc on a fine round, when O'Meara's approach shot ran over the green and rolled down onto the road. Requiring two strokes to chip to within five feet, O'Meara then two-putted for a double bogey. "I feel pleased but also let down because I had a very reasonable chance of tying the course record or breaking it," said O'Meara.

But O'Meara's disappointment was nothing compared to that of the host country. Indeed, short of neglecting to wear anything under his kilt on a blustery day, it is hard to imagine anything embarrassing a Scotsman more than what transpired at St. Andrews. After winning the Cup last year for the first time in 11 years, Scotland lost 2–1 in the opening round to India, a country which had never before even qualified for the event. Colin Montgomerie, who blew up to a 79 to give Gaurav Ghei of India a one-stroke win, did not win a single match all week. Great Scot, indeed.

The following week, in Surrey, England, Ernie Els of South Africa tapped in a two-footer on the 16th hole to beat Vijay Singh of Fiji 3 and 2 and win the World Match Play Championship. "The first thing I'd better do is buy a couple of rounds in the bar," said Els, who claimed his third straight world match play title on the same weekend he probably lost the unofficial title of golf's next big star. "I didn't play

Derian Hatcher and the Stars were an early surprise, winning seven straight.

DAVID E. KLUTHO

all that great today." En route to the title, Els managed to win both narrowly and handily, coming from six holes down to beat Steve Stricker of the U.S. in the quarterfinals, and ousting Mark Brooks 10 and 8 in the semifinals.

ICE HOCKEY

Whetting hockey fans' appetites for the NHL season was the World Cup of Hockey. In the best-of-three final, the U.S. came from one game down to beat Canada 5–2 in the final at the Molson Arena in Montreal. The U.S. scored four goals in the final 3:18 of the game, stunning the favored Canadians. "It's a crushed locker room right now," said Wayne Gretzky, fighting back tears. "It's probably a crushed country. It's devastating."

Gretzky's signing with the New York Rangers and consequent reunion with his former Edmonton Oilers teammate Mark Messier was one of the big stories of the early NHL season. Not that their reunion bore immediate fruit: The Rangers went winless in their first five games before beating Calgary 5–4 on October 14 to go 1-3-2.

The league's early surprise was the great start of the Dallas Stars, who did not even reach the playoffs last year. The Stars won their first six games, thanks largely to the pair of Mike Modano and Pat Verbeek, who between them had four goals and 11 assists in that stretch. The league's only undefeated team over the same period was the Florida Panthers (4-0-3). The Phoenix Coyotes, who last year were the Winnipeg Jets, started the season 3-3-1 and figured only to get better with the addition of Jeremy Roenick, who signed a five-year, $20 million contract on October 14.

HORSE RACING

It was not the send-off owner Allen Paulson had envisioned for his star horse, Cigar, but it will have to do. On October 26, in the Breeders' Cup Classic at Woodbine Racecourse in Etobicoke,

Ontario, Alphabet Soup, a 19–1 longshot, with Chris McCarron in the saddle, beat Louis Quatorze by a nose, running the mile and a quarter in 2:01. The great Cigar finished third, amid talk of his retiring to stud.

"The horse can't go on forever," said Paulson. "He didn't disgrace himself. It's probably time to go to stud, unless somebody puts up some big carrot out there. We might take another look at it. We'll see what Billy [Mott, Cigar's trainer] thinks of it."

Said Mott, "Retire him."

This was Cigar's first third-place finish in the two years since he switched to dirt. In that time, he won 17 of 20 starts, including an American-record tying 16 straight races. Cigar's third-place prize money left his career earnings $185 short of $10 million.

Here are the results of other Breeders' Cup races:

• In the 1 1/16-mile race for Juvenile Fillies, Storm Song, Craig Perrett up, gave trainer Nick Zito his first Breeders' Cup win, beating Love That Jazz by 4 1/2 lengths, in 1:43 3/5.

• After getting shut out of the winner's circle in 12 previous Breeders' Cup races, jockey Corey Nakatani rallied Lit de Justice from last place to a 1 1/4-length win over Paying Dues in the six-furlong Sprint. The triumph made Jenine Sahadi the first female trainer to win a Breeders' Cup race, and gave Nakatani an emotional win, which he dedicated to his sister, Dawn, who was found strangled to death in her Los Angeles apartment earlier in the month.

BOB MARTIN

2:08:51, while his countrywoman, Marian Sutton, ran 2:30:41 to win the women's race.

TENNIS

Sixteen-year-old Martina Hingis, the latest in a long line of tennis prodigies, captured her first WTA title by upsetting Anke Huber 6–2, 3–6, 6–3 in the Porsche Grand Prix in Filderstadt, Germany, on October 13. Hingis, who had just cracked the top ten in the world rankings the previous week, won a Porsche for her efforts, but alas cannot use her new toy in her native Switzerland, where the driving age is 18.

The following weekend Jana Novotna ended Hingis's nine-match winning streak, beating her 6–2, 6–2 to win the European Indoors title in Zurich. "I don't think I'm as mentally fit as I was earlier," said Hingis.

On October 27 Boris Becker snapped Pete Sampras's 21-match winning streak with a come-from-behind win in the Eurocard Open, in Stuttgart. Becker, who was playing in just his third tournament after returning from a wrist injury suffered in June, had 29 aces en route to his 3–6, 6–3, 3–6, 6–3, 6–3 win.

TRIATHLON

Luc Van Lierde set a record for the 140.6-mile Ironman Triathlon course in Kailua-Kona, Hawaii, despite having to serve a three-minute penalty at the start of the run. Competing in his first Ironman, the 27-year-old Belgian swam 2.4 miles, biked 112 and ran 26.2 in 8:04:11 to snip 3:34 off Mark Allen's three-year-old course record. Van Lierde finished the bike portion of the race right behind Thomas Hellriegel of Germany, the eventual runner-up, but had to spend three minutes in the penalty box for drafting. He caught Hellriegel for good with a mile and a half to go.

Paula Newby-Fraser, who after collapsing with a quarter mile to go in last year's race said she was retiring from Ironman competition, changed her mind and won her eighth title, in 9:06:49. Newby-Fraser, who also had to serve a three-minute penalty at the start of the run, passed Natascha Badmann of Switzerland at the 22-mile mark.

"I've got an angel on my shoulder, and Dawn is her name," he said.

• Riding Jewel Princess, which is trained by his father-in-law, Wallace Dollase, Nakatani scored his second win in a row, in the 1⅛-mile Distaff. Jewel Princess covered the mile and a sixteenth in 1:48⅖ to beat Serena's Song by a length and a half.

• Da Hoss, with Gary Stevens up, surprised the favored European horses by winning the Mile, clocking 1:35⅘ to beat Spinning World by a length and a half.

• In the Juvenile race, for two-year-old colts, Boston Harbor, with Jerry Bailey up, went wire-to-wire to give D. Wayne Lukas his fifth win in the Juvenile and his record 13th Breeders' Cup victory overall. Boston Harbor ran the 1¹⁄₁₆-mile race in 1:43⅗ to beat Acceptable by a neck.

• In the Turf race, European horses went 1-2-3-4, as English jockey Walter Swinburn ended an 0–19 streak by riding the Irish horse Pilsudski to a 1¼-length win over Singspiel.

MARATHON

On October 20, England's Paul Evans, the runner-up in the 1995 New York City Marathon, easily won the Chicago Marathon in a time of

Year in Sport

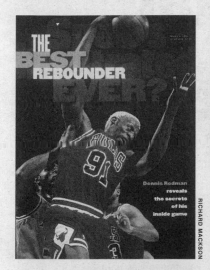

THE **BEST** REBOUNDER EVER?

Dennis Redman reveals the secrets of his inside game

RICHARD MACKSON

Sports Illustrated

Smashing!

The Sweet 16 is packed with powerhouses, including breakthrough Texas Tech

EL RICHARDSON/WASHINGTON POST

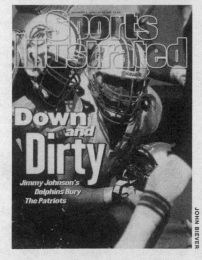

Sports Illustrated

Down and Dirty

Jimmy Johnson's Dolphins Bury The Patriots

JOHN BIEVER

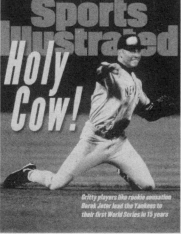

Sports Illustrated

Holy Cow!

Gritty players like rookie sensation Derek Jeter lead the Yankees to their first World Series in 15 years

AL TIELEMANS

The Flame Shines On

The heroes of 1996 were the spectators and athletes who revived the Olympic spirit after the bombing in Atlanta

by Gerry Callahan

KERRI STRUG wasn't the only person in Atlanta who choked back the pain and ended up a hero in 1996; she was just the one who started the trend. When Strug vaulted out of the shadows and into history, she was held up as a symbol of courage and determination, an Olympic fairytale come to life. It was an honor she richly deserved, of course, but it was one she would have to share with two million other resilient souls who descended upon Atlanta for the Summer Games. In the end, the entire city played hurt, and won. It was the performance of the year in sports, hands down.

Games are typically viewed as diversions from real life, mindless ways to escape the grind for a few hours at the end of a hard day, but when a terrorist's bomb exploded in Centennial Park early in the morning of July 27, killing two people and blowing a hole in the heart of the largest Olympiad ever, it was clear that this time there was no escape. This grand global celebration would forever be linked with the bomb, the deaths, the pain, the tragedy. The Olympic athletes and all those around the world who cheered them answered this killer's call with an even stronger display of human spirit. All the split magazine covers that appeared after the explosion—triumph versus tragedy—were not mere attempts by editors to market the melodrama. For all those in Atlanta, the challenge was palpable, and the response was instinctive. After many prayers and moments of silence, the applause grew louder, the spirit stronger, and the Games continued. One cruel and cowardly deed was countered by unforgettable displays of guts and resolve, and so it was that many Olympic athletes ran, jumped and vaulted their way into the headlines, easing some of the pain along the way. The crowds were there to give them a boost. The whole city came up big, just like 87-pound Strug. Triumph beat tragedy.

Although they got bumped off the stage by the Olympics, there were plenty of memorable performances in 1996: Michael Jordan got his touch back and wore a championship ring again while his tattooed teammate Dennis Rodman got in touch with his feminine side and wore a dress. The Atlanta Braves squared off with the New York Yankees in the World Series—the

MANNY MILLAN

Jordan rose to new heights—even for him—in winning his fourth NBA title.

team of the '90s versus history's most venerable franchise. The Dallas Cowboys won their third Super Bowl in four years and then lost their star receiver, Michael Irvin, for five games when he was found in a hotel room full of trouble. The Browns left Cleveland, and the Wiz arrived in Kansas City. The league that brought them, Major League Soccer, staged a wiz-bang finish to its first season in a driving rainstorm in Foxboro, Mass., with D.C. United taking the title 3–2 in overtime against the Los Angeles

Galaxy. The City of Angels, meanwhile, still had no football team but did have Shaquille O'Neal, who it hoped would restore NBA glory. The Avalanche beat the Panthers in the Stanley Cup finals. Where have you gone, Toe Blake?

Mike Tyson regained the heavyweight title and raked in millions without ever facing an opponent as tough as the prison oatmeal. Nebraska won its second straight national title, but not without tarnishing coach Tom Osborne's once impeccable reputation. Kentucky was the best college basketball team in the land; its jayvee squad may have been No. 2. Northwestern finally

The terrifying blast left blood on the park's commemorative bricks.

won; Cigar finally lost. Tiger Woods turned pro, signed a reported $60 million worth of endorsement deals and won the fifth and seventh tournaments he entered.

As always, the passing year seemed to introduce more money, more drugs, more lawyers and more madness to the sports world, and the Atlanta Olympics were certainly no exception. This time the Olympic rings were southern fried and served with Coke and a swoosh, and if you couldn't get tickets to the basketball games, you could always get drunk and ride the Ferris wheel. The city had all the ambience of a frat party, which seemed embarrassing at first glance. Then after a few days you remembered that parties can be fun, and so, for the most part, were these Games.

The party atmosphere was in full flower in Centennial Park on July 27, when an overflow crowd was enjoying a free concert before the bomb went off. Unthinkable

chaos ensued, and for a day or two, it seemed order would never be restored to the streets. Bomb threats prompted evacuations around the city. Security clamped down everywhere. Everyone walked a little lighter, even though their hearts were a good deal heavier.

The park remained closed for three days, then reopened with yet another made-for-TV ceremony. The *Today Show* broadcast live a few feet from the hole that was left after the explosion. Katie Couric sat with Richard Jewell, the beefy security guard who went from hero to suspect to .... To what? What is he now? Do we know? Will we ever? All we know is that he has returned to the talk-show circuit.

Athletes often talk about the need to block out distractions—or, as they prefer to say in the '90s, to *stay focused*. But this—getting back to the Games amid the bomb threats and intense security—was almost too much to ask. Here were these Olympians, in the most significant competition of their lives, facing an unimaginable dis-

Shannon MacMillan's overtime goal put the U.S. in the Olympic final.

traction. *You mean there might be, like, bombs in the arena?* Clearly the intention of the perpetrator was not to murder a couple of people at a concert but to kill an entire Olympics. But these Olympics refused to die.

Athletes and spectators alike did their part. While the unheralded Strug appeared out of nowhere to seize the Olympic spotlight, Michael Johnson had the more difficult task of performing directly under its glare and against his own supernatural standards. Johnson was expected to win gold in the 200 and the 400, which he did. He was not expected to eclipse his own world record in the 200 by .34 seconds, an achievement that seemed to knock the wind out of the nearly 80,000 in attendance. Looking at the 19.32 appear on the huge digital clock was akin to watching Bob Beamon soar through the air in Mexico City. *Did he just do what I think he did?* Johnson had taken his sport where it had never gone before, and it was something to see.

A few days earlier the crowd had been nearly as stunned when Carl Lewis, at age 35, captured his fourth straight Olympic long jump gold and the ninth gold medal of his incomparable career. Lewis had barely made the Olympic team, but when the big moment arrived, the legend not only outjumped his competitors, he outwilled them. Once he completed a jump of 27' 10¾", the other long jumpers, including the highly touted Mike Powell of the U.S., were lucky if they could take off their warmups without fouling. Lewis's legs might not have been as strong as they once were, but his mind was still cold steel.

But then the man now arguably the greatest track athlete of all time failed to exit the Olympic stage gracefully. He stumbled over his ego one last time. Sensing public sentiment was behind him after his performance in the long jump, Lewis lobbied for a spot on the 4 x 100 relay team, an event for which he had failed to qualify. Why now? He wanted a 10th gold medal to cap off his brilliant career. Of course he would have to supplant someone who had earned a spot on the team to get it. A debate raged for a few days, but in the end Lewis was left off the U.S. team, which wound up taking second place. Donovan Bailey, the gold medalist in the 100 meters, led Canada to the gold.

The U.S., it seemed, did not lose much else. In the final standings, the Americans captured 101 medals, including 44 golds. Germany was a distant second. While the U.S. men's basketball team once again won the gold without breaking a sweat, they weren't even the most popular American Dream Team in Atlanta. The U.S. women roundballers, who traveled and played together for the 14 months leading up to the Olympics, capped off a 60–0 world tour with a victory in the gold medal game, the final event of the Atlanta Games. Led by the phenomenal Lisa Leslie, the American women played unselfishly on the court and gave graciously of their time off the court. Who said the Dream Team would not be good for the game? These woman were terrific.

American women also dominated the softball diamond, the soccer field and the pool. Led by veteran shortstop Dot Richardson, the U.S. took the inaugural Olympic softball gold medal with a tense 3–1 victory over China, which played frustrated bridesmaid to the U.S. in soccer as well. Before a record crowd of 76,481 in Athens, Ga., with its star, and arguably the world's greatest player, Mia Hamm, playing injured, the U.S. prevailed 2–1 to take the first women's soccer gold medal. While the great Janet Evans finished her Olympic swimming career without a medal, there appeared to be a number of worthy successors to her throne. Brooke Bennett was the most obvious as she won gold in the 800—with Evans finishing sixth—but there were others, including Amy Van Dyken with four golds, as the American women swept the swimming competition.

But even the Americans were splashed aside by the outrageously dominant performance of Irish swimmer Michelle Smith. Amid the swirl of accusations of steroid use, the 26-year-old Smith won three gold medals and a bronze and fended off her inquisitors with the same defiant spunk that she displayed in the pool.

While the Olympics brought us the usual array of fresh new faces, much of the remaining 50 weeks of the sports calendar was dominated by familiar champions. The Cowboys and the Cornhuskers repeated as champions in '96, and the Bulls, with the incomparable Jordan back in the fold, regained the crown they had lost when he stepped aside in 1993. If anything, Jordan enhanced his reputation: Has any athlete ever accomplished what he did in '96?

It was his first full season back with the Bulls since his brief stint in minor league baseball, and at age 33, it may have been his finest. He won his fourth MVP, passing Magic and Larry in that category, and his eighth scoring title, passing Wilt Chamberlain. The Houston Rockets had won two straight titles, but clearly they were just keeping the crown warm for Jordan. Without a dominant center or a pure point guard, the Bulls won a record 72 regular-season games, then 15 of 18 in the postseason, including a 4–2 triumph over Seattle in the Finals. They were as dominant as NBC's Thursday-night lineup. They didn't play games; they gave seminars.

And in the middle of the clinic was the freak show. In a development that seemed to say more about celebrity than sports, Jordan shared top billing with a monument to self-promotion, not to mention self-mutilation. When Rodman wasn't wearing women's clothes, he wasn't wearing any clothes, appearing nude on the jacket of his best-selling book. On the court he remained a rebounding machine, leading the league for the fifth time. He got along with Jordan and Scottie Pippen and waited until the end of most games before removing his shoes. Off the court he garnered more tabloid headlines than Princess Di.

After the end of the '95–96 season, Jordan, Rodman and Phil Jackson all signed one-year contracts, assuring the team at least one more run at a title. Jordan's deal was for a reported $25 million. For one year. Many athletes were considered overpaid in '96, but even with the new deal, Jordan was not one of them. Shaquille O'Neal was. Jerry West showered Shaq with gold, and he donned Lakers yellow. The contract: seven years, $121 million. We were left to ponder how much the big guy will be worth when he actually wins something.

The Dallas Cowboys won something in '96: another Super Bowl, their third in four years, a truly remarkable run in this era of free agency and salary caps. So how come this team seemed more confused than Margot Kidder? In the off-season Irvin was found by police in an Irving, Tex., hotel room with two topless dancers and an array

Ireland's Smith made waves both in and out of the Olympic pool.

of controlled substances. His words to the cops when they confronted him were, "Can I tell you who I am?" Turned out he was the guy who got bounced for the first five games of the '96 regular season, three of which were Cowboy losses.

The Green Bay Packers, meanwhile, became the real America's Team. Brett Favre won the 1995–96 MVP award and after undergoing treatment for an addiction to pain killers, helped the Packers to a 6–1 start in '96–97. Jimmy Johnson took over for Don Shula in Miami. The Browns moved to Baltimore, became the Ravens and introduced the ugliest uniforms in the NFL. Almost as ugly as the feelings for Art Modell in the city of Cleveland.

Something odd happened in major league baseball in 1996. They played a full season, no strikes, no lockouts, no walkouts, no self-inflicted gunshot wounds to the feet. For a change, Donald Fehr was not on TV more than that annoying Infiniti guy. It was, in fact, a highly entertaining year between the lines, unless you are a big fan of low

ERAs and two-hour-and-20-minute games. Major league baseball may have to offer counseling to every player who didn't hit 30 home runs and drive in 110 RBIs. It must have been traumatic. A shocking 43 major leaguers hit 30, including Baltimore leadoff man Brady Anderson, who hit 50, 29 more than his previous career high. For a while it appeared that Mark McGwire had a legit shot at 62, but then, who didn't? Ken Griffey Jr. hit a career-high 49 with 140 RBIs and wasn't even the most valuable player on his team. Shortstop Alex Rodriguez, who turned 21 in July, crammed a career into his first full season, finishing with 36 homers, 123 RBIs and a batting title.

Naturally, baseball had its usual dose of deviant behavior in '96. Kelsey Grammer has an easier time dealing with success. Every time baseball appears to be on top of the world again, it finds a way to screw up. This time it literally spit in the face of authority. As some wonderful pennant races were about to give way to the playoffs, Baltimore star Roberto Alomar punctuated an argument with umpire John Hirschbeck by expectorating in the man's face. Alomar followed this up by mentioning Hirschbeck's deceased son, and American League president Gene Budig, showing all the spine of a jellyfish, suspended Alomar for five games—beginning in the '97 regular season. It set off a firestorm of controversy and confirmed an old baseball adage: The game must be great if it continues to survive the fools who run it.

Alomar's Orioles were ousted by the Yankees, who brought the World Series back to the Bronx for the first time in 15 years. They would square off against the Braves in a Series steeped in history, tradition and no shortage of grainy black-and-white footage, which was something that couldn't be said about the '96 Stanley Cup. The poor folks in Quebec City had to endure a triple hip check: First the Nordiques moved to Colorado, where they were renamed "the Avalanche," then they—make that "it"—won the Cup. At least the Denver fans didn't throw rubber avalanches on the ice every time their team scored. The upstart Florida Panthers may have failed to win the Cup, but in just their third year in the NHL, they did accomplish something: Their fans started the most annoying custom in sports, tossing rubber rats on the ice and delaying the game after each goal. Thankfully, the practice was banned in the off-season.

The Kentucky basketball program, which was banned from postseason play by the NCAA in 1990 and '91, returned to glory under the steady guidance of coach Rick Pitino. The Wildcats went 10 deep, and ran at their opposition like the heroes in the movie *Braveheart*, almost intimidating other teams off the floor. Pitino's team lost to his alma mater, UMass, early in the season, and avenged the loss in the Final Four. Marcus Camby of UMass was the best college player in the country, and Georgetown's Allen Iverson, who went first in the NBA draft, was up there, too. But at times it seemed as if the next six or eight names on the list were playing for Pitino in Lexington. After the season Pitino turned down a reported $30 million offer to take over the New Jersey Nets, choosing to stay in the college ranks. The job went to John Calipari of UMass.

While it is difficult to say which athletes

PATRICK MURPHY-RACEY

Pitino choreographed every step of the Wildcats' return to glory.

gave us the most memorable moments in '96, the list of the most forgettable performers is easy to compile: just take all the guys who got in the ring with Mike Tyson. In September, Don King finally found the perfect opponent for his meal ticket. Tyson didn't even have to *hit* Bruce Seldon to get a first-round knockout. To sum up the state of boxing in '96, a woman, Christy Martin, generated more excitement in the ring than Tyson. In February, Tommy Morrison revealed that he had tested positive for HIV and gracefully announced his retirement, only to reinstate himself in October.

Golf changed completely in '96. Oh, some things followed tradition: Greg Norman, for instance, blew a six-stroke lead on the final day of the Masters and lost to Nick Faldo. But at the Greater Milwaukee Open in late August, a kid named Tiger Woods teed off as a professional for the first time, and five weeks later, on the first hole of a playoff against Davis Love III in the Las Vegas Invitational, he won a tournament. Two weeks after that, he won another one. Contrary to his shameful debut TV commercial, Woods isn't just welcome on any course in America. There is no one else they would rather see. We have seen the future of golf, and it has the face of a 12-year-old but the eyes of a Tiger.

Tennis, still waiting for a Tiger of its own, often seemed about as suspenseful as an Iranian election. Steffi Graf won her 21st Grand Slam title and lost just three matches all year. Pete Sampras collected his eighth Grand Slam and lost his coach and friend Tim Gullikson, who died of brain cancer. Most of the top players chose to pass on the Olympics, which left the door open for camera pitchman Andre Agassi, who won the gold in men's singles.

Also this year: Dwight Gooden came back—with a no-hitter, no less—Tommy Lasorda retired, and Magic Johnson came

Blue Dodger: Lasorda reluctantly ended his 47-year baseball career.

back and retired—again. Ryne Sandberg returned. Ozzie Smith retired. Wrestler Dave Schultz was shot and killed by a benefactor of USA Wrestling whose behavior had long been questionable. Skater Sergei Grinkov was tragically felled by a heart ailment, and legendary Yankee broadcaster Mel Allen died. As always, the good shared the sports stage with the bad and the ugly, although Marge Schott was supposedly banned from baseball yet again.

The next 12 months will surely bring more of the same, but the Summer Olympics won't return to the United States anytime soon. And the tidal wave of humanity that flooded Atlanta for two weeks may never be seen again. Too dangerous, they said. Too crazy. Too chaotic. It was all those things, to be sure, but it was also a competition that at least two million people will never forget. Triumph took on tragedy, and won. It wasn't even close.

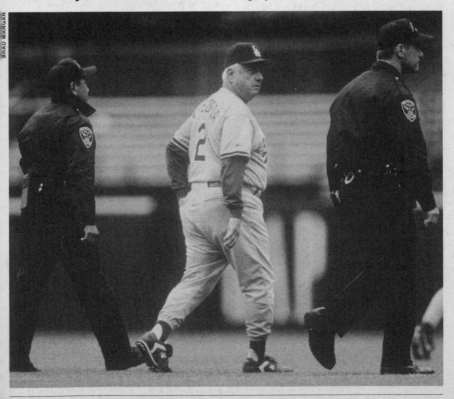

Baseball

Oct 23, 1995—Former Oakland A's manager Tony La Russa signs a two-year contract to manage the St. Louis Cardinals. Three days later Buck Showalter announces he will not return to manage the Yankees.

Oct 31—Ryne Sandberg, the nine-time Gold Glove–winning second baseman who retired on June 13, 1994, announces he will return to the Chicago Cubs to play the 1996 season.

Nov 2—Former St. Louis Cardinals manager Joe Torre signs a two-year contract to manage the New York Yankees. Earlier in the week, Ray Knight takes over as skipper of the Cincinnati Reds, whose former manager, Davey Johnson, signs on with Baltimore.

Nov 6—Seattle Mariners manager Lou Piniella, who guided his team from a 13-game August deficit to their first division title, is named American League Manager of the Year. The following day Don Baylor of the Colorado Rockies, who made the playoffs in just their third year of existence, wins the National League Manager of the Year award.

Nov 8—Outfielder Marty Cordova, who hit 24 home runs and drove in 84 runs for last-place Minnesota, is named AL Rookie of the Year. The following day pitcher Hideo Nomo becomes the fourth consecutive Dodger to be named the NL Rookie of the Year. Nomo was 13–6 with a 2.54 ERA and is the first Japanese player to win a prominent major league award.

Nov 13—Atlanta Braves pitcher Greg Maddux wins an unprecedented fourth consecutive NL Cy Young Award. Maddux, whose election is unanimous, was 19–2 with a 1.63 ERA. The following day Randy Johnson of the Seattle Mariners, who won 18 of 20 decisions and led the league in both ERA (2.48) and strikeouts (294), wins the American League Cy Young Award.

Nov 15—Barry Larkin, who hit .319 with 66 RBIs and 51 stolen bases for the Cincinnati Reds, becomes the first shortstop in 33 years to win the NL Most Valuable Player Award. The following day Boston slugger Mo Vaughn, who hit 39 home runs with 126 RBIs, wins the AL MVP award.

Nov 30—The New York Yankees decide not to exercise the $1.8 million option for 1996 in Darryl Strawberry's contract, buying the slugger out for $175,000.

Dec 3—The Atlanta Braves re-sign All-Star first baseman Fred McGriff to a four-year, $20 million contract. Two days later the Minnesota Twins sign Paul Molitor, who grew up in St. Paul, to a one-year, $2 million deal.

Dec 7—First baseman Tino Martinez, a lifelong Yankee fan who has spent his career with Seattle, has one of the more eventful days of his life as his wife gives birth to a girl, Victoria; he turns 28; and he signs a five-year, $20 million contract to play for the Bronx Bombers.

JOHN IACONO

Strawberry got yet another chance in New York.

Dec 13—In a flurry of free-agent signings totaling more than $57 million, second baseman Craig Biggio remains with the Houston Astros; pitcher Jack McDowell departs the Yankees for Cleveland and a two-year, $10 million contract; Randy Myers goes from Chicago (NL) to Baltimore for a $6 million, two-year contract; and former Chicago White Sox leadoff man Lance Johnson signs a two-year, $5 million deal with the New York Mets.

Dec 21—Division rivals New York and Baltimore each make key free-agent acquisitions as the Yankees re-sign pitcher David Cone—outbidding the Orioles for him—to a three-year deal worth over $17 million, and Baltimore lands six-time All-Star second baseman Roberto Alomar for three years and $18 million.

Jan 31, 1996—Ken Griffey Jr. becomes baseball's highest-paid player when he signs a four-year, $34 million contract extension with the Seattle Mariners.

Feb 8—Forty-four-year-old Dave Winfield, who began his career in 1973 with San Diego and collected 3,110 hits and 465 home runs while going on to play for New York (AL), California, Toronto, Minnesota and Cleveland, announces his retirement.

Feb 14—The St. Louis Cardinals acquire veteran closer Dennis Eckersley from the Oakland A's in exchange for a minor league reliever.

Feb 19—Charles O. Finley, 77, the iconoclastic owner of the Oakland A's from 1960–80, dies of heart disease.

March 5—The Veterans Committee elects four men—pitcher Jim Bunning, who played 17 seasons with Detroit and Philadelphia; manager Earl Weaver, who was ejected from 91 games while winning six AL East titles in 17 seasons as manager of the Orioles; pitcher Bill Foster, who was regarded as the best lefthander in the Negro Leagues; and turn-of-the-century Baltimore manager Ned Hanlon—to baseball's Hall of Fame in Cooperstown.

March 21—Major league owners approve by a 26–1 vote (with one abstention) an interim revenue-sharing plan. The plan, which would provide small market teams with up to $4 million in additional revenue during the '96 season, awaits approval by the players' union.

March 31—For the first time ever, major league baseball stages a regular-season game in March as the Chicago White Sox and the Seattle Mariners kick off the season with a Sunday-night tilt in the Kingdome. The Mariners win 3–2 in 12 innings.

April 1—Baseball's proper April opening—with afternoon games scheduled league-wide—is darkened by the death of umpire John McSherry, who is working home plate in Cincinnati when he collapses after the seventh pitch of the Reds–Expos game and dies an hour later.

April 1—Opening day in Cleveland—with the Indians set to square off against the Yankees—is *snowed* out.

April 10—New York beats Kansas City 7–3 at Yankee Stadium, where the temperature drops to 36° and snow dusts the field before the final out is recorded.

April 24—The Minnesota Twins—not the Vikings—defeat the Detroit Tigers—not the Lions—24–11 in Minnesota. The football-style score typifies baseball's first month, which features Ruthian offense. Four days earlier Texas had routed Baltimore 26–7, and five days later Montreal pounds Colorado 21–9.

April 27—San Francisco Giants outfielder Barry Bonds hits the 300th home run of his career in the third inning of a 6–3 victory over Florida, placing him—alongside his father Bobby, godfather Willie Mays and Andre Dawson—in the exclusive 300–300 club of players with at least 300 home runs and 300 stolen bases.

April 30—Barry Bonds reaches another milestone, tying the major league record of 11 home runs in the month of April by hitting two round-trippers, one of them a grand slam, against San Diego. Baltimore's Brady Anderson and Gary Sheffield of the Marlins have also tied the mark.

April 30—The Yankees and the Orioles break the record for the longest nine-inning game in a 13–10 slugfest, won by New York, that lasts 4 hours, 21 minutes, eclipsing the mark of 4:18 set by the Dodgers and Giants on Oct. 2, 1962.

May 2—An earthquake measuring 4.8 on the Richter scale rumbles through the Seattle Kingdome, causing the Mariners-Cleveland game to be suspended in the bottom of the seventh inning.

May 5—Cincinnati outfielder Eric Davis becomes the 18th major leaguer to hit a grand slam in consecutive games when he hits his second in as many days during the Reds' 12–6 victory over the Giants.

May 7—Centerfielder Brett Butler of the Los Angeles Dodgers, a 16-year veteran in the major leagues, announces that doctors have found a cancerous tumor in his throat. On May 21 he will undergo surgery to remove the tumor, then face six weeks of radiation therapy.

May 7—The New York Yankees announce that pitcher David Cone has a treatable aneurysm—the abnormal ballooning of a blood vessel—in his right (pitching) arm. Cone, 4–1 with a league-leading 2.03 ERA, is placed on the 15-day disabled list until further evaluation.

May 11—Al Leiter of the Florida Marlins throws the year's first no-hitter as the Marlins blank the Rockies 11–0.

May 14—Dwight Gooden, the New York Yankees righthander who missed part of 1994 and all of '95 because of a drug-related suspension, wins his second game since returning to the majors in grand style, pitching a no-hitter in the Yankees' 2–0 win over Seattle.

May 18—St. Louis Cardinals first baseman John Mabry hits for the cycle in the Redbirds' 9–8 loss to Colorado.

May 22—The Colorado Rockies announce that pitcher Bret Saberhagen will have reconstructive surgery on his right shoulder, a procedure that will most likely keep him out of baseball for over a year.

May 26—Former Los Angeles Dodgers infielder Mike Sharperson is killed in a one-car accident in Las Vegas.

June 4—Kris Benson, a righthander for Clemson University, goes to the Pittsburgh Pirates as the first pick of the major league draft.

June 6—The league announces that Marge Schott, the subject of recent controversy for her inflammatory racial remarks, must relinquish day-to-day control of the Reds or face indefinite suspension. Schott agrees to the terms on June 12.

June 6—For only the second time in major league history a player hits for the cycle and a team turns a triple play in the same game, as Boston's John Valentin wields the hot bat and the White Sox complete their first triple killing in 10 years in the 7–4 Red Sox victory.

June 16—Legendary Yankees announcer Mel Allen, 83, dies of an undisclosed ailment at his home in Greenwich, Conn.

June 19—Seattle centerfielder Ken Griffey Jr. breaks his right hand during the Mariners' 9–2 loss to Toronto, joining eight other Mariners on the DL.

June 19—The St. Louis Cardinals' 14-time All-Star shortstop Ozzie Smith, who many consider to be the greatest defensive shortstop of all time, announces that he will retire at season's end.

July 7—The Yankees re-sign outfielder Darryl Strawberry, who had spent the past two months with the St. Paul Saints of the independent Northern League.

July 9—Dodgers catcher Mike Piazza hits a home run and an RBI double and is named MVP as the National League wins the All-Star game 6–0.

July 12—Citing irreversible vision loss, Kirby Puckett of the Minnesota Twins announces his retirement. In 12 years the stocky outfielder hit .318 and played for two World Series-winning teams.

July 29—Tommy Lasorda announces his retirement, for health reasons, after 47 years in the Dodger organization. The Dodgers won two World Series, four pennants and seven division titles in Lasorda's 20 seasons as manager.

Aug 11—Representatives of baseball's owners and players emerge after a series of weekend meetings saying they have made "considerable progress" toward labor peace.

Aug 14—Florida Marlins outfielder Andre Dawson, who played 21 years in the majors with Montreal, Chicago (NL) and Boston, announces his retirement, effective after the season.

Aug 16—The San Diego Padres and New York Mets square off in Monterrey, Mexico, in the first major league game outside the U.S. and Canada.

Smith brought his long and brilliant career to a close.

CHUCK SOLOMON

Great Expectorations: Alomar's unseemly behavior caused a flap.

Aug 19—The Texas Rangers set an AL record with their 15th consecutive errorless game.

Sept 2—Boston's Mike Greenwell drives in all of his team's runs in the Red Sox' 9–8 victory over Seattle. In New York, David Cone returns from surgery to remove an aneurysm in his arm and pitches seven no-hit innings in the Yankees' 5–0 win over Oakland.

Sept 6—Eddie Murray of the Orioles hits his 500th career home run to join Hank Aaron and Willie Mays as the only players with at least 3,000 hits and 500 homers.

Sept 8—Dodgers catcher Mike Piazza hits his 33rd home run of the year, and the 4,459th of major league baseball's year, breaking the record set in 1987.

Sept 10—Los Angeles's Brett Butler, who made an emotional return from cancer surgery the previous week, breaks his hand in a 5–4 win over the Reds and is out for the year.

Sept 15—The A's Mark McGwire hits his 50th home run of the year in a 9–8 Oakland loss to Cleveland, while the Mets' Todd Hundley breaks Roy Campanella's 1953 record for homers by a catcher, belting his 41st in a 6–5 win over Atlanta.

Sept 16—Minnesoa's Paul Molitor gets his 3,000th career hit in a 6–5 Twins loss to the Royals.

Sept 17—Dodgers ace Hideo Nomo pitches a no-hitter at home run-friendly Coors Field as Los Angeles taps the Rockies 9–0. In Chicago, the Indians clinch the AL Central, qualifying for the postseason for the second straight year, a first in the franchise's 96-year history.

Sept 17—Jim Leyland announces he will resign as Pittsburgh manager at the end of the year.

Sept 18—Boston's Roger Clemens strikes out 20 Detroit Tigers in a 4–0 Red Sox victory, tying his own major league record.

Sept 24—The St Louis Cardinals clinch the NL Central. The following day the New York Yankees clinch their first AL East title since 1981.

Sept 27—Baltimore second baseman Roberto Alomar spits in the face of umpire John Hirschbeck after being ejected from a game in

CHUCK SOLOMON

Toronto for arguing a strike call. When the league defers his suspension until next season, umpires vote to boycott the playoffs. The umps are eventually forced to work by a court injunction while Alomar plays a key role in Baltimore's playoff run.

Sept 29—The San Diego Padres win the NL West with an 11-inning, 2–0 win over the Dodgers, who become the wild-card team with the defeat. In Detroit, Tigers shortstop Alan Trammell announces his retirement.

Oct 5—The Orioles down the Indians 4–3 in 12 innings to win their divisional playoff 3–1. In Texas, the Yankees win 6–4, eliminating the Rangers in four games.

Oct 5—St. Louis defeats San Diego 7–5 while the Braves down the Dodgers 5–2. The winners will meet for the NL Pennant after sweeping their divisional playoffs.

Oct 13—The New York Yankees defeat Baltimore 6–4 to win the ALCS in five games and advance to the World Series for the first time since 1981.

Oct 17—The Atlanta Braves, who had trailed 3–1 in the series, rout the Cardinals 15–0 in Game 7 of the NLCS and head to the World Series for the second year in a row. Braves starter Tom Glavine joins the offensive outburst with a three-run triple in the first inning.

Oct 26—The New York Yankees beat the Braves 3–2 to complete a turnaround from a two-games-to-none deficit and win the World Series. After losing Game 1, 12–1, and Game 2, 4–0, at home, the Bombers sweep three from the Braves in Atlanta, including an 8–6 win in Game 4 in which they rally from six runs behind. New York closer John Wetteland, who saves all four Series victories, is named MVP. It is the 23rd World Series title in Yankees history, tying New York with the Montreal Canadiens (23 Stanley Cups) as the professional sports teams with the most championships.

Boxing

Nov 4, 1995—Riddick Bowe stops Evander Holyfield in the eighth round of their fight in Las Vegas. It is the third meeting between the two heavyweights, with Bowe winning twice.

Nov 17—Promoter Don King leaves a New York city courtroom a free man after his trial for wire-fraud ends in a hung jury.

Dec 9—Frans Botha of South Africa wins the IBF heavyweight title in Stuttgart with a split decision over Germany's Axel Schulz.

Dec 16—Mike Tyson knocks out Buster Mathis Jr. in the third round of their non-title bout in Philadelphia.

Jan 12, 1996—Super middleweight Roy Jones Jr. furthers his claim to the title of best pound-for-pound fighter in the world with a second round TKO of Merqui Sosa in Madison Square Garden.

Jan 30—Dan Duva, 44, a boxing promoter for nearly 20 years, dies in New York after a long battle with cancer.

Feb 15—Heavyweight Tommy Morrison holds a press conference in Tulsa to announce that he has tested positive for the virus that causes AIDS. Saying he "blew it with irresponsible, irrational, immature decisions," he ends his seven-year career. Morrison learned of the positive test just hours before he was to meet Arthur Weathers in a scheduled 10-round bout in Las Vegas.

March 16—Heavyweight Mike Tyson wins the WBC crown in Las Vegas with a third-round TKO of Frank Bruno.

March 27—Frans Botha loses the IBF title he won in December after a U.S. District Court judge disqualifies him based on his positive test for steroids following the victory.

May 10—British heavyweight Lennox Lewis wins a disputed majority decision over Ray Mercer in their non-title fight in New York.

June 7—In the year's only compelling bout, rising star Oscar De La Hoya strips veteran Julio César Chávez of his WBC junior welterweight title with a bloody, fourth-round TKO in Las Vegas. De La Hoya, 23, runs his record to 22–0 with the victory while the 33-year-old Chávez drops to 97-2-1.

June 15—Roy Jones Jr. completes a historic, if somewhat gimmicky, double in Jacksonville when he plays point guard in an afternoon game with the Jacksonville Barracudas of the USBL, then defends his IBF super middleweight title against Canada's Eric Lucas later that night. For the record, he scores five points in the game, and wins the bout by TKO in the 11th round.

June 16—Forty-six-year-old heavyweight Larry Holmes knocks out Anthony Willis, 27, in the eighth round of their bout in Bay St. Louis, Miss. Says Holmes following the victory: "This was my last hurrah."

De La Hoya ripped the once-mighty Chávez.

June 22—Michael Moorer takes a split decision from Axel Schulz in Dortmund, Germany, to win the IBF heavyweight title.

July 11—A non-title fight in Madison Square Garden between heavyweights Riddick Bowe and Andrew Golota of Poland ends in a riot after Golota is disqualified in the seventh round for repeated low blows. Bowe's cornermen go after Golota, who appeared to be winning the bout when it was stopped, and the Garden erupts in a chair-flinging melee that lasts over 20 minutes.

Sept 7—Mike Tyson rocks Bruce Seldon in the first round of their WBA title bout in Las Vegas. Though no one watching sees the blow, Seldon staggers, then is finished off by a Tyson left. Tyson now holds the WBA and WBC belts.

Sept 20—Pernell (Sweet Pea) Whitaker retains his WBC welterweight title with a 12-round decision over Wilfredo Rivera in Miami.

Sept 24—Mike Tyson relinquishes his WBC heavyweight title rather than obey a court order that he fight WBC No. 1 contender Lennox Lewis. In a contract signed before the Bruce Seldon bout, Tyson had agreed to give up the WBC crown if he stopped Seldon to win the WBA title.

College Basketball

Nov 20, 1995—The nation's top two women's teams fall in the Women's Basketball Hall of Fame Tipoff Classic in Knoxville, Tenn., as No. 1 Connecticut loses 83–81 in overtime to No. 5 Louisiana Tech, and No. 2 Virginia is blown out by No. 6 Tennessee, 78–51.

Nov 29—For the second straight year Massachusetts begins its season by knocking off the No. 1 team in the country. The Minutemen defeat top-ranked Kentucky 92–82 in the Great Eight tournament in Auburn Hills, Michigan. In their opener the previous season UMass upset then–No. 1 Arkansas.

Nov 25—Despite 40 points by Georgetown sophomore guard Allen Iverson, Arizona defeats the Hoyas 92–79 to win the preseason National Invitation Tournament in New York City.

Dec 4—With three victories over three ranked opponents, including defending national champion UCLA, Kansas claims the top spot in the polls.

Dec 13—Temple upsets previously unbeaten crosstown rival Villanova, 62–56, in the Philadelphia Spectrum, knocking the Wildcats (7–1) out of the second spot in the national polls.

Jan 2, 1996—The fourth-ranked Tennessee women defeat No. 18 Florida 87–67 for their 69th consecutive home victory, breaking the Division I record set by Auburn from 1986–91.

Jan 14—Marcus Camby, the star center for top-ranked Massachusetts, collapses minutes before the Minutemen are to take the court against St. Bonaventure. He is hospitalized overnight and after a battery of tests prove inconclusive the incident is eventually termed "an isolated episode of altered consciousness."

Jan 19—The Tennessee women's team knocks off second-ranked Vanderbilt 85–82, then follows that victory with a 77–72 triumph over No. 1 Louisiana Tech two days later.

Jan 21—Cincinnati (12–0) falls 70–68 to

Iverson sailed from Georgetown to the NBA.

conference rival Alabama-Birmingham, and surprising Penn State (13–0) loses to Michigan, 67–66, leaving only Massachusetts (16–0) with an unblemished record.

Feb 7—Former UCLA point guard Henry Bibby takes over the head coaching position at USC. The exiting coach, Charlie Parker, improved the team's record from 7–21 the previous year to 11–10, but is nevertheless fired by athletic director Mike Garrett.

Feb 11—Arizona defeats Cincinnati 79–76 on a 65-foot, last second shot by Wildcat Miles Simon.

College Basketball *(Cont.)*

Feb 22—The NCAA suspends Villanova guard Kerry Kittles for his team's final three regular season games for making unauthorized use of a university telephone credit card number.

March 14—March Madness produces its seemingly annual stunning upset as Princeton, seeded 13th, gives retiring coach Pete Carril an ideal sendoff by upsetting fourth seed and defending national champion UCLA, 43–41. The winning bucket comes on Carril's signature play, the backdoor pass. In the West region, 12th seed Drexel upsets Memphis 75–63.

March 17—Unsung Texas Tech proves its 28–1 regular season record is legitimate by trouncing North Carolina 92–73 in the second round of the East regional. Tech forward Darvin Ham breaks the backboard with a dunk in the first half of the game.

March 18—The Sweet 16 for the women's tournament is set as Tennessee qualifies for the 15th time in 15 years by beating Ohio State 97–65. They join such mainstays as defending champs Connecticut, Louisiana Tech and Stanford. San Francisco beats Duke in Durham 64–60 to become the first 12th seed ever to reach the final 16, and No.11 seed Stephen F. Austin advances past Clemson 93–88 in overtime.

March 24—Mississippi State completes a surprising run to the Final Four by upsetting No. 2 seed Cincinnati 73–63 in the Southeast regional final. The Bulldogs will play Syracuse; Kentucky and Massachusetts will decide the other finalist. In the women's tournament Tennessee survives a scare from Virginia to win 52–46 and advance to the semifinals against Connecticut. Stanford and Georgia will square off in the other bracket.

March 28—Nebraska defeats St. Joseph's (Pa.) 60–56 to win the National Invitation Tournament in New York City.

March 31—Tennessee defeats Georgia 83–65 to win the women's national championship. The title is the fourth for Vols coach Pat Summitt; only John Wooden has more.

April 1—Kentucky overcomes 29 points and 10 rebounds by Syracuse forward John Wallace to defeat the Orangemen 76–67 and win the men's NCAA tournament. Kentucky senior guard Tony Delk pours in seven three-pointers and is named the Outstanding Player of the Final Four.

April 3—Georgia Tech freshman point guard Stephon Marbury announces he will enter June's NBA draft. He will be joined in the ensuing months by, among others, Connecticut junior Ray Allen, UMass junior Marcus Camby and Georgetown sophomore Allen Iverson.

College Football

Oct 24, 1995—Coach Tom Osborne announces that Nebraska running back Lawrence Phillips, who has admitted to assaulting Nebraska basketball player Kate McEwen, his ex-girlfriend, will be reinstated to the team.

Oct 28—Nebraska emerges from its cloud of off-field controversy to rout Colorado 44–21 in Boulder, running their record to 8–0 and extending their winning streak to 21 games, currently the longest in major college football. In the Big Ten, Northwestern (7–1) all but guarantees itself a spot in a bowl game with a 17–14 comeback victory over Illinois, and Ohio State holds the No. 4 national ranking with a 56–35 drubbing of Iowa.

Nov 2—Twentieth-ranked Virginia stuns No. 2 Florida State 33–28, handing the Seminoles their first ACC loss after 29 victories.

Nov 4—Northwestern proves its No. 5 ranking is deserved, downing Penn State 21–10 in Evanston.

Nov 11—Ohio State running back Eddie George makes his case for the Heisman—loudly—by rushing for a school-record 314 yards, catching four passes and scoring three touchdowns in the Buckeyes' rout of Iowa.

Nov 11—One of three unbeaten teams in Division I-A, Toledo makes a bid for national recognition as it crushes Akron 41–7 to clinch the Mid-American Conference title and run its record to 9-0-1.

Nov 18—UCLA coach Terry Donahue becomes the alltime Pacific 10 conference leader in coaching wins as the Bruins down archrival USC 24–10. The win also clinches an Aloha Bowl bid for UCLA (7–4).

Nov 18—Alex Van Dyke of Nevada breaks Howard Twilley's 30-year-old NCAA record for receiving yards in a season when he catches 13 passes for 314 yards in a 45–28 victory over San Jose State. His season total stands at 1,874 yards, compared to Twilley's 1,779.

Nov 25—Michigan stuns previously unbeaten, second-ranked Ohio State 31–23 in Ann Arbor, shattering the Buckeye's national title hopes and clearing the way for Northwestern (10–1) to go to its first Rose Bowl since 1948.

Nov 25—Florida quarterback Danny Wuerffel and Iowa State running back Troy Davis crowd the Heisman Trophy picture, which also includes Nebraska quarterback Tommie Frazier and running back Eddie George of Ohio State. Wuerffel throws for 443 yards and four touchdowns as Florida routs Florida State, while Davis finishes the season 2,010 rushing yards. Only four other backs—Marcus Allen (1981), Mike

Rozier ('83), Barry Sanders ('88) and Rashaan Salaam ('94)—have broken the 2,000-yard barrier in a season; all four won the Heisman.

Dec 2—The Southwest Conference closes the curtain on 81 years of competition as Texas beats Texas A&M 16–6, and Houston beats Rice 18–17 in the conference's final games. Baylor, Texas, Texas A&M and Texas Tech will join the new Big 12 conference (formerly the Big Eight) in 1996, with the remaining SWC teams moving to the Western Athletic Conference.

Dec 2—Florida defeats Arkansas 34–3 in the SEC title game to complete a perfect 12–0 regular season. Nebraska, which blanked Oklahoma 37–0 the previous week, finishes 11–0. The two will meet in the Fiesta Bowl on Jan. 2, marking just the third time in history that the regular season has produced two unbeaten, untied teams, ranked them 1-2 in the nation and paired them in a bowl.

Dec 2—Army comes from behind to nip Navy 14–13 and seal their fourth victory in a row against the Midshipmen, the series' longest streak in 48 years.

Dec 9—Ohio State running back Eddie George wins the 1995 Heisman Trophy, outpointing Nebraska quarterback Tommie Frazier 1,460 to 1,196. In other awards presented during the week UCLA's Jonathan Ogden wins the Outland Trophy as the nation's top interior lineman, Florida's Danny Wuerffel wins the Davey O'Brien quarterback award, and Illinois linebacker Kevin Hardy wins the Butkus Award.

Dec 9—North Alabama rolls over Pittsburg (KS) State 27–7 in Florence, Ala., to claim its third straight NCAA Division II title, a feat unprecedented at any level of college football. In the Amos Alonzo Stagg Bowl for the Division III national crown, Wisconsin-LaCrosse routs Rowan (N.J.) 36–7 to complete a perfect 14–0 season.

Dec 14—Northwestern coach Gary Barnett wins the Bear Bryant Award as college football coach of the year.

Dec 16—Montana nips Marshall 22–20 on a 25-yard field goal with 39 seconds remaining to win the Division I-AA national title game. Montana's quarterback, Dave Dickenson, later wins the Walter Payton Award as the top I-AA player in the nation, and the Grizzlies coach, Don Read, is named coach of the year.

Dec 27—Toledo defeats Nevada 40–37 in the Las Vegas Bowl to finish the season at 11-0-1. The game goes to overtime, showcasing college football's brand new bowl tiebreaker system. Toledo wins the overtime coin toss and elects to go on defense, where it holds Nevada, taking possession on the Toledo 25, to a field goal. Toledo then takes over at the Nevada 25 and scores a TD in four plays for the win.

Foes rarely got hold of Heisman winner George.

Jan 1, 1996—Tennessee surprises Ohio State 20–14 in the Citrus Bowl to complete an 11–1 season. Florida State (10–2) upends Notre Dame 31–26 in the Orange Bowl and Colorado (10–2) rips Oregon 38–6 to win the Cotton Bowl.

Jan 2—The much-anticipated Fiesta Bowl clash between No. 1 Nebraska and No. 2 Florida comes to an anticlimax in Tempe, Ariz., as the Cornhuskers embarrass the Gators 62–24 to complete their second straight undefeated season.

Jan 3—Both the Associated Press and the *USA Today*/CNN polls rank 12–0 Nebraska No. 1, giving coach Tom Osborne his second consecutive national title in 22 years as a head coach. The 12–1 Gators finish second in the AP poll but third in the coaches' rankings, where Tennessee (11–1) claims the No. 2 spot.

Jan 2—The University of Texas announces that it is considering legal action against Ron Weaver, 30, who faked his identity to regain college eligibility and play cornerback for the Longhorns in 1995–96. Weaver, who used the social security number of another man to assume a new identity, could be sued for the cost of his scholarship.

Feb 15—The NCAA Rules Committee votes to

institute a tiebreaker in all Division I-A games, effective this year. The new system, which was used in bowl games following the 1995 season, gives each team one possession, starting on the 25-yard line. The game ends when the score is no longer tied after each team has had a chance on offense, or after any score by the defense.

March 8—The NCAA places Mississippi State on probation for one year following an investigation that uncovered improper payments to players by a booster and an assistant coach. The program also faces scholarship reductions and limitations on official recruiting visits.

March 19—Florida State escapes with a light sentence of one year's probation without sanctions as the NCAA issues its ruling on a 1993 scandal involving Seminole players and sports agents.

April 13—Miami linebacker Marlin Barnes and a friend, Timwanika Lumpkins, are found beaten to death in a Coral Gables, Fla., campus apartment. The murders are later determined to be acts of domestic violence unrelated to campus security.

April 17—In a move intended to ease NCAA sanctions against its football program, Michigan State announces that it will forfeit all five of its 1994 victories for using an ineligible player.

April 18—Two days before he is expected to be selected in the NFL draft, former Nebraska quarterback Brook Berringer is killed in a plane crash north of Lincoln, Neb.

May 20—Alabama loses another football scholarship—the 14th the Tide has forfeited for the upcoming year—for failing to notify the NCAA of loans guaranteed to players by a Birmingham, Ala., tire dealer.

July 1—Miami's troubled football program is hit by further scandal as coach Butch Davis suspends linebackers James Burgess and Jeffrey Taylor for the 1996 season for their roles in the June 19 assault of Miami track star Maxwell Voce. They will sit out the '96 season along with Miami receiver Jammi German, who was previously charged in the same incident.

July 22—Representatives of college conferences announce that, beginning in 1998, the Big Ten and Pacific 10 champions, currently committed to playing in the Rose Bowl, will be able to move to another bowl if doing so will create a No. 1 versus No. 2 matchup.

Aug 24—Brigham Young and Texas A&M launch the 1996–97 season in the Pigskin Classic at Provo, Utah. The unranked Cougars stun the No. 12 Aggies 41–37 as quarterback Steve Sarkisian throws for 536 yards and six TDs.

Aug 25—Penn State meets Southern Cal in the Kickoff Classic at Giants Stadium in East Rutherford, N.J. The eighth-ranked Nittany Lions rout the No. 6 Trojans 24–7 behind sophomore tailback Curtis Enis's 241 rushing yards.

Sept 7—Eighteenth-ranked Northwestern, which scored one of last season's early upsets with its victory over Notre Dame, finds the tables turned as it falls to unranked Wake Forest 28–27.

Sept 14—Michigan avenges its famous 1994 Hail Mary defeat to Colorado with a 20–13 victory in Boulder over the fifth-ranked Buffaloes. On the game's final play, Colorado quarterback Koy Detmer launches another prayer to the end zone—where it is tipped away by Michigan.

Sept 16—Citing violations involving recruiting, academics and ethics, the NCAA places the Michigan State program on four years' probation.

Sept 21—The season's first Game of the Century turns out to be less than advertised as the top-ranked Florida Gators beat No. 2 Tennessee 35–29 before a NCAA-record crowd of 107,608 in Knoxville. The game is not nearly as close as the score might indicate as Florida intercepts Volunteer quarterback Peyton Manning four times while building a 35–0 lead.

Sept 21—Arizona State stuns unbeaten two-time defending national champion Nebraska 19–0 in Tempe.

Sept 28—Iowa State's Heisman Trophy candidate Troy Davis rushes for 378 yards and four touchdowns against Missouri. His rushing total is the third highest in Division I history.

Oct 5—Ohio State establishes itself as the team to beat in the Big Ten with a 38–7 trouncing of fourth-ranked Penn State. The win moves the Buckeyes (4–0) to No. 2 in the national polls.

Oct 19—Florida State (5–0) rocks No. 6 Miami 34–16 to claim the No. 2 ranking from Ohio State, a narrow winner over 27-point underdog Wisconsin.

Golf

Oct 29, 1995—Despite shooting a three-over-par 73 in the final round, Billy Mayfair wins the year-ending $3 million Tour Championship in Tulsa. Corey Pavin and Steve Elkington, both of whom also shot final-round 73s, tie for second.

Nov 20—Annika Sorenstam wins the Rolex Player of the Year Award and the Vare Trophy for lowest scoring average, joining Nancy Lopez as the only LPGA players to accomplish that double the year after winning the Rookie of the Year Award.

Dec 6—U.S. Women's Open champion Annika Sorenstam and Greg Norman, who had nine

Top 10 finishes in 16 tournaments, are named 1995 Players of the Year by the Golf Writers Association of America.

Jan 7, 1996—Mark O'Meara holds off Nick Faldo to win the season-opening Mercedes Championships in Carlsbad, Calif.

March 7—Twenty-six-year-old PGA rookie Tim Herron ties the Honda Classic tournament record with a 10-under-par 62 in the first round at Eagle Trace in Coral Springs, Fla.

Mar 31—Hall of Famer Patty Sheehan finally wins the Dinah Shore when she two putts from 126 feet on the final hole for a one-stroke victory.

April 7—Jack Nicklaus collects his 100th professional victory at the Senior Tour Tradition in Scottsdale, Ariz. He shoots a second straight 65 in the final round to defeat Hale Irwin.

April 14—Entering the final round of the Masters with a six-stroke lead over Nick Faldo, Greg Norman suffers one of the most excruciating collapses in golf history. He shoots a 78, relinquishing his lead and falling five strokes behind eventual winner Faldo.

May 12—Long-hitting Brit Laura Davies wins her second LPGA Championship in three years with a final round 70 in Wilmington, Del.

June 2—Annika Sorenstam wins her second consecutive U.S. Women's Open. In Dublin, Ohio, Tom Watson ends a nine-year winless stretch by winning the Memorial.

June 16—Steve Jones taps in for par on the final hole to win the U.S. Open by one stroke over Davis Love III and Tom Lehman, who bogeys the last hole.

Viva Las Vegas: Woods wins his first.

July 7—Dave Stockton holds off a charging Hale Irwin to win the U.S. Senior Open by two strokes.

July 21—Rebounding from his tough loss at the U.S. Open, Tom Lehman wins the 125th British Open at Royal Lytham and St. Anne's by two shots over Ernie Els and Mark McCumber.

Aug 4—Laura Davies shoots a 66 and passes 10 golfers on the final day to win the du Maurier Classic in Edmonton.

Aug 11—PGA Tour money leader Mark Brooks wins his third tournament of the year at the PGA Championship in Louisville.

Aug 25—Tiger Woods wins an unprecedented third straight U.S. Amateur Championship, rallying from two strokes back with three holes to play to defeat Steve Scott of the University of Florida. Two days later the 20-year-old announces his decision to turn pro.

Sept 15—Fred Couples sinks a 25-foot birdie putt to defeat Vijay Singh and propel the U.S to a one-point Presidents Cup victory over the International team.

Sept 15—LPGA rookie Karrie Webb, 21, wins her third tournament of the year, shooting a final round 69 to take the Safeco Classic and wrest the tour money lead from Laura Davies.

Sept 22—The U.S. wins nine of 12 singles matches to retain the Solheim Cup 17–11 over a European team featuring Laura Davies and Annika Sorenstam.

Oct 7—Since placing 60th in his pro debut in Milwaukee on Aug. 29, Tiger Woods has steadily improved, placing 11th, fifth and third in successive tournaments. At the Las Vegas Invitational he continues the upward trend, seizing his first pro victory in a sudden death playoff with Davis Love III.

Oct 13—Tiger Woods ties for third at the Texas Open, earning $81,000 and moving to 34th on the season money list. The top 30 earners qualify for the $3 million Tour Championship Oct. 24–27 in Tulsa.

Oct 20—The legend of Tiger Woods grows as the sensational rookie wins the Disney World/ Oldsmobile Classic with a 21-under-par performance. He finishes tied with Taylor Smith, but Smith is disqualified for using an illegal putter. Woods, who easily qualifies for the Tour Championship with the victory, has won two of the seven tournaments he has entered.

Oct 27, 1995—Mario Lemieux, who returned this season after a 17-month bout with Hodgkin's disease, scores three goals in Pittsburgh's 7–5 win over the New York Islanders, giving him 500 career goals in 605 games. The Penguins superstar is the second-fastest to reach the milestone, trailing Wayne Gretzky, who needed 575 games to score 500.

Nov 1—With hat tricks in his previous two games, Pittsburgh's Mario Lemieux heads to Tampa with a chance to become the first player ever to notch three in a row. He scores no goals but passes off for six assists—one shy of the NHL record—as the Penguins rout the Lightning 10–0.

Yzerman and Detroit won a record 62 games.

Nov 6—Paul Holmgren is dismissed as coach of the Hartford Whalers, who began the season 4–0 but slipped to 5-6-1.

Nov 6—Rangers center Mark Messier registers his 500th career goal as New York defeats Calgary 4–2.

Nov 7—The defending champion Devils, who had talked of moving to Nashville, decide to remain in New Jersey, signing a 12-year lease to stay in the Meadowlands Arena.

Nov 9—Pavel Bure of the Vancouver Canucks is lost for the season after suffering a torn ligament in his right knee during a game against Chicago.

Dec 6—Patrick Roy is traded by Montreal to the Colorado Avalanche in a five-player deal. Roy, who won two Stanley Cups with the Canadiens, exchanged angry words with coach Mario Tremblay following an 11–1 loss to Detroit on Dec. 2. As he skated off the ice he reportedly told team president Ronald Corey, "I've just played my last game for the Canadiens."

Dec 13—Detroit's Paul Coffey becomes the first NHL defenseman to tally 1,000 career assists when he sets up Igor Larionov's first period goal in the Red Wings' 3–1 win over Chicago.

Jan 2, 1996—The New York Rangers announce that goalie Mike Richter will be sidelined for four weeks with a strained groin muscle.

Jan 10—Scotty Bowman earns his 943rd career victory and coaches his 1,613th game, both records, as his Detroit Red Wings blank Dallas 4–0.

Jan 22—Defenseman Ray Bourque of the Boston Bruins scores the winning goal with 38 seconds remaining and is named MVP of the All-Star Game as the Eastern Conference defeats the Western Conference 5–4.

Feb 19—Patrick Roy becomes the second-youngest goalie to reach 300 wins as Colorado defeats the Edmonton Oilers 7–5.

Feb 27—The Los Angeles Kings complete a long-rumored deal with the St. Louis Blues, exchanging Wayne Gretzky, who will be a free agent at season's end, for Patrice Tardif, Craig Johnson, Roman Vopat and two future draft picks.

March 6—Chris Osgood becomes the third goalie to score a goal in an NHL game as he tallies an empty-netter for Detroit, capping a 4–2 win over Hartford.

March 11—With seventy-four-year-old Maurice (Rocket) Richard among the luminaries in attendance, the Montreal Canadiens drop the puck for the last time in the Montreal Forum, their home for the past 72 years. Montreal wins the final game on Forum ice 4–1 over Dallas.

March 14—The Rangers and Kings complete a deal involving seven players, with New York acquiring Jari Kurri, Marty McSorley and Shane Churla in exchange for Ray Ferraro, Ian Laperriere, Nathan La Fayette, prospect Mattias Norstrom and a draft pick.

March 20—Though the NHL doesn't list consecutive goaltending starts as a record, the league announces that Grant Fuhr is the first to make 71 straight starts in a single season as he takes the net against the Dallas Stars. Fuhr's streak is ended at 76 when he hurts his knee in Detroit on March 31.

April 10—The Detroit Red Wings defeat the Winnipeg Jets 5–2 to run their record to 60-13-7, tying the NHL record for wins in a season set by the 1976–77 Montreal Canadiens.

April 11—With a 3–2 victory over Hartford, the Boston Bruins clinch their 29th straight playoff berth, a professional sports record.

April 13—The defending champion New Jersey Devils fail to make the playoffs when they fall to last-place Ottowa 5–2 at home. They are the first Stanley Cup winners to miss the playoffs the following year since the 1969–70 Montreal Canadiens.

April 14—The Detroit Red Wings close the regular season with a 5–1 win against Dallas for a record 62nd victory.

April 15—The NHL announces that league attendance surpassed 17 million for the first time, with the Chicago Blackhawks becoming the first club ever to average more than 20,000 fans per game.

April 17—The Florida Panthers, who missed the playoffs by a single point in each of the franchise's first two seasons, win their first ever playoff game, downing Boston 6–3.

April 24—Petr Nedved scores for Pittsburgh at 19:15 of the fourth overtime to give the Penguins a 3–2 victory over Washington, evening their Eastern Conference series 2–2. Penguins goalie Ken Wregget stops Joe Juneau on a penalty shot—the first ever in overtime of a playoff game—in the second extra session.

April 28—The Winnipeg Jets play their last game in the Winnipeg Arena, losing 6–1 to Detroit in the sixth and final game of the Western Conference quarterfinals. The Jets will begin play next season as the Phoenix Coyotes.

May 16—Thirteen-year veteran Steve Yzerman scores at 1:15 of the second overtime, lifting the Red Wings to a 1–0 victory over St. Louis in Game 7 of the Western Conference semifinal.

May 29—Led by Joe Sakic's two goals and one assist, the Colorado Avalanche defeat top-seeded Detroit—which went 62-13-7 in the regular season—4–1 to win the Western Conference final in six games and earn the franchise's first trip to the Stanley Cup final.

June 1—The Florida Panthers advance to the Stanley Cup final in just their third year as a franchise, defeating Pittsburgh 3–1 in Game 7 of the Eastern Conference final. The Panthers hold Pittsburgh's high-scoring duo of Mario Lemieux and Jaromir Jagr to a combined total of two goals in the series.

June 3—Claude Lemieux of the Colorado Avalanche, who was MVP of the 1995 playoffs, is suspended for the first two games of the Stanley Cup final for his hit on Detroit's Kris Draper in Game 6 of the Western Conference final. Draper suffered a broken jaw, a broken nose and a deep facial laceration when he was slammed into the boards.

June 5—The Stanley Cup final begins as the Colorado Avalanche beat the Florida Panthers 3–1. Avalanche goalie Patrick Roy stops 25 shots and center Mike Ricci keys a three-goal second period.

June 6—Colorado trounces Florida 8–1 to take a 2–0 lead in the Stanley Cup final. The Avalanche's Peter Forsberg becomes the sixth player in Finals history to score three goals in one period when he records a hat trick in the first period. Joe Sakic ties the Stanley Cup record for assists in a game with four.

June 10—Colorado secures its first Stanley Cup

Sakic led Colorado to its first Stanley Cup title.

championship with a thrilling 1–0 victory over Florida in triple overtime. Patrick Roy stops 63 shots and his counterpart for Florida, John Vanbiesbrouck, turns aside 55, but is beaten on the 56th by Colorado defenseman Uwe Krupp at 4:31 of the third overtime. Colorado's Joe Sakic, who led all playoff scorers with 34 points, including an NHL-record six game-winning goals, wins the Conn Smythe Trophy as MVP of the playoffs.

June 10—Former Boston Bruin Bobby Orr's Stanley Cup-winning overtime goal against St. Louis in 1970 is voted the NHL's Greatest Moment. Orr's goal was captured in a famous photograph of the legendary defenseman sailing, parellel to the ice, through the crease.

June 19—Pittsburgh's Mario Lemieux, in his first year back after battling Hodgkin's disease, wins the regular season MVP award.

July 21—The New York Rangers sign free agent Wayne Gretzky, 35, to a two-year, $8 million contract.

Sept 5—Citing a degenerative hip condition, Cam Neely of the Boston Bruins retires after 13 NHL seasons.

Sept 14—The U.S. beats Canada 5–2 in Montreal to win the World Cup of Hockey final two games to one. The victory ranks with the 1980 Olympic gold medal triumph as the greatest in U.S. hockey history. "It's a crushed locker room,"

said Canada's Wayne Gretzky afterwards. "It's probably a crushed country. It's devastating."

Oct 15—The Phoenix Coyotes sign former Blackhawks center Jeremy Roenick to a five-year, $20 million contract.

Oct 19—The Dallas Stars defeat Toronto 2–0 to run their record to 7–1, tops in the NHL this season.

Horse Racing

Oct 28, 1995—Cigar runs through the mud at Belmont and into modern racing history when he wins the $3 million Breeders' Cup Classic by 2½ lengths over L'Carriere. The victory completes an undefeated season and secures a single-season earnings record of $4,819,800 for the five-year-old bay.

Oct 28—Mike Smith rides Unbridled's Song to victory in the Breeders' Cup Juvenile at Belmont Park, while Jerry Bailey drives My Flag through the stretch to win the Juvenile Fillies. In the Sprint, Desert Stormer leads from wire to wire with Kent Desormeaux up; favored filly Ridgewood Pearl of Ireland leads a 1-2-3 sweep for Europe in the Mile; and Northern Spur, also from Ireland, wins the Turf.

Jan 11, 1996—Cigar is the unanimous choice for champion older horse as the Eclipse Awards are announced; the five-year-old's owner, trainer and jockey—Allen Paulson, Bill Mott and Jerry

Editor's Note gave Lukas his third straight Belmont.

Bailey, respectively—also win Eclipses.

Feb 24—Built for Pleasure, whose odds are 143–1, beats Kentucky Derby favorite Unbridled's Song by a neck to win the Fountain of Youth Stakes.

March 16—Unbridled's Song firmly reestablishes himself as a Derby favorite with a 5¾-length victory in the Florida Derby.

March 27—Cigar wins the richest purse ever at the $4 million Dubai World Cup, holding off Soul of the Matter to win by half a length. The victory is Cigar's 14th in a row.

April 6—Cavonnier, a 10–1 fifth choice, wins the $1 million Santa Anita Derby.

April 13—Unbridled's Song wins the Wood Memorial, his final tuneup for the Kentucky Derby.

May 4—Grindstone defeats Cavonnier by a nose to win the Kentucky Derby's first photo finish since 1959. The injured Unbridled's Song finishes fifth.

MICHAEL MARTEN

Horse Racing *(Cont.)*

May 18—Bumped off of his Kentucky Derby mount, Prince of Thieves, by trainer D. Wayne Lukas, jockey Pat Day rides Louis Quatorze to victory in the 121st running of the Preakness Stakes. The win, Day's third straight in the Preakness and fifth overall, ends Lukas's streak of Triple Crown victories at six.

June 8—Editor's Note bests Skip Away by a length to win the 128th running of the Belmont Stakes, handing trainer D. Wayne Lukas his third straight victory in the race.

July 13—Cigar wins the $1.1 million dollar Citation Challenge in Chicago for his 16th consecutive victory, tying the modern record. In his next race, on Aug. 10 at the Pacific Classic, Cigar's streak is ended by 39–1 long shot Dare and Go.

Aug 3—Continentalvictory becomes the first filly to win the first two legs of trotting's Triple Crown when she wins the $1.2 million Hambletonian.

Sept 19—Harness driver Jack Moiseyev wins the second Little Brown Jug of his career.

Sept 28—Jockey Frankie Dettori wins a record seven times in one day at London's Ascot racetrack, at accumulative odds of 25,095–1. His astonishing day costs bookmakers at least $47 million, one third of their annual profit.

Oct 2—Just two days before her bid to become the first filly in U.S. horse racing to win a triple crown, Continentalvictory is scratched from the Kentucky Futurity. A combination of injury and surging hormones leads to the move.

Oct 5—Three-year-old colt Skip Away stuns Cigar by a head to win the $1 million Jockey Club Gold Cup at Belmont Park.

Motor Sports

Oct 29, 1995—Having already clinched his second straight F1 championship, Germany's Michael Schumacher ties Nigel Mansell's record of nine wins in a season by taking the Japanese Grand Prix in Suzuka. He fails to break the record when he crashes in the Nov. 12 season finale.

Nov 12—Dale Earnhardt wins the NASCAR season finale in Atlanta but Jeff Gordon, needing only to avoid a last-place finish to secure his first Winston Cup title, places 32nd and finishes 34 points ahead of Earnhardt for the season. Gordon, 24, becomes NASCAR's second-youngest champion; Bill Rexford won the 1950 season title when he was 23.

Dec 18—IndyCar owners, who have been feuding since summer with the new Indy Racing League, announce they will stage their own race opposite the Indianapolis 500. Titled the U.S. 500, the race will go off on May 26 at Michigan International Speedway.

Jan 27, 1996—The Indy Racing League, established by Indianapolis Motor Speedway president Tony George, makes its debut in Orlando with the Indy 200. Buzz Calkins, 25, wins the race in his Reynard-Ford.

Feb 18—Holding off a surging Dale Earnhardt over the final mile, Dale Jarrett wins his second Daytona 500 in four years.

Feb 25—Dale Earnhardt and Jarrett again duel to the finish, this time of the Rockingham 500, with Earnhardt coming out on top for a share of the season points lead.

Feb 25—CART founder Roger Penske and Indy Motor Speedway president Tony George meet to discuss ways to bridge the chasm that has split IndyCar racing. They emerge from their informal sessions without progress.

March 3—Jimmy Vasser wins IndyCar's season-opening Grand Prix of Miami.

March 10—Former IndyCar champion Jacques Villeneuve makes his Formula One debut at the Australian Grand Prix, finishing second to Damon Hill of Great Britain.

March 24—Defending Winston Cup champion Jeff Gordon continues to surge after a slow start to his season, winning the Darlington 400 over Dale Jarrett, who clips the wall with nine laps to go. The win is Gordon's second in three weeks. He wins the following weekend in the rain-shortened Bristol 500.

April 7—Damon Hill wins his third straight F1 race, defeating Williams-Renault teammate Jacques Villeneuve by 12 seconds at the Argentina Grand Prix.

April 21—Terry Labonte starts his 514th consecutive NASCAR race at the Martinsville 500, breaking Richard Petty's record. Rusty Wallace takes the checkered flag.

May 17—Six days after winning the pole position for his 15th Indy 500, Scott Brayton is killed during a practice run when a flat tire sends his car into the wall at 230 mph.

May 26—Buddy Lazier, who suffered 16 fractures in his lower back and pelvis during a crash two months earlier, wins the 80th Indy 500.

May 26—Season points leader Jimmy Vasser picks his way through a 12-car crash at the start of the race to win the inaugural U.S. 500 in Michigan.

July 14—On a tragic day in which eight drivers are killed during races around the world, IndyCar rookie Jeff Krosnoff dies in a crash after touching wheels with Stefan Johansson's car in the Toronto Molson-Indy.

July 30—Emerson Fittipaldi undergoes a successful five-hour operation to repair a fractured vertebra in his neck suffered two days earlier in the crash-filled Brooklyn 500 in Michigan.

Aug 18—Dale Jarrett enters the Winston Cup title picture when he wins the Brooklyn 400 at Michigan International Speedway to pull within 137 points of season leader Terry Labonte.

Sept 1—Dale Jarrett misses a chance at a $1 million bonus when he hits an oil spot on the 46th lap of the Southern 500. The Winston Million is awarded to any driver who wins three of NASCAR's four premier events; Jarrett had won the Daytona 500 and the World 600 in Charlotte,

N.C. Jeff Gordon wins the race for his seventh victory of the season.

Sept 8—Jimmy Vasser wraps up the CART PPG Cup season title when he finishes fourth at the Grand Prix of Monterey.

Sept 29—NASCAR runs for the last time at North Wilkesboro (N.C.) Speedway after holding 72 races there. Jeff Gordon wins for his 10th victory of the season, increasing his points lead to 111 over Terry Labonte.

Oct 13—Damon Hill clinches his first Formula One championship in style, winning the season-ending Japanese Grand Prix at Suzuka.

Olympics

Dec 13, 1995—NBC pays $2.3 billion for the U.S. television rights to the 2004, 2006 and 2008 Olympic Games, adding those to the three Olympics the network already owned (1996, 2000 and 2002).

Jan 3, 1996—North Korea becomes the 197th country to accept an invitation to take part in the 1996 Olympics, making the Atlanta Games the first in the postwar era with perfect attendance.

Jan 17—F. Don Miller, executive director of the United States Olympic Committee from 1973 to 1984, dies of cancer at the age of 75.

Jan 26—Charles Jewtraw, who won the first event at the first Winter Olympic Games, dies at the age of 95 in Hobe Sound, Fla. Jewtraw won the gold medal in 500-meter speedskating at the 1924 Games in Chamonix, France.

April 14—The final two spots on Dream Team III, the U.S. men's Olympic basketball team, go to an expected choice, Sacramento King guard Mitch Richmond, and an unexpected one, Phoenix Sun forward Charles Barkley, a veteran of Dream Team I.

April 14—At meetings in San Diego, the USOC's board of directors votes unanimously to pass the world's toughest anti-doping program, under which athletes in all 41 Olympic and Pan-American sports will be subject to no-notice, out-of-competition testing.

May 8—The International Olympic Committee announces that it will require all Olympic athletes to waive their legal rights and agree to take any Olympic disputes—including disputes over the results of drug testing—to a 12-member arbitration panel for a binding ruling.

May 19—The Olympic torch arrives in Prague, Okla., the birthplace of Jim Thorpe, where it is cheered by 200 people and carried up to the place where Thorpe was born in 1888 by his granddaughter, Dagmar Thorpe.

June 13—It is announced that 400-meter

PETER READ MILLER

Lewis grabbed his ninth career gold in Atlanta.

hurdler Danny Harris tested positive for cocaine at a meet in Rio de Janeiro on May 5. Since the positive test is Harris's second—he served a two-year suspension from 1992 through '94—Harris now faces a lifetime suspension from the sport.

June 16—Unlucky Kim Batten, the world record holder in the 400-meter hurdles, overcomes a late March ankle injury and makes the U.S. Olympic team, winning her specialty in 53.81.

June 16—Venus Lacy, the 6'4" center who played college basketball at Louisiana Tech, beats out Kara Wolters to become the 12th and final player named to the U.S. women's Olympic basketball team.

June 17—The saga of injury-prone Mary Slaney

takes a happy turn when she kicks to a second-place finish (behind Lynn Jennings) in the 5,000 meters at the U.S. Olympic Trials. The 37-year-old Slaney's time is 15:29.39.

June 18—Gymnast Dominique Moceanu announces that she will not compete in the following week's Olympic trials in Boston due to a four-inch stress fracture in her right leg. Moceanu, 14, plans to petition to be included on the U.S. team in Atlanta, as does five-time Olympic medalist Shannon Miller, who has an injured left wrist. The following day USA Gymnastics rules that that route to the Olympics will at least be possible. The body plans to weigh the pair's scores from U.S. nationals, which ended June 8, against those of trials competitors.

June 19—Thirty-four-year-old Carl Lewis finishes third in the long jump at the U.S. Olympic Trials in Atlanta with a jump of 27' 2¾". Finishing ahead of Lewis are world record–holder Mike Powell (27' 6½") and Joe Greene (a wind-aided 27' 4½").

June 23—Michael Johnson sets his first world outdoor record, running 200 meters in 19.66 to snip .06 off Pietro Mennea's 17-year-old record.

July 19—The Summer Olympic Games commence in Atlanta, with U.S. basketball player Teresa Edwards taking the Olympic oath on behalf of the athletes during the Opening Ceremony.

July 20—The U.S. men's basketball team steamrolls Argentina 96–68, but the most exciting game is Lithuania's 83–81 win over Croatia in double overtime. At the Georgia Tech Aquatic Center, it is a night of firsts in more ways than one. Michelle Smith of Ireland captures her country's first swimming medal, winning the 400 individual medley in a time of 4:39.18. Fred DeBurghgraeve sets a world record for the 100 breaststroke (1:00.60) in the morning prelims and then captures Belgium's first swimming gold in the final with a time of 1:00.65. Danyon Loader wins New Zealand's first swimming gold, in the 200 freestyle. China's Le Jingyi win the women's 100 free in 54.50.

July 21—In morning prelims at the pool, Penelope Heyns of South Africa breaks her own world record for the 100 breaststroke, clocking 1:07.02. At night Heyns wins the gold medal in 1:07.72. Tom Dolan wins the U.S.'s first gold medal of the Games, edging University of Michigan teammate Eric Namesnik 4:14.90 to 4:15.25 in the 400 individual medley. Dennis Hall of the U.S. wins the silver medal in the 125½-pound class of Greco-Roman wrestling, losing 4–1 in the final to Yuri Melnichenko of Kazakhstan. Cyclist Jeannie Longo-Ciprelli of France, 37, easily wins the women's road race.

July 22—At the Georgia Tech Aquatic Center

Michelle Smith of Ireland wins her second gold medal, clocking 4:07.25 for the 400 free. In the men's 100 free Aleksandr Popov of Russia edges Gary Hall of the U.S. 48.74 to 48.81. U.S. teammates Beth Botsford and Whitney Hedgepeth finish 1–2 in the 100 backstroke, while the U.S. 400 freestyle relay team of Jenny Thompson, Catherine Fox, Angel Martino and Amy Van Dyken also wins the gold. Elsewhere, the Russian men win the team gold in gymnastics, and the Pocket Hercules, Naim Suleymanoglu, wins his third weightlifting gold, lifting a world-record 738 pounds in the 141-pound class.

July 23—In the Games' most dramatic moment so far, gritty Kerri Strug lands her second vault on a badly sprained ankle, takes a few agonized hops and then falls to the floor in tears, to be carried off the floor by Bela Karolyi. She earns 9.712 points to remove all doubt that the U.S. team would win the gold medal. At the Georgia Tech Aquatic Center, Amy Van Dyken of the U.S. edges Liu Limin of China in the 100 butterfly, and her U.S. teammate Jeff Rouse easily takes the gold in the 100 backstroke, in 54.10. The U.S. men's 400 freestyle relay team of Jon Olsen, Josh Davis, Bradley Schumacher and Gary Hall Jr., wins the gold, as does breaststroker Penelope Heyns of South Africa in the 200 breast.

July 24—Michelle Smith of Ireland wins her third gold medal in swimming, taking the women's 200 individual medley in 2:13.93. Denis Pankratov of Russia hammers the world record for the 100 butterfly, clocking 52.27 to win the gold medal. Li Xiaoshuang of China wins the men's all-around title in gymnastics, with Alexei Nemov of Russia second and defending champion Vitaly Scherbo of Belarus third.

July 25—The U.S. is shut out of the medals in the women's all-around gymnastics competition, as Lilia Podkopayeva of the Ukraine takes the gold ahead of Gina Gogean of Romania. In the pool Brooke Bennett, a 16-year-old from Plant City, Florida, wins the 800 freestyle in 8:27.89. In the 50 free Aleksandr Popov of Russia again beats Gary Hall Jr. of the U.S., 22.13 to 22.26.

July 26—Track and field competition gets under way at Olympic Stadium with Randy Barnes, the world record holder in the shot put, beating his U.S. teammate John Godina with a final throw of 70' 11". On the final day of swimming, Amy Van Dyken wins her second individual gold medal, edging Le Jingyi of China in the 50 free, 24.87 to 24.90. Van Dyken's U.S. teammates Brad Bridgewater and Tripp Schwenk go 1–2 in the 200 backstroke, while the U.S. men's 400 medley relay team set a world record of 3:34.84 in easily winning the gold.

July 27—At about 1:12 A.M. a pipe bomb

explodes in Centennial Park in downtown Atlanta. The blast kills Alice Hawthorne, a 44-year-old mother from Albany, Ga., and injures scores of others. A Turkish photographer dies of a heart attack while rushing to report on the blast. The following morning, officials decide that the Games will go on. That night, Donovan Bailey of Canada wins the men's 100-meter dash in a world record 9.84. Gail Devers of the U.S. narrowly wins the women's 100 as the photo shows that she has dipped her left shoulder across the line a fraction of an inch ahead of Merlene Ottey of Jamaica, who must be content with the silver medal and clocking the same time as Devers, a 10.94. Devers's significant other, Kenny Harrison, wins the triple jump with a leap of 59' 4¼".

July 28—Fatuma Roba of Ethiopia easily wins the women's marathon, running most of the way by herself to finish in 2:26:05. Wang Junxia of China wins the women's 5,000 in 14:59.88, as co-favorite Sonia O'Sullivan drops out. Charles Austin of the U.S. wins the men's high jump, clearing 7' 10". Ghadaa Shouaa of Syria takes the women's heptathlon with a score of 6,780 points. Elsewhere, the U.S. baseball team mounts a comeback but still falls to Cuba 10–8.

July 29—On his third attempt in the long jump, Carl Lewis, at age 35, leaps 27' 10¾", a jump that will stand up for Lewis's fourth gold medal in the long jump, tying him with discus thrower Al Oerter as the only track and field athletes to win four golds in the same event. Minutes before the conclusion of the long jump, Michael Johnson wins the 400 in an Olympic record 43.49 but is overshadowed by Lewis. Allen Johnson of the U.S. takes the 110-meter hurdles, running 12.95 to teammate Mark Crear's 13.09. Tiny Haile Gebrselassie of Ethiopia hangs on to beat Paul Tergat of Kenya in the 10,000. The U.S. women's softball team earns a shot at the gold medal by beating China 1–0 behind Lisa Fernandez's three-hit, 13-strikeout performance. Veteran U.S. gymnast Shannon Miller wins the gold medal in the balance beam, earning a score of 9.862. Jair Lynch of the U.S. gets the silver in the parallel bars. Xiong Ni of China completes his collection of Olympic diving medals by beating teammate Yu Zhuocheng in the 3-meter springboard.

July 30—Centennial Park reopens in the morning. Dot Richardson's two-run homer down the right field line gives the U.S. a 3–1 victory over China and the inaugural gold medal in the new Olympic sport of women's softball. The U.S. women's volleyball team loses to Cuba 15–1, 15–10, 15–12 and drops from medal contention.

July 31—Vebjørn Rodal of Norway wins the fastest 800 in Olympic history, in 1:42.58. Gail Devers once again fails to finish off a 100 dash and hurdles double, finishing fourth behind

Russian-born Lyudmila Enquist, now competing for Sweden. Deon Hemmings of Jamaica runs 52.82 to beat U.S. teammates Kim Batten and Tonja Buford-Bailey in the 400 hurdles. Elsewhere, Fu Mingxia of China becomes the first woman to sweep the Olympic diving golds in 36 years when she wins the 3-meter springboard event. Cyclist Pascal Richard of Switzerland wins the 137.8-mile road race by a bike's length over Denmark's Rolf Soernsen. U.S. wrestlers Kendall Cross and Kurt Angle win gold medals in the 125½-pound and 220-pound weight classes, respectively.

Aug 1—In the most scintillating performance of the Games, Michael Johnson completes his 200/400 double in astonishing fashion, destroying his six-week-old record for the 200 with a time of 19.32. Marie-José Pérec completes the same double by winning the 200 in a relatively slow 22.12. Decathlete Dan O'Brien holds off young German Frank Buseman by throwing a personal best of 219' 6" in the ninth event, the javelin, and then clocking a brave 44:45.89 in the event he likes least, the 1500. In baseball semifinals, Japan beats the U.S. 11–2 and Cuba beats Nicaragua 8–1, relegating the U.S. to the bronze medal match against Nicaragua. Tiffeny Milbrett scores in the 68th minute to give the U.S. women's soccer team a 2–1 victory over China before the largest crowd ever to watch a women's game—76,481 people packed into Sanford Stadium in Athens, Ga.

Aug 2—Omar Linares hits three home runs to lift Cuba to a 13–9 win over Japan in the gold medal baseball game. The U.S. baseball team completes a disappointing Olympic tournament by beating Nicaragua 10–3 for the bronze medal. In freestyle wrestling Tom Brands wins the gold medal in the 136.5-pound class. Lindsay Davenport of the U.S. wins the gold in women's singles tennis. The gold in team synchronized swimming goes to the U.S., as does the gold in men's team archery. At Olympic Stadium, 34-year-old Jackie Joyner-Kersee rallies with a final jump of 22' 11" to take the bronze medal in the long jump behind surprise winner Chioma Ajunwa of Nigeria.

Aug 3—At Olympic Stadium the U.S. men's 4 x 100 relay team, distracted all week by the debate over whether or not to include Carl Lewis, finishes a distant second to Canada. The U.S. sweep the women's 4 x 100 relay plus both 4 x 400's. In the men's 1500, Noureddine Morceli of Algeria survives a mid-race crash that brings down his top rival, Hicham El Guerrouj, and goes on to win his first Olympic gold, in 3:35.78. Svetlana Masterkova of Russia wins her second gold medal, in the women's 1500, in 4:00.83, and Venuste Niyongabo of Burundi wins the men's 5,000 in 13:07.96. Andre Agassi wins the gold medal in men's singles tennis, beating Sergei Bruguera of Spain 6–2, 6–3, 6–1. Felix Savón of Cuba outpoints David Defiagbon of Canada 20–2 to claim his second straight Olympic boxing gold medal in the 200-pound division. Dream Team III fights off Yugoslavia 95–69 to win the gold medal in men's basketball. Cuba wins the gold in women's volleyball.

Aug 4—Fighting in the 156-pound division, David Reid becomes the only U.S. boxer to win a gold medal, knocking out Alfredo Duvergel of Cuba while trailing 16–6 in the third round. Josia

Thugwane wins the closest marathon in Olympic history, finishing the tough Atlanta course in 2:12:36, only three seconds ahead of Lee Bong-ju of South Korea. In the championship game, the U.S. women's basketball team gets 29 points from Lisa Leslie and crushes Brazil 111–87 to win the gold medal. In closing ceremonies featuring B.B. King, Little Richard, Tito Puente, Trisha Yearwood, Gloria Estefan and Wynton Marsalis, the Atlanta Games draw to a close. The U.S. tops the medals chart with 101 medals, 44 of them gold.

Pro Basketball

JOHN BIEVER

Free agency abounded but Miller stayed put.

Dec 4—NBA referees vote 27–26 to accept the league's final job proposal.

Dec 6—The league announces that Dallas Maverick forward Roy Tarpley has tested positive for alcohol for the third time and bans him, nullifying his five-year, $23 million contract.

Dec 7—Denver guard Mahmoud Abdul-Rauf scores an NBA season-high 51 points in the Nuggets' 124–119 win over Utah.

Dec 12—NBA referees show up for work for the first time since the beginning of the season.

Dec 17—Orlando's Shaquille O'Neal scores 32 points with 11 rebounds but his return is spoiled by the Toronto Raptors, who beat the Magic 110–93.

Dec 18—The 6–14 Minnesota Timberwolves fire coach Bill Blair and replace him with general manager Flip Saunders.

Dec 19—Pat Riley returns to New York as the coach of the Miami Heat, and the Knicks make him pay, whipping the Heat 89–70.

Jan 9, 1996—The Toronto Raptors set an NBA record by not making one of their three free-throw attempts in their 92–91 loss to the Charlotte Hornets.

Oct 24, 1995—Orlando's Shaquille O'Neal injures his right thumb during the Magic's 106–91 preseason win over the Miami Heat. He will not be able to play for six to eight weeks.

Nov 1—NBA referees reject a league proposal that would have given them a 15% pay increase, making them sports' highest-paid officials.

Nov 3—The Miami Heat get Alonzo Mourning, Pete Myers and LeRon Ellis from the Charlotte Hornets in a trade for Glen Rice, Khalid Reeves, Matt Geiger and a 1996 first-round draft pick.

Nov 30—The New Jersey Nets trade Derrick Coleman, Sean Higgins and Rex Walters to the Philadelphia 76ers for Shawn Bradley, Tim Perry and Greg Graham.

Jan 16—The Phoenix Suns, who have a record of 14–19, replace coach Paul Westphal with Cotton Fitzsimmons.

Jan 30—Magic Johnson ends his 4½-year retirement, scoring 19 points and getting eight rebounds and 10 assists in the Lakers' 128–118 win over Golden State.

Jan 30—The Chicago Bulls beat the Houston Rockets 98–87 to go 13–0 for Jan., becoming the seventh NBA team to go undefeated for an entire calendar month.

Feb 5—The Basketball Hall of Fame names six inductees, including George Gervin, Gail Goodrich, David Thompson, George Yardley, Nancy Lieberman-Cline and the late Yugoslav star Kresimir Cosic.

Feb 8—The New York Knicks trade forwards Charles Smith and Monty Williams to the San Antonio Spurs for forward J.R. Reid, forward/center Brad Lohaus and a first-round draft pick.

Feb 11—At the NBA All-Star Game, Michael Jordan wins MVP honors by shooting 8 for 11 and finishing with 20 points and four rebounds while leading the East to a 129–118 win over the West.

Feb 12—NBA owners take less than two minutes to approve a five-year contract for commissioner David Stern that is worth more than $40 million.

Feb 19—Charles Barkely grabs his 10,000th rebound in the Phoenix Suns' 98–94 overtime defeat of the Vancouver Grizzlies to become the 10th NBA player to accumulate 20,000 points and 10,000 rebounds.

Feb 20—In the fourth quarter of the Utah Jazz's defeat of the Boston Celtics, John Stockton makes two steals to become the NBA's alltime leader in steals, with 2,311, one more than Maurice Cheeks.

Feb 20—By beating the Philadelphia 76ers 123–104, the Orlando Magic set a league record by winning their 28th straight home game this season.

Feb 21—A record for futility is tied when the Philadelphia 76ers score just 57 points in losing to the Miami Heat, who score 66. The 76ers, who are 10–41, make only 22 of 69 field goals and commit 19 turnovers.

Feb 22—The Miami Heat trade forward Kevin Willis and guard Bimbo Coles to Golden State for guard Tim Hardaway and forward Chris Gatling, and deal Billy Owens and Kevin Gamble to Sacramento for Walt Williams and Tyrone Corbin. Elsewhere, Minnesota sends Christian Laettner and Sean Rooks to Atlanta for Andrew Lang and Spud Webb.

Feb 25—Portland guard Rod Strickland fails to show up for a game against Detroit and is suspended indefinitely by the Trail Blazers.

Feb 25—New York Knick forward J.R. Reid elbows Phoenix forward A.C. Green in the face, and the following day is suspended for two games and fined $10,000.

Feb 27—The Chicago Bulls notch their 50th victory earlier in the season than any other team, beating Minnesota 120–99.

March 4—Rod Strickland returns to the Portland Trail Blazers after a six-game suspension that cost him $166,830.

March 8—The New York Knicks fire coach Don Nelson, replacing him with Jeff VanGundy.

March 10—The Orlando Magic win their 39th straight home game, an NBA record, by beating the Phoenix Suns 122–106 at Orlando Arena.

March 12—The league suspends Mahmoud Abdul-Rauf indefinitely for refusing, because of his Islamic faith, to stand during the national anthem. Two days later a compromise is reached when Abdul-Rauf says he will stand and pray during the anthem.

March 16—After earning his third ejection of the season in a game with New Jersey, Chicago Bull bad boy Dennis Rodman headbutts referee Ted Bernhardt. The league suspends him for six games and fines him $20,000.

March 26—The Orlando Magic lose their first home game since March 14, 1995, when they are blown out by the Los Angeles Lakers 113–91.

April 7—Robert Parish of Charlotte, 42, plays in his 1,561st NBA game, a 93–89 Hornet win over Cleveland, breaking Kareem Abdul-Jabbar's league record.

April 8—The Charlotte Hornets snap Chicago's NBA-record home win streak at 44, beating the Bulls 98–97.

April 9—In Denver, Los Angeles Laker point guard Nick Van Exel shoves referee Ronnie Garretson onto the scoring table after getting ejected in a 98–91 Laker loss to the Nuggets. He is suspended for seven games and fined $25,000.

April 14—The Chicago Bulls win their 69th game, tying the NBA record for wins in a season, when they whip Cleveland 98–72.

April 14—Laker superstar Magic Johnson bumps referee Scott Foster during a game with the Phoenix Suns and the following day is suspended for three games and fined $62,500.

April 16—The Chicago Bulls beat the Milwaukee Bucks 86–80 to win their record-breaking 70th game of the season.

April 18—Dennis Scott makes an NBA-record 11 three-point shots (in 17 attempts) to lead the Orlando Magic past Atlanta 119–104.

April 21—The Chicago Bulls finish their season with a 103–93 win over Washington that makes their record 72–10.

April 22—The Toronto Raptors fire coach Brendan Malone, replacing him with assistant coach Darrell Walker, and the New Jersey Nets fire Butch Beard. No replacement is named.

April 29—Kobe Bryant announces that he plans to go right from Lower Merion (Pa.) High to the NBA.

May 7—Phil Jackson, who coached the Chicago Bulls to a record 72–10 season, wins NBA Coach of the Year honors.

May 12—The Seattle Sonics knock the two-time defending champion Houston Rockets out of the playoffs, beating them 114–107.

May 13—The Philadelphia 76ers fire coach John Lucas after the team goes 42–122 over the past two seasons.

May 14—Magic Johnson announces he's retiring again.

May 15—Damon Stoudamire, who averaged 19 points and 9.3 assists for the expansion Toronto Raptors, wins Rookie of the Year honors.

May 20—Michael Jordan wins MVP honors for a fourth time, by a record margin.

May 27—Chicago knocks Orlando out of the playoffs, beating them 106–101 behind Michael Jordan's 45 points.

June 2—Seattle ousts Utah, beating the Jazz 90–86.

June 6—The New Jersey Nets announce the hiring of UMass coach John Calipari.

June 13—Denver trades Mahmoud Abdul-Rauf to Sacramento for Sarunas Marciulionis and the 37th pick in the draft. The Nuggets also trade Jalen Rose, Reggie Williams and the 10th pick to Indiana for Mark Jackson and Ricky Pierce.

June 16—The Chicago Bulls win the NBA title, beating Seattle 87–75 in the sixth game of the NBA finals. Michael Jordan, who has averaged 27.3 points per game, wins MVP honors.

June 20—Phil Jackson signs a one-year, $2.5 million contract with the Bulls.

June 26—The Philadelphia 76ers make Allen Iverson the first pick in the NBA draft.

July 13—Michael Jordan signs a $25 million, one-year contract with the Bulls.

July 15—Atlanta signs center Dikembe Mutombo to a five-year deal worth $50 million.

July 18—Shaquille O'Neal signs a seven-year, $121 million contract with the Los Angeles Lakers.

July 31—The NBA disapproves Juwan Howard's $100 million contract with Miami on the grounds that it violates the league's salary cap.

Aug 5—The Chicago Bulls announce the signing of Dennis Rodman to a one-year deal worth slightly less than $10 million.

Aug 18—The Houston Rockets obtain Charles Barkley and Sam Cassell from the Phoenix Suns for Robert Horry, Mark Bryant and Chucky Brown.

Sept 25—Robert Parish, 43, signs a two-year contract with Chicago and thus starts his NBA-record 21st season.

Sept 30—On the day Indiana opens training camp, Reggie Miller, the last of the marquee NBA free agents, signs a four-year, $36 million contract.

Pro Football

Oct 29, 1995—Jerry Rice of the San Francisco 49ers surpasses James Lofton as the leading NFL pass receiver of all time by grabbing eight passes for 108 yards, bringing his career total to 14,040, 36 yards more than Lofton.

Oct 29—The Carolina Panthers defeat New England 20–17 for their third victory of the season, more than any first-year expansion team ever.

Oct 29—Jets kicker Nick Lowery, with a field goal and one PAT, becomes the third player in NFL history to score more than 16,000 points.

Nov 6—Cleveland owner Art Modell announces his intention to move the Browns to Baltimore in time for the 1996 season. A new stadium with 108 private suites and 7,500 club seats, a favorable 30-year lease with the city and up to $75 million in moving expenses are the major incentives from the city of Baltimore, whose beloved Colts had departed for Indianapolis in 1984.

Nov 5—Carolina engineers the upset of the season, defeating the Niners 13–7.

Nov 6—Dallas owner Jerry Jones files an antitrust suit against the NFL as a response to the NFL's earlier lawsuit against him, in which the league charged that Jones's deals with Pepsi and Nike violated the NFL Properties agreement.

Nov 12—In a 34–17 loss to New England, Miami's Dan Marino throws for 333 yards—his 51st 300-yard game of his career—to surpass Fran Tarkenton's alltime career passing record of 47,003

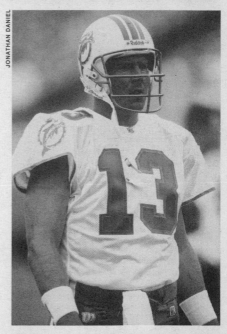

Marino notched a couple more passing records.

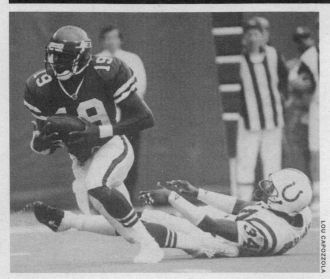

LOU CAPOZZOLA

Johnson went No. 1 in the NFL draft in April.

Aikman engineers a last-gasp drive to set up the winning field goal as time expires for a 21–20 win over the Giants. Emmitt Smith scores his 24th rushing TD of the season, tying John Riggins for the alltime mark.

Dec 24—In the NFL's final weekend, the Eagles lose to Chicago 20–14, thereby clinching the NFC East for the Cowboys and a wild-card berth for themselves. Detroit, which had beaten Tampa Bay on Saturday, and Atlanta, which upsets San Francisco 28–27, are the other NFC wild-card teams. Green Bay defeats the Steelers 24–19 to clinch the NFC Central. In the AFC, Indianapolis and San Diego, which both won on Saturday, as well as Miami, which beats St. Louis 41–22, are the wild-card teams.

Dec 25—Dallas beats Arizona 37–13 behind the running of Emmitt Smith, who scores his 25th rushing TD of the season, breaking John Riggins's alltime mark. The victory gives the Cowboys an NFC–best record of 12–4 and guarantees them home-field advantage throughout the NFC playoffs.

Dec 26—After a disappointing 4–12 season for the Cardinals, Arizona owner Bill Bidwill fires head coach Buddy Ryan.

Dec 26—Philadelphia coach Ray Rhodes is named NFL Coach of the Year after leading the previously woeful Eagles to a 10–6 record and an NFC playoff spot. Rhodes, the third black head coach in modern NFL history, is the first to be so honored.

Dec 27—After losing seven of their last nine games, the Tampa Bay Bucs fire head coach Sam Wyche.

Dec 30—Philadelphia rolls over Detroit 58–37 and Buffalo eliminates Miami 37–22 in the first day of the NFL playoffs.

Dec 31—Green Bay beats Atlanta 37–20 and Indianapolis defeats San Diego 35–20 to complete the first round of the NFL playoffs.

Jan 1, 1996—Green Bay's Brett Favre is named the NFL MVP. Favre, who threw for 38 TDS and 4,413 yards, led the Pack to its first division title since 1972.

yards. Marino's total at game's end stands at 47,299.

Nov 12—The St. Louis Rams defeat the Carolina Panthers 28–17 in their first game in their new stadium, the Trans World Dome.

Nov 19—The Baltimore Stallions beat the Calgary Stampede 37–20 to win the CFL's Grey Cup.

Nov 26—Dan Marino notches another career passing record, throwing four TD passes in a 36–28 loss to Indianapolis to surpass Fran Tarkenton and become the alltime leader in touchdown passes, with 346.

Dec 3—Pittsburgh clinches the AFC Central title and runs its winning streak to six games by beating Houston 21–7. Marcus Allen runs for 124 yards and a TD to lead Kansas City to the AFC West title with a 29–23 win over Oakland.

Dec 10—Dallas coach Barry Switzer is severely criticized after he orders the Cowboys to go for the first down on fourth-and-inches from the Dallas 29 with two minutes left in their game against the Eagles and the score tied. The Cowboys fail to get the yardage and four plays later Philadelphia's Gary Anderson kicks a field goal to give the Eagles a 20–17 win. Another kicker is also in the news as Atlanta's Morten Andersen becomes the first kicker to make three field goals of over 50 yards in a game, with boots of 52, 51, 55 and 55 yards in the Falcons' 19–14 win over New Orleans.

Dec 17—Buffalo clinches the AFC East with a 23–20 win over Miami and San Francisco backs into the NFC West title when surprising Carolina defeats Atlanta 21–17 for its seventh win of the season. Dallas barely averts disaster as Troy

Jan 4—Don Shula, the alltime coaching leader with 347 wins, calls its quits in Miami after a disappointing 9–7 season that included losses in seven of the Dolphins' last 12 games.

Jan 7—Wild-card Indianapolis shocks AFC Central winner Kansas City 10–7. The Colts are greatly aided by three missed field goals by Kansas City kicker Lin Elliott. In the NFC, Dallas seems to be peaking in the playoffs, easily disposing of Philadelphia 30–11.

Jan 6—Pittsburgh looks very strong in defeating Buffalo 40–21 in the AFC, while Green Bay advances to the NFC title game with a 27–17 win over the 49ers.

Jan 11—Jimmie Johnson signs a four-year, $8 million contract to replace Don Shula as head coach in Miami.

Jan 14—In the first half of the NFC title game, Green Bay gets a blocked punt and a 73-yard TD bomb from Brett Favre to Robert Brooks to stay in the game with Dallas; the Pack even noses in front 27–24 in the third quarter. But in the end it is the Cowboys who prevail, grinding out a 90-yard drive capped by an Emmitt Smith five-yard dive into the end zone to go in front for good in the 38–27 Dallas win. In the AFC title game, a 37-yard pass from Neil O'Donnell to Ernie Mills puts the Steelers in position for the winning TD, a one-yard plunge by Bam Morris, in Pittsburgh's 20–16 victory over Indianapolis.

Jan 22—Tampa Bay names Tony Dungy as its head coach, making Dungy the third black head coach currently active in the NFL.

Jan 27—Offensive lineman Lou Creekmur, tackle Dan Dierdorf, coach Joe Gibbs, wide receiver Charlie Joiner and defensive back Mel Renfro are elected to the Pro Football Hall of Fame.

Jan 28—Dallas wins its third Super Bowl in four years, defeating the Pittsburgh Steelers 27–17. The Steelers trim a 13-point deficit to three in the fourth quarter but Pittsburgh's Neil O'Donnell throws a critical interception to Dallas's Larry Brown, who returns the ball 33 yards to set up the TD by Emmitt Smith that puts the game away for the Cowboys. Brown, who intercepted three passes on the day, is named the game's MVP.

Feb 2—The CFL's effort to expand Canadian football into the U.S. ends as Grey Cup winner Baltimore announces its intention to move to Montreal and four other U.S. franchises announce that they are folding.

Feb 4—The NFC defeats the AFC 20–13 in the Pro Bowl.

Feb 7—Arizona hires Vince Tobin to replace Buddy Ryan as head coach.

Feb 11—The Colts hire Lindy Infante as their new head coach, replacing Ted Marchibroda, who was fired the previous week.

Feb 14—Art Modell fires Bill Belichick as the head coach of his still unnamed franchise in Baltimore. The following day he will name Ted Marchibroda as the new coach.

Feb 20—Deion Sanders announces that he is giving up his baseball career to concentrate his fulltime energies on football. On the same day teammate and Super Bowl MVP Larry Brown signs a five-year, $12.5 million contract with Oakland.

Feb 29—Free agent Neil O'Donnell signs a five-year, $25 million contract with the New York Jets, making him the fourth highest paid player in the NFL.

March 4—Cornelius Bennett signs a four-year, $13.6 million contract with Atlanta, making him the highest paid player in Falcons history.

March 11—NFL owners vote to approve the move of the Cleveland Browns to Baltimore.

March 12—Four-time Super Bowl winner Ronnie Lott announces his retirement after 15 seasons in which he was named to the Pro Bowl 10 times.

April 16—John Elway signs a five-year, $29.5 million contract with Denver that could allow him to finish his career with the Broncos.

April 21—The New York Jets make wide receiver Keyshawn Johnson from USC the No. 1 selection in the NFL draft. Johnson is one of five wide receivers taken in the first round.

April 23—Dan Marino signs a three-year, $17.9 million contract extension that makes him the third-highest paid player in the NFL, behind Troy Aikman and Drew Bledsoe.

April 30—NFL owners approve the Houston Oilers' plan to move to Nashville for the 1998 season.

May 14—Green Bay quarterback Brett Favre voluntarily enters the NFL substance abuse program to fight an addiction to painkillers.

June 14—Receiver Brian Blades is convicted of manslaughter in the accidental shooting of his cousin Charles Blades in a drunken dispute over a gun.

June 14—Dallas wide receiver Michael Irvin is indicted on charges of felony cocaine possession and misdemeanor marijuana possession stemming from an incident in March in which Irvin, former Cowboys tight end Alfredo Roberts and two women were allegedly found in a motel room with marijuana, cocaine and drug paraphernalia.

June 17—Broward County Circuit Court Judge Susan Lebow issues an order for a directed verdict of not guilty in the case of Brian Blades, overturning the jury's conviction of Blades just three days earlier. The judge's ruling is based on her conclusion that there is not sufficient evidence to support a guilty verdict.

June 23—The Scottish Claymores defeat the Frankfurt Galaxy 32–27 to win the World League of American Football championship game in Edinburgh, Scotland. The attendance of 38,892 fans is a record for the young league.

July 25—One week after Michael Irvin pled no contest to a felony cocaine-possession charge, the NFL suspends the wide receiver for five games. Irvin, who was sentenced to four years of probation, 800 hours of community service and a fine of $10,000, can play in preseason games but is barred from the team facility when the regular season begins.

Aug 13—Emmitt Smith signs an eight-year, $48 million contract with Dallas.

Aug 28—Jerry Rice becomes the highest-paid 49er by signing a seven-year, $32 million contract with San Francisco.

Sept 1—On Opening Day in the NFL, the former Cleveland Browns, now the Baltimore Ravens, win their first game by defeating Oakland 19–14.

Oct 6—Neil O'Donnell, signed by the Jets to a $25 million contract in the offseason, goes down with a separated shoulder in a 34–13 loss to Oakland and will miss up to six weeks for the winless Jets.

Oct 13—Jets kicker Nick Lowery kicks a 20-yard field goal early in the fourth quarter to pass Jan Stenerud's alltime career mark of 346 field goals.

Oct 21—Head coach David Shula is fired in Cincinnati, and in New Orleans head coach Jim Mora resigns.

Oct 21—As of our press date, a surprising trio of teams share the NFL's best record, at 6–1: Washington, Green Bay and Denver.

Oct 22—Unable to make a trade for Jeff George, the Atlanta Falcons unceremoniously waive the star quarterback who had feuded through the season with head coach June Jones.

Soccer

Nov 21, 1995—Doug Logan, 52, with a background in entertainment and arena business, is introduced in New York as the first commissioner of Major League Soccer.

Dec 14—Major League Soccer (MLS) announces the acquisition of Colombian superstar Carlos Valderrama.

Jan 3, 1996—Bruce Arena leaves the University of Virginia, where he won four straight NCAA titles, to take the head-coaching position with D.C. United of MLS.

Jan 9—MLS signs U.S. national team star Eric Wynalda.

Jan 21—Rebounding from a 1–0 loss to Brazil in the semis, the U.S. rolls over Guatemala 3–0 to claim third place in the Gold Cup. Eric Wynalda scores his 22nd career goal in the 35th minute, making him the national team's alltime leading scorer.

Feb 4—The U.S. women's national team splits a pair of games in South Florida with world champion Norway. In Friday's game in Tampa, the U.S. prevails 3–2, but Norway rebounds in Sunday's game, taking a 2–1 win before a U.S.–record crowd of 8,975 in Tampa.

Feb 5—MLS announces the signing of U.S. national team defender Marcelo Balboa. The following day in New York, former Saint Louis University star Brian McBride becomes the league's first draft pick.

April 6—MLS makes its debut as Eric Wynalda scores in the 88th minute to lead the San Jose Clash to a 1–0 victory over D.C. United before 31,683 at Spartan Stadium.

April 13—In its first full weekend of games MLS exceeds attendance expectations league-wide, with the highlight coming in Pasadena, where 69,255 fans watch the Los Angeles Galaxy defeat the New York/New Jersey MetroStars 2–1.

April 15—Actor Andrew Shue survives the Los Angeles Galaxy's final regular season cut and will continue his second career as a reserve midfielder with the team.

May 2—The Kansas City Wiz rallies from a two-goal deficit with four goals in the final 25 minutes to defeat the Columbus Crew 6–4.

May 18—Michelle Akers scores in the 63rd minute to lift the U.S. to a 1–0 triumph over China and the U.S. Women's Cup title.

May 26—The U.S. men down Scotland 2–1 in New Britain, Conn.

May 28—The New York/New Jersey MetroStars hire coach Carlos Queiroz, 43, formerly of Sporting Lisbon, one of Portugal's top clubs.

June 16—In the final game of U.S. Cup '96, Mexico and the U.S. play to a 2–2 tie before 92,216 at the Rose Bowl. Mexico wins the tournament with a 1-0-2 record.

June 26—Germany defeats England on penalty kicks after a 1–1 tie in the semifinals of the European Championships. In the other semifinal, the Czech Republic also advances on penalties after holding France to a 0–0 tie.

June 30—Substitute Oliver Bierhoff scores in the fourth minute of overtime to give Germany a 2–1 triumph over the Czech Republic in the final of the European Championship.

June 30—The Colorado Rapids defeat Los Angeles 2–1, handing the Galaxy their first loss of the season after 12 wins.

July 7—Raul Diaz Arce scores four goals as D.C. United routs the Dallas Burn 6–1 in RFK Stadium.

July 14—Defender Steve Pittman scores the winning goal as the Eastern Conference defeats the Western Conference 3–2 in the inaugural MLS All-Star Game at Giants Stadium. A crowd of 78,416 watches the game, which forms a doubleheader with the Brazil–FIFA World All-Stars game.

July 20—Shannon MacMillan scores in the 100th minute of the Olympic semifinal to give the U.S. a 2–1 sudden-death victory over Norway and a berth in the first-ever women's Olympic gold medal game.

STEPHAN DUNN

Campos and the Galaxy soared to the MLS title game.

Aug 1—With a crowd of 76,481 looking on in Georgia's Sanford Stadium, the U.S. women defeat China 2–1 to win the inaugural women's Olympic gold medal game. Tiffeny Milbrett scores the game winner in the 68th minute on a pass from Joy Fawcett.

Aug 9—Dallas Sidekicks veteran Tatu breaks Steve Zungul's indoor soccer career scoring record when he scores his 716th career goal against Sacramento.

Aug 13—New England Revolution defender Alexi Lalas, who has been feuding with coach Frank Stapleton for months, asks MLS, which owns all player contracts, to trade him.

Aug 15—Escondido, Calif., native Jovan Kirovski, 20, signs a four-year contract with German Bundesliga champion Borussia Dortmund. In England, U.S. goalkeeper Kasey Keller moves from second division Millwall to Premier League team Leicester City for a $1.39 million transfer fee.

Sept 7—The Rochester Rhinos of the second-division A-League stun the Tampa Bay Mutiny, one of the top teams in MLS, 4–3 in overtime in the quarterfinals of the U.S. Open Cup.

Sept 12—Martin Vasquez's second-half goal gives the Tampa Bay Mutiny a 2–1 victory over the New England Revolution and the MLS Eastern Conference title.

Sept 19—The Los Angeles Galaxy clinch the MLS Western Conference title with a 2–1 win over the Dallas Burn.

Sept 21—In a battle for the final Eastern Conference playoff berth, the Columbus Crew beats New England 1–0 before a crowd of 38,633

in Foxboro Stadium. The win completes the Crew's 9–1 run over the last two months of the season.

Sept 24—The New York/New Jersey MetroStars and D.C. United meet in the first MLS playoff game, with the MetroStars taking a 3–2 shootout victory at Giants Stadium.

Sept 25—U.S. Soccer and MLS announce the scheduled January start of Project 40, a program that will gather the top 40 18- and 19-year-olds in the country for a three-month training camp, after which 30 of them will receive developmental contracts with MLS.

Oct 12—D.C. United, which began the season 1–6, completes a two-game sweep of the Mutiny with a 2–1 win in Tampa and advances to the MLS title game.

Oct 13—With a 2–1 shootout victory over Kansas City, the Los Angeles Galaxy sweep the Wiz out of the playoffs and advance to the MLS title game.

Oct 19—Tampa Bay midfielder Carlos Valderrama is named Most Valuable Player of the MLS regular season. His coach, Thomas Rongen, is named coach of the year, while his teammate Steve Ralston wins the rookie of the year award.

Oct 20—MLS Cup '96 pits the Los Angeles Galaxy against D.C. United in a driving rainstorm in Foxboro, Mass, where, despite the weather, a crowd of 34,643 turns out. D.C. United battles back from a 2-goal deficit with goals by substitutes Tony Sanneh and Shawn Medved, then wins in sudden-death overtime on a header by Eddie Pope. Marco Etcheverry, who assists on all three D.C. goals, is named MVP of the game.

Sampras finished strong at the U.S. Open.

Nov 19, 1995—In the ATP Tour World Championship, Steffi Graf caps a dominant year by defeating Anke Huber 6-1, 2-6, 6-1, 4-6, 6-3 to finish the season ranked No. 1 with a record of 47–2. In the men's final, Boris Becker beats Michael Chang 7-6 (7-3), 6-0, 7-6 (7-5). In spite of his loss to Chang in the semifinals, Pete Sampras finishes the season ranked first.

Nov 26—Conchita Martinez defeats Mary Joe Fernandez 6-3, 6-4 to clinch a 3-2 Federation Cup win over the U.S. It is the fourth Federation Cup victory for Spain in six years.

Dec 3—Fighting off painful leg cramps, Pete Sampras defeats Yevgeny Kafelnikov to clinch the Davis Cup title for the U.S.

Jan 20, 1996—Pete Sampras is upset in the third round of the Australian Open by local favorite Mark Phillippoussis.

Jan 27—Monica Seles wins her fourth Australian Open and her first major in four years by beating Anke Huber 6-4, 6-1. Steffi Graf, recovering from foot surgery, is absent.

Jan 28—Boris Becker defeats Michael Chang 6-2, 6-4, 2-6, 6-2 to win his second Australian Open.

March 16—Steffi Graf, sidelined for three months, returns to the women's tour and defeats Conchita Martinez 7-6 (7-5), 7-6 (7-5) to win the Evert Cup final.

April 7—Petr Korda of the Czech Republic beats MaliVai Washington of the U.S. in the Davis Cup quarterfinals to eliminate the U.S. Absent from the competition are Pete Sampras and Andre Agassi.

April 17—Steffi Graf's father, Peter, in jail since August, is charged with evading $13 million in taxes and failing to declare up to $28 million of his daughter's income.

May 10—Fifteen-year-old Martina Hingis achieves the upset of her career, defeating Steffi Graf in the quarterfinals of the Italian Open. She will lose the final two days later to Conchita Martinez, 6-2, 6-3.

May 29—Andre Agassi commits 63 unforced errors and loses to unseeded Chris Woodruff in five sets.

June 8—Steffi Graf outlasts Arantxa Sánchez Vicario 6-3, 6-7 (4-7), 10-8 to win the French Open and capture her 19th Grand Slam singles title, putting her tied on the alltime list with Helen Wills Moody. Only Margaret Smith Court, with 24, has won more.

June 9—Yevgeny Kafelnikov becomes the first Russian to win a Grand Slam singles title, defeating Michael Stich 7-6 (7-4), 7-5, 7-6 (7-4).

June 24—Andre Agassi falls early again in a major, this time losing at Wimbledon to unseeded Doug Flach in the first round. Michael Chang and Jim Courier also fall victim to the upset bug.

July 6—Steffi Graf beats Arantxa Sánchez Vicario for her seventh Wimbledon title and 20th career Grand Slam singles title.

July 7—Richard Krajicek beats MaliVai Washington 6-3, 6-4, 6-3 in a Wimbledon final that for the first time features two unseeded players.

Sept 2—Martina Hingis pulls off her second major upset of the year, defeating Arantxa Sánchez Vicario in the fourth round of the U.S. Open.

Sept 8—For the first time in U.S. Open history, the men's and women's finals are held on the same day. Both matches feature the top two seeds in the draw. Steffi Graf continues to dominate the women's game, beating Monica Seles 7-5, 6-4 while Pete Sampras eliminates Michael Chang 6-1, 6-4, 7-6 (7-3). It was the first major of the year for Sampras, for Graf her third in three attempts.

Sept 29—Monica Seles anchors a healthy U.S. team to a dominant 5-0 Federation Cup victory over defending champion Spain.

Oct 13—Martina Hingis, now 16, wins her first WTA event, defeating Anke Huber 6-2, 3-6, 6-3 in the Porsche Grand Prix.

Oct 24—Gabriela Sabatini announces her retirement. Sabatini, who won the U.S. Open in 1990, earned more than $8 million in her 11-year career.

Nov 1, 1995—Bowler David Ozio defeats Walter Ray Williams Jr. to win the $60,000 AMF Dick Weber Classic.

Nov 12—Mexico's German Silva wins his second consecutive New York Marathon, completing the 26.2-mile course in 2 hours, 11 minutes. Tecla Loroupe of Kenya repeats as women's champion with a time of 2 hours, 28 minutes, six seconds.

Nov 18—Michelle Mullen defeats Cheryl Daniels 202–189 to win the Sam's Town Invitational bowling tournament in Las Vegas.

Nov 20—Olympic pairs skating champion Sergei Grinkov collapses and dies during a morning practice with his wife, Ekaterina Gordeeva, in Lake Placid, NY. The cause of death is later determined to be a massive heart attack caused by a blocked artery and high blood pressure.

Dec 1—The Notre Dame women's soccer team knocks off nine-time defending national champions North Carolina with a 1–0 victory in the semifinals of the NCAA tournament. Two days later, Notre Dame wins the national championship with a 1–0 triple overtime victory against Portland.

Dec 2—U.S. downhiller Picabo Street picks up where she left off the previous year, winning the season-opening race at Lake Louise, Alberta for her sixth consecutive victory. Street's streak is second only to Annemarie Moser-Pröll's 11-victory run from 1972–74.

Dec 10—Wisconsin beats Duke—which had ended Virginia's four-year run of national titles in the semifinals—2–0 to claim the NCAA title in men's soccer.

Dec 19—Italy's Alberto Tomba celebrates his 29th birthday by winning his first World Cup slalom race of the season in Madonna di Campiglio, Italy.

Jan 7, 1996—Alberto Tomba wins his third consecutive World Cup slalom race in Flachau, Austria.

Jan 20—Rudy Galindo, who had quit skating for eight months for financial reasons, returns to competition and earns two perfect scores to win the U.S. Figure Skating Championships in his native San Jose, Calif.

Jan 20—Michelle Kwan wins her first U.S. Figure Skating Championship.

Jan 26—U.S. Olympic wrestler David Schultz, 36, is shot and killed on the grounds of the Foxcatcher estate in Newton Square, Penn., which served as a training facility for USA Wrestling. On Jan. 28, John du Pont, who ran the estate, is arrested for the attack and later declared mentally unfit to stand trial.

Feb 4—Ethiopia's Haile Gebrselassie breaks the 3,000-meter indoor track record, running

Galindo returns to the rink in fine style, winning the U.S. Figure Skating Championships in January.

MANNY MILLAN

7:30.72, almost 4½ seconds faster than the previous mark.

Feb 18—Picabo Street becomes the first U.S. woman to win the downhill at the World Championships when she registers a time of 1:54.06 in Sierra Nevada, Spain, easily beating runner-up Katja Seizinger of Germany.

Feb 25—Alberto Tomba wins two gold medals at the World Championships in Sierra Nevada. Tomba, who had guaranteed a medal, won the giant slalom two days earlier, then rallied from a .81-second deficit to capture the slalom.

March 10—George Mason University ends Arkansas's NCAA record run of 12 consecutive indoor track championships when it takes the 1996 title in Indianapolis.

March 12—Jeff King wins his second Iditarod Trail Sled Dog Race, reaching the finish line in Nome, Alaska, after nine days, five hours and 43 minutes. The victory brings him $50,000 and a new truck.

March 21—Todd Eldredge wins the world figure skating championship in Edmonton, becoming the first U.S. man to do so since Brian Boitano in 1988.

March 23—Michelle Kwan wins the world figure skating title at the age of 15, becoming the third youngest champion in her sport.

April 15—Germany's Uta Pippig wins a women's-record third straight Boston Marathon, completing the race in 2 hours, 27 minutes, 12 seconds. Moses Tanui of Kenya, who finished second to Cosmas Ndeti last year, prevents Ndeti from winning an unprecedented fourth consecutive Boston title with his 2:09:16 performance.

April 27—Bowler Dave D'Entremont defeats Dave Arnold 215–202 to win the Brunswick World Tournament of Champions in Chicago.

May 7—Jackson State becomes the first historically black college to reach the NCAA Division I men's golf tournament. The Tigers, who narrowly missed going to the tournament the last three years, won eight of the 12 tournaments they entered in 1996.

May 12—Lance Armstrong becomes the first repeat winner of the Tour DuPont, capping the victory by winning the 12th and final leg for his record fifth stage victory in the race.

May 21—The Florida University women's tennis team concludes a perfect 31–0 season by defeating Stanford 5–2 for the NCAA championship. In the men's tournament,

Stanford wins its 14th title, knocking off top seed UCLA 4–1 in the final.

May 27—Princeton University wins its third NCAA Division I lacrosse title in five years when attackman Jesse Hubbard scores 34 seconds into sudden-death overtime to give the Tigers a 13–12 victory.

June 1—Ato Boldon of UCLA wins the NCAA 100-meter final in 9.92, a meet record and the fastest time in the world this year.

June 2—Stanford sophomore Tiger Woods survives a final-round 80 to win the NCAA men's individual golf title in Dublin, Ohio.

June 2—Dave Villwock wins the 93rd APBA Gold Cup in Detroit, the premier event in Unlimited Hydroplane racing.

June 8—Louisiana State wins the College World Series with a home run by second baseman Warren Morris on the game's final pitch. It is the first time in the 50-year history of the CWS that the title has been decided with a home run.

July 21—Denmark's Bjarne Riis wins the Tour de France, stopping Spain's Miguel Induráin in his bid for an unprecedented sixth consecutive Tour triumph.

Aug 14—Russia's Svetlana Masterkova sets a women's world record in the mile, running 4:12.56 in Zurich. She wins $50,000 and a 2.2-pound gold bar for the record.

Aug 24—Kao-Hsiung, Taiwan, wins the 50th Little League Baseball World Series, trouncing the team from Cranston, R.I. 13–3. It is the 17th little league title and second in a row for Taiwan.

Sept 8—Nebraska, which started women's soccer in 1994, upsets sixth-ranked Duke 3–1 in Durham, N.C. In the following week's poll, the Cornhuskers are ranked 12th.

Sept 9—U.S. high jumper Charles Austin, who won the gold medal in Atlanta, joins four other Olympic champions at the Solidarity for Sarajevo track meet in the rebuilt Kosevo Stadium. To the delight of the 50,000 spectators who are admitted for free, Austin wins his event with a leap of 7' 5¼".

Sept 16—Olympic track and field star Jackie Joyner-Kersee announces that she will join the Richmond Rage of the American Basketball League, a women's pro circuit which begins play in October.

Oct 8—Lance Armstrong, 25, the greatest active cyclist in the United States, announces that he has been diagnosed with testicular cancer that has spread to his abdomen and lungs. Doctors rate his chances of survival at 65%-85%.

Baseball

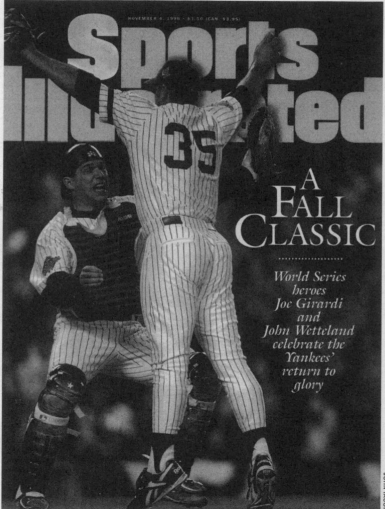

NOVEMBER 4, 1996 • $3.50 (CAN. $3.95)

Sports Illustrated

A FALL CLASSIC

World Series
heroes
Joe Girardi
and
John Wetteland
celebrate the
Yankees'
return to
glory

JOHN IACONO

Destiny's Darlings

A pinch of luck and a healthy dose of solid play propelled the Yankees to the title in baseball's power-happy 1996 season

by Tim Kurkjian

THE BRAVES never had a chance. They were trying to defend their World Series title against a very good, very gritty, very deep Yankee team. And they were up against destiny. Destiny always wins, it can overcome overwhelming odds, it can even beat one of the best pitching rotations in history.

The Yankees won the 1996 World Series in six games over the Braves because the gods of baseball looked down at the post-season and decided that one of the game's best guys, Yankee manager Joe Torre, who played and managed in more games (4,272) than anyone without going to the World Series, would go this year, and would win. This wasn't a certainty until the day before Game 6, the clincher, when Torre's older brother, Frank, received the heart transplant for which he had been waiting three months. The man who performed the operation was named Dr. Oz. Was there any doubt it was destiny?

No. How else can one explain how the Yankees could lose the first two games at Yankee Stadium by a combined score of 16–1, then win the next four—three on the road—to seize the Series? Or how the

Braves' fabulous starting rotation could post a 1.51 ERA in the Series, and lose? Or how Yankee first baseman Tino Martinez, the club leader in RBIs (117) this year, could go the entire post-season without an RBI, yet the Yanks went 11–4 in October? Or how New York reserve catcher Jim Leyritz, who thought he'd be playing almost anywhere but New York this season, could provide the biggest hit of the Series, a three-run homer that turned a certain Braves' win in Game 4 into a devastating loss from which they never recovered? Or how Yankee outfielder Darryl Strawberry suddenly played like a Gold Glover while Atlanta centerfielder Marquis Grissom, a four-time Gold Glover, could drop a fly ball, leading to a key loss in Game 5? Or how Yankee reliever Graeme Lloyd, the beleaguered left-hander who was almost booed out of Yankee Stadium in September, could become Sparky Lyle in October? Or how every managerial move Torre made, even the ones that seemed crazy, worked perfectly?

Destiny.

"People were praying harder for us," Torre said.

Pettitte redeemed his Game 1 stinker by twirling an unforgettable gem in Game 5.

Miraculously, the Yankees, the hated Yankees in so many parts of the country, became the sentimental favorite because of their determination, their classy manager and his ailing brother. So there was a celebration across the land on the night of Oct. 26—a full moon was out, of course—when the Yankees beat the great Greg Maddux, 3–2, in Game 6 to win their first world championship in 18 years. It ended when closer John Wetteland, the Series MVP, notched his fourth save of the Series by getting Atlanta's Mark Lemke to foul out to third base with the tying run at second and the winning run at first.

"We could have packed it in when we went to Atlanta, but we never gave up, our hearts are as big as the twin towers," said Yankee third baseman Wade Boggs, who took a victory ride around Yankee Stadium on a police horse after Game 6.

Early on, it didn't look encouraging. The Braves won Game 1, 12–1, behind John Smoltz, but the star of the game was leftfielder Andruw Jones. In the second inning, he became the youngest player (19) to hit a home run in a World Series when he belted a two-run homer off Andy Pettitte. In the third, he crashed a three-run shot, joining Oakland's Gene Tenace (1972) as the only players in history to homer in their first two Series at bats. "He has no idea what he just did," Braves shortstop Jeff Blauser said of Jones, who was born and raised in Curaçao in the Netherlands Antilles.

The Braves won Game 2, 4–0, behind Maddux, who made 82 pitches in eight innings—only 20 of them balls—in one of the most dominant pitching performances in World Series history. Can a man pitch any better? "No," said Braves pitching coach Leo Mazzone. "Yes," said former pitcher Don Sutton, a 324-game winner. "But only him [Maddux]." Even Maddux, who never gets caught up in his own brilliance, said of his start, "I will take that one to the grave."

The Series turned for the first time in the sixth inning of Game 3. New York starter David Cone loaded the bases with one out, clinging to a 2–0 lead and desperately hoping to get through six, then turn the game over to the league's best pitcher in 1996, reliever Mariano Rivera. Cone gave up a run, but finished the inning with a lead.

JOHN BIEVER

Facing Smoltz—who led the NL with 276 Ks—was a losing proposition.

Rivera, Lloyd and Wetteland made it stand up in a 5–2 win. "The sixth inning," said Torre, "*was* the World Series."

The turnaround that followed in Game 4, made for one of the most remarkable Series games ever played. Atlanta led 6–0 after five behind Denny Neagle, but the Yankees scored three runs in the sixth. Then in the eighth against Braves ace closer Mark Wohlers, Leyritz hit a three-run home run to tie the score. A maze of fascinating managerial moves followed, capped by Atlanta manager Bobby Cox's decision to walk Bernie Williams intentionally with two out, runners at first and second, score tied in the 10th. Boggs, a career .333 hitter, a future Hall of Famer and the last non-pitcher used by Torre in the game, pinch-hit against Steve Avery. With a batting eye as precise as anyone's in the last 40 years, Boggs drew a walk, forcing home the go-ahead run. "Bernie Williams carried them in the playoffs, and he's knocked the hell out of us," Cox said of his decision. "It was the smart thing to do. It would have been stupid not to walk Bernie Williams."

The Yankees added another run for an 8–6 win. It tied for the second-greatest comeback ever in a World Series, and the greatest in 40 years. It was so bizarre, so shocking, even Boggs said "it is starting to get spooky now."

Pettitte threw a gem for 8⅓ innings in Game 5, out-dueling Smoltz, who struck out 10 in eight innings of a 1–0 loss. The only run scored in the fourth when Grissom dropped a fly ball hit by Charlie Hayes (Grissom was shielded by rightfielder Jermaine Dye on the play, but took full blame for the error). Hayes then scored on Cecil Fielder's rocket double.

Two nights later, as Frank Torre rested comfortably with a new heart, the Yanks were champs.

They had advanced to the World Series by beating the Orioles in five games in the American League Championship Series, a victory they might not have achieved without the very real help of their devoted fans. In the eighth inning of Game 1 with Baltimore leading 4–3, Yankee shortstop Derek Jeter hit a towering fly ball to right field off Armando Benitez. As Oriole rightfielder Tony Tarasco stood poised at the wall to catch the ball, a fan—12-year-old Jeff Maier from Old Tappan, N.J.—reached over the wall and scooped the ball into the stands. It was clearly fan interference, but rightfield umpire Rich Garcia called it a home run. The Orioles went berserk, but the call stood. Garcia admitted that he missed the call after watching the TV replay after the game, but it was too late. The score was tied, Maier was a local hero and the Yankees went on to win 5–4 on Bernie Williams' homer in the 11th off Randy Myers.

The Yankees lost Game 2 at home but went to Baltimore and won Game 3 thanks in part to a Buckner-esque gaffe by Baltimore third baseman Todd Zeile, then wrapped up the AL crown with successive wins of 8–4 and 6–4. They scored five unearned runs in the finale because of an error by Oriole second baseman Roberto Alomar. To some, it was a sign of baseball justice. In the final weekend of the regular season, Alomar spat in umpire John

The mighty McGwire belted 52 home runs in just 423 at bats.

PETER READ MILLER

Hirschbeck's face after being ejected from a game in Toronto. Alomar was suspended for five games—beginning at the start of the 1997 season—by AL president Gene Budig. Major league umpires were so outraged by the leniency of the penalty, they threatened to strike the playoffs and World Series unless Alomar's suspension was ruled immediate. Only a judge's order forced the umpires to work, but the ugly incident dominated the first two rounds of the playoffs.

The Braves returned to the World Series after a wild seven-game series against St. Louis. The Cardinals lost the opener but won the next three—in Game 4, they overcame a 3–0 deficit in the seventh inning, tied the score, then won 4–3 on Brian Jordan's homer in the eighth inning. The celebration on the field, led by Cards closer Dennis Eckersley (who got the save), was excessive, said the Braves. So they went out and taught the Cardinals a lesson. In Game 5 in St. Louis, the Braves won, 14–0—the largest margin of victory ever for an LCS game. In Game 6 in Atlanta, Maddux pitched masterfully in a 3–1 win. In Game 7, the Braves scored six in the first inning—three on pitcher Tom Glavine's bases-loaded triple—and rolled to a 15–0 win.

The team many had expected to join the Braves as repeat pennant winners, the Indians—winners of more games (99) than any team in baseball this season—were knocked out by the Orioles in a bizarre four-game playoff series. The '96 Central Division champs had to open the playoffs with two games in Baltimore, and lost them both,

10–4 and 7–4. The Tribe won Game 3 at Jacobs Field, 9–4, on Albert Belle's grand slam off Armando Benitez in the seventh. But in a gripping Game 4, the Orioles tied the score 3–3 in the ninth on a two-out RBI single by Alomar off Jose Mesa, then won it in the 12th, 4–3, on a homer by Alomar off Mesa. Given the pressure Alomar was under for the Hirschbeck controversy, and the merciless booing he received every time he came to the plate, those were arguably the most remarkable back-to-back at-bats in post-season history.

The Rangers Juan Gonzalez made some remarkable post-season at-bats against the Yankees, bombing the Bombers with five home runs in the four game series, but it wasn't enough as New York recovered from a Game 1 loss to sweep the next three. Williams hit two homers in Game 4 to lead the Yankees back from a 4–0 deficit. It was the first post-season appearance in the 25-year history of the Rangers, but it ended when their bullpen helped lose three winnable games.

In the NL, the Braves swept the wild-card Dodgers behind tremendous pitching from Smoltz, Maddux and Glavine. The Cardinals swept the West Division champion Padres,

49

but it was a more difficult task. St. Louis won the first two at home, then overcame two homers by Padres third baseman Ken Caminiti to win Game 3 in San Diego, 7–5, on Brian Jordan's two-run homer in the ninth. Cardinals closer Eckersley, 42, saved all three wins.

As for the regular season, it was as irregular as perhaps any in major league history.

It began tragically on Opening Day when John McSherry, a National League umpire for 25 years, collapsed and died of a heart attack on the field in the first inning at Cincinnati's Riverfront Stadium. The game was postponed, as it should have been, but Reds owner Marge Schott expressed disappointment over the decision. More insensitive remarks on a variety of topics soon followed from Schott, leading to her three-year suspension as chief operating officer of the team.

It was a season full of heartache. Dodger centerfielder Brett Butler was diagnosed with throat cancer in early May, underwent three months of torturous treatment, yet somehow returned to the lineup in September. Four days later, he broke his left hand, and was lost for the season. On May 10 Yankees pitcher David Cone underwent surgery to repair an aneurysm in his right shoulder, seemingly finishing his season and threatening his career. Yet he returned to pitch in September, and no-hit the A's for seven innings in his first start back. In June Dodgers manager Tommy Lasorda suffered a mild heart attack. On July 29 he resigned the position he had held for 20 years. Twins centerfielder Kirby Puckett, the game's most popular player, did not play in '96, and was forced to retire because of irreversible damage to his right eye.

Puckett left the game with a Hall of Fame resume: .318 average, 2,304 hits, 207 homers, two World Series rings and a history of playing his best in big games. Someday he will be joined in Cooperstown by another Twin, Paul Molitor, who secured his spot by banging out 225 hits—at 40, he's the oldest player ever to lead the AL in hits—to run his career total to 3,014. Molitor hit .341 in 1996, the third-highest average ever for a 40-year-old. He also drove in 113 runs, making him the first AL player since 1950 to drive in 100 runs with fewer than 10 homers. By belting his 500th career homer, Baltimore's Eddie Murray also guaranteed himself a place in the Hall, joining Willie Mays and Hank Aaron as the only players to amass 500 homers and 3,000 hits.

It was a busy summer for Cooperstown because so many records—all of them offensive—were smashed in 1996. The 28 teams hit a total of 4,962 home runs, obliterating the record of 4,458 set in the juiced-ball year of 1987. The Orioles hit 257, breaking the record (240) of the '61 Yankees, who are now fourth on the list, behind the 1996 editions of the Mariners (245) and the A's (243).

"It was like arena baseball," said Yankees manager Torre.

Oakland first baseman Mark McGwire bashed 52 homers (in 423 at-bats!) and Baltimore centerfielder Brady Anderson—whose previous career high was 21—hit 50. Sixteen players hit 40 or more—eight more than the record set in 1961. The Colorado Rockies had three of them—Andres Galarraga, Ellis Burks and Vinny Castilla—to join the 1973 Atlanta Braves as the only teams in history to have three 40–home run men in a season. Mets catcher Todd Hundley hit 41, the most ever by a catcher, breaking Roy Campanella's record of 40. Forty-three players hit 30 or more—15 more than the record set in 1987.

One of the 40-homer men, Giants left fielder Barry Bonds (42 homers), also stole 40 bases, making him the second 40–40 man in history (Jose Canseco was the first in 1988).

But it wasn't just homers, it was uncontrollable hitting (especially in the AL) of all kinds. The last team to score 900 runs in a season was the 1953 Brooklyn Dodgers; in '96, the Mariners (993), Rockies (961), Indians (952), Orioles (949), Rangers (928) and Red Sox (928) all did it. Seven teams scored 20 or more runs in a game, tying a major league record. Twenty-nine times this year, a team scored in double figures and *lost*.

Seattle's Alex Rodriguez, 21, became the third youngest player ever to win a batting

V.J. LOVERO

Bonds joined Canseco in the 40–40 club; they are its only members.

4.34 mark—15 years ago, that would have been the *highest* in the league. The pitiful Tiger staff posted an ERA of 6.38, the highest by any team since the St. Louis Browns in 1939, and set a major league record by allowing 241 homers. The NL pitching was better, but hardly impressive. The league ERA was 4.22—the first time it has ever been over 4.00 for four straight seasons.

There were, however, some sparkling pitching performances. Florida's Kevin Brown had an ERA of 1.89. Atlanta's John Smoltz won 24 games. Florida's Al Leiter no-hit the Rockies May 11. Earlier that day, he had gone to a Chinese restaurant for lunch. His fortune cookie read: SOON YOU'LL BE SITTING ON TOP OF THE WORLD. "I'm keeping that fortune in my wallet forever," he said. On May 14, the Yankees's Doc Gooden, who missed all of 1995 due to a drug suspension, threw a no-hitter against the Mariners. The third no-hitter was thrown Sept. 17 by the Dodgers's Hideo Nomo, and it came at Denver's Coors Field, arguably the greatest hitter's park of all time. "I've seen it all now," said Dodger pitcher Tom Candiotti. "I saw a no-hitter at Coors Field." That same week, Boston's Roger Clemens did something equally astounding: he struck out 20 batters in a nine-inning game, tying the record that he set in 1986. Even though he did it against the horrendous Tigers it was breathtaking to watch.

So were the pennant races.

The Orioles won 11 of their first 13 games and appeared headed to their first AL title in 13 years, then completely fell apart for three months. "We were a terrible team for a long

title (.358), and the first shortstop to do so since Lou Boudreau in 1944. San Diego's Tony Gwynn (.353) won his seventh batting title; in baseball history, only Honus Wagner (eight) and Ty Cobb (12) have won more times. Gwynn won despite finishing with 498 plate appearances, four fewer than the requisite amount to qualify for a batting title. He was awarded the batting crown because of Rule 10.23a, which states that if a player doesn't have enough plate appearances to qualify, but still has the highest average in the league after adding enough hitless at-bats to reach the league minimum, he wins the batting title. The rule had never been invoked.

The brunt of all of the Louisville slugging in 1996 was borne by the pitchers, who cried most of the season that the ball was juiced. "Look at this ball," said Expos pitching coach Joe Kerrigan, massaging a ball with both hands. "Feel how hard it is. Feel how tight the seams are. This isn't the ball we were using a few years ago." The AL ERA was 4.99. The league leader, the Indians, had a

time," said pitcher Mike Mussina. They trailed the Yankees by 12 games at the end of July, but cut it to two by early September. But the Yankees won two of three over Baltimore in a series Sept. 18–19 in New York, and won the East title by four games. The defending East champs, the Red Sox, lost 19 of their first 25, and never seriously entered the race.

The Indians stumbled early, opened a seven-game lead over the White Sox, then made a shocking trade July 29, sending second baseman Carlos Baerga (and infielder Alvaro Espinoza) to the Mets for infielders Jose Vizcaino and Jeff Kent. Indians brass claimed that Baerga—the leader of the 1995 World Series team—was such a liability defensively and had gotten so lazy in his work habits that he had to be moved. The Tribe played better after the trade, went 19–7 in September and cruised to the Central title by 14½ games over Chicago.

The Rangers were picked by most experts to finish third in the AL West, but no one expected the Angels to fold up like a card table. Manager Marcel Lachemann was so distressed by his inability to fire up his team, he resigned on Aug. 6 with the Angels 10 games behind the Rangers. The Mariners stayed in the race most of the season despite getting only eight starts from ace Randy Johnson, who was felled by a back injury. Seattle's relentless lineup, led by Rodriguez and centerfielder Ken Griffey Jr. (49 homers), out-slugged opponents all season, but in the end, the Ranger lineup was just as formidable, and had better pitching.

The Cardinals, behind super-intense manager Tony LaRussa, peaked over the final three months to finish six games ahead of Houston. The Padres won the NL West on the final day of the season, completing a three-game sweep of the Dodgers in Los Angeles with a 2–0 win in 11 innings. The Braves labored more than usual en route to their fifth straight trip to the postseason, finishing eight games ahead of the upstart Expos. In spring training, some felt the young Mets would be a wild-card contender in the NL East, but injuries to their young pitching staff killed that hope before the season began. The Mets finished 71–91, and manager Dallas Green was gone by August. Of course, by season's end, most folks had forgotten there was more than one manager in the Big Apple.

TOM DIPACE

Twenty-one-year-old Rodriguez hit .358 with 36 home runs and 123 RBIs.

Final Standings

National League

EASTERN DIVISION

Team	Won	Lost	Pct	GB	Home	Away
Atlanta	96	66	.593	—	56–25	40–41
Montreal	88	74	.543	8	50–31	38–43
Florida	80	82	.494	16	52–29	28–53
New York	71	91	.438	25	42–37	29–52
Philadelphia	67	95	.414	29	35–46	32–49

CENTRAL DIVISION

Team	Won	Lost	Pct	GB	Home	Away
St Louis	88	74	.543	—	48–33	40–41
Houston	82	80	.506	6	48–33	34–47
Cincinnati	81	81	.500	7	46–35	35–46
Chicago	76	86	.469	12	43–38	33–48
Pittsburgh	73	89	.451	15	36–44	37–45

WESTERN DIVISION

Team	Won	Lost	Pct	GB	Home	Away
San Diego	91	71	.562	—	45–36	46–35
Los Angeles	90	72	.556	1	47–34	43–38
Colorado	83	79	.512	8	55–26	28–53
San Francisco	68	94	.420	23	38–44	30–50

American League

EASTERN DIVISION

Team	Won	Lost	Pct	GB	Home	Away
New York	92	70	.568	—	49–31	43–39
Baltimore	88	74	.543	4	43–38	45–36
Boston	85	77	.525	7	47–34	38–43
Toronto	74	88	.457	18	35–46	39–42
Detroit	53	109	.327	39	27–54	26–55

CENTRAL DIVISION

Team	Won	Lost	Pct	GB	Home	Away
Cleveland	99	62	.615	—	51–29	48–33
Chicago	85	77	.525	14½	44–37	41–40
Milwaukee	80	82	.494	19½	38–43	42–39
Minnesota	78	84	.481	21½	39–43	39–41
Kansas City	75	86	.466	24	37–43	38–43

WESTERN DIVISION

Team	Won	Lost	Pct	GB	Home	Away
Texas	90	72	.556	—	50–31	40–41
Seattle	85	76	.528	4½	43–38	42–38
Oakland	78	84	.481	12	40–41	38–43
California	70	91	.435	19½	44–37	27–53

1996 Playoffs

National League Divisional Playoffs

Oct 1 ....San Diego 1 at St Louis 3
Oct 3 ....San Diego 4 at St Louis 5

Oct 5 ....St Louis 7 at San Diego 5

(St Louis won series 3–0.)

Oct 2 ....Atlanta 2 at Los Angeles 1 (10 innings)
Oct 3 ....Atlanta 3 at Los Angeles 2

Oct 5 ....Los Angeles 2 at Atlanta 5

(Atlanta won series 3–0.)

National League Championship Series

Oct 9 ....St Louis 2 at Atlanta 4
Oct 10 ....St Louis 8 at Atlanta 3
Oct 12 ....Atlanta 2 at St Louis 3
Oct 13 ....Atlanta 3 at St Louis 4

Oct 14 ....Atlanta 14 at St Louis 0
Oct 16 ....St Louis 1 at Atlanta 3
Oct 17 ....St Louis 0 at Atlanta 15

(Atlanta won series 4–3.)

GAME 1

St Louis	0	1	0	0	0	0	1	0	0	—2
Atlanta	0	0	0	0	2	0	0	2	x	—4

WP—Smoltz. **LP**—Petkovsek. **Save**—Wohlers.
E—St Louis: Alicea (2). **LOB**—St Louis 5, Atlanta 7.
2B—St Louis: Andy Benes (1); Atlanta: Grissom (1).
3B—St Louis: Jordan (1). **SB**—Atlanta: C. Jones (1).
T—2:35. **A**—48,686.
Recap: After giving up a triple in the second inning to Brian Jordan and allowing the runner to score on a wild pitch, John Smoltz settled down to pick up his second win of the postseason, striking out six over eight innings. Javier Lopez singled in the bottom of the eighth to break a 2–2 tie and drive in the winning runs.

GAME 2

St Louis	1	0	2	0	0	0	5	0	0	—8
Atlanta	0	0	2	0	0	1	0	0	0	—3

WP—Stottlemyre. **LP**—Maddux.

GAME 2 (CONT.)

E—St Louis: Clayton (1), Gallego (1); Atlanta: Grissom (2), C. Jones (1). **LOB**—St Louis 6, Atlanta 7. **2B**—St Louis: Gant (2), Jordan (1), Pagnozzi (1). **HR**—St Louis: Gaetti (2). **SB**—St Louis: Clayton (1); Atlanta: Grissom (1). **Sac**—St Louis: Sweeney (bunt), Lankford (fly). **GIDP**—St Louis: Gaetti. **T**—2:53. **A**—52,067.
Recap: St. Louis's 38-year-old third baseman Gary Gaetti broke the game open in the seventh with a grand slam against Greg Maddux, who had never before yielded eight runs in a game in his career. Todd Stottlemyre gave up four hits and struck out eight.

GAME 3

Atlanta	1	0	0	0	0	0	1	0	—2
St Louis	2	0	0	0	0	1	0	0	x	—3

WP—Osborne. **LP**—Glavine.
E—Atlanta: Blauser (1). **LOB**—Atlanta 9, St Louis 4.
2B—Atlanta: Lopez (1). **HR**—St Louis: Gant 2 (3).

National League Championship Series *(Cont.)*

GAME 3 *(CONT.)*

Sac—Atlanta: C. Jones (fly), Dye (fly). **GIDP**—St Louis: Gallego. **T**—2:46. **A**—56,769.

Recap: Ron Gant exacted revenge from his former team, the Braves, who released him following a 1993 motorbike accident in which he broke his ankle. His homers in the first and sixth innings provided all the offense the Cardinals needed as Donovan Osborne held the Braves to two runs in seven innings.

GAME 4

Atlanta	0	1	0		0	0	2		0	0	0	—3
St Louis	0	0	0		0	0	0		3	1	x	—4

WP—Eckersley. **LP**—McMichael.
E—Atlanta: McGriff (1). **LOB**—Atlanta 7, St Louis 5. **2B**—Atlanta: C. Jones (1), Dye (1). **3B**—St Louis: Young (1). **HR**—Atlanta: Klesko (2), Lemke (1); St Louis: Jordan (2). **CS**—Atlanta: Dye (1). **Sac**—Atlanta: Neagle (bunt). **GIDP**—Atlanta: McGriff, Klesko. **T**—3:17. **A**—56,764.

Recap: Atlanta scored two runs to take a 3–0 lead in the sixth with a home run by Mark Lemke and a double by Chipper Jones, chasing St Louis starter Andy Benes. The Cardinals answered with three runs in the seventh, powered by Dmitri Young's two-out triple. Brian Jordan provided the winning margin with a homer in the eighth, and Dennis Eckersley pitched 1⅓ scoreless innings for the win.

GAME 5

Atlanta	5	2	0		3	1	0		0	1	2	—14
St Louis	0	0	0		0	0	0		0	0	0	—0

WP—Smoltz. **LP**—Stottlemyre.
LOB—Atlanta 11, St Louis 8. **2B**—Atlanta: Lemke (2), C. Jones (2), Lopez 2 (3). **3B**—Atlanta: Blauser (1). **HR**—Atlanta: Lopez (2), McGriff (2). **SB**—Atlanta: Grissom (3). **GIDP**—Atlanta: Smoltz. **T**—2:57. **A**—56,782.

Recap: Atlanta scored five runs on seven hits in the first inning to send St Louis starter Todd Stottlemyre to an early shower. After the fourth inning the Braves led 10–0. Almost lost in Atlanta's 22-hit explosion was the strong pitching of John Smoltz, who went seven innings, striking out six and issuing just one walk. Smoltz also joined the feast at the plate, collecting two hits and driving in a run.

GAME 6

St Louis	0	0	0		0	0	0		0	1	0	—1
Atlanta	0	1	0		0	1	0		0	1	x	—3

WP—Maddux. **LP**—Alan Benes.
E—St Louis: Petkovsek (1). **LOB**—St Louis 5, Atlanta 9. **2B**—Atlanta: Lopez (4). **SB**—Atlanta: Lopez (2). **Sac**—Atlanta: Maddux (bunt), Dye (fly). **T**—2:41. **A**—52,067.

Recap: Greg Maddux rebounded from his subpar Game 2 outing to shut down the Cardinals for 7⅔ innings while striking out seven and walking none.

GAME 7

St Louis	0	0	0		0	0	0		0	0	0	—0
Atlanta	6	0	0		4	0	3		2	0	x	—15

WP—Glavine. **LP**—Osborne.
E—St Louis: McGee (2), Clayton (2). **LOB**—St Louis 1, Atlanta 8. **2B**—Atlanta: Lemke (3), Lopez (5). **3B**—Atlanta: Glavine (1), McGriff (1). **HR**—Atlanta: Lopez (1), A. Jones (1), McGriff (2). **CS**—St Louis: Clayton (2). **GIDP**—St Louis: Jordan, Alicea. **T**—2:25. **A**—52,067.

Recap: The Braves reprised their Game 5 outburst, again starting the festivities in the first inning when they scored six runs on five hits off Donovan Osborne. Tom Glavine gave up just three hits in seven innings while, like Smoltz in Game 5, contributing at the plate as well, belting a three-run triple in the first inning. Atlanta's Javier Lopez, who hit .542 with six RBIs for the series, won the MVP award.

American League Divisional Playoffs

Oct 1 ....Cleveland 4 at Baltimore 10	Oct 4 ....Baltimore 4 at Cleveland 9
Oct 2 ....Cleveland 4 at Baltimore 7	Oct 5 ....Baltimore 4 at Cleveland 3 (12 innings)

(Baltimore won series 3–0.)

Oct 1 ....Texas 6 at New York 2	Oct 4 ....New York 3 at Texas 2
Oct 2 ....Texas 4 at New York 5 (12 innings)	Oct 5 ....New York 6 at Texas 4

(New York won series 3–1.)

American League Championship Series

Oct 9 ....Baltimore 4 at New York 5 (11 innings)	Oct 12 ....New York 8 at Baltimore 4
Oct 10 ....Baltimore 5 at New York 3	Oct 13 ....New York 6 at Baltimore 4
Oct 11 ....New York 5 at Baltimore 2	

(New York won series 4–1.)

GAME 1

Baltimore	0	1	1		1	0	1		0 0 0	0	0	—4
New York	1	1	0		0	0	0		1 1 0	0	1	—5

WP—Rivera. **LP**—Myers.
E—Baltimore: Alomar (1). **LOB**—Baltimore 11, New York 13. **2B**—Baltimore: C. Ripken (4), Anderson (1); New York: Raines (1), Williams (1). **HR**—Baltimore: Anderson (3), Palmeiro (2); New York: Jeter (1), Williams (4). **SB**—New York: Jeter (1). **Sac**—Baltimore: Surhoff (fly). **GIDP**—New York: Raines. **T**—4:23. **A**—56,495.

Recap: Twelve-year-old Jeff Maier reached out and grabbed a place in Yankee lore when he deflected Derek Jeter's eighth-inning fly to right into the stands. The hit was ruled a home run, tying the game. New York's Bernie Williams won it with a homer in the bottom of the 11th.

American League Championship Series *(Cont.)*

GAME 2

Baltimore	0	0	2	0	0	0	2	1	0	—5
New York	2	0	0	0	0	0	1	0	0	—3

WP—Wells. **LP**—Nelson. **Save**—Benitez.
E—New York: Duncan (1). **LOB**—Baltimore 10, New York 11. **2B**—Baltimore: Alomar (1), New York: Duncan (1). **3B**—New York: Girardi (1). **HR**—Baltimore: Zeile (1), Palmeiro (3). **Sac**—Baltimore: Alomar (fly). **GIDP**—New York: Fielder, Duncan. **T**—4:13. **A**—56,432.
Recap: Baltimore's David Wells won his 10th game in 11 career starts at Yankee Stadium. In the third, Todd Zeile's two-run homer tied the game for the Orioles; Rafael Palmeiro added two more with a shot in the seventh. Armando Benitez retired Cecil Fielder and Tino Martinez with two runners on in the ninth to save the victory.

GAME 3

New York	0	0	0	1	0	0	0	4	0	—5
Baltimore	2	0	0	0	0	0	0	0	0	—2

WP—Key. **LP**—Mussina. **Save**—Wetteland.
E—Baltimore: C. Ripken (1), Zeile (3). **LOB**—New York 1, Baltimore 5. **2B**—New York: Jeter (2), Martinez (1). **HR**—New York: Fielder (2); Baltimore: Zeile (2). **GIDP**—New York: Duncan, Girardi; Baltimore: Surhoff. **T**—2:50. **A**—48,635.
Recap: Todd Zeile hit a two-run homer in the first inning to give the Orioles a 2–0 lead, but then made a three-base throwing error in the eighth to allow the Yankees to score the go-head run. The next batter, Cecil Fielder, hit a two-run homer.

GAME 4

New York	2	1	0	2	0	0	0	3	0	—8
Baltimore	1	0	1	2	0	0	0	0	0	—4

WP—Weathers. **LP**—Coppinger.
LOB—New York 3, Baltimore 10. **2B**—New York: Jeter (3), Duncan (2), Williams (2), Baltimore: Alomar (2). **HR**—New York: Williams (5), Strawberry 2 (2), O'Neill (1); Baltimore: Hoiles (1). **Sac**—Baltimore: Palmeiro (fly). **T**—3:45. **A**—48,974.
Recap: Bernie Williams put New York on the board with a two-run homer in the first. Yankee starter Kenny Rogers gave up five hits and four runs in three innings, but New York never trailed, thanks to two home runs by Darryl Strawberry and one by Paul O'Neill.

GAME 5

New York	0	0	6	0	0	0	0	0	0	—6
Baltimore	0	0	0	0	0	1	0	1	2	—4

WP—Pettitte. **LP**—Erickson.
E—Baltimore: Alomar (2). **LOB**—New York 8, Baltimore 2. **2B**—New York: Williams (3). **HR**—New York: Leyritz (1), Fielder (3), Strawberry (3); Baltimore: Zeile (3), Murray (1), Bonilla (3). **SB**—New York: Jeter (2), Williams (2). **GIDP**—New York: O'Neill. **T**—2:57. **A**—48,718.
Recap: Jim Leyritz, Cecil Fielder and Darryl Strawberry all homered in the third and Andy Pettitte pitched eight strong innings as New York held on to advance to its first World Series since 1981.

Composite Box Scores

National League Championship Series

ATLANTA

BATTING	AB	R	H	HR	RBI	Avg
Belliard	6	0	4	0	2	.667
Lopez	24	8	13	2	6	.542
Neagle	2	0	1	0	0	.500
Lemke	27	4	12	1	5	.444
C. Jones	25	6	11	0	4	.440
Grissom	35	7	10	1	3	.286
Smoltz	7	1	2	0	1	.286
Klesko	16	1	4	1	3	.250
Mordecai	4	1	1	0	0	.250
McGriff	28	6	7	2	7	.250
A. Jones	9	3	2	1	3	.222
Dye	28	2	6	0	4	.214
Blauser	17	5	3	0	2	.176
Glavine	6	0	1	0	3	.167
5 others	15	0	0	0	0	.000
Totals	249	44	77	8	43	.309

PITCHING	G	IP	H	BB	SO	ERA
Wohlers	3	3	0	0	4	0.00
Bielecki	3	3	0	1	5	0.00
Smoltz	2	15	12	3	12	1.20
Glavine	2	13	10	0	9	2.08
Neagle	2	7⅔	2	3	8	2.35
Maddux	2	14⅓	15	2	10	2.51
McMichael	3	2	4	1	3	9.00
3 others	4	3	2	1	2	0.00
Totals	6	61	45	11	53	1.92

ST. LOUIS

BATTING	AB	R	H	HR	RBI	Avg
Clayton	20	4	7	0	1	.350
McGee	15	0	5	0	0	.333
Gaetti	24	1	7	1	4	.292
Young	7	1	2	0	2	.286
Mabry	23	1	6	0	0	.261
Andy Benes	4	0	1	0	0	.250
Gant	25	3	6	2	4	.240
Jordan	25	3	6	1	2	.240
Pagnozzi	19	1	3	0	1	.158
Gallego	14	1	2	0	0	.143
Sweeney	4	0	0	0	0	.000
Lankford	13	1	0	0	1	.000
8 others	28	1	0	0	0	.000
Totals	221	18	45	4	15	.204

PITCHING	G	IP	H	BB	SO	ERA
Eckersley	3	3⅓	2	0	4	0.00
Mathews	2	⅔	2	1	2	0.00
Fossas	5	4⅓	1	3	1	2.08
Alan Benes	2	6⅓	3	2	5	2.84
Andy Benes	3	15⅓	19	3	9	5.28
Petkovsek	6	7⅓	11	3	7	7.36
Honeycutt	5	4	5	3	3	9.00
Jackson	1	3	7	3	3	9.00
Osborne	2	7⅔	12	4	6	9.39
Stottlemyre	3	8	15	3	11	12.38
Totals	7	60	77	25	51	6.60

American League Championship Series

NEW YORK

BATTING	AB	R	H	HR	RBI	Avg
Williams	19	6	9	2	6	.474
Jeter	24	5	10	1	1	.417
Strawberry	12	4	5	3	5	.417
O'Neill	11	1	3	1	2	.273
Raines	15	2	4	0	0	.267
Girardi	12	1	3	0	0	.250
Leyritz	8	1	2	1	2	.250
Duncan	15	0	3	0	0	.200
Sojo	5	0	1	0	0	.200
Martinez	22	3	4	0	0	.182
Fielder	18	3	3	2	8	.167
Hayes	7	0	1	0	0	.143
Boggs	15	1	2	0	0	.133
Totals	183	27	50	10	24	.273

PITCHING	G	IP	H	BB	SO	ERA
Rivera	2	4	6	1	5	0.00
Lloyd	2	1⅔	0	0	1	0.00
Weathers	2	3	3	0	0	0.00
Key	1	8	3	1	5	2.25
Cone	1	6	5	5	5	3.00
Pettitte	2	15	10	5	7	3.60
Wetteland	4	4	2	1	5	4.50
Nelson	2	2⅓	5	0	2	11.57
Rogers	1	3	5	2	3	12.00
Totals	5	47	39	15	33	3.64

BALTIMORE

BATTING	AB	R	H	HR	RBI	Avg
Incaviglia	2	1	1	0	0	.500
Zeile	22	3	8	3	5	.364
Murray	15	1	4	1	2	.267
Surhoff	15	0	4	0	2	.267
C. Ripken	20	1	5	0	0	.250
Palmeiro	17	4	4	2	4	.235
Alomar	23	2	5	0	1	.217
Anderson	21	5	4	1	1	.190
Hoiles	12	1	2	1	2	.167
Parent	6	0	1	0	0	.167
Bonilla	20	1	1	1	2	.050
2 others	3	0	0	0	0	.000
Totals	176	19	39	9	19	.222

PITCHING	G	IP	H	BB	SO	ERA
Mathews	3	2⅓	0	2	3	0.00
Rhodes	3	2	2	0	2	0.00
Myers	3	4	4	3	2	2.25
Erickson	2	11⅓	14	4	8	2.38
Mills	3	2⅓	3	1	3	3.86
Wells	1	6⅔	8	3	6	4.05
Orosco	4	2	2	1	2	4.50
Mussina	1	7⅓	8	2	6	5.87
Benitez	3	2⅓	3	3	2	7.71
Coppinger	1	5⅓	6	1	3	8.44
Totals	5	46	50	20	37	4.11

1996 World Series

Oct 20 ....Atlanta 12 at New York 1
Oct 21 ....Atlanta 4 at New York 0
Oct 22 ....New York 5 at Atlanta 2
Oct 23 ....New York 8 at Atlanta 6
Oct 24 ....New York 1 at Atlanta 0
Oct 26 ....Atlanta 2 at New York 3

(New York won series 4–2.)

GAME 1

Atlanta	0	2	6	0	1	3	0	0	0	—12
New York	0	0	0	0	1	0	0	0	0	—1

WP—Smoltz. **LP**—Pettitte.
E—New York: Duncan (1). **LOB**—Atlanta 3, New York 8. **2B**—New York: Boggs (1). **HR**—Atlanta: McGriff (1), A. Jones 2 (2). **SB**—Atlanta: C. Jones (1). **Sac**—Atlanta: Lemke (bunt), C. Jones (fly). **T**—3:02. **A**—56,365.
Recap: Nineteen-year-old Andruw Jones became the youngest player to homer in a Series, getting two as the Braves shellacked the Yankees in the worst loss for the Bronx Bombers in 34 World Series.

GAME 2

Atlanta	1	0	1	0	1	1	0	0	0	—4
New York	0	0	0	0	0	0	0	0	0	—0

WP—Maddux. **LP**—Key.
E—New York: Raines (1). **LOB**—Atlanta 7, New York 6. **2B**—Atlanta: Grissom (1), Lemke (1), C. Jones (1), Pendleton (1); New York: O'Neill (1). **CS**—New York: Raines (1). **Sac**—Atlanta: Lemke (bunt), McGriff (fly). **GIDP**—Atlanta: J. Lopez, Blauser; New York: Boggs. **T**—2:44. **A**—56,340.
Recap: A brilliant performance by four-time Cy Young Award winner Greg Maddux, who limited the Yankees to six hits and no walks over eight innings, while Fred McGriff got his record 15th RBI of the post-season.

GAME 3

New York	1	0	0	1	0	0	0	3	0	—5
Atlanta	0	0	0	0	0	1	0	1	0	—2

WP—Cone. **LP**—Glavine. **S**—Wetteland.
E—New York: Jeter (1); Atlanta: Blauser (1). **LOB**—Yankees 9, Atlanta 7. **2B**—New York: Fielder (1). **3B**—Atlanta: Grissom (1). **HR**—New York: Williams (1). **CS**—Atlanta: A. Jones (1), Polonia (1). **Sac**—New York: Jeter (bunt), Girardi (bunt). **GIDP**—Atlanta: Lemke. **T**—3:22. **A**—51,843.
Recap: Solid pitching from David Cone, who had spent most of the season recovering from surgery for an aneurysm, and relievers Mariano Rivera and John Wetteland earned the Yankees their first '96 Series win. Bernie Williams overcame a 0–7 Series slump with a two-run homer in the eighth and a second-inning RBI.

GAME 4

New York	0 0 0	0 0 3	0 3 0	2	—8
Atlanta	0 4 1	0 1 0	0 0 0	0	—6

WP—Lloyd. **LP**—Avery. **Save**—Wetteland. **E**—Klesko (1), Dye (1). **LOB**—Yankees 13, Atlanta 8 8. **2B**—Atlanta: Grissom (2), A. Jones (1). **HR**—Atlanta: McGriff (2); New York: Leyritz (1). **Sac**—Atlanta: Dye (bunt), Neagle (bunt), J. Lopez (fly). **GIDP**—New York: B. Williams; Atlanta: McGriff. **T**—4:17. **A**—51,881.

Recap: The Yankees overcame a 6–0 deficit to tie the game with Jim Leyritz's 3-run homer against Mark Wohlers in the eighth. Yankee manager Joe Torre called on seven pitchers, five pinch-hitters and a pinch-runner to win the longest World Series game ever.

GAME 5

Yankees	0 0 0	1 0 0	0 0 0	—1
Atlanta	0 0 0	0 0 0	0 0 0	—0

WP—Pettitte. **LP**—Smoltz. **Save**—Wetteland. **E**—New York: Jeter (2); Atlanta: Grissom (1). **LOB**—Yankees 8, Atlanta 7. **2B**—New York: Fielder (2); Atlanta: C. Jones (2). **SB**—New York: Duncan (1), Leyritz (1); Atlanta: Grissom (1), A. Jones (1). **CS**—Atlanta: A. Jones (2). **GIDP**—Atlanta: C. Jones, Lopez. **T**—2:54. **A**—51,881.

Recap: In the last game ever to be played at Atlanta–Fulton County Stadium, Yankee pitcher Andy Pettitte dominated the Braves with a five-hitter over 8⅓ innings. The sole Yankee run came on Cecil Fielder's double in the fourth after Marquis Grissom's two-base error; the injured Paul O'Neill made a fine catch for the final out.

GAME 6

Atlanta	0 0 0	1 0 0	0 0 1	—2
New York	0 0 3	0 0 0	0 0 x	—3

WP—Key. **LP**—Maddux. **Save**—Wetteland. **E**—New York: Duncan (2). **LOB**—Atlanta 9, New York, 4. **2B**—Atlanta: C. Jones (3), Blauser (1); Yankees: O'Neill (2). **3B**—New York: Girardi (1). **SB**—New York: Jeter (1), Williams (1). **CS**—Atlanta: Pendleton (1); New York: Jeter, O'Neill. **T**—2:53. **A**—56,375.

Recap: The Yankees won a miraculous, come-from-behind 23rd title by proving that Greg Maddux was, indeed, human: He had one bad inning, the third, but it was enough to give the Yankees the lead and, eventually, the win. A tense ninth inning found Atlanta down 3–2 with runners on first and third and two outs, but John Wetteland, who was named MVP with a record four saves in the World Series, got Mark Lemke out on a popup.

1996 World Series Composite Box Score

ATLANTA

BATTING	AB	R	H	HR	RBI	Avg
Smoltz	2	0	1	0	0	.500
Grissom	27	4	12	0	5	.444
A. Jones	20	4	8	2	6	.400
McGriff	20	4	6	2	6	.300
C. Jones	21	3	6	0	3	.286
Lemke	26	2	6	0	2	.231
Pendleton	9	1	2	0	0	.222
Lopez	21	3	4	0	1	.190
Blauser	18	2	3	0	1	.167
Dye	17	0	2	0	1	.118
Klesko	10	2	1	0	1	.100
Mordecai	1	0	0	0	0	.000
Glavine	1	1	0	0	0	.000
4 others	8	0	0	0	0	.000
Totals	201	26	51	4	26	.254

PITCHING	G	IP	H	BB	SO	ERA
Bielecki	2	3	0	3	6	0.00
Clontz	3	1⅔	1	1	2	0.00
Wade	2	⅔	0	1	0	0.00
Smoltz	2	14	6	8	14	0.64
Glavine	1	7	4	3	8	1.29
Maddux	2	15⅓	14	1	5	1.72
Neagle	2	6	5	4	3	3.00
Avery	1	⅔	1	3	0	3.50
Wohlers	4	4⅓	7	2	4	6.23
McMichael	2	1	5	0	1	27.00
Totals	6	54	43	26	43	2.33

NEW YORK

BATTING	AB	R	H	HR	RBI	Avg
Rogers	1	0	1	0	0	1.000
Sojo	5	0	3	0	1	.600
Fielder	23	1	9	0	2	.391
Boggs	11	0	3	0	2	.273
Leyritz	8	1	3	1	3	.375
Jeter	20	5	5	0	1	.250
Strawberry	16	0	3	0	1	.188
Raines	14	2	3	0	0	.214
Hayes	16	2	3	0	1	.188
Martinez	11	0	1	0	0	.091
O'Neill	12	0	2	0	0	.167
Williams	24	3	4	1	4	.167
Duncan	19	1	1	0	0	.053
Girardi	10	1	2	0	1	.200
5 others	9	0	0	0	0	.000
Totals	199	18	43	2	16	.216

PITCHING	G	IP	H	BB	SO	ERA
Nelson	3	4⅓	1	1	5	0.00
Lloyd	4	2⅔	0	4	4	0.00
Cone	1	6	4	4	3	1.50
Rivera	4	5⅔	4	3	4	1.59
Wetteland	5	4⅓	4	1	4	2.08
Weathers	3	3	2	3	3	3.00
Key	2	11⅓	15	5	1	3.97
Boehringer	2	5	5	0	5	5.40
Pettitte	2	10⅔	11	4	5	5.90
Rogers	1	2	5	2	0	22.50
Totals	6	55	51	23	36	3.93

National League Batting

BATTING AVERAGE

Tony Gwynn, SD .... .353
Ellis Burks, Col .... .344
Mike Piazza, LA .... .336
Lance Johnson, NY .... .333
Mark Grace, Chi .... .331
Ken Caminiti, SD .... .326
Eric Young, Col .... .324
Bernard Gilkey, NY .... .317
Jeff Bagwell, Hou .... .315
Gary Sheffield, Fla .... .314

HITS

Lance Johnson, NY 227
Ellis Burks, Col 211
Marquis Grissom, Atl 207
Mark Grudzielanek, Mtl........201
Dante Bichette, Col..............198
Steve Finley, SD..................195
Vinny Castilla, Col................191
Andres Galarraga, Col........190
Al Martin, Pitt.......................189
Raul Mondesi, LA 188

DOUBLES

Jeff Bagwell, Hou...................48
Ellis Burks, Col......................45
Steve Finley, SD....................45
Bernard Gilkey, NY................44
Henry Rodriguez, Mtl.............42

TRIPLES

Lance Johnson, NY 21
Marquis Grissom, Atl 10
Thomas Howard, Cin 10
Steve Finley, SD......................9
Delino Deshields, LA 8
Ellis Burks, Col.......................8
Ray Lankford, StL 8

HOME RUNS

Andres Galarraga, Col..........47
Gary Sheffield, Fla 42
Barry Bonds, SF....................42
Todd Hundley, NY 41
Vinny Castilla, Col.................40
Sammy Sosa, Chi 40
Ken Caminiti, SD....................40
Ellis Burks, Col......................40
Mike Piazza, LA 36
Henry Rodriguez, Mtl.............36

RUNS SCORED

Ellis Burks, Col.....................142
Steve Finley, SD...................126
Barry Bonds, SF...................122
Andres Galarraga, Col.........119
Gary Sheffield, Fla 118
Lance Johnson, NY 117
Barry Larkin, Cin..................117
Dante Bichette, Col..............114
Chipper Jones, Atl 114
Craig Biggio, Hou 113
Eric Young, Col 113

TOTAL BASES

Ellis Burks, Col.....................392
Andres Galarraga, Col.........376
Steve Finley, SD...................348
Vinny Castilla, Col................345
Ken Caminiti, SD..................339

STOLEN BASES

Eric Young, Col 53
Lance Johnson, NY 50
Delino DeShields, LA.............48
Barry Bonds, SF....................40
Al Martin, Pitt.........................38

RUNS BATTED IN

Andres Galarraga, Col.........150
Dante Bichette, Col..............141
Ken Caminiti, SD..................130
Barry Bonds, SF...................129
Ellis Burks, Col.....................128
Jeff Bagwell, Hou..................120
Gary Sheffield, Fla 120
Bernard Gilkey, NY 117
Vinny Castilla, Col................113
Derek Bell, Hou....................113

SLUGGING PERCENTAGE

Ellis Burks, Col .... .639
Gary Sheffield, Fla .... .624
Ken Caminiti, SD................ .621
Barry Bonds, SF.................. .615
Andres Galarraga, Col........ .601

ON-BASE PERCENTAGE

Gary Sheffield, Fla 465
Barry Bonds, SF...................461
Jeff Bagwell, Hou..................451
Mike Piazza, LA 422
Rickey Henderson, SD 410
Barry Larkin, Cin 410

BASES ON BALLS

Barry Bonds, SF....................151
Gary Sheffield, Fla 142
Jeff Bagwell, Hou..................135
Rickey Henderson, SD 125
Barry Larkin, Cin 96

National League Pitching

EARNED RUN AVERAGE

Kevin Brown, Fla.................1.89
Greg Maddux, Atl 2.72
Al Leiter, Fla.......................2.93
John Smoltz, Atl 2.94
Tom Glavine, Atl 2.98
Steve Trachsel, Chi............3.03
Curt Schilling, Phil..............3.19
Hideo Nomo, LA 3.19
Jeff Fassero, Mtl 3.30
Ismael Valdes, LA...............3.32

SAVES

Jeff Brantley, Cinn 44
Todd Worrell, LA...................44
Trevor Hoffman, SD 42
Mark Wohlers, Atl..................39
Mel Rojas, Mtl 36
Rod Beck, SF.........................35
Robb Nen, Fla........................35
Ricky Bottalico, Phil..............34
Dennis Eckersley, StL...........30
John Franco, NY 28

WINS

John Smoltz, Atl 24
Andy Benes, Stl 18
Kevin Ritz, Col 17
Kevin Brown, Fla....................17
Hideo Nomo, LA 16
Shane Reynolds, Hou 16
Denny Neagle, Atl..................16
Al Leiter, Fla...........................16
Seven tied with 15.

GAMES PITCHED

Brad Clontz, Atl......................81
Bob Patterson, Chi.................79
Mark Dewey, SF.....................78
Jeff Shaw, Cin........................78
Mark Wohlers, Atl...................77

INNINGS PITCHED

John Smoltz, Atl..................253⅔
Greg Maddux, Atl 245
Shane Reynolds, Hou 239
Jaime Navarro, Chi.............236⅔
Tom Glavine, Atl 235⅓

STRIKEOUTS

John Smoltz, Atl 276
Hideo Nomo, LA 234
Pedro Martinez, Mtl...............222
Jeff Fassero, Mtl 222
Darryl Kile, Hou.....................219
Shane Reynolds, Hou 204
Al Leiter, Fla..........................200
Todd Stottlemyre, StL 194
Joey Hamilton, SD 184
Curt Schilling, Phil.................182

COMPLETE GAMES

Curt Schilling, Phil....................8
John Smoltz, Atl 6
Jeff Fassero, Mtl 5
Greg Maddux, Atl 5
Kevin Brown, Fla......................5
Todd Stottlemyre, StL 5

SHUTOUTS

Kevin Brown, Fla......................3
Seven tied with two.

American League Batting

BATTING AVERAGE

Alex Rodriguez, Sea .... .358
Frank Thomas, Chi.......... .349
Paul Molitor, Minn .... .341
Chuck Knoblauch, Minn .... .341
Rusty Greer, Tex............. .332
Dave Nilsson, Mil............... .331
Roberto Alomar, Balt .... .328
Edgar Martinez, Sea......... .327
Kevin Seitzer, Clev............. .326
Mo Vaughn, Bos .... .326

HITS

Paul Molitor, Min 225
Alex Rodriguez, Sea...........215
Kenny Lofton, Cle 210
Mo Vaughn, Bos 207
Chuck Knoblauch, Minn 197
Roberto Alomar, Balt 193
Ivan Rodriguez, Tex............192
Albert Belle, Clev 187
Kevin Seitzer, Clev..............187
Jeff Cirillo, Mil 184
Darryl Hamilton, Tex 184
Frank Thomas, Chi..............184

DOUBLES

Alex Rodriguez, Sea.............54
Edgar Martinez, Sea 52
Ivan Rodriguez, Tex.............47
Jeff Cirillo, Mil......................46
Marty Cordova, Minn 46

TRIPLES

Chuck Knoblauch, Minn 14
Fernando Vina, Mil................10
Dave Martinez, Chi..................8
Ozzie Guillen, Chi...................8
Paul Molitor, Minn 8
Jose Offerman, KC 8

HOME RUNS

Mark McGwire, Oak..............52
Brady Anderson, Balt 50
Ken Griffey Jr, Sea...............49
Albert Belle, Clev 48
Juan Gonzalez, Tex 47
Mo Vaughn, Bos 44
Jay Buhner, Sea 44
Frank Thomas, Chi...............40
Rafael Palmeiro, Balt 39
Cecil Fielder, NY..................39

RUNS SCORED

Alex Rodriguez, Sea............141
Chuck Knoblauch, Minn 140
Kenny Lofton, Cle 132
Roberto Alomarm Balt 132
Ken Griffey Jr, Sea..............125
Albert Belle, Clev 124
Jim Thome, Clev 122
Edgar Martinez, Sea 121
Tony Phillips, Chi 119
Mo Vaughn, Bos 118

TOTAL BASES

Alex Rodriguez, Sea 379
Albert Belle, Clev 375
Mo Vaughn, Bos 370
Brady Anderson, Bal 369
Juan Gonzalez, Tex 348

STOLEN BASES

Kenny Lofton, Clev 75
Tom Goodwin, KC 66
Otis Nixon, Tor 54
Chuck Knoblauch, Minn 45
Omar Vizquel, Clev...............35

RUNS BATTED IN

Albert Belle, Clev 148
Juan Gonzalez, Tex.............144
Mo Vaughn, Bos 143
Rafael Palmeiro, Balt 142
Ken Griffey Jr, Sea..............140
Jay Buhner, Sea 138
Frank Thomas, Chi..............134
Alex Rodriguez, Sea............123
John Jaha, Mil......................118
Tino Martinez, NY 117
Cecil Fielder, NY.................117

SLUGGING PERCENTAGE

Mark McGwire, Oak........... .730
Juan Gonzalez, Tex.......... .643
Brady Anderson, Balt .... .637
Alex Rodriguez, Sea......... .631
Ken Griffey Jr, Sea............ .628

ON-BASE PERCENTAGE

Mark McGwire, Oak.............467
Edgar Martinez, Sea............464
Frank Thomas, Chi...............459
Jim Thome, Clev..................450
Chuck Knoblauch, Min 448

BASES ON BALLS

Tony Phillips, Chi 125
Edgar Martinez, Sea............123
Jim Thome, Clev 123
Mark McGwire, Oak.............116
Frank Thomas, Chi..............109

American League Pitching

EARNED RUN AVERAGE

Juan Guzman, Tor 2.93
Pat Hentgen, Tor.................3.22
Charles Nagy, Clev.............3.41
Alex Fernandez, Chi 3.45
Kevin Appier, KC 3.62
Ken Hill, Tex........................3.63
Roger Clemens, Bos............3.63
Andrew Pettitte, NY.............3.87
Ben McDonald, Mil 3.90
Tim Belcher, KC..................3.92

SAVES

John Wetteland, NY 43
Jose Mesa, Clev 39
Roberto Hernandez, Chi........38
Troy Percival, Cal 36
Mike Fetters, Mil....................32
Michael Timlin, Tor................31
Heathcliff Slocumb, Bos 31
Mike Henneman, Tex.............31
Randy Myers, Balt 31
Jeff Montgomery, KC.............24

WINS

Andrew Pettitte, NY................21
Pat Hentgen, Tor...................20
Mike Mussina, Balt................19
Charles Nagy, Clev................17
Alex Fernandez, Chi 16
Ken Hill, Tex.........................16
Bobby Witt, Tex 16
Five tied with 15.

GAMES PITCHED

Eddie Guardado, Min 83
Mike Myers, Det....................83
Mike Stanton, Tex 81
Heathcliff Slocumb, Bos 75
Jeff Nelson, NY 73
Mike Jackson, Sea................73

INNINGS PITCHED

Pat Hentgen, Tor 265⅔
Alex Fernandez, Chi 258
Ken Hill, Tex 250⅔
Mike Mussina, Balt 243⅓
Roger Clemens, Bos 242⅔

STRIKEOUTS

Roger Clemens, Bos............257
Chuck Finley, Cal.................215
Kevin Appier, KC 207
Mike Mussina, Balt...............204
Alex Fernandez, Chi 200
Wilson Alvarez, Chi..............181
Pat Hentgen, Tor..................177
Tom Gordon, Bos 171
Ken Hill, Tex.........................170
Charles Nagy, Clev...............167

COMPLETE GAMES

Pat Hentgen, Tor..................10
Ken Hill, Tex...........................7
Roger Pavlik, Tex....................7
Four tied with six.

SHUTOUTS

Pat Hentgen, Tor.....................3
Ken Hill, Tex............................3
Rich Robertson, Minn 3
Roger Clemens, Bos...............2
Felipe Lira, Det 2

1996 Team Statistics

National League

TEAM BATTING	BA	AB	R	H	TB	2B	3B	HR	RBI	SB	BB	SO
Colorado	.287	5590	961	1607	2641	297	37	221	909	201	527	1110
Atlanta	.270	5614	773	1514	2425	264	28	197	735	83	530	1032
New York	.270	5618	746	1515	2319	269	47	147	697	97	447	1072
St Louis	.267	5503	759	1468	2239	283	31	142	711	149	495	1094
Pittsburgh	.266	5665	776	1509	2306	317	33	138	738	127	511	987
San Diego	.265	5655	771	1499	2273	285	24	147	718	110	601	1016
Houston	.262	5508	753	1445	2185	295	29	129	703	180	555	1052
Montreal	.262	5506	741	1441	2236	297	27	148	696	108	492	1077
Florida	.257	5498	688	1413	2163	240	30	150	650	99	553	1123
Cincinnati	.256	5455	778	1398	2302	259	36	191	733	172	603	1135
Philadelphia	.256	5499	650	1405	2128	249	39	132	604	117	536	1094
San Francisco	.253	5533	752	1400	2145	245	21	153	707	113	615	1188
Los Angeles	.252	5538	703	1396	2128	216	33	150	661	123	516	1189
Chicago	.251	5531	772	1388	2216	266	19	175	725	107	522	1086

TEAM PITCHING	ERA	W	L	Sho	CG	SV	Inn	H	R	ER	BB	SO
Los Angeles	3.46	90	72	9	6	50	1466⅓	1378	652	567	534	1213
Atlanta	3.52	96	66	9	14	46	1469	1372	648	577	451	1245
San Diego	3.72	91	71	11	5	47	1489	1394	682	617	506	1194
Montreal	3.78	88	74	7	11	43	1440⅓	1352	668	605	482	1204
Florida	3.95	80	82	13	8	41	1443	1385	703	633	598	1051
St Louis	3.97	88	74	11	13	43	1452⅓	1380	706	642	539	1050
New York	4.22	71	91	10	10	41	1440	1517	779	675	532	999
Cincinnati	4.32	81	81	8	6	52	1443	1447	773	695	591	1089
Chicago	4.36	76	86	11	10	34	1456⅓	1447	771	705	546	1027
Houston	4.37	82	80	4	13	35	1447	1541	792	704	539	1164
Philadelphia	4.48	67	95	6	12	42	1423⅓	1463	790	710	510	1043
Pittsburgh	4.61	73	89	7	5	37	1454⅓	1603	833	749	479	1046
San Francisco	4.71	68	94	8	9	35	1442⅓	1520	862	757	570	998
Colorado	5.59	83	79	5	5	34	1422⅔	1597	964	885	624	932

American League

TEAM BATTING	BA	AB	R	H	TB	2B	3B	HR	RBI	SB	BB	SO
Cleveland	.293	5681	952	1665	2700	335	23	218	904	159	671	843
Minnesota	.288	5673	877	1633	2413	332	47	118	812	143	576	958
New York	.288	5628	871	1621	2456	293	28	162	830	95	632	909
Seattle	.287	5668	993	1625	2739	343	18	245	954	90	670	1052
Texas	.284	5703	928	1622	2672	323	32	221	890	83	660	1041
Boston	.283	5756	928	1631	2627	307	31	209	882	91	642	1020
Chicago	.281	5644	898	1586	2520	284	33	195	860	105	701	927
Milwaukee	.279	5659	894	1577	2494	304	40	178	845	101	623	985
California	.276	5682	762	1571	2451	256	24	192	727	53	527	973
Baltimore	.274	5689	949	1557	2685	299	29	257	914	76	645	915
Kansas City	.266	5543	746	1477	2208	286	38	123	689	195	529	944
Oakland	.265	5630	861	1492	2546	283	21	243	822	57	640	1114
Toronto	.259	5599	766	1451	2354	302	35	177	712	116	529	1105
Detroit	.256	5530	783	1413	2324	257	21	204	741	87	546	1268

TEAM PITCHING	ERA	W	L	Sho	CG	SV	Inn	H	R	ER	BB	SO
Cleveland	4.34	99	62	9	13	46	1452⅓	1530	769	702	484	1033
Chicago	4.52	85	77	5	7	43	1461	1529	794	735	616	1039
Kansas City	4.55	75	86	8	17	37	1450	1563	786	733	460	925
Toronto	4.57	74	88	7	19	35	1445⅔	1476	809	735	610	1033
New York	4.65	92	70	9	6	53	1440	1469	787	744	610	1139
Texas	4.65	90	72	6	19	43	1449⅓	1569	799	750	582	976
Boston	4.98	85	77	5	17	37	1458	1606	921	810	722	1166
Baltimore	5.14	88	74	2	13	44	1468⅔	1604	903	841	597	1047
Milwaukee	5.14	80	82	5	6	42	1447⅓	1570	899	831	635	846
Oakland	5.20	78	84	5	7	34	1456⅓	1638	900	842	644	884
Seattle	5.21	85	76	4	4	34	1431⅔	1562	895	829	605	1000
Minnesota	5.28	78	84	5	13	31	1439⅔	1561	900	848	581	959
California	5.30	70	91	8	12	38	1439	1546	943	849	662	1052
Detroit	6.38	53	109	4	10	22	1432⅔	1699	1103	1015	784	957

National League Team-by-Team Statistical Leaders

Atlanta Braves

BATTING	BA	G	AB	R	H	TB	2B	3B	HR	RBI	SB	BB	SO
Justice, David	.321	40	140	23	45	72	9	0	6	25	1	21	22
Jones, Chipper	.309	157	598	114	185	317	32	5	30	110	14	87	88
Grissom, Marquis	.308	158	671	106	207	328	32	10	23	74	28	41	73
McGriff, Fred	.295	159	617	81	182	305	37	1	28	107	7	68	116
Lopez, Javy	.282	138	489	56	138	228	19	1	23	69	1	28	84
Klesko, Ryan	.282	153	528	90	149	280	21	4	34	93	6	68	129
Dye, Jermaine	.281	98	292	32	82	134	16	0	12	37	1	8	67
Perez, Eddie	.256	68	156	19	40	63	9	1	4	17	0	8	19
Lemke, Mark	.255	135	498	64	127	159	17	0	5	37	5	53	48
Blauser, Jeff	.245	83	265	48	65	111	14	1	10	35	6	40	54
Whiten, Mark	.243	96	272	45	66	111	13	1	10	38	15	49	87
Mordecai, Mike	.241	66	108	12	26	37	5	0	2	8	1	9	24
Pendleton, Terry	.238	153	568	51	135	196	26	1	11	75	2	41	111
Jones, Andruw	.217	31	106	11	23	47	7	1	5	13	3	7	29
Smith, Dwight	.203	101	153	16	31	45	5	0	3	16	1	17	42

PITCHING	ERA	W	L	G	GS	CG	SV	INN	H	R	ER	BB	SO
Bielecki, Mike	2.63	4	3	40	5	0	2	75⅓	63	24	22	33	71
Maddux, Greg	2.72	15	11	35	35	5	0	245	225	85	74	28	172
Borbon, Pedro	2.75	3	0	43	0	0	1	36	26	12	11	7	31
Smoltz, John	2.94	24	8	35	35	6	0	253⅔	199	93	83	55	276
Wade, Terrell	2.97	5	0	44	8	0	1	69⅔	57	28	23	47	79
Glavine, Tom	2.98	15	10	36	36	1	0	235⅓	222	91	78	85	181
Wohlers, Mark	3.03	2	4	77	0	0	39	77⅓	71	30	26	21	100
McMichael, Greg	3.22	5	3	73	0	0	2	86⅔	84	37	31	27	78
Neagle, Denny	3.50	16	9	33	33	2	0	221⅓	226	93	86	48	149
Avery, Steve	4.47	7	10	24	23	1	0	131	146	70	65	40	86
Clontz, Brad	5.69	6	3	81	0	0	1	80⅔	78	53	51	33	49

Chicago Cubs

BATTING	BA	G	AB	R	H	TB	2B	3B	HR	RBI	SB	BB	SO
Grace, Mark	.331	142	547	88	181	249	39	1	9	75	2	62	41
Houston, Tyler	.317	79	142	21	45	65	9	1	3	27	3	9	27
McRae, Brian	.276	157	624	111	172	265	32	5	17	66	37	73	84
Sosa, Sammy	.273	124	498	84	136	281	21	2	40	100	18	34	134
Gonzalez, Luis	.271	146	483	70	131	214	30	4	15	79	9	61	49
Servais, Scott	.265	129	445	42	118	171	20	0	11	63	0	30	75
Magadan, Dave	.254	78	169	23	43	62	10	0	3	17	0	29	23
Sandberg, Ryne	.244	150	554	85	135	246	28	4	25	92	12	54	116
Hernandez, Jose	.242	131	331	52	80	126	14	1	10	41	4	24	97
Gomez, Leo	.238	136	362	44	86	156	19	0	17	56	1	53	94
Bullett, Scott	.212	109	165	26	35	49	5	0	3	16	7	10	54
Sanchez, Rey	.211	95	289	28	61	73	9	0	1	12	7	22	42
Timmons, Ozzie	.200	65	140	18	28	53	4	0	7	16	1	15	3

PITCHING	ERA	W	L	G	GS	CG	SV	INN	H	R	ER	BB	SO
Bottenfield, Kent	2.63	3	5	48	0	0	1	61⅔	59	25	18	19	33
Wendell, Turk	2.84	4	5	70	0	0	18	79⅓	58	26	25	44	75
Adams, Terry	2.94	3	6	69	0	0	4	101	84	36	33	49	78
Trachsel, Steve	3.03	13	9	31	31	3	0	205	181	82	69	62	132
Patterson, Bob	3.13	3	3	79	0	0	8	54⅔	46	19	19	22	53
Navarro, Jaime	3.92	15	12	35	35	4	0	236⅔	244	116	103	72	158
Campbell, Kevin	4.46	3	1	13	5	0	0	36⅓	29	19	18	10	19
Myers, Randy	4.68	2	1	45	0	0	0	67⅓	61	38	35	38	50
Jones, Doug	5.01	2	2	28	0	0	2	32⅓	41	20	18	7	26
Castillo, Frank	5.28	7	16	33	33	1	0	182⅓	209	112	107	46	139
Telemaco, Amaury	5.46	5	7	25	17	0	0	97⅓	108	67	59	31	64
Foster, Kevin	6.21	7	6	17	16	1	0	87	98	63	60	35	53
Bullinger, Jim	6.54	6	10	37	20	1	1	129⅓	144	101	94	68	90

National League Team-by-Team Statistical Leaders *(Cont.)*

Cincinnati Reds

BATTING	BA	G	AB	R	H	TB	2B	3B	HR	RBI	SB	BB	SO
Mitchell, Kevin	.325	37	114	18	37	66	11	0	6	26	0	26	16
Morris, Hal	.313	142	528	82	165	253	32	4	16	80	7	50	76
Larkin, Barry	.298	152	517	117	154	293	32	4	33	89	36	96	52
Taubensee, Eddie	.291	108	327	46	95	151	20	0	12	48	3	26	64
Davis, Eric	.287	129	415	81	119	217	20	0	26	83	23	70	121
Harris, Lenny	.285	125	302	33	86	122	17	2	5	32	14	21	31
Howard, Thomas	.272	121	360	50	98	155	19	10	6	42	6	17	51
Sabo, Chris	.256	54	125	15	32	50	7	1	3	16	2	18	27
Sanders, Reggie	.251	81	287	49	72	133	17	1	14	33	24	44	86
Branson, Jeff	.244	129	311	34	76	127	16	4	9	37	2	31	67
Greene, Willie	.244	115	287	48	70	142	5	5	19	63	0	36	88
Oliver, Joe	.242	106	289	31	70	117	12	1	11	46	2	28	54
Boone, Bret	.233	142	520	56	121	184	21	3	12	69	3	31	100
Goodwin, Tom	.228	49	136	20	31	34	3	0	0	5	15	19	34
Owens, Eric	.200	88	205	26	41	47	6	0	0	9	16	23	38

PITCHING	ERA	W	L	G	GS	CG	SV	INN	H	R	ER	BB	SO
Brantley, Jeff	2.41	1	2	66	0	0	44	71	54	21	19	28	76
Shaw, Jeff	2.49	8	6	78	0	0	4	104⅔	99	34	29	29	69
Smiley, John	3.64	13	14	35	34	2	0	217⅓	207	100	88	54	171
Carrasco, Hector	3.75	4	3	56	0	0	0	74⅓	58	37	31	45	59
Burba, Dave	3.83	11	13	34	33	0	0	195	179	96	83	97	148
Service, Scott	3.94	1	0	34	1	0	0	48	51	21	21	18	46
Portugal, Mark	3.98	8	9	27	26	1	0	156	146	77	69	42	93
Smith, Lee	4.06	3	4	43	0	0	2	44⅓	49	20	20	23	35
Morgan, Mike	4.63	6	11	23	23	0	0	130⅓	146	72	67	47	74
Salkeld, Roger	5.20	8	5	29	19	1	0	116	114	69	67	54	82
Ruffin, Johnny	5.49	1	3	49	0	0	0	62⅓	71	42	38	37	69
Jarvis, Kevin	5.98	8	9	24	20	2	0	120⅓	152	93	80	43	63
Schourek, Pete	6.01	4	5	12	12	0	0	67⅓	79	48	45	24	54

Colorado Rockies

BATTING	BA	G	AB	R	H	TB	2B	3B	HR	RBI	SB	BB	SO
Burks, Ellis	.344	156	613	142	211	392	45	8	40	128	32	61	114
Young, Eric	.324	144	568	113	184	239	23	4	8	74	53	47	31
Bichette, Dante	.313	159	633	114	198	336	39	3	31	141	31	45	105
Castilla, Vinny	.304	160	629	97	191	345	34	0	40	113	7	35	88
Galarraga, Andres	.304	159	626	119	190	376	39	3	47	150	18	40	157
McCracken, Quinton	.290	124	283	50	82	116	13	6	3	40	17	32	62
Reed, Jeff	.284	116	341	34	97	143	20	1	8	37	2	43	65
Weiss, Walt	.282	155	517	89	146	194	20	2	8	48	10	80	78
Walker, Larry	.276	83	272	58	75	155	18	4	18	58	18	20	58
VanderWal, John	.252	104	151	20	38	63	6	2	5	31	2	19	38
Decker, Steve	.245	67	147	24	36	45	3	0	2	20	1	18	29
Anthony, Eric	.243	79	185	32	45	89	8	0	12	22	0	32	56
Owens, Jayhawk	.239	73	180	31	43	66	9	1	4	17	4	27	56
Bates, Jason	.206	88	160	19	33	46	8	1	1	9	2	23	34

PITCHING	ERA	W	L	G	GS	CG	SV	INN	H	R	ER	BB	SO
Reed, Steve	3.96	4	3	70	0	0	0	75	66	38	33	19	51
Holmes, Darren	3.97	5	4	62	0	0	1	77	78	41	34	28	73
Ruffin, Bruce	4.00	7	5	71	0	0	24	69⅔	55	35	31	29	74
Wright, Jamey	4.93	4	4	16	15	0	0	91⅓	105	60	50	41	45
Reynoso, Armando	4.96	8	9	30	30	0	0	168⅔	195	97	93	49	88
Ritz, Kevin	5.28	17	11	35	35	2	0	213	236	135	125	105	105
Thompson, Mark	5.30	9	11	34	28	3	0	169⅔	189	109	100	74	99
Painter, Lance	5.86	4	2	34	1	0	0	50⅔	56	37	33	25	48
Freeman, Marvin	6.04	7	9	26	23	0	0	129⅔	151	100	87	57	71
Leskanic, Curt	6.23	7	5	70	0	0	6	73⅔	82	51	51	38	76
Bailey, Roger	6.24	2	3	24	11	0	1	83⅔	94	64	58	52	45

National League Team-by-Team Statistical Leaders *(Cont.)*

Florida Marlins

BATTING	BA	G	AB	R	H	TB	2B	3B	HR	RBI	SB	BB	SO
Sheffield, Gary	.314	161	519	118	163	324	33	1	42	120	16	142	66
Renteria, Edgar	.309	106	431	68	133	172	18	3	5	31	16	33	68
Conine, Jeff	.293	157	597	84	175	289	32	2	26	95	1	62	121
Colbrunn, Greg	.286	141	511	60	146	224	26	2	16	69	4	25	76
Arias, Alex	.277	100	224	27	62	86	11	2	3	26	2	17	28
White, Devon	.274	146	552	77	151	251	37	6	17	84	22	38	99
Castillo, Luis	.262	41	164	26	43	50	2	1	1	8	17	14	46
Abbott, Kurt	.253	109	320	37	81	137	18	7	8	33	3	22	99
Veras, Quilvio	.253	73	253	40	64	86	8	1	4	14	8	51	42
Orsulak, Joe	.221	120	217	23	48	62	6	1	2	19	1	16	38
Tavarez, Jesus	.219	98	114	14	25	28	3	0	0	6	5	7	18
Johnson, Charles	.218	120	386	34	84	138	13	1	13	37	1	40	91
Grebeck, Craig	.211	50	95	8	20	24	1	0	1	9	0	4	14

PITCHING	ERA	W	L	G	GS	CG	SV	INN	H	R	ER	BB	SO
Brown, Kevin	1.89	17	11	32	32	5	0	233	187	60	49	33	159
Nen, Robb	1.95	5	1	75	0	0	35	83	67	21	18	21	92
Leiter, Al	2.93	16	12	33	33	2	0	215⅓	153	74	70	119	200
Hutton, Mark	3.67	5	1	13	9	0	0	56⅓	47	23	23	18	31
Burkett, John	4.32	6	10	24	24	1	0	154	154	84	74	42	108
Powell, Jay	4.54	4	3	67	0	0	2	71⅓	71	41	36	36	52
Weathers, Dave	4.54	2	2	31	8	0	0	71⅓	85	41	36	28	40
Valdes, Mark	4.81	1	3	11	8	0	0	48¾	63	32	26	23	13
Mathews, Terry	4.91	2	4	57	0	0	4	55	59	33	30	27	49
Rapp, Pat	5.10	8	16	30	29	0	0	162⅓	184	95	92	91	86
Perez, Yorkis	5.29	3	4	64	0	0	0	47⅔	51	28	28	31	47

Houston Astros

BATTING	BA	G	AB	R	H	TB	2B	3B	HR	RBI	SB	BB	SO
Bagwell, Jeff	.315	162	568	111	179	324	48	2	31	120	21	135	114
Biggio, Craig	.288	162	605	113	174	251	24	4	15	75	25	75	72
Gutierrez, Ricky	.284	89	218	28	62	75	8	1	1	15	6	23	42
Berry, Sean	.281	132	431	55	121	212	38	1	17	95	12	23	58
Hunter, Brian	.276	132	526	74	145	191	27	2	5	35	35	17	92
Eusebio, Tony	.270	58	152	15	41	55	7	2	1	19	0	18	20
Cangelosi, John	.263	108	262	49	69	91	11	4	1	16	17	44	41
Mouton, James	.263	122	300	40	79	105	15	1	3	34	21	38	55
Bell, Derek	.263	158	627	84	165	262	40	3	17	113	29	40	123
Miller, Orlando	.256	139	468	63	120	195	62	2	15	58	3	14	116
Spiers, Bill	.252	122	218	27	55	85	10	1	6	26	7	20	34
May, Derrick	.251	109	259	24	65	98	12	3	5	33	2	30	33
Cedeno, Andujar	.231	52	156	11	36	49	2	1	3	18	3	11	33
Manwaring, Kurt	.229	86	227	14	52	64	9	0	1	18	0	19	40

PITCHING	ERA	W	L	G	GS	CG	SV	INN	H	R	ER	BB	SO
Wagner, Billy	2.44	2	2	37	0	0	9	51⅔	28	16	14	30	67
Hampton, Mike	3.59	10	10	27	27	2	0	160⅓	175	79	64	49	101
Reynolds, Shane	3.65	16	10	35	35	4	0	239	227	103	97	44	204
Darwin, Danny	3.77	10	11	34	25	0	0	164⅔	160	79	69	27	96
Kile, Darryl	4.19	12	11	35	33	4	0	219	233	113	102	97	219
Jones, Todd	4.40	6	3	51	0	0	17	57⅓	61	30	28	32	44
Wall, Donne	4.56	9	8	26	23	2	0	150	170	84	76	34	99
Drabek, Doug	4.57	7	9	30	30	1	0	175⅓	208	102	89	60	137
Brocail, Doug	4.58	1	5	23	4	0	0	53	58	31	27	23	34
Young, Anthony	4.59	3	3	28	0	0	0	33⅓	36	18	17	22	19
Hernandez, Xavier	4.62	5	5	61	0	0	6	78	77	45	40	28	81
Morman, Alvin	4.93	4	1	53	0	0	0	42	43	24	23	24	31

National League Team-by-Team Statistical Leaders (Cont.)

Los Angeles Dodgers

BATTING	BA	G	AB	R	H	TB	2B	3B	HR	RBI	SB	BB	SO
Piazza, Mike	.336	148	547	87	184	308	16	0	36	105	0	81	93
Mondesi, Raul	.297	157	634	98	188	314	40	7	24	88	14	32	122
Hollandsworth, Todd	.291	149	478	64	139	209	26	4	12	59	21	41	93
Kirby, Wayne	.271	65	188	23	51	66	10	1	1	11	4	17	17
Clark, Dave	.270	107	226	28	61	101	12	2	8	36	2	34	53
Butler, Brett	.267	34	131	22	35	38	1	1	0	8	8	9	22
Blowers, Mike	.265	92	317	31	84	125	19	2	6	38	0	37	77
Karros, Eric	.260	154	608	84	158	291	29	1	34	111	8	53	121
Gagne, Greg	.255	128	428	48	109	156	13	2	10	55	4	50	93
Cedeno, Roger	.246	86	211	26	52	71	11	1	2	18	5	24	47
Wallach, Tim	.228	45	162	14	37	54	3	1	4	22	0	12	32
DeShields, Delino	.224	154	581	73	130	173	12	8	5	41	48	53	124
Hansen, Dave	.221	80	104	7	23	24	1	0	0	6	0	11	22
Curtis, Chad	.212	43	104	20	22	33	5	0	2	9	2	17	15
Fonville, Chad	.204	103	201	34	41	47	4	1	0	13	7	17	31

PITCHING	ERA	W	L	G	GS	CG	SV	INN	H	R	ER	BB	SO
Guthrie, Mark	2.22	2	3	66	0	0	1	73	65	21	18	22	56
Radinsky, Scott	2.41	5	1	58	0	0	1	52⅓	52	19	14	17	48
Osuna, Antonio	3.00	9	6	73	0	0	4	84	65	33	28	32	85
Worrell, Todd	3.03	4	6	72	0	0	44	65⅓	70	29	22	15	66
Nomo, Hideo	3.19	16	11	33	33	3	0	228⅓	180	93	81	85	234
Valdes, Ismael	3.32	15	7	33	33	0	0	225	219	94	83	54	173
Martinez, Ramon	3.42	15	6	28	27	2	0	168⅔	153	76	64	86	134
Astacio, Pedro	3.44	9	8	35	32	0	0	211¾	207	86	81	67	130
Park, Chan Ho	3.64	5	5	48	10	0	0	108⅔	82	48	44	71	119
Candiotti, Tom	4.49	9	11	28	27	1	0	152⅓	172	91	76	43	79
Eischen, Joey	4.78	0	1	28	0	0	0	43⅓	48	25	23	20	36

Montreal Expos

BATTING	BA	G	AB	R	H	TB	2B	3B	HR	RBI	SB	BB	SO
Grudzielanek, Mark	.306	153	657	99	201	261	34	4	6	49	33	26	83
White, Rondell	.293	88	334	35	98	143	19	4	6	41	14	22	53
Segui, David	.286	115	416	69	119	184	30	1	11	58	4	60	54
Lansing, Mike	.285	159	641	99	183	260	40	2	11	53	23	44	85
Alou, Moises	.281	143	540	87	152	247	28	2	21	96	9	49	83
Santangelo, F.P.	.277	152	393	54	109	160	20	5	7	56	5	49	61
Rodriguez, Henry	.276	143	532	81	147	299	42	1	36	103	2	37	160
Fletcher, Darrin	.266	127	394	41	105	163	22	0	12	57	0	27	42
Obando, Sherman	.247	89	178	30	44	77	9	0	8	22	2	22	48
Floyd, Cliff	.242	117	227	29	55	96	15	4	6	26	7	30	52
Webster, Lenny	.230	78	174	18	40	56	10	0	2	17	0	25	21
Andrews, Shane	.227	127	375	43	85	161	15	2	19	64	3	35	119
Silvestri, Dave	.204	86	162	16	33	40	4	0	1	17	2	34	41

PITCHING	ERA	W	L	G	GS	CG	SV	INN	H	R	ER	BB	SO
Rojas, Mel	3.22	7	4	74	0	0	36	81	56	30	29	28	92
Manuel, Barry	3.24	4	1	53	0	0	0	86	70	34	31	26	62
Juden, Jeff	3.27	5	0	58	0	0	0	74⅓	61	35	27	34	61
Fassero, Jeff	3.30	15	11	34	34	5	0	231⅔	217	95	85	55	222
Paniagua, Jose	3.53	2	4	13	11	0	0	51	55	24	20	23	27
Martinez, Pedro	3.70	13	10	33	33	4	0	216⅔	189	100	89	70	222
Urbina, Ugueth	3.71	10	5	33	17	0	0	114	102	54	47	44	108
Daal, Omar	4.02	4	5	64	6	0	0	87⅓	74	40	39	37	82
Cormier, Rheal	4.17	7	10	33	27	1	0	159⅔	165	80	74	41	100
Veres, Dave	4.17	6	3	68	0	0	4	77⅓	85	39	36	32	81
Dyer, Mike	4.40	5	5	70	1	0	2	75⅔	79	40	37	34	51
Leiter, Mark	4.92	8	12	35	34	2	0	205	219	128	112	69	164

New York Mets

BATTING	BA	G	AB	R	H	TB	2B	3B	HR	RBI	SB	BB	SO
Johnson, Lance	.333	160	682	117	227	327	31	21	9	69	50	33	40
Gilkey, Bernard	.317	153	571	108	181	321	44	3	30	117	17	73	125
Espinoza, Alvaro	.306	48	134	19	41	64	7	2	4	16	0	4	19
Vizcaino, Jose	.303	96	363	47	110	137	12	6	1	32	9	28	58
Ochoa, Alex	.294	82	282	37	83	120	19	3	4	33	4	17	30
Kent, Jeff	.290	89	335	45	97	146	20	1	9	39	4	21	56
Huskey, Butch	.278	118	414	43	115	180	16	2	15	60	1	27	77
Mayne, Brent	.263	70	99	9	26	35	6	0	1	6	0	12	22
Alfonzo, Edgardo	.261	123	368	36	96	127	15	2	4	40	2	25	56
Hundley, Todd	.259	153	540	85	140	297	32	1	41	112	1	79	146
Ordonez, Rey	.257	151	502	51	129	152	12	4	1	30	1	22	53
Brogna, Rico	.255	55	188	18	48	81	10	1	7	30	0	19	50
Jones, Chris	.242	89	149	22	36	55	7	0	4	18	1	12	42
Everett, Carl	.240	101	192	29	46	59	8	1	1	16	6	21	53
Petagine, Roberto	.232	50	99	10	23	38	3	0	4	17	0	9	27

PITCHING	ERA	W	L	G	GS	CG	SV	INN	H	R	ER	BB	SO
Franco, John	1.83	4	3	51	0	0	28	54	54	15	11	21	48
Mlicki, Dave	3.30	6	7	51	2	0	1	90	95	46	33	33	83
Clark, Mark	3.43	14	11	32	32	2	0	212⅓	217	98	81	48	142
DiPoto, Jerry	4.19	7	2	57	0	0	0	77⅓	91	44	36	45	52
Harnisch, Pete	4.21	8	12	31	31	2	0	194⅔	195	103	91	61	114
Byrd, Paul	4.24	1	2	38	0	0	0	46⅔	48	22	22	21	31
Jones, Bobby	4.42	12	8	31	31	3	0	195⅔	219	102	96	46	116
Person, Robert	4.52	4	5	27	32	0	0	89⅔	26	50	45	35	76
Henry, Doug	4.68	2	8	58	0	0	9	75	82	48	39	36	58
Isringhausen, Jason	4.77	6	14	27	27	2	0	171⅓	190	103	91	73	114
Wilson, Paul	5.38	5	12	26	26	1	0	149	157	102	89	71	109

Philadelphia Phillies

BATTING	BA	G	AB	R	H	TB	2B	3B	HR	RBI	SB	BB	SO
Eisenreich, Jim	.361	113	338	45	122	161	24	3	3	41	11	31	32
Amaro, Ruben	.316	61	117	14	37	53	10	0	2	15	0	9	18
Jefferies, Gregg	.292	104	404	59	118	162	17	3	7	51	20	36	21
Sefcik, Kevin	.284	44	116	10	33	44	5	3	0	9	3	9	16
Jordan, Kevin	.282	43	131	15	37	56	10	0	3	12	2	5	20
Otero, Ricky	.273	104	411	54	112	143	11	7	2	32	16	34	30
Zeile, Todd	.268	134	500	61	134	218	24	0	20	80	1	67	88
Doster, Dave	.267	39	105	14	28	39	8	0	1	8	0	7	21
Santiago, Benito	.264	136	481	71	127	242	21	2	30	85	2	49	104
Dykstra, Lenny	.261	40	134	21	35	56	6	3	3	13	3	26	25
Rolen, Scott	.254	37	130	10	33	52	7	0	4	18	0	13	27
Stocker, Kevin	.254	119	394	46	100	149	22	6	5	41	6	43	89
Lieberthal, Mike	.253	50	166	21	42	71	8	0	7	23	0	10	30
Morandini, Mickey	.250	140	539	64	135	180	24	6	3	32	26	49	87
Incaviglia, Pete	.234	99	269	33	63	122	7	2	16	42	2	30	82

PITCHING	ERA	W	L	G	GS	CG	SV	INN	H	R	ER	BB	SO
Ryan, Ken	2.43	3	5	62	0	0	8	89	71	32	24	45	70
Schilling, Curt	3.19	9	10	26	26	8	0	183⅓	149	69	65	50	182
Bottalico, Ricky	3.19	4	5	61	0	0	34	67⅔	47	24	24	23	74
Parrett, Jeff	3.39	3	3	51	0	0	0	66⅓	64	25	25	31	64
Fernandez, Sid	3.43	3	6	11	11	0	0	63	50	25	24	26	77
Grace, Mike	3.49	7	2	12	12	1	0	80	72	33	31	16	49
Borland, Toby	4.07	7	3	69	0	0	0	90⅔	83	51	41	43	76
Springer, Russ	4.66	3	10	51	7	0	0	96⅔	106	60	50	38	94
Mulholland, Terry	4.66	8	7	21	21	3	0	133⅓	157	74	69	21	52
Williams, Mike	5.44	6	14	32	29	0	0	167	188	107	101	67	103
Mimbs, Mike	5.53	3	9	21	17	0	0	99⅓	116	66	61	41	56
Hunter, Rich	6.49	3	7	14	14	0	0	69¼	84	54	50	33	32

National League Team-by-Team Statistical Leaders (Cont.)

Pittsburgh Pirates

BATTING	BA	G	AB	R	H	TB	2B	3B	HR	RBI	SB	BB	SO
Martin, Al	.300	155	630	101	189	285	40	1	18	72	38	54	116
Kendall, Jason	.300	130	414	54	124	166	23	5	3	42	5	35	30
Osik, Keith	.293	48	140	18	41	60	14	1	1	14	1	14	22
Merced, Orlando	.287	120	453	69	130	207	24	1	17	80	8	51	74
Garcia, Carlos	.285	101	390	66	111	155	18	4	6	44	16	23	58
Johnson, Mark	.274	127	343	55	94	157	24	0	13	47	6	44	64
King, Jeff	.271	155	591	91	160	294	36	4	30	111	15	70	95
Liriano, Nelson	.267	112	217	23	58	85	14	2	3	30	2	14	22
Allensworth, Jermaine	.262	61	229	32	60	89	9	3	4	31	11	23	50
Wehner, John	.259	86	139	19	36	53	9	1	2	13	1	8	22
Bell, Jay	.250	151	527	65	132	206	29	3	13	71	6	54	108
Hayes, Charlie	.248	128	459	51	114	169	21	2	10	62	6	36	78
Kingery, Mike	.246	117	276	32	68	93	12	2	3	27	2	23	29

PITCHING	ERA	W	L	G	GS	CG	SV	INN	H	R	ER	BB	SO
Wilkins, Marc	3.84	4	3	47	2	0	1	75	75	36	32	36	32
Lieber, Jon	3.99	9	5	51	15	0	1	142	156	70	63	28	94
Cordova, Francisco	4.09	4	7	59	6	0	12	99	103	49	45	20	95
Plesac, Dan	4.09	6	5	73	0	0	11	70⅓	67	35	32	24	76
Ruebel, Matt	4.60	1	1	26	7	0	1	58⅔	64	38	30	25	22
Loaiza, Esteban	4.96	2	3	10	10	1	0	52⅔	65	32	29	19	32
Smith, Zane	5.08	4	6	16	16	1	0	83⅓	104	53	47	21	47
Morel, Ramon	5.36	2	1	29	0	0	0	42	57	27	25	19	22
Wagner, Paul	5.40	4	8	16	15	1	0	81⅔	86	49	49	39	81
Peters, Chris	5.63	2	4	16	10	0	0	64	72	43	40	25	28
Schmidt, Jason	5.70	5	6	19	17	1	0	96⅓	108	67	61	53	74
Miceli, Dan	5.78	2	10	44	9	0	1	85⅔	99	65	55	45	66
Ericks, John	5.79	4	5	28	4	0	8	46⅔	56	35	30	19	46
Christiansen, Jason	6.70	3	3	33	0	0	0	44⅓	56	34	33	19	38

St. Louis Cardinals

BATTING	BA	G	AB	R	H	TB	2B	3B	HR	RBI	SB	BB	SO
Jordan, Brian	.310	140	513	82	159	248	36	1	17	104	22	29	84
McGee, Willie	.307	123	309	52	95	129	15	2	5	41	5	18	60
Mabry, John	.297	151	543	63	161	234	30	2	13	74	3	37	84
Smith, Ozzie	.282	82	227	36	64	84	10	2	2	18	7	25	9
Clayton, Royce	.277	129	491	64	136	182	20	4	6	35	33	33	89
Lankford, Ray	.275	149	545	100	150	265	36	8	21	86	35	79	133
Gaetti, Gary	.274	141	522	71	143	247	27	4	23	80	2	35	97
Pagnozzi, Tom	.270	119	407	48	110	172	23	0	13	55	4	24	78
Sweeney, Mark	.265	98	170	32	45	63	9	0	3	22	3	33	29
Alicea, Luis	.258	129	380	54	98	145	26	3	5	42	11	52	78
Gant, Ron	.246	122	419	74	103	211	14	2	30	82	13	73	98
Sheaffer, Danny	.227	79	198	10	45	66	9	3	2	20	3	9	25
Bell, David	.214	62	145	12	31	40	6	0	1	9	1	10	22
Gallego, Mike	.210	51	143	12	30	32	2	0	0	4	0	12	31

PITCHING	ERA	W	L	G	GS	CG	SV	INN	H	R	ER	BB	SO
Fossas, Tony	2.68	0	4	65	0	0	2	47	43	19	14	21	36
Honeycutt, Rick	2.85	2	1	61	0	0	4	47⅓	42	15	15	7	30
Bailey, Cory	3.00	5	2	51	0	0	0	57	57	21	19	30	38
Mathews, T.J.	3.01	2	6	67	0	0	6	83⅔	62	32	28	32	80
Eckersley, Dennis	3.30	0	6	63	0	0	30	60	65	26	22	6	49
Osborne, Dovovan	3.53	13	9	30	30	2	0	198⅔	191	87	78	57	134
Petkovsek, Mark	3.55	11	2	48	6	0	0	88⅔	83	37	35	35	45
Benes, Andy	3.83	18	10	36	34	3	1	230⅓	215	107	98	77	160
Stottlemyre, Mel	3.87	14	11	34	33	5	0	223⅓	191	100	96	93	194
Jackson, Danny	4.46	1	1	13	4	0	0	36⅓	33	18	18	16	27
Benes, Alan	4.90	13	10	34	32	3	0	191	192	120	104	89	131

National League Team-by-Team Statistical Leaders *(Cont.)*

San Diego Padres

BATTING	BA	G	AB	R	H	TB	2B	3B	HR	RBI	SB	BB	SO
Gwynn, Tony	.353	116	451	67	159	199	27	2	3	50	11	39	17
Caminiti, Ken	.326	146	546	109	178	339	37	2	40	130	11	78	99
Flaherty, John	.303	72	264	22	80	119	12	0	9	41	2	9	36
Finley, Steve	.298	161	655	126	195	348	45	9	30	95	22	56	88
Livingstone, Scott	.297	102	172	20	51	63	4	1	2	20	0	9	22
Cianfrocco, Archi	.281	79	192	21	54	79	13	3	2	32	1	8	56
Joyner, Wally	.277	121	433	59	120	175	29	1	8	65	5	69	71
Johnson, Brian	.272	82	243	18	66	105	13	1	8	35	0	4	36
Gomez, Chris	.262	89	328	32	86	113	16	1	3	29	2	39	64
Newfield, Marc	.251	84	191	27	48	74	11	0	5	26	1	16	44
Reed, Jody	.244	146	495	45	121	147	20	0	2	49	2	59	53
Henderson, Rickey	.241	148	465	110	112	160	17	2	9	29	37	125	90
Vaughn, Greg	.206	43	141	20	29	64	3	1	10	22	4	24	31

PITCHING	ERA	W	L	G	GS	CG	SV	INN	H	R	ER	BB	SO
Hoffman, Trevor	2.25	9	5	70	0	0	42	88	50	23	22	31	111
Bochtler, Doug	3.02	2	4	63	0	0	3	65⅔	45	25	22	39	68
Worrell, Tim	3.05	9	7	50	11	0	1	121	109	45	41	39	99
Ashby, Andy	3.23	9	5	24	24	1	0	150⅔	147	60	54	34	85
Sanders, Scott	3.38	9	5	46	16	0	0	144	117	58	54	48	157
Valenzuela, Fernando	3.62	13	8	33	31	0	0	171⅔	177	78	69	67	95
Florie, Bryce	4.01	2	2	39	0	0	0	49⅓	45	24	22	27	51
Hamilton, Joey	4.17	15	9	34	33	3	0	211⅔	206	100	98	83	184
Tewksbury, Bob	4.31	10	10	36	33	1	0	206⅔	224	116	99	43	126
Bergman, Sean	4.37	6	8	41	14	0	0	113⅓	119	63	55	33	85
Blair, Willie	4.60	2	6	60	0	0	1	88	80	52	45	29	67

San Francisco Giants

BATTING	BA	G	AB	R	H	TB	2B	3B	HR	RBI	SB	BB	SO
Mueller, Bill	.330	55	200	31	66	83	15	1	0	19	0	24	26
Bonds, Barry	.308	158	517	122	159	318	27	3	42	129	40	151	76
Williams, Matt	.302	105	404	69	122	206	16	1	22	85	1	39	95
Dunston, Shawon	.300	82	287	27	86	117	12	2	5	25	8	13	40
Hill, Glenallen	.280	98	379	56	106	189	26	0	19	67	6	33	95
Wilson, Gary	.271	41	118	10	32	40	2	0	2	12	0	12	27
Javier, Stan	.270	71	274	44	74	105	25	0	2	22	14	25	51
Carreon, Mark	.260	81	292	40	76	131	22	3	9	51	2	22	33
Benard, Marvin	.248	135	488	89	121	161	17	4	5	27	25	59	84
Wilkins, Rick	.243	136	411	53	100	164	18	2	14	59	0	67	121
Aurilia, Rich	.239	105	518	27	76	94	7	1	3	26	4	25	52
Lampkin, Tom	.232	66	177	26	41	67	8	0	6	29	1	20	22
Scarsone, Steve	.219	105	283	28	62	91	12	1	5	23	2	25	91
McCarty, David	.217	91	175	16	38	59	3	0	6	24	2	18	43
Thompson, Robby	.211	63	227	35	48	76	11	1	5	21	2	24	69

PITCHING	ERA	W	L	G	GS	CG	SV	INN	H	R	ER	BB	SO
Beck, Rod	3.34	0	9	63	0	0	35	62	56	23	23	10	48
Bautista, Jose	3.36	3	4	37	1	0	0	69⅔	66	32	26	15	28
Estes, Shawn	3.60	3	5	11	11	0	0	70	63	13	28	39	60
Rueter, Kirk	3.97	6	8	20	19	0	0	102	109	50	45	27	46
Dewey, Mark	4.21	6	3	78	0	0	0	83⅓	79	40	39	41	57
Gardner, Mark	4.42	12	7	30	28	4	0	179⅓	200	105	88	57	145
Watson, Allen	4.61	8	12	29	29	2	0	185⅔	189	105	95	69	128
Fernandez, Osvaldo	4.61	7	13	30	28	2	0	171⅔	193	95	88	57	106
Scott, Tim	4.64	5	7	65	0	0	1	66	65	36	34	30	47
Van Landingham, W.	5.40	9	14	32	32	0	0	181⅔	196	125	109	78	97
DeLucia, Rich	5.84	3	6	56	0	0	0	61⅔	62	44	40	31	55
Bourgeois, Steve	6.30	1	3	15	5	0	0	40	60	35	28	21	17

American League Team-by-Team Statistical Leaders

Baltimore Orioles

BATTING

	BA	G	AB	R	H	TB	2B	3B	HR	RBI	SB	BB	SO
Alomar, Roberto	.328	153	588	132	193	310	43	4	22	94	17	90	65
Anderson, Brady	.297	149	579	117	172	369	37	5	50	110	21	76	106
Surhoff, B.J.	.292	143	537	74	157	259	27	6	21	82	0	47	79
Palmeiro, Rafael	.289	162	626	110	181	342	40	2	39	142	8	95	96
Bonilla, Bobby	.287	159	595	107	171	292	27	5	28	116	1	75	85
Ripken, Cal Jr.	.278	163	640	94	178	298	40	1	26	102	1	59	78
Murray, Eddie	.260	152	566	69	147	236	21	1	22	79	4	61	87
Hoiles, Chris	.258	127	407	64	105	193	13	0	25	73	0	57	97
Smith, Mark	.244	27	78	9	19	33	2	0	4	10	0	3	20
Polonia, Luis	.240	58	175	25	42	54	4	1	2	14	8	10	20
Ripken, Billy	.230	57	135	19	31	45	8	0	2	12	0	9	18
Devereaux, Mike	.229	127	323	49	74	113	11	2	8	34	8	34	53
Parent, Mark	.226	56	137	17	31	65	7	0	9	23	0	5	37
Hammonds, Jeffrey	.226	71	248	38	56	95	10	1	9	27	3	23	53

PITCHING

	ERA	W	L	G	GS	CG	SV	INN	H	R	ER	BB	SO
Orosco, Jesse	3.40	3	1	66	0	0	0	55⅔	42	22	21	28	52
Myers, Randy	3.53	4	4	62	0	0	31	58⅔	60	24	23	29	74
Rhodes, Arthur	4.08	9	1	28	2	0	1	53	48	28	24	23	62
McDowell, Roger	4.25	1	1	41	0	0	4	59⅓	69	32	28	23	20
Mills, David	4.28	3	2	49	0	0	3	54⅔	40	26	26	35	50
Mussina, Mike	4.81	19	11	36	36	4	0	243⅓	264	137	130	69	204
Krivda, Rick	4.96	3	5	22	11	0	0	81⅔	89	48	45	39	54
Erickson, Scott	5.02	13	12	34	34	6	0	222⅓	262	137	124	66	100
Wells, David	5.14	11	14	34	34	3	0	224⅓	247	132	128	51	130
Coppinger, Rocky	5.18	10	6	23	22	0	0	125	126	76	72	60	104
Haynes, Jimmy	8.29	3	6	26	11	0	1	89	122	84	82	58	65

Boston Red Sox

BATTING

	BA	G	AB	R	H	TB	2B	3B	HR	RBI	SB	BB	SO
Jefferson, Reggie	.347	122	386	67	134	229	30	4	19	74	0	25	89
Vaughn, Mo	.326	161	635	118	207	370	29	1	44	143	2	95	154
Mitchell, Kevin	.304	27	92	9	28	38	4	0	2	13	0	11	14
Valentin, John	.296	131	527	84	156	230	29	3	13	59	9	63	59
Greenwell, Mike	.295	77	295	35	87	160	20	1	7	44	4	18	27
Canseco, Jose	.289	96	360	68	104	212	22	1	28	82	3	63	82
Naehring, Tim	.288	116	430	77	124	191	16	0	17	65	2	49	63
Cordero, Wil	.288	59	198	29	57	80	14	0	3	37	2	11	31
Frye, Jeff	.286	105	419	74	120	163	27	2	4	41	18	54	57
Haselman, Bill	.274	77	237	33	65	104	13	1	8	34	4	19	52
Selby, Bill	.274	40	95	12	26	39	4	0	3	6	1	9	11
Stanley, Mike	.270	121	397	73	107	201	20	1	24	69	2	69	62
Bragg, Darrem	.261	127	417	74	109	169	26	2	10	47	14	69	74
O'Leary, Troy	.260	149	497	68	129	212	28	5	15	81	3	47	80
Tinsley, Lee	.245	92	192	28	47	64	6	1	3	14	6	13	56
Malave, Jose	.235	41	102	12	24	39	3	0	4	17	0	2	25

PITCHING

	ERA	W	L	G	GS	CG	SV	INN	H	R	ER	BB	SO
Slocumb, Heathcliff	3.02	5	5	75	0	0	31	83⅓	68	31	28	55	88
Brandenburg, Mark	3.43	5	5	55	0	0	0	76	76	35	29	33	66
Clemens, Roger	3.63	10	13	34	34	6	0	242⅔	216	106	98	106	257
Maddux, Mike	4.48	3	2	23	7	0	0	64⅓	76	37	32	27	32
Garces, Rich	4.91	3	2	37	0	0	0	44	42	26	24	33	55
Wakefield, Tim	5.14	14	13	32	32	6	0	211⅔	238	151	121	90	140
Sele, Aaron	5.32	7	11	29	29	1	0	157⅓	192	110	93	67	137
Hudson, Joe	5.40	3	5	36	0	0	1	45	57	35	27	32	19
Gordon, Tom	5.59	12	9	34	34	4	0	215⅔	249	143	134	105	171
Mahomes, Pat	6.91	3	4	31	5	0	2	57⅓	72	46	44	33	36
Eshelman, Vaughn	7.08	6	3	39	10	0	0	87⅔	112	79	69	58	59

American League Team-by-Team Statistical Leaders *(Cont.)*

California Angels

BATTING	BA	G	AB	R	H	TB	2B	3B	HR	RBI	SB	BB	SO
Hudler, Rex	.311	92	302	60	94	168	20	3	16	40	14	9	54
Edmonds, Jim	.304	114	431	73	131	246	28	3	27	66	4	46	101
Davis, Chili	.292	145	530	73	155	263	24	0	28	95	5	86	99
Fabragas, Jorge	.287	90	254	18	73	85	6	0	2	26	0	17	27
Salmon, Tim	.286	156	581	90	166	291	27	4	30	98	4	93	125
Anderson, Garret	.285	150	607	79	173	246	33	2	12	72	7	27	84
Velarde, Randy	.285	136	530	82	151	226	27	3	14	54	7	70	118
Erstad, Darin	.284	57	208	34	59	78	5	1	4	20	3	17	29
Snow, J.T.	.257	155	575	69	148	221	20	1	17	67	1	56	96
DiSarcina, Gary	.256	150	536	62	137	186	26	4	5	48	2	21	36
Arias, George	.238	84	252	19	60	88	8	1	6	28	2	16	50
Wallach, Tim	.237	57	190	23	45	76	7	0	8	20	1	18	47

PITCHING	ERA	W	L	G	GS	CG	SV	INN	H	R	ER	BB	SO
Percival, Troy	2.31	0	2	62	0	0	36	74	38	20	19	31	100
Holtz, Mike	2.45	3	3	30	0	0	0	29⅓	21	11	8	19	31
James, Mike	2.67	5	5	69	0	0	1	81	62	27	24	42	65
McElroy, Chuck	2.95	5	1	40	0	0	0	36⅔	32	12	12	13	32
Harris, Pep	3.90	2	0	11	3	0	0	32⅓	31	16	14	17	20
Finley, Chuck	4.16	15	16	35	35	4	0	238	241	124	110	94	215
Dickson, Jason	4.57	1	4	7	7	0	0	43⅓	52	22	22	18	20
Langston, Mark	4.82	6	5	18	18	2	0	123⅓	116	68	66	45	83
Boskie, Shawn	5.32	12	11	37	28	1	0	189⅓	226	126	112	67	133
Springer, Dennis	5.51	5	6	20	15	2	0	94⅔	91	65	58	43	64
Grimsley, Jason	6.84	5	7	35	20	2	0	130⅓	150	110	99	74	82
Gohr, Greg	7.24	5	9	32	16	0	1	115⅔	163	96	93	44	75
Abbott, Jim	7.48	2	18	27	23	1	0	142	171	128	118	78	58

Chicago White Sox

BATTING	BA	G	AB	R	H	TB	2B	3B	HR	RBI	SB	BB	SO
Martin, Norberto	.350	70	140	30	49	59	7	0	1	14	10	6	17
Thomas, Frank	.349	141	527	110	184	330	26	0	40	134	1	109	70
Martinez, Dave	.318	146	440	85	140	206	20	8	10	53	15	52	52
Slaught, Don	.313	76	243	25	76	104	10	0	6	36	0	15	22
Baines, Harold	.311	143	495	80	154	249	29	0	22	95	3	73	62
Mouton, Lyle	.294	87	214	25	63	94	8	1	7	39	3	22	50
Ventura, Robin	.287	158	586	96	168	305	31	2	34	105	1	78	81
Phillips, Tony	.277	153	581	119	161	232	29	3	12	63	13	125	132
Durham, Ray	.275	156	557	79	153	226	33	5	10	65	30	58	95
Cedeno, Andujar	.272	89	301	46	82	104	12	2	2	20	6	15	64
Guillen, Ozzie	.263	150	499	62	131	183	24	8	4	45	6	10	27
Snopek, Chris	.260	46	104	18	27	53	6	1	6	18	0	6	16
Borders, Pat	.258	50	151	12	39	58	4	0	5	14	0	8	27
Tartabull, Danny	.254	132	472	58	120	230	23	3	27	101	1	64	128
Lewis, Darren	.228	141	337	55	77	105	12	2	4	53	21	45	40
Karkovice, Ron	.220	111	355	44	78	130	22	0	10	38	0	24	93

PITCHING	ERA	W	L	G	GS	CG	SV	INN	H	R	ER	BB	SO
Hernandez, Roberto	1.91	6	5	72	0	0	38	84⅔	65	21	18	38	85
Darwin, Danny	2.93	0	1	22	0	0	0	30⅔	26	10	10	9	15
Thomas, Larry	3.23	2	3	57	0	0	0	30⅔	32	11	11	14	20
Fernandez, Alex	3.45	16	10	35	35	6	0	258	248	110	99	72	200
Castillo, Tony	3.60	5	4	55	0	0	2	95	95	45	38	24	57
Alvarez, Wilson	4.22	15	10	35	35	0	0	217⅓	216	106	102	97	181
Baldwin, James	4.42	11	6	28	28	0	0	169	168	88	83	57	127
Simas, Bill	4.58	2	8	64	0	0	2	72⅔	75	39	37	39	65
Tapani, Kevin	4.59	13	10	34	34	1	0	225⅓	236	123	115	76	150
Keyser, Brian	4.98	1	2	28	0	0	1	59⅔	78	35	33	28	19
Karchner, Matt	5.76	7	4	50	0	0	1	59⅓	61	42	38	41	46
Magrane, Joe	6.88	1	5	19	8	0	0	53⅔	70	45	41	25	21
McCaskill, Kirk	6.97	5	5	29	4	0	0	51⅔	72	41	40	31	28

Cleveland Indians

BATTING	BA	G	AB	R	H	TB	2B	3B	HR	RBI	SB	BB	SO
Giles, Brian	.355	51	121	26	43	74	14	1	5	27	3	19	13
Seitzer, Kevin	.328	154	573	85	187	267	35	3	13	78	6	87	79
Carreon, Mark	.324	38	142	16	46	64	12	0	2	14	1	11	9
Franco, Julio	.322	112	432	72	139	203	20	1	14	76	8	61	82
Lofton, Kenny	.317	154	662	132	210	295	35	4	14	67	75	61	82
Thome, Jim	.311	151	505	122	157	309	28	5	38	116	2	123	141
Belle, Albert	.311	158	602	124	187	375	38	3	48	148	11	99	87
Ramirez, Manny	.309	152	550	94	170	320	45	3	33	112	8	85	104
Vizquel, Omar	.297	151	542	98	161	226	36	1	9	64	35	56	42
Vizcaino, Jose	.285	48	179	23	51	60	5	2	0	13	6	7	24
Baerga, Carlos	.267	100	424	54	113	168	25	0	10	55	1	16	25
Alomar, Sandy Jr.	.263	127	418	53	110	166	23	0	11	50	1	19	42
Pena, Tony	.195	67	174	14	34	41	4	0	1	27	0	15	25

PITCHING	ERA	W	L	G	GS	CG	SV	INN	H	R	ER	BB	SO
Plunk, Eric	2.43	3	2	56	0	0	2	77⅔	56	21	21	34	85
Shuey, Paul	2.85	5	2	42	0	0	4	53⅔	45	19	17	26	44
Assenmacher, Paul	3.09	4	2	63	0	0	1	46⅔	46	18	16	14	44
Nagy, Charles	3.41	17	5	32	32	5	0	222	217	89	84	61	167
Mesa, Jose	3.73	2	7	69	0	0	39	72⅓	69	32	30	28	64
Hershiser, Orel	4.24	15	9	33	33	1	0	206	238	115	97	58	125
Martinez, Dennis	4.50	9	6	20	20	1	0	112	122	63	56	37	48
Ogea, Chad	4.79	10	6	29	21	1	0	146⅓	151	82	78	42	101
McDowell, Jack	5.11	13	9	30	30	5	0	192	214	119	109	67	141
Tavarez, Julian	5.36	4	7	51	4	0	0	80⅓	101	49	48	22	46
Lopez, Albie	6.39	5	4	13	10	0	0	62	80	47	44	22	45
Mercker, Kent	6.98	4	6	24	12	0	0	69⅔	83	60	54	38	29

Detroit Tigers

BATTING	BA	G	AB	R	H	TB	2B	3B	HR	RBI	SB	BB	SO
Higginson, Bobby	.320	130	440	75	141	254	35	0	26	81	6	65	66
Pride, Curtis	.300	95	267	52	80	137	17	5	10	31	11	31	63
Nevin, Phil	.292	38	120	15	35	64	5	0	8	19	1	8	39
Lewis, Mark	.270	145	545	69	147	216	30	3	11	55	6	42	109
Easley, Damion	.268	49	112	14	30	44	2	0	4	17	3	10	25
Fryman, Travis	.268	157	616	90	165	269	32	3	22	100	4	57	118
Curtis, Chad	.263	104	400	65	105	157	20	1	10	37	16	53	73
Bartee, Kimera	.253	110	217	32	55	66	6	1	1	14	20	17	77
Clark, Tony	.250	100	376	56	94	189	14	0	27	72	0	29	127
Ausmus, Brad	.248	75	226	30	56	80	12	0	4	22	3	26	45
Sierra, Ruben	.247	142	518	61	128	194	26	2	12	72	4	60	83
Nieves, Melvin	.246	120	431	71	106	209	23	4	24	60	1	44	158
Trammell, Alan	.233	66	193	16	45	50	2	0	1	16	6	10	27
Williams, Eddie	.200	77	215	22	43	66	5	0	6	26	0	18	50

PITCHING	ERA	W	L	G	GS	CG	SV	INN	H	R	ER	BB	SO
Lewis, Richie	4.18	4	6	72	0	0	2	90⅓	78	45	42	65	78
Thompson, Justin	4.58	1	6	11	11	0	0	59	62	35	30	31	44
Olivares, Omar	4.89	7	11	25	25	4	0	160	169	90	87	75	81
Myers, Mike	5.01	1	5	83	0	0	6	64⅔	70	41	36	34	69
Sager, A.J.	5.01	4	5	22	9	0	0	79	91	46	44	29	52
Olson, Gregg	5.02	3	0	43	0	0	8	43	43	25	24	28	29
Cummings, John	5.12	3	3	21	0	0	0	31⅔	36	20	18	20	24
Lira, Felipe	5.22	6	14	32	32	3	0	194⅔	204	123	113	66	113
Lima, Jose	5.70	5	6	39	4	0	3	72⅔	87	48	46	22	59
Williams, Brian	6.77	3	10	40	17	2	2	121	145	107	91	85	72
Keagle, Greg	7.39	3	6	26	6	0	0	87⅔	104	76	72	68	70
Van Poppel, Todd	9.06	3	9	37	15	1	1	99⅓	139	107	100	62	53

Kansas City Royals

BATTING	BA	G	AB	R	H	TB	2B	3B	HR	RBI	SB	BB	SO
Offerman, Jose	.303	151	561	85	170	234	33	8	5	47	24	74	98
Randa, Joe	.303	110	337	36	102	146	24	1	6	47	13	26	47
Roberts, Bip	.283	90	339	39	96	121	21	2	0	52	12	25	38
Goodwin, Tom	.282	143	524	80	148	173	14	4	1	35	66	39	79
Sweeney, Mike	.279	50	165	23	46	68	10	0	4	24	1	18	21
MacFarlane, Mike	.274	112	379	58	104	189	24	2	19	54	3	31	57
Lockhart, Keith	.273	138	433	49	118	178	33	3	7	55	11	30	40
Damon, Johnny	.271	145	517	61	140	190	22	5	6	50	25	31	64
Tucker, Mike	.260	108	339	55	88	150	18	4	12	53	10	40	69
Paquette, Craig	.259	118	429	61	111	194	15	1	22	67	5	23	101
Hamelin, Bob	.255	89	239	31	61	104	14	1	9	40	5	54	58
Young, Kevin	.242	55	132	20	32	62	6	0	8	23	3	11	32
Vitiello, Joe	.241	85	257	29	62	103	15	1	8	40	2	38	69
Howard, David	.219	143	420	51	92	128	14	5	4	48	5	40	74

PITCHING	ERA	W	L	G	GS	CG	SV	INN	H	R	ER	BB	SO
Rosado, Jose	3.21	8	6	16	16	2	0	106⅔	101	39	38	20	04
Appier, Kevin	3.02	14	11	32	32	5	0	211⅓	192	87	85	75	207
Belcher, Tim	3.92	15	11	35	35	4	0	238⅔	262	117	104	68	113
Montgomery, Jeff	4.26	4	6	48	0	0	24	63⅓	59	31	30	19	45
Haney, Chris	4.70	10	14	35	35	4	0	228	267	136	119	51	115
Jacome, Jason	4.72	0	4	49	2	0	1	47⅔	67	27	25	22	32
Linton, Doug	5.02	7	9	21	18	0	0	104	111	65	58	26	87
Gubicza, Mark	5.13	4	12	19	19	2	0	119⅓	132	70	68	34	55
Pichardo, Hipolito	5.43	3	5	57	0	0	3	68	74	41	41	26	43
Pugh, Tim	5.45	0	1	19	1	0	0	36⅓	42	24	22	12	27
Magnante, Mike	5.67	2	2	38	0	0	0	54	58	38	34	24	32
Valera, Julio	6.46	3	2	31	2	0	1	61⅓	75	44	44	27	31

Milwaukee Brewers

BATTING	BA	G	AB	R	H	TB	2B	3B	HR	RBI	SB	BB	SO
Nilsson, Dave	.331	123	453	81	150	238	33	2	17	84	2	57	68
Cirillo, Jeff	.325	158	566	101	184	285	46	5	15	83	4	58	69
Newfield, Marc	.307	49	179	21	55	91	15	0	7	31	0	11	26
Jaha, John	.300	148	543	108	163	295	28	1	34	118	3	85	118
Vina, Fernando	.283	140	554	94	157	217	19	10	7	46	16	38	35
Vaughn, Greg	.280	102	375	78	105	214	16	0	31	95	5	58	99
Loretta, Mark	.279	73	154	20	43	49	3	0	1	13	2	14	15
Mieske, Matt	.278	127	374	46	104	176	24	3	14	64	1	26	76
Burnitz, Jeromy	.265	94	200	38	53	94	14	0	9	40	4	33	47
Valentin, Jose	.259	154	552	90	143	262	33	7	24	95	17	66	145
Williams, Gerald	.252	125	325	43	82	124	19	4	5	34	10	19	57
Levis, Jesse	.236	104	233	27	55	66	6	1	1	21	0	38	15
Hulse, David	.222	81	117	18	26	29	3	0	0	6	4	8	16
Matheny, Mike	.204	106	313	31	64	107	15	2	8	46	3	14	80

PITCHING	ERA	W	L	G	GS	CG	SV	INN	H	R	ER	BB	SO
Fetters, Mike	3.38	3	3	61	0	0	32	61⅓	65	28	23	26	53
Jones, Doug	3.41	5	0	24	0	0	1	31⅔	31	13	12	13	34
McDonald, Ben	3.90	12	10	35	35	2	0	221⅓	228	104	96	67	146
Wickman, Bob	4.42	7	1	70	0	0	0	95⅔	106	50	47	44	75
Eldred, Cal	4.46	4	4	15	15	0	0	84⅔	82	43	42	38	50
Karl, Scott	4.86	13	9	32	32	3	0	207⅓	220	124	112	72	121
Miranda, Angel	4.94	7	6	46	12	0	1	109⅓	116	68	60	69	78
Vanegmond, Tim	5.27	3	5	12	9	0	0	54⅔	58	35	32	23	33
D'Amico, Jeffrey	5.44	6	6	17	17	0	0	86	88	53	52	31	53
Sparks, Steve	6.60	4	7	20	13	1	0	88⅔	103	66	65	52	21
Garcia, Frank	6.66	4	4	37	2	0	4	75⅔	84	58	56	21	40
Potts, Mike	7.15	1	2	24	0	0	1	45⅓	58	39	36	30	21

Minnesota Twins

BATTING	BA	G	AB	R	H	TB	2B	3B	HR	RBI	SB	BB	SO
Molitor, Paul	.341	161	660	99	225	309	41	8	9	113	18	56	72
Knoblauch, Chuck	.341	153	578	140	197	299	35	14	13	72	45	98	74
Kelly, Roberto	.323	98	322	41	104	147	17	4	6	47	10	23	53
Cordova, Marty	.309	145	569	97	176	272	46	1	16	111	11	53	96
Coomer, Ron	.296	95	233	34	69	119	12	1	12	41	3	17	24
Becker, Rich	.291	148	525	92	153	228	31	4	12	71	19	68	118
Myers, Greg	.286	97	329	37	94	140	22	3	6	47	0	19	52
Stahoviak, Scott	.284	130	405	72	115	190	30	3	13	61	3	59	114
Hale, Chip	.276	85	87	8	24	32	5	0	1	16	0	10	6
Meares, Pat	.267	152	517	66	138	202	26	7	8	67	9	17	90
Lawton, Matt	.258	79	252	34	65	92	7	1	6	42	4	28	28
Walbeck, Matt	.223	63	215	25	48	64	10	0	2	24	3	9	34
Reboulet, Jeff	.222	107	234	20	52	61	9	0	0	23	4	25	34

PITCHING	ERA	W	L	G	GS	CG	SV	INN	H	R	ER	BB	SO
Trombley, Mike	3.01	5	1	43	0	0	6	68⅔	61	24	23	25	57
Naulty, Dan	3.79	3	2	49	0	0	4	57	43	26	24	35	56
Radke, Brad	4.46	11	16	35	35	3	0	232	231	125	115	57	148
Stevens, Dave	4.66	3	3	49	0	0	11	58	58	31	30	25	29
Rodriguez, Frank	5.05	13	14	38	33	3	2	206⅔	218	129	116	78	110
Robertson, Rich	5.12	7	17	36	31	5	0	186½	197	116	106	116	114
Guardado, Eddie	5.25	6	5	83	0	0	4	73⅔	61	45	43	33	74
Aguilera, Rick	5.42	8	6	19	19	2	0	111⅓	124	69	67	27	83
Hansell, Greg	5.69	3	0	50	0	0	3	74½	83	48	47	31	46
Parra, Jose	6.04	5	5	27	5	0	0	70	88	48	47	27	50
Aldred, Scott	6.21	6	9	36	25	0	0	165½	194	125	114	68	111

New York Yankees

BATTING	BA	G	AB	R	H	TB	2B	3B	HR	RBI	SB	BB	SO
Duncan, Mariano	.340	109	400	62	136	200	34	3	8	56	4	9	77
Jeter, Derek	.314	157	582	104	183	250	25	6	10	78	14	48	102
Boggs, Wade	.311	132	501	80	156	195	29	2	2	41	1	67	32
Williams, Bernie	.305	143	551	108	168	295	26	7	29	102	17	82	72
O'Neill, Paul	.302	150	546	89	165	259	35	1	19	91	0	102	76
Girardi, Joe	.294	124	422	55	124	158	22	3	2	45	13	30	55
Martinez, Tino	.292	155	595	82	174	277	28	0	25	117	2	68	85
Raines, Tim	.284	59	201	45	57	94	10	0	9	33	10	34	29
Leyritz, Jim	.264	88	265	23	70	101	10	0	7	40	2	30	68
Strawberry, Darryl	.262	63	202	35	53	99	13	0	11	36	6	31	55
Fielder, Cecil	.252	160	591	85	149	286	20	0	39	117	2	87	139
Listach, Pat	.240	87	317	51	76	99	16	2	1	33	25	36	51
Sojo, Luis	.220	95	287	23	63	78	10	1	1	21	2	11	17
Aldrete, Mike	.213	63	108	16	23	47	6	0	6	20	0	14	19
Fox, Andy	.196	113	189	26	37	50	4	0	3	13	11	20	28

PITCHING	ERA	W	L	G	GS	CG	SV	INN	H	R	ER	BB	SO
Rivera, Melido	2.09	8	3	61	0	0	5	107⅔	73	25	25	34	130
Wetteland, John	2.83	2	3	62	0	0	43	63⅔	54	23	20	21	69
Cone, David	2.88	7	2	11	11	1	0	72	50	25	23	34	71
Pettitte, Andy	3.87	21	8	35	34	2	0	221	229	105	95	72	162
Lloyd, Graeme	4.29	2	6	65	0	0	0	56⅔	61	30	27	22	30
Nelson, Jeff	4.36	4	4	73	0	0	2	74½	75	38	36	36	91
Rogers, Kenny	4.68	12	8	30	30	2	0	179	179	97	93	83	92
Gooden, Dwight	5.01	11	7	29	29	1	0	170⅔	169	101	95	88	126
Hutton, Mark	5.04	0	2	12	2	0	0	30½	32	19	17	18	25
Mecir, Jim	5.13	1	1	26	0	0	0	40¼	42	24	23	23	38
Boehringer, Brian	5.44	2	4	15	3	0	0	46⅓	46	28	28	21	37
Bones, Ricky	6.22	7	14	36	24	0	0	152	184	115	105	68	63
Mendoza, Ramiro	6.79	4	5	12	11	0	0	53	80	43	40	10	34

American League Team-by-Team Statistical Leaders *(Cont.)*

Oakland Athletics

BATTING	BA	G	AB	R	H	TB	2B	3B	HR	RBI	SB	BB	SO
McGwire, Mark	.312	130	423	104	132	309	21	0	52	113	0	116	112
Brosius, Scott	.304	114	428	73	130	221	25	0	22	71	7	59	85
Batista, Tony	.298	74	238	38	71	103	10	2	6	25	7	19	49
Giambi, Jason	.291	140	536	84	156	258	40	1	20	79	0	51	95
Berroa, Geronimo	.290	153	586	101	170	312	32	1	36	106	0	47	122
Stairs, Matt	.277	61	137	21	38	75	5	1	10	23	1	19	23
Steinbach, Terry	.272	145	514	79	140	272	25	1	35	100	0	49	115
Herrera, Jose	.269	108	320	44	86	121	15	1	6	30	6	20	59
Mashore, Damon	.267	50	105	20	28	46	7	1	3	12	4	16	31
Gates, Brent	.263	64	247	26	65	94	19	2	2	30	1	18	35
Munoz, Pedro	.256	34	121	17	31	54	5	0	6	18	0	9	31
Young, Ernie	.242	141	462	72	112	196	19	4	19	64	7	52	118
Bournigal, Rafael	.242	88	252	33	61	79	14	2	0	18	4	16	19
Bordick, Mike	.240	155	525	46	126	167	18	4	5	54	5	52	59
Plantier, Phil	.212	73	231	29	49	80	8	1	7	31	2	28	56

PITCHING	ERA	W	L	G	GS	CG	SV	INN	H	R	ER	BB	SO
Mohler, Mike	3.67	6	3	72	0	0	7	81	79	36	33	41	64
Groom, Buddy	3.84	5	0	72	1	0	2	77⅓	85	37	33	34	57
Adams, Willie	4.01	3	4	12	12	1	0	76⅓	76	39	34	23	68
Corsi, Jim	4.03	6	0	57	0	0	3	73⅔	71	33	33	34	43
Prieto, Ariel	4.15	6	7	21	21	2	0	125⅔	130	66	58	54	75
Taylor, Billy	4.33	6	3	55	0	0	17	60⅓	52	30	29	25	67
Telgheder, Dave	4.65	4	7	16	14	1	0	79⅓	92	42	41	26	43
Reyes, Carlos	4.78	7	10	46	10	0	0	122⅓	134	71	65	61	78
Wengert, Don	5.58	7	11	36	25	1	0	161⅓	200	102	100	60	75
Wojciechowski, Steve	5.65	5	5	16	15	0	0	79⅔	97	57	50	28	30
Wasdin, John	5.96	8	7	25	21	1	0	131⅓	145	96	87	50	75
Johns, Doug	5.98	6	12	40	23	1	1	158	187	112	105	69	71

Seattle Mariners

BATTING	BA	G	AB	R	H	TB	2B	3B	HR	RBI	SB	BB	SO
Rodriguez, Alex	.358	146	601	141	215	379	54	1	36	123	15	59	104
Martinez, Edgar	.327	139	499	122	163	297	52	2	26	103	3	123	84
Griffey, Ken Jr	.303	140	545	125	165	342	26	2	49	140	16	78	104
Whiten, Mark	.300	40	140	31	42	85	7	0	12	33	2	21	40
Amaral, Rich	.292	118	312	69	91	111	11	3	1	29	25	47	55
Cora, Joey	.291	144	530	90	154	221	37	6	6	45	5	35	32
Sorrento, Paul	.289	143	471	67	136	239	32	1	23	93	0	57	103
Wilson, Dan	.285	138	491	51	140	218	24	0	18	83	1	32	88
Buhner, Jay	.271	150	564	107	153	314	29	0	44	138	0	84	159
Hunter, Brian	.268	75	198	21	53	84	10	0	7	28	0	15	43
Hollins, Dave	.262	149	516	88	135	212	29	0	16	78	6	84	117
Strange, Doug	.235	88	183	19	43	61	7	1	3	23	1	14	31
Davis, Russ	.234	51	167	24	39	63	9	0	5	18	2	17	50

PITCHING	ERA	W	L	G	GS	CG	SV	INN	H	R	ER	BB	SO
Jackson, Mike	3.63	1	1	73	0	0	6	72	61	32	29	24	70
Johnson, Randy	3.67	5	0	14	8	0	1	61⅓	48	27	25	25	85
Moyer, Jamie	3.98	13	3	34	21	0	0	160⅔	177	86	71	46	79
Davis, Tim	4.01	2	2	40	0	0	0	42⅔	43	21	19	17	34
Charlton, Norm	4.04	4	7	70	0	0	20	75⅔	68	37	34	38	73
Carmona, Rafael	4.28	8	3	53	1	0	1	90⅓	93	47	43	55	62
Torres, Salomon	4.59	3	3	10	7	1	0	49	44	27	25	23	36
Mulholland, Terry	4.67	5	4	12	12	0	0	69⅓	75	38	36	28	34
Wells, Bob	5.30	12	7	36	16	1	0	130⅔	141	78	77	46	94
Hitchcock, Sterling	5.35	13	9	35	35	0	0	196⅔	245	131	117	73	132
Wolcott, Bob	5.73	7	10	30	28	1	0	149⅓	179	101	95	54	78
Ayala, Bobby	5.88	6	3	50	0	0	3	67⅓	65	45	44	25	61

American League Team-by-Team Statistical Leaders *(Cont.)*

Texas Rangers

BATTING	BA	G	AB	R	H	TB	2B	3B	HR	RBI	SB	BB	SO
Greer, Rusty	.332	139	542	96	180	287	41	6	18	100	9	62	86
Gonzalez, Juan	.314	134	541	89	170	348	33	2	47	144	2	45	82
Valle, Dave	.302	42	86	14	26	43	6	1	3	17	0	9	17
Rodriguez, Ivan	.300	153	639	116	192	302	47	3	19	86	5	38	55
Hamilton, Darryl	.293	148	627	94	184	239	29	4	6	51	15	54	66
McLemore, Mark	.290	147	517	84	150	196	23	4	5	46	27	87	69
Clark, Will	.284	117	436	69	124	190	25	1	13	72	2	64	67
Buford, Damon	.283	90	145	30	41	68	9	0	6	20	8	15	34
Palmer, Dean	.280	154	582	98	163	307	26	2	38	107	2	59	145
Newson, Warren	.255	91	235	34	60	106	14	1	10	31	3	37	82
Elster, Kevin	.252	157	515	79	130	238	32	2	24	99	4	32	138
Tettleton, Mickey	.246	143	491	78	121	221	26	1	24	83	2	95	137

PITCHING	ERA	W	L	G	GS	CG	SV	INN	H	R	ER	BB	SO
Vosberg, Ed	3.27	1	1	52	0	0	8	44	51	17	16	21	32
Russell, Jeff	3.38	3	3	55	0	0	3	56	58	22	21	22	23
Hill, Ken	3.63	16	10	35	35	7	0	250⅔	250	110	101	95	170
Stanton, Mike	3.66	4	4	81	0	0	1	78⅔	78	32	32	27	60
Burkett, John	4.06	5	2	10	10	1	0	68⅔	75	33	31	16	47
Cook, Dennis	4.09	5	2	60	0	0	0	70⅓	53	34	32	35	64
Oliver, Darren	4.66	14	6	30	30	1	0	173⅔	190	97	90	76	112
Pavelick, Roger	5.19	15	8	34	34	7	0	201	216	120	116	81	127
Gross, Kevin	5.22	11	8	28	19	1	0	129⅓	151	78	75	50	78
Witt, Bobby	5.41	16	12	33	32	2	0	199⅔	235	129	120	96	157
Henneman, Mike	5.79	0	7	49	0	0	31	42	41	28	27	17	34
Heredia, Gil	5.89	2	5	44	0	0	1	73⅓	91	50	48	14	43

Toronto Blue Jays

BATTING	BA	G	AB	R	H	TB	2B	3B	HR	RBI	SB	BB	SO
Perez, Robert	.327	86	202	30	66	82	10	0	2	21	3	8	17
Nixon, Otis	.286	125	496	87	142	162	15	1	1	29	54	71	68
Green, Shawn	.280	132	422	52	118	189	32	3	11	45	5	33	75
Olerud, John	.274	125	398	59	109	188	25	0	18	61	1	60	37
Delgado, Carlos	.270	138	488	68	132	239	28	2	25	92	0	58	139
Brumfield, Jacob	.256	90	308	52	79	138	19	2	12	52	12	24	58
Samuel, Juan	.255	69	188	34	48	86	8	3	8	26	9	15	65
Carter, Joe	.253	157	625	84	158	297	35	7	30	107	7	44	106
Perez, Tomas	.251	91	295	24	74	98	13	4	1	19	1	25	29
Sprague, Ed	.247	159	591	88	146	293	35	2	36	101	0	60	146
O'Brien, Charlie	.238	109	324	33	77	133	17	0	13	44	0	29	68
Gonzalez, Alex	.235	147	527	64	124	206	30	5	14	64	16	45	127
Martinez, Angel	.227	76	229	17	52	76	9	3	3	18	0	16	58

PITCHING	ERA	W	L	G	GS	CG	SV	INN	H	R	ER	BB	SO
Crabtree, Tim	2.54	5	3	53	0	0	1	67⅓	59	26	19	22	57
Guzman, Juan	2.93	11	8	27	27	4	0	187⅔	158	68	61	53	165
Spoljaric, Paul	3.08	2	2	28	0	0	1	38	30	17	13	19	38
Hentgen, Pat	3.22	20	10	35	35	10	0	265⅔	238	105	95	94	177
Timlin, Mike	3.65	1	6	59	0	0	31	56⅔	47	25	23	18	52
Risley, Bill	3.89	0	1	25	0	0	0	41⅔	33	20	18	25	29
Flener, Huck	4.58	3	2	15	11	0	0	70⅔	68	40	36	33	44
Williams, Woody	4.73	4	5	12	10	1	0	59	64	33	31	21	43
Hanson, Erik	5.41	13	17	35	35	4	0	214⅔	243	143	129	102	156
Quantrill, Paul	5.43	5	14	38	20	0	0	134⅓	172	90	81	51	86
Brow, Scott	5.59	1	0	18	1	0	0	38⅔	45	25	24	25	23
Janzen, Marty	7.33	4	6	15	11	0	0	73⅔	95	65	60	38	47

The World Series

Results

1903 ....Boston (A) 5, Pittsburgh (N) 3	1950 ....New York (A) 4, Philadelphia (N) 0
1904 ....No series	1951 ....New York (A) 4, New York (N) 2
1905 ....New York (N) 4, Philadelphia (A) 1	1952 ....New York (A) 4, Brooklyn (N) 3
1906 ....Chicago (A) 4, Chicago (N) 2	1953 ....New York (A) 4, Brooklyn (N) 2
1907 ....Chicago (N) 4, Detroit (A) 0; 1 tie	1954 ....New York (N) 4, Cleveland (A) 0
1908 ....Chicago (N) 4, Detroit (A) 1	1955 ....Brooklyn (N) 4, New York (A) 3
1909 ....Pittsburgh (N) 4, Detroit (A) 3	1956 ....New York (A) 4, Brooklyn (N) 3
1910 ....Philadelphia (A) 4, Chicago (N) 1	1957 ....Milwaukee (N) 4, New York (A) 3
1911 ....Philadelphia (A) 4, New York (N) 2	1958 ....New York (A) 4, Milwaukee (N) 3
1912 ....Boston (A) 4, New York (N) 3; 1 tie	1959 ....Los Angeles (N) 4, Chicago (A) 2
1913 ....Philadelphia (A) 4, New York (N) 1	1960 ....Pittsburgh (N) 4, New York (A) 3
1914 ....Boston (N) 4, Philadelphia (A) 0	1961 ....New York (A) 4, Cincinnati (N) 1
1915 ....Boston (A) 4, Philadelphia (N) 1	1962 ....New York (A) 4, San Francisco (N) 3
1916 ....Boston (A) 4, Brooklyn (N) 1	1963 ....Los Angeles (N) 4, New York (A) 0
1917 ....Chicago (A) 4, New York (N) 2	1964 ....St Louis (N) 4, New York (A) 3
1918 ....Boston (A) 4, Chicago (N) 2	1965 ....Los Angeles (N) 4, Minnesota (A) 3
1919 ....Cincinnati (N) 5, Chicago (A) 3	1966 ....Baltimore (A) 4, Los Angeles (N) 0
1920 ....Cleveland (A) 5, Brooklyn (N) 2	1967 ....St Louis (N) 4, Boston (A) 3
1921 ....New York (N) 5, New York (A) 3	1968 ....Detroit (A) 4, St Louis (N) 3
1922 ....New York (N) 4, New York (A) 0; 1 tie	1969 ....New York (N) 4, Baltimore (A) 1
1923 ....New York (A) 4, New York (N) 2	1970 ....Baltimore (A) 4, Cincinnati (N) 1
1924 ....Washington (A) 4, New York (N) 3	1971 ....Pittsburgh (N) 4, Baltimore (A) 3
1925 ....Pittsburgh (N) 4, Washington (A) 3	1972 ....Oakland (A) 4, Cincinnati (N) 3
1926 ....St Louis (N) 4, New York (A) 3	1973 ....Oakland (A) 4, New York (N) 3
1927 ....New York (A) 4, Pittsburgh (N) 0	1974 ....Oakland (A) 4, Los Angeles (N) 1
1928 ....New York (A) 4, St Louis (N) 0	1975 ....Cincinnati (N) 4, Boston (A) 3
1929 ....Philadelphia (A) 4, Chicago (N) 1	1976 ....Cincinnati (N) 4, New York (A) 0
1930 ....Philadelphia (A) 4, St Louis (N) 2	1977 ....New York (A) 4, Los Angeles (N) 2
1931 ....St Louis (N) 4, Philadelphia (A) 3	1978 ....New York (A) 4, Los Angeles (N) 2
1932 ....New York (A) 4, Chicago (N) 0	1979 ....Pittsburgh (N) 4, Baltimore (A) 3
1933 ....New York (N) 4, Washington (A) 1	1980 ....Philadelphia (N) 4, Kansas City (A) 2
1934 ....St Louis (N) 4, Detroit (A) 3	1981 ....Los Angeles (N) 4, New York (A) 2
1935 ....Detroit (A) 4, Chicago (N) 2	1982 ....St Louis (N) 4, Milwaukee (A) 3
1936 ....New York (A) 4, New York (N) 2	1983 ....Baltimore (A) 4, Philadelphia (N) 1
1937 ....New York (A) 4, New York (N) 1	1984 ....Detroit (A) 4, San Diego (N) 1
1938 ....New York (A) 4, Chicago (N) 0	1985 ....Kansas City (A) 4, St Louis (N) 3
1939 ....New York (A) 4, Cincinnati (N) 0	1986 ....New York (N) 4, Boston (A) 3
1940 ....Cincinnati (N) 4, Detroit (A) 3	1987 ....Minnesota (A) 4, St Louis (N) 3
1941 ....New York (A) 4, Brooklyn (N) 1	1988 ....Los Angeles (N) 4, Oakland (A) 1
1942 ....St Louis (N) 4, New York (A) 1	1989 ....Oakland (A) 4, San Francisco (N) 0
1943 ....New York (A) 4, St Louis (N) 1	1990 ....Cincinnati (N) 4, Oakland (A) 0
1944 ....St Louis (N) 4, St Louis (A) 2	1991 ....Minnesota (A) 4, Atlanta (N) 3
1945 ....Detroit (A) 4, Chicago (N) 3	1992 ....Toronto (A) 4, Atlanta (N) 2
1946 ....St Louis (N) 4, Boston (A) 3	1993 ....Toronto (A) 4, Philadelphia (N) 2
1947 ....New York (A) 4, Brooklyn (N) 3	1994 ....Series canceled due to players' strike
1948 ....Cleveland (A) 4, Boston (N) 2	1995 ....Atlanta (N) 4, Cleveland (A) 2
1949 ....New York (A) 4, Brooklyn (N) 1	1996 ....New York (A) 4, Atlanta (N) 2

Buckner's Rock-and-Roll Savior

Ghosts die hard in Red Sox country, and no specter has haunted fans more for the past 10 years than former Boston first baseman Bill Buckner's. In the 10th inning of the sixth game of the 1986 World Series, Buckner let a ground ball dribble between his legs, completing a collapse that cost the Sox a chance to win their first Series since 1918.

Now the Boston-based roots-rock band Slide has released its debut CD, *Forgiving Buckner*. "The title is about salvation," says Wolf Wortis, the band's singer and songwriter. "For a Red Sox fan to be able to forgive Bill Buckner means that the fan is ready to move on with life." Slide isn't a sports-rock gimmick band, but the group does draw metaphors from baseball. Its guitar-heavy track *Cool Papa Bell*, for example, doesn't refer to the legendary Negro Leagues speedster directly, but it does carry the underlying theme that "being good on the base paths, knowing when to take chances and when not to, is analagous to what you need to get through life."

Ultimately Slide thinks Buckner should be remembered for more than his notorious blunder. That's why it gave the disc a catalog number that ends with 2715, the number of hits Buckner had in his 22-year career.

Most Valuable Players

1955	Johnny Podres, Bklyn	1977	Reggie Jackson, NY (A)
1956	Don Larsen, NY (A)	1978	Bucky Dent, NY (A)
1957	Lew Burdette, Mil	1979	Willie Stargell, Pitt
1958	Bob Turley, NY (A)	1980	Mike Schmidt, Phil
1959	Larry Sherry, LA	1981	Ron Cey, LA
1960	Bobby Richardson, NY (A)		Pedro Guerrero, LA
1961	Whitey Ford, NY (A)		Steve Yeager, LA
1962	Ralph Terry, NY (A)	1982	Darrell Porter, StL
1963	Sandy Koufax, LA	1983	Rick Dempsey, Balt
1964	Bob Gibson, StL	1984	Alan Trammell, Det
1965	Sandy Koufax, LA	1985	Bret Saberhagen, KC
1966	Frank Robinson, Balt	1986	Ray Knight, NY (N)
1967	Bob Gibson, StL	1987	Frank Viola, Minn
1968	Mickey Lolich, Det	1988	Orel Hershiser, LA
1969	Donn Clendenon, NY (N)	1989	Dave Stewart, Oak
1970	Brooks Robinson, Balt	1990	Jose Rijo, Cin
1971	Roberto Clemente, Pitt	1991	Jack Morris, Minn
1972	Gene Tenace, Oak	1992	Pat Borders, Tor
1973	Reggie Jackson, Oak	1993	Paul Molitor, Tor
1974	Rollie Fingers, Oak	1994	Series canceled due to strike
1975	Pete Rose, Cin	1995	Tom Glavine, Atl
1976	Johnny Bench, Cin	1996	John Wetteland, NY

Career Batting Leaders (Minimum 50 at bats)

GAMES

Yogi Berra	75
Mickey Mantle	65
Elston Howard	54
Hank Bauer	53
Gil McDougald	53
Phil Rizzuto	52
Joe DiMaggio	51
Frankie Frisch	50
Pee Wee Reese	44
Roger Maris	41
Babe Ruth	41

AT BATS

Yogi Berra	259
Mickey Mantle	230
Joe DiMaggio	199
Frankie Frisch	197
Gil McDougald	190
Hank Bauer	188
Phil Rizzuto	183
Elston Howard	171
Pee Wee Reese	169
Roger Maris	152

HITS

Yogi Berra	71
Mickey Mantle	59
Frankie Frisch	58
Joe DiMaggio	54
Pee Wee Reese	46
Hank Bauer	46
Phil Rizzuto	45
Gil McDougald	45
Lou Gehrig	43
Eddie Collins	42
Babe Ruth	42
Elston Howard	42

BATTING AVERAGE

Pepper Martin	.418
Paul Molitor	.418
Marquis Grissom	.404
Lou Brock	.391
Thurman Munson	.373
George Brett	.373
Hank Aaron	.364
Frank Baker	.363
Roberto Clemente	.362
Lou Gehrig	.361

HOME RUNS

Mickey Mantle	18
Babe Ruth	15
Yogi Berra	12
Duke Snider	11
Reggie Jackson	10
Lou Gehrig	10
Frank Robinson	8
Bill Skowron	8
Joe DiMaggio	8
Goose Goslin	7
Hank Bauer	7
Gil McDougald	7

RUNS BATTED IN

Mickey Mantle	40
Yogi Berra	39
Lou Gehrig	35
Babe Ruth	33
Joe DiMaggio	30
Bill Skowron	29
Duke Snider	26
Reggie Jackson	24
Bill Dickey	24
Hank Bauer	24
Gil McDougald	24

RUNS

Mickey Mantle	42
Yogi Berra	41
Babe Ruth	37
Lou Gehrig	30
Joe DiMaggio	27
Roger Maris	26
Elston Howard	25
Gil McDougald	23
Jackie Robinson	22
Gene Woodling	21
Reggie Jackson	21
Duke Snider	21
Phil Rizzuto	21
Hank Bauer	21

STOLEN BASES

Lou Brock	14
Eddie Collins	14
Frank Chance	10
Davey Lopes	10
Phil Rizzuto	10
Honus Wagner	9
Frankie Frisch	9
Johnny Evers	8
Pepper Martin	7
Joe Morgan	7
Rickey Henderson	7

TOTAL BASES

Mickey Mantle	123
Yogi Berra	117
Babe Ruth	96
Lou Gehrig	87
Joe DiMaggio	84
Duke Snider	79
Hank Bauer	75
Reggie Jackson	74
Frankie Frisch	74
Gil McDougald	72

Career Batting Leaders *(Cont.)*

SLUGGING AVERAGE		STRIKEOUTS	
Reggie Jackson	.755	Mickey Mantle	54
Babe Ruth	.744	Elston Howard	37
Lou Gehrig	.731	Duke Snider	33
Al Simmons	.658	Babe Ruth	30
Lou Brock	.655	Gil McDougald	29
Paul Molitor	.636	Bill Skowron	26
Pepper Martin	.636	Hank Bauer	25
Hank Greenberg	.624	Reggie Jackson	24
Charlie Keller	.611	Bob Meusel	24
Jimmie Foxx	.609	Frank Robinson	23
Dave Henderson	.606	George Kelly	23
		Tony Kubek	23
		Joe DiMaggio	23

Career Pitching Leaders (Minimum 25 innings pitched*)

GAMES		LOSSES		COMPLETE GAMES	
Whitey Ford	22	Whitey Ford	8	Christy Mathewson	10
Rollie Fingers	16	Eddie Plank	5	Chief Bender	9
Allie Reynolds	15	Schoolboy Rowe	5	Bob Gibson	8
Bob Turley	15	Joe Bush	5	Red Ruffing	7
Clay Carroll	14	Rube Marquard	5	Whitey Ford	7
Clem Labine	13	Christy Mathewson	5	George Mullin	6
Waite Hoyt	12			Eddie Plank	6
Catfish Hunter	12	**SAVES**		Art Nehf	6
Art Nehf	12	Rollie Fingers	6	Waite Hoyt	6
Paul Derringer	11	Allie Reynolds	4		
Carl Erskine	11	Johnny Murphy	4	**STRIKEOUTS**	
Rube Marquard	11	John Wetteland	4	Whitey Ford	94
Christy Mathewson	11	Roy Face	3	Bob Gibson	92
Vic Raschi	11	Herb Pennock	3	Allie Reynolds	62
		Kent Tekulve	3	Sandy Koufax	61
INNINGS PITCHED		Firpo Marberry	3	Red Ruffing	61
Whitey Ford	146	Will McEnaney	3	Chief Bender	59
Christy Mathewson	101⅔	Todd Worrell	3	George Earnshaw	56
Red Ruffing	85⅔	Tug McGraw	3	Waite Hoyt	49
Chief Bender	85			Christy Mathewson	48
Waite Hoyt	83⅔	**EARNED RUN AVERAGE**		Bob Turley	46
Bob Gibson	81	Jack Billingham	.36		
Art Nehf	79	Harry Brecheen	.83	**BASES ON BALLS**	
Allie Reynolds	77	Babe Ruth	.87	Whitey Ford	34
Jim Palmer	65	Sherry Smith	.89	Allie Reynolds	32
Catfish Hunter	63	Sandy Koufax	.95	Art Nehf	32
		Hippo Vaughn	1.00	Jim Palmer	31
WINS		Monte Pearson	1.01	Bob Turley	29
Whitey Ford	10	Christy Mathewson	1.15	Paul Derringer	27
Bob Gibson	7	Babe Adams	1.29	Red Ruffing	27
Red Ruffing	7	Eddie Plank	1.32	Don Gullett	26
Allie Reynolds	7			Burleigh Grimes	26
Lefty Gomez	6	**SHUTOUTS**		Vic Raschi	25
Chief Bender	6	Christy Mathewson	4		
Waite Hoyt	6	Three Finger Brown	3		
Jack Coombs	5	Whitey Ford	3		
Three Finger Brown	5	Bill Hallahan	2		
Herb Pennock	5	Lew Burdette	2		
Christy Mathewson	5	Bill Dinneen	2		
Vic Raschi	5	Sandy Koufax	2		
Catfish Hunter	5	Allie Reynolds	2		
		Art Nehf	2		
		Bob Gibson	2		

*Except saves, which has no minimum requirement.

Alltime Team Rankings (by championships)

Team	W	L	Appearances	Pctg.	Most Recent	Last Championship
NY Yankees	23	11	34	.676	1996	1996
St Louis Cardinals	9	6	15	.600	1987	1982
Phil/K.C./Oakland A's	9	5	14	.643	1990	1989
Brooklyn/L.A. Dodgers	6	12	18	.333	1988	1988
NY/San Francisco Giants	5	11	16	.313	1989	1954
Boston Red Sox	5	4	9	.556	1986	1918
Cincinnati Reds	5	4	9	.556	1990	1990
Pittsburgh Pirates	5	2	7	.714	1979	1979
Detroit Tigers	4	5	9	.444	1984	1984
St Louis/Baltimore Orioles	3	4	7	.429	1983	1983
Washington/Minnesota Twins	3	3	6	.500	1991	1991
Bost/Mil/Atlanta Braves	3	5	8	.375	1996	1995
Chicago Cubs	2	8	10	.200	1945	1908
Chicago White Sox	2	2	4	.500	1959	1917
Cleveland Indians	2	2	4	.500	1995	1948
NY Mets	2	1	3	.667	1986	1986
Toronto Blue Jays	2	0	2	1.000	1993	1993
Philadelphia Phillies	1	4	5	.200	1993	1980
Kansas City Royals	1	1	2	.500	1985	1985
Seattle/Milwaukee Brewers	0	1	1	.000	1982	—
San Diego Padres	0	1	1	.000	1984	—

League Championship Series

National League

1969	New York (E) 3, Atlanta (W) 0
1970	Cincinnati (W) 3, Pittsburgh (E) 0
1971	Pittsburgh (E) 3, San Francisco (W) 1
1972	Cincinnati (W) 3, Pittsburgh (E) 2
1973	New York (E) 3, Cincinnati (W) 2
1974	Los Angeles (W) 3, Pittsburgh (E) 1
1975	Cincinnati (W) 3, Pittsburgh (E) 0
1976	Cincinnati (W) 3, Philadelphia (E) 0
1977	Los Angeles (W) 3, Philadelphia (E) 1
1978	Los Angeles (W) 3, Philadelphia (E) 1
1979	Pittsburgh (E) 3, Cincinnati (W) 0
1980	Philadelphia (E) 3, Houston (W) 2
1981	Los Angeles (W) 3, Montreal (E) 2
1982	St Louis (E) 3, Atlanta (W) 0
1983	Philadelphia (E) 3, Los Angeles (W) 1
1984	San Diego (W) 3, Chicago (E) 2
1985	St Louis (E) 4, Los Angeles (W) 2
1986	New York (E) 4, Houston (W) 2
1987	St Louis (E) 4, San Francisco (W) 3
1988	Los Angeles (W) 4, New York (E) 3
1989	San Francisco (W) 4, Chicago (E) 1
1990	Cincinnati (W) 4, Pittsburgh (E) 2
1991	Atlanta (W) 4, Pittsburgh (E) 3
1992	Atlanta (W) 4, Pitsburgh (E) 3
1993	Philadelphia (E) 4, Atlanta (W) 2
1994	Playoffs canceled due to players' strike
1995	Atlanta (E) 4, Cincinnati (C) 0
1996	Atlanta (E) 4, St Louis (C) 3

American League

1969	Baltimore (E) 3, Minnesota (W) 0
1970	Baltimore (E) 3, Minnesota (W) 0
1971	Baltimore (E) 3, Oakland (W) 0
1972	Oakland (W) 3, Detroit (E) 2
1973	Oakland (W) 3, Baltimore (E) 2
1974	Oakland (W) 3, Baltimore (E) 1
1975	Boston (E) 3, Oakland (W) 0
1976	New York (E) 3, Kansas City (W) 2
1977	New York (E) 3, Kansas City (W) 2
1978	New York (E) 3, Kansas City (W) 1
1979	Baltimore (E) 3, California (W) 1
1980	Kansas City (W) 3, New York (E) 0
1981	New York (E) 3, Oakland (W) 0
1982	Milwaukee (E) 3, California (W) 2
1983	Baltimore (E) 3, Chicago (W) 1
1984	Detroit (E) 3, Kansas City (W) 0
1985	Kansas City (W) 4, Toronto (E) 3
1986	Boston (E) 4, California (W) 3
1987	Minnesota (W) 4, Detroit (E) 1
1988	Oakland (W) 4, Boston (E) 0
1989	Oakland (W) 4, Toronto (E) 1
1990	Oakland (W) 4, Boston (E) 0
1991	Minnesota (W) 4, Toronto (E) 1
1992	Toronto (E) 4, Oakland (W) 2
1993	Toronto (E) 4, Chicago (W) 2
1994	Playoffs canceled due to players' strike
1995	Cleveland (C) 4, Seattle (W) 2
1996	New York (E) 4, Baltimore (WC) 1

NLCS Most Valuable Player

1977	Dusty Baker, LA	
1978	Steve Garvey, LA	
1979	Willie Stargell, Pitt	
1980	Manny Trillo, Phil	
1981	Burt Hooton, LA	
1982	Darrell Porter, StL	
1983	Gary Matthews, Phil	
1984	Steve Garvey, SD	
1985	Ozzie Smith, StL	
1986	Mike Scott, Hou	
1987	Jeffrey Leonard, SF	
1988	Orel Hershiser, LA	
1989	Will Clark, SF	
1990	Randy Myers, Cin	
	Rob Dibble, Cin	
1991	Steve Avery, Atl	
1992	John Smoltz, Atl	
1993	Curt Schilling, Phil	
1994	Playoffs canceled	
1995	Mike Devereaux, Atl	
1996	Javier Lopez, Atl	

League Championship Series (Cont.)

ALCS Most Valuable Player

1980........Frank White, KC	1986........Marty Barrett, Bos	1992........Roberto Alomar, Tor
1981........Graig Nettles, NY	1987........Gary Gaetti, Minn	1993........Dave Stewart, Tor
1982........Fred Lynn, Calif	1988........Dennis Eckersley, Oak	1994........Playoffs canceled
1983........Mike Boddicker, Balt	1989........Rickey Henderson, Oak	1995........Orel Hershiser, Clev
1984........Kirk Gibson, Det	1990........Dave Stewart, Oak	1996........Bernie Williams, NY
1985........George Brett, KC	1991........Kirby Puckett, Minn	

The All Star Game

Results

Date	Winner	Score	Site
7-6-33	American	4-2	Comiskey Park, Chi
7-10-34	American	9-7	Polo Grounds, NY
7-8-35	American	4-1	Municipal Stadium, Clev
7-7-36	National	4-3	Braves Field, Bos
7-7-37	American	8-3	Griffith Stadium, Wash
7-6-38	National	4-1	Crosley Field, Cin
7-11-39	American	3-1	Yankee Stadium, NY
7-10-40	National	4-0	Sportsman's Park, StL
7-8-41	American	7-5	Briggs Stadium, Det
7-6-42	American	3-1	Polo Grounds, NY
7-13-43	American	5-3	Shibe Park, Phil
7-11-44	National	7-1	Forbes Field, Pitt
1945	No game due to wartime travel restrictions		
7-9-46	American	12-0	Fenway Park, Bos
7-8-47	American	2-1	Wrigley Field, Chi
7-13-48	American	5-2	Sportsman's Park, StL
7-12-49	American	11-7	Ebbets Field, Bklyn
7-11-50	National	4-3	Comiskey Park, Chi
7-10-51	National	8-3	Briggs Stadium, Det
7-8-52	National	3-2	Shibe Park, Phil
7-14-53	National	5-1	Crosley Field, Cin
7-13-54	American	11-9	Municipal Stadium, Clev
7-12-55	National	6-5	County Stadium, Mil
7-10-56	National	7-3	Griffith Stadium, Wash
7-9-57	American	6-5	Busch Stadium, StL
7-8-58	American	4-3	Memorial Stadium, Balt
7-7-59	National	5-4	Forbes Field, Pitt
8-3-59	American	5-3	Memorial Coliseum, LA
7-11-60	National	5-3	Municipal Stadium, KC
7-13-60	National	6-0	Yankee Stadium, NY
7-11-61	National	5-4	Candlestick Park, SF
7-31-61	Tie*	1-1	Fenway Park, Bos
7-10-62	National	3-1	D.C. Stadium, Wash
7-30-62	American	9-4	Wrigley Field, Chi
7-9-63	National	5-3	Municipal Stadium, Clev
7-7-64	National	7-4	Shea Stadium, NY
7-13-65	National	6-5	Metropolitan Stadium, Minn
7-12-66	National	2-1	Busch Stadium, StL
7-11-67	National	2-1	Anaheim Stadium, Anaheim
7-9-68	National	1-0	Astrodome, Hou
7-23-69	National	9-3	R.F.K. Memorial Stadium, Wash
7-14-70	National	5-4	Riverfront Stadium, Cin
7-13-71	American	6-4	Tiger Stadium, Det
7-25-72	National	4-3	Atlanta Stadium, Atl
7-24-73	National	7-1	Royals Stadium, KC
7-23-74	National	7-2	Three Rivers Stadium, Pitt
7-15-75	National	6-3	County Stadium, Mil
7-13-76	National	7-1	Veterans Stadium, Phil
7-19-77	National	7-5	Yankee Stadium, NY
7-11-78	National	7-3	Jack Murphy Stadium, SD
7-17-79	National	7-6	Kingdome, Sea
7-8-80	National	4-2	Dodger Stadium, LA
8-9-81	National	5-4	Municipal Stadium, Clev
7-13-82	National	4-1	Olympic Stadium, Mtl
7-6-83	American	13-3	Comiskey Park, Chi

Results (Cont.)

Date	Winner	Score	Site
7-10-84	National	3-1	Candlestick Park, SF
7-16-85	National	6-1	Metrodome, Minn
7-15-86	American	3-2	Astrodome, Hou
7-14-87	National	2-0	Oakland Coliseum, Oak
7-12-88	American	2-1	Riverfront Stadium, Cin
7-11-89	American	5-3	Anaheim Stadium, Anaheim
7-10-90	American	2-0	Wrigley Field, Chi
7-9-91	American	4-2	SkyDome, Toronto
7-14-92	American	13-6	Jack Murphy Stadium, SD
7-13-93	American	9-3	Camden Yards, Balt
7-12-94	National	8-7	Three Rivers Stadium, Pitt
7-11-95	National	3-2	The Ballpark in Arlington, TX
7-9-96	National	6-0	Veterans Stadium, Phil

*Game called because of rain after 9 innings.

Most Valuable Players

1962	Maury Wills, LA	NL
	Leon Wagner, LA	AL
1963	Willie Mays, SF	NL
1964	Johnny Callison, Phil	NL
1965	Juan Marichal, SF	NL
1966	Brooks Robinson, Balt	AL
1967	Tony Perez, Cin	NL
1968	Willie Mays, SF	NL
1969	Willie McCovey, SF	NL
1970	Carl Yastrzemski, Bos	AL
1971	Frank Robinson, Balt	AL
1972	Joe Morgan, Cin	NL
1973	Bobby Bonds, SF	NL
1974	Steve Garvey, LA	NL
1975	Bill Madlock, Chi	NL
	Jon Matlack, NY	NL
1976	George Foster, Cin	NL
1977	Don Sutton, LA	NL
1978	Steve Garvey, LA	NL
1979	Dave Parker, Pitt	NL
1980	Ken Griffey, Cin	NL
1981	Gary Carter, Mtl	NL
1982	Dave Concepcion, Cin	NL
1983	Fred Lynn, Calif	AL
1984	Gary Carter, Mtl	NL
1985	LaMarr Hoyt, SD	NL
1986	Roger Clemens, Bos	AL
1987	Tim Raines, Mtl	NL
1988	Terry Steinbach, Oak	AL
1989	Bo Jackson, KC	AL
1990	Julio Franco, Tex	AL
1991	Cal Ripken Jr, Balt	AL
1992	Ken Griffey Jr, Sea	AL
1993	Kirby Puckett, Minn	AL
1994	Fred McGriff, Atl	NL
1995	Jeff Conine, Fla	NL
1996	Mike Piazza, LA	NL

The Regular Season

Most Valuable Players

NATIONAL LEAGUE

Year	Name and Team	Position	Noteworthy
1911	Wildfire Schulte, Chi	Outfield	21 HR†, 121 RBI†, .300
1912	*Larry Doyle, NY	Second base	10 HR, 90 RBI, .330
1913	Jake Daubert, Bklyn	First base	52 RBI, .350†
1914	*Johnny Evers, Bos	Second base	F.A. .976†, .279
1915-23	No selection		
1924	Dazzy Vance, Bklyn	Pitcher	28†-6, 2.16 ERA†, 262 K†
1925	Rogers Hornsby, StL	Second base, Manager	39 HR†, 143 RBI†, .403†
1926	*Bob O'Farrell, StL	Catcher	7 HR, 68 RBI, .293
1927	*Paul Waner, Pitt	Outfield	237 hits†, 131 RBI†, .380†
1928	*Jim Bottomley, StL	First base	31 HR†, 136 RBI†, .325
1929	*Rogers Hornsby, Chi	Second base	39 HR, 149 RBI, 156 runs†, .380
1930	No selection		
1931	*Frankie Frisch, StL	Second base	4 HR, 82 RBI, 28 SB†, .311
1932	Chuck Klein, Phil	Outfield	38 HR†, 137 RBI, 226 hits†, .348
1933	*Carl Hubbell, NY	Pitcher	23†-12, 1.66 ERA†, 10 SO†
1934	*Dizzy Dean, StL	Pitcher	30†-7, 2.66 ERA, 195 K†
1935	*Gabby Hartnett, Chi	Catcher	13 HR, 91 RBI, .344
1936	*Carl Hubbell, NY	Pitcher	26†-6, 2.31 ERA†
1937	Joe Medwick, StL	Outfield	31 HR‡, 154 RBI†, 111 runs†, .374†
1938	Ernie Lombardi, Cin	Catcher	19 HR, 95 RBI, .342†

*Played for pennant or, after 1968, division winner. †Led league. ‡Tied for league lead.

Most Valuable Players *(Cont.)*

NATIONAL LEAGUE *(Cont.)*

Year	Name and Team	Position	Noteworthy
1939	*Bucky Walters, Cin	Pitcher	27†-11, 2.29 ERA†, 137 K‡
1940	*Frank McCormick, Cin	First base	19 HR, 127 RBI, 191 hits†, .309
1941	*Dolph Camilli, Bklyn	First base	34 HR†, 120 RBI†, .285
1942	*Mort Cooper, StL	Pitcher	22†-7, 1.78 ERA†, 10 SO†
1943	*Stan Musial, StL	Outfield	13 HR, 81 RBI, 220 hits†, .357†
1944	*Marty Marion, StL	Shortstop	F.A. .972†, 63 RBI
1945	*Phil Cavarretta, Chi	First base	6 HR, 97 RBI, .355†
1946	*Stan Musial, StL	First base, Outfield	103 RBI, 124 runs†, 228 hits†, .365†
1947	Bob Elliott, Bos	Third base	22 HR, 113 RBI, .317
1948	Stan Musial, StL	Outfield	39 HR, 131 RBI†, .376†
1949	*Jackie Robinson, Bklyn	Second base	16 HR, 124 RBI, 37 SB†, .342†
1950	*Jim Konstanty, Phil	Pitcher	16-7, 22 saves†, 2.66 ERA
1951	Roy Campanella, Bklyn	Catcher	33 HR, 108 RBI, .325
1952	Hank Sauer, Chi	Outfield	37 HR‡, 121 RBI†, .270
1953	*Roy Campanella, Bklyn	Catcher	41 HR, 142 RBI†, .312
1954	*Willie Mays, NY	Outfield	41 HR, 110 RBI, 13 3B†, .345†
1955	*Roy Campanella, Bklyn	Catcher	32 HR, 107 RBI, .318
1956	*Don Newcombe, Bklyn	Pitcher	27†-7, 3.06 ERA
1957	*Hank Aaron, Mil	Outfield	44 HR†, 132 RBI†, .322
1958	Ernie Banks, Chi	Shortstop	47 HR†, 129 RBI†, .313
1959	Ernie Banks, Chi	Shortstop	45 HR, 143 RBI†, .304
1960	*Dick Groat, Pitt	Shortstop	2 HR, 50 RBI, .325†
1961	*Frank Robinson, Cin	Outfield	37 HR, 124 RBI, .323
1962	Maury Wills, LA	Shortstop	104 SB†, 208 hits, .299, GG
1963	*Sandy Koufax, LA	Pitcher	25‡-5, 1.88 ERA†, 306 K†
1964	*Ken Boyer, StL	Third Base	24 HR, 119 RBI†, .295
1965	Willie Mays, SF	Outfield	52 HR†, 112 RBI, .317, GG
1966	Roberto Clemente, Pitt	Outfield	29 HR, 119 RBI, 202 hits, .317, GG
1967	*Orlando Cepeda, StL	First base	25 HR, 111 RBI†, .325
1968	*Bob Gibson, StL	Pitcher	22-9, 1.12 ERA†, 268 K†, 13 SO†, GG
1969	Willie McCovey, SF	First base	45 HR†, 126 RBI†, .320
1970	*Johnny Bench, Cin	Catcher	45 HR†, 148 RBI†, .293, GG
1971	Joe Torre, StL	Third base	24 HR, 137 RBI†, .363†
1972	*Johnny Bench, Cin	Catcher	40 HR†, 125 RBI†, .270, GG
1973	*Pete Rose, Cin	Outfield	5 HR, 64 RBI, .338†, 230 hits†
1974	*Steve Garvey, LA	First base	21 HR, 111 RBI, 200 hits, .312, GG
1975	*Joe Morgan, Cin	Second base	17 HR, 94 RBI, 67 SB, .327, GG
1976	*Joe Morgan, Cin	Second base	27 HR, 111 RBI, 60 SB, .320, GG
1977	George Foster, Cin	Outfield	52 HR†, 149 RBI†, .320
1978	Dave Parker, Pitt	Outfield	30 HR, 117 RBI, .334†, GG
1979	Keith Hernandez, StL	First base	11 HR, 105 RBI, 210 hits, .344†, GG
	*Willie Stargell, Pitt	First base	32 HR, 82 RBI, .281
1980	*Mike Schmidt, Phil	Third base	48 HR†, 121 RBI†, .286, GG
1981	Mike Schmidt, Phil	Third base	31 HR†, 91 RBI†, 78 runs†, .316, GG
1982	*Dale Murphy, Atl	Outfield	36 HR, 109 RBI‡, .281, GG
1983	Dale Murphy, Atl	Outfield	36 HR, 121 RBI†, .302, GG
1984	*Ryne Sandberg, Chi	Second base	19 HR, 84 RBI, 114 runs†, .314, GG
1985	*Willie McGee, StL	Outfield	10 HR, 82 RBI, 18 3B†, .353†, GG
1986	Mike Schmidt, Phil	Third base	37 HR†, 119 RBI†, .290, GG
1987	Andre Dawson, Chi	Outfield	49 HR†, 137 RBI†, .287, GG
1988	*Kirk Gibson, LA	Outfield	25 HR, 76 RBI, 106 runs, .290
1989	*Kevin Mitchell, SF	Outfield	47 HR†, 125 RBI†, .291
1990	*Barry Bonds, Pitt	Outfield	33 HR, 114 RBI, .301
1991	*Terry Pendleton, Atl	Third base	23 HR, 86 RBI, .319†
1992	Barry Bonds, SF	Outfield	34 HR, 103 RBI, .311
1993	Barry Bonds, SF	Outfield	46 HR†, 123 RBI†, .336
1994	Jeff Bagwell, Hou	First base	39 HR, 116 RBI†, .368
1995	*Barry Larkin, Cin	Shortstop	15 HR, 66 RBI, 51 SB, .319

*Played for pennant or, after 1968, division winner. †Led league. ‡Tied for league lead.

Most Valuable Players *(Cont.)*

AMERICAN LEAGUE

Year	Name and Team	Position	Noteworthy
1911	Ty Cobb, Det	Outfield	8 HR, 144 RBI†, 24 3B†, .420†
1912	*Tris Speaker, Bos	Outfield	10 HR‡, 98 RBI, 53 2B†, .383
1913	Walter Johnson, Wash	Pitcher	36†-7, 1.09 ERA†, 11 SO†, 243 K†
1914	*Eddie Collins, Phil	Second base	2 HR, 85 RBI, 122 runs†, .344
1915-21	No selection		
1922	George Sisler, StL	First base	8 HR, 105 RBI, 246 hits‡, .420†
1923	*Babe Ruth, NY	Outfield	41 HR†, 131 RBI†, .393
1924	*Walter Johnson, Wash	Pitcher	23†-7, 2.72 ERA†, 158 K†
1925	*Roger Peckinpaugh, Wash	Shortstop	4 HR, 64 RBI, .294
1926	George Burns, Clev	First base	114 RBI, 216 hits‡, 64 2B†, .358
1927	*Lou Gehrig, NY	First base	47 HR, 175 RBI†, 52 2B†, .373
1928	Mickey Cochrane, Phil	Catcher	10 HR, 57 RBI, .293
1929	No selection		
1930	No selection		
1931	*Lefty Grove, Phil	Pitcher	31†-4, 2.06 ERA†, 175 K†
1932	Jimmie Foxx, Phil	First base	58 HR†, 169 RBI†, 151 runs†, .364
1933	Jimmie Foxx, Phil	First base	48 HR†, 163 RBI†, .356†
1934	*Mickey Cochrane, Det	Catcher	2 HR, 76 RBI, .320
1935	*Hank Greenberg, Det	First base	36 HR†, 170 RBI†, 203 hits, .328
1936	*Lou Gehrig, NY	First base	49 HR†, 152 RBI, 167 runs†, .354
1937	Charlie Gehringer, Det	Second base	14 HR, 96 RBI, 133 runs, .371†
1938	Jimmie Foxx, Bos	First base	50 HR†, 175 RBI†, .349†
1939	*Joe DiMaggio, NY	Outfield	30 HR, 126 RBI, .381†
1940	*Hank Greenberg, Det	Outfield	41 HR†, 150 RBI†, 50 2B†, .340
1941	*Joe DiMaggio, NY	Outfield	30 HR, 125 RBI†, .357
1942	*Joe Gordon, NY	Second base	18 HR, 103 RBI, .322
1943	*Spud Chandler, NY	Pitcher	20†-4, 1.64 ERA†, 5 SO‡
1944	Hal Newhouser, Det	Pitcher	29†-9, 2.22 ERA†, 187 K†
1945	*Hal Newhouser, Det	Pitcher	25†-9, 1.81 ERA†, 8 SO†, 212 K†
1946	*Ted Williams, Bos	Outfield	38 HR, 123 RBI, 142 runs†, .342
1947	*Joe DiMaggio, NY	Outfield	20 HR, 97 RBI, .315
1948	*Lou Boudreau, Clev	Shortstop	18 HR, 106 RBI, .355
1949	Ted Williams, Bos	Outfield	43 HR†, 159 RBI‡, 150 runs†, .343
1950	*Phil Rizzuto, NY	Shortstop	125 runs, 200 hits, .324
1951	*Yogi Berra, NY	Catcher	27 HR, 88 RBI, .294
1952	Bobby Shantz, Phil	Pitcher	24†-7, 2.48 ERA
1953	Al Rosen, Clev	Third base	43 HR†, 145 RBI†, 115 runs†, .336
1954	Yogi Berra, NY	Catcher	22 HR, 125 RBI, .307
1955	*Yogi Berra, NY	Catcher	27 HR, 108 RBI, .272
1956	*Mickey Mantle, NY	Outfield	52 HR†, 130 RBI†, 132 runs†, .353†
1957	*Mickey Mantle, NY	Outfield	34 HR, 94 RBI, 121 runs†, .365
1958	Jackie Jensen, Bos	Outfield	35 HR, 122 RBI†, .286
1959	*Nellie Fox, Chi	Second base	2 HR, 70 RBI, .306, GG
1960	*Roger Maris, NY	Outfield	39 HR, 112 RBI†, .283, GG
1961	*Roger Maris, NY	Outfield	61 HR†, 142 RBI†, .269
1962	*Mickey Mantle, NY	Outfield	30 HR, 89 RBI, .321, GG
1963	*Elston Howard, NY	Catcher	28 HR, 85 RBI, .287, GG
1964	Brooks Robinson, Balt	Third base	28 HR, 118 RBI†, .317, GG
1965	*Zoilo Versalles, Minn	Shortstop	126 runs†, 45 2B‡, 12 3B†, GG
1966	*Frank Robinson, Balt	Outfield	49 HR†, 122 RBI†, 122 runs†, .316†
1967	*Carl Yastrzemski, Bos	Outfield	44 HR‡, 121 RBI†, 112 runs†, .326†, GG
1968	*Denny McLain, Det	Pitcher	31†-6, 1.96 ERA, 280 K
1969	*Harmon Killebrew, Minn	Third base, First base	49 HR†, 140 RBI†, .276
1970	*Boog Powell, Balt	First base	35 HR, 114 RBI, .297
1971	*Vida Blue, Oak	Pitcher	24-8, 1.82 ERA†, 8 SO†, 301 K
1972	Dick Allen, Chi	First base	37 HR†, 113 RBI†, .308
1973	*Reggie Jackson, Oak	Outfield	32 HR†, 117 RBI†, 99 runs†, .293
1974	Jeff Burroughs, Tex	Outfield	25 HR, 118 RBI†, .301
1975	*Fred Lynn, Bos	Outfield	21 HR, 105 RBI, 103 runs†, .331, GG
1976	*Thurman Munson, NY	Catcher	17 HR, 105 RBI, .302
1977	Rod Carew, Minn	First base	100 RBI, 128 runs†, 239 hits†, .388†
1978	Jim Rice, Bos	Outfield, designated hitter	46 HR†, 139 RBI†, 213 hits†, .315

Most Valuable Players (Cont.)

AMERICAN LEAGUE (Cont.)

Year	Name and Team	Position	Noteworthy
1979	*Don Baylor, Calif	Outfield, designated hitter	36 HR, 139 RBI†, 120 runs†, .296
1980	*George Brett, KC	Third base	24 HR, 118 RBI, .390†
1981	*Rollie Fingers, Mil	Pitcher	6-3, 28 saves†, 1.04 ERA
1982	*Robin Yount, Mil	Shortstop	29 HR, 114 RBI, 210 hits†, .331, GG
1983	*Cal Ripken, Balt	Shortstop	27 HR, 102 RBI, 121 runs†, 211 hits†, .318
1984	*Willie Hernandez, Det	Pitcher	9-3, 32 saves, 1.92 ERA
1985	Don Mattingly, NY	First base	35 HR, 145 RBI†, 48 2B†, .324, GG
1986	*Roger Clemens, Bos	Pitcher	24†-4, 2.48 ERA†, 238 K
1987	George Bell, Tor	Outfield	47 HR, 134 RBI†, .308
1988	*Jose Canseco, Oak	Outfield	42 HR†, 124 RBI†, 40 SB, .307
1989	Robin Yount, Mil	Outfield	21 HR, 103 RBI, 101 runs, .318
1990	*Rickey Henderson, Oak	Outfield	28 HR, 119 runs†, 65 SB†, .325
1991	Cal Ripken Jr, Balt	Shortstop	34 HR, 114 RBI, .323
1992	Dennis Eckersley, Oak	Pitcher	7-1, 1.91 ERA, 51 saves
1993	Frank Thomas, Chi	First base	41 HR, 128 RBI, .017
1994	Frank Thomas, Chi	First base	38 HR, 101 RBI, .353
1995	*Mo Vaughn, Bos	First base	39 HR, 126 RBI, .300

*Played for pennant or, after 1968, division winner. †Led league. ‡Tied for league lead.

Notes: 2B=doubles; 3B=triples; F.A.=fielding average; GG=won Gold Glove, award begun in 1957; K=strikeouts; SO=shutouts; SB=stolen bases.

Rookies of the Year

NATIONAL LEAGUE	AMERICAN LEAGUE
1947* ... Jackie Robinson, Bklyn (1B)	1949 ... Roy Sievers, StL (OF)
1948* ... Alvin Dark, Bos (SS)	1950 ... Walt Dropo, Bos (1B)
1949 ... Don Newcombe, Bklyn (P)	1951 ... Gil McDougald, NY (3B)
1950 ... Sam Jethroe, Bos (OF)	1952 ... Harry Byrd, Phil (P)
1951 ... Willie Mays, NY (OF)	1953 ... Harvey Kuenn, Det (SS)
1952 ... Joe Black, Bklyn (P)	1954 ... Bob Grim, NY (P)
1953 ... Junior Gilliam, Bklyn (2B)	1955 ... Herb Score, Clev (P)
1954 ... Wally Moon, StL (OF)	1956 ... Luis Aparicio, Chi (SS)
1955 ... Bill Virdon, StL (OF)	1957 ... Tony Kubek, NY (OF, SS)
1956 ... Frank Robinson, Cin (OF)	1958 ... Albie Pearson, Wash (OF)
1957 ... Jack Sanford, Phil (P)	1959 ... Bob Allison, Wash (OF)
1958 ... Orlando Cepeda, SF (1B)	1960 ... Ron Hansen, Balt (SS)
1959 ... Willie McCovey, SF (1B)	1961 ... Don Schwall, Bos (P)
1960 ... Frank Howard, LA (OF)	1962 ... Tom Tresh, NY (SS)
1961 ... Billy Williams, Chi (OF)	1963 ... Gary Peters, Chi (P)
1962 ... Ken Hubbs, Chi (2B)	1964 ... Tony Oliva, Minn (OF)
1963 ... Pete Rose, Cin (2B)	1965 ... Curt Blefary, Balt (OF)
1964 ... Dick Allen, Phil (3B)	1966 ... Tommie Agee, Chi (OF)
1965 ... Jim Lefebvre, LA (2B)	1967 ... Rod Carew, Minn (2B)
1966 ... Tommy Helms, Cin (2B)	1968 ... Stan Bahnsen, NY (P)
1967 ... Tom Seaver, NY (P)	1969 ... Lou Piniella, KC (OF)
1968 ... Johnny Bench, Cin (C)	1970 ... Thurman Munson, NY (C)
1969 ... Ted Sizemore, LA (2B)	1971 ... Chris Chambliss, Clev (1B)
1970 ... Carl Morton, Mont (P)	1972 ... Carlton Fisk, Bos (C)
1971 ... Earl Williams, Atl (C)	1973 ... Al Bumbry, Balt (OF)
1972 ... Jon Matlack, NY (P)	1974 ... Mike Hargrove, Tex (1B)
1973 ... Gary Matthews, SF (OF)	1975 ... Fred Lynn, Bos (OF)
1974 ... Bake McBride, StL (OF)	1976 ... Mark Fidrych, Det (P)
1975 ... John Montefusco, SF (P)	1977 ... Eddie Murray, Balt (DH)
1976 ... Pat Zachry, Cin (P)	1978 ... Lou Whitaker, Det (2B)
Butch Metzger, SD (P)	1979 ... Alfredo Griffin, Tor (SS)
1977 ... Andre Dawson, Mont (OF)	John Castino, Minn (3B)
1978 ... Bob Horner, Atl (3B)	1980 ... Joe Charboneau, Clev (OF)
1979 ... Rick Sutcliffe, LA (P)	1981 ... Dave Righetti, NY (P)
1980 ... Steve Howe, LA (P)	1982 ... Cal Ripken, Balt (SS)
1981 ... Fernando Valenzuela, LA (P)	1983 ... Ron Kittle, Chi (OF)
1982 ... Steve Sax, LA (2B)	

*Just one selection for both leagues.

Rookies of the Year *(Cont.)*

NATIONAL LEAGUE *(Cont.)*

1983 ....Darryl Strawberry, NY (OF)
1984 ....Dwight Gooden, NY (P)
1985 ....Vince Coleman, StL (OF)
1986 ....Todd Worrell, StL (P)
1987 ....Benito Santiago, SD (C)
1988 ....Chris Sabo, Cin (3B)
1989 ....Jerome Walton, Chi (OF)
1990 ....Dave Justice, Atl (OF)
1991 ....Jeff Bagwell, Hou (3B)
1992 ....Eric Karros, LA (1B)
1993 ....Mike Piazza, LA (C)
1994 ....Raul Mondesi, LA (OF)
1995 ....Hideo Nomo, LA (P)

AMERICAN LEAGUE *(Cont.)*

1984 ....Alvin Davis, Sea (1B)
1985 ....Ozzie Guillen, Chi (SS)
1986 ....Jose Canseco, Oak (OF)
1987 ....Mark McGwire, Oak (1B)
1988 ....Walt Weiss, Oak (SS)
1989 ....Gregg Olson, Balt (P)
1990 ....Sandy Alomar Jr, Clev (C)
1991 ....Chuck Knoblauch, Minn (2B)
1992 ....Pat Listach, Mil (SS)
1993 ....Tim Salmon, Calif (OF)
1994 ....Bob Hamelin, Minn (DH)
1995 ....Marty Cordova, Minn (OF)

Cy Young Award

Year	W-L	Sv	ERA	Year	W-L	Sv	ERA
1956....*Don Newcombe, Bklyn (NL)	27-7	0	3.06	1962....Don Drysdale, LA (NL)	25-9	1	2.83
1957....Warren Spahn, Mil (NL)	21-11	3	2.69	1963....*Sandy Koufax, LA (NL)	25-5	0	1.88
1958....Bob Turley, NY (AL)	21-7	1	2.97	1964....Dean Chance, LA (AL)	20-9	4	1.65
1959....Early Wynn, Chi (AL)	22-10	0	3.17	1965....Sandy Koufax, LA (NL)	26-8	2	2.04
1960....Vernon Law, Pitt (NL)	20-9	0	3.08	1966....Sandy Koufax, LA (NL)	27-9	0	1.73
1961....Whitey Ford, NY (AL)	25-4	0	3.21				

NATIONAL LEAGUE				AMERICAN LEAGUE			
Year	W-L	Sv	ERA	Year	W-L	Sv	ERA
1967.....Mike McCormick, SF	22-10	0	2.85	1967.....Jim Lonborg, Bos	22-9	0	3.16
1968.....*Bob Gibson, StL	22-9	0	1.12	1968.....*Denny McLain, Det	31-6	0	1.96
1969.....Tom Seaver, NY	25-7	0	2.21	1969.....Denny McLain, Det	24-9	0	2.80
1970.....Bob Gibson, StL	23-7	0	3.12	.....Mike Cuellar, Balt	23-11	0	2.38
1971.....Ferguson Jenkins, Chi	24-13	0	2.77	1970.....Jim Perry, Minn	24-12	0	3.03
1972.....Steve Carlton, Phil	27-10	0	1.97	1971.....*Vida Blue, Oak	24-8	0	1.82
1973.....Tom Seaver, NY	19-10	0	2.08	1972.....Gaylord Perry, Clev	24-16	1	1.92
1974.....Mike Marshall, LA	15-12	21	2.42	1973.....Jim Palmer, Balt	22-9	1	2.40
1975.....Tom Seaver, NY	22-9	0	2.38	1974.....Catfish Hunter, Oak	25-12	0	2.49
1976.....Randy Jones, SD	22-14	0	2.74	1975.....Jim Palmer, Balt	23-11	1	2.09
1977.....Steve Carlton, Phil	23-10	0	2.64	1976.....Jim Palmer, Balt	22-13	0	2.51
1978.....Gaylord Perry, SD	21-6	0	2.72	1977.....Sparky Lyle, NY	13-5	26	2.17
1979.....Bruce Sutter, Chi	6-6	37	2.23	1978.....Ron Guidry, NY	25-3	0	1.74
1980.....Steve Carlton, Phil	24-9	0	2.34	1979.....Mike Flanagan, Balt	23-9	0	3.08
1981.....Fernando Valenzuela, LA	13-7	0	2.48	1980.....Steve Stone, Balt	25-7	0	3.23
1982.....Steve Carlton, Phil	23-11	0	3.10	1981.....*Rollie Fingers, Mil	6-3	28	1.04
1983.....John Denny, Phil	19-6	0	2.37	1982.....Pete Vuckovich, Mi	18-6	0	3.34
1984.....†Rick Sutcliffe, Chi	16-1	0	2.69	1983.....LaMarr Hoyt, Chi	24-10	0	3.66
1985.....Dwight Gooden, NY	24-4	0	1.53	1984.....*Willie Hernandez, Det	9-3	32	1.92
1986.....Mike Scott, Hou	18-10	0	2.22	1985.....Bret Saberhagen, KC	20-6	0	2.87
1987.....Steve Bedrosian, Phil	5-3	40	2.83	1986.....*Roger Clemens, Bos	24-4	0	2.48
1988.....Orel Hershiser, LA	23-8	1	2.26	1987.....Roger Clemens, Bos	20-9	0	2.97
1989.....Mark Davis, SD	4-3	44	1.85	1988.....Frank Viola, Minn	24-7	0	2.64
1990.....Doug Drabek, Pitt	22-6	0	2.76	1989.....Bret Saberhagen, KC	23-6	0	2.16
1991.....Tom Glavine, Atl	20-11	0	2.55	1990.....Bob Welch, Oak	27-6	0	2.95
1992.....Greg Maddux, Chi	20-11	0	2.18	1991.....Roger Clemens, Bos	18-10	0	2.62
1993.....Greg Maddux, Atl	20-10	0	2.36	1992.....*Dennis Eckersley, Oak	7-1	51	1.91
1994.....Greg Maddux, Atl	16-6	0	1.56	1993.....Jack McDowell, Chi	22-10	0	3.37
1995.....Greg Maddux, Atl	19-2	0	1.63	1994.....David Cone, KC	16-4	0	2.94
				1995.....Randy Johnson, Sea	18-2	0	2.48

*Pitchers who won the MVP and Cy Young awards in the same season.

†NL games only. Sutcliffe pitched 15 games with Cleveland before being traded to the Cubs.

Career Individual Batting

GAMES

Pete Rose	3562
Carl Yastrzemski	3308
Hank Aaron	3298
Ty Cobb	3035
Stan Musial	3026
Willie Mays	2992
Dave Winfield	2973
Eddie Murray	2971
Rusty Staub	2951
Brooks Robinson	2896
Robin Yount	2856
Al Kaline	2834
Eddie Collins	2826
Reggie Jackson	2820
Frank Robinson	2808
Honus Wagner	2792
Tris Speaker	2789
Tony Perez	2777
Mel Ott	2730
George Brett	2707

AT BATS

Pete Rose	14053
Hank Aaron	12364
Carl Yastrzemski	11988
Ty Cobb	11434
Eddie Murray	11169
Robin Yount	11008
Dave Winfield	11003
Stan Musial	10972
Willie Mays	10881
Brooks Robinson	10654
Honus Wagner	10430
George Brett	10349
Lou Brock	10332
Luis Aparicio	10230
Tris Speaker	10195
Al Kaline	10116
Rabbit Maranville	10078
Frank Robinson	10006
Eddie Collins	9949
Andre Dawson	9927

HOME RUNS

Hank Aaron	755
Babe Ruth	714
Willie Mays	660
Frank Robinson	586
Harmon Killebrew	573
Reggie Jackson	563
Mike Schmidt	548
Mickey Mantle	536
Jimmie Foxx	534
Ted Williams	521
Willie McCovey	521
Eddie Mathews	512
Ernie Banks	512
Mel Ott	511
Eddie Murray	501
Lou Gehrig	493
Willie Stargell	475
Stan Musial	475
Dave Winfield	465
Carl Yastrzemski	452

HITS

Pete Rose	4256
Ty Cobb	4189
Hank Aaron	3771
Stan Musial	3630
Tris Speaker	3514
Carl Yastrzemski	3419
Honus Wagner	3415
Eddie Collins	3312
Willie Mays	3283
Nap Lajoie	3242
Eddie Murray	3218
George Brett	3154
Paul Waner	3152
Robin Yount	3142
Dave Winfield	3110
Rod Carew	3053
Lou Brock	3023
Paul Molitor	3011
Al Kaline	3007
Roberto Clemente	3000

BATTING AVERAGE

Ty Cobb	.366
Rogers Hornsby	.358
Joe Jackson	.356
Ed Delahanty	.346
Tris Speaker	.345
Ted Williams	.344
Billy Hamilton	.344
Dan Brouthers	.342
Babe Ruth	.342
Harry Heilmann	.342
Pete Browning	.341
Willie Keeler	.341
Bill Terry	.341
George Sisler	.340
Lou Gehrig	.340
Jesse Burkett	.338
Nap Lajoie	.338
Tony Gwynn	.337
Riggs Stephenson	.336
Al Simmons	.334

RUNS

Ty Cobb	2246
Babe Ruth	2174
Hank Aaron	2174
Pete Rose	2165
Willie Mays	2062
Stan Musial	1949
Lou Gehrig	1888
Tris Speaker	1882
Mel Ott	1859
Rickey Henderson	1829
Frank Robinson	1829
Eddie Collins	1821
Carl Yastrzemski	1816
Ted Williams	1798
Charlie Gehringer	1774
Jimmie Foxx	1751
Honus Wagner	1736
Jesse Burkett	1720
Cap Anson	1719
Willie Keeler	1719

DOUBLES

Tris Speaker	792
Pete Rose	746
Stan Musial	725
Ty Cobb	724
George Brett	665
Nap Lajoie	657
Carl Yastrzemski	646
Honus Wagner	640
Hank Aaron	624
Paul Waner	605
Robin Yount	583
Charlie Gehringer	574
Eddie Murray	553
Paul Molitor	544
Harry Heilmann	542
Rogers Hornsby	541
Joe Medwick	540
Dave Winfield	540
Al Simmons	539
Lou Gehrig	534

TRIPLES

Sam Crawford	309
Ty Cobb	295
Honus Wagner	252
Jake Beckley	243
Roger Connor	233
Tris Speaker	222
Fred Clarke	220
Dan Brouthers	205
Joe Kelley	194
Paul Waner	191
Bid McPhee	188
Eddie Collins	186
Ed Delahanty	185
Sam Rice	184
Jesse Burkett	182
Edd Roush	182
Ed Konetchy	181
Buck Ewing	178
Rabbit Maranville	177
Stan Musial	177

BASES ON BALLS

Babe Ruth	2056
Ted Williams	2019
Joe Morgan	1865
Carl Yastrzemski	1845
Mickey Mantle	1733
Mel Ott	1708
Rickey Henderson	1675
Eddie Yost	1614
Darrell Evans	1605
Stan Musial	1599
Pete Rose	1566
Harmon Killebrew	1559
Lou Gehrig	1508
Mike Schmidt	1507
Eddie Collins	1499
Willie Mays	1464
Jimmie Foxx	1452
Eddie Mathews	1444
Frank Robinson	1420
Hank Aaron	1402

Career Individual Batting *(Cont.)*

RUNS BATTED IN		STOLEN BASES		TOTAL BASES	
Hank Aaron	2297	Rickey Henderson	1186	Hank Aaron	6856
Babe Ruth	2213	Lou Brock	938	Stan Musial	6134
Lou Gehrig	1995	Billy Hamilton	912	Willie Mays	6066
Stan Musial	1951	Ty Cobb	892	Ty Cobb	5854
Ty Cobb	1937	Tim Raines	787	Babe Ruth	5793
Jimmie Foxx	1922	Vince Coleman	752	Pete Rose	5752
Willie Mays	1903	Eddie Collins	744	Carl Yastrzemski	5539
Eddie Murray	1899	Arlie Latham	739	Frank Robinson	5373
Cap Anson	1879	Max Carey	738	Eddie Murray	5344
Mel Ott	1860	Honus Wagner	722	Dave Winfield	5221
Carl Yastrzemski	1844	Joe Morgan	689	Tris Speaker	5101
Ted Williams	1839	Willie Wilson	668	Lou Gehrig	5060
Dave Winfield	1833	Tom Brown	657	George Brett	5044
Al Simmons	1827	Bert Campaneris	649	Mel Ott	5041
Frank Robinson	1812	George Davis	616	Jimmie Foxx	4956
Honus Wagner	1732	Dummy Hoy	594	Ted Williams	4884
Reggie Jackson	1702	Maury Wills	586	Honus Wagner	4862
Tony Perez	1652	George Van Haltren	583	Al Kaline	4852
Ernie Banks	1636	Ozzie Smith	580	Reggie Jackson	4834
Goose Goslin	1609	Hugh Duffy	574	Andre Dawson	4787

SLUGGING AVERAGE		PINCH HITS		STRIKEOUTS	
Babe Ruth	.690	Manny Mota	150	Reggie Jackson	2597
Ted Williams	.634	Smoky Burgess	145	Willie Stargell	1936
Lou Gehrig	.632	Greg Gross	143	Mike Schmidt	1883
Jimmie Foxx	.609	Jose Morales	123	Tony Perez	1867
Hank Greenberg	.605	Jerry Lynch	116	Dave Kingman	1816
Joe DiMaggio	.579	Red Lucas	114	Bobby Bonds	1757
Rogers Hornsby	.577	Steve Braun	113	Dale Murphy	1748
Johnny Mize	.562	Terry Crowley	108	Lou Brock	1730
Stan Musial	.559	Denny Walling	108	Mickey Mantle	1710
Willie Mays	.557	Gates Brown	107	Harmon Killebrew	1699
Mickey Mantle	.557	Mike Lum	103	Dwight Evans	1697
Hank Aaron	.555	Jim Dwyer	102	Dave Winfield	1686
Ken Griffey Jr.	.549	Rusty Staub	100	Lee May	1570
Ralph Kiner	.548	Larry Biittner	95	Dick Allen	1556
Barry Bonds	.548	Vic Davalillo	95	Willie McCovey	1550
Hack Wilson	.545	Jerry Hairston	94	Dave Parker	1537
Mark McGwire	.544	Dave Philley	93	Frank Robinson	1532
Chuck Klein	.543	Joel Youngblood	93	Lance Parrish	1527
Duke Snider	.540	Jay Johnstone	92	Willie Mays	1526
Frank Robinson	.537	Ed Kranepool	90	Rick Monday	1513
		Elmer Valo	90		

The 30–30 Club (30 HR, 30 SB in single season)

NATIONAL LEAGUE

Year		HR	SB	Year		HR	SB
1956	Willie Mays, NY Giants	36	40	1990	Barry Bonds, Pitt	33	52
1957	Willie Mays, NY Giants	35	38	1991	Ron Gant, Atl	32	34
1963	Hank Aaron, Milwaukee	44	31	1991	Howard Johnson, NY	38	30
1969	Bobby Bonds, SF	32	45	1992	Barry Bonds, Pitt	34	39
1973	Bobby Bonds, SF	39	43	1993	Sammy Sosa, Chi	33	36
1983	Dale Murphy, Atl	36	30	1995	Barry Bonds, SF	33	31
1987	Eric Davis, Cin	37	50	1995	Sammy Sosa, Chi	36	34
1987	Darryl Strawberry, NY	39	36	1996	Barry Bonds, SF	42	40
1987	Howard Johnson, NY	36	32	1996	Ellis Burks, Col	40	32
1989	Howard Johnson, NY	36	41	1996	Barry Larkin, Cin	33	36
1990	Ron Gant, Atl	32	33	1996	Dante Bichette, Col	31	31

AMERICAN LEAGUE

Year		HR	SB	Year		HR	SB
1922	Kenny Williams, St L	39	37	1978	Bobby Bonds, Chi/Tex	31	43
1970	Tommy Harper, Mil	31	38	1987	Joe Carter, Clev	32	31
1975	Bobby Bonds, NY	32	30	1988	Jose Canseco, Oak	42	40
1977	Bobby Bonds, Cal	37	41				

Career Individual Pitching

GAMES

Hoyt Wilhelm	1070
Kent Tekulve	1050
Goose Gossage	1002
Lee Smith	997
Lindy McDaniel	987
Dennis Eckersley	964
Rollie Fingers	944
Gene Garber	931
Cy Young	906
Sparky Lyle	899
Jim Kaat	898
Jesse Orosco	885
Jeff Reardon	880
Don McMahon	874
Phil Niekro	864
Charlie Hough	858
Roy Face	848
Tug McGraw	824
Nolan Ryan	807
Walter Johnson	802

INNINGS PITCHED

Cy Young	7356.2
Pud Galvin	5941.1
Walter Johnson	5914.2
Phil Niekro	5404.1
Nolan Ryan	5386.0
Gaylord Perry	5350.1
Don Sutton	5282.1
Warren Spahn	5243.2
Steve Carlton	5217.1
Grover Alexander	5190.0
Kid Nichols	5056.1
Tim Keefe	5047.1
Bert Blyleven	4970.0
Mickey Welch	4802.0
Tom Seaver	4782.2
Christy Mathewson	4780.2
Tommy John	4710.1
Robin Roberts	4688.2
Early Wynn	4564.0
John Clarkson	4536.1

WINS

Cy Young	511
Walter Johnson	417
Grover Alexander	373
Christy Mathewson	373
Warren Spahn	363
Kid Nichols	361
Pud Galvin	360
Tim Keefe	342
Steve Carlton	329
John Clarkson	328
Eddie Plank	326
Nolan Ryan	324
Don Sutton	324
Phil Niekro	318
Gaylord Perry	314
Tom Seaver	311
Charley Radbourn	309
Mickey Welch	307
Lefty Grove	300
Early Wynn	300

LOSSES

Cy Young	316
Pud Galvin	308
Nolan Ryan	292
Walter Johnson	279
Phil Niekro	274
Gaylord Perry	265
Don Sutton	256
Jack Powell	254
Eppa Rixey	251
Bert Blyleven	250
Robin Roberts	245
Warren Spahn	245
Steve Carlton	244
Early Wynn	244
Jim Kaat	237
Frank Tanana	236
Gus Weyhing	232
Tommy John	231
Bob Friend	230
Ted Lyons	230

WINNING PERCENTAGE

Dave Foutz	.690
Whitey Ford	.690
Bob Caruthers	.688
Lefty Grove	.680
Vic Raschi	.667
Larry Corcoran	.665
Christy Mathewson	.665
Sam Leever	.660
Sal Maglie	.657
Sandy Koufax	.655
Johnny Allen	.654
Ron Guidry	.651
Lefty Gomez	.649
John Clarkson	.648
Three Finger Brown	.648
Dwight Gooden	.646
Dizzy Dean	.644
Grover Alexander	.642
Jim Palmer	.638

SAVES

Lee Smith	473
Jeff Reardon	367
Dennis Eckersley	353
Rollie Fingers	341
John Franco	323
Tom Henke	311
Goose Gossage	310
Bruce Sutter	300
Randy Myers	274
Dave Righetti	252
Dan Quisenberry	244
Doug Jones	242
Jeff Montgomery	242
Sparky Lyle	238
Hoyt Wilhelm	227
Gene Garber	218
Dave Smith	216
Rick Aguilera	211
Bobby Thigpen	201
Roy Face	193
Mike Henneman	193

EARNED RUN AVERAGE

Ed Walsh	1.82
Addie Joss	1.89
Three Finger Brown	2.06
John Ward	2.10
Christy Mathewson	2.13
Rube Waddell	2.16
Walter Johnson	2.17
Orval Overall	2.23
Tommy Bond	2.25
Ed Reulbach	2.28
Will White	2.28
Jim Scott	2.30
Eddie Plank	2.35
Larry Corcoran	2.36
Eddie Cicotte	2.38
Ed Killian	2.38
George McQuillan	2.00
Doc White	2.39
Nap Rucker	2.42
Terry Larkin	2.43
Jim McCormick	2.43
Jeff Tesreau	2.43

SHUTOUTS

Walter Johnson	110
Grover Alexander	90
Christy Mathewson	79
Cy Young	76
Eddie Plank	69
Warren Spahn	63
Nolan Ryan	61
Tom Seaver	61
Bert Blyleven	60
Don Sutton	58
Pud Galvin	57
Ed Walsh	57
Bob Gibson	56
Three Finger Brown	55
Steve Carlton	55
Jim Palmer	53
Gaylord Perry	53
Juan Marichal	52
Rube Waddell	50
Vic Willis	50

COMPLETE GAMES

Cy Young	749
Pud Galvin	639
Tim Keefe	554
Walter Johnson	531
Kid Nichols	531
Mickey Welch	525
Charley Radbourn	489
John Clarkson	485
Tony Mullane	468
Jim McCormick	466
Gus Weyhing	448
Grover Alexander	437
Christy Mathewson	434
Jack Powell	422
Eddie Plank	410
Will White	394
Amos Rusie	392
Vic Willis	388
Warren Spahn	382
Jim Whitney	377

Career Individual Pitching (Cont.)

STRIKEOUTS

Nolan Ryan	5714
Steve Carlton	4136
Bert Blyleven	3701
Tom Seaver	3640
Don Sutton	3574
Gaylord Perry	3534
Walter Johnson	3509
Phil Niekro	3342
Ferguson Jenkins	3192
Bob Gibson	3117
Jim Bunning	2855
Mickey Lolich	2832
Cy Young	2803
Frank Tanana	2773
Roger Clemens	2590
Warren Spahn	2583
Bob Feller	2581
Jerry Koosman	2556
Tim Keefe	2543
Christy Mathewson	2502

BASES ON BALLS

Nolan Ryan	2795
Steve Carlton	1833
Phil Niekro	1809
Early Wynn	1775
Bob Feller	1764
Bobo Newsom	1732
Amos Rusie	1704
Charlie Hough	1665
Gus Weyhing	1566
Red Ruffing	1541
Bump Hadley	1442
Warren Spahn	1434
Earl Whitehill	1431
Tony Mullane	1408
Sad Sam Jones	1396
Jack Morris	1390
Tom Seaver	1390
Gaylord Perry	1379
Mike Torrez	1371
Walter Johnson	1363

Alltime Winningest Managers

CAREER

	W	L	Pct	Yrs		W	L	Pct	Yrs
Connie Mack	3755	3967	.486	53	Ralph Houk	1627	1539	.514	20
John McGraw	2810	1987	.586	33	Fred Clarke	1609	1189	.575	19
Sparky Anderson	2238	1855	.547	26	Dick Williams	1592	1474	.519	21
Bucky Harris	2168	2228	.493	29	Tommy Lasorda	1589	1434	.526	20
Joe McCarthy	2155	1346	.616	24	Earl Weaver	1506	1080	.582	17
Walter Alston	2063	1634	.558	23	Clark Griffith	1491	1367	.522	20
Leo Durocher	2015	1717	.540	24	Miller Huggins	1431	1149	.555	17
Casey Stengel	1942	1868	.510	25	Al Lopez	1412	1012	.583	17
Gene Mauch	1907	2044	.483	26	Jimmy Dykes	1406	1541	.477	21
Bill McKechnie	1904	1737	.523	25	Wilbert Robertson	1402	1407	.499	19

REGULAR SEASON

	W	L	Pct	Yrs		W	L	Pct	Yrs
Connie Mack	3731	3948	.486	53	Ralph Houk	1619	1531	.514	20
John McGraw	2784	1959	.587	33	Fred Clarke	1602	1181	.576	19
Sparky Anderson	2194	1834	.545	26	Dick Williams	1571	1451	.520	21
Bucky Harris	2157	2218	.493	29	Tommy Lasorda	1558	1404	.526	20
Joe McCarthy	2125	1333	.615	24	Earl Weaver	1480	1060	.583	17
Walter Alston	2040	1613	.558	23	Clark Griffith	1491	1367	.522	20
Leo Durocher	2008	1709	.540	24	Miller Huggins	1413	1134	.555	17
Casey Stengel	1905	1842	.508	25	Al Lopez	1410	1004	.584	17
Gene Mauch	1902	2037	.483	26	Jimmy Dykes	1406	1541	.477	21
Bill McKechnie	1896	1723	.524	25	Wilbert Robertson	1399	1398	.500	19

WORLD SERIES

	W	L	T	Pct	App	WS		W	L	T	Pct	App	WS
Casey Stengel	37	26	0	.587	10	7	Bucky Harris	11	10	0	.524	3	2
Joe McCarthy	30	13	0	.698	9	7	Billy Southworth	11	11	0	.500	4	2
John McGraw	26	28	2	.482	9	2	Earl Weaver	11	13	0	.458	4	1
Connie Mack	24	19	0	.558	8	5	Whitey Herzog	10	11	0	.476	3	1
Walter Alston	20	20	0	.500	7	4	Bill Carrigan	8	2	0	.800	2	2
Miller Huggins	18	15	1	.544	6	3	Danny Murtaugh	8	6	0	.571	2	2
Sparky Anderson	16	12	0	.571	5	3	Ralph Houk	8	8	0	.500	3	2
Tommy Lasorda	12	11	0	.522	4	2	Bill McKechnie	8	14	0	.364	4	2
Dick Williams	12	14	0	.462	4	2	Tom Kelly	8	6	0	.571	2	2
Frank Chance	11	9	1	.548	4	2							

Individual Batting (Single Season)

HITS

George Sisler, 1920.............257
Lefty O'Doul, 1929...............254
Bill Terry, 1930....................254
Al Simmons, 1925................253
Rogers Hornsby, 1922.........250
Chuck Klein, 1930 250
Ty Cobb, 1911 248
George Sisler, 1922.............246
Heinie Manush, 1928...........241
Babe Herman, 1930 241

BATTING AVERAGE

Hugh Duffy, 1894................ .440
Tip O'Neill, 1887 .... .435
Ross Barnes, 1876 .... .429
Nap Lajoie, 1901 .... .426
Willie Keeler, 1897 .... .424
Rogers Hornsby, 1924......... .424
George Sisler, 1922........... .420
Ty Cobb, 1911 .... .420
Fred Dunlap, 1884............. .412
Ed Delahanty, 1899 .... .410

DOUBLES

Earl Webb, 1931 67
George Burns, 1926 64
Joe Medwick, 1936................64
Hank Greenberg, 1934...........63
Paul Waner, 1932 62
Charlie Gehringer, 1936 60
Tris Speaker, 1923................59
Chuck Klein, 1930 59
Billy Herman, 1936 57
Billy Herman, 1935 57

TOTAL BASES

Babe Ruth, 1921...................457
Rogers Hornsby, 1922.........450
Lou Gehrig, 1927.................447
Chuck Klein, 1930 445
Jimmie Foxx, 1932...............438
Stan Musial, 1948................429
Hack Wilson, 1930...............423
Chuck Klein, 1932................420
Lou Gehrig, 1930.................419
Joe DiMaggio, 1937 418

TRIPLES

Chief Wilson, 1912.................36
Dave Orr, 1886 31
Heinie Reitz, 1894.................31
Perry Werden, 1893...............29
Harry Davis, 1897..................28
George Davis, 1893................27
Sam Thompson, 1894............27
Jimmy Williams, 1899 27
John Reilly, 1890 26
George Treadway, 1894........26
Joe Jackson, 1912.................26
Sam Crawford, 1914..............26
Kiki Cuyler, 1925....................26

HOME RUNS

Roger Maris, 1961 61
Babe Ruth, 1927....................60
Babe Ruth, 1921....................59
Jimmie Foxx, 1932................58
Hank Greenberg, 1938..........58
Hack Wilson, 1930................56
Babe Ruth, 1920....................54
Babe Ruth, 1928....................54
Ralph Kiner, 1949 54
Mickey Mantle, 1961.............54

RUNS BATTED IN

Hack Wilson, 1930...............190
Lou Gehrig, 1931.................184
Hank Greenberg, 1937........183
Lou Gehrig, 1927.................175
Jimmie Foxx, 1938...............175
Lou Gehrig, 1930.................174
Babe Ruth, 1921...................171
Chuck Klein, 1930 170
Hank Greenberg, 1935........170
Jimmie Foxx, 1932...............169

STRIKEOUTS

Bobby Bonds, 1970.............189
Bobby Bonds, 1969............187
Rob Deer, 1987....................186
Pete Incaviglia, 1986...........185
Cecil Fielder, 1990...............182
Mike Schmidt, 1975.............180
Rob Deer, 1986 179
Dave Nicholson, 1963 175
Gorman Thomas, 1979........175
Jose Canseco, 1986............175
Rob Deer, 1991 175

RUNS

Billy Hamilton, 1894 192
Tom Brown, 1891..................177
Babe Ruth, 1921...................177
Tip O'Neill, 1887 167
Lou Gehrig, 1936..................167
Billy Hamilton, 1895..............166
Willie Keeler, 1894................165
Joe Kelley, 1894...................165
Arlie Latham, 1887...............163
Babe Ruth, 1928...................163
Lou Gehrig, 1931..................163

STOLEN BASES

Hugh Nicol, 1887..................138
Rickey Henderson, 1982......130
Arlie Latham, 1887................129
Lou Brock, 1974...................118
Charlie Comiskey, 1887.......117
John Ward, 1887...................111
Billy Hamilton, 1889..............111
Billy Hamilton, 1891..............111
Vince Coleman, 1985 110
Arlie Latham, 1888................109
Vince Coleman, 1987 109

BASES ON BALLS

Babe Ruth, 1923...................170
Ted Williams, 1947 162
Ted Williams, 1949 162
Ted Williams, 1946 156
Eddie Yost, 1956 151
Eddie Joost, 1949................149
Babe Ruth, 1920...................148
Eddie Stanky, 1945..............148
Jimmy Wynn, 1969 148
Jimmy Sheckard, 1911........147

SLUGGING AVERAGE

Babe Ruth, 1920.................. .847
Babe Ruth, 1921.................. .846
Babe Ruth, 1927.................. .772
Lou Gehrig, 1927................. .765
Babe Ruth, 1923.................. .764
Rogers Hornsby, 1925........ .756
Jeff Bagwell, 1994 .... .750
Jimmie Foxx, 1932............... .749
Babe Ruth, 1924................. .739
Babe Ruth, 1926................. .737

A Flat-out "I Do"

Injuries have long plagued Jose Canseco's baseball career, and they had an impact on his nuptials as well. While recovering from back surgery, Canseco married Jessica Seikaly at his Fort Lauderdale-area home on Aug. 27. The small group of friends in attendance witnessed an exceptionally private ceremony. "We had to get married in bed," Canseco reported. "I couldn't get out."

Individual Pitching (Single Season)

GAMES

Mike Marshall, 1974..............106
Kent Tekulve, 1979................94
Mike Marshall, 1973................92
Kent Tekulve, 1978................91
Wayne Granger, 1969 90
Mike Marshall, 1979................90
Kent Tekulve, 1987................90
Mark Eichhorn, 1987..............89
Wilbur Wood, 1968 88
Rob Murphy, 1987 87

GAMES STARTED

Will White, 1879 75
Jim Galvin, 1883 75
Jim McCormick, 1880............74
Charley Radbourn, 1884 73
Guy Hecker, 1884..................73
Jim Galvin, 1884 72
John Clarkson, 1889..............72
Bill Hutchison, 1892..............71
John Clarkson, 1885..............70
Matt Kilroy, 1887....................69

INNINGS PITCHED

Will White, 1878 ....680.0
Charley Radbourn, 1884...678.2
Guy Hecker, 1884............670.2
Jim McCormick, 1880........657.2
Jim Galvin, 1883 ....656.1
Jim Galvin, 1884 ....636.1
Charley Radbourn, 1883...632.1
Bill Hutchison, 1892..........627.0
John Clarkson, 1885.........623.0
Jim Devlin, 1876 ....622.0

WINS

Charley Radbourn, 1884 59
John Clarkson, 1885..............53
Guy Hecker, 1884..................52
John Clarkson, 1889..............49
Charley Radbourn, 1883 48
Charlie Buffinton, 1884 48
Al Spalding, 1876 47
John Ward, 1879 47
Jim Galvin, 1883 46
Jim Galvin, 1884 46
Matt Kilroy, 1887..................46

LOSSES

John Coleman, 1883..............48
Will White, 1880 42
Larry McKeon, 1884 41
George Bradley, 1879..........40
Jim McCormick, 1879............40
Henry Porter, 1888................37
Kid Carsey, 1891 37
George Cobb, 1892................37
Stump Weidman, 1886 36
Bill Hutchison, 1892..............36

WINNING PERCENTAGE

Roy Face, 1959..................947
Johnny Allen, 1937 .... .938
Greg Maddux, 1995 .... .905
Randy Johnson, 1995......... .900
Ron Guidry, 1978.............. .893
Freddie Fitzsimmons, 1940.... .889
Lefty Grove, 1931 .... .886
Bob Stanley, 1978 .... .882
Preacher Roe, 1951............. .880
Fred Goldsmith, 1880......... .875
Tom Seaver, 1981.............. .875

SAVES

Bobby Thigpen, 1990............57
Randy Myers, 1993................53
Dennis Eckersley, 1992..........51
Dennis Eckersley, 1990.........48
Rod Beck, 1993 48
Lee Smith, 1991....................47
Lee Smith, 1993....................46
Dave Righetti, 1986 46
Bryan Harvey, 1991 46
Jose Mesa, 1995 46
Six tied with 45.

EARNED RUN AVERAGE

Tim Keefe, 1880..................0.86
Dutch Leonard, 1914..........0.96
Three Finger Brown, 1906....1.04
Bob Gibson, 1968................1.12
Christy Mathewson, 1909 ...1.14
Walter Johnson, 1913..........1.14
Jack Pfiester, 1907 ....1.15
Addie Joss, 1908................1.16
Carl Lundgren, 1907...........1.17
Denny Driscoll, 1882 ....1.21

SHUTOUTS

George Bradley, 1876 16
Grover Alexander, 1916 16
Jack Coombs, 1910..............13
Bob Gibson, 1968..................13
Jim Galvin, 1884 12
Ed Morris, 1886 12
Grover Alexander, 1915 12
Tommy Bond, 1879 11
Charley Radbourn, 1884 11
Dave Foutz, 1886..................11
Christy Mathewson, 1908 11
Ed Walsh, 1908....................11
Walter Johnson, 1913............11
Sandy Koufax, 1963 11
Dean Chance, 1964..............11

COMPLETE GAMES

Will White, 1879 75
Charley Radbourn, 1884 73
Jim McCormick, 1880............72
Jim Galvin, 1883 72
Guy Hecker, 1884..................72
Jim Galvin, 1884 71
Tim Keefe, 1883....................68
John Clarkson, 1885..............68
John Clarkson, 1889..............68
Bill Hutchison, 1892..............67

STRIKEOUTS

Matt Kilroy, 1886..................513
Toad Ramsey, 1886..............499
Hugh Daily, 1884..................483
Dupee Shaw, 1884 451
Charley Radbourn, 1884 441
Charlie Buffinton, 1884 417
Guy Hecker, 1884..................385
Nolan Ryan, 1973................383
Sandy Koufax, 1965 382
Bill Sweeney, 1884 374

BASES ON BALLS

Amos Rusie, 1890................289
Mark Baldwin, 1889..............274
Amos Rusie, 1892................267
Amos Rusie, 1891................262
Mark Baldwin, 1890..............249
Jack Stivetts, 1891................232
Mark Baldwin, 1891..............227
Phil Knell, 1891....................226
Bob Barr, 1890 219
Amos Rusie 1893................218

Manager of the Year

NATIONAL LEAGUE	AMERICAN LEAGUE
1983 ....Tommy Lasorda, LA	1983 ....Tony La Russa, Chi
1984 ....Jim Frey, Chi	1984 ....Sparky Anderson, Det
1985 ....Whitey Herzog, StL	1985 ....Bobby Cox, Tor
1986 ....Hal Lanier, Hou	1986 ....John McNamara, Bos
1987 ....Buck Rodgers, Mtl	1987 ....Sparky Anderson, Det
1988 ....Tommy Lasorda, LA	1988 ....Tony La Russa, Oak
1989 ....Don Zimmer, Chi	1989 ....Frank Robinson, Balt
1990 ....Jim Leyland, Pitt	1990 ....Jeff Torborg, Chi
1991 ....Bobby Cox, Atl	1991 ....Tom Kelly, Minn
1992 ....Jim Leyland, Pitt	1992 ....Tony La Russa, Oak
1993 ....Dusty Baker, SF	1993 ....Gene Lamont, Chi
1994 ....Felipe Alou, Mtl	1994 ....Buck Showalter, NY
1995 ....Don Baylor, Col	1995 ....Lou Piniella, Sea

Individual Batting (Single Game)

MOST RUNS

7 ....Guy Hecker, Lou   Aug 15, 1886

MOST HITS

7 ....Wilbert Robinson, Balt   June 10, 1892
Rennie Stennett, Pitt   Sept 16, 1975

MOST HOME RUNS

4 ....Bobby Lowe, Bos (N)   May 30, 1894
Ed Delahanty, Phil   July 13, 1896
Lou Gehrig, NY (A)   June 3, 1932
Gil Hodges, Bklyn   Aug 31, 1950
Joe Adcock, Mil (N)   July 31, 1954
Rocky Colavito, Clev   June 10, 1959
Willie Mays, SF   April 30, 1961
Bob Horner, Atl   July 6, 1986
Mark Whiten, StL   Sept 7, 1993

MOST GRAND SLAMS

2 ....Tony Lazzeri, NY (A)   May 24, 1936
Jim Tabor, Bos (A)   July 4, 1939
Rudy York, Bos (A)   July 27, 1946
Jim Gentile, Balt   May 9, 1961
Tony Cloninger, Atl   July 3, 1966
Jim Northrup, Det   June 24, 1968
Frank Robinson, Balt   June 26, 1970
Robin Ventura, Chi (A)   Sept 4, 1995

MOST RBI

12 .....Jim Bottomley, StL   Sept 16, 1924
Mark Whiten, StL   Sept 7, 1993

Individual Batting (Single Inning)

MOST RUNS

3 ....Tommy Burns, Chi (N)   Sept 6, 1883, 7th inning
Ned Williamson, Chi (N)   Sept 6, 1883, 7th inning
Sammy White, Bos (A)   June 18, 1953, 7th inning

MOST HITS

3 ....Tommy Burns, Chi (N)   Sept 6, 1883, 7th inning
Fred Pfeiffer, Chi (N)   Sept 6, 1883, 7th inning
Ned Williamson, Chi (N)   Sept 6, 1883, 7th inning
Gene Stephens, Bos (A)   June 18, 1953, 7th inning

MOST RBI

6 ....Fred Merkle, NY (N)   May 13, 1911 (RBIs not officially adopted until 1920)
Bob Johnson, Phil (A)   Aug 29, 1937
Tom McBride, Bos (A)   Aug 4, 1945
Joe Astroth, Phil (A)   Sept 23, 1950
Gil McDougald, NY (A)   May 3, 1951
Sam Mele, Chi (A)   June 10, 1952
Jim Lemon, Wash   Sept 5, 1959
Jim Ray Hart, SF   July 8, 1970
Andre Dawson, Mont   Sept 24, 1985
Dale Murphy, Atl   July 27, 1989
Carlos Quintana, Bos (A)   July 30, 1991

Note: All single game hitting records for nine-inning game.

Individual Pitching (Single Game)

MOST INNINGS PITCHED

26	Leon Cadore, Bklyn	May 1, 1920, tie 1-1
	Joe Oeschger, Bos (N)	May 1, 1920, tie 1-1

MOST RUNS ALLOWED

24	Al Travers, Det	May 18, 1912 (only major league game)

MOST HITS ALLOWED

36	Jack Wadsworth, Lou	Aug 17, 1894

MOST STRIKEOUTS

20	Roger Clemens, Bos (A)	April 29, 1986
20	Roger Clemens, Bos (A)	Sept 18, 1996

MOST WALKS ALLOWED

16	Bill George, NY (N)	May 30, 1887
	George Van Haltren, Chi (N)	June 27, 1887
	Henry Gruber, Clev	Apr 19, 1890
	Bruno Haas, Phil (A)	June 2, 1915

MOST WILD PITCHES

6	J.R. Richard, Hou	April 10, 1979
	Phil Niekro, Atl	Aug 14, 1979
	Bill Gullickson, Mtl	April 10, 1982

Individual Pitching (Single Inning)

MOST RUNS ALLOWED

13	Lefty O'Doul, Bos (A)	July 7, 1923

MOST WALKS ALLOWED

8	Dolly Gray, Wash	Aug 28, 1909

MOST WILD PITCHES

4	Walter Johnson, Wash	Sept 21, 1914
	Phil Niekro, Atl	Aug 14, 1979

Miscellaneous

LONGEST GAME, BY INNINGS

26	Brooklyn 1, Boston 1	May 1, 1920

LONGEST NINE-INNING GAME, BY TIME

4:21	New York 13, Baltimore 10 April 30, 1996

Baseball Hall of Fame

Players

	Position	Career	Selected		Position	Career	Selected
Hank Aaron	OF	1954-76	1982	Jack Chesbro	P	1899-1909	1946
Grover Alexander	P	1911-30	1938	Fred Clarke	OF	1894-1915	1945
Cap Anson	1B	1876-97	1939	John Clarkson	P	1882-94	1963
Luis Aparicio	SS	1956-73	1984	Roberto Clemente	OF	1955-72	1973
Luke Appling	SS	1930-50	1964	Ty Cobb	OF	1905-28	1936
Richie Ashburn	OF	1948-62	1995	Mickey Cochrane	C	1925-37	1947
Earl Averill	OF	1929-41	1975	Eddie Collins	2B	1906-30	1939
Frank Baker	3B	1908-22	1955	Jimmy Collins	3B	1895-1908	1945
Dave Bancroft	SS	1915-30	1971	Earle Combs	OF	1924-35	1970
Ernie Banks	SS-1B	1953-71	1977	Roger Connor	1B	1880-97	1976
Jake Beckley	1B	1888-1907	1971	Stan Coveleski	P	1912-28	1969
Cool Papa Bell*	OF		1974	Sam Crawford	OF	1899-1917	1957
Johnny Bench	C	1967-83	1989	Joe Cronin	SS	1926-45	1956
Chief Bender	P	1903-25	1953	Candy Cummings	P	1872-77	1939
Yogi Berra	C	1946-65	1972	Kiki Cuyler	OF	1921-38	1968
Jim Bottomley	1B	1922-37	1974	Ray Dandridge*	3B		1987
Lou Boudreau	SS	1938-52	1970	Leon Day*	P		1995
Roger Bresnahan	C	1897-1915	1945	Dizzy Dean	P	1930-47	1953
Lou Brock	OF	1961-79	1985	Ed Delahanty	OF	1888-1903	1945
Dan Brouthers	1B	1879-1904	1945	Bill Dickey	C	1928-46	1954
Three Finger Brown	P	1903-16	1949	Martin Dihigo*	P-OF		1977
Jim Bunning	P	1955-1971	1996	Joe DiMaggio	OF	1936-51	1955
Jesse Burkett	OF	1890-1905	1946	Bobby Doerr	2B	1937-51	1986
Roy Campanella	C	1948-57	1969	Don Drysdale	P	1956-69	1984
Rod Carew	1B-2B	1967-85	1991	Hugh Duffy	OF	1888-1906	1945
Max Carey	OF	1910-29	1961	Johnny Evers	2B	1902-29	1939
Steve Carlton	P	1965-88	1994	Buck Ewing	C	1880-97	1946
Frank Chance	1B	1898-1914	1946	Red Faber	P	1914-33	1964
Oscar Charleston*	OF		1976	Bob Feller	P	1936-56	1962

Note: Career dates indicate first and last appearances in the majors.
*Elected on the basis of his career in the Negro leagues.

Players (Cont.)

	Position	Career	Selected
Rick Ferrell	C	1929-47	1984
Rollie Fingers	P	1968-85	1992
Elmer Flick	OF	1898-1910	1963
Whitey Ford	P	1950-67	1974
Bill Foster*	P		1996
Jimmie Foxx	1B	1925-45	1951
Frankie Frisch	2B	1919-37	1947
Pud Galvin	P	1879-92	1965
Lou Gehrig	1B	1923-39	1939
Charlie Gehringer	2B	1924-42	1949
Bob Gibson	P	1959-75	1981
Josh Gibson*	C		1972
Lefty Gomez	P	1930-43	1972
Goose Goslin	OF	1921-38	1968
Hank Greenberg	1B	1930-47	1956
Burleigh Grimes	P	1916-34	1964
Lefty Grove	P	1925-41	1947
Chick Hafey	OF	1924-37	1971
Jesse Haines	P	1918-37	1970
Billy Hamilton	OF	1888-1901	1961
Gabby Hartnett	C	1922-41	1955
Harry Heilmann	OF	1914-32	1952
Billy Herman	2B	1931-47	1975
Harry Hooper	OF	1909-25	1971
Rogers Hornsby	2B	1915-37	1942
Waite Hoyt	P	1918-38	1969
Carl Hubbell	P	1928-43	1947
Catfish Hunter	P	1965-79	1987
Monte Irvin*	OF	1949-56	1973
Reggie Jackson	OF	1967-87	1993
Travis Jackson	SS	1922-36	1982
Ferguson Jenkins	P	1965-83	1991
Hugh Jennings	SS	1891-1918	1945
Judy Johnson*	3B		1975
Walter Johnson	P	1907-27	1936
Addie Joss	P	1902-10	1978
Al Kaline	OF	1953-74	1980
Tim Keefe	P	1880-93	1964
Willie Keeler	OF	1892-1910	1939
George Kell	3B	1943-57	1983
Joe Kelley	OF	1891-1908	1971
George Kelly	1B	1915-32	1973
King Kelly	C	1878-93	1945
Harmon Killebrew	1B-3B	1954-75	1984
Ralph Kiner	OF	1946-55	1975
Chuck Klein	OF	1928-44	1980
Sandy Koufax	P	1955-66	1972
Nap Lajoie	2B	1896-1916	1937
Tony Lazzeri	2B	1926-39	1991
Bob Lemon	P	1941-58	1976
Buck Leonard*	1B		1977
Fred Lindstrom	3B	1924-36	1976
Pop Lloyd*	SS-1B		1977
Ernie Lombardi	C	1931-47	1986
Ted Lyons	P	1923-46	1955
Mickey Mantle	OF	1951-68	1974
Heinie Manush	OF	1923-39	1964
Rabbit Maranville	SS-2B	1912-35	1954
Juan Marichal	P	1960-75	1983
Rube Marquard	P	1908-25	1971
Eddie Mathews	3B	1952-68	1978
Christy Mathewson	P	1900-16	1936
Willie Mays	OF	1951-73	1979
Tommy McCarthy	OF	1884-96	1946
Willie McCovey	1B	1959-80	1986
Joe McGinnity	P	1899-1908	1946
Joe Medwick	OF	1932-48	1968
Johnny Mize	1B	1936-53	1981
Joe Morgan	2B	1963-84	1990
Stan Musial	OF-1B	1941-63	1969
Hal Newhouser	P	1939-55	1992
Kid Nichols	P	1890-1906	1949
Jim O'Rourke	OF	1876-1904	1945
Mel Ott	OF	1926-47	1951
Satchel Paige*	P	1948-65	1971
Jim Palmer	P	1965-84	1990
Herb Pennock	P	1912-34	1948
Gaylord Perry	P	1962-83	1991
Eddie Plank	P	1901-17	1946
Charley Radbourn	P	1880-91	1939
Pee Wee Reese	SS	1940-58	1984
Sam Rice	OF	1915-35	1963
Eppa Rixey	P	1912-33	1963
Phil Rizzuto	SS	1941-56	1994
Robin Roberts	P	1948-66	1976
Brooks Robinson	3B	1955-77	1983
Frank Robinson	OF	1956-76	1982
Jackie Robinson	2B	1947-56	1962
Edd Roush	OF	1913-31	1962
Red Ruffing	P	1924-47	1967
Amos Rusie	P	1889-1901	1977
Babe Ruth	OF	1914-35	1936
Ray Schalk	C	1912-29	1955
Mike Schmidt	3B	1972-89	1995
Red Schoendienst	2B	1945-63	1989
Tom Seaver	P	1967-86	1992
Joe Sewell	SS	1920-33	1977
Al Simmons	OF	1924-44	1953
George Sisler	1B	1915-30	1939
Enos Slaughter	OF	1938-59	1985
Duke Snider	OF	1947-64	1980
Warren Spahn	P	1942-65	1973
Al Spalding	P	1871-78	1939
Tris Speaker	OF	1907-28	1937
Willie Stargell	OF-1B	1962-82	1988
Bill Terry	1B	1923-36	1954
Sam Thompson	OF	1885-1906	1974
Joe Tinker	SS	1902-16	1946
Pie Traynor	3B	1920-37	1948
Dazzy Vance	P	1915-35	1955
Arky Vaughan	SS	1932-48	1985
Rube Waddell	P	1897-1910	1946
Honus Wagner	SS	1897-1917	1936
Bobby Wallace	SS	1894-1918	1953
Ed Walsh	P	1904-17	1946
Lloyd Waner	OF	1927-45	1967
Paul Waner	OF	1926-45	1952
John Ward	2B-P	1878-94	1964
Mickey Welch	P	1880-92	1973
Zach Wheat	OF	1909-27	1959
Hoyt Wilhelm	P	1952-72	1985
Billy Williams	OF	1959-76	1987
Ted Williams	OF	1939-60	1966
Vic Willis	P	1898-1910	1995
Hack Wilson	OF	1923-34	1979
Early Wynn	P	1939-63	1972
Carl Yastrzemski	OF	1961-83	1989
Cy Young	P	1890-1911	1937
Ross Youngs	OF	1917-26	1972

Baseball Hall of Fame *(Cont.)*

Umpires

	Year Selected
Al Barlick	1989
Jocko Conlan	1974
Tom Connolly	1953
Billy Evans	1973
Cal Hubbard	1976
Bill Klem	1953
Bill McGowan	1992

Pioneers/Executives

	Year Selected
Ed Barrow (manager-executive)	1953
Morgan Bulkeley (executive)	1937
Alexander Cartwright (executive)	1938
Henry Chadwick (writer-executive)	1938
Happy Chandler (commissioner)	1982
Charles Comiskey (manager-executive)	1939
Rube Foster (player-manager-executive)	1981
Ford Frick (commissioner-executive)	1970
Warren Giles (executive)	1979
Will Harridge (executive)	1972
William Hulbert (executive)	1995
Ban Johnson (executive)	1937
Kenesaw M. Landis (commissioner)	1944
Larry MacPhail (executive)	1978
Branch Rickey (manager-executive)	1967
Al Spalding (player-executive)	1939
Bill Veeck (owner)	1991
George Weiss (executive)	1971
George Wright (player-manager)	1937
Harry Wright (player-manager-executive)	1953
Tom Yawkey (executive)	1980

Managers

	Years Managed	Year Selected
Walt Alston	1954-76	1983
Leo Durocher	1939-73	1994
Clark Griffith	1901-20	1946
Bucky Harris	1924-56	1975
Ned Hanlon	1899-1907	1996
Miller Huggins	1913-29	1964
Al Lopez	1951-69	1977
Connie Mack	1894-1950	1937
Joe McCarthy	1926-50	1957
John McGraw	1899-1932	1937
Bill McKechnie	1915-46	1962
Wilbert Robinson	1902-31	1945
Casey Stengel	1934-65	1966

THEY SAID IT

Devon White, the Florida Marlins' centerfielder, after being booed for dropping a fly: "I look up in the stands and I see them miss fly balls too."

Notable Achievements

No-Hit Games, 9 Innings or More
NATIONAL LEAGUE

Date		Pitcher and Game
1876	July 15	George Bradley, StL vs Hart 2-0
1880	June 12	John Richmond, Wor vs Clev 1-0 (perfect game)
	June 17	Monte Ward, Prov vs Buff 5-0 (perfect game)
	Aug 19	Larry Corcoran, Chi vs Bos 6-0
	Aug 20	Pud Galvin, Buff at Wor 1-0
1882	Sep 20	Larry Corcoran, Chi vs Wor 5-0
	Sep 22	Tim Lovett, Bklyn vs NY 4-0
1883	July 25	Hoss Radbourn, Prov at Clev 8-0
	Sep 13	Hugh Daily, Clev at Phil 1-0
1884	June 27	Larry Corcoran, Chi vs Prov 6-0
	Aug 4	Pud Galvin, Buff at Det 18-0
1885	July 27	John Clarkson, Chi at Prov 4-0
	Aug 29	Charles Ferguson, Phil vs Prov 1-0
1891	July 31	Amos Rusie, NY vs Bklyn 6-0
	June 22	Tom Lovett, Bklyn vs NY 4-0
1892	Aug 6	Jack Stivetts, Bos vs Bklyn 11-0
	Aug 22	Alex Sanders, Lou vs Balt 6-2
	Oct 15	Bumpus Jones, Cin vs Pitt 7-1 (first major league game)
1893	Aug 16	Bill Hawke, Balt vs Wash 5-0

Date		Pitcher and Game
1897	Sep 18	Cy Young, Clev vs Cin 6-0
1898	Apr 22	Ted Breitenstein, Cin vs Pitt 11-0
	Apr 22	Jim Hughes, Balt vs Bos 8-0
	July 8	Frank Donahue, Phil vs Bos 5-0
	Aug 21	Walter Thornton, Chi vs Bklyn 2-0
1899	May 25	Deacon Phillippe, Lou vs NY 7-0
	Aug 7	Vic Willis, Bos vs Wash 7-1
1900	July 12	Noodles Hahn, Cin vs Phil 4-0
1901	July 15	Christy Mathewson, NY at StL 5-0
1903	Sep 18	Chick Fraser, Phil at Chi 10-0
1904	June 11	Bob Wicker, Chi at NY 1-0 (hit in 10th; won in 12th)
1905	June 13	Christy Mathewson, NY at Chi 1-0
1906	May 1	John Lush, Phil at Bklyn 6-0
	July 20	Mal Eason, Bklyn at StL 2-0
	Aug 1	Harry McIntire, Bklyn vs Pitt 0-1 (hit in 11th; lost in 13th)
1907	May 8	Frank Pfeffer, Bos vs Cin 6-0
	Sep 20	Nick Maddox, Pitt vs Bklyn 2-1
1908	July 4	George Wiltse, NY vs Phil 1-0 (10 innings)
	Sep 5	Nap Rucker, Bklyn vs Bos 6-0

No-Hit Games, 9 Innings or More *(Cont.)*

NATIONAL LEAGUE *(Cont.)*

Date	Pitcher and Game	Date	Pitcher and Game
1909......Apr 15	Leon Ames, NY vs Bklyn 0-3 (hit in 10th; lost in 13th)	1965 Sept 9	Sandy Koufax, LA vs Chi 1-0 (perfect game)
1912......Sept 6	Jeff Tesreau, NY at Phil 3-0	1967......June 18	Don Wilson, Hou vs Atl 2-0
1914......Sept 9	George Davis, Bos vs Phil 7-0	1968......July 29	George Culver, Cin at Phil 6-1
1915......Apr 15	Rube Marquard, NY vs Bklyn 2-0	Sept 17	Gaylord Perry, SF vs StL 1-0
Aug 31	Jimmy Lavender, Chi at NY 2-0	Sept 18	Ray Washburn, StL at SF 2-0
1916......June 16	Tom Hughes, Bos vs Pitt 2-0	1969......Apr 17	Bill Stoneman, Mtl at Phil 7-0
1917......May 2	Jim Vaughn, Chi vs Cin 0-1 (hit in 10th; lost in 10th)	Apr 30	Jim Maloney, Cin vs Hou 10-0
May 2	Fred Toney, Cin at Chi 1-0 (10 innings)	May 1	Don Wilson, Hou at Cin 4-0
		Aug 19	Ken Holtzman, Chi vs Atl 3-0
1919......May 11	Hod Eller, Cin vs StL 6-0	Sept 20	Bob Moose, Pitt at NY 4-0
1922......May 7	Jesse Barnes, NY vs Phil 6-0	1970......June 12	Dock Ellis, Pitt at SD 2-0
1924......July 17	Jesse Haines, StL vs Bos 5-0	July 20	Bill Singer, LA vs Phil 5-0
1925......Sept 13	Dazzy Vance, Bklyn vs Phil 10-1	1971......June 3	Ken Holtzman, Chi at Cin 1-0
1929......May 8	Carl Hubbell, NY vs Pitt 11-0	June 23	Rick Wise, Phil at Cin 4-0
1934......Sept 21	Paul Dean, StL vs Bklyn 3-0	Aug 14	Bob Gibson, StL at Pitt 11-0
1938......June 11	Johnny Vander Meer, Cin vs Bos 3-0	1972......Apr 16	Burt Hooton, Chi vs Phil 4-0
June 15	Johnny Vander Meer, Cin at Bklyn 6-0	Sept 2	Milt Pappas, Chi vs SD 8-0
		Oct 2	Bill Stoneman, Mtl vs NY 7-0
1940......Apr 30	Tex Carleton, Bklyn at Cin, 3-0	1973......Aug 5	Phil Niekro, Atl vs SD 9-0
1941......Aug 30	Lon Warneke, StL at Cin 2-0	1975......Aug 24	Ed Halicki, SF vs NY 6-0
1944......Apr 27	Jim Tobin, Bos vs Bklyn 2-0	1976......July 9	Larry Dierker, Hou vs Mtl 6-0
May 15	Clyde Shoun, Cin vs Bos 1-0	Aug 9	John Candelaria, Pitt vs LA 2-0
1946......Apr 23	Ed Head, Bklyn vs Bos 5-0	Sept 29	John Mtlefusco, SF at Atl 9-0
1947......June 18	Ewell Blackwell, Cin vs Bos 6-0	1978......Apr 16	Bob Forsch, StL vs Phil 5-0
1948......Sept 9	Rex Barney, Bklyn at NY 2-0	June 16	Tom Seaver, Cin vs StL 4-0
1950......Aug 11	Vern Bickford, Bos vs Bklyn 7-0	1979......Apr 7	Ken Forsch, Hou vs Atl 6-0
1951......May 6	Cliff Chambers, Pitt at Bos 3-0	1980......June 27	Jerry Reuss, LA at SF 8-0
1952......June 19	Carl Erskine, Bklyn vs Chi 5-0	1981......May 10	Charlie Lea, Mtl vs SF 4-0
1954......June 12	Jim Wilson, Mil vs Phil 2-0	Sept 26	Nolan Ryan, Hou vs LA 5-0
1955......May 12	Sam Jones, Chi vs Pitt 4-0	1983......Sept 26	Bob Forsch, StL vs Mtl 3-0
1956......May 12	Carl Erskine, Bklyn vs NY 3-0	1986......Sept 25	Mike Scott, Hou vs SF 2-0
Sept 25	Sal Maglie, Bklyn vs Phil 5-0	1988......Sept 16	Tom Browning, Cin vs LA 1-0 (perfect game)
1959......May 26	Harvey Haddix, Pitt at Mil 0-1 (hit in 13th; lost in 13th)	1990......June 29	Fernando Valenzuela, LA vs StL 6-0
		1990......Aug 15	Terry Mulholland, Phil vs SF 6-0
1960......May 15	Don Cardwell, Chi vs StL 4-0	1991......May 23	Tommy Greene, Phil at Mtl 2-0
Aug 18	Lew Burdette, Mil vs Phil 1-0	July 26	Mark Gardner, Mtl at LA 0-1 (hit in 10th, lost in 10th)
Sept 16	Warren Spahn, Mil vs Phil 4-0		
1961......Apr 28	Warren Spahn, Mil vs SF 1-0	July 28	Dennis Martinez, Mtl at LA 2-0 (perfect game)
1962......June 30	Sandy Koufax, LA vs NY 5-0		
1963......May 11	Sandy Koufax, LA vs SF 8-0	Sept 11	Kent Mercker (6), Mark Wohlers (2), and Alejandro Pena (1), Atl at SD 1-0
May 17	Don Nottebart, Hou vs Phil 4-1		
June 15	Juan Marichal, SF vs Hou 1-0	1992......Aug 17	Kevin Gross, LA vs SF 2-0
1964......Apr 23	Ken Johnson, Hou vs Cin 0-1	1993......Sept 8	Darryl Kile, Hou vs NY 7-1
June 4	Sandy Koufax, LA at Phil 3-0	1994......Apr 8	Kent Mercker, Atl vs LA 6-0
June 21	Jim Bunning, Phil at NY 6-0 (perfect game)	1995......June 3	Pedro Martinez, Mtl vs SD 1-0 (perfect through 9, hit in 10th)
1965......June 14	Jim Maloney, Cin vs NY 0-1 (hit in 11th; lost in 11th)	July 14	Ramon Martinez, LA vs Fla 7-0
		1996......May 11	Al Leiter, Fla vs Colorado 11-0
1965......Aug 19	Jim Maloney, Cin at Chi 1-0 (10 innings)	Sept 17	Hideo Nomo, LA at Colorado 9-0

Note: Includes the games struck from the record book on September 4, 1991, when baseball's committee on statistical accuracy voted to define no-hitters as games of 9 innings or more that end with a team getting no hits.

AMERICAN LEAGUE

Date	Pitcher and Game	Date	Pitcher and Game
1901......May 9	Earl Moore, Clev vs Chi 2-4 (hit in 10th; lost in 10th)	1905......July 22	Weldon Henley, Phil at StL 6-0
		Sept 6	Frank Smith, Chi at Det 15-0
1902......Sept 20	Jimmy Callahan, Chi vs Det 3-0	Sept 27	Bill Dinneen, Bos at StL 2-0
1904......May 5	Cy Young, Bos vs Phil 3-0 (perfect game)	1908......June 30	Cy Young, Bos at NY 8-0
		Sept 18	Bob Rhoades, Clev vs Bos 2-1
Aug 17	Jesse Tannehill, Bos at Chi 6-0	Sept 20	Frank Smith, Chi vs Phil 1-0

No-Hit Games, 9 Innings or More *(Cont.)*

AMERICAN LEAGUE *(Cont.)*

Date	Pitcher and Game	Date	Pitcher and Game
1908......Oct 2	Addie Joss, Clev vs Chi 1-0 (perfect game)	1965......Sept 16	Dave Morehead, Bos vs Clev 2-0
1910......Apr 20	Addie Joss, Clev at Chi 1-0	1966......June 10	Sonny Siebert, Clev vs Wash 2-0
May 12	Chief Bender, Phil vs Clev 4-0	1967......Apr 30	Steve Barber (8⅔) and Stu Miller (⅓), Balt vs Det 1-2
Aug 30	Tom Hughes, NY vs Clev 0-5 (hit in 10th; lost in 11th)	Aug 25	Dean Chance, Minn at Clev 2-1
1911......July 29	Joe Wood, Bos vs StL 5-0	Sept 10	Joel Horlen, Chi vs Det 6-0
Aug 27	Ed Walsh, Chi vs Bos 5-0	1968......Apr 27	Tom Phoebus, Balt vs Bos 6-0
1912......July 4	George Mullin, Det vs StL 7-0	May 8	Catfish Hunter, Oak vs Minn 4-0 (perfect game)
Aug 30	Earl Hamilton, StL at Det 5-1	1969......Aug 13	Jim Palmer, Balt vs Oak 8-0
1914......May 14	Jim Scott, Chi at Wash 0-1 (hit in 10th; lost in 10th)	1970......July 3	Clyde Wright, Calif vs Oak 4-0
May 31	Joe Benz, Chi vs Clev 6-1	Sept 21	Vida Blue, Oak vs Minn 6-0
1916......June 21	George Foster, Bos vs NY 2-0	1973......Apr 27	Steve Busby, KC at Det 3-0
Aug 26	Joe Bush, Phil vs Clev 5-0	May 15	Nolan Ryan, Calif at KC 3-0
Aug 30	Dutch Leonard, Bos vs StL 4-0	July 15	Nolan Ryan, Calif at Det 6-0
1917......Apr 14	Ed Cicotte, Chi at StL 11-0	July 30	Jim Bibby, Tex at Oak 6-0
Apr 24	George Mogridge, NY at Bos 2-1	1974......June 19	Steve Busby, KC at Mil 2-0
May 5	Ernie Koob, StL vs Chi 1-0	July 19	Dick Bosman, Clev vs Oak 4-0
May 6	Bob Groom, StL vs Chi 3-0	Sept 28	Nolan Ryan, Calif vs Minn 4-0
June 23	Ernie Shore, Bos vs Wash 4-0 (perfect game)	1975......June 1	Nolan Ryan, Calif vs Balt 1-0
1918......June 3	Dutch Leonard, Bos at Det 5-0	Sept 28	Vida Blue (5), Glenn Abbott and Paul Lindblad (1), Rollie Fingers (2), Oak vs Calif 5-0
1919......Sept 10	Ray Caldwell, Clev at NY 3-0	1976......July 28	John Odom (5) and Francisco Barrios (4), Chi at Oak 2-1
1920......July 1	Walter Johnson, Wash at Bos 1-0		
1922......Apr 30	Charlie Robertson, Chi at Det 2-0 (perfect game)	1977......May 14	Jim Colborn, KC vs Tex 6-0
1923......Sept 4	Sam Jones, NY at Phil 2-0	May 30	Dennis Eckersley, Clev vs Calif 1-0
Sept 7	Howard Ehmke, Bos at Phil 4-0	Sept 22	Bert Blyleven, Tex at Calif 6-0
1926......Aug 21	Ted Lyons, Chi at Bos 6-0	1981......May 15	Len Barker, Clev vs Tor 3-0 (perfect game)
1931......Apr 29	Wes Ferrell, Clev vs StL 9-0	1983......July 4	Dave Righetti, NY vs Bos 4-0
Aug 8	Bob Burke, Wash vs Bos 5-0	Sept 29	Mike Warren, Oak vs Chi 3-0
1934......Sept 18	Bobo Newsom, StL vs Bos 1-2 (hit in 10th; lost in 10th)	1984......Apr 7	Jack Morris, Det at Chi 4-0
1935......Aug 31	Vern Kennedy, Chi vs Clev 5-0	Sept 30	Mike Witt, Calif at Tex 1-0 (perfect game)
1937......June 1	Bill Dietrich, Chi vs StL 8-0	1986......Sept 19	Joe Cowley, Chi at Calif 7-1
1938......Aug 27	Mtle Pearson, NY vs Clev 13-0	1987......Apr 15	Juan Nieves, Mil at Balt 7-0
1940......Apr 16	Bob Feller, Clev at Chi 1-0 (opening day)	1990......Apr 11	Mark Langston (7), Mike Witt (2), Calif vs Sea 1-0
1945......Sept 9	Dick Fowler, Phil vs StL 1-0	June 2	Randy Johnson, Sea vs Det 2-0
1946......Apr 30	Bob Feller, Clev at NY 1-0	June 11	Nolan Ryan, Tex at Oak 5-0
1947......July 10	Don Black, Clev vs Phil 3-0	June 29	Dave Stewart, Oak at Tor 5-0
Sep 3	Bill McCahan, Phil vs Wash 3-0	1990......July 1	Andy Hawkins, NY at Chi 0-4 (pitched 8 innings of 9-inning game)
1948......June 30	Bob Lemon, Clev at Det 2-0	Sept 2	Dave Stieb, Tor at Clev 3-0
1951......July 1	Bob Feller, Clev vs Det 2-1	1991......May 1	Nolan Ryan, Tex vs Tor 3-0
July 12	Allie Reynolds, NY at Clev 1-0	July 13	Bob Milacki (6), Mike Flanagan (1), Mark Williamson (1), and Gregg Olson (1), Balt at Oak 2-0
Sept 28	Allie Reynolds, NY vs Bos 8-0		
1952......May 15	Virgil Trucks, Det vs Wash 1-0	Aug 11	Wilson Alvarez, Chi at Balt 7-0
Aug 25	Virgil Trucks, Det at NY 1-0	Aug 26	Bret Saberhagen, KC vs Chi 7-0
1953......May 6	Bobo Holloman, StL vs Phil 6-0 (first major league start)	1993......Apr 22	Chris Bosio, Sea vs Bos 7-0
1956......July 14	Mel Parnell, Bos vs Chi 4-0	Sept 4	Jim Abbott, NY vs Clev 4-0
1966......Oct 8	Don Larsen, NY (A) vs Bklyn (N) 2-0 (World Series) (perfect game)	1994......Apr 27	Scott Erickson, Minn vs Mil 6-0
1957......Aug 20	Bob Keegan, Chi vs Wash 6-0	July 28	Kenny Rogers, Texas vs Calif 4-0 (perfect game)
1958......July 20	Jim Bunning, Det at Bos 3-0	1996......May 14	Dwight Gooden, NY vs Seattle 2-0
Sept 20	Hoyt Wilhelm, Balt vs NY 1-0		
1962......May 5	Bo Belinsky, LA vs Balt 2-0		
June 26	Earl Wilson, Bos vs LA 2-0		
Aug 1	Bill Monbouquette, Bos at Chi 1-0		
Aug 26	Jack Kralick, Minn vs KC 1-0		

Longest Hitting Streaks

NATIONAL LEAGUE				AMERICAN LEAGUE		
Player and Team	Year	G		Player and Team	Year	G
Willie Keeler, Balt	1897	44		Joe DiMaggio, NY	1941	56
Pete Rose, Cin	1978	44		George Sisler, StL	1922	41
Bill Dahlen, Chi	1894	42		Ty Cobb, Det	1911	40
Tommy Holmes, Bos	1945	37		Paul Molitor, Mil	1987	39
Billy Hamilton, Phil	1894	36		Ty Cobb, Det	1917	35
Fred Clarke, Lou	1895	35		Ty Cobb, Det	1912	34
Benito Santiago, SD	1987	34		George Sisler, StL	1925	34
George Davis, NY	1893	33		John Stone, Det	1930	34
Rogers Hornsby, StL	1922	32		George McQuinn, StL	1938	34
Ed Delahanty, Phil	1899	31		Dom DiMaggio, Bos	1949	34
Willie Davis, LA	1969	31		Hal Chase, NY	1907	33
Rico Carty, Atl	1970	31		Heinie Manush, Wash	1933	33
				Nap Lajoie, Clev	1906	31
				Sam Rice, Wash	1924	31
				Ken Landreaux, Minn	1980	31

Triple Crown Hitters

NATIONAL LEAGUE					AMERICAN LEAGUE				
Player and Team	Year	HR	RBI	BA	Player and Team	Year	HR	RBI	BA
Paul Hines, Prov	1878	4	50	.358	Nap Lajoie, Phil	1901	14	125	.422
Hugh Duffy, Bos	1894	18	145	.438	Ty Cobb, Det	1909	9	115	.377
Heinie Zimmerman*, Chi	1912	14	103	.372	Jimmie Foxx, Phil	1933	48	163	.356
Rogers Hornsby, StL	1922	42	152	.401	Lou Gehrig, NY	1934	49	165	.363
	1925	39	143	.403	Ted Williams, Bos	1942	36	137	.356
Chuck Klein, Phil	1933	28	120	.368		1947	32	114	.343
Joe Medwick, StL	1937	31	154	.374	Mickey Mantle, NY	1956	52	130	.353
					Frank Robinson, Balt	1966	49	122	.316
					Carl Yastrzemski, Bos	1967	44	121	.326

*Zimmerman ranked first in RBIs as calculated by Ernie Lanigan, but only third as calculated by Information Concepts Inc.

Triple Crown Pitchers

NATIONAL LEAGUE						AMERICAN LEAGUE				
Player and Team	Year	W	L	SO	ERA	Player and Team	Year	W	L	SO	ERA
Tommy Bond, Bos	1877	40	17	170	2.11	Cy Young, Bos	1901	33	10	158	1.62
Hoss Radbourn, Prov	1884	60	12	441	1.38	Rube Waddell, Phil	1905	26	11	287	1.48
Tim Keefe, NY	1888	35	12	333	1.74	Walter Johnson, Wash	1913	36	7	303	1.09
John Clarkson, Bos	1889	49	19	284	2.73		1918	23	13	162	1.27
Amos Rusie, NY	1894	36	13	195	2.78		1924	23	7	158	2.72
Christy Mathewson, NY	1905	31	8	206	1.27	Lefty Grove, Phil	1930	28	5	209	2.54
	1908	37	11	259	1.43		1931	31	4	175	2.06
Grover Alexander, Phil	1915	31	10	241	1.22	Lefty Gomez, NY	1934	26	5	158	2.33
	1916	33	12	167	1.55		1937	21	11	194	2.33
	1917	30	13	201	1.86	Hal Newhouser, Det	1945	25	9	212	1.81
Hippo Vaughn, Chi	1918	22	10	148	1.74						
Grover Alexander, Chi	1920	27	14	173	1.91						
Dazzy Vance, Bklyn	1924	28	6	262	2.16						
Bucky Walters, Cin	1939	27	11	137	2.29						
Sandy Koufax, LA	1963	25	5	306	1.88						
	1965	26	8	382	2.04						
	1966	27	9	317	1.73						
Steve Carlton, Phil	1972	27	10	310	1.97						
Dwight Gooden, NY	1985	24	4	268	1.53						

THEY SAID IT

Joe Torre, New York Yankees manager and father of an infant daughter, on whether nighttime feedings disturb his sleep: "I'm 55 years old. I get up three times a night to go to the bathroom. The baby is on my schedule."

Consecutive Games Played, 500 or More Games

Cal Ripken Jr	2315*	Frank McCormick	652
Lou Gehrig	2130	Sandy Alomar Sr	648
Everett Scott	1307	Eddie Brown	618
Steve Garvey	1207	Roy McMillan	585
Billy Williams	1117	George Pinckney	577
Joe Sewell	1103	Steve Brodie	574
Stan Musial	895	Aaron Ward	565
Eddie Yost	829	Candy LaChance	540
Gus Suhr	822	Buck Freeman	535
Nellie Fox	798	Fred Luderus	533
Pete Rose	745	Clyde Milan	511
Dale Murphy	740	Charlie Gehringer	511
Richie Ashburn	730	Vada Pinson	508
Ernie Banks	717	Tony Cuccinello	504
Earl Averill	673	Charlie Gehringer	504
Pete Rose	678	Omar Moreno	503

*Streak in progress at the end of the 1996 season.

Unassisted Triple Plays

Player and Team	Date	Pos	Opp	Opp Batter
Neal Ball, Clev	7-19-09	SS	Bos	Amby McConnell
Bill Wambsganss, Clev	10-10-20	2B	Bklyn	Clarence Mitchell
George Burns, Bos	9-14-23	1B	Clev	Frank Brower
Ernie Padgett, Bos	10-6-23	SS	Phil	Walter Holke
Glenn Wright, Pitt	5-7-25	SS	StL	Jim Bottomley
Jimmy Cooney, Chi	5-30-27	SS	Pitt	Paul Waner
Johnny Neun, Det	5-31-27	1B	Clev	Homer Summa
Ron Hansen, Wash	7-30-68	SS	Clev	Joe Azcue
Mickey Morandini, Phil	9-20-92	2B	Pitt	Jeff King
John Valentin, Bos	7-15-94	SS	Minn	Marc Newfield

National League

Pennant Winners

Year	Team	Manager	W	L	Pct	GA
1900	Brooklyn	Ned Hanlon	82	54	.603	4½
1901	Pittsburgh	Fred Clarke	90	49	.647	7½
1902	Pittsburgh	Fred Clarke	103	36	.741	27½
1903	Pittsburgh	Fred Clarke	91	49	.650	6½
1904	New York	John McGraw	106	47	.693	13
1905	New York	John McGraw	105	48	.686	9
1906	Chicago	Frank Chance	116	36	.763	20
1907	Chicago	Frank Chance	107	45	.704	17
1908	Chicago	Frank Chance	99	55	.643	1
1909	Pittsburgh	Fred Clarke	110	42	.724	6½
1910	Chicago	Frank Chance	104	50	.675	13
1911	New York	John McGraw	99	54	.647	7½
1912	New York	John McGraw	103	48	.682	10
1913	New York	John McGraw	101	51	.664	12½
1914	Boston	George Stallings	94	59	.614	10½
1915	Philadelphia	Pat Moran	90	62	.592	7
1916	Brooklyn	Wilbert Robinson	94	60	.610	2½
1917	New York	John McGraw	98	56	.636	10
1918	Chicago	Fred Mitchell	84	45	.651	10½
1919	Cincinnati	Pat Moran	96	44	.686	9
1920	Brooklyn	Wilbert Robinson	93	61	.604	7
1921	New York	John McGraw	94	59	.614	4
1922	New York	John McGraw	93	61	.604	7
1923	New York	John McGraw	95	58	.621	4½
1924	New York	John McGraw	93	60	.608	1½

Pennant Winners (Cont.)

Year	Team	Manager	W	L	Pct	GA
1925	Pittsburgh	Bill McKechnie	95	58	.621	8½
1926	St Louis	Rogers Hornsby	89	65	.578	2
1927	Pittsburgh	Donie Bush	94	60	.610	1½
1928	St Louis	Bill McKechnie	95	59	.617	2
1929	Chicago	Joe McCarthy	98	54	.645	10½
1930	St Louis	Gabby Street	92	62	.597	2
1931	St Louis	Gabby Street	101	53	.656	13
1932	Chicago	Charlie Grimm	90	64	.584	4
1933	New York	Bill Terry	91	61	.599	5
1934	St Louis	Frankie Frisch	95	58	.621	2
1935	Chicago	Charlie Grimm	100	54	.649	4
1936	New York	Bill Terry	92	62	.597	5
1937	New York	Bill Terry	95	57	.625	3
1938	Chicago	Gabby Hartnett	89	63	.586	2
1939	Cincinnati	Bill McKechnie	97	57	.630	4½
1940	Cincinnati	Bill McKechnie	100	53	.654	12
1941	Brooklyn	Leo Durocher	100	54	.649	2½
1942	St Louis	Billy Southworth	106	48	.688	2
1943	St Louis	Billy Southworth	105	49	.682	18
1944	St Louis	Billy Southworth	105	49	.682	14½
1945	Chicago	Charlie Grimm	98	56	.636	3
1946	St Louis*	Eddie Dyer	98	58	.628	2
1947	Brooklyn	Burt Shotton	94	60	.610	5
1948	Boston	Billy Southworth	91	62	.595	6½
1949	Brooklyn	Burt Shotton	97	57	.630	1
1950	Philadelphia	Eddie Sawyer	91	63	.591	2
1951	New York†	Leo Durocher	98	59	.624	1
1952	Brooklyn	Chuck Dressen	96	57	.627	4½
1953	Brooklyn	Chuck Dressen	105	49	.682	13
1954	New York	Leo Durocher	97	57	.630	5
1955	Brooklyn	Walt Alston	98	55	.641	13½
1956	Brooklyn	Walt Alston	93	61	.604	1
1957	Milwaukee	Fred Haney	95	59	.617	8
1958	Milwaukee	Fred Haney	92	62	.597	8
1959	Los Angeles‡	Walt Alston	88	68	.564	2
1960	Pittsburgh	Danny Murtaugh	95	59	.617	7
1961	Cincinnati	Fred Hutchinson	93	61	.604	4
1962	San Francisco#	Al Dark	103	62	.624	1
1963	Los Angeles	Walt Alston	99	63	.611	6
1964	St Louis	Johnny Keane	93	69	.574	1
1965	Los Angeles	Walt Alston	97	65	.599	2
1966	Los Angeles	Walt Alston	95	67	.586	1½
1967	St Louis	Red Schoendienst	101	60	.627	10½
1968	St Louis	Red Schoendienst	97	65	.599	9
1969	New York (E)††	Gil Hodges	100	62	.617	8
1970	Cincinnati (W)††	Sparky Anderson	102	60	.630	14½
1971	Pittsburgh (E)††	Danny Murtaugh	97	65	.599	7
1972	Cincinnati (W)††	Sparky Anderson	95	59	.617	10½
1973	New York (E)††	Yogi Berra	82	79	.509	1½
1974	Los Angeles (W)††	Walt Alston	102	60	.630	4
1975	Cincinnati (W)††	Sparky Anderson	108	54	.667	20
1976	Cincinnati (W)††	Sparky Anderson	102	60	.630	10
1977	Los Angeles (W)††	Tommy Lasorda	98	64	.605	10
1978	Los Angeles (W)††	Tommy Lasorda	95	67	.586	2½
1979	Pittsburgh (E)††	Chuck Tanner	98	64	.605	2
1980	Philadelphia (E)††	Dallas Green	91	71	.562	1
1981	Los Angeles (W)††	Tommy Lasorda	63	47	.573	**
1982	St Louis (E)††	Whitey Herzog	92	70	.568	3
1983	Philadelphia (E)††	Pat Corrales/Paul Owens	90	72	.556	6
1984	San Diego (W)††	Dick Williams	92	70	.568	12

*Defeated Brooklyn, two games to none, in playoff for pennant. †Defeated Brooklyn, two games to one, in playoff for pennant. ‡Defeated Milwaukee, two games to none, in playoff for pennant. #Defeated Los Angeles, two games to one, in playoff for pennant. ††Won Championship Series **First half 36-21; second half 27-26, in season split by strike; defeated Houston in playoff for Western Division title.

Pennant Winners (Cont.)

Year	Team	Manager	W	L	Pct	GA
1985	St Louis (E)††	Whitey Herzog	101	61	.623	3
1986	New York (E)††	Dave Johnson	108	54	.667	21½
1987	St Louis (E)††	Whitey Herzog	95	67	.586	3
1988	Los Angeles (W)††	Tommy Lasorda	94	67	.584	7
1989	San Francisco (W)††	Roger Craig	92	70	.568	3
1990	Cincinnati (W)††	Lou Piniella	91	71	.562	5
1991	Atlanta (W)††	Bobby Cox	94	68	.580	1
1992	Atlanta (W)††	Bobby Cox	98	64	.605	8
1993	Philadelphia (E)††	Jim Fregosi	97	65	.599	3
1994	Season ended Aug. 11 due to players' strike					
1995	Atlanta (E)††	Bobby Cox	90	54	.625	21
1996	Atlanta (E)††	Bobby Cox	96	66	.593	8

††Won Championship Series

Leading Batsmen

Year	Player and Team	BA	Year	Player and Team	BA
1900	Honus Wagner, Pitt	.381	1931	Chick Hafey, StL	.349
1901	Jesse Burkett, StL	.382	1932	Lefty O'Doul, Bklyn	.368
1902	Ginger Beaumtl, Pitt	.357	1933	Chuck Klein, Phil	.368
1903	Honus Wagner, Pitt	.355	1934	Paul Waner, Pitt	.362
1904	Honus Wagner, Pitt	.349	1935	Arky Vaughan, Pitt	.385
1905	Cy Seymour, Cin	.377	1936	Paul Waner, Pitt	.373
1906	Honus Wagner, Pitt	.339	1937	Joe Medwick, StL	.374
1907	Honus Wagner, Pitt	.350	1938	Ernie Lombardi, Cin	.342
1908	Honus Wagner, Pitt	.354	1939	Johnny Mize, StL	.349
1909	Honus Wagner, Pitt	.339	1940	Debs Garms, Pitt	.355
1910	Sherry Magee, Phil	.331	1941	Pete Reiser, Bklyn	.343
1911	Honus Wagner, Pitt	.334	1942	Ernie Lombardi, Bos	.330
1912	Heinie Zimmerman, Chi	.372	1943	Stan Musial, StL	.357
1913	Jake Daubert, Bklyn	.350	1944	Dixie Walker, Bklyn	.357
1914	Jake Daubert, Bklyn	.329	1945	Phil Cavarretta, Chi	.355
1915	Larry Doyle, NY	.320	1946	Stan Musial, StL	.365
1916	Hal Chase, Cin	.339	1947	Harry Walker, StL-Phil	.363
1917	Edd Roush, Cin	.341	1948	Stan Musial, StL	.376
1918	Zach Wheat, Bklyn	.335	1949	Jackie Robinson, Bklyn	.342
1919	Edd Roush, Cin	.321	1950	Stan Musial, StL	.346
1920	Rogers Hornsby, StL	.370	1951	Stan Musial, StL	.355
1921	Rogers Hornsby, StL	.397	1952	Stan Musial, StL	.336
1922	Rogers Hornsby, StL	.401	1953	Carl Furillo, Bklyn	.344
1923	Rogers Hornsby, StL	.384	1954	Willie Mays, NY	.345
1924	Rogers Hornsby, StL	.424	1955	Richie Ashburn, Phil	.338
1925	Rogers Hornsby, StL	.403	1956	Hank Aaron, Mil	.328
1926	Bubbles Hargrave, Cin	.353	1957	Stan Musial, StL	.351
1927	Paul Waner, Pitt	.380	1958	Richie Ashburn, Phil	.350
1928	Rogers Hornsby, Bos	.387	1959	Hank Aaron, Mil	.355
1929	Lefty O'Doul, Phil	.398	1960	Dick Groat, Pitt	.325
1930	Bill Terry, NY	.401	1961	Roberto Clemente, Pitt	.351

Birnam Wood to Dunsinane

Red Sox fans have suffered plenty of disappointments since 1975, but the sting of that year's World Series will never go away. Boston lost a seven-game heart-wrencher to the Cincinnati Reds, the hometown team of current Red Sox third baseman Tim Naehring, who was eight at the time and rooted for the Reds. These days Naehring is helping to finance the construction of a scaled-down (to about 90%) replica of Fenway Park that will be used by high schools and youth leagues. Forgive the Boston faithful if they find Naehring's gesture somewhat traitorous: The mock Fenway is being built in Cincinnati.

Leading Batsmen *(Cont.)*

Year	Player and Team	BA	Year	Player and Team	BA
1962	Tommy Davis, LA	.346	1980	Bill Buckner, Chi	.324
1963	Tommy Davis, LA	.326	1981	Bill Madlock, Pitt	.341
1964	Roberto Clemente, Pitt	.339	1982	Al Oliver, Mtl	.331
1965	Roberto Clemente, Pitt	.329	1983	Bill Madlock, Pitt	.323
1966	Matty Alou, Pitt	.342	1984	Tony Gwynn, SD	.351
1967	Roberto Clemente, Pitt	.357	1985	Willie McGee, StL	.353
1968	Pete Rose, Cin	.335	1986	Tim Raines, Mtl	.334
1969	Pete Rose, Cin	.348	1987	Tony Gwynn, SD	.370
1970	Rico Carty, Atl	.366	1988	Tony Gwynn, SD	.313
1971	Joe Torre, StL	.363	1989	Tony Gwynn, SD	.336
1972	Billy Williams, Chi	.333	1990	Willie McGee, StL	.335
1973	Pete Rose, Cin	.338	1991	Terry Pendleton, Atl	.319
1974	Ralph Garr, Atl	.353	1992	Gary Sheffield, SD	.330
1975	Bill Madlock, Chi	.354	1993	Andres Galarraga, Col	.370
1976	Bill Madlock, Chi	.339	1994	Tony Gwynn, SD	.394
1977	Dave Parker, Pitt	.338	1995	Tony Gwynn, SD	.368
1978	Dave Parker, Pitt	.334	1996	Tony Gwynn, SD	.353
1979	Keith Hernandez, StL	.344			

Leaders in Runs Scored

Year	Player and Team	Runs	Year	Player and Team	Runs
1900	Roy Thomas, Phil	131	1939	Billy Werber, Cin	115
1901	Jesse Burkett, StL	139	1940	Arky Vaughan, Pitt	113
1902	Honus Wagner, Pitt	105	1941	Pete Reiser, Bklyn	117
1903	Ginger Beaumont, Pitt	137	1942	Mel Ott, NY	118
1904	George Browne, NY	99	1943	Arky Vaughan, Bklyn	112
1905	Mike Donlin, NY	124	1944	Bill Nicholson, Chi	116
1906	Honus Wagner, Pitt	103	1945	Eddie Stanky, Bklyn	128
	Frank Chance, Chi	103	1946	Stan Musial, StL	124
1907	Spike Shannon, NY	104	1947	Johnny Mize, NY	137
1908	Fred Tenney, NY	101	1948	Stan Musial, StL	135
1909	Tommy Leach, Pitt	126	1949	Pee Wee Reese, Bklyn	132
1910	Sherry Magee, Phil	110	1950	Earl Torgeson, Bos	120
1911	Jimmy Sheckard, Chi	121	1951	Stan Musial, StL	124
1912	Bob Bescher, Cin	120		Ralph Kiner, Pitt	124
1913	Tommy Leach, Chi	99	1952	Stan Musial, StL	105
	Max Carey, Pitt	99		Solly Hemus, StL	105
1914	George Burns, NY	100	1953	Duke Snider, Bklyn	132
1915	Gavvy Cravath, Phil	89	1954	Stan Musial, StL	120
1916	George Burns, NY	105		Duke Snider, Bklyn	120
1917	George Burns, NY	103	1955	Duke Snider, Bklyn	126
1918	Heinie Groh, Cin	88	1956	Frank Robinson, Cin	122
1919	George Burns, NY	86	1957	Hank Aaron, Mil	118
1920	George Burns, NY	115	1958	Willie Mays, SF	121
1921	Rogers Hornsby, StL	131	1959	Vada Pinson, Cin	131
1922	Rogers Hornsby, StL	141	1960	Bill Bruton, Mil	112
1923	Ross Youngs, NY	121	1961	Willie Mays, SF	129
1924	Frankie Frisch, NY	121	1962	Frank Robinson, Cin	134
	Rogers Hornsby, StL	121	1963	Hank Aaron, Mil	121
1925	Kiki Cuyler, Pitt	144	1964	Dick Allen, Phil	125
1926	Kiki Cuyler, Pitt	113	1965	Tommy Harper, Cin	126
1927	Lloyd Waner, Pitt	133	1966	Felipe Alou, Atl	122
	Rogers Hornsby, NY	133	1967	Hank Aaron, Atl	113
1928	Paul Waner, Pitt	142		Lou Brock, StL	113
1929	Rogers Hornsby, Chi	156	1968	Glenn Beckert, Chi	98
1930	Chuck Klein, Phil	158	1969	Bobby Bonds, SF	120
1931	Bill Terry, NY	121		Pete Rose, Cin	120
	Chuck Klein, Phil	121	1970	Billy Williams, Chi	137
1932	Chuck Klein, Phil	152	1971	Lou Brock, StL	126
1933	Pepper Martin, StL	122	1972	Joe Morgan, Cin	122
1934	Paul Waner, Pitt	122	1973	Bobby Bonds, SF	131
1935	Augie Galan, Chi	133	1974	Pete Rose, Cin	110
1936	Arky Vaughan, Pitt	122	1975	Pete Rose, Cin	112
1937	Joe Medwick, StL	111	1976	Pete Rose, Cin	130
1938	Mel Ott, NY	116	1977	George Foster, Cin	124

Leader in Runs Scored (Cont.)

Year	Player and Team	Runs	Year	Player and Team	Runs
1978	Ivan DeJesus, Chi	104	1988	Brett Butler, SF	109
1979	Keith Hernandez, StL	116	1989	Howard Johnson, NY	104
1980	Keith Hernandez, StL	111		Will Clark, SF	104
1981	Mike Schmidt, Phil	78		Ryne Sandberg, Chi	104
1982	Lonnie Smith, StL	120	1990	Ryne Sandberg, Chi	116
1983	Tim Raines, Mtl	133	1991	Brett Butler, LA	112
1984	Ryne Sandberg, Chi	114	1992	Barry Bonds, Pitt	109
1985	Dale Murphy, Atl	118	1993	Lenny Dykstra, Phil	143
1986	Von Hayes, Phil	107	1994	Jeff Bagwell, Hou	104
	Tony Gwynn, SD	107	1995	Craig Biggio, Hou	123
1987	Tim Raines, Mtl	123	1996	Ellis Burks, Col	142

Leaders in Hits

Year	Player and Team	Hits	Year	Player and Team	Hits
1900	Willie Keeler, Bklyn	208	1947	Tommy Holmes, Bos	191
1901	Jesse Burkett, StL	228	1948	Stan Musial, StL	230
1902	Ginger Beaumont, Pitt	194	1949	Stan Musial, StL	207
1903	Ginger Beaumont, Pitt	209	1950	Duke Snider, Bklyn	199
1904	Ginger Beaumont, Pitt	185	1951	Richie Ashburn, Phil	221
1905	Cy Seymour, Cin	219	1952	Stan Musial, StL	194
1906	Harry Steinfeldt, Chi	176	1953	Richie Ashburn, Phil	205
1907	Ginger Beaumont, Bos	187	1954	Don Mueller, NY	212
1908	Honus Wagner, Pitt	201	1955	Ted Kluszewski, Cin	192
1909	Larry Doyle, NY	172	1956	Hank Aaron, Mil	200
1910	Honus Wagner, Pitt	178	1957	Red Schoendienst, NY-Mil	200
	Bobby Byrne, Pitt	178	1958	Richie Ashburn, Phil	215
1911	Doc Miller, Bos	192	1959	Hank Aaron, Mil	223
1912	Heinie Zimmerman, Chi	207	1960	Willie Mays, SF	190
1913	Gavvy Cravath, Phil	179	1961	Vada Pinson, Cin	208
1914	Sherry Magee, Phil	171	1962	Tommy Davis, LA	230
1915	Larry Doyle, NY	189	1963	Vada Pinson, Cin	204
1916	Hal Chase, Cin	184	1964	Roberto Clemente, Pitt	211
1917	Heinie Groh, Cin	182		Curt Flood, StL	211
1918	Charlie Hollocher, Chi	161	1965	Pete Rose, Cin	209
1919	Ivy Olson, Bklyn	164	1966	Felipe Alou, Atl	218
1920	Rogers Hornsby, StL	218	1967	Roberto Clemente, Pitt	209
1921	Rogers Hornsby, StL	235	1968	Felipe Alou, Atl	210
1922	Rogers Hornsby, StL	250		Pete Rose, Cin	210
1923	Frankie Frisch, NY	223	1969	Matty Alou, Pitt	231
1924	Rogers Hornsby, StL	227	1970	Pete Rose, Cin	205
1925	Jim Bottomley, StL	227		Billy Williams, Chi	205
1926	Eddie Brown, Bos	201	1971	Joe Torre, StL	230
1927	Paul Waner, Pitt	237	1972	Pete Rose, Cin	198
1928	Freddy Lindstrom, NY	231	1973	Pete Rose, Cin	230
1929	Lefty O'Doul, Phil	254	1974	Ralph Garr, Atl	214
1930	Bill Terry, NY	254	1975	Dave Cash, Phil	213
1931	Lloyd Waner, Pitt	214	1976	Pete Rose, Cin	215
1932	Chuck Klein, Phil	226	1977	Dave Parker, Pitt	215
1933	Chuck Klein, Phil	223	1978	Steve Garvey, LA	202
1934	Paul Waner, Pitt	217	1979	Garry Templeton, StL	211
1935	Billy Herman, Chi	227	1980	Steve Garvey, LA	200
1936	Joe Medwick, StL	223	1981	Pete Rose, Phil	140
1937	Joe Medwick, StL	237	1982	Al Oliver, Mtl	204
1938	Frank McCormick, Cin	209	1983	Jose Cruz, Hou	189
1939	Frank McCormick, Cin	209		Andre Dawson, Mtl	189
1940	Stan Hack, Chi	191	1984	Tony Gwynn, SD	213
	Frank McCormick, Cin	191	1985	Willie McGee, StL	216
1941	Stan Hack, Chi	186	1986	Tony Gwynn, SD	211
1942	Enos Slaughter, StL	188	1987	Tony Gwynn, SD	218
1943	Stan Musial, StL	220	1988	Andres Galarraga, Mtl	184
1944	Stan Musial, StL	197	1989	Tony Gwynn, SD	203
	Phil Cavarretta, Chi	197	1990	Brett Butler, SF	192
1945	Tommy Holmes, Bos	224		Lenny Dykstra, Phil	192
1946	Stan Musial, StL	228	1991	Terry Pendleton, Atl	187

Leaders in Hits *(Cont.)*

Year	Player and Team	Hits	Year	Player and Team	Hits
1992	Terry Pendleton, Atl	199	1995	Dante Bichette, Col	197
	Andy Van Slyke, Pitt	199		Tony Gwynn, SD	197
1993	Lenny Dykstra, Phil	194	1996	Lance Johnson, NY	227
1994	Tony Gwynn, SD	165			

Home Run Leaders

Year	Player and Team	HR	Year	Player and Team	HR
1900	Herman Long, Bos	12	1947	Ralph Kiner, Pitt	51
1901	Sam Crawford, Cin	16		Johnny Mize, NY	51
1902	Tommy Leach, Pitt	6	1948	Ralph Kiner, Pitt	40
1903	Jimmy Sheckard, Bklyn	9		Johnny Mize, NY	40
1904	Harry Lumley, Bklyn	9	1949	Ralph Kiner, Pitt	54
1905	Fred Odwell, Cin	9	1950	Ralph Kiner, Pitt	47
1906	Tim Jordan, Bklyn	12	1951	Ralph Kiner, Pitt	42
1907	Dave Brain, Bos	10	1952	Ralph Kiner, Pitt	37
1908	Tim Jordan, Bklyn	12		Hank Sauer, Chi	37
1909	Red Murray, NY	7	1953	Eddie Mathews, Mil	47
1910	Fred Beck, Bos	10	1954	Ted Kluszewski, Cin	49
	Wildfire Schulte, Chi	10	1955	Willie Mays, NY	51
1911	Wildfire Schulte, Chi	21	1956	Duke Snider, Bklyn	43
1912	Heinie Zimmerman, Chi	14	1957	Hank Aaron, Mil	44
1913	Gavvy Cravath, Phil	19	1958	Ernie Banks, Chi	47
1914	Gavvy Cravath, Phil	19	1959	Eddie Mathews, Mil	46
1915	Gavvy Cravath, Phil	24	1960	Ernie Banks, Chi	41
1916	Dave Robertson, NY	12	1961	Orlando Cepeda, SF	46
	Cy Williams, Chi	12	1962	Willie Mays, SF	49
1917	Dave Robertson, NY	12	1963	Hank Aaron, Mil	44
	Gavvy Cravath, Phil	12		Willie McCovey, SF	44
1918	Gavvy Cravath, Phil	8	1964	Willie Mays, SF	47
1919	Gavvy Cravath, Phil	12	1965	Willie Mays, SF	52
1920	Cy Williams, Phil	15	1966	Hank Aaron, Atl	44
1921	George Kelly, NY	23	1967	Hank Aaron, Atl	39
1922	Rogers Hornsby, StL	42	1968	Willie McCovey, SF	36
1923	Cy Williams, Phil	41	1969	Willie McCovey, SF	45
1924	Jack Fournier, Bklyn	27	1970	Johnny Bench, Cin	45
1925	Rogers Hornsby, StL	39	1971	Willie Stargell, Pitt	48
1926	Hack Wilson, Chi	21	1972	Johnny Bench, Cin	40
1927	Hack Wilson, Chi	30	1973	Willie Stargell, Pitt	44
	Cy Williams, Phil	30	1974	Mike Schmidt, Phil	36
1928	Hack Wilson, Chi	31	1975	Mike Schmidt, Phil	38
	Jim Bottomley, StL	31	1976	Mike Schmidt, Phil	38
1929	Chuck Klein, Phil	43	1977	George Foster, Cin	52
1930	Hack Wilson, Chi	56	1978	George Foster, Cin	40
1931	Chuck Klein, Phil	31	1979	Dave Kingman, Chi	48
1932	Chuck Klein, Phil	38	1980	Mike Schmidt, Phil	48
	Mel Ott, NY	38	1981	Mike Schmidt, Phil	31
1933	Chuck Klein, Phil	28	1982	Dave Kingman, NY	37
1934	Ripper Collins, StL	35	1983	Mike Schmidt, Phil	40
	Mel Ott, NY	35	1984	Dale Murphy, Atl	36
1935	Wally Berger, Bos	34		Mike Schmidt, Phil	36
1936	Mel Ott, NY	33	1985	Dale Murphy, Atl	37
1937	Mel Ott, NY	31	1986	Mike Schmidt, Phil	37
	Joe Medwick, StL	31	1987	Andre Dawson, Chi	49
1938	Mel Ott, NY	36	1988	Darryl Strawberry, NY	39
1939	Johnny Mize, StL	28	1989	Kevin Mitchell, SF	47
1940	Johnny Mize, StL	43	1990	Ryne Sandberg, Chi	40
1941	Dolph Camilli, Bklyn	34	1991	Howard Johnson, NY	38
1942	Mel Ott, NY	30	1992	Fred McGriff, SD	35
1943	Bill Nicholson, Chi	29	1993	Barry Bonds, SF	46
1944	Bill Nicholson, Chi	33	1994	Matt Williams, SF	43
1945	Tommy Holmes, Bos	28	1995	Dante Bichette, Col	40
1946	Ralph Kiner, Pitt	23	1996	Andres Galarraga, Col	47

Runs Batted In Leaders

Year	Player and Team	RBI	Year	Player and Team	RBI
1900	Elmer Flick, Phil	110	1949	Ralph Kiner, Pitt	127
1901	Honus Wagner, Pitt	126	1950	Del Ennis, Phil	126
1902	Honus Wagner, Pitt	91	1951	Monte Irvin, NY	121
1903	Sam Mertes, NY	104	1952	Hank Sauer, Chi	121
1904	Bill Dahlen, NY	80	1953	Roy Campanella, Bklyn	142
1905	Cy Seymour, Cin	121	1954	Ted Kluszewski, Cin	141
1906	Jim Nealon, Pitt	83	1955	Duke Snider, Bklyn	136
	Harry Steinfeldt, Chi	83	1956	Stan Musial, StL	109
1907	Sherry Magee, Phil	85	1957	Hank Aaron, Mil	132
1908	Honus Wagner, Pitt	109	1958	Ernie Banks, Chi	129
1909	Honus Wagner, Pitt	100	1959	Ernie Banks, Chi	143
1910	Sherry Magee, Phil	123	1960	Hank Aaron, Mil	126
1911	Wildfire Schulte, Chi	121	1961	Orlando Cepeda, SF	142
1912	Heinie Zimmerman, Chi	103	1962	Tommy Davis, LA	153
1913	Gavvy Cravath, Phil	128	1963	Hank Aaron, Mil	130
1914	Sherry Magee, Phil	103	1964	Ken Boyer, StL	119
1915	Gavvy Cravath, Phil	115	1965	Deron Johnson, Cin	130
1916	Heinie Zimmerman, Chi-NY	83	1966	Hank Aaron, Atl	127
1917	Heinie Zimmerman, NY	102	1967	Orlando Cepeda, StL	111
1918	Sherry Magee, Phil	76	1968	Willie McCovey, SF	105
1919	Hi Myers, Bklyn	73	1969	Willie McCovey, SF	126
1920	George Kelly, NY	94	1970	Johnny Bench, Cin	148
	Rogers Hornsby, StL	94	1971	Joe Torre, StL	137
1921	Rogers Hornsby, StL	126	1972	Johnny Bench, Cin	125
1922	Rogers Hornsby, StL	152	1973	Willie Stargell, Pitt	119
1923	Irish Meusel, NY	125	1974	Johnny Bench, Cin	129
1924	George Kelly, NY	136	1975	Greg Luzinski, Phil	120
1925	Rogers Hornsby, StL	143	1976	George Foster, Cin	121
1926	Jim Bottomley, StL	120	1977	George Foster, Cin	149
1927	Paul Waner, Pitt	131	1978	George Foster, Cin	120
1928	Jim Bottomley, StL	136	1979	Dave Winfield, SD	118
1929	Hack Wilson, Chi	159	1980	Mike Schmidt, Phil	121
1930	Hack Wilson, Chi	190	1981	Mike Schmidt, Phil	91
1931	Chuck Klein, Phil	121	1982	Dale Murphy, Atl	109
1932	Don Hurst, Phil	143		Al Oliver, Mtl	109
1933	Chuck Klein, Phil	120	1983	Dale Murphy, Atl	121
1934	Mel Ott, NY	135	1984	Gary Carter, Mtl	106
1935	Wally Berger, Bos	130		Mike Schmidt, Phil	106
1936	Joe Medwick, StL	138	1985	Dave Parker, Cin	125
1937	Joe Medwick, StL	154	1986	Mike Schmidt, Phil	119
1938	Joe Medwick, StL	122	1987	Andre Dawson, Chi	137
1939	Frank McCormick, Cin	128	1988	Will Clark, SF	109
1940	Johnny Mize, StL	137	1989	Kevin Mitchell, SF	125
1941	Dolph Camilli, Bklyn	120	1990	Matt Williams, SF	122
1942	Johnny Mize, NY	110	1991	Howard Johnson, NY	117
1943	Bill Nicholson, Chi	128	1992	Darren Daulton, Phil	109
1944	Bill Nicholson, Chi	122	1993	Barry Bonds, SF	123
1945	Dixie Walker, Bklyn	124	1994	Jeff Bagwell, Hou	116
1946	Enos Slaughter, StL	130	1995	Dante Bichette, Col	128
1947	Johnny Mize, NY	138	1996	Andres Galarraga, Col	150
1948	Stan Musial, StL	131			

He Couldn't *Buy* a Home Run

Actor Charlie Sheen paid $6,537.50 to buy most of the seats behind the left-field fence in Anaheim Stadium for a game in April, hoping to catch a home run ball. Sheen and three friends sat alone, 20 rows up, and watched the California Angels–Detroit Tigers game, on the chance that someone—preferably Tigers slugger Cecil Fielder—might postmark a round-tripper to their vicinity. "I didn't want to crawl over the paying public," said Sheen, the hell-raising star of *Hot Shots! Part Deux* and other cinematic landmarks, in explaining why he bought up the 2,615 seats. "I wanted to avoid the violence." Alas, no one homered and the Sheen crew went ball-less.

And to think what $6,500 used to buy the erstwhile Heidi Fleiss client.

Leading Base Stealers

Year	Player and Team	SB	Year	Player and Team	SB
1900	George Van Haltren, NY	45	1953	Bill Bruton, Mil	26
	Patsy Donovan, StL	45	1954	Bill Bruton, Mil	34
1901	Honus Wagner, Pitt	48	1955	Bill Bruton, Mil	35
1902	Honus Wagner, Pitt	43	1956	Willie Mays, NY	40
1903	Jimmy Sheckard, Bklyn	67	1957	Willie Mays, NY	38
	Frank Chance, Chi	67	1958	Willie Mays, SF	31
1904	Honus Wagner, Pitt	53	1959	Willie Mays, SF	27
1905	Billy Maloney, Chi	59	1960	Maury Wills, LA	50
	Art Devlin, NY	59	1961	Maury Wills, LA	35
1906	Frank Chance, Chi	57	1962	Maury Wills, LA	104
1907	Honus Wagner, Pitt	61	1963	Maury Wills, LA	40
1908	Honus Wagner, Pitt	53	1964	Maury Wills, LA	53
1909	Bob Bescher, Cin	54	1965	Maury Wills, LA	94
1910	Bob Bescher, Cin	70	1966	Lou Brock, StL	74
1911	Bob Bescher, Cin	80	1967	Lou Brock, StL	52
1912	Bob Bescher, Cin	67	1968	Lou Brock, Stl	62
1913	Max Carey, Pitt	61	1969	Lou Brock, StL	53
1914	George Burns, NY	62	1970	Bobby Tolan, Cin	57
1915	Max Carey, Pitt	36	1971	Lou Brock, StL	64
1916	Max Carey, Pitt	63	1972	Lou Brock, StL	63
1917	Max Carey, Pitt	46	1973	Lou Brock, StL	70
1918	Max Carey, Pitt	58	1974	Lou Brock, StL	118
1919	George Burns, NY	40	1975	Davey Lopes, LA	77
1920	Max Carey, Pitt	52	1976	Davey Lopes, LA	63
1921	Frankie Frisch, NY	49	1977	Frank Taveras, Pitt	70
1922	Max Carey, Pitt	51	1978	Omar Moreno, Pitt	71
1923	Max Carey, Pitt	51	1979	Omar Moreno, Pitt	77
1924	Max Carey, Pitt	49	1980	Ron LeFlore, Mtl	97
1925	Max Carey, Pitt	46	1981	Tim Raines, Mtl	71
1926	Kiki Cuyler, Pitt	35	1982	Tim Raines, Mtl	78
1927	Frankie Frisch, StL	48	1983	Tim Raines, Mtl	90
1928	Kiki Cuyler, Chi	37	1984	Tim Raines, Mtl	75
1929	Kiki Cuyler, Chi	43	1985	Vince Coleman, StL	110
1930	Kiki Cuyler, Chi	37	1986	Vince Coleman, StL	107
1931	Frankie Frisch, StL	28	1987	Vince Coleman, StL	109
1932	Chuck Klein, Phil	20	1988	Vince Coleman, StL	81
1933	Pepper Martin, StL	26	1989	Vince Coleman, StL	65
1934	Pepper Martin, StL	23	1990	Vince Coleman, StL	77
1935	Augie Galan, Chi	22	1991	Marquis Grissom, Mtl	76
1936	Pepper Martin, StL	23	1992	Marquis Grissom, Mtl	78
1937	Augie Galan, Chi	23	1993	Chuck Carr, Flor	58
1938	Stan Hack, Chi	16	1994	Craig Biggio, Hou	39
1939	Stan Hack, Chi	17	1995	Quilvio Veras, Fla	56
	Lee Handley, Pitt	17	1996	Eric Young, Col	53
1940	Lonny Frey, Cin	22			
1941	Danny Murtaugh, Phil	18			
1942	Pete Reiser, Bklyn	20			
1943	Arky Vaughan, Bklyn	20			
1944	Johnny Barrett, Pitt	28			
1945	Red Schoendienst, StL	26			
1946	Pete Reiser, Bklyn	34			
1947	Jackie Robinson, Bklyn	29			
1948	Richie Ashburn, Phil	32			
1949	Jackie Robinson, Bklyn	37			
1950	Sam Jethroe, Bos	35			
1951	Sam Jethroe, Bos	35			
1952	Pee Wee Reese, Bklyn	30			

THEY SAID IT

Sterling Hitchcock, former New York Yankee pitcher who moved to the Seattle Mariners, on whether he misses pinstripes: "Polyester is polyester."

Leading Pitchers—Winning Percentage

Year	Pitcher and Team	W	L	Pct	Year	Pitcher and Team	W	L	Pct
1900	Jesse Tannehill, Pitt	20	6	.769	1949	Preacher Roe, Bklyn	15	6	.714
1901	Jack Chesbro, Pitt	21	10	.677	1950	Sal Maglie, NY	18	4	.818
1902	Jack Chesbro, Pitt	28	6	.824	1951	Preacher Roe, Bklyn	22	3	.880
1903	Sam Leever, Pitt	25	7	.781	1952	Hoyt Wilhelm, NY	15	3	.833
1904	Joe McGinnity, NY	35	8	.814	1953	Carl Erskine, Bklyn	20	6	.769
1905	Sam Leever, Pitt	20	5	.800	1954	Johnny Antonelli, NY	21	7	.750
1906	Ed Reulbach, Chi	19	4	.826	1955	Don Newcombe, Bklyn	20	5	.800
1907	Ed Reulbach, Chi	17	4	.810	1956	Don Newcombe, Bklyn	27	7	.794
1908	Ed Reulbach, Chi	24	7	.774	1957	Bob Buhl, Mil	18	7	.720
1909	Christy Mathewson, NY	25	6	.806	1958	Warren Spahn, Mil	22	11	.667
	Howie Camnitz, Pitt	25	6	.806		Lew Burdette, Mil	20	10	.667
1910	King Cole, Chi	20	4	.833	1959	Roy Face, Pitt	18	1	.947
1911	Rube Marquard, NY	24	7	.774	1960	Ernie Broglio, StL	21	9	.700
1912	Claude Hendrix, Pitt	24	9	.727	1961	Johnny Podres, LA	18	5	.783
1913	Bert Humphries, Chi	16	4	.800	1962	Bob Purkey, Cin	23	5	.821
1914	Bill James, Bos	26	7	.788	1963	Ron Perranoski, LA	16	3	.842
1915	Grover Alexander, Phil	31	10	.756	1964	Sandy Koufax, LA	19	5	.792
1916	Tom Hughes, Bos	16	3	.842	1965	Sandy Koufax, LA	26	8	.765
1917	Ferdie Schupp, NY	21	7	.750	1966	Juan Marichal, SF	25	6	.806
1918	Claude Hendrix, Chi	19	7	.731	1967	Dick Hughes, StL	16	6	.727
1919	Dutch Ruether, Cin	19	6	.760	1968	Steve Blass, Pitt	18	6	.750
1920	Burleigh Grimes, Bklyn	23	11	.676	1969	Tom Seaver, NY	25	7	.781
1921	Bill Doak, StL	15	6	.714	1970	Bob Gibson, StL	23	7	.767
1922	Pete Donohue, Cin	18	9	.667	1971	Don Gullett, Cin	16	6	.727
1923	Dolf Luque, Cin	27	8	.771	1972	Gary Nolan, Cin	15	5	.750
1924	Emil Yde, Pitt	16	3	.842	1973	Tommy John, LA	16	7	.696
1925	Bill Sherdel, StL	15	6	.714	1974	Andy Messersmith, LA	20	6	.769
1926	Ray Kremer, Pitt	20	6	.769	1975	Don Gullett, Cin	15	4	.789
1927	Larry Benton, Bos-NY	17	7	.708	1976	Steve Carlton, Phil	20	7	.741
1928	Larry Benton, NY	25	9	.735	1977	John Candelaria, Pitt	20	5	.800
1929	Charlie Root, Chi	19	6	.760	1978	Gaylord Perry, SD	21	6	.778
1930	Freddie Fitzsimmons, NY	19	7	.731	1979	Tom Seaver, Cin	16	6	.727
1931	Paul Derringer, StL	18	8	.692	1980	Jim Bibby, Pitt	19	6	.760
1932	Lon Warneke, Chi	22	6	.786	1981*	Tom Seaver, Cin	14	2	.875
1933	Ben Cantwell, Bos	20	10	.667	1982	Phil Niekro, Atl	17	4	.810
1934	Dizzy Dean, StL	30	7	.811	1983	John Denny, Phil	19	6	.760
1935	Bill Lee, Chi	20	6	.769	1984	Rick Sutcliffe, Chi	16	1	.941
1936	Carl Hubbell, NY	26	6	.813	1985	Orel Hershiser, LA	19	3	.864
1937	Carl Hubbell, NY	22	8	.733	1986	Bob Ojeda, NY	18	5	.783
1938	Bill Lee, Chi	22	9	.710	1987	Dwight Gooden, NY	15	7	.682
1939	Paul Derringer, Cin	25	7	.781	1988	David Cone, NY	20	3	.870
1940	Freddie Fitzsimmons, Bklyn	16	2	.889	1989	Mike Bielecki, Chi	18	7	.720
1941	Elmer Riddle, Cin	19	4	.826	1990	Doug Drabeck, Pitt	22	6	.786
1942	Larry French, Bklyn	15	4	.789	1991	John Smiley, Pitt	20	8	.714
1943	Mort Cooper, StL	21	8	.724		Jose Rijo, Cin	15	6	.714
1944	Ted Wilks, StL	17	4	.810	1992	Bob Tewksbury, StL	16	5	.762
1945	Harry Brecheen, StL	15	4	.789	1993	Tom Glavine, Atl	22	6	.786
1946	Murray Dickson, StL	15	6	.714	1994	Ken Hill, Mtl	16	5	.762
1947	Larry Jansen, NY	21	5	.808	1995	Greg Maddux, Atl	19	2	.905
1948	Harry Brecheen, StL	20	7	.741	1996	John Smoltz, Atl	24	8	.750

*1981 percentages based on 10 or more victories. Note: Percentages based on 15 or more victories in all other years.

Leading Pitchers—Earned-Run Average

Year	Player and Team	ERA	Year	Player and Team	ERA
1900	Rube Waddell, Pitt	2.37	1911	Christy Mathewson, NY	1.99
1901	Jesse Tannehill, Pitt	2.18	1912	Jeff Tesreau, NY	1.96
1902	Jack Taylor, Chi	1.33	1913	Christy Mathewson, NY	2.06
1903	Sam Leever, Pitt	2.06	1914	Bill Doak, StL	1.72
1904	Joe McGinnity, NY	1.61	1915	Grover Alexander, Phil	1.22
1905	Christy Mathewson, NY	1.27	1916	Grover Alexander, Phil	1.55
1906	Three Finger Brown, Chi	1.04	1917	Grover Alexander, Phil	1.83
1907	Jack Pfiester, Chi	1.15	1918	Hippo Vaughn, Chi	1.74
1908	Christy Mathewson, NY	1.43	1919	Grover Alexander, Chi	1.72
1909	Christy Mathewson, NY	1.14	1920	Grover Alexander, Chi	1.91
1910	George McQuillan, Phil	1.60	1921	Bill Doak, StL	2.58

Leading Pitchers—Earned-Run Average (Cont.)

Year	Player and Team	ERA	Year	Player and Team	ERA
1922	Rosy Ryan, NY	3.00	1960	Mike McCormick, SF	2.70
1923	Dolf Luque, Cin	1.93	1961	Warren Spahn, Mil	3.01
1924	Dazzy Vance, Bklyn	2.16	1962	Sandy Koufax, LA	2.54
1925	Dolf Luque, Cin	2.63	1963	Sandy Koufax, LA	1.88
1926	Ray Kremer, Pitt	2.61	1964	Sandy Koufax, LA	1.74
1927	Ray Kremer, Pitt	2.47	1965	Sandy Koufax, LA	2.04
1928	Dazzy Vance, Bklyn	2.09	1966	Sandy Koufax, LA	1.73
1929	Bill Walker, NY	3.08	1967	Phil Niekro, Atl	1.87
1930	Dazzy Vance, Bklyn	2.61	1968	Bob Gibson, StL	1.12
1931	Bill Walker, NY	2.26	1969	Juan Marichal, SF	2.10
1932	Lon Warneke, Chi	2.37	1970	Tom Seaver, NY	2.81
1933	Carl Hubbell, NY	1.66	1971	Tom Seaver, NY	1.76
1934	Carl Hubbell, NY	2.30	1972	Steve Carlton, Phil	1.98
1935	Cy Blanton, Pitt	2.59	1973	Tom Seaver, NY	2.08
1936	Carl Hubbell, NY	2.31	1974	Buzz Capra, Atl	2.28
1937	Jim Turner, Bos	2.38	1975	Randy Jones, SD	2.24
1938	Bill Lee, Chi	2.66	1976	John Denny, StL	2.52
1939	Bucky Walters, Cin	2.29	1977	John Candelaria, Pitt	2.34
1940	Bucky Walters, Cin	2.48	1978	Craig Swan, NY	2.43
1941	Elmer Riddle, Cin	2.24	1979	J.R. Richard, Hou	2.71
1942	Mort Cooper, StL	1.77	1980	Don Sutton, LA	2.21
1943	Howie Pollet, StL	1.75	1981	Nolan Ryan, Hou	1.69
1944	Ed Heusser, Cin	2.30	1982	Steve Rogers, Mtl	2.40
1945	Hank Borowy, Chi	2.14	1983	Atlee Hammaker, SF	2.25
1946	Howie Pollet, StL	2.10	1984	Alejandro Pena, LA	2.48
1947	Warren Spahn, Bos	2.33	1985	Dwight Gooden, NY	1.53
1948	Harry Brecheen, StL	2.24	1986	Mike Scott, Hou	2.22
1949	Dave Koslo, NY	2.50	1987	Nolan Ryan, Hou	2.76
1950	Jim Hearn, StL-NY	2.49	1988	Joe Magrane, StL	2.18
1951	Chet Nichols, Bos	2.88	1989	Scott Garrelts, SF	2.28
1952	Hoyt Wilhelm, NY	2.43	1990	Danny Darwin, Hou	2.21
1953	Warren Spahn, Mil	2.10	1991	Dennis Martinez, Mtl	2.39
1954	Johnny Antonelli, NY	2.29	1992	Bill Swift, SF	2.08
1955	Bob Friend, Pitt	2.84	1993	Greg Maddux, Atl	2.36
1956	Lew Burdette, Mil	2.71	1994	Greg Maddux, Atl	1.56
1957	Johnny Podres, Bklyn	2.66	1995	Greg Maddux, Atl	1.63
1958	Stu Miller, SF	2.47	1996	Kevin Brown, Fla	1.89
1959	Sam Jones, SF	2.82			

Note: Based on 10 complete games through 1950, then 154 innings until National League expanded in 1962, when it became 162 innings. In strike-shortened 1981, one inning per game required.

Leading Pitchers—Strikeouts

Year	Player and Team	SO	Year	Player and Team	SO
1900	Rube Waddell, Pitt	133	1921	Burleigh Grimes, Bklyn	136
1901	Noodles Hahn, Cin	233	1922	Dazzy Vance, Bklyn	134
1902	Vic Willis, Bos	226	1923	Dazzy Vance, Bklyn	197
1903	Christy Mathewson, NY	267	1924	Dazzy Vance, Bklyn	262
1904	Christy Mathewson, NY	212	1925	Dazzy Vance, Bklyn	221
1905	Christy Mathewson, NY	206	1926	Dazzy Vance, Bklyn	140
1906	Fred Beebe, Chi-StL	171	1927	Dazzy Vance, Bklyn	184
1907	Christy Mathewson, NY	178	1928	Dazzy Vance, Bklyn	200
1908	Christy Mathewson, NY	259	1929	Pat Malone, Chi	166
1909	Orval Overall, Chi	205	1930	Bill Hallahan, StL	177
1910	Christy Mathewson, NY	190	1931	Bill Hallahan, StL	159
1911	Rube Marquard, NY	237	1932	Dizzy Dean, StL	191
1912	Grover Alexander, Phil	195	1933	Dizzy Dean, StL	199
1913	Tom Seaton, Phil	168	1934	Dizzy Dean, StL	195
1914	Grover Alexander, Phil	214	1935	Dizzy Dean, StL	182
1915	Grover Alexander, Phil	241	1936	Van Lingle Mungo, Bklyn	238
1916	Grover Alexander, Phil	167	1937	Carl Hubbell, NY	159
1917	Grover Alexander, Phil	200	1938	Clay Bryant, Chi	135
1918	Hippo Vaughn, Chi	148	1939	Claude Passeau, Phil-Chi	137
1919	Hippo Vaughn, Chi	141		Bucky Walters, Cin	137
1920	Grover Alexander, Chi	173	1940	Kirby Higbe, Phil	137

Leading Pitchers—Strikeouts *(Cont.)*

Year	Player and Team	SO	Year	Player and Team	SO
1941	Johnny Vander Meer, Cin	202	1969	Ferguson Jenkins, Chi	273
1942	Johnny Vander Meer, Cin	186	1970	Tom Seaver, NY	283
1943	Johnny Vander Meer, Cin	174	1971	Tom Seaver, NY	289
1944	Bill Voiselle, NY	161	1972	Steve Carlton, Phil	310
1945	Preacher Roe, Pitt	148	1973	Tom Seaver, NY	251
1946	Johnny Schmitz, Chi	135	1974	Steve Carlton, Phil	240
1947	Ewell Blackwell, Cin	193	1975	Tom Seaver, NY	243
1948	Harry Brecheen, StL	149	1976	Tom Seaver, NY	235
1949	Warren Spahn, Bos	151	1977	Phil Niekro, Atl	262
1950	Warren Spahn, Bos	191	1978	J.R. Richard, Hou	303
1951	Warren Spahn, Bos	164	1979	J.R. Richard, Hou	313
	Don Newcombe, Bklyn	164	1980	Steve Carlton, Phil	286
1952	Warren Spahn, Bos	183	1981	Fernando Valenzuela, LA	180
1953	Robin Roberts, Phil	198	1982	Steve Carlton, Phil	286
1954	Robin Roberts, Phil	185	1983	Steve Carlton, Phil	275
1955	Sam Jones, Chi	198	1984	Dwight Gooden, NY	276
1956	Sam Jones, Chi	176	1985	Dwight Gooden, NY	268
1957	Jack Sanford, Phil	188	1986	Mike Scott, Hou	306
1958	Sam Jones, StL	225	1987	Nolan Ryan, Hou	270
1959	Don Drysdale, LA	242	1988	Nolan Ryan, Hou	228
1960	Don Drysdale, LA	246	1989	Jose DeLeon, StL	201
1961	Sandy Koufax, LA	269	1990	David Cone, NY	233
1962	Don Drysdale, LA	232	1991	David Cone, NY	241
1963	Sandy Koufax, LA	306	1992	John Smoltz, Atl	215
1964	Bob Veale, Pitt	250	1993	Jose Rijo, Cin	227
1965	Sandy Koufax, LA	382	1994	Andy Benes, SD	189
1966	Sandy Koufax, LA	317	1995	Hideo Nomo, LA	236
1967	Jim Bunning, Phil	253	1996	John Smoltz, Atl	276
1968	Bob Gibson, StL	268			

Leading Pitchers—Saves

Year	Player and Team	SV	Year	Player and Team	SV
1947	Hugh Casey, Bklyn	18	1972	Clay Carroll, Cin	37
1948	Harry Gumpert, Cin	17	1973	Mike Marshall, Mtl	13
1949	Ted Wilks, StL	9	1974	Mike Marshall, LA	21
1950	Jim Konstanty, Phil	22	1975	Al Hrabosky, StL	22
1951	Ted Wilks, StL, Pitt	13		Rawly Eastwick, Cin	22
1952	Al Brazle, StL	16	1976	Rawly Eastwick, Cin	26
1953	Al Brazle, StL	18	1977	Rollie Fingers, SD	35
1954	Jim Hughes, Bklyn	24	1978	Rollie Fingers, SD	37
1955	Jack Meyer, Phil	16	1979	Bruce Sutter, Chi	37
1956	Clem Labine, Bklyn	19	1980	Bruce Sutter, Chi	28
1957	Clem Labine, Bklyn	17	1981	Bruce Sutter, StL	25
1958	Roy Face, Pitt	20	1982	Bruce Sutter, StL	36
1959	Lindy McDaniel, StL	15	1983	Lee Smith, Chi	29
	Don McMahon, Mil	15	1984	Bruce Sutter, StL	45
1960	Lindy McDaniel, StL	26	1985	Jeff Reardon, Mtl	41
1961	Stu Miller, SF	17	1986	Todd Worrell, StL	36
	Roy Face, Pitt	17	1987	Steve Bedrosian, Phil	40
1962	Roy Face, Pitt	28	1988	John Franco, Cin	39
1963	Lindy McDaniel, Chi	22	1989	Mark Davis, SD	44
1964	Hal Woodeshick, Hou	23	1990	John Franco, NY	33
1965	Ted Abernathy, Chi	31	1991	Lee Smith, StL	47
1966	Phil Regan, LA	21	1992	Lee Smith, StL	42
1967	Ted Abernathy, Cin	28	1993	Randy Myers, Chi	53
1968	Phil Regan, Chi, LA	25	1994	John Franco, NY	30
1969	Fred Gladding, Hou	29	1995	Randy Myers, Chi	38
1970	Wayne Granger, Cin	35	1996	Jeff Brantley, Cin	44
1971	Dave Giusti, Pitt	30		Todd Worrell, LA	44

American League

Pennant Winners

Year	Team	Manager	W	L	Pct	GA
1901	Chicago	Clark Griffith	83	53	.610	4
1902	Philadelphia	Connie Mack	83	53	.610	5
1903	Boston	Jimmy Collins	91	47	.659	14½
1904	Boston	Jimmy Collins	95	59	.617	1½
1905	Philadelphia	Connie Mack	92	56	.622	2
1906	Chicago	Fielder Jones	93	58	.616	3
1907	Detroit	Hughie Jennings	92	58	.613	1½
1908	Detroit	Hughie Jennings	90	63	.588	½
1909	Detroit	Hughie Jennings	98	54	.645	3½
1910	Philadelphia	Connie Mack	102	48	.680	14½
1911	Philadelphia	Connie Mack	101	50	.669	13½
1912	Boston	Jake Stahl	105	47	.691	14
1913	Philadelphia	Connie Mack	96	57	.627	6½
1914	Philadelphia	Connie Mack	99	53	.651	8½
1915	Boston	Bill Carrigan	101	50	.669	2½
1916	Boston	Bill Carrigan	91	63	.591	2
1917	Chicago	Pants Rowland	100	54	.649	9
1918	Boston	Ed Barrow	75	51	.605	2½
1919	Chicago	Kid Gleason	88	52	.629	3½
1920	Cleveland	Tris Speaker	98	56	.636	2
1921	New York	Miller Huggins	98	55	.641	4½
1922	New York	Miller Huggins	94	60	.610	1
1923	New York	Miller Huggins	98	54	.645	16
1924	Washington	Bucky Harris	92	62	.597	2
1925	Washington	Bucky Harris	96	55	.636	8½
1926	New York	Miller Huggins	91	63	.591	3
1927	New York	Miller Huggins	110	44	.714	19
1928	New York	Miller Huggins	101	53	.656	2½
1929	Philadelphia	Connie Mack	104	46	.693	18
1930	Philadelphia	Connie Mack	102	52	.662	8
1931	Philadelphia	Connie Mack	107	45	.704	13½
1932	New York	Joe McCarthy	107	47	.695	13
1933	Washington	Joe Cronin	99	53	.651	7
1934	Detroit	Mickey Cochrane	101	53	.656	7
1935	Detroit	Mickey Cochrane	93	58	.616	3
1936	New York	Joe McCarthy	102	51	.667	19½
1937	New York	Joe McCarthy	102	52	.662	13
1938	New York	Joe McCarthy	99	53	.651	9½
1939	New York	Joe McCarthy	106	45	.702	17
1940	Detroit	Del Baker	90	64	.584	1
1941	New York	Joe McCarthy	101	53	.656	17
1942	New York	Joe McCarthy	103	51	.669	9
1943	New York	Joe McCarthy	98	56	.636	13½
1944	St Louis	Luke Sewell	89	65	.578	1
1945	Detroit	Steve O'Neill	88	65	.575	1½
1946	Boston	Joe Cronin	104	50	.675	12
1947	New York	Bucky Harris	97	57	.630	12
1948	Cleveland†	Lou Boudreau	97	58	.626	1
1949	New York	Casey Stengel	97	57	.630	1
1950	New York	Casey Stengel	98	56	.636	3
1951	New York	Casey Stengel	98	56	.636	5
1952	New York	Casey Stengel	95	59	.617	2
1953	New York	Casey Stengel	99	52	.656	8½
1954	Cleveland	Al Lopez	111	43	.721	8
1955	New York	Casey Stengel	96	58	.623	3
1956	New York	Casey Stengel	97	57	.630	9
1957	New York	Casey Stengel	98	56	.636	8
1958	New York	Casey Stengel	92	62	.597	10
1959	Chicago	Al Lopez	94	60	.610	5
1960	New York	Casey Stengel	97	57	.630	8
1961	New York	Ralph Houk	109	53	.673	8
1962	New York	Ralph Houk	96	66	.593	5
1963	New York	Ralph Houk	104	57	.646	10½
1964	New York	Yogi Berra	99	63	.611	1
1965	Minnesota	Sam Mele	102	60	.630	7

Pennant Winners (Cont.)

Year	Team	Manager	W	L	Pct	GA
1966	Baltimore	Hank Bauer	97	63	.606	9
1967	Boston	Dick Williams	92	70	.568	1
1968	Detroit	Mayo Smith	103	59	.636	12
1969	Baltimore (E)‡	Earl Weaver	109	53	.673	19
1970	Baltimore (E)‡	Earl Weaver	108	54	.667	15
1971	Baltimore (E)‡	Earl Weaver	101	57	.639	12
1972	Oakland (W)‡	Dick Williams	93	62	.600	5½
1973	Oakland (W)‡	Dick Williams	94	68	.580	6
1974	Oakland (W)‡	Al Dark	90	72	.556	5
1975	Boston (E)‡	Darrell Johnson	95	65	.594	4½
1976	New York (E)‡	Billy Martin	97	62	.610	10½
1977	New York (E)‡	Billy Martin	100	62	.617	2½
1978	New York (E)†‡	Billy Martin, Bob Lemon	100	63	.613	1
1979	Baltimore (E)‡	Earl Weaver	102	57	.642	8
1980	Kansas City (W)‡	Jim Frey	97	65	.599	14
1981	New York (E)‡	Gene Michael, Bob Lemon	59	48	.551	#
1982	Milwaukee (E)‡	Buck Rodgers, Harvey Kuenn	95	67	.586	1
1983	Baltimore (E)‡	Joe Altobelli	98	64	.605	6
1984	Detroit (E)‡	Sparky Anderson	104	58	.642	15
1985	Kansas City (W)‡	Dick Howser	91	71	.562	1
1986	Boston (E)‡	John McNamara	95	66	.590	5½
1987	Minnesota (W)‡	Tom Kelly	85	77	.525	2
1988	Oakland (W)‡	Tony La Russa	104	58	.642	13
1989	Oakland (W)‡	Tony La Russa	99	63	.611	7
1990	Oakland (W)‡	Tony La Russa	103	59	.636	9
1991	Minnesota (W)‡	Tom Kelly	95	67	.586	8
1992	Toronto‡	Cito Gaston	96	66	.593	4
1993	Toronto‡	Cito Gaston	95	67	.586	7
1994	Season ended Aug. 11 due to players' strike					
1995	Cleveland (C)‡	Mike Hargrove	100	44	.694	30
1996	New York (E)‡	Joe Torre	92	70	.568	4

†Defeated Boston in one-game playoff. ‡Won championship series.
#First half 34-22; second 25-26, in season split by strike; defeated Milwaukee in playoff for Eastern Divison title.

Leading Batsmen

Year	Player and Team	BA	Year	Player and Team	BA
1901	Nap Lajoie, Phil	.422	1925	Harry Heilmann, Det	.393
1902	Ed Delahanty, Wash	.376	1926	Heinie Manush, Det	.378
1903	Nap Lajoie, Clev	.355	1927	Harry Heilmann, Det	.398
1904	Nap Lajoie, Clev	.381	1928	Goose Goslin, Wash	.379
1905	Elmer Flick, Clev	.306	1929	Lew Fonseca, Clev	.369
1906	George Stone, StL	.358	1930	Al Simmons, Phil	.381
1907	Ty Cobb, Det	.350	1931	Al Simmons, Phil	.390
1908	Ty Cobb, Det	.324	1932	Dale Alexander, Det-Bos	.367
1909	Ty Cobb, Det	.377	1933	Jimmie Foxx, Phil	.356
1910	Nap Lajoie, Clev*	.383	1934	Lou Gehrig, NY	.363
1911	Ty Cobb, Det	.420	1935	Buddy Myer, Wash	.349
1912	Ty Cobb, Det	.410	1936	Luke Appling, Chi	.388
1913	Ty Cobb, Det	.390	1937	Charlie Gehringer, Det	.371
1914	Ty Cobb, Det	.368	1938	Jimmie Foxx, Bos	.349
1915	Ty Cobb, Det	.369	1939	Joe DiMaggio, NY	.381
1916	Tris Speaker, Clev	.386	1940	Joe DiMaggio, NY	.352
1917	Ty Cobb, Det	.383	1941	Ted Williams, Bos	.406
1918	Ty Cobb, Det	.382	1942	Ted Williams, Bos	.356
1919	Ty Cobb, Det	.384	1943	Luke Appling, Chi	.328
1920	George Sisler, StL	.407	1944	Lou Boudreau, Clev	.327
1921	Harry Heilmann, Det	.394	1945	Snuffy Stirnweiss, NY	.309
1922	George Sisler, StL	.420	1946	Mickey Vernon, Wash	.353
1923	Harry Heilmann, Det	.403	1947	Ted Williams, Bos	.343
1924	Babe Ruth, NY	.378	1948	Ted Williams, Bos	.369

*League president Ban Johnson declared Ty Cobb batting champion with a .385 average, beating Lajoie's .384. However, subsequent research has led to the revision of Lajoie's average to .383 and Cobb's to .382.

Leading Batsmen *(Cont.)*

Year	Player and Team	BA	Year	Player and Team	BA
1949	George Kell, Det	.343	1973	Rod Carew, Minn	.350
1950	Billy Goodman, Bos	.354	1974	Rod Carew, Minn	.364
1951	Ferris Fain, Phil	.344	1975	Rod Carew, Minn	.359
1952	Ferris Fain, Phil	.327	1976	George Brett, KC	.333
1953	Mickey Vernon, Wash	.337	1977	Rod Carew, Minn	.388
1954	Bobby Avila, Clev	.341	1978	Rod Carew, Minn	.333
1955	Al Kaline, Det	.340	1979	Fred Lynn, Bos	.333
1956	Mickey Mantle, NY	.353	1980	George Brett, KC	.390
1957	Ted Williams, Bos	.388	1981	Carney Lansford, Bos	.336
1958	Ted Williams, Bos	.328	1982	Willie Wilson, KC	.332
1959	Harvey Kuenn, Det	.353	1983	Wade Boggs, Bos	.361
1960	Pete Runnels, Bos	.320	1984	Don Mattingly, NY	.343
1961	Norm Cash, Det	.361	1985	Wade Boggs, Bos	.368
1962	Pete Runnels, Bos	.326	1986	Wade Boggs, Bos	.357
1963	Carl Yastrzemski, Bos	.321	1987	Wade Boggs, Bos	.363
1964	Tony Oliva, Minn	.323	1988	Wade Boggs, Bos	.366
1965	Tony Oliva, Minn	.321	1989	Kirby Puckett, Minn	.339
1966	Frank Robinson, Balt	.316	1990	George Brett, KC	.329
1967	Carl Yastrzemski, Bos	.326	1991	Julio Franco, Tex	.341
1968	Carl Yastrzemski, Bos	.301	1992	Edgar Martinez, Sea	.343
1969	Rod Carew, Minn	.332	1993	John Olerud, Tor	.363
1970	Alex Johnson, Calif	.329	1994	Paul O'Neill, NY	.359
1971	Tony Oliva, Minn	.337	1005	Edgar Martinez, Sea	.356
1972	Rod Carew, Minn	.318	1996	Alex Rodriguez, Sea	.358

Leaders in Runs Scored

Year	Player and Team	Runs	Year	Player and Team	Runs
1901	Nap Lajoie, Phil	145	1939	Red Rolfe, NY	139
1902	Dave Fultz, Phil	110	1940	Ted Williams, Bos	134
1903	Patsy Dougherty, Bos	108	1941	Ted Williams, Bos	135
1904	Patsy Dougherty, Bos-NY	113	1942	Ted Williams, Bos	141
1905	Harry Davis, Phil	92	1943	George Case, Wash	102
1906	Elmer Flick, Clev	98	1944	Snuffy Stirnweiss, NY	125
1907	Sam Crawford, Det	102	1945	Snuffy Stirnweiss, NY	107
1908	Matty McIntyre, Det	105	1946	Ted Williams, Bos	142
1909	Ty Cobb, Det	116	1947	Ted Williams, Bos	125
1910	Ty Cobb, Det	106	1948	Tommy Henrich, NY	138
1911	Ty Cobb, Det	147	1949	Ted Williams, Bos	150
1912	Eddie Collins, Phil	137	1950	Dom DiMaggio, Bos	131
1913	Eddie Collins, Phil	125	1951	Dom DiMaggio, Bos	113
1914	Eddie Collins, Phil	122	1952	Larry Doby, Clev	104
1915	Ty Cobb, Det	144	1953	Al Rosen, Clev	115
1916	Ty Cobb, Det	113	1954	Mickey Mantle, NY	129
1917	Donie Bush, Det	112	1955	Al Smith, Clev	123
1918	Ray Chapman, Clev	84	1956	Mickey Mantle, NY	132
1919	Babe Ruth, Bos	103	1957	Mickey Mantle, NY	121
1920	Babe Ruth, NY	158	1958	Mickey Mantle, NY	127
1921	Babe Ruth, NY	177	1959	Eddie Yost, Det	115
1922	George Sisler, StL	134	1960	Mickey Mantle, NY	119
1923	Babe Ruth, NY	151	1961	Mickey Mantle, NY	132
1924	Babe Ruth, NY	143		Roger Maris, NY	132
1925	Johnny Mostil, Chi	135	1962	Albie Pearson, LA	115
1926	Babe Ruth, NY	139	1963	Bob Allison, Minn	99
1927	Babe Ruth, NY	158	1964	Tony Oliva, Minn	109
1928	Babe Ruth, NY	163	1965	Zoilo Versalles, Minn	126
1929	Charlie Gehringer, Det	131	1966	Frank Robinson, Balt	122
1930	Al Simmons, Phil	152	1967	Carl Yastrzemski, Bos	112
1931	Lou Gehrig, NY	163	1968	Dick McAuliffe, Det	95
1932	Jimmie Foxx, Phil	151	1969	Reggie Jackson, Oak	123
1933	Lou Gehrig, NY	138	1970	Carl Yastrzemski, Bos	125
1934	Charlie Gehringer, Det	134	1971	Don Buford, Balt	99
1935	Lou Gehrig, NY	125	1972	Bobby Murcer, NY	102
1936	Lou Gehrig, NY	167	1973	Reggie Jackson, Oak	99
1937	Joe DiMaggio, NY	151	1974	Carl Yastrzemski, Bos	93
1938	Hank Greenberg, Det	144	1975	Fred Lynn, Bos	103

Leaders in Runs Scored (Cont.)

Year	Player and Team	Runs	Year	Player and Team	Runs
1976	Roy White, NY	104	1988	Wade Boggs, Bos	128
1977	Rod Carew, Minn	128	1989	Rickey Henderson, NY-Oak	113
1978	Ron LeFlore, Det	126		Wade Boggs, Bos	113
1979	Don Baylor, Calif	120	1990	Rickey Henderson, Oak	119
1980	Willie Wilson, KC	133	1991	Paul Molitor, Mil	133
1981	Rickey Henderson, Oak	89	1992	Tony Phillips, Det	114
1982	Paul Molitor, Mil	136	1993	Rafael Palmeiro, Tex	124
1983	Cal Ripken, Balt	121	1994	Frank Thomas, Chi	106
1984	Dwight Evans, Bos	121	1995	Albert Belle, Clev	121
1985	Rickey Henderson, NY	146		Edgar Martinez, Sea	121
1986	Rickey Henderson, NY	130	1996	Alex Rodriguez, Sea	141
1987	Paul Molitor, Mil	114			

Leaders in Hits

Year	Player and Team	Hits	Year	Player and Team	Hits
1901	Nap Lajoie, Phil	229	1944	Snuffy Stirnweiss, NY	205
1902	Piano Legs Hickman, Bos-Clev	194	1945	Snuffy Stirnweiss, NY	195
1903	Patsy Dougherty, Bos	195	1946	Johnny Pesky, Bos	208
1904	Nap Lajoie, Clev	211	1947	Johnny Pesky, Bos	207
1905	George Stone, StL	187	1948	Bob Dillinger, StL	207
1906	Nap Lajoie, Clev	214	1949	Dale Mitchell, Clev	203
1907	Ty Cobb, Det	212	1950	George Kell, Det	218
1908	Ty Cobb, Det	188	1951	George Kell, Det	191
1909	Ty Cobb, Det	216	1952	Nellie Fox, Chi	192
1910	Nap Lajoie, Clev	227	1953	Harvey Kuenn, Det	209
1911	Ty Cobb, Det	248	1954	Nellie Fox, Chi	201
1912	Ty Cobb, Det	227		Harvey Kuenn, Det	201
1913	Joe Jackson, Clev	197	1955	Al Kaline, Det	200
1914	Tris Speaker, Bos	193	1956	Harvey Kuenn, Det	196
1915	Ty Cobb, Det	208	1957	Nellie Fox, Chi	196
1916	Tris Speaker, Clev	211	1958	Nellie Fox, Chi	187
1917	Ty Cobb, Det	225	1959	Harvey Kuenn, Det	198
1918	George Burns, Phil	178	1960	Minnie Minoso, Chi	184
1919	Ty Cobb, Det	191	1961	Norm Cash, Det	193
	Bobby Veach, Det	191	1962	Bobby Richardson, NY	209
1920	George Sisler, StL	257	1963	Carl Yastrzemski, Bos	183
1921	Harry Heilmann, Det	237	1964	Tony Oliva, Minn	217
1922	George Sisler, StL	246	1965	Tony Oliva, Minn	185
1923	Charlie Jamieson, Clev	222	1966	Tony Oliva, Minn	191
1924	Sam Rice, Wash	216	1967	Carl Yastrzemski, Bos	189
1925	Al Simmons, Phil	253	1968	Bert Campaneris, Oak	177
1926	George Burns, Clev	216	1969	Tony Oliva, Minn	197
	Sam Rice, Wash	216	1970	Tony Oliva, Minn	204
1927	Earle Combs, NY	231	1971	Cesar Tovar, Minn	204
1928	Heinie Manush, StL	241	1972	Joe Rudi, Oak	181
1929	Dale Alexander, Det	215	1973	Rod Carew, Minn	203
	Charlie Gehringer, Det	215	1974	Rod Carew, Minn	218
1930	Johnny Hodapp, Clev	225	1975	George Brett, KC	195
1931	Lou Gehrig, NY	211	1976	George Brett, KC	215
1932	Al Simmons, Phil	216	1977	Rod Carew, Minn	239
1933	Heinie Manush, Wash	221	1978	Jim Rice, Bos	213
1934	Charlie Gehringer, Det	214	1979	George Brett, KC	212
1935	Joe Vosmik, Clev	216	1980	Willie Wilson, KC	230
1936	Earl Averill, Clev	232	1981	Rickey Henderson, Oak	135
1937	Beau Bell, StL	218	1982	Robin Yount, Mil	210
1938	Joe Vosmik, Bos	201	1983	Cal Ripken, Balt	211
1939	Red Rolfe, NY	213	1984	Don Mattingly, NY	207
1940	Rip Radcliff, StL	200	1985	Wade Boggs, Bos	240
	Barney McCosky, Det	200	1986	Don Mattingly, NY	238
	Doc Cramer, Bos	200	1987	Kirby Puckett, Minn	207
1941	Cecil Travis, Wash	218		Kevin Seitzer, KC	207
1942	Johnny Pesky, Bos	205	1988	Kirby Puckett, Minn	234
1943	Dick Wakefield, Det	200	1989	Kirby Puckett, Minn	215

Leaders in Hits (Cont.)

Year	Player and Team	Hits	Year	Player and Team	Hits
1990	Rafael Palmeiro, Tex	191	1994	Kenny Lofton, Clev	160
1991	Paul Molitor, Mil	216	1995	Lance Johnson, Chi	186
1992	Kirby Puckett, Minn	210	1996	Paul Molitor, Min	225
1993	Paul Molitor, Tor	211			

Home Run Leaders

Year	Player and Team	HR	Year	Player and Team	HR
1901	Nap Lajoie, Phil	13	1952	Larry Doby, Clev	32
1902	Socks Seybold, Phil	16	1953	Al Rosen, Clev	43
1903	Buck Freeman, Bos	13	1954	Larry Doby, Clev	32
1904	Harry Davis, Phil	10	1955	Mickey Mantle, NY	37
1905	Harry Davis, Phil	8	1956	Mickey Mantle, NY	52
1906	Harry Davis, Phil	12	1957	Roy Sievers, Wash	42
1907	Harry Davis, Phil	8	1958	Mickey Mantle, NY	42
1908	Sam Crawford, Det	7	1959	Rocky Colavito, Clev	42
1909	Ty Cobb, Det	9		Harmon Killebrew, Wash	42
1910	Jake Stahl, Bos	10	1960	Mickey Mantle, NY	40
1911	Frank Baker, Phil	9	1961	Roger Maris, NY	61
1912	Frank Baker, Phil	10	1962	Harmon Killebrew, Minn	48
	Tris Speaker, Bos	10	1963	Harmon Killebrew, Minn	45
1913	Frank Baker, Phil	13	1964	Harmon Killebrew, Minn	49
1914	Frank Baker, Phil	9	1965	Tony Conigliaro, Bos	32
1915	Braggo Roth, Chi-Clev	7	1966	Frank Robinson, Balt	49
1916	Wally Pipp, NY	12	1967	Harmon Killebrew, Minn	44
1917	Wally Pipp, NY	9		Carl Yastrzemski, Bos	44
1918	Babe Ruth, Bos	11	1968	Frank Howard, Wash	44
	Tilly Walker, Phil	11	1969	Harmon Killebrew, Minn	49
1919	Babe Ruth, Bos	29	1970	Frank Howard, Wash	44
1920	Babe Ruth, NY	54	1971	Bill Melton, Chi	33
1921	Babe Ruth, NY	59	1972	Dick Allen, Chi	37
1922	Ken Williams, StL	39	1973	Reggie Jackson, Oak	32
1923	Babe Ruth, NY	41	1974	Dick Allen, Chi	32
1924	Babe Ruth, NY	46	1975	Reggie Jackson, Oak	36
1925	Bob Meusel, NY	33		George Scott, Mil	36
1926	Babe Ruth, NY	47	1976	Graig Nettles, NY	32
1927	Babe Ruth, NY	60	1977	Jim Rice, Bos	39
1928	Babe Ruth, NY	54	1978	Jim Rice, Bos	46
1929	Babe Ruth, NY	46	1979	Gorman Thomas, Mil	45
1930	Babe Ruth, NY	49	1980	Reggie Jackson, NY	41
1931	Babe Ruth, NY	46		Ben Oglivie, Mil	41
	Lou Gehrig, NY	46	1981	Tony Armas, Oak	22
1932	Jimmie Foxx, Phil	58	1981	Dwight Evans, Bos	22
1933	Jimmie Foxx, Phil	48		Bobby Grich, Calif	22
1934	Lou Gehrig, NY	49		Eddie Murray, Balt	22
1935	Jimmie Foxx, Phil	36	1982	Reggie Jackson, Calif	39
	Hank Greenberg, Det	36		Gorman Thomas, Mil	39
1936	Lou Gehrig, NY	49	1983	Jim Rice, Bos	39
1937	Joe DiMaggio, NY	46	1984	Tony Armas, Bos	43
1938	Hank Greenberg, Det	58	1985	Darrell Evans, Det	40
1939	Jimmie Foxx, Bos	35	1986	Jesse Barfield, Tor	40
1940	Hank Greenberg, Det	41	1987	Mark McGwire, Oak	49
1941	Ted Williams, Bos	37	1988	Jose Canseco, Oak	42
1942	Ted Williams, Bos	36	1989	Fred McGriff, Tor	36
1943	Rudy York, Det	34	1990	Cecil Fielder, Det	51
1944	Nick Etten, NY	22	1991	Jose Canseco, Oak	44
1945	Vern Stephens, StL	24		Cecil Fielder, Det	44
1946	Hank Greenberg, Det	44	1992	Juan Gonzalez, Tex	43
1947	Ted Williams, Bos	32	1993	Juan Gonzalez, Tex	46
1948	Joe DiMaggio, NY	39	1994	Ken Griffey Jr, Sea	40
1949	Ted Williams, Bos	43	1995	Albert Belle, Clev	50
1950	Al Rosen, Clev	37	1996	Mark McGwire, Oak	52
1951	Gus Zernial, Chi-Phil	33			

Runs Batted In Leaders

Year	Player and Team	RBI	Year	Player and Team	RBI
1907	Ty Cobb, Det	116	1952	Al Rosen, Clev	105
1908	Ty Cobb, Det	108	1953	Al Rosen, Clev	145
1909	Ty Cobb, Det	107	1954	Larry Doby, Clev	126
1910	Sam Crawford, Det	120	1955	Ray Boone, Det	116
1911	Ty Cobb, Det	144		Jackie Jensen, Bos	116
1912	Frank Baker, Phil	133	1956	Mickey Mantle, NY	130
1913	Frank Baker, Phil	126	1957	Roy Sievers, Wash	114
1914	Sam Crawford, Det	104	1958	Jackie Jensen, Bos	122
1915	Sam Crawford, Det	112	1959	Jackie Jensen, Bos	112
	Bobby Veach, Det	112	1960	Roger Maris, NY	112
1916	Del Pratt, StL	103	1961	Roger Maris, NY	142
1917	Bobby Veach, Det	103	1962	Harmon Killebrew, Minn	126
1918	Bobby Veach, Det	78	1963	Dick Stuart, Bos	118
1919	Babe Ruth, Bos	114	1964	Brooks Robinson, Balt	118
1920	Babe Ruth, NY	137	1965	Rocky Colavito, Clev	108
1921	Babe Ruth, NY	171	1966	Frank Robinson, Balt	122
1922	Ken Williams, StL	155	1967	Carl Yastrzemski, Bos	121
1923	Babe Ruth, NY	131	1968	Ken Harrelson, Bos	109
1924	Goose Goslin, Wash	129	1969	Harmon Killebrew, Minn	140
1925	Bob Meusel, NY	138	1970	Frank Howard, Wash	126
1926	Babe Ruth, NY	145	1971	Harmon Killebrew, Minn	119
1927	Lou Gehrig, NY	175	1972	Dick Allen, Chi	113
1928	Babe Ruth, NY	142	1973	Reggie Jackson, Oak	117
	Lou Gehrig, NY	142	1974	Jeff Burroughs, Tex	118
1929	Al Simmons, Phil	157	1975	George Scott, Mil	109
1930	Lou Gehrig, NY	174	1976	Lee May, Balt	109
1931	Lou Gehrig, NY	184	1977	Larry Hisle, Minn	119
1932	Jimmie Foxx, Phil	169	1978	Jim Rice, Bos	139
1933	Jimmie Foxx, Phil	163	1979	Don Baylor, Calif	139
1934	Lou Gehrig, NY	165	1980	Cecil Cooper, Mil	122
1935	Hank Greenberg, Det	170	1981	Eddie Murray, Balt	78
1936	Hal Trosky, Clev	162	1982	Hal McRae, KC	133
1937	Hank Greenberg, Det	183	1983	Cecil Cooper, Mil	126
1938	Jimmie Foxx, Bos	175		Jim Rice, Bos	126
1939	Ted Williams, Bos	145	1984	Tony Armas, Bos	123
1940	Hank Greenberg, Det	150	1985	Don Mattingly, NY	145
1941	Joe DiMaggio, NY	125	1986	Joe Carter, Clev	121
1942	Ted Williams, Bos	137	1987	George Bell, Tor	134
1943	Rudy York, Det	118	1988	Jose Canseco, Oak	124
1944	Vern Stephens, StL	109	1989	Ruben Sierra, Tex	119
1945	Nick Etten, NY	111	1990	Cecil Fielder, Det	132
1946	Hank Greenberg, Det	127	1991	Cecil Fielder, Det	133
1947	Ted Williams, Bos	114	1992	Cecil Fielder, Det	124
1948	Joe DiMaggio, NY	155	1993	Albert Belle, Clev	129
1949	Ted Williams, Bos	159	1994	Kirby Puckett, Minn	112
	Vern Stephens, Bos	159	1995	Albert Belle, Clev	126
1950	Walt Dropo, Bos	144		Mo Vaughn, Bos	126
	Vern Stephens, Bos	144	1996	Albert Belle, Clev	148
1951	Gus Zernial, Chi-Phil	129			

Note: Runs Batted In not compiled before 1907; officially adopted in 1920.

Leading Base Stealers

Year	Player and Team	SB	Year	Player and Team	SB
1901	Frank Isbell, Chi	48	1910	Eddie Collins, Phil	81
1902	Topsy Hartsel, Phil	54	1911	Ty Cobb, Det	83
1903	Harry Bay, Clev	46	1912	Clyde Milan, Wash	88
1904	Elmer Flick, Clev	42	1913	Clyde Milan, Wash	75
	Harry Bay, Clev	42	1914	Fritz Maisel, NY	74
1905	Danny Hoffman, Phil	46	1915	Ty Cobb, Det	96
1906	Elmer Flick, Clev	39	1916	Ty Cobb, Det	68
	John Anderson, Wash	39	1917	Ty Cobb, Det	55
1907	Ty Cobb, Det	49	1918	George Sisler, StL	45
1908	Patsy Dougherty, Chi	47	1919	Eddie Collins, Chi	33
1909	Ty Cobb, Det	76	1920	Sam Rice, Wash	63

Leading Base Stealers (Cont.)

Year	Player and Team	SB	Year	Player and Team	SB
1921	George Sisler, StL	35	1959	Luis Aparicio, Chi	56
1922	George Sisler, StL	51	1960	Luis Aparicio, Chi	51
1923	Eddie Collins, Chi	49	1961	Luis Aparicio, Chi	53
1924	Eddie Collins, Chi	42	1962	Luis Aparicio, Chi	31
1925	John Mostil, Chi	43	1963	Luis Aparicio, Balt	40
1926	John Mostil, Chi	35	1964	Luis Aparicio, Balt	57
1927	George Sisler, StL	27	1965	Bert Campaneris, KC	51
1928	Buddy Myer, Bos	30	1966	Bert Campaneris, KC	52
1929	Charlie Gehringer, Det	27	1967	Bert Campaneris, KC	55
1930	Marty McManus, Det	23	1968	Bert Campaneris, Oak	62
1931	Ben Chapman, NY	61	1969	Tommy Harper, Sea	73
1932	Ben Chapman, NY	38	1970	Bert Campaneris, Oak	42
1933	Ben Chapman, NY	27	1971	Amos Otis, KC	52
1934	Bill Werber, Bos	40	1972	Bert Campaneris, Oak	52
1935	Bill Werber, Bos	29	1973	Tommy Harper, Bos	54
1936	Lyn Lary, StL	37	1974	Bill North, Oak	54
1937	Bill Werber, Phil	35	1975	Mickey Rivers, Calif	70
	Ben Chapman, Wash-Bos	35	1976	Bill North, Oak	75
1938	Frank Crosetti, NY	27	1977	Freddie Patek, KC	53
1939	George Case, Wash	51	1978	Ron LeFlore, Det	68
1940	George Case, Wash	35	1979	Willie Wilson, KC	83
1941	George Case, Wash	33	1980	Rickey Henderson, Oak	100
1942	George Case, Wash	44	1981	Rickey Henderson, Oak	56
1943	George Case, Wash	61	1982	Rickey Henderson, Oak	130
1944	Snuffy Stirnweiss, NY	55	1983	Rickey Henderson, Oak	108
1945	Snuffy Stirnweiss, NY	33	1984	Rickey Henderson, Oak	66
1946	George Case, Clev	28	1985	Rickey Henderson, NY	80
1947	Bob Dillinger, StL	34	1986	Rickey Henderson, NY	87
1948	Bob Dillinger, StL	28	1987	Harold Reynolds, Sea	60
1949	Bob Dillinger, StL	20	1988	Rickey Henderson, NY	93
1950	Dom DiMaggio, Bos	15	1989	Rickey Henderson, NY-Oak	77
1951	Minnie Minoso, Clev-Chi	31	1990	Rickey Henderson, Oak	65
1952	Minnie Minoso, Chi	22	1991	Rickey Henderson, Oak	58
1953	Minnie Minoso, Chi	25	1992	Kenny Lofton, Clev	66
1954	Jackie Jensen, Bos	22	1993	Kenny Lofton, Clev	70
1955	Jim Rivera, Chi	25	1994	Kenny Lofton, Clev	60
1956	Luis Aparicio, Chi	21	1995	Kenny Lofton, Clev	54
1957	Luis Aparicio, Chi	28	1996	Kenny Lofton, Clev	75
1958	Luis Aparicio, Chi	29			

Leading Pitchers—Winning Percentage

Year	Pitcher and Team	W	L	Pct	Year	Pitcher and Team	W	L	Pct
1901	Clark Griffith, Chi	24	7	.774	1924	Walter Johnson, Wash	23	7	.767
1902	Bill Bernhard, Phil-Clev	18	5	.783	1925	Stan Coveleski, Wash	20	5	.800
1903	Earl Moore, Clev	22	7	.759	1926	George Uhle, Clev	27	11	.711
1904	Jack Chesbro, NY	41	12	.774	1927	Waite Hoyt, NY	22	7	.759
1905	Jess Tannehill, Bos	22	9	.710	1928	General Crowder, StL	21	5	.808
1906	Eddie Plank, Phil	19	6	.760	1929	Lefty Grove, Phil	20	6	.769
1907	Wild Bill Donovan, Det	25	4	.862	1930	Lefty Grove, Phil	28	5	.848
1908	Ed Walsh, Chi	40	15	.727	1931	Lefty Grove, Phil	31	4	.886
1909	George Mullin, Det	29	8	.784	1932	Johnny Allen, NY	17	4	.810
1910	Chief Bender, Phil	23	5	.821	1933	Lefty Grove, Phil	24	8	.750
1911	Chief Bender, Phil	17	5	.773	1934	Lefty Gomez, NY	26	5	.839
1912	Smoky Joe Wood, Bos	34	5	.872	1935	Eldon Auker, Det	18	7	.720
1913	Walter Johnson, Wash	36	7	.837	1936	Monte Pearson, NY	19	7	.731
1914	Chief Bender, Phil	17	3	.850	1937	Johnny Allen, Clev	15	1	.938
1915	Smoky Joe Wood, Bos	15	5	.750	1938	Red Ruffing, NY	21	7	.750
1916	Eddie Cicotte, Chi	15	7	.682	1939	Lefty Grove, Phil	15	4	.789
1917	Reb Russell, Chi	15	5	.750	1940	Schoolboy Rowe, Det	16	3	.842
1918	Sad Sam Jones, Bos	16	5	.762	1941	Lefty Gomez, NY	15	5	.750
1919	Eddie Cicotte, Chi	29	7	.806	1942	Ernie Bonham, NY	21	5	.808
1920	Jim Bagby, Clev	31	12	.721	1943	Spud Chandler, NY	20	4	.833
1921	Carl Mays, NY	27	9	.750	1944	Tex Hughson, Bos	18	5	.783
1922	Joe Bush, NY	26	7	.788	1945	Hal Newhouser, Det	25	9	.735
1923	Herb Pennock, NY	19	6	.760	1946	Boo Ferriss, Bos	25	6	.806

Leading Pitchers—Winning Percentage *(Cont.)*

Year	Pitcher and Team	W	L	Pct	Year	Pitcher and Team	W	L	Pct
1947	Allie Reynolds, NY	19	8	.704	1972	Catfish Hunter, Oak	21	7	.750
1948	Jack Kramer, Bos	18	5	.783	1973	Catfish Hunter, Oak	21	5	.808
1949	Ellis Kinder, Bos	23	6	.793	1974	Mike Cuellar, Balt	22	10	.688
1950	Vic Raschi, NY	21	8	.724	1975	Mike Torrez, Balt	20	9	.690
1951	Bob Feller, Clev	22	8	.733	1976	Bill Campbell, Minn	17	5	.773
1952	Bobby Shantz, Phil	24	7	.774	1977	Paul Splittorff, KC	16	6	.727
1953	Ed Lopat, NY	16	4	.800	1978	Ron Guidry, NY	25	3	.893
1954	Sandy Consuegra, Chi	16	3	.842	1979	Mike Caldwell, Mil	16	6	.727
1955	Tommy Byrne, NY	16	5	.762	1980	Steve Stone, Balt	25	7	.781
1956	Whitey Ford, NY	19	6	.760	1981*	Pete Vuckovich, Mil	14	4	.778
1957	Dick Donovan, Chi	16	6	.727	1982	Pete Vuckovich, Mil	18	6	.750
	Tom Sturdivant, NY	16	6	.727		Jim Palmer, Balt	15	5	.750
1958	Bob Turley, NY	21	7	.750	1983	Richard Dotson, Chi	22	7	.759
1959	Bob Shaw, Chi	18	6	.750	1984	Doyle Alexander, Tor	17	6	.739
1960	Jim Perry, Clev	18	10	.643	1985	Ron Guidry, NY	22	6	.786
1961	Whitey Ford, NY	25	4	.862	1986	Roger Clemens, Bos	24	4	.857
1962	Ray Herbert, Chi	20	9	.690	1987	Roger Clemens, Bos	20	9	.690
1963	Whitey Ford, NY	24	7	.774	1988	Frank Viola, Minn	24	7	.774
1964	Wally Bunker, Balt	19	5	.792	1989	Bret Saberhagen, KC	23	6	.793
1965	Mudcat Grant, Minn	21	7	.750	1990	Bob Welch, Oak	27	6	.818
1966	Sonny Siebert, Clev	16	8	.667	1991	Scott Erickson, Minn	20	8	.714
1967	Joel Horlen, Chi	19	7	.731	1992	Mike Mussina, Balt	18	5	.783
1968	Denny McLain, Det	31	6	.838	1993	Jimmy Key, NY	18	6	.750
1969	Jim Palmer, Balt	16	4	.800	1994	Jimmy Key, NY	17	4	.810
1970	Mike Cuellar, Balt	24	8	.750	1995	Randy Johnson, Sea	18	2	.900
1971	Dave McNally, Balt	21	5	.808	1996	Charles Nagy, Clev	17	5	.773

*1981 percentages based on 10 or more victories. Note: Percentages based on 15 or more victories in all other years.

Leading Pitchers—Earned-Run Average

Year	Player and Team	ERA	Year	Player and Team	ERA
1913	Walter Johnson, Wash	1.14	1948	Gene Bearden, Clev	2.43
1914	Dutch Leonard, Bos	1.01	1949	Mel Parnell, Bos	2.78
1915	Smoky Joe Wood, Bos	1.49	1950	Early Wynn, Clev	3.20
1916	Babe Ruth, Bos	1.75	1951	Saul Rogovin, Det-Chi	2.78
1917	Eddie Cicotte, Chi	1.53	1952	Allie Reynolds, NY	2.07
1918	Walter Johnson, Wash	1.27	1953	Ed Lopat, NY	2.43
1919	Walter Johnson, Wash	1.49	1954	Mike Garcia, Clev	2.64
1920	Bob Shawkey, NY	2.46	1955	Billy Pierce, Chi	1.97
1921	Red Faber, Chi	2.47	1956	Whitey Ford, NY	2.47
1922	Red Faber, Chi	2.80	1957	Bobby Shantz, NY	2.45
1923	Stan Coveleski, Clev	2.76	1958	Whitey Ford, NY	2.01
1924	Walter Johnson, Wash	2.72	1959	Hoyt Wilhelm, Balt	2.19
1925	Stan Coveleski, Wash	2.84	1960	Frank Baumann, Chi	2.68
1926	Lefty Grove, Phil	2.51	1961	Dick Donovan, Wash	2.40
1927	Wilcy Moore, NY#	2.28	1962	Hank Aguirre, Det	2.21
1928	Garland Braxton, Wash	2.52	1963	Gary Peters, Chi	2.33
1929	Lefty Grove, Phil	2.81	1964	Dean Chance, LA	1.65
1930	Lefty Grove, Phil	2.54	1965	Sam McDowell, Clev	2.18
1931	Lefty Grove, Phil	2.06	1966	Gary Peters, Chi	1.98
1932	Lefty Grove, Phil	2.84	1967	Joe Horlen, Chi	2.06
1933	Monte Pearson, Clev	2.33	1968	Luis Tiant, Clev	1.60
1934	Lefty Gomez, NY	2.33	1969	Dick Bosman, Wash	2.19
1935	Lefty Grove, Bos	2.70	1970	Diego Segui, Oak	2.56
1936	Lefty Grove, Bos	2.81	1971	Vida Blue, Oak	1.82
1937	Lefty Gomez, NY	2.33	1972	Luis Tiant, Bos	1.91
1938	Lefty Grove, Bos	3.07	1973	Jim Palmer, Balt	2.40
1939	Lefty Grove, Bos	2.54	1974	Catfish Hunter, Oak	2.49
1940	Bob Feller, Clev†	2.62	1975	Jim Palmer, Balt	2.09
1941	Thornton Lee, Chi	2.37	1976	Mark Fidrych, Det	2.34
1942	Ted Lyons, Chi	2.10	1977	Frank Tanana, Calif	2.54
1943	Spud Chandler, NY	1.64	1978	Ron Guidry, NY	1.74
1944	Dizzy Trout, Det	2.12	1979	Ron Guidry, NY	2.78
1945	Hal Newhouser, Det	1.81	1980	Rudy May, NY	2.47
1946	Hal Newhouser, Det	1.94	1981	Steve McCatty, Oak	2.32
1947	Spud Chandler, NY	2.46	1982	Rick Sutcliffe, Clev	2.96

Leading Pitchers—Earned-Run Average (Cont.)

Year	Player and Team	ERA	Year	Player and Team	ERA
1983	Rick Honeycutt, Tex	2.42	1990	Roger Clemens, Bos	1.93
1984	Mike Boddicker, Balt	2.79	1991	Roger Clemens, Bos	2.62
1985	Dave Stieb, Tor	2.48	1992	Roger Clemens, Bos	2.41
1986	Roger Clemens, Bos	2.48	1993	Kevin Appier, KC	2.56
1987	Jimmy Key, Tor	2.76	1994	Steve Ontiveros, Oak	2.65
1988	Allan Anderson, Minn	2.45	1995	Randy Johnson, Sea	2.48
1989	Bret Saberhagen, KC	2.16	1996	Juan Guzman, Tor	2.93

Note: Based on 10 complete games through 1950, then, 154 innings until the American League expanded in 1961, when it became 162 innings. In strike-shortened 1981, one inning per game required. Earned runs not tabulated in American League prior to 1913.

#Wilcy Moore pitched only six complete games——he started 12——in 1927, but was recognized as leader because of 213 innings pitched.

†Ernie Bonham, New York, had 1.91 ERA and 10 complete games in 1940, but appeared in only 12 games and 99 innings, and Bob Feller was recognized as leader.

Leading Pitchers—Strikeouts

Year	Player and Team	SO	Year	Player and Team	SO
1901	Cy Young, Bos	159	1949	Virgil Trucks, Det	153
1902	Rube Waddell, Phil	210	1950	Bob Lemon, Clev	170
1903	Rube Waddell, Phil	301	1951	Vic Raschi, NY	164
1904	Rube Waddell, Phil	349	1952	Allie Reynolds, NY	160
1905	Rube Waddell, Phil	286	1953	Billy Pierce, Chi	186
1906	Rube Waddell, Phil	203	1954	Bob Turley, Balt	185
1907	Rube Waddell, Phil	226	1955	Herb Score, Clev	245
1908	Ed Walsh, Chi	269	1956	Herb Score, Clev	263
1909	Frank Smith, Chi	177	1957	Early Wynn, Clev	184
1910	Walter Johnson, Wash	313	1958	Early Wynn, Chi	179
1911	Ed Walsh, Chi	255	1959	Jim Bunning, Det	201
1912	Walter Johnson, Wash	303	1960	Jim Bunning, Det	201
1913	Walter Johnson, Wash	243	1961	Camilo Pascual, Minn	221
1914	Walter Johnson, Wash	225	1962	Camilo Pascual, Minn	206
1915	Walter Johnson, Wash	203	1963	Camilo Pascual, Minn	202
1916	Walter Johnson, Wash	228	1964	Al Downing, NY	217
1917	Walter Johnson, Wash	188	1965	Sam McDowell, Clev	325
1918	Walter Johnson, Wash	162	1966	Sam McDowell, Clev	225
1919	Walter Johnson, Wash	147	1967	Jim Lonborg, Bos	246
1920	Stan Coveleski, Clev	133	1968	Sam McDowell, Clev	283
1921	Walter Johnson, Wash	143	1969	Sam McDowell, Clev	279
1922	Urban Shocker, StL	149	1970	Sam McDowell, Clev	304
1923	Walter Johnson, Wash	130	1971	Mickey Lolich, Det	308
1924	Walter Johnson, Wash	158	1972	Nolan Ryan, Calif	329
1925	Lefty Grove, Phil	116	1973	Nolan Ryan, Calif	383
1926	Lefty Grove, Phil	194	1974	Nolan Ryan, Calif	367
1927	Lefty Grove, Phil	174	1975	Frank Tanana, Calif	269
1928	Lefty Grove, Phil	183	1976	Nolan Ryan, Calif	327
1929	Lefty Grove, Phil	170	1977	Nolan Ryan, Calif	341
1930	Lefty Grove, Phil	209	1978	Nolan Ryan, Calif	260
1931	Lefty Grove, Phil	175	1979	Nolan Ryan, Calif	223
1932	Red Ruffing, NY	190	1980	Len Barker, Clev	187
1933	Lefty Gomez, NY	163	1981	Len Barker, Clev	127
1934	Lefty Gomez, NY	158	1982	Floyd Bannister, Sea	209
1935	Tommy Bridges, Det	163	1983	Jack Morris, Det	232
1936	Tommy Bridges, Det	175	1984	Mark Langston, Sea	204
1937	Lefty Gomez, NY	194	1985	Bert Blyleven, Clev-Minn	206
1938	Bob Feller, Clev	240	1986	Mark Langston, Sea	245
1939	Bob Feller, Clev	246	1987	Mark Langston, Sea	262
1940	Bob Feller, Clev	261	1988	Roger Clemens, Bos	291
1941	Bob Feller, Clev	260	1989	Nolan Ryan, Tex	301
1942	Bobo Newsom, Wash	113	1990	Nolan Ryan, Tex	232
	Tex Hughson, Bos	113	1991	Roger Clemens, Bos	241
1943	Allie Reynolds, Clev	151	1992	Randy Johnson, Sea	241
1944	Hal Newhouser, Det	187	1993	Randy Johnson, Sea	308
1945	Hal Newhouser, Det	212	1994	Randy Johnson, Sea	204
1946	Bob Feller, Clev	348	1995	Randy Johnson, Sea	294
1947	Bob Feller, Clev	196	1996	Roger Clemens, Bos	257
1948	Bob Feller, Clev	164			

Leading Pitchers—Saves

Year	Player and Team	SV	Year	Player and Team	SV
1947	Joe Page, NY	17	1972	Sparky Lyle, NY	35
1948	Russ Christopher, Clev	17	1973	John Hiller, Det	38
1949	Joe Page, NY	29	1974	Terry Forster, Chi	24
1950	Mickey Harris, Wash	15	1975	Goose Gossage, Chi	26
1951	Ellis Kinder, Bos	14	1976	Sparky Lyle, NY	23
1952	Harry Dorish, Chi	11	1977	Bill Campbell, Bos	31
1953	Ellis Kinder, Bos	27	1978	Goose Gossage, NY	27
1954	Johnny Sain, NY	22	1979	Mike Marshall, Minn	32
1955	Ray Narleski, Clev	19	1980	Dan Quisenberry, KC	33
1956	George Zuverink, Bal	16	1981	Goose Gossage, NY	33
1957	Bob Grim, NY	19	1982	Rollie Fingers, Mil	28
1958	Ryne Duren, NY	20	1983	Dan Quisenberry, KC	35
1959	Turk Lown, Chi	15	1984	Dan Quisenberry, KC	45
1960	Mike Fornieles, Bos	14	1985	Dan Quisenberry, KC	37
	Johnny Klippstein, Clev	14	1986	Dave Righetti, NY	46
1961	Luis Arroyo, NY	29	1987	Tom Henke, Tor	34
1962	Dick Radatz, Bos	24	1988	Dennis Eckersley, Oak	45
1963	Stu Miller, Bal	27	1989	Jeff Russell, Tex	38
1964	Dick Radatz, Bos	29	1990	Bobby Thigpen, Chi	57
1965	Ron Kline, Wash	29	1991	Bryan Harvey, Cal	46
1966	Jack Aker, KC	32	1992	Dennis Eckersley, Oak	51
1967	Minnie Rojas, Cal	27	1993	Jeff Montgomery, KC	45
1968	Al Worthington, Minn	18		Duane Ward, Tor	45
1969	Ron Perranoski, Minn	31	1994	Lee Smith, Bal	33
1970	Ron Perranoski, Minn	34	1995	Jose Mesa, Clev	46
1971	Ken Sanders, Mil	31	1996	John Wetteland, NY	43

The Commissioners of Baseball

Kenesaw Mountain Landis ....Elected November 12, 1920. Served until his death on November 25, 1944.
Happy Chandler ....Elected April 24, 1945. Served until July 15, 1951.
Ford Frick ....Elected September 20, 1951. Served until November 16, 1965.
William Eckert ....Elected November 17, 1965. Served until December 20, 1968.
Bowie Kuhn ....Elected February 8, 1969. Served until September 30, 1984.
Peter Ueberroth ....Elected March 3, 1984. Took office October 1, 1984. Served through March 31, 1989.
A. Bartlett Giamatti ....Elected September 8, 1988. Took office April 1, 1989. Served until his death on September 1, 1989.
Francis Vincent Jr ....Appointed Acting Commissioner September 2, 1989. Elected Commissioner September 13, 1989. Served through September 7, 1992.
Allan H. (Bud) Selig ....Elected chairman of the executive council and given the powers of interim commissioner on September 9, 1992.

THEY SAID IT

Roger McDowell, Baltimore
Orioles reliever, on his recent
shoulder surgery performed by
orthopedist Lewis Yocum: "He lubed
it, oiled it, filtered it. I opted for the
new-car scent instead of apple
cinnamon."

Pro Football

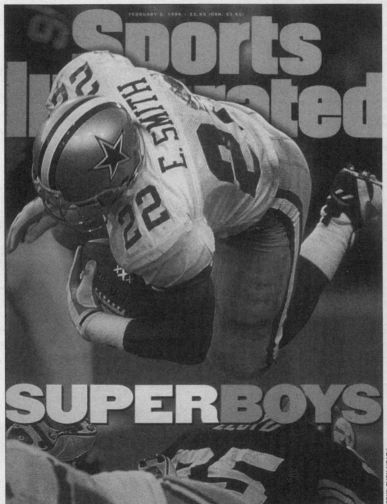

Passing Fancy

The Cowboys returned to the top, and offense was back in vogue as nearly every team sported a souped-up air attack

by Peter King

DID SOMEONE put helium in NFL footballs in 1995 or what?

Talk about the live-ball era. If Super Bowl XXX wasn't the high-scoring blowout that everyone predicted—Dallas beat Pittsburgh 27–17 for its third Super Bowl win in four years—the rest of the season certainly was. Let us count the ways the NFL exploded offensively in 1995:

• **Passing** Games averaged 441 passing yards, the most of all time. Four quarterbacks in the once ground-hugging NFC Central threw for more than 3,800 yards.

• **Receiving** In the 75 seasons prior to this one, eight players had years with 100 or more catches (two had done it twice). In 1995 alone nine players enjoyed 100-catch seasons—including the first running back to catch more than 100, Arizona fullback Larry Centers. Ram Isaac Bruce caught 119, and he didn't even make the Pro Bowl.

• **Points** In part due to the addition of 32 games involving the two expansion teams, the league scored 10,314 points, the first time the NFL has ever broken 10,000. Games averaged 43.0 points per game,

the most in a nonstrike season since 1985.

To understand this resurgence of offense, one must recognize that the NFL is a cyclical league. In back-to-back years a decade ago, the Super Bowl winners were the Bears, whose 46 defense was all the NFL rage, and the Giants, who played rock-solid defense and burn-the-clock offense. Chicago's Jim McMahon and New York's Phil Simms were very good NFL quarterbacks for those teams, but coaching philosophy and biting weather made them assist men, not big scorers, for their teams.

Today, with imaginative Bill Walsh disciples like Mike Shanahan in Denver and Mike Holmgren in Green Bay, and pass-happy offensive schemers such as Washington's Norv Turner and his like-thinking brother Ron in Chicago, the league's teams have turned decidedly toward the air. And no one's stopping them. Not with any consistency anyway.

In other words, as in baseball these days, the hitters are ahead of the pitchers. Way ahead.

How did this happen so quickly? Several reasons. First is that owners, for the most

Moore, who caught a record 123 passes, typified the new breed of NFL receiver.

part, have put offensive-minded coaches in power. Even the 49ers, who started this wave of superefficient offense, now find themselves looking to retool after being ousted in the 1995 playoffs by the new Green Bay machine, which was built by Bill Walsh–pupil Holmgren. The 49ers brought Walsh back to tutor their young offensive coordinator, Marc Trestman, and to work more closely with quarterbacks Steve Young and Elvis Grbac.

Another reason is that coaches are giving quarterbacks more responsibility than ever to beat defenses. The complexity and in-depth game planning that goes along with this responsibility is a double-edged sword, because many young players are not ready for it. In Washington, 1994 first-round pick Heath Shuler has struggled in his two NFL seasons, and he entered 1996 having to compete for his job against a former seventh-rounder, Gus Frerotte. Why? Largely because the Redskins' system has been

tough to learn. In college at Tennessee, Shuler had to learn about 200 pass plays in three years. In Game 16 of the 1995 NFL season alone, Washington's playbook had 144 pass plays, and quarterbacks coach Cam Cameron quizzed the quarterbacks on all of them two days before the game against Carolina. The quarterback who masters a system like this can set the heads of defensive backs spinning; but the one who struggles may find his own head swimming in X's and O's.

Reason No. 3 is simple: The receivers are monsters. When San Francisco sends 6'2" Jerry Rice and 6'4" J.J. Stokes into New Orleans' secondary these days, they'll have an average height advantage of half a foot over the three corners the Saints will throw at them: Eric Allen, Mark McMillian and 1996 rookie Alex Molden. Herman Moore and Cris Carter dueled for the NFL receptions record last year—Moore won, 123–122—using their 6'3" frames to catch passes with grace or upraised elbows, whichever the situation called for.

Last year Holmgren invited a *Sports Illus-*

Holmgren kept the Packer offense abuzz with fresh pass plays.

democracy there is in play-calling today:

"How do you like Double-Stutter Go?" Holmgren asks Favre.

"Love it," says Favre.

"Might be in the First 15," says Holmgren.

"O.K., flea-flicker."

"Second-and-one, first series," says Favre. "Come on, Mike! Let's go for the jugular."

trated writer and photographer to the Packers' camp for an unfiltered look at how a team gets ready for a game. The first thing an observer notices is the incredible offensive complexity. Holmgren stores all of the pass plays he has called in five years of Packer game-planning in a computer; there are more than 1,700 of these. "I want to have 10 new pass plays a week, every week," he said. "I just think that keeps it interesting for the guys. As long as you're not short-circuiting the quarterback, it keeps things fresh."

Indeed, NFL quarterbacks may be finding their circuits increasingly taxed. They have more power than they've ever had. Many signal-callers have carte blanche to audible at will on the field, and their input is often crucial to game plans. In Green Bay, for instance, Holmgren hosts a 90-minute Saturday morning meeting with three quarterbacks, offensive coordinator Sherm Lewis and two passing-game assistants. The level of input from Packer quarterback Brett Favre befits his status as the 1995 NFL Most Valuable Player. You can sense Holmgren's authority in the way he talks and in the way the other men defer to him. But you can also sense Favre's influence. Each Saturday before a game Holmgren meets with the group and begins to narrow down the list of his 15 favorite plays to use the next day. He calls it the First 15. The dialogue from these meetings often sounds like Russian, but it shows how much

For the record, the flea-flicker did not make it. But lots of plays Favre wanted did. Green Bay beat Minnesota 38–21 the next day, with Favre making a superb case for his impending MVP award: four touchdowns, no interceptions, 295 passing yards. It wasn't long ago (1993, to be exact) that Favre had a 24-interception season, and opposing coaches wondered if he would ever become patient and smart enough to efficiently run the West Coast offense that Holmgren took east from Walsh. But his last two seasons have been so collectively remarkable (71 touchdown passes, 27 interceptions) that Holmgren-Favre is shaping up as the best pairing since Walsh-Montana. Determined to keep the partnership on course, Favre sought treatment last spring for a dependency on painkillers brought about by years of playing hurt.

The 1995 season—and its controversial aftermath—will be remembered for five other major story lines. In order of importance:

1. Dallas ruled, but for how long? Instead of rejoicing in the moment, Dallas quarterback Troy Aikman looked beaten down when he went to an interview podium after the Cowboys' Super Bowl win over the Steelers in January 1996. "I've never been so happy for a season to end in my entire life," said Aikman. In piloting his third Super Bowl winner Aikman overcame his frosty relationship with coach Barry Switzer as well as charges from a former assistant

coach that he treated white players better than blacks. Indeed the Dallas celebration seemed more a sigh than a whoop-de-do. The one thing you couldn't take away from the Cowboys, though, was being the best team in a 30-team league despite everyone gunning for them and their Dallas maverick owner, Jerry Jones. The league sued Jones for $300 million in September 1995 for over-marketing the Cowboys in what it claimed were violations of the group-licensing agreements forged by NFL Properties. Jones responded with a $750 million countersuit. "We will prevail," he said.

It seemed like more people hated the Cowboys in 1995 than in their peak years of the '70s. "There is money, and there is class, and the two aren't synonymous," San Francisco president Carmen Policy said of Jerry Jones. Was it contempt, though, or envy? Jones and his former coach, Jimmy Johnson, constructed a marvelous team from 1989 to 1993, and club VP Stephen Jones, Jerry's

A third title brought relief rather than joy to the beleaguered Aikman.

son, did almost as good a job of keeping the team together by signing stars to slightly below-market contracts, allowing Dallas to fit more of them under the league's salary cap. The 1995 free-agent addition, cornerback Deion Sanders, promises to be a bigger factor in 1996 because he'll be a full-time two-way player. Dallas will most likely make him the third wideout to go along with his cornerback duties.

2. The Browns bolted to Baltimore. There are stunning stories, and then there is Art Modell sitting on an airport tarmac in Baltimore in October 1995, secretly signing a new lease to move the beloved Browns to Baltimore. "Like a thief in the night," Cleveland mayor Michael White said, "our NFL franchise has been snatched from the community [sic]." Modell claimed to be in such financial trouble that he had to guarantee personally a loan to sign free-agent wideout Andre Rison before the '95 season. He said he was $50 million in the red from operating the Browns and that moving to Baltimore was the only way he could ensure that the franchise would stay in the Modell family; the 70-year-old

BRAD MANGIN

Modell wants to leave the team to his son David. While Baltimore rejoiced, Cleveland wept. ART LIED! one sign screamed at the first Browns home game after the news broke, reminding Modell that he had said that he would never move the team. BENEDICT ART, another sign said.

Spinoffs of the Cleveland drama played out in several cities as franchise hopscotch reached a peak. The league stopped owner Ken Behring from moving the Seahawks from Seattle to Anaheim; Behring spent the spring of 1996 negotiating a deal to sell the team to computer magnate Paul Allen, a Washington native who would keep the team in Seattle. The Buccaneers, trumped on the Baltimore move by Modell, angled for a new stadium in Tampa. Houston

packed for Nashville, whose voters approved funding in May 1996 to build a state-of-the-art stadium to lure the Oilers in time for the 1998 season. The Bears quite likely would have moved to Gary, Ind., had not the voters there said no to funding a massive stadium. What all of this told a skeptical public is that no franchise—with the possible exception of the Giants, but who can tell these days?—is safe from plunderous owners and needy cities.

3. It's official: Dan Marino became the most prolific quarterback ever. In one memorable Dolphins season, Miami went 9–8, coach Don Shula stepped down, and Jimmy Johnson stepped into his job. And something else happened that history will long recall. Marino became the NFL's all-

Fairweather Johnson

In his Florida Keys home two days before Jimmy Johnson ended his self-imposed exile from coaching, the two-time Super Bowl–winning coach donned his reading glasses and looked over a player-and-salary-cap comparison between Tampa Bay and Miami, the two head coaching jobs that were his for the taking. Tampa had a huge advantage in draft choices (four in the top 45 of the 1996 draft, as opposed to Miami's one) and about $10 million more in salary-cap money to spend in 1996. "Miami's in tough shape, huh?" Johnson said.

He thought for a moment. "Tampa's young and hungry with a lot of picks and cap room. Miami's got some problems. But the one overriding thing is Dan Marino. For my sanity it'd be best to go to a place where the quarterback is a Hall of Famer, not a guy [Buc Trent Dilfer] I don't trust or have faith in."

Later that week the 52-year-old Johnson took the Dolphins job, succeeding the legendary Don Shula. Johnson was back in football after two years as a Fox TV analyst. "A decision of the heart, not of the mind," he said of bypassing Tampa for Miami. And by the team's first minicamp, in May, Johnson

pranced around the practice field, ranting and raving, even covering wide receiver O.J. McDuffie on one pass route. "Last year," said assistant coach Larry Seiple, a holdover from the Shula regime, "Coach Shula was hard on the players, but he was also a little laid-back. There just wasn't the same spark. Jimmy is a very hyper coach, active in all phases of the game. Enthusiasm, that's the biggest thing he brings."

Johnson left Fox for Miami, where he promised to restore past glory.

BILL FRAKES

Modell pondered the future in Baltimore, much to the chagrin of Browns fans.

time leader in touchdown passes, passing attempts, completions and yards. What makes Marino's accomplishments all the more remarkable is that of the 55 players who have caught at least one pass from him, it's likely that only one—Dan Marino—will make the Pro Football Hall of Fame. Number 4 on the alltime Marino receptions list is Jim Jensen, an unheralded former utility back for the Dolphins. "Joe Montana was a great player who won Super Bowls," said former Marino teammate Bryan Cox, now with Chicago. "But to say he was better than Dan Marino is an injustice. Look at Montana's supporting cast, all

Since Johnson left the Dallas Cowboys after winning his second straight Super Bowl in 1994, the football world spun on its axis a bit. The salary cap, which next year will allow each team to spend a maximum of $41 million in player salaries and prorated bonuses, would be new to Johnson, because the system took effect as he was leaving Dallas. You could almost feel the leaguewide smugness when Johnson took the job: Just wait until he has to build a team with the cap in mind, especially with such a cap-wrecked team as Miami. But Johnson didn't care. In fact, at the annual NFL meetings in March he told anyone who would listen that the Dolphins were the team to beat in the NFL in 1996.

"At Fox this year," he said, "most of the guys on the set would go back [to a lounge] to watch the games. I'd sit on the set, and they'd roll out a bank of TVs. I'd put sound from one game in one ear and sound from another game in the other, and I'd go from game to game, watching every one. So I think I have a better view of the league than I ever had when I was in Dallas. I know the players better, I know the trends better. So I think I'll be a better coach than I ever was before."

Two players were a couple of minutes late for Johnson's first Miami team meeting, and Johnson told the group that if anyone was ten seconds late for another meeting, don't bother walking through the door. That's the discipline Johnson—and many South Floridians—thought was lacking in the late Shula years. According to an agent for one Dolphin, several young players once left a team meeting last year to use their cellular phones and didn't return to the meeting. To be sure, beepers and cell phones will be checked at the door in this Dolphin era.

It says much about this sport, and about the region, that there wasn't much pining when Shula left the Dolphins. The place appreciated what he had done, but Miami hadn't won a Super Bowl in 22 years. Shula won big, but he hadn't won the big one since the Nixon administration. Johnson was a welcome bottom-line guy. "The history here is great, but if you know me, I don't give a crap about history. I care about now. Whoever can help us win a Super Bowl will be here. Because that's what we're going to do."

The man has done what he has predicted before. Why should now be any different?

built the best young offensive line in football, anchored by tackles Tony Boselli and Leon Searcy, and will be an offensive force if promising quarterback Mark Brunell reaches his potential.

5. The AFC just can't beat the NFC. In mid-1995 things looked good for the AFC, like the doormat of a conference would finally break its 11-game winless streak in the Super Bowl. The Chiefs had a seven-game winning streak. Oakland raced to an 8–2 record. The up-and-down Dolphins won the off-season free-agent sweepstakes and were terrific about every third week. Then in Oakland on Nov. 19, Dallas took a 24-point lead into the third quarter and whipped the Raiders 34–21. On Nov. 20 in Miami, the 49ers embarrassed the Dolphins 44–20. On Thanksgiving Day in Dallas, the Cowboys whipped the Chiefs 24–12. And, of course, the Cowboys went on to make it a dirty dozen losses for the AFC with their Super Bowl victory over Pittsburgh.

Why? Why does the NFC win 51% of its games against the AFC in the regular season over 12 years, but 100% of them in the biggest game of all? The AFC has turned the ball over inordinately, 40 times in the 12 losses, and the AFC has been outrushed by a 2-to-1 margin. "Rushing and turnovers are really the biggest keys to winning, I believe," Buffalo center Kent Hull said. "And the AFC has been inferior in both regards."

The AFC did have its moments. Indianapolis played valiantly and came within a failed Hail Mary pass of beating Pittsburgh to get to the Super Bowl. The Chiefs had the winningest season in the league. Pittsburgh scared Dallas. But after the most stunningly offensive season the NFL has seen in years, something very predictable happened: The best team won.

the Hall of Fame–type players. The guy had incredible teams around him."

4. The expansion teams were the best ever. Jacksonville and Carolina won 11 games between them, with a Week 16 loss to Washington preventing the Panthers from finishing at .500. Maybe the most amazing fact of 1995 was that Carolina coach Dom Capers built the league's seventh-best defense from scratch in one off-season. Capers and defensive coordinator Vic Fangio designed blitzes and unleashed them on any down where passing was even a remote option. "They know every blitz ever created out of the 3–4 defense, and they use them all," New Orleans guard Jim Dombrowski said after the Panthers stifled the Saints 20–3 in October. Jacksonville has

FOR THE RECORD·1995-1996

1995 NFL Final Standings

American Football Conference

EASTERN DIVISION

	W	L	T	Pct	Pts	OP
Buffalo	10	6	0	.625	350	335
†Indianapolis	9	7	0	.563	331	316
†Miami	9	7	0	.563	398	332
New England	6	10	0	.375	294	377
NY Jets	3	13	0	.188	233	384

CENTRAL DIVISION

	W	L	T	Pct	Pts	OP
Pittsburgh	11	5	0	.689	407	327
Cincinnati	7	9	0	.438	349	374
Houston	7	9	0	.438	348	324
Cleveland	5	11	0	.313	289	356
Jacksonville	4	12	0	.250	275	404

WESTERN DIVISION

	W	L	T	Pct	Pts	OP
Kansas City	13	3	0	.813	358	241
†San Diego	9	7	0	.563	321	323
Denver	8	8	0	.500	388	345
Seattle	8	8	0	.500	363	366
Oakland	8	8	0	.500	348	332

National Football Conference

EASTERN DIVISION

	W	L	T	Pct	Pts	OP
Dallas	12	4	0	.750	435	291
†Philadelphia	10	6	0	.615	318	338
Washington	6	10	0	.375	326	359
NY Giants	5	11	0	.313	290	340
Arizona	4	12	0	.250	275	422

CENTRAL DIVISION

	W	L	T	Pct	Pts	OP
Green Bay	11	5	0	.689	404	314
†Detroit	10	6	0	.625	436	336
Chicago	9	7	0	.563	392	360
Minnesota	8	8	0	.500	412	385
Tampa Bay	7	9	0	.438	238	335

WESTERN DIVISION

	W	L	T	Pct	Pts	OP
San Francisco	11	5	0	.688	457	258
†Atlanta	9	7	0	.563	362	349
St Louis	7	9	0	.438	309	418
Carolina	7	9	0	.438	289	325
New Orleans	7	9	0	.438	319	348

† Wild-card team.

1995-96 NFL Playoffs

AFC FIRST ROUND	AFC DIVISIONAL PLAYOFF	AFC CHAMPIONSHIP	NFC CHAMPIONSHIP	NFC DIVISIONAL PLAYOFF	NFC FIRST ROUND

SUPER BOWL XXX
January 28, 1996

Indianapolis 35 / San Diego 20

Indianapolis 10

Indianapolis 16

Kansas City 7

Miami 22 / Buffalo 37

Buffalo 21

Pittsburgh 20

Pittsburgh 40

DALLAS 27 / Pittsburgh 17

Philadelphia 11

Dallas 38

Dallas 30

Green Bay 27

Green Bay 27

San Francisco 17

Detroit 37 / Philadelphia 58

Atlanta 20 / Green Bay 37

NFL Playoff Box Scores

AFC Wild-card Games

Indianapolis	0	14	7	14—35
San Diego	3	7	7	3—20

FIRST QUARTER

San Diego: FG Carney 54, 5:32. Drive: 30 yards, 9 plays.

SECOND QUARTER

Indianapolis: Dilger 2 pass from Harbaugh (Blanchard kick), 0:57. Drive: 27 yards, 8 plays.
San Diego: Pupunu 6 pass from Humphries (Carney kick), 9:12. Drive: 68 yards, 18 plays.
Indianapolis: Crockett 33 run (Blanchard kick), 13:13. Drive: 80 yards, 8 plays.

THIRD QUARTER

San Diego: Jefferson 11 pass from Humphries (Carney kick), 10:40. Drive: 90 yards, 12 plays.
Indianapolis: Dawkins 42 pass from Harbaugh (Blanchard kick), 14:19. Drive: 81 yards, 7 plays.

FOURTH QUARTER

San Diego: FG Carney 30, 3:07. Drive: 55 yards, 8 plays.
Indianapolis: Crockett 66 run (Blanchard kick), 3:32. Drive: 66 yards, 1 play.
Indianapolis: Harbaugh 3 run (Blanchard kick), 8:05. Drive: 23 yards, 6 plays.
A: 61,182; T: 3:05.

Miami	0	0	0	22—22
Buffalo	10	14	3	10—37

FIRST QUARTER

Buffalo: Thomas 1 run (Christie kick), 5:02. Drive: 58 yards, 7 plays.
Buffalo: FG Christie 48, 7:58. Drive: 26 yards, 6 plays.

SECOND QUARTER

Buffalo: Holmes 21 run (Christie kick), 5:06. Drive: 68 yards, 4 plays.
Buffalo: Tasker 37 pass from Kelly (Christie kick), 7:39. Drive: 62 yards, 3 plays.

THIRD QUARTER

Buffalo: FG Christie 23, 13:57. Drive: 55 yards, 10 plays.

FOURTH QUARTER

Miami: McDuffie 5 pass from Marino (Stoyanovich kick), 1:07. Drive: 67 yards, 9 plays.
Buffalo: Tindale 44 run (Christie kick), 5:29. Drive: 61 yards, 3 plays.
Miami: Hill 45 pass from Marino (Stoyanovich kick), 6:59. Drive: 68 yards, 7 plays.
Buffalo: FG Christie 42, 10:24. Drive: 44 yards, 8 plays.
Miami: Kirby run (Marino pass to McDuffie for 2-point conversion), 12:51. Drive: 73 yards, 8 plays.
A: 73,103; T: 3:21.

NFC Wild-card Games

Detroit	7	0	14	16—37
Philadelphia	7	31	13	7—58

FIRST QUARTER

Philadelphia: Garner 15 run (Anderson kick), 9:53. Drive: 15 yards, 1 play.
Detroit: Sloan 32 pass from Mitchell (Hanson kick), 13:02. Drive: 77 yards, 7 plays.

SECOND QUARTER

Philadelphia: FG Anderson 21, 2:04. Drive: 57 yards, 8 plays.
Philadelphia: Barnett 22 pass from Peete (Anderson kick), 4:17. Drive: 39 yards, 3 plays.
Philadelphia: Wilburn 24 interception return (Anderson kick), 5:21.
Philadelphia: Watters 1 run (Anderson kick), 10:01. Drive: 31 yards, 8 plays.
Philadelphia: Carpenter 43 pass from Peete (Anderson kick), 15:00. Drive: 84 yards, 8 plays.

THIRD QUARTER

Philadelphia: Watters 45 pass from Peete (Anderson kick), 2:33. Drive: 50 yards, 3 plays.
Philadelphia: FG Anderson 31, 6:56. Drive: 39 yards, 6 plays.
Philadelphia: FG Anderson 39, 8:16. Drive: 1 yard, 4 plays.
Detroit: Moore 68 pass from Majkowski (Hanson kick), 9:16. Drive: 79 yards, 4 plays.
Detroit: Morton 7 pass from Majkowski (Hanson kick), 11:41. Drive: 30 yards, 5 plays.

FOURTH QUARTER

Philadelphia: Thomas 30 interception return (Anderson kick), 0:23.

FOURTH QUARTER (Cont.)

Detroit: Sloan 2 pass from Majkowski (Rivers run for 2-point conversion), 9:26. Drive: 69 yards, 7 plays.
Detroit: Rivers 1 run (Majkowski pass to Moore for 2-point conversion), 14:50. Drive: 75 yards, 10 plays.
A: 66,099; T: 3:23.

Atlanta	7	3	0	10—20
Green Bay	14	13	0	10—37

FIRST QUARTER

Atlanta: Metcalf 65 pass from George (Andersen kick), 2:59. Drive 64 yards, 2 plays.
Green Bay: Bennett 8 run (Jacke kick), 6:43. Drive: 48 yards, 8 plays.
Green Bay: Brooks 14 pass from Favre (Jacke kick), 11:35. Drive: 78 yards, 6 plays.

SECOND QUARTER

Atlanta: FG Andersen 31, 0:07. Drive: 60 yards, 7 plays.
Green Bay: Freeman 76 punt return (2-point conversion failed), 6:23.
Green Bay: Chmura 3 pass from Favre (Jacke kick), 14:11. Drive: 85 yards, 14 plays.

FOURTH QUARTER

Atlanta: Birden 27 pass from George (Andersen kick), 0:53. Drive: 80 yards, 11 plays.
Green Bay: Levens 17 pass from Favre (Jacke kick), 7:15. Drive: 70 yards, 12 plays.
Atlanta: FG Andersen 22, 10:54. Drive: 64 yards, 10 plays.
Green Bay: FG Jacke 25, 13:04. Drive: 26 yards, 6 plays.
A: 60,453; T: 3:15.

AFC Divisional Games

Indianapolis	0	7	3	0—10
Kansas City	7	0	0	0— 7

FIRST QUARTER

Kansas City: Dawson 20 pass from Bono (Elliott kick), 14:31. Drive: 62 yards, 5 plays.

SECOND QUARTER

Indianapolis: Turner 5 pass from Harbaugh (Blanchard kick), 8:11. Drive: 77 yards, 18 plays.

THIRD QUARTER

Indianapolis: FG Blanchard 30, 12:12. Drive: 35 yards, 9 plays.
A: 77,594; T: 3:08.

Buffalo	0	7	7	7—21
Pittsburgh	7	16	3	14—40

FIRST QUARTER

Pittsburgh: Williams 1 run (N. Johnson kick), 5:31. Drive: 76 yards, 9 plays.

SECOND QUARTER

Pittsburgh: Mills 10 pass from O'Donnell (N. Johnson kick), :42. Drive: 58 yards, 10 plays.
Pittsburgh: FG N. Johnson 45, 7:29. Drive: 16 yards, 5 plays.
Pittsburgh: FG N. Johnson 38, 10:38. Drive: -8 yards, 4 plays.
Buffalo: Thomas 1 run (Christie kick), 14:15. Drive: 49 yards, 4 plays.
Pittsburgh: FG N. Johnson 34, 14:35. Drive: 53 yards, 5 plays.

THIRD QUARTER

Pittsburgh: FG N. Johnson 34, 14:53. Drive: 53 yards, 5 plays.
Buffalo: Cline 2 pass from Van Pelt (Christie kick), 11:33. Drive: 42 yards, 4 plays.

FOURTH QUARTER

Buffalo: Thomas 9 pass from Kelly (Christie kick), 3:37. Drive: 36 yards, 6 plays.
Pittsburgh: Morris 13 run (N. Johnson kick), 8:44. Drive: 76 yards, 9 plays.
Pittsburgh: Morris 2 run (N. Johnson kick), 13:02. Drive: 23 yards, 4 plays.
A: 59,721; T: 3:19.

NFC Divisional Games

Philadelphia	0	3	0	8—11
Dallas	3	14	6	7—30

FIRST QUARTER

Dallas: FG Boniol 24, 8:47. Drive: 37 yards, 6 plays.

SECOND QUARTER

Philadelphia: FG Anderson 26, :03. Drive: 34 yards, 7 plays.
Dallas: Sanders 21 run (Boniol kick), 4:35. Drive: 70 yards, 7 plays.
Dallas: Smith 1 run (Boniol kick), 11:18. Drive: 79 yards, 6 plays.

THIRD QUARTER

Dallas: FG Boniol 18, 5:53. Drive: 59 yards, 10 plays.
Dallas: FG Boniol 51, 12:16. Drive: 25 yards, 9 plays.

FOURTH QUARTER

Dallas: Irvin 9 pass from Aikman (Boniol kick), 9:17. Drive: 21 yards, 3 plays.
Philadelphia: Cunningham 4 run (Cunningham pass to Johnson for 2-point conversion), 12:24. Drive: 65 yards, 9 plays.
A: 64,371; T: 2:59.

Green Bay	14	7	3	3—27
San Francisco	0	3	7	7—17

FIRST QUARTER

Green Bay: Newsome 31 fumble return (Jacke kick), 7:20.
Green Bay: Jackson 3 pass from Favre (Jacke kick), 10:47. Drive: 62 yards, 4 plays.

SECOND QUARTER

Green Bay: Chmura 13 pass from Favre (Jacke kick), 3:39. Drive: 72 yards, 7 plays.
San Francisco: FG Wilkins 21, 13:04. Drive: 76 yards, 12 plays.

THIRD QUARTER

San Francisco: Young 1 run (Wilkins kick), 7:14. Drive: 80 yards, 14 plays.
Green Bay: FG Jacke 27, 14:43. Drive: 49 yards, 7 plays.

FOURTH QUARTER

Green Bay: FG Jacke 26, 7:59. Drive: 31 yards, 10 plays.
San Francisco: Loville 2 run (Wilkins kick), 14:10. Drive: 47 yards, 11 plays.
A: 69,311; T: 3:16.

AFC Championship

Indianapolis............3	3	3	7—16
Pittsburgh..............3	7	3	7—20

FIRST QUARTER

Indianapolis: FG Blanchard 34, 2:43. Drive: 7 yards, 4 plays.
Pittsburgh: FG Johnson 31, 13:10. Drive: 40 yards, 11 plays.

SECOND QUARTER

Indianapolis: FG Blanchard 36, 2:52. Drive: 61 yards, 10 plays.
Pittsburgh: Stewart 5 pass from O'Donnell (Johnson kick), 14:47. Drive: 80 yards, 17 plays.

THIRD QUARTER

Indianapolis: FG Blanchard 37, 5:03. Drive: 51 yards, 10 plays.
Pittsburgh: FG Johnson 36, 14:17. Drive: 44 yards, 7 plays.

FOURTH QUARTER

Indianapolis: Turner 47 pass from Harbaugh (Blanchard kick), 6:14. Drive: 70 yards, 4 plays.
Pittsburgh: Morris 1 run (Johnson kick), 13:26. Drive: 67 yards, 8 plays.
A: 61,062; T: 2:59.

NFC Championship

Green Bay............10	7	10	0—27
Dallas...................14	10	0	14—38

FIRST QUARTER

Green Bay: FG Jacke 46, 1:10. Drive: -5 yards, 4 plays.
Dallas: Irvin 6 pass from Aikman (Boniol kick), 7:31. Drive: 80 yards, 11 plays.
Dallas: Irvin 4 pass from Aikman (Boniol kick), 12:40. Drive: 13 yards, 3 plays.
Green Bay: Brooks 73 pass from Favre (Jacke kick); 13:01. Drive: 73 yards, 1 play.

SECOND QUARTER

Green Bay: Jackson 24 pass from Favre (Jacke kick), 0:39. Drive: 35, yards, 3 plays.
Dallas: FG Boniol 34, 8:19. Drive: 60 yards, 13 plays.
Dallas: Smith 1 run (Boniol kick), 14:36. Drive: 99 yards, 11 plays.

THIRD QUARTER

Green Bay: FG Jacke 37, 3:31. Drive: 52 yards, 9 plays.
Green Bay: Brooks 1 pass from Favre (Jacke kick), 9:41. Drive: 79 yards, 8 plays.

FOURTH QUARTER

Dallas: Smith 5 run (Boniol kick), 2:36. Drive: 90 yards, 5 plays.
Dallas: Smith 16 run (Boniol kick), 5:32. Drive: 52 yards, 2 plays.
A: 65,135; T: 3:32.

Super Bowl Box Score

Dallas...................10	3	7	7—27
Pittsburgh..............0	7	0	10—17

FIRST QUARTER

Dallas: FG Boniol 42, 2:55. Drive: 47 yards, 7 plays. Key plays: Irvin 20 pass from Aikman to Dallas 49; E. Smith 23 run to Pitt 28. **Dallas 3–0.**
Dallas: Novacek 3 pass from Aikman (Boniol kick), 9:37. Drive: 75 yards, 8 plays. Key play: Sanders 47 pass from Aikman to Pitt 14. **Dallas 10–0.**

SECOND QUARTER

Dallas: FG Boniol 35, 8:57. Drive: 62 yards, 14 plays. Key play: Novacek 18 pass from Aikman to Pitt 16. **Dallas 13–0.**
Pittsburgh: Thigpen 6 pass from O'Donnell (N. Johnson kick), 14:47. Drive: 54 yards, 13 plays. Key plays: Hastings 19 pass from O'Donnell on 3rd-and-20 to Dallas 45; Stewart 3 run on 4th-and-1 to Dallas 42; Mills 17 pass from O'Donnell on 3rd-and-13 to Dallas 6. **Dallas 13–7.**

THIRD QUARTER

Dallas: E. Smith 1 run (Boniol kick), 8:18. Drive: 18 yards, 2 plays. Key play: L. Brown 44 int. return of O'Donnell pass to Pitt 18. **Dallas 20–7.**

FOURTH QUARTER

Pittsburgh: FG N. Johnson 46, 3:40. Drive: 52 yards, 11 plays. Key play: Mills 10 pass from O'Donnell, fumbled to Dallas 35, recovered by Bruener. **Dallas 20–10.**
Pittsburgh: Morris 1 run (N.Johnson kick), 8:24. Drive: 52 yards, 9 plays. Key plays: Figures onside kick rec. at Pitt 48; Hastings 11 pass from O'Donnell to Dallas 29. **Dallas 20–17.**
Dallas: E. Smith 4 run (Boniol kick), 11:17. Drive: 6 yards, 2 plays. Key play: L. Brown 33 int. return of O'Donnell pass to Pitt 6. **Dallas 27–17.**

A: 76,347; T: 3:24.

Super Bowl Box Score (Cont.)

Team Statistics

	Dallas	Pittsburgh
FIRST DOWNS	15	25
Rushing	5	9
Passing	10	15
Penalty	0	1
THIRD DOWN EFF	2-10	9-19
FOURTH DOWN EFF	1-1	2-4
TOTAL NET YARDS	254	310
Total plays	50	84
Avg gain	5.1	3.7
NET YARDS RUSHING	56	103
Rushes	25	31
Avg per rush	2.2	3.3
NET YARDS PASSING	198	207
Completed-Att.	15-23	28-49
Yards per pass	7.9	3.9
Sacked-yards lost	2-11	4-32
Had intercepted	0	3
PUNTS-Avg.	5 38.2	4-44.8
TOTAL RETURN YARDS	125	114
Punt returns	1-11	2-18
Kickoff returns	3-37	5-96
Interceptions	3-77	0-0
PENALTIES-Yds	5-25	2-15
FUMBLES-Lost	0-0	2-0
TIME OF POSSESSION	26:11	33:49

Passing

DALLAS

	Comp	Att	Yds	Int	TD
Aikman	15	23	209	0	1

PITTSBURGH

	Comp	Att	Yds	Int	TD
O'Donnell	28	49	239	3	1

Rushing

DALLAS

	No.	Yds	Lg	TD
E. Smith	18	49	23	2
Johnston	2	8	4	0
K. Williams	1	2	2	0
Aikman	4	-3	0	0

PITTSBURGH

	No.	Yds	Lg	TD
Morris	19	73	15	1
Pegram	6	15	4	0
Stewart	4	15	7	0
O'Donnell	1	0	0	0
J. Williams	1	0	0	0

Receiving

DALLAS

	No.	Yds	Lg	TD
Irvin	5	76	20	0
Novacek	5	50	19	1
K. Williams	2	29	22	0
Sanders	1	47	47	0
Johnston	1	4	4	0
E. Smith	1	3	3	0

PITTSBURGH

	No.	Yds	Lg	TD
Hastings	10	98	19	0
Mills	8	78	17	0
Thigpen	3	19	7	1
Morris	3	18	10	0
Holliday	2	19	10	0
J. Williams	2	7	5	0

Defense

DALLAS

	Tck	Ast	Int	Sack
Woodson	7	3	0	0
Jones	4	4	0	0
Case	6	1	0	0
Brown	5	2	2	0
Marion	5	2	1	0
Edwards	4	1	0	0
Tolbert	4	1	0	1
D. Smith	3	2	0	0
Carver	3	1	0	0
Haley	3	1	0	1
Bailey	4	0	0	0
Hennings	3	0	0	2
Maryland	3	0	0	0
Bates	3	1	0	0
Lett	2	1	0	0
Myles	1	0	0	0
Schwantz	2	1	0	0
Briggs	0	1	0	0
Hellestrae	1	0	0	0
Lang	1	0	0	0
C. Williams	1	0	0	0

PITTSBURGH

	Tck	Ast	Int	Sack
Kirkland	8	2	0	1
Lloyd	5	3	0	0
Lake	5	0	0	0
W. Williams	4	1	0	0
Perry	3	3	0	0
Steed	3	1	0	0
Bell	2	1	0	0
C. Brown	1	2	0	0
Greene	2	0	0	0
Olsavsky	1	1	0	0
Buckner	1	0	0	0
Seals	1	0	0	1
Flowers	2	0	0	0
Lester	0	1	0	0
McAfee	1	0	0	0
Strzelczyk	1	0	0	0
Thigpen	1	0	0	0
J. Williams	1	0	0	0

OFFENSE

Jerry Rice, San Francisco	Wide Receiver
Herman Moore, Detroit	Wide Receiver
Ben Coates, New England	Tight End
William Roaf, New Orleans	Tackle
Lomas Brown, Detroit	Tackle
Nate Newton, Dallas	Guard
Randall McDaniel, Minnesota	Guard
Dermontti Dawson, Pittsburgh	Center
Brett Favre, Green Bay	Quarterback
Emmitt Smith, Dallas	Running Back
Barry Sanders, Detroit	Running Back

DEFENSE

Reggie White, Green Bay	Defensive End
Bruce Smith, Buffalo	Defensive End
Chester McGlockton, Oakland	Defensive Tackle
John Randle, Minnesota	Nose Tackle
Bryce Paup, Buffalo	Outside Linebacker
Greg Lloyd, Pittsburgh	Outside Linebacker
Ken Norton, San Francisco	Inside Linebacker
Eric Davis, San Francisco	Cornerback
Aeneas Williams, Arizona	Cornerback
Merton Hanks, San Francisco	Safety
Darren Woodson, Dallas	Safety

SPECIALISTS

Morten Andersen, Atlanta	Kicker
Darren Bennett, San Diego	Punter
Brian Mitchell, Washington	Kick Returner

1995 AFC Team-by-Team Results

BUFFALO BILLS (10-6)			CINCINNATI BENGALS (7-9)			CLEVELAND BROWNS (5-11)		
7	at Denver	22	24	at Indianapolis	21	14	at New England	17
31	CAROLINA	9	24	JACKSONVILLE	17	22	TAMPA BAY	6
20	INDIANAPOLIS	14	21	at Seattle	24	14	at Houston	7
	OPEN DATE		28	HOUSTON	38	35	KANSAS CITY	17
22	at Cleveland	19	23	MIAMI	26	19	BUFFALO	22
29	NY JETS	10	16	at Tampa Bay	19	20	at Detroit	38
27	SEATTLE	21		OPEN DATE			OPEN DATE	
14	at New England	27	27	at Pittsburgh	9	15	JACKSONVILLE	23
6	at Miami	23	26	CLEVELAND	29	29	at Cincinatti	26
16	at Indianapolis	10	17	OAKLAND	20	10	HOUSTON	37
23	ATLANTA	17	32	at Houston	25	3	at Pittsburgh	20
28	at NY Jets	26	31	PITTSBURGH	49	20	GREEN BAY	31
25	NEW ENGLAND	35	17	at Jacksonville	13	17	PITTSBURGH	20
17	at San Francisco	27	10	at Green Bay	24	13	at San Diego	31
45	at St Louis	27	16	CHICAGO	10	11	at Minnesota	27
23	MIAMI	20	10	at Cleveland	26	26	CINCINNATI	10
17	HOUSTON	28	27	MINNESOTA	24	21	at Jacksonville	24
350		335	349		374	289		356

DENVER BRONCOS (8-8)

22	BUFFALO	7
21	at Dallas	31
38	WASHINGTON	31
6	at San Diego	17
10	at Seattle	27
37	at New England	3
27	OAKLAND	0
7	KANSAS CITY	21
	OPEN DATE	
38	ARIZONA	6
13	at Philadelphia	31
30	SAN DIEGO	27
33	at Houston	42
31	JACKSONVILLE	23
27	SEATTLE	31
17	at Kansas City	20
31	at Oakland	28
388		345

HOUSTON OILERS (7-9)

10	at Jacksonville	3
17	PITTSBURGH	34
7	CLEVELAND	14
38	at Cincinnati	28
16	JACKSONVILLE	17
17	at Minnesota	23
	OPEN DATE	
32	at Chicago	35
19	TAMPA BAY	7
37	at Cleveland	10
25	CINCINNATI	32
13	at Kansas City	20
42	DENVER	33
7	at Pittsburgh	21
17	DETROIT	24
23	NY JETS	6
28	at Buffalo	17
348		324

INDIANAPOLIS COLTS (9-7)

21	CINCINNATI	24
27	at NY Jets	24
14	at Buffalo	20
	OPEN DATE	
21	ST LOUIS	18
27	at Miami	24
18	SAN FRANCISCO	17
17	at Oakland	30
17	NY JETS	10
10	BUFFALO	16
14	at New Orleans	17
24	at New England	10
36	MIAMI	28
10	at Carolina	13
41	at Jacksonville	31
24	SAN DIEGO	27
10	NEW ENGLAND	7
331		316

JACKSONVILLE JAGUARS (4-12)

3	HOUSTON	10
17	at Cincinnati	24
10	at NY Jets	27
14	GREEN BAY	24
17	at Houston	16
20	PITTSBURGH	16
27	CHICAGO	30
23	at Cleveland	15
7	at Pittsburgh	24
	OPEN DATE	
30	SEATTLE	47
16	at Tampa Bay	17
13	CINCINNATI	17
23	at Denver	31
31	INDIANAPOLIS	41
0	at Detroit	44
24	CLEVELAND	21
275		404

KANSAS CITY CHIEFS (13-3)

34	at Seattle	10
20	NY GIANTS	17
23	OAKLAND	17
17	at Cleveland	35
24	at Arizona	3
29	SAN DIEGO	23
31	NEW ENGLAND	26
21	at Denver	7
	OPEN DATE	
24	WASHINGTON	3
22	at San Diego	7
20	HOUSTON	13
12	at Dallas	24
29	at Oakland	23
6	at Miami	13
20	DENVER	17
26	SEATTLE	3
358		241

MIAMI DOLPHINS (9-7)

52	NY JETS	14
20	at New England	3
23	PITTSBURGH	10
	OPEN DATE	
26	at Cincinnati	23
24	INDIANAPOLIS	27
30	at New Orleans	33
16	at NY Jets	17
23	BUFFALO	6
24	at San Diego	14
17	NEW ENGLAND	34
20	SAN FRANCISCO	44
28	at Indianapolis	36
21	ATLANTA	20
13	KANSAS CITY	6
20	at Buffalo	23
41	at St Louis	22
398		332

NEW ENGLAND PATRIOTS (6-10)

17	CLEVELAND	14
3	MIAMI	20
3	at San Francisco	28
	OPEN DATE	
17	at Atlanta	30
3	DENVER	37
26	at Kansas City	31
27	BUFFALO	14
17	CAROLINA	20
20	at NY Jets	7
34	at Miami	17
10	INDIANAPOLIS	24
35	at Buffalo	25
17	NEW ORLEANS	31
31	NY JETS	28
27	at Pittsburgh	41
7	at Indianapolis	10
294		377

NEW YORK JETS (3-13)

14	at Miami	52
24	INDIANAPOLIS	27
27	JACKSONVILLE	10
3	at Atlanta	13
10	OAKLAND	47
10	at Buffalo	29
15	at Carolina	26
10	MIAMI	16
10	at Indianapolis	17
7	NEW ENGLAND	20
	OPEN DATE	
26	BUFFALO	28
16	at Seattle	10
20	ST LOUIS	23
28	at New England	31
6	at Houston	23
0	NEW ORLEANS	12
233		384

OAKLAND RAIDERS (8-8)

17	SAN DIEGO	7
20	at Washington	8
17	at Kansas City	23
48	PHILADELPHIA	17
47	at NY Jets	10
34	SEATTLE	14
0	at Denver	27
30	INDIANAPOLIS	17
	OPEN DATE	
20	at Cincinnati	17
17	at NY Giants	13
21	DALLAS	34
6	at San Diego	12
23	KANSAS CITY	29
10	PITTSBURGH	29
10	at Seattle	44
28	DENVER	31
348		332

PITTSBURGH STEELERS (11-5)

23	DETROIT	20
34	at Houston	17
10	at Miami	23
24	MINNESOTA	44
31	SAN DIEGO	16
16	at Jacksonville	20
	OPEN DATE	
9	CINCINNATI	27
24	JACKSONVILLE	7
37	at Chicago	34
20	CLEVELAND	3
49	at Cincinnati	31
20	at Cleveland	17
21	HOUSTON	7
29	at Oakland	10
41	NEW ENGLAND	27
19	at Green Bay	24
407		**327**

SAN DIEGO CHARGERS (9-7)

7	at Oakland	17
14	SEATTLE	10
27	at Philadelphia	21
17	DENVER	6
16	at Pittsburgh	31
23	at Kansas City	29
9	DALLAS	23
35	at Seattle	25
	OPEN DATE	
14	MIAMI	24
7	KANSAS CITY	22
27	at Denver	30
12	OAKLAND	6
31	CLEVELAND	13
28	ARIZONA	25
27	at Indianapolis	24
27	at NY Giants	17
321		**323**

SEATTLE SEAHAWKS (8-8)

10	KANSAS CITY	34
10	at San Diego	14
24	CINCINNATI	21
	OPEN DATE	
27	DENVER	10
14	at Oakland	34
21	at Buffalo	27
25	SAN DIEGO	35
14	at Arizona	20
30	NY GIANTS	28
47	at Jacksonville	30
27	at Washington	20
10	NY JETS	16
26	PHILADELPHIA	14
31	at Denver	27
44	OAKLAND	10
3	at Kansas City	26
363		**366**

1995 NFC Team-by-Team Results

ARIZONA CARDINALS (4-12)

7	at Washington	27
19	PHILADELPHIA	31
20	at Detroit	17
20	at Dallas	34
3	KANSAS CITY	24
21	at NY Giants	27
24	WASHINGTON	20
	OPEN DATE	
20	SEATTLE	14
6	at Denver	38
24	MINNESOTA	30
7	at Carolina	27
40	ATLANTA	37
6	NY GIANTS	10
25	at San Diego	28
20	at Philadelphia	21
13	DALLAS	37
275		**422**

ATLANTA FALCONS (9-7)

23	CAROLINA	20
10	at San Francisco	41
27	at New Orleans	24
13	NY JETS	3
30	NEW ENGLAND	17
	OPEN DATE	
19	at St Louis	21
24	at Tampa Bay	21
13	DALLAS	28
34	DETROIT	22
17	at Buffalo	23
31	ST LOUIS	6
37	at Arizona	40
20	at Miami	21
19	NEW ORLEANS	14
17	at Carolina	21
28	SAN FRANCISCO	27
362		**349**

CAROLINA PANTHERS (7-9)

20	at Atlanta	23
9	at Buffalo	31
10	ST LOUIS	31
	OPEN DATE	
13	TAMPA BAY	20
27	at Chicago	31
26	NY JETS	15
20	NEW ORLEANS	3
20	at New England	17
13	at San Francisco	7
17	at St Louis	28
27	ARIZONA	7
26	at New Orleans	34
13	INDIANAPOLIS	10
10	SAN FRANCISCO	31
21	ATLANTA	17
17	at Washington	20
289		**325**

CHICAGO BEARS (9-7)

31	MINNESOTA	14
24	GREEN BAY	27
25	at Tampa Bay	6
28	at St Louis	34
	OPEN DATE	
31	CAROLINA	27
30	at Jacksonville	27
35	HOUSTON	32
14	at Minnesota	6
34	PITTSBURGH	37
28	at Green Bay	35
17	DETROIT	24
27	at NY Giants	24
7	at Detroit	27
10	at Cincinnati	16
31	TAMPA BAY	10
20	PHILADELPHIA	14
392		**360**

DALLAS COWBOYS (12-4)

35	at NY Giants	0
31	DENVER	21
23	at Minnesota	17
34	ARIZONA	20
23	at Washington	27
34	GREEN BAY	24
23	at San Diego	9
	OPEN DATE	
28	at Atlanta	13
34	PHILADELPHIA	12
20	SAN FRANCISCO	38
34	at Oakland	21
24	KANSAS CITY	12
17	WASHINGTON	24
17	at Philadelphia	20
21	NY GIANTS	20
37	at Arizona	13
435		**291**

DETROIT LIONS (10-6)

20	at Pittsburgh	23
10	at Minnesota	20
17	ARIZONA	20
27	SAN FRANCISCO	24
	OPEN DATE	
38	CLEVELAND	20
21	at Green Bay	30
30	WASHINGTON	36
24	GREEN BAY	16
22	at Atlanta	34
27	TAMPA BAY	24
24	at Chicago	17
44	MINNESOTA	38
27	CHICAGO	7
24	at Houston	17
44	JACKSONVILLE	0
37	at Tampa Bay	10
436		**336**

GREEN BAY PACKERS (11-5)

14	ST LOUIS	17
27	at Chicago	24
14	NY GIANTS	6
24	at Jacksonville	14
	OPEN DATE	
24	at Dallas	34
30	DETROIT	21
38	MINNESOTA	21
16	at Detroit	24
24	at Minnesota	27
35	CHICAGO	28
31	at Cleveland	20
35	TAMPA BAY	13
24	CINCINNATI	10
10	at Tampa Bay	13
34	at New Orleans	23
24	PITTSBURGH	19
404		314

MINNESOTA VIKINGS (8-8)

14	at Chicago	31
20	DETROIT	10
17	DALLAS	23
44	at Pittsburgh	24
	OPEN DATE	
23	HOUSTON	17
17	at Tampa Bay	20
21	at Green Bay	38
6	CHICAGO	14
27	Green Bay	24
30	at Arizona	24
43	NEW ORLEANS	24
38	at Detroit	44
31	TAMPA BAY	17
27	CLEVELAND	11
30	at San Francisco	37
24	at Cincinnati	27
412		385

NEW ORLEANS SAINTS (7-9)

22	SAN FRANCISCO	24
13	at St Louis	17
24	ATLANTA	27
29	at NY Giants	45
10	PHILADELPHIA	15
	OPEN DATE	
33	MIAMI	30
3	at Carolina	20
11	at San Francisco	7
19	ST LOUIS	10
17	INDIANAPOLIS	14
24	at Minnesota	43
34	CAROLINA	26
31	at New England	17
14	at Atlanta	19
23	GREEN BAY	34
12	at NY Jets	0
319		348

NEW YORK GIANTS (5-11)

0	DALLAS	35
17	at Kansas City	20
6	at Green Bay	14
45	NEW ORLEANS	29
6	at San Francisco	20
27	ARIZONA	21
14	PHILADELPHIA	17
	OPEN DATE	
24	at Washington	15
28	at Seattle	30
13	OAKLAND	17
19	at Philadelphia	28
24	CHICAGO	27
10	at Arizona	6
20	WASHINGTON	13
20	at Dallas	21
17	SAN DIEGO	27
290		340

PHILADELPHIA EAGLES (10-6)

6	TAMPA BAY	21
31	at Arizona	19
21	SAN DIEGO	27
17	at Oakland	48
15	at New Orleans	10
37	WASHINGTON	34
17	at NY Giants	14
	OPEN DATE	
20	ST LOUIS	9
12	at Dallas	34
31	DENVER	13
28	NY GIANTS	19
14	at Washington	7
14	at Seattle	26
20	DALLAS	17
21	ARIZONA	20
14	at Chicago	20
318		338

ST LOUIS RAMS (7-9)

17	at Green Bay	14
17	NEW ORLEANS	13
31	at Carolina	10
34	CHICAGO	28
18	at Indianapolis	21
	OPEN DATE	
21	ATLANTA	19
10	SAN FRANCISCO	44
9	at Philadelphia	20
10	at New Orleans	19
28	CAROLINA	17
6	at Atlanta	31
13	at San Francisco	41
23	at NY Jets	20
27	BUFFALO	45
23	WASHINGTON	35
22	MIAMI	41
309		418

SAN FRANCISCO 49ERS (11-5)

24	at New Orleans	22
41	ATLANTA	10
28	NEW ENGLAND	3
24	at Detroit	27
20	NY GIANTS	6
	OPEN DATE	
17	at Indianapolis	18
44	at St Louis	10
7	NEW ORLEANS	11
7	CAROLINA	13
38	at Dallas	20
44	at Miami	20
41	ST LOUIS	13
27	BUFFALO	17
31	at Carolina	10
37	MINNESOTA	30
27	at Atlanta	28
457		258

TAMPA BAY BUCCANEERS (7-9)

21	at Philadelphia	6
6	at Cleveland	22
6	CHICAGO	25
14	WASHINGTON	6
20	at Carolina	13
19	CINCINNATI	16
20	MINNESOTA	17
21	ATLANTA	24
7	at Houston	19
	OPEN DATE	
24	at Detroit	27
17	JACKSONVILLE	16
13	at Green Bay	35
17	at Minnesota	31
13	GREEN BAY	10
10	at Chicago	31
10	DETROIT	37
238		335

WASHINGTON REDSKINS (6-10)

27	ARIZONA	7
8	OAKLAND	20
31	at Denver	38
6	at Tampa Bay	14
27	DALLAS	23
34	at Philadelphia	37
20	at Arizona	24
36	DETROIT	30
15	NY GIANTS	24
3	at Kansas City	24
	OPEN DATE	
20	SEATTLE	27
14	PHILADELPHIA	14
24	at Dallas	17
13	at NY Giants	20
35	at St Louis	23
20	CAROLINA	17
326		359

American Football Conference

Scoring

TOUCHDOWNS	TD	Rush	Rec	Ret	Pts	KICKING	PAT	FG	Lg	Pts
Pickens, Cin	17	0	17	0	102	N. Johnson, Pitt	39/39	34/41	50	141
Warren, Sea	16	15	1	0	96	Elam, Den	39/39	31/38	56	132
Martin, NE	15	14	1	0	92	Christie, Buff	33/35	31/40	51	126
Faulk, Ind	14	11	3	0	84	Pelfrey, Cin	34/34	29/36	51	121
Miller, Den	14	0	14	0	84	Stoyanovich, Mia	37/37	27/34	51	118
Brooks, Buff	11	0	11	0	66	Del Greco, Hou	33/33	27/31	53	114
Brown, Oak	10	0	10	0	60	Stover, Cle	26/26	29/33	47	113
Parmalee, Mia	10	9	1	0	60	Peterson, Sea	40/40	23/28	49	109
Galloway, Sea	9	1	7	1	54	Elliott, KC	34/37	24/30	49	106
Jackson, Cle	9	0	9	0	54	Bahr, NE	27/27	23/33	55	96
Morris, Pitt	9	9	0	0	54					
Sanders, Hou	9	0	9	0	54					
Williams, Oak	9	9	0	0	54					

Passing

	Att	Comp	Pct Comp	Yds	Avg Gain	TD	Pct TD	Int	Pct Int	Lg	Rating Pts
Harbaugh, Ind	314	200	63.7	2575	8.20	17	5.4	5	1.6	52	100.7
Marino, Mia	482	309	64.1	3668	7.61	24	5.0	15	3.1	t67	90.8
Testaverde, Cle	392	241	61.5	2883	7.35	17	4.3	10	2.6	t70	87.8
Chandler, Hou	356	225	63.2	2460	6.91	17	4.8	10	2.8	t76	87.8
O'Donnell, Pitt	416	246	59.1	2970	7.14	17	4.1	7	1.7	t71	87.7
Elway, Den	542	316	58.3	3970	7.32	26	4.8	14	2.6	t62	86.4
Brunell, Jax	346	201	58.1	2168	6.27	15	4.3	7	2.0	45	82.6
Hostetler, Oak	286	172	60.1	1998	6.99	12	4.2	9	3.1	t80	82.2
Blake, Cin	567	326	57.5	3822	6.74	28	4.9	17	3.0	t88	82.1
Kelly, Buff	458	255	55.7	3130	6.83	22	4.8	13	2.8	t77	81.1

Pass Receiving

RECEPTIONS	No.	Yds	Avg	Lg	TD	YARDS	Yds	No.	Avg	Lg	TD
Pickens, Cin	99	1234	12.5	t68	17	Brown, Oak	1342	89	15.1	t80	10
Martin, SD	90	1224	13.6	t51	6	Thigpen, Pitt	1307	85	15.4	43	5
Brown, Oak	89	1342	15.1	t80	10	Pickens, Cin	1234	99	12.5	t68	17
Thigpen, Pitt	85	1307	15.4	43	5	Martin, SD	1224	90	13.6	t51	6
Coates, NE	84	915	10.9	35	6	Miller, Den	1079	59	18.3	t62	14
Blades, Sea	77	1001	13.0	49	4	Galloway, Sea	1039	67	15.5	t59	7
Murrell, NYJ	71	465	6.5	43	2	Blades, Sea	1001	77	13.0	49	4
Galloway, Sea	67	1039	15.5	t59	7	Brisby, NE	974	66	14.8	72	3
Brisby, NE	66	974	14.8	72	3	Coates, NE	915	84	10.9	35	6
Chrebet, NYJ	66	726	11.0	32	4	Fryar, Mia	910	62	14.7	t67	8
Kirby, Mia	66	618	9.4	46	3						

Rushing

	Att	Yds	Avg	Lg	TD
Martin, NE	368	1487	4.0	49	14
Warren, Sea	310	1346	4.3	52	15
Davis, Den	237	1117	4.7	t60	7
Williams, Oak	255	1114	4.4	60	9
Faulk, Ind	289	1078	3.7	40	11
T. Thomas, Buff	267	1005	3.8	49	6
R. Thomas, Hou	251	947	3.8	t74	5
Allen, KC	207	890	4.3	38	5
Parmalee, Mia	236	878	3.7	40	9
Pegram, Pitt	213	813	3.8	38	5

Total Yards from Scrimmage

	Total	Rush	Rec
Martin, NE	1748	1487	261
Warren, Sea	1593	1346	247
Faulk, Ind	1553	1078	475
Williams, Oak	1489	1114	375
Davis, Den	1484	1117	367
Brown, Oak	1342	0	1342
Thigpen, Pitt	1308	1	1307
Murrell, NYJ	1260	795	465
Pickens, Cin	1240	6	1234
T. Thomas, Buff	1225	1005	220

Interceptions

	No.	Yds	Lg	TD
W. Williams, Pitt	7	122	t63	1
D. Lewis, Hou	6	145	t98	1
Smith, NYJ	6	101	t49	1
Schulz, Buff	6	48	t32	1
McDaniel, Oak	6	46	t42	1
Four tied with 5.				

Sacks

Paup, Buff	17.5
Swilling, Oak	13.0
O'Neal, SD	12.5
N. Smith, KC	12.0
McGinest, NE	11.0

American Football Conference *(Cont.)*

Punting

	No.	Yds	Avg	Net Avg	TB	In 20	Lg	Blk	Ret	Ret Yds
Tuten, Sea	83	3735	45.0	36.5	8	21	73	0	48	549
Bennett, SD	72	3221	44.7	36.6	8	28	66	0	35	429
Aguiar, KC	91	3990	43.8	36.5	12	29	65	0	42	433
Barker, Jax	82	3591	43.8	39.6	5	19	63	0	45	323
Tupa, Cle	65	2831	43.6	36.2	9	18	64	0	34	296

Punt Returns

	No.	Yds	Avg	Lg	TD
Coleman, SD	28	326	11.6	t88	1
Burris, Buff	20	229	11.5	40	0
Milburn, Den	31	354	11.4	44	0
Vanover, KC	51	540	10.6	t86	1
Howard, Jax	24	246	10.3	40	0

Kickoff Returns

	No.	Yds	Avg	Lg	TD
Milburn, Den	47	1269	27.0	86	0
Carpenter, NYJ	21	553	26.3	58	0
Kaufman, Oak	22	572	26.0	t84	1
Vanover, KC	43	1095	25.5	t99	2
Meggett, NE	38	964	25.4	62	0

National Football Conference

Scoring

TOUCHDOWNS	TD	Rush	Rec	Ret	Pts
E. Smith, Dall	25	25	0	0	150
Rice, SF	17	1	15	1	104
Carter, Minn	17	0	17	0	102
Moore, Det	14	0	14	0	84
Bruce, StL	13	0	13	0	80
Loville, SF	13	10	3	0	80
R. Brooks, GB	13	0	13	0	78
Conway, Chi	12	0	12	0	72
Sanders, Det	12	11	1	0	72
Watters, Phi	12	11	1	0	72

KICKING	PAT	FG	Lg	Pts
Hanson, Det	48/48	28/34	56	132
Boniol, Dall	46/48	27/28	45	127
Andersen, Atl	29/30	31/37	59	122
Reveiz, Minn	44/44	26/36	51	122
Butler, Chi	45/45	23/31	47	114
Murray, Wash	33/33	27/36	52	114
G. Davis, Ariz	19/19	30/39	55	109
Kasay, Car	27/28	26/33	52	105
Anderson, Phi	32/33	22/30	43	98
Jacke, GB	43/43	17/23	51	94

Passing

	Att	Comp	Pct Comp	Yds	Avg Gain	TD	Pct TD	Int	Pct Int	Lg	Rating Pts
Favre, GB	570	359	63.0	4413	7.74	38	6.7	13	2.3	t99	99.5
Aikman, Dall	432	280	64.8	3304	7.65	16	3.7	7	1.6	50	93.6
Kramer, Chi	522	315	60.3	3838	7.35	29	5.6	10	1.9	t76	93.5
S. Young, SF	447	299	66.9	3200	7.16	20	4.5	11	2.5	57	92.3
Mitchell, Det	583	346	59.3	4338	7.44	32	5.5	12	2.1	t91	92.3
Moon, Minn	606	377	62.2	4228	6.98	33	5.4	14	2.3	t85	91.5
J. George, Atl	557	336	60.3	4143	7.44	24	4.3	11	2.0	t62	89.5
Everett, NO	567	345	60.8	3970	7.00	26	4.6	14	2.5	t70	87.0
Miller, StL	405	232	57.3	2623	6.48	18	4.4	15	3.7	72	76.2
Brown, NYG	456	254	55.7	2814	6.17	11	2.4	10	2.2	t57	73.1

Pass Receiving

RECEPTIONS	No.	Yds	Avg	Lg	TD
Moore, Det	123	1686	13.7	t69	14
Rice, SF	122	1848	15.1	t81	15
Carter, Minn	122	1371	11.2	t60	17
Bruce, StL	119	1781	15.0	72	13
Irvin, Dall	111	1603	14.4	50	10
Perriman, Det	108	1488	13.8	t91	9
Metcalf, Atl	104	1189	11.4	t62	8
R. Brooks, GB	102	1497	14.7	t99	13
Centers, Ariz	101	962	9.5	32	2
Loville, SF	87	662	7.6	31	3

YARDS	Yds	No.	Avg	Lg	TD
Rice, SF	1848	122	15.1	t81	15
Bruce, StL	1781	119	15.0	72	13
Moore, Det	1686	123	13.7	t69	14
Irvin, Dall	1603	111	14.4	50	10
R. Brooks, GB	1497	102	14.7	t99	13
Perriman, Det	1488	108	13.8	t91	9
Carter, Minn	1371	122	11.2	t60	17
Graham, Chi	1301	82	15.9	51	4
Metcalf, Atl	1189	104	11.4	t62	8
Reed, Minn	1167	72	16.2	t55	9

National Football Conference (Cont.)

Rushing

	Att	Yds	Avg	Lg	TD
E. Smith, Dall	377	1773	4.7	t60	25
Sanders, Det	314	1500	4.8	t75	11
Allen, Wash	338	1309	3.9	28	10
Watters, Phi	337	1293	3.8	57	11
Rhett, TB	332	1207	3.6	21	11
Hampton, NYG	306	1182	3.9	32	10
Heyward, Atl	236	1083	4.6	31	6
Salaam, Chi	296	1074	3.6	42	10
Hearst, Ariz	284	1070	3.8	38	1
Bennett, GB	316	1067	3.4	23	3

Total Yards from Scrimmage

	Total	Rush	Rec
E. Smith, Dall	2148	1773	375
Sanders, Det	1898	1500	398
Rice, SF	1884	36	1848
Bruce, StL	1798	17	1781
Bennett, GB	1715	1067	648
Watters, Phi	1707	1273	434
Moore, Det	1686	0	1686
Irvin, Dall	1603	0	1603
Allen, Wash	1541	1309	232
Perriman, Det	1536	48	1488

Interceptions

	No.	Yds	Lg	TD
O. Thomas, Minn	9	108	t45	1
Clay, Det	8	173	39	0
Thomas, Phi	7	104	t37	1
Six tied with 6.				

Sacks

Fuller, Phi	13.0
Martin, NO	13.0
Re. White, GB	12.0
Farr, StL	11.5
Flanigan, Chi	11.0
Harmon, Phi	11.0
Simmons, Ariz	11.0

Punting

	No.	Yds	Avg	Net Avg	TB	In 20	Lg	Blk	Ret	Ret Yds
Landeta, StL	83	3679	44.3	36.7	12	23	63	0	38	393
Feagles, Ariz	72	3150	43.8	38.2	8	20	60	0	32	242
Hutton, Phi	85	3682	43.3	33.7	13	20	63	1	38	527
Roby, TB	77	3296	42.8	36.2	7	23	61	1	41	335
Horan, NYG	72	3063	42.5	36.2	8	15	60	0	34	297

Punt Returns

	No.	Yds	Avg	Lg	TD
Palmer, Minn	26	342	13.2	t74	1
Mitchell, Wash	25	315	12.6	t59	1
Guliford, Car	43	475	11.0	t62	1
Carter, SF	30	309	10.3	t78	1
Jordan, GB	21	213	10.1	18	0
Edmonds, TB	29	293	10.1	45	0

Kickoff Returns

	No.	Yds	Avg	Lg	TD
Mitchell, Wash	55	1408	25.6	59	0
Ismail, Minn	42	1037	24.7	71	0
Hughes, NO	66	1617	24.5	83	0
Thomas, StL	32	752	23.5	46	0
Freeman, GB	24	556	23.2	45	0

1995 NFL Team Leaders

AFC Total Offense

	Total Yds	Yds Rush	Yds Pass	Time of Poss	Avg Pts/Game
Denver	6040	1995	4045	30:09	24.2
Pittsburgh	5769	1852	3917	32:36	25.4
Miami	5716	1506	4210	31:22	24.9
Oakland	5505	1932	3573	30:42	21.7
New England	5457	1866	3591	29:33	18.4
Seattle	5270	2178	3092	28:30	22.7
Kansas City	5242	2222	3020	31:08	22.4
San Diego	5213	1747	3466	29:34	20.1
Cincinnati	5192	1439	3753	26:57	21.8
Buffalo	5117	1993	3124	28:12	21.9
Cleveland	5076	1482	3594	28:25	18.1
Indianapolis	4919	1855	3064	31:37	20.7
Houston	4905	1664	3241	32:12	21.7
Jacksonville	4495	1705	2790	28:37	17.2
NY Jets	4067	1279	2788	29:14	14.6

AFC Total Defense

	Opp Total Yds	Opp Yds Rush	Opp Yds Pass	Avg PA/Game
Kansas City	4549	1327	3222	15.1
Pittsburgh	4561	1321	3240	20.4
Houston	4651	1526	3125	20.2
NY Jets	4756	2016	2740	24.0
Indianapolis	5027	1457	3570	19.7
San Diego	5074	1691	3383	20.2
Oakland	5104	1794	3310	20.7
Buffalo	5128	1626	3502	20.9
Denver	5193	1895	3298	21.6
Miami	5244	1675	3569	20.7
Jacksonville	5515	2003	3512	25.2
Cleveland	5648	1826	3822	22.2
Seattle	5669	2130	3539	22.9
New England	5764	1878	3886	23.6
Cincinnati	6349	2104	4245	23.4

NFC Total Offense

	Total Yds	Yds Rush	Yds Pass	Time of Poss	Avg Pts/Game
Detroit	6113	1753	4360	28:43	27.2
San Francisco	6087	1479	4608	31:55	28.6
Minnesota	5938	1733	4205	31:50	25.7
Dallas	5824	2201	3623	31:15	27.2
Green Bay	5750	1428	4322	31:12	25.2
Chicago	5673	1930	3743	29:55	24.5
Atlanta	5579	1393	4186	29:27	22.6
St Louis	5236	1431	3805	31:10	19.3
Washington	5184	1956	3228	28:42	20.4
New Orleans	5178	1390	3788	28:15	19.9
Arizona	4866	1363	3503	30:54	17.2
Philadelphia	4807	2121	2686	30:26	19.9
Carolina	4619	1573	3046	29:27	18.1
Tampa Bay	4542	1587	2955	28:35	14.9
NY Giants	4483	1833	2650	29:23	18.1

NFC Total Defense

	Opp Total Yds	Opp Yds Rush	Opp Yds Pass	Avg PA/Game
San Francisco	4398	1061	3337	16.1
Philadelphia	4638	1822	2816	21.1
Carolina	5027	1576	3451	20.3
Dallas	5044	1772	3272	18.2
St Louis	5118	1677	3441	26.1
Green Bay	5155	1515	3640	19.6
NY Giants	5293	2109	3184	21.2
Washington	5400	2132	3268	22.4
Chicago	5442	1441	4001	22.5
Minnesota	5451	1329	4122	24.1
New Orleans	5561	1838	3723	21.7
Detroit	5599	1795	3804	21.0
Arizona	5704	2249	3455	26.4
Tampa Bay	5712	1754	3958	20.9
Atlanta	6088	1547	4541	21.8

Takeaways/Giveaways

AFC

	Takeaways Int	Fum	Total	Giveaways Int	Fum	Total	Net Diff
Kansas City	16	17	33	10	11	21	12
Indianapolis	13	13	26	11	11	22	4
Buffalo	17	11	28	14	12	26	2
Pittsburgh	22	12	34	21	13	34	0
Houston	21	17	38	18	20	38	0
Oakland	11	22	33	21	13	34	-1
Miami	14	16	30	20	12	32	-2
San Diego	17	10	27	18	12	30	-3
Jacksonville	13	11	24	15	13	28	-4
New England	15	14	29	16	20	36	-7
Seattle	16	9	25	23	9	32	-7
Cleveland	17	7	24	20	11	31	-7
Cincinnati	12	12	24	18	14	32	-8
NY Jets	17	17	34	24	18	42	-8
Denver	8	13	21	14	16	30	-9

NFC

	Takeaways Int	Fum	Total	Giveaways Int	Fum	Total	Net Diff
Minnesota	25	15	40	16	13	29	11
Detroit	22	13	35	12	13	25	10
Atlanta	18	12	30	12	9	21	9
San Francisco	26	8	34	16	12	28	6
Washington	16	19	35	20	10	30	5
New Orleans	17	12	29	14	11	25	4
NY Giants	16	15	31	13	15	28	3
Chicago	16	13	29	10	16	26	3
Dallas	19	6	25	10	13	23	2
Philadelphia	19	19	38	19	17	36	2
Arizona	19	23	42	24	19	43	-1
St Louis	22	14	36	23	16	39	-3
Tampa Bay	14	16	30	20	14	34	-4
Carolina	21	16	37	25	16	41	-4
Green Bay	13	3	16	15	6	21	-5

Conference Rankings

American Football Conference

	Offense Total	Rush	Pass	Defense Total	Rush	Pass
Buffalo	10	4	10	8	5	8
Cincinnati	9	14	4	15	14	15
Cleveland	11	13	5	12	9	13
Denver	1	3	2	9	11	5
Houston	13	11	9	3	4	2
Indianapolis	12	7	12	5	3	12
Jacksonville	14	10	14	11	12	9
Kansas City	7	1	13	1	2	3
Miami	3	12	1	10	6	11
New England	5	6	6	14	10	14
NY Jets	15	15	15	4	13	1
Oakland	4	5	7	7	8	6
Pittsburgh	2	8	3	2	1	4
San Diego	8	9	8	6	7	7
Seattle	6	2	11	13	15	10

National Football Conference

	Offense Total	Rush	Pass	Defense Total	Rush	Pass
Arizona	11	15	10	13	15	8
Atlanta	7	13	5	15	5	15
Carolina	13	9	12	3	6	7
Chicago	6	4	8	9	3	13
Dallas	4	1	9	4	9	4
Detroit	1	6	2	12	10	11
Green Bay	5	12	3	6	4	9
Minnesota	3	7	4	10	2	14
New Orleans	10	14	7	11	12	10
NY Giants	15	5	15	7	13	2
Philadelphia	12	2	14	2	11	1
St Louis	8	11	6	5	7	6
San Francisco	2	10	1	1	1	5
Tampa Bay	14	8	13	14	8	12
Washington	9	3	11	8	14	3

Buffalo Bills

SCORING

	TD						
	Rush	Rec	Ret	PAT	FG	S	Pts
Christie	0	0	0	33/35	31/40	0	126
Brooks	0	11	0	0/0	0/0	0	66
T. Thomas	6	2	0	0/0	0/0	0	48
Holmes	4	0	0	0/0	0/0	0	24

Three tied with 18.

RUSHING

	No.	Yds	Avg	Lg	TD
T. Thomas	267	1005	3.8	49	6
Holmes	172	698	4.1	t38	4

PASSING

	Att	Comp	Pct Comp	Yds	Avg Gain	TD	Int	Rating Pts
Kelly	458	255	55.7	3130	6.83	22	13	81.1

RECEIVING

	No.	Yds	Avg	Lg	TD
Brooks	53	763	14.4	t51	11
L. Johnson	49	504	10.3	52	1
Copeland	42	646	15.4	t77	1
Armour	26	300	11.5	t28	3
T. Thomas	26	220	8.5	60	2

INTERCEPTIONS: Schulz, 6

PUNTING

	No.	Yds	Avg	Net Avg	TB	In 20	Lg	Blk
Mohr	86	3473	40.4	36.2	7	23	60	0

SACKS: Paup, 17.5

Cincinnati Bengals

SCORING

	TD						
	Rush	Rec	Ret	PAT	FG	S	Pts
Pelfrey	0	0	0	34/34	29/36	0	121
Pickens	0	17	0	0/0	0/0	0	102
Scott	0	5	0	0/0	0/0	0	30
To. McGee	0	4	0	0/0	0/0	0	24
Bieniemy	3	0	0	0/0	0/0	0	18
Green	2	1	0	0/0	0/0	0	18

RUSHING

	No.	Yds	Avg	Lg	TD
Green	171	661	3.9	t23	2
Bieniemy	98	381	3.9	27	3
Blake	53	309	5.8	30	2

PASSING

	Att	Comp	Pct Comp	Yds	Avg Gain	TD	Int	Rating Pts
Blake	567	326	57.5	3822	6.74	28	17	82.1

RECEIVING

	No.	Yds	Avg	Lg	TD
Pickens	99	1234	12.5	t68	17
To. McGee	55	754	13.7	41	4
Scott	52	821	15.8	t88	5
Bieniemy	43	424	9.9	33	0
Green	27	182	6.7	24	1

INTERCEPTIONS: Walker, 4

PUNTING

	No.	Yds	Avg	Net Avg	TB	In 20	Lg	Blk
Johnson	68	2861	42.1	38.6	4	26	61	0

SACKS: Copeland, 9

Cleveland Browns

SCORING

	TD						
	Rush	Rec	Ret	PAT	FG	S	Pts
Stover	0	0	0	26/26	29/33	0	113
Jackson	0	9	0	0/0	0/0	0	54
McCardell	0	4	0	0/0	0/0	0	24
Byner	2	2	0	0/0	0/0	0	24
Rison	0	3	0	0/0	0/0	0	18

RUSHING

	No.	Yds	Avg	Lg	TD
Hoard	136	547	4.0	25	0
Byner	115	432	3.8	23	2
White	62	163	2.6	11	1
Hunter	30	100	3.3	15	0

PASSING

	Att	Comp	Pct Comp	Yds	Avg Gain	TD	Int	Rating Pts
Testaverde	392	241	61.5	2883	7.35	17	10	87.8
Zeier	161	82	50.9	864	5.37	4	9	51.9

RECEIVING

	No.	Yds	Avg	Lg	TD
Byner	61	494	8.1	t29	2
McCardell	56	709	12.7	36	4
Rison	47	701	14.9	59	3
Jackson	44	714	16.2	t70	9
Kinchen	20	216	10.8	41	0

INTERCEPTIONS: S. Moore, 5

PUNTING

	No.	Yds	Avg	Net Avg	TB	In 20	Lg	Blk
Tupa	65	2831	43.6	36.2	9	18	64	0

SACKS: Pleasant, 8

Denver Broncos

SCORING

	TD						
	Rush	Rec	Ret	PAT	FG	S	Pts
Elam	0	0	0	39/39	31/38	0	132
Miller	0	14	0	0/0	0/0	0	84
Davis	7	1	0	0/0	0/0	0	48
Craver	5	1	0	0/0	0/0	0	36
Sharpe	0	4	0	0/0	0/0	0	24

RUSHING

	No.	Yds	Avg	Lg	TD
Davis	237	1117	4.7	t60	7
Craver	73	333	4.6	23	5
Milburn	49	266	5.4	29	0
Elway	41	176	4.3	25	1

PASSING

	Att	Comp	Pct Comp	Yds	Avg Gain	TD	Int	Rating Pts
Elway	542	316	58.3	3970	7.32	26	14	86.4
Millen	40	26	65.0	197	4.93	1	0	85.1

RECEIVING

	No.	Yds	Avg	Lg	TD
Sharpe	63	756	12.0	49	4
Miller	59	1079	18.3	t62	14
Davis	49	367	7.5	31	1
Craver	43	369	8.6	32	1
McCaffrey	39	477	12.2	35	2
Pritchard	33	441	13.4	t45	3

INTERCEPTIONS: Atwater, 3

PUNTING

	No.	Yds	Avg	Net Avg	TB	In 20	Lg	Blk
Rouen	52	2192	42.2	37.6	3	22	61	1

SACKS: Perry 6

Houston Oilers

SCORING

SCORING	Rush	TD Rec	Ret	PAT	FG	S	Pts
Del Greco	0	0	0	33/33	27/31	0	114
Sanders	0	9	0	0/0	0/0	0	54
Jeffires	0	8	0	0/0	0/0	0	48
R. Thomas	5	2	0	0/0	0/0	0	44
Butts	4	0	0	0/0	0/0	0	24

RUSHING	No.	Yds	Avg	Lg	TD
R. Thomas	251	947	3.8	t74	5
Brown	86	293	3.4	21	0
Butts	71	185	2.6	9	4

PASSING	Att	Comp	Pct Comp	Yds	Avg Gain	TD	Int	Rating Pts
Chandler	356	225	63.2	2450	6.91	17	10	87.8
Furrer	99	48	48.5	483	4.88	2	7	40.1
S. McNair	80	41	51.3	569	7.11	3	1	81.7

RECEIVING	No.	Yds	Avg	Lg	TD
Jeffires	61	684	11.2	t35	8
T. McNair	60	501	8.4	25	1
Wycheck	40	471	11.8	t36	1
R. Thomas	39	204	5.2	19	2
Sanders	35	823	23.5	t76	9

INTERCEPTIONS: D. Lewis, 6

PUNTING	No.	Yds	Avg	Net Avg	TB	In 20	Lg	Blk
Camarillo	77	3165	41.1	34.8	8	26	60	1

SACKS: Cook and Ford, 4.5

Jacksonville Jaguars

SCORING	Rush	TD Rec	Ret	PAT	FG	S	Pts
Hollis	0	0	0	27/28	20/27	0	87
W. Jackson	0	5	0	0/0	0/0	0	32
Smith	0	3	2	0/0	0/0	0	30
Brunell	4	0	0	0/0	0/0	0	24

Three tied with 18.

RUSHING	No.	Yds	Avg	Lg	TD
Stewart	137	525	3.8	22	2
Brunell	67	480	7.2	t27	4
Dunbar	110	361	3.3	26	2
Maston	41	186	4.5	21	0

PASSING	Att	Comp	Pct Comp	Yds	Avg Gain	TD	Int	Rating Pts
Brunell	346	201	58.1	2168	6.27	15	7	82.6
Beuerlein	142	71	50.0	952	6.70	4	7	60.5

RECEIVING	No.	Yds	Avg	Lg	TD
W. Jackson	53	589	11.1	45	5
Mitchell	41	527	12.9	35	2
Tillman	30	368	12.3	28	3
Givins	29	280	9.7	18	3
Howard	26	276	10.6	24	1

INTERCEPTIONS: Colon, 3

PUNTING	No.	Yds	Avg	Net Avg	TB	In 20	Lg	Blk
Barker	82	3591	43.8	38.6	5	19	63	0

SACKS: Smeenge, 4

Indianapolis Colts

SCORING	Rush	TD Rec	Ret	PAT	FG	S	Pts
Faulk	11	3	0	0/0	0/0	0	84
Blanchard	0	0	0	25/25	19/24	0	82
Turner	0	4	0	0/0	0/0	0	28
Dilger	0	4	0	0/0	0/0	0	24
Bailey	0	3	1	0/0	0/0	0	24

RUSHING	No.	Yds	Avg	Lg	TD
Faulk	289	1078	3.7	40	11
Potts	65	309	4.8	37	0
Harbaugh	52	235	4.5	21	2
Warren	47	152	3.2	42	1

PASSING	Att	Comp	Pct Comp	Yds	Avg Gain	TD	Int	Rating Pts
Harbaugh	314	200	63.7	2575	8.20	17	5	100.7
Erickson	83	50	60.2	586	7.06	3	4	73.7

RECEIVING	No.	Yds	Avg	Lg	TD
Faulk	56	475	8.5	34	3
Dawkins	52	784	15.1	52	3
Dilger	42	635	15.1	42	4
Turner	35	431	12.3	t47	4
Bailey	21	379	18.0	45	3
Potts	21	228	10.9	52	1

INTERCEPTIONS: Daniel and Ambrose, 3

PUNTING	No.	Yds	Avg	Net Avg	TB	In 20	Lg	Blk
Gardocki	63	2681	42.6	33.4	7	16	69	0

SACKS: Johnson, 4.5

Kansas City Chiefs

SCORING	Rush	TD Rec	Ret	PAT	FG	S	Pts
Elliot	0	0	0	34/37	24/30	0	106
Allen	5	0	0	0/0	0/0	0	30
Dawson	0	5	0	0/0	0/0	0	30
W. Davis	0	5	0	0/0	0/0	0	30
Bono	5	0	0	0/0	0/0	0	30
Vanover	0	2	3	0/0	0/0	0	30

RUSHING	No.	Yds	Avg	Lg	TD
Allen	207	890	4.3	38	5
Hill	155	667	4.3	27	1
Anders	58	398	6.9	44	2
Bono	28	113	4.0	t76	5

PASSING	Att	Comp	Pct Comp	Yds	Avg Gain	TD	Int	Rating Pts
Bono	520	293	56.3	3121	6.00	21	10	79.5

RECEIVING	No.	Yds	Avg	Lg	TD
Anders	55	349	6.3	28	1
Cash	42	419	10.0	t38	1
Dawson	40	513	12.8	t45	5
Slaughter	34	514	15.1	38	4
W. Davis	33	527	16.0	t60	5

INTERCEPTIONS: D. Carter, 4

PUNTING	No.	Yds	Avg	Net Avg	TB	In 20	Lg	Blk
Aguiar	91	3990	43.8	36.5	12	29	65	0

SACKS: N. Smith, 12

Miami Dolphins

SCORING

	TD Rush	Rec	Ret	PAT	FG	S	Pts
Stoyanovich	0	0	0	37/37	27/34	0	118
Parmalee	9	1	0	0/0	0/0	0	60
McDuffie	0	8	0	0/0	0/0	0	50
Fryar	0	8	0	0/0	0/0	0	48
Kirby	4	3	0	0/0	0/0	0	42

RUSHING

	No.	Yds	Avg	Lg	TD
Parmalee	236	878	3.7	40	9
Kirby	108	414	3.8	38	4
Spikes	32	126	3.9	t17	1

PASSING

	Att	Comp	Pct Comp	Yds	Avg Gain	TD	Int	Rating Pts
Marino	482	309	64.1	3668	7.61	24	15	90.8
Kosar	108	74	68.5	699	6.47	3	5	76.1

RECEIVING

	No.	Yds	Avg	Lg	TD
Kirby	66	618	9.4	46	3
Fryar	62	910	14.7	t67	8
McDuffie	62	819	13.2	48	8
Byars	51	362	7.1	26	2
Green	43	499	11.6	t31	3
Parmalee	39	345	8.8	35	1
Clark	37	525	14.2	t42	2

INTERCEPTIONS: Vincent, 5

PUNTING

	No.	Yds	Avg	Net Avg	TB	In 20	Lg	Blk
Kidd	57	2433	42.7	36.3	5	15	56	0

SACKS: Cox, 7.5

New England Patriots

SCORING

	TD Rush	Rec	Ret	PAT	FG	S	Pts
Bahr	0	0	0	27/27	23/33	0	96
Martin	14	1	0	0/0	0/0	0	92
Coates	0	6	0	0/0	0/0	0	36
Brisby	0	3	0	0/0	0/0	0	18

RUSHING

	No.	Yds	Avg	Lg	TD
Martin	368	1487	4.0	4.9	14
Meggett	60	250	4.2	25	2

PASSING

	Att	Comp	Pct Comp	Yds	Avg Gain	TD	Int	Rating Pts
Bledsoe	636	323	50.8	3507	5.51	13	16	63.7
Zolak	49	28	57.1	282	5.76	1	0	80.5

RECEIVING

	No.	Yds	Avg	Lg	TD
Coates	84	915	10.9	35	6
Brisby	66	974	14.8	72	3
Meggett	52	334	6.4	19	0
W. Moore	43	502	11.7	33	1
Martin	30	261	8.7	27	1

INTERCEPTIONS: V. Brown, 4

PUNTING

	No.	Yds	Avg	Net Avg	TB	In 20	Lg	Blk
O'Neill	41	1514	36.9	31.2	3	14	57	0
Wagner	37	1557	42.1	35.4	4	13	57	0

SACKS: McGinest, 11

New York Jets

SCORING

	TD Rush	Rec	Ret	PAT	FG	S	Pts
Lowery	0	0	0	24/24	17/21	0	75
Mitchell	0	5	0	0/0	0/0	0	30
Wilson	0	4	0	0/0	0/0	0	24
Chrebet	0	4	0	0/0	0/0	0	24
Murrell	1	2	0	0/0	0/0	0	18

RUSHING

	No.	Yds	Avg	Lg	TD
Murrell	192	795	4.1	30	1
B. Baxter	85	296	3.5	26	1
Moore	43	121	2.8	14	0

PASSING

	Att	Comp	Pct Comp	Yds	Avg Gain	TD	Int	Rating Pts
Esiason	389	221	56.8	2275	5.85	16	15	71.4
Brister	170	93	54.7	726	4.27	4	8	53.7

RECEIVING

	No.	Yds	Avg	Lg	TD
Murrell	71	465	6.5	43	2
Chrebet	66	726	11.0	32	4
Mitchell	45	497	11.0	t43	5
Wilson	41	484	11.8	24	4
Brady	26	252	9.7	29	2
B. Baxter	26	160	6.2	20	0

INTERCEPTIONS: Smith, 6

PUNTING

	No.	Yds	Avg	Net Avg	TB	In 20	Lg	Blk
Hansen	99	4090	41.3	31.9	10	23	67	1

SACKS: Douglas, 10

Oakland Raiders

SCORING

	TD Rush	Rec	Ret	PAT	FG	S	Pts
Jaeger	0	0	0	22/22	13/18	0	61
Brown	0	10	0	0/0	0/0	0	60
Williams	9	0	0	0/0	0/0	0	54
Ford	0	0	0	17/18	8/9	0	41

Four tied with 18.

RUSHING

	No.	Yds	Avg	Lg	TD
Williams	255	1114	4.4	60	9
Kaufman	108	490	4.5	28	1
Hostetler	31	119	3.8	18	0
Fenner	39	110	2.8	10	0

PASSING

	Att	Comp	Pct Comp	Yds	Avg Gain	TD	Int	Rating Pts
Hostetler	286	172	60.1	1998	6.99	12	9	82.2
Evans	175	100	57.1	1236	7.06	6	8	71.5
Hobert	80	44	55.0	540	6.75	6	4	80.2

RECEIVING

	No.	Yds	Avg	Lg	TD
Brown	89	1342	15.1	t80	10
Williams	54	375	6.9	28	0
Hobbs	38	612	16.1	t54	3
Fenner	35	252	7.2	23	3
Ismail	28	491	17.5	t73	3
Glover	26	220	8.5	25	3

INTERCEPTIONS: McDaniel, 6

PUNTING

	No.	Yds	Avg	Net Avg	TB	In 20	Lg	Blk
Gossett	75	3089	41.2	34.7	8	22	60	1

SACKS: Swilling, 13

Pittsburgh Steelers

SCORING	Rush	TD Rec	Ret	PAT	FG	S	Pts
N. Johnson	0	0	0	39/39	34/41	0	141
Morris	9	0	0	0/0	0/0	0	54
Mills	0	8	0	0/0	0/0	0	48
Pegram	5	1	0	0/0	0/0	0	38
Thigpen	0	5	0	0/0	0/0	0	30

RUSHING	No.	Yds	Avg	Lg	TD
Pegram	213	813	3.8	38	5
Morris	148	559	3.8	t30	9
McAfee	39	156	4.0	t22	1

PASSING	Att	Comp	Pct Comp	Yds	Avg Gain	TD	Int	Rating Pts
O'Donnell	416	246	59.1	2970	7.14	17	7	87.7
Tomczak	113	65	57.5	666	5.89	1	9	44.3
Miller	56	32	57.1	397	7.09	2	5	53.9

RECEIVING	No.	Yds	Avg	Lg	TD
Thigpen	85	1307	15.4	43	5
Hastings	48	502	10.5	36	1
Mills	39	679	17.4	t62	8
C. Johnson	38	432	11.4	33	0
Bruener	26	238	9.2	29	3
Pegram	26	206	7.9	22	1

INTERCEPTIONS: W. Williams, 7

PUNTING	No.	Yds	Avg	Net Avg	TB	In 20	Lg	Blk
Stark	59	2368	40.1	33.3	11	20	64	0

SACKS: K. Greene, 9

San Diego Chargers

SCORING	Rush	TD Rec	Ret	PAT	FG	S	Pts
Carney	0	0	0	32/33	21/26	0	95
Martin	0	6	0	0/0	0/0	0	36
Harmon	1	5	0	0/0	0/0	0	36
Means	5	0	0	0/0	0/0	0	30
Seay	0	3	0	0/0	0/0	0	20

RUSHING	No.	Yds	Avg	Lg	TD
Means	186	730	3.9	36	5
Hayden	128	470	3.7	20	3
Harmon	51	187	3.7	t48	1
Culver	47	155	3.3	17	3

PASSING	Att	Comp	Pct Comp	Yds	Avg Gain	TD	Int	Rating Pts
Humphries	478	282	59.0	3381	7.07	17	14	80.4
Gilbert	61	36	59.0	325	5.33	0	4	46.1

RECEIVING	No.	Yds	Avg	Lg	TD
Martin	90	1224	13.6	t51	6
Harmon	62	662	10.7	44	5
Jefferson	48	621	12.9	45	2
Seay	45	538	11.9	t38	3
Pupunu	35	315	9.0	26	0

INTERCEPTIONS: Harrison, 5

PUNTING	No.	Yds	Avg	Net Avg	TB	In 20	Lg	Blk
Bennett	72	3221	44.7	36.6	8	28	66	0

SACKS: O'Neal, 12.5

Seattle Seahawks

SCORING	Rush	TD Rec	Ret	PAT	FG	S	Pts
Peterson	0	0	0	40/40	23/28	0	109
Warren	15	1	0	0/0	0/0	0	96
Galloway	1	7	1	0/0	0/0	0	54
Strong	1	3	0	0/0	0/0	0	24
Blades	0	4	0	0/0	0/0	0	24

RUSHING	No.	Yds	Avg	Lg	TD
Warren	310	1346	4.3	52	15
Broussard	46	222	4.8	t21	1
L. Smith	36	215	6.0	68	0
Mirer	43	193	4.5	24	1

PASSING	Att	Comp	Pct Comp	Yds	Avg Gain	TD	Int	Rating Pts
Mirer	391	209	53.5	2564	6.56	13	20	63.7
Friesz	120	64	53.3	795	6.63	6	3	80.4

RECEIVING	No.	Yds	Avg	Lg	TD
Blades	77	1001	13.0	49	4
Galloway	67	1039	15.5	t59	7
Warren	35	247	7.1	t20	1
Crumpler	23	254	11.0	24	1

INTERCEPTIONS: Blackmon, 5

PUNTING	No.	Yds	Avg	Net Avg	TB	In 20	Lg	Blk
Tuten	83	3735	45.0	36.5	8	21	73	0

SACKS: Kennedy, 6.5

Lounge Acts

Big Boy's, a bar in Spooner, Wis., that's a hangout for Green Bay Packer fans, has a disturbing promotion designed to capitalize on the rivalry between the Pack and the hated Minnesota Vikings. When the teams play each other, Big Boy's holds a lottery in which customers draw the name of a Viking player. If the player gets a bloody nose during the game or is visited by a trainer on the field, the contest winner wins a shot of booze; if the player is helped off the field by two men, the reward is five drinks; if a stretcher is needed, the customer can stupefy himself with four hours' worth of alcohol.

After the two Green Bay–Minnesota games this season (the teams split), Big Boy's owner, Rick Johnson, has yet to spring for a 240-minute binge. However, he *has* given enough free drinks to waste an offensive line and, at times, has generously extended the house rules. "During the first game someone won five drinks for [Minnesota tackle] Korey Stringer," Johnson says. "Stringer was puking on the sideline." We don't know whether the winning drinker wound up puking, too. But we hope so.

Arizona Cardinals

SCORING	Rush	TD Rec	Ret	PAT	FG	S	Pts
G. Davis	0	0	0	19/19	30/39	0	109
R. Moore	0	5	0	0/0	0/0	0	32
Centers	2	2	0	0/0	0/0	0	24
Williams	0	0	3	0/0	0/0	0	18
Sanders	0	2	0	0/0	0/0	0	16

RUSHING	No.	Yds	Avg	Lg	TD
Hearst	284	1070	3.8	38	1
Centers	78	254	3.3	20	2

PASSING	Att	Comp	Pct Comp	Yds	Avg Gain	TD	Int	Rating Pts
Krieg	521	304	58.3	3554	6.82	16	21	72.6

RECEIVING	No.	Yds	Avg	Lg	TD
Centers	101	962	9.5	32	2
R. Moore	63	907	14.4	45	5
Sanders	52	883	17.0	48	2
Edwards	29	417	14.4	t28	2
Hearst	29	243	8.4	39	1

INTERCEPTIONS: Williams, 6

PUNTING	No.	Yds	Avg	Net Avg	TB	In 20	Lg	Blk
Feagles	72	3150	43.8	38.2	8	20	60	0

SACKS: Simmons, 11

Atlanta Falcons

SCORING	Rush	TD Rec	Ret	PAT	FG	S	Pts
Andersen	0	0	0	29/30	31/37	0	122
Mathis	0	9	0	0/0	0/0	0	60
Metcalf	1	8	1	0/0	0/0	0	60
Heyward	6	2	0	0/0	0/0	0	48
Emanuel	0	5	0	0/0	0/0	0	30

RUSHING	No.	Yds	Avg	Lg	TD
Heyward	236	1083	4.6	31	6
Anderson	39	161	4.1	13	1

PASSING	Att	Comp	Pct Comp	Yds	Avg Gain	TD	Int	Rating Pts
J. George	557	336	60.3	4143	7.44	24	11	89.5
Hebert	45	28	62.2	313	6.96	2	1	88.5

RECEIVING	No.	Yds	Avg	Lg	TD
Metcalf	104	1189	11.4	t62	8
Mathis	78	1039	13.3	t54	9
Emanuel	74	1039	14.0	52	5
Heyward	37	350	9.5	25	2
Birden	31	303	9.8	24	1

INTERCEPTIONS: Tuggle, Ross and Taylor, 3

PUNTING	No.	Yds	Avg	Net Avg	TB	In 20	Lg	Blk
Stryzinski	67	2759	41.2	36.2	5	21	64	0

SACKS: Doleman, 9

Carolina Panthers

SCORING	Rush	TD Rec	Ret	PAT	FG	S	Pts
Kasay	0	0	0	27/28	26/33	0	105
Green	0	6	0	0/0	0/0	0	36
Moore	4	0	0	0/0	0/0	0	24
Carrier	0	3	0	0/0	0/0	0	18
Collins	3	0	0	0/0	0/0	0	18
Metzelaars	0	3	0	0/0	0/0	0	18

RUSHING	No.	Yds	Avg	Lg	TD
Moore	195	740	3.8	t53	4
Griffith	65	197	3.0	15	1
Christian	41	158	3.9	17	0

PASSING	Att	Comp	Pct Comp	Yds	Avg Gain	TD	Int	Rating Pts
Collins	433	214	49.4	2717	6.27	14	19	61.9
Reich	84	37	44.0	441	5.25	2	2	58.7

RECEIVING	No.	Yds	Avg	Lg	TD
Carrier	66	1002	15.2	t66	3
Green	47	882	18.8	t89	6
Guliford	29	444	15.3	49	1
Christian	29	255	8.8	23	1
Metzelaars	20	171	8.6	27	3

INTERCEPTIONS: Maxie, 6

PUNTING	No.	Yds	Avg	Net Avg	TB	In 20	Lg	Blk
Barnhardt	95	3906	41.1	35.2	11	27	54	0

SACKS: Lathon, 8

Chicago Bears

SCORING	Rush	TD Rec	Ret	PAT	FG	S	Pts
Butler	0	0	0	45/45	23/31	0	114
Conway	0	12	0	0/0	0/0	0	72
Salaam	10	0	0	0/0	0/0	0	60
Jennings	0	6	0	0/0	0/0	0	36
Graham	0	4	0	0/0	0/0	0	24

RUSHING	No.	Yds	Avg	Lg	TD
Salaam	296	1074	3.6	42	10
Green	107	570	5.3	38	3

PASSING	Att	Comp	Pct Comp	Yds	Avg Gain	TD	Int	Rating Pts
Kramer	522	315	60.3	3838	7.35	29	10	93.5

RECEIVING	No.	Yds	Avg	Lg	TD
Graham	82	1301	15.9	51	4
Conway	62	1037	16.7	t76	12
T. Carter	40	329	8.2	27	1
Green	28	246	8.8	28	0
Jennings	25	217	8.7	20	6
Timpson	24	289	12.0	36	2
Wetnight	24	193	8.0	22	2

INTERCEPTIONS: Woolford, 4

PUNTING	No.	Yds	Avg	Net Avg	TB	In 20	Lg	Blk
Sauerbrun	55	2080	37.8	31.1	6	16	61	0

SACKS: Flanigan, 11

Dallas Cowboys

SCORING	Rush	Rec	TD Ret	PAT	FG	S	Pts
E. Smith	25	0	0	0/0	0/0	0	150
Boniol	0	0	0	46/48	27/28	0	127
Irvin	0	10	0	0/0	0/0	0	60
Novacek	0	5	0	0/0	0/0	0	32
Johnston	2	1	0	0/0	0/0	0	18

RUSHING	No.	Yds	Avg	Lg	TD
E. Smith	377	1773	4.7	t60	25
S. Williams	48	205	4.3	t44	1

PASSING	Att	Comp	Pct Comp	Yds	Avg Gain	TD	Int	Rating Pts
Aikman	432	280	64.8	3304	7.65	16	7	93.6
Wilson	57	38	66.7	691	6.86	1	3	70.1

RECEIVING	No.	Yds	Avg	Lg	TD
Irvin	111	1603	14.4	50	10
Novacek	62	705	11.4	t33	5
E. Smith	62	375	6.0	40	0
K. Williams	38	613	16.1	t48	2
Johnston	30	248	8.3	24	1

INTERCEPTIONS: Brown and Marion, 6

PUNTING	No.	Yds	Avg	Net Avg	TB	In 20	Lg	Blk
Jett	53	2166	40.9	34.5	6	17	58	0

SACKS: Hennings and Tolbert, 5.5

Green Bay Packers

SCORING	Rush	Rec	TD Ret	PAT	FG	S	Pts
Jacke	0	0	0	43/43	17/23	0	94
R. Brooks	0	13	0	0/0	0/0	0	78
Chmura	0	7	0	0/0	0/0	0	44
Bennett	3	4	0	0/0	0/0	0	42
Levens	3	4	0	0/0	0/0	0	42

RUSHING	No.	Yds	Avg	Lg	TD
Bennett	316	1067	3.4	23	3
Favre	39	181	4.6	40	3

PASSING	Att	Comp	Pct Comp	Yds	Avg Gain	TD	Int	Rating Pts
Favre	570	359	63.0	4413	7.74	38	13	99.5

RECEIVING	No.	Yds	Avg	Lg	TD
R. Brooks	102	1497	14.7	t99	13
Bennett	61	648	10.6	35	4
Chmura	54	679	12.6	33	7
Levens	48	434	9.0	27	4
Ingram	39	469	12.0	29	3
Morgan	31	344	11.1	t29	4

INTERCEPTIONS: Butler, 5

PUNTING	No.	Yds	Avg	Net Avg	TB	In 20	Lg	Blk
Hentrich	65	2740	42.2	34.6	7	26	61	2

SACKS: Re. White, 12

Detroit Lions

SCORING	Rush	Rec	TD Ret	PAT	FG	S	Pts
Hanson	0	0	0	48/48	28/34	0	132
Moore	0	14	0	0/0	0/0	0	84
Sanders	11	1	0	0/0	0/0	0	72
Perriman	0	9	0	0/0	0/0	0	56
Morton	0	8	0	0/0	0/0	0	48

RUSHING	No.	Yds	Avg	Lg	TD
Sanders	314	1500	4.8	t75	11
Mitchell	36	104	2.9	18	4

PASSING	Att	Comp	Pct Comp	Yds	Avg Gain	TD	Int	Rating Pts
Mitchell	583	346	59.3	4338	7.44	32	12	92.3

RECEIVING	No.	Yds	Avg	Lg	TD
Moore	123	1686	13.7	t69	14
Perriman	108	1488	13.8	t91	9
Sanders	48	398	8.3	40	1
Morton	44	590	13.4	t32	8

INTERCEPTIONS: Clay, 8

PUNTING	No.	Yds	Avg	Net Avg	TB	In 20	Lg	Blk
Royals	57	2393	42.0	31.0	6	15	69	2

SACKS: Scroggins, 9.5

Minnesota Vikings

SCORING	Rush	Rec	TD Ret	PAT	FG	S	Pts
Reveiz	0	0	0	44/44	26/36	0	122
Carter	0	17	0	0/0	0/0	0	102
Reed	0	9	0	0/0	0/0	0	54
R. Smith	5	0	0	0/0	0/0	0	32
Lee	2	1	0	0/0	0/0	0	18
Ismail	0	3	0	0/0	0/0	0	18

RUSHING	No.	Yds	Avg	Lg	TD
R. Smith	139	632	4.5	t58	5
Graham	110	406	3.7	26	2
Lee	69	371	5.4	t66	2

PASSING	Att	Comp	Pct Comp	Yds	Avg Gain	TD	Int	Rating Pts
Moon	606	377	62.2	4228	6.98	33	14	91.5

RECEIVING	No.	Yds	Avg	Lg	TD
Carter	122	1371	11.2	t60	17
Reed	72	1167	16.2	t55	9
Lee	71	558	7.9	33	1
Ismail	32	597	18.7	t85	3
Jordan	27	185	6.9	17	2

INTERCEPTIONS: O. Thomas, 9

PUNTING	No.	Yds	Avg	Net Avg	TB	In 20	Lg	Blk
Saxon	72	2948	40.9	33.1	6	21	60	0

SACKS: B. Thomas, 6

New Orleans Saints

	TD						
SCORING	Rush	Rec	Ret	PAT	FG	S	Pts
Brien	0	0	0	35/35	19/29	0	92
Early	0	8	0	0/0	0/0	0	48
Bates	7	0	0	0/0	0/0	0	42
Small	1	5	0	0/0	0/0	0	36
Lohmiller	0	0	0	11/13	8/14	0	35

RUSHING	No.	Yds	Avg	Lg	TD
Bates	244	951	3.9	t66	7
Zellars	50	162	3.2	11	2
Brown	49	159	3.2	t35	1

PASSING	Att	Comp	Pct Comp	Yds	Avg Gain	TD	Int	Rating
Everett	567	345	60.8	3970	7.00	26	14	87.0

RECEIVING	No.	Yds	Avg	Lg	TD
Early	81	1087	13.4	t70	8
Walls	57	694	12.2	29	4
Smith	45	466	10.4	43	3
Haynes	41	597	14.6	48	4
Small	38	461	12.1	t32	5
Brown	35	266	7.6	19	1

INTERCEPTIONS: Spencer, 4

PUNTING	No.	Yds	Avg	Net Avg	TB	In 20	Lg	Blk
Wilmsmeyer	73	2965	40.6	35.6	5	21	53	1

SACKS: Martin, 13

New York Giants

	TD						
SCORING	Rush	Rec	Ret	PAT	FG	S	Pts
Daluiso	0	0	0	28/28	20/28	0	88
Hampton	10	0	0	0/0	0/0	0	62
Sherrard	0	4	0	0/0	0/0	0	24
Brown	4	0	0	0/0	0/0	0	24
Wheatley	3	0	0	0/0	0/0	0	18
Calloway	0	3	0	0/0	0/0	0	18

RUSHING	No.	Yds	Avg	Lg	TD
Hampton	306	1182	3.9	32	10
Wheatley	78	245	3.1	t19	3
Brown	45	228	5.1	23	4

PASSING	Att	Comp	Pct Comp	Yds	Avg Gain	TD	Int	Rating Pts
Brown	456	254	55.7	2814	6.17	11	10	73.1

RECEIVING	No.	Yds	Avg	Lg	TD
Calloway	56	796	14.2	49	3
Sherrard	44	577	13.1	t57	4
Pierce	33	310	9.4	26	0
Walker	31	234	7.5	34	1

INTERCEPTIONS: Glenn and Sparks, 5

PUNTING	No.	Yds	Avg	Net Avg	TB	In 20	Lg	Blk
Horan	72	3063	42.5	36.2	8	15	60	0

SACKS: Strahan 7.5

Philadelphia Eagles

	TD						
SCORING	Rush	Rec	Ret	PAT	FG	S	Pts
Anderson	0	0	0	32/33	22/30	0	98
Watters	11	1	0	0/0	0/0	0	72
Garner	6	0	0	0/0	0/0	0	36
Barnett	0	5	0	0/0	0/0	0	32

RUSHING	No.	Yds	Avg	Lg	TD
Watters	337	1273	3.8	57	11
Garner	108	588	5.4	t55	6

PASSING	Att	Comp	Pct Comp	Yds	Avg Gain	TD	Int	Rating Pts
Peete	375	215	57.3	2326	6.20	8	14	67.3
Cunningham	121	69	57.0	605	5.00	3	5	61.5

RECEIVING	No.	Yds	Avg	Lg	TD
C. Williams	63	768	12.2	t37	2
Watters	62	434	7.0	24	1
Barnett	48	585	12.2	33	5
Carpenter	29	318	11.0	29	0
West	20	190	9.5	26	1
Martin	17	206	12.1	22	0

INTERCEPTIONS: Thomas, 7

PUNTING	No.	Yds	Avg	Net Avg	TB	In 20	Lg	Blk
Hutton	85	3682	43.3	33.7	13	20	63	1

SACKS: Fuller, 13

St Louis Rams

	TD						
SCORING	Rush	Rec	Ret	PAT	FG	S	Pts
Bruce	0	13	0	0/0	0/0	0	80
McLaughlin	0	0	0	17/17	8/16	0	41
Biasucci	0	0	0	13/14	9/12	0	40
Kinchen	0	4	0	0/0	0/0	0	24
Drayton	0	4	0	0/0	0/0	0	24

RUSHING	No.	Yds	Avg	Lg	TD
Bettis	183	637	3.5	41	3
Russell	66	203	3.1	18	0
Bailey	36	182	5.1	17	2
Robinson	40	165	4.1	37	0

PASSING	Att	Comp	Pct Comp	Yds	Avg Gain	TD	Int	Rating Pts
Miller	405	232	57.3	2623	6.48	18	15	76.2
Rypien	217	129	59.4	1448	6.67	9	8	77.9

RECEIVING	No.	Yds	Avg	Lg	TD
Bruce	119	1781	15.0	72	13
Drayton	47	458	9.7	31	4
Bailey	38	265	7.0	25	0
Kinchen	36	419	11.6	35	4
Hester	30	399	13.3	t38	3

INTERCEPTIONS: T. Wright, 6

PUNTING	No.	Yds	Avg	Net Avg	TB	In 20	Lg	Blk
Landeta	83	3679	44.3	36.7	12	23	63	0

SACKS: Farr, 11.5

San Francisco 49ers

SCORING	Rush	Rec	Ret	PAT	FG	S	Pts
Rice	1	15	1	0/0	0/0	0	104
Loville	10	3	0	0/0	0/0	0	80
Wilkins	0	0	0	27/29	12/13	0	63
Stokes	0	4	0	0/0	0/0	0	24

Three tied with 18.

RUSHING	No.	Yds	Avg	Lg	TD
Loville	218	723	3.3	27	10
S. Young	50	250	5.0	29	3
Floyd	64	237	3.7	23	2

PASSING	Att	Comp	Pct Comp	Yds	Avg Gain	TD	Int	Rating Pts
S. Young	447	299	66.9	3200	7.16	20	11	92.3
Grbac	183	127	69.4	1469	8.03	8	5	96.6

RECEIVING	No.	Yds	Avg	Lg	TD
Rice	122	1848	15.1	t81	15
Loville	87	662	7.6	31	3
Jones	60	595	9.9	39	3
Floyd	47	348	7.4	23	1
Stokes	38	517	13.6	t41	4
Taylor	29	387	13.3	40	2

INTERCEPTIONS: Drakeford and Hanks, 5

PUNTING	No.	Yds	Avg	Net Avg	TB	In 20	Lg	Blk
Thompson	57	2312	40.6	33.7	5	13	65	0

SACKS: Jackson, 9.5

Washington Redskins

SCORING	Rush	Rec	Ret	PAT	FG	S	Pts
Murray	0	0	0	33/33	27/36	0	114
Allen	10	1	0	0/0	0/0	0	66
Ellard	0	5	0	0/0	0/0	0	30
Logan	1	2	0	0/0	0/0	0	18
Mitchell	1	1	1	0/0	0/0	0	18
Shepherd	1	2	0	0/0	0/0	0	18

RUSHING	No.	Yds	Avg	Lg	TD
Allen	338	1309	3.9	28	10
Mitchell	46	301	6.5	t36	1

PASSING	Att	Comp	Pct Comp	Yds	Avg Gain	TD	Int	Rating Pts
Frerotte	396	199	50.3	2751	6.95	13	13	70.2
Shuler	125	66	52.8	745	5.96	3	7	55.6

RECEIVING	No.	Yds	Avg	Lg	TD
Ellard	56	1005	17.9	59	5
Mitchell	38	324	8.5	t22	1
Westbrook	34	522	15.4	45	1
Allen	31	232	7.5	24	1
Shepherd	29	486	16.8	t73	2
Logan	25	276	11.0	32	2

INTERCEPTIONS: Carter, 4

PUNTING	No.	Yds	Avg	Net Avg	TB	In 20	Lg	Blk
Turk	74	3140	42.4	37.7	9	29	60	0

SACKS: Harvey, 7.5

Tampa Bay Buccaneers

SCORING	Rush	Rec	Ret	PAT	FG	S	Pts
Husted	0	0	0	25/25	19/26	0	82
Rhett	11	0	0	0/0	0/0	0	66
Ellison	5	0	0	0/0	0/0	0	30

RUSHING	No.	Yds	Avg	Lg	TD
Rhett	332	1207	3.6	21	11
Ellison	26	218	8.4	75	5

PASSING	Att	Comp	Pct Comp	Yds	Avg Gain	TD	Int	Rating Pts
Dilfer	415	224	54.0	2774	6.68	4	18	60.1
Weldon	91	42	46.2	519	5.70	1	2	58.8

RECEIVING	No.	Yds	Avg	Lg	TD
Harris	62	751	12.1	33	1
Harper	46	633	13.8	49	2
Hawkins	41	493	12.0	47	0
Copeland	35	605	17.3	t64	2
Dawsey	30	372	12.4	26	0

INTERCEPTIONS: Mayhew, 5

PUNTING	No.	Yds	Avg	Net Avg	TB	In 20	Lg	Blk
Roby	77	3296	42.8	36.2	7	23	61	1

SACKS: Dotson, 5

Tampa Bay Profiteer

Back when grass was real, men bought NFL teams with fortunes made from honest industries such as steel and meat packing. Now comes the Dickensian tale of Malcolm Glazer, the Tampa Bay Buccaneer owner who got rich taxing puppies and kids.

Glazer operates trailer parks throughout upstate New York. For years this artful lodger had pinched inhabitants with monthly surcharges of $5 per pet and $3 per "additional occupant." Tenants groused, but it wasn't until Glazer agreed to cough up $192 million in January to buy the Bucs that they fought back. Now, as Tampa Bay fans accustomed to the penury of former owner Hugh Culverhous call Glazer a savior, trailer-park residents up north are calling him Scrooge. The tenants have filed a $100 million lawsuit charging "willful disregard of tenants' rights." They say that, despite the tax, Glazer didn't provide the amenities that kids and dogs are wont to use, such as playgrounds and grassy areas. Glazer dropped the fees last spring, but when he started spending millions on new free agents, he angered the mobile home folks even more. In Glazerbucks, wide receiver Alvin Harper, who signed a four-year, $10.66 million deal, is worth 3.5 million kid months, or 177,666 in dog years.

1996 NFL Draft

First two rounds of the 61st annual NFL Draft held April 20–21 in New York City.

First Round

Team	Selection	Position
1. ....NY Jets	Keyshawn Johnson, USC	WR
2. ....Jacksonville	Kevin Hardy, Illinois	LB
3. ....Arizona	Simeon Rice, Illinois	DE
4. ....Baltimore	Jonathan Ogden, UCLA	OT
5. ....NY Giants	Cedric Jones, Oklahoma	DE
6. ....St Louis	Lawrence Phillips, Nebraska	RB
7. ....New England	Terry Glenn, Ohio St	WR
8. ....Carolina	Tim Biakabutuka, Michigan	RB
9. ....Oakland	Rickey Dudley, Ohio St	TE
10. ......Cincinnati	Willie Anderson, Auburn	OT
11. ......New Orleans	Alex Molden, Oregon	DB
12. ......Tampa Bay	Regan Upshaw, California	DE
13. ......Chicago	Walt Harris, Mississippi St	DB
14. ......Houston	Eddie George, Ohio St	RB
15. ......Denver	John Mobley, Kutztown	LB
16. ......Minnesota	Duane Clemons, California	DE
17. ......Detroit	Reggie Brown, Texas A&M	LB
18. ......St Louis	Eddie Kennison, LSU	WR
19. ......Indianapolis	Marvin Harrison, Syracuse	WR
20. ......Miami	Daryl Gardener, Baylor	DT
21. ......Seattle	Pete Kendall, BC	OT
22. ......Tampa Bay	Marcus Jones, N Carolina	DT
23. ......Detroit	Jeff Hartings, Penn St	G
24. ......Buffalo	Eric Moulds, Mississippi St	WR
25. ......Philadelphia	Jermane Mayberry, Texas A&M-Kingsville	OT
26. ......Baltimore	Ray Lewis, Miami	LB
27. ......Green Bay	John Michels, USC	OT
28. ......Kansas City	Jerome Woods, Memphis	DB
29. ......Pittsburgh	Jamain Stephens, N Carolina A&T	OT
30. ......Washington	Andre Johnson, Penn St	OT

Second Round

Team	Selection	Position
31. ......NY Jets	Alex Van Dyke, Nevada	WR
32. ......Arizona	Leeland McElroy, Texas A&M	RB
33. ......Jacksonville	Tony Brackens, Texas	DE
34. ......NY Giants	Amani Toomer, Michigan	WR
35. ......Tampa Bay	Mike Alstott, Purdue	FB
36. ......New England	Lawyer Milloy, Washington	DB
37. ......Dallas	Kavika Pittman, McNeese St	DE
38. ......Houston	Bryant Mix, Alcorn St	DE
39. ......Cincinnati	Marco Battaglia, Rutgers	TE
40. ......New Orleans	Je'Rod Cherry, California	DB
41. ......San Diego	Bryan Still, Virginia Tech	WR
42. ......St Louis	Tony Banks, Michigan St	QB
43. ......Carolina	Muhsin Muhammad, Michigan St	WR
44. ......Denver	Tory James, LSU	DB
45. ......Minnesota	James Manley, Vanderbilt	DT
46. ......San Francisco	Israel Ifeanyi, USC	DE
47. ......Seattle	Fred Thomas, TN-Martin	DB
48. ......Houston	Jason Layman, Tennessee	G
49. ......Dallas	Randall Godfrey, Georgia	LB
50. ......San Diego	Patrick Sapp, Clemson	LB
51. ......Indianapolis	Dedric Mathis, Houston	DB
52. ......Chicago	Bobby Engram, Penn St	WR
53. ......Buffalo	Gabe Northern, LSU	DE
54. ......Philadelphia	Jason Dunn, Eastern KY	TE
55. ......Baltimore	DeRon Jenkins, Tennessee	DB
56. ......Green Bay	Derrick Mayes, Notre Dame	WR
57. ......Oakland	Lance Johnstone, Temple	LB
58. ......Kansas City	Reggie Tongue, Oregon St	DB
59. ......St Louis	Ernie Conwell, Washington	TE
60. ......Jacksonville	Michael Cheever, Georgia Tech	G
61. ......Philadelphia	Brian Dawkins, Clemson	DB

First Half Standings

	W	L	T	Pct	Pts/ Tm	Pts/ Opp
Scotland*	4	1	0	.800	102	63
Frankfurt	4	1	0	.800	137	101
Barcelona	3	2	0	.600	106	109
Amsterdam	2	3	0	.400	114	111
London	1	4	0	.200	67	118
Rhein	1	4	0	.200	82	106

*Clinched World Bowl '96 berth.

Final Standings

	W	L	T	Pct	Pts/ Tm	Pts/ Opp
Scotland	7	3	0	.700	206	159
Frankfurt*	6	4	0	.600	229	251
Amsterdam	5	5	0	.500	250	210
Barcelona	5	5	0	.500	192	220
London	4	6	0	.400	161	192
Rhein	3	7	0	.300	176	195

*Clinched World Bowl '96 berth.

1996 World Bowl

June 23, 1996 in Edinburgh, Scotland

Frankfurt Galaxy	7	7	6	7—27
Scottish Claymores	7	12	9	4—32

FIRST QUARTER

Scotland: Thomas 25 fumble return (Hastings kick), :11.

Frankfurt: Kearney 16 run (Kleinmann kick), 6:27.

SECOND QUARTER

Frankfurt: Bailey 2 pass from Pelluer (Kleinmann kick), 4:39.

Scotland: Murphy 6 pass from Ballard (kick failed), 14:02.

Scotland: Murphy 16 pass from Ballard (pass failed), 14:52.

THIRD QUARTER

Scotland: FG McCallum 46, 6:46.

Frankfurt: Bailey 32 pass from Pelluer (pass failed), 9:02.

Scotland: Murphy 71 pass from Ballard (kick failed), 8:42.

FOURTH QUARTER

Scotland: FG McCallum 50, 5:06.

Frankfurt: Bellamy 5 pass from Pelluer (Kleinmann kick), 12:10.

A: 38,892.

WLAF Individual Leaders

PASSING

	Att	Comp	Pct Comp	Yds	Avg Gain	TD	Pct TD	Int	Pct Int	Lg	Rating Pts
W. Furrer, Amsterdam	368	206	56.0	2689	7.31	20	5.4	13	3.5	48	82.6
S. Pelluer, Frankfurt	283	165	58.3	2136	7.55	11	3.9	12	4.2	90t	77.4
K. Holcomb, Barcelona	319	191	59.9	2382	7.47	14	4.4	16	5.0	87t	76.9
A. Kelly, Rhein	245	149	60.8	1333	5.44	9	3.7	7	2.9	44t	75.8
S. Matthews, Scotland	205	115	56.1	1560	7.61	9	4.4	10	4.9	52t	74.9

RECEIVING

RECEPTIONS	No.	Yds	Avg	Lg	TD	YARDS	Yds	No.	Avg	Lg	TD
B. Chamberlain, Rhein	58	685	11.8	32t	8	S. LaChapelle, Scot	1023	47	21.8	76	7
P. Bobo, Amsterdam	50	817	16.3	42t	4	P. Bobo, Amsterdam	817	50	16.3	42t	4
J. Kearney, Frankfurt	50	686	13.7	46t	6	J. Kearney, Frankfurt	686	50	13.7	46t	6
S. LaChapelle, Scot	47	1023	21.8	76	7	B. Chamberlain, Rhein	685	58	11.8	32t	8
B. Burnett, Barcelona	43	383	8.9	43	1	M. Bailey, Frankfurt	643	35	18.4	69	2

RUSHING

	Att	Yds	Avg	Lg	TD
S. Stacy, Scotland	208	780	3.8	43t	7
T. Vinson, London	105	516	4.9	67	3
C. Thompson, Bar	117	410	3.5	26	1
D. Clark, Rhein	84	399	4.8	23	3
T.C. Wright, Amster	80	379	4.7	22	2

Other Statistical Leaders

Points (TDs)	S. Stacy, Scotland	54
Points (Kicking)	S. Szeredy, Barcelona	42
Yards from Scrimmage	S. Stacy, Scotland	1097
Interceptions	K. McEntyre, London	5
	D.Studstill, London	5
	G. Coghill, Scotland	5
	J. Fuller, Scotland	5
Sacks	J. Drake, Scotland	8.0
Punting Avg.	S. Feexico, London	43.5
Punt Return Avg.	T.C. Wright, Amsterdam	16.0
Kickoff Return Avg.	B. Bryant, Amsterdam	24.1

NORTH DIVISION

	W	L	T	Pts	Pct	PF	PA
Calgary	15	3	0	30	.833	631	404
Edmonton	13	5	0	26	.722	599	359
British Columbia	10	8	0	20	.556	535	470
Hamilton	8	10	0	16	.444	427	509
Winnipeg	7	11	0	14	.389	404	653
Saskatchewan	6	12	0	12	.333	422	451
Toronto	4	14	0	8	.222	376	519
Ottawa	3	15	0	6	.167	348	685

SOUTH DIVISION

	W	L	T	Pts	Pct	PF	PA
Baltimore	15	3	0	30	.833	541	369
San Antonio	12	6	0	24	.667	630	457
Birmingham	10	8	0	20	.556	548	518
Memphis	9	9	0	18	.500	346	364
Shreveport	5	13	0	10	.278	465	514

Regular Season Statistical Leaders

Points (TDs)	Cory Philpot, B.C.	134
Points (Kicking)	Roman Anderson, S.A.	230
Yards (Rushing)	Mike Pringle, Baltimore	1791
Yards (Passing)	Matt Dunigan, Birmingham	4911
Yards (Receiving)	Dave Sapunjis, Calgary	1655
Receptions	Donald Narcisse, S.A.	123

1995 Playoff Results

DIVISION SEMIFINALS

North:	Hamilton 13, CALGARY 30
	British Columbia 15, EDMONTON 26
South:	Winnipeg 21, BALTIMORE 36
	Birmingham 9, SAN ANTONIO 52

DIVISION FINALS

North:	Edmonton 4, CALGARY 37
South:	San Antonio 11, BALTIMORE 21

1995 Grey Cup Championship

Nov. 19, 1995, at Taylor Field, Regina, Saskatchewan

Calgary Stampeders	6	7	7	0—20
Baltimore Stallions	7	16	8	6—37

A: 52,564

Congress at Work

Republicans and Democrats may haggle over things like health care and budgets, but when it comes to football, party lines dissolve. Indiana representatives Dan Burton, a Republican, and Andrew Jacobs, a Democrat, are cosponsoring a bill that would mandate the use of instant replay to review controversial calls in pro sports. They joined forces after the Indianapolis Colts lost 20-16 to the Pittsburgh Steelers in the AFC title game with the help of a blown call that gave Pittsburgh a touchdown.

The bill is called the What Really Happened Act of 1996. What's really happening, though, is that neither Burton nor Jacobs has nearly enough to do.

The Super Bowl

Results

	Date	Winner (Share)	Loser (Share)	Score	Site (Attendance)
I	1-15-67	Green Bay ($15,000)	Kansas City ($7,500)	35–10	Los Angeles (61,946)
II	1-14-68	Green Bay ($15,000)	Oakland ($7,500)	33–14	Miami (75,546)
III	1-12-69	NY Jets ($15,000)	Baltimore ($7,500)	16–7	Miami (75,389)
IV	1-11-70	Kansas City ($15,000)	Minnesota ($7,500)	23–7	New Orleans (80,562)
V	1-17-71	Baltimore ($15,000)	Dallas ($7,500)	16–13	Miami (79,204)
VI	1-16-72	Dallas ($15,000)	Miami ($7,500)	24–3	New Orleans (81,023)
VII	1-14-73	Miami ($15,000)	Washington ($7,500)	14–7	Los Angeles (90,182)
VIII	1-13-74	Miami ($15,000)	Minnesota ($7,500)	24–7	Houston (71,882)
IX	1-12-75	Pittsburgh ($15,000)	Minnesota ($7,500)	16–6	New Orleans (80,997)
X	1-18-76	Pittsburgh ($15,000)	Dallas ($7,500)	21–17	Miami (80,187)
XI	1-9-77	Oakland ($15,000)	Minnesota ($7,500)	32–14	Pasadena (103,438)
XII	1-15-78	Dallas ($18,000)	Denver ($9,000)	27–10	New Orleans (75,583)
XIII	1-21-79	Pittsburgh ($18,000)	Dallas ($9,000)	35–31	Miami (79,484)
XIV	1-20-80	Pittsburgh ($18,000)	Los Angeles ($9,000)	31–19	Pasadena (103,985)
XV	1-25-81	Oakland ($18,000)	Philadelphia ($9,000)	27–10	New Orleans (76,135)
XVI	1-24-82	San Francisco ($18,000)	Cincinnati ($9,000)	26–21	Pontiac, MI (81,270)
XVII	1-30-83	Washington ($36,000)	Miami ($18,000)	27–17	Pasadena (103,667)
XVIII	1-22-84	LA Raiders ($36,000)	Washington ($18,000)	38–9	Tampa (72,920)
XIX	1-20-85	San Francisco ($36,000)	Miami ($18,000)	38–16	Stanford (84,059)
XX	1-26-86	Chicago ($36,000)	New England ($18,000)	46–10	New Orleans (73,818)
XXI	1-25-87	NY Giants ($36,000)	Denver ($18,000)	39–20	Pasadena (101,063)
XXII	1-31-88	Washington ($36,000)	Denver ($18,000)	42–10	San Diego (73,302)
XXIII	1-22-89	San Francisco ($36,000)	Cincinnati ($18,000)	20–16	Miami (75,129)
XXIV	1-28-90	San Francisco ($36,000)	Denver ($18,000)	55–10	New Orleans (72,919)
XXV	1-27-91	NY Giants ($36,000)	Buffalo ($18,000)	20–19	Tampa (73,813)
XXVI	1-26-92	Washington ($36,000)	Buffalo ($18,000)	37–24	Minneapolis (63,130)
XXVII	1-31-93	Dallas ($36,000)	Buffalo ($18,000)	52–17	Pasadena (98,374)
XXVIII	1-30-94	Dallas ($38,000)	Buffalo ($23,500)	30–13	Atlanta (72,817)
XXIX	1-29-95	San Francisco ($42,000)	San Diego ($26,000)	49–26	Miami (74,107)
XXX	1-28-96	Dallas ($42,000)	Pittsburgh ($27,000)	27–17	Tempe, AZ (76,347)

Most Valuable Players

		Position
I	Bart Starr, GB	QB
II	Bart Starr, GB	QB
III	Joe Namath, NYJ	QB
IV	Len Dawson, KC	QB
V	Chuck Howley, Dall	LB
VI	Roger Staubach, Dall	QB
VII	Jake Scott, Mia	S
VIII	Larry Csonka, Mia	RB
IX	Franco Harris, Pitt	RB
X	Lynn Swann, Pitt	WR
XI	Fred Biletnikoff, Oak	WR
XII	Randy White, Dall	DT
	Harvey Martin, Dall	DE
XIII	Terry Bradshaw, Pitt	QB
XIV	Terry Bradshaw, Pitt	QB
XV	Jim Plunkett, Oak	QB
XVI	Joe Montana, SF	QB
XVII	John Riggins, Wash	RB
XVIII	Marcus Allen, Rai	RB
XIX	Joe Montana, SF	QB
XX	Richard Dent, Chi	DE
XXI	Phil Simms, NYG	QB
XXII	Doug Williams, Wash	QB
XXIII	Jerry Rice, SF	WR
XXIV	Joe Montana, SF	QB
XXV	Ottis Anderson, NYG	RB
XXVI	Mark Rypien, Wash	QB

Most Valuable Players (Cont.)

		Position
XXVII	Troy Aikman, Dall	QB
XXVIII	Emmitt Smith, Dall	RB
XXIX	Steve Young, SF	QB
XXX	Larry Brown, Dall	DB

Composite Standings

	W	L	Pct	Pts	Opp Pts
San Francisco 49ers	5	0	1.000	188	89
Green Bay Packers	2	0	1.000	68	24
NY Giants	2	0	1.000	59	39
Chicago Bears	1	0	1.000	46	10
NY Jets	1	0	1.000	16	7
Pittsburgh Steelers	4	1	.800	120	100
Oakland/LA Raiders	3	1	.750	111	66
Dallas Cowboys	5	3	.625	221	132
Washington Redskins	3	2	.600	122	103
Baltimore Colts	1	1	.500	23	29
Kansas City Chiefs	1	1	.500	33	42
Miami Dolphins	2	3	.400	74	103
LA Rams	0	1	.000	19	31
New England Patriots	0	1	.000	10	46
Philadelphia Eagles	0	1	.000	10	27
San Diego Chargers	0	1	.000	26	49
Cincinnati Bengals	0	2	.000	37	46
Buffalo Bills	0	4	.000	73	139
Denver Broncos	0	4	.000	50	163
Minnesota Vikings	0	4	.000	34	95

Career Leaders
Passing

	GP	Att	Comp	Pct Comp	Yds	Avg Gain	TD	Pct TD	Int	Pct Int	Lg	Rating Pts
Joe Montana, SF	4	122	83	68.0	1142	9.36	11	9.0	0	0.0	44	127.8
Jim Plunkett, Rai	2	46	29	63.0	433	9.41	4	8.7	0	0.0	t80	122.8
Terry Bradshaw, Pitt	4	84	49	58.3	932	11.10	9	10.7	4	4.8	t75	112.8
Troy Aikman, Dall	3	80	56	70.0	689	8.61	5	6.3	1	1.3	t56	111.9
Bart Starr, GB	2	47	29	61.7	452	9.62	3	6.4	1	2.1	t62	106.0
Roger Staubach, Dall	4	98	61	62.2	734	7.49	8	8.2	4	4.1	t45	95.4
Len Dawson, KC	2	44	28	63.6	353	8.02	2	4.5	2	4.5	t46	84.8
Bob Griese, Mia	3	41	26	63.4	295	7.20	1	2.4	2	4.9	t28	72.7
Dan Marino, Mia	1	50	29	58.0	318	6.36	1	2.0	2	4.0	30	66.9
Jim Kelly, Buff	4	145	81	55.9	829	5.72	2	1.4	7	4.8	61	57.2
Joe Theismann, Wash	2	58	31	53.4	386	6.66	2	3.4	4	6.9	60	57.1

Note: Minimum 40 attempts.

Rushing

	GP	Yds	Att	Avg	Lg	TD
Franco Harris, Pitt	4	354	101	3.5	25	4
Larry Csonka, Mia	3	297	57	5.2	9	2
Emmitt Smith, Dall	3	289	70	4.1	38	5
John Riggins, Wash	2	230	64	3.6	43	2
Timmy Smith, Wash	1	204	22	9.3	58	2
Thurman Thomas, Buff	4	204	52	3.9	31	4
Roger Craig, SF	3	198	52	3.8	18	2
Marcus Allen, Rai	1	191	20	9.6	t74	2
Tony Dorsett, Dall	2	162	31	5.2	29	1
Mark van Eeghen, Rai	2	148	36	4.1	11	0

Receiving

	GP	No.	Yds	Avg	Lg	TD
Jerry Rice, SF	3	28	512	18.3	t44	7
Andre Reed, Buff	4	27	323	11.9	40	0
Roger Craig, SF	3	20	212	10.6	40	2
Thurman Thomas, Buff	4	20	144	7.2	24	0
Tom Novacek, Dall	3	17	178	10.5	23	2
Lynn Swann, Pitt	4	16	364	22.8	t64	3
Michael Irvin, Dall	3	16	256	16.0	25	2
Chuck Foreman, Minn	3	15	139	9.3	26	0
Cliff Branch, Rai	3	14	181	12.9	50	3
Preston Pearson, Balt-Pitt-Dall	5	12	105	8.8	14	0
Don Beebe, Buff	3	12	171	14.3	43	2
Kenneth Davis, Buff	4	12	72	6.0	19	0

Single-Game Leaders

Scoring

	Pts
Roger Craig: XIX, San Francisco vs Miami (1 R, 2 P)	18
Jerry Rice: XXIV, San Francisco vs Denver (3 P); XXIX, SF vs San Diego (3 P)	18
Ricky Watters: XXIX, San Francisco vs San Diego (1 R, 2 P)	18

Touchdown Passes

	No.
Steve Young: XXIX, San Francisco vs San Diego	6
Joe Montana: XXIV, San Francisco vs Denver	5
Terry Bradshaw: XIII, Pittsburgh vs Dallas	4
Doug Williams: XXII, Washington vs Denver	4
Troy Aikman: XXVII, Dallas vs Buffalo	4

Four tied with 3.

Rushing Yards

	Yds
Timmy Smith: XXII, Washington vs Denver	204
Marcus Allen: XVIII, LA Raiders vs Washington	191
John Riggins: XVII, Washington vs Miami	166
Franco Harris: IX, Pittsburgh vs Minnesota	158
Larry Csonka: VIII, Miami vs Minnesota	145
Clarence Davis: XI, Oakland vs Minnesota	137
Thurman Thomas: XXV, Buffalo vs NY Giants	135
Emmitt Smith: XXVIII, Dallas vs Buffalo	132

Receiving Yards

	Yds
Jerry Rice: XXIII, San Francisco vs Cincinnati	215
Ricky Sanders: XXII, Washington vs Denver	193
Lynn Swann: X, Pittsburgh vs Dallas	161
Andre Reed: XXVII, Buffalo vs Dallas	152
Jerry Rice: XXIX, San Francisco vs San Diego	149
Jerry Rice: XXIV, San Francisco vs Denver	148
Max McGee: I, Green Bay vs Kansas City	138
George Sauer: III, NY Jets vs Baltimore	133

Receptions

	No.
Dan Ross: XVI, Cincinnati vs San Francisco	11
Jerry Rice: XXIII, San Francisco vs Cincinnati	11
Tony Nathan: XIX, Miami vs San Francisco	10
Jerry Rice: XXIX, San Francisco vs San Diego	10
Andre Hastings: XXX, Pittsburgh vs Dallas	10
Ricky Sanders: XXII, Washington vs Denver	9

Six tied with 8.

Passing Yards

	Yds
Joe Montana: XXIII, San Francisco vs Cincinnati	357
Doug Williams: XXII, Washington vs Denver	340
Joe Montana: XIX, San Francisco vs Miami	331
Steve Young: XXIX, San Francisco vs San Diego	325
Terry Bradshaw: XIII, Pittsburgh vs Dallas	318
Dan Marino: XIX, Miami vs San Francisco	318
Terry Bradshaw: XIV, Pittsburgh vs LA Rams	309
John Elway: XXI, Denver vs NY Giants	304

NFL Playoff History

1933
NFL championship Chicago Bears 23, NY Giants 21

1934
NFL championship NY Giants 30, Chicago Bears 13

1935
NFL championship Detroit 26, NY Giants 7

1936
NFL championship Green Bay 21, Boston 6

1937
NFL championship Washington 28, Chicago Bears 21

1938
NFL championship NY Giants 23, Green Bay 17

1939
NFL championship Green Bay 27, NY Giants 0

1940
NFL championship Chicago Bears 73, Washington 0

1941
W. div. playoff Chicago Bears 33, Green Bay 14
NFL championship Chicago Bears 37, NY Giants 9

1942
NFL championship Washington 14, Chicago Bears 6

1943
E. div. playoff Washington 28, NY Giants 0
NFL championship Chicago Bears 41, Washington 21

1944
NFL championship Green Bay 14, NY Giants 7

1945
NFL championship Cleveland 15, Washington 14

1946
NFL championship Chicago Bears 24, NY Giants 14

1947
E. div. playoff Philadelphia 21, Pittsburgh 0
NFL championship Chicago Cardinals 28, Philadelphia 21

1948
NFL championship Philadelphia 7, Chicago Cardinals 0

1949
NFL championship Philadelphia 14, Los Angeles 0

1950
Am. Conf. playoff Cleveland 8, NY Giants 3
Nat. Conf. playoff Los Angeles 24, Chicago Bears 14
NFL championship Cleveland 30, Los Angeles 28

1951
NFL championship Los Angeles 24, Cleveland 17

1952
Nat. Conf. playoff Detroit 31, Los Angeles 21
NFL championship Detroit 17, Cleveland 7

1953
NFL championship Detroit 17, Cleveland 16

1954
NFL championship Cleveland 56, Detroit 10

1955
NFL championship Cleveland 38, Los Angeles 14

1956
NFL championship NY Giants 47, Chicago Bears 7

1957
W. Conf. playoff Detroit 31, San Francisco 27
NFL championship Detroit 59, Cleveland 14

1958
E. Conf. playoff NY Giants 10, Cleveland 0
NFL championship Baltimore 23, NY Giants 17

1959
NFL championship Baltimore 31, NY Giants 16

1960
NFL championship Philadelphia 17, Green Bay 13
AFL championship Houston 24, LA Chargers 16

1961
NFL championship Green Bay 37, NY Giants 0
AFL championship Houston 10, San Diego 3

1962
NFL championship Green Bay 16, NY Giants 7
AFL championship Dallas Texans 20, Houston 17

1963
NFL championship Chicago 14, NY Giants 10
AFL E. div. playoff Boston 26, Buffalo 8
AFL championship San Diego 51, Boston 10

1964
NFL championship Cleveland 27, Baltimore 0
AFL championship Buffalo 20, San Diego 7

1965
NFL W. Conf. playoff Green Bay 13, Baltimore 10
NFL championship Green Bay 23, Cleveland 12
AFL championship Buffalo 23, San Diego 0

1966
NFL championship Green Bay 34, Dallas 27
AFL championship Kansas City 31, Buffalo 7

1967
NFL E. Conf. championship Dallas 52, Cleveland 14
NFL W. Conf. championship Green Bay 28, Los Angeles 7
NFL championship Green Bay 21, Dallas 17
AFL championship Oakland 40, Houston 7

1968
NFL E. Conf. championship Cleveland 31, Dallas 20
NFL W. Conf. championship Baltimore 24, Minnesota 14
NFL championship Baltimore 34, Cleveland 0
AFL W. div. playoff Oakland 41, Kansas City 6
AFL championship NY Jets 27, Oakland 23

1969

NFL E. Conf. championship	Cleveland 38, Dallas 14
NFL W. Conf. championship	Minnesota 23, Los Angeles 20
NFL championship	Minnesota 27, Cleveland 7
AFL div. playoffs	Kansas City 13, NY Jets 6
	Oakland 56, Houston 7
AFL championship	Kansas City 17, Oakland 7

1970

AFC div. playoffs	Baltimore 17, Cincinnati 0
	Oakland 21, Miami 14
AFC championship	Baltimore 27, Oakland 17
NFC div. playoffs	Dallas 5, Detroit 0
	San Francisco 17, Minnesota 14
NFC championship	Dallas 17, San Francisco 10

1971

AFC div. playoffs	Miami 27, Kansas City 24
	Baltimore 20, Cleveland 3
AFC championship	Miami 21, Baltimore 0
NFC div. playoffs	Dallas 20, Minnesota 12
	San Francisco 24, Washington 20
NFC championship	Dallas 14, San Francisco 3

1972

AFC div. playoffs	Pittsburgh 13, Oakland 7
	Miami 20, Cleveland 14
AFC championship	Miami 21, Pittsburgh 17
NFC div. playoffs	Dallas 30, San Francisco 28
	Washington 16, Green Bay 3
NFC championship	Washington 26, Dallas 3

1973

AFC div. playoffs	Oakland 33, Pittsburgh 14
	Miami 34, Cincinnati 16
AFC championship	Miami 27, Oakland 10
NFC div. playoffs	Minnesota 27, Washington 20
	Dallas 27, Los Angeles 16
NFC championship	Minnesota 27, Dallas 10

1974

AFC div. playoffs	Oakland 28, Miami 26
	Pittsburgh 32, Buffalo 14
AFC championship	Pittsburgh 24, Oakland 13
NFC div. playoffs	Minnesota 30, St Louis 14
	Los Angeles 19, Washington 10
NFC championship	Minnesota 14, Los Angeles 10

1975

AFC div. playoffs	Pittsburgh 28, Baltimore 10
	Oakland 31, Cincinnati 28
AFC championship	Pittsburgh 16, Oakland 10
NFC div. playoffs	Los Angeles 35, St Louis 23
	Dallas 17, Minnesota 14
NFC championship	Dallas 37, Los Angeles 7

1976

AFC div. playoffs	Oakland 24, New England 21
	Pittsburgh 40, Baltimore 14
AFC championship	Oakland 24, Pittsburgh 7
NFC div. playoffs	Minnesota 35, Washington 20
	Los Angeles 14, Dallas 12
NFC championship	Minnesota 24, Los Angeles 13

1977

AFC div. playoffs	Denver 34, Pittsburgh 21
	Oakland 37, Baltimore 31
AFC championship	Denver 20, Oakland 17

1977 *(Cont.)*

NFC div. playoffs	Dallas 37, Chicago 7
	Minnesota 14, Los Angeles 7
NFC championship	Dallas 23, Minnesota 6

1978

AFC 1st-rd. playoff	Houston 17, Miami 9
AFC div. playoffs	Houston 31, New England 14
	Pittsburgh 33, Denver 10
AFC championship	Pittsburgh 34, Houston 5
NFC 1st-rd. playoff	Atlanta 14, Philadelphia 13
NFC div. playoffs	Dallas 27, Atlanta 20
	Los Angeles 34, Minnesota 10
NFC championship	Dallas 28, Los Angeles 0

1979

AFC 1st-rd. playoff	Houston 13, Denver 7
AFC div. playoffs	Houston 17, San Diego 14
	Pittsburgh 34, Miami 14
AFC championship	Pittsburgh 27, Houston 13
NFC 1st-rd. playoff	Philadelphia 27, Chicago 17
NFC div. playoffs	Tampa Bay 24, Philadelphia 17
	Los Angeles 21, Dallas 19
NFC championship	Los Angeles 9, Tampa Bay 0

1980

AFC 1st-rd. playoff	Oakland 27, Houston 7
AFC div. playoffs	San Diego 20, Buffalo 14
	Oakland 14, Cleveland 12
AFC championship	Oakland 34, San Diego 27
NFC 1st-rd. playoff	Dallas 34, Los Angeles 13
NFC div. playoffs	Philadelphia 31, Minnesota 16
	Dallas 30, Atlanta 27
NFC championship	Philadelphia 20, Dallas 7

1981

AFC 1st-rd. playoff	Buffalo 31, NY Jets 27
AFC div. playoffs	San Diego 41, Miami 38
	Cincinnati 28, Buffalo 21
AFC championship	Cincinnati 27, San Diego 7
NFC 1st-rd. playoff	NY Giants 27, Philadelphia 21
NFC div. playoffs	Dallas 38, Tampa Bay 0
	San Francisco 38, NY Giants 24
NFC championship	San Francisco 28, Dallas 27

1982

AFC 1st-rd. playoffs	Miami 28, New England 13
	LA Raiders 27, Cleveland 10
	NY Jets 44, Cincinnati 17
	San Diego 31, Pittsburgh 28
AFC div. playoffs	NY Jets 17, LA Raiders 14
	Miami 34, San Diego 13
AFC championship	Miami 14, NY Jets 0
NFC 1st-rd. playoffs	Washington 31, Detroit 7
	Green Bay 41, St Louis 16
	Minnesota 30, Atlanta 24
	Dallas 30, Tampa Bay 17
NFC div. playoffs	Washington 21, Minnesota 7
	Dallas 37, Green Bay 26
NFC championship	Washington 31, Dallas 17

1983

AFC 1st-rd. playoff	Seattle 31, Denver 7
AFC div. playoffs	Seattle 27, Miami 20
	LA Raiders 38, Pittsburgh 10
AFC championship	LA Raiders 30, Seattle 14
NFC 1st-rd. playoff	LA Rams 24, Dallas 17
NFC div. playoffs	San Francisco 24, Detroit 23
	Washington 51, LA Rams 7
NFC championship	Washington 24, San Francisco 21

1984

AFC 1st-rd. playoff	Seattle 13, LA Raiders 7
AFC div. playoffs	Miami 31, Seattle 10
	Pittsburgh 24, Denver 17
AFC championship	Miami 45, Pittsburgh 28
NFC 1st-rd. playoff	NY Giants 16, LA Rams 13
NFC div. playoffs	San Francisco 21, NY Giants 10
	Chicago 23, Washington 19
NFC championship	San Francisco 23, Chicago 0

1985

AFC 1st-rd. playoff	New England 26, NY Jets 14
AFC div. playoffs	Miami 24, Cleveland 21
	New England 27, LA Raiders 20
AFC championship	New England 31, Miami 14
NFC 1st-rd. playoff	NY Giants 17, San Francisco 3
NFC div. playoffs	LA Rams 20, Dallas 0
	Chicago 21, NY Giants 0
NFC championship	Chicago 24, LA Rams 0

1986

AFC 1st-rd. playoff	NY Jets 35, Kansas City 15
AFC div. playoffs	Cleveland 23, NY Jets 20
	Denver 22, New England 17
AFC championship	Denver 23, Cleveland 20
NFC 1st-rd. playoff	Washington 19, LA Rams 7
NFC div playoffs	Washington 27, Chicago 13
	NY Giants 49, San Francisco 3
NFC championship	NY Giants 17, Washington 0

1987

AFC div. playoffs	Cleveland 38, Indianapolis 21
	Denver 34, Houston 10
AFC championship	Denver 38, Cleveland 33
NFC 1st-rd. playoff	Minnesota 44, New Orleans 10
NFC div playoffs	Minnesota 36, San Francisco 24
	Washington 21, Chicago 17
NFC championship	Washington 17, Minnesota 10

1988

AFC 1st-rd. playoff	Houston 24, Cleveland 23
AFC div. playoffs	Cincinnati 21, Seattle 13
	Buffalo 17, Houston 10
AFC championship	Cincinnati 21, Buffalo 10
NFC 1st-rd. playoff	Minnesota 28, LA Rams 17
NFC div. playoffs	Chicago 20, Philadelphia 12
	San Francisco 34, Minnesota 9
NFC championship	San Francisco 28, Chicago 3

1989

AFC 1st-rd. playoff	Pittsburgh 26, Houston 23
AFC div. playoffs	Cleveland 34, Buffalo 30
AFC div. playoffs	Denver 24, Pittsburgh 23
AFC championship	Denver 37, Cleveland 21
NFC 1st-rd. playoff	LA Rams 21, Philadelphia 7
NFC div. playoffs	LA Rams 19, NY Giants 13
	San Francisco 41, Minnesota 13
NFC championship	San Francisco 30, LA Rams 3

1990

AFC 1st-rd. playoffs	Miami 17, Kansas City 16
	Cincinnati 41, Houston 14
AFC div. playoffs	Buffalo 44, Miami 34
	LA Raiders 20, Cincinnati 10
AFC championship	Buffalo 51, LA Raiders 3
NFC 1st-rd. playoffs	Chicago 16, New Orleans 6
	Washington 20, Philadelphia 6
NFC div. playoffs	NY Giants 31, Chicago 3
	San Francisco 28, Washington 10
NFC championship	NY Giants 15, San Francisco 13

1991

AFC 1st-rd. playoffs	Houston 17, NY Jets 10
	Kansas City 10, LA Raiders 6
AFC div. playoffs	Denver 26, Houston 24
	Buffalo 37, Kansas City 14
AFC championship	Buffalo 10, Denver 7
NFC 1st-rd. playoffs	Atlanta 27, New Orleans 20
	Dallas 17, Chicago 13
NFC div. playoffs	Washington 24, Atlanta 7
	Detroit 38, Dallas 6
NFC championship	Washington 41, Detroit 10

1992

AFC 1st-rd. playoffs	San Diego 17, Kansas City 0
	Buffalo 41, Houston 38 (OT)
AFC div. playoffs	Buffalo 24, Pittsburgh 3
	Miami 31, San Diego 0
AFC championship	Buffalo 29, Miami 10
NFC 1st-rd. playoffs	Washington 24, Minnesota 7
	Philadelphia 36, New Orleans 20
NFC div. playoffs	San Francisco 20, Washington 13
	Dallas 34, Philadelphia 10
NFC championship	Dallas 30, San Francisco 20

1993

AFC 1st-rd. playoffs	LA Raiders 42, Denver 24
	Kansas City 27, Pittsburgh 24 (OT)
AFC div. playoffs	Buffalo 29, LA Raiders 23
	Kansas City 28, Houston 20
AFC championship	Buffalo 30, Kansas City 13
NFC 1st-rd. playoffs	NY Giants 17, Minnesota 10
	Green Bay 28, Detroit 24
NFC div. playoffs	San Francisco 44, NY Giants 3
	Dallas 27, Green Bay 17
NFC championship	Dallas 38, San Francisco 21

1994

AFC 1st-rd. playoffs	Miami 27, Kansas City 17
	Cleveland 20, New England 13
AFC div. playoffs	San Diego 22, Miami 21
	Pittsburgh 29, Cleveland 9
AFC championship	San Diego 17, Pittsburgh 13
NFC 1st-rd. playoffs	Green Bay 16, Detroit 12
	Chicago 35, Minnesota 18
NFC div. playoffs	Dallas 35, Green Bay 9
	San Francisco 44, Chicago 15
NFC championship	San Francisco 38, Dallas 28

1995

AFC 1st-rd. playoffs	Buffalo 37, Miami 22
	Indianapolis 35. San Diego 20
AFC div. playoffs	Pittsburgh 40, Buffalo 21
	Indianapolis 10, Kansas City 7
AFC championship	Pittsburgh 20, Indianapolis 16
NFC 1st-rd. playoffs	Philadelphia 58, Detroit 37
	Green Bay 37, Atlanta 20
NFC div. playoffs	Dallas 30, Philadelphia 11
	Green Bay 27, San Francisco 17
NFC championship	Dallas 38, Green Bay 27

Career Leaders

Scoring

	Yrs	TD	FG	PAT	Pts
George Blanda	26	9	335	943	2002
Jan Stenerud	19	0	373	580	1699
†Nick Lowery	17	0	366	536	1634
†Eddie Murray	18	0	325	498	1473
Pat Leahy	18	0	304	558	1470
†Gary Anderson	14	0	331	448	1441
†Morten Andersen	14	0	333	441	1440
Jim Turner	16	1	304	521	1439
†Matt Bahr	17	0	300	522	1422
Mark Moseley	16	0	300	482	1382
Jim Bakken	17	0	282	534	1380
Fred Cox	15	0	282	519	1365
†Norm Johnson	14	0	277	515	1354
Lou Groza	17	1	234	641	1349
Jim Breech	14	0	243	517	1246
Chris Bahr	14	0	241	490	1213
Gino Cappelletti	11	42	176	350	1130
Ray Wersching	15	0	222	456	1122
†Kevin Butler	11	0	243	387	1116
Don Cockroft	13	0	216	432	1080

Cappelletti's total includes four two-point conversions.

Rushing

	Yrs	Att	Yds	Avg	Lg	TD
Walter Payton	13	3,838	16,726	4.4	76	110
Eric Dickerson	11	2,996	13,259	4.4	85	90
Tony Dorsett	12	2,936	12,739	4.3	99	77
Jim Brown	9	2,359	12,312	5.2	80	106
Franco Harris	13	2,949	12,120	4.1	75	91
John Riggins	14	2,916	11,352	3.9	66	104
O.J. Simpson	11	2,404	11,236	4.7	94	61
†Marcus Allen	14	2,692	10,908	4.1	61	103
Ottis Anderson	14	2,562	10,273	4.0	76	81
†Barry Sanders	7	2,077	10,172	4.9	85	73
†Thurman Thomas	8	2,285	9,729	4.3	80	54
Earl Campbell	8	2,187	9,407	4.3	81	74
†Emmitt Smith	6	2,007	8,956	4.5	75	96
Jim Taylor	10	1,941	8,597	4.4	84	83
Joe Perry	14	1,737	8,378	4.8	78	53
Roger Craig	11	1,991	8,189	4.1	71	56
Gerald Riggs	10	1,989	8,188	4.1	58	69
†Herschel Walker	10	1,938	8,122	4.2	91	60
Larry Csonka	11	1,891	8,081	4.3	54	64
Freeman McNeil	12	1,798	8,074	4.5	69	38

Touchdowns

	Yrs	Rush	Pass Rec	Ret	Total TD
†Jerry Rice	11	9	146	1	156
Jim Brown	9	106	20	0	126
†Marcus Allen	14	103	21	1	125
Walter Payton	13	110	15	0	125
John Riggins	14	104	12	0	116
Lenny Moore	12	63	48	2	113
Don Hutson	11	3	99	3	105
Steve Largent	14	1	100	0	101
Franco Harris	13	91	9	0	100
†Emmitt Smith	6	96	4	0	100

	Yrs	Rush	Pass Rec	Ret	Total TD
Eric Dickerson	11	90	6	0	96
Jim Taylor	10	83	10	0	93
Tony Dorsett	12	77	13	1	91
Bobby Mitchell	11	18	65	8	91
Leroy Kelly	10	74	13	3	90
Charley Taylor	13	11	79	0	90
Don Maynard	15	0	88	0	88
Lance Alworth	11	2	85	0	87
Ottis Anderson	14	81	5	0	86
Paul Warfield	13	1	85	0	86

Combined Yards Gained

	Yrs	Total	Rush	Rec	Int Ret	Punt Ret	Kickoff Ret	Fum Ret
Walter Payton	13	21,803	16,726	4,538	0	0	539	0
Tony Dorsett	12	16,326	12,739	3,554	0	0	0	33
†Marcus Allen	14	15,957	10,908	5,055	0	0	0	−6
†Herschel Walker	10	15,881	8,122	4,621	0	0	3,138	0
†Jerry Rice	11	15,676	547	15,123	0	0	6	0
Jim Brown	9	15,459	12,312	2,499	0	0	648	0
Eric Dickerson	11	15,411	13,259	2,137	0	0	0	15
James Brooks	12	14,910	7,962	3,621	0	565	2,762	0
Franco Harris	13	14,622	12,120	2,287	0	0	233	−18
O.J. Simpson	11	14,368	11,236	2,142	0	0	990	0
James Lofton	16	14,277	246	14,004	0	0	0	27
†Henry Ellard	13	14,104	50	12,163	0	1,527	364	0
Bobby Mitchell	11	14,078	2,735	7,954	0	699	2,690	0
John Riggins	14	13,435	11,352	2,090	0	0	0	−7
Steve Largent	14	13,396	83	13,089	0	68	156	0
Ottis Anderson	14	13,364	10,273	3,062	0	0	0	29
†Thurman Thomas	8	13,351	9,729	3,622	0	0	0	0
Drew Hill	14	13,337	19	9,831	0	22	3,460	5
Greg Pruitt	12	13,262	5,672	3,069	0	2,007	2,514	0
Roger Craig	11	13,143	8,189	4,911	0	0	43	0

† Active player.

Career Leaders *(Cont.)*

Passing

PASSING EFFICIENCY*

	Yrs	Att	Comp	Pct Comp	Yds	Avg Gain	TD	Pct TD	Int	Pct Int	Rating Pts
†Steve Young	11	2,876	1,845	64.2	23,069	8.02	160	5.6	79	2.7	96.1
Joe Montana	15	5,391	3,409	63.2	40,551	7.52	273	5.1	139	2.6	92.3
†Dan Marino	13	6,531	3,913	59.9	48,841	7.48	352	5.4	200	3.1	88.4
†Brett Favre	5	2,150	1,342	62.4	14,825	6.90	108	5.0	66	3.1	86.8
†Jim Kelly	10	4,400	2,652	60.3	32,657	7.42	223	5.1	156	3.5	85.4
†Troy Aikman	7	2,713	1,704	62.8	19,607	7.23	98	3.6	85	3.1	83.5
Roger Staubach	11	2,958	1,685	57.0	22,700	7.67	153	5.2	109	3.7	83.4
Neil Lomax	8	3,153	1,817	57.6	22,771	7.22	136	4.3	90	2.9	82.7
Sonny Jurgensen	18	4,262	2,433	57.1	32,224	7.56	255	6.0	189	4.4	82.6
Len Dawson	19	3,741	2,136	57.1	28,711	7.67	239	6.4	183	4.9	82.6
†Dave Krieg	16	4,911	2,866	58.4	35,668	7.26	247	5.0	187	3.8	81.9
Ken Anderson	16	4,475	2,654	59.3	32,838	7.34	197	4.4	160	3.6	81.9
†Jeff Hostetler	10	1,792	1,036	57.8	12,983	7.24	66	3.7	47	2.6	81.8
†Neil O'Donnell	5	1,871	1,069	57.1	12,867	6.88	68	3.6	39	2.1	81.8
Danny White	13	2,950	1,761	59.7	21,959	7.44	155	5.3	132	4.5	81.7
†Bernie Kosar	11	3,333	1,970	59.1	23,093	6.93	123	3.7	87	2.6	81.6
†Warren Moon	12	5,753	3,380	58.8	42,177	7.33	247	4.3	199	3.5	81.5
†Boomer Esiason	12	4,680	2,661	56.9	34,149	7.30	223	4.8	168	3.6	80.8
Bart Starr	16	3,149	1,808	57.4	24,718	7.85	152	4.8	138	4.4	80.5
Ken O'Brien	10	3,602	2,110	58.6	25,094	6.97	128	3.6	98	2.7	80.4
Fran Tarkenton	18	6,467	3,686	57.0	47,003	7.27	342	5.3	266	4.1	80.4

*1,500 or more attempts. The passing ratings are based on performance standards established for completion percentage, interception percentage, touchdown percentage and average gain. Passers are allocated points according to how their marks compare with those standards.

YARDS

	Yrs	Att	Comp	Pct Comp	Yds		Yrs	Att	Comp	Pct Comp	Yds
†Dan Marino	13	6,531	3,913	59.9	48,841	Steve DeBerg	16	4,965	2,844	57.3	33,872
Fran Tarkenton	18	6,467	3,686	57.0	47,003	John Hadl	16	4,687	2,363	50.4	33,503
Dan Fouts	15	5,604	3,297	58.8	43,040	Phil Simms	14	4,647	2,576	55.4	33,462
†Warren Moon	12	5,753	3,380	58.8	42,177	Ken Anderson	16	4,475	2,654	59.3	32,838
†John Elway	13	5,926	3,346	56.5	41,706	†Jim Kelly	10	4,400	2,652	60.3	32,657
Joe Montana	15	5,391	3,409	63.2	40,551	Sonny Jurgensen	18	4,262	2,433	57.1	32,224
Johnny Unitas	18	5,186	2,830	54.6	40,239	†Jim Everett	10	4,384	2,538	57.9	31,583
†Dave Krieg	16	4,911	2,866	58.4	35,668	John Brodie	17	4,491	2,469	55.0	31,548
Jim Hart	19	5,076	2,593	51.1	34,665	Norm Snead	15	4,353	2,276	52.3	30,797
†Boomer Esiason	12	4,680	2,661	56.9	34,149	Joe Ferguson	18	4,519	2,369	52.4	29,817

TOUCHDOWNS

	No.		No.		No.
†Dan Marino	352	George Blanda	236	Ken Anderson	197
Fran Tarkenton	342	†John Elway	225	Joe Ferguson	196
Johnny Unitas	290	†Boomer Esiason	223	Bobby Layne	196
Joe Montana	273	†Jim Kelly	223	Norm Snead	196
Sonny Jurgensen	255	John Brodie	214	Ken Stabler	194
Dan Fouts	254	Terry Bradshaw	212	Steve DeBerg	193
†Dave Krieg	247	Y.A. Tittle	212	Bob Griese	192
†Warren Moon	247	Jim Hart	209	Sammy Baugh	187
John Hadl	244	Roman Gabriel	201	Craig Morton	183
Len Dawson	239	Phil Simms	199	Steve Grogan	182

† Active player.

Career Leaders (Cont.)
Receiving
RECEPTIONS

	Yrs	No.	Yds	Avg	Lg	TD		Yrs	No.	Yds	Avg	Lg	TD
†Jerry Rice	11	942	15,123	16.0	96	146	Drew Hill	14	634	9,831	15.5	81	60
†Art Monk	15	940	12,721	13.5	79	68	Don Maynard	15	633	11,834	18.7	87	88
Steve Largent	14	819	13,089	16.0	74	100	Raymond Berry	13	631	9,275	14.7	70	68
James Lofton	16	764	14,004	18.3	80	75	†Sterling Sharpe	8	658	8,890	13.5	76	69
Charlie Joiner	18	750	12,146	16.2	87	65	Harold Carmichael	14	590	8,985	15.2	85	79
†Andre Reed	11	748	10,703	14.3	83	75	Fred Biletnikoff	14	589	8,974	15.2	82	76
†Henry Ellard	13	723	12,163	16.8	81	59	Mark Clayton	11	582	8,974	15.4	78	85
†Gary Clark	11	699	10,856	15.5	84	65	Harold Jackson	16	579	10,372	17.9	79	76
Ozzie Newsome	13	662	7,980	12.1	74	47	†Cris Carter	9	571	7,204	12.6	80	66
Charley Taylor	13	649	9,110	14.0	88	79	†Ernest Givins	10	571	8,215	14.4	83	49

YARDS

	No.		No.		No.
†Jerry Rice	15,123	†Gary Clark	10,856	Charley Taylor	9,110
James Lofton	14,004	Stanley Morgan	10,716	Harold Carmichael	8,985
Steve Largent	13,089	†Andre Reed	10,703	Fred Biletnikoff	8,974
†Art Monk	12,721	Harold Jackson	10,372	Mark Clayton	8,974
†Henry Ellard	12,163	Lance Alworth	10,266	Wes Chandler	8,966
Charlie Joiner	12,146	Drew Hill	9,831	Roy Green	8,965
Don Maynard	11,834	Raymond Berry	9,275		

Sacks*

†Reggie White	157.0	Richard Dent	126.5
Lawrence Taylor	132.5	†Bruce Smith	126.5
†Rickey Jackson	128.0	*Officially compiled since 1982.	

Interceptions

	Yrs	No.	Yds	Avg	Lg	TD
Paul Krause	16	81	1185	14.6	81	3
Emlen Tunnell	14	79	1282	16.2	55	4
Dick (Night Train) Lane	14	68	1207	17.8	80	5
Ken Riley	15	65	596	9.2	66	5
Ronnie Lott	14	63	730	11.3	83	5

Punt Returns

	Yrs	No.	Yds	Avg	Lg	TD
George McAfee	8	112	1431	12.8	74	2
Jack Christiansen	8	85	1084	12.8	89	8
Claude Gibson	5	110	1381	12.6	85	3
Bill Dudley	9	124	1515	12.2	96	3
Rick Upchurch	9	248	3008	12.1	92	8

Note: 75 or more returns.

Punting

	Yrs	No.	Yds	Avg	Lg	Blk
Sammy Baugh	16	338	15,245	45.1	85	9
Tommy Davis	11	511	22,833	44.7	82	2
Yale Lary	11	503	22,279	44.3	74	4
Bob Scarpitto	8	283	12,408	43.8	87	4
Horace Gillom	7	385	16,872	43.8	80	5
Jerry Norton	11	358	15,671	43.8	78	2

Note: 250 or more punts.

Kickoff Returns

	Yrs	No.	Yds	Avg	Lg	TD
Gale Sayers	7	91	2781	30.6	103	6
Lynn Chandnois	7	92	2720	29.6	93	3
Abe Woodson	9	193	5538	28.7	105	5
Claude (Buddy) Young	6	90	2514	27.9	104	2
Travis Williams	5	102	2801	27.5	105	6

Note: 75 or more returns.

† Active player.

Lots of Rice but No Rison

What does Jerry Rice have in common with Kareem Abdul-Jabbar, Jesus Christ, Dan Marino Sr., Bernie Kosar Sr. and Terry Breitsprecher? All were named by NFL quarterbacks in an *SI* poll taken in September, 1995, which asked: If you had one pass left to throw, whom would you want on the receiving end? Both Dan Marino and Bernie Kosar chose their fathers, while 6' 8" Miami Dolphin teammate Dan McGwire singled out Abdul-Jabbar. Randall Cunningham named Jesus, "because he wouldn't drop it." And Breitsprecher was the choice of the Arizona Cardinals' Dave Krieg—he and Breitsprecher were a formidable combination at D.C. Everest High, in Schofield, Wis.

Rice was the overwhelming choice, receiving 28 of 53 votes. Conspicuously unchosen was Cleveland Brown Andre Rison, a four-time Pro Bowl selection who apparently lacks the mojo of Fred Biletnikoff, Steve Largent and Art Monk, legends who each drew one vote.

The most engaging reply came from New Orleans Saint Jim Everett, who said, "My wife." Congratulations, Christin, you're in good company.

Single-Season Leaders
Scoring

POINTS

	Year	TD	PAT	FG	Pts
Paul Hornung, GB	1960	15	41	15	176
Mark Moseley, Wash	1983	0	62	33	161
Gino Cappelletti, Bos	1964	7	38	25	155
Emmitt Smith, Dall	1995	25	0	0	150
Chip Lohmiller, Wash	1991	0	56	31	149
Gino Cappelletti, Bos	1961	8	48	17	147
Paul Hornung, GB	1961	10	41	15	146
Jim Turner, NYJ	1968	0	43	34	145
John Riggins, Wash	1983	24	0	0	144
Kevin Butler, Chi	1985	0	51	31	144

Note: Cappelletti's 1964 total includes a two-point conversion.

TOUCHDOWNS

	Year	Rush	Rec	Ret	Total
Emmitt Smith, Dall	1995	25	0	0	25
John Riggins, Wash	1983	24	0	0	24
O.J. Simpson, Buff	1975	16	7	0	23
Jerry Rice, SF	1987	1	22	0	23
Gale Sayers, Chi	1965	14	6	2	22
Emmitt Smith, Dall	1994	21	1	0	22

FIELD GOALS

	Year	Att	No.
Jeff Jaeger, LA Raiders	1993	44	35
Ali Haji-Sheikh, NYG	1983	42	35
Jim Turner, NYJ	1968	46	34
Jason Hanson, Det	1993	43	34
John Carney, SD	1994	38	34
Fuad Reveiz, Minn	1994	39	34
Norm Johnson, Pitt	1995	41	34

Rushing

YARDS GAINED

	Year	Att	Yds	Avg
Eric Dickerson, LA Rams	1984	379	2105	5.6
O.J. Simpson, Buff	1973	332	2003	6.0
Earl Campbell, Hou	1980	373	1934	5.2
Jim Brown, Cle	1963	291	1883	6.4
Barry Sanders, Det	1994	331	1883	5.7
Walter Payton, Chi	1977	339	1852	5.5
Eric Dickerson, LA Rams	1986	404	1821	4.5
O.J. Simpson, Buff	1975	329	1817	5.5
Eric Dickerson, LA Rams	1983	390	1808	4.6
Emmitt Smith, Dall	1995	377	1773	4.7

AVERAGE GAIN

	Year	Avg
Beattie Feathers, Chi	1934	8.44
Randall Cunningham, Phi	1990	7.98
Bobby Douglass, Chi	1972	6.87

TOUCHDOWNS

	Year	No.
Emmitt Smith, Dall	1995	25
John Riggins, Wash	1983	24
Emmitt Smith, Dall	1994	22
Joe Morris, NYG	1985	21
Jim Taylor, GB	1962	19
Earl Campbell, Hou	1979	19
Chuck Muncie, SD	1981	19

Passing

YARDS GAINED

	Year	Att	Comp	Pct	Yds
Dan Marino, Mia	1984	564	362	64.2	5084
Dan Fouts, SD	1981	609	360	59.1	4802
Dan Marino, Mia	1986	623	378	60.7	4746
Dan Fouts, SD	1980	589	348	59.1	4715
Warren Moon, Hou	1991	655	404	61.7	4690
Warren Moon, Hou	1990	584	362	62.0	4689
Neil Lomax, StL Cards	1984	560	345	61.6	4614
Drew Bledsoe, NE	1994	691	400	57.9	4555
Lynn Dickey, GB	1983	484	289	59.7	4458
Dan Marino, Mia	1994	615	385	62.6	4453

PASS RATING

	Year	Rat.
Steve Young, SF	1994	112.8
Joe Montana, SF	1989	112.4
Milt Plum, Cle	1960	110.4
Sammy Baugh, Wash	1945	109.9
Dan Marino, Mia	1984	108.9

TOUCHDOWNS

	Year	No.
Dan Marino, Mia	1984	48
Dan Marino, Mia	1986	44
Brett Favre, GB	1995	38
George Blanda, Hou	1961	36
Y. A. Tittle, NYG	1963	36

Single-Season Leaders *(Cont.)*
Receiving

RECEPTIONS

	Year	No.	Yds
Herman Moore, Det	1995	123	1686
Cris Carter, Minn	1994	122	1256
Jerry Rice, SF	1995	122	1848
Cris Carter, Minn	1995	122	1371
Isaac Bruce, StL Rams	1995	119	1781
Sterling Sharpe, GB	1993	112	1274
Jerry Rice, SF	1994	112	1499
Terance Mathis, Atl	1994	111	1342
Michael Irvin, Dall	1995	111	1603
Sterling Sharpe, GB	1992	108	1461
Brett Perriman, Det	1995	108	1488
Art Monk, Wash	1984	106	1372

YARDS GAINED

	Year	Yds
Jerry Rice, SF	1995	1848
Isaac Bruce, StL Rams	1995	1781
Charley Hennigan, Hou	1961	1746
Herman Moore, Det	1995	1686
Michael Irvin, Dall	1995	1603

TOUCHDOWNS

	Year	No.
Jerry Rice, SF	1987	22
Mark Clayton, Mia	1984	18
Sterling Sharpe, GB	1994	18

Six tied with 17.

All-Purpose Yards

	Year	Run	Rec	Ret	Total
Lionel James, SD	1985	516	1027	992	2535
Terry Metcalf, StL Cards	1975	816	378	1268	2462
Mack Herron, NE	1974	824	474	1146	2444
Gale Sayers, Chi	1966	1231	447	762	2440
Timmy Brown, Phi	1963	841	487	1100	2428
Tim Brown, LA Rai	1988	50	725	1542	2317
Marcus Allen, LA Rai	1985	1759	555	–6	2308
Timmy Brown, Phil	1962	545	849	912	2306
Gale Sayers, Chi	1965	867	507	898	2272
Eric Dickerson, LA Rams	1984	2105	139	15	2259
O.J. Simpson, Buff	1975	1817	426	0	2243

Interceptions

	Year	No.
Dick (Night Train) Lane, LA Rams	1952	14
Dan Sandifer, Wash	1948	13
Spec Sanders, NY Yanks	1950	13
Lester Hayes, Oak	1980	13

Punt Returns

	Year	Avg
Herb Rich, Balt	1950	23.0
Jack Christiansen, Det	1952	21.5
Dick Christy, NY Titans	1961	21.3
Bob Hayes, Dall	1968	20.8

Punting

	Year	No.	Yds	Avg
Sammy Baugh, Wash	1940	35	1799	51.4
Yale Lary, Det	1963	35	1713	48.9
Sammy Baugh, Wash	1941	30	1462	48.7
Yale Lary, Det	1961	52	2516	48.4
Sammy Baugh, Wash	1942	37	1783	48.2

Sacks

	Year	No.
Mark Gastineau, NYJ	1984	22
Reggie White, Phi	1987	21
Chris Doleman, Minn	1989	21
Lawrence Taylor, NYG	1986	20.5

Kickoff Returns

	Year	Avg
Travis Williams, GB	1967	41.1
Gale Sayers, Chi	1967	37.7
Ollie Matson, Chi Cardinals	1958	35.5
Jim Duncan, Balt	1970	35.4
Lynn Chandnois, Pitt	1952	35.2

Re-Poe Men

Art Modell's NFL franchise has metamorphosed from the Cleveland Browns into the Baltimore Ravens, named in tribute to the poem by one of Baltimore's famous residents, Edgar Allan Poe. It's likely the first franchise to honor lines of verse, and it made us think of the Dawg Pound's poor, forgotten souls and how one of them might lament Cleveland's fate.

THE MAVEN
Once upon a Sunday dreary, while I rooted, flush and beery,
In the Dawg Pound for the curious Cleveland Browns of yore —
While I shouted, madly waving, there came the words of someone raving
A man who said we weren't worth saving, razing us to save his store.
'Twas the voice of that heartless maven who took the Browns to Baltimore—
And said to Cleveland, "Nevermore."

—Kostya Kennedy

Single-Game Leaders

Scoring

POINTS

	Date	Pts
Ernie Nevers, Chi Cards vs Chi Bears	11-28-29	40
Dub Jones, Cle vs Chi Bears	11-25-51	36
Gale Sayers, Chi Bears vs SF	12-12-65	36
Paul Hornung, GB vs Balt	10-8-61	33

On Thanksgiving Day, 1929, Nevers scored all the Cardinals' points on six rushing TDs and four PATs. The Cards defeated Red Grange and the Bears, 40-6. Jones and Sayers each rushed for four touchdowns and scored two more on returns in their teams' victories. Hornung scored four touchdowns and kicked 6 PATs and a field goal in a 45-7 win over the Colts.

FIELD GOALS

	Date	No.
Jim Bakken, StL Cards vs Pitt	9-24-67	7
Rich Karlis, Minn vs LA Rams	11-5-89	7
Eight players tied with 6 FGs each.		

Bakken was 7 for 9, Karlis 7 for 7.

TOUCHDOWNS

	Date	No.
Ernie Nevers, Chi Cards vs Chi Bears	11-28-29	6
Dub Jones, Cle vs Chi Bears	11-25-51	6
Gale Sayers, Chi vs SF	12-12-65	6
Bob Shaw, Chi Cards vs Balt	10-2-50	5
Jim Brown, Cle vs Balt	11-1-59	5
Abner Haynes, Dall Texans vs Oak	11-26-61	5
Billy Cannon, Hous vs NY Titans	12-10-61	5
Cookie Gilchrist, Buff vs NYJ	12-8-63	5
Paul Hornung, GB vs Balt	12-12-65	5
Kellen Winslow, SD vs Oak	11-22-81	5
Jerry Rice, SF vs Atl	10-14-90	5

Rushing

YARDS GAINED

	Date	Yds
Walter Payton, Chi vs Minn	11-20-77	275
O.J. Simpson, Buff vs Det	11-25-76	273
O.J. Simpson, Buff vs NE	9-16-73	250
Willie Ellison, LA Rams vs NO	12-5-71	247
Cookie Gilchrist, Buff vs NYJ	12-8-63	243

CARRIES

	Date	No.
Jamie Morris, Wash vs Cin	12-17-88	45
Butch Woolfolk, NYG vs Phil	11-20-83	43
James Wilder, TB vs GB	9-30-84	43
James Wilder, TB vs Pitt	10-30-83	42
Franco Harris, Pitt vs Cin	10-17-76	41
Gerald Riggs, Atl vs LA Rams	11-17-85	41

TOUCHDOWNS

	Date	No.
Ernie Nevers, Cards vs Bears	11-28-29	6
Jim Brown, Clev vs Balt	11-1-59	5
Cookie Gilchrist, Buff vs NYJ	12-8-63	5

Passing

YARDS GAINED

	Date	Yds
Norm Van Brocklin, LA vs NY Yanks	9-28-51	554
Warren Moon, Hou vs KC	12-16-90	527
Dan Marino, Mia vs NYJ	10-23-88	521
Phil Simms, NYG vs Cin	10-13-85	513
Vince Ferragamo, LA Rams vs Chi	12-26-82	509
Y. A. Tittle, NYG vs Wash	10-28-62	505

COMPLETIONS

	Date	No.
Drew Bledsoe, NE vs Minn	11-13-94	45
Richard Todd, NYJ vs SF	9-21-80	42
Warren Moon, Hou vs Dall	11-10-91	41
Ken Anderson, Cin vs SD	12-20-82	40
Phil Simms, NYG vs Cin	10-13-85	40
Dan Marino, Mia vs Buff	11-16-86	39

Two tied with 38

TOUCHDOWNS

	Date	No.
Sid Luckman, Chi Bears vs NYG	11-14-43	7
Adrian Burk, Phi vs Wash	10-17-54	7
George Blanda, Hou vs NY Titans	11-19-61	7
Y. A. Tittle, NYG vs Wash	10-28-62	7
Joe Kapp, Minn vs Balt	9-28-69	7

Raider Raid

In a program targeting people with low credit ratings, three California banks will offer loans of as much as $25,000, at interest rates as high as 21.8%, to help Oakland Raider fans buy season tickets.

Single-Game Leaders *(Cont.)*
Receiving

YARDS GAINED

	Date	Yds
Flipper Anderson, LA Rams vs NO	11-26-89	336
Stephone Paige, KC vs SD	12-22-85	309
Jim Benton, Cle vs Det	11-22-45	303
Cloyce Box, Det vs Balt	12-3-50	302
Jerry Rice, SF vs Minn	12-18-95	289

TOUCHDOWNS

	Date	No.
Bob Shaw, Chi Cards vs Balt	10-2-50	5
Kellen Winslow, SD vs Oak	11-22-81	5
Jerry Rice, SF vs Atl	10-14-90	5

RECEPTIONS

	Date	No.
Tom Fears, LA Rams vs GB	12-3-50	18
Clark Gaines, NYJ vs SF	9-21-80	17
Sonny Randle, StL Cards vs NYG	11-4-62	16
Jerry Rice, SF vs LA Rams	11-20-94	16
Rickey Young, Minn vs NE	12-16-79	15
William Andrews, Atl vs Pitt	11-15-81	15
Andre Reed Buff vs GB	11-20-94	15
Isaac Bruce StL Rams vs Mia	12-24-95	15

All-Purpose Yards

	Date	Yds
Glyn Milburn, Den vs Sea	12-10-95	404
Billy Cannon, Hou vs NY Titans	12-10-61	373
Lionel James, SD vs LA Raiders	11-10-85	345
Timmy Brown, Phi vs StL	12-16-62	341
Gale Sayers, Chi vs Minn	12-18-66	339

Longest Plays

RUSHING

	Opponent	Year	Yds
Tony Dorsett, Dall	Minn	1983	99
Andy Uram, GB	Chi Cards	1939	97
Bob Gage, Pitt	Chi	1949	97
Jim Spitival, Balt	GB	1950	96
Bob Hoernschemeyer, Det	NY Yanks	1950	96

PASSING

	Opponent	Year	Yds
Frank Filchock to Andy Farkas, Washington	Pitt	1939	99
George Izo to Bobby Mitchell, Washington	Cle	1963	99
Karl Sweetan to Pat Studstill, Detroit	Balt	1966	99
Sonny Jurgensen to Gerry Allen, Washington	Chi	1968	99
Jim Plunkett to Cliff Branch, LA Raiders	Wash	1983	99
Ron Jaworski to Mike Quick, Philadelphia	Atl	1985	99
Stan Humphries to Tony Martin, San Diego	Sea	1994	99
Brett Favre to Robert Brooks, Green Bay	Chi	1995	99

FIELD GOALS

	Opponent	Year	Yds
Tom Dempsey, NO	Det	1970	63
Steve Cox, Cle	Cin	1984	60
Morten Andersen, NO	Chi	1991	60

PUNTS

	Opponent	Year	Yds
Steve O'Neal, NYJ	Den	1969	98
Joe Lintzenich, Chi	NYG	1931	94
Shawn McCarthy, NE	Buff	1991	93
Randall Cunningham, Phi	NYG	1989	91

INTERCEPTION RETURNS

	Opponent	Year	Yds
Vencie Glenn, SD	Den	1987	103
Louis Oliver, Mia	Buff	1992	103
Six players tied at 102			

KICKOFF RETURNS

	Opponent	Year	Yds
Al Carmichael, GB	Chi	1956	106
Noland Smith, KC	Den	1967	106
Roy Green, StL Cards	Dall	1979	106

PUNT RETURNS

	Opponent	Year	Yds
Robert Bailey, LA Rams	NO	1994	103
Gil LeFebvre, Cin	Brooklyn	1933	98
Charlie West, Min	Wash	1968	98
Dennis Morgan, Dall	StL Cards	1974	98
Terance Mathis, NYJ	Dall	1990	98

Rushing

Year	Player, Team	Att.	Yards	Avg.	TD
1932	Cliff Battles, Bos	148	576	3.9	3
1933	Jim Musick, Bos	173	809	4.7	5
1934	Beattie Feathers, Chicago Bears	101	1004	9.9	8
1935	Doug Russell, Chicago Cards	140	499	3.6	0
1936	Alphonse Leemans, NY	206	830	4.0	2
1937	Cliff Battles, Wash	216	874	4.0	5
1938	Byron White, Pitt	152	567	3.7	4
1939	Bill Osmanski, Chicago Bears	121	699	5.8	7
1940	Byron White, Det	146	514	3.5	5
1941	Clarence Manders, Bklyn	111	486	4.4	5
1942	Bill Dudley, Pitt	162	696	4.3	5
1943	Bill Paschal, NY	147	572	3.9	10
1944	Bill Paschal, NY	196	737	3.8	9
1945	Steve Van Buren, Phil	143	832	5.8	15
1946	Bill Dudley, Pitt	146	604	4.1	3
1947	Steve Van Buren, Phil	217	1008	4.6	13
1948	Steve Van Buren, Phil	201	945	4.7	10
1949	Steve Van Buren, Phil	263	1146	4.4	11
1950	Marion Motley, Clev	140	810	5.8	3
1951	Eddie Price, NY	271	971	3.6	7
1952	Dan Towler, LA	156	894	5.7	10
1953	Joe Perry, SF	192	1018	5.3	10
1954	Joe Perry, SF	173	1049	6.1	8
1955	Alan Ameche, Balt	213	961	4.5	9
1956	Rick Casares, Chicago Bears	234	1126	4.8	12
1957	Jim Brown, Clev	202	942	4.7	9
1958	Jim Brown, Clev	257	1527	5.9	17
1959	Jim Brown, Clev	290	1329	4.6	14
1960	Jim Brown, Clev, NFL	215	1257	5.8	9
	Abner Haynes, Dall Texans, AFL	156	875	5.6	9
1961	Jim Brown, Clev, NFL	305	1408	4.6	8
	Billy Cannon, Hou, AFL	200	948	4.7	6
1962	Jim Taylor, GB, NFL	272	1474	5.4	19
	Cookie Gilchrist, Buff, AFL	214	1096	5.1	13
1963	Jim Brown, Clev, NFL	291	1863	6.4	12
	Clem Daniels, Oak, AFL	215	1099	5.1	3
1964	Jim Brown, Clev, NFL	280	1446	5.2	7
	Cookie Gilchrist, Buff, AFL	230	981	4.3	6
1965	Jim Brown, Clev, NFL	289	1544	5.3	17
	Paul Lowe, SD, AFL	222	1121	5.0	7
1966	Jim Nance, Bos, AFL	299	1458	4.9	11
	Gale Sayers, Chi, NFL	229	1231	5.4	8
1967	Jim Nance, Bos, AFL	269	1216	4.5	7
	Leroy Kelly, Clev, NFL	235	1205	5.1	11
1968	Leroy Kelly, Clev, NFL	248	1239	5.0	16
	Paul Robinson, Cin, AFL	238	1023	4.3	8
1969	Gale Sayers, Chi, NFL	236	1032	4.4	8
	Dickie Post, SD, AFL	182	873	4.8	6
1970	Larry Brown, Wash, NFC	237	1125	4.7	5
	Floyd Little, Den, AFC	209	901	4.3	3
1971	Floyd Little, Den, AFC	284	1133	4.0	6
	John Brockington, GB, NFC	216	1105	5.1	4
1972	O.J. Simpson, Buff, AFC	292	1251	4.3	6
	Larry Brown, Wash, NFC	285	1216	4.3	8
1973	O.J. Simpson, Buff, AFC	332	2003	6.0	12
	John Brockington, GB, NFC	265	1144	4.3	3
1974	Otis Armstrong, Den, AFC	263	1407	5.3	9
	Lawrence McCutcheon, LA, NFC	236	1109	4.7	3
1975	O.J. Simpson, Buff, AFC	329	1817	5.5	16
	Jim Otis, StL, NFC	269	1076	4.0	5
1976	O.J. Simpson, Buff, AFC	290	1503	5.2	8
	Walter Payton, Chi, NFC	311	1390	4.5	13
1977	Walter Payton, Chi, NFC	339	1852	5.5	14
	Mark van Eeghen, Oak, AFC	324	1273	3.9	7
1978	Earl Campbell, Hou, AFC	302	1450	4.8	13
	Walter Payton, Chi, NFC	333	1395	4.2	11
1979	Earl Campbell, Hou, AFC	368	1697	4.6	19
	Walter Payton, Chi, NFC	369	1610	4.4	14
1980	Earl Campbell, Hou, AFC	373	1934	5.2	13
	Walter Payton, Chi, NFC	317	1460	4.6	6
1981	George Rogers, NO, NFC	378	1674	4.4	13
	Earl Campbell, Hou, AFC	361	1376	3.8	10
1982	Freeman McNeil, NY Jets, AFC	151	786	5.2	6
	Tony Dorsett, Dall, NFC	177	745	4.2	5
1983	Eric Dickerson, LA Rams, NFC	390	1808	4.6	18
	Curt Warner, Sea, AFC	335	1449	4.3	13
1984	Eric Dickerson, LA Rams, NFC	379	2105	5.6	14
	Earnest Jackson, SD, AFC	296	1179	4.0	8
1985	Marcus Allen, LA Raiders, AFC	380	1759	4.6	11
	Gerald Riggs, Atl, NFC	397	1719	4.3	10
1986	Eric Dickerson, LA Rams, NFC	404	1821	4.5	11
	Curt Warner, Sea, AFC	319	1481	4.6	13
1987	Charles White, LA Rams, NFC	324	1374	4.2	11
	Eric Dickerson, Ind, AFC	223	1011	4.5	5
1988	Eric Dickerson, Ind, AFC	388	1659	4.3	14
	Herschel Walker, Dall, NFC	361	1514	4.2	5
1989	Christian Okoye, KC, AFC	370	1480	4.0	12
	Barry Sanders, Det, NFC	280	1470	5.3	14
1990	Barry Sanders, Det, NFC	255	1304	5.1	13
	Thurman Thomas, Buff, AFC	271	1297	4.8	11
1991	Emmitt Smith, Dall, NFC	365	1563	4.3	12
	Thurman Thomas, Buff, AFC	288	1407	4.9	7
1992	Emmitt Smith, Dall, NFC	373	1713	4.6	18
	Barry Foster, Pitt, AFC	390	1690	4.3	11

Rushing *(Cont.)*

Year	Player, Team	Att.	Yards	Avg.	TD
1993	Emmitt Smith, Dall, NFC	283	1486	5.3	9
	Thurman Thomas, Buff, AFC	355	1315	3.7	6
1994	Barry Sanders, Det, NFC	331	1883	5.7	7
	Chris Warren, Sea, AFC	333	1545	4.6	9

Year	Player, Team	Att.	Yards	Avg.	TD
1995	Emmitt Smith, Dall, NFC	377	1773	4.7	25
	Curtis Martin, NE, AFC	368	1487	4.0	14

Passing

Year	Player, Team	Att.	Comp	Yards	TD	Int
1932	Arnie Herber, GB	101	37	639	9	9
1933	Harry Newman, NY	136	53	973	11	17
1934	Arnie Herber, GB	115	42	799	8	12
1935	Ed Danowski, NY	113	57	794	10	9
1936	Arnie Herber, GB	173	77	1239	11	13
1937	Sammy Baugh, Wash	171	81	1127	8	14
1938	Ed Danowski, NY	129	70	848	7	8
1939	Parker Hall, Clev	208	106	1227	9	13
1940	Sammy Baugh, Wash	177	111	1367	12	10
1941	Cecil Isbell, GB	206	117	1479	15	11
1942	Cecil Isbell, GB	268	146	2021	24	14
1943	Sammy Baugh, Wash	239	133	1754	23	19
1944	Frank Filchock, Wash	147	84	1139	13	9
1945	Sammy Baugh, Wash	182	128	1669	11	4
	Sid Luckman, Chicago Bears	217	117	1725	14	10
1946	Bob Waterfield, LA	251	127	1747	18	17
1947	Sammy Baugh, Wash	354	210	2938	25	15
1948	Tommy Thompson, Phil	246	141	1965	25	11
1949	Sammy Baugh, Wash	255	145	1903	18	14
1950	Norm Van Brocklin, LA	233	127	2061	18	14
1951	Bob Waterfield, LA	176	88	1566	13	10
1952	Norm Van Brocklin, LA	205	113	1736	14	17
1953	Otto Graham, Clev	258	167	2722	11	9
1954	Norm Van Brocklin, LA	260	139	2637	13	21
1955	Otto Graham, Clev	185	98	1721	15	8
1956	Ed Brown, Chicago Bears	168	96	1667	11	12
1957	Tommy O'Connell, Clev	110	63	1229	9	8
1958	Eddie LeBaron, Wash	145	79	1365	11	10
1959	Charlie Conerly, NY	194	113	1706	14	4
1960	Milt Plum, Clev, NFL	250	151	2297	21	5
	Jack Kemp, LA, AFL	406	211	3018	20	25
1961	George Blanda, Hou, AFL	362	187	3330	36	22
	Milt Plum, Clev, NFL	302	177	2416	18	10
1962	Len Dawson, Dall, AFL	310	189	2759	29	17
	Bart Starr, GB, NFL	285	178	2438	12	9
1963	Y.A. Tittle, NY, NFL	367	221	3145	36	14
	Tobin Rote, SD, AFL	286	170	2510	20	17
1964	Len Dawson, KC, AFL	354	199	2879	30	18
	Bart Starr, GB, NFL	272	163	2144	15	4
1965	Rudy Bukich, Chi, NFL	312	176	2641	20	9
	John Hadl, SD, AFL	348	174	2798	20	21
1966	Bart Starr, GB, NFL	251	156	2257	14	3
	Len Dawson, KC, AFL	284	159	2527	26	10
1967	Sonny Jurgensen, Wash, NFL	508	288	3747	31	16
	Daryle Lamonica, Oakland, AFL	425	220	3228	30	20

Year	Player, Team	Att.	Comp	Yards	TD	Int
1968	Len Dawson, KC, AFL	224	131	2109	17	9
	Earl Morrall, Balt, NFL	317	182	2909	26	17
1969	Sonny Jurgensen, Wash, NFL	442	274	3102	22	15
	Greg Cook, Cin, AFL	197	106	1854	15	11
1970	John Brodie, SF, NFC	378	223	2941	24	10
	Daryle Lamonica, Oak, AFC	356	179	2516	22	15
1971	Roger Staubach, Dall, NFC	211	126	1882	15	4
	Bob Griese, Mia, AFC	263	145	2089	19	9
1972	Norm Snead, NY, NFC	325	196	2307	17	12
	Earl Morrall, Mia, AFC	150	83	1360	11	7
1973	Roger Staubach, Dall, NFC	286	179	2428	23	15
	Ken Stabler, Oak, AFC	260	163	1997	14	10
1974	Ken Anderson, Cin, AFC	328	213	2667	18	10
	Sonny Jurgensen, Wash, NFC	167	107	1185	11	5
1975	Ken Anderson, Cin, AFC	377	228	3169	21	11
	Fran Tarkenton, Minn, NFC	425	273	2994	25	13
1976	Ken Stabler, Oak, AFC	291	194	2737	27	17
	James Harris, LA, NFC	158	91	1460	8	6
1977	Bob Griese, Mia, AFC	307	180	2252	22	13
	Roger Staubach, Dall, NFC	361	210	2620	18	9
1978	Roger Staubach, Dall, NFC	413	231	3190	25	16
	Terry Bradshaw, Pitt, AFC	368	207	2915	28	20
1979	Roger Staubach, Dall, NFC	461	267	3586	27	11
	Dan Fouts, SD, AFC	530	332	4082	24	24
1980	Brian Sipe, Clev, AFC	554	337	4132	30	14
	Ron Jaworski, Phi, NFC	451	257	3529	27	12
1981	Ken Anderson, Cin, AFC	479	300	3754	29	10
	Joe Montana, SF, NFC	488	311	3565	19	12
1982	Ken Anderson, Cin, AFC	309	218	2495	12	9
	Joe Theismann, Wash, NFC	252	161	2033	13	9
1983	Steve Bartkowski, Atl, NFC	432	274	3167	22	5
	Dan Marino, Mia AFC	296	173	2210	20	6
1984	Dan Marino, Mia, AFC	564	362	5084	48	17
	Joe Montana, SF, NFC	432	279	3630	28	10

Passing *(Cont.)*

Year	Player, Team	Att.	Comp	Yards	TD	Int
1985	Ken O'Brien, NY, AFC	488	297	3888	25	8
	Joe Montana, SF, NFC	494	303	3653	27	13
1986	Tommy Kramer, Minn, NFC	372	208	3000	24	10
	Dan Marino, Mia, AFC	623	378	4746	44	23
1987	Joe Montana, SF, NFC	398	266	3054	31	13
	Bernie Kosar, Clev, AFC	389	241	3033	22	9
1988	Boomer Esiason, Cin, AFC	388	223	3572	28	14
	Wade Wilson, Minn, NFC	332	204	2746	15	9
1989	Joe Montana, SF, NFC	386	271	3521	26	8
	Boomer Esiason, Cin, AFC	455	258	3525	28	11
1990	Jim Kelly, Buffalo, AFC	346	219	2829	24	9
	Phil Simms, NY, NFC	311	184	2284	15	4
1991	Steve Young, SF, NFC	279	180	2517	17	8
	Jim Kelly, Buff, AFC	474	304	3844	33	17
1992	Steve Young, SF, NFC	402	268	3465	25	7
	Warren Moon, Hou, AFC	346	224	2521	18	12
1993	Steve Young, SF, NFC	462	314	4023	29	16
	John Elway, Den, AFC	551	348	4030	25	10
1994	Steve Young, SF, NFC	461	324	3969	35	10
	Dan Marino, Mia, AFC	615	385	4453	30	17
1995	Brett Favre, GB, NFC	570	359	4413	38	13
	Jim Harbaugh, Ind, AFC	314	200	2575	17	5

Pass Receiving

Year	Player, Team	No.	Yds	Avg	TD
1932	Ray Flaherty, NY	21	350	16.7	3
1933	John Kelly, Brooklyn	22	246	11.2	3
1934	Joe Carter, Phil	16	238	14.9	4
	Morris Badgro, NY	16	206	12.9	1
1935	Tod Goodwin, NY	26	432	16.6	4
1936	Don Hutson, GB	34	536	15.8	8
1937	Don Hutson, GB	41	552	13.5	7
1938	Gaynell Tinsley, Chi Cards	41	516	12.6	1
1939	Don Hutson, GB	34	846	24.9	6
1940	Don Looney, Phil	58	707	12.2	4
1941	Don Hutson, GB	58	738	12.7	10
1942	Don Hutson, GB	74	1211	16.4	17
1943	Don Hutson, GB	47	776	16.5	11
1944	Don Hutson, GB	58	866	14.9	9
1945	Don Hutson, GB	47	834	17.7	9
1946	Jim Benton, LA	63	981	15.6	6
1947	Jim Keane, Chi Bears	64	910	14.2	10
1948	Tom Fears, LA	51	698	13.7	4
1949	Tom Fears, LA	77	1013	13.2	9
1950	Tom Fears, LA	84	1116	13.3	7
1951	Elroy Hirsch, LA	66	1495	22.7	17
1952	Mac Speedie, Clev	62	911	14.7	5
1953	Pete Pihos, Phil	63	1049	16.7	10
1954	Pete Pihos, Phil	60	872	14.5	10
	Billy Wilson, SF	60	830	13.8	5
1955	Pete Pihos, Phil	62	864	13.9	7
1956	Billy Wilson, SF	60	889	14.8	5
1957	Billy Wilson, SF	52	757	14.6	6
1958	Raymond Berry, Balt	56	794	14.2	9
	Pete Retzlaff, Phil	56	766	13.7	2
1959	Raymond Berry, Balt	66	959	14.5	14
1960	Lionel Taylor, Den, AFL	92	1235	13.4	12
	Raymond Berry, Baltimore, NFL	74	1298	17.5	10
1961	Lionel Taylor, Den, AFL	100	1176	11.8	4
	Jim Phillips, LA, NFL	78	1092	14.0	5
1962	Lionel Taylor, Den, AFL	77	908	11.8	4
	Bobby Mitchell, Wash, NFL	72	1384	19.2	11
1963	Lionel Taylor, Den, AFL	78	1101	14.1	10
	Bobby Joe Conrad, St. Louis, NFL	73	967	13.2	10
1964	Charley Hennigan, Houston, AFL	101	1546	15.3	8
	Johnny Morris, Chi, NFL	93	1200	12.9	10
1965	Lionel Taylor, Den, AFL	85	1131	13.3	6
	Dave Parks, SF, NFL	80	1344	16.8	12
1966	Lance Alworth, SD, AFL	73	1383	18.9	13
	Charley Taylor, Wash, NFL	72	1119	15.5	12
1967	George Sauer, NY, AFL	75	1189	15.9	6
	Charley Taylor, Wash, NFL	70	990	14.1	9
1968	Clifton McNeil, SF, NFL	71	994	14.0	7
	Lance Alworth, SD, AFL	68	1312	19.3	10
1969	Dan Abramowicz, NO, NFL	73	1015	13.9	7
	Lance Alworth, SD, AFL	64	1003	15.7	4
1970	Dick Gordon, Chi, NFC	71	1026	14.5	13
	Marlin Briscoe, Buff, AFC	57	1036	18.2	8
1971	Fred Biletnikoff, Oak, AFC	61	929	15.2	9
	Bob Tucker, NY, NFC	59	791	13.4	4
1972	Harold Jackson, Phil, NFC	62	1048	16.9	4
	Fred Biletnikoff, Oak, AFC	58	802	13.8	7
1973	Harold Carmichael, Phil, NFC	67	1116	16.7	9
	Fred Willis, Hou, AFC	57	371	6.5	1
1974	Lydell Mitchell, Balt, AFC	72	544	7.6	2
	Charles Young, Phil, NFC	63	696	11.0	3
1975	Chuck Foreman, Minn, NFC	73	691	9.5	9
	Reggie Rucker, Clev, AFC	60	770	12.8	3
	Lydell Mitchell, Balt, AFC	60	544	9.1	4
1976	MacArthur Lane, KC, AFC	66	686	10.4	1
	Drew Pearson, Dall, NFC	58	806	13.9	6
1977	Lydell Mitchell, Balt, AFC	71	620	8.7	4
	Ahmad Rashad, Minn, NFC	51	681	13.4	2

Pass Receiving *(Cont.)*

Year	Player, Team	No.	Yds	Avg	TD
1978	Rickey Young, Minn, NFC	88	704	8.0	5
	Steve Largent, Sea, AFC	71	1168	16.5	8
1979	Joe Washington, Balt, AFC	82	750	9.1	3
	Ahmad Rashad, Minn, NFC	80	1156	14.5	9
1980	Kellen Winslow, SD, AFC	89	1290	14.5	9
	Earl Cooper, SF, NFC	83	567	6.8	4
1981	Kellen Winslow, SD, AFC	88	1075	12.2	10
	Dwight Clark, SF, NFC	85	1105	13.0	4
1982	Dwight Clark, SF, NFC	60	913	15.2	5
	Kellen Winslow, SD, AFC	54	721	13.4	6
1983	Todd Christensen, LA, AFC	92	1247	13.6	12
	Roy Green, StL, NFC	78	1227	15.7	14
	Charlie Brown, Wash, NFC	78	1225	15.7	8
	Earnest Gray, NY, NFC	78	1139	14.6	5
1984	Art Monk, Wash, NFC	106	1372	12.9	7
	Ozzie Newsome, Clev, AFC	89	1001	11.2	5
1985	Roger Craig, SF, NFC	92	1016	11.0	6
	Lionel James, SD, AFC	86	1027	11.9	6
1986	Todd Christensen, Los Angeles, AFC	95	1153	12.1	8
	Jerry Rice, SF, NFC	86	1570	18.3	15
1987	J.T. Smith, StL, NFC	91	1117	12.3	8
	Al Toon, NY, AFC	68	976	14.4	5

Year	Player, Team	No.	Yds	Avg	TD
1988	Al Toon, NY, AFC	93	1067	11.5	5
	Henry Ellard, LA Rams, NFC	86	1414	16.4	10
1989	Sterling Sharpe, GB, NFC	90	1423	15.8	12
	Andre Reed, Buff, AFC	88	1312	14.9	9
1990	Jerry Rice, SF, NFC	100	1502	15.0	13
	Haywood Jeffires, Hou, AFC	74	1048	14.2	8
	Drew Hill, Hou, AFC	74	1019	13.8	5
1991	Haywood Jeffires, Hou, AFC	100	1181	11.8	7
	Michael Irvin, Dall, NFC	93	1523	16.4	8
1992	Sterling Sharpe, GB, NFC	108	1461	13.5	13
	Haywood Jeffires, Hou, AFC	90	913	10.1	9
1993	Sterling Sharpe, GB, NFC	112	1274	11.4	11
	Reggie Langhorne, Ind, AFC	85	1038	12.2	3
1994	Cris Carter, Minn, NFC	122	1256	10.3	7
	Ben Coates, NE, AFC	96	1174	12.2	7
1995	Herman Moore, Det, NFC	123	1686	13.7	14
	Carl Pickens, Cin, AFC	99	1234	12.5	17

Scoring

Year	Player, Team	TD	FG	PAT	TP
1932	Earl Clark, Portsmouth	6	3	10	55
1933	Ken Strong, NY	6	5	13	64
	Glenn Presnell, Ports	6	6	10	64
1934	Jack Manders, Chi	3	10	31	79
1935	Earl Clark, Det	6	1	16	55
1936	Earl Clark, Det	7	4	19	73
1937	Jack Manders, Chi	5	18	15	69
1938	Clarke Hinkle, GB	7	3	7	58
1939	Andy Farkas, Wash	11	0	2	68
1940	Don Hutson, GB	7	0	15	57
1941	Don Hutson, GB	12	1	20	95
1942	Don Hutson, GB	17	1	33	138
1943	Don Hutson, GB	12	3	36	117
1944	Don Hutson, GB	9	0	31	85
1945	Steve Van Buren, Phil	18	0	2	110
1946	Ted Fritsch, GB	10	9	13	100
1947	Pat Harder, Chicago Cards	7	7	39	102
1948	Pat Harder, Chicago Cards	6	7	53	110
1949	Pat Harder, Chicago Cards	8	3	45	102
	Gene Roberts, NY	17	0	0	102
1950	Doak Walker, Det	11	8	38	128
1951	Elroy Hirsch, LA	17	0	0	102

Year	Player, Team	TD	FG	PAT	TP
1952	Gordy Soltau, SF	7	6	34	94
1953	Gordy Soltau, SF	6	10	48	114
1954	Bobby Walston, Phil	11	4	36	114
1955	Doak Walker, Det	7	9	27	96
1956	Bobby Layne, Det	5	12	33	99
1957	Sam Baker, Wash	1	14	29	77
	Lou Groza, Clev	0	15	32	77
1958	Jim Brown, Clev	18	0	0	108
1959	Paul Hornung, GB	7	7	31	94
1960	Paul Hornung, GB, NFL	15	15	41	176
	Gene Mingo, Den, AFL	6	18	33	123
1961	Gino Cappelletti, Bos, AFL	8	17	48	147
	Paul Hornung, GB, NFL	10	15	41	146
1962	Gene Mingo, Den, AFL	4	27	32	137
	Jim Taylor, GB, NFL	19	0	0	114
1963	Gino Cappelletti, Bos, AFL	2	22	35	113
	Don Chandler, NY, NFL	0	18	52	106
1964	Gino Cappelletti, Bos, AFL	7	25	36	155
	Lenny Moore, Balt, NFL	20	0	0	120
1965	Gale Sayers, Chi, NFL	22	0	0	132
	Gino Cappelletti, Bos, AFL	9	17	27	132

Move Over, Knute

The New York Jets defeated the Seattle Seahawks at the Kingdome on Nov. 26, 1995 to raise their season record to 3–9. Some called it an upset, but others were sure that the moribund Jets would come through. Why? Because of the stirring message that New York owner Leon Hess had delivered a few days before the game, when he told the Jets, "Let's show them we're not a bunch of horses' asses."

Scoring *(Cont.)*

Year	Player, Team	TD	FG	PAT	TP
1966	Gino Cappelletti, Bos, AFL	6	16	35	119
	Bruce Gossett, LA, NFL	0	28	29	113
1967	Jim Bakken, StL, NFL	0	27	36	117
	George Blanda, Oak, AFL	0	20	56	116
1968	Jim Turner, NY, AFL	0	34	43	145
	Leroy Kelly, Clev, NFL	20	0	0	120
1969	Jim Turner, NY, AFL	0	32	33	129
	Fred Cox, Minn, NFL	0	26	43	121
1970	Fred Cox, Minn, NFC	0	30	35	125
	Jan Stenerud, KC, AFC	0	30	26	116
1971	Garo Yepremian, Mia, AFC	0	28	33	117
	Curt Knight, Wash, NFC	0	29	27	114
1972	Chester Marcol, GB, NFC	0	33	29	128
	Bobby Howfield, NY AFC	0	27	40	121
1973	David Ray, LA, NFC	0	30	40	130
	Roy Gerela, Pitt, AFC	0	29	36	123
1974	Chester Marcol, GB, NFC	0	25	19	94
	Roy Gerela, Pitt, AFC	0	20	33	93
1975	O.J. Simpson, Buff, AFC	23	0	0	138
	Chuck Foreman, Minn, NFC	22	0	0	132
1976	Toni Linhart, Balt, AFC	0	20	49	109
	Mark Moseley, Wash, NFC	0	22	31	97
1977	Errol Mann, Oak, AFC	0	20	39	99
	Walter Payton, Chi, NFC	16	0	0	96
1978	Frank Corral, LA, NFC	0	29	31	118
	Pat Leahy, NY, AFC	0	22	41	107
1979	John Smith, NE, AFC	0	23	46	115
	Mark Moseley, Wash, NFC	0	25	39	114
1980	John Smith, NE, AFC	0	26	51	129
	Ed Murray, Det, NFC	0	27	35	116
1981	Ed Murray, Det, NFC	0	25	46	121
	Rafael Septien, Dall, NFC	0	27	40	121
	Jim Breech, Cin, AFC	0	22	49	115
	Nick Lowery, KC, AFC	0	26	37	115
1982	Marcus Allen, LA, AFC	14	0	0	84
	Wendell Tyler, LA, NFC	13	0	0	78
1983	Mark Moseley, Wash, NFC	0	33	62	161
	Gary Anderson, Pitt, AFC	0	27	38	119
1984	Ray Wersching, SF, NFC	0	25	56	131
	Gary Anderson, Pitt, AFC	0	24	45	117
1985	Kevin Butler, Chi, NFC	0	31	51	144
	Gary Anderson, Pitt, AFC	0	33	40	139
1986	Tony Franklin, NE, AFC	0	32	44	140
	Kevin Butler, Chi, NFC	0	28	36	120
1987	Jerry Rice, SF, NFC	23	0	0	138
	Jim Breech, Cin, AFC	0	24	25	97
1988	Scott Norwood, Buff, AFC	0	32	33	129
	Mike Cofer, SF, NFC	0	27	40	121
1989	Mike Cofer, SF, NFC	0	29	49	136
	David Treadwell, Den, AFC	0	27	39	120
1990	Nick Lowery, KC, AFC	0	34	37	139
	Chip Lohmiller, Wash, NFC	0	30	41	131
1991	Chip Lohmiller, Wash, NFC	0	31	56	149
	Pete Stoyanovich, Mia, AFC	0	31	28	121
1992	Pete Stoyanovich, Mia, AFC	0	30	34	124
	Morten Anderson, NO, NFC	0	29	33	120
	Chip Lohmiller, Wash, NFC	0	30	30	120
1993	Jeff Jaeger, Rai, AFC	0	35	27	132
	Jason Hanson, Det, NFC	0	34	28	130
1994	John Carney, SD, AFC	0	34	33	135
	Fuad Reveiz, Minn, NFC	0	34	30	132
	Emmitt Smith, Dall, NFC	22	0	0	132
1995	Emmitt Smith, Dall, NFC	25	0	0	150
	Norm Johnson, Pitt, AFC	0	34	39	141

Pro Bowl Alltime Results

Date	Result
1-15-39	NY Giants 13, Pro All-Stars 10
1-14-40	Green Bay 16, NFL All-Stars 7
12-29-40	Chi Bears 28, NFL All-Stars 14
1-4-42	Chi Bears 35, NFL All-Stars 24
12-27-42	NFL All-Stars 17, Washington 14
1-14-51	A Conf 28, N Conf 27
1-12-52	N Conf 30, A Conf 13
1-10-53	N Conf 27, A Conf 7
1-17-54	East 20, West 9
1-16-55	West 26, East 19
1-15-56	East 31, West 30
1-13-57	West 19, East 10
1-12-58	West 26, East 7
1-11-59	East 28, West 21
1-17-60	West 38, East 21
1-15-61	West 35, East 31
1-7-62	AFL West 47, East 27
1-14-62	NFL West 31, East 30
1-13-63	AFL West 21, East 14
1-13-63	NFL East 30, West 20
1-12-64	NFL West 31, East 17
1-19-64	AFL West 27, East 24
1-10-65	NFL West 34, East 14
1-16-65	AFL West 38, East 14
1-15-66	AFL All-Stars 30, Buffalo 19
1-15-66	NFL East 36, West 7
1-21-67	AFL East 30, West 23
1-22-67	NFL East 20, West 10
1-21-68	AFL East 25, West 24
1-21-68	NFL East 38, East 20
1-19-69	AFL West 38, East 25
1-19-69	NFL West 10, East 7
1-17-70	AFL West 26, East 3
1-18-70	NFL West 16, East 13
1-24-71	NFC 27, AFC 6
1-23-72	AFC 26, NFC 13
1-21-73	AFC 33, NFC 28
1-20-74	AFC 15, NFC 13
1-20-75	NFC 17, AFC 10
1-26-76	NFC 23, AFC 20
1-17-77	AFC 24, NFC 14
1-23-78	NFC 14, AFC 13
1-29-79	NFC 13, AFC 7
1-27-80	NFC 37, AFC 27
2-1-81	NFC 21, AFC 7
1-31-82	AFC 16, NFC 13
2-6-83	NFC 20, AFC 19
1-29-84	NFC 45, AFC 3
1-27-85	AFC 22, NFC 14
2-2-86	NFC 28, AFC 24
2-1-87	AFC 10, NFC 6
2-7-88	AFC 15, NFC 6
1-29-89	NFC 34, AFC 3
2-4-90	NFC 27, AFC 21
2-3-91	AFC 23, NFC 21
2-2-92	NFC 21, AFC 15
2-7-93	AFC 23, NFC 20
2-6-94	NFC 17, AFC 3
2-5-95	AFC 41, NFC 13
2-4-96	NFC 20, AFC 13

Chicago All-Star Game Results

Date	Result (Attendance)	Date	Result (Attendance)
8-31-34	Chi Bears 0, All-Stars 0 (79,432)	8-10-56	Cleveland 26, All-Stars 0 (75,000)
8-29-35	Chi Bears 5, All-Stars 0 (77,450)	8-9-57	NY Giants 22, All-Stars 12 (75,000)
9-3-36	All-Stars 7, Detroit 7 (76,000)	8-15-58	All-Stars 35, Detroit 19 (70,000)
9-1-37	All-Stars 6, Green Bay 0 (84,560)	8-14-59	Baltimore 29, All-Stars 0 (70,000)
8-31-38	All-Stars 28, Washington 16 (74,250)	8-12-60	Baltimore 32, All-Stars 7 (70,000)
8-30-39	NY Giants 9, All-Stars 0 (81,456)	8-4-61	Philadelphia 28, All-Stars 14 (66,000)
8-29-40	Green Bay 45, All-Stars 28 (84,567)	8-3-62	Green Bay 42, All-Stars 20 (65,000)
8-28-41	Chi Bears 37, All-Stars 13 (98,203)	8-2-63	All-Stars 20, Green Bay 17 (65,000)
8-28-42	Chi Bears 21, All-Stars 0 (101,100)	8-7-64	Chicago 28, All-Stars 17 (65,000)
8-25-43	All-Stars 27, Washington 7 (48,471)	8-6-65	Cleveland 24, All-Stars 16 (68,000)
8-30-44	Chi Bears 24, All-Stars 21 (48,769)	8-5-66	Green Bay 38, All-Stars 0 (72,000)
8-30-45	Green Bay 19, All-Stars 7 (92,753)	8-4-67	Green Bay 27, All-Stars 0 (70,934)
8-23-46	All-Stars 16, Los Angeles 0 (97,380)	8-2-68	Green Bay 34, All-Stars 17 (69,917)
8-22-47	All-Stars 16, Chi Bears 0 (105,840)	8-1-69	NY Jets 26, All-Stars 24 (74,208)
8-20-48	Chi Cardinals 28, All-Stars 0 (101,220)	7-31-70	Kansas City 24, All-Stars 3 (69,940)
8-12-49	Philadelphia 38, All-Stars 0 (93,780)	7-30-71	Baltimore 24, All-Stars 17 (52,289)
8-11-50	All-Stars 17, Philadelphia 7 (88,885)	7-28-72	Dallas 20, All-Stars 7 (54,162)
8-17-51	Cleveland 33, All-Stars 0 (92,180)	7-27-73	Miami 14, All-Stars 3 (54,103)
8-15-52	Los Angeles 10, All-Stars 7 (88,316)	1974	No game
8-14-53	Detroit 24, All-Stars 10 (93,818)	8-1-75	Pittsburgh 21, All-Stars 14 (54,103)
8-13-54	Detroit 31, All-Stars 6 (93,470)	7-23-76	Pittsburgh 24, All-Stars 0 (52,895)
8-12-55	All-Stars 30, Cleveland 27 (75,000)		

Alltime Winningest NFL Coaches

Most Career Wins

			Regular Season				Career			
Coach	Yrs	Teams	W	L	T	Pct	W	L	T	Pct
Don Shula	33	Colts, Dolphins	328	156	6	.675	347	173	6	.665
George Halas	40	Bears	319	148	31	.672	324	151	31	.671
Tom Landry	29	Cowboys	250	162	6	.605	270	178	6	.601
Curly Lambeau	33	Packers, Cardinals, Redskins	226	132	22	.623	229	134	22	.623
Chuck Noll	23	Steelers	193	148	1	.566	209	156	1	.572
Chuck Knox	21	Rams, Bills, Seahawks	186	147	1	.558	193	158	1	.550
Paul Brown	21	Browns, Bengals	166	100	6	.621	170	108	6	.609
Bud Grant	18	Vikings	158	96	5	.620	168	108	5	.607
Steve Owen	23	Giants	151	100	17	.595	153	108	17	.582
†Dan Reeves	15	Broncos, Giants	135	96	1	.584	143	103	1	.581
Joe Gibbs	12	Redskins	124	60	0	.674	140	65	0	.683
†Marv Levy	15	Chiefs, Bills	127	96	0	.569	138	103	0	.573
Hank Stram	17	Chiefs, Saints	131	97	10	.571	136	100	10	.573
Weeb Ewbank	20	Colts, Jets	130	129	7	.502	134	130	7	.507
Sid Gillman	18	Rams, Chargers, Oilers	122	99	7	.550	123	104	7	.541
†M. Schottenheimer	12	Browns, Chiefs	116	66	1	.637	121	76	1	.614
George Allen	12	Rams, Redskins	116	47	5	.705	118	54	5	.681
Don Coryell	14	Cardinals, Chargers	111	83	1	.572	114	89	1	.561
John Madden	10	Raiders	103	32	7	.750	112	39	7	.731
Mike Ditka	11	Bears	106	62	0	.631	112	68	0	.622

Top Winning Percentages

	W	L	T	Pct		W	L	T	Pct
Vince Lombardi	105	35	6	.740	Don Shula	347	173	6	.665
John Madden	112	39	7	.731	Curly Lambeau	229	134	22	.623
Joe Gibbs	140	65	0	.683	Mike Ditka	112	68	0	.622
George Allen	118	54	5	.681	Bill Walsh	102	63	1	.617
George Halas	324	151	31	.671	†M. Schottenheimer	121	76	1	.614

Note: Minimum 100 victories.

†Active coach.

Alltime Number-One Draft Choices

Year	Team	Selection	Position
1936	Philadelphia	Jay Berwanger, Chicago	HB
1937	Philadelphia	Sam Francis, Nebraska	FB
1938	Cleveland	Corbett Davis, Indiana	FB
1939	Chicago Cardinals	Ki Aldrich, Texas Christian	C
1940	Chicago Cardinals	George Cafego, Tennessee	HB
1941	Chicago Bears	Tom Harmon, Michigan	HB
1942	Pittsburgh	Bill Dudley, Virginia	HB
1943	Detroit	Frank Sinkwich, Georgia	HB
1944	Boston	Angelo Bertelli, Notre Dame	QB
1945	Chicago Cardinals	Charley Trippi, Georgia	HB
1946	Boston	Frank Dancewicz, Notre Dame	QB
1947	Chicago Bears	Bob Fenimore, Oklahoma A&M	HB
1948	Washington	Harry Gilmer, Alabama	QB
1949	Philadelphia	Chuck Bednarik, Pennsylvania	C
1950	Detroit	Leon Hart, Notre Dame	E
1951	New York Giants	Kyle Rote, Southern Methodist	HB
1952	Los Angeles	Bill Wade, Vanderbilt	QB
1953	San Francisco	Harry Babcock, Georgia	E
1954	Cleveland	Bobby Garrett, Stanford	QB
1955	Baltimore	George Shaw, Oregon	QB
1956	Pittsburgh	Gary Glick, Colorado A&M	DB
1957	Green Bay	Paul Hornung, Notre Dame	HB
1958	Chicago Cardinals	King Hill, Rice	QB
1959	Green Bay	Randy Duncan, Iowa	QB
1960	Los Angeles	Billy Cannon, Louisiana St	RB
1961	Minnesota	Tommy Mason, Tulane	RB
	Buffalo (AFL)	Ken Rice, Auburn	G
1968	Minnesota	Ron Yary, Southern California	T
1969	Buffalo (AFL)	O.J. Simpson, Southern California	RB
1970	Pittsburgh	Terry Bradshaw, Louisiana Tech	QB
1971	New England	Jim Plunkett, Stanford	QB
1972	Buffalo	Walt Patulski, Notre Dame	DE
1973	Houston	John Matuszak, Tampa	DE
1974	Dallas	Ed Jones, Tennessee St	DE
1975	Atlanta	Steve Bartkowski, California	QB
1976	Tampa Bay	Lee Roy Selmon, Oklahoma	DE
1977	Tampa Bay	Ricky Bell, Southern California	RB
1978	Houston	Earl Campbell, Texas	RB
1979	Buffalo	Tom Cousineau, Ohio St	LB
1980	Detroit	Billy Sims, Oklahoma	RB
1981	New Orleans	George Rogers, South Carolina	RB
1982	New England	Kenneth Sims, Texas	DT
1983	Baltimore	John Elway, Stanford	QB
1984	New England	Irving Fryar, Nebraska	WR
1985	Buffalo	Bruce Smith, Virginia Tech	DE
1986	Tampa Bay	Bo Jackson, Auburn	RB
1987	Tampa Bay	Vinny Testaverde, Miami (FL)	QB
1988	Atlanta	Aundray Bruce, Auburn	LB
1989	Dallas	Troy Aikman, UCLA	QB
1990	Indianapolis	Jeff George, Illinois	QB
1991	Dallas	Russell Maryland, Miami (FL)	DT
1992	Indianapolis	Steve Emtman, Washington	DT
1993	New England	Drew Bledsoe, Washington St	QB
1994	Cincinnati	Dan Wilkinson, Ohio St	DT
1995	Cincinnati	Ki-Jana Carter, Penn St	RB
1996	New York Jets	Keyshawn Johnson, Southern California	WR

From 1947 through 1958, the first selection in the draft was a bonus pick, awarded to the winner of a random draw. That club, in turn, forfeited its last-round draft choice. The winner of the bonus choice was eliminated from future draws. The system was abolished after 1958, by which time all clubs had received a bonus choice.

Members of the Pro Football Hall of Fame

Herb Adderley
Lance Alworth
Doug Atkins
Morris (Red) Badgro
Lem Barney
Cliff Battles
Sammy Baugh
Chuck Bednarik
Bert Bell
Bobby Bell
Raymond Berry
Charles W. Bidwill, Sr.
Fred Biletnikoff
George Blanda
Mel Blount
Terry Bradshaw
Jim Brown
Paul Brown
Roosevelt Brown
Willie Brown
Buck Buchanan
Dick Butkus
Earl Campbell
Tony Canadeo
Joe Carr
Guy Chamberlin
Jack Christiansen
Earl (Dutch) Clark
George Connor
Jimmy Conzelman
Lou Creekmur
Larry Csonka
Al Davis
Willie Davis
Len Dawson
Dan Dierdorf
Mike Ditka
Art Donovan
Tony Dorsett
John (Paddy) Driscoll
Bill Dudley
Glen (Turk) Edwards
Weeb Ewbank
Tom Fears
Jim Finks
Ray Flaherty
Len Ford
Dan Fortmann
Dan Fouts
Frank Gatski
Bill George
Joe Gibbs
Frank Gifford
Sid Gillman
Otto Graham
Harold (Red) Grange
Bud Grant
Joe Greene
Forrest Gregg
Bob Griese
Lou Groza
Joe Guyon

George Halas
Jack Ham
John Hannah
Franco Harris
Ed Healey
Mel Hein
Ted Hendricks
Wilbur (Pete) Henry
Arnie Herber
Bill Hewitt
Clarke Hinkle
Elroy (Crazylegs) Hirsch
Paul Hornung
Ken Houston
Cal Hubbard
Sam Huff
Lamar Hunt
Don Hutson
Jimmy Johnson
John Henry Johnson
Charlie Joiner
David (Deacon) Jones
Stan Jones
Henry Jordan
Sonny Jurgensen
Leroy Kelly
Walt Kiesling
Frank (Bruiser) Kinard
Earl (Curly) Lambeau
Jack Lambert
Tom Landry
Dick (Night Train) Lane
Jim Langer
Willie Lanier
Steve Largent
Yale Lary
Dante Lavelli
Bobby Layne
Alphonse (Tuffy) Leemans
Bob Lilly
Larry Little
Vince Lombardi
Sid Luckman
Roy (Link) Lyman
John Mackey
Tim Mara
Gino Marchetti
George Preston Marshall
Ollie Matson
Don Maynard
George McAfee
Mike McCormack
Hugh McElhenny
Johnny (Blood) McNally
Mike Michalske
Wayne Millner
Bobby Mitchell
Ron Mix
Lenny Moore
Marion Motley
George Musso
Bronko Nagurski

Joe Namath
Earle (Greasy) Neale
Ernie Nevers
Ray Nitschke
Chuck Noll
Leo Nomellini
Merlin Olsen
Jim Otto
Steve Owen
Alan Page
Clarence (Ace) Parker
Jim Parker
Walter Payton
Joe Perry
Pete Pihos
Hugh (Shorty) Ray
Mel Renfro
Dan Reeves
John Riggins
Jim Ringo
Andy Robustelli
Art Rooney
Pete Rozelle
Bob St. Clair
Gale Sayers
Joe Schmidt
Tex Schramm
Lee Roy Selmon
Art Shell
O.J. Simpson
Jackie Smith
Bart Starr
Roger Staubach
Ernie Stautner
Jan Stenerud
Ken Strong
Joe Stydahar
Fran Tarkenton
Charley Taylor
Jim Taylor
Jim Thorpe
Y.A. Tittle
George Trafton
Charley Trippi
Emlen Tunnell
Clyde (Bulldog) Turner
Johnny Unitas
Gene Upshaw
Norm Van Brocklin
Steve Van Buren
Doak Walker
Bill Walsh
Paul Warfield
Bob Waterfield
Arnie Weinmeister
Randy White
Bill Willis
Larry Wilson
Kellen Winslow
Alex Wojciechowicz
Willie Wood

Champions of Other Leagues

Canadian Football League Grey Cup

Year	Results	Site	Attendance
1909	U of Toronto 26, Parkdale 6	Toronto	3,807
1910	U of Toronto 16, Hamilton Tigers 7	Hamilton	12,000
1911	U of Toronto 14, Toronto 7	Toronto	13,687
1912	Hamilton Alerts 11, Toronto 4	Hamilton	5,337
1913	Hamilton Tigers 44, Parkdale 2	Hamilton	2,100
1914	Toronto 14, U of Toronto 2	Toronto	10,500
1915	Hamilton Tigers 13, Toronto RAA 7	Toronto	2,808
1916-19	No game		
1920	U of Toronto 16, Toronto 3	Toronto	10,088
1921	Toronto 23, Edmonton 0	Toronto	9,558
1922	Queen's U 13, Edmonton 1	Kingston	4,700
1923	Queen's U 54, Regina 0	Toronto	8,629
1924	Queen's U 11, Balmy Beach 3	Toronto	5,978
1925	Ottawa Senators 24, Winnipeg 1	Ottawa	6,900
1926	Ottawa Senators 10, Toronto U 7	Toronto	8,276
1927	Balmy Beach 9, Hamilton Tigers 6	Toronto	13,676
1928	Hamilton Tigers 30, Regina 0	Hamilton	4,767
1929	Hamilton Tigers 14, Regina 3	Hamilton	1,906
1930	Balmy Beach 11, Regina 6	Toronto	3,914
1931	Montreal AAA 22, Regina 0	Montreal	5,112
1932	Hamilton Tigers 25, Regina 6	Hamilton	4,806
1933	Toronto 4, Sarnia 3	Sarnia	2,751
1934	Sarnia 20, Regina 12	Toronto	8,900
1935	Winnipeg 18, Hamilton Tigers 12	Hamilton	6,405
1936	Sarnia 26, Ottawa RR 20	Toronto	5,883
1937	Toronto 4, Winnipeg 3	Toronto	11,522
1938	Toronto 30, Winnipeg 7	Toronto	18,778
1939	Winnipeg 8, Ottawa 7	Ottawa	11,738
1940	Ottawa 12, Balmy Beach 5	Ottawa	1,700
1940	Ottawa 8, Balmy Beach 2	Toronto	4,998
1941	Winnipeg 18, Ottawa 16	Toronto	19,065
1942	Toronto RCAF 8, Winnipeg RCAF 5	Toronto	12,455
1943	Hamilton F Wild 23, Winnipeg RCAF 14	Toronto	16,423
1944	Montreal St H-D Navy 7, Hamilton F Wild 6	Hamilton	3,871
1945	Toronto 35, Winnipeg 0	Toronto	18,660
1946	Toronto 28, Winnipeg 6	Toronto	18,960
1947	Toronto 10, Winnipeg 9	Toronto	18,885
1948	Calgary 12, Ottawa 7	Toronto	20,013
1949	Montreal Als 28, Calgary 15	Toronto	20,087
1950	Toronto 13, Winnipeg 0	Toronto	27,101
1951	Ottawa 21, Saskatchewan 14	Toronto	27,341
1952	Toronto 21, Edmonton 11	Toronto	27,391
1953	Hamilton Ticats 12, Winnipeg 6	Toronto	27,313
1954	Edmonton 26, Montreal 25	Toronto	27,321
1955	Edmonton 34, Montreal 19	Vancouver	39,417
1956	Edmonton 50, Montreal 27	Toronto	27,425
1957	Hamilton 32, Winnipeg 7	Toronto	27,051
1958	Winnipeg 35, Hamilton 28	Vancouver	36,567
1959	Winnipeg 21, Hamilton 7	Toronto	33,133
1960	Ottawa 16, Edmonton 6	Vancouver	38,102
1961	Winnipeg 21, Hamilton 14	Toronto	32,651
1962	Winnipeg 28, Hamilton 27	Toronto	32,655
1963	Hamilton 21, British Columbia 10	Vancouver	36,545
1964	British Columbia 34, Hamilton 24	Toronto	32,655
1965	Hamilton 22, Winnipeg 16	Toronto	32,655
1966	Saskatchewan 29, Ottawa 14	Vancouver	36,553
1967	Hamilton 24, Saskatchewan 1	Ottawa	31,358
1968	Ottawa 24, Calgary 21	Toronto	32,655
1969	Ottawa 29, Saskatchewan 11	Montreal	33,172
1970	Montreal 23, Calgary 10	Toronto	32,669
1971	Calgary 14, Toronto 11	Vancouver	34,484
1972	Hamilton 13, Saskatchewan 10	Hamilton	33,993
1973	Ottawa 22, Edmonton 18	Toronto	36,653
1974	Montreal 20, Edmonton 7	Vancouver	34,450
1975	Edmonton 9, Montreal 8	Calgary	32,454

Canadian Football League Grey Cup *(Cont.)*

Year	Results	Site	Attendance
1976	Ottawa 23, Saskatchewan 20	Toronto	53,467
1977	Montreal 41, Edmonton 6	Montreal	68,318
1978	Edmonton 20, Montreal 13	Toronto	54,695
1979	Edmonton 17, Montreal 9	Montreal	65,113
1980	Edmonton 48, Hamilton 10	Toronto	54,661
1981	Edmonton 26, Ottawa 23	Montreal	52,478
1982	Edmonton 32, Toronto 16	Toronto	54,741
1983	Toronto 18, British Columbia 17	Vancouver	59,345
1984	Winnipeg 47, Hamilton 17	Edmonton	60,081
1985	British Columbia 37, Hamilton 24	Montreal	56,723
1986	Hamilton 39, Edmonton 15	Vancouver	59,621
1987	Edmonton 38, Toronto 36	Vancouver	59,478
1988	Winnipeg 22, British Columbia 21	Ottawa	50,604
1989	Saskatchewan 43, Hamilton 40	Toronto	54,088
1990	Winnipeg 50, Edmonton 11	Vancouver	46,968
1991	Toronto 36, Calgary 21	Winnipeg	51,985
1992	Calgary 24, Winnipeg 10	Toronto	45,863
1993	Edmonton 33, Winnipeg 23	Calgary	50,035
1994	British Columbia 26, Baltimore 23	Vancouver	55,097
1995	Baltimore 37, Calgary 20	Regina, Saskatchewan	52,564

In 1909, Earl Grey, the Governor-General of Canada, donated a trophy for the Rugby Football Championship of Canada. The trophy, which subsequently became known as the Grey Cup, was originally open only to teams registered with the Canada Rugby Union. Since 1954, it has been awarded to the winner of the Canadian Football League's championship game.

AMERICAN FOOTBALL LEAGUE I

Year	Champion	Record
1926	Philadelphia Quakers	7-2

AMERICAN FOOTBALL LEAGUE II

Year	Champion	Record
1936	Boston Shamrocks	8-3
1937	LA Bulldogs	8-0

AMERICAN FOOTBALL LEAGUE III

Year	Champion	Record
1940	Columbus Bullies	8-1-1
1941	Columbus Bullies	5-1-2

ALL-AMERICAN FOOTBALL CONFERENCE

Year	Championship Game
1946	Cleveland 14, NY Yankees 9
1947	Cleveland 14, NY Yankees 3
1948	Cleveland 49, Buffalo 7
1949	Cleveland 21, San Francisco 7

WORLD FOOTBALL LEAGUE

Year	World Bowl Championship
1974	Birmingham 22, Florida 21
1975	Disbanded midseason

UNITED STATES FOOTBALL LEAGUE

Year	Championship Game
1983	Michigan 24, Philadelphia 22, at Denver
1984	Philadelphia 23, Arizona 3, at Tampa
1985	Baltimore 28, Oakland 24, at East Rutherford

WORLD LEAGUE OF AMERICAN FOOTBALL

Year	Champion	Record
1992	Sacramento	8-2-0
1995	Frankfurt	6-4-0
1996	Scotland	7-3-0

College Football

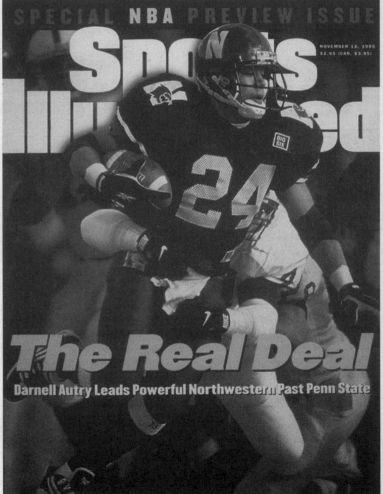

SPECIAL NBA PREVIEW ISSUE

Sports Illustrated

NOVEMBER 13, 1995
$2.95 (CAN. $3.95)

The Real Deal

Darnell Autry Leads Powerful Northwestern Past Penn State

DAMIAN STROHMEYER

The Last Dynasty?

Nebraska overcame off-field distractions and college football's increasing parity to win a second straight national title

by Tim Layden

AS NEBRASKA ran through the fall of 1995, taking down opponents like a scythe slicing through wild grass, it should have been obvious that the Cornhuskers were one of the greatest teams in college football history. At the end of the previous season they had given coach Tom Osborne his first national title, and they had followed that landmark year with 11 consecutive victories by an average score of 52–14. No game had been closer than 14 points.

But the public had been distracted from Nebraska's greatness by a string of off-the-field incidents that sullied the program's reputation and cast the Cornhuskers as outlaws rather than champions. Since the winter of 1994, five Nebraska players had been arrested, most publicly junior running back Lawrence Phillips, who in the early morning hours of Sept. 10, 1995, was charged with assault against his former girlfriend, a Nebraska basketball player named Kate McEwen. Phillips was suspended from the team and sat out six games. When he returned to play against Iowa State, attention focused on the merits of Osborne's decision to restore him to the team, rather than on the Cornhuskers' 21-game winning streak and No. 1 national ranking, which was achieved with a 44–21 victory over Colorado in Boulder the previous weekend.

The focus would shift, however, on the second night of 1996 when Nebraska took all of its talent, assembled and honed; all of its precision, so finely drilled; and all of its anger, bottled up and held for a long, difficult autumn, and unleashed it against No. 2 Florida in the Fiesta Bowl. In the first winner-take-all matchup of the new bowl alliance the Cornhuskers rushed for 524 yards, held the Gators to –28 yards on the ground, sacked Florida quarterback Danny Wuerffel seven times and won by the surreal final score of 62–24. Nebraska senior quarterback Tommie Frazier, the Cornhuskers' backbone throughout the season, rushed for 199 yards, passed for 105 and was named the game's Most Valuable Player.

Finally Nebraska's greatness had claimed center stage. The players, for their part,

Not even close: Frazier and Nebraska ran away from Florida in the Fiesta Bowl.

had known about it all along. "The truth is, we expected this to happen," said Nebraska junior strong safety Mike Minter, when the rout was finished. "All week in public we said the right things. But when we went to our hotel rooms, it was like, 'We're going to blow them out.'"

Nebraska was unusual for another reason. College football is as broad as the United States but has long been as tightly controlled as the Supreme Court. It is a game of traditional dynasties that stake places in the Top 10 and return to them each autumn. But 1995 was a season of change, symbolized by the dissolution of the Southwestern Conference, which sends four teams off to join the old Big Eight, creating another superconference next year, the Big 12. And, appropriately, there were new faces climbing among the elite and old reliables fighting them off like squatters. Nebraska was the exception, a runaway powerhouse from the old guard, entrenched and immovable.

There was just one other traditional power that seemed poised to roll into January alongside the Cornhuskers. Ohio State, which in coach John Cooper's seven years in Columbus had won 54 games but had never been to the Rose Bowl, won its first 11 games and rose to No. 2 behind Nebraska. The Buckeyes were a smooth offensive machine led by senior quarterback Bobby Hoying, tailback Eddie George and junior wide receiver Terry Glenn. In Hoying's first two years as a starter, he had thrown nearly as many interceptions (22) as touchdowns (27); in '95 he was second in the country in passing efficiency and threw for 28 touchdowns with just 11 interceptions. Glenn, who replaced All-America Joey Galloway, was sensational, catching 17 of Hoying's TD passes and injecting the Buckeyes' offense with electric potential on every play.

George was simply the rock on which the offense was built, a 6'3", 227-pound power back who, with relentless workouts, had crafted himself into a game-breaker. George rushed for 1,826 yards and won the

Heisman Trophy as the nation's outstanding player. The Buckeyes stamped themselves as championship material with a 45–26 win over Notre Dame in late September and then won at Penn State 28–25. Since the Rose Bowl does not belong to the bowl alliance, a repeat of 1994—when Penn State went unbeaten but did not get a shot at Nebraska, thereby finishing an empty No. 2—seemed possible.

At least it did until the last weekend of November. That was when Michigan upset the Buckeyes 31–23 in the game of the year behind junior running back Tshimanga Biakabutuka's career-high 313 rushing yards. "Think of how much that team lost today," former Michigan coach Bo Schembechler said after the game. Ohio State players were left in emotional shambles. "We've got to live with this, and it's going to be something," said Hoying. "I might not get over it." And with Ohio State's loss, Nebraska and Florida were left alone. And then only Nebraska.

But who would have thought that the Cornhuskers would share the New Year's weekend spotlight with surprise Rose Bowl participant Northwestern, a perennial Big Ten doormat that had won 37 games in the 20 previous seasons, and seemed more likely to give up football than to redefine it? It didn't matter in the least that USC beat the Wildcats in Pasadena, 41–32. They finished a remarkable 10–2 and remained the warmest story of the year. And who could have imagined that the second–most impressive major bowl winner would be Virginia Tech, champion of the Big East Conference and a 28–10 winner over Texas in the Sugar Bowl? The Hokies finished ranked No. 10 in the nation. No two teams proved more conclusively that in the new college football universe of fewer scholarships and tighter academic standards, the wealth of talent will be spread more widely. "College football, better play hard every

Sweet Serendipity

It began during preseason camp in August, when Northwestern coach Gary Barnett asked his players to stand in an auditorium and sing "High Hopes," as if that would somehow improve their lot. And it ended nearly four months later in another auditorium, where Northwestern players assembled to watch Michigan upset Ohio State, sending the Wildcats to their first Rose Bowl since 1949. Roses were delivered to the room, and Barnett said to his wife, Mary, "Fairy dust, it's fairy dust."

In between, Northwestern wrote the most compelling story in many college football seasons, a tale that defied reason and restored a measure of faith in the concept of the student-athlete. The Wildcats opened the season with a shocking 17–15 victory at Notre Dame, followed that with a 19–13 October upset of Michigan in Ann Arbor and in early November knocked off Penn State 21–10, in Evanston, prompting Joe Paterno to say, "They're my kind of football team."

The Wildcats finished the regular season at 10–1, a mind-boggling feat for a program that hadn't won more than four games in a season since 1971 and whose players have the second–highest average SAT scores (1,037, behind only Stanford) among NCAA Division I-A football programs. The very name—Northwestern—had become synonymous with futility and defeat. Now it represented a ray of hope, that it was possible to win with scholars in uniform.

At the core of this remarkable season was Barnett, who was hired before the 1992 season and won only eight games in his first three seasons. But even as Northwestern lost, Barnett peddled optimism. "The program needed awakening," he said. "We had to come in and light a fire." Introduced at a Northwestern basketball game in January of '92, he promised, "We're gonna take the Purple to Pasadena." He introduced a slogan: Expect victory.

week," said Florida State linebacker Todd Rebol.

Upsets became a regular weekend staple. Northwestern began its remarkable regular season with a 17–15 victory at Notre Dame and a month later knocked off Michigan 19–13. (In November the Wildcats beat Penn State 21–10, but at that point it no longer qualified as an upset). On the same weekend that Northwestern beat Michigan, Kansas shocked Colorado 40–24, and Texas Tech knocked off Texas A&M 14–7. By the time the bowls were finished, not only was Virginia Tech lodged at No. 10, but immediately in front of the Hokies, at Nos. 7–9, were Kansas State, Northwestern and Kansas. New kids in town, all of them.

And there were new faces, too, among the individual stars. Quicksilver tailback

Troy Davis of Iowa State, a sophomore who came to the plains from Miami, became just the fifth player in history to rush for more than 2,000 yards in a season—and the first of those not to win the Heisman. Alex Van Dyke, a wideout from Nevada, caught 129 passes for an NCAA-record 1,854 yards, breaking a 30-year-old mark set by Howard Twilley at Tulsa.

The old guard, meanwhile, failed to reach its accustomed level of domination. Notre Dame started the season with that shocking loss to Northwestern, then lost again at Ohio State before rallying for a 38–10 home victory against USC, which came into the game unbeaten and harboring hopes for a national championship. "This is the first time I've felt like this here, like I was part of a big-time victory as the Notre Dame quarterback," said Irish junior Ron Powlus, who has struggled against injury and mediocrity since arriving in South Bend in the

TODD ROSENBERG

No fairytale: Barnett took the Purple to Pasadena in the year's biggest surprise.

Dame," Barnett said. "That win just verified it." By the end of their miracle season, the Wildcats had taken on an air of sophistication and calm, as if they were, well, expecting victory. Even Barnett watched in occasional wonder. "Normally this type of thing has to evolve with time," he said after the Penn State win. "But we've just skipped first and second grades and gone on with it."

Ohio State's loss was serendipitous, fitting with the flow of the season. Northwestern lost to USC in the Rose Bowl, 41–32, but that defeat did little to kill the flavor of the season. "For one autumn," said senior placekicker Sam Valenzisi, "everything was the way it was supposed to be."

High hopes, indeed.

It all seemed ludicrous, but the players believed. "All of us bought into Coach Barnett's message, and it shows on the field," said All-America linebacker Pat Fitzgerald.

Progress was almost impossible to notice. In '94, a 3-3-1 start disintegrated into four consecutive losses by a total of 103 points. Yet before the Notre Dame opener, Barnett instructed his players not to carry him off the field after the victory. "This team believed in itself before Notre

fall of 1993. Alas, two weeks later against Navy, Powlus suffered a broken arm, and the Fighting Irish would end their season at 9–3, ranked No. 11, after a 31–26 loss to Florida State in the Orange Bowl.

The Seminoles, who in 1993 gave coach Bobby Bowden his first national championship, were ranked No. 1 for the first seven weeks of the season. They fell to No. 2 when Nebraska beat Colorado, and they dropped out of the national title race entirely with an upset loss at Virginia and a regular–season-ending 35–24 loss to Florida. "He killed me, he killed me and my boy in the same year," said Bowden after the loss, referring to Florida coach Steve Spurrier and his wins over FSU and Auburn, which is coached by Bowden's son, Terry.

It was a sobering year for the younger Bowden. He had taken over a probation-racked Auburn program in the fall of '93 and guided the Tigers to 20 consecutive wins before a tie with Georgia and a loss to Alabama closed the '94 season. But in '95 Auburn was upset early by LSU, crushed by Florida and finished 8–4. The only consolation for Tigers fans was indirect: a two-year probation slapped on rival Alabama by the NCAA, including the loss of 14 initial scholarships. The Crimson Tide finished 8–3 and lost to Tennessee for the first time since 1985. In all, it was a lousy year for college football in one of the states that cherishes the sport most.

There was, however, no more precipitous drop than Miami's. The Hurricanes had owned the '80s, rising from South Florida to win four national titles ('83, '87, '89, '91). But in the final years of the dynasty, there had been whispers of wrongdoing, and finally there were shouts. Under the cloud of an NCAA investigation that crippled recruiting, and with first-year coach Butch Davis replacing Dennis Erickson, Miami lost three of its first four games. The first was a 31–8 defeat at UCLA, after which junior center K.C. Jones said, "I'm embarrassed, real bad." A victory over Florida A&M followed, and then consecutive losses at Virginia Tech and Florida State. Yet before the season ended, Miami had set the stage for a swift renascence. Hurricane administrators lobbied the NCAA successfully, and the school was banned from the postseason for just one year. The team, meanwhile, finished with seven consecutive wins.

The state of Florida, however, clearly belonged to the Gators. They were hardly new to the national stage, having won 49 games in five years under the brash, confident Spurrier, who took over the program at his alma mater in 1990. Spurrier had installed a

Spurrier directed the Gators to an undefeated regular season.

Powlus (3) and Notre Dame upended Southern Cal's national title hopes.

wide-open passing game—the Fun 'n' Gun, it's called—and made 300-yard passing games seem ordinary. "It doesn't matter who you are, you can do well," said '95 back-up quarterback Eric Kresser. "Whoever is in there will put up numbers." But even as Florida accumulated talent and mastered Spurrier's offense, some team always seemed to have its number, to pin the one loss on the Gators that would keep them out of the national championship game.

In '92 Florida won the Southeastern Conference's Eastern Division but lost to eventual national champion Alabama in the SEC title game. A year later they won the SEC title but lost to Florida State. In '94 they lost at home to Auburn. No such problems in '95. The Gators chomped Ten-nessee 62–37 (the Volunteers would finish 11–1) and exorcised their Bowden family demons with wins over Auburn (49–38) and Florida State. Arkansas fell in the SEC title game 34–3. Wuerffel passed for 3,266 yards and 35 touchdowns and set an NCAA pass-efficiency record. The Gators would finally play for the national championship, and it was assumed that the Fiesta Bowl, the first title game under the alliance designed to find a true national champion, would be a classic.

That assumption would prove terribly wrong. The matchup was subjected to much cold analysis: Nebraska's raw strength against Florida's warp-speed offense. Could the Gators withstand the Cornhuskers' power? Likewise, could Nebraska stay with Florida's speed? As the second quarter began, the questions still seemed valid. Florida had answered

PETER READ MILLER

The Fiesta Bowl trophy offered ample consolation for Osborne's trying year.

Nebraska red, to soak up the victory. And it was Frazier who underscored the victory with the most remarkable run in many seasons. With the Cornhuskers holding a safe 42–18 lead, Frazier bulled through the right side for what seemed like a short gain. But despite four tacklers clinging to his back and legs, Frazier burst free along the right sideline and went 75 yards for a touchdown. As the third quarter expired, he stood alone at the back of the end zone, hands on hips. Losing the Heisman Trophy had disappointed him deeply, but he thrives on winning, and that was his salvation. "It's O.K.," he had said before the Fiesta Bowl. "I can still win the championship."

For Osborne it had been a trying year. "This has probably been the most difficult season I've ever had," he had said in the weeks leading up to the final game. The scrutiny attached to his players' troubles had aged him and forced him to explain himself too often. It had been difficult even for the coach to recognize the greatness of his own team. But on Jan. 2, under a desert sky in an era of widespread parity, the Huskers' superiority stood out like an oasis.

"This is the best team I've ever coached," Osborne said the next day, after the Cornhuskers had been voted No. 1 in both major polls. A cloud hung over them for much of the season, but history often omits peripheral details and preserves the larger images. If that is the case with the 1995 Nebraska Cornhuskers, they will surely be remembered not only as the best team that Osborne has coached, but one of the best that has ever played.

Nebraska's first touchdown with one of its own and taken a 10–6 lead.

By halftime there would be no more questions. "Things kind of snowballed," Osborne would say humbly later that night. It was a snowball the size of Jupiter. Nebraska scored three touchdowns in the second quarter, Kris Brown kicked two field goals, and Wuerffel was sacked for a safety by Jamel Williams. The score was 35–10, and the first true super bowl in college football history had taken on the look of an NFL Super Bowl blowout. "They were too good for us," Spurrier said, flogging himself and his program. "They clobbered us up and down the field, about everywhere. They were by far the best team I think we've played in my six years here."

The second half was an extended curtain call, a time for the Sun Devil Stadium crowd of 79,864, many of them dressed in

Final Polls

Associated Press

	Record	Pts	Head Coach	SI Preseason Rank
1 ....Nebraska (62)	12-0-0	1550	Tom Osborne	4
2 ....Florida	12-1-0	1474	Steve Spurrier	6
3 ....Tennessee	11-1-0	1428	Phillip Fulmer	9
4 ....Florida St	10-2-0	1311	Bobby Bowden	5
5 ....Colorado	10-2-0	1309	Rick Neuheisel	8
6 ....Ohio St	11-2-0	1161	John Cooper	22
7 ....Kansas St	10-2-0	1147	Bill Snyder	21
8 ....Northwestern	10-2-0	1124	Gary Barnett	79
9 ....Kansas	10-2-0	1029	Glen Mason	45
10 ....Virginia Tech	10-2-0	1015	Frank Beamer	32
11 ....Notre Dame	9-3-0	931	Lou Holtz	10
12 ....Southern Cal	9-2-1	886	John Robinson	1
13 ....Penn St	9-3-0	867	Joe Paterno	7
14 ....Texas	10-2-1	724	John Mackovic	20
15 ....Texas A&M	9-3-0	661	R.C. Slocum	3
16 ....Virginia	9-4-0	603	George Welsh	28
17 ....Michigan	9-4-0	474½	Lloyd Carr	14
18 ....Oregon	9-3-0	416	Mike Bellotti	36
19 ....Syracuse	9-3-0	382	Paul Pasqualoni	34
20 ....Miami (FL)	8-3-0	352	Butch Davis	13
21 ....Alabama	8-3-0	313	Gene Stallings	12
22 ....Auburn	8-4-0	276	Terry Bowden	2
23 ....Texas Tech	9-3-0	197	Spike Dykes	47
24 ....Toledo	11-0-1	170	Gary Pinkel	69
25 ....Iowa	8-4-0	133½	Hayden Fry	49

Note: As voted by panel of 62 sportswriters and broadcasters following bowl games (1st-place votes in parentheses).

USA Today/CNN

	Pts	Prev Rank		Pts	Prev Rank
1 ....Nebraska (62)	1550	1	14 ....Texas	768	6
2 ....Tennessee	1438	4	15 ....Texas A&M	703	18
3 ....Florida	1434	2	16 ....Syracuse	593	22
4 ....Colorado	1308	7	17 ....Virginia	585	19
5 ....Florida St	1280	8	18 ....Oregon	441	12
6 ....Kansas St	1129	10	19 ....Michigan	426	14
7 ....Northwestern	1121	3	20 ....Texas Tech	329	25
8 ....Ohio St	1105	5	21 ....Auburn	292	15
9 ....Virginia Tech	1101	11	22 ....Iowa	205	—
10 ....Kansas	994	13	23 ....East Carolina	163	—
11 ....Southern Cal	898	17	24 ....Toledo	150	—
12 ....Penn St	857	16	25 ....Louisiana St	110	—
13 ....Notre Dame	813	9			

Note: As voted by panel of 62 Division I-A head coaches; 25 points for 1st, 24 for 2nd, etc. (1st-place votes in parentheses).

Bowls and Playoffs

NCAA Division I-A Bowl Results

Date	Bowl	Result	Payout/Team ($)	Attendance
12-14-95 ....Las Vegas		Toledo 40, Nevada 37	175,000	11,127
12-25-95 ....Aloha		Kansas 51, UCLA 30	800,000	41,112
12-27-95 ....Copper		Texas Tech 55, Air Force 41	750,000	41,004
12-28-95 ....Alamo		Texas A&M 22, Michigan 20	1 million	64,597
12-29-95 ....Sun		Iowa 38, Washington 18	900,000	49,116
12-29-95 ....Independence		Louisiana St 45, Michigan St 26	750,000	48,835
12-29-95 ....Holiday		Kansas St 54, Colorado St 21	1.7 million	51,051
12-30-95 ....Liberty		East Carolina 19, Stanford 13	750,000	47,398

NCAA Division I-A Bowl Results *(Cont.)*

Date	Bowl	Result	Payout/Team ($)	Attendance
12-30-95	Carquest	North Carolina 20, Arkansas 10	1 million	34,428
12-30-95	Peach	Virginia 34, Georgia 27	1.13 million	70,825
12-31-95	Sugar	Virginia Tech 28, Texas 10	8.33 million	70,283
1-1-96	Outback	Penn St 43, Auburn 14	1.5 million	65,313
1-1-96	Gator	Syracuse 41, Clemson 0	1.3 million	67,940
1-1-96	Citrus	Tennessee 20, Ohio St 14	3 million	70,797
1-1-96	Cotton	Colorado 38, Oregon 6	2.5 million	58,214
1-1-96	Rose	Southern Cal 41, Northwestern 32	8.2 million	100,102
1-1-96	Orange	Florida St 31, Notre Dame 26	8.33 million	72,198
1-2-96	Fiesta	Nebraska 62, Florida 24	8.58 million	79,864

NCAA Division I-AA Championship Boxscore

Montana	3	7	2	10—22
Marshall	0	3	7	10—20

FIRST QUARTER

Montana: Andy Larson 48 field goal, 6:09.

SECOND QUARTER

Marshall: Tim Openlander 39 field goal, 12:54.
Montana: Matt Wells 24 pass from Dave Dickenson (Larson kick), 0:59.

THIRD QUARTER

Marshall: Chris Parker 10 run (Openlander kick), 9:46.
Montana: Safety, Chad Pennington intentional grounding in end zone.

FOURTH QUARTER

Montana: Wells 1 pass from Dickenson (Larson kick), 12:30.

FOURTH QUARTER *(Cont.)*

Marshall: Openlander 21 field goal, 10:50.
Marshall: Parker 26 run (Openlander kick), 4:45.
Montana: Larson 25 field goal, 0:39.

	Montana	Marshall
First downs	21	17
Rushing yardage	49	112
Passing yardage	281	246
Return yardage	23	0
Passes (comp-att-int)	29-48-1	23-41-1
Punts (no.-avg)	8-28.1	5-37.0
Fumbles (no.-lost)	0-0	4-1
Penalties (no.-yards)	4-18	12-109

Att: 32,106.

Small College Championship Summaries

NCAA DIVISION II

First round: Ferris St 36, Millersville 26; New Haven 27, Edinboro 12; North Alabama 38, Albany St (GA) 28; Carson-Newman 37, West Georgia 26; Pittsburg St 36, Northern Colorado 17; North Dakota St 41, North Dakota 10; Texas A&M-Kingsville 59, Fort Hays St 28; Portland St 56, East Texas St 35.
Quarterfinals: Ferris St 17, New Haven 9; North Alabama 38, Carson-Newman 7; Pittsburg St 9, North Dakota St 7; Texas A&M-Kingsville 30, Portland St 3.
Semifinals: North Alabama 45, Ferris St 7; Pittsburg St 28, Texas A&M-Kingsville 25 (OT).
Championship: 12-9-95 Florence, AL

Pittsburg St	0	0	0	7— 7
North Alabama	7	14	0	6—27

NCAA DIVISION III

First round: Mount Union 52, Hanover 18; Wheaton (IL) 63, Wittenberg 41; WI-La Crosse 45, Concordia-M'head 7; WI-River Falls 10, Central (IA) 7; Wash&Jeff 35, Emory & Henry 16; Lycoming 31, Widener 27; Rowan 46, Buffalo St 7; Union (NY) 24, Plymouth St 7.
Quarterfinals: Mount Union 40, Wheaton (IL) 14; WI-La Crosse 28, WI-River Falls 14; Wash&Jeff 48, Lycoming 0; Rowan 38, Union (NY) 7.
Semifinals: WI-La Crosse 20, Mount Union 17; Rowan 28, Wash&Jeff 15.
Championship: 12-9-95 Salem, VA

Rowan	7	0	0	0— 7
Wisconsin-La Crosse	0	16	7	13—36

NAIA DIVISION I PLAYOFFS

Semifinals: Central St (OH) 49, Western Montana 21; Northeastern St (OK) 17, Arkansas-Pine Bluff 14.
Championship: 12-2-95 Tahlequah, OK

Central St (OH)	7	10	7	13—37
Northeastern St (OK)	7	0	0	0— 7

NAIA DIVISION II PLAYOFFS

First round: Findlay (OH) 21, Pacific Lutheran (WA) 14; Malone (OH) 24, Geneva (PA) 23; Sioux Falls (SD) 41, Hastings (NE) 23; Bethany (KS) 30, Benedictine (KS) 29; Lambuth (TN) 49, Clinch Valley (VA) 0; Mary (ND) 14, Dickinson St (ND) 8; Hardin-Simmons (TX) 17, Howard Payne (TX) 6; Central Washington 28, Western Washington 21.
Quarterfinals: Findlay (OH) 15, Malone (OH) 7; Lambuth (TN) 63, Bethany (KS) 28; Central Washington 40, Hardin-Simmons (TX) 20; Mary (ND) 42, Sioux Falls (SD) 17.
Semifinals: Findlay (OH) 63, Lambuth (TN) 13; Central Washington 48, Mary (ND) 7.
Championship: 12-16-95 Tacoma, WA

Central Washington	0	14	7	0—21
Findlay (OH)	0	7	7	7—21

Awards

Heisman Memorial Trophy

Player/School	Class	Pos	1st	2nd	3rd	Total
Eddie George, Ohio St ....Sr		RB	268	248	160	1,460
Tommie Frazier, Nebraska ....Sr		QB	218	192	158	1,196
Danny Wuerffel, Florida ....Jr		QB	185	152	128	987
Darnell Autry, Northwestern ....So		RB	87	78	118	535
Troy Davis, Iowa St ....So		RB	41	80	119	402
Peyton Manning, Tennessee ....So		QB	10	21	37	109
Keyshawn Johnson, Southern Cal....Sr		WR	9	10	12	59
Tshimanga Biakabutuka, Michigan...Jr		RB	1	11	6	31
Warrick Dunn, Florida St ....Jr		RB	2	3	17	29
Bobby Hoying, Ohio St ....Sr		QB	0	9	10	28

Note: Former Heisman winners and the media vote, with ballots allowing for 3 names (3 points for 1st, 2 for 2nd, 1 for 3rd).

Offensive Players of the Year

Maxwell Award (Player)..............................Eddie George, Ohio St, RB
Walter Camp Player of the Year (Back) .....Eddie George, Ohio St, RB
Davey O'Brien Award (QB) ....Danny Wuerffel, Florida, QB
Doak Walker Award (RB) ....Eddie George, Ohio St, RB

Other Awards

Vince Lombardi/Rotary Award (Lineman)..Orlando Pace, Ohio St, OT
Outland Trophy (Interior lineman) ....Jonathan Ogden, UCLA, OT
Butkus Award (Linebacker).........................Kevin Hardy, Illinois, LB
Jim Thorpe Award (Defensive back)..........Greg Myers, Colorado St, DB
Sporting News Player of the Year ....Tommie Frazier, Nebraska, QB
Walter Payton Award (Div I-AA Player) ......Dave Dickenson, Montana, QB
Harlon Hill Trophy (Div II Player) ....Ronald McKinnon, N Alabama, LB

Coaches' Awards

Walter Camp Award ....Gary Barnett, Northwestern
Eddie Robinson Award (Div I-AA) ....Houston Nutt, Murray St
Bobby Dodd Award ....Gary Barnett, Northwestern
Bear Bryant Award ....Gary Barnett, Northwestern

AFCA COACHES OF THE YEAR

Division I-A ....Gary Barnett, Northwestern
Division I-AA ....Don Read, Montana
Division II and NAIA Division I....................Bobby Wallace, North Alabama
Division III and NAIA Division II..................Roger Harring, WI-LaCrosse

Football Writers Association of America All-America Team

OFFENSE

Terry Glenn, Ohio St, Jr.......................Wide receiver
Keyshawn Johnson, Southern Cal, Sr ...Wide receiver
Marco Battaglia, Rutgers, Sr ....Tight end
Dan Neil, Texas, Jr ....OL
Jason Odom, Florida, Sr ....OL
Jonathan Ogden, UCLA, Sr ....OL
Orlando Pace, Ohio St, So ....OL
Clay Shiver, Florida St, Sr....................Center
Tommie Frazier, Nebraska, Sr.............Quarterback
Eddie George, Ohio St, Sr..................Running back
Karim Abdul-Jabbar, UCLA, Jr ....Running back
Michael Reeder, Texas Christian, So ....PK
Marvin Harrison, Syracuse, Sr.............Kick returner

DEFENSE

Tony Brackens, Texas, Jr....................DL
Cornell Brown, Virginia Tech, Jr..........DL
Tedy Bruschi, Arizona, Sr....................DL
Cedric Jones, Oklahoma, Sr ....DL
Pat Fitzgerald, Northwestern, Jr..........Linebacker
Kevin Hardy, Illinois, Sr ....Linebacker
Zach Thomas, Texas Tech, Sr ....Linebacker
Kevin Abrams, Syracuse, Jr................Defensive back
Chris Canty, Kansas St, So ....Defensive back
Marcus Coleman, Texas Tech, Sr ......Defensive back
Lawyer Milloy, Washington, Jr.............Defensive back
Will Brice, Virginia, Jr ....Punter

Division I-A

ATLANTIC COAST CONFERENCE

	Conference			Full Season			
	W	L	T	W	L	T	Pct
Florida St	7	1	0	10	2	0	.833
Virginia	7	1	0	9	4	0	.692
Clemson	6	2	0	8	4	0	.667
Georgia Tech	5	3	0	6	5	0	.545
Maryland	4	4	0	6	5	0	.545
N Carolina	4	4	0	7	5	0	.583
N Carolina St	2	6	0	3	8	0	.273
Duke	1	7	0	3	8	0	.273
Wake Forest	0	8	0	1	10	0	.091

BIG EAST CONFERENCE

	Conference			Full Season			
	W	L	T	W	L	T	Pct
Virginia Tech	6	1	0	10	2	0	.833
Miami (FL)	6	1	0	8	3	0	.727
Syracuse	5	2	0	9	3	0	.750
W Virginia	4	3	0	5	6	0	.455
Boston College	4	3	0	4	8	0	.333
Rutgers	2	5	0	4	7	0	.364
Temple	1	6	0	1	10	0	.091
Pittsburgh	0	7	0	2	9	0	.182

BIG EIGHT CONFERENCE

	Conference			Full Season			
	W	L	T	W	L	T	Pct
Nebraska	7	0	0	12	0	0	1.000
Colorado	5	2	0	10	2	0	.833
Kansas	5	2	0	10	2	0	.833
Kansas St	5	2	0	10	2	0	.833
Oklahoma	2	5	0	5	5	1	.500
Oklahoma St	2	5	0	4	8	0	.333
Missouri	1	6	0	3	8	0	.273
Iowa St	1	6	0	3	8	0	.273

BIG TEN CONFERENCE

	Conference			Full Season			
	W	L	T	W	L	T	Pct
Northwestern	8	0	0	10	2	0	.833
Ohio St	7	1	0	11	2	0	.846
Michigan	5	3	0	9	4	0	.692
Penn St	5	3	0	9	3	0	.750
Michigan St	4	3	1	6	5	1	.542
Iowa	4	4	0	8	4	0	.667
Illinois	3	4	1	5	5	1	.500
Wisconsin	3	4	1	4	5	2	.455
Purdue	2	5	1	4	6	1	.409
Minnesota	1	7	0	3	8	0	.273
Indiana	0	8	0	2	9	0	.182

BIG WEST CONFERENCE

	Conference			Full Season			
	W	L	T	W	L	T	Pct
Nevada	6	0	0	9	3	0	.750
SW Louisiana	4	2	0	6	5	0	.545
Utah St	4	2	0	4	7	0	.364
Arkansas St	3	3	0	6	5	0	.545
New Mexico St	3	3	0	4	7	0	.364
N Illinois	3	3	0	3	8	0	.273
Louisiana Tech	2	4	0	5	6	0	.455
Pacific	2	4	0	3	8	0	.273
San Jose St	2	4	0	3	8	0	.273
UNLV	1	5	0	2	9	0	.182

Division I-A *(Cont.)*

MID-AMERICAN CONFERENCE

	Conference			Full Season			
	W	L	T	W	L	T	Pct
Toledo	7	0	1	11	0	1	.958
Miami (OH)	6	1	1	8	2	1	.773
Ball St	6	2	0	7	4	0	.636
W Michigan	6	2	0	7	4	0	.636
E Michigan	5	3	0	6	5	0	.545
Bowling Green	3	5	0	5	6	0	.455
Central Michigan	2	6	0	4	7	0	.364
Akron	2	6	0	2	9	0	.182
Ohio	1	6	1	2	8	1	.227
Kent	0	7	1	1	9	1	.136

PACIFIC-10 CONFERENCE

	Conference			Full Season			
	W	L	T	W	L	T	Pct
Southern Cal	6	1	1	9	2	1	.792
Washington	6	1	1	7	4	1	.625
Oregon	6	2	0	9	3	0	.750
Stanford	5	3	0	7	4	1	.625
UCLA	4	4	0	7	5	0	.583
Arizona	4	4	0	6	5	0	.545
Arizona St	4	4	0	6	5	0	.545
California	2	6	0	3	8	0	.273
Washington St	2	6	0	3	8	0	.273
Oregon St	0	8	0	1	10	0	.091

SOUTHEASTERN CONFERENCE

	Conference			Full Season*			
EAST	W	L	T	W	L	T	Pct
Florida	8	0	0	12	1	0	.923
Tennessee	7	1	0	11	1	0	.917
Georgia	3	5	0	6	6	0	.500
S Carolina	2	5	1	4	6	1	.409
Kentucky	2	6	0	4	7	0	.364
Vanderbilt	1	7	0	2	9	0	.182
WEST							
Arkansas	6	2	0	8	5	0	.615
Auburn	5	3	0	8	4	0	.667
Alabama	5	3	0	8	3	0	.727
Louisiana St	4	3	1	7	4	1	.625
Mississippi	3	5	0	6	5	0	.545
Mississippi St	1	7	0	3	8	0	.273

*Full season record includes SEC Championship Game in which Florida defeated Arkansas, 34-3, on Dec 2.

SOUTHWEST ATHLETIC CONFERENCE

	Conference			Full Season			
	W	L	T	W	L	T	Pct
Texas	7	0	0	10	2	1	.808
Texas Tech	5	2	0	9	3	0	.750
Texas A&M	5	2	0	9	3	0	.750
Baylor	5	2	0	7	4	0	.636
Texas Christian	3	4	0	6	5	0	.545
Rice	1	6	0	2	8	1	.227
Houston	2	5	0	2	9	0	.182
SMU	0	7	0	1	10	0	.091

Division I-A *(Cont.)*

WESTERN ATHLETIC CONFERENCE

	Conference			Full Season			
	W	L	T	W	L	T	Pct
Colorado St	6	2	0	8	4	0	.667
Air Force	6	2	0	8	5	0	.615
Utah	6	2	0	7	4	0	.636
Brigham Young	6	2	0	7	4	0	.636
San Diego St	5	3	0	8	4	0	.667
Wyoming	4	4	0	6	5	0	.545
Fresno St	2	6	0	5	7	0	.417
New Mexico	2	6	0	4	7	0	.364
Hawaii	2	6	0	4	8	0	.333
UTEP	1	7	0	2	10	0	.167

INDEPENDENTS

	Full Season			
	W	L	T	Pct
Notre Dame	9	3	0	.750
E Carolina	9	3	0	.750
Louisville	7	4	0	.636
Cincinnati	6	5	0	.545
S Mississippi	6	5	0	.545
Army	5	5	1	.500
Navy	5	6	0	.455
Tulsa	4	7	0	.364
Memphis	3	8	0	.273
N Texas	2	9	0	.182
Tulane	2	9	0	.182
NE Louisiana	2	9	0	.182

Division I-AA

BIG SKY CONFERENCE

	Conference			Full Season			
	W	L	T	W	L	T	Pct
Montana	6	1	0	13	2	0	.867
Boise St	4	3	0	7	4	0	.636
N Arizona	4	3	0	7	4	0	.636
Idaho	4	3	0	6	5	0	.545
Weber St	4	3	0	6	5	0	.545
Idaho St	3	4	0	6	5	0	.545
Montana St	2	5	0	5	6	0	.455
E Washington	1	6	0	3	8	0	.273

GATEWAY COLLEGIATE ATHLETIC CONFERENCE

	Conference			Full Season			
	W	L	T	W	L	T	Pct
E Illinois	5	1	0	10	2	0	.833
N Iowa	5	1	0	8	5	0	.615
Indiana St	3	3	0	7	4	0	.636
Illinois St	3	3	0	5	6	0	.455
S Illinois	2	4	0	5	6	0	.455
W Illinois	2	4	0	4	7	0	.364
SW Missouri St	1	5	0	4	7	0	.364

Division I-AA (Cont.)

IVY GROUP

	Conference			Full Season			
	W	L	T	W	L	T	Pct
Princeton	5	1	1	8	1	1	.850
Pennsylvania	5	2	0	7	3	0	.700
Cornell	5	2	0	6	4	0	.600
Dartmouth	4	2	1	7	2	1	.750
Columbia	3	4	0	3	6	1	.350
Brown	2	5	0	5	5	0	.500
Yale	2	5	0	3	7	0	.300
Harvard	1	6	0	2	8	0	.200

MID-EASTERN ATHLETIC CONFERENCE

	Conference			Full Season			
	W	L	T	W	L	T	Pct
Florida A&M	6	0	0	9	3	0	.750
Delaware St	5	1	0	6	5	0	.545
S Carolina St	4	2	0	6	4	0	.600
Howard	2	4	0	6	5	0	.545
N Carolina A&T	2	4	0	4	7	0	.364
Bethune-Cookman	2	4	0	3	8	0	.273
Morgan St	0	6	0	1	10	0	.091
Hampton*	—	—	—	8	3	0	.727

*Hampton was not eligible for the MEAC title.

OHIO VALLEY CONFERENCE

	Conference			Full Season			
	W	L	T	W	L	T	Pct
Murray St	8	0	0	11	1	0	.917
Eastern Kentucky	7	1	0	9	3	0	.750
Middle Tennessee St	6	2	0	7	4	0	.636
SE Missouri St	5	3	0	5	6	0	.455
TN-Martin	4	4	0	5	6	0	.455
Austin Peay	2	6	0	3	8	0	.273
Tennessee Tech	2	6	0	3	8	0	.273
Morehead St	1	7	0	2	8	0	.200
Tennessee St	1	7	0	2	9	0	.182

PATRIOT LEAGUE

	Conference			Full Season			
	W	L	T	W	L	T	Pct
Lehigh	5	0	0	8	3	0	.727
Bucknell	4	1	0	7	4	0	.636
Lafayette	3	2	0	4	6	1	.409
Fordham	2	3	0	4	6	1	.409
Holy Cross	1	4	0	2	9	0	.182
Colgate	0	5	0	0	11	0	.000

SOUTHERN CONFERENCE

	Conference			Full Season			
	W	L	T	W	L	T	Pct
Appalachian St	8	0	0	12	1	0	.923
Marshall	7	1	0	12	3	0	.800
Georgia Southern	5	3	0	9	4	0	.692
Furman	5	3	0	6	5	0	.545
Virginia Military	3	5	0	4	7	0	.364
E Tennessee St	4	4	0	4	7	0	.364
Tenn-Chattanooga	2	6	0	4	7	0	.364
W Carolina	2	6	0	3	7	0	.300
Citadel	0	8	0	2	9	0	.182

Division I-AA (Cont.)

SOUTHLAND CONFERENCE

	Conference			Full Season			
	W	L	T	W	L	T	Pct
McNeese St	5	0	0	13	1	0	.929
SF Austin St	4	1	0	11	2	0	.846
Northwestern St	2	3	0	6	5	0	.545
Sam Houston St	2	3	0	5	5	0	.500
SW Texas St	2	3	0	4	7	0	.364
Nicholls St	0	5	0	0	11	0	.000

SOUTHWESTERN ATHLETIC CONFERENCE

	Conference			Full Season			
	W	L	T	W	L	T	Pct
Jackson St	7	0	0	9	3	0	.750
Southern	6	1	0	11	1	0	.917
Alabama St	5	2	0	8	3	0	.727
Grambling	4	3	0	5	6	0	.455
Alcorn St	3	4	0	4	7	0	.364
Mississippi Valley	2	5	0	2	9	0	.182
Texas Southern	1	6	0	2	8	0	.200
Prairie View	0	7	0	0	11	0	.000

YANKEE CONFERENCE

	Conference			Full Season			
MID-ATLANTIC	W	L	T	W	L	T	Pct
Delaware	8	0	0	11	2	0	.846
James Madison	6	2	0	8	4	0	.667
Richmond	5	3	0	7	3	1	.682
William & Mary	5	3	0	7	4	0	.636
Northeastern	2	6	0	4	7	0	.364
Villanova	2	6	0	3	8	0	.273
NEW ENGLAND							
Rhode Island	6	2	0	7	4	0	.636
Connecticut	5	3	0	8	3	0	.727
New Hampshire	4	4	0	6	5	0	.545
Massachusetts	3	5	0	6	5	0	.545
Boston University	1	7	0	3	8	0	.273
Maine	1	7	0	3	8	0	.273

INDEPENDENTS

	Full Season			
	W	L	T	Pct
Troy St	11	1	0	.917
Hofstra	10	2	0	.833
Wagner	8	1	0	.889
St Mary's (CA)	8	2	0	.800
Liberty	8	3	0	.727
Monmouth (NJ)	7	3	0	.700
Jacksonville St	7	4	0	.636
Samford	7	4	0	.636
Robert Morris	6	4	0	.600
Towson St	6	4	0	.600
Central Florida	6	5	0	.545
AL-Birmingham	5	6	0	.455
Wofford	4	7	0	.364
Buffalo	3	8	0	.273
Youngstown St	3	8	0	.273
W Kentucky	2	8	0	.200
Central Connecticut St	2	8	0	.200
Davidson	1	8	1	.150
Charleston Southern	1	10	0	.091
St Francis (PA)	0	10	0	.000

Division I-A

SCORING

	Class	GP	TD	XP	FG	Pts	Pts/Game
Eddie George, Ohio St	Sr	12	24	0	0	144	12.00
George Jones, San Diego St	Jr	12	23	0	0	138	11.50
Wasean Tait, Toledo	Jr	11	20	0	0	120	10.91
Scott Greene, Michigan St	Sr	10	17	2	0	104	10.40
Byron Hanspard, Texas Tech	So	11	18	0	0	108	9.82
Leeland McElroy, Texas A&M	Jr	10	16	0	0	96	9.60
Beau Morgan, Air Force	Jr	12	19	0	0	114	9.50
Terry Glenn, Ohio St	Jr	11	17	2	0	104	9.45
Stephen Davis, Auburn	Sr	11	17	0	0	102	9.27
Moe Williams, Kentucky	Jr	11	17	0	0	102	9.27

FIELD GOALS

	Class	GP	FGA	FG	Pct	FG/Game
Michael Reeder, Texas Christian	So	11	25	23	.920	2.09
Rafael Garcia, Virginia	Jr	12	27	20	.741	1.67
Dan Pulsipher, Utah	Jr	11	22	17	.773	1.55
Eric Abrams, Stanford	Sr	11	18	16	.889	1.45
Eric Richards, Cincinnati	So	11	24	16	.667	1.45
Brett Conway, Penn St	Jr	11	24	16	.667	1.45
Jeff Hall, Tennessee	Fr	11	25	16	.640	1.45

TOTAL OFFENSE

			Rushing		Passing		Total Offense			
	Class	GP	Car	Net	Att	Yds	Yds	Yds/Play	TDR*	Yds/Game
Mike Maxwell, Nevada	Sr	9	34	12	409	3611	3623	8.18	34	402.56
Cody Ledbetter, New Mex St	Sr	11	90	223	453	3501	3724	6.86	32	338.55
Steve Sarkisian, Brigham Young	Jr	11	82	-167	385	3437	3270	7.00	22	297.27
Charlie Batch, Eastern Mich	Jr	11	61	52	421	3177	3229	6.70	24	293.55
Danny Wuerffel, Florida	Jr	11	46	-141	325	3266	3125	8.42	37	284.09
Steve Taneyhill, S Carolina	Sr	11	66	-38	389	3094	3056	6.72	29	277.82
Billy Blanton, San Diego St	Jr	12	69	24	389	3300	3324	7.26	23	277.00
Tony Graziani, Oregon	Jr	10	70	238	389	2491	2729	5.95	17	272.90
Peyton Manning, Tennessee	So	11	41	6	380	2954	2960	7.03	27	269.09
Marcus Cranell, E Carolina	Jr	11	94	201	447	2751	2952	5.46	24	268.36

*Touchdowns responsible for are TDs scored and passed for.

RUSHING

	Class	GP	Car	Yds	Avg	TD	Yds/Game
Troy Davis, Iowa St	So	11	345	2010	5.8	15	182.73
Wasean Tait, Toledo	Jr	11	357	1905	5.3	20	173.18
George Jones, San Diego St	Jr	12	305	1842	6.0	23	153.50
Darnell Autry, Northwestern	So	11	355	1675	4.7	14	152.27
Eddie George, Ohio St	Sr	12	303	1826	6.0	23	152.17
Deland McCullough, Miami (Ohio)	Sr	11	321	1627	5.1	14	147.91
Moe Williams, Kentucky	Jr	11	294	1600	5.4	17	145.45
Tshimanga Biakabutuka, Michigan	Jr	12	279	1724	6.2	12	143.67
Karim Abdul-Jabbar, UCLA	Jr	10	270	1419	5.3	11	141.90
Charles Talley, Northern Illinois	Jr	11	285	1540	5.4	7	140.00

What Jinx?

Never mind that it was a fantasy cover that ran during the baseball strike and celebrated an impending Chicago Cubs' World Series victory. Or that the cover appeared two summers ago. Or that SI ranked Northwestern 79th before the start of this past season. Splashed across the top of SI's Nov. 7, 1994, "cover" was the headline 8–0 NORTHWESTERN LOCKS UP ROSE BOWL BID. Indeed, with Ohio State's 31–23 loss at Michigan on November 25, the Wildcats (all right, they were 10–1, not 8–0) sealed their first trip to Pasadena since 1949. Remember, you heard it here first.

Division I-A (Cont.)

PASSING EFFICIENCY

	Class	GP	Att	Comp	Pct Comp	Yds	Yds/Att	TD	Int	Rating Pts
Danny Wuerffel, Florida	Jr	11	325	210	64.62	3266	10.05	35	10	178.4
Bobby Hoying, Ohio St	Sr	12	303	192	63.37	3023	9.98	28	11	170.4
Donovan McNabb, Syracuse	Fr	11	207	128	61.84	1991	9.62	16	6	162.3
Mike Maxwell, Nevada	Sr	9	409	277	67.73	3611	8.83	33	17	160.2
Matt Miller, Kansas St	Sr	11	240	154	64.17	2059	8.58	22	11	157.3
Steve Taneyhill, S Carolina	Sr	11	389	261	67.10	3094	7.95	29	9	153.9
Jim Arellanes, Fresno St	Jr	9	172	102	59.30	1539	8.95	13	6	152.4
Donald Sellers, New Mexico	Jr	10	195	121	62.05	1693	8.68	11	3	150.5
Steve Sarkisian, Brigham Young	Jr	11	385	250	64.94	3437	8.93	20	14	149.8
Josh Wallwork, Wyoming	Jr	10	271	163	60.15	2363	8.72	21	13	149.4

Note: Minimum 15 attempts per game.

RECEPTIONS PER GAME

	Class	GP	No.	Yds	TD	R/Game
Alex Van Dyke, Nevada	Sr	11	129	1854	16	11.73
Kevin Alexander, Utah St	Sr	11	92	1400	6	8.36
Chad Mackey, Louisiana Tech	Jr	11	90	1255	9	8.18
Keyshawn Johnson, Southern Cal	Sr	11	90	1218	6	8.18
Will Blackwell, San Diego St	So	11	86	1207	8	7.82

RECEIVING YARDS PER GAME

	Class	GP	No.	Yds	TD	Yds/Game
Alex Van Dyke, Nevada	Sr	11	129	1854	16	168.55
Marcus Harris, Wyoming	Jr	11	78	1423	14	129.36
Kevin Alexander, Utah St	Sr	11	92	1400	6	127.27
Terry Glenn, Ohio St	Jr	11	57	1316	17	119.64
Chad Mackey, Louisiana Tech	Jr	11	90	1255	9	114.09

ALL-PURPOSE RUNNERS

	Class	GP	Rush	Rec	PR	KOR	Yds	Yds/Game
Troy Davis, Iowa St	So	11	2010	159	0	297	2466	224.18
Alex Van Dyke, Nevada	Sr	11	6	1854	0	583	2443	222.09
Wasean Tait, Toledo	Jr	11	1905	183	0	0	2088	189.82
Eddie George, Ohio St	Sr	12	1826	399	0	0	2225	185.42
Abu Wilson, Utah St	Sr	11	1476	375	0	153	2004	182.18

INTERCEPTIONS

	Class	GP	No.	Yds	TD	Int/Game
Willie Smith, Louisiana Tech	Jr	10	8	65	0	.80
Chris Canty, Kansas St	So	11	8	117	2	.73
Sean Andrews, Navy	So	11	8	30	0	.73
Sam Madison, Louisville	Jr	11	7	136	0	.64
Plez Atkins, Iowa	So	10	6	97	2	.60
Harold Lusk, Utah	Jr	10	6	40	0	.60
Kevin Abrams, Syracuse	Jr	10	6	13	0	.60

PUNTING

	Class	No.	Avg
Brad Maynard, Ball St	Jr	66	46.53
Brian Gragert, Wyoming	Sr	40	45.20
Greg Ivy, Oklahoma St	Sr	66	44.65
Chad Kessler, Louisiana St	So	47	44.09

Note: Minimum of 3.6 per game.

PUNT RETURNS

	Class	No.	Yds	TD	Avg
James Dye, Brigham Young	Jr	20	438	2	21.90
Brian Roberson, Fresno St	Jr	19	346	1	18.21
Marvin Harrison, Syracuse	Sr	22	369	2	16.77
Greg Myers, Colorado St	Sr	35	555	3	15.86
Paul Guidry, UCLA	Jr	24	370	1	15.42

Note: Minimum 1.2 per game.

Division I-A (Cont.)

KICKOFF RETURNS

	Class	No.	Yds	TD	Avg
Robert Tate, Cincinnati	Jr	15	515	1	34.33
Winslow Oliver, New Mexico	Sr	21	666	1	31.71
Damon Dunn, Stanford	So	19	539	1	28.37
Steve Clay, Eastern Mich.	Sr	14	395	1	28.21
Emmett Mosley, Notre Dame	Jr	15	419	0	27.93

Note: Minimum of 1.2 per game.

Division I-A Single-Game Highs

RUSHING AND PASSING

Rushing and passing plays: 82—Rusty LaRue, Wake Forest, Oct 28 (vs Duke).
Rushing and passing yards: 559—Cody Ledbetter, New Mexico St, Nov 18 (vs UNLV).
Rushing plays: 49—Robert Holcomb, Illinois, Sept 23 (vs East Carolina).
Net rushing yards: 314—Eddie George, Ohio St, Nov 11 (vs Illinois).
Passes attempted: 78—Rusty LaRue, Wake Forest, Oct 28 (vs Duke).
Passes completed: 55—Rusty LaRue, Wake Forest, Oct 28 (vs Duke).
Passing yards: 552—Mike Maxwell, Nevada, Oct 28 (vs UNLV).

RECEIVING AND RETURNS

Passes caught: 18—Alex Van Dyke, Nevada, Sept 23 (vs Toledo); Oct 28 (vs UNLV).
Receiving yards: 314—Alex Van Dyke, Nevada, Nov 18 (vs San Jose St).
Punt return yards: 225—Chris McCranie, Georgia, Sept 2 (vs South Carolina).
Kickoff return yards: 190—Eddie Kennison, Louisiana St, Sept 2 (vs Texas A&M).

Division I-AA

SCORING

	Class	GP	TD	XP	FG	Pts	Pts/Game
Alcede Surtain, Alabama St	Sr	11	21	6	0	132	12.00
Tim Hall, Robert Morris	Sr	10	20	0	0	120	12.00
Derrick Cullors, Murray St	Sr	11	20	0	0	120	10.91
William Murrell, Eastern Kentucky	Jr	10	18	0	0	108	10.80
Kito Lockwood, Wagner	Sr	7	12	2	0	74	10.57

FIELD GOALS

	Class	GP	FGA	FG	Pct	FG/Game
David Ettinger, Hofstra	Jr	11	33	22	.667	2.00
Todd Kurz, Illinois St	Jr	11	25	19	.760	1.73
Tom Allison, Indiana St	Sr	11	23	18	.783	1.64
Gerald Carlson, Buffalo	Jr	11	22	17	.773	1.55
David Dearmas, Connecticut	Sr	11	23	17	.739	1.55

TOTAL OFFENSE

			Rushing				Passing		Total Offense			
	Class	GP	Car	Gain	Loss	Net	Att	Yds	Yds	Yds/Play	TDR*	Yds/Game
Dave Dickenson, Montana	Sr	11	89	322	289	33	455	4176	4209	7.74	41	382.64
Kevin Foley, Boston Univ	Jr	11	53	46	226	-180	476	3192	3012	5.69	17	273.82
Kharon Brown, Hofstra	Sr	11	151	1133	156	977	320	1860	2837	6.02	24	257.91
Jason McCullough, Brown	Jr	10	82	328	177	151	351	2406	2557	5.91	25	255.70
Bob Aylsworth, Lehigh	Sr	11	54	93	182	-89	400	2899	2810	6.19	27	255.45

*Touchdowns responsible for are TDs scored and passed for.

RUSHING

	Class	GP	Car	Yds	Avg	TD	Yds/Game
Reggie Greene, Siena	So	9	273	1461	5.4	11	162.33
Derrick Cullors, Murray St	Sr	11	269	1765	6.6	16	160.45
Tim Hall, Robert Morris	Sr	10	239	1572	6.6	16	157.20
Arnold Mickens, Butler	Sr	10	354	1558	4.4	11	155.80
Kito Lockwood, Wagner	Sr	7	212	1018	4.8	10	145.43

Division I-AA (Cont.)

PASSING EFFICIENCY

	Class	GP	Att	Comp	Pct Comp	Yds	Yds/Att	TD	Int	Rating Pts
Brian Kadel, Dayton	Sr	11	183	115	62.84	1880	10.27	18	6	175.0
Dave Dickenson, Montana	Sr	11	455	309	67.91	4176	9.18	38	9	168.6
Leo Hamlett, Delaware	Jr	11	174	95	54.60	1849	10.63	15	6	165.4
Chris Berg, Northern Iowa	Sr	10	206	113	54.85	2144	10.41	15	6	160.5
Jeff Lewis, Northern Arizona	Sr	10	313	209	66.77	2426	7.75	22	3	153.2

Note: Minimum 15 attempts per game.

RECEPTIONS PER GAME

	Class	GP	No.	Yds	TD	R/Game
Ed Mantie, Boston University	Sr	11	81	943	1	7.36
Pokey Eckford, Weber St	Sr	11	77	1074	6	7.00
Brian Klingerman, Lehigh	Sr	11	77	1040	10	7.00
Miles Macik, Pennsylvania	Sr	10	68	816	5	6.80
Lenny Harris, TN-Martin	Jr	8	53	790	5	6.63

RECEIVING YARDS PER GAME

	Class	GP	No.	Yds	TD	Yds/Game
Dedric Ward, Northern Iowa	Jr	10	44	1164	12	116.40
Mick Oliver, Cal St-Sacramento	Sr	9	45	907	11	100.78
Kamil Loud, Cal Poly SLO	So	11	57	1098	9	99.98
Lenny Harris, TN-Martin	Jr	8	53	790	5	98.75
Pokey Eckford, Weber St	Sr	11	77	1074	6	97.64

ALL-PURPOSE RUNNERS

	Class	GP	Rush	Rec	PR	KOR	Yds*	Yds/Game
Reggie Greene, Siena	So	9	1461	77	53	363	1954	217.11
Derrick Cullors, Murray St	Sr	11	1765	312	0	201	2278	207.09
C. Matthews, Northwestern St	Jr	11	1384	194	145	554	2277	207.00
Claude Mathis, SW Texas St	So	11	1286	315	352	308	2261	205.55
Joey Stockton, Western Kentucky	So	10	46	863	147	934	1990	199.00

*Includes interception return yards.

INTERCEPTIONS

	Class	GP	No.	Yds	TD	Int/Game
Picasso Nelson, Jackson St	Sr	9	8	71	0	.89
Damani Leech, Princeton	So	10	8	17	0	.80
William Hampton, Murray St	Jr	11	8	280	4	.73
Mark Wallrapp, Yale	Sr	10	7	65	0	.70
Doug Knopp, Cornell	Sr	10	7	18	0	.70

PUNTING

	Class	No.	Avg
Kevin O'Leary, Northern Arizona	Sr	44	42.75
Marc Collins, Eastern Kentucky	Sr	43	42.72
Josh Siefken, Tenn-Chattanooga	Sr	60	41.40
C. Vanwoerkom, Southern Utah	Sr	62	41.13

Note: Minimum 3.6 per game.

Division II

SCORING

	Class	GP	TD	XP	FG	Pts	Pts/Game
Antonio Leroy, Albany St (GA)	Jr	11	24	0	0	144	13.1
Chris Perry, Adams St	Sr	10	21	4	0	130	13.0
Fred Lane, Lane	Jr	10	20	6	0	126	12.6
Chris Pulliams, Ferris St	Jr	10	21	0	0	126	12.6
Sedrick Robinson, KY-Wesleyan	Jr	10	17	14	0	116	11.6

FIELD GOALS

	Class	GP	FGA	FG	Pct	FG/Game
Jon Ruff, Indiana (PA)	Sr	11	23	18	78.3	1.64
David Dell, East Texas St	Fr	11	26	17	65.4	1.55
Eric Myers, WV-Wesleyan	Jr	10	22	15	68.2	1.50
Scott Doyle, Chadron St	Sr	10	22	14	63.6	1.40
Mike Foster, Mesa St	So	10	20	14	70.0	1.40
Jason Lipke, Ferris St	Sr	10	20	14	70.0	1.40

TOTAL OFFENSE

	Class	GP	Yds	Yds/Game
Aaron Sparrow, Norfolk St	Sr	10	3300	330.0
Lance Funderburk, Valdosta St	Jr	11	3549	322.6
Scott Otis, Glenville St	Sr	10	2043	294.3
Pat Graham, Augustana (SD)	Jr	10	2830	283.0
Bob McLaughlin, Lock Haven	Sr	11	3092	281.1

RUSHING

	Class	GP	Car	Yds	TD	Yds/Game
Richard Huntley, Winston-Salem	Sr	10	273	1889	16	188.9
Fred Lane, Lane	Jr	10	273	1833	19	183.3
Randy Martin, St Cloud St	Jr	9	265	1426	10	158.4
Chris Pulliams, Ferris St	Jr	10	262	1489	19	148.9
Steve Papin, Portland St	Sr	11	257	1619	18	147.2

PASSING EFFICIENCY

	Class	GP	Att	Comp	Pct Comp	Yds	TD	Int	Rating Pts
Shawn Behr, Fort Hays St	Sr	11	318	191	60.0	3158	31	6	171.9
Bill Love, Ferris St	Sr	10	271	170	62.7	2469	19	4	159.4
Jarrod Furgason, Fairmont St	So	10	349	222	63.6	2696	35	8	157.0
Greg Moylan, Millersville	Jr	10	275	175	63.6	2310	22	6	156.2
Chris Shipe, Humboldt St	Jr	9	224	149	66.5	2025	9	5	151.3

Note: Minimum 15 attempts per game.

RECEPTIONS PER GAME

	Class	GP	No.	Yds	TD	Rec/Game
Sean Pender, Valdosta St	Jr	11	111	983	2	10.1
Jarett Vito, Emporia St	Fr	10	94	932	7	9.4
Chris Perry, Adams St	Sr	10	88	1719	21	8.8
Jon Spinosa, Lock Haven	Sr	10	80	613	0	8.0
Carlos Ferralls, Glenville St	So	10	80	1252	17	8.0

RECEIVING YARDS PER GAME

	Class	GP	No.	Yds	TD	Yds/Game
Chris Perry, Adams St	Sr	10	88	1719	21	171.9
Carlos Ferralls, Glenville St	So	10	80	1252	17	125.2
James Roe, Norfolk St	Sr	10	64	1248	15	124.8
Michael Dritlein, Washburn	Sr	10	48	1112	8	111.2
Sedrick Robinson, KY-Wesleyan	Jr	10	64	1105	17	110.5

Division II (Cont.)

INTERCEPTIONS

	Class	GP	No.	Yds	Int/Game
Chenelle Jones, Western NM	Sr	8	7	61	.9
Telley Priester, Virginia St	So	10	8	104	.8

Six tied with .7 Int/Game.

PUNTING

	Class	No.	Avg
Jon Mason, W Texas A&M	Sr	54	45.5
Jason Van Dyke, Adams St	Fr	54	42.9
John McGhee, Indiana (PA)	Sr	41	42.0
Brian Moorman, Pittsburg St	Fr	45	41.5
Jack Hankins, W Alabama	Sr	63	41.3
Kevin Thornewell, TX A&M-Kingsville	So	41	41.3

Note: Minimum 3.6 per game.

Division III

SCORING

	Class	GP	TD	XP	FG	Pts	Pts/Game
Anthony Jones, La Verne	Sr	8	19	4	0	118	14.8
Rob Marchitello, Maine Maritime	Sr	8	19	0	0	114	14.3
Darnell Morgan, Chapman	Sr	9	21	0	0	126	14.0
Scott Tumilty, Augustana (IL)	Sr	9	19	0	0	114	12.7
Kurt Barth, Eureka	So	10	18	15	0	123	12.3

FIELD GOALS

	Class	GP	FGA	FG	Pct	FG/Game
Dennis Unger, Albright	So	10	20	16	80.0	1.60
Roger Egbert, Union (NY)	Jr	9	21	12	57.1	1.33
Eddie Rhodes, Blackburn	Jr	8	13	10	76.9	1.25
Dave McQuilkin, Maine Maritime	So	9	16	11	68.8	1.22
David Johnston, Trenton St	Sr	10	17	11	64.7	1.10

TOTAL OFFENSE

	Class	GP	Yds	Yds/Game
Terry Peebles, Hanover	Sr	10	3981	398.1
John Furmaniak, Eureka	Sr	10	3503	350.3
Jon Nielsen, Claremont-M-S	Sr	9	2848	316.4
Eric Noble, Wilmington (OH)	Sr	9	2642	293.6
Jason Falk, Alma	Sr	9	2638	293.1

RUSHING

	Class	GP	Car	Yds	TD	Yds/Game
Brad Olson, Lawrence	So	9	242	1760	16	195.6
Anthony Jones, La Verne	Sr	8	200	1453	19	181.6
Rob Marchitello, Maine Maritime	Sr	8	292	1413	19	176.6
Jamall Pollock, Williams	Sr	8	216	1319	7	164.9
Fredrick Nanhed, Cal Lutheran	Fr	9	242	1380	10	153.3

PASSING EFFICIENCY

	Class	GP	Att	Comp	Pct Comp	Yds	TD	Int	Rating Pts
Bill Borchert, Mount Union	So	10	225	160	71.1	2270	30	4	196.3
Jason Baer, Washington & Jefferson	Jr	8	146	95	65.0	1536	19	3	192.3
Mike Donnelly, Wittenberg	Jr	10	153	92	60.1	1480	15	2	171.1
Kyle Adamson, Allegheny	So	10	209	142	67.9	2039	17	8	169.1
Brian Nelson, Wartburg	Jr	10	171	95	55.5	1600	19	3	167.3

Note: Minimum 15 attempts per game.

Division III (Cont.)

RECEPTIONS PER GAME

	Class	GP	No.	Yds	TD	Rec/Game
Ben Fox, Hanover	Sr	9	95	1087	15	10.6
Mike Cook, Claremont-M-S	Jr	9	83	993	7	9.2
Todd Bloom, Hardin-Simmons	So	9	72	744	4	8.0
Mike Gundersdorf, Wilkes	Jr	10	79	1269	8	7.9
Jake Doran, FDU-Madison	Sr	9	70	1201	11	7.8

RECEIVING YARDS PER GAME

	Class	GP	No.	Yds	TD	Yds/Game
Kurt Barth, Eureka	So	10	68	1337	18	133.7
Jake Doran, FDU-Madison	Sr	9	70	1201	11	133.4
Burnell Roques, Claremont-M-S	Sr	9	64	1169	14	129.9
Mike Gundersdorf, Wilkes	Jr	10	79	1269	8	126.9
Ben Fox, Hanover	Sr	9	95	1087	15	120.8

INTERCEPTIONS

	Class	GP	No.	Yds	Int/Game
LeMonde Zachary, St Lawrence	Fr	7	7	109	1.0
Mike Susi, Lebanon Valley	Sr	8	8	153	1.0
Jim Wallace, Ripon	Jr	10	9	149	.9
Mike Brouwer, Franklin	Sr	10	9	17	.9
Chris Nalley, Washington (MO)	Jr	10	9	50	.9
Keith Murphy, Western N. Eng.	Jr	7	6	79	.9

PUNTING

	Class	No.	Avg
Jeff Shea, Cal Lutheran	So	43	45.0
Mario Acosta, Chapman	So	38	40.2
Tyler Laughery, Claremont-M-S	Jr	39	39.6
David Heggie, Guilford	So	39	39.3
Drew Thomas, Washington & Lee	Sr	33	38.7

Note: Minimum 3.6 per game.

1995 NCAA Division I-A Team Leaders

Offense

SCORING

	GP	Pts	Avg
Nebraska	11	576	52.4
Florida St	11	532	48.4
Florida	12	534	44.5
Nevada	11	484	44.0
Auburn	11	424	38.5
Ohio St	12	461	38.4
Tennessee	11	411	37.4
Colorado	11	406	36.9
Kansas St	11	402	36.5
South Carolina	11	401	36.5

RUSHING

	GP	Car	Yds	Avg	TD	Yds/Game
Nebraska	11	627	4398	7.0	51	399.8
Air Force	12	672	3989	5.9	36	332.4
Army	11	699	3632	5.2	36	330.2
Clemson	11	611	2855	4.7	24	259.5
Toledo	11	564	2690	4.8	32	244.5
Notre Dame	11	562	2572	4.6	29	233.8
Navy	11	574	2570	4.5	21	233.4
Purdue	11	522	2567	4.9	25	233.4
Iowa St	11	506	2513	5.0	23	228.5
Northern Illinois	11	546	2497	4.6	18	227.0

TOTAL OFFENSE

	GP	Plays	Yds	Avg	TD*	Yds/Game
Nevada	11	917	6263	6.8	63	569.36
Nebraska	11	855	6119	7.2	69	556.27
Florida St	11	885	6067	6.9	71	551.55
Florida	12	867	6413	7.4	72	534.42
Ohio St	12	865	5887	6.8	60	490.58
Colorado	11	809	5353	6.6	48	486.64
San Diego St	12	883	5785	6.6	51	482.08
New Mexico St	11	811	5248	6.5	46	477.09
Auburn	11	788	5049	6.4	54	459.00
Fresno St	12	899	5479	6.1	47	456.58

*Defensive and special teams TDs not included.

Offense *(Cont.)*

PASSING

	GP	Att	Comp	Yds	Pct Comp	Yds/Att	TD	Int	Yds/Game
Nevada	11	509	337	4579	66.2	9.0	39	22	416.3
Florida	12	457	287	4330	62.8	9.5	48	12	360.8
Florida St	11	465	297	3616	63.9	7.8	36	14	328.7
New Mexico St	11	454	260	3540	57.3	7.8	30	20	321.8
Brigham Young	11	388	252	3469	64.9	8.9	20	14	315.4
South Carolina	11	420	282	3373	67.1	8.0	32	10	306.6
Eastern Michigan	11	441	254	3323	57.6	7.5	23	19	302.1
Colorado	11	366	222	3269	60.7	8.9	28	11	297.2
Fresno St	12	432	247	3483	57.2	8.1	25	17	290.3
Wake Forest	11	483	289	3073	59.8	6.4	19	18	279.4

Single-Game Highs

Points scored: 77—Florida St, Sept 16 (vs North Carolina St);
Nebraska, Sept 16 (vs Arizona St); South Carolina, Oct 7
(vs Kent); Virginia Tech, Oct 14 (vs Akron).
Net rushing yards: 624—Nebraska, Nov 4 (vs Iowa St).
Passing yards: 552—Nevada, Oct 28 (vs UNLV).
Total yards: 797—Florida St, Sept 2 (vs Duke).
Fewest total yards allowed: 39—Miami (OH), Nov 18 (vs Akron).
Passes attempted: 78—Wake Forest, Oct 28 (vs Duke).
Passes completed: 55—Wake Forest, Oct 28 (vs Duke).

Defense

SCORING

	GP	Pts	Avg
Northwestern	11	140	12.7
Kansas St.	11	145	13.2
Texas A&M	11	148	13.5
Nebraska	11	150	13.6
Virginia Tech	11	155	14.1
Louisiana St	11	160	14.5
Louisville	11	165	15.0
Miami (OH)	11	165	15.0
Baylor	11	166	15.1
Clemson	11	178	16.2

TOTAL DEFENSE

	GP	Plays	Yds	Avg	Yds/Game
Kansas St	11	673	2759	4.1	250.8
Miami (OH)	11	738	2764	3.7	251.3
Texas A&M	11	773	2835	3.7	257.7
Ball St	11	712	2850	4.0	259.1
Baylor	11	709	2903	4.1	263.9
N Carolina	11	729	2940	4.0	267.3
Arizona	11	739	2976	4.0	270.5
Western Michigan	11	686	3092	4.5	281.1
Alabama	11	727	3125	4.3	284.1
Virginia Tech	11	782	3145	4.0	285.9

RUSHING

	GP	Car	Yds	Avg	TD	Yds/Game
Virginia Tech	11	429	851	2.0	7	77.4
Nebraska	11	341	862	2.5	6	78.4
Michigan	12	419	1081	2.6	12	90.1
Georgia Tech	11	372	1003	2.7	17	91.2
Arkansas	12	424	1251	3.0	15	104.3
Alabama	11	380	1158	3.0	9	105.3
Oregon	11	416	1163	2.8	15	105.7
Texas A&M	11	444	1164	2.6	8	105.8
Oklahoma	11	424	1200	2.8	11	109.1
Virginia	12	424	1310	3.1	15	109.1

TURNOVER MARGIN

		Turnovers Gained			Turnovers Lost			Margin/
	GP	Fum	Int	Total	Fum	Int	Total	Game
Toledo	11	16	18	34	6	6	12	2.00
Louisville	11	17	24	41	12	8	20	1.91
Northwestern	11	16	16	32	6	6	12	1.82
Florida St	11	18	16	34	6	14	20	1.27
Nebraska	11	8	20	28	9	6	15	1.18
Washington	11	12	16	28	9	6	15	1.18

PASSING EFFICIENCY

	GP	Att	Comp	Yds	Pct Comp	Yds/Att	TD	Pct TD	Int	Pct Int	Rating Pts
Miami (OH)	11	303	137	1544	45.21	5.10	11	3.63	22	7.26	85.48
Texas A&M	11	329	150	1671	45.59	5.08	8	2.43	13	3.95	88.38
Texas Tech	11	372	153	2020	41.13	5.43	14	3.76	15	4.03	91.10
Ball St	11	303	128	1469	42.24	4.85	14	4.62	10	3.30	91.62
Baylor	11	310	148	1661	47.74	5.36	7	2.26	13	4.19	91.81
Louisiana St	11	343	158	1907	46.06	5.56	8	2.33	13	3.79	92.88
E Carolina	11	332	157	1988	47.29	5.99	7	2.11	19	5.72	93.10
Cincinnati	11	347	162	2011	46.69	5.80	11	3.17	20	5.76	94.30
Louisville	11	350	175	2130	50.00	6.09	8	2.29	24	6.86	94.95
Miami (FL)	11	302	145	1631	48.01	5.40	10	3.31	12	3.97	96.36

National Champions

Year	Champion	Record	Bowl Game	Head Coach
1883	Yale	8-0-0	No bowl	Ray Tompkins (Captain)
1884	Yale	9-0-0	No bowl	Eugene L. Richards (Captain)
1885	Princeton	9-0-0	No bowl	Charles DeCamp (Captain)
1886	Yale	9-0-1	No bowl	Robert N. Corwin (Captain)
1887	Yale	9-0-0	No bowl	Harry W. Beecher (Captain)
1888	Yale	13-0-0	No bowl	Walter Camp
1889	Princeton	10-0-0	No bowl	Edgar Poe (Captain)
1890	Harvard	11-0-0	No bowl	George A. Stewart/George C. Adams
1891	Yale	13-0-0	No bowl	Walter Camp
1892	Yale	13-0-0	No bowl	Walter Camp
1893	Princeton	11-0-0	No bowl	Tom Trenchard (Captain)
1894	Yale	16-0-0	No bowl	William C. Rhodes
1895	Pennsylvania	14-0-0	No bowl	George Woodruff
1896	Princeton	10-0-1	No bowl	Garrett Cochran
1897	Pennsylvania	15-0-0	No bowl	George Woodruff
1898	Harvard	11-0-0	No bowl	W. Cameron Forbes
1899	Harvard	10-0-1	No bowl	Benjamin H. Dibblee
1900	Yale	12-0-0	No bowl	Malcolm McBride
1901	Michigan	11-0-0	Won Rose	Fielding Yost
1902	Michigan	11-0-0	No bowl	Fielding Yost
1903	Princeton	11-0-0	No bowl	Art Hillebrand
1904	Pennsylvania	12-0-0	No bowl	Carl Williams
1905	Chicago	11-0-0	No bowl	Amos Alonzo Stagg
1906	Princeton	9-0-1	No bowl	Bill Roper
1907	Yale	9-0-1	No bowl	Bill Knox
1908	Pennsylvania	11-0-1	No bowl	Sol Metzger
1909	Yale	10-0-0	No bowl	Howard Jones
1910	Harvard	8-0-1	No bowl	Percy Houghton
1911	Princeton	8-0-2	No bowl	Bill Roper
1912	Harvard	9-0-0	No bowl	Percy Houghton
1913	Harvard	9-0-0	No bowl	Percy Houghton
1914	Army	9-0-0	No bowl	Charley Daly
1915	Cornell	9-0-0	No bowl	Al Sharpe
1916	Pittsburgh	8-0-0	No bowl	Pop Warner
1917	Georgia Tech	9-0-0	No bowl	John Heisman
1918	Pittsburgh	4-1-0	No bowl	Pop Warner
1919	Harvard	9-0-1	Won Rose	Bob Fisher
1920	California	9-0-0	Won Rose	Andy Smith
1921	Cornell	8-0-0	No bowl	Gil Dobie
1922	Cornell	8-0-0	No bowl	Gil Dobie
1923	Illinois	8-0-0	No bowl	Bob Zuppke
1924	Notre Dame	10-0-0	Won Rose	Knute Rockne
1925	Alabama (H)	10-0-0	Won Rose	Wallace Wade
	Dartmouth (D)	8-0-0	No bowl	Jesse Hawley
1926	Alabama (H)	9-0-1	Tied Rose	Wallace Wade
	Stanford (D)(H)	10-0-1	Tied Rose	Pop Warner
1927	Illinois	7-0-1	No bowl	Bob Zuppke
1928	Georgia Tech (H)	10-0-0	Won Rose	Bill Alexander
	Southern Cal (D)	9-0-1	No bowl	Howard Jones
1929	Notre Dame	9-0-0	No bowl	Knute Rockne
1930	Notre Dame	10-0-0	No bowl	Knute Rockne
1931	Southern Cal	10-1-0	Won Rose	Howard Jones
1932	Southern Cal (H)	10-0-0	Won Rose	Howard Jones
	Michigan (D)	8-0-0	No bowl	Harry Kipke
1933	Michigan	7-0-1	No bowl	Harry Kipke
1934	Minnesota	8-0-0	No bowl	Bernie Bierman
1935	Minnesota (H)	8-0-0	No bowl	Bernie Bierman
	Southern Meth (D)	12-1-0	Lost Rose	Matty Bell
1936	Minnesota	7-1-0	No bowl	Bernie Bierman
1937	Pittsburgh	9-0-1	No bowl	Jock Sutherland
1938	Texas Christian (AP)	11-0-0	Won Sugar	Dutch Meyer
	Notre Dame (D)	8-1-0	No bowl	Elmer Layden
1939	Southern Cal (D)	8-0-2	Won Rose	Howard Jones
	Texas A&M (AP)	11-0-0	Won Sugar	Homer Norton

Year	Champion	Record	Bowl Game	Head Coach
1940	Minnesota	8-0-0	No bowl	Bernie Bierman
1941	Minnesota	8-0-0	No bowl	Bernie Bierman
1942	Ohio St	9-1-0	No bowl	Paul Brown
1943	Notre Dame	9-1-0	No bowl	Frank Leahy
1944	Army	9-0-0	No bowl	Red Blaik
1945	Army	9-0-0	No bowl	Red Blaik
1946	Notre Dame	8-0-1	No bowl	Frank Leahy
1947	Notre Dame	9-0-0	No bowl	Frank Leahy
	Michigan*	10-0-0	Won Rose	Fritz Crisler
1948	Michigan	9-0-0	No bowl	Bennie Oosterbaan
1949	Notre Dame	10-0-0	No bowl	Frank Leahy
1950	Oklahoma	10-1-0	Lost Sugar	Bud Wilkinson
1951	Tennessee	10-1-0	Lost Sugar	Bob Neyland
1952	Michigan St	9-0-0	No bowl	Biggie Munn
1953	Maryland	10-1-0	Lost Orange	Jim Tatum
1954	Ohio St	10-0-0	Won Rose	Woody Hayes
	UCLA (UPI)	9-0-0	No bowl	Red Sanders
1955	Oklahoma	11-0-0	Won Orange	Bud Wilkinson
1956	Oklahoma	10-0-0	No bowl	Bud Wilkinson
1957	Auburn	10-0-0	No bowl	Shug Jordan
	Ohio St (UPI)	9-1-0	Won Rose	Woody Hayes
1958	Louisiana St	11-0-0	Won Sugar	Paul Dietzel
1959	Syracuse	11-0-0	Won Cotton	Ben Schwartzwalder
1960	Minnesota	8-2-0	Lost Rose	Murray Warmath
1961	Alabama	11-0-0	Won Sugar	Bear Bryant
1962	Southern Cal	11-0-0	Won Rose	John McKay
1963	Texas	11-0-0	Won Cotton	Darrell Royal
1964	Alabama	10-1-0	Lost Orange	Bear Bryant
1965	Alabama	9-1-1	Won Orange	Bear Bryant
	Michigan St (UPI)	10-1-0	Lost Rose	Duffy Daugherty
1966	Notre Dame	9-0-1	No bowl	Ara Parseghian
1967	Southern Cal	10-1-0	Won Rose	John McKay
1968	Ohio St	10-0-0	Won Rose	Woody Hayes
1969	Texas	11-0-0	Won Cotton	Darrell Royal
1970	Nebraska	11-0-1	Won Orange	Bob Devaney
	Texas (UPI)	10-1-0	Lost Cotton	Darrell Royal
1971	Nebraska	13-0-0	Won Orange	Bob Devaney
1972	Southern Cal	12-0-0	Won Rose	John McKay
1973	Notre Dame	11-0-0	Won Sugar	Ara Parseghian
	Alabama (UPI)	11-1-0	Lost Sugar	Bear Bryant
1974	Oklahoma	11-0-0	No bowl	Barry Switzer
	Southern Cal (UPI)	10-1-1	Won Rose	John McKay
1975	Oklahoma	11-1-0	Won Orange	Barry Switzer
1976	Pittsburgh	12-0-0	Won Sugar	Johnny Majors
1977	Notre Dame	11-1-0	Won Cotton	Dan Devine
1978	Alabama	11-1-0	Won Sugar	Bear Bryant
	Southern Cal (UPI)	12-1-0	Won Rose	John Robinson
1979	Alabama	12-0-0	Won Sugar	Bear Bryant
1980	Georgia	12-0-0	Won Sugar	Vince Dooley
1981	Clemson	12-0-0	Won Orange	Danny Ford
1982	Penn St	11-1-0	Won Sugar	Joe Paterno
1983	Miami (FL)	11-1-0	Won Orange	Howard Schnellenberger
1984	Brigham Young	13-0-0	Won Holiday	LaVell Edwards
1985	Oklahoma	11-1-0	Won Orange	Barry Switzer
1986	Penn St	12-0-0	Won Fiesta	Joe Paterno
1987	Miami (FL)	12-0-0	Won Orange	Jimmy Johnson
1988	Notre Dame	12-0-0	Won Fiesta	Lou Holtz
1989	Miami (FL)	11-1-0	Won Sugar	Dennis Erickson
1990	Colorado	11-1-1	Won Orange	Bill McCartney
	Georgia Tech (UPI)	11-0-1	Won Citrus	Bobby Ross
1991	Miami (FL)	12-0-0	Won Orange	Dennis Erickson
	Washington (CNN)	12-0-0	Won Rose	Don James
1992	Alabama	13-0-0	Won Sugar	Gene Stallings
1993	Florida St	12-1-0	Won Orange	Bobby Bowden
1994	Nebraska	13-0-0	Won Orange	Tom Osborne
1995	Nebraska	12-0-0	Won Fiesta	Tom Osborne

*The AP, which had voted Notre Dame No. 1, took a second vote, giving the national title to Michigan after its 49-0 win over Southern Cal in the Rose Bowl.

Note: Selectors: Helms Athletic Foundation (H) 1883-1935, The Dickinson System (D) 1924-40, The Associated Press (AP) 1936-present, United Press International (UPI) 1958-90, and USA Today/CNN (CNN) 1991-present.

Results of Major Bowl Games

Rose Bowl

1-1-02	Michigan 49, Stanford 0
1-1-16	Washington St 14, Brown 0
1-1-17	Oregon 14, Pennsylvania 0
1-1-18	Mare Island 19, Camp Lewis 7
1-1-19	Great Lakes 17, Mare Island 0
1-1-20	Harvard 7, Oregon 6
1-1-21	California 28, Ohio St 0
1-2-22	Washington & Jefferson 0, California 0
1-1-23	Southern Cal 14, Penn St 3
1-1-24	Navy 14, Washington 14
1-1-25	Notre Dame 27, Stanford 10
1-1-26	Alabama 20, Washington 19
1-1-27	Alabama 7, Stanford 7
1-2-28	Stanford 7, Pittsburgh 6
1-1-29	Georgia Tech 8, California 7
1-1-30	Southern Cal 47, Pittsburgh 14
1-1-31	Alabama 24, Washington St 0
1-1-32	Southern Cal 21, Tulane 12
1-2-33	Southern Cal 35, Pittsburgh 0
1-1-34	Columbia 7, Stanford 0
1-1-35	Alabama 29, Stanford 13
1-1-36	Stanford 7, Southern Meth 0
1-1-37	Pittsburgh 21, Washington 0
1-1-38	California 13, Alabama 0
1-2-39	Southern Cal 7, Duke 3
1-1-40	Southern Cal 14, Tennessee 0
1-1-41	Stanford 21, Nebraska 13
1-1-42	Oregon St 20, Duke 16
1-1-43	Georgia 9, UCLA 0
1-1-44	Southern Cal 29, Washington 0
1-1-45	Southern Cal 25, Tennessee 0
1-1-46	Alabama 34, Southern Cal 14
1-1-47	Illinois 45, UCLA 14
1-1-48	Michigan 49, Southern Cal 0
1-1-49	Northwestern 20, California 14
1-2-50	Ohio St 17, California 14
1-1-51	Michigan 14, California 6
1-1-52	Illinois 40, Stanford 7
1-1-53	Southern Cal 7, Wisconsin 0
1-1-54	Michigan St 28, UCLA 20
1-1-55	Ohio St 20, Southern Cal 7
1-2-56	Michigan St 17, UCLA 14
1-1-57	Iowa 35, Oregon St 19
1-1-58	Ohio St 10, Oregon 7
1-1-59	Iowa 38, California 12
1-1-60	Washington 44, Wisconsin 8
1-2-61	Washington 17, Minnesota 7
1-1-62	Minnesota 21, UCLA 3
1-1-63	Southern Cal 42, Wisconsin 37
1-1-64	Illinois 17, Washington 7
1-1-65	Michigan 34, Oregon St 7
1-1-66	UCLA 14, Michigan St 12
1-2-67	Purdue 14, Southern Cal 13
1-1-68	Southern Cal 14, Indiana 3
1-1-69	Ohio St 27, Southern Cal 16
1-1-70	Southern Cal 10, Michigan 3
1-1-71	Stanford 27, Ohio St 17
1-1-72	Stanford 13, Michigan 12
1-1-73	Southern Cal 42, Ohio St 17
1-1-74	Ohio St 42, Southern Cal 21
1-1-75	Southern Cal 18, Ohio St 17
1-1-76	UCLA 23, Ohio St 10
1-1-77	Southern Cal 14, Michigan 6
1-2-78	Washington 27, Michigan 20
1-1-79	Southern Cal 17, Michigan 10
1-1-80	Southern Cal 17, Ohio St 16
1-1-81	Michigan 23, Washington 6
1-1-82	Washington 28, Iowa 0
1-1-83	UCLA 24, Michigan 14
1-2-84	UCLA 45, Illinois 9
1-1-85	Southern Cal 20, Ohio St 17
1-1-86	UCLA 45, Iowa 28
1-1-87	Arizona St 22, Michigan 15
1-1-88	Michigan St 20, Southern Cal 17
1-1-89	Michigan 22, Southern Cal 14
1-1-90	Southern Cal 17, Michigan 10
1-1-91	Washington 46, Iowa 34
1-1-92	Washington 34, Michigan 14
1-1-93	Michigan 38, Washington 31
1-1-94	Wisconsin 21, UCLA 16
1-2-95	Penn St 38, Oregon 20
1-1-96	Southern Cal 41, Northwestern 32

City: Pasadena. Stadium: Rose Bowl, capacity 100,375.

Playing Sites: Tournament Park (1902, 1916-22), Rose Bowl (1923-41, since 1943), Duke Stadium, Durham, NC (1942).

Orange Bowl

1-1-35	Bucknell 26, Miami (FL) 0
1-1-36	Catholic 20, Mississippi 19
1-1-37	Duquesne 13, Mississippi St 12
1-1-38	Auburn 6, Michigan St 0
1-2-39	Tennessee 17, Oklahoma 0
1-1-40	Georgia Tech 21, Missouri 7
1-1-41	Mississippi St 14, Georgetown 7
1-1-42	Georgia 40, Texas Christian 26
1-1-43	Alabama 37, Boston College 21
1-1-44	Louisiana St 19, Texas A&M 14
1-1-45	Tulsa 26, Georgia Tech 12
1-1-46	Miami (FL) 13, Holy Cross 6
1-1-47	Rice 8, Tennessee 0
1-1-48	Georgia Tech 20, Kansas 14
1-1-49	Texas 41, Georgia 28
1-2-50	Santa Clara 21, Kentucky 13
1-1-51	Clemson 15, Miami (FL) 14
1-1-52	Georgia Tech 17, Baylor 14
1-1-53	Alabama 61, Syracuse 6
1-1-54	Oklahoma 7, Maryland 0
1-1-55	Duke 34, Nebraska 7
1-2-56	Oklahoma 20, Maryland 6
1-1-57	Colorado 27, Clemson 21
1-1-58	Oklahoma 48, Duke 21
1-1-59	Oklahoma 21, Syracuse 6
1-1-60	Georgia 14, Missouri 0
1-2-61	Missouri 21, Navy 14
1-1-62	Louisiana St 25, Colorado 7
1-1-63	Alabama 17, Oklahoma 0
1-1-64	Nebraska 13, Auburn 7
1-1-65	Texas 21, Alabama 17
1-1-66	Alabama 39, Nebraska 28
1-2-67	Florida 27, Georgia Tech 12

Note: The Fiesta, Orange and Sugar Bowls are joined by the new Bowl Alliance. The Alliance reserves six berths: one each for the champions of the SEC, Big Eight, Big East and ACC and two at-large, one of which is guaranteed to Notre Dame if it is ranked in the top 10 in one of the two polls. Of the six teams, the two highest-ranked go to the Fiesta Bowl in 1996, the Sugar Bowl in 1997, and the Orange Bowl in 1998. The champions of the Big Ten and Pac-10 go to the Rose Bowl; the champions of the Big West and Mid-American go to the Las Vegas Bowl; and the champion of the WAC plays the third-place finisher of the Big 12 in the Holiday Bowl. No other Bowls tie up conference champions.

Results of Major Bowl Games *(Cont.)*

Orange Bowl *(Cont.)*

1-1-68..............Oklahoma 26, Tennessee 24
1-1-69..............Penn St 15, Kansas 14
1-1-70..............Penn St 10, Missouri 3
1-1-71..............Nebraska 17, Louisiana St 12
1-1-72..............Nebraska 38, Alabama 6
1-1-73..............Nebraska 40, Notre Dame 6
1-1-74..............Penn St 16, Louisiana St 9
1-1-75..............Notre Dame 13, Alabama 11
1-1-76..............Oklahoma 14, Michigan 6
1-1-77..............Ohio St 27, Colorado 10
1-2-78..............Arkansas 31, Oklahoma 6
1-1-79..............Oklahoma 31, Nebraska 24
1-1-80..............Oklahoma 24, Florida St 7
1-1-81..............Oklahoma 18, Florida St 17
1-1-82..............Clemson 22, Nebraska 15
1-1-83..............Nebraska 21, Louisiana St 20
1-2-84..............Miami (FL) 31, Nebraska 30
1-1-85..............Washington 28, Oklahoma 17
1-1-86..............Oklahoma 25, Penn St 10
1-1-87..............Oklahoma 42, Arkansas 8
1-1-88..............Miami (FL) 20, Oklahoma 14
1-2-89..............Miami (FL) 23, Nebraska 3
1-1-90..............Notre Dame 21, Colorado 6
1-1-91..............Colorado 10, Notre Dame 9
1-1-92..............Miami (FL) 22, Nebraska 0
1-1-93..............Florida St 27, Nebraska 14
1-1-94..............Florida St 18, Nebraska 16
1-1-95..............Nebraska 24, Miami (FL) 17
1-1-96..............Florida St 31, Notre Dame 26

City: Miami. Stadium: Orange Bowl, capacity 74,224.

Sugar Bowl

1-1-35..............Tulane 20, Temple 14
1-1-36..............Texas Christian 3, Louisiana St 2
1-1-37..............Santa Clara 21, Louisiana St 14
1-1-38..............Santa Clara 6, Louisiana St 0
1-2-39..............Texas Christian 15, Carnegie Tech 7
1-1-40..............Texas A&M 14, Tulane 13
1-1-41..............Boston Col 19, Tennessee 13
1-1-42..............Fordham 2, Missouri 0
1-1-43..............Tennessee 14, Tulsa 7
1-1-44..............Georgia Tech 20, Tulsa 18
1-1-45..............Duke 29, Alabama 26
1-1-46..............Oklahoma St 33, St Mary's (CA) 13
1-1-47..............Georgia 20, N Carolina 10
1-1-48..............Texas 27, Alabama 7
1-1-49..............Oklahoma 14, N Carolina 6
1-2-50..............Oklahoma 35, Louisiana St 0
1-1-51..............Kentucky 13, Oklahoma 7
1-1-52..............Maryland 28, Tennessee 13
1-1-53..............Georgia Tech 24, Mississippi 7
1-1-54..............Georgia Tech 42, W Virginia 19
1-1-55..............Navy 21, Mississippi 0
1-2-56..............Georgia Tech 7, Pittsburgh 0
1-1-57..............Baylor 13, Tennessee 7
1-1-58..............Mississippi 39, Texas 7
1-1-59..............Louisiana St 7, Clemson 0
1-1-60..............Mississippi 21, Louisiana St 0
1-2-61..............Mississippi 14, Rice 6
1-1-62..............Alabama 10, Arkansas 3
1-1-63..............Mississippi 17, Arkansas 13
1-1-64..............Alabama 12, Mississippi 7
1-1-65..............Louisiana St 13, Syracuse 10
1-1-66..............Missouri 20, Florida 18
1-2-67..............Alabama 34, Nebraska 7
1-1-68..............Louisiana St 20, Wyoming 13

Sugar Bowl *(Cont.)*

1-1-69..............Arkansas 16, Georgia 2
1-1-70..............Mississippi 27, Arkansas 22
1-1-71..............Tennessee 34, Air Force 13
1-1-72..............Oklahoma 40, Auburn 22
12-31-72..........Oklahoma 14, Penn St 0
12-31-73..........Notre Dame 24, Alabama 23
12-31-74..........Nebraska 13, Florida 10
12-31-75..........Alabama 13, Penn St 6
1-1-77..............Pittsburgh 27, Georgia 3
1-2-78..............Alabama 35, Ohio St 6
1-1-79..............Alabama 14, Penn St 7
1-1-80..............Alabama 24, Arkansas 9
1-1-81..............Georgia 17, Notre Dame 10
1-1-82..............Pittsburgh 24, Georgia 20
1-1-83..............Penn St 27, Georgia 23
1-2-84..............Auburn 9, Michigan 7
1-1-85..............Nebraska 28, Louisiana St 10
1-1-86..............Tennessee 35, Miami (FL) 7
1-1-87..............Nebraska 30, Louisiana St 15
1-1-88..............Syracuse 16, Auburn 16
1-2-89..............Florida St 13, Auburn 7
1-1-90..............Miami (FL) 33, Alabama 25
1-1-91..............Tennessee 23, Virginia 22
1-1-92..............Notre Dame 39, Florida 28
1-1-93..............Alabama 34, Miami (FL) 13
1-1-94..............Florida 41, West Virginia 7
1-2-95..............Florida St 23, Florida 17
12-31-95..........Virginia Tech 28, Texas 10

City: New Orleans. Stadium: Louisiana Superdome, capacity 78,000.

Playing Sites: Tulane Stadium (1935-74), Louisiana Superdome (since 1975).

Cotton Bowl

1-1-37..............Texas Christian 16, Marquette 6
1-1-38..............Rice 28, Colorado 14
1-2-39..............St. Mary's (CA) 20, Texas Tech 13
1-1-40..............Clemson 6, Boston Col 3
1-1-41..............Texas A&M 13, Fordham 12
1-1-42..............Alabama 29, Texas A&M 21
1-1-43..............Texas 14, Georgia Tech 7
1-1-44..............Texas 7, Randolph Field 7
1-1-45..............Oklahoma St 34, Texas Christian 0
1-1-46..............Texas 40, Missouri 27
1-1-47..............Arkansas 0, Louisiana St 0
1-1-48..............SMU 13, Penn St 13
1-1-49..............SMU 21, Oregon 13
1-2-50..............Rice 27, N Carolina 13
1-1-51..............Tennessee 20, Texas 14
1-1-52..............Kentucky 20, Texas Christian 7
1-1-53..............Texas 16, Tennessee 0
1-1-54..............Rice 28, Alabama 6
1-1-55..............Georgia Tech 14, Arkansas 6
1-2-56..............Mississippi 14, Texas Christian 13
1-1-57..............Texas Christian 28, Syracuse 27
1-1-58..............Navy 20, Rice 7
1-1-59..............Texas Christian 0, Air Force 0
1-1-60..............Syracuse 23, Texas 14
1-2-61..............Duke 7, Arkansas 6
1-1-62..............Texas 12, Mississippi 7
1-1-63..............Louisiana St 13, Texas 0
1-1-64..............Texas 28, Navy 6
1-1-65..............Arkansas 10, Nebraska 7
1-1-66..............Louisiana St 14, Arkansas 7
12-31-66..........Georgia 24, SMU 9
1-1-68..............Texas A&M 20, Alabama 16

Cotton Bowl (Cont.)

1-1-69 ....Texas 36, Tennessee 13
1-1-70 ....Texas 21, Notre Dame 17
1-1-71 ....Notre Dame 24, Texas 11
1-1-72 ....Penn St 30, Texas 6
1-1-73 ....Texas 17, Alabama 13
1-1-74 ....Nebraska 19, Texas 3
1-1-75 ....Penn St 41, Baylor 20
1-1-76 ....Arkansas 31, Georgia 10
1-1-77 ....Houston 30, Maryland 21
1-2-78 ....Notre Dame 38, Texas 10
1-1-79 ....Notre Dame 35, Houston 34
1-1-80 ....Houston 17, Nebraska 14
1-1-81 ....Alabama 30, Baylor 2
1-1-82 ....Texas 14, Alabama 12
1-1-83 ....SMU 7, Pittsburgh 3
1-2-84 ....Georgia 10, Texas 9
1-1-85 ....Boston Col 45, Houston 28
1-1-86 ....Texas A&M 36, Auburn 16
1-1-87 ....Ohio St 28, Texas A&M 12
1-1-88 ....Texas A&M 35, Notre Dame 10
1-2-89 ....UCLA 17, Arkansas 3
1-1-90 ....Tennessee 31, Arkansas 27
1-1-91 ....Miami (FL) 46, Texas 3
1-1-92 ....Florida St 10, Texas A&M 2
1-1-93 ....Notre Dame 28, Texas A&M 3
1-1-94 ....Notre Dame 24, Texas A&M 21
1-2-95 ....Southern Cal 55, Texas Tech 14
1-1-96 ....Colorado 38, Oregon 6

City: Dallas. Stadium: Cotton Bowl, capacity 68,252.

Sun Bowl

1-1-36 ....Hardin-Simmons 14, New Mexico St 14
1-1-37 ....Hardin-Simmons 34, UTEP 6
1-1-38 ....W Virginia 7, Texas Tech 6
1-2-39 ....Utah 26, New Mexico 0
1-1-40 ....Catholic 0, Arizona St 0
1-1-41 ....Case Reserve 26, Arizona St 13
1-1-42 ....Tulsa 6, Texas Tech 0
1-1-43 ....2nd Air Force 13, Hardin-Simmons 7
1-1-44 ....Southwestern (TX) 7, New Mexico 0
1-1-45 ....Southwestern (TX) 35, New Mexico 0
1-1-46 ....New Mexico 34, Denver 24
1-1-47 ....Cincinnati 18, Virginia Tech 6
1-1-48 ....Miami (OH) 13, Texas Tech 12
1-1-49 ....W Virginia 21, UTEP 12
1-2-50 ....UTEP 33, Georgetown 20
1-1-51 ....West Texas St 14, Cincinnati 13
1-1-52 ....Texas Tech 25, Pacific 14
1-1-53 ....Pacific 26, Southern Miss 7
1-1-54 ....UTEP 37, Southern Miss 14
1-1-55 ....UTEP 47, Florida St 20
1-2-56 ....Wyoming 21, Texas Tech 14
1-1-57 ....George Washington 13, UTEP 0
1-1-58 ....Louisville 34, Drake 20
12-31-58 ....Wyoming 14, Hardin-Simmons 6
12-31-59 ....New Mexico St 28, N Texas 8
12-31-60 ....New Mexico St 20, Utah St 13
12-30-61 ....Villanova 17, Wichita St 9
12-31-62 ....W Texas St 15, Ohio 14
12-31-63 ....Oregon 21, SMU 14
12-26-64 ....Georgia 7, Texas Tech 0
12-31-65 ....UTEP 13, Texas Christian 12
12-24-66 ....Wyoming 28, Florida St 20
12-30-67 ....UTEP 14, Mississippi 7
12-28-68 ....Auburn 34, Arizona 10
12-20-69 ....Nebraska 45, Georgia 6

Sun Bowl (Cont.)

12-19-70 ....Georgia Tech 17, Texas Tech 9
12-18-71 ....Louisiana St 33, Iowa St 15
12-30-72 ....N Carolina 32, Texas Tech 28
12-29-73 ....Missouri 34, Auburn 17
12-28-74 ....Mississippi St 26, N Carolina 24
12-26-75 ....Pittsburgh 33, Kansas 19
1-2-77 ....Texas A&M 37, Florida 14
12-31-77 ....Stanford 24, Louisiana St 14
12-23-78 ....Texas 42, Maryland 0
12-22-79 ....Washington 14, Texas 7
12-27-80 ....Nebraska 31, Mississippi St 17
12-26-81 ....Oklahoma 40, Houston 14
12-25-82 ....N Carolina 26, Texas 10
12-24-83 ....Alabama 28, SMU 7
12-22-84 ....Maryland 28, Tennessee 27
12-28-85 ....Georgia 13, Arizona 13
12-25-86 ....Alabama 28, Washington 6
12-25-87 ....Oklahoma St 35, W Virginia 33
12-24-88 ....Alabama 29, Army 28
12-30-89 ....Pittsburgh 31, Texas A&M 28
12-31-90 ....Michigan 17, Southern Cal 16
12-31-91 ....UCLA 6, Illinois 3
12-31-92 ....Baylor 20, Arizona 15
12-24-93 ....Oklahoma 41, Texas Tech 10
12-30-94 ....Texas 35, N Carolina 31
12-29-95 ....Iowa 38, Washington 18

City: El Paso. Stadium: Sun Bowl, capacity 52,000.

Name Changes: Sun Bowl (1936-86; 94-), John Hancock Sun Bowl (1987-88), John Hancock Bowl (1989-93).

Playing Sites: Kidd Field (1936-62), Sun Bowl (since 1963).

Gator Bowl

1-1-46 ....Wake Forest 26, S Carolina 14
1-1-47 ....Oklahoma 34, N Carolina St 13
1-1-48 ....Maryland 20, Georgia 20
1-1-49 ....Clemson 24, Missouri 23
1-2-50 ....Maryland 20, Missouri 7
1-1-51 ....Wyoming 20, Washington & Lee 7
1-1-52 ....Miami (FL) 14, Clemson 0
1-1-53 ....Florida 14, Tulsa 13
1-1-54 ....Texas Tech 35, Auburn 13
12-31-54 ....Auburn 33, Baylor 13
12-31-55 ....Vanderbilt 25, Auburn 13
12-29-56 ....Georgia Tech 21, Pittsburgh 14
12-28-57 ....Tennessee 3, Texas A&M 0
12-27-58 ....Mississippi 7, Florida 3
1-2-60 ....Arkansas 14, Georgia Tech 7
12-31-60 ....Florida 13, Baylor 12
12-30-61 ....Penn St 30, Georgia Tech 15
12-29-62 ....Florida 17, Penn St 7
12-28-63 ....N Carolina 35, Air Force 0
1-2-65 ....Florida St 36, Oklahoma 19
12-31-65 ....Georgia Tech 31, Texas Tech 21
12-31-66 ....Tennessee 18, Syracuse 12
12-30-67 ....Penn St 17, Florida St 17
12-28-68 ....Missouri 35, Alabama 10
12-27-69 ....Florida 14, Tennessee 13
1-2-71 ....Auburn 35, Mississippi 28
12-31-71 ....Georgia 7, N Carolina 3
12-30-72 ....Auburn 24, Colorado 3
12-29-73 ....Texas Tech 28, Tennessee 19
12-30-74 ....Auburn 27, Texas 3
12-29-75 ....Maryland 13, Florida 0
12-27-76 ....Notre Dame 20, Penn St 9
12-30-77 ....Pittsburgh 34, Clemson 3
12-29-78 ....Clemson 17, Ohio St 15
12-28-79 ....N Carolina 17, Michigan 15

Gator Bowl (Cont.)

12-29-80 ....Pittsburgh 37, S Carolina 9
12-28-81 ....N Carolina 31, Arkansas 27
12-30-82 ....Florida St 31, W Virginia 12
12-30-83 ....Florida 14, Iowa 6
12-28-84 ....Oklahoma St 21, S Carolina 14
12-30-85 ....Florida St 34, Oklahoma St 23
12-27-86 ....Clemson 27, Stanford 21
12-31-87 ....Louisiana St 30, S Carolina 13
1-1-89 ....Georgia 34, Michigan St 27
12-30-89 ....Clemson 27, W Virginia 7
1-1-91 ....Michigan 35, Mississippi 3
12-29-91 ....Oklahoma 48, Virginia 14
12-31-92 ....Florida 27, N Carolina St 10
12-31-93 ....Alabama 24, North Carolina 10
12-30-94 ....Tennessee 45, Virginia Tech 23
1-1-96 ....Syracuse 41, Clemson 0

City: Jacksonville, FL. Stadium: Gator Bowl, capacity 76,676.

Florida Citrus Bowl

1-1-47 ....Catawba 31, Maryville (TN) 6
1-1-48 ....Catawba 7, Marshall 0
1-1-49 ....Murray St 21, Sul Ross St 21
1-2-50 ....St Vincent 7, Emory & Henry 6
1-1-51 ....Morris Harvey 35, Emory & Henry 14
1-1-52 ....Stetson 35, Arkansas St 20
1-1-53 ....E Texas St 33, Tennessee Tech 0
1-1-54 ....E Texas St 7, Arkansas St 7
1-1-55 ....NE-Omaha 7, Eastern Kentucky 6
1-2-56 ....Juniata 6, Missouri Valley 6
1-1-57 ....W Texas St 20, Southern Miss 13
1-1-58 ....E Texas St 10, Southern Miss 9
12-27-58 ....E Texas St 26, Missouri Valley 7
1-1-60 ....Middle Tennessee St 21, Presbyterian 12
12-30-60 ....Citadel 27, Tennessee Tech 0
12-29-61 ....Lamar 21, Middle Tennessee St 14
12-22-62 ....Houston 49, Miami (OH) 21
12-28-63 ....Western Kentucky 27, Coast Guard 0
12-12-64 ....E Carolina 14, Massachusetts 13
12-11-65 ....E Carolina 31, Maine 0
12-10-66 ....Morgan St 14, West Chester 6
12-16-67 ....TN-Martin 25, West Chester 8
12-27-68 ....Richmond 49, Ohio 42
12-26-69 ....Toledo 56, Davidson 33
12-28-70 ....Toledo 40, William & Mary 12
12-28-71 ....Toledo 28, Richmond 3
12-29-72 ....Tampa 21, Kent St 18
12-22-73 ....Miami (OH) 16, Florida 7
12-21-74 ....Miami (OH) 21, Georgia 10
12-20-75 ....Miami (OH) 20, S Carolina 7
12-18-76 ....Oklahoma St 49, Brigham Young 21
12-23-77 ....Florida St 40, Texas Tech 17
12-23-78 ....N Carolina St 30, Pittsburgh 17
12-22-79 ....Louisiana St 34, Wake Forest 10
12-20-80 ....Florida 35, Maryland 20
12-19-81 ....Missouri 19, Southern Miss 17
12-18-82 ....Auburn 33, Boston Col 26
12-17-83 ....Tennessee 30, Maryland 23
12-22-84 ....Georgia 17, Florida St 17
12-28-85 ....Ohio St 10, Brigham Young 7
1-1-87 ....Auburn 16, Southern Cal 7
1-1-88 ....Clemson 35, Penn St 10
1-2-89 ....Clemson 13, Oklahoma 6
1-1-90 ....Illinois 31, Virginia 21
1-1-91 ....Georgia Tech 45, Nebraska 21
1-1-92 ....California 37, Clemson 13
1-1-93 ....Georgia 21, Ohio State 14

Florida Citrus Bowl (Cont.)

1-1-94 ....Penn State 31, Tennessee 13
1-2-95 ....Alabama 24, Ohio St 17
1-1-96 ....Tennessee 20, Ohio St 14

City: Orlando, FL. Stadium: Florida Citrus Bowl, capacity 70,968.

Name Change: Tangerine Bowl (1947-82).

Playing Sites: Tangerine Bowl (1947-72, 1974-82); Florida Field, Gainesville (1973); Orlando Stadium (1983-85); Florida Citrus Bowl-Orlando (since 1986). Tangerine Bowl, Orlando Stadium and Florida Citrus Bowl-Orlando are identical site.

Liberty Bowl

12-19-59 ....Penn St 7, Alabama 0
12-17-60 ....Penn St 41, Oregon 12
12-16-61 ....Syracuse 15, Miami (FL) 14
12-15-62 ....Oregon St 6, Villanova 0
12-21-63 ....Mississippi St 16, N Carolina St 12
12-19-64 ....Utah 32, W Virginia 6
12-18-65 ....Mississippi 13, Auburn 7
12-10-66 ....Miami (FL) 14, Virginia Tech 7
12-16-67 ....N Carolina St 14, Georgia 7
12-14-68 ....Mississippi 34, Virginia Tech 17
12-13-69 ....Colorado 47, Alabama 33
12-12-70 ....Tulane 17, Colorado 3
12-20-71 ....Tennessee 14, Arkansas 13
12-18-72 ....Georgia Tech 31, Iowa St 30
12-17-73 ....N Carolina St 31, Kansas 18
12-16-74 ....Tennessee 7, Maryland 3
12-22-75 ....Southern Cal 20, Texas A&M 0
12-20-76 ....Alabama 36, UCLA 6
12-19-77 ....Nebraska 21, N Carolina 17
12-23-78 ....Missouri 20, Louisiana St 15
12-22-79 ....Penn St 9, Tulane 6
12-27-80 ....Purdue 28, Missouri 25
12-30-81 ....Ohio St 31, Navy 28
12-29-82 ....Alabama 21, Illinois 15
12-29-83 ....Notre Dame 19, Boston Col 18
12-27-84 ....Auburn 21, Arkansas 15
12-27-85 ....Baylor 21, Louisiana St 7
12-29-86 ....Tennessee 21, Minnesota 14
12-29-87 ....Georgia 20, Arkansas 17
12-28-88 ....Indiana 34, S Carolina 10
12-28-89 ....Mississippi 42, Air Force 29
12-27-90 ....Air Force 23, Ohio St 11
12-29-91 ....Air Force 38, Mississippi St 15
12-31-92 ....Mississippi 13, Air Force 0
12-28-93 ....Louisville 18, Michigan St 7
12-31-94 ....Illinois 30, E Carolina 0
12-30-95 ....East Carolina 19, Stanford 13

City: Memphis (since 1965). Stadium: Liberty Bowl Memorial Stadium, capacity 63,068.

Playing Sites: Philadelphia (Municipal Stadium, 1959-63), Atlantic City (Convention Center, 1964).

Bluebonnet Bowl (Discontinued)

12-19-59 ....Clemson 23, Texas Christian 7
12-17-60 ....Texas 3, Alabama 3
12-16-61 ....Kansas 33, Rice 7
12-22-62 ....Missouri 14, Georgia Tech 10
12-21-63 ....Baylor 14, LSU 7
12-19-64 ....Tulsa 14, Mississippi 7
12-18-65 ....Tennessee 27, Tulsa 6
12-17-66 ....Texas 19, Mississippi 0
12-23-67 ....Colorado 31, Miami (FL) 21
12-31-68 ....SMU 28, Oklahoma 27

Results of Major Bowl Games *(Cont.)*

Bluebonnet Bowl *(Cont.)*

12-31-69.........Houston 36, Auburn 7
12-31-70.........Alabama 24, Oklahoma 24
12-31-71.........Colorado 29, Houston 17
12-30-72.........Tennessee 24, LSU 17
12-29-73.........Houston 47, Tulane 7
12-23-74.........N Carolina St 31, Houston 31
12-27-75.........Texas 38, Colorado 21
12-31-76.........Nebraska 27, Texas Tech 24
12-31-77.........Southern Cal 47, Texas A&M 28
12-31-78.........Stanford 25, Georgia 22
12-31-79.........Purdue 27, Tennessee 22
12-31-80.........N Carolina 16, Texas 7
12-31-81.........Michigan 33, UCLA 14
12-31-82.........Arkansas 28, Florida 24
12-31-83.........Oklahoma St 24, Baylor 14
12-31-84.........W Virginia 31, Texas Christian 14
12-31-85.........Air Force 24, Texas 16
12-31-86.........Baylor 21, Colorado 9
12-31-87.........Texas 32, Pittsburgh 27
City: Houston. Playing sites: Rice Stadium (1959-67; 1985-86), Astrodome (1968-84, 1987).
Name change: Astro-Bluebonnet Bowl (1968-76).

Peach Bowl

12-30-68.........Louisiana St 31, Florida St 27
12-30-69.........W Virginia 14, S Carolina 3
12-30-70.........Arizona St 48, N Carolina 26
12-30-71.........Mississippi 41, Georgia Tech 18
12-29-72.........N Carolina St 49, W Virginia 13
12-28-73.........Georgia 17, Maryland 16
12-28-74.........Vanderbilt 6, Texas Tech 6
12-31-75.........W Virginia 13, N Carolina St 10
12-31-76.........Kentucky 21, N Carolina 0
12-31-77.........N Carolina St 24, Iowa St 14
12-25-78.........Purdue 41, Georgia Tech 21
12-31-79.........Baylor 24, Clemson 18
1-2-81.............Miami (FL) 20, Virginia Tech 10
12-31-81.........W Virginia 26, Florida 6
12-31-82.........Iowa 28, Tennessee 22
12-30-83.........Florida St 28, N Carolina 3
12-31-84.........Virginia 27, Purdue 24
12-31-85.........Army 31, Illinois 29
12-31-86.........Virginia Tech 25, N Carolina St 24
1-2-88.............Tennessee 27, Indiana 22
12-31-88.........N Carolina St 28, Iowa 23
12-30-89.........Syracuse 19, Georgia 18
12-29-90.........Auburn 27, Indiana 23
1-1-92.............E Carolina 37, N Carolina St 34
1-2-93.............North Carolina 21, Mississippi St 17
12-31-93.........Clemson 14, Kentucky 13
1-1-95.............N Carolina St 28, Mississippi St 24
12-30-95.........Virginia 34, Georgia 27
City: Atlanta. Stadium: Georgia Dome, capacity 71,233.
Playing Sites: Grant Field (1968-70), Atlanta-Fulton County Stadium (1971-92), Georgia Dome (since 1993).

Fiesta Bowl

12-27-71.........Arizona St 45, Florida St 38
12-23-72.........Arizona St 49, Missouri 35
12-21-73.........Arizona St 28, Pittsburgh 7
12-28-74.........Oklahoma St 16, Brigham Young 6
12-26-75.........Arizona St 17, Nebraska 14
12-25-76.........Oklahoma 41, Wyoming 7
12-25-77.........Penn St 42, Arizona St 30
12-25-78.........Arkansas 10, UCLA 10
12-25-79.........Pittsburgh 16, Arizona 10

Fiesta Bowl *(Cont.)*

12-26-80.........Penn St 31, Ohio St 19
1-1-82.............Penn St 26, Southern Cal 10
1-1-83.............Arizona St 32, Oklahoma 21
1-2-84.............Ohio St 28, Pittsburgh 23
1-1-85.............UCLA 39, Miami (FL) 37
1-1-86.............Michigan 27, Nebraska 23
1-2-87.............Penn St 14, Miami (FL) 10
1-1-88.............Florida St 31, Nebraska 28
1-2-89.............Notre Dame 34, W Virginia 21
1-1-90.............Florida St 41, Nebraska 17
1-1-91.............Louisville 34, Alabama 7
1-1-92.............Penn St 42, Tennessee 17
1-1-93.............Syracuse 26, Colorado 22
1-1-94.............Arizona 29, Miami (FL) 0
1-2-95.............Colorado 41, Notre Dame 24
1-2-96.............Nebraska 62, Florida 24
City: Tempe, AZ. Stadium: Sun Devil Stadium, capacity 74,000.

Independence Bowl

12-13-76.........McNeese St 20, Tulsa 16
12-17-77.........Louisiana Tech 24, Louisville 14
12-16-78.........E Carolina 35, Louisiana Tech 13
12-15-79.........Syracuse 31, McNeese St 7
12-13-80.........Southern Miss 16, McNeese St 14
12-12-81.........Texas A&M 33, Oklahoma St 16
12-11-82.........Wisconsin 14, Kansas St 3
12-10-83.........Air Force 9, Mississippi 3
12-15-84.........Air Force 23, Virginia Tech 7
12-21-85.........Minnesota 20, Clemson 13
12-20-86.........Mississippi 20, Texas Tech 17
12-19-87.........Washington 24, Tulane 12
12-23-88.........Southern Miss 38, UTEP 18
12-16-89.........Oregon 27, Tulsa 24
12-15-90.........Louisiana Tech 34, Maryland 34
12-29-91.........Georgia 24, Arkansas 15
12-31-92.........Wake Forest 39, Oregon 35
12-31-93.........Virginia Tech 45, Indiana 20
12-28-94.........Virginia 20, Texas Christian 10
12-29-95.........Louisiana St 45, Michigan St 26
City: Shreveport, LA. Stadium: Independence Stadium, capacity 40,000.

All-American Bowl (Discontinued)

12-22-77.........Maryland 17, Minnesota 7
12-20-78.........Texas A&M 28, Iowa St 12
12-29-79.........Missouri 24, S Carolina 14
12-27-80.........Arkansas 34, Tulane 15
12-31-81.........Mississippi St 10, Kansas 0
12-31-82.........Air Force 36, Vanderbilt 28
12-22-83.........W Virginia 20, Kentucky 16
12-29-84.........Kentucky 20, Wisconsin 19
12-31-85.........Georgia Tech 17, Michigan St 14
12-31-86.........Florida St 27, Indiana 13
12-22-87.........Virginia 22, Brigham Young 16
12-29-88.........Florida 14, Illinois 10
12-28-89.........Texas Tech 49, Duke 21
12-28-90...........N Carolina St 31, S Mississippi 27
City: Birmingham, AL. Stadium: Legion Field.
Name Change: Hall of Fame Classic (1977-84).

Holiday Bowl

12-22-78.........Navy 23, Brigham Young 16
12-21-79.........Indiana 38, Brigham Young 37
12-19-80.........Brigham Young 46, SMU 45
12-18-81.........Brigham Young 38, Washington St 36
12-17-82.........Ohio St 47, Brigham Young 17
12-23-83.........Brigham Young 21, Missouri 17
12-21-84.........Brigham Young 24, Michigan 17
12-22-85.........Arkansas 18, Arizona St 17
12-30-86.........Iowa 39, San Diego St 38
12-30-87.........Iowa 20, Wyoming 19
12-30-88.........Oklahoma St 62, Wyoming 14
12-29-89.........Penn St 50, Brigham Young 39
12-29-90.........Texas A&M 65, Brigham Young 14
12-30-91.........Iowa 13, Brigham Young 13
12-30-92.........Hawaii 27, Illinois 17
12-30-93.........Ohio St 28, Brigham Young 21
12-30-94.........Michigan 24, Colorado St 14
12-29-95.........Kansas St 54, Colorado St 21

City: San Diego. Stadium: Jack Murphy Stadium, capacity 61,820.

Las Vegas Bowl

12-19-81.........Toledo 27, San Jose St 25
12-18-82.........Fresno St 29, Bowling Green 28
12-17-83.........Northern Illinois 20, Cal St-Fullerton 13
12-15-84.........UNLV 30, Toledo 13*
12-14-85.........Fresno St 51, Bowling Green 7
12-13-86.........San Jose St 37, Miami (OH) 7
12-12-87.........Eastern Michigan 30, San Jose St 27
12-10-88.........Fresno St 35, Western Michigan 30
12-9-89.........Fresno St 27, Ball St 6
12-8-90.........San Jose St 48, Central Michigan 24
12-14-91.........Bowling Green 28, Fresno St 21
12-18-92.........Bowling Green 35, Nevada 34
12-17-93.........Utah St 42, Ball St 33
12-15-94.........UNLV 52, Central Michigan 24
12-14-95.........Toledo 40, Nevada 37

* Toledo won later by forfeit.

City: Las Vegas (since 1992). Stadium: Sam Boyd Silver Bowl Stadium, capacity 32,000.
Name change: California Bowl (1981-91).
Playing sites: Fresno, CA (Bulldog Stadium, 1981-91), Las Vegas.

Aloha Bowl

12-25-82.........Washington 21, Maryland 20
12-26-83.........Penn St 13, Washington 10
12-29-84.........SMU 27, Notre Dame 20
12-28-85.........Alabama 24, Southern Cal 3
12-27-86.........Arizona 30, N Carolina 21
12-25-87.........UCLA 20, Florida 16
12-25-88.........Washington St 24, Houston 22
12-25-89.........Michigan St 33, Hawaii 13
12-25-90.........Syracuse 28, Arizona 0
12-25-91.........Georgia Tech 18, Stanford 17
12-25-92.........Kansas 23, Brigham Young 20
12-25-93.........Colorado 41, Fresno St 30
12-25-94.........Boston College 12, Kansas St 7
12-25-95.........Kansas 51, UCLA 30

City: Honolulu. Stadium: Aloha Stadium, capacity 50,000.

Freedom Bowl (Discontinued)

12-16-84.........Iowa 55, Texas 17
12-30-85.........Washington 20, Colorado 17
12-30-86.........UCLA 31, Brigham Young 10
12-30-87.........Arizona St 33, Air Force 28
12-29-88.........Brigham Young 20, Colorado 17
12-30-89.........Washington 34, Florida 7
12-29-90.........Colorado St 32, Oregon 31
12-30-91.........Tulsa 28, San Diego St 17
12-29-92.........Fresno St 24, Southern Cal 7
12-30-93.........Southern Cal 28, Utah 21
12-29-94.........Utah 16, Arizona 13

City: Anaheim. Stadium: Anaheim Stadium.

Outback Bowl

12-23-86.........Boston College 27, Georgia 24
1-2-88.............Michigan 28, Alabama 24
1-2-89.............Syracuse 23, Louisiana St 10
1-1-90.............Auburn 31, Ohio St 14
1-1-91.............Clemson 30, Illinois 0
1-1-92.............Syracuse 24, Ohio St 17
1-1-93.............Tennessee 38, Boston College 23
1-1-94.............Michigan 42, N Carolina St 7
1-2-95.............Wisconsin 34, Duke 20
1-1-96.............Penn St 43, Auburn 14

City: Tampa. Stadium: Tampa Bay Stadium, capacity 74,301.
Name change: Hall of Fame Bowl (1986-95).

Copper Bowl

12-31-89.........Arizona 17, N Carolina St 10
12-31-90.........California 17, Wyoming 15
12-31-91.........Indiana 24, Baylor 0
12-29-92.........Washington St 31, Utah 28
12-29-93.........Kansas St 52, Wyoming 17
12-29-94.........Brigham Young 31, Oklahoma 6
12-27-95.........Texas Tech 55, Air Force 41

City: Tucson. Stadium: Arizona Stadium, capacity 55,900.

Carquest Bowl

12-28-90.........Florida St 24, Penn St 17
12-28-91.........Alabama 30, Colorado 25
1-1-93.............Stanford 24, Penn St 3
1-1-94.............Boston College 31, Virginia 13
1-2-95.............S Carolina 24, W Virginia 21
12-30-95.........N Carolina 20, Arkansas 10

City: Miami. Stadium: Joe Robbie, capacity 74,913.
Name Change: Blockbuster Bowl (1990-93).

Alamo Bowl

12-31-93.........California 37, Iowa 3
12-31-94.........Washington St 10, Baylor 3
12-28-95.........Texas A&M 22, Michigan 20

City: San Antonio, TX. Stadium: Alamodome, capacity 65,000.

1936

		Record	Coach
1.	Minnesota	7-1-0	Bernie Bierman
2.	Louisiana St	9-0-1	Bernie Moore
3.	Pittsburgh	7-1-1	Jack Sutherland
4.	Alabama	8-0-1	Frank Thomas
5.	Washington	7-1-1	Jimmy Phelan
6.	Santa Clara	7-1-0	Buck Shaw
7.	Northwestern	7-1-0	Pappy Waldorf
8.	Notre Dame	6-2-1	Elmer Layden
9.	Nebraska	7-2-0	Dana X. Bible
10.	Pennsylvania	7-1-0	Harvey Harman
11.	Duke	9-1-0	Wallace Wade
12.	Yale	7-1-0	Ducky Pond
13.	Dartmouth	7-1-1	Red Blaik
14.	Duquesne	7-2-0	John Smith
15.	Fordham	5-1-2	Jim Crowley
16.	Texas Christian	8-2-2	Dutch Meyer
17.	Tennessee	6-2-2	Bob Neyland
18.	Arkansas	7-3-0	Fred Thomsen
19.	Navy	6-3-0	Tom Hamilton
20.	Marquette	7-1-0	Frank Murray

1937

		Record	Coach
1.	Pittsburgh	9-0-1	Jack Sutherland
2.	California	9-0-1	Stub Allison
3.	Fordham	7-0-1	Jim Crowley
4.	Alabama	9-0-0	Frank Thomas
5.	Minnesota	6-2-0	Bernie Bierman
6.	Villanova	8-0-1	Clipper Smith
7.	Dartmouth	7-0-2	Red Blaik
8.	Louisiana St	9-1-0	Bernie Moore
9.	Notre Dame	6-2-1	Elmer Layden
	Santa Clara	8-0-0	Buck Shaw
11.	Nebraska	6-1-2	Biff Jones
12.	Yale	6-1-1	Ducky Pond
13.	Ohio St	6-2-0	Francis Schmidt
14.	Holy Cross	8-0-2	Eddie Anderson
	Arkansas	6-2-2	Fred Thomsen
16.	Texas Christian	4-2-2	Dutch Meyer
17.	Colorado	8-0-0	Bunnie Oakes
18.	Rice	5-3-2	Jimmy Kitts
19.	N Carolina	7-1-1	Ray Wolf
20.	Duke	7-2-1	Wallace Wade

1938

		Record	Coach
1.	Texas Christian	10-0-0	Dutch Meyer
2.	Tennessee	10-0-0	Bob Neyland
3.	Duke	9-0-0	Wallace Wade
4.	Oklahoma	10-0-0	Tom Stidham
5.	#Notre Dame	8-1-0	Elmer Layden
6.	Carnegie Tech	7-1-0	Bill Kern
7.	Southern Cal	8-2-0	Howard Jones
8.	Pittsburgh	8-2-0	Jack Sutherland
9.	Holy Cross	8-1-0	Eddie Anderson
10.	Minnesota	6-2-0	Bernie Bierman
11.	Texas Tech	10-0-0	Pete Cawthon
12.	Cornell	5-1-1	Carl Snavely

1938 (Cont.)

		Record	Coach
13.	Alabama	7-1-1	Frank Thomas
14.	California	10-1-0	Stub Allison
15.	Fordham	6-1-2	Jim Crowley
16.	Michigan	6-1-1	Fritz Crisler
17.	Northwestern	4-2-2	Pappy Waldorf
18.	Villanova	8-0-1	Clipper Smith
19.	Tulane	7-2-1	Red Dawson
20.	Dartmouth	7-2-0	Red Blaik

#Selected No. 1 by the Dickinson System.

1939

		Record	Coach
1.	Texas A&M	10-0-0	Homer Norton
2.	Tennessee	10-0-0	Bob Neyland
3.	#Southern Cal	7-0-2	Howard Jones
4.	Cornell	8-0-0	Carl Snavely
5.	Tulane	8-0-1	Red Dawson
6.	Missouri	8-1-0	Don Faurot
7.	UCLA	6-0-4	Babe Horrell
8.	Duke	8-1-0	Wallace Wade
9.	Iowa	6-1-1	Eddie Anderson
10.	Duquesne	8-0-1	Buff Donelli
11.	Boston College	9-1-0	Frank Leahy
12.	Clemson	8-1-0	Jess Neely
13.	Notre Dame	7-2-0	Elmer Layden
14.	Santa Clara	5-1-3	Buck Shaw
15.	Ohio St	6-2-0	Francis Schmidt
16.	Georgia Tech	7-2-0	Bill Alexander
17.	Fordham	6-2-0	Jim Crowley
18.	Nebraska	7-1-1	Biff Jones
19.	Oklahoma	6-2-1	Tom Stidham
20.	Michigan	6-2-0	Fritz Crisler

#Selected No. 1 by the Dickinson System.

1940

		Record	Coach
1.	Minnesota	8-0-0	Bernie Bierman
2.	Stanford	9-0-0	C. Shaughnessy
3.	Michigan	7-1-0	Fritz Crisler
4.	Tennessee	10-0-0	Bob Neyland
5.	Boston College	10-0-0	Frank Leahy
6.	Texas A&M	8-1-0	Homer Norton
7.	Nebraska	8-1-0	Biff Jones
8.	Northwestern	6-2-0	Pappy Waldorf
9.	Mississippi St	9-0-1	Allyn McKeen
10.	Washington	7-2-0	Jimmy Phelan
11.	Santa Clara	6-1-1	Buck Shaw
12.	Fordham	7-1-0	Jim Crowley
13.	Georgetown	8-1-0	Jack Hagerty
14.	Pennsylvania	6-1-1	George Munger
15.	Cornell	6-2-0	Carl Snavely
16.	SMU	8-1-1	Matty Bell
17.	Hard.-Simmons	9-0-0	Abe Woodson
18.	Duke	7-2-0	Wallace Wade
19.	Lafayette	9-0-0	Hooks Mylin
20.	—		

Only 19 teams selected.

Note: Except where indicated with an asterisk, the polls from 1936 through 1964 were taken before the bowl games and those from 1965 through the present were taken after the bowl games.

1941

		Record	Coach
1.	Minnesota	8-0-0	Bernie Bierman
2.	Duke	9-0-0	Wallace Wade
3.	Notre Dame	8-0-1	Frank Leahy
4.	Texas	8-1-1	Dana X. Bible
5.	Michigan	6-1-1	Fritz Crisler
6.	Fordham	7-1-0	Jim Crowley
7.	Missouri	8-1-0	Don Faurot
8.	Duquesne	8-0-0	Buff Donelli
9.	Texas A&M	9-1-0	Homer Norton
10.	Navy	7-1-1	Swede Larson
11.	Northwestern	5-3-0	Pappy Waldorf
12.	Oregon St	7-2-0	Lon Stiner
13.	Ohio St	6-1-1	Paul Brown
14.	Georgia	8-1-1	Wally Butts
15.	Pennsylvania	7-1-1	George Munger
16.	Mississippi St	8-1-1	Allyn McKeen
17.	Mississippi	6-2-1	Harry Mehre
18.	Tennessee	8-2-0	John Barnhill
19.	Washington St	6-4-0	Babe Hollingbery
20.	Alabama	8-2-0	Frank Thomas

1942

		Record	Coach
1.	Ohio St	9-1-0	Paul Brown
2.	Georgia	10-1-0	Wally Butts
3.	Wisconsin	8-1-1	H. Stuhldreher
4.	Tulsa	10-0-0	Henry Frnka
5.	Georgia Tech	9-1-0	Bill Alexander
6.	Notre Dame	7-2-2	Frank Leahy
7.	Tennessee	8-1-1	John Barnhill
8.	Boston College	8-1-0	Denny Myers
9.	Michigan	7-3-0	Fritz Crisler
10.	Alabama	7-3-0	Frank Thomas
11.	Texas	8-2-0	Dana X. Bible
12.	Stanford	6-4-0	Marchie Schwartz
13.	UCLA	7-3-0	Babe Horrell
14.	William & Mary	9-1-1	Carl Voyles
15.	Santa Clara	7-2-0	Buck Shaw
16.	Auburn	6-4-1	Jack Meagher
17.	Washington St	6-2-2	Babe Hollingbery
18.	Mississippi St	8-2-0	Allyn McKeen
19.	Minnesota	5-4-0	George Hauser
	Holy Cross	5-4-1	Ank Scanlon
	Penn St	6-1-1	Bob Higgins

1943

		Record	Coach
1.	Notre Dame	9-1-0	Frank Leahy
2.	Iowa Pre-Flight	9-1-0	Don Faurot
3.	Michigan	8-1-0	Fritz Crisler
4.	Navy	8-1-0	Billick Whelchel
5.	Purdue	9-0-0	Elmer Burnham
6.	Great Lakes	10-2-0	Tony Hinkle
7.	Duke	8-1-0	Eddie Cameron
8.	Del Monte P-F	7-1-0	Bill Kern
9.	Northwestern	6-2-0	Pappy Waldorf
10.	March Field	9-1-0	Paul Schissler
11.	Army	7-2-1	Red Balik

1943 *(Cont.)*

		Record	Coach
12.	Washington	4-0-0	Ralph Welch
13.	Georgia Tech	7-3-0	Bill Alexander
14.	Texas	7-1-0	Dana X. Bible
15.	Tulsa	6-0-1	Henry Frnka
16.	Dartmouth	6-1-0	Earl Brown
17.	Bainbridge NTS	7-0-0	Joe Maniaci
18.	Colorado College	7-0-0	Hal White
19.	Pacific	7-2-0	Amos A. Stagg
20.	Pennsylvania	6-2-1	George Munger

1944

		Record	Coach
1.	Army	9-0-0	Red Blaik
2.	Ohio St	9-0-0	Carroll Widdoes
3.	Randolph Field	11-0-0	Frank Tritico
4.	Navy	6-3-0	Oscar Hagberg
5.	Bainbridge NTS	9-0-0	Joe Maniaci
6.	Iowa Pre-Flight	10-1-0	Jack Meagher
7.	Southern Cal	7-0-2	Jeff Cravath
8.	Michigan	8-2-0	Fritz Crisler
9.	Notre Dame	8-2-0	Ed McKeever
10.	March Field	7-1-2	Paul Schissler
11.	Duke	5-4-0	Eddie Cameron
12.	Tennessee	8-0-1	John Barnhill
13.	Georgia Tech	8-2-0	Bill Alexander
	Norman P-F	6-0-0	John Gregg
15.	Illinois	5-4-1	Ray Eliot
16.	El Toro Marines	8-1-0	Dick Hanley
17.	Great Lakes	9-2-1	Paul Brown
18.	Fort Pierce	9-0-0	Hamp Pool
19.	St. Mary's P-F	4-4-0	Jules Sikes
20.	2nd Air Force	7-2-1	Bill Reese

1945

		Record	Coach
1.	Army	9-0-0	Red Blaik
2.	Alabama	9-0-0	Frank Thomas
3.	Navy	7-1-1	Oscar Hagberg
4.	Indiana	9-0-1	Bo McMillan
5.	Oklahoma A&M	8-0-0	Jim Lookabaugh
6.	Michigan	7-3-0	Fritz Crisler
7.	St. Mary's (CA)	7-1-0	Jimmy Phelan
8.	Pennsylvania	6-2-0	George Munger
9.	Notre Dame	7-2-1	Hugh Devore
10.	Texas	9-1-0	Dana X. Bible
11.	Southern Cal	7-3-0	Jeff Cravath
12.	Ohio St	7-2-0	Carroll Widdoes
13.	Duke	6-2-0	Eddie Cameron
14.	Tennessee	8-1-0	John Barnhill
15.	Louisiana St	7-2-0	Bernie Moore
16.	Holy Cross	8-1-0	John DeGrosa
17.	Tulsa	8-2-0	Henry Frnka
18.	Georgia	8-2-0	Wally Butts
19.	Wake Forest	4-3-1	Peahead Walker
20.	Columbia	8-1-0	Lou Little

1946

		Record	Coach
1.	Notre Dame	8-0-1	Frank Leahy
2.	Army	9-0-1	Red Blaik
3.	Georgia	10-0-0	Wally Butts
4.	UCLA	10-0-0	B. LaBrucherie
5.	Illinois	7-2-0	Ray Eliot
6.	Michigan	6-2-1	Fritz Crisler
7.	Tennessee	9-1-0	Bob Neyland
8.	Louisiana St	9-1-0	Bernie Moore
9.	N Carolina	8-1-1	Carl Snavely
10.	Rice	8-2-0	Jess Neely
11.	Georgia Tech	8-2-0	Bobby Dodd
12.	Yale	7-1-1	Howard Odell
13.	Pennsylvania	6-2-0	George Munger
14.	Oklahoma	7-3-0	Jim Tatum
15.	Texas	8-2-0	Dana X. Bible
16.	Arkansas	6-3-1	John Barnhill
17.	Tulsa	9-1-0	J.O. Brothers
18.	N Carolina St	8-2-0	Beattie Feathers
19.	Delaware	9-0-0	Bill Murray
20.	Indiana	6-3-0	Bo McMillan

1947

		Record	Coach
1.	Notre Dame	9-0-0	Frank Leahy
2.	#Michigan	9-0-0	Fritz Crisler
3.	SMU	9-0-1	Matty Bell
4.	Penn St	9-0-0	Bob Higgins
5.	Texas	9-1-0	Blair Cherry
6.	Alabama	8-2-0	Red Drew
7.	Pennsylvania	7-0-1	George Munger
8.	Southern Cal	7-1-1	Jeff Cravath
9.	N Carolina	8-2-0	Carl Snavely
10.	Georgia Tech	9-1-0	Bobby Dodd
11.	Army	5-2-2	Red Blaik
12.	Kansas	8-0-2	George Sauer
13.	Mississippi	8-2-0	Johnny Vaught
14.	William & Mary	9-1-0	Rube McCray
15.	California	9-1-0	Pappy Waldorf
16.	Oklahoma	7-2-1	Bud Wilkinson
17.	N Carolina St	5-3-1	Beattie Feathers
18.	Rice	6-3-1	Jess Neely
19.	Duke	4-3-2	Wallace Wade
20.	Columbia	7-2-0	Lou Little

#The AP, which had voted Notre Dame No. 1 before the bowl games, took a second vote, giving the title to Michigan after its 49-0 win over Southern Cal in the Rose Bowl.

1948

		Record	Coach
1.	Michigan	9-0-0	Bennie Oosterbaan
2.	Notre Dame	9-0-1	Frank Leahy
3.	N Carolina	9-0-1	Carl Snavely
4.	California	10-0-0	Pappy Waldorf
5.	Oklahoma	9-1-0	Bud Wilkinson
6.	Army	8-0-1	Red Blaik
7.	Northwestern	7-2-0	Bob Voigts
8.	Georgia	9-1-0	Wally Butts
9.	Oregon	9-1-0	Jim Aiken

1948 (Cont.)

		Record	Coach
10.	SMU	8-1-1	Matty Bell
11.	Clemson	10-0-0	Frank Howard
12.	Vanderbilt	8-2-1	Red Sanders
13.	Tulane	9-1-0	Henry Frnka
14.	Michigan St	6-2-2	Biggie Munn
15.	Mississippi	8-1-0	Johnny Vaught
16.	Minnesota	7-2-0	Bernie Bierman
17.	William & Mary	6-2-2	Rube McCray
18.	Penn St	7-1-1	Bob Higgins
19.	Cornell	8-1-0	Lefty James
20.	Wake Forest	6-3-0	Peahead Walker

1949

		Record	Coach
1.	Notre Dame	10-0-0	Frank Leahy
2.	Oklahoma	10-0-0	Bud Wilkinson
3.	California	10-0-0	Pappy Waldorf
4.	Army	9-0-0	Red Blaik
5.	Rice	9-1-0	Jess Neely
6.	Ohio St	6-1-2	Wes Fesler
7.	Michigan	0-2-1	Bernie Oosterbaan
8.	Minnesota	7-2-0	Bernie Bierman
9.	Louisiana St	8-2-0	Gaynell Tinsley
10.	Pacific	11-0-0	Larry Siemering
11.	Kentucky	9-2-0	Bear Bryant
12.	Cornell	8-1-0	Lefty James
13.	Villanova	8-1-0	Jim Leonard
14.	Maryland	8-1-0	Jim Tatum
15.	Santa Clara	7-2-1	Len Casanova
16.	N Carolina	7-3-0	Carl Snavely
17.	Tennessee	7-2-1	Bob Neyland
18.	Princeton	6-3-0	Charlie Caldwell
19.	Michigan St	6-3-0	Biggie Munn
20.	Missouri	7-3-0	Don Faurot
	Baylor	8-2-0	Bob Woodruff

1950

		Record	Coach
1.	Oklahoma	10-0-0	Bud Wilkinson
2.	Army	8-1-0	Red Blaik
3.	Texas	9-1-0	Blair Cherry
4.	Tennessee	10-1-0	Bob Neyland
5.	California	9-0-1	Pappy Waldorf
6.	Princeton	9-0-0	Charlie Caldwell
7.	Kentucky	10-1-0	Bear Bryant
8.	Michigan St	8-1-0	Biggie Munn
9.	Michigan	5-3-1	Bennie Oosterhaan
10.	Clemson	8-0-1	Frank Howard
11.	Washington	8-2-0	Howard Odell
12.	Wyoming	9-0-0	Bowden Wyatt
13.	Illinois	7-2-0	Ray Eliot
14.	Ohio St	6-3-0	Wes Fesler
15.	Miami (FL)	9-0-1	Andy Gustafson
16.	Alabama	9-2-0	Red Drew
17.	Nebraska	6-2-1	Bill Glassford
18.	Wash & Lee	8-2-0	George Barclay
19.	Tulsa	9-1-1	J.O. Brothers
20.	Tulane	6-2-1	Henry Frnka

1951

		Record	Coach
1.	Tennessee	10-0-0	Bob Neyland
2.	Michigan St	9-0-0	Biggie Munn
3.	Maryland	9-0-0	Jim Tatum
4.	Illinois	8-0-1	Ray Eliot
5.	Georgia Tech	10-0-1	Bobby Dodd
6.	Princeton	9-0-0	Charlie Caldwell
7.	Stanford	9-1-0	Chuck Taylor
8.	Wisconsin	7-1-1	Ivy Williamson
9.	Baylor	8-1-1	George Sauer
10.	Oklahoma	8-2-0	Bud Wilkinson
11.	Texas Christian	6-4-0	Dutch Meyer
12.	California	8-2-0	Pappy Waldorf
13.	Virginia	8-1-0	Art Guepe
14.	San Francisco	9-0-0	Joe Kuharich
15.	Kentucky	7-4-0	Bear Bryant
16.	Boston Univ.	6-4-0	Buff Donelli
17.	UCLA	5-3-1	Red Sanders
18.	Washington St	7-3-0	Forest Evashevski
19.	Holy Cross	8-2-0	Eddie Anderson
20.	Clemson	7-2-0	Frank Howard

1952

		Record	Coach
1.	Michigan St	9-0-0	Biggie Munn
2.	Georgia Tech	11-0-0	Bobby Dodd
3.	Notre Dame	7-2-1	Frank Leahy
4.	Oklahoma	8-1-1	Bud Wilkinson
5.	Southern Cal	9-1-0	Jess Hill
6.	UCLA	8-1-0	Red Sanders
7.	Mississippi	8-0-2	Johnny Vaught
8.	Tennessee	8-1-1	Bob Neyland
9.	Alabama	9-2-0	Red Drew
10.	Texas	8-2-0	Ed Price
11.	Wisconsin	6-2-1	Ivy Williamson
12.	Tulsa	8-1-1	J.O. Brothers
13.	Maryland	7-2-0	Jim Tatum
14.	Syracuse	7-2-0	Ben Schwartzwalder
15.	Florida	7-3-0	Bob Woodruff
16.	Duke	8-2-0	Bill Murray
17.	Ohio St	6-3-0	Woody Hayes
18.	Purdue	4-3-2	Stu Holcomb
19.	Princeton	8-1-0	Charlie Caldwell
20.	Kentucky	5-4-2	Bear Bryant

1953

		Record	Coach
1.	Maryland	10-0-0	Jim Tatum
2.	Notre Dame	9-0-1	Frank Leahy
3.	Michigan St	8-1-0	Biggie Munn
4.	Oklahoma	8-1-1	Bud Wilkinson
5.	UCLA	8-1-0	Red Sanders
6.	Rice	8-2-0	Jess Neely
7.	Illinois	7-1-1	Ray Eliot
8.	Georgia Tech	8-2-1	Bobby Dodd
9.	Iowa	5-3-1	Forest Evashevski
10.	West Virginia	8-1-0	Art Lewis
11.	Texas	7-3-0	Ed Price

1953 *(Cont.)*

		Record	Coach
12.	Texas Tech	10-1-0	DeWitt Weaver
13.	Alabama	6-2-3	Red Drew
14.	Army	7-1-1	Red Blaik
15.	Wisconsin	6-2-1	Ivy Williamson
16.	Kentucky	7-2-1	Bear Bryant
17.	Auburn	7-2-1	Shug Jordan
18.	Duke	7-2-1	Bill Murray
19.	Stanford	6-3-1	Chuck Taylor
20.	Michigan	6-3-0	Bennie Oosterbaan

1954

		Record	Coach
1.	Ohio St	9-0-0	Woody Hayes
2.	#UCLA	9-0-0	Red Sanders
3.	Oklahoma	10-0-0	Bud Wilkinson
4.	Notre Dame	9-1-0	Terry Brennan
5.	Navy	7-2-0	Eddie Erdelatz
6.	Mississippi	9-1-0	Johnny Vaught
7.	Army	7-2-0	Red Blaik
8.	Maryland	7-2-1	Jim Tatum
9.	Wisconsin	7-2-0	Ivy Williamson
10.	Arkansas	8-2-0	Bowden Wyatt
11.	Miami (FL)	8-1-0	Andy Gustafson
12.	West Virginia	8-1-0	Art Lewis
13.	Auburn	7-3-0	Shug Jordan
14.	Duke	7-2-1	Bill Murray
15.	Michigan	6-3-0	Bennie Oosterbaan
16.	Virginia Tech	8-0-1	Frank Moseley
17.	Southern Cal	8-3-0	Jess Hill
18.	Baylor	7-3-0	George Sauer
19.	Rice	7-3-0	Jess Neely
20.	Penn St	7-2-0	Rip Engle

#Selected No. 1 by UP.

1955

		Record	Coach
1.	Oklahoma	10-0-0	Bud Wilkinson
2.	Michigan St	8-1-0	Duffy Daugherty
3.	Maryland	10-0-0	Jim Tatum
4.	UCLA	9-1-0	Red Sanders
5.	Ohio St	7-2-0	Woody Hayes
6.	Texas Christian	9-1-0	Abe Martin
7.	Georgia Tech	8-1-1	Bobby Dodd
8.	Auburn	8-1-1	Shug Jordan
9.	Notre Dame	8-2-0	Terry Brennan
10.	Mississippi	9-1-0	Johnny Vaught
11.	Pittsburgh	7-3-0	John Michelosen
12.	Michigan	7-2-0	Bennie Oosterbaan
13.	Southern Cal	6-4-0	Jess Hill
14.	Miami (FL)	6-3-0	Andy Gustafson
15.	Miami (OH)	9-0-0	Ara Parseghian
16.	Stanford	6-3-1	Chuck Taylor
17.	Texas A&M	7-2-1	Bear Bryant
18.	Navy	6-2-1	Eddie Erdelatz
19.	West Virginia	8-2-0	Art Lewis
20.	Army	6-3-0	Red Blaik

1956

		Record	Coach
1.	Oklahoma	10-0-0	Bud Wilkinson
2.	Tennessee	10-0-0	Bowden Wyatt
3.	Iowa	8-1-0	Forest Evashevski
4.	Georgia Tech.	9-1-0	Bobby Dodd
5.	Texas A&M	9-0-1	Bear Bryant
6.	Miami (FL)	8-1-1	Andy Gustafson
7.	Michigan	7-2-0	Bennie Oosterbaan
8.	Syracuse	7-1-0	Ben Schwartzwalder
9.	Michigan St	7-2-0	Duffy Daugherty
10.	Oregon St	7-2-1	Tommy Prothro
11.	Baylor	8-2-0	Sam Boyd
12.	Minnesota	6-1-2	Murray Warmath
13.	Pittsburgh	7-2-1	John Michelosen
14.	Texas Christian	7-3-0	Abe Martin
15.	Ohio St	6-3-0	Woody Hayes
16.	Navy	6-1-2	Eddie Erdelatz
17.	Geo Washington	7-1-1	Gene Sherman
18.	Southern Cal	8-2-0	Jess Hill
19.	Clemson	7-1-2	Frank Howard
20.	Colorado	7-2-1	Dallas Ward
	Penn St	6-2-1	Rip Engle

1957

		Record	Coach
1.	Auburn	10-0-0	Shug Jordan
2.	#Ohio St	8-1-0	Woody Hayes
3.	Michigan St	8-1-0	Duffy Daugherty
4.	Oklahoma	9-1-0	Bud Wilkinson
5.	Navy	8-1-1	Eddie Erdelatz
6.	Iowa	7-1-1	Forest Evashevski
7.	Mississippi	8-1-1	Johnny Vaught
8.	Rice	7-3-0	Jess Neely
9.	Texas A&M	8-2-0	Bear Bryant
10.	Notre Dame	7-3-0	Terry Brennan
11.	Texas	6-3-1	Darrell Royal
12.	Arizona St	10-0-0	Dan Devine
13.	Tennessee	7-3-0	Bowden Wyatt
14.	Mississippi St	6-2-1	Wade Walker
15.	N Carolina St	7-1-2	Earle Edwards
16.	Duke	6-2-2	Bill Murray
17.	Florida	6-2-1	Bob Woodruff
18.	Army	7-2-0	Red Blaik
19.	Wisconsin	6-3-0	Milt Brunt
20.	VMI	9-0-1	John McKenna

#Selected No. 1 by UP.

1958

		Record	Coach
1.	Louisiana St	10-0-0	Paul Dietzel
2.	Iowa	7-1-1	Forest Evashevski
3.	Army	8-0-1	Red Blaik
4.	Auburn	9-0-1	Shug Jordan
5.	Oklahoma	9-1-0	Bud Wilkinson
6.	Air Force	9-0-1	Ben Martin
7.	Wisconsin	7-1-1	Milt Bruhn
8.	Ohio St	6-1-2	Woody Hayes
9.	Syracuse	8-1-0	Ben Schwartzwalder

1958 *(Cont.)*

		Record	Coach
10.	Texas Christian	8-2-0	Abe Martin
11.	Mississippi	8-2-0	Johnny Vaught
12.	Clemson	8-2-0	Frank Howard
13.	Purdue	6-1-2	Jack Mollenkopf
14.	Florida	6-3-1	Bob Woodruff
15.	S Carolina	7-3-0	Warren Giese
16.	California	7-3-0	Pete Elliott
17.	Notre Dame	6-4-0	Terry Brennan
18.	SMU	6-4-0	Bill Meek
19.	Oklahoma St	7-3-0	Cliff Speegle
20.	Rutgers	8-1-0	John Stiegman

1959

		Record	Coach
1.	Syracuse	10-0-0	Ben Schwartzwalder
2.	Mississippi	9-1-0	Johnny Vaught
3.	Louisiana St	9-1-0	Paul Dietzel
4.	Texas	9-1-0	Darrell Royal
5.	Georgia	9-1-0	Wally Butts
6.	Wisconsin	7-2-0	Milt Bruhn
7.	Texas Christian	8-2-0	Abe Martin
8.	Washington	9-1-0	Jim Owens
9.	Arkansas	8-2-0	Frank Broyles
10.	Alabama	7-1-2	Bear Bryant
11.	Clemson	8-2-0	Frank Howard
12.	Penn St	8-2-0	Rip Engle
13.	Illinois	5-3-1	Ray Eliot
14.	Southern Cal	8-2-0	Don Clark
15.	Oklahoma	7-3-0	Bud Wilkinson
16.	Wyoming	9-1-0	Bob Devaney
17.	Notre Dame	5-5-0	Joe Kuharich
18.	Missouri	6-4-0	Dan Devine
19.	Florida	5-4-1	Bob Woodruff
20.	Pittsburgh	6-4-0	John Michelosen

1960

		Record	Coach
1.	Minnesota	8-1-0	Murray Warmath
2.	Mississippi	9-0-1	Johnny Vaught
3.	Iowa	8-1-0	Forest Evashevski
4.	Navy	9-1-0	Wayne Hardin
5.	Missouri	9-1-0	Dan Devine
6.	Washington	9-1-0	Jim Owens
7.	Arkansas	8-2-0	Frank Broyles
8.	Ohio St	7-2-0	Woody Hayes
9.	Alabama	8-1-1	Bear Bryant
10.	Duke	7-3-0	Bill Murray
11.	Kansas	7-2-1	Jack Mitchell
12.	Baylor	8-2-0	John Bridgers
13.	Auburn	8-2-0	Shug Jordan
14.	Yale	9-0-0	Jordan Oliver
15.	Michigan St	6-2-1	Duffy Daugherty
16.	Penn St	6-3-0	Rip Engle
17.	New Mexico St	10-0-0	Warren Woodson
18.	Florida	8-2-0	Ray Graves
19.	Syracuse	7-2-0	Ben Schwartzwalder
	Purdue	4-4-1	Jack Mollenkopf

1961

		Record	Coach
1.	Alabama	10-0-0	Bear Bryant
2.	Ohio St	8-0-1	Woody Hayes
3.	Texas	9-1-0	Darrell Royal
4.	Louisiana St	9-1-0	Paul Dietzel
5.	Mississippi	9-1-0	Johnny Vaught
6.	Minnesota	7-2-0	Murray Warmath
7.	Colorado	9-1-0	Sonny Grandelius
8.	Michigan St	7-2-0	Duffy Daugherty
9.	Arkansas	8-2-0	Frank Broyles
10.	Utah St	9-0-1	John Ralston
11.	Missouri	7-2-1	Dan Devine
12.	Purdue	6-3-0	Jack Mollenkopf
13.	Georgia Tech	7-3-0	Bobby Dodd
14.	Syracuse	7-3-0	Ben Schwartzwalder
15.	Rutgers	9-0-0	John Bateman
16.	UCLA	7-3-0	Bill Barnes
17.	Rice	7-3-0	Jess Neely
	Penn St	7-3-0	Rip Engle
	Arizona	8-1-1	Jim LaRue
20.	Duke	7-3-0	Bill Murray

1962

		Record	Coach
1.	Southern Cal	10-0-0	John McKay
2.	Wisconsin	8-1-0	Milt Bruhn
3.	Mississippi	9-0-0	Johnny Vaught
4.	Texas	9-0-1	Darrell Royal
5.	Alabama	9-1-0	Bear Bryant
6.	Arkansas	9-1-0	Frank Broyles
7.	Louisiana St	8-1-1	Charlie McClendon
8.	Oklahoma	8-2-0	Bud Wilkinson
9.	Penn St	9-1-0	Rip Engle
10.	Minnesota	6-2-1	Murray Warmath
11-20: UPI			
11.	Georgia Tech	7-2-1	Bobby Dodd
12.	Missouri	7-1-2	Dan Devine
13.	Ohio St	6-3-0	Woody Hayes
14.	Duke	8-2-0	Bill Murray
	Washington	7-1-2	Jim Owens
16.	Northwestern	7-2-0	Ara Parseghian
	Oregon St	8-2-0	Tommy Prothro
18.	Arizona St	7-2-1	Frank Kush
	Miami (FL)	7-3-0	Andy Gustafson
	Illinois	2-7-0	Pete Elliott

1963

		Record	Coach
1.	Texas	10-0-0	Darrell Royal
2.	Navy	9-1-0	Wayne Hardin
3.	Illinois	7-1-1	Pete Elliott
4.	Pittsburgh	9-1-0	John Michelosen
5.	Auburn	9-1-0	Shug Jordan
6.	Nebraska	9-1-0	Bob Devaney
7.	Mississippi	7-0-2	Johnny Vaught
8.	Alabama	8-2-0	Bear Bryant
9.	Oklahoma	8-2-0	Bud Wilkinson
10.	Michigan St	6-2-1	Duffy Daugherty
11-20: UPI			
11.	Mississippi St	6-2-2	Paul Davis
12.	Syracuse	8-2-0	Ben Schwartzwalder

1963 *(Cont.)*

		Record	Coach
13.	Arizona St	8-1-0	Frank Kush
14.	Memphis St	9-0-1	Billy J. Murphy
15.	Washington	6-4-0	Jim Owens
16.	Penn St	7-3-0	Rip Engle
	Southern Cal	7-3-0	John McKay
	Missouri	7-3-0	Dan Devine
19.	N Carolina	8-2-0	Jim Hickey
20.	Baylor	7-3-0	John Bridgers

1964

		Record	Coach
1.	Alabama	10-0-0	Bear Bryant
2.	Arkansas	10-0-0	Frank Broyles
3.	Notre Dame	9-1-0	Ara Parseghian
4.	Michigan	8-1-0	Bump Elliott
5.	Texas	9-1-0	Darrell Royal
6.	Nebraska	9-1-0	Bob Devaney
7.	Louisiana St	7-2-1	Charlie McClendon
8.	Oregon St	8-2-0	Tommy Prothro
9.	Ohio St	7-2-0	Woody Hayes
10.	Southern Cal	7-3-0	John McKay
11-20: UPI			
11.	Florida St	8-1-1	Bill Peterson
12.	Syracuse	7-3-0	Ben Schwartzwalder
13.	Princeton	9-0-0	Dick Colman
14.	Penn St	6-4-0	Rip Engle
	Utah	8-2-0	Ray Nagel
16.	Illinois	6-3-0	Pete Elliott
	New Mexico	9-2-0	Bill Weeks
18.	Tulsa	8-2-0	Glenn Dobbs
19.	Missouri	6-3-1	Dan Devine
20.	Mississippi	5-4-1	Johnny Vaught
	Michigan St	4-5-1	Duffy Daugherty

1965

		Record	Coach
1.	Alabama	9-1-1	Bear Bryant
2.	#Michigan St	10-1-0	Duffy Daugherty
3.	Arkansas	10-1-0	Frank Broyles
4.	UCLA	8-2-1	Tommy Prothro
5.	Nebraska	10-1-0	Bob Devaney
6.	Missouri	8-2-1	Dan Devine
7.	Tennessee	8-1-2	Doug Dickey
8.	Louisiana St	8-3-0	Charlie McClendon
9.	Notre Dame	7-2-1	Ara Parseghian
10.	Southern Cal	7-2-1	John McKay
11-20: UPI†			
11.	Texas Tech	8-2-0	J.T. King
12.	Ohio St	7-2-0	Woody Hayes
13.	Florida	7-3-0	Ray Graves
14.	Purdue	7-2-1	Jack Mollenkopf
15.	Georgia	6-4-0	Vince Dooley
16.	Tulsa	8-2-0	Glenn Dobbs
17.	Mississippi	6-4-0	Johnny Vaught
18.	Kentucky	6-4-0	Charlie Bradshaw
19.	Syracuse	7-3-0	Ben Schwartzwalder
20.	Colorado	6-2-2	Eddie Crowder

#Selected No. 1 by UPI.

Note: Except where indicated with an asterisk, the polls from 1936 through 1964 were taken before the bowl games and those from 1965 through the present were taken after the bowl games. Additionally, the AP ranked only ten teams in its polls from 1962–67; positions 11–20 from those years are from the UPI poll.

1966*

		Record	Coach
1.	Notre Dame	9-0-1	Ara Parseghian
2.	Michigan St	9-0-1	Duffy Daugherty
3.	Alabama	10-0-0	Bear Bryant
4.	Georgia	9-1-0	Vince Dooley
5.	UCLA	9-1-0	Tommy Prothro
6.	Nebraska	9-1-0	Bob Devaney
7.	Purdue	8-2-0	Jack Mollenkopf
8.	Georgia Tech	9-1-0	Bobby Dodd
9.	Miami (FL)	7-2-1	Charlie Tate
10.	SMU	8-2-0	Hayden Fry

11-20: UPI

		Record	Coach
11.	Florida	8-2-0	Ray Graves
12.	Mississippi	8-2-0	Johnny Vaught
13.	Arkansas	8-2-0	Frank Broyles
14.	Tennessee	7-3-0	Doug Dickey
15.	Wyoming	9-1-0	Lloyd Eaton
16.	Syracuse	8-2-0	Ben Schwartzwalder
17.	Houston	8-2-0	Bill Yeoman
18.	Southern Cal	7-3-0	John McKay
19.	Oregon St	7-3-0	Dee Andros
20.	Virginia Tech	8-1-1	Jerry Claiborne

1967*

		Record	Coach
1.	Southern Cal	9-1-0	John McKay
2.	Tennessee	9-1-0	Doug Dickey
3.	Oklahoma	9-1-0	Chuck Fairbanks
4.	Indiana	9-1-0	John Pont
5.	Notre Dame	8-2-0	Ara Parseghian
6.	Wyoming	10-0-0	Lloyd Eaton
7.	Oregon St	7-2-1	Dee Andros
8.	Alabama	8-1-1	Bear Bryant
9.	Purdue	8-2-0	Jack Mollenkopf
10.	Penn St	8-2-0	Joe Paterno

11-20: UPI†

		Record	Coach
11.	UCLA	7-2-1	Tommy Prothro
12.	Syracuse	8-2-0	Ben Schwartzwalder
13.	Colorado	8-2-0	Eddie Crowder
14.	Minnesota	8-2-0	Murray Warmath
15.	Florida St	7-2-1	Bill Peterson
16.	Miami (FL)	7-3-0	Charlie Tate
17.	N Carolina St	8-2-0	Earle Edwards
18.	Georgia	7-3-0	Vince Dooley
19.	Houston	9-2-0	Bill Yeoman
20.	Arizona St	8-2-0	Frank Kush

†UPI ranked Penn St 11th and did not rank Alabama, which was on probation.

1968

		Record	Coach
1.	Ohio St	10-0-0	Woody Hayes
2.	Penn St	11-0-0	Joe Paterno
3.	Texas	9-1-1	Darrell Royal
4.	Southern Cal	9-1-1	John McKay
5.	Notre Dame	7-2-1	Ara Parseghian
6.	Arkansas	10-1-0	Frank Broyles
7.	Kansas	9-2-0	Pepper Rodgers
8.	Georgia	8-1-2	Vince Dooley
9.	Missouri	8-3-0	Dan Devine

1968 *(Cont.)*

		Record	Coach
10.	Purdue	8-2-0	Jack Mollenkopf
11.	Oklahoma	7-4-0	Chuck Fairbanks
12.	Michigan	8-2-0	Bump Elliott
13.	Tennessee	8-2-1	Doug Dickey
14.	SMU	8-3-0	Hayden Fry
15.	Oregon St	7-3-0	Dee Andros
16.	Auburn	7-4-0	Shug Jordan
17.	Alabama	8-3-0	Bear Bryant
18.	Houston	6-2-2	Bill Yeoman
19.	Louisiana St	8-3-0	Charlie McClendon
20.	Ohio University	10-1-0	Bill Hess

1969

		Record	Coach
1.	Texas	11-0-0	Darrell Royal
2.	Penn St	11-0-0	Joe Paterno
3.	Southern Cal	10-0-1	John McKay
4.	Ohio St	8-1-0	Woody Hayes
5.	Notre Dame	8-2-1	Ara Parseghian
6.	Missouri	9-2-0	Dan Devine
7.	Arkansas	9-2-0	Frank Broyles
8.	Mississippi	8-3-0	Johnny Vaught
9.	Michigan	8-3-0	Bo Schembechler
10.	Louisiana St	9-1-0	Charlie McClendon
11.	Nebraska	9-2-0	Bob Devaney
12.	Houston	9-2-0	Bill Yeoman
13.	UCLA	8-1-1	Tommy Prothro
14.	Florida	9-1-1	Ray Graves
15.	Tennessee	9-2-0	Doug Dickey
16.	Colorado	8-3-0	Eddie Crowder
17.	West Virginia	10-0-1	Jim Carlen
18.	Purdue	8-2-0	Jack Mollenkopf
19.	Stanford	7-2-1	John Ralston
20.	Auburn	8-3-0	Shug Jordan

1970

		Record	Coach
1.	Nebraska	11-0-1	Bob Devaney
2.	Notre Dame	10-1-0	Ara Parseghian
3.	#Texas	10-1-0	Darrell Royal
4.	Tennessee	11-0-1	Bill Battle
5.	Ohio St	9-1-0	Woody Hayes
6.	Arizona St	11-0-0	Frank Kush
7.	Louisiana St	9-3-0	Charlie McClendon
8.	Stanford	9-3-0	John Ralston
9.	Michigan	9-1-0	Bo Schembechler
10.	Auburn	9-2-0	Shug Jordan
11.	Arkansas	9-2-0	Frank Broyles
12.	Toledo	12-0-0	Frank Lauterbur
13.	Georgia Tech	9-3-0	Bud Carson
14.	Dartmouth	9-0-0	Bob Blackman
15.	Southern Cal	6-4-1	John McKay
16.	Air Force	9-3-0	Ben Martin
17.	Tulane	8-4-0	Jim Pittman
18.	Penn St	7-3-0	Joe Paterno
19.	Houston	8-3-0	Bill Yeoman
20.	Oklahoma	7-4-1	Chuck Fairbanks
	Mississippi	7-4-0	Johnny Vaught

#Selected No. 1 by UPI.

1971

		Record	Coach
1.	Nebraska	13-0-0	Bob Devaney
2.	Oklahoma	11-1-0	Chuck Fairbanks
3.	Colorado	10-2-0	Eddie Crowder
4.	Alabama	11-1-0	Bear Bryant
5.	Penn St.	11-1-0	Joe Paterno
6.	Michigan	11-1-0	Bo Schembechler
7.	Georgia	11-1-0	Vince Dooley
8.	Arizona St.	11-1-0	Frank Kush
9.	Tennessee	10-2-0	Bill Battle
10.	Stanford	9-3-0	John Ralston
11.	Louisiana St	9-3-0	Charlie McClendon
12.	Auburn	9-2-0	Shug Jordan
13.	Notre Dame	8-2-0	Ara Parseghian
14.	Toledo	12-0-0	John Murphy
15.	Mississippi	10-2-0	Billy Kinard
16.	Arkansas	8-3-1	Frank Broyles
17.	Houston	9-3-0	Bill Yeoman
18.	Texas	8-3-0	Darrell Royal
19.	Washington	8-3-0	Jim Owens
20.	Southern Cal	6-4-1	John McKay

1972

		Record	Coach
1.	Southern Cal	12-0-0	John McKay
2.	Oklahoma	11-1-0	Chuck Fairbanks
3.	Texas	10-1-0	Darrell Royal
4.	Nebraska	9-2-1	Bob Devaney
5.	Auburn	10-1-0	Shug Jordan
6.	Michigan	10-1-0	Bo Schembechler
7.	Alabama	10-2-0	Bear Bryant
8.	Tennessee	10-2-0	Bill Battle
9.	Ohio St	9-2-0	Woody Hayes
10.	Penn St.	10-2-0	Joe Paterno
11.	Louisiana St	9-2-1	Charlie McClendon
12.	North Carolina	11-1-0	Bill Dooley
13.	Arizona St.	10-2-0	Frank Kush
14.	Notre Dame	8-3-0	Ara Parseghian
15.	UCLA	8-3-0	Pepper Rodgers
16.	Colorado	8-4-0	Eddie Crowder
17.	N Carolina St.	8-3-1	Lou Holtz
18.	Louisville	9-1-0	Lee Corso
19.	Washington St	7-4-0	Jim Sweeney
20.	Georgia Tech	7-4-1	Bill Fulcher

1973

		Record	Coach
1.	Notre Dame	11-0-0	Ara Parseghian
2.	Ohio St	10-0-1	Woody Hayes
3.	Oklahoma	10-0-1	Barry Switzer
4.	#Alabama	11-1-0	Bear Bryant
5.	Penn St.	12-0-0	Joe Paterno
6.	Michigan	10-0-1	Bo Schembechler
7.	Nebraska	9-2-1	Tom Osborne
8.	Southern Cal	9-2-1	John McKay
9.	Arizona St.	11-1-0	Frank Kush
	Houston	11-1-0	Bill Yeoman
11.	Texas Tech	11-1-0	Jim Carlen
12.	UCLA	9-2-0	Pepper Rodgers

1973 *(Cont.)*

		Record	Coach
13.	Louisiana St	9-3-0	Charlie McClendon
14.	Texas	8-3-0	Darrell Royal
15.	Miami (OH)	11-0-0	Bill Mallory
16.	N Carolina St.	9-3-0	Lou Holtz
17.	Missouri	8-4-0	Al Onofrio
18.	Kansas	7-4-1	Don Fambrough
19.	Tennessee	8-4-0	Bill Battle
20.	Maryland	8-4-0	Jerry Claiborne
	Tulane	9-3-0	Bennie Ellender

#Selected No. 1 by UPI.

1974

		Record	Coach
1.	Oklahoma	11-0-0	Barry Switzer
2.	#Southern Cal	10-1-1	John McKay
3.	Michigan	10-1-0	Bo Schembechler
4.	Ohio St	10-2-0	Woody Hayes
5.	Alabama	11-1-0	Bear Bryant
6.	Notre Dame	10-2-0	Ara Parseghian
7.	Penn St.	10-2-0	Joe Paterno
8.	Auburn	10-2-0	Shug Jordan
9.	Nebraska	9-3-0	Tom Osborne
10.	Miami (OH)	10-0-1	Dick Crum
11.	N Carolina St.	9-2-1	Lou Holtz
12.	Michigan St	7-3-1	Denny Stolz
13.	Maryland	8-4-0	Jerry Claiborne
14.	Baylor	8-4-0	Grant Teaff
15.	Florida	8-4-0	Doug Dickey
16.	Texas A&M	8-3-0	Emory Ballard
17.	Mississippi St	9-3-0	Bob Tyler
	Texas	8-4-0	Darrell Royal
19.	Houston	8-3-1	Bill Yeoman
20.	Tennessee	7-3-2	Bill Battle

#Selected No. 1 by UPI.

1975

		Record	Coach
1.	Oklahoma	11-1-0	Barry Switzer
2.	Arizona St.	12-0-0	Frank Kush
3.	Alabama	11-1-0	Bear Bryant
4.	Ohio St	11-1-0	Woody Hayes
5.	UCLA	9-2-1	Dick Vermeil
6.	Texas	10-2-0	Darrell Royal
7.	Arkansas	10-2-0	Frank Broyles
8.	Michigan	8-2-2	Bo Schembechler
9.	Nebraska	10-2-0	Tom Osborne
10.	Penn St.	9-3-0	Joe Paterno
11.	Texas A&M	10-2-0	Emory Bellard
12.	Miami (OH)	11-1-0	Dick Crum
13.	Maryland	9-2-1	Jerry Claiborne
14.	California	8-3-0	Mike White
15.	Pittsburgh	8-4-0	Johnny Majors
16.	Colorado	9-3-0	Bill Mallory
17.	Southern Cal	8-4-0	John McKay
18.	Arizona	9-2-0	Jim Young
19.	Georgia	9-3-0	Vince Dooley
20.	West Virginia	9-3-0	Bobby Bowden

1976

		Record	Coach
1.	Pittsburgh	12-0-0	Johnny Majors
2.	Southern Cal	11-1-0	John Robinson
3.	Michigan	10-2-0	Bo Schembechler
4.	Houston	10-2-0	Bill Yeoman
5.	Oklahoma	9-2-1	Barry Switzer
6.	Ohio St	9-2-1	Woody Hayes
7.	Texas A&M	10-2-0	Emory Bellard
8.	Maryland	11-1-0	Jerry Claiborne
9.	Nebraska	9-3-1	Tom Osborne
10.	Georgia	10-2-0	Vince Dooley
11.	Alabama	9-3-0	Bear Bryant
12.	Notre Dame	9-3-0	Dan Devine
13.	Texas Tech	10-2-0	Steve Sloan
14.	Oklahoma St	9-3-0	Jim Stanley
15.	UCLA	9-2-1	Terry Donahue
16.	Colorado	8-4-0	Bill Mallory
17.	Rutgers	11-0-0	Frank Burns
18.	Kentucky	9-3-0	Fran Curci
19.	Iowa St	8-3-0	Earle Bruce
20.	Mississippi St	9-2-0	Bob Tyler

1977

		Record	Coach
1.	Notre Dame	11-1-0	Dan Devine
2.	Alabama	11-1-0	Bear Bryant
3.	Arkansas	11-1-0	Lou Holtz
4.	Texas	11-1-0	Fred Akers
5.	Penn St	11-1-0	Joe Paterno
6.	Kentucky	10-1-0	Fran Curci
7.	Oklahoma	10-2-0	Barry Switzer
8.	Pittsburgh	9-2-1	Jackie Sherrill
9.	Michigan	10-2-0	Bo Schembechler
10.	Washington	10-2-0	Don James
11.	Ohio St	9-3-0	Woody Hayes
12.	Nebraska	9-3-0	Tom Osborne
13.	Southern Cal	8-4-0	John Robinson
14.	Florida St	10-2-0	Bobby Bowden
15.	Stanford	9-3-0	Bill Walsh
16.	San Diego St	10-1-0	Claude Gilbert
17.	N Carolina	8-3-1	Bill Dooley
18.	Arizona St	9-3-0	Frank Kush
19.	Clemson	8-3-1	Charley Pell
20.	Brigham Young	9-2-0	LaVell Edwards

1978

		Record	Coach
1.	Alabama	11-1-0	Bear Bryant
2.	#Southern Cal	12-1-0	John Robinson
3.	Oklahoma	11-1-0	Barry Switzer
4.	Penn St	11-1-0	Joe Paterno
5.	Michigan	10-2-0	Bo Schembechler
6.	Clemson	11-1-0	Charley Pell
7.	Notre Dame	9-3-0	Dan Devine
8.	Nebraska	9-3-0	Tom Osborne
9.	Texas	9-3-0	Fred Akers
10.	Houston	9-3-0	Bill Yeoman
11.	Arkansas	9-2-1	Lou Holtz
12.	Michigan St	8-3-0	Darryl Rogers

1978 (Cont.)

		Record	Coach
13.	Purdue	9-2-1	Jim Young
14.	UCLA	8-3-1	Terry Donahue
15.	Missouri	8-4-0	Warren Powers
16.	Georgia	9-2-1	Vince Dooley
17.	Stanford	8-4-0	Bill Walsh
18.	N Carolina St	9-3-0	Bo Rein
19.	Texas A&M	8-4-0	Emory Bellard (4-2) Tom Wilson (4-2)
20.	Maryland	9-3-0	Jerry Claiborne

#Selected No. 1 by UPI.

1979

		Record	Coach
1.	Alabama	12-0-0	Bear Bryant
2.	Southern Cal	11-0-1	John Robinson
3.	Oklahoma	11-1-0	Barry Switzer
4.	Ohio St	11-1-0	Earle Bruce
5.	Houston	11-1-0	Bill Yeoman
6.	Florida St	11-1-0	Bobby Bowden
7.	Pittsburgh	11-1-0	Jackie Sherrill
8.	Arkansas	10-2-0	Lou Holtz
9.	Nebraska	10-2-0	Tom Osborne
10.	Purdue	10-2-0	Jim Young
11.	Washington	10-1-0	Don James
12.	Texas	9-3-0	Fred Akers
13.	Brigham Young	11-1-0	LaVell Edwards
14.	Baylor	8-4-0	Grant Teaff
15.	N Carolina	8-3-1	Dick Crum
16.	Auburn	8-3-0	Doug Barfield
17.	Temple	10-2-0	Wayne Hardin
18.	Michigan	8-4-0	Bo Schembechler
19.	Indiana	8-4-0	Lee Corso
20.	Penn St	8-4-0	Joe Paterno

1980

		Record	Coach
1.	Georgia	12-0-0	Vince Dooley
2.	Pittsburgh	11-1-0	Jackie Sherrill
3.	Oklahoma	10-2-0	Barry Switzer
4.	Michigan	10-2-0	Bo Schembechler
5.	Florida St	10-2-0	Bobby Bowden
6.	Alabama	10-2-0	Bear Bryant
7.	Nebraska	10-2-0	Tom Osborne
8.	Penn St	10-2-0	Joe Paterno
9.	Notre Dame	9-2-1	Dan Devine
10.	N Carolina	11-1-0	Dick Crum
11.	Southern Cal	8-2-1	John Robinson
12.	Brigham Young	12-1-0	LaVell Edwards
13.	UCLA	9-2-0	Terry Donahue
14.	Baylor	10-2-0	Grant Teaff
15.	Ohio St	9-3-0	Earle Bruce
16.	Washington	9-3-0	Don James
17.	Purdue	9-3-0	Jim Young
18.	Miami (FL)	9-3-0	H. Schnellenberger
19.	Mississippi St	9-3-0	Emory Bellard
20.	SMU	8-4-0	Ron Meyer

1981

		Record	Coach
1.	Clemson	12-0-0	Danny Ford
2.	Texas	10-1-1	Fred Akers
3.	Penn St	10-2-0	Joe Paterno
4.	Pittsburgh	11-1-0	Jackie Sherrill
5.	SMU	10-1-0	Ron Meyer
6.	Georgia	10-2-0	Vince Dooley
7.	Alabama	9-2-1	Bear Bryant
8.	Miami (FL)	9-2-0	H. Schnellenberger
9.	N Carolina	10-2-0	Dick Crum
10.	Washington	10-2-0	Don James
11.	Nebraska	9-3-0	Tom Osborne
12.	Michigan	9-3-0	Bo Schembechler
13.	Brigham Young	11-2-0	LaVell Edwards
14.	Southern Cal	9-3-0	John Robinson
15.	Ohio St	9-3-0	Earle Bruce
16.	Arizona St	9-2-0	Darryl Rogers
17.	West Virginia	9-3-0	Don Nehlen
18.	Iowa	8-4-0	Hayden Fry
19.	Missouri	8-4-0	Warren Powers
20.	Oklahoma	7-4-1	Barry Switzer

1982

		Record	Coach
1.	Penn St	11-1-0	Joe Paterno
2.	SMU	11-0-1	Bobby Collins
3.	Nebraska	12-1-0	Tom Osborne
4.	Georgia	11-1-0	Vince Dooley
5.	UCLA	10-1-1	Terry Donahue
6.	Arizona St	10-2-0	Darryl Rogers
7.	Washington	10-2-0	Don James
8.	Clemson	9-1-1	Danny Ford
9.	Arkansas	9-2-1	Lou Holtz
10.	Pittsburgh	9-3-0	Foge Fazio
11.	Louisiana St	8-3-1	Jerry Stovall
12.	Ohio St	9-3-0	Earle Bruce
13.	Florida St	9-3-0	Bobby Bowden
14.	Auburn	9-3-0	Pat Dye
15.	Southern Cal	8-3-0	John Robinson
16.	Oklahoma	8-4-0	Barry Switzer
17.	Texas	9-3-0	Fred Akers
18.	N Carolina	8-4-0	Dick Crum
19.	West Virginia	9-3-0	Don Nehlen
20.	Maryland	8-4-0	Bobby Ross

1983

		Record	Coach
1.	Miami (FL)	11-1-0	H. Schnellenberger
2.	Nebraska	12-1-0	Tom Osborne
3.	Auburn	11-1-0	Pat Dye
4.	Georgia	10-1-1	Vince Dooley
5.	Texas	11-1-0	Fred Akers
6.	Florida	9-2-1	Charlie Pell
7.	Brigham Young	11-1-0	LaVell Edwards
8.	Michigan	9-3-0	Bo Schembechler
9.	Ohio St	9-3-0	Earle Bruce
10.	Illinois	10-2-0	Mike White
11.	Clemson	9-1-1	Danny Ford

1983 *(Cont.)*

		Record	Coach
12.	SMU	10-2-0	Bobby Collins
13.	Air Force	10-2-0	Ken Hatfield
14.	Iowa	9-3-0	Hayden Fry
15.	Alabama	8-4-0	Ray Perkins
16.	West Virginia	9-3-0	Don Nehlen
17.	UCLA	7-4-1	Terry Donahue
18.	Pittsburgh	8-3-1	Foge Fazio
19.	Boston College	9-3-0	Jack Bicknell
20.	E Carolina	8-3-0	Ed Emory

1984

		Record	Coach
1.	Brigham Young	13-0-0	LaVell Edwards
2.	Washington	11-1-0	Don James
3.	Florida	9-1-1	Chas Pell (0-1-1)
			Galen Hall (9-0)
4.	Nebraska	10-2-0	Tom Osborne
5.	Boston College	10-2-0	Jack Bicknell
6.	Oklahoma	9-2-1	Barry Switzer
7.	Oklahoma St	10-2-0	Pat Jones
8.	SMU	10-2-0	Bobby Collins
9.	UCLA	9-3-0	Terry Donahue
10.	Southern Cal	10-3-0	Ted Tollner
11.	South Carolina	10-2-0	Joe Morrison
12.	Maryland	9-3-0	Bobby Ross
13.	Ohio St	9-3-0	Earle Bruce
14.	Auburn	9-4-0	Pat Dye
15.	Louisiana St	8-3-1	Bill Arnsparger
16.	Iowa	8-4-1	Hayden Fry
17.	Florida St	7-3-2	Bobby Bowden
18.	Miami (FL)	8-5-0	Jimmy Johnson
19.	Kentucky	9-3-0	Jerry Claiborne
20.	Virginia	8-2-2	George Welsh

1985

		Record	Coach
1.	Oklahoma	11-1-0	Barry Switzer
2.	Michigan	10-1-1	Bo Schembechler
3.	Penn St	11-1-0	Joe Paterno
4.	Tennessee	9-1-2	Johnny Majors
5.	Florida	9-1-1	Galen Hall
6.	Texas A&M	10-2-0	Jackie Sherrill
7.	UCLA	9-2-1	Terry Donahue
8.	Air Force	12-1-0	Fisher DeBerry
9.	Miami (FL)	10-2-0	Jimmy Johnson
10.	Iowa	10-2-0	Hayden Fry
11.	Nebraska	9-3-0	Tom Osborne
12.	Arkansas	10-2-0	Ken Hatfield
13.	Alabama	9-2-1	Ray Perkins
14.	Ohio St	9-3-0	Earle Bruce
15.	Florida St	9-3-0	Bobby Bowden
16.	Brigham Young	11-3-0	LaVell Edwards
17.	Baylor	9-3-0	Grant Teaff
18.	Maryland	9-3-0	Bobby Ross
19.	Georgia Tech	9-2-1	Bill Curry
20.	Louisiana St	9-2-1	Bill Arnsparger

1986

		Record	Coach
1.	Penn St.	12-0-0	Joe Paterno
2.	Miami (FL)	11-1-0	Jimmy Johnson
3.	Oklahoma	11-1-0	Barry Switzer
4.	Arizona St.	10-1-1	John Cooper
5.	Nebraska	10-2-0	Tom Osborne
6.	Auburn	10-2-0	Pat Dye
7.	Ohio St	10-3-0	Earle Bruce
8.	Michigan	11-2-0	Bo Schembechler
9.	Alabama	10-3-0	Ray Perkins
10.	Louisiana St	9-3-0	Bill Arnsparger
11.	Arizona	9-3-0	Larry Smith
12.	Baylor	9-3-0	Grant Teaff
13.	Texas A&M	9-3-0	Jackie Sherrill
14.	UCLA	8-3-1	Terry Donahue
15.	Arkansas	9-3-0	Ken Hatfield
16.	Iowa	9-3-0	Hayden Fry
17.	Clemson	8-2-2	Danny Ford
18.	Washington	8-3-1	Don James
19.	Boston College	9-3-0	Jack Bicknell
20.	Virginia Tech.	9-2-1	Bill Dooley

1987

		Record	Coach
1.	Miami (FL)	12-0-0	Jimmy Johnson
2.	Florida St.	11-1-0	Bobby Bowden
3.	Oklahoma	11-1-0	Barry Switzer
4.	Syracuse	11-0-1	Dick MacPherson
5.	Louisiana St	10-1-1	Mike Archer
6.	Nebraska	10-2-0	Tom Osborne
7.	Auburn	9-1-2	Pat Dye
8.	Michigan St	9-2-1	George Perles
9.	UCLA	10-2-0	Terry Donahue
10.	Texas A&M	10-2-0	Jackie Sherrill
11.	Oklahoma St	10-2-0	Pat Jones
12.	Clemson	10-2-0	Danny Ford
13.	Georgia	9-3-0	Vince Dooley
14.	Tennessee	10-2-1	Johnny Majors
15.	S Carolina	8-4-0	Joe Morrison
16.	Iowa	10-3-0	Hayden Fry
17.	Notre Dame	8-4-0	Lou Holtz
18.	Southern Cal	8-4-0	Larry Smith
19.	Michigan	8-4-0	Bo Schembechler
20.	Arizona St.	7-4-1	John Cooper

1988

		Record	Coach
1.	Notre Dame	12-0-0	Lou Holtz
2.	Miami (FL)	11-1-0	Jimmy Johnson
3.	Florida St.	11-1-0	Bobby Bowden
4.	Michigan	9-2-1	Bo Schembechler
5.	West Virginia	11-1-0	Don Nehlen
6.	UCLA	10-2-0	Terry Donahue
7.	Southern Cal	10-2-0	Larry Smith
8.	Auburn	10-2-0	Pat Dye
9.	Clemson	10-2-0	Danny Ford
10.	Nebraska	11-2-0	Tom Osborne
11.	Oklahoma St	10-2-0	Pat Jones
12.	Arkansas	10-2-0	Ken Hatfield
13.	Syracuse	10-2-0	Dick MacPherson
14.	Oklahoma	9-3-0	Barry Switzer
15.	Georgia	9-3-0	Vince Dooley

1988 (Cont.)

		Record	Coach
16.	Washington St	9-3-0	Dennis Erickson
17.	Alabama	9-3-0	Bill Curry
18.	Houston	9-3-0	Jack Pardee
19.	Louisiana St	8-4-0	Mike Archer
20.	Indiana	8-3-1	Bill Mallory

1989

		Record	Coach
1.	Miami (FL)	11-1-0	Dennis Erickson
2.	Notre Dame	12-1-0	Lou Holtz
3.	Florida St	10-2-0	Bobby Bowden
4.	Colorado	11-1-0	Bill McCartney
5.	Tennessee	11-1-0	Johnny Majors
6.	Auburn	10-2-0	Pat Dye
7.	Michigan	10-2-0	Bo Schembechler
8.	Southern Cal	9-2-1	Larry Smith
9.	Alabama	10-2-0	Bill Curry
10.	Illinois	10-2-0	John Mackovic
11.	Nebraska	10-2-0	Tom Osborne
12.	Clemson	10-2-0	Danny Ford
13.	Arkansas	10-2-0	Ken Hatfield
14.	Houston	9-2-0	Jack Pardee
15.	Penn St	8-3-1	Joe Paterno
16.	Michigan St	8-4-0	George Perles
17.	Pittsburgh	8-3-1	Mike Gottfried
18.	Virginia	10-3-0	George Welsh
19.	Texas Tech	9-3-0	Spike Dykes
20.	Texas A&M	8-4-0	R.C. Slocum
21.	West Virginia	8-3-1	Don Nehlen
22.	Brigham Young	10-3-0	LaVell Edwards
23.	Washington	8-4-0	Don James
24.	Ohio St	8-4-0	John Cooper
25.	Arizona	8-4-0	Dick Tomey

1990

		Record	Coach
1.	Colorado	11-1-1	Bill McCartney
2.	#Georgia Tech	11-0-1	Bobby Ross
3.	Miami (FL)	10-2-0	Dennis Erickson
4.	Florida St	10-2-0	Bobby Bowden
5.	Washington	10-2-0	Don James
6.	Notre Dame	9-3-0	Lou Holtz
7.	Michigan	9-3-0	Gary Moeller
8.	Tennessee	9-2-2	Johnny Majors
9.	Clemson	10-2-0	Ken Hatfield
10.	Houston	10-1-0	John Jenkins
11.	Penn St	9-3-0	Joe Paterno
12.	Texas	10-2-0	David McWilliams
13.	Florida	9-2-0	Steve Spurrier
14.	Louisville	10-1-1	H. Schnellenberger
15.	Texas A&M	9-3-1	R.C. Slocum
16.	Michigan St	8-3-1	George Perles
17.	Oklahoma	8-3-0	Gary Gibbs
18.	Iowa	8-4-0	Hayden Fry
19.	Auburn	8-3-1	Pat Dye
20.	Southern Cal	8-4-1	Larry Smith
21.	Mississippi	9-3-0	Billy Brewer
22.	Brigham Young	10-3-0	LaVell Edwards
23.	Virginia	8-4-0	George Welsh
24.	Nebraska	9-3-0	Tom Osborne
25.	Illinois	8-4-0	John Mackovic

#Selected No. 1 by UPI.

†Beginning in 1989, the Associated Press expanded its final poll to 25 teams.

1991

		Record	Coach
1.	Miami (FL)	12-0-0	Dennis Erickson
2.	#Washington	12-0-0	Don James
3.	Penn St.	11-2-0	Joe Paterno
4.	Florida St	11-2-0	Bobby Bowden
5.	Alabama	11-1-0	Gene Stallings
6.	Michigan	10-2-0	Gary Moeller
7.	Florida	10-2-0	Steve Spurrier
8.	California	10-2-0	Bruce Snyder
9.	E Carolina	11-1-0	Bill Lewis
10.	Iowa	10-1-1	Hayden Fry
11.	Syracuse	10-2-0	Paul Pasqualoni
12.	Texas A&M	10-2-0	R.C. Slocum
13.	Notre Dame	10-3-0	Lou Holtz
14.	Tennessee	9-3-0	Johnny Majors
15.	Nebraska	9-2-1	Tom Osborne
16.	Oklahoma	9-3-0	Gary Gibbs
17.	Georgia	9-3-0	Ray Goff
18.	Clemson	9-2-1	Ken Hatfield
19.	UCLA	9-3-0	Terry Donahue
20.	Colorado	8-3-1	Bill McCartney
21.	Tulsa	10-2-0	David Rader
22.	Stanford	8-4-0	Dennis Green
23.	Brigham Young	8-3-2	LaVell Edwards
24.	N Carolina St	9-3-0	Dick Sheridan
25.	Air Force	10-3-0	Fisher DeBerry

#Selected No. 1 by USA Today/ CNN.

1992

		Record	Coach
1.	Alabama	13-0-0	Gene Stallings
2.	Florida St	11-1-0	Bobby Bowden
3.	Miami	11-1-0	Dennis Erickson
4.	Notre Dame	10-1-1	Lou Holtz
5.	Michigan	9-0-3	Gary Moeller
6.	Syracuse	10-2-0	Paul Pasqualoni
7.	Texas A&M	12-1-0	R.C. Slocum
8.	Georgia	10-2-0	Ray Goff
9.	Stanford	10-3-0	Bill Walsh
10.	Florida	9-4-0	Steve Spurrier
11.	Washington	9-3-0	Don James
12.	Tennessee	9 3 0	Johnny Majors
13.	Colorado	9-2-1	Bill McCartney
14.	Nebraska	9-3-0	Tom Osborne
15.	Washington St	9-3-0	Mike Price
16.	Mississippi	9-3-0	Billy Brewer
17.	N Carolina St	9-3-1	Dick Sheridan
18.	Ohio St	8-3-1	John Cooper
19.	N Carolina	9-3-0	Mack Brown
20.	Hawaii	11-2-0	Bob Wagner
21.	Boston College	8-3-1	Tom Coughlin
22.	Kansas	8-4-0	Glen Mason
23.	Mississippi St	7-5-0	Jackie Sherrill
24.	Fresno St	9-4-0	Jim Sweeney
25.	Wake Forest	8-4-0	Bill Dooley

1993

		Record	Coach
1.	Florida St	12-1-0	Bobby Bowden
2.	Notre Dame	11-1-0	Lou Holtz
3.	Nebraska	11-1-0	Tom Osborne
4.	Auburn	11-0-0	Terry Bowden
5.	Florida	11-2-0	Steve Spurrier
6.	Wisconsin	10-1-1	Barry Alvarez
7.	West Virginia	11-1-0	Don Nehlen
8.	Penn St.	10-2-0	Joe Paterno
9.	Texas A&M	10-2-0	R.C. Slocum
10.	Arizona	10-2-0	Dick Tomey
11.	Ohio St	10-1-1	John Cooper
12.	Tennessee	9-2-1	Phil Fulmer

1993 (Cont.)

		Record	Coach
13.	Boston College	9-3-0	Tom Coughlin
14.	Alabama	9-3-1	Gene Stallings
15.	Miami	9-3-0	Dennis Erickson
16.	Colorado	8-3-1	Bill McCartney
17.	Oklahoma	9-3-0	Gary Gibbs
18.	UCLA	8-4-0	Terry Donahue
19.	N Carolina	10-3-0	Mack Brown
20.	Kansas St	9-2-1	Bill Snyder
21.	Michigan	8-4-0	Gary Moeller
22.	Virginia Tech	9-3-0	Frank Beamer
23.	Clemson	9-3-0	Ken Hatfield
24.	Louisville	9-3-0	H. Schnellenberger
25.	California	9-4-0	Keith Gilbertson

1994

		Record	Coach
1.	Nebraska	13-0-0	Tom Osborne
2.	Penn St.	12-0-0	Joe Paterno
3.	Colorado	11-1-0	Bill McCartney
4.	Florida St	10-1-1	Bobby Bowden
5.	Alabama	12-1-0	Gene Stallings
6.	Miami (FL)	10-2-0	Dennis Erickson
7.	Florida	10-2-1	Steve Spurrier
8.	Texas A&M	10-0-1	R.C. Slocum
9.	Auburn	9-1-1	Terry Bowden
10.	Utah	10-2-0	Ron McBride
11.	Oregon	9-4-0	Rich Brooks
12.	Michigan	8-4-0	Gary Moeller
13.	Southern Cal	8-3-1	John Robinson
14.	Ohio St	9-4-0	John Cooper
15.	Virginia	9-3-0	George Welsh
16.	Colorado St	10-2-0	Sonny Lubick
17.	N Carolina St	9-3-0	Mike O'Cain
18.	Brigham Young	10-3-0	LaVell Edwards
19.	Kansas St	9-3-0	Bill Snyder
20.	Arizona	8-4-0	Dick Tomey
21.	Washington St	8-4-0	Mike Price
22.	Tennessee	8-4-0	Phillip Fulmer
23.	Boston College	7-4-1	Dan Henning
24.	Mississippi St	8-4-0	Jackie Sherrill
25.	Texas	8-4-0	John Mackovic

1995

		Record	Coach
1.	Nebraska	12-0-0	Tom Osborne
2.	Florida	12-1-0	Steve Spurrier
3.	Tennessee	11-1-0	Phillip Fulmer
4.	Florida St	10-2-0	Bobby Bowden
5.	Colorado	10-2-0	Rick Neuheisel
6.	Ohio St	11-2-0	John Cooper
7.	Kansas St	10-2-0	Bill Snyder
8.	Northwestern	10-2-0	Gary Barnett
9.	Kansas	10-2-0	Glen Mason
10.	Virginia Tech	10-2-0	Frank Beamer
11.	Notre Dame	9-3-0	Lou Holtz
12.	Southern Cal	9-2-1	John Robinson
13.	Penn St.	9-3-0	Joe Paterno
14.	Texas	10-2-1	John Mackovic
15.	Texas A&M	9-3-0	S.C. Slocum
16.	Virginia	9-4-0	George Welsh
17.	Michigan	9-4-0	Lloyd Carr
18.	Oregon	9-3-0	Mike Bellotti
19.	Syracuse	9-3-0	Paul Pasqualoni
20.	Miami (FL)	8-3-0	Butch Davis
21.	Alabama	8-3-0	Gene Stallings
22.	Auburn	8-4-0	Terry Bowden
23.	Texas Tech	9-3-0	Spike Dykes
24.	Toledo	11-0-1	Gary Pinkel
25.	Iowa	8-4-0	Hayden Fry

Division I-AA

Year	Winner	Runner-Up	Score
1978	Florida A&M	Massachusetts	35–28
1979	Eastern Kentucky	Lehigh	30–7
1980	Boise St	Eastern Kentucky	31–29
1981	Idaho St	Eastern Kentucky	34–23
1982	Eastern Kentucky	Delaware	17–14
1983	Southern Illinois	Western Carolina	43–7
1984	Montana St	Louisiana Tech	19–6
1985	Georgia Southern	Furman	44–42
1986	Georgia Southern	Arkansas St	48–21
1987	NE Louisiana	Marshall	43–42
1988	Furman	Georgia Southern	17–12
1989	Georgia Southern	SF Austin St	37–34
1990	Georgia Southern	NV-Reno	36–13
1991	Youngstown St	Marshall	25–17
1992	Marshall	Youngstown St	31–28
1993	Youngstown St	Marshall	17–5
1994	Youngstown St	Boise St	28–14
1995	Montana	Marshall	22–20

Division II

Year	Winner	Runner-Up	Score
1973	Louisiana Tech	Western Kentucky	34–0
1974	Central Michigan	Delaware	54–14
1975	Northern Michigan	Western Kentucky	16–14
1976	Montana St	Akron	24–13
1977	Lehigh	Jacksonville St	33–0
1978	Eastern Illinois	Delaware	10–9
1979	Delaware	Youngstown St	38–21
1980	Cal Poly SLO	Eastern Illinois	21–13
1981	SW Texas St	N Dakota St	42–13
1982	SW Texas St	UC-Davis	34–9
1983	N Dakota St	Central St (OH)	41–21
1984	Troy St	N Dakota St	18–17
1985	N Dakota St	N Alabama	35–7
1986	N Dakota St	S Dakota	27–7
1987	Troy St	Portland St	31–17
1988	N Dakota St	Portland St	35–21
1989	Mississippi College	Jacksonville St	3–0
1990	N Dakota St	Indiana (PA)	51–11
1991	Pittsburg St	Jacksonville St	23–6
1992	Jacksonville St	Pittsburg St	17–13
1993	N Alabama	Indiana (PA)	41–34
1994	N Alabama	Texas A&M-Kingsville	16–10
1995	N Alabama	Pittsburg St	27–7

Division III

Year	Winner	Runner-Up	Score
1973	Wittenberg	Juniata	41–0
1974	Central (IA)	Ithaca	10–8
1975	Wittenberg	Ithaca	28–0
1976	St John's (MN)	Towson St	31–28
1977	Widener	Wabash	39–36
1978	Baldwin-Wallace	Wittenberg	24–10
1979	Ithaca	Wittenberg	14–10
1980	Dayton	Ithaca	63–0
1981	Widener	Dayton	17–10
1982	W Georgia	Augustana (IL)	14–0
1983	Augustana (IL)	Union (NY)	21–17
1984	Augustana (IL)	Central (IA)	21–12
1985	Augustana (IL)	Ithaca	20–7
1986	Augustana (IL)	Salisbury St	31–3
1987	Wagner	Dayton	19–3
1988	Ithaca	Central (IA)	39–24
1989	Dayton	Union (NY)	17–7
1990	Allegheny	Lycoming	21–14 (OT)
1991	Ithaca	Dayton	34–20
1992	WI-LaCrosse	Washington & Jefferson	16–12
1993	Mount Union	Rowan	34–24
1994	Albion	Washington & Jefferson	38–15
1995	WI-LaCrosse	Rowan	36–7

NAIA Divisional Championships

Division I

Year	Winner	Runner-Up	Score
1956	St Joseph's (IN)/ Montana St		0–0
1957	Pittsburg St (KS)	Hillsdale (MI)	27–26
1958	Northeastern Oklahoma	Northern Arizona	19–13
1959	Texas A&I	Lenoir-Rhyne (NC)	20–7
1960	Lenoir-Rhyne (NC)	Humboldt St (CA)	15–14
1961	Pittsburg St (KS)	Linfield (OR)	12–7
1962	Central St (OK)	Lenoir-Rhyne (NC)	28–13
1963	St John's (MN)	Prairie View (TX)	33–27
1964	Concordia-Moorhead/ Sam Houston		7–7
1965	St John's (MN)	Linfield (OR)	33–0
1966	Waynesburg (PA)	WI-Whitewater	42–21
1967	Fairmont St (WV)	Eastern Washington	28–21
1968	Troy St (MI)	Texas A&I	43–35
1969	Texas A&I	Concordia-Moorhead (MN)	32–7
1970	Texas A&I	Wofford (SC)	48–7
1971	Livingston (AL)	Arkansas Tech	14–12
1972	E Texas St	Carson-Newman (TN)	21–18
1973	Abilene Christian	Elon (NC)	42–14
1974	Texas A&I	Henderson St (AR)	34–23
1975	Texas A&I	Salem (WV)	37–0
1976	Texas A&I	Central Arkansas	26–0
1977	Abilene Christian	Southwestern Oklahoma	24–7
1978	Angelo St (TX)	Elon (NC)	34–14
1979	Texas A&I	Central St (OK)	20–14
1980	Elon (NC)	Northeastern Oklahoma	17–10
1981	Elon (NC)	Pittsburg St	3–0
1982	Central St (OK)	Mesa (CO)	14–11
1983	Carson-Newman (TN)	Mesa (CO)	36–28
1984	Carson-Newman (TN)/ Central Arkansas		19–19
1985	Central Arkansas/ Hillsdale (MI)		10–10
1986	Carson-Newman (TN)	Cameron (OK)	17–0
1987	Cameron (OK)	Carson-Newman (TN)	30–2
1988	Carson-Newman (TN)	Adams St (CO)	56–21
1989	Carson-Newman (TN)	Emporia St (KS)	34–20
1990	Central St (OH)	Mesa St (CO)	38–16
1991	Central Arkansas	Central St (OH)	19–16
1992	Central St (OH)	Gardner-Webb (NC)	19–16
1993	East Central (OK)	Glenville St (WV)	49–35
1994	Northeastern St (OK)	Arkansas-Pine Bluff	13–12
1995	Central St (OH)	Northeastern St (OK)	37–7

Division II

Year	Winner	Runner-Up	Score
1970	Westminster (PA)	Anderson (IN)	21–16
1971	California Lutheran	Westminster (PA)	30–14
1972	Missouri Southern	Northwestern (IA)	21–14
1973	Northwestern (IA)	Glenville St (WV)	10–3
1974	Texas Lutheran	Missouri Valley	42–0
1975	Texas Lutheran	California Lutheran	34–8
1976	Westminster (PA)	Redlands (CA)	20–13
1977	Westminster (PA)	California Lutheran	17–9
1978	Concordia-Moorhead (MN)	Findlay (OH)	7–0
1979	Findlay (OH)	Northwestern (IA)	51–6
1980	Pacific Lutheran	Wilmington (OH)	38–10
1981	Austin Coll./ Conc.-Moorhead (MN)		24–24
1982	Linfield (OR)	William Jewell (MO)	33–15
1983	Northwestern (IA)	Pacific Lutheran	25–21
1984	Linfield (OR)	Northwestern (IA)	33–22
1985	WI-La Crosse	Pacific Lutheran	24–7
1986	Linfield (OR)	Baker (KS)	17–0
1987	Pacific Lutheran	WI-Stevens Point*	16–16
1988	Westminster (PA)	WI-La Crosse	21–14
1989	Westminster (PA)	WI-La Crosse	51–30
1990	Peru St (NE)	Westminster (PA)	17–7
1991	Georgetown (KY)	Pacific Lutheran	28–20
1992	Findlay (OH)	Linfield (OR)	26–13
1993	Pacific Lutheran (WA)	Westminster (PA)	50–20
1994	Westminster (PA)	Pacific Lutheran	27–7
1995	Findlay (OH)/ Central Washington		21–21

*Forfeited 1987 season due to use of an ineligible player.

Awards

Heisman Memorial Trophy

Awarded to the best college player by the Downtown Athletic Club of New York City. The trophy is named after John W. Heisman, who coached Georgia Tech to the national championship in 1917 and later served as DAC athletic director.

Year	Winner, College, Position Winner's Season Statistics	Runner-Up, College
1935	**Jay Berwanger, Chicago, HB** Rush: 119 Yds: 577 TD: 6	Monk Meyer, Army
1936	**Larry Kelley, Yale, E** Rec: 17 Yds: 372 TD: 6	Sam Francis, Nebraska
1937	**Clint Frank, Yale, HB** Rush: 157 Yds: 667 TD: 11	Byron White, Colorado
1938	**†Davey O'Brien, Texas Christian, QB** Att/Comp: 194/110 Yds: 1733 TD: 19	Marshall Goldberg, Pittsburgh
1939	**Nile Kinnick, Iowa, HB** Rush: 106 Yds: 374 TD: 5	Tom Harmon, Michigan
1940	**Tom Harmon, Michigan, HB** Rush: 191 Yds: 852 TD: 16	John Kimbrough, Texas A&M
1941	**†Bruce Smith, Minnesota, HB** Rush: 98 Yds: 480 TD: 6	Angelo Bertelli, Notre Dame
1942	**Frank Sinkwich, Georgia, HB** Att/Comp: 166/84 Yds: 1392 TD: 10	Paul Governali, Columbia
1943	**Angelo Bertelli, Notre Dame, QB** Att/Comp: 36/25 Yds: 511 TD: 10	Bob Odell, Pennsylvania
1944	**Les Horvath, Ohio State, QB** Rush: 163 Yds: 924 TD: 12	Glenn Davis, Army
1945	***†Doc Blanchard, Army, FB** Rush: 101 Yds: 718 TD: 13	Glenn Davis, Army
1946	**Glenn Davis, Army, HB** Rush: 123 Yds: 712 TD: 7	Charley Trippi, Georgia
1947	**†John Lujack, Notre Dame, QB** Att/Comp: 109/61 Yds: 777 TD: 9	Bob Chappuis, Michigan
1948	***Doak Walker, Southern Methodist, HB** Rush: 108 Yds: 532 TD: 8	Charlie Justice, N Carolina
1949	**†Leon Hart, Notre Dame, E** Rec: 19 Yds: 257 TD: 5	Charlie Justice, N Carolina
1950	***Vic Janowicz, Ohio St, HB** Att/Comp: 77/32 Yds: 561 TD: 12	Kyle Rote, Southern Methodist
1951	**Dick Kazmaier, Princeton, HB** Rush: 149 Yds: 861 TD: 9	Hank Lauricella, Tennessee
1952	**Billy Vessels, Oklahoma, HB** Rush: 167 Yds: 1072 TD: 17	Jack Scarbath, Maryland
1953	**John Lattner, Notre Dame, HB** Rush: 134 Yds: 651 TD: 6	Paul Giel, Minnesota
1954	**Alan Ameche, Wisconsin, FB** Rush: 146 Yds: 641 TD: 9	Kurt Burris, Oklahoma
1955	**Howard Cassady, Ohio St, HB** Rush: 161 Yds: 958 TD: 15	Jim Swink, Texas Christian
1956	**Paul Hornung, Notre Dame, QB** Att/Comp: 111/59 Yds: 917 TD: 3	Johnny Majors, Tennessee
1957	**John David Crow, Texas A&M, HB** Rush: 129 Yds: 562 TD: 10	Alex Karras, Iowa
1958	**Pete Dawkins, Army, HB** Rush: 78 Yds: 428 TD: 6	Randy Duncan, Iowa
1959	**Billy Cannon, Louisiana St, HB** Rush: 139 Yds: 598 TD: 6	Rich Lucas, Penn St
1960	**Joe Bellino, Navy, HB** Rush: 168 Yds: 834 TD: 18	Tom Brown, Minnesota
1961	**Ernie Davis, Syracuse, HB** Rush: 150 Yds: 823 TD: 15	Bob Ferguson, Ohio St
1962	**Terry Baker, Oregon St, QB** Att/Comp: 203/112 Yds: 1738 TD: 15	Jerry Stovall, Louisiana St
1963	***Roger Staubach, Navy, QB** Att/Comp: 161/107 Yds: 1474 TD: 7	Billy Lothridge, Georgia Tech
1964	**John Huarte, Notre Dame, QB** Att/Comp: 205/114 Yds: 2062 TD: 16	Jerry Rhome, Tulsa

Heisman Memorial Trophy (Cont.)

Year	Winner, College, Position Winner's Season Statistics	Runner-Up, College
1965	**Mike Garrett, Southern Cal, HB** Rush: 267 Yds: 1440 TD: 16	Howard Twilley, Tulsa
1966	**Steve Spurrier, Florida, QB** Att/Comp: 291/179 Yds: 2012 TD: 16	Bob Griese, Purdue
1967	**Gary Beban, UCLA, QB** Att/Comp: 156/87 Yds: 1359 TD: 8	O.J. Simpson, Southern Cal
1968	**O.J. Simpson, Southern Cal, HB** Rush: 383 Yds: 1880 TD: 23	Leroy Keyes, Purdue
1969	**Steve Owens, Oklahoma, FB** Rush: 358 Yds: 1523 TD: 23	Mike Phipps, Purdue
1970	**Jim Plunkett, Stanford, QB** Att/Comp: 358/191 Yds: 2715 TD: 18	Joe Theismann, Notre Dame
1971	**Pat Sullivan, Auburn, QB** Att/Comp: 281/162 Yds: 2012 TD: 20	Ed Marinaro, Cornell
1972	**Johnny Rodgers, Nebraska, FL** Rec: 55 Yds: 942 TD: 17	Greg Pruitt, Oklahoma
1973	**John Cappelletti, Penn St, HB** Rush: 286 Yds: 1522 TD: 17	John Hicks, Ohio St
1974	***Archie Griffin, Ohio St, HB** Rush: 256 Yds: 1695 TD: 12	Anthony Davis, Southern Cal
1975	**Archie Griffin, Ohio St, HB** Rush: 262 Yds: 1450 TD: 4	Chuck Muncie, California
1976	**†Tony Dorsett, Pittsburgh, HB** Rush: 370 Yds: 2150 TD: 21	Ricky Bell, Southern Cal
1977	**Earl Campbell, Texas, FB** Rush: 267 Yds: 1744 TD: 19	Terry Miller, Oklahoma St
1978	***Billy Sims, Oklahoma, HB** Rush: 231 Yds: 1762 TD: 20	Chuck Fusina, Penn St
1979	**Charles White, Southern Cal, HB** Rush: 332 Yds: 1803 TD: 19	Billy Sims, Oklahoma
1980	**George Rogers, S Carolina, HB** Rush: 324 Yds: 1894 TD: 14	Hugh Green, Pittsburgh
1981	**Marcus Allen, Southern Cal, HB** Rush: 433 Yds: 2427 TD: 23	Herschel Walker, Georgia
1982	***Herschel Walker, Georgia, HB** Rush: 335 Yds: 1752 TD: 17	John Elway, Stanford
1983	**Mike Rozier, Nebraska, HB** Rush: 275 Yds: 2148 TD: 29	Steve Young, Brigham Young
1984	**Doug Flutie, Boston College, QB** Att/Comp: 396/233 Yds: 3454 TD: 27	Keith Byars, Ohio St
1985	**Bo Jackson, Auburn, HB** Rush: 278 Yds: 1786 TD: 17	Chuck Long, Iowa
1986	**Vinny Testaverde, Miami (FL), QB** Att/Comp: 276/175 Yds: 2557 TD: 26	Paul Palmer, Temple
1987	**Tim Brown, Notre Dame, WR** Rec: 39 Yds: 846 TD: 7	Don McPherson, Syracuse
1988	***Barry Sanders, Oklahoma St, RB** Rush: 344 Yds: 2628 TD: 39	Rodney Peete, Southern Cal
1989	***Andre Ware, Houston, QB** Att/Comp: 578/365 Yds: 4699 TD: 46	Anthony Thompson, Indiana
1990	***Ty Detmer, Brigham Young, QB** Att/Comp: 562/361 Yds: 5188 TD: 41	Raghib Ismail, Notre Dame
1991	***Desmond Howard, Michigan, WR** Rec: 61 Yds: 950 TD: 23	Casey Weldon, Florida St
1992	**Gino Torretta, Miami (FL), QB** Att/Comp: 402/228 Yds: 3060 TD: 19	Marshall Faulk, San Diego St
1993	**†Charlie Ward, Florida St, QB** Att/Comp: 380/264 Yds: 3032 TD: 27	Heath Shuler, Tennessee
1994	**Rashaan Salaam, Colorado, RB** Rush: 298 Yds: 2055 TD: 24	Ki-Jana Carter, Penn St
1995	**Eddie George, Ohio State, RB** Rush: 303 Yds: 1826 TD: 23	Tommie Frazier, Nebraska

*Juniors (all others seniors). †Winners who played for national championship teams the same year.

Note: Former Heisman winners and national media cast votes, with ballots allowing for three names (3 points for first, 2 for second and 1 for third).

Jim Thorpe Award

Given to the best defensive back of the year, the award is presented by the Jim Thorpe Athletic Club of Oklahoma City.

Year	Player, College	Year	Player, College
1986	Thomas Everett, Baylor	1991	Terrell Buckley, Florida St
1987	Bennie Blades, Miami (FL)	1992	Deon Figures, Colorado
	Rickey Dixon, Oklahoma	1993	Antonio Langham, Alabama
1988	Deion Sanders, Florida St	1994	Chris Hudson, Colorado
1989	Mark Carrier, Southern Cal	1995	Greg Myers, Colorado St
1990	Darryl Lewis, Arizona		

Outland Trophy

Given to the outstanding interior lineman, selected by the Football Writers Association of America.

Year	Player, College, Position	Year	Player, College, Position
1946	George Connor, Notre Dame, T	1971	Larry Jacobson, Nebraska, DT
1947	Joe Steffy, Army, G	1972	Rich Glover, Nebraska, MG
1948	Bill Fischer, Notre Dame, G	1973	John Hicks, Ohio St, OT
1949	Ed Bagdon, Michigan St, G	1974	Randy White, Maryland, DE
1950	Bob Gain, Kentucky, T	1975	Lee Roy Selmon, Oklahoma, DT
1951	Jim Weatherall, Oklahoma, T	1976	*Ross Browner, Notre Dame, DE
1952	Dick Modzelewski, Maryland, T	1977	Brad Shearer, Texas, DT
1953	J.D. Roberts, Oklahoma, G	1978	Greg Roberts, Oklahoma, G
1954	Bill Brooks, Arkansas, G	1979	Jim Ritcher, N Carolina St, C
1955	Calvin Jones, Iowa, G	1980	Mark May, Pittsburgh, OT
1956	Jim Parker, Ohio St, G	1981	*Dave Rimington, Nebraska, C
1957	Alex Karras, Iowa, T	1982	Dave Rimington, Nebraska, C
1958	Zeke Smith, Auburn, G	1983	Dean Steinkuhler, Nebraska, G
1959	Mike McGee, Duke, T	1984	Bruce Smith, Virginia Tech, DT
1960	Tom Brown, Minnesota, G	1985	Mike Ruth, Boston Col, NG
1961	Merlin Olsen, Utah St, T	1986	Jason Buck, Brigham Young, DT
1962	Bobby Bell, Minnesota, T	1987	Chad Hennings, Air Force, DT
1963	Scott Appleton, Texas, T	1988	Tracy Rocker, Auburn, DT
1964	Steve DeLong, Tennessee, T	1989	Mohammed Elewonibi, Brigham Young, G
1965	Tommy Nobis, Texas, G	1990	Russell Maryland, Miami (FL), DT
1966	Loyd Phillips, Arkansas, T	1991	*Steve Emtman, Washington, DT
1967	Ron Yary, Southern Cal, T	1992	Will Shields, Nebraska, G
1968	Bill Stanfill, Georgia, T	1993	Rob Waldrop, Arizona, NG
1969	Mike Reid, Penn St, DT	1994	Zach Wiegert, Nebraska, G
1970	Jim Stillwagon, Ohio St, MG	1995	Jonathan Ogden, UCLA, OT

*Juniors (all others seniors).

Vince Lombardi/Rotary Award

Given to the outstanding college lineman of the year, the award is sponsored by the Rotary Club of Houston.

Year	Player, College, Position	Year	Player, College, Position
1970	Jim Stillwagon, Ohio St, MG	1983	Dean Steinkuhler, Nebraska, G
1971	Walt Patulski, Notre Dame, DE	1984	Tony Degrate, Texas, DT
1972	Rich Glover, Nebraska, MG	1985	Tony Casillas, Oklahoma, NG
1973	John Hicks, Ohio St, OT	1986	Cornelius Bennett, Alabama, LB
1974	Randy White, Maryland, DT	1987	Chris Spielman, Ohio St, LB
1975	Lee Roy Selmon, Oklahoma, DT	1988	Tracy Rocker, Auburn, DT
1976	Wilson Whitley, Houston, DT	1989	Percy Snow, Michigan St, LB
1977	Ross Browner, Notre Dame, DE	1990	Chris Zorich, Notre Dame, NG
1978	Bruce Clark, Penn St, DT	1991	Steve Emtman, Washington, DT
1979	Brad Budde, Southern Cal, G	1992	Marvin Jones, Florida St, LB
1980	Hugh Green, Pittsburgh, DE	1993	Aaron Taylor, Notre Dame, OT
1981	Kenneth Sims, Texas, DT	1994	Warren Sapp, Miami (FL), DT
1982	Dave Rimington, Nebraska, C	1995	Orlando Pace, Ohio St, OT

Butkus Award

Given to the top collegiate linebacker, the award was established by the Downtown Athletic Club of Orlando and named for college hall of famer Dick Butkus of Illinois.

Year	Player, College	Year	Player, College
1985	Brian Bosworth, Oklahoma	1991	Erick Anderson, Michigan
1986	Brian Bosworth, Oklahoma	1992	Marvin Jones, Florida St
1987	Paul McGowan, Florida St	1993	Trev Alberts, Nebraska
1988	Derrick Thomas, Alabama	1994	Dana Howard, Illinois
1989	Percy Snow, Michigan St	1995	Kevin Hardy, Illinois
1990	Alfred Williams, Colorado		

Davey O'Brien National Quarterback Award

Given to the No. 1 quarterback in the nation by the Davey O'Brien Educational and Charitable Trust of Fort Worth. Named for Texas Christian Hall of Fame quarterback Davey O'Brien (1936-38).

Year	Player, College	Year	Player, College
1981	Jim McMahon, Brigham Young	1989	Andre Ware, Houston
1982	Todd Blackledge, Penn St	1990	Ty Detmer, Brigham Young
1983	Steve Young, Brigham Young	1991	Ty Detmer, Brigham Young
1984	Doug Flutie, Boston College	1992	Gino Torretta, Miami (FL)
1985	Chuck Long, Iowa	1993	Charlie Ward, Florida St
1986	Vinny Testaverde, Miami (FL)	1994	Kerry Collins, Penn St
1987	Don McPherson, Syracuse	1995	Danny Wuerffel, Florida
1988	Troy Aikman, UCLA		

Note: Originally known as the Davey O'Brien Memorial Trophy, honoring the outstanding football player in the Southwest as follows: 1977—Earl Campbell, Texas, RB; 1978—Billy Sims, Oklahoma, RB; 1979—Mike Singletary, Baylor, LB; 1980—Mike Singletary, Baylor, LB.

Maxwell Award

Given to the nation's outstanding college football player by the Maxwell Football Club of Philadelphia.

Year	Player, College, Position	Year	Player, College, Position
1937	Clint Frank, Yale, HB	1967	Gary Beban, UCLA, QB
1938	Davey O'Brien, Texas Christian, QB	1968	O.J. Simpson, Southern Cal, RB
1939	Nile Kinnick, Iowa, HB	1969	Mike Reid, Penn St, DT
1940	Tom Harmon, Michigan, HB	1970	Jim Plunkett, Stanford, QB
1941	Bill Dudley, Virginia, HB	1971	Ed Marinaro, Cornell, RB
1942	Paul Governali, Columbia, QB	1972	Brad Van Pelt, Michigan St, DB
1943	Bob Odell, Pennsylvania, HB	1973	John Cappelletti, Penn St, RB
1944	Glenn Davis, Army, HB	1974	Steve Joachim, Temple, QB
1945	Doc Blanchard, Army, FB	1975	Archie Griffin, Ohio St, RB
1946	Charley Trippi, Georgia, HB	1976	Tony Dorsett, Pittsburgh, RB
1947	Doak Walker, Southern Meth, HB	1977	Ross Browner, Notre Dame, DE
1948	Chuck Bednarik, Pennsylvania, C	1978	Chuck Fusina, Penn St, QB
1949	Leon Hart, Notre Dame, E	1979	Charles White, Southern Cal, RB
1950	Reds Bagnell, Pennsylvania, HB	1980	Hugh Green, Pittsburgh, DE
1951	Dick Kazmaier, Princeton, HB	1981	Marcus Allen, Southern Cal, RB
1952	John Lattner, Notre Dame, HB	1982	Herschel Walker, Georgia, RB
1953	John Lattner, Notre Dame, HB	1983	Mike Rozier, Nebraska, RB
1954	Ron Beagle, Navy, E	1984	Doug Flutie, Boston College, QB
1955	Howard Cassady, Ohio St, HB	1985	Chuck Long, Iowa, QB
1956	Tommy McDonald, Oklahoma, HB	1986	Vinny Testaverde, Miami (FL), QB
1957	Bob Reifsnyder, Navy, T	1987	Don McPherson, Syracuse, QB
1958	Pete Dawkins, Army, HB	1988	Barry Sanders, Oklahoma St, RB
1959	Rich Lucas, Penn St, QB	1989	Anthony Thompson, Indiana, RB
1960	Joe Bellino, Navy, HB	1990	Ty Detmer, Brigham Young, QB
1961	Bob Ferguson, Ohio St, FB	1991	Desmond Howard, Michigan, WR
1962	Terry Baker, Oregon St, QB	1992	Gino Torretta, Miami (FL), QB
1963	Roger Staubach, Navy, QB	1993	Charlie Ward, Florida St, QB
1964	Glenn Ressler, Penn St, C	1994	Kerry Collins, Penn St, QB
1965	Tommy Nobis, Texas, LB	1995	Eddie George, Ohio St, RB
1966	Jim Lynch, Notre Dame, LB		

Walter Payton Player of the Year Award

Given to the top Division I-AA football player, the award is sponsored by Sports Network and voted on by Division I-AA sports information directors.

Year	Player, College, Position
1987	Kenny Gamble, Colgate, RB
1988	Dave Meggett, Towson St, RB
1989	John Friesz, Idaho, QB
1990	Walter Dean, Grambling, RB
1991	Jamie Martin, Weber St, QB
1992	Michael Payton, Marshall, QB
1993	Doug Nussmeier, Idaho, QB
1994	Steve McNair, Alcorn St, QB
1995	Dave Dickenson, Montana, QB

The Harlon Hill Trophy

Given to the outstanding NCAA Division II college football player, the award is sponsored by the National Harlon Hill Awards Committee, Florence, AL.

Year	Player, College, Position
1986	Jeff Bentrim, N Dakota St, QB
1987	Johnny Bailey, Texas A&I, RB
1988	Johnny Bailey, Texas A&I, RB
1989	Johnny Bailey, Texas A&I, RB
1990	Chris Simdorn, N Dakota St, QB
1991	Ronnie West, Pittsburg St, WR
1992	Ronald Moore, Pittsburg St, RB
1993	Roger Graham, New Haven, RB
1994	Chris Hatcher, Valdosta St, QB
1995	Ronald McKinnon, N Alabama, LB

NCAA Division I-A Individual Records

Career

SCORING

Most Points Scored: 423 — Roman Anderson, Houston, 1988-91
Most Points Scored per Game: 12.1 — Marshall Faulk, San Diego St, 1991-93
Most Touchdowns Scored: 65 — Anthony Thompson, Indiana, 1986-89
Most Touchdowns Scored per Game: 2.0 — Marshall Faulk, San Diego St, 1991-93
Most Touchdowns Scored, Rushing: 64 — Anthony Thompson, Indiana, 1986-89
Most Touchdowns Scored, Passing: 121 — Ty Detmer, Brigham Young, 1988-91
Most Touchdowns Scored, Receiving: 43 — Aaron Turner, Pacific, 1989-92
Most Touchdowns Scored, Interception Returns: 5 — Ken Thomas, San Jose St, 1979-82; Jackie Walker, Tennessee, 1969-71
Most Touchdowns Scored, Punt Returns: 7 — Johnny Rodgers, Nebraska, 1970-72; Jack Mitchell, Oklahoma, 1946-48
Most Touchdowns Scored, Kickoff Returns: 6 — Anthony Davis, Southern Cal, 1972-74

TOTAL OFFENSE

Most Plays: 1795 — Ty Detmer, Brigham Young, 1988-91
Most Plays per Game: 48.5 — Doug Gaynor, Long Beach St, 1984-85
Most Yards Gained: 14,665 — Ty Detmer, Brigham Young, 1988-91 (15,031 passing, -366 rushing)
Most Yards Gained per Game: 320.9 — Chris Vargas, Nevada, 1992-93
Most 300+ Yard Games: 33 —Ty Detmer, Brigham Young, 1988-91

RUSHING

Most Rushes: 1215 — Steve Bartalo, Colorado St, 1983-86 (4813 yds)
Most Rushes per Game: 34.0 — Ed Marinaro, Cornell, 1969-71
Most Yards Gained: 6082 — Tony Dorsett, Pittsburgh, 1973-76
Most Yards Gained per Game: 174.6 — Ed Marinaro, Cornell, 1969-71
Most 100+ Yard Games: 33 — Tony Dorsett, Pittsburgh, 1973-76; Archie Griffin, Ohio St, 1972-75
Most 200+ Yard Games: 11 — Marcus Allen, Southern Cal, 1978-81

SPECIAL TEAMS

Highest Punt Return Average: 23.6 — Jack Mitchell, Oklahoma, 1946-48
Highest Kickoff Return Average: 36.2 — Forrest Hall, San Francisco, 1946-47
Highest Average Yards per Punt: 46.3 — Todd Sauerbrun, West Virginia, 1991-94

PASSING

Highest Passing Efficiency Rating: 162.7 — Ty Detmer, Brigham Young, 1988-91 (1530 attempts, 958 completions, 65 interceptions, 15,031 yards, 121 TD passes)
Most Passes Attempted: 1,530 — Ty Detmer, Brigham Young, 1988-91
Most Passes Attempted per Game: 39.6 — Mike Perez, San Jose St, 1986-87
Most Passes Completed: 958 — Ty Detmer, Brigham Young, 1988-91
Most Passes Completed per Game: 25.9 — Doug Gaynor, Long Beach St, 1984-85
Highest Completion Percentage: 65.2 — Steve Young, Brigham Young, 1981-83
Most Yards Gained: 15,031 — Ty Detmer, Brigham Young, 1988-91
Most Yards Gained per Game: 326.7 — Ty Detmer, Brigham Young, 1988-91

RECEIVING

Most Passes Caught: 266 — Aaron Turner, Pacific, 1989-92
Most Passes Caught per Game: 10.5 — Emmanuel Hazard, Houston, 1989-90
Most Yards Gained: 4,357— Ryan Yarborough, Wyoming, 1990-93
Most Yards Gained per Game: 140.9 — Alex Van Dyke, Nevada, 1994-95
Highest Average Gain per Reception: 25.7 — Wesley Walker, California, 1973-75

ALL-PURPOSE RUNNING

Most Plays: 1347 — Steve Bartalo, Colorado St, 1983-86 (1215 rushes, 132 receptions)
Most Yards Gained: 7172 — Napoleon McCallum, Navy, 1981-85 (4179 rushing, 796 receiving, 858 punt returns, 1339 kickoff returns)
Most Yards Gained per Game: 237.8 — Ryan Benjamin, Pacific, 1990-92
Highest Average Gain per Play: 17.4 — Anthony Carter, Michigan, 1979-82.

INTERCEPTIONS

Most Passes Intercepted: 29 — Al Brosky, Illinois, 1950-52
Most Passes Intercepted per Game: 1.1 — Al Brosky, Illinois, 1950-52
Most Yards on Interception Returns: 501 — Terrell Buckley, Florida St, 1989-91
Highest Average Gain per Interception: 26.5 — Tom Pridemore, W Virginia, 1975-77

Single Season

SCORING

Most Points Scored: 234 — Barry Sanders, Oklahoma St, 1988
Most Points Scored per Game: 21.27 — Barry Sanders, Oklahoma St, 1988
Most Touchdowns Scored: 39 — Barry Sanders, Oklahoma St, 1988
Most Touchdowns Scored, Rushing: 37 — Barry Sanders, Oklahoma St, 1988
Most Touchdowns Scored, Passing: 54 — David Klingler, Houston, 1990
Most Touchdowns Scored, Receiving: 22 — Emmanuel Hazard, Houston, 1989
Most Touchdowns Scored, Interception Returns: 3 — by many players
Most Touchdowns Scored, Punt Returns: 4 — James Henry, Southern Miss, 1987; Golden Richards, Brigham Young, 1971; Cliff Branch, Colorado, 1971
Most Touchdowns Scored, Kickoff Returns: 3 — Leland McElroy, Texas A&M, 1993; Terance Mathis, New Mexico, 1989; Willie Gault, Tennessee, 1980; Anthony Davis, Southern Cal, 1974; Stan Brown, Purdue, 1970; Forrest Hall, San Francisco, 1946

TOTAL OFFENSE

Most Plays: 704 — David Klingler, Houston, 1990
Most Yards Gained: 5221 — David Klingler, Houston, 1990
Most Yards Gained per Game: 474.6 — David Klingler, Houston, 1990
Most 300+ Yard Games: 12 — Ty Detmer, Brigham Young, 1990

RUSHING

Most Rushes: 403 — Marcus Allen, Southern Cal, 1981
Most Rushes per Game: 39.6 — Ed Marinaro, Cornell, 1971
Most Yards Gained: 2628 — Barry Sanders, Oklahoma St, 1988
Most Yards Gained per Game: 238.9 — Barry Sanders, Oklahoma St, 1988
Most 100+ Yard Games: 11 — By 12 players, most recently Darnell Autry, Northwestern, 1995; Wasean Tait, Toledo, 1995.

PASSING

Highest Passing Efficiency Rating: 178.4 — Danny Wuerffel, Florida, 1995 (325 attempts, 210 completions, 10 interceptions, 3266 yards, 35 TD passes)
Most Passes Attempted: 643 — David Klingler, Houston, 1990
Most Passes Attempted per Game: 58.5 — David Klingler, Houston, 1990
Most Passes Completed: 374 — David Klingler, Houston, 1990
Most Passes Completed per Game: 34.0 — David Klingler, Houston, 1990
Highest Completion Percentage: 71.3 — Steve Young, Brigham Young, 1983
Most Yards Gained: (12 games) 5188 — Ty Detmer, Brigham Young, 1990; (11 games) 5140 — David Klingler, Houston, 1990
Most Yards Gained per Game: 467.3 — David Klingler, Houston, 1990

RECEIVING

Most Passes Caught: 142 — Emmanuel Hazard, Houston, 1989
Most Passes Caught per Game: 13.4 — Howard Twilley, Tulsa, 1965
Most Yards Gained: 1854 — Alex Van Dyke, Nevada, 1995.
Most Yards Gained per Game: 177.9 — Howard Twilley, Tulsa, 1965
Highest Average Gain per Reception: 27.9 — Elmo Wright, Houston, 1968 (min. 30 receptions)

ALL-PURPOSE RUNNING

Most Plays: 432 — Marcus Allen, Southern Cal, 1981
Most Yards Gained: 3250 — Barry Sanders, Oklahoma St, 1988
Most Yards Gained per Game: 295.5 — Barry Sanders, Oklahoma St, 1988
Highest Average Gain per Play: 18.5 — Henry Bailey, UNLV, 1992

INTERCEPTIONS

Most Passes Intercepted: 14 — Al Worley, Washington, 1968
Most Yards on Interception Returns: 302 — Charles Phillips, Southern Cal, 1974
Highest Average Gain per Interception: 50.6 — Norm Thompson, Utah, 1969

SPECIAL TEAMS

Highest Punt Return Average: 25.9 — Bill Blackstock, Tennessee, 1951
Highest Kickoff Return Average: 38.2 — Forrest Hall, San Francisco, 1946
Highest Average Yards per Punt: 49.8 — Reggie Roby, Iowa, 1981

THEY SAID IT

Dick Tomey, Arizona football coach, on the hiring of the cerebral Homer Smith as offensive coordinator: "You won't find many football coaches with degrees from Princeton, Harvard and Stanford. Actually, you won't find many professors here with degrees from Princeton, Harvard and Stanford."

Single Game

SCORING

Most Points Scored: 48 — Howard Griffith, Illinois, 1990 (vs Southern Illinois)
Most Field Goals: 7 — Dale Klein, Nebraska, 1985 (vs Missouri); Mike Prindle, Western Michigan, 1984 (vs Marshall)
Most Extra Points (Kick): 13 — Derek Mahoney, Fresno St, 1991 (vs New Mexico); Terry Leiweke, Houston, 1968 (vs Tulsa)
Most Extra Points (2-Pts): 6 — Jim Pilot, New Mexico St, 1961 (vs Hardin-Simmons)

TOTAL OFFENSE

Most Yards Gained: 732 — David Klingler, Houston, 1990 (vs Arizona St)

RUSHING

Most Yards Gained: 396 — Tony Sands, Kansas, 1991 (vs Missouri)

RUSHING (Cont.)

Most Touchdowns Rushed: 8 — Howard Griffith, Illinois, 1990 (vs Southern Illinois)

PASSING

Most Passes Completed: 55 — Rusty LaRue, Wake Forest, 1995 (vs Duke)
Most Yards Gained: 716 — David Klingler, Houston, 1990 (vs Arizona St)
Most Touchdowns Passed: 11 — David Klingler, Houston, 1990 [vs Eastern Washington (I-AA)]

RECEIVING

Most Passes Caught: 23 — Randy Gatewood, UNLV, 1994 (vs Idaho)
Most Yards Gained: 363 — Randy Gatewood, UNLV, 1994 (vs Idaho)
Most Touchdown Catches: 6 — Tim Delaney, San Diego St, 1969 (vs New Mexico St)

NCAA Division I-AA Individual Records

Career

SCORING

Most Points Scored: 385 — Marty Zendejas, NV-Reno, 1984-87
Most Touchdowns Scored: 61 — Sherriden May, Idaho, 1992-94
Most Touchdowns Scored, Rushing: 55 — Kenny Gamble, Colgate, 1984-87
Most Touchdowns Scored, Passing: 139 — Willie Totten, Mississippi Valley, 1982-85
Most Touchdowns Scored, Receiving: 50 — Jerry Rice, Mississippi Valley, 1981-84

PASSING

Highest Passing Efficiency Rating: 170.8 — Shawn Knight, William & Mary, 1991-94
Most Passes Attempted: 1,680 — Steve McNair, Alcorn St, 1991-94
Most Passes Completed: 938 — Neil Lomax, Portland St, 1977-80
Most Passes Completed per Game: 24.3 — Tom Proudian, Iona, 1993-95
Highest Completion Percentage: 66.9 — Jason Garrett, Princeton, 1987-88

PASSING (CONT.)

Most Yards Gained: 14,496 — Steve McNair, Alcorn St, 1991-94
Most Yards Gained per Game: 345.1 — Steve McNair, Alcorn St, 1991-94

RUSHING

Most Rushes: 1,027 — Erik Marsh, Lafayette, 1991-94
Most Rushes per Game: 38.2 — Arnold Mickens, Butler, 1994-95
Most Yards Gained: 5,333 — Frank Hawkins, NV-Reno, 1977-80
Most Yards Gained per Game: 124.3 — Kenny Gamble, Colgate, 1984-87

RECEIVING

Most Passes Caught: 301 — Jerry Rice, Mississippi Valley, 1981-84
Most Yards Gained: 4,693 — Jerry Rice, Mississippi Valley, 1981-84
Most Yards Gained per Game: 114.5 — Jerry Rice, Mississippi Valley, 1981-84
Highest Average Gain per Reception: 24.3 — John Taylor, Delaware St, 1982-85

Single Season

SCORING

Most Points Scored: 170 — Geoff Mitchell, Weber St, 1991
Most Touchdowns Scored: 28 — Geoff Mitchell, Weber St, 1991
Most Touchdowns Scored, Rushing: 24 — Geoff Mitchell, Weber St, 1991
Most Touchdowns Scored, Passing: 56 — Willie Totten, Mississippi Valley, 1984
Most Touchdowns Scored, Receiving: 27 — Jerry Rice, Mississippi Valley, 1984

PASSING

Highest Passing Efficiency Rating: 204.6 — Shawn Knight, William & Mary, 1993

PASSING (CONT.)

Most Passes Attempted: 530 — Steve McNair, Alcorn St, 1994
Most Passes Completed: 324 — Willie Totten, Mississippi Valley, 1984
Most Passes Completed per Game: 32.4 — Willie Totten, Mississippi Valley, 1984
Highest Completion Percentage: 68.2 — Jason Garrett, Princeton, 1988; Dave Dickenson, Montana, 1994
Most Yards Gained: 4,863 — Steve McNair, Alcorn St, 1994
Most Yards Gained per Game: 455.7 — Willie Totten, Mississippi Valley, 1984

Single Season *(Cont.)*

RUSHING

Most Rushes: 409 — Arnold Mickens, Butler, 1994
Most Rushes per Game: 40.9 — Arnold Mickens, Butler, 1994
Most Yards Gained: 2255 — Arnold Mickens, Butler, 1994
Most Yards Gained per Game: 225.5 — Arnold Mickens, Butler, 1994

RECEIVING

Most Passes Caught: 115 — Brian Forster, Rhode Island, 1985
Most Yards Gained: 1,682 — Jerry Rice, Mississippi Valley, 1984
Most Yards Gained per Game: 168.2 — Jerry Rice, Mississippi Valley, 1984
Highest Average Gain per Reception: 26.5 — Dedric Ward, Northern Iowa, 1995 (min. 30 receptions)

Single Game

SCORING

Most Points Scored: 36 — By five players, most recently Erwin Matthews, Richmond, 1987 (vs Massachusetts)
Most Field Goals: 8 — Goran Lingmerth, Northern Arizona, 1986 (vs Idaho)

PASSING

Most Passes Completed: 48 — Clayton Millis, Cal St-Northridge, 1995 (vs St Mary's [CA])
Most Yards Gained: 649 — Steve McNair, Alcorn St, 1994 (vs Southern-BR)
Most Touchdowns Passed: 9 — Willie Totten, Mississippi Valley, 1984 (vs Kentucky St)

RUSHING

Most Yards Gained: 364 — Tony Vinson, Towson St, 1993 (vs Bucknell)
Most Touchdowns Rushed: 6 — Gene Lake, Delaware St, 1984 (vs. Howard); Gill Fenerty, Holy Cross, 1983 (vs Columbia); Henry Odom, S Carolina St, 1980 (vs Morgan St)

RECEIVING

Most Passes Caught: 24 — Jerry Rice, Mississippi Valley, 1983 (vs Southern-BR)
Most Yards Gained: 370 — Michael Lerch, Princeton, 1991 (vs Brown)
Most Touchdown Catches: 5 — Four players, most recently by Rod Marshall, Northern Arizona, 1995 (vs Abilene Christian)

NCAA Division II Individual Records

Career

SCORING

Most Points Scored: 464 — Walter Payton, Jackson St, 1971-74
Most Touchdowns Scored: 72 — Shawn Graves, Wofford, 1989-92
Most Touchdowns Scored, Rushing: 72 — Shawn Graves, Wofford, 1989-92
Most Touchdowns Scored, Passing: 116 — Chris Hatcher, Valdosta St, 1991-94
Most Touchdowns Scored, Receiving: 49 — Bruce Cerone, Yankton/Emporia St, 1966-69

PASSING

Highest Passing Efficiency Rating: 164.0 — Chris Petersen, UC-Davis, 1985-86
Most Passes Attempted: 1,719 — Bob McLaughlin, Lock Haven, 1992-95
Most Passes Completed: 1,001 — Chris Hatcher, Valdosta St, 1991-94
Most Passes Completed per Game: 25.7 — Chris Hatcher, Valdosta St, 1991-94
Highest Completion Percentage: 69.6 — Chris Peterson, UC-Davis, 1985-86
Most Yards Gained: 10,878 — Chris Hatcher, Valdosta St, 1991-94
Most Yards Gained per Game: 312.1 — Grady Benton, West Texas A&M, 1994-95

RUSHING

Most Rushes: 1,072 — Bernie Peeters, Luther, 1968-71
Most Rushes per Game: 29.8 — Bernie Peeters, Luther, 1968-71
Most Yards Gained: 6,320 — Johnny Bailey, Texas A&I*, 1986-89
Most Yards Gained per Game: 162.1 — Johnny Bailey, Texas A&I*, 1986-89

RECEIVING

Most Passes Caught: 261 — Jon Spinosa, Lock Haven, 1992-95
Most Yards Gained: 4,468 — James Roe, Norfolk St, 1992-95
Most Yards Gained per Game: 160.8 — Chris George, Glenville St, 1993-94
Highest Average Gain per Reception: 22.8 — Tyrone Johnson, Western St (CO), 1990-93

*Became Texas A&M-Kingsville in 1993

Single Season

SCORING

Most Points Scored: 178 — Terry Metcalf, Long Beach St, 1971
Most Touchdowns Scored: 29 — Terry Metcalf, Long Beach St, 1971
Most Touchdowns Scored, Rushing: 28 — Terry Metcalf, Long Beach St, 1971
Most Touchdowns Scored, Passing: 50 — Chris Hatcher, Valdosta St, 1994
Most Touchdowns Scored, Receiving: 21 — Chris Perry, Adams St, 1995

PASSING

Highest Passing Efficiency Rating: 210.1 — Boyd Crawford, College of Idaho, 1953
Most Passes Attempted: 544 — Lance Funderburk, Valdosta St, 1995
Most Passes Completed: 356 — Lance Funderburk, Valdosta St, 1995
Most Passes Completed per Game: 32.4 — Lance Funderburk, Valdosta St, 1995
Highest Completion Percentage: 74.6 — Chris Hatcher, Valdosta St, 1994
Most Yards Gained: 3,757 — Perry Klein, LIU-CW Post, 1993
Most Yards Gained per Game: 393.4 — Grady Benton, W Texas A&M, 1994

RUSHING

Most Rushes: 385 — Joe Gough, Wayne St (MI), 1994
Most Rushes per Game: 38.6 — Mark Perkins, Hobart, 1968
Most Yards Gained: 2,011 — Johnny Bailey, Texas A&I, 1986
Most Yards Gained per Game: 188.9 —Richard Huntley, Winston Salem, 1995

RECEIVING

Most Passes Caught: 119 — Brad Bailey, W Texas A&M, 1994
Most Yards Gained: 1,876 — Chris George, Glenville St, 1993
Most Yards Gained per Game: 187.6 — Chris George, Glenville St, 1993
Highest Average Gain per Reception: 32.5 — Tyrone Johnson, Western St, 1991 (min. 30 receptions)

Single Game

SCORING

Most Points Scored: 48 — Paul Zaeske, N Park, 1968 (vs N Central); Junior Wolf, Panhandle St, 1958 [vs St Mary (KS)]
Most Field Goals: 6 — Steve Huff, Central Missouri St, 1985 (vs SE Missouri St)

PASSING

Most Passes Completed: 45 — Chris Hatcher, Valdosta St,1993 (vs W Georgia; vs Miss. College)
Most Yards Gained: 614 — Alfred Montez, W New Mexico, 1994 (vs W Texas A&M); Perry Klein, LI-C.W. Post, 1993 (vs Salisbury St)
Most Touchdowns Passed: 10 — Bruce Swanson, N Park, 1968 (vs N Central)

RUSHING

Most Yards Gained: 382 — Kelly Ellis, Northern Iowa, 1979 (vs Western Illinois)
Most Touchdowns Rushed: 8 — Junior Wolf, Panhandle St, 1958 [vs St Mary (KS)]

RECEIVING

Most Passes Caught: 23 — Chris George, Glenville St, 1994 (vs W VA Wesleyan); Barry Wagner, Alabama A&M, 1989 (vs Clark Atlanta)
Most Yards Gained: 370 — Barry Wagner, Alabama A&M, 1989 (vs Clark Atlanta)
Most Touchdown Catches: 8 — Paul Zaeske, N Park, 1968 (vs N Central)

NCAA Division III Individual Records

Career

SCORING

Most Points Scored: 528 — Carey Bender, Coe, 1991-94
Most Touchdowns Scored: 86 — Carey Bender, Coe, 1991-94
Most Touchdowns Scored, Rushing: 76 — Joe Dudek, Plymouth St, 1982-85
Most Touchdowns Scored, Passing: 115 — Jim Ballard, Wilmington (OH)1990; Mt Union (OH) 91-93
Most Touchdowns Scored, Receiving: 55 — Chris Bisaillon, Illinois Wesleyan, 1989-92

RUSHING

Most Rushes: 1,152 — Anthony Russo, St John's (NY), 1990-93
Most Rushes per Game: 32.7 — Chris Sizemore, Bridgewater (VA), 1972-74
Most Yards Gained: 6,125 — Carey Bender, Coe, 1991-94
Most Yards Gained per Game: 175.1 — Ricky Gales, Simpson, 1988-89

Career *(Cont.)*

PASSING

Highest Passing Efficiency Rating: 159.5 — Jim Ballard, Wilmington (OH)1990; Mt Union (OH) 91-93
Most Passes Attempted: 1,696 — Kirk Baumgartner, WI-Stevens Point, 1986-89
Most Passes Completed: 883 — Kirk Baumgartner, WI-Stevens Point, 1986-89
Most Passes Completed per Game: 24.9 — Keith Bishop, Illinois Wesleyan, 1981; Wheaton (IL), 1983-85
Highest Completion Percentage: 62.2 — Brian Moore, Baldwin-Wallace, 1981-84
Most Yards Gained: 13,028 — Kirk Baumgartner, WI-Stevens Point, 1986-89
Most Yards Gained per Game: 317.8 — Kirk Baumgartner, WI-Stevens Point, 1986-89

RECEIVING

Most Passes Caught: 287 — Matt Newton, Principia (IL), 1990-93
Most Yards Gained: 3,846 — Dale Amos, Franklin & Marshall, 1986-89
Most Yards Gained per Game: 110.5 — Matt Newton, Principia (IL), 1990-93
Highest Average Gain per Reception: 20.6 — Rodd Patten, Framingham St, 1990-93

Single Season

SCORING

Most Points Scored: 194 — Carey Bender, Coe, 1994
Most Points Scored per Game: 19.4 — Carey Bender, Coe, 1994
Most Touchdowns Scored: 32 — Carey Bender, Coe, 1994
Most Touchdowns Scored, Rushing: 29 — Carey Bender, Coe, 1994
Most Touchdowns Scored, Passing: 39 — Kirk Baumgartner, WI-Stevens Point, 1989
Most Touchdowns Scored, Receiving: 20 — John Aromando, Trenton St, 1983

RUSHING

Most Rushes: 380 — Mike Birosak, Dickinson, 1989
Most Rushes per Game: 38.0 — Mike Birosak, Dickinson, 1989
Most Yards Gained: 2,243 — Carey Bender, Coe, 1994
Most Yards Gained per Game: 224.3 — Carey Bender, Coe, 1994

PASSING

Highest Passing Efficiency Rating: 225.0 — Mike Simpson, Eureka, 1994
Most Passes Attempted: 527 — Kirk Baumgartner, WI-Stevens Point, 1988
Most Passes Completed: 276 — Kirk Baumgartner, WI-Stevens Point, 1988
Most Passes Completed per Game: 29.1 — Keith Bishop, Illinois Wesleyan, 1985
Highest Completion Percentage: 73.4 — Mike Simpson, Eureka, 1994
Most Yards Gained: 3,828 — Kirk Baumgartner, WI-Stevens Point, 1988
Most Yards Gained per Game: 369.2 — Kirk Baumgartner, WI-Stevens Point, 1989

RECEIVING

Most Passes Caught: 106 — Theo Blanco, WI-Stevens Point, 1987
Most Yards Gained: 1,693 — Sean Munroe, Mass-Boston, 1992
Most Yards Gained per Game: 188.1 — Sean Munroe, Mass-Boston 1992
Highest Average Gain per Reception: 26.9 — Marty Redlawsk, Concordia (IL), 1985

Single Game

SCORING

Most Field Goals: 6 — Jim Hever, Rhodes, 1984 (vs Millsaps)

PASSING

Most Passes Completed: 50 — Tim Lynch, Hofstra, 1991 (vs Fordham)
Most Yards Gained: 602 — Tom Stallings, St Thomas (MN), 1993 (vs Bethel)
Most Touchdowns Passed: 8 — Steve Austin, Mass-Boston, 1992 (vs Framingham St); Kirk Baumgartner, WI-Stevens Point, 1989 (vs WI-Superior); John Koz, Baldwin-Wallace, 1993 (vs Ohio Northern)

RUSHING

Most Yards Gained: 417 — Carey Bender, Coe, 1993 (vs Grinnell)
Most Touchdowns Rushed: 8 — Carey Bender, Coe, 1994 (vs Beloit)

RECEIVING

Most Passes Caught: 23 — Sean Munroe, Mass-Boston, 1992 (vs Mass-Maritime)
Most Yards Gained: 332 — Sean Munroe, Mass-Boston, 1992 (vs Mass-Maritime)
Most Touchdown Catches: 5 — By 12 players, most recently Vurnell Roques, Claremont M.S., 1995 (vs Occidental)

Career

Scoring

POINTS (KICKERS)

	Years	Pts
Roman Anderson, Houston	1988-91	423
Carlos Huerta, Miami (FL)	1988-91	397
Jason Elam, Hawaii	1988-92	395
Derek Schmidt, Florida St	1984-87	393
Luis Zendejas, Arizona St	1981-84	368

POINTS (NON-KICKERS)

	Years	Pts
Anthony Thompson, Indiana	1986-89	394
Marshall Faulk, San Diego St	1991-93	376
Tony Dorsett, Pittsburgh	1973-76	356
Glenn Davis, Army	1943-46	354
Art Luppino, Arizona	1953-56	337

POINTS PER GAME (NON-KICKERS)

	Years	Pts/Game
Marshall Faulk, San Diego St	1991-93	12.1
Ed Marinaro, Cornell	1969-71	11.8
Bill Burnett, Arkansas	1968-70	11.3
Steve Owens, Oklahoma	1967-69	11.2
Eddie Talboom, Wyoming	1948-50	10.8

Total Offense

YARDS GAINED

	Years	Yds
Ty Detmer, Brigham Young	1988-91	14,665
Doug Flutie, Boston Col	1981-84	11,317
Eric Zeier, Georgia	1991-94	10,841
Alex Van Pelt, Pittsburgh	1989-92	10,814
Stoney Case, New Mexico	1991-94	10,651

YARDS PER GAME

	Years	Yds/Game
Chris Vargas, Nevada	1992-93	320.9
Ty Detmer, Brigham Young	1988-91	318.8
Mike Perez, San Jose St	1986-87	309.1
Doug Gaynor, Long Beach St	1984-85	305.0
Tony Eason, Illinois	1981-82	299.5

Rushing

YARDS GAINED

	Years	Yds
Tony Dorsett, Pittsburgh	1973-76	6,082
Charles White, Southern Cal	1976-79	5,598
Herschel Walker, Georgia	1980-82	5,259
Archie Griffin, Ohio St	1972-75	5,177
Darren Lewis, Texas A&M	1987-90	5,012

YARDS PER GAME

	Years	Yds/Game
Ed Marinaro, Cornell	1969-71	174.6
O.J. Simpson, Southern Cal	1967-68	164.4
Herschel Walker, Georgia	1980-82	159.4
LeShon Johnson, N Illinois	1992-93	150.6
Marshall Faulk, San Diego St	1991-93	148.0

TOUCHDOWNS RUSHING

	Years	TD
Anthony Thompson, Indiana	1986-89	64
Marshall Faulk, San Diego St	1991-93	57
Steve Owens, Oklahoma	1967-69	56
Tony Dorsett, Pittsburgh	1973-76	55
Ed Marinaro, Cornell	1969-71	50

Passing

PASSING EFFICIENCY

	Years	Rating
Ty Detmer, Brigham Young	1988-91	162.7
Jim McMahon, Brigham Young	1977-78, 80-81	156.9
Steve Young, Brigham Young	1982, 84-86	149.8
Robbie Bosco, Brigham Young	1981-83	149.4
Mike Maxwell, Nevada	1993-95	148.5

Note: Minimum 500 completions.

YARDS GAINED

	Years	Yds
Ty Detmer, Brigham Young	1988-91	15,031
Todd Santos, San Diego St	1984-87	11,425
Eric Zeier, Georgia	1991-94	11,153
Alex Van Pelt, Pittsburgh	1989-92	10,913
Kevin Sweeney, Fresno St	1982-86	10,623

Note: Minimum 500 completions.

COMPLETIONS

	Years	Comp
Ty Detmer, Brigham Young	1988-91	958
Todd Santos, San Diego St	1984-87	910
Brian McClure, Bowling Green	1982-85	900
Eric Wilhelm, Oregon St	1989-92	870
Alex Van Pelt, Pittsburgh	1989-92	845

Note: Minimum 500 completions.

TOUCHDOWNS PASSING

	Years	TD
Ty Detmer, Brigham Young	1988-91	121
David Klingler, Houston	1988-91	92
Troy Kopp, Pacific	1989-92	87
Jim McMahon, Brigham Young	1977-78, 80-81	84
Joe Adams, Tennessee St	1977-80	81

Receiving

CATCHES

	Years	No.
Aaron Turner, Pacific	1989-92	266
Terance Mathis, New Mexico	1985-87, 89	263
Mark Templeton, Long Beach St	1983-86	262
Howard Twilley, Tulsa	1963-65	261
David Williams, Illinois	1983-85	245

CATCHES PER GAME

	Years	No./Game
Emmanuel Hazard, Houston	1989-90	10.5
Alex Van Dyke, Nevada	1994-95	10.3
Howard Twilley, Tulsa	1963-65	10.0
Jason Phillips, Houston	1987-88	9.4
Bryan Reeves, Nevada	1992-93	8.2

YARDS GAINED

	Years	Yds
Ryan Yarborough, Wyoming	1990-93	4,357
Aaron Turner, Pacific	1989-92	4,345
Terance Mathis, New Mexico	1985-87, 89	4,254
Marc Zeno, Tulane	1984-87	3,725
Ron Sellers, Florida St	1966-68	3,598

TOUCHDOWN CATCHES

	Years	TD
Aaron Turner, Pacific	1989-92	43
Ryan Yarborough, Wyoming	1990-93	42
Clarkston Hines, Duke	1986-89	38
Terance Mathis, New Mexico	1985-87, 89	36
Elmo Wright, Houston	1968-70	34

Career (Cont.)

All-Purpose Running

YARDS GAINED	Years	Yds
Napoleon McCallum, Navy	1981-85	7172
Darrin Nelson, Stanford	1977-78, 80-81	6885
Terance Mathis, New Mexico	1985-87, 89	6691
Tony Dorsett, Pittsburgh	1973-76	6615
Paul Palmer, Temple	1983-86	6609

YARDS PER GAME	Years	Yds/Game
Ryan Benjamin, Pacific	1990-92	237.8
Sheldon Canley, San Jose St	1988-90	205.8
Howard Stevens, Louisville	1971-72	193.7
O.J. Simpson, Southern Cal	1967-68	192.9
Alex Van Dyke, Nevada	1994-95	188.5

Interceptions

PLAYER/SCHOOL	Years	Int
Al Brosky, Illinois	1950-52	29
John Provost, Holy Cross	1972-74	27
Martin Bayless, Bowling Green	1980-83	27
Tom Curtis, Michigan	1967-69	25
Tony Thurman, Boston Col	1981-84	25
Tracy Saul, Texas Tech	1989-92	25

Punting Average

PLAYER/SCHOOL	Years	Avg
Todd Sauerbrun, W Virginia	1991-94	46.3
Reggie Roby, Iowa	1979-82	45.6
Greg Montgomery, Michigan St	1985-87	45.4
Tom Tupa, Ohio St	1984-87	45.2
Barry Helton, Colorado	1984-87	44.9

Note: At least 150 punts kicked.

Punt Return Average

PLAYER/SCHOOL	Years	Avg
Jack Mitchell, Oklahoma	1946-48	23.6
Gene Gibson, Cincinnati	1949-50	20.5
Eddie Macon, Pacific	1949-51	18.9
Jackie Robinson, UCLA	1939-40	18.8
Mike Fuller, Auburn	1972-74	17.7
Bobby Dillon, Texas	1949-51	17.7

Note: At least 1.2 punt returns per game.

Kickoff Return Average

PLAYER/SCHOOL	Years	Avg
Anthony Davis, Southern Cal	1972-74	35.1
Overton Curtis, Utah St	1957-58	31.0
Fred Montgomery, New Mexico St	1991-92	30.5
Altie Taylor, Utah St	1966-68	29.3
Stan Brown, Purdue	1968-70	28.8
Henry White, Colgate	1974-77	28.8

Note: At least 1.2 kickoff returns per game. Min. 30 returns.

Tempering the Cornhuskers

In the aftermath of Lawrence Phillips's assault of his former girlfriend (SI, Sept. 18 et seq.), comes the news that Nebraska football players have been tutored in anger control by actor turned lay psychologist Tom Laughlin. Film buffs may be scratching their heads. Laughlin is best known for his portrayals of Billy Jack, the "mysterious half-breed Green Beret" who, in two 1970s films, made the world safer for flower power by chopping, kicking and shooting his way through waves of rednecks. "When [people] tell me I have to control my violent temper, I try, I really try," he tells a group of toughs in *Billy Jack*. But sometimes, he adds wearily, "I just go berserk!" Which he proceeds to do in graphic and bloody fashion. Now, about that Dom DeLuise appetite-control seminar....

Single Season

Scoring

POINTS	Year	Pts
Barry Sanders, Oklahoma St	1988	234
Mike Rozier, Nebraska	1983	174
Lydell Mitchell, Penn St	1971	174
Art Luppino, Arizona	1954	166
Bobby Reynolds, Nebraska	1950	157

FIELD GOALS	Year	FG
John Lee, UCLA	1984	29
Paul Woodside, W Virginia	1982	28
Luis Zendejas, Arizona St	1983	28
Fuad Reveiz, Tennessee	1982	27

Note: Four tied with 25 each.

All-Purpose Running

YARDS GAINED	Year	Yds
Barry Sanders, Oklahoma St	1988	3250
Ryan Benjamin, Pacific	1991	2995
Mike Pringle, Fullerton St	1989	2690
Paul Palmer, Temple	1986	2633
Ryan Benjamin, Pacific	1992	2597

All-Purpose Running (Cont.)

YARDS PER GAME	Year	Yds/Game
Barry Sanders, Oklahoma St	1988	295.5
Ryan Benjamin, Pacific	1991	249.6
Byron (Whizzer) White, Colorado	1937	246.3
Mike Pringle, Fullerton St	1989	244.6
Paul Palmer, Temple	1986	239.4

Total Offense

YARDS GAINED	Year	Yds
David Klingler, Houston	1990	5221
Ty Detmer, Brigham Young	1990	5022
Andre Ware, Houston	1989	4661
Jim McMahon, Brigham Young	1980	4627
Ty Detmer, Brigham Young	1989	4433

YARDS PER GAME	Year	Yds/Game
David Klingler, Houston	1990	474.6
Andre Ware, Houston	1989	423.7
Ty Detmer, Brigham Young	1990	418.5
Mike Maxwell, Nevada	1995	402.6
Steve Young, Brigham Young	1983	395.1

Single Season *(Cont.)*

Rushing

YARDS GAINED

	Year	Yds
Barry Sanders, Oklahoma St	1988	2628
Marcus Allen, Southern Cal	1981	2342
Mike Rozier, Nebraska	1983	2148
Rashaan Salaam, Colorado	1994	2055
Troy Davis, Iowa St	1995	2010

YARDS PER GAME

	Year	Yds/Game
Barry Sanders, Oklahoma St	1988	238.9
Marcus Allen, Southern Cal	1981	212.9
Ed Marinaro, Cornell	1971	209.0
Rashaan Salaam, Colorado	1994	186.8
Troy Davis, Iowa St	1995	182.7

TOUCHDOWNS RUSHING

	Year	TD
Barry Sanders, Oklahoma St	1988	37
Mike Rozier, Nebraska	1983	29
Ed Marinaro, Cornell	1971	24
Anthony Thompson, Indiana	1988	24
Anthony Thompson, Indiana	1989	24
Rashaan Salaam, Colorado	1994	24

Passing

PASSING EFFICIENCY

	Year	Rating
Danny Wuerffel, Florida	1995	178.4
Jim McMahon, Brigham Young	1980	176.9
Ty Detmer, Brigham Young	1989	175.6
Trent Dilfer, Fresno St	1993	173.1
Kerry Collins, Penn St	1994	172.9

YARDS GAINED

	Year	Yds
Ty Detmer, Brigham Young	1990	5188
David Klingler, Houston	1990	5140
Andre Ware, Houston	1989	4699
Jim McMahon, Brigham Young	1980	4571
Ty Detmer, Brigham Young	1989	4560

COMPLETIONS

	Year	Att	Comp
David Klingler, Houston	1990	643	374
Andre Ware, Houston	1989	578	365
Ty Detmer, Brigham Young	1990	562	361
Robbie Bosco, Brigham Young	1985	511	338
Chris Vargas, Nevada	1993	490	331

TOUCHDOWNS PASSING

	Year	TD
David Klingler, Houston	1990	54
Jim McMahon, Brigham Young	1980	47
Andre Ware, Houston	1989	46
Ty Detmer, Brigham Young	1990	41
Dennis Shaw, San Diego St	1969	39

Receiving

CATCHES

	Year	GP	No.
Emmanuel Hazard, Houston	1989	11	142
Howard Twilley, Tulsa	1965	10	134
Alex Van Dyke, Nevada	1995	11	129
Jason Phillips, Houston	1988	11	108
Fred Gilbert, Houston	1991	11	106

CATCHES PER GAME

	Year	No.	No./Game
Howard Twilley, Tulsa	1965	134	13.4
Emmanuel Hazard, Houston	1989	142	12.9
Alex Van Dyke, Nevada	1995	129	11.7
Jason Phillips, Houston	1988	108	9.8
Chris Penn, Tulsa	1993	105	9.6
Fred Gilbert, Houston	1991	106	9.6

YARDS GAINED

	Year	Yds
Alex Van Dyke, Nevada	1995	1854
Howard Twilley, Tulsa	1965	1779
Emmanuel Hazard, Houston	1989	1689
Aaron Turner, Pacific	1991	1604
Chris Penn, Tulsa	1993	1578

TOUCHDOWN CATCHES

	Year	TD
Emmanuel Hazard, Houston	1989	22
Desmond Howard, Michigan	1991	19
Aaron Turner, Pacific	1991	18
Dennis Smith, Utah	1989	18
Tom Reynolds, San Diego St	1969	18

Single Game

Scoring

POINTS

	Opponent	Year	Pts
Howard Griffith, Illinois	Southern Illinois	1990	48
Marshall Faulk, San Diego St	Pacific	1991	44
Jim Brown, Syracuse	Colgate	1956	43
Showboat Boykin, Mississippi	Mississippi St	1951	42
Fred Wendt, UTEP*	New Mexico St	1948	42

*UTEP was Texas Mines in 1948.

FIELD GOALS

	Opponent	Year	FG
Dale Klein, Nebraska	Missouri	1985	7
Mike Prindle, Western Michigan	Marshall	1984	7

Note: Klein's distances were 32-22-43-44-29-43-43.
Prindle's distances were 32-44-42-23-48-41-27.

Single Game *(Cont.)*

Total Offense

YARDS GAINED	Opponent	Year	Yds
David Klingler, Houston	Arizona St	1990	732
Matt Vogler, Texas Christian	Houston	1990	696
David Klingler, Houston	Texas Christian	1990	625
Scott Mitchell, Utah	Air Force	1988	625
Jimmy Klingler, Houston	Rice	1992	612

Passing

YARDS GAINED	Opponent	Year	Yds
David Klingler, Houston	Arizona St	1990	716
Matt Vogler, Texas Christian	Houston	1990	690
Scott Mitchell, Utah	Air Force	1988	631
Jeremy Leach, New Mexico	Utah	1989	622
Dave Wilson, Illinois	Ohio St	1980	621

COMPLETIONS	Opponent	Year	Comp
Rusty LaRue, Wake Forest	Duke	1995	55
Rusty LaRue, Wake Forest	NC St	1995	50
David Klingler, Houston	SMU	1990	48
Jimmy Klingler, Houston	Rice	1992	46
Scott Milanovich, Maryland	Florida St	1995	46

TOUCHDOWNS PASSING	Opponent	Year	TD
David Klingler, Houston	E. Wash	1990	11

Note: Klingler's TD passes were 5-48-29-7-3-7-40-10-7-8-51.

Rushing

YARDS GAINED	Opponent	Year	Yds
Tony Sands, Kansas	Missouri	1991	396
Marshall Faulk, San Diego St	Pacific	1991	386
Anthony Thompson, Indiana	Wisconsin	1989	377
Mike Pringle, California St-Fullerton	New Mexico St	1989	357
Rueben Mayes, Washington St	Oregon	1984	357

TOUCHDOWNS RUSHING	Opponent	Year	TD
Howard Griffith, Illinois	Southern Illinois	1990	8

Note: Griffith's TD runs were 5-51-7-41-5-18-5-3.

Receiving

CATCHES	Opponent	Year	No.
Randy Gatewood, UNLV	Idaho	1994	23
Jay Miller, Brigham Young	New Mexico	1973	22
Rick Eber, Tulsa	Idaho St	1967	20
Emmanuel Hazard, Hou	Texas Christian	1989	19
Emmanuel Hazard, Hou	Texas	1989	19
Ron Fair, Arizona St	Washington St	1989	19
Howard Twilley, Tulsa	Colorado St	1965	19

YARDS GAINED	Opponent	Year	Yds
Randy Gatewood, UNLV	Idaho	1994	363
Chuck Hughes, UTEP*	N Texas St	1965	349
Rick Eber, Tulsa	Idaho St	1967	322
Harry Wood, Tulsa	Idaho St	1967	318
Jeff Evans, New Mexico St	Southern IL	1978	316

*UTEP was Texas Western in 1965.

TOUCHDOWN CATCHES	Opponent	Year	TD
Tim Delaney, San Diego St	New Mexico St	1969	6

Note: Delaney's TD catches were 2-22-34-31-30-9.

Longest Plays *(since 1941)*

RUSHING	Opponent	Year	Yds
Gale Sayers, Kansas	Nebraska	1963	99
Max Anderson, Arizona St	Wyoming	1967	99
Ralph Thompson, W Texas St	Wichita St	1970	99
Kelsey Finch, Tennessee	Florida	1977	99

PASSING	Opponent	Year	Yds
Fred Owens to Jack Ford, Portland	St Mary's (CA)	1947	99
Bo Burris to Warren McVea, Houston	Washington St	1966	99
Colin Clapton to Eddie Jenkins, Holy Cross	Boston U	1970	99
Terry Peel to Robert Ford, Houston	Syracuse	1970	99
Terry Peel to Robert Ford, Houston	San Diego St	1972	99
Cris Collinsworth to Derrick Gaffney, Florida	Rice	1977	99
Scott Ankrom to James Maness, Texas Christian	Rice	1984	99
Gino Toretta to Horace Copeland, Miami	Arkansas	1991	99
John Paci to Thomas Lewis, Indiana	Penn St	1993	99

FIELD GOALS	Opponent	Year	Yds
Steve Little, Arkansas	Texas	1977	67
Russell Erxleben, Texas	Rice	1977	67
Joe Williams, Wichita St	Southern IL	1978	67
Tony Franklin, Texas A&M	Baylor	1976	65
Tony Franklin, Texas A&M	Baylor	1976	64
Russell Erxleben, Texas	Oklahoma	1977	64

PUNTS	Opponent	Year	Yds
Pat Brady, Nevada*	Loyola (CA)	1950	99
George O'Brien, Wisconsin	Iowa	1952	96
John Hadl, Kansas	Oklahoma	1959	94
Carl Knox, Texas Christian	Oklahoma	1947	94
Preston Johnson, SMU	Pittsburgh	1940	94

*Nevada was Nevada-Reno in 1950.

DIVISION I-A WINNINGEST TEAMS
Alltime Winning Percentage

	Yrs	W	L	T	Pct	GP	Bowl Record
Notre Dame	107	738	219	42	.760	999	12-8-0
Michigan	116	756	250	36	.743	1,042	13-14-0
Alabama	101	711	241	44	.736	996	27-17-3
Oklahoma	101	670	251	53	.715	974	20-11-1
Texas	103	705	279	33	.709	1,017	17-17-2
Ohio St	106	679	271	53	.703	1,003	13-15-0
Southern Cal	103	647	258	54	.703	959	25-13-0
Nebraska	106	698	290	40	.698	1,028	16-18-0
Penn St	109	695	294	41	.695	1,030	20-10-2
Tennessee	99	655	281	53	.689	989	20-16-0
Florida St	49	335	179	17	.647	531	16-7-2
Central Michigan	95	493	265	36	.644	794	3-2-0
Washington	106	576	318	50	.637	944	12-9-1
Miami (OH)	107	559	315	44	.633	918	5-2-0
Army	106	597	341	51	.629	989	2-1-0
Georgia	102	601	343	54	.629	998	15-14-3
Louisiana St	102	584	336	47	.628	967	12-16-1
Arizona St	83	453	268	24	.624	745	9-5-1
Auburn	103	575	340	47	.622	962	12-10-2
Colorado	106	578	351	36	.618	965	8-12-0
Miami (FL)	69	429	265	19	.615	713	10-11-0
Bowling Green	77	403	251	52	.608	706	2-3-0
Michigan St	99	532	339	44	.605	915	5-7-0
UCLA	77	449	291	37	.602	777	10-9-1
Minnesota	112	561	375	43	.595	979	2-3-0

Note: Includes bowl games.

Alltime Victories

Michigan	756	Georgia	601	N Carolina	563
Notre Dame	738	Syracuse	599	Georgia Tech	562
Alabama	711	Army	597	Arkansas	562
Texas	705	Louisiana St	584	Minnesota	561
Nebraska	698	Colorado	578	Miami (OH)	559
Penn St	695	Washington	576	Navy	554
Ohio St	679	Auburn	575	Rutgers	539
Oklahoma	670	Pittsburgh	571	Clemson	538
Tennessee	655	W Virginia	569	California	536
Southern Cal	647	Texas A&M	568	Michigan St	532

NUMBER ONE VS NUMBER TWO

The number 1 and number 2 teams, according to the Associated Press Poll, have met 30 times, including 11 bowl games, since the poll's inception in 1936. The number 1 teams have a 18-10-2 record in these matchups. Notre Dame (4-3-2) has played in 9 of the games.

Date	Results	Stadium
10-9-43	No. 1 Notre Dame 35, No. 2 Michigan 12	Michigan (Ann Arbor)
11-20-43	No. 1 Notre Dame 14, No. 2 Iowa Pre-Flight 13	Notre Dame (South Bend)
12-2-44	No. 1 Army 23, No. 2 Navy 7	Municipal (Baltimore)
11-10-45	No. 1 Army 48, No. 2 Notre Dame 0	Yankee (New York
12-1-45	No. 1 Army 32, No. 2 Navy 13	Municipal (Philadelphia)
11-9-46	No. 1 Army 0, No. 2 Notre Dame 0	Yankee (New York)
1-1-63	No. 1 Southern Cal 42, No. 2 Wisconsin 37 (Rose Bowl)	Rose Bowl (Pasadena)
10-12-63	No. 2 Texas 28, No. 1 Oklahoma 7	Cotton Bowl (Dallas)
1-1-64	No. 1 Texas 28, No. 2 Navy 6 (Cotton Bowl)	Cotton Bowl (Dallas)
11-19-66	No. 1 Notre Dame 10, No. 2 Michigan St 10	Spartan (East Lansing)
9-28-68	No. 1 Purdue 37, No. 2 Notre Dame 22	Notre Dame (South Bend)
1-1-69	No. 1 Ohio St 27, No. 2 Southern Cal 16 (Rose Bowl)	Rose Bowl (Pasadena)
12-6-69	No. 1 Texas 15, No. 2 Arkansas 14	Razorback (Fayetteville)
11-25-71	No. 1 Nebraska 35, No. 2 Oklahoma 31	Owen Field (Norman)
1-1-72	No. 1 Nebraska 38, No. 2 Alabama 6 (Orange Bowl)	Orange Bowl (Miami)
1-1-79	No. 2 Alabama 14, No. 1 Penn St 7 (Sugar Bowl)	Sugar Bowl (New Orleans)
9-26-81	No. 1 Southern Cal 28, No. 2 Oklahoma 24	Coliseum (Los Angeles)
1-1-83	No. 2 Penn St 27, No. 1 Georgia 23 (Sugar Bowl)	Sugar Bowl (New Orleans)

NUMBER ONE VS NUMBER TWO *(Cont.)*

Date	Results	Stadium
10-19-85	No. 1 Iowa 12, No. 2 Michigan 10	Kinnick (Iowa City)
9-27-86	No. 2 Miami (FL) 28, No. 1 Oklahoma 16	Orange Bowl (Miami)
1-2-87	No. 2 Penn St 14, No. 1 Miami (FL) 10 (Fiesta Bowl)	Fiesta Bowl (Tempe)
11-21-87	No. 2 Oklahoma 17, No. 1 Nebraska 7	Memorial (Lincoln)
1-1-88	No. 2 Miami (FL) 20, No. 1 Oklahoma 14 (Orange Bowl)	Orange Bowl (Miami)
11-26-88	No. 1 Notre Dame 27, No. 2 Southern Cal 10	Coliseum (Los Angeles)
9-16-89	No. 1 Notre Dame 24, No. 2 Michigan 19	Michigan (Ann Arbor)
11-16-91	No. 2 Miami (FL) 17, No. 1 Florida St 16	Campbell (Tallahassee)
1-1-93	No. 2 Alabama 34, No. 1 Miami (FL) 13	Superdome (New Orleans)
11-13-93	No. 2 Notre Dame 31, No. 1 Florida St 24	Notre Dame (South Bend)
1-1-94	No. 1 Florida St 18, No. 2 Nebraska 16 (Orange Bowl)	Orange Bowl (Miami)
1-2-96	No. 1 Nebraska 62, No. 2 Florida 24 (Fiesta Bowl)	Sun Devil (Tempe)

Longest Winning Streaks

Wins	Team	Yrs	Ended by	Score
47	Oklahoma	1953-57	Notre Dame	7–0
39	Washington	1908-14	Oregon St	0–0
37	Yale	1890-93	Princeton	6–0
37	Yale	1887-89	Princeton	10–0
35	Toledo	1969-71	Tampa	21–0
34	Pennsylvania	1894-96	Lafayette	6–4
31	Oklahoma	1948-50	Kentucky	13–7
31	Pittsburgh	1914-18	Cleveland Naval Reserve	10–9
31	Pennsylvania	1896-98	Harvard	10–0
30	Texas	1968-70	Notre Dame	24–11
29	Miami (FL)	1990-93	Alabama	34–13
29	Michigan	1901-03	Minnesota	6–6

Longest Unbeaten Streaks

No.	W	T	Team	Yrs	Ended by	Score
63	59	4	Washington	1907-17	California	27–0
56	55	1	Michigan	1901-05	Chicago	2–0
50	46	4	California	1920-25	Olympic Club	15–0
48	47	1	Oklahoma	1953-57	Notre Dame	7–0
48	47	1	Yale	1885-89	Princeton	10–0
47	42	5	Yale	1879-85	Princeton	6–5
44	42	2	Yale	.1894-96	Princeton	24–6
42	39	3	Yale	1904-08	Harvard	4–0
39	37	2	Notre Dame	1946-50	Purdue	28–14
37	36	1	Oklahoma	1972-75	Kansas	23–3
37	37	0	Yale	1890-93	Princeton	6–0
35	35	0	Toledo	1969-71	Tampa	21–0
35	34	1	Minnesota	1903-05	Wisconsin	16–12
34	33	1	Nebraska	1912-16	Kansas	7–3
34	34	0	Pennsylvania	1894-96	Lafayette	6–4
34	32	2	Princeton	1884-87	Harvard	12–0
34	29	5	Princeton	1877-82	Harvard	1–0
33	30	3	Tennessee	1926-30	Alabama	18–6
33	31	2	Georgia Tech	1914-18	Pittsburgh	32–0
33	30	3	Harvard	1911-15	Cornell	10–0
32	31	1	Nebraska	1969-71	UCLA	20–17
32	30	2	Army	1944-47	Columbia	21–20
32	31	1	Harvard	1898-1900	Yale	28–0
31	30	1	Alabama	1991-93	Louisiana St	17–13
31	30	1	Penn St	1967-70	Colorado	41–13
31	30	1	San Diego St	1967-70	Long Beach St	27–11
31	29	2	Georgia Tech	1950-53	Notre Dame	27–14
31	31	0	Oklahoma	1948-50	Kentucky	13–7
31	31	0	Pittsburgh	1919-22	Cleveland Naval	10–9
31	31	0	Pennsylvania	1896-98	Harvard	10–0

Note: Includes bowl games.

Longest Losing Streaks

Losses		Seasons	Ended Against	Score
44	Columbia	1983-88	Princeton	16–14
34	Northwestern	1979-82	Northern Illinois	31–6
28	Virginia	1958-61	William & Mary	21–6
28	Kansas St	1945-48	Arkansas St	37–6
27	Eastern Michigan	1980-82	Kent St	9–7

Longest Series

GP	Opponents (Series Leader Listed First)	Record	First Game	GP	Opponents (Series Leader Listed First)	Record	First Game
105	Minnesota-Wisconsin	57-40-8	1890	96	Navy-Army	44-45-7	1890
104	Missouri-Kansas	48-47-9	1891	93	Clemson-S Carolina	55-34-4	1896
102	Nebraska-Kansas	78-21-3	1892	93	Kansas-Kansas St	61-27-5	1902
102	Texas Christian-Baylor	47-48-7	1899	93	Oklahoma-Kansas	62-25-6	1903
102	Texas-Texas A&M	65-32-5	1894	93	Utah-Utah St	62-27-4	1892
100	N Carolina-Virginia	55-41-4	1892	92	Louisiana St-Tulane*	63-22-7	1893
100	Miami (OH)-Cincinnati	54-39-7	1888	92	Michigan-Ohio St	52-34-6	1897
99	Auburn-Georgia	47-44-8	1892	92	Mississippi-Miss St	53-33-6	1901
99	Oregon-Oregon St	49-40-10	1894	92	Penn St-Pittsburgh†	47-41-4	1893
98	Purdue-Indiana	59-33-6	1891				
98	Stanford-California	48-39-11	1892				

†Have not met since 1992. *Disputed series record. Tulane claims 23-61-7 record.

NCAA Coaches' Records

ALLTIME WINNINGEST DIVISION I-A COACHES

By Percentage

Coach (Alma Mater)	Colleges Coached	Yrs	W	L	T	Pct
Knute Rockne (Notre Dame '14)†	Notre Dame 1918-30	13	105	12	5	.881
Frank W. Leahy (Notre Dame '31)†	Boston Col 1939-40; Notre Dame 1941-43, 1946-53	13	107	13	9	.864
George W. Woodruff (Yale 1889)†	Pennsylvania 1892-01; Illinois 1903; Carlisle 1905	12	142	25	2	.846
Barry Switzer (Arkansas '60)	Oklahoma 1973-88	16	157	29	4	.837
Percy D. Haughton (Harvard 1899)†	Cornell 1899-1900; Harvard 1908-16; Columbia 1923-24	13	96	17	6	.832
Bob Neyland (Army '16)†	Tennessee 1926-34, 1936-40, 1946-52	21	173	31	12	.829
Fielding (Hurry Up) Yost (Lafayette 1897)†	Ohio Wesleyan 1897; Nebraska 1898; Kansas 1899; Stanford 1900; Michigan 1901-23, 1925-26	29	196	36	12	.828
Tom Osborne (Hastings '59)*	Nebraska 1973-present	23	231	47	3	.827
Bud Wilkinson (Minnesota '37)†	Oklahoma 1947-63	17	145	29	4	.826
Jock Sutherland (Pittsburgh '18)†	Lafayette 1919-23; Pittsburgh 1924-38	20	144	28	14	.812
Bob Devaney (Alma, MI '39)†	Wyoming 1957-61; Nebraska 1962-72	16	136	30	7	.806
Frank W. Thomas (Notre Dame '23)†	Chattanooga 1925-28; Alabama 1931-42, 1944-46	19	141	33	9	.795
Joe Paterno (Brown '50)*	Penn St 1966-present	30	278	72	3	.792
Henry L. Williams (Yale 1891)†	Army 1891; Minnesota 1900-21	23	141	34	12	.786
John Robinson (Oregon '58)*	Southern Cal 1976-82; Southern Cal; 1993-present	10	92	24	4	.783

*Active coach. †Hall of Fame member.

Note: Minimum 10 years as head coach at Division I institutions; record at 4-year colleges only; bowl games included; ties computed as half won, half lost.

ALLTIME WINNINGEST DIVISION I-A COACHES (Cont.)

By Victories

	Yrs	W	L	T	Pct		Yrs	W	L	T	Pct
Paul (Bear) Bryant	38	323	85	17	.780	*LaVell Edwards	24	214	80	3	.726
Glenn (Pop) Warner	44	319	106	32	.733	*Hayden Fry	34	213	161	10	.568
Amos Alonzo Stagg	57	314	199	35	.605	*Lou Holtz	26	208	92	7	.689
*Joe Paterno	30	278	72	3	.792	Jess Neely	40	207	176	19	.539
*Bobby Bowden	30	259	81	4	.759	Warren Woodson	31	203	95	14	.673
Woody Hayes	33	238	72	10	.759	Vince Dooley	25	201	77	10	.715
Bo Schembechler	27	234	65	8	.775	Eddie Anderson	39	201	128	15	.606
*Tom Osborne	23	231	47	3	.827						

Most Bowl Victories

	W	L	T		W	L	T
*Joe Paterno	17	8	1	Terry Donahue	8	4	1
Paul (Bear) Bryant	15	12	2	Barry Switzer	8	5	0
*Bobby Bowden	15	3	1	Darrell Royal	8	7	1
Jim Wacker	13	2	0	Vince Dooley	8	10	2
Don James	10	5	0	*John Robinson	7	1	0
*Lou Holtz	10	8	2	Bob Devaney	7	3	0
John Vaught	10	8	0	Dan Devine	7	3	0
*Tom Osborne	10	13	0	Earle Bruce	7	5	0
Bobby Dodd	9	4	0	Charlie McClendon	7	6	0
*Johnny Majors	9	7	0	*Active coach.			

WINNINGEST ACTIVE DIVISION I-A COACHES
By Percentage

						Bowls		
Coach, College	Yrs	W	L	T	Pct#	W	L	T
Tom Osborne, Nebraska	23	231	47	3	.827	10	13	0
R.C. Slocum, Texas A&M	7	68	15	2	.823	2	4	0
Joe Paterno, Penn St	30	278	72	3	.792	17	8	1
John Robinson, Southern Cal	10	92	24	4	.783	7	1	0
Bobby Bowden, Florida St	30	259	81	4	.759	15	3	1
Steve Spurrier, Florida	9	81	26	2	.752	2	4	0
LaVell Edwards, Brigham Young	24	214	80	3	.726	6	12	1
Danny Ford, Arkansas	14	105	41	5	.712	6	2	0
Lou Holtz, Notre Dame	26	208	92	7	.689	10	8	2
John Cooper, Ohio State	19	146	69	6	.674	3	7	0

#Bowl games included in overall record. Ties computed as half win, half loss.

Note: Minimum 5 years as Division I-A head coach; record at 4-year colleges only.

Hootie & the Blowhards

Because of the stiff sanctions the NCAA has levied against the Alabama football program (*SI*, Aug.14, 1995), Crimson Tide athletic director Cecil (Hootie) Ingram resigned late last summer. As he took his leave he said, "No tradition at Alabama is more cherished than that of winning within the rules."

Hold that line. The Southeastern Conference has been accused again and again of being the nation's cheatingest. There was the 1990 study in which sociologist Allen Sack asked former college football players whether they had received any improper benefits or inducements; this year's survey by the Seattle *Post-Intelligencer* in which college basketball coaches were asked which league is most riddled with improprieties; and the numbing frequency with which SEC schools have been paraded before the NCAA's Committee on Infractions. It would be naive to think that all other SEC teams took liberties with the rules but 'Bama didn't. Most telling, Bear Bryant himself owned up to the Tide's wrongdoing. Bryant liked to say that, while he avoided personal involvement in the purchase of talent, he wasn't reluctant to direct boosters to pay the prevailing rate.

In light of all this, Ingram might have simply said, "No tradition at Alabama is more cherished than that of winning," and left it at that.

WINNINGEST ACTIVE DIVISION I-A COACHES (Cont.)
By Victories

Joe Paterno, Penn St	278	
Bobby Bowden, Florida St	259	
Tom Osborne, Nebraska	231	
LaVell Edwards, Brigham Young	214	
Hayden Fry, Iowa	213	
Lou Holtz, Notre Dame	208	
Jim Sweeney, Fresno St	196	
Johnny Majors, Tennessee, Pitt	181	

Don Nehlen, W Virginia	168
Al Molde, W Michigan	166
Bill Mallory, Indiana	164
Jim Wacker, Minnesota	156
George Welsh, Virginia	153
John Cooper, Ohio St	146
Jackie Sherrill, Mississippi St	133
Jim Hess, New Mexico St	133

WINNINGEST ACTIVE DIVISION I-AA COACHES
By Percentage

Coach, College	Yrs	W	L	T	Pct*
Roy Kidd, Eastern Kentucky	32	266	94	8	.734
Terry Allen, Northern Iowa	7	63	24	0	.724
Eddie Robinson, Grambling	53	402	149	15	.724
Tubby Raymond, Delaware	30	250	97	3	.719
Bobby Keasler, McNeese St	6	53	21	2	.711
Steve Tosches, Princeton	9	61	27	2	.689
Jim Tressel, Youngstown St	10	87	41	2	.677
Houston Markham, Alabama St	9	62	31	5	.658
Cardell Jones, Alcorn St	5	34	18	3	.645
Bill Hayes, N Carolina A&T	20	141	78	2	.643

*Playoff games included.

Note: Minimum 5 years as a Division I-A and/or Division I-AA head coach; record at 4-year colleges only.

By Victories

Eddie Robinson, Grambling	402	
Roy Kidd, Eastern Kentucky	266	
Tubby Raymond, Delaware	250	
Carmen Cozza, Yale	177	
Ron Randleman, Sam Houston St	166	

Bill Bowes, New Hampshire	158
Willie Jeffries, S Carolina St	148
Bill Hayes, N Carolina A&T	141
James Donnelly, Middle Tennessee St	139
Jimmye Laycock, William & Mary	105

WINNINGEST ACTIVE DIVISION II COACHES
By Percentage

Coach, College	Yrs	W	L	T	Pct*
Chuck Broyles, Pittsburg St	6	69	8	2	.886
Peter Yetten, Bentley	8	59	14	1	.804
Rocky Hager, N Dakota St	9	85	21	1	.799
Ken Sparks, Carson-Newman	16	149	40	2	.785
Ron Taylor, Quincy	6	43	15	2	.733
Bob Cortese, Fort Hays St	16	127	45	6	.730
Danny Hale, Bloomsburg	8	62	23	1	.727
Mike Isom, Central Arkansas	6	47	18	4	.710
Gene Carpenter, Millersville	27	184	74	6	.708
Frank Cignetti, Indiana (PA)	14	117	48	1	.708
Tom Hollman, Edinboro	12	85	35	3	.703
Bobby Wallace, N Alabama	8	67	28	1	.703

*Ties computed as half win, half loss. Playoff games included.

Note: Minimum 5 years as a college head coach; record at 4-year colleges only.

By Victories

Jim Malosky, MN-Duluth	243	
Ron Harms, Texas A&M-Kingsville*	186	
Gene Carpenter, Millersville	184	
Dick Lowry, Hillsdale	166	
Willard Bailey, Virginia Union	158	

Bud Elliott, E New Mexico	149
Douglas Porter, Fort Valley St	149
Ken Sparks, Carson-Newman	149
Claire Boroff, NE-Kearney	146
Robert Ford, Albany (NY)	139

*Formerly Texas A&I.

WINNINGEST ACTIVE DIVISION III COACHES
By Percentage

Coach, College	Yrs	W	L	T	Pct*
Ken O'Keefe, Allegheny	6	60	7	1	.890
Dick Farley, Williams	9	60	9	3	.854
Larry Kehres, Mt Union	10	96	16	3	.848
Ron Schipper, Central (IA)	35	280	64	3	.811
John Luckhardt, Washington & Jefferson	14	118	28	2	.804
Vic Clark, Thomas More	6	47	13	0	.783
Roger Harring, WI-LaCrosse	27	232	62	7	.782
Bob Packard, Baldwin-Wallace	15	117	33	2	.776
Pete Schmidt, Albion	13	95	26	4	.776
John Gagliardi, St John's (MN)	47	325	99	11	.760

*Ties computed as half won, half lost. Playoff games included.

Note: Minimum 5 years as a college head coach; record at 4-year colleges only.

By Victories

John Gagliardi, St John's (MN)	325	Don Miller, Trinity (CT)	160
Ron Schipper, Central (IA)	280	Joe McDaniel, Centre	155
Roger Harring, WI-LaCrosse	232	Peter Mazzaferro, Bridgewater (MA)	151
Jim Christopherson, Concordia-M'head	189	Tom Gilburg, Franklin & Marshall	136
Frank Girardi, Lycoming	169	Don Canfield, St Olaf	119

NAIA Coaches' Records

WINNINGEST ACTIVE NAIA COACHES
By Percentage

Coach, College	Yrs	W	L	T	Pct*
Ted Kessinger, Bethany (KS)	20	164	37	1	.814
Gene Nicholson, Westminster (PA)	5	43	12	2	.772
Frosty Westering, Pacific Lutheran	32	242	76	7	.755
Hank Biesiot, Dickinson State, (ND)	20	125	45	1	.734
Dick Strahm, Findlay (OH)	21	152	58	5	.719
Dick Lowry, Hillsdale (MI)	21	166	70	3	.701
Jimmie Keeling, Hardin-Simmons (TX)	6	45	21	0	.682
Rob Smith, Western Washington	7	45	21	1	.679
Bob Petrino, Carroll (MT)	25	143	73	1	.661
Vic Wallace, Lambuth (TN)	15	103	54	5	.651

*Playoff games included.

Note: Minimum five years as a collegiate head coach and includes record against four-year institutions only.

By Victories

Frosty Westering, Pacific Lutheran	242	Bill Ramseyer, Clinch Valley (VA)	141
Dick Lowry, Hillsdale (MI)	166	Hank Biesiot, Dickinson State (ND)	125
Ted Kessinger, Bethany (KS)	164	Larry Wilcox, Benedictine (KS)	106
Dick Strahm, Findlay (OH)	152	Vic Wallace, Lambuth (TN)	103
Bob Petrino, Carroll (MT)	143	Jim Dennison, Walsh (OH)	87

Pro Basketball

JUNE 17, 1996 · $3.50
(CAN. $3.95)

Bull Winner

BARRY GOSSAGE/NBA PHOTOS

A League of Their Own

The rest of the NBA faded to gray as Chicago raced to an unprecedented 72 regular-season wins and its fourth title of the decade

by Phil Taylor

THEY DID not settle for mere dominance, or for simply winning another title. The Chicago Bulls didn't just leave their imprint upon the 1995–96 NBA season, they owned it. The year was theirs, as surely as if they had purchased it as a piece of clay and molded it to their liking. Did anyone else even play? The rest of the teams in the league seemed to fade to gray, as if they were the Washington Generals to the Bulls' Harlem Globetrotters, serving as little more than the canvas on which Chicago painted its masterpiece of a year. The Bulls dispatched all comers with almost frightening efficiency on their way to a record-setting 72–10 regular-season record, and they cruised through the postseason, winning 15 of their 18 games. It became clear almost from the beginning of the season that they were competing more against history than against any current opponent, that Chicago was the only team that mattered.

There were other story lines, to be sure. The legendary Magic Johnson pulled his retired jersey down from the rafters of the Great Western Forum and returned to the Los Angeles Lakers. Denver Nuggets guard Mahmoud Abdul-Rauf, a Muslim, caused a brief national stir when he refused to stand respectfully for the playing of the national anthem, citing religious reasons. All-Star center Alonzo Mourning was traded from the Charlotte Hornets to the Miami Heat, where he and new coach Pat Riley, who himself had bolted from the New York Knicks with a year left on his contract, tried to revitalize a moribund franchise. In other years any one of those developments might have been the most talked-about story of the season, but not in a year when the Bulls were capturing the public's attention in almost every way possible. They were in the sports columns, with Michael Jordan playing with renewed brilliance, and in the gossip columns, with Dennis Rodman becoming a pop-culture icon and hobnobbing with a varied list of celebrities ranging from rock group Pearl Jam to model Cindy Crawford to talk-show host Oprah Winfrey.

On the court Jordan proved again that he has no peer, not just by leading the league in scoring but by restoring to the Bulls the con-

MANNY MILLAN

of the movie *Space Jam*, which he was acting in, to make sure he would be able to work out rigorously and regularly. By the time he returned for the start of the 1995–96 season, he was back in peak basketball condition and ready to reclaim his status as the game's best player. "People were talking about Hakeem [Olajuwon] or Scottie [Pippen] as maybe being the best player in basketball," Jordan said after the Bulls gained a measure of revenge against Orlando by sweeping them in the Eastern Conference finals. "Well, I stopped all that conversation."

But if Jordan, who won his fourth regular-season Most Valuable Player award and his fourth playoff MVP, reestablished himself as the best player in the game, he had new competition for the title of the league's most talked-about player. His eccentric new teammate, the cross-dressing, heavily tattooed Rodman, captured the public's fancy with his ever-changing hair colors and his wild antics, which included head-butting referee Ted Bernhardt. The season began with the Bulls taking the calculated gamble of trading backup center Will Perdue for Rodman, who had worn out his welcome with the San Antonio Spurs with his repeated lateness and insubordination. There were those who thought that he would prove to be a similar distraction for the Bulls, but the

fident swagger they had been missing since he retired after the 1992–93 season. Jordan's return at midseason in 1995 had ended when the Bulls were eliminated by the Orlando Magic in the Eastern Conference semifinals, and he had looked disturbingly mortal in that series, making several late-game miscues. He used that rare failure as motivation the following summer, going so far as to have a gymnasium built on the set

RICHARD MACKSON

crowd favorite, not just at the Bulls' United Center but with fans around the country. Before the season was over Rodman had a raunchy best-selling autobiography on the market, *Bad as I Wanna Be*, for which he appeared on the cover perched nude on a motorcycle with nothing but a strategically placed basketball keeping the shot from being X-rated. He made a much talked-about appearance on *Saturday Night Live* during the playoffs and later signed a deal to appear in his own series on MTV. He was a commercial pitchman for everything from fast food to hotels, and his face even stopped traffic. A 32-foot-high mural of Rodman's head, which was to be repainted every time he changed his hair color, had to be removed from the side of a Chicago building because rubbernecking on the Kennedy Expressway was slowing down the morning commute. But the most memorable off-the-court moment of Rodman's remarkable year came in May, when he arrived for a book-signing at a downtown Chicago bookstore dressed in drag, complete with eyeshadow and lipstick. "Dennis is the only power forward in the league," teammate John Salley said, "who really knows how to accessorize." (The ribald rebounder later announced that he would be married at New York's Rockefeller Center only to turn up on the big day dressed as a blond bride, pen in hand to sign not a marriage license but more copies of his autobiography.)

strong personalities of Jordan, forward Scottie Pippen and coach Phil Jackson helped keep Rodman well behaved, at least by his standards. Jackson in particular seemed to develop a rapport with Rodman, one that may have started before the Bulls made the trade, on the day that Rodman saw Jackson arrive on a motorcycle to meet with him. It was exactly the right sign to the rebellious Rodman that he had found a coach who would understand him.

He rewarded Jackson and the Bulls with an inspired performance that lasted the entire season. Rodman led the league with 14.9 rebounds per game and quickly became a

By January the season had become little more than a search for a serious challenger to the Bulls, and when Johnson came out of retirement to rejoin the Lakers, it appeared that they might fit that description. Johnson, who had retired before the 1991–92 season when he discovered he was HIV-positive, returned on Jan. 30 and quickly showed that he was still capable of being an impact player despite his 3½-year layoff. A few things were different—he was a 250-pound power forward instead of the 220-pound point guard he had been in his previous incarnation—but a great many things were exactly the same. Johnson brought his infectious smile and his creative passing to the Lakers who, initially at least, benefited from both. Los Angeles, 24–18 when Johnson returned, went 29–11 the rest of the way to finish with 53 wins, but by the later stages of the regular season, it was clear that Johnson's return was not going as smoothly as it appeared on the surface.

Laker forward Cedric Ceballos, the team's leading scorer and co-captain, abruptly left the team without notice and did not return until four days later, after being spotted waterskiing in the resort town of Lake Havasu, Ariz. He apologized for going AWOL and said it was due to an unspecified family crisis, but Lakers players acknowledged that it was far more likely that Ceballos had left because

Unhappy campers: The Three J's couldn't make it work in the Big D.

he was unhappy that Johnson's return had cut into his playing time.

Ceballos played well and without incident after his return, but there were still problems in the Lakers' locker room stemming from Johnson's return. Ultimately it was Johnson himself who was the most unhappy, especially during the Lakers' first-round playoff loss to the Houston Rockets. Immediately after that series, Johnson said publicly what he had been hinting at for weeks—that he was not satisfied being a sixth man and playing most of his minutes at power forward. He wanted to return to his point guard position for nearly half the time and be free to run the Lakers' offense again. The Lakers were not willing to take the reins away from their fine young point guard, Nick Van Exel, which was the main reason that Johnson decided during the off-season to end his experiment and retire once again.

The Lakers weren't the only team with unhappy players. Portland Trail Blazers guard Rod Strickland, who had been at odds with coach P.J. Carlesimo for more than a year, left the team without permission in February when the Blazers didn't comply with his demand to be traded. Strickland, one of the top point guards in the league, eventually

PHIL HUBER

DAVID WALBERG

returned to help lead Portland into the play-offs, but his disdain for Carlesimo never lessened, and the Blazers traded him to the Washington Bullets after the season. The Dallas Mavericks, considered one of the most promising young teams in the league at the start of the season, saw their hopes fall apart, mostly due to friction among their three stars: point guard Jason Kidd, shooting guard Jim Jackson and small forward Jamal Mashburn. "These guys are known as the Three J's, but it's the fourth J that could bring them down—jealousy," said Dallas coach Dick Motta, who resigned after the season. Jackson and Mashburn were the primary combatants during the season, arguing mostly over each other's shot selection, but Kidd and Jackson became the main event during the off-season, with Kidd threatening to sit out the following year unless Jackson

Summer Blockbusters

The summer of 1996 may be remembered as the first time the NBA off-season was more entertaining than the regular season. It was as if some of the best players in the league were playing an expensive game of musical chairs, and when the music stopped there were dozens of famous faces in new places.

It was the summer of free agents, the most volatile summer in NBA history in terms of player movement. Center Shaquille O'Neal left the Orlando Magic to sign a seven-year, $121 million contract with the Los Angeles Lakers. Another of the league's top centers, Dikembe Mutombo, waved goodbye to the Denver Nuggets when the Atlanta Hawks lured him with a five-year, $50 million deal. Forward Juwan Howard bolted from the Washington Bullets to sign with the Miami Heat, but when the NBA ruled that the Heat had exceeded its salary cap to sign him, Howard returned to the Bullets, signing a seven-year contract worth $105 million.

Some major moves took place the old-fashioned way, by trades. The Phoenix Suns sent Charles Barkley to the Houston Rockets for four players, including guard Sam Cassell and forward Robert Horry, and the Charlotte Hornets traded Larry Johnson to the New York Knicks for Anthony Mason and Brad Lohaus. "Almost every team in the league has had a big-time shake-up except the Bulls," Barkley said. "There's going to be a lot of fans buying programs next season so they know who to root for."

But will the fans be rooting as loudly as always or will they begin to resent the truckloads of money that players are now earning? Even in the megabucks world of professional sports, some of the numbers are mind-boggling. In addition to the dollars O'Neal, Howard and Mutombo commanded, several teams paid dearly to retain their stars. The Seattle SuperSonics re-signed guard Gary Payton for seven years and $85 million. Center Alonzo Mourning agreed to stay with the Miami

was traded, a move Motta's replacement, Jim Cleamons, refused to make.

But although there were players who were at odds with coaches and with each other, there was still a generous amount of rancor left to be aimed at its usual target, the referees. The antagonism went even further than in most other years, with three players—Rodman, Van Exel and Johnson—all being suspended in the space of four weeks for bumping referees. Rodman's head bump of Bernhardt was hardly out of the ordinary for him, but Van Exel's forearm that knocked Ronnie Garretson onto the scorer's table was more troubling, and when the always cheerful Johnson lost his temper and chest-bumped Scott Foster, it was almost mind-boggling. Was it an epidemic? "I don't think so," Johnson said after the season. "I think it was three isolated cases that just happened to come up in a short space of time. I don't think refs are going to

have to start wearing flak jackets or anything." Even so, league officials were poised to come down hard on future offenders.

Most of the unhappiness in Denver came not from the players but from the fans, and it was directed at Abdul-Rauf, who gave radio talk-show hosts days worth of fodder when it came to the public's attention that he was not standing at attention for the national anthem, as is required under the standard players' contract. Abdul-Rauf, who changed his name from Chris Jackson when he became a Muslim, contended that the American flag was a "symbol of tyranny and oppression," and as such, his faith would not allow him to pay respect to it. Abdul-Rauf's stand—or refusal to stand—quickly became a national issue, with some people arguing that he should be allowed to do as he wished during the anthem under his right to freedom of expression, and many others branding him unpatriotic. Abdul-Rauf finally reached a compromise with the league, agreeing to stand

BILL FRAKES

The Real Deal got one from the Lakers: $121 million for seven years.

years, $35 million from Seattle) and P.J. Brown (five years, $37 million from Miami) became awfully wealthy as well. "Players are getting what the market will bear," McIlvaine said. "It's up to us now to earn our money, to show that we're worth the investment teams made in us. If we don't, I'm sure the fans will let us know about it."

But before they can boo or cheer anyone, the fans will have to reacquaint themselves with a dramatically different league, in which several teams have given themselves major makeovers. Free agency now appears to be the fastest, most effective way to rebuild in the NBA, so the summer of '96 could become the norm. Perhaps fans shouldn't spend too much money on scorecards in this new, free-spending NBA. By next summer they probably won't be worth the paper they're printed on.

Heat for $105 million over seven years. Money was tossed around so freely that when the Chicago Bulls re-signed Michael Jordan for $30 million for one season, it was considered a bargain.

And it wasn't just stars who broke the bank in the summer of '96. Lesser-known free agents such as Jim McIlvaine (seven

LOU CAPOZZOLA

opponents almost as easily, defeating the New York Knicks in five games before sweeping Orlando to advance to the NBA Finals against the Seattle SuperSonics, who despite losing to the Bulls in six games, finally shed their tag as underachievers. The Sonics had suffered upset losses in the first round of the playoffs the previous two years after compiling gaudy regular-season records. They atoned for those failures by defeating the Sacramento Kings in the first round, then sweeping the defending champion Houston Rockets, and finally outlasting the persistent Utah Jazz in a tense seven-game series.

But in a sense the Sonics' finest hour came against the Bulls. After losing the first three games of the series, it was widely assumed Seattle would go quietly in Game 4, but the Sonics fought back to win the next two games to send the series back to Chicago and give the Bulls the closest thing to a real scare they had experienced all season. Chicago was up to the task, however, and they wrapped up the title with an 87–75 Game 6 victory that put the championship trophy back in Jordan's arms.

The rest of the league had to settle for other, lesser rewards. Damon Stoudamire, the 5'10" point guard who was booed on draft night in Toronto when the Raptors announced they had chosen him with the ninth pick, changed those boos to cheers with a solid first year that earned him the Rookie of the Year award. One of Stoudamire's closest challengers was nine years older than he was, 31-year-old Lithuanian center Arvydas Sabonis of Portland, a longtime international star who finally made his way to the NBA. Seattle point guard Gary Payton was voted Defensive Player of the Year and led an All-Defensive team that was otherwise dominated by Bulls—Jordan, Rodman and Pippen.

But then, everything was dominated by Chicago in the '95–96 season. The championship trophy that Jordan cradled in his arms on that June night represented an entire year, a year the Bulls grabbed hold of from the opening tip-off, and never let go.

and pray during the anthem. But he remained a controversial figure in Denver, and the Nuggets traded him to the Sacramento Kings in June.

But that was a minor trade compared to the deal that sent Mourning from Charlotte to Miami early in the season. Mourning, a two–time All-Star, was to become a free agent following the season, and negotiations had broken down with the Hornets over a new contract. When Hornets owner George Shinn became convinced he would not be able to meet Mourning's contract demands, he traded him to the Heat for swingman Glen Rice, guard Khalid Reeves and center Matt Geiger. It was a blockbuster deal that, in the short run at least, didn't do a great deal for either team. The Hornets finished 41–41 and missed the playoffs, and after an impressive start with Mourning, the Heat simmered to a 42–40 finish. Miami reached the playoffs but were quickly swept by the Bulls.

Chicago finished off its other postseason

FOR THE RECORD·1995-1996

NBA Final Standings

Eastern Conference

ATLANTIC DIVISION

Team	W	L	Pct	GB
Orlando	60	22	.732	—
New York	47	35	.573	13
Miami	42	40	.512	18
Washington	39	43	.476	21
Boston	33	49	.402	27
New Jersey	30	52	.366	30
Philadelphia	18	64	.220	42

CENTRAL DIVISION

Team	W	L	Pct	GB
Chicago	72	10	.878	—
Indiana	52	30	.634	20
Cleveland	47	35	.573	25
Atlanta	46	36	.561	26
Detroit	46	36	.561	26
Charlotte	41	41	.500	31
Milwaukee	25	57	.305	47
Toronto	21	61	.256	51

Western Conference

MIDWEST DIVISION

Team	W	L	Pct	GB
San Antonio	59	23	.720	—
Utah	55	27	.671	4
Houston	48	34	.585	11
Denver	35	47	.427	24
Minnesota	26	56	.317	33
Dallas	26	56	.317	33
Vancouver	15	67	.183	44

PACIFIC DIVISION

Team	W	L	Pct	GB
Seattle	64	18	.780	—
LA Lakers	53	29	.646	11
Portland	44	38	.537	20
Phoenix	41	41	.500	23
Sacramento	39	43	.476	25
Golden State	36	46	.439	28
LA Clippers	29	53	.354	35

1996 NBA Playoffs

EASTERN CONFERENCE | WESTERN CONFERENCE

1st ROUND | SEMIFINALS | FINALS | FINALS | SEMIFINALS | 1st ROUND

NBA FINALS

CHICAGO (4-2)

Eastern Conference:
- Chicago / Miami → Chicago (3-0)
- Cleveland / New York → New York (3-0)
- Chicago (4-1)
- Orlando / Detroit → Orlando (3-0)
- Indiana / Atlanta → Atlanta (3-2)
- Orlando (4-1)
- Chicago (4-0)

Western Conference:
- Seattle / Sacramento → Seattle (3-1)
- LA Lakers / Houston → Houston (3-1)
- Seattle (4-0)
- San Antonio / Phoenix → San Antonio (3-1)
- Utah / Portland → Utah (3-2)
- Utah (4-2)
- Seattle (4-3)

1996 NBA Playoff Results

Eastern Conference First Round

Apr 26	Miami	85	at Chicago	102
Apr 28	Miami	75	at Chicago	106
May 1	Chicago	112	at Miami	91

Chicago won series 3–0.

Apr 26	Detroit	92	at Orlando	112
Apr 28	Detroit	77	at Orlando	92
Apr 30	Orlando	101	at Detroit	98

Orlando won series 3–0.

Apr 25	Atlanta	92	at Indiana	80
Apr 27	Atlanta	94	at Indiana	102*
Apr 29	Indiana	83	at Atlanta	90
May 2	Indiana	83	at Atlanta	75
May 5	Atlanta	89	at Indiana	87

Atlanta won series 3–2.

Apr 25	New York	106	at Cleveland	83
Apr 27	New York	84	at Cleveland	80
May 1	Cleveland	76	at New York	81

New York won series 3–0.

Western Conference First Round

Apr 26	Sacramento	85	at Seattle	97
Apr 28	Sacramento	90	at Seattle	81
Apr 30	Seattle	96	at Sacramento	89
May 2	Seattle	101	at Sacramento	87

Seattle won series 3–1.

Apr 26	Phoenix	98	at San Antonio	120
Apr 28	Phoenix	105	at San Antonio	110
May 1	San Antonio	93	at Phoenix	94
May 3	San Antonio	116	at Phoenix	98

San Antonio won series 3–1.

Apr 25	Portland	102	at Utah	110
Apr 27	Portland	90	at Utah	105
Apr 29	Utah	91	at Portland	94*
May 1	Utah	90	at Portland	98
May 5	Portland	64	at Utah	102

Utah won series 3–2.

Apr 25	Houston	87	at LA Lakers	83
Apr 27	Houston	94	at LA Lakers	104
Apr 30	LA Lakers	98	at Houston	104
May 2	LA Lakers	94	at Houston	102

Houston won series 3–1.

Eastern Conference Semifinals

May 5	New York	84	at Chicago	91
May 7	New York	80	at Chicago	91
May 11	Chicago	99	at New York	102*
May 12	Chicago	94	at New York	91
May 14	New York	81	at Chicago	94

Chicago won series 4–1.

May 8	Atlanta	105	at Orlando	117
May 10	Atlanta	94	at Orlando	120
May 12	Orlando	103	at Atlanta	96
May 13	Orlando	99	at Atlanta	104
May 15	Atlanta	88	at Orlando	96

Orlando won series 4–1.

Western Conference Semifinals

May 4	Houston	75	at Seattle	108
May 6	Houston	101	at Seattle	105
May 10	Seattle	115	at Houston	112
May 12	Seattle	114	at Houston	107*

Seattle won series 4–0.

May 7	Utah	95	at San Antonio	75
May 9	Utah	77	at San Antonio	88
May 11	San Antonio	75	at Utah	105
May 12	San Antonio	86	at Utah	101
May 14	Utah	87	at San Antonio	98
May 16	San Antonio	81	at Utah	108

Utah won series 4–2.

Eastern Conference Finals

May 19	Orlando	83	at Chicago	121
May 21	Orlando	88	at Chicago	93
May 25	Chicago	86	at Orlando	67
May 27	Chicago	106	at Orlando	101

Chicago won series 4–0.

Western Conference Finals

May 18	Utah	72	at Seattle	102
May 20	Utah	87	at Seattle	91
May 24	Seattle	76	at Utah	96
May 26	Seattle	88	at Utah	86
May 28	Utah	98	at Seattle	95*
May 30	Seattle	83	at Utah	118
June 2	Utah	86	at Seattle	90

Seattle won series 4–3.

Finals

June 5	Seattle	90	at Chicago	107
June 7	Seattle	88	at Chicago	92
June 9	Chicago	108	at Seattle	86
June 12	Chicago	86	at Seattle	107

| June 14 | Chicago | 78 | at Seattle | 89 |
| June 16 | Seattle | 75 | at Chicago | 87 |

Chicago won series 4–2.

*Overtime game.

NBA Finals Composite Box Score

CHICAGO BULLS

Player	GP	Field Goals		3-Pt FG		Free Throws		Rebounds		A	Stl	TO	BS	Avg	Hi
		FGM	Pct	FGM	FGA	FTM	Pct	Off	Total						
Jordan	6	51	41.5	6	19	56	83.6	10	32	25	10	18	1	27.3	36
Pippen	6	34	34.3	9	39	17	70.8	20	49	32	14	11	8	15.7	21
Kukoc	6	30	42.3	10	32	8	80.0	12	29	21	5	11	2	13.0	18
Longley	6	27	57.4	0	0	16	72.7	8	23	13	3	15	11	11.7	19
Rodman	6	17	48.6	0	0	11	57.9	41	88	15	5	11	1	7.5	10
Harper	6	12	37.5	4	13	11	91.7	4	13	10	4	3	2	6.5	15
Kerr	6	10	30.3	4	22	6	85.7	2	5	5	1	4	0	5.0	8
Brown	6	6	50.0	3	6	2	50.0	1	2	5	4	3	0	2.8	9
Wennington	6	8	66.7	0	0	1	50.0	2	3	1	0	2	0	2.8	6
Buechler	6	2	22.2	0	6	0	00.0	0	0	1	4	2	0	0.7	2
Salley	5	0	00.0	0	0	0	—	1	1	2	0	0	0	0.0	0
Total	6	197	41.6	36	137	128	75.7	101	245	130	50	80	25	93.0	108

SEATTLE SUPERSONICS

Player	GP	Field Goals		3-Pt FG		Free Throws		Rebounds		A	Stl	TO	BS	Avg	Hi
		FGM	Pct	FGM	FGA	FTM	Pct	Off	Total						
Kemp	6	49	55.1	0	1	42	85.7	26	60	13	8	24	12	23.3	32
Payton	6	40	44.4	9	27	19	73.1	6	38	42	9	15	0	18.0	23
Schrempf	6	35	44.3	7	18	21	87.5	9	30	15	3	16	1	16.3	23
Hawkins	6	25	45.5	6	22	24	92.3	7	21	6	7	12	1	13.3	21
Perkins	6	23	37.7	4	17	17	81.0	9	28	12	3	10	0	11.2	17
McMillan	4	3	42.9	3	5	2	100.0	0	11	6	2	3	0	2.8	8
Wingate	6	5	50.0	1	2	4	100.0	1	2	0	0	3	0	2.5	5
Askew	4	2	22.2	1	5	2	100.0	0	10	2	2	8	0	1.8	5
Johnson	3	2	33.3	0	0	0	—	6	7	1	1	0	1	1.3	2
Brickowski	6	2	22.2	1	5	0	—	2	12	3	1	4	1	0.8	5
Snow		0	00.0	0	0	0	—	0	2	1	0	1	0	0.0	0
Scheffler	4	0	00.0	0	0	0	—	1	2	0	0	0	0	0.0	0
Total	6	186	44.5	32	102	131	85.1	67	223	101	36	96	16	89.2	107

NBA Finals Box Scores

Game 1

SEATTLE 90

SEATTLE	Min	FG M-A	FT M-A	Reb O-T	A	PF	S	TO	TP
Kemp	41	9-14	14-16	5-8	2	6	2	7	32
Schrempf	35	3-8	6-6	3-8	3	4	1	2	13
Johnson	9	1-2	0-0	0-0	0	1	1	0	2
Hawkins	35	2-9	5-5	0-3	1	2	0	1	9
Payton	47	6-17	1-4	2-10	6	5	1	3	13
Perkins	37	5-14	1-1	4-5	2	3	1	3	14
McMillan	6	0-0	0-0	0-1	1	0	0	0	0
Askew	25	1-4	2-2	0-6	1	4	0	1	5
Brickowski	2	0-0	0-0	0-0	0	2	0	0	0
Wingate	2	0-0	2-2	0-0	0	2	0	0	2
Snow	1	0-0	0-0	0-0	0	0	0	0	0
Totals	240	27-68	31-36	14-41	16	29	6	17	90

Percentages: FG—.397, FT—.861. 3-pt goals: 5-16, .313 (Schrempf 1-2, Hawkins 0-3, Payton 0-3, Perkins 3-5, Askew 1-3). Team rebounds: 9. Blocked shots: 2 (Kemp, Johnson).

CHICAGO 107

CHICAGO	Min	FG M-A	FT M-A	Reb O-T	A	PF	S	TO	TP
Pippen	44	5-15	8-9	5-7	3	3	3	0	21
Rodman	36	3-6	1-2	3-13	2	5	1	2	7
Longley	26	5-12	4-5	1-1	1	4	0	1	14
Harper	30	6-10	2-2	3-5	7	4	2	1	15
Jordan	41	9-18	9-10	0-7	2	4	2	2	28
Kerr	12	0-5	0-0	0-0	0	0	0	0	0
Kukoc	27	7-13	2-3	3-4	4	3	1	0	18
Brown	3	0-1	0-0	0-0	0	0	0	0	0
Wennington	10	2-2	0-0	2-3	0	0	0	0	4
Buechler	9	0-4	0-0	0-0	1	2	0	1	0
Salley	2	0-0	0-0	0-0	0	2	0	0	0
Totals	240	37-86	26-31	17-40	20	27	9	7	107

Percentages: FG—.430, FT—.839. 3-pt goals: 7-26, .269 (Pippen 3-8, Harper 1-3, Jordan 1-4, Kerr 0-3, Kukoc 2-5, Buechler 0-3). Team rebounds: 10. Blocked shots: 9 (Longley 4, Pippen 3, Harper, Jordan). A: 24,544. Officials: J. Crawford, D. Crawford, Salvatore.

Game 2

SEATTLE 88

SEATTLE	Min	FG M-A	FT M-A	Reb O-T	A	PF	S	TO	TP
Kemp	40	8-18	13-16	8-13	2	3	1	3	29
Schrempf	41	5-14	4-4	1-2	3	5	0	2	15
Johnson	8	1-4	0-0	6-7	1	5	0	0	2
Hawkins	39	6-11	3-5	0-2	0	5	2	3	16
Payton	45	6-15	0-0	0-5	3	5	1	1	13
Perkins	33	5-10	3-4	1-4	0	3	0	3	13
Askew	22	0-1	0-0	0-4	1	3	2	4	0
Wingate	5	0-0	0-0	0-1	0	1	0	0	0
Brickowski	5	0-1	0-0	0-1	0	0	0	0	0
Snow	2	0-1	0-0	0-0	0	0	0	0	0
Totals	240	31-75	23-29	16-39	10	30	6	16	88

Percentages: FG—.413, FT—.793. 3-pt goals: 3-15, .200 (Kemp 0-1, Schrempf 1-3, Hawkins 1-5, Payton 1-4, Perkins 0-1, Askew 0-1). Team rebounds: 7. Blocked shots: 4 (Kemp 4).

CHICAGO 92

CHICAGO	Min	FG M-A	FT M-A	Reb O-T	A	PF	S	TO	TP
Pippen	38	8-16	5-8	3-7	2	3	2	3	21
Rodman	42	3-6	4-6	11-20	0	4	0	4	10
Longley	25	1-5	0-1	0-3	5	2	3	2	2
Harper	33	2-8	7-8	1-4	1	2	0	0	12
Jordan	43	9-22	10-16	2-6	8	3	2	2	29
Kukoc	24	4-12	1-2	3-5	5	2	0	1	11
Wennington	2	0-0	0-0	0-0	0	0	0	0	0
Buechler	5	1-1	0-0	0-0	0	1	2	0	2
Salley	7	0-0	0-0	0-0	1	4	0	0	0
Kerr	13	1-6	1-1	0-0	0	2	0	0	3
Brown	8	1-1	0-0	0-0	2	1	2	2	2
Totals	240	30-77	28-42	20-45	22	27	10	15	92

Percentages: FG—.390, FT—.667. 3-pt goals: 4-21, .190 (Pippen 0-4, Harper 1-4, Jordan 1-2, Kukoc 2-7, Kerr 0-4). Team rebounds: 20. Blocked shots: 5 (Pippen 2, Longley 2, Kukoc).
A: 24,544. Officials: E. T. Rush, Kersey, Hollins.

Game 3

CHICAGO 108

CHICAGO	Min	FG M-A	FT M-A	Reb O-T	A	PF	S	TO	TP
Pippen	40	5-14	1-3	2-8	9	3	3	0	12
Rodman	31	1-3	3-6	3-10	2	5	1	2	5
Longley	28	8-13	3-4	2-3	2	5	0	2	19
Kukoc	37	4-11	5-5	1-7	7	3	1	0	14
Jordan	41	11-23	11-11	2-3	5	1	2	3	36
Kerr	25	3-4	1-1	0-2	2	2	1	1	8
Harper	1	0-0	0-0	0-0	0	0	0	0	0
Wennington	15	3-4	0-0	0-0	1	4	0	0	6
Brown	10	2-2	1-2	0-0	0	3	0	1	6
Buechler	8	1-2	0-0	0-0	0	1	1	0	2
Salley	4	0-0	0-0	0-0	0	2	0	0	0
Totals	240	38-76	25-34	10-33	28	29	9	9	108

Percentages: FG—.500, FT—.735. 3-pt goals: 7-15, .467 (Pippen 1-4, Kukoc 1-3, Jordan 3-4, Kerr 1-2, Brown 1-1, Buechler 0-1). Team rebounds: 13. Blocked shots: 2 (Longley 2).

SEATTLE 86

SEATTLE	Min	FG M-A	FT M-A	Reb O-T	A	PF	S	TO	TP
Kemp	42	6-6	6-6	1-4	0	5	0	5	14
Schrempf	41	7-15	5-6	1-5	3	3	0	3	20
Johnson	3	0-0	0-0	0-0	0	0	0	0	0
Hawkins	40	2-6	7-7	0-1	2	4	1	2	12
Payton	45	7-15	5-6	2-7	9	2	3	3	19
Perkins	27	2-4	5-6	1-6	0	2	0	1	9
Askew	10	1-3	0-0	0-0	0	3	0	3	2
Brickowski	14	2-4	0-0	2-7	0	5	0	2	5
Wingate	12	2-5	0-0	0-0	0	3	0	1	5
Scheffler	3	0-0	0-0	0-0	0	0	0	0	0
Snow	3	0-1	0-0	0-2	0	2	0	0	0
Totals	240	27-60	28-31	7-32	14	29	3	20	86

Percentages: FG—.450, FT—.903. 3-pt goals: 4-16, .250 (Schrempf 1-5, Hawkins 1-3, Payton 0-3, Perkins 0-1, Askew 0-1, Brickowski 1-2, Wingate 1-1). Team rebounds: 5. Blocked shots: 4 (Kemp 4).
A: 17,072. Officials: Evans, Bavetta, Javie.

Game 4

CHICAGO 86

CHICAGO	Min	FG M-A	FT M-A	Reb O-T	A	PF	S	TO	TP
Pippen	40	4-17	0-0	3-11	8	5	1	3	9
Rodman	41	4-6	0-0	8-14	4	5	0	1	8
Longley	25	5-8	2-2	1-3	3	5	0	1	12
Harper	13	1-3	0-0	0-1	0	1	0	0	2
Jordan	38	6-19	11-13	1-3	2	3	1	4	23
Kukoc	30	6-11	0-0	0-1	1	3	1	6	14
Kerr	22	1-6	2-2	1-1	1	0	0	1	5
Wennington	7	2-4	0-0	0-0	0	1	0	0	4
Buechler	7	0-1	0-0	0-0	0	0	1	1	0
Salley	1	0-0	0-0	0-0	1	0	0	0	0
Brown	8	3-5	1-2	1-2	1	2	0	1	7
Totals	240	32-80	16-19	15-36	22	24	5	17	86

Percentages: FG—.400, FT—.842. 3-pt goals: 6-24, .250 (Pippen 1-8, Harper 0-1, Jordan 0-2, Kukoc 2-5, Kerr 1-4, Buechler 0-1, Brown 2-3). Team rebounds: 10. Blocked shots: 3 (Pippen 2, Longley).

SEATTLE 107

SEATTLE	Min	FG M-A	FT M-A	Reb O-T	A	PF	S	TO	TP
Kemp	33	12-17	1-1	3-11	3	4	2	1	25
Schrempf	42	6-13	1-2	2-5	3	1	1	2	14
Brickowski	16	0-0	0-0	0-2	0	5	1	2	0
Hawkins	37	6-9	4-4	3-6	2	3	1	1	18
Payton	44	9-16	0-3	0-3	11	4	2	2	21
Wingate	17	1-2	2-2	0-0	0	3	0	1	4
Perkins	33	7-13	2-2	0-3	3	2	0	2	17
McMillan	14	2-3	2-2	0-3	3	2	0	1	8
Scheffler	3	0-1	0-0	1-2	0	0	0	1	0
Snow	1	0-0	0-0	0-0	0	0	0	1	0
Totals	240	41-73	16-19	9-35	25	24	7	13	107

Percentages: FG—.562, FT—.842. 3-pt goals: 9-17, .529 (Schrempf 1-2, Hawkins 2-3, Payton 3-6, Perkins 1-3, McMillan 2-3). Team rebounds: 5. Blocked shots: 1 (Kemp).
A: 17,072. Officials: Mathis, J. Crawford, Oakes.

Game 5

CHICAGO 78

CHICAGO	Min	FG M-A	FT M-A	Reb O-T	A	PF	S	TO	TP
Pippen	44	5-20	3-4	5-8	5	4	1	2	14
Rodman	37	2-5	2-2	5-12	2	5	0	2	6
Longley	34	3-3	5-7	0-5	4	4	0	2	11
Kukoc	37	5-13	0-0	2-9	3	3	1	2	11
Jordan	43	11-22	4-5	2-4	1	3	1	2	26
Wennington	6	1-2	1-2	0-0	0	2	0	2	3
Harper	1	0-0	0-0	0-0	0	0	0	0	0
Kerr	24	2-8	2-3	0-1	2	3	0	1	7
Brown	10	0-2	0-0	0-0	1	3	0	0	0
Salley	1	0-1	0-0	1-1	0	0	0	0	0
Buechler	3	0-1	0-0	0-0	0	0	0	0	0
Totals	240	29-77	17-23	15-40	18	27	3	13	78

Percentages: FG—.377, FT—.739. 3-pt goals: 3-26, .115 (Pippen 1-8, Kukoc 1-5, Jordan 0-4, Kerr 1-7, Brown 0-1, Buechler 0-1). Team rebounds: 11. Blocked shots: 2 (Pippen, Longley).

SEATTLE 89

SEATTLE	Min	FG M-A	FT M-A	Reb O-T	A	PF	S	TO	TP
Kemp	46	8-16	6-8	3-10	3	4	0	4	22
Schrempf	39	5-12	2-2	1-5	1	2	0	2	13
Brickowski	17	0-1	0-0	0-2	3	3	0	0	0
Hawkins	38	7-14	5-5	3-5	1	3	1	2	21
Payton	46	7-18	7-8	2-9	6	3	1	1	23
Perkins	28	1-6	5-6	0-4	2	3	1	0	7
McMillan	21	1-1	0-0	0-6	2	4	1	1	3
Wingate	3	0-1	0-0	0-0	0	1	0	0	0
Scheffler	1	0-0	0-0	0-0	0	0	0	0	0
Snow	1	0-0	0-0	0-0	0	0	0	0	0
Totals	240	29-69	25-29	9-41	17	23	4	10	89

Percentages: FG—.420, FT—.862. 3-pt goals: 6-14, .429 (Schrempf 1-1, Brickowski 0-1, Hawkins 2-4, Payton 2-6, McMillan 1-1, Wingate 0-1). Team rebounds: 6. Blocked shots: 2 (Schrempf, Hawkins). A: 17,072. Officials: E.T. Rush, Kersey, Hollins.

Game 6

SEATTLE 75

SEATTLE	Min	FG M-A	FT M-A	Reb O-T	A	PF	S	TO	TP
Kemp	40	8-17	2-2	6-14	3	6	3	4	18
Schrempf	40	9-17	3-4	1-5	2	3	1	5	23
Brickowski	14	0-3	0-0	0-0	1	1	0	0	0
Hawkins	41	2-6	0-0	1-4	0	4	2	3	4
Payton	47	7-10	2-2	0-4	7	3	2	5	19
Perkins	32	3-14	1-2	3-6	5	0	1	1	7
McMillan	10	0-3	0-0	0-1	0	0	1	1	0
Wingate	9	2-2	0-0	1-1	0	3	0	1	4
Askew	5	0-1	0-0	0-0	0	0	0	0	0
Scheffler	1	0-0	0-0	0-0	0	0	0	0	0
Snow	1	0-0	0-0	0-0	1	0	0	0	0
Totals	240	31-73	8-10	12-35	19	20	10	20	75

Percentages: FG—.425, FT—.800. 3-pt goals: 5-24, .208 (Schrempf 2-5, Brickowski 0-2, Hawkins 0-4, Payton 3-5, Perkins 0-7, McMillan 0-1). Team rebounds: 8. Blocked shots: 3 (Kemp 2, Brickowski).

CHICAGO 87

CHICAGO	Min	FG M-A	FT M-A	Reb O-T	A	PF	S	TO	TP
Pippen	42	7-17	0-0	2-8	5	4	4	3	17
Rodman	38	4-9	1-3	11-19	5	4	3	0	9
Longley	32	5-6	2-3	4-8	0	0	1	6	12
Harper	38	3-11	2-2	0-3	2	1	2	2	10
Jordan	43	5-19	11-12	3-9	7	3	2	5	22
Kukoc	22	4-11	0-0	3-3	1	0	1	2	10
Kerr	17	3-4	0-0	1-1	0	1	0	1	7
Buechler	1	0-0	0-0	0-0	0	0	0	0	0
Wennington	2	0-0	0-0	0-0	0	0	0	0	0
Brown	5	0-0	0-0	0-0	0	2	1	0	0
Totals	240	31-78	16-20	24-51	20	15	14	19	87

Percentages: FG—.397, FT—.800. 3-pt goals: 9-25, .360 (Pippen 3-7, Harper 2-5, Jordan 1-3, Kukoc 2-7, Kerr 1-2, Brown 0-1). Team rebounds: 1. Blocked shots: 4 (Rodman, Longley, Harper, Kukoc). A: 24,544. Officials: Evans, Bavetta, Javie.

NBA Awards

All-NBA Teams

FIRST TEAM	SECOND TEAM	THIRD TEAM
G Michael Jordan, Chicago	Gary Payton, Seattle	Mitch Richmond, Sacramento
G Anfernee Hardaway, Orlando	John Stockton, Utah	Reggie Miller, Indiana
C David Robinson, San Antonio	Hakeem Olajuwon, Houston	Shaquille O'Neal, Orlando
F Scottie Pippen, Chicago	Shawn Kemp, Seattle	Charles Barkley, Phoenix
F Karl Malone, Utah	Grant Hill, Detroit	Juwan Howard, Washington

Master Lock NBA All-Defensive Teams

FIRST TEAM	SECOND TEAM
G Gary Payton, Seattle	Mookie Blaylock, Atlanta
G Michael Jordan, Chicago	Bobby Phills, Cleveland
C David Robinson, San Antonio	Hakeem Olajuwon, Houston
F Scottie Pippen, Chicago	Horace Grant, Orlando
F Dennis Rodman, Chicago	Derrick McKey, Indiana

All-Rookie Teams
(Chosen Without Regard to Position)

FIRST TEAM	SECOND TEAM
Damon Stoudamire, Toronto	Kevin Garnett, Minnesota
Joe Smith, Golden State	Bryant Reeves, Vancouver
Jerry Stackhouse, Philadelphia	Brent Barry, LA Clippers
Antonio McDyess, Denver	Rasheed Wallace, Washington
Arvydas Sabonis, Portland	Tyus Edney, Sacramento
Michael Finley, Phoenix	

NBA Individual Leaders

Scoring

	GP	Pts	Avg
Michael Jordan, Chi	82	2491	30.4
Hakeem Olajuwon, Hou	72	1936	26.9
Shaquille O'Neal, Orl	54	1434	26.6
Karl Malone, Utah	82	2106	25.7
David Robinson, SA	82	2051	25.0
Charles Barkley, Pho	71	1649	23.2
Alonzo Mourning, Mia	70	1623	23.2
Mitch Richmond, Sac	81	1872	23.1
Patrick Ewing, NY	76	1711	22.5
Juwan Howard, Wash	81	1789	22.1

Rebounds

	GP	Reb	Avg
Dennis Rodman, Chi	64	952	14.9
David Robinson, SA	82	1000	12.2
Dikembe Mutombo, Den	74	871	11.8
Charles Barkley, Pho	71	821	11.6
Shawn Kemp, Sea	79	904	11.4
Hakeem Olajuwon, Hou	72	784	10.9
Patrick Ewing, NY	76	806	10.6
Alonzo Mourning, Mia	70	727	10.4
Loy Vaught, LA Clippers	80	808	10.1
Jayson Williams, NJ	80	803	10.0

Assists

	GP	Assists	Avg
John Stockton, Utah	82	916	11.2
Jason Kidd, Dall	81	783	9.7
Avery Johnson, SA	82	789	9.6
Rod Strickland, Port	67	640	9.6
Damon Stoudamire, Tor	70	653	9.3
Kevin Johnson, Pho	56	517	9.2
Kenny Anderson, Cha	69	575	8.3
Tim Hardaway, Mia	80	640	8.0
Mark Jackson, Ind	81	635	7.8
Gary Payton, Sea	81	608	7.5

Field-Goal Percentage

	FGA	FGM	Pct
Gheorghe Muresan, Wash	798	466	.584
Chris Gatling, Mia	567	326	.575
Shaquille O'Neal, Orl	1033	592	.573
Anthony Mason, NY	798	449	.563
Shawn Kemp, Sea	937	526	.561
Dale Davis, Ind	599	334	.558
Arvydas Sabonis, Port	723	394	.545
Brian Williams, LA Clippers	766	416	.543
Chucky Brown, Hou	555	300	.541
John Stockton, Utah	818	440	.538

Free-Throw Percentage

	FTA	FTM	Pct
Mahmoud Abdul-Rauf, Den	157	146	.930
Jeff Hornacek, Utah	290	259	.893
Terrell Brandon, Cle	381	338	.887
Dana Barros, Bos	147	130	.884
Brent Price, Wash	191	167	.874
Hersey Hawkins, Sea	283	247	.873
Mitch Richmond, Sac	491	425	.866
Reggie Miller, Ind	498	430	.863
Tim Legler, Wash	153	132	.863
Spud Webb, Minn	145	125	.862

Three-Point Field-Goal Percentage

	FGA	FGM	Pct
Tim Legler, Wash	245	128	.522
Steve Kerr, Chi	237	122	.515
Hubert Davis, NY	267	127	.476
B.J. Armstrong, GS	207	98	.473
Jeff Hornacek, Utah	223	104	.466
Brent Price, Wash	301	139	.462
Bobby Phills, Cle	211	93	.441
Terry Dehere, LA Clippers	316	139	.440
Mitch Richmond, Sac	515	225	.437
Allan Houston, Det	447	191	.427

Steals

	GP	Steals	Avg
Gary Payton, Sea	81	231	2.85
Mookie Blaylock, Atl	81	212	2.62
Michael Jordan, Chi	82	180	2.20
Jason Kidd, Dall	81	175	2.16
Alvin Robertson, Tor	77	166	2.16
Anfernee Hardaway, Orl	82	166	2.02
Eric Murdock, Van	73	135	1.85
Eddie Jones, LA Lakers	70	129	1.84
Hersey Hawkins, Sea	82	149	1.82
Tom Gugliotta, Minn	78	139	1.78

Blocked Shots

	GP	BS	Avg
Dikembe Mutombo, Den	74	332	4.49
Shawn Bradley, NJ	79	288	3.65
David Robinson, SA	82	271	3.30
Hakeem Olajuwon, Hou	72	207	2.88
Alonzo Mourning, Mia	70	189	2.70
Elden Campbell, LA Lakers	82	212	2.59
Patrick Ewing, NY	76	184	2.42
Gheorghe Muresan, Wash	76	172	2.26
Shaquille O'Neal, Orl	54	115	2.13
Jim McIlvaine, Wash	80	166	2.08

NBA Team Statistics

Offense

Team	Field Goals		3-Pt Field Goals		Free Throws		Rebounds		A	Stl	Scoring
	FGM	Pct	3FGM	Pct	FTM	Pct	Off	Total			Avg
Chicago	3293	47.8	544	40.3	1495	74.6	1247	3658	2033	745	105.2
Seattle	3074	48.0	581	36.4	1843	76.0	954	3403	1999	882	104.5
Orlando	3203	48.2	622	37.8	1543	69.1	966	3367	2080	663	104.5
Phoenix	3159	47.3	327	33.2	1907	77.1	1009	3510	2001	623	104.3
Boston	3163	45.6	539	37.1	1630	71.4	1050	3477	1792	653	103.6
San Antonio	3148	47.7	518	39.2	1663	73.6	937	3523	2044	645	103.4
LA Lakers	3216	48.0	477	35.1	1529	74.6	995	3298	2080	722	102.9
Charlotte	3108	47.0	584	38.4	1631	77.0	987	3243	1907	582	102.8
Dallas	3124	42.0	735	36.0	1426	72.2	1408	3787	1913	642	102.5
Washington	3202	48.4	493	40.7	1511	72.8	930	3257	1815	592	102.5
Utah	3129	48.8	377	37.2	1769	76.8	993	3366	2139	667	102.5
Houston	3078	46.4	637	36.2	1611	76.5	919	3374	1982	645	102.5
Golden State	3056	45.6	447	37.3	1775	75.9	1173	3458	1889	706	101.6
Sacramento	2971	45.7	462	38.7	1759	73.1	1114	3459	1829	643	99.5
LA Clippers	3126	47.2	509	37.0	1392	70.2	979	3169	1672	703	99.4
Portland	3064	45.8	480	35.3	1537	66.2	1160	3737	1760	594	99.3
Indiana	2979	48.0	363	37.3	1823	75.5	1010	3272	1917	579	99.3
Atlanta	2985	44.8	566	35.5	1523	75.7	1182	3330	1609	771	98.3
Minnesota	2974	45.9	279	32.6	1797	77.7	985	3256	1867	650	97.9
Denver	3001	45.1	397	34.6	1614	74.3	1057	3544	1851	521	97.7
Toronto	3084	46.7	414	35.4	1412	72.3	1071	3284	1927	745	97.5
New York	3003	47.1	485	37.7	1480	75.7	829	3278	1822	645	97.2
Miami	2902	45.7	552	37.9	1553	71.0	999	3494	1752	574	96.5
Milwaukee	3034	46.7	357	33.8	1412	73.8	973	3137	1755	582	95.6
Detroit	2810	45.9	545	40.4	1657	75.1	884	3324	1610	506	95.4
Philadelphia	2796	43.6	492	34.2	1662	73.4	1031	3192	1629	643	94.5
New Jersey	2881	42.7	250	33.5	1672	74.5	1350	3853	1752	627	93.7
Cleveland	2761	46.0	596	37.7	1355	76.3	867	2922	1818	674	91.1
Vancouver	2772	42.8	372	32.9	1446	72.4	957	3127	1706	728	89.8

Defense (Opponent's Statistics)

Team	Field Goals		3-Pt Field Goals		Free Throws		Rebounds		Stl	Scoring	
	FGM	Pct	3FGM	Pct	FTM	Pct	Off	Total		Avg	Diff
Cleveland	2674	46.2	513	38.8	1400	75.9	874	3041	504	88.5	+2.6
Detroit	2827	44.3	505	36.6	1458	71.5	964	3232	556	92.9	+2.5
Chicago	2880	44.8	437	35.0	1424	71.7	981	3117	595	92.9	+12.2
New York	2859	44.2	442	33.7	1621	74.0	995	3420	653	94.9	+2.3
Miami	2734	43.4	446	36.1	1878	75.2	982	3297	662	95.0	+1.4
Utah	2747	44.5	550	38.5	1820	75.1	936	3085	584	95.9	+6.6
Indiana	2841	45.2	493	36.0	1703	74.0	1004	3055	663	96.1	+3.2
Seattle	2873	43.8	533	34.8	1654	71.6	1074	3329	758	96.7	+7.8
Portland	2953	44.2	472	34.8	1574	74.0	932	3248	708	97.0	+2.4
Atlanta	3044	47.4	479	36.0	1392	74.6	1054	3346	580	97.1	+1.2
San Antonio	3017	43.9	441	33.0	1485	73.0	1109	3582	604	97.1	+6.3
New Jersey	3006	45.4	543	38.4	1476	74.0	1028	3383	665	97.9	-4.2
LA Lakers	3118	45.8	442	36.7	1395	73.8	1146	3462	588	98.5	+4.5
Orlando	3060	45.4	496	36.6	1499	73.6	1087	3452	644	99.0	+5.6
Vancouver	3080	47.5	459	37.4	1561	73.3	1102	3652	698	99.8	-10.0
Denver	3091	45.9	453	36.7	1600	76.0	934	3319	617	100.4	-2.7
Houston	3178	46.0	482	35.9	1423	70.7	1126	3625	670	100.7	+1.7
Milwaukee	3084	48.0	514	39.7	1590	72.5	998	3303	648	100.9	-5.3
Washington	3061	46.0	377	34.2	1822	76.6	1105	3475	696	101.5	+1.1
Sacramento	2987	46.2	461	37.9	1950	75.1	1056	3368	767	102.3	-2.7
LA Clippers	3090	47.8	444	37.2	1824	74.6	1034	3396	689	103.0	-3.6
Golden State	3206	47.5	477	36.5	1564	74.6	1114	3406	698	103.1	-1.5
Minnesota	3086	46.9	530	38.0	1761	74.4	1036	3353	725	103.2	-5.4
Charlotte	3254	48.9	530	39.6	1440	73.6	953	3311	536	103.4	-0.6
Phoenix	3217	47.1	551	36.9	1540	73.9	1003	3385	586	104.0	+0.3
Philadelphia	3284	48.3	526	37.0	1472	74.1	1164	3642	723	104.5	-10.0
Toronto	3146	47.5	519	36.7	1799	74.5	1098	3372	766	105.0	-7.5
Boston	3296	48.1	415	35.7	1767	74.7	1040	3630	667	107.0	-3.4
Dallas	3403	49.2	470	39.4	1535	73.2	1087	3813	702	107.5	-4.9

NBA Team-by-Team Statistical Leaders

Atlanta Hawks

Player	GP	Min	FGM	Pct	FGA	FGM	FTM	Pct	Off	Total	A	Stl	TO	BS	Avg
			Field Goals		3-Pt FG		Free Throws		Rebounds						
Smith 80	80	2856	494	43.2	423	140	318	82.6	124	326	224	68	151	17	18.1
Laettner 74	74	2495	442	48.7	39	9	324	81.8	184	538	197	71	187	71	16.4
Blaylock..........81	81	2893	455	40.5	623	231	127	74.7	110	332	478	212	188	17	15.7
Long 82	82	3008	395	47.1	86	31	257	76.3	248	788	183	108	157	34	13.1
Augmon...........77	77	2294	362	49.1	4	1	251	79.2	137	304	137	106	138	31	12.7
Norman............34	34	770	127	46.5	84	33	17	35.4	40	132	63	15	46	16	8.9
Ehlo 79	79	1758	253	42.8	221	82	81	78.6	65	256	138	85	104	9	8.5
Rooks 65	65	1117	144	50.5	7	1	135	66.8	81	255	47	23	80	42	6.5
Henderson.......79	79	1416	192	44.2	3	0	119	59.5	164	356	51	44	87	43	6.4
Jordan 24	24	247	36	50.7	0	0	22	57.9	23	52	29	12	19	7	3.9
Bullard 46	46	460	66	40.7	72	26	16	80.0	18	60	18	17	24	11	3.8
Hawks 82	82	19,730	2,985	44.8	1,595	566	1,523	75.7	1,182	3,330	1,609	771	1,228	319	98.3
Opponents......82	82	19,730	3,044	47.4	1,329	479	1,392	74.6	1,054	3,346	1,841	580	1,405	338	97.1

Boston Celtics

Player	GP	Min	FGM	Pct	FGA	FGM	FTM	Pct	Off	Total	A	Stl	TO	BS	Avg
			Field Goals		3-Pt FG		Free Throws		Rebounds						
Radja...............53	53	1984	426	50.0	0	0	191	69.5	113	522	83	48	117	81	19.7
Fox...................81	81	2588	421	45.4	272	99	196	77.2	158	450	369	113	216	41	14.0
Barros.............80	80	2328	379	47.0	368	150	130	88.4	21	192	306	58	120	3	13.0
Wesley............82	82	2104	338	45.9	272	116	217	75.3	68	264	390	100	159	11	12.3
Day 79	79	1807	299	36.6	302	100	224	78.0	70	224	107	81	109	51	11.7
Williams 64	64	1470	241	44.1	10	3	200	67.1	92	217	70	56	88	11	10.7
Brown..............65	65	1591	246	39.9	220	68	135	85.4	36	136	146	80	74	12	10.7
Minor 78	78	1761	320	50.0	27	7	99	76.2	93	257	146	36	78	11	9.6
Montross.........61	61	1432	196	56.6	0	0	50	37.6	119	352	43	19	83	29	7.2
Ellison............69	69	1431	145	49.2	0	0	75	64.1	151	451	62	39	84	99	5.3
Burrough 61	61	495	64	37.6	0	0	61	65.6	45	109	15	15	40	10	3.1
Lister..............64	64	735	51	48.6	0	0	41	64.1	67	280	19	6	48	42	2.2
Celtics 82	82	19,905	3,163	45.6	1,453	539	1,630	71.4	1,050	3,477	1,792	653	1,302	406	103.6
Opponents.....82	82	19,905	3,296	48.1	1,162	415	1,767	74.7	1,040	3,630	1,916	667	1,314	489	107.0

Charlotte Hornets

Player	GP	Min	FGM	Pct	FGA	FGM	FTM	Pct	Off	Total	A	Stl	TO	BS	Avg
			Field Goals		3-Pt FG		Free Throws		Rebounds						
Rice 79	79	3142	610	47.1	403	171	319	83.7	86	378	232	91	163	19	21.6
Johnson...........81	81	3274	583	47.6	183	67	427	75.7	249	683	355	55	182	43	20.5
Anderson.........69	69	2344	349	41.8	256	92	260	76.9	63	203	575	111	146	14	15.2
Curry...............82	82	2371	441	45.3	406	164	146	85.4	68	264	176	108	130	25	14.5
Burrell.............20	20	693	92	44.7	98	37	42	75.0	26	98	47	27	43	13	13.2
Geiger.............77	77	2349	357	53.6	8	3	149	72.7	201	649	60	46	137	63	11.2
Goldwire 42	42	621	76	40.2	83	33	46	76.7	8	43	112	16	63	0	5.5
Adams..............21	21	329	37	44.6	41	14	26	74.3	5	22	67	21	25	4	5.4
Hancock...........63	63	838	112	52.3	3	1	47	64.4	40	98	47	28	56	5	4.3
Zidek 71	71	888	105	42.3	0	0	71	76.3	69	183	16	9	38	7	4.0
Parish 74	74	1086	120	49.8	0	0	50	70.4	89	303	29	21	50	54	3.9
Myers..............71	71	1092	91	36.8	58	14	80	65.6	35	140	145	34	81	17	3.9
Addison...........53	53	516	77	46.7	9	0	17	77.3	25	90	30	9	27	9	3.2
Hornets 82	82	19,880	3,108	47.0	1,520	584	1,631	77.0	987	3,243	1,907	582	1,241	277	102.8
Opponents 82	82	19,880	3,254	48.9	1,340	530	1,440	73.6	953	3,311	2,049	536	1,215	368	103.4

Chicago Bulls

Player	GP	Min	Field Goals		3-Pt FG		Free Throws		Rebounds		A	Stl	TO	BS	Avg
			FGM	Pct	FGA	FGM	FTM	Pct	Off	Total					
Jordan 82		3090	916	49.5	260	111	548	83.4	148	543	352	180	197	42	30.4
Pippen 77		2825	563	46.3	401	150	220	67.9	152	496	452	133	207	57	19.4
Kukoc 81		2103	386	49.0	216	87	206	77.2	115	323	287	64	114	28	13.1
Longley..........62		1641	242	48.2	0	0	80	77.7	104	318	119	22	114	84	9.1
Kerr................82		1919	244	50.6	237	122	78	92.9	25	110	192	63	42	2	8.4
Harper 80		1886	234	46.7	104	28	98	70.5	74	213	208	105	73	32	7.4
Rodman..........64		2088	146	48.0	27	3	56	52.8	356	952	160	36	138	27	5.5
Wennington 71		1065	169	49.3	1	1	37	86.0	58	174	46	21	37	16	5.3
Salley.............42		673	63	45.0	0	0	59	69.4	46	140	54	19	55	27	4.4
Buechler 74		740	112	46.3	90	40	14	63.6	45	111	56	34	39	7	3.8
Simpkins.........60		685	77	48.1	1	1	61	62.9	66	156	38	9	56	8	3.6
Edwards 28		274	41	37.3	0	0	16	61.5	15	40	11	1	21	8	3.5
Caffey.............57		545	71	43.8	1	0	40	58.8	51	111	24	12	48	7	3.2
Brown 68		671	78	40.6	11	1	28	60.9	17	66	73	57	31	12	2.7
Bulls 82		**19,730**	**3,293**	**47.8**	**1,349**	**544**	**1,495**	**74.6**	**1,247**	**3,648**	**2,033**	**745**	**1,175**	**345**	**105.2**
Opponents 82		**19,730**	**2,880**	**44.8**	**1,249**	**437**	**1,424**	**71.7**	**981**	**3,117**	**1,592**	**595**	**1,405**	**312**	**92.9**

Cleveland Cavaliers

Player	GP	Min	Field Goals		3-Pt FG		Free Throws		Rebounds		A	Stl	TO	BS	Avg
			FGM	Pct	FGA	FGM	FTM	Pct	Off	Total					
Brandon..........75		2570	510	46.5	235	91	338	88.7	47	248	487	132	142	33	19.3
Mills 80		3060	454	46.8	210	79	218	82.9	112	443	188	73	121	52	15.1
Phills 72		2530	386	46.7	211	93	186	77.5	62	261	271	102	126	27	14.6
Ferry 82		2680	422	45.9	363	143	103	76.9	71	309	191	57	122	37	13.3
Majerle............82		2367	303	40.5	414	146	120	71.0	70	305	214	81	93	34	10.6
Hill 44		929	130	51.2	0	0	81	60.0	94	244	33	31	64	20	7.8
Cage................82		2631	220	55.6	1	0	50	54.3	288	729	53	87	54	79	6.0
Sura 79		1150	148	41.1	78	27	99	70.2	34	135	233	56	115	21	5.3
Miner 19		136	23	44.2	10	2	13	100.0	4	12	8	0	14	0	3.2
Crotty..............58		617	51	44.7	27	8	62	86.1	20	54	102	22	51	6	3.0
Lang 41		367	41	53.2	2	0	34	72.3	17	53	12	14	24	12	2.8
Amaechi...........28		357	29	41.4	0	0	19	57.6	13	52	9	6	34	11	2.8
Marshall...........34		208	24	35.3	30	7	22	62.9	9	26	7	8	7	2	2.3
Cavs................82		**19,830**	**2,761**	**46.0**	**1,582**	**596**	**1,355**	**76.3**	**867**	**2,922**	**1,818**	**674**	**1,073**	**340**	**91.1**
Opponents......82		**19,830**	**2,674**	**46.2**	**1,322**	**513**	**1,400**	**75.9**	**874**	**3,041**	**1,818**	**504**	**1,282**	**336**	**88.5**

Dallas Mavericks

Player	GP	Min	Field Goals		3-Pt FG		Free Throws		Rebounds		A	Stl	TO	BS	Avg
			FGM	Pct	FGA	FGM	FTM	Pct	Off	Total					
Mashburn 18		669	145	37.9	102	35	97	72.9	37	97	50	14	55	3	23.4
Jackson............82		2820	569	43.5	333	121	345	82.5	173	410	235	47	191	22	19.6
McCloud...........79		2846	530	41.4	678	257	180	80.4	116	379	212	113	166	38	18.9
Kidd.................81		3034	493	38.1	396	133	229	69.2	203	553	783	175	328	26	16.6
Dumas..............67		1284	274	41.8	207	74	154	59.9	58	115	99	42	77	13	11.6
Jones...............68		2322	327	44.6	39	14	102	76.7	260	737	132	54	109	27	11.3
Harris...............61		1016	183	46.1	125	47	68	78.2	41	122	79	35	46	3	7.9
Brooks 69		716	134	45.7	62	25	59	85.5	11	41	100	42	43	3	5.1
Meyer 72		1266	145	43.9	11	3	70	68.6	114	319	57	20	67	32	5.0
Davis 28		501	55	50.9	0	0	27	57.4	43	117	21	10	25	4	4.9
Parks 64		869	101	40.9	26	7	41	66.1	66	216	29	25	31	32	3.9
Wood 62		772	75	43.1	62	20	38	76.0	51	154	34	19	24	10	3.4
Williams 65		1806	87	40.7	1	0	24	34.3	234	521	85	48	78	122	3.0
Mavericks.......82		**19,930**	**3,124**	**42.0**	**2,039**	**735**	**1,426**	**72.2**	**1,408**	**3,787**	**1,913**	**642**	**1,270**	**342**	**102.5**
Opponents......82		**19,930**	**3,403**	**49.2**	**1,193**	**470**	**1,535**	**73.2**	**1,087**	**3,813**	**1,978**	**702**	**1,348**	**531**	**107.5**

Denver Nuggets

Player	GP	Min	FGM	Pct	FGA	FGM	FTM	Pct	Off	Total	A	Stl	TO	BS	Avg
			Field Goals		**3-Pt FG**		**Free Throws**		**Rebounds**						
Abdul-Rauf	57	2029	414	43.4	309	121	146	93.0	26	138	389	64	115	3	19.2
D. Ellis	81	2626	459	47.9	364	150	136	76.0	88	315	139	57	98	7	14.9
Stith	82	2810	379	41.6	148	41	320	84.4	125	400	241	114	157	16	13.6
McDyess	76	2280	427	48.5	4	0	166	68.3	229	572	75	54	154	114	13.4
MacLean	56	1107	233	42.6	49	14	145	73.2	62	205	89	21	68	5	11.2
Mutombo	74	2713	284	49.9	1	0	246	69.5	249	871	108	38	150	332	11.0
L. Ellis	45	1269	189	43.8	22	4	89	60.1	93	322	74	36	83	33	10.5
Rose	80	2134	290	48.0	108	32	191	64.9	46	260	495	53	234	39	10.0
Hammonds	71	1045	127	47.4	0	0	88	76.5	85	223	23	23	48	13	4.8
Williams	52	817	94	37.0	89	20	33	84.6	25	122	74	34	51	21	4.6
Overton	55	607	67	37.6	26	8	40	72.7	8	63	106	13	40	5	3.3
Fish	18	134	21	58.3	0	0	10	52.6	10	21	8	3	3	7	2.9
Grant	31	527	35	35.4	34	8	5	83.3	7	34	97	22	30	2	2.7
Nuggets	**82**	**19,830**	**3,001**	**45.1**	**1,148**	**397**	**1,614**	**74.3**	**1,057**	**3,544**	**1,851**	**521**	**1,265**	**597**	**97.7**
Opponents	**82**	**19,830**	**3,091**	**45.9**	**1,235**	**453**	**1,600**	**76.0**	**934**	**3,319**	**1,875**	**617**	**1,130**	**418**	**100.4**

Detroit Pistons

Player	GP	Min	FGM	Pct	FGA	FGM	FTM	Pct	Off	Total	A	Stl	TO	BS	Avg
			Field Goals		**3-Pt FG**		**Free Throws**		**Rebounds**						
Hill	80	3260	564	46.2	26	5	485	75.1	127	783	548	100	263	48	20.2
Houston	82	3072	564	45.3	447	191	298	82.3	54	300	250	61	233	16	19.7
Thorpe	82	2841	452	53.0	4	0	257	71.0	211	688	158	53	195	39	14.2
Dumars	67	2193	255	42.6	298	121	162	82.2	28	138	265	43	97	3	11.8
Mills	82	1656	283	41.9	207	82	121	77.1	108	352	98	42	98	20	9.4
Hunter	80	2138	239	38.1	289	117	84	70.0	44	194	188	84	80	18	8.5
Curry	46	783	73	45.3	53	20	45	72.6	27	85	27	24	24	2	4.6
Ratliff	75	1305	128	55.7	1	0	85	70.8	110	297	13	16	56	116	4.5
Reid	69	997	106	56.7	0	0	51	66.2	78	203	11	47	41	40	3.8
Macon	23	287	29	43.3	15	7	9	81.8	10	22	16	15	9	0	3.2
West	47	682	61	48.4	0	0	28	62.2	49	133	6	6	35	37	3.2
Leckner	18	155	18	62.1	0	0	8	61.5	8	34	1	2	11	4	2.4
Roe	49	372	32	35.6	9	2	24	75.0	30	78	15	10	17	8	1.8
Pistons	**82**	**19,830**	**2,810**	**45.9**	**1,350**	**545**	**1,657**	**75.1**	**884**	**3,324**	**1,610**	**506**	**1,215**	**352**	**95.4**
Opponents	**82**	**19,830**	**2,827**	**44.3**	**1,380**	**505**	**1,458**	**71.5**	**964**	**3,232**	**1,729**	**556**	**1,153**	**385**	**92.9**

Golden State Warriors

Player	GP	Min	FGM	Pct	FGA	FGM	FTM	Pct	Off	Total	A	Stl	TO	BS	Avg
			Field Goals		**3-Pt FG**		**Free Throws**		**Rebounds**						
Sprewell	78	3064	515	42.8	282	91	352	78.9	124	380	328	127	222	45	18.9
Smith	82	2821	469	45.8	28	10	303	77.3	300	717	79	85	138	134	15.3
Mullin	55	1617	269	49.9	150	59	137	85.6	44	159	194	75	122	32	13.3
Armstrong	82	2262	340	46.8	207	98	234	83.9	22	184	401	68	128	6	12.3
Seikaly	64	1813	285	50.2	3	2	204	72.3	166	499	71	40	180	69	12.1
Coles	81	2615	318	40.9	254	88	168	79.6	49	260	422	94	171	17	11.0
Willis	75	2135	325	45.6	9	1	143	70.8	208	638	53	32	161	41	10.6
Kersey	76	1620	205	41.0	17	3	97	66.0	154	363	114	91	75	45	6.7
Marshall	62	934	125	39.8	94	28	64	77.1	65	213	49	22	48	31	5.5
Barry	68	712	91	49.2	93	44	31	83.8	17	63	85	33	42	11	3.8
Rozier	59	723	79	58.5	2	0	26	47.3	71	171	22	19	40	30	3.1
DeClercq	22	203	24	48.0	1	0	11	57.9	18	39	9	7	4	5	2.7
Warriors	**82**	**19,755**	**3,056**	**45.6**	**1,199**	**447**	**1,775**	**75.9**	**1,173**	**3,458**	**1,889**	**706**	**1,343**	**470**	**101.6**
Opponents	**82**	**19,755**	**3,206**	**47.5**	**1,308**	**477**	**1,564**	**74.6**	**1,114**	**3,406**	**2,098**	**698**	**1,375**	**385**	**103.1**

Houston Rockets

Player	GP	Min	Field Goals FGM	Pct	3-Pt FG FGA	FGM	Free Throws FTM	Pct	Rebounds Off	Total	A	Stl	TO	BS	Avg
Olajuwon	72	2797	768	51.4	14	3	397	72.4	176	784	257	113	247	207	26.9
Drexler	52	1997	331	43.3	235	78	265	78.4	97	373	302	105	134	24	19.3
Cassell	61	1682	289	43.9	210	73	235	82.5	51	188	278	53	157	4	14.5
Horry	71	2634	300	41.0	388	142	111	77.6	97	412	281	116	160	109	12.0
Elie	45	1386	180	50.4	127	41	98	85.2	47	155	138	45	59	11	11.1
Mack	31	868	121	42.2	135	54	39	84.8	18	98	79	22	28	9	10.8
Bryant	71	1587	242	54.3	2	0	127	71.8	131	351	52	31	85	19	8.6
Brown	82	2019	300	54.1	8	1	104	69.3	134	441	89	47	94	38	8.6
Smith	68	1617	201	43.3	238	91	87	82.1	21	96	245	47	100	3	8.5
Recasner	63	1275	149	41.5	191	81	57	86.4	31	144	170	23	61	5	6.9
Breaux	54	570	59	36.6	46	15	28	62.2	22	60	24	11	30	8	3.0
Chilcutt	74	651	73	40.8	98	37	17	85.4	2	156	26	19	22	14	2.7
Rockets	82	19,805	3,078	46.4	1,761	637	1,611	76.5	919	3,374	1,982	645	1,245	476	102.5
Opponents	82	19,805	3,178	46.0	1,344	482	1,423	70.7	1,126	3,625	1,945	670	1,224	400	100.7

Indiana Pacers

Player	GP	Min	Field Goals FGM	Pct	3-Pt FG FGA	FGM	Free Throws FTM	Pct	Rebounds Off	Total	A	Stl	TO	BS	Avg
Miller	76	2621	504	47.3	410	168	430	86.3	38	214	253	77	189	13	21.1
Smits	63	1901	466	52.1	5	1	231	78.8	119	433	110	21	160	45	18.5
McKey	75	2440	346	48.6	68	17	170	76.9	123	361	262	83	143	44	11.7
D. Davis	78	2617	334	55.8	0	0	135	46.7	252	709	76	56	119	112	10.3
Jackson	81	2643	296	47.3	149	64	150	78.5	66	307	635	100	201	5	10.0
Pierce	76	1404	264	44.7	104	35	174	84.9	40	136	101	57	93	6	9.7
A. Davis	82	2092	236	49.0	2	1	246	71.3	188	501	43	33	87	66	8.8
Johnson	62	1002	180	41.3	128	45	70	88.6	45	153	69	20	56	4	7.7
Best	59	571	69	42.3	25	8	75	83.3	11	44	97	20	63	3	3.7
Ferrell	54	591	80	48.2	8	0	42	73.7	32	93	30	23	34	3	3.7
Workman	77	1164	101	39.0	71	23	54	74.0	27	124	213	65	93	4	3.6
Schintzius	33	297	49	44.5	0	0	13	61.9	23	78	14	9	19	12	3.4
Caldwell	51	327	46	55.4	0	0	18	50.0	42	110	6	9	35	5	2.2
Pacers	82	19,755	2,979	48.0	973	363	1,823	75.5	1,010	3,272	1,917	579	1,335	323	99.3
Opponents	82	19,755	2,841	45.2	1,368	493	1,703	74.0	1,004	3,055	1,726	663	1,259	420	96.1

Los Angeles Clippers

Player	GP	Min	Field Goals FGM	Pct	3-Pt FG FGA	FGM	Free Throws FTM	Pct	Rebounds Off	Total	A	Stl	TO	BS	Avg
Vaught	80	2966	571	52.5	19	7	149	72.7	204	808	112	87	158	40	16.2
Williams	65	2157	416	54.3	6	1	196	73.4	149	492	122	70	190	55	15.8
Dehere	82	2018	315	45.9	316	139	247	75.5	41	143	350	54	191	16	12.4
Richardson	63	2013	281	42.3	245	94	78	74.3	35	158	340	77	95	13	11.7
Rogers	67	1950	306	47.7	153	49	113	62.8	113	286	167	75	144	35	11.6
Sealy	62	1601	272	41.5	100	21	147	79.9	76	240	116	84	113	28	11.5
Barry	79	1898	283	47.4	296	123	111	81.8	38	168	230	95	120	22	10.1
Murray	77	1816	257	44.7	116	37	99	75.0	89	246	84	61	108	25	8.4
Roberts	51	795	141	46.4	0	0	74	55.6	42	162	41	15	48	39	7.0
Piatkowski	65	784	98	40.5	114	38	67	81.7	40	103	48	24	45	10	4.6
Harvey	55	821	83	37.1	2	0	38	45.8	69	200	15	27	44	47	3.7
Outlaw	80	985	107	57.5	3	0	72	44.4	87	200	50	44	45	91	3.6
Tower	34	305	32	44.4	1	0	18	69.2	22	51	5	4	16	11	2.4
Clippers	82	19,730	3,126	47.2	1,374	509	1,392	70.2	979	3,169	1,672	703	1,355	411	99.4
Opponents	82	19,730	3,090	47.8	1,195	444	1,824	74.6	1,034	3,396	1,658	689	1,357	401	103.0

Los Angeles Lakers

Player	GP	Min	Field Goals		3-Pt FG		Free Throws		Rebounds		A	Stl	TO	BS	Avg
			FGM	Pct	FGA	FGM	FTM	Pct	Off	Total					
Ceballos 78	2628	638	53.0	184	51	329	80.4	215	536	119	94	167	22	21.2
Van Exel 74	2513	396	41.7	403	144	163	79.9	29	181	509	70	156	10	14.9
Johnson...........32	958	137	46.6	58	22	172	85.6	40	183	220	26	103	13	14.6
Campbell.........82	2699	447	50.3	5	0	249	71.3	162	623	181	88	137	212	13.9
Divac 79	2470	414	51.3	18	3	189	64.1	198	679	261	76	199	131	12.9
Jones...............70	2184	337	49.2	227	83	136	73.9	45	233	246	129	99	45	12.8
Peeler 73	1608	272	45.2	254	105	61	70.9	45	137	118	59	56	10	9.7
Threatt 82	1687	241	45.8	169	50	54	76.1	20	95	269	68	74	11	7.3
Lynch...............76	1012	117	43.0	13	4	53	66.3	82	209	51	47	40	10	3.8
Roberts 33	317	48	49.5	14	4	22	78.6	18	47	26	16	24	4	3.7
Strong.............63	746	72	42.6	9	1	69	81.2	60	178	32	18	20	12	3.4
Blount 57	715	79	47.3	2	0	65	56.8	69	170	42	25	47	35	3.2
Lakers..............82	**19,680**	**3,216**	**48.0**	**1,359**	**477**	**1,529**	**74.6**	**995**	**3,298**	**2,080**	**722**	**1,163**	**516**	**102.9**
Opponents.....82	**19,680**	**3,118**	**45.8**	**1,203**	**442**	**1,395**	**73.8**	**1,146**	**3,462**	**2,006**	**588**	**1,334**	**483**	**98.5**

Miami Heat

Player	GP	Min	Field Goals		3-Pt FG		Free Throws		Rebounds		A	Stl	TO	BS	Avg
			FGM	Pct	FGA	FGM	FTM	Pct	Off	Total					
Mourning 70	2671	563	52.3	30	9	488	68.5	218	727	159	70	262	189	23.2
Hardaway........80	2534	419	42.2	379	138	241	79.0	35	229	640	132	235	17	15.2
Chapman..........56	1865	289	42.6	337	125	83	73.5	22	145	166	45	79	10	14.0
Williams 73	2169	359	44.4	293	114	163	70.3	99	319	230	85	151	58	13.6
Danilovic..........19	542	83	45.1	78	34	55	76.4	12	46	47	15	37	3	13.4
Gatling.............71	1427	326	57.5	1	0	139	67.1	129	417	43	36	95	40	11.1
Thomas............74	1655	274	50.1	2	0	118	66.3	122	439	46	47	98	36	9.0
Askins..............75	1897	157	40.2	237	99	45	78.9	113	324	121	48	82	61	6.1
Lenard 30	323	53	37.6	101	36	34	79.1	12	52	31	6	23	1	5.9
Corbin.............71	1274	155	44.2	18	3	100	83.3	81	244	84	63	67	20	5.8
Malone.............32	510	76	39.4	16	5	29	90.6	8	40	26	16	22	0	5.8
Smith 59	938	116	42.3	116	38	28	60.9	30	95	154	37	66	10	5.1
Schayes...........32	399	32	34.0	0	0	37	80.4	29	89	9	11	23	16	3.2
Heat.................82	**19,780**	**2,902**	**45.7**	**1,458**	**552**	**1,553**	**71.0**	**999**	**3,494**	**1,752**	**574**	**1,394**	**439**	**96.5**
Opponents......82	**19,780**	**2,734**	**43.4**	**1,237**	**446**	**1,878**	**75.2**	**982**	**3,297**	**1,645**	**662**	**1,288**	**403**	**95.0**

Milwaukee Bucks

Player	GP	Min	Field Goals		3-Pt FG		Free Throws		Rebounds		A	Stl	TO	BS	Avg
			FGM	Pct	FGA	FGM	FTM	Pct	Off	Total					
Baker 82	3319	699	48.9	48	10	321	67.0	263	808	212	68	216	91	21.1
Robinson 82	3249	627	45.4	263	90	316	81.2	136	504	293	95	282	42	20.2
Douglas...........79	2335	345	50.4	110	40	160	73.1	55	180	436	63	194	5	11.3
Newman 82	2690	321	49.5	162	61	186	80.2	66	200	154	90	108	15	10.8
Benjamin 83	1896	294	49.8	3	0	140	72.2	141	539	64	45	144	85	8.8
Cummings........81	1777	270	46.2	7	1	104	65.0	162	445	89	56	69	30	8.0
Conlon 74	958	153	46.8	30	5	84	76.4	58	177	68	20	79	11	5.3
Mayberry 82	1705	153	42.0	189	75	41	60.3	21	90	302	64	89	10	5.1
Respert............62	845	113	38.7	122	42	35	83.3	28	74	68	32	42	4	4.9
Keys 69	816	87	41.8	71	22	36	83.7	41	125	65	32	33	14	3.4
Reynolds 19	191	21	39.6	10	1	13	61.9	13	33	12	15	16	6	2.9
Bucks...............82	**19,730**	**3,034**	**46.7**	**1,056**	**357**	**1,412**	**73.8**	**973**	**3,137**	**1,755**	**582**	**1,295**	**307**	**95.6**
Opponents......82	**19,730**	**3,084**	**48.0**	**1,296**	**514**	**1,590**	**72.5**	**998**	**3,303**	**1,940**	**648**	**1,212**	**373**	**100.9**

Minnesota Timberwolves

Player	GP	Min	Field Goals		3-Pt FG		Free Throws		Rebounds		A	Stl	TO	BS	Avg
			FGM	Pct	FGA	FGM	FTM	Pct	Off	Total					
Rider	75	2594	560	46.4	275	102	248	83.8	99	309	213	48	201	23	19.6
Gugliotta	78	2835	473	47.1	86	26	289	77.3	176	690	238	139	234	96	16.2
Lang	71	2365	353	44.7	5	1	125	80.1	153	455	65	42	124	126	11.7
Mitchell	78	2145	303	49.0	18	1	237	81.4	107	339	74	49	87	26	10.8
Garnett	80	2293	361	49.1	28	8	105	70.5	175	501	145	86	110	131	10.4
Porter	82	2072	269	44.2	226	71	164	78.5	36	212	452	89	173	15	9.4
Webb	77	1462	186	43.3	129	47	125	86.2	26	100	294	52	110	7	7.1
Martin	59	1149	147	40.6	69	20	101	84.2	16	82	217	53	107	3	7.0
West	73	1639	175	44.5	13	1	114	79.2	48	161	119	30	81	17	6.4
Riley	25	310	35	47.3	1	0	22	78.6	32	76	5	8	17	16	3.7
Davis	57	571	55	36.9	13	4	74	63.8	56	125	47	40	68	22	3.3
Allen	41	362	36	34.3	33	10	26	72.2	5	25	49	21	34	5	2.6
Bragg	53	369	65	45.0	0	0	23	56.1	38	79	8	17	26	8	2.5
T'wolves	**82**	**19,780**	**2,974**	**45.9**	**857**	**279**	**1,797**	**77.7**	**985**	**3,256**	**1,867**	**650**	**1,426**	**481**	**97.9**
Opponents	**82**	**19,780**	**3,086**	**46.9**	**1,393**	**530**	**1,761**	**74.4**	**1,036**	**3,353**	**1,966**	**725**	**1,343**	**498**	**103.2**

New Jersey Nets

Player	GP	Min	Field Goals		3-Pt FG		Free Throws		Rebounds		A	Stl	TO	BS	Avg
			FGM	Pct	FGA	FGM	FTM	Pct	Off	Total					
Gilliam	78	2856	576	47.4	1	0	277	79.1	241	713	140	73	177	53	18.3
Gill	47	1683	246	46.9	79	26	138	78.4	72	232	260	64	131	24	14.0
Childs	78	2408	324	41.6	259	95	259	85.2	51	245	548	111	230	8	12.8
Bradley	79	2329	387	44.3	4	1	169	68.7	221	638	36	49	179	288	11.9
Edwards	34	1007	142	36.4	104	42	68	81.0	14	75	71	54	68	7	11.6
Brown	81	2942	354	44.4	15	3	204	77.0	215	560	165	79	133	100	11.3
Williams	80	1858	279	42.3	7	2	161	59.2	342	803	47	35	106	57	9.0
Fleming	77	1747	227	43.3	28	3	133	75.1	49	170	255	41	122	5	7.7
O'Bannon	64	1253	156	39.0	56	10	77	71.3	65	168	63	44	62	11	6.2
Reeves	51	833	95	41.9	91	28	61	74.4	18	79	118	37	63	3	5.5
Graham	53	613	78	40.4	82	32	52	76.5	17	57	52	25	46	1	4.5
Dare	58	626	63	43.8	0	0	38	61.3	56	181	0	8	72	40	2.8
Mahorn	50	450	43	35.2	1	0	34	72.3	31	110	16	14	30	13	2.4
Perry	30	254	31	47.7	8	4	5	55.6	21	48	8	4	10	13	2.4
Nets	**82**	**19,905**	**2,881**	**42.7**	**746**	**250**	**1,672**	**74.5**	**1,350**	**3,853**	**1,752**	**627**	**1,375**	**571**	**93.7**
Opponents	**82**	**19,905**	**3,006**	**45.4**	**1,415**	**543**	**1,476**	**74.0**	**1,028**	**3,383**	**1,876**	**665**	**1,270**	**516**	**97.9**

New York Knickerbockers

Player	GP	Min	Field Goals		3-Pt FG		Free Throws		Rebounds		A	Stl	TO	BS	Avg
			FGM	Pct	FGA	FGM	FTM	Pct	Off	Total					
Ewing	76	2783	678	46.6	28	4	351	76.1	157	806	160	68	221	184	22.5
Mason	82	3457	449	56.3	0	0	298	72.0	220	764	363	69	211	34	14.6
Harper	82	2893	436	46.4	325	121	156	75.7	32	202	352	131	178	5	14.0
Starks	81	2491	375	44.3	396	143	131	75.3	31	237	315	103	156	11	12.6
Oakley	53	1775	211	47.1	26	7	175	83.3	162	460	137	58	104	14	11.4
Davis	74	1773	275	48.6	267	127	112	86.8	35	123	103	31	63	8	10.7
Anderson	76	2060	288	43.6	120	34	132	81.0	48	246	197	75	143	59	9.8
Reid	65	1313	160	49.4	1	0	107	75.4	73	255	42	43	79	17	6.6
Grant	47	596	88	48.6	24	8	48	82.8	12	52	69	39	45	3	4.9
Ward	62	787	87	39.9	99	33	37	68.5	29	102	132	54	79	6	3.9
Lohaus	55	598	71	40.6	122	51	4	80.0	7	64	44	10	20	17	3.6
H. Williams	44	571	62	40.8	4	1	13	65.0	15	90	27	14	22	33	3.1
Grandison	28	311	22	37.9	14	4	17	68.0	20	55	13	12	12	2	2.3
Knicks	**82**	**19,830**	**3,003**	**47.1**	**1,285**	**485**	**1,480**	**75.7**	**829**	**3,278**	**1,822**	**645**	**1,272**	**377**	**97.2**
Opponents	**82**	**19,830**	**2,859**	**44.2**	**1,311**	**442**	**1,621**	**74.0**	**995**	**3,420**	**1,671**	**653**	**1,293**	**281**	**94.9**

Orlando Magic

Player	GP	Min	Field Goals		3-Pt FG		Free Throws		Rebounds		A	Stl	TO	BS	Avg
			FGM	Pct	FGA	FGM	FTM	Pct	Off	Total					
O'Neal	54	1946	592	57.3	2	1	249	48.7	182	596	155	34	155	115	26.6
Hardaway	82	3015	623	51.3	283	89	445	76.7	129	354	582	166	229	41	21.7
Scott	82	3041	491	44.0	628	267	182	82.0	63	309	243	90	122	29	17.5
Anderson	77	2717	400	44.2	430	168	166	69.2	92	415	279	121	141	46	14.7
Grant	63	2286	347	51.3	6	1	152	73.4	178	580	170	62	64	74	13.4
Gattison	25	570	91	47.9	0	0	47	60.3	35	114	14	10	40	11	9.2
Shaw	75	1679	182	37.4	144	41	91	79.8	58	224	336	58	173	11	6.6
Royal	64	963	106	49.1	2	0	125	76.2	57	153	42	29	52	15	5.3
Wolf	64	1065	135	51.3	6	0	21	72.4	49	187	63	15	42	5	4.5
Thompson	33	246	48	46.6	64	25	19	70.4	4	24	31	12	24	0	4.2
Bowie	74	1078	128	47.1	31	12	40	87.0	40	123	105	34	55	10	4.2
Koncak	67	1288	84	48.0	9	3	32	56.1	63	272	51	27	41	44	3.0
Vaughn	33	266	27	33.8	1	0	10	55.6	33	80	8	6	18	15	1.9
Magic	82	19,855	3,203	48.2	1,645	622	1,543	69.1	966	3,367	2,080	663	1,160	406	104.5
Opponents	82	19,855	3,060	45.4	1,357	496	1,499	73.6	1,087	3,452	1,869	644	1,238	324	99.0

Philadelphia 76ers

Player	GP	Min	Field Goals		3-Pt FG		Free Throws		Rebounds		A	Stl	TO	BS	Avg
			FGM	Pct	FGA	FGM	FTM	Pct	Off	Total					
Stackhouse	72	2701	452	41.4	292	93	387	74.7	90	265	278	76	252	79	19.2
Weatherspoon	78	3096	491	48.4	2	0	318	74.6	237	753	158	112	179	108	16.7
Maxwell	75	2467	410	39.0	460	146	251	75.6	39	229	330	96	215	12	16.2
Ruffin	61	1551	263	40.6	284	104	148	81.3	21	132	269	43	149	2	12.8
Coleman	11	294	48	40.7	21	7	20	62.5	13	72	31	4	28	10	11.2
Massenburg	54	1463	214	49.5	3	0	111	70.7	127	352	30	28	73	20	10.0
Higgins	44	916	134	41.5	129	48	35	94.6	20	92	55	24	49	11	8.0
Pinckney	74	1710	171	51.0	3	0	136	76.0	189	458	72	64	77	28	6.5
Skiles	10	236	20	35.1	34	15	8	80.0	1	16	38	7	16	0	6.3
Alston	73	1614	198	51.2	3	1	55	49.1	127	302	61	56	59	52	6.2
Dumas	39	739	95	46.8	9	2	49	70.0	42	99	44	42	49	6	6.2
Sutton	48	655	85	39.2	117	47	35	76.1	8	50	102	25	62	2	5.3
Walters	44	610	61	41.2	66	22	42	80.8	13	55	106	25	41	4	4.2
Williams	13	193	15	51.7	2	0	10	83.3	13	46	5	6	8	7	3.1
Thompson	44	773	33	39.8	0	0	19	79.2	62	199	26	19	37	20	1.9
76ers	82	19,730	2,796	43.6	1,438	492	1,662	73.4	1,031	3,192	1,629	643	1,414	420	94.5
Opponents	82	19,730	3,284	48.3	1,421	526	1,472	74.1	1,164	3,642	2,109	723	1,288	469	104.5

Phoenix Suns

Player	GP	Min	Field Goals		3-Pt FG		Free Throws		Rebounds		A	Stl	TO	BS	Avg
			FGM	Pct	FGA	FGM	FTM	Pct	Off	Total					
Barkley	71	2632	580	50.0	175	49	440	77.7	243	821	262	114	218	56	23.2
Johnson	56	2007	342	50.7	57	21	342	85.9	42	221	517	82	170	13	18.7
Finley	82	3212	465	47.6	186	61	242	74.9	139	374	289	85	133	31	15.0
Manning	33	816	178	45.9	14	3	82	75.2	30	143	65	38	77	24	13.4
Person	82	2609	390	44.5	313	117	148	77.1	56	321	138	55	89	22	12.7
Tisdale	63	1152	279	49.5	0	0	114	76.5	55	214	58	15	63	36	10.7
Perry	81	1668	261	47.5	59	24	151	77.8	34	136	353	87	146	5	8.6
Green	82	2113	215	48.4	52	14	168	70.9	166	554	72	45	79	23	7.5
Williams	62	1652	180	45.3	1	0	95	73.1	129	372	62	46	62	90	7.3
Bennett	19	230	29	45.3	1	0	27	64.3	21	49	6	11	11	11	4.5
Carr	60	590	90	41.5	42	11	49	81.7	27	102	43	10	40	5	4.0
Rencher	36	405	33	33.0	29	9	31	67.4	9	44	54	16	43	2	2.9
Kleine	56	663	71	42.0	7	2	20	80.0	36	132	44	13	37	6	2.9
Suns	82	19,955	3,159	47.3	984	327	1,907	77.1	1,009	3,510	2,001	623	1,207	331	104.3
Opponents	82	19,955	3,217	47.1	1,492	551	1,540	73.9	1,003	3,385	2,088	586	1,191	420	104.0

Portland Trail Blazers

Player	GP	Min	Field Goals		3-Pt FG		Free Throws		Rebounds		A	Stl	TO	BS	Avg
			FGM	Pct	FGA	FGM	FTM	Pct	Off	Total					
C. Robinson	78	2980	553	42.3	471	178	360	66.4	123	443	190	86	194	68	21.1
Strickland	67	2526	471	46.0	111	38	276	65.2	89	297	640	97	255	16	18.7
Sabonis	73	1735	394	54.5	104	39	231	75.7	147	588	130	64	154	78	14.5
McKie	81	2259	337	46.7	117	38	152	76.4	86	304	205	92	135	21	10.7
Grant	76	2394	314	46.2	67	21	30	54.5	117	361	111	60	82	43	9.3
J. Robinson	76	1627	229	39.9	284	102	89	65.9	44	157	150	34	111	16	8.5
Trent	69	1219	220	51.3	9	0	78	55.3	84	238	50	25	92	11	7.5
Williams	70	1672	192	50.0	3	2	125	66.8	159	404	42	40	90	47	7.3
R. Robinson	43	715	92	41.6	79	30	33	64.7	19	78	142	26	72	5	5.7
Dudley	80	1924	162	45.3	1	0	80	51.0	239	720	37	41	79	100	5.1
Wingfield	44	487	60	38.2	63	19	26	76.5	45	104	28	20	31	6	3.8
Childress	28	250	25	31.6	47	13	22	81.5	1	19	32	8	28	1	3.0
Trail Blazers	**82**	**19,905**	**3,064**	**45.8**	**1,358**	**480**	**1,537**	**66.2**	**1,160**	**3,737**	**1,760**	**594**	**1,377**	**417**	**99.3**
Opponents	**82**	**19,905**	**2,953**	**44.2**	**1,355**	**472**	**1,574**	**74.0**	**932**	**3,248**	**1,817**	**708**	**1,192**	**409**	**97.0**

Sacramento Kings

Player	GP	Min	Field Goals		3-Pt FG		Free Throws		Rebounds		A	Stl	TO	BS	Avg
			FGM	Pct	FGA	FGM	FTM	Pct	Off	Total					
Richmond	81	2946	611	44.7	515	225	425	86.6	54	269	255	125	220	19	23.1
Grant	78	2398	427	50.7	17	4	262	73.2	175	545	127	40	185	103	14.4
Owens	62	1982	323	48.0	18	5	157	63.6	143	411	204	49	164	38	13.0
Polynice	81	2441	431	52.7	3	1	122	60.1	257	764	58	52	127	66	12.2
Marciulionis	53	1039	176	45.2	157	64	155	77.5	20	77	118	52	96	4	10.8
Edney	80	2481	305	41.2	144	53	197	78.2	63	201	491	89	192	3	10.8
Gamble	65	1325	152	40.1	114	44	38	79.2	21	113	100	35	43	8	5.9
Williamson	53	609	125	46.6	3	0	47	56.0	56	114	23	11	76	9	5.6
Smith	65	1384	144	60.5	1	1	68	38.4	143	389	110	47	72	46	5.5
Simmons	54	810	86	39.6	51	19	55	73.3	41	145	83	31	51	20	4.6
Houston	25	276	32	50.0	3	1	21	80.8	31	84	7	13	17	7	3.4
Causwell	73	1044	90	41.7	1	0	70	72.9	86	428	20	27	53	78	3.4
Hurley	72	1059	65	28.3	76	22	68	80.0	12	75	216	28	86	3	3.1
Kings	**82**	**19,755**	**2,971**	**45.8**	**1,194**	**462**	**1,759**	**73.1**	**1,114**	**3,459**	**1,829**	**643**	**1,442**	**436**	**99.5**
Opponents	**82**	**19,755**	**2,987**	**46.2**	**1,215**	**461**	**1,950**	**75.1**	**1,056**	**3,368**	**1,805**	**767**	**1,356**	**505**	**102.3**

San Antonio Spurs

Player	GP	Min	Field Goals		3-Pt FG		Free Throws		Rebounds		A	Stl	TO	BS	Avg
			FGM	Pct	FGA	FGM	FTM	Pct	Off	Total					
Robinson	82	3019	711	51.6	9	3	626	76.1	319	1000	247	111	190	271	25.0
Elliott	77	2901	525	46.6	392	161	326	77.1	69	396	211	69	198	33	20.0
Del Negro	82	2766	478	49.7	150	57	178	83.2	36	272	315	85	100	6	14.5
Johnson	82	3084	438	49.4	31	6	189	72.1	37	206	789	119	195	21	13.1
Person	80	2131	308	43.7	463	190	67	64.4	76	413	100	49	91	26	10.9
Smith	73	1716	244	42.2	15	2	119	73.0	133	362	65	50	106	80	8.3
Perdue	80	1396	122	52.3	1	0	67	53.6	175	485	33	28	86	75	5.2
Rivers	78	1235	108	37.2	137	47	48	75.0	30	138	123	73	57	21	4.0
Alexander	60	560	63	40.6	66	26	16	64.0	9	42	121	27	68	2	2.8
Williams	31	184	27	39.7	1	0	14	70.0	20	40	8	6	18	2	2.2
Herrera	44	393	40	41.2	1	0	5	29.4	30	81	16	9	29	8	1.9
Anderson	46	344	24	51.1	1	0	6	24.0	29	100	10	9	22	24	1.2
Spurs	**82**	**19,780**	**3,148**	**47.7**	**1,320**	**518**	**1,663**	**73.6**	**937**	**3,523**	**2,044**	**645**	**1,195**	**536**	**103.4**
Opponents	**82**	**19,780**	**3,017**	**43.9**	**1,337**	**441**	**1,485**	**73.0**	**1,109**	**3,582**	**1,849**	**604**	**1,257**	**428**	**97.1**

Seattle SuperSonics

Player	GP	Min	Field Goals		3-Pt FG		Free Throws		Rebounds		A	Stl	TO	BS	Avg
			FGM	Pct	FGA	FGM	FTM	Pct	Off	Total					
Kemp	79	2631	526	56.1	12	5	493	74.2	276	904	173	93	315	127	19.6
Payton	81	3162	618	48.4	299	98	229	74.8	104	339	608	231	260	19	19.3
Schrempf	63	2200	360	48.6	179	73	287	77.8	73	328	276	56	146	8	17.1
Hawkins	82	2823	443	47.3	380	146	247	87.3	86	297	218	149	164	14	15.6
Perkins	82	2169	325	40.8	363	129	191	79.3	101	367	120	83	82	48	11.8
Askew	69	1725	215	49.3	86	29	125	76.7	65	218	163	47	96	15	8.5
Johnson	81	1519	180	51.1	3	1	85	66.9	129	433	48	40	98	129	5.5
Brickowski	63	986	123	48.8	79	32	61	70.9	26	151	58	26	78	8	5.4
McMillan	55	1261	100	42.0	121	46	29	70.7	41	210	197	95	75	18	5.0
Wingate	60	695	88	41.5	34	15	32	78.0	17	56	58	20	42	4	3.7
Ford	28	139	30	37.5	25	4	26	76.5	12	24	5	8	6	1	3.2
Snow	43	389	42	42.0	10	2	29	59.2	9	43	73	28	38	0	2.7
Scheffler	35	181	24	53.3	5	1	9	47.4	15	33	2	6	8	2	1.7
SuperSonics	**82**	**19,880**	**3,074**	**48.0**	**1,596**	**581**	**1,843**	**76.0**	**954**	**3,403**	**1,999**	**882**	**1,441**	**393**	**104.5**
Opponents	**82**	**19,880**	**2,873**	**43.8**	**1,531**	**533**	**1,654**	**71.6**	**1,074**	**3,329**	**1,776**	**758**	**1,517**	**391**	**96.7**

Toronto Raptors

Player	GP	Min	Field Goals		3-Pt FG		Free Throws		Rebounds		A	Stl	TO	BS	Avg
			FGM	Pct	FGA	FGM	FTM	Pct	Off	Total					
Stoudamire	70	2865	481	42.6	337	133	236	79.2	59	281	653	98	267	19	19.0
Murray	82	2458	496	45.4	358	151	182	83.1	114	352	131	87	132	40	16.2
Miller	76	2516	418	52.6	11	0	146	66.1	177	562	219	108	202	143	12.9
Wright	57	1434	248	48.4	3	1	167	64.5	148	356	38	30	109	49	11.6
Robertson	77	2478	285	47.0	151	41	107	67.7	110	342	323	166	183	36	9.3
Rogers	56	1043	178	51.7	21	3	71	54.6	80	170	35	25	61	48	7.7
Tabak	67	1332	225	54.3	1	0	64	56.1	117	320	62	24	101	31	7.7
Christie	55	1036	150	44.5	106	46	69	74.2	34	154	117	70	95	19	7.5
Earl	42	655	117	42.4	3	0	82	71.9	51	129	27	18	49	37	7.5
Lewis	16	189	29	48.3	7	2	15	60.0	15	29	3	8	14	3	4.7
King	62	868	110	43.1	34	5	54	70.1	43	110	88	21	60	13	4.5
Esposito	30	282	36	36.0	56	13	31	79.5	4	16	23	7	39	6	3.9
Raptors	**82**	**19,830**	**3,084**	**46.7**	**1,168**	**414**	**1,412**	**72.3**	**1,071**	**3,284**	**1,927**	**745**	**1,544**	**493**	**97.5**
Opponents	**82**	**19,830**	**3,146**	**47.5**	**1,416**	**519**	**1,799**	**74.5**	**1,098**	**3,372**	**1,990**	**766**	**1,326**	**482**	**105.0**

Utah Jazz

Player	GP	Min	Field Goals		3-Pt FG		Free Throws		Rebounds		A	Stl	TO	BS	Avg
			FGM	Pct	FGA	FGM	FTM	Pct	Off	Total					
Malone	82	3113	789	51.9	40	16	512	72.3	175	804	345	138	199	56	25.7
Hornacek	82	2588	442	50.2	223	104	259	89.3	62	209	340	106	127	20	15.2
Stockton	82	2915	440	53.8	225	95	234	83.0	54	226	916	140	246	15	14.7
Morris	66	1424	265	43.7	197	63	98	77.2	100	229	77	63	71	20	10.5
Benoit	81	1961	255	43.9	192	64	87	77.7	90	383	82	43	71	49	8.2
Carr	80	1532	233	45.7	3	0	114	79.2	71	200	74	28	78	65	7.3
Keefe	82	1708	180	52.0	4	0	139	69.2	176	455	64	51	88	41	6.1
Spencer	71	1267	146	52.0	0	0	104	68.9	100	306	11	20	77	54	5.6
Eisley	65	961	104	43.0	62	14	65	84.4	22	78	146	29	77	3	4.4
Foster	73	803	107	43.9	8	1	61	84.7	53	178	25	7	58	22	3.8
Ostertag	57	661	86	47.3	0	0	36	66.7	57	175	5	5	25	63	3.6
Watson	16	217	18	41.9	7	3	9	69.2	5	27	24	8	17	2	3.0
Russell	59	577	56	39.4	40	14	48	71.6	28	90	29	29	36	8	2.9
Jazz	**82**	**19,780**	**3,129**	**48.8**	**1,013**	**377**	**1,769**	**76.8**	**993**	**3,366**	**2,139**	**667**	**1,215**	**418**	**102.5**
Opponents	**82**	**19,780**	**2,747**	**44.5**	**1,428**	**550**	**1,820**	**75.1**	**936**	**3,085**	**1,640**	**584**	**1,284**	**409**	**95.9**

Vancouver Grizzlies

Player	GP	Min	Field Goals		3-Pt FG		Free Throws		Rebounds		A	Stl	TO	BS	Avg
			FGM	Pct	FGA	FGM	FTM	Pct	Off	Total					
Anthony	69	2096	324	41.5	271	90	229	77.1	29	174	476	116	160	11	14.0
Reeves	77	2460	401	45.7	3	0	219	73.2	178	570	109	43	157	55	13.3
B. Edwards	82	2773	401	41.9	245	84	157	75.5	98	346	212	118	170	46	12.7
Scott	80	1894	271	40.1	221	74	203	83.5	40	192	123	63	100	22	10.2
Murdock	73	1673	244	41.6	145	45	114	79.7	26	169	327	135	132	9	8.9
King	80	1930	250	42.7	113	44	90	66.2	102	285	104	68	103	33	7.9
Wilkins	28	738	77	37.6	64	14	20	87.0	22	65	68	22	37	2	6.7
Moten	44	573	112	45.3	55	18	49	65.3	36	61	50	29	44	8	6.6
Amaya	54	1104	121	48.0	1	0	97	65.1	114	303	33	22	57	10	6.3
Avent	71	1586	179	38.4	0	0	57	74.0	108	355	69	30	107	42	5.8
Mobley	39	676	74	53.6	2	1	39	44.8	54	140	22	14	50	24	4.8
Manning	29	311	49	43.4	1	0	9	64.3	16	55	7	3	17	6	3.7
Turner	13	192	18	35.3	27	9	2	100.0	10	28	6	2	11	1	3.6
D. Edwards	31	519	32	35.2	4	0	29	76.3	35	87	39	10	29	18	3.0
Grizzlies	**82**	**19,880**	**2,772**	**42.8**	**1,129**	**372**	**1,446**	**72.4**	**957**	**3,127**	**1,706**	**728**	**1,347**	**333**	**89.8**
Opponents	**82**	**19,880**	**3,080**	**47.5**	**1,226**	**459**	**1,561**	**73.3**	**1,102**	**3,652**	**1,988**	**698**	**1,423**	**474**	**99.8**

Washington Bullets

Player	GP	Min	Field Goals		3-Pt FG		Free Throws		Rebounds		A	Stl	TO	BS	Avg
			FGM	Pct	FGA	FGM	FTM	Pct	Off	Total					
Webber	15	558	150	.543	34	15	41	.594	37	114	75	27	49	9	23.7
Howard	81	3294	733	.489	13	4	319	.749	188	660	360	67	303	39	22.1
Pack	31	1084	190	.428	98	26	154	.846	29	132	242	62	114	1	18.1
Cheaney	70	2324	426	.471	154	52	151	.706	67	239	154	67	129	18	15.1
Muresan	76	2242	466	.584	1	0	172	.619	248	728	56	52	143	172	14.5
Wallace	65	1788	275	.487	82	27	78	.650	93	303	85	42	103	54	10.1
B. Price	81	2042	252	.472	301	139	167	.874	38	228	416	78	153	4	10.0
Legler	77	1775	233	.507	245	128	132	.863	29	140	136	45	45	12	9.4
Eackles	55	1238	161	.427	128	54	98	.831	44	148	86	28	57	3	8.6
Whitney	21	335	45	.455	44	19	41	.932	2	33	51	18	23	1	7.1
Butler	61	858	88	.384	60	13	48	.578	29	118	67	41	67	12	3.9
McCann	62	653	76	.497	2	1	35	.473	46	143	24	21	42	15	3.0
McIlvaine	80	1195	62	.428	0	0	58	.552	66	230	11	21	36	166	2.3
Bullets	**82**	**19,805**	**3,202**	**48.4**	**1,212**	**493**	**1,511**	**72.8**	**930**	**3,257**	**1,815**	**592**	**1,327**	**506**	**102.5**
Opponents	**82**	**19,805**	**3,061**	**46.0**	**1,103**	**377**	**1,822**	**76.6**	**1,105**	**3,475**	**1,690**	**696**	**1,362**	**390**	**101.5**

Everything Is Not Jake

When the real NBA referees returned to work after last season's lockout, the realest ref wasn't among them. Jake O'Donnell, 58, called it quits in December 1995 after 28 years in the league, leaving the zebra fraternity, not to mention the NBA, much the poorer. In June of that year, Jake's 15-year-old son, Jim, with whom he had spent very little time over the years, moved into Jake's house in Jupiter, Fla. Now, Jake says, "I want to try and make it up to him."

Still, it's not hard to link O'Donnell's abrupt retirement with one or more of the following: the recent contentiousness between the ref's union and the NBA; O'Donnell's benching by the NBA for most of the 1995 playoffs; and his poor relationship with Darell Garretson, the league's chief of referees.

In happier times O'Donnell—who two months ago privately told NBA commissioner David Stern that he would retire when the labor situation was resolved—would have almost certainly stayed around for at least one more year. He was deeply stung in the 1994-95 season when the league didn't stand behind him after an incident involving Clyde Drexler of the Houston Rockets in Game 1 of the Western Conference semifinals. O'Donnell called two quick technicals on Drexler, with whom he had an acrimonious history, and then tossed him from the game. Not only did Rod Thorn, the NBA's vice president of operations, fail to assign O'Donnell to further playoff games, but he also rescinded Drexler's automatic $1,000 fine. "To be treated like that after my years of service was tough, I can't deny that," says O'Donnell. Although O'Donnell undoubtedly rushed to judgment in the Drexler episode, most of the time he kept control with a chatty, warn-first-and-blow-whistle-later style favored by old-fashioned refs. That soured his relationship with the flinty autocrat Garretson, who discourages refs from having contact with players and coaches.

Stern has told O'Donnell he wants him to stay close to the game, perhaps by conducting clinics or reffing some overseas exhibition games. O'Donnell has asked the commish for only one thing—not to give another referee his number, 11. Considering the recent bitterness between the NBA and the zebras, Stern would do well to honor that request.

1996 NBA Draft

The 1996 NBA Draft was held on June 26 in East Rutherford, NJ.

First Round

1. Allen Iverson, Philadelphia
2. Marcus Camby, Toronto
3. Shareef Abdur-Rahim, Vancouver
4. Stephon Marbury, Milwaukee (to Minnesota)
5. Ray Allen, Minnesota (to Milwaukee)
6. Antoine Walker, Boston
7. Lorenzen Wright, LA Clippers
8. Kerry Kittles, New Jersey
9. Samaki Walker, Dallas
10. Erick Dampier, Indiana
11. Todd Fuller, Golden State
12. Vitaly Potapenko, Cleveland
13. Kobe Bryant, Charlotte
14. Predrag Stojakovic, Sacramento
15. Steve Nash, Phoenix
16. Tony Delk, Charlotte
17. Jermaine O'Neal, Portland
18. John Wallace, New York
19. Walter McCarty, New York
20. Zydrunas Ilgauskas, Cleveland
21. Dontae Jones, New York
22. Roy Rogers, Vancouver
23. Efthimis Retzias, Denver
24. Derek Fisher, LA Lakers
25. Martin Muursepp, Utah (to Miami)
26. Jerome Williams, Detroit
27. Brian Evans, Orlando
28. Priest Lauderdale, Atlanta
29. Travis Knight, Chicago

Second Round

30. Othella Harrington, Houston
31. Mark Hendrickson, Philadelphia
32. Ryan Minor, Philadelphia
33. Moochie Norris, Milwaukee
34. Shawn Harvey, Dallas
35. Joseph Blair, Seattle
36. Doron Sheffer, LA Clippers
37. Jeff McInnis, Denver
38. Steve Hamer, Boston
39. Russ Millard, Phoenix
40. Marcus Mann, Golden State
41. Jason Sasser, Sacramento
42. Randy Livingston, Houston
43. Ben Davis, Phoenix
44. Malik Rose, Charlotte
45. Joe Vogel, Seattle
46. Marcus Brown, Portland
47. Ron Riley, Seattle
48. Jamie Feick, Philadelphia
49. Amal McCaskill, Orlando
50. Terrell Bell, Houston
51. Chris Robinson, Vancouver
52. Mark Pope, Indiana
53. Jeff Nordgaard, Milwaukee
54. Shandon Anderson, Utah
55. Ronnie Henderson, Washington
56. Reggie Geary, Cleveland
57. Drew Barry, Seattle
58. Darnell Robinson, Dallas

THEY SAID IT

Yinka Dare, the New Jersey Nets center, who was still looking for his first career assist after 45 games:
"I'm not going to rush it. I'm not going to force it."

Clean Out Those Lockers

The Naismith Basketball Hall of Fame in Springfield, Mass., received a boost in March 1996 when the Springfield city council approved a measure that, pending state approval, will fund an $80 million expansion of the hall. Maybe some of the money should go to pay for a cable hookup so the hall's curators can actually watch some games. One exhibit on the main floor, described by a hall official as "featuring 14 current stars of the NBA," includes full-sized lockers containing displays dedicated to the oft-injured Derrick Coleman, who is shown in a New Jersey Nets uniform, even though he was traded to the Philadelphia 76ers in November, and Toronto Raptors general manager Isiah Thomas, who retired as a player in 1994.

NBA Champions

Season	Winner	Series	Runner-Up	Winning Coach
1946-47	Philadelphia	4–1	Chicago	Eddie Gottlieb
1947-48	Baltimore	4–2	Philadelphia	Buddy Jeannette
1948-49	Minneapolis	4–2	Washington	John Kundla
1949-50	Minneapolis	4–2	Syracuse	John Kundla
1950-51	Rochester	4–3	New York	Les Harrison
1951-52	Minneapolis	4–3	New York	John Kundla
1952-53	Minneapolis	4–1	New York	John Kundla
1953-54	Minneapolis	4–3	Syracuse	John Kundla
1954-55	Syracuse	4–3	Ft Wayne	Al Cervi
1955-56	Philadelphia	4–1	Ft Wayne	George Senesky
1956-57	Boston	4–3	St Louis	Red Auerbach
1957-58	St Louis	4–2	Boston	Alex Hannum
1958-59	Boston	4–0	Minneapolis	Red Auerbach
1959-60	Boston	4–3	St Louis	Red Auerbach
1960-61	Boston	4–1	St Louis	Red Auerbach
1961-62	Boston	4–3	LA Lakers	Red Auerbach
1962-63	Boston	4–2	LA Lakers	Red Auerbach
1963-64	Boston	4–1	San Francisco	Red Auerbach
1964-65	Boston	4–1	LA Lakers	Red Auerbach
1965-66	Boston	4–3	LA Lakers	Red Auerbach
1966-67	Philadelphia	4–2	San Francisco	Alex Hannum
1967-68	Boston	4–2	LA Lakers	Bill Russell
1968-69	Boston	4–3	LA Lakers	Bill Russell
1969-70	New York	4–3	LA Lakers	Red Holzman
1970-71	Milwaukee	4–0	Baltimore	Larry Costello
1971-72	LA Lakers	4–1	New York	Bill Sharman
1972-73	New York	4–1	LA Lakers	Red Holzman
1973-74	Boston	4–3	Milwaukee	Tommy Heinsohn
1974-75	Golden State	4–0	Washington	Al Attles
1975-76	Boston	4–2	Phoenix	Tommy Heinsohn
1976-77	Portland	4–2	Philadelphia	Jack Ramsay
1977-78	Washington	4–3	Seattle	Dick Motta
1978-79	Seattle	4–1	Washington	Lenny Wilkens
1979-80	LA Lakers	4–2	Philadelphia	Paul Westhead
1980-81	Boston	4–2	Houston	Bill Fitch
1981-82	LA Lakers	4–2	Philadelphia	Pat Riley
1982-83	Philadelphia	4–0	LA Lakers	Billy Cunningham
1983-84	Boston	4–3	LA Lakers	K.C. Jones
1984-85	LA Lakers	4–2	Boston	Pat Riley
1985-86	Boston	4–2	Houston	K.C. Jones
1986-87	LA Lakers	4–2	Boston	Pat Riley
1987-88	LA Lakers	4–3	Detroit	Pat Riley
1988-89	Detroit	4–0	LA Lakers	Chuck Daly
1989-90	Detroit	4–1	Portland	Chuck Daly
1990-91	Chicago	4–1	LA Lakers	Phil Jackson
1991-92	Chicago	4–2	Portland	Phil Jackson
1992-93	Chicago	4–2	Phoenix	Phil Jackson
1993-94	Houston	4–3	New York	Rudy Tomjanovich
1994-95	Houston	4–0	Orlando	Rudy Tomjanovich
1995-96	Chicago	4–2	Seattle	Phil Jackson

NBA Finals Most Valuable Player

1969	Jerry West, LA	1983	Moses Malone, Phil
1970	Willis Reed, NY	1984	Larry Bird, Bos
1971	Kareem Abdul-Jabbar, Mil	1985	Kareem Abdul-Jabbar, LA Lakers
1972	Wilt Chamberlain, LA	1986	Larry Bird, Bos
1973	Willis Reed, NY	1987	Magic Johnson, LA Lakers
1974	John Havlicek, Bos	1988	James Worthy, LA Lakers
1975	Rick Barry, GS	1989	Joe Dumars, Det
1976	JoJo White, Bos	1990	Isiah Thomas, Det
1977	Bill Walton, Port	1991	Michael Jordan, Chi
1978	Wes Unseld, Wash	1992	Michael Jordan, Chi
1979	Dennis Johnson, Sea	1993	Michael Jordan, Chi
1980	Magic Johnson, LA	1994	Hakeem Olajuwon, Hou
1981	Cedric Maxwell, Bos	1995	Hakeem Olajuwon, Hou
1982	Magic Johnson, LA	1996	Michael Jordan, Chi

Most Valuable Player: Maurice Podoloff Trophy

Season	Player, Team	GP	Field Goals		3-Pt FG		Free Throws		Rebounds		A	Stl	BS	Avg
			FGM	Pct	FGM	Pct	FTM	Pct	Off	Total				
1955-56	Bob Pettit, StL	72	646	42.9	–	–	557	73.6	–	1,164	189	–	–	25.7
1956-57	Bob Cousy, Bos	64	478	37.8	–	–	363	82.1	–	309	478	–	–	20.6
1957-58	Bill Russell, Bos	69	456	44.2	–	–	230	51.9	–	1,564	202	–	–	16.6
1958-59	Bob Pettit, StL	72	719	43.8	–	–	667	75.9	–	1,182	221	–	–	29.2
1959-60	Wilt Chamberlain, Phil	72	1,065	46.1	–	–	577	58.2	–	1,941	168	–	–	37.6
1960-61	Bill Russell, Bos	78	532	42.6	–	–	258	55.0	–	1,868	264	–	–	16.9
1961-62	Bill Russell, Bos	76	575	45.7	–	–	286	59.5	–	1,891	341	–	–	18.9
1962-63	Bill Russell, Bos	78	511	43.2	–	–	287	55.5	–	1,843	348	–	–	16.8
1963-64	Oscar Robertson, Cin	79	840	48.3	–	–	800	85.3	–	783	868	–	–	31.4
1964-65	Bill Russell, Bos	78	429	43.8	–	–	244	57.3	–	1,878	410	–	–	14.1
1965-66	Wilt Chamberlain, Phil	79	1,074	54.0	–	–	501	51.3	–	1,943	414	–	–	33.5
1966-67	Wilt Chamberlain, Phil	81	785	68.3	–	–	386	44.1	–	1,957	630	–	–	24.1
1967-68	Wilt Chamberlain, Phil	82	819	59.5	–	–	354	38.0	–	1,952	702	–	–	24.3
1968-69	Wes Unseld, Balt	82	427	47.6	–	–	277	60.5	–	1,491	213	–	–	13.8
1969-70	Willis Reed, NY	81	702	50.7	–	–	351	75.6	–	1,126	161	–	–	21.7
1970-71	Kareem Abdul-Jabbar, Mil	82	1,063	57.7	–	–	470	69.0	–	1,311	272	–	–	31.7
1971-72	Kareem Abdul-Jabbar, Mil	81	1,159	57.4	–	–	504	68.9	–	1,346	370	–	–	34.8
1972-73	Dave Cowens, Bos	82	740	45.2	–	–	204	77.9	–	1,329	333	–	–	20.5
1973-74	Kareem Abdul-Jabbar, Mil	81	948	53.9	–	–	295	70.2	287	1,178	386	112	283	27.0
1974-75	Bob McAdoo, Buff	82	1,095	51.2	–	–	641	80.5	307	1,155	179	92	174	34.5
1975-76	Kareem Abdul-Jabbar, LA	82	914	52.9	–	–	447	70.3	272	1,383	413	119	338	37.7
1976-77	Kareem Abdul-Jabbar, LA	82	888	57.9	–	–	376	70.1	266	1,090	319	101	261	26.2
1977-78	Bill Walton, Port	58	460	52.2	–	–	177	72.0	118	766	291	60	146	18.9
1978-79	Moses Malone, Hou	82	716	54.0	–	–	599	73.9	587	1,444	147	79	119	24.8
1979-80	Kareem Abdul-Jabbar, LA	82	835	60.4	0	00.0	364	76.5	190	886	371	81	280	24.8
1980-81	Julius Erving, Phil	82	794	52.1	4	22.2	422	78.7	244	657	364	173	147	24.6
1981-82	Moses Malone, Hou	81	945	51.9	0	00.0	630	76.2	558	1,188	142	76	125	31.1
1982-83	Moses Malone, Phil	78	654	50.1	0	00.0	600	76.1	445	1,194	101	89	157	24.5
1983-84	Larry Bird, Bos	79	758	49.2	18	24.7	374	88.8	181	796	520	144	69	24.2
1984-85	Larry Bird, Bos	80	918	52.2	56	42.7	403	88.2	164	842	531	129	98	28.7
1985-86	Larry Bird, Bos	82	796	49.6	82	42.3	441	89.6	190	805	557	166	51	25.8
1986-87	Magic Johnson, LA Lakers	80	683	52.2	8	20.5	535	84.8	122	504	977	138	36	23.9
1987-88	Michael Jordan, Chi	82	1,069	53.5	7	13.2	723	84.1	139	449	485	259	131	35.0
1988-89	Magic Johnson, LA Lakers	77	579	50.9	59	31.4	513	91.1	111	607	988	138	22	22.5
1989-90	Magic Johnson, LA Lakers	79	546	48.0	106	38.4	567	89.0	128	522	907	132	34	22.3
1990-91	Michael Jordan, Chi	82	990	53.9	29	31.2	571	85.1	118	492	453	223	83	31.5
1991-92	Michael Jordan, Chi	80	943	51.9	27	27.0	491	83.2	91	511	489	182	75	30.1
1992-93	Charles Barkley, Pho	76	716	52.0	67	30.5	445	76.5	237	928	385	119	74	25.6
1993-94	Hakeem Olajuwon, Hou	80	894	52.8	8	42.1	388	71.6	229	955	287	128	297	27.3
1994-95	David Robinson, SA	81	788	53.0	6	30.0	656	77.4	234	877	236	134	262	27.6
1995-96	Michael Jordan, Chi	82	916	49.5	111	42.7	548	83.4	148	543	352	180	42	30.4

Coach of the Year: Arnold "Red" Auerbach Trophy

1962-63	Harry Gallatin, StL	1979-80	Bill Fitch, Bos
1963-64	Alex Hannum, SF	1980-81	Jack McKinney, Ind
1964-65	Red Auerbach, Bos	1981-82	Gene Shue, Wash
1965-66	Dolph Schayes, Phil	1982-83	Don Nelson, Mil
1966-67	Johnny Kerr, Chi	1983-84	Frank Layden, Utah
1967-68	Richie Guerin, StL	1984-85	Don Nelson, Mil
1968-69	Gene Shue, Balt	1985-86	Mike Fratello, Atl
1969-70	Red Holzman, NY	1986-87	Mike Schuler, Port
1970-71	Dick Motta, Chi	1987-88	Doug Moe, Den
1971-72	Bill Sharman, LA	1988-89	Cotton Fitzsimmons, Pho
1972-73	Tom Heinsohn, Bos	1989-90	Pat Riley, LA Lakers
1973-74	Ray Scott, Det	1990-91	Don Chaney, Hou
1974-75	Phil Johnson, KC-Oma	1991-92	Don Nelson, GS
1975-76	Bill Fitch, Clev	1992-93	Pat Riley, NY
1976-77	Tom Nissalke, Hou	1993-94	Lenny Wilkens, Atl
1977-78	Hubie Brown, Atl	1994-95	Del Harris, LA Lakers
1978-79	Cotton Fitzsimmons, KC	1995-96	Phil Jackson, Chi

Note: Award named after Auerbach in 1986.

Rookie of the Year: Eddie Gottlieb Trophy

1952-53...Don Meineke, FW
1953-54...Ray Felix, Balt
1954-55...Bob Pettit, Mil
1955-56...Maurice Stokes, Roch
1956-57...Tom Heinsohn, Bos
1957-58...Woody Sauldsberry, Phil
1958-59...Elgin Baylor, Minn
1959-60...Wilt Chamberlain, Phil
1960-61...Oscar Robertson, Cin
1961-62...Walt Bellamy, Chi
1962-63...Terry Dischinger, Chi
1963-64...Jerry Lucas, Cin
1964-65...Willis Reed, NY
1965-66...Rick Barry, SF
1966-67...Dave Bing, Det
1967-68...Earl Monroe, Balt

1968-69...Wes Unseld, Balt
1969-70...K. Abdul-Jabbar, Mil
1970-71...Dave Cowens, Bos
     Geoff Petrie, Port
1971-72...Sidney Wicks, Port
1972-73...Bob McAdoo, Buff
1973-74...Ernie DiGregorio, Buff
1974-75...Keith Wilkes, GS
1975-76...Alvan Adams, Pho
1976-77...Adrian Dantley, Buff
1977-78...Walter Davis, Pho
1978-79...Phil Ford, KC
1979-80...Larry Bird, Bos
1980-81...Darrell Griffith, Utah
1981-82...Buck Williams, NJ
1982-83...Terry Cummings, SD

1983-84...Ralph Sampson, Hou
1984-85...Michael Jordan, Chi
1985-86...Patrick Ewing, NY
1986-87...Chuck Person, Ind
1987-88...Mark Jackson, NY
1988-89...Mitch Richmond, GS
1989-90...David Robinson, SA
1990-91...Derrick Coleman, NJ
1991-92...Larry Johnson, Char
1992-93...Shaquille O'Neal, Orl
1993-94...Chris Webber, GS
1994-95...Jason Kidd, Dal
     Grant Hill, Det
1995-96...Damon Stoudamire, Tor

Defensive Player of the Year

1982-83.....................Sidney Moncrief, Mil
1983-84.....................Sidney Moncrief, Mil
1984-85.....................Mark Eaton, Utah
1985-86.....................Alvin Robertson, SA
1986-87.....................Michael Cooper, LA Lakers
1987-88.....................Michael Jordan, Chi
1988-89.....................Mark Eaton, Utah
1989-90.....................Dennis Rodman, Det
1990-91.....................Dennis Rodman, Det
1991-92.....................David Robinson, SA
1992-93.....................Hakeem Olajuwon, Hou
1993-94.....................Hakeem Olajuwon, Hou
1994-95.....................Dikembe Mutombo, Den
1995-96.....................Gary Payton, Sea

Sixth Man Award

1982-83.....................Bobby Jones, Phil
1983-84.....................Kevin McHale, Bos
1984-85.....................Kevin McHale, Bos
1985-86.....................Bill Walton, Bos
1986-87.....................Ricky Pierce, Mil
1987-88.....................Roy Tarpley, Dall
1988-89.....................Eddie Johnson, Pho
1989-90.....................Ricky Pierce, Mil
1990-91.....................Detlef Schrempf, Ind
1991-92.....................Detlef Schrempf, Ind
1992-93.....................Cliff Robinson, Port
1993-94.....................Dell Curry, Char
1994-95.....................Anthony Mason, NY
1995-96.....................Tony Kukoc, Chi

J. Walter Kennedy Citizenship Award

1974-75.....................Wes Unseld, Wash
1975-76.....................Slick Watts, Sea
1976-77.....................Dave Bing, Wash
1977-78.....................Bob Lanier, Det
1978-79.....................Calvin Murphy, Hou
1979-80.....................Austin Carr, Clev
1980-81.....................Mike Glenn, NY
1981-82.....................Kent Benson, Det
1982-83.....................Julius Erving, Phil
1983-84.....................Frank Layden, Utah
1984-85.....................Dan Issel, Den
1985-86.....................Michael Cooper, LA Lakers
     Rory Sparrow, NY
1986-87.....................Isiah Thomas, Det
1987-88.....................Alex English, Den
1988-89.....................Thurl Bailey, Utah

Kennedy Citizenship Award (Cont.)

1989-90.........................Glenn Rivers, Atl
1990-91.........................Kevin Johnson, Pho
1991-92.........................Magic Johnson, LA Lakers
1992-93.........................Terry Porter, Port
1993-94.........................Joe Dumars, Det
1994-95.........................Joe O'Toole, Atl
1995-96.........................Chris Dudley, Port

Most Improved Player

1985-86.........................Alvin Robertson, SA
1986-87.........................Dale Ellis, Sea
1987-88.........................Kevin Duckworth, Port
1988-89.........................Kevin Johnson, Pho
1989-90.........................Rony Seikaly, Mia
1990-91.........................Scott Skiles, Orl
1991-92.........................Pervis Ellison, Wash
1992-93.........................Chris Jackson, Den
1993-94.........................Don MacLean, Wash
1994-95.........................Dana Barros, Phil
1995-96.........................Gheorghe Muresan, Wash

Executive of the Year

1972-73.........................Joe Axelson, KC-Oma
1973-74.........................Eddie Donovan, Buff
1974-75.........................Dick Vertlieb, GS
1975-76.........................Jerry Colangelo, Pho
1976-77.........................Ray Patterson, Hou
1977-78.........................Angelo Drossos, SA
1978-79.........................Bob Ferry, Wash
1979-80.........................Red Auerbach, Bos
1980-81.........................Jerry Colangelo, Pho
1981-82.........................Bob Ferry, Wash
1982-83.........................Zollie Volchok, Sea
1983-84.........................Frank Layden, Utah
1984-85.........................Vince Boryla, Den
1985-86.........................Stan Kasten, Atl
1986-87.........................Stan Kasten, Atl
1987-88.........................Jerry Krause, Chi
1988-89.........................Jerry Colangelo, Pho
1989-90.........................Bob Bass, SA
1990-91.........................Bucky Buckwalter, Port
1991-92.........................Wayne Embry, Cle
1992-93.........................Jerry Colangelo, Pho
1993-94.........................Bob Whitsitt, Sea
1994-95.........................Jerry West, LA Lakers
1995-96.........................Jerry Krause, Chi

Selected by *The Sporting News.*

Scoring

MOST POINTS, CAREER

	Pts	Avg
Kareem Abdul-Jabbar	38,387	24.6
Wilt Chamberlain	31,419	30.1
Moses Malone	27,409	20.6
Elvin Hayes	27,313	21.0
Oscar Robertson	26,710	25.7
John Havlicek	26,395	20.8
Alex English	25,613	21.5
Dominique Wilkins	25,389	25.8
Jerry West	25,192	27.0
Michael Jordan	24,489	32.0

MOST POINTS, SEASON

Wilt Chamberlain, Phil	4,029	1961-62
Wilt Chamberlain, SF	3,586	1962-63
Michael Jordan, Chi	3,041	1986-87
Wilt Chamberlain, Phil	3,033	1960-61
Wilt Chamberlain, SF	2,948	1963-64
Michael Jordan, Chi	2,868	1987-88
Bob McAdoo, Buff	2,831	1974-75
Rick Barry, SF	2,775	1966-67
Michael Jordan, Chi	2,753	1989-90
Elgin Baylor, LA	2,719	1962-63

HIGHEST SCORING AVERAGE, CAREER

Michael Jordan	32.0	766 games
Wilt Chamberlain	30.1	1,045 games
Elgin Baylor	27.4	846 games
Jerry West	27.0	932 games
Bob Pettit	26.4	792 games
George Gervin	26.2	791 games
Karl Malone	26.0	898 games
Dominique Wilkins	25.8	984 games
Oscar Robertson	25.7	1,040 games
David Robinson	25.6	557 games

HIGHEST SCORING AVERAGE, SEASON

Wilt Chamberlain, Phil	50.4	1961-62
Wilt Chamberlain, SF	44.8	1962-63
Wilt Chamberlain, Phil	38.4	1960-61
Wilt Chamberlain, Phil	37.6	1959-60
Michael Jordan, Chi	37.1	1986-87
Wilt Chamberlain, SF	36.9	1963-64
Rick Barry, SF	35.6	1966-67
Michael Jordan, Chi	35.0	1987-88
Elgin Baylor, LA	34.8	1960-61

Note: Minimum 70 games.

MOST POINTS, GAME

Player, Team	Opp	Date
100 .... Wilt Chamberlain, Phi	NY	3/2/62
78 .... Wilt Chamberlain, Phi	LA	12/8/61
73 .... Wilt Chamberlain, Phi	Chi	1/13/62
73 .... Wilt Chamberlain, SF	NY	11/16/62
73 .... David Thompson, Den	Det	4/9/78
72 .... Wilt Chamberlain, SF	LA	11/3/62
71 .... David Robinson, SA	LAC	4/24/94
71 .... Elgin Baylor, LA	NY	11/15/60
70 .... Wilt Chamberlain, SF	Syr	3/10/63
69 .... Michael Jordan, Chi	Cle	3/28/90

Field-Goal Percentage

Highest Field Goal Percentage, Career: .599—Artis Gilmore
Highest Field Goal Percentage, Season: .727—Wilt Chamberlain, LA Lakers, 1972-73 (426/586)

Free-Throw Percentage

HIGHEST FREE-THROW PERCENTAGE, CAREER

Mark Price	.907
Rick Barry	.900
Calvin Murphy	.892
Scott Skiles	.890
Larry Bird	.886

Note: Minimum 1200 free throws made.

HIGHEST FREE-THROW PERCENTAGE, SEASON

Calvin Murphy, Hou	.958	1980-81
Mahmoud Abdul-Rauf, Den	.956	1993-94
Mark Price, Clev	.948	1992-93
Mark Price, Clev	.947	1991-92
Rick Barry, Hou	.946	1978-79

MOST FREE THROWS MADE, CAREER

	No.	Yrs	Pct
Moses Malone	8,531	19	.769
Oscar Robertson	7,694	14	.838
Jerry West	7,160	14	.814
Dolph Schayes	6,979	16	.844
Adrian Dantley	6,832	15	.818

Three-Point Field-Goal Percentage*

Most Three-Point Field Goals, Career: 1,269—Dale Ellis
Highest Three-Point Field-Goal Percentage, Career: .480—Steve Kerr
Most Three-Point Field Goals, Season: 267—Dennis Scott, Orl, 1995-96
Highest Three-Point Field Goal-Percentage, Season: .524—Steve Kerr, Chi, 1994-95
Most Three-Point Field Goals, Game: 11—Dennis Scott, Orlando vs Atlanta, 4/18/96

*First Year of Shot: 1979-80.

Steals

Most Steals, Career: 2,365—John Stockton
Most Steals, Season: 301—Alvin Robertson, San Antonio, 1985-86
Most Steals, Game: 11—Larry Kenon, San Antonio vs Kansas City, 12/26/76

THEY SAID IT

George Triantafillo, Dennis Rodman's bodyguard, on the necessity for unblinking vigilance: "Let's face it: When Dennis goes out, he doesn't blend in well."

NBA Alltime Individual Leaders (Cont.)

Rebounds

MOST REBOUNDS, CAREER

	No.	Yrs	Avg
Wilt Chamberlain	23,924	14	22.9
Bill Russell	21,620	13	22.5
Kareem Abdul-Jabbar	17,440	20	11.4
Elvin Hayes	16,279	16	12.5
Moses Malone	16,212	19	12.2
Nate Thurmond	14,464	14	15.0
Robert Parish	14,626	20	9.3
Walt Bellamy	14,241	14	13.7
Wes Unseld	13,769	13	14.0
Jerry Lucas	12,942	11	15.6

MOST REBOUNDS, SEASON

Wilt Chamberlain, Phil	2,149	1960-61
Wilt Chamberlain, Phil	2,052	1961-62
Wilt Chamberlain, Phil	1,957	1966-67
Wilt Chamberlain, Phil	1,952	1967-68
Wilt Chamberlain, SF	1,946	1962-63
Wilt Chamberlain, Phil	1,943	1965-66
Wilt Chamberlain, Phil	1,941	1959-60
Bill Russell, Bos	1,930	1963-64
Bill Russell, Bos	1,878	1964-65
Bill Russell, Bos	1,868	1960-61

MOST REBOUNDS, GAME

	Player, Team	Opp	Date
55	Wilt Chamberlain, Phi	Bos	11/24/60
51	Bill Russell, Bos	Syr	2/5/60
49	Bill Russell, Bos	Phi	11/16/57
49	Bill Russell, Bos	Det	3/11/65
45	Wilt Chamberlain, Phil	Syr	2/6/60
45	Wilt Chamberlain, Phil	LA	1/21/61

Assists

MOST ASSISTS, CAREER

John Stockton	11,310
Magic Johnson	10,141
Oscar Robertson	9,887
Isiah Thomas	9,061
Maurice Cheeks	7,392

MOST ASSISTS, SEASON

John Stockton, Utah	1,164	1990-91
John Stockton, Utah	1,134	1989-90
John Stockton, Utah	1,128	1987-88
John Stockton, Utah	1,126	1991-92
Isiah Thomas, Det	1,123	1984-85

MOST ASSISTS, GAME: 30—Scott Skiles, Orlando vs Denver, 12/30/90

Blocked Shots

MOST BLOCKED SHOTS, CAREER

Hakeem Olajuwon	3,190
Kareem Abdul-Jabbar	3,189
Mark Eaton	3,064
Wayne (Tree) Rollins	2,542

MOST BLOCKED SHOTS, SEASON

Mark Eaton, Utah	456	1984-85
Manute Bol, Wash	397	1985-86
Elmore Smith, LA	393	1973-74

MOST BLOCKED SHOTS, GAME: 17—Elmore Smith, LA Lakers vs Portland, 10/28/73

NBA Alltime Playoff Leaders

Scoring

MOST POINTS, CAREER

	Pts	Yrs	Avg
Kareem Abdul-Jabbar	5,762	18	24.3
Michael Jordan	4,717	11	33.9
Jerry West	4,457	13	29.1
Larry Bird	3,897	12	23.8
John Havlicek	3,776	13	22.0
Magic Johnson	3,701	13	19.5
Elgin Baylor	3,623	12	27.0
Wilt Chamberlain	3,607	13	22.5
Hakeem Olajuwon	3,202	11	27.8
Kevin McHale	3,182	13	18.8

*HIGHEST SCORING AVERAGE, CAREER

	Avg	Games
Michael Jordan	33.9	139
Jerry West	29.1	153
Hakeem Olajuwon	27.8	115
Karl Malone	27.3	97
Elgin Baylor	27.0	134

HIGHEST SCORING AVERAGE, CAREER (Cont.)

	Avg	Games
George Gervin	27.0	59
Dominique Wilkins	25.8	55
Bob Pettit	25.5	88
Shaquille O'Neal	25.3	36
Rick Barry	24.8	74

*Minimum of 25 games.

MOST POINTS, GAME

	Player, Team	Opp	Date
†63	Michael Jordan, Chi	Bos	4/20/86
61	Elgin Baylor, LA	Bos	4/14/62
56	Wilt Chamberlain, Phi	Syr	3/22/62
56	Michael Jordan, Chi	Mia	4/29/92
56	Charles Barkley, Pho	GS	5/4/94
55	Rick Barry, SF	Phi	4/18/67
55	Michael Jordan, Chi	Cle	5/1/88
55	Michael Jordan, Chi	Pho	4/16/95

†Double overtime game.

NBA Alltime Playoff Leaders (Cont.)

Rebounds

MOST REBOUNDS, CAREER

	No.	Yrs	Avg
Bill Russell	4,104	13	24.9
Wilt Chamberlain	3,913	13	24.5
Kareem Abdul-Jabbar	2,481	18	10.5
Wes Unseld	1,777	12	14.9
Robert Parish	1,761	15	9.7

MOST REBOUNDS, GAME

	Player, Team	Opp	Date
41	Wilt Chamberlain, Phi	Bos	4/5/67
40	Bill Russell, Bos	Phi	3/23/58
40	Bill Russell, Bos	StL	3/29/60
*40	Bill Russell, Bos	LA	4/18/62

Three tied at 39.

*Overtime game.

Assists

MOST ASSISTS, CAREER

	No.	Games
Magic Johnson	2,346	190
John Stockton	1,175	107
Larry Bird	1,062	164
Dennis Johnson	1,006	180
Isiah Thomas	987	111

MOST ASSISTS, GAME

	Player, Team	Opp	Date
24	Magic Johnson, LA	Pho	5/15/84
24	John Stockton, Utah	LAL	5/17/88
23	Magic Johnson, LA	Port	5/3/85
22	Doc Rivers, Atl	Bos	5/16/88

Four tied at 21.

Games played

K. Abdul-Jabbar	237
Danny Ainge	193
Magic Johnson	190
Robert Parish	182
Dennis Johnson	180
Byron Scott	175
John Havlicek	170
Kevin McHale	169
Michael Cooper	168
Bill Russell	165

Appearances

K. Abdul-Jabbar	18
Robert Parish	15
Dolph Schayes	15
Paul Silas	14
Wilt Chamberlain	13
Maurice Cheeks	13
Bob Cousy	13
Hal Greer	13
John Havlicek	13
Kevin McHale	13
Dennis Johnson	13
Bill Russell	13
Chet Walker	13
Jerry West	13

NBA Season Leaders

Scoring

1946-47	Joe Fulks, Phil	1389	1972-73	Nate Archibald, KC-Oma	34.0
1947-48	Max Zaslofsky, Chi	1007	1973-74	Bob McAdoo, Buff	30.6
1948-49	George Mikan, Minn	1698	1974-75	Bob McAdoo, Buff	34.5
1949-50	George Mikan, Minn	1865	1975-76	Bob McAdoo, Buff	31.1
1950-51	George Mikan, Minn	1932	1976-77	Pete Maravich, NO	31.1
1951-52	Paul Arizin, Phil	1674	1977-78	George Gervin, SA	27.2
1952-53	Neil Johnston, Phil	1564	1978-79	George Gervin, SA	29.6
1953-54	Neil Johnston, Phil	1759	1979-80	George Gervin, SA	33.1
1954-55	Neil Johnston, Phil	1631	1980-81	Adrian Dantley, Utah	30.7
1955-56	Bob Pettit, StL	1849	1981-82	George Gervin, SA	32.3
1956-57	Paul Arizin, Phil	1817	1982-83	Alex English, Den	28.4
1957-58	George Yardley, Det	2001	1983-84	Adrian Dantley, Utah	30.6
1958-59	Bob Pettit, StL	2105	1984-85	Bernard King, NY	32.9
1959-60	Wilt Chamberlain, Phil	2707	1985-86	Dominique Wilkins, Atl	30.3
1960-61	Wilt Chamberlain, Phil	3033	1986-87	Michael Jordan, Chi	37.1
1961-62	Wilt Chamberlain, Phil	4029	1987-88	Michael Jordan, Chi	35.0
1962-63	Wilt Chamberlain, SF	3586	1988-89	Michael Jordan, Chi	32.5
1963-64	Wilt Chamberlain, SF	2948	1989-90	Michael Jordan, Chi	33.6
1964-65	Wilt Chamberlain, SF-Phil	2534	1990-91	Michael Jordan, Chi	31.5
1965-66	Wilt Chamberlain, Phil	2649	1991-92	Michael Jordan, Chi	30.1
1966-67	Rick Barry, SF	2775	1992-93	Michael Jordan, Chi	32.6
1967-68	Dave Bing, Det	2142	1993-94	David Robinson, SA	29.8
1968-69	Elvin Hayes, SD	2327	1994-95	Shaquille O'Neal, Orl	29.3
1969-70	Jerry West, LA	*31.2	1995-96	Michael Jordan, Chi	30.4
1970-71	Kareem Abdul-Jabbar, Mil	31.7			
1971-72	Kareem Abdul-Jabbar, Mil	34.8			

*Based on per game average since 1969-70.

Rebounding

1950-51	Dolph Schayes, Syr	1080	1973-74	Elvin Hayes, Capital	18.1
1951-52	Larry Foust, FW	880	1974-75	Wes Unseld, Wash	14.8
	Mel Hutchins, Mil	880	1975-76	Kareem Abdul-Jabbar, LA	16.9
1952-53	George Mikan, Minn	1007	1976-77	Bill Walton, Port	14.4
1953-54	Harry Gallatin, NY	1098	1977-78	Len Robinson, NO	15.7
1954-55	Neil Johnston, Phil	1085	1978-79	Moses Malone, Hou	17.6
1955-56	Bob Pettit, StL	1164	1979-80	Swen Nater, SD	15.0
1956-57	Maurice Stokes, Roch	1256	1980-81	Moses Malone, Hou	14.8
1957-58	Bill Russell, Bos	1564	1981-82	Moses Malone, Hou	14.7
1958-59	Bill Russell, Bos	1612	1982-83	Moses Malone, Phil	15.3
1959-60	Wilt Chamberlain, Phil	1941	1983-84	Moses Malone, Phil	13.4
1960-61	Wilt Chamberlain, Phil	2149	1984-85	Moses Malone, Phil	13.1
1961-62	Wilt Chamberlain, Phil	2052	1985-86	Bill Laimbeer, Det	13.1
1962-63	Wilt Chamberlain, SF	1946	1986-87	Charles Barkley, Phil	14.6
1963-64	Bill Russell, Bos	1930	1987-88	Michael Cage, LA Clippers	13.0
1964-65	Bill Russell, Bos	1878	1988-89	Hakeem Olajuwon, Hou	13.5
1965-66	Wilt Chamberlain, Phil	1943	1989-90	Hakeem Olajuwon, Hou	14.0
1966-67	Wilt Chamberlain, Phil	1957	1990-91	David Robinson, SA	13.0
1967-68	Wilt Chamberlain, Phil	1952	1991-92	Dennis Rodman, Det	18.7
1968-69	Wilt Chamberlain, LA	1712	1992-93	Dennis Rodman, Det	18.3
1969-70	Elvin Hayes, SD	*16.9	1993-94	Dennis Rodman, SA	17.3
1970-71	Wilt Chamberlain, LA	18.2	1994-95	Dennis Rodman, SA	16.8
1971-72	Wilt Chamberlain, LA	19.2	1995-96	Dennis Rodman, Chi	14.9
1972-73	Wilt Chamberlain, LA	18.6			

*Based on per game average since 1969-70.

Assists

1946-47	Ernie Calverly, Prov	202	1971-72	Jerry West, LA	9.7
1947-48	Howie Dallmar, Phil	120	1972-73	Nate Archibald, KC-Oma	11.4
1948-49	Bob Davies, Roch	321	1973-74	Ernie DiGregorio, Buff	8.2
1949-50	Dick McGuire, NY	386	1974-75	Kevin Porter, Wash	8.0
1950-51	Andy Phillip, Phil	414	1975-76	Don Watts, Sea	8.1
1951-52	Andy Phillip, Phil	539	1976-77	Don Buse, Ind	8.5
1952-53	Bob Cousy, Bos	547	1977-78	Kevin Porter, NJ-Det	10.2
1953-54	Bob Cousy, Bos	578	1978-79	Kevin Porter, Det	13.4
1954-55	Bob Cousy, Bos	557	1979-80	Micheal Richardson, NY	10.1
1955-56	Bob Cousy, Bos	642	1980-81	Kevin Porter, Wash	9.1
1956-57	Bob Cousy, Bos	478	1981-82	Johnny Moore, SA	9.6
1957-58	Bob Cousy, Bos	463	1982-83	Magic Johnson, LA	10.5
1958-59	Bob Cousy, Bos	557	1983-84	Magic Johnson, LA	13.1
1959-60	Bob Cousy, Bos	715	1984-85	Isiah Thomas, Det	13.9
1960-61	Oscar Robertson, Cin	690	1985-86	Magic Johnson, LA Lakers	12.6
1961-62	Oscar Robertson, Cin	899	1986-87	Magic Johnson, LA Lakers	12.2
1962-63	Guy Rodgers, SF	825	1987-88	John Stockton, Utah	13.8
1963-64	Oscar Robertson, Cin	868	1988-89	John Stockton, Utah	13.6
1964-65	Oscar Robertson, Cin	861	1989-90	John Stockton, Utah	14.5
1965-66	Oscar Robertson, Cin	847	1990-91	John Stockton, Utah	14.2
1966-67	Guy Rodgers, Chi	908	1991-92	John Stockton, Utah	13.7
1967-68	Wilt Chamberlain, Phil	702	1992-93	John Stockton, Utah	12.0
1968-69	Oscar Robertson, Cin	772	1993-94	John Stockton, Utah	12.6
1969-70	Len Wilkens, Sea	*9.1	1994-95	John Stockton, Utah	12.3
1970-71	Norm Van Lier, Cin	10.1	1995-96	John Stockton, Utah	11.2

*Based on per game average since 1969-70.

Field-Goal Percentage

1946-47	Bob Feerick, Wash	40.1	1957-58	Jack Twyman, Cin	45.2
1947-48	Bob Feerick, Wash	34.0	1958-59	Ken Sears, NY	49.0
1948-49	Arnie Risen, Roch	42.3	1959-60	Ken Sears, NY	47.7
1949-50	Alex Groza, Ind	47.8	1960-61	Wilt Chamberlain, Phil	50.9
1950-51	Alex Groza, Ind	47.0	1961-62	Walt Bellamy, Chi	51.9
1951-52	Paul Arizin, Phil	44.8	1962-63	Wilt Chamberlain, SF	52.8
1952-53	Neil Johnston, Phil	45.2	1963-64	Jerry Lucas, Cin	52.7
1953-54	Ed Macauley, Bos	48.6	1964-65	Wilt Chamberlain, SF-Phil	51.0
1954-55	Larry Foust, FW	48.7	1965-66	Wilt Chamberlain, Phil	54.0
1955-56	Neil Johnston, Phil	45.7	1966-67	Wilt Chamberlain, Phil	68.3
1956-57	Neil Johnston, Phil	44.7	1967-68	Wilt Chamberlain, Phil	59.5

Field-Goal Percentage *(Cont.)*

1968-69	Wilt Chamberlain, LA	58.3	1982-83	Artis Gilmore, SA	62.6
1969-70	Johnny Green, Cin	55.9	1983-84	Artis Gilmore, SA	63.1
1970-71	Johnny Green, Cin	58.7	1984-85	James Donaldson, LA Clippers	63.7
1971-72	Wilt Chamberlain, LA	64.9	1985-86	Steve Johnson, SA	63.2
1972-73	Wilt Chamberlain, LA	72.7	1986-87	Kevin McHale, Bos	60.4
1973-74	Bob McAdoo, Buff	54.7	1987-88	Kevin McHale, Bos	60.4
1974-75	Don Nelson, Bos	53.9	1988-89	Dennis Rodman, Det	59.5
1975-76	Wes Unseld, Wash	56.1	1989-90	Mark West, Pho	62.5
1976-77	Kareem Abdul-Jabbar, LA	57.9	1990-91	Buck Williams, Port	60.2
1977-78	Bobby Jones, Den	57.8	1991-92	Buck Williams, Port	60.4
1978-79	Cedric Maxwell, Bos	58.4	1992-93	Cedric Ceballos, Pho	57.6
1979-80	Cedric Maxwell, Bos	60.9	1993-94	Shaquille O'Neal, Orl	59.9
1980-81	Artis Gilmore, Chi	67.0	1994-95	Chris Gatling, GS	63.3
1981-82	Artis Gilmore, Chi	65.2	1995-96	Gheorghe Muresan, Wash	58.4

Free-Throw Percentage

1946-47	Fred Scolari, Wash	81.1	1971-72	Jack Marin, Balt	89.4
1947-48	Bob Feerick, Wash	78.8	1972-73	Rick Barry, GS	90.2
1948-49	Bob Feerick, Wash	85.9	1973-74	Ernie DiGregorio, Buff	90.2
1949-50	Max Zaslofsky, Chi	84.3	1974-75	Rick Barry, GS	90.4
1950-51	Joe Fulks, Phil	85.5	1975-76	Rick Barry, GS	92.3
1951-52	Bob Wanzer, Roch	90.4	1976-77	Ernie DiGregorio, Buff	94.5
1952-53	Bill Sharman, Bos	85.0	1977-78	Rick Barry, GS	92.4
1953-54	Bill Sharman, Bos	84.4	1978-79	Rick Barry, Hou	94.7
1954-55	Bill Sharman, Bos	89.7	1979-80	Rick Barry, Hou	93.5
1955-56	Bill Sharman, Bos	86.7	1980-81	Calvin Murphy, Hou	95.8
1956-57	Bill Sharman, Bos	90.5	1981-82	Kyle Macy, Pho	89.9
1957-58	Dolph Schayes, Syr	90.4	1982-83	Calvin Murphy, Hou	92.0
1958-59	Bill Sharman, Bos	93.2	1983-84	Larry Bird, Bos	88.8
1959-60	Dolph Schayes, Syr	89.2	1984-85	Kyle Macy, Pho	90.7
1960-61	Bill Sharman, Bos	92.1	1985-86	Larry Bird, Bos	89.6
1961-62	Dolph Schayes, Syr	89.6	1986-87	Larry Bird, Bos	91.0
1962-63	Larry Costello, Syr	88.1	1987-88	Jack Sikma, Mil	92.2
1963-64	Oscar Robertson, Cin	85.3	1988-89	Magic Johnson, LA Lakers	91.1
1964-65	Larry Costello, Phil	87.7	1989-90	Larry Bird, Bos	93.0
1965-66	Larry Siegfried, Bos	88.1	1990-91	Reggie Miller, Ind	91.8
1966-67	Adrian Smith, Cin	90.3	1991-92	Mark Price, Clev	94.7
1967-68	Oscar Robertson, Cin	87.3	1992-93	Mark Price, Clev	94.8
1968-69	Larry Siegfried, Bos	86.4	1993-94	Mahmoud Abdul-Rauf, Den	95.6
1969-70	Flynn Robinson, Mil	89.8	1994-95	Spud Webb, Sac	93.4
1970-71	Chet Walker, Chi	85.9	1995-96	Mahmoud Abdul Rauf, Den	93.0

Three-Point Field-Goal Percentage

1979-80	Fred Brown, Sea	44.3*	1988-89	Jon Sundvold, Mia	52.2
1980-81	Brian Taylor, SD	38.3	1989-90	Steve Kerr, Clev	50.7
1981-82	Campy Russell, NY	43.9	1990-91	Jim Les, Sac	46.1
1982-83	Mike Dunleavy, SA	34.5	1991-92	Dana Barros, Sea	44.6
1983-84	Darrell Griffith, Utah	36.1	1992-93	B.J. Armstrong, Chi	45.3
1984-85	Byron Scott, LA Lakers	43.3	1993-94	Tracy Murray, Por	45.9
1985-86	Craig Hodges, Mil	45.1	1994-95	Steve Kerr, Chi	52.4
1986-87	Kiki Vandeweghe, Por	48.1	1995-96	Tim Legler, Wash	52.2
1987-88	Craig Hodges, Mil-Pho	49.1			

Steals

1973-74	Larry Steele, Por	2.68	1985-86	Alvin Robertson, SA	3.67
1974-75	Rick Barry, GS	2.85	1986-87	Alvin Robertson, SA	3.21
1975-76	Don Watts, Sea	3.18	1987-88	Michael Jordan, Chi	3.16
1976-77	Don Buse, Ind	3.47	1988-89	John Stockton, Utah	3.21
1977-78	Ron Lee, Pho	2.74	1989-90	Michael Jordan, Chi	2.77
1978-79	M.L. Carr, Det	2.46	1990-91	Alvin Robertson, Mil	3.04
1979-80	Micheal Richardson, NY	3.23	1991-92	John Stockton, Utah	2.98
1980-81	Magic Johnson, LA	3.43	1992-93	Michael Jordan, Chi	2.83
1981-82	Magic Johnson, LA	2.67	1993-94	Nate McMillan, Sea	2.96
1982-83	Micheal Richardson, GS-NJ	2.84	1994-95	Scottie Pippen, Chi	2.94
1983-84	Rickey Green, Utah	2.65	1995-96	Gary Payton, Sea	2.85
1984-85	Micheal Richardson, NJ	2.96			

NBA Season Leaders (Cont.)

Blocked Shots

1973-74...............Elmore Smith, LA	4.85	1985-86...............Manute Bol, Wash	4.96
1974-75...............Kareem Abdul-Jabbar, Mil	3.26	1986-87...............Mark Eaton, Utah	4.06
1975-76...............Kareem Abdul-Jabbar, LA	4.12	1987-88...............Mark Eaton, Utah	3.71
1976-77...............Bill Walton, Port	3.25	1988-89...............Manute Bol, GS	4.31
1977-78...............George Johnson, NJ	3.38	1989-90...............Hakeem Olajuwon, Hou	4.59
1978-79...............Kareem Abdul-Jabbar, LA	3.95	1990-91...............Hakeem Olajuwon, Hou	3.95
1979-80...............Kareem Abdul-Jabbar, LA	3.41	1991-92...............David Robinson, SA	4.49
1980-81...............George Johnson, SA	3.39	1992-93...............Hakeem Olajuwon, Hou	4.17
1981-82...............George Johnson, SA	3.12	1993-94...............Dikembe Mutombo, Den	4.10
1982-83...............Wayne Rollins, Atl	4.29	1994-95...............Dikembe Mutombo, Den	3.91
1983-84...............Mark Eaton, Utah	4.28	1995-96...............Dikembe Mutombo, Den	4.49
1984-85...............Mark Eaton, Utah	5.56		

NBA All-Star Game Results

Year	Result	Site	Winning Coach	Most Valuable Player
1951	East 111, West 94	Boston	Joe Lapchick	Ed Macauley, Bos
1952	East 108, West 91	Boston	Al Cervi	Paul Arizin, Phil
1953	West 79, East 75	Ft Wayne	John Kundla	George Mikan, Minn
1954	East 98, West 93 (OT)	New York	Joe Lapchick	Bob Cousy, Bos
1955	East 100, West 91	New York	Al Cervi	Bill Sharman, Bos
1956	West 108, East 94	Rochester	Charley Eckman	Bob Pettit, StL
1957	East 109, West 97	Boston	Red Auerbach	Bob Cousy, Bos
1958	East 130, West 118	St Louis	Red Auerbach	Bob Pettit, StL
1959	West 124, East 108	Detroit	Ed Macauley	Bob Pettit, StL
				Elgin Baylor, Minn
1960	East 125, West 115	Philadelphia	Red Auerbach	Wilt Chamberlain, Phil
1961	West 153, East 131	Syracuse	Paul Seymour	Oscar Robertson, Cin
1962	West 150, East 130	St Louis	Fred Schaus	Bob Pettit, StL
1963	East 115, West 108	Los Angeles	Red Auerbach	Bill Russell, Bos
1964	East 111, West 107	Boston	Red Auerbach	Oscar Robertson, Cin
1965	East 124, West 123	St Louis	Red Auerbach	Jerry Lucas, Cin
1966	East 137, West 94	Cincinnati	Red Auerbach	Adrian Smith, Cin
1967	West 135, East 120	San Francisco	Fred Schaus	Rick Barry, SF
1968	East 144, West 124	New York	Alex Hannum	Hal Greer, Phil
1969	East 123, West 112	Baltimore	Gene Shue	Oscar Robertson, Cin
1970	East 142, West 135	Philadelphia	Red Holzman	Willis Reed, NY
1971	West 108, East 107	San Diego	Larry Costello	Lenny Wilkens, Sea
1972	West 112, East 110	Los Angeles	Bill Sharman	Jerry West, LA
1973	East 104, West 84	Chicago	Tom Heinsohn	Dave Cowens, Bos
1974	West 134, East 123	Seattle	Larry Costello	Bob Lanier, Det
1975	East 108, West 102	Phoenix	K.C. Jones	Walt Frazier, NY
1976	East 123, West 109	Philadelphia	Tom Heinsohn	Dave Bing, Wash
1977	West 125, East 124	Milwaukee	Larry Brown	Julius Erving, Phil
1978	East 133, West 125	Atlanta	Billy Cunningham	Randy Smith, Buff
1979	West 134, East 129	Detroit	Lenny Wilkens	David Thompson, Den
1980	East 144, West 135 (OT)	Washington	Billy Cunningham	George Gervin, SA
1981	East 123, West 120	Cleveland	Billy Cunningham	Nate Archibald, Bos
1982	East 120, West 118	New Jersey	Bill Fitch	Larry Bird, Bos
1983	East 132, West 123	Los Angeles	Billy Cunningham	Julius Erving, Phil
1984	East 154, West 145 (OT)	Denver	K.C. Jones	Isiah Thomas, Det
1985	West 140, East 129	Indiana	Pat Riley	Ralph Sampson, Hou
1986	East 139, West 132	Dallas	K.C. Jones	Isiah Thomas, Det
1987	West 154, East 149 (OT)	Seattle	Pat Riley	Tom Chambers, Sea
1988	East 138, West 133	Chicago	Mike Fratello	Michael Jordan, Chi
1989	West 143, East 134	Houston	Pat Riley	Karl Malone, Utah
1990	East 130, West 113	Miami	Chuck Daly	Magic Johnson, LA Lakers
1991	East 116, West 114	Charlotte	Chris Ford	Charles Barkley, Phil
1992	West 153, East 113	Orlando	Don Nelson	Magic Johnson, LA Lakers
1993	West 135, East 132	Salt Lake City	Paul Westphal	Karl Malone, Utah
				John Stockton, Utah
1994	East 127, West 118	Minneapolis	Lenny Wilkens	Scottie Pippen, Chi
1995	West 139, East 112	Phoenix	Paul Westphal	Mitch Richmond, Sac
1996	East 129, West 118	San Antonio	Phil Jackson	Michael Jordan, Chi

Members of the Basketball Hall of Fame

Contributors

Senda Abbott (1984)
Forest C. (Phog) Allen (1959)
Clair F. Bee (1967)
Walter A. Brown (1965)
John W. Bunn (1964)
Bob Douglas (1971)
Al Duer (1981)
Clifford Fagan (1983)
Harry A. Fisher (1973)
Larry Fleisher (1991)
Edward Gottlieb (1971)
Luther H. Gulick (1959)
Lester Harrison (1979)
Ferenc Hepp (1980)
Edward J. Hickox (1959)

Paul D. (Tony) Hinkle (1965)
Ned Irish (1964)
R. William Jones (1964)
J. Walter Kennedy (1980)
Emil S. Liston (1974)
John B. McLendon (1978)
Bill Mokray (1965)
Ralph Morgan (1959)
Frank Morgenweck (1962)
James Naismith (1959)
Peter F. Newell (1978)
John J. O'Brien (1961)
Larry O'Brien (1991)
Harold G. Olsen (1959)
Maurice Podoloff (1973)

H.V. Porter (1960)
William A. Reid (1963)
Elmer Ripley (1972)
Lynn W. St. John (1962)
Abe Saperstein (1970)
Arthur A. Schabinger (1961)
Amos Alonzo Stagg (1959)
Boris Stankovic (1991)
Edward Steitz (1983)
Chuck Taylor (1968)
Oswald Tower (1959)
Arthur L. Trester (1961)
Clifford Wells (1971)
Lou Wilke (1982)

Players

Kareem Abdul-Jabbar (1995)
Nate (Tiny) Archibald (1991)
Paul J. Arizin (1977)
Thomas B. Barlow (1980)
Rick Barry (1986)
Elgin Baylor (1976)
John Beckman (1972)
Walt Bellamy (1993)
Sergei Belov (1992)
Dave Bing (1989)
Carol Blazejowski (1994)
Bennie Borgmann (1961)
Bill Bradley (1982)
Joseph Brennan (1974)
Al Cervi (1984)
Wilt Chamberlain (1978)
Charles (Tarzan) Cooper (1976)
Kresimir Cosic (1996)
Bob Cousy (1970)
Dave Cowens (1991)
Billy Cunningham (1985)
Bob Davies (1969)
Forrest S. DeBernardi (1961)
Dave DeBusschere (1982)
H. G. (Dutch) Dehnert (1968)
Anne Donovan (1995)
Paul Endacott (1971)
Julius Erving (1993)
Harold (Bud) Foster (1964)
Walter (Clyde) Frazier (1986)
Max (Marty) Friedman (1971)
Joe Fulks (1977)
Lauren (Laddie) Gale (1976)
Harry (the Horse) Gallatin (1991)
William Gates (1988)
George Gervin (1996)

Tom Gola (1975)
Gail Goodrich (1996)
Hal Greer (1981)
Robert (Ace) Gruenig (1963)
Clifford O. Hagan (1977)
Victor Hanson (1960)
John Havlicek (1983)
Connie Hawkins (1992)
Elvin Hayes (1989)
Tom Heinsohn (1985)
Nat Holman (1964)
Robert J. Houbregs (1986)
Chuck Hyatt (1959)
Dan Issel (1993)
Harry (Buddy) Jeannette (1994)
William C. Johnson (1976)
D. Neil Johnston (1989)
K.C. Jones (1988)
Sam Jones (1983)
Edward (Moose) Krause (1975)
Bob Kurland (1961)
Joe Lapchick (1966)
Nancy Lieberman-Cline (1996)
Clyde Lovellette (1987)
Jerry Lucas (1979)
Angelo (Hank) Luisetti (1959)
C. Edward Macauley (1960)
Peter P. Maravich (1986)
Slater Martin (1981)
Branch McCracken (1960)
Jack McCracken (1962)
Bobby McDermott (1987)
Dick McGuire (1993)
Ann Meyers (1993)
George L. Mikan (1959)
Vern Mikkelsen (1995)

Cheryl Miller (1995)
Earl Monroe (1989)
Calvin Murphy (1993)
Charles (Stretch) Murphy (1960)
H. O. (Pat) Page (1962)
Bob Pettit (1970)
Andy Phillip (1961)
Jim Pollard (1977)
Frank Ramsey (1981)
Willis Reed (1981)
Oscar Robertson (1979)
John S. Roosma (1961)
Bill Russell (1974)
John (Honey) Russell (1964)
Adolph Schayes (1972)
Ernest J. Schmidt (1973)
John J. Schommer (1959)
Barney Sedran (1962)
Uljana Semjonova (1993)
Bill Sharman (1975)
Christian Steinmetz (1961)
Lusia Harris Stewart (1992)
David Thompson (1996)
John A. (Cat) Thompson (1962)
Nate Thurmond (1984)
Jack Twyman (1982)
Wes Unseld (1987)
Robert (Fuzzy) Vandivier (1974)
Edward A. Wachter (1961)
Bill Walton (1993)
Robert F. Wanzer (1986)
Jerry West (1979)
Nera White (1992)
Lenny Wilkens (1988)
John R. Wooden (1960)
George (Bird) Yardley (1996)

Coaches

Harold Anderson (1984)
Red Auerbach (1968)
Sam Barry (1978)
Ernest A. Blood (1960)
Howard G. Cann (1967)
H. Clifford Carlson (1959)
Lou Carnesecca (1992)
Ben Carnevale (1969)
Everett Case (1981)
Denny Crum (1994)

Chuck Daly (1994)
Everett S. Dean (1966)
Edgar A. Diddle (1971)
Bruce Drake (1972)
Clarence Gaines (1981)
Jack Gardner (1983)
Amory T. (Slats) Gill (1967)
Aleksandr Gomelsky (1995)
Marv Harshman (1984)
Edgar S. Hickey (1978)

Howard A. Hobson (1965)
Red Holzman (1985)
Hank Iba (1968)
Alvin F. (Doggie) Julian (1967)
Frank W. Keaney (1960)
George E. Keogan (1961)
Bob Knight (1991)
John Kundla (1995)
Ward L. Lambert (1960)
Harry Litwack (1975)

Note: Year of election in parentheses.

Members of the Basketball Hall of Fame (Cont.)

Coaches (Cont.)

Kenneth D. Loeffler (1964)
A.C. (Dutch) Lonborg (1972)
Arad A. McCutchan (1980)
Al McGuire (1992)
Frank McGuire (1976)
Walter E. Meanwell (1959)
Raymond J. Meyer (1978)

Ralph Miller (1987)
Jack Ramsay (1992)
Cesare Rubini (1994)
Adolph F. Rupp (1968)
Leonard D. Sachs (1961)
Everett F. Shelton (1979)

Dean Smith (1982)
Fred R. Taylor (1985)
Bertha Teague (1984)
Margaret Wade (1984)
Stanley H. Watts (1985)
John R. Wooden (1972)

Referees

James E. Enright (1978)
George T. Hepbron (1960)
George Hoyt (1961)
Matthew P. Kennedy (1959)
Lloyd Leith (1982)
Zigmund J. Mihalik (1985)
John P. Nucatola (1977)
Ernest C. Quigley (1961)
J. Dallas Shirley (1979)
Earl Strom (1995)
David Tobey (1961)
David H. Walsh (1961)

Teams

Buffalo Germans (1961)
First Team (1959)
Original Celtics (1959)
Renaissance (1963)

Note: Year of election in parentheses.

ABA Champions

Year	Champion	Series	Loser	Winning Coach
1968	Pittsburgh Pipers	4–3	New Orleans Bucs	Vince Cazetta
1969	Oakland Oaks	4–1	Indiana Pacers	Alex Hannum
1970	Indiana Pacers	4–2	Los Angeles Stars	Bob Leonard
1971	Utah Stars	4–3	Kentucky Colonels	Bill Sharman
1972	Indiana Pacers	4–2	New York Nets	Bob Leonard
1973	Indiana Pacers	4–3	Kentucky Colonels	Bob Leonard
1974	New York Nets	4–1	Utah Stars	Kevin Loughery
1975	Kentucky Colonels	4–1	Indiana Pacers	Hubie Brown
1976	New York Nets	4–2	Denver Nuggets	Kevin Loughery

ABA Postseason Awards

Most Valuable Player

1967-68	Connie Hawkins, Pitt
1968-69	Mel Daniels, Ind
1969-70	Spencer Haywood, Den
1970-71	Mel Daniels, Ind
1971-72	Artis Gilmore, Ken
1972-73	Billy Cunningham, Car
1973-74	Julius Erving, NY
1974-75	Julius Erving, NY
	George McGinnis, Ind
1975-76	Julius Erving, NY

Rookie of the Year

1967-68	Mel Daniels, Minn
1968-69	Warren Armstrong, Oak
1969-70	Spencer Haywood, Den
1970-71	Charlie Scott, Vir
	Dan Issel, Ken
1971-72	Artis Gilmore, Ken
1972-73	Brian Taylor, NY
1973-74	Swen Nater, SA
1974-75	Marvin Barnes, SL
1975-76	David Thompson, Den

Coach of the Year

1967-68	Vince Cazetta, Pitt
1968-69	Alex Hannum, Oak
1969-70	Bill Sharman, LA
	Joe Belmont, Den
1970-71	Al Bianchi, Vir
1971-72	Tom Nissalke, Dall
1972-73	Larry Brown, Car
1973-74	Babe McCarthy, Ken
	Joe Mullaney, Utah
1974-75	Larry Brown, Den
1975-76	Larry Brown, Den

THEY SAID IT

Vlade Divac, the Yugoslav national team center, assessing his country's chances of beating Dream Team III in the 1996 summer Olympics:
"Second is not so bad."

ABA Season Leaders

Scoring

		GP	Pts	Avg
1967-68	...Connie Hawkins, Pitt	70	1875	26.8
1968-69	...Rick Barry, Oak	35	1190	34.0
1969-70	...Spencer Haywood, Den	84	2519	30.0
1970-71	...Dan Issel, Ken	83	2480	29.4
1971-72	...Charlie Scott, Vir	73	2524	34.6
1972-73	...Julius Erving, Vir	71	2268	31.9
1973-74	...Julius Erving, NY	84	2299	27.4
1974-75	...George McGinnis, Ind	79	2353	29.8
1975-76	...Julius Erving, NY	84	2462	29.3

Rebounds

1967-68	...............Mel Daniels, Minn	15.6
1968-69	...............Mel Daniels, Ind	16.5
1969-70	...............Spencer Haywood, Den	19.5
1970-71	...............Mel Daniels, Ind	18.0
1971-72	...............Artis Gilmore, Ken	17.8
1972-73	...............Artis Gilmore, Ken	17.5
1973-74	...............Artis Gilmore, Ken	18.3
1974-75	...............Swen Nater, SA	16.4
1975-76	...............Artis Gilmore, Ken	15.5

Assists

1967-68	................Larry Brown, NO	6.5
1968-69	................Larry Brown, Oak	7.1
1969-70	................Larry Brown, Wash	7.1
1970-71	................Bill Melchionni, NY	8.3
1971-72	................Bill Melchionni, NY	8.4
1972-73	................Bill Melchionni, NY	7.5
1973-74	................Al Smith, Den	8.2
1974-75	................Mack Calvin, Den	7.7
1975-76	................Don Buse, Ind	8.2

Steals

1973-74	................Ted McClain, Car	2.98
1974-75	................Brian Taylor, NY	2.80
1975-76	................Don Buse, Ind	4.12
1973-74	................Caldwell Jones, SD	4.00

Blocked Shots

1974-75	................Caldwell Jones, SD	3.24
1975-76	................Billy Paultz, SA	3.05

World Championship of Basketball

Year	Winner	Runner-Up	Score	Site
1950	.........................Argentina	United States	†	Rio de Janeiro
1954	.........................United States	Brazil	†	Rio de Janeiro
1959	.........................Brazil	United States	†	Santiago, Chile
1963	.........................Brazil	Yugoslavia	†	Rio de Janeiro
1967	.........................Soviet Union	Yugoslavia	†	Montevideo, Uruguay
1970	.........................Yugoslavia	Brazil	†	Ljubljana, Yugoslavia
1974	.........................Soviet Union	Yugoslavia	†	San Juan
1978	.........................Yugoslavia	Soviet Union	82-81 OT	Manila
1982	.........................Soviet Union	United States	95-94	Cali, Colombia
1986	.........................United States	Soviet Union	87-85	Madrid
1990	.........................Yugoslavia	Soviet Union	92-75	Buenos Aires
1994*	.........................United States	Russia	137-91	Toronto

*U.S. professionals began competing in 1994.
†Result determined by overall record in final round of competition.

THEY SAID IT

Paul Mokeski, coach of the CBA's Connecticut Pride and former NBA journeyman, after acquiring the playing rights to himself from the Quad City Thunder, where he served as player–assistant coach in 1992–93: "I picked up a great player. I'm very familiar with what he can do."

College Basketball

Sports Illustrated

APRIL 8, 1996 · $2.95 (CAN. $3.95)

Blue Heaven

Antoine Walker and Kentucky soar to the NCAA title

DAVID E. KLUTHO

Wildcat Strike

Despite the burden of lofty expectations, Kentucky won its sixth national title and the first for coach Rick Pitino

by Tim Crothers

AT A luncheon last fall in Kentucky, Wildcat coach Rick Pitino reminisced about his team's summer trip to Italy and then told an apocryphal story that is destined to become part of hoops lore in the Bluegrass State. "When I met the Pope, I leaned over and kissed his ring," Pitino said, a coy smile crossing his lips. "Then he looked at my hand to do the same, and he said, 'Oh, you don't have a ring.'"

It was brilliant coaching strategy. By teasing himself, kidding about his own failure to bring a national title to Kentucky in his first six seasons as coach, Pitino effectively stared down his own demons. The coach might also have hoped to douse expectations for the upcoming season. Fat chance. The incendiary combination of a Kentucky team brimming with talent and a streak of 17 seasons without an NCAA title induced manic behavior in Wildcats fans. Long before the season began, Kentucky travel agents had already started selling package tours to the Meadowlands, in East Rutherford, N.J., site of the '96 Final Four, and upon seeing Ken-

tucky ranked No. 2 in *Street & Smith*'s preseason yearbook, several Wildcats fanatics phoned the magazine's editors to demand, "How can you rank us so low?"

Even Pitino couldn't deny that he was blessed with one of the most talented rosters in the history of the sport, so stocked that he decided to institute a jayvee team at Kentucky to give everybody enough playing time. In fact, observers speculated that the best college basketball of the year might be played in Wildcats practices. But critics contended that Kentucky might actually have too much talent for its own good and that competing egos would destroy the team's chemistry. There also existed a lingering doubt that despite all the thoroughbreds, there wasn't a single true point guard in the lot. Finally, there was the burden on the players to meet the lofty expectations. "I tried to use pressure as a motivational force for my team," Pitino said. "Even if the players say it doesn't exist, every fan tells them, 'You've got to win it all.'"

Then a funny thing happened. This for-

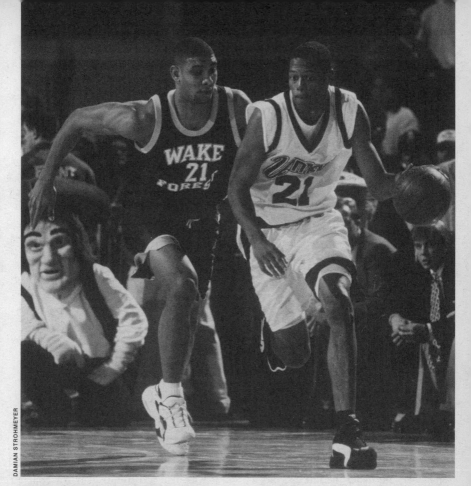

Camby rebounded from a mysterious collapse to guide UMass to the Final Four.

midable team—which many experts believed possessed a real chance at an undefeated season—didn't even have an undefeated first month, losing its second game of the year, 92–82, to Massachusetts on Nov. 28. Nobody realized it at the time, but, by shifting the focus onto other teams, the loss would work in Kentucky's favor. Having downed the Wildcats, the Minutemen soaked up most of the limelight, running off 26 straight wins to hold the No. 1 ranking through much of the season and acquiring what UMass coach John Calipari called "the golden 400-pound bull's-eye."

Somehow UMass kept its victory streak alive despite a four-game stretch without its star center, Marcus Camby, who collapsed and was rushed to the hospital semi-conscious just minutes before a Jan. 14 game at St. Bonaventure. Camby's condition was later described as an "isolated episode of altered consciousness." Considering his dominant play over the course of the season, it could be said that Camby often lapsed into this condition on the court as well.

UMass's undefeated season was finally spoiled on Feb. 24 by George Washington in an 86–76 stunner in Amherst. The upset was engineered by the combination

Despite his hardship off the court, Keady coached Purdue to a 26–6 mark.

BOB ROSATO

of the Colonials' 7'1" center Alexander Koul and 5'3" point guard Shawnta Rogers, running the most literal definition of the high-low offense in all of college basketball.

Iowa State was the long-shot story of the season. The Cyclones lost 10 players from their '95 team and were picked to languish in the basement of the Big Eight, but they finished second in the league behind Kansas and then upset the Jayhawks 56–55 in the championship game of the Big Eight tournament.

The season's other Cinderella sprung from State College, Pa., where Penn State finally shrugged off its image as just a football factory. The Nittany Lions lost their coach, Bruce Parkhill, who resigned unexpectedly in September, but under the tutelage of former assistant Jerry Dunn, the Lions roared to wins in 15 of their first 16 games. Penn State actually led the Big Ten conference standings into January, a surprise partly attributable to the weakness of the league.

Purdue would eventually win the Big Ten for the third straight year, despite a season of trauma for its coach, Gene Keady. The Boilermakers' coach endured a winter in which his father died and his daughter fell into a coma for three weeks. Purdue went on to lose 76–69 to Georgia in the second round of the NCAA tournament, but Keady, who guided the Boilers to a 26–6 record, was named coach of the year for the fifth time in his career.

It was also a difficult year for coach Charlie Parker, who was fired in February after guiding an undermanned Southern Cal team that had gone 7–21 the previous season to a respectable 11–10 record. Parker took charge of the team just two days before the start of the 1994–'95 season, when George Raveling, struggling to recover from a near-fatal auto accident, announced his retirement. Former UCLA Bruins guard Henry Bibby replaced Parker, and the Trojans didn't win another game all season, finishing at 11–16.

While the Kentucky men's team was quietly rolling through the season on its way to a title, the women of the SEC also soared over the competition to a monumental year. At one point eight of the conference's dozen teams were ranked in the Top 25. "I don't believe in coming back in another life, but if I did, I'd want to be a women's basketball coach, just in a different conference," said Mississippi coach Van Chancellor, whose team was among those ranked in the Top 25. "Sometimes I feel I'm out in the Atlantic on a little raft with only one paddle."

The league also showcased Georgia guard Saudia Roundtree, the nation's player of the year, and Tennessee's Chamique Holdsclaw, the freshman of the year. Not so coincidentally these two players would square off in the NCAA championship game, a contest especially notable because it would mark the first time that the women's final (23,291 fans) would outdraw the men's final (19,229). Tennessee came away with the title it was supposed to win the previous season when the Lady Vols lost to Connecticut in the NCAA finals. Holdsclaw, the rookie, scored 16 points and grabbed 14 rebounds in the 18-point victory, the second largest margin in NCAA women's championship history. The win also gave legendary Tennessee coach Pat Summitt her fourth NCAA title, making John Wooden the only coach with more. Summitt's sterling record of success—her career winning percentage is .818—even inspired Nashville musician Clifford Curry to record a song about her that was played over the local airwaves during the title run, a foot-stomping little ditty called "Pat Summitt, Dat Gummitt."

Back across the northern border, Kentucky would need only remember the UMass loss for much of its inspiration the rest of the way. At a team meeting following that game, the Cats' most eligible prima donna, sophomore forward Antoine Walker, stepped forward and said he would be willing to check his ego for the benefit of the team's goals. His teammates followed in lockstep.

The Cats showed their dominance during the regular season in several remarkable routs: a 64-point victory over Morehead State featuring more Kentucky dunks (11) than Eagles' baskets (nine), an 86-point first half against LSU in Baton Rouge and a game against Vanderbilt in which the Wildcats led 13–0 before the Commodores had so much as hit the rim. Still, there were the nitpickers who decried the school's change to denim-accessorized uniforms because the new blue looked dangerously close to the color worn at North Carolina. Said Pitino of his critics: "It's like you're having a great time in your life and someone asks, 'Any concern that you're going to die someday?'"

Kentucky plowed through the conference schedule, finishing 16–0 in the league without ever being seriously threatened. It was only the second time a team had survived SEC play without a loss. The conference tournament appeared to be a mere formality, but upstart Mississippi State stunned the Wildcats in the title game 84–73. Pitino, the master of spin control, had said before the Misisippi State game that "nothing good could come from a loss." But after the surprising defeat he told reporters, "I was glad we lost," because it would help his players refocus on their ultimate task, winning the national title.

The NCAA tournament provided its customary early-round thrills. Texas Tech forward Darvin Ham inspired his team to a victory over North Carolina in a second-round game in Richmond when he shattered a backboard with a ferocious dunk. Princeton provided its retiring coach, Pete Carril, with a memorable going-away present by defeating mighty defending national champion UCLA 43–41 in the opening round. The Tigers clinched the major upset with Carril's favorite play, the backdoor, in the final seconds.

The only juggernaut that cruised through the opening rounds was Kentucky, which unleashed its withering press, jokingly dubbed the "mother-in-law defense" because of its constant pressure and harassment, and won its first four tournament contests by an average of 28.3 points per game. Still, when the Wildcats arrived at the Final Four, they found themselves staring at the two teams that had handed them losses during the season, both by double digits.

Despite their victory over Kentucky, the Bulldogs still felt unappreciated, a sentiment further fueled when coach Richard Williams looked at his Final Four cap after winning the Southeast Regional. To his dismay Williams discovered that the hat read MISSISSIPPI rather than MISSISSIPPI STATE. After losing four of five games during a disappointing mid-January cold snap, Williams had turned around his team's fortunes by asking mercurial forward Dontae Jones to accept a more structured role. Jones, a high school dropout from Nashville who was only admitted to Mississippi State after picking up an astounding 36 credits during the previous summer, agreed to tone down his playground style. After adjusting his role, Jones would overshadow Bulldog stars Erick Dampier and Darryl Wilson during the march to the Meadowlands.

The Bulldogs faced Syracuse, another overachieving bunch, in the semifinals. The Orangemen had finished fourth in the Big East regular-season standings, but in senior forward John Wallace they possessed a player capable of carrying a team deep into the tournament ... if he showed up. Wallace missed the team flight on the eve of the Big Dance, claiming his alarm didn't go off, but turned up in time to nail the most exciting shot of the tournament, a lunging 20-foot jumper with 2.8 seconds remaining in overtime to beat Georgia in a third-round game. In the national semifinal game Wallace was high scorer with 21 points and guided Syracuse to a 77–69 victory, completing a most unlikely odyssey to the title game. The Orangemen left the court chanting their unique rallying cry: "'Cuse is in the house, oh my god, oh my god!"

A Ton of Bricks

Looking for a poster boy for the 1995–96 season? How about Tony Delk? Marcus Camby? Allen Iverson? Try Antric Klaiber. The 6'10" freshman center at the University of Connecticut missed the first 20 shots he attempted as a college player. Klaiber's miserable streak mercifully concluded on Dec. 30 against Hartford. On a dunk.

Klaiber most suitably represents what was the worst season for marksmanship in the last three decades of college basketball. "Shooting was really awful, and sometimes it was worse than that," said NBA scout Marty Blake, who witnessed as many college bricks as anybody last season. "I saw one game where a kid I was scouting went 2 for 12, and the only two shots he made were dunks."

And that wasn't even Klaiber, who was not alone in his purgatory. Nobody, it seems, could find the bottom of the net with much consistency. Morehead State lost to Kentucky 96–32 in a December game in Lexington while shooting just 13.8% in the contest. The Temple Owls, in a February game against UMass, missed 50 of their 63 shot attempts and all 16 heaves from beyond the three-point arc in a pathetic 59–35 drubbing. It speaks volumes that the Owls shot a meager 38.9% from the floor for the entire season and still defeated a No. 1 team (Kansas) and a No. 2 team (Villanova) along the way. Shooting was so horrendous that Delaware shot 29.6% against New Hampshire on Jan. 6 and won the game anyway. Virginia defeated Richmond on Dec. 9, despite shooting 5 for 29 in the second half.

For the season, field goal shooting among all Division I teams declined to a sorry 43.9%, the lowest since 1968–69. Three-point shooting, which has dropped every year since its introduction in 1986–87, fell to its deepest depression at just 34.2%. Even free throws dropped to a weak 67.4%, which, with the exception of 1994, was the lowest free-throw percentage since 1960.

Everybody has a theory for this ugly

UMass had its own slogan: Refuse to lose, and entering the Final Four they had indeed not lost to a ranked team all season. Nor had they faltered in any of their previous 26 games played away from Amherst. But Kentucky wouldn't take no for an answer. The Minutemen, who had appeared indefatigable during the regular season, finally looked weary in losing to the Wildcats 81–74.

On the eve of the final the onus sat heavily on Kentucky's shoulders. Wildcats center Mark Pope's nerves were so raw that while watching an episode of *Geraldo* about runaway kids he began sobbing uncontrollably. Pitino, on the other hand, continued to joke about the pressure, telling the story of an overnight letter sent by a doctor before the Wildcats left for the Meadowlands, which contained strategic suggestions for the team. "Thanks for your help," Pitino wrote back. "After the season I want to sit down with you and have a serious talk about how you're conducting surgery."

No doubt Pitino felt secure because of the solid foundation he knew he had laid a year earlier when the Wildcats lost to North Carolina in the Southeast Regional final. After that loss Pitino took his players, one by one, into a darkened hotel banquet room and tore down their egos until they were reduced

King of clang: Klaiber began his career as a Husky by going 0 for 20 from the field.

tices. But perhaps most important is the fundamental change in the way players approach the game and particularly a new emphasis on stylin'. "I went to the ABCD camp [for top high school players] last summer and after two days turned to someone and said, 'How many three-point shots have you seen made?'" asked Pittsburgh coach Ralph Willard. "The whole game for kids is to take it to the hole and try to dunk on somebody."

Said Utah coach Rick Majerus, "When have you seen a 17-foot jumper on *SportsCenter*?"

In this season of myopia, it seemed somehow fitting that Kentucky won the national title while shooting just 38.4% from the field against Syracuse, the lowest for a championship-game victor in 33 years.

shooting: an increase in three-point attempts, a renewed emphasis on defense, rushed offenses due to the ever dwindling shot clock. Also blamed for the increased bricklaying is limited practice time combined with a lack of emphasis on shooting jump shots during those prac-

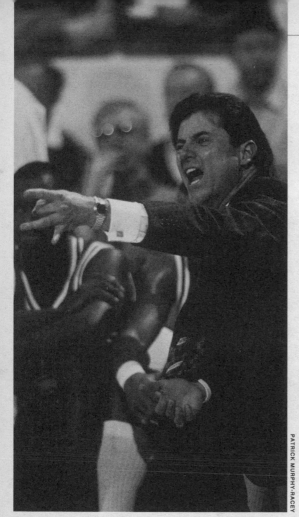
PATRICK MURPHY-RACEY

press caused 24 Syracuse turnovers. After falling behind by double digits in the opening half, Syracuse drew within two points twice in the second half, but both times Kentucky responded with an array of weapons, including a key Derek Anderson three-pointer and a crucial Walter McCarty tip-in down the stretch. Mostly, however, it was senior guard Tony Delk's seven three-pointers that overcame 29 points and 10 rebounds from Wallace and won Delk the Final Four's most outstanding player award.

After the game Pitino dubbed his team the Untouchables, as a testament to their ability to win despite the encumbrance of expectations. The players celebrated quietly, as if they had been anticipating their moment of triumph for an entire season. "I don't drink," Anderson said, "but I may buy myself a bottle of wine and just stare at it."

to rubble. Then in the locker room before the '96 championship game, Pitino completed the rebuilding process, explaining to each of his five starters why he would rather coach him than his Syracuse counterpart.

Kentucky's thoroughbreds thrived in an NCAA final better suited for mudders. In fact, due to a ferocious storm outside, there was rain leaking through the roof of the Meadowlands arena onto the court early in the first half. A withering Syracuse zone defense caused Kentucky to shoot just 28 for 73 from the floor, while the suffocating Wildcat

In the months immediately following the championship, Pitino would flirt with returning to the Meadowlands to coach the woeful New Jersey Nets. After a week of deliberation that left Kentucky fans breathless, Pitino eventually turned down the job, which was filled by Calipari, who signed for a reported $15 million over five years. Talk about your golden 400-pound bull's-eye.

For once Pitino, the carpetbagging coach, had resisted the temptation to take the money and run. Maybe it had something to do with his new ring.

NCAA Championship Game Box Score

Kentucky 76

KENTUCKY	Min	FG M-A	FT M-A	Reb O-T	A	PF	TP
Anderson	16	4-8	1-1	3-4	1	2	11
Walker	32	4-12	3-6	4-9	4	2	11
McCarty	19	2-6	0-0	5-7	3	3	4
Delk	37	8-20	1-2	1-7	2	2	24
Epps	35	0-6	0-0	1-4	7	1	0
Pope	27	1-6	2-2	1-3	2	3	4
Mercer	24	8-12	1-1	1-2	2	3	20
Sheppard	7	1-2	0-1	1-2	0	3	2
Edwards	3	0-1	0-0	0-0	1	0	0
Totals	200	28-73	8-13	17-38	22	19	76

Percentages: FG—.384, FT—.615. 3-pt goals: 12-27, .444 (Anderson 2-3, Walker 0-1, Delk 7-12, Epps 0-3, Pope 0-2, Mercer 3-4, Sheppard 0-1, Edwards 0-1). Team rebounds: 2. Blocked shots: 1 (Delk). Turnovers: 15 (Pope 4, Delk 3, Sheppard 3, Anderson 2, Edwards, Epps, McCarty). Steals: 11 (Walker 4, Anderson 3, Delk 2, Mercer, Pope).

Syracuse 67

SYRACUSE	Min	FG M-A	FT M-A	Reb O-T	A	PF	TP
Burgan	39	7-10	2-5	2-8	1	5	19
Wallace	38	11-19	5-5	3-10	1	5	29
Hill	28	3-9	1-1	2-10	1	2	7
Sims	39	2-5	1-2	1-2	7	2	6
Cipolla	35	3-8	0-0	0-1	2	1	6
Reafsnyder	13	0-1	0-0	0-4	0	0	0
Janulis	7	0-0	0-0	0-2	0	2	0
Nelson	1	0-0	0-0	0-0	0	0	0
Totals	200	26-52	9-13	8-37	12	17	67

Percentages: FG—.500, FT—.692. 3-pt goals: 6-15, .400 (Burgan 3-5, Wallace 2-3, Sims 1-4, Cipolla 0-3). Team rebounds: 1. Blocked shots: 2 (Wallace, Hill). Turnovers: 24 (Sims 7, Wallace 6, Burgan 5, Hill 3, Cipolla 2, Reafsnyder). Steals: 6 (Cipolla 4, Burgan, Sims).
Halftime: Kentucky 42, Syracuse 33. A: 19,229.
Officials: Clougherty, Thornley, Libbey.

Final AP Top 25

Poll taken before NCAA Tournament.

National Invitation Tournament Scores

First round: Rhode Island 82, Marist 77; College of Charleston 55, Tennessee 49; South Carolina 100, Davidson 73; Michigan St 64, Washington 50; Minnesota 68, St Louis 52; Missouri 89, Murray St 85; Illinois 73, Mount St Mary's (MD) 49; Wisconsin 55, Manhattan 42; Tulane 87, Auburn 73 (OT); Vanderbilt 86, AK-Little Rock 80; Alabama 72, Illinois 69; Fresno St 58, Miami (OH) 57; St Joseph's 82, Iona 78; Nebraska 91, Colorado St 83; Washington St 92, Gonzaga 73; Providence 91, Fairfield 79.
Second round: South Carolina 80, Vanderbilt 70; Tulane 84, Minnesota 65; Illinois St 77, Wisconsin 55; Alabama 72, Missouri 49; St Joseph's 82, Providence 62; Nebraska 82, Washington St 73; Fresno St 80, Michigan St 70; Rhode Island 62, College of Charleston 58 (OT).
Third round: Alabama 68, South Carolina 67; Tulane 83, Illinois State 72; St Joseph's 76, Rhode Island 59; Nebraska 83, Fresno St 71.
Semifinals: Nebraska 90, Tulane 78; St Joseph's 74, Alabama 69 (OT).
Championship: Nebraska 60, St Joseph's 56.
Consolation game: Tulane 87, Alabama 76.

1st ROUND

1 Connecticut 30-2
16 Colgate 15-14

8 Duke 18-12
9 E Michigan 24-5

5 Mississippi St 22-7
12 Virginia Comm. 24-8

4 UCLA 23-7
13 Princeton 21-6

6 Indiana 19-11
11 Boston College 18-10

3 Georgia Tech 22-11
14 Austin Peay 19-10

7 Temple 19-12
10 Oklahoma 17-12

2 Cincinnati 25-4
15 NC-Greensboro 20-9

1 Purdue 25-5
16 W Carolina 17-12

8 Georgia 19-9
9 Clemson 18-10

5 Memphis 22-7
12 Drexel 26-3

4 Syracuse 24-8
13 Montana St 21-8

6 Iowa 22-8
11 Geo Wash 21-8

3 Arizona 21-6
14 Valparaiso 21-10

7 Maryland 17-12
10 Santa Clara 19-8

2 Kansas 26-4
15 S Carolina St 22-7

2nd ROUND

Connecticut 68-59

Connecticut 95-81

E Michigan 75-60

Mississippi St 58-51

Mississippi St 63-41

Princeton 43-41

Boston College 64-51

Georgia Tech 90-79

Georgia Tech 100-89

Temple 61-43

Cincinnati 78-65

Cincinnati 66-61

Purdue 73-71

Georgia 76-69

Georgia 81-74

Drexel 75-63

Syracuse 69-58

Syracuse 88-55

Iowa 81-79

Arizona 87-73

Arizona 90-51

Santa Clara 91-79

Kansas 76-51

Kansas 92-54

REGIONALS

SOUTHEAST

Mississippi St 60-55

Mississippi St 73-63

Cincinnati 87-70

WEST

Syracuse 63-81

Syracuse 60-57

Kansas 83-80

Syracuse 77-69

NATIONAL CHAMPIONSHIP

KENTUCKY 76
SYRACUSE 67

Kentucky 81-74

EAST

Massachusetts 79-63

Massachusetts 86-62

Georgetown 98-90

MIDWEST

Kentucky 101-70

Kentucky 83-63

Wake Forest 60-59

2nd ROUND

Massachusetts 92-70

Massachusetts 79-74

Stanford 66-58

Arkansas 86-80

Arkansas 65-56

Marquette 68-44

N Carolina 83-62

Texas Tech 74-73

Texas Tech 92-73

New Mexico 69-48

Georgetown 93-56

Georgetown 73-62

Kentucky 110-72

Kentucky 84-60

Virginia Tech 61-48

Iowa St 74-64

Utah 72-43

Utah 73-67

Louisville 82-80

Louisville 68-64

Villanova 92-58

Texas 80-76

Wake Forest 65-62

Wake Forest 62-50

REGIONALS

1st ROUND

1 Massachusetts 31-1
16 Central Florida 11-18

8 Bradley 22-7
9 Stanford 19-8

5 Penn St 21-6
12 Arkansas 18-12

4 Marquette 22-7
13 Monmouth 20-9

6 N Carolina 21-10
11 New Orleans 21-8

3 Texas Tech 28-1
14 N Illinois 20-9

7 New Mexico 27-4
10 Kansas St 17-11

2 Georgetown 26-7
15 Miss. Valley St 22-6

1 Kentucky 28-2
16 San Jose St 13-16

8 WI-Green Bay 25-3
9 Virginia Tech 22-5

5 Iowa St 23-8
12 California 17-10

4 Utah 25-6
13 Canisius 19-10

6 Louisville 20-11
11 Tulsa 22-7

3 Villanova 25-6
14 Portland 19-10

7 Michigan 20-11
10 Texas 20-9

2 Wake Forest 23-5
15 NE Louisiana 16-13

NCAA Men's Division I Conference Standings

American West

	Conference			All Games		
	W	L	Pct	W	L	Pct
Cal Poly-SLO*	5	1	.833	16	13	.552
Southern Utah†	3	3	.500	15	13	.536
Cal St-Northridge	2	4	.333	7	20	.259
Cal St-Sacramento	2	4	.333	7	20	.259

Atlantic Coast

	Conference			All Games		
	W	L	Pct	W	L	Pct
Georgia Tech*	13	3	.813	24	12	.667
Wake Forest†	12	4	.750	26	6	.813
N Carolina	10	6	.625	21	11	.656
Duke	8	8	.500	18	13	.581
Maryland	8	8	.500	17	13	.567
Clemson	7	9	.438	18	11	.621
Virginia	6	10	.375	12	15	.444
Florida St	5	11	.313	13	14	.481
N Carolina St	3	13	.188	15	16	.484

Atlantic 10

EAST

	Conference			All Games		
	W	L	Pct	W	L	Pct
Massachusetts*†	15	1	.938	35	2	.946
Temple	12	4	.750	20	13	.606
St Joseph's (PA)	9	7	.563	19	13	.594
Rhode Island	8	8	.500	20	14	.588
St Bonaventure	4	12	.250	10	18	.357
Fordham	2	14	.125	4	23	.148

WEST

	Conference			All Games		
	W	L	Pct	W	L	Pct
Virginia Tech	13	3	.813	23	6	.793
George Washington	13	3	.813	21	8	.724
Xavier (OH)	8	8	.500	13	15	.464
Dayton	6	10	.375	15	14	.517
Duquesne	3	13	.188	9	18	.333
Lasalle	3	13	.188	6	24	.200

Big East

BIG EAST 7

	Conference			All Games		
	W	L	Pct	W	L	Pct
Georgetown	13	5	.722	29	8	.784
Syracuse	12	6	.667	29	9	.763
Providence	9	9	.500	18	12	.600
Miami (FL)	8	10	.444	15	13	.536
Seton Hall	7	11	.389	12	16	.429
Rutgers	6	12	.333	9	18	.333
Pittsburgh	5	13	.278	10	17	.370

BIG EAST 6

	Conference			All Games		
	W	L	Pct	W	L	Pct
Connecticut*†	17	1	.944	32	3	.914
Villanova	14	4	.778	26	7	.788
Boston College	10	8	.556	19	11	.633
W Virginia	7	11	.389	12	15	.444
St Johns	5	13	.278	11	16	.407
Notre Dame	4	14	.222	9	18	.333

Big Eight

	Conference			All Games		
	W	L	Pct	W	L	Pct
Kansas*	12	2	.857	29	5	.853
Iowa St†	9	5	.643	24	9	.727
Oklahoma	8	6	.571	17	13	.567
Oklahoma St	7	7	.500	17	10	.630
Kansas St	7	7	.500	17	12	.586
Missouri	6	8	.429	18	15	.545
Nebraska	4	10	.286	21	14	.600
Colorado	3	11	.214	9	18	.333

Big Sky

	Conference			All Games		
	W	L	Pct	W	L	Pct
Montana St*†	11	3	.786	21	9	.700
Montana	10	4	.714	20	8	.714
Weber St	10	4	.714	20	10	.667
Boise St	10	4	.714	15	13	.535
Idaho St	7	7	.500	11	15	.423
Idaho	5	9	.357	12	16	.429
Northern Arizona	3	11	.214	6	20	.231
Eastern Washington	0	14	.000	3	23	.115

Big South

	Conference			All Games		
	W	L	Pct	W	L	Pct
NC-Greensboro*†	11	3	.786	20	10	.667
NC-Asheville	9	5	.643	18	10	.643
Liberty	9	5	.643	17	12	.586
Charleston Southern	9	5	.643	15	13	.536
Radford	8	6	.571	14	13	.519
Winthrop	6	8	.429	7	19	.269
MD-Balt County	3	11	.214	5	22	.185
Coastal Carolina	1	13	.071	5	21	.192

Big Ten

	Conference			All Games		
	W	L	Pct	W	L	Pct
Purdue*	15	3	.833	26	6	.813
Penn St	12	6	.667	21	7	.750
Indiana	12	6	.667	19	12	.613
Iowa	11	7	.611	23	9	.719
Michigan	10	8	.556	20	12	.625
Minnesota	10	8	.556	19	13	.594
Michigan St	9	9	.500	16	16	.500
Wisconsin	8	10	.444	17	15	.531
Illinois	7	11	.389	18	13	.581
Ohio St	3	18	.143	10	17	.370
Northwestern	2	16	.111	7	20	.259

Big West

	Conference			All Games		
	W	L	Pct	W	L	Pct
Long Beach St*	12	6	.667	17	11	.607
UC-Irvine	11	7	.611	15	12	.556
Pacific	11	7	.611	15	12	.556
Utah St	10	8	.556	18	15	.545
Nevada	9	9	.500	16	13	.552
San Jose St†	9	9	.500	13	17	.433
New Mexico St	8	10	.444	11	15	.423
UC-Santa Barbara	8	10	.444	11	15	.423
UNLV	7	11	.389	10	16	.385
Cal St-Fullerton	5	13	.278	6	20	.231

*Conf. champ; †Conf. tourney winner.
Note: standings based on regular season conference play only; overall records include all tournament play.

Colonial Athletic Association

	Conference			All Games		
	W	L	Pct	W	L	Pct
VCU*†	14	2	.875	24	9	.727
Old Dominion	12	4	.750	18	13	.581
NC-Wilmington	9	7	.563	13	16	.448
E Carolina	8	8	.500	17	11	.607
American	8	8	.500	12	15	.444
George Mason	6	10	.375	11	16	.407
William & Mary	6	10	.375	10	16	.385
James Madison	6	10	.375	10	20	.333
Richmond	3	13	.188	8	20	.286

Conference USA

RED DIVISION

	Conference			All Games		
	W	L	Pct	W	L	Pct
Tulane	9	5	.643	22	10	.688
AL-Birmingham	6	8	.429	16	14	.533
Southern Mississippi	6	8	.429	12	15	.444
S Florida	2	12	.143	12	16	.429

WHITE DIVISION

	Conference			All Games		
	W	L	Pct	W	L	Pct
Memphis	11	3	.786	22	8	.733
Louisville	10	4	.714	22	12	.647
NC-Charlotte	6	8	.429	14	15	.483

BLUE DIVISION

	Conference			All Games		
	W	L	Pct	W	L	Pct
Cincinnati*†	11	3	.786	28	5	.848
Marquette	10	4	.714	23	8	.742
St Louis	4	10	.286	16	14	.533
DePaul	2	12	.143	11	18	.379

Ivy League

	Conference			All Games		
	W	L	Pct	W	L	Pct
Princeton*	13	2	.867	22	7	.759
Pennsylvania	12	3	.800	17	10	.630
Dartmouth	9	5	.643	16	10	.615
Harvard	7	7	.500	15	11	.577
Brown	5	9	.357	10	16	.385
Cornell	5	9	.357	10	16	.385
Yale	3	11	.214	8	18	.308
Columbia	3	11	.214	7	19	.269

Metro Atlantic

	Conference			All Games		
	W	L	Pct	W	L	Pct
Iona*	10	4	.714	21	8	.724
Fairfield	10	4	.714	20	10	.667
Manhattan	9	5	.643	17	12	.586
Loyola (MD)	8	6	.571	12	15	.444
Canisius†	7	7	.500	19	11	.633
Niagara	6	8	.429	13	15	.464
St Peter's	5	9	.357	15	12	.556
Siena	1	13	.071	5	22	.185

Mid-American

	Conference			All Games		
	W	L	Pct	W	L	Pct
Eastern Michigan*†	14	4	.778	25	6	.806
Western Michigan	13	5	.722	15	12	.556
Miami (OH)	12	6	.667	21	8	.724
Ball St	11	7	.611	16	12	.571
Ohio	11	7	.611	16	14	.533
Toledo	9	9	.500	18	14	.563
Bowling Green	9	9	.500	14	13	.519
Kent	8	10	.444	14	13	.519
Central Michigan	3	15	.167	6	20	.231
Akron	0	18	.000	3	23	.115

Mid-Continent

	Conference			All Games		
	W	L	Pct	W	L	Pct
Valparaiso*†	13	5	.722	21	11	.656
Western Illinois	12	6	.667	17	12	.586
NE Illinois	10	8	.556	14	13	.519
Buffalo	10	8	.556	13	14	.481
MO-Kansas City	10	8	.556	12	15	.444
Central Conn St	9	9	.500	13	15	.464
Eastern Illinois	9	9	.500	13	15	.464
Troy St	8	10	.444	11	16	.407
Youngstown St	7	11	.389	12	15	.444
Chicago St	2	16	.111	2	25	.074

Mid-Eastern Athletic

	Conference			All Games		
	W	L	Pct	W	L	Pct
S Carolina St*†	14	2	.875	22	8	.733
Coppin St	14	2	.875	19	10	.655
Bethune-Cookman	8	8	.500	12	15	.444
Delaware St	8	8	.500	11	17	.393
N Carolina A&T	7	9	.438	10	17	.370
MD-Eastern Shore	6	10	.375	11	16	.407
Howard	6	10	.375	7	20	.259
Morgan St	6	10	.375	7	20	.259
Florida A&M	3	13	.188	8	19	.296
Hampton	—			9	17	.346

Midwestern Collegiate

	Conference			All Games		
	W	L	Pct	W	L	Pct
WI-Green Bay*	16	0	1.000	25	4	.862
Butler	12	4	.750	19	8	.704
Northern Illinois†	10	6	.625	20	10	.667
Detroit	8	8	.500	18	11	.621
Wright St	8	8	.500	14	13	.519
IL-Chicago	5	11	.313	10	18	.357
WI-Milwaukee	5	11	.313	9	18	.333
Loyola (IL)	5	11	.313	8	19	.296
Cleveland St	3	13	.188	5	21	.192

*Conf. champ; †Conf. tourney winner.

Missouri Valley

	Conference			All Games		
	W	L	Pct	W	L	Pct
Bradley*	15	3	.833	22	8	.733
Illinois St	13	5	.722	22	12	.647
Tulsa†	12	6	.667	22	8	.733
SW Missouri St	11	7	.611	16	12	.571
Creighton	9	9	.500	14	15	.483
Evansville	9	9	.500	13	14	.481
Northern Iowa	8	10	.444	14	13	.519
Drake	8	10	.444	12	15	.444
Indiana St	6	12	.333	10	16	.385
Southern Illinois	4	14	.222	11	18	.379
Wichita St	4	14	.222	8	21	.276

North Atlantic

	Conference			All Games		
	W	L	Pct	W	L	Pct
Drexel*†	17	1	.944	27	4	.871
Boston U	13	5	.722	18	11	.621
Towson St	11	7	.611	16	12	.571
Delaware	11	7	.611	15	12	.556
Maine	11	7	.611	15	13	.536
Vermont	10	8	.556	12	15	.444
Hofstra	5	13	.278	9	18	.333
New Hampshire	5	13	.278	6	21	.222
Hartford	5	13	.278	6	22	.214
Northeastern	2	16	.111	4	24	.143

Northeast

	Conference			All Games		
	W	L	Pct	W	L	Pct
Mt St Mary's*	16	2	.889	21	8	.724
Marist	14	4	.778	22	7	.759
Monmouth (NJ) †	14	4	.778	20	10	.667
Rider	12	6	.667	19	11	.633
St Francis (PA)	11	7	.611	13	14	.481
Wagner	7	11	.389	10	17	.370
FDU	6	12	.333	7	20	.259
LIU-Brooklyn	5	13	.278	9	19	.321
St Francis (NY)	3	15	.167	9	18	.333
Robert Morris	2	16	.111	5	23	.179

Ohio Valley

	Conference			All Games		
	W	L	Pct	W	L	Pct
Murray St*	12	4	.750	19	10	.655
Tennessee St	11	5	.688	15	13	.536
Austin Peay†	10	6	.625	19	11	.633
Middle Tenn St	9	7	.563	15	12	.556
TN-Martin	9	7	.563	13	14	.481
Eastern Kentucky	7	9	.438	13	14	.481
Tennessee Tech	7	9	.438	13	15	.464
SE Missouri St	5	11	.313	8	19	.296
Morehead St	2	14	.125	7	20	.259

Pacific-10

	Conference			All Games		
	W	L	Pct	W	L	Pct
UCLA*	16	2	.889	23	8	.742
Arizona	13	5	.722	26	7	.788
Stanford	12	6	.667	20	9	.690
California	11	7	.611	17	11	.607
Washington	9	9	.500	16	12	.571
Oregon	9	9	.500	16	13	.552
Washington St	8	10	.444	17	12	.586
Arizona St	6	12	.333	11	16	.407
Southern Cal	4	14	.222	11	19	.367
Oregon St	2	16	.111	4	23	.148

Patriot

	Conference			All Games		
	W	L	Pct	W	L	Pct
Navy*	9	3	.750	15	12	.556
Colgate†	9	3	.750	15	15	.500
Bucknell	8	4	.667	17	11	.607
Holy Cross	8	4	.667	16	13	.552
Lafayette	4	8	.333	7	20	.259
Army	2	10	.167	7	20	.259
Lehigh	2	10	.167	4	23	.148

Southeastern

EAST

	Conference			All Games		
	W	L	Pct	W	L	Pct
Kentucky*	16	0	1.000	34	2	.944
Georgia	9	7	.563	21	10	.677
S Carolina	8	8	.500	19	12	.613
Vanderbilt	7	9	.438	18	14	.563
Tennessee	6	10	.375	14	15	.483
Florida	6	10	.375	12	16	.429

WEST

	Conference			All Games		
	W	L	Pct	W	L	Pct
Mississippi St†	10	6	.625	26	8	.765
Arkansas	9	7	.563	20	13	.606
Alabama	9	7	.563	19	13	.594
Auburn	6	10	.375	19	13	.594
Mississippi	6	10	.375	12	15	.444
LSU	4	12	.250	12	17	.414

*Conf. champ; †Conf. tourney winner.

Southern

NORTH

	Conference			All Games		
	W	L	Pct	W	L	Pct
Davidson*	14	0	1.000	25	5	.833
VMI	10	4	.714	18	10	.643
Marshall	8	6	.571	17	11	.607
Appalachian St	3	11	.214	8	20	.286
E Tennessee St	3	11	.214	7	20	.259

SOUTH

	Conference			All Games		
	W	L	Pct	W	L	Pct
Western Carolina†	10	4	.714	17	13	.567
TN-Chattanooga	9	5	.643	15	12	.556
Furman	6	8	.429	10	17	.370
The Citadel	5	9	.357	10	16	.385
Georgia Southern	2	12	.143	3	23	.115

Southland

	Conference			All Games		
	W	L	Pct	W	L	Pct
NE Louisiana*†	13	5	.722	16	14	.533
N Texas	12	6	.667	15	13	.536
TX-San Antonio	12	6	.667	14	14	.500
Stephen Austin	11	7	.611	17	11	.607
McNeese St	11	7	.611	15	12	.556
Sam Houston	9	9	.500	11	16	.407
SW Texas St	7	11	.389	11	15	.423
TX-Arlington	7	11	.389	11	15	.423
Nicholls St	5	13	.278	5	21	.192
Northwestern St	3	15	.167	5	21	.192

Southwest

	Conference			All Games		
	W	L	Pct	W	L	Pct
Texas Tech*†	14	0	1.000	30	2	.938
Houston	11	3	.786	17	10	.630
Texas	10	4	.714	21	10	.677
Texas Christian	6	8	.429	15	15	.500
Rice	5	9	.357	14	14	.500
Baylor	4	10	.286	9	18	.333
Texas A&M	3	11	.214	11	16	.407
SMU	3	11	.214	8	20	.286

Southwestern Athletic

	Conference			All Games		
	W	L	Pct	W	L	Pct
Miss Valley St*†	11	3	.786	22	7	.759
Jackson St	11	3	.786	16	13	.552
Southern	8	5	.615	17	11	.607
Texas Southern	7	7	.500	11	15	.423
Alcorn St	7	7	.500	10	15	.400
Grambling St	6	7	.462	12	16	.429
Alabama St	5	9	.357	9	18	.333
Prairie View	0	14	.000	4	23	.148

Sun Belt

	Conference			All Games		
	W	L	Pct	W	L	Pct
AK-Little Rock*	14	4	.778	23	7	.767
New Orleans†	14	4	.778	21	9	.700
Jacksonville	10	8	.556	15	13	.536
Western Kentucky	10	8	.556	13	14	.481
SW Louisiana	9	9	.500	16	12	.571
Lamar	7	11	.389	12	15	.444
S Alabama	7	11	.389	12	15	.444
Arkansas St	7	11	.389	9	18	.333
Louisiana Tech	6	12	.333	11	17	.393
TX-Pan American	6	12	.333	9	19	.321

Trans-America

EAST

	Conference			All Games		
	W	L	Pct	W	L	Pct
Coll of Charleston*	15	1	.938	25	4	.862
Campbell	11	5	.688	17	11	.607
Stetson	6	10	.375	10	17	.370
Central Florida†	6	10	.375	11	19	.367
Florida Int'l	6	11	.353	13	15	.464
Florida Atlantic	5	11	.313	9	18	.333

WEST

	Conference			All Games		
	W	L	Pct	W	L	Pct
Samford	11	5	.688	16	11	.593
SE Louisiana	11	5	.688	15	12	.556
Centenary	8	8	.500	11	16	.407
Mercer	8	9	.471	15	14	.517
Georgia St	6	10	.375	10	16	.385
Jacksonville St	4	12	.250	10	17	.370

West Coast

	Conference			All Games		
	W	L	Pct	W	L	Pct
Santa Clara*	10	4	.714	20	9	.690
Gonzaga	10	4	.714	21	9	.700
Loyola Marymount	8	6	.571	18	11	.621
San Francisco	8	6	.571	15	12	.556
Portland†	7	7	.500	19	11	.633
San Diego	6	8	.429	14	14	.500
St Mary's	5	9	.357	12	15	.444
Pepperdine	2	12	.143	10	18	.357

Western Athletic

	Conference			All Games		
	W	L	Pct	W	L	Pct
Utah*	15	3	.833	27	7	.794
New Mexico†	14	4	.778	28	5	.848
Fresno St	13	5	.722	22	11	.667
Colorado St	11	7	.611	18	12	.600
Brigham Young	9	9	.500	15	13	.536
San Diego St	8	10	.444	15	14	.517
Wyoming	8	10	.444	14	15	.483
Hawaii	7	11	.389	10	18	.357
UTEP	4	14	.222	13	15	.464
Air Force	1	17	.056	5	23	.179

Independents

	W	L	Pct
Oral Roberts	18	9	.667
Wofford	4	22	.154

*Conf. champ; †Conf. tourney winner.

Scoring

	Class	GP	Field Goals			3-Pt FG		Free Throws			Reb	Pts	Avg
			FGA	FG	Pct	FGA	FG	FTA	FT	Pct			
Kevin Granger, Texas Southern	Sr	24	392	194	49.5	86	30	290	230	79.3	168	648	27.0
Marcus Brown, Murray St	Sr	29	536	254	47.4	175	74	220	185	84.1	139	767	26.4
Bubba Wells, Austin Peay	Jr	30	568	312	54.9	78	34	173	131	75.7	219	789	26.3
JaFonde Williams, Hampton...............	Sr	26	534	220	41.2	228	83	183	146	79.8	103	669	25.7
Bonzi Wells, Ball St...........................	So	28	544	269	49.4	92	31	202	143	70.8	246	712	25.4
Anquell McCollum, Western Carolina...	Sr	30	566	257	45.4	241	99	166	138	83.1	159	751	25.0
Allen Iverson, Georgetown	So	37	650	312	48.0	238	87	317	215	67.8	141	926	25.0
Eddie Benton, Vermont......................	Sr	26	500	187	37.4	201	69	229	193	84.3	86	636	24.5
Matt Alosa, New Hampshire...............	Sr	26	476	199	41.8	220	76	180	150	83.3	79	624	24.0
Ray Allen, Connecticut	Jr	35	618	292	47.2	247	115	147	119	81.0	228	818	23.4
Michael Hart, Tennessee-Martin........	Sr	27	436	246	56.4	1	1	172	123	71.5	248	616	22.8
Tunji Awojobi, Boston University	Jr	29	435	253	58.2	23	3	211	149	70.6	314	658	22.7
Darren McLinton, James Madison......	Sr	30	501	213	42.5	294	122	154	132	85.7	65	680	22.7
Reggie Elliott, Mercer	Sr	29	555	226	40.7	190	54	188	150	79.8	186	656	22.6
Jeff Nordgaard, WI-Green Bay...........	Sr	29	500	277	55.4	25	8	131	93	71.0	183	655	22.6
Reggie Freeman, Texas	Jr	31	630	237	37.6	270	87	183	134	73.2	208	695	22.4
Anthony Harris, Hawaii	Sr	28	443	219	49.4	73	24	197	164	83.2	82	626	22.4
Jason Daisy, Northern Iowa................	Jr	27	425	208	48.9	162	68	163	119	73.0	107	603	22.3
Chris McGuthrie, Mt St Mary's (MD)...	Sr	29	524	229	43.7	261	102	108	87	80.6	70	647	22.3
John Wallace, Syracuse	Sr	38	599	293	48.9	88	37	291	222	76.3	329	845	22.2
Curtis McCants, George Mason.........	Jr	27	453	200	44.2	125	39	186	155	83.3	109	594	22.0
Sam Bowie, Southeastern LA	Sr	27	458	208	45.4	183	59	165	115	69.7	144	590	21.9
Craig Thames, Toledo	Sr	32	441	216	49.0	146	59	245	208	84.9	196	699	21.8
Ronnie Henderson, LSU	Jr	23	397	183	46.1	146	49	127	87	68.5	107	502	21.8
Marcus Mann, Mississippi Valley	Sr	29	415	251	60.5	2	1	197	126	64.0	394	629	21.7
Keith Van Horn, Utah..........................	Jr	32	439	236	53.8	132	54	188	160	85.1	283	626	21.4
Paul Marshall, Northeast LA	Sr	30	494	214	43.3	281	115	125	97	77.6	107	640	21.3
Troy Hudson, Southern Illinois...........	So	25	459	179	39.0	247	93	103	82	79.6	110	533	21.3
Ryan Minor, Oklahoma	Sr	30	521	217	41.7	191	62	174	143	82.2	229	639	21.3
Jimmy DeGraffenried, Weber St.........	Sr	30	374	214	57.2	100	47	188	162	86.2	199	637	21.2

REBOUNDS

	Class	GP	Reb	Avg
Marcus Mann, Mississippi Valley....	Sr	29	394	13.6
Malik Rose, Drexel	Sr	31	409	13.2
Adonal Foyle, Colgate.....................	So	29	364	12.6
Tim Duncan, Wake Forest...............	Jr	32	395	12.3
Scott Farley, Mercer........................	Sr	29	349	12.0
Chris Ensminger, Valparaiso	Sr	32	368	11.5
Thaddeous Delaney, Charleston (SC).............................	Jr	29	330	11.4
Alan Tomidy, Marist.........................	Sr	29	329	11.3
Quadre Lollis, Montana St	Sr	30	340	11.3
Kyle Snowden, Harvard	Jr	26	289	11.1

ASSISTS

	Class	GP	A	Avg
Raimonds Miglinieks, UC-Irvine......	Sr	27	230	8.5
Curtis McCants, George Mason......	Sr	27	223	8.3
Dan Pogue, Campbell	Sr	23	183	8.0
Pointer Williams, McNeese St.........	Sr	27	200	7.4
Lazarus Sims, Syracuse	Sr	38	281	7.4
Brevin Knight, Stanford	Jr	29	212	7.3
Phillip Turner, UC-Santa Barbara ...	Sr	26	190	7.3
Reggie Geary, Arizona	Sr	33	231	7.0
David Fizdale, San Diego	Sr	28	195	7.0
Aaron Hutchins, Marquette............	So	31	215	6.9

THREE-POINT FIELD GOALS MADE PER GAME

	Class	GP	FG	Avg
Dominick Young, Fresno St..............	Jr	29	120	4.1
Darren McLinton, James Madison...Sr		30	122	4.1
Keith Veney, Marshall.......................	Jr	28	111	4.0
Paul Marshall, Northeast LA.............	Sr	30	115	3.8
Troy Hudson, Southern IL	So	25	93	3.7
Mark Lueking, Army.........................	Sr	27	99	3.7
Troy Green, Southeastern LA...........	Fr	27	98	3.6
James Hannah, Grambling...............	Jr	28	101	3.6
David Sivulich, St Mary's (CA)	So	27	96	3.6
Eric Washington, Alabama...............	Jr	32	113	3.5

THREE-POINT FIELD-GOAL PERCENTAGE

	Class	GP	FGA	FG	Pct
Joe Stafford, Western Carolina ...	Jr	30	110	58	52.7
Ricky Peral, Wake Forest	Jr	32	100	51	51.0
Justyn Tebbs, Weber St.............	Sr	30	100	50	50.0
Aaron Brown, Central Michigan...Fr		26	104	51	49.0
Isaac Fontaine, Washington St...Jr		29	136	66	48.5
Mike Derocckis, Drexel..............	Fr	31	178	85	47.8
Mike Frensley, St Peter's	Sr	27	123	58	47.2
Pete Lisicky, Penn St.................	So	27	189	89	47.1
Jimmy DeGraffenried, Weber St ...Sr		30	100	47	47.0
Justin Jones, Utah St	So	33	165	77	46.7

Note: Minimum 1.5 made per game.

*Includes games played in tournaments.

STEALS

	Class	GP	S	Avg
Pointer Williams, McNeese St	Sr	27	118	4.4
Johnny Rhodes, Maryland	Sr	30	110	3.7
Roderick Taylor, Jackson St	Sr	29	106	3.7
Rasul Salahuddin, Long Beach St	Sr	28	101	3.6
Andrell Hoard, NE Illinois	Jr	27	97	3.6
Ben Larson, Cal Poly-SLO	Fr	29	100	3.4
Allen Iverson, Georgetown	So	37	124	3.4
Bonzi Wells, Ball St	So	28	87	3.1
Jerry McCullough, Pittsburgh	Sr	25	76	3.0
Edgar Padilla, Massachusetts	Jr	37	108	2.9

BLOCKED SHOTS

	Class	GP	BS	Avg
Keith Closs, Central Conn St	So	28	178	6.4
Adonal Foyle, Colgate	So	29	165	5.7
Roy Rogers, Alabama	Sr	32	156	4.9
Jerome James, Florida A&M	So	27	119	4.4
Alan Tomidy, Marist	Sr	29	113	3.9
Peter Aluma, Liberty	Jr	29	113	3.9
Marcus Camby, Massachusetts	Jr	33	128	3.9
Tim Duncan, Wake Forest	Jr	32	120	3.8
Calvin Booth, Penn St	Fr	28	101	3.6
Lorenzo Coleman, Tennessee Tech	Jr	28	96	3.4

FIELD-GOAL PERCENTAGE

	Class	GP	FGA	FG	Pct
Quadre Lollis, Montana St	Sr	30	314	212	67.5
Daniel Watts, Nevada	Sr	29	221	145	65.6
Lincoln Abrams, Centenary (LA)	Sr	27	286	187	65.4
Alexander Koul, Geo Wash	So	29	254	163	64.2
Terquin Mott, Coppin St	Jr	28	326	208	63.8
Antawn Jamison, N Carolina	Fr	32	322	201	62.4
Stanley Caldwell, Tennessee St	Sr	22	178	110	61.8
Greg Smith, Delaware	Jr	27	282	173	61.3
Marcus Mann, Mississippi Val	Sr	29	415	251	60.5
Curtis Fincher, Eastern KY	Sr	27	245	148	60.4

Note: Minimum 5 made per game.

FREE-THROW PERCENTAGE

	Class	GP	FTA	FT	Pct
Mike Dillard, Sam Houston St	Jr	25	68	63	92.6
Dion Cross, Stanford	Sr	29	88	81	92.0
Roderick Howard, NC-Charlotte	Jr	29	103	93	90.3
Geoff Billet, Rutgers	Fr	26	80	72	90.0
Steve Nash, Santa Clara	Sr	29	113	101	89.4
Derek Grimm, Missouri	Jr	33	113	100	88.5
Marcus Wilson, Evansville	Fr	25	85	75	88.2
Nod Carter, Middle Tenn St	Jr	27	118	104	88.1
Alhamisi Simms, MD-Balt Co	Fr	27	84	74	88.1
Jason Alexander, Stetson	Sr	27	140	123	87.9

Note: Minimum 2.5 made per game.

Single-Game Highs

POINTS

45 ....Marcus Brown, Murray St, Dec 16 (vs Washington [MO])
45 ....Eddie Benton, Vermont, Feb 2 (vs Hartford)

REBOUNDS

28 ....Marcus Mann, Mississippi Valley, Mar 9 (vs Jackson St)

ASSISTS

15 ....Steve Nash, Santa Clara, Dec 9 (vs Southern-BR)
15 ....Raimonds Miglinieks, UC-Irvine, Feb 10 (vs Cal St-Fullerton)
15 ....Colby Pierce, Austin Peay, Feb 12 (vs Tennessee Tech)
15 ....Kyle Kessel, Texas A&M, Feb 26 (vs Texas Christian)
15 ....Andre Owens, Oklahoma St, Feb 29 (vs Oklahoma)

THREE-POINT FIELD GOALS

12 ....David McMahan, Winthrop, Jan 15 (vs Coastal Carolina)

FREE THROWS

21 ....Steve Nash, Santa Clara, Jan 7 (vs St Mary's [CA])
19 ....Malik Rose, Drexel, Feb 5 (vs Hofstra)
19 ....Sidney Goodman, Coppin St, Feb 18 (vs N Carolina A&T)

STEALS

10 ....Bonzi Wells, Ball St, Jan 3 (vs Ohio)
10 ....Allen Iverson, Georgetown, Jan 13 (vs Miami [FL])

BLOCKED SHOTS

14 ....Roy Rogers, Alabama, Feb 10 (vs Georgia)
12 ....Keith Closs, Central Conn St, Jan 20 (vs Troy St)

SCORING OFFENSE

	GP	W	L	Pts	Avg		GP	W	L	Pts	Avg
Troy St	27	11	16	2551	94.5	Mississippi Valley	29	22	7	2486	85.7
Kentucky	36	34	2	3292	91.4	Southeastern LA	27	15	12	2296	85.0
Marshall	28	17	11	2560	91.4	Davidson	30	25	5	2528	84.3
George Mason	27	11	16	2443	90.5	VA Military	28	18	10	2358	84.2
Southern-BR	28	17	11	2521	90.0	Weber St	30	20	10	2524	84.1

SCORING DEFENSE

	GP	W	L	Pts	Avg		GP	W	L	Pts	Avg
Princeton	29	22	7	1498	51.7	Harvard	26	15	11	1581	60.8
WI-Green Bay	29	25	4	1620	55.9	Wake Forest	32	26	6	1963	61.3
S Alabama	27	12	15	1571	58.2	Manhattan	29	17	12	1802	62.1
Temple	33	20	13	1922	58.2	Charleston (SC)	29	25	4	1806	62.3
NC-Wilmington	29	13	16	1694	58.4	Massachusetts	37	35	2	2307	62.4

SCORING MARGIN

	Off	Def	Mar		Off	Def	Mar
Kentucky	91.4	69.4	22.1	Georgetown	83.3	68.8	14.5
Connecticut	86.2	64.7	17.9	Cincinnati	79.6	65.2	14.4
Drexel	82.6	66.3	16.3	Utah	76.7	63.9	12.9
Davidson	84.3	68.2	16.0	Texas Tech	82.2	69.4	12.8
Kansas	80.6	65.3	15.4	Massachusetts	74.8	62.4	12.5

FIELD-GOAL PERCENTAGE

	FGA	FG	Pct		FGA	FG	Pct
UCLA	1698	897	52.8	Marshall	1874	927	49.5
Colorado St	1683	851	50.6	New Mexico	1802	889	49.3
Coppin St	1650	828	50.2	Toledo	1670	822	49.2
Montana St	1800	898	49.9	N Carolina	1869	919	49.2
Weber St	1766	880	49.8	Arizona	1981	973	49.1

FIELD-GOAL PERCENTAGE DEFENSE

	FGA	FG	Pct		FGA	FG	Pct
Temple	1741	670	38.5	Massachusetts	2098	812	38.7
Marquette	1772	682	38.5	Cincinnati	1860	723	38.9
Mississippi St	2084	803	38.5	Tulsa	1728	677	39.2
Connecticut	2175	840	38.6	Wake Forest	1846	725	39.3
Kansas	2008	777	38.7	Virginia	1628	642	39.4

FREE-THROW PERCENTAGE

	FTA	FT	Pct		FTA	FT	Pct
Utah	828	649	78.4	Hawaii	732	550	75.1
Weber St	675	519	76.9	Stetson	464	347	74.8
Brigham Young	767	587	76.5	Samford	669	499	74.6
Stanford	736	558	75.8	Toledo	755	563	74.6
VA Military	623	469	75.3	WI-Green Bay	574	428	74.6

THREE-POINT FIELD GOALS MADE PER GAME

	GP	FG	Avg		GP	FG	Avg
Troy St	27	300	11.1	Southern-BR	28	252	9.0
Marshall	28	284	10.1	Auburn	32	287	9.0
N Carolina St	31	292	9.4	Pacific (CA)	27	241	8.9
Southern Ill	29	268	9.2	Mt St Mary's (MD)	29	255	8.8
Samford	27	243	9.0	St Mary's (CA)	27	233	8.6

THREE-POINT FIELD-GOAL PERCENTAGE

	GP	FGA	FG	Pct		GP	FGA	FG	Pct
Weber St	30	577	245	42.5	Western Carolina	30	503	204	40.6
Wake Forest	32	618	260	42.1	Evansville	27	444	180	40.5
Penn St	28	482	197	40.9	St Peter's	27	305	123	40.3
Connecticut	35	633	258	40.8	Miami (OH)	29	471	188	39.9
NC-Greensboro	30	503	205	40.8	Marshall	28	712	284	39.9

Note: Minimum 3.0 made per game.

NCAA Women's Championship Game Box Score

Tennessee 83

Tennessee	Min	FG M-A	FT M-A	Reb O-T	A	PF	TP
Holdsclaw	34	6-16	4-5	5-14	3	0	16
Conklin	23	5-8	0-0	0-4	3	2	14
Johnson	28	7-10	2-2	3-5	1	2	16
Marciniak	37	5-13	0-1	0-4	5	1	10
Davis	32	2-10	4-8	5-7	8	2	8
Smallwood	1	0-0	1-2	1-1	0	0	1
Milligan	1	0-1	0-0	0-0	0	0	0
Greene	1	0-1	0-0	0-0	0	0	0
Jolly	10	1-1	0-0	0-0	1	2	2
Laxton	12	2-7	0-0	2-3	0	1	4
Thompson	21	4-6	4-6	5-11	0	3	12
Totals	200	32-73	15-25	21-49	21	13	83

Percentages: FG—.438, FT—.600. 3-pt goals: 4-9, .444 (Conklin 4-5, Johnson 0-1, Marciniak 0-2, Davis 0-1). Team rebounds: 5. Blocked shots: None. Turnovers: 11 (Marciniak 4, Conklin 2, Thompson 2, Holdsclaw, Laxton, Johnson). Steals: 8 (Davis 4, Marciniak 2, Holdsclaw, Jolly).

Georgia 65

Georgia	Min	FG M-A	FT M-A	Reb O-T	A	PF	TP
Frett	37	10-18	4-4	6-16	0	1	25
Holland	33	4-12	1-1	1-1	5	4	11
Henderson	36	8-15	0-1	4-7	0	4	16
Roundtree	37	3-14	1-2	0-5	6	1	8
Powell	12	0-1	0-0	0-0	1	1	0
Irwin	16	1-3	0-0	0-2	1	0	3
Antvorskov	3	0-0	0-0	0-0	0	2	0
Thompson	1	0-0	0-0	0-1	1	0	0
Taylor	1	0-1	0-0	0-1	0	0	0
Bush	16	1-4	0-0	2-2	0	4	2
Walker	1	0-1	0-0	1-2	0	0	0
Decker	6	0-2	0-0	1-2	0	4	0
Walls	1	0-0	0-0	0-0	0	1	0
Totals	200	27-71	6-8	15-39	14	22	65

Percentages: FG—.380, FT—.750. 3-pt goals: 5-24, .208 (Frett 1-1, Holland 2-8, Roundtree 1-7, Powell 0-1, Irwin 1-3, Taylor 0-1, Bush 0-2, Decker 0-1). Team rebounds: None. Blocked shots: 2 (Henderson 2). Turnovers: 14 (Roundtree 6, Frett 2, Holland 2, Bush, Henderson, Irwin, Powell). Steals: 7 (Irwin 2, Roundtree 2, Frett, Holland, Powell). Halftime: Tennessee 42, Georgia 37. A: 23,291. Officials: Bell, Kantner, Palmer.

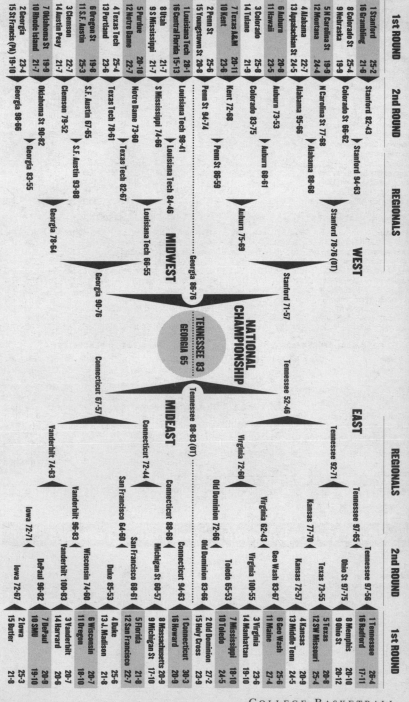

1996 NCAA Basketball Women's Division I Tournament

WEST

1st ROUND
- 1 Stanford 25-2
- 16 Grambling 21-6
- 8 Colorado St 25-4
- 9 Nebraska 19-9
- 5 N Carolina St 19-9
- 12 Montana 24-4
- 4 Alabama 22-7
- 13 Appalachian St 24-5
- 6 Auburn 20-8
- 11 Hawaii 23-5
- 3 Colorado 25-8
- 14 Tulane 21-9
- 7 Texas A&M 20-11
- 10 Kent 23-6
- 2 Penn St 25-6
- 15 Youngstown St 20-8
- 1 Louisiana Tech 28-1
- 16 Central Florida 15-13
- 8 Utah 21-7
- 9 S Mississippi 21-7
- 12 Notre Dame 20-10
- 12 Purdue 22-7
- 4 Texas Tech 25-4
- 13 Portland 23-6
- 5 Oregon St 19-8
- 11 S.F. Austin 25-3
- 3 Clemson 22-7
- 14 Austin Peay 21-7
- 7 Oklahoma St 19-9
- 10 Rhode Island 21-7
- 2 Georgia 23-4
- 15 St.Francis (PA) 19-10

2nd ROUND
- Stanford 82-43
- Stanford 94-63
- N Carolina St 77-68
- Alabama 95-66
- Auburn 73-53
- Colorado 83-75
- Kent 72-68
- Penn St 86-59
- Louisiana Tech 99-41
- S Mississippi 74-66
- Notre Dame 73-60
- Texas Tech 78-61
- S.F. Austin 67-65
- Clemson 79-52
- Oklahoma St 90-82
- Georgia 98-66

REGIONALS
- Stanford 94-63
- Stanford 78-76 (OT)
- Auburn 68-61
- Auburn 75-69
- Louisiana Tech 84-46
- Louisiana Tech 66-55
- S.F. Austin 93-88
- Georgia 78-64
- Georgia 83-55

MIDWEST

- Georgia 86-76
- Stanford 71-57
- Georgia 90-76

NATIONAL CHAMPIONSHIP

TENNESSEE 83
GEORGIA 65

Tennessee 52-46

Connecticut 67-57

EAST

REGIONALS
- Tennessee 97-65
- Tennessee 92-71
- Kansas 77-70
- Virginia 62-43
- Connecticut 72-44
- San Francisco 64-60
- Vanderbilt 74-63
- Iowa 72-71

2nd ROUND
- Tennessee 97-56
- Ohio St 97-75
- Texas 73-55
- Geo Wash 83-67
- Virginia 100-55
- Toledo 65-53
- Old Dominion 72-56
- Connecticut 94-63
- Michigan St 60-57
- San Francisco 68-61
- Duke 85-53
- Wisconsin 74-60
- Vanderbilt 100-83
- DePaul 96-82
- Iowa 72-67

1st ROUND
- 1 Tennessee 26-4
- 16 Radford 17-11
- 8 Memphis 20-10
- 9 Ohio St 20-12
- 5 Texas 25-4
- 12 SW Missouri 25-4
- 4 Kansas 20-9
- 13 Middle Tenn 24-5
- 6 Geo Wash 25-6
- 11 Maine 27-4
- 3 Virginia 23-6
- 14 Manhattan 19-10
- 7 Mississippi 18-10
- 10 Toledo 24-5
- 2 Old Dominion 27-2
- 15 Holy Cross 23-9
- 1 Connecticut 30-3
- 16 Howard 20-9
- 8 Massachusetts 20-9
- 9 Michigan St 17-10
- 5 Florida 21-8
- 12 San Francisco 22-7
- 4 Duke 25-6
- 13 J. Madison 21-8
- 6 Wisconsin 20-7
- 11 Oregon 18-10
- 3 Vanderbilt 20-7
- 14 Harvard 20-6
- 7 DePaul 20-9
- 10 SMU 19-10
- 2 Iowa 25-3
- 15 Butler 21-8

MIDEAST

REGIONALS
- Tennessee 88-83 (OT)
- Virginia 72-60
- Connecticut 88-68
- Tennessee 88-83 (OT)

2nd ROUND
- Tennessee 97-56

1st ROUND

NCAA Women's Division I Individual Leaders

SCORING

Player and Team	Class	GP	TFG	3FG	FT	Pts	Avg
Cindy Blodgett, Maine	So	32	313	50	213	889	27.8
Gray C. Harris, Southeast MO St	Sr	27	255	1	202	713	26.4
Gina Somma, Manhattan	Sr	30	288	4	188	768	25.6
Shannon Johnson, S Carolina	Sr	28	238	82	133	691	24.7
Ashley Berggren, Illinois	So	28	251	12	175	689	24.6
Lara Webb, Lamar	So	29	247	41	174	709	24.4
Nadine Malcolm, Providence	Jr	26	212	19	185	628	24.2
Shalonda Enis, Alabama	Jr	32	296	29	145	766	23.9
Anita Maxwell, New Mexico St	Sr	30	286	1	138	711	23.7
Jenni Ruff, Washington St	Sr	29	227	28	203	685	23.6
Tanja Kostic, Oregon St	Sr	28	230	2	188	650	23.2
Charmonique Stallworth, Northern IL	Sr	22	204	0	100	508	23.1
Tina Thompson, Southern Cal	Jr	27	229	24	141	623	23.1
Natasha Parks, Coppin St	Sr	26	191	70	141	593	22.8
Latasha Byears, DePaul	Sr	30	281	2	119	683	22.8

REBOUNDS

Player and Team	Class	GP	Reb	Avg
Dana Wynne, Seton Hall	Jr	29	372	12.8
Deneka Knowles, Southeastern LA	Sr	26	318	12.2
Felecia Autry, Campbell	So	27	329	12.2
Erica Scott, Mississippi Valley	Sr	28	339	12.1
Timothea Clemmer, Wright St	Sr	27	316	11.7
Latasha Byears, DePaul	Sr	30	351	11.7
Natasha Rezek, Pennsylvania	Sr	26	302	11.6
Brandy Reed, Southern MS	So	26	301	11.6
Kathy Caldwell, New Hampshire	Sr	28	323	11.5
Laphelia Doss, Eastern KY	So	27	310	11.5

ASSISTS

Player and Team	Class	GP	A	Avg
Brenda Pantoja, Arizona	Sr	30	278	9.3
Heather Smith, Toledo	Sr	31	263	8.5
Tina Nicholson, Penn St	Sr	34	283	8.3
Dayna Smith, Rhode Island	Sr	29	233	8.0
Eliza Sokolowska, California	Sr	25	186	7.4
Krissy Holden, Indiana St	Jr	26	190	7.3
Lisa Branch, Texas A&M	Sr	32	231	7.2
Akia Hardy, Long Beach St	Sr	24	171	7.1
Patricia Penicheiro, Old Dominion	Jr	32	226	7.1
Jennifer Sutter, Eastern WA	Jr	27	189	7.0

FIELD-GOAL PERCENTAGE

Player and Team	Class	GP	FGA	FG	Pct
Deneka Knowles, Southeastern LA	Sr	26	276	199	72.1
Tyish Hall, Duke	Jr	33	330	216	65.5
Megan Boguslawski, Western MI	Sr	27	355	226	63.7
Katryna Gaither, Notre Dame	Jr	31	412	261	63.3
Kara Wolters, Connecticut	Jr	37	486	306	63.0
Barbara Farris, Tulane	So	31	284	178	62.7
Clarisse Machanguana, Old Dominion	Jr	32	367	230	62.7
Katrina Hannaford, Northwestern	Jr	32	318	199	62.6
Myndee Larsen, Southern UT	Jr	25	271	168	62.0
Carrie Templin, Kent	So	31	315	195	61.9

Note: Minimum 5 made per game.

FREE-THROW PERCENTAGE

Player and Team	Class	GP	FTA	FT	Pct
Kristin Mattox, Louisville	Sr	27	126	116	92.1
Tracey DeLong, Charleston (SC)	So	28	91	82	90.1
Marcie Byrd, Rhode Island	Sr	29	109	97	89.0
Julie Krommenhoek, Utah	So	29	85	75	88.2
Heather Fiore, Canisius	Jr	27	126	111	88.1
Suzanne Ressa, Santa Clara	Sr	27	91	80	87.9
Heather Prater, Middle TN St	Sr	30	104	91	87.5
Haylee Ahu, S Florida	Jr	27	79	69	87.3
Katie Smith, Ohio St	Sr	34	235	205	87.2
Amy Geren, Clemson	Fr	31	97	84	86.6

Note: Minimum 2.5 made per game.

NCAA Men's Division II Individual Leaders

SCORING

Player and Team	Class	GP	TFG	3FG	FT	Pts	Avg
Brett Beeson, Moorhead St	Sr	27	305	58	232	900	33.3
Carlos Knox, IU/PU-Indianapolis	Jr	29	301	70	255	927	32.0
Shawn Harvey, W Virginia St	Sr	24	233	65	119	650	27.1
Tyrone Mason, Edinboro	Sr	27	278	27	139	722	26.7
Dan Buie, Washburn	So	27	242	2	193	679	25.1
Raul Varela, Colorado Mines	Sr	27	202	86	179	669	24.8
Alan Rainge, Northwood	Sr	26	236	14	156	642	24.7
Tim Jones, Georgia College	Jr	27	234	62	123	653	24.2
Dathon Brown, Fort Valley St	Sr	23	181	45	146	553	24.0
Tyrone Hopkins, Central Oklahoma	Jr	29	234	37	175	680	23.4

NCAA Men's Division II Individual Leaders *(Cont.)*

REBOUNDS

Player and Team	Class	GP	Reb	Avg
J.J. Sims, W Georgia	Sr	28	374	13.4
Tommie Foster, Morris Brown	Sr	25	329	13.2
John Burke, LIU-Southampton	Sr	27	336	12.4
Andrew Betts, LIU-C.W. Post	So	29	349	12.0
Kevin Vulin, Sacred Heart	Sr	27	316	11.7
Otis Key, Lincoln (MO)	Sr	25	282	11.3
Kino Outlaw, Mount Olive	Sr	27	298	11.0
Kenisy Adair, Kennesaw St	Jr	26	282	10.8
Deron Rutledge, TX A&M-Kingsville	Sr	28	303	10.8
Kebu Stewart, Cal St-Bakersfield	Jr	27	289	10.7

ASSISTS

Player and Team	Class	GP	A	Avg
Bobby Banks, Metropolitan St	Sr	27	244	9.0
Danny Gimpel, Adelphi	Jr	29	236	8.1
Joe Jessen, St Andrews	Fr	27	217	8.0
Alex Mavroukas, Bentley	So	23	175	7.6
Candice Pickens, California (PA)	Sr	29	217	7.5
Michael McClain, MO-Rolla	Sr	29	217	7.5
Jamie Stevens, Montana St-Billings	So	27	202	7.5
Jay Driscoll, Quincy	So	27	196	7.3
Matt Stone, Keene St	Sr	22	159	7.2
Warren King, Seattle Pacific	Sr	27	192	7.1

FIELD-GOAL PERCENTAGE

Player and Team	Class	GP	FGA	FG	Pct
Kyle Kirby, IU/PU-Fort Wayne	So	26	195	133	68.2
Eliecer Ellis, American (P.R.)	Jr	21	168	111	66.1
John Dixon, Dist. of Columbia	Sr	22	180	116	64.4
J.J. Sims, W Georgia	Sr	28	285	181	63.5
Robert Misenko, Indiana (PA)	Sr	28	294	186	63.3
Demetris Montgomery, Lynn	Jr	25	233	147	63.1
Alonzo Goldston, Fort Hays St	Jr	29	384	242	63.0
Pat Grabner, MN-Duluth	Jr	25	261	164	62.8
Robert Jones, California (PA)	Jr	29	260	163	62.7
Ed Madec, Sonoma St	Sr	26	227	142	62.6

Note: Minimum 5 made per game.

FREE-THROW PERCENTAGE

Player and Team	Class	GP	FTA	FT	Pct
Paul Cluxton, Northern KY	Jr	27	87	81	93.1
Roger Suchy, Lewis	Sr	27	92	83	90.2
Rosendo Bryden, Pembroke St	Sr	27	185	166	89.7
Mike Brown, Georgia College	Sr	28	95	85	89.5
Ryan McCarty, WI-Parkside	Sr	24	103	92	89.3
Lance Luitjens, Northern St	Sr	27	120	107	89.2
John Hemenway, S Dakota	Sr	27	201	179	89.1
Mike Shue, Lock Haven	Jr	24	126	112	88.9
Dan Shanks, Coker	Jr	26	145	128	88.3
Desmond Greer, N Alabama	Jr	28	127	112	88.2

Note: Minimum 2.5 made per game.

NCAA Women's Division II Individual Leaders

SCORING

Player and Team	Class	GP	TFG	3FG	FT	Pts	Avg
LaTina Bullock, Norfolk	Jr	29	261	30	194	746	25.7
Melissa Grider, Missouri Southern St	Sr	28	210	80	216	716	25.6
Lindy Jones, IU/PU-Fort Wayne	Sr	27	224	49	190	687	25.4
Elena Shandrina, Western New Mexico	Sr	26	237	14	172	660	25.4
Vanessa Edwards, Metropolitan St	Sr	27	268	0	137	673	24.9
Faye Hagan, Cal St-Dom Hills	Sr	28	259	7	158	683	24.4
Teasha Murphy, Barton	Sr	26	254	4	108	620	23.8
Jennifer Clarkson, Abilene Christian	Sr	28	215	2	230	662	23.6
Mona Gaffney, Clarion	Sr	26	231	2	150	614	23.6
Kristen Skoglund, St Anselm	Sr	27	229	12	148	618	22.9

REBOUNDS

Player and Team	Class	GP	Reb	Avg
Kisha Conway, Francis Marion	Sr	27	423	15.7
Olivia Hill, Miles	Sr	26	385	14.8
Christine Richardson, Lynn	Jr	27	379	14.0
Melissa Upton, Paine	Jr	25	349	14.0
Trecia Lewis, Virginia St	Jr	24	311	13.0
Carrolyn Burke, Queens (NY)	Sr	22	285	13.0
Tiesha Grace, New Haven	Jr	28	362	12.9
April Lindsey, Tampa	Jr	27	342	12.7
Lachan Rodriquez, Savannah St	So	27	338	12.5
Marie Scott, Missouri Southern St	Jr	28	348	12.4

ASSISTS

Player and Team	Class	GP	A	Avg
Dinah Jowers, Pace	Sr	27	273	10.1
Hayley Lystlund, Augusta	Sr	28	281	10.0
Joanna Bernabei, W Liberty St	Jr	26	259	10.0
Tina Epps, Clark Atlanta	Sr	24	226	9.4
Lamonica Filer, Norfolk St	Sr	29	228	7.9
Lorraine Lynch, Dist of Columbia	Sr	24	178	7.4
Felicia Wright, Delta St	Jr	28	203	7.3
Stephanie Hall, Charleston (WV)	Sr	25	181	7.2
Carla Gladden, St Augustine's	Jr	26	186	7.2
Sydney Jackson, W Florida	Sr	27	192	7.1

NCAA Women's Division II Individual Leaders *(Cont.)*

FIELD-GOAL PERCENTAGE

Player and Team	Class	GP	FGA	FG	Pct
Deidre Williams, Valdosta St.....Sr		27	287	218	76.0
Angela Watson, Central AR ......Sr		29	277	192	69.3
Jennifer Clarkson,					
Abilene Christian..................Sr		28	333	215	64.6
Mona Gaffney, Clarion..............Sr		26	359	231	64.3
Christa Vaughn, Armstrong St...So		23	213	137	64.3
Stacy Johnson, Delta St ....Jr		28	399	253	63.4
Paulita Murrell, W Texas A&M...Sr		28	245	155	63.3
Kathy Kennedy, Valdosta St......Jr		27	275	172	62.5
Tarra Blackwell, FL Southern ...So		29	273	170	62.3
Leann Freeland, Southern IN ....Jr		27	366	225	61.5

Note: Minimum 5 made per game.

FREE-THROW PERCENTAGE

Player and Team	Class	GP	FTA	FT	Pct
Katie Murphy,					
IU/PU-Indianapolis................Sr		23	90	84	93.3
Sara Belanger, MN-Duluth........Sr		26	77	68	88.3
Esther King, Stonehill..............Sr		29	106	93	87.7
Kim Cummings, Bentley ....Sr		28	136	118	86.8
Denise Gallo, Pitt-Johnstown....Sr		27	209	180	86.1
Leah Sheets, IU/PU-Ft Wayne...So		27	93	80	86.0
Lindy Jones, IU/PU-Ft Wayne....Sr		27	222	190	85.6
Kristi Smith, Portland St ....Sr		27	82	70	85.4
Holly Logghe, Bemidji St ....Sr		27	87	73	83.9
Jan Robins, Southwest Baptist...Jr		29	117	98	83.8

Note: Minimum 2.5 made per game.

NCAA Men's Division III Individual Leaders

SCORING

Player and Team	Class	GP	TFG	3FG	FT	Pts	Avg
Ed Brands, Grinnell ....Sr		23	248	150	130	776	33.7
Rick Hughes, Thomas More........................Sr		25	253	8	146	660	26.4
Alex Butler, Rhode Island College...............Jr		24	223	62	104	612	25.5
David Stephens, Colby ....Sr		24	198	37	175	608	25.3
Jon D'Orlando, Endicott ....So		23	208	49	114	579	25.2
Craig Jones, Rochester Institute ....Jr		25	237	0	147	621	24.8
Antoine Harden, Eastern............................Sr		25	250	16	99	615	24.6
J.R. Shumate, Ohio Wesleyan.....................Sr		25	204	95	96	599	24.0
John Wassenbergh, St Joseph's (ME).........Sr		27	235	6	161	637	23.6
Jim McGilvery, Colby-Sawyer ....Sr		25	211	48	119	589	23.6

REBOUNDS

Player and Team	Class	GP	Reb	Avg
Craig Jones, Rochester Institute .....Jr		25	341	13.6
Kevin Braaten, Baldwin-Wallace.....Sr		27	361	13.4
Mark Harris, Coast Guard..............Sr		25	317	12.7
Ira Nicholson, Mt St Vincent...........Jr		19	238	12.5
Greg Belinfanti, NYU......................Sr		25	309	12.4
Antoine Harden, Eastern................Sr		25	308	12.3
Chris Kelly, Staten Island ....Jr		27	324	12.0
Mike Nukk, Maritime (NY) ....Fr		24	282	11.8
Justin Hackley, Salve Regina ....Sr		23	268	11.7
Jason Turner, Wilkes.....................Sr		26	300	11.5

ASSISTS

Player and Team	Class	GP	A	Avg
Andre Bolton, Chris. Newport.........Sr		27	260	9.6
Phil Dixon, Shenandoah..................Sr		26	248	9.5
Dax Kajiwara, Vassar.....................Sr		24	213	8.9
Chris Perrin, Simpson....................Jr		25	211	8.4
J.J. Siepierski, Washington (MO)....Jr		25	209	8.4
Adam Piandes, Bates ....Sr		24	200	8.3
Zach Goring, St Olaf ....Fr		24	197	8.2
Matt Nadelhoffer, Wheaton (IL).......Jr		25	197	7.9
Matt Grieser, Anderson..................Sr		25	189	7.6
Jeff Boyle, Grinnell........................Sr		23	166	7.2

FIELD-GOAL PERCENTAGE

Player and Team	Class	GP	FGA	FG	Pct
John Patraitis, Anna Maria ....So		27	352	248	70.5
Jason Light, Emory & Henry ....So		25	294	207	70.4
James Christopher, Webster ....Sr		25	192	131	68.2
Kipp Christianson,					
St John's (MN)......................Jr		23	268	179	66.8
Jason Hayes, Marietta..............Jr		28	285	187	65.6
Adam Doll, Simpson ....Fr		25	201	131	65.2
Jim South, Augsburg ....Sr		24	272	177	65.1
Scott MacDonald, Menlo ....Sr		25	346	223	64.5
Matt Chitwood, WI-River Falls...So		24	241	155	64.3
Rick Hughes, Thomas More .....Sr		25	394	253	64.2

Note: Minimum 5 made per game.

FREE-THROW PERCENTAGE

Player and Team	Class	GP	FTA	FT	Pct
Charlie Nanick, Scranton............Jr		25	103	96	93.2
Matt Labuda, Wilkes...................Sr		26	79	73	92.4
Mike Nogelo, Williams ....So		24	92	84	91.3
Keith Wolff, Trinity (CT)..............Sr		22	117	105	89.7
Josh Murphy, Heidelberg ....Jr		25	97	87	89.7
Chad Onofrio, Tufts ....Sr		24	103	92	89.3
Marcus Buckley, WI-Eau Claire...Sr		19	63	56	88.9
Rich Kuc, Utica ....Jr		22	79	70	88.6
Ryan Odom, Hampden-Sydney ...Sr		22	68	60	88.2
Gerald Ross, Susquehanna ......Jr		20	67	59	88.1

Note: Minimum 2.5 made per game.

SCORING

Player and Team	Class	GP	TFG	3FG	FT	Pts	Avg
Meegan Garrity, Clark (MA)	Jr	27	262	91	160	775	28.7
Katy Downs, Whittier	Jr	25	192	91	200	675	27.0
Annie Guzek, Dickinson	Sr	25	228	0	195	651	26.0
Leslee Rogers, La Verne	Sr	25	209	100	133	651	26.0
Rebecca Morris, Wentworth Institute	Jr	20	162	7	181	512	25.6
Peggie Sweeney, Pine Manor	Sr	26	202	3	256	663	25.5
Kari Tufte, Luther	Sr	24	235	1	97	568	23.7
Kim Huber, Allegheny	Sr	26	220	0	153	593	22.8
Julie Roe, Millikin	Jr	25	214	0	141	569	22.8
Jennifer Nish, Scranton	Jr	27	255	7	97	614	22.7

REBOUNDS

Player and Team	Class	GP	Reb	Avg
Sayunara Lopez, Lehman	Fr	22	387	17.6
Maia Johnson, Eastern	Fr	21	315	15.0
Jocelyn Naple, Russell Sage	So	22	321	14.6
Julie Anderson, Johns Hopkins	So	26	374	14.4
Karen Provinski, Rochester Inst.	Sr	24	340	14.2
Denise Brace, Albertus Magnus	So	27	380	14.1
Kerry Ceurvels, Salve Regina	So	24	337	14.0
Jen White, Neumann	Sr	24	336	14.0
Kamilah Byrd, Rutgers-Camden	Jr	23	322	14.0
Sara Whitefield, North Park	Fr	25	346	13.8

ASSISTS

Player and Team	Class	GP	A	Avg
Stefanie Teter, Mary Washington	Sr	23	196	8.5
Suzy Venet, Mount Union	So	27	205	7.6
Leslie Baldwin, Centre	Jr	25	187	7.5
Diana Devlin, Bates	Sr	24	177	7.4
Michelle Dailey, Daniel Webster	Fr	23	164	7.1
Nicole Albert, Cal Lutheran	Jr	26	182	7.0
Kristie Silvius, Savannah A&D	Sr	24	165	6.9
Ivette Correa, Salem St	Sr	22	143	6.5
Kara Ryczek, Trinity (CT)	Sr	23	146	6.3
Megan Dillon, Cabrini	Jr	25	157	6.3

FIELD-GOAL PERCENTAGE

Player and Team	Class	GP	FGA	FG	Pct
Kari Tufte, Luther	Sr	24	364	235	64.6
Rebecca Baker, Wilkes	So	23	274	175	63.9
Chris Holland, Principia	Jr	26	287	177	61.7
Marie Mullooly, Beloit	Jr	24	225	138	61.3
Lanett Stephan, Franklin	Sr	24	294	179	60.9
Erin Biehle, John Carroll	Fr	24	211	125	59.2
Stephanie Lodermeier, Augsburg	So	25	320	189	59.1
Sharon Laddey, Rowan	Sr	26	336	197	58.6
Micky Davis, Hardin-Simmons	So	24	329	191	58.1
Christy Williams, Howard Payne	Jr	24	350	202	57.7

Note: Minimum 5 made per game.

FREE-THROW PERCENTAGE

Player and Team	Class	GP	FTA	FT	Pct
Julie James, Luther	Jr	24	66	60	90.9
Jennifer Young, Bridgewater (VA)	So	25	74	65	87.7
Holly Maines, Westfield St	Fr	27	90	78	86.7
Tracy Handrahan, WI-River Falls	Sr	25	74	64	86.5
Sarah Clarke, Muhlenberg	Fr	26	107	92	86.0
Katie Stanton, Hartwick	Jr	24	131	112	85.5
Bryna Burda, Geneseo St	So	27	85	72	84.7
Kitri Peterson, Bethel (MN)	Sr	20	111	94	84.7
Anika Egli, Eastern Mennonite	Fr	25	89	75	84.3
Melissa Vandamme, Alma	Jr	26	151	127	84.1

Note: Minimum 2.5 made per game.

First Lady Wins an NC-er

The score last week from Joseph-Beth Booksellers in Lexington, Ky., was Hillary Rodham Clinton 2,000, Dick Vitale 600. That's the approximate number of people who queued up when this oddest of literary couples happened to be signing their books at separate tables in the store. Rodham Clinton was autographing her best-selling It Takes a Village, while Vitale was inking his Holding Court: Reflections on the Game I Love. The authors met briefly and exchanged inscribed copies. The First Lady wrote: "Best Wishes, Dick. Forever a fan." Dicky V. responded with: "I really respect any individual who faces the pressure on a daily basis. I truly have great respect for you. You're awesome, baby." At least he resisted the urge to call the first-time author a Diaper Dandy.

FOR THE RECORD·Year by Year

NCAA Men's Division I Championship Results

NCAA Final Four Results

Year	Winner	Score	Runner-up	Third Place	Fourth Place	Winning Coach
1939	Oregon	46-33	Ohio St	*Oklahoma	*Villanova	Howard Hobson
1940	Indiana	60-42	Kansas	*Duquesne	*Southern Cal	Branch McCracken
1941	Wisconsin	39-34	Washington St	*Pittsburgh	*Arkansas	Harold Foster
1942	Stanford	53-38	Dartmouth	*Colorado	*Kentucky	Everett Dean
1943	Wyoming	46-34	Georgetown	*Texas	*DePaul	Everett Shelton
1944	Utah	42-40 (OT)	Dartmouth	*Iowa St	*Ohio St	Vadal Peterson
1945	Oklahoma St	49-45	NYU	*Arkansas	*Ohio St	Hank Iba
1946	Oklahoma St	43-40	N Carolina	Ohio St	California	Hank Iba
1947	Holy Cross	58-47	Oklahoma	Texas	CCNY	Alvin Julian
1948	Kentucky	58-42	Baylor	Holy Cross	Kansas St	Adolph Rupp
1949	Kentucky	46-36	Oklahoma St	Illinois	Oregon St	Adolph Rupp
1950	CCNY	71-68	Bradley	N Carolina St	Baylor	Nat Holman
1951	Kentucky	68-58	Kansas St	Illinois	Oklahoma St	Adolph Rupp
1952	Kansas	80-63	St John's (NY)	Illinois	Santa Clara	Forrest Allen
1953	Indiana	69-68	Kansas	Washington	Louisiana St	Branch McCracken
1954	La Salle	92-76	Bradley	Penn St	Southern Cal	Kenneth Loeffler
1955	San Francisco	77-63	La Salle	Colorado	Iowa	Phil Woolpert
1956	San Francisco	83-71	Iowa	Temple	Southern Meth	Phil Woolpert
1957	N Carolina	54-53 (3OT)	Kansas	San Francisco	Michigan St	Frank McGuire
1958	Kentucky	84-72	Seattle	Temple	Kansas St	Adolph Rupp
1959	California	71-70	W Virginia	Cincinnati	Louisville	Pete Newell
1960	Ohio St	75-55	California	Cincinnati	NYU	Fred Taylor
1961	Cincinnati	70-65 (OT)	Ohio St	Vacated‡	Utah	Edwin Jucker
1962	Cincinnati	71-59	Ohio St	Wake Forest	UCLA	Edwin Jucker
1963	Loyola (IL)	60-58 (OT)	Cincinnati	Duke	Oregon St	George Ireland
1964	UCLA	98-83	Duke	Michigan	Kansas St	John Wooden
1965	UCLA	91-80	Michigan	Princeton	Wichita St	John Wooden
1966	UTEP	72-65	Kentucky	Duke	Utah	Don Haskins
1967	UCLA	79-64	Dayton	Houston	N Carolina	John Wooden
1968	UCLA	78-55	N Carolina	Ohio St	Houston	John Wooden
1969	UCLA	92-72	Purdue	Drake	N Carolina	John Wooden
1970	UCLA	80-69	Jacksonville	New Mexico St	St Bonaventure	John Wooden
1971	UCLA	68-62	Vacated‡	Vacated‡	Kansas	John Wooden
1972	UCLA	81-76	Florida St	N Carolina	Louisville	John Wooden
1973	UCLA	87-66	Memphis St	Indiana	Providence	John Wooden
1974	N Carolina St	76-64	Marquette	UCLA	Kansas	Norm Sloan
1975	UCLA	92-85	Kentucky	Louisville	Syracuse	John Wooden
1976	Indiana	86-68	Michigan	UCLA	Rutgers	Bob Knight
1977	Marquette	67-59	N Carolina	NV-Las Vegas	NC-Charlotte	Al McGuire
1978	Kentucky	94-88	Duke	Arkansas	Notre Dame	Joe Hall
1979	Michigan St	75-64	Indiana St	DePaul	Penn	Jud Heathcote
1980	Louisville	59-54	Vacated‡	Purdue	Iowa	Denny Crum
1981	Indiana	63-50	N Carolina	Virginia	Louisiana St	Bob Knight
1982	N Carolina	63-62	Georgetown	*Houston	*Louisville	Dean Smith
1983	N Carolina St	54-52	Houston	*Georgia	*Louisville	Jim Valvano
1984	Georgetown	84-75	Houston	*Kentucky	*Virginia	John Thompson
1985	Villanova	66-64	Georgetown	*St John's (NY)	Vacated‡	Rollie Massimino
1986	Louisville	72-69	Duke	*Kansas	*Louisiana St	Denny Crum
1987	Indiana	74-73	Syracuse	*NV-Las Vegas	*Providence	Bob Knight
1988	Kansas	83-79	Oklahoma	*Arizona	*Duke	Larry Brown
1989	Michigan	80-79 (OT)	Seton Hall	*Duke	*Illinois	Steve Fisher
1990	UNLV	103-73	Duke	*Arkansas	*Georgia Tech	Jerry Tarkanian
1991	Duke	72-65	Kansas	*UNLV	*N Carolina	Mike Krzyzewski
1992	Duke	71-51	Michigan	*Cincinnati	*Indiana	Mike Krzyzewski
1993	N Carolina	77-71	Michigan	*Kansas	*Kentucky	Dean Smith
1994	Arkansas	76-72	Duke	*Arizona	*Florida	Nolan Richardson
1995	UCLA	89-78	Arkansas	*N Carolina	*Oklahoma St	Jim Harrick
1996	Kentucky	76-67	Syracuse	*Massachusetts	*Mississippi St	Rick Pitino

*Tied for third place. ‡Student-athletes representing St Joseph's (PA) in 1961, Villanova in 1971, Western Kentucky in 1971, UCLA in 1980 and Memphis State in 1985 were declared ineligible subsequent to the tournament. Under NCAA rules, the teams' and ineligible student-athletes' records were deleted, and the teams' places in the standings were vacated.

NCAA Final Four MVPs

Year	Winner, School	GP	Field Goals		3-Pt FG		Free Throws		Reb	A	Stl	BS	Avg
			FGM	Pct	FGA	FGM	FTM	Pct					
1939	....None selected												
1940	....Marv Huffman, Indiana	2	7	—	—	—	4	—	—	—	—	—	9.0
1941	....John Kotz, Wisconsin	2	8	—	—	—	6	—	—	—	—	—	11.0
1942	....Howard Dallmar, Stanford	2	8	—	—	—	4	66.7	—	—	—	—	10.0
1943	....Ken Sailors, Wyoming	2	10	—	—	—	8	72.7	—	—	—	—	14.0
1944	....Arnie Ferrin, Utah	2	11	—	—	—	6	—	—	—	—	—	14.0
1945	....Bob Kurland, Oklahoma St	2	16	—	—	—	5	—	—	—	—	—	18.5
1946	....Bob Kurland, Oklahoma St	2	21	—	—	—	10	66.7	—	—	—	—	26.0
1947	....George Kaftan, Holy Cross	2	18	—	—	—	12	70.6	—	—	—	—	24.0
1948	....Alex Groza, Kentucky	2	16	—	—	—	5	—	—	—	—	—	18.5
1949	....Alex Groza, Kentucky	2	19	—	—	—	14	—	—	—	—	—	26.0
1950	....Irwin Dambrot, CCNY	2	12	42.9	—	—	4	50.0	—	—	—	—	14.0
1951	....None selected												
1952	....Clyde Lovellette, Kansas	2	24	—	—	—	18	—	—	—	—	—	33.0
1953	....*B.H. Horn, Kansas	2	17	—	—	—	17	—	—	—	—	—	25.5
1954	....Tom Gola, La Salle	2	12	—	—	—	14	—	—	—	—	—	19.0
1955	....Bill Russell, San Francisco	2	19	—	—	—	9	—	—	—	—	—	23.5
1956	....*Hal Lear, Temple	2	32	—	—	—	16	—	—	—	—	—	40.0
1957	....*Wilt Chamberlain, Kansas	2	18	51.4	—	—	19	70.4	25	—	—	—	32.5
1958	....*Elgin Baylor, Seattle	2	18	34.0	—	—	12	75.0	41	—	—	—	24.0
1959	....*Jerry West, West Virginia	2	22	66.7	—	—	22	68.8	25	—	—	—	33.0
1960	....Jerry Lucas, Ohio State	2	16	66.7	—	—	3	100.0	23	—	—	—	17.5
1961	....*Jerry Lucas, Ohio State	2	20	71.4	—	—	16	94.1	25	—	—	—	28.0
1962	....Paul Hogue, Cincinnati	2	23	63.9	—	—	12	63.2	38	—	—	—	29.0
1963	....Art Heyman, Duke	2	18	41.0	—	—	15	68.2	19	—	—	—	25.5
1964	....Walt Hazzard, UCLA	2	11	55.0	—	—	8	66.7	10	—	—	—	15.0
1965	....*Bill Bradley, Princeton	2	34	63.0	—	—	19	95.0	24	—	—	—	43.5
1966	....*Jerry Chambers, Utah	2	25	53.2	—	—	20	83.3	35	—	—	—	35.0
1967	....Lew Alcindor, UCLA	2	14	60.9	—	—	11	45.8	38	—	—	—	19.5
1968	....Lew Alcindor, UCLA	2	22	62.9	—	—	9	90.0	34	—	—	—	26.5
1969	....Lew Alcindor, UCLA	2	23	67.7	—	—	16	64.0	41	—	—	—	31.0
1970	....Sidney Wicks, UCLA	2	15	71.4	—	—	9	60.0	34	—	—	—	19.5
1971	....*†Howard Porter, Villanova	2	20	48.8	—	—	7	77.8	24	—	—	—	23.5
1972	....Bill Walton, UCLA	2	20	69.0	—	—	17	73.9	41	—	—	—	28.5
1973	....Bill Walton, UCLA	2	28	82.4	—	—	2	40.0	30	—	—	—	29.0
1974	....David Thompson, NC State	2	19	51.4	—	—	11	78.6	17	—	—	—	24.5
1975	....Richard Washington, UCLA	2	23	54.8	—	—	8	72.7	20	—	—	—	27.0
1976	....Kent Benson, Indiana	2	17	50.0	—	—	7	63.6	18	—	—	—	20.5
1977	....Butch Lee, Marquette	2	11	34.4	—	—	8	100.0	6	2	1	1	15.0
1978	....Jack Givens, Kentucky	2	28	65.1	—	—	8	66.7	17	4	1	3	32.0
1979	....Earvin Johnson, Michigan St	2	17	68.0	—	—	19	86.4	17	3	0	2	26.5
1980	....Darrell Griffith, Louisville	2	23	62.2	—	—	11	68.8	7	15	0	2	28.5
1981	....Isiah Thomas, Indiana	2	14	56.0	—	—	9	81.8	4	9	3	4	18.5
1982	....James Worthy, N Carolina	2	20	74.1	—	—	2	28.6	8	9	0	4	21.0
1983	....*Akeem Olajuwon, Houston	2	16	55.2	—	—	9	64.3	40	3	2	5	20.5
1984	....Patrick Ewing, Georgetown	2	8	57.1	—	—	2	100.0	18	1	1	15	9.0
1985	....Ed Pinckney, Villanova	2	8	57.1	—	—	12	75.0	15	6	3	0	14.0
1986	....Pervis Ellison, Louisville	2	15	60.0	—	—	6	75.0	24	2	3	1	18.0
1987	....Keith Smart, Indiana	2	14	63.6	1	0	7	77.8	7	7	0	2	17.5
1988	....Danny Manning, Kansas	2	25	55.6	1	0	6	66.7	17	4	8	9	28.0
1989	....Glen Rice, Michigan	2	24	49.0	16	7	4	100.0	16	1	0	3	29.5
1990	....Anderson Hunt, UNLV	2	19	61.3	16	9	2	50.0	4	9	1	1	24.5
1991	....Christian Laettner, Duke	2	12	54.5	1	1	21	91.3	17	2	1	2	23.0
1992	....Bobby Hurley, Duke	2	10	41.7	12	7	8	80.0	3	11	0	3	17.5
1993	....Donald Williams, N Carolina	2	15	65.2	14	10	10	100.0	4	2	2	0	25.0
1994	....Corliss Williamson, Arkansas	2	21	50.0	0	0	10	71.4	21	8	4	3	26.0
1995	....Ed O'Bannon, UCLA	2	16	45.7	8	3	10	76.9	25	3	7	1	22.5
1996	....Tony Delk, Kentucky	2	15	41.7	16	8	6	54.6	9	2	3	2	22.0

*Not a member of the championship-winning team.   †Record later vacated.

Best NCAA Tournament Single-Game Scoring Performances

Player and Team	Year	Round	FG	3FG	FT	TP
Austin Carr, Notre Dame vs Ohio	1970	1st	25	—	11	61
Bill Bradley, Princeton vs Wichita St.	1965	C*	22	—	14	58
Oscar Robertson, Cincinnati vs Arkansas	1958	C	21	—	14	56
Austin Carr, Notre Dame vs Kentucky	1970	2nd	22	—	8	52
Austin Carr, Notre Dame vs Texas Christian	1971	1st	20	—	12	52
David Robinson, Navy vs Michigan	1987	1st	22	0	6	50
Elvin Hayes, Houston vs Loyola (IL)	1968	1st	20	—	9	49
Hal Lear, Temple vs SMU	1956	C*	17	—	14	48
Austin Carr, Notre Dame vs Houston	1971	C	17	—	13	47
Dave Corzine, DePaul vs Louisville	1978	2nd	18	—	10	46

C regional third place; C* third-place game.

NIT Championship Results

Year	Winner	Score	Runner-up	Year	Winner	Score	Runner-up
1938	Temple	60-36	Colorado	1968	Dayton	61-48	Kansas
1939	Long Island U	44-32	Loyola (IL)	1969	Temple	89-76	Boston College
1940	Colorado	51-40	Duquesne	1970	Marquette	65-53	St John's (NY)
1941	Long Island U	56-42	Ohio U	1971	N Carolina	84-66	Georgia Tech
1942	W Virginia	47-45	W Kentucky	1972	Maryland	100-69	Niagara
1943	St John's (NY)	48-27	Toledo	1973	Virginia Tech	92-91 (OT)	Notre Dame
1944	St John's (NY)	47-39	DePaul	1974	Purdue	97-81	Utah
1945	DePaul	71-54	Bowling Green	1975	Princeton	80-69	Providence
1946	Kentucky	46-45	Rhode Island	1976	Kentucky	71-67	NC-Charlotte
1947	Utah	49-45	Kentucky	1977	St Bonaventure	94-91	Houston
1948	St Louis	65-52	NYU	1978	Texas	101-93	N Carolina St
1949	San Francisco	48-47	Loyola (IL)	1979	Indiana	53-52	Purdue
1950	CCNY	69-61	Bradley	1980	Virginia	58-55	Minnesota
1951	BYU	62-43	Dayton	1981	Tulsa	86-84 (OT)	Syracuse
1952	La Salle	75-64	Dayton	1982	Bradley	67-58	Purdue
1953	Seton Hall	58-46	St John's (NY)	1983	Fresno St	69-60	DePaul
1954	Holy Cross	71-62	Duquesne	1984	Michigan	83-63	Notre Dame
1955	Duquesne	70-58	Dayton	1985	UCLA	65-62	Indiana
1956	Louisville	93-80	Dayton	1986	Ohio St	73-63	Wyoming
1957	Bradley	84-83	Memphis St	1987	Southern Miss	84-80	La Salle
1958	Xavier (OH)	78-74 (OT)	Dayton	1988	Connecticut	72-67	Ohio St
1959	St John's (NY)	76-71 (OT)	Bradley	1989	St John's (NY)	73-65	St Louis
1960	Bradley	88-72	Providence	1990	Vanderbilt	74-72	St Louis
1961	Providence	62-59	St Louis	1991	Stanford	78-72	Oklahoma
1962	Dayton	73-67	St John's (NY)	1992	Virginia	81-76	Notre Dame
1963	Providence	81-66	Canisius	1993	Minnesota	62-61	Georgetown
1964	Bradley	86-54	New Mexico	1994	Villanova	80-73	Vanderbilt
1965	St John's (NY)	55-51	Villanova	1995	Virginia Tech	65-64 (OT)	Marquette
1966	BYU	97-84	NYU	1996	Nebraska	60-56	St Joseph's
1967	Southern Illinois	71-56	Marquette				

NCAA Men's Division I Season Leaders

Scoring Average

Year	Player and Team	Ht	Class	GP	FG	3FG	FT	Pts	Avg
1948	Murray Wier, Iowa	5-9	Sr	19	152	—	95	399	21.0
1949	Tony Lavelli, Yale	6-3	Sr	30	228	—	215	671	22.4
1950	Paul Arizin, Villanova	6-3	Sr	29	260	—	215	735	25.3
1951	Bill Mlkvy, Temple	6-4	Sr	25	303	—	125	731	29.2
1952	Clyde Lovellette, Kansas	6-9	Sr	28	315	—	165	795	28.4
1953	Frank Selvy, Furman	6-3	Jr	25	272	—	194	738	29.5
1954	Frank Selvy, Furman	6-3	Sr	29	427	—	355	1209	41.7
1955	Darrell Floyd, Furman	6-1	Jr	25	344	—	209	897	35.9
1956	Darrell Floyd, Furman	6-1	Sr	28	339	—	268	946	33.8
1957	Grady Wallace, S Carolina	6-4	Sr	29	336	—	234	906	31.2
1958	Oscar Robertson, Cincinnati	6-5	So	28	352	—	280	984	35.1
1959	Oscar Robertson, Cincinnati	6-5	Jr	30	331	—	316	978	32.6

Scoring Average (Cont.)

Year	Player and Team	Ht	Class	GP	FG	3FG	FT	Pts	Avg
1960	Oscar Robertson, Cincinnati	6-5	Sr	30	369	—	273	1011	33.7
1961	Frank Burgess, Gonzaga	6-1	Sr	26	304	—	234	842	32.4
1962	Billy McGill, Utah	6-9	Sr	26	394	—	221	1009	38.8
1963	Nick Werkman, Seton Hall	6-3	Jr	22	221	—	208	650	29.5
1964	Howard Komives, Bowling Green	6-1	Sr	23	292	—	260	844	36.7
1965	Rick Barry, Miami (FL)	6-7	Sr	26	340	—	293	973	37.4
1966	Dave Schellhase, Purdue	6-4	Sr	24	284	—	213	781	32.5
1967	Jim Walker, Providence	6-3	Sr	28	323	—	205	851	30.4
1968	Pete Maravich, Louisiana St	6-5	So	26	432	—	274	1138	43.8
1969	Pete Maravich, Louisiana St	6-5	Jr	26	433	—	282	1148	44.2
1970	Pete Maravich, Louisiana St	6-5	Sr	31	522	—	337	1381	44.5
1971	Johnny Neumann, Mississippi	6-6	So	23	366	—	191	923	40.1
1972	Dwight Lamar, Southwestern Louisiana	6-1	Jr	29	429	—	196	1054	36.3
1973	William Averitt, Pepperdine	6-1	Sr	25	352	—	144	848	33.9
1974	Larry Fogle, Canisius	6-5	So	25	326	—	183	835	33.4
1975	Bob McCurdy, Richmond	6-7	Sr	26	321	—	213	855	32.9
1976	Marshall Rodgers, TX-Pan American	6-2	Sr	25	361	—	197	919	36.8
1977	Freeman Williams, Portland St	6-4	Jr	26	417	—	176	1010	38.8
1978	Freeman Williams, Portland St	6-4	Sr	27	410	—	149	969	35.9
1979	Lawrence Butler, Idaho St	6-3	Sr	27	310	—	192	812	30.1
1980	Tony Murphy, Southern-BR	6-3	Sr	29	377	—	178	932	32.1
1981	Zam Fredrick, S Carolina	6-2	Sr	27	300	—	181	781	28.9
1982	Harry Kelly, Texas Southern	6-7	Jr	29	336	—	190	862	29.7
1983	Harry Kelly, Texas Southern	6-7	Sr	29	333	—	169	835	28.8
1984	Joe Jakubick, Akron	6-5	Sr	27	304	—	206	814	30.1
1985	Xavier McDaniel, Wichita St	6-8	Sr	31	351	—	142	844	27.2
1986	Terrance Bailey, Wagner	6-2	Jr	29	321	—	212	854	29.4
1987	Kevin Houston, Army	5-11	Sr	29	311	63	268	953	32.9
1988	Hersey Hawkins, Bradley	6-3	Sr	31	377	87	284	1125	36.3
1989	Hank Gathers, Loyola Marymount	6-7	Jr	31	419	0	177	1015	32.7
1990	Bo Kimble, Loyola Marymount	6-5	Sr	32	404	92	231	1131	35.3
1991	Kevin Bradshaw, U.S. Int'l	6-6	Sr	28	358	60	278	1054	37.6
1992	Brett Roberts, Morehead St	6-8	Sr	29	278	66	193	815	28.1
1993	Greg Guy, TX-Pan American	6-1	Jr	19	189	67	111	556	29.3
1994	Glenn Robinson, Purdue	6-8	Jr	34	368	79	215	1030	30.3
1995	Kurt Thomas, Texas Christian	6-9	Sr	27	288	3	202	781	28.9
1996	Kevin Granger, Texas Southern	6-3	Sr	24	194	30	230	648	27.0

Rebounds

Year	Player and Team	Ht	Class	GP	Reb	Avg
1951	Ernie Beck, Pennsylvania	6-4	So	27	556	20.6
1952	Bill Hannon, Army	6-3	So	17	355	20.9
1953	Ed Conlin, Fordham	6-5	So	26	612	23.5
1954	Art Quimby, Connecticut	6-5	Jr	26	588	22.6
1955	Charlie Slack, Marshall	6-5	Jr	21	538	25.6
1956	Joe Holup, George Washington	6-6	Sr	26	604	†.256
1957	Elgin Baylor, Seattle	6-6	Jr	25	508	†.235
1958	Alex Ellis, Niagara	6-5	Sr	25	536	†.262
1959	Leroy Wright, Pacific	6-8	Jr	26	652	†.238
1960	Leroy Wright, Pacific	6-8	Sr	17	380	†.234
1961	Jerry Lucas, Ohio St	6-8	Jr	27	470	†.198
1962	Jerry Lucas, Ohio St	6-8	Sr	28	499	†.211
1963	Paul Silas, Creighton	6-7	Sr	27	557	20.6
1964	Bob Pelkington, Xavier (OH)	6-7	Sr	26	567	21.8
1965	Toby Kimball, Connecticut	6-8	Sr	23	483	21.0
1966	Jim Ware, Oklahoma City	6-8	Sr	29	607	20.9
1967	Dick Cunningham, Murray St	6-10	Jr	22	479	21.8
1968	Neal Walk, Florida	6-10	Jr	25	494	19.8
1969	Spencer Haywood, Detroit	6-8	So	22	472	21.5
1970	Artis Gilmore, Jacksonville	7-2	Jr	28	621	22.2
1971	Artis Gilmore, Jacksonville	7-2	Sr	26	603	23.2
1972	Kermit Washington, American	6-8	Jr	23	455	19.8
1973	Kermit Washington, American	6-8	Sr	22	439	20.0
1974	Marvin Barnes, Providence	6-9	Sr	32	597	18.7
1975	John Irving, Hofstra	6-9	So	21	323	15.4

†From 1956-1962, title was based on highest individual recoveries out of total by both teams in all games.

Rebounds *(Cont.)*

Year	Player and Team	Ht	Class	GP	Reb	Avg
1976	Sam Pellom, Buffalo	6-8	So	26	420	16.2
1977	Glenn Mosley, Seton Hall	6-8	Sr	29	473	16.3
1978	Ken Williams, N Texas St	6-7	Sr	28	411	14.7
1979	Monti Davis, Tennessee St	6-7	Jr	26	421	16.2
1980	Larry Smith, Alcorn St	6-8	Sr	26	392	15.1
1981	Darryl Watson, Miss Valley	6-7	Sr	27	379	14.0
1982	LaSalle Thompson, Texas	6-10	Jr	27	365	13.5
1983	Xavier McDaniel, Wichita St	6-7	So	28	403	14.4
1984	Akeem Olajuwon, Houston	7-0	Jr	37	500	13.5
1985	Xavier McDaniel, Wichita St	6-8	Sr	31	460	14.8
1986	David Robinson, Navy	6-11	Jr	35	455	13.0
1987	Jerome Lane, Pittsburgh	6-6	So	33	444	13.5
1988	Kenny Miller, Loyola (IL)	6-9	Fr	29	395	13.6
1989	Hank Gathers, Loyola (CA)	6-7	Jr	31	426	13.7
1990	Anthony Bonner, St Louis	6-8	Sr	33	456	13.8
1991	Shaquille O'Neal, Louisiana St	7-1	So	28	411	14.7
1992	Popeye Jones, Murray St	6-8	Sr	30	431	14.4
1993	Warren Kidd, Middle Tenn St	6-9	Sr	26	386	14.8
1994	Jerome Lambert, Baylor	6-8	Jr	24	355	14.8
1995	Kurt Thomas, Texas Christian	6-9	Sr	27	393	14.6
1996	Marcus Mann, Mississippi Valley	6-8	Sr	29	394	13.6

Assists

Year	Player and Team	Class	GP	A	Avg
1984	Craig Lathen, IL-Chicago	Jr	29	274	9.45
1985	Rob Weingard, Hofstra	Sr	24	228	9.50
1986	Mark Jackson, St John's (NY)	Jr	36	328	9.11
1987	Avery Johnson, Southern-BR	Jr	31	333	10.74
1988	Avery Johnson, Southern-BR	Sr	30	399	13.30
1989	Glenn Williams, Holy Cross	Sr	28	278	9.93
1990	Todd Lehmann, Drexel	Sr	28	260	9.29
1991	Chris Corchiani, N Carolina St	Sr	31	299	9.65
1992	Van Usher, Tennessee Tech	Sr	29	254	8.76
1993	Sam Crawford, New Mex St	Sr	34	310	9.12
1994	Jason Kidd, California	So	30	272	9.06
1995	Nelson Haggerty, Baylor	Sr	28	284	10.10
1996	Raimonds Miglinieks, UC-Irvine	Sr	27	230	8.52

Blocked Shots

Year	Player and Team	Class	GP	BS	Avg
1986	David Robinson, Navy	Jr	35	207	5.91
1987	David Robinson, Navy	Sr	32	144	4.50
1988	Rodney Blake, St Joseph's (PA)	Sr	29	116	4.00
1989	Alonzo Mourning, Georgetown	Fr	34	169	4.97
1990	Kenny Green, Rhode Island	Sr	26	124	4.77
1991	Shawn Bradley, Brigham Young	Fr	34	177	5.21
1992	Shaquille O'Neal, Louisiana St	Jr	30	157	5.23
1993	Theo Ratliff, Wyoming	Jr	28	124	4.43
1994	Grady Livingston, Howard	Jr	26	115	4.42
1995	Keith Close, Central Conn St	Fr	26	139	5.35
1996	Keith Close, Central Conn St	So	28	178	6.36

Steals

Year	Player and Team	Class	GP	S	Avg
1986	Darron Brittman, Chicago St	Sr	28	139	4.96
1987	Tony Fairley, Charleston Sou	Sr	28	114	4.07
1988	Aldwin Ware, Florida A&M	Sr	29	142	4.90
1989	Kenny Robertson, Cleveland St	Jr	28	111	3.96
1990	Ronn McMahon, E Washington	Sr	29	130	4.48
1991	Van Usher, Tennessee Tech	Jr	28	104	3.71
1992	Victor Snipes, NE Illinois	So	25	86	3.44
1993	Jason Kidd, California	Fr	29	110	3.80
1994	Shawn Griggs, SW Louisiana	Sr	30	120	4.00
1995	Roderick Anderson, Texas	Sr	30	101	3.37
1996	Pointer Williams, McNeese St	Sr	27	118	4.37

Single-Game Records

SCORING HIGHS VS DIVISION I OPPONENT

Pts	Player and Team vs Opponent	Date
72	Kevin Bradshaw, U.S. Int'l vs Loyola Marymount	1-5-91
69	Pete Maravich, Louisiana St vs Alabama	2-7-70
68	Calvin Murphy, Niagara vs Syracuse	12-7-68
66	Jay Handlan, Washington & Lee vs Furman	2-17-51
66	Pete Maravich, Louisiana St vs Tulane	2-10-69
66	Anthony Roberts, Oral Roberts vs N Carolina A&T	2-19-77
65	Anthony Roberts, Oral Roberts vs Oregon	3-9-77
65	Scott Haffner, Evansville vs Dayton	2-18-89
64	Pete Maravich, Louisiana St vs Kentucky	2-21-70
63	Johnny Neumann, Mississippi vs Louisiana St	1-30-71
63	Hersey Hawkins, Bradley vs Detroit	2-22-88

SCORING HIGHS VS NON-DIVISION I OPPONENT

Pts	Player and Team vs Opponent	Date
100	Frank Selvy, Furman vs Newberry	2-13-54
85	Paul Arizin, Villanova vs Philadelphia NAMC	2-12-49
81	Freeman Williams, Portland St vs Rocky Mountain	2-3-78
73	Bill Mlkvy, Temple vs Wilkes	3-3-51
71	Freeman Williams, Portland St vs Southern Oregon	2-9-77

REBOUNDING HIGHS BEFORE 1973

Reb	Player and Team vs Opponent	Date
51	Bill Chambers, William & Mary vs Virginia	2-14-53
43	Charlie Slack, Marshall vs Morris Harvey	1-12-54
42	Tom Heinsohn, Holy Cross vs Boston College	3-1-55
40	Art Quimby, Connecticut vs Boston U	1-11-55
39	Maurice Stokes, St Francis (PA) vs John Carroll	1-28-55
39	Dave DeBusschere, Detroit vs Central Michigan	1-30-60
39	Keith Swagerty, Pacific vs UC-Santa Barbara	3-5-65

REBOUNDING HIGHS SINCE 1973

Reb	Player and Team vs Opponent	Date
34	David Vaughn, Oral Roberts vs Brandeis	1-8-73
33	Robert Parish, Centenary vs Southern Miss	1-22-73
32	Jervaughn Scales, Southern-BR vs Grambling	2-7-94
32	Durand Macklin, Louisiana St vs Tulane	11-26-76
31	Jim Bradley, Northern Illinois vs WI-Milwaukee	2-19-73
31	Calvin Natt, Northeast Louisiana vs Georgia Southern	12-29-76

ASSISTS

A	Player and Team vs Opponent	Date
22	Tony Fairley, Baptist vs Armstrong St	2-9-87
22	Avery Johnson, Southern-BR vs Texas Southern	1-25-88
22	Sherman Douglas, Syracuse vs Providence	1-28-89
21	Mark Wade, NV-Las Vegas vs Navy	12-29-86
21	Kelvin Scarborough, New Mexico vs Hawaii	2-13-87
21	Anthony Manuel, Bradley vs UC-Irvine	12-19-87
21	Avery Johnson, Southern-BR vs Alabama St	1-16-88

STEALS

S	Player and Team vs Opponent	Date
13	Mookie Blaylock, Oklahoma vs Centenary	12-12-87
13	Mookie Blaylock, Oklahoma vs Loyola Marymount	12-17-88
12	Kenny Robertson, Cleveland St vs Wagner	12-3-88
12	Terry Evans, Oklahoma vs Florida A&M	1-27-93
11	Darron Brittman, Chicago St vs McKendree	2-24-86
11	Darron Brittman, Chicago St vs St Xavier	2-8-86
11	Marty Johnson, Towson St vs Bucknell	2-17-88
11	Aldwin Ware, Florida A&M vs Tuskegee	2-24-88
11	Mark Macon, Temple vs Notre Dame	1-29-89
11	Carl Thomas, E Michigan vs Chicago St	2-20-91
11	Ron Arnold, St Francis (NY) vs Mt St Mary's (MD)	2-4-93
11	Tyus Edney, UCLA vs George Mason	12-22-94

Single-Game Records *(Cont.)*

BLOCKED SHOTS

BS	Player and Team vs Opponent	Date
14	David Robinson, Navy vs NC-Wilmington	1-4-86
14	Shawn Bradley, Brigham Young vs E Kentucky	12-7-90
14	Roy Rogers, Alabama vs Georgia	2-10-96
13	Kevin Roberson, Vermont vs New Hampshire	1-9-92
13	Jim McIlvaine, Marquette vs Northeastern (IL)	12-9-92
13	Keith Closs, Central Conn St vs St. Francis (PA)	12-21-94
12	David Robinson, Navy vs James Madison	1-9-86
12	Derrick Lewis, Maryland vs James Madison	1-28-87
12	Rodney Blake, St Joseph's (PA) vs Cleveland St	12-2-87
12	Walter Palmer, Dartmouth vs Harvard	1-9-88
12	Alan Ogg, AL-Birmingham vs Florida A&M	12-16-88
12	Dikembe Mutombo, Georgetown vs St John's (NY)	1-23-89
12	Shaquille O'Neal, Louisiana St vs Loyola Marymount	2-3-90
12	Cedric Lewis, Maryland vs S Florida	1-19-91
12	Ervin Johnson, New Orleans vs Texas A&M	12-29-92
12	Kurt Thomas, Texas Christian vs Texas A&M	2-25-95
12	Keith Closs, Central Conn St vs Troy St	1-20-96

Season Records

POINTS

Player and Team	Year	GP	FG	3FG	FT	Pts
Pete Maravich, Louisiana St	1970	31	522	—	337	1381
Elvin Hayes, Houston	1968	33	519	—	176	1214
Frank Selvy, Furman	1954	29	427	—	355	1209
Pete Maravich, Louisiana St	1969	26	433	—	282	1148
Pete Maravich, Louisiana St	1968	26	432	—	274	1138
Bo Kimble, Loyola Marymount	1990	32	404	92	231	1131
Hersey Hawkins, Bradley	1988	31	377	87	284	1125
Austin Carr, Notre Dame	1970	29	444	—	218	1106
Austin Carr, Notre Dame	1971	29	430	—	241	1101
Otis Birdsong, Houston	1977	36	452	—	186	1090

SCORING AVERAGE

Player and Team	Year	GP	FG	FT	Pts	Avg
Pete Maravich, Louisiana St	1970	31	522	337	1381	44.5
Pete Maravich, Louisiana St	1969	26	433	282	1148	44.2
Pete Maravich, Louisiana St	1968	26	432	274	1138	43.8
Frank Selvy, Furman	1954	29	427	355	1209	41.7
Johnny Neumann, Mississippi	1971	23	366	191	923	40.1
Freeman Williams, Portland St	1977	26	417	176	1010	38.8
Billy McGill, Utah	1962	26	394	221	1009	38.8
Calvin Murphy, Niagara	1968	24	337	242	916	38.2
Austin Carr, Notre Dame	1970	29	444	218	1106	38.1
Austin Carr, Notre Dame	1971	29	430	241	1101	38.0
Kevin Bradshaw, U.S. Int'l	1991	28	358	278	1054	37.6

REBOUNDS

Player and Team	Year	GP	Reb	Player and Team	Year	GP	Reb
Walt Dukes, Seton Hall	1953	33	734	Artis Gilmore, Jacksonville	1970	28	621
Leroy Wright, Pacific	1959	26	652	Tom Gola, La Salle	1955	31	618
Tom Gola, La Salle	1954	30	652	Ed Conlin, Fordham	1953	26	612
Charlie Tyra, Louisville	1956	29	645	Art Quimby, Connecticut	1955	25	611
Paul Silas, Creighton	1964	29	631	Bill Russell, San Francisco	1956	29	609
Elvin Hayes, Houston	1968	33	624	Jim Ware, Oklahoma City	1966	29	607

REBOUND AVERAGE BEFORE 1973

Player and Team	Year	GP	Reb	Avg
Charlie Slack, Marshall	1955	21	538	25.6
Leroy Wright, Pacific	1959	26	652	25.1
Art Quimby, Connecticut	1955	25	611	24.4
Charlie Slack, Marshall	1956	22	520	23.6
Ed Conlin, Fordham	1953	26	612	23.5

Season Records (Cont.)

REBOUND AVERAGE SINCE 1973

Player and Team	Year	GP	Reb	Avg
Kermit Washington, American	1973	22	439	20.0
Marvin Barnes, Providence	1973	30	571	19.0
Marvin Barnes, Providence	1974	32	597	18.7
Pete Padgett, NV-Reno	1973	26	462	17.8
Jim Bradley, Northern Illinois	1973	24	426	17.8

ASSISTS

Player and Team	Year	GP	A	Player and Team	Year	GP	A
Mark Wade, UNLV	1987	38	406	Sherman Douglas, Syracuse	1989	38	326
Avery Johnson, Southern-BR	1988	30	399	Sam Crawford, N Mex St	1993	34	310
Anthony Manuel, Bradley	1988	31	373	Greg Anthony, UNLV	1991	35	310
Avery Johnson, Southern-BR	1987	31	333	Reid Gettys, Houston	1984	37	309
Mark Jackson, St John's (NY)	1986	32	328	Carl Golston, Loyola (IL)	1985	33	305

ASSIST AVERAGE

Player and Team	Year	GP	A	Avg	Player and Team	Year	GP	A	Avg
Avery Johnson, Southern-BR	1988	30	399	13.3	Chris Corchiani, N Carolina St	1991	31	299	9.6
Anthony Manuel, Bradley	1988	31	373	12.0	Tony Fairley, Baptist	1987	28	270	9.6
Avery Johnson, Southern-BR	1987	31	333	10.7	Tyrone Bogues, Wake Forest	1987	29	276	9.5
Mark Wade, NV-Las Vegas	1987	38	406	10.7	Craig Neal, Georgia Tech	1988	32	303	9.5
Nelson Haggerty, Baylor	1995	28	284	10.1	Ron Weingard, Hofstra	1985	24	228	9.5
Glenn Williams, Holy Cross	1989	28	278	9.9					

FIELD-GOAL PERCENTAGE

Player and Team	Year	GP	FG	FGA	Pct
Steve Johnson, Oregon St	1981	28	235	315	74.6
Dwayne Davis, Florida	1989	33	179	248	72.2
Keith Walker, Utica	1985	27	154	216	71.3
Steve Johnson, Oregon St	1980	30	211	297	71.0
Oliver Miller, Arkansas	1991	38	254	361	70.4
Alan Williams, Princeton	1987	25	163	232	70.3
Mark McNamara, California	1982	27	231	329	70.2
Warren Kidd, Middle Tennessee St	1991	30	173	247	70.0
Pete Freeman, Akron	1991	28	175	250	70.0
Joe Senser, West Chester	1977	25	130	186	69.9
Lee Campbell, SW Missouri St	1990	29	192	275	69.8
Stephen Scheffler, Purdue	1990	30	173	248	69.8

Based on qualifiers for annual championship.

FREE-THROW PERCENTAGE

Player and Team	Year	GP	FT	FTA	Pct
Craig Collins, Penn St	1985	27	94	98	95.9
Rod Foster, UCLA	1982	27	95	100	95.0
Danny Basile, Marist	1994	27	84	89	94.4
Carlos Gibson, Marshall	1978	28	84	89	94.4
Jim Barton, Dartmouth	1986	26	65	69	94.2
Jack Moore, Nebraska	1982	27	123	131	93.9
Dandrea Evans, Troy St	1994	27	72	77	93.5
Rob Robbins, New Mexico	1990	34	101	108	93.5
Tommy Boyer, Arkansas	1962	23	125	134	93.3
Damon Goodwin, Dayton	1986	30	95	102	93.1
Brian Magid, George Washington	1980	26	79	85	92.9
Mike Joseph, Bucknell	1990	29	144	155	92.9

Based on qualifiers for annual championship.

Season Records *(Cont.)*

THREE-POINT FIELD-GOAL PERCENTAGE

Player and Team	Year	GP	3FG	3FGA	Pct
Glenn Tropf, Holy Cross	1988	29	52	82	63.4
Sean Wightman, Western Michigan	1992	30	48	76	63.2
Keith Jennings, E Tennessee St	1991	33	84	142	59.2
Dave Calloway, Monmouth (NJ)	1989	28	48	82	58.5
Steve Kerr, Arizona	1988	38	114	199	57.3
Reginald Jones, Prairie View	1987	28	64	112	57.1
Joel Tribelhorn, Colorado St	1989	33	76	135	56.3
Mike Joseph, Bucknell	1988	28	65	116	56.0
Brian Jackson, Evansville	1995	27	53	95	55.8
Christian Laettner, Duke	1992	35	54	97	55.7
Reginald Jones, Prairie View	1988	27	85	155	54.8

Based on qualifiers for annual championship.

STEALS

Player and Team	Year	GP	S
Mookie Blaylock, Oklahoma	1988	39	150
Aldwin Ware, Florida A&M	1988	29	142
Darron Brittman, Chicago St	1986	28	139
Nadav Henefeld, Connecticut	1990	37	138
Mookie Blaylock, Oklahoma	1989	35	131

BLOCKED SHOTS

Player and Team	Year	GP	BS
David Robinson, Navy	1986	35	207
Keith Closs, Central Conn St	1996	28	178
Shawn Bradley, BYU	1991	34	177
Alonzo Mourning, Georgetown	1989	34	169
Adonal Foyle, Colgate	1996	29	165

STEAL AVERAGE

Player and Team	Year	GP	S	Avg
Darron Brittman, Chicago St	1986	28	139	4.96
Aldwin Ware, Florida A&M	1988	29	142	4.90
Ronn McMahon, E Washington	1990	29	130	4.48
Pointer Williams, McNeese St	1996	27	118	4.37
Jim Paguaga, St Francis (NY)	1986	28	120	4.29

BLOCKED-SHOT AVERAGE

Player and Team	Year	GP	BS	Avg
Keith Closs, Central Conn St	1996	28	178	6.36
David Robinson, Navy	1986	35	207	5.91
Adonal Foyle, Colgate	1996	29	165	5.69
Keith Closs, Central Conn St	1995	26	139	5.34
Shaquille O'Neal, Louisiana St	1992	30	157	5.23

Career Records

POINTS

Player and Team	Ht	Final Year	GP	FG	3FG*	FT	Pts
Pete Maravich, Louisiana St	6-5	1970	83	1387	—	893	3667
Freeman Williams, Portland St	6-4	1978	106	1369	—	511	3249
Lionel Simmons, La Salle	6-7	1990	131	1244	56	673	3217
Alphonso Ford, Mississippi Valley	6-2	1993	109	1121	333	590	3165
Harry Kelly, Texas Southern	6-7	1983	110	1234	—	598	3066
Hersey Hawkins, Bradley	6-3	1988	125	1100	118	690	3008
Oscar Robertson, Cincinnati	6-5	1960	88	1052	—	869	2973
Danny Manning, Kansas	6-10	1988	147	1216	10	509	2951
Alfredrick Hughes, Loyola (IL)	6-5	1985	120	1226	—	462	2914
Elvin Hayes, Houston	6-8	1968	93	1215	—	454	2884
Larry Bird, Indiana St	6-9	1979	94	1154	—	542	2850
Otis Birdsong, Houston	6-4	1977	116	1176	—	480	2832
Kevin Bradshaw, Bethune-Cookman, U.S. Int'l	6-6	1991	111	1027	132	618	2804
Allan Houston, Tennessee	6-6	1993	128	902	346	651	2801
Hank Gathers, Southern Cal, Loyola Marymount	6-7	1990	117	1127	0	469	2723
Reggie Lewis, Northeastern	6-7	1987	122	1043	30 (1)	592	2708
Daren Queenan, Lehigh	6-5	1988	118	1024	29	626	2703
Byron Larkin, Xavier (OH)	6-3	1988	121	1022	51	601	2696
David Robinson, Navy	7-1	1987	127	1032	1	604	2669
Wayman Tisdale, Oklahoma	6-9	1985	104	1077	—	507	2661

*Listed is the number of three-pointers scored since it became the national rule in 1987; the number in the parentheses is number scored prior to 1987—these counted as three points in the game but counted as two-pointers in the national rankings. The three-pointers in the parentheses are not included in total points.

Career Records (Cont.)

SCORING AVERAGE

Player and Team	Final Year	GP	FG	FT	Pts	Avg
Pete Maravich, Louisiana St	1968	83	1387	893	3667	44.2
Austin Carr, Notre Dame	1971	74	1017	526	2560	34.6
Oscar Robertson, Cincinnati	1960	88	1052	869	2973	33.8
Calvin Murphy, Niagara	1970	77	947	654	2548	33.1
Dwight Lamar, Southwestern Louisiana	1973	57	768	326	1862	32.7
Frank Selvy, Furman	1954	78	922	694	2538	32.5
Rick Mount, Purdue	1970	72	910	503	2323	32.3
Darrell Floyd, Furman	1956	71	868	545	2281	32.1
Nick Werkman, Seton Hall	1964	71	812	649	2273	32.0
Willie Humes, Idaho St	1971	48	565	380	1510	31.5
William Averitt, Pepperdine	1973	49	615	311	1541	31.4
Elgin Baylor, Coll of Idaho, Seattle	1958	80	956	588	2500	31.3
Elvin Hayes, Houston	1968	93	1215	454	2884	31.0
Freeman Williams, Portland St	1978	106	1369	511	3249	30.7
Larry Bird, Indiana St	1979	94	1154	542	2850	30.3

REBOUNDS BEFORE 1973

Player and Team	Final Year	GP	Reb
Tom Gola, La Salle	1955	118	2201
Joe Holup, George Washington	1956	104	2030
Charlie Slack, Marshall	1956	88	1916
Ed Conlin, Fordham	1955	102	1884
Dickie Hemric, Wake Forest	1955	104	1802

REBOUNDS FOR CAREERS BEGINNING IN 1973 OR AFTER*

Player and Team	Final Year	GP	Reb
Derrick Coleman, Syracuse	1990	143	1537
Malik Rose, Drexel	1996	120	1514
Ralph Sampson, Virginia	1983	132	1511
Pete Padgett, NV-Reno	1976	104	1464
Lionel Simmons, La Salle	1990	131	1429

ASSISTS

Player and Team	Final Year	GP	A
Bobby Hurley, Duke	1993	140	1076
Chris Corchiani, N Carolina St	1991	124	1038
Keith Jennings, E Tennessee St	1991	127	983
Sherman Douglas, Syracuse	1989	138	960
Tony Miller, Marquette	1995	123	956

FIELD-GOAL PERCENTAGE

Player and Team	Final Year	FG	FGA	Pct
Ricky Nedd, Appalachian St	1994	412	597	69.0
Stephen Scheffler, Purdue	1990	408	596	68.5
Steve Johnson, Oregon St	1981	828	1222	67.8
Murray Brown, Florida St	1980	566	847	66.8
Lee Campbell, SW Missouri St	1990	411	618	66.5

Note: Minimum 400 field goals.

FREE-THROW PERCENTAGE

Player and Team	Final Year	FT	FTA	Pct
Greg Starrick, Kentucky, Southern Illinois	1972	341	375	90.9
Jack Moore, Nebraska	1982	446	495	90.1
Steve Henson, Kansas St	1990	361	401	90.0
Steve Alford, Indiana	1987	535	596	89.8
Bob Lloyd, Rutgers	1967	543	605	89.8

Note: Minimum 300 free throws.

*Freshmen became eligible for varsity play in 1973.

Career Records *(Cont.)*

THREE-POINT FIELD GOALS MADE

Player and Team	Final Year	GP	3FG
Doug Day, Radford	1993	117	401
Ronnie Schmitz, MO-Kansas City	1993	112	378
Mark Alberts, Akron	1993	103	375
Jeff Fryer, Loyola Marymount	1990	112	363
Dennis Scott, Georgia Tech	1990	99	351

THREE-POINT FIELD-GOAL PERCENTAGE

Player and Team	Final Year	3FG	3FGA	Pct
Tony Bennett, WI-Green Bay	1992	290	584	49.7
Keith Jennings, E Tennessee St	1991	223	452	49.3
Kirk Manns, Michigan St	1990	212	446	47.5
Tim Locum, Wisconsin	1991	227	481	47.2
David Olson, Eastern Illinois	1992	262	562	46.6

Note: Minimum 200 3-point field goals.

STEALS

Player and Team	Final Year	GP	S
Eric Murdock, Providence	1991	117	376
Gerald Walker, San Francisco	1996	111	344
Johnny Rhodes, Maryland	1996	122	344
Michael Anderson, Drexel	1988	115	341
Kenny Robertson, New Mexico, Clev St	1990	119	341

BLOCKED SHOTS

Player and Team	Final Year	GP	BS
Alonzo Mourning, Georgetown	1992	120	453
Theo Ratliff, Wyoming	1995	111	425
Rodney Blake, St Joseph's (PA)	1988	116	419
Shaquille O'Neal, Louisiana St	1992	90	412
Kevin Roberson, Vermont	1992	112	409

NCAA Men's Division I Team Leaders

Division I Team Alltime Wins

Team	First Year	Yrs	W	L	T
Kentucky	1903	93	1650	520	1
N Carolina	1911	86	1647	588	0
Kansas	1899	98	1596	708	0
St John's (NY)	1908	89	1519	682	0
Duke	1906	91	1492	740	0
Temple	1895	100	1455	793	0
Oregon St	1902	95	1434	950	0
Syracuse	1901	95	1432	670	0
Pennsylvania	1897	96	1425	806	2
Notre Dame	1898	91	1398	748	1
Indiana	1901	96	1388	744	0
UCLA	1920	77	1374	596	0
Washington	1896	94	1348	873	0
Western Kentucky	1915	77	1344	635	0
Purdue	1897	97	1337	738	0

Note: Years in Division I only.

Division I Alltime Winning Percentage

Team	First Year	Yrs	W	L	T	Pct
Kentucky	1903	93	1650	520	1	.760
N Carolina	1911	86	1647	588	0	.737
UNLV	1959	38	789	284	0	.735
UCLA	1920	77	1374	596	0	.698
Kansas	1899	98	1596	708	0	.693
St John's (NY)	1908	89	1519	682	0	.690
Syracuse	1901	95	1432	670	0	.681
Western Kentucky	1915	77	1344	635	0	.679
Duke	1906	91	1492	740	0	.669
DePaul	1924	73	1177	600	0	.662
Arkansas	1924	73	1250	648	0	.659
Louisville	1912	82	1299	687	0	.654
Notre Dame	1898	91	1398	748	1	.651
Indiana	1901	96	1388	744	0	.651
Weber St	1963	34	625	338	0	.649

Note: Minimum of 20 years in Division I.

NCAA Men's Division I Winning Streaks

Longest—Full Season

Team	Games	Years	Ended by
UCLA	88	1971-74	Notre Dame (71-70)
San Francisco	60	1955-57	Illinois (62-33)
UCLA	47	1966-68	Houston (71-69)
UNLV	45	1990-91	Duke (79-77)
Texas	44	1913-17	Rice (24-18)
Seton Hall	43	1939-41	LIU-Brooklyn (49-26)
LIU-Brooklyn	43	1935-37	Stanford (45-31)
UCLA	41	1968-69	Southern Cal (46-44)
Marquette	39	1970-71	Ohio St (60-59)
Cincinnati	37	1962-63	Wichita St (65-64)
N Carolina	37	1957-58	W Virginia (75-64)

Longest—Home Court

Team	Games	Years
Kentucky	129	1943-55
St Bonaventure	99	1948-61
UCLA	98	1970-76
Cincinnati	86	1957-64
Marquette	81	1967-73
Arizona	81	1945-51
Lamar	80	1978-84
Long Beach St	75	1968-74
NV-Las Vegas	72	1974-78
Arizona	71	1987-92
Cincinnati	68	1972-78

Longest—Regular Season

Team	Games	Years	Ended by
UCLA	76	1971-74	Notre Dame (71-70)
Indiana	57	1975-77	Toledo (59-57)
Marquette	56	1970-72	Detroit (70-49)
Kentucky	54	1952-55	Georgia Tech (59-58)
San Francisco	51	1955-57	Illinois (62-33)
Pennsylvania	48	1970-72	Temple (57-52)
Ohio St	47	1960-62	Wisconsin (86-67)
Texas	44	1913-17	Rice (24-18)
UCLA	43	1966-68	Houston (71-69)
LIU-Brooklyn	43	1935-37	Stanford (45-31)
Seton Hall	42	1939-41	LIU-Brooklyn (49-26)

NCAA Men's Division I Winningest Coaches

Active Coaches

WINS

Coach and Team	W
Dean Smith, N Carolina	851
James Phelan, Mt St Mary's (MD)	758
Don Haskins, UTEP	678
Norm Stewart, Missouri	678
Bob Knight, Indiana	678
Lefty Driesell, James Madison	667
Lou Henson, Illinois	663
Jerry Tarkanian, Fresno St	647
Denny Crum, Louisville	587
Eddie Sutton, Oklahoma St	570

Note: Minimum 5 years as a Division I head coach; includes record at 4-year colleges only.

WINNING PERCENTAGE

Coach and Team	Yrs	W	L	Pct
Jerry Tarkanian, Fresno St	25	647	133	.830
Roy Williams, Kansas	8	213	56	.792
Dean Smith, N Carolina	35	851	247	.775
Jim Boeheim, Syracuse	20	483	159	.752
Nolan Richardson, Arkansas	16	391	132	.748
John Chaney, Temple	24	540	188	.742
Bob Knight, Indiana	31	678	247	.733
Larry Hunter, Ohio	20	430	159	.730
Rick Pitino, Kentucky	14	317	119	.728
John Thompson, Georgetown	24	553	208	.727

Note: Minimum 5 years as a Division I head coach; includes record at 4-year colleges only.

Alltime Winningest Men's Division I Coaches

WINS

Coach (Team)	W
Adolph Rupp (Kentucky)	876
Dean Smith (N Carolina)	851
Hank Iba (NW Missouri St, Colorado, Oklahoma St)	767
Ed Diddle (Western Kentucky)	759
Phog Allen (Baker, Kansas, Haskell, Central Missouri St, Kansas)	746
Ray Meyer (DePaul)	724
Don Haskins (UTEP)	678
Norm Stewart (Missouri)	678
Bob Knight (Army, Indiana)	678
Lefty Driesell (Davidson, Maryland, James Madison)	667
John Wooden (Indiana St, UCLA)	664
Lou Henson (Hardin-Simmons, New Mexico St, Illinois)	663
Ralph Miller (Wichita St, Iowa, Oregon St)	657
Marv Harshman (Pacific Lutheran, Washington St, Washington)	654
Gene Bartow (C MO St, Valparaiso, Memphis St, Illinois, UCLA, UAB)	647
Jerry Tarkanian (Long Beach St, UNLV, Fresno St)	647

Note: Minimum 10 head coaching seasons in Division I.

Alltime Winningest Men's Division I Coaches (Cont.)
WINNING PERCENTAGE

Coach (Team)	Yrs	W	L	Pct
Jerry Tarkanian (Long Beach St 69-73, UNLV 74-92, Fresno St 95-)	25	647	133	.830
Clair Bee (Rider 29-31, LIU-Brooklyn 32-45, 46-51)	21	412	87	.826
Adolph Rupp (Kentucky 31-72)	41	876	190	.822
John Wooden (Indiana St 47-48, UCLA 49-75)	29	664	162	.804
Dean Smith (N Carolina 62-)	35	851	247	.775
Harry Fisher (Columbia 07-16, Army 22-23, 25)	13	147	44	.770
Frank Keaney (Rhode Island 21-48)	27	387	117	.768
George Keogan (St Louis 16, Allegheny 19, Valparaiso 20-21, Notre Dame 24-43)	24	385	117	.767
Jack Ramsay (St Joseph's [PA] 56-66)	11	231	71	.765
Vic Bubas (Duke 60-69)	10	213	67	.761
Jim Boeheim (Syracuse 77-)	20	483	159	.752
Nolan Richardson (Tulsa 81-85, Arkansas 86-)	16	391	132	.748
Charles "Chick" Davies (Duquesne 25-43, 47-48)	21	314	106	.748
Ray Mears (Wittenberg 57-62, Tennessee 63-77)	21	399	135	.747
John Chaney (Cheyney 73-82, Temple 83-)	24	540	188	.742
Phog Allen (Baker 06-08, Kansas 08-09, Haskell 09, Cent MO St 13-19, Kansas 20-56)	48	746	264	.739
Al McGuire (Belmont Abbey 58-64, Marquette 65-77)	20	405	143	.739
Everett Chase (N Carolina 37-46)	18	376	133	.739
Walter Meanwell (Wisconsin 12-17, 21-34; Missouri 18, 20)	22	280	101	.735
Bob Knight (Army 66-71, Indiana 72-)	31	678	247	.733

Note: Minimum 10 head coaching seasons in Division I.

NCAA Women's Division I Championship Results

Year	Winner	Score	Runner-up	Winning Coach
1982	Louisiana Tech	76–62	Cheyney	Sonja Hogg
1983	Southern Cal	69–67	Louisiana Tech	Linda Sharp
1984	Southern Cal	72–61	Tennessee	Linda Sharp
1985	Old Dominion	70–65	Georgia	Marianne Stanley
1986	Texas	97–81	Southern Cal	Jody Conradt
1987	Tennessee	67–44	Louisiana Tech	Pat Summitt
1988	Louisiana Tech	56–54	Auburn	Leon Barmore
1989	Tennessee	76–60	Auburn	Pat Summitt
1990	Stanford	88–81	Auburn	Tara VanDerveer
1991	Tennessee	70–67 (OT)	Virginia	Pat Summitt
1992	Stanford	78–62	Western Kentucky	Tara VanDerveer
1993	Texas Tech	84–82	Ohio State	Marsha Sharp
1994	N Carolina	60–59	Louisiana Tech	Sylvia Hatchell
1995	Connecticut	70–64	Tennessee	Geno Auriemma
1996	Tennessee	83–65	Georgia	Pat Summitt

NCAA Women's Division I Alltime Individual Leaders

Single-Game Records
SCORING HIGHS

Pts	Player and Team vs Opponent	Year
60	Cindy Brown, Long Beach St vs San Jose St	1987
58	Kim Perrot, SW Louisiana vs SE Louisiana	1990
58	Lorri Bauman, Drake vs SW Missouri St	1984
55	Patricia Hoskins, Mississippi Valley vs Southern-BR	1989
55	Patricia Hoskins, Mississippi Valley vs Alabama St	1989
54	Anjinea Hopson, Grambling vs Jackson St	1994
54	Mary Lowry, Baylor vs Texas	1994
54	Wanda Ford, Drake vs SW Missouri St	1986
53	Felisha Edwards, NE Louisiana vs Southern Mississippi	1991
53	Chris Starr, NV-Reno vs Cal St-Sacramento	1983
53	Sheryl Swoopes, Texas Tech vs Texas	1993

Single-Game Records *(Cont.)*

REBOUNDING HIGHS

Reb	Player and Team vs Opponent	Year
40	Deborah Temple, Delta St vs AL-Birmingham	1983
37	Rosina Pearson, Bethune-Cookman vs Florida Memorial	1985
33	Maureen Formico, Pepperdine vs Loyola (CA)	1985
31	Darlene Beale, Howard vs S Carolina St	1987
30	Cindy Bonforte, Wagner vs Queens (NY)	1983
30	Kayone Hankins, New Orleans vs. Nicholls St	1994
29	Gail Norris, Alabama St vs Texas Southern	1992
29	Joy Kellogg, Oklahoma City vs Oklahoma Christian	1984
29	Joy Kellogg, Oklahoma City vs UTEP	1984

Eight tied with 28.

ASSISTS

A	Player and Team vs Opponent	Year
23	Michelle Burden, Kent St vs Ball St	1991
22	Shawn Monday, Tennessee Tech vs Morehead St	1988
22	Veronica Pettry, Loyola (IL) vs Detroit	1989
22	Tine Freil, Pacific vs Wichita St	1991
21	Tine Freil, Pacific vs Fresno St	1992
21	Amy Bauer, Wisconsin vs Detroit	1989
21	Neacole Hall, Alabama St vs Southern-BR	1989

Four tied with 20.

Season Records

POINTS

Player and Team	Year	GP	FG	3FG	FT	Pts
Cindy Brown, Long Beach St	1987	35	362	—	250	974
Genia Miller, Cal St-Fullerton	1991	33	376	0	217	969
Sheryl Swoopes, Texas Tech	1993	34	356	32	211	955
Andrea Congreaves, Mercer	1992	28	353	77	142	925
Wanda Ford, Drake	1986	30	390	—	139	919
Barbara Kennedy, Clemson	1982	31	392	—	124	908
Patricia Hoskins, Mississippi Valley	1989	27	345	13	205	908
LaTaunya Pollard, Long Beach St	1983	31	376	—	155	907
Tina Hutchinson, San Diego St	1984	30	383	—	132	898
Cindy Blodgett, Maine	1996	32	313	50	213	889

SEASON SCORING AVERAGE

Player and Team	Year	GP	FG	3FG	FT	Pts	Avg
Patricia Hoskins, Mississippi Valley	1989	27	345	13	205	908	33.6
Andrea Congreaves, Mercer	1992	28	353	77	142	925	33.0
Deborah Temple, Delta St	1984	28	373	—	127	873	31.2
Andrea Congreaves, Mercer	1993	26	302	51	150	805	31.0
Wanda Ford, Drake	1986	30	390	—	139	919	30.6
Anucha Browne, Northwestern	1985	28	341	—	173	855	30.5
LeChandra LeDay, Grambling	1988	28	334	36	146	850	30.4
Kim Perrot, Southwestern Louisiana	1990	28	308	95	128	839	30.0
Tina Hutchinson, San Diego St	1984	30	383	—	132	898	29.9
Jan Jensen, Drake	1991	30	358	6	166	888	29.6
Genia Miller, Cal St-Fullerton	1991	33	376	0	217	969	29.4
Barbara Kennedy, Clemson	1982	31	392	—	124	908	29.3
LaTaunya Pollard, Long Beach St	1983	31	376	—	155	907	29.3
Lisa McMullen, Alabama St	1991	28	285	126	119	815	29.1
Tresa Spaulding, BYU	1987	28	347	—	116	810	28.9
Hope Linthicum, Central Conn St	1987	23	282	—	101	665	28.9

NCAA Women's Division I Alltime Individual Leaders *(Cont.)*

Season Records *(Cont.)*

REBOUNDS

Player and Team	Year	GP	Reb	Player and Team	Year	GP	Reb
Wanda Ford, Drake	1985	30	534	Rosina Pearson, Beth-Cookman	1985	26	480
Wanda Ford, Drake	1986	30	506	Patricia Hoskins, Miss Valley	1987	28	476
Anne Donovan, Old Dominion	1983	35	504	Cheryl Miller, Southern Cal	1985	30	474
Darlene Jones, Miss Valley	1983	31	487	Darlene Beale, Howard	1987	29	459
Melanie Simpson, Okla City	1982	37	481	Olivia Bradley, W Virginia	1985	30	458

REBOUND AVERAGE

Player and Team	Year	GP	Reb	Avg
Rosina Pearson, Bethune-Cookman	1985	26	480	18.5
Wanda Ford, Drake	1985	30	534	17.8
Katie Beck, E Tennessee St	1988	25	441	17.6
DeShawne Blocker, E Tenn St	1994	26	450	17.3
Patricia Hoskins, Mississippi Valley	1987	28	476	17.0
Wanda Ford, Drake	1986	30	506	16.9
Patricia Hoskins, Mississippi Valley	1989	27	440	16.3
Joy Kellogg, Oklahoma City	1984	23	373	16.2
Deborah Mitchell, Mississippi Coll	1983	28	447	16.0

FIELD-GOAL PERCENTAGE

Player and Team	Year	GP	FG	FGA	Pct
Renay Adams, Tennessee Tech	1991	30	185	258	71.7
Regina Days, Georgia Southern	1986	27	234	332	70.5
Kim Wood, WI-Green Bay	1994	27	188	271	69.4
Kelly Lyons, Old Dominion	1990	31	308	444	69.4
Alisha Hill, Howard	1995	28	194	281	69.0
Trina Roberts, Georgia Southern	1982	31	189	277	68.2
Lidiya Varbanova, Boise St	1991	22	128	188	68.1
LaFreda Deckard, North Texas	1995	27	147	217	67.7
Sharon McDowell, NC-Wilmington	1987	28	170	251	67.7
Lidiya Varbanova, Boise St	1992	29	228	338	67.5
Mary Raese, Idaho	1986	31	254	380	66.8
Lydia Sawney, Tennessee Tech	1983	27	167	250	66.8

Based on qualifiers for annual championship.

FREE-THROW PERCENTAGE

Player and Team	Year	GP	FT	FTA	Pct
Ginny Doyle, Richmond	1992	29	96	101	95.0
Linda Cyborski, Delaware	1991	29	74	79	93.7
Jennifer Howard, N Carolina St	1994	27	118	127	92.9
Keely Feeman, Cincinnati	1986	30	76	82	92.7
Amy Slowikowski, Kent St	1989	27	112	121	92.6
Lea Ann Parsley, Marshall	1990	28	96	104	92.3
Chris Starr, NV-Reno	1986	25	119	129	92.2
DeAnn Craft, Central Florida	1987	24	94	102	92.2
Tracey Sneed, La Salle	1988	30	151	165	91.5

Based on qualifiers for annual championship.

THEY SAID IT

Mary Hegarty, the women's basketball coach at Chapman University in Orange, Calif., addressing her Panthers after they had committed 20 turnovers and trailed Cal Baptist 30–17 at halftime: "Who are you, and where did you get those uniforms?"

Career Records

POINTS

Player and Team	Yrs	GP	Pts
Patricia Hoskins, Mississippi Valley	1985-89	110	3122
Lorri Bauman, Drake	1981-84	120	3115
Cheryl Miller, Southern Cal	1983-86	128	3018
Valorie Whiteside, Appalachian St	1984-88	116	2944
Joyce Walker, Louisiana St	1981-84	117	2906
Sandra Hodge, New Orleans	1981-84	107	2860
Andrea Congreaves, Mercer	1989-93	108	2796
Karen Pelphrey, Marshall	1983-86	114	2746
Cindy Brown, Long Beach St	1983-87	128	2696
Carolyn Thompson, Texas Tech	1981-84	121	2655
Sue Wicks, Rutgers	1984-88	125	2655

SCORING AVERAGE

Player and Team	Yrs	GP	FG	3FG	FT	Pts	Avg
Patricia Hoskins, Mississippi Valley	1985-89	110	1196	24	706	3122	28.4
Sandra Hodge, New Orleans	1981-84	107	1194	—	472	2860	26.7
Lorri Bauman, Drake	1981-84	120	1104	—	907	3115	26.0
Andrea Congreaves, Mercer	1989-93	108	1107	153	429	2796	25.9
Valorie Whiteside, Appalachian St	1984-88	116	1153	0	638	2944	25.4
Joyce Walker, Louisiana St	1981-84	117	1259	—	388	2906	24.8
Tarcha Hollis, Grambling	1988-91	85	904	3	247	2058	24.2
Karen Pelphrey, Marshall	1983-86	114	1175	—	396	2746	24.1
Erma Jones, Bethune-Cookman	1982-84	87	961	—	173	2095	24.1
Cheryl Miller, Southern Cal	1983-86	128	1159	—	700	3018	23.6

NCAA Men's Division II Championship Results

Year	Winner	Score	Runner-up	Third Place	Fourth Place
1957	Wheaton (IL)	89-65	Kentucky Wesleyan	Mount St Mary's (MD)	Cal St-Los Angeles
1958	S Dakota	75-53	St Michael's	Evansville	Wheaton (IL)
1959	Evansville	83-67	SW Missouri St	N Carolina A&T	Cal St-Los Angeles
1960	Evansville	90-69	Chapman	Kentucky Wesleyan	Cornell College
1961	Wittenberg	42-38	SE Missouri St	S Dakota St	Mount St Mary's (MD)
1962	Mount St Mary's (MD)	58-57 (OT)	Cal St-Sacramento	Southern Illinois	Nebraska Wesleyan
1963	S Dakota St	44-42	Wittenberg	Oglethorpe	Southern Illinois
1964	Evansville	72-59	Akron	N Carolina A&T	Northern Iowa
1965	Evansville	85-82 (OT)	Southern Illinois	N Dakota	St Michael's
1966	Kentucky Wesleyan	54-51	Southern Illinois	Akron	N Dakota
1967	Winston-Salem	77-74	SW Missouri St	Kentucky Wesleyan	Illinois St
1968	Kentucky Wesleyan	63-52	Indiana St	Trinity (TX)	Ashland
1969	Kentucky Wesleyan	75-71	SW Missouri St	†Vacated	Ashland
1970	Philadelphia Textile	76-65	Tennessee St	UC-Riverside	Buffalo St
1971	Evansville	97-82	Old Dominion	†Vacated	Kentucky Wesleyan
1972	Roanoke	84-72	Akron	Tennessee St	Eastern Mich
1973	Kentucky Wesleyan	78-76 (OT)	Tennessee St	Assumption	Brockport St
1974	Morgan St	67-52	SW Missouri St	Assumption	New Orleans
1975	Old Dominion	76-74	New Orleans	Assumption	TN-Chattanooga
1976	Puget Sound	83-74	TN-Chattanooga	Eastern Illinois	Old Dominion
1977	TN-Chattanooga	71-62	Randolph-Macon	N Alabama	Sacred Heart
1978	Cheyney	47-40	WI-Green Bay	Eastern Illinois	Central Florida
1979	N Alabama	64-50	WI-Green Bay	Cheyney	Bridgeport
1980	Virginia Union	80-74	New York Tech	Florida Southern	N Alabama
1981	Florida Southern	73-68	Mount St Mary's (MD)	Cal Poly-SLO	WI-Green Bay
1982	District of Columbia	73-63	Florida Southern	Kentucky Wesleyan	Cal St-Bakersfield
1983	Wright St	92-73	District of Columbia	*Cal St-Bakersfield	*Morningside
1984	Central Missouri St	81-77	St Augustine's	*Kentucky Wesleyan	*N Alabama
1985	Jacksonville St	74-73	S Dakota St	*Kentucky Wesleyan	*Mount St Mary's (MD)
1986	Sacred Heart	93-87	SE Missouri St	*Cheyney	*Florida Southern
1987	Kentucky Wesleyan	92-74	Gannon	*Delta St	*Eastern Montana
1988	Lowell	75-72	AK-Anchorage	Florida Southern	Troy St
1989	N Carolina Central	73-46	SE Missouri St	UC-Riverside	Jacksonville St

Year	Winner	Score	Runner-up	Third Place	Fourth Place
1990	........Kentucky Wesleyan	93-79	Cal St-Bakersfield	N Dakota	Morehouse
1991	........N Alabama	79-72	Bridgeport (CT)	*Cal St-Bakersfield	*Virginia Union
1992	........Virginia Union	100-75	Bridgeport (CT)	*Cal St-Bakersfield	*California (PA)
1993	........Cal St-Bakersfield	85-72	Troy St (AL)	*New Hampshire Coll	*Wayne St (MI)
1994	........Cal St-Bakersfield	92-86	Southern Indiana	*New Hampshire Coll	*Washburn
1995	........Southern Indiana	71-63	UC-Riverside	*Norfolk St	*Indiana (PA)
1996	........Fort Hays St	70-63	Northern Kentucky	*California (PA)	*Virginia Union

*Indicates tied for third. †Student-athletes representing American International in 1969 and Southwestern Louisiana in 1971 were declared ineligible subsequent to the tournament. Under NCAA rules, the teams' and ineligible student-athletes' records were deleted, and the teams' places in the final standings were vacated.

NCAA Men's Division II Alltime Individual Leaders

SINGLE-GAME SCORING HIGHS

Pts	Player and Team vs Opponent	Date
113	............................Bevo Francis, Rio Grande vs Hillsdale	1954
84	..............................Bevo Francis, Rio Grande vs Alliance	1954
82	..............................Bevo Francis, Rio Grande vs Bluffton	1954
80	..............................Paul Crissman, Southern Cal Col vs Pacific Christian	1966
77	..............................William English, Winston-Salem vs Fayetteville St	1968

Season Records

SCORING AVERAGE

Player and Team	Year	GP	FG	FT	Pts	Avg
Bevo Francis, Rio Grande..1954		27	444	367	1255	46.5
Earl Glass, Mississippi Industrial 1963		19	322	171	815	42.9
Earl Monroe, Winston-Salem......................................1967		32	509	311	1329	41.5
John Rinka, Kenyon...1970		23	354	234	942	41.0
Willie Shaw, Lane..1964		18	303	121	727	40.4

REBOUND AVERAGE

Player and Team	Year	GP	Reb	Avg
Tom Hart, Middlebury 1956		21	620	29.5
Tom Hart, Middlebury 1955		22	649	29.5
Frank Stronczek, American Int'l......................1966		26	717	27.6
R.C. Owens, College of Idaho 1954		25	677	27.1
Maurice Stokes, St Francis (PA) 1954		26	689	26.5

ASSISTS

Player and Team	Year	GP	A
Steve Ray, Bridgeport 1989		32	400
Steve Ray, Bridgeport 1990		33	385
Tony Smith, Pfeiffer.......................1992		35	349
Jim Ferrer, Bentley 1989		31	309
Brian Gregory, Oakland 1989		28	300

ASSIST AVERAGE

Player and Team	Year	GP	A	Avg
Steve Ray, Bridgeport 1989		32	400	12.5
Steve Ray, Bridgeport 1990		33	385	11.7
Demetri Beekman, Assumption...1993		23	264	11.5
Ernest Jenkins, NM Highlands....1995		27	291	10.8
Brian Gregory, Oakland 1989		28	300	10.7

FIELD-GOAL PERCENTAGE

Player and Team	Year	Pct
Todd Linder, Tampa.......................1987		75.2
Maurice Stafford, N Alabama.........1984		75.0
Matthew Cornegay, Tuskegee 1982		74.8
Brian Moten, W Georgia.................1992		73.4
Ed Phillips, Alabama A&M..............1968		73.3

FREE-THROW PERCENTAGE

Player and Team	Year	Pct
Billy Newton, Morgan St 1976		94.4
Kent Andrews, McNeese St 1968		94.4
Mike Sanders, Northern Colorado..1987		94.3
Jay Harrie, E Montana....................1994		93.5
Joe Cullen, Hartwick.......................1969		93.2

Career Records
POINTS

Player and Team	Yrs	Pts
Travis Grant, Kentucky St	1969-72	4045
Bob Hopkins, Grambling	1953-56	3759
Tony Smith, Pfeiffer	1989-92	3350
Earnest Lee, Clark Atlanta	1984-87	3298
Joe Miller, Alderson-Broaddus	1954-57	3294

CAREER SCORING AVERAGE

Player and Team	Yrs	GP	Pts	Avg
Travis Grant, Kentucky St	1969-72	121	4045	33.4
John Rinka, Kenyon	1967-70	99	3251	32.8
Florindo Vieira, Quinnipiac	1954-57	69	2263	32.8
Willie Shaw, Lane	1961-64	76	2379	31.3
Mike Davis, Virginia Union	1966-69	89	2758	31.0

REBOUND AVERAGE

Player and Team	Yrs	GP	Reb	Avg
Tom Hart, Middlebury	1953, 55-56	63	1738	27.6
Maurice Stokes, St Francis (PA)	1953-55	72	1812	25.2
Frank Stronczek, American Int'l	1965-67	62	1549	25.0
Bill Thieben, Hofstra	1954-56	76	1837	24.2
Hank Brown, Lowell Tech	1965-67	49	1129	23.0

ASSISTS

Player and Team	Yrs	A
Demetri Beekman, Assumption	1990-93	1044
Rob Paternostro, New Hamp Coll	1992-95	919
Gallagher Driscoll, St Rose	1989-92	878
Tony Smith, Pfeiffer	1989-92	828
Steve Ray, Bridgeport	1989-90	785

ASSIST AVERAGE

Player and Team	Yrs	GP	A	Avg
Steve Ray, Bridgeport	1989-90	65	785	12.1
Demetri Beekman, Assumption	1990-93	119	1044	8.8
Ernest Jenkins, NM Highlands	1992-95	84	699	8.3
Mark Benson, Texas A&I	1989-91	86	674	7.8
Pat Madden, Jacksonville St	1989-91	88	688	7.8

Note: Minimum 550 Assists.

FIELD-GOAL PERCENTAGE

Player and Team	Yrs	Pct
Todd Linder, Tampa	1984-87	70.8
Tom Schurfranz, Bellarmine	1989-92	70.2
Chad Scott, California (PA)	1991-94	70.0
Ed Phillips, Alabama, A&M	1968-71	68.9
Ulysses Hackett, SC-Spartanburg	1990-92	67.9

Note: Minimum 400 FGM.

FREE-THROW PERCENTAGE

Player and Team	Yrs	Pct
Kent Andrews, McNeese St	1967-69	91.6
Jon Hagen, Mankato St	1963-65	90.0
Dave Reynolds, Davis & Elkins	1986-89	89.3
Tony Budzik, Mansfield	1989-92	88.2
Terry Gill, New Orleans	1972-74	88.2

Note: Minimum 250 FTM.

NCAA Men's Division III Championship Results

Year	Winner	Score	Runner-up	Third Place	Fourth Place
1975	LeMoyne-Owen	57-54	Glassboro St	Augustana (IL)	Brockport St
1976	Scranton	60-57	Wittenberg	Augustana (IL)	Plattsburgh St
1977	Wittenberg	79-66	Oneonta St	Scranton	Hamline
1978	North Park	69-57	Widener	Albion	Stony Brook
1979	North Park	66-62	Potsdam St	Franklin & Marshall	Centre
1980	North Park	83-76	Upsala	Wittenberg	Longwood
1981	Potsdam St	67-65 (OT)	Augustana (IL)	Ursinus	Otterbein
1982	Wabash	83-62	Potsdam St	Brooklyn	Cal St-Stanislaus
1983	Scranton	64-63	Wittenberg	Roanoke	WI-Whitewater
1984	WI-Whitewater	103-86	Clark (MA)	DePauw	Upsala
1985	North Park	72-71	Potsdam St	Nebraska Wesleyan	Widener
1986	Potsdam St	76-73	LeMoyne-Owen	Nebraska Wesleyan	Jersey City St
1987	North Park	106-100	Clark (MA)	Wittenberg	Stockton St
1988	Ohio Wesleyan	92-70	Scranton	Nebraska Wesleyan	Hartwick
1989	WI-Whitewater	94-86	Trenton St	Southern Maine	Centre
1990	Rochester	43-42	DePauw	Washington (MD)	Calvin
1991	WI-Platteville	81-74	Franklin & Marshall	Otterbein	Ramapo (NJ)
1992	Calvin	62-49	Rochester	WI-Platteville	Jersey City St
1993	Ohio Northern	71-68	Augustana	Mass-Dartmouth	Rowan
1994	Lebanon Valley Coll	66-59 (OT)	New York University	Wittenberg	St Thomas (MN)
1995	WI-Platteville	69-55	Manchester	Rowan	Trinity (CT)
1996	Rowan	100-93	Hope (MI)	Illinois Wesleyan	Franklin & Marshall

NCAA Men's Division III Alltime Individual Leaders

SINGLE-GAME SCORING HIGHS

Pts	Player and Team vs Opponent	Year
69	Steve Diekmann, Grinnell vs Simpson	1995
63	Joe DeRoche, Thomas vs St Joseph's (ME)	1988
62	Shannon Lilly, Bishop vs Southwest Assembly of God	1983
61	Steve Honderd, Calvin vs Kalamazoo	1993
61	Dana Wilson, Husson vs Ricker	1974

Season Records

SCORING AVERAGE

Player and Team	Year	GP	FG	FT	Pts	Avg
Steve Diekmann, Grinnell	1995	20	223	162	745	37.3
Rickey Sutton, Lyndon St	1976	14	207	93	507	36.2
Shannon Lilly, Bishop	1983	26	345	218	908	34.9
Dana Wilson, Husson	1974	20	288	122	698	34.9
Rickey Sutton, Lyndon St	1977	16	223	112	558	34.9

REBOUND AVERAGE

Player and Team	Year	GP	Reb	Avg
Joe Manley, Bowie St	1976	29	579	20.0
Fred Petty, New Hampshire College	1974	22	436	19.8
Larry Williams, Pratt	1977	24	457	19.0
Charles Greer, Thomas	1977	17	318	18.7
Larry Parker, Plattsburgh St	1975	23	430	18.7

ASSISTS

Player and Team	Year	GP	A
Robert James, Kean	1989	29	391
Ricky Spicer, WI-Whitewater	1989	31	295
Joe Marcotte, New Jersey Tech	1995	30	292
Ron Torgalski, Hamilton	1989	26	275
Albert Kirchner, Mt St Vincent	1990	24	267

ASSIST AVERAGE

Player and Team	Year	GP	A	Avg
Robert James, Kean	1989	29	391	13.5
Albert Kirchner, Mt St Vincent	1990	24	267	11.1
Ron Torgalski, Hamilton	1989	26	275	10.6
Louis Adams, Rust	1989	22	227	10.3
Eric Johnson, Coe	1991	24	238	9.9

FIELD-GOAL PERCENTAGE

Player and Team	Year	Pct
Travis Weiss, St John's (MN)	1994	76.6
Pete Metzelaars, Wabash	1982	75.3
Tony Rychlec, Mass Maritime	1981	74.9
Tony Rychlec, Mass Maritime	1982	73.1
Russ Newnan, Menlo	1991	73.0

FREE-THROW PERCENTAGE

Player and Team	Year	Pct
Andy Enfield, Johns Hopkins	1991	95.3
Yudi Teichman, Yeshiva	1989	95.2
Chris Carideo, Widener	1992	95.2
Mike Scheib, Susquehanna	1977	94.1
Jason Prevenost, Middlebury	1994	93.8

Career Records

POINTS

Player and Team	Yrs	Pts
Andre Foreman, Salisbury St	1989-92	2940
Lamont Strothers, Chris Newport	1988-91	2709
Matt Hancock, Colby	1987-90	2678
Scott Fitch, Geneseo St	1990-94	2634
Greg Grant, Trenton St	1987-89	2611

CAREER SCORING AVERAGE

Player and Team	Yrs	GP	Avg
Dwain Govan, Bishop	1974-75	55	32.8
Dave Russell, Shepherd	1974-75	60	30.6
Rickey Sutton, Lyndon St	1976-79	80	29.7
John Atkins, Knoxville	1976-78	70	28.7
Steve Peknik, Windham	1974-77	76	27.6

REBOUND AVERAGE

Player and Team	Yrs	GP	Reb	Avg
Larry Parker, Plattsburgh St	1975-78	85	1482	17.4
Charles Greer, Thomas	1975-77	58	926	16.0
Willie Parr, LeMoyne-Owen	1974-76	76	1182	15.6
Michael Smith, Hamilton	1989-92	107	1632	15.2
Dave Kufeld, Yeshiva	1977-80	81	1222	15.1
Ed Owens, Hampden-Sydney	1977-80	77	1160	15.1

ASSIST AVERAGE

Player and Team	Yrs	Avg
Phil Dixon, Shenandoah	1993-96	8.6
Steve Artis, Chris. Newport	1990-93	8.1
David Genovese, Mt St Vincent	1992-95	7.5
Kevin Root, Eureka	1989-91	7.1
Dennis Jacobi, Bowdoin	1989-92	7.1

Hockey

Colorado Avalanche Special Collector's Edition

JUNE 17, 1996 · $5.95

Sports Illustrated

Champs!

Patrick Roy and the Avalanche Snare the Stanley Cup

JOHN BIEVER

A Trade for the Title

Anchored by the play of transplanted goalie Patrick Roy, Colorado made a surprising run to the Stanley Cup title

by Michael Farber

THE COLORADO Avalanche won the Stanley Cup around last call on the morning of June 11 when Uwe Krupp's shot eluded Florida Panther goalie John Vanbiesbrouck, but the defining moment in this championship season occurred six months earlier in another city, another country and another language.

In Montreal on Dec. 2, 1995, the Detroit Red Wings were using Canadiens goaltender Patrick Roy for target practice. For a future Hall of Famer to be humiliated by the visiting team is one thing, but when his own coach abets the humiliation, then something is definitely up. When Roy, an inveterate wise guy, acknowledged the sarcastic cheers at the Forum by raising his stick after a routine save, rookie coach Mario Tremblay decided his goalie could stand another heaping helping of humble pie. Tremblay finally yanked Roy in the second period, after the ninth Detroit goal, creating a clash of egos that would shift the balance of power in the NHL.

The goalie skated to the bench, exchanging if-looks-could-kill glares with Tremblay, then stomped past the coach before doubling back to inform Montreal president Ronald Corey, in his traditional seat behind the bench, that he had played his final game for the Canadiens. Montreal, acting with a strange dispatch considering that Roy had been their marquee player for a decade, made little attempt to smooth over the differences and traded the two-time Conn Smythe Trophy winner to Colorado four days later. Even before Roy made 63 saves to beat Florida 1–0 in triple overtime of Game 4 of the Stanley Cup final and complete the Avalanche sweep, it was clear that as piques go, Roy's would rank right up there with Pikes.

Roy's exile 2,000 miles west symbolized 1995–96 in the NHL, a season of movement. Jaromir Jagr, Ron Francis and Petr Nedved were brilliant in Pittsburgh, registering 367 points, but the most prominent line belonged to Allied Van. Doesn't anybody stay in one place anymore? The Stanley Cup champions themselves were transplants as the former Quebec Nordiques became the only NHL team to

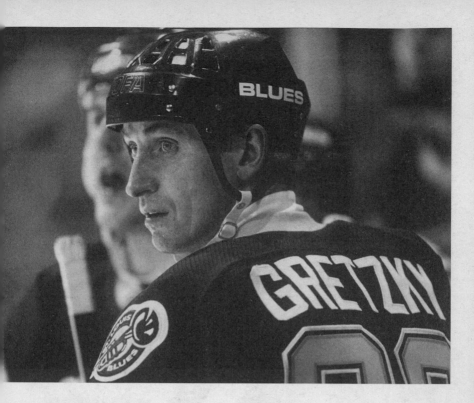

win a championship its first year in a city. There was helter-skelter player movement, and not just the usual small-print transactions, either. The 1995 Conn Smythe Trophy winner, Claude Lemieux, left New Jersey for Colorado at the start of the season, and nine former 50-goal scorers were traded during the year. Wayne Gretzky, the most prolific scorer in NHL history, moved twice, first from Los Angeles to St. Louis in February, and then to the New York Rangers in the off-season. The latter move reunites Gretzky with Mark Messier, kindling hope among the Ranger faithful that the pair will re-create their magic of a decade ago in Edmonton. (The acquisition of Gretzky made the Rangers early favorites to win the 1997 Stanley Cup.) There was plenty of movement in Florida, where arena workers in pest control suits hustled to clear the ice of plastic rats after each Panther goal, one of the new instant traditions in sport that began when Scott

The Rangers are hoping for a Roy-like impact from Gretzky.

Mellanby whacked a rat (a real one) in the Panther dressing room and then went out opening night and scored two goals—a "rat trick." Pittsburgh's Mario Lemieux, who had missed 1994–95 while recuperating from a chronically sore back and radiation treatments for Hodgkin's disease, returned to score his 500th goal and lead the NHL with 69 goals and 161 points; that was moving as well. And the Canadiens moved in mid-March, packing up the ghosts of 24 Stanley Cups past and heading east several blocks from the Forum, hockey's church, for the glitz and 135 corporate boxes of the Molson Centre. (Incidentally, there is glass behind the visitor's bench in the new arena but none behind the Canadiens', just in case the president and a Montreal goalie ever need to converse again.)

Only the Red Wings seemed inert, crashing

DAVID E. KLUTHO

Yzerman (left) would have traded his 500th career goal for a first title.

out of the Western Conference final against Colorado after setting a record with 62 regular-season wins. The 1990s Red Wings are like Hamlet: splendid but tragically flawed, full of promise but harboring a latent death wish. Since 1993 they have had ample talent, but they have been profligate in the postseason, tossing away their chances as gaily as their fans fling octopuses. This should have been their year. They had traded for Igor Larionov in October, and coach Scott Bowman had fashioned an all-Russian unit of Larionov, Sergei Fedorov, Slava Kozlov, Vladimir Konstantinov and Slava Fetisov that was so spectacular on the power play that the Joe Louis Arena

public-address system should have played "Sweet Georgia Brown." Detroit also had a stellar year from Steve Yzerman, who scored his 500th career goal, and solid goaltending from Chris Osgood, who scored his first. The Wings ran out of excuses in 1995–96 and with Colorado in ascendance, the dynasty that wasn't also ran out of time.

Avalanche general manager Pierre Lacroix has assembled a team with a feel of durability to it, a blend of experience and youth, skill and toughness that should keep

Colorado among the NHL elite into the next century. The core players—Joe Sakic, Peter Forsberg, Adam Deadmarsh and Sandis Ozolinsh—are all in their early to mid-20s. Sakic won the Conn Smythe Trophy with 18 goals in 22 playoff games following a 51-goal, 120-point regular season. And while Osgood of the Red Wings figured Sakic is the second-best player in the league behind Mario Lemieux, you can make a reasonable argument that he isn't even the best forward on the Avalanche. Forsberg, the 1994–95 Rookie of the Year, might not have Sakic's wrist shot, but he uses his strength to create room for himself offensively—he had 30 goals and 116 points in '95–96—and has developed into a superior defensive center. In addition to acquiring the disaffected Roy, Lacroix also traded for Claude Lemieux, who was embroiled in a contract dispute with New Jersey, and engineered a deal with San Jose for Ozolinsh, a flashy defenseman who often gives both teams good scoring chances but who quarterbacks his two-minute drill—the power play—as well as fellow Denverite John Elway runs his.

Of course what is obvious in 1996–97 was not last March when the Red Wings were joyriding through the NHL. In a fierce, playoff-style game at Denver that Colorado could use as a measuring stick, Detroit handled the Avalanche 4–2. Two weeks later in a rematch at Joe Louis Arena, Detroit floored the Avalanche 7–0, a Wing win that seemed especially instructive for the coming playoffs. Actually the only thing instructive was how meaningless the 82-game NHL regular season really is.

The first round of the playoffs was a better place to start the scavanger hunt for omens. Detroit needed six games to figure out Winnipeg Jet goalie Nikolai Khabibulin—a couple of games to pronounce his name correctly, a couple to get the puck past him—and while the hot goalie is a traditional playoff hazard, Detroit should have blown through the Jets without breaking a sweat. Meanwhile Roy, who had been slow to adjust to Colorado and its more offensive style, shut out Vancouver in

Game 3. But it wasn't the score (or lack of) as much as a postgame interview that grabbed the attention of veteran Roy watchers. Roy announced on TV that his father had given him some tips over the phone to help his concentration.

"Can you share those with us, Patrick?" Roy was asked.

"Can you keep a secret?"

"Yes."

"Well," Roy retorted, "so can I."

Roy was at his Bart Simpson–smart-alecky best throughout the playoffs. In a battle of quips with Chicago's Jeremy Roenick, Roy said he was having trouble hearing Roenick's rejoinders because his two Stanley Cup rings were blocking his ears. (Kids, do not try this with Dad's jewelry at home.) When told before the final that an Avalanche victory might annoy some fellow members of his West Palm Beach golf club—including Panther president Bill Torrey—hockey's bad boy smiled and said it was O.K., he could buy some new friends. "When Patrick is cocky," an admiring Torrey said, "you know you're in trouble."

Detroit found problems of its own in the second round against the Gretzky-fortified St. Louis Blues. When Gretzky was traded from Edmonton to Los Angeles in 1988, the deal was greeted with disbelief. When the Kings unloaded him in February, the move was greeted with a widespread sense of relief because the NHL seemed to be on hold and listening to Muzak for two months while Los Angeles tried to extricate itself from this muddle of rumor. Gretzky, soon to be an unrestricted free agent, was unhappy because the Kings didn't look like they would be Cup contenders anytime soon. But by going public with his disenchantment, the 35-year-old Gretzky, for the first time since he called the New Jersey Devils franchise Mickey Mouse in 1984, had become embroiled in a public-relations war he could not win. Initially Gretzky was optimistic about his move to St. Louis. Having good friend Brett Hull on his right wing seemed like Gretzky's chance to pad his point total, burnish his reputation and maybe earn a fifth Stanley Cup, but the

Sakic rapped home 18 goals during the playoffs, including six game winners.

blending of the NHL's most creative passer and most feared sniper was a disappointment. St. Louis coach and general manager Mike Keenan was critical of Gretzky during the playoffs—probably the deciding factor in Gretzky's decision to move on—as the Blues extended Detroit but lost Game 7, 1–0, in double overtime on Yzerman's goal.

The feeling around the NHL was that the right player had ended a classic match, but when Avalanche right wing Mike Keane won Game 1 of the Detroit–Colorado conference final late in the first overtime, the feeling—at least Osgood's feeling—was that the wrong player had scored. Keane, who was almost an oversight in the Roy deal even though he had been the Montreal captain, scored on a floater that the folks at *SportsCenter* would describe as a flutterball. Keane was peeved. "I saw the replays, and

that shot wasn't pink. It wasn't white. It was red," said Keane, referring to the *FoxTrax* puck that glowed red on your TV screen when shot hard, the technological innovation of the season that the network designed for those who have trouble following the puck (they are usually called football fans). As the teams engaged in the traditional handshake at center ice after the series, Osgood told Keane he had been lucky. Keane somehow kept his palm open instead of balling it into a fist, the only time any restraint was shown in the six games.

Emotions ran rampant inside and outside the rink during the Avalanche–Red Wing series, most of them revolving around Claude Lemieux. Lemieux had planted a rabbit punch on Kozlov during a first-period scrum in Game 3, prompting Bowman to scream postgame imprecations from the Detroit team bus at Lemieux, who was in the parking lot, headed toward his car with his wife and infant son. Lemieux ripped Bowman for cursing him in front of his family, a position that garnered him considerable sympathy in a chivalrous Denver press that was eager to overlook the fact that the chippy winger was an unlikely spokesman for propriety. The NHL suspended Lemieux for one game. When Lemieux cracked a defenseless Kris Draper into the boards in Game 6—Draper sustained a broken jaw—the NHL suspended Lemieux for the first two games of the finals against the rats-to-riches Panthers.

Because the NHL had tightened its rules concerning interference in the neutral zone —regulations that began to erode less than three months into the season—and because an untested Doug MacLean had replaced veteran Roger Neilson behind the bench, the Panthers were expected to slide after having missed the playoffs by a point their first two years. But from the moment Mellanby felled the rat, Florida showed its killer instinct. At first the Panthers were still a gimmick in search of a team. But while their pedigree would always be questioned, their grittiness in the tough Eastern Conference would not.

While the NHL's two best teams were in the West, the East remained a more physical and more competitive conference. Only three Western teams—Detroit, Colorado and Chicago—finished better than .500. Nine teams in the East were above that mark, including the defending Stanley Cup champion New Jersey Devils, who became the first team in 26 years to miss the postseason the year after winning the Stanley Cup (despite finishing with 86 points). The Eastern giants—the Rangers, Philadelphia and Pittsburgh—kept bumping each other off while the Panthers, despite a nine–game winless streak near the end of the season, kept honing a patient playoff style.

The Rangers, an experienced team built around Messier, cruised through December with an 11-3-3 record despite playing the 17 games in 31 days and wound up carrying a streak of 24 home games without a loss into late February. Messier seemed certain to score 50 goals—he last reached that milestone in 1982—but was injured in early April during the first game of a home-and-home series with Philadelphia and finished with 47 goals in 74 games. If Messier had yielded his title of fiercest forward in the game during the 1995 playoffs to the Flyers' Eric Lindros, he was in no hurry to give up his claim as the game's greatest leader.

Lindros, in his fourth season, seemed destined to carry the Flyers to a Stanley Cup final, but a team with a spotty second line and a defense that seems to find the most inopportune moments to implode is a terrific burden, even for a 6'4", 229-pounder with big skills and a mean streak. Lindros and John LeClair combined for 98 goals as the Flyers won the conference with 103 points, but they were often overshadowed by Lemieux and Jagr, whose 149 points constituted the best offensive season ever by a right wing. The NHL's equivalent of death and taxes had 310 points between them—playing on different lines. The Panthers, a generic team that had no forward with more than 70 points, looked unprepossessing in comparison.

But the Panthers eliminated Boston in five games, scoring a goal that would herald not only their own rise but a new era of defensemen. Bill Lindsay, a 12-goal man during the season, streaked around Bruin All-Star Ray Bourque in Game 5 and scored the winner, a sign that the NHL is about to undergo a changing of the rear guard. Bourque and Chris Chelios, the Norris Trophy winner for the third time, had standout seasons, but in the playoffs several youngsters—including Ozolinsh and Chris Pronger of St. Louis—showed they were ready to join, if not yet supplant, the greats.

Florida rookies Rhett Warrener and Ed Jovanovski were also among the impressive new defensemen. While Warrener kept his cool, Jovanovski gained attention for being a bit hot. When he and Lindros collided in the second round—and it happened seven times according to Florida's count—it looked like Popeye and Bluto going at each other. Lindros would tell Jovanovski, "You'll hear me coming," and the 19-year-old Jovanovski would reply, "Keep your head up." "Everybody says that,"

DAVID E. KLUTHO

Vanbiesbrouck stopped 55 shots in Game 6, only to be beaten on No. 56.

Jovanovski admitted. "I'm not much for comebacks." His actions said it all, however, and the Panthers surprised the Flyers in six games.

The Penguins also finished off the Rangers in five as Jagr and Lemieux scored 15 of the 21 Pittsburgh goals. Astoundingly, in seven games against Florida, the pair managed only two as checkers like Brian Skrudland and sharp goaltending by Vanbiesbrouck shackled them. The Panthers trailed 3–2 in the series, but had the moxie to win the last two, including the 3–1 clincher in Pittsburgh. The stumbling Penguin defense twice allowed Florida five goals in a game, a bonanza for a team that ranked only 12th in scoring during the season.

But against a better-balanced Avalanche team that displayed a refreshing commitment to defense—Keane was told defense wasn't the Avalanche's "karma" after the trade—Florida was overmatched. After losing Game 1 in Denver, MacLean tried to rally his players by photocopying and distributing a Denver newspaper column that caricatured his team as a blight on hockey. Psychology 101, Florida 0. In Game 2 the Panthers seemed more shaken than stirred as Colorado won 8–1, the second-most lopsided victory in Stanley Cup final history.

Colorado was ready for the rat infestation when the series shifted to Florida. Unlike Pittsburgh goalie Tom Barrasso, who had sought shelter in his net when the rain of rodents commenced, Roy kept skating in plain sight. After winning Game 3, 3–2, Roy said it was perfectly acceptable that Florida had nudged two past him because he couldn't stand the thought of fans returning home with unflung rats in their pockets. What a guy.

Roy, who moved into second place all-time with 86 playoff wins, must have had a change of heart by Game 4. He and Vanbiesbrouck combined to give the NHL its third-longest game in finals history and surely one of its best. Vanbiesbrouck stopped 55 shots until Krupp's wrist shot from inside the blue line snaked its way through traffic into the goal at 4:31 of the third overtime period. Sakic's six game-winning goals and 18 during the playoffs—second-highest in NHL history—made him a worthy Conn Smythe winner, but the Avalanche would not have won the Stanley Cup without a man who now ranks with the greatest money goalies. Six months after Montreal traded a goaltender who was just too willful, Roy's tantrum at the Forum was destined to go down in history as No. 1 on Colorado's list of greatest snits.

FOR THE RECORD·1995–1996

NHL Final Team Standings

Western Conference

CENTRAL DIVISION

	GP	W	L	T	GF	GA	Pts
Detroit	82	62	13	7	325	181	131
Chicago	82	40	28	14	273	220	94
Toronto	82	34	36	12	247	252	80
St Louis	82	32	34	16	219	248	80
Winnipeg	82	36	40	6	275	291	78
Dallas	82	26	42	14	227	280	66

PACIFIC DIVISION

	GP	W	L	T	GF	GA	Pts
Colorado	82	47	25	10	326	240	104
Calgary	82	34	37	11	241	240	79
Vancouver	82	32	35	15	278	278	79
Anaheim	82	35	39	8	234	247	78
Edmonton	82	30	44	8	239	304	68
Los Angeles	82	24	40	18	256	302	66
San Jose	82	20	55	7	252	357	47

Eastern Conference

NORTHEAST DIVISION

	GP	W	L	T	GF	GA	Pts
Pittsburgh	82	49	29	4	362	284	102
Boston	82	40	31	11	282	269	91
Montreal	82	40	32	10	265	248	90
Hartford	82	34	39	9	237	259	77
Buffalo	82	33	42	7	247	262	73
Ottawa	82	18	59	5	191	291	41

ATLANTIC DIVISION

	GP	W	L	T	GF	GA	Pts
Philadelphia	82	45	24	13	282	208	103
Rangers	82	41	27	14	272	237	96
Florida	82	41	31	10	258	230	92
Washington	82	39	32	11	234	204	89
Tampa Bay	82	38	32	12	238	248	88
Devils	82	37	33	12	215	202	86
Islanders	82	22	50	10	229	315	54

1996 Stanley Cup Playoffs

EASTERN CONFERENCE

QUARTERFINALS · SEMIFINALS · CONFERENCE FINAL

Tampa Bay
Philadelphia — Philadelphia (4–2)
Boston
Florida — Florida (4–1) — Florida (4–2)
Washington
Pittsburgh — Pittsburgh (4–2) — Florida (4–3)
Montreal
NY Rangers — NY Rangers (4–2) — Pittsburgh (4–1)

STANLEY CUP — Colorado (4–0)

WESTERN CONFERENCE

CONFERENCE FINAL · SEMIFINALS · QUARTERFINALS

Winnipeg
Detroit — Detroit (4–2) — Detroit (4–3)
St Louis
Toronto — St Louis (4–2) — Colorado (4–2)
Vancouver
Colorado — Colorado (4–2) — Colorado (4–2)
Calgary
Chicago — Chicago (4–0)

Stanley Cup Playoff Results

Conference Quarterfinals

EASTERN CONFERENCE

April 16	Tampa Bay	3	at Philadelphia	7	April 17	Washington	6	at Pittsburgh	4
April 18	Tampa Bay	2	at Philadelphia	1*	April 19	Washington	5	at Pittsburgh	3
April 21	Philadelphia	4	at Tampa Bay	5*	April 22	Pittsburgh	4	at Washington	1
April 23	Philadelphia	4	at Tampa Bay	1	April 24	Pittsburgh	3	at Washington	2**
April 25	Tampa Bay	1	at Philadelphia	4	April 26	Washington	1	at Pittsburgh	4
April 27	Philadelphia	6	at Tampa Bay	1	April 28	Pittsburgh	3	at Washington	2

Philadelphia won series 4–2.   Pittsburgh won series 4–2.

*Overtime game. **Quadruple overtime game.

Conference Quarterfinals *(Cont.)*

EASTERN CONFERENCE *(Cont.)*

April 16	Montreal	3	at NY Rangers	2*	April 17	Boston	3	at Florida	6
April 18	Montreal	5	at NY Rangers	3	April 22	Boston	2	at Florida	6
April 21	NY Rangers	2	at Montreal	1	April 24	Florida	4	at Boston	2
April 23	NY Rangers	4	at Montreal	3	April 25	Florida	2	at Boston	6
April 26	Montreal	2	at NY Rangers	3	April 27	Boston	3	at Florida	4
April 28	NY Rangers	5	at Montreal	3				

NY Rangers won series 4–2.   Florida won series 4–1.

WESTERN CONFERENCE

April 17	Winnipeg	1	at Detroit	4	April 16	Vancouver	2	at Colorado	5
April 19	Winnipeg	0	at Detroit	4	April 18	Vancouver	5	at Colorado	4
April 21	Detroit	1	at Winnipeg	4	April 20	Colorado	4	at Vancouver	0
April 23	Detroit	6	at Winnipeg	1	April 22	Colorado	3	at Vancouver	4
April 26	Winnipeg	3	at Detroit	1	April 25	Vancouver	4	at Colorado	5*
April 28	Detroit	4	at Winnipeg	1	April 27	Colorado	3	at Vancouver	2

Detroit won series 4–2.   Colorado won series 4–2.

April 17	Calgary	1	at Chicago	4	April 16	St Louis	3	at Toronto	1
April 19	Calgary	0	at Chicago	3	April 18	St Louis	4	at Toronto	5*
April 21	Chicago	7	at Calgary	5	April 21	Toronto	2	at St Louis	3*
April 23	Chicago	2	at Calgary	1#	April 23	Toronto	1	at St Louis	5

Chicago won series 4–0.

April 25	St Louis	4	at Toronto	5*
April 27	Toronto	1	at St Louis	2

St Louis won series 4–2.

Conference Semifinals

EASTERN CONFERENCE

May 2	Florida	2	at Philadelphia	0
May 4	Florida	2	at Philadelphia	3
May 7	Philadelphia	3	at Florida	1
May 9	Philadelphia	3	at Florida	4*
May 12	Florida	2	at Philadelphia	1†
May 14	Philadelphia	1	at Florida	4

Florida won series 4–2.

May 3	NY Rangers	3	at Pittsburgh	4
May 5	NY Rangers	6	at Pittsburgh	3
May 7	Pittsburgh	3	at NY Rangers	2
May 9	Pittsburgh	4	at NY Rangers	1
May 11	NY Rangers	3	at Pittsburgh	7

Pittsburgh won series 4–1.

WESTERN CONFERENCE

May 3	St Louis	2	at Detroit	3
May 5	St Louis	3	at Detroit	8
May 8	Detroit	4	at St Louis	5*
May 10	Detroit	0	at St Louis	1
May 12	St Louis	3	at Detroit	2
May 14	Detroit	4	at St Louis	2
May 16	St Louis	0	at Detroit	1†

Detroit won series 4–3.

May 2	Chicago	3	at Colorado	2*
May 4	Chicago	1	at Colorado	5
May 6	Colorado	3	at Chicago	4*
May 8	Colorado	3	at Chicago	2#
May 11	Chicago	1	at Colorado	4
May 13	Colorado	4	at Chicago	3†

Colorado won series 4–2.

Eastern Finals

May 18	Florida	5	at Pittsburgh	1
May 20	Florida	2	at Pittsburgh	3
May 24	Pittsburgh	2	at Florida	5
May 26	Pittsburgh	2	at Florida	1
May 28	Florida	0	at Pittsburgh	3
May 30	Pittsburgh	3	at Florida	4
June 1	Florida	3	at Pittsburgh	1

Florida won series 4–3.

Western Finals

May 19	Colorado	3	at Detroit	2*
May 21	Colorado	3	at Detroit	0
May 23	Detroit	6	at Colorado	4
May 25	Detroit	2	at Colorado	4
May 27	Colorado	2	at Detroit	5
May 29	Detroit	1	at Colorado	4

Colorado won series 4–2.

Stanley Cup Finals

June 4	Florida	1	at Colorado	3	June 8	Colorado	3	at Florida	2
June 6	Florida	1	at Colorado	8	June 10	Colorado	1	at Florida	0#

Colorado won series 4–0.

*Overtime game. †Double overtime game. #Triple overtime game.

Stanley Cup Championship Box Scores

Game 1

Florida..............1	0	0—1
Colorado 0	3	0—3

FIRST PERIOD

Scoring: 1, Fla, Fitzgerald 4 (Lindsay), 16:51. Penalties: Mellanby, Fla (roughing), 9:12; Skrudland, Fla (roughing), 9:21; Krupp, Col (high sticking), 13:46; Gusarov, Col (holding), 18:15.

SECOND PERIOD

Scoring: 2, Col, Young 3 (Deadmarsh, Lefebvre), 10:32. 3, Col, Ricci 6 (Keane, Ozolinsh), 12:21. 4, Col, Krupp 3 (Kamensky, Forsberg), 14:21. Penalties: Svehla, Fla (interference), 0:41; Lindsay, Fla (roughing), 7:56; Ricci, Col (roughing), 15:31; Svehla, Fla (roughing), 17:39; Ricci, Col (goalie interference), 18:30.

THIRD PERIOD

Scoring: None. Penalties: Sakic, Col (holding), 3:35; Carkner, Fla (slashing), 6:51; Vanbiesbrouck, Fla served by Sheppard (slashing), 9:55; Jovanovski, Fla (roughing), 19:42.

Shots on goal: Fla—12-6-8—26. Col—6-15-9—30. Power-play opportunities: Fla 0-of-5, Col 0-of-8. Goalies: Fla, Vanbiesbrouck (30 shots, 27 saves). Col, Roy (26 shots, 25 saves). A: 16,061. Referee: McCreary. Linesmen: Scapinello, Murphy.

Game 2

Florida..............1	0	0—1
Colorado 4	3	1—8

FIRST PERIOD

Scoring: 1, Col, Forsberg 8, 4:11. 2, Fla, Barnes 6 (power play) (Lowry, Jovanovski), 7:52. 3, Col, Corbet 2 (power play) (Young, Sakic), 10:43. 4, Col, Forsberg 9 (power play) (Sakic, Ozolinsh), 13:46. 5, Col, Forsberg 10 (power play) (Sakic, Deadmarsh), 15:05. Penalties: Deadmarsh, Col (roughing), 5:53; Lindsay, Fla (slashing), 8:55; Carkner, Fla (roughing), 12:51; Vanbiesbrouck, Fla served by Mellanby (interference), 14:50.

SECOND PERIOD

Scoring: 6, Col, Corbet 3, 4:37. 7, Col, Kamensky 10 (Gusarov, Deadmarsh), 5:08. 8, Col, Klemm 1 (Corbet, Krupp), 10:03. Penalties: Lefebvre, Col (holding), 6:26; Rychel, Col (roughing), 17:01.

THIRD PERIOD

Scoring: 9, Col, Klemm 2 (power play) (Sakic), 17:28. Penalties: Kamensky, Col (double high sticking minor), 3:11; Jovanovski, Fla (roughing), 7:28; Kamensky, Col (roughing), 7:28; Leschyshyn, Col (charging), 7:28; Jovanovski, Fla (fighting major), 9:39; Rychel, Col (instigator, fighting major, game misconduct), 9:39; Laus, Fla (goalie interference), 11:42; Mellanby, Fla (roughing), 16:09.

Shots on goal: Fla—8-15-5—28. Col—11-12-7—30. Power-play opportunities: Fla 1-of-7; Col 4-of-5. Goalies: Fla, Vanbiesbrouck (11 shots, 7 saves), Fitzpatrick (start of 2nd, 19 shots, 15 saves). Col, Roy (28 shots, 27 saves). A: 16,061. Referee: Koharski. Linesmen: Collins, Gauthier.

Game 3

Colorado 1	2	0—3
Florida..............2	0	0—2

FIRST PERIOD

Scoring: 1, Col, Lemieux 5 (Kamensky, Forsberg), 2:44. 2, Fla Sheppard 8 (power play) (Straka, Jovanovski), 9:14. 3, Fla, Niedermayer 5 (Mellanby, Garpenlov), 11:19. Penalties: Deadmarsh, Col (hooking), 7:40; Foote, Col (roughing), 12:49; Lowry, Fla (roughing), 12:49.

SECOND PERIOD

Scoring: 4, Col, Keane 3 (Foote, Gusarov), 1:38. 5, Col, Sakic 18 (Deadmarsh, Leschyshyn), 3:00. Penalties: None.

THIRD PERIOD

Scoring: None. Penalties: None.

Shots on goal: Col—6-10-6—22. Fla—16-13-5—34. Power-play opportunities: Col 0-of-0; Fla 1-of-1. Goalies: Col, Roy (34 shots, 32 saves). Fla, Vanbiesbrouck (22 shots, 19 saves). A: 14,703. Referee: Van Hellemond. Linesmen: Murphy, Scapinello.

Game 4

Colorado...........0	0	0	0	0	1—1
Florida 0	0	0	0	0	0—0

FIRST PERIOD
Scoring: None. Penalty: Svehla, Fla (roughing), 18:57.

SECOND PERIOD
Scoring: None. Penalties: Kamensky, Col (hooking), 5:21; Ozolinsh, Col (roughing), 5:21; Niedermayer, Fla (roughing), 5:21; Foote, Col (roughing), 9:28; Jovanovski, Fla (cross checking), 12:27; Leschyshyn, Col (hooking), 15:33; Ricci, Col (roughing), 18:05; Barnes, Fla (roughing), 18:05.

THIRD PERIOD
Scoring: None. Penalties: Vanbiesbrouck, Fla served by Sheppard (interference), 5:15; Lemieux, Col (high sticking), 6:29.

FIRST OVERTIME
Scoring: None. Penalties: Ozolinsh, Col (roughing), 13:04; Garpenlov, Fla (roughing), 13:04.

SECOND OVERTIME
Scoring: None. Penalties: Lemieux, Col (slashing), 9:57; Skrudland, Fla (slashing), 9:57.

THIRD OVERTIME
Scoring: 1, Col, Krupp 4 (unassisted), 4:31. Penalties: None.

Shots on goal: Col—9-10-10-11-12-4—56. Fla—10-17-8-7-18-3—63. Power-play opportunities: Col 0-of-3; Fla 0-of-4. Goalies: Col, Roy (63 shots, 63 saves). Fla, Vanbiesbrouck (56 shots, 55 saves). A: 14,703. Referee: McCreary. Linesmen: Collins, Gauthier.

Individual Playoff Leaders

Scoring

POINTS

Player and Team	GP	G	A	Pts	+/-	PM	Player and Team	GP	G	A	Pts	+/-	PM
Joe Sakic, Col................	22	18	16	34	10	14	Adam Deadmarsh, Col ...	22	5	12	17	8	25
Mario Lemieux, Pitt........	18	11	16	27	3	33	Ray Sheppard, Fla.........	21	8	8	16	4	0
Jaromir Jagr, Pitt...........	18	11	12	23	7	18	Stu Barnes, Fla..............	22	6	10	16	10	4
Valeri Kamensky, Col	22	10	12	22	11	28	Uwe Krupp, Col	22	4	12	16	5	33
Peter Forsberg, Col	22	10	11	21	10	18	Wayne Gretzky, StL........	13	2	14	16	2	0
Petr Nedved, Pitt...........	18	10	10	20	3	16	Scott Young, Col............	22	3	12	15	6	10
Steve Yzerman, Det.......	18	8	12	20	-1	4	Sergei Zubov, Pitt..........	18	1	14	15	9	26
Sergei Fedorov, Det.......	19	2	18	20	8	10	Shayne Corson, StL........	13	8	6	14	-1	22
Sandis Ozolinsh, Col	22	5	14	19	5	16	Paul Coffey, Det.............	17	5	9	14	-3	30
Dave Lowry, Fla.............	22	10	7	17	8	39	Nicklas Lidstrom, Det	19	5	9	14	2	10
Mike Ricci, Col...............	22	6	11	17	-1	18							

GOALS

Player and Team	GP	G
Joe Sakic, Col	22	11
Jaromir Jagr, Pitt	18	11
Mario Lemieux, Pitt..........	18	11
Petr Nedved, Pitt	18	10
Dave Lowry, Fla..............	22	10
Valeri Kamensky, Col	22	10
Peter Forsberg, Col	22	10

POWER PLAY GOALS

Player and Team	GP	PP
Adam Graves, NYR..........	10	6
Shayne Corson, StL.........	13	6
Dino Ciccarelli, Det	17	6
Joe Sakic, Col	22	6
Jaromir Jagr, Pitt	18	5

GAME-WINNING GOALS

Player and Team	GP	GW
Joe Sakic, Col	22	6
16 tied with two.		

SHORT-HANDED GOALS

Player and Team	GP	SH
Paul Coffey, Det	17	2
19 tied with one.		

ASSISTS

Player and Team	GP	A
Sergei Fedorov, Det	19	18
Mario Lemieux, Pitt..........	18	16
Joe Sakic, Col	22	16
Wayne Gretzky, StL.........	13	14
Sergei Zubov, Pitt...........	18	14
Sandis Ozolinsh, Col	22	14

PLUS/MINUS

Player and Team	GP	+/-
Alexei Gusarov, Col........	21	13
Adam Foote, Col	22	11
Valeri Kamensky, Col	22	11
Joe Sakic, Col	22	10
Peter Forsberg, Col	22	10

Goaltending (Minimum 420 minutes)

GOALS AGAINST AVERAGE

Player and Team	GP	Mins	GA	Avg
Ed Belfour, Chi	9	666	23	2.07
Patrick Roy, Col..............	22	1454	51	2.10
Chris Osgood, Det	15	936	33	2.12
Ron Hextall, Phil	12	760	27	2.13
J. Vanbiesbrouck, Fla	22	1332	50	2.25

SAVE PERCENTAGE

Player and Team	GP	Mins	GA	SA	Pct	W	L
J. Vanbiesbrouck, Fla..	22	1332	50	735	.932	12	10
Ken Wregget, Pitt	9	599	23	328	.930	7	2
Ed Belfour, Chi	9	666	23	323	.929	6	3
Tom Barrasso, Pitt	10	558	26	337	.922	4	5
Patrick Roy, Col.........	22	1454	51	649	.921	16	6

NHL Awards

Award	Player and Team
Hart Trophy (MVP)	Mario Lemieux, Pitt
Calder Trophy (top rookie)	Daniel Alfredsson, Ott
Vezina Trophy (top goaltender)	Jim Carey, Wash
Norris Trophy (top defenseman)	Chris Chelios, Chi
Lady Byng Trophy (for gentlemanly play)	Paul Kariya, Ana

Award	Player and Team
Selke Trophy (top defensive forward)	Sergei Fedorov, Det
Adams Award (top coach)	Scotty Bowman, Det
Jennings Trophy (goaltender on club allowing fewest goals)	Chris Osgood, Det / Mike Vernon, Det
Conn Smythe Trophy (playoff MVP)	Joe Sakic, Col

NHL Individual Leaders

Scoring

POINTS

Player and Team	GP	G	A	Pts	+/−	PM	Player and Team	GP	G	A	Pts	+/−	PM
Mario Lemieux, Pitt	70	69	92	161	10	54	Doug Weight, Edm	82	25	79	104	-19	95
Jaromir Jagr, Pitt	82	62	87	149	31	96	Wayne Gretzky, LA, Stl	80	23	79	102	-13	34
Joe Sakic, Col	82	51	69	120	14	44	Mark Messier, NYR	74	47	52	99	29	122
Ron Francis, Pitt	77	27	92	119	25	56	Petr Nedved, Pitt	80	45	54	99	37	68
Peter Forsberg, Col	82	30	86	116	26	47	Keith Tkachuk, Winn	76	50	48	98	11	156
Eric Lindros, Phil	73	47	68	115	26	163	John LeClair, Phil	82	51	46	97	21	64
Paul Kariya, Ana	82	50	58	108	9	20	Theoren Fleury, Cgy	80	46	50	96	17	112
Teemu Selanne, Winn, Ana	79	40	68	108	5	22	Pierre Turgeon, Mtl	80	38	58	96	19	44
Alexander Mogilny, Van	79	55	52	107	14	16	Steve Yzerman, Det	80	36	59	95	29	64
Sergei Fedorov, Det	78	39	68	107	49	48	V. Damphousse, Mtl	80	38	56	94	5	158

GOALS

Player and Team	GP	G
Mario Lemieux, Pitt	70	69
Jaromir Jagr, Pitt	82	62
Alexander Mogilny, Van	79	55
Peter Bondra, Wash	67	52
John LeClair, Phil	82	51
Joe Sakic, Col	82	51

GAME-WINNING GOALS

Player and Team	GP	GW
Jaromir Jagr, Pitt	82	12
Sergei Fedorov, Det	78	11
Claude Lemieux, Col	79	10
John LeClair, Phil	82	10
Paul Kariya, Ana	82	9

ASSISTS

Player and Team	GP	A
Mario Lemieux, Pitt	70	92
Ron Francis, Pitt	77	92
Jaromir Jagr, Pitt	82	87
Peter Forsberg, Col	82	86
Wayne Gretzky, LA, Stl	80	79
Doug Weight, Edm	82	79

POWER PLAY GOALS

Player and Team	GP	PP
Mario Lemieux, Pitt	70	31
Keith Tkachuk, Winn	76	20
Jaromir Jagr, Pitt	82	20
Paul Kariya, Ana	82	20
Scott Mellanby, Fla	79	19
John LeClair, Phil	82	19

SHORT-HANDED GOALS

Player and Team	GP	SHG
Mario Lemieux, Pitt	70	8
Dave Reid, Bos	63	6
Mats Sundin, Tor	76	6
Jamie Baker, SJ	77	6
Tom Fitzgerald, Fla	82	6
Joe Sakic, Col	82	6

PLUS/MINUS

Player and Team	GP	+/−
Vlad. Konstantinov, Det	81	60
Sergei Fedorov, Det	78	49
Viacheslav Fetisov, Det	69	37
Petr Nedved, Pitt	80	37
Vyacheslav Kozlov, Det	82	33

Goaltending
(Minimum 25 games)

GOALS AGAINST AVERAGE

Player and Team	GP	Mins	GA	Avg
Ron Hextall, Phil	53	3102	112	2.17
Chris Osgood, Det	50	2933	106	2.17
Jim Carey, Wash	71	4069	153	2.26
Mike Vernon, Det	32	1855	70	2.26
Martin Brodeur, NJ	77	4434	173	2.34

WINS

Player and Team	GP	Mins	W	L	T
Chris Osgood, Det	50	2933	39	6	5
Jim Carey, Wash	71	4069	35	24	9
Patrick Roy, Mtl, Col	61	3565	34	24	2
Bill Ranford, Edm, Bos	77	4322	34	30	9
Martin Brodeur, NJ	77	4434	34	30	12

SAVE PERCENTAGE

Player and Team	GP	GA	SA	Pct	W	L	T
Dominik Hasek, Buff	59	161	2011	.920	22	30	6
Daren Puppa, TB	57	131	1605	.918	29	16	9
Jeff Hackett, Chi	35	80	948	.915	18	11	4
Guy Hebert, Ana	59	157	1820	.914	28	23	5
Ron Hextall, Phil	53	112	1292	.913	31	13	7

SHUTOUTS

Player and Team	GP	Mins	SO	W	L	T
Jim Carey, Wash	71	4069	9	35	24	9
Martin Brodeur, NJ	77	4434	6	34	30	12
Chris Osgood, Det	50	2933	5	39	6	5
Daren Puppa, TB	57	3189	5	29	16	9
Jeff Hackett, Chi	35	2000	4	18	11	4
Ron Hextall, Phil	53	3102	4	31	13	7
Guy Hebert, Ana	59	3326	4	28	23	5
Sean Burke, Hart	66	3669	4	28	28	6

NHL Team-by-Team Statistical Leaders

Anaheim Mighty Ducks

SCORING

Player	GP	G	A	Pts	+/–	PM
Paul Kariya, L	82	50	58	108	9	20
Teemu Selanne, R	79	40	68	108	5	22
Roman Oksiuta, R	70	23	28	51	4	60
Steve Rucchin, C	64	19	25	44	3	12
Bobby Dollas, D	82	8	22	30	9	64
Joe Sacco, R	76	13	14	27	1	40
Anatoli Semenov, C	56	4	22	26	-1	24
Shaun Van Allen, C	49	8	17	25	13	41
Garry Valk, L	79	12	12	24	8	125
Jason York, D	79	3	21	24	-7	88
Fredrick Olausson, D	56	2	22	24	-7	38
Alex Hicks, C	64	10	11	21	11	37
Dave Karpa, D	72	3	16	19	-3	270
Patrik Carnback, R	34	6	12	18	3	34
Valeri Karpov, L	37	9	8	17	-1	10
Peter Douris, R	31	8	7	15	-3	9
*David Sacco, L	23	4	10	14	1	18
*Jean-Franc. Jomphe, R	31	2	12	14	7	39
*Denny Lambert, L	33	0	8	8	-2	55
Todd Ewen, R	53	4	3	7	-5	285
Ken Baumgartner, L	72	2	4	6	-5	193
*Jim Campbell, C	16	2	3	5	0	36

GOALTENDING

Player	GP	Mins	Avg	W	L	T	SO
Guy Hebert	59	3326	2.83	28	23	5	4
M. Schalenkov	30	1637	3.12	7	16	3	0
Team total	82	4982	2.97	35	39	8	4

*Rookie.

Boston Bruins

SCORING

Player	GP	G	A	Pts	+/–	PM
Adam Oates, C	70	25	67	92	16	18
Ray Bourque, D	82	20	62	82	31	58
Rick Tocchet, R	71	29	31	60	10	181
Jozef Stumpel, R	76	18	36	54	-8	14
Shawn McEachern, C	82	24	29	53	-5	34
Ted Donato, C	82	23	26	49	6	46
Cam Neely	49	26	20	46	3	31
Todd Elik, C	59	13	33	46	2	40
Dave Reid, L	63	23	21	44	14	4
Sandy Moger, R	80	15	14	29	-9	65
Steve Heinze, R	76	16	12	28	-3	43
Don Sweeney, D	77	4	24	28	-4	42
*Kyle McLaren, D	74	5	12	17	16	73
Tim Sweeney, R	41	8	8	16	4	14
Joe Mullen, R	37	8	7	15	-2	0
Rick Zombo, D	67	4	10	14	-7	53
Jon Rohloff, D	79	1	12	13	-8	59
Ron Sutter, C	18	5	7	12	10	24
Dean Chynoweth, D	49	2	6	8	-5	128
*Clayton Beddoes, C	39	1	6	7	-5	44

GOALTENDING

Player	GP	Mins	Avg	W	L	T	SO
†Bill Ranford	40	2307	2.83	21	12	4	1
*Robbie Tallas	1	60	3.00	1	0	0	0
*Scott Bailey	11	571	3.26	5	1	2	0
Craig Billington	27	1380	3.43	10	13	3	1
Blaine Lacher	12	671	3.93	3	5	2	0
Team total	82	4992	3.23	40	31	11	2

†Played 37 games with Edmonton.

Stan's Man

Every summer Pat Plunkett and his silent partner hit the road. Plunkett is one of four men employed year-round by the Hockey Hall of Fame in Toronto to watch over and protect the Stanley Cup. And though Plunkett is not one of the two men who get to carry the hallowed hardware onto the ice after the last game of the Stanley Cup finals, he is the one who takes Stanley on its annual victory tour. "I'm proud to do it," he says. "The Cup has helped me make friends and go places I otherwise wouldn't have gone."

During the season the Cup spends much of its time on display at the Hall, though it's often summoned by NHL teams for promotional use—and where it goes, so goes Plunkett. That's also true in the weeks after the finals, when each member of the winning team is allowed to spend a day with hockey's Holy Grail. As a result, Plunkett, 40, ends up toting Stanley to about three dozen parties, most of them hosted by players, in the U.S. and Canada. Plunkett carries the three-foot-tall, 34-pound Cup in a hard travel case lined with form-fitting foam.

In the summer of 1995 goalie Chris Terreri of the champion New Jersey Devils had Stanley (and Pat) flown in by helicopter at sunset to a seaside country club in Rhode Island; the arrival of the Cup (and Plunkett) was announced to the accompaniment of fireworks. Plunkett also brought the Cup to the White House for the Devils' victory ceremony. He was treated like a vaguely suspicious dignitary, getting ushered into Bill Clinton's presence with the team—but only after he and the Cup were X-rayed and sniffed by a dog.

Plunkett knew that the summer of '96 would be draining, with long days of travel and constant vigilance to make sure that the Cup, which has suffered dents and dings while in the hands of winning team members, wouldn't be damaged or stolen. "When you get tired or wonder why you're doing it, you just look at the names etched on the Cup," he says. "It reminds you of the sacrifice those players made, and it's hard to feel tired or jaded."

Buffalo Sabres

SCORING

Player	GP	G	A	Pts	+/–	PM
Pat LaFontaine, C	76	40	51	91	-8	36
Randy Burridge, L	74	25	33	58	0	30
Derek Plante, C	76	23	33	56	-4	28
Garry Galley, D	78	10	44	54	-2	81
Jason Dawe, L	67	25	25	50	-8	33
Brad May, L	79	15	29	44	6	295
Alexei Zhitnik, D	80	6	30	36	-25	58
Matthew Barnaby, L	73	15	16	31	-2	335
Mike Peca, C	68	11	20	31	-1	67
Donald Audette, R	23	12	13	25	0	18
*Brian Holzinger, C	58	10	10	20	-21	37
Mark Astley, D	60	2	18	20	-12	80
Darryl Shannon, D	74	4	13	17	15	92
Brent Hughes, L	76	5	10	15	-9	148
*Mike Wilson, D	58	4	8	12	13	41
Michal Grosek, L	23	6	4	10	-1	31
*Dane Jackson, R	22	5	4	9	3	41
Rob Ray, L	71	3	6	9	-8	287
Rob Conn, R	28	2	5	7	-9	18

GOALTENDING

Player	GP	Mins	Avg	W	L	T	SO
Dominik Hasek	59	3417	2.83	22	30	6	2
*Steve Shields	2	75	3.20	1	0	0	0
Andrei Trefilov	22	1094	3.51	8	8	1	0
John Blue	5	255	3.53	2	2	0	0
*Martin Biron	3	119	5.04	0	2	0	0
Team total	82	4976	3.16	33	42	7	2

Calgary Flames

SCORING

Player	GP	G	A	Pts	+/–	PM
Theoren Fleury, R	80	46	50	96	17	112
German Titov, C	82	28	39	67	9	24
Michael Nylander, C	73	17	38	55	0	20
Gary Roberts, L	35	22	20	42	15	78
*Cory Stillman, C	74	16	19	35	-5	41
James Patrick, D	80	3	32	35	3	30
Steve Chiasson, D	76	8	25	33	3	62
Zarley Zalapski, D	80	12	17	29	11	115
Mike Sullivan, C	81	9	12	21	-6	24
Corey Millen, C	44	7	14	21	8	18
Sandy McCarthy, R	75	9	7	16	-8	173
Pavel Torgajev, L	41	6	10	16	2	14
Ronnie Stern, R	52	10	5	15	2	111
Paul Kruse, L	75	3	12	15	-5	145
Dean Evason, C	67	7	7	14	-6	38
Bob Sweeney, C	72	7	7	14	-20	65
Tommy Albelin, D	73	1	13	14	1	18
Jocelyn Lemieux, R	67	5	7	12	-19	45
Jamie Huscroft, D	70	3	9	12	14	162
Sheldon Kennedy, R	41	3	7	10	3	36
Claude LaPointe, C	35	4	5	9	1	20
*Ed Ward, R	41	3	5	8	-2	44
*Marty Murray, C	15	3	3	6	-4	0

GOALTENDING

Player	GP	Mins	Avg	W	L	T	SO
Trevor Kidd	47	2570	2.78	15	21	8	3
Rick Tabaracci	43	2391	2.94	19	16	3	3
Team total	82	4984	2.89	34	37	11	6

Chicago Blackhawks

SCORING

Player	GP	G	A	Pts	+/–	PM	Player	GP	G	A	Pts	+/–	PM
Chris Chelios, D	81	14	58	72	25	140	Steve Smith, D	37	0	9	9	12	71
Jeremy Roenick, C	66	32	35	67	9	109	James Black, C	13	3	3	6	1	16
Gary Suter, D	82	20	47	67	3	80	Brent Grieve, L	28	2	4	6	5	28
Tony Amonte, R	81	31	32	63	10	62	Jim Cummins, R	52	2	4	6	-1	180
Bernie Nicholls, C	59	19	41	60	11	60	Enrico Ciccone, D	66	2	4	6	1	306
*Eric Daze, L	80	30	23	53	16	18	Steve Dubinsky, C	43	2	3	5	3	14
Joe Murphy, R	70	22	29	51	-3	86	Kip Miller, C	10	1	4	5	1	2
Denis Savard, C	69	13	35	48	20	102							
Murray Craven, L	66	18	29	47	20	36							
Bob Probert, R	78	19	21	40	15	237							
Brent Sutter, C	80	13	27	40	14	56							
Jeff Shantz, C	78	6	14	20	12	24							
Keith Carney, D	82	5	14	19	31	94							
Sergei Krivokrasov, R	46	6	10	16	10	32							
Eric Weinrich, D	77	5	10	15	14	65							

GOALTENDING

Player	GP	Mins	Avg	W	L	T	SO
Jim Waite	1	31	.00	0	0	0	0
Jeff Hackett	35	2000	2.40	18	11	4	4
Ed Belfour	50	2956	2.74	22	17	10	1
Team total	82	4999	2.64	40	28	14	5

*Rookie.

Colorado Avalanche

SCORING

Player	GP	G	A	Pts	+/–	PM
Joe Sakic, C	82	51	69	120	14	44
Peter Forsberg, C	82	30	86	116	26	47
Valeri Kamensky, L	81	38	47	85	14	85
Claude Lemieux, R	79	39	32	71	14	117
Scott Young, R	81	21	39	60	2	50
Sandis Ozolinsh, D	73	14	40	54	2	54
Adam Deadmarsh, C	78	21	27	48	20	142
Chris Simon, L	64	16	18	34	10	250
*Stephane Yelle, C	71	13	14	27	15	30
Mike Keane, R	73	10	17	27	-5	46
Craig Wolanin, D	75	7	20	27	25	50
Mike Ricci, C	62	6	21	27	1	52
Troy Murray, C	63	7	14	21	15	22
Alexei Gusarov, D	65	5	15	20	29	56
Curtis Leschyshyn, D	77	4	15	19	32	73
Dave Hannan, C	61	7	10	17	3	32
Adam Foote, D	73	5	11	16	27	88
Sylvain Lefebvre, D	75	5	11	16	26	49
*Jon Klemm, D	56	3	12	15	12	20
Rene Corbet, L	33	3	6	9	10	33
Warren Rychel, L	52	6	2	8	6	147

GOALTENDING

Player	GP	Mins	Avg	W	L	T	SO
†Patrick Roy	39	2305	2.68	22	15	1	1
Stephane Fiset	37	2107	2.93	22	6	7	1
Jocelyn Thibault	10	558	3.01	3	4	2	0
Team total	82	4982	2.89	47	25	10	2

†Played 22 games with Montreal.

Dallas Stars

SCORING

Player	GP	G	A	Pts	+/–	PM
Mike Modano, C	78	36	45	81	-12	63
Benoit Hogue, C	78	19	45	64	10	104
Greg Adams, L	66	22	21	43	-21	33
Brent Gilchrist, D	77	20	22	42	-11	36
Kevin Hatcher, D	74	15	26	41	-24	58
Brent Fedyk, L	65	20	14	34	-16	54
Joe Nieuwendyk, D	52	14	18	32	-17	41
Derian Hatcher, D	79	8	23	31	-12	129
Todd Harvey, C	69	9	20	29	-13	136
*Grant Marshall, R	70	9	19	28	0	111
*Jere Lehtinen, R	57	6	22	28	5	16
Mike Kennedy, L	61	9	17	26	-7	48
Grant Ledyard, D	73	5	19	24	-15	20
Guy Carbonneau, C	71	8	15	23	-2	38
Richard Matvichuk, D	73	6	16	22	4	71
Randy Wood, L	76	8	13	21	-15	62
Darryl Sydor, D	84	3	17	20	-12	75
Bill Huard, L	51	6	6	12	3	176
Mike Donnelly, L	24	2	5	7	-2	10

GOALTENDING

Player	GP	Mins	Avg	W	L	T	SO
Andy Moog	41	2228	2.99	13	19	7	1
Allan Bester	10	601	3.00	4	5	1	0
*Jordan Willis	1	19	3.16	0	1	0	0
Darcy Wakaluk	37	1875	3.39	9	16	5	1
E. Fernandez	5	249	4.58	0	1	1	0
Team total	82	4992	3.37	26	42	14	2

* Rookie.

Detroit Red Wings

SCORING

Player	GP	G	A	Pts	+/–	PM
Sergei Fedorov, C	78	39	68	107	49	48
Steve Yzerman, C	80	36	59	95	29	64
Paul Coffey, D	76	14	60	74	19	90
Vyacheslav Kozlov, C	82	36	37	73	33	70
Igor Larionov, C	73	22	51	73	31	34
Nicklas Lidstrom, D	81	17	50	67	29	20
Keith Primeau, L	74	27	25	52	19	168
Dino Ciccarelli, R	64	22	21	43	14	99
Viacheslav Fetisov, D	69	7	35	42	37	96
Greg Johnson, C	60	18	22	40	6	30
V. Konstantinov, D	81	14	20	34	60	139
Bob Errey, L	71	11	21	32	30	66
Darren McCarty, R	63	15	14	29	14	158
Doug Brown, R	62	12	15	27	11	4
Tim Taylor, C	72	11	14	25	11	39
Kris Draper, C	52	7	9	16	2	32
*Mathieu Dandenault, R	34	5	7	12	6	6
Marc Bergevin, D	70	1	9	10	7	33
Martin LaPointe, R	58	6	3	9	0	93
Kirk Maltby, R	55	3	6	9	-16	67
Mike Ramsey, D	47	2	4	6	17	35
Bob Rouse, D	58	0	6	6	5	48

GOALTENDING

Player	GP	Mins	Avg	W	L	T	S
*Kevin Hodson	4	163	1.10	2	0	0	1
Chris Osgood	50	2933	2.17	39	6	5	5
Mike Vernon	32	1855	2.26	21	7	2	3
Team total	82	4961	2.19	62	13	7	9

Edmonton Oilers

SCORING

Player	GP	G	A	Pts	+/–	PM
Doug Weight, C	82	25	79	104	-19	95
Zdeno Ciger, L	78	31	39	70	-15	41
Jason Arnott, C	64	28	31	59	-6	87
Mariusz Czerkawski, R	70	17	23	40	-4	18
David Oliver, R	80	20	19	39	-22	34
Todd Marchant, C	81	19	19	38	-19	66
*Miroslav Satan, L	62	18	17	35	0	22
Boris Mironov, D	78	8	24	32	-23	101
Jeff Norton, D	66	8	23	31	9	42
Dean McAmmond, L	53	15	15	30	6	23
Kelly Buchberger, L	82	11	14	25	-20	184
Scott Thornton, L	77	9	9	18	-25	149
Bryan Marchment, D	78	3	15	18	-7	202
Jiri Slegr, D	57	4	13	17	-1	.74
*David Roberts, L	34	3	10	13	-7	18
*Ryan Smyth, L	48	2	9	11	-10	28
Luke Richardson, D	82	2	9	11	-27	108
Kent Manderville, L	37	3	5	8	-5	38
Donald DuFresne, D	45	1	6	7	-4	20
*Brett Hauer, D	29	4	2	6	-11	30

GOALTENDING

Player	GP	Mins	Avg	W	L	T	SO
Fred Brathwaite	7	293	2.46	0	2	0	0
Curtis Joseph	34	1936	3.44	15	16	2	0
*Joaquin Gage	16	717	3.77	2	8	1	0
Bill Ranford	37	2015	3.81	13	18	5	1
Team total	82	4978	3.66	30	44	8	1

Florida Panthers

SCORING

Player	GP	G	A	Pts	+/–	PM
Scott Mellanby, R	79	32	38	70	4	160
Rob Niedermayer, C	82	26	35	61	1	107
Ray Sheppard, R	70	37	23	60	-19	16
Robert Svehla, D	81	8	49	57	-3	94
Johan Garpenlov, L	82	23	28	51	-10	36
Stu Barnes, C	72	19	25	44	-12	46
Martin Straka, R	77	13	30	43	-19	41
Jody Hull, R	78	20	17	37	5	25
Tom Fitzgerald, R	82	13	21	34	-3	75
Bill Lindsay, L	73	12	22	34	13	57
Jason Woolley, D	52	6	28	34	-9	32
Gord Murphy, D	70	8	22	30	5	30
*Radek Dvorak, L	77	13	14	27	5	20
Brian Skrudland, C	79	7	20	27	6	129
Dave Lowry, L	63	10	14	24	-2	36
Mike Hough, L	64	7	16	23	4	37
*Ed Jovanovski, D	70	10	11	21	-3	137
Terry Carkner, D	73	3	10	13	10	80
Magnus Svensson, D	27	2	9	11	-1	21
Geoff Smith, D	31	3	7	10	-4	20
Paul Laus, D	78	3	6	9	-2	236

GOALTENDING

Player	GP	Mins	Avg	W	L	T	SO
J. Vanbiesbrouck	57	3178	2.68	26	20	7	2
Mark Fitzpatrick	34	1786	2.96	15	11	3	0
Team total	82	4979	2.82	41	31	10	2

Hartford Whalers

SCORING

Player	GP	G	A	Pts	+/–	PM
Brendan Shanahan, L	74	44	34	78	2	125
Geoff Sanderson, L	81	34	31	65	0	40
Andrew Cassels, C	81	20	43	63	8	39
Nelson Emerson, R	81	29	29	58	-7	78
Jeff Brown, D	76	8	47	55	8	56
Andrei Nikolishin, C	61	14	37	51	-2	34
Robert Kron, R	77	22	28	50	-1	6
Paul Ranheim, L	73	10	20	30	-2	14
*Jeff O'Neill, C	65	8	19	27	-3	40
Glen Wesley, D	68	8	16	24	-9	88
Steven Rice, R	59	10	12	22	-4	47
Adam Burt, D	78	4	9	13	-4	121
Glen Featherstone, D	68	2	10	12	10	138
Kevin Dineen, R	46	2	9	11	-1	117
Gerald Diduck, D	79	1	9	10	7	88
*Sami Kapanen, L	35	5	4	9	0	6
Brad McCrimmon, D	58	3	6	9	15	62
Mark Janssens, C	81	2	7	9	-3	155
*Scott Daniels, L	53	3	4	7	-4	254
Kelly Chase, R	55	2	4	6	-4	230
Sean Burke, G	66	0	6	6	0	16

GOALTENDING

Player	GP	Mins	Avg	W	L	T	SO
*J. Muzzatti	22	1013	2.90	4	8	3	1
Jeff Reese	7	275	3.05	2	3	0	1
Sean Burke	66	3669	3.11	28	28	6	4
Team total	82	4979	3.12	34	39	9	6

Los Angeles Kings

SCORING

Player	GP	G	A	Pts	+/–	PM
Dimitri Khristich, L	76	27	37	64	0	44
Ray Ferraro, C	76	29	31	60	0	92
*Vitali Yachmenev, R	80	19	34	53	-3	16
Yanic Perreault, C	78	25	24	49	-11	16
Kevin Todd, C	74	16	27	43	6	38
Kevin Stevens, L	61	13	23	36	-10	71
Tony Granato, L	49	17	18	35	-5	46
Eric Lacroix, L	72	16	16	32	-11	110
*Craig Johnson, L	60	13	11	24	-8	36
Philippe Boucher, D	53	7	16	23	-26	31
Robert Lang, C	68	6	16	22	-15	10
Jaroslav Modry, D	73	4	17	21	-21	44
John Slaney, D	38	6	14	20	7	14
Ian Laperriere, C	71	6	11	17	-11	155
Gary Shuchuk, C	33	4	10	14	3	12
Vladimir Tsyplakov, L	23	5	5	10	1	4
Rob Cowie, D	46	5	5	10	-16	32
Doug Zmolek, D	58	2	5	7	-5	87
*Sean O'Donnell, D	71	2	5	7	3	127
*Aki Berg, D	51	0	7	7	-13	29
Nathan Lafayette, C	17	2	4	6	-4	8
Denis Tsygurov, D	18	1	5	6	0	22
Patrice Tardif, C	38	4	1	5	-11	49
*Barry Potomski, L	33	3	2	5	-7	104
Steven Finn, D	66	3	2	5	-12	126
*Jan Vopat, D	11	1	4	5	3	4

GOALTENDING

Player	GP	Mins	Avg	W	L	T	SO
*Jamie Storr	5	262	2.75	3	1	0	0
Kelly Hrudey	36	2077	3.26	7	15	10	0
*Byron Dafoe	47	2666	3.87	14	24	8	1
Team total	82	5025	3.61	24	40	18	1

* Rookie.

Montreal Canadiens

SCORING

Player	GP	G	A	Pts	+/–	PM
Pierre Turgeon, C	80	38	58	96	19	44
V. Damphousse, C	80	38	56	94	5	158
Mark Recchi, R	82	28	50	78	20	69
Martin Rucinsky, L	78	29	46	75	18	68
Andrei Kovalenko, R	77	28	28	56	20	49
*Saku Koivu, L	82	20	25	45	-7	40
*Valeri Bure, R	77	22	20	42	10	28
Patrice Brisebois, D	69	9	27	36	10	65
Brian Savage, L	75	25	8	33	-8	28
Vladimir Malakhov, D	61	5	23	28	7	79
Turner Stevenson, R	80	9	16	25	-2	167
Lyle Odelein, D	79	3	14	17	8	230
Stephane Quintal, D	68	2	14	16	-4	117
Benoit Brunet, L	26	7	8	15	-4	17
Peter Popovic, D	76	2	12	14	21	69
Oleg Petrov, R	36	4	7	11	-9	23
Marc Bureau, L	65	3	7	10	-3	46
*Chris Murray, R	48	3	4	7	5	163
*David Wilkie, D	24	1	5	6	-10	10
*Craig Rivet, D	19	1	4	5	4	54

GOALTENDING

Player	GP	Mins	Avg	W	L	T	SO
†J. Thibault	40	2334	2.83	23	13	3	3
#Pat Jablonski	23	1264	2.94	5	9	6	0
Patrick Roy	22	1260	2.95	12	9	1	1
*P. Labrecque	2	98	4.29	0	1	0	0
*Jose Theodore	1	9	6.67	0	0	0	0
Team total	82	4987	2.98	40	32	10	4

†Played 10 games with Colorado.

#Played one game with St. Louis.

New Jersey Devils

SCORING

Player	GP	G	A	Pts	+/–	PM
Phil Housley, D	81	17	51	68	-6	30
Steve Thomas, L	81	26	35	61	-2	98
Dave Andreychuk, L	76	28	29	57	-9	64
Bill Guerin, R	80	23	30	53	7	116
John MacLean, R	76	20	28	48	3	91
*Petr Sykora, C	63	18	24	42	7	32
Scott Niedermayer, D	79	8	25	33	5	46
Stephane Richer, R	73	20	12	32	-8	30
Bobby Holik, L	63	13	17	30	9	58
Scott Stevens, D	82	5	23	28	7	100
Brian Rolston, L	58	13	11	24	9	8
Neal Broten, C	55	7	16	23	-3	14
Shawn Chambers, D	64	2	21	23	1	18
Randy McKay, R	76	11	10	21	7	145
Valeri Zelepukin, L	61	6	9	15	-10	107
Mike Peluso, L	57	3	8	11	4	146
Bob Carpenter, L	52	5	5	10	-10	14
*Steve Sullivan, C	16	5	4	9	3	8
Sergei Brylin, C	50	4	5	9	-2	26
Ken Daneyko, D	80	2	4	6	-10	115
Reid Simpson, L	23	1	5	6	2	79
Kevin Dean, D	41	0	6	6	4	28

GOALTENDING

Player	GP	Mins	Avg	W	L	T	SO
*Corey Schwab	10	331	2.18	0	3	0	0
Martin Brodeur	77	4434	2.34	34	30	12	6
Chris Terreri	4	210	2.57	3	0	0	0
Team total	82	4995	2.43	37	33	12	6

New York Islanders

SCORING

Player	GP	G	A	Pts	+/–	PM		Player	GP	G	A	Pts	+/–	PM
Zigmund Palffy, R	81	43	44	87	-17	56		Brent Severyn, D	65	1	8	9	3	180
Travis Green, C	69	25	45	70	-20	42		*Dan Plante, R	73	5	3	8	-22	50
Marty McInnis, L	74	12	34	46	-11	39		Darius Kasparaitis, D	46	1	7	8	-12	93
*Todd Bertuzzi, R	76	18	21	39	-14	83		*Andrey Vasilyev, L	10	2	5	7	4	2
Alexander Semak, C	69	20	14	34	-4	68		Dennis Vaske, D	19	1	6	7	-13	21
Derek King, L	61	12	20	32	-10	23		Bob Beers, D	13	0	5	5	-2	10
Kenny Jonsson, D	66	4	26	30	7	32								
*Niklas Andersson, L	47	14	12	26	-3	12								
*Bryan McCabe, D	82	7	16	23	-24	156		**GOALTENDING**						
Patrick Flatley, R	56	8	9	17	-24	21			GP	Mins	Avg	W	L	T	SO
*Darby Hendrickson, C	62	7	10	17	-8	80		*Eric Fichaud	24	1234	3.31	7	12	2	1
Scott Lachance, D	55	3	10	13	-19	54		Jamie McLennan	13	636	3.68	3	9	1	0
Chris Luongo, D	74	3	7	10	-23	55		T. Soderstrom	51	2590	3.87	11	22	6	2
Pat Conacher, L	55	6	3	9	-13	18		*Tommy Salo	10	523	4.02	1	7	1	0
								Team total	82	4993	3.79	22	50	10	3

* Rookie.

New York Rangers

SCORING

Player	GP	G	A	Pts	+/-	PM
Mark Messier, C	74	47	52	99	29	122
Brian Leetch, D	82	15	70	85	12	30
Pat Verbeek, R	69	41	41	82	29	129
Luc Robitaille, L	77	23	46	69	13	80
Alexei Kovalev, R	81	24	34	58	5	98
Adam Graves, L	82	22	36	58	18	100
Jari Kurri, L	71	18	27	45	-16	39
Bruce Driver, D	66	3	34	37	2	42
Marty McSorley, D	68	10	23	33	-20	169
Sergei Nemchinov, C	78	17	15	32	9	38
Sergio Momesso, L	73	11	12	23	-13	142
*Niklas Sundstrom, L	82	9	12	21	2	14
Ulf Samuelsson, D	74	1	18	19	9	122
A. Karpovtsev, D	40	2	16	18	12	26
Doug Lidster, D	59	5	9	14	11	50
Jeff Beukeboom, D	82	3	11	14	19	220
*Darren Langdon, L	64	7	4	11	2	175
Shane Churla, R	55	4	6	10	-8	231
Kevin Lowe, D	53	1	5	6	20	76
Bill Berg, L	41	3	2	5	-6	41
Ken Gernander, C	10	2	3	5	-3	4

GOALTENDING

Player	GP	Mins	Avg	W	L	T	SO
*Jamie Ram	1	27	.00	0	0	0	0
Mike Richter	41	2396	2.68	24	13	3	3
Glenn Healy	44	2564	2.90	17	14	11	2
Team total	82	4995	2.85	41	27	14	5

Ottawa Senators

SCORING

Player	GP	G	A	Pts	+/-	PM
*Daniel Alfredsson, R	82	26	35	61	-18	28
Alexei Yashin, C	46	15	24	39	-15	28
Randy Cunneyworth, L	81	17	19	36	-31	130
Steve Duchesne, D	62	12	24	36	-23	42
Radek Bonk, C	76	16	19	35	-5	36
Tom Chorske, L	72	15	14	29	-9	21
Sean Hill, D	80	7	14	21	-26	94
Pavol Demitra, R	31	7	10	17	-3	6
Alexandre Daigle, C	50	5	12	17	-30	24
Ted Drury, C	42	9	7	16	-19	54
*Antti Tormanen, R	50	7	8	15	-15	28
*Trent McCleary, R	75	4	10	14	-15	68
Rob Gaudreau, C	52	8	5	13	-19	15
Stanislav Neckar, D	82	3	9	12	-16	54
David Archibald, C	44	6	4	10	-14	18
Michel Picard, L	17	2	6	8	-1	10
Lance Pitlick, D	28	1	6	7	-8	20
Troy Mallette, L	64	2	3	5	-7	171
Dennis Vial, D	64	1	4	5	-13	276

GOALTENDING

Player	GP	Mins	Avg	W	L	T	SO
†Damian Rhodes	36	2123	2.77	10	22	4	2
Don Beaupre	33	1770	3.73	6	23	0	1
*Mike Bales	20	1040	4.15	2	14	1	0
Team total	82	4953	3.53	18	59	5	3

†Played 11 games with Toronto.

* Rookie.

Philadelphia Flyers

SCORING

Player	GP	G	A	Pts	+/-	PM
Eric Lindros, C	73	47	68	115	26	163
John Leclair, L	82	51	46	97	21	64
Rod Brind'amour, C	82	26	61	87	20	110
Dale Hawerchuk, C	82	17	44	61	15	26
Pat Falloon, R	71	25	26	51	14	10
Eric Desjardins, D	80	7	40	47	19	45
Dan Quinn, C	63	13	32	45	-6	46
Mikael Renberg, R	51	23	20	43	8	45
Joel Otto, C	67	12	29	41	11	115
John Druce, R	77	13	16	29	-20	27
Petr Svoboda, D	73	1	28	29	28	105
Shjon Podein, L	79	15	10	25	25	89
Chris Therien, D	82	6	17	23	16	89
Rob Dimaio, R	59	6	15	21	0	68
Karl Dykhuis, D	82	5	15	20	12	101
Bob Corkum, C	76	9	10	19	3	34
Trent Klatt, R	71	7	12	19	2	44
Kerry Huffman, D	47	5	12	17	-18	69
Kevin Haller, D	69	5	9	14	18	92
Kjell Samuelsson, D	75	3	11	14	20	81
Patrick Juhlin, R	14	3	3	6	4	17

GOALTENDING

Player	GP	Mins	Avg	W	L	T	SO
Dominic Roussel	19	1075	2.34	11	7	0	1
Ron Hextall	31	1824	2.89	17	9	4	1
Team total	48	2906	2.73	28	16	4	2

Pittsburgh Penguins

SCORING

Player	GP	G	A	Pts	+/-	PM
Mario Lemieux, C	70	69	92	161	10	54
Jaromir Jagr, R	82	62	87	149	31	96
Ron Francis, C	77	27	92	119	25	56
Petr Nedved, C	80	45	54	99	37	68
Tomas Sandstrom, R	58	35	35	70	4	69
Sergei Zubov, D	64	11	55	66	28	22
Bryan Smolinski, C	81	24	40	64	6	69
Kevin Miller, R	81	28	25	53	-4	45
Dmitri Mironov, D	72	3	31	34	19	88
Glen Murray, R	69	14	15	29	4	57
Chris Joseph, D	70	5	14	19	6	71
Neil Wilkinson, D	62	3	14	17	12	120
*Dave Roche, L	71	7	7	14	-5	130
Chris Tamer, D	70	4	10	14	20	153
J.J. Daigneault, D	57	4	7	11	-6	53
Francois Leroux, D	66	2	9	11	2	161
*Joe Dziedzic, L	69	5	5	10	-5	68
*Richard Park, C	56	4	6	10	3	36
Dave McLlwain, C	19	2	5	7	-5	6
Brad Lauer, R	21	4	1	5	-5	6

GOALTENDING

Player	GP	Mins	Avg	W	L	T	SO
*P. De Rouville	1	60	3.00	1	0	0	0
Ken Wregget	38	2208	3.21	25	9	2	0
Wendell Young	10	497	3.26	3	6	0	0
Tom Barrasso	2	125	3.84	0	1	1	0
Team total	48	2901	3.27	29	16	3	0

St Louis Blues

SCORING

Player	GP	G	A	Pts	+/-	PM
Wayne Gretzky, C	80	23	79	102	-13	34
Brett Hull, R	70	43	40	83	4	30
Al MacInnis, D	82	17	44	61	5	88
Shayne Corson, L	77	18	28	46	3	192
Geoff Courtnall, L	69	24	16	40	-9	101
Brian Noonan, R	81	13	22	35	2	84
Yuri Khmylev, L	73	8	21	29	-17	40
Stephen Leach, R	73	11	17	28	-7	108
Stephane Matteau, L	78	11	15	26	-8	87
Chris Pronger, D	78	7	18	25	-18	110
Igor Kravchuk, D	66	7	16	23	-19	34
Adam Creighton, C	61	11	10	21	0	78
Peter Zezel, C	57	8	13	21	-2	12
Mike Hudson, C	59	5	12	17	2	55
Glenn Anderson, R	32	6	8	14	-11	33
Craig MacTavish, C	68	5	9	14	-9	70
Murray Baron, D	82	2	9	11	3	190
Rob Pearson, R	27	6	4	10	4	54
Charlie Huddy, D	64	5	5	10	-12	65
*Christer Olsson, D	26	2	8	10	-6	14
Ken Sutton, D	38	0	8	8	-13	43
Tony Twist, L	51	3	2	5	-1	100
*Roman Vopat, C	25	2	3	5	-8	48

GOALTENDING

Player	GP	Mins	Avg	W	L	T	SO
Grant Fuhr	79	4365	2.87	30	28	16	3
Bruce Racine	11	230	3.13	0	3	0	0
Jon Casey	9	395	3.80	2	3	0	0
Pat Jablonski	1	8	7.50	0	0	0	0
Team total	82	5003	2.97	32	34	16	3

San Jose Sharks

SCORING

Player	GP	G	A	Pts	+/-	PM
Owen Nolan, R	81	33	36	69	-33	146
Jeff Friesen, L	79	15	31	46	-19	42
Darren Turcotte, C	68	22	21	43	5	30
Ray Whitney, C	60	17	24	41	-23	16
*Marcus Ragnarsson, D	71	8	31	39	-24	42
Jamie Baker, C	77	16	17	33	-19	79
Ulf Dahlen, R	59	16	12	28	-21	27
Doug Bodger, D	73	4	24	28	-24	68
Chris Tancill, C	45	7	16	23	-12	20
*Shean Donovan, R	74	13	8	21	-17	39
Michal Sykora, D	79	4	16	20	-14	54
Yves Racine, D	57	1	19	20	-10	54
*Viktor Kozlov, R	62	6	13	19	-15	6
Jeff Odgers, L	78	12	4	16	-4	192
Andrei Nazarov, R	42	7	7	14	-15	62
*Ville Peltonen, L	31	2	11	13	-7	14
*Jan Caloun, R	11	8	3	11	4	0
*Dody Wood, C	32	3	6	9	0	138
Jay More, D	74	2	7	9	-32	147
Vlastimil Kroupa, D	27	1	7	8	-17	18
Jim Kyte, D	57	1	7	8	-12	146
Mike Rathje, D	27	0	7	7	-16	14
*Alexei Yegorov, R	9	3	2	5	-5	2
Tom Pederson, D	60	1	4	5	-9	40
Chris Terreri, G	50	0	5	5	0	4

GOALTENDING

Player	GP	Mins	Avg	W	L	T	SO
†Chris Terreri	46	2516	3.70	13	29	1	0
Arturs Irbe	22	1112	4.59	4	12	4	0
Wade Flaherty	24	1137	4.85	3	12	1	0
*Geoff Sarjeant	4	171	4.91	0	2	1	0
Team total	82	4959	4.32	20	55	4	0

†Played four games with New Jersey.

Tampa Bay Lightning

SCORING

Player	GP	G	A	Pts	+/-	PM
Brian Bradley, C	75	23	56	79	-11	77
Roman Hamrlik, D	82	16	49	65	-24	103
Alexander Selivanov, R	79	31	21	52	3	93
Petr Klima, R	67	22	30	52	-25	68
John Cullen, C	76	16	34	50	1	65
Brian Bellows, L	79	23	26	49	-14	39
Chris Gratton, C	82	17	21	38	-13	105
Rob Zamuner, L	72	15	20	35	11	62
Paul Ysebaert, L	55	16	15	31	-19	16
Shawn Burr, L	81	13	15	28	4	119
Bill Houlder, D	61	5	23	28	1	22
Mikael Andersson, L	64	8	11	19	0	2
Jason Wiemer, L	66	9	9	18	-9	81
Patrick Poulin, L	46	7	9	16	7	16
Cory Cross, D	75	2	14	16	4	66
*Aaron Gavey, C	73	8	4	12	-6	56
Michel Petit, D	54	4	8	12	-11	135
Igor Ulanov, D	64	3	9	12	11	116
David Shaw, D	66	1	11	12	5	64
John Tucker, R	63	3	7	10	-8	18

GOALTENDING

Player	GP	Mins	Avg	W	L	T	SO
Daren Puppa	57	3189	2.46	29	16	9	5
†Jeff Reese	19	994	3.26	7	7	1	0
J.C. Bergeron	12	595	4.24	2	6	2	0
*Derek Wilkinson	4	200	4.50	0	3	0	0
Team total	48	2906	2.97	17	28	3	2

†Played seven games with Hartford.

* Rookie.

Toronto Maple Leafs

SCORING

Player	GP	G	A	Pts	+/-	PM
Mats Sundin, C	76	33	50	83	8	46
Doug Gilmour, C	81	32	40	72	-5	77
Larry Murphy, D	82	12	49	61	-2	34
Wendel Clark, L	71	32	26	58	-5	76
Mike Gartner, R	82	35	19	54	5	52
Mathieu Schneider, D	78	13	41	54	-20	103
Dave Gagner, C	73	21	28	49	-19	103
Kirk Muller, C	51	13	19	32	-13	57
Todd Gill, D	74	7	18	25	-15	116
Dave Ellett, D	80	3	19	22	-10	59
Mike Craig, R	70	8	12	20	-8	42
*Todd Warriner, L	57	7	8	15	-11	26
Wayne Presley, R	80	6	8	14	3	85
Tie Domi, R	72	7	6	13	-3	297
Dimitri Yushkevich, D	69	1	10	1	-14	54
Nick Kypreos, L	61	4	5	9	1	107
Peter White, C	27	5	3	8	-14	0
Paul Dipietro, C	20	4	4	8	-3	4
Jamie Macoun, D	82	0	8	8	2	87
*Brandon Convery, C	11	5	2	7	-7	4

GOALTENDING

Player	GP	Mins	Avg	W	L	T	SO
Damian Rhodes	11	624	2.79	4	5	1	0
Felix Potvin	69	4009	2.87	30	26	11	2
†Don Beaupre	8	336	4.64	0	5	0	0
Team total	82	4989	3.03	34	36	12	2

†Played 33 games with Ottawa.

Vancouver Canucks

SCORING

Player	GP	G	A	Pts	+/-	PM
Alexander Mogilny, R	79	55	52	107	14	16
Trevor Linden, R	82	33	47	80	6	42
Cliff Ronning, C	79	22	45	67	16	42
Russ Courtnall, R	81	26	39	65	25	40
Martin Gelinas, L	81	30	26	56	8	59
Markus Naslund, R	76	22	33	55	20	42
Jyrki Lumme, D	80	17	37	54	-9	50
Esa Tikkanen, L	58	14	30	44	1	36
Jesse Belanger, C	72	20	21	41	-5	14
Mike Sillinger, R	74	14	24	38	-18	38
Bret Hedican, D	77	6	23	29	8	83
Dave Babych, D	53	3	21	24	-5	38
Leif Rohlin, D	56	6	16	22	0	32
Mike Ridley, C	37	6	15	21	-3	29
Josef Beranek, C	61	6	14	20	-11	60
Jim Dowd, C	66	5	15	20	-9	23
*Adrian Aucoin, D	49	4	14	18	8	34
Pavel Bure, L	15	6	7	13	-2	8
*Scott Walker, D	63	4	8	12	-7	137
Dana Murzyn, D	69	2	10	12	9	130
Frantisek Kucera, D	54	3	6	9	2	20
Gino Odjick, L	55	3	4	7	-16	181
Jim Sandlak, R	33	4	2	6	-3	6
*Brian Loney, R	12	2	3	5	2	6

GOALTENDING

Player	GP	Mins	Avg	W	L	T	SO
*Corey Hirsch	41	2338	2.93	17	14	6	1
Kirk McLean	45	2645	3.54	15	21	9	2
Team total	82	5003	3.33	32	35	15	3

Washington Capitals

SCORING

Player	GP	G	A	Pts	+/-	PM	Player	GP	G	A	Pts	+/-	PM
Michal Pivonka, C	73	16	65	81	18	36	Craig Berube, L	50	2	10	12	1	151
Peter Bondra, R	67	52	28	80	18	40	*Ken Klee, D	66	8	3	11	-1	60
Joe Juneau, C	80	14	50	64	-3	30	Mike Eagles, C	70	4	7	11	-1	75
Todd Krygier, L	76	15	33	48	-1	30	Joe Reekie, D	78	3	7	10	7	149
Steve Konowalchuk, C	70	23	22	45	13	92	*Jeff Nelson, C	33	0	7	7	3	16
Keith Jones, R	68	18	23	41	8	103	*Andrew Brunette, L	11	3	3	6	5	0
Sergei Gonchar, D	78	15	26	41	25	60	Jim Johnson, D	66	2	4	6	-3	34
Sylvain Cote, D	81	5	33	38	5	40	*Brendan Witt, D	48	2	3	5	-4	85
Dale Hunter, C	82	13	24	37	5	112							
Pat Peake, C	62	17	19	36	7	46							
Calle Johansson, D	78	10	25	35	13	50							
Kelly Miller, L	74	7	13	20	7	30							
*Stefan Ustorf, R	48	7	10	17	8	14							
Mark Tinordi, D	71	3	10	13	26	113							

GOALTENDING

Player	GP	Mins	Avg	W	L	T	SO
Jim Carey	71	4069	2.26	35	24	9	9
Olaf Kolzig	18	897	3.08	4	8	2	0
Team total	82	4990	2.45	39	32	11	9

* Rookie.

Winnipeg Jets

SCORING

Player	GP	G	A	Pts	+/-	PM	Player	GP	G	A	Pts	+/-	PM
Keith Tkachuk, L	76	50	48	98	11	156	*Shane Doan, R	74	7	10	17	-9	101
Craig Janney, C	84	20	62	82	-33	26	Craig Muni, D	72	1	7	8	-6	106
Alexei Zhamnov, C	58	22	37	59	-4	65	Jim McKenzie, L	73	4	2	6	-4	202
Teppo Numminen, D	74	11	43	54	-4	22	Jeff Finley, D	65	1	5	6	-2	81
Norm Maciver, D	71	7	46	53	6	58	Randy Gilhen, C	22	2	3	5	1	12
Igor Korolev, R	73	22	29	51	1	42							
Ed Olczyk, C	51	27	22	49	0	65							
Dallas Drake, C	69	19	20	39	-7	36							
Dave Manson, D	82	7	23	30	8	205							
Oleg Tverdovsky, D	82	7	23	30	-7	41							
Mike Eastwood, C	80	14	14	28	-14	20							
Mike Stapleton, C	58	10	14	24	-4	37							
Darrin Shannon, L	63	5	18	23	-5	28							
Kris King, L	81	9	11	20	-7	151							
*Deron Quint, D	51	5	13	18	-2	22							
*Chad Kilger, C	74	7	10	17	-4	34							

GOALTENDING

Player	GP	Mins	Avg	W	L	T	SO
*Scott Langkow	1	6	.00	0	0	0	0
N. Khabibulin	53	2914	3.13	26	20	3	2
†Dominic Roussel	7	285	3.37	2	2	0	0
Tim Cheveldae	30	1695	3.93	8	18	3	0
Tom Draper	1	34	5.29	0	0	0	0
Team total	82	4951	3.53	36	40	6	2

†Played nine games with Philadelphia.

* Rookie.

First Round

The opening round of the 1996 NHL draft was held on June 22 in St Louis.

Team	Selection	Position	Team	Selection	Position
1.....Ottawa	Chris Phillips	D	14...St Louis	Marty Reasoner	C
2.....San Jose	Andrei Zyuzin	D	15...Philadelphia	Daynus Zubrus	R
3.....NY Islanders	Jean-Pierre Dumont	R	16...Tampa Bay	Mario Larocque	D
4.....Washington	Alexandre Volchkov	R	17...Washington	Jaroslav Svejkovsky	R
5.....Dallas	Richard Jackman	D	18...Montreal	Matt Higgins	C
6.....Edmonton	Boyd Devereaux	C	19...Edmonton	Mathieu Descoteaux	D
7.....Buffalo	Erik Rasmussen	C/L	20...Florida	Marcus Nilsson	R
8.....Boston	Johnathan Aitken	D	21...San Jose	Marco Sturm	C
9.....Anaheim	Ruslan Salei	D	22...NY Rangers	Jeff Brown	D
10...New Jersey	Lance Ward	D	23...Pittsburgh	Craig Hillier	G
11...Phoenix	Dan Focht	D	24...Phoenix	Daniel Briere	C
12...Vancouver	Josh Holden	C	25...Colorado	Peter Ratchuk	D
13...Calgary	Derek Morris	D	26...Detroit	Jesse Wallin	D

The Antihero on Ice

The Old-Timers' Game played on January 19, 1996, during the NHL's All-Star weekend was dubbed a "Heroes of Hockey" contest, and participants such as Gordie Howe and Phil Esposito certainly fit the bill. A less likely "hero" was Dave Schultz, the former Philadelphia Flyer who made his living causing bloody terror on the ice. That Broad Street Bully totaled 2,294 penalty minutes—compared with only 79 goals—in a nine-year, four-team career, and thus would have been better suited for a game called, say, "Neroes of the NHL."

The Stanley Cup

Awarded annually to the team that wins the NHL's best-of-seven final-round playoffs. The Stanley Cup is the oldest trophy competed for by professional athletes in North America. It was donated in 1893 by Frederick Arthur, Lord Stanley of Preston.

Results

WINNERS PRIOR TO FORMATION OF NHL IN 1917

1892-93	Montreal A.A.A.
1893-94	Montreal A.A.A.
1894-95	Montreal Victorias
1895-96	Winnipeg Victorias (Feb)
1895-96	Montreal Victorias (Dec)
1896-97	Montreal Victorias
1897-98	Montreal Victorias
1898-99	Montreal Victorias (Feb)
1898-99	Montreal Shamrocks (Mar)
1899-1900	Montreal Shamrocks
1900-01	Winnipeg Victorias
1901-02	Winnipeg Victorias (Jan)
1901-02	Montreal A.A.A. (Mar)
1902-03	Montreal A.A.A. (Feb)
1902-03	Ottawa Silver Seven (Mar)
1903-04	Ottawa Silver Seven
1904-05	Ottawa Silver Seven
1905-06	Ottawa Silver Seven (Feb)
1905-06	Montreal Wanderers (Mar)
1906-07	Kenora Thistles (Jan)
1906-07	Montreal Wanderers (Mar)
1907-08	Montreal Wanderers
1908-09	Ottawa Senators
1909-10	Montreal Wanderers
1910-11	Ottawa Senators
1911-12	Quebec Bulldogs
1912-13	Quebec Bulldogs
1913-14	Toronto Blueshirts
1914-15	Vancouver Millionaires
1915-16	Montreal Canadiens
1916-17	Seattle Metropolitans

NHL WINNERS AND FINALISTS

Season	Champion	Finalist	GP in Final
1917-18	Toronto Arenas	Vancouver Millionaires	5
1918-19	No decision*	No decision*	5
1919-20	Ottawa Senators	Seattle Metropolitans	5
1920-21	Ottawa Senators	Vancouver Millionaires	5
1921-22	Toronto St Pats	Vancouver Millionaires	5
1922-23	Ottawa Senators	Vancouver Maroons, Edmonton Eskimos	2, 4
1923-24	Montreal Canadiens	Vancouver Maroons, Calgary Tigers	2, 2
1924-25	Victoria Cougars	Montreal Canadiens	4
1925-26	Montreal Maroons	Victoria Cougars	4
1926-27	Ottawa Senators	Boston Bruins	4
1927-28	New York Rangers	Montreal Maroons	5
1928-29	Boston Bruins	New York Rangers	2
1929-30	Montreal Canadiens	Boston Bruins	2
1930-31	Montreal Canadiens	Chicago Blackhawks	5
1931-32	Toronto Maple Leafs	New York Rangers	3
1932-33	New York Rangers	Toronto Maple Leafs	4
1933-34	Chicago Blackhawks	Detroit Red Wings	4
1934-35	Montreal Maroons	Toronto Maple Leafs	3
1935-36	Detroit Red Wings	Toronto Maple Leafs	4
1936-37	Detroit Red Wings	New York Rangers	5
1937-38	Chicago Blackhawks	Toronto Maple Leafs	4
1938-39	Boston Bruins	Toronto Maple Leafs	5
1939-40	New York Rangers	Toronto Maple Leafs	6
1940-41	Boston Bruins	Detroit Red Wings	4
1941-42	Toronto Maple Leafs	Detroit Red Wings	7
1942-43	Detroit Red Wings	Boston Bruins	4
1943-44	Montreal Canadiens	Chicago Blackhawks	4
1944-45	Toronto Maple Leafs	Detroit Red Wings	7
1945-46	Montreal Canadiens	Boston Bruins	5
1946-47	Toronto Maple Leafs	Montreal Canadiens	6
1947-48	Toronto Maple Leafs	Detroit Red Wings	4
1948-49	Toronto Maple Leafs	Detroit Red Wings	4
1949-50	Detroit Red Wings	New York Rangers	7
1950-51	Toronto Maple Leafs	Montreal Canadiens	5
1951-52	Detroit Red Wings	Montreal Canadiens	4
1952-53	Montreal Canadiens	Boston Bruins	5
1953-54	Detroit Red Wings	Montreal Canadiens	7
1954-55	Detroit Red Wings	Montreal Canadiens	7

NHL WINNERS AND FINALISTS *(Cont.)*

Season	Champion	Finalist	GP in Final
1955-56	Montreal Canadiens	Detroit Red Wings	5
1956-57	Montreal Canadiens	Boston Bruins	5
1957-58	Montreal Canadiens	Boston Bruins	6
1958-59	Montreal Canadiens	Toronto Maple Leafs	5
1959-60	Montreal Canadiens	Toronto Maple Leafs	4
1960-61	Chicago Blackhawks	Detroit Red Wings	6
1961-62	Toronto Maple Leafs	Chicago Blackhawks	6
1962-63	Toronto Maple Leafs	Detroit Red Wings	5
1963-64	Toronto Maple Leafs	Detroit Red Wings	7
1964-65	Montreal Canadiens	Chicago Blackhawks	7
1965-66	Montreal Canadiens	Detroit Red Wings	6
1966-67	Toronto Maple Leafs	Montreal Canadiens	6
1967-68	Montreal Canadiens	St Louis Blues	4
1968-69	Montreal Canadiens	St Louis Blues	4
1969-70	Boston Bruins	St Louis Blues	4
1970-71	Montreal Canadiens	Chicago Blackhawks	7
1971-72	Boston Bruins	New York Rangers	6
1972-73	Montreal Canadiens	Chicago Blackhawks	6
1973-74	Philadelphia Flyers	Boston Bruins	6
1974-75	Philadelphia Flyers	Buffalo Sabres	6
1975-76	Montreal Canadiens	Philadelphia Flyers	4
1976-77	Montreal Canadiens	Boston Bruins	4
1977-78	Montreal Canadiens	Boston Bruins	6
1978-79	Montreal Canadiens	New York Rangers	5
1979-80	New York Islanders	Philadelphia Flyers	6
1980-81	New York Islanders	Minnesota North Stars	5
1981-82	New York Islanders	Vancouver Canucks	4
1982-83	New York Islanders	Edmonton Oilers	4
1983-84	Edmonton Oilers	New York Islanders	5
1984-85	Edmonton Oilers	Philadelphia Flyers	5
1985-86	Montreal Canadiens	Calgary Flames	6
1986-87	Edmonton Oilers	Philadelphia Flyers	7
1987-88	Edmonton Oilers	Boston Bruins	4
1988-89	Calgary Flames	Montreal Canadiens	6
1989-90	Edmonton Oilers	Boston Bruins	5
1990-91	Pittsburgh Penguins	Minnesota North Stars	6
1991-92	Pittsburgh Penguins	Chicago Blackhawks	4
1992-93	Montreal Canadiens	Los Angeles Kings	5
1993-94	New York Rangers	Vancouver Canucks	7
1994-95	New Jersey Devils	Detroit Red Wings	4
1995-96	Colorado Avalanche	Florida Panthers	4

*In 1919 the Montreal Canadiens traveled to meet Seattle, the PCHL champions. After 5 games had been played—the teams were tied at 2 wins and 1 tie—the series was called off by the local Department of Health because of the influenza epidemic and the death of Canadian defenseman Joe Hall from influenza.

Conn Smythe Trophy

Awarded to the Most Valuable Player of the Stanley Cup playoffs, as selected by the Professional Hockey Writers Association. The trophy is named after the former coach, general manager, president and owner of the Toronto Maple Leafs.

1965	Jean Beliveau, Mtl	1981	Butch Goring, NYI
1966	Roger Crozier, Det	1982	Mike Bossy, NYI
1967	Dave Keon, Tor	1983	Bill Smith, NYI
1968	Glenn Hall, StL	1984	Mark Messier, Edm
1969	Serge Savard, Mtl	1985	Wayne Gretzky, Edm
1970	Bobby Orr, Bos	1986	Patrick Roy, Mtl
1971	Ken Dryden, Mtl	1987	Ron Hextall, Phil
1972	Bobby Orr, Bos	1988	Wayne Gretzky, Edm
1973	Yvan Cournoyer, Mtl	1989	Al MacInnis, Cgy
1974	Bernie Parent, Phil	1990	Bill Ranford, Edm
1975	Bernie Parent, Phil	1991	Mario Lemieux, Pitt
1976	Reggie Leach, Phil	1992	Mario Lemieux, Pitt
1977	Guy Lafleur, Mtl	1993	Patrick Roy, Mtl
1978	Larry Robinson, Mtl	1994	Brian Leetch, NYR
1979	Bob Gainey, Mtl	1995	Claude Lemieux, NJ
1980	Bryan Trottier, NYI	1996	Joe Sakic, Col

Alltime Stanley Cup Playoff Leaders

Points

	Yrs	GP	G	A	Pts		Yrs	GP	G	A	Pts
*Wayne Gretzky, Edm, LA, StL	15	193	112	250	362	Gordie Howe, Det, Hart	20	157	68	92	160
*Mark Messier, Edm, NYR	16	221	106	177	283	Bobby Smith, Minn, Mtl	13	184	64	96	160
*Jari Kurri, Edm, LA, NYR	13	185	105	125	230	*Doug Gilmour, StL, Cgy, Tor	12	136	49	111	160
*Glenn Anderson, four teams	15	225	93	121	214	Stan Mikita, Chi	18	155	59	91	150
*Paul Coffey, Edm, Pitt, LA, Det	14	172	58	128	186	*Mario Lemieux, Pitt	6	84	67	82	149
Bryan Trottier, NYI, Pitt	17	221	71	113	184	Brian Propp, Phil, Bos, Minn	13	160	64	84	148
Jean Beliveau, Mtl	17	162	79	97	176	*Ray Bourque, Bos	17	162	35	111	146
*Denis Savard, Chi, Mtl	15	163	66	107	173	Larry Robinson, Mtl, LA	20	227	28	116	144
Denis Potvin, NYI	14	185	56	108	164	Jacques Lemaire, Mtl	11	145	61	78	139
Mike Bossy, NYI	10	129	85	75	160	Phil Esposito, Chi, Bos, NYR	15	130	61	76	137

*Active player.

Goals

	Yrs	GP	G
*Wayne Gretzky, Edm, LA, StL	15	193	112
*Mark Messier, Edm, NYR	16	221	106
*Jari Kurri, Edm, LA, NYR	13	185	105
*Glenn Anderson, four teams	15	225	93
Mike Bossy, NYI	10	129	85
Maurice Richard, Mtl	15	133	82
Jean Beliveau, Mtl	17	162	79
*Dino Ciccarelli, Minn, Wash, Det	14	141	73
Bryan Trottier, NYI, Pitt	17	221	71
Gordie Howe, Det, Hart	20	157	68

*Active player.

Assists

	Yrs	GP	A
*Wayne Gretzky, Edm, LA, StL	15	193	250
*Mark Messier, Edm, NYR	16	221	177
*Paul Coffey, Edm, Pitt, LA, Det	14	172	128
*Jari Kurri, Edm, LA, NYR	13	185	125
*Glenn Anderson, four teams	15	225	121
Larry Robinson, Mtl, LA	20	227	116
Bryan Trottier, NYI, Pitt	17	221	113
*Ray Bourque, Bos	17	162	111
*Doug Gilmour, StL, Cgy, Tor	12	136	111
Denis Potvin, NYI	14	185	108

*Active player.

Goaltending

WINS	W	L	Pct
Billy Smith, LA, NYI	88	36	.710
*Patrick Roy, Mtl, Col	86	48	.642
Ken Dryden, Mtl	80	32	.714
*Grant Fuhr, five teams	78	36	.684
Jacques Plante, five teams	71	37	.657
*Andy Moog, Edm, Bos, Dall	61	48	.560
Turk Broda, Tor	58	42	.580
*Mike Vernon, Cgy, Det	57	41	.582
Terry Sawchuk, five teams	54	48	.529
*Tom Barrasso, Buff, Pitt	51	39	.567

*Active player.

SHUTOUTS	GP	W	SO
Clint Benedict, Ott, Mtl M	48	25	15
Jacques Plante, five teams	112	71	14
Turk Broda, Tor	101	58	13
Terry Sawchuk, five teams	106	54	12
Ken Dryden, Mtl	112	80	10

GOALS AGAINST AVG	Avg
George Hainsworth, Mtl, Tor	1.93
Turk Broda, Tor	1.98
Jacques Plante, five teams	2.17
*Patrick Roy, Mtl, Col	2.39
Ken Dryden, Mtl	2.40

Note: At least 50 games played.

Alltime Stanley Cup Standings

TEAM	W	L	Pct	TEAM	W	L	Pct
Montreal	376	239	.611	Calgary*	69	87	.442
Boston	228	242	.485	Buffalo	62	81	.434
Toronto	210	230	.477	Los Angeles	55	87	.387
Detroit	190	197	.491	Vancouver	54	70	.435
Chicago	185	210	.468	Washington	52	64	.448
NY Rangers	174	189	.479	Colorado**	51	51	.500
Philadelphia	132	118	.528	New Jersey†	47	40	.540
NY Islanders	128	90	.587	Winnipeg	19	43	.306
Edmonton	120	60	.667	Hartford	18	31	.367
St Louis	103	127	.448	Florida	12	10	.545
Dallas#	86	94	.478	San Jose	11	14	.440
Pittsburgh	85	70	.548	Tampa Bay	2	4	.333

*Atlanta Flames 1972-80. †Colorado Rockies 1976-82. #Minnesota North Stars 1967-93. **Quebec Nordiques 1979-95.
Note: Teams ranked by playoff victories.

Stanley Cup Coaching Records

Coach	Team	Yrs	Series			Games	Games			Cups	Pct
			Series	W	L	Games	W	L	T	Cups	Pct
Glen Sather	Edm	10	27	21	6	*126	89	37	0	4	.706
Toe Blake	Mtl	13	23	18	5	119	82	37	0	8	.689
†Jacques Lemaire	Mtl, NJ	4	12	9	3	67	42	25	0	1	.627
†Scott Bowman	Five teams	22	51	35	16	263	162	101	0	6	.616
Hap Day	Tor	9	14	10	4	80	49	31	0	5	.613
Al Arbour	StL, NYI	16	42	30	12	209	123	86	0	4	.589
†Mike Keenan	Phil, Chi, NYR, StL	11	28	18	10	160	91	69	0	1	.569
Fred Shero	Phil, NYR	8	21	15	6	108	61	47	0	2	.565
†Jacques Demers	Que, StL, Det, Mtl	9	19	11	8	104	57	47	0	1	.548
Bob Johnson	Cgy, Pitt	6	14	9	5	76	41	35	0	1	.539

*Does not include suspended game, May 24, 1988. †Active coach.
Note: Coaches ranked by winning percentage. Minimum: 65 games.

The 10 Longest Overtime Games

Date	Scorer	OT	Results	Series	Series Winner
3-24-36	Mud Bruneteau	116:30	Det 1 vs Mtl M 0	SF	Det
4-3-33	Ken Doraty	104:46	Tor 1 vs Bos 0	SF	Tor
4-24-96	Petr Nedved	79:15	Pitt 3 vs Wash 2	CQF	Pitt
3-23-43	Jack McLean	70:18	Tor 3 vs Det 2	SF	Det
3-28-30	Gus Rivers	68:52	Mtl 2 vs NYR 1	SF	Mtl
4-18-87	Pat LaFontaine	68:47	NYI 3 vs Wash 2	DSF	NYI
4-27-94	Dave Hannan	65:43	Buff 1 vs NJ 0	CQF	NJ
3-27-51	Maurice Richard	61:09	Mtl 3 vs Det 2	SF	Mtl
3-27-38	Lorne Carr	60:40	NYA 3 vs NYR 2	QF	NYA
3-26-32	Fred Cook	59:32	NYR 4 vs Mtl 3	SF	NYR

NHL Awards

Hart Memorial Trophy

Awarded annually "to the player adjudged to be the most valuable to his team." The original trophy was donated by Dr. David A. Hart, father of Cecil Hart, former manager-coach of the Montreal Canadiens. In the decade of the 1980s Wayne Gretzky won the award nine of 10 times.

	Winner	Key Statistics	Runner-Up
1924	Frank Nighbor, Ott	10 goals, 3 assists in 20 games	Sprague Cleghorn, Mtl
1925	Billy Burch, Ham	20 goals, 4 assists in 27 games	Howie Morenz, Mtl
1926	Nels Stewart, Mtl M	42 points in 36 games	Sprague Cleghorn, Mtl
1927	Herb Gardiner, Mtl	12 points in 44 games as defenseman	Bill Cook, NYR
1928	Howie Morenz, Mtl	33 goals, 18 assists	Roy Worters, Pitt
1929	Roy Worters, NYA	1.21 goals against, 13 shutouts	Ace Bailey, Tor
1930	Nels Stewart, Mtl M	39 goals, 16 assists	Lionel Hitchman, Bos
1931	Howie Morenz, Mtl	28 goals, 23 assists	Eddie Shore, Bos
1932	Howie Morenz, Mtl	24 goals, 25 assists	Ching Johnson, NYR
1933	Eddie Shore, Bos	27 assists in 48 games as defenseman	Bill Cook, NYR
1934	Aurel Joliat, Mtl	27 points	Lionel Conacher, Chi
1935	Eddie Shore, Bos	26 assists in 48 games as defenseman	Charlie Conacher, Tor
1936	Eddie Shore, Bos	16 assists in 46 games as defenseman	Hooley Smith, Mtl M
1937	Babe Siebert, Mtl	28 points	Lionel Conacher, Mtl M
1938	Eddie Shore, Bos	17 points in 47 games as defenseman	Paul Thompson, Chi
1939	Toe Blake, Mtl	led NHL in points (47)	Syl Apps, Tor
1940	Ebbie Goodfellow, Det	28 points	Syl Apps, Tor
1941	Bill Cowley, Bos	led NHL in assists (45) and points (62)	Dit Clapper, Bos
1942	Tom Anderson, Bos	41 points	Syl Apps, Tor
1943	Bill Cowley, Bos	led NHL in assists (45)	Doug Bentley, Chi
1944	Babe Pratt, Tor	57 points in 50 games	Bill Cowley, Bos
1945	Elmer Lach, Mtl	led NHL in assists (54) and points (80)	Maurice Richard, Mtl
1946	Max Bentley, Chi	61 points in 47 games	Gaye Stewart, Tor
1947	Maurice Richard, Mtl	led NHL in goals (45); 26 assists	Milt Schmidt, Bos
1948	Buddy O'Connor, NYR	60 points in 60 games	Frank Brimsek, Bos
1949	Sid Abel, Det	28 goals, 26 assists	Bill Durnan, Mtl

Hart Memorial Trophy *(Cont.)*

	Winner	Key Statistics	Runner-Up
1950	Charlie Rayner, NYR	6 shutouts	Ted Kennedy, Tor
1951	Milt Schmidt, Bos	61 points in 62 games	Maurice Richard, Mtl
1952	Gordie Howe, Det	led NHL in goals (47) and points (86)	Elmer Lach, Mtl
1953	Gordie Howe, Det	led NHL in goals (49) and points (95)	Al Rollins, Chi
1954	Al Rollins, Chi	5 shutouts	Red Kelly, Det
1955	Ted Kennedy, Tor	52 points	Harry Lumley, Tor
1956	Jean Beliveau, Mtl	led NHL in goals (47) and points (88)	Tod Sloan, Tor
1957	Gordie Howe, Det	led NHL in goals (44) and points (89)	Jean Beliveau, Mtl
1959	Andy Bathgate, NYR	74 points in 70 games	Gordie Howe, Det
1960	Gordie Howe, Det	45 assists, 73 points	Bobby Hull, Chi
1961	Bernie Geoffrion, Mtl	50 goals, 95 points	Johnny Bower, Tor
1962	Jacques Plante, Mtl	42 wins, 2.37 goals against	Doug Harvey, NYR
1963	Gordie Howe, Det	47 assists, 73 points	Stan Mikita, Chi
1964	Jean Beliveau, Mtl	50 assists, 78 points	Bobby Hull, Chi
1965	Bobby Hull, Chi	39 goals, 32 assists	Norm Ullman, Det
1966	Bobby Hull, Chi	led NHL in goals (54) and points (97)	Jean Beliveau, Mtl
1967	Stan Mikita, Chi	led NHL in assists (62) and points (97)	Ed Giacomin, NYR
1968	Stan Mikita, Chi	40 goals, 47 assists	Jean Beliveau, Mtl
1969	Phil Esposito, Bos	led NHL in assists (77) and points (126)	Jean Beliveau, Mtl
1970	Bobby Orr, Bos	led NHL in assists (87) and points (120)	Tony Esposito, Chi
1971	Bobby Orr, Bos	102 assists, 139 points	Tony Esposito, Chi
1972	Bobby Orr, Bos	80 assists, 117 points	Ken Dryden, Mtl
1973	Bobby Clarke, Phil	67 assists, 104 points	Phil Esposito, Bos
1974	Phil Esposito, Bos	led NHL in goals (68) and points (145)	Bernie Parent, Phil
1975	Bobby Clarke, Phil	89 assists, 116 points	Rogatien Vachon, LA
1976	Bobby Clarke, Phil	89 assists, 119 points	Denis Potvin, NYI
1977	Guy Lafleur, Mtl	led NHL in assists (80) and points (136)	Bobby Clarke, Phil
1978	Guy Lafleur, Mtl	led NHL in goals (60) and points (132)	Bryan Trottier, NYI
1979	Bryan Trottier, NYI	led NHL in assists (87) and points (134)	Guy Lafleur, Mtl
1980	Wayne Gretzky, Edm	51 goals, 86 assists	Marcel Dionne, LA
1981	Wayne Gretzky, Edm	led NHL in assists (109) and points (164)	Mike Liut, StL
1982	Wayne Gretzky, Edm	NHL-record 92 goals and 212 points	Bryan Trottier, NYI
1983	Wayne Gretzky, Edm	led NHL in goals (71) and points (196)	Pete Peeters, Bos
1984	Wayne Gretzky, Edm	led NHL in goals (87) and points (205)	Rod Langway, Wash
1985	Wayne Gretzky, Edm	led NHL in goals (73) and points (208)	Dale Hawerchuk, Winn
1986	Wayne Gretzky, Edm	NHL-record 163 assists and 215 points	Mario Lemieux, Pitt
1987	Wayne Gretzky, Edm	led NHL in assists (121) and points (183)	Ray Bourque, Bos
1988	Mario Lemieux, Pitt	led NHL in goals (70) and points (168)	Grant Fuhr, Edm
1989	Wayne Gretzky, LA	114 assists, 168 points	Mario Lemieux, Pitt
1990	Mark Messier, Edm	84 assists, 129 points	Ray Bourque, Bos
1991	Brett Hull, StL	led NHL in goals (86); 131 points	Wayne Gretzky, LA
1992	Mark Messier, NYR	72 assists, 107 points	Patrick Roy, Mtl
1993	Mario Lemieux, Pitt	69 goals, 91 assists in 60 games	Doug Gilmour, Tor
1994	Sergei Fedorov, Det	56 goals, 64 assists	Dominik Hasek, Buff
1995	Eric Lindros, Phil	29 goals, 41 assists in 46 games	Jaromir Jagr, Pitt
1996	Mario Lemieux, Pitt	led NHL in goals (69) and points (161)	Mark Messier, NYR

Art Ross Trophy

Awarded annually "to the player who leads the league in scoring points at the end of the regular season." The trophy was presented to the NHL in 1947 by Arthur Howie Ross, former manager-coach of the Boston Bruins. The tie-breakers, in order, are as follows: (1) player with most goals, (2) player with fewer games played, (3) player scoring first goal of the season. Bobby Orr is the only defenseman in NHL history to win this trophy, and he won it twice (1970 and 1975).

	Winner	Pts		Winner	Pts
1919	Newsy Lalonde, Mtl	44	1929	Ace Bailey, Tor	51
1920	Joe Malone, Que	30	1930	Cooney Weiland, Bos	32
1921	Newsy Lalonde, Mtl	48	1931	Howie Morenz, Mtl	73
1922	Punch Broadbent, Ott	41	1932	Harvey Jackson, Tor	51
1923	Babe Dye, Tor	46	1933	Bill Cook, NYR	53
1924	Cy Denneny, Ott	37	1934	Charlie Conacher, Tor	50
1925	Babe Dye, Tor	23	1935	Charlie Conacher, Tor	57
1926	Nels Stewart, Mtl M	44	1936	Sweeney Schriner, NYA	45
1927	Bill Cook, NYR	42	1937	Sweeney Schriner, NYA	46
1928	Howie Morenz, Mtl	37	1938	Gordie Drillon, Tor	52

Art Ross Trophy (Cont.)

	Winner	Pts		Winner	Pts
1939	Toe Blake, Mtl	47	1968	Stan Mikita, Chi	87
1940	Milt Schmidt, Bos	52	1969	Phil Esposito, Bos	126
1941	Bill Cowley, Bos	62	1970	Bobby Orr, Bos	120
1942	Bryan Hextall, NYR	56	1971	Phil Esposito, Bos	152
1943	Doug Bentley, Chi	73	1972	Phil Esposito, Bos	133
1944	Herb Cain, Bos	82	1973	Phil Esposito, Bos	130
1945	Elmer Lach, Mtl	80	1974	Phil Esposito, Bos	145
1946	Max Bentley, Chi	61	1975	Bobby Orr, Bos	135
1947	*Max Bentley, Chi	72	1976	Guy Lafleur, Mtl	125
1948	Elmer Lach, Mtl	61	1977	Guy Lafleur, Mtl	136
1949	Roy Conacher, Chi	68	1978	Guy Lafleur, Mtl	132
1950	Ted Lindsay, Det	78	1979	Bryan Trottier, NYI	134
1951	Gordie Howe, Det	86	1980	Marcel Dionne, LA	137
1952	Gordie Howe, Det	86	1981	Wayne Gretzky, Edm	164
1953	Gordie Howe, Det	95	1982	Wayne Gretzky, Edm	212
1954	Gordie Howe, Det	81	1983	Wayne Gretzky, Edm	196
1955	Bernie Geoffrion, Mtl	75	1984	Wayne Gretzky, Edm	205
1956	Jean Beliveau, Mtl	88	1985	Wayne Gretzky, Edm	208
1957	Gordie Howe, Det	89	1986	Wayne Gretzky, Edm	215
1958	Dickie Moore, Mtl	84	1987	Wayne Gretzky, Edm	183
1959	Dickie Moore, Mtl	96	1988	Mario Lemieux, Pitt	168
1960	Bobby Hull, Chi	81	1989	Mario Lemieux, Pitt	199
1961	Bernie Geoffrion, Mtl	95	1990	Wayne Gretzky, LA	142
1962	Bobby Hull, Chi	84	1991	Wayne Gretzky, LA	163
1963	Gordie Howe, Det	86	1992	Mario Lemieux, Pitt	131
1964	Stan Mikita, Chi	89	1993	Mario Lemieux, Pitt	160
1965	Stan Mikita, Chi	87	1994	Wayne Gretzky, LA	130
1966	Bobby Hull, Chi	97	1995	Jaromir Jagr, Pitt	70
1967	Stan Mikita, Chi	97	1996	Mario Lemieux, Pitt	161

Note: Listing includes scoring leaders prior to inception of Art Ross Trophy in 1947-48.

Lady Byng Memorial Trophy

Awarded annually "to the player adjudged to have exhibited the best type of sportsmanship and gentlemanly conduct combined with a high standard of playing ability." Lady Byng, who first presented the trophy in 1925, was the wife of Canada's Governor-General. She donated a second trophy in 1936 after the first was given permanently to Frank Boucher of the New York Rangers, who won it seven times in eight seasons. Stan Mikita, one of the league's most penalized players during his early years in the NHL, won the trophy twice late in his career (1967 and 1968).

1925	Frank Nighbor, Ott	1949	Bill Quackenbush, Det	1973	Gilbert Perreault, Buff
1926	Frank Nighbor, Ott	1950	Edgar Laprade, NYR	1974	John Bucyk, Bos
1927	Billy Burch, NYA	1951	Red Kelly, Det	1975	Marcel Dionne, Det
1928	Frank Boucher, NYR	1952	Sid Smith, Tor	1976	Jean Ratelle, NYR-Bos
1929	Frank Boucher, NYR	1953	Red Kelly, Det	1977	Marcel Dionne, LA
1930	Frank Boucher, NYR	1954	Red Kelly, Det	1978	Butch Goring, LA
1931	Frank Boucher, NYR	1955	Sid Smith, Tor	1979	Bob MacMillan, Atl
1932	Joe Primeau, Tor	1956	Earl Reibel, Det	1980	Wayne Gretzky, Edm
1933	Frank Boucher, NYR	1957	Andy Hebenton, NYR	1981	Rick Kehoe, Pitt
1934	Frank Boucher, NYR	1958	Camille Henry, NYR	1982	Rick Middleton, Bos
1935	Frank Boucher, NYR	1959	Alex Delvecchio, Det	1983	Mike Bossy, NYI
1936	Doc Romnes, Chi	1960	Don McKenney, Bos	1984	Mike Bossy, NYI
1937	Marty Barry, Det	1961	Red Kelly, Tor	1985	Jari Kurri, Edm
1938	Gordie Drillon, Tor	1962	Dave Keon, Tor	1986	Mike Bossy, NYI
1939	Clint Smith, NYR	1963	Dave Keon, Tor	1987	Joe Mullen, Cgy
1940	Bobby Bauer, Bos	1964	Ken Wharram, Chi	1988	Mats Naslund, Mtl
1941	Bobby Bauer, Bos	1965	Bobby Hull, Chi	1989	Joe Mullen, Cgy
1942	Syl Apps, Tor	1966	Alex Delvecchio, Det	1990	Brett Hull, StL
1943	Max Bentley, Chi	1967	Stan Mikita, Chi	1991	Wayne Gretzky, LA
1944	Clint Smith, Chi	1968	Stan Mikita, Chi	1992	Wayne Gretzky, LA
1945	Billy Mosienko, Chi	1969	Alex Delvecchio, Det	1993	Pierre Turgeon, NYI
1946	Toe Blake, Mtl	1970	Phil Goyette, StL	1994	Wayne Gretzky, LA
1947	Bobby Bauer, Bos	1971	John Bucyk, Bos	1995	Ron Francis, Pitt
1948	Buddy O'Connor, NYR	1972	Jean Ratelle, NYR	1996	Paul Kariya, Ana

James Norris Memorial Trophy

Awarded annually "to the defense player who demonstrates throughout the season the greatest all-around ability in the position." James Norris was the former owner-president of the Detroit Red Wings. Bobby Orr holds the record for most consecutive times winning the award (eight, 1968-1975).

1954 ......Red Kelly, Det	1969 ......Bobby Orr, Bos	1983 ......Rod Langway, Wash
1955 ......Doug Harvey, Mtl	1970 ......Bobby Orr, Bos	1984 ......Rod Langway, Wash
1956 ......Doug Harvey, Mtl	1971 ......Bobby Orr, Bos	1985 ......Paul Coffey, Edm
1957 ......Doug Harvey, Mtl	1972 ......Bobby Orr, Bos	1986 ......Paul Coffey, Edm
1958 ......Doug Harvey, Mtl	1973 ......Bobby Orr, Bos	1987 ......Ray Bourque, Bos
1959 ......Tom Johnson, Mtl	1974 ......Bobby Orr, Bos	1988 ......Ray Bourque, Bos
1960 ......Doug Harvey, Mtl	1975 ......Bobby Orr, Bos	1989 ......Chris Chelios, Mtl
1961 ......Doug Harvey, Mtl	1976 ......Denis Potvin, NYI	1990 ......Ray Bourque, Bos
1962 ......Doug Harvey, NYR	1977 ......Larry Robinson, Mtl	1991 ......Ray Bourque, Bos
1963 ......Pierre Pilote, Chi	1978 ......Denis Potvin, NYI	1992 ......Brian Leetch, NYR
1964 ......Pierre Pilote, Chi	1979 ......Denis Potvin, NYI	1993 ......Chris Chelios, Chi
1965 ......Pierre Pilote, Chi	1980 ......Larry Robinson, Mtl	1994 ......Ray Bourque, Bos
1966 ......Jacques Laperriere, Mtl	1981 ......Randy Carlyle, Pitt	1995 ......Paul Coffey, Det
1967 ......Harry Howell, NYR	1982 ......Doug Wilson, Chi	1996 ......Chris Chelios, Chi
1968 ......Bobby Orr, Bos		

Calder Memorial Trophy

Awarded annually "to the player selected as the most proficient in his first year of competition in the National Hockey League." Frank Calder was a former NHL president. Sergei Makarov, who won the award in 1989-1990, was the oldest recipient of the trophy, at 31. Players are no longer eligible for the award if they are 26 or older as of September 15th of the season in question.

1933 ......Carl Voss, Det	1955 ......Ed Litzenberger, Chi	1976 ......Bryan Trottier, NYI
1934 ......Russ Blinko, Mtl M	1956 ......Glenn Hall, Det	1977 ......Willi Plett, Atl
1935 ......Dave Schriner, NYA	1957 ......Larry Regan, Bos	1978 ......Mike Bossy, NYI
1936 ......Mike Karakas, Chi	1958 ......Frank Mahovlich, Tor	1979 ......Bobby Smith, Minn
1937 ......Syl Apps, Tor	1959 ......Ralph Backstrom, Mtl	1980 ......Ray Bourque, Bos
1938 ......Cully Dahlstrom, Chi	1960 ......Bill Hay, Chi	1981 ......Peter Stastny, Que
1939 ......Frank Brimsek, Bos	1961 ......Dave Keon, Tor	1982 ......Dale Hawerchuk, Winn
1940 ......Kilby MacDonald, NYR	1962 ......Bobby Rousseau, Mtl	1983 ......Steve Larmer, Chi
1941 ......Johnny Quilty, Mtl	1963 ......Kent Douglas, Tor	1984 ......Tom Barrasso, Buff
1942 ......Grant Warwick, NYR	1964 ......Jacques Laperriere, Mtl	1985 ......Mario Lemieux, Pitt
1943 ......Gaye Stewart, Tor	1965 ......Roger Crozier, Det	1986 ......Gary Suter, Cgy
1944 ......Gus Bodnar, Tor	1966 ......Brit Selby, Tor	1987 ......Luc Robitaille, LA
1945 ......Frank McCool, Tor	1967 ......Bobby Orr, Bos	1988 ......Joe Nieuwendyk, Cgy
1946 ......Edgar Laprade, NYR	1968 ......Derek Sanderson, Bos	1989 ......Brian Leetch, NYR
1947 ......Howie Meeker, Tor	1969 ......Danny Grant, Minn	1990 ......Sergei Makarov, Cgy
1948 ......Jim McFadden, Det	1970 ......Tony Esposito, Chi	1991 ......Ed Belfour, Chi
1949 ......Pentti Lund, NYR	1971 ......Gilbert Perreault, Buff	1992 ......Pavel Bure, Van
1950 ......Jack Gelineau, Bos	1972 ......Ken Dryden, Mtl	1993 ......Teemu Selanne, Winn
1951 ......Terry Sawchuk, Det	1973 ......Steve Vickers, NYR	1994 ......Martin Brodeur, NJ
1952 ......Bernie Geoffrion, Mtl	1974 ......Denis Potvin, NYI	1995 ......Peter Forsberg, Que
1953 ......Gump Worsley, NYR	1975 ......Eric Vail, Atl	1996 ......Daniel Alfredsson, Ott
1954 ......Camille Henry, NYR		

Vezina Trophy

Awarded annually "to the goalkeeper adjudged to be the best at his position." The trophy is named after Georges Vezina, an outstanding goalie for the Montreal Canadiens who collapsed during a game on November 28, 1925, and died four months later of tuberculosis. The general managers of the 21 NHL teams vote on the award.

1927 ......George Hainsworth, Mtl	1939 ......Frank Brimsek, Bos	1951 ......Al Rollins, Tor
1928 ......George Hainsworth, Mtl	1940 ......Dave Kerr, NYR	1952 ......Terry Sawchuk, Det
1929 ......George Hainsworth, Mtl	1941 ......Turk Broda, Tor	1953 ......Terry Sawchuk, Det
1930 ......Tiny Thompson, Bos	1942 ......Frank Brimsek, Bos	1954 ......Harry Lumley, Tor
1931 ......Roy Worters, NYA	1943 ......Johnny Mowers, Det	1955 ......Terry Sawchuk, Det
1932 ......Charlie Gardiner, Chi	1944 ......Bill Durnan, Mtl	1956 ......Jacques Plante, Mtl
1933 ......Tiny Thompson, Bos	1945 ......Bill Durnan, Mtl	1957 ......Jacques Plante, Mtl
1934 ......Charlie Gardiner, Chi	1946 ......Bill Durnan, Mtl	1958 ......Jacques Plante, Mtl
1935 ......Lorne Chabot, Chi	1947 ......Bill Durnan, Mtl	1959 ......Jacques Plante, Mtl
1936 ......Tiny Thompson, Bos	1948 ......Turk Broda, Tor	1960 ......Jacques Plante, Mtl
1937 ......Normie Smith, Det	1949 ......Bill Durnan, Mtl	1961 ......Johnny Bower, Tor
1938 ......Tiny Thompson, Bos	1950 ......Bill Durnan, Mtl	1962 ......Jacques Plante, Mtl

Vezina Trophy *(Cont.)*

1963	Glenn Hall, Chi	1974	Bernie Parent, Phil	1983	Pete Peeters, Bos
1964	Charlie Hodge, Mtl		Tony Esposito, Chi	1984	Tom Barrasso, Buff
1965	Terry Sawchuk, Tor	1975	Bernie Parent, Phil	1985	Pelle Lindbergh, Phil
	Johnny Bower, Tor	1976	Ken Dryden, Mtl	1986	John Vanbiesbrouck,
1966	Gump Worsley, Mtl	1977	Ken Dryden, Mtl		NYR
	Charlie Hodge, Mtl		Michel Larocque, Mtl	1987	Ron Hextall, Phil
1967	Glenn Hall, Chi	1978	Ken Dryden, Mtl	1988	Grant Fuhr, Edm
	Rogie Vachon, Mtl		Michel Larocque, Mtl	1989	Patrick Roy, Mtl
1969	Jacques Plante, StL	1979	Ken Dryden, Mtl	1990	Patrick Roy, Mtl
	Glenn Hall, StL		Michel Larocque, Mtl	1991	Ed Belfour, Chi
1970	Tony Esposito, Chi	1980	Bob Sauve, Buff	1992	Patrick Roy, Mtl
1971	Ed Giacomin, NYR		Don Edwards, Buff	1993	Ed Belfour, Chi
	Gilles Villemure, NYR	1981	Richard Sevigny, Mtl	1994	Dominik Hasek, Buff
1972	Tony Esposito, Chi		Denis Herron, Mtl	1995	Dominik Hasek, Buff
	Gary Smith, Chi		Michel Larocque, Mtl	1996	Jim Carey, Wash
1973	Ken Dryden, Mtl	1982	Bill Smith, NYI		

Selke Trophy

Awarded annually "to the forward who best excels in the defensive aspects of the game." The trophy is named after Frank J. Selke, the architect of the Montreal Canadians dynasty that won five consecutive Stanley Cups in the late '50s. The winner is selected by a vote of the Professional Hockey Writers Association.

1978	Bob Gainey, Mtl	1985	Craig Ramsay, Buff	1991	Dirk Graham, Chi
1979	Bob Gainey, Mtl	1986	Troy Murray, Chi	1992	Guy Carbonneau, Mtl
1980	Bob Gainey, Mtl	1987	Dave Poulin, Phil	1993	Doug Gilmour, Tor
1981	Bob Gainey, Mtl	1988	Guy Carbonneau, Mtl	1994	Sergei Fedorov, Det
1982	Steve Kasper, Bos	1989	Guy Carbonneau, Mtl	1995	Ron Francis, Pitt
1983	Bobby Clarke, Phil	1990	Rick Meagher, StL	1996	Sergei Fedorov, Det
1984	Doug Jarvis, Wash				

Adams Award

Awarded annually "to the NHL coach adjudged to have contributed the most to his team's success." The trophy is named in honor of Jack Adams, longtime coach and general manager of the Detroit Red Wings. The winner is selected by a vote of the National Hockey League Broadcasters' Association.

1974	Fred Shero, Phil	1982	Tom Watt, Winn	1990	Bob Murdoch, Winn
1975	Bob Pulford, LA	1983	Orval Tessier, Chi	1991	Brian Sutter, StL
1976	Don Cherry, Bos	1984	Bryan Murray, Wash	1992	Pat Quinn, Van
1977	Scott Bowman, Mtl	1985	Mike Keenan, Phil	1993	Pat Burns, Tor
1978	Bobby Kromm, Det	1986	Glen Sather, Edm	1994	Jacques Lemaire, NJ
1979	Al Arbour, NYI	1987	Jacques Demers, Det	1995	Marc Crawford, Que
1980	Pat Quinn, Phil	1988	Jacques Demers, Det	1996	Scotty Bowman, Det
1981	Red Berenson, StL	1989	Pat Burns, Mtl		

Can't Grant Him Hall Status

In mid-April of 1996, Grant Fuhr was back in the crease for the St. Louis Blues after having missed three games with a strained knee. That injury interrupted his NHL-record string of 76 straight starts in a season, an ironman performance for which he had received well-deserved attention during the season (SI, Feb. 19). But Fuhr was a long way from Ripken territory. After all, Fuhr wound up 426 games shy of the consecutive-game streak set by Hall of Fame goaltender Glenn Hall. Back in the days of the 70-game schedule, Hall—who regularly vomited from nervousness before games and who once said, "Playing goal is a winter of torture for me"—appeared in every game of every season from 1955–56 through '61–62 for the Detroit Red Wings and the Chicago Blackhawks. And Hall ran off his 502-game streak while fending off pucks without a mask. Once, playing for Detroit during the '57 postseason, he got smashed in the mouth with the puck. The game was delayed 30 minutes while he received 23 stitches. Then he returned, of course, and carried on.

Career Records

Alltime Point Leaders

	Player	Yrs	GP	G	A	Pts	Pts/game
1.	*Wayne Gretzky, Edm, LA, StL	17	1253	837	1771	2608	2.081
2.	Gordie Howe, Det, Hart	26	1767	801	1049	1850	1.047
3.	Marcel Dionne, Det, LA, NYR	18	1348	731	1040	1771	1.314
4.	Phil Esposito, Chi, Bos, NYR	18	1282	717	873	1590	1.240
5.	*Mark Messier, Edm, NYR	17	1201	539	929	1468	1.222
6.	Stan Mikita, Chi	22	1394	541	926	1467	1.052
7.	Bryan Trottier, NYI, Pitt	18	1279	524	901	1425	1.114
8.	*Paul Coffey, Edm, Pitt, LA, Det	16	1154	372	1038	1410	1.222
9.	*Dale Hawerchuk, Winn, Buff, StL, Phil	15	1137	506	869	1375	1.209
10.	*Mario Lemieux, Pitt	11	669	563	809	1372	2.051
11.	John Bucyk, Det, Bos	23	1540	556	813	1369	.889
12.	Guy Lafleur, Mtl, NYR, Que	17	1126	560	793	1353	1.202
13.	*Jari Kurri, Edm, LA, NYR	15	1099	583	758	1341	1.220
14.	Gilbert Perreault, Buff	17	1191	512	814	1326	1.113
15.	*Ray Bourque, Bos	17	1228	343	970	1313	1.069

*Active player.

Alltime Goal-Scoring Leaders

	Player	Yrs	GP	G	G/game
1.	*Wayne Gretzky, Edm, LA, StL	17	1253	837	.668
2.	Gordie Howe, Det, Hart	26	1767	801	.453
3.	Marcel Dionne, Det, LA, NYR	18	1348	731	.542
4.	Phil Esposito, Chi, Bos, NYR	18	1282	717	.559
5.	*Mike Gartner, Wash, Minn, NYR, Tor	17	1290	664	.515
6.	Bobby Hull, Chi, Winn, Hart	16	1063	610	.574
7.	*Jari Kurri, Edm, LA, NYR	15	1099	583	.530
8.	Mike Bossy, NYI	10	752	573	.762
9.	*Mario Lemieux, Pitt	11	669	563	.841
10.	Guy Lafleur, Mtl, NYR, Que	17	1126	560	.497

*Active player.

Alltime Assist Leaders

	Player	Yrs	GP	A	A/game
1.	*Wayne Gretzky, Edm, LA, StL	17	1253	1771	1.413
2.	Gordie Howe, Det, Hart	26	1767	1049	.594
3.	Marcel Dionne, Det, LA, NYR	18	1348	1040	.771
4.	*Paul Coffey, Edm, Pitt, LA, Det	16	1154	1038	.899
5.	*Ray Bourque, Bos	17	1228	970	.790
6.	*Mark Messier, Edm, NYR	17	1201	929	.773
7.	Stan Mikita, Chi	22	1394	926	.664
8.	Bryan Trottier, NYI, Pitt	18	1279	901	.704
9.	*Ron Francis, Hart, Pitt	15	1085	881	.812
10.	Phil Esposito, Chi, Bos, NYR	18	1282	873	.681

*Active player.

Alltime Penalty Minutes Leaders

	Player	Yrs	GP	PIM	Min/game
1.	Dave Williams, Tor, Van, Det, LA, Hart	14	962	3966	4.12
2.	*Dale Hunter, Que, Wash	16	1181	3218	2.72
3.	Chris Nilan, Mtl, NYR, Bos	13	688	3043	4.42
4.	*Tim Hunter, Cgy, Que, Van	15	769	3011	3.91
5.	*Marty McSorley, Pitt, Edm, LA, NYR	13	775	2892	3.73
6.	Willi Plett, Atl, Cgy, Minn, Bos	13	834	2572	3.08
7.	*Basil McRae, Que, Tor, Det, Minn, StL	15	568	2445	4.30
8.	*Rick Tocchet, Phil, Pitt, LA, Bos	12	788	2371	3.01
9.	*Jay Wells, LA, Phil, Buff, NYR, StL	17	1077	2346	2.18
10.	*Bob Probert, Det, Chi	10	552	2327	4.22

*Active player.

Goaltending Records

ALLTIME WIN LEADERS

Goaltender	W	L	T	Pct
Terry Sawchuk, five teams	447	330	173	.562
Jacques Plante, five teams	434	246	147	.614
Tony Esposito, Mtl, Chi	423	306	152	.566
Glenn Hall, Det, Chi, StL	407	327	163	.545
Rogie Vachon, Mtl, LA, Det, Bos	355	291	127	.541
Gump Worsley, NYR, Mtl, Minn	335	353	151	.489
Harry Lumley, five teams	333	326	143	.504
*Andy Moog, Edm, Bos, Dall	326	179	78	.626
*Grant Fuhr, five teams	320	223	87	.577
*Patrick Roy, Mtl, Col	311	190	67	.606

*Active player.

ACTIVE GOALTENDING LEADERS

Goaltender	W	L	T	Pct
Andy Moog, Edm, Bos, Dall	326	179	78	.626
Mike Vernon, Cgy, Det	288	168	57	.617
Mike Richter, NYR	149	91	28	.608
Patrick Roy, Mtl, Col	311	190	67	.606
Ed Belfour, Chi	190	123	50	.592
Grant Fuhr, five teams	320	223	87	.577
Tom Barrasso, Buff, Pitt	295	213	63	.572
Curtis Joseph, StL, Edm	152	112	36	.567
Ron Hextall, Phil, Que, NYI	234	174	53	.565
Daren Puppa, Buff, Tor, TB	167	138	45	.541

Note: Ranked by winning percentage; minimum 250 games played.

ALLTIME SHUTOUT LEADERS

Goaltender	Team	Yrs	GP	SO
Terry Sawchuk	Det, Bos, Tor, LA, NYR	21	971	103
George Hainsworth	Mtl, Tor	11	465	94
Glenn Hall	Det, Chi, StL	18	906	84
Jacques Plante	Mtl, NYR, StL, Tor, Bos	18	837	82
Tiny Thompson	Bos, Det	12	553	81
Alex Connell	Ott, Det, NYA, Mtl M	12	417	81
Tony Esposito	Mtl, Chi	16	886	76
Lorne Chabot	NYR, Tor, Mtl, Chi, Mtl M, NYA	11	411	73
Harry Lumley	Det, NYR, Chi, Tor, Bos	16	804	71
Roy Worters	Pitt Pir, NYA, *Mtl	12	484	66

*Played 1 game for Canadiens in 1929–30, not a shutout.

ALLTIME GOALS AGAINST AVERAGE LEADERS (PRE-1950)

Goaltender	Team	Yrs	GP	GA	GAA
George Hainsworth	Mtl, Tor	11	465	937	1.91
Alex Connell	Ott, Det, NYA, Mtl M	12	417	830	1.91
Chuck Gardiner	Chi	7	316	664	2.02
Lorne Chabot	NYR, Tor, Mtl, Chi, Mtl M, NYA	11	411	861	2.04
Tiny Thompson	Bos, Det	12	553	1183	2.08

ALLTIME GOALS AGAINST AVERAGE LEADERS (POST-1950)

Goaltender	Team	Yrs	GP	GA	GAA
Ken Dryden	Mtl	8	397	870	2.24
Jacques Plante	Mtl, NYR, StL, Tor, Bos	18	837	1965	2.38
Glenn Hall	Det, Chi, StL	18	906	2239	2.51
Terry Sawchuk	Det, Bos, Tor, LA, NYR	21	971	2401	2.52
Johnny Bower	NYR, Tor	15	552	1347	2.52

Note: Minimum 250 games played. Goals against average equals goals against per 60 minutes played.

Coaching Records

Coach	Team	Seasons	W	L	T	Pct
Scott Bowman	five teams	1967-87, 91–	975	434	245	.663
Toe Blake	Mtl	1955-68	500	255	159	.634
Glen Sather	Edm	1979-89, 93-94	464	268	110	.616
Fred Shero	Phil, NYR	1971-81	390	225	119	.612
Tommy Ivan	Det, Chi	1947-54, 56-58	288	174	111	.599
Mike Keenan	Phil, Chi, NYR, StL	1984–	455	301	98	.590
Pat Burns	Mtl, Tor	1988–	316	217	85	.580
Emile Francis	NYR, StL	1965-77, 81-83	393	273	112	.577
Bryan Murray	Wash, Det	1981-93	467	337	112	.571
Billy Reay	Tor, Chi	1957-59, 63-77	542	385	175	.571

Note: Minimum 600 regular-season games. Ranked by percentage.

Single-Season Records

Goals

Player	Season	GP	G	Player	Season	GP	G
Wayne Gretzky, Edm	1981-82	80	92	Wayne Gretzky, Edm	1982-83	80	71
Wayne Gretzky, Edm	1983-84	74	87	Brett Hull, StL	1991-92	73	70
Brett Hull, StL	1990-91	78	86	Mario Lemieux, Pitt	1987-88	77	70
Mario Lemieux, Pitt	1988-89	76	85	Bernie Nicholls, LA	1988-89	79	70
Alexander Mogilny, Buff	1992-93	77	76	Mario Lemieux, Pitt	1992-93	60	69
Phil Esposito, Bos	1970-71	78	76	Mario Lemieux, Pitt	1995-96	70	69
Teemu Selanne, Winn	1992-93	84	76	Mike Bossy, NYI	1978-79	80	69
Wayne Gretzky, Edm	1984-85	80	73	Phil Esposito, Bos	1973-74	78	68
Brett Hull, StL	1989-90	80	72	Jari Kurri, Edm	1985-86	78	68
Jari Kurri, Edm	1984-85	73	71	Mike Bossy, NYI	1980-81	79	68

Assists

Player	Season	GP	A	Player	Season	GP	A
Wayne Gretzky, Edm	1985-86	80	163	Wayne Gretzky, LA	1989-90	73	102
Wayne Gretzky, Edm	1984-85	80	135	Bobby Orr, Bos	1970-71	78	102
Wayne Gretzky, Edm	1982-83	80	125	Mario Lemieux, Pitt	1987-88	77	98
Wayne Gretzky, LA	1990-91	78	122	Adam Oates, Bos	1992-93	84	97
Wayne Gretzky, Edm	1986-87	79	121	Doug Gilmour, Tor	1992-93	83	95
Wayne Gretzky, Edm	1981-82	80	120	Pat LaFontaine, Buff	1992-93	84	95
Wayne Gretzky, Edm	1983-84	74	118	Mario Lemieux, Pitt	1985-86	79	93
Mario Lemieux, Pitt	1988-89	76	114	Peter Stastny, Que	1981-82	80	93
Wayne Gretzky, LA	1988-89	78	114	Wayne Gretzky, LA	1993-94	81	92
Wayne Gretzky, Edm	1987-88	64	109	Mario Lemieux, Pitt	1995-96	70	92
Wayne Gretzky, Edm	1980-81	80	109	Ron Francis, Pitt	1995-96	77	92

Points

Player	Season	G	A	Pts	Player	Season	G	A	Pts
Wayne Gretzky, Edm	1985-86	52	163	215	Wayne Gretzky, LA	1990-91	41	122	163
Wayne Gretzky, Edm	1981-82	92	120	212	Mario Lemieux, Pitt	1995-96	69	92	161
Wayne Gretzky, Edm	1984-85	73	135	208	Mario Lemieux, Pitt	1992-93	69	91	160
Wayne Gretzky, Edm	1983-84	87	118	205	Steve Yzerman, Det	1988-89	65	90	155
Mario Lemieux, Pitt	1988-89	85	114	199	Phil Esposito, Bos	1970-71	76	76	152
Wayne Gretzky, Edm	1982-83	71	125	196	Bernie Nicholls, LA	1988-89	70	80	150
Wayne Gretzky, Edm	1986-87	62	121	183	Wayne Gretzky, Edm	1987-88	40	109	149
Mario Lemieux, Pitt	1987-88	70	98	168	Pat LaFontaine, Buff	1992-93	53	95	148
Wayne Gretzky, LA	1988-89	54	114	168	Mike Bossy, NYI	1981-82	64	83	147
Wayne Gretzky, Edm	1980-81	55	109	164	Phil Esposito, Bos	1973-74	68	77	145

Points per Game

Player	Season	GP	Pts	Avg	Player	Season	GP	Pts	Avg
Wayne Gretzky, Edm	1983-84	74	205	2.77	Mario Lemieux, Pitt	1987-88	77	168	2.18
Wayne Gretzky, Edm	1985-86	80	215	2.69	Wayne Gretzky, LA	1988-89	78	168	2.15
Mario Lemieux, Pitt	1992-93	60	160	2.67	Wayne Gretzky, LA	1990-91	78	163	2.09
Wayne Gretzky, Edm	1981-82	80	212	2.65	Mario Lemieux, Pitt	1989-90	59	123	2.08
Mario Lemieux, Pitt	1988-89	76	199	2.62	Wayne Gretzky, Edm	1980-81	80	164	2.05
Wayne Gretzky, Edm	1984-85	80	208	2.60	Mario Lemieux, Pitt	1991-92	64	131	2.05
Wayne Gretzky, Edm	1982-83	80	196	2.45	Bill Cowley, Bos	1943-44	36	71	1.97
Wayne Gretzky, Edm	1987-88	64	149	2.33	Phil Esposito, Bos	1970-71	78	152	1.95
Wayne Gretzky, Edm	1986-87	79	183	2.32	Wayne Gretzky, LA	1989-90	73	142	1.95
Mario Lemieux, Pitt	1995-96	70	161	2.30	Steve Yzerman, Det	1988-89	80	155	1.94

Note: Minimum 50 points in one season.

Goals per Game

Player	Season	GP	G	Avg
Joe Malone, Mtl	1917-18	20	44	2.20
Cy Denneny, Ott	1917-18	22	36	1.64
Newsy Lalonde, Mtl	1917-18	14	23	1.64
Joe Malone, Que	1919-20	24	39	1.63
Newsy Lalonde, Mtl	1919-20	23	36	1.57
Joe Malone, Ham	1920-21	20	30	1.50
Babe Dye, Ham-Tor	1920-21	24	35	1.46
Cy Denneny, Ott	1920-21	24	34	1.42
Reg Noble, Tor	1917-18	20	28	1.40
Newsy Lalonde, Mtl	1920-21	24	33	1.38

Note: Minimum 20 goals in one season.

Assists per Game

Player	Season	GP	A	Avg
Wayne Gretzky, Edm	1985-86	80	163	2.04
Wayne Gretzky, Edm	1987-88	64	109	1.70
Wayne Gretzky, Edm	1984-85	80	135	1.69
Wayne Gretzky, Edm	1983-84	74	118	1.59
Wayne Gretzky, Edm	1982-83	80	125	1.56
Wayne Gretzky, LA	1990-91	78	122	1.56
Wayne Gretzky, Edm	1986-87	79	121	1.53
Mario Lemieux, Pitt	1992-93	60	91	1.52
Wayne Gretzky, Edm	1981-82	80	120	1.50
Mario Lemieux, Pitt	1988-89	76	114	1.50

Note: Minimum 35 assists in one season.

Shutout Leaders

	Season	SO	Length of Schedule
George Hainsworth, Mtl	1928-29	22	44
Alex Connell, Ott	1925-26	15	36
Alex Connell, Ott	1927-28	15	44
Hal Winkler, Bos	1927-28	15	44
Tony Esposito, Chi	1969-70	15	76
George Hainsworth, Mtl	1926-27	14	44
Clint Benedict, Mtl M	1926-27	13	44
Alex Connell, Ott	1926-27	13	44
George Hainsworth, Mtl	1927-28	13	44
John Roach, NYR	1928-29	13	44
Roy Worters, NYA	1928-29	13	44
Harry Lumley, Tor	1953-54	13	70
Tiny Thompson, Bos	1928-29	12	44
Lorne Chabot, Tor	1928-29	12	44
Chuck Gardiner, Chi	1930-31	12	44
Terry Sawchuk, Det	1951-52	12	70
Terry Sawchuk, Det	1953-54	12	70
Terry Sawchuk, Det	1954-55	12	70
Glenn Hall, Det	1955-56	12	70
Bernie Parent, Phil	1973-74	12	78

	Season	SO	Length of Schedule
Bernie Parent, Phil	1974-75	12	80
Lorne Chabot, NYR	1927-28	11	44
Harry Holmes, Det	1927-28	11	44
Clint Benedict, Mtl M	1928-29	11	44
Joe Miller, Pitt Pirates	1928-29	11	44
Tiny Thompson, Bos	1932-33	11	48
Terry Sawchuk, Det	1950-51	11	70
Lorne Chabot, NYR	1926-27	10	44
Roy Worters, Pitt Pirates	1927-28	10	44
Clarence Dolson, Det	1928-29	10	44
John Roach, Det	1932-33	10	48
Chuck Gardiner, Chi	1933-34	10	48
Tiny Thompson, Bos	1935-36	10	48
Frank Brimsek, Bos	1938-39	10	48
Bill Durnan, Mtl	1948-49	10	60
Gerry McNeil, Mtl	1952-53	10	70
Harry Lumley, Tor	1952-53	10	70
Tony Esposito, Chi	1973-74	10	78
Ken Dryden, Mtl	1976-77	10	80

Wins

	Season	Record
Bernie Parent, Phil	1973-74	47-13-12
Bernie Parent, Phil	1974-75	44-14-9
Terry Sawchuk, Det	1950-51	44-13-13
Terry Sawchuk, Det	1951-52	44-14-12
Tom Barasso, Pitt	1992-93	43-14-5
Ed Belfour, Chi	1990-91	43-19-7
Jacques Plante, Mtl	1955-56	42-12-10
Jacques Plante, Mtl	1961-62	42-14-14
Ken Dryden, Mtl	1975-76	42-10-8
Mike Richter, NYR	1993-94	42-12-6

Goals Against Average

(PRE-1950)

	Season	GP	GAA
George Hainsworth, Mtl	1928-29	44	0.92
George Hainsworth, Mtl	1927-28	44	1.05
Alex Connell, Ott	1925-26	36	1.12
Tiny Thompson, Bos	1928-29	44	1.18
Roy Worters, NYA	1928-29	38	1.21

(POST-1950)

	Season	GP	GAA
Tony Esposito, Chi	1971-72	48	1.77
Al Rollins, Tor	1950-51	40	1.77
Harry Lumley, Tor	1953-54	69	1.86
Jacques Plante, Mtl	1955-56	64	1.86
Jacques Plante, Tor	1970-71	40	1.88

Single-Game Records

Goals

	Date	G
Joe Malone, Que vs Tor	1-31-20	7
Newsy Lalonde, Mtl vs Tor	1-10-20	6
Joe Malone, Que vs Ott	3-10-20	6
Corb Denneny, Tor vs Ham	1-26-21	6
Cy Denneny, Ott vs Ham	3-7-21	6
Syd Howe, Det vs NYR	2-3-44	6
Red Berenson, StL vs Phil	11-7-68	6
Darryl Sittler, Tor vs Bos	2-7-76	6

Assists

	Date	A
Billy Taylor, Det vs Chi	3-16-47	7
Wayne Gretzky, Edm vs Wash	2-15-80	7
Wayne Gretzky, Edm vs Chi	12-11-85	7
Wayne Gretzky, Edm vs Que	2-14-86	7

Note: 19 tied with 6.

Points

	Date	G	A	Pts
Darryl Sittler, Tor vs Bos	2-7-76	6	4	10
Maurice Richard, Mtl vs Det	12-28-44	5	3	8
Bert Olmstead, Mtl vs Chi	1-9-54	4	4	8
Tom Bladon, Phil vs Clev	12-11-77	4	4	8
Bryan Trottier, NYI vs NYR	12-23-78	5	3	8
Peter Stastny, Que vs Wash	2-22-81	4	4	8
Anton Stastny, Que vs Wash	2-22-81	3	5	8
Wayne Gretzky, Edm vs NJ	11-19-83	3	5	8
Wayne Gretzky, Edm vs Minn	1-4-84	4	4	8
Paul Coffey, Edm vs Det	3-14-86	2	6	8
Mario Lemieux, Pitt vs StL	10-15-88	2	6	8
Bernie Nicholls, LA vs Tor	12-1-88	2	6	8
Mario Lemieux, Pitt vs NJ	12-31-88	5	3	8

NHL Season Leaders

Points

Season	Player and Club	Pts	Season	Player and Club	Pts
1917-18	Joe Malone, Mtl	44	1952-53	Gordie Howe, Det	95
1918-19	Newsy Lalonde, Mtl	30	1953-54	Gordie Howe, Det	81
1919-20	Joe Malone, Que	48	1954-55	Bernie Geoffrion, Mtl	75
1920-21	Newsy Lalonde, Mtl	41	1955-56	Jean Beliveau, Mtl	88
1921-22	Punch Broadbent, Ott	46	1956-57	Gordie Howe, Det	89
1922-23	Babe Dye, Tor	37	1957-58	Dickie Moore, Mtl	84
1923-24	Cy Denneny, Ott	23	1958-59	Dickie Moore, Mtl	96
1924-25	Babe Dye, Tor	44	1959-60	Bobby Hull, Chi	81
1925-26	Nels Stewart, Mtl M	42	1960-61	Bernie Geoffrion, Mtl	95
1926-27	Bill Cook, NY	37	1961-62	Andy Bathgate, NY	84
1927-28	Howie Morenz, Mtl	51		Bobby Hull, Chi	84
1928-29	Ace Bailey, Tor	32	1962-63	Gordie Howe, Det	86
1929-30	Cooney Weiland, Bos	73	1963-64	Stan Mikita, Chi	89
1930-31	Howie Morenz, Mtl	51	1964-65	Stan Mikita, Chi	87
1931-32	Harvey Jackson, Tor	53	1965-66	Bobby Hull, Chi	97
1932-33	Bill Cook, NY	50	1966-67	Stan Mikita, Chi	97
1933-34	Charlie Conacher, Tor	52	1967-68	Stan Mikita, Chi	87
1934-35	Charlie Conacher, Tor	57	1968-69	Phil Esposito, Bos	126
1935-36	Sweeney Schriner, NYA	45	1969-70	Bobby Orr, Bos	120
1936-37	Sweeney Schriner, NYA	46	1970-71	Phil Esposito, Bos	152
1937-38	Gord Drillon, Tor	52	1971-72	Phil Esposito, Bos	133
1938-39	Hector Blake, Mtl	47	1972-73	Phil Esposito, Bos	130
1939-40	Milt Schmidt, Bos	52	1973-74	Phil Esposito, Bos	145
1940-41	Bill Cowley, Bos	62	1974-75	Bobby Orr, Bos	135
1941-42	Bryan Hextall, NY	54	1975-76	Guy Lafleur, Mtl	125
1942-43	Doug Bentley, Chi	73	1976-77	Guy Lafleur, Mtl	136
1943-44	Herb Cain, Bos	82	1977-78	Guy Lafleur, Mtl	132
1944-45	Elmer Lach, Mtl	80	1978-79	Bryan Trottier, NYI	134
1945-46	Max Bentley, Chi	61	1979-80	Marcel Dionne, LA	137
1946-47	Max Bentley, Chi	72		Wayne Gretzky, Edm	137
1947-48	Elmer Lach, Mtl	61	1980-81	Wayne Gretzky, Edm	164
1948-49	Roy Conacher, Chi	68	1981-82	Wayne Gretzky, Edm	212
1949-50	Ted Lindsay, Det	78	1982-83	Wayne Gretzky, Edm	196
1950-51	Gordie Howe, Det	86	1983-84	Wayne Gretzky, Edm	205
1951-52	Gordie Howe, Det	86	1984-85	Wayne Gretzky, Edm	208

NHL Season Leaders (Cont.)

Points (Cont.)

Season	Player and Club	Pts	Season	Player and Club	Pts
1985-86	Wayne Gretzky, Edm	215	1991-92	Mario Lemieux, Pitt	131
1986-87	Wayne Gretzky, Edm	183	1992-93	Mario Lemieux, Pitt	160
1987-88	Mario Lemieux, Pitt	168	1993-94	Wayne Gretzky, LA	130
1988-89	Mario Lemieux, Pitt	199	1994-95	Jaromir Jagr, Pitt	70
1989-90	Wayne Gretzky, LA	142	1995-96	Mario Lemieux, Pitt	161
1990-91	Wayne Gretzky, LA	163			

Goals

Season	Player and Club	G	Season	Player and Club	G
1917-18	Joe Malone, Mtl	44	1956-57	Gordie Howe, Det	44
1918-19	Odie Cleghorn, Mtl	23	1957-58	Dickie Moore, Mtl	36
1919-20	Joe Malone, Que	39	1958-59	Jean Beliveau, Mtl	45
1920-21	Babe Dye, Ham-Tor	35	1959-60	Bobby Hull, Chi	39
1921-22	Punch Broadbent, Ott	32		Bronco Horvath, Bos	39
1922-23	Babe Dye, Tor	26	1960-61	Bernie Geoffrion, Mtl	50
1923-24	Cy Denneny, Ott	22	1961-62	Bobby Hull, Chi	50
1924-25	Babe Dye, Tor	38	1962-63	Gordie Howe, Det	38
1925-26	Nels Stewart, Mtl	34	1963-64	Bobby Hull, Chi	43
1926-27	Bill Cook, NY	33	1964-65	Norm Ullman, Det	42
1927-28	Howie Morenz, Mtl	33	1965-66	Bobby Hull, Chi	54
1928-29	Ace Bailey, Tor	22	1966-67	Bobby Hull, Chi	52
1929-30	Cooney Weiland, Bos	43	1967-68	Bobby Hull, Chi	44
1930-31	Bill Cook, NY	30	1968-69	Bobby Hull, Chi	58
1931-32	Charlie Conacher, Tor	34	1969-70	Phil Esposito, Bos	43
	Bill Cook, NY	34	1970-71	Phil Esposito, Bos	76
1932-33	Bill Cook, NY	28	1971-72	Phil Esposito, Bos	66
1933-34	Charlie Conacher, Tor	32	1972-73	Phil Esposito, Bos	55
1934-35	Charlie Conacher, Tor	36	1973-74	Phil Esposito, Bos	68
1935-36	Charlie Conacher, Tor	23	1974-75	Phil Esposito, Bos	61
	Bill Thoms, Tor	23	1975-76	Guy Lafleur, Mtl	56
1936-37	Larry Aurie, Det	23	1976-77	Steve Shutt, Mtl	60
	Nels Stewart, Bos-NYA	23	1977-78	Guy Lafleur, Mtl	60
1937-38	Gord Drill, Tor	26	1978-79	Mike Bossy, NYI	69
1938-39	Roy Conacher, Bos	26	1979-80	Charlie Simmer, LA	56
1939-40	Bryan Hextall, NY	24		Blaine Stoughton, Hart	56
1940-41	Bryan Hextall, NY	26	1980-81	Mike Bossy, NYI	68
1941-42	Lynn Patrick, NY	32	1981-82	Wayne Gretzky, Edm	92
1942-43	Doug Bentley, Chi	43	1982-83	Wayne Gretzky, Edm	71
1943-44	Doug Bentley, Chi	38	1983-84	Wayne Gretzky, Edm	87
1944-45	Maurice Richard, Mtl	50	1984-85	Wayne Gretzky, Edm	73
1945-46	Gaye Stewart, Tor	37	1985-86	Jari Kurri, Edm	68
1946-47	Maurice Richard, Mtl	50	1986-87	Wayne Gretzky, Edm	62
1947-48	Ted Lindsay, Det	33	1987-88	Mario Lemieux, Pitt	70
1948-49	Sid Abel, Det	28	1988-89	Mario Lemieux, Pitt	85
1949-50	Maurice Richard, Mtl	43	1989-90	Brett Hull, StL	72
1950-51	Gordie Howe, Det	43	1990-91	Brett Hull, StL	78
1951-52	Gordie Howe, Det	47	1991-92	Brett Hull, StL	70
1952-53	Gordie Howe, Det	49	1992-93	Alexander Mogilny, Buff	76
1953-54	Maurice Richard, Mtl	37		Teemu Selanne, Winn	76
1954-55	Bernie Geoffrion, Mtl	38	1993-94	Pavel Bure, Van	60
	Maurice Richard, Mtl	38	1994-95	Peter Bondra, Wash	34
1955-56	Jean Beliveau, Mtl	47	1995-96	Mario Lemieux, Pitt	69

Assists

Season	Player and Club	A	Season	Player and Club	A
1917-18	statistic not kept		1959-60	Bobby Hull, Chi	42
1918-19	Newsy Lalonde, Mtl	9	1960-61	Jean Beliveau, Mtl	58
1919-20	Corbett Denneny, Tor	12	1961-62	Andy Bathgate, NY	56
1920-21	Louis Berlinquette, Mtl	9	1962-63	Henri Richard, Mtl	50
1921-22	Punch Broadbench, Ott	14	1963-64	Andy Bathgate, NY-Tor	58
1922-23	Babe Dye, Tor	11	1964-65	Stan Mikita, Chi	59
1923-24	Billy Boucher, Mtl	6	1965-66	Stan Mikita, Chi	48
1924-25	Cy Denneny, Ott	15		Bobby Rousseau, Mtl	48
1925-26	Cy Denneny, Ott	12		Jean Beliveau, Mtl	48
1926-27	Dick Irvin, Chi	18	1966-67	Stan Mikita, Chi	62
1927-28	Howie Morenz, Mtl	18	1967-68	Phil Esposito, Bos	49
1928-29	Frank Boucher, NY	16	1968-69	Phil Esposito, Bos	77
1929-30	Frank Boucher, NY	36	1969-70	Bobby Orr, Bos	87
1930-31	Joe Primeau, Tor	36	1970-71	Bobby Orr, Bos	102
1931-32	Joe Primeau, Tor	37	1971-72	Bobby Orr, Bos	80
1932-33	Frank Boucher, NY	28	1972-73	Phil Esposito, Bos	75
1933-34	Joe Primeau, Tor	32	1973-74	Bobby Orr, Bos	89
1934-35	Art Chapman, NYA	28	1974-75	Bobby Clarke, Phil	89
1935-36	Art Chapman, NYA	28		Bobby Orr, Bos	89
1936-37	Syl Apps, Tor	29	1975-76	Bobby Clarke, Phil	89
1937-38	Syl Apps, Tor	29	1976-77	Guy Lafleur, Mtl	80
1938-39	Bill Cowley, Bos	34	1977-78	Bryan Trottier, NYI	77
1939-40	Milt Schmidt, Bos	30	1978-79	Bryan Trottier, NYI	87
1940-41	Bill Cowley, Bos	45	1979-80	Wayne Gretzky, Edm	86
1941-42	Phil Watson, NY	37	1980-81	Wayne Gretzky, Edm	109
1942-43	Bill Cowley, Bos	45	1981-82	Wayne Gretzky, Edm	120
1943-44	Clint Smith, Chi	49	1982-83	Wayne Gretzky, Edm	125
1944-45	Elmer Lach, Mtl	54	1983-84	Wayne Gretzky, Edm	118
1945-46	Elmer Lach, Mtl	34	1984-85	Wayne Gretzky, Edm	135
1946-47	Billy Taylor, Det	46	1985-86	Wayne Gretzky, Edm	163
1947-48	Doug Bentley, Chi	37	1986-87	Wayne Gretzky, Edm	121
1948-49	Doug Bentley, Chi	43	1987-88	Wayne Gretzky, Edm	109
1949-50	Ted Lindsay, Det	55	1988-89	Wayne Gretzky, LA	114
1950-51	Gordie Howe, Det	43		Mario Lemieux, Pitt	114
	Ted Kennedy, Tor	43	1989-90	Wayne Gretzky, LA	102
1951-52	Elmer Lach, Mtl	50	1990-91	Wayne Gretzky, LA	122
1952-53	Gordie Howe, Det	46	1991-92	Wayne Gretzky, LA	90
1953-54	Gordie Howe, Det	48	1992-93	Adam Oates, Bos	97
1954-55	Bert Olmstead, Mtl	48	1993-94	Wayne Gretzky, LA	92
1955-56	Bert Olmstead, Mtl	56	1994-95	Ron Francis, Pitt	48
1956-57	Ted Lindsay, Det	55	1995-96	Mario Lemieux, Pitt	92
1957-58	Henri Richard, Mtl	52		Ron Francis, Pitt	92
1958-59	Dickie Moore, Mtl	55			

Goalies Fear to View Lemieux

He had had Hodgkin's disease (in remission) and a chronically bad back, so there was a chance he had lost some strength. He was a well-worn 31 years old, so there was a chance he had lost some speed. And because of his maladies he missed all of the 1994-95 season, so there was a chance he'd lost some of his sharpness.

But none of that seemed to matter to NHL goalies when the subject turned to Pittsburgh Penguin superstar Mario Lemieux. Asked at the outset of the '95-96 season whom they would least like bearing down on them with the puck, 15 of the 29 keepers who responded chose Lemieux, who scored his 500th career goal on October 26, 1995. "He's a big man with speed, he's shifty and he's got a long reach," said Vancouver Canuck goalie Kirk McLean. "He can shoot when it looks like he's deking." Others cited Lemieux's patience, vision and experience. Of the other snipers mentioned—Vancouver's Pavel Bure (second, with four votes), the Detroit Red Wings' Sergei Fedorov, Pittsburgh's Jaromir Jagr, the New York Rangers' Alexei Kovalev and the Winnipeg Jets' Teemu Selanne—only Fleury is not European.

And the smooth-skating Canadian with whom Lemieux is often compared? Wayne Gretzky, 34 and definitely not as strong or as fast as he once was, did not get a mention.

Goals Against Average

Season	Goaltender and Club	GP	Min	GA	SO	Avg
1917-18	Georges Vezina, Mtl	21	1282	84	1	3.93
1918-19	Clint Benedict, Ott	18	1113	53	2	2.86
1919-20	Clint Benedict, Ott	24	1444	64	5	2.66
1920-21	Clint Benedict, Ott	24	1457	75	2	3.09
1921-22	Clint Benedict, Ott	24	1508	84	2	3.34
1922-23	Clint Benedict, Ott	24	1478	54	4	2.19
1923-24	Georges Vezina, Mtl	24	1459	48	3	1.97
1924-25	Georges Vezina, Mtl	30	1860	56	5	1.81
1925-26	Alex Connell, Ott	36	2251	42	15	1.12
1926-27	Clint Benedict, Mtl M	43	2748	65	13	1.42
1927-28	George Hainsworth, Mtl	44	2730	48	13	1.05
1928-29	George Hainsworth, Mtl	44	2800	43	22	0.92
1929-30	Tiny Thompson, Bos	44	2680	98	3	2.19
1930-31	Roy Worters, NYA	44	2760	74	8	1.61
1931-32	Chuck Gardiner, Chi	48	2989	92	4	1.85
1932-33	Tiny Thompson, Bos	48	3000	88	11	1.76
1933-34	Wilf Cude, Det-Mtl	30	1920	47	5	1.47
1934-35	Lorne Chabot, Chi	48	2940	88	8	1.80
1935-36	Tiny Thompson, Bos	48	2930	82	10	1.68
1936-37	Normie Smith, Det	48	2980	102	6	2.05
1937-38	Tiny Thompson, Bos	48	2970	89	7	1.80
1938-39	Frank Brimsek, Bos	43	2610	68	10	1.56
1939-40	Dave Kerr, NYR	48	3000	77	8	1.54
1940-41	Turk Broda, Tor	48	2970	99	5	2.00
1941-42	Frank Brimsek, Bos	47	2930	115	3	2.35
1942-43	Johnny Mowers, Det	50	3010	124	6	2.47
1943-44	Bill Durnan, Mtl	50	3000	109	2	2.18
1944-45	Bill Durnan, Mtl	50	3000	121	1	2.42
1945-46	Bill Durnan, Mtl	40	2400	104	4	2.60
1946-47	Bill Durnan, Mtl	60	3600	138	4	2.30
1947-48	Turk Broda, Tor	60	3600	143	5	2.38
1948-49	Bill Durnan, Mtl	60	3600	126	10	2.10
1949-50	Bill Durnan, Mtl	64	3840	141	8	2.20
1950-51	Al Rollins, Tor	40	2367	70	5	1.77
1951-52	Terry Sawchuk, Det	70	4200	133	12	1.90
1952-53	Terry Sawchuk, Det	63	3780	120	9	1.90
1953-54	Harry Lumley, Tor	69	4140	128	13	1.86
1954-55	Harry Lumley, Tor	69	4140	134	8	1.94
	Terry Sawchuk, Det	68	4060	132	12	1.94
1955-56	Jacques Plante, Mtl	64	3840	119	7	1.86
1956-57	Jacques Plante, Mtl	61	3660	123	9	2.02
1957-58	Jacques Plante, Mtl	57	3386	119	9	2.11
1958-59	Jacques Plante, Mtl	67	4000	144	9	2.16
1959-60	Jacques Plante, Mtl	69	4140	175	3	2.54
1960-61	Johnny Bower, Tor	58	3480	145	2	2.50
1961-62	Jacques Plante, Mtl	70	4200	166	4	2.37
1962-63	Jacques Plante, Mtl	56	3320	138	5	2.49
1963-64	Johnny Bower, Tor	51	3009	106	5	2.11
1964-65	Johnny Bower, Tor	34	2040	81	3	2.38
1965-66	Johnny Bower, Tor	35	1998	75	3	2.25
1966-67	Glenn Hall, Chi	32	1664	66	2	2.38
1967-68	Gump Worsley, Mtl	40	2213	73	6	1.98
1968-69	Jacques Plante, StL	37	2139	70	5	1.96
1969-70	Ernie Wakely, StL	30	1651	58	4	2.11
1970-71	Jacques Plante, Tor	40	2329	73	4	1.88
1971-72	Tony Esposito, Chi	48	2780	82	9	1.77
1972-73	Ken Dryden, Mtl	54	3165	119	6	2.26
1973-74	Bernie Parent, Phil	73	4314	136	12	1.89
1974-75	Bernie Parent, Phil	68	4041	137	12	2.03
1975-76	Ken Dryden, Mtl	62	3580	121	8	2.03
1976-77	Michael Larocque, Mtl	26	1525	53	4	2.09
1977-78	Ken Dryden, Mtl	52	3071	105	5	2.05
1978-79	Ken Dryden, Mtl	47	2814	108	5	2.30

Goals Against Average (Cont.)

Season	Goaltender and Club	GP	Min	GA	SO	Avg
1979-80	Bob Sauve, Buff	32	1880	74	4	2.36
1980-81	Richard Sevigny, Mtl	33	1777	71	2	2.40
1981-82	Denis Herron, Mtl	27	1547	68	3	2.64
1982-83	Pete Peeters, Bos	62	3611	142	8	2.36
1983-84	Pat Riggin, Wash	41	2299	102	4	2.66
1984-85	Tom Barrasso, Buff	54	3248	144	5	2.66
1985-86	Bob Froese, Phil	51	2728	116	5	2.55
1986-87	Brian Hayward, Mtl	37	2178	102	1	2.81
1987-88	Pete Peeters, Wash	35	1896	88	2	2.78
1988-89	Patrick Roy, Mtl	48	2744	113	4	2.47
1989-90	Patrick Roy, Mtl	54	3173	134	3	2.53
	Mike Liut, Hart-Wash	37	2161	91	4	2.53
1990-91	Ed Belfour, Chi	74	4127	170	4	2.47
1991-92	Patrick Roy, Mtl	67	3935	155	5	2.36
1992-93	*Felix Potvin, Tor	48	2781	116	2	2.50
1993-94	Dominik Hasek, Buff	58	3358	109	7	1.95
1994-95	Dominik Hasek, Buff	41	2416	85	5	2.11
1995-96	Ron Hextall, Phil	53	3102	112	4	2.17
	Chris Osgood, Det	50	2933	106	5	2.17

*Rookie.

Penalty Minutes

Season	Player and Club	GP	PIM	Season	Player and Club	GP	PIM
1918-19	Joe Hall, Mtl	17	85	1957-58	Lou Fontinato, NYR	70	152
1919-20	Cully Wilson, Tor	23	79	1958-59	Ted Lindsay, Chi	70	184
1920-21	Bert Corbeau, Mtl	24	86	1959-60	Carl Brewer, Tor	67	150
1921-22	Sprague Cleghorn, Mtl	24	63	1960-61	Pierre Pilote, Chi	70	165
1922-23	Billy Boucher, Mtl	24	52	1961-62	Lou Fontinato, Mtl	54	167
1923-24	Bert Corbeau, Tor	24	55	1962-63	Howie Young, Det	64	273
1924-25	Billy Boucher, Mtl	30	92	1963-64	Vic Hadfield, NYR	69	151
1925-26	Bert Corbeau, Tor	36	121	1964-65	Carl Brewer, Tor	70	177
1926-27	Nels Stewart, Mtl M	44	133	1965-66	Reggie Fleming, Bos-NYR	69	166
1927-28	Eddie Shore, Bos	44	165	1966-67	John Ferguson, Mtl	67	177
1928-29	Red Dutton, Mtl M	44	139	1967-68	Barclay Plager, StL	49	153
1929-30	Joe Lamb, Ott	44	119	1968-69	Forbes Kennedy, Phil-Tor	77	219
1930-31	Harvey Rockburn, Det	42	118	1969-70	Keith Magnuson, Chi	76	213
1931-32	Red Dutton, NYA	47	107	1970-71	Keith Magnuson, Chi	76	291
1932-33	Red Horner, Tor	48	144	1971-72	Brian Watson, Pitt	75	212
1933-34	Red Horner, Tor	42	126	1972-73	Dave Schultz, Phil	76	259
1934-35	Red Horner, Tor	46	125	1973-74	Dave Schultz, Phil	73	348
1935-36	Red Horner, Tor	43	167	1974-75	Dave Schultz, Phil	76	472
1936-37	Red Horner, Tor	48	124	1975-76	Steve Durbano, Pitt-KC	69	370
1937-38	Red Horner, Tor	47	82	1976-77	Dave Williams, Tor	77	338
1938-39	Red Horner, Tor	48	85	1977-78	Dave Schultz, LA-Pitt	74	405
1939-40	Red Horner, Tor	30	87	1978-79	Dave Williams, Tor	77	298
1940-41	Jimmy Orlando, Det	48	99	1979-80	Jimmy Mann, Winn	72	287
1941-42	Jimmy Orlando, Det	48	81	1980-81	Dave Williams, Van	77	343
1942-43	Jimmy Orlando, Det	40	89	1981-82	Paul Baxter, Pitt	76	409
1943-44	Mike McMahon, Mtl	42	98	1982-83	Randy Holt, Wash	70	275
1944-45	Pat Egan, Bos	48	86	1983-84	Chris Nilan, Mtl	76	338
1945-46	Jack Stewart, Det	47	73	1984-85	Chris Nilan, Mtl	77	358
1946-47	Gus Mortson, Tor	60	133	1985-86	Joey Kocur, Det	59	377
1947-48	Bill Barilko, Tor	57	147	1986-87	Tim Hunter, Cgy	73	361
1948-49	Bill Ezinicki, Tor	52	145	1987-88	Bob Probert, Det	74	398
1949-50	Bill Ezinicki, Tor	67	144	1988-89	Tim Hunter, Cgy	75	375
1950-51	Gus Mortson, Tor	60	142	1989-90	Basil McRae, Minn	66	351
1951-52	Gus Kyle, Bos	69	127	1990-91	Bob Ray, Buff	66	350
1952-53	Maurice Richard, Mtl	70	112	1991-92	Mike Peluso, Chi	63	408
1953-54	Gus Mortson, Chi	68	132	1992-93	Marty McSorley, LA	81	399
1954-55	Fern Flaman, Bos	70	150	1993-94	Tie Domi, Winn	81	347
1955-56	Lou Fontinato, NYR	70	202	1994-95	Enrico Ciccone, TB	41	225
1956-57	Gus Mortson, Chi	70	147	1995-96	Matthew Barnaby, Buff	73	335

NHL All-Star Game

First played in 1947, this game was scheduled before the start of the regular season and used to match the defending Stanley Cup champions against a squad made up of league All-Stars from other teams. In 1966 the games were moved to mid-season, although there was no game that year. The format changed to a conference versus conference showdown in 1969.

Results

Year	Site	Score	MVP	Attendance
1947	Toronto	All-Stars 4, Toronto 3	None named	14,169
1948	Chicago	All-Stars 3, Toronto 1	None named	12,794
1949	Toronto	All-Stars 3, Toronto 1	None named	13,541
1950	Detroit	Detroit 7, All-Stars 1	None named	9,166
1951	Toronto	1st team 2, 2nd team 2	None named	11,469
1952	Detroit	1st team 1, 2nd team 1	None named	10,680
1953	Montreal	All-Stars 3, Montreal 1	None named	14,153
1954	Detroit	All-Stars 2, Detroit 2	None named	10,689
1955	Detroit	Detroit 3, All-Stars 1	None named	10,111
1956	Montreal	All-Stars 1, Montreal 1	None named	13,095
1957	Montreal	All-Stars 5, Montreal 3	None named	13,003
1958	Montreal	Montreal 6, All-Stars 3	None named	13,989
1959	Montreal	Montreal 6, All-Stars 1	None named	13,818
1960	Montreal	All-Stars 2, Montreal 1	None named	13,949
1961	Chicago	All-Stars 3, Chicago 1	None named	14,534
1962	Toronto	Toronto 4, All-Stars 1	Eddie Shack, Tor	14,236
1963	Toronto	All-Stars 3, Toronto 3	Frank Mahovlich, Tor	14,034
1964	Toronto	All-Stars 3, Toronto 2	Jean Beliveau, Mtl	14,232
1965	Montreal	All-Stars 5, Montreal 2	Gordie Howe, Det	13,529
1967	Montreal	Montreal 3, All-Stars 0	Henri Richard, Mtl	14,284
1968	Toronto	Toronto 4, All-Stars 3	Bruce Gamble, Tor	15,753
1969	Montreal	East 3, West 3	Frank Mahovlich, Det	16,260
1970	St Louis	East 4, West 1	Bobby Hull, Chi	16,587
1971	Boston	West 2, East 1	Bobby Hull, Chi	14,790
1972	Minnesota	East 3, West 2	Bobby Orr, Bos	15,423
1973	NY Rangers	East 5, West 4	Greg Polis, Pitt	16,986
1974	Chicago	West 6, East 4	Garry Unger, StL	16,426
1975	Montreal	Wales 7, Campbell 1	Syl Apps Jr, Pitt	16,080
1976	Philadelphia	Wales 7, Campbell 5	Pete Mahovlich, Mtl	16,436
1977	Vancouver	Wales 4, Campbell 3	Rick Martin, Buff	15,607
1978	Buffalo	Wales 3, Campbell 2 (OT)	Billy Smith, NYI	16,433
1980	Detroit	Wales 6, Campbell 3	Reg Leach, Phil	21,002
1981	Los Angeles	Campbell 4, Wales 1	Mike Liut, StL	15,761
1982	Washington	Wales 4, Campbell 2	Mike Bossy, NYI	18,130
1983	NY Islanders	Campbell 9, Wales 3	Wayne Gretzky, Edm	15,230
1984	NJ Devils	Wales 7, Campbell 6	Don Maloney, NYR	18,939
1985	Calgary	Wales 6, Campbell 4	Mario Lemieux, Pitt	16,825
1986	Hartford	Wales 4, Campbell 3 (OT)	Grant Fuhr, Edm	15,100
1988	St Louis	Wales 6, Campbell 5 (OT)	Mario Lemieux, Pitt	17,878
1989	Edmonton	Campbell 9, Wales 5	Wayne Gretzky, LA	17,503
1990	Pittsburgh	Wales 12, Campbell 7	Mario Lemieux, Pitt	16,236
1991	Chicago	Campbell 11, Wales 5	Vince Damphousse, Tor	18,472
1992	Philadelphia	Campbell 10, Wales 6	Brett Hull, StL	17,380
1993	Montreal	Wales 16, Campbell 6	Mike Gartner, NYR	17,137
1994	NY Rangers	East 9, West 8	Mike Richter, NYR	18,200
1996	Boston	East 5, West 4	Ray Bourque, Bos	17,565

Note: The Challenge Cup, a series between the NHL All-Stars and the Soviet Union, was played instead of the All-Star Game in 1979. Eight years later, Rendez-Vous '87, a two-game series matching the Soviet Union and the NHL All-Stars, replaced the All-Star Game. The 1995 NHL All-Star game was cancelled due to a labor dispute.

Hockey Hall of Fame

Located in Toronto, the Hockey Hall of Fame was officially opened on August 26, 1961. The current chairman is Ian (Scotty) Morrison, a former NHL referee. There are, at present, 304 members of the Hockey Hall of Fame—208 players, 83 "builders," and 13 on-ice officials. To be eligible, player and referee/linesman candidates should have been out of the game for three years, but the Hall's Board of Directors can make exceptions.

Players

Sid Abel (1969)
Jack Adams (1959)
Charles (Syl) Apps (1961)
George Armstrong (1975)
Irvine (Ace) Bailey (1975)
Donald H. (Dan) Bain (1945)
Hobey Baker (1945)
Bill Barber (1990)
Marty Barry (1965)
Andy Bathgate (1978)
Jean Beliveau (1972)
Clint Benedict (1965)
Douglas Bentley (1964)
Max Bentley (1966)
Hector (Toe) Blake (1966)
Leo Boivin (1986)
Dickie Boon (1952)
Mike Bossy (1991)
Emile (Butch) Bouchard (1966)
Frank Boucher (1958)
George (Buck) Boucher (1960)
Johnny Bower (1976)
Russell Bowie (1945)
Frank Brimsek (1966)
Harry L. (Punch) Broadbent (1962)
Walter (Turk) Broda (1967)
John Bucyk (1981)
Billy Burch (1974)
Harry Cameron (1962)
Gerry Cheevers (1985)
Francis (King) Clancy (1958)
Aubrey (Dit) Clapper (1947)
Bobby Clarke (1987)
Sprague Cleghorn (1958)
Neil Colville (1967)
Charlie Conacher (1961)
Lionel Conacher (1994)
Alex Connell (1958)
Bill Cook (1952)
Fred (Bun) Cook (1995)
Arthur Coulter (1974)
Yvan Cournoyer (1982)
Bill Cowley (1968)
Samuel (Rusty) Crawford (1962)
Jack Darragh (1962)
Allan M. (Scotty) Davidson (1950)
Clarence (Hap) Day (1961)
Alex Delvecchio (1977)
Cy Denneny (1959)
Marcel Dionne (1992)
Gordie Drillon (1975)
Charles Drinkwater (1950)
Ken Dryden (1983)
Woody Dumart (1992)

Thomas Dunderdale (1974)
Bill Durnan (1964)
Mervyn A. (Red) Dutton (1958)
Cecil (Babe) Dye (1970)
Phil Esposito (1984)
Tony Esposito (1988)
Arthur F. Farrell (1965)
Ferdinand (Fern) Flaman (1990)
Frank Foyston (1958)
Frank Frederickson (1958)
Bill Gadsby (1970)
Bob Gainey (1992)
Chuck Gardiner (1945)
Herb Gardiner (1958)
Jimmy Gardner (1962)
Bernie (Boom Boom) Geoffrion (1972)
Eddie Gerard (1945)
Ed Giacomin (1987)
Rod Gilbert (1982)
Hamilton (Billy) Gilmour (1962)
Frank (Moose) Goheen (1952)
Ebenezer R. (Ebbie) Goodfellow (1963)
Mike Grant (1950)
Wilfred (Shorty) Green (1962)
Si Griffis (1950)
George Hainsworth (1961)
Glenn Hall (1975)
Joe Hall (1961)
Doug Harvey (1973)
George Hay (1958)
William (Riley) Hern (1962)
Bryan Hextall (1969)
Harry (Hap) Holmes (1972)
Tom Hooper (1962)
George (Red) Horner (1965)
Miles (Tim) Horton (1977)
Gordie Howe (1972)
Syd Howe (1965)
Harry Howell (1979)
Bobby Hull (1983)
John (Bouse) Hutton (1962)
Harry M. Hyland (1962)
James (Dick) Irvin (1958)
Harvey (Busher) Jackson (1971)
Ernest (Moose) Johnson (1952)
Ivan (Ching) Johnson (1958)
Tom Johnson (1970)
Aurel Joliat (1947)
Gordon (Duke) Keats (1958)
Leonard (Red) Kelly (1969)
Ted (Teeder) Kennedy (1966)
Dave Keon (1986)
Elmer Lach (1966)

Guy Lafleur (1988)
Edouard (Newsy) Lalonde (1950)
Jacques Laperriere (1987)
Guy LaPointe (1993)
Edgar Laprade (1993)
Jean (Jack) Laviolette (1962)
Hugh Lehman (1958)
Jacques Lemaire (1984)
Percy LeSueur (1961)
Herbert A. Lewis (1989)
Ted Lindsay (1966)
Harry Lumley (1980)
Lanny McDonald (1992)
Frank McGee (1945)
Billy McGimsie (1962)
George McNamara (1958)
Duncan (Mickey) MacKay (1952)
Frank Mahovlich (1981)
Joe Malone (1950)
Sylvio Mantha (1960)
Jack Marshall (1965)
Fred G. (Steamer) Maxwell (1962)
Stan Mikita (1983)
Dicky Moore (1974)
Patrick (Paddy) Moran (1958)
Howie Morenz (1945)
Billy Mosienko (1965)
Frank Nighbor (1947)
Reg Noble (1962)
Herbert (Buddy) O'Connor (1988)
Harry Oliver (1967)
Bert Olmstead (1985)
Bobby Orr (1979)
Bernie Parent (1984)
Brad Park (1988)
Lester Patrick (1947)
Lynn Patrick (1980)
Gilbert Perreault (1990)
Tommy Phillips (1945)
Pierre Pilote (1975)
Didier (Pit) Pitre (1962)
Jacques Plante (1978)
Denis Potvin (1991)
Walter (Babe) Pratt (1966)
Joe Primeau (1963)
Marcel Pronovost (1978)
Bob Pulford (1991)
Harvey Pulford (1945)
Hubert (Bill) Quackenbush (1976)
Frank Rankin (1961)
Jean Ratelle (1985)

Hockey Hall of Fame (Cont.)

Players (Cont.)

Claude (Chuck) Rayner (1973)
Kenneth Reardon (1966)
Henri Richard (1979)
Maurice (Rocket) Richard
   (1961)
George Richardson (1950)
Gordon Roberts (1971)
Larry Robinson (1995)
Art Ross (1945)
Blair Russel (1965)
Ernest Russell (1965)
Jack Ruttan (1962)
Serge Savard (1986)
Terry Sawchuk (1971)
Fred Scanlan (1965)
Milt Schmidt (1961)
Dave (Sweeney) Schriner
   (1962)
Earl Seibert (1963)
Oliver Seibert (1961)
Eddie Shore (1947)
Steve Shutt (1993)
Albert C. (Babe) Siebert (1964)
Harold (Bullet Joe) Simpson
   (1962)
Daryl Sittler (1989)
Alfred E. Smith (1962)
Billy Smith (1993)
Clint Smith (1991)
Reginald (Hooley) Smith (1972)
Thomas Smith (1973)
Allan Stanley (1981)
Russell (Barney) Stanley
   (1962)
John (Black Jack) Stewart
   (1964)
Nels Stewart (1962)
Bruce Stuart (1961)
Hod Stuart (1945)
Frederic (Cyclone) (O.B.E.)
   Taylor (1947)
Cecil R. (Tiny) Thompson
   (1959)
Vladislav Tretiak (1989)
Harry J. Trihey (1950)
Norm Ullman (1982)
Georges Vezina (1945)
Jack Walker (1960)
Marty Walsh (1962)
Harry Watson (1994)
Harry E. Watson (1962)
Ralph (Cooney) Weiland (1971)
Harry Westwick (1962)
Fred Whitcroft (1962)
Gordon (Phat) Wilson (1962)
Lorne (Gump) Worsley (1980)
Roy Worters (1969)

Builders

Charles Adams (1960)
Weston W. Adams (1972)
Thomas (Frank) Ahearn (1962)
John (Bunny) Ahearne (1977)
Montagu Allan (C.V.O.) (1945)
Keith Allen (1992)
Harold Ballard (1977)
David Bauer (1989)
John Bickell (1978)
Scott Bowman (1991)
George V. Brown (1961)
Walter A. Brown (1962)
Frank Buckland (1975)
Jack Butterfield (1980)
Frank Calder (1947)
Angus D. Campbell (1964)
Clarence Campbell (1966)
Joe Cattarinich (1977)
Joseph (Leo) Dandurand
   (1963)
Francis Dilio (1964)
George S. Dudley (1958)
James A. Dunn (1968)
Robert Alan Eagleson (1989)
Emile Francis (1982)
Jack Gibson (1976)
Tommy Gorman (1963)
Frank Griffiths (1993)
William Hanley (1986)
Charles Hay (1974)
James C. Hendy (1968)
Foster Hewitt (1965)
William Hewitt (1947)
Fred J. Hume (1962)
George (Punch) Imlach (1984)
Tommy Ivan (1974)
William M. Jennings (1975)
Bob Johnson (1992)
Gordon W. Juckes (1979)
John Kilpatrick (1960)
Seymour Knox III (1993)
George Leader (1969)
Robert LeBel (1970)
Thomas F. Lockhart (1965)
Paul Loicq (1950)
Frederic McLaughlin (1963)
John Mariucci (1985)
Frank Mathers (1992)
John (Jake) Milford (1984)
Hartland Molson (1973)
Francis Nelson (1947)
Bruce A. Norris (1969)
James Norris, Sr. (1958)
James D. Norris (1962)
William M. Northey (1947)
John O'Brien (1962)
Brian O'Neill (1994)

Builders (Cont.)

Fred Page (1993)
Frank Patrick (1958)
Allan W. Pickard (1958)
Rudy Pilous (1985)
Norman (Bud) Poile (1990)
Samuel Pollock (1978)
Donat Raymond (1958)
John Robertson (1947)
Claude C. Robinson (1947)
Philip D. Ross (1976)
Gunther Sabetzki (1995)
Frank J. Selke (1960)
Harry Sinden (1983)
Frank D. Smith (1962)
Conn Smythe (1958)
Edward M. Snider (1988)
Lord Stanley of Preston
   (G.C.B.) (1945)
James T. Sutherland (1947)
Anatoli V. Tarasov (1974)
Bill Torrey (1995)
Lloyd Turner (1958)
William Tutt (1978)
Carl Potter Voss (1974)
Fred C. Waghorn (1961)
Arthur Wirtz (1971)
Bill Wirtz (1976)
John A. Ziegler, Jr. (1987)
Neil Armstrong (1991)

Referees/Linesmen

John Ashley (1981)
William L. Chadwick (1964)
John D'Amico (1993)
Chaucer Elliott (1961)
George Hayes (1988)
Robert W. Hewitson (1963)
Fred J. (Mickey) Ion (1961)
Matt Pavelich (1987)
Mike Rodden (1962)
J. Cooper Smeaton (1961)
Roy (Red) Storey (1967)
Frank Udvari (1973)

Note: Year of election to the Hall of Fame is in parentheses after the member's name.

Tennis

Sports Illustrated

Peter the Great

Pete Sampras wins his fourth U.S. Open

MANNY MILLAN

Simply the Best

Though troubled by off-court turmoil, Pete Sampras and Steffi Graf held serve as tennis's titans

by Alexander Wolff

TWO VERY familiar twentysomethings spent the year imposing themselves on a tennis world long since inured to their dominance. Steffi Graf won every Grand Slam tournament she entered, leaving her with 21 for her career and putting her, at age 27, well within reach of Margaret Court's record of 24. Meanwhile Pete Sampras spent more time than any other man atop the computer rankings. But inasmuch as Sampras measures himself at season's end not by some enumerative printout but by Slams won, all that mattered was this: At the U.S. Open he won his eighth Grand Slam title, placing him, at 25, only four shy of Roy Emerson's mark.

That, on the surface, was the tennis year—two wondrously talented players advancing ineluctably through the primes of their careers. But to fully fathom the handiwork of Graf and Sampras, one must avert one's eyes from the court, away from her maddening slice backhand and his confounding first serve, to parallel stories being played out off it. The press treated these two extracurricular tales as melodrama, but

to the respective champions ensnared in them, they were psychodramas. And that neither Graf nor Sampras was undone by the mental strain of these backstories— each of which featured the tennis person closest to them—only caused their achievements to stand out more boldly in relief.

Graf's father, Peter—her mentor, coach and Svengali—had spent all of the year in a prison cell in Mannheim, awaiting trial in a German court on charges of failing to pay taxes on some $28 million of his daughter's winnings. The trial actually began during the second week of the U.S. Open, a trick of timing that very nearly caused Graf to opt out of the final Grand Slam event of the season. But she played anyway and proved why, in a women's game fraught with sudden flameouts and ill-fated comebacks, she has been a model of Teutonic stolidity. A year earlier she had fled the interview room in tears after winning the same event, so unnerving were her father's legal troubles. But after her 7–5, 6–4 defeat of Monica Seles in the finals at Flushing Meadow, with the most ornery thunder-

Graf extended her career Grand Slam total to 21, just three shy of Court's record.

storm mustering around her, she let out a scream, as if she were mocking the gods. "You go through different emotions when you win," she would say moments later, after fleeing the rainswept stadium court. "Sometimes you feel like crying. Sometimes you feel like screaming. Today I was definitely in the screaming mode."

For Sampras, the death in May of his longtime coach and confidant, former pro Tim Gullikson, of brain cancer, was a storm cloud in its own right, hanging over his Grand Slam season. Again and again Sampras tried to win one for his late friend, beginning with the Australian Open (where he lost in the third round to hometown favorite Mark Philipoussis), continuing at the French (where he was ushered out in the semis by eventual champion Yevgeny Kafelnikov) and again at the Slam that he had won three straight times, Wimbledon (where that event's ultimate titlist, Richard Krajicek, upset him in the quarters).

MANNY MILLAN

"I've thought about not having Tim in my life," Sampras had said shortly before Gullikson's death. "And though it's hard saying it, I might not care if I win or lose." For a while he seemed not to care. At the funeral, where he served as a pallbearer, Sampras tried reading a eulogy, but couldn't finish. He made a gift of his 1993 Wimbledon platter to Gullikson's family and pulled out of the next two tour events, repairing to Tampa, where for a couple of weeks he couldn't bring himself to train.

But the player Gullikson liked to call the game's "gold standard" noticed the French Open looming on the calendar, and that was the one Grand Slam he had never won, the tournament Gullikson and he had been shooting for—the sport's great test on clay, the surface least suited to Sampras's serve-and-volley game. Though he wouldn't triumph there this year either, Sampras was gallant at Roland Garros, winning five-set matches from two-time French Open champion Sergi Bruguera, fellow hard-serving American Todd Martin and another two-time winner in Paris, Jim Courier, before Kafelnikov took him out. At Wimbledon he stumbled, but then every other favorite did too, in an event marked by the exit of a record 10 seeded players in the first week and the first-ever men's final involving two

Hingis had plenty to smile about at the U.S. Open, where she reached three semis.

me," Sampras said. "But I can play for myself now."

In other respects, "ex-" marked the tennis year:

• There was the extended: the new 29-inch rackets. Other than the prototypical weekend hacker, who suddenly had at his or her disposal more power, spin and control, no player benefited more from these "power sticks" than the 5'9" Chang, who rose to No. 2 in the rankings while reaching the finals of two of his last four Grand Slam events. As testimony to the benefit of his new prosthesis, Chang served up 16 aces while beating Andre Agassi in their U.S. Open semifinal and began routinely zinging first serves up to 125 mph after a career stuck around 110.

unseeded players, Krajicek and MaliVai Washington.

It took until September, and the U.S. Open, for Sampras to win his Grand Slam for Gully. No moment better stood for Gullikson's spirit than Sampras's performance in the quarterfinals against Spain's Alex Corretja. After nearly four hours on the stadium court, Sampras became ill two points into the fifth-set tiebreaker. He upchucked behind the baseline, then served—and won—a point with puke streaming from his nostrils. "If it was a boxing match, the ref would have called it," Sampras would say afterward. "Thank god we're not boxing."

He went on to win the final 6–1, 6–4, 7–6 over Michael Chang on the very day that Gullikson would have celebrated his 45th birthday. Sampras had finally carved out the strokes of an epitaph. "Tim's still with

"It's almost as if I'm gaining a little bit of height," Chang said. To keep such rangy boomers as Martin, Krajicek and Goran Ivanisevic from picking up 32-inch rackets and becoming all but unreturnable, the International Tennis Federation moved quickly to limit rackets to 29 inches, effective Jan. 1, 1997.

• There were outsized expectations for three 15-year-olds—Switzerland's Martina Hingis, Russia's Anna Kournikova and Venus Williams of the U.S.—who just beat new WTA rules, designed to keep teenage girls from joining Andrea Jaeger and Jennifer Capriati in the phenom graveyard, which limit the extent to which those 17 and under can play the tour. The most advanced of this tyro trio was Hingis, who reached the semifinals of the U.S. Open not only in singles, where she lost to Graf 7–5, 6–3, but in doubles and mixed doubles as well.

• There was the excruciating: the pain in Monica Seles's shoulder, which sidelined her for 15 weeks and left her so vulnerable that she lost to Jana Novotna in the French and in the Olympics.

• There were the exceptions to the Graf-Sampras rule: At the Australian Open, which she had won in 1991, '92 and '93 before taking a knife in her back from unemployed German lathe operator Günther Parche, Seles won another women's crown, while Boris Becker took his first Grand Slam title in five years.

• There was exhibitionism, delivered at Wimbledon by 23-year-old pizza vendor Melissa Johnson, who, moments before the men's final, dashed onto Centre Court wearing nothing but (in the spirit of pizza vending) an apron. This occasioned the following veddy, veddy British statement from the panjandrums of the All England Lawn Tennis Club: "Whilst we do not wish to condone the practice, it did at least provide some light amusement for our loyal and patient supporters, who have had a trying time during the recent bad weather."

• There was excessive exposure: John McEnroe, under contract to USA, NBC and CBS, jabbered and yapped on more networks than a typical presidential candidate.

• There was the regal exit of Stefan Edberg, whose swaybacked serve and classic volleys graced 54 straight Grand Slam events, six of which the phlegmatic Swede wound up winning. Though only 30, he had sunk steadily in the rankings and figured the time had come to bow out. "If I'm going to be out there, I want to be in the top 10 and really have a chance of winning a Grand Slam," Edberg said. "I've been on the tour now for many, many years. It's time for me to go now, before it's too late." Of course, if the examples of his countrymen Bjorn Borg and Mats Wilander are any guide, Edberg will get restless in retirement and imprudently launch a comeback.

• There was exurban splendor at the Atlanta Olympics; some 16 miles from the hurly-burly of the Games, at bucolic Stone Moun-tain Park, three of the four golds went to American entrants—Agassi and Lindsay Davenport in singles and the team of Mary Joe Fernandez and Gigi Fernandez in women's doubles. The Woodies of Oz, Australia's Mark Woodforde and Todd Woodbridge, won the men's doubles, and Leander Paes of India, with his bronze, delivered to the world's second-most-populous country only its 15th Olympic medal in 48 years.

• And there was excitation—the ongoing controversies over the rankings on both the men's and the women's tours. As a result of having been forced off the circuit by Parche's attack, Seles had been decreed the co–No. 1 player upon her return, and after six tournaments was granted a special ranking formula that will persist into 1997. This arrangement seemed more and more outdated as the season progressed, given the way Graf ruled, and Seles graciously acknowledged as much after losing the U.S. Open final. "Steffi clearly is number one," she said. "Everyone can see that."

On the men's side, the rankings controversy first centered on Thomas Muster. He's the laconic Austrian clay-courter from Arnold Schwarzenegger's home province and nicknamed the Mus-Terminator, who held the top spot briefly in February and March, largely because he had won virtually every dirt-track event he entered. But few in the game considered him much more than a one-trick pony. "I don't see him as number one in the world on anything but clay," said Sampras. "And I think people know that." After Muster failed to win the crown jewel of mud wrestles, the French, he never again threatened to retake the top spot, and the controversy died down.

Roland Garros went to Kafelnikov, the 22-year-old Russian who figured in the year's other ranking contretemps: a near-revolt by male pros after the U.S. Tennis Association at first ignored the ATP rankings in determining the seedings for the U.S. Open, and then "redrew" the tournament bracket when the players, believing the draw was being rejiggered to please

BOB MARTIN

incarcerated her father, and that injuries nagged her for much of the season. Said Chanda Rubin, the American upstart whom Graf slapped down in the finals of March's Lipton International, "With someone like Arantxa [Sánchez Vicario] or Monica, there's just not quite the same oppressiveness as Graf."

As for Sampras, though he needed that U.S. Open title at the end of the season to meet his own criteria for a successful year, he had foreshadowed how he would end the season. Back in December, playing under the guidance of Gully's twin brother, Tom, the U.S. team captain, against Russia in the Davis Cup final in Moscow, he had strung together three remarkable days of tennis. Following a 3½-hour, five-set singles defeat of Andrei Chesnokov, he cramped up and had to be carried off the court. Yet Sampras came back the next day to team with Martin to win the doubles. And the next day, with the U.S. leading Russia two matches to one, he dispatched Kafelnikov in straight sets.

American television, threatened a boycott of future Grand Slam events. Kafelnikov, the No. 4 player in the world, who was somehow seeded seventh for the Open, bolted in a huff nonetheless, pointing out that, given the draw, none of the three top Americans—Sampras (No. 1 in the world), Chang (then No. 3) and Agassi (then No. 8)—could meet before the semifinals.

In the end, none of these spats would really matter. Sampras and Graf had the whole thing wired. Graf lost three matches all year. She has now spent nearly seven years—half of her career—in her aerie atop the rankings. Nowadays if Fraulein Forehand so much as enters a Slam, she wins it: Injuries kept her out of the last two Australian Opens, but she's six for her last six Grand Slams otherwise. "It's an incredible achievement by itself," she said, scarcely needing to add that it was even more incredible given that she hadn't been entirely cleared of the legal troubles that

When Sampras was named at the last minute to replace Agassi, Kafelnikov had rather undiplomatically suggested that Sampras would be the lesser opponent, especially in a short series involving doubles and played on clay.

"I guess they don't know Pete," said Tom Gullikson. "I would take him on my side for one-on-one tennis, two-on-two, three-on-three, any surface. I would take him for golf."

As it was, Sampras and Graf only had tennis—and their own complicated emotions—to worry about. But lord over both, both ultimately did.

FOR THE RECORD·1995–1996

1996 Grand Slam Champions

Australian Open
Men's Singles

	Winner	Finalist	Score
Quarterfinals	Mark Woodforde ....Thomas Enqvist (7)		6-4, 6-4, 6-4
	Boris Becker (4) ....Yevgeny Kafelnikov (6)		6-4, 7-6 (11-9), 6-1
	Michael Chang (5) ....Mikael Tillstrom		6-0, 6-2, 6-4
	Andre Agassi (2) ....Jim Courier (8)		6-7 (7-9), 2-6, 6-3, 6-4, 6-2
Semifinals	Boris Becker...........................Mark Woodforde		6-4, 6-2, 6-0
	Michael Chang.......................Andre Agassi		6-1, 6-4, 7-6 (7-1)
Final	Boris Becker...........................Michael Chang		6-2, 6-4, 2-6, 6-2

Women's Singles

	Winner	Finalist	Score
Quarterfinals	Amanda Coetzer (16)..............Martina Hingis		7-5, 4-6, 6-1
	Anke Huber (8).......................Conchita Martinez (2)		4-6, 6-2, 6-1
	Chanda Rubin (13)..................Arantxa Sánchez Vicario (3)		6-4, 2-6, 16-14
	Monica Seles (1) ....Iva Majoli (7)		6-1, 6-2
Semifinals	Anke Huber ....Amanda Coetzer		4-6, 6-4, 6-2
	Monica Seles..........................Chanda Rubin		6-7 (2-7), 6-1, 7-5
Final	Monica Seles..........................Anke Huber		6-4, 6-1

Doubles

	Winner	Finalist	Score
Men's Final	Stefan Edberg/.......................Sebastien Lareau/ Petr Korda	Alex O'Brien	7-5, 7-5, 4-6, 6-1
Women's Final	Chanda Rubin/.......................Lindsay Davenport/ Arantxa Sánchez Vicario (8)	Gigi Fernandez (3)	7-5, 2-6, 6-4
Mixed Final	Larisa Neilend/.......................Nicole Arendt/ Mark Woodforde (1)	Luke Jensen	4-6, 7-5, 6-0

French Open
Men's Singles

	Winner	Finalist	Score
Quarterfinals	Pete Sampras (1) ....Jim Courier (7)		6-7 (4-7), 4-6, 6-4, 6-4, 6-4
	Yevgeny Kafelnikov (6) ....Richard Krajicek (13)		6-3, 6-4, 6-7 (4-7), 6-2
	Marc Rosset (14).....................Bernd Karbacher		4-6, 4-6, 6-3, 7-5, 6-0
	Michael Stich (15) ....Cedric Pioline		6-4, 4-6, 6-3, 6-2
Semifinals	Yevgeny Kafelnikov.................Pete Sampras		7-6 (7-4), 6-0, 6-2
	Michael Stich ....Marc Rosset		6-3, 6-4, 6-2
Final	Yevgeny Kafelnikov.................Michael Stich		7-6 (7-4), 7-5, 7-6 (7-4)

Women's Singles

	Winner	Finalist	Score
Quarterfinals	Steffi Graf (1)..........................Iva Majoli (5)		6-3, 6-1
	Conchita Martinez (3)..............Lindsay Davenport (9)		6-1, 6-3
	Jana Novotna (10)...................Monica Seles (1)		7-6 (9-7), 6-3
	Arantxa Sánchez Vicario (4) ...Karina Habsudova		6-2, 6-7 (4-7), 10-8
Semifinals	Steffi Graf ....Conchita Martinez		6-3, 6-1
	Arantxa Sánchez Vicario.........Jana Novotna		6-3, 7-5
Final	Steffi Graf ....Arantxa Sánchez Vicario		6-3, 6-7 (4-7), 10-8

Note: Seedings in parentheses.

French Open *(Cont.)*
Doubles

	Winner	Finalist	Score
Men's Final	Yevgeny Kafelnikov/	Guy Forget/	6-2, 6-3
	Daniel Vacek (7)	Jakob Hlasek (5)	
Women's Final	Lindsay Davenport/	Gigi Fernandez/	6-2, 6-1
	Mary Joe Fernandez (4)	Natasha Zvereva (2)	
Mixed Final	Patricia Tarabini/	Nicole Arendt/	6-2, 6-2
	Javier Frana	Luke Jensen	

Wimbledon
Men's Singles

	Winner	Finalist	Score
Quarterfinals	Richard Krajicek	Pete Sampras (1)	7-5, 7-6 (7-3), 6-4
	Jason Stoltenberg	Goran Ivanisevic (4)	6-3, 7-6 (7-3), 6-7 (3-7), 7-6 (7-3)
	Todd Martin (13)	Tim Henman	7-6 (7-5), 7-6 (7-2), 6-4
	MaliVai Washington	Alex Radulescu	6-7 (5-7), 7-6 (7-1), 5-7, 7-6 (7-3), 6-4
Semifinals	Richard Krajicek	Jason Stoltenberg	7 5, 6 2, 6-1
	MaliVai Washington	Todd Martin	5-7, 6-4, 6-7, 6-3, 10-8
Final	Richard Krajicek	MaliVai Washington	6-3, 6-4, 6-3

Women's Singles

	Winner	Finalist	Score
Quarterfinals	Kimiko Date (12)	Mary Pierce (13)	3-6, 6-3, 6-1
	Steffi Graf (1)	Jana Novotna (6)	6-3, 6-2
	Meredith McGrath	Mary Joe Fernandez (9)	6-3, 6-1
	Arantxa Sánchez Vicario (4)	Judith Wiesner	6-4, 6-0
Semifinals	Steffi Graf	Kimiko Date	6-2, 2-6, 6-3
	Arantxa Sánchez Vicario	Meredith McGrath	6-1, 6-1
Final	Steffi Graf	Arantxa Sánchez Vicario	6-3, 7-5

Doubles

	Winner	Finalist	Score
Men's Final	Todd Woodbridge/	Byron Black/	4-6, 6-1, 6-3, 6-2
	Mark Woodforde (1)	Grant Connell (3)	
Women's Final	Martina Hingis/	Meredith McGrath/	5-7, 7-5, 6-1
	Helena Sukova (8)	Larisa Neiland (4)	
Mixed Final	Helena Sukova/	Larisa Neiland/	1-6, 6-3, 6-2
	Cyril Suk (7)	Mark Woodforde (1)	

U.S. Open
Men's Singles

	Winner	Finalist	Score
Quarterfinals	Pete Sampras (1)	Alex Corretja	7-6 (7-5), 5-7, 5-7, 6-4, 7-6 (9-7)
	Goran Ivanisevic (4)	Stefan Edberg	6-3, 6-4, 7-6 (11-9)
	Andre Agassi (6)	Thomas Muster (3)	6-2, 7-5, 4-6, 6-2
	Michael Chang (2)	Javier Sanchez	7-5, 6-3, 6-7 (2-7), 6-3
Semifinals	Pete Sampras	Goran Ivanisevic	6-3, 6-4, 6-7 (9-11), 6-3
	Michael Chang	Andre Agassi	6-3, 6-2, 6-2
Final	Pete Sampras	Michael Chang	6-1, 6-4, 7-6 (7-3)

Note: Seedings in parentheses.

U.S. Open *(Cont.)*

Women's Singles

	Winner	Finalist	Score
Quarterfinals	Steffi Graf (1)	Judith Wiesner	7-5, 6-3
	Martina Hingis (16)	Jana Novotna (7)	7-6 (7-1), 6-4
	Conchita Martinez (4)	Linda Wild	7-6 (8-6), 6-0
	Monica Seles (2)	Amanda Coetzer	6-0, 6-3
Semifinals	Steffi Graf	Martina Hingis	7-5, 6-3
	Monica Seles	Conchita Martinez	6-4, 6-3
Final	Steffi Graf	Monica Seles	7-5, 6-4

Doubles

	Winner	Finalist	Score
Men's Final	Todd Woodbridge/ Mark Woodforde (1)	Paul Haarhuis/ Jacco Eltingh (8)	4-6, 7-6 (7-5), 7-6 (7-2)
Women's Final	Gigi Fernandez/ Natasha Zvereva (2)	Jana Novotna/ Arantxa Sánchez Vicario (1)	1-6, 6-1, 6-4
Mixed Final	Lisa Raymond/ Patrick Galbraith (3)	Manon Bollegraf/ Rick Leach (4)	7-6 (8-6), 7-6 (7-4)

Note: Seedings in parentheses.

Major Tournament Results

Men's Tour (late 1995)

Date	Tournament	Site	Winner	Finalist	Score
Sept 11-17	Romanian Open	Bucharest	Thomas Muster	Gilbert Schaller	6-4, 6-3
Sept 25-Oct 1	Swiss Indoors	Basel	Jim Courier	Jan Siemerink	6-7 (2-7), 7-6 (7-5), 5-7, 6-2, 7-5
Oct 9-15	Seiko Super Tennis	Tokyo	Michael Chang	Mark Philippoussis	5-7, 6-4, 6-4
Oct 16-22	Grand Prix de Tennis	Lyon, France	Wayne Ferreira	Pete Sampras	7-6 (7-2), 5-7, 6-3
Oct 23-29	Eurocard Open	Essen, Germany	Thomas Muster	MaliVai Washington	7-6 (8-6), 2-6, 6-3, 6-4
Oct 30-Nov 5	Paris Open	Paris	Pete Sampras	Boris Becker	7-6 (7-5), 6-4, 6-4
Nov 6-12	Stockholm Open	Stockholm	Thomas Enqvist	Arnaud Boetsch	7-5, 6-4
Nov 14-19	ATP Tour World Championships	Frankfurt	Boris Becker	Michael Chang	7-6 (7-3), 6-0, 7-6 (7-5)

Men's Tour (through September 29, 1996)

Date	Tournament	Site	Winner	Finalist	Score
Jan 15-28	Australian Open	Melbourne	Boris Becker	Michael Chang	6-2, 6-4, 2-6, 6-2
Feb 12-18	Dubai Open	Dubai, United Arab Emirates	Goran Ivanisevic	Alberto Costa	6-4, 6-3
Feb 19-25	European Championship	Antwerp, Belgium	Michael Stich	Goran Ivanisevic	6-3, 6-2, 7-6 (7-5)
Feb 19-25	Kroger St. Jude	Memphis	Pete Sampras	Todd Martin	6-4, 7-6 (7-2)
Feb 26-Mar 3	Italian Indoors	Milan	Goran Ivanisevic	Marc Rosset	6-3, 7-6 (7-3)
Feb 26-Mar 3	U.S. Indoor	Philadelphia	Jim Courier	Chris Woodruff	6-4, 6-3
Mar 4-10	ABM/AMRO World	Rotterdam, Netherlands	Goran Ivanisevic	Yevgeny Kafelnikov	6-4, 3-6, 6-3
Mar 11-17	Champions Cup	Indian Wells, California	Michael Chang	Paul Haarhuis	7-5, 6-1, 6-1
Mar 21-31	Lipton Championships	Key Biscayne, Florida	Andre Agassi	Goran Ivanisevic	3-0, 40-0 retired
Apr 15-21	Japan Open	Tokyo	Pete Sampras	Richey Reneberg	6-4, 7-5
Apr 15-21	Barcelona Open	Barcelona	Thomas Muster	Marcelo Rios	6-3, 4-6, 6-4, 6-1
Apr 22-28	Monte Carlo Open	Monte Carlo, Monaco	Thomas Muster	Alberto Costa	6-3, 5-7, 4-6, 6-3, 6-2
May 6-12	German Open	Hamburg	Roberto Carretero	Alex Corretja	2-6, 6-4, 6-4, 6-4
May 13-19	Italian Open	Rome	Thomas Muster	Richard Krajicek	6-2, 6-4, 3-6, 6-3
May 27-June 9	French Open	Paris	Yevgeny Kafelnikov	Michael Stich	7-6 (7-4), 7-5, 7-6 (7-4)

Men's Tour (through September 29, 1996) *(Cont.)*

Date	Tournament	Site	Winner	Finalist	Score
June 17-23	Gerry Weber Open	Halle, Germany	Nicklas Kulti	Yevgeny Kafelnikov	6-7 (5-7), 6-3, 6-4
June 24-July 7	Wimbledon	Wimbledon	Richard Krajicek	MaliVai Washington	6-3, 6-4, 6-3
July 15-21	Mercedes Cup	Stuttgart	Thomas Muster	Yevgeny Kafelnikov	6-2, 6-2, 6-4
July 23-Aug 3	Atlanta Olympics	Atlanta	Andre Agassi	Sergi Bruguera	6-2, 6-3, 6-1
Aug 5-11	ATP Championship	Cincinnati	Andre Agassi	Michael Chang	7-6 (7-4), 6-4
Aug 12-18	RCA Championships	Indianapolis	Pete Sampras	Goran Ivanisevic	7-6 (7-3), 7-5
Aug 12-18	PilotPen International	New Haven	Alex O'Brien	Jan Siemerink	7-6 (8-6), 6-4
Aug 19-25	du Maurier Open	Toronto	Wayne Ferreira	Todd Woodbridge	6-2, 6-4
Aug 26-Sept 8	U.S. Open	New York	Pete Sampras	Michael Chang	6-1, 6-4, 7-6 (7-3)
Sept 23-29	Swiss Indoors	Basel, Switzerland	Pete Sampras	Hendrik Dreekmann	7-5, 6-2, 6-0

Women's Tour (late 1995)

Date	Tournament	Site	Winner	Finalist	Score
Sept 18-24	Nichirei International Ladies Championships	Tokyo	Mary Pierce	Arantxa Sánchez Vicario	6-3, 6-3
Sept 25-Oct 1	Sparkassen Cup	Leipzig	Anke Huber	Magdalena Maleeva	walkover
Oct 2-8	European Indoors	Zurich	Iva Majoli	Mary Pierce	6-4, 6-4
Oct 9-15	Porsche Tennis Grand Prix	Filderstadt, Germany	Iva Majoli	Gabriela Sabatini	6-4, 7-6 (7-4)
Oct 17-22	Brighton International	Brighton, England	Mary Joe Fernandez	Amanda Coetzer	6-4, 7-5
Oct 30-Nov 5	Bank of the West Classic	Oakland, CA	Magdalena Maleeva	Ai Sugiyama	6-3, 6-4
Nov 6-12	Advanta Championships	Philadelphia	Steffi Graf-	Lori McNeil	6-1, 4-6, 6-3
Nov 13-19	WTA Tour Championships	New York	Steffi Graf	Anke Huber	6-1, 2-6, 6-1, 4-6, 6-3

Women's Tour (through October 6, 1996)

Date	Tournament	Site	Winner	Finalist	Score
Jan 8-14	Peters International	Sydney	Monica Seles	Lindsay Davenport	4-6, 7-6 (9-7), 6-3
Jan 15-27	Australian Open	Melbourne	Monica Seles	Anke Huber	6-4, 6-1
Jan 30-Feb 4	Pan Pacific Open	Tokyo	Iva Majoli	Arantxa Sánchez Vicario	6-4, 6-1
Feb 13-18	Open Gaz de France	Paris	Julie Halard-Decugis	Iva Majoli	7-5, 7-6 (7-4)
Feb 19-25	Nokia Grand Prix	Essen, Ger.	Iva Majoli	Jana Novotna	7-5, 1-6, 7-6 (8-6)
Mar 8-16	State Farm Evert Cup	Indian Wells, California	Steffi Graf	Conchita Martinez	7-6 (7-5), 7-6 (7-5)
Mar 21-31	Lipton Championships	Key Biscayne, Florida	Steffi Graf	Chanda Rubin	6-1, 6-3
Apr 1-7	Family Circle Cup	Hilton Head, S Carolina	Arantxa Sánchez Vicario	Barbara Paulus	6-2, 2-6, 6-2
Apr 8-14	Bausch & Lomb Championships	Amelia Island, Florida	Irina Spirlea	Mary Pierce	6-7 (7-9), 6-4, 6-3
Apr 30-May 5	Hamburg Open Cup	Hamburg	Arantxa Sánchez Vicario	Conchita Martinez	4-6, 7-6 (7-4), 6-0
May 6-12	Italian Open	Rome	Conchita Martinez	Martina Hingis	6-2, 6-3
May 13-19	German Open	Berlin	Steffi Graf	Karina Habsudova	4-6, 6-2, 7-5
May 21-25	Open Ford International Championships of Spain	Madrid	Jana Novotna	Magdalena Maleeva	4-6, 6-4, 6-3
May 27-June 8	French Open	Paris	Steffi Graf	Arantxa Sánchez Vicario	6-3, 6-7 (4-7) 10-8
June 17-22	Direct Line Insurance Int'l Championships	Eastbourne, England	Monica Seles	Mary Joe Fernandez	6-0, 6-2
June 24-July 6	Wimbledon Championships	Wimbledon	Steffi Graf	Arantxa Sánchez Vicario	6-3, 7-5

Women's Tour (through October 6, 1996) *(Cont.)*

Date	Tournament	Site	Winner	Finalist	Score
July 23-Aug 2	Atlanta Olympics	Atlanta	Lindsay Davenport	Arantxa Sánchez Vicario	7-6 (8-6), 6-2
Aug 5-11	du Maurier Open	Montreal	Monica Seles	Arantxa Sánchez Vicario	6-1, 7-6 (7-2)
Aug 12-18	Acura Classic	Manhattan Beach, Cal.	Lindsay Davenport	Anke Huber	6-2, 6-3
Aug 19-25	Toshiba Tennis Classic	San Diego	Kimiko Date	Arantxa Sánchez Vicario	3-6, 6-3, 6-0
Aug 26-Sept 8	U.S. Open	New York	Steffi Graf	Monica Seles	7-5, 6-4
Sept 16-22	Nichirei International Ladies Open	Tokyo	Monica Seles	Arantxa Sánchez Vicario	6-1, 6-4
Sept 30-Oct 6	Sparkassen Cup	Leipzig	Anke Huber	Iva Majoli	5-7, 6-3, 6-1

1995 Singles Leaders

Men

Rank	Player	Tournament Wins	Match Record	Earnings ($)
1	Pete Sampras	5	72-16	5,415,066
2	Andre Agassi	7	73-9	2,975,738
3	Thomas Muster	12	86-18	2,887,979
4	Boris Becker	2	54-18	3,712,358
5	Michael Chang	4	65-18	2,555,870
6	Yevgeny Kafelnikov	4	73-32	1,841,561
7	Thomas Enqvist	5	63-23	1,819,398
8	Jim Courier	4	61-22	1,202,769
9	Wayne Ferreira	4	58-26	1,276,216
10	Goran Ivanisevic	1	46-24	3,777,862
11	Richard Krajicek	2	41-26	925,822
12	Michael Stich	1	47-19	853,974
13	Sergi Bruguera	0	40-19	2,058,044
14	Arnaud Boetsch	1	45-33	607,535
15	Marc Rosset	2	40-22	570,786
16	Andrei Medvedev	1	41-26	922,692
17	Magnus Larsson	0	35-15	702,245
18	Todd Martin	1	47-25	1,455,558
19	Paul Haarhuis	1	34-25	1,005,587
20	Gilbert Schaller	1	43-30	426,568

Note: Compiled by the Association of Tennis Professionals (ATP).

Women

Rank	Player	Tournament Wins	Match Record	Earnings ($)
1	Steffi Graf	9	47-2	2,538,620
*1	Monica Seles	1	11-1	397,010
2	Conchita Martinez	6	63-10	1,186,845
3	Arantxa Sánchez Vicario	2	49-15	1,073,169
4	Kimiko Date	1	41-12	607,113
5	Mary Pierce	2	37-16	680,088
6	Magdalena Maleeva	0	35-11	484,951
7	Gabriela Sabatini	1	44-17	594,808
8	Mary Joe Fernandez	2	31-15	427,659
9	Iva Majoli	2	29-12	467,871
10	Anke Huber	1	42-17	607,922
11	Jana Novotna	1	30-12	394,523
12	Lindsay Davenport	1	33-13	319,914
13	Brenda Schultz-McCarthy	2	41-16	411,906
14	Natasha Zvereva	0	31-17	400,017
15	Chanda Rubin	1	43-19	326,523
16	Martina Hingis	0	22-13	147,154
17	Naoko Sawamatsu	0	24-13	168,407
18	Amy Frazier	1	28-15	193,139
19	Amanda Coetzer	2	34-22	263,256
20	Lisa Raymond	0	25-16	176,438

*Co-ranked number one for her first six tournaments.
Note: Compiled by the Women's Tennis Association (WTA).

National Team Competition

1995 Davis Cup World Group Final

United States d. Russia 3-2, Dec 1-3 in Moscow
  Pete Sampras (U.S.) d. Andrei Chesnokov (Rus) 3-6, 6-4, 6-3, 6-7 (5-7), 6-4
  Yevgeny Kafelnikov (Rus) d. Jim Courier (U.S.) 7-6, 7-5, 6-3
  Pete Sampras/Todd Martin (Swe) d. Yevgeny Kafelnikov/Andrei Olhovskiy (Rus) 7-5, 6-4, 6-3
  Pete Sampras (U.S.) d. Yevgeny Kafelnikov (Rus) 6-2, 6-4, 7-6 (7-4)
  Andrei Chesnokov (Rus) d. Jim Courier (U.S.) 6-7 (1-7), 7-5, 6-0

1996 Davis Cup World Group Tournament

FIRST ROUND

Italy d. Russia 3-2
South Africa d. Austria 3-2
Germany d. Switzerland 5-0
France d. Denmark 5-0
India d. Netherlands 3-2
Sweden d. Belgium 4-1
Czech Republic d. Hungary 5-0
United States d. Mexico 5-0

QUARTER FINAL ROUND

Italy d. South Africa 4-1
France d. Germany 5-0
Sweden d. India 5-0
Czech Republic d. United States 3-2

SEMIFINALS

France d. Italy 3-2
  Andrea Gaudenzi (Italy) d. Cedric Pioline (France) 5-7, 6-1, 7-6 (7-4), 6-3
  Renzo Furlan (Italy) d. Arnaud Boetsch (France) 7-5, 1-6, 6-3, 7-6 (7-5)
  Guy Forget/Guillaume Raoux (France) d. Andrea Gaudenzi/Diego Nargiso (Italy) 6-3, 6-4, 6-2
  Cedric Pioline (France) d. Renzo Furlan (Italy) 6-3, 2-6, 6-2, 6-4
  Arnaud Boetsch (France) d. Andrea Gaudenzi (Italy) 6-4, 6-2, 7-6 (10-8)

Sweden d. Czech Republic 4-1
  Thomas Enqvist (Swe) d. Petr Korda (Cze) 6-4, 6-3, 7-6 (11-9)
  Stefan Edberg (Swe) d. Daniel Vacek (Cze) 7-6 (7-2) 7-5, 4-6, 6-3
  Petr Korda/Daniel Vacek (Cze) d. Jonas Bjorkman/Nicklas Kulti (Swe) 4-6, 6-3, 6-4, 6-4
  Thomas Enqvist (Swe) d. Daniel Vacek (Cze) 6-3 6-7 (3-7), 4-6, 7-5, 6-3
  Stefan Edberg (Swe) d. Petr Korda (Cze) 4-6, 6-2, 7-5

FINAL: France versus Sweden to be held Nov 29-Dec 1 in Malmo, Sweden.

1996 Federation Cup World Group Tournament

FIRST ROUND

Japan d. Germany 3-2
Spain d. South Africa 3-2
France d. Argentina 3-2
United States d. Austria 3-2

SEMIFINALS

United States d. Japan 5-0
  Lindsay Davenport (U.S.) d. Kimiko Date (Japan) 6-2, 6-1
  Monica Seles (U.S.) d. Ai Sugiyama (Japan) 6-2, 6-2
  Monica Seles (U.S.) d. Kimiko Date (Japan) 6-0, 6-2
  Lindsay Davenport (U.S.) d. Ai Sugiyama (Japan) 7-6 (10-8), 7-5
  Lindsay Davenport/Linda Wild (U.S.) d. Ai Sugiyama/Kyoko Nagatsuka (Japan) 6-2, 6-1

Spain d. France 3-2
  Conchita Martinez (Spain) d. Julie Halard-Decugis (France) 1-6, 6-4, 6-2
  Mary Pierce (France) d. Arantxa Sánchez Vicario (Spain) 6-3, 6-4
  Conchita Martinez (Spain) d. Mary Pierce (France) 7-5, 6-1
  Julie Halard-Decugis (France) d. Arantxa Sánchez Vicario (Spain) 2-6, 6-4, 7-5
  Conchita Martinez/Arantxa Sánchez Vicario (Spain) d. Julie Halard-Decugis/Nathalie Tauziat (France) 6-4, 2-1 retired

FINAL

United States d. Spain 5-0, Sept 28-29 in Atlantic City
  Monica Seles (U.S.) d. Conchita Martinez (Spain) 6-2, 6-4
  Lindsay Davenport (U.S.) d. Arantxa Sánchez Vicario (Spain) 7-5, 6-1
  Monica Seles (U.S.) d. Arantxa Sánchez Vicario (Spain) 3-6, 6-3, 6-1
  Lindsay Davenport (U.S.) d. Gala Leon Garcia (Spain) 7-5, 6-2
  Mary Joe Fernandez/Lindsay Davenport (U.S.) d. Virginia Ruano Pascual/Gala Leon Garcia (Spain) 6-1, 6-4

Grand Slam Tournaments

MEN

Australian Championships

Year	Winner	Finalist	Score
1905	Rodney Heath	A. H. Curtis	4-6, 6-3, 6-4, 6-4
1906	Tony Wilding	H. A. Parker	6-0, 6-4, 6-4
1907	Horace M. Rice	H. A. Parker	6-3, 6-4, 6-4
1908	Fred Alexander	A. W. Dunlop	3-6, 3-6, 6-0, 6-2, 6-3
1909	Tony Wilding	E. F. Parker	6-1, 7-5, 6-2
1910	Rodney Heath	Horace M. Rice	6-4, 6-3, 6-2
1911	Norman Brookes	Horace M. Rice	6-1, 6-2, 6-3
1912	J. Cecil Parke	A. E. Beamish	3-6, 6-3, 1-6, 6-1, 7-5
1913	E. F. Parker	H. A. Parker	2-6, 6-1, 6-2, 6-3
1914	Pat O'Hara Wood	G. L. Patterson	6-4, 6-3, 5-7, 6-1
1915	Francis G. Lowe	Horace M. Rice	4-6, 6-1, 6-1, 6-4
1916-18	No tournament		
1919	A. R. F. Kingscote	E. O. Pockley	6-4, 6-0, 6-3
1920	Pat O'Hara Wood	Ron Thomas	6-3, 4-6, 6-8, 6-1, 6-3
1921	Rhys H. Gemmell	A. Hedeman	7-5, 6-1, 6-4
1922	Pat O'Hara Wood	Gerald Patterson	6-0, 3-6, 3-6, 6-3, 6-2
1923	Pat O'Hara Wood	C. B. St John	6-1, 0-1, 0-3
1924	James Anderson	R. E. Schlesinger	6-3, 6-4, 3-6, 5-7, 6-3
1925	James Anderson	Gerald Patterson	11-9, 2-6, 6-2, 6-3
1926	John Hawkes	J. Willard	6-1, 6-3, 6-1
1927	Gerald Patterson	John Hawkes	3-6, 6-4, 3-6, 18-16, 6-3
1928	Jean Borotra	R. O. Cummings	6-4, 6-1, 4-6, 5-7, 6-3
1929	John C. Gregory	R. E. Schlesinger	6-2, 6-2, 5-7, 7-5
1930	Gar Moon	Harry C. Hopman	6-3, 6-1, 6-3
1931	Jack Crawford	Harry C. Hopman	6-4, 6-2, 2-6, 6-1
1932	Jack Crawford	Harry C. Hopman	4-6, 6-3, 3-6, 6-3, 6-1
1933	Jack Crawford	Keith Gledhill	2-6, 7-5, 6-3, 6-2
1934	Fred Perry	Jack Crawford	6-3, 7-5, 6-1
1935	Jack Crawford	Fred Perry	2-6, 6-4, 6-4, 6-4
1936	Adrian Quist	Jack Crawford	6-2, 6-3, 4-6, 3-6, 9-7
1937	Vivian B. McGrath	John Bromwich	6-3, 1-6, 6-0, 2-6, 6-1
1938	Don Budge	John Bromwich	6-4, 6-2, 6-1
1939	John Bromwich	Adrian Quist	6-4, 6-1, 6-3
1940	Adrian Quist	Jack Crawford	6-3, 6-1, 6-2
1941-45	No tournament		
1946	John Bromwich	Dinny Pails	5-7, 6-3, 7-5, 3-6, 6-2
1947	Dinny Pails	John Bromwich	4-6, 6-4, 3-6, 7-5, 8-6
1948	Adrian Quist	John Bromwich	6-4, 3-6, 6-3, 2-6, 6-3
1949	Frank Sedgman	Ken McGregor	6-3, 6-3, 6-2
1950	Frank Sedgman	Ken McGregor	6-3, 6-4, 4-6, 6-1
1951	Richard Savitt	Ken McGregor	6-3, 2-6, 6-3, 6-1
1952	Ken McGregor	Frank Sedgman	7-5, 12-10, 2-6, 6-2
1953	Ken Rosewall	Mervyn Rose	6-0, 6-3, 6-4
1954	Mervyn Rose	Rex Hartwig	6-2, 0-6, 6-4, 6-2
1955	Ken Rosewall	Lew Hoad	9-7, 6-4, 6-4
1956	Lew Hoad	Ken Rosewall	6-4, 3-6, 6-4, 7-5
1957	Ashley Cooper	Neale Fraser	6-3, 9-11, 6-4, 6-2
1958	Ashley Cooper	Mal Anderson	7-5, 6-3, 6-4
1959	Alex Olmedo	Neale Fraser	6-1, 6-2, 3-6, 6-3
1960	Rod Laver	Neale Fraser	5-7, 3-6, 6-3, 8-6, 8-6
1961	Roy Emerson	Rod Laver	1-6, 6-3, 7-5, 6-4
1962	Rod Laver	Roy Emerson	8-6, 0-6, 6-4, 6-4
1963	Roy Emerson	Ken Fletcher	6-3, 6-3, 6-1
1964	Roy Emerson	Fred Stolle	6-3, 6-4, 6-2
1965	Roy Emerson	Fred Stolle	7-9, 2-6, 6-4, 7-5, 6-1
1966	Roy Emerson	Arthur Ashe	6-4, 6-8, 6-2, 6-3
1967	Roy Emerson	Arthur Ashe	6-4, 6-1, 6-1
1968	Bill Bowrey	Juan Gisbert	7-5, 2-6, 9-7, 6-4
1969*	Rod Laver	Andres Gimeno	6-3, 6-4, 7-5

*Became Open (amateur and professional) in 1969.

Australian Championships (Cont.)

Year	Winner	Finalist	Score
1970	Arthur Ashe	Dick Crealy	6-4, 9-7, 6-2
1971	Ken Rosewall	Arthur Ashe	6-1, 7-5, 6-3
1972	Ken Rosewall	Mal Anderson	7-6, 6-3, 7-5
1973	John Newcombe	Onny Parun	6-3, 6-7, 7-5, 6-1
1974	Jimmy Connors	Phil Dent	7-6, 6-4, 4-6, 6-3
1975	John Newcombe	Jimmy Connors	7-5, 3-6, 6-4, 7-5
1976	Mark Edmondson	John Newcombe	6-7, 6-3, 7-6, 6-1
1977 (Jan)	Roscoe Tanner	Guillermo Vilas	6-3, 6-3, 6-3
1977 (Dec)	Vitas Gerulaitis	John Lloyd	6-3, 7-6, 5-7, 3-6, 6-2
1978	Guillermo Vilas	John Marks	6-4, 6-4, 3-6, 6-3
1979	Guillermo Vilas	John Sadri	7-6, 6-3, 6-2
1980	Brian Teacher	Kim Warwick	7-5, 7-6, 6-3
1981	Johan Kriek	Steve Denton	6-2, 7-6, 6-7, 6-4
1982	Johan Kriek	Steve Denton	6-3, 6-3, 6-2
1983	Mats Wilander	Ivan Lendl	6-1, 6-4, 6-4
1984	Mats Wilander	Kevin Curren	6-7, 6-4, 7-6, 6-2
1985 (Dec)	Stefan Edberg	Mats Wilander	6-4, 6-3, 6-3
1987 (Jan)	Stefan Edberg	Pat Cash	6-3, 6-4, 3-6, 5-7, 6-3
1988	Mats Wilander	Pat Cash	6-3, 6-7, 3-6, 6-1, 8-6
1989	Ivan Lendl	Miloslav Mecir	6-2, 6-2, 6-2
1990	Ivan Lendl	Stefan Edberg	4-6, 7-6, 5-2 ret
1991	Boris Becker	Ivan Lendl	1-6, 6-4, 6-4, 6-4
1992	Jim Courier	Stefan Edberg	6-3, 3-6, 6-4, 6-2
1993	Jim Courier	Stefan Edberg	6-2, 6-1, 2-6, 7-5
1994	Pete Sampras	Todd Martin	7-6 (7-4), 6-4, 6-4
1995	Andre Agassi	Pete Sampras	4-6, 6-1, 7-6 (8-6), 6-4
1996	Boris Becker	Michael Chang	6-2, 6-4, 2-6, 6-2

French Championships

Year	Winner	Finalist	Score
1925†	Rene Lacoste	Jean Borotra	7-5, 6-1, 6-4
1926	Henri Cochet	Rene Lacoste	6-2, 6-4, 6-3
1927	Rene Lacoste	Bill Tilden	6-4, 4-6, 5-7, 6-3, 11-9
1928	Henri Cochet	Rene Lacoste	5-7, 6-3, 6-1, 6-3
1929	Rene Lacoste	Jean Borotra	6-3, 2-6, 6-0, 2-6, 8-6
1930	Henri Cochet	Bill Tilden	3-6, 8-6, 6-3, 6-1
1931	Jean Borotra	Claude Boussus	2-6, 6-4, 7-5, 6-4
1932	Henri Cochet	Giorgio de Stefani	6-0, 6-4, 4-6, 6-3
1933	Jack Crawford	Henri Cochet	8-6, 6-1, 6-3
1934	Gottfried von Cramm	Jack Crawford	6-4, 7-9, 3-6, 7-5, 6-3
1935	Fred Perry	Gottfried von Cramm	6-3, 3-6, 6-1, 6-3
1936	Gottfried von Cramm	Fred Perry	6-0, 2-6, 6-2, 2-6, 6-0
1937	Henner Henkel	Henry Austin	6-1, 6-4, 6-3
1938	Don Budge	Roderick Menzel	6-3, 6-2, 6-4
1939	Don McNeill	Bobby Riggs	7-5, 6-0, 6-3
1940	No tournament		
1941‡	Bernard Destremau	n/a	n/a
1942‡	Bernard Destremau	n/a	n/a
1943‡	Yvon Petra	n/a	n/a
1944‡	Yvon Petra	n/a	n/a
1945‡	Yvon Petra	Bernard Destremau	7-5, 6-4, 6-2
1946	Marcel Bernard	Jaroslav Drobny	3-6, 2-6, 6-1, 6-4, 6-3
1947	Joseph Asboth	Eric Sturgess	8-6, 7-5, 6-4
1948	Frank Parker	Jaroslav Drobny	6-4, 7-5, 5-7, 8-6
1949	Frank Parker	Budge Patty	6-3, 1-6, 6-1, 6-4
1950	Budge Patty	Jaroslav Drobny	6-1, 6-2, 3-6, 5-7, 7-5
1951	Jaroslav Drobny	Eric Sturgess	6-3, 6-3, 6-3
1952	Jaroslav Drobny	Frank Sedgman	6-2, 6-0, 3-6, 6-4
1953	Ken Rosewall	Vic Seixas	6-3, 6-4, 1-6, 6-2
1954	Tony Trabert	Arthur Larsen	6-4, 7-5, 6-1
1955	Tony Trabert	Sven Davidson	2-6, 6-1, 6-4, 6-2
1956	Lew Hoad	Sven Davidson	6-4, 8-6, 6-3

†1925 was the first year that entries were accepted from all countries.

‡From 1941 to 1945 the event was called Tournoi de France and was closed to all foreigners.

French Championships (Cont.)

Year	Winner	Finalist	Score
1957	Sven Davidson	Herbie Flam	6-3, 6-4, 6-4
1958	Mervyn Rose	Luis Ayala	6-3, 6-4, 6-4
1959	Nicola Pietrangeli	Ian Vermaak	3-6, 6-3, 6-4, 6-1
1960	Nicola Pietrangeli	Luis Ayala	3-6, 6-3, 6-4, 4-6, 6-3
1961	Manuel Santana	Nicola Pietrangeli	4-6, 6-1, 3-6, 6-0, 6-2
1962	Rod Laver	Roy Emerson	3-6, 2-6, 6-3, 9-7, 6-2
1963	Roy Emerson	Pierre Darmon	3-6, 6-1, 6-4, 6-4
1964	Manuel Santana	Nicola Pietrangeli	6-3, 6-1, 4-6, 7-5
1965	Fred Stolle	Tony Roche	3-6, 6-0, 6-2, 6-3
1966	Tony Roche	Istvan Gulyas	6-1, 6-4, 7-5
1967	Roy Emerson	Tony Roche	6-1, 6-4, 2-6, 6-2
1968*	Ken Rosewall	Rod Laver	6-3, 6-1, 2-6, 6-2
1969	Rod Laver	Ken Rosewall	6-4, 6-3, 6-4
1970	Jan Kodes	Zeljko Franulovic	6-2, 6-4, 6-0
1971	Jan Kodes	Ilie Nastase	8-6, 6-2, 2-6, 7-5
1972	Andres Gimeno	Patrick Proisy	4-6, 6-3, 6-1, 6-1
1973	Ilie Nastase	Nikki Pilic	6-3, 6-3, 6-0
1974	Bjorn Borg	Manuel Orantes	6-7, 6-0, 6-1, 6-1
1975	Bjorn Borg	Guillermo Vilas	6-2, 6-3, 6-4
1976	Adriano Panatta	Harold Solomon	6-1, 6-4, 4-6, 7-6
1977	Guillermo Vilas	Brian Gottfried	6-0, 6-3, 6-0
1978	Bjorn Borg	Guillermo Vilas	6-1, 6-1, 6-3
1979	Bjorn Borg	Victor Pecci	6-3, 6-1, 6-7, 6-4
1980	Bjorn Borg	Vitas Gerulaitis	6-4, 6-1, 6-2
1981	Bjorn Borg	Ivan Lendl	6-1, 4-6, 6-2, 3-6, 6-1
1982	Mats Wilander	Guillermo Vilas	1-6, 7-6, 6-0, 6-4
1983	Yannick Noah	Mats Wilander	6-2, 7-5, 7-6
1984	Ivan Lendl	John McEnroe	3-6, 2-6, 6-4, 7-5, 7-5
1985	Mats Wilander	Ivan Lendl	3-6, 6-4, 6-2, 6-2
1986	Ivan Lendl	Mikael Pernfors	6-3, 6-2, 6-4
1987	Ivan Lendl	Mats Wilander	7-5, 6-2, 3-6, 7-6
1988	Mats Wilander	Henri Leconte	7-5, 6-2, 6-1
1989	Michael Chang	Stefan Edberg	6-1, 3-6, 4-6, 6-4, 6-2
1990	Andres Gomez	Andre Agassi	6-3, 2-6, 6-4, 6-4
1991	Jim Courier	Andre Agassi	3-6, 6-4, 2-6, 6-1, 6-4
1992	Jim Courier	Petr Korda	7-5, 6-2, 6-1
1993	Sergi Bruguera	Jim Courier	6-4, 2-6, 6-2, 3-6, 6-3
1994	Sergi Bruguera	Alberto Berasategui	6-3, 7-5, 2-6, 6-1
1995	Thomas Muster	Michael Chang	7-5, 6-2, 6-4
1996	Yevgeny Kafelnikov	Michael Stich	7-6 (7-4), 7-5, 7-6 (7-4)

*Became Open (amateur and professional) in 1968 but closed to contract professionals in 1972.

Wimbledon Championships

Year	Winner	Finalist	Score
1877	Spencer W. Gore	William C. Marshall	6-1, 6-2, 6-4
1878	P. Frank Hadow	Spencer W. Gore	7-5, 6-1, 9-7
1879	John T. Hartley	V. St Leger Gould	6-2, 6-4, 6-2
1880	John T. Hartley	Herbert F. Lawford	6-0, 6-2, 2-6, 6-3
1881	William Renshaw	John T. Hartley	6-0, 6-1, 6-1
1882	William Renshaw	Ernest Renshaw	6-1, 2-6, 4-6, 6-2, 6-2
1883	William Renshaw	Ernest Renshaw	2-6, 6-3, 6-3, 4-6, 6-3
1884	William Renshaw	Herbert F. Lawford	6-0, 6-4, 9-7
1885	William Renshaw	Herbert F. Lawford	7-5, 6-2, 4-6, 7-5
1886	William Renshaw	Herbert F. Lawford	6-0, 5-7, 6-3, 6-4
1887	Herbert F. Lawford	Ernest Renshaw	1-6, 6-3, 3-6, 6-4, 6-4
1888	Ernest Renshaw	Herbert F. Lawford	6-3, 7-5, 6-0
1889	William Renshaw	Ernest Renshaw	6-4, 6-1, 3-6, 6-0
1890	William J. Hamilton	William Renshaw	6-8, 6-2, 3-6, 6-1, 6-1
1891	Wilfred Baddeley	Joshua Pim	6-4, 1-6, 7-5, 6-0
1892	Wilfred Baddeley	Joshua Pim	4-6, 6-3, 6-3, 6-2
1893	Joshua Pim	Wilfred Baddeley	3-6, 6-1, 6-3, 6-2
1894	Joshua Pim	Wilfred Baddeley	10-8, 6-2, 8-6
1895	Wilfred Baddeley	Wilberforce V. Eaves	4-6, 2-6, 8-6, 6-2, 6-3
1896	Harold S. Mahoney	Wilfred Baddeley	6-2, 6-8, 5-7, 8-6, 6-3

Wimbledon Championship *(Cont.)*

Year	Winner	Finalist	Score
1897	Reggie F. Doherty	Harold S. Mahoney	6-4, 6-4, 6-3
1898	Reggie F. Doherty	H. Laurie Doherty	6-3, 6-3, 2-6, 5-7, 6-1
1899	Reggie F. Doherty	Arthur W. Gore	1-6, 4-6, 6-2, 6-3, 6-3
1900	Reggie F. Doherty	Sidney H. Smith	6-8, 6-3, 6-1, 6-2
1901	Arthur W. Gore	Reggie F. Doherty	4-6, 7-5, 6-4, 6-4
1902	H. Laurie Doherty	Arthur W. Gore	6-4, 6-3, 3-6, 6-0
1903	H. Laurie Doherty	Frank L. Riseley	7-5, 6-3, 6-0
1904	H. Laurie Doherty	Frank L. Riseley	6-1, 7-5, 8-6
1905	H. Laurie Doherty	Norman E. Brookes	8-6, 6-2, 6-4
1906	H. Laurie Doherty	Frank L. Riseley	6-4, 4-6, 6-2, 6-3
1907	Norman E. Brookes	Arthur W. Gore	6-4, 6-2, 6-2
1908	Arthur W. Gore	H. Roper Barrett	6-3, 6-2, 4-6, 3-6, 6-4
1909	Arthur W. Gore	M. J. G. Ritchie	6-8, 1-6, 6-2, 6-2, 6-2
1910	Anthony F. Wilding	Arthur W. Gore	6-4, 7-5, 4-6, 6-2
1911	Anthony F. Wilding	H. Roper Barrett	6-4, 4-6, 2-6, 6-2 ret
1912	Anthony F. Wilding	Arthur W. Gore	6-4, 6-4, 4-6, 6-4
1913	Anthony F. Wilding	Maurice E. McLoughlin	8-6, 6-3, 10-8
1914	Norman E. Brookes	Anthony F. Wilding	6-4, 6-4, 7-5
1915-18	No tournament		
1919	Gerald L. Patterson	Norman E. Brookes	6-3, 7-5, 6-2
1920	Bill Tilden	Gerald L. Patterson	2-6, 6-3, 6-2, 6-4
1921	Bill Tilden	Brian I. C. Norton	4-6, 2-6, 6-1, 6-0, 7-5
1922	Gerald L. Patterson	Randolph Lycett	6-3, 6-4, 6-2
1923	Bill Johnston	Francis T. Hunter	6-0, 6-3, 6-1
1924	Jean Borotra	Rene Lacoste	6-1, 3-6, 6-1, 3-6, 6-4
1925	Rene Lacoste	Jean Borotra	6-3, 6-3, 4-6, 8-6
1926	Jean Borotra	Howard Kinsey	8-6, 6-1, 6-3
1927	Henri Cochet	Jean Borotra	4-6, 4-6, 6-3, 6-4, 7-5
1928	Rene Lacoste	Henri Cochet	6-1, 4-6, 6-4, 6-2
1929	Henri Cochet	Jean Borotra	6-4, 6-3, 6-4
1930	Bill Tilden	Wilmer Allison	6-3, 9-7, 6-4
1931	Sidney B. Wood Jr	Francis X. Shields	walkover
1932	Ellsworth Vines	Henry Austin	6-4, 6-2, 6-0
1933	Jack Crawford	Ellsworth Vines	4-6, 11-9, 6-2, 2-6, 6-4
1934	Fred Perry	Jack Crawford	6-3, 6-0, 7-5
1935	Fred Perry	Gottfried von Cramm	6-2, 6-4, 6-4
1936	Fred Perry	Gottfried von Cramm	6-1, 6-1, 6-0
1937	Don Budge	Gottfried von Cramm	6-3, 6-4, 6-2
1938	Don Budge	Henry Austin	6-1, 6-0, 6-3
1939	Bobby Riggs	Elwood Cooke	2-6, 8-6, 3-6, 6-3, 6-2
1940-45	No tournament		
1946	Yvon Petra	Geoff E. Brown	6-2, 6-4, 7-9, 5-7, 6-4
1947	Jack Kramer	Tom P. Brown	6-1, 6-3, 6-2
1948	Bob Falkenburg	John Bromwich	7-5, 0-6, 6-2, 3-6, 7-5
1949	Ted Schroeder	Jaroslav Drobny	3-6, 6-0, 6-3, 4-6, 6-4
1950	Budge Patty	Frank Sedgman	6-1, 8-10, 6-2, 6-3
1951	Dick Savitt	Ken McGregor	6-4, 6-4, 6-4
1952	Frank Sedgman	Jaroslav Drobny	4-6, 6-3, 6-2, 6-3
1953	Vic Seixas	Kurt Nielsen	9-7, 6-3, 6-4
1954	Jaroslav Drobny	Ken Rosewall	13-11, 4-6, 6-2, 9-7
1955	Tony Trabert	Kurt Nielsen	6-3, 7-5, 6-1
1956	Lew Hoad	Ken Rosewall	6-2, 4-6, 7-5, 6-4
1957	Lew Hoad	Ashley Cooper	6-2, 6-1, 6-2
1958	Ashley Cooper	Neale Fraser	3-6, 6-3, 6-4, 13-11
1959	Alex Olmedo	Rod Laver	6-4, 6-3, 6-4
1960	Neale Fraser	Rod Laver	6-4, 3-6, 9-7, 7-5
1961	Rod Laver	Chuck McKinley	6-3, 6-1, 6-4
1962	Rod Laver	Martin Mulligan	6-2, 6-2, 6-1
1963	Chuck McKinley	Fred Stolle	9-7, 6-1, 6-4
1964	Roy Emerson	Fred Stolle	6-4, 12-10, 4-6, 6-3
1965	Roy Emerson	Fred Stolle	6-2, 6-4, 6-4
1966	Manuel Santana	Dennis Ralston	6-4, 11-9, 6-4
1967	John Newcombe	Wilhelm Bungert	6-3, 6-1, 6-1
1968*	Rod Laver	Tony Roche	6-3, 6-4, 6-2

*Became Open (amateur and professional) in 1968 but closed to contract professionals in 1972.

Wimbledon Championships *(Cont.)*

Year	Winner	Finalist	Score
1969	Rod Laver	John Newcombe	6-4, 5-7, 6-4, 6-4
1970	John Newcombe	Ken Rosewall	5-7, 6-3, 6-2, 3-6, 6-1
1971	John Newcombe	Stan Smith	6-3, 5-7, 2-6, 6-4, 6-4
1972	Stan Smith	Ilie Nastase	4-6, 6-3, 6-3, 4-6, 7-5
1973	Jan Kodes	Alex Metreveli	6-1, 9-8, 6-3
1974	Jimmy Connors	Ken Rosewall	6-1, 6-1, 6-4
1975	Arthur Ashe	Jimmy Connors	6-1, 6-1, 5-7, 6-4
1976	Bjorn Borg	Ilie Nastase	6-4, 6-2, 9-7
1977	Bjorn Borg	Jimmy Connors	3-6, 6-2, 6-1, 5-7, 6-4
1978	Bjorn Borg	Jimmy Connors	6-2, 6-2, 6-3
1979	Bjorn Borg	Roscoe Tanner	6-7, 6-1, 3-6, 6-3, 6-4
1980	Bjorn Borg	John McEnroe	1-6, 7-5, 6-3, 6-7, 8-6
1981	John McEnroe	Bjorn Borg	4-6, 7-6, 7-6, 6-4
1982	Jimmy Connors	John McEnroe	3-6, 6-3, 6-7, 7-6, 6-4
1983	John McEnroe	Chris Lewis	6-2, 6-2, 6-2
1984	John McEnroe	Jimmy Connors	6-1, 6-1, 6-2
1985	Boris Becker	Kevin Curren	6-3, 6-7, 7-6, 6-4
1986	Boris Becker	Ivan Lendl	6-4, 6-3, 7-5
1987	Pat Cash	Ivan Lendl	7-6, 6-2, 7-5
1988	Stefan Edberg	Boris Becker	4-6, 7-6, 6-4, 6-2
1989	Boris Becker	Stefan Edberg	6-0, 7-6, 6-4
1990	Stefan Edberg	Boris Becker	6-2, 6-2, 3-6, 3-6, 6-4
1991	Michael Stich	Boris Becker	6-4, 7-6, 6-4
1992	Andre Agassi	Goran Ivanisevic	6-7, 6-4, 6-4, 1-6, 6-4
1993	Pete Sampras	Jim Courier	7-6 (7-3), 7-6 (8-6), 3-6, 6-3
1994	Pete Sampras	Goran Ivanisevic	7-6 (7-2), 7-6 (7-5), 6-0
1995	Pete Sampras	Boris Becker	6-7 (5-7), 6-2, 6-4, 6-2
1996	Richard Krajicek	MaliVai Washington	6-3, 6-4, 6-3

Note: Prior to 1922 the tournament was run on a challenge-round system. The previous year's winner "stood out" of an All Comers event, which produced a challenger to play him for the title.

United States Championships

Year	Winner	Finalist	Score
1881	Richard D. Sears	W. E. Glyn	6-0, 6-3, 6-2
1882	Richard D. Sears	C. M. Clark	6-1, 6-4, 6-0
1883	Richard D. Sears	James Dwight	6-2, 6-0, 9-7
1884	Richard D. Sears	H. A. Taylor	6-0, 1-6, 6-0, 6-2
1885	Richard D. Sears	G. M. Brinley	6-3, 4-6, 6-0, 6-3
1886	Richard D. Sears	R. L. Beeckman	4-6, 6-1, 6-3, 6-4
1887	Richard D. Sears	H. W. Slocum Jr	6-1, 6-3, 6-2
1888‡	H. W. Slocum Jr	H. A. Taylor	6-4, 6-1, 6-0
1889	H. W. Slocum Jr	Q. A. Shaw	6-3, 6-1, 4-6, 6-2
1890	Oliver S. Campbell	H. W. Slocum Jr	6-2, 4-6, 6-3, 6-1
1891	Oliver S. Campbell	Clarence Hobart	2-6, 7-5, 7-9, 6-1, 6-2
1892	Oliver S. Campbell	Frederick H. Hovey	7-5, 3-6, 6-3, 7-5
1893‡	Robert D. Wrenn	Frederick H. Hovey	6-4, 3-6, 6-4, 6-4
1894	Robert D. Wrenn	M. F. Goodbody	6-8, 6-1, 6-4, 6-4
1895	Frederick H. Hovey	Robert D. Wrenn	6-3, 6-2, 6-4
1896	Robert D. Wrenn	Frederick H. Hovey	7-5, 3-6, 6-0, 1-6, 6-1
1897	Robert D. Wrenn	Wilberforce V. Eaves	4-6, 8-6, 6-3, 2-6, 6-2
1898‡	Malcolm D. Whitman	Dwight F. Davis	3-6, 6-2, 6-2, 6-1
1899	Malcolm D. Whitman	J. Parmly Paret	6-1, 6-2, 3-6, 7-5
1900	Malcolm D. Whitman	William A. Larned	6-4, 1-6, 6-2, 6-2
1901‡	William A. Larned	Beals C. Wright	6-2, 6-8, 6-4, 6-4
1902	William A. Larned	Reggie F. Doherty	4-6, 6-2, 6-4, 8-6
1903	H. Laurie Doherty	William A. Larned	6-0, 6-3, 10-8
1904‡	Holcombe Ward	William J. Clothier	10-8, 6-4, 9-7
1905	Beals C. Wright	Holcombe Ward	6-2, 6-1, 11-9
1906	William J. Clothier	Beals C. Wright	6-3, 6-0, 6-4
1907‡	William A. Larned	Robert LeRoy	6-2, 6-2, 6-4
1908	William A. Larned	Beals C. Wright	6-1, 6-2, 8-6
1909	William A. Larned	William J. Clothier	6-1, 6-2, 5-7, 1-6, 6-1
1910	William A. Larned	Thomas C. Bundy	6-1, 5-7, 6-0, 6-8, 6-1

‡No challenge round played.

United States Championships *(Cont.)*

Year	Winner	Finalist	Score
1911	William A. Larned	Maurice E. McLoughlin	6-4, 6-4, 6-2
1912†	Maurice E. McLoughlin	Bill Johnson	3-6, 2-6, 6-2, 6-4, 6-2
1913†	Maurice E. McLoughlin	Richard N. Williams	6-4, 5-7, 6-3, 6-1
1914	Richard N. Williams	Maurice E. McLoughlin	6-3, 8-6, 10-8
1915	Bill Johnston	Maurice E. McLoughlin	1-6, 6-0, 7-5, 10-8
1916	Richard N. Williams	Bill Johnston	4-6, 6-4, 0-6, 6-2, 6-4
1917#	R. L. Murray	N. W. Niles	5-7, 8-6, 6-3, 6-3
1918	R. L. Murray	Bill Tilden	6-3, 6-1, 7-5
1919	Bill Johnston	Bill Tilden	6-4, 6-4, 6-3
1920	Bill Tilden	Bill Johnston	6-1, 1-6, 7-5, 5-7, 6-3
1921	Bill Tilden	Wallace F. Johnson	6-1, 6-3, 6-1
1922	Bill Tilden	Bill Johnston	4-6, 3-6, 6-2, 6-3, 6-4
1923	Bill Tilden	Bill Johnston	6-4, 6-1, 6-4
1924	Bill Tilden	Bill Johnston	6-1, 9-7, 6-2
1925	Bill Tilden	Bill Johnston	4-6, 11-9, 6-3, 4-6, 6-3
1926	Rene Lacoste	Jean Borotra	6-4, 6-0, 6-4
1927	Rene Lacoste	Bill Tilden	11-9, 6-3, 11-9
1928	Henri Cochet	Francis T. Hunter	4-6, 6-4, 3-6, 7-5, 6-3
1929	Bill Tilden	Francis T. Hunter	3-6, 6-3, 4-6, 6-2, 6-4
1930	John H. Doeg	Francis X. Shields	10-8, 1-6, 6-4, 16-14
1931	Ellsworth Vines	George M. Lott Jr	7-9, 6-3, 9-7, 7-5
1932	Ellsworth Vines	Henri Cochet	6-4, 6-4, 6-4
1933	Fred Perry	Jack Crawford	6-3, 11-13, 4-6, 6-0, 6-1
1934	Fred Perry	Wilmer L. Allison	6-4, 6-3, 1-6, 8-6
1935	Wilmer L. Allison	Sidney B. Wood Jr	6-2, 6-2, 6-3
1936	Fred Perry	Don Budge	2-6, 6-2, 8-6, 1-6, 10-8
1937	Don Budge	Gottfried von Cramm	6-1, 7-9, 6-1, 3-6, 6-1
1938*	Don Budge	Gene Mako	6-3, 6-8, 6-2, 6-1
1939	Bobby Riggs	Welby van Horn	6-4, 6-2, 6-4
1940	Don McNeill	Bobby Riggs	4-6, 6-8, 6-3, 6-3, 7-5
1941	Bobby Riggs	Francis Kovacs II	5-7, 6-1, 6-3, 6-3
1942	Ted Schroeder	Frank Parker	8-6, 7-5, 3-6, 4-6, 6-2
1943	Joseph R. Hunt	Jack Kramer	6-3, 6-8, 10-8, 6-0
1944	Frank Parker	William F. Talbert	6-4, 3-6, 6-3, 6-3
1945	Frank Parker	William F. Talbert	14-12, 6-1, 6-2
1946	Jack Kramer	Tom P. Brown	9-7, 6-3, 6-0
1947	Jack Kramer	Frank Parker	4-6, 2-6, 6-1, 6-0, 6-3
1948	Pancho Gonzales	Eric W. Sturgess	6-2, 6-3, 14-12
1949	Pancho Gonzales	Ted Schroeder	16-18, 2-6, 6-1, 6-2, 6-4
1950	Arthur Larsen	Herbie Flam	6-3, 4-6, 5-7, 6-4, 6-3
1951	Frank Sedgman	Vic Seixas	6-4, 6-1, 6-1
1952	Frank Sedgman	Gardnar Mulloy	6-1, 6-2, 6-3
1953	Tony Trabert	Vic Seixas	6-3, 6-2, 6-3
1954	Vic Seixas	Rex Hartwig	3-6, 6-2, 6-4, 6-4
1955	Tony Trabert	Ken Rosewall	9-7, 6-3, 6-3
1956	Ken Rosewall	Lew Hoad	4-6, 6-2, 6-3, 6-3
1957	Mal Anderson	Ashley J. Cooper	10-8, 7-5, 6-4
1958	Ashley J. Cooper	Mal Anderson	6-2, 3-6, 4-6, 10-8, 8-6
1959	Neale Fraser	Alex Olmedo	6-3, 5-7, 6-2, 6-4
1960	Neale Fraser	Rod Laver	6-4, 6-4, 9-7
1961	Roy Emerson	Rod Laver	7-5, 6-3, 6-2
1962	Rod Laver	Roy Emerson	6-2, 6-4, 5-7, 6-4
1963	Rafael Osuna	Frank Froehling III	7-5, 6-4, 6-2
1964	Roy Emerson	Fred Stolle	6-4, 6-2, 6-4
1965	Manuel Santana	Cliff Drysdale	6-2, 7-9, 7-5, 6-1
1966	Fred Stolle	John Newcombe	4-6, 12-10, 6-3, 6-4
1967	John Newcombe	Clark Graebner	6-4, 6-4, 8-6
1968*	Arthur Ashe	Tom Okker	14-12, 5-7, 6-3, 3-6, 6-3
1968**	Arthur Ashe	Bob Lutz	4-6, 6-3, 8-10, 6-0, 6-4
1969	Rod Laver	Tony Roche	7-9, 6-1, 6-3, 6-2
1969**	Stan Smith	Bob Lutz	9-7, 6-3, 6-1
1970	Ken Rosewall	Tony Roche	2-6, 6-4, 7-6, 6-3
1971	Stan Smith	Jan Kodes	3-6, 6-3, 6-2, 7-6

*Became Open (amateur and professional) in 1968.
†Challenge round abolished; #National Patriotic Tournament; **Amateur event held.

United States Championships (Cont.)

Year	Winner	Finalist	Score
1972	Ilie Nastase	Arthur Ashe	3-6, 6-3, 6-7, 6-4, 6-3
1973	John Newcombe	Jan Kodes	6-4, 1-6, 4-6, 6-2, 6-3
1974	Jimmy Connors	Ken Rosewall	6-1, 6-0, 6-1
1975	Manuel Orantes	Jimmy Connors	6-4, 6-3, 6-3
1976	Jimmy Connors	Bjorn Borg	6-4, 3-6, 7-6, 6-4
1977	Guillermo Vilas	Jimmy Connors	2-6, 6-3, 7-6, 6-0
1978	Jimmy Connors	Bjorn Borg	6-4, 6-2, 6-2
1979	John McEnroe	Vitas Gerulaitis	7-5, 6-3, 6-3
1980	John McEnroe	Bjorn Borg	7-6, 6-1, 6-7, 5-7, 6-4
1981	John McEnroe	Bjorn Borg	4-6, 6-2, 6-4, 6-3
1982	Jimmy Connors	Ivan Lendl	6-3, 6-2, 4-6, 6-4
1983	Jimmy Connors	Ivan Lendl	6-3, 6-7, 7-5, 6-0
1984	John McEnroe	Ivan Lendl	6-3, 6-4, 6-1
1985	Ivan Lendl	John McEnroe	7-6, 6-3, 6-4
1986	Ivan Lendl	Miloslav Mecir	6-4, 6-2, 6-0
1987	Ivan Lendl	Mats Wilander	6-7, 6-0, 7-6, 6-4
1988	Mats Wilander	Ivan Lendl	6-4, 4-6, 6-3, 5-7, 6-4
1989	Boris Becker	Ivan Lendl	7-6, 1-6, 6-3, 7-6
1990	Pete Sampras	Andre Agassi	6-4, 6-3, 6-2
1991	Stefan Edberg	Jim Courier	6-2, 6-4, 6-0
1992	Stefan Edberg	Pete Sampras	3-6, 6-4, 7-6, 6-2
1993	Pete Sampras	Cedric Pioline	6-4, 6-4, 6-3
1994	Andre Agassi	Michael Stich	6-1, 7-6 (7-5), 7-5
1995	Pete Sampras	Andre Agassi	6-4, 6-3, 4-6, 7-5
1996	Pete Sampras	Michael Chang	6-1, 6-4, 7-6 (7-3)

WOMEN

Australian Championships

Year	Winner	Finalist	Score
1922	Margaret Molesworth	Esna Boyd	6-3, 10-8
1923	Margaret Molesworth	Esna Boyd	6-1, 7-5
1924	Sylvia Lance	Esna Boyd	6-3, 3-6, 6-4
1925	Daphne Akhurst	Esna Boyd	1-6, 8-6, 6-4
1926	Daphne Akhurst	Esna Boyd	6-1, 6-3
1927	Esna Boyd	Sylvia Harper	5-7, 6-1, 6-2
1928	Daphne Akhurst	Esna Boyd	7-5, 6-2
1929	Daphne Akhurst	Louise Bickerton	6-1, 5-7, 6-2
1930	Daphne Akhurst	Sylvia Harper	10-8, 2-6, 7-5
1931	Coral Buttsworth	Margorie Crawford	1-6, 6-3, 6-4
1932	Coral Buttsworth	Kathrine Le Messurier	9-7, 6-4
1933	Joan Hartigan	Coral Buttsworth	6-4, 6-3
1934	Joan Hartigan	Margaret Molesworth	6-1, 6-4
1935	Dorothy Round	Nancye Wynne Bolton	1-6, 6-1, 6-3
1936	Joan Hartigan	Nancye Wynne Bolton	6-4, 6-4
1937	Nancye Wynne Bolton	Emily Westacott	6-3, 5-7, 6-4
1938	Dorothy Bundy	D. Stevenson	6-3, 6-2
1939	Emily Westacott	Nell Hopman	6-1, 6-2
1940	Nancye Wynne Bolton	Thelma Coyne	5-7, 6-4, 6-0
1941-45	No tournament		
1946	Nancye Wynne Bolton	Joyce Fitch	6-4, 6-4
1947	Nancye Wynne Bolton	Nell Hopman	6-3, 6-2
1948	Nancye Wynne Bolton	Marie Toomey	6-3, 6-1
1949	Doris Hart	Nancye Wynne Bolton	6-3, 6-4
1950	Louise Brough	Doris Hart	6-4, 3-6, 6-4
1951	Nancye Wynne Bolton	Thelma Long	6-1, 7-5
1952	Thelma Long	H. Angwin	6-2, 6-3
1953	Maureen Connolly	Julia Sampson	6-3, 6-2
1954	Thelma Long	J. Staley	6-3, 6-4
1955	Beryl Penrose	Thelma Long	6-4, 6-3
1956	Mary Carter	Thelma Long	3-6, 6-2, 9-7
1957	Shirley Fry	Althea Gibson	6-3, 6-4
1958	Angela Mortimer	Lorraine Coghlan	6-3, 6-4
1959	Mary Carter-Reitano	Renee Schuurman	6-2, 6-3

Australian Championships *(Cont.)*

Year	Winner	Finalist	Score
1960	Margaret Smith	Jan Lehane	7-5, 6-2
1961	Margaret Smith	Jan Lehane	6-1, 6-4
1962	Margaret Smith	Jan Lehane	6-0, 6-2
1963	Margaret Smith	Jan Lehane	6-2, 6-2
1964	Margaret Smith	Lesley Turner	6-3, 6-2
1965	Margaret Smith	Maria Bueno	5-7, 6-4, 5-2 ret
1966	Margaret Smith	Nancy Richey	Default
1967	Nancy Richey	Lesley Turner	6-1, 6-4
1968	Billie Jean King	Margaret Smith	6-1, 6-2
1969*	Margaret Smith Court	Billie Jean King	6-4, 6-1
1970	Margaret Smith Court	Kerry Melville Reid	6-3, 6-1
1971	Margaret Smith Court	Evonne Goolagong	2-6, 7-6, 7-5
1972	Virginia Wade	Evonne Goolagong	6-4, 6-4
1973	Margaret Smith Court	Evonne Goolagong	6-4, 7-5
1974	Evonne Goolagong	Chris Evert	7-6, 4-6, 6-0
1975	Evonne Goolagong	Martina Navratilova	6-3, 6-2
1976	Evonne Goolagong Cawley	Renata Tomanova	6-2, 6-2
1977 (Jan)	Kerry Melville Reid	Dianne Balestrat	7-5, 6-2
1977 (Dec)	Evonne Goolagong Cawley	Helen Gourlay	6-3, 6-0
1978	Chris O'Neil	Betsy Nagelsen	6-3, 7-6
1979	Barbara Jordan	Sharon Walsh	6-3, 6-3
1980	Hana Mandlikova	Wendy Turnbull	6-0, 7-5
1981	Martina Navratilova	Chris Evert Lloyd	6-7, 6-4, 7-5
1982	Chris Evert Lloyd	Martina Navratilova	6-3, 2-6, 6-3
1983	Martina Navratilova	Kathy Jordan	6-2, 7-6
1984	Chris Evert Lloyd	Helena Sukova	6-7, 6-1, 6-3
1985 (Dec)	Martina Navratilova	Chris Evert Lloyd	6-2, 4-6, 6-2
1987 (Jan)	Hana Mandlikova	Martina Navratilova	7-5, 7-6
1988	Steffi Graf	Chris Evert	6-1, 7-6
1989	Steffi Graf	Helena Sukova	6-4, 6-4
1990	Steffi Graf	Mary Joe Fernandez	6-3, 6-4
1991	Monica Seles	Jana Novotna	5-7, 6-3, 6-1
1992	Monica Seles	Mary Joe Fernandez	6-2, 6-3
1993	Monica Seles	Steffi Graf	4-6, 6-3, 6-2
1994	Steffi Graf	Arantxa Sánchez Vicario	6-0, 6-2
1995	Mary Pierce	Arantxa Sánchez Vicario	6-3, 6-2
1996	Monica Seles	Anke Huber	6-4, 6-1

*Became Open (amateur and professional) in 1969.

French Championships

Year	Winner	Finalist	Score
1925†	Suzanne Lenglen	Kathleen McKane	6-1, 6-2
1926	Suzanne Lenglen	Mary K. Browne	6-1, 6-0
1927	Kea Bouman	Irene Peacock	6-2, 6-4
1928	Helen Wills	Eileen Bennett	6-1, 6-2
1929	Helen Wills	Simone Mathieu	6-3, 6-4
1930	Helen Wills Moody	Helen Jacobs	6-2, 6-1
1931	Cilly Aussem	Betty Nuthall	8-6, 6-1
1932	Helen Wills Moody	Simone Mathieu	7-5, 6-1
1933	Margaret Scriven	Simone Mathieu	6-2, 4-6, 6-4
1934	Margaret Scriven	Helen Jacobs	7-5, 4-6, 6-1
1935	Hilde Sperling	Simone Mathieu	6-2, 6-1
1936	Hilde Sperling	Simone Mathieu	6-3, 6-4
1937	Hilde Sperling	Simone Mathieu	6-2, 6-4
1938	Simone Mathieu	Nelly Landry	6-0, 6-3
1939	Simone Mathieu	Jadwiga Jedrzejowska	6-3, 8-6
1940-45	No tournament		
1946	Margaret Osborne	Pauline Betz	1-6, 8-6, 7-5
1947	Patricia Todd	Doris Hart	6-3, 3-6, 6-4
1948	Nelly Landry	Shirley Fry	6-2, 0-6, 6-0
1949	Margaret Osborne duPont	Nelly Adamson	7-5, 6-2
1950	Doris Hart	Patricia Todd	6-4, 4-6, 6-2

†1925 was the first year that entries were accepted from all countries.

French Championships *(Cont.)*

Year	Winner	Finalist	Score
1951	Shirley Fry	Doris Hart	6-3, 3-6, 6-3
1952	Doris Hart	Shirley Fry	6-4, 6-4
1953	Maureen Connolly	Doris Hart	6-2, 6-4
1954	Maureen Connolly	Ginette Bucaille	6-4, 6-1
1955	Angela Mortimer	Dorothy Knode	2-6, 7-5, 10-8
1956	Althea Gibson	Angela Mortimer	6-0, 12-10
1957	Shirley Bloomer	Dorothy Knode	6-1, 6-3
1958	Zsuzsi Kormoczi	Shirley Bloomer	6-4, 1-6, 6-2
1959	Christine Truman	Zsuzsi Kormoczi	6-4, 7-5
1960	Darlene Hard	Yola Ramirez	6-3, 6-4
1961	Ann Haydon	Yola Ramirez	6-2, 6-1
1962	Margaret Smith	Lesley Turner	6-3, 3-6, 7-5
1963	Lesley Turner	Ann Haydon Jones	2-6, 6-3, 7-5
1964	Margaret Smith	Maria Bueno	5-7, 6-1, 6-2
1965	Lesley Turner	Margaret Smith	6-3, 6-4
1966	Ann Jones	Nancy Richey	6-3, 6-1
1967	Francoise Durr	Lesley Turner	4-6, 6-3, 6-4
1968*	Nancy Richey	Ann Jones	5-7, 6-4, 6-1
1969	Margaret Smith Court	Ann Jones	6-1, 4-6, 6-3
1970	Margaret Smith Court	Helga Niessen	6-2, 6-4
1971	Evonne Goolagong	Helen Gourlay	6-3, 7-5
1972	Billie Jean King	Evonne Goolagong	6-3, 6-3
1973	Margaret Smith Court	Chris Evert	6-7, 7-6, 6-4
1974	Chris Evert	Olga Morozova	6-1, 6-2
1975	Chris Evert	Martina Navratilova	2-6, 6-2, 6-1
1976	Sue Barker	Renata Tomanova	6-2, 0-6, 6-2
1977	Mima Jausovec	Florenza Mihai	6-2, 6-7, 6-1
1978	Virginia Ruzici	Mima Jausovec	6-2, 6-2
1979	Chris Evert Lloyd	Wendy Turnbull	6-2, 6-0
1980	Chris Evert Lloyd	Virginia Ruzici	6-0, 6-3
1981	Hana Mandlikova	Sylvia Hanika	6-2, 6-4
1982	Martina Navratilova	Andrea Jaeger	7-6, 6-1
1983	Chris Evert Lloyd	Mima Jausovec	6-1, 6-2
1984	Martina Navratilova	Chris Evert Lloyd	6-3, 6-1
1985	Chris Evert Lloyd	Martina Navratilova	6-3, 6-7, 7-5
1986	Chris Evert Lloyd	Martina Navratilova	2-6, 6-3, 6-3
1987	Steffi Graf	Martina Navratilova	6-4, 4-6, 8-6
1988	Steffi Graf	Natalia Zvereva	6-0, 6-0
1989	Arantxa Sánchez Vicario	Steffi Graf	7-6, 3-6, 7-5
1990	Monica Seles	Steffi Graf	7-6, 6-4
1991	Monica Seles	Arantxa Sánchez Vicario	6-3, 6-4
1992	Monica Seles	Steffi Graf	6-2, 3-6, 10-8
1993	Steffi Graf	Mary Joe Fernandez	4-6, 6-2, 6-4
1994	Arantxa Sánchez Vicario	Mary Pierce	6-4, 6-4
1995	Steffi Graf	Arantxa Sánchez Vicario	7-5, 4-6, 6-0
1996	Steffi Graf	Arantxa Sánchez Vicario	6-3, 6-7 (4-7), 10-8

*Became Open (amateur and professional) in 1968 but closed to contract professionals in 1972.

Wimbledon Championships

Year	Winner	Finalist	Score
1884	Maud Watson	Lilian Watson	6-8, 6-3, 6-3
1885	Maud Watson	Blanche Bingley	6-1, 7-5
1886	Blanche Bingley	Maud Watson	6-3, 6-3
1887	Charlotte Dod	Blanche Bingley	6-2, 6-0
1888	Charlotte Dod	Blanche Bingley Hillyard	6-3, 6-3
1889	Blanche Bingley Hillyard	n/a	n/a
1890	Lena Rice	n/a	n/a
1891	Charlotte Dod	n/a	n/a
1892	Charlotte Dod	Blanche Bingley Hillyard	6-1, 6-1
1893	Charlotte Dod	Blanche Bingley Hillyard	6-8, 6-1, 6-4
1894	Blanche Bingley Hillyard	n/a	n/a
1895	Charlotte Cooper	n/a	
1896	Charlotte Cooper	Mrs. W. H. Pickering	6-2, 6-3
1897	Blanche Bingley Hillyard	Charlotte Cooper	5-7, 7-5, 6-2

Wimbledon Championships *(Cont.)*

Year	Winner	Finalist	Score
1898	Charlotte Cooper	n/a	n/a
1899	Blanche Bingley Hillyard	Charlotte Cooper	6-2, 6-3
1900	Blanche Bingley Hillyard	Charlotte Cooper	4-6, 6-4, 6-4
1901	Charlotte Cooper Sterry	Blanche Bingley Hillyard	6-2, 6-2
1902	Muriel Robb	Charlotte Cooper Sterry	7-5, 6-1
1903	Dorothea Douglass	n/a	n/a
1904	Dorothea Douglass	Charlotte Cooper Sterry	6-0, 6-3
1905	May Sutton	Dorothea Douglass	6-3, 6-4
1906	Dorothea Douglass	May Sutton	6-3, 9-7
1907	May Sutton	Dorothea Douglass Lambert Chambers	6-1, 6-4
1908	Charlotte Cooper Sterry	n/a	n/a
1909	Dora Boothby	n/a	n/a
1910	Dorothea Douglass Lambert Chambers	Dora Boothby	6-2, 6-2
1911	Dorothea Douglass Lambert Chambers	Dora Boothby	6-0, 6-0
1912	Ethel Larcombe	n/a	n/a
1913	Dorothea Douglass Lambert Chambers		
1914	Dorothea Douglass Lambert Chambers	Ethel Larcombe	7-5, 6-4
1915-18	No tournament		
1919	Suzanne Lenglen	Dorothea Douglass Lambert Chambers	10-8, 4-6, 9-7
1920	Suzanne Lenglen	Dorothea Douglass Lambert Chambers	6-3, 6-0
1921	Suzanne Lenglen	Elizabeth Ryan	6-2, 6-0
1922	Suzanne Lenglen	Molla Mallory	6-2, 6-0
1923	Suzanne Lenglen	Kathleen McKane	6-2, 6-2
1924	Kathleen McKane	Helen Wills	4-6, 6-4, 6-2
1925	Suzanne Lenglen	Joan Fry	6-2, 6-0
1926	Kathleen McKane Godfree	Lili de Alvarez	6-2, 4-6, 6-3
1927	Helen Wills	Lili de Alvarez	6-2, 6-4
1928	Helen Wills	Lili de Alvarez	6-2, 6-3
1929	Helen Wills	Helen Jacobs	6-1, 6-2
1930	Helen Wills Moody	Elizabeth Ryan	6-2, 6-2
1931	Cilly Aussem	Hilde Kranwinkel	7-5, 7-5
1932	Helen Wills Moody	Helen Jacobs	6-3, 6-1
1933	Helen Wills Moody	Dorothy Round	6-4, 6-8, 6-3
1934	Dorothy Round	Helen Jacobs	6-2, 5-7, 6-3
1935	Helen Wills Moody	Helen Jacobs	6-3, 3-6, 7-5
1936	Helen Jacobs	Hilde Kranwinkel Sperling	6-2, 4-6, 7-5
1937	Dorothy Round	Jadwiga Jedrzejowska	6-2, 2-6, 7-5
1938	Helen Wills Moody	Helen Jacobs	6-4, 6-0
1939	Alice Marble	Kay Stammers	6-2, 6-0
1940-45	No tournament		
1946	Pauline Betz	Louise Brough	6-2, 6-4
1947	Margaret Osborne	Doris Hart	6-2, 6-4
1948	Louise Brough	Doris Hart	6-3, 8-6
1949	Louise Brough	Margaret Osborne duPont	10-8, 1-6, 10-8
1950	Louise Brough	Margaret Osborne duPont	6-1, 3-6, 6-1
1951	Doris Hart	Shirley Fry	6-1, 6-0
1952	Maureen Connolly	Louise Brough	6-4, 6-3
1953	Maureen Connolly	Doris Hart	8-6, 7-5
1954	Maureen Connolly	Louise Brough	6-2, 7-5
1955	Louise Brough	Beverly Fleitz	7-5, 8-6
1956	Shirley Fry	Angela Buxton	6-3, 6-1
1957	Althea Gibson	Darlene Hard	6-3, 6-2
1958	Althea Gibson	Angela Mortimer	8-6, 6-2
1959	Maria Bueno	Darlene Hard	6-4, 6-3
1960	Maria Bueno	Sandra Reynolds	8-6, 6-0
1961	Angela Mortimer	Christine Truman	4-6, 6-4, 7-5
1962	Karen Hantze Susman	Vera Sukova	6-4, 6-4

Wimbledon Championships (Cont.)

Year	Winner	Finalist	Score
1963	Margaret Smith	Billie Jean Moffitt	6-3, 6-4
1964	Maria Bueno	Margaret Smith	6-4, 7-9, 6-3
1965	Margaret Smith	Maria Bueno	6-4, 7-5
1966	Billie Jean King	Maria Bueno	6-3, 3-6, 6-1
1967	Billie Jean King	Ann Haydon Jones	6-3, 6-4
1968*	Billie Jean King	Judy Tegart	9-7, 7-5
1969	Ann Haydon Jones	Billie Jean King	3-6, 6-3, 6-2
1970	Margaret Smith Court	Billie Jean King	14-12, 11-9
1971	Evonne Goolagong	Margaret Smith Court	6-4, 6-1
1972	Billie Jean King	Evonne Goolagong	6-3, 6-3
1973	Billie Jean King	Chris Evert	6-0, 7-5
1974	Chris Evert	Olga Morozova	6-0, 6-4
1975	Billie Jean King	Evonne Goolagong Cawley	6-0, 6-1
1976	Chris Evert	Evonne Goolagong Cawley	6-3, 4-6, 8-6
1977	Virginia Wade	Betty Stove	4-6, 6-3, 6-1
1978	Martina Navratilova	Chris Evert	2-6, 6-4, 7-5
1979	Martina Navratilova	Chris Evert Lloyd	6-4, 6-4
1980	Evonne Goolagong Cawley	Chris Evert Lloyd	6-1, 7-6
1981	Chris Evert Lloyd	Hana Mandlikova	6-2, 6-2
1982	Martina Navratilova	Chris Evert Lloyd	6-1, 3-6, 6-2
1983	Martina Navratilova	Andrea Jaeger	6-0, 6-3
1984	Martina Navratilova	Chris Evert Lloyd	7-6, 6-2
1985	Martina Navratilova	Chris Evert Lloyd	4-6, 6-3, 6-2
1986	Martina Navratilova	Hana Mandlikova	7-6, 6-3
1987	Martina Navratilova	Steffi Graf	7-5, 6-3
1988	Steffi Graf	Martina Navratilova	5-7, 6-2, 6-1
1989	Steffi Graf	Martina Navratilova	6-2, 6-7, 6-1
1990	Martina Navratilova	Zina Garrison	6-4, 6-1
1991	Steffi Graf	Gabriela Sabatini	6-4, 3-6, 8-6
1992	Steffi Graf	Monica Seles	6-2, 6-1
1993	Steffi Graf	Jana Novotna	7-6 (8-6), 1-6, 6-4
1994	Conchita Martinez	Martina Navratilova	6-4, 3-6, 6-3
1995	Steffi Graf	Arantxa Sánchez Vicario	4-6, 6-1, 7-5
1996	Steffi Graf	Arantxa Sánchez Vicario	6-3, 7-5

*Became Open (amateur and professional) in 1968 but closed to contract professionals in 1972.

Note: Prior to 1922 the tournament was run on a challenge round system. The previous year's winner "stood out" of an All Comers event, which produced a challenger to play her for the title.

United States Championships

Year	Winner	Finalist	Score
1887	Ellen Hansell	Laura Knight	6-1, 6-0
1888	Bertha L. Townsend	Ellen Hansell	6-3, 6-5
1889	Bertha L. Townsend	Louise Voorhes	7-5, 6-2
1890	Ellen C. Roosevelt	Bertha L. Townsend	6-2, 6-2
1891	Mabel Cahill	Ellen C. Roosevelt	6-4, 6-1, 4-6, 6-3
1892	Mabel Cahill	Elisabeth Moore	5-7, 6-3, 6-4, 4-6, 6-2
1893	Aline Terry	Alice Schultze	6-1, 6-3
1894	Helen Hellwig	Aline Terry	7-5, 3-6, 6-0, 3-6, 6-3
1895	Juliette Atkinson	Helen Hellwig	6-4, 6-2, 6-1
1896	Elisabeth Moore	Juliette Atkinson	6-4, 4-6, 6-2, 6-2
1897	Juliette Atkinson	Elisabeth Moore	6-3, 6-3, 4-6, 3-6, 6-3
1898	Juliette Atkinson	Marion Jones	6-3, 5-7, 6-4, 2-6, 7-5
1899	Marion Jones	Maud Banks	6-1, 6-1, 7-5
1900	Myrtle McAteer	Edith Parker	6-2, 6-2, 6-0
1901	Elisabeth Moore	Myrtle McAteer	6-4, 3-6, 7-5, 2-6, 6-2
1902**	Marion Jones	Elisabeth Moore	6-1, 1-0 retired
1903	Elisabeth Moore	Marion Jones	7-5, 8-6
1904	May Sutton	Elisabeth Moore	6-1, 6-2
1905	Elisabeth Moore	Helen Homans	6-4, 5-7, 6-1
1906	Helen Homans	Maud Barger-Wallach	6-4, 6-3
1907	Evelyn Sears	Carrie Neely	6-3, 6-2
1908	Maud Barger-Wallach	Evelyn Sears	6-3, 1-6, 6-3

**Five-set final abolished.

United States Championship *(Cont.)*

Year	Winner	Finalist	Score
1909	Hazel Hotchkiss	Maud Barger-Wallach	6-0, 6-1
1910	Hazel Hotchkiss	Louise Hammond	6-4, 6-2
1911	Hazel Hotchkiss	Florence Sutton	8-10, 6-1, 9-7
1912†	Mary K. Browne	Eleanora Sears	6-4, 6-2
1913	Mary K. Browne	Dorothy Green	6-2, 7-5
1914	Mary K. Browne	Marie Wagner	6-2, 1-6, 6-1
1915	Molla Bjurstedt	Hazel Hotchkiss Wightman	4-6, 6-2, 6-0
1916	Molla Bjurstedt	Louise Hammond Raymond	6-0, 6-1
1917‡	Molla Bjurstedt	Marion Vanderhoef	4-6, 6-0, 6-2
1918	Molla Bjurstedt	Eleanor Goss	6-4, 6-3
1919	Hazel Hotchkiss Wightman	Marion Zinderstein	6-1, 6-2
1920	Molla Bjurstedt Mallory	Marion Zinderstein	6-3, 6-1
1921	Molla Bjurstedt Mallory	Mary K. Browne	4-6, 6-4, 6-2
1922	Molla Bjurstedt Mallory	Helen Wills	6-3, 6-1
1923	Helen Wills	Molla Bjurstedt Mallory	6-2, 6-1
1924	Helen Wills	Molla Bjurstedt Mallory	6-1, 6-3
1925	Helen Wills	Kathleen McKane	3-6, 6-0, 6-2
1926	Molla Bjurstedt Mallory	Elizabeth Ryan	4-6, 6-4, 9-7
1927	Helen Wills	Betty Nuthall	6-1, 6-4
1928	Helen Wills	Helen Jacobs	6-2, 6-1
1929	Helen Wills	Phoebe Holcroft Watson	6-4, 6-2
1930	Betty Nuthall	Anna McCune Harper	6-1, 6-4
1931	Helen Wills Moody	Eileen Whitingstall	6-4, 6-1
1932	Helen Jacobs	Carolin Babcock	6-2, 6-2
1933	Helen Jacobs	Helen Wills Moody	8-6, 3-6, 3-0 retired
1934	Helen Jacobs	Sarah Palfrey	6-1, 6-4
1935	Helen Jacobs	Sarah Palfrey Fabyan	6-2, 6-4
1936	Alice Marble	Helen Jacobs	4-6, 6-3, 6-2
1937	Anita Lizane	Jadwiga Jedrzejowska	6-4, 6-2
1938	Alice Marble	Nancye Wynne	6-0, 6-3
1939	Alice Marble	Helen Jacobs	6-0, 8-10, 6-4
1940	Alice Marble	Helen Jacobs	6-2, 6-3
1941	Sarah Palfrey Cooke	Pauline Betz	7-5, 6-2
1942	Pauline Betz	Louise Brough	4-6, 6-1, 6-4
1943	Pauline Betz	Louise Brough	6-3, 5-7, 6-3
1944	Pauline Betz	Margaret Osborne	6-3, 8-6
1945	Sarah Palfrey Cooke	Pauline Betz	3-6, 8-6, 6-4
1946	Pauline Betz	Patricia Canning	11-9, 6-3
1947	Louise Brough	Margaret Osborne	8-6, 4-6, 6-1
1948	Margaret Osborne duPont	Louise Brough	4-6, 6-4, 15-13
1949	Margaret Osborne duPont	Doris Hart	6-4, 6-1
1950	Margaret Osborne duPont	Doris Hart	6-4, 6-3
1951	Maureen Connolly	Shirley Fry	6-3, 1-6, 6-4
1952	Maureen Connolly	Doris Hart	6-3, 7-5
1953	Maureen Connolly	Doris Hart	6-2, 6-4
1954	Doris Hart	Louise Brough	6-8, 6-1, 8-6
1955	Doris Hart	Patricia Ward	6-4, 6-2
1956	Shirley Fry	Althea Gibson	6-3, 6-4
1957	Althea Gibson	Louise Brough	6-3, 6-2
1958	Althea Gibson	Darlene Hard	3-6, 6-1, 6-2
1959	Maria Bueno	Christine Truman	6-1, 6-4
1960	Darlene Hard	Maria Bueno	6-4, 10-12, 6-4
1961	Darlene Hard	Ann Haydon	6-3, 6-4
1962	Margaret Smith	Darlene Hard	9-7, 6-4
1963	Maria Bueno	Margaret Smith	7-5, 6-4
1964	Maria Bueno	Carole Graebner	6-1, 6-0
1965	Margaret Smith	Billie Jean Moffitt	8-6, 7-5
1966	Maria Bueno	Nancy Richey	6-3, 6-1
1967	Billie Jean King	Ann Haydon Jones	11-9, 6-4
1968*	Virginia Wade	Billie Jean King	6-4, 6-4
1968#	Margaret Smith Court	Maria Bueno	6-2, 6-2
1969	Margaret Smith Court	Nancy Richey	6-2, 6-2
1969#	Margaret Smith Court	Virginia Wade	4-6, 6-3, 6-0

*Became Open (amateur and professional) in 1968.
†Challenge round abolished; ‡National Patriotic Tournament; #Amateur event held.

United States Championship (Cont.)

Year	Winner	Finalist	Score
1970	Margaret Smith Court	Rosie Casals	6-2, 2-6, 6-1
1971	Billie Jean King	Rosie Casals	6-4, 7-6
1972	Billie Jean King	Kerry Melville	6-3, 7-5
1973	Margaret Smith Court	Evonne Goolagong	7-6, 5-7, 6-2
1974	Billie Jean King	Evonne Goolagong	3-6, 6-3, 7-5
1975	Chris Evert	Evonne Goolagong Cawley	5-7, 6-4, 6-2
1976	Chris Evert	Evonne Goolagong Cawley	6-3, 6-0
1977	Chris Evert	Wendy Turnbull	7-6, 6-2
1978	Chris Evert	Pam Shriver	7-6, 6-4
1979	Tracy Austin	Chris Evert Lloyd	6-4, 6-3
1980	Chris Evert Lloyd	Hana Mandlikova	5-7, 6-1, 6-1
1981	Tracy Austin	Martina Navratilova	1-6, 7-6, 7-6
1982	Chris Evert Lloyd	Hana Mandlikova	6-3, 6-1
1983	Martina Navratilova	Chris Evert Lloyd	6-1, 6-3
1984	Martina Navratilova	Chris Evert Lloyd	4-6, 6-4, 6-4
1985	Hana Mandlikova	Martina Navratilova	7-6, 1-6, 7-6
1986	Martina Navratilova	Helena Sukova	6-3, 6-2
1987	Martina Navratilova	Steffi Graf	7-6, 6-1
1988	Steffi Graf	Gabriela Sabatini	6-3, 3-6, 6-1
1989	Steffi Graf	Martina Navratilova	3-6, 6-4, 6-2
1990	Gabriela Sabatini	Steffi Graf	6-2, 7-6
1991	Monica Seles	Martina Narvatilova	7-6, 6-1
1992	Monica Seles	Arantxa Sánchez Vicario	6-3, 6-2
1993	Steffi Graf	Helena Sukova	6-3, 6-3
1994	Arantxa Sánchez Vicario	Steffi Graf	1-6, 7-6 (7-3), 6-4
1995	Steffi Graf	Monica Seles	7-6 (8-6), 0-6, 6-3
1996	Steffi Graf	Monica Seles	7-5, 7-4

Grand Slams

Singles

Don Budge, 1938
Maureen Connolly, 1953
Rod Laver, 1962, 1969
Margaret Smith Court, 1970
Steffi Graf, 1988

Doubles

Frank Sedgman and Ken McGregor, 1951
Martina Navratilova and Pam Shriver, 1984
Maria Bueno and two partners: Christine Truman
   (Australian), Darlene Hard (French, Wimbledon
   and U.S. Championships), 1960

Mixed Doubles

Margaret Smith and Ken Fletcher, 1963
Owen Davidson and two partners: Lesley Turner
   (Australian), Billie Jean King (French, Wimbledon
   and U.S. Championships), 1967

THEY SAID IT

*Roger Maltbie, the NBC golf analyst,
after watching former tennis great
Ivan Lendl hit five balls into a water
hazard on the 18th hole of a
celebrity golf tournament: "Grass
isn't his best surface."*

Alltime Grand Slam Champions

MEN

Player	Aus. S-D-M	French S-D-M	Wim. S-D-M	U.S. S-D-M	Total
Roy Emerson	6-3-0	2-6-0	2-3-0	2-4-0	28
John Newcombe	2-5-0	0-3-0	3-6-0	2-3-1	25
Frank Sedgman	2-2-2	0-2-2	1-3-2	2-2-2	22
Bill Tilden	†	0-0-1	3-1-0	7-5-4	21
Rod Laver	3-4-0	2-1-1	4-1-2	2-0-0	20
John Bromwich	2-8-1	0-0-0	0-2-2	0-3-1	19
Jean Borotra	1-1-1	1-5-2	2-3-1	0-0-1	18
Fred Stolle	0-3-1	1-2-0	0-2-3	1-3-2	18
Ken Rosewall	4-3-0	2-2-0	0-2-0	2-2-1	18
Neale Fraser	0-3-1	0-3-0	1-2-0	2-3-3	18
Adrian Quist	3-10-0	0-1-0	0-2-0	0-1-0	17
John McEnroe	0-0-0	0-0-1	3-4-0	4-5-0	17
Jack Crawford	4-4-3	1-1-1	1-1-1	0-0-0	17

†Did not compete.

WOMEN

Player	Aus. S-D-M	French S-D-M	Wim. S-D-M	U.S. S-D-M	Total
Margaret Smith Court	11-8-2	5-4-4	3-2-5	5-5-8	62
Martina Navratilova	3-8-0	2-7-2	9-7-3	4-9-2	56
Billie Jean King	1-0-1	1-1-2	6-10-4	4-5-4	39
Doris Hart	1-1-2	2-5-3	1-4-5	2-4-5	35
Helen Wills Moody	†	4-2-0	8-3-1	7-4-2	31
Louise Brough	1-1-0	0-3-0	4-5-4	1-8-3	30**
Margaret Osborne duPont	†	2-3-0	1-5-1	3-8-6	29**
Elizabeth Ryan	†	0-4-0	0-12-7	0-1-2	26
*Steffi Graf	4-0-0	5-0-0	7-1-0	5-0-0	22
Pam Shriver	0-7-0	0-4-1	0-5-0	0-5-0	22
Chris Evert	2-0-0	7-2-0	3-1-0	6-0-0	21
Darlene Hard	†	1-3-2	0-4-3	2-6-0	21
Suzanne Lenglen	†	2-2-2#	6-6-3	0-0-0	21
Nancye Wynne Bolton	6-10-4	0-0-0	0-0-0	0-0-0	20
Maria Bueno	0-1-0	0-1-1	3-5-0	4-4-0	19
Thelma Coyne Long	2-12-4	0-0-1	0-0-0	0-0-0	19

*Active player. †Did not compete.

#Suzanne Lenglen also won four singles titles at the French Championships before 1925, when competition was first opened to entries from all nations

**During the war years 1940-45, with competition in the U.S. Championships thinned due to wartime constraints, Louise Brough Clapp also won four doubles titles 1942-45 and one mixed doubles title in 1942; and Margaret Osborne duPont won five doubles titles in 1941-45 and three mixed doubles titles 1943-45.

Alltime Grand Slam Singles Champions

MEN

Player	Aus.	French	Wim.	U.S.	Total
Roy Emerson	6	2	2	2	12
Bjorn Borg	0	6	5	0	11
Rod Laver	3	2	4	2	11
Bill Tilden	†	0	3	7	10
*Pete Sampras	1	0	3	4	8
Jimmy Connors	1	0	2	5	8
Ivan Lendl	2	3	0	3	8
Fred Perry	1	1	3	3	8
Ken Rosewall	4	2	0	2	8
Henri Cochet	†	4	2	1	7
Rene Lacoste	†	3	2	2	7
Bill Larned	†	†	0	7	7
John McEnroe	0	0	3	4	7
John Newcombe	2	0	3	2	7
Willie Renshaw	†	†	7	†	7
Dick Sears	†	†	0	7	7

*Active player. †Did not compete.

Alltime Grand Slam Singles Champions *(Cont.)*

WOMEN

Player	Aus.	French	Wim.	U.S.	Total
Margaret Smith Court	11	5	3	5	24
*Steffi Graf	4	5	7	5	21
Helen Wills Moody	†	4	8	7	19
Chris Evert	2	7	3	6	18
Martina Navratilova	3	2	9	4	18
Billie Jean King	1	1	6	4	12
Maureen Connolly	1	2	3	3	9
*Monica Seles	4	3	0	2	9
Suzanne Lenglen	†	2#	6	0	8
Molla Bjurstedt Mallory	†	†	0	8	8
Maria Bueno	0	0	3	4	7
Evonne Goolagong	4	1	2	0	7
Dorothea D.L. Chambers	†	†	7	0	7
Nancye Wynne Bolton	6	0	0	0	6
Louise Brough	1	0	4	1	6
Margaret Osborne duPont	†	2	1	3	6
Doris Hart	1	2	1	2	6
Blanche Bingley Hillyard	†	†	6	†	6

*Active player. †Did not compete.
#Suzanne Lenglen also won four singles titles at the French Championships before 1925, when competition was first opened to entries from all nations.

National Team Competition

Davis Cup

Started in 1900 as the International Lawn Tennis Challenge Trophy by America's Dwight Davis, the runner-up in the 1898 U.S. Championships. A Davis Cup meeting between two countries is known as a tie and is a three-day event consisting of two singles matches, followed by one doubles match and then two more singles matches. The United States boasts the greatest number of wins (31), followed by Australia (20).

Year	Winner	Finalist	Site	Score
1900	United States	Great Britain	Boston	3-0
1901	No tournament			
1902	United States	Great Britain	New York	3-2
1903	Great Britain	United States	Boston	4-1
1904	Great Britain	Belgium	Wimbledon	5-0
1905	Great Britain	United States	Wimbledon	5-0
1906	Great Britain	United States	Wimbledon	5-0
1907	Australasia	Great Britain	Wimbledon	3-2
1908	Australasia	United States	Melbourne	3-2
1909	Australasia	United States	Sydney	5-0
1910	No tournament			
1911	Australasia	United States	Christchurch, NZ	5-0
1912	Great Britain	Australasia	Melbourne	3-2
1913	United States	Great Britain	Wimbledon	3-2
1914	Australasia	United States	New York	3-2
1915-18	No tournament			
1919	Australasia	Great Britain	Sydney	4-1
1920	United States	Australasia	Auckland, NZ	5-0
1921	United States	Japan	New York	5-0
1922	United States	Australasia	New York	4-1
1923	United States	Australasia	New York	4-1
1924	United States	Australia	Philadelphia	5-0
1925	United States	France	Philadelphia	5-0
1926	United States	France	Philadelphia	4-1
1927	France	United States	Philadelphia	3-2
1928	France	United States	Paris	4-1
1929	France	United States	Paris	3-2
1930	France	United States	Paris	4-1
1931	France	Great Britain	Paris	3-2

Davis Cup *(Cont.)*

Year	Winner	Finalist	Site	Score
1932	France	United States	Paris	3-2
1933	Great Britain	France	Paris	3-2
1934	Great Britain	United States	Wimbledon	4-1
1935	Great Britain	United States	Wimbledon	5-0
1936	Great Britain	Australia	Wimbledon	3-2
1937	United States	Great Britain	Wimbledon	4-1
1938	United States	Australia	Philadelphia	3-2
1939	Australia	United States	Philadelphia	3-2
1940-45	No tournament			
1946	United States	Australia	Melbourne	5-0
1947	United States	Australia	New York	4-1
1948	United States	Australia	New York	5-0
1949	United States	Australia	New York	4-1
1950	Australia	United States	New York	4-1
1951	Australia	United States	Sydney	3-2
1952	Australia	United States	Adelaide	4-1
1953	Australia	United States	Melbourne	3-2
1954	United States	Australia	Sydney	3-2
1955	Australia	United States	New York	5-0
1956	Australia	United States	Adelaide	5-0
1957	Australia	United States	Melbourne	3-2
1958	United States	Australia	Brisbane	3-2
1959	Australia	United States	New York	3-2
1960	Australia	Italy	Sydney	4-1
1961	Australia	Italy	Melbourne	5-0
1962	Australia	Mexico	Brisbane	5-0
1963	United States	Australia	Adelaide	3-2
1964	Australia	United States	Cleveland	3-2
1965	Australia	Spain	Sydney	4-1
1966	Australia	India	Melbourne	4-1
1967	Australia	Spain	Brisbane	4-1
1968	United States	Australia	Adelaide	4-1
1969	United States	Romania	Cleveland	5-0
1970	United States	West Germany	Cleveland	5-0
1971	United States	Romania	Charlotte, NC	3-2
1972	United States	Romania	Bucharest	3-2
1973	Australia	United States	Cleveland	5-0
1974	South Africa	India	*	walkover
1975	Sweden	Czechoslovakia	Stockholm	3-2
1976	Italy	Chile	Santiago	4-1
1977	Australia	Italy	Sydney	3-1
1978	United States	Great Britain	Palm Springs	4-1
1979	United States	Italy	San Francisco	5-0
1980	Czechoslovakia	Italy	Prague	4-1
1981	United States	Argentina	Cincinnati	3-1
1982	United States	France	Grenoble	4-1
1983	Australia	Sweden	Melbourne	3-2
1984	Sweden	United States	Gothenburg	4-1
1985	Sweden	West Germany	Munich	3-2
1986	Australia	Sweden	Melbourne	3-2
1987	Sweden	India	Gothenburg	5-0
1988	West Germany	Sweden	Gothenburg	4-1
1989	West Germany	Sweden	Stuttgart	3-2
1990	United States	Australia	St Petersburg	3-2
1991	France	United States	Lyon	3-1
1992	United States	Switzerland	Fort Worth, TX	3-1
1993	Germany	Australia	Dusseldorf	4-1
1994	Sweden	Russia	Moscow	4-1
1995	United States	Russia	Moscow	3-2

*India refused to play the final in protest over South Africa's governmental policy of apartheid.
Note: Prior to 1972 the challenge-round system was in effect, with the previous year's winner "standing out" of the competition until the finals. A straight 16-nation tournament has been held since 1981.

Federation Cup

The Federation Cup was started in 1963 by the International Lawn Tennis Federation (now the ITF). Until 1991 all entrants gathered at one site at one time for a tournament that was concluded within one week. Since 1995 the Fed Cup, as it is now called, has been contested in three rounds by a World Group of eight nations. A meeting between two countries now consists of four singles and one doubles matches. The United States boasts the greatest number of wins (15), followed by Australia (7).

Year	Winner	Finalist	Site	Score
1963	United States	Australia	London	2-1
1964	Australia	United States	Philadelphia	2-1
1965	Australia	United States	Melbourne	2-1
1966	United States	West Germany	Turin	3-0
1967	United States	Great Britain	West Berlin	2-0
1968	Australia	Netherlands	Paris	3-0
1969	United States	Australia	Athens	2-1
1970	Australia	Great Britain	Freiburg	3-0
1971	Australia	Great Britain	Perth	3-0
1972	South Africa	Great Britain	Johannesburg	2-1
1973	Australia	South Africa	Bad Homburg	3-0
1974	Australia	United States	Naples	2-1
1975	Czechoslovakia	Australia	Aix-en-Provence	3-0
1976	United States	Australia	Philadelphia	2-1
1977	United States	Australia	Eastbourne, UK	2-1
1978	United States	Australia	Melbourne	2-1
1979	United States	Australia	Madrid	3-0
1980	United States	Australia	West Berlin	3-0
1981	United States	Great Britain	Nagoya	3-0
1982	United States	West Germany	Santa Clara	3-0
1983	Czechoslovakia	West Germany	Zurich	2-1
1984	Czechoslovakia	Australia	Sao Paulo	2-1
1985	Czechoslovakia	United States	Tokyo	2-1
1986	United States	Czechoslovakia	Prague	3-0
1987	West Germany	United States	Vancouver	2-1
1988	Czechoslovakia	USSR	Melbourne	2-1
1989	United States	Spain	Tokyo	3-0
1990	United States	USSR	Atlanta	2-1
1991	Spain	United States	Nottingham	2-1
1992	Germany	Spain	Frankfurt	2-1
1993	Spain	Australia	Frankfurt	3-0
1994	Spain	United States	Frankfurt	3-0
1995	Spain	United States	Valencia, Spain	3-2
1996	United States	Spain	Atlantic City	5-0

Romanian Politics Gets Nasty

As a tennis player, Ilie Nastase was known as much for his guile and guff as he was for the dazzling skills that made him the world's best player in 1973. So it is fitting that now, at 49, he has become a political player in his homeland of Romania. In December 1995 Nasty was elected to the national council that plots strategy for the ruling Social Democracy Party.

Nastase devised his own strategy during his heyday, one that at turns angered and enthralled the tennis world. "I want to play the game inside out and upside down," Nastase once said, and he did exactly that. He regularly disrupted matches by refusing to play for several minutes (invaluble filibuster experience) and also taunted opponents and flipped the bird to the crowd (excellent preparation for legislative debate). During one tantrum he slammed a ball at an official.

There has always been a bit of the ingratiating politician in Nastase, who could charm his peers even after rankling them. When his shenanigans had led the normally coolheaded Arthur Ashe to call him an "ass," he brought Ashe a bouquet. Now, with his swagger and good looks, Nastase will attempt to aid the Social Democrats, Romania's most prominent party since the overthrow of the country's Communist regime in 1989. A former army officer who speaks five languages, Nastase remains an alluring figure in Romania, particularly in Bucharest, the capital city, where he grew up the son of a bank cashier and where he now owns a restaurant and sports club. "It's a very clean city," Nastase once said. "Lots of chickies, too. Everybody drinks beer and Pepsi and has a good time."

Nastase said that he wouldn't run for any office in Romania's general elections in 1996. But he has always been unpredictable. And now that he's back in the public eye, people are once again wondering: What will Nasty do next?

Rankings

ATP Computer Year-End Top 10
MEN

1973

1 ....Ilie Nastase
2 ....John Newcombe
3 ....Jimmy Connors
4 ....Tom Okker
5 ....Stan Smith
6 ....Ken Rosewall
7 ....Manuel Orantes
8 ....Rod Laver
9 ....Jan Kodes
10 ..Arthur Ashe

1974

1 ....Jimmy Connors
2 ....John Newcombe
3 ....Bjorn Borg
4 ....Rod Laver
5 ....Guillermo Vilas
6 ....Tom Okker
7 ....Arthur Ashe
8 ....Ken Rosewall
9 ....Stan Smith
10 ..Ilie Nastase

1975

1 ....Jimmy Connors
2 ....Guillermo Vilas
3 ....Bjorn Borg
4 ....Arthur Ashe
5 ....Manuel Orantes
6 ....Ken Rosewall
7 ....Ilie Nastase
8 ....John Alexander
9 ....Roscoe Tanner
10 ..Rod Laver

1976

1 ....Jimmy Connors
2 ....Bjorn Borg
3 ....Ilie Nastase
4 ....Manuel Orantes
5 ....Raul Ramirez
6 ....Guillermo Vilas
7 ....Adriano Panatta
8 ....Harold Solomon
9 ....Eddie Dibbs
10 ..Brian Gottfried

1977

1 ....Jimmy Connors
2 ....Guillermo Vilas
3 ....Bjorn Borg
4 ....Vitas Gerulaitis
5 ....Brian Gottfried
6 ....Eddie Dibbs
7 ....Manuel Orantes
8 ....Raul Ramirez
9 ....Ilie Nastase
10 ..Dick Stockton

1978

1 ....Jimmy Connors
2 ....Bjorn Borg
3 ....Guillermo Vilas
4 ....John McEnroe
5 ....Vitas Gerulaitis
6 ....Eddie Dibbs
7 ....Brian Gottfried
8 ....Raul Ramirez
9 ....Harold Solomon
10 ..Corrado Barazzutti

1979

1 ....Bjorn Borg
2 ....Jimmy Connors
3 ....John McEnroe
4 ....Vitas Gerulaitis
5 ....Roscoe Tanner
6 ....Guillermo Vilas
7 ....Arthur Ashe
8 ....Harold Solomon
9 ....Jose Higueras
10 ..Eddie Dibbs

1980

1 ....Bjorn Borg
2 ....John McEnroe
3 ....Jimmy Connors
4 ....Gene Mayer
5 ....Guillermo Vilas
6 ....Ivan Lendl
7 ....Harold Solomon
8 ....Jose-Luis Clerc
9 ....Vitas Gerulaitis
10 ..Eliot Teltscher

1981

1 ....John McEnroe
2 ....Ivan Lendl
3 ....Jimmy Connors
4 ....Bjorn Borg
5 ....Jose-Luis Clerc
6 ....Guillermo Vilas
7 ....Gene Mayer
8 ....Eliot Teltscher
9 ....Vitas Gerulaitis
10 ..Peter McNamara

1982

1 ....John McEnroe
2 ....Jimmy Connors
3 ....Ivan Lendl
4 ....Guillermo Vilas
5 ....Vitas Gerulaitis
6 ....Jose-Luis Clerc
7 ....Mats Wilander
8 ....Gene Mayer
9 ....Yannick Noah
10 ..Peter McNamara

1983

1 ....John McEnroe
2 ....Ivan Lendl
3 ....Jimmy Connors
4 ....Mats Wilander
5 ....Yannick Noah
6 ....Jimmy Arias
7 ....Jose Higueras
8 ....Jose-Luis Clerc
9 ....Kevin Curren
10 ..Gene Mayer

1984

1 ....John McEnroe
2 ....Jimmy Connors
3 ....Ivan Lendl
4 ....Mats Wilander
5 ....Andres Gomez
6 ....Anders Jarryd
7 ....Henrik Sundstrom
8 ....Pat Cash
9 ....Eliot Teltscher
10 ..Yannick Noah

1985

1 ....Ivan Lendl
2 ....John McEnroe
3 ....Mats Wilander
4 ....Jimmy Connors
5 ....Stefan Edberg
6 ....Boris Becker
7 ....Yannick Noah
8 ....Anders Jarryd
9 ....Miloslav Mecir
10 ..Kevin Curren

1986

1 ....Ivan Lendl
2 ....Boris Becker
3 ....Mats Wilander
4 ....Yannick Noah
5 ....Stefan Edberg
6 ....Henri Leconte
7 ....Joakim Nystrom
8 ....Jimmy Connors
9 ....Miloslav Mecir
10 ..Andres Gomez

1987

1 ....Ivan Lendl
2 ....Stefan Edberg
3 ....Mats Wilander
4 ....Jimmy Connors
5 ....Boris Becker
6 ....Miloslav Mecir
7 ....Pat Cash
8 ....Yannick Noah
9 ....Tim Mayotte
10 ..John McEnroe

ATP Computer Year-End Top 10 *(Cont.)*
MEN *(CONT.)*

1988
1 ....Mats Wilander
2 ....Ivan Lendl
3 ....Andre Agassi
4 ....Boris Becker
5 ....Stefan Edberg
6 ....Kent Carlsson
7 ....Jimmy Connors
8 ....Jakob Hlasek
9 ....Henri Leconte
10 ..Tim Mayotte

1989
1 ....Ivan Lendl
2 ....Boris Becker
3 ....Stefan Edberg
4 ....John McEnroe
5 ....Michael Chang
6 ....Brad Gilbert
7 ....Andre Agassi
8 ....Aaron Krickstein
9 ....Alberto Mancini
10 ..Jay Berger

1990
1 ....Stefan Edberg
2 ....Boris Becker
3 ....Ivan Lendl
4 ....Andre Agassi
5 ....Pete Sampras
6 ....Andres Gomez
7 ....Thomas Muster
8 ....Emilio Sanchez
9 ....Goran Ivanisevic
10 ..Brad Gilbert

1991
1 ....Stefan Edberg
2 ....Jim Courier
3 ....Boris Becker
4 ....Michael Stich
5 ....Ivan Lendl
6 ....Pete Sampras
7 ....Guy Forget
8 ....Karel Novacek
9 ....Petr Korda
10 ..Andre Agassi

1992
1 ....Jim Courier
2 ....Stefan Edberg
3 ....Pete Sampras
4 ....Goran Ivanisevic
5 ....Boris Becker
6 ....Michael Chang
7 ....Petr Korda
8 ....Ivan Lendl
9 ....Andre Agassi
10 ..Richard Krajicek

1993
1 ....Pete Sampras
2 ....Michael Stich
3 ....Jim Courier
4 ....Sergi Bruguera
5 ....Stefan Edberg
6 ....Andrei Medvedev
7 ....Goran Ivanisevic
8 ....Michael Chang
9 ....Thomas Muster
10 ..Cedric Pioline

1994
1 ....Pete Sampras
2 ....Andre Agassi
3 ....Boris Becker
4 ....Sergi Bruguera
5 ....Goran Ivanisevic
6 ....Michael Chang
7 ....Stefan Edberg
8 ....Alberto Berasategui
9 ....Michael Stich
10 ..Todd Martin

1995
1 ....Pete Sampras
2 ....Andre Agassi
3 ....Thomas Muster
4 ....Boris Becker
5 ....Michael Chang
6 ....Yevgeny Kafelnikov
7 ....Thomas Enqvist
8 ....Jim Courier
9 ....Wayne Ferreira
10 ..Goran Ivanisevic

WTA Computer Year-End Top 10
WOMEN

1973
1 ....Margaret Smith Court
2 ....Billie Jean King
3 ....Evonne Goolagong
4 ....Chris Evert
5 ....Rosie Casals
6 ....Virginia Wade
7 ....Kerry Reid
8 ....Nancy Gunter
9 ....Julie Heldman
10 ..Helga Masthoff

1974
1 ....Billie Jean King
2 ....Evonne Goolagong
3 ....Chris Evert
4 ....Virginia Wade
5 ....Julie Heldman
6 ....Rosie Casals
7 ....Kerry Reid
8 ....Olga Morozova
9 ....Lesley Hunt
10 ..Francoise Durr

1975
1 ....Chris Evert
2 ....Billie Jean King
3 ....Evonne Goolagong Cawley
4 ....Martina Navratilova
5 ....Virginia Wade
6 ....Margaret Smith Court
7 ....Olga Morozova
8 ....Nancy Gunter
9 ....Francoise Durr
10 ..Rosie Casals

1976
1 ....Chris Evert
2 ....Evonne Goolagong Cawley
3 ....Virginia Wade
4 ....Martina Navratilova
5 ....Sue Barker
6 ....Betty Stove
7 ....Dianne Balestrat
8 ....Mima Jausovec
9 ....Rosie Casals
10 ..Francoise Durr

1977
1 ....Chris Evert
2 ....Billie Jean King
3 ....Martina Navratilova
4 ....Virginia Wade
5 ....Sue Barker
6 ....Rosie Casals
7 ....Betty Stove
8 ....Dianne Balestrat
9 ....Wendy Turnbull
10 ..Kerry Reid

1978
1 ....Martina Navratilova
2 ....Chris Evert
3 ....Evonne Goolagong Cawley
4 ....Virginia Wade
5 ....Billie Jean King
6 ....Tracy Austin
7 ....Wendy Turnbull
8 ....Kerry Reid
9 ....Betty Stove
10 ..Dianne Balestrat

WTA Computer Year-End Top 10 (Cont.)

WOMEN (CONT.)

1979

1 ....Martina Navratilova
2 ....Chris Evert Lloyd
3 ....Tracy Austin
4 ....Evonne Goolagong Cawley
5 ....Billie Jean King
6 ....Dianne Balestrat
7 ....Wendy Turnbull
8 ....Virginia Wade
9 ....Kerry Reid
10 ..Sue Barker

1980

1 ....Chris Evert Lloyd
2 ....Tracy Austin
3 ....Martina Navratilova
4 ....Hana Mandlikova
5 ....Evonne Goolagong Cawley
6 ....Billie Jean King
7 ....Andrea Jaeger
8 ....Wendy Turnbull
9 ....Pam Shriver
10 ..Greer Stevens

1981

1 ....Chris Evert Lloyd
2 ....Tracy Austin
3 ....Martina Navratilova
4 ....Andrea Jaeger
5 ....Hana Mandlikova
6 ....Sylvia Hanika
7 ....Pam Shriver
8 ....Wendy Turnbull
9 ....Bettina Bunge
10 ..Barbara Potter

1982

1 ....Martina Navratilova
2 ....Chris Evert Lloyd
3 ....Andrea Jaeger
4 ....Tracy Austin
5 ....Wendy Turnbull
6 ....Pam Shriver
7 ....Hana Mandlikova
8 ....Barbara Potter
9 ....Bettina Bunge
10 ..Sylvia Hanika

1983

1 ....Martina Navratilova
2 ....Chris Evert Lloyd
3 ....Andrea Jaeger
4 ....Pam Shriver
5 ....Sylvia Hanika
6 ....Jo Durie
7 ....Bettina Bunge
8 ....Wendy Turnbull
9 ....Tracy Austin
10 ..Zina Garrison

1984

1 ....Martina Navratilova
2 ....Chris Evert Lloyd
3 ....Hana Mandlikova
4 ....Pam Shriver
5 ....Wendy Turnbull
6 ....Manuela Maleeva
7 ....Helena Sukova
8 ....Claudia Kohde-Kilsch
9 ....Zina Garrison
10 ..Kathy Jordan

1985

1 ....Martina Navratilova
2 ....Chris Evert Lloyd
3 ....Hana Mandlikova
4 ....Pam Shriver
5 ....Claudia Kohde-Kilsch
6 ....Steffi Graf
7 ....Manuela Maleeva
8 ....Zina Garrison
9 ....Helena Sukova
10 ..Bonnie Gadusek

1986

1 ....Martina Navratilova
2 ....Chris Evert Lloyd
4 ....Hana Mandlikova
5 ....Helena Sukova
6 ....Pam Shriver
7 ....Claudia Kohde-Kilsch
8 ....Manuela Maleeva
9 ....Kathy Rinaldi
10 ..Gabriela Sabatini

1987

1 ....Steffi Graf
2 ....Martina Navratilova
3 ....Chris Evert
4 ....Pam Shriver
5 ....Hana Mandlikova
6 ....Gabriela Sabatini
7 ....Helena Sukova
8 ....Manuela Maleeva
9 ....Zina Garrison
10 ..Claudia Kohde-Kilsch

1988

1 ....Steffi Graf
2 ....Martina Navratilova
3 ....Chris Evert
4 ....Gabriela Sabatini
5 ....Pam Shriver
6 ....Manuela Maleeva-Fragniere
7 ....Natalia Zvereva
8 ....Helena Sukova
9 ....Zina Garrison
10 ..Barbara Potter

1989

1 ....Steffi Graf
2 ....Martina Navratilova
3 ....Gabriela Sabatini
4 ....Zina Garrison
5 ....Arantxa Sánchez Vicario
6 ....Monica Seles
7 ....Conchita Martinez
8 ....Helena Sukova
9 ....Manuela Maleeva-Fragniere
10 ..*Chris Evert

1990

1 ....Steffi Graf
2 ....Monica Seles
3 ....Martina Navratilova
4 ....Mary Joe Fernandez
5 ....Gabriela Sabatini
6 ....Katerina Maleeva
7 ....Arantxa Sánchez Vicario
8 ....Jennifer Capriati
9 ....Manuela Maleeva-Fragniere
10 ..Zina Garrison

1991

1 ....Monica Seles
2 ....Steffi Graf
3 ....Gabriela Sabatini
4 ....Martina Navratilova
5 ....Arantxa Sánchez Vicario
6 ....Jennifer Capriati
7 ....Jana Novotna
8 ....Mary Joe Fernandez
9 ....Conchita Martinez
10 ..Manuela Maleeva-Fragniere

1992

1 ....Monica Seles
2 ....Steffi Graf
3 ....Gabriela Sabatini
4 ....Arantxa Sánchez Vicario
5 ....Martina Navratilova
6 ....Mary Joe Fernandez
7 ....Jennifer Capriati
8 ....Conchita Martinez
9 ....Manuela Maleeva-Fragniere
10 ..Jana Novotna

1993

1 ....Steffi Graf
2 ....Arantxa Sánchez Vicario
3 ....Martina Navratilova
4 ....Conchita Martinez
5 ....Gabriela Sabatini
6 ....Jana Novotna
7 ....Mary Joe Fernandez
8 ....Monica Seles
9 ....Jennifer Capriati
10 ..Anke Huber

*When Chris Evert announced her retirement at the 1989 United States Open, she was ranked 4 in the world. That was her last official series tournament.

WTA Computer Year-End Top 10 (Cont.)
WOMEN (CONT.)

1994
1 ....Steffi Graf
2 ....Arantxa Sánchez Vicario
3 ....Conchita Martinez
4 ....Jana Novotna
5 ....Mary Pierce
6 ....Lindsay Davenport
7 ....Gabriela Sabatini
8 ....Martina Navratilova
9 ....Kimiko Date
10 ..Natasha Zvereva

1995
1 ....Steffi Graf (co-No. 1)
1 ....Monica Seles (co-No. 1)
2 ....Conchita Martinez
3 ....Arantxa Sánchez Vicario
4 ....Kimiko Date
5 ....Mary Pierce
6 ....Magdalena Maleeva
7 ....Gabriela Sabatini
8 ....Mary Joe Fernandez
9 ....Iva Majoli
10 ..Anke Huber

Prize Money

Top 25 Men's Career Prize Money Leaders

Note: From arrival of Open tennis in 1968 through October 6, 1996.

	Earnings ($)
Pete Sampras	23,614,350
Ivan Lendl	21,262,417
Stefan Edberg	20,532,861
Boris Becker	20,243,822
Michael Chang	13,204,026
Goran Ivanisevic	13,137,650
John McEnroe	12,539,622
Andre Agassi	12,317,063
Jim Courier	12,154,705
Michael Stich	12,104,156
Sergi Bruguera	9,499,201
Jimmy Connors	8,641,040
Thomas Muster	8,105,134
Mats Wilander	7,973,256
Petr Korda	7,311,121
Guy Forget	5,574,268
Brad Gilbert	5,507,745
Jakob Hlasek	5,490,470
Wayne Ferreira	5,390,983
Anders Jarryd	5,376,517
Emilio Sanchez	5,301,460
Mark Woodforde	5,124,509
David Wheaton	5,045,419
Guillermo Vilas	4,923,882
Yevgeny Kafelnikov	4,850,932

Top 25 Women's Career Prize Money Leaders

Note: From arrival of Open tennis in 1968 through October 6, 1996.

	Earnings ($)
Martina Navratilova	20,344,061
Steffi Graf	19,307,816
Arantxa Sánchez Vicario	11,208,976
Chris Evert	8,896,195
Monica Seles	8,872,740
Gabriela Sabatini	8,766,305
Conchita Martinez	5,988,916
Helena Sukova	5,895,089
Jana Novotna	5,845,335
Pam Shriver	5,441,586
Natasha Zvereva	5,282,038
Zina Garrison Jackson	4,572,421
Gigi Fernandez	4,197,874
Mary Joe Fernandez	3,990,439
Hana Mandlikova	3,340,959
Manuela Maleeva-Fragniere	3,244,811
Larisa Neiland	3,178,904
Lori McNeil	3,145,449
Wendy Turnbull	2,769,024
Anke Huber	2,472,815
Nathalie Tauziat	2,374,887
Mary Pierce	2,337,870
Claudia Kohde-Kilsch	2,227,043
Katerina Maleeva	2,217,816
Brenda Schultz-McCarthy	2,049,172

Yet Another Sign That the Apocalypse Is Upon Us

Tennis Extra Magazine, a 30-minute syndicated show that debuted in April, hired as its host presidential brother Roger Clinton.

Open Era Overall Wins

Men's Career Leaders—Singles Titles Won

The top tournament-winning men from the institution of Open tennis in 1968 through October 6, 1996.

	W		W
Jimmy Connors	109	Stefan Edberg	41
Ivan Lendl	94	Stan Smith	39
John McEnroe	77	Andre Agassi	34
Bjorn Borg	62	Arthur Ashe	33
Guillermo Vilas	62	Mats Wilander	33
Ilie Nastase	57	John Newcombe	32
Rod Laver	47	Manuel Orantes	32
Boris Becker	46	Ken Rosewall	32
Pete Sampras	43	Tom Okker	31
Thomas Muster	42	Vitas Gerulaitis	27

Women's Career Leaders—Singles Titles Won

The top tournament-winning women from the institution of Open tennis in 1968 through October 6, 1996.

	W		W
Martina Navratilova	167	Conchita Martinez	30
Chris Evert	157	Tracy Austin	29
Steffi Graf	101	Hana Mandlikova	27
Evonne Goolagong Cawley	88	Gabriela Sabatini	27
Margaret Court	79	Nancy Richey	25
Billie Jean King	67	Arantxa Sánchez Vicario	24
Virginia Wade	55	Kerry Melville Reid	22
Monica Seles	38	Sue Barker	21
Helga Masthoff	37	Pam Shriver	21
Olga Morozova	31	Julie Heldman	20

Annual ATP/WTA Champions

Men—ATP Tour World Championship

Year	Player	Year	Player
1970	Stan Smith	1984	John McEnroe
1971	Ilie Nastase	1985	John McEnroe
1972	Ilie Nastase	1986 (Jan)	Ivan Lendl
1973	Ilie Nastase	1986 (Dec)	Ivan Lendl
1974	Guillermo Vilas	1987	Ivan Lendl
1975	Ilie Nastase	1988	Boris Becker
1976	Manuel Orantes	1989	Stefan Edberg
1977	Not held	1990	Andre Agassi
1978	Jimmy Connors	1991	Pete Sampras
1979	John McEnroe	1992	Boris Becker
1980	Bjorn Borg	1993	Michael Stich
1981	Bjorn Borg	1994	Pete Sampras
1982	Ivan Lendl	1995	Boris Becker
1983	Ivan Lendl		

Note: Event held twice in 1986.

Women—WTA Tour Championship

Year	Player	Year	Player
1972	Chris Evert	1985	Martina Navratilova
1973	Chris Evert	1986 (Mar)	Martina Navratilova
1974	Evonne Goolagong	1986 (Nov)	Martina Navratilova
1975	Chris Evert	1987	Steffi Graf
1976	Evonne Goolagong	1988	Gabriela Sabatini
1977	Chris Evert	1989	Steffi Graf
1978	Martina Navratilova	1990	Monica Seles
1979	Martina Navratilova	1991	Monica Seles
1980	Tracy Austin	1992	Monica Seles
1981	Martina Navratilova	1993	Steffi Graf
1982	Sylvia Hanika	1994	Gabriela Sabatini
1983	Martina Navratilova	1995	Steffi Graf
1984*	Martina Navratilova		

*Since 1984 the final has been best-of-five sets.
Note: Event held twice in 1986.

Serving Tennis Wrong

It would be easy for Americans to look back contentedly at the Olympic tennis competition, inasmuch as the U.S. won gold in three of the four events. But some Americans, including women's singles champion Lindsay Davenport, found the experience unsatisfying, and the International Tennis Federation (ITF), which oversees the Olympic tournament, should heed their grousing. "This is so bogus," says Davenport of a format featuring the usual looking-out-for-number-one, single-elimination slog characteristic of the rest of the tennis calendar. "We do everything as a team, eat together and room together, and then we go off and play separate matches."

Olympic tennis sorely needs a team element to distinguish it from ordinary tour stops, but the ITF can hardly be counted on to come up with a fresh format for the Sydney Games in 2000. The sport's international governing body can't even work out enough of a truce in its feud with the ATP to keep the men's tour from holding tournaments during the Olympic fortnight.

Any of several alternative formats would enliven the Olympic competition. Round-robin play using the simple Van Alen scoring system—31 points wins the match, just as 21 points wins a game in table tennis—would treat Olympic spectators, who typically aren't hard-core tennis fans, to shorter matches and the chance to see more players on a given day. The World Team Tennis format, in which matches consist of one set in each of five categories (men's and women's singles, men's and women's doubles, and mixed doubles), with the winner determined by total games won, would make each point more meaningful. Mixed doubles, in particular, would underscore that tennis is that rarest of sports, one in which men and women can compete together.

At the very least the ITF should identify players' nationalities on the scoreboard, and establish some parallel team competition, as gymnastics has, for the world's dozen or so most powerful tennis nations. The aforementioned changes would exalt the team over the individual and thereby enrich the sport. Without them, this Admiral Stockdale of Olympic events will continue to raise the questions, What is it? Why is it here?

Pauline Betz Addie (1965)
George T. Adee (1964)
Fred B. Alexander (1961)
Wilmer L. Allison (1963)
Manuel Alonso (1977)
Arthur Ashe (1985)
Juliette Atkinson (1974)
Tracy Austin (1992)
Lawrence A. Baker Sr (1975)
Maud Barger-Wallach (1958)
Angela Mortimer Barrett (1993)
Karl Behr (1969)
Bjorn Borg (1987)
Jean Borotra (1976)
Maureen Connolly Brinker(1968)
John Bromwich (1984)
Norman Everard Brookes (1977)
Mary K. Browne (1957)
Jacques Brugnon (1976)
J. Donald Budge (1964)
Maria E. Bueno (1978)
May Sutton Bundy (1956)
Mabel E. Cahill (1976)
Rosie Casals (1996)
Oliver S. Campbell (1955)
Malcolm Chace (1961)
Dorothea Douglass
   Chambers (1981)
Philippe Chatrier (1992)
Louise Brough Clapp (1967)
Clarence Clark (1983)
Joseph S. Clark (1955)
William J. Clothier (1956)
Henri Cochet (1976)
Arthur W. (Bud) Collins Jr (1994)
Ashley Cooper (1991)
Margaret Smith Court (1979)
Gottfried von Cramm (1977)
Jack Crawford (1979)
Joseph F. Cullman III (1990)
Allison Danzig (1968)
Sarah Palfrey Danzig (1963)
Dwight F. Davis (1956)
Charlotte Dod (1983)
John H. Doeg (1962)
Lawrence Doherty (1980)
Reginald Doherty (1980)
Jaroslav Drobny (1983)
Margaret Osborne duPont
   (1967)
James Dwight (1955)
Roy Emerson (1982)
Pierre Etchebaster (1978)
Chris Evert (1995)
Robert Falkenburg (1974)
Neale Fraser (1984)
Shirley Fry-Irvin (1970)
Charles S. Garland (1969)

Althea Gibson (1971)
Kathleen McKane Godfree
   (1978)
Richard A. Gonzales (1968)
Evonne Goolagong Cawley
   (1988)
Bryan M. Grant Jr (1972)
David Gray (1985)
Clarence Griffin (1970)
King Gustaf V of Sweden
   (1980)
Harold H. Hackett (1961)
Ellen Forde Hansell (1965)
Darlene R. Hard (1973)
Doris J. Hart (1969)
Gladys M. Heldman (1979)
W. E. (Slew) Hester Jr (1981)
Bob Hewitt (1992)
Lew Hoad (1980)
Harry Hopman (1978)
Fred Hovey (1974)
Joseph R. Hunt (1966)
Lamar Hunt (1993)
Francis T. Hunter (1961)
Helen Hull Jacobs (1962)
William Johnston (1958)
Ann Haydon Jones (1985)
Perry Jones (1970)
Billie Jean King (1987)
Jan Kodes (1990)
John A. Kramer (1968)
Rene Lacoste (1976)
Al Laney (1979)
William A. Larned (1956)
Arthur D. Larsen (1969)
Rod G. Laver (1981)
Suzanne Lenglen (1978)
Dorothy Round Little (1986)
George M. Lott Jr (1964)
Gene Mako (1973)
Molla Bjurstedt Mallory (1958)
Hana Mandlikova (1994)
Alice Marble (1964)
Alastair B. Martin (1973)
Dan Maskell (1996)
William McChesney Martin (1982)
Chuck McKinley (1986)
Maurice McLoughlin (1957)
Frew McMillan (1992)
W. Donald McNeill (1965)
Elisabeth H. Moore (1971)
Gardnar Mulloy (1972)
R. Lindley Murray (1958)
Julian S. Myrick (1963)
Ilie Nastase (1991)
John D. Newcombe (1986)
Arthur C. Nielsen Sr (1971)
Alex Olmedo (1987)

Rafael Osuna (1979)
Mary Ewing Outerbridge (1981)
Frank A. Parker (1966)
Gerald Patterson (1989)
Budge Patty (1977)
Theodore R. Pell (1966)
Fred Perry (1975)
Tom Pettitt (1982)
Nicola Pietrangeli (1986)
Adrian Quist (1984)
Dennis Ralston (1987)
Ernest Renshaw (1983)
William Renshaw (1983)
Vincent Richards (1961)
Bobby Riggs (1967)
Helen Wills Moody Roark
   (1959)
Anthony D. Roche (1986)
Ellen C. Roosevelt (1975)
Ken Rosewall (1980)
Elizabeth Ryan (1972)
Manuel Santana (1984)
Richard Savitt (1976)
Frederick R. Schroeder (1966)
Eleonora Sears (1968)
Richard D. Sears (1955)
Frank Sedgman (1979)
Pancho Segura (1984)
Vic Seixas Jr (1971)
Francis X. Shields (1964)
Betty Nuthall Shoemaker (1977)
Henry W. Slocum Jr (1955)
Stan Smith (1987)
Fred Stolle (1985)
William F. Talbert (1967)
Bill Tilden (1959)
Lance Tingay (1982)
Ted Tinling (1986)
Bertha Townsend Toulmin
   (1974)
Tony Trabert (1970)
James H. Van Alen (1965)
John Van Ryn (1963)
Guillermo Vilas (1991)
Ellsworth Vines (1962)
Virginia Wade (1989)
Marie Wagner (1969)
Holcombe Ward (1956)
Watson Washburn (1965)
Malcolm D. Whitman (1955)
Hazel Hotchkiss Wightman
   (1957)
Anthony Wilding (1978)
Richard Norris Williams II
   (1957)
Sidney B. Wood (1964)
Robert D. Wrenn (1955)
Beals C. Wright (1956)

Note: Years in parentheses are dates of induction.

Golf

APRIL 22, 1996 · $2.95 (CAN. $3.80)

AGONY
at
AUGUSTA
— Greg Norman —

JOHN BIEVER

A Child Shall Lead Them

In a strange and wondrous year, the star of the golf firmament was a 20-year-old amateur-turned-pro named Tiger Woods

by Rick Reilly

A 20-YEAR-old kid made $60,002,544 at the Milwaukee Open.

A man lost a playoff in a TV tower.

A man lost a playoff after leaving the course.

A man won the national championship by reading a book, and ....

A shark got eaten alive.

That's what kind of year it was in golf in 1996. And yet at the same time, it was one of golf's most memorable. That was thanks to the 20-year-old who became not only the Story of the Year, but also the PGA Tour Rookie of the Year, the Endorsement King of the Year, the Most Controversial Nike Ad of the Year and the Amateur for the Ages—Tiger Woods.

Woods, skinny as a 1-iron but twice as steely, ended his remarkable amateur career by coming from behind to win his third straight U.S. Amateur title, then turned pro and six weeks later won his first tournament and qualified for his PGA card with a win in Las Vegas. That Amateur three-peat is a feat no player in history can meet—not Jack Nicklaus (two in three years), not Ben Hogan (none), not lifelong amateur Bobby Hogan (none), not lifelong amateur Bobby Jones (five, but never three in a row) and not Arnold Palmer (one). Even more breathtaking, it was Woods's sixth straight USGA title; he won three straight U.S. Junior Amateurs before he was old enough to play the varsity version. His match-play record in those six events was a spiffy 42–3.

But this one at Pumpkin Ridge, just outside Portland, was unforgettable. To win a U.S. Amateur, you do not just have to play one great round, or two; you must win for seven straight days. Come down with a little flying elbow or have a small argument with your putter and it's over. But Woods and his titanium composure breezed through everybody until the finals, when he ran into Steve Scott, the 19-year-old University of Florida wunderkind who suddenly found he was riding a Tiger—5 up with 16 holes to play.

Fifteen thousand chaperoned the underage twosome that day—the biggest crowd at an amateur since Bobby Jones won his Grand Slam at Merion in Philadelphia in 1930. Woods was still 2 down with three to play when he sank an eight-footer for a birdie on the 34th hole, then stared down a 35-footer on, yes, the 35th hole, and somehow

Woods's Amateur win and smashing pro debut gave golf a shot of adrenaline.

ROBERT BECK

drained that to pull even. When they tied the 36th and 37th and Scott bogeyed the 38th, all Woods needed was an 18-inch putt for his title. The hug Tiger put on his dad that day was twice as long as Dave Letterman ever put on Goldie Hawn.

Looking back on it, he'd hit 28 of his last 29 greens, fired a bogeyless 65 on the final 18 holes (to Scott's respectable two-under 70) and didn't even know it. "Given the circumstances," Woods said when told what he'd done, "that has to be the best I've ever played."

Three days later he was a pro, signing a package of endorsement deals with Nike and Titleist and who knows who else, that were valued as high as $60 million, and nobody was saying he wasn't worth it. The only problem marketing Tiger is hardly a problem at all—which golden path do you take? Do you market him as the longest player in the game? (At the B.C. Open you couldn't have built a decent-sized toolshed between his ball and what he had left for his second shot on the 350-yard par 4s.) As the one with the most talent? As the pro from Generation X? As the next Nicklaus? As the black Nicklaus?

Nike decided to start with the latter, in a haymaker debut ad that introduced Tiger as a person who, despite his considerable achievements, can't play on some American courses because of "the color of my skin."

Baloney, said golf. Baloney, said golf writers. All true, said Woods. "Semantics," said the author of the ad, Weiden and Kennedy's Jim Riswold. "Obviously Tiger could probably get on any course he wanted. But could

any 20-year-old black man? No way. That's the point."

Whatever Woods was going to be, it was clear right from the beginning that he was going to become it in a hurry. Using his seven possible sponsor exemptions, he set out on a crash-course final closeout PGA Tour cash grab to try to earn enough money to land in the top 125 and earn his PGA card for 1997. He finished tied for 60th at the Milwaukee Open, finished 11th in the Canadian Open, then stunned the game by leading after three rounds at Quad Cities. Eventually he took a quadruple bogey 8 on the final day—putting the quad in Quad Cities—to finish tied for fifth. Then he finished tied for third at the B.C. Open. Then he *won* the Las Vegas Invitational. In five weeks he'd made $437,194, earned a two-year tour exemption, got into next year's

Lehman met every challenge, including Royal Lytham's treacherous bunkers.

Masters and placed himself 40th on the PGA money list. With two tournaments to go he was even conceivably within range of the $600,000 or so he would need to qualify for the year-ending Tour championship. Can you get stock in this kid?

Whatever becomes of him in his long professional career, may he never have a day like Greg (Shark) Norman did at the 1996 Masters. This was the Masters that was supposed to be his, the 39-regular green jacket that had gotten away from him so many times before—to Nicklaus in '86, to Larry Mize in '87, to Ben Crenshaw in '95. This time there seemed to be none of that. By Saturday night he had dominated the azaleas and the field, practically lapped it, posting a 63 on Friday and leading second-place Nick Faldo, his nemesis, by six shots going into the Sunday that promised to be his.

But by the end of that Sunday he had thrown a lead sale. He gave all six of those shots away and five more besides. He had turned the most gorgeous grounds in golf into a kind of funeral parlor in which men shook their heads and stared at their shoes and women wiped away tears. Faldo reeled him in slowly and surely—four strokes on the front nine, three more on Amen Cor-

ner—until Norman chunk-hooked an ugly six-iron into the pond at the 16th on his way to another double bogey. He had taken his coronation parade and driven it off a pier.

The victory ceremony on the 18th green was more like a dirge. "I feel so badly for Greg," said Faldo. "Just very sorry." Thus, Norman takes his place at the head of the table of great Masters' goats—Ken Venturi in 1956 (blew a four-shot lead as an amateur), Roberto De Vicenzo in 1968 (signed an incorrect card), Ed Sneed in 1979 (bogeyed the last three holes) and Scott Hoch in 1989 (missed a three-footer to win). Faldo, meanwhile, kept his usual reservation at the annual champions dinner. It was his third green jacket in eight years, the sixth major of his career, the most of any golfer in the '80s and '90s. "Well," said a brave Norman afterward, "I screwed up. It's all on me. I know that. But losing this Masters championship is not the end of the world.... I'll wake up tomorrow morning and I'll breathe. [Pause.] I hope."

Compared to that, the annual screamfest known as the U.S. Open was the company picnic. Steve Jones, back from a three-year absence from golf after a brutal motorcycle accident, somehow won the U.S. Open at Oakland Hills in suburban Detroit with a ridiculously accurate driver, the wrong grip (necessitated by the accident; he called it the "reverse overlap Vardon Jones grip") and inspiration from a book written about the most famous comeback golfer of all—Ben Hogan.

Jones (the two-time Colorado sand-greens champion, no less), outlasted his good friend Tom Lehman and Davis Love, who missed a tiddler on 18, by one shot to win not just his first major but also his first tournament in seven years. Afterward—to the great beer-spewing delight of a Mr. Curt Sampson—Jones credited Sampson's biography of Hogan for it. "I read that and I realized just how little I practice," he said. "I really don't think I could've won without that book."

Sales skyrocketed, and Jones became the first U.S. Open champion who had to qualify to get in since Orville Moody in 1969. He also kept alive the Open's new reputation as the Schwab's Drugstore of golf, the place where a guy can get his big break. Jones became the fifth straight Open champion who had never before won a major—Tom Kite in 1992, Lee Janzen in 1993, Ernie Els in 1994, Corey Pavin in 1995 and now Jones in 1996.

Both Pavin and Jones had stepped on Lehman's balding head to accept the trophy—Lehman losing to Pavin at the end at Shinnecock—and Lehman had also lost a crusher to José María Olazábal in the 1994 Masters. And so Lehman was beginning to look like he might be buried in a silver coffin if something good didn't happen soon. So in July, when Lehman took a six-shot lead over (gulp) Faldo into Sunday morning at the British Open at Royal Lytham and St. Anne's, there wasn't a soul in Blackpool, England, who wasn't thinking, uh-oh.

The difference is that Lehman was no Norman. Norman never went through the kinds of balata hell that Lehman went through—the Duluth Opens, the Cheyenne Classics, the sleeping in your car because you can't afford the room at the Red Roof Inn. Norman was never the Hogan tour Player of the Year at 33 years old the way Lehman was. Norman wasn't just five years from filling out a job application that would've had him renting skis to University of Minnesota students in the winter, and only one year from precancerous polyp–removal surgery on his colon. There was a certain grit to Lehman that you just don't see that often, a bulldog in Dockers, who seems to get his teeth into something and doesn't like to let go. This was one bone he didn't want to let go. "That was always my greatest fear," Lehman said. "To die and have it written on my tombstone: 'Here lies Tom Lehman. He couldn't win the Big One.'"

At one point, on the 7th that Sunday, with Faldo stiffing every iron in close, a well-lubricated Brit yelled out, "Remember Augusta!" and another followed with, sarcastically, "Knock it in, Greg!" That only seemed to set the bulldog jaw tighter. "No offense to Greg," Lehman said. "But they were calling me a choker. I wanted to sink that putt just to show them." He didn't, but he made a lot of other ones and hung on for a two-shot victory. That night in his hotel room, when he was fast asleep, somebody should have said, "Here lies Tom Lehman. Relieved as hell."

The strangest victory of all was won by Mark Brooks at the PGA Championship at Valhalla in Louisville, Ky. The leader in the clubhouse was local boy Kenny Perry, only the problem was, Perry wasn't in the clubhouse at all. He was in the CBS-TV tower as Brooks played his final two holes, needing a birdie somewhere to tie Perry and force a playoff. Perry chatted amiably on-air with Venturi. He schmoozed with Jim Nantz. He gave expert commentary as Brooks played the 17th. Commercial. Come back. Perry is *still* there as Brooks plays the 18th. Perry is STILL there when Brooks makes a birdie out of the bunker. Wow. Playoff. Suddenly it occurs to Perry that maybe he should've been staying warm, hitting a few balls, taking a few putts, that sort of thing. Instead, he came down the tower ladder and straight into the playoff, swung like a man with lumbago and lost to Brooks on the very first hole.

Amazingly, Perry didn't regret leaving his first real chance at a major in the tower. "I probably should have had my butt down on the practice range," he said. "But that TV time was good for me. I've been around 10 years out here and, shoot, nobody knows who I am."

Everybody knows who Tom Watson is, and most know that he hadn't won on Tour in nine years. That ended gloriously in 1996 with Watson's thrilling victory at Jack Nicklaus's Memorial Tournament in Dublin, Ohio. This was a giant sigh of a victory, a great exhale for a legend, because Watson had so doggedly refused to change his golfing ways. Clearly one of the best ball-strikers on the PGA Tour these last nine years—"I've never hit it better than I am right now," he said in 1994—his putter had been possessed by a poltergeist, and it was painful to watch. Watson refused to go to a long

BOB MARTIN

the second Presidents Cup, an America versus Every Other Continent Besides Europe semicontrived TV-driven rivalry that somehow is catching on despite its crass intentions. It was won by America's Fred Couples, who also struck the victorious shots two years before to win for the U.S. Couples made a flat 25-foot putt on the 17th hole at the Robert Trent Jones course outside Washington, D.C., in the last match on the course to defeat Fiji's Vijay Singh. When the ball dropped, Couples danced, whooped and threw other people's hats in celebration. Things finally quieted down, then Singh missed a 15-footer that would have sent the match to the last hole. "He stepped on my line," said the Eeyorish Singh, though almost nobody was listening.

Still, the gloomiest face of the year belonged to Jesper Parnevik of Sweden, who had just enough points to make a Saturday playoff at the International in Castle Rock, Colo. This was a bottom-of-the-pile playoff, three out of four go home, one can stay and play on Sunday for all the cash. But Parnevik didn't know he was in the playoff. Parnevik thought he had one point too few and left the course, resigned to take his chances at the next Tour stop. By the time he was told of his mistake it was too late. Of course, this is what comes of wearing your hat like that.

So that was 1996, and you wonder what 1997 will think up. For sure, a whole lot of the attention will be heaped on the kid with the longest drive, the brightest smile and now, the fattest wallet—Eldrick (Tiger) Woods. But on this one September day in 1996, after a simple practice round, Woods was not thinking of any of those things. He was thinking of how cool it was to get a free courtesy car.

Because it's free? a reporter asked.

"No," said Woods.

Because it's luxurious?

"No," he said.

Why then?

"Because the rental-car place wouldn't let me have a car. I'm not 21."

Next thrill: beer!

putter, refused to putt cross-handed, refused to check into Dave Pelz rehab. When Watson made a dicey downhill 12-footer on the 18th to win at Muirfield after so long, it was, at last, vindication. Watson could only smile, but Nicklaus himself summed it up: "I think it's the most thrilling win of any I've seen or accomplished myself in 10 years, since I won at Augusta in '86.... It means an awful lot for the game of golf."

Nineteen ninety-six meant a lot to the near-record nine first-time winners on the PGA Tour, including three in a row in March—Tim Herron at Honda, Paul Goydos at Bay Hill and Scott McCarron at New Orleans—known forevermore as the March of Anonymity.

It also meant a lot to the United States for its women to win the Solheim Cup on foreign soil in late September. The Solheim is the women's version of the Ryder Cup, the one the American men lost the year before. Americans had also lost the Walker and Curtis cups. A fourth in the Solheim would have been an embarrassing four in a row, but it didn't happen, thanks mainly to Michelle McGann's stunning upset of the U.S. Steel of women's golf, Laura Davies.

The American men made up for last year's Ryder Cup loss by taking a thrilling victory in

Men's Majors

The Masters

**Augusta National GC; Augusta, GA
(par 72; 6,925 yds) April 11-14**

Player	Score	Earnings ($)
Nick Faldo	69-67-73-67—276	450,000
Greg Norman	63-69-71-78—281	270,000
Phil Mickelson	65-73-72-72—282	170,000
Frank Nobilo	71-71-72-69—283	120,000
Scott Hoch	67-73-73-71—284	95,000
Duffy Waldorf	72-71-69-72—284	95,000
Corey Pavin	75-66-73-71—285	77,933
Jeff Maggert	71-73-72-69—285	77,993
Davis Love III	72-71-74-68—285	77,993
David Frost	70-68-74-74—286	65,000
Scott McCarron	70-70-72-74—286	65,000
Ernie Els	71-71-72-73—287	52,500
Bob Tway	67-72-76-72—287	52,500
Lee Janzen	68-75-71-73—287	52,500
Fred Couples	78-68-71-71—288	43,750
Mark Calcavecchia	71-73-71-73 288	43,750
John Huston	71-71-71-76—289	40,000
David Duval	73-72-69-76—290	32,600
Nick Price	71-75-70-74—290	32,600
Paul Azinger	70-74-76-60—290	32,600
Mark O'Meara	72-71-75-72—290	32,500
Tom Lehman	75-70-72-73—290	32,500

U.S. Open

**Oakland Hills CC; Bloomfield Hills, MI
(par 70; 6,974 yds) June 13-16**

Player	Score	Earnings ($)
Steve Jones	74-66-69-69—278	425,000
Davis Love III	71-69-70-69—279	204,801
Tom Lehman	71-72-65-71—279	204,801
John Morse	68-74-68-70—280	111,235
Ernie Els	72-67-72-70—281	84,965
Jim Furyk	72-69-70-70—281	84,965
Scott Hoch	73-71-71-67—282	66,295
Vijay Singh	71-72-70-69—282	66,295
Ken Green	73-67-72-70—282	66,295
Lee Janzen	68-75-71-69—283	52,591
Greg Norman	73-66-74-70—283	52,591
Colin Montgomerie	70-72-69-72—283	52,591
Dan Forsman	72-71-70-71—284	43,725
Tom Watson	70-71-71-72—284	43,725
Frank Nobilo	69-71-70-74—284	43,725
Nick Faldo	72-71-72-70—285	33,188
David Berganio	69-72-72-72—285	33,188
Mark O'Meara	72-73-68-72—285	33,188
Mark Brooks	76-68-69-72—285	33,188
John Cook	70-71-71-73—285	33,188
Stewart Cink	69-73-70-73—285	33,188
Sam Torrance	71-69-71-74—285	33,188

British Open

**Royal Lytham & St Anne's; Lytham,
England; (par 71; 6,892 yds) July 18-21**

Player	Score	Earnings ($)
Tom Lehman	67-67-64-73—271	310,000
Mark McCumber	67-69-71-66—273	193,750
Ernie Els	68-67-71-67—273	193,750
Nick Faldo	68-68-68-70—274	116,250
Jeff Maggert	69-70-72-65—276	77,500
Mark Brooks	67-70-68-71—276	77,500
Peter Hedblom	70-65-75-67—277	54,250
Greg Norman	71-68-71-67—277	54,250
Greg Turner	72-69-68-68—277	54,250
Fred Couples	67-70-69-71—277	54,250
Alexander Cejka	73-67-71-67—278	41,850
Darren Clarke	70-68-69-71—278	41,850
Vijay Singh	69-67-69-73—278	41,850
Mark McNulty	69-71-70-69—279	31,388
David Duval	76-67-66-70—279	31,388
Paul McGinley	69-65-74-71—279	31,388
Shigeki Maruyama	68-70-69-72—279	31,388
Michael Welch	71-68-73-68—280	24,025
Padraig Harrington	68-68-73-71—280	24,025
Loren Roberts	67-69-72-72—280	24,025
Rocco Mediate	69-70-69-72—280	24,025

PGA Championship

**Valhalla GC; Louisville, KY
(par 72; 7,144 yds) August 8-11**

Player	Score	Earnings ($)
*Mark Brooks	68-70-69-70—277	430,000
Kenny Perry	66-72-71-68—277	260,000
Tommy Tolles	69-71-71-67—278	140,000
Steve Elkington	67-74-67-70—278	140,000
Justin Leonard	71-66-72-70—279	86,667
Jesper Parnevik	73-67-69-70—279	86,667
Vijay Singh	69-69-69-72—279	86,667
Frank Nobilo	69-72-71-68—280	57,500
Per Johansson	72-71-66-69—280	57,500
Larry Mize	71-70-69-70—280	57,500
Lee Janzen	68-71-71-70—280	57,500
Nick Price	68-71-69-72—280	57,500
Phil Mickelson	67-67-74-72—280	57,500
Joey Sindelar	73-72-69-67—281	39,000
Tom Lehman	71-71-69-70—281	39,000
Mike Brisky	71-69-69-72—281	39,000
D.A. Weibring	71-73-71-67—282	27,286
Tom Watson	69-71-73-69—282	27,286
Brad Faxon	72-68-73-69—282	27,286
Jim Furyk	70-70-73-69—282	27,286
David Edwards	69-71-72-70—282	27,286
Greg Norman	68-72-69-73—282	27,286
Russ Cochran	68-72-65-77—282	27,286

* won on first playoff hole

Men's Tour Results

Late 1995 PGA Tour Events

Tournament	Final Round	Winner	Score/ Under Par	Earnings ($)
Kapalua International	Nov 5	Jim Furyk	271/–17	180,000
World Cup of Golf	Nov 12	Fred Couples/Davis Love III	543/–33	200,000 each
JC Penney Classic	Dec 3	Davis Love III/Beth Daniel	257/–27	162,500 each

1996 PGA Tour Events

Tournament	Final Round	Winner	Score/ Under Par	Earnings ($)
Mercedes Championships	Jan 7	Mark O'Meara	271/–17	180,000
Nortel Open	Jan 14	Phil Mickelson	273/–14	225,000
Bob Hope Classic	Jan 21	Mark Brooks	337/–23	234,000
Phoenix Open	Jan 27	Phil Mickelson*	269/–15	234,000
Buick Invitational	Feb 11	Davis Love III	269/–19	216,000
Hawaiian Open	Feb 18	Jim Furyk*	277/–11	216,000
Nissan Los Angeles Open	Feb 25	Craig Stadler	278/–6	216,000
Doral Open	Mar 3	Greg Norman	269/–19	324,000
Honda Classic	Mar 10	Tim Herron	271/–17	234,000
Bay Hill Invitational	Mar 17	Paul Goydos	275/–13	216,000
Freeport-McDermott Classic	Mar 24	Scott McCarron	275/–13	216,000
Players Championship	Mar 31	Fred Couples	270/–18	630,000
BellSouth Classic	Apr 7	Paul Stankowski*	280/–8	234,000
The Masters	Apr 14	Nick Faldo	276/–12	450,000
MCI Classic	Apr 21	Loren Roberts	265/–19	252,000
Greater Greensboro Open	Apr 28	Mark O'Meara	274/–14	324,000
Houston Open	May 5	Mark Brooks*	274/–14	270,000
Byron Nelson Classic	May 12	Phil Mickelson	265/–15	270,000
The Colonial	May 19	Corey Pavin	272/–8	270,000
Kemper Open	May 26	Steve Stricker	270/–14	270,000
The Memorial	June 2	Tom Watson	274/–14	324,000
Buick Classic	June 9	Ernie Els	271/–13	216,000
U.S. Open	June 16	Steve Jones	278/-2	425,000
St. Jude Classic	June 23	John Cook	258/–26	243,000
Greater Hartford Open	June 30	D.A. Weibring	270/–10	270,000
Western Open	July 7	Steve Stricker	270/–18	360,000
Michelob Championship	July 14	Scott Hoch	265/–19	225,000
British Open	July 21	Tom Lehman	271/–13	310,000
Deposit Guaranty Classic	July 21	Willie Wood	268/–20	180,000
New England Classic	July 28	John Cook	268/–16	216,000
Buick Open	Aug 4	Justin Leonard	266/–22	216,000
PGA Championship	Aug 11	Mark Brooks*	277/–11	430,000
The International	Aug 18	Clarence Rose*	+31 ‡	288,000
World Series of Golf	Aug 25	Phil Mickelson	274/–6	378,000
Greater Vancouver Open	Aug 25	Guy Boros	272/–12	180,000
Greater Milwaukee Open	Sept 1	Loren Roberts*	265/–19	216,000
Canadian Open #	Sept 8	Dudley Hart	202/–14	270,000
Quad City Classic	Sept 15	Ed Fiori	268/–12	216,000
B.C. Open #	Sept 22	Fred Funk	197/–16	180,000
Buick Challenge #	Sept 29	Michael Bradley*	134/–10	180,000
Las Vegas Invitational	Oct 6	Tiger Woods*	332/–27	297,000
Texas Open	Oct 13	David Ogrin	275/–13	216,000

*Won sudden-death playoff. #Tournament shortened by rain. ‡Revised Stableford scoring.

Women's Majors

Nabisco Dinah Shore

Mission Hills CC; Rancho Mirage, CA
(par 72; 6,460 yds) March 28-31

Player	Score	Earnings ($)
Patty Sheehan	71-72-67-71—281	135,000
Kelly Robbins	71-72-71-68—282	64,158
Meg Mallon	71-70-71-70—282	64,158
Annika Sorenstam	67-72-73-70—282	64,158
Amy Fruhwirth	71-73-68-71—283	32,305
Karrie Webb	72-70-70-71—283	32,305
Brandie Burton	75-67-68-73—283	32,305
Hollis Stacy	69-71-74-70—284	23,550
Kris Tschetter	71-74-70-70—285	21,285
Deb Richard	73-71-73-69—286	16,212
Liselotte Neumann	73-69-75-69—286	16,212
Val Skinner	74-71-71-70—286	16,212
Rosie Jones	72-67-75-72—286	16,212
Tracy Hanson	69-69-74-74—286	16,212
Nancy Lopez	73-72-73-69—287	12,114
Missie McGeorge	74-70-74-69—287	12,114
Joan Pitcock	71-74-71-71—287	12,114
Laura Davies	72-70-70-75—287	12,114
Marianne Morris	76-71-71-70—288	10,189
Stephanie Farwig	71-73-73-71—288	10,189
Tracy Kerdyk	67-72-77-72—288	10,189
Juli Inkster	70-70-74-74—288	10,189

LPGA Championship#

DuPont Country Club; Wilmington, DE
(par 71; 6,386 yds) May 10-12

Player	Score	Earnings ($)
Laura Davies	72-71-70—213	180,000
Julie Piers	72-72-70—214	111,711
Penny Hammel	73-72-70—215	72,461
Jane Crafter	75-68-72—215	72,461
Judy Dickinson	71-74-71—216	37,800
Juli Inkster	70-73-73—216	37,800
Shirley Furlong	70-73-73—216	37,800
Val Skinner	73-69-74—216	37,800
Hiromi Kobayashi	71-70-75—216	37,800
Michelle Dobek	72-75-70—217	22,342
Patty Sheehan	72-74-71—217	22,342
Meg Mallon	69-75-73—217	22,342
Kristi Albers	72-71-74—217	22,342
Lisa Kiggens	75-70-73—218	17,058
Betsy King	72-72-74—218	17,058
Jill Briles-Hinton	73-69-76—218	17,058
Annika Sorenstam	69-73-76—218	17,058
Carin Hj Hoch	73-74-72—219	13,080
Kris Tschetter	75-71-73—219	13,080
Kathryn Marshall	73-73-73—219	13,080
Sherri Steinhauer	74-71-74—219	13,080
Deb Richard	74-70-75—219	13,080
Amy Benz	73-71-75—219	13,080
Nancy Lopez	70-73-76—219	13,080
Kelly Robbins	69-71-79—219	13,080

#Shortened to 54 holes due to rain.

U.S. Women's Open

Pine Needles GC, Southern Pines, NC
(par 70; 6,207 yds) May 30-June 2

Player	Score	Earnings ($)
Annika Sorenstam	70-67-69-66—272	212,500
Kris Tschetter	70-74-68-66—278	125,000
Pat Bradley	74-70-67-69—280	60,373
Jane Geddes	71-69-70-70—280	60,373
Brandie Burton	70-70-69-71—280	60,373
Laura Davies	74-68-70-69—281	40,077
Catrin Nilsmark	72-73-68-69—282	35,995
Cindy Rarick	73-70-72-68—283	29,584
Val Skinner	74-68-71-70—283	29,584
Liselotte Neumann	74-69-70-70—283	29,584
Tammie Green	72-70-69-72—283	29,584
Jenny Lidback	70-76-68-70—284	24,654
Alison Nicholas	74-70-74-67—285	23,243
Patty Sheehan	74-71-72-69—286	19,664
Stefania Croce	72-70-74-70—286	19,664
Cindy Schreyer	74-70-70-72—286	19,664
Maggie Will	71-72-70-73—286	19,664
Michele Redman	70-73-69-74—286	19,664
Cathy Johnston-Forbes	72-75-71-69—287	14,375
Meg Mallon	77-72-68-70—287	14,375
Wendy Ward	76-68-71-72—287	14,375
Karrie Webb	74-73-68-72—287	14,375
Beth Daniel	69-78-68-72—287	14,375
Mayumi Hirase	74-69-69-75—287	14,375

du Maurier Ltd. Classic

Edmonton CC; Edmonton, Alberta
(par 72; 6,324 yds) August 1-4

Player	Score	Earnings ($)
Laura Davies	71-70-70-66—277	150,000
Nancy Lopez	68-71-69-71—279	80,513
Karrie Webb	65-68-74-72—279	80,513
Meg Mallon	72-65-69-74—280	52,837
Pat Hurst	69-70-68-74—281	42,772
Lisolette Neumann	69-74-67-73—283	32,456
Annika Sorenstam	71-70-69-73—283	32,456
Kathy Postlewait	72-68-70-74—284	24,909
Dana Dormann	69-70-71-74—284	24,909
Amy Fruhwirth	70-71-71-73—285	20,128
Rosie Jones	70-71-68-76—285	20,128
Catriona Matthew	71-73-72-70—286	14,808
Chris Greatrex	74-69-71-72—286	14,808
Juli Inkster	73-72-68-73—286	14,808
Emilee Klein	71-73-69-73—286	14,808
Barb Mucha	68-74-71-73—286	14,808
Marta Figueras-Dotti	70-71-72-73—286	14,808
Val Skinner	71-72-69-74—286	14,808
Judy Dickinson	73-70-73-71—287	11,574
Jan Stephenson	73-71-70-73—287	11,574
Joan Pitcock	73-67-71-76—287	11,574

Women's Tour Results

Late 1995 LPGA Tour Events

Tournament	Final Round	Winner	Score/ Under Par	Earnings ($)
JC Penney Classic ....Dec 3		Davis Love III/Beth Daniel	257/–27	162,500 each

1996 LPGA Tour Events

Tournament	Final Round	Winner	Score/ Under Par	Earnings ($)
Tournament of Champions.....................Jan 14		Liselotte Neumann	275/–13	117,500
HEALTHSOUTH Inaugural ....Jan 21		Karrie Webb*	209/–7	67,500
Hawaiian Open ....Feb 24		Meg Mallon	212/–4	90,000
Ping/Welch's Championship ....Mar 17		Liselotte Neumann	276/–12	67,500
Standard Register/Ping ....Mar 24		Laura Davies	284/–8	105,000
Nabisco Dinah Shore ....Mar 31		Patty Sheehan	281/–7	135,000
Twelve Bridges Classic.........................Apr 7		Kelly Robbins*	273/–11	75,000
Chick-Fil-A Championship ....Apr 21		Barb Mucha	208/–8	82,500
Sara Lee Classic ....Apr 28		Meg Mallon	210/–6	90,000
Titleholders Championship ....May 5		Karrie Webb	272/–16	180,000
McDonald's LPGA Championship # ....May 12		Laura Davies	213/even	180,000
Corning Classic...................................May 26		Rosie Jones	276/–12	90,000
U.S. Women's Open...............................June 2		Annika Sorenstam	272/–8	212,500
Oldsmobile Classic ....June 9		Michelle McGann*	272/–16	90,000
Edina Realty Classic ....June 16		Liselotte Neumann*	207/–9	82,500
Rochester International # ....June 23		Dottie Pepper	206/–10	90,000
ShopRite Classic ....June 30		Dottie Pepper	202/–11	112,500
Jamie Farr Kroger Classic ....July 7		Joan Pitcock	204/–9	86,250
Youngstown-Warren Classic...................July 14		Michelle McGann	200/–16	90,000
Friendly's Classic ....July 21		Dottie Pepper	279/–9	75,000
Heartland Classic ....July 28		Vicki Fergon	276/–12	82,500
du Maurier Ltd. Classic ....Aug 4		Laura Davies	277/–11	150,000
Ping/Welch's Championship ....Aug 11		Emilee Klein	273/–15	75,000
British Open ....Aug 18		Emilee Klein	277/–15	127,500
Star Bank Classic ....Aug 25		Laura Davies	204/–12	82,500
State Farm Rail Classic ....Sept 2		Michelle McGann*	202/–14	86,250
Safeway Golf Championship ....Sept 8		Dottie Pepper	202/–14	82,500
Safeco Classic ....Sept 15		Karrie Webb	277/–11	82,500
Fieldcrest Classic.................................Sept 29		Trish Johnson	288/–18	75,000
Big Apple Classic ....Oct 6		Caroline Pierce	211/–2	108,750
Betsy King LPGA Classic.......................Oct 13		Annika Sorenstam	270/–18	90,000

* Won sudden-death playoff. #Shortened due to rain.

Senior Men's Tour Results

Late 1995 Senior Tour Events

Tournament	Final Round	Winner	Score/ Under Par	Earnings ($)
Maui Kaanapali Classic ....Oct 29		Bob Charles*	204/–9	90,000
Emerald Coast Classic #.........................Nov 5		Raymond Floyd*	135/–7	150,000
Senior TOUR Championship ....Nov 12		Jim Colbert	282/–6	262,000

1996 Senior Tour Events

Tournament	Final Round	Winner	Score/ Under Par	Earnings ($)
Tournament of Champions.....................Jan 21		John Bland	207/–9	151,000
Royal Caribbean Classic ....Feb 4		Bob Murphy	203/–10	127,500
Greater Naples Challenge ....Feb 11		Al Geiberger	202/–14	90,000
Suncoast Classic ....Feb 18		Jack Nicklaus	211/–2	112,500
American Express Invitational.................Feb 25		Hale Irwin	197/–19	135,000

1996 Senior Tour Events (Cont.)

Tournament	Final Round	Winner	Score/ Under Par	Earnings ($)
FHP Healthcare Classic	Mar 3	Walt Morgan*	199/–11	120,000
Toshiba Senior Classic	Mar 17	Jim Colbert	201/–12	150,000
The Dominion Seniors	Mar 31	Tom Weiskopf	207/–9	97,500
The Tradition	Apr 7	Jack Nicklaus	272/–16	150,000
PGA Seniors' Championship	Apr 21	Hale Irwin	280/–8	198,000
Las Vegas Classic	Apr 28	Jim Colbert*	207/–9	150,000
Paine Webber Invitational	May 5	Graham Marsh	206/–10	120,000
Nationwide Championship	May 12	Jim Colbert	206/–10	180,000
NFL Senior Classic	May 19	Bob Murphy	202/–14	142,500
BellSouth Classic	May 26	Isao Aoki	202/–14	180,000
Bruno's Memorial Classic	June 2	John Bland*	208/–8	157,000
Pittsburgh Senior Classic	June 9	Tom Weiskopf	205/–11	165,000
Canadian Senior Open	June 16	Charles Coody	271/–9	165,000
Bell Atlantic Classic	June 23	Dale Douglass*	206/–4	135,000
Kroger Senior Classic	July 30	Isao Aoki	198/–15	135,000
U.S. Senior Open	July 7	Dave Stockton	277/–11	212,500
Senior Players Championship	July 14	Raymond Floyd	275/–13	225,000
Burnet Senior Classic	July 21	Vicente Fernandez	205/–11	187,500
Ameritech Senior Classic	July 28	Walt Morgan	205/–11	165,000
VFW Senior Championship	Aug 4	Dave Eichelberger	200/–10	135,000
First of America Classic	Aug 11	Dave Stockton	206/–10	127,500
Long Island Classic	Aug 18	John Bland	202/–14	120,000
Bank of Boston Classic	Aug 25	Jim Dent	204/–12	120,000
Franklin Quest Senior Classic	Sept 1	Graham Marsh	202/–14	120,000
Boone Valley Classic	Sept 8	Gibby Gilbert*	203/–10	180,000
Bank One Classic	Sept 15	Mike Hill	207/–9	90,000
Brickyard Crossing Championship #	Sept 22	Jimmy Powell	134/–10	112,500
Vantage Championship	Sept 29	Jim Colbert	204/–12	225,000
Ralph's Senior Classic	Oct 6	Gil Morgan	202/–11	120,000
The Transamerica	Oct 13	John Bland	204/–12	97,500

*Won sudden-death playoff. #Shortened due to rain.

Amateur Results

Tournament	Final Round	Winner	Score	Runner-Up
Women's Amateur Public Links	June 23	Heather Graff	5 & 4	Lauri Berles
Men's Amateur Public Links	July 20	Tim Hogarth	8 & 7	Jeff Thomas
Junior Amateur	July 27	Shane McMenamy	19 holes	Charles Howell
Girls' Junior	Aug 3	Dorothy Delasin	5 & 4	Grace Park
Women's Amateur	Aug 10	Kelli Kuehne	2 & 1	Marisa Baena
Men's Amateur	Aug 25	Tiger Woods	38 holes	Steve Scott
Women's Mid-Amateur	Sept 29	Ellen Port	2 & 1	Kerry Postillion
Men's Mid-Amateur	Oct 3	John Miller	3 & 2	Randal Lewis
Senior Women	Sept 13	Gayle Borthwick	226 (+10)	Marlene Streit
Senior Men	Sept 12	O. Gordon Brewer	2 up	Heyward Sullivan

International Results

Tournament	Final Round	Winner	Score	Runner-Up
Curtis Cup	June 22	GB/Ireland	11½–6½	United States
Presidents Cup	Sept 15	United States	16½–15½	International
Solheim Cup	Sept 22	United States	17–11	Europe

PGA Tour Final 1996 Money Leaders

Name	Events	Best Finish	Scoring Average*	Money ($)
Tom Lehman	24	1 (2)	69.32	1,780,159
Phil Mickelson	23	1 (4)	70.23	1,697,799
Mark Brooks	31	1 (2)	70.39	1,429,396
Steve Stricker	24	1 (2)	70.10	1,383,739
Mark O'Meara	23	1 (2)	69.69	1,255,749
Fred Couples	19	1	69.57	1,248,694
Davis Love III	25	1	69.81	1,211,139
Brad Faxon	23	2 (4)	69.94	1,055,050
Scott Hoch	28	1	70.02	1,039,564
David Duval	25	2 (2)	70.16	977,079

*Adjusted for average score of field in each tournament entered.

LPGA Tour Final 1995 Money Leaders

Name	Events	Best Finish	Scoring Average	Money ($)
Annika Sorenstam	19	1 (3)	71.00	666,533
Laura Davies	17	1 (2)	71.37	530,349
Kelly Robbins	24	1	71.66	527,655
Dottie Mochrie	25	1 (2)	71.13	521,000
Betsy King	26	1	71.24	481,149
Beth Daniel	25	1	71.33	480,124
Michelle McGann	23	1 (2)	71.56	449,296
Meg Mallon	25	2 (2)	71.28	434,986
Val Skinner	26	1	71.95	430,248
Rosie Jones	26	1	71.64	426,957

Senior Tour Final 1995 Money Leaders

Name	Events	Best Finish	Scoring Average	Money ($)
Jim Colbert	34	1 (4)	70.33	1,444,386
Raymond Floyd	21	1 (3)	69.47	1,419,545
Dave Stockton	34	1 (2)	69.85	1,415,847
Bob Murphy	28	1 (4)	69.87	1,241,524
Isao Aoki	23	1	69.67	1,041,766
J.C. Snead	28	1 (2)	70.68	978,137
Lee Trevino	29	1 (2)	70.03	943,993
Graham Marsh	27	1	70.15	849,350
Tom Wargo	33	1	70.78	844,687
Hale Irwin	12	1 (2)	68.85	799,175

Amen Corner

In the spring there were two robberies and one attempted robbery at the Shelby Park Golf Course in Nashville. In each case, gun-wielding youths preyed on golfers by jumping out of trees that stand along a railroad track near the 16th tee. A tip from the pros: When playing Shelby, save that mulligan for the back nine.

AL TIELEMANS

A Daryl Johnston dive set up a field goal in Dallas's 27–17 defeat of Pittsburgh in Super Bowl XXX.

Reggie White and the Packers' spirits soared as Green Bay beat the 49ers 27-17 in the playoffs.

Penn State's Stephen Pitts—like so many of Northwestern's favored opponents—got buried.

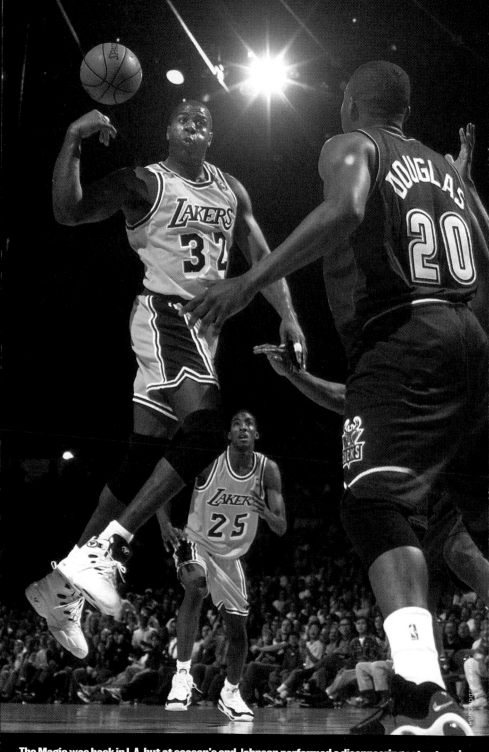

The Magic was back in L.A. but at season's end Johnson performed a disappearing act yet again.

The flamboyant Dennis Rodman landed in Chicago and helped the Bulls to a historic 72–10 season.

Ray Allen—graceful but deadly—led Connecticut to the round of 16 in the NCAA tournament.

Walter McCarty and Kentucky won the battle of the boards against Syracuse in the NCAA title game

Gritty Steffi Graf shook off injury and offcourt distractions to win her seventh Wimbledon title.

BOB MARTIN

DAVID E. KLUTHO

Mike Vernon and the Red Wings lost Game 3 of their playoff series against St. Louis on this goal in OT.

Snubbed by trainer D. Wayne Lukas, Pat Day won the Preakness anyway aboard Louis Quatorze.

JOHN BIEVER

Tiger Woods won his third straight U.S. Amateur, turned pro and promptly earned his PGA Tour card.

Michael Johnson was the Golden Boy of the Games, winning an unprecedented 200-400 double.

BILL FRAKES

Tiffeny Milbrett (16), Tisha Venturini (15) and the U.S. team played heady ball for the Olympic gold

Seattle's Alex Rodriguez was solid in the field and a sensation at the plate, leading the AL in batting

Albert Belle—explosive on and off the field—had another productive season for Cleveland.

Mike Tyson's continuing comeback included a three-round battering of WBC champ Frank Bruno.

Men's Golf

THE MAJOR TOURNAMENTS
The Masters

Year	Winner	Score	Runner-Up
1934	Horton Smith	284	Craig Wood
1935	Gene Sarazen* (144)	282	Craig Wood (149) (only 36-hole playoff)
1936	Horton Smith	285	Harry Cooper
1937	Byron Nelson	283	Ralph Guldahl
1938	Henry Picard	285	Ralph Guldahl, Harry Cooper
1939	Ralph Guldahl	279	Sam Snead
1940	Jimmy Demaret	280	Lloyd Mangrum
1941	Craig Wood	280	Byron Nelson
1942	Byron Nelson* (69)	280	Ben Hogan (70)
1943-45	No tournament		
1946	Herman Keiser	282	Ben Hogan
1947	Jimmy Demaret	281	Byron Nelson, Frank Stranahan
1948	Claude Harmon	279	Cary Middlecoff
1949	Sam Snead	282	Johnny Bulla, Lloyd Mangrum
1950	Jimmy Demaret	283	Jim Ferrier
1951	Ben Hogan	280	Skee Riegel
1952	Sam Snead	286	Jack Burke Jr
1953	Ben Hogan	274	Ed Oliver Jr
1954	Sam Snead* (70)	289	Ben Hogan (71)
1955	Cary Middlecoff	279	Ben Hogan
1956	Jack Burke Jr	289	Ken Venturi
1957	Doug Ford	282	Sam Snead
1958	Arnold Palmer	284	Doug Ford, Fred Hawkins
1959	Art Wall Jr	284	Cary Middlecoff
1960	Arnold Palmer	282	Ken Venturi
1961	Gary Player	280	Charles R. Coe, Arnold Palmer
1962	Arnold Palmer* (68)	280	Gary Player (71), Dow Finsterwald (77)
1963	Jack Nicklaus	286	Tony Lema
1964	Arnold Palmer	276	Dave Marr, Jack Nicklaus
1965	Jack Nicklaus	271	Arnold Palmer, Gary Player
1966	Jack Nicklaus* (70)	288	Tommy Jacobs (72), Gay Brewer, Jr (78)
1967	Gay Brewer Jr	280	Bobby Nichols
1968	Bob Goalby	277	Roberto DeVicenzo
1969	George Archer	281	Billy Casper, George Knudson, Tom Weiskopf
1970	Billy Casper* (69)	279	Gene Littler (74)
1971	Charles Coody	279	Johnny Miller, Jack Nicklaus
1972	Jack Nicklaus	286	Bruce Crampton, Bobby Mitchell, Tom Weiskopf
1973	Tommy Aaron	283	J. C. Snead
1974	Gary Player	278	Tom Weiskopf, Dave Stockton
1975	Jack Nicklaus	276	Johnny Miller, Tom Weiskopf
1976	Ray Floyd	271	Ben Crenshaw
1977	Tom Watson	276	Jack Nicklaus
1978	Gary Player	277	Hubert Green, Rod Funseth, Tom Watson
1979†	Fuzzy Zoeller* (4-3)	280	Ed Sneed (4-4), Tom Watson (4-4)
1980	Seve Ballesteros	275	Gibby Gilbert, Jack Newton
1981	Tom Watson	280	Johnny Miller, Jack Nicklaus
1982	Craig Stadler* (4)	284	Dan Pohl (5)
1983	Seve Ballesteros	280	Ben Crenshaw, Tom Kite
1984	Ben Crenshaw	277	Tom Watson
1985	Bernhard Langer	282	Curtis Strange, Seve Ballesteros, Ray Floyd
1986	Jack Nicklaus	279	Greg Norman, Tom Kite
1987	Larry Mize* (4-3)	285	Seve Ballesteros (5), Greg Norman (4-4)
1988	Sandy Lyle	281	Mark Calcavecchia
1989	Nick Faldo* (5-3)	283	Scott Hoch (5-4)
1990	Nick Faldo* (4-4)	278	Ray Floyd (4-x)
1991	Ian Woosnam	277	José María Olazábal
1992	Fred Couples	275	Ray Floyd
1993	Bernhard Langer	277	Chip Beck

The Masters (Cont.)

Year	Winner	Score	Runner-Up
1994 ....José María Olazábal		279	Tom Lehman
1995 ....Ben Crenshaw		274	Davis Love III
1996 ....Nick Faldo		276	Greg Norman

*Winner in playoff. Playoff scores are in parentheses. †Playoff cut from 18 holes to sudden death.
Note: Played at Augusta National Golf Club, Augusta, GA.

United States Open Championship

Year	Winner	Score	Runner-Up	Site
1895........Horace Rawlins		†173	Willie Dunn	Newport GC, Newport, RI
1896........James Foulis		†152	Horace Rawlins	Shinnecock Hills GC, Southampton, NY
1897........Joe Lloyd		†162	Willie Anderson	Chicago GC, Wheaton, IL
1898........Fred Herd		328	Alex Smith	Myopia Hunt Club, Hamilton, MA
1899........Willie Smith		315	George Low	Baltimore CC, Baltimore
			Val Fitzjohn	
			W. H. Way	
1900........Harry Vardon		313	John H. Taylor	Chicago GC, Wheaton, IL
1901........Willie Anderson* (85)		331	Alex Smith (86)	Myopia Hunt Club, Hamilton, MA
1902........Laurie Auchterlonie		307	Stewart Gardner	Garden City GC, Garden City, NY
1903........Willie Anderson* (82)		307	David Brown (84)	Baltusrol GC, Springfield, NJ
1904........Willie Anderson		303	Gil Nicholls	Glen View Club, Golf, IL
1905........Willie Anderson		314	Alex Smith	Myopia Hunt Club, Hamilton, MA
1906........Alex Smith		295	Willie Smith	Onwentsia Club, Lake Forest, IL
1907........Alex Ross		302	Gil Nicholls	Philadelphia Cricket Club, Chestnut Hill, PA
1908........Fred McLeod* (77)		322	Willie Smith (83)	Myopia Hunt Club, Hamilton, MA
1909........George Sargent		290	Tom McNamara	Englewood GC, Englewood, NJ
1910........Alex Smith* (71)		298	John McDermott (75)	Philadelphia Cricket Club, Chestnut Hill, PA
			Macdonald Smith (77)	
1911........John McDermott* (80)		307	Mike Brady (82)	Chicago GC, Wheaton, IL
			George Simpson (85)	
1912........John McDermott		294	Tom McNamara	CC of Buffalo, Buffalo
1913........Francis Ouimet* (72)		304	Harry Vardon (77)	The Country Club, Brookline, MA
			Edward Ray (78)	
1914........Walter Hagen		290	Chick Evans	Midlothian CC, Blue Island, IL
1915........Jerry Travers		297	Tom McNamara	Baltusrol GC, Springfield, NJ
1916........Chick Evans		286	Jock Hutchison	Minikahda Club, Minneapolis
1917-18 ..No tournament				
1919........Walter Hagen* (77)		301	Mike Brady (78)	Brae Burn CC, West Newton, MA
1920........Edward Ray		295	Harry Vardon	Inverness CC, Toledo
			Jack Burke	
			Leo Diegel	
			Jock Hutchison	
1921........Jim Barnes		289	Walter Hagen	Columbia CC, Chevy Chase, MD
			Fred McLeod	
1922........Gene Sarazen		288	John L. Black	Skokie CC, Glencoe, IL
			Bobby Jones	
1923........Bobby Jones* (76)		296	Bobby Cruickshank (78)	Inwood CC, Inwood, NY
1924........Cyril Walker		297	Bobby Jones	Oakland Hills CC, Birmingham, MI
1925........W. MacFarlane* (75-72)		291	Bobby Jones (75-73)	Worcester CC, Worcester, MA
1926........Bobby Jones		293	Joe Turnesa	Scioto CC, Columbus, OH
1927........Tommy Armour* (76)		301	Harry Cooper (79)	Oakmont CC, Oakmont, PA
1928........Johnny Farrell* (143)		294	Bobby Jones (144)	Olympia Fields CC, Matteson, IL
1929........Bobby Jones* (141)		294	Al Espinosa (164)	Winged Foot GC, Mamaroneck, NY
1930........Bobby Jones		287	Macdonald Smith	Interlachen CC, Hopkins, MN
1931........Billy Burke* (149-148)		292	George Von Elm	Inverness Club, Toledo
			(149-149)	
1932........Gene Sarazen		286	Phil Perkins	Fresh Meadows CC, Flushing, NY
			Bobby Cruickshank	
1933........Johnny Goodman		287	Ralph Guldahl	North Shore CC, Glenview, IL
1934........Olin Dutra		293	Gene Srazen	Merion Cricket Club, Ardmore, PA
1935........Sam Parks Jr		299	Jimmy Thompson	Oakmont CC, Oakmont, PA
1936........Tony Manero		282	Harry Cooper	Baltusrol GC (Upper Course), Springfield, NJ
1937........Ralph Guldahl		281	Sam Snead	Oakland Hills CC, Birmingham, MI
1938........Ralph Guldahl		284	Dick Metz	Cherry Hills CC, Denver, CO
1939........Byron Nelson* (68-70)		284	Craig Wood (68-73)	Philadelphia CC, Philadelphia
			Denny Shute (76)	

United States Open Championship *(Cont.)*

Year	Winner	Score	Runner-Up	Site
1940	Lawson Little* (70)	287	Gene Sarazen (73)	Canterbury GC, Cleveland
1941	Craig Wood	284	Denny Shute	Colonial Club, Fort Worth
1942-45	No tournament			
1946	Lloyd Mangrum* (72-72)	284	Vic Ghezzi (72-73) Byron Nelson (72-73)	Canterbury GC, Cleveland
1947	Lew Worsham* (69)	282	Sam Snead (70)	St Louis CC, Clayton, MO
1948	Ben Hogan	276	Jimmy Demaret	Riviera CC, Los Angeles
1949	Cary Middlecoff	286	Sam Snead Clayton Heafner	Medinah CC, Medinah, IL
1950	Ben Hogan* (69)	287	Lloyd Mangrum (73) George Fazio (75)	Merion GC, Ardmore, PA
1951	Ben Hogan	287	Clayton Heafner	Oakland Hills CC, Birmingham, MI
1952	Julius Boros	281	Ed Oliver	Northwood CC, Dallas
1953	Ben Hogan	283	Sam Snead	Oakmont CC, Oakmont, PA
1954	Ed Furgol	284	Gene Littler	Baltusrol GC (Lower Course), Springfield, NJ
1955	Jack Fleck* (69)	287	Ben Hogan (72)	Olympic Club (Lake Course), San Francisco
1956	Cary Middlecoff	281	Ben Hogan Julius Boros	Oak Hill CC, Rochester, NY
1957	Dick Mayer* (72)	282	Cary Middlecoff (79)	Inverness Club, Toledo
1958	Tommy Bolt	283	Gary Player	Southern Hills CC, Tulsa
1959	Billy Casper	282	Bob Rosburg	Winged Foot GC, Mamaroneck, NY
1960	Arnold Palmer	280	Jack Nicklaus	Cherry Hills CC, Denver
1961	Gene Littler	281	Bob Goalby Doug Sanders	Oakland Hills CC, Birmingham, MI
1962	Jack Nicklaus* (71)	283	Arnold Palmer (74)	Oakmont CC, Oakmont, PA
1963	Julius Boros* (70)	293	Jacky Cupit (73) Arnold Palmer (76)	The Country Club, Brookline, MA
1964	Ken Venturi	278	Tommy Jacobs	Congressional CC, Washington, DC
1965	Gary Player* (71)	282	Kel Nagle (74)	Bellerive CC, St Louis
1966	Billy Casper* (69)	278	Arnold Palmer (73)	Olympic Club (Lake Course), San Francisco
1967	Jack Nicklaus	275	Arnold Palmer	Baltusrol GC (Lower Course), Springfield, NJ
1968	Lee Trevino	275	Jack Nicklaus	Oak Hill CC, Rochester, NY
1969	Orville Moody	281	Deane Beman Al Geiberger Bob Rosburg	Champions GC (Cypress Creek Course), Houston
1970	Tony Jacklin	281	Dave Hill	Hazeltine GC, Chaska, MN
1971	Lee Trevino* (68)	280	Jack Nicklaus (71)	Merion GC (East Course), Ardmore, PA
1972	Jack Nicklaus	290	Bruce Crampton	Pebble Beach GL, Pebble Beach, CA
1973	Johnny Miller	279	John Schlee	Oakmont CC, Oakmont, PA
1974	Hale Irwin	287	Forrest Fezler	Winged Foot GC, Mamaroneck, NY
1975	Lou Graham* (71)	287	John Mahaffey (73)	Medinah CC, Medinah, IL
1976	Jerry Pate	277	Tom Weiskopf Al Geiberger	Atlanta Athletic Club, Duluth, GA
1977	Hubert Green	278	Lou Graham	Southern Hills CC, Tulsa
1978	Andy North	285	Dave Stockton J. C. Snead	Cherry Hills CC, Denver
1979	Hale Irwin	284	Gary Player Jerry Pate	Inverness Club, Toledo
1980	Jack Nicklaus	272	Isao Aoki	Baltusrol GC (Lower Course), Springfield, NJ
1981	David Graham	273	George Burns Bill Rogers	Merion GC, Ardmore, PA
1982	Tom Watson	282	Jack Nicklaus	Pebble Beach GL, Pebble Beach, CA
1983	Larry Nelson	280	Tom Watson	Oakmont CC, Oakmont, PA
1984	Fuzzy Zoeller* (67)	276	Greg Norman (75)	Winged Foot GC, Mamaroneck, NY
1985	Andy North	279	Dave Barr T. C. Chen Denis Watson	Oakland Hills CC, Birmingham, MI
1986	Ray Floyd	279	Lanny Wadkins Chip Beck	Shinnecock Hills GC, Southampton, NY
1987	Scott Simpson	277	Tom Watson	Olympic Club (Lake Course), San Francisco
1988	Curtis Strange* (71)	278	Nick Faldo (75)	The Country Club, Brookline, MA
1989	Curtis Strange	278	Chip Beck Mark McCumber Ian Woosnam	Oak Hill CC, Rochester, NY
1990	Hale Irwin* (74) (3)	280	Mike Donald (74) (4)	Medinah CC, Medinah, IL

U.S. Open (Cont.)

Year	Winner	Score	Runner-Up	Site
1991	Payne Stewart (75)	282	Scott Simpson (77)	Hazeltine GC, Chaska, MN
1992	Tom Kite	285	Jeff Sluman	Pebble Beach GL, Pebble Beach, CA
1993	Lee Janzen	272	Payne Stewart	Baltusrol GC, Springfield, NJ
1994	Ernie Els*	279	Loren Roberts	Oakmont CC, Oakmont, PA
			Colin Montgomerie	
1995	Corey Pavin	280	Greg Norman	Shinnecock Hills GC, Southampton, NY
1996	Steve Jones	278	Davis Love III	Oakland Hills CC, Birmingham, MI
			Tom Lehman	

*Winner in playoff. Playoff scores are in parentheses. The 1990 playoff went to one hole of sudden death after an 18-hole playoff. In the 1994 playoff, Montgomerie was eliminated after 18 playoff holes, and Els beat Roberts on the 20th.
†Before 1898, 36 holes. From 1898 on, 72 holes.

British Open

Year	Winner	Score	Runner-Up	Site
1860†	Willie Park	174	Tom Morris Sr	Prestwick, Scotland
1861‡	Tom Morris Sr	163	Willie Park	Prestwick, Scotland
1862	Tom Morris Sr	163	Willie Park	Prestwick, Scotland
1863	Willie Park	168	Tom Morris Sr	Prestwick, Scotland
1864	Tom Morris, Sr	160	Andrew Strath	Prestwick, Scotland
1865	Andrew Strath	162	Willie Park	Prestwick, Scotland
1866	Willie Park	169	David Park	Prestwick, Scotland
1867	Tom Morris Sr	170	Willie Park	Prestwick, Scotland
1868	Tom Morris Jr	154	Tom Morris Sr	Prestwick, Scotland
1869	Tom Morris Jr	157	Tom Morris Sr	Prestwick, Scotland
1870	Tom Morris Jr	149	David Strath	Prestwick, Scotland
			Bob Kirk	
1871	No tournament			
1872	Tom Morris Jr	166	David Strath	Prestwick, Scotland
1873	Tom Kidd	179	Jamie Anderson	St Andrews, Scotland
1874	Mungo Park	159	No record	Musselburgh, Scotland
1875	Willie Park	166	Bob Martin	Prestwick, Scotland
1876	Bob Martin#	176	David Strath	St Andrews, Scotland
1877	Jamie Anderson	160	Bob Pringle	Musselburgh, Scotland
1878	Jamie Anderson	157	Robert Kirk	Prestwick, Scotland
1879	Jamie Anderson	169	Andrew Kirkaldy	St Andrews, Scotland
			James Allan	
1880	Robert Ferguson	162	No record	Musselburgh, Scotland
1881	Robert Ferguson	170	Jamie Anderson	Prestwick, Scotland
1882	Robert Ferguson	171	Willie Fernie	St Andrews, Scotland
1883	Willie Fernie*	159	Robert Ferguson	Musselburgh, Scotland
1884	Jack Simpson	160	Douglas Rolland	Prestwick, Scotland
			Willie Fernie	
1885	Bob Martin	171	Archie Simpson	St Andrews, Scotland
1886	David Brown	157	Willie Campbell	Musselburgh, Scotland
1887	Willie Park, Jr	161	Bob Martin	Prestwick, Scotland
1888	Jack Burns	171	Bernard Sayers	St Andrews, Scotland
			David Anderson	
1889	Willie Park Jr* (158)	155	Andrew Kirkaldy (163)	Musselburgh, Scotland
1890	John Ball	164	Willie Fernie	Prestwick, Scotland
1891	Hugh Kirkaldy	166	Andrew Kirkaldy	St Andrews, Scotland
			Willie Fernie	
1892	Harold Hilton	**305	John Ball	Muirfield, Scotland
			Hugh Kirkaldy	
1893	William Auchterlonie	322	John E. Laidlay	Prestwick, Scotland
1894	John H. Taylor	326	Douglas Rolland	Royal St George's, England
1895	John H. Taylor	322	Alexander Herd	St Andrews, Scotland
1896	Harry Vardon* (157)	316	John H. Taylor (161)	Muirfield, Scotland
1897	Harold Hilton	314	James Braid	Hoylake, England
1898	Harry Vardon	307	Willie Park Jr	Prestwick, Scotland
1899	Harry Vardon	310	Jack White	Royal St George's, England
1900	John H. Taylor	309	Harry Vardon	St Andrews, Scotland
1901	James Braid	309	Harry Vardon	Muirfield, Scotland
1902	Alexander Herd	307	Harry Vardon	Hoylake, England
1903	Harry Vardon	300	Tom Vardon	Prestwick, Scotland

British Open (Cont.)

Year	Winner	Score	Runner-Up	Site
1904	Jack White	296	John H. Taylor	Royal St George's, England
1905	James Braid	318	John H. Taylor Rolland Jones	St Andrews, Scotland
1906	James Braid	300	John H. Taylor	Muirfield, Scotland
1907	Arnaud Massy	312	John H. Taylor	Hoylake, England
1908	James Braid	291	Tom Ball	Prestwick, Scotland
1909	John H. Taylor	295	James Braid Tom Ball	Deal, England
1910	James Braid	299	Alexander Herd	St Andrews, Scotland
1911	Harry Vardon	303	Arnaud Massy	Royal St George's, England
1912	Ted Ray	295	Harry Vardon	Muirfield, Scotland
1913	John H. Taylor	304	Ted Ray	Hoylake, England
1914	Harry Vardon	306	John H. Taylor	Prestwick, Scotland
1915-19	No tournament			
1920	George Duncan	303	Alexander Herd	Deal, England
1921	Jock Hutchison* (150)	296	Roger Wethered (159)	St Andrews, Scotland
1922	Walter Hagen	300	George Duncan Jim Barnes	Royal St George's, England
1923	Arthur G. Havers	295	Walter Hagen	Troon, Scotland
1924	Walter Hagen	301	Ernest Whitcombe	Hoylake, England
1925	Jim Barnes	300	Archie Compston Ted Ray	Prestwick, Scotland
1926	Bobby Jones	291	Al Watrous	Royal Lytham & St Anne's, England
1927	Bobby Jones	285	Aubrey Boomer	St Andrews, Scotland
1928	Walter Hagen	292	Gene Sarazen	Royal St George's, England
1929	Walter Hagen	292	Johnny Farrell	Muirfield, Scotland
1930	Bobby Jones	291	Macdonald Smith Leo Diegel	Hoylake, England
1931	Tommy Armour	296	Jose Jurado	Carnoustie, Scotland
1932	Gene Sarazen	283	Macdonald Smith	Prince's, England
1933	Denny Shute* (149)	292	Craig Wood (154)	St Andrews, Scotland
1934	Henry Cotton	283	Sidney F. Brews	Royal St George's, England
1935	Alfred Perry	283	Alfred Padgham	Muirfield, Scotland
1936	Alfred Padgham	287	James Adams	Hoylake, England
1937	Henry Cotton	290	Reginald A. Whitcombe	Carnoustie, Scotland
1938	Reginald A. Whitcombe	295	James Adams	Royal St George's, England
1939	Richard Burton	290	Johnny Bulla	St Andrews, Scotland
1940-45	No tournament			
1946	Sam Snead	290	Bobby Locke Johnny Bulla	St Andrews, Scotland
1947	Fred Daly	293	Reginald W. Horne Frank Stranahan	Hoylake, England
1948	Henry Cotton	294	Fred Daly	Muirfield, Scotland
1949	Bobby Locke* (135)	283	Harry Bradshaw (147)	Royal St George's, England
1950	Bobby Locke	279	Roberto DeVicenzo	Troon, Scotland
1951	Max Faulkner	285	Tony Cerda	Portrush, Ireland
1952	Bobby Locke	287	Peter Thomson	Royal Lytham & St Anne's, England
1953	Ben Hogan	282	Frank Stranahan Dai Rees Peter Thomson Tony Cerda	Carnoustie, Scotland
1954	Peter Thomson	283	Sidney S. Scott Dai Rees Bobby Locke	Royal Birkdale, England
1955	Peter Thomson	281	John Fallon	St Andrews, Scotland
1956	Peter Thomson	286	Flory Van Donck	Hoylake, England
1957	Bobby Locke	279	Peter Thomson	St Andrews, Scotland
1958	Peter Thomson* (139)	278	Dave Thomas (143)	Royal Lytham & St Anne's, England
1959	Gary Player	284	Fred Bullock Flory Van Donck	Muirfield, Scotland
1960	Kel Nagle	278	Arnold Palmer	St Andrews, Scotland
1961	Arnold Palmer	284	Dai Rees	Royal Birkdale, England
1962	Arnold Palmer	276	Kel Nagle	Troon, Scotland
1963	Bob Charles* (140)	277	Phil Rodgers (148)	Royal Lytham & St Anne's, England
1964	Tony Lema	279	Jack Nicklaus	St Andrews, Scotland

British Open (Cont.)

Year	Winner	Score	Runner-Up	Site
1965	Peter Thomson	285	Brian Huggett Christy O'Connor	Southport, England
1966	Jack Nicklaus	282	Doug Sanders Dave Thomas	Muirfield, Scotland
1967	Robert DeVicenzo	278	Jack Nicklaus	Hoylake, England
1968	Gary Player	289	Jack Nicklaus Bob Charles	Carnoustie, Scotland
1969	Tony Jacklin	280	Bob Charles	Royal Lytham & St Anne's, England
1970	Jack Nicklaus* (72)	283	Doug Sanders (73)	St Andrews, Scotland
1971	Lee Trevino	278	Lu Liang Huan	Royal Birkdale, England
1972	Lee Trevino	278	Jack Nicklaus	Muirfield, Scotland
1973	Tom Weiskopf	276	Johnny Miller	Troon, Scotland
1974	Gary Player	282	Peter Oosterhuis	Royal Lytham & St Anne's, England
1975	Tom Watson* (71)	279	Jack Newton (72)	Carnoustie, Scotland
1976	Johnny Miller	279	Jack Nicklaus Seve Ballesteros	Royal Birkdale, England
1977	Tom Watson	268	Jack Nicklaus	Turnberry, Scotland
1978	Jack Nicklaus	281	Ben Crenshaw Tom Kite Ray Floyd Simon Owen	St Andrews, Scotland
1979	Seve Ballesteros	283	Ben Crenshaw Jack Nicklaus	Royal Lytham & St Anne's, England
1980	Tom Watson	271	Lee Trevino	Muirfield, Scotland
1981	Bill Rogers	276	Bernhard Langer	Royal St George's, England
1982	Tom Watson	284	Nick Price Peter Oosterhuis	Royal Troon, Scotland
1983	Tom Watson	275	Andy Bean	Royal Birkdale, England
1984	Seve Ballesteros	276	Tom Watson Bernhard Langer	St Andrews, Scotland
1985	Sandy Lyle	282	Payne Stewart	Royal St George's, England
1986	Greg Norman	280	Gordon Brand	Turnberry, Scotland
1987	Nick Faldo	279	Paul Azinger Rodger Davis	Muirfield, Scotland
1988	Seve Ballesteros	273	Nick Price	Royal Lytham & St Anne's, England
1989††	Mark Calcavecchia* (4-3-3-3)	275	Wayne Grady (4-4-4-4) Greg Norman (3-3-4-x)	Royal Troon, Scotland
1990	Nick Faldo	270	Payne Stewart Mark McNulty	St Andrews, Scotland
1991	Ian Baker-Finch	272	Mike Harwood	Royal Birkdale, England
1992	Nick Faldo	272	John Cook	Muirfield, Scotland
1993	Greg Norman	267	Nick Faldo	Royal St George's, England
1994	Nick Price*	268	Jesper Parnevik	Turnberry, Scotland
1995	John Daly* (4-3-4-4)	282	C. Rocca (5-4-7-3)	St Andrews, Scotland
1996	Tom Lehman	271	Mark McCumber Ernie Els	Royal Lytham & St Anne's, England

*Winner in playoff. Playoff scores are in parentheses. †The first event was open only to professional golfers.

‡The second annual open was open to amateurs and pros. #Tied, but refused playoff.

**Championship extended from 36 to 72 holes. ††Playoff cut from 18 holes to 4 holes.

PGA Championship

Year	Winner	Score	Runner-Up	Site
1916	Jim Barnes	1 up	Jock Hutchison	Siwanoy CC, Bronxville, NY
1917-18	No tournament			
1919	Jim Barnes	6 & 5	Fred McLeod	Engineers CC, Roslyn, NY
1920	Jock Hutchison	1 up	J. Douglas Edgar	Flossmoor CC, Flossmoor, IL
1921	Walter Hagen	3 & 2	Jim Barnes	Inwood CC, Far Rockaway, NY
1922	Gene Sarazen	4 & 3	Emmet French	Oakmont CC, Oakmont, PA
1923	Gene Sarazen	1 up 38 holes	Walter Hagen	Pelham CC, Pelham, NY
1924	Walter Hagen	2 up	Jim Barnes	French Lick CC, French Lick, IN
1925	Walter Hagen	6 & 5	William Mehlhorn	Olympia Fields CC, Olympia Fields, IL
1926	Walter Hagen	5 & 3	Leo Diegel	Salisbury GC, Westbury, NY
1927	Walter Hagen	1 up	Joe Turnesa	Cedar Crest CC, Dallas

PGA Championship *(Cont.)*

Year	Winner	Score	Runner-Up	Site
1928	Leo Diegel	6 & 5	Al Espinosa	Five Farms CC, Baltimore
1929	Leo Diegel	6 & 4	Johnny Farrell	Hillcrest CC, Los Angeles
1930	Tommy Armour	1 up	Gene Sarazen	Fresh Meadow CC, Flushing, NY
1931	Tom Creavy	2 & 1	Denny Shute	Wannamoisett CC, Rumford, RI
1932	Olin Dutra	4 & 3	Frank Walsh	Keller GC, St Paul
1933	Gene Sarazen	5 & 4	Willie Goggin	Blue Mound CC, Milwaukee
1934	Paul Runyan	1 up	Craig Wood	Park CC, Williamsville, NY
1935	Johnny Revolta	5 & 4	Tommy Armour	Twin Hills CC, Oklahoma City
		38 holes		
1936	Denny Shute	3 & 2	Jimmy Thomson	Pinehurst CC, Pinehurst, NC
1937	Denny Shute	1 up	Harold McSpaden	Pittsburgh FC, Aspinwall, PA
		37 holes		
1938	Paul Runyan	8 & 7	Sam Snead	Shawnee CC, Shawnee-on-Delaware, PA
1939	Henry Picard	1 up	Byron Nelson	Pomonok CC, Flushing, NY
		37 holes		
1940	Byron Nelson	1 up	Sam Snead	Hershey CC, Hershey, PA
1941	Vic Ghezzi	1 up	Byron Nelson	Cherry Hills CC, Denver
		38 holes		
1942	Sam Snead	2 & 1	Jim Turnesa	Seaview CC, Atlantic City
1943	No tournament			
1944	Bob Hamilton	1 up	Byron Nelson	Manito G & CC, Spokane, WA
1945	Byron Nelson	4 & 3	Sam Byrd	Morraine CC, Dayton
1946	Ben Hogan	6 & 4	Ed Oliver	Portland GC, Portland, OR
1947	Jim Ferrier	2 & 1	Chick Harbert	Plum Hollow CC, Detroit
1948	Ben Hogan	7 & 6	Mike Turnesa	Norwood Hills CC, St Louis
1949	Sam Snead	3 & 2	Johnny Palmer	Hermitage CC, Richmond
1950	Chandler Harper	4 & 3	Henry Williams Jr	Scioto CC, Columbus, OH
1951	Sam Snead	7 & 6	Walter Burkemo	Oakmont CC, Oakmont, PA
1952	Jim Turnesa	1 up	Chick Harbert	Big Spring CC, Louisville
1953	Walter Burkemo	2 & 1	Felice Torza	Birmingham CC, Birmingham, MI
1954	Chick Harbert	4 & 3	Walter Burkemo	Keller GC, St Paul
1955	Doug Ford	4 & 3	Cary Middlecoff	Meadowbrook CC, Detroit
1956	Jack Burke	3 & 2	Ted Kroll	Blue Hill CC, Boston
1957	Lionel Hebert	2 & 1	Dow Finsterwald	Miami Valley CC, Dayton
1958	Dow Finsterwald	276	Billy Casper	Llanerch CC, Havertown, PA
1959	Bob Rosburg	277	Jerry Barber	Minneapolis GC, St Louis Park, MN
			Doug Sanders	
1960	Jay Hebert	281	Jim Ferrier	Firestone CC, Akron
1961	Jerry Barber* (67)	277	Don January (68)	Olympia Fields CC, Olympia Fields, IL
1962	Gary Player	278	Bob Goalby	Aronimink GC, Newton Square, PA
1963	Jack Nicklaus	279	Dave Ragan Jr	Dallas Athletic Club, Dallas
1964	Bobby Nichols	271	Jack Nicklaus	Columbus CC, Columbus, OH
			Arnold Palmer	
1965	Dave Marr	280	Billy Casper	Laurel Valley CC, Ligonier, PA
			Jack Nicklaus	
1966	Al Geiberger	280	Dudley Wysong	Firestone CC, Akron
1967	Don January* (69)	281	Don Massengale (71)	Columbine CC, Littleton, CO
1968	Julius Boros	281	Bob Charles	Pecan Valley CC, San Antonio
			Arnold Palmer	
1969	Ray Floyd	276	Gary Player	NCR CC, Dayton
1970	Dave Stockton	279	Arnold Palmer	Southern Hills CC, Tulsa
			Bob Murphy	
1971	Jack Nicklaus	281	Billy Casper	PGA Natl GC, Palm Beach Gardens, FL
1972	Gary Player	281	Tommy Aaron	Oakland Hills CC, Birmingham, MI
			Jim Jamieson	
1973	Jack Nicklaus	277	Bruce Crampton	Canterbury GC, Cleveland
1974	Lee Trevino	276	Jack Nicklaus	Tanglewood GC, Winston-Salem, NC
1975	Jack Nicklaus	276	Bruce Crampton	Firestone CC, Akron
1976	Dave Stockton	281	Ray Floyd	Congressional CC, Bethesda, MD
			Don January	
1977†	Lanny Wadkins* (4-4-4)	282	Gene Littler (4-4-5)	Pebble Beach GL, Pebble Beach, CA
1978	John Mahaffey* (4-3)	276	Jerry Pate (4-4)	Oakmont CC, Oakmont, PA
			Tom Watson (4-5)	
1979	David Graham* (4-4-2)	272	Ben Crenshaw (4-4-4)	Oakland Hills CC, Birmingham, MI
1980	Jack Nicklaus	274	Andy Bean	Oak Hill CC, Rochester, NY

PGA Championship (Cont.)

Year	Winner	Score	Runner-Up	Site
1981 ....Larry Nelson	273	Fuzzy Zoeller	Atlanta Athletic Club, Duluth, GA
1982 ....Raymond Floyd	272	Lanny Wadkins	Southern Hills CC, Tulsa
1983 ....Hal Sutton	274	Jack Nicklaus	Riviera CC, Pacific Palisades, CA
1984 ....Lee Trevino	273	Gary Player	Shoal Creek, Birmingham, AL
			Lanny Wadkins	
1985 ....Hubert Green	278	Lee Trevino	Cherry Hills CC, Denver
1986 ....Bob Tway	276	Greg Norman	Inverness CC, Toledo
1987 ....Larry Nelson* (4)	287	Lanny Wadkins (5)	PGA Natl GC, Palm Beach Gardens, FL
1988 ....Jeff Sluman	272	Paul Azinger	Oak Tree GC, Edmond, OK
1989 ....Payne Stewart	276	Mike Reid	Kemper Lakes GC, Hawthorn Woods, IL
1990 ....Wayne Grady	282	Fred Couples	Shoal Creek, Birmingham, AL
1991 ....John Daly	276	Bruce Lietzke	Crooked Stick GC, Carmel, IN
1992 ....Nick Price	278	Jim Gallagher Jr	Bellerive CC, St. Louis
1993 ....Paul Azinger* (4-4)	272	Greg Norman (4-5)	Inverness CC, Toledo, OH
1994 ....Nick Price	269	Corey Pavin	Southern Hills CC, Tulsa, OK
1995 ....Steve Elkington* (3)	267	Colin Montgomerie (4)	Riviera CC, Pacific Palisades, CA
1996 ....Mark Brooks* (3)	277	Kenny Perry (x)	Valhalla GC, Louisville, KY

*Winner in playoff. Playoff scores are in parentheses. †Playoff changed from 18 holes to sudden death.

Alltime Major Championship Winners

	Masters	U.S. Open	British Open	PGA Champ.	U.S. Amateur	British Amateur	Total
†Jack Nicklaus 6	4	3	5	2	0	20
Bobby Jones.....................0	4	3	0	5	1	13
Walter Hagen 0	2	4	5	0	0	11
Ben Hogan..........................2	4	1	2	0	0	9
†Gary Player 3	1	3	2	0	0	9
John Ball 0	0	1	0	0	8	9
†Arnold Palmer 4	1	2	0	1	0	8
*Tom Watson 2	1	5	0	0	0	8
Harold Hilton 0	0	2	0	1	4	7
Gene Sarazen.....................1	2	1	3	0	0	7
Sam Snead 3	0	1	3	0	0	7
Harry Vardon 0	1	6	0	0	0	7
†Lee Trevino 0	2	2	2	0	0	6
*Nick Faldo 3	0	3	0	0	0	6

*Active PGA player. †Active Senior PGA player.

Alltime Multiple Professional Major Winners

MASTERS	U.S. OPEN (Cont.)	BRITISH OPEN (Cont.)	PGA CHAMPIONSHIP
Jack Nicklaus 6	Hale Irwin 3	Walter Hagen 4	Walter Hagen 5
Arnold Palmer.............4	Julius Boros.................2	Bobby Locke 4	Jack Nicklaus 5
Jimmy Demaret 3	Billy Casper 2	Tom Morris Sr 4	Gene Sarazen 3
Nick Faldo 3	Ralph Guldahl 2	Tom Morris Jr 4	Sam Snead..................3
Gary Player.................3	Walter Hagen 2	Willie Park...................4	Jim Barnes 2
Sam Snead.................3	John McDermott.........2	Jamie Anderson.........3	Leo Diegel..................2
Seve Ballesteros.........2	Cary Middlecoff..........2	Seve Ballesteros.........3	Raymond Floyd 2
Ben Crenshaw.............2	Andy North 2	Henry Cotton 3	Ben Hogan 2
Ben Hogan 2	Gene Sarazen 2	Nick Faldo 3	Byron Nelson...............2
Bernhard Langer 2	Alex Smith 2	Robert Ferguson 3	Larry Nelson 2
Byron Nelson..............2	Curtis Strange 2	Bobby Jones 3	Gary Player.................2
Horton Smith...............2	Lee Trevino.................2	Jack Nicklaus 3	Paul Runyan 2
Tom Watson 2		Gary Player.................3	Denny Shute...............2
	BRITISH OPEN	Harold Hilton 2	Dave Stockton 2
U.S. OPEN	Harry Vardon...............6	Bob Martin 2	Lee Trevino.................2
	James Braid 5	Greg Norman 2	
Willie Anderson 4	J.H. Taylor 5	Arnold Palmer.............2	
Ben Hogan 4	Peter Thomson 5	Willie Park Jr 2	
Bobby Jones 4	Tom Watson 5	Lee Trevino.................2	
Jack Nicklaus 4			

THE PGA TOUR

Most Career Wins

	Wins		Wins		Wins
Sam Snead	81	Billy Casper	51	Tom Watson	33
Jack Nicklaus	70	Walter Hagen	40	Horton Smith	32
Ben Hogan	63	Cary Middlecoff	40	Harry Cooper	31
Arnold Palmer	60	Gene Sarazen	38	Jimmy Demaret	31
Byron Nelson	52	Lloyd Mangrum	36	Leo Diegel	30

Season Money Leaders

		Earnings ($)			Earnings ($)
1934	Paul Runyan	6,767.00	1966	Billy Casper	121,944.92
1935	Johnny Revolta	9,543.00	1967	Jack Nicklaus	188,998.08
1936	Horton Smith	7,682.00	1968	Billy Casper	205,168.67
1937	Harry Cooper	14,138.69	1969	Frank Beard	164,707.11
1938	Sam Snead	19,534.49	1970	Lee Trevino	157,037.63
1939	Henry Picard	10,303.00	1971	Jack Nicklaus	244,490.50
1940	Ben Hogan	10,655.00	1972	Jack Nicklaus	320,542.26
1941	Ben Hogan	18,358.00	1973	Jack Nicklaus	308,362.10
1942	Ben Hogan	13,143.00	1974	Johnny Miller	353,021.59
1943	No statistics compiled		1975	Jack Nicklaus	298,149.17
1944	Byron Nelson (war bonds)	37,967.69	1976	Jack Nicklaus	266,438.57
1945	Byron Nelson (war bonds)	63,335.66	1977	Tom Watson	310,653.16
1946	Ben Hogan	42,556.16	1978	Tom Watson	362,428.93
1947	Jimmy Demaret	27,936.83	1979	Tom Watson	462,636.00
1948	Ben Hogan	32,112.00	1980	Tom Watson	530,808.33
1949	Sam Snead	31,593.83	1981	Tom Kite	375,698.84
1950	Sam Snead	35,758.83	1982	Craig Stadler	446,462.00
1951	Lloyd Mangrum	26,088.83	1983	Hal Sutton	426,668.00
1952	Julius Boros	37,032.97	1984	Tom Watson	476,260.00
1953	Lew Worsham	34,002.00	1985	Curtis Strange	542,321.00
1954	Bob Toski	65,819.81	1986	Greg Norman	653,296.00
1955	Julius Boros	63,121.55	1987	Curtis Strange	925,941.00
1956	Ted Kroll	72,835.83	1988	Curtis Strange	1,147,644.00
1957	Dick Mayer	65,835.00	1989	Tom Kite	1,395,278.00
1958	Arnold Palmer	42,607.50	1990	Greg Norman	1,165,477.00
1959	Art Wall	53,167.60	1991	Corey Pavin	979,430.00
1960	Arnold Palmer	75,262.85	1992	Fred Couples	1,344,188.00
1961	Gary Player	64,540.45	1993	Nick Price	1,478,557.00
1962	Arnold Palmer	81,448.33	1994	Nick Price	1,499,927.00
1963	Arnold Palmer	128,230.00	1995	Greg Norman	1,654,959.00
1964	Jack Nicklaus	113,284.50	1996	Tom Lehman	1,780,159.00
1965	Jack Nicklaus	140,752.14			

Note: Total money listed from 1968 through 1974. Official money listed from 1975 on.

Career Money Leaders‡

	Earnings ($)		Earnings ($)		Earnings ($)
1. Greg Norman	9,592,829	18. Davis Love III	5,623,890	35. Lee Janzen	3,910,397
2. Tom Kite	9,337,998	19. Scott Hoch	5,465,898	36. Jeff Sluman	3,860,431
3. Payne Stewart	7,389,479	20. David Frost	5,458,172	37. John Mahaffey	3,828,008
4. Nick Price	7,338,119	21. Jack Nicklaus	5,440,357	38. Bob Tway	3,815,540
5. Fred Couples	7,188,408	22. Jay Haas	5,426,821	39. Loren Roberts	3,809,733
6. Corey Pavin	7,175,523	23. Ray Floyd	5,194,044	40. Steve Pate	3,661,591
7. Tom Watson	7,072,113	24. Gil Morgan	4,991,433	41. David Edwards	3,646,275
8. Paul Azinger	6,957,324	25. Fuzzy Zoeller	4,918,771	42. D.A. Weibring	3,612,373
9. Ben Crenshaw	6,845,235	26. Mark McCumber	4,799,702	43. Joey Sindelar	3,565,399
10. Curtis Strange	6,791,618	27. Scott Simpson	4,768,955	44. Brad Faxon	3,537,539
11. Mark O'Meara	6,126,466	28. Larry Mize	4,584,287	45. Lee Trevino	3,478,450
12. Lanny Wadkins	6,028,855	29. Jim Gallagher, Jr	4,583,940	46. John Huston	3,408,018
13. Craig Stadler	6,008,753	30. Peter Jacobsen	4,547,564	47. Billy Mayfair	3,397,626
14. Mark Calcavecchia	5,866,716	31. Steve Elkington	4,525,487	48. Tim Simpson	3,351,476
15. Hale Irwin	5,845,024	32. Hal Sutton	4,486,587	49. Ken Green	3,347,802
16. Chip Beck	5,755,844	33. John Cook	4,461,954	50. Larry Nelson	3,313,938
17. Bruce Lietzke	5,710,262	34. Wayne Levi	4,237,387		

‡Statistics through 10/31/95.

Year by Year Statistical Leaders

SCORING AVERAGE

1980	Lee Trevino	69.73
1981	Tom Kite	69.80
1982	Tom Kite	70.21
1983	Raymond Floyd	70.61
1984	Calvin Peete	70.56
1985	Don Pooley	70.36
1986	Scott Hoch	70.08
1987	David Frost	70.09
1988	Greg Norman	69.38
1989	Payne Stewart	69.485†
1990	Greg Norman	69.10
1991	Fred Couples	69.59
1992	Fred Couples	69.38
1993	Greg Norman	68.90
1994	Greg Norman	68.81
1995	Greg Norman	69.06
1996	Tom Lehman	69.32

Note: Scoring average per round, with adjustments made at each round for the field's course scoring average.

DRIVING DISTANCE

		Yds
1980	Dan Pohl	274.3
1981	Dan Pohl	280.1
1982	Bill Calfee	275.3
1983	John McComish	277.4
1984	Bill Glasson	276.5
1985	Andy Bean	278.2
1986	Davis Love III	285.7
1987	John McComish	283.9
1988	Steve Thomas	284.6
1989	Ed Humenik	280.9
1990	Tom Purtzer	279.6
1991	John Daly	288.9
1992	John Daly	283.4
1993	John Daly	288.9
1994	Davis Love III	283.8
1995	John Daly	289.0
1996	John Daly	288.8

Note: Average computed by charting distance of two tee shots on a predetermined par-four or par-five hole (one on front nine, one on back nine).

DRIVING ACCURACY

1980	Mike Reid	79.5
1981	Calvin Peete	81.9
1982	Calvin Peete	84.6
1983	Calvin Peete	81.3
1984	Calvin Peete	77.5
1985	Calvin Peete	80.6
1986	Calvin Peete	81.7
1987	Calvin Peete	83.0
1988	Calvin Peete	82.5
1989	Calvin Peete	82.6
1990	Calvin Peete	83.7
1991	Hale Irwin	78.3

DRIVING ACCURACY (Cont.)

1992	Doug Tewell	82.3
1993	Doug Tewell	82.5
1994	David Edwards	81.6
1995	Fred Funk	81.3
1996	Fred Funk	78.7

Note: Percentage of fairways hit on number of par-four and par-five holes played; par-three holes excluded.

GREENS IN REGULATION

1980	Jack Nicklaus	72.1
1981	Calvin Peete	73.1
1982	Calvin Peete	72.4
1983	Calvin Peete	71.4
1984	Andy Bean	72.1
1985	John Mahaffey	71.9
1986	John Mahaffey	72.0
1987	Gil Morgan	73.3
1988	John Adams	73.9
1989	Bruce Lietzke	72.6
1990	Doug Tewell	70.9
1991	Bruce Lietzke	73.3
1992	Tim Simpson	74.0
1993	Fuzzy Zoeller	73.6
1994	Bill Glasson	73.0
1995	Lenny Clements	72.3
1996	Fred Couples	71.8
	Mark O'Meara	71.8

Note: Average of greens reached in regulation out of total holes played; hole is considered hit in regulation if any part of the ball rests on the putting surface in two shots less than the hole's-five hit in two shots is one green in regulation.

PUTTING

1980	Jerry Pate	28.81
1981	Alan Tapie	28.70
1982	Ben Crenshaw	28.65
1983	Morris Hatalsky	27.96
1984	Gary McCord	28.57
1985	Craig Stadler	28.627†
1986	Greg Norman	1.736
1987	Ben Crenshaw	1.743
1988	Don Pooley	1.729
1989	Steve Jones	1.734
1990	Larry Rinker	1.7467†
1991	Jay Don Blake	1.7326†
1992	Mark O'Meara	1.731
1993	David Frost	1.739
1994	Loren Roberts	1.737
1995	Jim Furyk	1.708
1996	Brad Faxon	1.709

Note: Average number of putts taken on greens reached in regulation; prior to 1986, based on average number of putts per 18 holes.

ALL-AROUND

1987	Dan Pohl	170
1988	Payne Stewart	170
1989	Paul Azinger	250
1990	Paul Azinger	162
1991	Scott Hoch	283
1992	Fred Couples	256
1993	Gil Morgan	252
1994	Bob Estes	227
1995	Justin Leonard	323
1996	Fred Couples	214

Note: Addition of the places of standing from the other seven statistical categories; the player with the number closest to zero leads.

SAND SAVES

1980	Bob Eastwood	65.4
1981	Tom Watson	60.1
1982	Isao Aoki	60.2
1983	Isao Aoki	62.3
1984	Peter Oosterhuis	64.7
1985	Tom Purtzer	60.8
1986	Paul Azinger	63.8
1987	Paul Azinger	63.2
1988	Greg Powers	63.5
1989	Mike Sullivan	66.0
1990	Paul Azinger	67.2
1991	Ben Crenshaw	64.9
1992	Mitch Adcock	66.9
1993	Ken Green	64.4
1994	Corey Pavin	65.4
1995	Billy Mayfair	68.6
1996	Gary Rusnak	64.0

Note: Percentage of up-and-down efforts from greenside sand traps only; fairway bunkers excluded.

PAR BREAKERS

1980	Tom Watson	.213
1981	Bruce Lietzke	.225
1982	Tom Kite	.2154†
1983	Tom Watson	.211
1984	Craig Stadler	.220
1985	Craig Stadler	.218
1986	Greg Norman	.248
1987	Mark Calcavecchia	.221
1988	Ken Green	.236
1989	Greg Norman	.224
1990	Greg Norman	.219

Note: Average based on total birdies and eagles scored out of total holes played. Discontinued as an official category after 1990.

† Number had to be carried to extra decimal place to determine winner.

Year by Year Statistical Leaders *(Cont.)*

EAGLES

1980	Dave Eichelberger	16	1985	Larry Rinker	14	1991	Andy Bean	15
1981	Bruce Lietzke	12	1986	Joey Sindelar	16	1992	Dan Forsman	18
1982	Tom Weiskopf	10	1987	Phil Blackmar	20	1993	Davis Love III	15
	J. C. Snead	10	1988	Ken Green	21	1994	Davis Love III	18
	Andy Bean	10	1989	Lon Hinkle	14	1995	Kelly Gibson	16
1983	Chip Beck	15		Duffy Waldorf	14	1996	Tom Watson	97.2
1984	Gary Hallberg	15	1990	Paul Azinger	14			

Note: Total of eagles scored from 1980-1995. Since 1996 winner determined by number of holes played per eagle.

BIRDIES

1980	Andy Bean	388	1986	Joey Sindelar	415	1992	Jeff Sluman	417
1981	Vance Heafner	388	1987	Dan Forsman	409	1993	John Huston	426
1982	Andy Bean	392	1988	Dan Forsman	465	1994	Brad Bryant	397
1983	Hal Sutton	399	1989	Ted Schulz	415	1995	Steve Lowery	410
1984	Mark O'Meara	419	1990	Mike Donald	401	1996	Fred Couples	4.20
1985	Joey Sindelar	411	1991	Scott Hoch	446			

Note: Total of birdies scored from 1980-95. Since 1996, winner determined by average number of birdies per round.

PGA Player of the Year Award

1948	Ben Hogan	1965	Dave Marr	1982	Tom Watson
1949	Sam Snead	1966	Billy Casper	1983	Hal Sutton
1950	Ben Hogan	1967	Jack Nicklaus	1984	Tom Watson
1951	Ben Hogan	1968	Not awarded	1985	Lanny Wadkins
1952	Julius Boros	1969	Orville Moody	1986	Bob Tway
1953	Ben Hogan	1970	Billy Casper	1987	Paul Azinger
1954	Ed Furgol	1971	Lee Trevino	1988	Curtis Strange
1955	Doug Ford	1972	Jack Nicklaus	1989	Tom Kite
1956	Jack Burke	1973	Jack Nicklaus	1990	Wayne Levi
1957	Dick Mayer	1974	Johnny Miller	1991	Fred Couples
1958	Dow Finsterwald	1975	Jack Nicklaus	1992	Fred Couples
1959	Art Wall	1976	Jack Nicklaus	1993	Nick Price
1960	Arnold Palmer	1977	Tom Watson	1994	Nick Price
1961	Jerry Barber	1978	Tom Watson	1995	Greg Norman
1962	Arnold Palmer	1979	Tom Watson	1996	Tom Lehman
1963	Julius Boros	1980	Tom Watson		
1964	Ken Venturi	1981	Bill Rogers		

Vardon Trophy: Scoring Average

Year	Winner	Avg	Year	Winner	Avg	Year	Winner	Avg
1937	Harry Cooper	*500	1960	Billy Casper	69.95	1979	Tom Watson	70.27
1938	Sam Snead	520	1961	Arnold Palmer	69.85	1980	Lee Trevino	69.73
1939	Byron Nelson	473	1962	Arnold Palmer	70.27	1981	Tom Kite	69.80
1940	Ben Hogan	423	1963	Billy Casper	70.58	1982	Tom Kite	70.21
1941	Ben Hogan	494	1964	Arnold Palmer	70.01	1983	Raymond Floyd	70.61
1942-46	No award		1965	Billy Casper	70.85	1984	Calvin Peete	70.56
1947	Jimmy Demaret	69.90	1966	Billy Casper	70.27	1985	Don Pooley	70.36
1948	Ben Hogan	69.30	1967	Arnold Palmer	70.18	1986	Scott Hoch	70.08
1949	Sam Snead	69.37	1968	Billy Casper	69.82	1987	Don Pohl	70.25
1950	Sam Snead	69.23	1969	Dave Hill	70.34	1988	Chip Beck	69.46
1951	Lloyd Mangrum	70.05	1970	Lee Trevino	70.64	1989	Greg Norman	69.49
1952	Jack Burke	70.54	1971	Lee Trevino	70.27	1990	Greg Norman	69.10
1953	Lloyd Mangrum	70.22	1972	Lee Trevino	70.89	1991	Fred Couples	69.59
1954	E. J. Harrison	70.41	1973	Bruce Crampton	70.57	1992	Fred Couples	69.38
1955	Sam Snead	69.86	1974	Lee Trevino	70.53	1993	Nick Price	69.11
1956	Cary Middlecoff	70.35	1975	Bruce Crampton	70.51	1994	Greg Norman	68.81
1957	Dow Finsterwald	70.30	1976	Don January	70.56	1995	Steve Elkington	69.62
1958	Bob Rosburg	70.11	1977	Tom Watson	70.32	1996	Tom Lehman	69.32
1959	Art Wall	70.35	1978	Tom Watson	70.16			

*Point system used, 1937-41.

Note: As of 1988, based on minimum of 60 rounds per year. Adjusted for average score of field in tournaments entered.

Alltime PGA Tour Records*

Scoring

90 HOLES

325—(67-67-64-65-62) by Tom Kite, at four courses, La Quinta, CA, in winning the 1993 Bob Hope Classic (35 under par).

72 HOLES

257—(60-68-64-65) by Mike Souchak, at Brackenridge Park GC, San Antonio, to win 1955 Texas Open (27 under par).

54 HOLES

Opening rounds

189—(64-62-63) by John Cook, at the TPC at Southwind, Memphis, TN, en route to winning the 1996 St Jude Classic.

Consecutive rounds

189—(63-63-63) by Chandler Harper in the last three rounds to win the 1954 Texas Open at Brackenridge Park GC, San Antonio.

189—(64-62-63) by John Cook, at the TPC at Southwind, Memphis, TN, in the first three rounds of the 1996 St Jude Classic.

36 HOLES

Opening rounds

126—(64-62) by Tommy Bolt, at Cavalier Yacht & CC, Virginia Beach, VA, in 1954 Virginia Beach Open.

126—(64-62) by Paul Azinger, at Oak Hills CC, San Antonio, in the 1989 Texas Open.

126—(64-62) by John Cook, at the TPC at Southwind, Memphis, TN, in the 1996 St Jude Classic.

126—(64-62) by Rick Fehr, at the Las Vegas Hilton CC/TPC at Summerlin, Las Vegas, in the 1996 Las Vegas Invitational.

Consecutive rounds

125—(64–61) by Gay Brewer in the middle rounds of the 1967 Pensacola Open, which he won, at Pensacola CC, Pensacola, FL.

125—(63-62) by Ron Streck in the last two rounds to win the 1978 Texas Open at Oak Hills CC, San Antonio.

125—(62-63) by Blaine McCallister in the middle two rounds in winning the 1988 Hardee's Golf Classic at Oakwood CC, Coal Valley, IL.

125—(62-63) by John Cook, in the middle two rounds in winning the 1996 St Jude Classic at the TPC at Southwind, Memphis, TN.

18 HOLES

59—by Al Geiberger, at Colonial Country Club, Memphis, in second round in winning the 1977 Memphis Classic.

59—by Chip Beck, at Sunrise Golf Club, Las Vegas, in third round of the 1991 Las Vegas Invitational.

9 HOLES

27—by Mike Souchak, at Brackenridge Park GC, San Antonio, on par-35 second nine of first round in the 1955 Texas Open.

27—by Andy North at En-Joie GC, Endicott, NY, on par-34 second nine of first round in the 1975 BC Open.

MOST CONSECUTIVE ROUNDS UNDER 70

19—Byron Nelson in 1945.

MOST BIRDIES IN A ROW

8—Bob Goalby at Pasadena GC, St Petersburg, FL, during fourth round in winning the 1961 St Petersburg Open.

Scoring (Cont.)

MOST BIRDIES IN A ROW (Cont.)

8—Fuzzy Zoeller, at Oakwood CC, Coal Valley, IL, during first round of 1976 Quad Cities Open.

8—Dewey Arnette, Warwick Hills GC, Grand Blanc, MI, during first round of the 1987 Buick Open.

MOST BIRDIES IN A ROW TO WIN

5—Jack Nicklaus to win 1978 Jackie Gleason Inverrary Classic (last 5 holes).

Wins

MOST CONSECUTIVE YEARS WINNING AT LEAST ONE TOURNAMENT

17—Jack Nicklaus, 1962-78.
17—Arnold Palmer, 1955-71.
16—Billy Casper, 1956-71.

MOST CONSECUTIVE WINS

11—Byron Nelson, from Miami Four Ball, March 8-11, 1945, through Canadian Open, August 2-4, 1945.

MOST WINS IN A SINGLE EVENT

8—Sam Snead, Greater Greensboro Open, 1938, 1946, 1949, 1950, 1955, 1956, 1960, and 1965.

MOST CONSECUTIVE WINS IN A SINGLE EVENT

4—Walter Hagen, PGA Championships, 1924-27.

MOST WINS IN A CALENDAR YEAR

18—Byron Nelson, 1945

MOST YEARS BETWEEN WINS

12—Howard Twitty, 1980–93.

MOST YEARS FROM FIRST WIN TO LAST

29—Sam Snead, 1936-65.
29—Ray Floyd, 1963-92.

YOUNGEST WINNERS

John McDermott, 19 years and 10 months, 1911 US Open.

OLDEST WINNER

Sam Snead, 52 years and 10 months, 1965 Greater Greensboro Open.

WIDEST WINNING MARGIN: STROKES

16—Bobby Locke, 1948 Chicago Victory National Championship.

Putting

FEWEST PUTTS, ONE ROUND

18—Andy North, at Kingsmill GC, in second round of 1990 Anheuser Busch Golf Classic.

18—Kenny Knox, at Harbour Town GL, in first round of 1989 MCI Heritage Classic.

18—Mike McGee, at Colonial CC, in first round of 1987 Federal Express St Jude Classic.

18—Sam Trahan, at Whitemarsh Valley CC, in final round of 1979 IVB Philadelphia Golf Classic.

18—Jim McGovern, at TPC at Southwind, in second round of 1992 Federal Express St. Jude Classic.

FEWEST PUTTS, FOUR ROUNDS

93—Kenny Knox, in 1989 MCI Heritage Classic at Harbour Town GL.

*Through 10/13/96.

THE MAJOR TOURNAMENTS

LPGA Championship

Year	Winner	Score	Runner-Up	Site
1955	Beverly Hanson† (4 and 3)	220	Louise Suggs	Orchard Ridge CC, Ft Wayne, IN
1956	Marlene Hagge* (5)	291	Patty Berg (6)	Forest Lake CC, Detroit
1957	Louise Suggs	285	Wiffi Smith	Churchill Valley CC, Pittsburgh
1958	Mickey Wright	288	Fay Crocker	Churchill Valley CC, Pittsburgh
1959	Betsy Rawls	288	Patty Berg	Sheraton Hotel CC, French Lick, IN
1960	Mickey Wright	292	Louise Suggs	Sheraton Hotel CC, French Lick, IN
1961	Mickey Wright	287	Louise Suggs	Stardust CC, Las Vegas
1962	Judy Kimball	282	Shirley Spork	Stardust CC, Las Vegas
1963	Mickey Wright	294	Mary Lena Faulk Mary Mills Louise Suggs	Stardust CC, Las Vegas
1964	Mary Mills	278	Mickey Wright	Stardust CC, Las Vegas
1965	Sandra Haynie	279	Clifford A. Creed	Stardust CC, Las Vegas
1966	Gloria Ehret	282	Mickey Wright	Stardust CC, Las Vegas
1967	Kathy Whitworth	284	Shirley Englehorn	Pleasant Valley CC, Sutton, MA
1968	Sandra Post* (68)	294	Kathy Whitworth (75)	Pleasant Valley CC, Sutton, MA
1969	Betsy Rawls	293	Susie Berning Carol Mann	Concord GC, Kiameshia Lake, NY
1970	Shirley Englehorn* (74)	285	Kathy Whitworth (78)	Pleasant Valley CC, Sutton, MA
1971	Kathy Whitworth	288	Kathy Ahern	Pleasant Valley CC, Sutton, MA
1972	Kathy Ahern	293	Jane Blalock	Pleasant Valley CC, Sutton, MA
1973	Mary Mills	288	Betty Burfeindt	Pleasant Valley CC, Sutton, MA
1974	Sandra Haynie	288	JoAnne Carner	Pleasant Valley CC, Sutton, MA
1975	Kathy Whitworth	288	Sandra Haynie	Pine Ridge GC, Baltimore
1976	Betty Burfeindt	287	Judy Rankin	Pine Ridge GC, Baltimore
1977	Chako Higuchi	279	Pat Bradley Sandra Post Judy Rankin	Bay Tree Golf Plantation, N. Myrtle Beach, SC
1978	Nancy Lopez	275	Amy Alcott	Jack Nicklaus GC, Kings Island, OH
1979	Donna Caponi	279	Jerilyn Britz	Jack Nicklaus GC, Kings Island, OH
1980	Sally Little	285	Jane Blalock	Jack Nicklaus GC, Kings Island, OH
1981	Donna Caponi	280	Jerilyn Britz Pat Meyers	Jack Nicklaus GC, Kings Island, OH
1982	Jan Stephenson	279	JoAnne Carner	Jack Nicklaus GC, Kings Island, OH
1983	Patty Sheehan	279	Sandra Haynie	Jack Nicklaus GC, Kings Island, OH
1984	Patty Sheehan	272	Beth Daniel Pat Bradley	Jack Nicklaus GC, Kings Island, OH
1985	Nancy Lopez	273	Alice Miller	Jack Nicklaus GC, Kings Island, OH
1986	Pat Bradley	277	Patty Sheehan	Jack Nicklaus GC, Kings Island, OH
1987	Jane Geddes	275	Betsy King	Jack Nicklaus GC, Kings Island, OH
1988	Sherri Turner	281	Amy Alcott	Jack Nicklaus GC, Kings Island, OH
1989	Nancy Lopez	274	Ayako Okamoto	Jack Nicklaus GC, Kings Island, OH
1990	Beth Daniel	280	Rosie Jones	Bethesda CC, Bethesda, MD
1991	Meg Mallon	274	Pat Bradley Ayako Okamoto	Bethesda CC, Bethesda, MD
1992	Betsy King	267	Karen Noble	Bethesda CC, Bethesda, MD
1993	Patty Sheehan	275	Lauri Merten	Bethesda CC, Bethesda, MD
1994	Laura Davies	279	Alice Ritzman	DuPont CC, Wilmington, DE
1995	Kelly Robbins	274	Laura Davies	DuPont CC, Wilmington, DE
1996	Laura Davies	213†	Julie Piers	DuPont CC, Wilmington, DE

*Won in playoff. Playoff scores are in parentheses. 1956 was sudden death; 1968 and 1970 were 18-hole playoffs.
†Won match play final. #Shortened due to rain.

U.S. Women's Open

Year	Winner	Score	Runner-Up	Site
1946	Patty Berg	5 & 4	Betty Jameson	Spokane CC, Spokane, WA
1947	Betty Jameson	295	Sally Sessions	Starmount Forest CC, Greensboro, NC
			Polly Riley	
1948	Babe Zaharias	300	Betty Hicks	Atlantic City CC, Northfield, NJ
1949	Louise Suggs	291	Babe Zaharias	Prince George's G & CC, Landover, MD
1950	Babe Zaharias	291	Betsy Rawls	Rolling Hills CC, Wichita, KS
1951	Betsy Rawls	293	Louise Suggs	Druid Hills GC, Atlanta
1952	Louise Suggs	284	Marlene Bauer	Bala GC, Philadelphia
			Betty Jameson	
1953	Betsy Rawls* (71)	302	Jackie Pung (77)	CC of Rochester, Rochester, NY
1954	Babe Zaharias	291	Betty Hicks	Salem CC, Peabody, MA
1955	Fay Crocker	299	Mary Lena Faulk	Wichita CC, Wichita, KS
			Louise Suggs	
1956	Kathy Cornelius* (75)	302	Barbara McIntire (82)	Northland CC, Duluth, MN
1957	Betsy Rawls	299	Patty Berg	Winged Foot GC, Mamaroneck, NY
1958	Mickey Wright	290	Louise Suggs	Forest Lake CC, Detroit
1959	Mickey Wright	287	Louise Suggs	Churchill Valley CC, Pittsburgh
1960	Betsy Rawls	292	Joyce Ziske	Worcester CC, Worcester, MA
1961	Mickey Wright	293	Betsy Rawls	Baltusrol GC (Lower Course), Springfield, NJ
1962	Murle Breer	301	Jo Ann Prentice	Dunes GC, Myrtle Beach, SC
			Ruth Jessen	
1963	Mary Mills	289	Sandra Haynie	Kenwood CC, Cincinnati
			Louise Suggs	
1964	Mickey Wright* (70)	290	Ruth Jessen (72)	San Diego CC, Chula Vista, CA
1965	Carol Mann	290	Kathy Cornelius	Atlantic City CC, Northfield, NJ
1966	Sandra Spuzich	297	Carol Mann	Hazeltine Natl GC, Chaska, MN
1967	Catherine LaCoste	294	Susie Berning	Hot Springs GC (Cascades Course),
			Beth Stone	Hot Springs, VA
1968	Susie Berning	289	Mickey Wright	Moslem Springs GC, Fleetwood, PA
1969	Donna Caponi	294	Peggy Wilson	Scenic Hills CC, Pensacola, FL
1970	Donna Caponi	287	Sandra Haynie	Muskogee CC, Muskogee, OK
			Sandra Spuzich	
1971	JoAnne Carner	288	Kathy Whitworth	Kahkwa CC, Erie, PA
1972	Susie Berning	299	Kathy Ahern	Winged Foot GC, Mamaroneck, NY
			Pam Barnett	
			Judy Rankin	
1973	Susie Berning	290	Gloria Ehret	CC of Rochester, Rochester, NY
			Shelley Hamlin	
1974	Sandra Haynie	295	Carol Mann	La Grange CC, La Grange, IL
			Beth Stone	
1975	Sandra Palmer	295	JoAnne Carner	Atlantic City CC, Northfield, NJ
			Sandra Post	
			Nancy Lopez	
1976	JoAnne Carner* (76)	292	Sandra Palmer (78)	Rolling Green CC, Springfield, PA
1977	Hollis Stacy	292	Nancy Lopez	Hazeltine Natl GC, Chaska, MN
1978	Hollis Stacy	289	JoAnne Carner	CC of Indianapolis, Indianapolis
			Sally Little	
1979	Jerilyn Britz	284	Debbie Massey	Brooklawn CC, Fairfield, CT
			Sandra Palmer	
1980	Amy Alcott	280	Hollis Stacy	Richland CC, Nashville
1981	Pat Bradley	279	Beth Daniel	La Grange CC, La Grange, IL
1982	Janet Anderson	283	Beth Daniel	Del Paso CC, Sacramento
			Sandra Haynie	
			Donna White	
			JoAnne Carner	
1983	Jan Stephenson	290	JoAnne Carner	Cedar Ridge CC, Tulsa
			Patty Sheehan	
1984	Hollis Stacy	290	Rosie Jones	Salem CC, Peabody, MA
1985	Kathy Baker	280	Judy Dickinson	Baltusrol GC (Upper Course), Springfield, NJ
1986	Jane Geddes* (71)	287	Sally Little (73)	NCR GC, Dayton
1987	Laura Davies* (71)	285	Ayako Okamoto (73)	Plainfield CC, Plainfield, NJ
			JoAnne Carner (74)	
1988	Liselotte Neumann	277	Patty Sheehan	Baltimore CC, Baltimore
1989	Betsy King	278	Nancy Lopez	Indianwood G & CC, Lake Orion, MI
1990	Betsy King	284	Patty Sheehan	Atlanta Athletic Club, Duluth, GA

U.S. Women's Open *(Cont.)*

Year	Winner	Score	Runner-Up	Site
1991	Meg Mallon	283	Pat Bradley	Colonial Club, Fort Worth
1992	Patty Sheehan* (72)	280	Juli Inkster	Oakmont CC, Oakmont, PA
1993	Lauri Merten	280	Donna Andrew	Crooked Stick, Carmel, IN
			Helen Alfredsson	
1994	Patty Sheehan	277	Tammie Green	Indianwood G & CC, Lake Orion, MI
1995	Annika Sorenstam	278	Meg Mallon	The Broadmoor GC, Colorado Springs, CO
1996	Annika Sorenstam	272	Kris Tschetter	Pine Needles GC, Southern Pines, NC

*Winner in playoff. 18-hole playoff scores are in parentheses.

Dinah Shore

Year	Winner	Score	Runner-Up
1972	Jane Blalock	213	Carol Mann, Judy Rankin
1973	Mickey Wright	284	Joyce Kazmierski
1974	Jo Ann Prentice*	289	Jane Blalock, Sandra Haynie
1975	Sandra Palmer	283	Kathy McMullen
1976	Judy Rankin	285	Betty Burfeindt
1977	Kathy Whitworth	289	JoAnne Carner, Sally Little
1978	Sandra Post*	283	Penny Pulz
1979	Sandra Post	276	Nancy Lopez
1980	Donna Caponi	275	Amy Alcott
1981	Nancy Lopez	277	Carolyn Hill
1982	Sally Little	278	Hollis Stacy, Sandra Haynie
1983	Amy Alcott	282	Beth Daniel, Kathy Whitworth
1984	Juli Inkster*	280	Pat Bradley
1985	Alice Miller	275	Jan Stephenson
1986	Pat Bradley	280	Val Skinner
1987	Betsy King*	283	Patty Sheehan
1988	Amy Alcott	274	Colleen Walker
1989	Juli Inkster	279	Tammie Green, JoAnne Carner
1990	Betsy King	283	Kathy Postlewait, Shirley Furlong
1991	Amy Alcott	273	Dottie Mochrie
1992	Dottie Mochrie*	279	Juli Inkster
1993	Helen Alfredsson	284	Amy Benz, Tina Barrett, Betsy King
1994	Donna Andrews	276	Laura Davies
1995	Nanci Bowen	285	Susie Redman
1996	Patti Sheehan	281	Kelly Robbins, Meg Mallon, Annika Sorenstam

*Winner in sudden-death playoff.

Note: Designated fourth major in 1983.

Played at Mission Hills CC, Rancho Mirage, CA.

du Maurier Classic

Year	Winner	Score	Runner-Up	Site
1973	Jocelyne Bourassa*	214	Sandra Haynie	Montreal GC, Montreal
			Judy Rankin	
1974	Carole Jo Callison	208	JoAnne Carner	Candiac GC, Montreal
1975	JoAnne Carner*	214	Carol Mann	St George's CC, Toronto
1976	Donna Caponi*	212	Judy Rankin	Cedar Brae G & CC, Toronto
1977	Judy Rankin	214	Pat Meyers	Lachute G & CC, Montreal
			Sandra Palmer	
1978	JoAnne Carner	278	Hollis Stacy	St George's CC, Toronto
1979	Amy Alcott	285	Nancy Lopez	Richelieu Valley CC, Montreal
1980	Pat Bradley	277	JoAnne Carner	St George's CC, Toronto
1981	Jan Stephenson	278	Nancy Lopez	Summerlea CC, Dorion, Quebec
			Pat Bradley	
1982	Sandra Haynie	280	Beth Daniel	St George's CC, Toronto
1983	Hollis Stacy	277	JoAnne Carner	Beaconsfield GC, Montreal
			Alice Miller	
1984	Juli Inkster	279	Ayako Okamoto	St George's G & CC, Toronto
1985	Pat Bradley	278	Jane Geddes	Beaconsfield CC, Montreal

du Maurier Classic (Cont.)

Year	Winner	Score	Runner-Up	Site
1986	Pat Bradley*	276	Ayako Okamoto	Board of Trade CC, Toronto
1987	Jody Rosenthal	272	Ayako Okamoto	Islesmere GC, Laval, Quebec
1988	Sally Little	279	Laura Davies	Vancouver GC, Coquitlam, British Columbia
1989	Tammie Green	279	Pat Bradley Betsy King	Beaconsfield GC, Montreal
1990	Cathy Johnston	276	Patty Sheehan	Westmount G & CC, Kitchener, Ontario
1991	Nancy Scranton	279	Debbie Massey	Vancouver GC, Coquitlam, British Columbia
1992	Sherri Steinhauer	277	Judy Dickinson	St. Charles CC, Winnipeg, Manitoba
1993	Brandie Burton	277	Betsy King	London Hunt and CC, London, Ontario
1994	Martha Nause	279	Michelle McGann	Ottawa Hunt and GC, Ottawa, Ont.
1995	Jenny Lidback	280	Liselotte Neumann	Beaconsfield GC, Pointe-Claire, Quebec
1996	Laura Davies	277	Nancy Lopez, Karrie Webb	Edmonton CC, Edmonton, Alberta

*Winner in sudden-death playoff.

Note: Designated third major in 1979.

Alltime Major Championship Winners

	LPGA	U.S. Open	Dinah Shore	du Maurier	#Ttitleholders	†Western	U.S. Am	British Am	Total
Patty Berg	0	1	0	0	7	7	1	0	16
Mickey Wright	4	4	0	0	2	3	0	0	13
Louise Suggs	1	2	0	0	4	4	1	1	13
Babe Zaharias	0	3	0	0	3	4	1	1	12
Betsy Rawls	2	4	0	0	0	2	0	0	8
*JoAnne Carner	0	2	0	0	0	0	5	0	7
Kathy Whitworth	3	0	0	0	2	1	0	0	6
*Pat Bradley	1	1	1	3	0	0	0	0	6
*Juli Inkster	0	0	2	1	0	0	3	0	6
*Patty Sheehan	3	2	1	0	0	0	0	0	6
Glenna Vare	0	0	0	0	0	0	6	0	6

*Active LPGA player.

#Major from 1937–1972. †Major from 1937–1967.

Alltime Multiple Professional Major Winners

LPGA

Mickey Wright	4
Nancy Lopez	3
Patty Sheehan	3
Kathy Whitworth	3
Donna Caponi	2
Sandra Haynie	2
Mary Mills	2
Betsy Rawls	2

U.S. OPEN

Betsy Rawls	4
Mickey Wright	4
Susie Maxwell Berning	3

U.S. OPEN (Cont.)

Hollis Stacy	3
Babe Zaharias	3
JoAnne Carner	2
Donna Caponi	2
Betsy King	2
Patty Sheehan	2
Louise Suggs	2

DINAH SHORE

Amy Alcott	3
Juli Inkster	2
Betsy King	2

DU MAURIER

Pat Bradley	3
JoAnne Carner	2

TITLEHOLDERS

Patty Berg	7
Louise Suggs	4
Babe Zaharias	3
Dorothy Kirby	2
Marilynn Smith	2
Kathy Whitworth	2
Mickey Wright	2

WESTERN OPEN

Patty Berg	7
Louise Suggs	4
Babe Zaharias	4
Mickey Wright	3
June Beebe	2
Opal Hill	2
Betty Jameson	2
Betsy Rawls	2

THE LPGA TOUR

Most Career Wins†

	Wins		Wins		Wins
Kathy Whitworth	88	JoAnne Carner	42	Babe Zaharias	31
Mickey Wright	82	Sandra Haynie	42	*Betsy King	30
Patty Berg	57	Carol Mann	38	Amy Alcott	29
Betsy Rawls	55	*Patty Sheehan	35	Jane Blalock	29
Louise Suggs	50	*Beth Daniel	32	Judy Rankin	26
*Nancy Lopez	47	*Pat Bradley	31		

*Active LPGA player. †Through 10/13/96.

Season Money Leaders

		Earnings ($)			Earnings ($)
1950	Babe Zaharias	14,800	1973	Kathy Whitworth	82,864
1951	Babe Zaharias	15,087	1974	JoAnne Carner	87,094
1952	Betsy Rawls	14,505	1975	Sandra Palmer	76,374
1953	Louise Suggs	19,816	1976	Judy Rankin	150,734
1954	Patty Berg	16,011	1977	Judy Rankin	122,890
1955	Patty Berg	16,492	1978	Nancy Lopez	189,814
1956	Marlene Hagge	20,235	1979	Nancy Lopez	197,489
1957	Patty Berg	16,272	1980	Beth Daniel	231,000
1958	Beverly Hanson	12,639	1981	Beth Daniel	206,998
1959	Betsy Rawls	26,774	1982	JoAnne Carner	310,400
1960	Louise Suggs	16,892	1983	JoAnne Carner	291,404
1961	Mickey Wright	22,236	1984	Betsy King	266,771
1962	Mickey Wright	21,641	1985	Nancy Lopez	416,472
1963	Mickey Wright	31,269	1986	Pat Bradley	492,021
1964	Mickey Wright	29,800	1987	Ayako Okamoto	466,034
1965	Kathy Whitworth	28,658	1988	Sherri Turner	350,851
1966	Kathy Whitworth	33,517	1989	Betsy King	654,132
1967	Kathy Whitworth	32,937	1990	Beth Daniel	863,578
1968	Kathy Whitworth	48,379	1991	Pat Bradley	763,118
1969	Carol Mann	49,152	1992	Dottie Mochrie	693,335
1970	Kathy Whitworth	30,235	1993	Betsy King	595,992
1971	Kathy Whitworth	41,181	1994	Laura Davies	687,201
1972	Kathy Whitworth	65,063	1995	Annika Sorenstam	666,533

Career Money Leaders†

		Earnings ($)			Earnings ($)			Earnings ($)
1.	Betsy King	5,510,481.50	11.	Rosie Jones	2,872,347.97	21.	Val Skinner	2,075,022.75
2.	Pat Bradley	5,393,933.03	12.	Meg Mallon	2,800,254.00	22.	Chris Johnson	1,949,194.50
3.	Beth Daniel	5,135,807.80	13.	Ayako Okamoto	2,741,741.85	23.	Deb Richard	1,924,253.00
4.	Patty Sheehan	5,121,437.01	14.	Juli Inkster	2,495,817.23	24.	Dawn Coe-Jones	1,918,458.57
5.	Nancy Lopez	4,478,135.83	15.	Jan Stephenson	2,427,142.00	25.	Michelle McGann	1,908,464.00
6.	Dottie Pepper	3,675,617.00	16.	Colleen Walker	2,281,470.71	26.	D. Ammaccapane	1,878,974.00
7.	Amy Alcott	3,242,555.14	17.	Liselotte Neumann	2,248,392.00	27.	Brandie Burton	1,789,975.00
8.	Laura Davies	3,043,489.00	18.	Tammie Green	2,208,218.00	28.	Sherri Steinhauer	1,769,819.00
9.	Jane Geddes	2,925,992.30	19.	Hollis Stacy	2,127,736.99	29.	Sally Little	1,765,027.80
10.	JoAnne Carner	2,885,707.63	20.	Judy Dickinson	2,102,048.92	30.	Kathy Whitworth	1,731,770.01

†Through 10/13/96.

LPGA Player of the Year

1966	Kathy Whitworth	1976	Judy Rankin	1986	Pat Bradley
1967	Kathy Whitworth	1977	Judy Rankin	1987	Ayako Okamoto
1968	Kathy Whitworth	1978	Nancy Lopez	1988	Nancy Lopez
1969	Kathy Whitworth	1979	Nancy Lopez	1989	Betsy King
1970	Sandra Haynie	1980	Beth Daniel	1990	Beth Daniel
1971	Kathy Whitworth	1981	JoAnne Carner	1991	Pat Bradley
1972	Kathy Whitworth	1982	JoAnne Carner	1992	Dottie Mochrie
1973	Kathy Whitworth	1983	Patty Sheehan	1993	Betsy King
1974	JoAnne Carner	1984	Betsy King	1994	Beth Daniel
1975	Sandra Palmer	1985	Nancy Lopez	1995	Annika Sorenstam

Vare Trophy: Best Scoring Average

	Avg			Avg			Avg
1953......Patty Berg	75.00	1968......Carol Mann	72.04	1983......JoAnne Carner	71.41
1954......Babe Zaharias	75.48	1969......Kathy Whitworth	72.38	1984......Patty Sheehan	71.40
1955......Patty Berg	74.47	1970......Kathy Whitworth	72.26	1985......Nancy Lopez	70.73
1956......Patty Berg	74.57	1971......Kathy Whitworth	72.88	1986......Pat Bradley	71.10
1957......Louise Suggs	74.64	1972......Kathy Whitworth	72.38	1987......Betsy King	71.14
1958......Beverly Hanson	74.92	1973......Judy Rankin	73.08	1988......Colleen Walker	71.26
1959......Betsy Rawls	74.03	1974......JoAnne Carner	72.87	1989......Beth Daniel	70.38
1960......Mickey Wright	73.25	1975......JoAnne Carner	72.40	1990......Beth Daniel	70.54
1961......Mickey Wright	73.55	1976......Judy Rankin	72.25	1991......Pat Bradley	70.76
1962......Mickey Wright	73.67	1977......Judy Rankin	72.16	1992......Dottie Mochrie	70.80
1963......Mickey Wright	72.81	1978......Nancy Lopez	71.76	1993......Nancy Lopez	70.83
1964......Mickey Wright	72.46	1979......Nancy Lopez	71.20	1994......Beth Daniel	70.90
1965......Kathy Whitworth	72.61	1980......Amy Alcott	71.51	1995......Annika Sorenstam	71.00
1966......Kathy Whitworth	72.60	1981......JoAnne Carner	71.75		
1967......Kathy Whitworth	72.74	1982......JoAnne Carner	71.49		

Alltime LPGA Tour Records†

Scoring

72 HOLES

268—(66-67-69-66) by Nancy Lopez to win at the Willow Creek GC, High Point, NC, in the 1985 Henredon Classic (20 under par).

268—(67-63-70-68) by Beth Daniel to win at the Walnut Hills CC, E. Lansing, MI, in the 1994 Oldsmobile Classic (20 under par).

54 HOLES

197—(67-65-65) by Pat Bradley to win at the Rail GC, Springfield, Ill., in the 1991 Rail Charity Golf Classic (19 under par).

36 HOLES

129—(64-65) by Judy Dickinson at Pasadena Yacht & CC, St Petersburg, in the 1985 S&H Golf Classic (15 under par).

18 HOLES

62—by Mickey Wright at Hogan Park GC, Midland, TX, in the first round in winning the 1964 Tall City Open (9 under par).

62—by Vicki Fergon at Almaden G & CC, San Jose, CA, in the second round of the 1984 San Jose Classic (11 under par).

62—by Laura Davies at the Rail Golf Club, Springfield, Ill., in the first round of the 1991 Rail Charity Golf Classic (10 under par).

62—by Hollis Stacy at Meridian Valley Country Club, Seattle, WA, in the second round of the 1992 Safeco Classic (10 under par).

9 HOLES

28—by Mary Beth Zimmerman at Rail GC, 1984 Rail Charity Golf Classic, Springfield, IL (par 36). Zimmerman shot 64.

†Through 10/13/96.

Scoring *(Cont.)*

9 HOLES *(Cont.)*

28—by Pat Bradley at Green Gables CC, Denver, 1984 Columbia Savings Classic (par 35). Bradley shot 65.

28—by Muffin Spencer-Devlin at Knollwood CC, Elmsford, NY, in winning the 1985 MasterCard International Pro-Am (par 35). Spencer-Devlin shot 64.

28—by Peggy Kirsch at Squaw Creek CC, Vienna, OH, in the 1991 Phar-Mor (par 35).

28—by Renee Heiken at Highland Meadows CC, Sylvania, OH, in the 1996 Jamie Farr Kroger Classic (par 34).

MOST CONSECUTIVE ROUNDS UNDER 70

9—Beth Daniel, in 1990.

MOST BIRDIES IN A ROW

8—Mary Beth Zimmerman at Rail GC in Springfield, IL, in the second round of the 1984 Rail Charity Classic. Zimmerman shot 64 (8 under par).

Wins

MOST CONSECUTIVE WINS IN SCHEDULED EVENTS

4—Mickey Wright, in 1962.
4—Mickey Wright, in 1963.
4—Kathy Whitworth, in 1969.

MOST CONSECUTIVE WINS IN ENTERED TOURNAMENTS

5—Nancy Lopez, in 1987.

MOST WINS IN A CALENDAR YEAR

13—Mickey Wright, in 1963.

WIDEST WINNING MARGIN, STROKES

14—Louise Suggs, 1949 US Women's Open.
14—Cindy Mackey, 1986 MasterCard Int'l Pro-Am.

U.S. Senior Open

Year	Winner	Score	Runner-Up	Site
1980	Roberto DeVicenzo	285	William C. Campbell	Winged Foot GC, Mamaroneck, NY
1981	Arnold Palmer* (70)	289	Bob Stone (74)	Oakland Hills CC, Birmingham, MI
			Billy Casper (77)	
1982	Miller Barber	282	Gene Littler	Portland GC, Portland, OR
			Dan Sikes, Jr	
1983	Billy Casper* (75) (3)	288	Rod Funseth (75) (4)	Hazeltine GC, Chaska, MN
1984	Miller Barber	286	Arnold Palmer	Oak Hill CC, Rochester, NY
1985	Miller Barber	285	Roberto DeVicenzo	Edgewood Tahoe GC, Stateline, NV
1986	Dale Douglass	279	Gary Player	Scioto CC, Columbus, OH
1987	Gary Player	270	Doug Sanders	Brooklawn CC, Fairfield, CT
1988	Gary Player* (68)	288	Bob Charles (70)	Medinah CC, Medinah, IL
1989	Orville Moody	279	Frank Beard	Laurel Valley GC, Ligonier, PA
1990	Lee Trevino	275	Jack Nicklaus	Ridgewood CC, Paramus, NJ
1991	Jack Nicklaus (65)	282	Chi Chi Rodriguez (69)	Oakland Hills CC, Birmingham, MI
1992	Larry Laoretti	275	Jim Colbert	Saucon Valley CC, Bethlehem, PA
1993	Jack Nicklaus	278	Tom Weiskopf	Cherry Hills CC, Englewood, CO
1994	Simon Hobday	274	Jim Albus	Pinehurst Resort & CC, Pinehurst, NC
1995	Tom Weiskopf	275	Jack Nicklaus	Congressional CC, Bethesda, MD
1996	Dave Stockton	277	Hale Irwin	Canterbury GC, Beachwood, OH

*Winner in playoff. Playoff scores are in parentheses. The 1983 playoff went to one hole of sudden death after an 18-hole playoff.

SENIOR TOUR

Season Money Leaders

Year	Winner	Earnings ($)	Year	Winner	Earnings ($)
1980	Don January	44,100	1988	Bob Charles	533,929
1981	Miller Barber	83,136	1989	Bob Charles	725,887
1982	Miller Barber	106,890	1990	Lee Trevino	1,190,518
1983	Don January	237,571	1991	Mike Hill	1,065,657
1984	Don January	328,597	1992	Lee Trevino	1,027,002
1985	Peter Thomson	386,724	1993	Dave Stockton	1,175,944
1986	Bruce Crampton	454,299	1994	Dave Stockton	1,402,519
1987	Chi Chi Rodriguez	509,145	1995	Jim Colbert	1,444,386

Career Money Leaders†

		Earnings ($)			Earnings ($)
1.	Lee Trevino	6,532,149	17.	Jim Albus	3,556,257
2.	Bob Charles	6,443,518	18.	J.C. Snead	3,505,167
3.	Jim Colbert	6,313,902	19.	Harold Henning	3,303,350
4.	Chi Chi Rodriguez	5,677,319	20.	Rocky Thompson	3,300,746
5.	Dave Stockton	5,596,917	21.	Orville Moody	3,187,609
6.	Mike Hill	5,545,040	22.	Charles Coody	3,144,630
7.	George Archer	5,264,385	23.	Tom Wargo	3,049,442
8.	Ray Floyd	4,957,160	24.	Don January	2,991,569
9.	Jim Dent	4,770,983	25.	Simon Hobday	2,896,036
10.	Dale Douglass	4,756,286	26.	Gibby Gilbert	2,788,865
11.	Gary Player	4,242,242	27.	Jimmy Powell	2,744,224
12.	Bruce Crampton	3,971,312	28.	Walter Zembriski	2,693,496
13.	Bob Murphy	3,893,992	29.	Don Bies	2,473,531
14.	Al Geiberger	3,838,533	30.	Kermit Zarley	2,353,364
15.	Isao Aoki	3,646,288			
16.	Miller Barber	3,624,712	†Through 10/13/96.		

Most Career Wins†

	Wins		Wins
Lee Trevino	26	Gary Player	18
Miller Barber	24	Mike Hill	18
Bob Charles	22	George Archer	17
Don January	22	Jim Colbert	17
Chi Chi Rodriguez	22	Raymond Floyd	13
Bruce Crampton	19	Dave Stockton	13

†Through 10/13/96.

MAJOR MEN'S AMATEUR CHAMPIONSHIPS

U.S. Amateur

Year	Winner	Score	Runner-Up	Site
1895	Charles B. Macdonald	12 & 11	Charles E. Sands	Newport GC, Newport, RI
1896	H. J. Whigham	8 & 7	J.G Thorp	Shinnecock Hills GC, Southampton, NY
1897	H. J. Whigham	8 & 6	W. Rossiter Betts	Chicago GC, Wheaton, IL
1898	Findlay S. Douglas	5 & 3	Walter B. Smith	Morris County GC, Morristown, NJ
1899	H. M. Harriman	3 & 2	Findlay S. Douglas	Onwentsia Club, Lake Forest, IL
1900	Walter Travis	2 up	Findlay S. Douglas	Garden City GC, Garden City, NY
1901	Walter Travis	5 & 4	Walter E. Egan	CC of Atlantic City, NJ
1902	Louis N. James	4 & 2	Eben M. Byers	Glen View Club, Golf, IL
1903	Walter Travis	5 & 4	Eben M. Byers	Nassau CC, Glen Cove, NY
1904	H. Chandler Egan	8 & 6	Fred Herreshoff	Baltusrol GC, Springfield, NJ
1905	H. Chandler Egan	6 & 5	D.E. Sawyer	Chicago GC, Wheaton, IL
1906	Eben M. Byers	2 up	George S. Lyon	Englewood GC, Englewood, NJ
1907	Jerry Travers	6 & 5	Archibald Graham	Euclid Club, Cleveland, OH
1908	Jerry Travers	8 & 7	Max H. Behr	Garden City GC, Garden City, NY
1909	Robert A. Gardner	4 & 3	H. Chandler Egan	Chicago GC, Wheaton, IL
1910	William C. Fownes Jr	4 & 3	Warren K. Wood	The Country Club, Brookline, MA
1911	Harold Hilton	1 up	Fred Herreshoff	The Apawamis Club, Rye, NY
1912	Jerry Travers	7 & 6	Charles Evans Jr.	Chicago GC, Wheaton, IL
1913	Jerry Travers	5 & 4	John G. Anderson	Garden City GC, Garden City, NY
1914	Francis Ouimet	6 & 5	Jerry Travers	Ekwanok CC, Manchester, VT
1915	Robert A. Gardner	5 & 4	John G. Anderson	CC of Detroit, Grosse Pt. Farms, MI
1916	Chick Evans	4 & 3	Robert A. Gardner	Merion Cricket Club, Haverford, PA
1917-18	No tournament			
1919	S. Davidson Herron	5 & 4	Bobby Jones	Oakmont CC, Oakmont, PA
1920	Chick Evans	7 & 6	Francis Ouimet	Engineers' CC, Roslyn, NY
1921	Jesse P. Guilford	7 & 6	Robert A. Gardner	St. Louis CC, Clayton, MO
1922	Jess W. Sweetser	3 & 2	Chick Evans	The Country Club, Brookline, MA
1923	Max R. Marston	1 up	Jess W. Sweetser	Flossmoor CC, Flossmoor, IL
1924	Bobby Jones	9 & 8	George Von Elm	Merion Cricket Club, Ardmore, PA
1925	Bobby Jones	8 & 7	Watts Gunn	Oakmont CC, Oakmont, PA
1926	George Von Elm	2 & 1	Bobby Jones	Baltusrol GC, Springfield, NJ
1927	Bobby Jones	8 & 7	Chick Evans	Minikahda Club, Minneapolis
1928	Bobby Jones	10 & 9	T. Phillip Perkins	Brae Burn CC, West Newton, MA
1929	Harrison R. Johnston	4 & 3	Dr. O.F. Willing	Del Monte G & CC, Pebble Beach, CA
1930	Bobby Jones	8 & 7	Eugene V. Homans	Merion Cricket Club, Ardmore, PA
1931	Francis Ouimet	6 & 5	Jack Westland	Beverly CC, Chicago, IL
1932	C. Ross Somerville	2 & 1	John Goodman	Baltimore CC, Timonium, MD
1933	George T. Dunlap Jr	6 & 5	Max R. Marston	Kenwood CC, Cincinnati, OH
1934	Lawson Little	8 & 7	David Goldman	The Country Club, Brookline, MA
1935	Lawson Little	4 & 2	Walter Emery	The Country Club, Cleveland, OH
1936	John W. Fischer	1 up	Jack McLean	Garden City GC, Garden City, NY
1937	John Goodman	2 up	Raymond E. Billows	Alderwood CC, Portland, OR
1938	William P. Turnesa	8 & 7	B. Patrick Abbott	Oakmont CC, Oakmont, PA
1939	Marvin H. Ward	7 & 5	Raymond E. Billows	North Shore CC, Glenview, IL
1940	Richard D. Chapman	11 & 9	W. McCullough Jr	Winged Foot GC, Mamaroneck, NY
1941	Marvin H. Ward	4 & 3	B. Patrick Abbott	Omaha Field Club, Omaha, NE
1942-45	No tournament			
1946	Ted Bishop	1 up	Smiley L. Quick	Baltusrol GC, Springfield, NJ
1947	Skee Riegel	2 & 1	John W. Dawson	Del Monte G & CC, Pebble Beach, CA
1948	William P. Turnesa	2 & 1	Raymond E. Billows	Memphis CC, Memphis, TN
1949	Charles R. Coe	11 & 10	Rufus King	Oak Hill CC, Rochester, NY
1950	Sam Urzetta	1 up	Frank Stranahan	Minneapolis GC, Minneapolis, MN
1951	Billy Maxwell	4 & 3	Joseph F. Gagliardi	Saucon Valley CC, Bethlehem, PA
1952	Jack Westland	3 & 2	Al Mengert	Seattle GC, Seattle, WA
1953	Gene Littler	1 up	Dale Morey	Oklahoma City G & CC, Oklahoma City
1954	Arnold Palmer	1 up	Robert Sweeny	CC of Detroit, Grosse Pt. Farms, MI
1955	E. Harvie Ward Jr	9 & 8	Wm. Hyndman III	CC of Virginia, Richmond, VA
1956	E. Harvie Ward Jr	5 & 4	Charles Kocsis	Knollwood Club, Lake Forest, IL
1957	Hillman Robbins Jr	5 & 4	Dr. Frank M. Taylor	The Country Club, Brookline, MA
1958	Charles R. Coe	5 & 4	Tommy Aaron	Olympic Club, San Francisco, CA
1959	Jack Nicklaus	1 up	Charles R. Coe	Broadmoor GC, Colorado Springs, CO
1960	Deane Beman	6 & 4	Robert W. Gardner	St. Louis CC, Clayton, MO
1961	Jack Nicklaus	8 & 6	H. Dudley Wysong	Pebble Beach GL, Pebble Beach, CA

U.S. Amateur (Cont.)

Year	Winner	Score	Runner-Up	Site
1962	Labron E. Harris Jr	1 up	Downing Gray	Pinehurst CC, Pinehurst, NC
1963	Deane Beman	2 & 1	Richard H. Sikes	Wakonda Club, Des Moines, IA
1964	William C. Campbell	1 up	Edgar M. Tutwiler	Canterbury GC, Cleveland, OH
1965	Robert J. Murphy Jr	291	Robert B. Dickson	Southern Hills, CC, Tulsa, OK
1966	Gary Cowan	285-75	Deane Beman	Merion GC, Ardmore, PA
1967	Robert B. Dickson	285	Marvin Giles III	Broadmoor GC, Colorado Springs, CO
1968	Bruce Fleisher	284	Marvin Giles III	Scioto CC, Columbus, OH
1969	Steven N. Melnyk	286	Marvin Giles III	Oakmont CC, Oakmont, PA
1970	Lanny Wadkins	279	Tom Kite	Waverley CC, Portland, OR
1971	Gary Cowan	280	Eddie Pearce	Wilmington CC, Wilmington DE
1972	Marvin Giles III	285	two tied	Charlotte CC, Charlotte, NC
1973	Craig Stadler	6 & 5	David Strawn	Inverness Club, Toledo, OH
1974	Jerry Pate	2 & 1	John P. Grace	Ridgewood CC, Ridgewood, NJ
1975	Fred Ridley	2 up	Keith Fergus	CC of Virginia, Richmond, VA
1976	Bill Sander	8 & 6	C. Parker Moore Jr	Bel Air CC, Los Angeles, CA
1977	John Fought	9 & 8	Doug Fischesser	Aronimink GC, Newton Square, PA
1978	John Cook	5 & 4	Scott Hoch	Plainfield CC, Plainfield, NJ
1979	Mark O'Meara	8 & 7	John Cook	Canterbury GC, Cleveland, OH
1980	Hal Sutton	9 & 8	Bob Lewis	CC of North Carolina, Pinehurst, NC
1981	Nathaniel Crosby	1 up	Brian Lindley	Olympic Club, San Francisco, CA
1982	Jay Sigel	8 & 7	David Tolley	The Country Club, Brookline, MA
1983	Jay Sigel	8 & 7	Chris Perry	North Shore CC, Glenviedw IL
1984	Scott Verplank	4 & 3	Sam Randolph	Oak Tree GC, Edmond, OK
1985	Sam Randolph	1 up	Peter Persons	Montclair GC, West Orange, NJ
1986	Buddy Alexander	5 & 3	Chris Kite	Shoal Creek, Shoal Creek AL
1987	Bill Mayfair	4 & 3	Eric Rebmann	Jupiter Hills Club, Jupiter, FL
1988	Eric Meeks	7 & 6	Danny Yates	Va. Hot Springs G & CC, VA
1989	Chris Patton	3 & 1	Danny Green	Merion GC, Ardmore, PA
1990	Phil Mickelson	5 & 4	Manny Zerman	Cherry Hills CC, Englewood, CO
1991	Mitch Voges	7 & 6	Manny Zerman	The Honors Course, Ooltewah, TN
1992	Justin Leonard	8 & 7	Tom Scherrer	Muirfield Village GC, Dublin, OH
1993	John Harris	5 & 3	Danny Ellis	Champions GC, Houston, TX
1994	Tiger Woods	2 up	Trip Kuehne	TPC-Sawgrass, Ponte Vedre, FL
1995	Tiger Woods	2 up	Buddy Marucci	Newport Country Club, Newport, RI
1996	Tiger Woods	38 holes	Steve Scott	Pumpkin Ridge GC, Cornelius, OR

Note: All stroke play from 1965 to 1972.

U.S. Junior Amateur

1948 ... Dean Lind	1965 ... James Masserio	1982 ... Rich Marik
1949 ... Gay Brewer	1966 ... Gary Sanders	1983 ... Tim Straub
1950 ... Mason Rudolph	1967 ... John Crooks	1984 ... Doug Martin
1951 ... Tommy Jacobs	1968 ... Eddie Pearce	1985 ... Charles Rymer
1952 ... Don Bisplinghoff	1969 ... Aly Trompas	1986 ... Brian Montgomery
1953 ... Rex Baxter	1970 ... Gary Koch	1987 ... Brett Quigley
1954 ... Foster Bradley	1971 ... Mike Brannan	1988 ... Jason Widener
1955 ... William Dunn	1972 ... Bob Byman	1989 ... David Duval
1956 ... Harlan Stevenson	1973 ... Jack Renner	1990 ... Mathew Todd
1957 ... Larry Beck	1974 ... David Nevatt	1991 ... Tiger Woods
1958 ... Buddy Baker	1975 ... Brett Mullin	1992 ... Tiger Woods
1959 ... Larry Lee	1976 ... Madden Hatcher, III	1993 ... Tiger Woods
1960 ... Bill Tindall	1977 ... Willie Wood Jr	1994 ... Terry Noe
1961 ... Charles McDowell	1978 ... Don Hurter	1995 ... D. Scott Hailes
1962 ... Jim Wiechers	1979 ... Jack Larkin	1996 ... Shane McMenamy
1963 ... Gregg McHatton	1980 ... Eric Johnson	
1964 ... Johnny Miller	1981 ... Scott Erickson	

Note: Event is for amateur golfers younger than 18 years of age.

Mid-Amateur Championship

1981 ... Jim Holtgrieve	1987 ... Jay Sigel	1993 ... Jeff Thomas
1982 ... William Hoffer	1988 ... David Eger	1994 ... Tim Jackson
1983 ... Jay Sigel	1989 ... James Taylor	1995 ... Jerry Courville Jr
1984 ... Mike Podolak	1990 ... Jim Stuart	1996 ... John Miller
1985 ... Jay Sigel	1991 ... Jim Stuart	
1986 ... Bill Loeffler	1992 ... Danny Yates	

Note: Event is for amateur golfers at least 25 years of age.

British Amateur

1887 ....H. G. Hutchinson	1925 ....R. Harris	1964 ....C. Clark
1888 ....John Ball	1926 ....Jess Sweetser	1965 ....M. Bonallack
1889 ............J.E. Laidlay	1927 ....Dr. W. Tweddell	1966 ............C.R. Cole
1890 ....John Ball	1928 ............T.P. Perkins	1967 ....R. Dickson
1891 ............J.E. Laidlay	1929 ............C.J.H. Tolley	1968 ....M. Bonallack
1892 ....John Ball	1930 ....Robert T. Jones Jr.	1969 ....M. Bonallack
1893 ....Peter Anderson	1931 ....E. Martin Smith	1970 ....M. Bonallack
1894 ....John Ball	1932 ....J. DeForest	1971 ....Steve Melnyk
1895 ............L.M.B. Melville	1933 ....M. Scott	1972 ....Trevor Homer
1896 ............F.G. Tait	1934 ....W. Lawson Little	1973 ....R. Siderowf
1897 ............A.J.T. Allan	1935 ....W. Lawson Little	1974 ....Trevor Homer
1898 ............F.G. Tait	1936 ....H. Thomson	1975 ....M. Giles
1899 ....John Ball	1937 ....R. Sweeney Jr.	1976 ....R. Siderowf
1900 ............H.H. Hilton	1938 ............C.R. Yates	1977 ....P. McEvoy
1901 ............H.H. Hilton	1939 ............A.T. Kyle	1978 ....P. McEvoy
1902 ....C. Hutchings	1940–45 ....not held	1979 ....J. Sigel
1903 ....R. Maxwell	1946 ....J. Bruen	1980 ....D. Evans
1904 ............W.J. Travis	1947 ....Willie D. Turnesa	1981 ....P. Ploujoux
1905 ............A.G. Barry	1948 ....Frank R. Stranahan	1982 ....M. Thompson
1906 ....James Robb	1949 ............S.M. McReady	1983 ....A. Parkin
1907 ....John Ball	1950 ....Frank R. Stranahan	1984 ............J.M. Olazabal
1908 ............E.A. Lassen	1951 ....Richard D. Chapman	1985 ....G. McGimpsey
1909 ....R. Maxwell	1952 ............E.H. Ward	1986 ....D. Curry
1910 ....John Ball	1953 ............J.B. Carr	1987 ....P. Mayo
1911 ............H.H. Hilton	1954 ............D.W. Bachli	1988 ....C. Hardin
1912 ....John Ball	1955 ............J.W. Conrad	1989 ....S. Dodd
1913 ............H.H. Hilton	1956 ............J.C. Beharrel	1990 ....R. Muntz
1914 ............J.L.C. Jenkins	1957 ....R. Reid Jack	1991 ....G. Wolstenholme
1915-19 ....not held	1958 ............J.B. Carr	1992 ....S. Dundas
1920 ............C.J.H. Tolley	1959 ....Deane Beman	1993 ....I. Pyman
1921 ............W.I. Hunter	1960 ............J.B. Carr	1994 ....L. James
1922 ............E.W.E. Holderness	1961 ....M. Bonallack	1995 ....G. Sherry
1923 ............R.H. Wethered	1962 ....R. Davies	1996 ....W. Bladon
1924 ............E.W.E. Holderness	1963 ....M. Lunt	

Amateur Public Links

1922 ....Edmund R. Held	1949 ....Kenneth J. Towns	1974 ....Charles Barenaba
1923 ....Richard J. Walsh	1950 ....Stanley Bielat	1975 ....Randy Barenaba
1924 ....Joseph Coble	1951 ....Dave Stanley	1976 ....Eddie Mudd
1925 ....Raymond J. McAuliffe	1952 ....Omer L. Bogan	1977 ....Jerry Vidovic
1926 ....Lester Bolstad	1953 ....Ted Richards Jr.	1978 ....Dean Prince
1927 ....Carl F. Kauffmann	1954 ....Gene Andrews	1979 ....Dennis Walsh
1928 ....Carl F. Kauffmann	1955 ....Sam D. Kocsis	1980 ....Jodie Mudd
1929 ....Carl F. Kauffmann	1956 ....James H. Buxbaum	1981 ....Jodie Mudd
1930 ....Robert E. Wingate	1957 ....Don Essig III	1982 ....Billy Tuten
1931 ....Charles Ferrera	1958 ....Daniel D. Sikes Jr.	1983 ....Billy Tuten
1932 ............R.L. Miller	1959 ....William A. Wright	1984 ....Bill Malley
1933 ....Charles Ferrera	1960 ....Verne Callison	1985 ....Jim Sorenson
1934 ....David A. Mitchell	1961 ....Richard H. Sikes	1986 ....Bill Mayfair
1935 ....Frank Strafaci	1962 ....Richard H. Sikes	1987 ....Kevin Johnson
1936 ....B. Patrick Abbott	1963 ....Robert Lunn	1988 ....Ralph Howe III
1937 ....Bruce N. McCormick	1964 ....William McDonald	1989 ....Tim Hobby
1938 ....Al Leach	1965 ....Arne Dokka	1990 ....Michael Combs
1939 ....Andrew Szwedko	1966 ....Lamont Kaser	1991 ....David Berganio Jr.
1940 ....Robert C. Clark	1967 ....Verne Callison	1992 ....Warren Schulte
1941 ....William M. Welch Jr.	1968 ....Gene Towry	1993 ....David Berganio Jr.
1942–45 ....not held	1969 ....John M. Jackson Jr.	1994 ....Guy Yamamoto
1946 ....Smiley L. Quick	1970 ....Robert Risch	1995 ....Chris Wollmann
1947 ....Wilfred Crossley	1971 ....Fred Haney	1996 ....Tim Hogarth
1948 ....Michael R. Ferentz	1972 ....Bob Allard	
	1973 ....Stan Stopa	

U.S. Senior Golf

1955 ....J. Wood Platt	1969 ....Curtis Person Sr	1983 ....William Hyndman III
1956 ....Frederick J. Wright	1970 ....Gene Andrews	1984 ....Bob Rawlins
1957 ....J. Clark Espie	1971 ....Tom Draper	1985 ....Lewis W. Oehmig
1958 ....Thomas C. Robbins	1972 ....Lewis W. Oehmig	1986 ....Bo Williams
1959 ....J. Clark Espie	1973 ....William Hyndman III	1987 ....John Richardson
1960 ....Michael Cestone	1974 ....Dale Morey	1988 ....Clarence Moore
1961 ....Dexter H. Daniels	1975 ....William F. Colm	1989 ....Bo Williams
1962 ....Merrill L. Carlsmith	1976 ....Lewis W. Oehmig	1990 ....Jackie Cummings
1963 ....Merrill L. Carlsmith	1977 ....Dale Morey	1991 ....Bill Bosshard
1964 ....William D. Higgins	1978 ....K. K. Compton	1992 ....Clarence Moore
1965 ....Robert B. Kiersky	1979 ....William C. Campbell	1993 ....Joe Ungvary
1966 ....Dexter H. Daniels	1980 ....William C. Campbell	1994 ....O. Gordon Brewer
1967 ....Ray Palmer	1981 ....Ed Updegraff	1995 ....James Stahl Jr
1968 ....Curtis Person Sr	1982 ....Alton Duhon	1996 ....O. Gordon Brewer

Event is for golfers at least 55 years of age.

MAJOR WOMEN'S AMATEUR CHAMPIONSHIPS

U.S. Women's Amateur

Year	Winner	Score	Runner-Up	Site
1895 ....Mrs. Charles S. Brown		132	Nellie Sargent	Meadow Brook Club, Hempstead, NY
1896 ....Beatrix Hoyt		2 & 1	Mrs. Arthur Turnure	Morris Couty GC, Morristown, NJ
1897 ....Beatrix Hoyt		5 & 4	Nellie Sargent	Essex County Club, Manchester, MA
1898 ....Beatrix Hoyt		5 &3	Maude Wetmore	Ardsley Club, Ardsley-on-Hudson, NY
1899 ....Ruth Underhill		2 & 1	Margaret Fox	Philadelphia CC, Philadelphia, PA
1900 ....Frances C. Griscom		6 & 5	Margaret Curtis	Shinnecock Hills GC, Shinnecock Hills, NY
1901 ....Genevieve Hecker		5 &3	Lucy Herron	Baltusrol GC, Springfield, NJ
1902 ....Genevieve Hecker		4 & 3	Louisa A. Wells	The Country Club, Brookline, MA
1903 ....Bessie Anthony		7 & 6	J. Anna Carpenter	Chicago GC, Wheaton, IL
1904 ....Georgianna M. Bishop		5 &3	Mrs. E.F. Sanford	Merion Cricket Club, Haverford, PA
1905 ....Pauline Mackay		1 up	Margaret Curtis	Morris County GC, Convent, NJ
1906 ....Harriot S. Curtis		2 & 1	Mary B. Adams	Brae Burn CC, West Newton, MA
1907 ....Margaret Curtis		7 & 6	Harriot S. Curtis	Midlothian GC, Blue Island, IL
1908 ....Katherine C. Harley		6 & 5	Mrs. T.H. Polhemus	Chevy Chase Club, Chevy Chase, MD
1909 ....Dorothy I. Campbell		3 & 2	Nonna Barlow	Merion Cricket Club, Haverford, PA
1910 ....Dorothy I. Campbell		2 & 1	Mrs. G.M. Martin	Homewood CC, Flossmoor, IL
1911 ....Margaret Curtis		5 &3	Lillian B. Hyde	Baltusrol GC, Springfield, NJ
1912 ....Margaret Curtis		3 & 2	Nonna Barlow	Essex County Club, Manchester, MA
1913 ....Gladys Ravenscroft		2 up	Marion Hollins	Wilmington CC, Wilmington, DE
1914 ....Katherine Harley		1 up	Elaine V. Rosenthal	Nassau CC, Glen Cove, NY
1915 ....Florence Vanderbeck		3 & 2	Margaret Gavin	Onwentsia Club, Lake Forest, IL
1916 ....Alexa Stirling		2 & 1	Mildred Caverly	Belmont Springs CC, Waverley, MA
1917-18 ......No tournament				
1919 ....Alexa Stirling		6 & 5	Margaret Gavin	Shawnee CC, Shawnee-on Delaware, PA
1920 ....Alexa Stirling		5 & 4	Dorothy Campbell	Mayfield CC, Cleveland, OH
1921 ....Marion Hollins		5 & 4	Alexa Stirling	Hollywood GC, Deal, NJ
1922 ....Glenna Collett		5 & 4	Margaret Gavin	Greenbriar GC, White Sulphur Springs, WV
1923 ....Edith Cummings		3 & 2	Alexa Stirling	Westchester-Biltmore CC, Rye, NY
1924 ....Dorothy Campbell		7 & 6	Mary K. Browne	Rhode Island CC, Nyatt, RI
1925 ....Glenna Collett		9 & 8	Alexa Stirling	St. Louis CC, Clayton, MO
1926 ....Helen Stetson		3 & 1	Elizabeth Goss	Merion Cricket Club, Ardmore, PA
1927 ....Miriam Burns Horn		5 & 4	Maureen Orcutt	Cherry Valley Club, Garden City, NY
1928 ....Glenna Collett		13 & 12	Virginia Van Wie	Va. Hot Springs G & TC, Hot Springs, VA
1929 ....Glenna Collett		4 & 3	Leona Pressler	Oakland Hills CC, Birmingham, MI
1930 ....Glenna Collett		6 & 5	Virginia Van Wie	Los Angeles CC, Beverly Hills, CA
1931 ....Helen Hicks		2 & 1	Glenna Collet Vare	CC of Buffalo, Williamsville, NY
1932 ....Virginia Van Wie		10 & 8	Glenna Collet Vare	Salem CC, Peabody, MA
1933 ....Virginia Van Wie		4 & 3	Helen Hicks	Exmoor CC, Highland Park, IL
1934 ....Virginia Van Wie		2 & 1	Dorothy Traung	Whitemarsh Valley CC, Chestnut Hill, PA
1935 ....Glenna Collett Vare		3 & 2	Patty Berg	Interlachen CC, Hopkins, MN
1936 ....Pamela Barton		4 & 3	Maureen Orcutt	Canoe Brook CC, Summit, NJ
1937 ....Estelle Lawson		7 & 6	Patty Berg	Memphis CC, Memphis, TN
1938 ....Patty Berg		6 & 5	Estelle Lawson	Westmoreland CC, Wilmette, IL
1939 ....Betty Jameson		3 & 2	Dorothy Kirby	Wee Burn Club, Darien, CT

U.S. Women's Amateur (Cont.)

Year	Winner	Score	Runner-Up	Site
1940	Betty Jameson	6 & 5	Jane S. Cothran	Del Monte G & CC, Pebble Beach, CA
1941	Elizabeth Hicks	5 & 3	Helen Sigel	The Country Club, Brookline, MA
1942-45	No tournament			
1946	Babe Zaharias	11 & 9	Clara Sherman	Southern Hills CC, Tulsa, OK
1947	Louise Suggs	2 up	Dorothy Kirby	Franklin Hills CC, Franklin, MI
1948	Grace S. Lenczyk	4 & 3	Helen Sigel	Del Monte G & CC, Pebble Beach, CA
1949	Dorothy Porter	3 & 2	Dorothy Kielty	Merion GC, Ardmore, PA
1950	Beverly Hanson	6 & 4	Mae Murray	Atlanta AC, Atlanta, GA
1951	Dorothy Kirby	2 & 1	Claire Doran	Town & CC, St. Paul, MN
1952	Jacqueline Pung	2 & 1	Shirley McFedters	Waverley CC, Portland, OR
1953	Mary Lena Faulk	3 & 2	Polly Riley	Rhode Island CC, West Barrington, RI
1954	Barbara Romack	4 & 2	Miickey Wright	Allegheny CC, Sewickley, PA
1955	Patricia A. Lesser	7 & 6	Jane Nelson	Myers Park CC, Charlotte, NC
1956	Marlene Stewart	2 & 1	JoAnne Gunderson	Meridian Hills CC, Indianapolis, IN
1957	JoAnne Gunderson	8 & 6	Ann Casey Johnstone	Del Paso CC, Sacramento, CA
1958	Anne Quast	3 & 2	Barbara Romack	Wee Burn CC, Darien, CT
1959	Barbara McIntire	4 & 3	Joanne Goodwin	Congressional CC, Washington, D.C.
1960	JoAnne Gunderson	6 & 5	Jean Ashley	Tulsa CC, Tulsa, OK
1961	Anne Quast Sander	14 & 13	Phyllis Preuss	Tacoma G & CC, Tacoma, WA
1962	JoAnne Gunderson	9 & 8	Anne Baker	CC of Rochester, Rochester, NY
1963	Anne Quast Sander	2 & 1	Peggy Conley	Taconic CC, Williamstown, MA
1964	Barbara McIntire	3 & 2	JoAnne Gunderson	Prairie Dunes CC, Hutchinson, KS
1965	Jean Ashley	5 & 4	Anne Quast Sander	Lakewood CC, Denver, CO
1966	JoAnne Gunderson	1 up	Marlene Stewart Streit	Sewickley Heights GC, Sewickley, PA
1967	Mary Lou Dill	5 & 4	Jean Ashley	Annandale GC, Pasadena, CA
1968	JoAnne Gunderson Carner	5 & 4	Anne Quast Sander	Birmingham CC, Birmingham, MI
1969	Catherine Lacoste	3 & 2	Shelley Hamling	Las Colinas CC, Irving, TX
1970	Martha Wilkinson	3 & 2	Cynthia Hall	Wee Burn CC, Darien, CT
1971	Laura Baugh	1 up	Beth Barry	Atlanta CC, Atlanta, GA
1972	Mary Budke	5 & 4	Cynthia Hill	St. Louis CC, St. Louis, MO
1973	Carol Semple	1 up	Anne Quast Sander	Montclair GC, Montclair, NJ
1974	Cynthia Hill	5 & 4	Carol Semple	Broadmoor GC, Seattle, WA
1975	Beth Daniel	3 & 2	Donna Horton	Brae Burn CC, West Newton, MA
1976	Donna Horton	2 & 1	Marianne Bretton	Del Paso CC, Sacramento, CA
1977	Beth Daniel	3 & 1	Cathy Sherk	Cincinnati CC, Cincinnati, OH
1978	Cathy Sherk	4 & 3	Judith Oliver	Sunnybrook GC, Plymouth Meeting, PA
1979	Carolyn Hill	7 & 6	Patty Sheehan	Memphis CC, Memphis, TN
1980	Juli Inkster	2 up	Patti Rizzo	Prairie Dunes CC, Hutchinson, KS
1981	Juli Inkster	1 up	Lindy Goggin	Waverley CC, Portland, OR
1982	Juli Inkster	4 & 3	Cathy Hanlon	Broadmoor GC, Colorado Springs, CO
1983	Joanne Pacillo	2 & 1	Sally Quinlan	Canoe Brook CC, Summit, NJ
1984	Deb Richard	1 up	Kimberly Williams	Broadmoor GC, Seattle, WA
1985	Michiko Hattori	5 & 4	Cheryl Stacy	Fox Chapel CC, Pittsburgh, PA
1986	Kay Cockerill	9 & 7	Kathleen McCarthy	Pasatiempo GC, Santa Cruz, CA
1987	Kay Cockerill	3 & 2	Tracy Kerdyk	Rhode Island CC, Barrington, RI
1988	Pearl Sinn	6 & 5	Karen Noble	Minikahda Club, Miinneapolis, MN
1989	Vicki Goetze	4 & 3	Brandie Burton	Pinehurst CC (No. 2), Pinehurst, NC
1990	Pat Hurst	37 holes	Stephanie Davis	Canoe Brook CC, Summit, NJ
1991	Amy Fruhwirth	5 & 4	Heidi Voorhees	Prairie Dunes CC, Hutchinson, KN
1992	Vicki Goetz	1-up	Annika Sorensteam	Kemper Lakes GC, Hawthorne Hills, IL
1993	Jill McGill	1-up	Sarah Ingram	San Diego CC, Chula Vista, CA
1994	Wendy Ward	2 & 1	Jill McGill	The Homestead, Hot Springs, WV
1995	Kelli Kuehne	4 & 3	Anne-Marie Knight	The Country Club, Brookline, MA
1996	Kelli Kuehne	2 & 1	Marisa Baena	Firethorn GC, Lincoln, NE

Girls' Junior Championship

1949 ....Marlene Bauer	1966 ....Claudia Mayhew	1983 ....Kim Saiki
1950 ....Patricia Lesser	1967 ....Elizabeth Story	1984 ....Cathy Mockett
1951 ....Arlene Brooks	1968 ....Peggy Harmon	1985 ....Dana Lofland
1952 ....Mickey Wright	1969 ....Hollis Stacy	1986 ....Pat Hurst
1953 ....Millie Meyerson	1970 ....Hollis Stacy	1987 ....Michelle McGann
1954 ....Margaret Smith	1971 ....Hollis Stacy	1988 ....Jamille Jose
1955 ....Carole Jo Kabler	1972 ....Nancy Lopez	1989 ....Brandie Burton
1956 ....JoAnne Gunderson	1973 ....Amy Alcott	1990 ....Sandrine Mendiburu
1957 ....Judy Eller	1974 ....Nancy Lopez	1991 ....Emilee Klein
1958 ....Judy Eller	1975 ....Dayna Benson	1992 ....Jamie Koizumi
1959 ....Judy Rand	1976 ....Pilar Dorado	1993 ....Kellee Booth
1960 ....Carol Sorenson	1977 ....Althea Tome	1962 ....Maureen Orcutt
1961 ....Mary Lowell	1978 ....Lori Castillo	1963 ....Sis Choate
1962 ....Mary Lou Daniel	1979 ....Penny Hammel	1994 ....Kelli Kuehne
1963 ....Janis Ferraris	1980 ....Laurie Rinker	1995 ....Marcy Newton
1964 ....Peggy Conley	1981 ....Kay Cornelius	1996 ....Dorothy Delasin
1965 ....Gail Sykes	1982 ....Heather Farr	

Women's British Amateur

1893 ....Lady Margaret Scott	1927 ....Miss Thion de la Chaume	1961 ....M. Spearman
1894 ....Lady Margaret Scott		1962 ....M. Spearman
1895 ....Lady Margaret Scott	1928 ....Miss N. Le Blan	1963 ....B. Varangot
1896 ....Miss Pascoe	1929 ....Miss J. Wethered	1964 ....C. Sorenson
1897 ....Miss E.C. Orr	1930 ....Miss D. Fishwick	1965 ....B. Varangot
1898 ....Miss L. Thomson	1931 ....Miss E. Wilson	1966 ....E. Chadwick
1899 ....Miss M. Hezlet	1932 ....Miss E. Wilson	1967 ....E. Chadwick
1900 ....Miss Adair	1933 ....Miss E. Wilson	1968 ....B. Varangot
1901 ....Miss Graham	1934 ....Mrs. A.M. Holm	1975 ....C. Lacoste
1902 ....Miss M. Hezlet	1935 ....Miss W. Morgan	1976 ....D. Oxley
1903 ....Miss Adair	1936 ....Miss P. Barton	1977 ....A. Uzielli
1904 ....Miss L. Dod	1937 ....Miss J. Anderson	1978 ....E. Kennedy
1905 ....Miss B. Thompson	1938 ....Mrs. A.M. Holm	1979 ....M. Madill
1906 ....Mrs. Kennon	1939 ....Miss P. Barton	1980 ....A. Quast
1907 ....Miss M. Hezlet	1940–45 ....not held	1981 .............I.C. Robertson
1908 ....Miss M. Titterton	1946 ............G.W. Hetherington	1982 ....K. Douglas
1909 ....Miss D. Campbell	1947 ....B. Zaharias	1983 ....J. Thornhill
1910 ....Miss Grant Suttie	1948 ....L. Suggs	1984 ....J. Rosenthal
1911 ....Miss D. Campbell	1949 ....F. Stephens	1985 ....L. Beman
1912 ....Miss G. Ravenscroft	1950 ....Vicomtesse de Saint Sauveur	1986 ....M. McGuire
1913 ....Miss M. Dodd		1987 ....J. Collingham
1914 ....Miss C. Leitch	1951 ............P.J. MacCann	1988 ....J. Furby
1915–19 ....not held	1952 ....M. Paterson	1989 ....H. Dobson
1920 ....Miss C. Leitch	1953 ....M. Stewart	1990 ....J. Hall
1921 ....Miss C. Leitch	1954 ....F. Stephens	1991 ....V. Michaud
1922 ....Miss J. Wethered	1955 ....J. Valentine	1992 ....P. Pedersen
1923 ....Miss D. Chambers	1956 ....M. Smith	1993 ....Catriona Lambert
1924 ....Miss J. Wethered	1957 ....P. Garvey	1994 ....Emma Duggleby
1925 ....Miss J. Wethered	1958 ....J. Valentine	1995 ....Julie Hall
1926 ....Miss C. Leitch	1959 ....E. Price	1996 ....Kelli Kuehne
	1960 ....B. McIntyre	

Women's Amateur Public Links

1977 ....Kelly Fuiks	1984 ....Heather Farr	1990 ....Cathy Mockett
1978 ....Kelly Fuiks	1985 ....Danielle Ammaccapane	1991 ....Tracy Hanson
1979 ....Lori Castillo		1992 ....Amy Fruhwirth
1980 ....Lori Castillo	1986 ....Cindy Schreyer	1993 ....Connie Masterson
1981 ....Mary Enright	1987 ....Tracy Kerdyk	1994 ....Jill McGill
1982 ....Nancy Taylor	1988 ....Pearl Sinn	1995 ....Jo Jo Robertson
1983 ....Kelli Antolock	1989 ....Pearl Sinn	1996 ....Heather Graff

Amateur Golf (Cont.)

U.S. Senior Women's Amateur

1964 ....Loma Smith	1975 ....Alberta Bower	1986 ....Connie Guthrie
1965 ....Loma Smith	1976 ....Cecile H. Maclaurin	1987 ....Anne Sander
1966 ....Maureen Orcutt	1977 ....Dorothy Porter	1988 ....Lois Hodge
1967 ....Marge Mason	1978 ....Alice Dye	1989 ....Anne Sander
1968 ....Carolyn Cudone	1979 ....Alice Dye	1990 ....Anne Sander
1969 ....Carolyn Cudone	1980 ....Dorothy Porter	1991 ....Phyllis Preuss
1970 ....Carolyn Cudone	1981 ....Dorothy Porter	1992 ....Rosemary Thompson
1971 ....Carolyn Cudone	1982 ....Edean Ihlanfeldt	1993 ....Anne Sander
1972 ....Carolyn Cudone	1983 ....Dorothy Porter	1994 ....Marlene Streit
1973 ....Gwen Hibbs	1984 ....Constance Guthrie	1995 ....Jean Smith
1974 ....Justine Cushing	1985 ....Marlene Streit	1996 ....Gayle Borthwick

Women's Mid-Amateur Championship

1987	Cindy Scholefield
1988	Martha Lang
1989	Robin Weiss
1990	Carol Semple Thompson
1991	Sarah LeBrun Ingram
1992	Marion Mamey-McInerney
1993	Sarah Ingram
1994	Sarah Ingram
1995	Ellen Port
1996	Ellen Port

International Golf

Ryder Cup Matches

Year	Results	Site
1927	United States 9½, Great Britain 2½	Worcester CC, Worcester, MA
1929	Great Britain 7, United States 5	Moortown GC, Leeds, England
1931	United States 9, Great Britain 3	Scioto CC, Columbus, OH
1933	Great Britain 6½, United States 5½	Southport and Ainsdale Courses, Southport, England
1935	United States 9, Great Britain 3	Ridgewood CC, Ridgewood, NJ
1937	United States 8, Great Britain 4	Southport and Ainsdale Courses, Southport, England
1939-1945	No tournament	
1947	United States 11, Great Britain 1	Portland GC, Portland, OR
1949	United States 7, Great Britain 5	Ganton GC, Scarborough, England
1951	United States 9½, Great Britain 2½	Pinehurst CC, Pinehurst, NC
1953	United States 6½, Great Britain 5½	Wentworth Club, Surrey, England
1955	United States 8, Great Britain 4	Thunderbird Ranch & CC, Palm Springs, CA
1957	Great Britain 7½, United States 4½	Lindrick GC, Yorkshire, England
1959	United States 8½, Great Britain 3½	Eldorado CC, Palm Desert, CA
1961	United States 14½, Great Britain 9½	Royal Lytham & St Anne's GC, St Anne's-on-the-Sea, England
1963	United States 23, Great Britain 9	East Lake CC, Atlanta
1965	United States 19½, Great Britain 12½	Royal Birkdale GC, Southport, England
1967	United States 23½, Great Britain 8½	Champions GC, Houston
1969	United States 16, Great Britain 16	Royal Birkdale GC, Southport, England
1971	United States 18½, Great Britain 13½	Old Warson CC, St Louis
1973	United States 19, Great Britain 13	Hon Co of Edinburgh Golfers, Muirfield, Scotland
1975	United States 21, Great Britain 11	Laurel Valley GC, Ligonier, PA
1977	United States 12½, Great Britain 7½	Royal Lytham & St Anne's GC, St Anne's-on-the-Sea, England
1979	United States 17, Europe 11	Greenbrier, White Sulphur Springs, WV
1981	United States 18½, Europe 9½	Walton Heath GC, Surrey, England
1983	United States 14½, Europe 13½	PGA National GC, Palm Beach Gardens, FL
1985	Europe 16½, United States 11½	Belfry GC, Sutton Coldfield, England
1987	Europe 15, United States 13	Muirfield GC, Dublin, OH
1989	Europe 14, United States 14	Belfry GC, Sutton Coldfield, England
1991	United States 14½, Europe 13½	Ocean Course, Kiawah Island, SC
1993	United States 15, Europe 13	Belfry GC, Sutton Coldfield, England
1995	Europe 14½, United States 13½	Oak Hill CC, Rochester, NY

Team matches held every odd year between US professionals and those of Great Britain/Europe (since 1979, prior to which was US vs GB). Team members selected on basis of finishes in PGA and European tour events.

Walker Cup Matches

Year	Results	Site
1922	United States 8, Great Britain 4	Nat. Golf Links of America, Southampton, NY
1923	United States 6, Great Britain 5	St. Andrews, Scotland
1924	United States 9, Great Britain 3	Garden City GC, Garden City, NY
1926	United States 6, Great Britain 5	St. Andrews, Scotland
1928	United States 11, Great Britain 1	Chicago GC, Wheaton, IL
1930	United States 10, Great Britain 2	Royal St. George GC, Sandwich, England
1932	United States 8, Great Britain 1	The Country Club, Brookline, MA
1934	United States 9, Great Britain 2	St. Andrews, Scotland
1936	United States 9, Great Britain 0	Pine Valley GC, Clementon, NJ
1938	Great Britain 7, United States 4	St. Andrews, Scotland
1940-46	No tournament	
1947	United States 8, Great Britain 4	St. Andrews, Scotland
1949	United States 10, Great Britain 2	Winged Foot GC, Mamaroneck, NY
1951	United States 6, Great Britain 3	Birkdale GC, Southport, England
1953	United States 9, Great Britain 3	The Kittansett Club, Marion, MA
1955	United States 10, Great Britain 2	St. Andrews, Scotland
1957	United States 8, Great Britain 3	Minikahda Club, Minneapolis, MN
1959	United States 9, Great Britain 3	Muirfield, Scotland
1961	United States 11, Great Britain 1	Seattle GC, Seattle, WA
1963	United States 12, Great Britain 8	Ailsa Course, Turnberry, Scotland
1965	Great Britain 11, United States 11	Baltimore CC, Five Farms, Baltimore, MD
1967	United States 13, Great Britain 7	Royal St. George's GC, Sandwich, England
1969	United States 10, Great Britain 8	Milwaukee CC, Milwaukee, WI
1971	Great Britain 13, United States 11	St. Andrews, Scotland
1973	United States 14, Great Britain 10	The Country Club, Brookline, MA
1975	United States 15½, Great Britain 8½	St. Andrews, Scotland
1977	United States 16, Great Britain 8	Shinnecock Hills GC, Southampton, NY
1979	United States 15½, Great Britain 8½	Muirfield, Scotland
1981	United States 15, Great Britain 9	Cypress Point Club, Pebble Beach, CA
1983	United States 13½, Great Britain 10½	Royal Liverpool GC, Hoylake, England
1985	United States 13, Great Britain 11	Pine Valley GC, Pine Valley, NJ
1987	United States 16½, Great Britain 7½	Sunningdale GC, Berkshire, England
1989	Great Britain 12½, United States 11½	Peachtree Golf Club, Atlanta, GA
1991	United States 14, Great Britain 10	Portmarnock GC, Dublin, Ireland
1993	United States 19, Great Britain 5	Interlachen CC, Edina, MN
1995	Great Britain/Ireland 14, United States 10	Royal Porthcawl, Porthcawl, Wales

Men's amateur team competition every other year between United States and Great Britain. US team members selected by USGA.

Curtis Cup Matches

Year	Results	Site
1932	United States 5½, British Isles 3½	Wentworth GC, Wentworth, England
1934	United States 6½, British Isles 2½	Chevy Chase Club, Chevy Chase, MD
1936	United States 4½, British Isles 4½	King's Course, Gleneagles, Scotland
1938	United States 5½, British Isles 3½	Essex CC, Manchester, MA
1940-46	No tournament	
1948	United States 6½, British Isles 2½	Birkdale GC, Southport, England
1950	United States 7½, British Isles 1½	CC of Buffalo, Williamsville, NY
1952	British Isles 5, United States 4	Muirfield, Scotland
1954	United States 6, British Isles 3	Merion GC, Ardmore, PA
1956	British Isles 5, United States 4	Prince's GC, Sandwich Bay, England
1958	British Isles 4½, United States 4½	Brae Burn CC, West Newton, Mass.
1960	United States 6½, British Isles 2½	Lindrick GC, Worksop, England
1962	United States 8, British Isles 1	Broadmoor CG, Colorado Springs,CO
1964	United States 10½, British Isles 7½	Royal Porthcawl GC, Porthcawl, South Wales
1966	United States 13, British Isles 5	Va. Hot Springs G & TC, Hot Springs, VA
1968	United States 10½, British Isles 7½	Royal County Down GC, Newcastle, N. Ire.
1970	United States 11½, British Isles 6½	Brae Burn CC, West Newton, MA
1972	United States 10, British Isles 8	Western Gailes, Ayrshire, Scotland
1974	United States 13, British Isles 5	San Francisco GC, San Francisco, CA
1976	United States 11½, British Isles 6½	Royal Lytham & St. Anne's GC, England

Curtis Cup Matches (Cont.)

Year	Results	Site
1978	United States 12, British Isles 6	Apawamis Club, Rye, NY
1980	United States 13, British Isles 5	St. Pierre G & CC, Chepstow, Wales
1982	United States 14½, British Isles 3½	Denver CC, Denver, CO
1984	United States 9½, British Isles 8½	Muirfield, Scotland
1986	British Isles 13, United States 5	Prairie Dunes CC, Hutchinson, KS
1988	British Isles 11, United States 7	Royal St. George's GC, Sandwich, England
1990	United States 14, British Isles 4	Somerset Hills CC, Bernardsville, NJ
1992	Great Britain/Ireland 10, United States 8	Royal Liverpool GC, Hoylake, England
1994	Great Britain/Ireland 9, United States 9	The Honors Course, Ooltewah, TN
1996	Great Britain/Ireland 11½, United States 6½	Killarney Golf & Fishing Club, Killarney, Ireland

Women's amateur team competition every other year between the United States and Great Britain. US team members selected by USGA.

Norman Invasion

A few days after Greg Norman's spectacular collapse in the final round of the Masters, sportswriter Frank Deford mused on National Public Radio about the impact Norman's nationally televised disintegration might one day have on the English language. "In my old dictionary from 2005," Deford said, "is the word *normanfy*, sometimes referred to in the vernacular as to 'pull a norman.'" Well, Webster's needn't wait until the next century to officially define *norman* as "the squandering, under pressure, of a large lead or advantage"—on both sides of the Atlantic, Norman's name is already being used in that sense. On April 17 London's *Daily Mirror* ran in bold type Newcastle United soccer striker Les Ferdinand's pledge, WE WON'T DO A NORMAN! before a critical match. The same day Jay Mariotti of the *Chicago Sun-Times* assessed the shaky but triumphant performance of his city's Bulls in their record-setting 70th victory of the season that came against the Milwaukee Bucks: "At least they didn't do a Norman." The Masters disaster has even given Norman's name political currency. Looking back on the 1992 presidential race, in which the incumbent at one point led challenger Bill Clinton 54% to 34% in the polls, syndicated columnist John Hall referred to "President Bush's Greg Norman–like collapse."

Boxing

Sports Illustrated

APRIL 15, 1996

$2.95 (CAN. $3.95)

THE LADY IS A

CHAMP

BOXING'S
NEW SENSATION,
Christy Martin

BRIAN SMITH

Close to the Edge

Novelty acts, flaccid competition and one full-fledged riot pushed boxing ever further from the mainstream of sport

by Richard Hoffer

THERE WAS an unpleasant feeling in 1996 that boxing, while never mainstream, was becoming sport's sideshow, one cheesy circus act after another. This isn't to say it wasn't entertaining, in its low-rent way, just that it wasn't always credible. Maybe it's enough to know that by year's end the game's two most popular performers were the Coal Miner's Daughter and the hairless ecto-morph known as Butterbean. Both of them were fun, of course, but neither was practicing the sweet science as we remember it.

Most everything seemed to be about novelty, some of it intentional, some not. The fighter everybody regarded as the best, pound-for-pound, avoided any dangerous bouts in the year and concentrated on his basketball career instead. Indeed, his 1996 highlight was a doubleheader: a game of pro hoops followed by a fight with a ridiculously undermanned opponent. Only cumulatively were the performances exciting.

And the guy everybody thought was the most talented heavyweight in the world made most of his headlines as the center-piece of a Madison Square Garden brawl, a riot that did little to dissuade anyone that the sport had been taken over by gangsters, thugs and hoodlums.

As for Mike Tyson's comeback, which was supposed to lead boxing out of its doldrums, that became more and more difficult to take seriously as well. Going into his fight with Evander Holyfield in November, he had put together just eight rounds in his post-prison career, and, through no fault of his own, each one of them was worse than the last. This is what we waited for? In September, Tyson wafting a right hand at WBA champion Bruce Seldon and the fighter going down face first, seemingly untouched, in the first round? Tyson's opposition was so progressively feeble throughout the year that not even he could have been heartened by his increasingly swift dispatches. The ticket buyers couldn't have been encouraged either; they cried fix at the Seldon debacle.

This may have been the year, in fact, that weeded out the game's real fans. Anybody who comes back for more is devoted to the sport beyond any measure of rational behavior.

V.J. LOVERO

There was, really, just one good fight, one event that delivered exactly as it should have, one single sign of hope. Oscar De La Hoya, the gold medal winner from the Barcelona Olympics, came through with one of the most vicious performances seen in years, the kind of bloodletting that might have moved critics even if it had been held in a bullring. It was a pivotal fight, not just in De La Hoya's career, but in boxing history, because it established him as the rightful heir to Sugar Ray Leonard. He always had the charisma, but, watching him slice and dice the formerly formidable Julio César Chávez in just four rounds, it was now possible to believe he had the fighter's instinct to go with his flair.

It was a magnificent display, but not simply because Chávez had been reduced to a public form of arterial spray. De La Hoya's resolution in the face of such a legend as Chávez satisfied a lot of doubters who had been wondering just how committed to boxing the young star was. De La Hoya, though just 23 at the time of the fight, had already been talking about retirement, saying he much preferred a life of golf, and perhaps

De La Hoya cut up his idol Chávez in the year's only impressive bout.

the study of architecture, to so gruesome a sport as this. The continued lack of fan support among Latinos, who back brawlers over defensive geniuses like De La Hoya, disturbed him, too.

Yet here he was, boxing's cover boy, calmly eviscerating Chávez and liking it. De La Hoya, having added Chávez's 140-pound title to his growing résumé, promised he would not be doing this for ever, opting for the career model of Leonard over Chávez. He was going to be the sport's next executive boxer. Chávez, meanwhile, was effectively interred in his 100th bout, which was not his farewell fight after all. Mexican tax authorities finished their investigation of his finances late in 1996 and compelled him to fight at least once more—on De La Hoya's undercard— with the $1 million purse going directly to the government.

Elsewhere, the sport was not so electric. Roy Jones, everybody's favorite fighter since he won the super middleweight title from

Golota fought Bowe's cornermen in the fiasco that typified the season.

afterthought, she burst upon the boxing scene when her March bout with Deirdre Gogarty appeared on the pay-per-view broadcast of Tyson's fight with Frank Bruno. It did not escape anyone's attention that Martin's fight was the more exciting of the two, with more blood and guts than fans had grown accustomed to. Like Butterbean, Martin was soon off on the talk-show circuit, where she was promoted foremost as a lady, feminine out of the ring, however fierce and technically sound within. The combination played surprisingly well. Perfectly schooled by her husband, Jim, her boxing withstood any patronizing from her masculine counterparts and at the same time removed her from the politics of gender. However, as the year wore on it became apparent that there still wasn't women's boxing, there was only Christy Martin, and she would never be more than an undercard attraction because of that.

James Toney two years ago, frustrated his fans (and his contractual network, HBO) by failing to appear in even one megafight. It may be true, as Jones contends, that he is too good to suffer true competition in his weight class. However, a condescending stunt like his afternoon pro basketball game/late-night fight with Eric Lucas in June, will not satisfy his constituency forever. Anyway, after scoring just five points (and making three turnovers) in the Jacksonville Barracudas' game that day, it looks like he shouldn't quit his night job just yet.

A far more desperate gimmick was former toughman Eric Esch, who became a marketing phenomenon strictly on the basis of his girth and nickname. At 300 pounds and completely bald, the Butterbean is a fearsome looking creature. However, not even promoter Bob Arum was pretending he was anything more than the dietary heir to George Foreman. Genial and hard-hitting, and entirely artless, Butterbean has always been more comfortable on the talk-show host's couch than in the ring, where he lumbers menacingly but not very effectively. The proclaimed king of the four-rounders couldn't even make good on that claim, losing early in the year. But his popularity was not much diminished, and he was booked well into the future, four rounders all.

At least Christy Martin can fight. Developed on Don King bills as an undercard

There were other bright spots in boxing, of a more traditional nature, particularly Naseem Hamed, the Yemeni "prince" who was tearing through the featherweight division in England, cocky and quotable—"I've got charisma, mouth, the gift of gab, everything." But as ever, most attention tilted toward the heavyweights, and, as ever, the news in that division was rarely good.

It seemed there was just one disaster after another. The worst, certainly, was erstwhile contender Tommy Morrison who, despite a loss to Lennox Lewis, was poised to take advantage of the Mike Tyson bonanza. But before the popular slugger could take his place on the gravy train of Tyson opponents, a Nevada drug test in February revealed he'd been infected with HIV. Stunned by the news (he was set to appear on one of King's cards in Las Vegas as part of his buildup), he returned to his home near Tulsa and bravely considered his past and his future. In front of an assembly of the media, he revealed a poorly kept secret, that he had had a wildly promiscuous lifestyle, and he promised responsibility for his actions. Indeed, he hoped to devote his life to public service, offering his "stupidity" as an example. "I thought I was Superman," he said. "I have never been more wrong in my life."

Similarly sad, but without the possibility of any redemption, was the ugliness that followed Riddick Bowe's Madison Square Garden fight with Andrew Golota in July. This was not the kind of event that you'd have wanted your children to see, and not just because of Golota's repeated low blows. Golota, who seemed to be winning the bout, was finally disqualified for one of those blows in the seventh round. Then, with Bowe writhing in his corner, the real fun began. The aftermath was a full-blown riot, led by Bowe's corner, lasting several minutes longer than the main event, injuring 22 people and doing more damage to Golota than Bowe did.

As Bowe's career has been studded with these catastrophes, it was only natural to blame his manager, the fiery Rock Newman. But there was plenty of blame to go around, most of it in Bowe's corner, which was discovered to be a refuge of scoundrels the likes of which was shocking even for boxing. The brawl had a depressing effect on the sport— the image of Golota's trainer, veteran Lou Duva, leaving the arena on a stretcher (he was O.K.) led many newscasts—and a similar effect on Bowe's career. Weighing 252 pounds and poorly prepared for the fight, he slipped a little further on everyone's wish list. Instead, everyone was talking about Golota.

They might have been talking about Tyson, but his comeback continued to be tainted by mismatches, and although his Holyfield fight would undoubtedly be a marquee event, his box office appeal was weakening. Following his September fight with Seldon, during which he won his second title (he would later forfeit his first due to the usual politics), it became obvious that a Tyson fight, unlike one of Butter-

bean's, was no longer guaranteed entertainment.

Unfortunately, the brevity of his fights could not be laid to any growing fierceness on Tyson's part. Instead, it was a result of a total loss of spirit on his opponents' part. Following Tyson's two title fights, essentially fainting fits for two so-called champions, the startlingly inept Peter McNeeley was recast as a warrior. He may have lasted just 89 seconds for Tyson's coming-out party the year before, but at least he distinguished himself by trying.

Tyson's fight with Buster Mathis Jr. at the end of 1995 loomed as the first real test, because Mathis was at least a tried professional with genuine boxing skills. The fight had been postponed from its November date when Tyson hurt his thumb and hastily put together in Philadelphia just weeks later. Whatever would happen, and a lot of people thought they knew, nobody could say they were cheated. The fight was to be televised free on the Fox network.

Tyson was powerful in that fight, flattening Mathis in the third. But the three champions, assembled at ringside for the fight so they might better look like ducks in a row, insisted they were unimpressed. "I saw some weaknesses," said Bruno, holder of the WBC title. Though he'd been stopped by Tyson six years before, Bruno was extremely confident. "I can't wait," he said.

Yet when his turn came, Bruno held up no better than McNeeley or Mathis under Tyson's barrage. In their March fight Bruno appeared exceedingly nervous, crossing himself a dozen times on the walk to the ring. In it, the massively muscled Bruno (27 pounds heavier than Tyson) outright panicked, forgetting to jab and just generally giving way to his challenger.

It was hard to say that Tyson had returned to the form he last enjoyed as a champion six years before, so little opposition did Bruno provide. But Tyson did everything he could have, or even should have. He staggered and cut Bruno in the first round, rocked him again in the second, then pummeled him with a 13-punch sequence in the third round that left him limp against the ropes. Bruno, the most

Seldon (right) was the weakest in a line of feeble Tyson foes.

saw his left jab collapsed into a worthless stub. Finally Tyson, missing with a left, apparently hit Seldon on the back of the head with a right. Nobody really saw it, no matter how many replays were shown, but Seldon speculated that Tyson had "hit a nerve." Whatever. Seldon fell face first. Upon rising he was hit with a Tyson left, a punch many people, with the exception of Seldon, actually saw.

legitimate of the three challengers, had offered nothing, but at least Tyson reacted as of old, as a dangerous predator.

If the champions couldn't complicate Tyson's consolidation of the championships, the courts could. Lewis sued to become a Tyson opponent, and promoter King was forced to pay him $4 million in step-aside money so that Tyson could pursue the titles. However, the courts and sanctioning bodies could not be forced into so easy an agreement, and it appeared that the title Tyson had just won would be taken as soon as he fought anyone but Lewis.

Indeed, he fought WBA champion Seldon next, and this would prove to be the biggest sham of them all. Seldon, who had won the title vacated by George Foreman the year before, was nobody's idea of a champion. Earlier in his career he had lost to every important heavyweight he had faced—Oliver McCall, Bowe and Tony Tubbs. But he had a style that might give Tyson problems. His jab was effective, and he was a skilled boxer. The question was, could he frustrate Tyson?

He could barely stand up in his own corner. Entering the ring with a forced grin, Seldon had a chance to circle the ring for no longer than a minute, during which time he

Seldon was down and out less than two minutes into the first round. "He's a destroyer," said Seldon later.

Tyson seemed satisfied with the result, as if he were now his old fearsome self. "I am punching pretty hard these days," he said. But few others outside his camp believed anything at all had been proved. And nobody outside his camp thought they had seen a good show.

It was not a promising time for boxing, not least because the Olympics failed for the first time to generate any interest at all in the sport. NBC refused to televise the bouts during prime time, and it may have been just as well, as only unheralded light middleweight David Reid got a gold medal for the home team. The remaining U.S. boxers turned out to be overhyped and underdeveloped, more mouth than chin when it came to the medal rounds.

The only glorious moment in boxing, and it wasn't really boxing, was the appearance of Muhammad Ali at the Games as he lit the torch with his shaking hand. The crowd went wild at the sight of him. It was hard to imagine that the sport was producing another legend who, 30 years from now, would earn the cheers Ali did that night. Actually, it was impossible to imagine.

FOR THE RECORD·1995-1996

Current Champions

Division	Weight Limit	WBC Champion	WBA Champion	IBF Champion
Heavyweight	None	vacant	Mike Tyson	Michael Moorer
Cruiserweight	190	Marcelo Dominguez	Nate Miller	Alphonso Washington
Light heavyweight	175	Fabrice Tiozzo	Virgil Hill	Henry Maske
Super middleweight	168	Vincenzo Nardiello	Frank Liles	Roy Jones
Middleweight	160	Keith Holmes	William Joppy	Bernard Hopkins
Junior middleweight	154	Terry Norris	Laurent Boudouani	Terry Norris
Welterweight	147	Pernell Whitaker	Ike Quartey	Felix Trinidad
Junior welterweight	140	Oscar De La Hoya	Frankie Randall	Kostya Tszyu
Lightweight	135	Jean-Baptiste Mendy	Orzubek Nazarov	Phillip Holiday
Junior lightweight	130	Azumah Nelson	Choi Yong-Soo	Arturo Gatti
Featherweight	126	Luisito Espinosa	Wilfredo Vazquez	Tom Johnson
Junior featherweight	122	Daniel Zaragoza	Antonio Cermeno	Vuyani Bungu
Bantamweight	118	S. Singmanassak	Nana Yaw Konadu	Mbulelo Botile
Junior bantamweight	115	Hiroshi Kawashima	Yokthai Sith-Oar	Danny Romero
Flyweight	112	Yuri Arbachakov	Saen Sow Ploenchit	Mark Johnson
Junior flyweight	108	Saman Sor Jaturong	Keiji Yamaguchi	Michael Carbajal
Strawweight	105	Ricardo Lopez	Rosendo Alvarez	Ratanapol Sow Voraphin

Note: WBC = World Boxing Council; WBA = World Boxing Association; IBF = International Boxing Federation

Championship and Major Fights of 1995 and 1996

Abbreviations: WBC=World Boxing Council; WBA= World Boxing Association; IBF=International Boxing Federation; KO=knockout; TKO=technical knockout; Dec=decision; Split=split decision; Disq=disqualification.

Heavyweight

Date	Winner	Loser	Result	Title	Site
Dec 9	Frans Botha	Axel Schulz	Split 12	IBF	Stuttgart
Dec 16	Mike Tyson	Buster Mathis Jr.	KO 3	—	Philadelphia
Mar 16	Mike Tyson	Frank Bruno	TKO 3	WBC	Las Vegas
June 22	Michael Moorer	Axel Schulz	Split 12	IBF	Dortmund, Germany
Sept 7	Mike Tyson	Bruce Seldon	TKO 1	WBA	Las Vegas

Cruiserweight

Date	Winner	Loser	Result	Title	Site
Oct 24	Marcelo Dominguez	Sergei Kobozev	Split 12	WBC	Levallois-Perret, France
Jan 13	Nate Miller	Reynaldo Gimenez	TKO 4	WBA	Miami
Mar 23	Nate Miller	Brian LaSpada	TKO 9	WBA	Miami
July 5	Marcelo Dominguez	Patrice Aouissi	TKO 9	WBC	Hyeres, France
Aug 31	Nate Miller	James Heath	TKO 7	WBA	Dublin
Aug 31	Adolpho Washington	Torsten May	Dec 12	IBF	Palma de Mallorca, Sp

Light Heavyweight

Date	Winner	Loser	Result	Title	Site
Oct 14	Henry Maske	Graciano Rocchigiani	Dec 12	IBF	Munich
Jan 13	Fabrice Tiozzo	Eric Lucas	Dec 12	WBC	St Etienne, France
Feb 17	Henry Maske	Duran Williams	Dec 12	IBF	Dortmund, Germany
Apr 20	Virgil Hill	Louis Del Valle	Dec 12	WBA	Grand Forks, ND
May 25	Henry Maske	John Scully	Dec 12	IBF	Leipzig, Germany

Super Middleweight

Date	Winner	Loser	Result	Title	Site
Dec 9	Frank Liles	Mauricio Amaral	Dec 12	WBA	Stuttgart, Germany
Mar 2	Thulane Malinga	Nigel Benn	Split 12	WBC	Newcastle, England
June 8	Frank Liles	Tom Littles	TKO 3	WBA	Newcastle, England
June 15	Roy Jones	Eric Lucas	TKO 11	IBF	Jacksonville, FL
July 6	Vincenzo Nardiello	Thulane Malinga	Split 12	WBC	Manchester, England

Middleweight

Date	Winner	Loser	Result	Title	Site
Oct 13	Jorge Castro	Reggie Johnson	Split 12	WBA	Chubut, Argentina
Dec 19	Shinji Takehara	Jorge Castro	Dec 12	WBA	Tokyo
Jan 27	Bernard Hopkins	Steve Frank	TKO 1	IBF	Phoenix, AZ
Mar 16	Keith Holmes	Quincy Taylor	TKO 9	WBC	Las Vegas
Mar 16	Bernard Hopkins	Joe Lipsey Jr	KO 4	IBF	Las Vegas
June 24	William Joppy	Shinji Takehara	TKO 9	WBA	Yokohama, Japan
July 16	Bernard Hopkins	William James	TKO 11	IBF	Atlantic City

Junior Middleweight (Super Welterweight)

Date	Winner	Loser	Result	Title	Site
Sept 16	Terry Norris	David Gonzales	TKO 9	WBC	Las Vegas
Dec 16	Julio César Vasquez	Carl Daniels	TKO 11	WBA	Philadelphia
Dec 16	Terry Norris	Paul Vaden	Dec 12	WBC/IBF	Philadelphia
Jan 27	Terry Norris	Jorge Luis Vado	TKO 2	IBF	Phoenix, AZ
Feb 24	Terry Norris	Vincent Pettway	TKO 8	WBC/IBF	Richmond, VA
Aug 21	Laurent Boudouani	Julio César Vasquez	KO 5	WBA	Le Cannet-Rocheville, Fr
Sept 7	Terry Norris	Alex Rios	TKO 5	WBC/IBF	Las Vegas

Welterweight

Date	Winner	Loser	Result	Title	Site
Nov 18	Pernell Whitaker	Jake Rodriguez	KO 6	WBC	Atlantic City
Nov 18	Felix Trinidad	Larry Barnes	TKO 4	IBF	Atlantic City
Feb 10	Felix Trinidad	Rodney Moore	TKO 4	IBF	Las Vegas
Apr 12	Pernell Whitaker	Wilfredo Rivera	Split 12	WBC	Cupecoy Bay, St Maar
Apr 12	Ike Quartey	Vincent Phillips	TKO 3	WBA	Cupecoy Bay, St Maar
May 18	Felix Trinidad	Freddie Pendleton	KO 5	IBF	Las Vegas
Sept 7	Felix Trinidad	Ray Lovato	TKO 6	IBF	Las Vegas
Sept 20	Pernell Whitaker	Wilfredo Rivera	Dec 12	WBC	Miami

Junior Welterweight (Super Lightweight)

Date	Winner	Loser	Result	Title	Site
Jan 13	Juan Martin Coggi	Frankie Randall	Tech 5	WBA	Miami
Jan 20	Kostya Tszyu	Hugo Pineda	TKO 11	IBF	Parramatta, Australia
May 24	Kostya Tszyu	Corey Johnson	KO 4	IBF	Sydney, Australia
June 7	Oscar De La Hoya	Julio César Chávez	TKO 4	WBC	Las Vegas
Aug 16	Frankie Randall	Juan Martin Coggi	Dec 12	WBA	Buenos Aires
Sept 14	Kostya Tszyu	Jan Bergman	KO 6	IBF	Newcastle, Australia

Lightweight

Date	Winner	Loser	Result	Title	Site
Nov 4	Phillip Holiday	Rocky Martinez	Dec 12	IBF	Sun City, South Africa
Nov 14	Orzubek Nazarov	Dindo Canoy	Dec 12	WBA	Iwaki City, Japan
Feb 17	Phillip Holiday	John Lark	TKO 10	IBF	Hammanskraal, S.A.
Apr 15	Orzubek Nazarov	Adrianus Taroreh	KO 4	WBA	Tokyo
Apr 20	Jean-Baptiste Mendy	Lamar Murphy	Dec 12	WBC	Levallois-Perret, France
May 18	Phillip Holiday	Jeff Fenech	TKO 2	IBF	Melbourne, Australia

Junior Lightweight (Super Featherweight)

Date	Winner	Loser	Result	Title	Site
Oct 21	Choi Yong-Soo	Victor Hugo Paz	TKO 10	WBA	Salta, Argentina
Dec 1	Azumah Nelson	Gabriel Ruelas	TKO 5	WBC	Indio, CA
Dec 15	Arturo Gatti	Tracy Patterson	Dec 12	IBF	New York City
Jan 27	Choi Yong-Soo	Yamato Mitani	Dec 12	WBA	Tokyo
Mar 23	Arturo Gatti	Wilson Rodriguez	KO 6	IBF	New York City
May 11	Choi Yong-Soo	Orlando Soto	TKO 8	WBA	Chejudo, S Korea
June 1	Azumah Nelson	James Leija	TKO 6	WBC	Las Vegas

Featherweight

Date	Winner	Loser	Result	Title	Site
Dec 9	Tom Johnson	Jose Badillo	Dec 12	IBF	Stuttgart, Germany
Dec 11	Luisito Espinosa	Manuel Medina	Dec 12	WBC	Tokyo
Jan 27	Eloy Rojas	Miguel Arrozal	Dec 12	WBA	Phoenix, AR
Mar 1	Luisito Espinosa	Alejandro Gonzalez	KO 4	WBC	Guadalajara, Mexico
Mar 2	Tom Johnson	Ever Beleno	TKO 12	IBF	Newcastle, England
Apr 27	Tom Johnson	Claudio Martinet	KO 7	IBF	Antibes, France
May 18	Wilfredo Vazquez	Eloy Rojas	TKO 11	WBA	Las Vegas
July 6	Luisito Espinosa	Cesar Soto	Dec 12	WBC	Manila
Aug 31	Tom Johnson	Ramon Guzman	Dec 12	IBF	Dublin

Junior Featherweight (Super Bantamweight)

Date	Winner	Loser	Result	Title	Site
Nov 6	Daniel Zaragoza	Hector Acero-Sanchez	Split 12	WBC	Inglewood, CA
Nov 26	Antonio Cermeno	Jesus Salud	Dec 12	WBA	Maracay, Venezuela
Jan 23	Vuyani Bungu	Johnny Lewus	Dec 12	IBF	Biloxi, MS
Mar 3	Daniel Zaragoza	Joichiro Tatsuyoshi	TKO 11	WBC	Yokohama, Japan
Mar 23	Antonio Cermeno	Yober Ortega	Dec 12	WBA	Miami
Apr 15	Vuyani Bungu	Pablo Ozuna	KO 2	IBF	Hammanskraal, S.A.
July 20	Daniel Zaragoza	Tsuyoshi Harada	TKO 7	WBC	Osaka, Japan
Aug 20	Vuyani Bungu	Jesus Salud	Dec 12	IBF	Hammanskraal, S.A.

Bantamweight

Date	Winner	Loser	Result	Title	Site
Nov 25	Mbulelo Botile	Reynaldo Hurtado	TKO 2	IBF	East London, S.A.
Dec 2	Wayne McCullough	Johnni Bredahl	TKO 8	WBC	Belfast
Jan 28	Nana Yaw Konadu	Veerapol Sahaprom	TKO 2	WBA	Kanchanaburi, Thai.
Mar 30	Wayne McCullough	Jose Luis Bueno	Split 12	WBC	Dublin
Apr 2	Mbulelo Botile	Ancee Gedeon	KO 11	IBF	Providence, RI
June 29	Mbulelo Botile	Marlon Arlos	TKO 8	IBF	East London, S.A.
Aug 10	S. Singmanassak	Jose Luis Bueno	TKO 5	WBC	Phitsanulok, Thailand

Junior Bantamweight (Super Flyweight)

Date	Winner	Loser	Result	Title	Site
Nov 8	Hiroshi Kawashima	Boy Aruan	TKO 3	WBC	Tokyo
Nov 25	Alimi Goitia	Aquiles Guzman	TKO 5	WBA	Isla Margarita, Venez.
Feb 10	Carlos Salazar	Antonello Melis	TKO 6	IBF	Rome
Feb 24	Alimi Goitia	Lee Hyung-Chul	TKO 12	WBA	Kwangyang, S Korea
Apr 27	Hiroshi Kawashima	Cecilio Espino	Dec 12	WBC	Tokyo
Apr 27	Harold Grey	Carlos Salazar	Dec 12	IBF	Cartagena, Colombia
Apr 29	Alimi Goitia	Satoshi Iida	TKO 5	WBA	Nagoya, Japan
Aug 24	Yokthai Sith-Oar	Alimi Goitia	TKO 8	WBA	Kamphaeng Phet, Thai.
Aug 24	Danny Romero	Harold Grey	KO 2	IBF	Albuquerque, NM

Flyweight

Date	Winner	Loser	Result	Title	Site
Oct 17	Saen Sow Ploenchit	Hiroki Ioka	TKO 10	WBA	Osaka, Japan
Jan 14	Saen Sow Ploenchit	Chang Young-Soon	Dec 12	WBA	Nonsaburi, Thailand
Feb 5	Yuri Arbachakov	Raul Juarez	Dec 12	WBC	Osaka, Japan
Mar 24	Saen Sow Ploenchit	Leo Gamez	Split 12	WBA	Rangsit, Thailand
May 4	Mark Johnson	Francisco Tejedor	KO 1	IBF	Anaheim, CA
Aug 5	Mark Johnson	Raul Juarez	TKO 8	IBF	Inglewood, CA
Aug 26	Yuri Arbachakov	Takato Toguchi	TKO 9	WBC	Tokyo
Sept 8	Saen Sow Ploenchit	A. Makhmoutov	Dec 12	WBA	Nakhon Phanom, Thai.

Junior Flyweight

Date	Winner	Loser	Result	Title	Site
Nov 12	Saman Sor Jaturong	Yuichi Hosono	KO 4	WBC	Ratchaburi, Thailand
Jan 13	Carlos Murillo	Choi Hi-Yong	Dec 12	WBA	Miami
Mar 15	Carlos Murillo	Jose Garcia	TKO 10	WBA	Panama City
Mar 16	Michael Carbajal	Melchor Cob Castro	Dec 12	IBF	Las Vegas
Apr 27	Saman Sor Jaturong	Joma Gamboa	TKO 7	WBC	Maha Sarakham, Thai.
May 21	Keiji Yamaguchi	Carlos Murillo	Split 12	WBA	Osaka, Japan
Aug 10	Saman Sor Jaturong	Shiro Yahiro	TKO 9	WBC	Phitsanulok, Thailand
Aug 13	Keiji Yamaguchi	Carlos Murillo	Dec 12	WBA	Osaka, Japan
Sept 13	Michael Carbajal	Julio Coronell	TKO 8	IBF	Des Moines, IA

Strawweight (Mini Flyweight)

Date	Winner	Loser	Result	Title	Site
Oct 29	Ratanapal Sow Voraphin	Jack Russell	KO 2	IBF	Suphan Buri, Thailand
Dec 2	Rosendo Alvarez	Chana Porpaoin	Split 12	WBA	Sakaew, Thailand
Dec 30	Ratanapal Sow Voraphin	Osvaldo Guerrero	TKO 6	IBF	Chiang Mai, Thailand
Mar 16	Ricardo Lopez	Ala Villamor	KO 8	WBC	Las Vegas
Mar 30	Rosendo Alvarez	Kermin Guardia	KO 3	WBA	Managua, Nicaragua
May 18	Ratanapal Sow Voraphin	Jun Arlos	Dec 12	IBF	Yala, Thailand
June 15	Rosendo Alvarez	Eric Chavez	Dec 12	WBA	Sendai City, Japan
June 29	Ricardo Lopez	Kittichai Preecha	KO 3	WBC	Indio, CA
July 13	Ratanapal Sow Voraphin	Jun Orhaliza	KO 3	IBF	Chiang Mai, Thailand

Bad Decisions

In moves tasteless by even the standards of the sport they cover, both *Boxing Illustrated* and *KO* selected as their 1995 Fight of the Year the bout that put former middleweight champion Gerald McClellan into a coma and left him handicapped. While the latter publication at least admitted to "ambivalence drifting toward guilt" for its choice, *BI* cited, without irony, the "continually explosive action" involving McClellan and Nigel Benn in "the Britisher's 11th-round [sic] knockout" (the bout went only 10).

"There were four or five fights to choose from," said *BI* associate editor Gregory Juckett of the balloting, in which editors and correspondents overwhelmingly picked Benn-McClellan. "I'm just looking at the fight itself, and it was a war."

FOR THE RECORD·Year by Year

World Champions

Sanctioning bodies: the National Boxing Association (NBA), the New York State Athletic Commission (NY), the World Boxing Association (WBA), the World Boxing Council (WBC), and the International Boxing Federation (IBF).

Heavyweights
(Weight: Unlimited)

Champion	Reign	Champion	Reign	Champion	Reign
John L. Sullivan	1885-92	Floyd Patterson	1960-62	Greg Page* WBA	1984-85
James J. Corbett	1892-97	Sonny Liston	1962-64	Michael Spinks	1985-87
Bob Fitzsimmons	1897-99	Muhammad Ali	1964-70	Tim Witherspoon* WBA	1986
James J. Jeffries	1899-1905†	Ernie Terrell* WBA	1965-67	Trevor Berbick* WBC	1986
Marvin Hart	1905-06	Joe Frazier* NY	1968-70	Mike Tyson* WBC	1986-87
Tommy Burns	1906-08	Jimmy Ellis* WBA	1968-70	James Bonecrusher	
Jack Johnson	1908-15	Joe Frazier	1970-73	Smith* WBA	1986-87
Jess Willard	1915-19	George Foreman	1973-74	Tony Tucker* IBF	1987
Jack Dempsey	1919-26	Muhammad Ali	1974-78	Mike Tyson	1987-90
Gene Tunney	1926-28	Leon Spinks	1978	Buster Douglas	1990
Max Schmeling	1930-32	Ken Norton* WBC	1978	Evander Holyfield	1990-92
Jack Sharkey	1932-33	Larry Holmes* WBC	1978-80	Lennox Lewis* WBC	1993-95
Primo Carnera	1933-34	Muhammad Ali	1978-79†	Riddick Bowe	1992-93
Max Baer	1934-35	John Tate* WBA	1979-80	Evander Holyfield	1993-94
James J. Braddock	1935-37	Mike Weaver* WBA	1980-82	Michael Moorer	1994
Joe Louis	1937-49†	Larry Holmes	1980-85	George Foreman	1994-95
Ezzard Charles	1949-51	Michael Dokes* WBA	1982-83	Frank Bruno* WBC	1995-96
Jersey Joe Walcott	1951-52	Gerrie Coetzee* WBA	1983-84	Bruce Seldon* WBA	1995-96
Rocky Marciano	1952-56†	Tim Witherspoon* WBC	1984	Mike Tyson WBA	1996-
Ingemar Johansson	1959-60	Pinklon Thomas* WBC	1984-86	Michael Moorer* IBF	1996-

Cruiserweights
(Weight Limit: 190 pounds)

Champion	Reign	Champion	Reign	Champion	Reign
Marvin Camel* WBC	1980	Evander Holyfield * WBA	1986-88	Bobby Czyz* WBA	1991-92†
Carlos De Leon* WBC	1980-82	Ricky Parkey* IBF	1986-87	Anaclet Wamba* WBC	1991-95
Ossie Ocasio* WBA	1982-84	Evander Holyfield*		James Pritchard* IBF	1991
S.T. Gordon* WBC	1982-83	WBA/IBF	1987-88	James Warring* IBF	1991-92
Carlos De Leon* WBC	1983-85	Evander Holyfield	1988†	Alfred Cole* IBF	1992-96
Marvin Camel* IBF	1983-84	Toufik Belbouli* WBA	1989	Orlin Norris* WBA	1993-95
Lee Roy Murphy* IBF	1984-86	Robert Daniels* WBA	1989-91	Nate Miller* WBA	1995-
Piet Crous* WBA	1984-85	Carlos De Leon* WBC	1989-90	Marcelo	
Alfonso Ratliff* WBC	1985	Glenn McCrory* IBF	1989-90	Dominguez* WBC	1995-
Dwight Braxton* WBA	1985-86	Jeff Lampkin* IBF	1990	Alph. Washington* IBF	1996-
Bernard Benton* WBC	1985-86	Massimiliano			
Carlos De Leon* WBC	1986-88	Duran* WBC	1990-91		

Note: Division called Junior Heavyweight by the WBA.

Light Heavyweights
(Weight Limit: 175 pounds)

Champion	Reign	Champion	Reign	Champion	Reign
Jack Root	1903	George Nichols* NBA	1932	Dick Tiger	1966-68
George Gardner	1903	Bob Godwin* NBA	1933	Bob Foster	1968-74†
Bob Fitzsimmons	1903-05	Bob Olin	1934-35	Vicente Rondon* WBA	1971-72
Philadelphia Jack		John Henry Lewis	1935-38	John Conteh* WBC	1974-77
O'Brien	1905-12†	Melio Bettina	1939	Victor Galindez* WBA	1974-78
Jack Dillon	1914-16	Billy Conn	1939-40†	Miguel A. Cuello* WBC	1977-78
Battling Levinsky	1916-20	Anton Christoforidis	1941	Mate Parlov* WBC	1978
Georges Carpentier	1920-22	Gus Lesnevich	1941-48	Mike Rossman* WBA	1978-79
Battling Siki	1922-23	Freddie Mills	1948-50	Marvin Johnson* WBC	1978-79
Mike McTigue	1923-25	Joey Maxim	1950-52	Matthew Saad	
Paul Berlenbach	1925-26	Archie Moore	1952-62†	Muhammad* WBC	1979-81
Jack Delaney	1926-27†	Harold Johnson* NBA	1961	Marvin Johnson* WBA	1979-80
Jimmy Slattery* NBA	1927	Harold Johnson	1962-63	Eddie Mustapha	
Tommy Loughran	1927-29	Willie Pastrano	1963-65	Muhammad* WBA	1980-81
Maxie Rosenbloom	1930-34	Jose Torres	1965-66	Michael Spinks* WBA	1981-83

*Champion not generally recognized. †Champion retired or relinquished title.

Light Heavyweights *(Cont.)*

Champion	Reign
Dwight Muhammad Qawi* WBC	1981-83
Michael Spinks	1983-85†
J. B. Williamson* WBC	1985-86
Slobodan Kacar* IBF	1985-86
Marvin Johnson* WBA	1986-87
Dennis Andries* WBC	1986-87
Bobby Czyz* IBF	1986-87

Champion	Reign
Leslie Stewart* WBA	1987
Virgil Hill* WBA	1987
Pr Charles Williams* IBF	1987-93
Thomas Hearns* WBC	1987†
Donny Lalonde* WBC	1987-88
Sugar Ray Leonard* WBC	1988
Dennis Andries* WBC	1989
Jeff Harding* WBC	1989-90

Champion	Reign
Dennis Andries* WBC	1990-91
Thomas Hearns* WBC	1991-92
Jeff Harding* WBC	1991-94
Iran Barkley* WBA	1992
Virgil Hill* WBA	1992-
Henry Maske* IBF	1993-
Mike McCallum* WBC	1994-95
Fabrice Tiozzo* WBC	1995-

Super Middleweights
(Weight Limit: 168 pounds)

Champion	Reign
Murray Sutherland* IBF	1984
Chong-Pal Park* IBF	1984-87
Chong-Pal Park* WBA	1987-88
G. Rocchigiani* IBF	1988-89
F. Obelmejias* WBA	1988-89
Ray Leonard* WBC	1988-90†
In-Chul Baek* WBA	1989-90

Champion	Reign
Lindell Holmes* IBF	1990-91
C. Tiozzo* WBA	1990-91
Mauro Galvano* WBC	1990-92
Victor Cordova* WBA	1991
Darrin Van Horn* IBF	1991-92
Iran Barkley *WBA	1992
Nigel Benn* WBC	1992-96

Champion	Reign
James Toney* IBF	1992-94
Michael Nunn* WBA	1992-94
Steve Little* WBA	1994
Frank Liles* WBA	1994-
Roy Jones* IBF	1994-
Thulane Malinga* WBC	1996
V. Nardiello* WBC	1996-

Middleweights
(Weight Limit: 160 pounds)

Champion	Reign
Jack Dempsey	1884-91
Bob Fitzsimmons	1891-97
Kid McCoy	1897-98
Tommy Ryan	1898-1907
Stanley Ketchel	1908
Billy Papke	1908
Stanley Ketchel	1908-10
Frank Klaus	1913
George Chip	1913-14
Al McCoy	1914-17
Mike O'Dowd	1917-20
Johnny Wilson	1920-23
Harry Greb	1923-26
Tiger Flowers	1926
Mickey Walker	1926-31†
Gorilla Jones	1931-32
Marcel Thil	1932-37
Fred Apostoli	1937-39
Al Hostak* NBA	1938
Solly Krieger* NBA	1938-39
Al Hostak* NBA	1939-40
Ceferino Garcia	1939-40
Ken Overlin	1940-41
Tony Zale* NBA	1940-41
Billy Soose	1941
Tony Zale	1941-47

Champion	Reign
Rocky Graziano	1947-48
Tony Zale	1948
Marcel Cerdan	1948-49
Jake La Motta	1949-51
Sugar Ray Robinson	1951
Randy Turpin	1951
Sugar Ray Robinson	1951-52
Bobo Olson	1953-55
Sugar Ray Robinson	1955-57
Gene Fullmer	1957
Sugar Ray Robinson	1957
Carmen Basilio	1957-58
Sugar Ray Robinson	1958-60
Gene Fullmer* NBA	1959-62
Paul Pender	1960-61
Terry Downes	1961-62
Paul Pender	1962-63
Dick Tiger* WBA	1962-63
Dick Tiger	1963
Joey Giardello	1963-65
Dick Tiger	1965-66
Emile Griffith	1966-67
Nino Benvenuti	1967
Emile Griffith	1967-68
Nino Benvenuti	1968-70
Carlos Monzon	1970-77†

Champion	Reign
Rodrigo Valdez* WBC	1974-76
Rodrigo Valdez	1977-78
Hugo Corro	1978-79
Vito Antuofermo	1979-80
Alan Minter	1980
Marvin Hagler	1980-87
Sugar Ray Leonard	1987
Frank Tate* IBF	1987-88
Sumbu Kalambay* WBA	1987-89
Thomas Hearns* WBC	1987-88
Iran Barkley* WBC	1988-89
Michael Nunn* IBF	1988-91
Roberto Duran* WBC	1989-90
Mike McCallum* WBA	1989-91
Julian Jackson* WBC	1990-93
James Toney* IBF	1991-93
Reggie Johnson* WBA	1992-94
Roy Jones* IBF	1993-95†
G. McClellan* WBC	1993-95†
Jorge Castro* WBA	1994-95
Shinji Takehara* WBA	1995-96
Jullian Jackson*WBC	1995
Quincy Taylor* WBC	1995-96
Bernard Hopkins* IBF	1995-
Keith Holmes* WBC	1996-
William Joppy* WBA	1996-

Junior Middleweights
(Weight Limit: 154 pounds)

Champion	Reign
Emile Griffith (EBU)	1962-63
Dennis Moyer	1962-63
Ralph Dupas	1963
Sandro Mazzinghi	1963-65
Nino Benvenuti	1965-66
Ki-Soo Kim	1966-68
Sandro Mazzinghi	1968
Freddie Little	1969-70
Carmelo Bossi	1970-71
Koichi Wajima	1971-74
Oscar Albarado	1974-75

Champion	Reign
Koichi Wajima	1975
Miguel de Oliveira* WBC	1975-76
Jae-Do Yuh	1975-76
Elisha Obed* WBC	1975-76
Koichi Wajima	1976
Jose Duran	1976
Eckhard Dagge* WBC	1976-77
Miguel Angel Castellini	1976-77
Eddie Gazo	1977-78
Rocky Mattioli* WBC	1977-79
Masashi Kudo	1978-79

Champion	Reign
Maurice Hope* WBC	1979-81
Ayub Kalule	1979-81
Wilfred Benitez* WBC	1981-82
Sugar Ray Leonard	1981-82
Tadashi Mihara* WBA	1981-82
Davey Moore* WBA	1982-83
Thomas Hearns* WBA	1982-84
Roberto Duran* WBA	1983-84
Mark Medal* IBF	1984
Thomas Hearns	1984-86
Mike McCallum* WBA	1984-87

*Champion not generally recognized. †Champion retired or relinquished title.

Junior Middleweights *(Cont.)*

Champion	Reign	Champion	Reign	Champion	Reign
Carlos Santos* IBF	1984-86	Robert Hines* IBF	1988-89	Julio C. Vasquez* WBA	1992-95
Buster Drayton* IBF	1986-87	Darrin Van Horn* IBF	1989	Simon Brown* WBC	1994
Duane Thomas* WBC	1986-87	Rene Jacquot* WBC	1989	Terry Norris *WBC	1994-
Matthew Hilton* IBF	1987-88	John Mugabi* WBC	1989-90	Vincent Pettway* IBF	1994-95
Lupe Aquino* WBC	1987	Gianfranco Rosi* IBF	1989-94	Paul Vaden* IBF	1995
Gianfranco Rosi* WBC	1987-88	Terry Norris* WBC	1990-94	Carl Daniels* WBA	1995
Julian Jackson* WBA	1987-90	Gilbert Dele* WBA	1991	Terry Norris WBC,IBF	1995-
Donald Curry* WBC	1988-89	Vinny Pazienza* WBA	1991-92	L. Boudouani *WBA	1996-

Note: Division called Super Welterweight by the WBC.

Welterweights
(Weight Limit: 147 pounds)

Champion	Reign	Champion	Reign	Champion	Reign
Paddy Duffy	1888-90	Young Corbett III	1933	John H. Stracey	1975-76
Mysterious Billy Smith	1892-94	Jimmy McLarnin	1933-34	Carlos Palomino	1976-79
Tommy Ryan	1894-98	Barney Ross	1934	Pipino Cuevas* WBA	1976-80
Mysterious Billy Smith	1898-1900	Jimmy McLarnin	1934-35	Wilfredo Benitez	1979
Rube Ferns	1900	Barney Ross	1935-38	Sugar Ray Leonard	1979-80
Matty Matthews	1900-01	Henry Armstrong	1938-40	Roberto Duran	1980
Rube Ferns	1901	Fritzie Zivic	1940-41	Thomas Hearns* WBA	1980-81
Joe Walcott	1901-04	Red Cochrane	1941-46	Sugar Ray Leonard	1980-82
The Dixie Kid	1904-05	Marty Servo	1946	Donald Curry* WBA	1983-85
Honey Mellody	1906-07	Sugar Ray Robinson	1946-51†	Milton McCrory* WBC	1983-85
Twin Sullivan	1907-08	Johnny Bratton	1951	Donald Curry	1985-86
Jimmy Gardner	1908	Kid Gavilan	1951-54	Lloyd Honeyghan	1986-87
Jimmy Clabby	1910-11	Johnny Saxton	1954-55	Jorge Vaca WBC	1987-88
Waldemar Holberg	1914	Tony DeMarco	1955	Lloyd Honeyghan WBC	1988-89
Tom McCormick	1914	Carmen Basilio	1955-56	Mark Breland* WBA	1987
Matt Wells	1914-15	Johnny Saxton	1956	Marlon Starling* WBA	1987-88
Mike Glover	1915	Carmen Basilio	1956-57	Tomas Molinares* WBA	1988-89
Jack Britton	1915	Virgil Akins	1958	Simon Brown* IBF	1988-91
Ted "Kid" Lewis	1915-16	Don Jordan	1958-60	Mark Breland* WBA	1989-90
Jack Britton	1916-17	Kid Paret	1960-61	Marlon Starling* WBC	1989-90
Ted "Kid" Lewis	1917-19	Emile Griffith	1961	Aaron Davis* WBA	1990-91
Jack Britton	1919-22	Kid Paret	1961-62	Maurice Blocker* WBC	1990-91
Mickey Walker	1922-26	Emile Griffith	1962-63	Meldrick Taylor* WBA	1991-1992
Pete Latzo	1926-27	Luis Rodriguez	1963	Simon Brown* WBC	1991
Joe Dundee	1927-29	Emile Griffith	1963-66	Buddy McGirt* WBC	1991-1993
Jackie Fields	1929-30	Curtis Cokes	1966-69	Felix Trinidad* IBF	1992-
Young Jack Thompson	1930	Jose Napoles	1969-70	Pernell Whitaker WBC	1993-
Tommy Freeman	1930-31	Billy Backus	1970-71	Crisanto Espana* WBA	1992-94
Young Jack Thompson	1931	Jose Napoles	1971-75	Ike Quartey* WBA	1994-
Lou Brouillard	1931-32	Hedgemon Lewis* NY	1972-73		
Jackie Fields	1932-33	Angel Espada* WBA	1975-76		

Junior Welterweights
(Weight Limit: 140 pounds)

Champion	Reign	Champion	Reign	Champion	Reign
Pinkey Mitchell	1922-25	Eddie Perkins	1963-65	Saoul Mamby* WBC	1980-82
Red Herring	1925	Carlos Hernandez	1965-66	Aaron Pryor* WBA	1980-83
Mushy Callahan	1926-30	Sandro Lopopolo	1966-67	Leroy Haley* WBC	1982-83
Jack (Kid) Berg	1930-31	Paul Fujii	1967-68	Aaron Pryor* IBF	1983-85
Tony Canzoneri	1931-32	Nicolino Loche	1968-72	Bruce Curry* WBC	1983-84
Johnny Jadick	1932-33	Pedro Adigue* WBC	1968-70	Johnny Bumphus* WBA	1984
Sammy Fuller*	1932-33	Bruno Arcari* WBC	1970-74	Bill Costello* WBC	1984-85
Battling Shaw	1933	Alfonso Frazer	1972	Gene Hatcher* WBA	1984-85
Tony Canzoneri	1933	Antonio Cervantes	1972-76	Ubaldo Sacco* WBA	1985-86
Barney Ross	1933-35	Perico Fernandez* WBC	1974-75	Lonnie Smith* WBC	1985-86
Tippy Larkin	1946	S. Muangsurin* WBC	1975-76	Patrizio Oliva* WBA	1986-87
Carlos Ortiz	1959-60	Wilfred Benitez	1976-79	Gary Hinton* IBF	1986
Duilio Loi	1960-62	M. Velasquez* WBC	1976	Rene Arredondo* WBC	1986
Eddie Perkins	1962	S. Muangsurin* WBC	1976-78	Tsuyoshi Hamada* WBC	1986-87
Duilio Loi	1962-63	A. Cervantes* WBA	1977-80	Joe Louis Manley* IBF	1986-87
Roberto Cruz* WBA	1963	Sang-Hyun Kim* WBC	1978-80	Terry Marsh* IBF	1987

*Champion not generally recognized. †Champion retired or relinquished title.

Junior Welterweights *(Cont.)*

Champion	Reign	Champion	Reign	Champion	Reign
Juan Coggi* WBA	1987-90	Juan Coggi* WBA	1991	Frankie Randall* WBC	1994
Rene Arredondo* WBC	1987	Edwin Rosario* WBA	1991-92	Frankie Randall* WBA	1994-96
R. Mayweather* WBC	1987-89	Rafael Pineda* IBF	1991-92	Juan Coggi* WBA	1996
James McGirt* IBF	1988	Akinobu Hiranaka* WBA	1992	Julio César Chávez WBC	1994-96
Meldrick Taylor* IBF	1988-90	Pernell Whitaker*† IBF	1992-93	Kostya Tszyu* IBF	1995-
Julio César Chávez* WBC	1989-94	Charles Murray* IBF	1993-94	Frankie Randall* WBA	1996-
Julio César Chávez* IBF	1990-91	Jake Rodriguez* IBF	1994-95	Oscar De La Hoya WBC	1996-
Loreto Garza* WBA	1990-91	Juan Coggi* WBA	1993-94		

Lightweights
(Weight Limit: 135 pounds)

Champion	Reign	Champion	Reign	Champion	Reign
Jack McAuliffe	1886-94	Juan Zurita* NBA	1944-45	Edwin Rosario* WBC	1983-84
Kid Lavigne	1896-99	Ike Williams	1947-51	Choo Choo Brown* IBF	1984
Frank Erne	1899-1902	James Carter	1951-52	L. Bramble* WBA	1984-86
Joe Gans	1902-04	Lauro Salas	1952	Jose Luis Ramirez* WBC	1984-85
Jimmy Britt	1904-05	James Carter	1952-54	Harry Arroyo* IBF	1984-85
Battling Nelson	1905-06	Paddy DeMarco	1954	Jimmy Paul* IBF	1985-86
Joe Gans	1906-08	James Carter	1954-55	Hector Camacho* WBC	1985-86
Battling Nelson	1908-10	Wallace Smith	1955-56	Greg Haugen* IBF	1986-87
Ad Wolgast	1910-12	Joe Brown	1956-62	Edwin Rosario* WBA	1986-87
Willie Ritchie	1912-14	Carlos Ortiz	1962-65	Julio César Chávez* WBA	1987-88
Freddie Wolsh	1915-17	Ismael Laguna	1965	Jose Luis Ramirez* WBC	1987-88
Benny Leonard	1917-25†	Carlos Ortiz	1965-68	Julio César Chávez	1988-89
Jimmy Goodrich	1925	Carlos Teo Cruz	1968-69	Vinny Pazienza* IBF	1987-88
Rocky Kansas	1925-26	Mando Ramos	1969-70	Greg Haugen* IBF	1988-89
Sammy Mandell	1926-30	Ismael Laguna	1970	P. Whitaker* WBC, IBF	1989-90
Al Singer	1930	Ken Buchanan	1970-72	Edwin Rosario* WBA	1989-90
Tony Canzoneri	1930-33	Roberto Duran	1972-79†		1991-92
Barney Ross	1933-35†	Chango Carmona* WBC	1972	Juan Nazario* WBA	1990
Tony Canzoneri	1935-36	Rodolfo Gonzalez* WBC	1972-74	P. Whitaker* WBA, WBC	1990-92
Lou Ambers	1936-38	Ishimatsu Suzuki* WBC	1974-76	Pernell Whitaker* IBF	1991-92
Henry Armstrong	1938-39	Esteban DeJesus* WBC	1976-78	Julio César Chávez* IBF	1990-91
Lou Ambers	1939-40	Jim Watt* WBC	1979-81	Julio César Chávez* WBC	1990-92
Sammy Angott* NBA	1940-41	Ernesto Espana* WBA	1979-80	Miguel Gonzalez* WBC	1992-95
Lew Jenkins	1940-41	Hilmer Kenty* WBA	1980-81	Joey Gamache WBA	1992-93
Sammy Angott	1941-42†	Sean O'Grady* WBA	1981	Dingaan Thobela* WBA	1993
Beau Jack* NY	1942-43	Claude Noel* WBA	1981	Fred Pendleton* IBF	1993-94
Bob Montgomery* NY	1943	Alexis Arguello* WBC	1981-82	Orzubek Nazarov* WBA	1994-
Sammy Angott* NBA	1943-44	Arturo Frias* WBA	1981-82	Rafael Ruelas* IBF	1994-95
Beau Jack* NY	1943-44	Ray Mancini* WBA	1982-84	Phillip Holiday* IBF	1995-
Bob Montgomery* NY	1944-47	Alexis Arguello	1982-83	Jean B. Mendy* WBC	1996-

Junior Lightweights
(Weight Limit: 130 pounds)

Champion	Reign	Champion	Reign	Champion	Reign
Johnny Dundee	1921-23	Ben Villaflor	1973-76	Alfredo Layne* WBA	1986
Jack Bernstein	1923	Kuniaki Shibata* WBC	1974-75	Brian Mitchell* WBA	1986-91
Johnny Dundee	1923-24	Alfredo Escalera* WBC	1975-78	Rocky Lockridge* IBF	1987-88
Steve (Kid) Sullivan	1924-25	Samuel Serrano	1976-80	Azumah Nelson* WBC	1988-94
Mike Ballerino	1925	Alexis Arguello* WBC	1978-80	Tony Lopez* IBF	1988-89
Tod Morgan	1925-29	Yasutsune Uehara	1980-81	Juan Molina* IBF	1989-90
Benny Bass	1929-31	Rafael Limon* WBC	1980-81	Tony Lopez* IBF	1990-91
Kid Chocolate	1931-33	C. Boza-Edwards* WBC	1981	Joey Gamache WBA	1991
Frankie Klick	1933-34	Samuel Serrano	1981-83	Brian Mitchell* IBF	1991
Sandy Saddler	1949-50	R. Navarrete* WBC	1981-82	Genaro Hernandez* WBA	1991-95
Harold Gomes	1959-60	Rafael Limon* WBC	1982	James Leija* WBC	1994
Gabriel (Flash) Elorde	1960-67	Bobby Chacon* WBC	1982-83	Juan Molina* IBF	1991-95
Yoshiaki Numata	1967	Roger Mayweather	1983-84	Gabriel Ruelas* WBC	1994-95
Hiroshi Kobayashi	1967-71	Hector Camacho* WBC	1983-84	Eddie Hopson* IBF	1995
Rene Barrientos* WBC	1969-70	Rocky Lockridge	1984-85	Tracy Patterson* IBF	1995
Yoshiaki Numata* WBC	1970-71	Hwan-Kil Yuh* IBF	1984-85	Azumah Nelson* WBC	1995-
Alfredo Marcano	1971-72	Julio César Chávez* IBF	1984-87	Choi Yong-Soo* WBA	1995-
R. Arredondo* WBC	1971-74	Lester Ellis* IBF	1985	Arturo Gatti* IBF	1995-
Ben Villaflor	1972-73	Wilfredo Gomez	1985-86		
Kuniaki Shibata	1973	Barry Michael* IBF	1985-87		

*Champion not generally recognized. †Champion retired or relinquished title.

Featherweights
(Weight Limit: 126 pounds)

Champion	Reign	Champion	Reign	Champion	Reign
Torpedo Billy Murphy	1890	Joey Archibald	1941	Danny Lopez WBC	1976-80
Young Griffo	1890-92	Richie Lamos* NBA	1941	Rafael Ortega* WBA	1977
George Dixon	1892-97	Chalky Wright	1941-42	Cecilio Lastra* WBA	1977-78
Solly Smith	1897-98	Jackie Wilson* NBA	1941-43	Eusebio Pedroza* WBA	1978-85
Dave Sullivan	1898	Willie Pep	1942-48	S. Sanchez WBC	1980-82
George Dixon	1898-1900	Jackie Callura* NBA	1943	Juan LaPorte* WBC	1982-84
Terry McGovern	1900-01	Phil Terranova* NBA	1943-44	Wilfredo Gomez* WBC	1984
Young Corbett II	1901-04	Sal Bartolo* NBA	1944-46	Min-Keun Oh* IBF	1984-85
Jimmy Britt	1904	Sandy Saddler	1948-49	Azumah Nelson* WBC	1984-88
Tommy Sullivan	1904-05	Willie Pep	1949-50	Barry McGuigan* WBA	1985-86
Abe Attell	1906-12	Sandy Saddler	1950-57†	Ki Young Chung* IBF	1985-86
Johnny Kilbane	1912-23	Kid Bassey	1957-59	Steve Cruz* WBA	1986-87
Eugene Criqui	1923	Davey Moore	1959-63	Antonio Rivera* IBF	1986-88
Johnny Dundee	1923-24	Sugar Ramos	1963-64	A. Esparragoza* WBA	1987-91
"Kid" Kaplan	1925-26	Vicente Saldivar	1964-67†	Calvin Grove* IBF	1988
Benny Bass	1927-28	Paul Rojas* WBA	1968	Jorge Paez* IBF	1988-91
Tony Canzoneri	1928	Jose Legra* WBC	1968-69	Jeff Fenech* WBC	1988-90†
Andre Routis	1928-29	Shozo Saijyo* WBA	1968-71	Marcos Villasana* WBC	1990-91
Battling Battalino	1929-32	J. Famechon* WBC	1969-70	Paul Hodkinson* WBC	1991-93
Tommy Paul* NBA	1932-33	Vicente Saldivar WBC	1970	Troy Dorsey* IBF	1991
Kid Chocolate* NY	1932-33	Kuniaki Shibata WBC	1970-72	Manuel Medina* IBF	1991-93
Freddie Miller* NBA	1933-36	Antonio Gomez* WBA	1971-72	Yung Kyun Park* WBA	1991-93
Mike Beloise* NY	1936-37	C. Sanchez WBC	1972	Gregorio Vargas* WBC	1993
Petey Sarron* NBA	1936-37	Ernesto Marcel* WBA	1972-74	Tom Johnson* IBF	1993-
Maurice Holtzer	1937-38	Jose Legra WBC	1972-73	Eloy Rojas* WBA	1993-96
Henry Armstrong	1937-38	Eder Jofre WBC	1973-74	Kevin Kelley* WBC	1993-95
Joey Archibald* NY	1938-39	Ruben Olivares* WBA	1974	A. Gonzalez* WBC	1995
Leo Rodak* NBA	1938-39	Bobby Chacon* WBC	1974-75	Manuel Medina* WBC	1995-95
Joey Archibald	1939-40	Alexis Arguello WBA	1974-76	Luisito Espinosa* WBC	1995-
Petey Scalzo* NBA	1940-41	Ruben Olivares* WBC	1975	Wilfredo Vazquez* WBA	1996-
Harry Jeffra	1940-41	Poison Kotey* WBC	1975-76		

Junior Featherweights
(Weight Limit: 122 pounds)

Champion	Reign	Champion	Reign	Champion	Reign
Jack (Kid) Wolfe*	1922-23	Victor Callejas* WBA	1984-86	Fabrice Benichou* IBF	1989-90
Carl Duane*	1923-24	Juan (Kid) Meza* WBC	1984-85	Jesus Salud* WBA	1989-90
Rigoberto Riasco* WBC	1976	Ji-Won Kim* IBF	1985-86	Welcome Ncita* IBF	1990-92
Royal		Lupe Pintor* WBC	1985-86	Paul Banke* WBC	1990
Kobayashi* WBC	1976	Samart		Luis Mendoza* WBA	1990-91
Dong-Kyun Yum* WBC	1976-79	Payakaroon* WBC	1986-87	Rual Perez* WBA	1992
Wilfredo Gomez* WBC	1977-83	Seung-Hoon Lee* IBF	1987-88	Pedro Decima* WBC	1990-91
Soo-Hwan Hong* WBA	1977-78	Louie Espinoza* WBA	1987	K. Hatanaka* WBC	1991
Ricardo Cardona* WBA	1978-80	Jeff Fenech* WBC	1987	Daniel Zaragoza* WBC	1991-92
Leo Randolph* WBA	1980	Julio Gervacio* WBA	1987-88	Tracy Patterson* WBC	1992-94
Sergio Palma* WBA	1980-82	Daniel Zaragoza* WBC	1988-90	Kennedy McKinney* IBF	1993-94
Leonardo Cruz* WBA	1982-84	Jose Sanabria* IBF	1988-89	Wilfredo Vasquez* WBA	1992-95
Jaime Garza* WBC	1983	Bernardo		Vuyani Bungu* IBF	1994-
Bobby Berna* IBF	1983-84	Pinango* WBA	1988	H. Acero Sanchez* WBC	1994-95
Loris Stecca* WBA	1984	Juan Jose		Antonio Cermeno* WBA	1995-
Seung-Il Suh* IBF	1984-85	Estrada* WBA	1988-89	Daniel Zaragoza* WBC	1995-

Bantamweights
(Weight Limit: 118 pounds)

Champion	Reign	Champion	Reign	Champion	Reign
Spider Kelly	1887	Frankie Neil	1903-4	Pete Herman	1917-20
Hughey Boyle	1887-88	Joe Bowker	1904-5	Joe Lynch	1920-21
Spider Kelly	1889	Jimmy Walsh	1905-6	Pete Herman	1921
Chappie Moran	1889-90	Owen Moran	1907-8	Johnny Buff	1921-22
George Dixon	1890-91	Monte Attell*	1909-10	Joe Lynch	1922-24
Pedlar Palmer*	1895-99	Frankie Conley	1910-11	Abe Goldstein	1924
Terry McGovern	1899-1900	Johnny Coulon	1911-14	Cannonball Martin	1924-25
Harry Harris	1901-2	Kid Williams	1914-17	Phil Rosenberg	1925-27
Harry Forbes	1902-3	Kewpie Ertle*	1915	Bud Taylor NBA	1927-28

*Champion not generally recognized. †Champion retired or relinquished title.

Bantamweights (Cont.)

Champion	Reign	Champion	Reign	Champion	Reign
Bushy Graham* NY	1928-29	Ruben Olivares	1969-70	Kaokor Galaxy* WBA	1988
Panama Al Brown	1929-35	Chucho Castillo	1970-71	Moon Sung-Kil* WBA	1988-89
Sixto Escobar* NBA	1934-35	Ruben Olivares	1971-72	Kaokor Galaxy* WBA	1989
Baltazar Sangchilli	1935-36	Rafael Herrera	1972	Raul Perez* WBC	1988-91
Lou Salica* NBA	1935	Enrique Pinder	1972-73	O. Canizales* IBF	1988-95
Sixto Escobar* NBA	1935-36	Romeo Anaya	1973	Luisito Espinosa* WBA	1989-91
Tony Marino	1936	Rafael Herrera* WBC	1973-74	Israel Contreras* WBA	1991-92
Sixto Escobar	1936-37	Soo-Hwan Hong	1974-75	Eddie Cook* WBA	1992-93
Harry Jeffra	1937-38†	Rodolfo Martinez* WBC	1974-76	Greg Richardson* WBC	1991
Sixto Escobar	1938-39	Alfonso Zamora	1975-77	J. Tatsuyoshi, WBC	1991-92
Georgie Pace NBA	1939-40	Carlos Zarate* WBC	1976-79	Victor Rabanales* WBC	1992-93
Lou Salica	1940-42	Jorge Lujan	1977-80	Jung-Il Byun* WBC	1993
Manuel Ortiz	1942-47	Lupe Pintor* WBC	1979-83	Jorge Julio WBA	1993
Harold Dade	1947	Julian Solis	1980	Yasuei Yakushiji* WBC	1993-95
Manuel Ortiz	1947-50	Jeff Chandler	1980-84	Junior Jones WBA*	1994
Vic Toweel	1950-52	Albert Davila* WBA	1983-85	John M. Johnson* WBA	1994
Jimmy Carruthers	1952-54†	Richard Sandoval	1984-86	D. Chuvatana*WBA	1994-95
Robert Cohen	1954-56	Satoshi Shingaki* IBF	1984-85	V. Sahaprom* WBA	1995-96
Paul Macias* NBA	1955-57	Jeff Fenech* IBF	1985	W. McCullough* WBC	1995-96
Mario D'Agata	1956-57	Daniel Zaragoza* WBC	1985	Harold Mestre* IBF	1995
Alphonse Halimi	1957-59	Miguel Lora* WBC	1985-88	Mbuleo Botile* IBF	1995-
Joe Becerra	1959-60†	Gaby Canizales	1986	N. Y. Konadu* WBC	1996-
Eder Jofre	1961-65	Bernardo Pinango	1986-87	S. Singmanassak* WBC	1996-
Fighting Harada	1965-68	W. Vasquez* WBA	1987-88		
Lionel Rose	1968-69	Kevin Seabrooks* IBF	1987-88		

Junior Bantamweights
(Weight Limit: 115 pounds)

Champion	Reign	Champion	Reign	Champion	Reign
Rafael Orono* WBC	1980-81	Gilberto Roman* WBC	1986-87	Katsuya Onizuka* WBA	1993-94
Chul-Ho Kim* WBC	1981-82	Ellyas Pical* IBF	1986	Lee Hyung-Chul* WBA	1994-95
Gustavo Ballas* WBA	1981	Santos Laciar* WBC	1987	Jose Luis Bueno* WBC	1993-94
Rafael Pedroza* WBA	1981-82	Tae-Il Chang* IBF	1987	Hiroshi Kawashima*WBC	1994
Jiro Watanabe* WBA	1982-84	Sugar Rojas* WBC	1987-88	Harold Grey* IBF	1994-95
Rafael Orono* WBC	1982-83	Ellyas Pical* IBF	1987-89	Alimi Goitia* WBA	1995-96
Payao Poontarat* WBC	1983-84	Gilberto Roman* WBC	1988-89	Yokthai Sith-Oar* WBA	1996-
Joo-Do Chun* IBF	1983-85	Juan Polo Perez* IBF	1989-90	Carlos Salazar* IBF	1995-96
Jiro Watanabe	1984-86	Nana Konadu* WBC	1989-90	Harold Grey* IBF	1996
Kaosai Galaxy* WBA	1984	Sung-Kil Moon* WBC	1990-93	Danny Romero* IBF	1996-
Ellyas Pical* IBF	1985-86	Robert Quiroga* IBF	1990-93		
Cesar Polanco* IBF	1986	Julio Borboa* IBF	1993-94		

Flyweights
(Weight Limit: 112 pounds)

Champion	Reign	Champion	Reign	Champion	Reign
Sid Smith	1913	Rinty Monaghan	1948-50	Erbito Salavarria	1970-73
Bill Ladbury	1913-14	Terry Allen	1950	B. Gonzalez* WBA	1972
Percy Jones	1914	Dado Marino	1950-52	V. Borkorsor* WBC	1972-73
Joe Symonds	1914-16	Yoshio Shirai	1953-54	Venice Borkorsor	1973
Jimmy Wilde	1916-23	Pascual Perez	1954-60	Chartchai Chionoi* WBA	1973-74
Pancho Villa	1923-25	Pone Kingpetch	1960-62	B. Gonzalez* WBA	1973-74
Fidel LaBarba	1925-27†	Masahiko Harada	1962-63	Shoji Oguma* WBC	1974-75
Frenchy Belanger NBA	1927-28	Pone Kingpetch	1963	S. Hanagata* WBA	1974-75
Izzy Schwartz NY	1927-29	Hiroyuki Ebihara	1963-64	Miguel Canto* WBC	1975-79
Frankie Genaro NBA	1928-29	Pone Kingpetch	1964-65	Erbito Salavarria* WBA	1975-76
Spider Pladner NBA	1929	Salvatore Burrini	1965-66	Alfonso Lopez* WBA	1976
Frankie Genaro NBA	1929-31	H. Accavallo* WBA	1966-68	G. Espadas* WBA	1976-78
Midget Wolgast* NY	1930-35	Walter McGowan	1966	B. Gonzalez* WBA	1978-79
Young Perez NBA	1931-32	Chartchai Chionoi	1966-69	Chan-Hee Park* WBC	1979-80
Jackie Brown NBA	1932-35	Efren Torres	1969-70	Luis Ibarra* WBA	1979-80
Benny Lynch	1935-38	Hiroyuki Ebihara* WBA	1969	Tae-Shik Kim* WBA	1980
Small Montana* NY	1935-37	B. Villacampo* WBA	1969-70	Shoji Oguma* WBC	1980-81
Peter Kane	1938-43	Chartchai Chionoi	1970	Peter Mathebula* WBA	1980-81
Little Dado* NY	1938-40	B. Chartvanchai* WBA	1970	Santos Laciar* WBA	1981
Jackie Paterson	1943-48	Masao Ohba* WBA	1970-73	Antonio Avelar* WBC	1981-82

*Champion not generally recognized. †Champion retired or relinquished title.

Flyweights *(Cont.)*

Champion	Reign
Luis Ibarra* WBA	1981
Juan Herrera* WBA	1981-82
P. Cardona* WBC	1982
Santos Laciar* WBA	1982-85
Freddie Castillo* WBC	1982
E. Mercedes* WBC	1982-83
Charlie Magri* WBC	1983
Frank Cedeno* WBC	1983-84
Soon-Chun Kwon* IBF	1983-85
Koji Kobayashi* WBC	1984
Gabriel Bernal* WBC	1984
Sot Chitalada* WBC	1984-88
Hilario Zapate* WBA	1985-87

Champion	Reign
Chong-Kwan	
Chung* IBF	1985-86
Bi-Won Chung* IBF	1986
Hi-Sup Shin* IBF	1986-87
Dodie Penalosa* IBF	1987
Fidel Bassa* WBA	1987-89
Choi-Chang Ho* IBF	1987-88
Rolando Bohol* IBF	1988
Yong-Kang Kim* WBC	1988-89
Duke McKenzie* IBF	1988-89
Sot Chitalada* WBC	1989-91
Dave McAuley* IBF	1989-92
Jesus Rojas* WBA	1989-90

Champion	Reign
Yul-Woo Lee* WBA	1990
L. Tamakuma* WBA	1990-91
M. Kittikasem* WBC	1991-92
Yuri Arbachakov* WBC	1992-
Yong Kang Kim* WBA	1991-92
Rodolfo Blanco* IBF	1992-93
P. Sithbangprachan* IBF	1993-95
David Griman* WBA	1992-94
S. S. Ploenchit* WBA	1994-
Francisco Tejedor* IBF	1995
Danny Romero* IBF	1995-96
Mark Johnson* IBF	1996-

Junior Flyweights
(Weight Limit: 108 pounds)

Champion	Reign
Franco Udella* WBC	1975
Jaime Rios* WBA	1975-76
Luis Estaba* WBC	1975-78
Juan Guzman* WBA	1976
Yoko Gushiken* WBA	1976-81
Freddy Castillo* WBC	1978
Netrnoi Vorasingh* WBC	1978
Sung-Jun Kim* WBC	1978-80
Shigeo Nakajima* WBC	1980
Hilario Zapata* WBC	1980-82
Pedro Flores* WBA	1981
Hwan-Jin Kim* WBA	1981
Katsuo Tokashiki* WBA	1981-83
Amado Urzua* WBC	1982
Tadashi Tomori* WBC	1982

Champion	Reign
Hilario Zapata* WBC	1982-83
Jung-Koo Chang* WBC	1983-88
Lupe Madera* WBA	1983-84
Dodie Penalosa* IBF	1983-86
Francisco Quiroz* WBA	1984-85
Joey Olivo* WBA	1985
Myung-Woo Yuh* WBA	1985-91
Jum-Hwan Choi* IBF	1986-88
Tacy Macalos* IBF	1988-89
German Torres* WBC	1988-89
Yul-Woo Lee* WBC	1989
Muangchai	
Kittikasem* IBF	1989-90
Humberto	
Gonzalez* WBC	1989-90

Champion	Reign
Michael Carbajal* IBF	1990-94
R. Pascua* WBC	1990
M. C. Castro* WBC	1991
H. Gonzalez* WBC	1991-93
Hirokia Ioka* WBA	1991-92
Michael Carbajal, WBC	1993-94
Myung-Woo Yuh* WBA	1993
Leo Gamez* WBA	1993-95
H. Gonzalez* WBC, IBF	1994-95
Choi Hi-Yong* WBA	1995-96
S. Sor Jaturong* WBC, IBF	1995-96
Carlos Murillo* WBA	1996
Keiji Yamaguchi* WBA	1996-
Michael Carbajal* IBF	1996-
S. Sor Jaturong* WBC	1995-

Strawweights
(Weight Limit: 105 pounds)

Champion	Reign
Franco Udella* WBC	1975
Jaime Rios* WBA	1975-76
Luis Estaba* WBC	1975-78
Juan Guzman* WBA	1976
Yoko Gushiken* WBA	1976-81
Freddy Castillo* WBC	1978
Netrnoi Vorasingh* WBC	1978
Sung-Jun Kim* WBC	1978-80
Shigeo Nakajima* WBC	1980
Hilario Zapata* WBC	1980-82
Pedro Flores* WBA	1981
Hwan-Jin Kim* WBA	1981

Champion	Reign
Katsuo Tokashiki* WBA	1981-83
Amado Urzua* WBC	1982
Tadashi Tomori* WBC	1982
Hilario Zapata* WBC	1982-83
Jung-Koo Chang* WBC	1983-88
Lupe Madera* WBA	1983-84
Dodie Penalosa* IBF	1983-86
Francisco Quiroz* WBA	1984-85
Joey Olivo* WBA	1985
Myung-Woo Yuh* WBA	1985-93
Jum-Hwan Choi* IBF	1986-88
Tacy Macalos* IBF	1988-89

Champion	Reign
German Torres* WBC	1988-89
Yul-Woo Lee* WBC	1989
M. Kittikasem* IBF	1989-90
H. Gonzalez* WBC	1989-90
Michael Carbajal* IBF	1990
Rolando Pascua* WBC	1990
M. C. Castro* WBC	1991
Ricardo Lopez* WBC	1990-
R. S. Voraphin* IBF	1992-
Chana Porpaoin* WBA	1993-95
Rosendo Alvarez* WBA	1995-

*Champion not generally recognized.

Alltime Career Leaders
Total Bouts

Name	Years Active	Bouts	Name	Years Active	Bouts
Len Wickwar	1928-47	463	Maxie Rosenbloom	1923-39	299
Jack Britton	1905-30	350	Harry Greb	1913-26	298
Johnny Dundee	1910-32	333	Young Stribling	1921-33	286
Billy Bird	1920-48	318	Battling Levinsky	1910-29	282
George Marsden	1928-46	311	Ted (Kid) Lewis	1909-29	279

Note: Based on records in *The Ring Record Book* and *Boxing Encyclopedia.*

Most Knockouts

Name	Years Active	KOs	Name	Years Active	KOs
Archie Moore	1936-63	130	Sandy Saddler	1944-56	103
Young Stribling	1921-33	126	Sam Langford	1902-26	102
Billy Bird	1920-48	125	Henry Armstrong	1931-45	100
George Odwell	1930-45	114	Jimmy Wilde	1911-23	98
Sugar Ray Robinson	1940-65	110	Len Wickwar	1928-47	93

Note: Based on records in *The Ring Record Book* and *Boxing Encyclopedia*.

World Heavyweight Championship Fights

Date	Winner	Wgt	Loser	Wgt	Result	Site
Sept 7, 1892	James J. Corbett*	178	John L. Sullivan	212	KO 21	New Orleans
Jan 25, 1894	James J. Corbett	184	Charley Mitchell	158	KO 3	Jacksonville, FL
Mar 17, 1897	Bob Fitzsimmons*	167	James J. Corbett	183	KO 14	Carson City, NV
June 9, 1899	James J. Jeffries*	206	Bob Fitzsimmons	167	KO 11	Coney Island, NY
Nov 3, 1899	James J. Jeffries	215	Tom Sharkey	183	Ref 25	Coney Island, NY
Apr 6, 1900	James J. Jeffries	n/a	Jack Finnegan	n/a	KO 1	Detroit
May 11, 1900	James J. Jeffries	218	James J. Corbett	188	KO 23	Coney Island, NY
Nov 15, 1901	James J. Jeffries	211	Gus Ruhlin	194	TKO 6	San Francisco
July 25, 1902	James J. Jeffries	219	Bob Fitzsimmons	172	KO 8	San Francisco
Aug 14, 1903	James J. Jeffries	220	James J. Corbett	190	KO 10	San Francisco
Aug 25, 1904	James J. Jeffries	219	Jack Munroe	186	TKO 2	San Francisco
July 3, 1905	Marvin Hart*	190	Jack Root	171	KO 12	Reno
Feb 23, 1906	Tommy Burns*	180	Marvin Hart	188	Ref 20	Los Angeles
Oct 2, 1906	Tommy Burns	n/a	Jim Flynn	n/a	KO 15	Los Angeles
Nov 28, 1906	Tommy Burns	172	Jack O'Brien	163½	Draw 20	Los Angeles
May 8, 1907	Tommy Burns	180	Jack O'Brien	167	Ref 20	Los Angeles
Jul 4, 1907	Tommy Burns	181	Bill Squires	180	KO 1	Colma, CA
Dec 2, 1907	Tommy Burns	177	Gunner Moir	204	KO 10	London
Feb 10, 1908	Tommy Burns	n/a	Jack Palmer	n/a	KO 4	London
Mar 17, 1908	Tommy Burns	n/a	Jem Roche	n/a	KO 1	Dublin
Apr 18, 1908	Tommy Burns	n/a	Jewey Smith	n/a	KO 5	Paris
June 13, 1908	Tommy Burns	184	Bill Squires	183	KO 8	Paris
Aug 24, 1908	Tommy Burns	181	Bill Squires	184	KO 13	Sydney
Sept 2, 1908	Tommy Burns	183	Bill Lang	187	KO 6	Melbourne
Dec 26, 1908	Jack Johnson*	192	Tommy Burns	168	TKO 14	Sydney
Mar 10, 1909	Jack Johnson	n/a	Victor McLaglen	n/a	ND 6	Vancouver
May 19, 1909	Jack Johnson	205	Jack O'Brien	161	ND 6	Philadelphia
June 30, 1909	Jack Johnson	207	Tony Ross	214	ND 6	Pittsburgh
Sept 9, 1909	Jack Johnson	209	Al Kaufman	191	ND 10	San Francisco
Oct 16, 1909	Jack Johnson	205½	Stanley Ketchel	170¼	KO 12	Colma, CA
July 4, 1910	Jack Johnson	208	James J. Jeffries	227	KO 15	Reno
July 4, 1912	Jack Johnson	195½	Jim Flynn	175	TKO 9	Las Vegas
Dec 19, 1913	Jack Johnson	n/a	Jim Johnson	n/a	Draw 10	Paris
June 27, 1914	Jack Johnson	221	Frank Moran	203	Ref 20	Paris
Apr 5, 1915	Jess Willard*	230	Jack Johnson	205½	KO 26	Havana
Mar 25, 1916	Jess Willard	225	Frank Moran	203	ND 10	New York City
July 4, 1919	Jack Dempsey*	187	Jess Willard	245	TKO 4	Toledo, OH
Sept 6, 1920	Jack Dempsey	185	Billy Miske	187	KO 3	Benton Harbor, MI
Dec 14, 1920	Jack Dempsey	188¼	Bill Brennan	197	KO 12	New York City
July 2, 1921	Jack Dempsey	188	Georges Carpentier	172	KO 4	Jersey City
July 4, 1923	Jack Dempsey	188	Tommy Givvons	175½	Ref 15	Shelby, MT
Sept 14, 1923	Jack Dempsey	192½	Luis Firpo	216½	KO 2	New York City
Sept 23, 1926	Gene Tunney*	189½	Jack Dempsey	190	UD 10	Philadelphia
Sept 22, 1927	Gene Tunney	189½	Jack Dempsey	192½	UD 10	Chicago
July 26, 1928	Gene Tunney	192	Tom Heeney	203½	TKO 11	New York City
June 12, 1930	Max Schmeling*	188	Jack Sharkey	197	Foul 4	New York City
July 3, 1931	Max Schmeling	189	Young Stribling	186½	TKO 15	Cleveland
June 21, 1932	Jack Sharkey*	205	Max Schmeling	188	Split 15	Long Island City
June 29, 1933	Primo Carnera*	260½	Jack Sharkey	201	KO 6	Long Island City
Oct 22, 1933	Primo Carnera	259½	Paulino Uzcudun	229¼	UD 15	Rome
Mar 1, 1934	Primo Carnera	270	Tommy Loughran	184	UD 15	Miami
June 14, 1934	Max Baer*	209½	Primo Carnera	263¼	TKO 11	Long Island City
June 13, 1935	James J. Braddock*	193¾	Max Baer	209½	UD 15	Long Island City
June 22, 1937	Joe Louis	197¼	James J. Braddock	197	KO 8	Chicago
Aug 30, 1937	Joe Louis	197	Tommy Farr	204¼	UD 15	New York City
Feb 23, 1938	Joe Louis	200	Nathan Mann	193½	KO 3	New York City

Date	Winner	Wgt	Loser	Wgt	Result	Site
Apr 1, 1938	Joe Louis	202½	Harry Thomas	196	KO 5	Chicago
June 22, 1938	Joe Louis	198¼	Max Schmeling	193	KO 1	New York City
Jan 25, 1939	Joe Louis	200¼	John Henry Lewis	180¾	KO 1	New York City
Apr 17, 1939	Joe Louis	201¼	Jack Roper	204¾	KO 1	Los Angeles
June 28, 1939	Joe Louis	200¾	Tony Galento	233¾	TKO 4	New York City
Sept 20, 1939	Joe Louis	200	Bob Pastor	183	KO 11	Detroit
Feb 9, 1940	Joe Louis	203	Arturo Godoy	202	Split 15	New York City
Mar 29, 1940	Joe Louis	201½	Johnny Paychek	187½	KO 2	New York City
June 20, 1940	Joe Louis	199	Arturo Godoy	201¼	TKO 8	New York City
Dec 16, 1940	Joe Louis	202¼	Al McCoy	180¾	TKO 6	Boston
Jan 31, 1941	Joe Louis	202½	Red Burman	188	KO 5	New York City
Feb 17, 1941	Joe Louis	203½	Gus Dorazio	193½	KO 2	Philadelphia
Mar 21, 1941	Joe Louis	202	Abe Simon	254½	TKO 13	Detroit
Apr 8, 1941	Joe Louis	203½	Tony Musto	199½	TKO 9	St Louis
May 23, 1941	Joe Louis	201½	Buddy Baer	237½	Disq 7	Washington, DC
June 18, 1941	Joe Louis	199½	Billy Conn	174	KO 13	New York City
Sept 29, 1941	Joe Louis	202¼	Lou Nova	202½	TKO 6	New York City
Jan 9, 1942	Joe Louis	206¾	Buddy Baer	250	KO 1	New York City
Mar 27, 1942	Joe Louis	207½	Abe Simon	255½	KO 6	New York City
June 9, 1946	Joe Louis	207	Billy Conn	187	KO 8	New York City
Sept 18, 1946	Joe Louis	211	Tami Mauriello	198½	KO 1	New York City
Dec 5, 1947	Joe Louis	211½	Jersey Joe Walcott	194½	Split 15	New York City
June 25, 1948	Joe Louis	213½	Jersey Joe Walcott	194¾	KO 11	New York City
June 22, 1949	Ezzard Charles*	181¾	Jersey Joe Walcott	195½	UD 15	Chicago
Aug 10, 1949	Ezzard Charles	180	Gus Lesnevich	182	TKO 8	New York City
Oct 14, 1949	Ezzard Charles	182	Pat Valentino	188½	KO 8	San Francisco
Aug 15, 1950	Ezzard Charles	183¼	Freddie Beshore	184½	TKO 14	Buffalo
Sept 27, 1950	Ezzard Charles	184½	Joe Louis	218	UD 15	New York City
Dec 5, 1950	Ezzard Charles	185	Nick Barone	178½	KO 11	Cincinnati
Jan 12, 1951	Ezzard Charles	185	Lee Oma	193	TKO 10	New York City
Mar 7, 1951	Ezzard Charles	186	Jersey Joe Walcott	193	UD 15	Detroit
May 30, 1951	Ezzard Charles	182	Joey Maxim	181½	UD 15	Chicago
July 18, 1951	Jersey Joe Walcott*	194	Ezzard Charles	182	KO 7	Pittsburgh
June 5, 1952	Jersey Joe Walcott	196	Ezzard Charles	191½	UD 15	Philadelphia
Sept 23, 1952	Rocky Marciano*	184	Jersey Joe Walcott	196	KO 13	Philadelphia
May 15, 1953	Rocky Marciano	184½	Jersey Joe Walcott	197¾	KO 1	Chicago
Sept 24, 1953	Rocky Marciano	185	Roland LaStarza	184¾	TKO 11	New York City
June 17, 1954	Rocky Marciano	187½	Ezzard Charles	185½	UD 15	New York City
Sept 17, 1954	Rocky Marciano	187	Ezzard Charles	192½	KO 8	New York City
May 16, 1955	Rocky Marciano	189	Don Cockell	205	TKO 9	San Francisco
Sept 21, 1955	Rocky Marciano	188¼	Archie Moore	188	KO 9	New York City
Nov 30, 1956	Floyd Patterson*	182¼	Archie Moore	187¾	KO 5	Chicago
July 29, 1957	Floyd Patterson	184	Tommy Jackson	192½	TKO 10	New York City
Aug 22, 1957	Floyd Patterson	187¼	Pete Rademacher	202	KO 6	Seattle
Aug 18, 1958	Floyd Patterson	184½	Roy Harris	194	TKO 13	Los Angeles
May 1, 1959	Floyd Patterson	182½	Brian London	206	KO 11	Indianapolis
June 26, 1959	Ingemar Johansson*	196	Floyd Patterson	182	TKO 3	New York City
June 20, 1960	Floyd Patterson*	190	Ingemar Johansson	194¾	KO 5	New York City
Mar 13, 1961	Floyd Patterson	194¾	Ingemar Johansson	206½	KO 6	Miami Beach
Dec 4, 1961	Floyd Patterson	188½	Tom McNeeley	197	KO 4	Toronto
Sept 25, 1962	Sonny Liston*	214	Floyd Patterson	189	KO 1	Chicago
July 22, 1963	Sonny Liston	215	Floyd Patterson	194½	KO 1	Las Vegas
Feb 25, 1964	Cassius Clay*	210½	Sonny Liston	218	TKO 7	Miami Beach
Mar 5, 1965	Ernie Terrell WBA*	199	Eddie Machen	192	UD 15	Chicago
May 25, 1965	Muhammad Ali	206	Sonny Liston	215¼	KO 1	Lewiston, ME
Nov 1, 1965	Ernie Terrell WBA*	206	George Chuvalo	209	UD 15	Toronto
Nov 22, 1965	Muhammad Ali	210	Floyd Patterson	196¾	TKO 12	Las Vegas
Mar 29, 1966	Muhammad Ali	214½	George Chuvalo	216	UD 15	Toronto
May 21, 1966	Muhammad Ali	201½	Henry Cooper	188	TKO 6	London
June 28, 1966	Ernie Terrell WBA*	209½	Doug Jones	187½	UD 15	Houston
Aug 6, 1966	Muhammad Ali	209½	Brian London	201½	KO 3	London
Sept 10, 1966	Muhammad Ali	203½	Karl Mildenberger	194¼	TKO 12	Frankfurt
Nov 14, 1966	Muhammad Ali	212¾	Cleveland Williams	210½	TKO 3	Houston
Feb 6, 1967	Muhammad Ali	212¼	Ernie Terrell WBA	212½	UD 15	Houston
Mar 22, 1967	Muhammad Ali	211½	Zora Folley	202½	KO 7	New York City
Mar 4, 1968	Joe Frazier*	204½	Buster Mathis	243½	TKO 11	New York City
Apr 27, 1968	Jimmy Ellis*	197	Jerry Quarry	195	Maj 15	Oakland
June 24, 1968	Joe Frazier NY*	203½	Manuel Ramos	208	TKO 2	New York City

World Heavyweight Championship Fights *(Cont.)*

Date	Winner	Wgt	Loser	Wgt	Result	Site
Aug 14, 1968	Jimmy Ellis WBA*	198	Floyd Patterson	188	Ref 15	Stockholm
Dec 10, 1968	Joe Frazier NY*	203	Oscar Bonavena	207	UD 15	Philadelphia
Apr 22, 1969	Joe Frazier NY*	204½	Dave Zyglewicz	190½	KO 1	Houston
June 23, 1969	Joe Frazier NY*	203½	Jerry Quarry	198½	TKO 8	New York City
Feb 16, 1970	Joe Frazier NY*	205	Jimmy Ellis WBA	201	TKO 5	New York City
Nov 18, 1970	Joe Frazier*	209	Bob Foster	188	KO 2	Detroit
Mar 8, 1971	Joe Frazier*	205½	Muhammad Ali	215	UD 15	New York City
Jan 15, 1972	Joe Frazier	215½	Terry Daniels	195	TKO 4	New Orleans
May 26, 1972	Joe Frazier	217½	Ron Stander	218	TKO 5	Omaha
Jan 22, 1973	George Foreman*	217½	Joe Frazier	214	TKO 2	Kingston, Jam.
Sept 1, 1973	George Foreman	219½	Jose Roman	196½	KO 1	Tokyo
Mar 26, 1974	George Foreman	224¼	Ken Norton	212¾	TKO 2	Caracas
Oct 30, 1974	Muhammad Ali*	216-½	George Foreman	220	KO 8	Kinshasa, Zaire
Mar 24, 1975	Muhammad Ali	223½	Chuck Wepner	225	TKO 15	Cleveland
May 16, 1975	Muhammad Ali	224½	Ron Lyle	219	TKO 11	Las Vegas
July 1, 1975	Muhammad Ali	224½	Joe Bugner	230	UD 15	Kuala Lumpur, Malaysia
Oct 1, 1975	Muhammad Ali	224½	Joe Frazier	215	TKO 15	Manila
Feb 20, 1976	Muhammad Ali	226	Jean Pierre Coopman	206	KO 5	San Juan
Apr 30, 1976	Muhammad Ali	230	Jimmy Young	209	UD 15	Landover, MD
May 24, 1976	Muhammad Ali	230	Richard Dunn	206½	TKO 5	Munich
Sept 28, 1976	Muhammad Ali	221	Ken Norton	217½	UD 15	New York City
May 16, 1977	Muhammad Ali	221¼	Alfredo Evangelista	209¼	UD 15	Landover, MD
Sept 29, 1977	Muhammad Ali	225	Earnie Shavers	211¼	UD 15	New York City
Feb 15, 1978	Leon Spinks*	197¼	Muhammad Ali	224¼	Split 15	Las Vegas
June 9, 1978	Larry Holmes*	209	Ken Norton WBC	220	Split 15	Las Vegas
Sept 15, 1978	Muhammad Ali*	221	Leon Spinks	201	UD 15	New Orleans
Nov 10, 1978	Larry Holmes WBC*	214	Alfredo Evangelista	208¼	KO 7	Las Vegas
Mar 23, 1979	Larry Holmes WBC*	214	Osvaldo Ocasio	207	TKO 7	Las Vegas
June 22, 1979	Larry Holmes WBC*	215	Mike Weaver	202	TKO 12	New York City
Sept 28, 1979	Larry Holmes WBC*	210	Earnie Shavers	211	TKO 11	Las Vegas
Oct 20, 1979	John Tate*	240	Gerrie Coetzee	222	UD 15	Pretoria
Feb 3, 1980	Larry Holmes WBC*	213½	Lorenzo Zanon	215	TKO 6	Las Vegas
Mar 31, 1980	Mike Weaver*	232	John Tate WBA	232	KO 15	Knoxville
Mar 31, 1980	Larry Holmes WBC*	211	Leroy Jones	254½	TKO 8	Las Vegas
July 7, 1980	Larry Holmes WBC*	214¼	Scott LeDoux	226	TKO 7	Minneapolis
Oct 2, 1980	Larry Holmes WBC*	211¼	Muhammad Ali	217½	TKO 11	Las Vegas
Oct 25, 1980	Mike Weaver WBA*	210	Gerrie Coetzee	226½	KO 13	Sun City, S.A.
Apr 11, 1981	Larry Holmes	215	Trevor Berbick	215½	UD 15	Las Vegas
June 12, 1981	Larry Holmes	212¼	Leon Spinks	200¼	TKO 3	Detroit
Oct 3, 1981	Mike Weaver WBA*	215	James Quick Tillis	209	UD 15	Rosemont, IL
Nov 6, 1981	Larry Holmes	213¼	Renaldo Snipes	215¾	TKO 11	Pittsburgh
June 11, 1982	Larry Holmes	212½	Gerry Cooney	225½	TKO 13	Las Vegas
Nov 26, 1982	Larry Holmes	217½	Tex Cobb	234¼	UD 15	Houston
Dec 10, 1982	Michael Dokes*	216	Mike Weaver WBA	209¾	TKO 1	Las Vegas
Mar 27, 1983	Larry Holmes	221	Lucien Rodriguez	209	UD 12	Scranton, PA
May 20, 1983	Michael Dokes WBA*	223	Mike Weaver	218½	Draw 15	Las Vegas
May 20, 1983	Larry Holmes	213	Tim Witherspoon	219½	Split 12	Las Vegas
Sept 10, 1983	Larry Holmes	223	Scott Frank	211¼	TKO 5	Atlantic City
Sept 23, 1983	Gerrie Coetzee*	215	Michael Dokes WBA	217	KO 10	Richfield, OH
Nov 25, 1983	Larry Holmes	219	Marvis Frazier	200	TKO 1	Las Vegas
Mar 9, 1984	Tim Witherspoon	220¼	Greg Page	239½	Maj 12	Las Vegas
Aug 31, 1984	Pinklon Thomas*	216	Tim Witherspoon WBC	217	Maj 12	Las Vegas
Nov 9, 1984	Larry Holmes IBF	221½	James Smith	227	TKO 12	Las Vegas
Dec 1, 1984	Greg Page*	236½	Gerrie Coetzee WBA	218	KO 8	Sun City, S.A.
Mar 15, 1985	Larry Holmes	223½	David Bey	233¼	TKO 10	Las Vegas
Apr 29, 1985	Tony Tubbs*	229	Greg Page WBA	239½	UD 15	Buffalo
May 20, 1985	Larry Holmes	224¼	Carl Williams	215	UD 15	Las Vegas
June 15, 1985	Pinklon Thomas*	220¼	Mike Weaver	221¼	KO 8	Las Vegas
Sept 21, 1985	Michael Spinks*	200	Larry Holmes IBF	221½	UD 15	Las Vegas
Jan 17, 1986	Tim Witherspoon	227	Tony Tubbs WBA	229	Maj 15	Atlanta
Mar 22, 1986	Trevor Berbick*	218½	Pinklon Thomas WBC	222¾	UD 15	Las Vegas
Apr 19, 1986	Michael Spinks	205	Larry Holmes	223	Split 15	Las Vegas
July 19, 1986	Tim Witherspoon*	234¾	Frank Bruno	228	TKO 11	Wembley, Eng.
Sept 6, 1986	Michael Spinks	201	Steffen Tangstad	214¾	TKO 4	Las Vegas
Nov 22, 1986	Mike Tyson*	221¼	Trevor Berbick WBC	218½	TKO 2	Las Vegas
Dec 12, 1986	James Smith*	228½	Tim Witherspoon WBA	233½	TKO 1	New York City
Mar 7, 1987	Mike Tyson WBC*	219	James Smith WBA	233	UD 12	Las Vegas

World Heavyweight Championship Fights *(Cont.)*

Date	Winner	Wgt	Loser	Wgt	Result	Site
May 30, 1987	Mike Tyson*	218¾	Pinklon Thomas	217¾	TKO 6	Las Vegas
May 30, 1987	Tony Tucker	222¼	Buster Douglas	227¼	TKO 10	Las Vegas
June 15, 1987	Michael Spinks	208¾	Gerry Cooney	238	TKO 5	Atlantic City
Aug 1, 1987	Mike Tyson*	221	Tony Tucker IBF	221	UD 12	Las Vegas
Oct 16, 1987	Mike Tyson*	216	Tyrell Biggs	228¾	TKO 7	Atlantic City
Jan 22, 1988	Mike Tyson*	215¾	Larry Holmes	225¾	TKO 4	Atlantic City
Mar 20, 1988	Mike Tyson*	216¼	Tony Tubbs	238¼	KO 2	Tokyo
June 27, 1988	Mike Tyson*	218¼	Michael Spinks	212¼	KO 1	Atlantic City
Feb 25, 1989	Mike Tyson	218	Frank Bruno	228	TKO 5	Las Vegas
July 21, 1989	Mike Tyson	219¼	Carl Williams	218	TKO 1	Atlantic City
Feb 10, 1990	Buster Douglas*	231½	Mike Tyson	220½	KO 10	Tokyo
Oct 25, 1990	Evander Holyfield	208	Buster Douglas	246	KO 3	Las Vegas
Apr 19, 1991	Evander Holyfield	212	George Foreman	257	UD 12	Atlantic City
Nov 23, 1991	Evander Holyfield	210	Bert Cooper	215	TKO 7	Atlanta
June 19, 1992	Evander Holyfield	210	Larry Holmes	233	UD 12	Las Vegas
Nov 13, 1992	Riddick Bowe	235	Evander Holyfield	205	UD 12	Las Vegas
Feb 6, 1993	Riddick Bowe	243	Michael Dokes	244	KO 1	New York City
May 8, 1993	Lennox Lewis	235	Tony Tucker	235	UD 12	Las Vegas
May 22, 1993	Riddick Bowe	244	Jesse Ferguson	224	KO 2	Washington, DC
Oct 2, 1993	Lennox Lewis	229	Frank Bruno	233	KO 7	London
Nov 6, 1993	Evander Holyfield	217	Riddick Bowe	246	Split 12	Las Vegas
Apr 22, 1994	Michael Moorer	214	Evander Holyfield	214	Split 12	Las Vegas
May 6, 1994	Lennox Lewis	235	Phil Jackson	218	TKO 8	Atlantic City
Nov 6, 1994	George Foreman	250	Michael Moorer	222	KO 10	Las Vegas
Mar 11, 1995	Riddick Bowe	241	Herbie Hide	214	KO 6	Las Vegas
Apr 8, 1995	Oliver McCall	231	Larry Holmes	236	UD 12	Las Vegas
Apr 8, 1995	Bruce Seldon	236	Tony Tucker	243	TKO 7	Las Vegas
Apr 22, 1995	George Foreman	256	Axel Schulz	221	Split 12	Las Vegas
Jun 17, 1995	Riddick Bowe	243	Jorge Luis Gonzalez	237	KO 6	Las Vegas
Aug 19, 1995	Bruce Seldon	234	Joe Hipp	233	TKO 10	Las Vegas
Sept 2, 1995	Frank Bruno	247¾	Oliver McCall	234¾	UD 12	London
Dec 9, 1995	Frans Botha	237	Axel Shulz	223	Split 12	Stuttgart
Mar 16, 1996	Mike Tyson	220	Frank Bruno	247	TKO 3	Las Vegas
June 22, 1996	Michael Moorer	222¼	Axel Shulz	222¾	Split 12	Dortmund, Ger.
Sept 7, 1996	Mike Tyson	219	Bruce Seldon	229	TKO 1	Las Vegas

*Champion not generally recognized. KO=knockout; TKO=technical knockout; UD=unanimous decision; Split=split decision; Ref=referee's decision; Disq=disqualification; ND=no decision.

Ring Magazine Fighter and Fight of the Year

Year	Fighter
1928	Gene Tunney
1929	Tommy Loughran
1930	Max Schmeling
1932	Jack Sharkey
1933	No award
1934	T. Canzoneri/B. Ross
1935	Barney Ross
1936	Joe Louis
1937	Henry Armstrong
1938	Joe Louis
1939	Joe Louis
1940	Billy Conn
1941	Joe Louis
1942	Ray Robinson
1943	Fred Apostoli
1944	Beau Jack

Note: No fight of the year named until 1945

Year	Fighter	Fight	Winner	Site
1945	Willie Pep	Rocky Graziano-Freddie Cochrane	Rocky Graziano	New York City
1946	Tony Zale	Tony Zale-Rocky Graziano	Tony Zale	New York City
1947	Gus Lesnevich	Rocky Graziano-Tony Zale	Rocky Graziano	Chicago
1948	Ike Williams	Marcel Cerdan-Tony Zale	Marcel Cerdan	Jersey City
1949	Ezzard Charles	Willie Pep-Sandy Saddler	Willie Pep	New York City
1950	Ezzard Charles	Jake LaMotta-Laurent Dauthuille	Jake LaMotta	Detroit
1951	Ray Robinson	Jersey Joe Walcott-Ezzard Charles	Jersey Joe Walcott	Pittsburgh
1952	Rocky Marciano	Rocky Marciano-Jersey Joe Walcott	Rocky Marciano	Philadelphia
1953	Carl Olson	Rocky Marciano-Roland LaStarza	Rocky Marciano	New York City
1954	Rocky Marciano	Rocky Marciano-Ezzard Charles	Rocky Marciano	New York City
1955	Rocky Marciano	Carmen Basilio-Tony DeMarco	Carmen Basilio	Boston
1956	Floyd Patterson	Carmen Basilio-Johnny Saxton	Carmen Basilio	Syracuse
1957	Carmen Basilio	Carmen Basilio-Ray Robinson	Carmen Basilio	New York City
1958	Ingemar Johansson	Ray Robinson-Carmen Basilio	Ray Robinson	Chicago
1959	Ingemar Johansson	Gene Fullmer-Carmen Basilio	Gene Fullmer	San Francisco
1960	Floyd Patterson	Floyd Patterson-Ingemar Johansson	Floyd Patterson	New York City
1961	Joe Brown	Joe Brown-Dave Charnley	Joe Brown	London
1962	Dick Tiger	Joey Giardello-Henry Hank	Joey Giardello	Philadelphia
1963	Cassius Clay	Cassius Clay-Doug Jones	Cassius Clay	New York City

Year	Fighter	Fight	Winner	Site
1964	Emile Griffith	Cassius Clay-Sonny Liston	Cassius Clay	Miami Beach
1965	Dick Tiger	Floyd Patterson-George Chuvalo	Floyd Patterson	New York City
1966	No award	Jose Torres-Eddie Cotton	Jose Torres	Las Vegas
1967	Joe Frazier	Nino Benvenuti-Emile Griffith	Nino Benvenuti	New York City
1968	Nino Benvenuti	Dick Tiger-Frank DePaula	Dick Tiger	New York City
1969	Jose Napoles	Joe Frazier-Jerry Quarry	Joe Frazier	New York City
1970	Joe Frazier	Carlos Monzon-Nino Benvenuti	Carlos Monzon	Rome
1971	Joe Frazier	Joe Frazier-Muhammad Ali	Joe Frazier	New York City
1972	Muhammad Ali Carlos Monzon	Bob Foster-Chris Finnegan	Bob Foster	London
1973	George Foreman	George Foreman-Joe Frazier	George Foreman	Kingston, Jam.
1974	Muhammad Ali	Muhammad Ali-George Foreman	Muhammad Ali	Kinshasa, Zaire
1975	Muhammad Ali	Muhammad Ali-Joe Frazier	Muhammad Ali	Manila
1976	George Foreman	George Foreman-Ron Lyle	George Foreman	Las Vegas
1977	Carlos Zarate	Joe Young-George Foreman	Joe Young	San Juan
1978	Muhammad Ali	Leon Spinks-Muhammad Ali	Leon Spinks	Las Vegas
1979	Ray Leonard	Danny Lopez-Tony Ayala	Danny Lopez	San Antonio
1980	Thomas Hearns	Saad Muhammad-Danny Lopez	Saad Muhammad	McAfee, NJ
1981	Ray Leonard Salvador Sanchez	Ray Leonard-Tonny Hearns	Ray Leonard	Las Vegas
1982	Larry Holmes	Bobby Chacon-Rafael Limon	Bobby Chacon	Sacramento
1983	Marvin Hagler	Bobby Chacon-Cornelius Boza-Edwards	Bobby Chacon	Las Vegas
1984	Thomas Hearns	Jose Luis Ramirez-Edwin Rosario	Jose Luis Ramirez	San Juan
1985	Donald Curry Marvin Hagler	Marvin Hagler-Tommy Hearns	Marvin Hagler	Las Vegas
1986	Mike Tyson	Stevie Cruz-Barry McGuigan	Stevie Cruz	Las Vegas
1987	Evander Holyfield	Ray Leonard-Marvin Hagler	Ray Leonard	Las Vegas
1988	Mike Tyson	Tony Lopez-Rocky Lockridge	Tony Lopez	Inglewood, CA
1989	Pernell Whitaker	Roberto Duran-Iran Barkley	Roberto Duran	Atlantic City
1990	Julio César Chávez	Julio César Chávez-Meldrick Taylor	Julio César Chávez	Las Vegas
1991	James Toney	Robert Quiroga-Kid Akeem Anifowoshe	Robert Quiroga	San Antonio
1992	Riddick Bowe	Riddick Bowe-Evander Holyfield	Riddick Bowe	Las Vegas
1993	Michael Carbajal	Michael Carbajal-Humberto Gonzalez	Michael Carbajal	Las Vegas
1994	Roy Jones	Jorge Castro-John David Jackson	Jorge Castro	Monterrey, Mex.
1995	Oscar De La Hoya	Saman Sor Jaturong-Chiquita Gonzalez	Saman Sor Jaturong	Inglewood, CA

U.S. Olympic Gold Medalists

LIGHT FLYWEIGHT

| 1984 | Paul Gonzales |

FLYWEIGHT

1904	George Finnegan
1920	Frank Di Gennara
1024	Fidel LaBarba
1952	Nathan Brooks
1976	Leo Randolph
1984	Steve McCrory

BANTAMWEIGHT

| 1904 | Oliver Kirk |
| 1988 | Kennedy McKinney |

FEATHERWEIGHT

1904	Oliver Kirk
1924	John Fields
1984	Meldrick Taylor

LIGHTWEIGHT

1904	Harry Spanger
1920	Samuel Mosberg
1968	Ronald W. Harris
1976	Howard Davis
1984	Pernell Whitaker
1992	Oscar De La Hoya

LIGHT WELTERWEIGHT

1952	Charles Adkins
1972	Ray Seales
1976	Ray Leonard
1984	Jerry Page

WELTERWEIGHT

1904	Albert Young
1932	Edward Flynn
1984	Mark Breland

LIGHT MIDDLEWEIGHT

1960	Wilbert McClure
1984	Frank Tate
1996	David Reid

MIDDLEWEIGHT

1904	Charles Mayer
1932	Carmen Bath
1952	Floyd Patterson
1960	Edward Crook
1976	Michael Spinks

LIGHT HEAVYWEIGHT

1920	Eddie Eagan
1952	Norvel Lee
1956	James Boyd
1960	Cassius Clay
1976	Leon Spinks
1988	Andrew Maynard

HEAVYWEIGHT

| 1984 | Henry Tillman |
| 1988 | Ray Mercer |

SUPER HEAVYWEIGHT

1904	Samuel Berger
1952	H. Edward Sanders
1956	T. Peter Rademacher
1964	Joe Frazier
1968	George Foreman
1984	Tyrell Biggs

Horse Racing

Sports Illustrated

Vintage Cigar

Cigar strides to victory in the $4 million Dubai World Cup

BILL FRAKES

Making History

Several horses chased greatness in 1996, but only Cigar captured it, completing a record 16-race win streak

by William F. Reed

IN A CURIOUS and historic twist, some of the most important American horse racing stories of 1996 occurred outside the country. The year's most riveting race, one for the ages, took place on March 27 in Dubai, a Persian Gulf state halfway around the world. Then on Oct. 26 in Toronto, the Breeders' Cup, Ltd., held its $11 million program outside the U.S. for the first time since its inception in 1984. These events were proof that with every passing year the racing world shrinks. Even so, many Americans still believe that world spins around the Kentucky Derby, held at Churchill Downs every year since 1875.

The Derby's 122nd edition produced one of the more intriguing—and controversial—stories in the race's history. Had you wandered past Barn 33 at Churchill Downs on the morning of Saturday, May 4, to check on the status of Unbridled's Song, you would have seen this sign outside his stall: UNBRIDLED'S SONG DOING GREAT!!!! The message was the final deception of perhaps the strangest week a Derby favorite has ever undergone.

When Unbridled's Song, a gray son of 1990 Derby winner Unbridled, arrived at Churchill Downs on Thursday, April 18, he was accompanied by enough baggage to sway the back of a normal steed. No Derby favorite had won the roses since Spectacular Bid in 1979. No winner of the Breeders' Cup Juvenile, the race last fall that catapulted Unbridled's Song into the favorite's role, had ever come back to win the Derby. No winner of the Wood Memorial, the colt's final Derby tune-up, had prevailed in Louisville since Pleasant Colony in 1981.

Whenever any of this was mentioned to Ernie Paragallo, the colt's brash young owner, he responded with a sneer or a shrug. In the fall of 1995—*before* the Breeders' Cup Juvenile—Paragallo predicted that Unbridled's Song would win the Triple Crown the following year. The colt started slowly in '96 but then destroyed a strong field in the Florida Derby to reclaim the favorite's role—and make Paragallo look prescient.

Then came his glorified workout in the Wood. After that race, as Paragallo stood on the track waiting for jockey Mike Smith to

Unbridled's Song (11) was surrounded by rumors—but no roses—at the Derby.

bring Unbridled's Song to the winner's circle, he even upped the ante.

"I don't think he's going to lose again," Paragallo said.

"Ever?" asked an incredulous turf writer.

"Ever," Paragallo said.

No such talk emitted from Jim Ryerson, who found himself caught in trainer's hell. He couldn't tell his boss to shut up, yet he also knew how tough it is to win the Derby. So Ryerson tried to keep a low profile—no easy task for the trainer of the Derby favorite—and concentrate on keeping Unbridled's Song, a high-strung sort, from coming unglued as Derby Day approached.

Alas, for the trainer, the questions about his colt's fragile psyche gave way to more serious questions about his soundness. On the Saturday before the Derby, Ryerson announced that Unbridled's Song had suffered an injury to his left front hoof in the Wood. He tried to downplay it, but it was a hard sell. When Ryerson also announced that the colt had been training with a protective "bar shoe," on the hoof, the Churchill backstretch turned into Rumor Central. By the Tuesday before the race, in fact, the

overwhelming consensus was that Unbridled's Song would have to be scratched.

But then came the miracle—or at least what was interpreted as a miracle. Early Wednesday morning, Unbridled's Song, with Smith in the saddle, went out and worked a half mile, equipped with yet another form of bar shoe, in an astonishing 46 seconds. He had risen, Lazarus-like, from the dead. After the workout Smith couldn't stop smiling. "I feel like I've already won the Derby," he said. That night, however, the colt's wildly fluctuating stock took another dive when he drew what was considered to be the worst post position in the field: No. 20, on the extreme outside. Naturally Paragallo said he wasn't worried. But Ryerson looked more and more like a man who needed about a case of Rolaids.

The media, which is starved for hard news in the days leading up to the Derby, jumped on the story with such force that Churchill Downs officials set up a podium outside Barn 33 so Ryerson could hold a state-of-the-horse address every day. That was a Derby first, as was the announcement that an Internet site had been established for Unbridled's Song on the World Wide Web. By Derby Day the site had reportedly received over 27,000 hits from 'net jockeys.

Nose to Grindstone: Bailey won the Derby's first photo finish since '59.

ished fifth. Grindstone, teamed with jockey Jerry Bailey, snatched the win away from Cavonnier in the very last stride, giving the Derby its first photo finish since 1959.

To nobody's surprise Paragallo's reaction to the race was to engage in some revisionist history regarding his colt's sizzling work on Wednesday. "He might have left his race on the track," Paragallo said. Ryerson agreed. "He was definitely quicker [in the work] than we wanted him to go," the trainer said. "Those things happen. He gets into that big stride, and a 110-pound jockey can't slow him up."

As dusk descended on Churchill Downs, the message board outside Barn 33 was updated to read, WE'LL BE BACK. But that turned out to be just a case of wishful thinking.

In the aftermath of the Derby, Bailey, the rider of both 1995 Horse of the Year Cigar and Derby-winner Grindstone, was the hottest jockey in racing. As Bailey's friendly rival, Chris McCarron, put it, "It seems that everything Jerry touches turns to gold these days." But five days after the Derby, when it was announced that Grindstone was being retired to stud because of a bone chip in his right front knee, Bailey was suddenly without a mount for the Preakness, the second jewel in the Triple Crown.

That put trainer D. Wayne Lukas, winner of a record six consecutive Triple Crown races, in a quandary. He didn't want a rival trainer to sign up Bailey, yet he knew that Bailey wouldn't agree to ride Victory Speech, the weakest of his three Preakness horses, in the Baltimore classic. So on May 10 Lukas tempted fate by naming Bailey to replace Pat Day on Prince of Thieves, which created something of an uproar. Day had won three

And then there was that message board outside the barn, set up in the vain hope of taking some of the media glare off Ryerson. The final announcement was that, for the sake of balance, Unbridled's Song would run with bar shoes on both front hooves.

The Derby betting reflected the questions that surrounded Unbridled's Song. He was made the favorite because he had the best credentials in the field, yet his final odds of 7–2—unusually high for a favorite—indicated the public's concern about the historical jinxes, the bar shoe, the post position and the colt's nerves.

Before the race Ryerson used every trick imaginable to insulate his colt from the Derby inferno. He kept him in the barn until the last possible moment, brought him to the track by an alternate post route and took him out of the prerace post parade when he bucked at the roar that greeted the ending of "My Old Kentucky Home."

Considering the unique circumstances, Unbridled's Song ran a creditable race. He broke cleanly, secured a good position near the lead heading into the first turn and was in perfect stalking position through the first six furlongs. Turning for home he had the lead. But then he veered sharply to the outside, opening a huge hole that Cavonnier drove through to take the lead in midstretch. At the wire Unbridled's Song fin-

times—twice for Lukas—in the previous 10 runnings of the Preakness. Yet Lukas is a "now" trainer, and Day hadn't done much for him lately.

But by the Sunday before the Preakness, Day and his agent, Larry (Doc) Danner, had worked out a deal with Nick Zito for Day to get the mount on Louis Quatorze, who ran only 16th in the Derby. Yet Day was strangely confident. He told Danner, "I'll wave at you from the winner's circle tomorrow." He did, too. On another Day's day at the Preakness, Pat electrified the crowd of 85,122 by sending Louis Quatorze straight to the lead and staying there, the first wire-to-wire winner since Aloma's Ruler in 1982. And get this: The winning time of 1:53⅗ for 1³⁄₁₆ mile tied the stakes record. For Day and Danner, the win was made even sweeter by the fact that Bailey finished seventh aboard Prince of Thieves.

Day's third consecutive Preakness win stopped Lukas's Triple Crown winning streak. "I'm not happy to see Wayne's streak end," said the diplomatic Day, "but I'm glad that my streak continued."

But Lukas regained the upper hand three weeks later. Editor's Note finally fulfilled his potential by outdueling Skip Away in the Belmont, giving Lukas his third consecutive win in the mile-and-a-half classic. The win also ended a nine-race losing streak for Editor's Note and secured for his owner, William T. Young, who also owned Grindstone, two legs of the 1996 Triple Crown.

The favorites going into the Aug. 24 Travers Stakes at Saratoga were Louis Quatorze, Editor's Note and Skip Away. So, naturally, the race was won by Will's Way, a late-blooming colt who had missed the Triple Crown series and was making only his sixth career start. Coming from off the pace, Will's Way outlasted Louis Quatorze in a prolonged stretch duel. Skip Away finished third. No cigar—or Cigar comparisons—for Skip Away.

The Travers winner was trained by Bond, James Bond, who playfully affixes 007 to his saddlecloths, tack boxes, water buckets and stall webbings. Had the Travers crowd included more movie fans, Will's Way probably wouldn't have gone off as the fifth choice in the six-betting-entry field. Heck, every movie fan worth his Milk Duds knows that when James Bond gets involved, strange and improbable things happen.

The fictional Bond, known for his sophistication and worldliness, would certainly have felt comfortable at the year's signature event. The race in Dubai will always be remembered as the one in which Cigar proved conclusively that he deserves to be ranked among the alltime greats.

A bay son of Palace Music, out of Solar Slew, Cigar carried a 12-race winning streak into his 6-year-old year, and everywhere he went owner Allen Paulson received plaudits from racing fans for resisting the temptation to retire him to stud in favor of continuing his chase of the game's legends.

In his first start of 1996, Cigar notched consecutive victory No. 13 in the Donn Handicap at Gulfstream Park. That put him only three victories away from tying the immortal Citation's 16-race winning streak in 1948 and 1950 (he didn't run in 1949 because of an injury), a 20th-century record for North American thoroughbreds.

After the Donn, the next objective for Paulson and trainer Bill Mott was the Santa Anita Handicap on March 2. But an abscessed hoof kept Cigar out of that race and pointing instead for the $4 million Dubai World Cup, a new event that the horse-loving Dubai oil shiekhs dreamed up to attract the world's best horses to their homeland and, in the process, to expose the international media to the finer points of their culture.

The way some racing experts saw it, the risks of going to Dubai more than outweighed the rewards. Why risk Cigar's streak—and his reputation—in a race that smelled like an ambush? Besides the lengthy trip, Cigar would have to make his first post-injury start over an unfamiliar surface (sand) and against one of the strongest international fields to be assembled outside the Breeders' Cup. But the same sort of optimism and sportsmanship that led Paulson to bring back Cigar for one more year prevailed in the Dubai decision. Cigar already had an

Despite being snubbed by Lukas, Day (6) seized his third straight Preakness.

winner's circle, the Arlington crowd gave a wild and sustained tribute to the World's Horse. During the streak Cigar had competed at nine tracks in seven states and two nations, at several distances, using tactics ranging from being on the lead to coming from off it, and on surfaces stretching from mud to sand.

And then came the end.

On Aug. 10 at Del Mar, the lovely oceanside track just north of San Diego, Cigar sought the record-breaking 17th consecutive victory. An excited crowd of 44,181 sent him off as the 1–10 favorite. But early in the race Bailey allowed himself to be drawn into a speed duel with Dramatic Gold and Siphon. The sizzling fractions were :45⅖ for a half mile, 1:09⅕ for six furlongs and 1:33⅗ for a mile. "Too fast," said Mott as he studied the teletimer.

So that set the race up perfectly for Dare and Go, a 39–1 shot who came from off the torrid pace to blow past Cigar in the stretch and take a 3½-length victory. Dare and Go was trained by Mandella, the trainer of Soul of the Matter, the horse who had run so valiantly against Cigar in Dubai.

"You can go only so fast and still have anything left," said Mott. "We became the victim of that today. The fact is, we finished second. It's all history now, and we can't do it over. A good horse won the race … but I still think Cigar ranks as one of the alltime greats."

At the Breeders' Cup in Canada, greatness was everyone's favorite topic. Some certified it, others began the quest for it. In racing, you never know. Maybe Unbridled's Song had as much talent as Cigar. But greatness in racing demands equal measures of good luck, intelligent management and the ability to find a way to win. And that will always be the same, no matter how worldly the sport becomes.

unbeaten year and a Horse of the Year title to his credit. What was there to lose at that point except a horse race?

Because of the difference in time zones, the Dubai Cup was broadcast in the morning in the U.S., and Cigar fans from coast to coast flocked into simulcasting outlets and off-track-betting parlors to see if their hero could fulfill Paulson's dreams. At the eighth pole Soul of the Matter, an American-based star owned by songwriter Burt Bacharach and trained by Richard Mandella, made a threatening move to Cigar's flank. But Cigar dug in for Bailey, fought back and prevailed by a long neck. It was such an electrifying performance that giddy trade publications upgraded Cigar's status from America's Horse to the World's Horse.

Cigar returned to the races on June 1, scoring an easy win in the Massachusetts Handicap to run his victory streak to 15, one shy of Citation's modern record. The next stop was Arlington Park outside Chicago, where track owner Richard Duchossois had dreamed up a made-for-Cigar race entitled the Citation Challenge and put up a $1.1 million purse.

The race was held on July 13, and an estimated 35,000 fans came out to see if Cigar could make history. They didn't go home disappointed. Racing five wide on both turns, Cigar surged to the lead in the turn for home and drew off to a four-length victory over Dramatic Gold. When Cigar returned to the

FOR THE RECORD·1995–1996

THOROUGHBRED RACING

The Triple Crown

122nd Kentucky Derby

May 4, 1996. Grade I, 3-year-olds; 8th race, Churchill Downs, Louisville. All 126 lbs. Distance: 1¼ miles. Stakes value: $1,169,800; Winner: $869,800; Second: $170,000; Third: $85,000; Fourth: $45,000. Track: Fast. Off: 5:34 p.m. Winner: Grindstone (Dark Bay or Brown Colt, 1993, Unbridled-Buzz My Bell by Drone); Times: 0:22⅕, 0:46, 1:10, 1:35, 2:01. Won: Driving. Breeder: Overbrook Farm.

Horse	Finish-PP	Margin	Jockey/Owner
Grindstone	1-15	nose	Jerry Bailey/William T. Young
Cavonnier	2-4	3½	Chris McCarron/Walter Family Trust
Prince of Thieves	3-10	neck	Pat Day/Peter Mitchell
Halo Sunshine	4-5	nose	Craig Perret/Henry Pabst
Unbridled's Song	5-19	3½	Mike Smith/Paraneck Stable
Editor's Note	6-17	head	Gary Stevens/Overbrook Farm
Blow Out	7-1	1½	Patrick Johnson/L. W. Heiligbrodt, R. E. Keefer, Walter New
Alyrob	8-12	1½	Corey Nakatani/Four Star Stable
Diligence	9-3	2½	Kent Desormeaux/Kinsman Stable
Victory Speech	10-2	1¼	Jose Santos/Michael Tabor and Mrs. John Magnier
Corker	11-9	2½	Cory Black/A. B. Hancock III, Bert Kinerk, Robert McNair
Skip Away	12-16	½	Shane Sellers/Carolyn H. Hine
Zarb's Magic	13-7	½	Ron Ardoin/Foxwood Plantation, Inc.
Semoran	14-6	3½	Russell Baze/Donald R. Dizney and James E. English
In Contention	15-8	2	Tony Black/Noreen Carpenito
Louis Quatorze	16-11	2½	Chris Antley/Condren, Hofmann, Cornacchia
Matty G	17-18	neck	Alex Solis/Double J. Farm
Honour and Glory	18-13	2½	Aaron Gryder/Michael Tabor
Built for Pleasure	19-14	—	John Velazquez/Thomas H. Heard Jr

121st Preakness Stakes

May 18, 1996. Grade I, 3-year-olds; 10th race, Pimlico Race Course, Baltimore. All 126 lbs. Distance: 1³⁄₁₆ miles; Stakes value: $704,800; Winner: $458,120; Second: $140,960; Third: $70,480; Fourth: $35,240. Track: Fast. Off: 5:33 p.m. Winner: Louis Quatorze (Bay Colt, 1993, Sovereign Dancer-On to Royalty by On to Glory); Times: 0:23, 0:46⅕, 1:09⅘, 1:34⅘, 1:53⅗. Won: Driving. Breeder: Georgia E Hofmann.

Horse	Finish-PP	Margin	Jockey/Owner
Louis Quatorze	1-6	3¼	Pat Day/W. J. Condren, G. E. Hofmann, J. M. Cornacchia
Skip Away	2-11	3	Shane Sellers/Carolyn H. Hine
Editor's Note	3-10	2½	Gary Stevens/Overbrook Farm
Cavonnier	4-2	neck	Chris McCarron/Walter Family Trust
Victory Speech	5-3	2	Rene Douglas/Michael Tabor and Mrs. John Magnier
In Contention	6-4	7	Alex Solis/Noreen Carpenito
Prince of Thieves	7-9	7½	Jerry Bailey/Peter Mitchell
Allied Forces	8-1	5½	Richard Migliore/Ahmed Al Tayar
Secreto de Estado	9-5	nose	Cornelio Velazquez/Robert Perez
Tour's Big Red	10-12	¾	Joe Bravo/William E. Penn
Mixed Count	11-8	8	Edgar Prado/Leonard Pearlstein
Feather Box	12-7	—	John Velazquez/Buckland Farm

128th Belmont Stakes

June 8, 1996. Grade I, 3-year-olds; 9th race, Belmont Park, Elmont, NY. All 126 lbs. Distance: 1½ miles. Stakes purse: $729,800; Winner: $437,880; Second: $145,960; Third: $80,278; Fourth: $43,788; Fifth: 21,894. Track: Fast. Off: 5:33 p.m. Winner: Editor's Note (Chestnut Colt, 1993, Forty Niner-Beware of the Cat by Caveat); Times: 0:23⅗, 46⅘, 1:10⅘, 1:35⅘, 2:02, 2:28⅘. Won: Driving. Breeder: Fawn Leap Farm.

Horse	Finish-PP	Margin	Jockey/Owner
Editor's Note	1-7	1	Rene Douglas/William T. Young
Skip Away	2-13	4	Jose Santos/Carolyn H. Hine
My Flag (121 lbs)	3-9	6	Mike Smith/Ogden Phipps
Louis Quatorze	4-12	2	Pat Day/W. J. Condren, G. E. Hofmann, J. M. Cornacchia
Prince of Thieves	5-8	8	Jerry Bailey/Peter Mitchell and Charles Grimm
Rocket Flash	6-4	1	Eddie Maple/Henryk de Kwiatkowski
Natural Selection	7-2	2	Robbie Davis/Buckram Oak Farm
Jamies First Punch	8-5	2	John Velazquez/Zimpom Stable
In Contention	9-11	16	Joe Bravo/Noreen Carpenito
Traffic Circle	10-10	6½	Jorge Chavez/C. P. Kimmel, P. J. Solondz, Candy Stables
Saratoga Dandy	11-1	neck	Robbie Davis/W. J. Condren and J. M. Cornacchia
Appealing Skier	12-8	—	Richard Migliore/New Farm

South Salem and Cavonnier did not finish.

Major Stakes Races

Late 1995

Date	Race	Track	Distance	Winner	Jockey/Trainer	Purse ($)
Oct 6	The Meadowlands Cup Handicap	Meadowlands	1⅛ miles	Peaks and Valleys	Julie Krone/ J. Day	500,000
Oct 7	Jockey Club Gold Cup	Belmont Park	1¼ miles	Cigar	Jerry Bailey/ William Mott	750,000
Oct 7	Turf Classic Invitational	Belmont Park	1½ miles	Turk Passer	John Velazquez/ F. Schulhofer	500,000
Oct 7	Moet Champagne Stakes	Belmont Park	1 1/16 miles	Maria's Mon	Robbie Davis/ R. Schosberg	500,000
Oct 7	Beldame Stakes	Belmont Park	1⅛ miles	Serena's Song	Gary Stevens/ D. Wayne Lukas	250,000
Oct 8	Spinster Stakes	Keeneland	1⅛ miles	Inside Information	Mike Smith/ C. McCaughey	300,000
Oct 8	Oak Tree Invitational	Santa Anita	1⅛ miles	Northern Spur	Chris McCarron/ Ron McAnally	300,000
Oct 17	Rothman's International	Woodbine	1½ miles	Lassigny	Pat Day/ William Mott	1,088,750
Oct 28	Breeders' Cup Classic	Belmont Park	1¼ miles	Cigar	Jerry Bailey/ William Mott	3,000,000
Oct 28	Breeders' Cup Turf	Belmont Park	1½ miles	Northern Spur	Chris McCarron/ Ron McAnally	2,000,000
Oct 28	Breeders' Cup Juvenile Fillies	Belmont Park	1 1/16 miles	My Flag	Jerry Bailey/ C. McCaughey	1,000,000
Oct 28	Breeders' Cup Sprint	Belmont Park	6 furlongs	Desert Stormer	K. Desmormeaux/ F. Lyons	1,000,000
Oct 28	Breeders' Cup Distaff	Belmont Park	1⅛ miles	Inside Information	Mike Smith/ C. McCaughey	1,000,000
Oct 28	Breeders' Cup Mile	Belmont Park	1 mile	Ridgewood Pearl	Johnnie Murtaugh/ J. Oxx	1,000,000
Oct 28	Breeders' Cup Juvenile	Belmont Park	1 1/16 miles	Unbridled's Song	Mike Smith/ J. Ryerson	1,000,000
Nov 12	Yellow Ribbon Stakes	Santa Anita	1¼ miles	Alpride	Chris McCarron/ Ron McAnally	600,000
Nov 26	Matriarch Stakes	Hollywood	1¼ miles	Duda	Jerry Bailey/ William Mott	700,000

1996 (Through September 14)

Date	Race	Track	Distance	Winner	Jockey/Trainer	Purse ($)
Feb 3	San Antonio Handicap	Santa Anita	1⅛ miles	Alphabet Soup	Chris Antley D. Hofmans	304,900
Feb 4	Strub Stakes	Santa Anita	1¼ miles	Helmsman	Chris McCarron/ W. Dollase	500,000
Feb 10	Donn Handicap	Gulfstream Park	1⅛ miles	Cigar	Jerry Bailey/ William Mott	300,000
Feb 11	La Canada Stakes	Santa Anita	1⅛ miles	Jewel Princess	Alex Solis/ W. Dollase	209,900
Feb 19	San Luis Obispo Handicap	Santa Anita	1⅛ miles	Windsharp	E. Delahoussaye/ W. Dollase	210,800
Feb 24	Fountain of Youth Stakes	Gulfstream Park	1 1/16 miles	Built for Pleasure	Gary Boulanger/ T. Heard	200,000
Mar 2	Gulfstream Park Handicap	Gulfstream Park	1¼ miles	Wekiva Springs	Jerry Bailey/ William Mott	500,000
Mar 9	Crown Royal Pan Am Handicap	Gulfstream Park	1½ miles	Celtic Arms	Mike Smith/ D. Cecil	300,000
Mar 16	Florida Derby	Gulfstream Park	1⅛ miles	Unbridled's Song	Mike Smith/ J. Ryerson	500,000
Mar 17	San Felipe Stakes	Santa Anita	1 1/16 miles	Odyle	Corey Nakatani/ J. Gonzales	252,400
Mar 17	Louisianna Derby	Fair Grounds	1 1/16 miles	Grindstone	Jerry Bailey/ D. Wayne Lukas	370,000
Mar 23	Remington Park Derby	Remington Park	1 1/16 miles	Semoran	Rudy Baze/ B. Baffert	300,000
Mar 27	Dubai World Cup	Nad Al Sheba	1¼ miles	Cigar	Jerry Bailey/ William Mott	4,000,000
Mar 30	Jim Beam Stakes	Turfway Park	1⅛ miles	Roar	Mike Smith/ C. McGaughey	600,000

1996 (Through September 14) *(Cont.)*

Date	Race	Track	Distance	Winner	Jockey/Trainer	Purse ($)
Mar 30	Gotham Stakes	Aqueduct	1 mile	Romano Gucci	Julie Krone/ R. Dutrow	201,200
Apr 6	Santa Anita Derby	Santa Anita	1⅛ miles	Cavonnier	Chris McCarron/ B. Baffert	1,000,000
Apr 6	Oaklawn Handicap	Oaklawn Park	1⅛ miles	Geri	Jerry Bailey/ William Mott	750,000
Apr 12	Apple Blossom Handicap	Oaklawn Park	1¹⁄₁₆ miles	Twice the Vice	Chris McCarron/ R. Ellis	500,000
Apr 13	Blue Grass Stakes	Keeneland	1⅛ miles	Skip Away	Shane Sellers/ H. Hine	700,000
Apr 13	Wood Memorial Stakes	Aqueduct	1⅛ miles	Unbridled's Song	Mike Smith/ J. Ryerson	500,000
Apr 13	Arkansas Derby	Oaklawn Park	1⅛ miles	Zarb's Magic	Ronald Ardoin/ B. Thomas	500,000
Apr 20	Ashland Stakes	Keeneland	1¹⁄₁₆ miles	My Flag	Jerry Bailey/ C. McGaughey	540,750
Apr 20	Santa Barbara Handicap	Santa Anita	1¼ miles	Auriette	Kent Desormeaux/ G. Jones	310,900
Apr 21	San Juan Capistrano Invitational Handicap	Santa Anita	1¾ miles	Raintrap	Alex Solis/ R. Frankel	400,000
May 3	Kentucky Oaks	Churchill Downs	1⅛ miles	Pike Place Dancer	Corey Nakatani/ J. Hollendorfer	500,000
May 4	Kentucky Derby	Churchill Downs	1¼ miles	Grindstone	Jerry Bailey/ D. Wayne Lukas	1,000,000
May 11	Pimlico Special	Pimlico	1³⁄₁₆ miles	Star Standard	Pat Day/ Nick Zito	582,000
May 11	Illinois Derby	Sportsman Park	1⅛ miles	Natural Selection	Randy Romero/ M. Moubarak	500,000
May 18	The Preakness Stakes	Pimlico	1³⁄₁₆ miles	Louis Quatorze	Pat Day/ Nick Zito	704,800
May 27	Metropolitan Handicap	Belmont Park	1 mile	Honour and Glory	John Velazquez/ D. Wayne Lukas	400,000
May 27	Hollywood Turf	Hollywood Park	1¼ miles	Sandpit	Corey Nakatani/ Richard Mandella	500,000
June 1	Massachusetts Handicap	Suffolk Downs	1⅛ miles	Cigar	Jerry Bailey/ William Mott	500,000
June 2	Californian Stakes	Hollywood Park	1⅛ miles	Tinners Way	E. Delahoussaye/ R. Frankel	248,234
June 8	Belmont Stakes	Belmont Park	1½ miles	Editor's Note	Rene Douglas/ D. Wayne Lukas	729,800
June 8	Vodafone Derby	Epsom, Eng.	1½ miles	Shaamit	Michael Hills/ W. Haggas	1,297,975
June 15	Brooklyn Handicap	Belmont Park	1⅛ miles	Wekiva Springs	Mike Smith/ William Mott	300,000
June 16	Shoemaker Breeders' Cup Mile	Hollywood Park	1 mile	Fastness	Corey Nakatani/ J. Sahadi	680,000
June 22	Caesars International Stakes	Atlantic City	1³⁄₁₆ miles	Sandpit	Corey Nakatani/ Richard Mandella	500,000
June 23	Ohio Derby	Thistledowns	1⅛ miles	Skip Away	Jose Santos/ S. Hines	300,000
June 30	Hollywood Gold Cup	Hollywood Park	1¼ miles	Siphon	David Flores/ Richard Mandella	1,000,000
July 7	Beverly Hills Handicap	Hollywood Park	1¾ miles	Different	Chris McCarron/ Ron McAnally	273,000
July 7	Queen's Plate	Woodbine	1¼ miles	Victor Cooley	Emile Ramsammy/ M. Frostad	425,800
July 13	Arlington Citation Challenge Handicap	Arlington	1⅛ miles	Cigar	Jerry Bailey/ William Mott	1,075,000
July 14	Delaware Handicap	Delaware Park	1¼ miles	Urbane	Alex Solis/ R. Bradshaw	302,400
July 20	Frank J. DeFrancis Memorial Dash Stakes	Laurel	6 furlongs	Lite the Fuse	Julie Krone/ R. Dutrow	300,000
July 21	Caesars Palace Turf Champ	Atlantic City	1⅛ miles	Talloires	Kent Desormeaux/ Richard Mandella	700,000
July 21	Swaps Stakes	Hollywood Park	1⅛ miles	Victory Speech	Jerry Bailey/ D. Wayne Lukas	500,000

1996 (Through September 14) *(Cont.)*

Date	Race	Track	Distance	Winner	Jockey/Trainer	Purse ($)
July 21 ....American Derby		Arlington Park	1³⁄₁₆ miles	Jaunatxo	Jose Diaz/ L. Roussel	300,000
Aug 3 ......Whitney Handicap		Saratoga	1⅛ miles	Mahogany Hall	Jose Santos/ J. Baker	350,000
Aug 3 ......Ramona Handicap		Del Mar	1⅛ miles	Matiara	Corey Nakatani/ Richard Mandella	313,500
Aug 4 ......Haskell Invitational Handicap		Monmouth Park	1⅛ miles	Skip Away	Jose Santos/ S. Hines	750,000
Aug 4 ......Eddie Read Handicap		Del Mar	1⅛ miles	Fastness	Corey Nakatani/ J. Sahadi	313,000
Aug 10 ....Pacific Classic Stakes		Del Mar	1¼ miles	Dare and Go	Alex Solis/ Richard Mandella	1,000,000
Aug 10 ....Sword Dancer Invitational Handicap		Saratoga	1½ miles	Broadway Flyer	Mike Smith/ William Mott	250,000
Aug 17 ....Alabama Stakes		Saratoga	1¼ miles	Yanks Music	John Velazquez/ L O'Brien	250,000
Aug 18 ....Del Mar Invitational Oaks		Del Mar	1⅛ miles	Antespend	Chris Antley/ Ron McAnally	250,000
Aug 23 ....John A. Morris Handicap		Saratoga	1¼ miles	Urbane	Alex Solis/ R. Bradshaw	300,000
Aug 24 ....Travers Stakes		Saratoga	1¼ miles	Will's Way	Jorge Chavez/ James Bond	750,000
Aug 24 ....Beverly D. Stakes		Arlington Park	1³⁄₁₆ miles	Timarida	John Murtaugh/ J. Oxx	500,000
Aug 25 ....Arlington Million		Arlington Park	1¼ miles	Mecke	Robbie Davis/ E. Tortora	1,000,000
Aug 25 ....Secretariat Stakes		Arlington Park	1¼ miles	Marlin	Shane Sellers/ D. Wayne Lukas	500,000
Aug 25 ....Philip H. Iselan Handicap		Monmouth Park	1¹⁄₁₆ miles	Smart Strike	Craig Perret/ M. Frostad	300,000
Sept 1 .....Chula Vista Handicap		Del Mar	1¾ miles	Different	Chris McCarron/ Ron McAnally	303,200
Sept 2 .....Del Mar Invitational Derby		Del Mar	1⅛ miles	Rainbow Blues	Corey Nakatani/ C. Whittingham	300,000
Sept 14 ...Woodward Stakes		Belmont Park	1⅛ miles	Cigar	Jerry Bailey/ William Mott	500,000

1995 Statistical Leaders

Horses

Horse	Starts	1st	2nd	3rd	Purses ($)	Horse	Starts	1st	2nd	3rd	Purses ($)
Cigar....................10		10	0	0	4,819,800	Northern Spur..........4		2	0	1	1,265,000
Thunder Gulch 10		7	0	1	2,644,080	Awad 15		4	3	0	1,209,851
Serena's Song 13		9	2	0	1,524,920	Inside Information....8		7	1	0	1,160,408
Sandpit 9		4	3	0	1,420,537	Ridgewood Pearl.....6		5	1	0	1,158,704
Peaks and Valleys...8		5	2	0	1,323,750	Mecke...................14		2	4	4	988,750

Jockeys

Jockey	Mounts	1st	2nd	3rd	Purses ($)	Win Pct	$ Pct*
Jerry Bailey....................1,265		287	193	144	16,308,230	.23	.49
Corey Nakatani...............1,399		304	222	202	14,919,358	.22	.52
Gary Stevens 1,018		222	154	146	14,533,404	.22	.51
Pat Day 1,148		240	233	166	11,754,611	.21	.56
Mike Smith 1,362		263	191	198	11,707,395	.19	.48
Chris McCarron 922		166	165	138	11,306,397	.18	.51
Kent Desormeaux...........1,177		236	201	167	10,839,904	.20	.51
Eddie Delahoussaye 1,097		171	173	179	9,272,306	.16	.48
Alex Solis 1,448		211	193	231	8,753,520	.15	.44
Jorge Chavez 1,393		249	189	188	8,558,462	.18	.45

*Percentage in the Money (1st, 2nd, and 3rd).

Trainers

Trainer	Starts	1st	2nd	3rd	Purses ($)	Win Pct	$ Pct*
D. Wayne Lukas	840	194	114	91	12,842,865	.23	.47
William Mott	654	161	101	84	11,781,350	.25	.53
Ron McAnally	438	68	88	67	6,511,962	.15	.51
Richard Mandella	323	70	57	50	6,066,561	.22	.55
Robert Frankel	339	80	43	52	6,006,493	.24	.52
Shug McGaughey	283	63	59	44	5,131,039	.22	.59
Jerry Hollendorfer	916	205	166	142	3,586,698	.22	.56
Gary Jones	309	53	46	50	3,351,130	.17	.48
H. Allen Jerkens	430	68	64	66	3,238,894	.16	.46
Nick Zito	354	46	58	53	3,225,750	.13	.44

*Percentage in the Money (1st, 2nd, and 3rd).

Owners

Owner	Starts	1st	2nd	3rd	Purses ($)
Allen E. Paulson	409	86	62	58	7,232,967
John Franks	1,112	196	179	150	4,501,456
Frank H. Stronach	534	96	103	76	3,932,288
Juddmonte Farms	206	50	22	33	3,724,597
Golden Eagle Farm	568	91	99	78	3,314,777
Michael Tabor	34	15	3	5	3,198,011
Robert & Beverly Lewis	171	37	15	16	3,033,790
Pin Oak Stable	113	36	25	12	2,433,155
Overbrook Farm	251	62	39	34	2,317,707
Mr & Mrs Martin Wygod	188	54	34	23	2,204,007

HARNESS RACING

Major Stakes Races

Late 1995

Date	Race	Location	Winner	Driver/Trainer	Purse ($)
Oct 20	BC Two-year-old Filly Trot	Garden State Park	Continentalvictory	Michel LaChance/ Ronald S. Gurfien	300,000
Oct 20	BC Two-year-old Colt/Gelding Pace	Garden State Park	John Street North	Jack Moiseyev/ Jeffrey N. Webster	500,000
Oct 21	BC Two-year-old Colt/Gelding Trot	Garden State Park	Armbro Officer	Steve Condren/ Robert A. McIntosh	347,800
Oct 21	BC Two-year-old Filly Pace	Garden State Park	Paige Nicole Q	John Campbell/ Charles A. Sylvester	470,300
Nov 3	BC Three-year-old Filly Trot	Woodbine	Lookout Victory	Sonny Patterson/ Per Karl Eriksson	446,900
Nov 3	BC Three-year-old Filly Pace	Woodbine	Headline Hanover	Doug Brown/ Stewart M. Firlotte	467,500
Nov 3	BC Three-year-old Colt/Gelding Trot	Woodbine	Abundance	Bill O'Donnell/ John E. Ducharme	515,625
Nov 3	BC Three-year-old Colt/Gelding Pace	Woodbine	Jenna's Beach Boy	Bill Fahy/ Joseph J. Holoway	605,500
Nov 18	Governor's Cup	Garden State Park	Live or Die	Steve Condren/ Robert A. McIntosh	600,000

Major Stakes Races (Cont.)

1996 (Through September 19)

Date	Race	Location	Winner	Driver/Trainer	Purse ($)
June 22	North America Cup	Woodbine	Arizona Jack	John Campbell/ Gary S. Machiz	1,000,000
July 6	Yonkers Trot	Yonkers	Continentalvictory	Michel LaChance/ Ronald S. Gurfein	334,700
July 13	Meadowlands Pace	Meadowlands	Hot Lead	George Brennan/ Brian K. Magie Jr	1,000,000
July 30	Peter Haughton Memorial	Meadowlands	Yankee Glide	Berndt Lindstedt/ James E. Keller	500,000
July 31	Merrie Annabelle Final	Meadowlands	Vernon Blue Chip	Michel LaChance/ Ronald S. Gurfein	350,600
Aug 3	Hambletonian	Meadowlands	Continentalvictory	Michel LaChance/ Ronald S. Gurfein	1,000,000
Aug 3	Hambletonian Oaks	Meadowlands	Moni Maker	Wally Hennessey/ William J. Andrews	300,000
Aug 9	BC Three and up TK Trot	Meadowlands	CR Kay Suzie	Rod Allen/ Charles E. Perry	500,000
Aug 9	BC Three and up Mare Pace	Meadowlands	She's A Great Lady	John Campbell/ Joseph J. Holloway	300,000
Aug 9	BC Three and up Horse/Gelding Pace	Meadowlands	Jenna's Beach Boy	Rod Allen/ Joseph J. Holloway	300,000
Aug 10	Sweetheart	Meadowlands	Stienam's Place	Jack Moiseyev/ Bruce L. Riegle	665,400
Aug 10	Woodrow Wilson	Meadowlands	Jeremys Gambit	Michel LaChance/ Noel M. Daley	800,000
Aug 10	Adios Final	Ladbroke at The Meadows	Electric Yankee	Michel LaChance/ Brendan Johnson	163,852
Aug 24	Cane Pace	Yonkers	Scoot to Power	Cat Manzi/ Jonas L. Stutaman	326,429
Aug 31	World Trotting Derby	Du Quoin	Continentalvictory	Michel LaChance/ Ronald S. Gurfein	334,700
Sept 19	Little Brown Jug	Delaware	Armbro Operative	Jack Moiseyev/ Brendan Johnson	347,020

Major Races

The Hambletonian

Ran at the Delaware County Fair, in Delaware, OH, on August 3, 1996.

Horse	Driver	PP	¼	½	¾	Stretch-Margin	Finish-Margin
Continentalvictory	Michel LaChance	1	1	1	1	1-½	1-½
Lindy Lane	William O'Donnell	2	3	2	2	2-½	2-½
Running Sea	Walter Hennessey	4	4	4	5	3-2½	3-4
Kramer Boy	Jack Moiseyev	5	5	5	3	4-4	4-5¼
Armbro Officer	Steve Condren	7	7	5	6	5-8	5-10
Freezing Cold	Berndt Lindstedt	6	6	6	7	6-9	6-10½
Steeler Spur	Richard Stillings	9	8	7	8	7-11½	7-12
Tony Oaks	S. O. Noble III	8	2	3	4	8-19½	8-29
Act of Grace	John Campbell	X3	9	9	9	9-dis	9-dis

Pine Man was scratched.

Time: 0:28⅕, 0:55⅗, 1:25⅕, 1:52⅗; Fast

Major Races (Cont.)

The Little Brown Jug

Ran at the Meadowlands, in East Rutherford, NJ, on September 19, 1996.

Horse	Driver	PP	¼	½	¾	Stretch-Margin	Finish-Margin
Armbro Operative	Jack Moiseyev	2	3	3	1	1-5	1-2
A Stud Named Sue	George Brennan	5	6	6	5	2-5	2-2
Mattduff	Douglas Brown	9	5	5	4	3-5½	3-5½
Scoot to Power	John Campbell	6	7	7	6	5-7¼	4-6
Mattropolis	Brad Hanners	1	2	2	3	6-8¼	5-7¼
Bubba Gump	Anthony Morgan	7	8	8	7	7-8¾	6-8
Armbro Oliver`	Mike Saftic	4	4	4	8	8-9¾	7-8
All Star Hanna	Howard Parker	8	9	9	9	9-10¾	8-9
Firm Belief	Michel LaChance	3	1	1	2	4-7	9-11

Time: 0:26⅕, 0:55, 1:23⅗, 1:52⅗; Fast

1995 Statistical Leaders

1995 Leading Moneywinners by Age, Sex and Gait

Division	Horse	Starts	1st	2nd	3rd	Earnings ($)
2-Year-Old Pacing Colts	A Stud Name Sue	12	9	2	0	870,787
2-Year-Old Pacing Fillies	On Her Way	11	4	3	3	477,593
3-Year-Old Pacing Colts	David's Pass	13	5	2	1	1,452,362
3-Year-Old Pacing Fillies	She's A Great Lady	25	14	4	1	610,930
Aged Pacing Horses	Pacific Rocket	27	16	4	2	724,555
Aged Pacing Mares	Ellamony	22	18	1	2	527,890
2-Year-Old Trotting Colts	Armbro Officer	9	3	3	0	277,134
2-Year-Old Trotting Fillies	Continentalvictory	17	10	3	0	432,810
3-Year-Old Trotting Colts	Tagliabue	13	5	5	2	869,600
3-Year-Old Trotting Fillies	CR Kay Suzie	13	10	0	1	610,535
Aged Trotting Horses	S J's Photo	18	9	4	3	682,565
Aged Trotting Mares	Giant Mermaid	18	5	4	2	134,575

Drivers

Driver	Earnings ($)	Driver	Earnings ($)
John Campbell	9,469,797	Luc Oulette	5,014,167
Michel LaChance	6,442,205	Steve Condren	4,469,631
Jack Moiseyev	6,282,295	Tony Morgan	4,439,134
Doug Brown	5,969,611	Ron Pierce	4,044,756
Catello Manzi	5,048,885	Bill Fahy	3,950,904

Queen of the Nags

Rose Hamburger is 105 years old and loves her new job. So do readers of the *New York Post*, for whom Hamburger has been providing a daily "best bet" at Aqueduct since December 1995. "She's good," says *Post* sports editor Greg Gallo, "right there with our best handicappers."

Born on Dec. 29, 1890, in New York City, Hamburger moved to Baltimore when she was 25 and began playing the ponies sometime before World War I. "I look at speed figures, check the owner, trainer and jockey, and then, by some magic, I make my pick," she says. After belonging to the Maryland Jockey Club for 45 years and witnessing every Preakness from 1915 to '88 (her most memorable: Man o' War's win in '20 and Secretariat's in '73), Hamburger returned to New York and became a conspicuous fixture at the Aqueduct rail. When she turned 100, the *Racing Form* ran a feature on her. When she turned 102, Aqueduct named its eighth race that day the Happy 102nd Rose. When she turned 105, Gallo gave her a job.

Though Hamburger hasn't been getting to the track so often in recent months, Gallo figures Gamblin' Rose, as the paper bills her, is a bargain working from home. "She gets subscriptions to the *Form* and the *Post*, and we throw in a few bucks," says Gallo. "Nobody has a lifetime contract here, but I'd say she's in pretty good shape."

[Rose Hamburger died on Aug. 6, 1996, after a brief bout with pneumonia. Her final pick, Capote Bell in the eighth race at Saratoga on July 27, came home a winner.]

THOROUGHBRED RACING

Kentucky Derby

Run at Churchill Downs, Louisville, KY, on the first Saturday in May.

Year	Winner (Margin)	Jockey	Second	Third	Time
1875	Aristides (1)	Oliver Lewis	Volcano	Verdigris	2:37¾
1876	Vagrant (2)	Bobby Swim	Creedmoor	Harry Hill	2:38¼
1877	Baden-Baden (2)	William Walker	Leonard	King William	2:38
1878	Day Star (2)	Jimmie Carter	Himyar	Leveler	2:37¼
1879	Lord Murphy (1)	Charlie Shauer	Falsetto	Strathmore	2:37
1880	Fonso (1)	George Lewis	Kimball	Bancroft	2:37½
1881	Hindoo (4)	Jimmy McLaughin	Lelex	Alfambra	2:40
1882	Apollo (½)	Babe Hurd	Runnymede	Bengal	2:40¼
1883	Leonatus (3)	Billy Donohue	Drake Carter	Lord Raglan	2:43
1884	Buchanan (2)	Isaac Murphy	Loftin	Audrain	2:40¼
1885	Joe Cotton (Neck)	Erskine Henderson	Bersan	Ten Booker	2:37¼
1886	Ben Ali (½)	Paul Duffy	Blue Wing	Free Knight	2:36½
1887	Montrose (2)	Isaac Lewis	Jim Gore	Jacobin	2:39¼
1888	MacBeth II (1)	George Covington	Gallifet	White	2:38¼
1889	Spokane (Nose)	Thomas Kiley	Proctor Knott	Once Again	2:34½
1890	Riley (2)	Isaac Murphy	Bill Letcher	Robespierre	2:45
1891	Kingman (1)	Isaac Murphy	Balgowan	High Tariff	2:52¼
1892	Azra (Nose)	Alonzo Clayton	Huron	Phil Dwyer	2:41½
1893	Lookout (5)	Eddie Kunze	Plutus	Boundless	2:39¼
1894	Chant (2)	Frank Goodale	Pearl Song	Sigurd	2:41
1895	Halma (3)	Soup Perkins	Basso	Laureate	2:37½
1896	Ben Brush (Nose)	Willie Simms	Ben Eder	Semper Ego	2:07¼
1897	Typhoon II (Head)	Buttons Garner	Ornament	Dr. Catlett	2:12½
1898	Plaudit (Neck)	Willie Simms	Lieber Karl	Isabey	2:09
1899	Manuel (2)	Fred Taral	Corsini	Mazo	2:12
1900	Lieut. Gibson (4)	Jimmy Boland	Florizar	Thrive	2:06¼
1901	His Eminence (2)	Jimmy Winkfield	Sannazarro	Driscoll	2:07¾
1902	Alan-a-Dale (Nose)	Jimmy Winkfield	Inventor	The Rival	2:08¾
1903	Judge Himes (¾)	Hal Booker	Early	Bourbon	2:09
1904	Elwood (½)	Frankie Prior	Ed Tierney	Brancas	2:08½
1905	Agile (3)	Jack Martin	Ram's Horn	Layson	2:10¾
1906	Sir Huon (2)	Roscoe Troxler	Lady Navarre	James Reddick	2:08⅕
1907	Pink Star (2)	Andy Minder	Zal	Ovelando	2:12⅗
1908	Stone Street (1)	Arthur Pickens	Sir Cleges	Dunvegan	2:15⅕
1909	Wintergreen (4)	Vincent Powers	Miami	Dr. Barkley	2:08⅕
1910	Donau (½)	Fred Herbert	Joe Morris	Fighting Bob	2:06⅖
1911	Meridian (¾)	George Archibald	Governor Gray	Colston	2:05
1912	Worth (Neck)	Carroll H. Schilling	Duval	Flamma	2:09⅖
1913	Donerail (½)	Roscoe Goose	Ten Point	Gowell	2:04⅘
1914	Old Rosebud (8)	John McCabe	Hodge	Bronzewing	2:03⅖
1915	Regret (2)	Joe Notter	Pebbles	Sharpshooter	2:05⅖
1916	George Smith (Neck)	Johnny Loftus	Star Hawk	Franklin	2:04
1917	Omar Khayyam (2)	Charles Borel	Ticket	Midway	2:04⅗
1918	Exterminator (1)	William Knapp	Escoba	Viva America	2:10⅘
1919	Sir Barton (5)	Johnny Loftus	Billy Kelly	Under Fire	2:09⅘
1920	Paul Jones (Head)	Ted Rice	Upset	On Watch	2:09
1921	Behave Yourself (Head)	Charles Thompson	Black Servant	Prudery	2:04⅕
1922	Morvich (½)	Albert Johnson	Bet Mosie	John Finn	2:04⅗
1923	Zev (1½)	Earl Sande	Martingale	Vigil	2:05⅖
1924	Black Gold (½)	John Mooney	Chilhowee	Beau Butler	2:05⅕
1925	Flying Ebony (1½)	Earl Sande	Captain Hal	Son of John	2:07⅗
1926	Bubbling Over (5)	Albert Johnson	Bagenbaggage	Rock Man	2:03⅘
1927	Whiskery (Head)	Linus McAtee	Osmond	Jock	2:06
1928	Reigh Count (3)	Chick Lang	Misstep	Toro	2:10⅖
1929	Clyde Van Dusen (2)	Linus McAtee	Naishapur	Panchio	2:10⅘
1930	Gallant Fox (2)	Earl Sande	Gallant Knight	Ned O.	2:07⅗
1931	Twenty Grand (4)	Charles Kurtsinger	Sweep All	Mate	2:01⅘
1932	Burgoo King (5)	Eugene James	Economic	Stepenfetchit	2:05⅕
1933	Brokers Tip (Nose)	Don Meade	Head Play	Charley O.	2:06⅘

Kentucky Derby (Cont.)

Year	Winner (Margin)	Jockey	Second	Third	Time
1934	Cavalcade (2½)	Mack Garner	Discovery	Agrarian	2:04
1935	Omaha (1½)	Willie Saunders	Roman Soldier	Whiskolo	2:05
1936	Bold Venture (Head)	Ira Hanford	Brevity	Indian Broom	2:03⅗
1937	War Admiral (1¾)	Charles Kurtsinger	Pompoon	Reaping Reward	2:03⅕
1938	Lawrin (1)	Eddie Arcaro	Dauber	Can't Wait	2:04⅘
1939	Johnstown (8)	James Stout	Challedon	Heather Broom	2:03⅗
1940	Gallahadion (1½)	Carroll Bierman	Bimelech	Dit	2:05
1941	Whirlaway (8)	Eddie Arcaro	Staretor	Market Wise	2:01⅖
1942	Shut Out (2½)	Wayne Wright	Alsab	Valdina Orphan	2:04⅖
1943	Count Fleet (3)	John Longden	Blue Swords	Slide Rule	2:04
1944	Pensive (4½)	Conn McCreary	Broadcloth	Stir Up	2:04⅕
1945	Hoop Jr. (6)	Eddie Arcaro	Pot o' Luck	Darby Dieppe	2:07
1946	Assault (8)	Warren Mehrtens	Spy Song	Hampden	2:06⅗
1947	Jet Pilot (Head)	Eric Guerin	Phalanx	Faultless	2:06⅘
1948	Citation (3½)	Eddie Arcaro	Coaltown	My Request	2:05⅖
1949	Ponder (3)	Steve Brooks	Capot	Palestinian	2:04⅕
1950	Middleground (1¼)	William Boland	Hill Prince	Mr. Trouble	2:01⅗
1951	Count Turf (4)	Conn McCreary	Royal Mustang	Ruhe	2:02⅗
1952	Hill Gail (2)	Eddie Arcaro	Sub Fleet	Blue Man	2:01⅗
1953	Dark Star (Head)	Hank Moreno	Native Dancer	Invigorator	2:02
1954	Determine (1½)	Ray York	Hasty Road	Hasseyampa	2:03
1955	Swaps (1½)	Bill Shoemaker	Nashua	Summer Tan	2:01⅘
1956	Needles (¾)	Dave Erb	Fabius	Come On Red	2:03⅖
1957	Iron Liege (Nose)	Bill Hartack	Gallant Man	Round Table	2:02⅕
1958	Tim Tam (½)	Ismael Valenzuela	Lincoln Road	Noureddin	2:05
1959	Tomy Lee (Nose)	Bill Shoemaker	Sword Dancer	First Landing	2:02⅕
1960	Venetian Way (3½)	Bill Hartack	Bally Ache	Victoria Park	2:02⅖
1961	Carry Back (¾)	John Sellers	Crozier	Bass Clef	2:04
1962	Decidedly (2¼)	Bill Hartack	Roman Line	Ridan	2:00⅖
1963	Chateaugay (1¼)	Braulio Baeza	Never Bend	Candy Spots	2:01⅘
1964	Northern Dancer (Neck)	Bill Hartack	Hill Rise	The Scoundrel	2:00
1965	Lucky Debonair (Neck)	Bill Shoemaker	Dapper Dan	Tom Rolfe	2:01⅕
1966	Kauai King (½)	Don Brumfield	Advocator	Blue Skyer	2:02
1967	Proud Clarion (1)	Bobby Ussery	Barbs Delight	Damascus	2:00⅗
1968	Forward Pass (Disq.)	Ismael Valenzuela	Francie's Hat	T.V. Commercial	2:02⅕
1969	Majestic Prince (Neck)	Bill Hartack	Arts and Letters	Dike	2:01⅘
1970	Dust Commander (5)	Mike Manganello	My Dad George	High Echelon	2:03⅖
1971	Canonero II (3¾)	Gustavo Avila	Jim French	Bold Reason	2:03⅕
1972	Riva Ridge (3¼)	Ron Turcotte	No Le Hace	Hold Your Peace	2:01⅘
1973	Secretariat (2½)	Ron Turcotte	Sham	Our Native	1:59⅖
1974	Cannonade (2¼)	Angel Cordero Jr	Hudson County	Agitate	2:04
1975	Foolish Pleasure (1¾)	Jacinto Vasquez	Avatar	Diabolo	2:02
1976	Bold Forbes (1)	Angel Cordero Jr	Honest Pleasure	Elocutionist	2:01⅗
1977	Seattle Slew (1¾)	Jean Cruguet	Run Dusty Run	Sanhedrin	2:02⅕
1978	Affirmed (1½)	Steve Cauthen	Alydar	Believe It	2:01⅕
1979	Spectacular Bid (2¾)	Ronald J. Franklin	General Assembly	Golden Act	2:02⅖
1980	Genuine Risk (1)	Jacinto Vasquez	Rumbo	Jaklin Klugman	2:02
1981	Pleasant Colony (¾)	Jorge Velasquez	Woodchopper	Partez	2:02
1982	Gato Del Sol (2½)	Eddie Delahoussaye	Laser Light	Reinvested	2:02⅕
1983	Sunny's Halo (2)	Eddie Delahoussaye	Desert Wine	Caveat	2:02⅕
1984	Swale (3¼)	Laffit Pincay Jr	Coax Me Chad	At the Threshold	2:02⅖
1985	Spend A Buck (5)	Angel Cordero Jr	Stephan's Odyssey	Chief's Crown	2:00⅕
1986	Ferdinand (2¼)	Bill Shoemaker	Bold Arrangement	Broad Brush	2:02⅘
1987	Alysheba (¾)	Chris McCarron	Bet Twice	Avies Copy	2:03⅖
1988	Winning Colors (Neck)	Gary Stevens	Forty Niner	Risen Star	2:02⅕
1989	Sunday Silence (2½)	Pat Valenzuela	Easy Goer	Awe Inspiring	2:05
1990	Unbridled (3½)	Craig Perret	Summer Squall	Pleasant Tap	2:02
1991	Strike the Gold (1¾)	Chris Antley	Best Pal	Mane Minister	2:03
1992	Lil E. Tee (1)	Pat Day	Casual Lies	Dance Floor	2:03
1993	Sea Hero (2½)	Jerry Bailey	Prairie Bayou	Wild Gale	2:02⅖
1994	Go for Gin (2½)	Chris McCarron	Strodes Creek	Blumin Affair	2:03⅗
1995	Thunder Gulch (2¼)	Gary Stevens	Tejano Run	Timber Country	2:01⅕
1996	Grindstone (Nose)	Jerry Bailey	Cavonnier	Prince of Thieves	2:01

Note: Distance: 1½ miles (1875-95), 1¼ miles (1896-present).

Preakness

Run at Pimlico Race Course, Baltimore, Md., two weeks after the Kentucky Derby.

Year	Winner (Margin)	Jockey	Second	Third	Time
1873	Survivor (10)	G. Barbee	John Boulger	Artist	2:43
1874	Culpepper (¾)	W. Donohue	King Amadeus	Scratch	2:56½
1875	Tom Ochiltree (2)	L. Hughes	Viator	Bay Final	2:43½
1876	Shirley (4)	G. Barbee	Rappahannock	Algerine	2:44¾
1877	Cloverbrook (4)	C. Holloway	Bombast	Lucifer	2:45½
1878	Duke of Magenta (6)	C. Holloway	Bayard	Albert	2:41¾
1879	Harold (3)	L. Hughes	Jericho	Rochester	2:40½
1880	Grenada (¾)	L. Hughes	Oden	Emily F.	2:40½
1881	Saunterer (½)	T. Costello	Compensation	Baltic	2:40½
1882	Vanguard (Neck)	T. Costello	Heck	Col Watson	2:44½
1883	Jacobus (4)	G. Barbee	Parnell		2:42½
1884	Knight of Ellerslie (2)	S. Fisher	Welcher		2:39½
1885	Tecumseh (2)	Jim McLaughlin	Wickham	John C.	2:49
1886	The Bard (3)	S. Fisher	Eurus	Elkwood	2:45
1887	Dunboyne (1)	W. Donohue	Mahoney	Raymond	2:39½
1888	Refund (3)	F. Littlefield	Judge Murray	Glendale	2:49
1889	Buddhist (8)	W. Anderson	Japhet		2:17½
1890*	Montague (3)	W. Martin	Philosophy	Barrister	2:36¾
1894	Assignee (3)	Fred Taral	Potentate	Ed Kearney	1:49¼
1895	Belmar (1)	Fred Taral	April Fool	Sue Kittie	1:50½
1896	Margrave (1)	H. Griffin	Hamilton II	Intermission	1:51
1897	Paul Kauvar (1½)	C. Thorpe	Elkins	On Deck	1:51¼
1898	Sly Fox (2)	C. W. Simms	The Huguenot	Nuto	1:49⅗
1899	Half Time (1)	R. Clawson	Filigrane	Lackland	1:47
1900	Hindus (Head)	H. Spencer	Sarmation	Ten Candles	1:48⅖
1901	The Parader (2)	F. Landry	Sadie S.	Dr. Barlow	1:47⅕
1902	Old England (Nose)	L. Jackson	Major Daingerfield	Namtor	1:45⅘
1903	Flocarline (½)	W. Gannon	Mackey Dwyer	Rightful	1:44⅘
1904	Bryn Mawr (1)	E. Hildebrand	Wotan	Dolly Spanker	1:44⅕
1905	Cairngorm (Head)	W. Davis	Kiamesha	Coy Maid	1:45⅘
1906	Whimsical (4)	Walter Miller	Content	Larabie	1:45
1907	Don Enrique (1)	G. Mountain	Ethon	Zambesi	1:45⅖
1908	Royal Tourist (4)	E. Dugan	Live Wire	Robert Cooper	1:46⅖
1909	Effendi (1)	Willie Doyle	Fashion Plate	Hilltop	1:39⅘
1910	Layminster (½)	R. Estep	Dalhousie	Sager	1:40⅗
1911	Watervale (1)	E. Dugan	Zeus	The Nigger	1:51
1912	Colonel Holloway (5)	C. Turner	Bwana Tumbo	Tipsand	1:56⅗
1913	Buskin (Neck)	J. Butwell	Kleburne	Barnegat	1:53⅖
1914	Holiday (¾)	A. Schuttinger	Brave Cunarder	Defendum	1:53⅘
1915	Rhine Maiden (1½)	Douglas Hoffman	Half Rock	Runes	1:58
1916	Damrosch (1½)	Linus McAtee	Greenwood	Achievement	1:54⅘
1917	Kalitan (2)	E. Haynes	Al M. Dick	Kentucky Boy	1:54⅖
1918	War Cloud (¾)	Johnny Loftus	Sunny Slope	Lanius	1:53⅗
1918	Jack Hare, Jr (2)	C. Peak	The Porter	Kate Bright	1:53⅖
1919	Sir Barton (4)	Johnny Loftus	Eternal	Sweep On	1:53
1920	Man o' War (1½)	Clarence Kummer	Upset	Wildair	1:51⅗
1921	Broomspun (¾)	F. Coltiletti	Polly Ann	Jeg	1:54⅕
1922	Pillory (Head)	L. Morris	Hea	June Grass	1:51⅗
1923	Vigil (1¼)	B. Marinelli	General Thatcher	Rialto	1:53⅗
1924	Nellie Morse (1½)	J. Merimee	Transmute	Mad Play	1:57⅕
1925	Coventry (4)	Clarence Kummer	Backbone	Almadel	1:59
1926	Display (Head)	J. Maiben	Blondin	Mars	1:59⅘
1927	Bostonian (½)	A. Abel	Sir Harry	Whiskery	2:01⅗
1928	Victorian (Nose)	Sonny Workman	Toro	Solace	2:00⅕
1929	Dr. Freeland (1)	Louis Schaefer	Minotaur	African	2:01⅗
1930	Gallant Fox (¾)	Earl Sande	Crack Brigade	Snowflake	2:00⅗
1931	Mate (1½)	G. Ellis	Twenty Grand	Ladder	1:59
1932	Burgoo King (Head)	E. James	Tick On	Boatswain	1:59⅘
1933	Head Play (4)	Charles Kurtsinger	Ladysman	Utopian	2:02
1934	High Quest (Nose)	R. Jones	Cavalcade	Discovery	1:58⅕
1935	Omaha (6)	Willie Saunders	Firethorn	Psychic Bid	1:58⅖
1936	Bold Venture (Nose)	George Woolf	Granville	Jean Bart	1:59
1937	War Admiral (Head)	Charles Kurtsinger	Pompoon	Flying Scot	1:58⅖
1938	Dauber (7)	M. Peters	Cravat	Menow	1:59⅘

Preakness (Cont.)

Year	Winner (Margin)	Jockey	Second	Third	Time
1939	Challedon (1¼)	George Seabo	Gilded Knight	Volitant	1:59⅘
1940	Bimelech (3)	F. A. Smith	Mioland	Gallahadion	1:58⅗
1941	Whirlaway (5½)	Eddie Arcaro	King Cole	Our Boots	1:58⅘
1942	Alsab (1)	B. James	Requested Sun Again	(dead heat for second)	1:57
1943	Count Fleet (8)	Johnny Longden	Blue Swords	Vincentive	1:57⅖
1944	Pensive (¾)	Conn McCreary	Platter	Stir Up	1:59⅕
1945	Polynesian (2½)	W. D. Wright	Hoop Jr	Darby Dieppe	1:58⅘
1946	Assault (Neck)	Warren Mehrtens	Lord Boswell	Hampden	2:01⅖
1947	Faultless (1¼)	Doug Dodson	On Trust	Phalanx	1:59
1948	Citation (5½)	Eddie Arcaro	Vulcan's Forge	Boyard	2:02⅖
1949	Capot (Head)	Ted Atkinson	Palestinian	Noble Impulse	1:56
1950	Hill Prince (5)	Eddie Arcaro	Middleground	Dooley	1:59⅕
1951	Bold (7)	Eddie Arcaro	Counterpoint	Alerted	1:56⅖
1952	Blue Man (3½)	Conn McCreary	Jampol	One Count	1:57⅖
1953	Native Dancer (Neck)	Eric Guerin	Jamie K.	Royal Bay Gem	1:57⅘
1954	Hasty Road (Neck)	Johnny Adams	Correlation	Hasseyampa	1:57⅖
1955	Nashua (1)	Eddie Arcaro	Saratoga	Traffic Judge	1:54⅗
1956	Fabius (¾)	Bill Hartack	Needles	No Regrets	1:58⅖
1957	Bold Ruler (2)	Eddie Arcaro	Iron Liege	Inside Tract	1:56⅕
1958	Tim Tam (1½)	I. Valenzuela	Lincoln Road	Gone Fishin'	1:57⅕
1959	Royal Orbit (4)	William Harmatz	Sword Dancer	Dunce	1:57
1960	Bally Ache (4)	Bobby Ussery	Victoria Park	Celtic Ash	1:57⅗
1961	Carry Back (¾)	Johnny Sellers	Globemaster	Crozier	1:57⅗
1962	Greek Money (Nose)	John Rotz	Ridan	Roman Line	1:56⅕
1963	Candy Spots (3½)	Bill Shoemaker	Chateaugay	Never Bend	1:56⅕
1964	Northern Dancer (2¼)	Bill Hartack	The Scoundrel	Hill Rise	1:56⅘
1965	Tom Rolfe (Neck)	Ron Turcotte	Dapper Dan	Hail to All	1:56⅕
1966	Kauai King (1¾)	Don Brumfield	Stupendous	Amberoid	1:55⅖
1967	Damascus (2¼)	Bill Shoemaker	In Reality	Proud Clarion	1:55⅕
1968	Forward Pass (6)	I. Valenzuela	Out of the Way	Nodouble	1:56⅘
1969	Majestic Prince (Head)	Bill Hartack	Arts and Letters	Jay Ray	1:55⅗
1970	Personality (Neck)	Eddie Belmonte	My Dad George	Silent Screen	1:56⅕
1971	Canonero II (1½)	Gustavo Avila	Eastern Fleet	Jim French	1:54
1972	Bee Bee Bee (1¼)	Eldon Nelson	No Le Hace	Key to the Mint	1:55⅗
1973	Secretariat (2½)	Ron Turcotte	Sham	Our Native	1:54⅖
1974	Little Current (7)	Miguel Rivera	Neapolitan Way	Cannonade	1:54⅗
1975	Master Derby (1)	Darrel McHargue	Foolish Pleasure	Diabolo	1:56⅖
1976	Elocutionist (3)	John Lively	Play the Red	Bold Forbes	1:55
1977	Seattle Slew (1½)	Jean Cruguet	Iron Constitution	Run Dusty Run	1:54⅖
1978	Affirmed (Neck)	Steve Cauthen	Alydar	Believe It	1:54⅖
1979	Spectacular Bid (5½)	Ron Franklin	Golden Act	Screen King	1:54⅕
1980	Codex (4¾)	Angel Cordero Jr	Genuine Risk	Colonel Moran	1:54⅕
1981	Pleasant Colony (1)	Jorge Velasquez	Bold Ego	Paristo	1:54⅗
1982	Aloma's Ruler (½)	Jack Kaenel	Linkage	Cut Away	1:55⅖
1983	Deputed Testamony (2¾)	Donald Miller Jr	Desert Wine	High Honors	1:55⅖
1984	Gate Dancer (1½)	Angel Cordero Jr	Play On	Fight Over	1:53⅗
1985	Tank's Prospect (Head)	Pat Day	Chief's Crown	Eternal Prince	1:53⅖
1986	Snow Chief (4)	Alex Solis	Ferdinand	Broad Brush	1:54⅘
1987	Alysheba (½)	Chris McCarron	Bet Twice	Cryptoclearance	1:55⅘
1988	Risen Star (1¼)	E. Delahoussaye	Brian's Time	Winning Colors	1:56⅕
1989	Sunday Silence (Nose)	Pat Valenzuela	Easy Goer	Rock Point	1:53⅘
1990	Summer Squall (2¼)	Pat Day	Unbridled	Mister Frisky	1:53⅗
1991	Hansel (Head)	Jerry Bailey	Corporate Report	Mane Minister	1:54
1992	Pine Bluff (¾)	Chris McCarron	Alydeed	Casual Lies	1:55⅗
1993	Prairie Bayou (½)	Mike Smith	Cherokee Run	El Bakan	1:56⅗
1994	Tabasco Cat (¾)	Pat Day	Go For Gin	Concern	1:56⅖
1995	Timber Country (½)	Pat Day	Oliver's Twist	Thunder Gulch	1:54⅖
1996	Louis Quatorze (3¼)	Pat Day	Skip Away	Editor's Note	1:53⅖

*Preakness was not run 1891-1893. In 1918, it was run in two divisions.

Note: Distance: 1½ miles (1873-88), 1¼ miles (1889), 1½ miles (1890), 1 1/16 miles (1894-1900), 1 mile and 70 yards (1901-1907), 1 1/16 miles (1908), 1 mile (1909-10), 1⅛ miles (1911-24), 1 3/16 miles (1925-present).

Belmont

Run at Belmont Park, Elmont, NY, three weeks after the Preakness Stakes. Held previously at two locations in the Bronx, NY: Jerome Park (1867–1889) and Morris Park (1890–1904).

Year	Winner (Margin)	Jockey	Second	Third	Time
1867	Ruthless (Head)	J. Gilpatrick	De Courcy	Rivoli	3:05
1868	General Duke (2)	R. Swim	Northumberland	Fannie Ludlow	3:02
1869	Fenian (Unknown)	C. Miller	Glenelg	Invercauld	3:04¼
1870	Kingfisher (½)	E. Brown	Foster	Midday	2:59½
1871	Harry Bassett (3)	W. Miller	Stockwood	By-the-Sea	2:56
1872	Joe Daniels (¾)	James Rowe	Meteor	Shylock	2:58¼
1873	Springbok (4)	James Rowe	Count d'Orsay	Strachino	3:01¾
1874	Saxon (Neck)	G. Barbee	Grinstead	Aaron Pennington	2:39½
1875	Calvin (2)	R. Swim	Aristides	Milner	2:40¼
1876	Algerine (Head)	W. Donahue	Fiddlestick	Barricade	2:40½
1877	Cloverbrook (1)	C. Holloway	Loiterer	Baden-Baden	2:46
1878	Duke of Magenta (2)	L. Hughes	Bramble	Sparta	2:43½
1879	Spendthrift (5)	S. Evans	Monitor	Jericho	2:42¾
1880	Grenada (½)	L. Hughes	Ferncliffe	Turenne	2:47
1881	Saunterer (Neck)	T. Costello	Eole	Baltic	2:47
1882	Forester (5)	James McLaughlin	Babcock	Wyoming	2:43
1883	George Kinney (2)	James McLaughlin	Trombone	Renegade	2:42½
1884	Panique (½)	James McLaughlin	Knight of Ellerslie	Himalaya	2:42
1885	Tyrant (3½)	Paul Duffy	St Augustine	Tecumseh	2:43
1886	Inspector B (1)	James McLaughlin	The Bard	Linden	2:41
1887	Hanover (28-32)	James McLaughlin	Oneko		2:43½
1888	Sir Dixon (12)	James McLaughlin	Prince Royal		2:40¼
1889	Eric (Head)	W. Hayward	Diable	Zephyrus	2:47
1890	Burlington (1)	S. Barnes	Devotee	Padishah	2:07¾
1891	Foxford (Neck)	E. Garrison	Montana	Laurestan	2:08¾
1892	Patron (Unknown)	W. Hayward	Shellbark		2:17
1893	Comanche (Head)(21)	Willie Simms	Dr. Rice	Rainbow	1:53¼
1894	Henry of Navarre (2-4)	Willie Simms	Prig	Assignee	1:56½
1895	Belmar (Head)	Fred Taral	Counter Tenor	Nanki Pooh	2:11½
1896	Hastings (Neck)	H. Griffin	Handspring	Hamilton II	2:24½
1897	Scottish Chieftain (1)	J. Scherrer	On Deck	Octagon	2:23¼
1898	Bowling Brook (8)	P. Littlefield	Previous	Hamburg	2:32
1899	Jean Bereaud (Head)	R. R. Clawson	Half Time	Glengar	2:23
1900	Ildrim (Head)	N. Turner	Petrucio	Missionary	2:21½
1901	Commando (½)	H. Spencer	The Parader	All Green	2:21
1902	Masterman (2)	John Bullmann	Ranald	King Hanover	2:22½
1903	Africander (2)	John Bullmann	Whorler	Red Knight	2:23⅕
1904	Delhi (3½)	George Odom	Graziallo	Rapid Water	2:06⅗
1905	Tanya (1/2)	E. Hildebrand	Blandy	Hot Shot	2:08
1906	Burgomaster (4)	L. Lyne	The Quail	Accountant	2:20
1907	Peter Pan (1)	G. Mountain	Superman	Frank Gill	Unknown
1908	Colin (Head)	Joe Notter	Fair Play	King James	Unknown
1909	Joe Madden (8)	E. Dugan	Wise Mason	Donald MacDonald	2:21⅗
1910*	Sweep (6)	J. Butwell	Duke of Ormonde		2:22
1913	Prince Eugene (½)	Roscoe Troxler	Rock View	Flying Fairy	2:18
1914	Luke McLuke (8)	M. Buxton	Gainer	Charlestonian	2:20
1915	The Finn (4)	G. Byrne	Half Rock	Pebbles	2:18⅖
1916	Friar Rock (3)	E. Haynes	Spur	Churchill	2:22
1917	Hourless (10)	J. Butwell	Skeptic	Wonderful	2:17⅘
1918	Johren (2)	Frank Robinson	War Cloud	Cum Sah	2:20⅖
1919	Sir Barton (5)	Johnny Loftus	Sweep On	Natural Bridge	2:17⅖
1920	Man o' War (20)	Clarence Kummer	Donnacona		2:14⅕
1921	Grey Lag (3)	Earl Sande	Sporting Blood	Leonardo II	2:16⅘
1922	Pillory (2)	C. H. Miller	Snob II	Hea	2:18⅘
1923	Zev (1½)	Earl Sande	Chickvale	Rialto	2:19
1924	Mad Play (2)	Earl Sande	Mr. Mutt	Modest	2:18⅘
1925	American Flag (8)	Albert Johnson	Dangerous	Swope	2:16⅘
1926	Crusader (1)	Albert Johnson	Espino	Haste	2:32⅕
1927	Chance Shot (1½)	Earl Sande	Bois de Rose	Flambino	2:32⅖
1928	Vito (3)	Clarence Kummer	Genie	Diavolo	2:33⅕

Belmont (Cont.)

Year	Winner (Margin)	Jockey	Second	Third	Time
1929	Blue Larkspur (¾)	Mack Garner	African	Jack High	2:32⅘
1930	Gallant Fox (3)	Earl Sande	Whichone	Questionnaire	2:31⅗
1931	Twenty Grand (10)	Charles Kurtsinger	Sun Meadow	Jamestown	2:29⅗
1932	Faireno (1½)	T. Malley	Osculator	Flag Pole	2:32⅘
1933	Hurryoff (1½)	Mack Garner	Nimbus	Union	2:32⅗
1934	Peace Chance (6)	W. D. Wright	High Quest	Good Goods	2:29⅕
1935	Omaha (1½)	Willie Saunders	Firethorn	Rosemont	2:30⅗
1936	Granville (Nose)	James Stout	Mr. Bones	Hollyrood	2:30
1937	War Admiral (3)	Charles Kurtsinger	Sceneshifter	Vamoose	2:28⅗
1938	Pasteurized (Neck)	James Stout	Dauber	Cravat	2:29⅖
1939	Johnstown (5)	James Stout	Belay	Gilded Knight	2:29⅗
1940	Bimelech (¾)	F. A. Smith	Your Chance	Andy K	2:29⅗
1941	Whirlaway (2½)	Eddie Arcaro	Robert Morris	Yankee Chance	2:31
1942	Shut Out (2)	Eddie Arcaro	Alsab	Lochinvar	2:29⅕
1943	Count Fleet (25)	Johnny Longden	Fairy Manhurst	Deseronto	2:28⅕
1944	Bounding Home (½)	G. L. Smith	Pensive	Bull Dandy	2:32⅕
1945	Pavot (5)	Eddie Arcaro	Wildlife	Jeep	2:30⅕
1946	Assault (3)	Warren Mehrtens	Natchez	Cable	2:30⅘
1947	Phalanx (5)	R. Donoso	Tide Rips	Tailspin	2:29⅖
1948	Citation (8)	Eddie Arcaro	Better Self	Escadru	2:28⅕
1949	Capot (½)	Ted Atkinson	Ponder	Palestinian	2:30⅕
1950	Middleground (1)	William Boland	Lights Up	Mr. Trouble	2:28⅗
1951	Counterpoint (4)	D. Gorman	Battlefield	Battle Morn	2:29
1952	One Count (2½)	Eddie Arcaro	Blue Man	Armageddon	2:30⅕
1953	Native Dancer (Neck)	Eric Guerin	Jamie K.	Royal Bay Gem	2:38⅗
1954	High Gun (Neck)	Eric Guerin	Fisherman	Limelight	2:30⅘
1955	Nashua (9)	Eddie Arcaro	Blazing Count	Portersville	2:29
1956	Needles (Neck)	David Erb	Career Boy	Fabius	2:29⅘
1957	Gallant Man (8)	Bill Shoemaker	Inside Tract	Bold Ruler	2:26⅗
1958	Cavan (6)	Pete Anderson	Tim Tam	Flamingo	2:30⅕
1959	Sword Dancer (¾)	Bill Shoemaker	Bagdad	Royal Orbit	2:28⅖
1960	Celtic Ash (5½)	Bill Hartack	Venetian Way	Disperse	2:29⅗
1961	Sherluck (2¼)	Braulio Baeza	Globemaster	Guadalcanal	2:29⅕
1962	Jaipur (Nose)	Bill Shoemaker	Admiral's Voyage	Crimson Satan	2:28⅘
1963	Chateaugay (2½)	Braulio Baeza	Candy Spots	Choker	2:30⅕
1964	Quadrangle (2)	Manuel Ycaza	Roman Brother	Northern Dancer	2:28⅖
1965	Hail to All (Neck)	John Sellers	Tom Rolfe	First Family	2:28⅖
1966	Amberold (2½)	William Boland	Buffle	Advocator	2:29⅗
1967	Damascus (2½)	Bill Shoemaker	Cool Reception	Gentleman James	2:28⅘
1968	Stage Door Johnny (1¼)	Hellodoro Gustines	Forward Pass	Call Me Prince	2:27⅕
1969	Arts and Letters (5½)	Braulio Baeza	Majestic Prince	Dike	2:28⅘
1970	High Echelon (¾)	John L. Rotz	Needles N Pins	Naskra	2:34
1971	Pass Catcher (¾)	Walter Blum	Jim French	Bold Reason	2:30⅖
1972	Riva Ridge (7)	Ron Turcotte	Ruritania	Cloudy Dawn	2:28
1973	Secretariat (31)	Ron Turcotte	Twice a Prince	My Gallant	2:24
1974	Little Current (7)	Miguel A. Rivera	Jolly Johu	Cannonade	2:29⅕
1975	Avatar (Neck)	Bill Shoemaker	Foolish Pleasure	Master Derby	2:28⅕
1976	Bold Forbes (Neck)	Angel Cordero Jr	McKenzie Bridge	Great Contractor	2:29
1977	Seattle Slew (4)	Jean Cruguet	Run Dusty Run	Sanhedrin	2:29⅗
1978	Affirmed (Head)	Steve Cauthen	Alydar	Darby Creek Road	2:26⅘
1979	Coastal (3¼)	Ruben Hernandez	Golden Act	Spectacular Bid	2:28⅗
1980	Temperence Hill (2)	Eddie Maple	Genuine Risk	Rockhill Native	2:29⅘
1981	Summing (Neck)	George Martens	Highland Blade	Pleasant Colony	2:29
1982	Conquistador Cielo (14½)	Laffit Pincay, Jr	Gato Del Sol	Illuminate	2:28⅕
1983	Caveat (3½)	Laffit Pincay Jr	Slew o'Gold	Barberstown	2:27⅘
1984	Swale (4)	Laffit Pincay Jr	Pine Circle	Morning Bob	2:27⅕
1985	Creme Fraiche (½)	Eddie Maple	Stephan's Odyssey	Chief's Crown	2:27
1986	Danzig Connection (1¼)	Chris McCarron	Johns Treasure	Ferdinand	2:29⅘
1987	Bet Twice (14)	Craig Perret	Cryptoclearance	Gulch	2:28⅕

Belmont (*Cont.*)

Year	Winner (Margin)	Jockey	Second	Third	Time
1988	Risen Star (14¾)	Eddie Delahoussaye	Kingpost	Brian's Time	2:26⅖
1989	Easy Goer (8)	Pat Day	Sunday Silence	Le Voyageur	2:26
1990	Go and Go (8¼)	Michael Kinane	Thirty Six Red	Baron de Vaux	2:27⅕
1991	Hansel (Head)	Jerry Bailey	Strike the Gold	Mane Minister	2:28
1992	A.P. Indy (¾)	Eddie Delahoussaye	My Memoirs	Pine Bluff	2:26
1993	Colonial Affair (2¼)	Julie Krone	Kissin Kris	Wild Gale	2:29⅘
1994	Tabasco Cat (2)	Pat Day	Go For Gin	Strodes Creek	2:26⅘
1995	Thunder Gulch (2)	Gary Stevens	Star Standard	Citadeed	2:32
1996	Editor's Note (1)	Rene Douglas	Skip Away	My Flag	2:28⅘

*Race not held in 1911-1912.

Note: Distance: 1 mile 5 furlongs (1867-89), 1¼ miles (1890-1905), 1⅜ miles (1906-25), 1½ miles (1926-present).

Triple Crown Winners

Year	Horse	Jockey	Owner	Trainer
1919	Sir Barton	John Loftus	J. K. L. Ross	H. G. Bedwell
1930	Gallant Fox	Earle Sande	Belair Stud	James Fitzsimmons
1935	Omaha	William Saunders	Belair Stud	James Fitzsimmons
1937	War Admiral	Charles Kurtsinger	Samuel D. Riddle	George Conway
1941	Whirlaway	Eddie Arcaro	Calumet Farm	Ben Jones
1943	Count Fleet	John Longden	Mrs J. D. Hertz	Don Cameron
1946	Assault	Warren Mehrtens	King Ranch	Max Hirsch
1948	Citation	Eddie Arcaro	Calumet Farm	Jimmy Jones
1973	Secretariat	Ron Turcotte	Meadow Stable	Lucien Laurin
1977	Seattle Slew	Jean Cruguet	Karen L. Taylor	William H. Turner Jr
1978	Affirmed	Steve Cauthen	Harbor View Farm	Laz Barrera

Awards

Horse of the Year

Year	Horse	Owner	Trainer	Breeder
1936	Granville	Belair Stud	James Fitzsimmons	Belair Stud
1937	War Admiral	Samuel D. Riddle	George Conway	Mrs. Samuel D. Riddle
1938	Seabiscuit	Charles S. Howard	Tom Smith	Wheatley Stable
1939	Challedon	William L. Brann	Louis J. Schaefer	Branncastle Farm
1940	Challedon	William L. Brann	Louis J. Schaefer	Branncastle Farm
1941	Whirlaway	Calumet Farm	Ben Jones	Calumet Farm
1942	Whirlaway	Calumet Farm	Ben Jones	Calumet Farm
1943	Count Fleet	Mrs. John D. Hertz	Don Cameron	Mrs. John D. Hertz
1944	Twilight Tear	Calumet Farm	Ben Jones	Calumet Farm
1945	Busher	Louis B. Mayer	George Odom	Idle Hour Stock Farm
1946	Assault	King Ranch	Max Hirsch	King Ranch
1947	Armed	Calumet Farm	Jimmy Jones	Calumet Farm
1948	Citation	Calumet Farm	Jimmy Jones	Calumet Farm
1949	Capot	Greentree Stable	John M. Gaver Sr	Greentree Stable
1950	Hill Prince	C. T. Chenery	Casey Hayes	C. T. Chenery
1951	Counterpoint	C. V. Whitney	Syl Veitch	C. V. Whitney
1952	One Count	Mrs. W. M. Jeffords	O. White	W. M. Jeffords
1953	Tom Fool	Greentree Stable	John M. Gaver Sr	D. A. Headley
1954	Native Dancer	A. G. Vanderbilt	Bill Winfrey	A. G. Vanderbilt
1955	Nashua	Belair Stud	James Fitzsimmons	Belair Stud
1956	Swaps	Ellsworth-Galbreath	Mesh Tenney	R. Ellsworth
1957	Bold Ruler	Wheatley Stable	James Fitzsimmons	Wheatley Stable
1958	Round Table	Kerr Stables	Willy Molter	Claiborne Farm
1959	Sword Dancer	Brookmeade Stable	Elliott Burch	Brookmeade Stable
1960	Kelso	Bohemia Stable	C. Hanford	Mrs. R. C. duPont
1961	Kelso	Bohemia Stable	C. Hanford	Mrs. R. C. duPont
1962	Kelso	Bohemia Stable	C. Hanford	Mrs. R. C. duPont
1963	Kelso	Bohemia Stable	C. Hanford	Mrs. R. C. duPont
1964	Kelso	Bohemia Stable	C. Hanford	Mrs. R. C. duPont
1965	Roman Brother	Harbor View Stable	Burley Parke	Ocala Stud
1966	Buckpasser	Ogden Phipps	Eddie Neloy	Ogden Phipps

Horse of the Year (Cont.)

Year	Horse	Owner	Trainer	Breeder
1967	Damascus	Mrs. E. W. Bancroft	Frank Y. Whiteley Jr	Mrs. E. W. Bancroft
1968	Dr. Fager	Tartan Stable	John A. Nerud	Tartan Farms
1969	Arts and Letters	Rokeby Stable	Elliott Burch	Paul Mellon
1970	Fort Marcy	Rokeby Stable	Elliott Burch	Paul Mellon
1971	Ack Ack	E. E. Fogelson	Charlie Whittingham	H. F. Guggenheim
1972	Secretariat	Meadow Stable	Lucien Laurin	Meadow Stud
1973	Secretariat	Meadow Stable	Lucien Laurin	Meadow Stud
1974	Forego	Lazy F Ranch	Sherrill W. Ward	Lazy F Ranch
1975	Forego	Lazy F Ranch	Sherrill W. Ward	Lazy F Ranch
1976	Forego	Lazy F Ranch	Frank Y. Whiteley Jr	Lazy F Ranch
1977	Seattle Slew	Karen L. Taylor	Billy Turner Jr	B. S. Castleman
1978	Affirmed	Harbor View Farm	Laz Barrera	Harbor View Farm
1979	Affirmed	Harbor View Farm	Laz Barrera	Harbor View Farm
1980	Spectacular Bid	Hawksworth Farm	Bud Delp	Mmes. Gilmore and Jason
1981	John Henry	Dotsam Stable	Ron McAnally and Lefty Nickerson	Golden Chance Farm
1982	Conquistador Cielo	H. de Kwiatkowski	Woody Stephens	L. E. Landoli
1983	All Along	Daniel Wildenstein	P. L. Biancone	Dayton
1984	John Henry	Dotsam Stable	Ron McAnally	Golden Chance Farm
1985	Spend a Buck	Hunter Farm	Cam Gambolati	Irish Hill Farm & R. W. Harper
1986	Lady's Secret	Mr. & Mrs. Eugene Klein	D. Wayne Lukas	R. H. Spreen
1987	Ferdinand	Mrs. H. B. Keck	Charlie Whittingham	H. B. Keck
1988	Alysheba	D. & P. Scharbauer	Jack Van Berg	Preston Madden
1989	Sunday Silence	Gaillard, Hancock, & Whittingham	Charlie Whittingham	Oak Cliff Thoroughbreds
1990	Criminal Type	Calumet Farm	D. Wayne Lukas	Calumet Farm
1991	Black Tie Affair	Jeffrey Sullivan	Ernie Poulos	Stephen D. Peskoff
1992	A.P. Indy	Tomonori Tsurumaki	Neil Drysdale	W.S. Farish & W.S. Kilroy
1993	Kotashaan	La Presle Farm	Richard Mandella	La Presle Farm
1994	Holy Bull	Jimmy Croll	Jimmy Croll	Pelican Stable
1995	Cigar	Allen E. Paulson	William Mott	Allen E. Paulson

Note: From 1936 to 1970, the *Daily Racing Form* annually selected a "Horse of the Year." In 1971 the *Daily Racing Form*, with the Thoroughbred Racing Association and the National Turf Writers Association, jointly created the Eclipse Awards.

Eclipse Award Winners

	2-YEAR-OLD COLT	2-YEAR-OLD FILLY	3-YEAR-OLD COLT
1971	Riva Ridge	Numbered Account	Canonero II
1972	Secretariat	La Prevoyante	Key to the Mint
1973	Protagonist	Talking Picture	Secretariat
1974	Foolish Pleasure	Ruffian	Little Current
1975	Honest Pleasure	Dearly Precious	Wajima
1976	Seattle Slew	Sensational	Bold Forbes
1977	Affirmed	Lakeville Miss	Seattle Slew
1978	Spectacular Bid	Candy Eclair / It's in the Air	Affirmed
1979	Rockhill Native	Smart Angle	Spectacular Bid
1980	Lord Avie	Heavenly Cause	Temperence Hill
1981	Deputy Minister	Before Dawn	Pleasant Colony
1982	Roving Boy	Landaluce	Conquistador Cielo
1983	Devil's Bag	Althea	Slew o' Gold
1984	Chief's Crown	Outstandingly	Swale
1985	Tasso	Family Style	Spend A Buck
1986	Capote	Brave Raj	Snow Chief
1987	Forty Niner	Epitome	Alysheba
1988	Easy Goer	Open Mind	Risen Star
1989	Rhythm	Go for Wand	Sunday Silence
1990	Fly So Free	Meadow Star	Unbridled
1991	Arazi	Pleasant Stage	Hansel
1992	Gilded Time	Eliza	A.P. Indy
1993	Dehere	Phone Chatter	Prairie Bayou
1994	Timber Country	Flanders	Holy Bull
1995	Maria's Mon	Golden Attraction	Thunder Gulch

Eclipse Award Winners *(Cont.)*

3-YEAR-OLD FILLY

1971 ....Turkish Trousers
1972 ....Susan's Girl
1973 ....Desert Vixen
1974 ....Chris Evert
1975 ....Ruffian
1976 ....Revidere
1977 ....Our Mims
1978 ....Tempest Queen
1979 ....Davona Dale
1980 ....Genuine Risk
1981 ....Wayward Lass
1982 ....Christmas Past
1983 ....Heartlight No. One
1984 ....Life's Magic
1985 ....Mom's Command
1986 ....Tiffany Lass
1987 ....Sacahuista
1988 ....Winning Colors
1989 ....Open Mind
1990 ....Go for Wand
1991 ....Dance Smartly
1992 ....Saratoga Dew
1993 ....Hollywood Wildcat
1994 ....Heavenly Prize
1995 ....Serena's Song

OLDER COLT, HORSE OR GELDING

1971 ....Ack Ack (5)
1972 ....Autobiography (4)
1973 ....Riva Ridge (4)
1974 ....Forego (4)
1975 ....Forego (5)
1976 ....Forego (6)
1977 ....Forego (7)
1978 ....Seattle Slew (4)
1979 ....Affirmed (4)
1980 ....Spectacular Bid (4)
1981 ....John Henry (6)
1982 ....Lemhi Gold (4)
1983 ....Bates Motel (4)
1984 ....Slew o'Gold (4)
1985 ....Vanlandingham (4)
1986 ....Turkoman (4)
1987 ....Ferdinand (4)
1988 ....Alysheba (4)
1989 ....Blushing John (4)
1990 ....Criminal Type (5)
1991 ....Black Tie Affair (5)
1992 ....Pleasant Tap (5)
1993 ....Bertrando (4)
1994 ....The Wicked North (5)
1995 ....Cigar (5)

OLDER FILLY OR MARE

1971 ....Shuvee (5)
1972 ....Typecast (6)
1973 ....Susan's Girl (4)
1974 ....Desert Vixen (4)
1975 ....Susan's Girl (6)
1976 ....Proud Delta (4)
1977 ....Cascapedia (4)
1978 ....Late Bloomer (4)
1979 ....Waya (4)

Note: Number in parentheses is horse's age.

OLDER FILLY OR MARE *(Cont.)*

1980 ....Glorious Song (4)
1981 ....Relaxing (5)
1982 ....Track Robbery (6)
1983 ....Ambassador of Luck (4)
1984 ....Princess Rooney (4)
1985 ....Life's Magic (4)
1986 ....Lady's Secret (4)
1987 ....North Sider (5)
1988 ....Personal Ensign (4)
1989 ....Bayakoa (5)
1990 ....Bayakoa (6)
1991 ....Queena (5)
1992 ....Paseana (5)
1993 ....Paseana (5)
1994 ....Sky Beauty (4)
1995 ....Inside Information (4)

CHAMPION TURF HORSE

1971 .....Run the Gantlet (3)
1972 .....Cougar II (6)
1973 .....Secretariat (3)
1974 .....Dahlia (4)
1975 .....Snow Knight (4)
1976 .....Youth (3)
1977 .....Johnny D (3)
1978 .....Mac Diarmida (3)

CHAMPION MALE TURF HORSE

1979 .....Bowl Game (5)
1980 .....John Henry (5)
1981 .....John Henry (6)
1982 .....Perrault (5)
1983 .....John Henry (8)
1984 .....John Henry (9)
1985 .....Cozzene (4)
1986 .....Manila (3)
1987 .....Theatrical (5)
1988 .....Sunshine Forever (3)
1989 .....Steinlen (6)
1990 .....Itsallgreektome (3)
1991 .....Tight Spot (4)
1992 .....Sky Classic (5)
1993 .....Kotashaan (5)
1994 .....Paradise Creek (5)
1995 .....Northern Spur (4)

CHAMPION FEMALE TURF HORSE

1979 .....Trillion (5)
1980 .....Just a Game II (4)
1981 .....De La Rose (3)
1982 .....April Run (4)
1983 .....All Along (4)
1984 .....Royal Heroine (4)
1985 .....Pebbles (4)
1986 .....Estrapade (6)
1987 .....Miesque (3)
1988 .....Miesque (4)
1989 .....Brown Bess (7)
1990 .....Laugh and Be Merry (5)
1991 .....Miss Alleged (4)
1992 .....Flawlessly (4)
1993 .....Flawlessly (5)
1994 .....Hatoof (5)
1995 .....Possibly Perfect (5)

STEEPLECHASE OR HURDLE HORSE

1971 .....Shadow Brook (7)
1972 .....Soothsayer (5)
1973 .....Athenian Idol (5)
1974 .....Gran Kan (8)
1975 .....Life's Illusion (4)
1976 .....Straight & True (6)
1977 .....Cafe Prince (7)
1978 .....Cafe Prince (8)
1979 .....Martie's Anger (4)
1980 .....Zaccio (4)
1981 .....Zaccio (5)
1982 .....Zaccio (6)
1983 .....Flatterer (4)
1984 .....Flatterer (5)
1985 .....Flatterer (6)
1986 .....Flatterer (7)
1987 .....Inlander (6)
1988 .....Jimmy Lorenzo (6)
1989 .....Highland Bud (4)
1990 .....Morley Street (7)
1991 .....Morley Street (8)
1992 .....Lonesome Glory (4)
1993 .....Lonesome Glory (5)
1994 .....Warm Spell (6)
1995 .....Lonesome Glory (7)

SPRINTER

1971 .....Ack Ack (5)
1972 .....Chou Croute (4)
1973 .....Shecky Greene (3)
1974 .....Forego (4)
1975 .....Gallant Bob (3)
1976 .....My Juliet (4)
1977 .....What a Summer (4)
1978 .....Dr. Patches (4)
............J. O. Tobin (4)
1979 .....Star de Naskra (4)
1980 .....Plugged Nickel (3)
1981 .....Guilty Conscience (5)
1982 .....Gold Beauty (3)
1983 .....Chinook Pass (4)
1984 .....Eillo (4)
1985 .....Precisionist (4)
1986 .....Smile (4)
1987 .....Groovy (4)
1988 .....Gulch (4)
1989 .....Safely Kept (3)
1990 .....Housebuster (3)
1991 .....Housebuster (4)
1992 .....Rubiano (5)
1993 .....Cardmania (7)
1994 .....Cherokee Run (4)
1995 .....Not Surprising (5)

OUTSTANDING OWNER

1971 .....Mr. & Mrs. E. E. Fogleson
1974 .....Dan Lasater
1975 .....Dan Lasater
1976 .....Dan Lasater
1977 .....Maxwell Gluck
1978 .....Harbor View Farm
1979 .....Harbor View Farm
1980 .....Mr. & Mrs. Bertram Firestone

Eclipse Award Winners *(Cont.)*

OUTSTANDING OWNER *(Cont.)*

1981.....Dotsam Stable
1982.....Viola Sommer
1983.....John Franks
1984.....John Franks
1985.....Mr. & Mrs. Eugene Klein
1986.....Mr. & Mrs. Eugene Klein
1987.....Mr. & Mrs. Eugene Klein
1988.....Ogden Phipps
1989.....Ogden Phipps
1990.....Frances Genter
1991.....Sam-Son Farm
1992.....Juddmonte Farms
1993.....John Franks
1994.....John Franks
1995.....Allen E. Paulson

OUTSTANDING TRAINER

1971.....Charlie Whittingham
1972.....Lucien Laurin
1973.....H. Allen Jerkens
1974.....Sherrill Ward
1975.....Steve DiMauro
1976.....Lazaro Barrera
1977.....Lazaro Barrera
1978.....Lazaro Barrera
1979.....Lazaro Barrera
1980.....Bud Delp
1981.....Ron McAnally
1982.....Charlie Whittingham
1983.....Woody Stephens
1984.....Jack Van Berg
1985.....D. Wayne Lukas
1986.....D. Wayne Lukas
1987.....D. Wayne Lukas
1988.....Claude R. McGaughey III
1989.....Charlie Whittingham
1990.....Carl Nafzger
1991.....Ron McAnally
1992.....Ron McAnally
1993.....Bobby Frankel
1994.....D. Wayne Lukas
1995.....William Mott

OUTSTANDING JOCKEY

1971.....Laffit Pincay Jr
1972.....Braulio Baeza
1973.....Laffit Pincay Jr
1974.....Laffit Pincay Jr
1975.....Braulio Baeza
1976.....Sandy Hawley
1977.....Steve Cauthen
1978.....Darrel McHargue

OUTSTANDING JOCKEY *(Cont.)*

1979.....Laffit Pincay Jr
1980.....Chris McCarron
1981.....Bill Shoemaker
1982.....Angel Cordero Jr
1983.....Angel Cordero Jr
1984.....Pat Day
1985.....Laffit Pincay Jr
1986.....Pat Day
1987.....Pat Day
1988.....Jose Santos
1989.....Kent Desormeaux
1990.....Craig Perret
1991.....Pat Day
1992.....Kent Desormeaux
1993.....Mike Smith
1994.....Mike Smith
1995.....Jerry Bailey

OUTSTANDING APPRENTICE JOCKEY

1971.....Gene St. Leon
1972.....Thomas Wallis
1973.....Steve Valdez
1974.....Chris McCarron
1975.....Jimmy Edwards
1976.....George Martens
1977.....Steve Cauthen
1978.....Ron Franklin
1979.....Cash Asmussen
1980.....Frank Lovato Jr
1981.....Richard Migliore
1982.....Alberto Delgado
1983.....Declan Murphy
1984.....Wesley Ward
1985.....Art Madrid Jr
1986.....Allen Stacy
1987.....Kent Desormeaux
1988.....Steve Capanas
1989.....Michael Luzzi
1990.....Mark Johnston
1991.....Mickey Walls
1992.....Jesus A. Bracho
1993.....Juan Umana
1994.....Dale Beckner
1995.....Ramon Perez

OUTSTANDING BREEDER

1974.....John W. Galbreath
1975.....Fred W. Hooper
1976.....Nelson Bunker Hunt
1977.....Edward Plunket Taylor
1978.....Harbor View Farm

OUTSTANDING BREEDER *(Cont.)*

1979.....Claiborne Farm
1980.....Mrs. Henry D. Paxson
1981.....Golden Chance Farm
1982.....Fred W. Hooper
1983.....Edward Plunket Taylor
1984.....Claiborne Farm
1985.....Nelson Bunker Hunt
1986.....Paul Mellon
1987.....Nelson Bunker Hunt
1988.....Ogden Phipps
1989.....North Ridge Farm
1990.....Calumet Farm
1991.....John and Betty Mabee
1992.....William S. Farish III
1993.....Allen Paulson
1994.....William T. Young
1995.....Juddmonte Farms

AWARD OF MERIT

1976.....Jack J. Dreyfus
1977.....Steve Cauthen
1978.....Ogden Phipps
1979.....Frank E. Kilroe
1980.....John D. Schapiro
1981.....Bill Shoemaker
1984.....John Gaines
1985.....Keene Daingerfield
1986.....Herman Cohen
1987.....J. B. Faulconer
1988.....John Forsythe
1989.....Michael P. Sandler
1991.....Fred W. Hooper
1994.....Alfred G. Vanderbilt

SPECIAL AWARD

1971.....Robert J. Kleberg
1974.....Charles Hatton
1976.....Bill Shoemaker
1980.....John T. Landry
          Pierre E. Bellocq (Peb)
1984.....C. V. Whitney
1985.....Arlington Park
1987.....Anheuser-Busch
1988.....Edward J. DeBartolo Sr
1989.....Richard Duchossois
1994.....John Longden
          Edward Arcaro

Note: Special Award and Award of Merit not presented annually. For long-term and/or outstanding service to the industry.

Breeders' Cup

Location: Hollywood Park (CA) 1984, 1987; Aqueduct Racetrack (NY) 1985; Santa Anita Park (CA) 1986, 1993; Churchill Downs (KY) 1988, 1991, 1995; Gulfstream Park (FL) 1989, 1992; Belmont Park (NY) 1990.

Juveniles

Year	Winner (Margin)	Jockey	Second	Third	Time
1984	Chief's Crown (¾)	Don MacBeth	Tank's Prospect	Spend a Buck	1:36⅕
1985	Tasso (Nose)	Laffit Pincay Jr	Storm Cat	Scat Dancer	1:36⅕
1986	Capote (1¼)	Laffit Pincay Jr	Qualify	Alysheba	1:43⅘
1987	Success Express (1¾)	Jose Santos	Regal Classic	Tejano	1:35⅕
1988	Is It True (1¼)	Laffit Pincay Jr	Easy Goer	Tagel	1:46⅗
1989	Rhythm (2)	Craig Perret	Grand Canyon	Slavic	1:43⅗
1990	Fly So Free (3)	Jose Santos	Take Me Out	Lost Mountain	1:43⅖
1991	Arazi (4¾)	Pat Valenzuela	Bertrando	Snappy Landing	1:44⅗
1992	Gilded Time (¾)	Chris McCarron	It'sali'lknownfact	River Special	1:43⅖
1993	Brocco (5)	Gary Stevens	Blumin Affair	Tabasco Cat	1:42⅘
1994	Timber Country (½)	Pat Day	Eltish	Tejano Run	1:44⅖
1995	Unbridled's Song (Neck)	Mike Smith	Hennessy	Editor's Note	1:41⅗

Note: One mile (1984–85, 87); 1$\frac{1}{16}$ miles (1986 and since 1988).

Juvenile Fillies

Year	Winner (Margin)	Jockey	Second	Third	Time
1984	Outstandingly*	Walter Guerra	Dusty Heart	Fine Spirit	1:37⅘
1985	Twilight Ridge (1)	Jorge Velasquez	Family Style	Steal a Kiss	1:35⅘
1986	Brave Raj (5½)	Pat Valenzuela	Tappiano	Saros Brig	1:43⅕
1987	Epitome (Nose)	Pat Day	Jeanne Jones	Dream Team	1:36⅖
1988	Open Mind (1¾)	Angel Cordero Jr	Darby Shuffle	Lea Lucinda	1:46⅗
1989	Go for Wand (2¾)	Randy Romero	Sweet Roberta	Stella Madrid	1:44⅕
1990	Meadow Star (5)	Jose Santos	Private Treasure	Dance Smartly	1:44
1991	Pleasant Stage (Neck)	Eddie Delahoussaye	La Spia	Cadillac Women	1:46⅖
1992	Eliza (1½)	Pat Valenzuela	Educated Risk	Boots 'n Jackie	1:42⅘
1993	Phone Chatter (Head)	Laffit Pincay	Sardula	Heavenly Prize	1:43
1994	Flanders (Head)	Pat Day	Serena's Song	Stormy Blues	1:45⅕
1995	My Flag (½)	Jerry Bailey	Cara Rafaela	Golden Attraction	1:42⅖

*In 1984, winner Fran's Valentine was disqualified for interference in the stretch and placed 10th.
Note: One mile (1984–85, 87); 1$\frac{1}{16}$ miles (1986 and since 1988).

Sprint

Year	Winner (Margin)	Jockey	Second	Third	Time
1984	Eillo (Nose)	Craig Perret	Commemorate	Fighting Fit	1:10⅕
1985	Precisionist (¾)	Chris McCarron	Smile	Mt. Livermore	1:08⅖
1986	Smile (1¼)	Jacinto Vasquez	Pine Tree Lane	Bedside Promise	1:08⅖
1987	Very Subtle (4)	Pat Valenzuela	Groovy	Exclusive Enough	1:08⅘
1988	Gulch (¾)	Angel Cordero Jr	Play the King	Afleet	1:10⅖
1989	Dancing Spree (Neck)	Angel Cordero Jr	Safely Kept	Dispersal	1:09
1990	Safely Kept (Neck)	Craig Perret	Dayjur	Black Tie Affair	1:09⅗
1991	Sheikh Albadou (Neck)	Pat Eddery	Pleasant Tap	Robyn Dancer	1:09⅕
1992	Thirty Slews (Neck)	Eddie Delahoussaye	Meafara	Rubiano	1:08⅕
1993	Cardmania (Neck)	Eddie Delahoussaye	Meafara	Gilded Time	1:08⅗
1994	Cherokee Run (Head)	Mike Smith	Soviet Problem	Cardmania	1:09⅖
1995	Desert Stormer (Neck)	Kent Desormeaux	Mr. Greeley	Lit de Justice	1:09

Note: Six furlongs (since 1984).

Breeders' Cup *(Cont.)*

Mile

Year	Winner (Margin)	Jockey	Second	Third	Time
1984	Royal Heroine (1½)	Fernando Toro	Star Choice	Cozzene	1:32⅗
1985	Cozzene (2¼)	Walter Guerra	Al Mamoon*	Shadeed	1:35
1986	Last Tycoon (Head)	Yves St-Martin	Palace Music	Fred Astaire	1:35⅕
1987	Miesque (3½)	Freddie Head	Show Dancer	Sonic Lady	1:32⅘
1988	Miesque (4)	Freddie Head	Steinlen	Simply Majestic	1:38⅗
1989	Steinlen (¾)	Jose Santos	Sabona	Most Welcome	1:37⅕
1990	Royal Academy (Neck)	Lester Piggott	Itsallgreektome	Priolo	1:35⅕
1991	Opening Verse (2¼)	Pat Valenzuela	Val de Bois	Star of Cozzene	1:37⅖
1992	Lure (3)	Mike Smith	Paradise Creek	Brief Truce	1:32⅘
1993	Lure (2¼)	Mike Smith	Ski Paradise	Fourstars Allstar	1:33⅖
1994	Barathea (Head)	Frankie Dettori	Johann Quatz	Unfinished Symph	1:34⅖
1995	Ridgewood Pearl (2)	John Murtagh	Fastness	Sayyedati	1:43⅗

*2nd place finisher Palace Music was disqualified for interference and placed 9th.

Distaff

Year	Winner (Margin)	Jockey	Second	Third	Time
1984	Princess Rooney (7)	Eddie Delahoussaye	Life's Magic	Adored	2:02⅖
1985	Life's Magic (6¼)	Angel Cordero Jr	Lady's Secret	Dontstop Themusic	2:02
1986	Lady's Secret (2½)	Pat Day	Fran's Valentine	Outstandingly	2:01⅕
1987	Sacahuista (2¼)	Randy Romero	Clabber Girl	Oueee Bebe	2:02⅘
1988	Personal Ensign (Nose)	Randy Romero	Winning Colors	Goodbye Halo	1:52
1989	Bayakoa (1½)	Laffit Pincay Jr	Gorgeous	Open Mind	1:47⅖
1990	Bayakoa (6¾)	Laffit Pincay Jr	Colonial Waters	Valay Maid	1:49⅕
1991	Dance Smarty (½)	Pat Day	Versailles Treaty	Brought to Mind	1:50⅘
1992	Paseana (4)	Chris McCarron	Versailles Treaty	Magical Maiden	1:48
1993	Hollywood Wildcat (Nose)	Eddie Delahoussaye	Paseana	Re Toss	1:48⅕
1994	One Dreamer (Neck)	Gary Stevens	Heavenly Prize	Miss Dominique	1:50⅗
1995	Inside Information (13½)	Mike Smith	Heavenly Prize	Lakeway	1:46

Note: 1¼ miles (1984-87); 1⅛ miles (since 1988).

Turf

Year	Winner (Margin)	Jockey	Second	Third	Time
1984	Lashkari (Neck)	Yves St-Martin	All Along	Raami	2:25⅕
1985	Pebbles (Neck)	Pat Eddery	Strawberry Rd II	Mourjane	2:27
1986	Manila (Neck)	Jose Santos	Theatrical	Estrapade	2:25⅖
1987	Theatrical (½)	Pat Day	Trempolino	Village Star II	2:24⅖
1988	Great Communicator (½)	Ray Sibille	Sunshine Forever	Indian Skimmer	2:35⅕
1989	Prized (Head)	Eddie Delahoussaye	Sierra Roberta	Star Lift	2:28
1990	In the Wings (½)	Gary Stevens	With Approval	El Senor	2:29⅗
1991	Miss Alleged (2)	Eric Legrix	Itsallgreektome	Quest for Fame	2:30⅘
1992	Fraise (Nose)	Pat Valenzuela	Sky Classic	Quest For Fame	2:24
1993	Kotashaan (½)	Kent Desormeaux	Bien Bien	Luazar	2:25
1994	Tikkanen (1½)	Mike Smith	Hatoof	Paradise Creek	2:26⅖
1995	Northern Spur (Neck)	Chris McCarron	Freedom Cry	Carnegie	2:42

Note: 1½ miles.

Classic

Year	Winner (Margin)	Jockey	Second	Third	Time
1984	Wild Again (Head)	Pat Day	Slew o' Gold*	Gate Dancer	2:03⅖
1985	Proud Truth (Head)	Jorge Velasquez	Gate Dancer	Turkoman	2:00⅘
1986	Skywalker (1¼)	Laffit Pincay Jr	Turkoman	Precisionist	2:00⅖
1987	Ferdinand (Nose)	Bill Shoemaker	Alysheba	Judge Angelucci	2:01⅖
1988	Alysheba (Nose)	Chris McCarron	Seeking the Gold	Waquoit	2:04⅘
1989	Sunday Silence (½)	Chris McCarron	Easy Goer	Blushing John	2:00⅕
1990	Unbridled (1)	Pat Day	Ibn Bey	Thirty Six Red	2:02⅕
1991	Black Tie Affair (1¼)	Jerry Bailey	Twilight Agenda	Unbridled	2:02⅘
1992	A.P. Indy (2)	Eddie Delahoussaye	Pleasant Tap	Jolypha	2:00⅕
1993	Arcangues (2)	Jerry Bailey	Bertrando	Kissin Kris	2:00⅘
1994	Concern (Neck)	Jerry Bailey	Tabasco Cat	Dramatic Gold	2:02⅖
1995	Cigar (2½)	Jerry Bailey	L'Carriere	Unaccounted For	1:59⅖

*2nd place finisher Gate Dancer was disqualified for interference and placed 3rd.
Note: 1¼ miles.

England's Triple Crown Winners

England's Triple Crown consists of the Two Thousand Guineas, held at Newmarket; the Epsom Derby, held at Epsom Downs; and the St. Leger Stakes, held at Doncaster.

Year	Horse	Owner	Year	Horse	Owner
1853	West Australian	Mr. Bowes	1900	Diamond Jubilee	Prince of Wales
1865	Gladiateur	F. DeLagrange	1903	*Rock Sand	J. Miller
1866	Lord Lyon	R. Sutton	1915	Pommern	S. Joel
1886	*Ormonde	Duke of Westminster	1917	Gay Crusader	Mr. Fairie
1891	Common	†F. Johnstone	1918	Gainsborough	Lady James Douglas
1893	Isinglass	H. McCalmont	1935	*Bahram	Aga Khan
1897	Galtee More	J. Gubbins	1970	‡Nijinsky II	C. W. Engelhard
1899	Flying Fox	Duke of Westminster			

*Imported into United States. †Raced in name of Lord Alington in Two Thousand Guineas. ‡Canadian-bred.

Annual Leaders

Horse—Money Won

Year	Horse	Age	Starts	1st	2nd	3rd	Winnings ($)
1919	Sir Barton	3	13	8	3	2	88,250
1920	Man o'War	3	11	11	0	0	166,140
1921	Morvich	2	11	11	0	0	115,234
1922	Pillory	3	7	4	1	1	95,654
1923	Zev	3	14	12	1	0	272,008
1924	Sarzen	3	12	8	1	1	95,640
1925	Pompey	2	10	7	2	0	121,630
1926	Crusader	3	15	9	4	0	166,033
1927	Anita Peabody	2	7	6	0	1	111,905
1928	High Strung	2	6	5	0	0	153,590
1929	Blue Larkspur	3	6	4	1	0	153,450
1930	Gallant Fox	3	10	9	1	0	308,275
1931	Gallant Flight	2	7	7	0	0	219,000
1932	Gusto	3	16	4	3	2	145,940
1933	Singing Wood	2	9	3	2	2	88,050
1934	Cavalcade	3	7	6	1	0	111,235
1935	Omaha	3	9	6	1	2	142,255
1936	Granville	3	11	7	3	0	110,295
1937	Seabiscuit	4	15	11	2	2	168,580
1938	Stagehand	3	15	8	2	3	189,710
1939	Challedon	3	15	9	2	3	184,535
1940	Bimelech	3	7	4	2	1	110,005
1941	Whirlaway	3	20	13	5	2	272,386
1942	Shut Out	3	12	8	2	0	238,872
1943	Count Fleet	3	6	6	0	0	174,055
1944	Pavot	2	8	8	0	0	179,040
1945	Busher	3	13	10	2	1	273,735
1946	Assault	3	15	8	2	3	424,195
1947	Armed	6	17	11	4	1	376,325
1948	Citation	3	20	19	1	0	709,470
1949	Ponder	3	21	9	5	2	321,825
1950	Noor	5	12	7	4	1	346,940
1951	Counterpoint	3	15	7	2	1	250,525
1952	Crafty Admiral	4	16	9	4	1	277,225
1953	Native Dancer	3	10	9	1	0	513,425
1954	Determine	3	15	10	3	2	328,700
1955	Nashua	3	12	10	1	1	752,550
1956	Needles	3	8	4	2	0	440,850
1957	Round Table	3	22	15	1	3	600,383
1958	Round Table	4	20	14	4	0	662,780
1959	Sword Dancer	3	13	8	4	0	537,004
1960	Bally Ache	3	15	10	3	1	445,045
1961	Carry Back	3	16	9	1	3	565,349
1962	Never Bend	2	10	7	1	2	402,969
1963	Candy Spots	3	12	7	2	1	604,481
1964	Gun Bow	4	16	8	4	2	580,100
1965	Buckpasser	2	11	9	1	0	568,096

Note: Annual leaders on pages 484-488 courtesy of *The American Racing Manual*, a publication of Daily Racing Form, Inc.

Horse—Money Won *(Cont.)*

Year	Horse	Age	Starts	1st	2nd	3rd	Winnings ($)
1966	Buckpasser	3	14	13	1	0	669,078
1967	Damascus	3	16	12	3	1	817,941
1968	Forward Pass	3	13	7	2	0	546,674
1969	Arts and Letters	3	14	8	5	1	555,604
1970	Personality	3	18	8	2	1	444,049
1971	Riva Ridge	2	9	7	0	0	503,263
1972	Droll Role	4	19	7	3	4	471,633
1973	Secretariat	3	12	9	2	1	860,404
1974	Chris Evert	3	8	5	1	2	551,063
1975	Foolish Pleasure	3	11	5	4	1	716,278
1976	Forego	6	8	6	1	1	401,701
1977	Seattle Slew	3	7	6	0	1	641,370
1978	Affirmed	3	11	8	2	0	901,541
1979	Spectacular Bid	3	12	10	1	1	1,279,334
1980	Temperence Hill	3	17	8	3	1	1,130,452
1981	John Henry	6	10	8	0	0	1,798,030
1982	Perrault	5	8	4	1	2	1,197,400
1983	All Along	4	7	4	1	1	2,138,963
1984	Slew o'Gold	4	6	5	1	0	2,627,944
1985	Spend A Buck	3	7	5	1	1	3,552,704
1986	Snow Chief	3	9	6	1	1	1,875,200
1987	Alysheba	3	10	3	3	1	2,511,156
1988	Alysheba	4	9	7	1	0	3,808,600
1989	Sunday Silence	3	9	7	2	0	4,578,454
1990	Unbridled	3	11	4	3	2	3,718,149
1991	Dance Smartly	3	8	8	0	0	2,876,821
1992	A.P. Indy	3	7	5	0	1	2,622,560
1993	Kotashaan	3	10	6	3	0	2,619,014
1994	Paradise Creek	5	11	8	2	1	2,610,187
1995	Cigar	5	10	10	0	0	4,819,800

Trainer—Money Won

Year	Trainer	Wins	Winnings ($)	Year	Trainer	Wins	Winnings ($)
1908	James Rowe, Sr	50	284,335	1940	Silent Tom Smith	14	269,200
1909	Sam Hildreth	73	123,942	1941	Plain Ben Jones	70	475,318
1910	Sam Hildreth	84	148,010	1942	John M. Gaver Sr	48	406,547
1911	Sam Hildreth	67	49,418	1943	Plain Ben Jones	73	267,915
1912	John F. Schorr	63	58,110	1944	Plain Ben Jones	60	601,660
1913	James Rowe, Sr	18	45,936	1945	Silent Tom Smith	52	510,655
1914	R. C. Benson	45	59,315	1946	Hirsch Jacobs	99	560,077
1915	James Rowe, Sr	19	75,596	1947	Jimmy Jones	85	1,334,805
1916	Sam Hildreth	39	70,950	1948	Jimmy Jones	81	1,118,670
1917	Sam Hildreth	23	61,698	1949	Jimmy Jones	76	978,587
1918	H. Guy Bedwell	53	80,296	1950	Preston Burch	96	637,754
1919	H. Guy Bedwell	63	208,728	1951	John M. Gaver Sr	42	616,392
1920	L. Feustal	22	186,087	1952	Plain Ben Jones	29	662,137
1921	Sam Hildreth	85	262,768	1953	Harry Trotsek	54	1,028,873
1922	Sam Hildreth	74	247,014	1954	Willie Molter	136	1,107,860
1923	Sam Hildreth	75	392,124	1955	Sunny Jim Fitzsimmons	66	1,270,055
1924	Sam Hildreth	77	255,608	1956	Willie Molter	142	1,227,402
1925	G. R. Tompkins	30	199,245	1957	Jimmy Jones	70	1,150,910
1926	Scott P. Harlan	21	205,681	1958	Willie Molter	69	1,116,544
1927	W. H. Bringloe	63	216,563	1959	Willie Molter	71	847,290
1928	John F. Schorr	65	258,425	1960	Hirsch Jacobs	97	748,349
1929	James Rowe, Jr	25	314,881	1961	Jimmy Jones	62	759,856
1930	Sunny Jim Fitzsimmons	47	397,355	1962	Mesh Tenney	58	1,099,474
1931	Big Jim Healey	33	297,300	1963	Mesh Tenney	40	860,703
1932	Sunny Jim Fitzsimmons	68	266,650	1964	Bill Winfrey	61	1,350,534
1933	Humming Bob Smith	53	135,720	1965	Hirsch Jacobs	91	1,331,628
1934	Humming Bob Smith	43	249,938	1966	Eddie Neloy	93	2,456,250
1935	Bud Stotler	87	303,005	1967	Eddie Neloy	72	1,776,089
1936	Sunny Jim Fitzsimmons	42	193,415	1968	Eddie Neloy	52	1,233,101
1937	Robert McGarvey	46	209,925	1969	Elliott Burch	26	1,067,936
1938	Earl Sande	15	226,495	1970	Charlie Whittingham	82	1,302,354
1939	Sunny Jim Fitzsimmons	45	266,205	1971	Charlie Whittingham	77	1,737,115

Trainer—Money Won (Cont.)

Year	Trainer	Wins	Winnings ($)	Year	Trainer	Wins	Winnings ($)
1972	Charlie Whittingham	79	1,734,020	1984	D. Wayne Lukas	131	5,835,921
1973	Charlie Whittingham	85	1,865,385	1985	D. Wayne Lukas	218	11,155,188
1974	Pancho Martin	166	2,408,419	1986	D. Wayne Lukas	259	12,345,180
1975	Charlie Whittingham	93	2,437,244	1987	D. Wayne Lukas	343	17,502,110
1976	Jack Van Berg	496	2,976,196	1988	D. Wayne Lukas	318	17,842,358
1977	Laz Barrera	127	2,715,848	1989	D. Wayne Lukas	305	16,103,998
1978	Laz Barrera	100	3,307,164	1990	D. Wayne Lukas	267	14,508,871
1979	Laz Barrera	98	3,608,517	1991	D. Wayne Lukas	289	15,942,223
1980	Laz Barrera	99	2,969,151	1992	D. Wayne Lukas	230	9,806,436
1981	Charlie Whittingham	74	3,993,302	1993	Robert Frankel	79	8,883,252
1982	Charlie Whittingham	63	4,587,457	1994	D. Wayne Lukas	147	9,247,457
1983	D. Wayne Lukas	78	4,267,261	1995	D. Wayne Lukas	194	12,842,865

Jockey—Money Won

Year	Jockey	Mts	1st	2nd	3rd	Pct	Winnings ($)
1919	John Loftus	177	65	36	24	.37	252,707
1920	Clarence Kummer	353	87	79	48	.25	292,376
1921	Earl Sande	340	112	69	59	.33	263,043
1922	Albert Johnson	297	43	57	40	.14	345,054
1923	Earl Sande	430	122	89	79	.28	569,394
1924	Ivan Parke	844	205	175	121	.24	290,395
1925	Laverne Fator	315	81	54	44	.26	305,775
1926	Laverne Fator	511	143	90	86	.28	361,435
1927	Earl Sande	179	49	33	19	.27	277,877
1928	Pony McAtee	235	55	43	25	.23	301,295
1929	Mack Garner	274	57	39	33	.21	314,975
1930	Sonny Workman	571	152	88	79	.27	420,438
1931	Charles Kurtsinger	519	93	82	79	.18	392,095
1932	Sonny Workman	378	87	48	55	.23	385,070
1933	Robert Jones	471	63	57	70	.13	226,285
1934	Wayne D. Wright	919	174	154	114	.19	287,185
1935	Silvio Coucci	749	141	125	103	.19	319,760
1936	Wayne D. Wright	670	100	102	73	.15	264,000
1937	Charles Kurtsinger	765	120	94	106	.16	384,202
1938	Nick Wall	658	97	94	82	.15	385,161
1939	Basil James	904	191	165	105	.21	353,333
1940	Eddie Arcaro	783	132	143	112	.17	343,661
1941	Don Meade	1164	210	185	158	.18	398,627
1942	Eddie Arcaro	687	123	97	89	.18	481,949
1943	John Longden	871	173	140	121	.20	573,276
1944	Ted Atkinson	1539	287	231	213	.19	899,101
1945	John Longden	778	180	112	100	.23	981,977
1946	Ted Atkinson	1377	233	213	173	.17	1,036,825
1947	Douglas Dodson	646	141	100	75	.22	1,429,949
1948	Eddie Arcaro	726	188	108	98	.26	1,686,230
1949	Steve Brooks	906	209	172	110	.23	1,316,817
1950	Eddie Arcaro	888	195	153	144	.22	1,410,160
1951	Bill Shoemaker	1161	257	197	161	.22	1,329,890
1952	Eddie Arcaro	807	188	122	109	.23	1,859,591
1953	Bill Shoemaker	1683	485	302	210	.29	1,784,187
1954	Bill Shoemaker	1251	380	221	142	.30	1,876,760
1955	Eddie Arcaro	820	158	126	108	.19	1,864,796
1956	Bill Hartack	1387	347	252	184	.25	2,343,955
1957	Bill Hartack	1238	341	208	178	.28	3,060,501
1958	Bill Shoemaker	1133	300	185	137	.26	2,961,693
1959	Bill Shoemaker	1285	347	230	159	.27	2,843,133
1960	Bill Shoemaker	1227	274	196	158	.22	2,123,961
1961	Bill Shoemaker	1256	304	186	175	.24	2,690,819
1962	Bill Shoemaker	1126	311	156	128	.28	2,916,844
1963	Bill Shoemaker	1203	271	193	137	.22	2,526,925
1964	Bill Shoemaker	1056	246	147	133	.23	2,649,553
1965	Braulio Baeza	1245	270	200	201	.22	2,582,702
1966	Braulio Baeza	1341	298	222	190	.22	2,951,022
1967	Braulio Baeza	1064	256	184	127	.24	3,088,888
1968	Braulio Baeza	1089	201	184	145	.18	2,835,108

Jockey—Money Won *(Cont.)*

Year	Jockey	Mts	1st	2nd	3rd	Pct	Winnings ($)
1969	Jorge Velasquez	1442	258	230	204	.18	2,542,315
1970	Laffit Pincay Jr	1328	269	208	187	.20	2,626,526
1971	Laffit Pincay Jr	1627	380	288	214	.23	3,784,377
1972	Laffit Pincay Jr	1388	289	215	205	.21	3,225,827
1973	Laffit Pincay Jr	1444	350	254	209	.24	4,093,492
1974	Laffit Pincay Jr	1278	341	227	180	.27	4,251,060
1975	Braulio Baeza	1190	196	208	180	.16	3,674,398
1976	Angel Cordero Jr	1534	274	273	235	.18	4,709,500
1977	Steve Cauthen	2075	487	345	304	.23	6,151,750
1978	Darrel McHargue	1762	375	294	263	.21	6,188,353
1979	Laffit Pincay Jr	1708	420	302	261	.25	8,183,535
1980	Chris McCarron	1964	405	318	282	.20	7,666,100
1981	Chris McCarron	1494	326	251	207	.22	8,397,604
1982	Angel Cordero Jr	1838	397	338	227	.22	9,702,520
1983	Angel Cordero Jr	1792	362	296	237	.20	10,116,807
1984	Chris McCarron	1565	356	276	218	.23	12,038,213
1985	Laffit Pincay Jr	1409	289	246	183	.21	13,415,049
1986	Jose Santos	1636	329	237	222	.20	11,329,297
1987	Jose Santos	1639	305	268	208	.19	12,407,355
1988	Jose Santos	1867	370	287	265	.20	14,877,298
1989	Jose Santos	1459	285	238	220	.20	13,847,003
1990	Gary Stevens	1504	283	245	202	.19	13,881,198
1991	Chris McCarron	1440	265	228	206	.18	14,441,083
1992	Kent Desormeaux	1568	361	260	208	.23	14,193,006
1993	Mike Smith	1,510	343	235	214	.23	14,008,148
1994	Mike Smith	1,484	317	250	196	.21	15,979,820
1995	Jerry Bailey	1,265	287	193	144	.23	16,308,230

Jockey—Races Won

Year	Jockey	Mts	1st	2nd	3rd	Pct
1895	J. Perkins	762	192	177	129	.25
1896	J. Scherrer	1093	271	227	172	.24
1897	H. Martin	803	173	152	116	.21
1898	T. Burns	973	277	213	149	.28
1899	T. Burns	1064	273	173	266	.26
1900	C. Mitchell	874	195	140	139	.23
1901	W. O'Connor	1047	253	221	192	.24
1902	J. Ranch	1069	276	205	181	.26
1903	G.C. Fuller	918	229	152	122	.25
1904	E. Hildebrand	1169	297	230	171	.25
1905	D. Nicol	861	221	143	136	.26
1906	W. Miller	1384	388	300	199	.28
1907	W. Miller	1194	334	226	170	.28
1908	V. Powers	1260	324	204	185	.26
1909	V. Powers	704	173	121	114	.25
1910	G. Garner	947	200	188	153	.20
1911	T. Koerner	813	162	133	112	.20
1912	P. Hill	967	168	141	129	.17
1913	M. Buxton	887	146	131	136	.16
1914	J. McTaggart	787	157	132	106	.20
1915	M. Garner	775	151	118	90	.19
1916	F. Robinson	791	178	131	124	.23
1917	W. Crump	803	151	140	101	.19
1918	F. Robinson	864	185	140	108	.21
1919	C. Robinson	896	190	140	126	.21
1920	J. Butwell	721	152	129	139	.21
1921	C. Lang	696	135	110	105	.19
1922	M. Fator	859	188	153	116	.22
1923	I. Parke	718	173	105	95	.24
1924	I. Parke	844	205	175	121	.24
1925	A. Mortensen	987	187	145	138	.19
1926	R. Jones	1172	190	163	152	.16
1927	L. Hardy	1130	207	192	151	.18
1928	J. Inzelone	1052	155	152	135	.15
1929	M. Knight	871	149	132	133	.17

Jockey—Races Won (Cont.)

Year	Jockey	Mts	1st	2nd	3rd	Pct
1930	H.R. Riley	861	177	145	123	.21
1931	H. Roble	1174	173	173	155	.15
1932	J. Gilbert	1050	212	144	160	.20
1933	J. Westrope	1224	301	235	166	.25
1934	M. Peters	1045	221	179	147	.21
1935	C. Stevenson	1099	206	169	146	.19
1936	B. James	1106	245	195	161	.22
1937	J. Adams	1265	260	186	177	.21
1938	J. Longden	1150	236	168	171	.21
1939	D. Meade	1284	255	221	180	.20
1940	E. Dew	1377	287	201	180	.21
1941	D. Meade	1164	210	185	158	.18
1942	J. Adams	1120	245	185	150	.22
1943	J. Adams	1069	228	159	171	.21
1944	T. Atkinson	1539	287	231	213	.19
1945	J.D. Jessop	1085	290	182	168	.27
1946	T. Atkinson	1377	233	213	173	.17
1947	J. Longden	1327	316	250	195	.24
1948	J. Longden	1197	319	233	161	.27
1949	G. Glisson	1347	270	217	181	.20
1950	W. Shoemaker	1640	388	266	230	.24
1951	C. Burr	1319	310	232	192	.24
1952	A. DeSpirito	1482	390	247	212	.26
1953	W. Shoemaker	1683	485	302	210	.29
1954	W. Shoemaker	1251	380	221	142	.30
1955	W. Hartack	1702	417	298	215	.25
1956	W. Hartack	1387	347	252	184	.25
1957	W. Hartack	1238	341	208	178	.28
1958	W. Shoemaker	1133	300	185	137	.26
1959	W. Shoemaker	1285	347	230	159	.27
1960	W. Hartack	1402	307	247	190	.22
1961	J. Sellers	1394	328	212	227	.24
1962	R. Ferraro	1755	352	252	226	.20
1963	W. Blum	1704	360	286	215	.21
1964	W. Blum	1577	324	274	170	.21
1965	J. Davidson	1582	319	228	190	.20
1966	A. Gomez	996	318	173	142	.32
1967	J. Velasquez	1939	438	315	270	.23
1968	A. Cordero Jr.	1662	345	278	219	.21
1969	L. Snyder	1645	352	290	243	.21
1970	S. Hawley	1908	452	313	265	.24
1971	L Pincay Jr.	1627	380	288	214	.23
1972	S. Hawley	1381	367	269	200	.27
1973	S. Hawley	1925	515	336	292	.27
1974	C.J. McCarron	2199	546	392	297	.25
1975	C.J. McCarron	2194	458	389	305	.21
1976	S. Hawley	1637	413	245	201	.25
1977	S. Cauthen	2075	487	345	304	.23
1978	E. Delahoussaye	1666	384	285	238	.23
1979	D. Gall	2146	479	396	326	.22
1980	C.J. McCarron	1964	405	318	282	.20
1981	D. Gall	1917	376	305	297	.20
1982	Pat Day	1870	399	326	255	.21
1983	Pat Day	1725	454	321	251	.26
1984	Pat Day	1694	399	296	259	.24
1985	C.W. Antley	2335	469	371	288	.20
1986	Pat Day	1417	429	246	202	.30
1987	Kent Desormeaux	2207	450	370	294	.28
1988	Kent Desormeaux	1897	474	295	276	.25
1989	Kent Desormeaux	2312	598	385	309	.25
1990	Pat Day	1421	364	265	222	.26
1991	Pat Day	1405	430	256	213	.31
1992	Russell Baze	1691	433	296	237	.25
1993	Russell Baze	1579	410	297	225	.26
1994	Russell Baze	1588	415	301	266	.26
1995	Russell Baze	1531	445	310	232	.29

Jockey	Years Riding	Mts	1st	2nd	3rd	Win Pct	Winnings ($)
Bill Shoemaker (1990)	42	40,350	8,833	6,136	4,987	.219	123,375,524
Laffit Pincay	30	41,713	8,440	6,811	5,770	.202	192,484,910
Angel Cordero (1992)	31	38,646	7,057	6,136	5,359	.183	164,561,227
David Gall	39	39,283	6,910	6,065	5,710	.176	22,431,714
Jorge Velasquez	33	40,280	6,751	6,105	5,692	.168	123,252,413
Pat Day	23	30,499	6,705	5,192	4,262	.220	149,339,825
Larry Snyder (1994)	35	35,681	6,388	5,030	3,440	.179	47,207,289
Sandy Hawley	29	30,760	6,357	4,731	4,061	.207	85,382,333
Carl Gambardella (1994)	39	39,018	6,349	5,953	5,353	.163	29,389,041
Chris McCarron	21	30,354	6,338	5,036	4,173	.209	195,660,204
John Longden (1966)	40	32,413	6,032	4,914	4,273	.186	24,665,800
Earlie Fires	31	39,411	5,808	4,903	4,697	.147	69,205,127
Eddie Delahoussaye	26	34,291	5,633	4,959	4,786	.164	152,317,592
Russell Baze	22	28,096	5,434	4,461	3,900	.193	73,933,645
Jacinto Vasquez	36	37,303	5,223	4,717	4,506	.140	80,526,130
Eddie Arcaro (1961)	31	24,092	4,779	3,807	3,302	.198	30,039,543
Don Brumfield (1989)	37	33,223	4,573	4,076	3,758	.138	43,567,861
Steve Brooks (1975)	34	30,330	4,451	4,219	3,658	.147	18,239,817
Walter Blum (1975)	22	28,673	4,382	3,913	3,350	.153	26,197,189
Eddie Maple	28	33,032	4,311	4,395	4,226	.130	101,928,775
Ron Ardoin	23	25,991	4,285	3,466	3,070	.165	41,728,827
Bill Hartack (1974)	22	21,535	4,272	3,370	2,871	.198	26,466,758
Avelino Gomez (1980)	34	17,028	4,081	2,947	2,405	.240	11,777,297
Craig Perret	29	24,682	4,079	3,564	3,285	.165	91,525,276
Rodolfo Baez	22	24,353	4,004	3,592	3,484	.164	23,475,169

Note: Records go through June 30, 1996 and include available statistics for races ridden in foreign countries. Figures in parentheses after jockey's name indicate last year in which he rode.

Leading jockeys courtesy of *The American Racing Manual*, a publication of Daily Racing Form, Inc.

National Museum of Racing Hall of Fame

HORSES

Ack Ack (1986, 1966)
Affectionately (1989, 1960)
Affirmed (1980, 1975)
All Along (1990, 1979)
Alsab (1976, 1939)
Alydar (1989, 1975)
Alysheba (1993, 1984)
American Eclipse (1970, 1814)
Armed (1963, 1941)
Artful (1956, 1902)
Arts and Letters (1994, 1966)
Assault (1964, 1943)
Battleship (1969, 1927)
Bed o' Roses (1976, 1947)
Beldame (1956, 1901)
Ben Brush (1955, 1893)
Bewitch (1977, 1945)
Bimelech (1990, 1937)
Black Gold (1989, 1921)
Black Helen (1991, 1932)
Blue Larkspur (1957, 1926)
Bold Ruler (1973, 1954)
Bon Nouvel (1976, 1960)
Boston (1955, 1833)
Broomstick (1956, 1901)
Buckpasser (1970, 1963)
Busher (1964, 1942)
Bushranger (1967, 1930)
Cafe Prince (1985, 1970)
Carry Back (1975, 1958)
Cavalcade (1993, 1931)

Challedon (1977, 1936)
Chris Evert (1988, 1971)
Cicada (1967, 1959)
Citation (1959, 1945)
Coaltown (1983, 1945)
Colin (1956, 1905)
Commando (1956, 1898)
Count Fleet (1961, 1940)
Crusader (1995, 1923)
Dahlia (1981, 1970)
Damascus (1974, 1964)
Dark Mirage (1974, 1965)
Davona Dale (1985, 1976)
Desert Vixen (1979, 1970)
Devil Diver (1980, 1939)
Discovery (1969, 1931)
Domino (1955, 1891)
Dr. Fager (1971, 1964)
Eight Thirty (1994, 1936)
Elkridge (1966, 1938)
Emperor of Norfolk (1988, 1885)
Equipoise (1957, 1928)
Exterminator (1957, 1915)
Fairmount (1985, 1921)
Fair Play (1956, 1905)
Fashion (1980, 1837)
Firenze (1981, 1884)
Flatterer (1994, 1979)
Foolish Pleasure (1995, 1972)
Forego (1979, 1970)
Gallant Bloom (1977, 1966)

Gallant Fox (1957, 1927)
Gallant Man (1987, 1954)
Gallorette (1962, 1942)
Gamely (1980, 1964)
Genuine Risk (1986, 1977)
Go For Wand (1996, 1987)
Good and Plenty (1956, 1900)
Grey Lag (1957, 1918)
Hamburg (1986, 1895)
Hanover (1955, 1884)
Henry of Navarre (1985, 1891)
Hill Prince (1991, 1947)
Hindoo (1955, 1878)
Imp (1965, 1894)
Jay Trump (1971, 1957)
John Henry (1990, 1975)
Johnstown (1992, 1936)
Jolly Roger (1965, 1922)
Kelso (1967, 1957)
Kentucky (1983, 1861)
Kingston (1955, 1884)
Lady's Secret (1992, 1982)
La Prevoyante (1995, 1970)
L'Escargot (1977, 1963)
Lexington (1955, 1850)
Longfellow (1971, 1867)
Luke Blackburn (1956, 1877)
Majestic Prince (1988, 1966)
Man o' War (1957, 1917)
Miss Woodford (1967, 1880)
Myrtlewood (1979, 1932)

Note: Years of election and foaling in parentheses.

HORSES *(Cont.)*

Nashua (1965, 1952)
Native Dancer (1963, 1950)
Native Diver (1978, 1959)
Neji (1966, 1950)
Northern Dancer (1976, 1961)
Oedipus (1978, 1946)
Old Rosebud (1968, 1911)
Omaha (1965, 1932)
Pan Zareta (1972, 1910)
Parole (1984, 1873)
Personal Ensign (1993, 1984)
Peter Pan (1956, 1904)
Princess Doreen (1982, 1921)
Princess Rooney (1991, 1980)
Real Delight (1987, 1949)
Regret (1957, 1912)
Reigh Count (1978, 1923)
Roamer (1981, 1911)
Roseben (1956, 1901)

Round Table (1972, 1954)
Ruffian (1976, 1972)
Ruthless (1975, 1864)
Salvator (1955, 1886)
Sarazen (1957, 1921)
Seabiscuit (1958, 1933)
Searching (1978, 1952)
Seattle Slew (1981, 1974)
Secretariat (1974, 1970)
Shuvee (1975, 1966)
Silver Spoon (1978, 1956)
Sir Archy (1955, 1805)
Sir Barton (1957, 1916)
Slew o' Gold (1992, 1980)
Spectacular Bid (1982, 1976)
Stymie (1975, 1941)
Sun Beau (1996, 1925)
Sunday Silence (1996, 1986)
Susan's Girl (1976, 1969)

Swaps (1966, 1952)
Sword Dancer (1977, 1956)
Sysonby (1956, 1902)
Ta Wee (1994, 1967)
Ten Broeck (1982, 1872)
Tim Tam (1985, 1955)
Tom Fool (1960, 1949)
Top Flight (1966, 1929)
Tosmah (1984, 1961)
Twenty Grand (1957, 1928)
Twilight Tear (1963, 1941)
Two Lea (1982, 1946)
War Admiral (1958, 1934)
Whirlaway (1959, 1938)
Whisk Broom II (1979, 1907)
Zaccio (1990, 1976)
Zev (1983, 1920)

HARNESS RACING

Major Races

Hambletonian

Year	Winner	Driver	Year	Winner	Driver
1926	Guy McKinney	Nat Ray	1962	A. C.'s Viking	Sanders Russell
1927	Iosola's Worthy	Marvin Childs	1963	Speedy Scot	Ralph Baldwin
1928	Spenser	W. H. Leese	1964	Ayres	J. Simpson, Sr
1929	Walter Dear	Walter Cox	1965	Egyptian Candor	Del Cameron
1930	Hanover's Bertha	Tom Berry	1966	Kerry Way	Frank Ervin
1931	Calumet Butler	R. D. McMahon	1967	Speedy Streak	Del Cameron
1932	The Marchioness	William Caton	1968	Nevele Pride	Stanley Dancer
1933	Mary Reynolds	Ben White	1969	Lindy's Pride	H. Beissinger
1934	Lord Jim	Doc Parshall	1970	Timothy T.	J. Simpson, Jr
1935	Greyhound	Sep Palin	1971	Speedy Crown	H. Beissinger
1936	Rosalind	Ben White	1972	Super Bowl	Stanley Dancer
1937	Shirley Hanover	Henry Thomas	1973	Flirth	Ralph Baldwin
1938	McLin Hanover	Henry Thomas	1974	Christopher T.	Bill Haughton
1939	Peter Astra	Doc Parshall	1975	Bonefish	Stanley Dancer
1940	Spencer Scott	Fred Egan	1976	Steve Lobell	Bill Haughton
1941	Bill Gallon	Lee Smith	1977	Green Speed	Bill Haughton
1942	The Ambassador	Ben White	1978	Speedy Somolli	H. Beissinger
1943	Volo Song	Ben White	1979	Legend Hanover	George Sholty
1944	Yankee Maid	Henry Thomas	1980	Burgomeister	Bill Haughton
1945	Titan Hanover	H. Pownall Sr	1981	Shiaway St. Pat	Ray Remmen
1946	Chestertown	Thomas Berry	1982	Speed Bowl	Tom Haughton
1947	Hoot Mon	Sep Palin	1983	Duenna	Stanley Dancer
1948	Demon Hanover	Harrison Hoyt	1984	Historic Freight	Ben Webster
1949	Miss Tilly	Fred Egan	1985	Prakas	Bill O'Donnell
1950	Lusty Song	Del Miller	1986	Nuclear Kosmos	Ulf Thoresen
1951	Mainliner	Guy Crippen	1987	Mack Lobell	John Campbell
1952	Sharp Note	Bion Shively	1988	Armbro Goal	John Campbell
1953	Helicopter	Harry Harvey	1989	Park Avenue Joe*	Ron Waples
1954	Newport Dream	Del Cameron		Probe*	Bill Fahy
1955	Scott Frost	Joe O'Brien	1990	Harmonious	John Campbell
1956	The Intruder	Ned Bower	1991	Giant Victory	Jack Moiseyev
1957	Hickory Smoke	J. Simpson Sr	1992	Alf Palema	Mickey McNichol
1958	Emily's Pride	Flave Nipe	1993	American Winner	Ron Pierce
1959	Diller Hanover	Frank Ervin	1994	Victory Dream	Michel LaChance
1960	Blaze Hanover	Joe O'Brien	1995	Tagliabue	John Campbell
1961	Harlan Dean	James Arthur	1996	Continentalvictory	Michel LaChance

*Park Avenue Joe and Probe dead-heated for win. Park Avenue finished first in the summary 2-1-1 to Probe's 1-9-1 finish.
Note: Run at 1 mile since 1947.

Little Brown Jug

Year	Winner	Driver	Year	Winner	Driver
1946	Ensign Hanover	Wayne Smart	1972	Strike Out	Keith Waples
1947	Forbes Chief	Del Cameron	1973	Melvin's Woe	Joe O'Brien
1948	Knight Dream	Frank Safford	1974	Armbro Omaha	Bill Haughton
1949	Good Time	Frank Ervin	1975	Seatrain	Ben Webster
1950	Dudley Hanover	Del Miller	1976	Keystone Ore	Stanley Dancer
1951	Tar Heel	Del Cameron	1977	Governor Skipper	John Chapman
1952	Meadow Rice	Wayne Smart	1978	Happy Escort	William Popfinger
1953	Keystoner	Frank Ervin	1979	Hot Hitter	Herve Filion
1954	Adios Harry	Morris MacDonald	1980	Niatross	Clint Galbraith
1955	Quick Chief	Bill Haughton	1981	Fan Hanover	Glen Garnsey
1956	Noble Adios	John Simpson Sr	1982	Merger	John Campbell
1957	Torpid	John Simpso Sr	1983	Ralph Hanover	Ron Waples
1958	Shadow Wave	Joe O'Brien	1984	Colt Fortysix	Chris Boring
1959	Adios Butler	Clint Hodgins	1985	Nihilator	Bill O'Donnell
1960	Bullet Hanover	John Simpson Sr	1986	Barberry Spur	Bill O'Donnell
1961	Henry T. Adios	Stanley Dancer	1987	Jaguar Spur	Dick Stillings
1962	Lehigh Hanover	Stanley Dancer	1988	B. J. Scoot	Michel Lachance
1963	Overtrick	John Patterson	1989	Goalie Jeff	Michel Lachance
1964	Vicar Hanover	Bill Haughton	1990	Beach Towel	Ray Remmen
1965	Bret Hanover	Frank Ervin	1991	Precious Bunny	Jack Moiseye
1966	Romeo Hanover	George Sholty	1992	Fake Left	Ron Waples
1967	Best of All	James Hackett	1993	Life Sign	John Campbell
1968	Rum Customer	Bill Haughton	1994	Magical Mike	Michel Lachance
1969	Laverne Hanover	Bill Haughton	1995	Nick's Fantasy	John Campbell
1970	Most Happy Fella	Stanley Dancer	1996	Armbro Operative	Jack Moiseyev
1971	Nansemond	Herve Filion			

Breeders' Crown

1984

Div	Winner	Driver
2PC	Dragon's Lair	Jeff Mallet
2PF	Amneris	John Campbell
3PC	Troublemaker	Bill O'Donnell
3PF	Naughty But Nice	Tommy Haughton
2TC	Workaholic	Berndt Lindstedt
2TF	Conifer	George Sholty
3TC	Baltic Speed	Jan Nordin
3TF	Fancy Crown	Bill O'Donnell

1985

Div	Winner	Driver
2PC	Robust Hanover	John Campbell
2PF	Caressable	Herve Filion
3PC	Nihilator	Bill O'Donnell
3PF	Stienam	Buddy Gilmour
2TC	Express Ride	John Campbell
2TF	JEF's Spice	Mickey McNichol
3TC	Prakas	John Campbell
3TF	Armbro Devona	Bill O'Donnell
AP	Division Street	Michel Lachance
AT	Sandy Bowl	John Campbell

1986

Div	Winner	Driver
2PC	Sunset Warrior	Bill Gale
2PF	Halcyon	Ray Remmen
3PC	Masquerade	Richard Silverman
3PF	Glow Softly	Ron Waples
2TC	Mack Lobell	John Campbell
2TF	Super Flora	Ron Waples
3TC	Sugarcane Hanover	Ron Waples
3TF	JEF's Spice	Bill O'Donnell
APM	Samshu Bluegrass	Michel Lachance
ATM	Grades Singing	Herve Filion
APH	Forrest Skipper	Lucien Fontaine
ATH	Nearly Perfect	Mickey McNichol

1987

Div	Winner	Driver
2PC	Camtastic	Bill O'Donnell
2PF	Leah Almahurst	Bill Fahy
3PC	Call For Rain	Clint Galbraith
3PF	Pacific	Tom Harmer
2TC	Defiant One	Howard Beissinger
2TF	Nan's Catch	Berndt Lindstedt
3TC	Mack Lobell	John Campbell
3TF	Armbro Fling	George Sholty
APM	Follow My Star	John Campbell
ATM	Grades Singing	Olle Goop
APH	Armbro Emerson	Walter Whelan
ATH	Sugarcane Hanover	Ron Waples

Note: 2=Two-year-old; T=Trotter; C=Colt; 3=Three-year-old; P=Pacer; F=Filly; A=Aged; H=Horse; M=Mare.

Breeders' Crown *(Cont.)*

1988

Div	Winner	Driver
2PC	Kentucky Spur	Dick Stillings
2PF	Central Park West	John Campbell
3PC	Camtastic	Bill O'Donnell
3PF	Sweet Reflection	Bill O'Donnell
2TC	Valley Victory	Bill O'Donnell
2TF	Peace Corps	John Campbell
3TC	Firm Tribute	Mark O'Mara
3TF	Nalda Hanover	Mickey McNichol
APM	Anniecrombie	Dave Magee
ATM	Armbro Flori	Larry Walker
APH	Call For Rain	Clint Galbraith
ATH	Mack Lobell	John Campbell

1989

Div	Winner	Driver
2PC	Till We Meet Again	Mickey McNichol
2PF	Town Pro	Doug Brown
3PC	Goalie Jeff	Michel LaChance
3PF	Cheery Hello	John Campbell
2TC	Royal Troubador	Carl Allen
2TF	Delphi's Lobell	Ron Waples
3TC	Esquire Spur	Dick Stillings
3TF	Pace Corps	John Campbell
APM	Armbro Feather	John Kopas
ATM	Grades Singing	Olle Goop
APH	Matt's Scooter	Michel LaChance
ATH	Delray Lobell	John Campbell

1990

Div	Winner	Driver
2PC	Artsplace	John Campbell
2PF	Miss Easy	John Campbell
3PC	Beach Towel	Ray Remmen
3PF	Town Pro	Doug Brown
2TC	Crysta's Best	Dick Richardson Jr
2TF	Jean Bi	Jan Nordin
3TC	Embassy Lobell	Michel LaChance
3TF	Me Maggie	Berndt Lindstedt
APM	Caesar's Jackpot	Bill Fahy
ATM	Peace Corps	Stig Johansson
APH	Bay's Fella	Paul MacDonell
ATH	No Sex Please	Ron Waples

1991

Div	Winner	Driver
2PC	Digger Almahurst	Doug Brown
2PF	Hazleton Kay	John Campbell
3PC	Three Wizzards	Bill Gale
3PF	Miss Easy	John Campbell
2TC	King Conch	Bill Gale
2TF	Armbro Keepsake	John Campbell
3TC	Giant Victory	Ron Pierce
3TF	Twelve Speed	Ron Waples
APM	Delinquent Account	Bill O'Donnell
ATM	Me Maggie	Berndt Lindstedt
APH	Camluck	Michel LaChance
ATH	Billyjojimbob	Paul MacDonell

1992

Div	Winner	Driver
2PC	Village Jiffy	Ron Waples
2PF	Immortality	John Campbell
3PC	Kingsbridge	Roger Mayotte
3PF	So Fresh	John Campbell
2TC	Giant Chill	John Patterson, Jr
2TF	Winky's Goal	Cat Manzi
3TC	Baltic Striker	Michel LaChance
3TF	Imperfection	Michel LaChance
APM	Shady Daisy	Ron Pierce
ATM	Peace Corps	Torbjorn Jansson
APH	Artsplace	John Campbell
ATH	No Sex Please	Ron Waples

1993

Div	Winner	Driver
2PC	Expensive Scooter	Jack Moiseyev
2PF	Electric Scooter	Mike LaChance
3PC	Life Sign	John Campbell
3PF	Immortality	John Campbell
2TC	Westgate Crown	John Campbell
2TF	Gleam	Jimmy Takter
3TC	Pine Chip	John Campbell
3TF	Expressway Hanover	Per Henriksen
APM	Swing Back	Kelly Sheppard
ATM	Lifetime Dream	Paul MacDonnell
APH	Staying Together	Bill O'Donnell
ATH	Earl	Chris Christoforou Jr

1994

Div	Winner	Driver
2PC	Jenna's Beach Boy	Bill Fahy
2PF	Yankee Cashmere	Peter Wrenn
3PC	Magical Mike	Michel LaChance
3PF	Hardie Hanover	Tim Twaddle
2TC	Eager Seelster	Teddy Jacobs
2TF	Lookout Victory	John Patterson
3TC	Incredible Abe	Italo Tamborrino
3TF	Imageofa Clear Day	Bill O'Donnell
APM	Shady Daisy	Michel LaChance
ATM	Armbro Keepsake	Stig Johansson
APH	Village Jiffy	Paul MacDonell
ATH	Pine Chip	John Campbell

1995

Div	Winner	Driver
2PC	John Street North	Jack Moiseyev
2PF	Paige Nicole Q	John Campbell
3PC	Jenna's Beach Boy	Bill Fahy
3PF	Headline Hanover	Doug Brown
2TC	Armbro Officer	Steve Condren
2TF	Continentalvictory	Michel LaChance
3TC	Abundance	Bill O'Donnell
3TF	Lookout Victory	Sonny Patterson
APM	Ellamony	Mike Saftic
ATM	CR Kay Suzie	Rod Allen
APH	Thatll Be Me	Roger Mayotte
ATH	Panifesto	Luc Ouellette

Note: 2=Two-year-old; T=Trotter; C=Colt; 3=Three-year-old; P=Pacer; F=Filly; A=Aged; H=Horse; M=Mare.

Triple Crown Winners

Trotting

Trotting's Triple Crown consists of the Hambletonian (first run in 1926), the Kentucky Futurity (first run in 1893), and the Yonkers Trot (known as the Yonkers Futurity when it began in 1955).

Year	Horse	Owner	Breeder	Trainer & Driver
1955	Scott Frost	S.A. Camp Farms	Est of W. N. Reynolds	Joe O'Brien
1963	Speedy Scot	Castleton Farms	Castleton Farms	Ralph Baldwin
1964	Ayres	Charlotte Sheppard	Charlotte Sheppard	John Simpson Sr
1968	Nevele Pride	Nevele Acres & Lou Resnick	Mr & Mrs E. C. Quin	Stanley Dancer
1969	Lindy's Pride	Lindy Farm	Hanover Shoe Farms	Howard Beissinger
1972	Super Bowl	Rachel Dancer & Rose Hild Breeding Farm	Stoner Creek Stud	Stanley Dancer

Pacing

Pacing's Triple Crown consists of the Cane Pace (called the Cane Futurity when it began in 1955), the Little Brown Jug (first run in 1946), and the Messenger Stake (first run in 1956).

Year	Horse	Owner	Breeder	Trainer/Driver
1959	Adios Butler	Paige West & Angelo Pellillo	R. C. Carpenter	Paige West/Clint Hodgins
1965	Bret Hanover	Richard Downing	Hanover Shoe Farms	Frank Ervin
1966	Romeo Hanover	Lucky Star Stables & Morton Finder	Hanover Shoe Farms	Jerry Silverman/ William Meyer (Cane) & George Sholty (Jug & Messenger)
1968	Rum Customer	Kennilworth Farms & L. C. Mancuso	Mr. & Mrs. R. C. Larkin	Bill Haughton
1970	Most Happy Fella	Egyptian Acres Stable	Stoner Creek Stud	Stanley Dancer
1980	Niatross	Niagara Acres, C. Galbraith & Niatross Stables	Niagara Acres	Clint Galbraith
1983	Ralph Hanover	Waples Stable, Pointsetta Stable, Grant's Direct Stable & P. J. Baugh	Hanover Shoe Farms	Stew Firlotte/Ron Waples

Awards

Horse of the Year

Year	Horse	Gait	Owner
1947	Victory Song	T	Castleton Farm
1948	Rodney	T	R. H. Johnston
1949	Good Time	P	William Cane
1950	Proximity	T	Ralph and Gordon Verhurst
1951	Pronto Don	T	Hayes Fair Acres Stable
1952	Good Time	P	William Cane
1953	Hi Lo's Forbes	P	Mr. and Mrs. Earl Wagner
1954	Stenographer	T	Max Hempt
1955	Scott Frost	T	S. A. Camp Farms
1956	Scott Frost	T	S. A. Camp Farms
1957	Torpid	P	Sherwood Farm
1958	Emily's Pride	T	Walnut Hall and Castleton Farms
1959	Bye Bye Byrd	P	Mr. and Mrs. Rex Larkin
1960	Adios Butler	P	Adios Butler Syndicate
1961	Adios Butler	P	Adios Butler Syndicate
1962	Su Mac Lad	T	I. W. Berkemeyer
1963	Speedy Scot	T	Castleton Farm
1964	Bret Hanover	P	Richard Downing
1965	Bret Hanover	P	Richard Downing
1966	Bret Hanover	P	Richard Downing
1967	Nevele Pride	T	Nevele Acres
1968	Nevele Pride	T	Nevele Acres, Louis Resnick
1969	Nevele Pride	T	Nevele Acres, Louis Resnick
1970	Fresh Yankee	T	Duncan MacDonald
1971	Albatross	P	Albatross Stable
1972	Albatross	P	Amicable Stable
1973	Sir Dalrae	P	A La Carte Racing Stable
1974	Delmonica Hanover	T	Delvin Miller, W. Arnold Hanger
1975	Savoir	T	Allwood Stable
1976	Keystone Ore	P	Mr. and Mrs. Stanley Dancer, Rose Hild Farms, Robert Jones
1977	Green Speed	T	Beverly Lloyds
1978	Abercrombie	P	Shirley Mitchell, L. Keith Bulen
1979	Niatross	P	Niagara Acres, Clint Galbraith
1980	Niatross	P	Niatross Syndicate, Niagara Acres, Clint Galbraith
1981	Fan Hanover	P	Dr. J. Glen Brown
1982	Cam Fella	P	Norm Clements, Norm Faulkner
1983	Cam Fella	P	JEF's Standardbred, Norm Clements, Norm Faulkner

Horse of the Year *(Cont.)*

Year	Horse	Gait	Owner
1984	Fancy Crown	T	Fancy Crown Stable
1985	Nihilator	P	Wall Street-Nihilator Syndicate
1986	Forrest Skipper	P	Forrest L. Bartlett
1987	Mack Lobell	T	One More Time Stable and Fair Wind Farm
1988	Mack Lobell	T	John Erik Magnusson
1989	Matt's Scooter	P	Gordon and Illa Rumpel, Charles Jurasvinski
1990	Beach Towel	P	Uptown Stables
1991	Precious Bunny	P	R. Peter Heffering
1992	Artsplace	P	George Segal
1993	Staying Together	P	Robert Hamather
1994	Cam's Card Shark	P	Jeffrey S. Snyder
1995	CR Kay Suzie	T	Carl & Rod Allen Stable, Inc.

Note: Balloting is conducted by the U.S Trotting Association for the U.S. Harness Writers Association.

Leading Drivers—Money Won

Year	Driver	Winnings ($)	Year	Driver	Winnings ($)
1946	Thomas Berry	121,933	1971	Herve Filion	1,915,945
1947	H. C. Fitzpatrick	133,675	1972	Herve Filion	2,473,265
1948	Ralph Baldwin	153,222	1973	Herve Filion	2,233,303
1949	Clint Hodgins	184,108	1974	Herve Filion	3,474,315
1950	Del Miller	306,813	1975	Carmine Abbatiello	2,275,093
1951	John Simpson Sr	333,316	1976	Herve Filion	2,278,634
1952	Bill Haughton	311,728	1977	Herve Filion	2,551,058
1953	Bill Haughton	374,527	1978	Carmine Abbatiello	3,344,457
1954	Bill Haughton	415,577	1979	John Campbell	3,308,984
1955	Bill Haughton	599,455	1980	John Campbell	3,732,306
1956	Bill Haughton	572,945	1981	Bill O'Donnell	4,065,608
1957	Bill Haughton	586,950	1982	Bill O'Donnell	5,755,067
1958	Bill Haughton	816,659	1983	John Campbell	6,104,082
1959	Bill Haughton	771,435	1984	Bill O'Donnell	9,059,184
1960	Del Miller	567,282	1985	Bill O'Donnell	10,207,372
1961	Stanley Dancer	674,723	1986	John Campbell	9,515,055
1962	Stanley Dancer	760,343	1987	John Campbell	10,186,495
1963	Bill Haughton	790,086	1988	John Campbell	11,148,565
1964	Stanley Dancer	1,051,538	1989	John Campbell	9,738,450
1965	Bill Haughton	889,943	1990	John Campbell	11,620,878
1966	Stanley Dancer	1,218,403	1991	Jack Moiseyev	9,568,468
1967	Bill Haughton	1,305,773	1992	John Campbell	8,202,108
1968	Bill Haughton	1,654,463	1993	John Campbell	9,926,482
1969	Del Insko	1,635,463	1994	John Campbell	9,834,139
1970	Herve Filion	1,647,837	1995	John Campbell	9,469,797

Motor Sports

Sports Illustrated

Daytona Dale

Dale Jarrett celebrates his Daytona win
with daughters Natalee and Karsyn.

GEORGE TIEDEMANN

Tarnished Tradition

In a year of off-track turmoil, the Indy 500's loss was NASCAR's gain—for now

by Ed Hinton

UPHEAVAL ABOUNDED in North American motor racing in 1996. It was the year Indy Car racing tore itself asunder and enfeebled the Indianapolis 500 itself. It was the year NASCAR headed uptown, abandoned its bootlegger roots, established itself indisputably as America's premier motor sport—and yet left open the potential for splits of its own in the future.

The driving performances, all told, weren't very memorable. Which was just as well, in that any outstanding job on the track would have been lost in the deluge of politics, power-struggling and financial maneuvering.

Nowhere was the driving mediocrity more evident than in Formula One, where Damon Hill, apparently on his way to the 1996 title, was nevertheless fired by his team, Williams, for his unspectacular performance.

NASCAR's Winston Cup season points race became a four-man cavalry charge down the stretch, with Terry Labonte, Jeff Gordon, Dale Jarrett and Dale Earnhardt vying for the title. NASCAR ballyhooed that as an exciting fight for the championship, but the flip side was that the chase was close because none of the four had a truly outstanding year.

The seasons of Gordon and Jarrett, if combined, would have made one spectacu-lar year. Jarrett won the three most prestigious races—the Daytona 500, the Coca-Cola 600 in Charlotte and the Brickyard 400. With a win in the Southern 500 in Darlington, S.C., Jarrett also could have collected the Winston Select Million jackpot. But that race went to Gordon, giving him the most wins on the tour, seven, as the Winston Cup circuit entered the traditional stretch drive of autumn. But Gordon had a somewhat roller-coaster year, with wretched finishes or DNFs often falling as valleys between wins or second-place finishes.

CART's PPG Cup championship went to Jimmy Vasser, who dominated the spring with four wins, but went winless after the May 26 U.S. 500. Vasser's early-season success was largely attributable to the superiority of his Honda engine over the Ford Cosworth that propelled Michael Andretti and the Ilmor Mercedes that powered Al Unser Jr. Vasser's championship hopes survived his long winless spell because Unser Jr. had an atypically awful season, and Andretti made a late charge but could not make up for early inconsistency.

Little noted nor long remembered is that two guys named Buzz Calkins and Scott Sharp tied for the first season champi-

After winning the pole for his 15th Indy, Brayton was killed during a practice run.

onship of the new Indy Racing League, the counterrevolutionary organization that turned a rift into a gaping schism. That championship was decided in only three races.

Each of the warring factions in Indy Car racing suffered its share of tragedy. Veteran Scott Brayton died on May 17 of head injuries suffered in a crash during practice for the Indy 500, which is now under the IRL umbrella. Rookie Jeff Krosnoff was killed in a horrific crash near the end of CART's "Molson Indy" race through the streets of Toronto on July 14.

Drag racing suffered its first driver fatality in 11 years on Aug. 31 when Blaine Johnson, who was leading the NHRA in Top Fuel points, was killed during the U.S. Nationals at Indianapolis Raceway Park. The next day at the Nationals, motorcyclist Elmer Trett was killed during an exhibition run.

Most of all, the year will be remembered for the enormous split in Indy Car racing. The team owners of CART on one side and Indianapolis Motor Speedway president Tony George on the other had been saber-rattling since George came to power in 1990. George wanted to return Indy Car racing to simpler technology: more oval track racing as opposed to road courses, and emphasis on bringing up young American drivers from the heartland forms of racing like sprint cars and midgets. CART was committed to high technology and road racing, and was becoming more and more dominated by foreign drivers.

But at its crux the dispute is all about control of the Indy Car branch of motor sports. Only historical perspective reveals the entire iceberg: George's grandfather, Tony Hulman, bought Indianapolis Motor Speedway in 1946. Hulman was credited with saving the 500 and nurturing it back to status as the world's most renowned motor race. Hulman died in 1977, while George was still a teenager. Within a year CART was organized and a year after that the team owners, led by Roger Penske and U.E. (Pat) Patrick, broke away from the Speedway's puppet sanctioning body, the United States Auto Club and joined CART. CART members were banned from that year's Indy 500, but CART owners went to court and won reinstatement. From then through 1995, CART essentially controlled

GEORGE TIEDEMANN

George waged war with CART team owners for control of Indy Car racing.

all of Indy Car racing, except for the Indy 500 itself. CART teams raced at Indy each year via an uneasy detente but ran their own series of races the rest of the time.

George ascended to the presidency of the Speedway in 1990, at the age of 30, and became the track's first truly forceful leader since his grandfather. George believed the Speedway should have more control over the form of racing it birthed in 1911, and he set out to regain it.

In '96 George began running races for his new Indy Racing League, and used the 500 itself to try to coerce CART members to his side. That brought all-out war.

George reserved 25 of the Indianapolis 500's 33 starting spots—traditionally open to all comers who were fast enough—for members of the IRL. CART owners furiously claimed that they were being shut out. They scheduled their own race, the U.S. 500, for Michigan International Speedway on May 26, in direct opposition to the 80th running of the Indy 500.

George staged the first race for the IRL in January on a hastily constructed track at Disney World. CART teams, as promised, refused to participate in Orlando or at the IRL's other pre–Indy 500 event, in Phoenix. They didn't earn any IRL points and were automatically out of the running for the reserved starting spots at Indianapolis.

So come what once was America's favorite time of the racing season, the Month of May at Indianapolis, the CART teams established a rebel camp in Michigan, claiming that's where the "stars and cars of Indianapolis" would be on May 26.

Meanwhile, Indianapolis Motor Speedway was inhabited by a motley contingent of older race cars and mostly unknown drivers. Only one former Indy 500 champion, 1990 winner Arie Luyendyk, entered the '96 race. The CART camp predicted disaster at Indy due to the old cars and inexperienced drivers running at top speeds.

But when disaster did come to Indy, it was not at all according to CART's forecast. Brayton, after winning the pole on May 11, was killed during a practice session six days later when his right rear tire was punctured, sending his Lola-Menard car slamming into the concrete wall in Turn 2. Brayton was a veteran of 14 Indy 500 starts and was in a Lola-Menard that even the CART barons admitted was well-prepared.

If all the squabbling represented Indy Car civil war, then May 26 was the fateful day, its Battle of Gettysburg: The rebel U.S. 500 vs. the established Indy 500. Nobody won the battle, but CART emerged as a loser of sorts. Its race drew an announced 110,879 to Michigan, but its drivers took an immediate pratfall when 12 cars piled up approaching the starting line before the green flag even fell. The melee began a moment before what should have been the start when pole sitter Vasser touched wheels with Andrian Fernandez. No one was seriously injured, but this was all doubly embarrassing to CART after its predictions of catastrophe at Indianapolis.

CART rules allowed the teams to give themselves a multimillion-dollar mulligan, offering all 12 drivers involved in the crash the option of switching to backup cars for the new start. Nine did that, three made repairs to their primary cars, and Fernandez scratched. Vasser, hardly a household name, went on to win. Traditional stars such as Unser Jr., Andretti and Emerson Fittipaldi weren't factors at Michigan, so the notion of "the stars and cars of Indianapolis" essentially backfired for CART.

Over at the Brickyard, Indy held its own, drawing a full house, though not quite the usual overflow crowd of 400,000-plus. The Indy start, in contrast to the race in Michigan, was so clean as to be dull at first—the field tiptoed through the first lap before reaching record speeds in excess of 230 mph. Not until the late stages of the race did any serious crashes occur at Indy. Veteran Lyn St. James suffered a fractured wrist during her collision with rookie Scott Harrington, and on the final lap Roberto Güerrero spun and collided with Allesandro Zampedri and Eliseo Salazar. Zampedri's car landed upside down, and he suffered severe injuries to his legs.

When unheralded Buddy Lazier emerged as the winner, one of motor racing's most compelling stories of the human spirit came to national attention. Lazier drove the race in terrible pain, still recovering from 16 fractures and 25 chips in his lower backbone and tailbone, suffered in a crash at Phoenix in March. "A month ago I could barely walk on crutches, so this win is extra sweet," said the erstwhile skier from Vail,

Colo., who had to be lifted from his car in Victory Lane.

New technical rules for the IRL in 1997, which apply to the Indy 500, made the divorce from CART appear final. The only way CART teams could return to the Brickyard would be with special, Indy-only cars that couldn't be used on the CART tour.

So deep questions remained regarding the very survival of Indy Car racing as a form of motor sport. Could George make the IRL series significant enough, quickly enough, to return the Indy 500 to more than a shell of itself, a has-been event rife with no-names? And could CART's other races remain prestigious for long in the public eye without participation in the sport's cornerstone event, the Indy 500?

All in all, the Indy Car tumult left NASCAR stock car racing in clear command of American motor sports enthusiasm. Not that this was anything new—it had been so, de facto, for years—but it became obvious to the general public in '96. The last vestige of Indy Car racing supremacy was that the Indy 500, all by itself, had outshone NASCAR racing in the U.S. That glitter dimmed in '96. And for the third straight year, the new NASCAR race at Indianapolis Motor Speedway, the Brickyard 400, sold out. NASCAR television ratings skyrocketed to more than triple the average of Indy Car ratings. Indeed, ESPN sources say live NASCAR Winston Cup races outrate everything else the sports network carries except live NFL games. And NASCAR Winston Cup racing drew nearly six million spectators in '96, tripling its attendance of only six years ago.

More importantly, NASCAR prepared to pen-

TOM LYNN

Unsung Lazier (front) prevailed at Indy despite 16 fractures in his back.

France (right) promised that NASCAR would keep its house in order.

etrate larger, more sophisticated markets. The '97 schedule includes races in the Dallas–Fort Worth and Los Angeles areas, and a second race at the enormously popular New Hampshire International Speedway, 70 miles north of Boston.

But NASCAR has lost something along the way.

"It has lost what got it here," said living legend Junior Johnson, the ex–moonshine runner turned driver turned car owner, who retired in 1996. "It got here on the strength of the people who had the willpower and honesty that America is made out of. Now, it's running solely on money."

Johnson saw NASCAR leaving its foundations. Wild and colorful drivers were being replaced by vanilla spokesmen for corporate sponsors, and grassroots tracks were being abandoned for uptown venues. Johnson spoke from his farm 12 miles from little North Wilkesboro Speedway in the traditional moonshine hills of North Carolina. Both he and NASCAR began racing there in 1947, when starting fields were heavily spiced with Johnson's moonshine-running peers. North Wilkesboro was NASCAR's longest-running track. But NASCAR's elite Winston Cup series, the one Johnson helped to build, said adios with two races there in '96 and will race no more at North Wilkesboro.

The track was bought by two rival wheeler-dealers, Bruton Smith, who paid $6 million, and Bob Bahre, who chipped in $8 million, solely so they could cannibalize it for its Winston Cup dates. After much squabbling Smith took Wilkesboro's spring date to his new Texas Motor Speedway, and Bahre took the fall date for a second Winston Cup race at his New Hampshire International Speedway.

Smith, as president of Speedway Motorsports Inc., controls the tracks at Charlotte; Atlanta; Bristol, Tenn.; and Dallas–Fort Worth. He is now tied with International Speedway Corp., the track-owning arm of NASCAR, in number of tracks controlled. And Smith shows no signs of slowing down, saying privately that he'll probably build a track in Illinois, and he is even looking at possibilities in the New York City area.

What is he up to?

"People [inside racing] know Bruton—so they don't know," quips Richard Petty.

Smith vehemently denies that he has any plans to start a rival league to NASCAR, but he admits that he is at least getting in the position to do so.

"But if I did, it would damage what we have," he says. "I don't want to do that. I'm interested in building NASCAR, because the bigger it gets, the better it is for me."

"All I can tell you," says NASCAR president Bill France Jr., "is what Bruton said … that he loves us and is with us forever. Isn't that what he said? Bruton's all right. Everything will be all right."

Smith is pretty important, says Smith. "When I took this sport to Wall Street [he listed Speedway Motorsports Inc. on the New York Stock Exchange in 1995], it awakened a lot in the world. It awakened the board rooms of the Fortune 500 companies. You bring the financial clout into this sport, great things happen."

Indeed, major corporations seem to be climbing over one another to get in on the NASCAR promotional bonanza.

Should NASCAR itself ever come up for sale, "I'd be the first in line," Smith admits. "But I think the France family has run a damn good ship."

Stay tuned.

FOR THE RECORD·1995–1996

Indy Racing League

Indianapolis 500

Results of the 80th running of the Indianapolis 500 and final round of the inaugural Indy Racing League season. Held Sunday, May 26, 1996, at the 2.5-mile Indianapolis Motor Speedway in Indianapolis, IN. Distance, 500 miles; starters, 33; time of race, 3:22:46; average speed, 147.956 mph; margin of victory, .7 second; caution flags, 10 for 59 laps; lead changes, 15 among 5 drivers.

TOP 10 FINISHERS

Pos	Driver (start pos.)	Car	Qual. Speed	Laps	Status
1	Buddy Lazier (5)	Reynard-Ford	231.468	200	running
2	Davy Jones (2)	Lola-Mercedes	232.882	200	running
3	Richie Hearn (15)	Reynard-Ford	226.521	200	running
4	Alessandro Zampedri (7)	Lola-Ford	229.595	199	accident
5	Roberto Guerrero (6)	Reynard-Ford	231.373	198	accident
6	Eliseo Salazar (3)	Lola-Ford	232.684	197	accident
7	Danny Ongais (33)	Lola-Menard	233.718	197	running
8	Hideshi Matsuda (30)	Lola-Ford	226.856	197	running
9	Robbie Buhl (23)	Lola-Ford	226.217	197	running
10	Scott Sharp (21)	Lola-Ford	231.201	194	accident

1996 Indy Racing League Results

Date	Race	Winner (start pos.)	Car	Avg Speed
Jan 27	Indy 200	Buzz Calkins (5)	Reynard-Ford	128.325
Mar 24	Dura-Lube 200	Arie Luyendyk (1)	Reynard-Ford	117.368
May 26	Indianapolis 500	Buddy Lazier (5)	Reynard-Ford	147.956

1996 Championship Final Standings

Driver	Starts	Highest Finish	Pts
Buzz Calkins	3	1	246
Scott Sharp	3	2	246
Robbie Buhl	3	3	240
Richie Hearn	3	3	237
Roberto Guerrero	3	5	237

Championship Auto Racing Teams

U.S. 500

Results of the inaugural running of the U.S. 500 and 6th round of the 1996 Indy Car World Series. Held Sunday, May 26, 1996 at the 2-mile Michigan International Speedway in Brooklyn, MI. Distance, 500 miles; starters, 26; time of race, 3:11:49; average speed, 156.403 mph; margin of victory, 11 seconds; caution flags, 12 for 69 laps; lead changes, 11 among 7 drivers.

TOP 10 FINISHERS

Pos	Driver (start pos.)	Car	Qual. Speed	Laps	Status
1	Jimmy Vasser (1)	Reynard-Honda	232.025	250	running
2	Mauricio Gugelmin (14)	Reynard-Ford Cosworth	225.625	250	running
3	Roberto Moreno (20)	Lola-Ford Cosworth	221.447	249	running
4	Andre Ribeiro (6)	Lola-Honda	229.710	249	running
5	Mark Blundell (19)	Reynard-Ford Cosworth	221.487	249	running
6	Eddie Lawson (18)	Lola-Mercedes	221.618	249	running
7	Paul Tracy (7)	Penske-Mercedes	228.980	248	running
8	Al Unser Jr (5)	Penske-Mercedes	230.213	246	running
9	Gil de Ferran (13)	Reynard-Honda	225.957	245	running
10	Emerson Fittipaldi (8)	Penske-Mercedes	227.816	241	running

1996 Indy Car World Series Results

Date	Event	Winner (start pos.)	Car	Avg Speed
Mar 3	Grand Prix of Miami	Jimmy Vasser (3)	Reynard-Honda	109.399
Mar 17	Rio 400	Andre Ribeiro (3)	Lola-Honda	117.927
Mar 31	IndyCar Australia	Jimmy Vasser (1)	Reynard-Honda	90.218
Apr 14	Grand Prix of Long Beach	Jimmy Vasser (3)	Reynard-Honda	96.281
Apr 28	Nazareth Grand Prix	Michael Andretti (5)	Lola-Ford Cosworth	140.953
May 26	U.S. 500	Jimmy Vasser (1)	Reynard-Honda	156.403
June 2	Milwaukee 200	Michael Andretti (5)	Lola-Ford Cosworth	128.282
June 9	Detroit Grand Prix	Michael Andretti (9)	Lola-Ford Cosworth	75.136
June 23	Portland 200	*Alex Zanardi (1)	Reynard-Honda	103.837
June 30	Grand Prix of Cleveland	Gil de Ferran (7)	Reynard-Honda	133.736
July 14	Indy Toronto	Adrian Fernandez (3)	Lola-Honda	97.598
July 28	Michigan 500	Andre Ribeiro (8)	Lola-Honda	152.627
Aug 11	Mid-Ohio 200	*Alex Zanardi (1)	Reynard-Honda	104.358
Aug 18	Elkhart Lake 200	Michael Andretti (3)	Lola-Ford Cosworth	102.947
Sept 1	Indy Vancouver	Michael Andretti (2)	Lola-Ford Cosworth	94.374
Sept 8	Grand Prix of Monterey	*Alex Zanardi (1)	Reynard-Honda	102.687

*Rookie.

1996 Championship Final Standings

Driver	Starts	Wins	Pts
Jimmy Vasser	16	4	154
Michael Andretti	16	5	132
*Alex Zanardi	16	3	132
Al Unser Jr.	16	0	125
Christian Fittipaldi	16	0	110
Gil de Ferran	16	1	104
Bobby Rahal	16	0	102
Bryan Herta	16	0	86
*Greg Moore	16	0	84
Scott Pruett	16	0	82

*Rookie.

National Association for Stock Car Auto Racing

Daytona 500

Results of the opening round of the 1996 Winston Cup series. Held Sunday, February 18, at the 2.5-mile high-banked Daytona International Speedway.

Distance, 500 miles; starters, 43; time of race, 3:14:25; average speed, 154.308 mph; margin of victory, .12 second; caution flags, 6 for 26 laps; lead changes, 32 among 15 drivers.

TOP 10 FINISHERS

Pos	Driver (start pos.)	Car	Laps	Winnings ($)
1	Dale Jarrett (7)	Ford	200	360,775
2	Dale Earnhardt (1)	Chevrolet	200	215,065
3	Ken Schrader (4)	Chevrolet	200	169,547
4	Mark Martin (15)	Ford	200	118,840
5	Jeff Burton (16)	Ford	200	91,702
6	Wally Dallenbach (9)	Ford	200	96,720
7	Ted Musgrave (20)	Ford	200	82,712
8	Bill Elliott (21)	Ford	200	78,155
9	Ricky Rudd (10)	Ford	200	79,987
10	Michael Waltrip (11)	Ford	200	74,255

Late 1995 Winston Cup Series Results

Date	Track/Distance	Winner (start pos.)	Car	Avg Speed	Winnings ($)
Oct 8	Charlotte 500	Mark Martin (5)	Ford	145.358	105,650
Oct 22	Rockingham 400	Ward Burton (3)	Pontiac	114.778	70,250
Oct 29	Phoenix 500K	Ricky Rudd (29)	Ford	102.128	78,260
Nov 12	Atlanta 500	Dale Earnhardt (11)	Chevrolet	163.633	141,850

Note: Distances are in miles unless followed by * (laps) or K (kilometers).

1996 Winston Cup Series Results (through September 22)

Date	Track/Distance	Winner (start pos.)	Car	Avg Speed	Winnings ($)
Feb 18	Daytona 500	Dale Jarrett (7)	Ford	154.308	360,775
Feb 25	Rockingham 400	Dale Earnhardt (18)	Chevrolet	113.959	83,840
Mar 3	Richmond 400*	Jeff Gordon (2)	Chevrolet	102.750	92,400
Mar 10	Atlanta 500	Dale Earnhardt (18)	Chevrolet	161.298	91,050
Mar 24	Darlington 400	Jeff Gordon (2)	Chevrolet	124.792	97,310
Mar 31	Bristol 500*	Jeff Gordon (8)	Chevrolet	91.308	93,765
Apr 14	N Wilkesboro 400*	Terry Labonte (1)	Chevrolet	96.370	229,025
Apr 21	Martinsville 500*	Rusty Wallace (5)	Ford	81.410	59,245
Apr 28	Talladega 500	Sterling Marlin (4)	Chevrolet	149.999	109,845
May 5	Sonoma 300K	Rusty Wallace (7)	Ford	77.673	58,395
May 26	World 600	Dale Jarrett (15)	Ford	147.581	165,250
June 2	Dover Downs 500	Jeff Gordon (1)	Chevrolet	122.741	138,730
June 9	Pocono 500	Jeff Gordon (1)	Chevrolet	139.104	96,980
June 16	Michigan 400	Rusty Wallace (18)	Ford	166.033	71,380
July 6	Daytona 400	Sterling Marlin (2)	Chevrolet	161.602	106,565
July 14	New Hampshire 300*	Ernie Irvan (6)	Ford	98.930	112,625
July 21	Pocono 500	Rusty Wallace (13)	Ford	144.892	59,165
July 28	Talladega 500	Jeff Gordon (2)	Chevrolet	133.387	272,550
Aug 3	Indianapolis 400	Dale Jarrett (24)	Ford	139.508	564,035
Aug 11	Watkins Glen 90*	Geoff Bodine (13)	Ford	92.334	88,740
Aug 18	Michigan 400	Dale Jarrett (11)	Ford	139.792	83,195
Aug 24	Bristol 500*	Rusty Wallace (5)	Ford	91.267	77,090
Sept 1	Southern 500	Jeff Gordon (2)	Chevrolet	135.757	99,630
Sept 7	Richmond 400	Ernie Irvan (16)	Ford	105.469	86,665
Sept 15	Dover 500	Jeff Gordon (3)	Chevrolet	105.646	153,630
Sept 22	Martinsville 500*	Jeff Gordon (10)	Chevrolet	82.223	93,825

Note: Distances are in miles unless followed by * (laps) or K (kilometers).

1995 Winston Cup Final Standings

Driver	Car	Starts	Wins	Pts
Jeff Gordon	Chevy	31	7	4614
Dale Earnhardt	Chevy	31	5	4580
Sterling Marlin	Chevy	31	3	4361
Mark Martin	Ford	31	4	4320
Rusty Wallace	Ford	31	2	4240
Terry Labonte	Chevy	31	3	4146
Ted Musgrave	Ford	31	0	3949
Bill Elliott	Ford	31	0	3746
Ricky Rudd	Ford	31	1	3734
Bobby Labonte	Chevy	31	3	3718

1995 Winston Cup Driver Winnings

Driver	Winnings ($)
Jeff Gordon	4,347,343
Dale Earnhardt	3,154,241
Sterling Marlin	2,253,502
Mark Martin	1,893,519
Rusty Wallace	1,642,837
Terry Labonte	1,558,659
Bobby Labonte	1,413,682
Dale Jarrett	1,363,158
Ricky Rudd	1,337,703
Ted Musgrave	1,147,445

Formula One Grand Prix Racing

1996 Formula One Results (through September 22)

Date	Grand Prix	Winner	Car	Time
Mar 10	Australia	Damon Hill	Williams Renault	1:32:50.491
Mar 31	Brazil	Damon Hill	Williams Renault	1:49:52.976
Apr 7	Argentina	Damon Hill	Williams Renault	1:54:55.322
Apr 28	Europe	Jacques Villeneuve	Williams Renault	1:33:26.473
May 5	San Marino	Damon Hill	Williams Renault	1:35:26.156
May 19	Monaco	Oliver Panis	Ligier Mugen Honda	2:00:45.629
June 2	Spain	Michael Schumacher	Ferrari	1:59:49.307
June 16	Canada	Damon Hill	Williams Renault	1:36:03.465
June 30	France	Damon Hill	Williams Renault	1:36:28.795
July 14	Great Britain	Jacques Villeneuve	Williams Renault	1:33:00.874
July 28	Germany	Damon Hill	Williams Renault	1:21:43.417
Aug 11	Hungary	Jacques Villeneuve	Williams Renault	1:46:21.134
Aug 25	Belgium	Michael Schumacher	Ferrari	1:28:15.125
Sept 8	Italy	Michael Schumacher	Ferrari	1:17:43.632
Sept 22	Portugal	Jacques Villeneuve	Williams Renault	1:40:22.915

Formula One Grand Prix Racing (Cont.)

1995 World Championship Final Standings

Drivers compete in Grand Prix races for the title of World Driving Champion. Below are the top 10 results from the 1995 season. Points are awarded for places 1-6 as follows: 10-6-4-3-2-1.

Driver, Country	Starts	Wins	Car	Pts
Michael Schumacher, Germany	17	9	Benetton Renault	102
Damon Hill, Great Britain	17	4	Williams Renault	69
David Coulthard, Great Britain	17	1	Williams Renault	49
Johnny Herbert, Great Britain	17	2	Bennetton Renault	45
Jean Alesi, France	17	1	Ferrari	42
Gerhard Berger, Austria	17	0	Ferrari	31
Mika Hakkinen, Finland	15	0	McLaren Mercedes	13
Olivier Panis, France	17	0	Ligier Mugen Honda	16
Heinz-Harald Frentzen, Germany	17	0	Sauber Ford	15
Mark Blundell, Great Britain	15	0	McLaren Mercedes	13

International Motor Sports Association

The 24 Hours of Daytona

Held at the Daytona International Speedway on February 3-4, 1996, the 24 Hours of Daytona annually serves as the opening round of the International Motor Sports Association's racing season.

Place	Drivers	Car (Class)	Distance
1	Wayne Taylor, Scott Sharp, Jim Pace	Oldsmobile (WSC)	697 laps (103.32 mph)
2	Massimiliano Papis, Gianpiero Moretti, Bob Wollek, Didier Theys	Ferrari (WSC)	697 laps
3	Tim McAdam, Barry Waddell, Butch Hamlet, Jim Downing	Mazda Kudzu (WSC)	649 laps
4	Enzo Calderari, Ferdinand de Lesseps, Lilian Bryner, Ulrich Richter	Porsche (GTS-2)	649 laps
5	Ross Bentley, Franck Freon, Lee Payne	Oldsmobile (WSC)	645 laps

1996 World SportsCar Championship Results (through September 1)

Date	Race	Winner(s)	Car
Feb 3-4	24 Hours of Daytona	Wayne Taylor, Scott Sharp, Jim Pace	Oldsmobile
Mar 16	12 Hours of Sebring	Wayne Taylor, Eric van de Poele, Jim Pace	Oldsmobile
Apr 21	Grand Prix of Atlanta	Max Papis, Gianpiero Moretti	Ferrari
May 5	Texas Grand Prix	Wayne Taylor, Jim Pace	Oldsmobile
May 27	Lime Rock Grand Prix	Gianpiero Moretti, Max Papis	Ferrari
June 9	Six Hours of the Glen	Max Papis, Gianpiero Moretti	Ferrari
July 14	California Grand Prix	Wayne Taylor, Scott Sharp	Oldsmobile
Aug 25	Mosport 500	John Paul Jr, Butch Leitzinger	Ford
Sept 1	Grand Prix of Dallas	Butch Leitzinger	Ford

1996 Supreme GTS-1 Results (through September 1)

Date	Race	Winner(s)	Car
Feb 3-4	24 Hours of Daytona	Charles Morgan, Rob Morgan, Joe Pezza, Jon Gooding, Irv Hoerr	Oldsmobile
Mar 16	12 Hours of Sebring	Hans Stuck, Bill Adam	Porsche
Apr 21	Grand Prix of Atlanta	Irv Hoerr, Darin Brassfield	Oldsmobile
May 5	Texas Grand Prix	Irv Hoerr, Darin Brassfield	Oldsmobile
May 27	Lime Rock Grand Prix	Irv Hoerr	Oldsmobile
June 9	Six Hours of the Glen	Irv Hoerr, Darin Brassfield, Brian Cunningham, Brian Devries	Oldsmobile
July 14	California Grand Prix	Darin Brassfield, Irv Hoerr	Oldsmobile
Aug 25	Mosport 500	Irv Hoerr	Oldsmobile
Sept 1	Grand Prix of Dallas	Darin Brassfield	Oldsmobile

International Motor Sports Association *(Cont.)*

1995 World SportsCar Championship Final Standings

Driver	Pts
Fermin Velez	262
James Weaver	260
Mauro Baldi	245
Wayne Taylor	232
Jim Pace	231
Butch Leitzinger	188
Roger Mandeville	147
Henry Camferdam	147
Leigh Miller	121
Gianpiero Moretti	118

24 Hours of Le Mans

Held at LeMans, France, on June 15-16, 1996, the 24 Hours of LeMans is the most prestigious international event in endurance racing.

Place	Drivers	Car	Distance
1	Manuel Reuter, Davy Jones, Alexander Wurz	TWR Porsche	354 laps (2,991.3 mi)
2	Hans-Joachim Stuck, Thierry Boutsen, Bob Wollek	Porsche AG	353
3	Yannick Dalmas, Karl Wendlinger, Scott Goodyear	Porsche AG	341
4	John Nielsen, Thomas Bscher, Peter Kox	McLaren BMW	338
5	Pierre Henri Raphanel, Lindsay Owen Jones, David Brabham	McLaren BMW	335
6	Andy Wallace, Olivier Grouillard, Derek Bell	McLaren BMW	328
7	Henri Pescarolo, Franck LaGorce, Ammanuel Collard	Courage Porsche C36	327
8	Nelson Piquet, Johnny Cecotto, Danny Sullivan	McLaren BMW	324
9	Ray Bellm, James Weaver, JJ Lehto	McLaren BMW	323
10	Price Cobb, Mark Dismore, Shawn Hendricks	Chrysler Viper	320

National Hot Rod Association

1996 Results (through September 15)

TOP FUEL

Date	Race, Site	Winner	Time	Speed
Feb 1-4	Winternationals, Pomona, CA	Blaine Johnson	4.736	299.70
Feb 22-25	ATSCO Nationals, Phoenix	Kenny Bernstein	4.705	305.39
Mar 28-31	Slick 50 Nationals, Houston	Kenny Bernstein	4.663	306.95
Apr 18-21	Fram Nationals, Atlanta	Larry Dixon	6.043	232.73
May 2-5	Virginia Nationals, Richmond	Shelly Anderson	4.779	298.90
June 6-9	Pontiac Nationals, Columbus, OH	Cory McClenathan	4.817	306.43
June 20-23	Pennzoil Nationals, Memphis	Mike Dunn	4.897	295.85
July 4-7	Western Auto Nationals, Topeka, KS	Scott Kalitta	4.664	314.68
July 13-21	Mile-High Nationals, Denver	Eddie Hill	4.845	288.92
July 26-29	Autolite Nationals, Sonoma, CA	Blaine Johnson	4.671	306.01
Aug 2-4	Northwest Nationals, Seattle	Shelly Anderson	4.663	308.00
Aug 15-18	Champion Auto Nationals, Brainerd, MN	Kenny Bernstein	4.733	302.82
Sept 12-15	Keystone Nationals, Reading, PA	Kenny Bernstein	4.675	305.81

1996 Results (through September 15)
FUNNY CAR

Date	Race, Site	Winner	Time	Speed
Feb 1-4	Winternationals, Pomona, CA	Al Hofmann	5.054	302.72
Feb 22-25	ATSCO Nationals, Phoenix	John Force	5.196	285.85
Mar 28-31	Slick 50 Nationals, Houston	John Force	5.056	294.98
Apr 18-21	Fram Nationals, Atlanta	Tony Pedregon	5.108	294.59
May 2-5	Virginia Nationals, Richmond	John Force	5.071	285.17
June 6-9	Pontiac Nationals, Columbus, OH	Chuck Etchells	5.178	287.63
June 20-23	Mid-South Nationals, Memphis	John Force	5.302	296.54
July 4-7	Western Auto Nationals, Topeka, KS	John Force	4.930	303.54
July 13-21	Mile-High Nationals, Denver	John Force	5.221	294.81
July 26-29	Autolite Nationals, Sonoma, CA	Cruz Pedregon	5.058	291.45
Aug 2-4	Northwest Nationals, Seattle	John Force	4.965	302.11
Aug 15-18	Champion Auto Nationals, Brainerd, MN	John Force	5.120	303.13
Sept 12-15	Keystone Nationals, Reading, PA	Jeff Arend	5.187	291.16

PRO STOCK

Date	Race, Site	Winner	Time	Speed
Feb 1-4	Winternationals, Pomona, CA	Jim Yates	7.041	195.48
Feb 22-25	ATSCO Nationals, Phoenix	Jim Yates	7.057	194.51
Mar 28-31	Slick 50 Nationals, Houston	Mike Edwards	7.029	196.46
Apr 18-21	Fram Nationals, Atlanta	Kurt Johnson	7.068	195.82
May 2-5	Virginia Nationals, Richmond	Warren Johnson	7.018	196.03
June 6-9	Pontiac Nationals, Columbus, OH	Chuck Harris	7.168	193.09
June 20-23	Mid-South Nationals, Memphis	Warren Johnson	7.221	192.84
July 4-7	Western Auto Nationals, Topeka, KS	Warren Johnson	7.104	194.38
July 13-21	Mile-High Nationals, Denver	Jim Yates	7.475	183.41
July 26-29	Autolite Nationals, Sonoma, CA	Warren Johnson	7.067	194.84
Aug 2-4	Northwest Nationals, Seattle	Mike Edwards	7.046	196.24
Aug 15-18	Champion Auto Nationals, Brainerd, MN	Warren Johnson	7.110	193.38
Sept 12-15	Keystone Nationals, Reading, PA	Jim Yates	6.957	197.45

1995 Standings

TOP FUEL

Driver	Wins	Pts
Scott Kalitta	6	1,575
Cory McClenathan	3	1,360
Larry Dixon	4	1,318
Mike Dunn	3	1,255
Blaine Johnson	1	1,237
Eddie Hill	1	983
Kenny Burnstein	0	949
Tommy Johnson Jr	0	859
Shelly Anderson	0	838
Joe Amato	0	775

FUNNY CAR

Driver	Wins	Pts
John Force	6	1,690
Al Hofmann	5	1,508
Cruz Pedragon	5	1,351
Chuck Etchells	2	1,202
KC Spurlock	0	956
Dean Skuza	0	937
Whit Bazemore	0	884
Gary Clapshaw	1	831
Gary Densham	0	757
Jim Epler	0	714

PRO STOCK

Driver	Wins	Pts
Warren Johnson	7	1,675
Jim Yates	1	1,370
Kurt Johnson	2	1,198
Steve Schmidt	2	1,066
Jerry Eckman	0	978
Mark Pawuk	1	903
Bob Glidden	1	807
George Marnell	0	784
Larry Morgan	0	682
Chuck Harris	0	680

Indianapolis 500

First held in 1911, the Indianapolis 500—200 laps of the 2.5-mile Indianapolis Motor Speedway Track (called the Brickyard in honor of its original pavement)—has grown to become the most famous auto race in the world. Held on Memorial Day weekend, it annually draws the largest crowd of any sporting event in the world.

Year	Winner (Start Position)	Car	Avg MPH	Pole Winner	MPH
1911	Ray Harroun (28)	Marmon Wasp	74.590	Lewis Strang	Awarded pole
1912	Joe Dawson (7)	National	78.720	Gil Anderson	Drew pole
1913	Jules Goux (7)	Peugeot	75.930	Caleb Bragg	Drew pole
1914	Rene Thomas (15)	Delage	82.470	Jean Chassagne	Drew pole
1915	Ralph DePalma (2)	Mercedes	89.840	Howard Wilcox	98.90
1916	Dario Resta (4)	Peugeot	84.000	John Aitken	96.69
1917-18	No race				
1919	Howard Wilcox (2)	Peugeot	88.050	Rene Thomas	104.78
1920	Gaston Chevrolet (6)	Monroe	88.620	Ralph DePalma	99.15
1921	Tommy Milton (20)	Frontenac	89.620	Ralph DePalma	100.75
1922	Jimmy Murphy (1)	Murphy Special	94.480	Jimmy Murphy	100.50
1923	Tommy Milton (1)	H.C.S. Special	90.950	Tommy Milton	108.17
1924	L. L. Corum	Duesenberg Special	98.230	Jimmy Murphy	108.037
	Joe Boyer (21)				
1925	Peter DePaolo (2)	Duesenberg Special	101.130	Leon Duray	113.196
1926	Frank Lockhart (20)	Miller Special	95.904	Earl Cooper	111.735
1927	George Souders (22)	Duesenberg	97.545	Frank Lockhart	120.100
1928	Louis Meyer (13)	Miller Special	99.482	Leon Duray	122.391
1929	Ray Keech (6)	Simplex Piston Ring Special	97.585	Cliff Woodbury	120.599
1930	Billy Arnold (1)	Miller Hartz Special	100.448	Billy Arnold	113.268
1931	Louis Schneider (13)	Bowes Seal-Fast Special	96.629	Russ Snowberger	112.796
1932	Fred Frame (27)	Miller Hartz Special	104.144	Lou Moore	117.363
1933	Louis Meyer (6)	Tydol Special	104.162	Bill Cummings	118.524
1934	Bill Cummings (10)	Boyle Products Special	104.863	Kelly Petillo	119.329
1935	Kelly Petillo (22)	Gilmore Speedway Special	106.240	Rex Mays	120.736
1936	Louis Meyer (28)	Ring-Free Special	109.069	Rex Mays	119.664
1937	Wilbur Shaw (2)	Shaw-Gilmore Special	113.580	Bill Cummings	123.343
1938	Floyd Roberts (1)	Burd Piston Ring Special	117.200	Floyd Roberts	125.681
1939	Wilbur Shaw (3)	Boyle Special	115.035	Jimmy Snyder	130.138
1940	Wilbur Shaw (2)	Boyle Special	114.277	Rex Mays	127.850
1941	Floyd Davis	Noc-Out Hose Clamp Special	115.117	Mauri Rose	128.691
	Mauri Rose (17)				
1942-45	No race				
1946	George Robson (15)	Thorne Engineering Special	114.820	Cliff Bergere	126.471
1947	Mauri Rose (3)	Blue Crown Spark Plug Special	116.338	Ted Horn	126.564
1948	Mauri Rose (3)	Blue Crown Spark Plug Special	119.814	Rex Mays	130.577
1949	Bill Holland (4)	Blue Crown Spark Plug Special	121.327	Duke Nalon	132.939
1950	Johnnie Parsons (5)	Wynn's Friction Proofing	124.002	Walt Faulkner	134.343
1951	Lee Wallard (2)	Belanger Special	126.244	Duke Nalon	136.498
1952	Troy Ruttman (7)	Agajanian Special	128.922	Fred Agabashian	138.010
1953	Bill Vukovich (1)	Fuel Injection Special	128.740	Bill Vukovich	138.392
1954	Bill Vukovich (19)	Fuel Injection Special	130.840	Jack McGrath	141.033
1955	Bob Sweikert (14)	John Zink Special	128.209	Jerry Hoyt	140.045
1956	Pat Flaherty (1)	John Zink Special	128.490	Pat Flaherty	145.596
1957	Sam Hanks (13)	Belond Exhaust Special	135.601	Pat O'Connor	143.948
1958	Jim Bryan (7)	Belond AP Parts Special	133.791	Dick Rathmann	145.974
1959	Rodger Ward (6)	Leader Card 500 Roadster	135.857	Johnny Thomson	145.908
1960	Jim Rathmann (2)	Ken-Paul Special	138.767	Eddie Sachs	146.592
1961	A. J. Foyt (7)	Bowes Seal-Fast Special	139.130	Eddie Sachs	147.481
1962	Rodger Ward (2)	Leader Card 500 Roadster	140.293	Parnelli Jones	150.370
1963	Parnelli Jones (1)	Agajanian-Willard Special	143.137	Parnelli Jones	151.153
1964	A. J. Foyt (5)	Sheraton-Thompson Special	147.350	Jim Clark	158.828
1965	Jim Clark (2)	Lotus Ford	150.686	A. J. Foyt	161.233
1966	Graham Hill (15)	American Red Ball Special	144.317	Mario Andretti	165.899
1967	A. J. Foyt (4)	Sheraton-Thompson Special	151.207	Mario Andretti	168.982
1968	Bobby Unser (3)	Rislone Special	152.882	Joe Leonard	171.559
1969	Mario Andretti (2)	STP Oil Treatment Special	156.867	A. J. Foyt	170.568
1970	Al Unser (1)	Johnny Lightning 500 Special	155.749	Al Unser	170.221
1971	Al Unser (5)	Johnny Lightning Special	157.735	Peter Revson	178.696
1972	Mark Donohue (3)	Sunoco McLaren	162.962	Bobby Unser	195.940
1973	Gordon Johncock (11)	STP Double Oil Filters	159.036	Johnny Rutherford	198.413

Year	Winner (Start Position)	Car	Avg MPH	Pole Winner	MPH
1974	Johnny Rutherford (25)	McLaren	158.589	A. J. Foyt	191.632
1975	Bobby Unser (3)	Jorgensen Eagle	149.213	A. J. Foyt	193.976
1976	Johnny Rutherford (1)	Hy-Gain McLaren/Goodyear	148.725	Johnny Rutherford	188.957
1977	A. J. Foyt (4)	Gilmore Racing Team	161.331	Tom Sneva	198.884
1978	Al Unser (5)	FNCTC Chaparral Lola	161.361	Tom Sneva	202.156
1979	Rick Mears (1)	The Gould Charge	158.899	Rick Mears	193.736
1980	Johnny Rutherford (1)	Pennzoil Chaparral	142.862	Johnny Rutherford	192.256
1981	Bobby Unser (1)	Norton Spirit Penske PC-9B	139.084	Bobby Unser	200.546
1982	Gordon Johncock (5)	STP Oil Treatment	162.026	Rick Mears	207.004
1983	Tom Sneva (4)	Texaco Star	162.117	Teo Fabi	207.395
1984	Rick Mears (3)	Pennzoil Z-7	163.612	Tom Sneva	210.029
1985	Danny Sullivan (8)	Miller American Special	152.982	Pancho Carter	212.583
1986	Bobby Rahal (4)	Budweiser/Truesports/March	170.722	Rick Mears	216.828
1987	Al Unser (20)	Cummins Holset Turbo	162.175	Mario Andretti	215.390
1988	Rick Mears (1)	Penske-Chevrolet	144.809	Rick Mears	219.198
1989	Emerson Fittipaldi (3)	Penske-Chevrolet	167.581	Rick Mears	223.885
1990	Arie Luyendyk (3)	Domino's Pizza Chevrolet	185.981*	Emerson Fittipaldi	225.301†
1991	Rick Mears (1)	Penske-Chevrolet	176.457	Rick Mears	224.113
1992	Al Unser Jr (12)	G92-Chevrolet	134.477	Roberto Guerrero	232.482
1993	Emerson Fittipaldi (9)	Penske-Chevrolet	157.207	Arie Luyendyk	223.967
1994	Al Unser Jr (1)	Penske-Mercedes	160.872	Al Unser Jr	228.011
1995	Jacques Villeneuve (5)	Reynard-Ford	153.616	Scott Brayton	231.616
1996	Buddy Lazier (5)	Reynard-Ford	147.956	Tony Stewart	233.100

*Track record, winning time. †Track record, qualifying time.

Indianapolis 500 Rookie of the Year Award

1952 ....Art Cross	1968 ....Billy Vukovich	1984 ....Michael Andretti
1953 ....Jimmy Daywalt	1969 ....Mark Donohue*	............Roberto Guerrero
1954 ....Larry Crockett	1970 ....Donnie Allison	1985 ....Arie Luyendyk*
1955 ....Al Herman	1971 ....Denny Zimmerman	1986 ....Randy Lanier
1956 ....Bob Veith	1972 ....Mike Hiss	1987 ....Fabrizio Barbazza
1957 ....Don Edmunds	1973 ....Graham McRae	1988 ....Billy Vukovich III
1958 ....George Amick	1974 ....Pancho Carter	1989 ....Bernard Jourdain
1959 ....Bobby Grim	1975 ....Bill Puterbaugh	............Scott Pruett
1960 ....Jim Hurtubise	1976 ....Vern Schuppan	1990 ....Eddie Cheever
1961 ....Parnelli Jones*	1977 ....Jerry Sneva	1991 ....Jeff Andretti
............Bobby Marshman	1978 ....Rick Mears*	1992 ....Lyn St. James
1962 ....Jimmy McElreath	............Larry Rice	1993 ....Nigel Mansell
1963 ....Jim Clark*	1979 ....Howdy Holmes	1994 ....Jacques Villeneuve*
1964 ....Johnny White	1980 ....Tim Richmond	1995 ....Gil de Ferran
1965 ....Mario Andretti*	1981 ....Josele Garza	1996 ....Tony Stewart
1966 ....Jackie Stewart	1982 ....Jim Hickman	
1967 ....Denis Hulme	1983 ....Teo Fabi	*Future winner of Indy 500.

Championship Auto Racing Teams

Indy Car World Series Champions

From 1909 to 1955, this championship was awarded by the American Automobile Association (AAA), and from 1956 to 1979 by United States Auto Club (USAC). Since 1979, Championship Auto Racing Teams (CART) has conducted the championship.

1909 ....George Robertson	1924 ....Jimmy Murphy	1939 ....Wilbur Shaw
1910 ....Ray Harroun	1925 ....Peter DePaolo	1940 ....Rex Mays
1911 ....Ralph Mulford	1926 ....Harry Hartz	1941 ....Rex Mays
1912 ....Ralph DePalma	1927 ....Peter DePaolo	1942-45 ....No racing
1913 ....Earl Cooper	1928 ....Louis Meyer	1946 ....Ted Horn
1914 ....Ralph DePalma	1929 ....Louis Meyer	1947 ....Ted Horn
1915 ....Earl Cooper	1930 ....Billy Arnold	1948 ....Ted Horn
1916 ....Dario Resta	1931 ....Louis Schneider	1949 ....Johnnie Parsons
1917 ....Earl Cooper	1932 ....Bob Carey	1950 ....Henry Banks
1918 ....Ralph Mulford	1933 ....Louis Meyer	1951 ....Tony Bettenhausen
1919 ....Howard Wilcox	1934 ....Bill Cummings	1952 ....Chuck Stevenson
1920 ....Tommy Milton	1935 ....Kelly Petillo	1953 ....Sam Hanks
1921 ....Tommy Milton	1936 ....Mauri Rose	1954 ....Jimmy Bryan
1922 ....Jimmy Murphy	1937 ....Wilbur Shaw	1955 ....Bob Sweikert
1923 ....Eddie Hearne	1938 ....Floyd Roberts	1956 ....Jimmy Bryan

Indy Car World Series Champions *(Cont.)*

1957 ....Jimmy Bryan	1971 ....Joe Leonard	1984 ....Mario Andretti
1958 ....Tony Bettenhausen	1972 ....Joe Leonard	1985 ....Al Unser
1959 ....Rodger Ward	1973 ....Roger McCluskey	1986 ....Bobby Rahal
1960 ....A. J. Foyt	1974 ....Bobby Unser	1987 ....Bobby Rahal
1961 ....A. J. Foyt	1975 ....A. J. Foyt	1988 ....Danny Sullivan
1962 ....Rodger Ward	1976 ....Gordon Johncock	1989 ....Emerson Fittipaldi
1963 ....A. J. Foyt	1977 ....Tom Sneva	1990 ....Al Unser Jr
1964 ....A. J. Foyt	1978 ....Tom Sneva	1991 ....Michael Andretti
1965 ....Mario Andretti	1979 ....A. J. Foyt	1992 ....Bobby Rahal
1966 ....Mario Andretti	1979 ....Rick Mears	1993 ....Nigel Mansell
1967 ....A. J. Foyt	1980 ....Johnny Rutherford	1994 ....Al Unser Jr
1968 ....Bobby Unser	1981 ....Rick Mears	1995 ....Jacques Villeneuve
1969 ....Mario Andretti	1982 ....Rick Mears	1996 ....Jimmy Vasser
1970 ....Al Unser	1983 ....Al Unser	

Alltime Indy Car Leaders

WINS		WINNINGS ($)		POLE POSITIONS	
A. J. Foyt	67	*Al Unser Jr	15,240,093	Mario Andretti	67
Mario Andretti	52	*Bobby Rahal	14,044,508	A. J. Foyt	53
Al Unser	39	*Emerson Fittipaldi	12,937,375	Bobby Unser	49
Bobby Unser	35	*Michael Andretti	11,917,869	Rick Mears	38
*Michael Andretti	35	Mario Andretti	11,279,654	*Michael Andretti	30
*Al Unser Jr	31	Rick Mears	11,050,807	Al Unser	27
Rick Mears	29	Danny Sullivan	8,254,673	Johnny Rutherford	23
Johnny Rutherford	27	*Arie Luyendyk	7,092,188	Gordon Johncock	20
Rodger Ward	26	Al Unser	6,740,843	Rex Mays	19
Gordon Johncock	25	*Raul Boesel	5,544,137	Danny Sullivan	19
*Bobby Rahal	24	A. J. Foyt	5,357,589	*Bobby Rahal	18
Ralph DePalma	24	*Scott Brayton	4,807,214	*Emerson Fittipaldi	17
Tommy Milton	23	*Teo Fabi	4,573,131	Tony Bettenhausen	14
Tony Bettenhausen	22	Tom Sneva	4,392,993	Don Branson	14
*Emerson Fittipaldi	22	*Roberto Guerrero	4,275,163	Tom Sneva	14
Earl Cooper	20	Johnny Rutherford	4,209,232	Parnelli Jones	12
Jimmy Bryan	19	*Scott Goodyear	4,133,201	Danny Ongais	11
Jimmy Murphy	19	*Jaques Villeneuve	3,748,982	Rodger Ward	11
Ralph Mulford	17	*Paul Tracy	3,584,020		
Danny Sullivan	17	Gordon Johncock	3,431,414	Four tied with 10.	

*Active driver. Note: Leaders in wins and pole positions through 1996; leaders in winnings through 1995.

National Association for Stock Car Auto Racing

Stock Car Racing's Major Events

Winston offers a $1 million bonus to any driver to win 3 of NASCAR's top 4 events in the same season. These races are the richest (Daytona 500), the fastest (Talladega 500), the longest (World 600 at Charlotte) and the oldest (Southern 500 at Darlington). These events form the backbone of NASCAR racing. Only 3 drivers, LeeRoy Yarbrough (1969), David Pearson (1976) and Bill Elliott (1985), have scored the 3-track hat trick.

Daytona 500

Year	Winner	Car	Avg MPH	Pole Winner	MPH
1959	Lee Petty	Oldsmobile	135.520	Cotton Owens	143.198
1960	Junior Johnson	Chevrolet	124.740	Fireball Roberts	151.556
1961	Marvin Panch	Pontiac	149.601	Fireball Roberts	155.709
1962	Fireball Roberts	Pontiac	152.529	Fireball Roberts	156.995
1963	Tiny Lund	Ford	151.566	Johnny Rutherford	165.183
1964	Richard Petty	Plymouth	154.345	Paul Goldsmith	174.910
1965	Fred Lorenzen	Ford	141.539	Darel Dieringer	171.151
1966	Richard Petty	Plymouth	160.627	Richard Petty	175.165
1967	Mario Andretti	Ford	149.926	Curtis Turner	180.831
1968	Cale Yarborough	Mercury	143.251	Cale Yarborough	189.222
1969	LeeRoy Yarbrough	Ford	157.950	David Pearson	190.029
1970	Pete Hamilton	Plymouth	149.601	Cale Yarborough	194.015
1971	Richard Petty	Plymouth	144.462	A. J. Foyt	182.744
1972	A. J. Foyt	Mercury	161.550	Bobby Isaac	186.632
1973	Richard Petty	Dodge	157.205	Buddy Baker	185.662

Daytona 500 (Cont.)

Year	Winner	Car	Avg MPH	Pole Winner	MPH
1974	Richard Petty	Dodge	140.894	David Pearson	185.017
1975	Benny Parsons	Chevrolet	153.649	Donnie Allison	185.827
1976	David Pearson	Mercury	152.181	A. J. Foyt	185.943
1977	Cale Yarborough	Chevrolet	153.218	Donnie Allison	188.048
1978	Bobby Allison	Ford	159.730	Cale Yarborough	187.536
1979	Richard Petty	Oldsmobile	143.977	Buddy Baker	196.049
1980	Buddy Baker	Oldsmobile	177.602*	A. J. Foyt	195.020
1981	Richard Petty	Buick	169.651	Bobby Allison	194.624
1982	Bobby Allison	Buick	153.991	Benny Parsons	196.317
1983	Cale Yarborough	Pontiac	155.979	Ricky Rudd	198.864
1984	Cale Yarborough	Chevrolet	150.994	Cale Yarborough	201.848
1985	Bill Elliott	Ford	172.265	Bill Elliott	205.114
1986	Geoff Bodine	Chevrolet	148.124	Bill Elliott	205.039
1987	Bill Elliott	Ford	176.263	Bill Elliott	210.364†
1988	Bobby Allison	Buick	137.531	Ken Schrader	193.823
1989	Darrell Waltrip	Chevrolet	148.466	Ken Schrader	196.996
1990	Derrike Cope	Chevrolet	165.761	Ken Schrader	196.515
1991	Earnie Irvan	Chevrolet	148.148	Davey Allison	195.955
1992	Davey Allison	Ford	160.256	Sterling Marlin	192.213
1993	Dale Jarrett	Chevrolet	154.972	Kyle Petty	189.426
1994	Sterling Marlin	Chevrolet	156.931	Loy Allen Jr	190.158
1995	Sterling Marlin	Chevrolet	141.710	Dale Jarrett	193.498
1996	Dale Jarrett	Ford	154.308	Dale Earnhardt	189.510

*Track record, winning time. †Track record, qualifying time. Note: The Daytona 500, held annually in February, now opens the NASCAR season with 200 laps around the high-banked Daytona International Speedway.

World 600

Year	Winner	Car	Avg MPH	Pole Winner
1960	Joe Lee Johnson	Chevrolet	107.752	J.L. Johnson
1961	David Pearson	Pontiac	111.634	Richard Petty
1962	Nelson Stacy	Ford	125.552	Fireball Roberts
1963	Fred Lorenzen	Ford	132.418	Junior Johnson
1964	Jim Paschal	Plymouth	125.772	Junior Johnson
1965	Fred Lorenzen	Ford	121.772	Fred Lorenzon
1966	Marvin Panch	Plymouth	135.042	Paul Goldsmith
1967	Jim Paschal	Plymouth	135.832	Cale Yarborough
1968	Buddy Baker	Dodge	104.207	Donnie Allison
1969	Lee Yarbrough	Mercury	134.631	Donnie Allison
1970	Donnie Allison	Ford	129.680	Bobby Isaac
1971	Bobby Allison	Mercury	140.442	Charlie Glotzbach
1972	Buddy Baker	Dodge	142.255	Bobby Allison
1973	Buddy Baker	Dodge	134.890	Buddy Baker
1974	David Pearson	Mercury	135.720	David Pearson
1975	Richard Petty	Dodge	145.327	David Pearson
1976	David Pearson	Mercury	137.352	David Pearson
1977	Richard Petty	Dodge	137.636	David Pearson
1978	Darrell Waltrip	Chevrolet	138.355	David Pearson
1979	Darrell Waltrip	Chevrolet	136.674	Neil Bonnet
1980	Benny Parsons	Chevrolet	119.265	Cale Yarborough
1981	Bobby Allison	Buick	129.326	Neil Bonnet
1982	Neil Bonnett	Ford	130.508	David Pearson
1983	Neil Bonnett	Chevrolet	140.406	Buddy Baker
1984	Bobby Allison	Buick	129.233	Harry Gant
1985	Darrell Waltrip	Chevrolet	141.807	Bill Elliott
1986	Dale Earnhardt	Chevrolet	140.406	Geoff Bodine
1987	Kyle Petty	Ford	131.483	Bill Elliott
1988	Darrell Waltrip	Chevrolet	124.460	Davey Allison
1989	Darrell Waltrip	Chevrolet	144.077	Alan Kulwicki
1990	Rusty Wallace	Pontiac	137.650	Ken Schrader
1991	Davey Allison	Ford	138.951	Mark Martin
1992	Dale Earnhardt	Chevrolet	132.980	Bill Elliott
1993	Dale Earnhardt	Chevrolet	145.504	Ken Schrader
1994	Jeff Gordon	Chevrolet	139.445	Jeff Gordon
1995	Bobby Labonte	Chevrolet	151.952	Jeff Gordon
1996	Dale Jarrett	Ford	147.581	Jeff Gordon

Note: Held at the 1.5-mile high-banked Charlotte Motor Speedway on Memorial Day weekend.

Talladega 500

Year	Winner	Car	Avg MPH	Pole Winner	MPH
1969	Richard Brickhouse	Dodge	153.778	Charlie Glotzbach	199.466
1970	Pete Hamilton	Plymouth	158.517	Bobby Isaac	186.834
1971	Bobby Allison	Mercury	145.945	Davey Allison	187.323
1972	James Hylton	Mercury	148.728	Bobby Isaac	190.677
1973	Dick Brooks	Plymouth	145.454	Bobby Allison	187.064
1974	Richard Petty	Dodge	148.637	David Pearson	184.926
1975	Buddy Baker	Ford	130.892	Dave Marcis	191.340
1976	Dave Marcis	Dodge	157.547	Dave Marcis	190.651
1977	Davey Allison	Chevrolet	162.524	Benny Parsons	192.682
1978	Lennie Pond	Olds	174.700	Cale Yarborough	192.917
1979	Darrell Waltrip	Olds	161.229	Neil Bonnet	193.600
1980	Neil Bonnet	Mercury	166.894	Buddy Baker	198.545
1981	Ron Bouchard	Buick	156.737	Harry Gant	195.897
1982	Darrell Waltrip	Buick	168.157	Geoff Bodine	199.400
1983	Dale Earnhardt	Ford	170.611	Cale Yarborough	201.744
1984	Dale Earnhardt	Chevrolet	155.485	Cale Yarborough	202.474
1985	Cale Yarborough	Ford	148.772	Bill Elliott	207.578
1986	Bobby Hillin	Buick	151.552	Bill Elliott	209.005
1987	Bill Elliott	Ford	171.293	Bill Elliott	203.827
1988	Ken Schrader	Chevrolet	154.505	Darrell Waltrip	196.274
1989	Terry Labonte	Ford	157.354	Mark Martin	194.800
1990	Dale Earnhardt	Chevrolet	174.430	Dale Earnhardt	192.513
1991	Harry Gant	Olds	165.620	Sterling Marlin	192.085
1992	Ernie Irvan	Chevrolet	176.309	Sterling Marlin	190.586
1993	Dale Earnhardt	Chevrolet	153.858	Bill Elliott	192.397
1994	Jimmy Spencer	Ford	163.217	Dale Earnhardt	193.470
1995	Sterling Marlin	Chevrolet	173.188	Sterling Marlin	194.212
1996	Jeff Gordon	Chevrolet	133.387	Jeremy Mayfield	192.370

Note: Held at the 2.66-mile Talladega Superspeedway on the last weekend in July.

Southern 500

Year	Winner	Car	Avg MPH	Pole Winner
1950	Johnny Mantz	Plymouth	76.260	Wally Campbell
1951	Herb Thomas	Hudson	76.900	Marshall Teague
1952	Fonty Flock	Olds	74.510	Dick Rathman
1953	Buck Baker	Olds	92.780	Fonty Flock
1954	Herb Thomas	Hudson	94.930	Buck Baker
1955	Herb Thomas	Chevrolet	92.281	Tim Flock
1956	Curtis Turner	Ford	95.067	Buck Baker
1957	Speedy Thompson	Chevrolet	100.100	Paul Goldsmith
1958	Fireball Roberts	Chevrolet	102.590	Fireball Roberts
1959	Jim Reed	Chevrolet	111.836	Fireball Roberts
1960	Buck Baker	Pontiac	105.901	Cotton Owens
1961	Nelson Stacy	Ford	117.880	Fireball Roberts
1962	Larry Frank	Ford	117.965	Fireball Roberts
1963	Fireball Roberts	Ford	129.784	Fireball Roberts
1964	Buck Baker	Dodge	117.757	Richard Petty
1965	Ned Jarrett	Ford	115.924	Junior Johnson
1966	Darel Dieringer	Mercury	114.830	Lee Yarborough
1967	Richard Petty	Plymouth	131.933	David Pearson
1968	Cale Yarborough	Mercury	126.132	Charlie Glotzbach
1969	Lee Yarbrough	Ford	105.612	Cale Yarborough
1970	Buddy Baker	Dodge	128.817	David Pearson
1971	Bobby Allison	Mercury	131.398	Bobby Allison
1972	Bobby Allison	Chevrolet	128.124	David Pearson
1973	Cale Yarborough	Chevrolet	134.033	David Pearson
1974	Cale Yarborough	Chevrolet	111.075	Richard Petty
1975	Bobby Allison	Matador	116.825	David Pearson
1976	David Pearson	Mercury	120.534	David Pearson
1977	David Pearson	Mercury	106.797	Darrell Waltrip
1978	Cale Yarborough	Olds	116.828	David Pearson
1979	David Pearson	Chevrolet	126.259	Bobby Allison
1980	Terry Labonte	Chevrolet	115.210	Darrell Waltrip
1981	Neil Bonnett	Ford	126.410	Harry Gant
1982	Cale Yarborough	Buick	126.703	David Pearson
1983	Bobby Allison	Buick	123.343	Neil Bonnett

Southern 500 (Cont.)

Year	Winner	Car	Avg MPH	Pole Winner
1984	Harry Gant	Chevrolet	128.270	Harry Gant
1985	Bill Elliott	Ford	121.254	Bill Elliott
1986	Tim Richmond	Chevrolet	121.068	Tim Richmond
1987	Dale Earnhardt	Chevrolet	115.520	Davey Allison
1988	Bill Elliott	Ford	128.297	Bill Elliott
1989	Dale Earnhardt	Chevrolet	135.462	Alan Kulwicki
1990	Dale Earnhardt	Chevrolet	123.141	Dale Earnhardt
1991	Harry Gant	Olds	133.508	Davey Allison
1992	Darrell Waltrip	Chevrolet	129.114	Sterling Marlin
1993	Mark Martin	Ford	137.932	Ken Schrader
1994	Bill Elliott	Ford	127.915	Geoff Bodine
1995	Jeff Gordon	Chevrolet	121.231	John Andretti
1996	Jeff Gordon	Chevrolet	135.757	Dale Jarrett

Note: Held at the 1.366-mile Darlington Raceway on Labor Day weekend.

Winston Cup NASCAR Champions

Year	Driver	Car	Wins	Poles	Winnings ($)
1949	Red Byron	Oldsmobile	2	0	5,800
1950	Bill Rexford	Oldsmobile	1	0	6,175
1951	Herb Thomas	Hudson	7	4	18,200
1952	Tim Flock	Hudson	8	4	20,210
1953	Herb Thomas	Hudson	11	10	27,300
1954	Lee Petty	Dodge	7	3	26,706
1955	Tim Flock	Chrysler	18	19	33,750
1956	Buck Baker	Chrysler	14	12	29,790
1957	Buck Baker	Chevrolet	10	5	24,712
1958	Lee Petty	Olds	7	4	20,600
1959	Lee Petty	Plymouth	10	2	45,570
1960	Rex White	Chevrolet	6	3	45,260
1961	Ned Jarrett	Chevrolet	1	4	27,285
1962	Joe Weatherly	Pontiac	9	6	56,110
1963	Joe Weatherly	Mercury	3	6	58,110
1964	Richard Petty	Plymouth	9	8	98,810
1965	Ned Jarrett	Ford	13	9	77,966
1966	David Pearson	Dodge	14	7	59,205
1967	Richard Petty	Plymouth	27	18	130,275
1968	David Pearson	Ford	16	12	118,824
1969	David Pearson	Ford	11	14	183,700
1970	Bobby Isaac	Dodge	11	13	121,470
1971	Richard Petty	Plymouth	21	9	309,225
1972	Richard Petty	Plymouth	8	3	227,015
1973	Benny Parsons	Chevrolet	1	0	114,345
1974	Richard Petty	Dodge	10	7	299,175
1975	Richard Petty	Dodge	13	3	378,865
1976	Cale Yarborough	Chevrolet	9	2	387,173
1977	Cale Yarborough	Chevrolet	9	3	477,499
1978	Cale Yarborough	Oldsmobile	10	8	530,751
1979	Richard Petty	Chevrolet	5	1	531,292
1980	Dale Earnhardt	Chevrolet	5	0	588,926
1981	Darrell Waltrip	Buick	12	11	693,342
1982	Darrell Waltrip	Buick	12	7	873,118
1983	Bobby Allison	Buick	6	0	828,355
1984	Terry Labonte	Chevrolet	2	2	713,010
1985	Darrell Waltrip	Chevrolet	3	4	1,318,735
1986	Dale Earnhardt	Chevrolet	5	1	1,783,880
1987	Dale Earnhardt	Chevrolet	11	1	2,099,243
1988	Bill Elliott	Ford	6	6	1,574,639
1989	Rusty Wallace	Pontiac	6	4	2,247,950
1990	Dale Earnhardt	Chevrolet	9	4	3,083,056
1991	Dale Earnhardt	Chevrolet	4	0	2,396,685
1992	Alan Kulwicki	Ford	2	6	2,322,561
1993	Dale Earnhardt	Chevrolet	6	2	3,353,789
1994	Dale Earnhardt	Chevrolet	4	2	3,400,733
1995	Jeff Gordon	Chevrolet	7	8	4,347,343

Alltime NASCAR Leaders

WINS		WINNINGS ($)		POLE POSITIONS	
Richard Petty	200	*Dale Earnhardt	27,470,146	Richard Petty	127
David Pearson	105	*Bill Elliott	16,130,780	David Pearson	113
Bobby Allison	84	*Darrell Waltrip	15,084,911	Cale Yarborough	70
*Darrell Waltrip	84	*Rusty Wallace	13,904,662	*Darrell Waltrip	59
Cale Yarborough	83	*Terry Labonte	12,071,788	Bobby Allison	57
*Dale Earnhardt	70	*Mark Martin	11,343,942	Bobby Isaac	51
Lee Petty	54	*Ricky Rudd	11,034,692	*Bill Elliott	48
Ned Jarrett	50	*Geoff Bodine	10,218,558	Junior Johnson	47
Junior Johnson	50	*Jeff Gordon	9,104,752	Buck Baker	44
Herb Thomas	49	*Ken Schrader	8,587,505	Buddy Baker	40
Buck Baker	46	*Sterling Marlin	8,492,312	*Geoff Bodine	35
*Rusty Wallace	46	Harry Gant	8,456,094	Herb Thomas	38
*Bill Elliott	40	*Kyle Petty	7,810,469	Tim Flock	37
Tim Flock	40	Richard Petty	7,755,409	Fireball Roberts	37
Bobby Isaac	37	*Morgan Shepherd	7,254,652	Ned Jarrett	36
Fireball Roberts	32	*Dale Jarrett	7,173,384	Rex White	36

*Active drivers. Note: NASCAR leaders through September 22, 1996; leaders in winnings from modern era only.

Formula One Grand Prix Racing

World Driving Champions

Year	Winner	Car	Year	Winner	Car
1950	Guiseppe Farina, Italy	Alfa Romeo	1970	Jochen Rindt, Austria*	Lotus-Ford
1951	Juan-Manuel Fangio, Argentina	Alfa Romeo	1971	Jackie Stewart, Scotland	Tyrell-Ford
			1972	Emerson Fittipaldi, Brazil	Lotus-Ford
1952	Alberto Ascari, Italy	Ferrari	1973	Jackie Stewart, Scotland	Tyrell-Ford
1953	Alberto Ascari, Italy	Ferrari	1974	Emerson Fittipaldi, Brazil	McLaren-Ford
1954	Juan-Manuel Fangio, Argentina	Maserati/ Mercedes	1975	Niki Lauda, Austria	Ferrari
			1976	James Hunt, England	McLaren-Ford
1955	Juan-Manuel Fangio, Argentina	Mercedes	1977	Niki Lauda, Austria	Ferrari
			1978	Mario Andretti, U.S.	Lotus-Ford
1956	Juan-Manuel Fangio, Argentina	Ferrari	1979	Jody Scheckter, S Africa	Ferrari
			1980	Alan Jones, Australia	Williams-Ford
1957	Juan-Manuel Fangio, Argentina	Maserati	1981	Nelson Piquet, Brazil	Brabham-Ford
			1982	Keke Rosberg, Finland	Williams-Ford
1958	Mike Hawthorne, England	Ferrari	1983	Nelson Piquet, Brazil	Brabham-BMW
1959	Jack Brabham, Australia	Cooper-Climax	1984	Niki Lauda, Austria	McLaren-Porsche
1960	Jack Brabham, Australia	Cooper-Climax	1985	Alain Prost, France	McLaren-Porsche
1961	Phil Hill, United States	Ferrari	1986	Alain Prost, France	McLaren-Porsche
1962	Graham Hill, England	BRM	1987	Nelson Piquet, Brazil	Williams-Honda
1963	Jim Clark, Scotland	Lotus-Climax	1988	Ayrton Senna, Brazil	McLaren-Honda
1964	John Surtees, England	Ferrari	1989	Alain Prost, France	McLaren-Honda
1965	Jim Clark, Scotland	Lotus-Climax	1990	Ayrton Senna, Brazil	McLaren-Honda
1966	Jack Brabham, Australia	Brabham-Climax	1991	Ayrton Senna, Brazil	McLaren-Honda
1967	Denis Hulme, New Zealand	Brabham-Repco	1992	Nigel Mansell, Britain	Williams-Renault
			1993	Alain Prost, France	Williams-Renault
1968	Graham Hill, England	Lotus-Ford	1994	Michael Schumacher, Ger	Benetton-Ford
1969	Jackie Stewart, Scotland	Matra-Ford	1995	Michael Schumacher, Ger	Benetton-Renault

*The championship was awarded after Rindt was killed in practice for the Italian Grand Prix.

Formula One Grand Prix Racing (Cont.)

Alltime Grand Prix Winners

Driver	Wins	Driver	Wins
Alain Prost, France	51	Niki Lauda, Austria	25
Ayrton Senna, Brazil	41	Juan Manuel Fangio, Argentina	24
Nigel Mansell, Great Britain	31	Nelson Piquet, Brazil	23
Jackie Stewart, Great Britian	27	*Michael Schumacher, Germany	22
Jim Clark, Great Britain	25	*Damon Hill, Great Britain	20

*Active driver. Note: Grand Prix winners through September 22, 1996.

Alltime Grand Prix Pole Winners

Driver	Poles	Driver	Poles
Ayrton Senna, Brazil	65	Niki Lauda, Austria	24
Alain Prost, France	33	Nelson Piquet, Brazil	24
Jim Clark, Great Britain	33	*Damon Hill, Great Britian	20
Nigel Mansell, Great Britain	32	Mario Andretti, United States	18
Juan Manuel Fangio, Argentina	28	Rene Arnoux, France	18

*Active driver. Note: Pole winners through September 22, 1996.

International Motor Sports Association

The 24 Hours of Daytona

Year	Winner	Car	Avg Speed	Distance
1962	Dan Gurney	Lotus 19-Class SP11	104.101 mph	3 hrs (312.42 mi)
1963	Pedro Rodriguez	Ferrari-Class 12	102.074 mph	3 hrs (308.61 mi)
1964	Pedro Rodriguez/Phil Hill	Ferrari 250 LM	98.230 mph	2,000 km
1965	Ken Miles/Lloyd Ruby	Ford	99.944 mph	2,000 km
1966	Ken Miles/Lloyd Ruby	Ford Mark II	108.020 mph	24 hrs (2,570.63 mi)
1967	Lorenzo Bandini/Chris Amon	Ferrari 330 P4	105.688 mph	24 hrs (2,537.46 mi)
1968	Vic Elford/Jochen Neerpasch	Porsche 907	106.697 mph	24 hrs (2,565.69 mi)
1969	Mark Donohue/Chuck Parsons	Chevy Lola	99.268 mph	24 hrs (2,383.75 mi)
1970	Pedro Rodriguez/Leo Kinnunen	Porsche 917	114.866 mph	24 hrs (2,758.44 mi)
1971	Pedro Rodriguez/Jackie Oliver	Porsche 917K	109.203 mph	24 hrs (2,621.28 mi)
1972*	Mario Andretti/Jacky Ickx	Ferrari 312/P	122.573 mph	6 hrs (738.24 mi)
1973	Peter Gregg/Hurley Haywood	Porsche Carrera	106.225 mph	24 hrs (2,552.7 mi)
1974	(No race)			
1975	Peter Gregg/Hurley Haywood	Porsche Carrera	108.531 mph	24 hrs (2,606.04 mi)
1976†	Peter Gregg/Brian Redman/ John Fitzpatrick	BMW CSL	104.040 mph	24 hrs (2,092.8 mi)
1977	John Graves/Hurley Haywood/ Dave Helmick	Porsche Carrera	108.801 mph	24 hrs (2,615 mi)
1978	Rolf Stommelen/ Antoine Hezemans/Peter Gregg	Porsche Turbo	108.743 mph	24 hrs (2,611.2 mi)
1979	Ted Field/Danny Ongais/ Hurley Haywood	Porsche Turbo	109.249 mph	24 hrs (2,626.56 mi)
1980	Volkert Meri/Rolf Stommelen/ Reinhold Joest	Porsche Turbo	114.303 mph	24 hrs
1981	Bob Garretson/Bobby Rahal/ Brian Redman	Porsche Turbo	113.153 mph	24 hrs
1982	John Paul Jr/John Paul Sr/ Rolf Stommelen	Porsche Turbo	114.794 mph	24 hrs
1983	Preston Henn/Bob Wollek/ Claude Ballot-Lena/A. J. Foyt	Porsche Turbo	98.781 mph	24 hrs
1984	Sarel van der Merwe/ Graham Duxbury/Tony Martin	Porsche March	103.119 mph	24 hrs (2,476.8 mi)
1985	A. J. Foyt/Bob Wollek/ Al Unser Sr/Thierry Boutsen	Porsche 962	104.162 mph	24 hrs (2,502.68 mi)
1986	Al Holbert/Derek Bell/Al Unser Jr	Porsche 962	105.484 mph	24 hrs (2,534.72 mi)
1987	Chip Robinson/Derek Bell/ Al Holbert/Al Unser Jr	Porsche 962	111.599 mph	24 hrs (2,680.68 mi)
1988	Martin Brundle/John Nielsen/ Raul Boesel	Jaguar XJR-9	107.943 mph	24 hrs (2,591.68 mi)
1989	John Andretti/Derek Bell/ Bob Wollek	Porsche 962	92.009 mph	24 hrs (2,210.76 mi)

*Race shortened due to fuel crisis. †Course lengthened from 3.81 miles to 3.84 miles.

The 24 Hours of Daytona (Cont.)

Year	Winner	Car	Avg Speed	Distance
1990	Davy Jones/ Jan Lammers/ Andy Wallace	Jaguar XJR-12	112.857 mph	24 hrs (2,709.16 mi)
1991	Hurley Haywood/ John Winter/ Frank Jelinski/ Henri Pescarolo/ Bob Wollek	Porsche 962C	106.633 mph	24 hrs (2,559.64 mi)
1992	Massahiro Hasemi/ Kazuoyshi Hoshino/ Toshio Suzuki/ Anders Olofsson	Nissan R91CP	112.987 mph	24 hrs (2,712.72 mi)
1993	P.J. Jones/Mark Dismore/ Rocky Moran	Toyota Eagle MK III	103.537 mph	24 hrs (2,484.88 mi)
1994	Paul Gentilozzi/ Scott Pruett/ Butch Leitzinger/ Steve Millen	Nissan 300 ZX	104.80 mph	24 hrs (2,693.67 mi)
1995	Jurgen Lassig/ Christophe Buochut/ Giovanni Lavaggi/ Marco Werner	Porsche Spyder K8	102.28 mph	690 laps (2,456.4 mi)
1996	Wayne Taylor/ Scott Sharp/ Jim Pace	Oldsmobile Mark III	103.32 mph	697 laps (2,481.32 mi)

World SportsCar Champions*

Year	Winner	Car	Year	Winner	Car
1978	Peter Gregg	Porsche 935	1987	Chip Robinson	Porsche 962
1979	Peter Gregg	Porsche 935	1988	Geoff Brabham	Nissan GTP
1980	John Fitzpatrick	Porsche 935	1989	Geoff Brabham	Nissan GTP
1981	Brian Redman	Chevy Lola	1990	Geoff Brabham	Nissan GTP
1982	John Paul Jr	Chevy Lola	1991	Geoff Brabham	Nissan NPT
1983	Al Holbert	Chevy March	1992	Juan Fangio II	Toyota EGL MKIII
1984	Randy Lanier	Chevy March	1993	Juan Fangio II	Toyota EGL MKIII
1985	Al Holbert	Porsche 962	1994	Wayne Taylor	Mazda Kudzu
1986	Al Holbert	Porsche 962	1995	Fermin Velez	Ferrari 333 SP

*1978-93 champions raced in the GT series, which in 1994 was replaced by the World SportsCar series.

Alltime IMSA Leaders

WORLD SPORTSCAR WINS

James Weaver	6
Jeremy Dale	4
Fermin Velez	4
Gianpiero Moretti	3
Eliseo Salazar	3
Jay Cochran	2
Andy Evans	2
Wayne Taylor	2
Andy Wallace	2

Note: Leaders through 1995 season.

SUPREME GT SERIES WINS

Al Holbert	49
Peter Gregg	41
Irv Hoerr	33
Hurley Haywood	28
Geoff Brabham	26
Gene Felton	25
Parker Johnstone	25
Jim Downing	23
Don Devendorf	22
Tommy Riggins	22
Jack Baldwin	21
Bob Earl	21
Juan Fangio II	21

24 Hours of Le Mans

Year	Winning Drivers	Car
1923	André Lagache/René Léonard	Chenard & Walker
1924	John Duff/Francis Clement	Bentley 3-litre
1925	Gérard de Courcelles/André Rossignol	La Lorraine
1926	Robert Bloch/André Rossignol	La Lorraine
1927	J. Dudley Benjafield/Sammy Davis	Bentley 3-litre
1928	Woolf Barnato/Bernard Rubin	Bentley 4½
1929	Woolf Barnato/Sir Henry Birkin	Bentley Speed Six
1930	Woolf Barnato/Glen Kidston	Bentley Speed Six
1931	Earl Howe/Sir Henry Birkin	Alfa Romeo 8C-2300 sc
1932	Raymond Sommer/Luigi Chinetti	Alfa Romeo 8C-2300 sc
1933	Raymond Sommer/Tazio Nuvolari	Alfa Romeo 8C-2300 sc

Year	Winning Drivers	Car
1934	Luigi Chinetti/Philippe Etancelin	Alfa Romeo 8C-2300 sc
1935	John Hindmarsh/Louis Fontés	Lagonda M45R
1936	Race cancelled	
1937	Jean-Pierre Wimille/Robert Benoist	Bugatti 57G sc
1938	Eugene Chaboud/Jean Tremoulet	Delahaye 135M
1939	Jean-Pierre Wimille/Pierre Veyron	Bugatti 57G sc
1940-48	Races cancelled	
1949	Luigi Chinetti/Lord Selsdon	Ferrari 166MM
1950	Louis Rosier/Jean-Louis Rosier	Talbot-Lago
1951	Peter Walker/Peter Whitehead	Jaguar C
1952	Hermann Lang/Fritz Reiss	Mercedes-Benz 300 SL
1953	Tony Rolt/Duncan Hamilton	Jaguar C
1954	Froilan Gonzales/Maurice Trintignant	Ferrari 375
1955	Mike Hawthorn/Ivor Bueb	Jaguar D
1956	Ron Flockhart/Ninian Sanderson	Jaguar D
1957	Ron Flockhart/Ivor Buab	Jaguar D
1958	Olivier Gendebien/Phil Hill	Ferrari 250 TR58
1959	Carroll Shelby/Roy Salvadori	Aston Martin DBR1
1960	Olivier Gendebien/Paul Frãre	Ferrari 250 TR59/60
1961	Olivier Gendebien/Phil Hill	Ferrari 250 TR61
1962	Olivier Gendebien/Phil Hill	Ferrari 250P
1963	Lodovico Scarfiotti/Lorenzo Bandini	Ferrari 250P
1964	Jean Guichel/Nino Vaccarella	Ferrari 275P
1965	Jochen Rindt/Masten Gregory	Ferrari 250LM
1966	Chris Amon/Bruce McLaren	Ford Mk2
1967	Dan Gurney/A. J. Foyt	Ford Mk4
1968	Pedro Rodriguez/Lucien Bianchi	Ford GT40
1969	Jacky Ickx/Jackie Oliver	Ford GT40
1970	Hans Herrmann/Richard Attwood	Porsche 917
1971	Helmut Marko/Gijs van Lennep	Porsche 917
1972	Henri Pescarolo/Graham Hill	Matra-Simca MS670
1973	Henri Pescarolo/Gérard Larrousse	Matra-Simca MS670B
1974	Henri Pescarolo/Gérard Larrousse	Matra-Simca MS670B
1975	Jacky Ickx/Derek Bell	Mirage-Ford MB
1976	Jacky Ickx/Gijs van Lennep	Porsche 936
1977	Jacky Ickx/Jurgen Barth/Hurley Haywood	Porsche 936
1978	Jean-Pierre Jaussaud/Didier Pironi	Renault-Alpine A442
1979	Klaus Ludwig/Bill Whittington/Don Whittington	Porsche 935
1980	Jean-Pierre Jaussaud/Jean Rondeau	Rondeau-Ford M379B
1981	Jacky Ickx/Derek Bell	Porsche 936-81
1982	Jacky Ickx/Derek Bell	Porsche 956
1983	Vern Schuppan/Hurley Haywood/Al Holbert	Porsche 956-83
1984	Klaus Ludwig/Henri Pescarolo	Porsche 956B
1985	Klaus Ludwig/Paolo Barilla/John Winter	Porsche 956B
1986	Derek Bell/Hans-Joachim Stuck/Al Holbert	Porsche 962C
1987	Derek Bell/Hans-Joachim Stuck/Al Holbert	Porsche 962C
1988	Jan Lammers/Johnny Dumfries/Andy Wallace	Jaguar XJR9LM
1989	Jochen Mass/Manuel Reuter/Stanley Dickens	Sauber-Mercedes C9-88
1990	John Nielsen/Price Cobb/Martin Brundle	TWR Jaguar XJR-12
1991	Volker Weidler/Johnny Herbert/Bertrand Gachof	Mazda 787B
1992	Derek Warwick/Yannick Dalmas/Mark Blundell	Peugeot 905B
1993	Geoff Brabham/Christophe Bouchut/Eric Helary	Peugeot 905
1994	Yannick Dalmas/Hurley Haywood/Mauro Baldi	Porsche 962
1995	Yannick Dalmas/J.J. Lehto/Masanori Sekiya	McLaren BMW
1996	Manuel Reuter/Davy Jones/Alexander Wurz	TWR Porsche

Drag Racing: Milestone Performances

Top Fuel

ELAPSED TIME

Time (Sec.)	Driver	Date	Site
9.00	Jack Chrisman	Feb 18, 1961	Pomona, CA
8.97	Jack Chrisman	May 20, 1961	Empona, VA
7.96	Bobby Vodnick	May 16, 1964	Bayview, MD
6.97	Don Johnson	May 7, 1967	Carlsbad, CA
5.97	Mike Snively	Nov 17, 1972	Ontario, CA
5.78	Don Garlits	Nov 18, 1973	Ontario, CA
5.698	Gary Beck	Oct 10, 1975	Ontario, CA
5.573	Gary Beck	Oct 18, 1981	Irvine, CA
5.484	Gary Beck	Sept 6, 1982	Clermont, IN
5.391	Gary Beck	Oct 1, 1983	Fremont, CA
5.280	Darrell Gwynn	Sept 25, 1986	Ennis, TX
5.176	Darrell Gwynn	April 4, 1987	Ennis, TX
5.090	Joe Amato	Oct 1, 1987	Ennis, TX
4.990	Eddie Hill	April 9, 1988	Ennis, TX
4.881	Gary Ormsby	Sept 28, 1990	Topeka, KS
4.799	Cory McClenathan	Sept 19, 1992	Mohnton, PA
4.762	Cory McClenathan	Oct 3, 1993	Topeka, KS
4.690	Michael Brotherton	May 20, 1994	Englishtown, NJ
4.592	Blaine Johnson	July 6, 1996	Topeka, KS

SPEED

MPH	Driver	Date	Site
180.36	Connie Kalitta	Sept 3, 1962	Indianapolis
190.26	Don Garlits	Sept 21, 1963	East Haddam, CT
201.34	Don Garlits	Aug 1, 1964	Great Meadows, NJ
211.26	Donny Milani	May 15, 1965	Sacramento, CA
223.32	Don Cook	Apr 24, 1965	Fremont, CA
230.17	James Warren	Apr 10, 1967	Fresno, CA
243.24	Don Garlits	March 18, 1973	Gainesville, FL
250.69	Don Garlits	Oct 11, 1975	Ontario, CA
260.11	Joe Amato	March 18, 1984	Gainesville, FL
272.56	Don Garlits	March 23, 1986	Gainesville, FL
282.13	Joe Amato	Sept 5, 1987	Clermont, IN
291.54	Connie Kalitta	Feb 11, 1989	Pomona, CA
301.70	Kenny Bernstein	March 20, 1992	Gainesville, FL
311.86	Kenny Bernstein	Oct 30, 1994	Pomona, CA
315.67	Scott Kalitta	July 5, 1996	Topeka, KS

Funny Car

ELAPSED TIME

Time (Sec.)	Driver	Date	Site
6.92	Leroy Goldstein	Sept 3, 1970	Clermont, IN
5.987	Don Prudhomme	Oct 12, 1975	Ontario, CA
5.868	Raymond Beadle	July 16, 1981	Englishtown, NJ
5.799	Tom Anderson	Sept 3, 1982	Clermont, IN
5.637	Don Prudhomme	Sept 4, 1982	Clermont, IN
5.588	Rick Johnson	Feb 3, 1985	Pomona, CA
5.425	Kenny Bernstein	Sept 26, 1986	Ennis, TX
5.397	Kenny Bernstein	April 5, 1987	Ennis, TX
5.255	Ed McCulloch	April 17, 1988	Ennis, TX
5.193	Don Prudhomme	March 2, 1989	Baytown, TX
5.077	Cruz Pedregon	Sept 20, 1992	Mohnton, PA
4.987	Chuck Etcholis	Oct 2, 1993	Topeka, KS
4.889	John Force	July 6, 1996	Topeka, KS

SPEED

MPH	Driver	Date	Site
200.44	Gene Snow	August, 1968	Houston, TX
250.00	Don Prudhomme	May 23, 1982	Baton Rouge, LA
260.11	Kenny Bernstein	March 18, 1984	Gainesville, FL
271.41	Kenny Bernstein	Aug 30, 1986	Indianapolis
280.72	Mike Dunn	Oct 2, 1987	Ennis, TX

Funny Car (Cont.)

SPEED (CONT.)

MPH	Driver	Date	Site
290.13	Jim White	Oct 11, 1991	Ennis, TX
291.82	Jim White	Oct 25, 1991	Pomona, CA
300.40	Jim Epler	Oct 3, 1993	Topeka, KS
311.20	Cruz Pedragon	July 7, 1996	Topeka, KS

Pro Stock

ELAPSED TIME

Time (Sec.)	Driver	Date	Site
7.778	Lee Shepherd	March 12, 1982	Gainesville, FL
7.655	Lee Shepherd	Oct 1, 1982	Fremont, CA
7.557	Bob Glidden	Feb 2, 1985	Pomona, CA
7.497	Bob Glidden	Sep 13, 1985	Maple Grove, PA
7.377	Bob Glidden	Aug 28, 1986	Clermont, IN
7.294	Frank Sanchez	Oct 7, 1988	Baytown, TX
7.184	Darrell Alderman	Oct 12, 1990	Ennis, TX
7.099	Scott Geoffrion	Sept 19, 1992	Mohnton, PA
6.988	Kurt Johnson	May 20, 1994	Englishtown, NJ
6.947	Jim Yates	Sept 15, 1996	Mohnton, PA

SPEED

MPH	Driver	Date	Site
181.08	Warren Johnson	Oct 1, 1982	Fremont, CA
190.07	Warren Johnson	Aug 29, 1986	Clermont, IN
191.32	Bob Glidden	Sep 4, 1987	Clermont, IN
192.18	Warren Johnson	Oct 13, 1990	Ennis, TX
193.21	Bob Glidden	July 28, 1991	Sonoma, CA
194.51	Warren Johnson	July 31, 1992	Sonoma, CA
195.99	Warren Johnson	May 21, 1993	Englishtown, NJ
196.24	Warren Johnson	Mar 19, 1993	Gainesville, FL
197.15	Warren Johnson	Apr 23, 1994	Commerce, GA
199.15	Warren Johnson	Mar 10, 1995	Baytown, TX

Alltime Drag Racing Leaders

NATIONAL EVENT WINS

*Bob Glidden	85
*Warren Johnson	59
*John Force	59
Don Prudhomme	49
*Kenny Bernstein	46
*David Schultz	41
Don Garlits	35
*Joe Amato	35
*John Myers	29
Lee Shepherd	26
Darrell Alderman	26

BEST WON-LOST RECORD (WINNING PCT)

*John Myers	221-49 (.819)
*David Schultz	263-59 (.817)
*Bob Glidden	788-219 (.783)
Darrell Alderman	187-59 (.756)
*John Force	475-174 (.732)
*Warren Johnson	545-203 (.729)
*Cruz Pedregon	168-82 (.672)
*Joe Amato	383-192 (.666)
*Kenny Bernstein	412-211 (.661)
*Scott Geoffrion	139-74 (.653)

*Active driver. Note: Drag racing leaders through September 15, 1996.

Bowling

Sports Illustrated

Super Soper

**Butch Soper
wins the
PBA Nationals
in Toledo**

Happy Endings

A slew of long-suffering veterans demonstrated the power of persistence with thrilling triumphs in 1996

by Franz Lidz

THIS YEAR'S sign that the apocalypse is upon us: To attract the young and hip, a bowling center in Plover, Wis., installed two indoor beach volleyball courts.

This *decade*'s sign that the apocalypse is upon us: To attract the dazed and confused, the Brunswick Corporation unveiled Cosmic Bowling, in which keglers aim at fluorescent pins through a shifting fog of artificial smoke and strobe lights amid the thumping of heavy-metal music.

In a year that saw the PBA update its corporate logo from 1953 to, say, 1965, bowling went Hollywood, '90s-style. The movie *Kingpin* rolled into neighborhood cineplexes in July, veered straight into the gutter and disappeared faster than you could say "comb-over." Hailed as the best film about the sport since *Slime Ball Bowl-O-Rama*, *Kingpin* centered on corn-fed amateur champ Roy Munson, who wins his first pro tournament by beating veteran Ernie McCracken at the 1979 Odor Eaters Championships. McCracken exacts revenge by talking Roy into hustling some locals and then leaving him to the angry victims, who grind off Roy's bowling hand in a ball

return. Seventeen years later a broken-down Roy meets an Amish naïf named Ishmael (Go ahead, call him Ishmael) and enters him in a $1 million tournament in Reno. Can anybody guess Ishmael's opponent in the climactic finals? Those of you who haven't yet divined *Kingpin*'s outcome should rent *Rocky II* or *The Color of Money* or *The Karate Kid* or any of the other 15,321 or so mentor-training-a-novice sports flicks.

To gain a measure of redemption, the big winners on the 1996 pro tour had to wait almost as long as Roy Munson. Sometimes longer. During his 25 years on the pro tour, Butch Soper had never even qualified for the finals of a PBA major. In fact, he had not won anything since the 1990 Kessler Open. Yet he triumphed at the PBA nationals in Toledo, defeating arch-nemesis Walter Ray Williams 226–210. Four years ago Soper lay comatose and near death with a ruptured colon. "I don't remember anything," he recalled of his 17 days in an intensive care ward. "The doctor took me into his office later and said, 'Butch, I do a lot of these operations, and I wouldn't have given you more than a 10 percent chance of

COURTESY OF WOMEN'S INTERNATIONAL BOWLING CONGRESS

living.' Kind of wakes you up—know what I mean?"

As a kind of contemporary Rip Van Winkle, Dave D'Entremont shook off 14 years of slumber to win the Tournament of Champions in Chicago. Since joining the tour in 1982, the 34-year-old D'Entremont had spent more time lugging 55-gallon steel drums on a Cleveland loading dock than lofting 16-pound bowling balls in PBA alleys. His prospects weren't looking any brighter in Chicago. With 16 match games left, he was idling in 21st place. The turnaround was abrupt. "I came in on Friday and found my shot," he said. "It was right in my wheelhouse. I let 'em rip." He ripped through the field to qualify fifth for the arena final. The ripping continued at Harper College Athletic Center in Palatine, where D'Entremont rolled over Justin Hromek, Bryan Goebel and Danny Wiseman to make the final. But two frames into the deciding match against Dave Arnold, he appeared doomed. D'Entremont flagged a spare in the opening frame and left a 2-4-10 split in the second. He came into frame 3 trailing by 20. Needing only a mark in the 10th to win, Arnold left an impossible 4-6-7 split. Needing a strike and nine pins in the 10th to win, D'Entremont struck out. Of the 215–202 victory, D'Entremont said, "This is a vindication for everything bad that has happened to me on TV during my whole career. Every bad break, atoned for in one clean sweep."

Ernie Schlegel's sweeping victory in the American Bowling Congress Masters in Salt Lake City could have been dubbed *The Kid Not in the Hall*. The 53-year-old Bicentennial Kid came into Salt Lake ticked at not being voted into the ABC Hall of Fame for the third straight year. "I felt my credentials were much better than anyone else's on the ballot," he said flatly. "I should have won unanimously." Schlegel backed up his talk by steamrolling Mike Aulby 236–200 in the title match. By beating the 1995 Bowler of the Year, Schlegel became the oldest Mas-

ters champ in history. "It's up to the people who love me and the people who hate me," he said. "If this doesn't get me into the Hall of Fame, the people who vote should have their heads examined."

Of all the '96 champs, none was more long-suffering than Lisa Wagner, the 1980s female Bowler of the Decade. Though Wagner had won more tournaments than any woman in bowling history, she had never finished better than seventh at the WIBC Queens. Qualifying fourth in the stepladder finals of the Buffalo event, she buffaloed three opponents to reach the final. There she faced Tammy Turner, who had won her last two tournaments and was flattening her match-play opposition with a 220 average. By terminating the Taminator 231–226, Wagner won $12,675, the traditional Queens tiara and the hand of boyfriend Brian Billert. "Will you marry me?" he asked during the televised awards ceremony.

"You bet," said Wagner.

Just like in the movies.

The Majors

MEN

Brunswick World Tournament of Champions

CHAMPIONSHIP ROUND

Bowler	Games	Total	Earnings ($)
Dave D'Entremont	4	971	60,000
Dave Arnold	1	202	33,000
Danny Wiseman	1	224	24,000
Bryan Goebel	1	227	18,000
Justin Hromek	1	246	12,000

Playoff Results: D'Entremont def. Hromek, 259-246; D'Entremont def. Goebel, 258-227; D'Entremont def. Wiseman, 239-224; D'Entremont def. Arnold, 215-202.

Held at Brunswick Deer Park Lanes, Lake Zurich, IL, April 21–27, 1996.

ABC Masters Tournament

CHAMPIONSHIP ROUND

Bowler	Games	Total	Earnings ($)
Ernie Schlegel	1	236	50,600
Mike Aulby	2	422	27,500
Joe Firpo	3	733	20,800
Rohn Morton	1	236	15,500
Bob Belmont	1	191	11,000

Playoff Results: Firpo def. Belmont, 278-191; Firpo def. Morton, 267-236; Aulby def. Firpo, 222-188; Schlegel def. Aulby, 236-200.

Held at Salt Palace, Salt Lake City, UT, April 30–May 4, 1996.

PBA National Championship

CHAMPIONSHIP ROUND

Bowler	Games	Total	Earnings ($)
Butch Soper	2	442	30,000
Walter Ray Williams Jr	1	210	16,000
Justin Hromek	2	431	8,000
Tim Criss	2	473	6,500
Mark Williams	1	179	5,500

Playoff Results: Criss def. Mark Williams, 268-179; Hromek def. Criss, 217-205; Soper def. Hromek, 216-214; Soper def. Williams Jr, 226-210.

Qualifying and match play held at Ducats Imperial Lanes, Toledo, OH; finals held at Savage Hall, Unversity of Toledo; June 1-8, 1996.

1995 BPAA United States Open

CHAMPIONSHIP ROUND

Bowler	Games	Total	Earnings ($)
Dave Husted	1	266	46,000
Paul Koehler	2	523	24,000
Steve Hoskins	3	743	14,000
Parker Bohn III	1	216	10,500
Dave D'Entremont	1	212	8,500

Playoff Results: Hoskins def. D'Entremont, 231-212; Hoskins def. Bohn, 256-216; Koehler def. Hoskins, 278-256; Husted def. Koehler, 266-245.

Held at Bowl One, Troy, MI, April 2-8, 1995.

WOMEN

Sam's Town Invitational

CHAMPIONSHIP ROUND

Bowler	Games	Total	Earnings ($)
Michelle Mullen	1	202	18,000
Cheryl Daniels	2	421	9,000
Kim Adler	3	638	5,000
Wendy Macpherson	1	189	4,500
Leanne Barrette	1	182	3,800

Playoff Results: Adler def. Barrette, 204-182; Adler def. Macpherson, 234-189; Daniels def. Adler, 232-200; Mullen def. Daniels, 202-189.

Held at Sam's Town Bowling Center, Las Vegas, NV, Nov 11-18, 1995.

WIBC Queens

CHAMPIONSHIP ROUND

Bowler	Games	Total	Earnings ($)
Lisa Wagner	4	863	12,675
Tammy Turner	1	226	7,250
Sandra Ranallo	1	194	4,175
Jeanne Naccarato	1	195	3,250
Diana Teeters	1	165	2,250

Playoff Results: Wagner def. Teeters, 202-165; Wagner def. Naccarato, 214-195; Wagner def. Ranallo, 214-195; Wagner def. Turner, 231-226.

Held at Thruway Lanes, Buffalo, NY, May 14-18, 1996.

1995 BPAA United States Open

CHAMPIONSHIP ROUND

Bowler	Games	Total	Earnings ($)
Cheryl Daniels	2	458	18,000
Tish Johnson	1	180	9,000
Diana Teeters	3	694	7,000
Wendy Macpherson	1	183	5,000
Sandra Jo Shiery	1	212	4,000

Playoff Results: Teeters def. Shiery 247-212; Teeters def. Macpherson 225-183; Daniels def. Teeters 223-222; Daniels def. Johnson 235-180.

Championship round held at National Sports Center, Blaine, MN, Oct 6, 1995.

Spare Time Legislation

Last spring we told you about a pair of Indiana congressmen who were sponsoring a bill to mandate the use of instant replay to review close calls in pro sports (*SI*, March 18, 1996). Well, they're not the only lawmakers working hard in the public's interest. Florida state senator Howard Forman has introduced a bowling safety act that would regulate "the duties of bowling-center operators, bowlers, spectators and other customers" in the Sunshine State. The bill, which according to Forman is intended to curb rising insurance costs, calls for the posting of a sign in bowling alleys warning of "the risks that are inherent in bowling and in being in a bowling center." It also includes this valuable tip to keglers: "When bowling, maintain reasonable control of the bowling ball." In the summer of '96 the bill was up for discussion before the judiciary committee, where we trust it won't veer into gutter politics.

PBA Tour Results

1995 Fall Tour

Date	Event	Winner	Earnings ($)	Runner-Up
Sept 21–24	Oronamin C Japan Cup*	Amleto Monacelli	50,000	Dave D'Entremont
Sept 30–Oct 4	Indianapolis Open	Jason Couch	17,500	Richard Wolfe
Oct 7–11	Greater Detroit Open	Brian Voss	17,500	Justin Hromek
Oct 14–18	Great Lakes Classic	Danny Wiseman	17,500	John Mazza
Oct 21–25	Rochester Open	Walter Ray Williams Jr	17,500	David Traber
Oct 28–Nov 1	AMF Dick Weber Classic	David Ozio	60,000	Walter Ray Williams Jr
Nov 3–8	Bayer/Brunswick Touring Players Championship	Ernie Schlegel	40,000	Randy Pedersen
Dec 8–10	PBA National Resident Pro Championship*	Ray Edwards	6,800	Ted Hannahs
Dec 8–10	Merit Mixed Doubles Championship	Butch Soper & Kim Canady	40,000	Eric Forkel & Robin Romeo

1996 Winter Tour

Date	Event	Winner	Earnings ($)	Runner-Up
Jan 22–26	Peoria Open	Wayne Webb	19,000	Bob Learn Jr
Jan 20–Feb 2	Columbia 300 Open	C.K. Moore	22,000	Butch Soper
Feb 6–9	Reno Open	Dave Arnold	16,000	Walter Ray Williams Jr
Feb 12–16	Oregon Open	Brian Voss	19,000	Dave Wodka
Feb 18–23	Track Synergy Open	Walter Ray Williams Jr	22,000	Brain LeClair
Feb 25–Mar 1	Tucson Open	Bryan Goebel	16,000	Ricky Ward

1996 Spring Tour

Date	Event	Winner	Earnings ($)	Runner-Up
Mar 5–9	ACDelco Classic	Tom Baker	48,000	Bob Learn Jr
Mar 11–16	Showboat Invitational	Walter Ray Williams Jr	37,000	Brian LeClair
Mar 17–23	Quaker State 250	Steve Wilson	48,000	Jimmy Keeth
Mar 26–30	Comfort Inn Classic	Steve Hoskins	50,000	Brian Voss
Apr 2–6	Flagship Open	Bob Learn Jr	30,000	Randy Pedersen
Apr 9–13	Brunswick Johnny Petraglia Open	Walter Ray Williams Jr	34,000	Steve Jaros
Apr 16–20	Bud Light Championship	Philip Ringener	40,000	Joe Firpo
Apr 21–27	Brunswick World Tournament of Champions	Dave D'Entremont	60,000	Dave Arnold
Apr 30–May 4	ABC Masters*	Ernie Schlegel	50,600	Mike Aulby
May 15–18	IOF Foresters Open	David Traber	45,000	Jess Stayrook
May 21–25	Greater Baltimore Open	Mike Aulby	19,000	Walter Ray Williams Jr
May 29–June 1	Greater Hartford Open	Dennis Horan	19,000	C.K. Moore
June 1–8	PBA National Championship	Butch Soper	30,000	Walter Ray Williams Jr
June 9–15	Greater Detroit Open	Doug Kent	19,000	Jeff Zaffino
June 18–22	Kingpin Classic	Jess Stayrook	27,000	Butch Soper

1995 Senior Fall Tour

Date	Event	Winner	Earnings ($)	Runner-Up
Sept 15–19	Naples PBA Senior Open	Tommie Evans	10,000	John Handegard
Sept 22–26	St Petersburg/Clearwater Senior Open	Don Helling	10,000	Larry Laub
Sept 20–Oct 4	Palm Beach Senior Classic	John Hricsina	10,000	Avery LeBlanc

*Not an official PBA Tour event.

1996 Senior Tour (through Aug 30)

Date	Event	Winner	Earnings ($)	Runner-Up
Mar 11–15	Greater Albany Senior Open	John Handegard	8,000	Ron Winger
Apr 19–25	Ladies and Legends	Mike Kench & Liz Johnson	15,000	Pete Couture & Carolyn Dorin
June 30–July 4	Seattle Senior Open	Hobo Boothe	9,000	Earl Anthony
July 7–12	Northwestern Senior Classic	Gary Mage	9,000	John Handegard
July 14–18	Tri-Cities Senior Open	Gary Dickinson	9,000	Bruce Forsland
July 28–Aug 3	Showboat Senior Invitational	John Denton	20,000	Earl Anthony
Aug 5–9	Reno Senior Open	Pete Couture	8,500	Roger Tramp
Aug 11–17	ABC Senior Masters	Dave Davis	60,000	John Hatz
Aug 18–22	Pontiac Osteopathic Hospital Senior Open	Gary Dickinson	10,000	Bobby Knipple
Aug 24–30	PBA Senior Championship	Dale Eagle	16,000	Roy Buckley

LPBT Tour Results

1995 Fall Tour

Date	Event	Winner	Earnings ($)	Runner-Up
Sept 29–Oct-6	BPAA US Open	Cheryl Daniels	18,000	Tish Johnson
Oct 8–12	Brunswick Three Rivers Open	Sandra Jo Shiery	12,000	Tammy Turner
Oct 14–19	Columbia 300 Delaware Open	Marianne DiRuppo	12,800	Cheryl Daniels
Oct 21–26	Hammer Eastern Open	Kim Adler	12,000	Anne Marie Duggan
Oct 29–Nov 2	Lady Ebonite Classic	Aleta Sill	12,000	Tish Johnson
Nov 4–9	Hammer Players Championship	Anne Marie Duggan	16,000	Kim Adler
Nov 11–18	Sam's Town Invitational	Michelle Mullen	18,000	Cheryl Daniels
Dec 7–10	Merit Mixed Doubles Championship	Kim Canady & Butch Soper	40,000	Robin Romeo & Eric Forkel

1996 Winter Tour

Date	Event	Winner	Earnings ($)	Runner-Up
Feb 3–8	Clabber Girl Greater Terre Haute Open	Jackie Sellars	10,000	Darris Street
Feb 10–15	Claremore Classic	Cindy Coburn-Carroll	9,000	Tish Johnson
Feb 18–22	Lubbock Open	Leanne Barrette	9,000	Cheryl Daniels
Feb 25–29	Treasure Chest Classic	Sandra Jo Shiery	10,000	Debbie McMullen
Mar 2–7	South Texas Open	Dana Miller-Mackie	9,000	Tish Johnson
Mar 9–14	Texas Border Shoot Out	Wendy Macpherson	9,000	Jackie Sellars

1996 Spring Tour

Date	Event	Winner	Earnings ($)	Runner-Up
Apr 19–25	Ladies and Legends	Liz Johnson & Mike Kench	15,000	Carolyn Dorin & Pete Couture
Apr 28–May 1	Storm Doubles	Laura Moriarty	14,000	Tammy Turner
May 4–9	Omaha Lancers	Tammy Turner	11,000	Wendy Macpherson
May 14–18	WIBC Queens*	Lisa Wagner	12,675	Tammy Turner

1996 Summer Tour

Date	Event	Winner	Earnings ($)	Runner-Up
July 14–18	Greater Little Rock Classic	Wendy Macpherson	9,000	Marianne DiRuppo
July 22–26	Greater Charleston Open	Aleta Sill	9,000	Tammy Turner
July 28–Aug 1	Franklin Virginia Open	Jackie Sellars	9,000	Marianne DiRuppo

*Not an official LPBT Tour event.

PBA

MONEY LEADERS

Name	Titles	Tournaments	Earnings ($)
Mike Aulby	1	27	285,192
Dave D'Entremont	2	30	271,245
Walter Ray Williams Jr	1	26	254,020
Jess Stayrook	2	29	206,130
David Ozio	1	24	171,905

AVERAGE

Name	Games	Pinfall	Average
Mike Aulby	928	209,257	225.49
Walter Ray Williams Jr	937	209,551	223.64
Norm Duke	831	185,014	222.64
Mark Williams	1017	225,250	221.48
Parker Bohn III	999	221,019	221.24

Seniors

MONEY LEADERS

Name	Titles	Tournaments	Earnings ($)
John Handegard	1	12	63,133
Dave Davis	1	9	52,600
Tommy Evans	3	11	48,016
Pete Couture	0	10	39,875
Avery Le Blanc	0	11	39,155

AVERAGE

Name	Games	Pinfall	Average
Tommy Evans	400	89,600	224.00
John Handegard	492	109,386	222.33
Pete Couture	443	98,390	222.10
Larry Laub	441	97,836	221.85
Gary Dickinson	476	104,506	219.55

LPBT

MONEY LEADERS

Name	Titles	Tournaments	Earnings ($)
Tish Johnson	2	22	123,440
Anne Marie Duggan	2	22	116,847
Cheryl Daniels	2	22	112,335
Kim Adler	2	22	96,291
Aleta Sill	2	22	80,931

AVERAGE

Name	Games	Pinfall	Average
Anne Marie Duggan	787	169,827	215.79
Tish Johnson	836	179,957	215.26
Cheryl Daniels	762	162,862	213.73
Carol Norman	829	176,917	213.41
Wendy Macpherson	567	120,198	211.99

FOR THE RECORD · Year by Year

Men's Majors

BPAA United States Open

Year	Winner	Score	Runner-Up	Site
1942	John Crimmins	265.09-262.33	Joe Norris	Chicago
1943	Connie Schwoegler	not available	Frank Benkovic	Chicago
1944	Ned Day	315.21-298.21	Paul Krumske	Chicago
1945	Buddy Bomar	304.46-296.16	Joe Wilman	Chicago
1946	Joe Wilman	310.27-305.37	Therman Gibson	Chicago
1947	Andy Varipapa	314.16-308.04	Allie Brandt	Chicago
1948	Andy Varipapa	309.23-309.06	Joe Wilman	Chicago
1949	Connie Schwoegler	312.31-307.27	Andy Varipapa	Chicago
1950	Junie McMahon	318.37-307.17	Ralph Smith	Chicago
1951	Dick Hoover	305.29-304.07	Lee Jouglard	Chicago
1952	Junie McMahon	309.29-305.41	Bill Lillard	Chicago
1953	Don Carter	304.17-297.36	Ed Lubanski	Chicago
1954	Don Carter	308.02-307.25	Bill Lillard	Chicago
1955	Steve Nagy	307.17-303.34	Ed Lubanski	Chicago
1956	Bill Lillard	304.30-304.22	Joe Wilman	Chicago
1957	Don Carter	308.49-305.45	Dick Weber	Chicago
1958	Don Carter	311.03-308.09	Buzz Fazio	Minneapolis
1959	Billy Welu	311.48-310.26	Ray Bluth	Buffalo
1960	Harry Smith	312.24-308.12	Bob Chase	Omaha
1961	Bill Tucker	318.49-309.11	Dick Weber	San Bernardino, CA
1962	Dick Weber	299.34-297.38	Roy Lown	Miami Beach
1963	Dick Weber	642-591	Billy Welu	Kansas City, MO
1964	Bob Strampe	714-616	Tommy Tuttle	Dallas
1965	Dick Weber	608-586	Jim St. John	Philadelphia
1966	Dick Weber	684-681	Nelson Burton Jr	Lansing, MI
1967	Les Schissler	613-610	Pete Tountas	St. Ann, MO
1968	Jim Stefanich	12,401-12,104	Billy Hardwick	Garden City, NY
1969	Billy Hardwick	12,585-11,463	Dick Weber	Miami
1970	Bobby Cooper	12,936-12,307	Billy Hardwick	Northbrook, IL
1971	Mike Limongello	397 (2 games)	Teata Semiz	St. Paul, MN
1972	Don Johnson	233 (1 game)	George Pappas	New York City
1973	Mike McGrath	712 (3 games)	Earl Anthony	New York City
1974	Larry Laub	749 (3 games)	Dave Davis	New York City
1975	Steve Neff	279 (1 game)	Paul Colwell	Grand Prairie, TX
1976	Paul Moser	226 (1 game)	Jim Frazier	Grand Prairie, TX
1977	Johnny Petraglia	279 (1 game)	Bill Spigner	Greensboro, NC
1978	Nelson Burton Jr	873 (4 games)	Jeff Mattingly	Greensboro, NC
1979	Joe Berardi	445 (2 games)	Earl Anthony	Windsor Locks, CT
1980	Steve Martin	930 (4 games)	Earl Anthony	Windsor Locks, CT
1981	Marshall Holman	684 (3 games)	Mark Roth	Houston
1982	Dave Husted	1011 (4 games)	Gil Sliker	Houston
1983	Gary Dickinson	214 (1 game)	Steve Neff	Oak Lawn, IL
1984	Mark Roth	244 (1 game)	Guppy Troup	Oak Hill, IL
1985	Marshall Holman	233 (1 game)	Wayne Webb	Venice, FL
1986	Steve Cook	467 (2 games)	Frank Ellenburg	Venice, FL
1987	Del Ballard Jr	525 (2 games)	Pete Weber	Tacoma, WA
1988	Pete Weber	929 (4 games)	Marshall Holman	Atlantic City, NJ
1989	Mike Aulby	429 (2 games)	Jim Pencak	Edmond, OK
1990	Ron Palombi Jr	269 (1 game)	Amleto Monacelli	Indianapolis
1991	Pete Weber	956 (4 games)	Mark Thayer	Indianapolis
1992	Robert Lawrence	667 (3 games)	Scott Devers	Canandaigua, NY
1993	Del Ballard Jr	505 (2 games)	Walter Ray Williams Jr	Canandaigua, NY
1994	Justin Hromek	267 (1 game)	Parker Bohn III	Troy, MI
1995	Dave Husted	266 (1 game)	Paul Koehler	Troy, MI

Note: From 1942 to 1970, the tournament was called the BPAA All-Star. Peterson scoring was used from 1942 through 1962. Under this system, the winner of an individual match game gets one point, plus one point for each 50 pins knocked down. From 1963 through 1967, a three-game championship was held between the two top qualifiers. From 1968 through 1970 total pinfall determined the winner. From 1971 to the present, five qualifiers compete for the championship.

PBA National Championship

Year	Winner	Score	Runner-Up	Site
1960	Don Carter	6512 (30 games)	Ronnie Gaudern	Memphis
1961	Dave Soutar	5792 (27 games)	Morrie Oppenheim	Cleveland
1962	Carmen Salvino	5369 (25 games)	Don Carter	Philadelphia
1963	Billy Hardwick	13,541 (61 games)	Ray Bluth	Long Island, NY
1964	Bob Strampe	13,979 (61 games)	Ray Bluth	Long Island, NY
1965	Dave Davis	13,895 (61 games)	Jerry McCoy	Detroit
1966	Wayne Zahn	14,006 (61 games)	Nelson Burton Jr	Long Island, NY
1967	Dave Davis	421 (2 games)	Pete Tountas	New York City
1968	Wayne Zahn	14,182 (60 games)	Nelson Burton Jr	New York City
1969	Mike McGrath	13,670 (60 games)	Bill Allen	Garden City, NY
1970	Mike McGrath	660 (3 games)	Dave Davis	Garden City, NY
1971	Mike Limongello	911 (4 games)	Dave Davis	Paramus, NJ
1972	Johnny Guenther	12,986 (56 games)	Dick Ritger	Rochester, NY
1973	Earl Anthony	212 (1 game)	Sam Flanagan	Oklahoma City
1974	Earl Anthony	218 (1 game)	Mark Roth	Downey, CA
1975	Earl Anthony	245 (1 game)	Jim Frazier	Downey, CA
1976	Paul Colwell	191 (1 game)	Dave Davis	Seattle
1977	Tommy Hudson	206 (1 game)	Jay Robinson	Seattle
1978	Warren Nelson	453 (2 games)	Joseph Groskind	Reno
1979	Mike Aulby	727 (3 games)	Earl Anthony	Las Vegas
1980	Johnny Petraglia	235 (1 game)	Gary Dickinson	Sterling Heights, MI
1981	Earl Anthony	242 (1 game)	Ernie Schlegel	Toledo, OH
1982	Earl Anthony	233 (1 game)	Charlie Tapp	Toledo, OH
1983	Earl Anthony	210 (1 game)	Mike Durbin	Toledo, OH
1984	Bob Chamberlain	961 (4 games)	Dan Eberl	Toledo, OH
1985	Mike Aulby	476 (2 games)	Steve Cook	Toledo, OH
1986	Tom Crites	190 (1 game)	Mike Aulby	Toledo, OH
1987	Randy Pedersen	759 (3 games)	Amleto Monacelli	Toledo, OH
1988	Brian Voss	246 (1 game)	Todd Thompson	Toledo, OH
1989	Pete Weber	221 (1 game)	Dave Ferraro	Toledo, OH
1990	Jim Pencak	900 (4 games)	Chris Warren	Toledo, OH
1991	Mike Miller	450 (2 games)	Norm Duke	Toledo, OH
1992	Eric Forkel	833 (4 games)	Bob Vespi	Toledo, OH
1993	Ron Palombi Jr	237 (1 game)	Eugene McCune	Toledo, OH
1994	David Traber	196 (1 game)	Dale Traber	Toledo, OH
1995	Scott Alexander	246 (1 game)	Wayne Webb	Toledo, OH
1996	Butch Soper	442 (2 games)	Walter Ray Williams Jr	Toledo, OH

Note: Totals from 1963-66, 1968-69 and 1972 include bonus pins.

Tournament of Champions

Year	Winner	Score	Runner-Up	Site
1965	Billy Hardwick	484 (2 games)	Dick Weber	Akron, OH
1966	Wayne Zahn	595 (3 games)	Dick Weber	Akron, OH
1967	Jim Stefanich	227 (1 game)	Don Johnson	Akron, OH
1968	Dave Davis	213 (1 game)	Don Johnson	Akron, OH
1969	Jim Godman	266 (1 game)	Jim Stefanich	Akron, OH
1970	Don Johnson	299 (1 game)	Dick Ritger	Akron, OH
1971	Johnny Petraglia	245 (1 game)	Don Johnson	Akron, OH
1972	Mike Durbin	775 (3 games)	Tim Harahan	Akron, OH
1973	Jim Godman	451 (2 games)	Barry Asher	Akron, OH
1974	Earl Anthony	679 (3 games)	Johnny Petraglia	Akron, OH
1975	Dave Davis	448 (2 games)	Barry Asher	Akron, OH
1976	Marshall Holman	441 (2 games)	Billy Hardwick	Akron, OH
1977	Mike Berlin	434 (2 games)	Mike Durbin	Akron, OH
1978	Earl Anthony	237 (1 game)	Teata Semiz	Akron, OH
1979	George Pappas	224 (1 game)	Dick Ritger	Akron, OH
1980	Wayne Webb	750 (3 games)	Gary Dickinson	Akron, OH
1981	Steve Cook	287 (1 game)	Pete Couture	Akron, OH
1982	Mike Durbin	448 (2 games)	Steve Cook	Akron, OH
1983	Joe Berardi	865 (4 games)	Henry Gonzalez	Akron, OH
1984	Mike Durbin	950 (4 games)	Mike Aulby	Akron, OH
1985	Mark Williams	616 (3 games)	Bob Handley	Akron, OH
1986	Marshall Holman	233 (1 game)	Mark Baker	Akron, OH
1987	Pete Weber	928 (4 games)	Jim Murtishaw	Akron, OH
1988	Mark Williams	237 (1 game)	Tony Westlake	Fairlawn, OH

Tournament of Champions *(Cont.)*

Year	Winner	Score	Runner-Up	Site
1989	Del Ballard Jr	490 (2 games)	Walter Ray Williams Jr	Fairlawn, OH
1990	Dave Ferraro	226 (1 game)	Tony Westlake	Fairlawn, OH
1991	David Ozio	476 (2 games)	Amleto Monacelli	Fairlawn, OH
1992	Marc McDowell	471 (2 games)	Don Genalo	Fairlawn, OH
1993	George Branham III	227 (1 game)	Parker Bohn III	Fairlawn, OH
1994	Norm Duke	422 (2 games)	Eric Forkel	Fairlawn, OH
1995	Mike Aulby	502 (2 games)	Bob Spaulding	Lake Zurich, IL
1996	Dave D'Entremont	971 (4 games)	Dave Arnold	Lake Zurich, IL

ABC Masters Tournament

Year	Winner	Scoring Avg	Runner-Up	Site
1951	Lee Jouglard	201.8	Joe Wilman	St. Paul, MN
1952	Willard Taylor	200.32	Andy Varipapa	Milwaukee
1953	Rudy Habetler	200.13	Ed Brosius	Chicago
1954	Eugene Elkins	205.19	W. Taylor	Seattle
1955	Buzz Fazio	204.13	Joe Kristof	Ft. Wayne, IN
1956	Dick Hoover	209.9	Ray Bluth	Rochester, NY
1957	Dick Hoover	216.39	Bill Lillard	Ft. Worth, TX
1958	Tom Hennessy	209.15	Lou Frantz	Syracuse, NY
1959	Ray Bluth	214.26	Billy Golembiewski	St. Louis, MO
1960	Billy Golembiewski	206.13	Steve Nagy	Toledo, OH
1961	Don Carter	211.18	Dick Hoover	Detroit
1962	Billy Golembiewski	223.12	Ron Winger	Des Moines, IA
1963	Harry Smith	219.3	Bobby Meadows	Buffalo
1964	Billy Welu	227	Harry Smith	Oakland, CA
1965	Billy Welu	202.12	Don Ellis	St. Paul, MN
1966	Bob Strampe	219.80	Al Thompson	Rochester, NY
1967	Lou Scalia	216.9	Bill Johnson	Miami Beach
1968	Pete Tountas	220.15	Buzz Fazio	Cincinnati
1969	Jim Chestney	223.2	Barry Asher	Madison, WI
1970	Don Glover	215.10	Bob Strampe	Knoxville, TN
1971	Jim Godman	229.8	Don Johnson	Detroit
1972	Bill Beach	220.27	Jim Godman	Long Beach, CA
1973	Dave Soutar	218.61	Dick Ritger	Syracuse, NY
1974	Paul Colwell	234.17	Steve Neff	Indianapolis
1975	Eddie Ressler	213.51	Sam Flanagan	Dayton, OH
1976	Nelson Burton Jr	220.79	Steve Carson	Oklahoma City
1977	Earl Anthony	218.21	Jim Godman	Reno
1978	Frank Ellenburg	200.61	Earl Anthony	St. Louis
1979	Doug Myers	202.9	Bill Spigner	Tampa, FL
1980	Neil Burton	206.69	Mark Roth	Louisville
1981	Randy Lightfoot	218.3	Skip Tucker	Memphis
1982	Joe Berardi	207.12	Ted Hannahs	Baltimore
1983	Mike Lastowski	212.65	Pete Weber	Niagara Falls, NY
1984	Earl Anthony	212.5	Gil Sliker	Reno
1985	Steve Wunderlich	210.4	Tommy Kress	Tulsa, OK
1986	Mark Fahy	206.5	Del Ballard Jr	Las Vegas
1987	Rick Steelsmith	210.7	Brad Snell	Niagara Falls, NY
1988	Del Ballard Jr	219.1	Keith Smith	Jacksonville, FL
1989	Mike Aulby	218.5	Mike Edwards	Wichita
1990	Chris Warren	231.6	David Ozio	Reno
1991	Doug Kent	226.8	George Branham III	Toledo, OH
1992	Ken Johnson	230.0	Dave D'Entremont	Corpus Christi, TX
1993	Norm Duke	245.68	Patrick Allen	Tulsa, OK
1994	Steve Fehr	213.09	Steve Anderson	Greenacres, FL
1995	Mike Aulby	230.7	Mark Williams	Reno
1996	Ernie Schlegel	221.2	Mike Aulby	Salt Lake City

Women's Majors

BPAA United States Open

Year	Winner	Score	Runner-Up	Site
1949	Marion Ladewig	113.26-104.26	Catherine Burling	Chicago
1950	Marion Ladewig	151.46-146.06	Stephanie Balogh	Chicago
1951	Marion Ladewig	159.17-148.03	Sylvia Wene	Chicago
1952	Marion Ladewig	154.39-142.05	Shirley Garms	Chicago
1953	Not held			
1954	Marion Ladewig	148.29-143.01	Sylvia Wene	Chicago
1955	Sylvia Wene	142.30-141.11	Sylvia Fanta	Chicago
1955	Anita Cantaline	144.40-144.13	Doris Pórter	Chicago
1956	Marion Ladewig	150.16-145.41	Marge Merrick	Chicago
1957	Not held			
1958	Merle Matthews	145.09-143.14	Marion Ladewig	Minneapolis
1959	Marion Ladewig	149.33-143.00	Donna Zimmerman	Buffalo
1960	Sylvia Wene	144.14-143.26	Marion Ladewig	Omaha
1961	Phyllis Notaro	144.13-143.12	Hope Riccilli	San Bernardino, CA
1962	Shirley Garms	138.44-135.49	Joy Abel	Miami Beach
1963	Marion Ladewig	586-578	Bobbie Shaler	Kansas City, MO
1964	LaVerne Carter	683-609	Evelyn Teal	Dallas
1965	Ann Slattery	597-550	Sandy Hooper	Philadelphia
1966	Joy Abel	593-538	Bette Rockwell	Lansing, MI
1967	Gloria Bouvia	578-516	Shirley Garms	St. Ann, MO
1968	Dotty Fothergill	9,000-8,187	Doris Coburn	Garden City, NY
1969	Dotty Fothergill	8,284-8,258	Kayoka Suda	Miami
1970	Mary Baker	8,730-8,465	Judy Cook	Northbrook, IL
1971	Paula Carter	5,660-5,650	June Llewellyn	Kansas City, MO
1972	Lorrie Nichols	5,272-5,189	Mary Baker	Denver
1973	Millie Martorella	5,553-5,294	Patty Costello	Garden City, NY
1974	Patty Costello	219-216	Betty Morris	Irving, TX
1975	Paula Carter	6,500-6,352	Lorrie Nichols	Toledo, OH
1976	Patty Costello	11,341-11,281	Betty Morris	Tulsa, OK
1977	Betty Morris	10,511-10,358	Virginia Norton	Milwaukee
1978	Donna Adamek	236-202	Vesma Grinfelds	Miami
1979	Diana Silva	11,775-11,718	Bev Ortner	Phoenix
1980	Pat Costello	223-199	Shinobu Saitoh	Rockford, IL
1981	Donna Adamek	201-190	Nikki Gianulias	Rockford, IL
1982	Shinobu Saitoh	12,184-12,028	Robin Romeo	Hendersonville, TN
1983	Dana Miller-Mackie	247-200	Aleta Sill	St. Louis
1984	Karen Ellingsworth	236-217	Lorrie Nichols	St. Louis
1985	Pat Mercatani	214-178	Nikki Gianulias	Topeka, KS
1986	Wendy Macpherson	265-179	Lisa Wagner	Topeka, KS
1987	Carol Norman	206-179	Cindy Coburn	Mentor, OH
1988	Lisa Wagner	226-218	Lorrie Nichols	Winston-Salem, NC
1989	Robin Romeo	187-163	Michelle Mullen	Addison, IL
1990	Dana Miller-Mackie	190-189	Tish Johnson	Dearborn Heights, MI
1991	Anne Marie Duggan	196-185	Leanne Barrette	Fountain Valley, CA
1992	Tish Johnson	216-213	Aleta Sill	Fountain Valley, CA
1993	Dede Davidson	213-194	Dana Miller-Mackie	Garland, TX
1994	Aleta Sill	229-170	Anne Marie Duggan	Wichita
1995	Cheryl Daniels	235-180	Tish Johnson	Blaine, MN

Note: From 1942 to 1970, the tournament was called the BPAA All-Star. Peterson scoring was used from 1949 through 1962. Under this system, the winner of an individual match game gets one point, plus one point for each 50 pins knocked down. From 1963 through 1967, a three-game championship was held between the two top qualifiers. From 1968 through 1973, 1975-77, 1979 and 1982, total pinfall determined the winner. In the other years, five qualifiers competed in a playoff for the championship, with the final match listed above.

WIBC Queens

Year	Winner	Score	Runner-Up	Site
1961	Janet Harman	794-776	Eula Touchette	Fort Wayne, IN
1962	Dorothy Wilkinson	799-794	Marion Ladewig	Phoenix
1963	Irene Monterosso	852-803	Georgette DeRosa	Memphis
1964	D. D. Jacobson	740-682	Shirley Garms	Minneapolis
1965	Betty Kuczynski	772-739	LaVerne Carter	Portland, OR
1966	Judy Lee	771-742	Nancy Peterson	New Orleans
1967	Millie Ignizio	840-809	Phyllis Massey	Rochester, NY
1968	Phyllis Massey	884-853	Marian Spencer	San Antonio
1969	Ann Feigel	832-765	Millie Ignizio	San Diego
1970	Millie Ignizio	807-797	Joan Holm	Tulsa, OK
1971	Millie Ignizio	809-778	Katherine Brown	Atlanta
1972	Dotty Fothergill	890-841	Maureen Harris	Kansas City, MO
1973	Dotty Fothergill	804-791	Judy Soutar	Las Vegas
1974	Judy Soutar	939-705	Betty Morris	Houston
1975	Cindy Powell	758-674	Patty Costello	Indianapolis
1976	Pam Buckner	214-178	Shirley Sjostrom	Denver
1977	Dana Stewart	175-167	Vesma Grinfelds	Milwaukee
1978	Loa Boxberger	197-176	Cora Fiebig	Miami
1979	Donna Adamek	216-181	Shinobu Saitoh	Tucson, AZ
1980	Donna Adamek	213-165	Cheryl Robinson	Seattle
1981	Katsuko Sugimoto	166-158	Virginia Norton	Baltimore
1982	Katsuko Sugimoto	160-137	Nikki Gianulias	St. Louis
1983	Aleta SIll	214-188	Dana Miller-Mackie	Las Vegas
1984	Kazue Inahashi	248-222	Aleta Sill	Niagara Falls, NY
1985	Aleta Sill	279-192	Linda Graham	Toledo, OH
1986	Cora Fiebig	223-177	Barbara Thorberg	Orange County, CA
1987	Cathy Alameida	850-817	Lorrie Nichols	Hartford, CT
1988	Wendy Macpherson	213-199	Leanne Barrette	Reno/Carson City, NV
1989	Carol Gianotti	207-177	Sandra Jo Shiery	Bismarck-Mandan, ND
1990	Patty Ann	207-173	Vesma Grinfelds	Tampa, FL
1991	Dede Davidson	231-159	Jeanne Maiden	Cedar Rapids, IA
1992	Cindy Coburn-Carroll	184-170	Dana Miller-Mackie	Lansing, MI
1993	Jan Schmidt	201-163	Pat Costello	Baton Rouge, LA
1994	Anne Marie Duggan	224-177	Wendy Macpherson-Papanos	Salt Lake City
1995	Sandra Postma	226-187	Carolyn Dorin	Tucson, AZ
1996	Lisa Wagner	231-226	Tammy Turner	Buffalo, NY

Sam's Town Invitational

Year	Winner	Score	Runner-Up	Site
1984	Aleta Sill	238 (1 game)	Cheryl Daniels	Las Vegas, NV
1985	Patty Costello	236 (1 game)	Robin Romeo	Las Vegas, NV
1986	Aleta Sill	238 (1 game)	Dina Wheeler	Las Vegas, NV
1987	Debbie Bennett	880 (4 games)	Lorrie Nichols	Las Vegas, NV
1988	Donna Adamek	634 (3 games)	Robin Romeo	Las Vegas, NV
1989	Tish Johnson	210 (1 game)	Dede Davidson	Las Vegas, NV
1990	Wendy Macpherson	900 (4 games)	Jeanne Maiden	Las Vegas, NV
1991	Lorrie Nichols	469 (2 games)	Dana Miller-Mackie	Las Vegas, NV
1992	Tish Johnson	279 (1 game)	Robin Romeo	Las Vegas, NV
1993	Robin Romeo	194 (1 game)	Tammy Turner	Las Vegas, NV
1994	Tish Johnson	178 (1 game)	Carol Gianotti	Las Vegas, NV
1995	Michelle Mullen	202 (1 game)	Cheryl Daniels	Las Vegas, NV

PWBA Championships

1960	Marion Ladewig	1971	Patty Costello
1961	Shirley Garms	1972	Patty Costello
1962	Stephanie Balogh	1973	Betty Morris
1963	Janet Harman	1974	Pat Costello
1964	Betty Kuczynski	1975	Pam Buckner
1965	Helen Duval	1976	Patty Costello
1966	Joy Abel	1977	Vesma Grinfelds
1967	Betty Mivalez	1978	Toni Gillard
1968	Dotty Fothergill	1979	Cindy Coburn
1969	Dotty Fothergill	1980	Donna Adamek
1970	Bobbe North		

Men's Awards

BWAA Bowler of the Year

1942 ....Johnny Crimmins	1961 ....Dick Weber	1978 ....Mark Roth
1943 ....Ned Day	1962 ....Don Carter	1979 ....Mark Roth
1944 ....Ned Day	1963 ....Dick Weber,	1980 ....Wayne Webb
1945 ....Buddy Bomar	Billy Hardwick (PBA)*	1981 ....Earl Anthony
1946 ....Joe Wilman	1964 ....Billy Hardwick,	1982 ....Earl Anthony
1947 ....Buddy Bomar	Bob Strampe (PBA)*	1983 ....Earl Anthony
1948 ....Andy Varipapa	1965 ....Dick Weber	1984 ....Mark Roth
1949 ....Connie Schwoegler	1966 ....Wayne Zahn	1985 ....Mike Aulby
1950 ....Junie McMahon	1967 ....Dave Davis	1986 ....Walter Ray Williams Jr
1951 ....Lee Jouglard	1968 ....Jim Stefanich	1987 ....Marshall Holman
1952 ....Steve Nagy	1969 ....Billy Hardwick	1988 ....Brian Voss
1953 ....Don Carter	1970 ....Nelson Burton Jr	1989 ....Mike Aulby,
1954 ....Don Carter	1971 ....Don Johnson	Amleto Monacelli (PBA)*
1955 ....Steve Nagy	1972 ....Don Johnson	1990 ....Amleto Monacelli
1956 ....Bill Lillard	1973 ....Don McCune	1991 ....David Ozio
1957 ....Don Carter	1974 ....Earl Anthony	1992 ....Dave Ferraro
1958 ....Don Carter	1975 ....Earl Anthony	1993 ....Walter Ray Williams Jr
1959 ....Ed Lubanski	1976 ....Earl Anthony	1994 ....Norm Duke
1960 ....Don Carter	1977 ....Mark Roth	1995 ....Mike Aulby

*The PBA began selecting a player of the year in 1963. Its selection has been the same as the BWAA's in all but three years.

Women's Awards

BWAA Bowler of the Year

1948 ....Val Mikiel	1965 ....Betty Kuczynski	1982 ....Nikki Gianulias
1949 ....Val Mikiel	1966 ....Joy Abel	1983 ....Lisa Wagner
1950 ....Marion Ladewig	1967 ....Millie Martorella	1984 ....Aleta Sill
1951 ....Marion Ladewig	1968 ....Dotty Fothergill	1985 ....Aleta Sill,
1952 ....Marion Ladewig	1969 ....Dotty Fothergill	Patty Costello (LPBT)*
1953 ....Marion Ladewig	1970 ....Mary Baker	1986 ....Lisa Wagner,
1954 ....Marion Ladewig	1971 ....Paula Sperber Carter	Jeanne Madden (LPBT)*
1955 ....Marion Ladewig	1972 ....Patty Costello	1987 ....Betty Morris
1956 ....Sylvia Martin	1973 ....Judy Soutar	1988 ....Lisa Wagner
1957 ....Anita Cantaline	1974 ....Betty Morris	1989 ....Robin Romeo
1958 ....Marion Ladewig	1975 ....Judy Soutar	1990 ....Tish Johnson,
1959 ....Marion Ladewig	1976 ....Patty Costello	Leanne Barrette (LPBT)*
1960 ....Sylvia Martin	1977 ....Betty Morris	1991 ....Leanne Barrette
1961 ....Shirley Garms	1978 ....Donna Adamek	1992 ....Tish Johnson
1962 ....Shirley Garms	1979 ....Donna Adamek	1993 ....Lisa Wagner
1963 ....Marion Ladewig	1980 ....Donna Adamek	1994 ....Anne Marie Duggan
1964 ....LaVerne Carter	1981 ....Donna Adamek	1995 ....Tish Johnson

*The LPBT began selecting a player of the year in 1983. Its selection has been the same as the BWAA's in all but three years.

Career Leaders

Earnings

MEN		WOMEN	
Pete Weber	$1,746,041	Aleta Sill	$737,862
Mike Aulby	$1,656,505	Tish Johnson	$721,886
Marshall Holman	$1,655,256	Lisa Wagner	$624,043
Walter Ray Williams Jr	$1,530,829	Robin Romeo	$582,274
Mark Roth	$1,484,948	Anne Marie Duggan	$530,776

Titles

MEN		WOMEN	
Earl Anthony	41	Lisa Wagner	29
Mark Roth	34	Patty Costello	25
Don Johnson	26	Aleta Sill	25
Dick Weber	26	Tish Johnson	21
Mike Aulby	23	Donna Adamek	19

Note: Leaders through the end of 1995.

Soccer

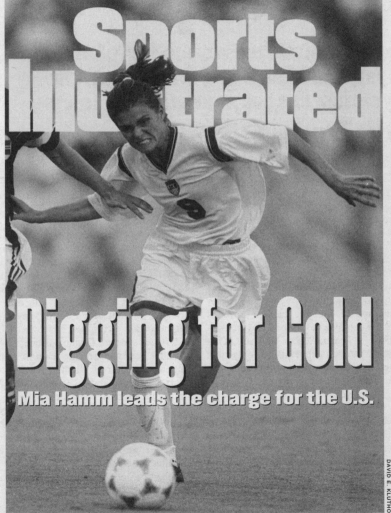

Sports Illustrated

Digging for Gold

Mia Hamm leads the charge for the U.S.

Playing For Keeps

As MLS completed a successful maiden voyage and the U.S. women lit up the Olympics, soccer seemed here to stay

by Hank Hersch

THE PROOF was in the counting. The eye-opening, head-snapping, mind-boggling nature of U.S. soccer in 1996 could be measured by two sets of five digits, like a pair of feet (in cleats?) that have left tracks that will last for the ages: 76,481—the number of fans in Athens, Ga., on Aug. 1, when the U.S. women's team claimed the first Olympic soccer gold medal in the history of the Summer Games; and 17,416—the average crowd at any of the 160 matches in the inaugural season of Major League Soccer. Both sets of figures far exceeded expectations; only time will tell which one will mean more to the growth of the sport.

For the players on the women's side, certainly, the shouts of "U.S.A! U.S.A!" from a packed house on a sultry night at Sanford Stadium were the most heartwarming appreciation they could have received for their years of success in obscurity. In 1991 they had won the first-ever women's world cup, beating Norway in the final in Guanzhou, China. In the '95 tournament in Sweden they drew slightly more media attention, finishing third behind Norway and Germany. And yet until the Games began, the largest crowd they had ever drawn on local soil had been for a Feb. 4 game in Jacksonville. The gate: 8,975.

But through the magic of the Olympics the women's team achieved a prominence it might never have reached otherwise. Soccer fans from around the world and the fervid if far-flung supporters of the women's team conspired to make its tickets hotly desired. Where once the players couldn't get arrested, now a fleet of nine motorcycle cops was needed to escort their bus to the stadium in Orlando for their Olympic opener.

Still it remained for the team to respond under this welter of attention, and nothing short of gold would do. The U.S. Soccer Federation made that much clear, offering the players performance bonuses only if they finished first. That stance prompted a brief strike in December '95 by nine team members, and while the USSF eventually relented—extending a bonus package that included compensation for a silver medal—the nearly $4 million it pumped into the Olympic effort over a two-year period was not a bet to place or show.

The U.S. advanced through the first round of competition with a 2-0-1 record, their only

Wynalda's game winner in the MLS opener was voted goal of the year.

blemish a 0–0 tie with China. (The men's team, meanwhile, failed to advance out of its tough round-robin group, going 1-1-1.) U.S. striker Mia Hamm, arguably the best female player in the world, sat out that China draw with an injured left ankle, and coach Tony DiCicco worried about her status for the semifinal against archrival Norway.

Before a crowd of 64,196, Hamm not only answered the call but also bedeviled Norway with her creativity and speed. Despite being fouled seven times, she helped the U.S. to a 28–8 edge in shots on goal. Yet for all the Yanks' dominance, they trailed 1–0 until the 76th minute, when a hand ball by Norway in the 18-yard box led to Michelle Akers's tying penalty kick. That sent the game into sudden-death overtime.

DiCicco had not inserted midfielder Shannon MacMillan during regulation play. In fact, he had barely included MacMillan on his roster at all. The 1995 college player of the year at Portland State had been left off the most recent World Cup team because of a broken left toe. Then in December, DiCicco told her she was not among his final 25 for the Olympics. Said MacMillan of this latest unkind cut, "I lost it leaving that meeting, I lost it in my car, I lost it at the airport in Portland when my friends picked me up. I thought my career was over."

But after the lockout over bonuses later that month, DiCicco brought her back to fill in. Given another look, MacMillan stuck, and as the semifinal match against Norway extended into overtime, she yearned to go in. Three minutes after finally entering the game, she ended it. Taking a pinpoint pass from midfielder Julie Foudy, MacMillan tucked the ball into the left corner of the net in the 100th minute. Thus the U.S. would face China, which defeated Brazil 3–2 in the other semifinal, for the inaugural championship. "This is where we wanted to be, the gold medal game," Hamm said. "It took everything from every single person on this team to get there."

Once the game started, the 24-year-old

Hamm had to take everything and then some. Hers were now compound maladies: the throbbing ankle, an injured groin from practice the day before and foul after foul against her by China. Despite setting up the game's first goal in the 18th minute when she banged a shot off the post and MacMillan put away the ricochet, Hamm wondered at halftime, with the score 1–1, if she might be slowing down her team.

Goalkeeper Briana Scurry was quick to reject that notion: "I told her, 'Mia, we need you. You have 45 minutes of your entire life to do this, and if you do it, you'll never regret it.' Mia's impact on a game is tremendous even when she isn't 100 percent. The Chinese have to worry about her, which means someone else might get loose."

That is precisely what happened in the 68th minute, when Hamm found defender Joy Fawcett on a run down the right wing. Fawcett centered to an unmarked Tiffeny Milbrett, who beat two defenders and goalkeeper Gao Hong from five yards out. Hamm went off on a stretcher with a minute to play. She was carried back onto the field seconds later to celebrate a 2–1 victory as the largest crowd ever to see a women's soccer match roared its approval.

The only downside of the team's epic moment was that the rest of the nation barely got to share it. NBC chose not to air the final live, and its coverage of the tournament consisted of four segments totaling 20 minutes. Still, the Athens turnout turned on enough sponsors to begin discussion of a women's professional league in the States. "Our goal is to try to reach a bigger audience," Foudy said. "It's a step-by-step progression. Some are baby steps. Others are like this one."

For men's soccer in the U.S. there was one huge step to go: the creation of a bona fide professional league. Such a league was a condition set by the Fédération Internationale de Football Association (FIFA) when it awarded the 1994 World Cup to the U.S. on July 4, 1988. A first division was supposed to be up and running before the Cup; after the task of putting on the tournament proved more difficult than expected, its start was put off until 1995, then '96. And when MLS was finally unveiled on April 6 in San Jose, it was far from clear whether the interest piqued by the World Cup two years earlier could be recaptured.

MLS's most recent predecessor, the North American Soccer League, had provided 17 years of world-class competition before disbanding in 1984. The NASL reeled in such luminaries from overseas as Pelé, Franz Beckenbauer and Giorgio Chinaglia, and jammed NFL stadiums with overflow crowds. On the other hand, it failed to develop local talent by favoring foreign journeymen over U.S. prospects, never secured a reliable TV deal and allowed the richest clubs to spend

GEORGE TIEDEMANN

El Diablo's fiendish passing created all three D.C. United goals in the final.

the opposition, and thus the league, into oblivion.

The new league, mindful that pro soccer could not afford to go boom and bust again, took into account the NASL's mistakes. Players would sign contracts with MLS and then be allotted to the 10 franchises; the teams would each have a salary cap of $1.135 million; no more than four foreign players would be included on any roster. For TV exposure, MLS signed sweetheart deals with ESPN and Univision that, when combined with local broadcasts, ensured that 94% of the games would be on the tube. The league's approach, emphasizing long-term growth over short-term gratification, attracted a handful of deep-pocketed owners and sponsors who coughed up over $50 million.

But the other questions remained: Would the league's gimmickry—shoot-outs at the end of regulation to break ties, nicknames like the Wiz (Kansas City), Burn (Dallas) and Galaxy (Los Angeles), game time kept on the stadium clock—turn off aficionados? Could the largely homegrown talent, sprinkled with stars such as midfielder Carlos Valderrama of Colombia, Roberto Donadoni of Italy and goalkeeper Jorge Campos of Mexico, play attractive soccer? And, most important, would the teams draw crowds? League officials hoped for an average attendance of 10,000. "All we knew was, we were throwing a party," said Dallas general manager Billy Hicks. "We didn't know who was coming. We didn't know if anyone was coming."

What happened over the next few weeks was something beyond the dreams of MLS's most Pollyannaish pooh-bahs. For starters, the opener at Spartan Stadium in San Jose attracted a packed house of 31,683, who watched Eric Wynalda, the U.S. national team's alltime leading scorer, curl the league's first goal into the upper right corner of visiting D.C. United's net in the 88th minute to lift the Clash to a 1–0 victory. A week later in Los Angeles police had to cut off traffic that stacked up for miles around the Rose Bowl, and 69,255 eventually wedged their way into the debut of Campos and the Galaxy. More than 92,000 turned up for another Rose Bowl game, 35,000 paid to see the Burn at the Cotton Bowl on Cinco de Mayo, and over 78,000 greeted the All-Star Game in East Rutherford, N.J.

"For the first time," said All-Star midfielder Tab Ramos of the New York/New Jersey MetroStars, "soccer has a chance to be part of our culture." Indeed, by midseason the MLS Web site was receiving 25,000 hits a day; Campos, Ramos and New England defender Alexi Lalas had appeared on Kellogg's cereal boxes; action figures were in the works. In the greenroom before Lalas was to make an appearance on David Letterman, comedian Bill Murray told him, "Nice shootout win in Columbus [Ohio] the other night."

In the face of all the fanfare MLS commissioner Doug Logan was cautiously optimistic. "We've certainly exceeded our expectations," he said in September. "We're 80 percent above our projections on attendance. Our TV partners are very happy, our sponsors are very happy and we're all very pleased with the level of play. But remember: No one gets a degree at the end of their freshman year."

They do get grades, though, and amid all the high marks, some franchises were barely passing. Despite having the league's best record (20–12) behind Valderrama and fleet U.S. forward Roy Lassiter, the season's top scorer, Tampa Bay finished ninth in attendance. Colorado, too, struggled at the gate and joined New England as the only teams to miss the playoffs. Nor did the refereeing always pass muster, as inconsistent calls drove some of the most levelheaded veterans to the brink of madness.

And while the caliber of play was surprisingly high, the league did feel it necessary to allow each club another foreigner in 1997. Further, in recognition of the limitations col-

lege soccer places on player development (forbidding off-season club ball), the USSF earmarked $1.5 million to institute Project 40 in January. The program would isolate the top 40 18- and 19-year-olds in the U.S. and invite them to a three-month training camp, after which 30 of them would be offered "developmental contracts" with MLS.

It was a product of the college game—in fact, a player who continued to attend school between practices and games—who would score the final goal of the league's first season. After two best-of-three playoff rounds among the eight qualifying teams, the Galaxy and D.C. United reached the finale, MLS Cup '96, on Oct. 20. A nasty nor'easter drenched the pitch at Foxboro, Mass., and threatened to put a damper on the season's climax. But despite the weather, 34,643 of the faithful showed up in a driving rain at the neutral site to shiver and cheer. "What fans," Logan said afterward. "I don't know what other sport in the world has the staying power of these fans."

One could also marvel at the staying power of United, which began the season 2–8 but rallied to finish second in the East. United found itself down 2–nil in the final after Galaxy goals by Eduardo (el Tanque) Hurtado in the fifth minute and Chris Armas in the 55th. But D.C. coach Bruce Arena made two second-half substitutions and both scored—midfielder Tony Sanneh in the 70th minute and midfielder Shawn Medved in the 82nd—to even the score and send the game into sudden-death overtime.

Just 3:25 into OT, United midfielder Marco (el Diablo) Etcheverry swung a gorgeous left-footed corner kick into the penalty area, where defender Eddie Pope, a former North Carolina star, blasted a header from six yards out past Campos. Three goals in 21 minutes, sparked by the magic of Bolivia's Etcheverry, the game's MVP, had lifted the D.C. side to the first MLS title, 3–2. Afterward team captain and U.S. national team star John Harkes, relishing the crowd and the competition, had to feel satisfied with his decision to leave England to play at home. "Soccer fever is alive in the United States," Harkes said, "and it's going to stay."

Major League Soccer

Final Standings

EASTERN CONFERENCE							WESTERN CONFERENCE						
Team	Won	Lost	Pts	GF	GA	SOW	Team	Won	Lost	Pts	GF	GA	SOW
†Tampa Bay...20	12	58	66	51	1		†Los Angeles..19	13	49	59	49	4
*D.C. United...16	16	46	62	56	1		*Dallas...........17	15	41	50	48	5
*MetroStars 15	17	39	45	47	3		*Kansas City ..17	15	41	61	63	5
*Columbus 15	17	37	59	60	4		*San Jose.......15	17	39	50	50	3
New England ..15	17	33	43	56	6		Colorado 11	21	29	44	59	2

†Conference champion. *Clinched playoff berth.

Note: Three points for a win; one point for a shootout win. GF= goals for in regulation. GA= goals against in regulation. SOW=shootout win; shootout wins are a subset of total wins.

1996 Playoffs

Eastern Conference Semifinals

Sept 24............D.C. United 2 at MetroStars 3 (SO)   Oct 2 ....MetroStars 1 at D.C. United 2
Sept 27............MetroStars 0 at D.C. United 1
(D.C. United won series 2–1.)

Sept 25............Tampa Bay 2 at Columbus 0   Oct 2 ....Columbus 1 at Tampa Bay 4
Sept 28............Columbus 2 at Tampa Bay 1
(Tampa Bay won series 2–1.)

Eastern Conference Finals

Oct 10 ....Tampa Bay 1 at D.C. United 4   Oct 12 .............D.C. United 2 at Tampa Bay 1
(D.C. United won series 2–0.)

Western Conference Semifinals

Sept 26............Dallas 2 at Kansas City 3   Oct 2 ....Kansas City 3 at Dallas 2 (SO)
Sept 29............Kansas City 1 at Dallas 2
(Kansas City won series 2–1.)

Sept 26............Los Angeles 0 at San Jose 1   Oct 2 ....San Jose 0 at Los Angeles 2
Sept 29............San Jose 0 at Los Angeles 2
(Los Angeles won series 2–1.)

Western Conference Finals

Oct 10 ....Kansas City 1 at Los Angeles 2   Oct 13 ....Los Angeles 2 at Kansas City 1 (SO)
(Los Angeles won series 2–0.)

SO= shootout.

MLS Cup '96

FOXBORO, MASS., OCTOBER 20, 1996

Los Angeles 1	1	0	—2
D.C. United...........................0	2	1	—3

Goals: Hurtado (5), Armas (56); Sanneh (73), Medved (82), Pope (94).
Los Angeles—Campos, Vanney, Fraser, Semioli, Salcedo (Onalfo 77), Cienfuegos, Armas, Jones, Hurtado, Noamouz, Karapetyan (Razov 76).
D.C. United—Simpson, Peay, Pope, Agoos, Gori (Medved 70), Maessner (Sanneh 59), Williams, Harkes, Etcheverry, Diaz Arce, Moreno.

Att: 34,643.

1996 MLS Leaders

POINTS

Player, Team	GP	G	A	Pts
Roy Lassiter, Tampa Bay	30	27	4	58
Preki, Kansas City	32	18	13	49
Eduardo Hurtado, LA	26	21	7	49
Raul Diaz Arce, D.C.	28	23	2	48
Brian McBride, Columbus	28	17	3	37

ASSISTS

Player, Team	GP	A
Marco Etcheverry, D.C.	26	19
Carlos Valderrama, Tampa Bay	23	17
Eric Wynalda, San Jose	27	13
Preki, Kansas City	32	13
Mauricio Cienfuegos, Los Angeles	28	11

GOALS

Player, Team	GP	G
Roy Lassiter, Tampa Bay	30	27
Raul Diaz Arce, D.C.	28	23
Eduardo Hurtado, Los Angeles	26	21
Preki, Kansas City	32	18
Brian McBride, Columbus	30	17

GOALS-AGAINST-AVERAGE LEADERS

Player, Team	GAA
Jorge Campos, Los Angeles	1.20
Tony Meola, MetroStars	1.31
Mark Dodd, Dallas	1.46
Mark Dougherty, Tampa Bay	1.68
Aidan Heaney, New England	1.70

International Competition

1996 U.S. Men's National Team Results

Date	Opponent	Site	Result	U.S. Goals
Jan 13	Trinidad & Tobago	Anaheim, CA	3–2 W	Wynalda (2), Moore
Jan 16	El Salvador	Anaheim, CA	2–0 W	Wynalda, Balboa
Jan 18	Brazil	Los Angeles	0–1 L	none
Jan 21	Guatemala	Los Angeles	3–0 W	Wynalda, Agoos, Kirovski
May 26	Scotland	New Britain, CT	2–1 W	Wynalda, Jones
June 9	Ireland	Foxboro, MA	2–1 W	Ramos, Reyna
June 12	Bolivia	Washington, D.C.	0–2 L	none
June 16	Mexico	Pasadena, CA	2–2 T	Wynalda, Dooley
Aug 30	El Salvador	Los Angeles	3–1 W	Moore (2), Wynalda

Record through Oct. 11, 1996: 6-2-1

1996 U.S. Women's National Team Results

Date	Opponent	Site	Result	U.S. Goals
Jan 14	Russia*	Campinas, Brazil	8–1 W	Foudy (2), Parlow (2), Akers, Gabarra, Milbrett, MacMillan
Jan 16	Brazil*	Campinas, Brazil	3–2 W	Hamm, Gabarra, Milbrett
Jan 18	Ukraine*	Campinas, Brazil	6–0 W	Garrett (3), MacMillan, Grubb, Milbrett
Jan 20	Brazil*	Campinas, Brazil	1–1 T	Milbrett
Feb 2	Norway	Tampa	3–2 W	Hamm, Akers, Milbrett
Feb 4	Norway	Jacksonville, FL	1–2 L	Chastain
Feb 10	Denmark	Orlando	2–1 W	Lilly, Overbeck
Feb 15	Sweden	San Antonio, TX	3–0 W	MacMillan, Venturini, Hamm
Feb 17	Sweden	Houston	3–0 W	Venturini, Milbrett, Parlow
Mar 14	Germany	Decatur, GA	6–0 W	Overbeck, Parlow, Hamm, Chastain, Milbrett (2)
Mar 16	Germany	Davidson, NC	2–0 W	Milbrett, Lilly
Mar 20	Holland	Fullerton, CA	6–0 W	Venturini (2), Foudy, Lilly (2), Akers
Mar 26	France	St Louis	4–1 W	Akers, Lilly, Parlow (2)
Mar 28	France	Indianapolis	8–2 W	Hamm (4), MacMillan, Milbrett, Akers, Gabarra
May 12	Canada#	Worcester, MA	6–0 W	Foudy, Milbrett, MacMillan, Gabarra, Parlow, Roberts
May 16	Japan#	Horsham, PA	4–0 W	Venturini, Lilly (2), Gabarra
May 18	China#	Washington, D.C.	1–0 W	Akers
July 4	Australia	Tampa	2–1 W	Venturini, Parlow
July 6	Australia	Pensacola, FL	2–1 W	Venturini, Lilly
July 21	Denmark**	Orlando	3–0 W	Venturini, Hamm, Milbrett
July 23	Sweden**	Orlando	2–1 W	Venturini, MacMillan
July 25	China**	Miami	0–0 T	none
July 28	Norway**	Athens, GA	2–1 W	Akers, MacMillan
Aug 1	China**	Athens, GA	2–1 W	MacMillan, Milbrett

*Brazil Soccer Cup. #U.S. Women's Cup. **Olympic Soccer tournament. Record through Oct. 11, 1996: 21-1-2

1996 European Championship

Country	GP	W	L	T	G	GA	Pts
GROUP A							
England†	3	2	0	1	7	2	7
Netherlands†	3	1	1	1	3	4	4
Scotland	3	1	1	1	1	2	4
Switzerland	3	0	2	1	1	4	1

Country	GP	W	L	T	G	GA	Pts
GROUP B							
France†	3	2	0	1	5	2	7
Spain†	3	1	0	2	4	3	5
Bulgaria	3	1	1	1	3	4	4
Romania	3	0	3	0	1	4	0

Country	GP	W	L	T	G	GA	Pts
GROUP C							
Germany†	3	2	0	1	5	0	7
Czech Rep†	3	1	1	1	5	6	4
Italy	3	1	1	1	3	3	4
Russia	3	0	2	1	4	8	1

Country	GP	W	L	T	G	GA	Pts
GROUP D							
Portugal†	3	2	0	1	5	1	7
Croatia†	3	2	1	0	4	3	6
Denmark	3	1	1	1	4	3	4
Turkey	3	0	3	0	0	5	0

†Advanced to quarterfinals

EURO '96 FINAL

*Advanced on penalty kick shootout.

FINAL
WEMBLEY, JUNE 30, 1996

Germany	0	1	1	—2
Czech Republic	0	1	0	—1

Goals: Bierhoff (73, 95); Berger (pen. 59)
Germany—Kopke, Helmer, Sammer, Scholl (Bierhoff 69), Hassler, Kuntz, Babbel, Ziege, Klinsmann, Strunz, Ellts (Bode 45).
Czech Republic—Kouba, Suchoparek, Nedved, Kadlec, Nemec, Poborski (Smicer 88), Kuka, Bejbl, Berger, Hornak, Rada.

Att: 73, 611

Snapshots from Abroad

With the launch of Major League Soccer in April 1995, 12 members of the 1994 U.S. World Cup team returned home to help pro soccer succeed on these shores. But several top-flight U.S. players, most notably midfielder Claudio Reyna, remain abroad, getting the kind of experience that only a league with a strong tradition can provide.

In 1995–96 Reyna started several games for Bayer Leverkusen in the rugged first division of the German Bundesliga, where his U.S. teammate Thomas Dooley also plays, for Schalke. Reyna rejoined the team for the '96-97 season with the hope of cracking the starting lineup for good. Another player anxious to shine at the highest level is 20-year-old California native Jovan Kirovski, who has 16 appearances for the national team. Kirovski left his parents' home in Escondido at the age of 16 to play for the Manchester United reserves, for whom he scored 20 goals in 21 games in '95–96. Denied his work permit in the summer of '96, he left England to sign with prestigious German club Borussia Dortmund, the 1995–96 Bundesliga champion. Injuries to starters provided Kirovski with opportunities to play, and he did not squander them, scoring his first goal in October '96.

In goalkeeper–rich England, U.S. netminder Kasey Keller moved from Millwall to Premier League club Leicester City for a $1.4 million transfer fee, while one of his rivals for the starting U.S. job, Juergen Sommer, played for First Division club Queens Park Rangers. Ernie Stewart, the striker who scored the United States's second goal in its 2–1 win over Colombia in the 1994 World Cup, plays for NAC Breda of the Dutch First Division.

International Club Competition

1995 Toyota Cup Final

Competition between winners of European Cup and Libertadores Cup.

TOKYO: NOV 28, 1995

Ajax (Netherlands) 0   0   0   0—0
Gremio (Brazil) 0   0   0   0—0

Goals: None. Ajax won 4–3 on penalties.

Att: 60,000

Ajax: Van Der Sar, Reiziger, Blind, F. De Boer, Finidi George, Bogarde, R. De Boer, Davids, Litmanen (Reuser, 95), Kluivert, Overmars (Kanu, 69).
Gremio: Danrlei, Arce, Rivarola, Adilson, Roger, Goiano, Dinho, Arilson (Luciano, 62), Carlos Miguel (Gelson, 97), Paulo Nunes, Jardel (Magno, 79).

European Cup-Winners' Cup

Cup winners of countries belonging to UEFA.

BRUSSELS: MAY 8, 1996

Paris St Germain (Fr) 1   0   —1
Rapid Vienna (Austria) ...0   0   —0

Goal: N'Gotty (29).

Att: 37,500

Paris St Germain: Lama, Fournier (Llacer, 80), N'Gotty, Roche, Le Guen, Colleter, Bravo, Guerin, Djorkaeff, Rai (Dely Valdes, 12), Loko.
Rapid Vienna: Konsel, Hatz, Guggi, Ivanov, Schoettel, Stoeger, Stumpf (Barisic, 46), Marasek, Jancker, Kuehbauer, Heraf.

UEFA Cup

Competition between teams other than league champions and cup-winners from UEFA.

(SECOND LEG) BORDEAUX: MAY 15, 1996

Bayern Munich (Ger) 0   3   —3
Bordeaux (France) 0   1   —1

Goals: Dutuel (75); Scholl (53), Kostadinov (65), Klinsmann (79) (aggregate: Bayern Munich, 5–1).

Att: 36,000

Bayern Munich: Kahn, Babbel, Ziegee, Strunz, Helmer, Frey (Zickler, 60), Scholl, Sforza, Klinsmann, Matthaeus, Kostadinov (Witeczek, 75).
Bordeaux: Huard, Bancarel, Lizarazu (Ancelin, 32), Friis-Hansen, Dogon, Lucas (Grenet, 79), Zidane, Croci (Dutuel, 57), Tholot, Witschge, Dugarry.

European Cup

League champions of the countries belonging to UEFA (Union of European Football Associations).

ROME: MAY 22, 1996

Juventus(Italy) 1   0   —1
Ajax (Netherlands) 1   0   —1

Goals: Ravanelli (13); Litmanen (41). Juventus wins 4–2 on penalties.

Att: 67,000.

Juventus: Peruzzi, Ferrara, Pessotto, Torricelli, Vierchowod, Paulo Sauso (Di Livio, 57), Deschamps, Conte (Jugovic, 44), Vialli, Del Piero, Ravanelli (Padovano, 78).
Ajax: Van Der Sar, Silooy, Blind, F. De Boer (Scholten, 69), Bogarde, R. De Boer (Wooter, 91), Finidi George, Davids, Kanu, Litmanen, Musampa (Kluivert, 46).

Libertadores Cup

Competition between champion clubs and runners-up of 10 South American National Associations.

(SECOND LEG) BUENOS AIRES: JUNE 26, 1996

River Plate (Arg) 1   1   —2
America Cali (Col) 0   0   —0

Goals: Crespo (6, 59).

Att: 76,000.

River Plate: Burgos, Diaz, Ayala, Rivarola, Altamirano, Escudero (Gomez, 74), Almeyda, Cedres, Ortega (Sorin, 88), Francescoli, Crespo (Gallardo, 86).
America Cali: Cordoba, Bermudez, Asprilla, Dinas, Cabrera, Berti, Mazziri, Escobar, Oviedo, Zambrano, De Avila.

1995–96 League Champions—Europe

Country	League Champion	Cup Winner
Albania	Tirana	Tirana
Armenia	Piounik Yerevan	Kotalki Abovyan
Austria	Rapid Vienna	Sturm Graz
Belarus	Dinamo Minsk	KPC Mozyr
Belgium	F.C. Bruges	F.C. Bruges
Bulgaria	Slavia Sofia	Slavia Sofia
Croatia	Croatia Zagreb	Croatia Zagreb
Cyprus	Apoel Nicosia	Apoel Nicosia
Czech Republic	Slavia Prague	Sparta Prague
Denmark	Brondby	Aarhus
England	Manchester United	Manchester United
Estonia	Lantana Tallinn	Lantana Tallinn
Faroe Islands	GI Gotu	HB Thorshavn
Finland	Haka Valkeakoski	My-Pa Anjalankoski
France	Auxerre	Auxerre
Georgia	Dinamo Tiflis	Dinamo Tiflis
Germany	Borussia Dortmund	Kaiserslautern

League Champions—Europe (Cont.)

Country	League Champion	Cup Winner
Greece	Panathinaikos	AEK Athens
Holland	Ajax	PSV Eindhoven
Hungary	Ferencvaros	Kispest Honved
Iceland	IA Akranes	KR Reykjavik
Ireland	St Patrick's	St Patrick's
Israel	Maccabi Tel Aviv	Rishon Le-Zion
Italy	A.C. Milan, Juventus	Fiorentina
Latvia	Skonto Riga	Skonto Riga
Liechtenstein	FC Vaduz	FC Vaduz
Lithuania	Inkaras-Grifas Kaunus	Kareda Siaullai
Luxembourg	Jeunesse Esch	Union Luxembourg
Macedonia	Sileks Kratovo	Sloga Skopje
Malta	Sliema Wanderers	FC Valetta
Moldova	Zimbru Chisinau	FC Constructorul
Northern Ireland	FC Porta Down	Glentoran
Norway	Rosenborg Trandheim	Brann Bergen
Poland	Widzew Lodz	Ruch Chorzow
Portugal	FC Porto	Benfica
Romania	Steaua Bucharest	Steaua Bucharest
Russia	Spartak Vladikavkaz	Lok. Moscow
Scotland	Glasgow Rangers	Glasgow Rangers
Slovakia	Slovan Bratislava	Chamion Humenne
Slovenia	NK HIT Gorica	Olympia Ljubijana
Spain	Atletico Madrid	Atletico Madrid
Sweden	IFK Göteborg	AIK Stockholm
Switzerland	Grasshopper	F.C. Sion
Turkey	Fenerbahce	Galatasaray
Ukraine	Dinamo Kiev	Dinamo Kiev
Wales	Bangor City	Liansantflraid
Yugoslavia	Partizan Belgrade	Red Star

A-League

1996 Final Standings

Team	W	L	SOW	GF	GA	Pts
Montreal Impact	17	6	4	40	18	55
Colorado Foxes	14	11	2	55	33	44
Seattle Sounders	12	11	4	35	25	40
Rochester Rhinos	11	13	3	44	42	36
Vancouver 86ers	10	14	3	38	38	33
New York Fever	6	18	3	30	40	21
Atlanta Ruckus	3	19	0	14	60	9

Note: Three points for a win; one point for a shootout win. GF= goals for in regulation. GA= goals against in regulation. SOW=shootout win.

Playoff Results: Four teams—Montreal, Colorado, Seattle and Rochester—qualified for the playoffs. Rochester defeated Montreal two games to one and Seattle defeated Colorado two games to one in the semifinal round; Seattle defeated Rochester 2–0 in the A-League Championship game.

SCORING LEADERS

Player, Team	G	A	Pts
Wolde Harris, Colorado	17	8	42
Doug Miller, Rochester	18	2	38
Domenic Mobilio, Vancouver	14	4	32
Leenin Steenkamp, Rochester	9	5	23
Carsten Siersbaek, Colorado	7	8	22

ASSISTS LEADERS

Player, Team	A
Wolde Harris, Colorado	8
Carsten Siersbaek, Colorado	8
Lloyd Barker, Montreal	7
Hector Marinaro, Rochester	7
Lee Tschantret, New York	7

GOALS LEADERS

Player, Team	G
Doug Miller, Rochester	18
Wolde Harris, Colorado	17
Domenic Mobilio, Vancouver	14
Leenin Steenkamp, Rochester	9
Eddy Burdusco, Montreal	8

GOALS-AGAINST-AVERAGE LEADERS

Player, Team	GAA
Paolo Ceccarelli, Montreal	0.65
Marcus Hahnemann, Seattle	0.91
Trey Harrington, Colorado	1.23
Paul Dolan, Vancouver	1.27
Azmi, New York	1.38

The World Cup

Results

Year	Champion	Score	Runner-Up	Winning Coach
1930	Uruguay	4-2	Argentina	Alberto Supicci
1934	Italy	2-1	Czechoslovakia	Vittorio Pozzo
1938	Italy	4-2	Hungary	Vittorio Pozzo
1950	Uruguay	2-1	Brazil	Juan Lopez
1954	West Germany	3-2	Hungary	Sepp Herberger
1958	Brazil	5-2	Sweden	Vicente Feola
1962	Brazil	3-1	Czechoslovakia	Aymore Moreira
1966	England	4-2	West Germany	Alf Ramsey
1970	Brazil	4-1	Italy	Mario Zagalo
1974	West Germany	2-1	Netherlands	Helmut Schoen
1978	Argentina	3-1	Netherlands	César Menotti
1982	Italy	3-1	West Germany	Enzo Bearzot
1986	Argentina	3-2	West Germany	Carlos Bilardo
1990	West Germany	1-0	Argentina	Franz Beckenbauer
1994	Brazil	0-0 (3-2)	Italy	Carlos Alberto Parreira

Alltime World Cup Participation

Of the 58 nations which have taken part in the World Cup, only Brazil has competed in each of the 15 tournaments held to date. West Germany or an undivided Germany (1934, '38 and '94) have played in 14 World Cups.

	Matches	W	T	L	Goals For	Goals Against
Brazil	73	49	13	11	159	68
*Germany	73	42	16	15	154	97
Italy	61	35	14	12	97	59
Argentina	52	26	9	17	90	65
England	41	18	12	11	55	38
†Russia	34	16	6	12	60	40
Uruguay	37	15	8	14	61	52
France	34	15	5	14	71	56
Yugoslavia	33	15	5	13	55	42
Hungary	32	15	3	14	87	57
Spain	37	15	9	13	53	44
Poland	25	13	5	7	39	29
Sweden	37	13	7	17	62	60
Austria	26	12	2	12	40	43
Czechoslovakia	30	11	5	14	44	45
Netherlands	25	11	6	8	43	29
Belgium	29	9	4	16	37	53
Mexico	33	7	8	18	31	68
Chile	21	7	3	11	26	32
Portugal	9	6	0	3	19	12
Romania	17	6	4	7	26	29
Switzerland	22	6	3	13	33	51
United States	14	4	1	9	17	33
Scotland	20	4	6	10	23	35
Peru	15	4	3	8	19	31
Bulgaria	22	3	7	12	21	42
Northern Ireland	13	3	5	5	13	23
Paraguay	11	3	4	4	16	25
Cameroon	11	3	4	4	11	21
Denmark	4	3	0	1	10	6
Nigeria	4	2	0	2	7	4
East Germany	6	2	2	2	5	5
Costa Rica	4	2	0	2	4	6
Saudi Arabia	4	2	0	2	5	6
Colombia	10	2	2	6	13	20
Algeria	6	2	1	3	6	10
Wales	5	1	3	1	4	4
Morocco	7	1	3	3	5	8
Republic of Ireland	9	1	5	3	4	7
Tunisia	3	1	1	1	3	2
North Korea	4	1	1	2	5	9
Cuba	3	1	1	1	5	12
Turkey	3	1	0	2	10	11
Norway	4	1	1	2	2	3
Israel	3	1	0	2	1	3
Honduras	3	0	2	1	2	3
Egypt	4	0	2	2	3	6
Kuwait	3	0	1	2	2	6
Australia	3	0	1	2	0	5
Iran	3	0	1	2	2	8
South Korea	11	0	3	8	9	34
Dutch East Indies	1	0	0	1	0	6
Iraq	3	0	0	3	1	4
Canada	3	0	0	3	0	5
United Arab Emirates	3	0	0	3	2	11
New Zealand	3	0	0	3	2	12
Haiti	3	0	0	3	2	14
Zaire	3	0	0	3	0	14
Bolivia	6	0	1	5	1	20
El Salvador	6	0	0	6	1	22
Greece	3	0	0	3	0	8

*Includes West Germany 1950-90. †Includes USSR 1930-1990.
Note: Matches decided by penalty kicks are shown as drawn games.

World Cup Final Box Scores

URUGUAY 1930

Uruguay...........1	3	—4
Argentina.........2	0	—2

FIRST HALF

Scoring: 1, Uruguay, Dorado (12); 2, Argentina, Peucelle (20); 3, Argentina, Stabile (37).

SECOND HALF

Scoring: 4, Uruguay, Cea (57); 5, Uruguay, Iriarte (68); 6, Uruguay, Castro (89).

Argentina: Botosso, Della Toree, Paternoster, Evaristo, J., Monti, Suarez, Peucelle, Varallo, Stabile, Ferreira, Evaristo, M.

Uruguay: Ballesteros, Nasazzi, Mascheroni, Andrade, Fernandez, Gestido, Dorado, Scarone, Castro, Cea, Iriarte.

Referee: Langenus (Belgium).

FRANCE 1938

Italy...................3	1	—4
Hungary............1	1	—2

FIRST HALF

Scoring: 1, Italy, Colaussi (5); 2, Hungary, Titkos (7); 3, Italy, Piola (16); 4, Italy, Piola (35).

SECOND HALF

Scoring: 5, Hungary, Sarosi (70); 6, Italy, Colaussi (82).

Italy: Olivieri, Foni, Rava, Serantoni, Andreolo, Locatelli, Biavati, Meazza, Piola, Ferrari, Colaussi.

Hungary: Szabo; Polger, Biro, Szalay, Szucs, Lazar, Sas, Vincze, Sarosi, Zsengeller, Titkos.

Referee: Capdeville (France).

SWITZERLAND 1954

W Germany 2	1	—3
Hungary............2	0	—2

FIRST HALF

Scoring: 1, Hungary, Puskas (6); 2, Hungary, Czibor (8); 3, W Germ, Morlock (10); 4, W Germ, Rahn (18).

SECOND HALF

Scoring: 5, W Germ, Rahn (84).

West Germany: Turek; Posipal, Kohlmeyer, Eckel, Liebrich, Mai, Rahn, Morlock, Walter, O., Walter, F., Schaefer.

Hungary: Grosics; Buzansky, Lantos, Bozsik, Lorant, Zakarias, Czibor, Kocsis, Hidegkuti, Puskas, Toth.

Referee: Ling (England).

ITALY 1934

Italy..................0	1	1—2
Czechoslovakia ..0	1	0—1

SECOND HALF

Scoring: 1, Czech., Puc (70); 2, Italy, Orsi (80).

OVERTIME

Scoring: 3, Italy, Schiavio (95).

Italy: Combi, Monzeglio, Allemandi, Ferraris Monti, Monti, Bertolini, Guaita, Meazza, Schiavio, Ferrari, Orsi.

Czechoslovakia: Planicka, Zenisek, Ctyroky, Kostalek, Cambal, Cambal, Krcil, Junek, Svoboda, Sobotka, Nejedly, Puc.

Referee: Eklind (Sweden).

BRAZIL 1950

Uruguay 0	2	—2
Brazil................0	1	—1

SECOND HALF

Scoring: 1, Brazil, Friaca (47); 2, Uruguay, Schiaffino (66); 3, Uruguay, Ghiggia (79).

Uruguay: Maspoli, Gonzales, Tejera, Gambretta, Varela, Andrade, Ghiggia, Perez, Miguez, Schiffiano, Moran

Brazil: Barbosa, Augusto, Juvenal, Bauer, Banilo, Bigode, Friaca, Zizinho, Ademir, Jair, Chico.

Referee: Reader (England).

SWEDEN 1958

Brazil.................2	3	—5
Sweden.............1	1	—2

FIRST HALF

Scoring:1, Sweden, Liedholm (3); 2, Brazil, Vava (9); 3, Brazil, Vava (32).

SECOND HALF

Scoring: 4, Brazil, Pelé (55); 5, Brazil, Zagalo (68); 6, Sweden Simonsson (80); 7, Brazil, Pelé (90).

Brazil: Glymar, Santos, D., Santos, N., Zito, Bellini, Orlando, Garrincha, Didi, Vava, Pelé, Zagalo.

Sweden: Svensson, Bergmark, Axbom, Boerjesson, Gustavsson, Parling, Hamrin, Gren, Simonsson, Liedholm, Skoglund.

Referee: Guigue (France).

CHILE 1962

Brazil............................1	2	—3
Czechoslovakia 1	0	—1

FIRST HALF

Scoring: 1, Czech, Masopust (15); 2, Brazil, Amarildo (17).

SECOND HALF

Scoring: 3, Brazil, Zito (68); 4, Brazil, Vava (77).

Brazil: Glymar; Santos, D., Santos, N., Zito, Mauro, Zozimo, Garrincha, Didi, Vava, Amarildo, Zagalo.

Czechoslovakia: Schroiff, Tichy, Novak, Pluskal, Popluhar, Masopust, Pospichal, Scherer, Kvasnak, Kadraba, Jelinek.

Referee: Latychev (USSR).

World Cup Final Box Scores *(Cont.)*

ENGLAND 1966

England............1   1   2——4
W. Germany.........1   1   0——2

FIRST HALF

Scoring: 1, Germany, Haller (12); 2, England, Hurst, (18).

SECOND HALF

Scoring: 3, England, Peters (78); 4, Germany, Weber (90).

OVERTIME

Scoring: 5, England, Hurst (101); 6, England, Hurst (120).

England: Banks, Cohen, Wilson, Stiles, Charlton, J., Moore, Ball, Hurst, Hunt, Charlton, R., Peters.

W. Germany: Tilkowski, Hottges, Schmellinger, Beckenbauer, Schulz, Weber, Held, Haller, Seeler, Overath, Emmerich.

Referee: Dienst (Switzerland).

W. GERMANY 1974

W. Germany 2   0 ——2
Netherlands.....1   0 ——1

FIRST HALF

Scoring: 1, The Netherlands, Neeskens, PK, (1); 2, W. Germany, Breitner, PK, (26); 3, W. Germany, Muller, (44).

W. Germany: Maier, Vogts, Beckenbauer, Schwarzenbeck, Breitner, Hoeness, Bonhof, Overath, Grabowski, Muller, Holzenbein.

The Netherlands: Jongbloed, Suurbier, Rijsbergen (de Jong), Haan, Krol, Jansen, Neeskens, van Hanagem, Cruyff, Rensenbrink (van der Kerkhof).

Referee: Taylor (England).

ITALY 1982

Italy...................0   3 ——3
W. Germany 0   1 ——1

SECOND HALF

Scoring: 1, Italy, Rossi (57); 2, Italy, Tardelli (68); 3, Italy, Altobelli (81); 4, Germany, Breitner (83).

Italy: Zoff, Bergomi, Scirea, Collovati, Cabrini, Oriali, Gentile, Tardelli, Conti, Rossi, Graziani (Altobelli), Causio).

W. Germany: Schumacher, Kaltz, Stielike, Foerster, K., Foerster, B., Dremmler (Hrubesch), Breitner, Briegel, Rummenigge (Mueller), Fishcher (Littbrarski).

Referee: Coelho (Brazil).

MEXICO 1970

Brazil.................1   3 ——4
Italy...................1   0 ——1

FIRST HALF

Scoring: 1, Brazil, Pelé (18); 2, Italy, Boninsegna (32).

SECOND HALF

Scoring: 3, Brazil, Gerson (65); 4, Brazil, Jairzinho (70); 5, Brazil, Alberto (86).

Brazil: Feliz, Alberto, Brito, Wilson, Piazza, Everaldo, Clodoaldo, Gerson, Jairzinho, Tostao, Pelé, Rivelino.

Italy: Albertosi, Burgnich, Cera, Rosato, Facchetti, Bertini (Juliano), Mazzola, De Sisti, Domenghini, Boninsegna (Rivera), Riva.

Referee: Glockner (E. Germany).

ARGENTINA 1978

Argentina.........1   0   2——3
Netherlands 0   1   0——1

FIRST HALF

Scoring: 1, Argentina, Kempes (38).

SECOND HALF

Scoring: 2, The Netherlands, Nanninga (81).

OVERTIME

Scoring: 3, Arg., Kempes (104); 4, Arg., Bertoni (114).

Argentina: Fillol, Olguin, Galvan, Passarella, Tarantini, Ardiles (Larrosa), Gallego, Kempes, Bertoni, Luque, Ortiz (Houseman).

The Netherlands: Jongbloed, Jansen (Suurbier), Krol, Brandts, Poortvliet, Neeskens, Haan, van der Kerkhoff, W., van der Kerkhoff, R., Rep (Nanninga), Rensenbrink.

Referee: Gonella (Italy).

MEXICO 1986

Argentina.........1   2 ——3
W. Germany 0   2 ——2

FIRST HALF

Scoring: 1, Argentina, Brown (22).

SECOND HALF

Scoring: 2, Arg., Valdano (55); 3, W. Germ., Rummenigge (73); 4, W. Germ., Voller (81); 5, Arg., Burruchaga (83).

Argentina: Pumpido, Brown, Cuciuffo, Ruggeri, Olarticoecha, Bastista, Giusti, Burruchaga (90, Trobbiani), Enrique, Maradona, Valdona.

W. Germany: Schumacher, Jakobs, Forster, Eder, Brehme, Matthaus, Berthold, Magath (62 Hoeness), Briegel, Rummenigge, Allofs (46 Voller).

Referee: Filho (Brazil).

World Cup Final Box Scores *(Cont.)*

ITALY 1990

W Germany.........0		1——1
Argentina..............0		0——0

UNITED STATES 1994

Italy...................0	0	0——0
Brazil....................0	0	0——0

SECOND HALF

Scoring: 1, W. Germany, Brehme, PK, (84).

W. Germany: Illgner, Brehme, Kohler, Augenthaler, Buchwald, Berthold (Reuter), Littbarski, Haessler, Mattaeus, Voeller, Klinsmann.

Argentina: Goychoechea, Lorenzo, Serrizuela, Sensini, Ruggeri (Monzon), Simon, Basualdo, Burruchag (Calderon), Maradona, Troglio, Dezottir.

Referee: Coelho (Brazil).

Scoring: None. Shootout goals: Italy—2: Albertini, Evani; Brazil—3: Romario, Branco, Dunga.

Italy: Pagliuca, Benarrivo, Maldini, Baresi, Mussi (Apolloni) 35), Albertini, D. Baggio (Evani 95), Berti, Donadoni, Baggio, Massaro,

Brazil: Taffarel, Jorginho (Cafu 21), Branco, Aldair, Santos, Silva, Dunga, Zinho (Viola 106), Mazinho, Bebeto, Romario

Referee: Sandor Puhl (Hungary).

Alltime Leaders

GOALS

Player, Nation	Tournaments	Goals	Player, Nation	Tournaments	Goals
Gerd Muller, West Germany	.....1970, '74	14	Ademir, Brazil	1950	9
Just Fontaine, France	1958	13	Eusebio, Portugal	1966	9
Pelé, Brazil	...................................1958, '62, '66, '70	12	Jairzinho, Brazil	...................1970, '74	9
Sandor Kocsis, Hungary	1954	11	Paolo Rossi, Italy	...................1982, '86	9
Teofilo Cubillas, Peru	................1970, '78	10	Karl-Heinz Rummenigge,		
Gregorz Lato, Poland	...............1974, '78, '82	10	W. Germany	..............................1978, '82, '86	9
Helmut Rahn, West Germany	...1954, '58	10	Uwe Seeler, West Germany	......1958, '62, '66, '70	9
Gary Lineker, England	..............1986, '90	10	Vava, Brazil	................................1958, '62	9

LEADING SCORER, CUP BY CUP

Year	Player, Nation	Goals	Year	Player, Nation	Goals
1930	..........Guillermo Stabile, Argentina	8	1962	..........Leonel Sanchez, Chile	4
1934	..........Oldrich Nejedly, Czechoslovakia	5		Vava, Brazil	
1938	..........Leonidas da Silva, Brazil	8	1966	..........Eusebio Ferreira, Portugal	9
1950	..........Ademir de Menenzes, Brazil	9	1970	..........Gerd Mueller, West Germany	10
1954	..........Sandor Kocsis, Hungary	11	1974	..........Gregorz Lato, Poland	7
1958	..........Just Fontaine, France	13	1978	..........Mario Kempes, Argentina	6
1962	..........Florian Albert, Hungary	4	1982	..........Paolo Rossi, Italy	6
	Valentin Ivanov, USSR		1986	..........Gary Lineker, England	6
	Garrincha, Brazil		1990	..........Salvatore Schillaci, Italy	6
	Drazan Jerkovic, Yugoslavia		1994	..........Hristo Stoitchkov, Bulgaria	6
				Oleg Salenko, Russia	

Most Goals, Individual, One Game

Goals	Player, Nation	Score	Date
5	....................................Oleg Salenko, Russia	Russia-Cameroon, 6-1	6-28-94
4	....................................Leonidas, Brazil	Brazil-Poland, 6-5	6-5-38
4	....................................Ernest Willimowski, Poland	Brazil-Poland, 6-5	6-5-38
4	....................................Gustav Wetterstrïm, Sweden	Sweden-Cuba, 8-0	6-12-38
4	....................................Juan Alberto Schiaffino, Uruguay	Uruguay-Bolivia, 8-0	7-2-50
4	....................................Ademir, Brazil	Brazil-Sweden, 7-1	7-9-50
4	....................................Sandor Kocsis, Hungary	Hungary-West Germany, 8-3	6-20-54
4	....................................Just Fontaine, France	France-West Germany, 6-3	6-28-58
4	....................................Eusebio, Portugal	Portugal-No. Korea, 5-3	7-23-66
4	....................................Emilio Butragueño, Spain	Spain-Denmark, 5-1	6-18-86

Note: 30 players have scored 31 World Cup hat tricks. Gerd Muller of West Germany is the only man to have two World Cup hat tricks, both in 1970. The last hat tricks were 6-23-90, Tomas Skuhravy (Czech) vs. Costa Rica and Michel (Spain) vs. So. Korea, 6-17-90.

Attendance and Goal Scoring, Year by Year

Year	Site	No. of Games	Goals	Goals/Game	Attendance	Avg Att
1930 ....Uruguay		18	70	3.89	434,500	24,139
1934 ....Italy		17	70	4.12	395,000	23,235
1938 ....France		18	84	4.67	483,000	26,833
1950 ....Brazil		22	88	4.00	1,337,000	60,773
1954 ....Switzerland		26	140	5.38	943,000	36,269
1958 ....Sweden		35	126	3.60	868,000	24,800
1962 ....Chile		32	89	2.78	776,000	24,250
1966 ....England		32	89	2.78	1,614,677	50,459
1970 ....Mexico		32	95	2.97	1,673,975	52,312
1974 ....West Germany		38	97	2.55	1,774,022	46,685
1978 ....Argentina		38	102	2.68	1,610,215	42,374
1982 ....Spain		52	146	2.80	1,856,277	35,698
1986 ....Mexico		52	132	2.54	2,441,731	46,956
1990 ....Italy		52	115	2.21	2,514,443	48,354
1994 ....United States		52	140	2.69	3,567,415	68,604
Totals		516	1583	3.07	22,289,255	43,196

The United States in the World Cup

URUGUAY 1930: FINAL COMPETITION

Date	Opponent	Result	Scoring
7-13-30 ..Belgium		3-0 W	US: McGhee 2, Patenaude
7-17-30 ..Paraguay		3-0 W	US: Patenaude 2, Florie
7-26-30 ...Argentina		1-6 L	ARG: Monti 2, Scopelli 2, Stabile 2 US: Brown.

ITALY 1934: FINAL COMPETITION

Date	Opponent	Result	Scoring
5-27-34 ..Italy		1-7 L	US: Donelli ITA: Schiavio 3, Orsi 2, Meazza, Ferrari

BRAZIL 1950: FINAL COMPETITION

Date	Opponent	Result	Scoring
6-25-50 ..Spain		1-3 L	US: Pariani SPN: Igoa, Basora, Zarra
6-29-50 ..England		1-0 W	US: Gaetjens.
7-2-50 ....Chile		2-5 L	US: Wallace, Maca CHL: Robledo, Cremaschi 3, Prieto

ITALY 1990: FINAL COMPETITION

Date	Opponent	Result	Scoring
6-10-90 ..Czechoslovakia	1-5 L		US: Caligiuri Czech: Skuhravy 2, Hasek, Bilek, Luhovy
6-14-90 ..Italy		0-1 L	Italy: Giannini
6-19-90 ..Austria		1-2 L	US: Murray Austria: Rodax, Ogris

UNITED STATES 1994: FINAL COMPETITION

Date	Opponent	Result	Scoring
6-18-94 ..Switzerland		1-1 T	US: Wynalda Sui: Bregy
6-22-94 ..Colombia		2-1 W	US: Escobar (own goal), Stewart Colombia: Valencia
6-26-94 ..Romania		1-0 L	Romania: Petrescu
7-4-94 ....Brazil		1-0 L	Brazil: Bebeto

International Competition

European Championship

Official name: the European Football Championship. Held every four years since 1960.

Year	Champion	Score	Runner-up	Year	Champion	Score	Runner-up
1960 ......USSR		2–1	Yugoslavia	1980 ......West Germany		2–1	Belgium
1964 ......Spain		2–1	USSR	1984 ......France		2–0	Spain
1968 ......Italy		2–0	Yugoslavia	1988 ......Holland		2–0	USSR
1972 ......West Germany		3–0	USSR	1992 ......Denmark		2–0	Germany
1976 ......Czechoslovakia*		2–2	West Germany	1996 ......Germany		2–1	Czech Republic

*Won on penalty kicks.

Under-20 World Championship

Year	Host	Champion	Runner-Up
1977	Tunisia	USSR	Mexico
1979	Japan	Argentina	USSR
1981	Australia	W. Germany	Qatar
1983	Mexico	Brazil	Argentina
1985	USSR	Brazil	Spain
1987	Chile	Yugoslavia	W. Germany
1989	Saudi Arabia	Portugal	Nigeria
1991	Portugal	Portugal	Brazil
1993	Australia	Brazil	Ghana
1995	Qatar	Argentina	Brazil

Under-17 World Championship

1985	Nigeria
1987	USSR
1989	Saudi Arabia
1991	Ghana

Under-17 *(Cont.)*

1993	Nigeria
1995	Ghana

Pan American Games

1951	Argentina
1955	Argentina
1959	Argentina
1963	Brazil
1967	Mexico
1971	Argentina
1975	Brazil-Mexico (tie)
1979	Brazil
1983	Uruguay
1987	Brazil
1991	United States
1995	Argentina

South American Championship (Copa America)

Year	Champion	Host	Year	Champion	Host
1916	Uruguay	Argentina	1947	Argentina	Ecuador
1917	Uruguay	Uruguay	1949	Brazil	Brazil
1919	Brazil	Brazil	1953	Paraguay	Peru
1920	Uruguay	Chile	1955	Argentina	Chile
1921	Argentina	Argentina	1956	Uruguay	Uruguay
1922	Brazil	Brazil	1957	Argentina	Peru
1923	Uruguay	Uruguay	1958	Argentina	Argentina
1924	Uruguay	Uruguay	1959	Uruguay	Ecuador
1925	Argentina	Argentina	1963	Bolivia	Bolivia
1926	Uruguay	Chile	1967	Uruguay	Uruguay
1927	Argentina	Peru	1975	Peru	Various sites
1929	Argentina	Argentina	1979	Paraguay	Various sites
1935	Uruguay	Peru	1983	Uruguay	Various sites
1937	Argentina	Argentina	1987	Uruguay	Argentina
1939	Peru	Peru	1989	Brazil	Brazil
1941	Argentina	Chile	1990	Brazil	Argentina
1942	Uruguay	Uruguay	1991	Argentina	Chile
1945	Argentina	Chile	1993	Argentina	Ecuador
1946	Argentina	Argentina	1995	Uruguay	Uruguay

Awards

European Footballer of the Year

Year	Player	Team	Year	Player	Team
1956	Stanley Matthews	Blackpool	1973	Johan Cruyff	Barcelona
1957	Alfredo Di Stefano	Real Madrid	1974	Johan Cruyff	Barcelona
1958	Raymond Kopa	Real Madrid	1975	Oleg Blokhin	Dynamo Kiev
1959	Alfredo Di Stefano	Real Madrid	1976	Franz Beckenbauer	Bayern Munich
1960	Luis Suarez	Barcelona	1977	Allan Simonsen	Borussia Moenchengladbach
1961	Omar Sivori	Juventus			
1962	Josef Masopust	Dukla Prague	1978	Kevin Keegan	SV Hamburg
1963	Lev Yashin	Moscow Dynamo	1979	Kevin Keegan	SV Hamburg
1964	Denis Law	Manchester United	1980	Karl-Heinz Rummenigge	Bayern Munich
1965	Eusebio	Benfica			
1966	Bobby Charlton	Manchester United	1981	Karl-Heinz Rummenigge	Bayern Munich
1967	Florian Albert	Ferencvaros			
1968	George Best	Manchester United	1982	Paolo Rossi	Juventus
1969	Gianni Rivera	AC Milan	1983	Michel Platini	Juventus
1970	Gerd Mueller	Bayern Munich	1984	Michel Platini	Juventus
1971	Johan Cruyff	Ajax	1985	Michel Platini	Juventus
1972	Franz Beckenbauer	Bayern Munich	1986	Igor Belanov	Dynamo Kiev
			1987	Ruud Gullit	AC Milan

European Footballer of the Year *(Cont.)*

1988	Marco Van Basten	AC Milan	1992	Marco Van Basten	AC Milan
1989	Marco Van Basten	AC Milan	1993	Roberto Baggio	Juventus
1990	Lothar Matthaeus	Inter Milan	1994	Hristo Stoichkov	Barcelona
1991	Jean-Pierre Papin	Olympique Marseille	1995	George Weah	AC Milan

African Footballer of the Year

Year	Player	Nation	Year	Player	Nation
1970	Salif Keita	Mali	1984	ThÇophile Abega	Cameroon
1971	Ibrahim Sunday	Ghana	1985	Mohamed Timoumi	Morocco
1972	Chérif Souleyman	Guinea	1986	Badou Zaki	Morocco
1973	Tshimimu Bwanga	Zaire	1987	Rabah Madjer	Algeria
1974	Paul Moukila	Congo	1988	Kalusha Bwalya	Zambia
1975	Ahmed Faras	Morocco	1989	George Weah	Liberia
1976	Roger Milla	Cameroon	1990	Roger Milla	Cameroon
1977	Dhiab Tarak	Tunisia	1991	Abedi Pele	Ghana
1978	Abdul Razak	Ghana	1992	Abedi Pele	Ghana
1979	Thomas Nkono	Cameroon	1993	Rashidi Yekini	Nigeria
1980	Jean Manga Onguene	Cameroon	1994	George Weah	Liberia
1981	Lakhdar Belloumi	Algeria	1995	George Weah	Liberia
1982	Thomas Nkono	Cameroon			
1983	Mahmoud Al-Khatib	Egypt			

Selected by *France Football*.

South American Player of the Year

Year	Player	Team	Year	Player	Team
1971	Tostao	Cruzeiro	1984	Enzo Francescoli	River Plate
1972	Teofilo Cubillas	Alianza Lima	1985	Julio Cesar Romero	Fluminense
1973	Pelé	Santos	1986	Antonio Alzamendi	River Plate
1974	Elias Figueroa	Internacional	1987	Carlos Valderrama	Deportivo Cali
1975	Elias Figueroa	Internacional	1988	Ruben Paz	Racing Buenos Aires
1976	Elias Figueroa	Internacional	1989	Bebeto	Vasco da Gama
1977	Zico	Flamengo	1990	Raul Amarilla	Olimpia
1978	Mario Kempes	Valencia	1991	Oscar Ruggeri	Velez Sarsfield
1979	Diego Maradona	Argentinos Juniors	1992	Rai	Sao Paulo
1980	Diego Maradona	Boca Juniors	1993	Carlos Valderrama	Junior Barranquilla
1981	Zico	Flamengo	1994	Cafu	Sao Paulo
1982	Zico	Flamengo	1995	Enzo Francescoli	River Plate
1983	Socrates	Corinthians			

Selected by Uruguayan magazine *El Pais*.

International Club Competition

Toyota Cup

Competition between winners of European Champion Clubs' Cup and Libertadores Cup.

1960...Real Madrid, Spain	1972...Ajax, Holland	1984...Independiente, Argentina
1961...Penarol, Uruguay	1973...Independiente, Argentina	1985...Juventus, Italy
1962...Santos, Brazil	1974...Atletico de Madrid, Spain	1986...River Plate, Argentina
1963...Santos, Brazil	1975...No tournament	1987...Porto, Portugal
1964...Inter, Italy	1976...Bayern Munich	1988...Nacional, Uruguay
1965...Inter, Italy	1977...Boca Juniors, Argentina	1989...Milan, Italy
1966...Penarol, Uruguay	1978...No tournament	1990...Milan, Italy
1967...Racing Club, Argentina	1979...Olimpia, Paraguay	1991...Red Star Belgrade, Yugos.
1968...Estudiantes, Argentina	1980...Nacional, Uruguay	1992...Sao Paulo, Brazil
1969...Milan, Italy	1981...Flamengo, Brazil	1993...Sao Paulo, Brazil
1970...Feyenoord, Netherlands	1982...Penarol, Uruguay	1994...Velez Sarsfield, Argentina
1971...Nacional, Uruguay	1983...Gremio, Brazil	1995...Ajax Amsterdam, Netherlands

Note: Until 1968 a best-of-three-games format decided the winner. After that a two-game/total-goal format was used until Toyota became the sponsor in 1980, moved the game to Tokyo, and switched the format to a one game championship. The European Cup runner-up substituted for the winner in 1971, 1973, 1974, and 1979.

European Cup

1956...Real Madrid, Spain	1961...Benfica, Portugal	1966...Real Madrid, Spain
1957...Real Madrid, Spain	1962...Benfica, Portugal	1967...Celtic, Scotland
1958...Real Madrid, Spain	1963...AC Milan, Italy	1968...Manchester United, England
1959...Real Madrid, Spain	1964...Inter-Milan, Italy	1969...AC Milan, Italy
1960...Real Madrid, Spain	1965...Inter-Milan, Italy	

European Cup (Cont.)

1970...Feyenoord, Netherlands
1971...Ajax Amsterdam, Netherlands
1972...Ajax Amsterdam, Netherlands
1973...Ajax Amsterdam, Netherlands
1974...Bayern Munich, West Germany
1975...Bayern Munich, West Germany
1976...Bayern Munich, West Germany

1977...Liverpool, England
1978...Liverpool, England
1979...Nottingham Forest, England
1980...Nottingham Forest, England
1981...Liverpool, England
1982...Aston Villa, England
1983...SV Hamburg, West Germany
1984...Liverpool, England
1985...Juventus, Italy

1986...Steaua Bucharest, Romania
1987...Porto, Portugal
1988...P.S.V. Eindhoven, Netherlands
1989...AC Milan, Italy
1990...AC Milan, Italy
1991....Red Star Belgrade, Yugoslav.
1992...Barcelona, Spain
1993...Olympique Marseille, France
1994...AC Milan, Italy
1995...Ajax Amsterdam, Netherlands
1996...Juventus, Italy

Note: On four occasions the European Cup winner has refused to play in the Intercontinental Cup (now Toyota Cup) and has been replaced by the runner-up: Panathinaikos (Greece) in 1971, Juventus (Italy) in 1973, Atletico Madrid (Spain) in 1974, and Malmo (Sweden) in 1979.

Libertadores Cup

Competition between champion clubs and runners-up of 10 South American National Associations.

1960...Penarol, Uruguay
1961...Penarol, Uruguay
1962...Santos, Brazil
1963...Santos, Brazil
1964...Independiente, Argentina
1965...Independiente, Argentina
1966...Penarol, Uruguay
1967...Racing Club, Argentina
1968...Estudiantes, Argentina
1969...Estudiantes, Argentina
1970...Estudiantes, Argentina
1971...Nacional, Uruguay
1972...Independiente, Argentina

1973...Independiente, Argentina
1974...Independiente, Argentina
1975...Independiente, Argentina
1976...Cruzeiro, Brazil
1977...Boca Juniors, Argentina
1978...Boca Juniors, Argentina
1979...Olimpia, Paraguay
1980...Nacional, Uruguay
1981...Flamengo, Brazil
1982...Penarol, Uruguay
1983...Gremio, Brazil
1984...Independiente, Argentina
1985...Argentinos Juniors, Arg

1986...River Plate, Argentina
1987...Penarol, Uruguay
1988...Nacional, Uruguay
1989...Atletico Nacional, Colombia
1990...Olimpia, Paraguay
1991...Colo Colo, Chile
1992...Sao Paulo, Brazil
1993...Sao Paulo, Brazil
1994...Velez Sarsfield, Argentina
1995...Gremio, Brazil
1996...River Plate, Argentina

UEFA Cup

Competition between teams other than league champions and cup winners from the Union of European Football Associations.

1958...Barcelona, Spain
1959...No tournament
1960...Barcelona, Spain
1961...AS Roma, Italy
1962...Valencia, Spain
1963...Valencia, Spain
1964...Real Zaragoza, Spain
1965...Ferencvaros, Hungary
1966...Barcelona, Spain
1967...Dynamo Zagreb, Yugoslavia
1968...Leeds United, England
1969...Newcastle United, England
1970...Arsenal, England
1971...Leeds United, England

1972...Tottenham Hotspur, England
1973...Liverpool, England
1974...Feyenoord, Netherlands
1975...Borussia Monchengladbach, West Germany
1976...Liverpool, England
1977...Juventus, Italy
1978...P.S.V. Eindhoven, Netherlands
1979...Borussia Monchengladbach, West Germany
1980...Eintracht Frankfurt, West Germany
1981...Ipswich Town, England
1982...I.F.K. Gothenburg, Sweden

1983...Anderlecht, Belgium
1984...Tottenham Hotspur, England
1985...Real Madrid, Spain
1986...Real Madrid, Spain
1987...I.F.K. Gothenburg, Sweden
1988...Bayer Leverkusen, West Germany
1989...Naples, Italy
1990...Juventus, Italy
1991...Inter-Milan, Italy
1992...Torino, Italy
1993...Juventus, Italy
1994...Internazionale, Italy
1995...Parma, Italy
1996...Bayern Munich, Germany

European Cup-Winners' Cup

Competition between cup winners of countries belonging to UEFA.

1961...A.C. Fiorentina, Italy
1962...Atletico Madrid, Spain
1963...Tottenham Hotspur, England
1964...Sporting Lisbon, Portugal
1965...West Ham United, England
1966...Borussia Dortmund, West Germany
1967...Bayern Munich, West Germany

1968...A.C. Milan, Italy
1969...Slovan Bratislava, Czechoslovakia
1970...Manchester City, England
1971...Chelsea, England
1972...Glasgow Rangers, Scotland
1973...A.C. Milan, Italy
1974...Magdeburg, East Germany
1975...Dynamo Kiev, USSR

1976...Anderlecht, Belgium
1977...S.V. Hamburg, West Germany
1978...Anderlecht, Belgium
1979...Barcelona, Spain
1980...Valencia, Spain
1981...Dynamo Tbilisi, USSR
1982...Barcelona, Spain
1983...Aberdeen, Scotland
1984...Juventus, Italy

European Cup-Winners' Cup *(Cont.)*

1985...Everton, England	1989...Barcelona, Spain	1993...Parma, Italy
1986...Dynamo Kiev, USSR	1990...Sampdoria, Italy	1994...Arsenal, England
1987...Ajax Amsterdam, Netherlands	1991...Manchester United, England	1995...Real Zaragoza, Spain
1988...Mechelen, Belgium	1992...Werder Bremen, Germany	1996...Paris St Germain, France

Major League Soccer

Results

Year	Champion	Score	Runner-up	Regular Season MVP
1996 ...........................D.C. United		3–2	Los Angeles	Carlos Valderrama, TB

Major Indoor Soccer League

Results

Called the Major Soccer League from 1990–92. Folded in 1992.

	Champion	Series	Runner-Up	Championship Series MVP
1979	NY Arrows	2–0	Philadelphia	Shep Messing, NY
1980	NY Arrows	7–4	Houston	Steve Zungul, NY
1981	NY Arrows	6–5	St Louis	Steve Zungul, NY
1982	NY Arrows	3–2	St Louis	Steve Zungul, NY
1983	San Diego	3–2	Baltimore	Juli Veee, SD
1984	Baltimore	4–1	St Louis	Scott Manning, Balt
1985	San Diego	4–1	Baltimore	Steve Zungul, SD
1986	San Diego	4–3	Minnesota	Brian Quinn, SD
1987	Dallas	4–3	Tacoma	Tatu, Dall
1988	San Diego	4–0	Cleveland	Hugo Perez, SD
1989	San Diego	4–3	Baltimore	Victor Nogueira, SD
1990	San Diego	4–2	Baltimore	Brian Quinn, SD
1991	San Diego	4–2	Cleveland	Ben Collins, SD
1992	San Diego	4–2	Dallas	Thomas Usiyan, SD

Championship format: 1979, best-of-three-games series; 1980-81, one-game championship; 1982-83, best-of-five-games series; 1984–92, best-of-seven-games series.

Statistical Leaders

SCORING

Year	Player, Team	Points
1978-79	Fred Grgurev, Phil	74
1979-80	Steve Zungul, NY	136
1980-81	Steve Zungul, NY	152
1981-82	Steve Zungul, NY	163
1982-83	Steve Zungul, NY	122
1983-84	Stan Stamenkovic, Balt	97
1984-85	Steve Zungul, SD	136
1985-86	Steve Zungul, Tac	115
1986-87	Tatu, Dall	111
1987-88	Erik Rasmussen, Wich	112
1988-89	Preci, Tac	104
1989-90	Tatu, Dall	113
1990-91	Tatu, Dall	144
1991-92	Zoran Karic, Clev	102

ASSISTS

Year	Player, Team	Assists
1978-79	Fred Grgurev, Phil	28
1979-80	Steve Zungul, NY	46
1980-81	Jorgen Kristensen, Wich	52
1981-82	Steve Zungul, NY	60
1982-83	Stan Stamenkovic, Mem	65
1983-84	Stan Stamenkovic, Balt	63

ASSISTS *(CONT.)*

Year	Player, Team	Assists
1984-85	Steve Zungul, SD	68
1985-86	Steve Zungul, Tac	60
1986-87	Kai Haaskivi, Clev	55
1987-88	Preki, Tac	58
1988-89	Preki, Tac	53
1989-90	Jan Goossens, KC	55
1990-91	Tatu, Dall	66
1991-92	Zoran Karic, Clev	63

GOALS

Year	Player, Team	Goals
1978-79	Fred Grgurev, Phil	46
1979-80	Steve Zungul, NY	90
1980-81	Steve Zungul, NY	108
1981-82	Steve Zungul, NY/GB	103
1982-83	Steve Zungul, NY/GB	75
1983-84	Mark Liveric, NY	58
1984-85	Steve Zungul, SD	68
1985-86	Erik Rasmussen, Wich	67
1986-87	Tatu, Dall	73
1987-88	Hector Marinaro, Minn	58
1988-89	Preki, Tac	51
1989-90	Tatu, Dall	64
1990-91	Tatu, Dall	78
1991-92	Hector Marinaro, Clev	53

Statistical Leaders *(Cont.)*

TOP GOALKEEPERS

Year	Player, Team	Goals Agst Avg	Year	Player, Team	Goals Agst Avg
1978-79	Paul Hammond, Hous	4.16	1985-86	Keith Van Eron, Balt	3.66
1979-80	Sepp Gantenhammer, Hous	4.42	1986-87	Tino Lettieri, Minn	3.38
1980-81	Enzo DiPede, Chi	4.06	1987-88	Zoltan Toth, SD	2.94
1981-82	Slobo Liijevski, StL	3.85*	1988-89	Victor Nogueira, SD	2.86
1982-83	Zoltan Toth, NY	4.01	1989-90	Joe Papaleo, Dall	3.34
1983-84	Slobo Liijevski, StL	3.67	1990-91	Victor Nogueira, SD	4.37
1984-85	Scott Manning, Balt	3.89	1991-92	Victor Nogueira, SD	4.60

North American Soccer League

Formed in 1968 by the merger of the National Professional Soccer League and the USA League, both of which had begun operations a year earlier. The NPSL's lone champion was the Oakland Clippers. The USA League, which brought entire teams in from Europe, was won in 1967 by the LA Wolves, who were the English League's Wolverhampton Wanderers.

Year	Champion	Score	Runner-Up	Regular Season MVP
1968	Atlanta	0–0, 3–0	San Diego	John Kowalik, Chi
1969	Kansas City	No game	Atlanta	Cirilio Fernandez, KC
1970	Rochester	3–0,1–3	Washington	Carlos Metidieri, Roch
1971	Dallas	1–2, 4–1, 2–0	Atlanta	Carlos Metidieri, Roch
1972	NY	2–1	St Louis	Randy Horton, NY
1973	Philadelphia	2–0	Dallas	Warren Archibald, Mia
1974	Los Angeles	4–3*	Miami	Peter Silvester, Balt
1975	Tampa Bay	2–0	Portland	Steve David, Miami
1976	Toronto	3–0	Minnesota	Pelé, NY
1977	NY	2–1	Seattle	Franz Beckenbauer, NY
1978	NY	3–1	Tampa Bay	Mike Flanagan, NE
1979	Vancouver	2–1	Tampa Bay	Johan Cruyff, LA
1980	NY	3–0	Ft Lauderdale	Roger Davies, Sea
1981	Chicago	1–0*	NY	Giorgio Chinaglia, NY
1982	NY	1–0	Seattle	Peter Ward, Sea
1983	Tulsa	2–0	Toronto	Roberto Cabanas, NY
1984	Chicago	2–1, 3–2	Toronto	Steve Zungul, SJ

*Shootout.

Championship Format: 1968 & 1970: Two games/total goals. 1971 & 1984: Best-of-three game series. 1972-1983: One game championship. Title in 1969 went to the regular season champion.

Statistical Leaders

SCORING

Year	Player/Team	Pts	Year	Player/Team	Pts
1968	John Kowalik, Chi	69	1977	Steven David, LA	58
1969	Kaiser Motaung, Atl	36	1978	Giorgio Chinaglia, NY	79
1970	Kirk Apostolidis, Dall	35	1979	Oscar Fabbiani, Tampa Bay	58
1971	Carlos Metidieri, Roch	46	1980	Giorgio Chinaglia, NY	77
1972	Randy Horton, NY	22	1981	Giorgio Chinaglia, NY	74
1973	Kyle Rote, Dall	30	1982	Giorgio Chinaglia, NY	55
1974	Paul Child, San Jose	36	1983	Roberto Cabanas, NY	66
1975	Steven David, Miami	52	1984	Slavisa Zungul, Golden Bay	50
1976	Giorgio Chinaglia, NY	49			

A-League

Year	Champion	Score	Runner-Up	Regular Season MVP
1991	San Francisco	1–3, 2–0 (1–0 on penalty kicks)	Albany	Jean Harbor, MD
1992	Colorado	1–0	Tampa Bay	Taifour Diane, CO
1993	Colorado	3–1 (OT)	Los Angeles	Taifour Diane, CO
1994	Montreal	1–0	Colorado	Paulinho, LA
1995	Seattle	1–2 (SO), 3–0, 2–1 (SO)	Atlanta	Peter Hattrup, Seattle
1996	Seattle	2–0	Rochester	Wolde Harris, CO

Note: Also known as the American Professional Soccer League.

NCAA Sports

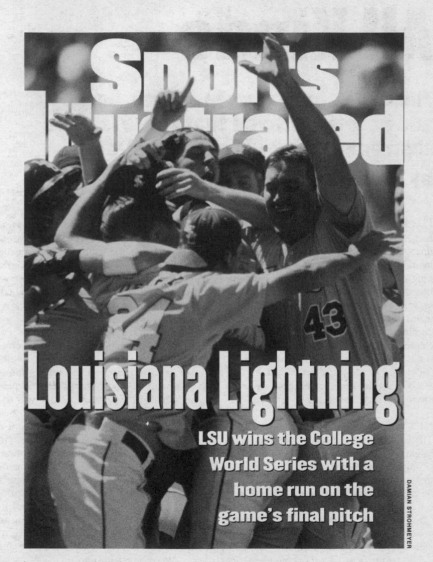

Sports Illustrated

Louisiana Lightning

LSU wins the College
World Series with a
home run on the
game's final pitch

DAMIAN STROHMEYER

It Takes All Kinds

The NCAA champions in soccer, hockey and baseball proved that there is more than one way to win a national title

by Hank Hersch

EACH NCAA season is a marathon race; each championship game merely the finish line. After grueling months of games and injuries and practice after practice, the winning team is often only remembered for how it appeared in the final moments of the season, when the title was at stake. Some teams win comfortably and seem suddenly dominant; some grind their way home to create an image of abiding toughness; some conjure up an almost electrical aura by seizing victory at the last possible instant. The 1995–96 season saw each of these scenarios enacted as its teams of destiny emerged.

MEN'S SOCCER

The score belied the extent of Wisconsin's hegemony. On a cold (33°) and windy (15 mph gusts) December day in Richmond, the Badgers stormed past Duke 2–0 to win the school's first soccer championship. "Don't call us a fluke," said midfielder Mike Gentile. "Don't call us a Cinderella team." Duke coach John Rennie wouldn't and didn't. "I think the better team won," he said.

The triumph had its shocking elements, nonetheless. Consider that Wisconsin had never before marched past even the quarterfinals, that Duke had knocked off powerhouse Virginia in the semis, that entering the championship game the winning goalkeeper had played all of 231 minutes over four years at Madison and that the Badgers rallying cry at the Final Four was the less-than-hearty, "We're here, we might as well win it all."

But in its first appearance in the national spotlight, Wisconsin proved to be monumentally unshakable. The reason: its defense, which featured tenacious man-to-man marking and remarkable quickness in support. The victory over Duke was the Badgers' fifth straight shutout in five tournament games; no team had ever kept a clean sheet for so long in the NCAAs. (In 1976 San Francisco was not scored upon, but the tournament lasted only four rounds then.) Wisconsin's defense became such a prominent subject of discussion that the Badgers became, well, defensive about it. "We've been attacking all year," Gentile said. "I don't know what else we have to prove to anyone. We didn't change for any team. We didn't adjust to them. We went out to impose ourselves on them."

Hansen put the Badgers on the board in the ninth minute of the title game.

All-America sweeper Scott Lamphear, who spearheaded the D, was quicker to calculate the value of the shutout streak. "You can't get less than zero," he said. "I think I learned that in third-grade math."

It was in an eighth-grade gym class in Livonia, Mich., that Lamphear, Gentile and forward Travis Roy first met. Eight years later, as seniors and four-year starters at Madison, they would constitute the nucleus of the championship team. "Scott is very tough, strong, skillful," Wisconsin coach Jim Launder has said. "Mike is very good all-around, does a lot of the little things. Travis was a defender as a youth but is very good around the goal."

In the semis at Richmond, the playmaking Gentile set up Lars Hansen in front of the net in the 64th minute for the goal that cinched a 1–0 victory over Portland. Duke, meanwhile, was holding off Virginia 3–2, thwarting the Cavaliers in their bid for a sixth title in seven years. The Blue Devils extended themselves greatly in upsetting

their archrivals, and they had less to give against Wisconsin. "It wasn't as much physically … as being emotionally drained," said Duke midfielder Jay Heaps. "Physically, I think we were there."

For their part the Badgers certainly had fresh legs in goal for the final. Jon Belskis, a 6'4", 215-pound junior from Hanover Park, Ill., had seen no game action since walking on in 1992 until starter Todd Wilson dislocated his left elbow on Nov. 26. Belskis's first start was a 2–0 shutout of SMU in the NCAA quarterfinals. He would not yield a goal throughout the tournament. "Coming in as a walk-on, I never minded being a backup," Belskis said. "I knew someday I'd probably get my shot. I just wanted to be ready when it came."

With a crowd of 21,319 looking on, Wisconsin essentially put away the final in the ninth minute as Roy's shot after a corner kick found Hansen at the six-yard line, where he redirected the ball past Duke keeper John Morton. In the 63rd minute junior defender Chad Cole settled a goal-mouth scramble by driving the ball home from 12 yards out. It was Cole's first goal of the sea-

All-Tournament Turco turned aside 38 of 40 shots during the Final Four.

son. "I always think offensive-minded," he said. "I just decided I was going to save the best for last."

Wisconsin continued to pepper Morton, who was credited with 10 saves to Belskis's two. "You don't expect to be in a shooting gallery in a national championship game, but when you get down—and our team likes to go forward—we start to go forward even more," Morton said. Still, the Devils could not break the zero barrier that Wisconsin had imposed on its last six opponents dating back to the regular season. After allowing a penalty kick goal to Marquette on Oct. 22, the Badgers (20-4-1) surrendered just two scores in 933 minutes, a goals-allowed average of 0.19.

"In the beginning of the year we set goals," said Launder, in his 14th year at Madison. "We wanted to win the Big Ten and then go to the Final Four. And then, almost as an afterthought, we said, 'While we're there, we might as well win it all.'" And the Badgers did, going away.

MEN'S HOCKEY

Before the title game against Colorado College in Cincinnati, overtime in the NCAA tournament had not been kind to Michigan. The Wolverines had played sudden death six times and died five. Their last two OT

experiences had not only been mortal, they had also been mortifying: a 5–4 loss to Lake Superior State in 1994 and a 4–3 loss to Maine in '95, the latter a semifinal disaster that took three extra periods and set a record as the longest game in tournament history. "I had confidence the last few years going into overtime," said defenseman Steven Halko, Michigan's senior captain. "We just didn't get the bounce."

There was ample reason to believe that things might bounce better for the Wolverines in 1996. They had balance, finishing their 34-7-2 season third nationally in both power play efficiency (29.1%) and penalty killing (86.2%). They had a devastating attack, led by junior center Brendan Morrison (28 goals, 44 assists), a Hobey Baker Award finalist. And they had defense, the last line of which consisted of sophomore goalie Marty Turco, who ranked second in the country in goals-against average (2.20).

Above all, they had resolve. "Our day will come," read the reminder on coach Red Berenson's desk, and the Wolverines to a man believed that, even as the tournament draw unfolded. To reach the finals and then to win, they would have to defeat three of the most formidable programs in hockey—Minnesota, Boston University and Colorado College—in three cities over three March weekends. Throw in Lake Superior State, whom the Wolverines defeated just prior to the NCAAs, and you have a final foursome with a combined 122-25-11 record.

The only way for the Wolverines to negotiate such a daunting gantlet was to make their own breaks, and they did. No break was more bold, more monumental—or more amazing—than the one junior right wing Mike Legg made against Minnesota in the second round. Michigan trailed the Golden Gophers 2-1 with 7:06 to play in the second period when Legg scored what one *ESPN* wag called, "The most amazing goal in college hockey history ... we're not exaggerating." Standing behind the Minnesota net, Legg squatted down, scooped the puck onto the edge of his stick blade, stepped to the left around the net and then whipped the puck, lacrosse-style, over the stunned goalie's shoulder. "I'm just in awe," said Michigan right wing Bill Muckalt. "I've seen him do it a lot in practice, but it took a lot of guts to try it in a game."

The shot seen 'round the nightly highlights came with a message. "A lot of people have said that we've flopped in the past," Legg said. "But that's not fair to this team. We haven't flopped yet." The Wolverines then fired an equally portentous salvo in the semis. Behind 17 saves by Turco, they blanked defending national champion BU, four–zip, the first time the Terriers had ever been shut out in NCAA tournament play.

Through the first two periods of the title game against Colorado College, Turco remained almost as firm between the pipes. While Michigan could muster a mere seven shots, Turco faced eight in the second period alone, when the Tigers took advantage of four power plays and scored twice to lead 2-1. Turco speared one point-blank blast with his glove at the 12-minute mark to keep the game tight. "That could have put it away," CC forward Jay McNeill would say later. "We felt like we had the game in hand, and we didn't bury them when we had the chance."

Legg drew Michigan even, scoring on a rebound in the third period. And some 13 minutes later the Wolverines once again entered into the extra session that had meant extra agony the past two years. This time, though, with 3:35 elapsed,

Muckalt drove a shot off goalie Ryan Bach's pad. The puck deflected to Morrison, who was swooping in on the back door. "The puck was rolling, and it seemed to take forever to get to me," he would say. With Bach sprawled out, the net wide open, Morrison had a chance to secure Michigan's record eighth college hockey championship, to give Berenson his 300th victory in 12 seasons at Ann Arbor, to clinch the Wolverines' first title since 1963–64 and to dispatch all the ghosts of overtimes past.

The final score: Michigan 3, Colorado College 2. Afterward Muckalt would look at Morrison, the tournament's Most Outstanding Player, and laugh. "It took you long enough to put it in, Mo," he said.

BASEBALL

Could what LSU coach Skip Bertman fondly called those "god-awful yellow shirts" have been stitched by wizards? Did pitcher Brian Daugherty's omnipresent three-foot rainstick wrapped in purple-and-gold tape and inscribed with STICKIN' IT TO OMAHA and WTLG (for "win the last game") double as a magic wand? Surely the Tigers' miraculous victory in Omaha, the most stunning in the 50-year history of the College World Series, was the work of some sorcerer. And indeed it was: an unassuming zoology major battling injuries and batting ninth, dressed in god-awful yellow and waving his own aluminum magic wand.

In the end—or rather, on the brink of the end—with two out in the bottom of the ninth, second baseman Warren Morris stepped to the plate with the Tigers trailing Miami 8–7 and a runner on. A 5'11", 170-pound junior, Morris had missed two-thirds of the season after undergoing surgery on a broken right wrist. He had just returned for the NCAA South II Regional, 29 days after his operation. All Morris hoped to do was make contact as he faced the first pitch from Hurricane relief ace Robbie Morrison. "I just tried to think of it as an intrasquad game and I had to get the runner in from third," Morris said.

To that point the Tigers' life in Omaha had been charmed. Clad in their lucky—if

Morris (right) couldn't have picked a better moment for his first homer of the year.

in Miami, who had scored 29 times in their previous two games. Before a record crowd of 23,905 the Hurricanes went up 7–3, but the Tigers scored two runs apiece in the seventh and eighth to draw even. The Hurricanes responded with a run off reliever Patrick Coogan in the top of the ninth. Senior designated hitter Brad Wilson led off the bottom of the inning with a double, but Morrison got right-fielder Justin Bowles to ground out and fanned catcher Tim Lanier. That brought up Morris. In the anxious LSU dugout, Coogan had heard someone say, "Warren hasn't gotten a home run all year."

Of all the talismans the Tigers had trotted out, none was as reliable as Morris: The 22 times he had been healthy enough to make the lineup in 1996, LSU had won. Bertman deemed the injuries that sidelined him "the saddest thing that's ever happened to LSU." With a clean rip at a Morrison hanging curveball, Morris delivered the saddest thing that has ever happened to Miami, a scorching shot down the rightfield line that landed three rows into the bleachers. The LSU bench erupted while the Miami players sank to their knees in tears. "I just hit it on the good part of the bat, and emotion took care of the rest of it," Morris would say. "I felt like it was happening to someone else."

In half a century no CWS champion had ever won with a home run on the game's last pitch. This one provided the Tigers with their third national title in six seasons. "This is the greatest championship I've ever been a part of, and that includes [the '88 Olympics in] Korea," said Bertman. "To end it that way, that was something you fantasize about." WTLG, indeed.

gaudy—gold unis, they had held off Wichita State 9–8 thanks to a pair of brilliant plays by sophomore centerfielder Mike Koerner. Not only did he make a running, one-handed catch with the bases loaded, he also convinced junior pitcher Kevin Shipp to go ahead and bring his spikes to Rosenblatt Stadium, just in case. Shipp, who was scheduled to make LSU's next start, wound up dousing the Shockers' comeback attempt with one inning of clutch relief.

To reach the title game the Tigers had to twice get past Florida, which had swept their four-game series in the regular season. LSU took the first game 9–4, then tripped the Gators 2–1 behind the seven-hit pitching of All-America southpaw Eddie Yarnall. In 19 previous wins over eight years at the CWS, LSU had never scored fewer than five runs. "This is not our best type of game," Bertman said. "Our best is 14–12. We don't steal or bunt or hit-and-run. We stand back."

LSU had a fellow practitioner of bashball

NCAA Team Champions

Fall 1995

Cross-Country

MEN

	Champion	Runner-Up
Division I:	Arkansas	Northern Arizona
Division II:	Western St	Central Missouri St
Division III:	Williams	N Central

WOMEN

	Champion	Runner-Up
Division I:	Providence	Colorado
Division II:	Adams St	Abilene Christian
Division III:	Cortland St	WI-Oshkosh

Field Hockey

WOMEN

	Champion	Runner-Up
Division I:	N Carolina	Maryland
Division II	Lock Haven	Bloomsburg
Division III:	Trenton St	Messiah College

Football

MEN

	Champion	Runner-Up
Division I-A:	Nebraska	Florida
Division I-AA:	Montana	Marshall
Division II:	N Alabama	Pittsburg St
Division III:	WI-La Crosse	Rowan

Soccer

MEN

	Champion	Runner-Up
Division I:	Wisconsin	Duke
Division II:	Southern Connecticut St	SC-Spartanburg
Division III:	Williams	Methodist

WOMEN

	Champion	Runner-Up
Division I:	Notre Dame	Portland
Division II:	Franklin Pierce	Barry
Division III:	UC-San Diego	Methodist (NC)

Volleyball

WOMEN

	Champion	Runner-Up
Division I:	Nebraska	Texas
Division II:	Barry	Northern Michigan
Division III:	Washington (MO)	Cal Lutheran

Water Polo

MEN

Champion	Runner-Up
UCLA	California

Winter 1995-1996

Basketball

MEN

	Champion	Runner-Up
Division I:	Kentucky	Syracuse
Division II:	Fort Hays St	Northern Kentucky
Division III:	Rowan	Hope

WOMEN

	Champion	Runner-Up
Division I:	Tennessee	Georgia
Division II:	N Dakota St	Shippensburg
Division III:	WI-Oshkosh	Mount Union

Fencing

Champion	Runner-Up
Penn St	Notre Dame

Gymnastics

MEN

Champion	Runner-Up
Ohio St	California

WOMEN

Alabama	UCLA

Ice Hockey

MEN

	Champion	Runner-Up
Division I:	Michigan	Colorado College
Division II:	AL-Huntsville	Bemidji St
Division III:	Middlebury	Rochester IT

Rifle

Champion	Runner-Up
West Virginia	Air Force

Skiing

Champion	Runner-Up
Utah	Denver

Swimming and Diving

MEN

	Champion	Runner-Up
Division I:	Texas	Auburn
Division II:	Oakland (MI)	Cal St-Bakersfield
Division III:	Kenyon	Denison

WOMEN

	Champion	Runner-Up
Division I:	Stanford	SMU
Division II:	Air Force	Oakland (MI)
Division III:	Kenyon	UC-San Diego

Wrestling

MEN

	Champion	Runner-Up
Division I:	Iowa	Iowa St
Division II:	Pittsburgh-Johnstown	Central Oklahoma
Division III:	Wartburg	Augsburg

NCAA Team Champions (Cont.)

Indoor Track

MEN

	Champion	Runner-Up
Division I:	George Mason	Nebraska
Division II:	Abilene Christian	St Augustine's
Division III:	Lincoln (PA)	Mount Union

WOMEN

	Champion	Runner-Up
Division I:	Louisiana St	Georgia
Division II:	Abilene Christian	St Augustine's
Division III:	WI-Oshkosh	Lincoln (PA)

Spring 1996

Baseball

	Champion	Runner-Up
Division I:	Louisiana St	Miami (FL)
Division II:	Kennesaw St	St Joseph's (IN)
Division III:	William Paterson	Cal Lutheran

Golf

MEN

	Champion	Runner-Up
Division I:	Arizona St	UNLV
Division II:	Florida Southern	SC-Aiken
Division III:	Methodist (NC)	Skidmore

WOMEN

	Champion	Runner-Up
Division I:	Arizona	San Jose St
Divisions II and III:	Methodist (NC)	Rollins

Lacrosse

MEN

	Champion	Runner-Up
Division I:	Princeton	Virginia
Division II:	LIU-C.W. Post	Adelphi
Division III:	Nazareth	Washington (MD)

WOMEN

	Champion	Runner-Up
National Collegiate:	Maryland	Virginia
Division III:	Trenton St	Middlebury

Softball

	Champion	Runner-Up
Division I:	Arizona	Washington
Division II:	Kennesaw St	NE-Omaha
Division III:	Trenton St	Chapman

Tennis

MEN

	Champion	Runner-Up
Division I:	Stanford	UCLA
Division II:	Lander (SC)	Rollins
Division III:	UC-Santa Cruz	Emory

WOMEN

	Champion	Runner-Up
Division I:	Florida	Stanford
Division II:	Armstrong St	Abilene Christian
Division III:	Emory	Washington & Lee

Spring 1996 (Cont.)
Outdoor Track

MEN

	Champion	Runner-Up
Division I:	Arkansas	George Mason
Division II:	Abilene Christian	St Augustine's
Division III:	Lincoln (PA)	Williams

WOMEN

	Champion	Runner-Up
Division I:	Louisiana St	Texas
Division II:	Abilene Christian	St Augustine's
Division III:	WI-Oshkosh	Lincoln (PA)

Volleyball

MEN

Champion	Runner-Up
UCLA	Hawaii

NCAA Division I Individual Champions

Fall 1995

Cross-Country

MEN

Champion	Runner-Up
Godfrey Siamusiye, Arkansas	Mark Carroll, Providence

WOMEN

Champion	Runner-Up
Kathy Butler, Wisconsin	Amy Skieresz, Arizona

Winter 1995-1996

Fencing

MEN

	Champion	Runner-Up
Sabre	Maxim Pekarev, Princeton	Serge Lilov, Penn St
Foil	Thorstein Becker, Wayne St (MI)	Greg Chang, Harvard
Épée	Jeremy Kahn, Duke	George Hentea, St John's (NY)

WOMEN

	Champion	Runner-Up
Foil	Olga Kalinovskaya, Penn St	Sara Walsh, Notre Dame
Épée	Nicole Dygert, St John's (NY)	Lauren O'Brien, Stanford

Gymnastics

MEN

	Champion	Runner-Up
All-around	Blaine Wilson, Ohio St	Keith Wiley, Stanford
Vault	Jay Thornton, Iowa	Ian Bachrach, Stanford
Parallel bars	Jamie Ellis, Stanford	Jay Thornton, Iowa
	Blaine Wilson, Ohio St	
Horizontal bar	Carl Imhauser, Temple	Ian Bachrach, Stanford
		David Kruse, California
Floor exercise	Ian Bachrach, Stanford	Jay Thornton, Iowa
Pommel horse	Drew Durbin, Ohio St	Kendall Schiess, New Mexico
Rings	Scott McCall, William & Mary	Ted Harris, Nebraska
	Blaine Wilson, Ohio St	

Gymnastics *(Cont.)*

WOMEN

	Champion	Runner-Up
All-around	Meredith Willard, Alabama	Kristen Guise, Florida
Balance beam	Summer Reid, Utah	Karin Lichey, Georgia
		Lori Strong, Georgia
		Stella Umeh, UCLA
Uneven bars	Stephanie Woods, Alabama	Jenni Beathard, Georgia
		Heather Bennett, Oregon St
Floor exercise	Heidi Hornbeek, Arizona	Danielle Adams, Alabama
	Kim Kelly, Alabama	
Vault	Leah Brown, Georgia	Jenny Hansen, Kentucky

Skiing

MEN

	Champion	Runner-Up
Slalom	Mattias Erlandsson, New Mexico	Jimmy Renstroem, New Mexico
Giant slalom	Andrew Hare, Utah	Alain Britt-Cote, Utah
10-kilometer freestyle	Thorodd Bakken, Vermont	Tor Arne Haugen, Utah
20-kilometer classical	Geir Skari, Denver	Vidar Lofshus, Denver

WOMEN

	Champion	Runner-Up
Slalom	Roberta Pergher, Denver	Christl Hager, Utah
Giant slalom	Jennifer Collins, Dartmouth	Caroline Gedde-Dahl, Colorado
5-kilometer freestyle	Lisbeth Johnson, Denver	Cecilie Risvoll, Vermont
10-kilometer classical	Lisbeth Johnson, Denver	Heidi Selenes, Utah

Wrestling

	Champion	Runner-Up
118 lb	Sheldon Thomas, Clarion	Jason Nurre, Iowa St
126 lb	Sanshiro Abe, Penn St	Dwight Hinson, Iowa St
134 lb	Cary Kolat, Lock Haven	Steve St John, Arizona St
142 lb	Bill Zadick, Iowa	John Hughes, Penn St
150 lb	Chris Bono, Iowa St	Charlie Becks, Ohio St
158 lb	Joe Williams, Iowa	Ernest Benion, Illinois
167 lb	Daryl Weber, Iowa	Mark Branch, Oklahoma St
177 lb	Les Gutches, Oregon St	Reese Andy, Wyoming
190 lb	John Kading, Oklahoma	Paschal Duru, Cal St-Bakersfield
Heavyweight	Jeff Walter, Wisconsin	Justin Harty, N Carolina

Swimming and Diving

MEN

	Champion	Time	Runner-Up	Time
50-yard freestyle	Francisco Sanchez, Arizona St	19.35	Ricky Busquets, Tennessee	19.45
100-yard freestyle	Ricky Busquets, Tennessee	42.64	Francisco Sanchez, Arizona St	42.89
200-yard freestyle	Bela Szabados, Florida Atlantic	1:34.33	John Piersma, Michigan	1:34.70
500-yard freestyle	Tom Dolan, Michigan	4:12.77	John Piersma, Michigan	4:14.55
1650-yard freestyle	Tom Dolan, Michigan	14:38.37	Kevin Radvany, Stanford	14:53.73
100-yard backstroke	Ryan Berube, SMU	46.15	Neil Walker, Texas	46.60
200-yard backstroke	Ryan Berube, SMU	1:41.23	Brad Bridgewater, Southern Cal	1:41.88
100-yard breaststroke	Jeremy Linn, Tennessee	53.04	Matthew Buck, Georgia	53.47
200-yard breaststroke	Matthew Buck, Georgia	1:56.62	Jeremy Linn, Tennessee	1:56.78
100-yard butterfly	Martin Pepper, Arizona	46.74	Jason Lancaster, Michigan	47.01
200-yard butterfly	Ugur Taner, California	1:43.22	Tom Malchow, Michigan	1:44.64
200-yard IM	Ryan Berube, SMU	1:44.85	Scott Tucker, Auburn	1:45.61
400-yard IM	Tom Dolan, Michigan	3:41.44	Matt Hooper, Texas	3:45.50

	Champion	Pts	Runner-Up	Pts
1-meter diving†	Pat Bogart, Minnesota	564.90	Evan Stewart, Tennessee	556.50
3-meter diving†	Chris Mantilla, Miami (FL)	648.00	Bryan Gillooly, Miami (FL)	644.35
Platform†	Bryan Gillooly, Miami (FL)	789.75	Tyce Routson, Miami (FL)	783.25

†Scoring based on 22 dives.

NCAA Division I Individual Champions *(Cont.)*

Swimming and Diving *(Cont.)*

WOMEN

	Champion	Time	Runner-Up	Time
50-yard freestyle	Nicole DeMan, Tennessee	22.59	Jessica Tong, Stanford	22.81
100-yard freestyle	Claudia Franco, Stanford	49.04	Martina Moravcova, SMU	49.23
200-yard freestyle	Martina Moravcova, SMU	1:44.64	Lindsay Benko, Southern Cal	1:46.17
500-yard freestyle	Lindsay Benko, Southern Cal	4:42.46	Annette Salmeen, UCLA	4:42.95
1650-yard freestyle	Mimosa McNerney, Florida	16:06.23	Kerri Hale, Michigan	16:12.95
100-yard backstroke	Jessica Tong, Stanford	54.40	Maureen McLaren, Stanford	54.66
200-yard backstroke	Lindsay Benko, Southern Cal	1:55.78	Lia Oberstar, SMU	1:56.00
100-yard breaststroke	Penny Heyns, Nebraska	1:00.27	Katie McClelland, SMU	1:01.30
200-yard breaststroke	Kristine Quance, Southern Cal	2:09.57	Penny Heyns, Nebraska	2:09.71
100-yard butterfly	Lisa Coole, Georgia	54.21	Tanya Schuh, Minnesota	54.37
200-yard butterfly	Annette Salmeen, UCLA	1:55.84	Tori DeSilvia, Tennessee	1:57.90
200-yard IM	Kristine Quance, Southern Cal	1:57.58	Martina Moravcova, SMU	1:58.80
400-yard IM	Kristine Quance, Southern Cal	4:06.60	Allison Wagner, Florida	4:11.69

	Champion	Pts	Runner-Up	Pts
1-meter diving#	Kimiko Hirai, Indiana	443.35	Elizabeth Leake, Kentucky	435.75
3-meter diving†	Michelle Rojohn, Kansas	567.95	Becky Ruehl, Cincinnati	552.65
Platform†	Becky Ruehl, Cincinnati	636.05	Megan Gardner, Stanford	612.50

#Scoring based on 20 dives. †Scoring based on 22 dives.

Indoor Track

MEN

	Champion	Mark	Runner-Up	Mark
55-meter dash	Tim Harden, Kentucky	6.06	Obadele Thompson, UTEP	6.08
55-meter hurdles	Darius Pemberton, Houston	7.14	Jeff Jackson, Baylor	7.18
200-meter dash	Obadele Thompson, UTEP	20.36*	Rohsaan Griffin, Louisiana St	20.69
400-meter dash	Greg Haughton, George Mason	45.87	Marlon Ramsey, Baylor	45.96
800-meter run	Einars Tupuritis, Wichita St	1:45.80*	Alex Morgan, George Mason	1:46.70
Mile run	Julius Achon, George Mason	4:02.83	Jonah Kiptarus, Nebraska	4:03.59
3,000-meter run	Ryan Wilson, Arkansas	7:51.66	Robert Gary, Ohio St	7:52.63
5,000-meter run	Jason Casiano, Wisconsin	13:50.08	Godfrey Siamusiye, Arkansas	13:50.49
High jump	Michael Roberson, McNeese St	7 ft 5 in	Itai Margalit, Kansas St	7 ft 3¾ in
Long jump	Andrew Owusu, Alabama	25 ft 11 in	Mike Alridge, Louisiana St	25 ft 10 in
Triple jump	Robert Howard, Arkansas	54 ft 10¾ in	Ndabe Mdhlongwa, SW La	54 ft 5¼ in
Shot put	Jonathan Ogden, UCLA	63 ft 8¾ in	Mark Parlin, UCLA	61 ft 9¾ in
Pole vault	Lawrence Johnson, Tennessee	18 ft 6½ in	Daren McDonough, Illinois	18 ft 2½ in
35-pound wt throw	Ryan Butler, Wyoming	71 ft 1½ in	Mark McGehearty, BC	68 ft 9 in

WOMEN

	Champion	Mark	Runner-Up	Mark
55-meter dash	D'Andre Hill, Louisiana St	6.69	Debbie Ferguson, Georgia	6.77
55-meter hurdles	Kim Carson, Louisiana St	7.44	Tonya Williams, Illinois	7.62
200-meter dash	Debbie Ferguson, Georgia	23.17	D'Andre Hill, Louisiana St	23.24
400-meter dash	Monique Hennagan, N Carolina	52.57	Ryan Tolbert, Vanderbilt	52.75
800-meter run	Kristi Kloster, Kansas	2:04.91	Dawn Williams, AR-Little Rock	2:04.91
Mile run	Joline Staeheli, Georgetown	4:36.96	Trine Pilskog, Arkansas	4:38.58
3,000-meter run	Melody Fairchild, Oregon	9:07.25	Milena Glusac, Oregon	9:13.31
5,000-meter run	Marie McMahon, Providence	15:42.71	Kathy Butler, Wisconsin	15:51.91
High jump	Najuma Fletcher, Pittsburgh	6 ft ¾ in	Corissa Yasen, Purdue	6 ft ¾ in
Long jump	Angee Henry, Nebraska	20 ft 11¼ in	Nicole Devonish, Texas	20 ft 10½ in
Triple jump	Nicola Martial, Nebraska	44 ft 8¼ in	Suzette Lee, Louisiana St	44 ft 8 in
Shot put	Valeyta Althouse, UCLA	57 ft 11 in	Teri Steer, SMU	56 ft 4½ in
20-pound wt throw	Dawn Ellerbe, S Carolina	67 ft 10¼ in	Lisa Misipeka, S Carolina	62 ft 3¼ in

*Meet record.

Rifle

	Champion	Pts	Runner-Up	Pts
Smallbore	Joe Johnson, Navy	1170	Trevor Gathman, W Virginia	1169
Air rifle	Trevor Gathman, W Virginia	394	Bobbie Breyen, Air Force	391

Spring 1996

Golf

MEN

Champion	Score	Runner-Up	Score
Tiger Woods, Stanford	285	Rory Sabbatini, Arizona	289

WOMEN

Champion	Score	Runner-Up	Score
Marisa Baena, Arizona	296	Kellee Booth, Arizona St	303

Outdoor Track

MEN

	Champion	Mark	Runner-Up	Mark
100-meter dash	Ato Bolden, UCLA	9.92*	Tim Harden, Kentucky	10.10
200-meter dash	Roshaan Griffin, Louisiana St	20.24	Gentry Bradley, UCLA	20.48
400-meter dash	Davian Clarke, Miami (FL)	45.29	Greg Haughton, George Mason	45.43
800-meter run	Einars Tupuritis, Wichita St	1:45.08	Marko Koers, Illinois	1:45.22
1,500-meter run	Marko Koers, Illinois	3:37.57	Jonah Kiptarus, Nebraska	3:38.08
3,000-met. steeple	Dmitry Drozdov, Iowa St	8:32.01	Pascal Dobert, Wisconsin	8:34.11
5,000-meter run	Alan Culpepper, Colorado	13:47.26	Godfrey Siamusiye, Arkansas	13:48.86
10,000-meter run	Godfrey Siamusiye, Arkansas	28:56.39	Jason Bunston, Arkansas	28:56.55
110-meter hurdles	Dominique Arnold, Washington St	13.46	Reggie Torian, Wisconsin	13.57
400-meter hurdles	Neil Gardner, Michigan	49.27	Ian Weakly, George Mason	49.68
High jump	Eric Bishop, N Carolina	7 ft 6 in	Matt Hemingway, Arkansas	7 ft 5 in
Pole vault	Lawrence Johnson, Tennessee	19 ft 1 in*	David Cox, Fresno St	18 ft 2½ in
Long jump	Richard Duncan, Texas	26 ft ½ in	Eric Bowers, Georgia Tech	25 ft 10¼ in
Triple jump	Robert Howard, Arkansas	56 ft 1¾ in	Ndabe Mdhlongwa, SW La.	55 ft 2¾ in
Shot put	Andy Bloom, Wake Forest	65 ft ½ in	Chima Ugwu, Arizona	63 ft 3¼ in
Discus throw	Andy Bloom, Wake Forest	211 ft 1 in	Alex Tammert, SMU	204 ft 2 in
Hammer throw	Balazs Kiss, Southern Cal	265 ft 3 in*	Bengt Johannson, Southern Cal	229 ft 1 in
Javelin throw	Pal Arne Fagernes, Arizona St	259 ft 8 in	Mats Nilsson, Alabama	251 ft 6 in
Decathlon	Victor Houston, Auburn	7766 pts	Ross Bomben, California	7752 pts

WOMEN

	Champion	Mark	Runner-Up	Mark
100-meter dash	D'Andre Hill, Louisiana St	11.03	Zundra Feagin, Louisiana St	11.20
200-meter dash	Zundra Feagin, Louisiana St	22.44	D'Andre Hill, Louisiana St	22.49
400-meter dash	Suziann Reid, Texas	52.16	Toya Brown, Texas	52.25
800-meter run	Monique Hennagan, N Carolina	2:03.27	Lorrieann Adams, Arizona St	2:03.82
1,500-meter run	Miesha Marzell, Georgetown	4:17.92	Kelly Smith, Colorado	4:18.77
3,000-meter run	Kathy Butler, Wisconsin	9:16.19	Emebet Shiferaw, Southern Cal	9:17.18
5,000-meter run	Jennifer Rhines, Villanova	16:05.85	Katie Swords, SMU	16:11.42
10,000-meter run	Katie Swords, SMU	32:56.63	Kate Landau, Georgetown	33:08.57
100-meter hurdles	Kim Carson, Louisiana St	12.82	Tonya Williams, Illinois	12.97
400-meter hurdles	Tonya Williams, Illinois	54.56*	Ryan Tolbert, Vanderbilt	54.91
High jump	Amy Acuff, UCLA	6 ft 4¼ in	Kajsa Bergqvist, SMU	6 ft 3¼ in
Long jump	Angee Henry, Nebraska	21 ft 11½ in	Nicole Devonish, Texas	21 ft 3¼ in
Triple jump	Suzette Lee, Louisiana	45 ft 1 in	Trecia Smith, Pittsburgh	44 ft 6¾ in
Shot put	Teri Steer, SMU	59 ft	Valeyta Althouse, UCLA	58 ft 8 in
Discus throw	Anna Soderberg, Northern AZ	195 ft 3 in	Suzy Powell, UCLA	193 ft 7 in
Hammer throw	Dawn Ellerbe, S Carolina	209 ft 2 in*	Lisa Misipeka, S Carolina	199 ft 11 in
Javelin throw	Windy Dean, SMU	186 ft 1 in	Tanya Simonsen, Minnesota	167 ft 7 in
Heptathlon	Corissa Yasen, Purdue	5765 pts	Nicole Haynes, Southern Cal	5613 pts

*Meet record. w=wind-aided.

Tennis

MEN

	Champion	Score	Runner-Up
Singles	Cecil Mamiit, Southern Cal	(6-2, 4-6, 6-3)	Fredrik Bergh, Fresno St
Doubles	Justin Gimelstob & Srdjan Muskatirovic, UCLA	(6-7 (3), 6-4, 6-4)	Ashley Fisher & Jason Weir-Smith, Texas Christian

WOMEN

	Champion	Score	Runner-Up
Singles	Jill Craybas, Florida	(5-7, 6-3, 6-3)	Kylie Hunt, Kansas
Doubles	Dawn Buth & Stephanie Nickitas, Florida	(6-1, 6-3)	Cristina Moros & Farley Taylor, Texas

FOR THE RECORD·Year by Year

CHAMPIONSHIP RESULTS

Baseball

DIVISION I

Year	Champion	Coach	Score	Runner-Up	Most Outstanding Player
1947	California*	Clint Evans	8-7	Yale	No award
1948	Southern Cal	Sam Barry	9-2	Yale	No award
1949	Texas*	Bibb Falk	10-3	Wake Forest	Charles Teague, Wake Forest, 2B
1950	Texas	Bibb Falk	3-0	Washington St	Ray VanCleef, Rutgers, CF
1951	Oklahoma*	Jack Baer	3-2	Tennessee	Sidney Hatfield, Tennessee, P-1B
1952	Holy Cross	Jack Barry	8-4	Missouri	James O'Neill, Holy Cross, P
1953	Michigan	Ray Fisher	7-5	Texas	J.L. Smith, Texas, P
1954	Missouri	John "Hi" Simmons	4-1	Rollins	Tom Yewcic, Michigan St, C
1955	Wake Forest	Taylor Sanford	7-6	Western Michigan	Tom Borland, Oklahoma St, P
1956	Minnesota	Dick Siebert	12-1	Arizona	Jerry Thomas, Minnesota, P
1957	California*	George Wolfman	1-0	Penn St	Cal Emery, Penn St, P-1B
1958	Southern Cal	Rod Dedeaux	8-7†	Missouri	Bill Thom, Southern Cal, P
1959	Oklahoma St	Toby Greene	5-3	Arizona	Jim Dobson, Oklahoma St, 3B
1960	Minnesota	Dick Siebert	2-1‡	Southern Cal	John Erickson, Minnesota, 2B
1961	Southern Cal*	Rod Dedeaux	1-0	Oklahoma St	Littleton Fowler, Oklahoma St, P
1962	Michigan	Don Lund	5-4	Santa Clara	Bob Garibaldi, Santa Clara, P
1963	Southern Cal	Rod Dedeaux	5-2	Arizona	Bud Hollowell, Southern Cal, C
1964	Minnesota	Dick Siebert	5-1	Missouri	Joe Ferris, Maine, P
1965	Arizona St	Bobby Winkles	2-1#	Ohio St	Sal Bando, Arizona St, 3B
1966	Ohio St	Marty Karow	8-2	Oklahoma St	Steve Arlin, Ohio St, P
1967	Arizona St	Bobby Winkles	11-2	Houston	Ron Davini, Arizona St, C
1968	Southern Cal*	Rod Dedeaux	4-3	Southern Illinois	Bill Seinsoth, Southern Cal, 1B
1969	Arizona St	Bobby Winkles	10-1	Tulsa	John Dolinsek, Arizona St, LF
1970	Southern Cal	Rod Dedeaux	2-1	Florida St	Gene Ammann, Florida St, P
1971	Southern Cal	Rod Dedeaux	7-2	Southern Illinois	Jerry Tabb, Tulsa, 1B
1972	Southern Cal	Rod Dedeaux	1-0	Arizona St	Russ McQueen, Southern Cal, P
1973	Southern Cal*	Rod Dedeaux	4-3	Arizona St	Dave Winfield, Minnesota, P-OF
1974	Southern Cal	Rod Dedeaux	7-3	Miami (FL)	George Milke, Southern Cal, P
1975	Texas	Cliff Gustafson	5-1	S Carolina	Mickey Reichenbach, Texas, 1B
1976	Arizona	Jerry Kindall	7-1	Eastern Michigan	Steve Powers, Arizona, P-DH
1977	Arizona St	Jim Brock	2-1	S Carolina	Bob Horner, Arizona St, 3B
1978	Southern Cal*	Rod Dedeaux	10-3	Arizona St	Rod Boxberger, Southern Cal, P
1979	Cal St-Fullerton	Augie Garrido	2-1	Arkansas	Tony Hudson, Cal St-Fullerton, P
1980	Arizona	Jerry Kindall	5-3	Hawaii	Terry Francona, Arizona, LF
1981	Arizona St	Jim Brock	7-4	Oklahoma St	Stan Holmes, Arizona St, LF
1982	Miami (FL)*	Ron Fraser	9-3	Wichita St	Dan Smith, Miami (FL), P
1983	Texas*	Cliff Gustafson	4-3	Alabama	Calvin Schiraldi, Texas, P
1984	Cal St-Fullerton	Augie Garrido	3-1	Texas	John Fishel, Cal St-Fullerton, LF
1985	Miami (FL)	Ron Fraser	10-6	Texas	Greg Ellena, Miami (FL), DH
1986	Arizona	Jerry Kindall	10-2	Florida St	Mike Senne, Arizona, LF
1987	Stanford	Mark Marquess	9-5	Oklahoma St	Paul Carey, Stanford, RF
1988	Stanford	Mark Marquess	9-4	Arizona St	Lee Plemel, Stanford, P
1989	Wichita St	Gene Stephenson	5-3	Texas	Greg Brummett, Wichita St, P
1990	Georgia	Steve Webber	2-1	Oklahoma St	Mike Rebhan, Georgia, P
1991	Louisiana St	Skip Bertman	6-3	Wichita St	Gary Hymel, Louisiana St, C
1992	Pepperdine	Andy Lopez	3-2	Cal St-Fullerton	Phil Nevin, Cal St-Fullerton, 3B
1993	Louisiana St	Skip Bertman	8-0	Wichita St	Todd Walker, Louisiana St, 2B
1994	Oklahoma	Larry Cochell	13-5	Georgia Tech	Chip Glass, Oklahoma, CF
1995	Cal St-Fullerton*	Augie Garrido	11-5	Southern Cal	Mark Kotsay, Cal St-Fullerton, CF-P
1996	Louisiana St*	Skip Bertman	9-8	Miami (FL)	Pat Burrell, Miami (FL), 3B

*Undefeated teams in College World Series play. †12 innings. ‡10 innings. #15 innings.

DIVISION II

Year	Champion	Year	Champion	Year	Champion
1968	Chapman*	1974	UC-Irvine	1980	Cal Poly-Pomona*
1969	Illinois St*	1975	Florida Southern	1981	Florida Southern*
1970	Cal St-Northridge	1976	Cal Poly-Pomona	1982	UC-Riverside*
1971	Florida Southern	1977	UC-Riverside	1983	Cal Poly-Pomona*
1972	Florida Southern	1978	Florida Southern	1984	Cal St-Northridge
1973	UC-Irvine*	1979	Valdosta St	1985	Florida Southern*

Baseball *(Cont.)*

DIVISION II *(Cont.)*

Year	Champion	Year	Champion	Year	Champion
1986	.........Troy St	1990	.........Jacksonville St	1994	.........Central Missouri St
1987	.........Troy St*	1991	.........Jacksonville St	1995	.........Florida Southern*
1988	.........Florida Southern*	1992	.........Tampa*	1996	.........Kennesaw St*
1989	.........Cal Poly-SLO	1993	.........Tampa		

DIVISION III

Year	Champion	Year	Champion	Year	Champion
1976	.........Cal St-Stanislaus	1983	.........Marietta	1990	.........Eastern Connecticut St
1977	.........Cal St-Stanislaus	1984	.........Ramapo	1991	.........Southern Maine
1978	.........Glassboro St	1985	.........WI-Oshkosh	1992	.........William Paterson
1979	.........Glassboro St	1986	.........Marietta	1993	.........Montclair St
1980	.........Ithaca	1987	.........Montclair St	1994	.........WI-Oshkosh
1981	.........Marietta	1988	.........Ithaca	1995	.........La Verne
1982	.........Eastern Connecticut St	1989	.........NC Wesleyan	1996	.........William Paterson

*Undefeated teams in final series.

Cross-Country

Men

DIVISION I

Year	Champion	Coach	Pts	Runner-Up	Pts	Individual Champion	Time
1938	...Indiana	Earle Hayes	51	Notre Dame	61	Greg Rice, Notre Dame	20:12.9
1939	...Michigan St	Lauren Brown	54	Wisconsin	57	Walter Mehl, Wisconsin	20:30.9
1940	...Indiana	Earle Hayes	65	Eastern Michigan	68	Gilbert Dodds, Ashland	20:30.2
1941	...Rhode Island	Fred Tootell	83	Penn St	110	Fred Wilt, Indiana	20:30.1
1942	...Indiana	Earle Hayes	57			Oliver Hunter, Notre Dame	20:18.0
	Penn St	Charles Werner	57				
1943	...No meet						
1944	...Drake	Bill Easton	25	Notre Dame	64	Fred Feiler, Drake	21:04.2
1945	...Drake	Bill Easton	50	Notre Dame	65	Fred Feiler, Drake	21:14.2
1946	...Drake	Bill Easton	42	NYU	98	Quentin Brelsford, Ohio Wesleyan	20:22.9
1947	...Penn St	Charles Werner	60	Syracuse	72	Jack Milne, N Carolina	20:41.1
1948	...Michigan St	Karl Schlademan	41	Wisconsin	69	Robert Black, Rhode Island	19:52.3
1949	...Michigan St	Karl Schlademan	59	Syracuse	81	Robert Black, Rhode Island	20:25.7
1950	...Penn St	Charles Werner	53	Michigan St	55	Herb Semper Jr, Kansas	20:31.7
1951	...Syracuse	Robert Grieve	80	Kansas	118	Herb Semper Jr, Kansas	20:09.5
1952	...Michigan St	Karl Schlademan	65	Indiana	68	Charles Capozzoli, Georgetown	19:36.7
1953	...Kansas	Bill Easton	70	Indiana	82	Wes Santee, Kansas	19:43.5
1954	...Oklahoma St	Ralph Higgins	61	Syracuse	118	Allen Frame, Kansas	19:54.2
1955	...Michigan St	Karl Schlademan	46	Kansas	68	Charles Jones, Iowa	19:57.4
1956	...Michigan St	Karl Schlademan	28	Kansas	88	Walter McNew, Texas	19:55.7
1957	...Notre Dame	Alex Wilson	121	Michigan St	127	Max Truex, Southern Cal	19:12.3
1958	...Michigan St	Francis Dittrich	79	Western Michigan	104	Crawford Kennedy, Michigan State	20:07.1
1959	...Michigan St	Francis Dittrich	44	Houston	120	Al Lawrence, Houston	20:35.7
1960	...Houston	John Morriss	54	Michigan St	80	Al Lawrence, Houston	19:28.2
1961	...Oregon St	Sam Bell	68	San Jose St	82	Dale Story, Oregon St	19:46.6
1962	...San Jose St	Dean Miller	58	Villanova	69	Tom O'Hara, Loyola (IL)	19:20.3
1963	...San Jose St	Dean Miller	53	Oregon	68	Victor Zwolak, Villanova	19:35.0
1964	...W Michigan	George Dales	86	Oregon	116	Elmore Banton, Ohio	20:07.5
1965	...W Michigan	George Dales	81	Northwestern	114	John Lawson, Kansas	29:24.0
1966	...Villanova	James Elliott	79	Kansas St	155	Gerry Lindgren, Washington St	29:01.4
1967	...Villanova	James Elliott	91	Air Force	96	Gerry Lindgren, Washington St	30:45.6
1968	...Villanova	James Elliott	78	Stanford	100	Michael Ryan, Air Force	29:16.8
1969	...UTEP	Wayne Vandenburg	74	Villanova	88	Gerry Lindgren, Washington St	28:59.2
1970	...Villanova	James Elliott	85	Oregon	86	Steve Prefontaine, Oregon	28:00.2
1971	...Oregon	Bill Dellinger	83	Washington St	122	Steve Prefontaine, Oregon	29:14.0

Men (Cont.)

DIVISION I (Cont.)

Year	Champion	Coach	Pts	Runner-Up	Pts	Individual Champion	Time
1977	Oregon	Bill Dellinger	100	UTEP	105	Henry Rono, Washington St	28:33.5
1972	Tennessee	Stan Huntsman	134	E Tennessee St	148	Neil Cusack, E Tennessee St	28:23.0
1973	Oregon	Bill Dellinger	89	UTEP	157	Steve Prefontaine, Oregon	28:14.0
1974	Oregon	Bill Dellinger	77	Western Kentucky	110	Nick Rose, W Kentucky	29:22.0
1975	UTEP	Ted Banks	88	Washington St	92	Craig Virgin, Illinois	28:23.3
1976	UTEP	Ted Banks	62	Oregon	117	Henry Rono, Washington St	28:06.6
1977	Oregon	Bill Dellinger	100	UTEP	105	Henry Rono, Washington St	28:33.5
1978	UTEP	Ted Banks	56	Oregon	72	Alberto Salazar, Oregon	29:29.7
1979	UTEP	Ted Banks	86	Oregon	93	Henry Rono, Washington St	28:19.6
1980	UTEP	Ted Banks	58	Arkansas	152	Suleiman Nyambui, UTEP	29:04.0
1981	UTEP	Ted Banks	17	Providence	109	Mathews Motshwarateu, UTEP	28:45.6
1982	Wisconsin	Dan McClimon	59	Providence	138	Mark Scrutton, Colorado	30:12.6
1983	Vacated			Wisconsin	164	Zakarie Barie, UTEP	29:20.0
1984	Arkansas	John McDonnell	101	Arizona	111	Ed Eyestone, Brigham Young	29:28.8
1985	Wisconsin	Martin Smith	67	Arkansas	104	Timothy Hacker, Wisconsin	29:17.88
1986	Arkansas	John McDonnell	69	Dartmouth	141	Aaron Ramirez, Arizona	30:27.53
1987	Arkansas	John McDonnell	87	Dartmouth	119	Joe Falcon, Arkansas	29:14.97
1988	Wisconsin	Martin Smith	105	Northern Arizona	160	Robert Kennedy, Indiana	29:20.0
1989	Iowa St	Bill Bergan	54	Oregon	72	John Nuttall, Iowa St	29:30.55
1990	Arkansas	John McDonnell	68	Iowa St	96	Jonah Koech, Iowa St	29:05.0
1991	Arkansas	John McDonnell	52	Iowa St	114	Sean Dollman, Western Ky	30:17.1
1992	Arkansas	John McDonnell	46	Wisconsin	87	Bob Kennedy, Indiana	30:15.3
1993	Arkansas	John McDonnell	31	Brigham Young	153	Josephat Kapkory, Wash St	29:32.4
1994	Iowa St	Bill Bergan	65	Colorado	88	Martin Keino, Arizona	30:08.7
1995	Arkansas	John McDonnell	100	Northern Arizona	142	Godfrey Siamusiye, Arkansas	30:09

DIVISION II

Year	Champion	Year	Champion	Year	Champion
1958	Northern Illinois	1971	Cal St-Fullerton	1984	SE Missouri St
1959	S Dakota St	1972	N Dakota St	1985	S Dakota St
1960	Central St (OH)	1973	S Dakota St	1986	Edinboro
1961	Southern Illinois	1974	SW Missouri St	1987	Edinboro
1962	Central St (OH)	1975	UC-Irvine	1988	Edinboro/ Mankato St
1963	Emporia St	1976	UC-Irvine	1989	S Dakota St
1964	Kentucky St	1977	Eastern Illinois	1990	Edinboro
1965	San Diego St	1978	Cal Poly-SLO	1991	MA-Lowell
1966	San Diego St	1979	Cal Poly-SLO	1992	Adams St
1967	San Diego St	1980	Humboldt St	1993	Adams St
1968	Eastern Illinois	1981	Millersville	1994	Adams St
1969	Eastern Illinois	1982	Eastern Washington	1995	Western St
1970	Eastern Michigan	1983	Cal Poly-Pomona		

DIVISION III

Year	Champion	Year	Champion	Year	Champion
1973	Ashland	1981	North Central	1989	WI-Oshkosh
1974	Mount Union	1982	North Central	1990	WI-Oshkosh
1975	North Central	1983	Brandeis	1991	Rochester
1976	North Central	1984	St Thomas (MN)	1992	North Central
1977	Occidental	1985	Luther	1993	North Central
1978	North Central	1986	St Thomas (MN)	1994	Williams
1979	North Central	1987	North Central	1995	Williams
1980	Carleton	1988	WI-Oshkosh		

Women

DIVISION I

Year	Champion	Coach	Pts	Runner-Up	Pts	Individual Champion	Time
1981	Virginia	John Vasvary	36	Oregon	83	Betty Springs, N Carolina St	16:19.0
1982	Virginia	Martin Smith	48	Stanford	91	Lesley Welch, Virginia	16:39.7
1983	Oregon	Tom Heinonen	95	Stanford	98	Betty Springs, N Carolina St	16:30.7
1984	Wisconsin	Peter Tegen	63	Stanford	89	Cathy Branta, Wisconsin	16:15.6
1985	Wisconsin	Peter Tegen	58	Iowa St	98	Suzie Tuffey, N Carolina St	16:22.5
1986	Texas	Terry Crawford	62	Wisconsin	64	Angela Chalmers, N Arizona	16:55.49
1987	Oregon	Tom Heinonen	97	N Carolina St	99	Kimberly Betz, Indiana	16:10.85

Women *(Cont.)*

DIVISION I *(Cont.)*

Year	Champion	Coach	Pts	Runner-Up	Pts	Individual Champion	Time
1988	Kentucky	Don Weber	75	Oregon	128	Michelle Dekkers, Indiana	16:30.0
1989	Villanova	Marty Stern	99	Kentucky	168	Vicki Huber, Villanova	15:59.86
1990	Villanova	Marty Stern	82	Providence	172	Sonia O'Sullivan, Villanova	16:06.0
1991	Villanova	Marty Stern	85	Arkansas	168	Sonia O'Sullivan, Villanova	16:30.3
1992	Villanova	Marty Stern	123	Arkansas	130	Carole Zajac, Villanova	17:01.9
1993	Villanova	Marty Stern	66	Arkansas	71	Carole Zajac, Villanova	16:40.3
1994	Villanova	John Marshall	75	Michigan	108	Jennifer Rhines, Villanova	16:31.2
1995	Providence	Ray Treacy	88	Colorado	123	Kathy Butler, Wisconsin	16:51

DIVISION II

Year	Champion	Year	Champion	Year	Champion
1981	S Dakota St	1986	Cal Poly-SLO	1991	Cal Poly-SLO
1982	Cal Poly-SLO	1987	Cal Poly-SLO	1992	Adams St
1983	Cal Poly-SLO	1988	Cal Poly-SLO	1993	Adams St
1984	Cal Poly-SLO	1989	Cal Poly-SLO	1994	Adams St
1985	Cal Poly-SLO	1990	Cal Poly-SLO	1995	Adams St

DIVISION III

Year	Champion	Year	Champion	Year	Champion
1981	Central (IA)	1987	St Thomas (MN)	1992	Cortland St
1982	St Thomas (MN)		WI-Oshkosh	1993	Cortland St
1983	WI-La Crosse	1988	WI-Oshkosh	1994	Cortland St
1984	St Thomas (MN)	1989	Cortland St	1995	Cortland St
1985	Franklin & Marshall	1990	Cortland St		
1986	St Thomas (MN)	1991	WI-Oshkosh		

Fencing

Men's and Women's Combined

TEAM CHAMPIONS

Year	Champion	Coach	Pts	Runner-Up	Pts
1990	Penn St	Emmanuil Kaidanov	36	Columbia-Barnard	35
1991	Penn St	Emmanuil Kaidanov	4700	Columbia-Barnard	4200
1992	Columbia-Barnard	George Kolombatovich Aladar Kogler	4150	Penn St	3646
1993	Columbia-Barnard	George Kolumbatovich Aladar Kogler	4525	Penn St	4500
1994	Notre Dame	Michael DeCicco	4350	Penn St	4075
1995	Penn St	Emmanuil Kaidanov	440	St John's (NY)	413
1996	Penn St	Emmanuil Kaidanov	1500	Notre Dame	1190

Men

TEAM CHAMPIONS

Year	Champion	Coach	Pts	Runner-Up	Pts
1941	Northwestern	Henry Zettleman	28½	Illinois	27
1942	Ohio St	Frank Riebel	34	St John's (NY)	33½
1943-1946	No tournament				
1947	NYU	Martinez Castello	72	Chicago	50½
1948	CCNY	James Montague	30	Navy	28
1949	Army	Servando Velarde	63		
	Rutgers	Donald Cetrulo	63		
1950	Navy	Joseph Fiems	67½	NYU	66½
				Rutgers	66½
1951	Columbia	Servando Velarde	69	Pennsylvania	64
1952	Columbia	Servando Velarde	71	NYU	69
1953	Pennsylvania	Lajos Csiszar	94	Navy	86
1954	Columbia	Irving DeKoff	61		
	NYU	Hugo Castello	61		
1955	Columbia	Irving DeKoff	62	Cornell	57
1956	Illinois	Maxwell Garret	90	Columbia	88
1957	NYU	Hugo Castello	65	Columbia	64
1958	Illinois	Maxwell Garret	47	Columbia	43

Men (Cont.)

TEAM CHAMPIONS (Cont.)

Year	Champion	Coach	Pts	Runner-Up	Pts
1959	Navy	Andre Deladrier	72	NYU	65
1960	NYU	Hugo Castello	65	Navy	57
1961	NYU	Hugo Castello	79	Princeton	68
1962	Navy	Andre Deladrier	76	NYU	74
1963	Columbia	Irving DeKoff	55	Navy	50
1964	Princeton	Stan Sieja	81	NYU	79
1965	Columbia	Irving DeKoff	76	NYU	74
1966	NYU	Hugo Castello	5-0	Army	5-2
1967	NYU	Hugo Castello	72	Pennsylvania	64
1968	Columbia	Louis Bankuti	92	NYU	87
1969	Pennsylvania	Lajos Csiszar	54	Harvard	43
1970	NYU	Hugo Castello	71	Columbia	63
1971	NYU	Hugo Castello	68		
	Columbia	Louis Bankuti	68		
1972	Detroit	Richard Perry	73	NYU	70
1973	NYU	Hugo Castello	76	Pennsylvania	71
1974	NYU	Hugo Castello	92	Wayne St (MI)	87
1975	Wayne St (MI)	Istvan Danosi	89	Cornell	83
1976	NYU	Herbert Cohen	79	Wayne St (MI)	77
1977	Notre Dame	Michael DeCicco	114*	NYU	114
1978	Notre Dame	Michael DeCicco	121	Pennsylvania	110
1979	Wayne St (MI)	Istvan Danosi	119	Notre Dame	108
1980	Wayne St (MI)	Istvan Danosi	111	Pennsylvania	106
				MIT	106
1981	Pennsylvania	Dave Micahnik	113	Wayne St (MI)	111
1982	Wayne St (MI)	Istvan Danosi	85	Clemson	77
1983	Wayne St (MI)	Aladar Kogler	86	Notre Dame	80
1984	Wayne St (MI)	Gil Pezza	69	Penn St	50
1985	Wayne St (MI)	Gil Pezza	141	Notre Dame	140
1986	Notre Dame	Michael DeCicco	151	Columbia	141
1987	Columbia	George Kolombatovich	86	Pennsylvania	78
1988	Columbia	George Kolombatovich	90	Notre Dame	83
		Aladar Kogler			
1989	Columbia	George Kolombatovich	88	Penn St	85
		Aladar Kogler			

*Tie broken by a fence-off. Note: Beginning in 1990, men's and women's combined teams competed for the national championship.

INDIVIDUAL CHAMPIONS

	Foil	Sabre	Épée
1941	Edward McNamara, Northwestern	William Meyer, Dartmouth	G.I I. Boland, Illinois
1942	Byron Kreiger, Wayne St (MI)	Andre Deladrier, St. John's (NY)	Ben Burtt, Ohio St
1943-46	No Tournament		
1947	Abraham Balk, NYU	Oscar Parsons, Temple	Abraham Balk, NYU
1948	Albert Axelrod, CCNY	James Day, Navy	William Bryan, Navy
1949	Ralph Tedesco, Rutgers	Alex Treves, Rutgers	Richard C. Bowman, Army
1950	Robert Nielsen, Columbia	Alex Treves, Rutgers	Thomas Stuart, Navy
1951	Robert Nielsen, Columbia	Chamberless Johnston, Princeton	Daniel Chafetz, Columbia
1952	Harold Goldsmith, CCNY	Frank Zimolzak, Navy	James Wallner, NYU
1953	Ed Nober, Brooklyn	Robert Parmacek, Pennsylvania	Jack Tori, Pennsylvania
1954	Robert Goldman, Pennsylvania	Steve Sobel, Columbia	Henry Kolowrat, Princeton
1955	Herman Velasco, Illinois	Barry Pariser, Columbia	Donald Tadrawski, Notre Dame
1956	Ralph DeMarco, Columbia	Gerald Kaufman, Columbia	Kinmont Hoitsma, Princeton
1957	Bruce Davis, Wayne St (MI)	Bernie Balaban, NYU	James Margolis, Columbia
1958	Bruce Davis, Wayne St (MI)	Art Schankin, Illinois	Roland Wommack, Navy
1959	Joe Paletta, Navy	Al Morales, Navy	Roland Wommack, Navy
1960	Gene Glazer, NYU	Mike Desaro, NYU	Gil Eisner, NYU
1961	Herbert Cohen, NYU	Israel Colon, NYU	Jerry Halpern, NYU
1962	Herbert Cohen, NYU	Barton Nisonson, Columbia	Thane Hawkins, Navy
1963	Jay Lustig, Columbia	Bela Szentivanyi, Wayne St (MI)	Larry Crum, Navy
1964	Bill Hicks, Princeton	Craig Bell, Illinois	Paul Pesthy, Rutgers
1965	Joe Nalven, Columbia	Howard Goodman, NYU	Paul Pesthy, Rutgers

Fencing (Cont.)

Men (Cont.)

INDIVIDUAL CHAMPIONS (Cont.)

Foil	Sabre	Épée
1966....Al Davis, NYU	Paul Apostol, NYU	Bernhardt Hermann, Iowa
1967....Mike Gaylor, NYU	Todd Makler, Pennsylvania	George Masin, NYU
1968...Gerard Esponda, San Francisco	Todd Makler, Pennsylvania	Don Sieja, Cornell
1969....Anthony Kestler, Columbia	Norman Braslow, Pennsylvania	James Wetzler, Pennsylvania
1970....Walter Krause, NYU	Bruce Soriano, Columbia	John Nadas, Case Reserve
1971....Tyrone Simmons, Detroit	Bruce Soriano, Columbia	George Szunyogh, NYU
1972....Tyrone Simmons, Detroit	Bruce Soriano, Columbia	Ernesto Fernandez, Pennsylvania
1973....Brooke Makler, Pennsylvania	Peter Westbrock, NYU	Risto Hurme, NYU
1974....Greg Benko, Wayne St (MI)	Steve Danosi, Wayne St (MI)	Risto Hurme, NYU
1975....Greg Benko, Wayne St (MI)	Yuri Rabinovich, Wayne St (MI)	Risto Hurme, NYU
1976....Greg Benko, Wayne St (MI)	Brian Smith, Columbia	Randy Eggleton, Pennsylvania
1977....Pat Gerard, Notre Dame	Mike Sullivan, Notre Dame	Hans Wieselgren, NYU
1978....Ernest Simon, Wayne St (MI)	Mike Sullivan, Notre Dame	Bjorne Vaggo, Notre Dame
1979....Andrew Bonk, Notre Dame	Yuri Rabinovich, Wayne St (MI)	Carlos Songini, Cleveland St
1980....Ernest Simon, Wayne St (MI)	Paul Friedberg, Pennsylvania	Gil Pezza, Wayne St (MI)
1981....Ernest Simon, Wayne St (MI)	Paul Friedberg, Pennsylvania	Gil Pezza, Wayne St (MI)
1982....Alexander Flom, George Mason	Neil Hick, Wayne St (MI)	Peter Schifrin, San Jose St
1983....Demetrios Valsamis, NYU	John Friedberg, North Carolina	Ola Harstrom, Notre Dame
1984....Charles Higgs-Coulthard, Notre Dame	Michael Lofton, NYU	Ettore Bianchi, Wayne St (MI)
1985....Stephan Chauvel, Wayne St (MI)	Michael Lofton, NYU	Ettore Bianchi, Wayne St (MI)
1986....Adam Feldman, Penn St	Michael Lofton, NYU	Chris O'Loughlin, Pennsylvania
1987....William Mindel, Columbia	Michael Lofton, NYU	James O'Neill, Harvard
1988....Marc Kent, Columbia	Robert Cottingham, Columbia	Jon Normile, Columbia
1989....Edward Mufel, Penn St	Peter Cox, Penn St	Jon Normile, Columbia
1990....Nick Bravin, Stanford	David Mandell, Columbia	Jubba Beshin, Notre Dame
1991....Ben Atkins, Columbia	Vitali Nazlimov, Penn St	Marc Oshima, Columbia
1992....Nick Bravin, Stanford	Tom Strzalkowski, Penn St	Harald Bauder, Wayne St
1993....Nick Bravin, Stanford	Tom Strzalkowski, Penn St	Ben Atkins, Columbia
1994....Kwame van Leeuwen, Harvard	Tom Strzalkowski, Penn St	Harald Winkman, Princeton
1995....Sean McClain, Stanford	Paul Palestis, NYU	Mike Gattner, Lawrence
1996....Thorstein Becker, Wayne St (MI)	Maxim Pekarev, Princeton	Jeremy Kahn, Duke

Women

TEAM CHAMPIONS

Year	Champion	Coach	Rec	Runner-Up	Rec
1982	Wayne St (MI)	Istvan Danosi	7-0	San Jose St	6-1
1983	Penn St	Beth Alphin	5-0	Wayne St (MI)	3-2
1984	Yale	Henry Harutunian	3-0	Penn St	2-1
1985	Yale	Henry Harutunian	3-0	Pennsylvania	2-1
1986	Pennsylvania	David Micahnik	3-0	Notre Dame	2-1
1987	Notre Dame	Yves Auriol	3-0	Temple	2-1
1988	Wayne St (MI)	Gil Pezza	3-0	Notre Dame	2-1
1989	Wayne St (MI)	Gil Pezza	3-0	Columbia-Barnard	2-1

Note: Beginning in 1990, men's and women's combined teams competed for the national championship.

INDIVIDUAL CHAMPIONS

Foil	Foil (Cont.)
1982................Joy Ellingson, San Jose St	1992................Olga Cheryak, Penn St
1983................Jana Angelakis, Penn St	1993................Olga Kalinovskaya, Penn St
1984................Mary Jane O'Neill, Pennsylvania	1994................Olga Kalinovskaya, Penn St
1985................Caitlin Bilodeaux, Columbia-Barnard	1995................Olga Kalinovskaya, Penn St
1986................Molly Sullivan, Notre Dame	1996................Olga Kalinovskaya, Penn St
1987................Caitlin Bilodeaux, Columbia-Barnard	
1988................Molly Sullivan, Notre Dame	**Épée**
1989................Yasemin Topcu, Wayne St (MI)	1995................Tina Loven, St John's (NY)
1990................Tzu Moy, Columbia-Barnard	1996................Nicole Dygert, St John's (NY)
1991................Heidi Piper, Notre Dame	Note: The women's épée competition was added in 1995.

Field Hockey

DIVISION I

Year	Champion	Coach	Score	Runner-Up
1981	Connecticut	Diane Wright	4-1	Massachusetts
1982	Old Dominion	Beth Anders	3-2	Connecticut
1983	Old Dominion	Beth Anders	3-1 (3 OT)	Connecticut
1984	Old Dominion	Beth Anders	5-1	Iowa
1985	Connecticut	Diane Wright	3-2	Old Dominion
1986	Iowa	Judith Davidson	2-1 (2 OT)	New Hampshire
1987	Maryland	Sue Tyler	2-1 (OT)	N Carolina
1988	Old Dominion	Beth Anders	2-1	Iowa
1989	N Carolina	Karen Shelton	2-1 (3 OT)*	Old Dominion
1990	Old Dominion	Beth Anders	5-0	N Carolina
1991	Old Dominion	Beth Anders	2-0	N Carolina
1992	Old Dominion	Beth Anders	4-0	Iowa
1993	Maryland	Missy Meharg	2-1 (3 OT)*	N Carolina
1994	James Madison	Christy Morgan	2-1 (3 OT)*	N Carolina
1995	N Carolina	Karen Shelton-Scroggs	5-1	Maryland

*Penalty strokes.

DIVISION II *(DISCONTINUED, THEN RENEWED)*

Year	Champion	Coach	Score	Runner-Up
1981	Pfeiffer	Ellen Briggs	5-3	Bentley
1982	Lock Haven	Sharon E. Taylor	4-1	Bloomsburg
1983	Bloomsburg	Jan Hutchinson	1-0	Lock Haven
1992	Lock Haven	Sharon E. Taylor	3-1	Bloomsburg
1993	Bloomsburg	Jan Hutchison	2-1 (2 OT)	Lock Haven
1994	Lock Haven	Sharon E. Taylor	2-1	Bloomsburg
1995	Lock Haven	Sharon E. Taylor	1-0	Bloomsburg

DIVISION III

Year	Champion	Year	Champion	Year	Champion
1981	Trenton St	1986	Salisbury St	1991	Trenton St
1982	Ithaca	1987	Bloomsburg	1992	William Smith
1983	Trenton St	1988	Trenton St	1993	Cortland St
1984	Bloomsburg	1989	Lock Haven	1994	Cortland St
1985	Trenton St	1990	Trenton St	1995	Trenton St

Golf

Men

DIVISION I
Results, 1897-1938

Year	Champion	Site	Individual Champion
1897	Yale	Ardsley Casino	Louis Bayard Jr, Princeton
1898	Harvard (spring)		John Reid Jr, Yale
1898	Yale (fall)		James Curtis, Harvard
1899	Harvard		Percy Pyne, Princeton
1900	No tournament		
1901	Harvard	Atlantic City	H. Lindsley, Harvard
1902	Yale (spring)	Garden City	Charles Hitchcock Jr, Yale
1902	Harvard (fall)	Morris County	Chandler Egan, Harvard
1903	Harvard	Garden City	F. O. Reinhart, Princeton
1904	Harvard	Myopia	A. L. White, Harvard
1905	Yale	Garden City	Robert Abbott, Yale
1906	Yale	Garden City	W. E. Clow Jr, Yale
1907	Yale	Nassau	Ellis Knowles, Yale
1908	Yale	Brae Burn	H. H. Wilder, Harvard
1909	Yale	Apawamis	Albert Seckel, Princeton
1910	Yale	Essex County	Robert Hunter, Yale
1911	Yale	Baltusrol	George Stanley, Yale
1912	Yale	Ekwanok	F. C. Davison, Harvard
1913	Yale	Huntingdon Valley	Nathaniel Wheeler, Yale
1914	Princeton	Garden City	Edward Allis, Harvard

Men (Cont.)

DIVISION I (Cont.)

Results, 1897-1938 (Cont.)

Year	Champion	Site	Individual Champion
1915	Yale	Greenwich	Francis Blossom, Yale
1916	Princeton	Oakmont	J. W. Hubbell, Harvard
1917-18	No tournament		
1919	Princeton	Merion	A. L. Walker Jr, Columbia
1920	Princeton	Nassau	Jess Sweetster, Yale
1921	Dartmouth	Greenwich	Simpson Dean, Princeton
1922	Princeton	Garden City	Pollack Boyd, Dartmouth
1923	Princeton	Siwanoy	Dexter Cummings, Yale
1924	Yale	Greenwich	Dexter Cummings, Yale
1925	Yale	Montclair	Fred Lamprecht, Tulane
1926	Yale	Merion	Fred Lamprecht, Tulane
1927	Princeton	Garden City	Watts Gunn, Georgia Tech
1928	Princeton	Apawamis	Maurice McCarthy, Georgetown
1929	Princeton	Hollywood	Tom Aycock, Yale
1930	Princeton	Oakmont	G. T. Dunlap Jr, Princeton
1931	Yale	Olympia Fields	G. T. Dunlap Jr, Princeton
1932	Yale	Hot Springs	J. W. Fischer, Michigan
1933	Yale	Buffalo	Walter Emery, Oklahoma
1934	Michigan	Cleveland	Charles Yates, Georgia Tech
1935	Michigan	Congressional	Ed White, Texas
1936	Yale	North Shore	Charles Kocsis, Michigan
1937	Princeton	Oakmont	Fred Haas Jr, Louisiana St
1938	Stanford	Louisville	John Burke, Georgetown

Results, 1939-1996

Year	Champion	Coach	Score	Runner-Up	Score	Host or Site	Individual Champion
1939	Stanford	Eddie Twiggs	612	Northwestern	614	Wakonda	Vincent D'Antoni, Tulane
				Princeton	614		
1940	Princeton	Walter Bourne	601			Ekwanok	Dixon Brooke, Virginia
	Louisiana St	Mike Donahue	601				
1941	Stanford	Eddie Twiggs	580	Louisiana St	599	Ohio St	Earl Stewart, Louisiana St
1942	Louisiana St	Mike Donahue	590			Notre Dame	Frank Tatum Jr
	Stanford	Eddie Twiggs	590				
1943	Yale	William Neale Jr	614	Michigan	618	Olympia Fields	Wallace Ulrich, Carleton
1944	Notre Dame	George Holderith	311	Minnesota	312	Inverness	Louis Lick, Minnesota
1945	Ohio St	Robert Kepler	602	Northwestern	621	Ohio St	John Lorms, Ohio St
1946	Stanford	Eddie Twiggs	619	Michigan	624	Princeton	George Hamer, Georgia
1947	Louisiana St	T. P. Heard	606	Duke	614	Michigan	Dave Barclay, Michigan
1948	San Jose St	Wilbur Hubbard	579	Louisiana St	588	Stanford	Bob Harris, San Jose St
1949	N Texas	Fred Cobb	590	Purdue	600	Iowa St	Harvie Ward, N Carolina
				Texas	600		
1950	N Texas	Fred Cobb	573	Purdue	577	New Mexico	Fred Wampler, Purdue
1951	N Texas	Fred Cobb	588	Ohio St	589	Ohio St	Tom Nieporte, Ohio St
1952	N Texas	Fred Cobb	587	Michigan	593	Purdue	Jim Vickers, Oklahoma
1953	Stanford	Charles Finger	578	N Carolina	580	Broadmoor	Earl Moeller, Oklahoma St
1954	Southern Meth	Graham Ross	572	N Texas	573	Houston, Rice	Hillman Robbins, Memphis St
1955	Louisiana St	Mike Barbato	574	N Texas	583	Tennessee	Joe Campbell, Purdue
1956	Houston	Dave Williams	601	N Texas	602	Ohio St	Rick Jones, Ohio St
				Purdue	602		

Men (Cont.)
DIVISION I (Cont.)
Results, 1939-1995 (Cont.)

Year	Champion	Coach	Score	Runner-Up	Score	Host or Site	Individual Champion
1957	Houston	Dave Williams	602	Stanford	603	Broadmoor	Rex Baxter Jr, Houston
1958	Houston	Dave Williams	570	Oklahoma St	582	Williams	Phil Rodgers, Houston
1959	Houston	Dave Williams	561	Purdue	571	Oregon	Dick Crawford, Houston
1960	Houston	Dave Williams	603	Purdue	607	Broadmoor	Dick Crawford, Houston
				Oklahoma St	607		
1961	Purdue	Sam Voinoff	584	Arizona St	595	Lafayette	Jack Nicklaus, Ohio St
1962	Houston	Dave Williams	588	Oklahoma St	598	Duke	Kermit Zarley, Houston
1963	Oklahoma St	Labron Harris	581	Houston	582	Wichita St	R. H. Sikes, Ark
1964	Houston	Dave Williams	580	Oklahoma St	587	Broadmoor	Terry Small, San Jose St
1965	Houston	Dave Williams	577	Cal St-LA	587	Tennessee	Marty Fleckman, Houston
1966	Houston	Dave Williams	582	San Jose St	586	Stanford	Bob Murphy, Florida
1967	Houston	Dave Williams	585	Florida	588	Shawnee, PA	Hale Irwin, Colorado
1968	Florida	Buster Bishop	1154	Houston	1156	New Mexico St	Grier Jones, Oklahoma St
1969	Houston	Dave Williams	1223	Wake Forest	1232	Broadmoor	Bob Clark, Cal St-LA
1970	Houston	Dave Williams	1172	Wake Forest	1182	Ohio St	John Mahaffey, Houston
1971	Texas	George Hannon	1144	Houston	1151	Arizona	Ben Crenshaw, Texas
1972	Texas	George Hannon	1146	Houston	1159	Cape Coral	Ben Crenshaw, Texas; Tom Kite, Texas
1973	Florida	Buster Bishop	1149	Oklahoma St	1159	Oklahoma St	Ben Crenshaw, Texas
1974	Wake Forest	Jess Haddock	1158	Florida	1160	San Diego St	Curtis Strange, Wake Forest
1975	Wake Forest	Jess Haddock	1156	Oklahoma St	1189	Ohio St	Jay Haas, Wake Forest
1976	Oklahoma St	Mike Holder	1166	Brigham Young	1173	New Mexico	Scott Simpson, Southern Cal
1977	Houston	Dave Williams	1197	Oklahoma St	1205	Colgate	Scott Simpson, Southern Cal
1978	Oklahoma St	Mike Holder	1140	Georgia	1157	Oregon	David Edwards, Oklahoma St
1979	Ohio St	James Brown	1189	Oklahoma St	1191	Wake Forest	Gary Hallberg, Wake Forest
1980	Oklahoma St	Mike Holder	1173	Brigham Young	1177	Ohio St	Jay Don Blake, Utah St
1981	Brigham Young	Karl Tucker	1161	Oral Roberts	1163	Stanford	Ron Commans, Southern Cal
1982	Houston	Dave Williams	1141	Oklahoma St	1151	Pinehurst	Billy Ray Brown, Houston
1983	Oklahoma St	Mike Holder	1161	Texas	1168	Fresno St	Jim Carter, Arizona St
1984	Houston	Dave Williams	1145	Oklahoma St	1146	Houston	John Inman, N Carolina
1985	Houston	Dave Williams	1172	Oklahoma St	1175	Florida	Clark Burroughs, Ohio St
1986	Wake Forest	Jess Haddock	1156	Oklahoma St	1160	Wake Forest	Scott Verplank, Oklahoma St
1987	Oklahoma St	Mike Holder	1160	Wake Forest	1176	Ohio St	Brian Watts, Oklahoma St

Men *(Cont.)*

DIVISION I *(Cont.)*

Results, 1939-1995 *(Cont.)*

Year	Champion	Coach	Score	Runner-Up	Score	Host or Site	Individual Champion
1988 ....UCLA	Eddie Merrins	1176	UTEP	1179	Southern Cal	E. J. Pfister,
				Oklahoma	1179		Oklahoma St
				Oklahoma St	1179		
1989 ....Oklahoma	Gregg Grost	1139	Texas	1158	Oklahoma	Phil Mickelson,
						Oklahoma St	Arizona St
1990 ....Arizona St	Steve Loy	1155	Florida	1157	Florida	Phil Mickelson,
							Arizona St
1991 ....Oklahoma St	Mike Holder	1161	N Carolina	1168	San Jose St	Warren Schutte,
							UNLV
1992 ....Arizona	Rick LaRose	1129	Arizona St	1136	New Mexico	Phil Mickelson,
							Arizona St
1993 ....Florida	Buddy Alexander	1145	Georgia Tech	1146	Kentucky	Todd Demsey,
							Arizona St
1994 ....Stanford	Wally Goodwin	1129	Texas	1133	McKinney, TX	Justin Leonard,
							Texas
1995 ....Oklahoma St*	Mike Holder	1156	Stanford	1156	Ohio St	Chip Spratlin,
							Auburn
1996 ....Arizona St	Randy Lein	1186	UNLV	1189	TN-Chattanooga	Tiger Woods,
							Stanford

*Won sudden death playoff. Notes: Match play, 1897-1964; par-70 tournaments held in 1969, 1973 and 1989; par-71 tournaments held in 1968, 1981 and 1988; all other championships par-72 tournaments. Scores are based on 4 rounds instead of 2 after 1967.

DIVISION II

Year	Champion	Year	Champion	Year	Champion
1963 ....SW Missouri St		1975 ....UC-Irvine		1987 ....Tampa	
1964 ....Southern Illinois		1976 ....Troy St		1988 ....Tampa	
1965 ....Middle Tennessee St		1977 ....Troy St		1989 ....Columbus	
1966 ....Cal St-Chico		1978 ....Columbus		1990 ....Florida Southern	
1967 ....Lamar		1979 ....UC-Davis		1991 ....Florida Southern	
1968 ....Lamar		1980 ....Columbus		1992 ....Columbus	
1969 ....Cal St-Northridge		1981 ....Florida Southern		1993 ....Abilene Christian	
1970 ....Rollins		1982 ....Florida Southern		1994 ....Columbus	
1971 ....New Orleans		1983 ....SW Texas St		1995 ....Florida Southern	
1972 ....New Orleans		1984 ....Troy St		1996 ....Florida Southern	
1973 ....Cal St-Northridge		1985 ....Florida Southern			
1974 ....Cal St-Northridge		1986 ....Florida Southern			

Note: Par-71 tournaments held in 1967,1970, 1976-78, 1985 and 1988; par-70 tournament held in 1996; and all other championships par-72 tournaments.

DIVISION III

Year	Champion	Year	Champion	Year	Champion
1975 ....Wooster		1983 ....Allegheny		1991 ....Methodist (NC)	
1976 ....Cal St-Stanislaus		1984 ....Cal St-Stanislaus		1992 ....Methodist (NC)	
1977 ....Cal St-Stanislaus		1985 ....Cal St-Stanislaus		1993 ....UC-San Diego	
1978 ....Cal St-Stanislaus		1986 ....Cal St-Stanislaus		1994 ....Methodist (NC)	
1979 ....Cal St-Stanislaus		1987 ....Cal St-Stanislaus		1995 ....Methodist (NC)	
1980 ....Cal St-Stanislaus		1988 ....Cal St-Stanislaus		1996 ....Methodist (NC)	
1981 ....Cal St-Stanislaus		1989 ....Cal St-Stanislaus			
1982 ....Rampano		1990 ....Methodist (NC)			

Note: All championships par-72 except for 1986 and 1988, which were par-71; fourth round of 1975 championships canceled as a result of bad weather; first round of 1988 championships canceled as a result of rain.

Women

DIVISION I

Year	Champion	Coach	Score	Runner-Up	Score	Individual Champion
1982 .....Tulsa	Dale McNamara	1191	Texas Christian	1227	Kathy Baker, Tulsa
1983 .....Texas Christian	Fred Warren	1193	Tulsa	1196	Penny Hammel, Miami (FL)
1984 .....Miami (FL)	Lela Cannon	1214	Arizona St	1221	Cindy Schreyer, Georgia
1985 .....Florida	Mimi Ryan	1218	Tulsa	1233	Danielle Ammaccapane,
						Arizona St

Golf (Cont.)

Women (Cont.)
DIVISION I (Cont.)

Year	Champion	Coach	Score	Runner-Up	Score	Individual Champion
1986	Florida	Mimi Ryan	1180	Miami (FL)	1188	Page Dunlap, Florida
1987	San Jose St	Mark Gale	1187	Furman	1188	Caroline Keggi, New Mexico
1988	Tulsa	Dale McNamara	1175	Georgia	1182	Melissa McNamara, Tulsa
				Arizona	1182	
1989	San Jose St	Mark Gale	1208	Tulsa	1209	Pat Hurst, San Jose St
1990	Arizona St	Linda Vollstedt	1206	UCLA	1222	Susan Slaughter, Arizona
1991	UCLA*	Jackie Steinmann	1197	San Jose St	1197	Annika Sorenstam, Arizona
1992	San Jose St	Mark Gale	1171	Arizona	1175	Vicki Goetze, Georgia
1993	Arizona St	Linda Vollstedt	1187	Texas	1189	Charlotta Sorenstam, Texas
1994	Arizona St	Linda Vollstedt	1189	Southern Cal	1205	Emilee Klein, Arizona St
1995	Arizona St	Linda Vollstedt	1155	San Jose St	1181	Kristel Mourgue d'Algue, Arizona St
1996	Arizona*	Rick LaRose	1240	San Jose St	1240	Marisa Baena, Arizona

*Won sudden death playoff. Note: Par-74 tournaments held in 1983 and 1988; par-72 tournament held in 1990; all other championships par-73 tournaments.

Gymnastics

Men
TEAM CHAMPIONS

Year	Champion	Coach	Pts	Runner-Up	Pts
1938	Chicago	Dan Hoffer	22	Illinois	18
1939	Illinois	Hartley Price	21	Army	17
1940	Illinois	Hartley Price	20	Navy	17
1941	Illinois	Hartley Price	68.5	Minnesota	52.5
1942	Illinois	Hartley Price	39	Penn St	30
1943-47	No tournament				
1948	Penn St	Gene Wettstone	55	Temple	34.5
1949	Temple	Max Younger	28	Minnesota	18
1950	Illinois	Charley Pond	26	Temple	25
1951	Florida St	Hartley Price	26	Illinois	23.5
				Southern Cal	23.5
1952	Florida St	Hartley Price	89.5	Southern Cal	75
1953	Penn St	Gene Wettstone	91.5	Illinois	68
1954	Penn St	Gene Wettstone	137	Illinois	68
1955	Illinois	Charley Pond	82	Penn St	69
1956	Illinois	Charley Pond	123.5	Penn St	67.5
1957	Penn St	Gene Wettstone	88.5	Illinois	80
1958	Michigan St	George Szypula	79		
	Illinois	Charley Pond	79		
1959	Penn St	Gene Wettstone	152	Illinois	87.5
1960	Penn St	Gene Wettstone	112.5	Southern Cal	65.5
1961	Penn St	Gene Wettstone	88.5	Southern Illinois	80.5
1962	Southern Cal	Jack Beckner	95.5	Southern Illinois	75
1963	Michigan	Newton Loken	129	Southern Illinois	73
1964	Southern Illinois	Bill Meade	84.5	Southern Cal	69.5
1965	Penn St	Gene Wettstone	68.5	Washington	51.5
1966	Southern Illinois	Bill Meade	187.200	California	185.100
1967	Southern Illinois	Bill Meade	189.550	Michigan	187.400
1968	California	Hal Frey	188.250	Southern Illinois	188.150
1969	Iowa	Mike Jacobson	161.175	Penn St	160.450
	Michigan*	Newton Loken		Colorado St	
1970	Michigan	Newton Loken	164.150	Iowa St	164.050
				New Mexico St	
1971	Iowa St	Ed Gagnier	319.075	Southern Illinois	316.650
1972	Southern Illinois	Bill Meade	315.925	Iowa St	312.325
1973	Iowa St	Ed Gagnier	325.150	Penn St	323.025
1974	Iowa St	Ed Gagnier	326.100	Arizona St	322.050
1975	California	Hal Frey	437.325	Louisiana St	433.700
1976	Penn St	Gene Wettstone	432.075	Louisiana St	425.125

Men (Cont.)
TEAM CHAMPIONS (CONT.)

Year	Champion	Coach	Pts	Runner-Up	Pts
1977	Indiana St	Roger Counsil	434.475		
	Oklahoma	Paul Ziert	434.475		
1978	Oklahoma	Paul Ziert	439.350	Arizona St	437.075
1979	Nebraska	Francis Allen	448.275	Oklahoma	446.625
1980	Nebraska	Francis Allen	563.300	Iowa St	557.650
1981	Nebraska	Francis Allen	284.600	Oklahoma	281.950
1982	Nebraska	Francis Allen	285.500	UCLA	281.050
1983	Nebraska	Francis Allen	287.800	UCLA	283.900
1984	UCLA	Art Shurlock	287.300	Penn St	281.250
1985	Ohio St	Michael Willson	285.350	Nebraska	284.550
1986	Arizona St	Don Robinson	283.900	Nebraska	283.600
1987	UCLA	Art Shurlock	285.300	Nebraska	284.750
1988	Nebraska	Francis Allen	288.150	Illinois	287.150
1989	Illinois	Yoshi Hayasaki	283.400	Nebraska	282.300
1990	Nebraska	Francis Allen	287.400	Minnesota	287.300
1991	Oklahoma	Greg Buwick	288.025	Penn St	285.500
1992	Stanford	Sadao Hamada	289.575	Nebraska	288.950
1993	Stanford	Sadao Hamada	276.500	Nebraska	275.500
1994	Nebraska	Francis Allen	288.250	Stanford	285.925
1995	Stanford	Sadao Hamada	232.400	Nebraska	231.525
1996	Ohio St	Peter Kormann	232.150	California	231.775

*Trampoline.

INDIVIDUAL CHAMPIONS

ALL-AROUND

1938 .....Joe Giallombardo, Illinois
1939 .....Joe Giallombardo, Illinois
1940 .....Joe Giallombardo, Illinois
Paul Fina, Illinois
1941 .....Courtney Shanken, Chicago
1942 .....Newt Loken, Minnesota
1948 .....Ray Sorenson, Penn St
1949 .....Joe Kotys, Kent
1950 .....Joe Kotys, Kent
1951 .....Bill Roetzheim, Florida St
1952 .....Jack Beckner, Southern Cal
1953 .....Jean Cronstedt, Penn St
1954 .....Jean Cronstedt, Penn St
1955 .....Karl Schwenzfeier, Penn St
1956 .....Don Tonry, Illinois
1957 .....Armando Vega, Penn St
1958 .....Abie Grossfeld, Illinois
1959 .....Armando Vega, Penn St
1960 .....Jay Werner, Penn St
1961 .....Gregor Weiss, Penn St
1962 .....Robert Lynn, Southern Cal
1963 .....Gil Larose, Michigan
1964 .....Ron Barak, Southern Cal
1965 .....Mike Jacobson, Penn St
1966 .....Steve Cohen, Penn St
1967 .....Steve Cohen, Penn St
1968 .....Makoto Sakamoto, USC
1969 .....Mauno Nissinen, Wash
1970 .....Yoshi Hayasaki, Wash
1971 .....Yoshi Hayasaki, Wash
1972 .....Steve Hug, Stanford
1973 .....Steve Hug, Stanford
Marshall Avener, Penn St
1974 .....Steve Hug, Stanford
1975 .....Wayne Young, BYU
1976 .....Peter Kormann, Southern
Conn St
1977 .....Kurt Thomas, Indiana St

1978 .....Bart Conner, Oklahoma
1979 .....Kurt Thomas, Indiana St
1980 .....Jim Hartung, Nebraska
1981 .....Jim Hartung, Nebraska
1982 .....Peter Vidmar, UCLA
1983 .....Peter Vidmar, UCLA
1984 .....Mitch Gaylord, UCLA
1985 .....Wes Suter, Nebraska
1986 .....Jon Louis, Stanford
1987 .....Tom Schlesinger, Nebraska
1988 .....Vacated†
1989 .....Patrick Kirsey, Nebraska
1990 .....Mike Racanelli, Ohio St
1991 .....John Roethlisberger, Minn
1992 .....John Roethlisberger, Minn
1993 .....John Roethlisberger, Minn
1994 .....Dennis Harrison, Nebraska
1995 .....Richard Grace, Nebraska
1996 .....Blaine Wilson, Ohio St

HORIZONTAL BAR

1938 .....Bob Sears, Army
1939 .....Adam Walters, Temple
1940 .....Norm Boardman, Temple
1941 .....Newt Loken, Minnesota
1942 .....Norm Boardman, Temple
1948 .....Joe Calvetti, Illinois
1949 .....Bob Stout, Temple
1950 .....Joe Kotys, Kent
1951 .....Bill Roetzheim, Florida St
1952 .....Charles Simms, USC
1953 .....Hal Lewis, Navy
1954 .....Jean Cronstedt, Penn St
1955 .....Carlton Rintz, Michigan St
1956 .....Ronnie Amster, Florida St
1957 .....Abie Grossfeld, Illinois
1958 .....Abie Grossfeld, Illinois
1959 .....Stanley Tarshis, Mich St
1960 .....Stanley Tarshis, Mich St
1961 .....Bruno Klaus, Southern Ill

1962 .....Robert Lynn, USC
1963 .....Gil Larose, Michigan
1964 .....Ron Barak, USC
1965 .....Jim Curzi, Michigan St
Mike Jacobsen, Penn St
1966 .....Rusty Rock, Cal St-
Northridge
1967 .....Rich Grigsby, Cal St-
Northridge
1968 .....Makoto Sakamoto, USC
1969 .....Bob Manna, New Mexico
1970 .....Yoshi Hayasaki, Wash
1971 .....Brent Simmons, Iowa St
1972 .....Tom Lindner, Souhern Ill
1973 .....Jon Aitken, New Mexico
1974 .....Rick Banley, Indiana St
1975 .....Rich Larsen, Iowa St
1976 .....Tom Beach, California
1977 .....John Hart, UCLA
1978 .....Mel Cooley, Washington
1979 .....Kurt Thomas, Indiana St
1980 .....Philip Cahoy, Nebraska
1981 .....Philip Cahoy, Nebraska
1982 .....Peter Vidmar, UCLA
1983 .....Scott Johnson, Nebraska
1984 .....Charles Lakes, Illinois
1985 .....Dan Hayden, Arizona St
Wes Suter, Nebraska
1986 .....Dan Hayden, Arizona St
1987 .....David Moriel, UCLA
1988 .....Vacated†
1989 .....Vacated†
1990 .....Chris Waller, UCLA
1991 .....Luis Lopez, New Mexico
1992 .....Jair Lynch, Stanford
1993 .....Steve McCain, UCLA
1994 .....Jim Foody, UCLA
1995 .....Rick Kieffer, Nebraska
1996 .....Carl Imhauser, Temple

Men (Cont.)
INDIVIDUAL CHAMPIONS (CONT.)

PARALLEL BARS

1938.....Erwin Beyer, Chicago
1939.....Bob Sears, Army
1940.....Bob Hanning, Minnesota
1941.....Caton Cobb, Illinois
1942.....Hal Zimmerman, Penn St
1948.....Ray Sorenson, Penn St
1949.....Joe Kotys, Kent
     Mel Stout, Michigan St
1950.....Joe Kotys, Kent
1951.....Jack Beckner, USC
1952.....Jack Beckner, USC
1953.....Jean Cronstedt, Penn St
1954.....Jean Cronstedt, Penn St
1955.....Carlton Rintz, Michigan St
1956.....Armando Vega, Penn St
1957.....Armando Vega, Penn St
1958.....Tad Muzyczko, Mich St
1959.....Armando Vega, Penn St
1960.....Robert Lynn, Southern Cal
1961.....Fred Tijerina, Southern Ill
     Jeff Cardinalli, Springfield
1962.....Robert Lynn, Southern Cal
1963.....Arno Lascari, Michigan
1964.....Ron Barak, Southern Cal
1965.....Jim Curzi, Michigan St
1966.....Jim Curzi, Michigan St
1967.....Makoto Sakamoto, USC
1968.....Makoto Sakamoto, USC
1969.....Ron Rapper, Michigan
1970.....Ron Rapper, Michigan
1971.....Brent Simmons, Iowa St
     Tom Dunn, Penn St
1972.....Dennis Mazur, Iowa St
1973.....Steve Hug, Stanford
1974.....Steve Hug, Stanford
1975.....Yoichi Tomita, Long
     Beach St
1976.....Gene Whelan, Penn St
1977.....Kurt Thomas, Indiana St
1978.....John Corritore, Michigan
1979.....Kurt Thomas, Indiana St
1980.....Philip Cahoy, Nebraska
1981.....Philip Cahoy, Nebraska
     Peter Vidmar, UCLA
     Jim Hartung, Nebraska
1982.....Jim Hartung, Nebraska
1983.....Scott Johnson, Nebraska
1984.....Tim Daggett, UCLA
1985.....Dan Hayden, Arizona St
     Noah Riskin, Ohio St
     Seth Riskin, Ohio St
1986.....Dan Hayden, Arizona St
1987.....Kevin Davis, Nebraska
     Tom Schlesinger, Nebraska
1988.....Kevin Davis, Nebraska
1989.....Vacated†
1990.....Patrick Kirksey, Nebraska
1991.....Scott Keswick, UCLA
     John Roethlisberger, Minn
1992.....Dom Minicucci, Temple
1993.....Jair Lynch, Stanford
1994.....Richard Grace, Nebraska
1995.....Richard Grace, Nebraska
1996.....Jamie Ellis, Stanford
     Blaine Wilson, Ohio St

VAULT

1938.....Erwin Beyer, Chicago
1939.....Marv Forman, Illinois
1940.....Earl Shanken, Chicago
1941.....Earl Shanken, Chicago
1942.....Earl Shanken, Chicago
1948.....Jim Peterson, Minnesota
1962.....Bruno Klaus, Southern Ill
1963.....Gil Larose, Michigan
1964.....Sidney Oglesby, Syracuse
1965.....Dan Millman, California
1966.....Frank Schmitz, S Illinois
1967.....Paul Mayer, S Illinois
1968.....Bruce Colter, Cal St-Los
     Angeles
1969.....Dan Bowles, California
     Jack McCarthy, Illinois
1970.....Doug Boger, Arizona
1971.....Pat Mahoney, Cal St-
     Northridge
1972.....Gary Morava, Southern Ill
1973.....John Crosby, S Conn St
1974.....Greg Goodhue, Oklahoma
1975.....Tom Beach, California
1976.....Sam Shaw, Cal St-
     Fullerton
1977.....Steve Wejmar, Wash
1978.....Ron Galimore, Louisiana St
1979.....Leslie Moore, Oklahoma
1980.....Ron Galimore, Iowa St
1981.....Ron Galimore, Iowa St
1982.....Randall Wickstrom, Cal
     Steve Elliott, Nebraska
1983.....Chris Riegel, Nebraska
     Mark Oates, Oklahoma
1984.....Chris Riegel, Nebraska
1985.....Derrick Cornelius,
     Cortland St
1986.....Chad Fox, New Mexico
1987.....Chad Fox, New Mexico
1988.....Chad Fox, New Mexico
1989.....Chad Fox, New Mexico
1990.....Brad Hayashi, UCLA
1991.....Adam Carton, Penn St
1992.....Jason Hebert, Syracuse
1993.....Steve Wiegel, N Mexico
1994.....Steve McCain, UCLA
1995.....Ian Bachrach, Stanford
1996.....Jay Thornton, Iowa

POMMEL HORSE

1938.....Erwin Beyer, Chicago
1939.....Erwin Beyer, Chicago
1940.....Harry Koehnemann, Illinois
1941.....Caton Cobb, Illinois
1942.....Caton Cobb, Illinois
1948.....Steve Greene, Penn St
1949.....Joe Berenato, Temple
1950.....Gene Rabbitt, Syracuse
1951.....Joe Kotys, Kent
1952.....Frank Bare, Illinois
1953.....Carlton Rintz, Michigan St
1954.....Robert Lawrence, Penn St
1955.....Carlton Rintz, Michigan St
1956.....James Brown, Cal St-
     Los Angeles

1957.....John Davis, Illinois
1958.....Bill Buck, Iowa
1959.....Art Shurlock, California
1960.....James Fairchild, California
1961.....James Fairchild, California
1962.....Mike Aufrecht, Illinois
1963.....Russ Mills, Yale
1964.....Russ Mills, Yale
1965.....Bob Elsinger, Springfield
1966.....Gary Hoskins, Cal St-
     Los Angeles
1967.....Keith McCanless, Iowa
1968.....Jack Ryan, Colorado
1969.....Keith McCanless, Iowa
1970.....Russ Hoffman, Iowa St
     John Russo, Wisconsin
1971.....Russ Hoffman, Iowa St
1972.....Russ Hoffman, Iowa St
1973.....Ed Slezak, Indiana St
1974.....Ted Marcy, Stanford
1975.....Ted Marcy, Stanford
1976.....Ted Marcy, Stanford
1977.....Chuck Walter, New Mexico
1978.....Mike Burke, Northern Ill
1979.....Mike Burke, Northern Ill
1980.....David Stoldt, Illinois
1981.....Mark Bergman, California
     Steve Jennings, New Mexico
1982.....Peter Vidmar, UCLA
     Steve Jennings, New Mexico
1983.....Doug Kieso, Northern Ill
1984.....Tim Daggett, UCLA
1985.....Tony Pineda, UCLA
1986.....Curtis Holdsworth, UCLA
1987.....Li Xiao Ping, Cal St-
     Fullerton
1988.....Vacated†
     Mark Sohn, Penn St
1989.....Mark Sohn, Penn St
     Chris Waller, UCLA
1990.....Mark Sohn, Penn St
1991.....Mark Sohn, Penn St
1992.....Che Bowers, Nebraska
1993.....John Roethlisberger, Minn
1994.....Jason Bertram, California
1995.....Drew Durbin, Ohio St
1996.....Drew Durbin, Ohio St

FLOOR EXERCISE

1941.....Lou Fina, Illinois
1953.....Bob Sullivan, Illinois
1954.....Jean Cronstedt, Penn St
1955.....Don Faber, UCLA
1956.....Jamile Ashmore, Florida St
1957.....Norman Marks, Cal St-
     Los Angeles
1958.....Abie Grossfeld, Illinois
1959.....Don Tonry, Illinois
1960.....Ray Hadley, Illinois
1961.....Robert Lynn, Southern Cal
1962.....Robert Lynn, Southern Cal
1963.....Tom Seward, Penn St
     Mike Henderson, Michigan
1964.....Rusty Mitchell, S Illinois
1965.....Frank Schmitz, S Illinois
1966.....Frank Schmitz, S Illinois

Men (Cont.)

INDIVIDUAL CHAMPIONS (CONT.)

FLOOR EXERCISE (Cont.)

1967.....Dave Jacobs, Michigan
1968.....Toby Towson, Michigan St
1969.....Toby Towson, Michigan St
1970.....Tom Proulx, Colorado St
1971.....Stormy Eaton, New Mexico
1972.....Odessa Lovin, Oklahoma
1973.....Odessa Lovin, Oklahoma
1974.....Doug Fitzjarrell, Iowa St
1975.....Kent Brown, Arizona St
1976.....Bob Robbins, Colorado St
1977.....Ron Galimore, Louisiana St
1978.....Curt Austin, Iowa St
1979.....Mike Wilson, Oklahoma
     Bart Conner, Oklahoma
1980.....Steve Elliott, Nebraska
1981.....James Yuhashi, Oregon
1982.....Steve Elliott, Nebraska
1983.....Scott Johnson, Nebraska
     David Branch, Arizona St
     Donnie Hinton, Arizona St
1984.....Kevin Ekburg, Northern Ill
1985.....Wes Suter, Nebraska
1986.....Jerry Burrell, Arizona St
     Brian Ginsberg, UCLA
1987.....Chad Fox, New Mexico

1988.....Chris Wyatt, Temple
1989.....Jody Newman, Arizona St
1990.....Mike Racanelli, Ohio St
1991.....Brad Hayashi, UCLA
1992.....Brian Winkler, Michigan
1993.....Richard Grace, Nebraska
1994.....Mark Booth, Stanford
1995.....Jay Thornton, Iowa
1996.....Ian Bachrach, Stanford

RINGS

1959.....Armando Vega, Penn St
1960.....Sam Garcia, Southern Cal
1961.....Fred Orlofsky, Southern Ill
1962.....Dale Cooper, Michigan St
1963.....Dale Cooper, Michigan St
1964.....Chris Evans, Arizona St
1965.....Glenn Gailis, Iowa
1966.....Ed Gunny, Michigan St
1967.....Josh Robison, California
1968.....Pat Arnold, Arizona
1969.....Paul Vexler, Penn St
     Ward Maythaler, Iowa St
1970.....Dave Seal, Indiana St
1971.....Charles Ropiequet, S Illinois
1972.....Dave Seal, Indiana St

1973.....Bob Mahorney, Indiana St
1974.....Keith Heaver, Iowa St
1975.....Keith Heaver, Iowa St
1976.....Doug Wood, Iowa St
1977.....Doug Wood, Iowa St
1978......Scott McEldowney, Oregon
1979.....Kirk Mango, Northern Ill
1980.....Jim Hartung, Nebraska
1981.....Jim Hartung, Nebraska
1982.....Jim Hartung, Nebraska
1983.....Alex Schwartz, UCLA
1984.....Tim Daggett, UCLA
1985.....Mark Diab, Iowa St
1986.....Mark Diab, Iowa St
1987.....Paul O'Neill, Houst Baptist
1988.....Paul O'Neill, New Mexico
1989.....Vacated†
     Paul O'Neill, New Mexico
1990.....Wayne Cowden, Penn St
1991.....Adam Carton, Penn St
1992.....Scott Keswick, UCLA
1993.....Chris LaMorte, N Mexico
1994.....Chris LaMorte, N Mexico
1995.....Dave Frank, Temple
1996.....Scott McCall, William&Mary
     Blaine Wilson, Ohio St

† Championships won by Miguel Rubio (All Around, 1988; Horizontal Bar, 1988-89) and Alfonso Rodriguez (Pommel Horse, 1988; Rings, 1989; Parallel Bars, 1989) were vacated by action of the NCAA Committee on Infractions.

DIVISION II (DISCONTINUED)

Year	Champion	Coach	Pts	Runner-Up	Pts
1968	Cal St-Northridge	Bill Vincent	179.400	Springfield	178.050
1969	Cal St-Northridge	Bill Vincent	151.800	Southern Connecticut St	145.075
1970	Northwestern Louisiana	Armando Vega	160.250	Southern Connecticut St	159.300
1971	Cal St-Fullerton	Dick Wolfe	158.150	Springfield	156.987
1972	Cal St-Fullerton	Dick Wolfe	160.550	Southern Connecticut St	153.050
1973	Southern Connecticut St	Abe Grossfeld	160.750	Cal St-Northridge	158.700
1974	Cal St-Fullerton	Dick Wolfe	309.800	Southern Connecticut St	309.400
1975	Southern Connecticut St	Abe Grossfeld	411.650	IL-Chicago	398.800
1976	Southern Connecticut St	Abe Grossfeld	419.200	IL-Chicago	388.850
1977	Springfield	Frank Wolcott	395.950	Cal St-Northridge	381.250
1978	IL-Chicago	C. Johnson/A. Gentile	406.850	Cal St-Northridge	400.400
1979	IL-Chicago	Clarence Johnson	418.550	WI-Oshkosh	385.650
1980	WI-Oshkosh	Ken Allen	260.550	Cal St-Chico	256.050
1981	WI-Oshkosh	Ken Allen	209.500	Springfield	201.550
1982	WI-Oshkosh	Ken Allen	216.050	East Stroudsburg	211.200
1983	East Stroudsburg	Bruno Klaus	258.650	WI-Oshkosh	257.850
1984	East Stroudsburg	Bruno Klaus	270.800	Cortland St	246.350

Women

TEAM CHAMPIONS

Year	Champion	Coach	Pts	Runner-Up	Pts
1982	Utah	Greg Marsden	148.60	Cal St-Fullerton	144.10
1983	Utah	Greg Marsden	184.65	Arizona St	183.30
1984	Utah	Greg Marsden	186.05	UCLA	185.55
1985	Utah	Greg Marsden	188.35	Arizona St	186.60
1986	Utah	Greg Marsden	186.95	Arizona St	186.70
1987	Georgia	Suzanne Yoculan	187.90	Utah	187.55
1988	Alabama	Sarah Patterson	190.05	Utah	189.50
1989	Georgia	Suzanne Yoculan	192.65	UCLA	192.60
1990	Utah	Greg Marsden	194.900	Alabama	194.575
1991	Alabama	Sarah Patterson	195.125	Utah	194.375
1992	Utah	Greg Marsden	195.650	Georgia	194.600

Women (Cont.)

TEAM CHAMPIONS *(CONT.)*

Year	Champion	Coach	Pts	Runner-Up	Pts
1993	Georgia	Suzanne Yoculan	198.000	Alabama	196.825
1994	Utah	Greg Marsden	196.400	Alabama	196.350
1995	Utah	Greg Marsden	196.650	Alabama	196.425
				Michigan	196.425
1996	Alabama	Sarah Patterson	198.025	UCLA	197.475

INDIVIDUAL CHAMPIONS

ALL-AROUND

1982.....Sue Stednitz, Utah
1983.....Megan McCunniff, Utah
1984......Megan McCunniff-Marsden, Utah
1985.......Penney Hauschild, Alabama
1986.......Penney Hauschild, Alabama
Jackie Brummer, Arizona St
1987.....Kelly Garrison-Steves, Oklahoma
1988.....Kelly Garrison-Steves, Oklahoma
1989.....Corrinne Wright, Georgia
1990.....Dee Dee Foster, Alabama
1991.....Hope Spivey, Georgia
1992.....Missy Marlowe, Utah
1993.....Jenny Hansen, Kentucky
1994.....Jenny Hansen, Kentucky·
1995.....Jenny Hansen, Kentucky
1996.....Meredith Willard, Alabama

VAULT

1982.....Elaine Alfano, Utah
1983.....Elaine Alfano, Utah
1984.....Megan Marsden, Utah
1985.....Elaine Alfano, Utah
1986.....Kim Neal, Arizona St
Pam Loree, Penn St
1987.....Yumi Mordre, Washington
1988.....Jill Andrews, UCLA
1989.....Kim Hamilton, UCLA
1990.....Michele Bryant, Nebraska
1991.....Anna Basaldva, Arizona
1992.....Tammy Marshall, Massachusetts
Heather Stepp, Georgia
Kristein Kenoyer, Utah
1993.....Heather Stepp, Georgia
1994.....Jenny Hansen, Kentucky
1995.....Jenny Hansen, Kentucky
1996.....Leah Brown, Georgia

BALANCE BEAM

1982.....Sue Stednitz, Utah
1983.....Julie Goewey, Cal St-Fullerton
1984.....Heidi Anderson, Oregon St
1985.....Lisa Zeis, Arizona St
1986.....Jackie Brummer, Arizona St
1987.....Yumi Mordre, Washington
1988.....Kelly Garrison-Steves, Oklahoma
1989.....Jill Andrews, UCLA
Joy Selig, Oregon St
1990.....Joy Selig, Oregon St
1991.....Missy Marlowe, Utah
1992.....Missy Marlowe, Utah
Dana Dobransky, Alabama
1993.....Dana Dobransky, Alabama
1994.....Jenny Hansen, Kentucky
1995.....Jenny Hansen, Kentucky
1996.....Summer Reid, Utah

FLOOR EXERCISE

1982.....Mary Ayotte-Law, Oregon St
1983.....Kim Neal, Arizona St
1984.....Maria Anz, Florida
1985.....Lisa Mitzel, Utah
1986.....Lisa Zeis, Arizona St
Penney Hauschild, Alabama
1987.....Kim Hamilton, UCLA
1988.....Kim Hamilton, UCLA
1989.....Corrinne Wright, Georgia
Kim Hamilton, UCLA
1990.....Joy Selig, Oregon St
1991.....Hope Spivey, Georgia
1992.....Missy Marlowe, Utah

1993.....Heather Stepp, Georgia
Tammy Marshall, UMass
Amy Durham, Oregon St
1994.....Hope Spivey-Sheeley, Georgia
1995.....Jenny Hansen, Kentucky
Stella Umeh, UCLA
Leslie Angeles, Georgia
1996.....Heidi Hornbeek, Arizona
Kim Kelly, Alabama

UNEVEN BARS

1982.....Lisa Shirk, Pittsburgh
1983.....Jeri Cameron, Arizona St
1984.....Jackie Brummer, Arizona St
1985.....Penney Hauschild, Alabama
1986.....Lucy Wener, Georgia
1987.....Lucy Wener, Georgia
1988.....Kelly Garrison-Steves, Oklahoma
1989.....Lucy Wener, Georgia
1990.....Marie Roethlisberger, Minnesota
1991.....Kelly Macy, Georgia
1992.....Missy Marlowe, Utah
1993.....Agina Simpkins, Georgia
Beth Wymer, Michigan
1994.....Sandy Woolsey, Utah
Beth Wymer, Michigan
Lori Strong, Georgia
1995.....Beth Wymer, Michigan
1996.....Stephanie Woods, Alabama

DIVISION II *(DISCONTINUED)*

Year	Champion	Coach	Pts	Runner-Up	Pts
1982	Cal St-Northridge	Donna Stuart	138.10	Jacksonville St	134.05
1983	Denver	Dan Garcia	174.80	Cal St-Northridge	174.35
1984	Jacksonville St	Robert Dillard	173.40	SE Missouri St	171.45
1985	Jacksonville St	Robert Dillard	176.85	SE Missouri St	173.95
1986	Seattle Pacific	Laurel Tindall	175.80	Jacksonville St	175.15

Ice Hockey

DIVISION I

Year	Champion	Coach	Score	Runner-Up	Most Outstanding Player
1948	Michigan	Vic Heyliger	8-4	Dartmouth	Joe Riley, Dartmouth, F
1949	Boston Col	John Kelley	4-3	Dartmouth	Dick Desmond, Dartmouth, G
1950	Colorado Col	Cheddy Thompson	13-4	Boston U	Ralph Bevins, Boston U, G
1951	Michigan	Vic Heyliger	7-1	Brown	Ed Whiston, Brown, G
1952	Michigan	Vic Heyliger	4-1	Colorado Col	Kenneth Kinsley, Colorado Col, G
1953	Michigan	Vic Heyliger	7-3	Minnesota	John Matchefts, Michigan, F
1954	Rensselaer	Ned Harkness	5-4 (OT)	Minnesota	Abbie Moore, Rensselaer, F
1955	Michigan	Vic Heyliger	5-3	Colorado Col	Philip Hilton, Colorado Col, D
1956	Michigan	Vic Heyliger	7-5	Michigan Tech	Lorne Howes, Michigan, G
1957	Colorado Col	Thomas Bedecki	13-6	Michigan	Bob McCusker, Colorado Col, F
1958	Denver	Murray Armstrong	6-2	N Dakota	Murray Massier, Denver, F
1959	N Dakota	Bob May	4-3 (OT)	Michigan St	Reg Morelli, N Dakota, F
1960	Denver	Murray Armstrong	5-3	Michigan Tech	Bob Marquis, Boston U, F
1961	Denver	Murray Armstrong	12-2	St Lawrence	Barry Urbanski, Boston U, G
1962	Michigan Tech	John MacInnes	7-1	Clarkson	Louis Angotti, Michigan Tech, F
1963	N Dakota	Barney Thorndycraft	6-5	Denver	Al McLean, N Dakota, F
1964	Michigan	Allen Renfrew	6-3	Denver	Bob Gray, Michigan, G
1965	Michigan Tech	John MacInnes	8-2	Boston Col	Gary Milroy, Michigan Tech, F
1966	Michigan St	Amo Bessone	6-1	Clarkson	Gaye Cooley, Michigan St, G
1967	Cornell	Ned Harkness	4-1	Boston U	Walt Stanowski, Cornell, D
1968	Denver	Murray Armstrong	4-0	N Dakota	Gerry Powers, Denver, G
1969	Denver	Murray Armstrong	4-3	Cornell	Keith Magnuson, Denver, D
1970	Cornell	Ned Harkness	6-4	Clarkson	Daniel Lodboa, Cornell, D
1971	Boston U	Jack Kelley	4-2	Minnesota	Dan Brady, Boston U, G
1972	Boston U	Jack Kelley	4-0	Cornell	Tim Regan, Boston U, G
1973	Wisconsin	Bob Johnson	4-2	Vacated	Dean Talafous, Wisconsin, F
1974	Minnesota	Herb Brooks	4-2	Michigan Tech	Brad Shelstad, Minnesota, G
1975	Michigan Tech	John MacInnes	6-1	Minnesota	Jim Warden, Michigan Tech, G
1976	Minnesota	Herb Brooks	6-4	Michigan Tech	Tom Vanelli, Minnesota, F
1977	Wisconsin	Bob Johnson	6-5 (OT)	Michigan	Julian Baretta, Wisconsin, G
1978	Boston U	Jack Parker	5-3	Boston Col	Jack O'Callahan, Boston U, D
1979	Minnesota	Herb Brooks	4-3	N Dakota	Steve Janaszak, Minnesota, G
1980	N Dakota	John Gasparini	5-2	Northern Michigan	Doug Smail, N Dakota, F
1981	Wisconsin	Bob Johnson	6-3	Minnesota	Marc Behrend, Wisconsin, G
1982	N Dakota	John Gasparini	5-2	Wisconsin	Phil Sykes, N Dakota, F
1983	Wisconsin	Jeff Sauer	6-2	Harvard	Marc Behrend, Wisconsin, G
1984	Bowling Green	Jerry York	5-4 (OT)	MN-Duluth	Gary Kruzich, Bowling Green, G
1985	Rensselaer	Mike Addesa	2-1	Providence	Chris Terreri, Providence, G
1986	Michigan St	Ron Mason	6-5	Harvard	Mike Donnelly, Michigan St, F
1987	N Dakota	John Gasparini	5-3	Michigan St	Tony Hrkac, N Dakota, F
1988	Lake Superior St	Frank Anzalone	4-3 (OT)	St Lawrence	Bruce Hoffort, Lake Superior St, G
1989	Harvard	Bill Cleary	4-3 (OT)	Minnesota	Ted Donato, Harvard, F
1990	Wisconsin	Jeff Sauer	7-3	Colgate	Chris Tancill, Wisconsin, F
1991	N Michigan	Rick Comley	8-7 (3OT)	Boston U	Scott Beattie, N Michigan, F
1992	Lake Superior St	Jeff Jackson	4-2	Wisconsin	Paul Constantin, Lake Superior St, F
1993	Maine	Shawn Walsh	5-4	Lake Superior St	Jim Montgomery, Maine, F
1994	Lake Superior St	Jeff Jackson	9-1	Boston U	Sean Tallaire, Lake Superior St, F
1995	Boston U	Jack Parker	6-2	Maine	Chris O'Sullivan, Boston U, F
1996	Michigan	Red Berenson	3-2 (OT)	Colorado Col	Brendan Morrison, Michigan, F

DIVISION II *(DISCONTINUED, THEN RENEWED)*

Year	Champion	Coach	Score	Runner-Up
1978	Merrimack	Thom Lawler	12-2	Lake Forest
1979	Lowell	Bill Riley Jr	6-4	Mankato St
1980	Mankato St	Don Brose	5-2	Elmira
1981	Lowell	Bill Riley Jr	5-4	Plattsburgh St
1982	Lowell	Bill Riley Jr	6-1	Plattsburgh St
1983	Rochester Inst	Brian Mason	4-2	Bemidji St
1984	Bemidji St	R.H. (Bob) Peters	14-4*	Merrimack
1993	Bemidji St	R.H. (Bob) Peters	15-6*	Mercyhurst
1994	Bemidji St	R.H. (Bob) Peters	7-6*	AL-Huntsville
1995	Bemidji St	R.H. (Bob) Peters	11-6*	Mercyhurst
1996	AL-Huntsville	Doug Ross	10-1*	Bemidji St

*Two-game, total-goal series.

DIVISION III

Year	Champion	Coach	Score	Runner-Up
1984	Babson	Bob Riley	8-0	Union (NY)
1985	Rochester Inst	Bruce Delventhal	5-1	Bemidji St
1986	Bemidji St	R.H. (Bob) Peters	8-5	Vacated
1987	Vacated			Oswego St
1988	WI-River Falls	Rick Kozuback	7-1, 3-5, 3-0	Elmira
1989	WI-Stevens Point	Mark Mazzoleni	3-3, 3-2	Rochester Inst
1990	WI-Stevens Point	Mark Mazzoleni	10-1, 3-6, 1-0	Plattsburgh St
1991	WI-Stevens Point	Mark Mazzoleni	6-2	Mankato St
1992	Plattsburgh St	Bob Emery	7-3	WI-Stevens Point
1993	WI-Stevens Point	Joe Baldarotta	4-3	WI-River Falls
1994	WI-River Falls	Dean Talafous	6-4	WI-Superior
1995	Middlebury	Bill Beaney	1-0	Fredonia St
1996	Middlebury	Bill Beaney	3-2	Rochester IT

Lacrosse

Men

DIVISION I

Year	Champion	Coach	Score	Runner-Up
1971	Cornell	Richie Moran	12-6	Maryland
1972	Virginia	Glenn Thiel	13-12	Johns Hopkins
1973	Maryland	Bud Beardmore	10-9 (2 OT)	Johns Hopkins
1974	Johns Hopkins	Bob Scott	17-12	Maryland
1975	Maryland	Bud Beardmore	20-13	Navy
1976	Cornell	Richie Moran	16-13 (OT)	Maryland
1977	Cornell	Richie Moran	16-8	Johns Hopkins
1978	Johns Hopkins	Henry Ciccarone	13-8	Cornell
1979	Johns Hopkins	Henry Ciccarone	15-9	Maryland
1980	Johns Hopkins	Henry Ciccarone	9-8 (2 OT)	Virginia
1981	N Carolina	Willie Scroggs	14-13	Johns Hopkins
1982	N Carolina	Willie Scroggs	7-5	Johns Hopkins
1983	Syracuse	Roy Simmons Jr	17-16	Johns Hopkins
1984	Johns Hopkins	Don Zimmerman	13-10	Syracuse
1985	Johns Hopkins	Don Zimmerman	11-4	Syracuse
1986	N Carolina	Willie Scroggs	10-9 (OT)	Virginia
1987	Johns Hopkins	Don Zimmerman	11-10	Cornell
1988	Syracuse	Roy Simmons Jr	13-8	Cornell
1989	Syracuse	Roy Simmons Jr	13-12	Johns Hopkins
1990	Syracuse	Roy Simmons Jr	21-9	Loyola (MD)
1991	N Carolina	Dave Klarmann	18-13	Towson St
1992	Princeton	Bill Tierney	10-9	Syracuse
1993	Syracuse	Roy Simmons Jr	13-12	N Carolina
1994	Princeton	Bill Tierney	9-8 (OT)	Virginia
1995	Syracuse	Roy Simmons Jr	13-9	Maryland
1996	Princeton	Bill Tierney	13-12 (OT)	Virginia

DIVISION II (DISCONTINUED, THEN RENEWED)

Year	Champion	Coach	Score	Runner-Up
1974	Towson St	Carl Runk	18-17 (OT)	Hobart
1975	Cortland St	Chuck Winters	12-11	Hobart
1976	Hobart	Jerry Schmidt	18-9	Adelphi
1977	Hobart	Jerry Schmidt	23-13	Washington (MD)
1978	Roanoke	Paul Griffin	14-13	Hobart
1979	Adelphi	Paul Doherty	17-12	MD-Baltimore County
1980	MD-Baltimore County	Dick Watts	23-14	Adelphi
1981	Adelphi	Paul Doherty	17-14	Loyola (MD)
1993	Adelphi	Kevin Sheehan	11-7	LIU-C.W. Post
1994	Springfield	Keith Bugbee	15-12	New York Tech
1995	Adelphi	Sandy Kapatos	12-10	Springfield
1996	LIU-C.W. Post	Tom Postel	15-10	Adelphi

Men (Cont.)
DIVISION III

Year	Champion	Coach	Score	Runner-Up
1980	Hobart	Dave Urick	11-8	Cortland St
1981	Hobart	Dave Urick	10-8	Cortland St
1982	Hobart	Dave Urick	9-8 (OT)	Washington (MD)
1983	Hobart	Dave Urick	13-9	Roanoke
1984	Hobart	Dave Urick	12-5	Washington (MD)
1985	Hobart	Dave Urick	15-8	Washington (MD)
1986	Hobart	Dave Urick	13-10	Washington (MD)
1987	Hobart	Dave Urick	9-5	Ohio Wesleyan
1988	Hobart	Dave Urick	18-9	Ohio Wesleyan
1989	Hobart	Dave Urick	11-8	Ohio Wesleyan
1990	Hobart	B.J. O'Hara	18-6	Washington (MD)
1991	Hobart	B.J. O'Hara	12-11	Salisbury St
1992	Nazareth (NY)	Scott Nelson	13-12	Hobart
1993	Hobart	B.J. O'Hara	16-10	Ohio Wesleyan
1994	Salisbury St	Jim Berkman	15-9	Hobart
1995	Salisbury St	Jim Berkman	22-13	Nazareth
1996	Nazareth	Scott Nelson	11-10 (OT)	Washington (MD)

Women
DIVISION I

Year	Champion	Coach	Score	Runner-Up
1982	Massachusetts	Pamela Hixon	9-6	Trenton St
1983	Delaware	Janet Smith	10-7	Temple
1984	Temple	Tina Sloan Green	6-4	Maryland
1985	New Hampshire	Marisa Didio	6-5	Maryland
1986	Maryland	Sue Tyler	11-10	Penn St
1987	Penn St	Susan Scheetz	7-6	Temple
1988	Temple	Tina Sloan Green	15-7	Penn St
1989	Penn St	Susan Scheetz	7-6	Harvard
1990	Harvard	Carole Kleinfelder	8-7	Maryland
1991	Virginia	Jane Miller	8-6	Maryland
1992	Maryland	Cindy Timchal	11-10	Harvard
1993	Virginia	Jane Miller	8-6 (OT)	Princeton
1994	Princeton	Chris Sailer	10-7	Virginia
1995	Maryland	Cindy Timchal	13-5	Princeton
1996	Maryland	Cindy Timchal	10-5	Virginia

DIVISION III

Year	Champion	Score	Runner-Up	Year	Champion	Score	Runner-Up
1985	Trenton St	7-4	Ursinus	1991	Trenton St	7-6	Ursinus
1986	Ursinus	12-10	Trenton St	1992	Trenton St	5-3	William Smith
1987	Trenton St	8-7 (OT)	Ursinus	1993	Trenton St	10-9	William Smith
1988	Trenton St	14-11	William Smith	1994	Trenton St	29-11	William Smith
1989	Ursinus	8-6	Trenton St	1995	Trenton St	14-13	William Smith
1990	Ursinus	7-6	St Lawrence	1996	Trenton St	15-8	Middlebury

Rifle

Men's and Women's Combined

						Individual Champions	
Year	Champion	Coach	Score	Runner-Up	Score	Air Rifle	Smallbore
1980	Tennessee Tech	James Newkirk	6201	W Virginia	6150	Rod Fitz-Randolph, Tennessee Tech	Rod Fitz-Randolph, Tennessee Tech
1981	Tennessee Tech	James Newkirk	6139	W Virginia	6136	John Rost, W Virginia	Kurt Fitz-Randolph, Tennessee Tech
1982	Tennessee Tech	James Newkirk	6138	W Virginia	6136	John Rost, W Virginia	Kurt Fitz-Randolph, Tennessee Tech
1983	W Virginia	Edward Etzel	6166	Tennessee Tech	6148	Ray Slonena, Tennessee Tech	David Johnson, W Virginia
1984	W Virginia	Edward Etzel	6206	East Tennessee St	6142	Pat Spurgin, Murray St	Bob Broughton, W Virginia

						Individual Champions	
Year	Champion	Coach	Score	Runner-Up	Score	Air Rifle	Smallbore
1985	Murray St	Elvis Green	6150	W Virginia	6149	Christian Heller, W Virginia	Pat Spurgin, Murray St
1986	W Virginia	Edward Etzel	6229	Murray St	6163	Marianne Wallace, Murray St	Mike Anti, W Virginia
1987	Murray St	Elvis Green	6205	W Virginia	6203	Rob Harbison, TN-Martin	Web Wright, W Virginia
1988	W Virginia	Greg Perrine	6192	Murray St	6183	Deena Wigger, Murray St	Web Wright, W Virginia
1989	W Virginia	Edward Etzel	6234	S Florida	6180	Michelle Scarborough, S Florida	Deb Sinclair, AK-Fairbanks
1990	W Virginia	Marsha Beasley	6205	Navy	6101	Gary Hardy, W Virginia	Michelle Scarborough, S Florida
1991	W Virginia	Marsha Beasley	6171	Alaska-Fairbanks	6110	Ann Pfiffner, W Virginia	Soma Dutta, UTEP
1991	W Virginia	Marsha Beasley	6171	Alaska-Fairbanks	6110	Ann Pfiffner, W Virginia	Soma Dutta, UTEP
1992	W Virginia	Marsha Beasley	6214	Alaska-Fairbanks	6166	Ann Pfiffner, W Virginia	Tim Manges, W Virginia
1993	W Virginia	Marsha Beasley	6179	Alaska-Fairbanks	6169	Trevor Gathman, W Virginia	Eric Uptagrafft, W Virginia
1994	AK-Fairbanks	Randy Pitney	6194	W Virginia	6187	Nancy Napolski, Kentucky	Cory Brunetti, AK-Fairbanks
1995	W Virginia	Marsha Beasley	6241	Air Force	6187	Benji Belden, Murray St	Oleg Selezner, AK-Fairbanks
1996	W Virginia	Marsha Beasley	6179	Air Force	6168	Trevor Gathman, W Virginia	Joe Johnson, Navy

Skiing

Men's and Women's Combined

Year	Champion	Coach	Pts	Runner-Up	Pts	Host or Site
1954	Denver	Willy Schaeffler	384.0	Seattle	349.6	NV-Reno
1955	Denver	Willy Schaeffler	567.05	Dartmouth	558.935	Norwich
1956	Denver	Willy Schaeffler	582.01	Dartmouth	541.77	Winter Park
1957	Denver	Willy Schaeffler	577.95	Colorado	545.29	Ogden Snow Basin
1958	Dartmouth	Al Merrill	561.2	Denver	550.6	Dartmouth
1959	Colorado	Bob Beattie	549.4	Denver	543.6	Winter Park
1960	Colorado	Bob Beattie	571.4	Denver	568.6	Bridger Bowl
1961	Denver	Willy Schaeffler	376.19	Middlebury	366.94	Middlebury
1962	Denver	Willy Schaeffler	390.08	Colorado	374.30	Squaw Valley
1963	Denver	Willy Schaeffler	384.6	Colorado	381.6	Solitude
1964	Denver	Willy Schaeffler	370.2	Dartmouth	368.8	Franconia Notch
1965	Denver	Willy Schaeffler	380.5	Utah	378.4	Crystal Mountain
1966	Denver	Willy Schaeffler	381.02	Western Colorado	365.92	Crested Butte
1967	Denver	Willy Schaeffler	376.7	Wyoming	375.9	Sugarloaf Mountain
1968	Wyoming	John Cress	383.9	Denver	376.2	Mount Werner
1969	Denver	Willy Schaeffler	388.6	Dartmouth	372.0	Mount Werner
1970	Denver	Willy Schaeffler	386.6	Dartmouth	378.8	Cannon Mountain
1971	Denver	Peder Pytte	394.7	Colorado	373.1	Terry Peak
1972	Colorado	Bill Marolt	385.3	Denver	380.1	Winter Park
1973	Colorado	Bill Marolt	381.89	Wyoming	377.83	Middlebury
1974	Colorado	Bill Marolt	176	Wyoming	162	Jackson Hole
1975	Colorado	Bill Marolt	183	Vermont	115	Fort Lewis
1976	Colorado	Bill Marolt	112			Bates
	Dartmouth	Jim Page	112			
1977	Colorado	Bill Marolt	179	Wyoming	154.5	Winter Park
1978	Colorado	Bill Marolt	152.5	Wyoming	121.5	Cannon Mountain
1979	Colorado	Tim Hinderman	153	Utah	130	Steamboat Springs
1980	Vermont	Chip LaCasse	171	Utah	151	Lake Placid and Stowe
1981	Utah	Pat Miller	183	Vermont	172	Park City
1982	Colorado	Tim Hinderman	461	Vermont	436.5	Lake Placid
1983	Utah	Pat Miller	696	Vermont	650	Bozeman
1984	Utah	Pat Miller	750.5	Vermont	684	New Hampshire
1985	Wyoming	Tim Ameel	764	Utah	744	Bozeman

Skiing (Cont.)

Year	Champion	Coach	Pts	Runner-Up	Pts	Host or Site
1986 .....Utah	Pat Miller	612	Vermont	602	Vermont
1987 .....Utah	Pat Miller	710	Vermont	627	Anchorage
1988 .....Utah	Pat Miller	651	Vermont	614	Middlebury
1989 .....Vermont	Chip LaCasse	672	Utah	668	Jackson Hole
1990 .....Vermont	Chip LaCasse	671	Utah	571	Vermont
1991 .....Colorado	Richard Rokos	713	Vermont	682	Park City
1992 .....Vermont	Chip LaCasse	693.5	New Mexico	642.5	New Hampshire
1993 .....Utah	Pat Miller	783	Vermont	700.5	Steamboat Springs
1994 .....Vermont	Chip LaCasse	688	Utah	667	Sugarloaf, ME
1995 .....Colorado	Richard Rokos	720.5	Utah	711	New Hampshire
1996 .....Utah	Pat Miller	719	Denver	635½	Montana St

Soccer

Men
DIVISION I

Year	Champion	Coach	Score	Runner-Up
1959 ....St Louis	Bob Guelker	5-2	Bridgeport
1960 ....St Louis	Bob Guelker	3-2	Maryland
1961 ....West Chester	Mel Lorback	2-0	St Louis
1962 ....St Louis	Bob Guelker	4-3	Maryland
1963 ....St Louis	Bob Guelker	3-0	Navy
1964 ....Navy	F. H. Warner	1-0	Michigan St
1965 ....St Louis	Bob Guelker	1-0	Michigan St
1966 ....San Francisco	Steve Negoesco	5-2	LIU-Brooklyn
1967 ....Michigan St	Gene Kenney	0-0	Game called
St Louis	Harry Keough		due to inclement weather
1968 ....Maryland	Doyle Royal	2-2 (2 OT)	
Michigan St	Gene Kenney		
1969 ....St Louis	Harry Keough	4-0	San Francisco
1970 ....St Louis	Harry Keough	1-0	UCLA
1971 ....Vacated		3-2	St Louis
1972 ....St Louis	Harry Keough	4-2	UCLA
1973 ....St Louis	Harry Keough	2-1 (OT)	UCLA
1974 ....Howard	Lincoln Phillips	2-1 (4 OT)	St Louis
1975 ....San Francisco	Steve Negoesco	4-0	SIU-Edwardsville
1976 ....San Francisco	Steve Negoesco	1-0	Indiana
1977 ....Hartwick	Jim Lennox	2-1	San Francisco
1978 ....Vacated		2-0	Indiana
1979 ....SIU-Edwardsville	Bob Guelker	3-2	Clemson
1980 ....San Francisco	Steve Negoesco	4-3 (OT)	Indiana
1981 ....Connecticut	Joe Morrone	2-1 (OT)	Alabama A&M
1982 ....Indiana	Jerry Yeagley	2-1 (8 OT)	Duke
1983 ....Indiana	Jerry Yeagley	1-0 (2 OT)	Columbia
1984 ....Clemson	I. M. Ibrahim	2-1	Indiana
1985 ....UCLA	Sigi Schmid	1-0 (8 OT)	American
1986 ....Duke	John Rennie	1-0	Akron
1987 ....Clemson	I. M. Ibrahim	2-0	San Diego St
1988 ....Indiana	Jerry Yeagley	1-0	Howard
1989 ....Santa Clara	Steve Sampson	1-1 (2 OT)	
Virginia	Bruce Arena		
1990 ....UCLA	Sigi Schmid	1-0 (OT)	Rutgers
1991 ....Virginia	Bruce Arena	0-0*	Santa Clara
1992 ....Virginia	Bruce Arena	2-0	San Diego
1993 ....Virginia	Bruce Arena	2-0	S Carolina
1994 ....Virginia	Bruce Arena	1-0	Indiana
1995 ....Wisconsin	Jim Launder	2-0	Duke

*Under a rule passed in 1991, the NCAA determined that when a score is tied after regulation and overtime, and the championship is determined by penalty kicks, the official score will be 0-0.

Men (Cont.)

DIVISION II

Year	Champion	Year	Champion	Year	Champion
1972	SIU-Edwardsville	1980	Lock Haven	1988	Florida Tech
1973	MO-St Louis	1981	Tampa	1989	New Hampshire Col
1974	Adelphi	1982	Florida Intl	1990	Southern Connecticut St
1975	Baltimore	1983	Seattle Pacific	1991	Florida Tech
1976	Loyola (MD)	1984	Florida Intl	1992	Southern Connecticut St
1977	Alabama A&M	1985	Seattle Pacific	1993	Seattle Pacific
1978	Seattle Pacific	1986	Seattle Pacific	1994	Tampa
1979	Alabama A&M	1987	Southern Connecticut St	1995	Southern Connecticut St

DIVISION III

Year	Champion	Year	Champion	Year	Champion
1974	Brockport St	1982	NC-Greensboro	1990	Glassboro St
1975	Babson	1983	NC-Greensboro	1991	UC-San Diego
1976	Brandeis	1984	Wheaton (IL)	1992	Kean
1977	Lock Haven	1985	NC-Greensboro	1993	UC-San Diego
1978	Lock Haven	1986	NC-Greensboro	1994	Bethany (WV)
1979	Babson	1987	NC-Greensboro	1995	Williams
1980	Babson	1988	UC-San Diego		
1981	Glassboro St	1989	Elizabethtown		

Women

DIVISION I

Year	Champion	Coach	Score	Runner-Up
1982	N Carolina	Anson Dorrance	2-0	Central Florida
1983	N Carolina	Anson Dorrance	4-0	George Mason
1984	N Carolina	Anson Dorrance	2-0	Connecticut
1985	George Mason	Hank Leung	2-0	N Carolina
1986	N Carolina	Anson Dorrance	2-0	Colorado Col
1987	N Carolina	Anson Dorrance	1-0	Massachusetts
1988	N Carolina	Anson Dorrance	4-1	N Carolina St
1989	N Carolina	Anson Dorrance	2-0	Colorado Col
1990	N Carolina	Anson Dorrance	6-0	Connecticut
1991	N Carolina	Anson Dorrance	3-1	Wisconsin
1992	N Carolina	Anson Dorrance	9-1	Duke
1993	N Carolina	Anson Dorrance	6-0	George Mason
1994	N Carolina	Anson Dorrance	5-0	Notre Dame
1995	Notre Dame	Chris Petrucelli	1-0	Portland

DIVISION II

Year	Champion
1988	Cal St-Hayward
1989	Barry
1990	Sonoma St
1991	Cal St-Dominguez Hills
1992	Barry
1993	Barry
1994	Franklin Pierce
1995	Franklin Pierce

DIVISION III

Year	Champion
1986	Rochester
1987	Rochester
1988	William Smith
1989	UC-San Diego
1990	Ithaca
1991	Ithaca
1992	Cortland St
1993	Trenton St
1994	Trenton St
1995	UC-San Diego

Softball

DIVISION I

Year	Champion	Coach	Score	Runner-Up
1982	UCLA*	Sharron Backus	2-0†	Fresno St
1983	Texas A&M	Bob Brock	2-0‡	Cal St-Fullerton
1984	UCLA	Sharron Backus	1-0#	Texas A&M
1985	UCLA	Sharron Backus	2-1**	Nebraska
1986	Cal St-Fullerton*	Judi Garman	3-0	Texas A&M
1987	Texas A&M	Bob Brock	4-1	UCLA
1988	UCLA	Sharron Backus	3-0	Fresno St
1989	UCLA*	Sharron Backus	1-0	Fresno St
1990	UCLA	Sharron Backus	2-0	Fresno St
1991	Arizona	Mike Candrea	5-1	UCLA
1992	UCLA*	Sharron Backus	2-0	Arizona
1993	Arizona	Mike Candrea	1-0	UCLA
1994	Arizona	Mike Candrea	4-0	Cal St-Northridge
1995	UCLA*	Sharron Backus/ Sue Enquist	4-2	Arizona
1996	Arizona*	Mike Candrea	6-4	Washington

*Undefeated teams in final series. †8 innings. ‡12 innings. #13 innings. **9 innings.

DIVISION II

Year	Champion	Year	Champion	Year	Champion
1982	Sam Houston St	1987	Cal St-Northridge	1992	Missouri Southern
1983	Cal St-Northridge	1988	Cal St-Bakersfield	1993	Florida Southern
1984	Cal St-Northridge	1989	Cal St-Bakersfield	1994	Merrimack
1985	Cal St-Northridge	1990	Cal St-Bakersfield	1995	Kennesaw St
1986	SF Austin St	1991	Augustana (SD)	1996	Kennesaw St

DIVISION III

Year	Champion	Year	Champion	Year	Champion
1982	Sam Houston St	1987	Trenton St*	1993	Central (IA)
1982	Eastern Connecticut St*	1988	Central (IA)	1994	Trenton St
1983	Trenton St	1989	Trenton St*	1995	Chapman
1984	Buena Vista*	1990	Eastern Connecticut St	1996	Trenton St*
1985	Eastern Connecticut St	1991	Central (IA)		
1986	Eastern Connecticut St	1992	Trenton St		

*Undefeated teams in final series.

Swimming and Diving

Men

DIVISION I

Year	Champion	Coach	Pts	Runner-Up	Pts
1937	Michigan	Matt Mann	75	Ohio St	39
1938	Michigan	Matt Mann	46	Ohio St	45
1939	Michigan	Matt Mann	65	Ohio St	58
1940	Michigan	Matt Mann	45	Yale	42
1941	Michigan	Matt Mann	61	Yale	58
1942	Yale	Robert J. H. Kiphuth	71	Michigan	39
1943	Ohio St	Mike Peppe	81	Michigan	47
1944	Yale	Robert J. H. Kiphuth	39	Michigan	38
1945	Ohio St	Mike Peppe	56	Michigan	48
1946	Ohio St	Mike Peppe	61	Michigan	37
1947	Ohio St	Mike Peppe	66	Michigan	39
1948	Michigan	Matt Mann	44	Ohio St	41
1949	Ohio St	Mike Peppe	49	Iowa	35
1950	Ohio St	Mike Peppe	64	Yale	43
1951	Yale	Robert J. H. Kiphuth	81	Michigan St	60
1952	Ohio St	Mike Peppe	94	Yale	81
1953	Yale	Robert J. H. Kiphuth	96½	Ohio St	73½
1954	Ohio St	Mike Peppe	94	Michigan	67
1955	Ohio St	Mike Peppe	90	Yale	51
				Michigan	51
1956	Ohio St	Mike Peppe	68	Yale	54
1957	Michigan	Gus Stager	69	Yale	61

Men (Cont.)

DIVISION I (Cont.)

Year	Champion	Coach	Pts	Runner-Up	Pts
1958	Michigan	Gus Stager	72	Yale	63
1959	Michigan	Gus Stager	137½	Ohio St	44
1960	Southern Cal	Peter Daland	87	Michigan	73
1961	Michigan	Gus Stager	85	Southern Cal	62
1962	Ohio St	Mike Peppe	92	Southern Cal	46
1963	Southern Cal	Peter Daland	81	Yale	77
1964	Southern Cal	Peter Daland	96	Indiana	91
1965	Southern Cal	Peter Daland	285	Indiana	278½
1966	Southern Cal	Peter Daland	302	Indiana	286
1967	Stanford	Jim Gaughran	275	Southern Cal	260
1968	Indiana	James Counsilman	346	Yale	253
1969	Indiana	James Counsilman	427	Southern Cal	306
1970	Indiana	James Counsilman	332	Southern Cal	235
1971	Indiana	James Counsilman	351	Southern Cal	260
1972	Indiana	James Counsilman	390	Southern Cal	371
1973	Indiana	James Counsilman	358	Tennessee	294
1974	Southern Cal	Peter Daland	339	Indiana	338
1975	Southern Cal	Peter Daland	344	Indiana	274
1976	Southern Cal	Peter Daland	398	Tennessee	237
1977	Southern Cal	Peter Daland	385	Alabama	204
1978	Tennessee	Ray Bussard	307	Auburn	185
1979	California	Nort Thornton	287	Southern Cal	227
1980	California	Nort Thornton	234	Texas	220
1981	Texas	Eddie Reese	259	UCLA	189
1982	UCLA	Ron Ballatore	219	Texas	210
1983	Florida	Randy Reese	238	Southern Meth	227
1984	Florida	Randy Reese	287½	Texas	277
1985	Stanford	Skip Kenney	403½	Florida	302
1986	Stanford	Skip Kenney	404	California	335
1987	Stanford	Skip Kenney	374	Southern Cal	296
1988	Texas	Eddie Reese	424	Southern Cal	369½
1989	Texas	Eddie Reese	475	Stanford	396
1990	Texas	Eddie Reese	506	Southern Cal	423
1991	Texas	Eddie Reese	476	Stanford	420
1992	Stanford	Skip Kenney	632	Texas	356
1993	Stanford	Skip Kenney	520½	Michigan	396
1994	Stanford	Skip Kenney	566½	Texas	445
1995	Michigan	Jon Urbanchek	561	Stanford	475
1996	Texas	Eddie Reese	479	Auburn	443½

DIVISION II

Year	Champion	Year	Champion	Year	Champion
1963	SW Missouri St	1975	Cal St-Northridge	1987	Cal St-Bakersfield
1964	Bucknell	1976	Cal St-Chico	1988	Cal St-Bakersfield
1965	San Diego St	1977	Cal St-Northridge	1989	Cal St-Bakersfield
1966	San Diego St	1978	Cal St-Northridge	1990	Cal St-Bakersfield
1967	UC-Santa Barbara	1979	Cal St-Northridge	1991	Cal St-Bakersfield
1968	Long Beach St	1980	Oakland (MI)	1992	Cal St-Bakersfield
1969	UC-Irvine	1981	Cal St-Northridge	1993	Cal St-Bakersfield
1970	UC-Irvine	1982	Cal St-Northridge	1994	Oakland (MI)
1971	UC-Irvine	1983	Cal St-Northridge	1995	Oakland (MI)
1972	Eastern Michigan	1984	Cal St-Northridge	1996	Oakland (MI)
1973	Cal St-Chico	1985	Cal St-Northridge		
1974	Cal St-Chico	1986	Cal St-Bakersfield		

DIVISION III

Year	Champion	Year	Champion	Year	Champion
1975	Cal St-Chico	1983	Kenyon	1991	Kenyon
1976	St Lawrence	1984	Kenyon	1992	Kenyon
1977	Johns Hopkins	1985	Kenyon	1993	Kenyon
1978	Johns Hopkins	1986	Kenyon	1994	Kenyon
1979	Johns Hopkins	1987	Kenyon	1995	Kenyon
1980	Kenyon	1988	Kenyon	1996	Kenyon
1981	Kenyon	1989	Kenyon		
1982	Kenyon	1990	Kenyon		

Women
DIVISION I

Year	Champion	Coach	Pts	Runner-Up	Pts
1982	Florida	Randy Reese	505	Stanford	383
1983	Stanford	George Haines	418½	Florida	389½
1984	Texas	Richard Quick	392	Stanford	324
1985	Texas	Richard Quick	643	Florida	400
1986	Texas	Richard Quick	633	Florida	586
1987	Texas	Richard Quick	648½	Stanford	631½
1988	Texas	Richard Quick	661	Florida	542½
1989	Stanford	Richard Quick	610½	Texas	547
1990	Texas	Mark Schubert	632	Stanford	622½
1991	Texas	Mark Schubert	746	Stanford	653
1992	Stanford	Richard Quick	735½	Texas	651
1993	Stanford	Richard Quick	649½	Florida	421
1994	Stanford	Richard Quick	512	Texas	421
1995	Stanford	Richard Quick	497½	Michigan	478½
1996	Stanford	Richard Quick	478	SMU	397

DIVISION II

Year	Champion	Year	Champion	Year	Champion
1982	Cal St-Northridge	1987	Cal St-Northridge	1992	Oakland (MI)
1983	Clarion	1988	Cal St-Northridge	1993	Oakland (MI)
1984	Clarion	1989	Cal St-Northridge	1994	Oakland (MI)
1985	S Florida	1990	Oakland (MI)	1995	Air Force
1986	Clarion	1991	Oakland (MI)	1996	Air Force

DIVISION III

Year	Champion	Year	Champion	Year	Champion
1982	Williams	1987	Kenyon	1992	Kenyon
1983	Williams	1988	Kenyon	1993	Kenyon
1984	Kenyon	1989	Kenyon	1994	Kenyon
1985	Kenyon	1990	Kenyon	1995	Kenyon
1986	Kenyon	1991	Kenyon	1996	Kenyon

Tennis

Men
INDIVIDUAL CHAMPIONS 1883-1945

Year	Champion	Year	Champion
1883	Joseph Clark, Harvard (spring)	1906	Robert LeRoy, Columbia
1883	Howard Taylor, Harvard (fall)	1907	G. Peabody Gardner, Jr, Harvard
1884	W. P. Knapp, Yale	1908	Nat Niles, Harvard
1885	W. P. Knapp, Yale	1909	Wallace Johnson, Pennsylvania
1886	G. M. Brinley, Trinity (CT)	1910	R. A. Holden, Jr, Yale
1887	P. S. Sears, Harvard	1911	E. H. Whitney, Harvard
1888	P. S. Sears, Harvard	1912	George Church, Princeton
1889	R. P. Huntington, Jr, Yale	1913	Richard Williams II, Harvard
1890	Fred Hovey, Harvard	1914	George Church, Princeton
1891	Fred Hovey, Harvard	1915	Richard Williams II, Harvard
1892	William Larned, Cornell	1916	G. Colket Caner, Harvard
1893	Malcolm Chace, Brown	1917-18	No tournament
1894	Malcolm Chace, Yale	1919	Charles Garland, Yale
1895	Malcolm Chace, Yale	1920	Lascelles Banks, Yale
1896	Malcolm Whitman, Harvard	1921	Philip Neer, Stanford
1897	S. G. Thompson, Princeton	1922	Lucien Williams, Yale
1898	Leo Ware, Harvard	1923	Carl Fischer, Philadelphia Osteo
1899	Dwight Davis, Harvard	1924	Wallace Scott, Washington
1900	Raymond Little, Princeton	1925	Edward Chandler, California
1901	Fred Alexander, Princeton	1926	Edward Chandler, California
1902	William Clothier, Harvard	1927	Wilmer Allison, Texas
1903	E. B. Dewhurst, Pennsylvania	1928	Julius Seligson, Lehigh
1904	Robert LeRoy, Columbia	1929	Berkeley Bell, Texas
1905	E. B. Dewhurst, Pennsylvania	1930	Clifford Sutter, Tulane

Men (Cont.)

INDIVIDUAL CHAMPIONS 1883-1945 (Cont.)

1931......................Keith Gledhill, Stanford		1939......................Frank Guernsey, Rice	
1932......................Clifford Sutter, Tulane		1940......................Donald McNeil, Kenyon	
1933......................Jack Tidball, UCLA		1941......................Joseph Hunt, Navy	
1934......................Gene Mako, Southern Cal		1942......................Frederick Schroeder, Jr, Stanford	
1935......................Wilbur Hess, Rice		1943......................Pancho Segura, Miami (FL)	
1936......................Ernest Sutter, Tulane		1944......................Pancho Segura, Miami (FL)	
1937......................Ernest Sutter, Tulane		1945......................Pancho Segura, Miami (FL)	
1938......................Frank Guernsey, Rice			

DIVISION I

Year	Champion	Coach	Pts	Runner-Up	Pts	Individual Champion
1946	....Southern Cal	William Moyle	9	William & Mary	6	Robert Falkenburg, Southern Cal
1947	....William & Mary	Sharvey G. Umbeck	10	Rice	4	Gardner Larned, William & Mary
1948	....William & Mary	Sharvey G. Umbeck	6	San Francisco	5	Harry Likas, San Francisco
1949	....San Francisco	Norman Brooks	7	Rollins/Tulane/	4	Jack Tuero, Tulane
				Washington		
1950	....UCLA	William Ackerman	11	California	5	Herbert Flam, UCLA
				Southern Cal	5	
1951	....Southern Cal	Louis Wheeler	9	Cincinnati	7	Tony Trabert, Cincinnati
1952	....UCLA	J. D. Morgan	11	California	5	Hugh Stewart, Southern Cal
				Southern Cal	5	
1953	....UCLA	J. D. Morgan	11	California	6	Hamilton Richardson, Tulane
1954	....UCLA	J. D. Morgan	15	Southern Cal	10	Hamilton Richardson, Tulane
1955	....Southern Cal	George Toley	12	Texas	7	Jose Aguero, Tulane
1956	....UCLA	J. D. Morgan	15	Southern Cal	14	Alejandro Olmedo, Southern Cal
1957	....Michigan	William Murphy	10	Tulane	9	Barry MacKay, Michigan
1958	....Southern Cal	George Toley	13	Stanford	9	Alejandro Olmedo, Southern Cal
1959	....Notre Dame	Thomas Fallon	8			Whitney Reed, San Jose St
	Tulane	Emmet Pare	8			
1960	....UCLA	J. D. Morgan	18	Southern Cal	8	Larry Nagler, UCLA
1961	....UCLA	J. D. Morgan	17	Southern Cal	16	Allen Fox, UCLA
1962	....Southern Cal	George Toley	22	UCLA	12	Rafael Osuna, Southern Cal
1963	....Southern Cal	George Toley	27	UCLA	19	Dennis Ralston, Southern Cal
1964	....Southern Cal	George Toley	26	UCLA	25	Dennis Ralston, Southern Cal
1965	....UCLA	J. D. Morgan	31	Miami (FL)	13	Arthur Ashe, UCLA
1966	....Southern Cal	George Toley	27	UCLA	23	Charles Pasarell, UCLA
1967	....Southern Cal	George Toley	28	UCLA	23	Bob Lutz, Southern Cal
1968	....Southern Cal	George Toley	31	Rice	23	Stan Smith, Southern Cal
1969	....Southern Cal	George Toley	35	UCLA	23	Joaquin Loyo-Mayo, Southern Cal
1970	....UCLA	Glenn Bassett	26	Trinity (TX)	22	Jeff Borowiak, UCLA
				Rice	22	
1971	....UCLA	Glenn Bassett	35	Trinity (TX)	27	Jimmy Connors, UCLA
1972	....Trinity (TX)	Clarence Mabry	36	Stanford	30	Dick Stockton, Trinity (TX)
1973	....Stanford	Dick Gould	33	Southern Cal	28	Alex Mayer, Stanford
1974	....Stanford	Dick Gould	30	Southern Cal	25	John Whitlinger, Stanford
1975	....UCLA	Glenn Bassett	27	Miami (FL)	20	Bill Martin, UCLA
1976	....Southern Cal	George Toley	21			Bill Scanlon, Trinity (TX)
	UCLA	Glenn Bassett	21			
1977	....Stanford	Dick Gould		Trinity (TX)		Matt Mitchell, Stanford
1978	....Stanford	Dick Gould		UCLA		John McEnroe, Stanford
1979	....UCLA	Glenn Bassett		Trinity (TX)		Kevin Curren, Texas
1980	....Stanford	Dick Gould		California		Robert Van't Hof, Southern Cal
1981	....Stanford	Dick Gould		UCLA		Tim Mayotte, Stanford
1982	....UCLA	Glenn Bassett		Pepperdine		Mike Leach, Michigan
1983	....Stanford	Dick Gould		Southern Meth		Greg Holmes, Utah
1984	....UCLA	Glenn Bassett		Stanford		Mikael Pernfors, Georgia
1985	....Georgia	Dan Magill		UCLA		Mikael Pernfors, Georgia
1986	....Stanford	Dick Gould		Pepperdine		Dan Goldie, Stanford
1987	....Georgia	Dan Magill		UCLA		Andrew Burrow, Miami (FL)
1988	....Stanford	Dick Gould		Louisiana St		Robby Weiss, Pepperdine
1989	....Stanford	Dick Gould		Georgia		Donni Leaycraft, Louisiana St
1990	....Stanford	Dick Gould		Tennessee		Steve Bryan, Texas
1991	....Southern Cal	Dick Leach		Georgia		Jared Palmer, Stanford
1992	....Stanford	Dick Gould		Notre Dame		Alex O'Brien, Stanford

Men (Cont.)
DIVISION I (Cont.)

Year	Champion	Coach	Pts	Runner-Up	Pts	Individual Champion
1993	Southern Cal	Dick Leach		Georgia		Chris Woodruff, Tennessee
1994	Southern Cal	Dick Leach		Stanford		Mark Merklein, Florida
1995	Stanford	Dick Gould		Mississippi		Sargis Sargsian, Arizona St
1996	Stanford	Dick Gould		UCLA		Cecil Mamiit, Southern Cal

Note: Prior to 1977, individual wins counted in the team's total points. In 1977, a dual-match single-elimination team championship was initiated, eliminating the point system.

DIVISION II

Year	Champion	Year	Champion	Year	Champion
1963	Cal St-LA	1975	UC-Irvine/San Diego	1987	Chapman
1964	Cal St-LA/S Illinois	1976	Hampton	1988	Chapman
1965	Cal St-LA	1977	UC-Irvine	1989	Hampton
1966	Rollins	1978	SIU-Edwardsville	1990	Cal Poly-SLO
1967	Long Beach St	1979	SIU-Edwardsville	1991	Rollins
1968	Fresno St	1980	SIU-Edwardsville	1992	UC-Davis
1969	Cal St-Northridge	1981	SIU-Edwardsville	1993	Lander (SC)
1970	UC-Irvine	1982	SIU-Edwardsville	1994	Lander (SC)
1971	UC-Irvine	1983	SIU-Edwardsville	1995	Lander (SC)
1972	UC-Irvine/ Rollins	1984	SIU-Edwardsville	1996	Lander (SC)
1973	UC-Irvine	1985	Chapman		
1974	San Diego	1986	Cal Poly-SLO		

DIVISION III

Year	Champion	Year	Champion	Year	Champion
1976	Kalamazoo	1983	Redlands	1991	Kalamazoo
1977	Swarthmore	1984	Redlands	1992	Kalamazoo
1978	Kalamazoo	1985	Swarthmore	1993	Kalamazoo
1979	Redlands	1986	Kalamazoo	1994	Washington (MD)
1980	Gustavus Adolphus	1987	Kalamazoo	1995	UC-Santa Cruz
1981	Claremont-M-S	1988	Washington & Lee	1996	UC-Santa Cruz
	Swarthmore	1989	UC-Santa Cruz		
1982	Gustavus Adolphus	1990	Swarthmore		

Women
DIVISION I

Year	Champion	Coach	Runner-Up	Individual Champion
1982	Stanford	Frank Brennan	UCLA	Alycia Moulton, Stanford
1983	Southern Cal	Dave Borelli	Trinity (TX)	Beth Herr, Southern Cal
1984	Stanford	Frank Brennan	Southern Cal	Lisa Spain, Georgia
1985	Southern Cal	Dave Borelli	Miami (FL)	Linda Gates, Stanford
1986	Stanford	Frank Brennan	Southern Cal	Patty Fendick, Stanford
1987	Stanford	Frank Brennan	Georgia	Patty Fendick, Stanford
1988	Stanford	Frank Brennan	Florida	Shaun Stafford, Florida
1989	Stanford	Frank Brennan	UCLA	Sandra Birch, Stanford
1990	Stanford	Frank Brennan	Florida	Debbie Graham, Stanford
1991	Stanford	Frank Brennan	UCLA	Sandra Birch, Stanford
1992	Florida	Andy Brandi	Texas	Lisa Raymond, Florida
1993	Texas	Jeff Moore	Stanford	Lisa Raymond, Florida
1994	Georgia	Jeff Wallace	Stanford	Angela Lettiere, Georgia
1995	Texas	Jeff Moore	Florida	Keri Phebus, UCLA
1996	Florida	Andy Brandi	Stanford	Jill Craybas, Florida

DIVISION II

Year	Champion	Year	Champion	Year	Champion
1982	Cal St-Northridge	1987	SIU-Edwardsville	1992	Cal Poly-Pomona
1983	TN-Chattanooga	1988	SIU-Edwardsville	1993	UC-Davis
1984	TN-Chattanooga	1989	SIU-Edwardsville	1994	N Florida
1985	TN-Chattanooga	1990	UC-Davis	1995	Armstrong St
1986	SIU-Edwardsville	1991	Cal Poly-Pomona	1996	Armstrong St

Women *(Cont.)*

DIVISION III

Year	Champion	Year	Champion	Year	Champion
1982	Occidental	1987	UC-San Diego	1992	Pomona-Pitzer
1983	Principia	1988	Mary Washington	1993	Kenyon
1984	Davidson	1989	UC-San Diego	1994	UC San Diego
1985	UC-San Diego	1990	Gustavus Adolphus	1995	Kenyon
1986	Trenton St	1991	Mary Washington	1996	Emory

Indoor Track and Field

Men

DIVISION I

Year	Champion	Coach	Pts	Runner-Up	Pts
1965	Missouri	Tom Botts	14	Oklahoma St	12
1966	Kansas	Bob Timmons	14	Southern Cal	13
1967	Southern Cal	Vern Wolfe	26	Oklahoma	17
1968	Villanova	Jim Elliott	35	Southern Cal	25
1969	Kansas	Bob Timmons	41½	Villanova	33
1970	Kansas	Bob Timmons	27½	Villanova	26
1971	Villanova	Jim Elliott	22	UTEP	19¼
1972	Southern Cal	Vern Wolfe	19	Bowling Green/ Mich St	18
1973	Manhattan	Fred Dwyer	18	Kansas/Kent St/UTEP	12
1974	UTEP	Ted Banks	19	Colorado	18
1975	UTEP	Ted Banks	36	Kansas	17½
1976	UTEP	Ted Banks	23	Villanova	15
1977	Washington St	John Chaplin	25½	UTEP	25
1978	UTEP	Ted Banks	44	Auburn	38
1979	Villanova	Jim Elliott	52	UTEP	51
1980	UTEP	Ted Banks	76	Villanova	42
1981	UTEP	Ted Banks	76	Southern Meth	51
1982	UTEP	John Wedel	67	Arkansas	30
1983	Southern Meth	Ted McLaughlin	43	Villanova	32
1984	Arkansas	John McDonnell	38	Washington St	28
1985	Arkansas	John McDonnell	70	Tennessee	29
1986	Arkansas	John McDonnell	49	Villanova	22
1987	Arkansas	John McDonnell	39	Southern Meth	31
1988	Arkansas	John McDonnell	34	Illinois	29
1989	Arkansas	John McDonnell	34	Florida	31
1990	Arkansas	John McDonnell	44	Texas A&M	36
1991	Arkansas	John McDonnell	34	Georgetown	27
1992	Arkansas	John McDonnell	53	Clemson	46
1993	Arkansas	John McDonnell	66	Clemson	30
1994	Arkansas	John McDonnell	83	UTEP	45
1995	Arkansas	John McDonnell	59	GMU/Tennessee	26
1996	George Mason	John Cook	39	Nebraska	31½

DIVISION II

Year	Champion	Year	Champion	Year	Champion
1985	SE Missouri St	1989	St Augustine's	1993	Abilene Christian
1986	not held	1990	St Augustine's	1994	Abilene Christian
1987	St Augustine's	1991	St Augustine's	1995	St Augustine's
1988	Abil Christ/ St August	1992	St Augustine's	1996	Abilene Christian

DIVISION III

Year	Champion	Year	Champion	Year	Champion
1985	St Thomas (MN)	1989	North Central	1993	WI-La Crosse
1986	Frostburg St	1990	Lincoln (PA)	1994	WI-La Crosse
1987	WI-La Crosse	1991	WI-La Crosse	1995	Lincoln (PA)
1988	WI-La Crosse	1992	WI-La Crosse	1996	Lincoln (PA)

Women

DIVISION I

Year	Champion	Coach	Pts	Runner-Up	Pts
1983	Nebraska	Gary Pepin	47	Tennessee	44
1984	Nebraska	Gary Pepin	59	Tennessee	48
1985	Florida St	Gary Winckler	34	Texas	32
1986	Texas	Terry Crawford	31	Southern Cal	26
1987	Louisiana St	Loren Seagrave	49	Tennessee	30
1988	Texas	Terry Crawford	71	Villanova	52
1989	Louisiana St	Pat Henry	61	Villanova	34
1990	Texas	Terry Crawford	50	Wisconsin	26
1991	Louisiana St	Pat Henry	48	Texas	39
1992	Florida	Bev Kearney	50	Stanford	26
1993	Louisiana St	Pat Henry	49	Wisconsin	44
1994	Louisiana St	Pat Henry	48	Alabama	29
1995	Louisiana St	Pat Henry	40	UCLA	37
1996	Louisiana St	Pat Henry	52	Georgia	34

DIVISION II

Year	Champion	Year	Champion	Year	Champion
1985	St Augustine's	1989	Abilene Christian	1993	Abilene Christian
1986	not held	1990	Abilene Christian	1994	Abilene Christian
1987	St Augustine's	1991	Abilene Christian	1995	Abilene Christian
1988	Abilene Christian	1992	Alabama A&M	1996	Abilene Christian

DIVISION III

Year	Champion	Year	Champion	Year	Champion
1985	MA-Boston	1989	Christopher Newport	1993	Lincoln (PA)
1986	MA-Boston	1990	Christopher Newport	1994	WI-Oshkosh
1987	MA-Boston	1991	Cortland St	1995	WI-Oshkosh
1988	Christopher Newport	1992	Christopher Newport	1996	WI-Oshkosh

Outdoor Track and Field

Men

DIVISION I

Year	Champion	Coach	Pts	Runner-Up	Pts
1921	Illinois	Harry Gill	20†	Notre Dame	16†
1922	California	Walter Christie	28†	Penn St	19†
1923	Michigan	Stephen Farrell	29†	Mississippi St	16
1924	No meet				
1925	Stanford*	R. L. Templeton	31†		
1926	Southern Cal*	Dean Cromwell	27†		
1927	Illinois*	Harry Gill	35†		
1928	Stanford	R. L. Templeton	72	Ohio St	31
1929	Ohio St	Frank Castleman	50	Washington	42
1930	Southern Cal	Dean Cromwell	55†	Washington	40
1931	Southern Cal	Dean Cromwell	77†	Ohio St	31†
1932	Indiana	Billy Hayes	56	Ohio St	49†
1933	Louisiana St	Bernie Moore	58	Southern Cal	54
1934	Stanford	R. L. Templeton	63	Southern Cal	54†
1935	Southern Cal	Dean Cromwell	74†	Ohio St	40†
1936	Southern Cal	Dean Cromwell	103†	Ohio St	73
1937	Southern Cal	Dean Cromwell	62	Stanford	50
1938	Southern Cal	Dean Cromwell	67†	Stanford	38
1939	Southern Cal	Dean Cromwell	86	Stanford	44†
1940	Southern Cal	Dean Cromwell	47	Stanford	28†
1941	Southern Cal	Dean Cromwell	81†	Indiana	50
1942	Southern Cal	Dean Cromwell	85†	Ohio St	44†
1943	Southern Cal	Dean Cromwell	46	California	39
1944	Illinois	Leo Johnson	79	Notre Dame	43
1945	Navy	E. J. Thomson	62	Illinois	48†
1946	Illinois	Leo Johnson	78	Southern Cal	42†
1947	Illinois	Leo Johnson	59†	Southern Cal	34†

Men (Cont.)

DIVISION I (Cont.)

Year	Champion	Coach	Pts	Runner-Up	Pts
1948	Minnesota	James Kelly	46	Southern Cal	41†
1949	Southern Cal	Jess Hill	55†	UCLA	31
1950	Southern Cal	Jess Hill	49†	Stanford	28
1951	Southern Cal	Jess Mortenson	56	Cornell	40
1952	Southern Cal	Jess Mortenson	66†	San Jose St	24†
1953	Southern Cal	Jess Mortenson	80	Illinois	41
1954	Southern Cal	Jess Mortenson	66†	Illinois	31†
1955	Southern Cal	Jess Mortenson	42	UCLA	34
1956	UCLA	Elvin Drake	55†	Kansas	51
1957	Villanova	James Elliott	47	California	32
1958	Southern Cal	Jess Mortenson	48†	Kansas	40†
1959	Kansas	Bill Easton	73	San Jose St	48
1960	Kansas	Bill Easton	50	Southern Cal	37
1961	Southern Cal	Jess Mortenson	65	Oregon	47
1962	Oregon	William Bowerman	85	Villanova	40†
1963	Southern Cal	Vern Wolfe	61	Stanford	42
1964	Oregon	William Bowerman	70	San Jose St	40
1965	Oregon	William Bowerman	32		
	Southern Cal	Vern Wolfe	32		
1966	UCLA	Jim Bush	81	Brigham Young	33
1967	Southern Cal	Vern Wolfe	86	Oregon	40
1968	Southern Cal	Vern Wolfe	58	Washington St	57
1969	San Jose St	Bud Winter	48	Kansas	45
1970	Brigham Young	Clarence Robison	35		
	Kansas	Bob Timmons	35		
	Oregon	William Bowerman	35		
1971	UCLA	Jim Bush	52	Southern Cal	41
1972	UCLA	Jim Bush	82	Southern Cal	49
1973	UCLA	Jim Bush	56	Oregon	31
1974	Tennessee	Stan Huntsman	60	UCLA	56
1975	UTEP	Ted Banks	55	UCLA	42
1976	Southern Cal	Vern Wolfe	64	UTEP	44
1977	Arizona St	Senon Castillo	64	UTEP	50
1978	UCLA/UTEP	Jim Bush/Ted Banks	50		
1979	UTEP	Ted Banks	64	Villanova	48
1980	UTEP	Ted Banks	69	UCLA	46
1981	UTEP	Ted Banks	70	Southern Meth	57
1982	UTEP	John Wedel	105	Tennessee	94
1983	SMU	Ted McLaughlin	104	Tennessee	102
1984	Oregon	Bill Dellinger	113	Washington St	94½
1985	Arkansas	John McDonnell	61	Washington St	46
1986	Southern Meth	Ted McLaughlin	53	Washington St	52
1987	UCLA	Bob Larsen	81	Texas	28
1988	UCLA	Bob Larsen	82	Texas	41
1989	Louisiana St	Pat Henry	53	Texas A&M	51
1990	Louisiana St	Pat Henry	44	Arkansas	36
1991	Tennessee	Doug Brown	51	Washington St	42
1992	Arkansas	John McDonnell	60	Tennessee	46½
1993	Arkansas	John McDonnell	69	LSU/Ohio St	45
1994	Arkansas	John McDonnell	83	UTEP	45
1995	Arkansas	John McDonnell	61½	UCLA	55
1996	Arkansas	John McDonnell	55	George Mason	40

*Unofficial championship. †Fraction of a point.

Men *(Cont.)*

DIVISION II

Year	Champion	Year	Champion	Year	Champion
1963	MD-Eastern Shore	1974	Eastern Illinois	1985	Abilene Christian
1964	Fresno St		Norfolk St	1986	Abilene Christian
1965	San Diego St	1975	Cal St-Northridge	1987	Abilene Christian
1966	San Diego St	1976	UC-Irvine	1988	Abilene Christian
1967	Long Beach St	1977	Cal St-Hayward	1989	St Augustine's
1968	Cal Poly-SLO	1978	Cal St-LA	1990	St Augustine's
1969	Cal Poly-SLO	1979	Cal Poly-SLO	1991	St Augustine's
1970	Cal Poly-SLO	1980	Cal Poly-SLO	1992	St Augustine's
1971	Kentucky St	1981	Cal Poly-SLO	1993	St Augustine's
1972	Eastern Michigan	1982	Abilene Christian	1994	St Augustine's
1973	Norfolk St	1983	Abilene Christian	1995	St Augustine's
		1984	Abilene Christian	1996	Abilene Christian

DIVISION III

Year	Champion	Year	Champion	Year	Champion
1974	Ashland	1982	Glassboro St	1990	Lincoln (PA)
1975	Southern-N Orleans	1983	Glassboro St	1991	WI-La Crosse
1976	Southern-N Orleans	1984	Glassboro St	1992	WI-La Crosse
1977	Southern-N Orleans	1985	Lincoln (PA)	1993	WI-La Crosse
1978	Occidental	1986	Frostburg St	1994	North Central
1979	Slippery Rock	1987	Frostburg St	1995	Lincoln (PA)
1980	Glassboro St	1988	WI-La Crosse	1996	Lincoln (PA)
1981	Glassboro St	1989	North Central		

Women

DIVISION I

Year	Champion	Coach	Pts	Runner-Up	Pts
1982	UCLA	Scott Chisam	153	Tennessee	126
1983	UCLA	Scott Chisam	116½	Florida St	108
1984	Florida St	Gary Winckler	145	Tennessee	124
1985	Oregon	Tom Heinonen	52	Florida St/LSU	46
1986	Texas	Terry Crawford	65	Alabama	55
1987	Louisiana St	Loren Seagrave	62	Alabama	53
1988	Louisiana St	Loren Seagrave	61	UCLA	58
1989	Louisiana St	Pat Henry	86	UCLA	47
1990	Louisiana St	Pat Henry	53	UCLA	46
1991	Louisiana St	Pat Henry	78	Texas	67
1992	Louisiana St	Pat Henry	87	Florida	81
1993	Louisiana St	Pat Henry	93	Wisconsin	44
1994	Louisiana St	Pat Henry	86	Texas	43
1995	Louisiana St	Pat Henry	69	UCLA	58
1996	Louisiana St	Pat Henry	81	Texas	52

DIVISION II

Year	Champion	Year	Champion	Year	Champion
1982	Cal Poly-SLO	1987	Abilene Christian	1992	Alabama A&M
1983	Cal Poly-SLO	1988	Abilene Christian	1993	Alabama A&M
1984	Cal Poly-SLO	1989	Cal Poly-SLO	1994	Alabama A&M
1985	Abilene Christian	1990	Cal Poly-SLO	1995	Abilene Christian
1986	Abilene Christian	1991	Cal Poly-SLO	1996	Abilene Christian

DIVISION III

Year	Champion	Year	Champion	Year	Champion
1982	Central (IA)	1987	Chris. Newport	1992	Chris. Newport
1983	WI-La Crosse	1988	Chris. Newport	1993	Lincoln (PA)
1984	WI-La Crosse	1989	Chris. Newport	1994	Chris. Newport
1985	Cortland St	1990	WI-Oshkosh	1995	WI-Oshkosh
1986	MA-Boston	1991	WI-Oshkosh	1996	WI-Oshkosh

Volleyball

Men

Year	Champion	Coach	Score	Runner-Up	Most Outstanding Player
1970	UCLA	Al Scates	3-0	Long Beach St	Dane Holtzman, UCLA
1971	UCLA	Al Scates	3-0	UC-Santa Barbara	Kirk Kilgore, UCLA
					Tim Bonynge, UC-Santa Barbara
1972	UCLA	Al Scates	3-2	San Diego St	Dick Irvin, UCLA
1973	San Diego St	Jack Henn	3-1	Long Beach St	Duncan McFarland, San Diego St
1974	UCLA	Al Scates	3-2	UC-Santa Barbara	Bob Leonard, UCLA
1975	UCLA	Al Scates	3-1	UC-Santa Barbara	John Bekins, UCLA
1976	UCLA	Al Scates	3-0	Pepperdine	Joe Mika, UCLA
1977	Southern Cal	Ernie Hix	3-1	Ohio St	Celso Kalache, Southern Cal
1978	Pepperdine	Marv Dunphy	3-2	UCLA	Mike Blanchard, Pepperdine
1979	UCLA	Al Scates	3-1	Southern Cal	Sinjin Smith, UCLA
1980	Southern Cal	Ernie Hix	3-1	UCLA	Dusty Dvorak, Southern Cal
1981	UCLA	Al Scates	3-2	Southern Cal	Karch Kiraly, UCLA
1982	UCLA	Al Scates	3-0	Penn St	Karch Kiraly, UCLA
1983	UCLA	Al Scates	3-0	Pepperdine	Ricci Luyties, UCLA
1984	UCLA	Al Scates	3-1	Pepperdine	Ricci Luyties, UCLA
1985	Pepperdine	Marv Dunphy	3-1	Southern Cal	Bob Ctvrtlik, Pepperdine
1986	Pepperdine	Rod Wilde	3-2	Southern Cal	Steve Friedman, Pepperdine
1987	UCLA	Al Scates	3-0	Southern Cal	Ozzie Volstad, UCLA
1988	Southern Cal	Bob Yoder	3-2	UC-Santa Barbara	Jen-Kai Liu, Southern Cal
1989	UCLA	Al Scates	3-1	Stanford	Matt Sonnichsen, UCLA
1990	Southern Cal	Jim McLaughlin	3-1	Long Beach St	Bryan Ivie, Southern Cal
1991	Long Beach St	Ray Ratelle	3-1	Southern Cal	Brent Hilliard, Long Beach St
1992	Pepperdine	Marv Dunphy	3-0	Stanford	Alon Grinberg, Pepperdine
1993	UCLA	Al Scates	3-0	Cal St-Northridge	Mike Sealy/Jeff Nygaard, UCLA
1994	Penn St	Tom Peterson	3-2	UCLA	Ramon Hernandez, Penn St
1995	UCLA	Al Scates	3-0	Penn St	Jeff Nygaard, UCLA
1996	UCLA	Al Scates	3-2	Hawaii	Yuval Katz, Hawaii

Women

DIVISION I

Year	Champion	Coach	Score	Runner-Up
1981	Southern Cal	Chuck Erbe	3-2	UCLA
1982	Hawaii	Dave Shoji	3-2	Southern Cal
1983	Hawaii	Dave Shoji	3-0	UCLA
1984	UCLA	Andy Banachowski	3-2	Stanford
1985	Pacific	John Dunning	3-1	Stanford
1986	Pacific	John Dunning	3-0	Nebraska
1987	Hawaii	Dave Shoji	3-1	Stanford
1988	Texas	Mick Haley	3-0	Hawaii
1989	Long Beach St	Brian Gimmillaro	3-0	Nebraska
1990	UCLA	Andy Banachowski	3-0	Pacific
1991	UCLA	Andy Banachowski	3-2	Long Beach St
1992	Stanford	Don Shaw	3-1	UCLA
1993	Long Beach St	Brian Gimmillaro	3-1	Penn St
1994	Stanford	Don Shaw	3-1	UCLA
1995	Nebraska	Terry Pettit	3-1	Texas

DIVISION II

Year	Champion	Year	Champion	Year	Champion
1981	Cal St-Sacramento	1986	UC-Riverside	1991	West Texas St
1982	UC-Riverside	1987	Cal St-Northridge	1992	Portland St
1983	Cal St-Northridge	1988	Portland St	1993	Northern Michigan
1984	Portland St	1989	Cal St-Bakersfield	1994	Northern Michigan
1985	Portland St	1990	West Texas St	1995	Barry

DIVISION III

Year	Champion	Year	Champion	Year	Champion
1981	UC-San Diego	1986	UC-San Diego	1991	Washington (MO)
1982	La Verne	1987	UC-San Diego	1992	Washington (MO)
1983	Elmhurst	1988	UC-San Diego	1993	Washington (MO)
1984	UC-San Diego	1989	Washington (MO)	1994	Washington (MO)
1985	Elmhurst	1990	UC-San Diego	1995	Washington (MO)

Water Polo

Year	Champion	Coach	Score	Runner-Up
1969	UCLA	Bob Horn	5-2	California
1970	UC-Irvine	Ed Newland	7-6 (3 OT)	UCLA
1971	UCLA	Bob Horn	5-3	San Jose St
1972	UCLA	Bob Horn	10-5	UC-Irvine
1973	California	Pete Cutino	8-4	UC-Irvine
1974	California	Pete Cutino	7-6	UC-Irvine
1975	California	Pete Cutino	9-8	UC-Irvine
1976	Stanford	Art Lambert	13-12	UCLA
1977	California	Pete Cutino	8-6	UC-Irvine
1978	Stanford	Dante Dettamanti	7-6 (3 OT)	California
1979	UC-Santa Barbara	Pete Snyder	11-3	UCLA
1980	Stanford	Dante Dettamanti	8-6	California
1981	Stanford	Dante Dettamanti	17-6	Long Beach St
1982	UC-Irvine	Ed Newland	7-4	Stanford
1983	California	Pete Cutino	10-7	Southern Cal
1984	California	Pete Cutino	9-8	Stanford
1985	Stanford	Dante Dettamanti	12-11 (2 OT)	UC-Irvine
1986	Stanford	Dante Dettamanti	9-6	California
1987	California	Pete Cutino	9-8 (OT)	Southern Cal
1988	California	Pete Cutino	14-11	UCLA
1989	UC-Irvine	Ed Newland	9-8	California
1990	California	Steve Heaston	8-7	Stanford
1991	California	Steve Heaston	7-6	UCLA
1992	California	Steve Heaston	12-11	Stanford
1993	Stanford	Dante Dettamanti	11-9	Southern Cal
1994	Stanford	Dante Dettamanti	14-10	Southern Cal
1995	UCLA	Guy Baker	10-8	California

Wrestling

DIVISION I

Year	Champion	Coach	Pts	Runner-Up	Pts	Most Outstanding Wrestler
1928	Oklahoma St*	E.C. Gallagher				
1929	Oklahoma St	E.C. Gallagher	26	Michigan	18	
1930	Oklahoma St*	E.C. Gallagher	27	Illinois	14	
1931	Oklahoma St*	E.C. Gallagher		Michigan		
1932	Indiana*	W.H. Thom		Oklahoma St		Edwin Belshaw, Indiana
1933	Oklahoma St*	E.C. Gallagher				Allan Kelley, Oklahoma St
	Iowa St*	Hugo Otopalik				Pat Johnson, Harvard
1934	Oklahoma St	E.C. Gallagher	29	Indiana	19	Ben Bishop, Lehigh
1935	Oklahoma St	E.C. Gallagher	36	Oklahoma	18	Ross Flood, Oklahoma St
1936	Oklahoma	Paul Keen	14	Central St (OK)	10	Wayne Martin, Oklahoma
				Oklahoma St	10	
1937	Oklahoma St	E.C. Gallagher	31	Oklahoma	13	Stanley Henson, Oklahoma St
1938	Oklahoma St	E.C. Gallagher	19	Illinois	15	Joe McDaniels, Oklahoma St
1939	Oklahoma St	E.C. Gallagher	33	Lehigh	12	Dale Hanson, Minnesota
1940	Oklahoma St	E.C. Gallagher	24	Indiana	14	Don Nichols, Michigan
1941	Oklahoma St	Art Griffith	37	Michigan St	26	Al Whitehurst, Oklahoma St
1942	Oklahoma St	Art Griffith	31	Michigan St	26	David Arndt, Oklahoma St
1943-45	No tournament					
1946	Oklahoma St	Art Griffith	25	Northern Iowa	24	Gerald Leeman, Northern Iowa
1947	Cornell	Paul Scott	32	Northern Iowa	19	William Koll, Northern Iowa
1948	Oklahoma St	Art Griffith	33	Michigan St	28	William Koll, Northern Iowa
1949	Oklahoma St	Art Griffith	32	Northern Iowa	27	Charles Hetrick, Oklahoma St
1950	Northern Iowa	David McCuskey	30	Purdue	16	Anthony Gizoni, Waynesburg
1951	Oklahoma	Port Robertson	24	Oklahoma St	23	Walter Romanowski, Cornell
1952	Oklahoma	Port Robertson	22	Northern Iowa	21	Tommy Evans, Oklahoma
1953	Penn St	Charles Speidel	21	Oklahoma	15	Frank Bettucci, Cornell
1954	Oklahoma St	Art Griffith	32	Pittsburgh	17	Tommy Evans, Oklahoma
1955	Oklahoma St	Art Griffith	40	Penn St	31	Edward Eichelberger, Lehigh
1956	Oklahoma St	Art Griffith	65	Oklahoma	62	Dan Hodge, Oklahoma
1957	Oklahoma	Port Robertson	73	Pittsburgh	66	Dan Hodge, Oklahoma
1958	Oklahoma St	Myron Roderick	77	Iowa St	62	Dick Delgado, Oklahoma
1959	Oklahoma St	Myron Roderick	73	Iowa St	51	Ron Gray, Iowa St
1960	Oklahoma	Thomas Evans	59	Iowa St	40	Dave Auble, Cornell

DIVISION I *(Cont.)*

Year	Champion	Coach	Pts	Runner-Up	Pts	Most Outstanding Wrestler
1961	Oklahoma St	Myron Roderick	82	Oklahoma	63	E. Gray Simons, Lock Haven
1962	Oklahoma St	Myron Roderick	82	Oklahoma	45	E. Gray Simons, Lock Haven
1963	Oklahoma	Thomas Evans	48	Iowa St	45	Mickey Martin, Oklahoma
1964	Oklahoma St	Myron Roderick	87	Oklahoma	58	Dean Lahr, Colorado
1965	Iowa St	Harold Nichols	87	Oklahoma St	86	Yojiro Uetake, Oklahoma St
1966	Oklahoma St	Myron Roderick	79	Iowa St	70	Yojiro Uetake, Oklahoma St
1967	Michigan St	Grady Peninger	74	Michigan	63	Rich Sanders, Portland St
1968	Oklahoma St	Myron Roderick	81	Iowa St	78	Dwayne Keller, Oklahoma St
1969	Iowa St	Harold Nichols	104	Oklahoma	69	Dan Gable, Iowa St
1970	Iowa St	Harold Nichols	99	Michigan St	84	Larry Owings, Washington
1971	Oklahoma St	Tommy Chesbro	94	Iowa St	66	Darrell Keller, Oklahoma St
1972	Iowa St	Harold Nichols	103	Michigan St	72½	Wade Schalles, Clarion
1973	Iowa St	Harold Nichols	85	Oregon St	72½	Greg Strobel, Oregon St
1974	Oklahoma	Stan Abel	69½	Michigan	67	Floyd Hitchcock, Bloomsburg
1975	Iowa	Gary Kurdelmeier	102	Oklahoma	77	Mike Frick, Lehigh
1976	Iowa	Gary Kurdelmeier	123½	Iowa St	85¾	Chuch Yagla, Iowa
1977	Iowa St	Harold Nichols	95½	Oklahoma St	88¾	Nick Gallo, Hofstra
1978	Iowa	Dan Gable	94½	Iowa St	94	Mark Churella, Michigan
1979	Iowa	Dan Gable	122½	Iowa St	88	Bruce Kinseth, Iowa
1980	Iowa	Dan Gable	110¾	Oklahoma St	87	Howard Harris, Oregon St
1981	Iowa	Dan Gable	129¾	Oklahoma	100¼	Gene Mills, Syracuse
1982	Iowa	Dan Gable	131¾	Iowa St	111	Mark Schultz, Oklahoma
1983	Iowa	Dan Gable	155	Oklahoma St	102	Mike Sheets, Oklahoma St
1984	Iowa	Dan Gable	123¾	Oklahoma St	98	Jim Zalesky, Iowa
1985	Iowa	Dan Gable	145¼	Oklahoma	98½	Barry Davis, Iowa
1986	Iowa	Dan Gable	158	Oklahoma	84¼	Marty Kistler, Iowa
1987	Iowa St	Jim Gibbons	133	Iowa	108	John Smith, Oklahoma St
1988	Arizona St	Bobby Douglas	93	Iowa	85½	Scott Turner, N Carolina St
1989	Oklahoma St	Joe Seay	91¼	Arizona St	70½	Tim Krieger, Iowa St
1990	Oklahoma St	Joe Seay	117¾	Arizona St	104¾	Chris Barnes, Oklahoma St
1991	Iowa	Dan Gable	157	Oklahoma St	108¾	Jeff Prescott, Penn St
1992	Iowa	Dan Gable	149	Oklahoma St	100½	Tom Brands, Iowa
1993	Iowa	Dan Gable	123¾	Penn St	87½	Terry Steiner, Iowa
1994	Oklahoma St	John Smith	94¾	Iowa	76½	Pat Smith, Oklahoma St
1995	Iowa	Dan Gable	134	Oregon St	77½	T.J. Jaworsky, N Carolina
1996	Iowa	Dan Gable	122½	Iowa St	78½	Les Gutches, Oregon St

*Unofficial champions.

DIVISION II

Year	Champion	Year	Champion	Year	Champion
1963	Western St (CO)	1975	Northern Iowa	1987	Cal St-Bakersfield
1964	Western St (CO)	1976	Cal St-Bakersfield	1988	N Dakota St
1965	Mankato St	1977	Cal St-Bakersfield	1989	Portland St
1966	Cal Poly-SLO	1978	Northern Iowa	1990	Portland St
1967	Portland St	1979	Cal St-Bakersfield	1991	NE-Omaha
1968	Cal Poly-SLO	1980	Cal St-Bakersfield	1992	Central Oklahoma
1969	Cal Poly-SLO	1981	Cal St-Bakersfield	1993	Central Oklahoma
1970	Cal Poly-SLO	1982	Cal St-Bakersfield	1994	Central Oklahoma
1971	Cal Poly-SLO	1983	Cal St-Bakersfield	1995	Central Oklahoma
1972	Cal Poly-SLO	1984	SIU-Edwardsville	1996	Pittsburgh-Johnstown
1973	Cal Poly-SLO	1985	SIU-Edwardsville		
1974	Cal Poly-SLO	1986	SIU-Edwardsville		

DIVISION III

Year	Champion	Year	Champion	Year	Champion
1974	Wilkes	1982	Brockport St	1990	Ithaca
1975	John Carroll	1983	Brockport St	1991	Augsburg
1976	Montclair St	1984	Trenton St	1992	Brockport
1977	Brockport St	1985	Trenton St	1993	Augsburg
1978	Buffalo	1986	Montclair St	1994	Ithaca
1979	Trenton St	1987	Trenton St	1995	Augsburg
1980	Brockport St	1988	St Lawrence	1996	Wartburg
1981	Trenton St	1989	Ithaca		

INDIVIDUAL CHAMPIONSHIP
RECORDS

Swimming and Diving

Men

Event	Time	Record Holder	Date
50-yard freestyle	19.14	David Fox, N Carolina St	3-25-93
100-yard freestyle	41.80	Matt Biondi, California	4-4-87
200-yard freestyle	1:33.03	Matt Biondi, California	4-3-87
500-yard freestyle	4:08.75	Tom Dolan, Michigan	3-23-95
1650-yard freestyle	14:29.31	Tom Dolan, Michigan	3-25-95
100-yard backstroke	45.43	Brian Retterer, Stanford	3-24-95
200-yard backstroke	1:40.64	Jeff Rouse, Stanford	3-28-92
100-yard breaststroke	52.48	Steve Lundquist, Southern Meth	3-25-83
200-yard breaststroke	1:53.77	Mike Barrowman, Michigan	3-24-90
100-yard butterfly	46.18	Lars Frolander, SMU	3-24-95
200-yard butterfly	1:41.78	Melvin Stewart, Tennessee	3-30-91
200-yard individual medley	1:43.52	Greg Burgess, Florida	3-25-93
400-yard individual medley	3:38.18	Tom Dolan, Michigan	3-24-95

Women

Event	Time	Record Holder	Date
50-yard freestyle	21.77	Amy Van Dyken, Colorado St	3-18-94
100-yard freestyle	47.61	Jenny Thompson, Stanford	3-21-92
200-yard freestyle	1:43.28	Nicole Haislett, Florida	3-20-92
500-yard freestyle	4:34.39	Janet Evans, Stanford	3-15-90
1650-yard freestyle	15:39.14	Janet Evans, Stanford	3-17-90
100-yard backstroke	53.98	Betsy Mitchell, Texas	3-21-92
200-yard backstroke	1:52.98	Whitney Hedgepeth, Texas	3-21-87
100-yard breaststroke	59.71	Beata Kaszuba, Arizona St	3-17-95
200-yard breaststroke	2:09.71	Beata Kaszuba, Arizona St	3-18-95
100-yard butterfly	51.75	Crissy Ahmann-Leighton, Arizona	3-20-92
200-yard butterfly	1:53.42	Summer Sanders, Stanford	3-21-92
200-yard individual medley	1:55.54	Summer Sanders, Stanford	3-20-92
400-yard individual medley	4:02.28	Summer Sanders, Stanford	3-20-92

Indoor Track and Field

Men

Event	Mark	Record Holder	Date
55-meter dash	6.00	Lee McRae, Pittsburgh	3-14-86
55-meter hurdles	7.07	Allen Johnson, N Carolina	3-13-92
200-meter dash	20.36	Obadele Thompson, UTEP	3-8-96
400-meter dash	45.79	Gabriel Luke, Rice	3-10-90
800-meter run	1:45.80	Einars Tupuritis, Wichita St	3-9 -96
Mile run	3:55.33	Kevin Sullivan, Michigan	3-11-95
3,000-meter run	7:50.90	Josephat Kapkory, Wash St	3-11-94
5,000-meter run	13:37.94	Jonah Koech, Iowa St	3-9-90
High jump	7 ft 9¼ in	Hollis Conway, Southwestern Louisiana	3-11-89
Pole vault	19 ft 1½ in	Lawrence Johnson, Tennessee	3-12-94
Long jump	27 ft 10 in	Carl Lewis, Houston	3-13-81
Triple jump	56 ft 9½ in	Keith Connor, Southern Meth	3-13-81
Shot put	69 ft 8½ in	Michael Carter, SMU	3-13-81
		Soren Tallhem, Brigham Young	3-9-85
35-pound weight throw	76 ft 5½ in	Robert Weir, SMU	3-11-83

Indoor Track and Field *(Cont.)*

Women

Event	Mark	Record Holder	Date
55-meter dash	6.56	Gwen Torrence, Georgia	3-14-87
55-meter hurdles	7.44	Lynda Tolbert, Arizona St	3-9-90
200-meter dash	22.90	Holly Hyche, Indiana St	3-11-94
400-meter dash	51.05	Maicel Malone, Arizona St	3-9-91
800-meter run	2:02.05	Amy Wickus, Wisconsin	3-11-94
Mile run	4:30.63	Suzy Favor, Wisconsin	3-11-89
3,000-meter run	8:54.98	Stephanie Herbst, Wisconsin	3-15-86
5,000-meter run	15:41.12	Jennifer Rhines, Villanova	3-10-95
High jump	6 ft 5½ in	Amy Acuff, UCLA	3-11-95
Long jump	22 ft 1 in	Daphne Saunders, Louisiana St	3-12-94
Triple jump	45 ft 9 in	Sheila Hudson, California	3-10-90
Shot put	57 ft 11¾ in	Regina Cavanaugh, Rice	3-14-86

Outdoor Track and Field

Men

Event	Mark	Record Holder	Date
100-meter dash	9.92	Ato Bolden, UCLA	6-1-96
200-meter dash	19.87	Lorenzo Daniel, Mississippi St	6-3-88
400-meter dash	44.00	Quincy Watts, Southern Cal	6-6-92
800-meter run	1:44.70	Mark Everett, Florida	6-1-90
1,500-meter run	3:35.30	Sydney Maree, Villanova	6-6-81
3,000-meter steeplechase	8:12.39	Henry Rono, Washington St	6-1-78
5,000-meter run	13:20.63	Sydney Maree, Villanova	6-2-79
10,000-meter run	28:01.30	Suleiman Nyambui, UTEP	6-1-79
110-meter high hurdles	13.22	Greg Foster, UCLA	6-2-78
400-meter intermediate hurdles	47.85	Kevin Young, UCLA	6-3-88
High jump	7 ft 9¾ in	Hollis Conway, Southwestern Louisiana	6-3-89
Pole vault	19 ft 1 in	Lawrence Johnson, Tennessee	5-29-96
Long jump	28 ft	Erick Walder, Arkansas	6-3-93
Triple jump	57 ft 7¾ in	Keith Connor, Southern Meth	6-5-82
Shot put	72 ft 2¼ in	John Godina, UCLA	6-3-95
Discus throw	220 ft	Kamy Keshmiri, Nevada	6-5-92
Hammer throw	265 ft 3 in	Balazs Kiss, Southern Cal	5-31-96
Javelin throw	266 ft 9 in	Todd Riech, Fresno St	6-3-94
Decathlon	8279 pts	Tito Steiner, Brigham Young	6-2/3-81

Women

Event	Mark	Record Holder	Date
100-meter dash	10.78	Dawn Sowell, Louisiana St	6-3-89
200-meter dash	22.04	Dawn Sowell, Louisiana St	6-2-89
400-meter dash	50.18	Pauline Davis, Alabama	6-3-89
800-meter run	1:59.11	Suzy Favor, Wisconsin	6-1-90
1,500-meter run	4:08.26	Suzy Favor, Wisconsin	6-2-90
3,000-meter run	8:47.35	Vicki Huber, Villanova	6-3-88
5,000-meter run	15:38.47	Annette Hand, Oregon	6-4-88
10,000-meter run	32:28.57	Sylvia Mosqueda, Cal St-LA	6-1-88
100-meter hurdles	12.70	Tananjalyn Stanley, Louisiana St	6-3-89
400-meter hurdles	54.56	Tonya Williams, Illinois	5-31-96
High jump	6 ft 5 in	Amy Acuff, UCLA	6-3-95
Long jump	22 ft 9¼ in	Sheila Echols, Louisiana St	6-5-87
Triple jump	46 ft ¾ in	Sheila Hudson, California	6-2-90
Shot put	59 ft 11¾ in	Valeyta Althouse, UCLA	6-1-95
Discus throw	209 ft 10 in	Leslie Deniz, Arizona St	6-4-83
Hammer throw	209 ft 2 in	Dawn Ellerbe, S Carolina	6-1-96
Javelin throw	206 ft 9 in	Karin Smith, Cal Poly-SLO	6-4-82
Heptathlon	6527 pts	Diane Guthrie-Gresham, George Mason	6-2/3-95

Olympics

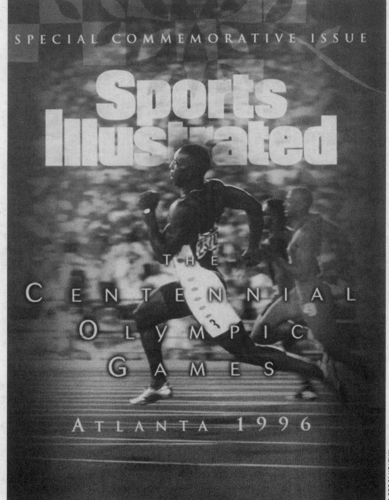

SPECIAL COMMEMORATIVE ISSUE

Sports Illustrated

THE
CENTENNIAL
OLYMPIC
GAMES

ATLANTA 1996

WALTER IOOSS JR

Five-Ring Circus

Though beset by hucksterism and widespread chaos, the Atlanta Games were still the greatest show on earth

by Richard Hoffer

ATLANTA IS famous for its ability to reinvent itself. Ever since Sherman torched it, the city has been in a constant state of urban renewal, always becoming something else, something newer and better, faster and bigger. But for a month or so last summer it suffered a languid lapse of Southern progress and became a kind of county fair, full of sideshows and carny rides, an entertainment throwback that seemed predicated on the world citizen's appetite for corn dogs and a need to ride the Ejection Seat.

It was the kind of low-rent circus that materializes out of nowhere, plywood game booths banged together overnight, petting zoos suddenly appearing under freeway interchanges, a rodeo arena overtaking a downtown parking lot. It was absurd and, in Olympic tradition, absolutely unheard of. Nobody in the 100 years of modern Olympics that these Games were supposed to celebrate could recall the host city becoming a shantytown in the service of its visitors. The international officials were aghast at Atlanta's idea of a party and, before the first event had been staged, complained of the clutter. And the media—with the possible exception of NBC—howled at the cheesiness of this cultural undressing.

But clutter, with a dash of chaos and a heaping helping of commercialism, was the persistent theme of these Games and Atlanta was making no apology for it. Clutter—and certainly commercialism—was even institutionalized in Centennial Olympic Park, a 21-acre plot in Atlanta's downtown that was given over entirely to the notion that people were interested in the history of corporate sponsors and would stand in line to drink beer at the world's longest bar (or, as it happened, drench themselves in the Olympic rings fountain). Inside the park, laid out over bricks engraved with the names of individual donors, "booths" duplicated the spirit of the shacks and tents beyond this official perimeter. They were just bigger, sturdier, and the logos were genuine.

LYNN JOHNSON

Aesthetically the entire setting was a disaster. The Atlanta skyline, a proud symbol of Southern rebirth, was reduced to a vista of Ferris wheels, lit by strings of lightbulbs. A city that had sought to distinguish itself by attracting corporate headquarters and becoming the business center of the South was now, in its bid for worldwide attention, achieving a perverse fame for its two-bit hucksterism, ma-and-pa ice cream booths lining the sidewalks, ribs here, trading pins there—and how about that Ejection Seat? It was a Georgian boardwalk, colorful all right, but not very dignified. It was a colossal sell-out.

And yet people—and there were more of them than for any Olympics, before and probably ever again—seemed to be having fun. Reports of computer snafus, in which some results were rendered useless, hardly affected the fans' enjoyment. And horrify-

Step right up: At times, the Atlanta Games resembled a county fair.

ing stories of transportation problems seemed limited to a few athletes (one contingent effectively had to hijack a bus to get to the event on time) and the journalists. Of course, the stories were too good not to print. Some of the vehicles, surplus rides from other cities, were in woeful condition. And the mostly rookie bus drivers dragooned from all parts of the South were so ill-equipped for the hordes, the traffic, the geography, that they couldn't help but produce memorable anecdotes: One junkyard pilot, faced with the prospect of freeway driving, broke down crying and abruptly abandoned her bus and passengers en route. A thousand bus rides, a thousand stories.

But in fact Atlanta was only overburdened

The 4' 9", 87-pound Strug delivered one of the Games' biggest moments.

in these particulars. The public transportation was certainly crowded beyond belief, but MARTA, the city's slick train system, worked all the same. And the facilities, some of them filled to bursting, rocked. For that matter, the streets were busy with T-shirt shoppers, and Centennial Park could only be negotiated elbow-to-elbow. As goofy as it all looked, it increasingly seemed elitist to criticize Atlanta for its taste.

And then, with the late-night bombing of Centennial Park scarcely a week into the Games, it became impossible to criticize Atlanta at all. The free nightly concert was sending power chords out among the usual throng when the pipe bomb went off, scattering the Olympics into infamy. One woman was killed in the blast, 111 people were injured, and there was now blood on the $35 donor bricks. The Games themselves were only briefly imperiled—the events were ruled safe enough to continue—but the park was closed, transformed in one ugly moment from a kind of town square into a crime scene. And the Olympic spirit, the one Atlanta had in mind in its unorthodox staging of a world party, was broken.

It was ironic that that random bombing, executed for no apparent purpose or particular cause (and by nobody who could be quickly apprehended), served to refocus the public's attention on what the Olympics are truly about. The park empty, the surrounding streets blockaded, it was finally understood that Atlanta had nothing more complicated than a good time on its Olympic agenda. There was, during the time the park was closed, a bereavement for that part of the Olympic spirit, the part that allows people to mingle, to eat ribs on the sidewalk, to have a good time. And that grief gave way to a fury, to a resolve to take back the sidewalks, take back the park. Three days after the bombing Atlanta was reborn yet one more time, and with a new appreciation. The park, scrubbed, reconsecrated, opened with a mournful trumpet that soon enough gave way to a rollicking gospel choir. This American defiance in the face of fear is the new patriotism, the new kind of chest-thumping in a world where medal counts don't mean much. We will party. We will eat corn dogs.

With that the bombing became a blip on the Olympic time line, never to be forgotten of course, but certainly not a historical spike like Munich. Atlanta was saved that. Even more, Atlanta and its Olympic park came to symbolize triumph over adversity. The park in particular, without pedigree or previous importance, was now a landmark. The international officials would continue to hold their noses, and worldly visitors might leave puzzled by America's apparent mainlining of Coca-Cola (the host beverage), but everybody else understood that Atlanta's effort was more purely American than anything ever held before. In this country, the Olympics insisted, we like sitcoms, state fairs and fast food, and we crowd carnivals somewhat more than we do museums. We can't help it. This was the Olympics for all the rest of us.

It was, in any case, an Olympics for a record crowd. The effort was populist through and through with the stated intent of attracting the most participation, both by athletes and fans. Every invited nation—197 countries—showed up. And there were 8.6 million ticket sales. Did MARTA seem a little crowded to you? Consider that the combined ticket sales of Los Angeles and Barcelona were only a half-million more than for the Atlanta Games alone.

This came at a cost of more than just aesthetics, though. Atlanta's decision to make the Games available on this scale required a huge investment for the large venues and made private financing necessary. This was the Logo Olympics, with corporate sponsors literally billboarding the Games to recoup their own investment. It was also responsible for much of the entrepreneurship around the Games, Atlanta having sold off rights for quick money. Again, the International Organizing Committee sniffed in disgust and by the end of the Olympics was promising that there would never be another Atlanta. Indeed, Sydney officials were assuring everybody they could that they were downscaling for their own 2000 party. Only six million tickets would be sold, and the financing of the venue construction would be undertaken by the Australian government, with almost all of the profits being returned to taxpayers.

So Sydney's Games will be different, maybe even better when viewed from the outside (or from a bus). But their organizers will be hard-pressed to provide the drama that was presented in Atlanta's venues. However Atlanta failed to satisfy its visitors, it had nothing to do with the athletes, who delivered time and again. They can usually be counted on to move us to tears, laughs and gasps. They practice four years at a clip just to amaze us.

Who was most amazing this time around? Hard to say. The track men produced their fair amount of headlines, and the Dream Team, an increasingly tired concept, still got attention (probably as much for the players' progress through Atlanta eateries as the ritual destruction of comparatively amateur competition), and the U.S. wrestlers, fighting through their own haze of grief, surprised folks. Yet it's fair to say that these Games belonged to the women. Swimmers and gymnasts as always; softball players, soccer players and basketball players like never before.

Of them all, though, diminutive Kerri Strug may be the enduring figure from these Games. Her famous limping vault would have been the keynote of any Olympics—especially as the media tends to mythologize women's gymnastics, much as it does figure skating—but at these besieged Games it was particularly striking, wonderfully appropriate. Like Atlanta itself, a gymnastics underdog had to overcome disaster to win one for the United States.

Who, having watched NBC's over-the-top videotaped version, doesn't know the story? Strug, 4'9" and just 87 pounds, was an afterthought on a team of more celebrated stars, one of them a 14-year-old with an autobiography already published. Strug's Olympic coach, Bela Karolyi, said, "She is just a little girl, who was never the roughest, toughest girl, always a little shy, always standing behind somebody else." Yet everybody she was used to standing behind was crashing off the vault in the team's final and most critical event. With the team desperately trying to hold off the Russians in the team competition to win their first ever gold medal, Shannon Miller had been scored low for a hop on her landing, and author Dominique Moceanu had crashed on her two tries. Strug, normally steady if unspectacular, was apparently contaminated by these lapses as she also staggered on her landing.

That blown vault was the least of her problems, though. Her left ankle had rolled over on her landing, and her leg was suddenly numb. "Do I have to do this again?" she asked Karolyi. Not only did she have to make one more vault, but according to Karolyi's quick math, she had to score a 9.6. No hops, no falls.

It was both horrible and wonderful to watch. She raced down the runway, soared over the horse and landed full-on, a grimace spreading across her face. The 18-year-old pro that she was, Strug hopped twice on one foot to acknowledge the judges and, that formality aside, collapsed on the mat.

Karolyi's arithmetic had been wrong: The U.S. would have won regardless of the outcome of Strug's final vault, but her 9.712 score was heroic beyond that detail. Even without the overwrought telecast or the supposed drama of the team victory, the moment had a heroic simplicity to it. Pretty good picture, too. It didn't hurt when Karolyi wrapped her, this waif, in his bear-like arms and carried her to the podium for the medal ceremonies. From that point she was off to endorsement land and a world of "tours" (just like the figure skaters), but nobody who saw it would ever forget her wincing vault or wonder what amateur athletics was really about.

All the female Olympians were rich with this desire to win. Teen Queens like Strug are always emerging from the Olympics, and this was no different, with Brooke Bennett supplanting the veteran (and former Teen Queen) Janet Evans as the new Distance Darling. This Olympics was different though in its celebration of women instead of girls. It was still fun to see swimmer Amanda Beard clutching her teddy bear, but it seemed less patronizing to cheer the women basketball players or the softball players or the soccer team. The U.S. softball team, in particular, went a long way in establishing the women as deserving equals in Olympic competition. The dinger-hitting doc named Dot Richardson and all her similarly tough-minded teammates were a sensation as the U.S. won a thrilling tournament, the first in Olympic history.

And in an Olympics where the concept of the Dream Team, the NBA all stars, lost some of its luster, the U.S. women hoopsters proved quite dreamy indeed. No knock on the men but these women were far more purposeful, having spent 14 months touring the world just to get ready for the Olympics. Polished and poised, they were a refreshing sight—and a hot ticket—as they completed a 60–0 run by winning the gold medal.

But, as in any Olympics where the motto remains *citius, altius, fortius*, track continued to generate attention. There were several stories generating dramatic questions: Could Carl Lewis still perform at the age of 35? Could Michael Johnson really double in the 200 and the 400? Was Dan O'Brien truly the world's greatest athlete? The answers turned out to be, yes, yes and yes.

The sight of Johnson sailing around the track in his gold shoes may have been the Olympics' most compelling spectacle. He won the 400 convincingly and then set an

WALTER IOOSS, JR.

"How did you all get in my dream?" Lewis asked after his gold-medal leap.

ninth of his remarkable Olympic career.

Johnson did have the night of his 200 triumph to himself, but thereafter Lewis resurrected himself in the news columns, shrewdly dominating the Games by his absence. There was quite a furor over whether Lewis, more popular with fans than with his teammates, should be part of the 4 x 100-meter relay. It was true that he could no longer successfully compete in the 100, had failed in the trials, and had neglected even to practice with the relay team. On the other hand, there was the matter of a possible 10th gold medal, which would tie Lewis with old-timer Ray Ewry as the Games' most golden ath-

astonishing world record in the 200 three days later. Johnson does not, contrary to the men's gold medalist in tennis, believe that image is everything; he maintains a sober, unquotable profile. But when he turned to look at the clock after his half lap and saw his time of 19.32, a third of a second off his old record, he was ready with a quote that captured the magnitude of his accomplishment. "I am rarely shocked by my own performance," he said in his basso profundo voice. "And I am shocked."

He may have had a lock on track and field goose bumps, but when it came to the stirring up of news he finished a distant second to veteran headline-monger Lewis. Johnson's 400 win had nearly been overshadowed by Lewis and his long jump of 27' 10¾" that same night. Lewis's leap was not a world record, not even close to a personal best. But it was the 35-year-old's fourth gold medal in the event and the

lete, a feat some wags argued Lewis should be granted a shot at for the good that dramatic moment would do the sport's sagging profile. Additionally, Lewis himself hinted, there was his experience in handling the baton on that final leg; and, besides, who did the world want to see whisking down that last straightaway, Lewis, a celebrity again after his long jump, or Dennis Mitchell?

Lewis conducted his campaign shrewdly, pretending to be apart from the fray, but more or less winking at the controversy. "People feel I have the right to run," he said, adding, "It's not coming from me." Fairness finally won out over public opinion, and Lewis was not allowed to get that 10th career medal at some other athlete's expense. The controversy seemed academic after the U.S. was beaten soundly in the event by a blistering anchor leg from Canadian Donovan Bailey, who had already won the 100 in world-record time.

OLYMPICS **607**

Lisa Leslie socked away 29 points in the gold medal game against Brazil.

surprised as anyone. Take wrestler Kurt Angle who—like all of wrestling really—had lost a father figure when former Olympian Dave Shultz was murdered at a wrestlers' training facility. Yet there was Angle at the Olympics, winning the 220-pound division by a margin so close that his Iranian opponent insisted on raising his own hand. Angle was a welter of emotions, happy and relieved of course, then anguished, remembering his departed friend. After the awards ceremony he suddenly put his hands over his face and said, "To tell you the truth, I don't feel very good right now."

The Olympics were shot through with such moments, and by the end of the Games it hardly seemed relevant where they happened or what went on outside the venues. It was hot, a little tawdry, the buses got lost a lot of the time, and a little too much attention was paid that damn Ejection Seat. Plus, there was the tragedy in Centennial Park. But there were all these people, racked by tears of despair and joy, gone goofy as they vented all that emotion. We were all reminded that it's a pretty volatile situation to be capped and shaken for four years of training, and that the resulting fizz, as usual, is pretty wonderful to witness.

As for the carnival atmosphere, it probably didn't hurt a bit that you could buy some barbecue out of a plywood booth on an Atlanta curbside, spill some sauce on your new Lithuanian basketball shirt, wash the rest down with a Coke and then risk it all in the Ejection Seat. It may even have been fun.

It was surprising, since the U.S. was hugely favored and had a long history of dominance in the event. But the Canadians' victory was so decisive, that no one, not even Michael Johnson, could have made up the difference.

At times these assorted furors seemed driven by shoe contracts (why did some athletes appear only at Nike press conferences?) and other commercial imperatives; and it was possible to become, or remain, cynical as the athletes, essentially professionals, pursued their own agendas. But, as always, there were small grace notes competing with, say, the Dream Team's boom box: sweet music amid the noise. Swimmer Angel Martino, for example, apologized for winning only the bronze in the 100-meter freestyle and then backstage draped the medal around the neck of a friend who was fighting cancer. Things like that. And when they happened, the athletes were as

1996 Summer Games

TRACK AND FIELD
Men

100 METERS
1. ..Donovan Bailey, Canada — 9.84 WR
2. ..Frankie Fredericks, Namibia — 9.89
3. ..Ato Boldon, Trinidad and Tobago — 9.90

200 METERS
1. ..Michael Johnson, United States — 19.32 WR
2. ..Frankie Fredericks, Namibia — 19.68
3. ..Ato Boldon, Trinidad and Tobago — 19.80

400 METERS
1. ..Michael Johnson, United States — 43.49 OR
2. ..Roger Black, Great Britain — 44.41
3. ..Davis Kamoga, Uganda — 44.53

800 METERS
1. ..Vebjoern Rodal, Norway — 1:42.58 OR
2. ..Hezekiel Sepeng, South Africa — 1:42.74
3. ..Fred Onyancha, Kenya — 1:42.79

1500 METERS
1. ..Noureddine Morceli, Algeria — 3:35.78
2. ..Fermin Cacho, Spain — 3:36.40
3. ..Stephen Kipkorir, Kenya — 3:36.72

5000 METERS
1. ..Venuste Niyongabo, Burundi — 13:07.96
2. ..Paul Bitok, Kenya — 13:08.16
3. ..Khalid Boulami, Morocco — 13:08.37

10,000 METERS
1. ..Haile Gebrselassie, Ethiopia — 27:07.34 OR
2. ..Paul Tergat, Kenya — 27:08.17
3. ..Salah Hissou, Morocco — 27:24.67

MARATHON
1. ..Josia Thugwane, South Africa — 2:12:36
2. ..Bong-Ju Lee, South Korea — 2:12:39
3. ..Eric Wainaina, Kenya — 2:12:44

110-METER HURDLES
1. ..Allen Johnson, United States — 12.95 OR
2. ..Mark Crear, United States — 13.09
3. ..Florian Schwarthoff, Germany — 13.17

400-METER HURDLES
1. ..Derrick Adkins, United States — 47.54
2. ..Samuel Matete, Zambia — 47.78
3. ..Calvin Davis, United States — 47.96

3000-METER STEEPLECHASE
1. ..Joseph Keter, Kenya — 8:07.12
2. ..Moses Kiptanui, Kenya — 8:08.33
3. ..Alessandro Lambruschini, Italy — 8:11.28

4 X 100 METER RELAY
1. ..Canada: Donovan Bailey, Robert Esmie, Glenroy Gilbert, Bruny Surin — 37.69
2. ..United States — 38.05
3. ..Brazil — 38.41

4 X 400 METER RELAY
1. ..United States: Alvin Harrison, Anthuan Maybank, Derek Mills, LaMont Smith — 2:55.99
2. ..Great Britain — 2:56.60
3. ..Jamaica — 2:59.42

20-KILOMETER WALK
1. ..Jefferson Pérez, Ecuador — 1:20:07
2. ..Ilya Markov, Russia — 1:20:16
3. ..Bernardo Segura, Mexico — 1:20:23

50-KILOMETER WALK
1. ..Robert Korzeniowski, Poland — 3:43:30
2. ..Mikhail Shchennikov, Russia — 3:43:46
3. ..Valentin Massana, Spain — 3:44:19

HIGH JUMP
1. ..Charles Austin, United States — 7 ft 10 in OR
2. ..Artur Partyka, Poland — 7 ft 9¼ in
3. ..Steve Smith, Great Britain — 7 ft 8½ in

POLE VAULT
1. ..Jean Galfione, France — 19 ft 5¼ in OR
2. ..Igor Trandenkov, Russia — 19 ft 5¼ in
3. ..Andrei Tivontchik, Germany — 19 ft 5¼ in

LONG JUMP
1. ..Carl Lewis, United States — 27 ft 10¾ in
2. ..James Beckford, Jamaica — 27 ft 2½ in
3. ..Joe Greene, United States — 27 ft ½ in

TRIPLE JUMP
1. ..Kenny Harrison, United States — 59 ft 4¼ in OR
2. ..Jonathan Edwards, Great Britain — 58 ft 8 in
3. ..Yoelvis Quesada, Cuba — 57 ft 2¾ in

SHOT PUT
1. ..Randy Barnes, United States — 70 ft 11 in
2. ..John Godina, United States — 68 ft 2½ in
3. ..Oleksandr Bagach, Ukraine — 68 ft ½ in

DISCUS THROW
1. ..Lars Riedel, Germany — 227 ft 8 in OR
2. ..Vladimir Dubrovshchik, Belarus — 218 ft 6 in
3. ..Vasiliy Kaptyukh, Belarus — 215 ft 10 in

HAMMER THROW
1. ..Balazs Kiss, Hungary — 266 ft 6 in
2. ..Lance Deal, United States — 266 ft 2 in
3. ..Oleksiy Krykun, Ukraine — 262 ft 6 in

JAVELIN
1. ..Jan Zelezny, Czech Republic — 289 ft 3 in
2. ..Steve Backley, Great Britain — 286 ft 10 in
3. ..Seppo Raty, Finland — 285 ft 4 in

DECATHLON
Pts
1. ..Dan O'Brien, United States — 8824 OR
2. ..Frank Busemann, Germany — 8706
3. ..Tomas Dvorak, Czech Republic — 8664

Note: OR=Olympic record. WR=world record. EOR=equals Olympic record. EWR=equals world record.

TRACK AND FIELD (Cont.)
Women

100 METERS
1. ..Gail Devers, United States   10.94
2. ..Merlene Ottey, Jamaica   10.94
3. ..Gwen Torrence, United States   10.96

200 METERS
1. ..Marie-José Pérec, France   22.12
2. ..Merlene Ottey, Jamaica   22.24
3. ..Mary Onyali, Nigeria   22.38

400 METERS
1. ..Marie-José Pérec, France   48.25 OR
2. ..Cathy Freeman, Australia   48.63
3. ..Falilat Ogunkoya, Nigeria   49.10

800 METERS
1. ..Svetlana Masterkova, Russia   1:57.73
2. ..Ana Fidelia Quirot, Cuba   1:58.11
3. ..Maria Mutola, Mozambique   1:58.71

1500 METERS
1. ..Svetlana Masterkova, Russia   4:00.83
2. ..Gabriela Szabo, Russia   4:01.54
3. ..Theresia Kiesl, Austria   4:03.02

5000 METERS
1. ..Wang Junxia, China   14:59.88
2. ..Pauline Konga, Kenya   15:03.49
3. ..Roberta Brunet, Italy   15:07.52

10,000 METERS
1. ..Fernanda Ribeiro, Portugal   31:01.63 OR
2. ..Wang Junxia, China   31:02.58
3. ..Gete Wami, Ethiopia   31:06.68

MARATHON
1. ..Fatuma Roba, Ethiopia   2:26:05
2 ...Valentina Yegorova, Russia   2:28:05
3. ..Yuko Arimori, Japan   2:28:39

100-METER HURDLES
1. ..Lyudmila Engqvist, Sweden   12.58
2. ..Brigita Bukovec, Slovenia   12.59
3. ..Patricia Girard-Leno, France   12.65

400-METER HURDLES
1. ..Deon Hemmings, Jamaica   52.82 OR
2. ..Kim Batten, United States   53.08
3. ..Tonja Buford-Bailey, United States   53.22

4 X 100 METER RELAY
1. ..United States: Chryste Gaines   41.95
    Gail Devers, Inger Miller, Gwen
    Torrence
2. ..Bahamas   42.14
3. ..Jamaica   42.24

4 X 400 METER RELAY
1. ..United States: Rochelle Stevens   3:20.91
    Maicel Malone, Kim Graham,
    Jearl Miles
2. ..Nigeria   3:21.04
3. ..Germany   3:21.41

10-KILOMETER WALK
1. ..Elena Nikolayeva, Russia   41:49 OR
2. ..Elisabetta Perrone, Italy   42:12
3. ..Wang Yan, China   42:19

HIGH JUMP
1. ..Stefka Kostadinova, Bulgaria   6 ft 8¾ in OR
2. ..Niki Bakogianni, Greece   6 ft 8 in
3. ..Inga Babakova, Ukraine   6 ft 7 in

LONG JUMP
1. ..Chioma Ajunwa, Nigeria   23 ft 4½ in
2. ..Fiona May, Italy   23 ft ½ in
3. ..Jackie Joyner-Kersee, United States   22 ft 11¾ in

TRIPLE JUMP
1. ..Inessa Kravets, Ukraine   50 ft 3½ in
2. ..Inna Lasovskaya, Russia   49 ft 1¾ in
3. ..Sarka Kasparkova, Czech Republic   49 ft 1¾ in

SHOT PUT
1. ..Astrid Kumbernuss, Germany   67 ft 5½ in
2. ..Sui Xinmei, China   65 ft 2¾ in
3. ..Irina Khudorozhkina, Russia   63 ft 6 in

DISCUS THROW
1. ..Ilke Wyludda, Germany   228 ft 6 in
2. ..Natalya Sadova, Russia   218 ft 1 in
3. ..Ellina Zvereva, Belarus   215 ft 4 in

JAVELIN
1. ..Heli Rantanen, Finland   222 ft 11 in
2. ..Louise McPaul, Australia   215 ft
3. ...Trine Hattestad, Norway   213 ft 2 in

HEPTATHLON
                        Pts
1. ..Ghada Shouaa, Syria   6780
2. ..Natasha Sazanovich, Belarus   6563
3. ..Denise Lewis, Great Britain   6489

BADMINTON

Men
SINGLES
1. ..Poul-Erik Hoyer-Larsen, Denmark
2. ..Dong Jiong, China
3. ..Rashid Sidek, Malaysia

DOUBLES
1. ..Rexy Mainaky & Ricky Subagja, Indonesia
2. ..Cheah Soon Kit & Yap Kim Hock, Malaysia
3. ..S. Antonius & Denny Kantono, Indonesia

Women
SINGLES
1. ..Bang Soo Hyun, South Korea
2. ..Mia Audina, Indonesia
3. ..Susi Susanti, Indonesia

DOUBLES
1. ...Ge Fei & Gu Jun, China
2. ..Gil Young Ah & Jang Hye Ock, South Korea
3. ..Qin Yiyuan & Tang Yongshu, China

Note: OR=Olympic record. WR=world record. EOR=equals Olympic record. EWR=equals world record.

BADMINTON *(Cont.)*

MIXED DOUBLES

1. ....Gil Young Ah & Kim Dong Moon, South Korea
2. ....Park Joo Bong & Ra Kyung Min, South Korea
3. ....Liu Jianjun & Sun Man, China

BASEBALL

1. ....Cuba
2. ....Japan
3. ....United States

CANOE/KAYAK

Men

C-1 FLATWATER 500 METERS
1.	...Martin Doktor, Czech Republic	1:49.93
2.	...Slavomir Knazovicky, Slovakia	1:50.51
3.	...Imre Pulai, Hungary	1:50.75

C-1 FLATWATER 1000 METERS
1.	...Martin Doktor, Czech Republic	3:54.41
2.	...Ivan Klementiev, Latvia	3:54.95
3.	...Gyorgy Zala, Hungary	3:56.36

C-2 FLATWATER 500 METERS
1.	...C. Horváth & G. Kolonics, Hungary	1:40.42
2.	...N. Shuravski & V. Reneischi, Moldova	1:40.45
3.	...G. Andriev & G. Obreja, Romania	1:41.33

C-2 FLATWATER 1000 METERS
1.	...A. Dittmer & G. Kirchbach, Germany	3:31.87
2.	...A. Borsan & M. Glavan, Romania	3:32.29
3.	...C. Horváth & G. Kolonics, Hungary	3:32.51

C-1 WHITEWATER SLALOM
		Pts
1.	...Michal Martikan, Slovakia	151.03
2.	...Lukas Pollert, Czech Republic	151.17
3.	...Patrice Estanguet, France	152.84

C-2 WHITEWATER SLALOM
		Pts
1.	...F. Adisson & W. Forgues, France	158.82
2.	...J. Rohan & M. Simek, Czech Republic	160.16
3.	...A. Ehrenberg & M. Senft, Germany	163.72

K-1 FLATWATER 500 METERS
1.	...Antonio Rossi, Italy	1:37.42
2.	...Knut Holmann, Norway	1:38.33
3.	...Piotr Markiewicz, Poland	1:38.61

K-1 FLATWATER 1000 METERS
1.	...Knut Holmann, Norway	3:25.78
2.	...Beniamino Bonomi, Italy	3:27.07
3.	...Clint Robinson, Australia	3:29.71

Men *(Cont.)*

K-2 FLATWATER 500 METERS
1.	...K. Bluhm & T. Gutsche, Germany	1:28.69
2.	...B. Bonomi & D. Scarpa, Italy	1:28.72
3.	...D. Collins & A. Trim, Australia	1:29.40

K-2 FLATWATER 1000 METERS
1.	...A. Rossi & D. Scarpa, Italy	3:09.19
2.	...K. Bluhm & T. Gutsche, Germany	3:10.51
3.	...M. Kazanov & A. Dushev, Bulgaria	3:11.20

K-4 FLATWATER 1000 METERS
1.	...Germany	2:51.52
2.	...Hungary	2:53.18
3.	...Russia	2:53.99

K-1 WHITEWATER SLALOM
		Pts
1.	...Oliver Fix, Germany	141.22
2.	...Andraz Vehovar, Slovenia	141.65
3.	...Thomas Becker, Germany	142.79

Women

K-1 FLATWATER 500 METERS
1.	...Rita Kóbán, Hungary	1:47.65
2.	...Caroline Brunet, Canada	1:47.89
3.	...Josefa Idem, Italy	1:48.73

K-2 FLATWATER 500 METERS
1.	...A. Andersson & S. Gunnarsson, Sweden	1:39.32
2.	...R. Portwich & B. Fischer, Germany	1:39.68
3.	...K. Borshert & A. Wood, Australia	1:40.64

K-4 FLATWATER 500 METERS
1.	...Germany	1:31.07
2.	...Switzerland	1:32.70
3.	...Sweden	1:32.91

K-1 WHITEWATER SLALOM
		Pts
1.	...Stepanka Hilgertova, Czech Republic	169.49
2.	...Dana Chladek, United States	169.49
3.	...Myriam Fox-Jerusalmi, France	171.00

BASKETBALL

Men

Final: United States 95, Yugoslavia 69
Lithuania (3rd)
United States: Charles Barkley, Anfernee Hardaway, Grant Hill, Karl Malone, Reggie Miller, Hakeem Olajuwon, Shaquille O'Neal, Scottie Pippen, Mitch Richmond, John Stockton, David Robinson, Gary Payton

Women

Final: United States 111, Brazil 87
Australia (3rd)
United States: Jennifer Azzi, Ruthie Bolton, Teresa Edwards, Lisa Leslie, Rebecca Lobo, Katrina McClain, Nikki McCray, Carla McGhee, Dawn Staley, Katy Steding, Sheryl Swoopes, Venus Lacey

BOXING

LIGHT FLYWEIGHT (106 LB)
1. Daniel Petrov, Bulgaria
2. Mansueto Velasco, Philippines
3. Oleg Kiryukhin, Ukraine
3. Rafael Lozano, Spain

FLYWEIGHT (112 LB)
1. Maikro Romero, Cuba
2. Bolat Zhumadilov, Kazakhstan
3. Zoltan Lunka, Germany
3. Albert Pakeev, Russia

BANTAMWEIGHT (119 LB)
1. István Kovács, Hungary
2. Arnaldo Mesa, Cuba
3. Vichairachanon Khadpo, Thailand
3. Raimkul Malakhbekov, Russia

FEATHERWEIGHT (125 LB)
1. Somluck Kamsing, Thailand
2. Serafim Todorov, Bulgaria
3. Pablo Chacon, Argentina
3. Floyd Mayweather, United States

LIGHTWEIGHT (132 LB)
1. Hocine Soltani, Algeria
2. Tontcho Tontchev, Bulgaria
3. Terrance Cauthen, United States
3. Leonard Doroftei, Romania

LIGHT WELTERWEIGHT (139 LB)
1. Hector Vinent, Cuba
2. Oktay Urkal, Germany
3. Fathi Missaoui, Tunisia
3. Bolat Niyazymbetov, Kazakhstan

WELTERWEIGHT (147 LB)
1. Oleg Saitov, Russia
2. Juan Hernández, Cuba
3. Daniel Santos, Puerto Rico
3. Marian Simion, Romania

LIGHT MIDDLEWEIGHT (156 LB)
1. David Reid, United States
2. Alfredo Duvergel, Cuba
3. Ermakhan Ibraimov, Kazakhstan
3. Karim Tulaganov, Uzbekistan

MIDDLEWEIGHT (165 LB)
1. Ariel Hernández, Cuba
2. Malik Beyleroglu, Turkey
3. Mohamed Bahari, Algeria
3. Rhoshii Wells, United States

LIGHT HEAVYWEIGHT (178 LB)
1. Vassili Jirov, Kazakhstan
2. Lee Seung Bao, South Korea
3. Antonio Tarver, United States
3. Thomas Ulrich, Germany

HEAVYWEIGHT (201 LB)
1. Félix Sávon, Cuba
2. David Defiagbon, Canada
3. Nate Jones, United States
3. Luan Krasniqi, Germany

SUPERHEAVYWEIGHT (201+ LB)
1. Vladimir Klitchko, Ukraine
2. Paea Wolfgram, Tonga
3. Duncan Dokiwari, Nigeria
3. Alexei Lezin, Russia

GYMNASTICS

Men

ALL-AROUND
		Pts
1.	Li Xiaoshuang, China	58.423
2.	Alexei Nemov, Russia	58.374
3.	Vitaly Scherbo, Belarus	58.197

HORIZONTAL BAR
		Pts
1.	Andreas Wecker, Germany	9.850
2.	Krasimir Dounev, Bulgaria	9.825
3.	Vitaly Scherbo, Belarus	9.800
3.	Fan Bin, China	9.800
3.	Alexei Nemov, Russia	9.800

PARALLEL BARS
		Pts
1.	Rustam Sharipov, Ukraine	9.837
2.	Jair Lynch, United States	9.825
3.	Vitaly Scherbo, Belarus	9.800

VAULT
		Pts
1.	Alexei Nemov, Russia	9.787
2.	Yeo Hong-Chul, South Korea	9.756
3.	Vitaly Scherbo, Belarus	9.724

POMMEL HORSE
		Pts
1.	Donghua Li, Switzerland	9.875
2.	Marius Urzica, Romania	9.825
3.	Alexei Nemov, Russia	9.787

Women

ALL-AROUND
		Pts
1.	Lilia Podkopayeva, Ukraine	39.255
2.	Gina Gogean, Romania	39.075
3.	Simona Amanar, Romania	39.067
3.	Lavinia Milosovici, Romania	39.067

VAULT
		Pts
1.	Simona Amanar, Romania	9.825
2.	Mo Huilan, China	9.768
3.	Gina Gogean, Romania	9.750

UNEVEN BARS
		Pts
1.	Svetlana Chorkina, Russia	9.850
2.	Bi Wenjing, China	9.837
2.	Amy Chow, United States	9.837

BALANCE BEAM
		Pts
1.	Shannon Miller, United States	9.862
2.	Lilia Podkopayeva, Ukraine	9.825
3.	Gina Gogean, Romania	9.787

FLOOR EXERCISE
		Pts
1.	Lilia Podkopayeva, Ukraine	9.887
2.	Simona Amanar, Romania	9.850
3.	Dominique Dawes, United States	9.837

GYMNASTICS (Cont.)

Men

RINGS

		Pts
1.	..........Yuri Chechi, Italy	9.887
2.	..........Szilveszter Csollany, Hungary	9.812
2.	..........Dan Burinca, Romania	9.812

FLOOR EXERCISE

		Pts
1.	..........Ioannis Melissanidis, Greece	9.850
2.	..........Li Xiaoshuang, China	9.837
3.	..........Alexei Nemov, Russia	9.800

TEAM COMBINED EXERCISES

		Pts
1.	..........Russia	576.778
2.	..........China	575.539
3.	..........Ukraine	571.541

Women

TEAM COMBINED EXERCISES

		Pts
1.	..........United States: Amanda Borden, Amy Chow, Dominique Dawes, Shannon Miller, Dominique Moceanu, Jaycie Phelps, Kerri Strug	389.225
2.	..........Russia	388.404
3.	..........Romania	388.246

RHYTHMIC ALL-AROUND

		Pts
1.	..........Ekaterina Serebrianskaya, Ukraine	39.683
2.	..........Janna Batyrchina, Russia	39.382
3.	..........Elena Vitrichenko, Ukraine	39.331

RHYTHMIC TEAM COMBINED EXERCISES

		Pts
1.	..........Spain	38.933
2.	..........Bulgaria	38.866
3.	..........Russia	38.365

SWIMMING

Men

50-METER FREESTYLE

1.	..Aleksandr Popov, Russia	22.13
2.	..Gary Hall Jr, United States	22.26
3.	..Fernando Scherer, Brazil	22.29

100-METER FREESTYLE

1.	..Aleksandr Popov, Russia	48.74
2.	..Gary Hall Jr, United States	48.81
3.	..Gustavo Borges, Brazil	49.02

200-METER FREESTYLE

1.	..Danyon Loader, New Zealand	1:47.63
2.	..Gustavo Borges, Brazil	1:48.08
3.	..Daniel Kowalski, Australia	1:48.25

400-METER FREESTYLE

1.	..Danyon Loader, New Zealand	3:47.97
2.	..Paul Palmer, Great Britain	3:49.00
3.	..Daniel Kowalski, Australia	3:49.39

1500-METER FREESTYLE

1.	..Kieren Perkins, Australia	14:56.40
2.	..Daniel Kowalski, Australia	15:02.43
3.	..Graeme Smith, Great Britain	15:02.48

100-METER BACKSTROKE

1.	..Jeff Rouse, United States	54.10
2.	..Rodolfo Falcon Cabrera, Cuba	54.98
3.	..Neisser Bent, Cuba	55.02

200-METER BACKSTROKE

1.	..Brad Bridgewater, United States	1:58.54
2.	..Tripp Schwenk, United States	1:58.99
3.	..Emanuele Merisi, Italy	1:59.18

100-METER BREASTSTROKE

1.	..Fred DeBurghgraeve, Belgium	1:00.65
2.	..Jeremy Linn, United States	1:00.77
3.	..Mark Warnecke, Germany	1:01.33

200-METER BREASTSTROKE

1.	..Norbert Rózsa, Hungary	2:12.57
2.	..Károly Güttler, Hungary	2:13.03
3.	..Andrei Korneyev, Russia	2:13.17

100-METER BUTTERFLY

1.	..Denis Pankratov, Russia	52.27 WR
2.	..Scott Miller, Australia	52.53
3.	..Vladislav Kulikov, Russia	53.13

200-METER BUTTERFLY

1.	..Denis Pankratov, Russia	1:56.51
2.	..Tom Malchow, United States	1:57.44
3.	..Scott Goodman, Australia	1:57.48

200-METER INDIVIDUAL MEDLEY

1.	..Attila Czene, Hungary	1:59.91 OR
2.	..Jani Sievinen, Finland	2:00.13
3.	..Curtis Myden, Canada	2:01.13

400-METER INDIVIDUAL MEDLEY

1.	..Tom Dolan, United States	4:14.90
2.	..Eric Namesnik, United States	4:15.25
3.	..Curtis Myden, Canada	4:16.28

4 X 100 METER MEDLEY RELAY

1.	..United States: Jeff Rouse, Mark Henderson, Gary Hall Jr, Jeremy Linn	3:34.84 WR
2.	..Russia	3:37.55
3.	..Australia	3:39.56

4 X 100 METER FREESTYLE RELAY

1.	..United States: Jon Olsen, Josh Davis, Bradley Schumacher, Gary Hall Jr	3:15.41 OR
2.	..Russia	3:17.06
3.	..Germany	3:17.20

4 X 200 METER FREESTYLE RELAY

1.	..United States: Ryan Berube, Joe Hudepohl, Bradley Schumacher, Jon Olsen	7:14.84
2.	..Sweden	7:17.56
3.	..Germany	7:17.71

Note: OR=Olympic record. WR=world record. EOR=equals Olympic record. EWR=equals world record.

SWIMMING (Cont.)
Women

50-METER FREESTYLE
1. ..Amy Van Dyken, United States — 24.87
2. ..Le Jingyi, China — 24.90
3. ..Sandra Volker, Germany — 25.14

100-METER FREESTYLE
1. ..Le Jingyi, China — 54.50 OR
2. ..Sandra Volker, Germany — 54.88
3. ..Angel Martino, United States — 54.93

200-METER FREESTYLE
1. ..Claudia Poll, Costa Rica — 1:58.16
2. ..Franziska van Almsick, Germany — 1:58.57
3. ..Dagmar Hase, Germany — 1:59.56

400-METER FREESTYLE
1. ..Michelle Smith, Ireland — 4:07.25
2. ..Dagmar Hase, Germany — 4:08.30
3. ..Kirsten Vlieghuis, Netherlands — 4:08.70

800-METER FREESTYLE
1. ..Brooke Bennett, United States — 8:27.89
2. ..Dagmar Hase, Germany — 8:29.91
3. ..Kirsten Vlieghuis, Netherlands — 8:30.84

100-METER BACKSTROKE
1. ..Beth Botsford, United States — 1:01.19
2. ..Whitney Hedgepeth, United States — 1:01.47
3. ..Marianne Kriel, South Africa — 1:02.12

200-METER BACKSTROKE
1. ..Krisztina Egerszegi, Hungary — 2:07.83
2. ..Whitney Hedgepeth, United States — 2:11.98
3. ..Cathleen Rund, Germany — 2:12.06

100-METER BREASTSTROKE
1. ..Penelope Heyns, South Africa — 1:07.73
2. ..Amanda Beard, United States — 1:08.09
3. ..Samantha Riley, Australia — 1:09.18

200-METER BREASTSTROKE
1. ..Penelope Heyns, South Africa — 2:25.41 OR
2. ..Amanda Beard, United States — 2:25.75
3. ..Agnes Kovacs, Hungary — 2:26.57

100-METER BUTTERFLY
1. ..Amy Van Dyken, United States — 59.13
2. ..Liu Limin, China — 59.14
3. ..Angel Martino, United States — 59.23

200-METER BUTTERFLY
1. ..Susan O'Neill, Australia — 2:07.76
2. ..Petria Thomas, Australia — 2:09.82
3. ..Michelle Smith, Ireland — 2:09.91

200-METER INDIVIDUAL MEDLEY
1. ..Michelle Smith, Ireland — 2:13.93
2. ..Marianne Limpert, Canada — 2:14.35
3. ..Lin Li, China — 2:14.74

400-METER INDIVIDUAL MEDLEY
1. ..Michelle Smith, Ireland — 4:39.18
2. ..Allison Wagner, United States — 4:42.03
3. ..Krisztina Egerszegi, Hungary — 4:42.53

4 X 100 METER MEDLEY RELAY
1. ..United States: Beth Botsford, — 4:02.88
Amanda Beard, Angel Martino,
Amy Van Dyken
2. ..Australia — 4:05.08
3. ..China — 4:07.34

4 X 100 METER FREESTYLE RELAY
1. ..United States: Jenny Thompson, — 3:39.29 OR
Catherine Fox, Angel Martino,
Amy Van Dyken
2. ..China — 3:40.48
3. ..Germany — 3:41.48

4 X 200 METER FREESTYLE RELAY
1. ..United States: Trina Jackson, — 7:59.87
Sheila Taormina, Cristina Teuscher,
Jenny Thompson
2. ..Germany — 8:01.55
3. ..Australia — 8:05.47

DIVING

Men		Women	
SPRINGBOARD	Pts	**SPRINGBOARD**	Pts
1. ....Xiong Ni, China	701.46	1. ....Fu Mingxia, China	547.68
2. ....Yu Zhuocheng, China	690.93	2. ....Irina Lashko, Russia	512.19
3. ....Mark Lenzi, United States	686.49	3. ....Annie Pelletier, Canada	509.64
PLATFORM	Pts	**PLATFORM**	Pts
1. ....Dmitri Sautin, Russia	692.34	1. ....Fu Mingxia, China	521.58
2. ....Jan Hempel, Germany	663.27	2. ....Annika Walter, Germany	479.22
3. ....Xiao Hailiang, China	658.20	3. ....Mary Ellen Clark, United States	472.95

INDIVIDUAL ARCHERY

Men	Women
1. ....Justin Huish, United States	1. ....Kim Kyung Wook, South Korea
2. ....Magnus Petersson, Sweden	2. ....He Ying, China
3. ....Oh Kyo Moon, South Korea	3. ....Olena Sadovnycha, Ukraine

Note: OR=Olympic record. WR=world record. EOR=equals Olympic record. EWR=equals world record.

TEAM ARCHERY

Men

1. ....United States
2. ....South Korea
3. ....Italy

Women

1. ....South Korea
2. ....Germany
3. ....Poland

CYCLING

Men

ROAD RACE

1. ..Pascal Richard, Switzerland	4:53:56
2. ..Rolf Sorensen, Denmark	4:53:56
3. ..Maximilian Sciandri, Great Britain	4:53:58

INDIVIDUAL TIME TRIAL

1. ..Miguel Indurain, Spain	1:04:05
2. ..Abraham Olano, Spain	1:04:17
3. ..Chris Boardman, Great Britain	1:04:36

1 KM TIME TRIAL

1. ..Florian Rousseau, France	1:02.712 OR
2. ..Erin Hartwell, United States	1:02.940
3. ..Takanobu Jumonji, Japan	1:03.261

4000 METER INDIVIDUAL PURSUIT

1. ..Andrea Collinelli, Italy	4:20.893
2. ..Philippe Ermenault, France	4:22.714
3. ..Bradley McGee, Australia	4:26.121

4000 METER TEAM PURSUIT

1. ..France: Christophe Capelle, Philippe Ermenault, Jean-Michel Monin, Francis Moreau, Herve Thuet	4:05.930
2. ..Russia	4:07.730
3. ..Australia	4:07.570

SPRINT

1. ..Jens Fiedler, Germany	10.664
2. ..Marty Nothstein, United States	11.074
3. ..Curt Harnett, Canada	10.947

Men (Cont.)

40 KM POINTS RACE

1. ..Silvio Martinello, Italy	37
2. ..Brian Walton, Canada	29
3. ..Stuart O'Grady, Australia	27

Women

ROAD RACE

1. ..Jeannie Longo-Ciprelli, France	2:36:13
2. ..Imelda Chiappa, Italy	2:36.38
3. ..Clara Hughes, Canada	2:36.44

INDIVIDUAL TIME TRIAL

1. ..Zulfiya Zabirova, Russia	36:40
2. ..Jeannie Longo-Ciprelli, France	37:00
3. ..Clara Hughes, Canada	37:13

3000 METER INDIVIDUAL PURSUIT

1. ..Antonella Bellutti, Italy	3:33.595
2. ..Marion Clignet, France	3:38.571
3. ..Judith Arndt, Germany	3:38.744

SPRINT

1. ..Felicia Ballanger, France	11.903
2. ..Michelle Ferris, Australia	12.096
3. ..Ingrid Haringa, Netherlands	12.074

24 KM POINTS RACE

1. ..Nathalie Lancien, France	24
2. ..Ingrid Haringa, Netherlands	23
3. ..Lucy Tyler Sharman, Australia	17

MOUNTAIN BIKING

Men

1. ......Bart Jan Brentjens, Netherlands	2:17:38
2. ......Thomas Frischkneckt, Switzerland	2:20:14
3. ......Miguel Martinez, France	2:20:36

Women

1. ......Paola Pezzo, Italy	1:50:51
2. ......Alison Sydor, Canada	1:51:58
3. ......Susan DeMattei, United States	1:52:36

EQUESTRIAN

3-DAY TEAM

1. ......Australia: Wendy Schaeffer, Phillip Dutton, Andrew Hoy, Darien Powers	203.850
2. ......United States	261.100
3. ......New Zealand	268.550

3-DAY INDIVIDUAL

1. ......Blyth Tait, New Zealand	56.80
2. ......Sally Clark, New Zealand	60.40
3. ......Kerry Millikin, United States	73.70

TEAM DRESSAGE

1. ......Germany: Isabell Werth, Monica Theodorescu, Martin Schaudt, Klaus Balkenhol	5553
2. ......The Netherlands	5437
3. ......United States	5309

INDIVIDUAL DRESSAGE

1. ......Isabell Werth, Germany	235.09
2. ......Anky van Grunsven, Netherlands	233.02
3. ......Sven Rothenberger, Netherlands	224.94

TEAM JUMPING

1. ......Germany: Ulrich Kirchoff, Lars Nieberg, Franke Sloothaak, Ludger Beerbaum	1.25
2. ......United States	12.00
3. ......Brazil	17.25

INDIVIDUAL JUMPING

1. ......Ulrich Kirchoff, Germany	1.00
2. ......Willi Melliger, Switzerland	4.00
3. ......Alexandra Ledermann, France	4.00

Note: OR=Olympic record. WR=world record. EOR=equals Olympic record. EWR=equals world record.

FENCING

Men

FOIL
1. ....Alessandro Puccini, Italy
2. ....Lionel Plumenail, France
3. ....Franck Boidin, France

SABRE
1. ....Stanislav Pozdniakov, Russia
2. ....Sergei Sharikov, Russia
3. ....Damien Touya, France

ÉPÉE
1. ....Aleksandr Beketov, Russia
2. ....Ivan Trevejo Perez, Cuba
3. ....Geza Imre, Hungary

TEAM FOIL
1. ....Russia
2. ....Poland
3. ....Cuba

TEAM SABRE
1. ....Russia
2. ....Hungary
3. ....Italy

Men *(Cont.)*

TEAM ÉPÉE
1. ....Italy
2. ....Russia
3. ....France

Women

FOIL
1. ....Laura Badea, Romania
2. ....Valentina Vezzali, Italy
3. ....Giovanna Trillini, Italy

ÉPÉE
1. ....Laura Flessel, France
2. ....Valerie Barlois, France
3. ....Gyöngyi Szalay, Hungary

TEAM FOIL
1. ....Italy
2. ....Romania
3. ....Germany

TEAM ÉPÉE
1. ....France
2. ....Italy
3. ....Russia

FIELD HOCKEY

Men
1. ....The Netherlands
2. ....Spain
3. ....Australia

Women
1. ....Australia
2. ....South Korea
3. ....The Netherlands

TEAM HANDBALL

Men
1. ....Croatia
2. ....Sweden
3. ....Spain

Women
1. ....Denmark
2. ....South Korea
3. ....Hungary

JUDO

Men

EXTRA-LIGHTWEIGHT
1. ....Tadahiro Nomura, Japan
2. ....Girolamo Giovinazzo, Italy
3. ....Dorjpalam Narmandakh, Mongolia
3. ....Richard Trautmann, Germany

HALF-LIGHTWEIGHT
1. ....Udo Quellmalz, Germany
2. ....Yukimasa Nakamura, Japan
3. ....Henrique Guimares, Brazil
3. ....Israel Hernandez Plana, Cuba

LIGHTWEIGHT
1. ....Kenzo Nakamura, Japan
2. ....Kwak Dae Sung, South Korea
3. ....Christophe Gagliano, France
3. ....James Pedro, United States

HALF-MIDDLEWEIGHT
1. ....Djamel Bouras, France
2. ....Toshihiko Koga, Japan
3. ....Cho In Chul, South Korea
3. ....Soso Liparteliani, Georgia

Women

EXTRA-LIGHTWEIGHT
1. ....Kye Sun Hi, North Korea
2. ....Ryoko Tamura, Japan
3. ....Amarilis Savón, Cuba
3. ....Yolanda Soler, Spain

HALF-LIGHTWEIGHT
1. ....Marie-Claire Restoux, France
2. ....Hyun Sook Hee, South Korea
3. ....Noriko Sugawara, Japan
3. ....Legna Verdecia, Cuba

LIGHTWEIGHT
1. ....Driulis González, Cuba
2. ....Jung Sun Yong, South Korea
3. ....Isabel Fernández, Spain
3. ....Marisbel Lomba, Belgium

HALF-MIDDLEWEIGHT
1. ....Yuko Emoto, Japan
2. ....Gella Vandecaveye, Belgium
3. ....Jenny Gal, Netherlands
3. ....Jung Sung Sook, South Korea

JUDO

Men *(Cont.)*	Women *(Cont.)*
MIDDLEWEIGHT	**MIDDLEWEIGHT**
1. Jeon Ki Young, South Korea	1. Cho Min Sun, South Korea
2. Armen Bagdasarov, Uzbekistan	2. Aneta Szczepanska, Poland
3. Mark Huizinga, Netherlands	3. Wang Xianbo, China
3. Marko Spittka, Germany	3. Claudia Zwiers, Netherlands
HALF-HEAVYWEIGHT	**HALF-HEAVYWEIGHT**
1. Pawel Nastula, Poland	1. Ulla Werbrouck, Belgium
2. Kim Min Soo, South Korea	2. Yoko Tanabe, Japan
3. Miguel Fernandes, Brazil	3. Ylenia Scapin, Italy
3. Stéphane Traineau, France	3. Diadenis Luna, Cuba
HEAVYWEIGHT	**HEAVYWEIGHT**
1. David Douillet, France	1. Sun Fuming, China
2. Ernesto Perez, Spain	2. Estela Rodriguez, Cuba
3. Harry van Barneveld, Belgium	3. Christine Cicot, France
3. Frank Möller, Germany	3. Johanna Hagn, Germany

MODERN PENTATHLON

1. Aleksandr Parygin, Kazakhstan
2. Eduard Zenovka, Russia
3. Janos Martinek, Hungary

ROWING

Men

SINGLE SCULLS		COXLESS PAIR	
1. Xeno Mueller, Switzerland	6:44.85	1. S. Redgrave & M. Pinsent, Great Britain	6:20.09
2. Derek Porter, Canada	6:47.45	2. D. Weightman & R. Scott, Australia	6:21.02
3. Thomas Lange, Germany	6:47.72	3. M. Andrieux & J. Rolland, France	6:22.15
DOUBLE SCULLS		**COXLESS FOUR**	
1. D. Tizzano & A. Abbagnale, Italy	6:16.98	1. Australia	6:06.37
2. K. Undset & S. Stoerseth, Norway	6:18.42	2. France	6:07.03
3. F. Kowal & S. Barathay, France	6:19.85	3. Britain	6:07.28
LIGHTWEIGHT DOUBLE SCULLS		**LIGHTWEIGHT COXLESS FOUR**	
1. M. Gier & M. Gier, Switzerland	6:23.47	1. Denmark	6:09.58
2. Van Der Linden & Aardewijn, Netherlands	6:26.48	2. Canada	6:10.13
3. A. Edwards & B. Hick, Australia	6:26.69	3. United States	6:12.29
QUADRUPLE SCULLS		**EIGHT-OARS**	
1. Germany	5:56.93	1. The Netherlands	5:42.74
2. United States	5:59.10	2. Germany	5:44.58
3. Australia	6:01.65	3. Russia	5:45.77

Women

SINGLE SCULLS		QUADRUPLE SCULLS	
1. Ekaterina Khodotovich, Belarus	7:32.21	1. Germany	6:27.44
2. Silken Laumann, Canada	7:35.15	2. Ukraine	6:30.36
3. Trine Hansen, Denmark	7:37.20	3. Canada	6:30.38
DOUBLE SCULLS		**COXLESS PAIR**	
1. M. McBean & K. Heddle, Canada	6:56.84	1. M. Still & K. Slatter, Australia	7:01.39
2. Cao Mianying & Zhang Xiuyun, China	6:58.35	2. M. Schwen & K. Kraft, United States	7:01.78
3. I. Eijs & E. Van Nes, Netherlands	6:58.72	3. C. Gosse & H. Cortin, France	7:03.82
LIGHTWEIGHT DOUBLE SCULLS		**EIGHT-OARS**	
1. C. Burcica & C. Macoviciuc, Romania	7:12.78	1. Romania	6:19.73
2. T. Bell & L. Burns, United States	7:14.65	2. Canada	6:24.05
3. R. Joyce & V. Lee, Australia	7:16.56	3. Belarus	6:24.44

SOCCER

Men	Women
1. Nigeria	1. United States
2. Argentina	2. China
3. Brazil	3. Norway

SOFTBALL

1. ....United States
2. ....China
3. ....Australia

SYNCHRONIZED SWIMMING

1. ....United States
2. ....Canada
3. ....Japan

SHOOTING

Men

RAPID-FIRE PISTOL

	Pts
1......Ralf Schumann, Germany	698
2......Emil Milev, Bulgaria	692.1
3......Vladimir Vokhmianin, Kazakhstan	691.5

FREE PISTOL

	Pts
1......Boris Kokorev, Russia	666.4
2......Igor Basinski, Belarus	662.0
3......Roberto Di Donna, Italy	661.8

AIR PISTOL

	Pts
1......Roberto Di Donna, Italy	684
2......Wang Yifu, China	684
3......Tanu Kiriakov, Bulgaria	683

RUNNING TARGET

	Pts
1......Yang Ling, China	685.8
2......Xiao Jun, China	679.8
3......Miroslav Janus, Czech Republic	678.4

SMALL-BORE RIFLE, THREE-POSITION

	Pts
1......Jean-Pierre Amat, France	1273.9
2......Sergei Beliaev, Kazakhstan	1272.3
3......Wolfram Waibel Jr, Austria	1269.6

SMALL-BORE RIFLE, PRONE

	Pts
1......Christian Klees, Germany	704.8
2......Sergei Beliaev, Kazakhstan	703.3
3......Jozef Gonci, Slovakia	701.9

AIR RIFLE

	Pts
1......Artem Khadzhibekov, Russia	695.7
2......Wolfram Waibel Jr, Austria	695.2
3......Jean-Pierre Amat, France	693.1

TRAP

	Pts
1......Michael Diamond, Australia	149
2......Josh Lakatos, United States	147
3......Lance Bade, United States	147

DOUBLE TRAP

	Pts
1......Russell Mark, Australia	189.0
2......Albano Pera, Italy	183.0
3......Zhang Bing, China	183.0

SKEET

	Pts
1......Ennio Falco, Italy	149.0
2......Miroslaw Rzepkowski, Poland	148.0
3......Andrea Benelli, Italy	147.0

Women

SPORT PISTOL

	Pts
1......Li Duihong, China	687.9
2......Diana Yorgova, Bulgaria	684.8
3......Marina Logvinenko, Russia	684.2

AIR PISTOL

	Pts
1......Olga Klochneva, Russia	490.1
2......Marina Logvinenko, Russia	488.5
3......Maria Grozdeva, Bulgaria	488.5

SMALL-BORE RIFLE, THREE-POSITION

	Pts
1......Aleksandra Ivosev, Yugoslavia	686.1
2......Irina Gerasimenok, Russia	680.1
3......Renata Mauer, Poland	679.8

AIR RIFLE

	Pts
1......Renata Mauer, Poland	497.6
2......Petra Horneber, Germany	497.4
3......Aleksandra Ivosev, Yugoslavia	497.2

DOUBLE TRAP

	Pts
1......Kim Rhode, United States	141.0
2......Susanne Kiermayer, Germany	139.0
3......Deserie Huddleston, Australia	139.0

TABLE TENNIS

Men

SINGLES

1. ....Liu Guoliang, China
2. ....Wang Tao, China
3. ....Joerg Rosskopf, Germany

DOUBLES

1. ....Kong Linghui & Liu Guoliang, China
2. ....Lu Lin & Wang Tao, China
3. ....Lee Chul Seung & Yoo Nam Kyu, South Korea

Women

SINGLES

1. ....Deng Yaping, China
2. ....Chen Jing, Taiwan
3. ....Qiao Hong, China

DOUBLES

1. ....Deng Yaping & Qiao Hong, China
2. ....Liu Wei & Qiao Yunping, China
3. ....Park Hae Jung & Ryu Ji Hae, South Korea

TENNIS

Men	Women
SINGLES	**SINGLES**

Men

SINGLES
1. ....Andre Agassi, United States
2. ....Sergi Bruguera, Spain
3. ....Leander Paes, India

DOUBLES
1. ....Todd Woodbridge &
      Mark Woodforde, Australia
2. ....Neil Broad &
      Tim Henman, Great Britain
3. ....Marc-Kevin Goellner &
      David Prinosil, Germany

Women

SINGLES
1. ....Lindsay Davenport, United States
2. ....Arantxa Sánchez Vicario, Spain
3. ....Jana Novotna, Czech Republic

DOUBLES
1. ....Gigi Fernandez &
      Mary Joe Fernandez, United States
2. ....Jana Novotna &
      Helena Sukova, Czech Republic
3. ....Conchita Martinez &
      Arantxa Sánchez Vicario, Spain

VOLLEYBALL

Men
1. ....The Netherlands
2. ....Italy
3. ....Yugoslavia

Women
1. ....Cuba
2. ....China
3. ....Brazil

BEACH VOLLEYBALL

Men
1. ....Karch Kiraly & Kent Steffes, United States
2. ....Michael Dodd & M. Whitmarsh, United States
3. ....John Child & Mark Heese, Canada

Women
1. ....S. Pires Tavares & J. Silva Cruz, Brazil
2. ....Monica Rodrigues & A. Samuel Ramos, Brazil
3. ....Natalie Cook & Kerri Ann Pottharst, Australia

WATER POLO

1. ....Spain
2. ....Croatia
3. ....Italy

WEIGHTLIFTING

119 POUNDS
1. ....Halil Mutlu, Turkey	633 lb OR
2. ....Zhang Xiangsen, China	616 lb
3. ....Sevdalin Minchev, Bulgaria	611 lb

130 POUNDS
1. ....Tang Ningsheng, China	678 lb OR
2. ....Leonidas Sabanis, Greece	672 lb
3. ....Nikolai Pechalov, Bulgaria	667 lb

141 POUNDS
1. ....Naim Suleymanoglu, Turkey	739 lb OR
2. ....Valerios Leonidis, Greece	733 lb
3. ....Xiao Jiangang, China	711 lb

154 POUNDS
1. ....Zhan Xugang, China	787 lb OR
2. ....Kim Myong Nam, North Korea	761 lb
3. ....Attila Feri, Hungary	750 lb

167.5 POUNDS
1. ....Pablo Lara, Cuba	809 lb
2. ....Yoto Yotov, Bulgaria	794 lb
3. ....Jon Chol, North Korea	787 lb

183 POUNDS
1. ....Pyrros Dimas, Greece	864 lb OR
2. ....Marc Huster, Germany	842 lb
3. ....Andrzej Cofalik, Poland	820 lb

200.5 POUNDS
1. ....Alexei Petrov, Russia	886 lb
2. ....Leonidas Kokas, Greece	860 lb
3. ....Oliver Caruso, Germany	860 lb

218 POUNDS
1. ....Kakhi Kakhiasvili, Greece	926 lb OR
2. ....Anatoli Khrapati, Kazakhstan	904 lb
3. ....Denis Gotfrid, Ukraine	886 lb

238 POUNDS
1. ....Timur Taimazov, Ukraine	948 lb
2. ....Sergey Syrtsov, Russia	926 lb
3. ....Nicu Vlad, Romania	926 lb

238+ POUNDS
1. ....Andrei Chemerkin, Russia	1008 lb OR
2. ....Ronny Weller, Germany	1003 lb
3. ....Stefan Botev, Australia	992 lb

FREESTYLE WRESTLING

105.5 POUNDS
1. ....Kim Il, North Korea
2. ....Armen Mkrchyan, Armenia
3. ....Alexis Vila, Cuba

114.5 POUNDS
1. ....Valentin Yordanov, Bulgaria
2. ....Namik Abdullayev, Azerbaijan
3. ....Maulen Mamyrov, Kazakhstan

125.5 POUNDS
1. ....Kendall Cross, United States
2. ....Guivi Sissaouri, Canada
3. ....Ri Yong Sam, North Korea

136.5 POUNDS
1. ....Tom Brands, United States
2. ....Jang Jae Sung, South Korea
3. ....Elbrus Tedeyev, Ukraine

Note: OR=Olympic Record. WR=World Record. EOR=Equals Olympic Record. EWR=Equals World Record.

FREESTYLE WRESTLING

149.5 POUNDS
1. ....Vadim Bogiev, Russia
2. ....Townsend Saunders, United States
3. ....Zaza Zazirov, Ukraine

163 POUNDS
1. ....Buvaysa Saytyev, Russia
2. ....Park Jang Soon, South Korea
3. ....Takuya Ota, Japan

180.5 POUNDS
1. ....Khadzhimurad Magomedov, Russia
2. ....Yang Hyun Mo, South Korea
3. ....Amir Reza Khadem Azghadi, Iran

198 POUNDS
1. ....Rasul Khadem, Iran
2. ....Makharbek Khadartsev, Russia
3. ....Eldari Kurtanidze, Georgia

220 POUNDS
1. ....Kurt Angle, United States
2. ....Abbas Jadidi, Iran
3. ....Arawat Sabejew, Germany

286 POUNDS
1. ....Mahmut Demir, Turkey
2. ....Alexei Medvedev, Belarus
3. ....Bruce Baumgartner, United States

GRECO-ROMAN WRESTLING

105.5 POUNDS
1. ....Sim Kwon Ho, South Korea
2. ....Aleksandr Pavlov, Belarus
3. ....Zafar Gouliev, Russia

114.5 POUNDS
1. ....Armen Nazarian, Armenia
2. ....Brandon Paulson, United States
3. ....Andrei Kalashnikov, Ukraine

125.5 POUNDS
1. ....Yuri Melnichenko, Kazakhstan
2. ....Dennis Hall, United States
3. ....Sheng Zetian, China

136.5 POUNDS
1. ....Wlodzimierz Zawadzki, Poland
2. ....Juan Luis Maren, Cuba
3. ....Mahmet Pirim, Turkey

149.5 POUNDS
1. ....Ryszard Wolny, Poland
2. ....Ghani Yalouz, France
3. ....Aleksandr Tretyakov, Russia

163 POUNDS
1. ....Filberto Azcuy, Cuba
2. ....Marko Asell, Finland
3. ....Jozef Tracz, Poland

180.5 POUNDS
1. ....Hamza Yerlikaya, Turkey
2. ....Thomas Zander, Germany
3. ....Valery Tsilent, Belarus

198 POUNDS
1. ....Vyacheslav Oleynyk, Ukraine
2. ....Jacek Fafinski, Poland
3. ....Maik Bullmann, Germany

220 POUNDS
1. ....Andrzej Wronski, Poland
2. ....Sergei Lishtvan, Belarus
3. ....Mikael Ljungberg, Sweden

286 POUNDS
1. ....Aleksandr Karelin, Russia
2. ....Matt Ghaffari, United States
3. ....Sergei Mureiko, Moldova

YACHTING

MEN'S 470
1. ....Ukraine
2. ....Great Britain
3. ....Portugal

MEN'S FINN
1. ....Mateusz Kusznierewicz, Poland
2. ....Sebastien Godefroid, Belgium
3. ....Roy Heiner, Netherlands

MEN'S BOARD
1. ....Nikolas Kaklamanakis, Greece
2. ....Carlos Espinola, Argentina
3. ....Gal Fridman, Israel

WOMEN'S 470
1. ....Spain
2. ....Japan
3. ....Ukraine

WOMEN'S EUROPE
1. ....Kristine Roug, Denmark
2. ....Margriet Matthijsse, Netherlands
3. ....Courtenay Becker-Dey, United States

WOMEN'S BOARD
1. ....Lee Lai Shan, Hong Kong
2. ....Barbara Kendall, New Zealnad
3. ....Alessandra Sensini, Italy

SOLING
1. ....Germany
2. ....Russia
3. ....United States

STAR
1. ....Torben Grael & Marcelo Ferreira, Brazil
2. ....Hans Wallen & Bobbie Lohse, Sweden
3. ....Colin Beashel & David Giles, Australia

TORNADO
1. ....J. Luis Ballester & Fernando Leon, Spain
2. ....M. Booth & A. Landenberger, Australia
3. ....Lars Grael & Kiko Pellicano, Brazil

LASER
1. ....Robert Scheidt, Brazil
2. ....Ben Ainslie, Great Britain
3. ....Peer Moberg, Norway

BIATHLON

Men			Women		
10 KILOMETERS			**7.5 KILOMETERS**		
1. ..Sergei Tchepikov, Russia		28:07.0	1. ..Myriam Bedard, Canada		26:08.8
2. ..Ricco Gross, Germany		28:13.0	2. ..Svetlana Paramygina, Belarus		26:09.9
3. ..Sergei Tarasov, Russia		28:27.4	3. ..Valentyna Tserbe, Ukraine		26:10.0
20 KILOMETERS			**15 KILOMETERS**		
1. ..Sergei Tarasov, Russia		57:25.3	1. ..Myriam Bedard, Canada		52:06.6
2. ..Frank Luck, Germany		57:28.7	2. ..Anne Briand, France		52:53.3
3. ..Sven Fischer, Germany		57:41.9	3. ..Ursula Disl, Germany		53:15.3
4 X 7.5 KILOMETER RELAY			**3 X 7.5 KILOMETER RELAY**		
1. ......Germany		1:30:22.1	1. ......Russia		1:47:19.5
2. ......Russia		1:31:23.6	2. ......Germany		1:51:16.5
3. ......France		1:32:31.3	3. ......France		1:52:28.3

BOBSLED

4-MAN BOB			2-MAN BOB		
1. ......Germany II		3:27.78	1. ......Switzerland		3:30.81
2. ......Switzerland		3:27.84	2. ......Switzerland II		3:30.86
3. ......Germany		3:28.01	3. ......Italy		3:31.01

ICE HOCKEY

1. ....Sweden
2. ....Canada
3. ....Finland

LUGE

Men			Women		
SINGLES			**SINGLES**		
1. ......Georg Hackl, Germany		3:21.571	1. ......Gerda Weissensteiner, Italy		3:15.517
2. ......Markus Prock, Austria		3:21.584	2. ......Susi Erdmann, Germany		3:16.276
3. ......Armin Zoggeler, Italy		3:21.833	3. ......Andrea Tagwerker, Austria		3:16.652
DOUBLES					
1. ......K. Brugger and W. Huber, Italy		1:36.720			
2. ......H. Raffl and N. Huber, Italy		1:36.769			
3. ......S. Krausse and J. Behrendt, Ger.		1:36.945			

FIGURE SKATING

Men	Women
Men	**Women**
1. ......Alexei Urmanov, Russia	1. ......Oksana Baiul, Ukraine
2. ......Elvis Stojko, Canada	2. ......Nancy Kerrigan, United States
3. ......Philippe Candeloro, France	3. ......Chen Lu, China
Pairs	**Ice Dancing**
1. ..Ekaterina Gordeeva and Sergei Grinkov, Russia	1. ..Oksana Gritschuk and Evgeni Platov, Russia
2. ..Natalia Mishkutienok and Artur Dmitriev, Russia	2. ..Maia Usova and Alexander Zhulin, Russia
3. ..Isabella Brasseur and Lloyd Eisler, Canada	3. ..Jayne Torvill and Christopher Dean, Great Britain

SPEED SKATING

Men			Women		
500 METERS			**500 METERS**		
1. ..Aleksandr Golubev, Russia		36.33 OR	1. ..Bonnie Blair, United States		39.25
2. ..Sergei Klevchenya, Russia		36.39	2. ..Susan Auch, Canada		39.61
3. ..Manabu Horii, Japan		36.53	3. ..Franziska Schenk, Germany		39.70
1000 METERS			**1000 METERS**		
1. ..Dan Jansen, United States		1:12.43 WR	1. ..Bonnie Blair, United States		1:18.74
2. ..Igor Zhelezovsky, Belarus		1:12.72	2. ..Anke Baier, Germany		1:20.12
3. ..Sergei Klevchenya, Russia		1:12.85	3. ..Qiaobo Ye, China		1:20.22

SPEED SKATING

Men (Cont.)

1500 METERS
1. ..Johann Olav Koss, Norway — 1:51.29 WR
2. ..Rintje Ritsma, The Netherlands — 1:54.85
3. ..Falko Zandstra, The Netherlands — 1:54.90

5000 METERS
1. ..Johann Olav Koss, Norway — 6:34.96 WR
2. ..Kjell Storelid, Norway — 6:42.68
3. ..Rintje Ritsma, Netherlands — 6:43.94

10,000 METERS
1. ..Johann Olav Koss, Norway — 13:30.55 WR
2. ..Kjell Storelid, Norway — 13:49.25
3. ..Bart Veldkamp, The Netherlands — 13:56.73

Women (Cont.)

1500 METERS
1. ..Emese Hunyady, Austria — 2:02.19
2. ..Svetlana Fedotkina, Russia — 2:02.69
3. ..Seiko Hashimoto, Japan — 2:06.88

3000 METERS
1. ..Gunda Niemann, Germany — 4:19.90
2. ..Heike Warnicke, Germany — 4:22.88
3. ..Emese Hunyady, Austria — 4:24.64

5000 METERS
1. ..Gunda Niemann, Germany — 7:31.57
2. ..Heike Warnicke, Germany — 7:37.59
3. ..Claudia Pechstein, Germany — 7:39.80

SHORT TRACK SPEED SKATING

Men

500 METERS
1. ..Chae Ji-Hoon, South Korea — 43.45
2. ..Mirko Vuillermin, Italy — 43.47
3. ..Nicholas Gooch, Great Britain — 43.68

1000 METERS
1. ...Ki-Hoon Kim, South Korea — 1:34.57
2. ..Ji-Hoon Chae, South Korea — 1:34.92
3. ..Marc Gagnon, Canada — DNF

5000-METER RELAY
1. ...Italy — 7:11.74 OR
2. ..United States — 7:13.37
3. ..Australia — 7:13.68

Women

500 METERS
1. ..Cathy Turner, United States — 45.98 OR
2. ..Yanmei Zhang, China — 46.44
3. ..Amy Peterson, United States — 46.76

1000 METERS
1. ..Chun Lee-Kyung, South Korea — 1:36.87
2. ..Nathalie Lambert, Canada — 1:36.97
3. ..Kim So-Hee, South Korea — 1:37.09

3000-METER RELAY
1. ...South Korea — 4:26.64 OR
2. ..Canada — 4:32.04
3. ..United States — 4:39.34

ALPINE SKIING

Men

DOWNHILL
1. ..Tommy Moe, United States — 1:45.75
2. ..Kjetil Andre Aamodt, Norway — 1:45.79
3. ..Edward Podivinsky, Canada — 1:45.87

SUPER GIANT SLALOM
1. ..Markus Wasmeier, Germany — 1:32.53
2. ..Tommy Moe, United States — 1:32.61
3. ..Kjetil Andre Aamodt, Norway — 1:32.93

GIANT SLALOM
1. ..Markus Wasmeier, Germany — 2:52.46
2. ..Urs Kaelin, Switzerland — 2:52.48
3. ..Christian Mayer, Austria — 2:52.58

SLALOM
1. ..Thomas Stangassinger, Austria — 2:02.02
2. ..Alberto Tomba, Italy — 2:02.17
3. ..Jure Kosir, Slovenia — 2:02.53

COMBINED
	Pts
1. ..Lasse Kjus, Norway	3:17.53
2. ..Kjell Andre Aamodt, Norway	3:18.55
3. ..Harald Strand Nilsen, Norway	3:19.14

Women

DOWNHILL
1. ..Katja Seizinger, Germany — 1:35.93
2. ..Picabo Street, United States — 1:36.59
3. ..Isolde Kostner, Italy — 1:36.85

SUPER GIANT SLALOM
1. ..Diann Roffe-Steinrotter, U.S. — 1:22.15
2. ..Svetlana Gladischeva, Russia — 1:22.44
3. ..Isolde Kostner, Italy — 1:22.45

GIANT SLALOM
1. ..Deborah Compagnoni, Italy — 2:30.97
2. ..Martina Ertl, Germany — 2:32.19
2. ..Vreni Schneider, Switzerland — 2:32.97

SLALOM
1. ..Vreni Schneider, Switzerland — 1:56.01
2. ..Elfriede Eder, Austria — 1:56.35
3. ..Katja Koren, Slovenia — 1:56.61

COMBINED
1. ..Pernilla Wiberg, Sweden — 3:05.16
2. ..Vreni Schneider, Switzerland — 3:05.29
3. ..Alenka Dovzan, Slovenia — 3:06.64

Note: OR=Olympic Record; WR=World Record; EOR=Equals Olympic Record; EWR=Equals World Record; WB=World Best.

ALPINE SKIING (Cont.)

FREESTYLE SKIING

Men

MOGUL

	Pts
1. ..Jean-Luc Brassard, Canada	27.24
2. ..Sergei Shoupletsov, Russia	26.90
3. ..Edgar Grospiron, France	26.64

AERIAL

	Pts
1. ..Andreas Schoenbaechler, Switz.	234.67
2. ..Philippe Laroche, Canada	228.63
3. ..Lloyd Langlois, Canada	222.44

Women

MOGUL

	Pts
1. ..Stine Lise Hattestad, Norway	25.97
2. ..Liz McIntyre, United States	25.89
3. ..Elizaveta Kojevnikova, Russia	25.81

AERIAL

	Pts
1. ..Lina Cherjazova, Uzbekistan	166.84
2. ..Marie Lindgren, Sweden	165.88
3. ..Hilde Synnove Lid, Norway	164.13

NORDIC SKIING

Men

10 KILOMETERS (CLASSICAL)

1. ..Bjorn Daehlie, Norway	24:20.1
2. ..Vladimir Smirnov, Russia	24:38.3
3. ..Marco Albarello, Italy	24:42.3

30 KILOMETERS (CLASSICAL)

1. ..Thomas Alsgaard, Norway	1:12:26.4
2. ..Bjorn Daehlie, Norway	1:13:13.6
3. ..Myka Myllyla, Finland	1:14:14.5

50 KILOMETERS (FREESTYLE)

1. ..Vladimir Smirnov, Kazakhstan	2:07:20.3
2. ..Myka Myllyla, Finland	2:08:41.9
3. ..Sture Sivertsen, Norway	2:08:49.0

15 KILOMETERS (FREESTYLE)

1. ..Bjorn Daehlie, Norway	1:00.08.8
2. ..Vladimir Smirnov, Kazakhstan	1:00:38.0
3. ..Silvio Fauner, Italy	1:01:48.6

4 X 10 KILOMETER RELAY (MIXED)

1. ....Italy	1:41:15.0
2. ....Norway	1:41:15.4
3. ....Finland	1:42:15.6

SKI JUMPING (NORMAL HILL)

	Pts
1. ..Espen Bredesen, Norway	282.0
2. ..Lasse Ottesen, Norway	268.0
3. ..Dieter Thoma, Germany	260.5

SKI JUMPING (LARGE HILL)

	Pts
1. ..Jens Weisflogg, Germany	274.5
2. ..Espen Bredesen, Norway	266.5
3. ..Andreas Goldberger, Austria	255.0

TEAM SKI JUMPING

	Pts
1. ....Germany	970.1
2. ....Japan	956.9
3. ....Austria	918.9

NORDIC COMBINED

	Pts
1. ....Fred B. Lundberg, Norway	457.970
2. ....Takanori Kono, Japan	446.345
3. ....Bjarte Engen Vik, Norway	446.175

TEAM COMBINED

	Pts
1. ....Japan	1368.860
2. ....Norway	1310.940
3. ....Switzerland	1275.240

Women

5 KILOMETERS (CLASSICAL)

1. ..Lyubov Egorova, Russia	14:08.8
2. ..Manuela Di Centa, Italy	14:28.3
3. ..Marja-Liisa Kirvesniemi, Finland	14:36.0

15 KILOMETERS (FREESTYLE)

1. ..Manuela Di Centa, Italy	39:44.5
2. ..Lyubov Egorova, Russia	41:03.0
3. ..Nina Gavriluk, Russia	41:10.4

10 KILOMETERS (FREESTYLE)

1. ..Lyubov Egorova, Russia	41:38.1
2. ..Maunela Di Centa, Italy	41:46.4
3. ..Stefania Belmondo, Italy	42:21.1

30 KILOMETERS (CLASSICAL)

1. ..Manuela Di Centa, Italy	1:25:41.6
2. ..Marit Wold, Norway	1:25:57.8
3. ..Marja-Liisa Kirvesniemi, Finland	1:26:13.6

4 X 5 KILOMETER RELAY (MIXED)

1. ....Russia	57:12.5
2. ....Norway	57:42.6
3. ....Italy	58:42.6

Olympic Games Locations and Dates

Summer

	Year	Site	Dates	Competitors			Most Medals	US Medals
				Men	Women	Nations		
I	1896	Athens, Greece	Apr 6-15	311	0	13	Greece (10-19-18—47)	11-6-2—19 (2nd)
II	1900	Paris, France	May 20-Oct 28	1319	11	22	France (29-41-32—102)	20-14-19—53 (2nd)
III	1904	St Louis, United States	July 1-Nov 23	681	6	12	United States (80-86-72—238)	
—	1906	Athens, Greece	Apr 22-May 28	77	7	20	France (15-9-16—40)	12-6-5—23 (4th)
IV	1908	London, Great Britain	Apr 27-Oct 31	1999	36	23	Britain (56-50-39—145)	23-12-12—47 (2nd)
V	1912	Stockholm, Sweden	May 5-July 22	2490	57	28	Sweden (24-24-17—65)	23-19-19—61 (2nd)
VI	1916	Berlin, Germany	Canceled because of war					
VII	1920	Antwerp, Belgium	Apr 20-Sep 12	2543	64	29	United States (41-27-28—96)	
VIII	1924	Paris, France	May 4-July 27	2956	136	44	United States (45-27-27—99)	
IX	1928	Amsterdam, Netherlands	May 17-Aug 12	2724	290	46	United States (22-18-16—56)	
X	1932	Los Angeles, United States	July 30-Aug 14	1281	127	37	United States (41-32-31—104)	
XI	1936	Berlin, Germany	Aug 1-16	3738	328	49	Germany (33-26-30—89)	24-20-12—56 (2nd)
XII	1940	Tokyo, Japan	Canceled because of war					
XIII	1944	London, Great Britain	Canceled because of war					
XIV	1948	London, Great Britain	July 29-Aug 14	3714	385	59	United States (38-27-19—84)	
XV	1952	Helsinki, Finland	July 19-Aug 3	4407	518	69	United States (40-19-17—76)	
XVI	1956	Melbourne, Australia*	Nov 22-Dec 8	2958	384	67	USSR (37-29-32—98)	32-25-17—74 (2nd)
XVII	1960	Rome, Italy	Aug 25-Sep 11	4738	610	83	USSR (43-29-31—103)	34-21-16—71 (2nd)
XVIII	1964	Tokyo, Japan	Oct 10-24	4457	683	93	United States (36-26-28—90)	
XIX	1968	Mexico City, Mexico	Oct 12-27	4750	781	112	United States (45-28-34—107)	
XX	1972	Munich, West Germany	Aug 26-Sep 10	5848	1299	122	USSR (50-27-22—99)	33-31-30—94 (2nd)
XXI	1976	Montreal, Canada	July 17-Aug 1	4834	1251	92†	USSR (49-41-35—125)	34-35-25—94 (3rd)
XXII	1980	Moscow, USSR	July 19-Aug 3	4265	1088	81‡	USSR (80-69-46—195)	Did not compete
XXIII	1984	Los Angeles, United States	July 28-Aug 12	5458	1620	141#	United States (83-61-30—174)	
XXIV	1988	Seoul, South Korea	Sep 17-Oct 2	7105	2476	160	USSR (55-31-46—132)	36-31-27—94 (3rd)
XXV	1992	Barcelona, Spain	July 25-Aug. 9	7555	3008	172	Unified Team (45-38-29—112)	37-34-37—108 (2nd)
XXVI	1996	Atlanta, United States	July 19-Aug 4	6984	3766	197	United States (44-32-25—101)	

*The equestrian events were held in Stockholm, Sweden, June 10-17, 1956.

†This figure includes Cameroon, Egypt, Morocco, and Tunisia, countries that boycotted the 1976 Olympics after some of their athletes had already competed.

‡The US was among 65 countries that refused to participate in the 1980 Summer Games in Moscow.

#The USSR, East Germany, and 14 other countries did not participate in the 1984 Summer Games in Los Angeles.

Winter

	Year	Site	Dates	Competitors			Most Medals	US Medals
				Men	Women	Nations		
I	1924	Chamonix, France	Jan 25-Feb 4	281	13	16	Norway (4-7-6—17)	1-2-1—4 (3rd)
II	1928	St Moritz, Switzerland	Feb 11-19	468	27	25	Norway (6-4-5—15)	2-2-2—6 (2nd)
III	1932	Lake Placid, United States	Feb 4-15	274	32	17	United States (6-4-2—12)	
IV	1936	Garmisch-Partenkirchen, Germany	Feb 6-16	675	80	28	Norway (7-5-3—15)	1-0-3—4 (T-5th)
—	1940	Garmisch-Partenkirchen, Germany	Canceled because of war					
—	1944	Cortina d'Ampezzo, Italy	Canceled because of war					
V	1948	St Moritz, Switzerland	Jan 30-Feb 8	636	77	28	Norway (4-3-3—10) Sweden (4-3-3—10) Switzerland (3-4-3—10)	3-4-2—9 (4th)
VI	1952	Oslo, Norway	Feb 14-25	623	109	30	Norway (7-3-6—16)	4-6-1—11 (2nd)
VII	1956	Cortina d'Ampezzo, Italy	Jan 26-Feb 5	686	132	32	USSR (7-3-6—16)	2-3-2—7 (T 4th)
VIII	1960	Squaw Valley, United States	Feb 18-28	521	144	30	USSR (7-5-9—21)	3-4-3—10 (2nd)
IX	1964	Innsbruck, Austria	Jan 29-Feb 9	986	200	36	USSR (11-8-6—25)	1-2-3—6 (7th)
X	1968	Grenoble, France	Feb 6-18	1081	212	37	Norway (6-6-2—14)	1-5-1—7 (T-7th)
XI	1972	Sapporo, Japan	Feb 3-13	1015	217	35	USSR (8-5-3—16)	3-2-3—8 (6th)
XII	1976	Innsbruck, Austria	Feb 4-15	900	228	37	USSR (13-6-8—27)	3-3-4—10 (T-3rd)
XIII	1980	Lake Placid, United States	Feb 14-23	833	234	37	USSR (10-6-6—22)	6-4-2—12 (3rd)
XIV	1984	Sarajevo, Yugoslavia	Feb 7-19	1002	276	49	USSR (6-10-9—25)	4-4-0—8 (T-5th)
XV	1988	Calgary, Canada	Feb 13-28	1128	317	57	USSR (11-9-9—29)	2-1-3—6 (T-8th)
XVI	1992	Albertville, France	Feb 8-23	1318	490	65	Germany (10-10-6—26)	5-4-2—11 (6th)
XVII	1994	Lillehammer, Norway	Feb 11-27	1302	542		Norway (10-11-5—26)	6-5-2—13 (T-5th)

Alltime Olympic Medal Winners

Summary

NATIONS

Nation	Gold	Silver	Bronze	Total	Nation	Gold	Silver	Bronze	Total
United States	832	634	553	2019	Australia	86	85	121	292
Soviet Union (1952–88)	395	319	296	1010	Japan	92	89	97	278
Great Britain	169	223	218	610	Romania	63	77	99	239
France	175	179	206	560	Poland	50	67	110	227
Sweden	132	151	174	457	Canada	48	78	90	216
Italy	166	135	144	445	The Netherlands	49	58	81	188
East Germany (1956–88)	159	150	136	445	Bulgaria	43	76	63	182
Hungary	142	129	155	426	Switzerland	46	69	59	174
Germany (1896–1936, 1992–)	124	121	134	379	China	52	63	49	164
					Denmark	38	60	57	155
West Germany (1952–88)	77	104	120	301	Czechoslovakia (1924–92)	49	49	44	142
Finland	99	80	113	292	Belgium	37	49	49	135

Summer (Cont.)

INDIVIDUALS — OVERALL

Men — Athlete, Nation	Sport	G	S	B	Tot
Nikolai Andrianov, USSR	Gym	7	5	3	15
Boris Shakhlin, USSR	Gym	7	4	2	13
Edoardo Mangiarotti, Italy	Fen	6	5	2	13
Takashi Ono, Japan	Gym	5	4	4	13
Paavo Nurmi, Finland	Track	9	3	0	12
Sawao Kato, Japan	Gym	8	3	1	12
Mark Spitz, United States	Swim	9	1	1	11
Matt Biondi, United States	Swim	8	2	1	11
Viktor Chukarin, USSR	Gym	7	3	1	11
Carl Osburn, United States	Shoot	5	4	2	11
Ray Ewry, United States	Track	10	0	0	10
Carl Lewis, United States	Track	9	1	0	10
Aladár Gerevich, Hungary	Fen	7	1	2	10
Akinori Nakayama, Japan	Gym	6	2	2	10
Vitaly Scherbo, UT/Belarus	Gym	6	0	4	10
Aleksandr Dityatin, USSR	Gym	3	6	1	10

Women — Athlete, Nation	Sport	G	S	B	Tot
Larissa Latynina, USSR	Gym	9	5	4	18
Vera Cáslavská, Czech	Gym	7	4	0	11
Agnes Keleti, Hungary	Gym	5	3	2	10
Polina Astaknova, USSR	Gym	5	2	3	10
Nadia Comaneci, Romania	Gym	5	3	1	9
Lyudmila Tourischeva, USSR	Gym	4	3	2	9
Kornelia Ender, E Germany	Swim	4	4	0	8
Dawn Fraser, Australia	Swim	4	4	0	8
Shirley Babashoff, United States	Swim	2	6	0	8
Sofia Muratova, USSR	Gym	2	2	4	8
Eight tied with seven.					

INDIVIDUALS — GOLD

Men

Ray Ewry, United States	10
Paavo Nurmi, Finland	9
Carl Lewis, United States	9
Mark Spitz, United States	9
Sawao Kato, Japan	8
Matt Biondi, United States	8
Nikolai Andrianov, USSR	7
Boris Shakhlin, USSR	7
Viktor Chukarin, USSR	7
Aladár Gerevich, Hungary	7

Women

Larissa Latynina, USSR	9
Vera Cáslavská, Czech	7
Kristin Otto, E Germany	6
Agnes Keleti, Hungary	5
Nadia Comaneci, Romania	5
Polina Astaknova, USSR	5
Krisztina Egerszegi, Hun	5
Jenny Thompson, United States	5
Kornelia Ender, E Germany	4
Dawn Fraser, Australia	4
Lyudmila Tourischeva, USSR	4
Evelyn Ashford, United States	4
Janet Evans, United States	4
Fanny Blankers-Koen, Neth	4
Betty Cuthbert, Australia	4
Pat McCormick, United States	4
Bärbel Eckert Wöckel, E Ger	4
Amy Van Dyken, United States	4

Winter

NATIONS

Nation	Gold	Silver	Bronze	Total
Norway	73	77	64	214
Soviet Union (1956–88)	78	57	59	194
United States	53	56	37	146
Austria	36	48	44	128
East Germany (1956–88)	43	39	36	118
Finland	36	45	42	123
Sweden	39	26	34	99
Italy	25	21	21	67
Germany (1928–36, 1992–)	23	21	17	61

INDIVIDUALS — OVERALL

Men — Athlete, Nation	Sport	G	S	B	Tot
Sixten Jernberg, Sweden	N Ski	4	3	2	9
Bjorn Dählie, Norway	N Ski	5	3	0	8
Clas Thunberg, Finland	S Skat	5	1	1	7
Ivar Ballangrud, Norway	S Skat	4	2	1	7
Veikko Hakulinen, Finland	N Ski	3	3	1	7
Eero Mäntyranta, Finland	N Ski	3	2	2	7
Bogdan Musiol, E Ger/Ger	Bob	1	5	1	7

Women — Athlete, Nation	Sport	G	S	B	Tot
Raisa Smetanina, USSR/UT	N Ski	4	5	1	10
Lyubov Egorova, UT/Russia	N Ski	6	3	0	9
Galina Kulakova, USSR	N Ski	4	2	2	8
Karin Kania, E Germany	S Skat	3	4	1	8
Marja-Liisa Kirvesniemi, Fin	N Ski	3	0	4	7
Andrea Ehrig, E Germany	S Skat	1	5	1	7

INDIVIDUALS — GOLD

Men

Bjorn Dählie, Nor	5
Clas Thunberg, Fin	5
Eric Heiden, U.S.	5
Sixten Jernberg, Swe	5
Ivar Ballangrud, Nor	4
Gunde Svan, Swe	4
Y. Grishin, USSR	4
Johann Ol. Koss, Nor	4
Matti Nykänen, Fin	4
A. Tikhonov, USSR	4
N. Zimyatov, USSR	4
T. Wassberg, Swe	4

Women

Lyubov Egorova, UT/Russia	6
L. Skoblikova, USSR	6
Bonnie Blair, U.S.	5
Raisa Smetanina, USSR/UT	4
G. Kulakova, USSR	4
Eight tied with three.	

TRACK AND FIELD
Men

100 METERS

1896	Thomas Burke, United States	12.0
1900	Frank Jarvis, United States	11.0
1904	Archie Hahn, United States	11.0
1906	Archie Hahn, United States	11.2
1908	Reginald Walker, South Africa	10.8 OR
1912	Ralph Craig, United States	10.8
1920	Charles Paddock, United States	10.8
1924	Harold Abrahams, Great Britain	10.6 OR
1928	Percy Williams, Canada	10.8
1932	Eddie Tolan, United States	10.3 OR
1936	Jesse Owens, United States	10.3
1948	Harrison Dillard, United States	10.3
1952	Lindy Remigino, United States	10.4
1956	Bobby Morrow, United States	10.5
1960	Armin Hary, West Germany	10.2 OR
1964	Bob Hayes, United States	10.0 EWR
1968	Jim Hines, United States	9.95 WR
1972	Valery Borzov, USSR	10.14
1976	Hasely Crawford, Trinidad	10.06
1980	Allan Wells, Great Britain	10.25
1984	Carl Lewis, United States	9.99
1988	Carl Lewis, United States*	9.92 WR
1992	Linford Christie, Great Britain	9.96
1996	Donovan Bailey, Canada	9.84 WR

*Ben Johnson, Canada, disqualified.

200 METERS

1900	John Walter Tewksbury, United States	22.2
1904	Archie Hahn, United States	21.6 OR
1906	Not held	
1908	Robert Kerr, Canada	22.6
1912	Ralph Craig, United States	21.7
1920	Allen Woodring, United States	22.0
1924	Jackson Scholz, United States	21.6
1928	Percy Williams, Canada	21.8
1932	Eddie Tolan, United States	21.2 OR
1936	Jesse Owens, United States	20.7 OR
1948	Mel Patton, United States	21.1
1952	Andrew Stanfield, United States	20.7
1956	Bobby Morrow, United States	20.6 OR
1960	Livio Berruti, Italy	20.5 EWR
1964	Henry Carr, United States	20.3 OR
1968	Tommie Smith, United States	19.83 WR
1972	Valery Borzov, USSR	20.00
1976	Donald Quarrie, Jamaica	20.23
1980	Pietro Mennea, Italy	20.19
1984	Carl Lewis, United States	19.80 OR
1988	Joe DeLoach, United States	19.75 OR
1992	Mike Marsh, United States	20.01
1996	Michael Johnson, United States	19.32 WR

400 METERS

1896	Thomas Burke, United States	54.2
1900	Maxey Long, United States	49.4 OR
1904	Harry Hillman, United States	49.2 OR
1906	Paul Pilgrim, United States	53.2
1908	Wyndham Halswelle, Great Britain	50.0
1912	Charles Reidpath, United States	48.2 OR
1920	Bevil Rudd, South Africa	49.6
1924	Eric Liddell, Great Britain	47.6 OR
1928	Ray Barbuti, United States	47.8
1932	William Carr, United States	46.2 WR

400 METERS *(Cont.)*

1936	Archie Williams, United States	46.5
1948	Arthur Wint, Jamaica	46.2
1952	George Rhoden, Jamaica	45.9
1956	Charles Jenkins, United States	46.7
1960	Otis Davis, United States	44.9 WR
1964	Michael Larrabee, United States	45.1
1968	Lee Evans, United States	43.86 WR
1972	Vincent Matthews, United States	44.66
1976	Alberto Juantorena, Cuba	44.26
1980	Viktor Markin, USSR	44.60
1984	Alonzo Babers, United States	44.27
1988	Steve Lewis, United States	43.87
1992	Quincy Watts, United States	43.50 OR
1996	Michael Johnson, United States	43.49 OR

800 METERS

1896	Edwin Flack, Australia	2:11
1900	Alfred Tysoe, Great Britain	2:01.2
1904	James Lightbody, United States	1:56 OR
1906	Paul Pilgrim, United States	2:01.5
1908	Mel Sheppard, United States	1:52.8 WR
1912	James Meredith, United States	1:51.9 WR
1920	Albert Hill, Great Britain	1:53.4
1924	Douglas Lowe, Great Britain	1:52.4
1928	Douglas Lowe, Great Britain	1:51.8 OR
1932	Thomas Hampson, Great Britain	1:49.8 WR
1936	John Woodruff, United States	1:52.9
1948	Mal Whitfield, United States	1:49.2 OR
1952	Mal Whitfield, United States	1:49.2 EOR
1956	Thomas Courtney, United States	1:47.7 OR
1960	Peter Snell, New Zealand	1:46.3 OR
1964	Peter Snell, New Zealand	1:45.1 OR
1968	Ralph Doubell, Australia	1:44.3 EWR
1972	Dave Wottle, United States	1:45.9
1976	Alberto Juantorena, Cuba	1:43.50 WR
1980	Steve Ovett, Great Britain	1:45.40
1984	Joaquim Cruz, Brazil	1:43.00 OR
1988	Paul Ereng, Kenya	1:43.45
1992	William Tanui, Kenya	1:43.66
1996	Vebjoern Rodal, Norway	1:42.58 OR

1500 METERS

1896	Edwin Flack, Australia	4:33.2
1900	Charles Bennett, Great Britain	4:06.2 WR
1904	James Lightbody, United States	4:05.4 WR
1906	James Lightbody, United States	4:12.0
1908	Mel Sheppard, United States	4:03.4 OR
1912	Arnold Jackson, Great Britain	3:56.8 OR
1920	Albert Hill, Great Britain	4:01.8
1924	Paavo Nurmi, Finland	3:53.6 OR
1928	Harry Larva, Finland	3:53.2 OR
1932	Luigi Beccali, Italy	3:51.2 OR
1936	Jack Lovelock, New Zealand	3:47.8 WR
1948	Henri Eriksson, Sweden	3:49.8
1952	Josef Barthel, Luxemburg	3:45.1 OR
1956	Ron Delany, Ireland	3:41.2 OR
1960	Herb Elliott, Australia	3:35.6 WR
1964	Peter Snell, New Zealand	3:38.1
1968	Kipchoge Keino, Kenya	3:34.9 OR
1972	Pekka Vasala, Finland	3:36.3
1976	John Walker, New Zealand	3:39.17
1980	Sebastian Coe, Great Britain	3:38.4
1984	Sebastian Coe, Great Britain	3:32.53 OR

Note: OR=Olympic Record; WR=World Record; EOR=Equals Olympic Record; EWR=Equals World Record; WB=World Best.

TRACK AND FIELD (Cont.)
Men (Cont.)

1500 METERS (Cont.)

1988	Peter Rono, Kenya	3:35.96
1992	Fermin Cacho, Spain	3:40.12
1996	Noureddine Morceli, Algeria	3:35.78

5000 METERS

1912	Hannes Kolehmainen, Finland	14:36.6 WR
1920	Joseph Guillemot, France	14:55.6
1924	Paavo Nurmi, Finland	14:31.2 OR
1928	Villie Ritola, Finland	14:38
1932	Lauri Lehtinen, Finland	14:30 OR
1936	Gunnar Höckert, Finland	14:22.2 OR
1948	Gaston Reiff, Belgium	14:17.6 OR
1952	Emil Zatopek, Czechoslovakia	14:06.6 OR
1956	Vladimir Kuts, USSR	13:39.6 OR
1960	Murray Halberg, New Zealand	13:43.4
1964	Bob Schul, United States	13:48.8
1968	Mohamed Gammoudi, Tunisia	14:05.0
1972	Lasse Viren, Finland	13:26.4 OR
1976	Lasse Viren, Finland	13:24.76
1980	Miruts Yifter, Ethiopia	13:21.0
1984	Said Aouita, Morocco	13:05.59 OR
1988	John Ngugi, Kenya	13:11.70
1992	Dieter Baumann, Germany	13:12.52
1996	Venuste Niyongabo, Burundi	13:07.96

10,000 METERS

1912	Hannes Kolehmainen, Finland	31:20.8
1920	Paavo Nurmi, Finland	31:45.8
1924	Vilho (Ville) Ritola, Finland	30:23.2 WR
1928	Paavo Nurmi, Finland	30:18.8 OR
1932	Janusz Kusocinski, Poland	30:11.4 OR
1936	Ilmari Salminen, Finland	30:15.4
1948	Emil Zatopek, Czechoslovakia	29:59.6 OR
1952	Emil Zatopek, Czechoslovakia	29:17.0 OR
1956	Vladimir Kuts, USSR	28:45.6 OR
1960	Pyotr Bolotnikov, USSR	28:32.2 OR
1964	Billy Mills, United States	28:24.4 OR
1968	Naftali Temu, Kenya	29:27.4
1972	Lasse Viren, Finland	27:38.4 WR
1976	Lasse Viren, Finland	27:40.38
1980	Miruts Yifter, Ethiopia	27:42.7
1984	Alberto Cova, Italy	27:47.54
1988	Brahim Boutaib, Morocco	27:21.46 OR
1992	Khalid Skah, Morocco	27:46.70
1996	Haile Gebrselassie, Ethiopia	27:07.34 OR

MARATHON

1896	Spiridon Louis, Greece	2:58:50
1900	Michel Theato, France	2:59:45
1904	Thomas Hicks, United States	3:28:53
1906	William Sherring, Canada	2:51:23.6
1908	John Hayes, United States	2:55:18.4 OR
1912	Kenneth McArthur, South Africa	2:36:54.8
1920	Hannes Kolehmainen, Finland	2:32:35.8 WB
1924	Albin Stenroos, Finland	2:41:22.6
1928	Boughera El Ouafi, France	2:32:57
1932	Juan Zabala, Argentina	2:31:36 OR
1936	Kijung Son, Japan (Korea)	2:29:19.2 OR
1948	Delfo Cabrera, Argentina	2:34:51.6
1952	Emil Zatopek, Czechoslovakia	2:23:03.2 OR
1956	Alain Mimoun O'Kacha, France	2:25:00.0
1960	Abebe Bikila, Ethiopia	2:15:16.2 WB
1964	Abebe Bikila, Ethiopia	2:12:11.2 WB
1968	Mamo Wolde, Ethiopia	2:20:26.4
1972	Frank Shorter, United States	2:12:19.8

MARATHON (Cont.)

1976	Waldemar Cierpinski, East Germany	2:09:55 OR
1980	Waldemar Cierpinski, East Germany	2:11:03.0
1984	Carlos Lopes, Portugal	2:09:21.0 OR
1988	Gelindo Bordin, Italy	2:10:32
1992	Hwang Young-Cho, S Korea	2:13:23
1996	Josia Thugwane, South Africa	2:12:36

Note: Marathon distances: 1896, 1904—40,000 meters; 1900—40,260 meters; 1906—41,860 meters; 1912—40,200 meters; 1920—42,750 meters; 1908 and since 1924—42,195 meters (26 miles, 385 yards).

110-METER HURDLES

1896	Thomas Curtis, United States	17.6
1900	Alvin Kraenzlein, United States	15.4 OR
1904	Frederick Schule, United States	16.0
1906	Robert Leavitt, United States	16.2
1908	Forrest Smithson, United States	15.0 WR
1912	Frederick Kelly, United States	15.1
1920	Earl Thomson, Canada	14.8 WR
1924	Daniel Kinsey, United States	15.0
1928	Sydney Atkinson, South Africa	14.8
1932	George Saling, United States	14.6
1936	Forrest Towns, United States	14.2
1948	William Porter, United States	13.9 OR
1952	Harrison Dillard, United States	13.7 OR
1956	Lee Calhoun, United States	13.5 OR
1960	Lee Calhoun, United States	13.8
1964	Hayes Jones, United States	13.6
1968	Willie Davenport, United States	13.3 OR
1972	Rod Milburn, United States	13.24 EWR
1976	Guy Drut, France	13.30
1980	Thomas Munkelt, East Germany	13.39
1984	Roger Kingdom, United States	13.20 OR
1988	Roger Kingdom, United States	12.98 OR
1992	Mark McKoy, Canada	13.12
1996	Allen Johnson, United States	12.95 OR

400-METER HURDLES

1900	John Walter Tewksbury, United States	57.6
1904	Harry Hillman, United States	53.0
1906	Not held	
1908	Charles Bacon, United States	55.0 WR
1912	Not held	
1920	Frank Loomis, United States	54.0 WR
1924	F. Morgan Taylor, United States	52.6
1928	David Burghley, Great Britain	53.4 OR
1932	Robert Tisdall, Ireland	51.7
1936	Glenn Hardin, United States	52.4
1948	Roy Cochran, United States	51.1 OR
1952	Charles Moore, United States	50.8 OR
1956	Glenn Davis, United States	50.1 EOR
1960	Glenn Davis, United States	49.3 EOR
1964	Rex Cawley, United States	49.6
1968	Dave Hemery, Great Britain	48.12 WR
1972	John Akii-Bua, Uganda	47.82 WR
1976	Edwin Moses, United States	47.64 WR
1980	Volker Beck, East Germany	48.70
1984	Edwin Moses, United States	47.75
1988	Andre Phillips, United States	47.19 OR
1992	Kevin Young, United States	46.78 WR
1996	Derrick Adkins, United States	47.54

TRACK AND FIELD (Cont.)

Men (Cont.)

3000-METER STEEPLECHASE

1920	Percy Hodge, Great Britain	10:00.4 OR
1924	Vilho (Ville) Ritola, Finland	9:33.6 OR
1928	Toivo Loukola, Finland	9:21.8 WR
1932	Volmari Iso-Hollo, Finland	10:33.4*
1936	Volmari Iso-Hollo, Finland	9:03.8 WR
1948	Thore Sjöstrand, Sweden	9:04.6
1952	Horace Ashenfelter, United States	8:45.4 WR
1956	Chris Brasher, Great Britain	8:41.2 OR
1960	Zdzislaw Krzyszkowiak, Poland	8:34.2 OR
1964	Gaston Roelants, Belgium	8:30.8 OR
1968	Amos Biwott, Kenya	8:51
1972	Kipchoge Keino, Kenya	8:23.6 OR
1976	Anders Gärderud, Sweden	8:08.2 WR
1980	Bronislaw Malinowski, Poland	8:09.7
1984	Julius Korir, Kenya	8:11.8
1988	Julius Kariuki, Kenya	8:05.51 OR
1992	Matthew Birir, Kenya	8:08.84
1996	Joseph Keter, Kenya	8:07.12

*About 3450 meters; extra lap by error.

4 X 100-METER RELAY

1912	Great Britain	42.4 OR
1920	United States	42.2 WR
1924	United States	41.0 EWR
1928	United States	41.0 EWR
1932	United States	40.0 WR
1936	United States	39.8 WR
1948	United States	40.6
1952	United States	40.1
1956	United States	39.5 WR
1960	West Germany	39.5 EWR
1964	United States	39.0 OR
1968	United States	38.2 WR
1972	United States	38.19 EWR
1976	United States	38.33
1980	USSR	38.26
1984	United States	37.83 WR
1988	USSR	38.19
1992	United States	37.40 WR
1996	Canada	37.69

4 X 400-METER RELAY

1908	United States	3:29.4
1912	United States	3:16.6 WR
1920	Great Britain	3:22.2
1924	United States	3:16.0 WR
1928	United States	3:14.2 WR
1932	United States	3:08.2 WR
1936	Great Britain	3:09.0
1948	United States	3:10.4 WR
1952	Jamaica	3:03.9 WR
1956	United States	3:04.8
1960	United States	3:02.2 WR
1964	United States	3:00.7 WR
1968	United States	2:56.16 WR
1972	Kenya	2:59.8
1976	United States	2:58.65
1980	USSR	3:01.1
1984	United States	2:57.91
1988	United States	2:56.16 EWR
1992	United States	2:55.74 WR
1996	United States	2:55.99

20-KILOMETER WALK

1956	Leonid Spirin, USSR	1:31:27.4
1960	Vladimir Golubnichiy, USSR	1:33:07.2
1964	Kenneth Mathews, Great Britain	1:29:34.0 OR
1968	Vladimir Golubnichiy, USSR	1:33:58.4
1972	Peter Frenkel, East Germany	1:26:42.4 OR
1976	Daniel Bautista, Mexico	1:24:40.6 OR
1980	Maurizio Damilano, Italy	1:23:35.5 OR
1984	Ernesto Canto, Mexico	1:23:13.0 OR
1988	Jozef Pribilinec, Czechoslovakia	1:19:57.0 OR
1992	Daniel Plaza, Spain	1:21:45.0
1996	Jefferson Pérez, Ecuador	1:20:07

50-KILOMETER WALK

1932	Thomas Green, Great Britain	4:50:10
1936	Harold Whitlock, Great Britain	4:30:41.4 OR
1948	John Ljunggren, Sweden	4:41:52
1952	Giuseppe Dordoni, Italy	4:28:07.8 OR
1956	Norman Read, New Zealand	4:30:42.8
1960	Donald Thompson, Great Britain	4:25:30 OR
1964	Abdon Parnich, Italy	4:11:12.4 OR
1968	Christoph Höhne, East Germany	4:20:13.6
1972	Bernd Kannenberg, West Germany	3:56:11.6 OR
1980	Hartwig Gauder, East Germany	3:49:24.0 OR
1984	Raul Gonzalez, Mexico	3:47:26.0 OR
1988	Viacheslav Ivanenko, USSR	3:38:29.0 OR
1992	Andrey Perlov, Unified Team	3:50:13
1996	Robert Korzeniowski, Poland	3:43:30

HIGH JUMP

1896	Ellery Clark, United States	5 ft 11¼ in
1900	Irving Baxter, United States	6 ft 2¾ in OR
1904	Samuel Jones, United States	5 ft 11 in
1906	Cornelius Leahy, Great Britain/Ireland	5 ft 10 in
1908	Harry Porter, United States	6 ft 3 in OR
1912	Alma Richards, United States	6 ft 4 in OR
1920	Richmond Landon, United States	6 ft 4 in OR
1924	Harold Osborn, United States	6 ft 6 in OR
1928	Robert W. King, United States	6 ft 4½ in
1932	Duncan McNaughton, Canada	6 ft 5½ in
1936	Cornelius Johnson, United States	6 ft 8 in OR
1948	John L. Winter, Australia	6 ft 6 in
1952	Walter Davis, United States	6 ft 8½ in OR
1956	Charles Dumas, United States	6 ft 11½ in OR
1960	Robert Shavlakadze, USSR	7 ft 1 in OR
1964	Valery Brumel, USSR	7 ft 1¾ in OR
1968	Dick Fosbury, United States	7 ft 4¼ in OR
1972	Yuri Tarmak, USSR	7 ft 3¾ in
1976	Jacek Wszola, Poland	7 ft 4½ in OR
1980	Gerd Wessig, East Germany	7 ft 8¾ in WR
1984	Dietmar Mögenburg, West Germany	7 ft 8½ in
1988	Gennadiy Avdeyenko, USSR	7 ft 9¾ in OR
1992	Javier Sotomayor, Cuba	7 ft 8 in.
1996	Charles Austin, United States	7 ft 10 in OR

POLE VAULT

1896	William Hoyt, United States	10 ft 10 in
1900	Irving Baxter, United States	10 ft 10 in
1904	Charles Dvorak, United States	11 ft 5¾ in
1906	Fernand Gonder, France	11 ft 5¾ in

Note: OR=Olympic Record; WR=World Record; EOR=Equals Olympic Record; EWR=Equals World Record; WB=World Best.

TRACK AND FIELD *(Cont.)*
Men *(Cont.)*

POLE VAULT *(Cont.)*

1908	Alfred Gilbert, United States	12 ft 2 in OR
	Edward Cooke Jr, United States	
1912	Harry Babcock, United States	12 ft 11½ in OR
1920	Frank Foss, United States	13 ft 5 in WR
1924	Lee Barnes, United States	12 ft 11½ in
1928	Sabin Carr, United States	13 ft 9¼ in OR
1932	William Miller, United States	14 ft 1¾ in OR
1936	Earle Meadows, United States	14 ft 3¼ in OR
1948	Guinn Smith, United States	14 ft 1¼ in
1952	Robert Richards, United States	14 ft 11 in OR
1956	Robert Richards, United States	14 ft 11½ in OR
1960	Don Bragg, United States	15 ft 5 in OR
1964	Fred Hansen, United States	16 ft 8¾ in OR
1968	Bob Seagren, United States	17 ft 8½ in OR
1972	Wolfgang Nordwig, East Germany	18 ft ½ in OR
1976	Tadeusz Slusarski, Poland	18 ft ½ in EOR
1980	Wladyslaw Kozakiewicz, Poland	18 ft 11½ in WR
1984	Pierre Quinon, France	18 ft 10¼ in
1988	Sergei Bubka, USSR	19 ft 4¼ in OR
1992	Maksim Tarasov, Unified Team	19 ft ¼ in
1996	Jean Galfione, France	19 ft 5 ¼ in OR

LONG JUMP

1896	Ellery Clark, United States	20 ft 10 in
1900	Alvin Kraenzlein, United States	23 ft 6¾ in OR
1904	Meyer Prinstein, United States	24 ft 1 in OR
1906	Meyer Prinstein, United States	23 ft 7½ in
1908	Frank Irons, United States	24 ft 6½ in OR
1912	Albert Gutterson, United States	24 ft 11¼ in OR
1920	William Peterssen, Sweden	23 ft 5½ in
1924	DeHart Hubbard, United States	24 ft 5 in
1928	Edward B. Hamm, United States	25 ft 4½ in OR
1932	Edward Gordon, United States	25 ft ¾ in
1936	Jesse Owens, United States	26 ft 5½ in OR
1948	William Steele, United States	25 ft 8 in
1952	Jerome Biffle, United States	24 ft 10 in
1956	Gregory Bell, United States	25 ft 8¼ in
1960	Ralph Boston, United States	26 ft 7¾ in OR
1964	Lynn Davies, Great Britain	26 ft 5¾ in
1968	Bob Beamon, United States	29 ft 2½ in WR
1972	Randy Williams, United States	27 ft ½ in
1976	Arnie Robinson, United States	27 ft 4¾ in
1980	Lutz Dombrowski, East Germany	28 ft ¼ in
1984	Carl Lewis, United States	28 ft ¼ in
1988	Carl Lewis, United States	28 ft 7½ in
1992	Carl Lewis, United States	28 ft 5 ½ in
1996	Carl Lewis, United States	27 ft 10¾ in

TRIPLE JUMP

1896	James Connolly, United States	44 ft 11¾ in
1900	Meyer Prinstein, United States	47 ft 5¾ in OR
1904	Meyer Prinstein, United States	47 ft 1 in
1906	Peter O'Connor, Great Britain/Ireland	46 ft 2¼ in
1908	Timothy Ahearne, Great Britain/Ireland	48 ft 11¼ in OR
1912	Gustaf Lindblom, Sweden	48 ft 5¼ in
1920	Vilho Tuulos, Finland	47 ft 7 in
1924	Anthony Winter, Australia	50 ft 11¼ in WR
1928	Mikio Oda, Japan	49 ft 11 in
1932	Chuhei Nambu, Japan	51 ft 7 in WR

TRIPLE JUMP *(Cont.)*

1936	Naoto Tajima, Japan	52 ft 6 in WR
1948	Arne Ahman, Sweden	50 ft 6¼ in
1952	Adhemar da Silva, Brazil	53 ft 2¾ in WR
1956	Adhemar da Silva, Brazil	53 ft 7¾ in OR
1960	Jozef Schmidt, Poland	55 ft 2 in
1964	Jozef Schmidt, Poland	55 ft 3½ in OR
1968	Viktor Saneyev, USSR	57 ft ¾ in WR
1972	Viktor Saneyev, USSR	56 ft 11¾ in
1976	Viktor Saneyev, USSR	56 ft 8¾ in
1980	Jaak Uudmae, USSR	56 ft 11¼ in
1984	Al Joyner, United States	56 ft 7½ in
1988	Khristo Markov, Bulgaria	57 ft 9½ in OR
1992	Mike Conley, United States	59 ft 7½ in
1996	Kenny Harrison, United States	59 ft 4¼ in OR

SHOT PUT

1896	Robert Garrett, United States	36 ft 9¾ in
1900	Richard Sheldon, United States	46 ft 3¼ in OR
1904	Ralph Rose, United States	48 ft 7 in WR
1906	Martin Sheridan, United States	40 ft 5¼ in
1908	Ralph Rose, United States	46 ft 7½ in
1912	Pat McDonald, United States	50 ft 4 in OR
1920	Ville Porhola, Finland	48 ft 7¼ in
1924	Clarence Houser, United States	49 ft 2¼ in
1928	John Kuck, United States	52 ft ¾ in WR
1932	Leo Sexton, United States	52 ft 6 in OR
1936	Hans Woellke, Germany	53 ft 1¾ in OR
1948	Wilbur Thompson, United States	56 ft 2 in OR
1952	Parry O'Brien, United States	57 ft ½ in OR
1956	Parry O'Brien, United States	60 ft 11¼ in OR
1960	William Nieder, United States	64 ft 6¾ in OR
1964	Dallas Long, United States	66 ft 8½ in OR
1968	Randy Matson, United States	67 ft 4¾ in
1972	Wladyslaw Komar, Poland	69 ft 6 in OR
1976	Udo Beyer, East Germany	69 ft ¾ in
1980	Vladimir Kiselyov, USSR	70 ft ½ in OR
1984	Alessandro Andrei, Italy	69 ft 9 in
1988	Ulf Timmermann, East Germany	73 ft 8¾ in OR
1992	Mike Stulce, United States	71 ft 2½ in
1996	Randy Barnes, United States	70 ft 11 in

DISCUS THROW

1896	Robert Garrett, United States	95 ft 7½ in
1900	Rudolf Bauer, Hungary	118 ft 3 in OR
1904	Martin Sheridan, United States	128 ft 10½ in OR
1906	Martin Sheridan, United States	136 ft
1908	Martin Sheridan, United States	134 ft 2 in OR
1912	Armas Taipele, Finland	148 ft 3 in OR
1920	Elmer Niklander, Finland	146 ft 7 in
1924	Clarence Houser, United States	151 ft 4 in OR
1928	Clarence Houser, United States	155 ft 3 in OR
1932	John Anderson, United States	162 ft 4 in OR
1936	Ken Carpenter, United States	165 ft 7 in OR
1948	Adolfo Consolini, Italy	173 ft 2 in OR
1952	Sim Iness, United States	180 ft 6 in OR
1956	Al Oerter, United States	184 ft 11 in OR
1960	Al Oerter, United States	194 ft 2 in OR
1964	Al Oerter, United States	200 ft 1 in OR
1968	Al Oerter, United States	212 ft 6 in OR
1972	Ludvik Danek, Czechoslovakia	211 ft 3 in
1976	Mac Wilkins, United States	221 ft 5 in OR
1980	Viktor Rashchupkin, USSR	218 ft 8 in

TRACK AND FIELD *(Cont.)*
Men *(Cont.)*

DISCUS THROW *(Cont.)*

1984...Rolf Dannenberg, West Germany	218 ft 6 in
1988...Jürgen Schult, East Germany	225 ft 9 in OR
1992...Romas Ubartas, Lithuania	213 ft 8 in
1996...Lars Riedel, Germany	227 ft 8 in OR

HAMMER THROW

1900...John Flanagan, United States	163 ft 1 in
1904...John Flanagan, United States	168 ft 1 in OR
1906...Not held	
1908...John Flanagan, United States	170 ft 4 in OR
1912...Matt McGrath, United States	179 ft 7 in OR
1920...Pat Ryan, United States	173 ft 5 in
1924...Fred Tootell, United States	174 ft 10 in
1928...Patrick O'Callaghan, Ireland	168 ft 7 in
1932...Patrick O'Callaghan, Ireland	176 ft 11 in
1936...Karl Hein, Germany	185 ft 4 in OR
1948...Imre Nemeth, Hungary	183 ft 11 in
1952...Jozsef Csermak, Hungary	197 ft 11 in WR
1956...Harold Connolly, United States	207 ft 3 in OR
1960...Vasily Rudenkov, USSR	220 ft 2 in OR
1964...Romuald Klim, USSR	228 ft 10 in OR
1968...Gyula Zsivotsky, Hungary	240 ft 8 in OR
1972...Anatoli Bondarchuk, USSR	247 ft 8 in OR
1976...Yuri Sedykh, USSR	254 ft 4 in OR
1980...Yuri Sedykh, USSR	268 ft 4 in WR
1984...Juha Tiainen, Finland	256 ft 2 in
1988...Sergei Litvinov, USSR	278 ft 2 in OR
1992...Andrey Abduvaliyev, Unified Team	270 ft 9 in
1996...Balazs Kiss, Hungary	266 ft 6 in

JAVELIN

1908...Erik Lemming, Sweden	179 ft 10 in
1912...Erik Lemming, Sweden	198 ft 11 in WR
1920...Jonni Myyrä, Finland	215 ft 10 in OR
1924...Jonni Myyrä, Finland	206 ft 6 in
1928...Eric Lundkvist, Sweden	218 ft 6 in OR
1932...Matti Jarvinen, Finland	238 ft 6 in OR
1936...Gerhard Stöck, Germany	235 ft 8 in
1948...Kai Hautavaara, Finland	228 ft 10½ in

JAVELIN *(Cont.)*

1952...Cy Young, United States	242 ft 1 in OR
1956...Egil Danielson, Norway	281 ft 2¼ in WR
1960...Viktor Tsibulenko, USSR	277 ft 8 in
1964...Pauli Nevala, Finland	271 ft 2 in
1968...Janis Lusis, USSR	295 ft 7 in OR
1972...Klaus Wolfermann, West Germany	296 ft 10 in OR
1976...Miklos Nemeth, Hungary	310 ft 4 in WR
1980...Dainis Kuta, USSR	299 ft 2⅜ in
1984...Arto Härkönen, Finland	284 ft 8 in
1988...Tapio Korjus, Finland	276 ft 6 in
1992...Jan Zelezny, Czechoslovakia	294 ft 2 in OR
1996...Jan Zelezny, Czech Rep	289 ft 3 in

DECATHLON

	Pts
1904 ...Thomas Kiely, Ireland	6036
1912...Jim Thorpe, United States*	8412 WR
1920...Helge Lövland, Norway	6803
1924...Harold Osborn, United States	7711 WR
1928...Paavo Yrjölä, Finland	8053.29 WR
1932...James Bausch, United States	8462 WR
1936...Glenn Morris, United States	7900 WR
1948...Robert Mathias, United States	7139
1952...Robert Mathias, United States	7887 WR
1956...Milton Campbell, United States	7937 OR
1960...Rafer Johnson, United States	8392 OR
1964...Willi Holdorf, West Germany	7887
1968...Bill Toomey, United States	8193 OR
1972...Nikolai Avilov, USSR	8454 WR
1976...Bruce Jenner, United States	8617 WR
1980...Daley Thompson, Great Britain	8495
1984...Daley Thompson, Great Britain	8798 EWR
1988...Christian Schenk, East Germany	8488
1992...Robert Zmelik, Czechoslovakia	8611
1996...Dan O'Brien, United States	8824 OR

*In 1913, Thorpe was disqualified for having played professional baseball in 1910. His record was restored in 1982.

Women

100 METERS

1928 ....Elizabeth Robinson, United States	12.2 EWR
1932 ....Stella Walsh, Poland	11.9 EWR
1936 ....Helen Stephens, United States	11.5
1948 ....Francina Blankers-Koen, Netherlands	11.9
1952 ....Marjorie Jackson, Australia	11.5 EWR
1956 ....Betty Cuthbert, Australia	11.5 EWR
1960 ....Wilma Rudolph, United States	11.0
1964 ....Wyomia Tyus, United States	11.4
1968 ....Wyomia Tyus, United States	11.0 WR
1972 ....Renate Stecher, East Germany	11.07
1976 ....Annegret Richter, West Germany	11.08
1980 ....Lyudmila Kondratyeva, USSR	11.06
1984 ....Evelyn Ashford, United States	10.97 OR
1988 ....Florence Griffith Joyner, United States	10.54
1992 ....Gail Devers, United States	10.82
1996 ....Gail Devers, United States	10.94

200 METERS

1948 ....Francina Blankers-Koen, Netherlands	24.4
1952 ....Marjorie Jackson, Australia	23.7
1956 ....Betty Cuthbert, Australia	23.4 EOR
1960 ....Wilma Rudolph, United States	24.0
1964 ....Edith McGuire, United States	23.0 OR
1968 ....Irena Szewinska, Poland	22.5 WR
1972 ....Renate Stecher, East Germany	22.40 EWR
1976 ....Bärbel Eckert, East Germany	22.37 OR
1980 ....Bärbel Wöckel (Eckert), East Germany	22.03 OR
1984 ....Valerie Brisco-Hooks, United States	21.81 OR
1988 ....Florence Griffith Joyner, United States	21.34 WR
1992 ....Gwen Torrence, United States	21.81
1996 ....Marie-José Pérec, France	22.12

Note: OR=Olympic Record; WR=World Record; EOR=Equals Olympic Record; EWR=Equals World Record; WB=World Best.

TRACK AND FIELD *(Cont.)*
Women *(Cont.)*

400 METERS

1964	Betty Cuthbert, Australia	52.0 OR
1968	Colette Besson, France	52.0 EOR
1972	Monika Zehrt, East Germany	51.08 OR
1976	Irena Szewinska, Poland	49.29 WR
1980	Marita Koch, East Germany	48.88 OR
1984	Valerie Brisco-Hooks, United States	48.83 OR
1988	Olga Bryzgina, USSR	48.65 OR
1992	Marie-José Pérec, France	48.83
1996	Marie-José Pérec, France	48.25 OR

800 METERS

1928	Lina Radke, Germany	2:16.8 WR
1932	Not held 1932–1956	
1960	Lyudmila Shevtsova, USSR	2:04.3 EWR
1964	Ann Packer, Great Britain	2:01.1 OR
1968	Madeline Manning, United States	2:00.9 OR
1972	Hildegard Falck, West Germany	1:58.55 OR
1976	Tatyana Kazankina, USSR	1:54.94 WR
1980	Nadezhda Olizarenko, USSR	1:53.42 WR
1984	Doina Melinte, Romania	1:57.6
1988	Sigrun Wodars, East Germany	1:56.10
1992	Ellen Van Langen, Netherlands	1:55.54
1996	Svetlana Masterkova, Russia	1:57.73

1500 METERS

1972	Lyudmila Bragina, USSR	4:01.4 WR
1976	Tatyana Kazankina, USSR	4:05.48
1980	Tatyana Kazankina, USSR	3:56.6 OR
1984	Gabriella Dorio, Italy	4:03.25
1988	Paula Ivan, Romania	3:53.96 OR
1992	Hassiba Boulmerka, Algeria	3:55.30
1996	Svetlana Masterkova, Russa	4:00.83

3000 METERS

1984	Maricica Puica, Romania	8:35.96 OR
1988	Tatyana Samolenko, USSR	8:26.53 OR
1992	Elena Romanova, Unified Team	8:46.04

5000 METERS

1996	Wang Junxia, China	14:57.88

10,000 METERS

1988	Olga Bondarenko, USSR	31:05.21 OR
1992	Derartu Tulu, Ethiopia	31:06.02
1996	Fernanda Ribeiro, Portugal	31:01.63 OR

MARATHON

1984	Joan Benoit, United States	2:24:52 OR
1988	Rosa Mota, Portugal	2:25:40
1992	Valentin Yegorova, Unified Team	2:32:41
1996	Fatuma Roba, Ethiopia	2:26:05

80-METER HURDLES

1932	Babe Didrikson, United States	11.7 WR
1936	Trebisonda Valla, Italy	11.7
1948	Francina Blankers-Koen, Netherlands	11.2 OR
1952	Shirley Strickland, Australia	10.9 WR
1956	Shirley Strickland, Australia	10.7 OR
1960	Irina Press, USSR	10.8
1964	Karin Balzer, East Germany	10.5
1968	Maureen Caird, Australia	10.3 OR

100-METER HURDLES

1972	Annelie Ehrhardt, East Germany	12.59 WR
1976	Johanna Schaller, East Germany	12.77
1980	Vera Komisova, USSR	12.56 OR
1984	Benita Fitzgerald-Brown, United States	12.84
1988	Yordanka Donkova, Bulgaria	12.38 OR
1992	Paraskevi Patoulidou, Greece	12.64
1996	Lyudmila Engqvist, Sweden	12.58

400-METER HURDLES

1984	Nawal el Moutawakel, Morocco	54.61 OR
1988	Debra Flintoff-King, Australia	53.17 OR
1992	Sally Gunnell, Great Britain	53.23
1996	Deon Hemmings, Jamaica	52.82 OR

4 X 100-METER RELAY

1928	Canada	48.4 WR
1932	United States	46.9 WR
1936	United States	46.9
1948	Netherlands	47.5
1952	United States	45.9 WR
1956	Australia	44.5 WR
1960	United States	44.5
1964	Poland	43.6
1968	United States	42.8 WR
1972	West Germany	42.81 EWR
1976	East Germany	42.55 OR
1980	East Germany	41.60 WR
1984	United States	41.65
1988	United States	41.98
1992	United States	42.11
1996	United States	41.95

4 X 400-METER RELAY

1972	East Germany	3:23 WR
1976	East Germany	3:19.23 WR
1980	USSR	3:20.02
1984	United States	3:18.29 OR
1988	USSR	3:15.18 WR
1992	Unified Team	3:20.20
1996	United States	3:20.91

10-KILOMETER WALK

1992	Chen Yueling, China	44:32
1996	Elena Nikolayeva, Russia	41:49 OR

HIGH JUMP

1928	Ethel Catherwood, Canada	5 ft 2½ in
1932	Jean Shiley, United States	5 ft 5¼ in WR
1936	Ibolya Csak, Hungary	5 ft 3 in
1948	Alice Coachman, United States	5 ft 6 in OR
1952	Esther Brand, South Africa	5 ft 5¾ in
1956	Mildred L. McDaniel, United States	5 ft 9¼ in WR
1960	Iolanda Balas, Romania	6 ft ¾ in OR
1964	Iolanda Balas, Romania	6 ft 2¾ in OR
1968	Miloslava Reskova, Czechoslovakia	5 ft 11½ in
1972	Ulrike Meyfarth, West Germany	6 ft 3½ in EWR
1976	Rosemarie Ackermann, East Germany	6 ft 4 in OR

TRACK AND FIELD (Cont.)
Women (Cont.)

HIGH JUMP (Cont.)

1980	Sara Simeoni, Italy	6 ft 5½ in OR
1984	Ulrike Meyfarth, West Germany	6 ft 7½ in OR
1988	Louise Ritter, United States	6 ft 8 in OR
1992	Heike Henkel, Germany	6 ft 7½
1996	Stefka Kostadinova, Bulgaria	6 ft 8¾ in OR

LONG JUMP

1948	Olga Gyarmati, Hungary	18 ft 8¼ in
1952	Yvette Williams, New Zealand	20 ft 5¾ in OR
1956	Elzbieta Krzeskinska, Poland	20 ft 10 in EWR
1960	Vyera Krepkina, USSR	20 ft 10¾ in OR
1964	Mary Rand, Great Britain	22 ft 2¼ in WR
1968	Viorica Viscopoleanu, Romania	22 ft 4½ in WR
1972	Heidemarie Rosendahl, West Germany	22 ft 3 in
1976	Angela Voigt, East Germany	22 ft ¾ in
1980	Tatyana Kolpakova, USSR	23 ft 2 in OR
1984	Anisoara Stanciu, Romania	22 ft 10 in
1988	Jackie Joyner-Kersee, United States	24 ft 3½ in OR
1992	Heike Drechsler, Germany	23 ft 5¼ in
1996	Chioma Ajunwa, Nigeria	23 ft 4½ in

TRIPLE JUMP

1996	Inessa Kravets, Ukraine	50 ft 3½ in

SHOT PUT

1948	Micheline Ostermeyer, France	45 ft 1½ in
1952	Galina Zybina, USSR	50 ft 1¾ in WR
1956	Tamara Tyshkevich, USSR	54 ft 5 in OR
1960	Tamara Press, USSR	56 ft 10 in OR
1964	Tamara Press, USSR	59 ft 6¼ in OR
1968	Margitta Gummel, East Germany	64 ft 4 in WR
1972	Nadezhda Chizhova, USSR	69 ft WR
1976	Ivanka Hristova, Bulgaria	69 ft 5¼ in OR
1980	Ilona Slupianek, E Germany	73 ft 6¼ in
1984	Claudia Losch, West Germany	67 ft 2¼ in
1988	Natalya Lisovskaya, USSR	72 ft 11¾ in
1992	Svetlana Kriveleva, Unified Team	69 ft 1¼ in
1996	Astrid Kumbernuss, Germany	67 ft 5½ in

DISCUS THROW

1928	Helena Konopacka, Poland	129 ft 11¾ in WR
1932	Lillian Copeland, United States	133 ft 2 in OR
1936	Gisela Mauermayer, Germany	156 ft 3 in OR
1948	Micheline Ostermeyer, France	137 ft 6 in
1952	Nina Romaschkova, USSR	168 ft 8 in OR

DISCUS THROW (Cont.)

1956	Olga Fikotova, Czechoslovakia	176 ft 1 in OR
1960	Nina Ponomaryeva, USSR	180 ft 9 in OR
1964	Tamara Press, USSR	187 ft 10 in OR
1968	Lia Manoliu, Romania	191 ft 2 in OR
1972	Faina Melnik, USSR	218 ft 7 in OR
1976	Evelin Schlaak, East Germany	226 ft 4 in OR
1980	Evelin Jahl (Schlaak), East Germany	229 ft 6 in OR
1984	Ria Stalman, Netherlands	214 ft 5 in
1988	Martina Hellmann, East Germany	237 ft 2 in OR
1992	Maritza Martén, Cuba	229 ft 10 in
1996	Ilke Wyludda, Germany	228 ft 6 in

JAVELIN THROW

1932	Babe Didrikson, United States	143 ft 4 in OR
1936	Tilly Fleischer, Germany	148 ft 3 in OR
1948	Herma Bauma, Austria	149 ft 6 in
1952	Dana Zatopkova, Czechoslovakia	165 ft 7 in
1956	Inese Jaunzeme, USSR	176 ft 8 in
1960	Elvira Ozolina, USSR	183 ft 8 in OR
1964	Mihaela Penes, Romania	198 ft 7 in
1968	Angela Nemeth, Hungary	198 ft
1972	Ruth Fuchs, East Germany	209 ft 7 in OR
1976	Ruth Fuchs, East Germany	216 ft 4 in OR
1980	Maria Colon, Cuba	224 ft 5 in OR
1984	Tessa Sanderson, Great Britain	228 ft 2 in OR
1988	Petra Felke, East Germany	245 ft OR
1992	Silke Renk, Germany	224 ft 2 in
1996	Heli Rantanen, Finland	222 ft 11 in

PENTATHLON

		Pts
1964	Irina Press, USSR	5246 WR
1968	Ingrid Becker, West Germany	5098
1972	Mary Peters, Great Britain	4801 WR*
1976	Siegrun Siegl, East Germany	4745
1980	Nadezhda Tkachenko, USSR	5083 WR

HEPTATHLON

		Pts
1984	Glynis Nunn, Australia	6390 OR
1988	Jackie Joyner-Kersee, United States	7291 WR
1992	Jackie Joyner-Kersee, United States	7044
1996	Ghada Shouaa, Syria	6780

Note: OR=Olympic Record; WR=World Record; EOR=Equals Olympic Record; EWR=Equals World Record; WB=World Best.

BASKETBALL

Men

1936
Final: United States 19, Canada 8
United States: Ralph Bishop, Joe Fortenberry, Carl Knowles, Jack Ragland, Carl Shy, William Wheatley, Francis Johnson, Samuel Balter, John Gibbons, Frank Lubin, Arthur Mollner, Donald Piper, Duane Swanson, Willard Schmidt

1948
Final: United States 65, France 21
United States: Cliff Barker, Don Barksdale, Ralph Beard, Lewis Beck, Vince Boryla, Gordon Carpenter, Alex Groza, Wallace Jones, Bob Kurland, Ray Lumpp, Robert Pitts, Jesse Renick, Bob Robinson, Ken Rollins

1952
Final: United States 36, USSR 25
United States: Charles Hoag, Bill Hougland, Melvin Dean Kelley, Bob Kenney, Clyde Lovellette, Marcus Freiberger, Victor Wayne Glasgow, Frank McCabe, Daniel Pippen, Howard Williams, Ronald Bontemps, Bob Kurland, William Lienhard, John Keller

1956
Final: United States 89, USSR 55
United States: Carl Cain, Bill Hougland, K. C. Jones, Bill Russell, James Walsh, William Evans, Burdette Haldorson, Ron Tomsic, Dick Boushka, Gilbert Ford, Bob Jeangerard, Charles Darling

1960
Final: United States 90, Brazil 63
United States: Jay Arnette, Walt Bellamy, Bob Boozer, Terry Dischinger, Jerry Lucas, Oscar Robertson, Adrian Smith, Burdette Haldorson, Darrall Imhoff, Allen Kelley, Lester Lane, Jerry West

1964
Final: United States 73, USSR 59
United States: Jim Barnes, Bill Bradley, Larry Brown, Joe Caldwell, Mel Counts, Richard Davies, Walt Hazzard, Lucius Jackson, John McCaffrey, Jeff Mullins, Jerry Shipp, George Wilson

1968
Final: United States 65, Yugoslavia 50
United States: John Clawson, Ken Spain, Jo-Jo White, Michael Barrett, Spencer Haywood, Charles Scott, William Hosket, Calvin Fowler, Michael Silliman, Glynn Saulters, James King, Donald Dee

1972
Final: USSR 51, United States 50
United States: Kenneth Davis, Doug Collins, Thomas Henderson, Mike Bantom, Bobby Jones, Dwight Jones, James Forbes, James Brewer, Tom Burleson, Tom McMillen, Kevin Joyce, Ed Ratleff

1976
Final: United States 95, Yugoslavia 74
United States: Phil Ford, Steve Sheppard, Adrian Dantley, Walter Davis, Quinn Buckner, Ernie Grunfield, Kenny Carr, Scott May, Michel Armstrong, Tom La Garde, Phil Hubbard, Mitch Kupchak

Men

1980
Final: Yugoslavia 86, Italy 77
U.S. participated in boycott.

1984
Final: United States 96, Spain 65
United States: Steve Alford, Leon Wood, Patrick Ewing, Vern Fleming, Alvin Robertson, Michael Jordan, Joe Kleine, Jon Koncak, Wayman Tisdale, Chris Mullin, Sam Perkins, Jeff Turner

1988
Final: USSR 76, Yugoslavia 63
United States (3rd): Mitch Richmond, Charles E. Smith, IV, Vernell Coles, Hersey Hawkins, Jeff Grayer, Charles D. Smith, Willie Anderson, Stacey Augmon, Dan Majerle, Danny Manning, J. R. Reid, David Robinson

1992
Final: United States 117, Croatia 85
United States: David Robinson, Christian Laettner, Patrick Ewing, Larry Bird, Scottie Pippen, Michael Jordan, Clyde Drexler, Karl Malone, John Stockton, Chris Mullin, Charles Barkley, Earvin Johnson

1996
Final: United States 95, Yugoslavia 69
United States: Charles Barkley, Anfernee Hardaway, Grant Hill, Karl Malone, Reggie Miller, Hakeem Olajuwon, Shaquille O'Neal, Scottie Pippen, Mitch Richmond, John Stockton, David Robinson, Gary Payton

Women

1976
Gold, USSR; Silver, United States*
United States: Cindy Brogdon, Susan Rojcewicz, Ann Meyers, Lusia Harris, Nancy Dunkle, Charlotte Lewis, Nancy Lieberman, Gail Marquis, Patricia Roberts, Mary Anne O'Connor, Patricia Head, Julienne Simpson

*In 1976 the women played a round-robin tournament, with the gold medal going to the team with the best record. The USSR won with a 5-0 record, and the USA, with a 3-2 record, was given the silver by virtue of a 95-79 victory over Bulgaria, which was also 3-2.

1980
Final: USSR 104, Bulgaria 73
U.S. participated in boycott.

1984
Final: United States 85, Korea 55
United States: Teresa Edwards, Lea Henry, Lynette Woodard, Anne Donovan, Cathy Boswell, Cheryl Miller, Janice Lawrence, Cindy Noble, Kim Mulkey, Denise Curry, Pamela McGee, Carol Menken-Schaudt

1988
Final: United States 77, Yugoslavia 70
United States: Teresa Edwards, Mary Ethridge, Cynthia Brown, Anne Donovan, Teresa Weatherspoon, Bridgette Gordon, Victoria Bullett, Andrea Lloyd, Katrina McClain, Jennifer Gillom, Cynthia Cooper, Suzanne McConnell

BASKETBALL *(Cont.)*
Women *(Cont.)*

1992
Final: Unified Team 76, China 66
United States (3rd): Teresa Edwards, Teresa Weatherspoon, Victoria Bullett, Katrina McClain, Cynthia Cooper, Suzanne McConnell, Daedra Charles, Clarissa Davis, Tammy Jackson, Vickie Orr, Carolyn Jones, Medina Dixon

1996
Final: United States 111, Brazil 87
United States: Jennifer Azzi, Ruthie Bolton, Teresa Edwards, Lisa Leslie, Rebecca Lobo, Katrina McClain, Nikki McCray, Carla McGhee, Dawn Staley, Katy Steding, Sheryl Swoopes, Venus Lacey

BOXING

LIGHT FLYWEIGHT (106 LB)
1968	Francisco Rodriguez, Venezuela
1972	Gyorgy Gedo, Hungary
1976	Jorge Hernandez, Cuba
1980	Shamil Sabyrov, USSR
1984	Paul Gonzalez, United States
1988	Ivailo Hristov, Bulgaria
1992	Rogelio Marcelo, Cuba
1996	Daniel Petrov, Bulgaria

FLYWEIGHT (112 LB)
1904	George Finnegan, United States
1906-1912	Not held
1920	Frank Di Gennara, United States
1924	Fidel LaBarba, United States
1928	Antal Kocsis, Hungary
1932	Istvan Enekes, Hungary
1936	Willi Kaiser, Germany
1948	Pascual Perez, Argentina
1952	Nathan Brooks, United States
1956	Terence Spinks, Great Britain
1960	Gyula Torok, Hungary
1964	Fernando Atzori, Italy
1968	Ricardo Delgado, Mexico
1972	Georgi Kostadinov, Bulgaria
1976	Leo Randolph, United States
1980	Peter Lessov, Bulgaria
1984	Steve McCrory, United States
1988	Kim Kwang Sun, South Korea
1992	Su Choi Chol, North Korea
1996	Maikro Romero, Cuba

BANTAMWEIGHT (119 LB)
1904	Oliver Kirk, United States
1906	Not held
1908	A. Henry Thomas, Great Britain
1912	Not held
1920	Clarence Walker, South Africa
1924	William Smith, South Africa
1928	Vittorio Tamagnini, Italy
1932	Horace Gwynne, Canada
1936	Ulderico Sergo, Italy
1948	Tibor Csik, Hungary
1952	Pentti Hamalainen, Finland
1956	Wolfgang Behrendt, East Germany
1960	Oleg Grigoryev, USSR
1964	Takao Sakurai, Japan
1968	Valery Sokolov, USSR
1972	Orlando Martinez, Cuba
1976	Yong Jo Gu, North Korea
1980	Juan Hernandez, Cuba
1984	Maurizio Stecca, Italy
1988	Kennedy McKinney, United States
1992	Joel Casamayor, Cuba
1996	István Kovács, Hungary

FEATHERWEIGHT (125 LB)
1904	Oliver Kirk, United States
1906	Not held
1908	Richard Gunn, Great Britain
1912	Not held
1920	Paul Fritsch, France
1924	John Fields, United States
1928	Lambertus van Klaveren, Netherlands
1932	Carmelo Robledo, Argentina
1936	Oscar Casanovas, Argentina
1948	Ernesto Formenti, Italy
1952	Jan Zachara, Czechoslovakia
1956	Vladimir Safronov, USSR
1960	Francesco Musso, Italy
1964	Stanislav Stephashkin, USSR
1968	Antonio Roldan, Mexico
1972	Boris Kousnetsov, USSR
1976	Angel Herrera, Cuba
1980	Rudi Fink, East Germany
1984	Meldrick Taylor, United States
1988	Giovanni Parisi, Italy
1992	Andreas Tews, Germany
1996	Somluck Kamsing, Thailand

LIGHTWEIGHT (132 LB)
1904	Harry Spanger, United States
1906	Not held
1908	Frederick Grace, Great Britain
1912	Not held
1920	Samuel Mosberg, United States
1924	Hans Nielsen, Denmark
1928	Carlo Orlandi, Italy
1932	Lawrence Stevens, South Africa
1936	Imre Harangi, Hungary
1948	Gerald Dreyer, South Africa
1952	Aureliano Bolognesi, Italy
1956	Richard McTaggart, Great Britain
1960	Kazimierz Pazdzior, Poland
1964	Jozef Grudzien, Poland
1968	Ronald Harris, United States
1972	Jan Szczepanski, Poland
1976	Howard Davis, United States
1980	Angel Herrera, Cuba
1984	Pernell Whitaker, United States
1988	Andreas Zuelow, East Germany
1992	Oscar De La Hoya, United States
1996	Hocine Soltani, Algeria

LIGHT WELTERWEIGHT (139 LB)
1952	Charles Adkins, United States
1956	Vladimir Yengibaryan, USSR
1960	Bohumil Nemecek, Czechoslovakia
1964	Jerzy Kulej, Poland
1968	Jerzy Kulej, Poland
1972	Ray Seales, United States
1976	Ray Leonard, United States

BOXING *(Cont.)*

LIGHT WELTERWEIGHT *(Cont.)*

1980 ....Patrizio Oliva, Italy
1984 ....Jerry Page, United States
1988 ....Viatcheslav Janovski, USSR
1992 ....Hector Vinent, Cuba
1996 ....Hector Vinent, Cuba

WELTERWEIGHT (147 LB)

1904 ....Albert Young, United States
1906-1912 ......Not held
1920 ....Albert Schneider, Canada
1924 ....Jean Delarge, Belgium
1928 ....Edward Morgan, New Zealand
1932 ....Edward Flynn, United States
1936 ....Sten Suvio, Finland
1948 ....Julius Torma, Czechoslovakia
1952 ....Zygmunt Chychla, Poland
1956 ....Nicolae Linca, Romania
1960 ....Giovanni Benvenuti, Italy
1964 ....Marian Kasprzyk, Poland
1968 ....Manfred Wolke, East Germany
1972 ....Emilio Correa, Cuba
1976 ....Jochen Bachfeld, East Germany
1980 ....Andres Aldama, Cuba
1984 ....Mark Breland, United States
1988 ....Robert Wangila, Kenya
1992 ....Michael Carruth, Ireland
1996 ....Oleg Saitov, Russia

LIGHT MIDDLEWEIGHT (156 LB)

1952 ....Laszlo Papp, Hungary
1956 ....Laszlo Papp, Hungary
1960 ....Wilbert McClure, United States
1964 ....Boris Lagutin, USSR
1968 ....Boris Lagutin, USSR
1972 ....Dieter Kottysch, West Germany
1976 ....Jerzy Rybicki, Poland
1980 ....Armando Martinez, Cuba
1984 ....Frank Tate, United States
1988 ....Park Si-Hun, South Korea
1992 ....Juan Lemus, Cuba
1996 ....David Reid, United States

MIDDLEWEIGHT (165 LB)

1904 ....Charles Mayer, United States
1908 ....John Douglas, Great Britain
1912 ....Not held
1920 ....Harry Mallin, Great Britain
1924 ....Harry Mallin, Great Britain
1928 ....Piero Toscani, Italy
1932 ....Carmen Barth, United States
1936 ....Jean Despeaux, France
1948 ....Laszlo Papp, Hungary
1952 ....Floyd Patterson, United States
1956 ....Gennady Schatkov, USSR
1960 ....Edward Crook, United States
1964 ....Valery Popenchenko, USSR
1968 ....Christopher Finnegan, Great Britain
1972 ....Vyacheslav Lemechev, USSR
1976 ....Michael Spinks, United States

MIDDLEWEIGHT *(Cont.)*

1980 ....Jose Gomez, Cuba
1984 ....Shin Joon Sup, South Korea
1988 ....Henry Maske, East Germany
1992 ....Ariel Hernandez, Cuba
1996 ....Ariel Hernandez, Cuba

LIGHT HEAVYWEIGHT (178 LB)

1920 ....Edward Eagan, United States
1924 ....Harry Mitchell, Great Britain
1928 ....Victor Avendano, Argentina
1932 ....David Carstens, South Africa
1936 ....Roger Michelot, France
1948 ....George Hunter, South Africa
1952 ....Norvel Lee, United States
1956 ....James Boyd, United States
1960 ....Cassius Clay, United States
1964 ....Cosimo Pinto, Italy
1968 ....Dan Poznyak, USSR
1972 ....Mate Parlov, Yugoslavia
1976 ....Leon Spinks, United States
1980 ....Slobodan Kacer, Yugoslavia
1984 ....Anton Josipovic, Yugoslavia
1988 ....Andrew Maynard, United States
1992 ....Torsten May, Germany
1996 ....Vassili Jirov, Kazakhstan

HEAVYWEIGHT (OVER 201 LB)

1904 ....Samuel Berger, United States
1906 ....Not held
1908 ....Albert Oldham, Great Britain
1912 ....Not held
1920 ....Ronald Rawson, Great Britain
1924 ....Otto von Porat, Norway
1928 ....Arturo Rodriguez Jurado, Argentina
1932 ....Santiago Lovell, Argentina
1936 ....Herbert Runge, Germany
1948 ....Rafael Inglesias, Argentina
1952 ....H. Edward Sanders, United States
1956 ....T. Peter Rademacher, United States
1960 ....Franco De Piccoli, Italy
1964 ....Joe Frazier, United States
1968 ....George Foreman, United States
1972 ....Teofilo Stevenson, Cuba
1976 ....Teofilo Stevenson, Cuba
1980 ....Teofilo Stevenson, Cuba

HEAVYWEIGHT (201* LB)

1984 ....Henry Tillman, United States
1988 ....Ray Mercer, United States
1992 ....Félix Sávon, Cuba
1996 ....Félix Sávon, Cuba

SUPER HEAVYWEIGHT (UNLIMITED)

1984 ....Tyrell Biggs, United States
1988 ....Lennox Lewis, Canada
1992 ....Roberto Balado, Cuba
1996 ....Vladimir Klitchko, Ukraine

*Until 1984 the heavyweight division was unlimited. With the addition of the super heavyweight division, a limit of 201 pounds was imposed.

SWIMMING

Men

50-METER FREESTYLE

1904 ....Zoltan Halmay, Hungary (50 yds) 28.0
1988 ....Matt Biondi, United States 22.14 WR
1992 ....Aleksandr Popov, Unified Team 22.30
1996 ....Aleksandr Popov, Russia 22.13

SWIMMING *(Cont.)*
Men *(Cont.)*

100-METER FREESTLYE

1896	Alfred Hajos, Hungary	1:22.2 OR
1904	Zoltan Halmay, Hungary (100 yds)	1:02.8
1906	Charles Daniels, United States	1:13.4
1908	Charles Daniels, United States	1:05.6 WR
1912	Duke Kahanamoku, United States	1:03.4
1920	Duke Kahanamoku, United States	1:00.4 WR
1924	John Weissmuller, United States	59.0 OR
1928	John Weissmuller, United States	58.6 OR
1932	Yasuji Miyazaki, Japan	58.2
1936	Ferenc Csik, Hungary	57.6
1948	Wally Ris, United States	57.3 OR
1952	Clarke Scholes, United States	57.4
1956	Jon Henricks, Australia	55.4 OR
1960	John Devitt, Australia	55.2 OR
1964	Don Schollander, United States	53.4 OR
1968	Mike Wenden, Australia	52.2 WR
1972	Mark Spitz, United States	51.22 WR
1976	Jim Montgomery, United States	49.99 WR
1980	Jörg Woithe, East Germany	50.40
1984	Rowdy Gaines, United States	49.80 OR
1988	Matt Biondi, United States	48.63 OR
1992	Aleksandr Popov, Unified Team	49.02
1996	Aleksandr Popov, Russia	48.74

200-METER FREESTYLE

1900	Frederick Lane, Australia	2:25.2 OR
1904	Charles Daniels, United States	2:44.2
1906	Not held 1906-1964	
1968	Michael Wenden, Australia	1:55.2 OR
1972	Mark Spitz, United States	1:52.78 WR
1976	Bruce Furniss, United States	1:50.29 WR
1980	Sergei Kopliakov, USSR	1:49.81 OR
1984	Michael Gross, West Germany	1:47.44 WR
1988	Duncan Armstrong, Australia	1:47.25 WR
1992	Evgueni Sadovyi, Unified Team	1:46.70 OR
1996	Danyon Loader, New Zealand	1:47.63

400-METER FREESTYLE

1896	Paul Neumann, Austria (500 yds)	8:12.6
1904	Charles Daniels, U.S. (440 yds)	6:16.2
1906	Otto Scheff, Austria (440 yds)	6:23.8
1908	Henry Taylor, Great Britain	5:36.8
1912	George Hodgson, Canada	5:24.4
1920	Norman Ross, United States	5:26.8
1924	John Weissmuller, United States	5:04.2 OR
1928	Albert Zorilla, Argentina	5:01.6 OR
1932	Buster Crabbe, United States	4:48.4 OR
1936	Jack Medica, United States	4:44.5 OR
1948	William Smith, United States	4:41.0 OR
1952	Jean Boiteux, France	4:30.7 OR
1956	Murray Rose, Australia	4:27.3 OR
1960	Murray Rose, Australia	4:18.3 OR
1964	Don Schollander, United States	4:12.2 WR
1968	Mike Burton, United States	4:09.0 OR
1972	Brad Cooper, Australia	4:00.27 OR
1976	Brian Goodell, United States	3:51.93 WR
1980	Vladimir Salnikov, USSR	3:51.31 OR
1984	George DiCarlo, United States	3:51.23 OR
1988	Uwe Dassler, East Germany	3:46.95 WR
1992	Evgueni Sadovyi, Unified Team	3:45.00 WR
1996	Danyon Loader, New Zealand	3:47.97

1500-METER FREESTYLE

1908	Henry Taylor, Great Britain	22:48.4 WR
1912	George Hodgson, Canada	22:00.0 WR

1500-METER FREESTYLE *(Cont.)*

1920	Norman Ross, United States	22:23.2
1924	Andrew Charlton, Australia	20:06.6 WR
1928	Arne Borg, Sweden	19:51.8 OR
1932	Kusuo Kitamura, Japan	19:12.4 OR
1936	Noboru Terada, Japan	19:13.7
1948	James McLane, United States	19:18.5
1952	Ford Konno, United States	18:30.3 OR
1956	Murray Rose, Australia	17:58.9
1960	John Konrads, Australia	17:19.6 OR
1964	Robert Windle, Australia	17:01.7 OR
1968	Mike Burton, United States	16:38.9 OR
1972	Mike Burton, United States	15:52.58 OR
1976	Brian Goodell, United States	15:02.40 WR
1980	Vladimir Salnikov, USSR	14:58.27 WR
1984	Michael O'Brien, United States	15:05.20
1988	Vladimir Salnikov, USSR	15:00.40
1992	Kieren Perkins, Australia	14:43.48 WR
1996	Kieren Perkins, Australia	14:56.40

100-METER BACKSTROKE

1904	Walter Brack, Germany (100 yds)	1:16.8
1908	Arno Bieberstein, Germany	1:24.6 WR
1912	Harry Hebner, United States	1:21.2
1920	Warren Kealoha, United States	1:15.2
1924	Warren Kealoha, United States	1:13.2 OR
1928	George Kojac, United States	1:08.2 WR
1932	Masaji Kiyokawa, Japan	1:08.6
1936	Adolph Kiefer, United States	1:05.9 OR
1948	Allen Stack, United States	1:06.4
1952	Yoshi Oyakawa, United States	1:05.4 OR
1956	David Thiele, Australia	1:02.2 OR
1960	David Thiele, Australia	1:01.9 OR
1964	Not held	
1968	Roland Matthes, East Germany	58.7 OR
1972	Roland Matthes, East Germany	56.58 OR
1976	John Naber, United States	55.49 WR
1980	Bengt Baron, Sweden	56.33
1984	Rick Carey, United States	55.79
1988	Daichi Suzuki, Japan	55.05
1992	Mark Tewksbury, Canada	53.98 WR
1996	Jeff Rouse, United States	54.10

200-METER BACKSTROKE

1900	Ernst Hoppenberg, Germany	2:47.0
1904	Not held 1904-1960	
1964	Jed Graef, United States	2:10.3 WR
1968	Roland Matthes, East Germany	2:09.6 OR
1972	Roland Matthes, East Germany	2:02.82 EWR
1976	John Naber, United States	1:59.19 WR
1980	Sandor Wladar, Hungary	2:01.93
1984	Rick Carey, United States	2:00.23
1988	Igor Polianski, USSR	1:59.37
1992	Martin Lopez-Zubero, Spain	1:58.47 OR
1996	Brad Bridgewater, United States	1:58.54

100-METER BREASTSTROKE

1968	Don McKenzie, United States	1:07.7 OR
1972	Nobutaka Taguchi, Japan	1:04.94 WR
1976	John Hencken, United States	1:03.11 WR
1980	Duncan Goodhew, Great Britain	1:03.44
1984	Steve Lundquist, United States	1:01.65 WR
1988	Adrian Moorhouse, Great Britain	1:02.04
1992	Nelson Diebel, United States	1:01.50 OR
1996	Fred DeBurghgraeve, Belgium	1:00.65

Note: OR=Olympic Record; WR=World Record; EOR=Equals Olympic Record; EWR=Equals World Record; WB=World Best.

SWIMMING (Cont.)
Men (Cont.)

200-METER BREASTSTROKE

1908	Frederick Holman, Great Britain	3:09.2 WR
1912	Walter Bathe, Germany	3:01.8 OR
1920	Haken Malmroth, Sweden	3:04.4
1924	Robert Skelton, United States	2:56.6
1928	Yoshiyuki Tsuruta, Japan	2:48.8 OR
1932	Yoshiyuki Tsuruta, Japan	2:45.4
1936	Tetsuo Hamuro, Japan	2:41.5 OR
1948	Joseph Verdeur, United States	2:39.3 OR
1952	John Davies, Australia	2:34.4 OR
1956	Masura Furukawa, Japan	2:34.7 OR
1960	William Mulliken, United States	2:37.4
1964	Ian O'Brien, Australia	2:27.8 WR
1968	Felipe Munoz, Mexico	2:28.7
1972	John Hencken, United States	2:21.55 WR
1976	David Wilkie, Great Britain	2:15.11 WR
1980	Robertas Zhulpa, USSR	2:15.85
1984	Victor Davis, Canada	2:13.34 WR
1988	Jozsef Szabo, Hungary	2:13.52
1992	Mike Barrowman, United States	2:10.16 WR
1996	Norbert Rózsa, Hungary	2:12.57

100-METER BUTTERFLY

1968	Doug Russell, United States	55.9 OR
1972	Mark Spitz, United States	54.27 WR
1976	Matt Vogel, United States	54.35
1980	Pär Arvidsson, Sweden	54.92
1984	Michael Gross, West Germany	53.08 WR
1988	Anthony Nesty, Suriname	53.00 OR
1992	Pablo Morales, United States	53.32
1996	Denis Pankratov, Russia	52.27 WR

200-METER BUTTERFLY

1956	William Yorzyk, United States	2:19.3 OR
1960	Michael Troy, United States	2:12.8 WR
1964	Kevin Berry, Australia	2:06.6 WR
1968	Carl Robie, United States	2:08.7
1972	Mark Spitz, United States	2:00.70 WR
1976	Mike Bruner, United States	1:59.23 WR
1980	Sergei Fesenko, USSR	1:59.76
1984	Jon Sieben, Australia	1:57.04 WR
1988	Michael Gross, West Germany	1:56.94 OR
1992	Melvin Stewart, United States	1:56.26 OR
1996	Denis Pankratov, Russia	1:56.51

200-METER INDIVIDUAL MEDLEY

1968	Charles Hickcox, United States	2:12.0 OR
1972	Gunnar Larsson, Sweden	2:07.17 WR
1984	Alex Baumann, Canada	2:01.42 WR
1988	Tamas Darnyi, Hungary	2:00.17 WR
1992	Tamas Darnyi, Hungary	2:00.76
1996	Attila Czene, Hungary	1:59.91 OR

400-METER INDIVIDUAL MEDLEY

1964	Richard Roth, United States	4:45.4 WR
1968	Charles Hickcox, United States	4:48.4
1972	Gunnar Larsson, Sweden	4:31.98 OR
1976	Rod Strachan, United States	4:23.68 WR
1980	Aleksandr Sidorenko, USSR	4:22.89 OR
1984	Alex Baumann, Canada	4:17.41 WR
1988	Tamas Darnyi, Hungary	4:14.75 WR
1992	Tamas Darnyi, Hungary	4:14.23 OR
1996	Tom Dolan United States	4:14.90

4 X 100-METER MEDLEY RELAY

Year	Team	Time
1960	United States	4:05.4 WR
1964	United States	3:58.4 WR
1968	United States	3:54.9 WR
1972	United States	3:48.16 WR
1976	United States	3:42.22 WR
1980	Australia	3:45.70
1984	United States	3:39.30 WR
1988	United States	3:36.93 WR
1992	United States	3:36.93 EWR
1996	United States	3:34.84 WR

4 X 100-METER FREESTYLE RELAY

Year	Team	Time
1964	United States	3:32.2 WR
1968	United States	3:31.7 WR
1972	United States	3:26.42 WR
1976-1980	Not held	
1984	United States	3:19.03 WR
1988	United States	3:16.53 WR
1992	United States	3:16.74
1996	United States	3:15.41 OR

4 X 200-METER FREESTYLE RELAY

Year	Team	Time
1906	Hungary (1000 m)	16:52.4
1908	Great Britain	10:55.6
1912	Australia/New Zealand	10:11.6 WR
1920	United States	10:04.4 WR
1924	United States	9:53.4 WR
1928	United States	9:36.2 WR
1932	Japan	8:58.4 WR
1936	Japan	8:51.5 WR
1948	United States	8:46.0 WR
1952	United States	8:31.1 OR
1956	Australia	8:23.6 WR
1960	United States	8:10.2 WR
1964	United States	7:52.1 WR
1968	United States	7:52.33
1972	United States	7:35.78 WR
1976	United States	7:23.22 WR
1980	USSR	7:23.50
1984	United States	7:15.69 WR
1988	United States	7:12.51 WR
1992	Unified Team	7:11.95 WR
1996	United States	7:14.84

Women

50-METER FREESTYLE

1988	Kristin Otto, East Germany	25.49 OR
1992	Yang Wenyi, China	24.79 WR
1996	Amy Van Dyken, United States	24.87

100-METER FREESTYLE

1912	Fanny Durack, Australia	1:22.2
1920	Ethelda Bleibtrey, United States	1:13.6 WR
1924	Ethel Lackie, United States	1:12.4
1928	Albina Osipowich, United States	1:11.0 OR
1932	Helene Madison, United States	1:06.8 OR

100-METER FREESTYLE (Cont.)

1936	Hendrika Mastenbroek, Netherlands	1:05.9 OR
1948	Greta Andersen, Denmark	1:06.3
1952	Katalin Szöke, Hungary	1:06.8
1956	Dawn Fraser, Australia	1:02.0 WR
1960	Dawn Fraser, Australia	1:01.2 OR
1964	Dawn Fraser, Australia	59.5 OR
1968	Jan Henne, United States	1:00.0
1972	Sandra Neilson, United States	58.59 OR

SWIMMING (Cont.)
Women (Cont.)

100-METER FREESTYLE (Cont.)

1976	Kornelia Ender, East Germany	55.65 WR
1980	Barbara Krause, East Germany	54.79 WR
1984	Carrie Steinseifer, United States	55.92
	Nancy Hogshead, United States	55.92
1988	Kristin Otto, East Germany	54.93
1992	Zhuang Yong, China	54.64 OR
1996	Le Jingyi, China	54.50 OR

200-METER FREESTYLE

1968	Debbie Meyer, United States	2:10.5 OR
1972	Shane Gould, Australia	2:03.56 WR
1976	Kornelia Ender, East Germany	1:59.26 WR
1980	Barbara Krause, East Germany	1:58.33 OR
1984	Mary Wayte, United States	1:59.23
1988	Heike Friedrich, East Germany	1:57.65 OR
1992	Nicole Haislett, United States	1:57.90
1996	Claudia Poll, Costa Rica	1:58.16

400-METER FREESTYLE

1924	Martha Norelius, United States	6:02.2 OR
1928	Martha Norelius, United States	5:42.8 WR
1932	Helene Madison, United States	5:28.5 WR
1936	Hendrika Mastenbroek, Netherlands	5:26.4 OR
1948	Ann Curtis, United States	5:17.8 OR
1952	Valeria Gyenge, Hungary	5:12.1 OR
1956	Lorraine Crapp, Australia	4:54.6 OR
1960	Chris von Saltza, United States	4:50.6 OR
1964	Virginia Duenkel, United States	4:43.3 OR
1968	Debbie Meyer, United States	4:31.8 OR
1972	Shane Gould, Australia	4:19.44 WR
1976	Petra Thümer, East Germany	4:09.89 WR
1980	Ines Diers, East Germany	4:08.76 WR
1984	Tiffany Cohen, United States	4:07.10 OR
1988	Janet Evans, United States	4:03.85 WR
1992	Dagmar Hase, Germany	4:07.18
1996	Michelle Smith, Ireland	4:07.25

800-METER FREESTYLE

1968	Debbie Meyer, United States	9:24.0 OR
1972	Keena Rothhammer, United States	8:53.68 WR
1976	Petra Thümer, East Germany	8:37.14 WR
1980	Michelle Ford, Australia	8:28.90 OR
1984	Tiffany Cohen, United States	8:24.95 OR
1988	Janet Evans, United States	8:20.20 OR
1992	Janet Evans, United States	8:25.52
1996	Brooke Bennett, United States	8:27.89

100-METER BACKSTROKE

1924	Sybil Bauer, United States	1:23.2 OR
1928	Marie Braun, Netherlands	1:22.0
1932	Eleanor Holm, United States	1:19.4
1936	Dina Senff, Netherlands	1:18.9
1948	Karen Harup, Denmark	1:14.4 OR
1952	Joan Harrison, South Africa	1:14.3
1956	Judy Grinham, Great Britain	1:12.9 OR
1960	Lynn Burke, United States	1:09.3 OR
1964	Cathy Ferguson, United States	1:07.7 WR
1968	Kaye Hall, United States	1:06.2 WR
1972	Melissa Belote, United States	1:05.78 OR
1976	Ulrike Richter, East Germany	1:01.83 OR
1980	Rica Reinisch, East Germany	1:00.86 WR
1984	Theresa Andrews, United States	1:02.55
1988	Kristin Otto, East Germany	1:00.89
1992	Krisztina Egerszegi, Hungary	1:00.68 OR
1996	Beth Botsford, United States	1:01.19

200-METER BACKSTROKE

1968	Pokey Watson, United States	2:24.8 OR
1972	Melissa Belote, United States	2:19.19 WR
1976	Ulrike Richter, East Germany	2:13.43 OR
1980	Rica Reinisch, East Germany	2:11.77 WR
1984	Jolanda De Rover, Netherlands	2:12.38
1988	Krisztina Egerszegi, Hungary	2:09.29 OR
1992	Krisztina Egerszegi, Hungary	2:07.06 OR
1996	Krisztina Egerszegi, Hungary	2:07.83

100-METER BREASTSTROKE

1968	Djurdjica Bjedov, Yugoslavia	1:15.8 OR
1972	Catherine Carr, United States	1:13.58 WR
1976	Hannelore Anke, East Germany	1:11.16
1980	Ute Geweniger, East Germany	1:10.22
1984	Petra Van Staveren, Netherlands	1:09.88 OR
1988	Tania Dangalakova, Bulgaria	1:07.95 OR
1992	Elena Roudkovskaia, Unified Team	1:08.00
1996	Penelope Heyns, South Africa	1:07.73

200-METER BREASTSTROKE

1924	Lucy Morton, Great Britain	3:33.2 OR
1928	Hilde Schrader, Germany	3:12.6
1932	Clare Dennis, Australia	3:06.3 OR
1936	Hideko Maehata, Japan	3:03.6
1948	Petronella Van Vliet, Netherlands	2:57.2
1952	Eva Szekely, Hungary	2:51.7 OR
1956	Ursula Happe, West Germany	2:53.1 OR
1960	Anita Lonsbrough, Great Britain	2:49.5 WR
1964	Galina Prozumenshikova, USSR	2:46.4 OR
1968	Sharon Wichman, United States	2:44.4 OR
1972	Beverly Whitfield, Australia	2:41.71 OR
1976	Marina Koshevaia, USSR	2:33.35 WR
1980	Lina Kaciusyte, USSR	2:29.54 OR
1984	Anne Ottenbrite, Canada	2:30.38
1988	Silke Hoerner, East Germany	2:26.71 WR
1992	Kyoko Iwasaki, Japan	2:26.65 OR
1996	Penelope Heyns, South Africa	2:25.41 OR

100-METER BUTTERFLY

1956	Shelley Mann, United States	1:11.0 OR
1960	Carolyn Schuler, United States	1:09.5 OR
1964	Sharon Stouder, United States	1:04.7 WR
1968	Lynn McClements, Australia	1:05.5
1972	Mayumi Aoki, Japan	1:03.34 WR
1976	Kornelia Ender, East Germany	1:00.13 EWR
1980	Caren Metschuck, East Germany	1:00.42
1984	Mary T. Meagher, United States	59.26
1988	Kristin Otto, East Germany	59.00 OR
1992	Qian Hong, China	58.62 OR
1996	Amy Van Dyken, United States	59.13

200-METER BUTTERFLY

1968	Ada Kok, Netherlands	2:24.7 OR
1972	Karen Moe, United States	2:15.57 WR
1976	Andrea Pollack, East Germany	2:11.41 OR
1980	Ines Geissler, East Germany	2:10.44 OR
1984	Mary T. Meagher, United States	2:06.90 OR
1988	Kathleen Nord, East Germany	2:09.51
1992	Summer Sanders, United States	2:08.67
1996	Susan O'Neill, Australia	2:07.76

200-METER INDIVIDUAL MEDLEY

1968	Claudia Kolb, United States	2:24.7 OR
1972	Shane Gould, Australia	2:23.07 WR
1976	Not held 1976-1980	
1984	Tracy Caulkins, United States	2:12.64 OR

Note: OR=Olympic Record; WR=World Record; EOR=Equals Olympic Record; EWR=Equals World Record; WB=World Best.

SWIMMING *(Cont.)*
Women *(Cont.)*

200-METER INDIVIDUAL MEDLEY *(Cont.)*

1988	Daniela Hunger, East Germany	2:12.59 OR
1992	Lin Li, China	2:11.65 WR
1996	Michelle Smith, Ireland	2:13.93

400-METER INDIVIDUAL MEDLEY

1964	Donna de Varona, United States	5:18.7 OR
1968	Claudia Kolb, United States	5:08.5 OR
1972	Gail Neall, Australia	5:02.97 WR
1976	Ulrike Tauber, East Germany	4:42.77 WR
1980	Petra Schneider, East Germany	4:36.29 WR
1984	Tracy Caulkins, United States	4:39.24
1988	Janet Evans, United States	4:37.76
1992	Krisztina Egerszegi, Hungary	4:36.54
1996	Michelle Smith, Ireland	4:39.18

4 X 100-METER MEDLEY RELAY

1960	United States	4:41.1 WR
1964	United States	4:33.9 WR
1968	United States	4:28.3 OR
1972	United States	4:20.75 WR
1976	East Germany	4:07.95 WR
1980	East Germany	4:06.67 WR
1984	United States	4:08.34
1988	East Germany	4:03.74 OR
1992	United States	4:02.54 WR
1996	United States	4:02.88

4 X 100-METER FREESTYLE RELAY

1912	Great Britain	5:52.8 WR
1920	United States	5:11.6 WR
1924	United States	4:58.8 WR
1928	United States	4:47.6 WR
1932	United States	4:38.0 WR
1936	Netherlands	4:36.0 OR
1948	United States	4:29.2 OR
1952	Hungary	4:24.4 WR
1956	Australia	4:17.1 WR
1960	United States	4:08.9 WR
1964	United States	4:03.8 WR
1968	United States	4:02.5 OR
1972	United States	3:55.19 WR
1976	United States	3:44.82 WR
1980	East Germany	3:42.71 WR
1984	United States	3:43.43
1988	East Germany	3:40.63 OR
1992	United States	3:39.46 WR
1996	United States	3:39.29 OR

4 X 200-METER FREESTYLE RELAY

1996	United States	7:59.87

Note: OR=Olympic Record; WR=World Record; EOR=Equals Olympic Record; EWR=Equals World Record; WB=World Best.

DIVING
Men

SPRINGBOARD

		Pts
1908	Albert Zürner, Germany	85.5
1912	Paul Günther, Germany	79.23
1920	Louis Kuehn, United States	675.40
1924	Albert White, United States	97.46
1928	Pete DesJardins, United States	185.04
1932	Michael Galitzen, United States	161.38
1936	Richard Degener, United States	163.57
1948	Bruce Harlan, United States	163.64
1952	David Browning, United States	205.29
1956	Robert Clotworthy, United States	159.56
1960	Gary Tobian, United States	170.00
1964	Kenneth Sitzberger, United States	159.90
1968	Bernie Wrightson, United States	170.15
1972	Vladimir Vasin, USSR	594.09
1976	Phil Boggs, United States	619.05
1980	Aleksandr Portnov, USSR	905.02
1984	Greg Louganis, United States	754.41
1988	Greg Louganis, United States	730.80
1992	Mark Lenzi, United States	676.53
1996	Xiong Ni, China	701.46

PLATFORM

		Pts
1904	George Sheldon, United States	12.66
1906	Gottlob Walz, Germany	156.0
1908	Hjalmar Johansson, Sweden	83.75
1912	Erik Adlerz, Sweden	73.94
1920	Clarence Pinkston, United States	100.67
1924	Albert White, United States	97.46
1928	Pete DesJardins, United States	98.74
1932	Harold Smith, United States	124.80
1936	Marshall Wayne, United States	113.58
1948	Sammy Lee, United States	130.05
1952	Sammy Lee, United States	156.28
1956	Joaquin Capilla, Mexico	152.44
1960	Robert Webster, United States	165.56
1964	Robert Webster, United States	148.58
1968	Klaus Dibiasi, Italy	164.18
1972	Klaus Dibiasi, Italy	504.12
1976	Klaus Dibiasi, Italy	600.51
1980	Falk Hoffmann, East Germany	835.65
1984	Greg Louganis, United States	710.91
1988	Greg Louganis, United States	638.61
1992	Sun Shuwei, China	677.31
1996	Dmitri Sautin, Russia	692.34

Women
SPRINGBOARD

		Pts
1920	Aileen Riggin, United States	539.90
1924	Elizabeth Becker, United States	474.50
1928	Helen Meany, United States	78.62
1932	Georgia Coleman, United States	87.52
1936	Marjorie Gestring, United States	89.27

		Pts
1948	Victoria Draves, United States	108.74
1952	Patricia McCormick, United States	147.30
1956	Patricia McCormick, United States	142.36
1960	Ingrid Krämer, East Germany	155.81

DIVING *(Cont.)*
Women *(Cont.)*

SPRINGBOARD *(Cont.)*

		Pts
1964	Ingrid Engel Krämer, East Germany	145.00
1968	Sue Gossick, United States	150.77
1972	Micki King, United States	450.03
1976	Jennifer Chandler, United States	506.19
1980	Irina Kalinina, USSR	725.91
1984	Sylvie Bernier, Canada	530.70
1988	Gao Min, China	580.23
1992	Gao Min, China	572.40
1996	Fu Mingxia, China	547.68

PLATFORM

		Pts
1912	Greta Johansson, Sweden	39.90
1920	Stefani Fryland-Clausen, Denmark	34.60
1924	Caroline Smith, United States	33.20

PLATFORM *(Cont.)*

		Pts
1928	Elizabeth B. Pinkston, United States	31.60
1932	Dorothy Poynton, United States	40.26
1936	Dorothy Poynton Hill, United States	33.93
1948	Victoria Draves, United States	68.87
1952	Patricia McCormick, United States	79.37
1956	Patricia McCormick, United States	84.85
1960	Ingrid Krämer, East Germany	91.28
1964	Lesley Bush, United States	99.80
1968	Milena Duchkova, Czechoslovakia	109.59
1972	Ulrika Knape, Sweden	390.00
1976	Elena Vaytsekhovskaya, USSR	406.59
1980	Martina Jäschke, East Germany	596.25
1984	Zhou Jihong, China	435.51
1988	Xu Yanmei, China	445.20
1992	Fu Mingxia, China	461.43
1996	Fu Mingxia, China	521.58

GYMNASTICS
Men

ALL-AROUND

		Pts
1900	Gustave Sandras, France	302
1904	Julius Lenhart, Austria	69.80
1906	Pierre Paysse, France	97
1908	Alberto Braglia, Italy	317.0
1912	Alberto Braglia, Italy	135.0
1920	Giorgio Zampori, Italy	88.35
1924	Leon Stukelj, Yugoslavia	110.340
1928	Georges Miez, Switzerland	247.500
1932	Romeo Neri, Italy	140.625
1936	Alfred Schwarzmann, Germany	113.100
1948	Veikko Huhtanen, Finland	229.70
1952	Viktor Chukarin, USSR	115.70
1956	Viktor Chukarin, USSR	114.25
1960	Boris Shakhlin, USSR	115.95
1964	Yukio Endo, Japan	115.95
1968	Sawao Kato, Japan	115.90
1972	Sawao Kato, Japan	114.65
1976	Nikolai Andrianov, USSR	116.65
1980	Aleksandr Dityatin, USSR	118.65
1984	Koji Gushiken, Japan	118.70
1988	Vladimir Artemov, USSR	119.125
1992	Vitaly Scherbo, Unified Team	59.025
1996	Li Xiaoshuang, China	58.423

HORIZONTAL BAR

		Pts
1896	Hermann Weingärtner, Germany	—
1900	Not held	
1904	Anton Heida, United States	40
1908	Not held 1908–1920	
1924	Leon Stukelj, Yugoslavia	19.73
1928	Georges Miez, Switzerland	19.17
1932	Dallas Bixler, United States	18.33
1936	Aleksanteri Saarvala, Finland	19.367
1948	Josef Stafler, Switzerland	19.85
1952	Jack Günthard, Switzerland	19.55
1956	Takashi Ono, Japan	19.60
1960	Takashi Ono, Japan	19.60
1964	Boris Shakhlin, USSR	19.625
1968	Akinori Nakayama, Japan	19.55
1972	Mitsuo Tsukahara, Japan	19.725

HORIZONTAL BAR *(Cont.)*

		Pts
1976	Mitsuo Tsukahara, Japan	19.675
1980	Stoyan Deltchev, Bulgaria	19.825
1984	Shinji Morisue, Japan	20.00
1988	Vladimir Artemov, USSR	19.90
1992	Trent Dimas, United States	9.875
1996	Andreas Wecker, Germany	9.850

PARALLEL BARS

		Pts
1896	Alfred Flatow, Germany	—
1900	Not held	
1904	George Eyser, United States	44
1908	Not held 1908–1920	
1924	August Güttinger, Switzerland	21.63
1928	Ladislav Vacha, Czechoslovakia	18.83
1932	Romeo Neri, Italy	18.97
1936	Konrad Frey, Germany	19.067
1948	Michael Reusch, Switzerland	19.75
1952	Hans Eugster, Switzerland	19.65
1956	Viktor Chukarin, USSR	19.20
1960	Boris Shakhlin, USSR	19.40
1964	Yukio Endo, Japan	19.675
1968	Akinori Nakayama, Japan	19.475
1972	Sawao Kato, Japan	19.475
1976	Sawao Kato, Japan	19.675
1980	Aleksandr Tkachyov, USSR	19.775
1984	Bart Conner, United States	19.95
1988	Vladimir Artemov, USSR	19.925
1992	Vitaly Scherbo, Unified Team	9.900
1996	Rustan Sharipov, Ukraine	9.837

VAULT

		Pts
1896	Karl Schumann, Germany	—
1900	Not held	
1904	George Eyser, United States	36
1908	Not held 1908–1920	
1924	Frank Kriz, United States	9.98
1928	Eugen Mack, Switzerland	9.58
1932	Savino Guglielmetti, Italy	18.03
1936	Alfred Schwarzmann, Germany	19.20
1948	Paavo Aaltonen, Finland	19.55

GYMNASTICS (Cont.)
Men (Cont.)

VAULT (Cont.)

		Pts
1952	Viktor Chukarin, USSR	19.20
1956	Helmut Bantz, Germany	18.85
1960	Takashi Ono, Japan	19.35
1964	Haruhiro Yamashita, Japan	19.60
1968	Mikhail Voronin, USSR	19.00
1972	Klaus Köste, East Germany	18.85
1976	Nikolai Andrianov, USSR	19.45
1980	Nikolai Andrianov, USSR	19.825
1984	Lou Yun, China	19.95
1988	Lou Yun, China	19.875
1992	Vitaly Scherbo, Unified Team	9.856
1996	Alexei Nemov, Russia	9.787

POMMEL HORSE

		Pts
1896	Louis Zutter, Switzerland	—
1900	Not held	
1904	Anton Heida, United States	42
1908	Not held 1908–1920	
1924	Josef Wilhelm, Switzerland	21.23
1928	Hermann Hänggi, Switzerland	19.75
1932	Istvan Pelle, Hungary	19.07
1936	Konrad Frey, Germany	19.333
1948	Paavo Aaltonen, Finland	19.35
1952	Viktor Chukarin, USSR	19.50
1956	Boris Shakhlin, USSR	19.25
1960	Eugen Ekman, Finland	19.375
1964	Miroslav Cerar, Yugoslavia	19.525
1968	Miroslav Cerar, Yugoslavia	19.325
1972	Viktor Klimenko, USSR	19.125
1976	Zoltan Magyar, Hungary	19.70
1980	Zoltan Magyar, Hungary	19.925
1984	Li Ning, China	19.95
1988	Dmitri Bilozerchev, USSR	19.95
1992	Vitaly Scherbo, Unified Team	9.925
1996	Donghua Li, Switzerland	9.875

RINGS

		Pts
1896	Ioannis Mitropoulos, Greece	—
1900	Not held	
1904	Hermann Glass, United States	45
1908	Not held 1908–1920	
1924	Francesco Martino, Italy	21.553
1928	Leon Stukelj, Yugoslavia	19.25
1932	George Gulack, United States	18.97
1936	Alois Hudec, Czechoslovakia	19.433
1948	Karl Frei, Switzerland	19.80
1952	Grant Shaginyan, USSR	19.75
1956	Albert Azaryan, USSR	19.35
1960	Albert Azaryan, USSR	19.725
1964	Takuji Haytta, Japan	19.475

RINGS (Cont.)

		Pts
1968	Akinori Nakayama, Japan	19.45
1972	Akinori Nakayama, Japan	19.35
1976	Nikolai Andrianov, USSR	19.65
1980	Aleksandr Dityatin, USSR	19.875
1984	Koji Gushiken, Japan	19.85
1988	Holger Behrendt, East Germany	19.925
1992	Vitaly Scherbo, Unified Team	9.937
1996	Yuri Chechi, Italy	9.887

FLOOR EXERCISE

		Pts
1932	Istvan Pelle, Hungary	9.60
1936	Georges Miez, Switzerland	18.666
1948	Ferenc Pataki, Hungary	19.35
1952	K. William Thoresson, Sweden	19.25
1956	Valentin Muratov, USSR	19.20
1960	Nobuyuki Aihara, Japan	19.45
1964	Franco Menichelli, Italy	19.45
1968	Sawao Kato, Japan	19.475
1972	Nikolai Andrianov, USSR	19.175
1976	Nikolai Andrianov, USSR	19.45
1980	Roland Brückner, East Germany	19.75
1984	Li Ning, China	19.925
1988	Sergei Kharkov, USSR	19.925
1992	Li Xiaoshuang, China	9.925
1996	Ioannis Melissanidis, Greece	9.850

TEAM COMBINED EXERCISES

		Pts
1904	Turngemeinde Philadelphia	374.43
1906	Norway	19.00
1908	Sweden	438
1912	Italy	265.75
1920	Italy	359.855
1924	Italy	839.058
1928	Switzerland	1718.625
1932	Italy	541.850
1936	Germany	657.430
1948	Finland	1358.30
1952	USSR	574.40
1956	USSR	568.25
1960	Japan	575.20
1964	Japan	577.95
1968	Japan	575.90
1972	Japan	571.25
1976	Japan	576.85
1980	USSR	598.60
1984	United States	591.40
1988	USSR	593.35
1992	Unified Team	585.45
1996	Russia	576.778

Women
ALL-AROUND

		Pts
1952	Maria Gorokhovskaya, USSR	76.78
1956	Larissa Latynina, USSR	74.933
1960	Larissa Latynina, USSR	77.031
1964	Vera Caslavska, Czechoslovakia	77.564
1968	Vera Caslavska, Czechoslovakia	78.25
1972	Lyudmila Tousischeva, USSR	77.025

		Pts
1976	Nadia Comaneci, Romania	79.275
1980	Yelena Davydova, USSR	79.15
1984	Mary Lou Retton, United States	79.175
1988	Yelena Shushunova, USSR	79.662
1992	Tatiana Gutsu, Unified Team	39.737
1996	Lilia Podkopayeva, Ukraine	39.255

GYMNASTICS *(Cont.)*
Women

VAULT

	Pts
1952 .....Yekaterina Kalinchuk, USSR	19.20
1956 .....Larissa Latynina, USSR	18.833
1960 .....Margarita Nikolayeva, USSR	19.316
1964 .....Vera Caslavska, Czechoslovakia	19.483
1968 .....Vera Caslavska, Czechoslovakia	19.775
1972 .....Karin Janz, East Germany	19.525
1976 .....Nelli Kim, USSR	19.80
1980 .....Natalya Shaposhnikova, USSR	19.725
1984 .....Ecaterina Szabo, Romania	19.875
1988 .....Svetlana Boginskaya, USSR	19.905
1992 .....Henrietta Onodi, Hungary	9.925
Lavinia Milosovici, Romania	9.925
1996 .....Simona Amanar, Romania	9.825

UNEVEN BARS

	Pts
1952 .....Margit Korondi, Hungary	19.40
1956 .....Agnes Keleti, Hungary	18.966
1960 .....Polina Astakhova, USSR	19.616
1964 .....Polina Astakhova, USSR	19.332
1968 .....Vera Caslavska, Czechoslovakia	19.65
1972 .....Karin Janz, East Germany	19.675
1976 .....Nadia Comaneci, Romania	20.00
1980 .....Maxi Gnauck, East Germany	19.875
1984 .....Ma Yanhong, China	19.95
1988 .....Daniela Silivas, Romania	20.00
1992 .....Lu Li, China	10.00
1996 .....Svetlana Chorkina, Russia	9.850

BALANCE BEAM

	Pts
1952 .....Nina Bocharova, USSR	19.22
1956 .....Agnes Keleti, Hungary	18.80
1960 .....Eva Bosakova, Czechoslovakia	19.283
1964 .....Vera Caslavska, Czechoslovakia	19.449
1968 .....Natalya Kuchinskaya, USSR	19.65
1972 .....Olga Korbut, USSR	19.40
1976 .....Nadia Comaneci, Romania	19.95
1980 .....Nadia Comaneci, Romania	19.80
1984 .....Simona Pauca, Romania	19.80
1988 .....Daniela Silivas, Romania	19.924
1992 .....Tatiana Lisenko, Unified Team	9.975
1996 .....Shannon Miller, United States	9.862

FLOOR EXERCISE

	Pts
1952 .....Agnes Keleti, Hungary	19.36
1956 .....Agnes Keleti, Hungary	18.733
1960 .....Larissa Latynina, USSR	19.583
1964 .....Larissa Latynina, USSR	19.599
1968 .....Vera Caslavska, Czechoslovakia	19.675
1972 .....Olga Korbut, USSR	19.575
1976 .....Nelli Kim, USSR	19.85
1980 .....Nadia Comaneci, Romania	19.875
1984 .....Ecaterina Szabo, Romania	19.975
1988 .....Daniela Silivas, Romania	19.937
1992 .....Lavinia Milosovici, Romania	10.00
1996 .....Lilia Podkopayeva, Ukraine	9.887

TEAM COMBINED EXERCISES

		Pts
1928 ....The Netherlands		316.75
1932 ....Not held		
1936 ....Germany		506.50
1948 ....Czechoslovakia		445.45
1952 ....USSR		527.03
1956 ....USSR		444.800
1960 ....USSR		382.320
1964 ....USSR		280.890
1968 ....USSR		382.85
1972 ....USSR		380.50
1976 ....USSR		466.00
1980 ....USSR		394.90
1984 ....Romania		392.02
1988 ....USSR		395.475
1992 ....Unified Team		395.666
1996 ....United States		389.225

RHYTHMIC ALL-AROUND

	Pts
1984 .....Lori Fung, Canada	57.95
1988 .....Marina Lobach, USSR	60.00
1992 .....Aleksandra Timoshenko, UTeam	59.037
1996 .....Ekaterina Serebrianskaya, Ukr	39.683

RHYTHMIC TEAM COMBINED EXERCISES

	Pts
1996 .....Spain	38.933

SOCCER
Men

1900 .....Great Britain	1928 .....Uruguay	1964 .....Hungary	1988 .....Soviet Union
1904 .....Canada	1936 .....Italy	1968 .....Hungary	1992 .....Spain
1908 .....Great Britain	1948 .....Sweden	1972 .....Poland	1996 .....Nigeria
1912 .....Great Britain	1952 .....Hungary	1976 .....East Germany	
1920 .....Belgium	1956 .....Soviet Union	1980 .....Czechoslovakia	
1924 .....Uruguay	1960 .....Yugoslavia	1984 .....France	

Women
1996 ....United States

BIATHLON

Men

10 KILOMETERS

1980	Frank Ullrich, East Germany	32:10.69
1984	Eirik Kvalfoss, Norway	30:53.8
1988	Frank-Peter Rötsch, W Germany	25:08.1
1992	Mark Kirchner, Germany	26:02.3
1994	Sergei Tchepikov, Russia	28:07.0

20 KILOMETERS

1960	Klas Lestander, Sweden	1:33:21.6
1964	Vladimir Melyanin, Soviet Union	1:20:26.8
1968	Magnar Solberg, Norway	1:13:45.9
1972	Magnar Solberg, Norway	1:15:55.5
1976	Nikolay Kruglov, Soviet Union	1:14:12.26
1980	Anatoliy Alyabiev, Soviet Union	1:08:16.31
1984	Peter Angerer, W Germany	1:11:52.7

20 KILOMETERS *(Cont.)*

1988	Frank-Peter Rötsch, W Germany	56:33.3
1992	Evgueni Redkine, Unified Team	57:34.4
1994	Sergei Tarasov, Russia	57:25.3

4 X 7.5-KILOMETER RELAY

1968	Soviet Union	2:13:02.4
1972	Soviet Union	1:51:44.92
1976	Soviet Union	1:57:55.64
1980	Soviet Union	1:34:03.27
1984	Soviet Union	1:38:51.7
1988	Soviet Union	1:22:30.0
1992	Germany	1:24:43.5
1994	Germany	1:30:22.1

Women

7.5 KILOMETERS

1992	Antissa Restzova, Unified Team	24:29.2
1994	Myriam Bedard, Canada	26:08.8

15 KILOMETERS

1992	Antje Misersky, Germany	51:47.2
1994	Myriam Bedard, Canada	52:06.6

3 X 7.5-KILOMETER RELAY

1992	France	1:15:55.6
1994	Russia	1:47:19.5

BOBSLED

4-MAN BOB

1924	Switzerland (Eduard Scherrer)	5:45.54
1928	United States (William Fiske) (5-man)	3:20.50
1932	United States (William Fiske)	7:53.68
1936	Switzerland (Pierre Musy)	5:19.85
1948	United States (Francis Tyler)	5:20.10
1952	Germany (Andreas Ostler)	5:07.84
1956	Switzerland (Franz Kapus)	5:10.44
1960	Not held	
1964	Canada (Victor Emery)	4:14.46
1968	Italy (Eugenio Monti) (2 runs)	2:17.39
1972	Switzerland (Jean Wicki)	4:43.07
1976	East Germany (Meinhard Nehmer)	3:40.43
1980	East Germany (Meinhard Nehmer)	3:59.92
1984	East Germany (Wolfgang Hoppe)	3:20.22
1988	Switzerland (Ekkehard Fasser)	3:47.51
1992	Austria (Ingo Appelt)	3:53.90
1994	Germany (Harold Czudaj)	3:27.78

Note: Driver in parentheses.

2-MAN BOB

1932	United States (Hubert Stevens)	8:14.74
1936	United States (Ivan Brown)	5:29.29
1948	Switzerland (Felix Endrich)	5:29.20
1952	Germany (Andreas Ostler)	5:24.54
1956	Italy (Lamberto Dalla Costa)	5:30.14
1960	Not held	
1964	Great Britain (Anthony Nash)	4:21.90
1968	Italy (Eugenio Monti)	4:41.54
1972	West Germany (Wolfgang Zimmerer)	4:57.07
1976	East Germany (Meinhard Nehmer)	3:44.42
1980	Switzerland (Erich Schärer)	4:09.36
1984	East Germany (Wolfgang Hoppe)	3:25.56
1988	USSR (Janis Kipours)	3:53.48
1992	Switzerland (Gustav Weder)	4:03.26
1994	Switzerland (Gustav Weder)	3:30.81

Note: Driver in parentheses.

ICE HOCKEY

1920*	Canada, United States, Czechoslovakia
1924	Canada, United States, Great Britain
1928	Canada, Sweden, Switzerland
1932	Canada, United States, Germany
1936	Great Britain, Canada, United States
1948	Canada, Czechoslovakia, Switzerland
1952	Canada, United States, Sweden
1956	USSR, United States, Canada
1960	United States, Canada, USSR
1964	USSR, Sweden, Czechoslovakia
1968	USSR, Czechoslovakia, Canada
1972	USSR, United States, Czechoslovakia
1976	USSR, Czechoslovakia, West Germany
1980	United States, USSR, Sweden
1984	USSR, Czechoslovakia, Sweden
1988	USSR, Finland, Sweden
1992	Unified Team, Canada, Czechoslovakia
1994	Sweden, Canada, Finland

*Competition held at summer games in Antwerp.
Note: Gold, silver, and bronze medals.

LUGE

Men

SINGLES			DOUBLES		
1964	Thomas Köhler, East Germany	3:26.77	1964	Austria	1:41.62
1968	Manfred Schmid, Austria	2:52.48	1968	East Germany	1:35.85
1972	Wolfgang Scheidel, W Germany	3:27.58	1972	East Germany	1:28.35
1976	Detlef Guenther, West Germany	3:27.688	1976	East Germany	1:25.604
1980	Bernhard Glass, West Germany	2:54.796	1980	East Germany	1:19.331
1984	Paul Hildgartner, Italy	3:04.258	1984	West Germany	1:23.620
1988	Jens Müller, West Germany	3:05.548	1988	East Germany	1:31.940
1992	Georg Hackl, Germany	3:02.363	1992	Germany	1:32.053
1994	Georg Hackl, Germany	3:21.571	1994	Italy	1:36.720

Women

SINGLES			SINGLES (Cont.)		
1964	Ortrun Enderlein, Germany	3:24.67	1984	Steffi Martin, East Germany	2:46.570
1968	Erica Lechner, Italy	2:28.66	1988	Steffi Walter (Martin) E Germany	3:03.973
1972	Anna-Maria Müller, East Germany	2:59.18	1992	Doris Neuner, Austria	3:06.696
1976	Margit Schumann, East Germany	2:50.621	1994	Gerda Weissensteiner, Italy	3:15.517
1980	Vera Zozulya, USSR	2:36.537			

FIGURE SKATING

Men

SINGLES		SINGLES (Cont.)	
1908*	Ulrich Salchow, Sweden	1968	Wolfgang Schwarz, Austria
1920†	Gillis Grafström, Sweden	1972	Ondrej Nepela, Czechoslovakia
1924	Gillis Grafström, Sweden	1976	John Curry, Great Britain
1928	Gillis Grafström, Sweden	1980	Robin Cousins, Great Britain
1932	Karl Schäfer, Austria	1984	Scott Hamilton, United States
1936	Karl Schäfer, Austria	1988	Brian Boitano, United States
1948	Dick Button, United States	1992	Victor Petrenko, Unified Team
1952	Dick Button, United States	1994	Alexei Urmanov, Russia
1956	Hayes Alan Jenkins, United States		
1960	David Jenkins, United States	*Competition held at summer games in London.
1964	Manfred Schnelldorfer, West Germany	†Competition held at summer games in Antwerp.

Women

SINGLES		SINGLES (Cont.)	
1908*	Madge Syers, Great Britain	1968	Peggy Fleming, United States
1920†	Magda Julin, Sweden	1972	Beatrix Schuba, Austria
1924	Herma Szabo-Planck, Austria	1976	Dorothy Hamill, United States
1928	Sonja Henie, Norway	1980	Anett Pötzsch, East Germany
1932	Sonja Henie, Norway	1984	Katarina Witt, East Germany
1936	Sonja Henie, Norway	1988	Katarina Witt, East Germany
1948	Barbara Ann Scott, Canada	1992	Kristi Yamaguchi, United States
1952	Jeanette Altwegg, Great Britain	1994	Oksana Baiul, Ukraine
1956	Tenley Albright, United States		
1960	Carol Heiss, United States	*Competition held at summer games in London.
1964	Sjoukje Dijkstra, Netherlands	†Competition held at summer games in Antwerp.

FIGURE SKATING *(Cont.)*

Mixed

PAIRS

1908* ..Anna Hübler & Heinrich Burger, Germany
1920#..Ludovika & Walter Jakobsson, Finland
1924....Helene Engelmann & Alfred Berger, Austria
1928....Andree Joly & Pierre Brunet, France
1932....Andree Brunet (Joly) & Pierre Brunet, France
1936....Maxi Herber & Ernst Baier, Germany
1948....Micheline Lannoy & Pierre Baugniet, Belgium
1952....Ria Falk and Paul Falk, West Germany
1956....Elisabeth Schwartz & Kurt Oppelt, Austria
1960....Barbara Wagner & Robert Paul, Canada
1964....Lyudmila Beloussova & Oleg Protopopov, USSR
1968....Lyudmila Beloussova & Oleg Protopopov, USSR
1972....Irina Rodnina & Alexei Ulanov, USSR
1976....Irina Rodnina & Aleksandr Zaitsev, USSR
1980....Irina Rodnina & Aleksandr Zaitsev, USSR
1984....Elena Valova & Oleg Vasiliev, USSR
1988....Ekaterina Gordeeva & Sergei Grinkov, USSR

PAIRS *(Cont.)*

1992....Natalia Michkouteniok & Artour Dmitriev, Unified Team
1994....Ekaterina Gordeeva and Sergei Grinkov, Russia

ICE DANCING

1976....Lyudmila Pakhomova & Aleksandr Gorshkov, USSR
1980....Natalia Linichuk & Gennadi Karponosov, USSR
1984....Jayne Torvill & Christopher Dean, Great Britain
1988....Natalia Bestemianova & Andrei Bukin, USSR
1992....Marina Klimova & Sergei Ponomarenko, Unified Team
1994....Oksana Gritschuk and Evgeni Platov, Russia

*Competition held at summer games in London.
#Competition held at summer games in Antwerp.

SPEED SKATING

Men

500 METERS

1924....Charles Jewtraw, United States	44.0	
1928....Clas Thunberg, Finland	43.4	OR
Bernt Evensen, Norway	43.4	OR
1932....John Shea, United States	43.4	EOR
1936....Ivar Ballangrud, Norway	43.4	EOR
1948....Finn Helgesen, Norway	43.1	OR
1952....Kenneth Henry, United States	43.2	
1956....Yevgeny Grishin, USSR	40.2	EWR
1960....Yevgeny Grishin, USSR	40.2	EWR
1964....Terry McDermott, United States	40.1	OR
1968....Erhard Keller, West Germany	40.3	
1972....Erhard Keller, West Germany	39.44	OR
1976....Yevgeny Kulikov, USSR	39.17	OR
1980....Eric Heiden, United States	38.03	OR
1984....Sergei Fokichev, USSR	38.19	
1988....Uwe-Jens Mey, East Germany	36.45	WR
1992....Uwe-Jens Mey, East Germany	37.14	
1994....Aleksandr Golubev, Russia	36.33	

1000 METERS

1976....Peter Mueller, United States 1:19.32
1980....Eric Heiden, United States 1:15.18 OR
1984....Gaetan Boucher, Canada 1:15.80
1988....Nikolai Gulyaev, USSR 1:13.03 OR
1992....Olaf Zinke, Germany 1:14.85
1994....Dan Jansen, United States 1:12.43 WR

1500 METERS

1924....Clas Thunberg, Finland 2:20.8
1928....Clas Thunberg, Finland 2:21.1
1932....John Shea, United States 2:57.5
1936....Charles Mathisen, Norway 2:19.2 OR
1948....Sverre Farstad, Norway 2:17.6 OR

1500 METERS *(Cont.)*

1952....Hjalmar Andersen, Norway	2:20.4	
1956....Yevgeny Grishin, USSR	2:08.6	WR
Yuri Mikhailov, USSR	2:08.6	WR
1960....Roald Aas, Norway	2:10.4	
Yevgeny Grishin, USSR	2:10.4	
1964....Ants Anston, USSR	2:10.3	
1968....Cornelis Verkerk, Netherlands	2:03.4	OR
1972....Ard Schenk, Netherlands	2:02.96	OR
1976....Jan Egil Storholt, Norway	1:59.38	OR
1980....Eric Heiden, United States	1:55.44	OR
1984....Gaetan Boucher, Canada	1:58.36	
1988....Andre Hoffmann, East Germany	1:52.06	WR
1992....Johann Olav Koss, Norway	1:54.81	
1994....Johann Olav Koss, Norway	1:51.29	WR

5000 METERS

1924....Clas Thunberg, Finland	8:39.0	
1928....Ivar Ballangrud, Norway	8:50.5	
1932....Irving Jaffee, United States	9:40.8	
1936....Ivar Ballangrud, Norway	8:19.6	OR
1948....Reidar Liaklev, Norway	8:29.4	
1952....Hjalmar Andersen, Norway	8:10.6	OR
1956....Boris Shilkov, USSR	7:48.7	OR
1960....Viktor Kosichkin, USSR	7:51.3	
1964....Knut Johannesen, Norway	7:38.4	OR
1968....Fred Anton Maier, Norway	7:22.4	WR
1972....Ard Schenk, Netherlands	7:23.61	
1976....Sten Stensen, Norway	7:24.48	
1980....Eric Heiden, United States	7:02.29	OR
1984....Sven Tomas Gustafson, Sweden	7:12.28	
1988....Tomas Gustafson, Sweden	6:44.63	WR
1992....Geir Karlstad, Norway	6:59.97	
1994....Johann Olav Koss, Norway	6:34.96	WR

Note: OR=Olympic Record; WR=World Record; EOR=Equals Olympic Record; EWR=Equals World Record; WB=World Best.

SPEED SKATING (Cont.)

Men (Cont.)

10,000 METERS		
1924	Julius Skutnabb, Finland	18:04.8
1928	Not held, thawing of ice	
1932	Irving Jaffee, United States	19:13.6
1936	Ivar Ballangrud, Norway	17:24.3 OR
1948	Ake Seyffarth, Sweden	17:26.3
1952	Hjalmar Andersen, Norway	16:45.8 OR
1956	Sigvard Ericsson, Sweden	16:35.9 OR
1960	Knut Johannesen, Norway	15:46.6 WR
1964	Jonny Nilsson, Sweden	15:50.1

10,000 METERS (Cont.)		
1968	Johnny Höglin, Sweden	15:23.6 OR
1972	Ard Schenk, Netherlands	15:01.35 OR
1976	Piet Kleine, Netherlands	14:50.59 OR
1980	Eric Heiden, United States	14:28.13 WR
1984	Igor Malkov, USSR	14:39.90
1988	Tomas Gustafson, Sweden	13:48.20 WR
1992	Bart Veldkamp, The Netherlands	14:12.12
1994	Johann Olav Koss, Norway	13:30.55 WR

Women

500 METERS		
1960	Helga Haase, East Germany	45.9
1964	Lydia Skoblikova, USSR	45.0 OR
1968	Lyudmila Titova, USSR	46.1
1972	Anne Henning, United States	43.33 OR
1976	Sheila Young, United States	42.76 OR
1980	Karin Enke, East Germany	41.78 OR
1984	Christa Rothenburger, East Germany	41.02 OR
1988	Bonnie Blair, United States	39.10 WR
1992	Bonnie Blair, United States	40.33
1994	Bonnie Blair, United States	39.25

1000 METERS		
1960	Klara Guseva, USSR	1:34.1
1964	Lydia Skoblikova, USSR	1:33.2 OR
1968	Carolina Geijssen, Netherlands	1:32.6 OR
1972	Monika Pflug, West Germany	1:31.40 OR
1976	Tatiana Averina, USSR	1:28.43 OR
1980	Natalya Petruseva, USSR	1:24.10 OR
1984	Karin Enke, East Germany	1:21.61 OR
1988	Christa Rothenburger, East Germany	1:17.65 WR
1992	Bonnie Blair, United States	1:21.90
1994	Bonnie Blair, United States	1:18.74

1500 METERS		
1960	Lydia Skoblikova, USSR	2:25.2 WR
1964	Lydia Skoblikova, USSR	2:22.6 OR
1968	Kaija Mustonen, Finland	2:22.4 OR
1972	Dianne Holum, United States	2:20.85 OR
1976	Galina Stepanskaya, USSR	2:16.58 OR
1980	Anne Borckink, Netherlands	2:10.95 OR
1984	Karin Enke, East Germany	2:03.42 WR
1988	Yvonne van Gennip, Netherlands	2:00.68 OR
1992	Jacqueline Boerner, Germany	2:05.87
1994	Emese Hunyady, Austria	2:02.19

3000 METERS		
1960	Lydia Skoblikova, USSR	5:14.3
1964	Lydia Skoblikova, USSR	5:14.9
1968	Johanna Schut, Netherlands	4:56.2 OR
1972	Christina Baas-Kaiser, Netherlands	4:52.14 OR
1976	Tatiana Averina, USSR	4:45.19 OR
1980	Bjorg Eva Jensen, Norway	4:32.13 OR
1984	Andrea Schöne, East Germany	4:24.79 OR
1988	Yvonne van Gennip, Netherlands	4:11.94 WR
1992	Gunda Niemann, Germany	4:19.90
1994	Svetlana Bazhanova, Russia	4:17.43

5000 METERS		
1988	Yvonne van Gennip, Netherlands	7:14.13 WR
1992	Gunda Niemann, Germany	7:31.57
1994	Claudia Pechstein, Germany	7:14.37

SHORT TRACK SPEED SKATING

Men

500 METERS		
1994	Chae Ji-Hoon, South Korea	43.54

1000 METERS		
1992	Kim Ki-Hoon, South Korea	1:30.76 WR
1994	Kim Ki-Hoon, South Korea	1:34.57

5000-METER RELAY		
1992	Korea	7:14.02 WR
1994	Italy	7:11.74 OR

Women

500 METERS		
1992	Cathy Turner, United States	47.04
1994	Cathy Turner, United States	45.98 OR

1000 METERS		
1994	Chun Lee-Kyung, South Korea	1:36.87

3000-METER RELAY		
1992	Canada	4:36.62
1994	South Korea	4:26.64 OR

ALPINE SKIING

Men

DOWNHILL

1948	Henri Oreiller, France	2:55.0
1952	Zeno Colo, Italy	2:30.8
1956	Anton Sailer, Austria	2:52.2
1960	Jean Vuarnet, France	2:06.0
1964	Egon Zimmermann, Austria	2:18.16
1968	Jean-Claude Killy, France	1:59.85
1972	Bernhard Russi, Switzerland	1:51.43
1976	Franz Klammer, Austria	1:45.73
1980	Leonhard Stock, Austria	1:45.50
1984	Bill Johnson, United States	1:45.59
1988	Pirmin Zurbriggen, Switzerland	1:59.63
1992	Patrick Ortlieb, Austria	1:50.37
1994	Tommy Moe, United States	1:45.75

SUPER GIANT SLALOM

1988	Franck Piccard, France	1:39.66
1992	Kjetil Andre Aamodt, Norway	1:13.04
1994	Markus Wasmeier, Germany	1:32.53

GIANT SLALOM

1952	Stein Eriksen, Norway	2:25.0
1956	Anton Sailer, Austria	3:00.1
1960	Roger Staub, Switzerland	1:48.3
1964	Francois Bonlieu, France	1:46.71
1968	Jean-Claude Killy, France	3:29.28
1972	Gustav Thöni, Italy	3:09.62
1976	Heini Hemmi, Switzerland	3:26.97
1980	Ingemar Stenmark, Sweden	2:40.74
1984	Max Julen, Switzerland	2:41.18
1988	Alberto Tomba, Italy	2:06.37
1992	Alberto Tomba, Italy	2:06.98
1994	Markus Wasmeier, Germany	2:52.46

SLALOM

1948	Edi Reinalter, Switzerland	2:10.3
1952	Othmar Schneider, Austria	2:00.0
1956	Anton Sailer, Austria	3:14.7
1960	Ernst Hinterseer, Austria	2:08.9
1964	Josef Stiegler, Austria	2:11.13
1968	Jean-Claude Killy, France	1:39.73
1972	Francisco Fernandez Ochoa, Spain	1:49.27
1976	Piero Gros, Italy	2:03.29
1980	Ingemar Stenmark, Sweden	1:44.26
1984	Phil Mahre, United States	1:39.41
1988	Alberto Tomba, Italy	1:39.47
1992	Finn Christian Jagge, Norway	1:44.39
1994	Thomas Stangassinger, Austria	2:02.02

*COMBINED

		Pts
1936	Franz Pfnür, Germany	99.25
1948	Henri Oreiller, France	3.27
1988	Hubert Strolz, Austria	36.55
1992	Josef Polig, Italy	14.58
1994	Lasse Kjus, Norway	3:17.53

*Beginning in 1994, scoring was based on time.

Women

DOWNHILL

1948	Hedy Schlunegger, Switzerland	2:28.3
1952	Trude Jochum-Beiser, Austria	1:47.1
1956	Madeleine Berthod, Switzerland	1:40.7
1960	Heidi Biebl, West Germany	1:37.6
1964	Christl Haas, Austria	1:55.39
1968	Olga Pall, Austria	1:40.87
1972	Marie-Theres Nadig, Switzerland	1:36.68
1976	Rosi Mittermaier, West Germany	1:46.16
1980	Annemarie Moser-Pröll, Austria	1:37.52
1984	Michela Figini, Switzerland	1:13.36
1988	Marina Kiehl, West Germany	1:25.86
1992	Kerrin Lee-Gartner, Canada	1:52.55
1994	Katja Seizinger, Germany	1:35.93

SUPER GIANT SLALOM

1988	Sigrid Wolf, Austria	1:19.03
1992	Deborah Compagnoni, Italy	1:21.22
1994	Diann Roffe-Steinrotter, U.S.	1:22.15

GIANT SLALOM

1952	Andrea Mead Lawrence, United States	2:06.8
1956	Ossi Reichert, West Germany	1:56.5
1960	Yvonne Rüegg, Switzerland	1:39.9
1964	Marielle Goitschel, France	1:52.24
1968	Nancy Greene, Canada	1:51.97
1972	Marie-Theres Nadig, Switzerland	1:29.90
1976	Kathy Kreiner, Canada	1:29.13
1980	Hanni Wenzel, Liechtenstein (2 runs)	2:41.66
1984	Debbie Armstrong, United States	2:20.98
1988	Vreni Schneider, Switzerland	2:06.49
1992	Pernilla Wiberg, Sweden	2:12.74
1994	Deborah Compagnoni, Italy	2:30.97

SLALOM

1948	Gretchen Fraser, United States	1:57.2
1952	Andrea Mead Lawrence, United States	2:10.6
1956	Renee Colliard, Switzerland	1:52.3
1960	Anne Heggtveigt, Canada	1:49.6
1964	Christine Goitschel, France	1:29.86
1968	Marielle Goitschel, France	1:25.86
1972	Barbara Cochran, United States	1:31.24
1976	Rosi Mittermaier, West Germany	1:30.54
1980	Hanni Wenzel, Liechtenstein	1:25.09
1984	Paoletta Magoni, Italy	1:36.47
1988	Vreni Schneider, Switzerland	1:36.69
1992	Petra Kronberger, Austria	1:32.68
1994	Vreni Schneider, Switzerland	1:56.01

*COMBINED

		Pts
1988	Anita Wachter, Austria	29.25
1992	Petra Kronberger, Austria	2.55
1994	Pernilla Wiberg, Sweden	3:05.16

NORDIC SKIING

Men

15 KILOMETERS (CLASSICAL)

1924	Thorlief Haug, Norway	*1:14:31.0
1928	Johan Gröttumsbraaten, Norway	†1:37:01.0
1932	Sven Utterström, Sweden	‡1:23:07.0
1936	Erik-August Larsson, Sweden	*14:38.0
1948	Martin Lundström, Sweden	*13:50.0
1952	Hallgeir Brenden, Norway	*1:34.0
1956	Hallgeir Brenden, Norway	49:39.0
1960	Haakon Brusveen, Norway	51:55.5
1964	Eero Mantyränta, Finland	50:54.1
1968	Harald Grönningen, Norway	47:54.2
1972	Sven-Ake Lundback, Sweden	45:28.24
1976	Nikolay Bajukov, Unified Team	43:58.47
1980	Thomas Wassberg, Sweden	41:57.63
1984	Gunde Swan, Sweden	41:25.6
1988	Michael Deviatyarov, USSR	41:18.9
1992	Vegard Ulvang, Norway	**27:36.0
1994	Bjorn Daehlie, Norway	**24:20.1

*Distance was 18 km; †Distance was 19.7 km;
‡Distance was 18.2 km; **Distance was 10 km.

30 KILOMETERS (CLASSICAL)

1956	Veikko Hakulinen, Finland	1:44:06.0
1960	Sixten Jernberg, Sweden	1:51:03.9
1964	Eero Mantyränta, Finland	1:30:50.7
1968	Franco Nones, Italy	1:35:39.2
1972	Viaceslav Vedenine, USSR	1:36:31.2
1976	Sergei Savelyev, USSR	1:30:29.38
1980	Nikolai Simyatov, USSR	1:27:02.80
1984	Nikolai Simyatov, USSR	1:28:56.3
1988	Alexey Prokororov, USSR	1:24:26.3
1992	Vegard Ulvang, Norway	1:22:27.8
1994	Thomas Alsgaard, Norway	1:12:26.4

50 KILOMETERS (FREESTYLE)

1924	Thorleif Haug, Norway	3:44:32.0
1928	Per Erik Hedlund, Sweden	4:52:03.0
1932	Veli Saarinen, Finland	4:28:00.0
1936	Elis Wiklund, Sweden	3:30:11.0
1948	Nils Karlsson, Sweden	3:47:48.0
1952	Veikko Hakulinen, Finland	3:33:33.0
1956	Sixten Jernberg, Sweden	2:50:27.0
1960	Kalevi Hämäläinen, Finland	2:59:06.3
1964	Sixten Jernberg, Sweden	2:43:52.6
1968	Olle Ellefsaeter, Norway	2:28:45.8
1972	Paal Tyldrum, Norway	2:43:14.75
1976	Ivar Formo, Norway	2:37:30.50
1980	Nikolai Simyatov, USSR	2:27:24.60
1984	Thomas Wassberg, Sweden	2:15:55.8
1988	Gunde Svan, Sweden	2:04:30.9
1992	Bjorn Dählie, Norway	2:03:41.5
1994	Vladimir Smirnov, Kazakhstan	2:07:20.3

15 KILOMETERS (FREESTYLE)

1992	Bjorn Dählie, Norway	1:05:37.9
1994	Bjorn Dählie, Norway	1:00:08.8

4 X 10 KILOMETER RELAY

1936	Finland	2:41:33.0
1948	Sweden	2:32:80.0
1952	Finland	2:20:16.0
1956	USSR	2:15:30.0
1960	Finland	2:18:45.6
1964	Sweden	2:18:34.6
1968	Norway	2:08:33.5
1972	USSR	2:04:47.94
1976	Finland	2:07:59.72
1980	USSR	1:57:03.46
1984	Sweden	1:55:06.3
1988	Sweden	1:43:58.6
1992	Norway	1:39:26.0
1994	Italy	1:41:15.0

SKI JUMPING (NORMAL HILL)

		Pts
1964	Veikko Kankkonen, Finland	229.90
1968	Jiri Raska, Czechoslovakia	216.5
1972	Yukio Kasaya, Japan	244.2
1976	Hans-Georg Aschenbach, East Germany	252.0
1980	Toni Innauer, Austria	266.3
1984	Jens Weissflog, East Germany	215.2
1988	Matti Nykänen, Finland	229.1
1992	Ernst Vettori, Austria	222.8
1994	Espen Bredesen, Norway	282.0

SKI JUMPING (LARGE HILL)

		Pts
1924	Jacob Tullin Thams, Norway	18.960
1928	Alf Andersen, Norway	19.208
1932	Birger Ruud, Norway	228.1
1936	Birger Ruud, Norway	232.0
1948	Petter Hugsted, Norway	228.1
1952	Arnfinn Bergmann, Norway	226.0
1956	Antti Hyvärinen, Finland	227.0
1960	Helmut Recknagel, East Germany	227.2
1964	Toralf Engan, Norway	230.70
1968	Vladimir Beloussov, USSR	231.3
1972	Wojciech Fortuna, Poland	219.9
1976	Karl Schnabl, Austria	234.8
1980	Jouko Tormanen, Finland	271.0
1984	Matti Nykänen, Finland	231.2
1988	Matti Nykänen, Finland	224.0
1992	Toni Nieminen, Finland	239.5
1994	Jens Weissflog, Germany	274.5

TEAM SKI JUMPING

		Pts
1988	Finland	634.4
1992	Finland	644.4
1994	Germany	970.1

NORDIC SKIING *(Cont.)*

Men *(Cont.)*

NORDIC COMBINED

	Pts
*1924 ..Thorleif Haug, Norway	18.906
*1928 ..Johan Gröttumsbraaten, Norway	17.833
1932....Johan Gröttumsbraaten, Norway	446.0
1936....Oddbjörn Hagen, Norway	430.30
1948....Heikki Hasu, Finland	448.80
1952....Simon Slattvik, Norway	451.621
1956....Sverre Stenersen, Norway	455.0
1960....Georg Thoma, West Germany	457.952
1964....Tormod Knutsen, Norway	469.28
1968....Frantz Keller, West Germany	449.04
1972....Ulrich Wehling, East Germany	413.34
1976....Ulrich Wehling, East Germany	423.39
1980....Ulrich Wehling, East Germany	432.20

NORDIC COMBINED *(Cont.)*

	Pts
1984....Tom Sandberg, Norway	422.595
1988....Hippolyt Kempf, Switzerland	432.230
1992....Fabrice Guy, France	426.47
1994....Fred B. Lundberg, Norway	457.970

TEAM NORDIC COMBINED

1988....West Germany	
1992....Japan	
1994....Japan	

*Different scoring system; 1924–1952 distance was 18 km; 1952–present, 15 km.

Women

5 KILOMETERS (CLASSICAL)

1964....Klaudia Boyarskikh, USSR	17:50.5
1968....Toini Gustafsson, Sweden	16:45.2
1972....Galina Kulakova, USSR	17:00.50
1976....Helena Takalo, Finland	15:48.69
1980....Raisa Smetanina, USSR	15:06.92
1984....Marja-Liisa Hamalainen, Finland	17:04.0
1988....Marjo Matikainen, Finland	15:04.0
1992....Marjut Lukkarinen, Finland	14:13.8
1994....Lyubova Egorova, Russia	14:08.8

10 KILOMETERS (CLASSICAL)

1952....Lydia Widemen, Finland	41:40.0
1956....Lyubov Kosyryeva, USSR	38:11.0
1960....Maria Gusakova, USSR	39:46.6
1964....Klaudia Boyarskikh, USSR	40:24.3
1968....Toini Gustafsson, Sweden	36:46.5
1972....Galina Kulakova, USSR	34:17.8
1976....Raisa Smetanina, USSR	30:13.41
1980....Barbara Petzold, East Germany	30:31.54
1984....Marja-Lisa Hamalainen, Finland	31:44.2
1988....Vida Ventsene, USSR	30:08.3

15 KILOMETERS (CLASSICAL)

1992....Lyubov Egorova, Unified Team	42:20.8
1994....Manuela Di Centa, Italy	39:44.5

20 KILOMETERS (FREESTYLE)

1984....Marja-Liisa Hamalainen, Finland	1:01:45.0
1988....Tamara Tikhonova, USSR	55:53.6

30 KILOMETERS (FREESTYLE)

1992....Stefania Belmondo, Italy	1:22:30.1
1994....Manuela Di Centa, Italy	1:25:41.6

10 KILOMETERS (FREESTYLE PURSUIT)

1992....Lyubov Egorova, Unified Team	40:07.7
1994....Lyubov Egorova, Russia	41:38.1

4 X 5-KILOMETER RELAY

1956....Finland	1:9:01.0
1960....Sweden	1:4:21.4
1964....USSR	59:20.0
1968....Norway	57:30.0
1972....USSR	48:46.15
1976....USSR	1:07:49.75
1980....East Germany	1:02:11.10
1984....Norway	1:06:49.7
1988....USSR	59:51.1
1992....Unified Team	59:34.8
1994....Russia	57:12.5

Note: 10 km (classical) changed to 15 km (classical) in 1992; 20 km (freestyle) changed to 30 km (freestyle).

FREESTYLE SKIING

Men
MOGUL

	Pts
1992....Edgar Grospiron, France	25.81
1994....Jean-Luc Brassard, Canada	27.24

AERIAL

	Pts
1994....Andreas Schoenbaechler, Swi	234.67

Women
MOGUL

	Pts
1992....Donna Weinbrecht, United States	23.69
1994....Stine Lise Hattestad, Norway	25.97

AERIAL

	Pts
1994....Lina Cherjazova, Uzbekistan	166.84

Track and Field

BILL FRAKES

Atlanta Burning

Michael Johnson torched the track in an unforgettable Olympic performance
by Merrell Noden

RARELY DOES an entire year's worth of track and field reach a climax as astonishing and unmistakable as this one did on Aug. 1, the day of the men's 200 final at the Atlanta Olympics. On that sultry evening Michael Johnson, running with the peculiar low knee lift and arched back that are his trademarks, sprinted down the homestretch like a man pursued by demons. Johnson's friend Denver Broncos cornerback Ray Crockett would later describe the sight best, telling Johnson that it had looked as if he were driving a car off the turn. By the time he had reached the finish, Johnson had put nearly five meters of red Mondo track between himself and runner-up Frankie Fredericks of Namibia.

The eye, knowing it had seen something amazing, jumped to the huge digital clock in the infield. It registered an incomprehensible number—19.32—a time so seemingly beyond the current reach of men that not even a man as ambitious and bold as Johnson had guessed it was attainable. "I am rarely shocked by my own performance," said Johnson, who had set the previous record of 19.66 six weeks earlier on this same track at the U.S. trials. "And I am shocked."

With that one race Johnson not only completed the first successful 200/400 double in Olympic history, he also wrested the crown of world's top track and field athlete from Carl Lewis. Not that Lewis surrendered it willingly. With his usual instinct for drama, Lewis had made the U.S. Olympic team in only one event, the long jump, and had done so by a mere inch; in the qualifying round at the Olympics he had needed his final jump to qualify for the final.

On July 29, four weeks after turning 35, Lewis won his fourth straight Olympic long jump title with a third-round leap of 27' 10¾". Among track and field athletes, only discus thrower Al Oerter had won four titles in the same event. With nine gold medals in all, Lewis has surely had the greatest career of any Olympic track and field athlete. But when the Olympic flame was finally extinguished, on Aug. 4, there was no doubt that Johnson had been the brightest star of these Games.

And that is saying something, for the Atlanta Games must rank among the greatest in history. Attendance was nothing short of phenomenal, averaging 77,638 for each session, including mornings. What a meet they saw! Among the athletes who merely underscored their greatness by winning gold medals were Noureddine Morceli in the 1,500, Haile Gebrselassie in the 10,000 and Dan O'Brien in the decathlon. Donovan Bailey of Canada set a world record in the 100, winning the most wide-open Olympic 100 in history in 9.84 seconds. Vebjørn Rodal of Norway won a titanic battle over the deepest 800 field ever: Norberto Tellez of Cuba ran 1:42.85—which was faster than all previous gold medalists—and finished fourth.

Like Johnson, Marie-José Pérec of France and Svetlana Masterkova of Russia achieved memorable doubles. The long-legged Pérec, a sometime runway model, became the first person to win two Olympic 400 titles, winning in 48.25—the fastest 400 in 10 years—then added the 200 gold, in 22.12. Masterkova, who had retired from the sport in 1994 to have a daughter, used her killer kick to win both the 800 and the 1,500. (After the Games, in Zurich, Masterkova set the only significant women's world record of the year, running the mile in 4:12.56.)

Prior to the Games it had looked as if their highlight might be the ongoing—and not always friendly—rivalry in the 100 between defending Olympic champion Gail Devers and world champion Gwen Torrence, who would be competing in front of her hometown crowd. Torrence beat Devers at the U.S. trials in June but pulled her thigh in doing so. At the Games, Torrence finished third and seemed relieved to have finished even that high. Devers crossed the line first in 10.94 seconds, beating Merlene Ottey in a photo finish.

The Games brought mixed joy to Devers. Though her boyfriend, Kenny Harrison, won

BILL FRAKES

Pérec glided to an unprecedented second Olympic 400 title.

the triple jump in an American record 59' 4¼", her training partner, Jackie Joyner-Kersee, strained her right hamstring in the first event of the heptathlon, the hurdles, and was pulled from the event by her husband and coach, Bob Kersee. Somehow she came back to compete in the long jump, where her best leap of 22' 11¾" placed her third.

With the business of winning medals completed, running fast was the clear aim of the post-Olympic season. Kenyans seemed to be everywhere, especially two who had missed the Olympics. Twenty-year-old Daniel Komen, who had finished fourth in the 5,000 at the Kenyan trials, made up for that disappointment by lowering the world record in the 3,000 from 7:25.11 to 7:20.67, a Johnsonesque improvement. Transplanted Kenyan Wilson Kipketer, ruled ineligible to compete in the Olympics for his adoptive Denmark, set his sights on Seb Coe's ancient 800 mark of 1:41.73. Kipketer broke 1:43 a record seven times this season, topped by a 1:41.83. Salah Hissou of Morocco, the bronze medalist in the 10,000, broke Gebrselassie's world record for that distance, clocking 26:38.08 in Brussels.

Somewhat surprisingly, Johnson did not set any further records. His post-Olympic season was delayed by a hamstring strain he suffered at the end of the 200. One wonders what new goals he will set for himself. Surely he will aim for Butch Reynolds's eight-year-old record in the 400, where Johnson's win streak has now reached 57, dating back to 1989. In truth, though, in the span of six glorious days, he did all he needed to do to earn a place with Lewis in the Olympic pantheon.

U.S. Olympic Trials

Atlanta, Ga., June 14–17, 19, 21–23, 1996

Men

100 METERS

1. ....Dennis Mitchell, Mizuno TC 9.92
2. ....Michael Marsh, Santa Monica TC 10.00
3. ....Jon Drummond, Nike 10.02

200 METERS

1. ....Michael Johnson, Nike Intl .....19.66 WR
2. ....Jeff Williams, Mizuno TC 20.03
3. ....Michael Marsh, Santa Monica TC ...20.04

400 METERS

1. ....Michael Johnson, Nike Intl 43.44
2. ....Butch Reynolds, Foot Locker AC 43.91
3. ....Alvin Harrison, Nike 44.09

800 METERS

1. ....Johnny Gray, Santa Monica TC 1:44.00
2. ....Brandon Rock, Powerade 1:44.84
3. ....Jose Parilla, adidas 1:44.86

1500 METERS

1. ....Paul McMullen, Asics 3:43.86
2. ....Jim Sorensen, Athletes in Action ..3:43.88
3. ....Jason Pyrah, Mizuno TC 3:44.08

STEEPLECHASE

1. ....Mark Croghan, adidas 8:18.80
2. ....Robert Gary, unat 8:19.26
3. ....Marc Davis, Nike 8:20.73

5000 METERS

1. ....Bob Kennedy, Nike Intl 13:46.17
2. ....Matt Giusto, Foot Locker AC 13:56.69
3. ....Ronnie Harris, Reebok E 13:57.49

10,000 METERS

1. ....Todd Williams, adidas 28:46.58
2. ....Joe LeMay, adidas RR 29:06.89
3. ....Dan Middleman, NYAC 29:13.81

110-METER HURDLES

1. ....Allen Johnson, Nike ....12.92 AR
2. ....Mark Crear, Reebok 13.05
3. ....Eugene Swift, InSport 13.21

400-METER HURDLES

1. ....Bryan Bronson, Powerade 47.98
2. ....Derrick Adkins, Reebok RC 48.18
3. ....Calvin Davis, Nike 48.32

20-KILOMETER WALK

1. ....Curt Clausen, Shore AC 1:29:50
2. ....Tim Seaman, La Grange TC 1:30:27
3. ....Gary Morgan, NYAC 1:31:00

HIGH JUMP

1. ....Charles Austin, unat ....7 ft 6½ in
2. ....Ed Broxterman, Kansas State ...7 ft 6½ in
3. ....Cameron Wright, unat ....7 ft 6½ in

POLE VAULT

1. ....Lawrence Johnson, Tennessee ..19 ft ¼ in
2. ....Jeff Hartwig, Bell Athletics ....19 ft ¼ in
3. ....Scott Huffman, Foot Locker AC ..18 ft 8¼ in

LONG JUMP

1. ....Mike Powell, Foot Locker AC ..27 ft 6½ in
2. ....Joe Greene, Goldwin TC ......27 ft 4½ in w
3. ....Carl Lewis, Santa Monica ....27 ft 2¾ in

TRIPLE JUMP

1. ....Kenny Harrison, Nike ....59 ft 1½ in w
2. ....Mike Conley, Foot Locker AC ..57 ft 7¾ in
3. ....Robert Howard, Arkansas ....56 ft 4¾ in

SHOT PUT

1. ....Randy Barnes, Goldwin TC .....70 ft 1½ in
2. ....John Godina, Reebok RC ....69 ft 6¼ in
3. ...........C.J. Hunter, Nike ....69 ft 1½ in

DISCUS THROW

1. ....Anthony Washington, USW ....216 ft 1 in
2. ....John Godina, Reebok RC ....211 ft 10 in
3. ....Adam Setliff, SSTC ....207 ft 7 in

HAMMER THROW

1. ....Lance Deal, NYAC ....249 ft 4 in
2. ....David Popejoy, NYAC ....243 ft 8 in
3. ....Kevin McMahon, Reebok E .....241 ft 5 in

JAVELIN THROW

1. ....Todd Riech, Nike ....268 ft 7 in
2. ....Tom Pukstys, adidas ....267 ft 8 in
3. ....Breaux Greer, unat ....262 ft 5 in

DECATHLON

1. ....Dan O'Brien, Foot Locker AC ...8726 pts.
2. ....Steve Fritz, Accusplit ....8636 pts.
3. ....Chris Huffins, Mizuno ....8546 pts.

MARATHON*

1. ....Bob Kempainen, Nike 2:12:45
2. ....Mark Coogan, New Balance 2:13:05
3. ....Keith Brantley, New Balance 2:13:22

WR=World record. AR=American record. w=wind aided. *Held Feb. 17, 1996 in Charlotte, N.C.

Women

100 METERS

1.	Gwen Torrence, Nike	10.82
2.	Gail Devers, Nike	10.91
3.	D'Andre Hill, Louisiana State	10.92

200 METERS

1.	Carlette Guidry, adidas	22.14
2.	Dannette Young-Stone, Reebok	22.18
3.	Inger Miller, unat	22.25

400 METERS

1.	Maicel Malone, Asics	50.52
2.	Jearl Miles, Reebok RC	50.61
3.	Kim Graham, Asics	50.87

800 METERS

1.	Meredith Rainey, Foot Locker AC	1:57.04
2.	Joetta Clark, Foot Locker AC	1:58.22
3.	Suzy Hamilton, Reebok	1:59.04

1500 METERS

1.	Regina Jacobs, Mizuno TC	4:08.67
2.	Juli Henner, Reebok E	4:09.49
3.	Vicki Huber, Asics	4:11.23

5,000 METERS

1.	Lynn Jennings, Nike	15:28.18
2.	Mary Slaney, Nike	15:29.39
3.	Amy Rudolph, Reebok	15:29:91

10,000 METERS

1.	Kate Fonshell, Asics	32:37.91
2.	Olga Appell, Reebok	32:43.79
3.	Joan Nesbit, New Balance	32:46.77

10,000 METER WALK

1.	Debbi Lawrence, NS	46:05
2.	Michelle Rohl, Park	46:37
3.	Victoria Herazo, Calif. Walkers	48:12

100-METER HURDLES

1.	Gail Devers, Nike I	12.62
2.	Lynda Goode, Goldwin	12.69
3.	Cheryl Dickey, unat	12.76

400-METER HURDLES

1.	Kim Batten, Reebok RC	53.81
2.	Tonja Buford-Bailey, Nike	53.92
3.	Sandra Farmer-Patrick, Nike	54.07

HIGH JUMP

1.	Tisha Waller, Goldwin	6 ft 4¾ in
2.	Connie Teabury, Goldwin	6 ft 4¾ in
3.	Amy Acuff, UCLA	6 ft 3½ in

LONG JUMP

1.	Jackie Joyner-Kersee, Honda	23 ft 1¼ in w
2.	Shana Williams, Nike	22 ft 9 in
3.	Marieke Veltman, Reebok	22 ft 7 in

TRIPLE JUMP

1.	Cynthea Rhodes, unat	46 ft 1½ in
2.	Sheila Hudson, Reebok	46 ft 1¼ in
3.	Diana Orrange, Nike	46 ft 5 in

SHOT PUT

1	Connie Price-Smith, Reebok RC	62 ft 7¾ in
2.	Ramona Pagel, Nike	61 ft ¼ in
3.	Dawn Dumble, Reebok	58 ft 2 in

DISCUS THROW

1.	Suzy Powell, UCLA	198 ft 9 in
2.	Lacy Barnes-Mileham, Nike	195 ft 9 in
3.	Aretha Hill, Washington	190 ft 5 in

JAVELIN

1	Nicole Carroll, unat	188 ft 11 in
2	Windy Dean, SMU	187 ft 4 in
3.	Lynda Lipson, Klub Keihas	184 ft 9 in

HEPTATHLON

1	Kelly Blair, Nike	6406 pts.
2	Jackie Joyner-Kersee, Honda	6403 pts.
3.	Sharon Hanson, unat	6352 pts.

MARATHON*

1	Jenny Spangler, Santa Monica TC	2:29:54
2	Linda Somers, adidas	2:30:06
3.	Anne Marie Lauck, Nike	2:31:18

w=wind aided. *Held Feb 10, 1996 in Columbia, S.C.

THEY SAID IT

Ruth Wysocki, the former U.S. Olympic distance runner, on her relationship with the Brooks footwear company: "In 1984 my shoe sponsor said it would take care of me for life. I guess I died in 1988."

USATF Indoor Championships

Atlanta, Ga., March 1–2, 1996

Men

60 METERS
1.	Donovan Powell, Jamaica	6.55
2.	Keith Williams, Griffin	6.56
3.	Michael Marsh, Santa Monica TC	6.60

200 METERS
1.	Kevin Little, USW	20.46
2.	Jeff Williams, unat	20.61
3.	Dave Dopek, Powerade	20.70

400 METERS
1.	Michael Johnson, Nike	44.66
2.	Derek Mills, Powerade	45.60
3.	Marlon Ramsey, Baylor	45.86

800 METERS
1.	Brandon Rock, Powerade	1:48.71
2.	David Kiptoo, Kenya	1:48.75
3.	Rich Kenah, Reebok E	1:49.20

MILE
1.	Steve Holman, Reebok	3:57.72
2.	Jason Pyrah, Mizuno TC	3:58.89
3.	Marcus O'Sullivan, Ireland	3:58.98

3,000 METERS
1.	Khalid Kairouani, Morocco	7:46.77
2.	Bob Kennedy, Nike	7:47.41
3.	Brian Baker, New Balance	7:47.47

60-METER HURDLES
1.	Courtney Hawkins, adidas	7.46
2.	Allen Johnson, Nike	7.50
3.	Derek Knight, Elite Athletes	7.65

5,000-METER WALK
1.	Allen James, Athletes in Action	20:02.59
2.	Gary Morgan, NYAC	20:06.02
3.	Curt Clausen, Shore AC	20:17.96

4 X 400 METER RELAY
1.	Ohio State (Clive Brooks, Adam Herrdon, Nikia Fenner, Marlon DeLeon)	3:09.19
2.	Texas-Arlington	3:09.20
3.	Texas Christian	3:09.84

DISTANCE MEDLEY RELAY
1.	Tennessee (Junior Sloan, Shane Begnaud, Mike Moran, Tony Cosey)	9:43.77
2.	NYAC	9:43.85
3.	Air Force	9:46.79

HIGH JUMP
1.	Charles Austin, unat	7 ft 9¼ in*
2.	Randy Jenkins, Nike	7 ft 5¾ in
3.	Hollis Conway, Reebok	7 ft 3¾ in

POLE VAULT
1.	Pat Manson, Goldwin TC	18 ft 8¼ in
2.	David Cox, unat	18 ft 6½ in
3.	Kory Tarpenning, Nike	18 ft 6½ in

LONG JUMP
1.	Erick Walder, adidas	26 ft 7 in
2.	Kareem Streete-Thompson, Nike	26 ft 1¾ in
3.	Mike Conley, Foot Locker AC	25 ft 11 in

TRIPLE JUMP
1.	LaMark Carter, Powerade	56 ft 2 in
2.	Desmond Hunt, unat	55 ft 2 in
3.	Jerome Romain, Dominican R	54 ft 11¼ in

SHOT PUT
1.	John Godina, Reebok	66 ft 9¾ in
2.	C.J. Hunter, Powerade	66 ft 5¼ in
3.	Ron Backes, NYAC	63 ft 7¾ in

35-POUND WEIGHT THROW
1.	Lance Deal, NYAC	83 ft 7¼ in
2.	Louis Chisari, NYAC	73 ft 7½ in
3.	Boris Stoikos, Canada	71 ft 3½ in

*Meet record.

Women

60 METERS

1.	Gwen Torrence, Mizuno TC	7.05
2.	Celena Mondie-Milner, Powerade	7.17
3.	Holli Hyche, adidas	7.24

200 METERS

1.	Gwen Torrence, Mizuno TC	22.33 AR
2.	Dannette Young, Reebok	22.71
3.	Carlette Guidry, adidas	22.97

400 METERS

1.	Maicel Malone, Asics	51.49
2.	Jearl Miles, Reebok	51.57
3.	Shanelle Porter, USW	52.06

800 METERS

1.	Joetta Clark, Foot Locker AC	2:00.90
2.	Julie Jenkins-Donley, unat	2:01.16
3.	Alisa Hill, unat	2:01.65

MILE

1.	Stephanie Best, Mountain West	4:34.67
2.	Sarah Thorsett, Powerade	4:35.00
3.	Kathy Franey, Nike	4:35.73

3,000 METERS

1.	Joan Nesbit, New Balance	8:56.01
2.	Amy Rudolph, Reebok	9:00.58
3.	Fran ten Bensel, New Balance	9:14.52

60-METER HURDLES

1.	Michelle Freeman, Jamaica	7.91
2.	Tonya Lawson, Anderson Intl	7.98
3.	Cheryl Dickey, Nike	8.08

3,000-METER WALK

1.	Michelle Rohl, Parkside AC	12:55.90
2.	Maryanne Torrellas, Abr	13:09.35
3.	Victoria Herazo, Calif. Walkers	13:12.29

4 X 400 METER RELAY

Final cancelled.
No. 1 qualifier: Louisiana St (LaTasha Stroman, Charlene Maulseed, Sheila Powell, Astia Walker)　3:36.37

DISTANCE MEDLEY RELAY

1.	Auburn (Amanda Patrick, Eusheka Bartley, Janet Trujillo, Rachel Sauder)	11:19.69
2.	Alabama	11:33.70
3.	North Carolina	11:34.02

HIGH JUMP

1.	Tisha Waller, Goldwin	6 ft 6¼ in
2.	Angela Bradburn, Powerade	6 ft 3½ in
3.	Clare Look-Jaeger, Nike	6 ft 3½ in

POLE VAULT

1.	Stacy Dragila, unat	13 ft 5¼ in AR
2.	Melissa Price, Fresno St	13 ft 1¼ in
3.	Kellie Suttle, Bell Athletics	12 ft 7¼ in

LONG JUMP

1.	Shana Williams, Nike	22 ft 3¼ in
2.	Marieke Veltman, Reebok	21 ft 2½ in
3.	DeDe Nathan, Nike	21 ft ¾ in

TRIPLE JUMP

1.	Sheila Hudson, Reebok	46 ft 7½ in
2.	Cynthea Rhodes, unat	45 ft 8½ in
3.	Carla Shannon, unat	44 ft 3¼ in

SHOT PUT

1.	Connie Price-Smith, Reebok	61 ft 9 in
2.	Ramona Pagel, Nike	58 ft 11½ in
3.	Valeyta Mahone, UCLA	58 ft 8½ in

20-POUND WEIGHT THROW

1.	Dawn Ellerbe, S Carolina	65 ft 1¼ in
2.	Lisa Misipeka, S Carolina	60 ft 7¼ in
3.	Gladys Nortey, Louisiana St	59 ft 1¼ in

AR=American record.

IAAF World Cross-Country Championships

Stellenbosch, South Africa, March 23, 1996

MEN (12,100 METERS; 7.5 MILES)

1.	Paul Tergat, Kenya	33:44
2.	Salah Hissou, Morocco	33:56
3.	Ismael Kirui, Kenya	33:57

WOMEN (6,350 METERS; 3.94 MILES)

1.	Gete Wami, Ethiopia	20:12
2.	Rose Cheruiwot, Kenya	20:18
3.	Naomi Mugo, Kenya	20:21

Major Marathons

New York City: November 12, 1995

MEN

1.	German Silva, Mexico	2:11:00
2.	Paul Evans, Great Britain	2:11:05
3.	William Koech, Kenya	2:11:19

WOMEN

1.	Tecla Loroupe, Kenya	2:28:06
2.	Manuela Machado, Portugal	2:30:37
3.	Lieve Slegers, Belgium	2:32:08

Tokyo: November 19, 1995

WOMEN ONLY

1.	Junko Asari, Japan	2:28:46
2.	Valentina Yegorova, Russia	2:28:48
3.	Mariko Hara, Japan	2:28:50

Fukuoka, Japan: December 3, 1995

MEN ONLY

1.	Luis dos Santos, Brazil	2:09:30
2.	Antonio Serrano, Spain	2:09:32
3.	Masaki Ohya, Japan	2:09:33

Honolulu: December 10, 1995

MEN

1.	Josia Thugwane, South Africa	2:16:08
2.	Benson Masya, Kenya	2:16:19
3.	Jimmy Muindi, Kenya	2:17:55

WOMEN

1.	Colleen de Reuck, South Africa	2:37:29
2.	Veronica Kanga, Kenya	2:39:35
3.	Carla Beurskens, Netherlands	2:42:27

Los Angeles: March 3, 1996

MEN

1.	Jose Luis Molina, Costa Rica	2:13:23
2.	Alfredo Vigueras, Mexico	2:13:26
3.	Julio Hernandez, Colombia	2:14:50

WOMEN

1.	Lyubov Klochko, Ukraine	2:30:30
2.	Lucia Rendon, Mexico	2:34:55
3.	Maria del Carmen Diaz, Mexico	2:35:18

Boston: April 15, 1996

MEN

1.	Moses Tanui, Kenya	2:09:16
2.	Ezekiel Bitok, Kenya	2:09:26
3.	Cosmas N'Deti, Kenya	2:09:51

WOMEN

1.	Uta Pippig, Germany	2:27:12
2.	Tecla Loroupe, Kenya	2:28:37
3.	Nobuko Fujimura, Japan	2:29:24

London: April 21, 1996

MEN

1.	Dionicio Ceron, Mexico	2:10:00
2.	Vincent Rousseau, Belgium	2:10:26
3.	Paul Evans, Great Britain	2:10:40

WOMEN

1.	Liz McColgan, Great Britain	2:27:54
2.	Joyce Chepchumba, Kenya	2:30:09
3.	Malgorzata Sobanska, Poland	2:30:17

Rotterdam: April 28, 1996

MEN

1.	Belayneh Dinsamo, Ethiopia	2:10:30
2.	Daisuke Tokunaga, Japan	2:10:30
3.	Philip Chirchir, Kenya	2:11:04

WOMEN

1.	Lieve Slegers, Belgium	2:28:06
2.	Maria del Carmen Diaz, Mexico	2:29:48
3.	Anne van Schuppen, Netherlands	2:31:26

FOR THE RECORD·Year by Year

TRACK AND FIELD

World Records

As of September 25, 1996. World outdoor records are recognized by the International Amateur Athletics Federation (IAAF).

Men

Event	Mark	Record Holder	Date	Site
100 meters	9.84	Donovan Bailey, Canada	7-27-96	Atlanta
200 meters	19.32	Michael Johnson, United States	8-1-96	Atlanta
400 meters	43.29	Butch Reynolds, United States	8-17-88	Zurich
800 meters	1:41.73	Sebastian Coe, Great Britain	6-10-81	Florence
1,000 meters	2:12.18	Sebastian Coe, Great Britain	7-11-81	Oslo
1,500 meters	3:27.37	Noureddine Morceli, Algeria	7-12-95	Nice, France
Mile	3:44.39	Noureddine Morceli, Algeria	9-5-93	Rieti, Italy
2,000 meters	4:47.88	Noureddine Morceli, Algeria	7-3-95	Paris
3,000 meters	7:20.67	Daniel Komen, Kenya	9-1-96	Rieti, Italy
Steeplechase	7:59.18	Moses Kiptanui, Kenya	8-16-95	Zurich
5,000 meters	12:44.39	Haile Gebrselassie, Ethiopia	8-16-95	Zurich
10,000 meters	26:38.08	Salah Hissou, Morocco	8-23-96	Brussels
20,000 meters	56:55.6	Arturo Barrios, Mexico	3-30-91	La Flâche, France
Hour	21,101 meters	Arturo Barrios, Mexico	3-30-91	La Flâche, France
25,000 meters	1:13:55.8	Toshihiko Seko, Japan	3-22-81	Christchurch, New Zealand
30,000 meters	1:29:18.8	Toshihiko Seko, Japan	3-22-81	Christchurch, New Zealand
Marathon	2:06:50	Belayneh Dinsamo, Ethiopia	4-17-88	Rotterdam
110-meter hurdles	12.91	Colin Jackson, Great Britain	8-20-93	Stuttgart, Germany
400-meter hurdles	46.78	Kevin Young, United States	8-6-92	Barcelona
20-kilometer walk	1:17:25.6	Bernardo Segura, Mexico	5-7-94	Bergen, Norway
30-kilometer walk	2:01:44.1	Maurizio Damilano, Italy	10-3-92	Cuneo, Italy
50-kilometer walk	3:40:58	Andrey Plotnikov, Russia	4-21-96	Sochi
4x100-meter relay	37.40	United States (Mike Marsh, Leroy Burrell, Dennis Mitchell, Carl Lewis)	8-8-92	Barcelona
		United States (Jon Drummond, Andre Cason, Dennis Mitchell, Leroy Burrell)	8-21-93	Stuttgart, Germany
4x200-meter relay	1:18.68	Santa Monica TC (Mike Marsh, Leroy Burrell, Floyd Heard, Carl Lewis)	4-17-94	Walnut, CA
4x400-meter relay	2:54.29	United States (Andrew Valmon, Quincy Watts, Butch Reynolds, Michael Johnson)	8-22-93	Stuttgart, Germany
4x800-meter relay	7:03.89	Great Britain (Peter Elliott, Garry Cook, Steve Cram, Sebastian Coe)	8-30-82	London
4x1500-meter relay	14:38.8	West Germany (Thomas Wessinghage, Harald Hudak, Michael Lederer, Karl Fleschen)	8-17-77	Cologne
High jump	8 ft ½ in	Javier Sotomayor, Cuba	7-27-93	Salamanca, Spain
Pole vault	20 ft 1¾ in	Sergei Bubka, Ukraine	7-31-94	Sestriere, Italy
Long jump	29 ft 4½ in	Mike Powell, United States	8-30-91	Tokyo
Triple jump	60 ft ¼ in	Jonathan Edwards, Great Britain	8-7-95	Göteborg, Sweden
Shot put	75 ft 10¼ in	Randy Barnes, United States	5-20-90	Westwood, CA
Discus throw	243 ft 0 in	Jürgen Schult, East Germany	6-6-86	Neubrandenburg, Germany
Hammer throw	284 ft 7 in	Yuri Syedikh, USSR	8-30-86	Stuttgart, Germany
Javelin throw	323 ft 1 in	Jan Zelezny, Czech Republic	5-25-96	Jena, Germany
Decathlon	8891 pts	Dan O'Brien, United States	9-4/5-92	Talence, France

Note: The decathlon consists of 10 events—the 100 meters, long jump, shot put, high jump and 400 meters on the first day; the 110-meter hurdles, discus, pole vault, javelin and 1500 meters on the second.

Women

Event	Mark	Record Holder	Date	Site
100 meters	10.49	Florence Griffith Joyner, United States	7-16-88	Indianapolis
200 meters	21.34	Florence Griffith Joyner, United States	9-29-88	Seoul
400 meters	47.60	Marita Koch, East Germany	10-6-85	Canberra, Australia
800 meters	1:53.28	Jarmila Kratochvílová, Czechoslovakia	7-26-83	Munich
1,000 meters	2:29.34	Maria Mutola, Mozambique	8-25-95	Brussels
1,500 meters	3:50.46	Qu Yunxia, China	9-11-93	Beijing
Mile	4:12.56	Svetlana Masterkova, Russia	8-14-96	Zurich
2,000 meters	5:25.36	Sonia O'Sullivan, Ireland	7-8-94	Edinburgh
3,000 meters	8:06.11	Wang Junxia, China	9-13-93	Beijing
5,000 meters	14:36.45	Fernanda Ribeiro, Portugal	7-22-95	Hechtel, Belgium
10,000 meters	29:31.78	Wang Junxia, China	9-8-93	Beijing
Hour	18,084 meters	Silvana Cruciata, Italy	5-4-81	Rome
20,000 meters	1:06:48.8	Izumi Maki, Japan	9-19-93	Amagasaki
25,000 meters	1:29:29.2	Karolina Szabó, Hungary	4-22-88	Budapest
30,000 meters	1:47:05.6	Karolina Szabó, Hungary	4-22-88	Budapest
Marathon	2:21:06	Ingrid Kristiansen, Norway	4-21-85	London
100-meter hurdles	12.21	Yordanka Donkova, Bulgaria	8-20-88	Stara Zagora, Bulgaria
400-meter hurdles	52.61	Kim Batten, United States	8-11-95	Göteborg, Sweden
5-kilometer walk	20:13.26	Kerry Saxby, Australia	2-25-96	Hobart, Australia
10-kilometer walk	41:04	Yelena Nikolayeva, Russia	4-20-96	Sochi
4x100-meter relay	41.37	East Germany (Silke Gladisch, Sabine Reiger, Ingrid Auerswald, Marlies Göhr)	10-6-85	Canberra, Australia
4x200-meter relay	1:28.15	East Germany (Marlies Göhr, Romy Müller, Bärbel Wöckel, Marita Koch)	8-9-80	Jena, East Germany
4x400-meter relay	3:15.17	USSR (Tatyana Ledovskaya, Olga Nazarova, Maria Pinigina, Olga Bryzgina)	10-1-88	Seoul
4x800-meter relay	7:50.17	USSR (Nadezhda Olizarenko, Lyubov Gurina, Lyudmila Borisova, Irina Podyalovskaya)	8-5-84	Moscow
High jump	6 ft 10¼ in	Stefka Kostadinova, Bulgaria	8-30-87	Rome
Pole vault	14 ft 7¼ in	Emma George, Australia	7-14-96	Sapporo
Long jump	24 ft 8¼ in	Galina Chistyakova, USSR	6-11-88	Leningrad
Triple jump	50 ft 10¼ in	Inessa Kravets, Ukraine	8-10-95	Göteborg, Sweden
Shot put	74 ft 3 in	Natalya Lisovskaya, USSR	6-7-87	Moscow
Discus throw	252 ft 0 in	Gabriele Reinsch, East Germany	7-9-88	Neubrandenburg, Germany
Hammer throw	227 ft 11 in	Olga Kuzenkova	2-17-96	Sydney
Javelin throw	262 ft 5 in	Petra Felke, East Germany	9-9-88	Potsdam, East Germany
Heptathlon	7291 pts	Jackie Joyner-Kersee, U.S.	9-23/24-88	Seoul

Note: The heptathlon consists of 7 events—the 100-meter hurdles, high jump, shot put and 200 meters on the first day; the long jump, javelin and 800 meters on the second.

Steppin' Out

Race walking, as some wag once put it, is like a contest to see who can whisper the loudest. Admittedly an esoteric discipline, walking has been part of the Games since 1906. These days, however, competing for spectator interest against more, well, *dynamic* events, walking is in danger of becoming irrevocably marginalized. Did anyone really expect fans still buzzing from Michael Johnson's 19.32 200-meter dash at the Olympics on the night of Aug. 1 to gear down for the following morning's 50-kilometer walk? That's 3 ½ hours of athletic whispering.

In the interest of promoting this sport, we offer the following modest proposal: The 100-meter walk. Think about it—the whole stadium on its feet as eight athletes burst from the blocks and wiggle their way down the track, leaning dramatically at the finish *less than a minute* later. If that works out, we could add the 110-meter walking hurdles, the walking triple jump, even the walking pole vault.

The sky's the limit. We just have to take that first step.

As of September 25, 1996. American outdoor records are recognized by USA Track and Field (USATF). WR=world record.

Men

Event	Mark	Record Holder	Date	Site
100 meters	9.85	Leroy Burrell	7-6-94	Lausanne
200 meters	19.32 WR	Michael Johnson	8-1-96	Atlanta
400 meters	43.29 WR	Butch Reynolds	8-17-88	Zurich
800 meters	1:42.60	Johnny Gray	8-28-85	Koblenz, Germany
1,000 meters	2:13.9	Rick Wohlhuter	7-30-74	Oslo
1,500 meters	3:29.77	Sydney Maree	8-25-85	Cologne
Mile	3:47.69	Steve Scott	7-7-82	Oslo
2,000 meters	4:52.44	Jim Spivey	9-15-87	Lausanne
3,000 meters	7:31.69	Bob Kennedy	8-23-96	Brussels
Steeplechase	8:09.17	Henry Marsh	8-28-85	Koblenz, Germany
5,000 meters	12:58.21	Bob Kennedy	8-14-96	Zurich
10,000 meters	27:20.56	Mark Nenow	9-5-86	Brussels
20,000 meters	58:25.0	Bill Rodgers	8-9-77	Boston
Hour	20,547 meters	Bill Rodgers	8-9-77	Boston
25,000 meters	1:14:11.8	Bill Rodgers	2-21-79	Saratoga, CA
30,000 meters	1:31:49	Bill Rodgers	2-21-79	Saratoga, CA
Marathon	2:10:04	Pat Petersen	4-23-89	London
110-meter hurdles	12.92	Roger Kingdom	8-16-89	Zurich
		Allen Johnson	6-23-96	Atlanta
		Allen Johnson	8-23-96	Brussels
400-meter hurdles	46.78 WR	Kevin Young	8-6-92	Barcelona
20-kilometer walk	1:24:26.9	Allen James	5-7-94	Fana, Norway
30-kilometer walk	2:21:40	Herm Nelson	9-7-91	Bellevue, WA
50-kilometer walk	3:59:41.2	Herm Nelson	6-9-96	Seattle
4x100-meter relay	37.40 WR	United States (Mike Marsh, Leroy Burrell, Dennis Mitchell, Carl Lewis)	8-8-92	Barcelona
		United States (Jon Drummond, Andre Cason, Dennis Mitchell, Leroy Burrell)	8-21-93	Stuttgart, Germany
4x200-meter relay	1:18.68 WR	Santa Monica Track Club (Mike Marsh, Leroy Burrell, Floyd Heard, Carl Lewis)	4-17-94	Walnut, CA
4x400-meter relay	2:54.29 WR	United States (Andrew Valmon, Quincy Watts, Butch Reynolds, Michael Johnson)	8-22-93	Stuttgart, Germany
4x800-meter relay	7:06.5	Santa Monica Track Club (James Robinson, David Mack, Earl Jones, Johnny Gray)	4-26-86	Walnut, CA
4x1,500-meter relay	14:46.3	National Team (Dan Aldredge, Andy Clifford, Todd Harbour, Tom Duits)	6-24-79	Bourges, France
High jump	7 ft 10½ in	Charles Austin	8-17-91	Zurich
Pole vault	19 ft 7½ in	Lawrence Johnson	5-25-96	Knoxville, TN
Long jump	29 ft 4½ in WR	Mike Powell	8-30-91	Tokyo
Triple jump	59 ft 4¼ in	Kenny Harrison	7-27-96	Atlanta
Shot put	75 ft 10¼ in WR	Randy Barnes	5-20-90	Westwood, CA
Discus throw	237 ft 4 in	Ben Plucknett	7-7-81	Stockholm
Hammer throw	270 ft 9 in	Lance Deal	9-7-96	Milan
Javelin throw	284 ft 10 in	Tom Pukstys	8-25-96	Sheffield, England
Decathlon	8891 pts WR	Dan O'Brien	9-4/5-92	Talence, France

Women

Event	Mark	Record Holder	Date	Site
100 meters	10.49 WR	Florence Griffith Joyner	7-16-88	Indianapolis
200 meters	21.34 WR	Florence Griffith Joyner	9-29-88	Seoul
400 meters	48.83	Valerie Brisco-Hooks	8-6-84	Los Angeles
800 meters	1:56.90	Mary Slaney	8-16-85	Bern, Switzerland
1,500 meters	3:57.12	Mary Slaney	7-26-83	Stockholm
Mile	4:16.71	Mary Slaney	8-21-85	Zurich
2,000 meters	5:32.7	Mary Slaney	8-3-84	Eugene, OR
3,000 meters	8:25.83	Mary Slaney	9-7-85	Rome
5,000 meters	14:56.04	Amy Rudolph	7-8-96	Stockholm
10,000 meters	31:19.89	Lynn Jennings	8-7-92	Barcelona
Marathon	2:21:21	Joan Samuelson	10-20-85	Chicago
100-meter hurdles	12.46	Gail Devers	8-20-93	Stuttgart, Germany
400-meter hurdles	52.61 WR	Kim Batten	8-11-95	Göteborg, Sweden
5,000-meter walk	21:28.17	Teresa Vaill	4-24-93	Philadelphia
10,000-meter walk	44:41.87	Michelle Rohl	7-26-94	St. Petersburg
4x100-meter relay	41.49	National Team (Michelle Finn, Gwen Torrence, Wenda Vereen, Gail Devers)	8-22-93	Stuttgart, Germany
4x200-meter relay	1:32.44	Vector Sports (Esther Jones, Cheryl Taplin, Inger Miller, Chryste Gaines)	4-6-96	Tempe, AZ
4x400-meter relay	3:15.51	Olympic Team (Denean Howard, Diane Dixon, Valerie Brisco, Florence Griffith Joyner)	10-1-88	Seoul
4x800-meter relay	8:17.09	Athletics West (Sue Addison, Lee Arbogast, Mary Decker, Chris Mullen)	4-24-83	Walnut, CA
High jump	6 ft 8 in	Louise Ritter	7-9-88	Austin, TX
		Louise Ritter	9-30-88	Seoul
Pole vault	13 ft 9¼ in	Stacy Dragila	6-19-96	Atlanta
Long jump	24 ft 7 in	Jackie Joyner-Kersee	5-22-94	New York City
			7-31-94	Sestriere, Italy
Triple jump	47 ft 3½ in	Sheila Hudson	7-8-96	Stockholm
Shot put	66 ft 2½ in	Ramona Pagel	6-25-88	San Diego
Discus throw	216 ft 10 in	Carol Cady	5-31-86	San Jose
Javelin throw	227 ft 5 in	Kate Schmidt	9-10-77	Fürth, West Germany
Heptathlon	7291 pts WR	Jackie Joyner-Kersee	9-23/24-88	Seoul

World and American Indoor Records

Men

As of September 25, 1996. American indoor records are recognized by USA Track and Field. World Indoor records are recognized by the International Amateur Athletics Federation (IAAF).

Event	Mark	Record Holder	Date	Site
50 meters	5.56	Donovan Bailey, Canadian (W)	2-9-96	Reno
	5.61	James Sanford (A)	2-20-81	San Diego
55 meters*	6.00	Lee McRae (A)	3-14-86	Oklahoma City
60 meters	6.41	Andre Cason (W, A)	2-14-92	Madrid
200 meters	19.92	Frankie Fredericks, Namibia (W)	2-18-96	Liévin, France
	20.40	Jeff Williams (A)	2-18-96	Liévin, France
400 meters	44.63	Michael Johnson (W, A)	3-4-95	Atlanta
800 meters	1:44.84	Paul Ereng, Kenya (W)	3-4-89	Budapest
	1:45.00	Johnny Gray (A)	3-8-92	Sindelfingen, Germany
1,000 meters	2:15.26	Noureddine Morceli, Algeria (W)	2-22-92	Birmingham, England
	2:18.19	Ocky Clark (A)	2-12-89	Stuttgart
1,500 meters	3:34.16	Noureddine Morceli, Algeria (W)	2-28-91	Seville
	3:38.12	Jeff Atkinson (A)	3-5-89	Budapest
Mile	3:49.78	Eamonn Coughlan, Ireland (W)	2-27-83	East Rutherford, NJ
	3:51.8	Steve Scott (A)	2-20-81	San Diego
3,000 meters	7:30.72	Haile Gebrselassie, Ethiopia (W)	2-4-96	Stuttgart, Germany
	7:39.94	Steve Scott (A)	2-10-89	East Rutherford, NJ

Men (Cont.)

Event	Mark	Record Holder	Date	Site
5,000 meters	13:10.98	Haile Gebrselassie, Ethiopia (W)	1-27-96	Sindelfingen, Germany
	13:20.55	Doug Padilla (A)	2-12-82	New York City
50-meter hurdles	6.25	Mark McKoy, Canada (W)	3-5-86	Kobe, Japan
	6.35	Greg Foster (A)	1-27-85	Rosemont, Illinois
	6.35	Greg Foster (A)	1-31-87	Ottawa, Ontario
55-meter hurdles*	6.89	Renaldo Nehemiah (A)	1-20-79	New York City
60-meter hurdles	7.30	Colin Jackson, Great Britain (W)	3-6-94	Sindelfingen, Germany
	7.36	Greg Foster (A)	1-16-87	Los Angeles
5,000-meter walk	18:07.08	Mikhail Shchennikov, Russia (W)	2-14-95	Moscow
	19:18.40	Tim Lewis (A)	3-7-87	Indianapolis
4x200-meter relay	1:22.11	Great Britain (W) (Linford Christie, Darren Braithwaite, Ade Mafe, John Regis)	3-3-91	Glasgow
	1:22.71	National Team (A) (Thomas Jefferson, Raymond Pierre, Antonio McKay Kevin Little)	3-3-91	Glasgow
4x400-meter relay	3:03.05	Germany (W) (Rico Lieder, Jens Carlowitz, Klaus Just, Thomas Schönlebe)	3-10-91	Seville
	3:03.24	National Team (A) (Raymond Pierre, Chip Jenkins, Andrew Valmon, Antonio McKay)	3-10-91	Seville
4x800-meter relay	7:17.8	Soviet Union (W) (Valeriy Taratynov, Stanislav Meshcherskikh, Aleksey Taranov, Viktor Semyashkin)	3-14-71	Sofia
	7:18.23	University of Florida (A) (Dedric Jones, Lewis Lacy, Stephen Adderly, Scott Peters)	3-14-92	Indianapolis
High jump	7 ft 11½ in	Javier Sotomayor, Cuba (W)	3-4-89	Budapest
	7 ft 10½ in	Hollis Conway (A)	3-10-91	Seville
Pole vault	20 ft 2 in	Sergei Bubka, Ukraine (W)	2-21-93	Donetsk, Ukraine
	19 ft 3¾ in	Billy Olsen (A)	1-25-86	Albuquerque
Long jump	28 ft 10¼ in	Carl Lewis (W, A)	1-27-84	New York City
Triple jump	58 ft 3¾ in	Leonid Voloshin (W)	2-6-94	Grenoble, France
	58 ft 3¼ in	Mike Conley (A)	2-27-87	New York City
Shot put	74 ft 4¼ in	Randy Barnes (W, A)	1-20-89	Los Angeles
Weight throw	84 ft 10¼ in	Lance Deal (W, A)	3-4-95	Atlanta
Pentathlon	4478 pts	Steve Fritz, United States (W, A)	1-14-95	Lawrence, KS
Heptathlon	6476 pts	Dan O'Brien (W, A)	3-13/14-93	Toronto

*No recognized world record

The Marabomber

Before traveling to Massachusetts to run in the 1996 Boston Marathon, Don Holshuh knew he would need a way to get his prerace warmup outfit back from the starting line in Hopkinton to his house in Keene, N.H. That's why Holshuh, a 47-year-old dermatologist, brought along two large, postage-paid, self-addressed envelopes and a couple of carnations. About an hour before the race, he gave one envelope full of clothing to a girl standing near the starting point and asked her to mail it, giving her a carnation for her trouble. Just before the start, he gave the other envelope and flower to a woman standing on a nearby lawn.

Holshuh's first bundle arrived two days later, but he had to wait more than a week for the other, which arrived somewhat tattered and bearing the return address of the Hopkinton police department. It turned out that the woman who took Holshuh's second envelope had, in the words of the department's Marilyn Palmer, "watched too many made-for-TV movies." Fearing that she had received a letter bomb, she dialed 911. The cops arrived and cordoned off the lawn until a bomb squad came to X-ray the package, revealing a pair of gloves and a mesh T-shirt inside. That undoubtedly produced a sigh of relief from the woman, who had reported to the police that the man had "handed her a package, then left the scene."

He and some 38,000 accomplices.

Women

Event	Mark	Record Holder	Date	Site
50 meters	5.96	Irina Privolova, Russia (W)	2-9-95	Madrid
	6.02	Gwen Torrence (A)	2-9-96	Reno, NV
55 meters*	6.56	Gwen Torrence (A)	3-14-87	Oklahoma City
60 meters	6.92	Irina Privalova, Russia (W)	2-11-93	Madrid
	6.92	Irina Privalova, Russia (W)	2-9-95	Madrid
	6.95	Gail Devers (A)	3-12-93	Toronto
200 meters	21.87	Merlene Ottey, Jamaica (W)	2-13-93	Liévin, France
	22.33	Gwen Torrence (A)	3-2-96	Atlanta
400 meters	49.59	Jarmila Kratochvilová, Czech.(W)	3-7-82	Milan
	50.64	Diane Dixon (A)	3-10-91	Seville
800 meters	1:56.40	Christine Wachtel, E Germany (W)	2-14-88	Vienna
	1:58.9	Mary Slaney (A)	2-22-80	San Diego
1,000 meters	2:31.23	Maria Mutola, Mozambique (W)	2-25-96	Stockholm
	2:37.60	Mary Slaney (A)	1-21-89	Portland
1,500 meters	4:00.27	Doina Melinte, Romania (W)	2-9-90	East Rutherford, NJ
	4:00.80	Mary Slaney (A)	2-8-80	New York City
Mile	4:17.14	Doina Melinte, Romania (W)	2-9-90	East Rutherford, NJ
	4:20.5	Mary Slaney (A)	2-19-82	San Diego
3,000 meters	8:33.82	Elly van Hulst, Netherlands (W)	3-4-89	Budapest
	8:40.45	Lynn Jennings (A)	2-23-90	New York City
5,000 meters	15:03.17	Liz McColgan, Scotland (W)	2-22-92	Birmingham, England
	15:22.64	Lynn Jennings (A)	1-7-90	Hanover, NH
50-meter hurdles	6.58	Cornelia Oschkenat, E Germany (W)	2-20-88	Berlin
	6.67	Jackie Joyner-Kersee (A)	2-10-95	Reno, NV
55-meter hurdles*	7.37	Jackie Joyner-Kersee (A)	2-3-89	New York City
60-meter hurdles	7.69	Lyudmila Narozhilenko, Russia (W)	2-4-90	Chelyabinsk, Russia
	7.81	Jackie Joyner-Kersee (A)	2-5-89	Fairfax, VA
3,000 meter walk	11:44.00	Yelena Ivanova, CIS (W)	2-7-92	Moscow
	12:20.79	Debbi Lawrence (A)	3-12-93	Toronto
4x200-meter relay	1:32.55	SC Eintracht Hamm, W Gemany (W) (Helga Arendt, Silke-Beate Knoll, Mechthild Kluth, Gisela Kinzel)	2-20-88	Dortmund, W Germany
	1:33.24	National Team (A) (Flirtisha Harris, Chryste Gaines, Terri Dendy, Michele Collins)	2-12-94	Glasgow
4x400-meter relay	3:27.22	Germany (W) (Sandra Seuser, Annett Hesselbarth, Katrin Schreiter, Grit Breuer)	3-10-91	Seville
	3:29.00	National Team (A) (Terri Dendy, Lillie Leatherwood, Jearl Miles, Diane Dixon)	3-10-91	Seville
4x800-meter relay	8:18.71	Russia (W) (Natalya Zaytseva, Olga Kuvnetsova, Yelena Afanasyeva, Yekaterina Podkopayeva)	2-4-94	Moscow
	8:25.50	Villanova (A) (Gina Procaccio, Debbie Grant, Michelle DiMuro, Celeste Halliday)	2-7-87	Gainesville, FL
High jump	6 ft 9½ in	Heike Henkel, Germany (W)	2-8-92	Karlsruhe, Germany
	6 ft 6¾ in	Coleen Sommer (A)	2-13-82	Ottawa
Long jump	24 ft 2¼ in	Heike Drechsler, E Germany (W)	2-13-88	Vienna
	23 ft 4¾ in	Jackie Joyner-Kersee (A)	3-5-94	Atlanta
Triple jump	49 ft 3⅜ in	Yolanda Chen, Russia (W)	3-11-95	Barcelona
	46 ft 8¼ in	Sheila Hudson-Strudwick (A)	3-4-95	Atlanta
Shot put	73 ft 10 in	Helena Fibingerová, Czech. (W)	2-19-77	Jablonec, Czech.
	65 ft ¾ in	Ramona Pagel (A)	2-20-87	Inglewood, CA
Weight throw*	68 ft 11¾ in	Dawn Ellerbe (A)	2-25-96	Lexington, KY
Pentathlon	4991 pts	Irina Byelova, CIS (W)	2-14/15-92	Berlin
	4632 pts	Kym Carter (A)	3-10-95	Barcelona

*No recognized world record

Historically, the Olympics have served as the outdoor world championships for track and field. In 1983 the International Amateur Athletic Federation (IAAF) instituted a separate World Championship meet, to be held every 4 years between the Olympics. The first was held in Helsinki in 1983, the second in Rome in 1987, the third in Tokyo in 1991, the fourth in Stuttgart, Germany, in 1993 and the fifth in Göteborg, Sweden, in 1995. In 1993 the IAAF began to hold the meet on a biennial basis.

Men

100 METERS

1983	Carl Lewis, United States	10.07
1987*	Carl Lewis, United States	9.93 WR
1991	Carl Lewis, United States	9.86 WR
1993	Linford Christie, Great Britain	9.87
1995	Donovan Bailey, Canada	9.97

200 METERS

1983	Calvin Smith, United States	20.14
1987	Calvin Smith United States	20.16
1991	Michael Johnson, United States	20.01
1993	Frank Fredericks, Namibia	19.85
1995	Michael Johnson, United States	19.79

400 METERS

1983	Bort Cameron, Jamaica	45.05
1987	Thomas Schoenlebe, E Germany	44.33
1991	Antonio Pettigrew, United States	44.57
1993	Michael Johnson, United States	43.65
1995	Michael Johnson, United States	43.39

800 METERS

1983	Willi Wulbeck, W Germany	1:43.65
1987	Billy Konchellah, Kenya	1:43.06
1991	Billy Konchellah, Kenya	1:43.99
1993	Paul Ruto, Kenya	1:44.71
1995	Wilson Kipketer, Denmark	1:45.08

1500 METERS

1983	Steve Cram, Great Britain	3:41.59
1987	Abdi Bile, Somalia	3:36.80
1991	Noureddine Morceli, Algeria	3:32.84
1993	Noureddine Morceli, Algeria	3:34.24
1995	Noureddine Morceli, Algeria	3:33.73

STEEPLECHASE

1983	Patriz Ilg, W Germany	8:15.06
1987	Francesco Panetta, Italy	8:08.57
1991	Moses Kiptanui, Kenya	8:12.59
1993	Moses Kiptanui, Kenya	8:06.36
1995	Moses Kiptanui, Kenya	8:04.16

5000 METERS

1983	Eamonn Coghlan, Ireland	13:28.53
1987	Said Aouita, Morocco	13:26.44
1991	Yobes Ondieki, Kenya	13:14.45
1993	Ismael Kirui, Kenya	13:02.75
1995	Ismael Kirui, Kenya	13:16.77

10,000 METERS

1983	Alberto Cova, Italy	28:01.04
1987	Paul Kipkoech, Kenya	27:38.63
1991	Moses Tanui, Kenya	27:38.74
1993	Haile Gebrselassie, Ethiopia	27:46.02
1995	Haile Gebrselassie, Ethiopia	27:12.95

MARATHON

1983	Rob de Castella, Australia	2:10:03
1987	Douglas Wakiihuri, Kenya	2:11:48
1991	Hiromi Taniguchi, Japan	2:14:57
1993	Mark Plaatjes, United States	2:13:57
1995	Martin Fiz, Spain	2:11:41

110-METER HURDLES

1983	Greg Foster, United States	13.42
1987	Greg Foster, United States	13.21
1991	Greg Foster, United States	13.06
1993	Colin Jackson, Great Britain	12.91 WR
1995	Allen Johnson, United States	13.00

400-METER HURDLES

1983	Edwin Moses, United States	47.50
1987	Edwin Moses, United States	47.46
1991	Samuel Matete, Zambia	47.64
1993	Kevin Young, United States	47.18
1995	Derrick Adkins, United States	47.98

20-KILOMETER WALK

1983	Ernesto Canto, Mexico	1:20:49
1987	Maurizio Damilano, Italy	1:20:45
1991	Maurizio Damilano, Italy	1:19:37
1993	Valentin Massana, Spain	1:22:31
1995	Michele Didoni, Italy	1:19:59

50-KILOMETER WALK

1983	Ronald Weigel, E Germany	3:43:08
1987	Hartwig Gauder, E Germany	3:40:53
1991	Aleksandr Potashov, USSR	3:53:09
1993	Jesus Angel Garcia, Spain	3:41:41
1995	Valentin Kononen, Finland	3:43:42

4 X 100 METER RELAY

1983	United States (Emmit King, Willie Gault, Calvin Smith, Carl Lewis)	37.86
1987	United States (Lee McRae, Lee McNeil, Harvey Glance, Carl Lewis)	37.90
1991	United States (Andre Cason Leroy Burrell, Dennis Mitchell Carl Lewis)	37.50 WR
1993	United States (Jon Drummond, Andre Cason, Dennis Mitchell, Leroy Burrell)	37.48
1995	Canada (Robert Esmie, Glenroy Gilbert, Bruny Surin, Donovan Bailey)	38.31

WR=World record.

*Ben Johnson, Canada, disqualified

Men *(Cont.)*

4 X 400 METER RELAY

1983	USSR (Sergei Lovachev, Alecksandr Troschilo, Nikolay Chernyetskilo, Viktor Markin)	3:00.79
1987	United States (Danny Everett Rod Haley, Antonio McKay, Butch Reynolds)	2:57.29
1991	Great Britain (Roger Black Derek Redmond, John Regis, Kriss Akabusi)	2:57.53
1993	United States (Andrew Valmon, Quincy Watts, Butch Reynolds, Michael Johnson)	2:54.29 WR
1995	United States (Marlon Ramsey, Derek Mills, Butch Reynolds, Michael Johnson)	2:57.32

HIGH JUMP

1983	Gennadi Avdeyenko, USSR	7 ft 7¼ in
1987	Patrik Sjoberg, Sweden	7 ft 9¾ in
1991	Charles Austin, United States	7 ft 9¾ in
1993	Javier Sotomayor, Cuba	7 ft 10½ in
1995	Troy Kemp, Bahamas	7 ft 9¼ in

POLE VAULT

1983	Sergei Bubka, USSR	18 ft 8¼ in
1987	Sergei Bubka, USSR	19 ft 2¼ in
1991	Sergei Bubka, USSR	19 ft 6¼ in
1993	Sergei Bubka, Ukraine	19 ft 8¼ in
1995	Sergei Bubka, Ukraine	19 ft 5 in

LONG JUMP

1983	Carl Lewis, United States	28 ft ¾ in
1987	Carl Lewis, United States	28 ft 5¼ in
1991	Mike Powell, U.S.	29 ft 4½ in WR
1993	Mike Powell, United States	28 ft 2¼ in
1995	Ivan Pedroso, Cuba	28 ft 6½ in

TRIPLE JUMP

1983	Zdzislaw Hoffmann, Poland	57 ft 2 in
1987	Khristo Markov, Bulgaria	58 ft 9 ½ in
1991	Kenny Harrison, United States	58 ft 4 in
1993	Mike Conley, United States	58 ft 7¼ in
1995	Jonathan Edwards, G.B.	60 ft ¼ in WR

SHOT PUT

1983	Edward Sarul, Poland	70 ft 2¼ in
1987	Werner Günthör, Switzerland	72 ft 11¼ in
1991	Werner Günthör, Switzerland	71 ft 1¼ in
1993	Werner Günthör, Switzerland	72 ft 1 in
1995	John Godina, United States	70 ft 5¼ in

DISCUS THROW

1983	Imrich Bugar, Czech.	222 ft 2 in
1987	Juergen Schult, E Germany	225 ft 6 in
1991	Lars Riedel, Germany	217 ft 2 in
1993	Lars Riedel, Germany	222 ft 2 in
1995	Lars Riedel, Germany	225 ft 7 in

HAMMER THROW

1983	Sergei Litvinov, USSR	271 ft 3 in
1987	Sergei Litvinov, USSR	272 ft 6 in
1991	Yuriy Sedykh, USSR	268 ft
1993	Andrey Abduvaliyev, Tajikistan	267 ft 10 in
1995	Andrey Abduvaliyev, Tajikistan	267 ft 7 in

JAVELIN THROW

1983	Detlef Michel, E Germany	293 ft 7 in
1987	Seppo Räty, Finland	274 ft 1 in
1991	Kimmo Kinnunen, Finland	297 ft 11 in
1993	Jan Zelezny, Czech Republic	282 ft 1 in
1995	Jan Zelezny, Czech Republic	293 ft 11 in

DECATHLON

1983	Daley Thompson, G Britain	8666 pts
1987	Torsten Voss, E Germany	8680 pts
1991	Dan O'Brien, United States	8812 pts
1993	Dan O'Brien, United States	8817 pts
1995	Dan O'Brien, United States	8695 pts

Women

100 METERS

1983	Marlies Gohr, E Germany	10.97
1987	Silke Gladisch, E Germany	10.90
1991	Katrin Krabbe, Germany	10.99
1993	Gail Devers, United States	10.82
1995	Gwen Torrence, United States	10.85

200 METERS

1983	Marita Koch, E Germany	22.13
1987	Silke Gladisch, E Germany	21.74
1991	Katrin Krabbe, Germany	22.09
1993	Merlene Ottey, Jamaica	21.98
1995	Merlene Ottey, Jamaica	22.12

400 METERS

1983	Jarmila Kratochvilova, Czech	47.99
1987	Olga Bryzgina, USSR	49.38
1991	Marie-José Pérec, France	49.13
1993	Jearl Miles, United States	49.82
1995	Marie-José Pérec, France	49.28

800 METERS

1983	Jarmila Kratochvilova, Czech	1:54.68
1987	Sigrun Wodars, E Germany	1:55.26
1991	Lilia Nurutdinova, USSR	1:57.50
1993	Maria Mutola, Mozambique	1:55.43
1995	Ana Quirot, Cuba	1:56.11

1500 METERS

1983	Mary Slaney, United States	4:00.90
1987	Tatyana Samolenko, USSR	3:58.56
1991	Hassiba Boulmerka, Algeria	4:02.21
1993	Dong Liu, China	4:00.50
1995	Hassiba Boulmerka, Algeria	4:02.42

3000 METERS*

1983	Mary Slaney, United States	8:34.62
1987	Tatyana Samolenko, USSR	8:38.73
1991	Tatyana Dorovskikh, USSR	8:35.82
1993	Qu Yunxia, China	8:28.71
1995	Sonia O'Sullivan, Ireland	14:46.47

WR=World record. * contested at 5,000 meters in 1995.

Women (Cont.)

10,000 METERS

1987	Ingrid Kristiansen, Norway	31:05.85
1991	Liz McColgan, Great Britain	31:14.31
1993	Wang Junxia, China	30:49:30
1995	Fernanda Ribeiro, Portugal	31:04.99

MARATHON

1983	Grete Waitz, Norway	2:28:09
1987	Rosa Mota, Portugal	2:25:17
1991	Wanda Panfil, Poland	2:29:53
1993	Junko Asari, Japan	2:30:03
1995	Manuela Machado, Portugal	2:25:39*

100-METER HURDLES

1983	Bettine Jahn, E Germany	12.35
1987	Ginka Zagorcheva, Bulgaria	12.34
1991	Lyudmila Narozhilenko, USSR	12.59
1993	Gail Devers, United States	12.46
1995	Gail Devers, United States	12.68

400-METER HURDLES

1983	Yekaterina Fesenko, USSR	54.14
1987	Sabine Busch, E Germany	53.62
1991	Tatyana Ledovskaya, USSR	53.11
1993	Sally Gunnell, Great Britain	52.74 WR
1995	Kim Batten, United States	52.61

10-KILOMETER WALK

1987	Irina Strakhova, USSR	44:12
1991	Alina Ivanova, USSR	42:57
1993	Sari Essayah, Finland	42:59
1995	Irina Stankina, Russia	42:13

4 X 100 METER RELAY

1983	East Germany (Silke Gladisch, Marita Koch, Ingrid Auerswald, Marlies Gohr)	41.76
1987	United States (Alice Brown, Diane Williams, Florence Griffith, Pam Marshall)	41.58
1991	Jamaica (Dalia Duhaney, Juliet Cuthbert, Beverley McDonald, Merlene Ottey)	41.94
1993	Russia (Olga Bogoslovskaya, Galina Malchugina, Natalya Voronova, Irina Privalova)	41.49
1995	United States (Celena Mondie-Milner, Carlette Guidry, Chryste Gaines, Gwen Torrence)	42.12

4 X 400 METER RELAY

1983	East Germany (Kerstin Walther, Sabine Busch, Marita Koch, Dagmar Rubsam)	3:19.73
1987	E Germany (Dagmar Neubauer, Kirsten Emmelmann, Petra Müller, Sabine Busch)	3:18.63

4 X 400 METER RELAY (Cont.)

1991	USSR (Tatyana Ledovskaya, Lyudmila Dzhigalova, Olga Nazarova, Olga Bryzgina)	3:18.43
1993	United States (Gwen Torrence, Maicel Malone, Natasha Kaiser-Brown, Jearl Miles)	3:16.71
1995	United States (Kim Graham, Rochelle Stevens, Camara Jones, Jearl Miles)	3:22.39

HIGH JUMP

1983	Tamara Bykova, USSR	6 ft 7 in
1987	Stefka Kostadinova, Bulgaria	6 ft 10¼ in
1991	Heike Henkel, Germany	6 ft 8¾ in
1993	Ioamnet Quintero, Cuba	6 ft 6¼ in
1995	Stefka Kostadinova, Bulgaria	6 ft 7 in

LONG JUMP

1983	Heike Daute, E Germany	23 ft 10¼ in
1987	Jackie Joyner-Kersee, U.S.	24 ft 1¾ in
1991	Jackie Joyner-Kersee, U.S.	24 ft ¼ in
1993	Heike Drechsler, Germany	23 ft 4 in
1995	Fiona May, Italy	22 ft 10¾ in w

TRIPLE JUMP

1993	Ana Biryukova, Russia	49 ft 6 ¼ in WR
1995	Inessa Kravets, Ukraine	50 ft 10¼ in WR

SHOT PUT

1983	Helena Fibingerova, Czech.	69 ft ¾ in
1987	Natalya Lisovskaya, USSR	69 ft 8¼ in
1991	Zhihong Huang, China	68 ft 4¼ in
1993	Zhihong Huang, China	67 ft 6 in
1995	Astrid Kumbernuss, Germany	69 ft 7½ in

DISCUS THROW

1983	Martina Opitz, E Germany	226 ft 2 in
1987	Martina Hellmann, E Germany	235 ft
1991	Tsvetanka Khristova, Bulgaria	233 ft
1993	Olga Burova, Russia	221 ft 1 in
1995	Ellina Zvereva, Belarus	225 ft 2 in

JAVELIN THROW

1983	Tiina Lillak, Finland	232 ft 4 in
1987	Fatima Whitbread, G Britain	251 ft 5 in
1991	Demei Xu, China	225 ft 8 in
1993	Trine Hattestad, Finland	227 ft
1995	Natalya Shikolenko, Belarus	221 ft 8 in

HEPTATHLON

1983	Ramona Neubert, E Germany	6714 pts
1987	Jackie Joyner-Kersee, U.S.	7128 pts
1991	Sabine Braun, Germany	6672 pts
1993	Jackie Joyner-Kersee, U.S.	6837 pts
1995	Ghada Shouaa, Syria	6651 pts

WR=World record. *400 meters short

Track & Field News Athlete of the Year

Each year (since 1959 for men and since 1974 for women) Track & Field News has chosen the outstanding athlete in the sport.

Men

Year	Athlete	Event
1959	Martin Lauer, West Germany	110-meter hurdles/Decathlon
1960	Rafer Johnson, United States	Decathlon
1961	Ralph Boston, United States	Long jump
1962	Peter Snell, New Zealand	800/1,500 meters
1963	C. K. Yang, Taiwan	Decathlon/Pole vault
1964	Peter Snell, New Zealand	800/1,500 meters
1965	Ron Clarke, Australia	5,000/10,000 meters
1966	Jim Ryun, United States	800/1,500 meters
1967	Jim Ryun, United States	1500 meters
1968	Bob Beamon, United States	Long jump
1969	Bill Toomey, United States	Decathlon
1970	Randy Matson, United States	Shot put
1971	Rod Milburn, United States	110-meter hurdles
1972	Lasse Viren, Finland	5,000/10,000 meters
1973	Ben Jipcho, Kenya	1,500/5,000 meters/Steeplechase
1974	Rick Wohlhuter, United States	800/1,500 meters
1975	John Walker, New Zealand	800/1,500 meters
1976	Alberto Juantorena, Cuba	400/800 meters
1977	Alberto Juantorena, Cuba	400/800 meters
1978	Henry Rono, Kenya	5,000/10,000 meters/Steeplechase
1979	Sebastian Coe, Great Britain	800/1,500 meters
1980	Edwin Moses, United States	400-meter hurdles
1981	Sebastian Coe, Great Britain	800/1500 meters
1982	Carl Lewis, United States	100/200 meters/Long jump
1983	Carl Lewis, United States	100/200 meters/Long jump
1984	Carl Lewis, United States	100/200 meters/Long jump
1985	Said Aouita, Morocco	1,500/5,000 meters
1986	Yuri Syedikh, USSR	Hammer throw
1987	Ben Johnson, Canada	100 meters
1988	Sergei Bubka, USSR	Pole vault
1989	Roger Kingdom, United States	110-meter hurdles
1990	Michael Johnson, United States	200/400 meters
1991	Sergei Bubka, CIS	Pole vault
1992	Kevin Young, United States	400-meter hurdles
1993	Noureddine Morceli, Algeria	1,500/mile/3,000
1994	Noureddine Morceli, Algeria	1,500/mile/3,000/5,000
1995	Haile Gebrselassie, Ethiopia	5,000/10,000

Women

Year	Athlete	Event
1974	Irena Szewinska, Poland	100/200/400 meters
1975	Faina Melnik, USSR	Shot put/Discus
1976	Tatyana Kazankina, USSR	800/1,500 meters
1977	Rosemarie Ackermann, East Germany	High jump
1978	Marita Koch, East Germany	100/200/400 meters
1979	Marita Koch, East Germany	100/200/400 meters
1980	Ilona Briesenick, East Germany	Shot put
1981	Evelyn Ashford, United States	100/200 meters
1982	Marita Koch, East Germany	100/200/400 meters
1983	Jarmila Kratochvilova, Czechoslovakia	200/400/800 meters
1984	Evelyn Ashford, United States	100 meters
1985	Marita Koch, East Germany	100/200/400 meters
1986	Jackie Joyner-Kersee, United States	Long jump/Heptathlon
1987	Jackie Joyner-Kersee, United States	100-meter hurdles/Long jump/Heptathlon
1988	Florence Griffith Joyner, United States	100/200 meters
1989	Ana Quirot, Cuba	400/800 meters
1990	Merlene Ottey, Jamaica	100/200 meters
1991	Heike Henkel, Germany	High jump
1992	Heike Drechsler, Germany	Long Jump
1993	Wang Junxia, China	1,500/3,000/10,000/marathon
1994	Jackie Joyner-Kersee, United States	100-meter hurdles/Long jump/Heptathlon
1995	Sonia O'Sullivan, Ireland	1,500/3,000/5,000

MARATHON

World Record Progression

Men

Record Holder	Time	Date	Site
John Hayes, United States	2:55:18.4	7-24-08	Shepherd's Bush, London
Robert Fowler, United States	2:52:45.4	1-1-09	Yonkers, NY
James Clark, United States	2:46:52.6	2-12-09	New York City
Albert Raines, United States	2:46:04.6	5-8-09	New York City
Frederick Barrett, Great Britain	2:42:31	5-26-09	Shepherd's Bush, London
Harry Green, Great Britain	2:38:16.2	5-12-13	Shepherd's Bush, London
Alexis Ahlgren, Sweden	2:36:06.6	5-31-13	Shepherd's Bush, London
Johannes Kolehmainen, Finland	2:32:35.8	8-22-20	Antwerp, Belgium
Albert Michelsen, United States	2:29:01.8	10-12-25	Port Chester, NY
Fusashige Suzuki, Japan	2:27:49	3-31-35	Tokyo
Yasuo Ikenaka, Japan	2:26:44	4-3-35	Tokyo
Kitei Son, Japan	2:26:42	11-3-35	Tokyo
Yun Bok Suh, Korea	2:25:39	4-19-47	Boston
James Peters, Great Britain	2:20:42.2	6-14-52	Chiswick, England
James Peters, Great Britain	2:18:40.2	6-13-53	Chiswick, England
James Peters, Great Britain	2:18:34.8	10-4-53	Turku, Finland
James Peters, Great Britain	2:17:39.4	6-26-54	Chiswick, England
Sergei Popov, USSR	2:15:17	8-24-58	Stockholm
Abebe Bikila, Ethiopia	2:15:16.2	9-10-60	Rome
Toru Terasawa, Japan	2:15:15.8	2-17-63	Beppu, Japan
Leonard Edelen, United States	2:14:28	6-15-63	Chiswick, England
Basil Heatley, Great Britain	2:13:55	6-13-64	Chiswick, England
Abebe Bikila, Ethiopia	2:12:11.2	6-21-64	Tokyo
Morio Shigematsu, Japan	2:12:00	6-12-65	Chiswick, England
Derek Clayton, Australia	2:09:36.4	12-3-67	Fukuoka, Japan
Derek Clayton, Australia	2:08:33.6	5-30-69	Antwerp, Belgium
Rob de Castella, Australia	2:08:18	12-6-81	Fukuoka, Japan
Steve Jones, Great Britain	2:08:05	10-21-84	Chicago
Carlos Lopes, Portugal	2:07:12	4-20-85	Rotterdam, Netherlands
Belayneh Dinsamo, Ethiopia	2:06:50	4-17-88	Rotterdam, Netherlands

Women

Record Holder	Time	Date	Site
Dale Greig, Great Britain	3:27:45	5-23-64	Ryde, England
Mildred Simpson, New Zealand	3:19:33	7-21-64	Auckland, New Zealand
Maureen Wilton, Canada	3:15:22	5-6-67	Toronto
Anni Pede-Erdkamp, West Germany	3:07:26	9-16-67	Waldniel, West Germany
Caroline Walker, United States	3:02:53	2-28-70	Seaside, OR
Elizabeth Bonner, United States	3:01:42	5-9-71	Philadelphia
Adrienne Beames, Australia	2:46:30	8-31-71	Werribee, Australia
Chantal Langlace, France	2:46:24	10-27-74	Neuf Brisach, France
Jacqueline Hansen, United States	2:43:54.5	12-1-74	Culver City, CA
Liane Winter, West Germany	2:42:24	4-21-75	Boston
Christa Vahlensieck, West Germany	2:40:15.8	5-3-75	Dülmen, West Germany
Jacqueline Hansen, United States	2:38:19	10-12-75	Eugene, OR
Chantal Langlace, France	2:35:15.4	5-1-77	Oyarzun, France
Christa Vahlensieck, West Germany	2:34:47.5	9-10-77	West Berlin, West Germany
Grete Waitz, Norway	2:32:29.9	10-22-78	New York City
Grete Waitz, Norway	2:27:32.6	10-21-79	New York City
Grete Waitz, Norway	2:25:41.3	10-26-80	New York City
Grete Waitz, Norway	2:25:29	4-17-83	London
Joan Benoit Samuelson, United States	2:22:43	4-18-83	Boston
Ingrid Kristiansen, Norway	2:21:06	4-21-85	London

Boston Marathon

The Boston Marathon began in 1897 as a local Patriot's Day event. Run every year but 1918 since then, it has grown into one of the world's premier marathons.

Men

Year	Winner	Time	Year	Winner	Time
1897	John J. McDermott, United States	2:55:10	1947	Yun Bok Suh, Korea	2:25:39
1898	Ronald J. McDonald, United States	2:42:00	1948	Gerard Cote, Canada	2:31:02
1899	Lawrence J. Brignolia, United States	2:54:38	1949	Karl Gosta Leandersson, Sweden	2:31:50
1900	James J. Caffrey, Canada	2:39:44	1950	Kee Yong Ham, Korea	2:32:39
1901	James J. Caffrey, Canada	2:29:23	1951	Shigeki Tanaka, Japan	2:27:45
1902	Sammy Mellor, United States	2:43:12	1952	Doroteo Flores, Guatemala	2:31:53
1903	John C. Lorden, United States	2:41:29	1953	Keizo Yamada, Japan	2:18:51
1904	Michael Spring, United States	2:38:04	1954	Veikko Karvonen, Finland	2:20:39
1905	Fred Lorz, United States	2:38:25	1955	Hideo Hamamura, Japan	2:18:22
1906	Timothy Ford, United States	2:45:45	1956	Antti Viskari, Finland	2:14:14
1907	Tom Longboat, Canada	2:24:24	1957	John J. Kelley, United States	2:20:05
1908	Thomas Morrissey, United States	2:25:43	1958	Franjo Mihalic, Yugoslavia	2:25:54
1909	Henri Renaud, United States	2:53:36	1959	Eino Oksanen, Finland	2:22:42
1910	Fred Cameron, Canada	2:28:52	1960	Paavo Kotila, Finland	2:20:54
1911	Clarence H. DeMar, United States	2:21:39	1961	Eino Oksanen, Finland	2:23:39
1912	Mike Ryan, United States	2:21:18	1962	Eino Oksanen, Finland	2:23:48
1913	Fritz Carlson, United States	2:25:14	1963	Aurele Vandendriessche, Belgium	2:18:58
1914	James Duffy, Canada	2:25:01	1964	Aurele Vandendriessche, Belgium	2:19:59
1915	Edouard Fabre, Canada	2:31:41	1965	Morio Shigematsu, Japan	2:16:33
1916	Arthur Roth, United States	2:27:16	1966	Kenji Kimihara, Japan	2:17:11
1917	Bill Kennedy, United States	2:28:37	1967	David McKenzie, New Zealand	2:15:45
1918	No race		1968	Amby Burfoot, United States	2:22:17
1919	Carl Linder, United States	2:29:13	1969	Yoshiaki Unetani, Japan	2:13:49
1920	Peter Trivoulidas, Greece	2:29:31	1970	Ron Hill, England	2:10:30
1921	Frank Zuna, United States	2:18:57	1971	Alvaro Mejia, Colombia	2:18:45
1922	Clarence H. DeMar, United States	2:18:10	1972	Olavi Suomalainen, Finland	2:15:39
1923	Clarence H. DeMar, United States	2:23:37	1973	Jon Anderson, United States	2:16:03
1924	Clarence H. DeMar, United States	2:29:40	1974	Neil Cusack, Ireland	2:13:39
1925	Chuck Mellor, United States	2:33:00	1975	Bill Rodgers, United States	2:09:55
1926	John C. Miles, Canada	2:25:40	1976	Jack Fultz, United States	2:20:19
1927	Clarence H. DeMar, United States	2:40:22	1977	Jerome Drayton, Canada	2:14:46
1928	Clarence H. DeMar, United States	2:37:07	1978	Bill Rodgers, United States	2:10:13
1929	John C. Miles, Canada	2:33:08	1979	Bill Rodgers, United States	2:09:27
1930	Clarence H. DeMar, United States	2:34:48	1980	Bill Rodgers, United States	2:12:11
1931	James (Hinky) Henigan, United States	2:46:45	1981	Toshihiko Seko, Japan	2:09:26
1932	Paul de Bruyn, Germany	2:33:36	1982	Alberto Salazar, United States	2:08:52
1933	Leslie Pawson, United States	2:31:01	1983	Gregory A. Meyer, United States	2:09:00
1934	Dave Komonen, Canada	2:32:53	1984	Geoff Smith, England	2:10:34
1935	John A. Kelley, United States	2:32:07	1985	Geoff Smith, England	2:14:05
1936	Ellison M. (Tarzan) Brown, United States	2:33:40	1986	Rob de Castella, Australia	2:07:51
1937	Walter Young, Canada	2:33:20	1987	Toshihiko Seko, Japan	2:11:50
1938	Leslie Pawson, United States	2:35:34	1988	Ibrahim Hussein, Kenya	2:08:43
1939	Ellison M. (Tarzan) Brown, United States	2:28:51	1989	Abebe Mekonnen, Ethiopia	2:09:06
1940	Gerard Cote, Canada	2:28:28	1990	Gelindo Bordin, Italy	2:08:19
1941	Leslie Pawson, United States	2:30:38	1991	Ibrahim Hussein, Kenya	2:11:06
1942	Bernard Joseph Smith, United States	2:26:51	1992	Ibrahim Hussein, Kenya	2:08:14
1943	Gerard Cote, Canada	2:28:25	1993	Cosmas N'Deti, Kenya	2:09:33
1944	Gerard Cote, Canada	2:31:50	1994	Cosmas N'Deti, Kenya	2:07:15
1945	John A. Kelley, United States	2:30:40	1995	Cosmas N'Deti, Kenya	2:09:22
1946	Stylianos Kyriakides, Greece	2:29:27	1996	Moses Tanui, Kenya	2:09:16

Women

Year	Winner	Time	Year	Winner	Time
1966	Roberta Gibb, United States	3:21:40*	1976	Kim Merritt, United States	2:47:10
1967	Roberta Gibb, United States	3:27:17*	1977	Miki Gorman, United States	2:48:33
1968	Roberta Gibb, United States	3:30:00*	1978	Gayle Barron, United States	2:44:52
1969	Sara Mae Berman, United States	3:22:46*	1979	Joan Benoit, United States	2:35:15
1970	Sara Mae Berman, United States	3:05:07*	1980	Jacqueline Gareau, Canada	2:34:28
1971	Sara Mae Berman, United States	3:08:30*	1981	Allison Roe, New Zealand	2:26:46
1972	Nina Kuscsik, United States	3:10:36	1982	Charlotte Teske, West Germany	2:29:33
1973	Jacqueline A. Hansen, United States	3:05:59	1983	Joan Benoit, United States	2:22:43
1974	Miki Gorman, United States	2:47:11	1984	Lorraine Moller, New Zealand	2:29:28
1975	Liane Winter, West Germany	2:42:24	1985	Lisa Larsen Weidenbach, United States	2:34:06

Women *(Cont.)*

Year	Winner	Time	Year	Winner	Time
1986	Ingrid Kristiansen, Norway	2:24:55	1992	Olga Markova, Russia	2:23:43
1987	Rosa Mota, Portugal	2:25:21	1993	Olga Markova, Russia	2:25:27
1988	Rosa Mota, Portugal	2:24:30	1994	Uta Pippig, Germany	2:21:45
1989	Ingrid Kristiansen, Norway	2:24:33	1995	Uta Pippig, Germany	2:25:11
1990	Rosa Mota, Portugal	2:25:24	1996	Uta Pippig, Germany	2:27:12
1991	Wanda Panfil, Poland	2:24:18	*Unofficial.		

Note: Over the years the Boston course has varied in length. The distances have been 24 miles, 1232 yards (1897-1923); 26 miles, 209 yards (1924-1926); 26 miles 385 yards (1927-1952); and 25 miles, 958 yards (1953-1956). Since 1957, the course has been certified to be the standard marathon distance of 26 miles, 385 yards.

New York City Marathon

From 1970 through 1975 the New York City Marathon was a small local race run in the city's Central Park. In 1976 it was moved to the streets of New York's five boroughs. It has since become one of the biggest and most prestigious marathons in the world.

Men

Year	Winner	Time	Year	Winner	Time
1970	Gary Muhrcke, United States	2:31:38	1983	Rod Dixon, New Zealand	2:08:59
1971	Norman Higgins, United States	2:22:54	1984	Orlando Pizzolato, Italy	2:14:53
1972	Sheldon Karlin, United States	2:27:52	1985	Orlando Pizzolato, Italy	2:11:34
1973	Tom Fleming, United States	2:21:54	1986	Gianni Poli, Italy	2:11:06
1974	Norbert Sander, United States	2:26:30	1987	Ibrahim Hussein, Kenya	2:11:01
1975	Tom Fleming, United States	2:19:27	1988	Steve Jones, Great Britain	2:08:20
1976	Bill Rodgers, United States	2:10:10	1989	Juma Ikangaa, Tanzania	2:08:01
1977	Bill Rodgers, United States	2:11:28	1990	Douglas Wakiihuri, Kenya	2:12:39
1978	Bill Rodgers, United States	2:12:12	1991	Salvador Garcia, Mexico	2:09:28
1979	Bill Rodgers, United States	2:11:42	1992	Willie Mtolo, South Africa	2:09:29
1980	Alberto Salazar, United States	2:09:41	1993	Andres Espinosa, Mexico	2:10:04
1981	Alberto Salazar, United States	2:08:13	1994	German Silva, Mexico	2:11:21
1982	Alberto Salazar, United States	2:09:29	1995	German Silva, Mexico	2:11:00

Women

Year	Winner	Time	Year	Winner	Time
1970	No finisher		1983	Grete Waitz, Norway	2:27:00
1971	Beth Bonner, United States	2:55:22	1984	Grete Waitz, Norway	2:29:30
1972	Nina Kuscsik, United States	3:08:41	1985	Grete Waitz, Norway	2:28:34
1973	Nina Kuscsik, United States	2:57:07	1986	Grete Waitz, Norway	2:28:06
1974	Katherine Switzer, United States	3:07:29	1987	Priscilla Welch, Great Britain	2:30:17
1975	Kim Merritt, United States	2:46:14	1988	Grete Waitz, Norway	2:28:07
1976	Miki Gorman, United States	2:39:11	1989	Ingrid Kristiansen, Norway	2:25:30
1977	Miki Gorman, United States	2:43:10	1990	Wanda Panfiil, Poland	2:30:45
1978	Grete Waitz, Norway	2:32:30	1991	Liz McColgan, Scotland	2:27:23
1979	Grete Waitz, Norway	2:27:33	1992	Lisa Ondieki, Australia	2:24:40
1980	Grete Waitz, Norway	2:25:41	1993	Uta Pippig, Germany	2:26:24
1981	Allison Roe, New Zealand	2:25:29	1994	Tecla Loroupe, Kenya	2:27:37
1982	Grete Waitz, Norway	2:27:14	1995	Tecla Loroupe, Kenya	2:28:06

CROSS COUNTRY

World Cross-Country Championships

Conducted by the International Amateur Athletic Federation (IAAF), this meet annually brings together the best runners in the world at every distance from the mile to the marathon to compete in the same cross-country race.

Men

Year	Winner	Winning Team	Year	Winner	Winning Team
1973	Pekka Paivarinta, Finland	Belgium	1978	John Treacy, Ireland	France
1974	Eric DeBeck, Belgium	Belgium	1979	John Treacy, Ireland	England
1975	Ian Stewart, Scotland	New Zealand	1980	Craig Virgin, United States	England
1976	Carlos Lopes, Portugal	England	1981	Craig Virgin, United States	Ethiopia
1977	Leon Schots, Belgium	Belgium	1982	Mohammed Kedir, Ethiopia	Ethiopia

Men *(Cont.)*

Year	Winner	Winning Team	Year	Winner	Winning Team
1983	Bekele Debele, Ethiopia	Ethiopia	1990	Khalid Skah, Morocco	Kenya
1984	Carlos Lopes, Portugal	Ethiopia	1991	Khalid Skah, Morocco	Kenya
1985	Carlos Lopes, Portugal	Ethiopia	1992	John Ngugi, Kenya	Kenya
1986	John Ngugi, Kenya	Kenya	1993	William Sigei, Kenya	Kenya
1987	John Ngugi, Kenya	Kenya	1994	William Sigei, Kenya	Kenya
1988	John Ngugi, Kenya	Kenya	1995	Paul Tergat, Kenya	Kenya
1989	John Ngugi, Kenya	Kenya	1996	Paul Tergat, Kenya	Kenya

Women

Year	Winner	Winning Team	Year	Winner	Winning Team
1973	Paola Cacchi, Italy	England	1985	Zola Budd, England	United States
1974	Paola Cacchi, Italy	England	1986	Zola Budd, England	England
1975	Julie Brown, United States	United States	1987	Annette Sergent, France	United States
1976	Carmen Valero, Spain	USSR	1988	Ingrid Kristiansen, Norway	USSR
1977	Carmen Valero, Spain	USSR	1989	Annette Sergent, France	USSR
1978	Grete Waitz, Norway	Romania	1990	Lynn Jennings, United States	USSR
1979	Grete Waitz, Norway	United States	1991	Lynn Jennings, United States	Kenya
1980	Grete Waitz, Norway	USSR	1992	Lynn Jennings, United States	Kenya
1981	Grete Waitz, Norway	USSR	1993	Albertina Dias, Portugal	Kenya
1982	Maricica Puica, Romania	USSR	1994	Helen Chepngeno, Kenya	Portugal
1983	Grete Waitz, Norway	United States	1995	Derartu Tulu, Ethiopia	Kenya
1984	Maricica Puica, Romania	United States	1996	Gete Wami, Ethiopia	Kenya

Notable Achievements

Longest Winning Streaks

MEN

Event	Name and Nationality	Streak	Years
100-meter dash	Bob Hayes, United States	49	1962–64
200-meter dash	Manfred Gemar, Germany	41	1956–60
400-meter run	Michael Johnson, United States	57	1989–
800-meter run	Mal Whitfield, United States	40	1951–54
1,500-meter run	Josy Barthel, Luxembourg	17	1952
1,500-meter run/mile	Steve Ovett, Great Britain	45	1977–80
Mile	Herb Elliott, Australia	35	1957–60
Steeplechase	Gaston Roelants, Belgium	45	1961–66
5,000-meter run	Emil Zátopek, Czechoslovakia	48	1949–52
10,000-meter run	Emil Zátopek, Czechoslovakia	38	1948–54
Marathon	Frank Shorter, United States	6	1971–73
110-meter hurdles	Jack Davis, United States	44	1952–55
400-meter hurdles	Edwin Moses, United States	107	1977–87
High jump	Ernie Shelton, United States	46	1953–55
Pole vault	Bob Richards, United States	50	1950–52
Long jump	Carl Lewis, United States	65	1981–91
Triple jump	Adhemar da Silva, Brazil	60	1950–56
Shot put	Parry O'Brien, United States	116	1952–56
Discus throw	Ricky Bruch, Sweden	54	1972–73
Hammer throw	Imre Nemeth, Hungary	73	1946–50
Javelin throw	Janis Lusis, USSR	41	1967–70
Decathlon	Bob Mathias, United States	11	1948–56

WOMEN

Event	Name and Nationality	Streak	Years
100-meter dash	Merlene Ottey, Jamaica	56	1987–91
200-meter dash	Irena Szewinska, Poland	38	1973–75
400-meter run	Irena Szewinska, Poland	36	1973–78
800-meter run	Ana Fidelia Quirot, Cuba	36	1987–90
1,500-meter run	Paula Ivan, Romania	15	1988–91
1,500-meter run/mile	Paula Ivan, Romania	19	1988–90
3,000-meter run	Mary Slaney, United States	10	1982–84
10,000-meter run	Ingrid Kristiansen, Norway	5	1985–87

Longest Winning Streaks *(Cont.)*

WOMEN *(Cont.)*

Event	Name and Nationality	Streak	Years
Marathon	Katrin Dörre, East Germany	10	1982–86
100-meter hurdles	Annelie Ernhardt, East Germany	44	1972–75
400-meter hurdles	Ann-Louise Skoglund, Sweden	18	1981–83
High jump	Iolanda Balas, Romania	140	1956–67
Long jump	Tatyana Shchelkanova, USSR	19	1964–66
Shot put	Nadezhda Chizhova, USSR	57	1969–73
Discus throw	Gisela Mauermeyer, Germany	65	1935–42
Javelin throw	Ruth Fuchs, East Germany	30	1972–73
Multi	Heide Rosendahl, West Germany	15	1969–72

Most Consecutive Years Ranked No. 1 in the World

MEN

No.	Name and Nationality	Event	Years
9	Victor Saneyev, USSR	Triple jump	1968–76
8	Bob Richards, United States	Pole vault	1949–56
8	Ralph Boston, United States	Long jump	1960–67
7	Emil Zátopek (Czech)	10,000-meter run	1948–54

WOMEN

No.	Name and Nationality	Event	Years
9	Iolanda Balas, Romania	High jump	1958–66
8	Ruth Fuchs, East Germany	Javelin throw	1972–79
7	Faina Melnick, USSR	Discus throw	1971–77

Major Barrier Breakers

MEN

Event	Mark	Name and Nationality	Date	Site
sub 10-second 100-meter dash	9.95	Jim Hines, United States	Oct. 14, 1968	Mexico City
sub 20-second 200-meter dash	19.83	Tommie Smith, United States	Oct. 16, 1968	Mexico City
sub 45-second 400-meter run	44.9	Otis Davis, United States	Sept. 6, 1960	Rome
sub 1:45 800-meter run	1:44.3	Peter Snell, New Zealand	Feb. 3, 1962	Christchurch, New Zealand
sub four minute mile	3:59.4	Roger Bannister, Great Britain	May 6, 1954	Oxford
sub 3:50 mile	3:49.4	John Walker, New Zealand	Aug. 12, 1975	Göteborg
sub 13-minute 5,000-meter run	12:58.39	Said Aouita, Morocco	July 22, 1986	Rome
sub 27:00 10,000-meter run	26:58.38	Yobes Ondieki, Kenya	July 10, 1993	Oslo
sub 13-second 110-meter hurdles	12.93	Renaldo Nehemiah, United States	Aug. 19, 1981	Zurich
sub 50-second 400-meter hurdles	49.5	Glenn Davis, United States	June 29, 1956	Los Angeles
7' high jump	7' ⅜"	Charles Dumas, United States	June 29, 1956	Los Angeles
8' high jump	8'	Javier Sotomayor, Cuba	July 29, 1989	San Juan
60' triple jump	60'¼"	Jonathan Edwards, Great Britain	Aug. 7, 1995	Göteborg
20' pole vault	20'	Sergei Bubka, USSR	March 15, 1991	San Sebastian, Spain
70' shot put	70' 7¼"	Randy Matson, United States	May 5, 1965	College Station, Texas
200' discus throw	200' 5"	Al Oerter, United States	May 18, 1962	Los Angeles
300' (new) javelin	300' 1"	Steve Backley, Great Britain	Jan. 25, 1992	Auckland, New Zealand

WOMEN

Event	Mark	Name and Nationality	Date	Site
sub 11-second 100-meter dash	10.88	Marlies Oelsner, East Germany	July 1, 1977	Dresden
sub 22-second 200-meter dash	21.71	Marita Koch, East Germany	June 10, 1979	Karl Marx Stadt
sub 50-second 400-meter run	49.9	Irena Szewinska, Poland	June 22, 1974	Warsaw
sub 2:00 800-meter run	1:59.1	Shin Geum Dan, North Korea	Nov. 12, 1963	Djakarta
sub 4:00 1500-meter run	3:56.0	Tatyana Kazankina, USSR	June 28, 1976	Podolsk, USSR

Major Barrier Breakers (Cont.)

WOMEN (Cont.)

Event	Mark	Name and Nationality	Date	Site
sub 4:20 mile	4:17.55	Mary Decker, United States	Feb. 16, 1980	Houston
sub 15:00 5,000-meter run	14:58.89	Ingrid Kristiansen, Norway	June 28, 1984	Oslo
sub 30:00 10,000-meter run	29:31.78	Wang Junxia, China	Sept. 8, 1993	Beijing
sub 2:30 marathon	2:27:33	Grete Waitz, Norway	Oct. 21, 1979	New York City
sub 13-second 100-meter hurdles	12.9	Karin Balzer, East Germany	Sept. 5, 1969	Berlin
6' high jump	6'	Iolanda Balas, Romania	Oct. 18, 1958	Budapest
70' shot put	70' 4½"	Nadyezhda Chizhova, USSR	Sept. 29, 1973	Varna, Bulgaria
200' discus throw	201'	Liesel Westermann, West Germany	Nov. 5, 1967	Sao Paulo
200' javelin throw	201' 4"	Elvira Ozolina, USSR	Aug. 27, 1964	Kiev
first 7,000-point heptathlon	7,148	Jackie Joyner-Kersee, U.S.	July 6–7, 1986	Moscow

Olympic Accomplishments

Oldest Olympic gold medalist—Patrick (Babe) McDonald, United States, 42 years, 26 days, 56-pound weight throw, 1920
Oldest Olympic medalist—Tebbs Lloyd Johnson, Great Britain, 48 years, 115 days, 1948 (bronze), 50K walk
Youngest Olympic gold medalist—Barbara Jones, United States, 15 years 123 days, 1952, 4 x 100 relay
Youngest gold medalist in individual event—Ulrike Meyfarth, West Germany, 16 years, 123 days, 1972, high jump

World Record Accomplishments*

Most world records equaled or set in a day—6, Jesse Owens, United States, 5/25/35, (9.4 100-yard dash; 26' 8¼" long jump; 20.3 200-meter dash and 220-yard dash; and 22.6 220-yard hurdles and 200-meter hurdles
Most records in a year—10, Gunder Hägg, Sweden, 1941-42, 1,500 to 5,000 meters
Most records in a career—35, Sergei Bubka, 1983-94, pole vault indoors and out
Longest span of record setting—11 years, 20 days, Irena Szewinska, Poland, 1965-76, 200-meter dash
Youngest person to set a set world record—Carolina Gisolf, Holland, 15 years, 5 days, 1928, high jump , 5' 3⅜"
Youngest man to set a world record—John Thomas, United States, 17 years, 355 days, 1959, high jump, 7' 1¼"
Oldest person to set world record—Carlos Lopes, Portugal, 38 years, 59 days, marathon, 2:07:12
Greatest percentage improvement—6.59, Bob Beamon, United States, 1968, long jump
Longest lasting record—long jump, 26' 8¼", Jesse Owens, United States, 25 years, 79 days (1935-60)
Highest clearance over head, men—23¼", Franklin Jacobs, United States (5' 8"), 1978
Highest clearance over head, woman—12¾", Yolanda Henry, United States (5' 6"), 1990
*Marks sanctioned by the IAAF

Welcome Home

Josia Thugwane's long run, it seems, is not yet finished. Thugwane, the 5' 2", 99-pound maintenance worker from the Koornfontein coal mines whose inspired stretch drive in the 1996 Olympic marathon made him South Africa's first black Olympic gold medalist, returned home in August of '96 to find himself the target of a rumored murder plot. Before leaving for the Games, Thugwane, 25, earned about $250 a month tending roads at the mines and lived with his wife and four children in a tin shack in the impoverished black settlement of Bethal. His victory brought him a bonus of $33,000 from the government and a new Mercedes, as well as several sponsorship offers, and upon his homecoming, friends warned him that local criminals were planning to rob and kill him. Thugwane, who in March of '96 had been grazed in the jaw by a bullet when he was the victim of a carjacking, took the warnings seriously. "I don't know who they are," he told the Johannesburg *Star*. "But if they say they will kill someone, they always do."

Thugwane moved his family into a protected house on the mines' property and started traveling with a government bodyguard. "The people in the township are saying I no longer want to be associated with them," he said. "They think I'm rich now. I fear for my wife and children. I don't care where I live. I just want to be safe."

Thugwane's plight is tragically representative of the new South Africa. Apartheid is gone, but poverty and resentment remain, and a spiraling crime rate is transforming the nation into the most murderous society in the world. Thugwane's victory has been hailed around the world as a symbol of hope and renewal for South Africa, but as the runner points out, "Medals won't matter to me if I'm dead."

Swimming

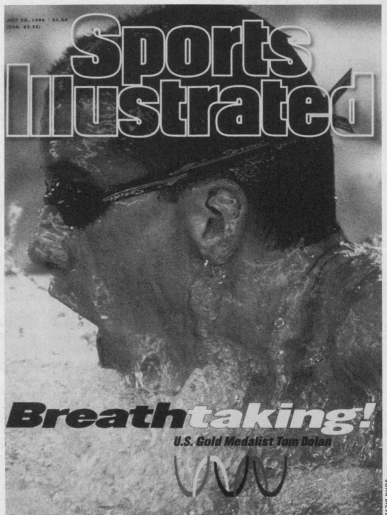

JULY 29, 1996 · $3.50
(CAN. $3.95)

Sports Illustrated

Breath*taking!*

U.S. Gold Medalist Tom Dolan

JOHN BIEVER

Wonder Women

In taking Atlanta by storm, Amy Van Dyken of the U.S. and Ireland's Michelle Smith each provoked a different kind of wonder

by Gerry Callahan

ON THE eve of the Atlanta Olympics, they were the most celebrated swimmers on the U.S. team: the tall, gutsy asthmatic who was hoping to bring home a pile of gold medals for the men's team and the smiling, well-spoken legend who would be the focus of the U.S. women's team. The man with the breathing difficulties, Tom Dolan, had a chance to win gold in four events and emerge as the next Mark Spitz, while the woman with the neon smile, Janet Evans, was after more than medals. She came to her third and final Olympic Games to win our hearts once again.

It's funny how things play out on the Olympic stage sometimes. In the end, the U.S. swimmers were indeed led by a courageous asthma-sufferer and a classy champion with big teeth and a bigger heart, but there was a surprising twist. The two heroes came in one tall, toothy, package. While Dolan stalled after one gold medal, and Evans sputtered in her Olympic swan song, 23-year-old sprinter Amy Van Dyken splashed into the picture, earning four gold medals and millions of new admirers.

Upon draping gold number four around her neck, Van Dyken, an outcast in her Colorado high school, held herself up as a model for awkward kids everywhere. Not because she had asthma. Just because she was a six-foot outsider who was now sitting on top of the world. Even in an Olympic year, there were few moments as sweet. "This is for all the nerds out there," said Van Dyken. "For all the kids out there who are struggling the way I was struggling, I hope I can be an inspiration to you." If they missed her in the Olympic pool, they could, of course, see her on a Wheaties box shortly after her remarkable performance.

Van Dyken recalled overhearing her high school teammates complaining that they couldn't win the relay with her on the team. In Atlanta the U.S. couldn't lose with Van Dyken. She was part of two winning relays and also won individual golds in the 50 free and the 100 butterfly, becoming the first U.S. woman ever to win four gold medals in one Games. Evans, meanwhile, failed to make the finals of the 400 and finished sixth in the 800, well behind winner Brooke Bennett, the 16-year-old phenom from Florida, who appeared to claim the

Nerd no more: Van Dyken's four gold medals landed her on the Wheaties box.

RICHARD MACKSON

throne as the new teen queen of distance swimming.

Van Dyken wasn't the only American who couldn't fit her winnings in her carry-on bag. Most of the prizes at the Georgia Tech Aquatic Center pool went to the home team. Jenny Thompson, competing in her second Olympics, won three gold medals, giving her five for her career, which ties her with Bonnie Blair for the most golds for an American woman. Thompson earned all five of her golds on relays. Angel Martino won four medals, two individual bronze and two relay golds, while Amanda Beard and Whitney Hedgepeth each won two silvers and Beard added a relay gold. By the end of the week, the gold-laden U.S. women looked like the Mr. T fan club.

The U.S. men, meanwhile, set a world record in the 4x100 medley relay. Gary Hall Jr., who anchored that relay, finished second to Russian rocket Aleksandr Popov in the 50 and the 100 but was only a fingertip away in both races. Even while losing, Hall seemed to emerge as the new cover boy for men's swimming in the U.S.

For the Americans, the gold medal stand was as crowded as MARTA, Atlanta's overloaded subway system. The U.S. won 26 medals in swimming, including 13 golds. Germany and Australia were distant runners-up in the swimming medal standings. Van Dyken alone took home more golds than China, Australia and Germany *combined*. The Chinese swimmers were especially disappointing, earning just one gold and lending weight to the theory that they could not compete without chemical additives.

The Chinese, in fact, were outperformed by one previously unknown woman from that well-known aquatics hotbed Ireland. While the Americans dominated the team competition, there was no doubt which individual stole the Atlanta show, in the pool and out. Ireland had never won an Olympic medal in swimming—the country, in fact, does not even have a 50-meter pool—but in dramatic fashion, 26-year-old Michelle Smith became the first. She won three golds and a bronze, setting off parties in her country and protests in Atlanta.

Smith passed all her drug tests, but rumors of possible cheating dogged her throughout her Olympic experience. Her husband and coach, Erik de Bruin, is a former Dutch discus thrower who had been suspended after a positive drug test in 1993. Her times had jumped dramatically in recent races, and then she won three Olympic events—the 200 IM, the 400 IM and the 400 freestyle—and prompted comparisons to everyone from Spitz to Secretariat to, yes, Ben Johnson. She was that impressive and that surprising.

The questions followed each race, but Smith's interrogators had no more luck than her rival swimmers. She remained defiant to the end, scoffing at any suggestion of steroid use and insisting that she had been tested more than any American swimmer. Whether she beat the best swimmers from around the world—or just beat the system—Smith left the insinuations in Atlanta and returned to a national celebration in her homeland. The United States may have dominated the Olympic competition, but in Ireland the sport of swimming was changed forever. There reportedly were plans to build a 50-meter pool.

FOR THE RECORD·1995–1996

1995–1996 Major Competitions

Men

SHORT COURSE METERS WORLD CHAMPIONSHIPS
Rio de Janeiro, Brazil, November 30–December 3, 1995

50 free ....Francisco Sanchez, Venezuela, 21.80
100 free.......Fernando Scherer, Brazil, 47.97
200 free........Gustavo Borges, Brazil, 1:45.55
400 free.......Daniel Kowalski, Australia, 3:45.14
1500 free.......Daniel Kowalski, Australia, 14:48.51
100 back......Rodolfo Falcon, Cuba, 53.12
200 back......Rodolfo Falcon, Cuba, 1:55.16
100 breast....Mark Warnecke, Germany, 59.89
200 breast....Wang Yiwu, China, 2:11.11
100 fly ....Scott Miller, Australia, 52.38
200 fly ....Scott Goodman, Australia, 1:54.79
200 IM ....Matthew Dunn, Australia, 1:56.86
400 IM ....Matthew Dunn, Australia, 4:08.02
400 m relay ..New Zealand, 3:35.69
400 f relay ....Brazil, 3:12.42
800 f relay ....Australia, 7:07.97

U.S. INDOOR CHAMPIONSHIPS
Orlando, Florida, February 8–11, 1996

50 free ....David Fox, Raleigh, 22.73
100 free.........David Fox, Raleigh, 50.66
200 free........Josh Davis, Athletes in Action, 1:50.47
400 free........Josh Davis, Athletes in Action, 3:55.63
800 free........Yann deFabrique, Bolles Sharks, 8:19.40
1500 free......Peter Wright, J. Wahoos, 15:31.97
100 back......Tripp Schwenk, unattached, 56.39
200 back......Tripp Schwenk, unattached, 2:02.57
100 breast....Seth Van Neerden, Ft Lauderdale, 1:03.24
200 breast....Norbert Rozsa, Hungary, 2:16.65
100 fly ....Peter Horvath, Hungary, 54.59
200 fly ....Attila Czene, Hungary, 1:59.47
200 IM ....Ron Karnaugh, Florida Aquatics, 2:03.13
400 IM ....Eric Namesnik, Club Wolverines, 4:23.06
400 m relay ..Sport Hungary, 3:47.09
400 f relay ....Fort Lauderdale B, 3:31.13
800 f relay ....Bolles, 7:44.07
1-m spgbd ...Dean Panaro, Ft Lauderdale
              Diving, 416.61
3-m spgbd ...Mark Lenzi, Kimball Divers, 692.67
Platform........David Pichler, Miami Diving, 622.50
3-m sync dv ..Kent Ferguson/David Pichler, 326.97
10-m sync plt..Mark Ruiz/Kongzheng Li, 293.13
Diving competitions held in Oxford, OH, April 17-21.

*Meet record.

U.S. OLYMPIC TRIALS
Indianapolis, Indiana, March 6–12, 1996

50 free..........Gary Hall, Jr, Phoenix, 22.27
100 free........Jon Olsen, unattached, 49.45
200 free.......John Piersma, Michigan, 1:48.97
400 free.......Tom Dolan, Michigan, 3:48.99
1500 free......Carlton Bruner, Club Wolverine,15:12.85
100 back   Tripp Schwenk, Sarasota YMCA, 54.94
200 back......Brad Bridgewater, USC, 1:59.15
100 breast....Jeremy Linn, Tennessee, 1:01.94
200 breast....Kurt Grote, Stanford, 2:14.22
100 fly ....John Hargis, Auburn, 53.42
200 fly ....Tom Malchow, Michigan, 1:57.39
200 IM ....Tom Dolan, Michigan, 2:00.20
400 IM ....Tom Dolan, Michigan, 4:12.72*
3-m spgbd ...Scott Donie, Miami Diving, 1,002.28
Platform........Patrick Jeffrey, Team Orlando, 1,147.71
Diving competitions held in Indianapolis, IN, June19-23.

U.S. OUTDOOR CHAMPIONSHIPS
Fort Lauderdale, Florida, August 12–16, 1996

50 free ....Bill Pilczuk, Auburn Aquatics, 22.68
100 free........Neil Walker, Verona Aquatics, 50.07
200 free.......Josh Davis, Athletes in Action, 1:49.18
400 free.......Josh Davis, Athletes in Action, 3:54.71
800 free........Lawrence Frostad, Mass Bay
              Marlins, 8:02.64
1500 free......Chris Thompson, Roseburg, 15:23.72
100 back......Lenny Krazelburg, Trojan SC, 56.11
200 back......Lenny Krazelburg, Trojan SC, 1:59.37
100 breast....Jarrod Marrs, Bengal Tiger, 1:03.41
200 breast....Tom Wilkens, Santa Clara, 2:15.82
100 fly ....Matt Hooper, Alamo Area, 54.00
200 fly ....Matt Hooper, Alamo Area, 1:59.64
200 IM ....Tom Wilkens, Santa Clara, 2:03.19
400 IM ....Tom Wilkens, Santa Clara, 4:18.76
400 m relay ..Athletes in Action, 3:47.12
400 f relay ....Athletes in Action, 3:25.47
800 f relay ....Mass Bay Marlins A, 7:34.52
1-m spgbd ...Troy Dumais, Trojan Dive Club, 411.00
3-m spgbd ...Troy Dumais, Trojan Dive Club, 672.51
Platform........Russ Bertram, Ft Lauderdale, 642.84
3-m sync dv ..Russ Bertram/Chris Mantilla, 269.52
10-m sync plt..Russ Bertram/Chris Mantilla, 262.35
Diving competitions held in Moultrie, GA, August 14-18.

FINA/KODAK DIVING GRAND PRIX
Fort Lauderdale, Florida, May 9–12, 1996

3-m spgbd ...Dmitry Sautin, Russia, 698.58
Platform........Dmitry Sautin, Russia, 658.77

Women

SHORT COURSE METERS WORLD CHAMPIONSHIPS
Rio de Janeiro, Brazil, November 30–December 3, 1995

50 free ....Le Jingyi, China, 24.62
100 free ....Le Jingyi, China, 53.23
200 free ......Claudia Poll, Costa Rica, 1:55.42 WR
400 free ......Claudia Poll, Costa Rica, 4:05.18
800 free ......Sarah Hardcastle, Great Britain, 8:26.46
100 back .....Misty Hyman, United States, 1:00.21
200 back .....Mette Jacobsen, Denmark, 2:08.18
100 breast ...Samantha Riley, Australia, 1:05.70 WR
200 breast ...Samantha Riley, Australia, 2:20.85 WR
100 fly..........Liu Limin, China, 58.66 WR
200 fly..........Susan O'Neill, Australia, 2:06.18*
200 IM ....Eli Overton, Australia, 2:11.67
400 IM ....Joanne Malar, Canada, 4:36.40
400 m relay ..Australia, 4:00.46
400 f relay ...China, 3:37.00
800 f relay ...Canada, 7:58.25

U.S. INDOOR CHAMPIONSHIPS
Orlando, Florida, February 8–11, 1996

50 free ....Angel Martino, Americus Blue Tide, 25.45
100 free ....Angel Martino, Americus Blue Tide, 55.39
200 free ......Suzu Chiba, GWSC, 1:59.20
400 free ......Brooke Bennett, BSTC Blue Wave, 4:12.66
800 free ......Brooke Bennett, BSTC Blue Wave, 8:30.54
1500 free ....Brooke Bennett, BSTC Blue Wave, 16:37.94
100 back .....Whitney Hedgepeth, Texas
                    Aquatics, 1:02.36
200 back .....Whitney Hedgepeth, Texas
                    Aquatics, 2:13.10
100 breast ...Jilen Siroky, Mecklenburg, 1:11.45
200 breast ...Riley Mants, Manta, 2:31.78
100 fly..........Richelle Depold, unattached, 1:01.10
200 fly..........Lauren Stinnett, Curl-Burke, 2:13.52
200 IM ....Shannon Cullen, Redlands, 2:18.81
400 IM ....Corrie Murphy, unattached, 4:50.75
400 m relay ..Mecklenburg, 4:21.96
400 f relay ....Phoenix, 3:52.12
800 f relay ....Phoenix, 8:19.27
1-m spgbd ..Reyne Borup, Ft Lauderdale
                    Diving, 267.66
3-m spgbd...Jenny Keim, Ft Lauderdale Diving, 497.97
Platform ....Becky Ruehl, unattached, 485.13
3-m sync .....Kim Stanfield/Kristen Walls, 268.80
10-m sync ...Patty Armstrong/Laura Wilkinson, 264.06
Diving competitions held in Oxford, OH, April 17-21.

WR=World record.   *Meet record.

U.S. OLYMPIC TRIALS
Indianapolis, Indiana, March 6–12, 1996

50 free ....Amy Van Dyken, unattached, 25.17
100 free ....Amy Van Dyken, unattached, 55.27
200 free ......Cristina Teuscher, Badger, 1:59.50
400 free ......Janet Evans, Trojan, 4:10.07
800 free ......Brooke Bennett, BSTC Blue Wave, 8:31.41
100 back .....Whitney Hedgepeth,
                    Texas Aquatics, 1:01.52
200 back .....Beth Botsford, North Baltimore, 2:10.66
100 breast ...Amanda Beard, Irvine Novas, 1:08.36
200 breast ...Amanda Beard, Irvine Novas, 2:26.25
100 fly..........Angel Martino, Americus Blue Tide, 59.63
200 fly..........Annette Salmeen, UCLA, 2:12.39
200 IM ....Allison Wagner, Florida, 2:13.71
400 IM ....Allison Wagner, Florida, 4:41.61
3-m spgbd ..Melisa Moses,
                    Clabadistas del Sol, 862.53
Platform   Mary Ellen Clark,
                    Ft Lauderdale Diving, 865.08
Diving competitions held in Indianapolis, IN, June 19-23.

U.S. OUTDOOR CHAMPIONSHIPS
Fort Lauderdale, Florida, August 12–16, 1996

50 free ....Liesl Kolbisen, Hillenbrand, 26.11
100 free ....Liesl Kolbisen, Hillenbrand, 56.50
200 free ......Lauren Thies, Multnomah AC, 2:01.45
400 free ......Jennifer Parmenter, Rose Bowl, 4:13.24
800 free ......Ashley Whitney, Bolles Sharkes, 8:36.62
1500 free .....Diana Munz, Lake Erie Silver
                    Dolphins, 16:36.64
100 back .....Lea Loveless, Badger, 1:02.50
200 back .....Lea Loveless, Badger, 2:12.11
100 breast ...Katie Hathaway, Mecklenburg, 1:09.86
200 breast ...Annemieke McReynolds, Scenic
                    City, 2:29.71
100 fly..........Misty Hyman, Afox, 59.68
200 fly..........Misty Hyman, Afox, 2:10.95
200 IM ....Jennifer Parmenter, Rose Bowl, 2:15.93
400 IM ....Jennifer Parmenter, Rose Bowl, 4:43.48
400 m relay ..Bolles Sharks A, 4:17.69
400 f relay ....Bolles Sharks A, 3:52.06
800 f relay ....Bolles Sharks A, 8:16.58
1-m spgbd ..Doris Glenn Easterly, Ft Lauderdale, 275.76
3-m spgbd ..Erica Sorgi, Mission Viejo
                    Matadors, 525.69
Platform ....Becky Ruehl, Cincinnati Stingrays, 517.02
3-m sync .....Patty Armstrong/Laura Wilkinson, 263.52
10-m sync ...Patty Armstrong/Laura Wilkinson, 298.05
Diving competitions held in Moultrie, GA, August 14-18.

FINA/KODAK DIVING GRAND PRIX
Fort Lauderdale, Florida, May 9–12, 1996

3-m spgbd ...Irina Lashko, Russia, 532.65
Platform........Vanessa Baker, Australia, 483.33

World and American Records Set in 1996

Men

Event	Mark	Record Holder	Date	Site
100 butterfly	52.27	Denis Pankratov, Russia (W)	7-24-96	Atlanta
100 breast	1:00.60	F. Deburghgraeve, Belgium (W)	7-20-96	Atlanta
	1:00.77	Jeremy Linn (A)	7-20-96	Atlanta
400 medley relay	3:34.84	United States (W, A) (Jeff Rouse, Jeremy Linn, Mark Henderson, Gary Hall, Jr)	7-26-96	Atlanta

Women

Event	Mark	Record Holder	Date	Site
50 freestyle	24.87	Amy Van Dyken (A)	7-26-96	Atlanta
100 breast	1:07.02	Penelope Heyns, S Africa (W)	7-21-96	Atlanta
	1:08.09	Amanda Beard (A)	7-21-96	Atlanta
400 freestyle relay	3:39.29	United States (A) (Angel Martino, Amy Van Dyken, Catherine Fox, Jenny Thompson)	7-22-96	Atlanta
800 freestyle relay	7:59.87	United States (A) (Trina Jackson, Cristina Teuscher, Sheila Taormina, Jenny Thompson)	7-25-96	Atlanta

Did She or Didn't She?

Stories of sudden success, such as the one carved out by Irish swimmer Michelle Smith in Atlanta, occasion long and anguished colloquies among the men and women credentialed to tell them. At what point is it fair to "put in play" questions of drugs? How much innuendo can be written into a news report about how Smith's physique grew and her times shrank precisely when she moved to the Netherlands, the seedbed of performance-enhancing substances like erythropoetin and human-growth hormone, for which chemical sleuths have no tests? Is it possible to ignore the fact that Smith's husband and coach, Erik de Bruin, a former Dutch discus thrower, is banned from competition by his sport's governing body, the IAAF, because of a positive test for performance-enhancing drugs?

These questions resonated last week for Irish journalist Paul Kimmage, who, during a four-year career as a professional cyclist in the late 1980s, witnessed and, on occasion, partook of the secret pharmacological culture of sports. The exposé he wrote after retiring, *A Rough Ride*, earned him the contempt of the cycling community, which literally turned its back on him when he began covering sports as a writer for Dublin's *Sunday Independent*. Kimmage agonized over what to express in print during the summer of 1996 but finally penned a story conveying his doubts that Smith did not use drugs, urging his fellow citizens to "take your heads out of the sand."

"I listen to people who are on the inside," says Kimmage, "and when people on the inside say this improvement is incredible for a 26-year-old woman, I'm suspicious. These people jumping up and down in the streets back home were the first to point the finger at the Chinese when they beat [Irish distance runner] Sonia O'Sullivan at the worlds three years ago. But when it's one of our own, they don't want to believe she'd do it. 'An Irish girl? Taking drugs?'"

Before he sat down to write his story, Kimmage called his wife, Ann, and voiced his questions about Ireland's Olympic hero. "You're not going to write all that, are you?" she said, knowing that if he did, she and Paul and their children, Evelyn, 6, and Eoin, 4, would be in for another turn in pariahdom, another rough ride. But write it he did.

When Kimmage got back to the Auld Sod that photo was still hanging in his office, the one of him riding in his last Tour de France, in 1989, scaling a peak in the Pyrenees. In the background is Johannes Draaijer, one of a spate of young Dutch cyclists who died of heart failure from 1987 to '90. No one in the sport doubts that some frightening, newfangled drug was responsible.

Kimmage could not bear to watch Smith win her third gold medal. He was in the press room, transcribing an interview, when the distant strains of the Irish national anthem told him she had won again. "I've never been so driven to write, but never been so afraid and sad," he said before sitting down to compose his Sunday sermon. "I don't know what the solution is." He found something to say, but it didn't make him or anyone else very happy.

—Alexander Wolff

World and American Records Through Aug. 31, 1996

MEN
Freestyle

Event	Time	Record Holder	Date	Site
50 meters	21.81	Tom Jager (W, A)	3-24-90	Nashville
100 meters	48.42	Alexander Popov, Russia (W)	6-18-94	Monte Carlo
		Matt Biondi (A)	8-10-88	Austin
200 meters	1:46.69	Giorgio Lamberti, Italy (W)	8-15-89	Bonn
	1:47.72	Matt Biondi (A)	8-8-88	Austin
400 meters	3:43.80	Kieran Perkins, Australia (W)	9-9-94	Rome
	3:48.06	Matt Cetlinski (A)	8-11-88	Austin
800 meters	7:46.00	Kieran Perkins, Australia (W)	8-24-94	Vancouver, B.C.
	7:52.45	Sean Killion (A)	7-27-87	Clovis, CA
1,500 meters	14:41.66	Kieran Perkins, Australia (W)	8-24-94	Vancouver, B.C.
	15:01.51	George DiCarlo (A)	6-30-84	·Indianapolis

Backstroke

Event	Time	Record Holder	Date	Site
100 meters	53.86*	Jeff Rouse (W, A)	7-31-92	Barcelona
200 meters	1:56.57	Martin Zubero, Spain (W)	11-23-91	Tuscaloosa, AL
	1:58.33	Tripp Schwenk (A)	8-1-95	Pasadena

*Set on first leg of relay.

Breaststroke

Event	Time	Record Holder	Date	Site
100 meters	1:00.60	F. Deburghgraeve, Belgium (W)	7-20-96	Atlanta
	1:00.77	Jeremy Linn (A)	7-20-96	Atlanta
200 meters	2:10.16	Mike Barrowman (W,A)	7-29-92	Barcelona

Butterfly

Event	Time	Record Holder	Date	Site
100 meters	52.27	Denis Pankratov, Russia (W)	7-24-96	Atlanta
	52.84	Pablo Morales (A)	6-23-86	Orlando, FL
200 meters	1:55.22	Denis Pankratov, Russia (W)	6-14-95	Canet, France
	1:55.69	Melvin Stewart (A)	1-12-91	Perth, Australia

Individual Medley

Event	Time	Record Holder	Date	Site
200 meters	1:59.36	Jani Sievinen, Finland (W)	9-11-94	Rome
	2:00.11	Dave Wharton (A)	8-20-89	Tokyo
400 meters	4:12.30	Tom Dolan (W, A)	9-6-94	Rome

Relays

Event	Time	Record Holder	Date	Site
400 meter medley	3:34.84	United States (W, A) (Jeff Rouse, Jeremy Linn, Mark Henderson, Gary Hall Jr)	7-26-96	Atlanta
400 meter freestyle	3:15.11	United States (W, A) (David Fox, Joe Hudepohl, Jon Olsen, Gary Hall Jr)	8-12-95	Atlanta
800 meter freestyle	7:11.95	EUN (W) (Dmitri Lepikov, Vladimir Taianovitch, Veniamin Taianovitch, Yevgeny Sadovyi)	7-27-92	Barcelona
	7:12.51	United States (A) (Troy Dalbey, Matt Cetlinski, Doug Gjertsen, Matt Biondi)	9-21-88	Seoul

WOMEN

Freestyle

Event	Time	Record Holder	Date	Site
50 meters	24.51	Li Jingyi, China (W)	9-11-94	Rome
	24.87	Amy Van Dyken (A)	7-26-96	Atlanta
100 meters	54.01	Li Jingyi, China (W)	9-5-94	Rome
	54.48	Jenny Thompson (A)	3-1-92	Indianapolis
200 meters	1:57.55	Franziska van Almsick, Germany (W)	9-6-94	Rome
	1:57.90	Nicole Haislett (A)	7-27-92	Barcelona
400 meters	4:03.85	Janet Evans (W, A)	9-22-88	Seoul
800 meters	8.16.22	Janet Evans (W, A)	8-20-89	Tokyo
1500 meters	15:52.10	Janet Evans (W, A)	3-26-88	Orlando, FL

Backstroke

Event	Time	Record Holder	Date	Site
100 meters	1:00.16	He Cihong, China (W)	9-10-94	Rome
	1:00.82†	Lea Loveless (A)	7-30-92	Barcelona
200 meters	2:06.62	Krisztina Egerszegi, Hungary (W)	8-26-91	Athens, Greece
	2:08.60	Betsy Mitchell (A)	6-27-86	Orlando, FL

Breaststroke

Event	Time	Record Holder	Date	Site
100 meters	1:07.02	Penelope Heyns, South Africa (W)	7-21-96	Atlanta
	1:08.09	Amanda Beard (A)	7-21-96	Atlanta
200 meters	2:24.76	Rebecca Brown (W)	3-16-94	Queensland, Aus.
	2:25.35	Anita Nall (A)	3-2-92	Indianapolis

Butterfly

Event	Time	Record Holder	Date	Site
100 meters	57.93	Mary T. Meagher (W, A)	8-16-81	Brown Deer, WI
200 meters	2:05.96	Mary T. Meagher (W, A)	8-13-81	Brown Deer, WI

Individual Medley

Event	Time	Record Holder	Date	Site
200 meters	2:11.65	Lin Li, China (W)	7-30-92	Barcelona
	2:11.91	Summer Sanders (A)	7-30-92	Barcelona
400 meters	4:36.10	Petra Schneider, East Germany (W)	8-1-82	Guayaquil, Ecuador
	4:37.58	Summer Sanders (A)	7-26-92	Barcelona

Relays

Event	Time	Record Holder	Date	Site
400 meter medley	4:01.67	China (W) (He Cihong, Dai Guohong, Liu Limin, Le Jingyi)	9-10-94	Rome
	4:02.54	United States (A) (Lea Loveless, Anita Nall, Crissy Ahmann-Leighton, Jenny Thompson)	7-30-92	Barcelona
400 meter freestyle	3:37.91	China (W) (Le Jingyi, Ying Shan, Le Ying, Lu Bin)	9-7-94	Rome
	3:39.29	United States (A) (Angel Martino, Amy Van Dyken, Catherine Fox, Jenny Thompson)	7-22-96	Atlanta
800 meter freestyle	7:55.47	East Germany (W) (Manuela Stellmach, Astrid Strauss, Anke Mohring, Heike Friedrich)	8-18-87	Strasbourg, France
	7:59.87	United States (A) (Trina Jackson, Cristina Teuscher, Sheila Taormina, Jenny Thompson)	7-25-96	Atlanta

†Time swum on leadoff leg of 400-meter medley relay. Note: Records through Aug. 31, 1996.

World Championships

Venues: Belgrade, Sep 4–9, 1973; Cali, Colombia, July 18–27, 1975; West Berlin, Aug 20–28, 1978; Guayaquil, Equador, Aug 1–7, 1982; Madrid, Aug 17–22, 1986; Perth, Australia, Jan 7–13, 1991; Rome, Sep 1–11, 1994.

MEN

50-meter Freestyle

1986	Tom Jager, United States	22.49‡
1991	Tom Jager, United States	22.16‡
1994	Alexander Popov, Russia	22.17

100-meter Freestyle

1973	Jim Montgomery, United States	51.70
1975	Andy Coan, United States	51.25
1978	David McCagg, United States	50.24
1982	Jorg Woithe, East Germany	50.18
1986	Matt Biondi, United States	48.94
1991	Matt Biondi, United States	49.18
1994	Alexander Popov, Russia	49.12

200-meter Freestyle

1973	Jim Montgomery, United States	1:53.02
1975	Tim Shaw, United States	1:52.04‡
1978	Billy Forrester, United States	1:51.02‡
1982	Michael Gross, West Germany	1:49.84
1986	Michael Gross, West Germany	1:47.92
1991	Giorgio Lamberti, Italy	1:47.27‡
1994	Antti Kasvio, Finland	1:47.32

400-meter Freestyle

1973	Rick DeMont, United States	3:58.18‡
1975	Tim Shaw, United States	3:54.88‡
1978	Vladimir Salnikov, USSR	3:51.94‡
1982	Vladimir Salnikov, USSR	3:51.30‡
1986	Rainer Henkel, West Germany	3:50.05
1991	Joerg Hoffman, Germany	3:48.04‡
1994	Kieran Perkins, Australia	3:43.80*

1500-meter Freestyle

1973	Stephen Holland, Australia	15:31.85
1975	Tim Shaw, United States	15:28.92‡
1978	Vladimir Salnikov, USSR	15:03.99‡
1982	Vladimir Salnikov, USSR	15:01.77‡
1986	Rainer Henkel, West Germany	15:05.31
1991	Joerg Hoffman, Germany	14:50.36*
1994	Kieran Perkins, Australia	14:50.52

100-meter Backstroke

1973	Roland Matthes, East Germany	57.47
1975	Roland Matthes, East Germany	58.15
1978	Bob Jackson, United States	56.36‡
1982	Dirk Richter, East Germany	55.95
1986	Igor Polianski, USSR	55.58‡
1991	Jeff Rouse, United States	55.23‡
1994	Martin Lopez Zubero, Spain	55.17‡

200-meter Backstroke

1973	Roland Matthes, East Germany	2:01.87‡
1975	Zoltan Varraszto, Hungary	2:05.05
1978	Jesse Vassallo, United States	2:02.16
1982	Rick Carey, United States	2:00.82‡
1986	Igor Polianski, USSR	1:58.78‡
1991	Martin Zubero, Spain	1:59.52
1994	Vladimir Selkov, Russia	1:57.42‡

100-meter Breaststroke

1973	John Hencken, United States	1:04.02‡
1975	David Wilkie, Great Britain	1:04.26‡
1978	Walter Kusch, West Germany	1:03.56‡
1982	Steve Lundquist, United States	1:02.75‡
1986	Victor Davis, Canada	1:02.71
1991	Norbert Rozsa, Hungary	1:01.45*
1994	Norbert Rozsa, Hungary	1:01.24‡

200-meter Breaststroke

1973	David Wilkie, Great Britain	2:19.28‡
1975	David Wilkie, Great Britain	2:18.23‡
1978	Nick Nevid, United States	2:18.37
1982	Victor Davis, Canada	2:14.77*
1986	Jozsef Szabo, Hungary	2:14.27‡
1991	Mike Barrowman, United States	2:11.23*
1994	Norbert Rozsa, Hungary	2:12.81

100-meter Butterfly

1973	Bruce Robertson, Canada	55.69
1975	Greg Jagenburg, United States	55.63
1978	Joe Bottom, United States	54.30
1982	Matt Gribble, United States	53.88‡
1986	Pablo Morales, United States	53.54‡
1991	Anthony Nesty, Suriname	53.29‡
1994	Rafal Szukala, Poland	53.51

200-meter Butterfly

1973	Robin Backhaus, United States	2:03.32
1975	Bill Forrester, United States	2:01.95‡
1978	Mike Bruner, United States	1:59.38‡
1982	Michael Gross, East Germany	1:58.85‡
1986	Michael Gross, East Germany	1:56.53‡
1991	Melvin Stewart, United States	1:55.69*
1994	Denis Pankratov, Russia	1:56.54

200-meter Individual Medley

1973	Gunnar Larsson, Sweden	2:08.36
1975	Andras Hargitay, Hungary	2:07.72
1978	Graham Smith, Canada	2:03.65*
1982	Alexander Sidorenko, USSR	2:03.30‡
1986	Tamás Darnyi, Hungary	2:01.57‡
1991	Tamás Darnyi, Hungary	1:59.36*
1994	Jani Sievin, Finland	1:58.16*

400-meter Individual Medley

1973	Andras Hargitay, Hungary	4:31.11
1975	Andras Hargitay, Hungary	4:32.57
1978	Jesse Vassallo, United States	4:20.05*
1982	Ricardo Prado, Brazil	4:19.78*
1986	Tamás Darnyi, Hungary	4:18.98‡
1991	Tamás Darnyi, Hungary	4:12.36*
1994	Tom Dolan, United States	4:12.30*

* World record; ‡Meet record.

MEN *(Cont.)*

400-meter Medley Relay

1973	United States (Mike Stamm, John Hencken, Joe Bottom, Jim Montgomery)	3:49.49
1975	United States (John Murphy, Rick Colella, Greg Jagenburg, Andy Coan)	3:49.00
1978	United States (Robert Jackson, Nick Nevid, Joe Bottom, David McCagg)	3:44.63
1982	United States (Rick Carey, Steve Lundquist, Matt Gribble, Rowdy Gaines)	3:40.84*
1986	United States (Dan Veatch, David Lundberg, Pablo Morales, Matt Biondi)	3:41.25
1991	United States (Jeff Rouse, Eric Wunderlich, Mark Henderson Matt Biondi)	3:39.66‡
1994	United States (Jeff Rouse, Eric Wunderlich, Mark Henderson, Gary Hall)	3:37.74‡

400-meter Freestyle Relay

1973	United States (Mel Nash, Joe Bottom, Jim Montgomery, John Murphy)	3:27.18
1975	United States (Bruce Furniss, Jim Montgomery, Andy Coan, John Murphy)	3:24.85
1978	United States (Jack Babashoff, Rowdy Gaines, Jim Montgomery, David McCagg)	3:19.74
1982	United States (Chris Cavanaugh, Robin Leamy, David McCagg, Rowdy Gaines)	3:19.26*
1986	United States (Tom Jager, Mike Heath, Paul Wallace, Matt Biondi)	3:19.89
1991	United States (Tom Jager, Brent Lang, Doug Gjertsen, Matt Biondi)	3:17.15‡
1994	United States (Jon Olsen, Josh Davis, Ugur Taner, Gary Hall)	3:16.90‡

800-meter Freestyle Relay

1973	United States (Kurt Krumpholz, Robin Backhaus, Rick Klatt, Jim Montgomery)	7:33.22*
1975	West Germany (Klaus Steinbach, Werner Lampe, Hans Joachim Geisler, Peter Nocke)	7:39.44
1978	United States (Bruce Furniss, Billy Forrester, Bobby Hackett, Rowdy Gaines)	7:20.82
1982	United States (Rich Saeger, Jeff Float, Kyle Miller, Rowdy Gaines)	7:21.09
1986	East Germany (Lars Hinneburg, Thomas Flemming, Dirk Richter, Sven Lodziewski)	7:15.91‡
1991	Germany (Peter Sitt, Steffan Zesner, Stefan Pfeiffer, Michael Gross)	7:13.50‡
1994	Sweden (Christer Waller, Tommy Werner, Lars Frolander, Anders Holmertz)	7:17.34

WOMEN

50-meter Freestyle

1986	Tamara Costache, Romania	25.28*
1991	Zhuang Yong, China	25.47
1994	Le Jingyi, China	24.51*

100-meter Freestyle

1973	Kornelia Ender, East Germany	57.54
1975	Kornelia Ender, East Germany	56.50
1978	Barbara Krause, East Germany	55.68‡
1982	Birgit Meineke, East Germany	55.79
1986	Kristin Otto, East Germany	55.05‡
1991	Nicole Haislett, United States	55.17
1994	Le Jingyi, China	54.01*

200-meter Freestyle

1973	Keena Rothhammer, United States	2:04.99
1975	Shirley Babashoff, United States	2:02.50
1978	Cynthia Woodhead, United States	1:58.53*
1982	Annemarie Verstappen, Netherlands	1:59.53‡
1986	Heike Friedrich, East Germany	1:58.26‡
1991	Hayley Lewis, Australia	2:00.48
1994	Franziska Van Almsick, Germany	1:56.78*

400-meter Freestyle

1973	Heather Greenwood, United States	4:20.28
1975	Shirley Babashoff, United States	4:22.70
1978	Tracey Wickham, Australia	4:06.28*
1982	Carmela Schmidt, East Germany	4:08.98
1986	Heike Friedrich, East Germany	4:07.45
1991	Janet Evans, United States	4:08.63
1994	Yang Aihua, China	4:09.64

800-meter Freestyle

1973	Novella Calligaris, Italy	8:52.97
1975	Jenny Turrall, Australia	8:44.75‡
1978	Tracey Wickham, Australia	8:24.94‡
1982	Kim Linehan, United States	8:27.48
1986	Astrid Strauss, East Germany	8:28.24
1991	Janet Evans, United States	8:24.05‡
1994	Janet Evans, United States	8:29.85

100-meter Backstroke

1973	Ulrike Richter, East Germany	1:05.42
1975	Ulrike Richter, East Germany	1:03.30‡
1978	Linda Jezek, United States	1:02.55‡

* World record; ‡Meet record.

WOMEN *(Cont.)*

100-meter Backstroke *(Cont.)*

1982....Kristin Otto, East Germany	1:01.30‡
1986....Betsy Mitchell, United States	1:01.74
1991....Krisztina Egerszegi, Hungary	1:01.78
1994....He Cihong, China	1:00.57

200-meter Backstroke

1973....Melissa Belote, United States	2:20.52
1975....Birgit Treiber, East Germany	2:15.46*
1978....Linda Jezek, United States	2:11.93*
1982....Cornelia Sirch, East Germany	2:09.91*
1986....Cornelia Sirch, East Germany	2:11.37
1991....Krisztina Egerszegi, Hungary	2:09.15‡
1994....He Cihong, China	2:07.40

100-meter Breaststroke

1973....Renate Vogel, East Germany	1:13.74
1975....Hannalore Anke, East Germany	1:12.72
1978....Julia Bogdanova, USSR	1:10.31*
1982....Ute Geweniger, East Germany	1:09.14‡
1986....Sylvia Gerasch, East Germany	1:08.11*
1991....Linley Frame, Australia	1:08.81
1994....Samantha Riley, Australia	1:07.96*

200-meter Breaststroke

1973....Renate Vogel, East Germany	2:40.01
1975....Hannalore Anke, East Germany	2:37.25‡
1978....Lina Kachushite, USSR	2:31.42*
1982....Svetlana Varganova, USSR	2:28.82‡
1986....Silke Hoerner, East Germany	2:27.40*
1991....Elena Volkova, USSR	2:29.53
1994....Samantha Riley, Australia	2:26.87‡

100-meter Butterfly

1973....Kornelia Ender, East Germany	1:02.53
1975....Kornelia Ender, East Germany	1:01.24*
1978....Joan Pennington, United States	1:00.20‡
1982....Mary T. Meagher, United States	59.41‡
1986....Kornelia Gressler, East Germany	59.51
1991....Qian Hong, China	59.68
1994....Liu Limin, China	58.98‡

200-meter Butterfly

1973....Rosemarie Kother, East Germany	2:13.76‡
1975....Rosemarie Kother, East Germany	2:15.92
1978....Tracy Caulkins, United States	2:09.87*
1982....Ines Geissler, East Germany	2:08.66‡
1986....Mary T. Meagher, United States	2:08.41‡
1991....Summer Sanders, United States	2:09.24
1994....Liu Limin, China	2:07.25‡

200-meter Individual Medley

1973....Andrea Huebner, East Germany	2:20.51
1975....Kathy Heddy, United States	2:19.80
1978....Tracy Caulkins, United States	2:14.07*
1982....Petra Schneider, East Germany	2:11.79
1986....Kristin Otto, East Germany	2:15.56
1991....Li Lin, China	2:13.40
1994....Lu Bin, China	2:12.34‡

* World record; ‡Meet record

400-meter Individual Medley

1973....Gudrun Wegner, East Germany	4:57.71
1975....Ulrike Tauber, East Germany	4:52.76‡
1978....Tracy Caulkins, United States	4:40.83*
1982....Petra Schneider, East Germany	4:36.10*
1986....Kathleen Nord, East Germany	4:43.75
1991....Lin Li, China	4:41.45
1994....Dai Guohong, China	4:39.14

400-meter Medley Relay

1973....East Germany (Ulrike Richter, Renate Vogel, Rosemarie Kother, Kornelia Ender)	4:16.84
1975....East Germany (Ulrike Richter, Hannelore Anke, Rosemarie Kother, Kornelia Ender)	4:14.74
1978....United States (Linda Jezek, Tracy Caulkins, Joan Pennington, Cynthia Woodhead)	4:08.21↓
1982....East Germany (Kristin Otto, Ute Gewinger, Ines Geissler, Birgit Meineke)	4:05.8*
1986....East Germany (Kathrin Zimmermann, Sylvia Gerasch, Kornelia Gressler, Kristin Otto)	4:04.82
1991....United States (Janie Wagstaff, Tracey McFarlane, Crissy Ahmann-Leighton, Nicole Haislett)	4:06.51
1994....China (He Cihong, Dai Guohong, Liu Limin, Lu Bin)	4:01.67*

400-meter Freestyle Relay

1973....East Germany (Kornelia Ender, Andrea Eife, Andrea Huebner, Sylvia Eichner)	3:52.45
1975....East Germany (Kornelia Ender, Barbara Krause, Claudia Hempel, Uto Bruokner)	3:49.37
1978....United States (Tracy Caulkins, Stephanie Elkins, Joan Pennington, Cynthia Woodhead)	3:43.43*
1982....East Germany (Birgit Meineke, Susanne Link, Kristin Otto, Caren Metschuk)	3:43.97
1986....East Germany (Kristin Otto, Manuela Stellmach, Sabine Schulze, Heike Friedrich)	3:40.57*
1991....United States (Nicole Haislett, Julie Cooper, Whitney Hedgepeth, Jenny Thompson)	3:43.26
1994....China (Le Jingyi, Ying Shan, Le Ying, Lu Bin)	3:37.91*

800-meter Freestyle Relay

1986....East Germany (Manuela Stellmach, Astrid Strauss, Nadja Bergknecht, Heike Friedrich)	7:59.33*
1991....Germany (Kerstin Kielgass, Manuela Stellmach, Dagmar Hase, Stephanie Ortwig)	8:02.56
1994....China (Le Ying, Yang Alhua, Zhou Guabin, Lu Bin)	7:57.96

World Diving Championships

MEN

1-meter Springboard

		Pts
1991	Edwin Jongejans, Holland	588.51
1994	Evan Stewart, Zimbabwe	382.14

3-meter Springboard

		Pts
1973	Phil Boggs, United States	618.57
1975	Phil Boggs, United States	597.12
1978	Phil Boggs, United States	913.95
1982	Greg Louganis, United States	752.67
1986	Greg Louganis, United States	750.06
1991	Kent Ferguson, United States	650.25
1994	Wu Zhuocheng, China	655.44

Platform

		Pts
1973	Klaus Dibiasi, Italy	559.53
1975	Klaus Dibiasi, Italy	547.98
1978	Greg Louganis, United States	844.11
1982	Greg Louganis, United States	634.26
1986	Greg Louganis, United States	668.58
1991	Sun Shuwei, China	626.79
1994	Dmitry Sautin, Russia	634.71

WOMEN

1-meter Springboard

		Pts
1991	Gao Min, China	478.26
1994	Chen Lixia, China	279.30

3-meter Springboard

		Pts
1973	Christa Koehler, East Germany	442.17
1975	Irina Kalinina, USSR	489.81
1978	Irina Kalinina, USSR	691.43
1982	Megan Neyer, United States	501.03
1986	Gao Min, China	582.90
1991	Gao Min, China	539.01
1994	Tan Shuping, China	548.49

Platform

		Pts
1973	Ulrike Knape, Sweden	406.77
1975	Janet Ely, United States	403.89
1978	Irina Kalinina, USSR	412.71
1982	Wendy Wyland, United States	438.79
1986	Chen Lin, China	449.67
1991	Fu Mingxia, China	426.51
1994	Fu Mingxia, China	434.04

THEY SAID IT

Margot Thien, U.S. synchronized swimmer who posed nude for a LIFE photo spread, on being recognized by fans: "I'm like, 'So what is it that you're recognizing?'"

Men

50-METER FREESTYLE

1988	Matt Biondi	22.14*

100-METER FREESTLYE

1906	Charles Daniels	1:13.4
1908	Charles Daniels	1:05.6*
1912	Duke Kahanamoku	1:03.4
1920	Duke Kahanamoku	1:00.4
1924	John Weissmuller	59.0‡
1928	John Weissmuller	58.6‡
1948	Wally Ris	57.3‡
1952	Clarke Scholes	57.4
1964	Don Schollander	53.4‡
1972	Mark Spitz	51.22*
1976	Jim Montgomery	49.99*
1984	Rowdy Gaines	49.80‡
1988	Matt Biondi	48.63‡

200-METER FREESTYLE

1904	Charles Daniels	2:44.2
1906	Not held 1906-1964	
1972	Mark Spitz	1:52.78*
1976	Bruce Furniss	1:50.29*

400-METER FREESTYLE

1904	Charles Daniels (440 yds)	6:16.2
1920	Norman Ross	5:26.8
1924	John Weissmuller	5:04.2‡
1932	Buster Crabbe	4:48.4‡
1936	Jack Medica	4:44.5‡
1948	William Smith	4:41.0‡
1964	Don Schollander	4:12.2*
1968	Mike Burton	4:09.0‡
1976	Brian Goodell	3:51.93*
1984	George DiCarlo	3:51.23‡

1500-METER FREESTYLE

1920	Norman Ross	22:23.2
1948	James McLane	19:18.5
1952	Ford Konno	18:30.3‡
1968	Mike Burton	16:38.9‡
1972	Mike Burton	15:52.58‡
1976	Brian Goodell	15:02.40*
1984	Michael O'Brien	15:05.20

100-METER BACKSTROKE

1912	Harry Hebner	1:21.2
1920	Warren Kealoha	1:15.2
1924	Warren Kealoha	1:13.2‡
1928	George Kojac	1:08.2*
1936	Adolph Kiefer	1:05.9‡
1948	Allen Stack	1:06.4
1952	Yoshi Oyakawa	1:05.4‡
1976	John Naber	55.49*
1984	Rick Carey	55.79
1996	Jeff Rouse	54.10

200-METER BACKSTROKE

1964	Jed Graef	2:10.3*
1976	John Naber	1:59.19*
1984	Rick Carey	2:00.23
1996	Brad Bridgewater	1:58.54

100-METER BREASTSTROKE

1968	Donald McKenzie	1:07.7‡
1976	John Hencken	1:03.11*
1984	Steve Lundquist	1:01.65 *
1992	Nelson Diebel	1:01.50‡

200-METER BREASTSTROKE

1924	Robert Skelton	2:56.6
1948	Joseph Verdeur	2:39.3‡
1960	William Mulliken	2:37.4
1972	John Hencken	2:21.55
1992	Mike Barrowman	2:10.16*

100-METER BUTTERFLY

1968	Douglas Russell	55.9‡
1972	Mark Spitz	54.27*
1976	Matt Vogel	54.35
1992	Pablo Morales	53.32

200-METER BUTTERFLY

1956	William Yorzyk	2:19.3‡
1960	Michael Troy	2.12.8*
1968	Carl Robie	2:08.7
1972	Mark Spitz	2:00.70*
1976	Mike Bruner	1:59.23*
1992	Melvin Stewart	1:56.26

200-METER INDIVIDUAL MEDLEY

1968	Charles Hickcox	2:12.0‡

400-METER INDIVIDUAL MEDLEY

1964	Richard Roth	4:45.4*
1968	Charles Hickcox	4:48.4
1976	Rod Strachan	4:23.68*
1996	Tom Dolan	4.:14.90

3-METER SPRINGBOARD DIVING

1920	Louis Kuehn	675.4 points
1924	Albert White	696.4
1928	Pete Desjardins	185.04
1932	Michael Galitzen	161.38
1936	Richard Degener	163.57
1948	Bruce Harlan	163.64
1952	David Browning	205.29
1956	Robert Clotworthy	159.56
1960	Gary Tobian	170.00
1964	Kenneth Sitzberger	159.90
1968	Bernard Wrightson	170.15
1976	Philip Boggs	619.05
1984	Greg Louganis	754.41
1988	Greg Louganis	730.80

PLATFORM DIVING

1904	George Sheldon	12.66 points
1920	Clarence Pinkston	100.67
1924	Albert White	97.46
1928	Pete Desjardins	98.74
1932	Harold Smith	124.80
1936	Marshall Wayne	113.58
1948	Sammy Lee	130.05
1952	Sammy Lee	156.28
1960	Robert Webster	165.56
1964	Robert Webster	148.58
1984	Greg Louganis	576.99
1988	Greg Louganis	638.61

* World record; ‡Meet (Olympic) record.

Women

50-METER FREESTYLE

1996	Amy Van Dyken	24.87

100-METER FREESTLYE

1920	Ethelda Bleibtrey	1:13.6*
1924	Ethel Lackie	1:12.4
1928	Albina Osipowich	1:11.0‡
1932	Helene Madison	1:06.8‡
1968	Jan Henne	1:00.0
1972	Sandra Neilson	58.59‡
1984	Carrio Steinseifer	55.92
	Nancy Hogshead	55.92

200-METER FREESTYLE

1968	Debbie Meyer	2:10.5‡
1984	Mary Wayte	1:59.23
1992	Nicole Haislett	1:57.90

400-METER FREESTYLE

1924	Martha Norelius	6:02.2‡
1928	Martha Norelius	5:42.8*
1932	Helene Madison	5:28.5*
1948	Ann Curtis	5:17.8‡
1960	Chris von Saltza	4:50.6
1964	Virginia Duenkel	4:43.3‡
1968	Debbie Meyer	4:31.8‡
1984	Tiffany Cohen	4:07.10‡
1988	Janet Evans	4:03.85*

800-METER FREESTYLE

1968	Debbie Meyer	9:24.0‡
1972	Keena Rothhammer	8:53.86*
1984	Tiffany Cohen	8:24.95‡
1988	Janet Evans	8:20.20‡
1992	Janet Evans	8:25.52
1996	Brooke Bennett	8:27.89

100-METER BACKSTROKE

1924	Sybil Bauer	1:23.2‡
1932	Eleanor Holm	1:19.4
1960	Lynn Burke	1:09.3‡
1964	Cathy Ferguson	1:07.7*
1968	Kaye Hall	1:06.2*
1972	Melissa Belote	1:05.78‡
1984	Theresa Andrews	1:02.55
1996	Beth Botsford	1:01.19

200-METER BACKSTROKE

1968	Pokey Watson	2:24.8‡
1972	Melissa Belote	2:19.19*

100-METER BREASTSTROKE

1972	Catherine Carr	1:13.58*

200-METER BREASTSTROKE

1968	Sharon Wichman	2:44.4‡

100-METER BUTTERFLY

1956	Shelley Mann	1:11.0‡
1960	Carolyn Schuler	1:09.5‡
1964	Sharon Stouder	1:04.7*
1984	Mary T. Meagher	59.26
1996	Amy Van Dyken	59.13

200-METER BUTTERFLY

1972	Karen Moe	2:15.57*
1984	Mary T. Meagher	2:06.90‡
1992	Summer Sanders	2:08.67

200-METER INDIVIDUAL MEDLEY

1968	Sharon Wichman	2:44.4‡
1984	Tracy Caulkins	2:12.64‡

400-METER INDIVIDUAL MEDLEY

1964	Donna De Varona	5:18.7‡
1968	Claudia Kolb	5:08.5‡
1984	Tracy Caulkins	4:39.24
1988	Janet Evans	4:37.76

3-METER SPRINGBOARD DIVING

1920	Aileen Riggin	539.9 points
1924	Elizabeth Becker	474.5
1928	Helen Meany	78.62
1932	Georgia Coleman	87.52
1936	Marjorie Gestring	89.27
1948	Victoria Draves	108.74
1952	Patricia McCormick	147.30
1956	Patricia McCormick	142.36
1968	Sue Gossick	150.77
1972	Micki King	450.03
1976	Jennifer Chandler	506.19

PLATFORM DIVING

1924	Caroline Smith	33.2 points
1928	Elizabeth Becker Pinkston	31.6
1932	Dorothy Poynton	40.26
1936	Dorothy Poynton Hill	33.93
1948	Victoria Draves	68.87
1952	Patricia McCormick	79.37
1956	Patricia McCormick	84.85
1964	Lesley Bush	99.80

* World record; ‡Meet (Olympic) record.

Barrier Breakers

MEN

Event	Barrier	Athlete and Nation	Time	Date
100 Freestyle	1:00	Johnny Weissmuller, United States	58.6	7-9-22
100 Freestyle	:50	James Montgomery, United States	49.99	7-25-76
200 Freestyle	2:00	Don Schollander, United States	1:58.8	7-27-63
200 Freestyle	1:50	Sergei Kopliakov, USSR	1:49.83	4-7-79
400 Freestyle	4:00	Rick DeMont, United States	3:58.18	9-6-73
400 Freestyle	3:50	Vladimir Salnikov, USSR	3:49.57	3-12-82
800 Freestyle	8:00	Vladimir Salnikov, USSR	7:56.49	3-23-79
1500 Freestyle	15:00	Vladimir Salnikov, USSR	14:58.27	7-22-80
100 Backstroke	1:00	Thompson Mann, United States	59.6	10-16-64
200 Backstroke	2:00	John Naber, United States	1:59.19	7-24-76
200 Breaststroke	2:30	Chester Jastremski, United States	2:29.6	8-19-61
100 Butterfly	1:00	Lance Larson, United States	59.0	6-29-60
200 Butterfly	2:00	Roger Pyttel, East Germany	1:59.63	6-3-76

WOMEN

Event	Barrier	Athlete and Nation	Time	Date
100 Freestyle	1:00	Dawn Fraser, Australia	59.9	10-27-62
200 Freestyle	2:00	Kornelia Ender, East Germany	1:59.78	6-2-76
400 Freestyle	4:30	Debbie Meyer, United States	4:29.0	8-18-67
800 Freestyle	10:00	Jane Cederqvist, Sweden	9:55.6	8-17-60
800 Freestyle	9:00	Ann Simmons, United States	8:59.4	9-10-71
1500 Freestyle	20:00	Ilsa Konrads, Australia	19:25.7	1-14-60
	16:00	Janet Evans, United States	15:52.10	3-26-88
200 Backstroke	2:30	Satoko Tanaka, Japan	2:29.6	2-10-63
100 Butterfly	1:00	Christine Knacke, East Germany	59.78	8-28-77
400 Individual Medley	5:00	Gudrun Wegner, East Germany	4:57.51	9-6-73

Olympic Achievements

MOST INDIVIDUAL GOLDS IN SINGLE OLYMPICS

MEN

No.	Athlete and Nation	Olympic Year	Events
4	Mark Spitz, United States	1972	100, 200 Free; 100, 200 Fly

WOMEN

No.	Athlete and Nation	Olympic Year	Events
4	Kristin Otto, East Germany	1988	50, 100 Free; 100 Back; 100 Fly
3	Debbie Meyer, United States	1968	200, 400, 800 Free
3	Shane Gould, Australia	1972	200, 400 Free; 200 IM
3	Kornelia Ender, East Germany	1976	100, 200 Free; 100 Fly
3	Janet Evans, United States	1988	400, 800 Free; 400 IM
3	Krisztina Egerszegi, Hungary	1992	100, 200 Back; 400 IM
3	Michelle Smith, Ireland	1996	400 free, 200 IM, 400 IM

Olympic Achievements (Cont.)

MOST INDIVIDUAL OLYMPIC GOLD MEDALS, CAREER

MEN

No.	Athlete and Nation	Olympic Years and Events
4	Charles Meldrum Daniels, United States	1904 (220, 440 Free); 1906 (100 Free,) 1908 (100 Free)
4	Roland Matthes, East Germany	1968 (100, 200 Back); 1972 (100, 200 Back)
4	Mark Spitz, United States	1972 (100, 200 Free; 100, 200 Fly)

WOMEN

No.	Athlete and Nation	Olympic Years and Events
4	Kristin Otto, East Germany	1988 (50 Free; 100 Free, Back and Fly)
4	Janet Evans, United States	1988 (400, 800 Free; 400 IM); 1992 (800 Free)
4	Krisztina Egerszegi, Hungary	1992 (100, 200 Back; 400 IM); 1996 (200 Back)

Most Olympic Gold Medals in a Single Olympics, Men—7, Mark Spitz, United States, 1972: 100, 200 Free; 100, 200 Fly; 4 x 100, 4 x 200 Free Relays; 4 x 100 Medley Relay

Most Olympic Gold Medals in a Single Olympics, Women—6, Kristin Otto, East Germany, 1988: 50, 100 Free; 100 Back; 100 Fly; 4 x 100 Free Relay; 4 x 100 Medley Relay

Most Olympic Medals in a Career, Men—
11, Matt Biondi, United States:1984 (one gold), '88 (five gold, one silver, one bronze), '92 (two gold, one silver)
11, Mark Spitz, United States: 1968 (two gold, one silver, one bronze), 1972 (seven gold)

Most Olympic Medals in Career, Women—
8, Dawn Fraser, Australia: 1956 (two gold, one silver), '60 (one gold, two silver), '64 (one gold, one silver)
8, Kornelia Ender, East Germany: 1972 (three silver), '76 (four gold, one silver)
8, Shirley Babashoff, United States: 1972 (one gold, two silver), '76 (one gold, four silver)

Winner, Same Event, Three Consecutive Olympics—Dawn Fraser, Australia, 100 Freestyle, 1956, '60, '64; Krisztina Egerszegi, Hungary, 200 Back, 1988, '92, '96.

Youngest Person to Win an Olympic Diving Gold—Marjorie Gestring, United States, 1936, 13 years, 9 months, springboard diving

Youngest Person to Win Olympic Swimming Gold—Krisztina Egerszegi, Hungary, 1988, 14 years, one month, 200 backstroke

World Record Achievements

Most World Records, Career, Women—42, Ragnhild Hveger, Denmark, 1936-42
Most World Records, Career, Men—32, Arne Borg, Sweden, 1921-29
Most Freestyle Records Held Concurrently—
5, Helene Madison, United States, 1931-33
5, Shane Gould, Australia, 1972
Most Consecutive Lowerings of a Record—10, Kornelia Ender, East Germany, 100 Freestyle, 7-13-73 to 7-19-76
Longest Duration of World Record—19 years, 359 days, 1:04.6 in 100 Free, Willy den Ouden, the Netherlands

Skiing

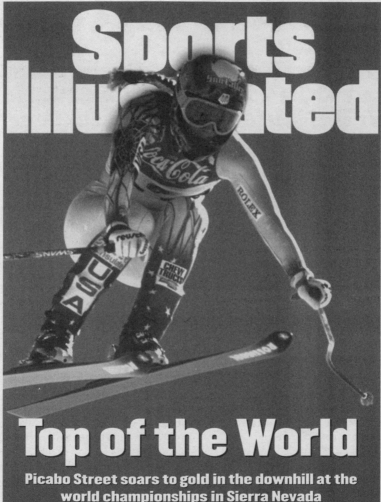

Top of the World

Picabo Street soars to gold in the downhill at the world championships in Sierra Nevada

Go Tell It on The Mountain

Its public profile waning, ski racing looked to spread the word about charismatic stars like Alberto Tomba and Picabo Street

by Michael Farber

SKI RACING, which many in the profession think needs a face-lift as much as it needs ski lifts, turned to its leading personalities in 1996. Katja Seizinger of Germany and Lasse Kjus of Norway won the overall World Cup titles, but it was the exuberant Alberto Tomba and Picabo Street who prevented their sport from entering the yawn of a new era. They are the king and queen of skiing with personalities as large as the mountains on which they race, and while there might be better all-around skiers, none of them possess their incredible knack of locating the spotlight on the world stage.

The stage in this case was Sierra Nevada, a remote resort in southeastern Spain, which, after a year's postponement because of a lack of snow, finally was host to the world championships. The Atlas Mountains of Morocco were visible across the Mediterranean from just above the start of the men's downhill, a fact Tomba noted in a prechampionships interview when he said the races might as well be held in Africa. Apparently he meant it as a joke, but the people of Andalusia weren't amused by Tomba's sense of geography. When the Italian team—minus Tomba—marched in the opening ceremonies, it was roundly jeered.

Tomba had never won a gold medal at the world championships, the one blank space on his overflowing résumé. Indeed, since he took the bronze in the giant slalom as a relative unknown in 1987, Tomba had skied indifferently at the worlds. But on a short, sheer, icy course lined with whistling Spaniards itching for his comeuppance, the maestro transformed negative energy into a bravura GS performance. On the second run Tomba slipped and wound up brushing the snow with his left buttock. Somehow he recovered and recaptured his rhythm, but he was pushing so hard to make up for the lost time he practically crossed the finish line on one ski. When he saw he had beaten the leaders, Swiss skiers Urs Kälin and Michael von Grünigen, the prerace favorite who had won five of the previous eight World Cup GS races, Tomba blew kisses to the crowd and then kissed the snow.

NORBERT SCHMIDT

Tomba won two golds at the world championships, but not many friends.

Two days later in front of a still less-than-universally-adoring mob of 12,000—a FORZA ITALIA sign stood next to an ANTI-TOMBA FAN CLUB banner—he eked out a second victory, in the slalom. Tomba led, but five skiers were waiting to take their second runs, and his chance of hanging on to a medal, let alone gold, was remote. But one by one, almost by magic if not fate, they either skied off course or failed to beat his time. The brash Tomba was overwhelmed. "When I won the two [1988 Olympic] gold medals in Calgary, it was all a party," he said. "My medals today are the award for suffering. I have been suffering, fighting for years. Nothing was handed to me."

Street hasn't had much handed to her, either, mostly because the American goes out and takes it with a frankness that is a breath of fresh air on the often musty circuit. "I learned something about myself this year," said Street, the two-time World Cup downhill champion who won three downhills on the circuit after taking six of nine in her breakthrough 1995 season. "When somebody beats me, I've realized it's something I've done more than anything they did. As long as I'm healthy, I'm the skier to beat."

Street wasn't particularly healthy at Sierra Nevada. While snowplowing down to the T bar during course inspection the day before the downhill, she hit some fresh powder and landed face first in the snow, knocking herself out for an instant. Her ribs hurt and her head throbbed, but the following day she cruised to victory by .57 of a second over Seizinger. Hilary Lindh was third in the race, her only podium finish of the winter.

Seizinger won seven races and took home her first World Cup overall title.

In the World Cup, Luc Alphand of France repeated as men's downhill champion, and Atle Skaardal gave Norway another title by winning the men's Super G, but it was the Street-Seizinger rivalry that enlivened a circuit that seems stuck in neutral. The Great White Circus of the '80s has become more of a series of diffuse carnivals, which set up sponsor tents and then leave town a few days later, scarcely leaving an imprint. Federation Internationale de Ski, the sport's governing body, came under attack from skiers and ski officials, who think it lacks the marketing savvy to compete with other sports in the '90s.

"It's a matter of time before the World Cup circuit is obsolete," said Tommy Moe, the 1994 Olympic gold medal champion who returned from a knee injury but couldn't crack the top 30 in any World Cup downhill. "As far as I can tell, right now all FIS is is a bunch of dudes in suits who make a lot of money." Echoed U.S. Skiing vice president Paul Major: "We have a flat sport right now. Alberto and Picabo should be thought of just like Michael Jordan. These are incredible athletes doing incredible things at incredible speeds, but the FIS is stuck in the mud with its marketing. We're not getting that message across."

In the Nordic combined—a discipline that pairs cross-country skiing with ski jumping—Todd Lodwick won a World Cup event in his hometown of Steamboat Springs, Colo., and then captured the world junior championship, the first medal for an American in the event since 1974.

FOR THE RECORD·1995-1996

World Cup Season Race Results

Men

Date	Event	Site	Winner
11-12-95	Giant Slalom	Tignes, France	Michael von Gruenigen, Switz
11-17-95	Giant Slalom	Vail, Colorado	Michael von Gruenigen, Switz
11-19-95	Slalom	Beaver Creek, Colorado	Michael Tritscher, Austria
11-25-95	Giant Slalom	Park City, Utah	Michael von Gruenigen, Switz
11-26-95	Slalom	Park City, Utah	Andrej Miklavc, Slovenia
12-1-95	Downhill	Vail, Colorado	Luc Alphand, France
12-2-95	Super G	Vail, Colorado	Lasse Kjus, Norway
12-9-95	Downhill	Val d'Isere, France	Luc Alphand, France
12-10-95	Super G	Val d'Isere, France	Atle Skaardal, Norway
12-16-95	Downhill	Val Gardena, Italy	Patrick Ortlieb, Austria
12-17-95	Giant Slalom	Alta Badia, Italy	Hans Knauss, Austria
12-19-95	Slalom	Madonna di Campiglio, Italy	Alberto Tomba, Italy
12-21-96	Giant Slalom	Kranjska Gora, Slovenia	Lasse Kjus, Norway
12-22-96	Slalom	Kranjska Gora, Slovenia	Alberto Tomba, Italy
12-29-95	Downhill	Bormio, Italy	Lasse Kjus, Norway
1-6-96	Giant Slalom	Flachau, Austria	Urs Kaelin, Switzerland
1-7-96	Slalom	Flachau, Austria	Alberto Tomba, Italy
1-13-96	Downhill	Kitzbühel, Austria	Guenther Mader, Austria
1-14-96	Slalom	Kitzbühel, Austria	Thomas Sykora, Austria
1-13/14-96	Combined	Kitzbühel, Austria	Guenther Mader, Austria
1-16-96	Giant Slalom	Adelboden, Switzerland	Michael von Gruenigen, Switz
1-19-96	Downhill	Veysonnaz, Switzerland	Bruno Kernen, Switzerland
1-20-96	Downhill	Veysonnaz, Switzerland	Bruno Kernen, Switzerland
1-21-96	Slalom	Veysonnaz, Switzerland	Sebastian Amiez, France
1-20/21-96	Combined	Veysonnaz, Switzerland	Marc Girardelli, Luxembourg
1-23-96	Super G	Valloire, France	Hans Knauss, Austria
1-27-96	Slalom	Sestriere, Italy	Mario Reiter, Austria
2-2-96	Downhill	Garmisch-Partenkirchen, Germany	Luc Alphand, France
2-5-96	Super G	Garmisch-Partenkirchen, Germany	Werner Perathoner, Italy
2-10-96	Giant Slalom	Hinterstoder, Austria	Michael von Gruenigen, Switz
3-3-96	Super G	Nagano, Japan	Peter Runggaldier, Italy
3-6-96	Downhill	Lillehammer, Norway	Lasse Kjus, Norway
3-7-96	Super G	Lillehammer, Norway	Kjetil Andre Aamodt, Norway
3-9-96	Giant Slalom	Lillehammer, Norway	Urs Kaelin, Switzerland
3-10-96	Slalom	Lillehammer, Norway	Thomas Sykora, Austria

Women

Date	Event	Site	Winner
11-16-95	Super G	Vail, Colorado	Martina Ertl, Germany
11-18-95	Slalom	Beaver Creek, Colorado	Elfi Eder, Austria
12-3-95	Downhill	Lake Louise, Alberta	Picabo Street, United States
12-7-95	Super G	Val d'Isere, France	Alexandra Meissnitzer, Austria
12-8-95	Giant Slalom	Val d'Isere, France	Martina Ertl, Germany
12-15-95	Downhill	St Anton, Austria	Katja Seizinger, Germany
12-16-95	Downhill	St Anton, Austria	Michaela Dorfmeister, Austria
12-17-95	Slalom	St Anton, Austria	Elfi Eder, Austria
12-16/17-95	Combined	St Anton, Austria	Anita Wachter, Austria
12-20-95	Super G	Veysonnaz, Switzerland	Alexandra Meissnitzer, Austria
12-21-95	Giant Slalom	Veysonnaz, Switzerland	Martina Ertl, Germany
12-22-95	Slalom	Veysonnaz, Switzerland	Pernilla Wiberg, Sweden
12-29-95	Slalom	Semmering, Austria	Pernilla Wiberg, Sweden
12-30-95	Slalom	Semmering, Austria	Elfi Eder, Austria
1-5-96	Giant Slalom	Maribor, Slovenia	Martina Ertl, Germany
1-6-96	Giant Slalom	Maribor, Slovenia	Katja Seizinger, Germany
1-7-96	Slalom	Maribor, Slovenia	Kristina Andersson, Sweden
1-13-96	Super G	Garmisch-Partenkirchen, Germany	Katja Seizinger, Germany
1-14-96	Slalom	Garmisch-Partenkirchen, Germany	Urska Hrovat, Slovenia
1-19-96	Downhill	Cortina d'Ampezzo, Italy	Picabo Street, United States
1-20-96	Downhill	Cortina d'Ampezzo, Italy	Isolde Kostner, Italy
1-21-96	Giant Slalom	Cortina d'Ampezzo, Italy	Anita Wachter, Austria
1-26-96	Slalom	Sestriere, Italy	Sonja Nef, Switzerland

Women *(Cont.)*

Date	Event	Site	Winner
1-28-96	Slalom	Serre Chevalier, France	Claudia Riegler, New Zealand
2-2-96	Super G	Val d'Isere, France	Katja Seizinger, Germany
2-3-96	Downhill	Val d'Isere, France	Katja Seizinger, Germany
2-4-96	Super G	Val d'Isere, France	Katja Seizinger, Germany
2-29-96	Downhill	Narvik, Norway	Picabo Street, United States
3-1-96	Downhill	Narvik, Norway	Warwara Zelenskaja, Russia
3-2-96	Giant Slalom	Narvik, Norway	Deborah Compagnoni, Italy
3-6-96	Downhill	Lillehammer, Norway	Heidi Zurbriggen, Switzerland
3-7-96	Super G	Lillehammer, Norway	Ingeborg Helen Marken, Norway
3-9-96	Giant Slalom	Lillehammer, Norway	Katja Seizinger, Germany
3-10-96	Slalom	Lillehammer, Norway	Karin Roten, Switzerland

World Cup Standings

Men

OVERALL
	Pts
Lasse Kjus, Norway	1216
Guenther Mader, Austria	991
Michael von Gruenigen, Switz	880
Luc Alphand, France	839
Alberto Tomba, Italy	766
Hans Knauss, Austria	748
Fredrick Nyberg, Sweden	673
Mario Reiter, Austria	667

DOWNHILL
	Pts
Luc Alphand, France	577
Guenther Mader, Austria	407
Patrick Ortlieb, Austria	359
Lasse Kjus, Norway	343
Bruno Kernen, Switzerland	325
Xavier Gigandet, Switzerland	274
Peter Runggaldier, Italy	261
Kristian Ghedina, Italy	237

SLALOM
	Pts
Sebastian Amiez, France	539
Alberto Tomba, Italy	490
Thomas Sykora, Austria	446
Mario Reiter, Austria	384
Jure Kosir, Slovenia	381
Andrej Miklavc, Slovenia	299
Finn Christian Jagge, Norway	256
Fabio DeCrignis, Italy	242
Yves Dimier, France	242
Christian Mayer, Austria	242

GIANT SLALOM
	Pts
Michael von Gruenigen, Switz	738
Urs Kaelin, Switzerland	601
Lasse Kjus, Norway	475
Fredrick Nyberg, Sweden	338
Hans Knauss, Austria	306
Mario Reiter, Austria	283
Steve Locher, Switzerland	283
Alberto Tomba, Italy	276
Christophe Saioni, France	276

SUPER G
	Pts
Atle Skaardal, Norway	312
Hans Knauss, Austria	267
Lasse Kjus, Norway	264
Luc Alphand, France	262
Peter Runggaldier, Italy	239
Richard Kroell, Austria	223
Fredrik Nyberg, Sweden	217
Kjetil Andre Aamodt, Norway	179

Women

OVERALL
	Pts
Katja Seizinger, Germany	1472
Martina Ertl, Germany	1059
Anita Wachter, Austria	1044
Isolde Kostner, Italy	905
Alexandra Meissnitzer, Austria	894
Picabo Street, United States	837
Heidi Zurbriggen, Switzerland	785
Pernilla Wiberg, Sweden	777

DOWNHILL
	Pts
Picabo Street, United States	640
Katja Seizinger, Germany	485
Isolde Kostner, Italy	449
Heidi Zurbriggen, Switzerland	449
Warwara Zelenskaja, Russia	424
Alexandra Meissnitzer, Austria	316
Renate Goetschl, Austria	308
Michaela Dorfmeister, Austria	298

SLALOM
	Pts
Elfi Eder, Austria	580
Urska Hrovat, Slovenia	440
Pernilla Wiberg, Sweden	414
Marianne Kjoerstad, Norway	398
Kristina Andersson, Sweden	360
Karin Roten, Switzerland	351
Martina Accola, Switzerland	346
Claudia Riegler, New Zealand	281

GIANT SLALOM
	Pts
Martina Ertl, Germany	485
Katja Seizinger, Germany	410
Anita Wachter, Austria	371
Sabina Panzanini, Italy	313
Sonja Nef, Switzerland	292
Deborah Compagnoni, Italy	280
Erika Hansson, Sweden	252
Karin Roten, Switzerland	214

SUPER G
	Pts
Katja Seizinger, Germany	545
Alexandra Meissnitzer, Austria	374
Martina Ertl, Germany	335
Isolde Kostner, Italy	291
Renate Goetschl, Austria	267
Michaela Dorfmeister, Austria	249
Heidi Zurbriggen, Switzerland	243
Anita Wachter, Austria	221

FOR THE RECORD · Year by Year

Event Descriptions

Downhill: A speed event entailing a single run on a course with a minimum vertical drop of 500 meters (800 for Men's World Cup) and very few control gates.
Slalom: A technical event in which times for runs on two courses are totaled to determine the winner. Skiers must make many quick, short turns through a combination of gates (55-75 gates for men, 40-60 for women) over a short course (140-220–meter vertical drop for men, 120-180 for women).

Giant Slalom: A faster technical event with fewer, more broadly spaced gates than in the slalom. Times for runs on two courses with vertical drops of 250-400 meters (250-300 for women) are combined to determine the winner.
Super G: A speed event that is a cross between the downhill and the giant slalom.
Combined: An event in which scores from designated slalom and downhill races are combined to determine finish order.

FIS World Championships

Sites

1931 ....Mürren, Switzerland	1936 ....Innsbruck, Austria
1932 ....Cortina d'Ampezzo, Italy	1937 ....Chamonix, France
1933 ....Innsbruck, Austria	1938 ....Engelberg, Switzerland
1934 ....St Moritz, Switzerland	1939 ....Zakopane, Poland
1935 ....Mürren, Switzerland	

Men

DOWNHILL

1931 ....Walter Prager, Switzerland	1936 ....Rudolf Rominger, Switzerland
1932 ....Gustav Lantschner, Austria	1937 ....Émile Allais, France
1933 ....Walter Prager, Switzerland	1938 ....James Couttet, France
1934 ....David Zogg, Switzerland	1939 ....Hans Lantschner, Germany
1935 ....Franz Zingerle, Austria	

SLALOM

1931 ....David Zogg, Switzerland	1936 ....Rudi Matt, Austria
1932 ....Friedrich Dauber, Germany	1937 ....Émile Allais, France
1933 ....Anton Seelos, Austria	1938 ....Rudolf Rominger, Switzerland
1934 ....Franz Pfnür, Germany	1939 ....Rudolf Rominger, Switzerland
1935 ....Anton Seelos, Austria	

Women

DOWNHILL

1931 ....Esme Mackinnon, Great Britain	1936 ....Evie Pinching, Great Britain
1932 ....Paola Wiesinger, Italy	1937 ....Christel Cranz, Germany
1933 ....Inge Wersin-Lantschner, Austria	1938 ....Lisa Resch, Germany
1934 ....Anni Rüegg, Switzerland	1939 ....Christel Cranz, Germany
1935 ....Christel Cranz, Germany	

SLALOM

1931 ....Esme Mackinnon, Great Britain	1936 ....Gerda Paumgarten, Austria
1932 ....Rösli Streiff, Switzerland	1937 ....Christel Cranz, Germany
1933 ....Inge Wersin-Lantschner, Austria	1938 ....Christel Cranz, Germany
1934 ....Christel Cranz, Germany	1939 ....Christel Cranz, Germany
1935 ....Anni Rüegg, Switzerland	

FIS World Alpine Ski Championships

Sites

1950.....Aspen, Colorado
1954.....Are, Sweden
1958.....Badgastein, Austria
1962.....Chamonix, France
1966.....Portillo, Chile
1970.....Val Gardena, Italy
1974.....St Moritz, Switzerland
1978.....Garmisch-Partenkirchen, West Germany

1982.....Schladming, Austria
1985.....Bormio, Italy
1987.....Crans-Montana, Switzerland
1989.....Vail, Colorado
1991.....Saalbach-Hinterglemm, Austria
1993.....Morioka-Shizukuishi, Japan
1996.....Sierra Nevada, Spain

Men
DOWNHILL

1950.............Zeno Colo, Italy
1954.............Christian Pravda, Austria
1958.............Toni Sailer, Austria
1962.............Karl Schranz, Austria
1966.............Jean-Claude Killy, France
1970.............Bernard Russi, Switzerland
1974.............David Zwilling, Austria
1978.............Josef Walcher, Austria

1982.............Harti Weirather, Austria
1985.............Pirmin Zurbriggen, Switzerland
1987.............Peter Müller, Switzerland
1989.............Hansjörg Tauscher, West Germany
1991.............Franz Heinzer, Switzerland
1993.............Urs Lehmann, Switzerland
1996.............Patrick Ortlieb, Austria

SLALOM

1950.............Georges Schneider, Switzerland
1954.............Stein Eriksen, Norway
1958.............Josl Rieder, Austria
1962.............Charles Bozon, France
1966.............Carlo Senoner, Italy
1970.............Jean-Noël Augert, France
1974.............Gustavo Thoeni, Italy
1978.............Ingemar Stenmark, Sweden

1982.............Ingemar Stenmark, Sweden
1985.............Jonas Nilsson, Sweden
1987.............Frank Wörndl, West Germany
1989.............Rudolf Nierlich, Austria
1991.............Marc Girardelli, Luxembourg
1993.............Kjetil André Aamodt, Norway
1996.............Alberto Tomba, Italy

GIANT SLALOM

1950.............Zeno Colo, Italy
1954.............Stein Eriksen, Norway
1958.............Toni Sailer, Austria
1962.............Egon Zimmermann, Austria
1966.............Guy Périllat, France
1970.............Karl Schranz, Austria
1974.............Gustavo Thoeni, Italy
1978.............Ingemar Stenmark, Sweden

1982.............Steve Mahre, United States
1985.............Markus Wasmaier, West Germany
1987.............Pirmin Zurbriggen, Switzerland
1989.............Rudolf Nierlich, Austria
1991.............Rudolf Nierlich, Austria
1993.............Kjetil André Aamodt, Norway
1996.............Alberto Tomba, Italy

COMBINED

1982.............Michel Vion, France
1985.............Pirmin Zurbriggen, Switzerland
1987.............Marc Girardelli, Luxembourg
1989.............Marc Girardelli, Luxembourg

1991.............Stefan Eberharter, Austria
1993.............Lasse Kjus, Norway
1996.............Marc Girardelli, Luxembourg

SUPER G

1987.............Pirmin Zurbriggen, Switzerland
1989.............Martin Hangl, Switzerland
1991.............Stefan Eberharter, Austria

1993.............Cancelled due to weather
1996.............Atle Skaardal, Norway

Women
DOWNHILL

1950.............Trude Beiser-Jochum, Austria
1954.............Ida Schopfer, Switzerland
1958.............Lucile Wheeler, Canada
1962.............Christl Haas, Austria
1966.............Erika Schinegger, Austria
1970.............Annerösli Zryd, Switzerland
1974.............Annemarie Moser-Pröll, Austria
1978.............Annemarie Moser-Pröll, Austria

1982.............Gerry Sorensen, Canada
1985.............Michela Figini, Switzerland
1987.............Maria Walliser, Switzerland
1989.............Maria Walliser, Switzerland
1991.............Petra Kronberger, Austria
1993.............Kate Pace, Canada
1996.............Picabo Street, United States

SLALOM

1950.............Dagmar Rom, Austria
1954.............Trude Klecker, Austria
1958.............Inger Bjornbakken, Norway
1962.............Marianne Jahn, Austria

1966.............Annie Famose, France
1970.............Ingrid Lafforgue, France
1974.............Hanni Wenzel, Liechtenstein
1978.............Lea Sölkner, Austria

Women (Cont.)

SLALOM (Cont.)

1982 ....Erika Hess, Switzerland	1991 ....Vreni Schneider, Switzerland
1985 ....Perrine Pelen, France	1993 ....Karin Buder, Austria
1987 ....Erika Hess, Switzerland	1996 ....Pernilla Wiberg, Sweden
1989 ....Mateja Svet, Yugoslavia	

GIANT SLALOM

1950 ....Dagmar Rom, Austria	1982 ....Erika Hess, Switzerland
1954 ....Lucienne Schmith-Couttet, France	1985 ....Diann Roffe, United States
1958 ....Lucile Wheeler, Canada	1987 ....Vreni Schneider, Switzerland
1962 ....Marianne Jahn, Austria	1989 ....Vreni Schneider, Switzerland
1966 ....Marielle Goitschel, France	1991 ....Pernilla Wiberg, Sweden
1970 ....Betsy Clifford, Canada	1993 ....Carole Merle, France
1974 ....Fabienne Serrat, France	1996 ....Deborah Compagnoni, Italy
1978 ....Maria Epple, West Germany	

COMBINED

1982 ....Erika Hess, Switzerland	1991 ....Chantal Bournissen, Switzerland
1985 ....Erika Hess, Switzerland	1993 ....Miriam Vogt, Germany
1987 ....Erika Hess, Switzerland	1996 ....Pernilla Wiberg, Sweden
1989 ....Tamara McKinney, United States	

SUPER G

1987 ....Maria Walliser, Switzerland	1993 ....Katja Seizinger, Germany
1989 ....Ulrike Maier, Austria	1996 ....Isolde Kostner, Italy
1991 ....Ulrike Maier, Austria	

Note: The 1995 FIS World Alpine Ski Championships were postponed to 1996 due to the lack of snow.

World Cup Season Title Holders

Men
OVERALL

1967 ....Jean-Claude Killy, France	1982 ....Phil Mahre, United States
1968 ....Jean-Claude Killy, France	1983 ....Phil Mahre, United States
1969 ....Karl Schranz, Austria	1984 ....Pirmin Zurbriggen, Switzerland
1970 ....Karl Schranz, Austria	1985 ....Marc Girardelli, Luxembourg
1971 ....Gustavo Thoeni, Italy	1986 ....Marc Girardelli, Luxembourg
1972 ....Gustavo Thoeni, Italy	1987 ....Pirmin Zurbriggen, Switzerland
1973 ....Gustavo Thoeni, Italy	1988 ....Pirmin Zurbriggen, Switzerland
1974 ....Piero Gros, Italy	1989 ....Marc Girardelli, Luxembourg
1975 ....Gustavo Thoeni, Italy	1990 ....Pirmin Zurbriggen, Switzerland
1976 ....Ingemar Stenmark, Sweden	1991 ....Marc Girardelli, Luxembourg
1977 ....Ingemar Stenmark, Sweden	1992 ....Paul Accola, Switzerland
1978 ....Ingemar Stenmark, Sweden	1993 ....Marc Girardelli, Luxembourg
1979 ....Peter Lüscher, Switzerland	1994 ....Kjetil André Aamodt, Norway
1980 ....Andreas Wenzel, Liechtenstein	1995 ....Alberto Tomba, Italy
1981 ....Phil Mahre, United States	1996 ....Lasse Kjus, Norway

DOWNHILL

1967 ....Jean-Claude Killy, France	1982 ....Steve Podborski, Canada
1968 ....Gerhard Nenning, Austria	Peter Müller, Switzerland
1969 ....Karl Schranz, Austria	1983 ....Franz Klammer, Austria
1970 ....Karl Schranz, Austria	1984 ....Urs Raber, Switzerland
Karl Cordin, Austria	1985 ....Helmut Höflehner, Austria
1971 ....Bernhard Russi, Switzerland	1986 ....Peter Wirnsberger, Austria
1972 ....Bernhard Russi, Switzerland	1987 ....Pirmin Zurbriggen, Switzerland
1973 ....Roland Collumbin, Switzerland	1988 ....Pirmin Zurbriggen, Switzerland
1974 ....Roland Collumbin, Switzerland	1989 ....Marc Girardelli, Luxembourg
1975 ....Franz Klammer, Austria	1990 ....Helmut Höflehner, Austria
1976 ....Franz Klammer, Austria	1991 ....Franz Heinzer, Switzerland
1977 ....Franz Klammer, Austria	1992 ....Franz Heinzer, Switzerland
1978 ....Franz Klammer, Austria	1993 ....Franz Heinzer, Switzerland
1979 ....Peter Müller, Switzerland	1994 ....Marc Girardelli, Luxembourg
1980 ....Peter Müller, Switzerland	1995 ....Luc Alphand, France
1981 ....Harti Weirather, Austria	1996 ....Luc Alphand, France

Men (Cont.)
SLALOM (Cont.)

1967 ....Jean-Claude Killy, France	1982 ....Phil Mahre, United States
1968 ....Domeng Giovanoli, Switzerland	1983 ....Ingemar Stenmark, Sweden
1969 ....Jean-Noël Augert, France	1984 ....Marc Girardelli, Luxembourg
1970 ....Patrick Russel, France	1985 ....Marc Girardelli, Luxembourg
Alain Penz, France	1986 ....Rok Petrovic, Yugoslavia
1971 ....Jean-Noël Augert, France	1987 ....Bojan Krizaj, Yugoslavia
1972 ....Jean-Noël Augert, France	1988 ....Alberto Tomba, Italy
1973 ....Gustavo Thoeni, Italy	1989 ....Armin Bittner, West Germany
1974 ....Gustavo Thoeni, Italy	1990 ....Armin Bittner, West Germany
1975 ....Ingemar Stenmark, Sweden	1991 ....Marc Girardelli, Luxembourg
1976 ....Ingemar Stenmark, Sweden	1992 ....Alberto Tomba, Italy
1977 ....Ingemar Stenmark, Sweden	1993 ....Tomas Fogdof, Sweden
1978 ....Ingemar Stenmark, Sweden	1994 ....Alberto Tomba, Italy
1979 ....Ingemar Stenmark, Sweden	1995 ....Alberto Tomba, Italy
1980 ....Ingemar Stenmark, Sweden	1996 ....Sebastien Amiez, France
1981 ....Ingemar Stenmark, Sweden	

GIANT SLALOM

1967 ....Jean-Claude Killy, France	1983 ....Phil Mahre, United States
1968 ....Jean-Claude Killy, France	1984 ....Ingemar Stenmark, Sweden
1969 ....Karl Schranz, Austria	Pirmin Zurbriggen, Switzerland
1970 ....Gustavo Thoeni, Italy	1985 ....Marc Girardelli, Luxembourg
1971 ....Patrick Russel, France	1986 ....Joël Gaspoz, Switzerland
1972 ....Gustavo Thoeni, Italy	1987 ....Joël Gaspoz, Switzerland
1973 ....Hans Hinterseer, Austria	Pirmin Zurbriggen, Switzerland
1974 ....Piero Gros, Italy	1988 ....Alberto Tomba, Italy
1975 ....Ingemar Stenmark, Sweden	1989 ....Pirmin Zurbriggen, Switzerland
1976 ....Ingemar Stenmark, Sweden	1990 ....Ole-Cristian Furuseth, Norway
1977 ....Heini Hemmi, Switzerland	Günther Mader, Austria
Ingemar Stenmark, Sweden	1991 ....Alberto Tomba, Italy
1978 ....Ingemar Stenmark, Sweden	1992 ....Alberto Tomba, Italy
1979 ....Ingemar Stenmark, Sweden	1993 ....Kjetil André Aamodt, Norway
1980 ....Ingemar Stenmark, Sweden	1994 ....Christian Mayer, Austria
1981 ....Ingemar Stenmark, Sweden	1995 ....Alberto Tomba, Italy
1982 ....Phil Mahre, United States	1996 ....Michael von Gruenigen, Switzerland

SUPER G

1986 ....Markus Wasmeier, West Germany	1992 ....Paul Accola, Switzerland
1987 ....Pirmin Zurbriggen, Switzerland	1993 ....Kjetil André Aamodt, Norway
1988 ....Pirmin Zurbriggen, Switzerland	1994 ....Jan Einar Thorsen, Norway
1989 ....Pirmin Zurbriggen, Switzerland	1995 ....Peter Runggaldier, Italy
1990 ....Pirmin Zurbriggen, Switzerland	1996 ....Atle Skaardal, Norway
1991 ....Franz Heinzer, Switzerland	

COMBINED

1979 ....Andreas Wenzel, Liechtenstein	1988 ....Hubert Strolz, Austria
1980 ....Andreas Wenzel, Liechtenstein	1989 ....Marc Girardelli, Luxembourg
1981 ....Phil Mahre, United States	1990 ....Pirmin Zurbriggen, Switzerland
1982 ....Phil Mahre, United States	1991 ....Marc Girardelli, Luxembourg
1983 ....Phil Mahre, United States	1992 ....Paul Accola, Switzerland
1984 ....Andreas Wenzel, Liechtenstein	1993 ....Marc Girardelli, Luxembourg
1985 ....Andreas Wenzel, Liechtenstein	1994 ....Kjetil-André Aamodt, Norway
1986 ....Markus Wasmeier, West Germany	1995 ....Marc Girardelli, Luxembourg
1987 ....Pirmin Zurbriggen, Switzerland	1996 ....Guenther Mader, Austria

Women
OVERALL

1967 ....Nancy Greene, Canada	1975 ....Annemarie Moser-Pröll, Austria
1968 ....Nancy Greene, Canada	1976 ....Rosi Mitermaier, West Germany
1969 ....Gertrud Gabl, Austria	1977 ....Lise-Marie Morerod, Switzerland
1970 ....Michèle Jacot, France	1978 ....Hanni Wenzel, Liechtenstein
1971 ....Annemarie Pröll, Austria	1979 ....Annemarie Moser-Pröll, Austria
1972 ....Annemarie Pröll, Austria	1980 ....Hanni Wenzel, Liechtenstein
1973 ....Annemarie Pröll, Austria	1981 ....Marie-Thérèse Nadig, Switzerland
1974 ....Annemarie Moser-Pröll, Austria	1982 ....Erika Hess, Switzerland

Women (Cont.)

OVERALL (Cont.)

1983 ....Tamara McKinney, United States	1990 ....Petra Kronberger, Austria
1984 ....Erika Hess, Switzerland	1991 ....Petra Kronberger, Austria
1985 ....Michela Figini, Switzerland	1992 ....Petra Kronberger, Austria
1986 ....Maria Walliser, Switzerland	1993 ....Anita Wachter, Austria
1987 ....Maria Walliser, Switzerland	1994 ....Vreni Schneider, Switzerland
1988 ....Michela Figini, Switzerland	1995 ....Vreni Schneider, Switzerland
1989 ....Vreni Schneider, Switzerland	1996 ....Katja Seizinger, Germany

DOWNHILL

1967 ....Marielle Goitschel, France	1982 ....Marie-Cecile Gros-Gaudenier, France
1968 ....Isabelle Mir, France	1983 ....Doris De Agostini, Switzerland
Olga Pall, Austria	1984 ....Maria Walliser, Switzerland
1969 ....Wiltrud Drexel, Austria	1985 ....Michela Figini, Switzerland
1970 ....Isabelle Mir, France	1986 ....Maria Walliser, Switzerland
1971 ....Annemarie Pröll, Austria	1987 ....Michela Figini, Switzerland
1972 ....Annemarie Pröll, Austria	1988 ....Michela Figini, Switzerland
1973 ....Annemarie Pröll, Austria	1989 ....Michela Figini, Switzerland
1974 ....Annemarie Moser-Pröll, Austria	1990 ....Katrin Gutensohn-Knopf, Germany
1975 ....Annemarie Moser-Pröll, Austria	1991 ....Chantal Bournissen, Switzerland
1976 ....Brigitte Totschnig, Austria	1992 ....Katja Seizinger, Germany
1977 ....Brigitte Totschnig Habersatter, Austria	1993 ....Katja Seizinger, Germany
1978 ....Annemarie Moser-Pröll, Austria	1994 ....Katja Seizinger, Germany
1979 ....Annemarie Moser-Pröll, Austria	1995 ....Picabo Street, United States
1980 ....Marie-Thérèse Nadig, Switzerland	1996 ....Picabo Street, United States
1981 ....Marie-Thérèse Nadig, Switzerland	

SLALOM

1967 ....Marielle Goitschel, France	1983 ....Erika Hess, Switzerland
1968 ....Marielle Goitschel, France	1984 ....Tamara McKinney, United States
1969 ....Gertrud Gabl, Austria	1985 ....Erika Hess, Switzerland
1970 ....Ingrid Lafforgue, France	1986 ....Roswitha Steiner, Austria
1971 ....Britt Lafforgue, France	Erika Hess, Switzerland
1972 ....Britt Lafforgue, France	1987 ....Corrine Schmidhauser, Switzerland
1973 ....Patricia Emonet, France	1988 ....Roswitha Steiner, Austria
1974 ....Christa Zechmeister, West Germany	1989 ....Vreni Schneider, Switzerland
1975 ....Lise-Marie Morerod, Switzerland	1990 ....Vreni Schneider, Switzerland
1976 ....Rosi Mittermaier, West Germany	1991 ....Petra Kronberger, Austria
1977 ....Lise-Marie Morerod, Switzerland	1992 ....Vreni Schneider, Switzerland
1978 ....Hanni Wenzel, Liechtenstein	1993 ....Vreni Schneider, Switzerland
1979 ....Regina Sackl, Austria	1994 ....Vreni Schneider, Switzerland
1980 ....Perrine Pelen, France	1995 ....Vreni Schneider, Switzerland
1981 ....Erika Hess, Switzerland	1996 ....Elfi Eder, Austria
1982 ....Erika Hess, Switzerland	

GIANT SLALOM

1967 ....Nancy Greene, Canada	1983 ....Tamara McKinney, United States
1968 ....Nancy Greene, Canada	1984 ....Erika Hess, Switzerland
1969 ....Marilyn Cochran, United States	1985 ....Maria Keihl, West Germany
1970 ....Michèle Jacot, France	Michela Figini, Switzerland
Françoise Macchi, France	1986 ....Vreni Schneider, Switzerland
1971 ....Annemarie Pröll, Austria	1987 ....Vreni Schneider, Switzerland
1972 ....Annemarie Pröll, Austria	Maria Walliser, Switzerland
1973 ....Monika Kaserer, Austria	1988 ....Mateja Svet, Yugoslavia
1974 ....Hanni Wenzel, Liechtenstein	1989 ....Vreni Schneider, Switzerland
1975 ....Annemarie Moser-Pröll, Austria	1990 ....Anita Wachter, Austria
1976 ....Lise-Marie Morerod, France	1991 ....Vreni Schneider, Switzerland
1977 ....Lise-Marie Morerod, France	1992 ....Carole Merle, France
1978 ....Lise-Marie Morerod, France	1993 ....Carole Merle, France
1979 ....Christa Kinshofer, West Germany	1994 ....Anita Wachter, Austria
1980 ....Hanni Wenzel, Liechtenstein	1995 ....Vreni Schneider, Switzerland
1981 ....Marie-Thérèse Nadig, Switzerland	1996 ....Martina Ertl, Germany
1982 ....Irene Epple, West Germany	

Women *(Cont.)*

SUPER G

1986	Maria Kiehl, West Germany	1992	Carole Merle, France
1987	Maria Walliser, Switzerland	1993	Katja Seizinger, Germany
1988	Michela Figini, Switzerland	1994	Katja Seizinger, Germany
1989	Carole Merle, France	1995	Katja Seizinger, Germany
1990	Carole Merle, France	1996	Katja Seizinger, Germany
1991	Carole Merle, France		

COMBINED

1979	Annemarie Moser-Pröll, Austria	1988	Brigitte Oertli, Switzerland
	Hanni Wenzel, Liechtenstein	1989	Brigitte Oertli, Switzerland
1980	Hanni Wenzel, Liechtenstein	1990	Anita Wachter, Austria
1981	Marie-Thérèse Nadig, Switzerland	1991	Sabine Ginther, Austria
1982	Irene Epple, West Germany	1992	Sabine Ginther, Austria
1983	Hanni Wenzel, Liechtenstein	1993	Anita Wachter, Austria
1984	Erika Hess, Switzerland	1994	Pernilla Wiberg, Sweden
1985	Brigitte Oertli, Switzerland	1995	Pernilla Wiberg, Sweden
1986	Maria Walliser, Switzerland	1996	Anita Wachter, Austria
1987	Brigitte Oertli, Switzerland		

World Cup Career Victories

Men

DOWNHILL

25	Franz Klammer, Austria
19	Peter Müller, Switzerland
15	Franz Heinzer, Switzerland

SLALOM

40	Ingemar Stenmark, Sweden
32	Alberto Tomba, Italy*
16	Marc Girardelli, Luxembourg*

GIANT SLALOM

46	Ingemar Stenmark, Sweden
15	Alberto Tomba, Italy*
11	Gustavo Thoeni, Italy
	Pirmin Zurbriggen, Switzerland

SUPER G

10	Pirmin Zurbriggen, Switzerland
7	Marc Girardelli, Luxembourg*
6	Markus Wasmeier, Germany

COMBINED

11	Phil Mahre, United States
	Pirmin Zurbriggen, Switzerland
	Marc Girardelli, Luxembourg*

Women

DOWNHILL

36	Annemarie Moser-Pröll, Austria
17	Michela Figini, Switzerland
14	Maria Walliser, Switzerland

SLALOM

33	Vreni Schneider, Switzerland
21	Erika Hess, Switzerland
15	Perrine Pelen, France

GIANT SLALOM

21	Vreni Schneider, Switzerland
16	Annemarie Moser-Pröll, Austria
14	Lise Marie Morerod, France

SUPER G

12	Carole Merle, France
10	Katja Seizinger, Germany*
3	Maria Kiehl, Germany
	Maria Walliser, Switzerland
	Sigrid Wolf, Austria

COMBINED

8	Hanni Wenzel, Lichtenstein
7	Annemarie Moser-Pröll, Austria
	Brigitte Oertli, Switzerland

*still active

U.S. Olympic Gold Medalists

Men

Year	Winner	Event
1980	Phil Mahre	Combined
1984	Bill Johnson	Downhill
1984	Phil Mahre	Slalom
1994	Tommy Moe	Downhill

Women

Year	Winner	Event
1948	Gretchen Fraser	Slalom
1952	Andrea Mead Lawrence	Slalom
1952	Andrea Mead Lawrence	Giant Slalom
1972	Barbara Ann Cochran	Slalom
1984	Debbie Armstrong	Giant Slalom
1994	Diann Roffe-Steinrotter	Super G

Figure Skating

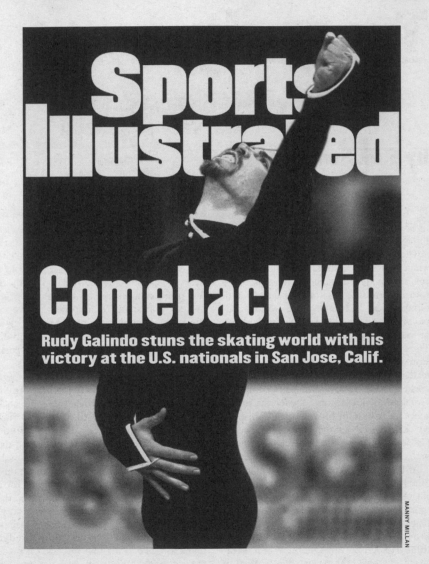

Sports Illustrated

Comeback Kid

Rudy Galindo stuns the skating world with his victory at the U.S. nationals in San Jose, Calif.

MANNY MILLAN

Triumph and Tragedy

The death of Sergei Grinkov cast a pall over an otherwise marvelous season

by E.M. Swift

IT WAS a year of heartbreaking tragedy and timeless triumph in figure skating, of breakthroughs by old faces and young ones.

The tragedy occurred on Nov. 20, 1995, when Russian pairs skater Sergei Grinkov collapsed and died of a heart attack during a routine training session in Lake Placid. Grinkov, just 28, had won four world championships and two Olympic gold medals with his partner and wife, Ekaterina Gordeeva. The couple, who had been skating professionally since winning their second gold medal in 1994, were generally considered the greatest in the history of the pairs event, and Grinkov's death cast a pall over the entire sport. A tribute in his honor in February, which featured a moving performance by Gordeeva skating alone, was the most memorable, and emotional, evening of the year.

At the U.S. nationals, which were held in San Jose, hometown boy Rudy Galindo staged one of the most stirring upsets the sport has ever seen. Galindo, a relative old-timer at 26, had previously been best known as a pairs skater, twice winning the U.S. pairs title with Kristi Yamaguchi. When Yamaguchi dissolved the partnership in 1990 to concentrate on her singles career, Galindo's fortunes took a nosedive. He missed out on both the 1992 and '94 Olympics and finished fifth, seventh and eighth in the last three U.S. nationals while skating solo. Broke and demoralized from the loss of his father to a heart attack and the AIDS-related deaths of two of his coaches and his brother, George, in a six-year span, Galindo nearly gave up the sport. He quit training for nearly eight months in 1995, supporting himself and his mother, with whom he lived in a trailer park, by giving skating lessons.

If the nationals had been held anywhere but San Jose, it's unlikely Galindo would have entered. But he decided to come back for one last try in front of the hometown fans. Coached by his sister, Laura, Galindo shocked the establishment and captured the hearts of figure skating fans by flawlessly skating both his short and long programs, upstaging defending champion Todd Eldredge. With his win Galindo became the fourth oldest U.S. men's champion in history.

A month later, at the world championships in Edmonton, the 24-year-old Eldredge thanked Galindo for that setback. "It made me go back and train and get my act together," the native of Chatham, Mass., said.

The peerless Grinkov and Gordeeva won two Olympic and four world titles.

He had planned to do a lucrative tour between the nationals and the worlds but canceled it after losing. The extra work paid off as Eldredge, skating with a speed and passion few had seen in him before, finally fulfilled the expectations that had hung over his head for so long. A two-time national champion by the age of 19, he had always come up short on the world stage. Until Edmonton. Skating as technically difficult a long program as a U.S. skater had ever attempted—two triple-triple combinations, eight triple jumps in all—Eldredge edged Russia's brilliant young star, 18-year-old Ilia Kulik, and the ever surprising Galindo, who finished third in his first singles appearance at the worlds.

In the ladies' singles the year belonged to 15-year-old Michelle Kwan, the charming Californian whose ascendency to the top of her sport had been predicted since she was a precocious 13-year-old. All she lacked was on-ice maturity and presence, attributes which only age and, well, makeup could provide. Seeking to persuade the judges that Kwan was no longer the little girl who had placed second at the U.S. nationals and fourth at the worlds in 1995, coach Frank Carroll jettisoned the ponytail of Kwan's girlhood in favor of the braided-bun look. He persuaded her parents to allow her to wear makeup when she skated. And he gave her a

mesmerizing long program in which she portrayed the temptress Salome. The result was that in 1996 Kwan matured into the complete package: elegant, athletic, graceful, disciplined and nerveless. She evolved into a flower with steel inside and steamrolled the competition at the U.S. nationals and the newly created Champions Series.

But it was Kwan's performance at the worlds that will be best remembered. China's Chen Lu, the defending ladies' champion, threw down a beautiful gauntlet by skating the performance of her life in the long program. An ethereal, long-limbed presence who breezes across the ice like a leaf on the wind, the 19-year-old Chen was so flawless that she was rewarded with the first two 6.0s of her career. To even have a chance Kwan had to be perfect, and even then there were no guarantees. "I said to myself, Just go for it," Kwan said later. "Go for everything. Why not?" Poised, assured, steadier on her landings than Chen, Kwan matched the Chinese champion jump for jump until she added an impromptu triple toe loop in the final seconds, her seventh triple of the night. It proved to be the difference.

Kwan, like Chen, was given two perfect 6.0s, but she won the first place votes of six judges, to Chen's three. It marked the first time since 1986, when Brian Boitano and Debi Thomas reigned, that the U.S. could boast of world champions in both the men's and ladies' singles.

FOR THE RECORD·1996

World Champions

Edmonton, Alberta, March 17–23

Women

1........Michelle Kwan, United States
2........Chen Lu, China
3........Irina Slutskaya, Russia

Men

1.........Todd Eldredge, United States
2.........Ilia Kulik, Russia
3.........Rudy Galindo, United States

Pairs

1........Marina Eltsova and Andrey Bushkov, Russia
2........Mandy Wotzel and Ingo Steuer, Germany
3........Jenni Meno and Todd Sand, United States

Dance

1.........Oksana Gritschuk and Evgeny Platov, Russia
2.........Anjelika Krylova and Oleg Ovsiannikov, Russia
3.........Shae-Lynn Bourne and Victor Kraatz, Canada

World Figure Skating Championships Medal Table

Country	Gold	Silver	Bronze	Total
Russia	2	2	1	5
United States	2	0	2	4
China	0	1	0	1
Germany	0	1	0	1
Canada	0	0	1	1

Champions of the United States

San Jose, California, January 13–20

Women

1......................Michelle Kwan, Los Angeles FSC
2......................Tonia Kwiatkowski, Winterhurst FSC
3......................Tara Lipinski, University of Delaware FSC

Men

1......................Rudy Galindo, St Moritz ISC
2......................Todd Eldredge, Detroit SC
3......................Dan Hollander, St Clair Shores FSC

Pairs

1......................Jenni Meno and Todd Sand,
Winterhurst FSC/Los Angeles FSC
2. ....Kyoko Ina and Jason Dungjen,
SC of New York
3......................Shelby Lyons and Brian Wells,
Broadmoor SC

Dance

1. ....Elizabeth Punsalan and Jerod Swallow,
Detroit SC
2......................Renee Rocca and Gorsha Sur,
Broadmoor SC
3......................Eve Chalom and Matthew Gates,
Detroit SC

Skating Terminology

Basic Skating Terms

Edges: The two sides of the skating blade, on either side of the grooved center. There is an inside edge, on the inner side of the leg; and an outside edge, on the outer side of the leg.

Free Foot, Hip, Knee, Side, Etc.: The foot a skater is not skating on at any one time is the free foot; everything on that side of the body is then called "free." (See also "skating foot.")

Free Skating (Freestyle): A 4- or 5-minute competition program of free-skating components, choreographed to music, with no set elements. Skating moves include jumps, spins, steps and other linking movements.

Skating Foot, Hip, Knee, Side, Etc.: Opposite of the free foot, hip, knee, side, etc. The foot a skater is skating on at any one time is the skating foot; everything on that side of the body is then called "skating."

Toe Picks (Toe Rakes): The teeth at the front of the skate blade, used primarily for certain jumps and spins.

Trace, Tracing: The line left on the ice by the skater's blade.

Jumps

Waltz: A beginner's jump, involving half a revolution in the air, taken from a forward outside edge and landed on the back outside edge of the other foot.

Toe Loop: A one-revolution jump taken off from and landed on the same back outside edge. This jump is similar to the loop jump except that the skater kicks the toe pick of the free leg into the ice upon takeoff, providing added power.

Toe Walley: A jump similar to the toe loop, except that the takeoff is from the inside edge.

Flip: A jump taken off with the toe pick of the free leg from a back inside edge and landed on a back outside edge, with one in-air revolution.

Lutz: A toe jump similar to the flip, taken off with the toe pick of the free leg from a backward outside edge. The skater enters the jump skating in one direction, and concludes the jump skating in the opposite direction. Usually performed in the corners of the rink. Named after founder Alois Lutz, who first completed the jump in Vienna, 1918.

Salchow: A one-, two- or three-revolution jump. The skater takes off from the back inside edge of one foot and lands backwards on the outside edge of the right foot, the opposite foot from which the skater took off. Named for its originator and first Olympic champion (1908), Sweden's Ulrich Salchow.

Axel: A combination of the waltz and loop jumps, including one-and-a-half revolutions. The only jump begun from a forward outside edge, the axel is landed on the back outside edge of the opposite foot. Named for its inventor, Norway's Axel Paulsen.

Spins

Spin: The rotation of the body in one place on the ice. Various spins are the back, fast or scratch, sit, camel, butterfly and layback.

Camel Spin: A spin with the skater in an arabesque position (the free leg at right angles to the leg on the ice).

Flying Camel Spin: A jump spin ending in the camel-spin position.

Flying Sit Spin: A jump spin in which the skater leaps off the ice, assumes a sitting position at the peak of the jump, lands and spins in a similar sitting position.

Pair Movements/Techniques

Death Spiral: One of the most dramatic moves in figure skating. The man, acting as the center of a circle, holds tightly to the hand of his partner and pulls her around him. The woman, gliding on one foot, achieves a position almost horizontal to the ice.

Lifts: The most spectacular moves in pairs skating. They involve any maneuver in which the man lifts the woman off the ice. The man often holds his partner above his head with one hand.

Throws: The man lifts the woman into the air and throws her away from him. She spins in the air and lands on one foot.

Twist: The man throws the woman into the air. She spins in the air (either a double- or triple-twist), and he catches her at the landing.

Compiled by the United States Figure Skating Assocation.

World Champions

Women

1906	Madge Sayers-Cave, Great Britain
1907	Madge Sayers-Cave, Great Britain
1908	Lily Kronberger, Hungary
1909	Lily Kronberger, Hungary
1910	Lily Kronberger, Hungary
1911	Lily Kronberger, Hungary
1912	Opika von Meray Horvath, Hungary
1913	Opika von Meray Horvath, Hungary
1914	Opika von Meray Horvath, Hungary
1915-21	No competition
1922	Herma Plank-Szabo, Austria
1923	Herma Plank-Szabo, Austria
1924	Herma Plank-Szabo, Austria
1925	Herma Jaross-Szabo, Austria
1926	Herma Jaross-Szabo, Austria
1927	Sonja Henie, Norway
1928	Sonja Henie, Norway
1929	Sonja Henie, Norway
1930	Sonja Henie, Norway
1931	Sonja Henie, Norway
1932	Sonja Henie, Norway
1933	Sonja Henie, Norway
1934	Sonja Henie, Norway
1935	Sonja Henie, Norway
1936	Sonja Henie, Norway
1937	Cecilia Colledge, Great Britain
1938	Megan Taylor, Great Britain
1939	Megan Taylor, Great Britain
1940-46	No competition
1947	Barbara Ann Scott, Canada
1948	Barbara Ann Scott, Canada
1949	Alena Vrzanova, Czechoslovakia
1950	Alena Vrzanova, Czechoslovakia
1951	Jeannette Altwegg, Great Britain
1952	Jacqueline duBief, France
1953	Tenley Albright, United States
1954	Gundi Busch, West Germany
1955	Tenley Albright, United States
1956	Carol Heiss, United States
1957	Carol Heiss, United States

Women *(Cont.)*

1956	Carol Heiss, United States	1977	Linda Fratianne, United States
1957	Carol Heiss, United States	1978	Annett Poetzsch, East Germany
1958	Carol Heiss, United States	1979	Linda Fratianne, United States
1959	Carol Heiss, United States	1980	Annett Poetzsch, East Germany
1960	Carol Heiss, United States	1981	Denise Biellmann, Switzerland
1961	No competition	1982	Elaine Zayak, United States
1962	Sjoukje Dijkstra, Netherlands	1983	Rosalynn Sumners, United States
1963	Sjoukje Dijkstra, Netherlands	1984	Katarina Witt, East Germany
1964	Sjoukje Dijkstra, Netherlands	1985	Katarina Witt, East Germany
1965	Petra Burka, Canada	1986	Debi Thomas, United States
1966	Peggy Fleming, United States	1987	Katarina Witt, East Germany
1967	Peggy Fleming, United States	1988	Katarina Witt, East Germany
1968	Peggy Fleming, United States	1989	Midori Ito, Japan
1969	Gabriele Seyfert, East Germany	1990	Jill Trenary, United States
1970	Gabriele Seyfert, East Germany	1991	Kristi Yamaguchi, United States
1971	Beatrix Schuba, Austria	1992	Kristi Yamaguchi, United States
1972	Beatrix Schuba, Austria	1993	Oksana Baiul, Ukraine
1973	Karen Magnussen, Canada	1994	Yuka Sato, Japan
1974	Christine Errath, East Germany	1995	Chen Lu, China
1975	Dianne DeLeeuw, Netherlands	1996	Michelle Kwan, United States
1976	Dorothy Hamill, United States		

Men

1896	Gilbert Fuchs, Germany	1953	Hayes Alan Jenkins, United States
1897	Gustav Hugel, Austria	1954	Hayes Alan Jenkins, United States
1898	Henning Grenander, Sweden	1955	Hayes Alan Jenkins, United States
1899	Gustav Hugel, Austria	1956	Hayes Alan Jenkins, United States
1900	Gustav Hugel, Austria	1957	David W. Jenkins, United States
1901	Ulrich Salchow, Sweden	1958	David W. Jenkins, United States
1902	Ulrich Salchow, Sweden	1959	David W. Jenkins, United States
1903	Ulrich Salchow, Sweden	1960	Alan Giletti, France
1904	Ulrich Salchow, Sweden	1961	No competition
1905	Ulrich Salchow, Sweden	1962	Donald Jackson, Canada
1906	Gilbert Fuchs, Germany	1963	Donald McPherson, Canada
1907	Ulrich Salchow, Sweden	1964	Manfred Schneldorfer, W Germany
1908	Ulrich Salchow, Sweden	1965	Alain Calmat, France
1909	Ulrich Salchow, Sweden	1966	Emmerich Danzer, Austria
1910	Ulrich Salchow, Sweden	1967	Emmerich Danzer, Austria
1911	Ulrich Salchow, Sweden	1968	Emmerich Danzer, Austria
1912	Fritz Kachler, Austria	1969	Tim Wood, United States
1913	Fritz Kachler, Austria	1970	Tim Wood, United States
1914	Gosta Sandhal, Sweden	1971	Andrej Nepela, Czechoslovakia
1915-21	No competition	1972	Andrej Nepela, Czechoslovakia
1922	Gillis Grafstrom, Sweden	1973	Andrej Nepela, Czechoslovakia
1923	Fritz Kachler, Austria	1974	Jan Hoffmann, East Germany
1924	Gillis Grafstrom, Sweden	1975	Sergei Volkov, USSR
1925	Willy Bockl, Austria	1976	John Curry, Great Britain
1926	Willy Bockl, Austria	1977	Vladimir Kovalev, USSR
1927	Willy Bockl, Austria	1978	Charles Tickner, United States
1928	Willy Bockl, Austria	1979	Vladimir Kovalev, USSR
1929	Gillis Grafstrom, Sweden	1980	Jan Hoffmann, East Germany
1930	Karl Schafer, Austria	1981	Scott Hamilton, United States
1931	Karl Schafer, Austria	1982	Scott Hamilton, United States
1932	Karl Schafer, Austria	1983	Scott Hamilton, United States
1933	Karl Schafer, Austria	1984	Scott Hamilton, United States
1934	Karl Schafer, Austria	1985	Aleksandr Fadeev, USSR
1935	Karl Schafer, Austria	1986	Brian Boitano, United States
1936	Karl Schafer, Austria	1987	Brian Orser, Canada
1937	Felix Kaspar, Austria	1988	Brian Boitano, United States
1938	Felix Kaspar, Austria	1989	Kurt Browning, Canada
1939	Graham Sharp, Great Britain	1990	Kurt Browning, Canada
1940-46	No competition	1991	Kurt Browning, Canada
1947	Hans Gerschwiler, Switzerland	1992	Viktor Petrenko, CIS
1948	Dick Button, United States	1993	Kurt Browning, Canada
1949	Dick Button, United States	1994	Elvis Stojko, Canada
1950	Dick Button, United States	1995	Elvis Stojko, Canada
1951	Dick Button, United States	1996	Todd Eldredge, United States
1952	Dick Button, United States		

Pairs

1908 ....Anna Hubler, Heinrich Burger, Germany
1909 ....Phyllis Johnson, James H. Johnson, Great Britain
1910 ....Anna Hubler, Heinrich Burger, Germany
1911 ....Ludowika Eilers, Walter Jakobsson, Germany/Finland
1912 ....Phyllis Johnson, James H. Johnson, Great Britain
1913 ....Helene Engelmann, Karl Majstrik, Germany
1914 ....Ludowika Jakobsson-Eilers, Walter Jakobsson-Eilers, Finland
1915-21 ......No competition
1922 ....Helene Engelmann, Alfred Berger, Germany
1923 ....Ludowika Jakobsson-Eilers, Walter Jakobsson-Eilers, Finland
1924 ....Helene Engelmann, Alfred Berger, Germany
1925 ....Herma Jaross-Szabo, Ludwig Wrede, Austria
1926 ....Andree Joly, Pierre Brunet, France
1927 ....Herma Jaross-Szabo, Ludwig Wrede, Austria
1928 ....Andree Joly, Pierre Brunet, France
1929 ....Lilly Scholz, Otto Kaiser, Austria
1930 ....Andree Brunet-Joly, Pierre Brunet-Joly, France
1931 ....Emilie Rotter, Laszlo Szollas, Hungary
1932 ....Andree Brunet-Joly, Pierre Brunet-Joly, France
1933 ....Emilie Rotter, Laszlo Szollas, Hungary
1934 ....Emilie Rotter, Laszlo Szollas, Hungary
1935 ....Emilie Rotter, Laszlo Szollas, Hungary
1936 ....Maxi Herber, Ernst Bajer, Germany
1937 ....Maxi Herber, Ernst Bajer, Germany
1938 ....Maxi Herber, Ernst Bajer, Germany
1939 ....Maxi Herber, Ernst Bajer, Germany
1940-46 ......No competition
1947 ....Micheline Lannoy, Pierre Baugniet, Belgium
1948 ....Micheline Lannoy, Pierre Baugniet, Belgium
1949 ....Andrea Kekessy, Ede Kiraly, Hungary
1950 ....Karol Kennedy, Peter Kennedy, United States
1951 ....Ria Baran Falk, Paul Falk, West Germany
1952 ....Ria Baran Falk, Paul Falk, West Germany
1953 ....Jennifer Nicks, John Nicks, Great Britain
1954 ....Frances Dafoe, Norris Bowden, Canada
1955 ....Frances Dafoe, Norris Bowden, Canada
1956 ....Sissy Schwarz, Kurt Oppelt, Austria
1957 ....Barbara Wagner, Robert Paul, Canada
1958 ....Barbara Wagner, Robert Paul, Canada
1959 ....Barbara Wagner, Robert Paul, Canada
1960 ....Barbara Wagner, Robert Paul, Canada
1961 ....No competition
1962 ....Maria Jelinek, Otto Jelinek, Canada
1963 ....Marika Kilius, Hans-Jurgen Baumler, West Germany
1964 ....Marika Kilius, Hans-Jurgen Baumler, West Germany

1965 ....Ljudmila Protopopov, Oleg Protopopov, USSR
1966 ....Ljudmila Protopopov, Oleg Protopopov, USSR
1967 ....Ljudmila Protopopov, Oleg Protopopov, USSR
1968 ....Ljudmila Protopopov, Oleg Protopopov, USSR
1969 ....Irina Rodnina, Alexsei Ulanov, USSR
1970...........Irina Rodnina, Alexsei Ulanov, USSR
1971 ....Irina Rodnina, Sergei Ulanov, USSR
1972 ....Irina Rodnina, Sergei Ulanov, USSR
1973 ....Irina Rodnina, Aleksandr Zaitsev, USSR
1974 ....Irina Rodnina, Aleksandr Zaitsev, USSR
1975 ....Irina Rodnina, Aleksandr Zaitsev, USSR
1976 ....Irina Rodnina, Aleksandr Zaitsev, USSR
1977 ....Irina Rodnina, Aleksandr Zaitsev, USSR
1978 ....Irina Rodnina, Aleksandr Zaitsev, USSR
1979 ....Tai Babilonia, Randy Gardner, United States
1980 ....Maria Cherkasova, Sergei Shakhrai, USSR
1981 ....Irina Vorobieva, Igor Lisovsky, USSR
1982 ....Sabine Baess, Tassilio Thierbach, East Germany
1983 ....Elena Valova, Oleg Vasiliev, USSR
1984 ....Barbara Underhill, Paul Martini, Canada
1985 ....Elena Valova, Oleg Vasiliev, USSR
1986...........Yekaterina Gordeeva, Sergei Grinkov, USSR
1987...........Yekaterina Gordeeva, Sergei Grinkov, USSR
1988 ....Elena Valova, Oleg Vasiliev, USSR
1989...........Yekaterina Gordeeva, Sergei Grinkov, USSR
1990...........Yekaterina Gordeeva, Sergei Grinkov, USSR
1991 ....Natalia Mishkutienok, Artur Dmitriev, USSR
1992 ....Natalia Mishkutienok, Artur Dmitriev, CIS
1993 ....Isabelle Brasseur, Lloyd Eisler, Canada
1994 ....Evgenia Shishkova, Vadim Naumov, Russia
1995 ....Hadka Kovarikova, Rene Novotny, Czech Republic
1996 ....Marina Eltsova, Andrey Buskhov, Russia

THEY SAID IT

Shawn Eckardt, Tonya Harding's 300-pound former bodyguard, on the first thing he planned to do upon his release from prison: "Get something to eat."

Dance

1950 ....Lois Waring, Michael McGean, United States	1972 ....Ljudmila Pakhomova, Aleksandr Gorshkov, USSR
1951 ....Jean Westwood, Lawrence Demmy, Great Britain	1973 ....Ljudmila Pakhomova, Aleksandr Gorshkov, USSR
1952 ....Jean Westwood, Lawrence Demmy, Great Britain	1974 ....Ljudmila Pakhomova, Aleksandr Gorshkov, USSR
1953 ....Jean Westwood, Lawrence Demmy, Great Britain	1975 ....Irina Moiseeva, Andreij Minenkov, USSR
1954 ....Jean Westwood, Lawrence Demmy, Great Britain	1976 ....Ljudmila Pakhomova, Aleksandr Gorshkov, USSR
1955 ....Jean Westwood, Lawrence Demmy, Great Britain	1977 ....Irina Moiseeva, Andreij Minenkov, USSR
1956 ....Pamela Wieght, Paul Thomas, Great Britain	1978 ....Natalia Linichuk, Gennadi Karponosov, USSR
1957 ....June Markham, Courtney Jones, Great Britain	1979 ....Natalia Linichuk, Gennadi Karponosov, USSR
1958 ....June Markham, Courtney Jones, Great Britain	1980 ....Krisztina Regoeczy, Andras Sallai, Hungary
1959 ....Doreen D. Denny, Courtney Jones, Great Britain	1981 ....Jayne Torvill, Christopher Dean, Great Britain
1960 ....Doreen D. Denny, Courtney Jones, Great Britain	1982 ....Jayne Torvill, Christopher Dean, Great Britain
1961 ....No competition	1983 ....Jayne Torvill, Christopher Dean, Great Britain
1962 ....Eva Romanova, Pavel Roman, Czechoslovakia	1984 ....Jayne Torvill, Christopher Dean, Great Britain
1963 ....Eva Romanova, Pavel Roman, Czechoslovakia	1985 ....Natalia Bestemianova, Andrei Bukin, USSR
1964 ....Eva Romanova, Pavel Roman, Czechoslovakia	1986 ....Natalia Bestemianova, Andrei Bukin, USSR
1965 ....Eva Romanova, Pavel Roman, Czechoslovakia	1987 ....Natalia Bestemianova, Andrei Bukin, USSR
1966 ....Diane Towler, Bernard Ford, Great Britain	1988 ....Natalia Bestemianova, Andrei Bukin, USSR
1967 ....Diane Towler, Bernard Ford, Great Britain	1989 ....Marina Klimova, Sergei Ponomarenko, USSR
1968 ....Diane Towler, Bernard Ford, Great Britain	1990 ....Marina Klimova, Sergei Ponomarenko, USSR
1969 ....Diane Towler, Bernard Ford, Great Britain	1991 ....Isabelle Duchesnay, Paul Duchesnay, France
1970 ....Ljudmila Pakhomova, Aleksandr Gorshkov, USSR	1992 ....Marina Klimova, Sergei Ponomarenko , CIS
1971 ....Ljudmila Pakhomova, Aleksandr Gorshkov, USSR	1993 ....Renee Roca, Gorsha Sur, United States
	1994 ....Oksana Gritschuk, Evgeny Platov, Russia
	1995 ....Oksana Gritschuk, Evgeny Platov, Russia
	1996 ....Oksana Gritschuk, Evgeny Platov, Russia

Champions of the United States

The championships held in 1914, 1918, 1920 and 1921 under the auspices of the International Skating Union of America were open to Canadians, although they were considered to be United States championships. Beginning in 1922, the championships have been held under the auspices of the United States Figure Skating Association.

Women

1914 ....Theresa Weld, SC of Boston	1934 ....Suzanne Davis, SC of Boston
1915-17 ......No competition	1935 ....Maribel Y. Vinson, SC of Boston
1918 ....Rosemary S. Beresford, New York SC	1936 ....Maribel Y. Vinson, SC of Boston
1919 ....No competition	1937 ....Maribel Y. Vinson, SC of Boston
1920 ....Theresa Weld, SC of Boston	1938 ....Joan Tozzer, SC of Boston
1921 ....Theresa Weld Blanchard, SC of Boston	1939 ....Joan Tozzer, SC of Boston
1922 ....Theresa Weld Blanchard, SC of Boston	1940 ....Joan Tozzer, SC of Boston
1923 ....Theresa Weld Blanchard, SC of Boston	1941 ....Jane Vaughn, Philadelphia SC & HS
1924 ....Theresa Weld Blanchard, SC of Boston	1942 ....Jane Vaughn Sullivan, Philadelphia SC & HS
1925 ....Beatrix Loughran, New York SC	1943...........Gretchen Van Zandt Merrill, SC of Boston
1926 ....Beatrix Loughran, New York SC	1944...........Gretchen Van Zandt Merrill, SC of Boston
1927 ....Beatrix Loughran, New York SC	1945...........Gretchen Van Zandt Merrill, SC of Boston
1928 ....Maribel Y. Vinson, SC of Boston	1946...........Gretchen Van Zandt Merrill, SC of Boston
1929 ....Maribel Y. Vinson, SC of Boston	1947...........Gretchen Van Zandt Merrill, SC of Boston
1930 ....Maribel Y. Vinson, SC of Boston	1948...........Gretchen Van Zandt Merrill, SC of Boston
1931 ....Maribel Y. Vinson, SC of Boston	1949 ....Yvonne Claire Sherman, SC of New York
1932 ....Maribel Y. Vinson, SC of Boston	1950 ....Yvonne Claire Sherman, SC of New York
1933 ....Maribel Y. Vinson, SC of Boston	

Women *(Cont.)*

1951 ....Sonya Klopfer, Junior SC of New York	1974 ....Dorothy Hamill, SC of New York
1952 ....Tenley E. Albright, SC of Boston	1975 ....Dorothy Hamill, SC of New York
1953 ....Tenley E. Albright, SC of Boston	1976 ....Dorothy Hamill, SC of New York
1954 ....Tenley E. Albright, SC of Boston	1977 ....Linda Fratianne, Los Angeles FSC
1955 ....Tenley E. Albright, SC of Boston	1978 ....Linda Fratianne, Los Angeles FSC
1956 ....Tenley E. Albright, SC of Boston	1979 ....Linda Fratianne, Los Angeles FSC
1957 ....Carol E. Heiss, SC of New York	1980 ....Linda Fratianne, Los Angeles FSC
1958 ....Carol E. Heiss, SC of New York	1981 ....Elaine Zayak, SC of New York
1959 ....Carol E. Heiss, SC of New York	1982 ....Rosalynn Sumners, Seattle SC
1960 ....Carol E. Heiss, SC of New York	1983 ....Rosalynn Sumners, Seattle SC
1961 ....Laurence R. Owen, SC of Boston	1984 ....Rosalynn Sumners, Seattle SC
1962 ....Barbara Roles Pursley, Arctic Blades FSC	1985 ....Tiffany Chin, San Diego FSC
1963 ....Lorraine G. Hanlon, SC of Boston	1986 ....Debi Thomas, Los Angeles FSC
1964 ....Peggy Fleming, Arctic Blades FSC	1987 ....Jill Trenary, Broadmoor SC
1965 ....Peggy Fleming, Arctic Blades FSC	1988 ....Debi Thomas, Los Angeles FSC
1966 ....Peggy Fleming, City of Colorado Springs	1989 ....Jill Trenary, Broadmoor SC
1967 ....Peggy Fleming, Broadmoor SC	1990 ....Jill Trenary, Broadmoor SC
1968 ....Peggy Fleming, Broadmoor SC	1991 ....Tonya Harding, Carousel FSC
1969 ....Janet Lynn, Wagon Wheel FSC	1992 ....Kristi Yamaguchi, St Moritz ISC
1970 ....Janet Lynn, Wagon Wheel FSC	1993 ....Nancy Kerrigan, Colonial FSC
1971 ....Janet Lynn, Wagon Wheel FSC	1994 ....Tonya Harding, Portland FSC
1972 ....Janet Lynn, Wagon Wheel FSC	1995 ....Nicole Bobek, Los Angeles FSC
1973 ....Janet Lynn, Wagon Wheel FSC	1996 ....Michelle Kwan, Los Angeles FSC

Men

1914 ....Norman M. Scott, WC of Montreal	1957 ....David Jenkins, Broadmoor SC
1915-17 ......No competition	1958 ....David Jenkins, Broadmoor SC
1918 ....Nathaniel W. Niles, SC of Boston	1959 ....David Jenkins, Broadmoor SC
1919 ....No competition	1960 ....David Jenkins, Broadmoor SC
1920 ....Sherwin C. Badger, SC of Boston	1961 ....Bradley R. Lord, SC of Boston
1921 ....Sherwin C. Badger, SC of Boston	1962 ....Monty Hoyt, Broadmoor SC
1922 ....Sherwin C. Badger, SC of Boston	1963 ....Thomas Litz, Hershey FSC
1923 ....Sherwin C. Badger, SC of Boston	1964 ....Scott Ethan Allen, SC of New York
1924 ....Sherwin C. Badger, SC of Boston	1965 ....Gary C. Visconti, Detroit SC
1925 ....Nathaniel W. Niles, SC of Boston	1966 ....Scott Ethan Allen, SC of New York
1926 ....Chris I. Christenson, Twin City FSC	1967 ....Gary C. Visconti, Detroit SC
1927 ....Nathaniel W. Niles, SC of Boston	1968 ....Tim Wood, Detroit SC
1928 ....Roger F. Turner, SC of Boston	1969 ....Tim Wood, Detroit SC
1929 ....Roger F. Turner, SC of Boston	1970 ....Tim Wood, City of Colorado Springs
1930 ....Roger F. Turner, SC of Boston	1971 ....John Misha Petkevich, Great Falls FSC
1931 ....Roger F. Turner, SC of Boston	1972 ....Kenneth Shelley, Arctic Blades FSC
1932 ....Roger F. Turner, SC of Boston	1973 ....Gordon McKellen, Jr, SC of Lake Placid
1933 ....Roger F. Turner, SC of Boston	1974 ....Gordon McKellen, Jr, SC of Lake Placid
1934 ....Roger F. Turner, SC of Boston	1975 ....Gordon McKellen, Jr, SC of Lake Placid
1935 ....Robin H. Lee, SC, New York	1976 ....Terry Kubicka, Arctic Blades FSC
1936 ....Robin H. Lee, SC, New York	1977 ....Charles Tickner, Denver FSC
1937 ....Robin H. Lee, SC, New York	1978 ....Charles Tickner, Denver FSC
1938 ....Robin H. Lee, Chicago FSC	1979 ....Charles Tickner, Denver FSC
1939 ....Robin H. Lee, St Paul FSC	1980 ....Charles Tickner, Denver FSC
1940 ....Eugene Turner, Los Angeles FSC	1981 ....Scott Hamilton, Philadelphia SC & HS
1941 ....Eugene Turner, Los Angeles FSC	1982 ....Scott Hamilton, Philadelphia SC & HS
1942 ....Robert Specht, Chicago FSC	1983 ....Scott Hamilton, Philadelphia SC & HS
1943 ....Arthur R. Vaughn, Jr, Philadelphia SC & HS	1984 ....Scott Hamilton, Philadelphia SC & HS
1944-45 ......No competition	1985 ....Brian Boitano, Peninsula FSC
1946 ....Dick Button, Philadelphia SC & HS	1986 ....Brian Boitano, Peninsula FSC
1947 ....Dick Button, Philadelphia SC & HS	1987 ....Brian Boitano, Peninsula FSC
1948 ....Dick Button, Philadelphia SC & HS	1988 ....Brian Boitano, Peninsula FSC
1949 ....Dick Button, Philadelphia SC & HS	1989 ....Christopher Bowman, Los Angeles FSC
1950 ....Dick Button, SC of Boston	1990 ....Todd Eldredge, Los Angeles FSC
1951 ....Dick Button, SC of Boston	1991 ....Todd Eldredge, Los Angeles FSC
1952 ....Dick Button, SC of Boston	1992 ....Christopher Bowman, Los Angeles FSC
1953 ....Hayes Alan Jenkins, Cleveland SC	1993 ....Scott Davis, Broadmoor SC
1954 ....Hayes Alan Jenkins, Broadmoor SC	1994 ....Scott Davis, Broadmoor SC
1955 ....Hayes Alan Jenkins, Broadmoor SC	1995 ....Todd Eldredge, Detroit SC
1956 ....Hayes Alan Jenkins, Broadmoor SC	1996 ....Rudy Galindo, St Moritz ISC

Pairs

1914 ......Jeanne Chevalier, Norman M. Scott,
WC of Montreal

1915-17 .No competition

1918 ......Theresa Weld, Nathaniel W. Niles,
SC of Boston

1919 ......No competition

1920 ......Theresa Weld, Nathaniel W. Niles,
SC of Boston

1921 ......Theresa Weld Blanchard, Nathaniel W.
Niles,SC of Boston

1922 ......Theresa Weld Blanchard, Nathaniel W.
Niles, SC of Boston

1923 ......Theresa Weld Blanchard, Nathaniel W.
Niles, SC of Boston

1924 ......Theresa Weld Blanchard, Nathaniel W.
Niles, SC of Boston

1925 ......Theresa Weld Blanchard, Nathaniel W.
Niles, SC of Boston

1926 ......Theresa Weld Blanchard, Nathaniel W.
Niles, SC of Boston

1927 ......Theresa Weld Blanchard, Nathaniel W.
Niles, SC of Boston

1928 ......Maribel Y. Vinson, Thornton L. Coolidge,
SC of Boston

1929 ......Maribel Y. Vinson, Thornton L. Coolidge,
SC of Boston

1930 ......Beatrix Loughran, Sherwin C. Badger,
SC of New York

1931 ......Beatrix Loughran, Sherwin C. Badger,
SC of New York

1932 ......Beatrix Loughran, Sherwin C. Badger,
SC of New York

1933 ......Maribel Y. Vinson, George E. B. Hill,
SC of Boston

1934 ......Grace E. Madden, James L. Madden,
SC of Boston

1935 ......Maribel Y. Vinson, George E. B. Hill,
SC of Boston

1936 ......Maribel Y. Vinson, George E. B. Hill,
SC of Boston

1937 ......Maribel Y. Vinson, George E. B. Hill,
SC of Boston

1938 ......Joan Tozzer, M. Bernard Fox, SC of Boston

1939 ......Joan Tozzer, M. Bernard Fox, SC of Boston

1940 ......Joan Tozzer, M. Bernard Fox, SC of Boston

1941 ......Donna Atwood, Eugene Turner, Mercury
FSC/Los Angeles FSC

1942 ......Doris Schubach, Walter Noffke,
Springfield Ice Birds

1943 ......Doris Schubach, Walter Noffke,
Springfield Ice Birds

1944 ......Doris Schubach, Walter Noffke,
Springfield Ice Birds

1945 ......Donna Jeanne Pospisil, Jean-Pierre Brunet,
SC of New York

1946 ......Donna Jeanne Pospisil, Jean-Pierre Brunet,
SC of New York

1947 ......Yvonne Claire Sherman, Robert J.
Swenning, SC of New York

1948 ......Karol Kennedy, Peter Kennedy, Seattle SC

1949 ......Karol Kennedy, Peter Kennedy, Seattle SC

1950 ......Karol Kennedy, Peter Kennedy,
Broadmoor SC

1951 ......Karol Kennedy, Peter Kennedy,
Broadmoor SC

1952 ......Karol Kennedy, Peter Kennedy,
Broadmoor SC

1953 ......Carole Ann Ormaca, Robin Greiner,
SC of Fresno

1954 ......Carole Ann Ormaca, Robin Greiner,
SC of Fresno

1955 ......Carole Ann Ormaca, Robin Greiner,
St Moritz ISC

1956 ......Carole Ann Ormaca, Robin Greiner,
St Moritz ISC

1957 ......Nancy Rouillard Ludington, Ronald
Ludington, Commonwealth FSC/
SC of Boston

1958 ......Nancy Rouillard Ludington, Ronald
Ludington, Commonwealth FSC/
SC of Boston

1959 ......Nancy Rouillard Ludington, Ronald
Ludington, Commonwealth FSC

1960 ......Nancy Rouillard Ludington, Ronald
Ludington, Commonwealth FSC

1961 ......Maribel Y. Owen, Dudley S. Richards,
SC of Boston

1962 ......Dorothyann Nelson, Pieter Kollen,
Village of Lake Placid

1963 ......Judianne Fotheringill, Jerry J. Fotheringill,
Broadmoor SC

1964 ......Judianne Fotheringill, Jerry J. Fotheringill,
Broadmoor SC

1965 ......Vivian Joseph, Ronald Joseph,
Chicago FSC

1966 ......Cynthia Kauffman, Ronald Kauffman,
Seattle SC

1967 ......Cynthia Kauffman, Ronald Kauffman,
Seattle SC

1968 ......Cynthia Kauffman, Ronald Kauffman,
Seattle SC

1969 ......Cynthia Kauffman, Ronald Kauffman,
Seattle SC

1970 ......Jo Jo Starbuck, Kenneth Shelley,
Arctic Blades FSC

1971 ......Jo Jo Starbuck, Kenneth Shelley,
Arctic Blades FSC

1972 ......Jo Jo Starbuck, Kenneth Shelley,
Arctic Blades FSC

1973 ......Melissa Militano, Mark Militano,
SC of New York

1974 ......Melissa Militano, Johnny Johns,
SC of New York/Detroit SC

1975 ......Melissa Militano, Johnny Johns,
SC of New York/Detroit SC

1976 ......Tai Babilonia, Randy Gardner,
Los Angeles FSC

1977 ......Tai Babilonia, Randy Gardner,
Los Angeles FSC

1978 ......Tai Babilonia, Randy Gardner,
Los Angeles FSC/Santa Monica FSC

1979 ......Tai Babilonia, Randy Gardner,
Los Angeles FSC/Santa Monica FSC

1980 ......Tai Babilonia, Randy Gardner,
Los Angeles FSC/Santa Monica FSC

1981 ......Caitlin Carruthers, Peter Carruthers,
SC of Wilmington

1982 ......Caitlin Carruthers, Peter Carruthers,
SC of Wilmington

1983 ......Caitlin Carruthers, Peter Carruthers,
SC of Wilmington

1984 ......Caitlin Carruthers, Peter Carruthers,
SC of Wilmington

Pairs *(Cont.)*

1985	Jill Watson, Peter Oppegard, Los Angeles FSC	1991	Natasha Kuchiki, Todd Sand, Los Angeles FSC
1986	Gillian Wachsman, Todd Waggoner, SC of Wilmington	1992	Calla Urbanski, Rocky Marval, U of Delaware FSC/SC of New York
1987	Jill Watson, Peter Oppegard, Los Angeles FSC	1993	Calla Urbanski, Rocky Marval, U of Delaware FSC/SC of New York
1988	Jill Watson, Peter Oppegard, Los Angeles FSC	1994	Jenni Meno, Todd Sand, Winterhurst FSC/Los Angeles FSC
1989	Kristi Yamaguchi, Rudy Galindo, St Moritz ISC	1995	Jenni Meno, Todd Sand, Winterhurst FSC/Los Angeles FSC
1990	Kristi Yamaguchi, Rudy Galindo, St Moritz ISC	1996	Jenni Meno, Todd Sand, Winterhurst FSC/Los Angeles FSC

Dance

1914 ......Waltz: Theresa Weld, Nathaniel W. Niles, SC of Boston
1915-19...No competition
1920 ......Waltz: Theresa Weld, Nathaniel W. Niles, SC of Boston
Fourteenstep: Gertrude Cheever Porter, Irving Brokaw, New York SC
1921 ......Waltz and Fourteenstep: Theresa Weld Blanchard, Nathaniel W. Niles, SC of Boston
1922 ......Waltz: Beatrix Loughran, Edward M. Howland, New York SC/SC of Boston
Fourteenstep: Theresa Weld Blanchard, Nathaniel W. Niles, SC of Boston
1923 ......Waltz: Mr. & Mrs. Henry W. Howe, New York SC
Fourteenstep: Sydney Goode, James B. Greene, New York SC
1924 ......Waltz: Rosaline Dunn, Frederick Gabel, New York SC
Fourteenstep: Sydney Goode, James B. Greene, New York SC
1925 ......Waltz and Fourteenstep: Virginia Slattery, Ferrier T. Martin, New York SC
1926 ......Waltz: Rosaline Dunn, Joseph K. Savage, New York SC
Fourteenstep: Sydney Goode, James B. Greene, New York SC
1927 ......Waltz and Fourteenstep: Rosaline Dunn, Joseph K. Savage, New York SC
1928 ......Waltz: Rosaline Dunn, Joseph K. Savage, New York SC
Fourteenstep: Ada Bauman Kelly, George T. Braakman, New York SC
1929 ......Waltz and Original Dance combined: Edith C. Secord, Joseph K. Savage, SC of New York
1930 ......Waltz: Edith C. Secord, Joseph K. Savage, SC of New York
Original: Clara Rotch Frothingham, George E. B. Hill, SC of Boston
1931 ......Waltz: Edith C. Secord, Ferrier T. Martin, SC of New York
Original: Theresa Weld Blanchard, Nathaniel W. Niles, SC of Boston
1932 ......Waltz: Edith C. Secord, Joseph K. Savage, SC of New York
Original: Clara Rotch Frothingham, George E. B. Hill, SC of Boston
1933 ......Waltz: Ilse Twaroschk, Frederick F. Fleishmann, Brooklyn FSC
Original: Suzanne Davis, Frederick Goodridge, SC of Boston

1934 ......Waltz: Nettie C. Prantel, Roy Hunt, SC of New York
Original: Suzanne Davis, Frederick Goodridge, SC of Boston
1935 ......Waltz: Nettie C. Prantel, Roy Hunt, SC of New York
1936 ......Marjorie Parker, Joseph K. Savage, SC of New York
1937 ......Nettie C. Prantel, Harold Hartshorne, SC of New York
1938 ......Nettie C. Prantel, Harold Hartshorne, SC, of New York
1939 ......Sandy Macdonald, Harold Hartshorne, SC of New York
1940 ......Sandy Macdonald, Harold Hartshorne, SC of New York
1941 ......Sandy Macdonald, Harold Hartshorne, SCNY
1942 ......Edith B. Whetstone, Alfred N. Richards, Jr, Philadelphia SC & HS
1943 ......Marcella May, James Lochead, Jr, Skate & Ski Club
1944 ......Marcella May, James Lochead, Jr, Skate & Ski Club
1945 ......Kathe Mehl Williams, Robert J. Swenning, SC of New York
1946 ......Anne Davies, Carleton C. Hoffner, Jr, Washington FSC
1947 ......Lois Waring, Walter H. Bainbridge, Jr, Baltimore FSC/Washigton FSC
1948 ......Lois Waring, Walter H. Bainbridge, Jr, Baltimore FSC/Washington FSC
1949 ......Lois Waring, Walter H. Bainbridge, Jr, Baltimore FSC/Washington FSC
1950 ......Lois Waring, Michael McGean, Baltimore FSC
1951 ......Carmel Bodel, Edward L. Bodel, St Moritz ISC
1952 ......Lois Waring, Michael McGean, Baltimore FSC
1953 ......Carol Ann Peters, Daniel C. Ryan, Washington FSC
1954 ......Carmel Bodel, Edward L. Bodel, St Moritz ISC
1955 ......Carmel Bodel, Edward L. Bodel, St Moritz ISC
1956 ......Joan Zamboni, Roland Junso, Arctic Blades FSC
1957 ......Sharon McKenzie, Bert Wright, Los Angeles FSC
1958 ......Andree Anderson, Donald Jacoby, Buffalo SC
1959 ......Andree Anderson Jacoby, Donald Jacoby, Buffalo SC

Dance *(Cont.)*

1960 ......Margie Ackles, Charles W. Phillips, Jr, Los Angeles FSC/Arctic Blades FSC	1979 ......Stacey Smith, John Summers, SC of Wilmington
1961 ......Diane C. Sherbloom, Larry Pierce, Los Angeles FSC/WC of Indianapolis	1980 ......Stacey Smith, John Summers, SC of Wilmington
1962 ......Yvonne N. Littlefield, Peter F. Betts, Arctic Blades FSC/ Paramount, CA	1981 ......Judy Blumberg, Michael Seibert, Broadmoor SC/ISC of Indianapolis
1963 ......Sally Schantz, Stanley Urban, SC of Boston/Buffalo SC	1982 ......Judy Blumberg, Michael Seibert, Broadmoor SC/ISC of Indianapolis
1964 ......Darlene Streich, Charles D. Fetter, Jr, WC of Indianapolis	1983 ......Judy Blumberg, Michael Seibert, Pittsburgh FSC
1965 ......Kristin Fortune, Dennis Sveum, Los Angeles FSC	1984 ......Judy Blumberg, Michael Seibert, Pittsburgh FSC
1966 ......Kristin Fortune, Dennis Sveum, Los Angeles FSC	1985 ......Judy Blumberg, Michael Seibert, Pittsburgh FSC
1967 ......Lorna Dyer, John Carrell, Broadmoor SC	1986 ......Renee Roca, Donald Adair, Genesee FSC/Academy FSC
1968 ......Judy Schwomeyer, James Sladky, WC of Indianapolis/Genesee FSC	1987 ......Suzanne Semanick, Scott Gregory, U of Delaware SC
1969 ......Judy Schwomeyer, James Sladky, WC of Indianapolis/Genesee FSC	1988 ......Suzanne Semanick, Scott Gregory, U of Delaware SC
1970 ......Judy Schwomeyer, James Sladky, WC of Indianapolis/Genesee FSC	1989 ......Susan Wynne, Joseph Druar, Broadmoor SC/Seattle SC
1971 ......Judy Schwomeyer, James Sladky, WC of Indianapolis/Genesee FSC	1990 ......Susan Wynne, Joseph Druar, Broadmoor SC/Seattle SC
1972 ......Judy Schwomeyer, James Sladky, WC of Indianapolis/Genesee FSC	1991 ......Elizabeth Punsalan, Jerod Swallow, Broadmoor SC
1973 ......Mary Karen Campbell, Johnny Johns, Lansing SC/Detroit SC	1992 ......April Sargent, Russ Witherby, Ogdensburg FSC/U of Delaware FSC
1974 ......Colleen O'Connor, Jim Millns, Broadmoor SC/City of Colorado Springs	1993 ......Renee Roca, Gorsha Sur, Broadmoor SC
1975 ......Colleen O'Connor, Jim Millns, Broadmoor SC	1994 ......Elizabeth Punsalan, Jerod Swallow, Broadmoor SC/Detroit SC
1976 ......Colleen O'Connor, Jim Millns, Broadmoor SC	1995 ......Renee Roca, Gorsha Sur, Broadmoor SC
1977 ......Judy Genovesi, Kent Weigle, SC of Hartford/Charter Oak FSC	1996 ......Elizabeth Punsalan, Jerod Swallow, Detroit SC
1978 ......Stacey Smith, John Summers, SC of Wilmington	

U.S. Olympic Gold Medalists

Women

1956	Tenley Albright	1976	Dorothy Hamill
1960	Carol Heiss	1992	Kristi Yamaguchi
1968	Peggy Fleming		

Men

1948	Richard Button	1960	David W. Jenkins
1952	Richard Button	1984	Scott Hamilton
1956	Hayes Alan Jenkins	1988	Brian Boitano

Special Achievements

Women successfully landing a triple Axel in competition:
 Midori Ito, Japan, 1988 free-skating competition at Aichi, Japan.
 Tonya Harding, United States, 1991 U.S. Figure Skating Championship.

Miscellaneous Sports

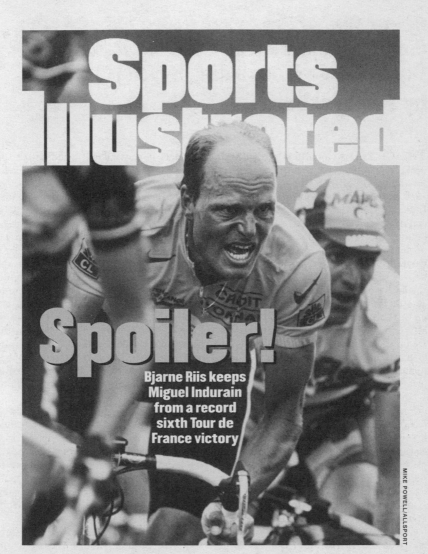

Sports Illustrated

Spoiler!

Bjarne Riis keeps Miguel Indurain from a record sixth Tour de France victory

MIKE POWELL/ALLSPORT

Great Dane

Bjarne Riis of Denmark, a 32-year-old who didn't turn pro until 1986, deposed five-time Tour de France king Miguel Indurain

by Tim Crothers

THE GIFTED scriptwriters at the Tour de France conceived a charming drama for their '96 edition. During the race's 17th stage, on the day after Miguel Indurain's 32nd birthday, the Spanish cycling legend would make a ceremonial detour into Spain to pedal through his hometown of Villava. He would be clad, naturally, in the leader's yellow jersey on his way to a historic sixth Tour triumph. It should have been a tour de force for the Tour de France. Alas, Miguel did not show up in the proper costume. On that July afternoon the yellow jersey belonged to Denmark's Bjarne Riis, who four days later would win the race, a Tour far less remarkable for what did not occur than for what did occur.

For the first time since 1990, Indurain did not win the Tour. He did not break the record with his sixth Tour victory. And for the first time in six years, King Miguel of Navarre did not return home from Paris to place his victory bouquet at the feet of the statue of the Virgin of Rosario, Villava's other patron saint.

In fact, from the outset, the 83rd Tour de France did not go according to plan. During the race's opening week, the midsummer weather in Holland, Belgium and France felt more like November in Buffalo. Rain. Cold. Wind. More rain. The Tour lost 31 riders in seven days, including the top American cyclist, Lance Armstrong, who quit in the sixth stage during a monsoon, afraid he might have contracted bronchitis.

The next day, in stage 7, Indurain, who has likened himself to a lizard because he rides better in hot weather, failed to eat and drink properly and suffered from a sugar deficiency. He "cracked" for the first time since he was a callow support rider in the late '80s, losing over three minutes to the charging Riis. "I could not believe it," said Richard Virenque of France, who finished third overall in the race. "We were all there with Indurain, and then, when we broke away, he just appeared to be cycling on the same piece of road. Truly, it was the most remarkable sight I have seen on the Tour."

The ninth stage actually had to be shortened because of snow, but nothing ruffled the imperturbable Riis as he slipped on *le maillot jaune* that afternoon and never relinquished it. "I remember we came to one mountain peak in a snowstorm," said Walter Godefroot, Riis's team manager. "All that Bjarne said to me was, 'Wow, what a wonderful view.'"

Trailing Riis by 4:38 with just eight stages remaining, Indurain was encouraged by a letter marked URGENT from Charly Gaul, the winner of the '58 Tour.

Chances are Indurain will take one more shot at the Tour victory mark.

Gaul wrote: "When I won the Tour I was a fifteen minutes behind three days before the end. It's not over yet. Good luck."

Spanish sportswriters began predicting the worst Danish tragedy this side of Hamlet. But they had shortchanged Riis, a late bloomer at age 32, who was raised by a single father, a cycling coach in their hometown of Herning. Bjarne didn't begin his professional cycling career until '86 and was initially content to ride in support of others, including two-time Tour winner Laurent Fignon of France. But after nearly retiring from the sport after a poor season in '88, he gradually gained confidence and ambition with age. Riis finished third in the Tour as a support rider for the Gewiss team in '95 and then switched to Telekom to try to win in '96, guided by advice from Fignon, his cycling guru.

Fignon preached an attacking style, leading Riis to stalk the defending champion so voraciously that the French press took to calling him *le carnassier*, the carnivore. The great Dane chewed up Indurain

and the rest of the field during the 16th stage, which concluded with a brutal 13-kilometer unyielding ascent to the Pyrenees ski resort at Hautacam. At the summit Riis had gained 90 seconds on his closest rivals. By the time he reached the Tour's final stages his lead was so secure that he could have won the race riding into Paris on a Schwinn 3-speed with training wheels.

Indurain would eventually finish 11th, 14:14 behind Riis, his worst result since '89. Among the theories for his downfall were the nasty weather and a weak support team, but in the end it was a simple question of horsepower. "My heart was willing," explained Indurain, "but my legs told me no."

Indurain will probably chase the victory record in at least one more Tour. Perhaps he can rediscover his form, but he understands his aura of invincibility is gone forever, erased by Riis's virtuoso performance, which reminded many of Indurain himself. "I struggle to believe that I actually won the Tour," Riis said. "To beat the great Indurain is like deposing a king."

The reign in Spain fell plainly to the Dane.

FOR THE RECORD·Year by Year

Archery

National Men's Champions

1879......Will H. Thompson	1919 ......Dr. Robert Elmer	1961 ......Clayton Sherman
1880 ......L. L. Pedinghaus	1920 ......Dr. Robert Elmer	1962 ......Charles Sandlin
1881 ......F. H. Walworth	1921 ......James Jiles	1963 ......Dave Keaggy, Jr.
1882 ......D. H. Nash	1922 ......Dr. Robert Elmer	1964 ......Dave Keaggy, Jr.
1883 ......Col. Robert Williams	1923 ......Bill Palmer	1965 ......George Slinzer
1884 ......Col. Robert Williams	1924 ......James Jiles	1966 ......Hardy Ward
1885 ......Col. Robert Williams	1925 ......Dr. Paul Crouch	1967 ......Ray Rogers
1886 ......W. A. Clark	1926 ......Stanley Spencer	1968 ......Hardy Ward
1887 ......W. A. Clark	1927 ......Dr. Paul Crouch	1969 ......Ray Rogers
1888 ......Lewis Maxson	1928 ......Bill Palmer	1970 ......Joe Thornton
1889 ......Lewis Maxson	1929 ......Dr. E. K. Roberts	1971 ......John Williams
1890 ......Lewis Maxson	1930 ......Russ Hoogerhyde	1972 ......Kevin Erlandson
1891 ......Lewis Maxson	1931 ......Russ Hoogerhyde	1973 ......Darrell Pace
1892 ......Lewis Maxson	1932 ......Russ Hoogerhyde	1974 ......Darrell Pace
1893 ......Lewis Maxson	1933 ......Ralph Miller	1975 ......Darrell Pace
1894 ......Lewis Maxson	1934 ......Russ Hoogerhyde	1976 ......Darrell Pace
1895 ......W. B. Robinson	1935 ......Gilman Keasey	1977 ......Rick McKinney
1896 ......Lewis Maxson	1936 ......Gilman Keasey	1978 ......Darrell Pace
1897 ......W. A. Clark	1937 ......Russ Hoogerhyde	1979 ......Rick McKinney
1898 ......Lewis Maxson	1938 ......Pat Chambers	1980 ......Rick McKinney
1899 ......M. C. Howell	1939 ......Pat Chambers	1981 ......Rick McKinney
1900 ......A. R. Clark	1940 ......Russ Hoogerhyde	1982 ......Rick McKinney
1901 ......Will H. Thompson	1941 ......Larry Hughes	1983 ......Rick McKinney
1902 ......Will H. Thompson	1946 ......Wayne Thompson	1984 ......Darrell Pace
1903 ......Will H. Thompson	1947 ......Jack Wilson	1985 ......Rick McKinney
1904 ......George Bryant	1948 ......Larry Hughes	1986 ......Rick McKinney
1905 ......George Bryant	1949 ......Russ Reynolds	1987 ......Rick McKinney
1906 ......Henry Richardson	1950 ......Stan Overby	1988 ......Jay Barrs
1907 ......Henry Richardson	1951 ......Russ Reynolds	1989 ......Ed Eliason
1908 ......Will H. Thompson	1952 ......Robert Larson	1990 ......Ed Eliason
1909 ......George Bryant	1953 ......Bill Glackin	1991 ......Ed Eliason
1910 ......Henry Richardson	1954 ......Robert Rhode	1992 ......Alan Rasor
1911 ......Dr. Robert Elmer	1955 ......Joe Fries	1993 ......Jay Barrs
1912 ......George Bryant	1956 ......Joe Fries	1994 ......Jay Barrs
1913 ......George Bryant	1957 ......Joe Fries	1995 ......Justin Huish
1914 ......Dr. Robert Elmer	1958 ......Robert Bitner	1996 ......Richard (Butch) Johnson
1915 ......Dr. Robert Elmer	1959 ......Wilbert Vetrovsky	
1916 ......Dr. Robert Elmer	1960 ......Robert Kadlec	

National Women's Champions

1879 ......Mrs. S. Brown	1902 ......Mrs. M. C. Howell	1927 ......Mrs. R. Johnson
1880 ......Mrs. T. Davies	1903 ......Mrs. M. C. Howell	1928 ......Beatrice Hodgson
1881 ......Mrs. A. H. Gibbes	1904 ......Mrs. M. C. Howell	1929 ......Audrey Grubbs
1882 ......Mrs. A. H. Gibbes	1905 ......Mrs. M. C. Howell	1930 ......Audrey Grubbs
1883 ......Mrs. M. C. Howell	1906 ......Mrs. E. C. Cook	1931 ......Dorothy Cummings
1884 ......Mrs. H. Hall	1907 ......Mrs. M. C. Howell	1932 ......Ilda Hanchette
1885 ......Mrs. M. C. Howell	1908 ......Harriet Case	1933 ......Madelaine Taylor
1886 ......Mrs. M. C. Howell	1909 ......Harriet Case	1934 ......Desales Mudd
1887 ......Mrs. A. M. Phillips	1910 ......J. V. Sullivan	1935 ......Ruth Hodgert
1888 ......Mrs. A. M. Phillips	1911 ......Mrs. J. S. Taylor	1936 ......Gladys Hammer
1889 ......Mrs. A. M. Phillips	1912 ......Mrs. Witwer Tayler	1937 ......Gladys Hammer
1890 ......Mrs. M. C. Howell	1913 ......Mrs. P. Fletcher	1938 ......Jean Tenney
1891 ......Mrs. M. C. Howell	1914 ......Mrs. B. P. Gray	1939 ......Belvia Carter
1892 ......Mrs. M. C. Howell	1915 ......Cynthia Wesson	1940 ......Ann Weber
1893 ......Mrs. M. C. Howell	1916 ......Cynthia Wesson	1941 ......Ree Dillinger
1894 ......Mrs. Albert Kern	1919 ......Dorothy Smith	1946 ......Ann Weber
1895 ......Mrs. M. C. Howell	1920 ......Cynthia Wesson	1947 ......Ann Weber
1896 ......Mrs. M. C. Howell	1921 ......Mrs. L. C. Smith	1948 ......Jean Lee
1897 ......Mrs. J. S. Baker	1922 ......Dorothy Smith	1949 ......Jean Lee
1898 ......Mrs. M. C. Howell	1923 ......Norma Pierce	1950 ......Jean Lee
1899 ......Mrs. M. C. Howell	1924 ......Dorothy Smith	1951 ......Jean Lee
1900 ......Mrs. M. C. Howell	1925 ......Dorothy Smith	1952 ......Ann Weber
1901 ......Mrs. C. E. Woodruff	1926 ......Dorothy Smith	1953 ......Ann Weber

National Women's Champions *(Cont.)*

1954 .....Luarette Young	1969 .....Doreen Wilber	1984 .....Ruth Rowe
1955 .....Ann Clark	1970 .....Nancy Myrick	1985 .....Terri Pesho
1956 .....Carole Meinhart	1971 .....Doreen Wilber	1986 .....Debra Ochs
1957 .....Carole Meinhart	1972 .....Ruth Rowe	1987 .....Terry Quinn
1958 .....Carole Meinhart	1973 .....Doreen Wilber	1988 .....Debra Ochs
1959 .....Carole Meinhart	1974 .....Doreen Wilber	1989 .....Debra Ochs
1960 .....Ann Clark	1975 .....Irene Lorensen	1990 .....Denise Parker
1961 .....Victoria Cook	1976 .....Luann Ryon	1991 .....Denise Parker
1962 .....Nancy Vonderheide	1977 .....Luann Ryon	1992 .....Sherry Block
1963 .....Nancy Vonderheide	1978 .....Luann Ryon	1993 .....Denise Parker
1964 .....Victoria Cook	1979 .....Lynette Johnson	1994 .....Judy Adams
1965 .....Nancy Pfeiffer	1980 .....Judi Adams	1995 .....Jessica Carlson
1966 .....Helen Thornton	1981 .....Debra Metzger	1996 .....Janet Dykman
1967 .....Ardelle Mills	1982 .....Luann Ryon	
1968 .....Victoria Cook	1983 .....Nancy Myrick	

Chess

World Champions

FIDE

1866-94....................Wilhelm Steinitz, Austria	1963-69....................Tigran Petrosian, USSR
1894 1021.................Emanuel Lasker, Germany	1969-72....................Boris Spassky, USSR
1921-27....................Jose Capablanca, Cuba	1972-75....................Bobby Fischer, United States
1927-35....................Alexander Alekhine, France	1975-85....................Anatoly Karpov, USSR
1935-37....................Max Euwe, Holland	1985-93....................*Gary Kasparov, USSR
1937-47....................Alexander Alekhine, France	1993.........................vacant
1948-57....................Mikhail Botvinnik, USSR	1994-........................Anatoly Karpov, Russia
1957-58....................Vassily Smyslov, USSR	*Kasparov stripped of title by FIDE in 1993.
1958-59....................Mikhail Botvinnik, USSR	
1960-61....................Mikhail Tal, USSR	**Professional Chess Association**
1961-63....................Mikhail Botvinnik, USSR	1993-........................Gary Kasparov

United States Champions

1857-71........Paul Morphy	1954-57........Arthur Bisguier	1984-85........Lev Alburt
1871-76........George Mackenzie	1957-61........Bobby Fischer	1986 ....Yasser Seirawan
1876-80........James Mason	1961-62........Larry Evans	1987 ....Joel Benjamin
1880-89........George Mackenzie	1962-68........Bobby Fischer	Nick DeFirmian
1889-90........Samuel Lipschutz	1968-69........Larry Evans	1988 ....Michael Wilder
1890 ....Jackson Showalter	1969-72........Samuel Reshevsky	1989 ....Roman
1890-91........Max Judd	1972-73........Robert Byrne	Dzindzichashvili
1891-92........Jackson Showalter	1973-74........Lubomir Kavale	Stuart Rachels
1892-94........Samuel Lipschutz	John Grefe	Yasser Seirawan
1894 ....Jackson Showalter	1974-77........Walter Browne	1990 ....Lev Alburt
1894-95........Albert Hodges	1978-80........Lubomir Kavalek	1991 ....Gata Kamski
1895-97........Jackson Showalter	1980-81........Larry Evans	1992 ....Patrick Wolff
1897-1906 ...Harry Pillsbury	Larry Christiansen	1993 ....Alex Yermolinsky
1906-09........Vacant	Walter Browne	A. Shabalov
1909-36........Frank Marshall	1981-83........Walter Browne	1994 ....Boris Gulko
1936-44........Samuel Reshevsky	Yasser Seirawan	1995 ....Patrick Wolff
1944-46........Arnold Denker	1983 ....Roman	Nick DeFirmian
1946-48........Samuel Reshevsky	Dzindzichashvili	Alexander Ivanov
1948-51........Herman Steiner	1983 ....Larry Christiansen	1996 ....Alex Yermolinsky
1951-54........Larry Evans	Walter Browne	

Curling

World Men's Champions

Year	Country, Skip	Year	Country, Skip	Year	Country, Skip
1972.....Canada, Crest Melesnuk		1978.....U.S., Bob Nichols		1985.....Canada, Al Hackner	
1973.....Sweden, Kjell Oscarius		1979.....Norway, Kristian Soerum		1986.....Canada, Ed Luckowich	
1974.....U.S., Bud Somerville		1980.....Canada, Rich Folk		1987.....Canada, Russ Howard	
1975.....Switzerland, Otto Danieli		1981.....Switzerland, Jurg Tanner		1988.....Norway, Eigil Ramsfjell	
1976.....U.S., Bruce Roberts		1982.....Canada, Al Hackner		1989.....Canada, Pat Ryan	
1977.....Sweden, Ragnar Kamp		1983.....Canada, Ed Werenich		1990.....Canada, Ed Werenich	
		1984.....Norway, Eigil Ramsfjell		1991.....Scotland, David Smith	

World Men's Champions (Cont.)

Year	Country, Skip	Year	Country, Skip	Year	Country, Skip
1992	Switzerland, Markus Eggler	1994	Canada, Rick Folk	1996	Canada, Jeff Stoughton
1993	Canada, Russ Howard	1995	Canada, Kerry Burtnyk		

World Women's Champions

Year	Country, Skip	Year	Country, Skip	Year	Country, Skip
1979	Switzerland, Gaby Casanova	1984	Canada, Connie Lallberte	1992	Sweden, Elisabet Johanssen
1980	Canada, Marj Mitchell	1985	Canada, Linda Moore	1993	Canada, Sandra Peterson
1981	Sweden, Elisabeth Hogstrom	1986	Canada, Marilyn Darte	1994	Canada, Sandra Peterson
1982	Denmark, Marianne Jorgenson	1987	Canada, Pat Sanders	1995	Sweden, Elisabet Gustafson
1983	Switzerland, Erika Mueller	1988	Germany, Andrea Schopp	1996	Canada, Marilyn Bodogh
		1989	Canada, Heather Houston		
		1990	Norway, Dordi Nordby		
		1991	Norway, Dordi Nordby		

U.S. Men's Champions

Year	Site	Winning Club	Skip
1957	Chicago, IL	Hibbing, MN	Harold Lauber
1958	Milwaukee, WI	Detroit, MI	Douglas Fisk
1959	Green Bay, WI	Hibbing, MN	Fran Kleffman
1960	Chicago, IL	Grafton, ND	Orvil Gilleshammer
1961	Grand Forks, ND	Seattle, WA	Frank Crealock
1962	Detroit, MI	Hibbing, MN	Fran Kleffman
1963	Duluth, MN	Detroit, MI	Mike Slyziuk
1964	Utica, NY	Duluth, MN	Robert Magle, Jr.
1965	Seattle, WA	Superior, WI	Bud Somerville
1966	Hibbing, MN	Fargo, ND	Joe Zbacnik
1967	Winchester, MA	Seattle, WA	Bruce Roberts
1968	Madison, WI	Superior, WI	Bud Somerville
1969	Grand Forks, ND	Superior, WI	Bud Somerville
1970	Ardsley, NY	Grafton, ND	Art Tallackson
1971	Duluth, MN	Edmore, ND	Dale Dalziel
1972	Wilmette, IL	Grafton, ND	Robert Labonte
1973	Colorado Springs, CO	Winchester, MA	Charles Reeves
1974	Schenectady, NY	Superior, WI	Bud Somerville
1975	Detroit, MI	Seattle, WA	Ed Risling
1976	Wausau, WI	Hibbing, MN	Bruce Roberts
1977	Northbrook, IL	Hibbing, MN	Bruce Roberts
1978	Utica, NY	Superior, WI	Bob Nichols
1979	Superior, WI	Bemidji, MN	Scott Baird
1980	Bemidji, MN	Hibbing, MN	Paul Pustovar
1981	Fairbanks, AK	Superior, WI	Bob Nichols
1982	Brookline, MA	Madison, WI	Steve Brown
1983	Colorado Springs, CO	Colorado Springs, CO	Don Cooper
1984	Hibbing, MN	Hibbing, MN	Bruce Roberts
1985	Mequon, WI	Wilmette, IL	Tim Wright
1986	Seattle, WA	Madison, WI	Steve Brown
1987	Lake Placid, NY	Seattle, WA	Jim Vukich
1988	St Paul, MN	Seattle, WA	Doug Jones
1989	Detroit, MI	Seattle, WA	Jim Vukich
1990	Superior, WI	Seattle, WA	Doug Jones
1991	Utica, NY	Madison, WI	Steve Brown
1992	Grafton, ND	Seattle, WA	Doug Jones
1993	St Paul, MN	Bemidji, MN	Scott Baird
1994	Duluth, MN	Bemidji, MN	Scott Baird
1995	Appleton, WI	Superior, WI	Tim Somerville
1996	Bemidji, MN	Superior, WI	Tim Somerville

U.S. Women's Champions

Year	Site	Winning Club	Skip
1977	Wilmette, IL	Hastings, NY	Margaret Smith
1978	Duluth, MN	Wausau, WI	Sandy Robarge
1979	Winchester, MA	Seattle, WA	Nancy Langley
1980	Seattle, WA	Seattle, WA	Sharon Kozal
1981	Kottle Moraine, WI	Seattle, WA	Nancy Langley

U.S. Women's Champions *(Cont.)*

Year	Site	Winning Club	Skip
1982	Bowling Green, OH	Oak Park, IL	Ruth Schwenker
1983	Grafton, ND	Seattle, WA	Nancy Langley
1984	Wauwatosa, WI	Duluth, MN	Amy Hatten
1985	Hershey, PA	Fairbanks, AK	Bev Birklid
1986	Chicago, IL	St Paul, MN	Gerri Tilden
1987	St Paul, MN	Seattle, WA	Sharon Good
1988	Darien, CT	Seattle, WA	Nancy Langley
1989	Detroit, MI	Rolla, ND	Jan Lagasse
1990	Superior, WI	Denver, CO	Bev Behnke
1991	Utica, NY	Houston, TX	Maymar Gemmell
1992	Grafton, ND	Madison, WI	Lisa Schoeneberg
1993	St Paul, MN	Denver, CO	Bev Behnke
1994	Duluth, MN	Denver, CO	Bev Behnke
1995	Appleton, WI	Madison, WI	Lisa Schoeneberg
1996	Bemidji, MN	Madison, WI	Lisa Schoeneberg

Cycling

Professional Road Race World Champions

1927 ....Alfred Binda, Italy
1928 ....George Ronsse, Belgium
1929 ....George Ronsse, Belgium
1930 ....Alfred Binda, Italy
1931 ....Learco Guerra, Italy
1932 ....Alfred Binda, Italy
1933 ....George Speicher, France
1934 ....Karel Kaers, Belgium
1935 ....Jean Aerts, Belgium
1936 ....Antonio Magne, France
1937 ....Elio Meulenberg, Belgium
1938 ....Marcel Kint, Belgium
No competition 1939-45
1946 ....Hans Knecht, Switzerland
1947 ....Theo. Middelkamp, Holland
1948 ....Alberic Schotte, Belgium
1949 ....Henri Van Steenbergen, Belgium
1950 ....Alberic Schotte, Belgium
1951 ....Ferdinand Kubler, Switzerland
1952 ....Heinz Mueller, Germany
1953 ....Fausto Coppi, Italy
1954 ....Louison Bobet, France
1955 ....Stan Ockers, Belgium

1956 ....Rik Van Steenbergen, Belgium
1957 ....Rik Van Steenbergen, Belgium
1958 ....Ercole Baldini, Italy
1959 ....Andre Darrigade, France
1960 ....Rik van Looy, Belgium
1961 ....Rik van Looy, Belgium
1962 ....Jean Stablenski, France
1963 ....Bennoni Beheyt, Belgium
1964 ....Jan Janssen, Holland
1965 ....Tommy Simpson, England
1966 ....Rudi Altig, West Germany
1967 ....Eddy Merckx, Belgium
1968 ....Vittorio Adorni, Italy
1969 ....Harm Ottenbros, Netherlands
1970 ....J.P. Monseré, Belgium
1971 ....Eddy Merckx, Belgium
1972 ....Marino Basso, Italy
1973 ....Felice Gimondi, Italy
1974 ....Eddy Merckx, Belgium
1975 ....Hennie Kuiper, Holland
1976 ....Freddy Maertens, Belgium
1977 ....Francesco Moser, Italy

1978 ....Gerri Knetemann, Holland
1979 ....Jan Raas, Holland
1980 ....Bernard Hinault, France
1981 ....Freddy Maertens, Belgium
1982 ....Giuseppe Saronni, Italy
1983 ....Greg LeMond, United States
1984 ....Claude Criquielion, Belgium
1985 ....Joop Zoetemelk, Holland
1986 ....Moreno Argentin, Italy
1987 ....Stephen Roche, Ireland
1988 ....Maurizio Fondriest, Italy
1989 ....Greg LeMond, United States
1990 ....Rudy Dhaenene, Belgium
1991 ....Gianni Bugno, Italy
1992 ....Gianni Bugno, Italy
1993 ....Lance Armstrong, United States
1994 ....Luc LeBlanc, France
1995 ....Abraham Olano, Spain

Tour DuPont Winners

Year	Winner	Time
1989	Dag Otto Lauritzen, Norway	33 hrs, 28 min, 48 sec
1990	Raul Alcala, Mexico	45 hrs, 20 min, 9 sec
1991	Erik Breukink, Holland	48 hrs, 56 min, 53 sec
1992	Greg LeMond, United States	44 hrs, 27 min, 43 sec
1993	Raul Alcala, Mexico	46 hrs, 42 min, 52 sec
1994	Viatcheslav Ekimov, Russia	47 hrs, 14 min, 29 sec
1995	Lance Armstrong, United States	46 hrs, 31 min, 16 sec
1996	Lance Armstrong, United States	48 hrs, 20 min, 5 sec

Tour de France Winners

Year	Winner	Time
1903	Maurice Garin, France	94 hrs, 33 min
1904	Henri Cornet, France	96 hrs, 5 min, 56 sec
1905	Louis Trousselier, France	110 hrs, 26 min, 58 sec
1906	Rene Pottier, France	Not available

Tour de France Winners *(Cont.)*

Year	Winner	Time
1907	Lucien Petit-Breton, France	158 hrs, 54 min, 5 sec
1908	Lucien Petit-Breton, France	Not available
1909	Francois Faber, Luxembourg	157 hrs, 1 min, 22 sec
1910	Octave Lapize, France	162 hrs, 41 min, 30 sec
1911	Gustave Garrigou, France	195 hrs, 37 min
1912	Odile Defraye, Belgium	190 hrs, 30 min, 28 sec
1913	Philippe Thys, Belgium	197 hrs, 54 min
1914	Philippe Thys, Belgium	200 hrs, 28 min, 48 sec
1915-18	No race	
1919	Firmin Lambot, Belgium	231 hrs, 7 min, 15 sec
1920	Philippe Thys, Belgium	228 hrs, 36 min, 13 sec
1921	Leon Scieur, Belgium	221 hrs, 50 min, 26 sec
1922	Firmin Lambot, Belgium	222 hrs, 8 min, 6 sec
1923	Henri Pelissier, France	222 hrs, 15 min, 30 sec
1924	Ottavio Bottechia, Italy	226 hrs, 18 min, 21 sec
1925	Ottavio Bottechia, Italy	219 hrs, 10 min, 18 sec
1926	Lucien Buysse, Belgium	238 hrs, 44 min, 25 sec
1927	Nicolas Frantz, Luxembourg	198 hrs, 16 min, 42 sec
1928	Nicolas Frantz, Luxembourg	192 hrs, 48 min, 58 sec
1929	Maurice Dewaele, Belgium	186 hrs, 39 min, 16 sec
1930	Andre Leducq, France	172 hrs, 12 min, 16 sec
1931	Antonin Magne, France	177 hrs, 10 min, 3 sec
1932	Andre Leducq, France	154 hrs, 12 min, 49 sec
1933	Georges Speicher, France	147 hrs, 51 min, 37 sec
1934	Antonin Magne, France	147 hrs, 13 min, 58 sec
1935	Romain Maes, Belgium	141 hrs, 32 min
1936	Sylvere Maes, Belgium	142 hrs, 47 min, 32 sec
1937	Roger Lapebie, France	138 hrs, 58 min, 31 sec
1938	Gino Bartali, Italy	148 hrs, 29 min, 12 sec
1939	Sylvere Maes, Belgium	132 hrs, 3 min, 17 sec
1940-46	No race	
1947	Jean Robic, France	148 hrs, 11 min, 25 sec
1948	Gino Bartali, Italy	147 hrs, 10 min, 36 sec
1949	Fausto Coppi, Italy	149 hrs, 40 min, 49 sec
1950	Ferdi Kubler, Switzerland	145 hrs, 36 min, 56 sec
1951	Hugo Koblet, Switzerland	142 hrs, 20 min, 14 sec
1952	Fausto Coppi, Italy	151 hrs, 57 min, 20 sec
1953	Louison Bobet, France	129 hrs, 23 min, 25 sec
1954	Louison Bobet, France	140 hrs, 6 min, 5 sec
1955	Louison Bobet, France	130 hrs, 29 min, 26 sec
1956	Roger Walkowiak, France	124 hrs, 1 min, 16 sec
1957	Jacques Anquetil, France	129 hrs, 46 min, 11 sec
1958	Charly Gaul, Luxembourg	116 hrs, 59 min, 5 sec
1959	Federico Bahamontes, Spain	123 hrs, 46 min, 45 sec
1960	Gastone Nencini, Italy	112 hrs, 8 min, 42 sec
1961	Jacques Anquetil, France	122 hrs, 1 min, 33 sec
1962	Jacques Anquetil, France	114 hrs, 31 min, 54 sec
1963	Jacques Anquetil, France	113 hrs, 30 min, 5 sec
1964	Jacques Anquetil, France	127 hrs, 9 min, 44 sec
1965	Felice Gimondi, Italy	116 hrs, 42 min, 6 sec
1966	Lucien Aimar, France	117 hrs, 34 min, 21 sec
1967	Roger Pingeon, France	136 hrs, 53 min, 50 sec
1968	Jan Janssen, Netherlands	133 hrs, 49 min, 32 sec
1969	Eddy Merckx, Belgium	116 hrs, 16 min, 2 sec
1970	Eddy Merckx, Belgium	119 hrs, 31 min, 49 sec
1971	Eddy Merckx, Belgium	96 hrs, 45 min, 14 sec
1972	Eddy Merckx, Belgium	108 hrs, 17 min, 18 sec
1973	Luis Ocana, Spain	122 hrs, 25 min, 34 sec
1974	Eddy Merckx, Belgium	116 hrs, 16 min, 58 sec
1975	Bernard Thevenet, France	114 hrs, 35 min, 31 sec
1976	Lucien Van Impe, Belgium	116 hrs, 22 min, 23 sec
1977	Bernard Thevenet, France	115 hrs, 38 min, 30 sec
1978	Bernard Hinault, France	108 hrs, 18 min
1979	Bernard Hinault, France	103 hrs, 6 min, 50 sec
1980	Joop Zoetemelk, Netherlands	109 hrs, 19 min, 14 sec
1981	Bernard Hinault, France	96 hrs, 19 min, 38 sec
1982	Bernard Hinault, France	92 hrs, 8 min, 46 sec

Tour de France Winners *(Cont.)*

Year	Winner	Time
1983	Laurent Fignon, France	105 hrs, 7 min, 52 sec
1984	Laurent Fignon, France	112 hrs, 3 min, 40 sec
1985	Bernard Hinault, France	113 hrs, 24 min, 23 sec
1986	Greg LeMond, United States	110 hrs, 35 min, 19 sec
1987	Stephen Roche, Ireland	115 hrs, 27 min, 42 sec
1988	Pedro Delgado, Spain	84 hrs, 27 min, 53 sec
1989	Greg LeMond, United States	87 hrs, 38 min, 35 sec
1990	Greg LeMond, United States	90 hrs, 43 min, 20 sec
1991	Miguel Induráin, Spain	101 hrs, 1 min, 20 sec
1992	Miguel Induráin, Spain	100 hrs, 49 min, 30 sec
1993	Miguel Induráin, Spain	95 hrs, 57 min, 9 sec
1994	Miguel Induráin, Spain	103 hrs, 38 min, 38 sec
1995	Miguel Induráin, Spain	92 hrs, 44 min, 59 sec
1996	Bjarne Riis, Denmark	95 hrs, 57 min, 16 sec

Sled Dog Racing

Iditarod

Year	Winner	Time	Year	Winner	Time
1973	Dick Wilmarth	20 days, 00:40:41	1985	Libby Riddles	18 days, 00:20:17
1974	Carl Huntington	20 days, 15:02:07	1986	Susan Butcher	11 days, 15:06:00
1975	Emmitt Peters	14 days, 14:43:45	1987	Susan Butcher	11 days, 02:05:13
1976	Gerald Riley	18 days, 22:58:17	1988	Susan Butcher	11 days, 11:41:40
1977	Rick Swenson	16 days, 16:27:13	1989	Joe Runyan	11 days, 05:24:34
1978	Dick Mackey	14 days, 18:52:24	1990	Susan Butcher	11 days, 01:53:23
1979	Rick Swenson	15 days, 10:37:47	1991	Rick Swenson	12 days, 16:34:39
1980	Joe May	14 days, 07:11:51	1992	Martin Buser	10 days, 19:17:15
1981	Rick Swenson	12 days, 08:45:02	1993	Jeff King	10 days, 15:38:15
1982	Rick Swenson	16 days, 04:40:10	1994	Martin Buser	10 days, 13:02:39
1983	Dick Mackey	12 days, 14:10:44	1995	Doug Swingley	9 days, 02:42:19
1984	Dean Osmar	12 days, 15:07:33	1996	Jeff King	9 days, 05:43:13

Fishing

Saltwater Fishing Records

Species	Weight	Where Caught	Date	Angler
Albacore	88 lb 2 oz	Gran Canaria, Canary Islands	Nov 19, 1977	Siegfried Dickemann
Amberjack, greater	155 lb 10 oz	Challenger Bank, Bermuda	June 24, 1981	Joseph Dawson
Amberjack, Pacific	104 lb	Baja California, Mexico	July 4, 1984	Richard Cresswell
Barracuda, great	85 lb	Christmas Island, Kiribati	April 11, 1992	John W. Helfrich
Barracuda, Mexican	21 lb	Phantom Isle, Costa Rica	Mar 27, 1987	E. Greg Kent
Barracuda, pickhandle	17 lb 4 oz	Sitra Channel, Arabian Gulf	Nov 21, 1985	Roger J. Cranswick
Bass, barred sand	13 lb 3 oz	Huntington Beach, CA	Aug 29, 1988	Robert Halal
Bass, black sea	9 lb 8 oz	Virginia Beach, VA	Jan 9, 1987	Joe Mizelle, Jr
Bass, European	20 lb 11 oz	Stes Maries de la Mer, France	May 6, 1986	Jean Baptiste Bayle
Bass, giant sea	563 lb 8 oz	Anacapa Island, CA	Aug 20, 1968	James D. McAdam, Jr
Bass, redeye	8 lb 12 oz	Apalatchicola River, FL	Jan 28, 1995	Carl W. Davis
Bass, striped	78 lb 8 oz	Atlantic City, NJ	Sep 21, 1982	Albert R. McReynolds
Bluefish	31 lb 12 oz	Hatteras Inlet, NC	Jan 30, 1972	James M. Hussey
Bonefish	19 lb	Zululand, South Africa	May 26, 1962	Brian W. Batchelor
Bonito, Atlantic	18 lb 4 oz	Faial Island, Azores	July 8, 1953	D. G. Higgs
Bonito, Pacific	14 lb 12 oz	Baja California, Mexico	Oct. 12, 1980	Jerome H. Rilling
Cabezon	23 lb	Juan De Fuca Strait, WA	Aug 4, 1990	Wesley Hunter
Cobia	135 lb 9 oz	Shark Bay, Australia	July 9, 1985	Peter W. Goulding
Cod, Atlantic	98 lb 12 oz	Isle of Shoals, NH	June 8, 1969	Alphonse Bielevich
Cod, Pacific	30 lb	Andrew Bay, AK	July 7, 1984	Donald R. Vaughn
Conger	133 lb 4 oz	South Devon, England	June 5, 1995	Vic Evans
Dolphin	87 lb	Papagallo Gulf, Costa Rica	Sep 25, 1976	Manuel Salazar
Drum, black	113 lb 1 oz	Lewes, DE	Sep 15, 1975	Gerald M. Townsend
Drum, red	94 lb 2 oz	Avon, NC	Nov 7, 1984	David Deuel
Eel, American	9 lb 4 oz	Cape May, NJ	Nov 9, 1995	Jeff Pennick
Eel, marbled	36 lb 1 oz	Durban, South Africa	June 10, 1984	Ferdie van Nooten

Saltwater Fishing Records (Cont.)

Species	Weight	Where Caught	Date	Angler
Flounder, southern	20 lb 9 oz	Nassau Sound, FL	Dec 23, 1983	Larenza W. Mungin
Flounder, summer	22 lb 7 oz	Montauk, NY	Sep 15, 1975	Charles Nappi
Grouper, warsaw	436 lb 12 oz	Destin, FL	Dec 22, 1985	Steve Haeusler
Halibut, Atlantic	255 lb 4 oz	Gloucester, MA	July 28, 1989	Sonny Manley
Halibut, California	53 lb 4 oz	Santa Rosa Island, CA	July 7, 1988	Russell J. Harmon
Halibut, Pacific	396 lb	Unalaska Bay, Bering Sea	June 21, 1995	Michael James Golat
Jack, crevalle	57 lb 5 oz	Barra do Kwanza, Angola	Oct 10, 1992	Cam Nicolson
Jack, horse-eye	24 lb 8 oz	Miami, FL	Dec 20, 1982	Tilo Schnau
Jack, Pacific crevalle	29 lb 8 oz	Playa Zancudo, Costa Rica	Jan 1, 1994	Ronald C. Snody
Jewfish	680 lb	Fernandina Beach, FL	May 20, 1961	Lynn Joyner
Kawakawa	29 lb	Isla Clarion, Mexico	Dec 17, 1986	Ronald Nakamura
Lingcod	69 lb	Langara Island, B.C.	June 16, 1992	Murray M. Homer
Mackerel, cero	17 lb 2 oz	Islamorada, FL	Apr 5, 1986	G. Michael Mills
Mackerel, king	90 lb	Key West, FL	Feb 16, 1976	Norton I. Thomton
Mackerel, narrowbarred	99 lb	Natal, South Africa	Mar 14, 1982	Michael J. Wilkinson
Mackerel, Spanish	13 lb	Ocracoke Inlet, NC	Nov 4, 1987	Robert Cranton
Marlin, Atlantic blue	1402 lb 2 oz	Vitoria, Brazil	Feb 29, 1992	Paulo R. A. Amorim
Marlin, black	1560 lb	Cabo Blanco, Peru	Aug 4, 1953	A. C. Glassell, Jr
Marlin, Pacific blue	1376 lb	Kaaiwi Point, HI	May 31, 1982	J. W. de Beaubien
Marlin, striped	494 lb	Tutukaka, New Zealand	Jan 16, 1986	Bill Boniface
Marlin, white	181 lb 14 oz	Vitoria, Brazil	Dec 8, 1979	Evandro Luiz Caser
Permit	53 lb 4 oz	Lake Worth, FL	Mar 25, 1994	Roy Brooker
Pollock	50 lb	Salstraumen, Norway	Nov 30, 1995	Thor Magnus-Lekang
Pompano, African	50 lb 8 oz	Daytona Beach, FL	Apr 21, 1990	Tom Sargent
Roosterfish	114 lb	La Paz, Mexico	June 1, 1960	Abe Sackheim
Runner, blue	8 lb 7 oz	Port Aransas, TX	Feb 13, 1995	Allen E. Windecker
Runner, rainbow	37 lb 9 oz	Isla Clarion, Mexico	Nov 21, 1991	Tom Pfleger
Sailfish, Atlantic	141 lb 1 oz	Luanda, Angola	Feb 19, 1994	Alfredo de Sousa
Sailfish, Pacific	221 lb	Santa Cruz Island, Ecuador	Feb 12, 1947	C. W. Stewart
Seabass, white	83 lb 12 oz	San Felipe, Mexico	Mar 31, 1953	L. C. Baumgardner
Seatrout, spotted	17 lb 7 oz	Ft. Pierce, FL	May 11, 1995	Craig F. Carson
Shark, bigeye thresher	802 lb	Tutukaka, New Zealand	Feb 8, 1981	Dianne North
Shark, blue	437 lb	Catherine Bay, NSW, Australia	Oct 2, 1976	Peter Hyde
Shark, grter hammrhd	991 lb	Sarasota, FL	May 30, 1982	Allen Ogle
Shark, Greenland	1708 lb 9 oz	Trondheimsfjord, Norway	Oct 18, 1987	Terje Nordtvedt
Shark, porbeagle	507 lb	Caithness, Scotland	Mar 9, 1993	Christopher Bennet
Shark, shortfin mako	1115 lb	Black River, Mauritius	Nov 16, 1988	Patrick Guillanton
Shark, tiger	1780 lb	Cherry Grove, SC	June 14, 1964	Walter Maxwell
Shark, tope	98 lb 8 oz	Santa Monica, CA	Oct 20, 1994	Freed Oakley
Shark, white	2664 lb	Ceduna, Australia	Apr 21, 1959	Alfred Dean
Skipjack, black	26 lb	Baja California, Mexico	Oct 23, 1991	Clifford K. Hamaishi
Snapper, cubera	121 lb 8 oz	Cameron, LA	July 5, 1982	Mike Hebert
Snook	53 lb 10 oz	Parismina Ranch, Costa Rica	Oct 18, 1978	Gilbert Ponzi
Spearfish	90 lb 13 oz	Madeira Island, Portugal	June 2, 1980	Joseph Larkin
Swordfish	1182 lb	Iquique, Chile	May 7, 1953	L. Marron
Tarpon	283 lb 4 oz	Sherbro Island, Sierra Leone	Apr 16, 1991	Yvon Victor Sebag
Tautog	24 lb	Wachapreague, VA	Aug 25, 1987	Gregory Bell
Tilapia	6 lb 5 oz	Lake Arenal, Costa Rica	Feb 10, 1995	Marvin C. Smith
Trevally, bigeye	18 lb 1 oz	Clipperton Island, France	May 12, 1990	Rebecca A. Mills
Trevally, giant	145 lb 8 oz	Maui, HI	Mar 28, 1991	Russell Mori
Tuna, Atlantic bigeye	375 lb 8 oz	Ocean City, MD	Aug 26, 1977	Cecil Browne
Tuna, blackfin	42 lb 10 oz	Duck Key, FL	May 21, 1995	Shawn Snyder
Tuna, bluefin	1496 lb	Aulds Cove, Nova Scotia	Oct 26, 1979	Ken Fraser
Tuna, longtail	79 lb 2 oz	Montague Island, NSW, Australia	Apr 12, 1982	Tim Simpson
Tuna, Pacific bigeye	435 lb	Cabo Blanco, Peru	Apr 17, 1957	Russel Lee
Tuna, skipjack	41 lb 14 oz	Pearl Beach, Mauritius	Nov 12, 1985	Edmund Heinzen
Tuna, southern bluefin	348 lb 5 oz	Whakatane, New Zealand	Jan 16, 1981	Rex Wood
Tuna, yellowfin	388 lb 12 oz	San Benedicto Is, Mexico	Apr 1, 1977	Curt Wiesenhutter
Tunny, little	35 lb 2 oz	Cape de Garde, Algeria	Dec 14, 1988	Jean Yves Chatard
Wahoo	155 lb 8 oz	San Salvador, Bahamas	Apr 3, 1990	William Bourne
Weakfish	19 lb 2 oz	Jones Beach Inlet, NY	Oct 11, 1984	Dennis Rooney
		Delaware Bay, Delaware	May 20, 1989	William E. Thomas
Yellowtail, California	79 lb 4 oz	Baja California, Mexico	July 2, 1991	Robert I. Welker
Yellowtail, southern	114 lb 10 oz	Tauranga, New Zealand	Feb 5, 1984	Mike Godfrey

Freshwater Fishing Records

Species	Weight	Where Caught	Date	Angler
Barramundi	63 lb 2 oz	Queensland, Australia	April 28, 1991	Scott Barnsley
Bass, largemouth	22 lb 4 oz	Montgomery Lake, GA	June 2, 1932	George W. Perry
Bass, peacock	27 lb	Rio Negro, Brazil	Dec 4,1994	Gerald "Doc" Lawson
Bass, rock	3 lb	York River, Ontario	Aug 1, 1974	Peter Gulgin
Bass, smallmouth	10 lb 8 oz	Hendricks Creek, KY	Apr 14, 1986	Paul E. Beal
Bass, Suwannee	3 lb 14 oz	Suwannee River, FL	Mar 2, 1985	Ronnie Everett
Bass, white	6 lb 13 oz	Orange, VA	July 31, 1989	Ronald Sprouse
Bass, whiterock	24 lb 3 oz	Leesville Lake, VA	May 12, 1989	David Lambert
Bass, yellow	2 lb 4 oz	Lake Monroe, IN	Mar 27, 1977	Donald L. Stalker
Bluegill	4 lb 12 oz	Ketona Lake, AL	Apr 9, 1950	T. S. Hudson
Bowfin	21 lb 8 oz	Florence, SC	Jan 29, 1980	Robert Harmon
Buffalo, bigmouth	70 lb 5 oz	Bastrop, LA	Apr 21, 1980	Delbert Sisk
Buffalo, black	55 lb 8 oz	Cherokee Lake, TN	May 3, 1984	Edward McLain
Buffalo, smallmouth	68 lb 8 oz	Lake Hamilton, AR	May 16, 1984	Jerry Dolezal
Bullhead, brown	5 lb 11oz	Cedar Creek, FL	Mar 28, 1995	Robert Bengis
Bullhead, yellow	4 lb 4 oz	Mormon Lake, AZ	May 11, 1984	Emily Williams
Burbot	18 lb 4 oz	Pickford, MI	Jan 31, 1980	Thomas Courtemanche
Carp	75 lb 11 oz	Lac de St Cassien, France	May 21, 1987	Leo van der Gugten
Catfish, blue	109 lb 4 oz	Moncks Corner, SC	Mar 14, 1991	George A. Lijewski
Catfish, channel	58 lb	Santee-Cooper Reservoir, SC	July 7, 1964	W. B. Whaley
Catfish, flathead	91 lb 4 oz	Lake Lewisville, TX	Mar 28, 1982	Mike Rogers
Catfish, white	18 lb 14 oz	Inverness, FL	Sep 21, 1991	Jim Miller
Char, Arctic	32 lb 9 oz	Tree River, Canada	July 30, 1981	Jeffrey Ward
Crappie, white	5 lb 3 oz	Enid Dam, MS	July 31, 1957	Fred L. Bright
Dolly Varden	18 lb 9 oz	Mashutuk River, AK	July 13, 1993	Richard B. Evans
Dorado	51 lb 5 oz	Corrientes, Argentina	Sep 27, 1984	Armando Giudice
Drum, freshwater	54 lb 8 oz	Nickajack Lake, TN	Apr 20, 1972	Benny E. Hull
Gar, alligator	279 lb	Rio Grande River, TX	Dec 2, 1951	Bill Valverde
Gar, Florida	21 lb 3 oz	Boca Raton, FL	June 3, 1981	Jeff Sabol
Gar, longnose	50 lb 5 oz	Trinity River, TX	July 30, 1954	Townsend Miller
Gar, shortnose	5 lb 12 oz	Rend Lake, IL	July 16, 1995	Donna K. Willmert
Gar, spotted	9 lb 12 oz	Lake Mexia, TX	Apr 7, 1994	Rick Rivard
Grayling, Arctic	5 lb 15 oz	Katseyedie River, Northwest Territories	Aug 16, 1967	Jeanne P. Branson
Inconnu	53 lb	Pah River, AK	Aug 20, 1986	Lawrence Hudnall
Kokanee	9 lb 6 oz	Okanagan Lake, Vernon, BC	June 18, 1988	Norm Kuhn
Muskellunge	67 lb 8 oz	Hayward, WI	July 24,1949	Cal Johnson
Muskellunge, tiger	51 lb 3 oz	Lac Vieux-Desert, WI, MI	July 16, 1919	John Knobla
Perch, Nile	191 lb 8 oz	Lake Victoria, Kenya	Sep 5, 1991	Andy Davison
Perch, white	4 lb 12 oz	Messalonskee Lake, ME	June 4, 1949	Mrs. Earl Small
Perch, yellow	4 lb 3 oz	Bordentown, NJ	May 1865	C. C. Abbot
Pickerel, chain	9 lb 6 oz	Homerville, GA	Feb 17, 1961	Baxley McQuaig, Jr
Pike, northern	55 lb 1 oz	Lake of Grefeern, West Germany	Oct 16, 1986	Lothar Louis
Redhorse, greater	9 lb 3 oz	Salmon River, Pulaski, NY	May 11, 1985	Jason Wilson
Redhorse, silver	11 lb 7 oz	Plum Creek, WI	May 29, 1985	Neal Long
Salmon, Atlantic	79 lb 2 oz	Tana River, Norway	1928	Henrik Henriksen
Salmon, chinook	97 lb 4 oz	Kenai River, AK	May 17, 1985	Les Anderson
Salmon, chum	35 lb	Edye Pass, Canada	July 11, 1995	Todd A. Johansson
Salmon, coho	33 lb 4 oz	Pulaski, NY	Sep 27, 1989	Jerry Lifton
Salmon, pink	13 lb 1 oz	Ontario, Canada	Sep 23, 1992	Ray Higaki
Salmon, sockeye	15 lb 3 oz	Kenai River, AK	Aug 9, 1987	Stan Roach
Sauger	8 lb 12 oz	Lake Sakakawea, ND	Oct 6, 1971	Mike Fischer
Shad, American	11 lb 4 oz	Connecticut River, MA	May 19, 1986	Bob Thibodo
Sturgeon, white	468 lb	Benicia, CA	July 9, 1983	Joey Pallotta III
Sunfish, green	2 lb 2 oz	Stockton Lake, MO	June 18, 1971	Paul M. Dilley
Sunfish, redbreast	1 lb 12 oz	Suwannee River, FL	May 29, 1984	Alvin Buchanan
Sunfish, redear	5 lb 3 oz	Sacramento, CA	June 27, 1994	Anthony H. White, Sr
Tigerfish, giant	97 lb	Zaire River, Kinshasa, Zaire	July 9, 1988	Raymond Houtmans
Trout, Apache	5 lb 3 oz	Apache Reservation, AZ	May 29, 1991	John Baldwin
Trout, brook	14 lb 8 oz	Nipigon River, Ontario	July 1916	W. J. Cook
Trout, brown	40 lb 4 oz	Heber Springs, AR	May 9, 1992	Howard L. Collins
Trout, bull	32 lb	Lake Pond Oreille, ID	Oct 27, 1949	N. L. Higgins
Trout, cutthroat	41 lb	Pyramid Lake, NV	Dec 1925	J. Skimmerhorn
Trout, golden	11 lb	Cook's Lake, WY	Aug 5, 1948	Charles S. Reed

Freshwater Fishing Records (Cont.)

Species	Weight	Where Caught	Date	Angler
Trout, lake	66 lb 8 oz	Great Bear Lake, Northwest Territories	July 19, 1991	Rodney Harback
Trout, rainbow	42 lb 2 oz	Bell Island, AK	June 22, 1970	David Robert White
Trout, tiger	20 lb 13 oz	Lake Michigan, WI	Aug 12, 1978	Pete M. Friedland
Walleye	25 lb	Old Hickory Lake, TN	Aug 2, 1960	Mabry Harper
Warmouth	2 lb 7 oz	Yellow River, Holt, FL	Oct 19, 1985	Tony D. Dempsey
Whitefish, lake	14 lb 6 oz	Meaford, Ontario	May 21, 1984	Dennis Laycock
Whitefish, mountain	5 lb 6 oz	Rioh River, Saskatchewan, Canada	June 15, 1988	John Bell
Whitefish, broad	9 lb	Tozitna River, AK	July 17, 1989	Al Mathews
Whitefish, round	6 lb	Putahow River, Manitoba	June 14, 1984	Allan J. Ristori
Zander	25 lb 2 oz	Trosa, Sweden	June 12, 1986	Harry Lee Tennison

Greyhound Racing

Annual Greyhound Race of Champions Winners*

Year	Winner (Sex)	Affiliation/Owner	Year	Winner	Affiliation/Owner
1982	DD's Jackie (F)	Wonderland Park/R.H. Walters, Jr.	1988	BB's Old Yellow (M)	Supplemental (Southland)/ Margie Bonita Hyers
1983	Comin' Attraction (F)	Rocky Mt Greyhound Park/ Bob Riggin	1989	Osh Kosh Juliet (F)	Tampa Greyhound Track/ William F. Pollard
1984	Fallon (F)	Tampa Greyhound Track/ E.J. Alderson	1990	Daring Don (M)	Interstate Kennel Club/ Perry Padrta
1985	Lady Delight (F)	Lincoln Greyhound Park/ Julian A. Gay	1991	Mo Kick (M)	Flagler Greyhound Track/ Eric M. Kennon
1986	Ben G Speedboat (M)	Multnomah Kennel Club/ Louis Bennett	1992	Dicky Vallie (M)	Dairyland Greyhound Track/ George Benjamin
1987	ET's Pesky (F)	Supplemental (Flagler)/ Emil Tanis	1993	Mega Morris (M)	Jacksonville Kennel Club/ Ferrell's Kennel

* The Greyhound Race of Champions has not been held since 1993.

Gymnastics

World Champions
MEN
All-Around

Year	Champion and Nation	Year	Champion and Nation
1903	Joseph Martinez, France	1966	Mikhail Voronin, USSR
1905	Marcel Lalue, France	1970	Eizo Kenmotsu, Japan
1907	Joseph Czada, Czechoslovakia	1974	Shigeru Kasamatsu, Japan
1909	Marcos Torres, France	1978	Nikolai Andrianov, USSR
1911	Ferdinand Steiner, Czechoslovakia	1979	Alexander Ditiatin, USSR
1913	Marcos Torres, France	1981	Yuri Korolev, USSR
1922	Peter Sumi, Yug./F. Pechacek, Czech.	1983	Dimitri Bilozertchev, USSR
1926	Peter Sumi, Yugoslavia	1985	Yuri Korolev, USSR
1930	Josip Primozic, Yugoslavia	1987	Dimitri Bilozertchev, USSR
1934	Eugene Mack, Switzerland	1989	Igor Korobchinsky, USSR
1938	Jan Gajdos, Czechoslovakia	1991	Grigori Misutin, CIS
1950	Walter Lehmann, Switzerland	1993	Vitaly Scherbo, Belarus
1954	Valentin Mouratov, USSR Victor Chukarin, USSR	1994	Ivan Ivankov, Belarus
1958	Boris Shaklin, USSR	1995	Li Xiaoshuang, China
1962	Yuri Titov, USSR		

Pommel Horse

Year	Champion and Nation	Year	Champion and Nation
1930	Josip Primozic, Yugoslavia	1950	Josef Stalder, Switzerland
1934	Eugene Mack, Switzerland	1954	Grant Chaguinjan, USSR
1938	Michael Reusch, Switzerland	1958	Boris Shaklin, USSR

World Champions (Cont.)
MEN (Cont.)
Pommel Horse (Cont.)

Year	Champion and Nation	Year	Champion and Nation
1962	Miroslav Cerar, Yugoslavia	1987	Zsolt Borkai, Hungary
1966	Miroslav Cerar, Yugoslavia		Dmitri Bilozertchev, USSR
1970	Miroslav Cerar, Yugoslavia	1989	Valentin Moguilny, USSR
1974	Zoltan Magyar, Hungary	1991	Valeri Belenki, USSR
1978	Zoltan Magyar, Hungary	1992	Pae Gil Su, North Korea/ Vitaly
1979	Zoltan Magyar, Hungary		Scherbo, CIS/ Li Jing, China
1981	Michael Mikolai, East Germany	1993	Pae Gil Su, North Korea
	Li Xiaoping, Chi	1994	Marius Urzica, Romania
1983	Dmitri Bilozertchev, USSR	1995	Li Donghua, Switzerland
1985	Valentin Moguilny, USSR	1996	Pae Gil Su, North Korea

Floor Exercise

Year	Champion and Nation	Year	Champion and Nation
1930	Josip Primozic, Yugoslavia	1979	Kurt Thomas, United States
1934	Georges Miesz, Switzerland		Roland Brucker, GDR
1938	Jan Gajdos, Czechoslovakia	1981	Yuri Korolev, USSR/ Li Yuejui, Chi
1950	Josef Staldor, Switzerland	1983	Tong Fei, China
1954	Valentin Mouratov, USSR	1985	Tong Fei, China
	Masao Takemoto, Japan	1987	Lou Yun, China
1958	Masao Takemoto, Japan	1989	Igor Korobchinsky, USSR
1962	Nobuyuki Aihara, Japan	1991	Igor Korobchinsky, USSR
	Yukio Endo, Japan	1993	Grigori Misutin, Ukraine
1966	Akinori Nakayama, Japan	1994	Vitaly Scherbo, Belarus
1970	Akinori Nakayama, Japan	1995	Vitaly Scherbo, Belarus
1974	Shigeru Kasamatsu, Japan	1996	Vitaly Scherbo, Belarus
1978	Kurt Thomas, United States		

Rings

Year	Champion and Nation	Year	Champion and Nation
1930	Emanuel Loffler, Czechoslovakia	1981	Alexander Ditiatin, USSR
1934	Alois Hudec, Czechoslovakia	1983	Dimitri Bilozertchev, USSR
1938	Alois Hudec, Czechoslovakia	1985	Li Ning, China/ Yuri Korolev, USSR
1950	Walter Lehmann, Switzerland	1987	Yuri Korolev, USSR
1954	Albert Azarian, USSR	1989	Andreas Aguilar, West Germany
1958	Albert Azarian, USSR	1991	Grigory Misutin, USSR
1962	Yuri Titov, USSR	1992	Vitaly Scherbo, CIS
1966	Mikhail Voronin, USSR	1993	Yuri Chechi, Italy
1970	Akinori Nakayama, Japan	1994	Yuri Chechi, Italy
1974	N. Andrianov, USSR/ D. Grecu, Rom.	1995	Yuri Chechi, Italy
1978	Nikolai Andrianov, USSR	1996	Yuri Chechi, Italy
1979	Alexander Ditiatin, USSR		

Parallel Bars

Year	Champion and Nation	Year	Champion and Nation
1930	Josip Primozic, Yugoslavia	1983	Vladimir Artemov, USSR
1934	Eugene Mack, Switzerland		Lou Yun, China
1938	Michael Reusch, Switzerland	1985	Sylvio Kroll, East Germany
1950	Hans Eugster, Switzerland		Valentin Moguilny, USSR
1954	Victor Chukarin, USSR	1987	Vladimir Artemov, USSR
1958	Boris Shaklin, USSR	1989	Li Jing, China
1962	Miroslav Cerar, Yugoslavia		Vladimir Artemov, USSR
1966	Sergei Diamidov, USSR	1991	Li Jing, China
1970	Akinori Nakayama, Japan	1992	Li Jin, China
1974	Eizo Kenmotsu, Japan		Alexei Voropaev, CIS
1978	Eizo Kenmotsu, Japan	1993	Vitaly Scherbo, Belarus
1979	Bart Conner, United States	1994	Huang Liping, China
1981	Koji Gushiken, Japan	1995	Vitaly Scherbo, Belarus
	Alexandr Ditiatin, USSR	1996	Rustam Sharipov, Ukraine

World Champions (Cont.)
MEN (Cont.)

High Bar

Year	Champion and Nation	Year	Champion and Nation
1930	Istvan Pelle, Hungary	1981	Alexander Takchev, USSR
1934	Ernst Winter, Germany	1983	Dimitri Bilozertchev, USSR
1938	Michael Reusch, Switzerland	1985	Tong Fei, China
1950	Paavo Aaltonen, Finland	1987	Dimitri Bilozertchev, USSR
1954	Valentin Mouratov, USSR	1989	Li Chunyang, China
1958	Boris Shaklin, USSR	1991	Li Chunyang, China/R. Buechner, Germ
1062	Takashi Ono, Japan	1992	Grigori Misutin, CIS
1966	Akinori Nakayama, Japan	1993	Sergei Kharkov, Russia
1970	Eizo Kenmotsu, Japan	1994	Vitaly Scherbo, Belarus
1974	Eberhard Gienger, West Germany	1995	Andreas Wecker, Germany
1978	Shigeru Kasamatsu, Japan	1996	Jesús Carballo, Spain
1979	Kurt Thomas, United States		

Vault

Year	Champion and Nation	Year	Champion and Nation
1934	Eugene Mack, Switzerland	1983	Arthur Akopian, USSR
1938	Eugene Mack, Switzerland	1985	Yuri Korolev, USSR
1950	Ernst Gebendinger, Switzerland	1987	Lou Yun, China
1954	Leo Sotornik, Czechoslovakia		Sylvio Kroll, East Germany
1958	Yuri Titov, USSR	1989	Joreg Behrend, East Germany
1962	Premysel Krbec, Czechoslovakia	1991	Yoo Ok Youl, South Korea
1966	Haruhiro Yamashita, Japan	1992	Yoo Ok Youl, South Korea
1970	Mitsuo Tsukahara, Japan	1993	Vitaly Scherbo, Belarus
1974	Shigeru Kasamatsu, Japan	1994	Vitaly Scherbo, Belarus
1978	Junichi Shimizu, Japan	1995	G. Misutin, Ukraine/A. Nemov, Russia
1979	Alexander Ditiatin, USSR	1996	Alexei Nemov, Russia
1981	Ralf-Peter Hemmann, East Germany		

WOMEN

All-Around

Year	Champion and Nation	Year	Champion and Nation
1934	Vlasta Dekanova, Czechoslovakia	1981	Olga Bicherova, USSR
1938	Vlasta Dekanova, Czechoslovakia	1983	Natalia Yurchenko, USSR
1950	Helena Rakoczy, Poland	1985	Elena Shoushounova, USSR
1954	Galina Roudiko, USSR		Oksana Omeliantchik, USSR
1958	Larissa Latynina, USSR	1987	Aurelia Dobre, Romania
1962	Larissa Latynina, USSR	1989	Svetlana Bouguinskaia, USSR
1966	Vera Caslavska, Czechoslovakia	1991	Kim Zmeskal, United States
1970	Ludmilla Tourischeva, USSR	1993	Shannon Miller, United States
1974	Ludmilla Tourischeva, USSR	1994	Shannon Miller, United States
1978	Elena Mukhina, USSR	1995	Lilia Podkopayeva, Ukraine
1979	Nelli Kim, USSR		

Floor Exercise

Year	Champion and Nation	Year	Champion and Nation
1950	Helena Rakoczy, Poland	1987	Elena Shoushounova, USSR
1954	Tamara Manina, USSR		Daniela Silivas, Romania
1958	Eva Bosakava, Czechoslovakia	1989	Svetlana Bouguinskaia, USSR
1962	Larissa Latynina, USSR		Daniela Silivas, Romania
1966	Natalia Kuchinskaya, USSR	1991	Cristina Bontas, Romania
1970	Ludmilla Tourischeva, USSR		Oksana Tchusovitina, USSR
1974	Ludmilla Tourischeva, USSR	1992	Kim Zmeskal, United States
1978	Nelli Kim, USSR	1993	Shannon Miller, United States
	Elena Mukhina, USSR	1994	Dina Kochetkova, Russia
1979	Emilia Eberle, Romania	1995	Gina Gogean, Romania
1981	Natalia Ilenko, USSR	1996	Gina Gogean, Romania
1983	Ecaterina Szabo, Romania		
1985	Oksana Omeliantchik, USSR		

World Champions (Cont.)
WOMEN (Cont.)

Uneven Bars

Year	Champion and Nation	Year	Champion and Nation
1950	Gertchen Kolar, Austria	1983	Maxi Gnauck, East Germany
	Anna Pettersson, Sweden	1985	Gabriele Fahnrich, East Germany
1954	Agnes Keleti, Hungary	1987	Daniela Silivas, Romania
1958	Larissa Latynina, USSR		Doerte Thuemmler, East Germany
1962	Irina Pervuschina, USSR	1989	Fan Di, China/ Daniela Silivas, Rom
1966	Natalia Kuchinskaya, USSR	1991	Gwang Suk Kim, North Korea
1970	Karin Janz, East Germany	1992	Lavinia Milosivici, Romania
1974	Annelore Zinke, East Germany	1993	Shannon Miller, United States
1978	Marcia Frederick, United States	1994	Luo Li, China
1979	Ma Yanhong, China	1995	Svetlana Chorkina, Russia
	Maxi Gnauck, East Germany	1996	Svetlana Chorkina, Russia
1981	Maxi Gnauck, East Germany		

Balance Beam

Year	Champion and Nation	Year	Champion and Nation
1950	Helena Rakoczy, Poland	1983	Olga Mostepanova, USSR
1954	Keiko Tanaka, Japan	1985	Daniela Silivas, Romania
1958	Larissa Latynina, USSR	1987	Aurelia Dobre, Romania
1962	Eva Bosakova, Czechoslovakia	1989	Daniela Silivas, Romania
1966	Natalia Kuchinskaya, USSR	1991	Svetlana Boguinskaia, USSR
1970	Erika Zuchold, East Germany	1992	Kim Zmeskal, United States
1974	Ludmilla Tourischeva, USSR	1993	Lavinia Milosovici, Romania
1978	Nadia Comaneci, Romania	1994	Shannon Miller, United States
1979	Vera Cerna, Czechoslovakia	1995	Mo Huilan, China
1981	Maxi Gnauck, East Germany	1996	Dina Kochetkova, Russia

Vault

Year	Champion and Nation	Year	Champion and Nation
1950	Helena Rakoczy, Poland	1983	Boriana Stoyanova, Bulgaria
1954	T Manina, USSR/ A Pettersson, Swe	1985	Elena Shoushounova, USSR
1958	Larissa Latynina, USSR	1987	Elena Shoushounova, USSR
1962	Vera Caslavska, Czechoslovakia	1989	Olesia Durnik, USSR
1966	Vera Caslavska, Czechoslovakia	1991	Lavinia Milosivici, Romania
1970	Erika Zuchold, East Germany	1992	Henrietta Onodi, Hungary
1974	Olga Korbut, USSR	1993	Elena Piskun, Belarus
1978	Nelli Kim, USSR	1994	Gina Gogean, Romania
1979	Dumitrita Turner, Romania	1995	L. Podkopayeva, Ukr./S. Amanar, Rom.
1981	Maxi Gnauck, East Germany	1996	Gina Gogean, Romania

National Champions

MEN

All-Around

Year	Champion	Year	Champion	Year	Champion
1963	Art Shurlock	1971	Yoshi Takei	1979	Bart Conner
1964	Rusty Mitchell	1972	Yoshi Takei	1980	Peter Vidmar
1965	Rusty Mitchell	1973	Marshall Avener	1981	Jim Hartung
1966	Rusty Mitchell	1974	John Crosby	1982	Peter Vidmar
1967	Katsuzoki Kanzaki	1975	Tom Beach	1983	Mitch Gaylord
1968	Yoshi Hayasaki		Bart Conner	1984	Mitch Gaylord
1969	Steve Hug	1976	Kurt Thomas	1985	Brian Babcock
1970	Makoto Sakamoto	1977	Kurt Thomas	1986	Tim Daggett
	Mas Watanabe	1978	Kurt Thomas	1987	Scott Johnson

National Champions *(Cont.)*

MEN *(Cont.)*

All-Around *(Cont.)*

Year	Champion	Year	Champion	Year	Champion
1988	Dan Hayden	1991	Chris Waller	1994	Scott Keswick
1989	Tim Ryan	1992	John Roethlisberger	1995	John Roethlisberger
1990	John Roethlisberger	1993	John Roethlisberger	1996	Blaine Wilson

Floor Exercise

Year	Champion	Year	Champion	Year	Champion
1963	Tom Seward	1973	John Crosby	1986	Robert Sundstrom
1964	Rusty Mitchell	1974	John Crosby	1987	John Sweeney
1965	Rusty Mitchell	1975	Peter Korman	1988	Mark Oates
1966	Dan Millman	1977	Ron Galimore		Charles Lakes
1967	Katsuzoki Kanzaki	1978	Kurt Thomas	1989	Mike Racanelli
	Ron Aure	1979	Ron Galimore	1990	Bob Stelter
1968	Katsuzoki Kanzaki	1980	Ron Galimore	1991	Mike Racanelli
1969	Steve Hug	1981	Jim Hartung	1992	Gregg Curtis
	Dave Thor	1982	Jim Hartung	1993	Kerry Huston
1970	Makoto Sakamoto	1983	Mitch Gaylord	1994	Jeremy Killen
1971	John Crosby	1984	Peter Vidmar	1995	Daniel Stover
1972	Yoshi Takei	1985	Mark Oates	1996	Jay Thornton

Pommel Horse

Year	Champion	Year	Champion	Year	Champion
1963	Larry Spiegel	1974	Marshall Avener	1987	Tim Daggett
1964	Sam Bailie	1975	Bart Conner	1988	Kevin Davis
1965	Jack Ryan	1977	Gene Whelan	1989	Kevin Davis
1966	Jack Ryan	1978	Jim Hartung	1990	Patrick Kirksey
1967	Paul Mayer	1979	Bart Conner	1991	Chris Waller
	Dave Doty	1980	Jim Hartung	1992	Chris Waller
1968	Katsuoki Kanzaki	1981	Jim Hartung	1993	Chris Waller
1969	Dave Thor	1982	Jim Hartung	1994	Mihai Begiu
1970	Mas Watanabe	1983	Bart Conner	1995	Mark Sohn
1971	Leonard Caling	1984	Tim Daggett	1996	Josh Stein
1972	Sadao Hamada	1985	Phil Cahoy		
1973	Marshall Avener	1986	Phil Cahoy		

Rings

Year	Champion	Year	Champion	Year	Champion
1963	Art Shurlock	1973	Jim Ivicek	1985	Dan Hayden
1964	Glen Gailis	1974	Tom Weeden	1986	Dan Hayden
1965	Glen Gailis	1975	Tom Beach	1987	Scott Johnson
1966	Glen Gailis	1977	Kurt Thomas	1988	Dan Hayden
1967	Fred Dennis	1978	Mike Silverstein	1989	Scott Keswick
	Don Hatch	1979	Bart Conner	1990	Scott Keswick
1968	Yoshi Hayasaki	1980	Jim Hartung	1991	Scott Keswick
1969	Fred Dennis	1981	Jim Hartung	1992	Tim Ryan
	Bob Emery	1982	Jim Hartung	1993	John Roethlisberger
1970	Makoto Sakamoto		Peter Vidmar	1994	Scott Keswick
1971	Yoshi Takei	1983	Mitch Gaylord	1995	Paul O'Neill
1972	Yoshi Takei	1984	Jim Hartung	1996	Kip Simons

Vault

Year	Champion	Year	Champion	Year	Champion
1963	Art Shurlock	1967	Jack Kenan	1971	Gary Morava
1964	Gary Hery		Sid Jensen	1972	Mike Kelley
1965	Brent Williams	1968	Rich Scorza	1973	Gary Morava
1966	Dan Millman	1969	Dave Butzman	1974	John Crosby
		1970	Makoto Sakamoto	1975	Tom Beach

Gymnastics (Cont.)

National Champions (Cont.)

MEN (Cont.)

Vault (Cont.)

Year	Champion	Year	Champion	Year	Champion
1977	Ron Galimore	1984	Chris Reigel	1990	Lance Ringnald
1978	Jim Hartung	1985	Scott Johnson	1991	Scott Keswick
1979	Ron Galimore		Mark Oates	1992	Trent Dimas
1980	Ron Galimore	1986	Scott Wilbanks	1993	Bill Roth
1981	Ron Galimore	1987	John Sweeney	1994	Keith Wiley
1982	Jim Hartung	1988	John Sweeney	1995	David St. Pierre
	Jim Mikus		Bill Paul	1996	Blaine Wilson
1983	Chris Reigel	1989	Bill Roth		

Parallel Bars

Year	Champion	Year	Champion	Year	Champion
1963	Tom Seward	1975	Bart Conner	1985	Tim Daggett
1964	Rusty Mitchell	1977	Kurt Thomas	1986	Tim Daggett
1965	Glen Gailis	1978	Bart Conner	1987	Scott Johnson
1966	Ray Hadley	1979	Bart Conner	1988	Dan Hayden
1967	Katsuzoki Kanzaki	1980	Phil Cahoy		Kevin Davis
	Tom Goldsborough		Larry Gerard	1989	Conrad Voorsanger
1968	Yoshi Hayasaki	1981	Bart Conner	1990	Trent Dimas
1969	Steve Hug	1982	Peter Vidmar	1991	Scott Keswick
1970	Makoto Sakamoto	1983	Mitch Gaylord	1992	Jair Lynch
1971	Brent Simmons	1984	Peter Vidmar	1993	Chainey Umphrey
1972	Yoshi Takei		Mitch Gaylord	1994	Steve McCain
1973	Marshall Avener		Tim Daggett	1995	John Roethlisberger
1974	Jim Ivicek			1996	Jair Lynch

High Bars

Year	Champion	Year	Champion	Year	Champion
1963	Art Shurlock	1975	Tom Beach	1986	Dan Hayden
1964	Glen Gailis	1977	Kurt Thomas		David Moriel
1965	Rusty Mitchell	1978	Kurt Thomas	1987	David Moriel
1966	Katsuzoki Kanzaki	1979	Yoichi Tomita	1988	Dan Hayden
1967	Katsuzoki Kanzaki	1980	Jim Hartung	1989	Tim Ryan
	Jerry Fontana	1981	Bart Conner	1990	Trent Dimas
1968	Yoshi Hayasaki	1982	Mitch Gaylord		Lance Ringnald
1969	Rich Grisby	1983	Mario McCutcheon	1991	Lance Ringnald
1970	Makoto Sakamoto	1984	Peter Vidmar	1992	Jair Lynch
1971	Yoshi Takei		Tim Daggett	1993	Steve McCain
1972	Tom Lindner		Mitch Gaylord	1994	Scott Keswick
1973	John Crosby	1985	Dan Hayden	1995	John Roethlisberger
1974	Brent Simmons			1996	Bill Roth

WOMEN

All-Around

Year	Champion	Year	Champion	Year	Champion
1963	Donna Schanezer	1973	Joan Moore Gnat	1985	Sabrina Mar
1965	Gail Daley	1974	Joan Moore Gnat	1986	Jennifer Sey
1966	Donna Schanezer	1975	Tammy Manville	1987	Kristie Phillips
1968	Linda Scott	1976	Denise Cheshire	1988	Phoebe Mills
1969	Joyce Tanac	1977	Donna Turnbow	1989	Brandy Johnson
	Schroeder	1978	Kathy Johnson	1990	Kim Zmeskal
1970	Cathy Rigby McCoy	1979	Leslie Pyfer	1991	Kim Zmeskal
1971	Joan Moore Gnat	1980	Julianne McNamara	1992	Kim Zmeskal
	Linda Metheny	1981	Tracee Talavera	1993	Shannon Miller
	Mulvihill	1982	Tracee Talavera	1994	Dominique Dawes
1972	Joan Moore Gnat	1983	Dianne Durham	1995	Dominique Moceanu
	Cathy Rigby McCoy	1984	Mary Lou Retton	1996	Shannon Miller

National Champions (Cont.)
WOMEN (Cont.)

Vault

Year	Champion	Year	Champion	Year	Champion
1963	Donna Schanezer	1974	Dianne Dunbar	1985	Yolanda Mavity
1965	Gail Daley	1975	Kolleen Casey	1986	Joyce Wilborn
1966	Donna Schanezer	1976	Debbie Wilcox	1987	Rhonda Faehn
1968	Terry Spencer	1977	Lisa Cawthron	1988	Rhonda Faehn
1969	Joyce Tanac Schroeder Cleo Carver	1978	Rhonda Schwandt Sharon Shapiro	1989	Brandy Johnson
1970	Cathy Rigby McCoy	1979	Chrcita Canary	1990	Brandy Johnson
1971	Joan Moore Gnat Adele Gleaves	1980	Julianne McNamara Beth Kline	1991	Kerri Strug
1972	Cindy Eastwood	1981	Kim Neal	1992	Kerri Strug
1973	Roxanne Pierce Mancha	1982	Yumi Mordre	1993	Dominique Dawes
		1983	Dianne Durham	1994	Dominique Dawes
		1984	Mary Lou Retton	1995	Shannon Miller
				1996	Dominique Dawes

Uneven Bars

Year	Champion	Year	Champion	Year	Champion
1963	Donna Schanezer	1974	Diane Dunbar	1987	Melissa Marlowe
1965	Irene Haworth	1975	Leslie Wolfsberger	1988	Chelle Stack
1966	Donna Schanezer	1976	Leslie Wolfsberger	1989	Chelle Stack
1968	Linda Scott	1977	Donna Turnbow	1990	Sandy Woolsey
1969	Joyce Tanac Schroeder Lisa Nelson	1978	Marcia Frederick	1991	Elisabeth Crandall
1970	Roxanne Pierce Mancha	1979	Marcia Frederick	1992	Dominique Dawes
1971	Joan Moore Gnat	1980	Marcia Frederick	1993	Shannon Miller
1972	Cathy Rigby McCoy	1981	Julianne McNamara	1994	Dominique Dawes
1973	Roxanne Pierce Mancha	1982	Marie Roethlisberger	1995	Dominique Dawes
		1983	Julianne McNamara	1996	Dominique Dawes
		1984	Julianne McNamara		
		1985	Sabrina Mar		
		1986	Marie Roethlisberger		

Balance Beam

Year	Champion	Year	Champion	Year	Champion
1963	Leissa Krol	1975	Kyle Gayner	1985	Kelly Garrison-Steves
1965	Gail Daley	1976	Carrie Englert	1988	Kelly Garrison-Steves
1966	Irene Haworth Linda Scott	1977	Donna Turnbow	1989	Brandy Johnson
1968	Linda Scott	1978	Christa Canary	1990	Betty Okino
1969	Lonna Woodward	1979	Heidi Anderson	1991	Shannon Miller
1970	Joyce Tanac Schroeder	1980	Kelly Garrison-Steves	1992	Kerri Strug Kim Zmeskal
1971	Linda Metheny Mulvihill	1981	Tracee Talavera	1993	Dominique Dawes
1972	Kim Chace	1982	Julianne McNamara	1994	Dominique Dawes
1973	Nancy Thies Marshall	1983	Dianne Durham	1995	Doni Thompson Monica Flammer
1974	Joan Moore Gnat	1984	Pam Bileck Tracee Talavera	1996	Dominique Dawes
		1986	Angie Denkins		
		1987	Kristie Phillips		

Floor Exercise

Year	Champion	Year	Champion	Year	Champion
1963	Donna Schanezer	1976	Carrie Englert	1988	Phoebe Mills
1965	Gail Daley	1977	Kathy Johnson	1989	Brandy Johnson
1966	Donna Schanezer	1978	Kathy Johnson	1990	Brandy Johnson
1968	Linda Scott	1979	Heidi Anderson	1991	Kim Zmeskal Dominique Dawes
1970	Cathy Rigby McCoy	1980	Beth Kline	1992	Kim Zmeskal
1971	Joan Moore Gnat Linda Metheny Mulvihill	1981	Michelle Goodwin	1993	Shannon Miller
1972	Joan Moore Gnat	1982	Amy Koopman	1994	Dominique Dawes
1973	Joan Moore Gnat	1983	Dianne Durham	1995	Dominique Dawes
1974	Joan Moore Gnat	1984	Mary Lou Retton	1996	Dominique Dawes
1975	Kathy Howard	1985	Sabrina Mar		
		1986	Yolanda Mavity		
		1987	Kristie Phillips		

Handball

National Four-Wall Champions

MEN

1919 .....Bill Ranft	1939 .....Joe Platak	1959 .....John Sloan	1979 .....Naty Alvarado
1920 .....Max Gold	1940 .....Joe Platak	1960 .....Jimmy Jacobs	1980 .....Naty Alvarado
1921 .....Carl Haedge	1941 .....Joe Platak	1961 .....John Sloan	1981 .....Fred Lewis
1922 .....Art Shinners	1942 .....Jack Clemente	1962 .....Oscar Obert	1982 .....Naty Alvarado
1923 .....Joe Murray	1943 .....Joe Platak	1963 .....Oscar Obert	1983 .....Naty Alvarado
1924 .....Maynard Laswe	1944 .....Frank Coyle	1964 .....Jimmy Jacobs	1984 .....Naty Alvarado
1925 .....Maynard Laswe	1945 .....Joe Platak	1965 .....Jimmy Jacobs	1985 .....Naty Alvarado
1926 .....Maynard Laswe	1946 .....Angelo Trutio	1966 .....Paul Haber	1986 .....Naty Alvarado
1927 .....George Nelson	1947 .....Gus Lewis	1967 .....Paul Haber	1987 .....Naty Alvarado
1928 .....Joe Griffin	1948 .....Gus Lewis	1968 .....Stuffy Singer	1988 .....Naty Alvarado
1929 .....Al Banuet	1949 .....Vic Hershkowitz	1969 .....Paul Haber	1989 .....Poncho Monreal
1930 .....Al Banuet	1950 .....Ken Schneider	1970 .....Paul Haber	1990 .....Naty Alvarado
1931 .....Al Banuet	1951 .....Walter Plakan	1971 .....Paul Haber	1991 .....John Bike
1932 .....Angelo Trutio	1952 .....Vic Hershkowitz	1972 .....Fred Lewis	1992 .....Octavio Silveyra
1933 .....Sam Atcheson	1953 .....Bob Brady	1973 .....Terry Muck	1993 .....David Chapman
1934 .....Sam Atcheson	1954 .....Vic Hershkowitz	1974 .....Fred Lewis	1994 .....Octavio Silveyra
1935 .....Joe Platak	1955 .....Jimmy Jacobs	1975 .....Fred Lewis	1995 .....David Chapman
1936 .....Joe Platak	1956 .....Jimmy Jacobs	1976 .....Fred Lewis	1996 .....David Chapman
1937 .....Joe Platak	1957 .....Jimmy Jacobs	1977 .....Naty Alvarado	
1938 .....Joe Platak	1958 .....John Sloan	1978 .....Fred Lewis	

WOMEN

1980 .....Rosemary Bellini	1985 .....Peanut Motal	1990 .....Anna Engele	1995 .....Anna Engele
1981 .....Rosemary Bellini	1986 .....Peanut Motal	1991 .....Anna Engele	1996 .....Anna Engele
1982 .....Rosemary Bellini	1987 .....Rosemary Bellini	1992 .....Lisa Fraser	
1983 .....Diane Harmon	1988 .....Rosemary Bellini	1993 .....Anna Engele	
1984 .....Rosemary Bellini	1989 .....Anna Engele	1994 .....Anna Engele	

National Three-Wall Champions

MEN

1950 .....Vic Hershkowitz	1962 .....Oscar Obert	1974 .....Fred Lewis	1986 .....Vern Roberts
1951 .....Vic Hershkowitz	1963 .....Marty Decatur	1975 .....Lou Russo	1987 .....Vern Roberts
1952 .....Vic Hershkowitz	1964 .....Marty Decatur	1976 .....Lou Russo	1988 .....Jon Kendler
1953 .....Vic Herskkowitz	1965 .....Carl Obert	1977 .....Fred Lewis	1989 .....John Bike
1954 .....Vic Hershkowitz	1966 .....Marty Decatur	1978 .....Fred Lewis	1990 .....Vince Munoz
1955 .....Vic Hershkowitz	1967 .....Carl Obert	1979 .....Naty Alvarado	1991 .....John Bike
1956 .....Vic Hershkowitz	1968 .....Marty Decatur	1980 .....Lou Russo	1992 .....John Bike
1957 .....Vic Hershkowitz	1969 .....Marty Decatur	1981 .....Naty Alvarado	1993 .....Eric Klarman
1958 .....Vic Hershkowitz	1970 .....Steve August	1982 .....Naty Alvarado	1994 .....David Chapman
1959 .....Jimmy Jacobs	1971 .....Lou Russo	1983 .....Naty Alvarado	1995 .....David Chapman
1960 .....Jimmy Jacobs	1972 .....Lou Russo	1984 .....Naty Alvarado	1996 .....Vince Munoz
1961 .....Jimmy Jacobs	1973 .....Paul Haber	1985 .....Vern Roberts	

WOMEN

1981 .....Allison Roberts	1985 .....Rosemary Bellini	1989 .....Rosemary Bellini	1993 .....Anna Engele
1982 .....Allison Roberts	1986 .....Rosemary Bellini	1990 .....Rosemary Bellini	1994 .....Anna Engele
1983 .....Allison Roberts	1987 .....Rosemary Bellini	1991 .....Rosemary Bellini	1995 .....Allison Roberts
1984 .....Rosemary Bellini	1988 .....Rosemary Bellini	1992 .....Anna Engele	1996 .....Anna Engele

World Four-Wall Champions

1984 ....Merv Deckert, Canada	1991 ....Pancho Monreal, United States
1986 ....Vern Roberts, United States	1994 ....David Chapman, United States
1988 ....Naty Alvarado, United States	

Lacrosse

United States Club Lacrosse Association Champions

1960 ......Mt Washington Club	1966 ......Mt Washington Club	1972 ......Carling
1961 ......Baltimore Lacrosse Club	1967 ......Mt Washington Club	1973 ......Long Island Athletic Club
1962 ......Mt Washington Club	1968 ......Long Island Athletic Club	1974 ......Long Island Athletic Club
1963 ......University Club	1969 ......Long Island Athletic Club	1975 ......Mt Washington Club
1964 ......Mt Washington Club	1970 ......Long Island Athletic Club	1976 ......Mt Washington Club
1965 ......Mt Washington Club	1971 ......Long Island Athletic Club	1977 ......Mt Washington Club

Lacrosse (Cont.)

United States Club Lacrosse Association Champions (Cont.)

1978 ......Long Island Athletic Club	1985 ......LI-Hofstra Lacrosse Club	1992 ......Maryland Lacrosse Club
1979 ......Maryland Lacrosse Club	1986 ......LI-Hofstra Lacrosse Club	1993 ......Mt Washington Club
1980 ......Long Island Athletic Club	1987 ......LI-Hofstra Lacrosse Club	1994 ......LI-Hofstra Lacrosse Club
1981 ......Long Island Athletic Club	1988 ......Maryland Lacrosse Club	1995 ......Mt Washington Club
1982 ......Maryland Lacrosse Club	1989 ......LI-Hofstra Lacrosse Club	1996 ......LI-Hofstra Lacrosse Club
1983 ......Maryland Lacrosse Club	1990 ......Mt Washington Club	
1984 ......Maryland Lacrosse Club	1991 ......Mt Washington Club	

Little League Baseball

Little League World Series Champions

Year	Champion	Runner-Up	Score	Year	Champion	Runner-Up	Score
1947	..Williamsport, PA	Lock Haven, PA	16-7	1972	..Taipei, Taiwan	Hammond, IN	6-0
1948	..Lock Haven, PA	St Petersburg, FL	6-5	1973	..Tainan City, Taiwan	Tucson, AZ	12-0
1949	..Hammonton, NJ	Pensacola, FL	5-0	1974	..Kao-Hsuing, Taiwan	El Cajun, CA	7-2
1950	..Houston, TX	Bridgeport, CT	2-1	1975	..Lakewood, NJ	Tampa, FL	4-3
1951	..Stamford, CT	Austin, TX	3-0	1976	..Tokyo, Japan	Campbell, CA	10-3
1952	..Norwalk, CT	Monongahela, PA	4-3	1977	..Kao-Hsuing, Taiwan	El Cajun, CA	7-2
1953	..Birmingham, AL	Schenectady, NY	1-0	1978	..Pin-Tung, Taiwan	Danville, CA	11-1
1954	..Schenectady, NY	Colton, CA	7-5	1979	..Hsien, Taiwan	Campbell, CA	2-1
1955	..Morrisville, PA	Merchantville, NJ	4-3	1980	..Hua Lian, Taiwan	Tampa, FL	4-3
1956	..Roswell, NM	Merchantville, NJ	3-1	1981	..Tai-Chung, Taiwan	Tampa, FL	4-2
1957	..Monterrrey, Mex.	LaMesa, CA	4-0	1982	..Kirkland, WA	Hsien, Taiwan	6-0
1958	..Monterrey, Mex.	Kankakee, IL	10-1	1983	..Marietta, GA	Barahona, D.Rep.	3-1
1959	..Hamtramck, MI	Auburn, CA	12-0	1984	..Seoul, S. Korea	Altamonte Sgs, FL	6-2
1960	..Levittown, PA	Ft Worth, TX	5-0	1985	..Seoul, S. Korea	Mexicali, Mex.	7-1
1961	..El Cajon, CA	El Campo, TX	4-2	1986	..Tainan Park, Taiwan	Tucson, AZ	12-0
1962	..San Jose, CA	Kankakee, IL	3-0	1987	..Hua Lian, Taiwan	Irvine, CA	21-1
1963	..Granada Hills, CA	Stratford, CT	2-1	1988	..Tai-Chung, Taiwan	Pearl City, HI	10-0
1964	..Staten Island, NY	Monterrey, Mex.	4-0	1989	..Trumbull, CT	Kaohsiung, Taiwan	5-2
1965	..Windsor Locks, CT	Stoney Creek, Can.	3-1	1990	..Taipei, Taiwan	Shippensburg, PA	9-0
1966	..Houston, TX	W.New York, NJ	8-2	1991	..Tai-Chung, Taiwan	San Ramon Vly, CA	11-0
1967	..West Tokyo, Japan	Chicago, IL	4-1	1992*	..Long Beach, CA	Zamboanga, Phil.	6-0
1968	..Osaka, Japan	Richmond, VA	1-0	1993	..Long Beach, CA	David Chiriqui, Pan.	3-2
1969	..Taipei, Taiwan	Santa Clara, CA	5-0	1994	..Maracaibo, Venez.	Northridge, CA	4-3
1970	..Wayne, NJ	Campbell, CA	2-0	1995	..Tainan, Taiwan	Sprint, TX	17-3
1971	..Tainan, Taiwan	Gary, IN	12-3	1996	..Kao-Hsuing, Taiwan	Cranston, RI	13-3

*Long Beach declared a 6-0 winner after the international tournament committee determined that Zamboanga City had used players that were not within its city limits.

Motor Boat Racing

American Power Boat Association Gold Cup Champions

Year	Boat	Driver	Avg MPH	Year	Boat	Driver		Avg MPH
1904	....Standard (June)	Carl Riotte	23.160	1917	....Miss Detroit II	Gar Wood		54.410
1904	....Vingt-et-Un II (Sep)	W. Sharpe Kilmer	24.900	1918	....Miss Detroit II	Gar Wood		51.619
1905	....Chip I	J. Wainwright	15.000	1919	....Miss Detroit III	Gar Wood		42.748
1906	....Chip II	J. Wainwright	25.000	1920	....Miss America I	Gar Wood		62.022
1907	....Chip II	J. Wainwright	23.903	1921	....Miss America I	Gar Wood		52.825
1908	....Dixie II	E. J. Schroeder	29.938	1922	....Packard Chriscraft	J. G. Vincent		40.253
1909	....Dixie II	E. J. Schroeder	29.590	1923	....Packard Chriscraft	Caleb Bragg		43.867
1910	....Dixie III	F. K. Burnham	32.473	1924	....Baby Bootlegger	Caleb Bragg		45.302
1911	....MIT II	J. H. Hayden	37.000	1925	....Baby Bootlegger	Caleb Bragg		47.240
1912	....P.D.Q. II	A. G. Miles	39.462	1926	....Greenwich Folly	George Townsend		47.984
1913	....Ankle Deep	Cas Mankowski	42.779	1927	....Greenwich Folly	George Townsend		47.662
1914	....Baby Speed Demon II	Jim Blackton & Bob Edgren	48.458	1928	...No race			
1915	....Miss Detroit	Johnny Milot & Jack Beebe	37.656	1929	....Imp	Richard Hoyt		48.662
1916	....Miss Minneapolis	Bernard Smith	48.860	1930	....Hotsy Totsy	Vic Kliesrath		52.673
				1931	....Hotsy Totsy	Vic Kliesrath		53.602

American Power Boat Association Gold Cup Champions (Cont.)

Year	Boat	Driver	Avg MPH	Year	Boat	Driver	Avg MPH
1932	Delphine IV	Bill Horn	57.775	1968	Miss Bardahl	Bill Shumacher	108.173
1933	El Lagarto	George Reis	56.260	1969	Miss Budweiser	Bill Sterett	98.504
1934	El Lagarto	George Reis	55.000	1970	Miss Budweiser	Dean Chenoweth	99.562
1935	El Lagarto	George Reis	55.056				
1936	Impshi	Kaye Don	45.735	1971	Miss Madison	Jim McCormick	98.043
1937	Notre Dame	Clell Perry	63.675	1972	Atlas Van Lines	Bill Muncey	104.277
1938	Alagi	Theo Rossi	64.340	1973	Miss Budweiser	Dean Chenoweth	99.043
1939	My Sin	Z. G. Simmons, Jr	66.133				
1940	Hotsy Totsy III	Sidney Allen	48.295	1974	Pay 'n Pak	George Henley	104.428
1941	My Sin	Z. G. Simmons, Jr	52.509	1975	Pay 'n Pak	George Henley	108.921
1942-45	No race			1976	Miss U.S.	Tom D'Eath	100.412
1946	Tempo VI	Guy Lombardo	68.132	1977	Atlas Van Lines	Bill Muncey	111.822
1947	Miss Peps V	Danny Foster	57.000	1978	Atlas Van Lines	Bill Muncey	111.412
1948	Miss Great Lakes	Danny Foster	46.845	1979	Atlas Van Lines	Bill Muncey	100.765
1949	My Sweetie	Bill Cantrell	73.612	1980	Miss Budweiser	Dean Chenoweth	106.932
1950	Slo-Mo-Shun IV	Ted Jones	78.216				
1951	Slo-Mo-Shun V	Lou Fageol	90.871	1981	Miss Budweiser	Dean Chenoweth	116.932
1952	Slo-Mo-Shun IV	Stan Dollar	79.923				
1953	Slo-Mo-Shun IV	Joe Taggart & Lou Fageol	99.108	1982	Atlas Van Lines	Chip Hanauer	120.050
				1983	Atlas Van Lines	Chip Hanauer	118.507
1954	Slo-Mo-Shun IV	Joe Taggart & Lou Fageol	92.613	1984	Atlas Van Lines	Chip Hanauer	130.175
				1985	Miller American	Chip Hanauer	120.643
1955	Gale V	Lee Schoenith	99.552	1986	Miller American	Chip Hanauer	116.523
1956	Miss Thriftaway	Bill Muncey	96.552	1987	Miller American	Chip Hanauer	127.620
1957	Miss Thriftaway	Bill Muncey	101.787	1988	Miss Circus Circus	Chip Hanauer & Jim Prevost	123.756
1958	Hawaii Kai III	Jack Regas	103.000				
1959	Maverick	Bill Stead	104.481	1989	Miss Budweiser	Tom D'Eath	131.209
1960	No race			1990	Miss Budweiser	Tom D'Eath	143.176
1961	Miss Century 21	Bill Muncey	99.678	1991	Winston Eagle	Mark Tate	137.771
1962	Miss Century 21	Bill Muncey	100.710	1992	Miss Budweiser	Chip Hanauer	136.282
1963	Miss Bardahl	Ron Musson	105.124	1993	Miss Budweiser	Chip Hanauer	141.195
1964	Miss Bardahl	Ron Musson	103.433	1994	Smokin' Joe Camel	Mark Tate	145.260
1965	Miss Bardahl	Ron Musson	103.132	1995	Miss Budweiser	Chip Hanauer	149.160
1966	Tahoe Miss	Mira Slovak	93.019	1996	PICO American Dream	Dave Villwock	149.328
1967	Miss Bardahl	Bill Shumacher	101.484				

Unlimited Hydroplane Racing Association Annual Champion Drivers

Year	Driver	Boats	Wins	Year	Driver	Boats	Wins
1947	Danny Foster	Miss Peps V	6	1972	Bill Muncey	Atlas Van Lines	6
1948	Dan Arena	Such Crust	2	1973	Mickey Remund	Pay 'n Pack	4
1949	Bill Cantrell	My Sweetie	7	1974	George Henley	Pay 'n Pack	7
1950	Dan Foster	Such Crust/DaphneX	2	1975	Billy Schumacher	Weisfield's	2
1951	Chuck Thompson	Miss Pepsi	5	1976	Bill Muncey	Atlas Van Lines	5
1952	Chuck Thompson	Miss Pepsi	3	1977	Mickey Remund	Miss Budweiser	3
1953	Lee Schoenith	Gale II	1	1978	Bill Muncey	Atlas Van Lines	6
1954	Lee Schoenith	Gale V	4	1979	Bill Muncey	Atlas Van Lines	7
1955	Lee Schoenith	Gale V/Wha Hoppen	1	1980	Dean Chenoweth	Miss Budweiser	5
1956	Russ Schleeh	Shanty I	3	1981	Dean Chenoweth	Miss Budweiser	6
1957	Jack Regas	Hawaii Kai III	5	1982	Chip Hanauer	Atlas Van Lines	5
1958	Mira Slovak	Bardah/Miss Buren	3	1983	Chip Hanauer	Atlas Van Lines	3
1959	Bill Stead	Maverick	5	1984	Jim Kropfeld	Miss Budweiser	6
1960	Bill Muncey	Miss Thriftway	4	1985	Chip Hanauer	Miller American	5
1961	Bill Muncey	Miss Century 21	4	1986	Jim Kropfeld	Miss Budweiser	3
1962	Bill Muncey	Miss Century 21	5	1987	Jim Kropfeld	Miss Budweiser	5
1963	Bill Cantrell	Gale V	0	1988	Tom D'Eath	Miss Budweiser	4
1964	Ron Musson	Miss Bardahl	4	1989	Chip Hanauer	Miss Circus Circus	3
1965	Ron Musson	Miss Bardahl	4	1990	Chip Hanauer	Miss Circus Circus	6
1966	Mira Slovak	Tahoe Miss	4	1991	Mark Tate	Winston/Oberto	3
1967	Bill Schumacher	Miss Bardahl	6	1992	Chip Hanauer	Miss Budweiser	7
1968	Bill Schumacher	Miss Bardahl	4	1993	Chip Hanauer	Miss Budweiser	7
1969	Bill Sterett, Sr	Miss Budweiser	4	1994	Mark Tate	Smokin' Joe Camel	2
1970	Dean Chenoweth	Miss Budweiser	4	1995	Mark Tate	Smokin' Joe Camel	4
1971	Dean Chenoweth	Miss Budweiser	2				

Motor Boat Racing (Cont.)

Unlimited Hydroplane Racing Association Annual Champion Boats

Year	Boat	Owner	Wins	Year	Boat	Owner	Wins
1970	Miss Budweiser	Little-Friedkin	4	1983	Atlas Van Lines	Muncey-Lucero	3
1971	Miss Budweiser	Little-Friedkin	2	1984	Miss Budweiser	Bernie Little	6
1972	Atlas Van Lines	Joe Schoenith	6	1985	Miller American	Muncey-Lucero	5
1973	Pay 'n Pak	Dave Heerensperger	4	1986	Miss Budweiser	Bernie Little	3
1974	Pay 'n Pak	Dave Heerensperger	7	1987	Miss Budweiser	Bernie Little	5
1975	Pay 'n Pak	Dave Heerensperger	5	1988	Miss Budweiser	Bernie Little	4
1976	Atlas Van Lines	Bill Muncey	5	1989	Miss Budweiser	Bernie Little	4
1977	Miss Budweiser	Bernie Little	3	1990	Circus Circus	Bill Bennett	6
1978	Atlas Van Lines	Bill Muncey	6	1991	Miss Budweiser	Bernie Little	4
1979	Atlas Van Lines	Bill Muncey	7	1992	Miss Budweiser	Bernie Little	7
1980	Miss Budweiser	Bernie Little	5	1993	Miss Budweiser	Bernie Little	7
1981	Miss Budweiser	Bernie Little	6	1994	Miss Budweiser	Bernie Little	4
1982	Atlas Van Lines	Fran Muncey	5	1995	Miss Budweiser	Bernie Little	5

Polo

United States Open Polo Champions

1904 ......Wanderers	1932 ......Templeton	1958 ......Dallas	1978 ......Abercrombie &
1905-09..Not contested	1933 ......Aurora	1959 ......Circle F	Kent
1910 ......Ranelagh	1934 ......Templeton	1960 ......Oak Brook—	1979 ......Retama
1911 ......Not contested	1935 ......Greentree	C.C.C.	1980 ......Southern Hills
1912 ......Cooperstown	1936 ......Greentree	1961 ......Milwaukee	1981 ......Rolex A & K
1913 ......Cooperstown	1937 ......Old Westbury	1962 ......Santa Barbara	1982 ......Retama
1914 ......Meadow Brook	1938 ......Old Westbury	1963 ......Tulsa	1983 ......Ft. Lauderdale
Magpies	1939 ......Bostwick Field	1964 ......Concar Oak	1984 ......Retama
1915 ......Not contested	1940 ......Aknusti	Brook	1985 ......Carter Ranch
1916 ......Meadow Brook	1941 ......Gulf Stream	1965 ......Oak Brook—	1986 ......Retama II
1917-18..Not contested	1942-45..Not contested	Santa Barbara	1987 ......Aloha
1919 ......Meadow Brook	1946 ......Mexico	1966 ......Tulsa	1988 ......Les Diables
1920 ......Meadow Brook	1947 ......Old Westbury	1967 ......Bunntyco—	Bleus
1921 ......Great Neck	1948 ......Hurricanes	Oak Brook	1989 ......Les Diables
1922 ......Argentine	1949 ......Hurricanes	1968 ......Midland	Bleus
1923 ......Meadow Brook	1950 ......Bostwick	1969 ......Tulsa Greenhill	1990 ......Les Diables
1924 ......Midwick	1951 ......Milwaukee	1970 ......Tulsa Greenhill	Bleus
1925 ......Orange County	1952 ......Beverly Hills	1971 ......Oak Brook	1991 ......Grant's Farm
1926 ......Hurricanes	1953 ......Meadow Brook	1972 ......Milwaukee	Manor
1927 ......Sands Point	1954 ......C.C.C.—	1973 ......Oak Brook	1992 ......Hanalei Bay
1928 ......Meadow Brook	Meadow Brook	1974 ......Milwaukee	1993 ......Gehache
1929 ......Hurricanes	1955 ......C.C.C.	1975 ......Milwaukee	1994 ......Aspen
1930 ......Hurricanes	1956 ......Brandywine	1976 ......Willow Bend	1995 ......Outback
1931 ......Santa Paula	1957 ......Detroit	1977 ......Retama	1996 ......Outback

Top-Ranked Players

The United States Polo Association ranks its registered players from minus 2 to plus 10 goals, with 10 Goal players being the game's best. At present, the USPA recognizes nine 10-Goal and ten 9-Goal players:

10-GOAL	9-GOAL
Mariano Aguerre (Greenwich)	A.D. Alberdi (Palm Beach)
Adolfo Cambiaso (Palm Beach)	Benjamin Araya (Palm Beach)
Carlos Gracida (Palm Beach)	Michael Vincen Azzaro (San Antonio)
Guillermo Gracida, Jr (Palm Beach)	Christian LaPrida (Palm Beach)
Bautista Heguy (Palm Beach)	Tomas Llorente (Palm Beach)
Gonzalo Heguy (Myopia)	Esteban Panelo (Palm Beach)
Marcos Heguy (Palm Beach)	Alfonso Pieres (Palm Beach)
Juan Ignacio Merlos (Palm Beach)	Owen R. Rinehart (Palm Beach)
Gonzalo Pieres (Palm Beach)	Ernesto Trotz (Palm Beach)
	Martin Zubia (Palm Beach)

Rodeo

All-Around

1929....Earl Thode	1948....Gerald Roberts	1965....Dean Oliver	1982....Chris Lybbert
1930....Clay Carr	1949....Jim Shoulders	1966....Larry Mahan	1983....Roy Cooper
1931....John Schneider	1950....Bill Linderman	1967....Larry Mahan	1984....Dee Picket
1932....Donald Nesbit	1951....Casey Tibbs	1968....Larry Mahan	1985....Lewis Feild
1933....Clay Carr	1952....Harry Tompkins	1969....Larry Mahan	1986....Lewis Feild
1934....Leonard Ward	1953....Bill Linderman	1970....Larry Mahan	1987....Lewis Feild
1935....Everett Bowman	1954....Buck Rutherford	1971....Phil Lyne	1988....Dave Appleton
1936....John Bowman	1955....Casey Tibbs	1972....Phil Lyne	1989....Ty Murray
1937....Everett Bowman	1956....Jim Shoulders	1973....Larry Mahan	1990....Ty Murray
1938....Burel Mulkey	1957....Jim Shoulders	1974....Tom Ferguson	1991....Ty Murray
1939....Paul Carney	1958....Jim Shoulders	1975....Tom Ferguson	1992....Ty Murray
1940....Fritz Truan	1959....Jim Shoulders	1976....Tom Ferguson	1993....Ty Murray
1941....Homer Pettigrew	1960....Harry Tompkins	1977....Tom Ferguson	1994....Ty Murray
1942....Gerald Roberts	1961....Benny Reynolds	1978....Tom Ferguson	1995....Joe Beaver
1943....Louis Brooks	1962....Tom Nesmith	1979....Tom Ferguson	
1944....Louis Brooks	1963....Dean Oliver	1980....Paul Tierney	
1947....Todd Whatley	1964....Dean Oliver	1981....Jimmie Cooper	

Saddle Bronc Riding

1929....Earl Thode	1948....Gene Pruett	1965....Shawn Davis	1982....Monty Henson
1930....Clay Carr	1949....Casey Tibbs	1966....Marty Wood	1983....B. Gjermundson
1931....Earl Thode	1950....Bill Linderman	1967....Shawn Davis	1984....B. Gjermundson
1932....Peter Knight	1951....Casey Tibbs	1968....Shawn Davis	1985....B. Gjermundson
1933....Peter Knight	1952....Casey Tibbs	1969....Bill Smith	1986....Bud Munroe
1934....Leonard Ward	1953....Casey Tibbs	1970....Dennis Reiners	1987....Clint Johnson
1935....Peter Knight	1954....Casey Tibbs	1971....Bill Smith	1988....Clint Johnson
1936....Peter Knight	1955....DebCopenhaver	1972....Mel Hyland	1989....Clint Johnson
1937....Burel Mulkey	1956....DebCopenhaver	1973....Bill Smith	1990....Robert Etbauer
1938....Burel Mulkey	1957....Alvin Nelson	1974....John McBeth	1991....Robert Etbauer
1939....Fritz Truan	1958....Marty Wood	1975....Monty Henson	1992....Billy Etbauer
1940....Fritz Truan	1959....Casey Tibbs	1976....Monty Henson	1993....Dan Mortensen
1941....Doff Aber	1960....Enoch Walker	1977....Bobby Berger	1994....Dan Mortensen
1942....Doff Aber	1961....Winston Bruce	1978....Joe Marvel	1995....Dan Mortensen
1943....Louis Brooks	1962....Kenny McLean	1979....Bobby Berger	
1944....Louis Brooks	1963....Guy Weeks	1980....Clint Johnson	
1947....Carl Olson	1964....Marty Wood	1981....B. Gjermundson	

Bareback Riding

1932....Smoky Snyder	1950....Jim Shoulders	1966....Paul Mayo	1982....Bruce Ford
1933....Nate Waldrum	1951....Casey Tibbs	1967....Clyde Vamvoras	1983....Bruce Ford
1934....Leonard Ward	1952....Harry Tompkins	1968....Clyde Vamvoras	1984....Larry Peabody
1935....Frank Schneider	1953....Eddy Akridge	1969....Gary Tucker	1985....Lewis Feild
1936....Smoky Snyder	1954....Eddy Akridge	1970....Paul Mayo	1986....Lewis Feild
1937....Paul Carney	1955....Eddy Akridge	1971....Joe Alexander	1987....Bruce Ford
1938....Pete Grubb	1956....Jim Shoulders	1972....Joe Alexander	1988....Marvin Garrett
1939....Paul Carney	1957....Jim Shoulders	1973....Joe Alexander	1989....Marvin Garrett
1940....Carl Dossey	1958....Jim Shoulders	1974....Joe Alexander	1990....Chuck Logue
1941....George Mills	1959....Jack Buschbom	1975....Joe Alexander	1991....Clint Corey
1942....Louis Brooks	1960....Jack Buschbom	1976....Joe Alexander	1992....Wayne Herman
1943....Bill Linderman	1961....Eddy Akridge	1977....Joe Alexander	1993....Deb Greenough
1944....Louis Brooks	1962....Ralph Buell	1978....Bruce Ford	1994....Marvin Garrett
1947....Larry Finley	1963....John Hawkins	1979....Bruce Ford	1995....Marvin Garrett
1948....Sonny Tureman	1964....Jim Houston	1980....Bruce Ford	
1949....Jack Buschbom	1965....Jim Houston	1981....J.C. Trujillo	

Bull Riding

1929....John Schneider	1932....Smokey Snyder	1936....Smokey Snyder	1941....Dick Griffith
1930....John Schneider	John Schneider	1937....Smokey Snyder	1942....Dick Griffith
1931....Smokey Snyder	1933....Frank Schneider	1938....Kid Fletcher	1943....Ken Roberts
1932....John Schneider	1934....Frank Schneider	1939....Dick Griffith	1944....Ken Roberts
	1935....Smokey Snyder	1940....Dick Griffith	1947....Wag Blessing

Bull Riding *(Cont.)*

1948....Harry Tompkins	1960....Harry Tompkins	1972....John Quintana	1984....Don Gay
1949....Harry Tompkins	1961....Ronnie Rossen	1973....Bobby Steiner	1985....Ted Nuce
1950....Harry Tompkins	1962....Freckles Brown	1974....Don Gay	1986....Tuff Hedeman
1951....Jim Shoulders	1963....Bill Kornell	1975....Don Gay	1987....Lane Frost
1952....Harry Tompkins	1964....Bob Wegner	1976....Don Gay	1988....Jim Sharp
1953....Todd Whatley	1965....Larry Mahan	1977....Don Gay	1989....Tuff Hedeman
1954....Jim Shoulders	1966....Ronnie Rossen	1978....Don Gay	1990....Jim Sharp
1955....Jim Shoulders	1967....Larry Mahan	1979....Don Gay	1991....Tuff Hedeman
1956....Jim Shoulders	1968....George Paul	1980....Don Gay	1992....Cody Custer
1957....Jim Shoulders	1969....Doug Brown	1981....Don Gay	1993....Ty Murray
1958....Jim Shoulders	1970....Gary Leffew	1982....Charles Sampson	1994....Daryl Mills
1959....Jim Shoulders	1971....Bill Nelson	1983....Cody Snyder	1995....Joromo Davis

Calf Roping

1929....Everett Bowman	1948....Toots Mansfield	1965....Glen Franklin	1982....Roy Cooper
1930....Jake McClure	1949....Troy Fort	1966....Junior Garrison	1983....Roy Cooper
1931....Herb Meyers	1950....Toots Mansfield	1967....Glen Franklin	1984....Roy Cooper
1932....Richard Merchant	1951....Don McLaughlin	1968....Glen Franklin	1985....Joe Beaver
1933....Bill McFarlane	1952....Don McLaughlin	1969....Dean Oliver	1986....Chris Lybbert
1934....Irby Mundy	1953....Don McLaughlin	1970....Junior Garrison	1987....Joe Beaver
1935....Everett Bowman	1954....Don McLaughlin	1971....Phil Lyne	1988....Joe Beaver
1936....Clyde Burk	1955....Dean Oliver	1972....Phil Lyne	1989....Rabe Rabon
1937....Everett Bowman	1956....Ray Wharton	1973....Ernie Taylor	1990....Troy Pruitt
1938....Burel Mulkey	1957....Don McLaughlin	1974....Tom Ferguson	1991....Fred Whitfield
1939....Toots Mansfield	1958....Dean Oliver	1975....Jeff Copenhaver	1992....Joe Beaver
1940....Toots Mansfield	1959....Jim Bob Altizer	1976....Roy Cooper	1993....Joe Beaver
1941....Toots Mansfield	1960....Dean Oliver	1977....Roy Cooper	1994....Herbert Theriot
1942....Clyde Burk	1961....Dean Oliver	1978....Roy Cooper	1995....Fred Whitfield
1943....Toots Mansfield	1962....Dean Oliver	1979....Paul Tierney	
1944....Clyde Burk	1963....Dean Oliver	1980....Roy Cooper	
1947....Troy Fort	1964....Dean Oliver	1981....Roy Cooper	

Steer Wrestling

1929....Gene Ross	1948....Homer Pettigrew	1965....Harley May	1982....Stan Williamson
1930....Everett Bowman	1949....Bill McGuire	1966....Jack Roddy	1983....Joel Edmondson
1931....Gene Ross	1950....Bill Linderman	1967....Roy Duvall	1984....John W. Jones
1932....Hugh Bennett	1951....Dub Phillips	1968....Jack Roddy	1985....Ote Berry
1933....Everett Bowman	1952....Harley May	1969....Roy Duvall	1986....Steve Duhon
1934....Shorty Ricker	1953....Ross Dollarhide	1970....John W. Jones	1987....Steve Duhon
1935....Everett Bowman	1954....James Bynum	1971....Billy Hale	1988....John W. Jones
1936....Jack Kerschner	1955....Benny Combs	1972....Roy Duvall	1989....John W. Jones
1937....Gene Ross	1956....Harley May	1973....Bob Marshall	1990....Ote Berry
1938....Everett Bowman	1957....Clark McEntire	1974....Tommy Puryear	1991....Ote Berry
1939....Harry Hart	1958....James Bynum	1975....F. Shepperson	1992....Mark Roy
1940....Homer Pettigrew	1959....Harry Charters	1976....Tom Ferguson	1993....Steve Duhon
1941....Hub Whiteman	1960....Bob A. Robinson	1977....Larry Ferguson	1994....Blaine Pederson
1942....Homer Pettigrew	1961....Jim Bynum	1978....Byron Walker	1995....Ote Berry
1943....Homer Pettigrew	1962....Tom Nesmith	1979....Stan Williamson	
1944....Homer Pettigrew	1963....Jim Bynum	1980....Butch Myers	
1947....Todd Whatley	1964....C.R. Boucher	1981....Byron Walker	

Team Roping

1929....Charles Maggini	1939....Asbury Schell	1949....Ed Yanez	1959....Jim Rodriguez, Jr
1930....Norman Cowan	1940....Pete Grubb	1950....Buck Sorrels	1960....Jim Rodriguez, Jr
1931....Arthur Beloat	1941....Jim Hudson	1951....Olan Sims	1961....Al Hooper
1932....Ace Gardner	1942....Verne Castro	1952....Asbury Schell	1962....Jim Rodriguez, Jr
1933....Roy Adams		Vic Castro	1953....Ben Johnson	1963....Les Hirdes
1934....Andy Jauregui	1943....Mark Hull	1954....Eddie Schell	1964....Bill Hamilton
1935....Lawrence Conltk		Leonard Block	1955....Vern Castro	1965....Jim Rodriguez, Jr
1936....John Rhodes	1944....Murphy Chaney	1956....Dale Smith	1966....Ken Luman
1937....Asbury Schell	1947....Jim Brister	1957....Dale Smith	1967....Joe Glenn
1938....John Rhodes	1948....Joe Glenn	1958....Ted Ashworth	1968....Art Arnold

Rodeo (Cont.)

Team Roping (Cont.)

1969....Jerold Camarillo	1977....Jerold Camarillo	1985....Jake Barnes	1993....Bobby Hurley
1970....John Miller	1978....Doyle Gellerman	1986....Clay O. Cooper	1994....Jake Barnes
1971....John Miller	1979....Allen Bach	1987....Clay O. Cooper	Clay O. Cooper
1972....Leo Camarillo	1980....Tee Woolman	1988....Jake Barnes	1995....Bobby Hurley
1973....Leo Camarillo	1981....Walt Woodard	1989....Jake Barnes	Allen Bach
1974....H.P. Evetts	1982....Tee Woolman	1990....Allen Bach	
1975....Leo Camarillo	1983....Leo Camarillo *	1991....Bob Harris	
1976....Leo Camarillo	1984....Dee Pickett	1992....Clay O. Cooper	

Steer Roping

1929....Charles Maggini	1946....Everett Shaw	1963....Don McLaughlin	1980....Guy Allen
1930....Clay Carr	1947....Ike Rude	1964....Sonny Davis	1981....Arnold Felts
1931....Andy Jauregui	1948....Everett Shaw	1965....Sonney Wright	1982....Guy Allen
1932....George Weir	1949....Shoat Webster	1966....Sonny Davis	1983....Roy Cooper
1933....John Bowman	1950....Shoat Webster	1967....Jim Bob Altizer	1984....Guy Allen
1934....John McEntire	1951....Everett Shaw	1968....Sonny Davis	1985....Jim Davis
1935.....Richard Merchant	1952....Buddy Neal	1969....Walter Arnold	1986....Jim Davis
1936....John Bowman	1953....Ike Rude	1970....Don McLaughlin	1987....Shaun Burchett
1937....Everett Bowman	1954....Shoat Webster	1971....Olin Young	1988....Shaun Burchett
1938....Hugh Bennett	1955....Shoat Webster	1972....Allen Keller	1989....Guy Allen
1939....Dick Truitt	1956....Jim Snively	1973....Roy Thompson	1990....Phil Lyne
1940....Clay Carr	1957....Clark McEntire	1974....Olin Young	1991....Guy Allen
1941....Ike Rude	1958....Clark McEntire	1975....Roy Thompson	1992....Guy Allen
1942....King Merrit	1959....Everett Shaw	1976....Marvin Cantrell	1993....Guy Allen
1943....Tom Rhodes	1960....Don McLaughlin	1977....Buddy Cockrell	1994....Guy Allen
1944....Tom Rhodes	1961....Clark McEntire	1978....Sonny Worrell	1995....Guy Allen
1945....Everett Shaw	1962....Everett Shaw	1979....Gary Good	

Note: In 1945-46 champions were crowned only in Steer Roping.

Rowing

National Collegiate Rowing Champions

MEN'S EIGHT

1982 ....Yale	1987 ....Harvard	1992 ....Harvard
1983 ....Harvard	1988 ....Harvard	1993 ....Brown
1984 ....Washington	1989 ....Harvard	1994 ....Brown
1985 ....Harvard	1990 ....Wisconsin	1995 ....Brown
1986 ....Wisconsin	1991 ....Pennsylvania	1996 ....Princeton

WOMEN'S EIGHT

1979 ....Yale	1985 ....Washington	1991 ....Boston University
1980 ....California	1986 ....Wisconsin	1992 ....Boston University
1981 ....Washington	1987 ....Washington	1993 ....Princeton
1982 ....Washington	1988 ....Washington	1994 ....Princeton
1983 ....Washington	1989 ....Cornell	1995 ....Princeton
1984 ....Washington	1990 ....Princeton	1996 ....Brown

Rugby

National Men's Club Championship

Year	Winner	Runner-Up	Year	Winner	Runner-Up
1979	Old Blues (CA)	St Louis Falcons	1988	Old Mission Beach AC	Milwaukee
1980	Old Blues (CA)	St. Louis Falcons	1989	Old Mission Beach AC	Philly/Whitemarsh
1981	Old Blues (CA)	Old Blue (NY)	1990	Denver Barbos	Old Blues (CA)
1982	Old Blues (CA)	Denver Barbos	1991	Old Mission Beach AC	Washington
1983	Old Blues (CA)	Dallas Harlequins	1992	Old Blues (CA)	Mystic River (MA)
1984	Dallas Harlequins	Los Angeles	1993	Old Mission Beach AC	Milwaukee
1985	Milwaukee	Denver Barbos	1994	Old Mission Beach AC	Life College (GA)
1986	Old Blues (CA)	Old Blue (NY)	1995	Potomac Athletic Club	Old Mission Beach
1987	Old Blues (CA)	Pittsburgh	1996	Old Mission Beach AC	Old Blues (CA)

National Men's Collegiate Championship

Year	Winner	Runner-Up	Year	Winner	Runner-Up
1980	California	Air Force	1989	Air Force	Long Beach
1981	California	Harvard	1990	Air Force	Army
1982	California	Life College	1991	California	Army
1983	California	Air Force	1992	California	Army
1984	Harvard	Colorado	1993	California	Air Force
1985	California	Maryland	1994	California	Navy
1986	California	Dartmouth	1995	California	Air Force
1987	San Diego State	Air Force	1996	California	Penn State
1988	California	Dartmouth			

World Cup Championship

Year	Winner	Runner-Up	Year	Winner	Runner-Up
1987	New Zealand	France	1995	South Africa	New Zealand
1991	Australia	England			

Sailing

America's Cup Champions

SCHOONERS AND J-CLASS BOATS

Year	Winner	Skipper	Series	Loser	Skipper
1851	America	Richard Brown			
1870	Magic	Andrew Comstock	1-0	Cambria, Great Britain	J. Tannock
1871	Columbia (2-1)	Nelson Comstock	4-1	Livonia, Great Britain	J. R. Woods
	Sappho (2-0)	Sam Greenwood			
1876	Madeleine	Josephus Williams	2-0	Countess of Dufferin, Canada	J. E. Ellsworth
1881	Mischief	Nathanael Clock	2-0	Atalanta, Canada	Alexander Cuthbert
1885	Puritan	Aubrey Crocker	2-0	Genesta, Great Britain	John Carter
1886	Mayflower	Martin Stone	2-0	Galatea, Great Britain	Dan Bradford
1887	Volunteer	Henry Haff	2-0	Thistle, Great Britain	John Barr
1893	Vigilant	William Hansen	3-0	Valkyrie II, Great Britain	William Granfield
1895	Defender	Henry Haff	3-0	Valkyrie III, Great Britain	William Granfield
1899	Columbia	Charles Barr	3-0	Shamrock I, Great Britain	Archie Hogarth
1901	Columbia	Charles Barr	3-0	Shamrock II, Great Britain	E. A. Sycamore
1903	Reliance	Charles Barr	3-0	Shamrock III, Great Britain	Bob Wringe
1920	Resolute	Charles F. Adams	3-2	Shamrock IV, Great Britain	William Burton
1930	Enterprise	Harold Vanderbilt	4-0	Shamrock V, Great Britain	Ned Heard
1934	Rainbow	Harold Vanderbilt	4-2	Endeavour, Great Britain	T. O. M. Sopwith
1937	Ranger	Harold Vanderbilt	4-0	Endeavour II, Great Britain	T. O. M. Sopwith

12-METER BOATS

Year	Winner	Skipper	Series	Loser	Skipper
1958	Columbia	Briggs Cunningham	4-0	Sceptre, Great Britain	Graham Mann
1962	Weatherly	Bus Mosbacher	4-1	Gretel, Australia	Jock Sturrock
1964	Constellation	Bob Bavier & Eric Ridder	4-0	Sovereign, Australia	Peter Scott
1967	Intrepid	Bus Mosbacher	4-0	Dame Pattie, Australia	Jock Sturrock
1970	Intrepid	Bill Ficker	4-1	Gretel II, Australia	Jim Hardy
1974	Courageous	Ted Hood	4-0	Southern Cross, Australia	John Cuneo
1977	Courageous	Ted Turner	4-0	Australia	Noel Robins
1980	Freedom	Dennis Conner	4-1	Australia	Jim Hardy
1983	Australia II	John Bertrand	4-3	Liberty, United States	Dennis Conner
1987	Stars & Stripes	Dennis Conner	4-0	Kookaburra III, Australia	Iain Murray

60-FOOT CATAMARAN VS 133-FOOT MONOHULL

Year	Winner	Skipper	Series	Loser	Skipper
1988	Stars & Stripes	Dennis Conner	2-0	New Zealand	David Barnes

75-FOOT MONOHULL (IACC)

Year	Winner	Skipper	Series	Loser	Skipper
1992	America[3]	Bill Koch	4-1	Il Moro di Venezia, Italy	Paul Cayard
1995	Black Magic I	Russell Coutts	5-0	Young America, United States	Dennis Conner

Note: Winning entries have been from the United States every year but two; in 1983 an Australian vessel won, and in 1995 a vessel from New Zealand won.

Shooting World Champions

Men

50M FREE RIFLE PRONE

1947 .....O. Sannes, Norway
1949 .....A.C. Jackson,
   United States
1952 .....A.C. Jackson,
   United States
1954 .....G. Boa, Canada
1958 .....M. Nordquist
1962 .....K. Wenk, West Germany
1966 .....D. Boyd, United States
1970 .....M. Fiess, S. Africa
1974 .....K. Bulan, Czech.
1978 .....A. Allan, Great Britain
1982 .....V. Danilschenko, USSR
1986 .....S. Bereczky, Hungary
1990 .....V. Bochkarev, USSR
1994 .....Venjie Li, China

AIR RIFLE

1966 .....G. Kümmet, W. Germany
1970 .....G. Kusterman, W. Germ.
1974 .....E. Pedzisz, Poland
1978 .....O. Schlipf, W. Germany
1979 .....K. Hillenbrand
1981 .....F. Bessy, France
1982 .....F. Rettkowski, E. Germ.
1983 .....P. Heberle, France
1985 .....P. Heberle, France
1986 .....H. Riederer, W. Germany
1987 .....K. Ivanov, USSR
1989 .....J. P. Amet, France
1990 .....H. Riederer, W. Germany
1994 .....Boris Polak, Israel

MEN'S TRAP

1929 .....De Lumniczer, Hungary
1930 .....M. Arie, United States
1931 .....Kiszkurno, Poland
1933 .....De Lumniczer, Hungary
1934 .....A. Montagh, Hungary
1935 .....R. Sack, W. Germany
1936 .....Kiszkurno, Poland
1937 .....K. Huber, Finland
1938 .....I. Strassburger, Hungary
1939 .....De Lumniczer, Hungary
1947 .....H. Liljedahl, Sweden
1949 .....F. Rocchi, Argentina
1950 .....C. Sala, Italy
1952 .....P.J. Grossi, Argentina
1954 .....C. Merlo, Italy
1958 .....F. Eisenlauer,
   United States
1959 .....H. Badravi, Egypt
1961 .....E. Mattarelli, Italy
1962 .....W. Zimenko, USSR
1965 .....J.E. Lire, Chile
1966 .....K. Jones, United States
1967 .....G. Rennard, Belgium
1969 .....E. Mattarelli, Italy
1970 .....M. Carrega, France
1971 .....M. Carrega, France
1973 .....A. Andrushkin, USSR
1974 .....M. Carrega, France
1975 .....J. Primrose, Canada
1977 .....E. Azkue, Spain
1978 .....E. Vallduvi, Spain
1979 .....M. Carrega, France
1981 .....A. Asanov, USSR
1982 .....L. Giovonnetti, Italy

MEN'S TRAP *(Cont.)*

1983 .....J. Primrose, Canada
1985 .....M. Bednarik, Czech.
1986 .....M. Benarik, Czech.
1987 .....D. Monakov, USSR
1989 .....M. Venturini, Italy
1990 .....J. Damne, E. Germany
1994 .....Dmitriy Monakov, Ukraine
1995 .....G. Pellielo, Italy

THREE POSITION RIFLE

1929 .....O. Ericsson, Sweden
1930 .....Petersen, Denmark
1931 .....Amundson, Norway
1933 .....De Lisle, France
1935 .....Leskinnen, Finland
1937 .....Mazoyer, France
1939 .....Steigelmann, Germany
1947 .....I. H. Erben, Sweden
1949 .....P. Janhonen, Finland
1952 .....Kongshaug, Norway
1954 .....A. Bugdanov, USSR
1958 .....Itkis, USSR
1962 .....G. Anderson,
   United States
1966 .....G. Anderson,
   United States
1970 .....Parkhimovitch, USSR
1974 .....L. Wigger, United States
1978 .....E. Svensson, Sweden
1982 .....K. Ivanov, USSR
1986 .....P. Heinz, W. Germany
1990 .....E. C. Lee, S. Korea
1994 .....Petr Kurka, Czech Republic

Women

THREE POSITION RIFLE

1966 .....M. Thompson,
   United States
1970 .....M. Thompson Murdock,
   United States
1974 .....A. Pelova, Bulgaria
1978 .....W. Oliver, United States
1982 .....M. Helbig, E. Germany
1986 .....V. Letcheva, Bulgaria
1990 .....V. Letcheva, Bulgaria
1994 .....A. Maloukhina, Russia

AIR RIFLE

1970 .....V. Cherkasque, USSR
1974 .....T. Ratkinova, USSR
1978 .....W. Oliver, United States
1979 .....K. Monez, United States
1981 .....S. Romaristova, USSR
1982 .....S. Lang, W. Germany
1983 .....M. Helbig, E. Germany

AIR RIFLE *(Cont.)*

1985 .....E. Forian, Hungary
1986 .....V. Letcheva, Bulgaria
1987 .....V. Letcheva, Bulgaria
1989 .....V. Letcheva, Bulgaria
1990 .....E. Joc, Hungary
1994 .....S. Pfeilschifter, Germany

SPORT PISTOL

1966 .....N. Rasskazova, USSR
1970 .....N. Stoljarova, USSR
1974 .....N. Stoljarova, USSR
1978 .....K. Dyer, United States
1982 .....P. Balogh, Hungary
1986 .....M. Dobrantcheva, USSR
1990 .....M. Logvinenko, Sov Union
1994 .....Soon Hee Boo, S. Korea

AIR PISTOL

1970 .....S. Carroll, United States
1974 .....Z. Simonian, USSR
1978 .....K. Hansson, Sweden
1979 .....R. Fox, United States
1981 .....N. Kalinina, USSR
1982 .....M. Dobrantcheva, USSR
1983 .....K. Bodin, Sweden
1985 .....M. Dobrantcheva, USSR
1986 .....A. Völker, E. Germany
1987 .....J. Brajkovic, Yugoslavia
1989 .....N. Salukvadse, USSR
1990 .....Jasna Sekaric, Yugoslavia
1994 .....Jasna Sekaric, IOP

Softball

Men
MAJOR FAST PITCH

1933..........J. L. Gill Boosters, Chicago	1965..........Sealmasters, Aurora, IL
1934..........Ke-Nash-A, Kenosha, WI	1966..........Clearwater (FL) Bombers
1935..........Crimson Coaches, Toledo, OH	1967..........Sealmasters, Aurora, IL
1936..........Kodak Park, Rochester, NY	1968..........Clearwater (FL) Bombers
1937..........Briggs Body Team, Detroit	1969..........Raybestos Cardinals, Stratford, CT
1938..........The Pohlers, Cincinnati	1970..........Raybestos Cardinals, Stratford, CT
1939..........Carr's Boosters, Covington, KY	1971..........Welty Way, Cedar Rapids, IA
1940..........Kodak Park, Rochester, NY	1972..........Raybestos Cardinals, Stratford, CT
1941..........Bendix Brakes, South Bend, IN	1973..........Clearwater (FL) Bombers
1942..........Deep Rock Oilers, Tulsa	1974..........Gianella Bros, Santa Rosa, CA
1943..........Hammer Air Field, Fresno	1975..........Rising Sun Hotel, Reading, PA
1944..........Hammer Air Field, Fresno	1976..........Raybestos Cardinals, Stratford, CT
1945..........Zollner Pistons, Fort Wayne, IN	1977..........Billard Barbell, Reading, PA
1946..........Zollner Pistons, Fort Wayne, IN	1978..........Billard Barbell, Reading, PA
1947..........Zollner Pistons, Fort Wayne, IN	1979..........McArdle Pontiac/Cadillac, Midland, MI
1948..........Briggs Beautyware, Detroit	1980..........Peterbilt Western, Seattle
1949..........Tip Top Tailors, Toronto	1981..........Archer Daniels Midland, Decatur, IL
1950..........Clearwater (FL) Bombers	1982..........Peterbilt Western, Seattle
1951..........Dow Chemical, Midland, MI	1983..........Franklin Cardinals, Stratford, CT
1952..........Briggs Beautyware, Detroit	1984..........California Kings, Merced, CA
1953..........Briggs Beautyware, Detroit	1985..........Pay'n Pak, Seattle
1954..........Clearwater (FL) Bombers	1986..........Pay'n Pak, Seattle
1955..........Raybestos Cardinals, Stratford, CT	1987..........Pay'n Pak, Seattle
1956..........Clearwater (FL) Bombers	1988..........TransAire, Elkhart, IN
1957..........Clearwater (FL) Bombers	1989..........Penn Corp, Sioux City, IA
1958..........Raybestos Cardinals, Stratford, CT	1990..........Penn Corp, Sioux City, IA
1959..........Sealmasters, Aurora, IL	1991..........Guanella Brothers, Rohnert Park, CA
1960..........Clearwater (FL) Bombers	1992..........Natl Health Care Disc, Sioux City, IA
1961..........Sealmasters, Aurora, IL	1993..........Natl Health Care Disc, Sioux City, IA
1962..........Clearwater (FL) Bombers	1994..........Decatur Pride, Decatur, IL
1963..........Clearwater (FL) Bombers	1995..........Decatur Pride, Decatur, IL
1964..........Burch Tool, Detroit	1996..........Green Bay (WI) All-Car

SUPER SLOW PITCH

1981..........Howard's/Western Steer, Denver, NC	1989..........Ritch's Salvage, Harrisburg, NC
1982..........Jerry's Catering, Miami, Fla.	1990..........Steele's Silver Bullets, Grafton, OH
1983..........Howard's/Western Steer, Denver, NC	1991..........Sunbelt/Worth, Centerville, GA
1984..........Howard's/Western Steer, Denver, NC	1992..........Ritch's Superior, Windsor Locks, CT
1985..........Steele's Sports, Grafton, OH	1993..........Ritch's Superior, Windsor Locks, CT
1986..........Steele's Sports, Grafton, OH	1994..........Bell Corp, Tampa, Fla.
1987..........Steele's Sports, Grafton, OH	1995..........Lighthouse Worth, Stone Mtn., GA
1988..........Starpath, Monticello, KY	1996..........Ritch's Superior, Windsor Locks, CT

MAJOR SLOW PITCH

1953..........Shields Construction, Newport, KY	1969..........Copper Hearth, Milwaukee
1954..........Waldneck's Tavern, Cincinnati	1970..........Little Caesar's, Southgate, MI
1955..........Lang Pet Shop, Covington, KY	1971..........Pile Drivers, Virginia Beach, VA
1956..........Gatliff Auto Sales, Newport, KY	1972..........Jiffy Club, Louisville, KY
1957..........Gatliff Auto Sales, Newport, KY	1973..........Howard's Furniture, Denver, NC
1958..........East Side Sports, Detroit	1974..........Howard's Furniture, Denver, NC
1959..........Yorkshire Restaurant, Newport, KY	1975..........Pyramid Cafe, Lakewood, OH
1960..........Hamilton Tailoring, Cincinnati	1976..........Warren Motors, Jacksonville, FL
1961..........Hamilton Tailoring, Cincinnati	1977..........Nelson Painting, Oklahoma City
1962..........Skip Hogan A.C., Pittsburgh	1978..........Campbell Carpets, Concord, CA
1963..........Gatliff Auto Sales, Newport, KY	1979..........Nelco Mfg Co, Oklahoma City
1964..........Skip Hogan A.C., Pittsburgh	1980..........Campbell Carpets, Concord, CA
1965..........Skip Hogan A.C., Pittsburgh	1981..........Elite Coating, Gordon, CA
1966..........Michael's Lounge, Detroit	1982..........Triangle Sports, Minneapolis
1967..........Jim's Sport Shop, Pittsburgh	1983..........No. 1 Electric & Heating, Gastonia, NC
1968..........County Sports, Levittown, NY	1984..........Lilly Air Systems, Chicago

Men *(Cont.)*

MAJOR SLOW PITCH *(Cont.)*

1985..........Blanton's, Fayetteville, NC	1991..........Riverside Paving, Louisville, KY
1986..........Non-Ferrous Metals, Cleveland	1992..........Vernon's, Jacksonville, FL
1987..........Starpath, Monticello, KY	1993..........Back Porch/Destin Roofing, Destin, FL
1988..........Bell Corp/FAF, Tampa, FL	1994..........Riverside RAM/Taylor Bros., Louisville, KY
1989..........Ritch's Salvage, Harrisburg, NC	1995..........Riverside/RAM/Taylor/TPS, Louisville, KY
1990..........New Construction, Shelbyville, IN	1996..........Bell 2/Robert's/Easton, Orlando, FL

Women
MAJOR FAST PITCH

1933..........Great Northerns, Chicago	1965..........Orange (CA) Lionettes
1934..........Hart Motors, Chicago	1966..........Raybestos Brakettes, Stratford, CT
1935..........Bloomer Girls, Cleveland	1967..........Raybestos Brakettes, Stratford, CT
1936..........Nat'l Screw & Mfg, Cleveland	1968..........Raybestos Brakettes, Stratford, CT
1937..........Nat'l Screw & Mfg, Cleveland	1969..........Orange (CA) Lionettes
1938..........J. J. Krieg's, Alameda, CA	1970..........Orange (CA) Lionettes
1939..........J. J. Krieg's, Alameda, CA	1971..........Raybestos Brakettes, Stratford, CT
1940..........Arizona Ramblers, Phoenix	1972..........Raybestos Brakettes, Stratford, CT
1941..........Higgins Midgets, Tulsa	1973..........Raybestos Brakettes, Stratford, CT
1942..........Jax Maids, New Orleans	1974..........Raybestos Brakettes, Stratford, CT
1943..........Jax Maids, New Orleans	1975..........Raybestos Brakettes, Stratford, CT
1944..........Lind & Pomeroy, Portland, OR	1976..........Raybestos Brakettes, Stratford, CT
1945..........Jax Maids, New Orleans	1977..........Raybestos Brakettes, Stratford, CT
1946..........Jax Maids, New Orleans	1978..........Raybestos Brakettes, Stratford, CT
1947..........Jax Maids, New Orleans	1979..........Sun City (AZ) Saints
1948..........Arizona Ramblers, Phoenix	1980..........Raybestos Brakettes, Stratford, CT
1949..........Arizona Ramblers, Phoenix	1981..........Orlando (FL) Rebels
1950..........Orange (CA) Lionettes	1982..........Raybestos Brakettes, Stratford, CT
1951..........Orange (CA) Lionettes	1983..........Raybestos Brakettes, Stratford, CT
1952..........Orange (CA) Lionettes	1984..........Los Angeles Diamonds
1953..........Betsy Ross Rockets, Fresno	1985..........Hi-Ho Brakettes, Stratford, CT
1954..........Leach Motor Rockets, Fresno	1986..........Southern California Invasion, Los Angeles
1955..........Orange (CA) Lionettes	1987..........Orange County Majestics, Anaheim, CA
1956..........Orange (CA) Lionettes	1988..........Hi-Ho Brakettes, Stratford, CT
1957..........Hacienda Rockets, Fresno	1989..........Whittier (CA) Raiders
1958..........Raybestos Brakettes, Stratford, CT	1990..........Raybestos Brakettes, Stratford, CT
1959..........Raybestos Brakettes, Stratford, CT	1991..........Raybestos Brakettes, Stratford, CT
1960..........Raybestos Brakettes, Stratford, CT	1992..........Raybestos Brakettes, Stratford, CT
1961..........Gold Sox, Whittier, CA	1993..........Redding Rebels, Redding, CA
1962..........Orange (CA) Lionettes	1994..........Redding Rebels, Redding, CA
1963..........Raybestos Brakettes, Stratford, CT	1995..........Redding Rebels, Redding, CA
1964..........Erv Lind Florists, Portland, OR	1996..........California Commotion, Woodland Hills, CA

MAJOR SLOW PITCH

1959..........Pearl Laundry, Richmond, VA	1978..........Bob Hoffman's Dots, Miami
1960..........Carolina Rockets, High Pt, NC	1979..........Bob Hoffman's Dots, Miami
1961..........Dairy Cottage, Covington, KY	1980..........Howard's Rubi-Otts, Graham, NC
1962..........Dana Gardens, Cincinnati	1981..........Tifton (GA) Tomboys
1963..........Dana Gardens, Cincinnati	1982..........Richmond (VA) Stompers
1964..........Dana Gardens, Cincinnati	1983..........Spooks, Anoka, MN
1965..........Art's Acres, Omaha	1984..........Spooks, Anoka, MN
1966..........Dana Gardens, Cincinnati	1985..........Key Ford Mustangs, Pensacola, FL
1967..........Ridge Maintenance, Cleveland	1986..........Sur-Way Tomboys, Tifton, GA
1968..........Escue Pontiac, Cincinnati	1987..........Key Ford Mustangs, Pensacola, FL
1969..........Converse Dots, Hialeah, FL	1988..........Spooks, Anoka, MN
1970..........Rutenschruder Floral, Cincinnati	1989..........Canaan's Illusions, Houston
1971..........Gators, Ft Lauderdale, FL	1990..........Spooks, Anoka, MN
1972..........Riverside Ford, Cincinnati	1991..........Kannan's Illusions, San Antonio, TX
1973..........Sweeney Chevrolet, Cincinnati	1992..........Universal Plastics, Cookeville, TN
1974..........Marks Brothers Dots, Miami	1993..........Universal Plastics, Cookeville, TN
1975..........Marks Brothers Dots, Miami	1994..........Universal Plastics, Cookeville, TN
1976..........Sorrento's Pizza, Cincinnati	1995..........Armed Forces, Sacramento, CA
1977..........Fox Valley Lassies, St Charles, IL	1996..........Spooks, Anoka, MN

Speed Skating

All-Around World Champions

MEN

1891 .....Joseph F. Donoghue, U.S.	1933 .....Hans Engnestangen, Nor.	1969 .....Dag Fornaes, Norway
1893 .....Jaap Eden, Neth.	1934 .....Bernt Evensen, Norway	1970 .....Ard Schenk, Neth.
1895 .....Jaap Eden, Neth.	1935 .....Michael Staksrud, Nor.	1971 .....Ard Schenk, Neth.
1896 .....Jaap Eden, Neth.	1936 .....Ivar Ballangrud, Norway	1972 .....Ard Schenk, Neth.
1897 .....Jack K. McCulloch, Can.	1937 .....Michael Staksrud, Nor.	1973 .....Göran Claeson, Sweden
1898 .....Peder Ostlund, Norway	1938 .....Ivar Ballangrud, Norway	1974 .....Sten Stensen, Norway
1899 .....Peder Ostlund, Norway	1939 .....Birger Wasenius, Finland	1975 .....Harm Kuipers, Neth.
1900 .....Edvard Engelsaas, Nor.	1947 .....Lassi Parkkinen, Finland	1976 .....Piet Kleine, Neth.
1901 .....Franz F. Wathan, Finland	1948 .....Odd Lundberg, Norway	1977 .....Eric Heiden, U.S.
1904 .....Sigurd Mathisen, Norway	1949 .....Kornel Pajor, Hungary	1978 .....Eric Heiden, U.S.
1905 .....C. Coen de Koning, Neth.	1950 .....Hjalmar Andersen, Nor.	1979 .....Eric Heiden, U.S.
1908 .....Oscar Mathisen, Norway	1951 .....Hjalmar Andersen, Nor.	1980 .....Hilbert van der Duin, Neth.
1909 .....Oscar Mathisen, Norway	1952 .....Hjalmar Andersen, Nor.	1981 .....Amund Sjobrand, Norway
1910 .....Nikolai Strunnikov, Russia	1953 .....Oleg Goncharenko, USSR	1982 .....Hilbert van der Duin, Neth.
1911 .....Nikolai Strunnikov, Russia	1954 .....Boris Shilkov, USSR	1983 .....Rolf Falk-Larssen, Nor.
1912 .....Oscar Mathisen, Norway	1955 .....Sigvard Ericsson, Swe.	1984 .....Oleg Bozhev, USSR
1913 .....Oscar Mathisen, Norway	1956 .....Oleg Goncharenko, USSR	1985 .....Hein Vergeer, Neth.
1914 .....Oscar Mathisen, Norway	1957 .....Knut Johannesen, Nor.	1986 .....Hein Vergeer, Neth.
1922 .....Harald Strom, Norway	1958 .....Oleg Goncharenko, USSR	1987 .....Nikolai Guliaev, USSR
1923 .....Klas Thunberg, Finland	1959 .....Juhani Järvinen, Finland	1988 .....Eric Flaim, U.S.
1924 .....Roald Larsen, Norway	1960 .....Boris Stenin, USSR	1989 .....Leo Visser, Neth.
1925 .....Klas Thunberg, Finland	1961 .....Henk van der Grift, Neth.	1990 .....Johann Olav Koss, Nor.
1926 .....Ivar Ballangrud, Norway	1962 .....Viktor Kosichkin, USSR	1991 .....Johann Olav Koss, Nor.
1927 .....Bernt Evensen, Norway	1963 .....Jonny Nilsson, Sweden	1992 .....Roberto Sighel, Italy
1928 .....Klas Thunberg, Finland	1964 .....Knut Johannesen, Nor.	1993 .....Falko Zandstra, Neth.
1929 .....Klas Thunberg, Finland	1965 .....Per Ivar Moe, Norway	1994 .....Johann Olav Koss, Nor.
1930 .....Michael Staksrud, Nor.	1966 .....Kees Verkerk, Neth.	1995 .....Rintje Ritsma, Neth.
1931 .....Klas Thunberg, Finland	1967 .....Kees Verkerk, Neth.	1996 .....Rintje Ritsma, Neth.
1932 .....Ivar Ballangrud, Norway	1968 .....Fred Anton Maier, Nor.	

WOMEN

1936 .....Kit Klein, U.S.	1961 .....Valentina Stenina, USSR	1980 .....Natalia Petruseva, USSR
1937 .....Laila Schou Nilsen, Nor.	1962 .....Inga Artamonova, USSR	1981 .....Natalia Petruseva, USSR
1938 .....Laila Schou Nilsen, Nor.	1963 .....Lidia Skoblikova, USSR	1982 .....Karin Busch, GDR
1939 .....Verné Lesche, Finland	1964 .....Lidia Skoblikova, USSR	1983 .....Andrea Schöne, GDR
1947 .....Verné Lesche, Finland	1965 .....Inga Artamonova, USSR	1984 .....Karin Enke-Busch, GDR
1948 .....Maria Isakova, USSR	1966 .....Valentina Stenina, USSR	1985 .....Andrea Schöne, GDR
1949 .....Maria Isakova, USSR	1967 .....Stien Kaiser, Neth.	1986 .....Karin Kania-Enke, GDR
1950 .....Maria Isakova, USSR	1968 .....Stien Kaiser, Neth.	1987 .....Karin Kania, GDR
1951 .....Eevi Huttunen, Finland	1969 .....Lasma Kauniste, USSR	1988 .....Karin Kania, GDR
1952 .....Lidia Selikhova, USSR	1970 .....Atje Keulen-Deelstra, Neth.	1989 .....Constanze Moser, GDR
1953 .....Khalida Shchegoleeva, USSR	1971 .....Nina Statkevich, USSR	1990 .....Jacqueline Börner, GDR
1954 .....Lidia Selikhova, USSR	1972 .....Atje Keulen-Deelstra, Neth.	1991 .....Gunda Kleemann, Ger.
1955 .....Rimma Zhukova, USSR	1973 .....Atje Keulen-Deelstra, Neth.	1992 .....Gunda Niemann-Kleemann, Germany
1956 .....Sofia Kondakova, USSR	1974 .....Atje Keulen-Deelstra, Neth.	1993 .....Gunda Niemann, Germany
1957 .....Inga Artamonova, USSR	1975 .....Karin Kessow, GDR	1994 .....Emese Hunyady, Austria
1958 .....Inga Artamonova, USSR	1976 .....Sylvia Burka, Canada	1995 .....Gunda Niemann, Germany
1959 .....Tamara Rylova, USSR	1977 .....Vera Bryndzej, USSR	1996 .....Gunda Niemann, Germany
1960 .....Valentina Stenina, USSR	1978 .....Tatiana Averina, USSR	
	1979 .....Beth Heiden, U.S.	

Squash

National Men's Champions

HARD BALL		HARD BALL *(Cont.)*		HARD BALL *(Cont.)*	
Year	Champion	Year	Champion	Year	Champion
1907 ....John A. Miskey		1912 ....Constantine Hutchins		1917 ....Stanley W. Pearson	
1908 ....John A. Miskey		1913 ....Morton L. Newhall		1918-19 .....No tournament	
1909 ....William L. Freeland		1914 ....Constantine Hutchins		1920 ....Charles C. Peabody	
1910 ....John A. Miskey		1915 ....Stanley W. Pearson		1921 ....Stanley W. Pearson	
1911 ....Francis S. White		1916 ....Stanley W. Pearson		1922 ....Stanley W. Pearson	

National Men's Champions (Cont.)

HARD BALL (Cont.)		HARD BALL (Cont.)		HARD BALL (Cont.)	
Year	Champion	Year	Champion	Year	Champion
1923	Stanley W. Pearson	1956	G. Diehl Mateer, Jr	1985	Kenton Jernigan
1924	Gerald Roberts	1957	Henri R. Salaun	1986	Hugh LaBossier
1925	W. Palmer Dixon	1958	Henri R. Salaun	1987	Frank J. Stanley IV
1926	W. Palmer Dixon	1959	Benjamin H.	1988	Scott Dulmage
1927	Myles Baker		Heckscher	1989	Rodolfo Rodriquez
1928	Herbert N. Rawlins Jr.	1960	G. Diehl Mateer, Jr	1990	Hector Barragan
1929	J. Lawrence Pool	1961	Henri R. Salaun	1991	Hector Barragan
1930	Herbert N. Rawlins Jr.	1962	Samuel P. Howe III	1992	Hector Barragan
1931	J. Lawrence Pool	1963	Benjamin H.	1993	Hector Barragan
1932	Beckman H. Pool		Heckscher	1994	Hector Barragan
1933	Beckman H. Pool	1964	Ralph E. Howe	1995	W. Keen Butcher
1934	Neil J. Sullivan II	1965	Stephen T. Vehslage	1996	W. Keen Butcher
1935	Donald Strachan	1966	Victor Niederhoffer		
1936	Germain G. Glidden	1967	Samuel P. Howe III	**SOFT BALL**	
1937	Germain G. Glidden	1968	Colin Adair	Year	Champion
1938	Germain G. Glidden	1969	Anil Nayar	1983	Kenton Jernigan
1939	Donald Strachan	1970	Anil Nayar	1984	Kenton Jernigan
1940	A. Willing Patterson	1971	Colin Adair	1985	Kenton Jernigan
1941	Charles M. P. Britton	1972	Victor Niederhoffer	1986	Darius Pandole
1942	Charles M. P. Britton	1973	Victor Niederhoffer	1987	Richard Hashim
1943-45	No tournament	1974	Victor Niederhoffer	1988	John Phelan
1946	Charles M. P. Britton	1975	Victor Niederhoffer	1989	Will Carlin
1947	Charles M. P. Britton	1976	Peter Briggs	1990	Syed Jafry
1948	Stanley W. Pearson, Jr	1977	Thomas E. Page	1991	Hector Barragan
1949	H. Hunter Lott, Jr	1978	Michael Desaulniers	1992	Phil Yarrow
1950	Edward J. Hahn	1979	Mario Sanchez	1993	Phil Yarrow
1951	Edward J. Hahn	1980	Michael Desaulniers	1994	Roberto Rosales
1952	Harry B. Conlon	1981	Mark Alger	1995	A. Martin Clark
1953	Ernest Howard	1982	John Nimick	1996	Mohsen Mir
1954	G. Diehl Mateer, Jr	1983	Kenton Jernigan		
1955	Henri R. Salaun	1984	Kenton Jernigan		

National Women's Champions

HARD BALL		HARD BALL (Cont.)		HARD BALL (Cont.)	
Year	Champion	Year	Champion	Year	Champion
1928	Eleanora Sears	1959	Betty Howe Constable	1986	Alicia McConnell
1929	Margaret Howe	1960	Margaret Varner	1987	Alicia McConnell
1930	Hazel Wightman	1961	Margaret Varner	1988	Alicia McConnell
1931	Ruth Banks	1962	Margaret Varner	1989	Demer Holleran
1932	Margaret Howe	1963	Margaret Varner	1990	Demer Holleran
1933	Susan Noel	1964	Ann Wetzel	1991	Demer Holleran
1934	Margaret Howe	1965	Joyce Davenport	1992	Demer Holleran
1935	Margot Lumb	1966	Betty Meade	1993	Demer Holleran
1936	Anne Page	1967	Betty Meade	1994	Demer Holleran
1937	Anne Page	1968	Betty Meade	Note: Tournament not held since 1994.	
1938	Cecile Bowes	1969	Joyce Davenport		
1939	Anne Page	1970	Nina Moyer	**SOFT BALL**	
1940	Cecile Bowes	1971	Carol Thesieres	Year	Champion
1941	Cecile Bowes	1972	Nina Moyer	1983	Alicia McConnell
1942-46	No tournament	1973	Gretchen Spruance	1984	Julie Harris
1947	Anne Page Homer	1974	Gretchen Spruance	1985	Sue Clinch
1948	Cecile Bowes	1975	Ginny Akabane	1986	Julie Harris
1949	Janet Morgan	1976	Gretchen Spruance	1987	Diana Staley
1950	Betty Howe	1977	Gretchen Spruance	1988	Sara Luther
1951	Jane Austin	1978	Gretchen Spruance	1989	Nancy Gengler
1952	Margaret Howe	1979	Heather McKay	1990	Joyce Maycock
1953	Margaret Howe	1980	Barbara Maltby	1991	Ellie Pierce
1954	Lois Dilks	1981	Barbara Maltby	1992	Demer Holleran
1955	Janet Morgan	1982	Alicia McConnell	1993	Demer Holleran
1956	Betty Howe Constable	1983	Alicia McConnell	1994	Demer Holleran
1957	Betty Howe Constable	1984	Alicia McConnell	1995	Ellie Pierce
1958	Betty Howe Constable	1985	Alicia McConnell	1996	Demer Holleran

Triathlon

Ironman Championship
MEN

Date	Winner	Time	Site
1978	Gordon Haller	11:46	Waikiki Beach
1979	Tom Warren	11:15:56	Waikiki Beach
1980	Dave Scott	9:24:33	Ala Moana Park
1981	John Howard	9:38:29	Kailua-Kona
1982	Scott Tinley	9:19:41	Kailua-Kona
1982	Dave Scott	9:08:23	Kailua-Kona
1983	Dave Scott	9:05:57	Kailua-Kona
1984	Dave Scott	8:54:20	Kailua-Kona
1985	Scott Tinley	8:50:54	Kailua-Kona
1986	Dave Scott	8:28:37	Kailua-Kona
1987	Dave Scott	8:34:13	Kailua-Kona
1988	Scott Molina	8:31:00	Kailua-Kona
1989	Mark Allen	8:09:15	Kailua-Kona
1990	Mark Allen	8:28:17	Kailua-Kona
1991	Mark Allen	8:18:32	Kailua-Kona
1992	Mark Allen	8:09:09	Kailua-Kona
1993	Mark Allen	8:07:46	Kailua-Kona
1994	Greg Welch	8:20:27	Kailua-Kona
1995	Mark Allen	8:20:34	Kailua-Kona

WOMEN

Date	Winner	Time	Site
1978	No finishers		
1979	Lyn Lemaire	12:55	Waikiki Beach
1980	Robin Beck	11:21:24	Ala Moana Park
1981	Linda Sweeney	12:00:32	Kailua-Kona
1982	Kathleen McCartney	11:09:40	Kailua-Kona
1982	Julie Leach	10:54:08	Kailua-Kona
1983	Sylviane Puntous	10:43:36	Kailua-Kona
1984	Sylviane Puntous	10:25:13	Kailua-Kona
1985	Joanne Ernst	10:25:22	Kailua-Kona
1986	Paula Newby-Fraser	9:49:14	Kailua-Kona
1987	Erin Baker	9:35:25	Kailua-Kona
1988	Paula Newby-Fraser	9:01:01	Kailua-Kona
1989	Paula Newby-Fraser	9:00:56	Kailua-Kona
1990	Erin Baker	9:13:42	Kailua-Kona
1991	Paula Newby-Fraser	9:07:52	Kailua-Kona
1992	Paula Newby-Fraser	8:55:29	Kailua-Kona
1993	Paula Newby-Fraser	8:58:23	Kailua-Kona
1994	Paula Newby-Fraser	9:20:14	Kailua-Kona
1995	Karen Smyers	9:16:46	Kailua-Kona

Note: The Ironman Championship was contested twice in 1982.

Volleyball

World Champions
MEN

Year	Winner	Runnerup	Site
1949	Soviet Union	Czechoslovakia	Prague, Czechoslovakia
1952	Soviet Union	Czechoslovakia	Moscow, Soviet Union
1956	Czechoslovakia	Soviet Union	Paris, France
1960	Soviet Union	Czechoslovakia	Rio de Janeiro, Brazil
1962	Soviet Union	Czechoslovakia	Moscow, Soviet Union
1966	Czechoslovakia	Romania	Prague, Czechoslovakia
1970	East Germany	Bulgaria	Sofia, Bulgaria
1974	Poland	Soviet Union	Mexico City
1978	Soviet Union	Italy	Rome, Italy
1982	Soviet Union	Brazil	Buenos Aires, Argentina
1986	United States	Soviet Union	Paris, France
1990	Italy	Cuba	Rio de Janeiro, Brazil
1994	Italy	Netherlands	Athens, Greece

World Champions *(Cont.)*

WOMEN

Year	Winner	Runnerup	Site
1952	Soviet Union	Poland	Moscow, Soviet Union
1956	Soviet Union	Romania	Paris, France
1960	Soviet Union	Japan	Rio de Janeiro, Brazil
1962	Japan	Soviet Union	Moscow, Soviet Union
1966	Japan	United States	Prague, Czechoslovakia
1970	Soviet Union	Japan	Sofia, Bulgaria
1974	Japan	Soviet Union	Mexico City
1978	Cuba	Japan	Rome, Italy
1982	China	Peru	Lima, Peru
1986	China	Cuba	Prague, Czechoslovakia
1990	Soviet Union	China	Beijing, China
1994	Cuba	Brazil	Sao Paulo, Brazil

U.S. Men's Open Champions—Gold Division

Year	Champion	Year	Champion
1928	Germantown, PA YMCA	1963	Hollywood, CA YMCA
1929	Hyde Park YMCA, IL	1964	Hollywood, CA YMCA Stars
1930	Hyde Park YMCA, IL	1965	Westside JCC, CA
1931	San Antonio, TX YMCA	1966	Sand & Sea Club, CA
1932	San Antonio, TX YMCA	1967	Fresno, CA VBC
1933	Houston, TX YMCA	1968	Westside JCC, Los Angeles, CA
1934	Houston, TX YMCA	1969	Los Angeles, CA YMCA
1935	Houston, TX YMCA	1970	Chart House, San Diego
1936	Houston, TX YMCA	1971	Santa Monica, CA YMCA
1937	Duncan YMCA, IL	1972	Chart House, San Diego
1938	Houston, TX YMCA	1973	Chuck's Steak, Los Angeles
1939	Houston, TX YMCA	1974	UC Santa Barbara, CA
1940	Los Angeles AC, CA	1975	Chart House, San Diego
1941	North Ave. YMCA, IL	1976	Maliabu, Los Angeles, CA
1942	North Ave. YMCA, IL	1977	Chuck's, Santa Barbara
1943-44	No championships	1978	Chuck's, Los Angeles
1945	North Ave. YMCA, IL	1979	Nautilus, Long Beach
1946	Pasadena, CA YMCA	1980	Olympic Club, San Francisco
1947	North Ave. YMCA, IL	1981	Nautilus, Long Beach
1948	Hollywood, CA YMCA	1982	Chuck's, Los Angeles
1949	Downtown YMCA, CA	1983	Nautilus Pacifica, CA
1950	Long Beach, CA YMCA	1984	Nautilus Pacifica, CA
1951	Hollywood, CA YMCA	1985	Molten/SSI Torrance, CA
1952	Hollywood, CA YMCA	1986	Molten, Torrance, CA
1953	Hollywood, CA YMCA	1987	Molten, Torrance, CA
1954	Stockton, CA YMCA	1988	Molten, Torrance, CA
1955	Stockton, CA YMCA	1989	Not held
1956	Hollywood, CA YMCA Stars	1990	Nike, Carson, CA
1957	Hollywood, CA YMCA Stars	1991	Offshore, Woodland Hills, CA
1958	Hollywood, CA YMCA Stars	1992	Creole Six Pack, Elmhurst, NY
1959	Hollywood, CA YMCA Stars	1993	Asics, Huntington Beach, CA
1960	Westside JCC, CA	1994	Asics/Paul Mitchell, Hunt. Beach, CA
1961	Hollywood, CA YMCA	1995	Shakter, Belagarad, Ukraine
1962	Hollywood, CA YMCA	1996	POL-AM-VBC, Brooklyn, NY

U.S. Women's Open Champions—Gold Division

Year	Champion	Year	Champion
1949	Eagles, Houston TX	1960	Mariners, Santa Monica, CA
1950	Voit #1, Santa Monica, CA	1961	Breakers, Long Beach, CA
1951	Eagles, Houston, TX	1962	Shamrocks, Long Beach, CA
1952	Voit #1, Santa Monica, CA	1963	Shamrocks, Long Beach, CA
1953	Voit #1, Los Angeles, CA	1964	Shamrocks, Long Beach, CA
1954	Houstonettes, Houston, TX	1965	Shamrocks, Long Beach, CA
1955	Mariners, Santa Monica, CA	1966	Renegades, Los Angeles, CA
1956	Mariners, Santa Monica, CA	1967	Shamrocks, Long Beach, CA
1957	Mariners, Santa Monica, CA	1968	Shamrocks, Long Beach, CA
1958	Mariners, Santa Monica, CA	1969	Shamrocks, Long Beach, CA
1959	Mariners, Santa Monica, CA	1970	Shamrocks, Long Beach, CA

U.S. Women's Open Champions—Gold Division (Cont.)

1971	Renegades, Los Angeles, CA	1985	Merrill Lynch, Arizona
1972	E Pluribus Unum, Houston	1986	Merrill Lynch, Arizona
1973	E Pluribus Unum, Houston	1987	Chrysler, Pleasanton, CA
1974	Renegades, Los Angeles, CA	1988	Chrysler, Hayward, CA
1975	Adidas, Norwalk, CA	1989	Plymouth, Hayward, CA
1976	Pasadena, TX	1990	Plymouth, Hayward, CA
1977	Spoilers, Hermosa, CA	1991	Fitness, Champaign, IL
1978	Nick's, Los Angeles, CA	1992	Nick's Kronies, Chicago, IL
1979	Mavericks, Los Angeles, CA	1993	Nick's Fishmarket, Chicago, IL
1980	NAVA, Fountain Valley, CA	1994	Nick's Fishmarket, Chicago, IL
1981	Utah State, Logan, UT	1995	Kittleman Assoc./Rudi's/Nick's, Chicago, IL
1982	Monarchs, Hilo, HI	1996	Pure Texas Nuts, Austin, TX
1983	Syntex, Stockton, CA		
1984	Chrysler, Palo Alto, CA		

Wrestling

United States National Champions

1983

FREESTYLE		FREESTYLE (Cont.)		GRECO-ROMAN (Cont.)	
105.5	Rich Salamone	220	Greg Gibson	149.5	Jim Martinez
114.5	Joe Gonzales	Hvy	Bruce Baumgartner	163	James Andre
125.5	Joe Corso	Team	Sunkist Kids	180.5	Steve Goss
136.5	Rich Dellagatta*			198	Steve Fraser*
149.5	Bill Hugent	**GRECO-ROMAN**		220	Dennis Koslowski
163	Lee Kemp	105.5	T. J. Jones	Hvy	No champion
180.5	Chris Campbell	114.5	Mark Fuller	Team	Minnesota Wrestling
198	Pete Bush	125.5	Rob Hermann		Club
		136.5	Dan Mello		

1984

FREESTYLE		FREESTYLE (Cont.)		GRECO-ROMAN (Cont.)	
105.5	Rich Salamone	220	Harold Smith	149.5	Jim Martinez*
114.5	Charlie Heard	Hvy	Bruce Baumgartner	163	John Matthews
125.5	Joe Corso	Team	Sunkist Kids	180.5	Tom Press
136.5	Rich Dellagatta*			198	Mike Houck
149.5	Andre Metzger	**GRECO-ROMAN**		220	No champion
163	Dave Schultz*	105.5	T. J. Jones	Hvy	No champion
180.5	Mark Schultz	114.5	Mark Fuller	Team	Adirondack
198	Steve Fraser	136.5	Dan Mello		Three-Style, WA

1985

FREESTYLE		FREESTYLE (Cont.)		GRECO-ROMAN (Cont.)	
105.5	Tim Vanni	220	Greg Gibson	136.5	Buddy Lee
114.5	Jim Martin	286	Bruce Baumgartner	149.5	Jim Martinez
125.5	Charlie Heard	Team	Sunkist Kids	163	David Butler
136.5	Darryl Burley	**GRECO-ROMAN**		180.5	Chris Catallo
149.5	Bill Nugent*	105.5	T. J. Jones	198	Mike Houck
163	Kenny Monday	114.5	Mark Fuller	220	Greg Gibson
180.5	Mike Sheets	125.5	Eric Seward*	286	Dennis Koslowski
198	Mark Schultz			Team	U.S. Marine Corps

1986

FREESTYLE		FREESTYLE (Cont.)		GRECO-ROMAN (Cont.)	
105.5	Rich Salamone	286	Bruce Baumgartner	136.5	Frank Famiano
114.5	Joe Gonzales	Team	Sunkist Kids (Div. I)	149.5	Jim Martinez
125.5	Kevin Darkus		Hawkeye Wrestling	163	David Butler*
136.5	John Smith		Club (Div. II)	180.5	Darryl Gholar
149.5	Andre Metzger*	**GRECO-ROMAN**		198	Derrick Waldroup
163	Dave Schultz	105.5	Eric Wetzel	220	Dennis Koslowski
180.5	Mark Schultz	114.5	Shawn Sheldon	286	Duane Koslowski
198	Jim Scherr	125.5	Anthony Amado	Team	U.S. Marine Corps (Div. I)
220	Dan Severn				U.S. Navy (Div. II)

United States National Champions (Cont.)

1987

FREESTYLE
105.5 ....Takashi Irie
114.5 ....Mitsuru Sato
125.5 ....Barry Davis
136.5 ....Takumi Adachi
149.5 ....Andre Metzger
163 ....Dave Schultz*
180.5 ....Mark Schultz
198 ....Jim Scherr
220 ....Bill Scherr

FREESTYLE (Cont.)
286 ....Bruce Baumgartner
Team ....Sunkist Kids (Div. I)
Team Foxcatcher (Div. II)

GRECO-ROMAN
105.5 ....Eric Wetzel
114.5 ....Shawn Sheldon
125.5 ....Eric Seward
136.5 ....Frank Famiano

GRECO-ROMAN (Cont.)
149.5 ....Jim Martinez
163 ....David Butler
180.5 ....Chris Catallo
198 ....Derrick Waldroup*
220 ....Dennis Koslowski
286 ....Duane Koslowski
Team........U.S. Marine Corp (Div. I)
U.S. Army (Div. II)

1988

FREESTYLE
105.5 ....Tim Vanni
114.5 ....Joe Gonzales
125.5 ....Kevin Darkus
136.5 ....John Smith*
149.5 ....Nate Carr
163 ....Kenny Monday
180.5 ....Dave Schultz
198 ....Melvin Douglas III
220 ....Bill Scherr

FREESTYLE (Cont.)
286 ....Bruce Baumgartner
Team ....Sunkist Kids (Div. I)
Team Foxcatcher (Div. II)

GRECO-ROMAN
105.5 ....T. J. Jones
114.5 ....Shawn Sheldon
125.5 ....Gogi Parseghian*
136.5 ....Dalen Wasmund

GRECO-ROMAN (Cont.)
149.5 ....Craig Pollard
163 ....Tony Thomas
180.5 ....Darryl Gholar
198 ....Mike Carolan
220 ....Dennis Koslowski
286 ....Duane Koslowski
Team........U.S. Marine Corps (Div. I)
Sunkist Kids (Div. II)

1989

FREESTYLE
105.5 ....Tim Vanni
114.5 ....Zeke Jones
125.5 ....Brad Penrith
136.5 ....John Smith
149.5 ....Nate Carr
163 ....Rob Koll
180.5 ....Rico Chiapparelli
198 ....Jim Scherr*
220 ....Bill Scherr

FREESTYLE (Cont.)
286 ....Bruce Baumgartner
Team ....Sunkist Kids (Div. I)
Team Foxcatcher (Div. II)

GRECO-ROMAN
105.5 ....Lew Dorrance
114.5 ....Mark Fuller
125.5 ....Gogi Parseghian
136.5 ....Isaac Anderson

GRECO-ROMAN (Cont.)
149.5 ....Andy Seras*
163 ....David Butler
180.5 ....John Morgan
198 ....Michial Foy
220 ....Steve Lawson
286 ....Craig Pittman
Team .......U.S. Marine Corps (Div. I)
Jets USA (Div. II)

1990

FREESTYLE
105.5 ....Rob Eiter
114.5 ....Zeke Jones
125,5 ....Joe Melchiore
136.5 ....John Smith
149.5 ....Nate Carr
163 ....Rob Koll
180.5 ....Royce Alger
198 ....Chris Campbell*
220 ....Bill Scherr

FREESTYLE (Cont.)
286 ....Bruce Baumgartner
Team ....Sunkist Kids (Div. I)
Team Foxcatcher (Div. II)

GRECO-ROMAN
105.5 ....Lew Dorrance
114.5 ....Sam Henson
125.5 ....Mark Pustelnik
136.5 ....Isaac Anderson

GRECO-ROMAN (Cont.)
149.5 ....Andy Seras
163 ....David Butler
180.5 ....Derrick Waldroup
198 ....Randy Couture*
220 ....Chris Tironi
286 ....Matt Ghaffari
Team ....Jets USA (Div. I)
California Jets (Div. II)

1991

FREESTYLE
105.5 ....Tim Vanni
114.5 ....Zeke Jones
125.5 ....Brad Penrith
136.5 ....John Smith*
149.5 ....Townsend Saunders
163 ....Kenny Monday
180.5 ....Kevin Jackson
198 ....Chris Campbell

FREESTYLE (Cont.)
220 ....Mark Coleman
286 ....Bruce Baumgartner
Team ....Sunkist Kids (Div. I)
Jets USA (Div. II)

GRECO-ROMAN
105.5 ....Eric Wetzel
114.5 ....Shawn Sheldon
125.5 ....Frank Famiano

GRECO-ROMAN (Cont.)
136.5 ....Buddy Lee
149.5 ....Andy Seras
163 ....Gordy Morgan
180.5 ....John Morgan*
198 ....Michial Foy
220 ....Dennis Koslowski
286 ....Craig Pittman
Team ....Jets USA (Div. I)
Sunkist Kids (Div. II)

*Outstanding wrestler

United States National Champions (Cont.)

1992

FREESTYLE		
105.5	Rob Eiter
114.5	Jack Griffin
125.5	Kendall Cross*
136.5	John Fisher
149.5	Matt Demaray
163	Greg Elinsky
180.5	Royce Alger
198	Dan Chaid
220	Bill Scherr

FREESTYLE (Cont.)
286 ....Bruce Baumgartner
Team ....Sunkist Kids (Div. I)
Team Foxcatcher (Div. II)

GRECO-ROMAN
105.5 ....Eric Wetzel
114.5 ......Mark Fuller
125.5 ....Dennis Hall
136.5 ......Buddy Lee*

GRECO-ROMAN (Cont.)
149.5 ....Rodney Smith
163 ....Travis West
180.5 ....John Morgan
198 ....Michial Foy
220 ....Dennis Koslowski
286 ....Matt Ghaffari
Team ....NY Athletic Club (Div. I)
Sunkist Kids (Div. II)

1993

FREESTYLE
105.5 ....Rob Eiter
114.5 ......Zeke Jones
125.5 ....Brad Penrith
136.5 ....Tom Brands
149.5 ....Matt Demaray
163 ....Dave Schultz*
180.5 ......Kevin Jackson
198 ....Melvin Douglas
220 ....Kirk Trost

FREESTYLE (Cont.)
286 ....Bruce Baumgartner
Team ....Sunkist Kids (Div. I)
Team Foxcatcher (Div. II)

GRECO-ROMAN
105.5 ....Eric Wetzel
114.5 ......Shawn Sheldon
125.5 ....Dennis Hall*
136.5 ....Shon Lewis

GRECO-ROMAN (Cont.)
149.5 ....Andy Seras
163 ....Gordy Morgan
180.5 ....Dan Henderson
198 ....Randy Couture
220 ....James Johnson
286 ....Matt Ghaffari
Team ....NY Athletic Club (Div. I)
Sunkist Kids (Div. II)

1994

FREESTYLE
105.5 ....Tim Vanni
114.5 ....Zeke Jones
125.5 ....Terry Brands
136.5 ....Tom Brands
149.5 ....Matt Demaray
163 ....Dave Schultz
180.5 ....Royce Alger
198 ....Melvin Douglas
220 ....Mark Kerr

FREESTYLE (Cont.)
286 ....Bruce Baumgartner*
Team ....Sunkist Kids (Div. I)
Team Foxcatcher (Div. II)

GRECO-ROMAN
105.5 ....Isaac Ramaswamy
114.5 ....Shawn Sheldon
125.5 ....Dennis Hall
136.5 ....Shon Lewis

GRECO-ROMAN (Cont.)
149.5 ....Andy Seras*
163 ....Gordy Morgan
180.5 ....Dan Henderson
198 ....Derrick Waldroup
220 ....James Johnson
286 ....Matt Ghaffari
Team ....Armed Forces (Div. I)
NY Athletic Club (Div. II)

1995

FREESTYLE
105.5 ....Rob Eiter
114.5 ....Lou Rosselli
125.5 ....Kendall Cross*
136.5 ....Tom Brands
149.5 ....Matt Demaray
163 ....Dave Schultz
180.5 ......Kevin Jackson
198 ....Melvin Douglas
220 ....Kurt Angle

FREESTYLE (Cont.)
286 ....Bruce Baumgartner
Team ....Sunkist Kids (Div. I)
Team Foxcatcher (Div. II)

GRECO-ROMAN
105.5 ....Isaac Ramaswamy
114.5 ....Shawn Sheldon
125.5 ....Dennis Hall*
136.5 ....Van Fronhofer

GRECO-ROMAN (Cont.)
149.5 ....Heath Sims
163 ....Matt Lindland
180.5 ....Marty Morgan
198 ....Michial Foy
220 ....James Johnson
286 ....Rulon Gardner
Team ....Armed Forces (Div. I)
Sunkist Kids (Div. II)

1996

FREESTYLE
105.5 ....Rob Eiter
114.5 ....Lou Rosselli
125.5 ....Kendall Cross
136.5 ....Tom Brands
149.5 ....Townsend Saunders
163 ....Kenny Monday
180.5 ....Les Gutches*
198 ....Melvin Douglas
220 ....Kurt Angle

FREESTYLE (Cont.)
286 ....Bruce Baumgartner
Team ....Sunkist Kids (Div. I)
NY Athletic Club (Div. II)

GRECO-ROMAN
105.5 ....Mujaahid Maynard
114.5 ....Shawn Sheldon
125.5 ....Dennis Hall*
136.5 ....Shon Lewis

GRECO-ROMAN (Cont.)
149.5 ....Rodney Smith
163 ....Keith Sieracki
180.5 ....Marty Morgan
198 ....Michial Foy
220 ....John Oostendrop
286 ....Matt Ghaffari
Team ....Armed Forces (Div. I)
Sunkist Kids (Div. II)

*Outstanding wrestler

The Sports Market

Sports Illustrated

A SUPER BOWL QUARTERBACK AND THE GREATEST HOCKEY PLAYER OF ALL TIME

JUMP TEAMS IN CONTROVERSIAL

MEGADEALS

IS NEIL O'DONNELL OVERPRICED?
IS WAYNE GRETZKY OVER THE HILL?

ROBERT BECK (GRETZKY), ROBERT ROGERS (O'DONNELL)

Funny Money

Sport's golden age continued as owners, cities and networks tossed billions around like so much Monopoly money

by E.M. Swift

AT SOME point surely the bubble will burst, and the wildly inflationary numbers that have driven sports salaries, ticket prices, television rights fees and franchise values to KingDome come will stabilize and begin a downward spiral. The golden age, like all golden ages, will come to an end, and reason and moderation will return to the business of sport. But that process did not begin in 1996, another year when sports fields were blanketed with funny-money that fell down on players like rain.

Examples? Where to begin? Amateur golfing sensation Tiger Woods turned professional and promptly signed endorsement deals with Nike and others that totaled $60 million, elevating him past such corporate pitchmen as Michael Jordan ($38 million in estimated 1997 endorsement income), Shaquille O'Neal ($23 million), Arnold Palmer ($16 million), Andre Agassi ($15.8 million) and Jack Nicklaus ($14.3 million), the man to whom Woods is so often compared. Imagine what will happen now that Woods has

proven the Nicklaus comparisons have some validity.

Athletes' salaries, meanwhile, kept growing at a rate that far outstripped those of any other segment of society. NBC conducted a poll that asked people which profession was most overpaid among the likes of doctors, lawyers, corporate executives, movie stars, Congressmen and athletes. The jocks won going away. While contracts of major league baseball players stayed relatively stable in 1996—years of strikes and lockouts have alienated older fans, while baseball's glacial pace of play has failed to attract young ones—new free agency rules in the NFL, NBA and NHL initiated bidding wars that have turned ordinary players into multimillionaires.

Neil O'Donnell, a workmanlike quarterback who had the good fortune of playing for the AFC champion Pittsburgh Steelers in 1995–96, was one such beneficiary. Despite his poor performance in the Super Bowl, the woeful New York Jets (3–13) signed O'Donnell to a five-year,

MANNY MILLAN

A bargain at any price, Jordan signed a record one-year, $25 million deal.

$25 million free-agent contract in February, which temporarily propelled him past such future Hall of Famers as Dan Marino, John Elway and Emmitt Smith in the NFL's salary picture. The early returns suggested that the Jets might just as well have saved their money. The return of Joe Willie Namath, this was not. With O'Donnell at the helm, the Jets started 0–6 and averaged just 12.5 points per game—then he went down with a shoulder separation. Marino and Elway, meanwhile, took advantage of the hot quarterback market by signing new deals that paid them each $5.9 million per year, making them the third and fourth best-remunerated players in the league, behind $6 million quarterbacks Drew Bledsoe and Troy Aikman.

Chicken feed compared to basketball salaries, which took a quantum leap forward, fueled by a wave of 150-plus free agents that washed up on the NBA's shores after the league's new collective bargaining agreement went into effect on July 11. At the top of the list, appropriately, was Michael Jordan, whose one-year, $25 million contract with the world champion Bulls—the highest single-season salary in the history of team sports—set the ceiling against which all others would be measured. To put that $25 million figure in some sort of perspective, 15 years ago Magic Johnson signed a 25-*year*, $25 million contract which was considered outlandish. The entire Chicago Bulls team was bought by Jerry Reinsdorf and his partners for $15 million in 1985, Jordan's rookie season. And the NBA's salary cap in 1996–97 is $24.3 million per team—a figure that clubs are only allowed to exceed in order to sign their own free agents. Of course, many would argue that Jordan can beat most teams all by himself, so his salary *should* be higher than the cap.

Few would argue that Jordan's raise was long overdue. The best player in NBA history was only the 31st best-compensated in

Modell enraged the city of Cleveland by absconding with its beloved Browns.

1995–96, when he played for just $3.85 million while leading the Bulls to their fourth championship in the past six years. Meanwhile, the Bulls, as usual, sold out every game at home, a 437-game streak that goes back to Nov. '87. They were also the NBA's top draw on the road. And they played in all five of the highest-rated TV games in the regular season—ratings that the NBA will use as leverage the next time commissioner David Stern sits down to negotiate a television contract. Jordan is worth every penny.

But what about the money being flung at some of the other wanna-be-like-Mike's? O'Neal, with more flop movies on his resume (one) than championship rings (0 college, 0 pro), jumped from the Orlando Magic to the L.A. Lakers for $120 million over seven years—a cool $17.1 million per, all of which must somehow fit beneath the Lakers' salary cap. Then Shaq issued the most hilarious quote of the year by claiming that his move was "not about money." What was it about, Kazaam? Better scripts?

Alonzo Mourning, another center who has never whiffed a title, signed for $16 million a year with Miami, where coach, G.M. and president Pat Riley was throwing millions around like Monopoly money. Riley also signed New Jersey Nets forward P.J. Brown (surely you've heard of P.J. Brown) to a seven-year, $36 million contract. But Riley got himself into hot water by then trying to add Washington's Juwan Howard to the mix for seven years and

$100.8 million. The NBA nixed the Howard move on the grounds that Miami was in violation of the league's salary cap, but the Bullets matched that $14 million a year offer in order to keep their young star—not bad scratch for a guy who's never played in the postseason. Even second-tier NBA players like Chris Gatling (!), who jumped from Miami to Dallas for five years and $22 million, are commanding salaries the likes of which Kareem Abdul-Jabbar and Julius Erving never dreamed. Has everyone in the NBA lost their marbles?

In a word: No. The NBA has been generating so much money that it literally doesn't seem to know what to do with it. With over $3 billion a year in licensing revenues, four-year television contracts with NBC and Turner Sports worth another $1.1 billion, and 92.4% attendance in its 29 arenas, the NBA is a growing, robust business that has been able to buy labor peace by sharing 59% of its gross revenues with its players. At all levels, domestically and internationally, basketball is hot, and its avowed goal of one day supplanting soccer as the world's most popular sport is beginning to look like an achievable dream.

The biggest problem facing the NFL was, once again, owner-styled free agency, as franchises continued to relocate, or threaten to relocate, in search of richer and richer stadium deals. Last year both the Rams and the Raiders left Los Angeles. This year Art Modell enraged the city of Cleveland by moving the Browns, a local institution for 50 years, to Baltimore, where they were renamed the Ravens. The move was especially galling since Clevelanders had consistently supported the team, through good years and bad, ever since Modell bought the Browns in 1961.

Between 1985 and '94 the Browns, who have never made the Super Bowl, placed in the top seven in NFL attendance every year, averaging over 71,500 fans a game. But the economics of the league are such that luxury boxes and concession revenues—not attendance—now determine who wins the battle of the bottom line. Modell had put himself in a financial hole thanks to some poor business deals, and Baltimore, desperate to once again land an NFL team after their beloved Colts departed in the dead of night in 1984, made him an offer that he couldn't—or didn't—refuse. The Maryland Stadium Authority gave the team up to $75 million in moving expenses, then promised to build the team a new 70,000-seat outdoor stadium, theirs to enjoy rent free, which is due to open in 1998. The new stadium will have 108 luxury boxes and 7,500 club seats. Modell gets to keep all ticket, concession, parking and stadium advertising revenues. As a kicker, the Baltimore folks devised a scheme to build the team a new $15 million training complex. All Modell has to do is pay stadium operating expenses, estimated to run about $3 million a year.

The deal, which is expected to add $30 million a year to Modell's bottom line, is idiot-proof—ideally suited to a businessman of his modest acumen. So sweet was its nectar that NFL owners in Houston, Tampa Bay, Arizona, Chicago, Cincinnati and Detroit immediately began contemplating moves to other cities—the Gary (Ind.) Bears?—attempting to blackmail their hometowns into either a) renegotiating their leases or b) building them a new stadium. The newest wrinkle in financing these stadiums is the sale of something called "personal seat licenses," which are being peddled to fans for as much as $5,000 each and give the personal seat licensee the right to then purchase a season ticket. Such a deal. Even P.T. Barnum, who knew there was one born every minute, would be amazed at the fleecing an NFL fan is willing to take.

Of course, it shouldn't come as news that money makes the sports world go round, and nowhere was that more apparent than during the Atlanta Olympics, an event that set new standards for unchecked, and often tasteless, commercialism. Scrambling to meet a $1.7 billion budget without the help of government financing, the Atlanta Committee for the Olympic Games (ACOG) went on a selling spree, hawking the rights to use the Olympic name on everything from television game shows to Vidalia onion sauces.

The result was a pantheon of disposable corporate monuments sprung up in downtown Atlanta, garish totems to the gods who were footing the bill for the Games. A prominent Atlanta skyscraper turned itself into a giant Swatch display case. Anheuser-Busch contributed a 17,300-square-foot sports bar to Centennial Olympic Park that, in the true spirit of the Olympic ideal, it named Bud World. Atlanta-based Coca-Cola, which many considered to be the real host of the Games, reportedly spent upward of $300 million on various Olympic-related promotions and projects, including a 12-acre downtown amusement park called Coca-Cola Olympic City that featured a six-story Coke bottle. Every bus,

every barricade, every streetlight in the city became a billboard for one of the corporate sponsors. Even small-time capitalists got in on the action, buying vending licenses from the city so they could sell T-shirts, caps, souvenirs and soft drinks from makeshift stands on every downtown sidewalk. The accumulated effect was that of transforming the host city of the Centennial Games into a giant, steamy mother of all flea markets. One hundred years after Baron Pierre de Coubertin had resurrected the Olympics, his friendly sporting competition between nations had metamorphosed into a gaudy shrine to global consumerism.

International Olympic Committee members sat up and took notice. Fearful that a good thing—corporate sponsorship and private funding—had gone too far, several prominent IOC members vowed that in the future, no city would be allowed to host the Games without some financial backing from its local and regional governments.

Payne's Games were an unqualified financial, if not aesthetic, success.

Financially, though, if not aesthetically, the Atlanta Games were an unqualified success. ACOG says it broke even on its $1.7 billion budget, and the city of Atlanta got a new baseball stadium and a downtown park, Centennial Park, out of the deal. NBC, which in 1993 bought the American television rights for $456 million during a depressed market, sold more than $600 million in advertising. U.S. television ratings for the Games were huge, which no doubt made NBC Sports president Dick Ebersol feel pretty smug. In a stunning coup that took rivals Fox, ABC and CBS off guard, Ebersol was able to lock up the American broadcasting rights for NBC to every Olympics between 2000 and 2008. (CBS will broadcast the 1998 Winter Games from Nagano, Japan.) The price tag for those five Olympiads? A staggering $3.55 billion.

The negotiations began in August 1995,

when Ebersol extended a take-it-or-leave-it offer to IOC president Juan Antonio Samaranch and VP Dick Pound for both the 2000 Games in Sydney ($705 million) and the 2002 Games in Salt Lake City ($545 million). Samaranch and Pound took it. Then Ebersol went back to the IOC in November and was able to sew up the rights to the 2004, 2006 and 2008 Games—the sites of which are not even determined yet—for an additional $2.3 billion, a figure he arrived at by adding a modest 3% annual increase to the fees that he negotiated for 2000 and 2002. Any profit that NBC makes after production expenses and rights payments will be split 50/50 with the IOC.

It was a masterstroke by the 48-year-old Ebersol, providing, of course, the Olympics maintain their current level of appeal. By 2008 NBC will have broadcast six of the last seven Olympiads and be identified by a generation of American viewers as the network that brought the Olympics

Three days after turning pro Woods swooshed into big endorsement dollars.

into their living rooms. The IOC, for its part, has gained a stable American broadcasting partner with a vested interest in promoting the Olympics year round, and, more important, long-range financial planning capability. Cities bidding to host future Games—the local organizing committees will receive 49% of the funds paid by NBC—will now know, years ahead of time, how much money they can expect from U.S. television, which will is still a crucial source of their funding.

Of course, one never can tell. Any year now the golden age of sports may come to a crashing halt, and NBC's multibillion dollar Olympic gamble may blow up in its face, like an O'Donnell pass being swatted down by big Leon Lett. By 2008 televised spelunking might be all the rage. Or virtual reality Jane Austen tea dances.

More likely, though, the insanity will continue long enough for Ebersol and NBC to make a tidy profit and for Woods to retire at age 29 and buy Costa Rica. It's only funny money, after all. He might just as well spend it.

Baseball Directory

Major League Baseball

Address: 350 Park Avenue
            New York, NY 10022
Telephone: (212) 339-7800
Acting Commissioner/Chairman of the Executive
  Council: Bud Selig
Executive Director, Public Relations: Richard Levin

Major League Baseball Players Association

Address: 12 East 49th Street, 24th Floor
            New York, NY 10017
Telephone: (212) 826-0808
Executive Director: Donald Fehr
Director of Marketing: Judy Heeter

American League

American League Office

Address: 350 Park Avenue
            New York, NY 10022
Telephone: (212) 339-7600
President: Dr. Gene Budig
VP of Media Affairs and Administration: Phyllis Merhige

Baltimore Orioles

Address: Oriole Park at Camden Yards
            333 W Camden Street
            Baltimore, MD 21201
Telephone: (410) 685-9800
Stadium (Capacity): Camden Yards (48,262)
Managing Partner/Owner: Peter G. Angelos
Vice Chairmen: Thomas Clancy and Joseph Foss
Manager: Davey Johnson
Director of Public Relations: John Maroon

Boston Red Sox

Address: 4 Yawkey Way
            Fenway Park
            Boston, MA 02215
Telephone: (617) 267-9440
Stadium (Capacity): Fenway Park (33,871)
Majority Owner/CEO: John Harrington
Consultant: Lou Gorman
Executive VP and GM: Daniel F. Duquette
Manager: Kevin Kennedy
Vice President, Public Relations: Dick Bresciani

California Angels

Address: P.O. Box 2000
            Anaheim Stadium
            Anaheim, CA 92803
Telephone: (714) 937-7200
Stadium (Capacity): Anaheim Stadium (64,573)
Owners: Gene Autry; Walt Disney Company
General Manager: Bill Bavasi
Interim Manager: John McNamara
Director of Communications: Bill Robertson

Chicago White Sox

Address: Comiskey Park
            333 West 35th Street
            Chicago, IL 60616
Telephone: (312) 924-1000
Stadium (Capacity): Comiskey Park (44,321)
Chairman: Jerry Reinsdorf
General Manager: Ron Schueler
Manager: Terry Bevington
Director of Publc Relations: Doug Abel

Cleveland Indians

Address: Jacobs Field
            2401 Ontario Street
            Cleveland, OH 44115-4003
Telephone: (216) 420-4200
Stadium (Capacity): Jacobs Field (42,865)
Chairman of the Board and CEO: Richard Jacobs
Executive VP and General Manager: John Hart
Manager: Mike Hargrove
Vice President, Public Relations: Bob DiBiasio

Detroit Tigers

Address: 2121 Trumbull Ave.
            Tiger Stadium
            Detroit, MI 48216
Telephone: (313) 962-4000
Stadium (Capacity): Tiger Stadium (52,416)
Owner: Mike Ilitch
CEO and President: John McHale
Manager: Buddy Bell
Director of Public Relations: Tyler Barnes

Kansas City Royals

Address: P.O. Box 419969
            Kansas City, MO 64141
Telephone: (816) 921-2200
Stadium (Capacity): Kauffman Stadium (40,625)
Chairman of the Board and CEO: David D. Glass
General Manager: Herk Robinson
Manager: Bob Boone
Vice President, Marketing and Communications: Mike
  Levy

Milwaukee Brewers

Address: P.O. Box 3099
            Milwaukee, WI 53201-3099
Telephone: (414) 933-4114
Stadium (Capacity): Milwaukee County Stadium
  (53,192)
President and Chief Executive Officer: Bud Selig
Senior VP, Baseball Operations: Sal Bando
Manager: Phil Garner
Media Relations: Jon Greenberg

Minnesota Twins

Address: Hubert H. Humphrey Metrodome
            501 Chicago Avenue South
            Minneapolis, MN 55415
Telephone: (612) 375-1366
Stadium (Capacity): Hubert H. Humphrey Metrodome
  (48,678)
Owner: Carl Pohlad
General Manager: Terry Ryan
Manager: Tom Kelly
Manager of Media Relations: Sean Harlin

New York Yankees

Address: Yankee Stadium
            Bronx, NY 10451
Telephone: (718) 293-4300
Stadium (Capacity): Yankee Stadium (57,545)
Principal Owner: George Steinbrenner
VP and Executive Consul: David Sussman
General Manager: Bob Watson
Manager: Joe Torre
Director of Media Relations and Publicity: Rick
  Cerrone

American League (Cont.)

Oakland Athletics
Address: 7677 Oakport St., 2nd floor
             Oakland, CA 94621
Telephone: (510) 638-4900
Stadium (Capacity): Oakland-Alameda County
Coliseum (48,000)
Owners: Steve Schott, Ken Hofmann
Executive VP and General Manager: Sandy Alderson
Manager: Art Howe
Baseball Information Manager: Mike Selleck

Seattle Mariners
Address: P.O. Box 4100
             Seattle, WA 98104
Telephone: (206) 628-3555
Stadium (Capacity): The Kingdome (59,166)
Chairman: John Ellis
General Manager: Woody Woodward
Manager: Lou Piniella
Director of Public Relations: Dave Aust

Texas Rangers
Address: P.O. Box 90111
             Arlington, TX 76004·
Telephone: (817) 273-5222
Stadium (Capacity): The Ballpark in Arlington (49,178)
General Partners: Rusty Rose and Thomas Schieffer
General Manager: Doug Melvin
Manager: Johnny Oates
Vice President, Public Relations: John Blake

Toronto Blue Jays
Address: SkyDome
             1 Blue Jays Way, Suite 3200
             Toronto, Ontario, Canada M5V 1J1
Telephone: (416) 341-1000
Stadium (Capacity): SkyDome (50,516)
Chairman of the Board: Peter N.T. Widdrington
President and CEO: Paul Beeston
Executive VP of Baseball Operations: Gord Ash
Manager: Cito Gaston
Director of Public Relations: Howard Starkman

National League

National League Office
Address: 350 Park Avenue
             New York, NY 10022
Telephone: (212) 339-7700
President: Leonard Coleman
Director of Public Relations: Ricky Clemons

Atlanta Braves
Address: P.O. Box 4064
             Atlanta, GA 30302
Telephone: (404) 522-7630
Stadium (Capacity): TBA
Owner: Ted Turner
General Manager: John Schuerholz
Manager: Bobby Cox
Director of Public Relations: Jim Schultz

Chicago Cubs
Address: Wrigley Field
             1060 West Addison
             Chicago, IL 60613
Telephone: (312) 404-2827
Stadium (Capacity): Wrigley Field (38,765)
President and CEO: Andrew B. MacPhail
Executive VP of Business Operations: Mark McGuire
General Manager: Ed Lynch
Manager: Jim Riggleman
Director of Media Relations: Sharon Panozzo

Cincinnati Reds
Address: 100 Cinergy Field
             Cincinnati, OH 45202
Telephone: (513) 421-4510
Stadium (Capacity): Cinergy Field (52,952)
General Partner: Marge Schott
General Manager: James G. Bowden
Manager: Ray Knight
Publicity Director: Mike Ringering

Colorado Rockies
Address: 2001 Blake Street
             Denver, CO 80205
Telephone: (303) 292-0200
Stadium (Capacity): Coors Field (50,249)
President: Jerry McMorris
Senior VP of Business Operations: Keli McGregor
General Manager/Executive VP: Bob Gebhard
Manager: Don Baylor
Director of Public Relations: Mike Swanson

Florida Marlins
Address: 2267 N.W. 199th Street
             Miami, FL 33056
Telephone: (305) 626-7400
Stadium (Capacity): Pro Player Stadium (46,000)
Owner: H. Wayne Huizenga
Vice President and General Manager: David
Dombrowski
Manager: John Boles
Director of Media Relations: Ron Colangelo

Houston Astros
Address: P.O. Box 288
             Houston, TX 77001
Telephone: (713) 799-9500
Stadium (Capacity): Astrodome (54,313)
Chairman: Drayton McLane Jr.
General Manager: Gerry Hunsicker
Manager: Terry Collins
Director of Media Relations: Rob Matwick

Los Angeles Dodgers
Address: 1000 Elysian Park Avenue
             Los Angeles, CA 90012-1199
Telephone: (213) 224-1500
Stadium (Capacity): Dodger Stadium (56,000)
President: Peter O'Malley
Executive Vice President: Fred Claire
Manager: Bill Russell
Director of Publicity: Jay Lucas

Montreal Expos
Address: P.O. Box 500
             Station M
             Montreal
             Quebec, Canada H1V 3P2
Telephone: (514) 253-3434
Stadium (Capacity): Olympic Stadium (46,500)
President: Claude Brochu
Vice President and General Manager: Jim Beattie
Manager: Felipe Alou
Director, Media Relations: Peter Loyello

National League (Cont.)

New York Mets
Address: Shea Stadium
        123-01 Roosevelt Ave.
        Flushing, NY 11368
Telephone: (718) 507-6387
Stadium (Capacity): Shea Stadium (55,601)
Chairman: Nelson Doubleday
President and CEO: Fred Wilpon
Executive VP of Baseball Operations: Joe McIlvaine
Manager: Bobby Valentine
Director of Media Relations: Jay Horwitz

Philadelphia Phillies
Address: P.O. Box 7575
        Philadelphia, PA 19101-7575
Telephone: (215) 463-6000
Stadium (Capacity): Veterans Stadium (62,268)
President: Bill Giles
General Manager: Lee Thomas
Manager: Jim Fregosi
Vice President, Public Relations: Larry Shenk

Pittsburgh Pirates
Address: P.O. Box 7000
        Pittsburgh, PA 15212
Telephone: (412) 323-5000
Stadium (Capacity): Three Rivers Stadium (48,044)
CEO and Managing General Partner: Kevin McClatchy
General Manager: Cam Bonifay
Manager: Jim Leyland
Director of Media Relations: Jim Trdinich

St. Louis Cardinals
Address: Busch Stadium
        250 Stadium Plaza
        St. Louis, MO 63102
Telephone: (314) 421-3060
Stadium (Capacity): Busch Stadium (57,673)
President and CEO: Mark Lamping
General Manager: Walt Jocketty
Manager: Tony LaRussa
Director of Media Relations: Brian Bartow

San Diego Padres
Address: P.O. Box 2000
        San Diego, CA 92112
Telephone: (619) 283-4494
Stadium (Capacity): San Diego/Jack Murphy Stadium
  (60,000)
Chairman: John Moores
General Manager: Kevin Towers
Manager: Bruce Bochy
Director of Media Relations: Roger Riley

San Francisco Giants
Address: 3Com Park
        San Francisco, CA 94124
Telephone: (415) 468-3700
Stadium (Capacity): 3Com Park (63,000)
President/Managing General Partner: Peter Magowan
General Manager: Bob Quinn
Manager: Dusty Baker
VP, Communications: Bob Rose

Pro Football Directory

National Football League
Address: 410 Park Avenue
        New York, New York 10022
Telephone: (212) 758-1500
Commissioner: Paul Tagliabue
Director of Communications: Greg Aiello

National Football League Players Association
Address: 2021 L Street, N.W.
        Washington, D.C. 20036
Telephone: (202) 463-2200
Executive Director: Gene Upshaw
Director, Public Relations: Frank Woschitz

National Conference

Arizona Cardinals
Address: P.O. Box 888
        Phoenix, AZ 85001
Telephone: (602) 379-0101
Stadium (Capacity): Sun Devil Stadium (73,377)
President and Owner: Bill Bidwill
Vice President: Larry Wilson
Acting General Manager: Bob Ferguson
Head Coach: Vince Tobin
Director of Public Relations: Paul Jensen

Atlanta Falcons
Address: 1 Falcon Place
        Suwanee, GA 30174
Telephone: (770) 945-1111
Stadium (Capacity): Georgia Dome (71,228)
Chairman of the Board: Rankin M. Smith Sr.
President: Taylor W. Smith
Director of Player Personnel: Ken Herock
Coach: June Jones
Publicity Director: Charlie Taylor

Carolina Panthers
Address: Ericsson Stadium
        800 South Mint St.
        Charlotte, NC 28202
Telephone: (704) 358-7000
Stadium (Capacity): Ericsson Stadium
  (72,520)
Founder and Owner: Jerry Richardson
President: Mike McCormack
General Manager: Bill Polian
Coach: Dom Capers
Director of Communications: Charlie Dayton

Chicago Bears
Address: 250 N. Washington Road
        Lake Forest, IL 60045
Telephone: (847) 295-6600
Stadium (Capacity): Soldier Field (66,946)
President: Michael McCaskey
Coach: Dave Wannstedt
Director of Public Relations: Bryan Harlan

National Conference *(Cont.)*

Dallas Cowboys
Address: One Cowboys Parkway
            Irving, TX 75063
Telephone: (214) 556-9900
Stadium (Capacity): Texas Stadium (65,921)
Owner, President and General Manager: Jerry Jones
Coach: Barry Switzer
Public Relations Director: Rich Dalrymple

Detroit Lions
Address: 1200 Featherstone Road
            Pontiac, MI 48342
Telephone: (810) 335-4131
Stadium (Capacity): Pontiac Silverdome (80,368)
Chairman and President: William Clay Ford
Executive Vice President and COO: Chuck Schmidt
Coach: Wayne Fontes
Director of Media Relations: Mike Murray

Green Bay Packers
Address: 1265 Lombardi Avenue
            Green Bay, WI 54304
Telephone: (414) 496-5700
Stadium (Capacity): Lambeau Field (60,790)
President: Bob Harlan
General Manager: Ron Wolf
Coach: Mike Holmgren
Public Relations Director: Lee Remmel

Minnesota Vikings
Address: 9520 Viking Drive
            Eden Prairie, MN 55344
Telephone: (612) 828-6500
Stadium (Capacity): HHH Metrodome (63,000)
President: Roger L. Headrick
VP of Administrative and Team Operations: Jeff Diamond
Coach: Dennis Green
Public Relations Director: David Pelletier

New Orleans Saints
Address: 5800 Airline Highway
            Metairie, LA 70003
Telephone: (504) 733-0255
Stadium (Capacity): Louisiana Superdome (64,992)
Owner: Tom Benson
VP of Football Operations: Bill Kuharich
Executive VP/General Manager: Bill Kuharich
VP/Head Coach: Jim Mora
Director of Media Relations: Rusty Kasmiersky

New York Giants
Address: Giants Stadium
            East Rutherford, NJ 07073
Telephone: (201) 935-8111
Stadium (Capacity): Giants Stadium (78,148)
President and co-CEO: Wellington T. Mara
Chairman and co-CEO: Preston Robert Tisch
Senior VP and General Manager: George Young
Coach: Dan Reeves
VP of Public Relations: Pat Hanlon

Philadelphia Eagles
Address: Veterans Stadium
            3501 South Broad Street
            Philadelphia, PA 19148
Telephone: (215) 463-2500
Stadium (Capacity): Veterans Stadium (65,352)
Owner: Jeffrey Lurie
Senior VP: Joe Banner
Senior VP/Chief Financial Officer: Mimi Box
Director of Football Operations: Dick Daniels
Coach: Ray Rhodes
Director of Public Relations: Ron Howard

St. Louis Rams
Address: One Rams Way
            St. Louis, MO 63045
Telephone: (314) 982-7267
Stadium (Capacity): Trans World Dome (66,000)
Owner and Chairman: Georgia Frontiere
Vice-Chairman and Owner: Stan Kroenke
President: John Shaw
Coach: Rich Brooks
Director of Public Relations: Rick Smith

San Francisco 49ers
Address: 4949 Centennial Boulevard
            Santa Clara, CA 95054
Telephone: (408) 562-4949
Stadium (Capacity): 3Com Park (70,207)
Owner: Edward J. DeBartolo Jr.
General Manager: Dwight Clark
Coach: George Seifert
Public Relations Director: Rodney Knox

Tampa Bay Buccaneers
Address: One Buccaneer Place
            Tampa, FL 33607
Telephone: (813) 870-2700
Stadium (Capacity): Houlihan's Stadium (74,321)
Owner: Malcolm Glazer
Coach: Tony Dungy
Director of Public Relations: Chip Namias

Washington Redskins
Address: 21300 Redskin Park Drive
            Ashburn, VA 20147
Telephone: (703) 478-8900
Stadium (Capacity): RFK Memorial Stadium (56,454)
Owner: Jack Kent Cooke
General Manager: Charley Casserly
Coach: Norv Turner
Director of Public Relations: Mike McCall

American Conference

Buffalo Bills
Address: One Bills Drive
            Orchard Park, NY 14127
Telephone: (716) 648-1800
Stadium (Capacity): Rich Stadium (80,024)
President: Ralph C. Wilson Jr.
Executive VP/General Manager: John Butler
Coach: Marv Levy
Director of Media Relations: Scott Berchtold

Baltimore Ravens
Address: 1101 Owings Mills Blvd.
            Owings Mills, MD 21117
Telephone: (410) 654-6200
Stadium (Capacity): Memorial Stadium (65,248)
President: Art Modell
Coach: Ted Marchibroda
VP and Director of Public Relations: Kevin Byrne

American Conference *(Cont.)*

Cincinnati Bengals
Address: One Bengals Drive
        Cincinnati, OH 45204
Telephone: (513) 621-3550
Stadium (Capacity): Cinergy Field (60,389)
President and General Manager: Mike Brown
Vice President: John Sawyer
Coach: Dave Shula
Director of Public Relations: Jack Brennan

Denver Broncos
Address: 13655 Broncos Parkway
        Englewood, CO 80112
Telephone: (303) 649-9000
Stadium (Capacity): Mile High Stadium (76,273)
President/CEO: Pat Bowlen
General Manager: John Beake
Coach: Mike Shanahan
Director of Media Relations: Jim Saccomano

Houston Oilers
Address: 8030 El Rio
        Houston, TX 77054
Telephone: (713) 881-3500
Stadium (Capacity): Astrodome (59,969)
President: K.S. (Bud) Adams, Jr.
General Manager: Floyd Reese
Coach: Jeff Fisher
Director of Media Relations: Dave Pearson

Indianapolis Colts
Address: P.O. Box 535000
        Indianapolis, IN 46253
Telephone: (317) 297-2658
Stadium (Capacity): RCA Dome (60,272)
President Emeritus: Robert Irsay
Senior Executive VP/General Manager/COO: Jim Irsay
Coach: Lindy Infante
Public Relations Director: Craig Kelley

Jacksonville Jaguars
Address: One Stadium Place
        Jacksonville, FL 32202
Telephone: (904) 633-6000
Stadium (Capacity): Jacksonville Municipal Stadium
(73,000)
Owner: J. Wayne Weaver
President and COO: David Seldin
Coach: Tom Coughlin
Executive Director of Communications: Dan Edwards

Kansas City Chiefs
Address: One Arrowhead Drive
        Kansas City, MO 64129
Telephone: (816) 924-9300
Stadium (Capacity): Arrowhead Stadium (79,101)
Founder: Lamar Hunt
CEO/President/General Manager: Carl Peterson
Coach: Marty Schottenheimer
Public Relations Director: Bob Moore

Miami Dolphins
Address: 7500 S.W. 30th Street
        Davie, FL 33314
Telephone: (305) 452-7000
Stadium (Capacity): Pro Player Stadium (75,235)
Chairman of the Board/Owner: H. Wayne Huizenga
President and COO: Eddie J. Jones
General Manager/Head Coach: Jimmy Johnson
Senior Director of Media Relations: Harvey Greene

New England Patriots
Address: Foxboro Stadium
        60 Washington St.
        Foxboro, MA 02035
Telephone: (508) 543-8200
Stadium (Capacity): Foxboro Stadium (60,292)
President and CEO: Robert K. Kraft
VP Owners Representative: Jonathan Kraft
VP Business Operations: Andy Wasynczuk
Coach: Bill Parcells
Dir. of Public and Community Relations: Donald Lowery

New York Jets
Address: 1000 Fulton Avenue
        Hempstead, NY 11550
Telephone: (516) 560-8100
Stadium (Capacity): Giants Stadium (77,716)
Chairman of the Board: Leon Hess
Director of Player Personnel: Dick Haley
Coach: Rich Kotite
Director of Public Relations: Frank Ramos

Oakland Raiders
Address: 1220 Harbor Bay Parkway
        Alameda, CA 94502
Telephone: (510) 864-5000
Stadium (Capacity): Oakland-Alameda County
Coliseum (62,500)
President of the General Partner: Al Davis
Coach: Mike White
Executive Assistant: Al LoCasale
Director of Public Relations: Mike Taylor

Pittsburgh Steelers
Address: Three Rivers Stadium
        300 Stadium Circle
        Pittsburgh, PA 15212
Telephone: (412) 323-1200
Stadium (Capacity): Three Rivers Stadium (59,600)
President: Dan Rooney
Director of Football Operations: Tom Donahoe
Coach: Bill Cowher
Media Relations Coordinator: Rob Boulware

San Diego Chargers
Address: San Diego Jack Murphy Stadium
        P.O. Box 609609
        San Diego, CA 92160
Telephone: (619) 280-2111
Stadium (Capacity): San Diego Jack Murphy Stadium
(61,863)
Chairman of the Board/President: Alex G. Spanos
General Manager: Bobby Beathard
Coach: Bobby Ross
Director of Public Relations: Bill Johnston

Seattle Seahawks
Address: 11220 N.E. 53rd Street
        Kirkland, WA 98033
Telephone: (206) 827-9777
Stadium (Capacity): The Kingdome (66,400)
Owner: Ken Behring
President: David Behring
Coach: Dennis Erickson
VP of Administration and Communications: Gary Wright
Director of Public Relations: Dave Neubert

Other Leagues

Canadian Football League
Address: 110 Eglinton Avenue West, 5th floor
            Toronto, Ontario M4R 1A3, Canada
Telephone: (416) 322-9650
Commissioner: Larry W. Smith
Communications Manager: Jim Neish

World League of American Football
Address: 410 Park Avenue
            New York, NY 10022
Telephone: (212) 758-1500
President: Oliver Luck (London)
Chief Operating Officer: Dick Regan (London)
Director of Communications: Pete Abitante

Pro Basketball Directory

National Basketball Association
Address: 645 Fifth Avenue
            New York, NY 10022
Telephone: (212) 826-7000
Commissioner: David Stern
Deputy Commissioner: Russell Granik
Group VP and GM, Communications Group: Brian McIntyre

National Basketball Association Players Association
Address: 1775 Broadway
            Suite 2401
            New York, NY 10019
Telephone: (212) 333-7510
Executive Director: William Hunter

Atlanta Hawks
Address: One CNN Center, South Tower
            Suite 405
            Atlanta, GA 30303
Telephone: (404) 827-3800
Arena (Capacity): The Omni (16,378)
Owner: Ted Turner
President: Stan Kasten
General Manager: Pete Babcock
Coach: Lenny Wilkens
Director of Media Relations: Arthur Triche

Boston Celtics
Address: 151 Merrimac Street
            Boston, MA 02114
Telephone: (617) 523-6050
Arena (Capacity): FleetCenter (18,600)
Owner and Chairman of the Board: Paul Gaston
President: Arnold (Red) Auerbach
Executive VP & General Manager: Jan Volk
Coach: M. L. Carr
Director of Public Relations: R. Jeffrey Twiss

Charlotte Hornets
Address: 100 Hive Drive
            Charlotte, NC 28217
Telephone: (704) 357-0252
Arena (Capacity): Charlotte Coliseum (24,042)
Owner: George Shinn
Coach: Dave Cowens
Director of Media Relations: Harold Kaufman

Chicago Bulls
Address: 1901 W. Madison
            Chicago, IL 60612
Telephone: (312) 455-4000
Arena (Capacity): United Center (21,711)
Chairman: Jerry Reinsdorf
General Manager: Jerry Krause
Coach: Phil Jackson
Director of Media Services: Tim Hallam

Cleveland Cavaliers
Address: One Center Court
            Cleveland, OH 44115
Telephone: (216) 420-2262
Arena (Capacity): Gund Arena (20,562)
Chairman: Gordon Gund
President/COO, Team Division: Wayne Embry
Coach: Mike Fratello
Director of Media Relations: Bob Zink

Dallas Mavericks
Address: Reunion Arena
            777 Sports Street
            Dallas, TX 75207
Telephone: (214) 748-1808
Arena (Capacity): Reunion Arena (17,502)
Owners: Ross Perot Jr, David McDavid, Frank Zaccanelli
VP of Basketball Operations: Keith Grant
Coach: Jim Cleamons
VP of Communications Kevin Sullivan

Denver Nuggets
Address: McNichols Sports Arena
            1635 Clay Street
            Denver, CO 80204
Telephone: (303) 893-6700
Arena (Capacity): McNichols Sports Arena (17,171)
Owners: Ascent Entertainment Group
President and Coach: Bernie Bickerstaff
General Manager: Todd Eley
Media Relations Director: Tommy Sheppard

Detroit Pistons
Address: The Palace of Auburn Hills
            Two Championship Drive
            Auburn Hills, MI 48326
Telephone: (810) 377-0100
Arena (Capacity): The Palace of Auburn Hills (21,454)
Owner: William M. Davidson
VP of Basketball Operations: Rick Sund
Coach: Doug Collins
VP, Public Relations: Matt Dobek

Golden State Warriors
Address: 1221 Broadway, 20th floor
            Oakland, CA 94612
Telephone: (510) 986-2200
Arena (Capacity): San Jose Arena (18,500)
Owner and CEO: Christopher Cohan
General Manager: Dave Twardzik
Coach: Rick Adelman
Director of Communications: Julie Marvel

Houston Rockets
Address: The Summit
            Ten Greenway Plaza
            Houston, TX 77046
Telephone: (713) 627-3865
Arena (Capacity): The Summit (16,285)
Owner: Leslie Alexander
Sr Executive VP of Business Operations: John Thomas
Sr Executive VP of Basketball Affairs: Robert Barr
Executive VP of Basketball Affairs: Carroll Dawson
Coach: Rudy Tomjanovich
Manager of Media Services: Tim Frank

Indiana Pacers
Address: 300 E. Market Street
            Indianapolis, IN 46204
Telephone: (317) 263-2100
Arena (Capacity): Market Square Arena (16,530)
Owners: Melvin Simon and Herbert Simon
President: Donnie Walsh
Coach: Larry Brown
Media Relations Director: David Benner

Los Angeles Clippers
Address: L.A. Memorial Sports Arena
            3939 S. Figueroa Street
            Los Angeles, CA 90037
Telephone: (213) 748-8000
Arena (Capacity): L.A. Memorial Sports Arena (16,021)
Owner: Donald T. Sterling
VP of Basketball Operations: Elgin Baylor
Coach: Bill Fitch
VP of Communications: Joe Safety

Los Angeles Lakers
Address: Great Western Forum
            3900 West Manchester Boulevard
            Inglewood, CA 90306
Telephone: (310) 419-3100
Arena (Capacity): The Great Western Forum (17,505)
Owner: Dr. Jerry Buss
General Manager: Jerry West
Coach: Del Harris
Director of Public Relations: John Black

Miami Heat
Address: Sun Trust International Center
            One S.E. 3rd Ave., Suite 2300
            Miami, FL 33131
Telephone: (305) 577-4328
Arena (Capacity): Miami Arena (15,200)
Managing General Partner: Mickey Arison
Executive VP/Business Operations: Pauline Winick
Executive VP/Basketball Operations: Dave Wohl
President and Coach: Pat Riley
Director of Public Relations: Wayne Witt

Milwaukee Bucks
Address: The Bradley Center
            1001 N. Fourth Street
            Milwaukee, WI 53203
Telephone: (414) 227-0500
Arena (Capacity): The Bradley Center (18,633)
Owner: Herb Kohl
General Manager: Mike Dunleavy
Coach: Chris Ford
Public Relations Director: Bill King II

Minnesota Timberwolves
Address: 600 First Avenue North
            Minneapolis, MN 55403
Telephone: (612) 673-1602
Arena (Capacity): Target Center (19,006)
Owner: Glen Taylor
VP of Basketball Operations: Kevin McHale
General Manager/Coach: Phil (Flip) Saunders
Manager of PR/Communications: Kent Wipf

New Jersey Nets
Address: 405 Murray Hill Parkway
            East Rutherford, NJ 07073
Telephone: (201) 935-8888
Arena (Capacity): Continental Airlines Arena (20,029)
Chairman/CEO: Henry Taub
Vice President of Basketball Operations and Coach:
  John Calipari
Director of Public Relations: John Mertz

New York Knickerbockers
Address: Madison Square Garden
            Two Pennsylvania Plaza
            New York, NY 10121
Telephone: (212) 465-6499
Arena (Capacity): Madison Square Garden (19,763)
Owner: ITT/Sheraton and Cablevision
President: David W. Checketts
President and General Manager: Ernie Grunfeld
Coach: Jeff Van Gundy
VP of Public Relations: Chris Weiller

Orlando Magic
Address: P.O. Box 76
            Orlando, FL 32802
Telephone: (407) 649-3200
Arena (Capacity): Orlando Arena (17,248)
Owner: Rich DeVos
General Manager: Pat Williams
Coach: Brian Hill
Senior Director of Communications: Alex Martins

Philadelphia 76ers
Address: Veterans Stadium
            P.O. Box 25040
            Broad Street and Pattison Avenue
            Philadelphia, PA 19147
Telephone: (215) 339-7600
Arena (Capacity): CoreStates Center (21,000)
Owner and President: Pat Croce
General Manager: Brad Greenberg
Coach: Johnny Davis
Public Relations Director: Jodi Silverman

Phoenix Suns
Address: P.O. Box 1369
            Phoenix, AZ 85001
Telephone: (602) 379-7867
Arena (Capacity): America West Arena (19,023)
Owner: Jerry Colangelo
Coach: Cotton Fitzsimmons
Media Relations Director: Julie Fie

Portland Trail Blazers
Address: One Center Court
            Suite 200
            Portland, OR 97227
Telephone: (503) 234-9291
Arena (Capacity): Rose Garden Arena (21,500)
Chairman of the Board: Paul Allen
President and General Manager: Bob Whitsitt
Coach: P.J. Carlesimo
Director of Sports Communication: John Christiansen

Sacramento Kings
Address: One Sports Parkway
Sacramento, CA 95834
Telephone: (916) 928-0000
Arena (Capacity): ARCO Arena (17,317)
Managing General Partner: Jim Thomas
VP of Basketball Operations: Geoff Petrie
Coach: Garry St. Jean
Director of Media Relations: Travis Stanley

San Antonio Spurs
Address: AlamoDome
100 Montana
San Antonio, TX 78203
Telephone: (210) 554-7787
Arena (Capacity): AlamoDome (20,662)
Chairman: Peter Holt
President and CEO: John C. Diller
Coach: Bob Hill
Director of Media Services: Tom James

Seattle Supersonics
Address: 190 Queen Anne Avenue North
Suite 200
Seattle, WA 98109
Telephone: (206) 281-5847
Arena (Capacity): KeyArena (17,100)
Owner: Barry Ackerley
President and General Manager: Wally Walker
Coach: George Karl
Director of Media Relations: Cheri White

Toronto Raptors
Address: 20 Bay Street, Suite 1702
Toronto, Ontario, Canada M5J 2N8
Telephone: (416) 214-2255
Arena (Capacity): SkyDome (25,356)
Owner: Bitove Investments, Inc., Slaight Investments
Inc., Bank of Nova Scotia, Isiah Thomas, the
Granovsky family, David Peterson
Executive VP of Basketball Operations: Isiah Thomas
Coach: Darrell Walker
Senior Manager, Sports Communication: Rick Kaplan

Utah Jazz
Address: 301 West So. Temple
Salt Lake City, UT 84101
Telephone: (801) 575-7800
Arena (Capacity): Delta Center (20,600)
Owner: Larry H. Miller
General Manager: R. Tim Howells
Coach: Jerry Sloan
Director of Media Relations: Kim Turner

Vancouver Grizzlies
Address: General Motors Place
800 Griffiths Way
Vancouver, B.C., Canada V6B 6G1
Telephone: (604) 899-4666
Arena (Capacity): General Motors Place (19,139)
Owner: Orca Bay Sports and Entertainment
General Manager: Stu Jackson
Coach: Brian Winters
Director of Media Relations: Steve Frost

Washington Bullets
Address: One Harry S. Truman Drive
Landover, MD 20785
Telephone: (301) 773-2255
Arena (Capacity): USAir Arena (18,756)
Owner: Abe Pollin
General Manager and Vice President: Wes Unseld
Coach: Jim Lynam
Director of Public Relations: Maureen Lewis

Other League

Continental Basketball Association
Address: 701 Market Street, Suite 140
St. Louis, MO 63101
Telephone: (314) 621-7222
Commissioner: Steve Patterson
VP of Public Relations: Brett Meister

Hockey Directory

National Hockey League
Address: 1251 Avenue of the Americas
47th floor
New York, NY 10020-1198
Telephone: (212) 789-2000
Commissioner: Gary Bettman
Senior VP and Chief Operating Officer: Steven Solomon
Vice President, Public Relations: Arthur Pincus

National Hockey League Players Association
Address: 777 Bay Street, Suite 2400
Toronto, Ontario, Canada M5G 2C8
Telephone: (416) 408-4040
Executive Director: Bob Goodenow

Mighty Ducks of Anaheim
Address: P.O. Box 61077
Anaheim, CA 92803-6177
Telephone: (714) 704-2700
Arena (Capacity): Arrowhead Pond of Anaheim (17,174)
Owner: Disney Sports Enterprises
General Manager: Jack Ferreira
Coach: Ron Wilson
Director of Media Relations: Bill Robertson

Boston Bruins
Address: One FleetCenter
Suite 250
Boston, MA 02114-1303
Telephone: (617) 624-1909
Arena (Capacity): FleetCenter (17,565)
Owner and Governor: Jeremy M. Jacobs
Alternative Governor, President and General
Manager: Harry Sinden
Coach: Steve Kasper
Director of Media Relations: Heidi Holland

Buffalo Sabres
Address: Marine Midland Arena
One Seymour H. Knox III Plaza
Buffalo, NY 14203
Telephone: (716) 855-4100
Arena (Capacity): Marine Midland Arena (18,500)
Chairman of the Board: Seymour H. Knox III
President and CEO: Douglas G. Moss
General Manager: John Muckler
Coach: Ted Nolan
Director of Public Relations: Jeff Holbrook

Calgary Flames
Address: Canadian Airlines Saddledome
555 Saddledome Drive, SE
Calgary, Alberta T2G 2W1
Telephone: (403) 777-2177
Arena (Capacity): Canadian Airlines Saddledome (20,000)
Owners: Grant A. Bartlett, Harley N. Hotchkiss, N. Murray Edwards, Ronald V. Joyce, Alvin G. Libin, Allan P. Markin, J.R. McCaig, Byron J. Seaman, Daryl K. Seaman
President: Ron Bremner
General Manager: Al Coates
Director of Hockey Operations: Al MacNeil
Coach: Pierre Page
Director of Public Relations: Rick Skaggs

Chicago Blackhawks
Address: United Center
1901 W. Madison Street
Chicago, IL 60612
Telephone: (312) 455-7000
Arena (Capacity): United Center (20,500)
President: William W. Wirtz
General Manager: Robert Pulford
Coach: Craig Hartsburg
Public Relations Director: Jim DeMaria

Colorado Avalanche
Address: McNichols Sports Arena
1635 Clay Street
Denver, CO 80204
Telephone: (303) 893-6700
Arena (Capacity): McNichols Sports Arena (16,061)
Owner: Ascent Entertainment Group
General Manager: Pierre Lacroix
Coach: Marc Crawford
Director of Press Relations: Jean Martineau

Dallas Stars
Address: 211 Cowboys Parkway
Irving, TX 75063
Telephone: (972) 868-2890
Arena (Capacity): Reunion Arena (16,924)
Owner: Thomas O. Hicks
General Manager: Bob Gainey
Coach: Ken Hitchcock
Director of Public Relations: Larry Kelly

Detroit Red Wings
Address: Joe Louis Sports Arena
600 Civic Center Drive
Detroit, MI 48226
Telephone: (313) 396-7544
Arena (Capacity): Joe Louis Sports Arena (19,875)
Senior Vice President: Jim Devellano
Director of Player Personnel and Head Coach: Scott Bowman
Assistant General Manager: Ken Holland
Director of Public Relations: TBA

Edmonton Oilers
Address: 11230 110th Street, 2nd floor
Edmonton, Alberta T5G 3G8
Telephone: (403) 474-8561
Arena (Capacity): Edmonton Coliseum (17,103)
Owner and Governor: Peter Pocklington
General Manager: Glen Sather
Coach: Ron Low
Director of Public Relations: Bill Tuele

Florida Panthers
Address: 100 Northeast Third Avenue, 2nd floor
Fort Lauderdale, FL 33301
Telephone: (954) 768-1900
Arena (Capacity): Miami Arena (14,703)
Owner: H. Wayne Huizenga
General Manager: Bryan Murray
Coach: Doug MacLean
Director of Media Relations: Greg Bouris

Hartford Whalers
Address: 242 Trumbull Street, 8th floor
Hartford, CT 06103
Telephone: (203) 728-3366
Arena (Capacity): Hartford Civic Center Veterans Memorial Coliseum (15,635)
Owner: KTR Hockey Ltd. Partnership
President and General Manager: Jim Rutherford
Assistant General Manager: Terry McDonnell
Coach: Paul Maurice
Director of Public Relations: Chris Brown

Los Angeles Kings
Address: The Great Western Forum
3900 West Manchester Boulevard
P.O. Box 17013
Inglewood, CA 90308
Telephone: (310) 419-3160
Arena (Capacity): The Great Western Forum (16,005)
President: Tim Leiweke
General Manager: Sam McMaster
Coach: Larry Robinson
Director of Public Relations: Nick Salata

Montreal Canadiens
Address: Molson Centre
1260 de la Gauchetiere West
Montreal, Quebec H3B 5E8
Telephone: (514) 932-2582
Arena (Capacity): Molson Centre (21,000)
Chairman of the Board, President and Governor: Ronald Corey
General Manager: Regean Houle
Coach: Mario Tremblay
Director of Communications: Donald Beauchamp

New Jersey Devils
Address: Continental Airlines Arena
P.O. Box 504
East Rutherford, NJ 07073
Telephone: (201) 935-6050
Arena (Capacity): Continental Airlines Arena (19,040)
Chairman: John J. McMullen
President and General Manager: Lou Lamoriello
Coach: Jacques Lemaire
Director of Public Relations: Mike Gilbert

New York Islanders
Address: Nassau Veterans' Memorial Coliseum
Uniondale, NY 11553
Telephone: (516) 794-4100
Arena (Capacity): Nassau Veterans' Memorial Coliseum (16,297)
Co-Chairmen: Robert Rosenthal, Stephen Walsh
General Manager and Coach: Mike Milbury
Media Relations Director: Ginger Killian

New York Rangers
Address: Madison Square Garden
             2 Pennsylvania Plaza
             New York, NY 10121
Telephone: (212) 465-6000
Arena (Capacity): Madison Square Garden (18,200)
Owner: ITT Cablevision
President and General Manager: Neil Smith
Coach: Colin Campbell
Director of Communications: John Rosasco

Ottawa Senators
Address: 301 Moodie Drive
             Suite 200
             Nepean, Ontario K2H 9C4
Telephone: (613) 721-0115
Arena (Capacity): The Corel Centre (18,500)
Founder: Bruce M. Firestone
Chairman and Governor: Rod Bryden
President and CEO: Roy Mlakar
General Manager: Pierre Gauthier
Coach: Jacques Martin
Director, Media Relations: Phil Legault

Philadelphia Flyers
Address: CoreStates Center
             One CoreStates Complex
             Philadelphia, PA 19148
Telephone: (215) 465-4500
Arena (Capacity): CoreStates Center (19,500)
Majority Owners: Ed Snider and family
Limited Partners: Sylvan and Fran Tobin
President and General Manager: Bob Clarke
Coach: Terry Murray
Vice President of Public Relations: Mark Piazza

Phoenix Coyotes
Address: One Renaissance Square
             2 North Central, Suite 1930
             Phoenix, AZ 85004
Telephone: (602) 379-2800
Arena (Capacity): America West Arena (TBA)
CEO and Governor: Richard Burke
President and Alternate Governor: Steven Gluckstern
Executive VP of Hockey Operations: Bobby Smith
General Manager: John Paddock
Coach: Don Hay
Director of Media and Player Relations: Richard Nairn

Pittsburgh Penguins
Address: Civic Arena
             300 Auditorium Place, Gate 9
             Pittsburgh, PA 15219
Telephone: (412) 642-1800
Arena (Capacity): Civic Arena (17,189)
Ownership: Howard Baldwin, Morris Belzberg,
  Thomas Ruta
General Manager: Craig Patrick
Coach: Eddie Johnston
Director of Media Relations: Steve Bovino

St. Louis Blues
Address: Kiel Center
             P.O. Box 66792
             St. Louis, MO 63166-6792
Telephone: (314) 622-2500
Arena (Capacity): Kiel Center (19,260)
President and CEO: Jack Quinn
General Manager and Coach: Mike Keenan
Director of Public Relations: Jeff Trammel

San Jose Sharks
Address: San Jose Arena
             525 West Santa Clara Street
             San Jose, CA 95113
Telephone: (408) 287-7070
Arena (Capacity): San Jose Arena (17,190)
Owners: George and Gordon Gund
Executive Vice President and General Manager: Dean
  Lombardi
Coach: Al Simms
Director of Media Relations: Ken Arnold

Tampa Bay Lightning
Address: 501 East Kennedy Boulevard
             Suite 175
             Tampa, FL 33602
Telephone: (813) 229-2658
Arena (Capacity): Ice Palace (19,500)
President: Steve Oto
General Manager: Phil Esposito
Coach: Terry Crisp
VP of Communications: Gerry Helper

Toronto Maple Leafs
Address: Maple Leaf Gardens
             60 Carlton Street
             Toronto, Ontario M5B 1L1
Telephone: (416) 977-1641
Arena (Capacity): Maple Leaf Gardens (15,728)
CEO: Steve A. Stavro
General Manager: Cliff Fletcher
Coach: Mike Murphy
Director of Business Operations and Communications:
  Bob Stellick

Vancouver Canucks
Address: General Motors Place
             800 Griffiths Way
             Vancouver, B.C. V6B 6G1
Telephone: (604) 899-4600
Arena (Capacity): General Motors Place (18,422)
Chairman and CEO: Arthur Griffiths
Vice Chairman: John E. McCaw Jr
President and C.O.O.: John Chaple
President, GM, and Alternate Governor: Pat Quinn
Coach: Tom Renney
Mgr. of Hockey Information: Devin Smith
Public and Community Relations Coordinator:
  Veronica Varhaug

Washington Capitals
Address: USAir Arena
             Landover, MD 20785
Telephone: (301) 386-7000
Arena (Capacity): USAir Arena (18,130)
Board of Directors: Abe Pollin, David P. Binderman,
  Stewart L. Binderman, James E. Cafritz, A. James
  Clark, Albert Cohen, J. Martin Irving, James T.
  Lewis, R. Robert Linowes, Arthur K. Mason, Dr.
  Jack Meshel, David M. Osnos, Richard M. Patrick
VP and General Manager: Dave Poile
Coach: Jim Schoenfeld
VP of Communications: Matt Williams

College Sports Directory

NATIONAL COLLEGIATE ATHLETIC ASSOCIATION (NCAA)
Address: 6201 College Boulevard
             Overland Park, KS 66211
Telephone: (913) 339-1906
Executive Director: Cedric Dempsey
Director of Public Information: Kathryn Reith

ATLANTIC COAST CONFERENCE
Address: P.O. Drawer ACC
             Greensboro, NC 27419-6999
Telephone: (910) 854-8787
Commissioner: Eugene F. Corrigan
Director of Media Relations: Brian Morrison

Clemson University
Address: Clemson, SC 29633
Nickname: Tigers
Telephone: (864) 656-2114
Football Stadium (Capacity): Clemson Memorial
  Stadium (81,473)
Basketball Arena (Capacity): Littlejohn Coliseum (11,020)
President: Constantine Curris
Athletic Director: Bobby Robinson
Football Coach: Tommy West
Basketball Coach: Rick Barnes
Sports Information Director: Tim Bourret

Duke University
Address: Durham, NC 27708
Nickname: Blue Devils
Telephone: (919) 684-2633
Football Stadium (Capacity): Wallace Wade Stadium
  (33,941)
Basketball Arena (Capacity): Cameron Indoor
  Stadium (9,314)
President: Nan Keohane
Athletic Director: Tom Butters
Football Coach: Fred Goldsmith
Basketball Coach: Mike Krzyzewski
Sports Information Director: Mike Cragg

Florida State University
Address: P.O. Box 2195
             Tallahassee, FL 32316
Nickname: Seminoles
Telephone: (904) 644-1403
Football Stadium (Capacity): Doak S. Campbell
  Stadium (77,500)
Basketball Arena (Capacity): Leon County Civic
  Center (12,500)
President: Sandy D'Alemberte
Athletic Director: Dave Hart
Football Coach: Bobby Bowden
Basketball Coach: Pat Kennedy
Sports Information Director: Rob Wilson

Georgia Tech
Address: 150 Bobby Dodd Way
             Atlanta, GA 30332
Nickname: Yellow Jackets
Telephone: (404) 894-5445
Football Stadium (Capacity): Bobby Dodd
  Stadium/Grant Field (46,000)
Basketball Arena (Capacity): Alexander Memorial
  Coliseum at McDonald's Center (10,000)
President: G. Wayne Clough
Athletic Director: Dr. Homer Rice
Football Coach: George O'Leary
Basketball Coach: Bobby Cremins
Sports Information Director: Mike Finn

University of Maryland
Address: P.O. Box 295
             College Park, MD 20741
Nickname: Terrapins
Telephone: (301) 314-7064
Football Stadium (Capacity): Byrd Stadium (48,055)
Basketball Arena (Capacity): Cole Fieldhouse
  (14,500)
President: Dr. William E. Kirwin
Athletic Director: Deborah Yow
Football Coach: Mark Duffner
Basketball Coach: Gary Williams
Sports Information Director: Chuck Walsh

University of North Carolina
Address: P.O. Box 2126
             Chapel Hill, NC 27514
Nickname: Tar Heels
Telephone: (919) 962-2123
Football Stadium (Capacity): Kenan Memorial
  Stadium (52,000)
Basketball Arena (Capacity): Dean E. Smith Center
  (21,572)
Chancellor: Dr. Michael K. Hooker
Athletic Director: John Swofford
Football Coach: Mack Brown
Basketball Coach: Dean Smith
Sports Information Director: Rick Brewer

North Carolina State University
Address: Box 8501
             Raleigh, NC 27695
Nickname: Wolfpack
Telephone: (919) 515-2102
Football Stadium (Capacity): Carter-Finley Stadium
  (52,000)
Basketball Arena (Capacity): Reynolds Coliseum
  (12,400)
Chancellor: Dr. Larry K. Monteith
Acting Athletic Director: Les Robinson
Football Coach: Mike O'Cain
Basketball Coach: Herb Sendek
Sports Information Director: Mark Bockelman

University of Virginia
Address: P.O. Box 3785
             Charlottesville, VA 22903
Nickname: Cavaliers
Telephone: (804) 982-5151
Football Stadium (Capacity): Scott Stadium (42,000)
Basketball Arena (Capacity): University Hall (8,500)
President: John Casteen III
Athletic Director: Terry Holland
Football Coach: George Welsh
Men's Basketball Coach: Jeff Jones
Women's Basketball Coach: Debbie Ryan
Sports Information Director: Rich Murray

Wake Forest University
Address: P.O. Box 7426
             Winston-Salem, NC 27109
Nickname: Demon Deacons
Telephone: (910) 759-5640
Football Stadium (Capacity): Groves Stadium
  (31,500)
Basketball Arena (Capacity): Lawrence Joel
  Memorial Coliseum (14,407)
President: Dr. Thomas K. Hearn Jr.
Athletic Director: Ron Wellman
Football Coach: Jim Caldwell
Basketball Coach: Dave Odom
Sports Information Director: John Justus

BIG EAST CONFERENCE

Address: 56 Exchange Terrace, 5th floor
Providence, RI 02903
Telephone: (401) 272-9108
Commissioner: Michael A. Tranghese
Associate Commissioner for Public Relations: John Paquette

Boston College

Address: Chestnut Hill, MA 02167
Nickname: Eagles
Telephone: (617) 552-3004
Football Stadium (Capacity): Alumni Stadium (44,500)
Basketball Arena (Capacity): Silvio O. Conte Forum (8,604)
President: Rev. William P. Leahy, S.J.
Athletic Director: Chet Gladchuk
Football Coach: Dan Henning
Basketball Coach: Jim O'Brien
Sports Information Director: Reid Oslin

University of Connecticut

Address: 2095 Hillside Road
Storrs, CT 06269-3078
Nickname: Huskies
Telephone: (203) 486-2725
Football Stadium (Capacity): Memorial Stadium (16,200)
Basketball Arena (Capacity): Gampel Pavilion (8,241)
President: Philip E. Austin
Athletic Director: Lew Perkins
Football Coach: Skip Holtz
Men's Basketball Coach: Jim Calhoun
Women's Basketball Coach: Geno Auriemma
Sports Information Director: Tim Tolokan
Note: Division I-AA football.

Georgetown University

Address: McDonough Arena
Box 571121
Washington, DC 20057-1121
Nickname: Hoyas
Telephone: (202) 687-2435
Football Stadium (Capacity): Kehoe Field (2,000)
Basketball Arena (Capacity): USAir Arena (19,035)
President: Rev. Leo J. O'Donovan, S.J.
Senior Athletic Director: Francis X. Rienzo
Athletic Director: Joseph Lang
Football Coach: Robert Benson
Basketball Coach: John Thompson
Sports Information Director: Bill Shapland (basketball), Bill Hurd
Note: Division I-AA football.

University of Miami

Address: One Hurricane Drive
Coral Gables, FL 33146
Nickname: Hurricanes
Telephone: (305) 284-3244
Football Stadium (Capacity): Orange Bowl (72,319)
Basketball Arena (Capacity): Miami Arena (15,508)
President: Edward Foote II
Athletic Director: Paul Dee
Football Coach: Butch Davis
Basketball Coach: Leonard Hamilton
Sports Information Director: Bob Burda

University of Pittsburgh

Address: Dept. of Athletics, P.O. Box 7436
Pittsburgh, PA 15213
Nickname: Panthers
Telephone: (412) 648-8240
Football Stadium (Capacity): Pitt Stadium (56,100)
Basketball Arena (Capacity): Fitzgerald Field House (6,798), Pittsburgh Civic Arena (16,798)
Chancellor: Mark A. Nordenberg
Athletic Director: Oval Jaynes
Football Coach: Johnny Majors
Basketball Coach: Ralph Willard
Sports Information Director: Ron Wall

Providence College

Address: River Avenue
Providence, RI 02918
Nickname: Friars
Telephone: (401) 865-2265
Basketball Arena (Capacity): Providence Civic Center (13,410)
President: Rev. Philip A. Smith, O.P.
Assistant VP for Athletics: John Marinatto
Basketball Coach: Pete Gillen
Sports Information Director: Tim Connor
Note: No football program.

Rutgers University

Address: P.O. Box 1149
Piscataway, NJ 08855-1149
Nickname: Scarlet Knights
Telephone: (908) 445-4200
Football Stadium (Capacity): Rutgers Stadium (42,000), Giants Stadium (76,000)
Basketball Arena (Capacity): Louis Brown Athletic Center (9,000)
President: Dr. Francis L. Lawrence
Athletic Director: Frederick Gruninger
Football Coach: Terry Shea
Basketball Coach: Bob Wenzel
Sports Information Director: Peter Kowalski

St. John's University

Address: 8000 Utopia Parkway
Jamaica, NY 11439
Nickname: Red Storm
Telephone: (718) 990-6367
Football Stadium (Capacity): St. John's Stadium (3,000)
Basketball Arena (Capacity): Alumni Hall (6,008), Madison Square Garden (19,876)
President: Very Rev. Donald J. Harrington, C.M.
Athletic Director: Edward J. Manetta Jr.
Football Coach: Bob Ricca
Basketball Coach: Fran Fraschilla
Sports Information Director: Dominic Scianna
Note: Division I-AA football.

Seton Hall University

Address: 400 South Orange Avenue
South Orange, NJ 07079
Nickname: Pirates
Telephone: (201) 761-9497
Basketball Arena (Capacity): Walsh Auditorium (3,200), The Meadowlands (20,029)
President: Monsignor Robert T. Sheeran
Athletic Director: Larry Keating
Basketball Coach: George Blaney
Sports Information Director: John Wooding
Note: No football program.

Syracuse University

Address: Manley Field House
            Syracuse, NY 13244-5020
Nickname: Orangemen
Telephone: (315) 443-2608
Football Stadium (Capacity): Carrier Dome (50,000)
Basketball Arena (Capacity): Carrier Dome (33,000)
Chancellor: Dr. Kenneth Shaw
Athletic Director: Jake Crouthamel
Football Coach: Paul Pasqualoni
Basketball Coach: Jim Boeheim
Sports Information Director: Larry Kimball

Temple University

Address: McGonigle Hall
            Philadelphia, PA 19122
Nickname: Owls
Telephone: (215) 204-7445
Football Stadium (Capacity): Veterans Stadium
(66,592)
Basketball Arena (Capacity): McGonigle Hall (3,900)
President: Peter J. Liacouras
Athletic Director: Dave O'Brien
Football Coach: Ron Dickerson
Basketball Coach: John Chaney
Sports Information Director: Scott Cathcart
Note: Plays football in Big East, basketball in Atlantic 10
Conference.

Villanova University

Address: 800 Lancaster Avenue
            Villanova, PA 19085
Nickname: Wildcats
Telephone: (610) 519-4110
Football Stadium (Capacity): Villanova Stadium (13,400)
Basketball Arena (Capacity): duPont Pavilion (6,500),
CoreStates Spectrum (18,497)
President: Rev. Edmund Dobbin, O.S.A.
Athletic Director: Gene DeFilippo
Football Coach: Andy Talley
Basketball Coach: Steve Lappas
Sports Information Director: Karen Frascona
Note: Division I-AA football.

Virginia Tech

Address: Jamerson Athletic Center
            Blacksburg, VA 24061
Nickname: Hokies
Telephone: (540) 231-6726
Football Stadium (Capacity): Lane Stadium/Worsham
Field (51,000)
Basketball Arena (Capacity): Cassell Coliseum (9,971)
President: Dr. Paul Torgersen
Athletic Director: Dave Braine
Football Coach: Frank Beamer
Basketball Coach: Bill Foster
Sports Information Director: Dave Smith
Note: Plays football in Big East, basketball in Atlantic 10.

West Virginia University

Address: P.O. Box 0877
            Morgantown, WV 26507-0877
Nickname: Mountaineers
Telephone: (304) 293-2821
Football Stadium (Capacity): Mountaineer Field
(63,500)
Basketball Arena (Capacity): WVU Coliseum (14,000)
President: David Hardesty
Athletic Director: Ed Pastilong
Football Coach: Don Nehlen
Basketball Coach: Gale Catlett
Sports Information Director: Shelley Poe

BIG TEN CONFERENCE

Address: 1500 West Higgins Road
            Park Ridge, IL 60068
Telephone: (847) 696-1010
Commissioner: James E. Delany
Assistant Commissioner: Mark Rudner

University of Illinois

Address: 1700 S 4th Street
            Champaign, IL 61820
Nickname: Fighting Illini
Telephone: (217) 333-1390
Football Stadium (Capacity): Memorial Stadium (72,292)
Basketball Arena (Capacity): Assembly Hall (16,153)
President: James Stukel
Athletic Director: Ronald Guenther
Football Coach: Lou Tepper
Basketball Coach: Lon Kruger
Sports Information Director: Dave Johnson

Indiana University

Address: 17th Street and Fee Lane/Assembly Hall
            Bloomington, IN 47405
Nickname: Hoosiers
Telephone: (812) 855-2421
Football Stadium (Capacity): Memorial Stadium
(52,354)
Basketball Arena (Capacity): Assembly Hall (17,357)
President: Myles Brand
Athletic Director: Clarence Doninger
Football Coach: Bill Mallory
Basketball Coach: Bob Knight
Sports Information Director: Kit Klingelhoffer

University of Iowa

Address: 205 Carver-Hawkeye Arena
            Iowa City, IA 52242
Nickname: Hawkeyes
Telephone: (319) 335-9411
Football Stadium (Capacity): Kinnick Stadium (70,397)
Basketball Arena (Capacity): Carver-Hawkeye Arena
(15,500)
President: Mary Sue Coleman
Athletic Director: Robert Bowlsby
Football Coach: Hayden Fry
Men's Basketball Coach: Tom Davis
Women's Basketball Coach: Angie Lee
Sports Information Director: Phil Haddy

University of Michigan

Address: 1000 S. State Street
            Ann Arbor, MI 48109
Nickname: Wolverines
Telephone: (313) 763-4423
Football Stadium (Capacity): Michigan Stadium
(102,501)
Basketball Arena (Capacity): Crisler Arena (13,562)
Interim President: Homer Neal
Athletic Director: Dr. Joseph Roberson
Football Coach: Lloyd Carr
Basketball Coach: Steve Fisher
Sports Information Director: Bruce Madej

Michigan State University

Address: East Lansing, MI 48824
Nickname: Spartans
Telephone: (517) 355-2271
Football Stadium (Capacity): Spartan Stadium (72,027)
Basketball Arena (Capacity): Jack Breslin Student Events Center (15,138)
President: M. Peter McPherson
Athletic Director: Merritt J. Norvell Jr., Ph.D.
Football Coach: Nick Saban
Basketball Coach: Tom Izzo
Sports Information Director: Ken Hoffman

University of Minnesota

Address: 208 Bierman Athletic Building Minneapolis, MN 55455
Nickname: Golden Gophers
Telephone: (612) 625-4090
Football Stadium (Capacity): Hubert H. Humphrey Metrodome (63,669)
Basketball Arena (Capacity): Williams Arena (14,300)
President: Nils Hasselmo
Athletic Director: McKinley Boston
Football Coach: Jim Wacker
Basketball Coach: Clem Haskins
Sports Information Director: Marc Ryan

Northwestern University

Address: 1501 Central Street Evanston, IL 60208
Nickname: Wildcats
Telephone: (847) 491-3205
Football Stadium (Capacity): Dyche Stadium (49,256)
Basketball Arena (Capacity): Welsh-Ryan Arena (8,117)
President: Henry S. Bienen
Athletic Director: Rick Taylor
Football Coach: Gary Barnett
Basketball Coach: Ricky Byrdsong
Director of Media Services: Brad Hurlbut

Ohio State University

Address: 410 Woody Hayes Drive, Room 124 Columbus, OH 43210
Nickname: Buckeyes
Telephone: (614) 292-6861
Football Stadium (Capacity): Ohio Stadium (91,470)
Basketball Arena (Capacity): St. John Arena (13,276)
President: Dr. E. Gordon Gee
Athletic Director: Andy Geiger
Football Coach: John Cooper
Basketball Coach: Randy Ayers
Sports Information Director: Steve Snapp

Penn State University

Address: 101 D Bryce Jordan Center University Park, PA 16802
Nickname: Nittany Lions
Telephone: (814) 865-1757
Football Stadium (Capacity): Beaver Stadium (93,967)
Basketball Arena (Capacity): Bryce Jordan Center (15,000)
President: Dr. Graham Spanier
Athletic Director: Tim Curley
Football Coach: Joe Paterno
Men's Basketball Coach: Jerry Dunn
Women's Basketball Coach: Rene Portland
Sports Information Director: Jeff Nelson

Purdue University

Address: Mackey Arena, Room 15 West Lafayette, IN 47907
Nickname: Boilermakers
Telephone: (317) 494-3200
Football Stadium (Capacity): Ross-Ade Stadium (67,861)
Basketball Arena (Capacity): Mackey Arena (14,123)
President: Dr. Steven C. Beering
Athletic Director: Morgan Burke
Football Coach: Jim Colletto
Basketball Coach: Gene Keady
Sports Information Director: Mark Adams

University of Wisconsin

Address: 1440 Monroe Street Madison, WI 53711
Nickname: Badgers
Telephone: (608) 262-1811
Football Stadium (Capacity): Camp Randall Stadium (77,745)
Basketball Arena (Capacity): UW Fieldhouse (11,895)
Chancellor: David Ward
Athletic Director: Pat Richter
Football Coach: Barry Alvarez
Basketball Coach: Dick Bennett
Sports Information Director: Steve Malchow

BIG TWELVE CONFERENCE

Address: 2201 Stemmons Freeway, 28th floor Dallas, TX 75207-2805
Telephone: (214) 742-1212
Commissioner: Steven J. Hatchell
Publicity Director: Bo Carter

Baylor University

Address: 150 Bear Run Waco, TX 76711
Nickname: Bears
Telephone: (817) 755-1234
Football Stadium (Capacity): Floyd Casey Stadium (50,000)
Basketball Arena (Capacity): Ferrell Center (10,080)
President: Robert Sloan
Athletic Director: Tom Stan
Football Coach: Chuck Reedy
Basketball Coach: Harry Miller
Sports Information Director: Maxey Parrish

University of Colorado

Address: Campus Box 357 Boulder, CO 80309
Nickname: Buffaloes
Telephone: (303) 492-5626
Football Stadium (Capacity): Folsom Field (51,748)
Basketball Arena (Capacity): Coors Event Center (11,198)
President: John Buechner
Interim Athletic Director: Dick Tharpe
Football Coach: Rick Neuheisel
Basketball Coach: Ricardo Patton
Sports Information Director: David Plati

Iowa State University

Address: 1802 S. Fourth
Jacobson Building
Ames, IA 50011
Nickname: Cyclones
Telephone: (515) 294-3372
Football Stadium (Capacity): Cyclone Stadium-Jack Trice Field (43,000)
Basketball Arena (Capacity): Hilton Coliseum (14,020)
President: Dr. Martin C. Jischke
Athletic Director: Gene Smith
Football Coach: Dan McCarney
Basketball Coach: Tim Floyd
Sports Information Director: Tom Kroeschell

University of Kansas

Address: Allen Field House, Room 104
Lawrence, KS 66045
Nickname: Jayhawks
Telephone: (913) 864-3417
Football Stadium (Capacity): Memorial Stadium (50,250)
Basketball Arena (Capacity): Allen Field House (16,300)
Chancellor: Robert Hemenway
Athletic Director: Dr. Bob Fredrick
Football Coach: Glen Mason
Men's Basketball Coach: Roy Williams
Women's Basketball Coach: Marian Washington
Sports Information Director: Doug Vance

Kansas State University

Address: 1800 College Ave., Suite 144
Manhattan, KS 66502
Nickname: Wildcats
Telephone: (913) 532-6735
Football Stadium (Capacity): KSU Stadium-Wagner Field (42,000)
Basketball Arena (Capacity): Bramlage Coliseum (13,500)
President: Dr. Jon Wefald
Athletic Director: Max Urick
Football Coach: Bill Snyder
Basketball Coach: Tom Asbury
Sports Information Director: Kent Brown

University of Missouri

Address: P.O. Box 677
Columbia, MO 65205
Nickname: Tigers
Telephone: (573) 882-3241
Football Stadium (Capacity): Faurot Field/Memorial Stadium (62,000)
Basketball Arena (Capacity): Hearnes Center (13,300)
Interim Chancellor: Dr. Richard Wallace
Athletic Director: Joe Castiglione
Football Coach: Larry Smith
Basketball Coach: Norm Stewart
Sports Information Director: Bob Brendel

University of Nebraska

Address: 116 South Stadium
Lincoln, NE 68588
Nickname: Cornhuskers
Telephone: (402) 472-2263
Football Stadium (Capacity): Memorial Stadium (72,700)
Basketball Arena (Capacity): Bob Devaney Sports Center (14,302)
President: L. Dennis Smith
Athletic Director: Bill Byrne
Football Coach: Tom Osborne
Basketball Coach: Danny Nee
Sports Information Director: Chris Anderson

University of Oklahoma

Address: 180 W. Brooks, Room 235
Norman, OK 73019
Nickname: Sooners
Telephone: (405) 325-8231
Football Stadium (Capacity): Memorial Stadium/Owen Field (75,004)
Basketball Arena (Capacity): Lloyd Noble Center (11,100)
President: David Boren
Athletic Director: Steve Owens
Football Coach: John Blake
Basketball Coach: Kelvin Sampson
Sports Information Director: Mike Prusinski

Oklahoma State University

Address: 202 Gallagher-Iba Arena
Stillwater, OK 74078
Nickname: Cowboys
Telephone: (405) 744-5749
Football Stadium (Capacity): Lewis Field (50,614)
Basketball Arena (Capacity): Gallagher-Iba Arena (6,381)
President: Dr. James Halligan
Athletic Director: Terry Don Phillips
Football Coach: Bob Simmons
Basketball Coach: Eddie Sutton
Sports Information Director: Steve Buzzard

University of Texas

Address: P.O. Box 7399
Austin, TX 78713
Nickname: Longhorns
Telephone: (512) 471-7437
Football Stadium (Capacity): Memorial Stadium (75,512)
Basketball Arena (Capacity): Erwin Special Events Center (16,231)
Chancellor: Dr. William Cunningham
Athletic Director: DeLoss Dodds
Football Coach: John Mackovic
Basketball Coach: Tom Penders
Sports Information Director: Dave Saba

Texas A&M University

Address: John Koldus Building
College Station, TX 77843
Nickname: Aggies
Telephone: (409) 845-3218
Football Stadium (Capacity): Kyle Field (70,210)
Basketball Arena (Capacity): G. Rollie White Coliseum (7,800)
President: Dr. Ray Bowen
Athletic Director: Wally Groff
Football Coach: R. C. Slocum
Basketball Coach: Tony Barone
Sports Information Director: Alan Cannon

Texas Tech University

Address: Box 43021
             Lubbock, TX 79409
Nickname: Red Raiders
Telephone: (806) 742-2770
Football Stadium (Capacity): Jones Stadium (50,500)
Basketball Arena (Capacity): Lubbock Municipal
   Coliseum (8,174)
President: Donald Harragan
Interim Athletic Director: Gerald Myers
Football Coach: Spike Dykes
Men's Basketball Coach: James Dickey
Women's Basketball Coach: Marsha Sharp
Sports Information Director: Richard Kilwien

BIG WEST CONFERENCE

Address: 2 Corporate Park, Suite 206
             Irvine, CA 92606
Telephone: (714) 261-2525
Commissioner: Dennis Farrell
Publicity Director: Dennis Bickmeyer

Boise State University

Address: 1910 University Drive
             Boise, ID 83725
Nickname: Broncos
Telephone: (208) 385-1981
Football Stadium (Capacity) Lyle Smith Field (23,000)
Basketball Arena (Capacity): BSU Pavilion (13,000)
President: Dr. Charles Ruck
Athletic Director: Gene Bleymaier
Football Coach: Ernest (Pokey) Allen
Basketball Coach: Rod Jensen
Sports Information Director: Max Corbet

Cal Poly San Luis Obispo

Address: One Grand Avenue
             San Luis Obispo, CA 93407
Nickname: Mustangs
Telephone: (805) 756-2923
Football Stadium (Capacity): Mustang Stadium (8,500)
Basketball Arena (Capacity): Mott Gym (3,500)
President: Dr. Warren J. Baker
Athletic Director: John McCutcheon
Football Coach: Andre Patterson
Basketball Coach: Jeff Schneider
Sports Information Director: Eric McDowell

University of California–Irvine

Address: Campus and University Drive
             Irvine, CA 92697
Nickname: Anteaters
Telephone: (714) 824-5614
Basketball Arena (Capacity): Bren Event Center (5,000)
President: Laurel Wilkening
Athletic Director: Dan Guerrero
Basketball Coach: Rod Baker
Sports Information Director: Bob Olson
Note: No football program.

University of California–Santa Barbara

Address: Department of Athletics
             Santa Barbara, CA 93106-5200
Nickname: Gauchos
Telephone: (805) 893-3428
Basketball Arena (Capacity): Thunderdome (6,000)
Chancellor: Henry Yang
Athletic Director: Gary Cunningham
Basketball Coach: Jerry Pimm
Sports Information Director: Bill Mahoney
Note: No football program.

California State University–Fullerton

Address: 800 North State College Boulevard
             P.O. Box 34080
             Fullerton, CA 92834-9480
Nickname: Titans
Telephone: (714) 773-2677
Basketball Arena (Capacity): Titan Gym (4,000)
President: Dr. Milton A. Gordon
Athletic Director: John Easterbrook
Basketball Coach: Bob Hawking
Sports Information Director: Mel Franks
Note: No football program.

University of Idaho

Address: Kibbie Activities Center
             Moscow, ID 83844-2302
Nickname: Vandals
Telephone: (208) 885-0211
Football Stadium (Capacity): Kibbie Dome (16,000)
Basketball Arena (Capacity): Kibbie Dome (10,000)
President: Dr. Robert Hoover
Interim Athletic Director: Kathy Clark
Football Coach: Chris Tormey
Basketball Coach: Kermit Davis
Sports Information Director: Sean Johnson

Long Beach State University

Address: 1250 Bellflower Boulevard
             Long Beach, CA 90840
Nickname: 49ers
Telephone: (310) 985-8569
Basketball Arena (Capacity): The Pyramid (5,000)
President: Dr. Robert C. Maxson
Athletic Director: Bill Shumard
Basketball Coach: Wayne Morgan
Sports Information Director: Randy Franz
Note: No football program.

University of Nevada—Reno

Address: Lawlor Annex, MS232
             Reno, NV 89557
Nickname: Wolfpacks
Telephone: (702) 784-4600
Football Stadium (Capacity): Mackay Stadium
   (31,500)
Basketball Arena (Capacity): Lawlor Event Center
   (11,500)
President: Joe Crowley
Athletic Director: Chris Ault
Football Coach: Jeff Tisdel
Basketball Coach: Pat Foster
Sports Information Director: Paul Stuart

New Mexico State University

Address: Box 30001, Dept. 3145
             Las Cruces, NM 88003
Nickname: Aggies
Telephone: (505) 646-4126
Football Stadium (Capacity): Aggie Memorial Stadium
   (30,343)
Basketball Arena (Capacity): Pan American Center
   (13,007)
President: Michael J. Orenduff
Athletic Director: Al Gonzales
Football Coach: Jim Hess
Basketball Coach: Neil McCarthy
Sports Information Director: Steve Shutt

University of North Texas

Address: P.O. Box 13917
Denton, TX 76203
Nickname: Eagles
Telephone: (817) 565-2664
Football Stadium (Capacity): Fouts Field (30,500)
Basketball Arena (Capacity): Super Pit (10,032)
President: Dr. Alfred F. Hurley
Athletic Director: Craig Helwig
Football Coach: Matt Simon
Basketball Coach: Tim Jankovich
Sports Information Director: TBA

University of the Pacific

Address: 3601 Pacific Avenue
Stockton, CA 95211
Nickname: Tigers
Telephone: (209) 946-2479
Football Stadium (Capacity): Amos Alonzo Stagg Memorial Stadium (30,000)
Basketball Arena (Capacity): A.G. Spanos Center (6,150)
President: Dr. Donald DeRosa
Interim Athletic Director: Cindy Spiro
Football Coach: Chuck Shelton
Basketball Coach: Bob Thomason
Sports Information Director: Mike Millerick
Note: No football program in 1996.

Utah State University

Address: Logan, UT 84322-7400
Nickname: Aggies
Telephone: (801) 797-1850
Football Stadium (Capacity): Romney Stadium (30,000)
Basketball Arena (Capacity): The Smith Spectrum (10,270)
President: Dr. George H. Emert
Athletic Director: Chuck Bell
Football Coach: John L. Smith
Basketball Coach: Larry Eustachy
Sports Information Director: TBA

CONFERENCE USA

Address: 35 East Wacker Drive, Suite 650
Chicago, IL 60601
Telephone: (312) 553-0483
Comissioner: Michael Slive
Media Relations Director: Brian Teter

University of Alabama-Birmingham

Address: UAB Arena
617 13th Street South
Birmingham, AL 35294
Nickname: Blazers
Telephone: (205) 934-7252
Football Stadium (Capacity): Legion Field (83,091)
Basketball Arena (Capacity): UAB Arena (8,500)
President: Dr. J. Claude Bennett
Athletic Director: Gene Bartow
Football Coach: Watson Brown
Basketball Coach: Murray Bartow
Sports Information Director: Grant Shingleton

University of Cincinnati

Address: Cincinnati, OH 45221-0021
Nickname: Bearcats
Telephone: (513) 556-5601
Football Stadium (Capacity): Nippert Stadium (35,500)
Basketball Arena (Capacity): Myrl Shoemaker Center (13,176)
President: Dr. Joseph A. Steger
Athletic Director: Gerald O'Dell
Football Coach: Rick Minter
Basketball Coach: Bob Huggins
Sports Information Director: Tom Hathaway

DePaul University

Address: 1011 West Belden Avenue
Chicago, IL 60614
Nickname: Blue Demons
Telephone: (312) 325-7526
Basketball Arena (Capacity): Rosemont Horizon (17,500)
President: Rev. John P. Minogue, C.M.
Athletic Director: Bill Bradshaw
Basketball Coach: Joey Meyer
Sports Information Director: John Lanctot
Note: No football program.

University of Houston

Address: 3100 Cullen Boulevard
Houston, TX 77204
Nickname: Cougars
Telephone: (713) 743-9370
Football Stadium (Capacity): Astrodome (65,000)
Basketball Arena (Capacity): Hofheinz Pavilion (10,060)
President: Dr. Glenn Goerke
Athletic Director: William C. Carr
Football Coach: Kim Helton
Basketball Coach: Alvin Brooks
Sports Information Director: Donna Turner

University of Louisville

Address: Louisville, KY 40292
Nickname: Cardinals
Telephone: (502) 852-5732
Football Stadium (Capacity): Cardinal Stadium (37,500)
Basketball Arena (Capacity): Freedom Hall (19,000)
President: Dr. John Schumaker
Athletic Director: William Olsen
Football Coach: Ron Cooper
Basketball Coach: Denny Crum
Sports Information Director: Kenny Klein

Marquette University

Address: P.O. Box 1881
Milwaukee, WI 53201-1881
Nickname: Golden Eagles
Telephone: (414) 288-7447
Basketball Arena (Capacity): Bradley Center (18,592)
President: Rev. Robert W. Wild, S.J.
Athletic Director: Bill Cords
Basketball Coach: Mike Deane
Sports Information Director: Kathleen Hohl
Note: No football program.

University of Memphis
Address: Memphis, TN 38152
Nickname: Tigers
Telephone: (901) 678-2337
Football Stadium (Capacity): Liberty Bowl Memorial
  Stadium/Rex Dockery Field (62,380)
Basketball Arena (Capacity): The Pyramid (20,142)
President: Dr. V. Lane Rawlins
Athletic Director: R.C. Johnson
Football Coach: Rip Scherer
Basketball Coach: Larry Finch
Sports Information Director: Bob Winn

University of North Carolina-Charlotte
Address: 9201 University City Boulevard
            UNC-Charlotte
            Belk Gymnasium
            Charlotte, NC 28223-0001
Nickname: 49ers
Telephone: (704) 547-4937
Basketball Arena (Capacity): Dale F. Halton Arena
  (9,100)
Chancellor: James H. Woodward
Athletic Director: Judy W. Rose
Basketball Coach: Melvin Watkins
Sports Information Director: Mark Colone
Note: No football program.

Saint Louis University
Address: 3672 West Pine Boulevard
            St. Louis, MO 63108
Nickname: Billikens
Telephone: (314) 977-3177
Basketball Arena (Capacity): Kiel Center (20,000)
President: Rev. Lawrence Biondi, S.J.
Athletic Director: Doug Woolard
Basketball Coach: Charlie Spoonhour
Sports Information Director: Doug McIlhagga
Note: No football program.

University of South Florida
Address: 4202 East Fowler Ave., PED 214
            Tampa, FL 33620
Nickname: Bulls
Telephone: (813) 974-2125
Basketball Arena (Capacity): Sun Dome (11,000)
President: Betty Castor
Athletic Director: Paul Griffin
Basketball Coach: Seth Greenberg
Sports Information Director: John Gerdes
Note: The football program will begin with the 1997 season.

University of Southern Mississippi
Address: P.O. Box 5161
            Hattiesburg, MS 39406
Nickname: Golden Eagles
Telephone: (601) 266-5017
Football Stadium (Capacity): M. M. Roberts Stadium
  (33,000)
Basketball Arena (Capacity): Reed Green Coliseum
  (8,095)
President: Dr. Aubrey K. Lucas
Athletic Director: H. C. Bill McLellan
Football Coach: Jeff Bower
Basketball Coach: James Green
Sports Information Director: Regie Napier

Tulane University
Address: James Wilson Jr. Center for
            Intercollegiate Athletics
            New Orleans, LA 70118
Nickname: Green Wave
Telephone: (504) 865-5501
Football Stadium (Capacity): Louisiana Superdome
  (71,000)
Basketball Arena (Capacity): Fogelman Arena (5,000)
President: Dr. Eamon Kelly
Athletic Director: Sandy Barbour
Football Coach: Eugene (Buddy) Teevens
Basketball Coach: Perry Clark
Sports Information Director: Lenny Vangilder

IVY LEAGUE
Address: 120 Alexander Street, Princeton, NJ 08544
Telephone: (609) 258-6426
Executive Director: Jeff Orleans
Publicity Director: Chuck Yrigoyen

Brown University
Address: 235 Hope Street, Providence, RI 02912
Nickname: Bears
Telephone: (401) 863-2211
Football Stadium (Capacity): Brown Stadium (20,000)
Basketball Arena (Capacity): Paul Bailey Pizzitola
  Memorial Sports Center (2,500)
President: Vartan Gregorian
Athletic Director: David Roach
Football Coach: Mark Whipple
Basketball Coach: Franklin Dobbs
Sports Information Director: Christopher Humm

Columbia University
Address: Dodge Physical Fitness Center
            New York, NY 10027
Nickname: Lions
Telephone: (212) 854-2538
Football Stadium (Capacity): Lawrence A. Wien
  Stadium at Baker Field (17,000)
Basketball Arena (Capacity): Levien Gymnasium (3,400)
President: Dr. George Rupp
Athletic Director: Dr. John Reeves
Football Coach: Ray Tellier
Basketball Coach: Armond Hill
Director of Athletic Communications: Brian Bodine

Cornell University
Address: Teagle Hall, Campus Road
            Ithaca, NY 14853
Nickname: Big Red
Telephone: (607) 255-5220
Football Stadium (Capacity): Schoellkopf Field (27,000)
Basketball Arena (Capacity): Newman Arena (4,750)
President: Hunter R. Rawlings III
Athletic Director: Charles Moore
Football Coach: Jim Hofher
Basketball Coach: Scott Thompson
Sports Information Director: Dave Wohlhueter

Dartmouth College
Address: 6083 Alumni Gym
            Hanover, NH 03755-3512
Nickname: Big Green
Telephone: (603) 646-2465
Football Stadium (Capacity): Memorial Field (20,416)
Basketball Arena (Capacity): Leede Arena (2,100)
President: James Freedman
Athletic Director: Richard G. Jaeger
Football Coach: John Lyons
Basketball Coach: Dave Faucher
Sports Information Director: Kathy Slattery

Harvard University

Address: 60 John F. Kennedy St.
             Cambridge, MA 02138
Nickname: Crimson
Telephone: (617) 495-2206
Football Stadium (Capacity): Harvard Stadium (37,967)
Basketball Arena (Capacity): Lavietes Pavilion (2,195)
President: Neil L. Rudentsine
Athletic Director: William J. Cleary Jr.
Football Coach: Tim Murphy
Basketball Coach: Frank Sullivan
Sports Information Director: John Veneziano

University of Pennsylvania

Address: Weightman Hall North
             235 South 33rd Street
             Philadelphia, PA 19104-6322
Nickname: Quakers
Telephone: (215) 898-6121
Football Stadium (Capacity): Franklin Field (60,546)
Basketball Arena (Capacity): The Palestra (8,700)
President: Dr. Judith Rodin
Athletic Director: Steven Bilsky
Football Coach: Al Bagnoli
Basketball Coach: Fran Dunphy
Director, Media Relations: Gail Stasulli Zachary
Director, Athletic Communications: Shaun May

Princeton University

Address: P.O. Box 71
             Jadwin Gym
             Princeton, NJ 08544
Nickname: Tigers
Telephone: (609) 258-3568
Football Stadium (Capacity): Palmer Stadium (45,725)
Basketball Arena (Capacity): Jadwin Gym (7,550)
President: Harold Shapiro
Athletic Director: Gary D. Walters
Football Coach: Steve Tosches
Basketball Coach: Bill Carmody
Sports Information Director: Kurt Kehl

Yale University

Address: Box 208216
             New Haven, CT 06520
Nickname: Bulldogs, Elis
Telephone: (203) 432-1456
Football Stadium (Capacity): Yale Bowl (64,269)
Basketball Arena (Capacity): John J. Lee
  Amphitheater (3,100)
President: Richard C. Levin
Athletic Director: Tom Beckett
Football Coach: Carmen Cozza
Basketball Coach: Dick Kuchen
Sports Information Director: Steve Conn

MID-AMERICAN CONFERENCE

Address: Four Seagate, Suite 102
             Toledo, OH 43604
Telephone: (419) 249-7177
Commissioner: Jerry Ippoliti
Publicity Director: Tom Lessig

Ball State University

Address: 2000 University Avenue
             Muncie, IN 47306
Nickname: Cardinals
Telephone: (317) 285-8225
Football Stadium (Capacity): Ball State University
  Stadium (21,581)
Basketball Arena (Capacity): University Arena
  (11,500)
President: Dr. John E. Worthen
Athletic Director: Andrea Seger
Football Coach: Bill Lynch
Basketball Coach: Ray McCallum
Sports Information Director: Joe Hernandez

Bowling Green University

Address: Bowling Green, OH 43403
Nickname: Falcons
Telephone: (419) 372-2401
Football Stadium (Capacity): Doyt L. Perry Stadium
  (30,599)
Basketball Arena (Capacity): Anderson Arena (5,000)
President: Dr. Sidney A. Ribeau
Athletic Director: Ron Zwierlein
Football Coach: Gary Blackney
Basketball Coach: Jim Larranga
Sports Information Director: Steve Barr

Central Michigan University

Address: Rose Center
             Mount Pleasant, MI 48859
Nickname: Chippewas
Telephone: (517) 774-3041
Football Stadium (Capacity): Kelly/Shorts Stadium
  (20,083)
Basketball Arena (Capacity): Rose Arena (6,000)
President: Leonard Plachta
Athletic Director: Herb Deromedi
Football Coach: Dick Flynn
Basketball Coach: Leonard Drake
Sports Information Director: Fred Stabley, Jr.

Eastern Michigan University

Address: Bowen Fieldhouse
             Ypsilanti, MI 48197
Nickname: Eagles
Telephone: (313) 487-0317
Football Stadium (Capacity): Rynearson Stadium
  (30,200)
Basketball Arena (Capacity): Bowen Arena (5,600)
President: Dr. William Shelton
Athletic Director: Tim Weiser
Football Coach: Rick Rasnick
Basketball Coach: TBA
Sports Information Director: James Streeter

Kent State University

Address: Kent, OH 44242
Nickname: Golden Flashes
Telephone: (330) 672-3120
Football Stadium (Capacity): Dix Stadium (30,520)
Basketball Arena (Capacity): Memorial Athletic and
  Convocation Center (6,034)
President: Dr. Carol A. Cartwright
Athletic Director: Laing Kennedy
Football Coach: Jim Corrigal
Basketball Coach: Gary Waters
Sports Information Director: Dale Gallagher

Miami University
Address: Millett Hall
Oxford, OH 45056
Nickname: Redskins
Telephone: (513) 529-3113
Football Stadium (Capacity): Yager Stadium (30,012)
Basketball Arena (Capacity): Millett Hall (9,200)
President: Dr. James Garland
Athletic Director: Eric Hyman
Football Coach: Randy Walker
Basketball Coach: Charlie Coles
Sports Information Director: John Estes

Ohio University
Address: P.O. Box 689
Convocation Center
Athens, OH 45701-2979
Nickname: Bobcats
Telephone: (614) 593-1174
Football Stadium (Capacity): Don Peden Stadium
(20,000)
Basketball Arena (Capacity): Convocation Center
(13,000)
President: Dr. Robert Glidden
Athletic Director: Thomas Boeh
Football Coach: Jim Grobe
Basketball Coach: Larry Hunter
Director of Media Services: George Mauzy

University of Toledo
Address: 2801 W. Bancroft St.
Toledo, OH 43606
Nickname: Rockets
Telephone: (419) 537-4184
Football Stadium (Capacity): Glass Bowl (26,248)
Basketball Arena (Capacity): Savage Hall (9,000)
President: Dr. Frank E. Horton
Athletic Director: Pete Liske
Football Coach: Gary Pinkel
Basketball Coach: Stan Joplin
Sports Information Director: Rod Brandt

Western Michigan University
Address: Kalamazoo, MI 49008
Nickname: Broncos
Telephone: (616) 387-4138
Football Stadium (Capacity): Waldo Stadium (30,062)
Basketball Arena (Capacity): University Arena (5,800)
President: Dr. Diether H. Haenicke
Athletic Director: James Weaver
Football Coach: Al Molde
Basketball Coach: Bob Donewald
Sports Information Director: John Beatty

PACIFIC-10 CONFERENCE
Address: 800 S. Broadway, Suite 400
Walnut Creek, CA 94596
Telephone: (510) 932-4411
Commissioner: Thomas C. Hansen
Publicity Director: Jim Muldoon

University of Arizona
Address: 229 McHale Center
Tuscon, AZ 85721
Nickname: Wildcats
Telephone: (602) 621-2211
Football Stadium (Capacity): Arizona Stadium (56,167)
Basketball Arena (Capacity): McHale Center (13,447)
President: Dr. Manuel Pacheco
Athletic Director: Jim Livengood
Football Coach: Dick Tomey
Basketball Coach: Lute Olson
Sports Information Director: Tom Duddleston

Arizona State University
Address: Tempe, AZ 85287
Nickname: Sun Devils
Telephone: (602) 965-6592
Football Stadium (Capacity): Sun Devil Stadium (73,656)
Basketball Arena (Capacity): University Activity
Center (14,287)
President: Lattie Coor
Athletic Director: Dr. Kevin White
Football Coach: Bruce Snyder
Basketball Coach: Bill Frieder
Sports Information Director: Mark Brand

University of California
Address: Berkeley, CA 94720
Nickname: Golden Bears
Telephone: (510) 642-5363
Football Stadium (Capacity): Memorial Stadium (74,909)
Basketball Arena (Capacity): Harmon Gym (6,578)
Chancellor: Chang-Lin Tien
Athletic Director: John Kasser
Football Coach: Steve Mariucci
Basketball Coach: Ben Braun
Sports Information Director: Kevin Reneau

University of California at Los Angeles
Address: P.O. Box 24044
Los Angeles, CA 90024
Nickname: Bruins
Telephone: (310) 206-6831
Football Stadium (Capacity): Rose Bowl (102,083)
Basketball Arena (Capacity): Pauley Pavilion (12,819)
Chancellor: Dr. Charles Young
Athletic Director: Peter T. Dalis
Football Coach: Bob Toledo
Basketball Coach: Jim Harrick
Sports Information Director: Marc Dellins

University of Oregon
Address: Len Casanova Athletic Center
2727 Leo Harris Parkway
Eugene, OR 97401
Nickname: Ducks
Telephone: (541) 346-4481
Football Stadium (Capacity): Autzen Stadium (41,698)
Basketball Arena (Capacity): McArthur Court (9,738)
President: David Frohnmayer
Athletic Director: William Moos
Football Coach: Mike Bellotti
Basketball Coach: Jerry Green
Co-Sports Information Directors: David Williford and
Jamie Klund

Oregon State University
Address: Gill Coliseum
Corvallis, OR 97331
Nickname: Beavers
Telephone: (541) 737-3720
Football Stadium (Capacity): Parker Stadium (36,345)
Basketball Arena (Capacity): Gill Coliseum (10,400)
President: Paul Risser
Athletic Director: Dutch Baughman
Football Coach: Jerry Pettibone
Basketball Coach: Eddie Payne
Sports Information Director: Hal Cowan

University of Southern California
Address: Los Angeles, CA 90089
Nickname: Trojans
Telephone: (213) 740-8480
Football Stadium (Capacity): Los Angeles Memorial
  Coliseum (94,159)
Basketball Arena (Capacity): Los Angeles Sports
  Arena (15,509)
President: Dr. Steven Sample
Athletic Director: Mike Garrett
Football Coach: John Robinson
Basketball Coach: Henry Bibby
Sports Information Director: Tim Tessalone

Stanford University
Address: Stanford, CA 94305
Nickname: Cardinal
Telephone: (415) 723-4418
Football Stadium (Capacity): Stanford Stadium (85,500)
Basketball Arena (Capacity): Maples Pavilion (7,500)
President: Gerhard Casper
Athletic Director: Dr. Ted Leland
Football Coach: Tyrone Willingham
Men's Basketball Coach: Mike Montgomery
Women's Basketball Coach: Tara Van Derveer
Sports Information Director: Gary Migdol

University of Washington
Address: UW Media Relations
            Graves Building, Box 354070
            Seattle, WA 98195-4070
Nickname: Huskies
Telephone: (206) 543-2230
Football Stadium (Capacity): Husky Stadium (72,500)
Basketball Arena (Capacity): Hec Edmundson
  Pavilion (8,000)
President: Richard L. McCormick
Athletic Director: Barbara Hedges
Football Coach: Jim Lambright
Basketball Coach: Bob Bender
Sports Information Director: Jim Daves

Washington State University
Address: P.O. Box 641602
            Pullman, WA 99164-1602
Nickname: Cougars
Telephone: (509) 335-0270
Football Stadium (Capacity): Martin Stadium (37,600)
Basketball Arena (Capacity): Friel Court (12,058)
President: Dr. Samuel H. Smith
Athletic Director: Rick Dickson
Football Coach: Mike Price
Basketball Coach: Kevin Eastman
Sports Information Director: Rod Commons

SOUTHEASTERN CONFERENCE
Address: 2201 Civic Center Boulevard
            Birmingham, AL 35203
Telephone: (205) 458-3000
Commissioner: Roy Kramer
Publicity Director: Mark Whitworth

University of Alabama
Address: P.O. Box 870391
            323 Paul Bryant Drive
            Tuscaloosa, AL 35487
Nickname: Crimson Tide
Telephone: (205) 348-6084
Football Stadium (Capacity): Bryant-Denny Stadium
  (70,123)
Basketball Arena (Capacity): Coleman Coliseum
  (15,043)
President: Dr. Andrew Sorensen
Athletic Director: Bob Bockrath
Football Coach: Gene Stallings
Men's Basketball Coach: David Hobbs
Women's Basketball Coach: Rick Moody
Sports Information Director: Larry White

University of Arkansas
Address: Broyles Athletic Center
            Fayetteville, AR 72701
Nickname: Razorbacks
Telephone: (501) 575-2751
Football Stadium (Capacity): Razorback Stadium
  (51,000); War Memorial Stadium (53,727)
Basketball Arena (Capacity): Bud Walton Arena
  (19,002)
Chancellor: Dr. Dan Ferritor
Athletic Director: Frank Broyles
Football Coach: Danny Ford
Basketball Coach: Nolan Richardson
Sports Information Director: Rick Schaeffer

Auburn University
Address: P.O. Box 351
            Auburn, AL 36831-0351
Nickname: Tigers
Telephone: (334) 844-9800
Football Stadium (Capacity): Jordan Hare Stadium
  (85,214)
Basketball Arena (Capacity): Beard-Eaves Memorial
  Coliseum (13,500)
President: Dr. William V. Muse
Athletic Director: David Housel
Football Coach: Terry Bowden
Men's Basketball Coach: Cliff Ellis
Women's Basketball Coach: Joe Ciampi
Sports Information Director: Kent Partridge

University of Florida
Address: P.O. Box 14485
            Gainesville, FL 32604
Nickname: Gators
Telephone: (352) 375-4683
Football Stadium (Capacity): Ben Hill Griffin Stadium
  at Florida Field (84,000)
Basketball Arena (Capacity): Stephen C. O'Connell
  Center (12,000)
President: Dr. John Lombardi
Athletic Director: Jeremy Foley
Football Coach: Steve Spurrier
Basketball Coach: Billy Donovan
Sports Information Director: John Humenik

University of Georgia

Address: P.O. Box 1472
Athens, GA 30603-1472
Nickname: Bulldogs
Telephone: (706) 542-1621
Football Stadium (Capacity): Sanford Stadium (86,117)
Basketball Arena (Capacity): The Coliseum (10,512)
President: Dr. Charles Knapp
Athletic Director: Vince Dooley
Football Coach: Jim Donnan
Men's Basketball Coach: Tubby Smith
Women's Basketball Coach: Andy Landers
Sports Information Director: Claude Felton

University of Kentucky

Address: Memorial Coliseum
Lexington, KY 40506
Nickname: Wildcats
Telephone: (606) 257-3838
Football Stadium (Capacity): Commonwealth Stadium (57,800)
Basketball Arena (Capacity): Rupp Arena (23,000)
President: Dr. Charles Wethington Jr.
Athletic Director: C. M. Newton
Football Coach: Bill Curry
Basketball Coach: Rick Pitino
Sports Information Director: Tony Neeley

Louisiana State University

Address: P.O. Box 25095
Baton Rouge, LA 70894
Nickname: Fighting Tigers
Telephone: (504) 388-8226
Football Stadium (Capacity): Tiger Stadium (79,940)
Basketball Arena (Capacity): Pete Maravich
Assembly Center (14,164)
Chancellor: Dr. William E. Davis
Athletic Director: Joe Dean
Football Coach: Gerry DiNardo
Men's Basketball Coach: Dale Brown
Women's Basketball Coach: Sue Gunther
Sports Information Director: Herb Vincent

University of Mississippi

Address: P.O. Box 217
University, MS 38677
Nickname: Rebels
Telephone: (601) 232-7522
Football Stadium (Capacity): Vaught-Hemingway
Stadium (42,577)
Basketball Arena (Capacity): C. M. (Tad) Smith
Coliseum (8,135)
Chancellor: Dr. Robert C. Khayat
Athletic Director: Pete Boone
Football Coach: Tommy Tuberville
Basketball Coach: Rob Evans
Sports Information Director: Langston Rogers

Mississippi State University

Address: P.O. Drawer 5308
Mississippi St., MS 39762
Nickname: Bulldogs
Telephone: (601) 325-2703
Football Stadium (Capacity): Scott Field (41,200)
Basketball Arena (Capacity): Humphrey Coliseum (9,149)
President: Dr. Donald Zacharias
Athletic Director: Larry Templeton
Football Coach: Jackie Sherrill
Basketball Coach: Richard Williams
Sports Information Director: Mike Nemeth

University of South Carolina

Address: Rex Enright Athletic Center
1300 Rosewood Drive
Columbia, SC 29208
Nickname: Gamecocks
Telephone: (803) 777-5204
Football Stadium (Capacity): Williams-Brice Stadium (80,250)
Basketball Arena (Capacity): Frank McGuire Arena (12,401)
President: Dr. John Palms
Athletic Director: Dr. Mike McGee
Football Coach: Brad Scott
Basketball Coach: Eddie Fogler
Sports Information Director: Kerry Tharp

University of Tennessee

Address: P.O. Box 15016
Knoxville, TN 37901
Nickname: Volunteers
Telephone: (423) 974-1212
Football Stadium (Capacity): Neyland Stadium (102,544)
Basketball Arena (Capacity): Thompson Boling Arena
and Assembly Center (24,535)
President: Dr. Joseph F. Johnson
Athletic Director: Doug Dickey
Football Coach: Phillip Fulmer
Men's Basketball Coach: Kevin O'Neill
Women's Basketball Coach: Pat Summitt
Sports Information Director: Bud Ford

Vanderbilt University

Address: P.O. Box 120158
Nashville, TN 37212
Nickname: Commodores
Telephone: (615) 322-4121
Football Stadium (Capacity): Vanderbilt Stadium (41,000)
Basketball Arena (Capacity): Memorial Gym (15,311)
Chancellor: Joe B. Wyatt
Athletic Director: Todd Turner
Football Coach: Rod Dowhower
Basketball Coach: Jan Van Breda Kolff
Sports Information Director: Rod Williamson

WESTERN ATHLETIC CONFERENCE

Address: 9250 East Costilla Avenue, Suite 300
Englewood, CO 80112
Telephone: (303) 799-9221
Commissioner: Karl Benson
Publicity Director: Jeff Hurd

Air Force

Address: USAF Academy, CO 80840-9500
Nickname: Falcons
Telephone: (719) 333-4008
Football Stadium (Capacity): Falcon Stadium (52,260)
Basketball Arena (Capacity): Clune Arena (6,007)
President: Lt. Gen. Paul E. Stein
Athletic Director: Col. Randall W. Spetman
Football Coach: Fisher DeBerry
Basketball Coach: Reggie Minton
Sports Information Director: David Kellogg

Brigham Young University
Address: 30 Smith Field House
              Provo, UT 84602
Nickname: Cougars
Telephone: (801) 378-4911
Football Stadium (Capacity): Cougar Stadium (65,000)
Basketball Arena (Capacity): Marriott Center (23,000)
President: Merrill J. Bateman
Athletic Director: Rondo Fehlberg
Football Coach: LaVell Edwards
Basketball Coach: Roger Reid
Sports Information Director: Ralph Zobell

Colorado State University
Address: Moby Arena
              Fort Collins, CO 80523
Nickname: Rams
Telephone: (970) 491-5300
Football Stadium (Capacity): Hughes Stadium (30,000)
Basketball Arena (Capacity): Moby Arena (9,001)
President: Dr. Albert C. Yates
Athletic Director: Tom Jurich
Football Coach: Sonny Lubick
Basketball Coach: Stew Morrill
Sports Information Director: Gary Ozello

Fresno State University
Address: 5305 N. Campus Drive, Room 153
              Fresno, CA 93740-0027
Nickname: Bulldogs
Telephone: (209) 278-2643
Football Stadium (Capacity): Bulldog Stadium
(41,031)
Basketball Arena (Capacity): Selland Arena (10,159)
President: Dr. John Welty
Athletic Director: Dr. Al Bohl
Football Coach: Jim Sweeney
Basketball Coach: Jerry Tarkanian
Sports Information Director: Dave Haglund

University of Hawaii
Address: 1355 Lower Campus Road
              Honolulu, HI 96822-2370
Nickname: Rainbow Warriors
Telephone: (808) 956-8111
Football Stadium (Capacity): Aloha Stadium (50,000)
Basketball Arena (Capacity): Special Events Arena
(10,225)
President: Dr. Kenneth Mortimer
Athletic Director: Hugh Yoshida
Football Coach: Fred von Appen
Basketball Coach: Riley Wallace
Interim Sports Information Director: Lois Manin

University of Nevada at Las Vegas
Address: 4505 Maryland Parkway
              Las Vegas, NV 89154
Nickname: Rebels
Telephone: (702) 895-3207
Football Stadium (Capacity): Sam Boyd Stadium
(32,000)
Basketball Arena (Capacity): Thomas and Mack
Center (18,500)
President: Dr. Carol C. Harter
Athletic Director: Charles Cavagnaro
Football Coach: Jeff Horton
Basketball Coach: Bill Bayno
Sports Information Director: Jim Gemma

University of New Mexico
Address: 1414 University S.E.
              Albuquerque, NM 87131
Nickname: Lobos
Telephone: (505) 277-6375
Football Stadium (Capacity): University Stadium (30,646)
Basketball Arena (Capacity): University Arena—The
Pit (18,100)
President: Dr. Richard Peck
Athletic Director: Rudy Davalos
Football Coach: Dennis Franchione
Basketball Coach: Dave Bliss
Sports Information Director: Greg Remington

Rice University
Address: 6100 Main, MS548
              Houston, TX 77005-1892
Nickname: Owls
Telephone: (713) 527-4034
Football Stadium (Capacity): Rice Stadium (70,000)
Basketball Arena (Capacity): Autry Court (5,000)
President: Malcolm Gillis
Athletic Director: Bobby May
Football Coach: Ken Hatfield
Basketball Coach: Willis Wilson
Sports Information Director: Bill Cousins

San Diego State University
Address: San Diego, CA 92182-4309
Nickname: Aztecs
Telephone: (619) 594-5547
Football Stadium (Capacity): San Diego Jack Murphy
Stadium (61,104)
Basketball Arena (Capacity): San Diego Sports
Arena (13,741)
President: Dr. Stephen Weber
Athletic Director: Rick Bay
Football Coach: Ted Tollner
Basketball Coach: Fred Trenkle
Sports Information Director: John Rosenthal

San Jose State University
Address: One Washington Square
              San Jose, CA 95192-0062
Nickname: Spartans
Telephone: (408) 924-1200
Football Stadium (Capacity): Spartan Stadium
(31,218)
Basketball Arena (Capacity): Event Center (4;600)
President: Dr. Robert L. Caret
Athletic Director: Dr. Tom Brennan
Football Coach: John Ralston
Basketball Coach: Stan Morrison
Sports Information Director: Lawrence Fan

Southern Methodist University
Address: SMU Box 216
              Dallas, TX 75275
Nickname: Mustangs
Telephone: (214) 768-2883
Football Stadium (Capacity): Cotton Bowl (68,252)
Basketball Arena (Capacity): Moody Coliseum (9,007)
President: R. Gerald Turner
Athletic Director: Jim Copeland
Football Coach: Tom Rossley
Basketball Coach: Mike Dement
Sports Information Director: Jon Jackson

University of Texas at El Paso
Address: 201 Baltimore
             El Paso, TX 79902
Nickname: Miners
Telephone: (915) 747-5347
Football Stadium (Capacity): Sun Bowl (53,000)
Basketball Arena (Capacity): Special Events Center
   (12,222)
President: Dr. Diana Natalicio
Athletic Director: John Thompson
Football Coach: Charlie Bailey
Basketball Coach: Don Haskins
Sports Information Director: Gary Richter

Texas Christian University
Address: P.O. Box 297600
             Fort Worth, TX 76129
Nickname: Horned Frogs
Telephone: (817) 921-7969
Football Stadium (Capacity): Amon G. Carter Stadium
   (46,000)
Basketball Arena (Capacity): Daniel-Meyer Coliseum
   (7,166)
Chancellor: Dr. William E. Tucker
Athletic Director: Frank Windegger
Football Coach: Pat Sullivan
Basketball Coach: Billy Tubbs
Sports Information Director: Glen Stone

University of Tulsa
Address: 600 S. College
             Tulsa, OK 74104
Nickname: Golden Hurricane
Telephone: (918) 631-2395
Football Stadium (Capacity): Skelley Stadium (40,385)
Basketball Arena (Capacity): Tulsa Convention
   Center (8,659)
President: Robert Lawless
Interim Athletic Director: Judy MacLeod
Football Coach: Dave Rader
Basketball Coach: Steve Robinson
Sports Information Director: Don Tomkalski

University of Utah
Address: Jon M. Huntsman Center
             Salt Lake City, UT 84112
Nickname: Utes
Telephone: (801) 581-8171
Football Stadium (Capacity): Rice Stadium (35,000)
Basketball Arena (Capacity): Jon M. Huntsman
   Center (15,000)
President: Dr. Arthur K. Smith
Athletic Director: Dr. Chris Hill
Football Coach: Ron McBride
Basketball Coach: Rick Majerus
Media Relations Director: Bruce Woodbury
Sports Information Director: Liz Abel

University of Wyoming
Address: P.O. Box 3414
             Laramie, WY 82071-3414
Nickname: Cowboys
Telephone: (307) 766-2292
Football Stadium (Capacity): War Memorial Stadium
   (33,500)
Basketball Arena (Capacity): Arena-Auditorium (15,028)
President: Dr. Terry Roark
Athletic Director: Lee Moon
Football Coach: Joe Tiller
Basketball Coach: Joby Wright
Sports Information Director: Kevin McKinney

INDEPENDENTS

Army
Address: West Point, NY 10996
Nickname: Cadets/Black Knights
Telephone: (914) 938-3303
Football Stadium (Capacity): Michie Stadium (39,929)
Basketball Arena (Capacity): Cristl Arena (5,043)
Superintendent: Lt. Gen. Daniel W. Christman
Athletic Director: Al Vanderbush
Football Coach: Bob Sutton
Basketball Coach: Dino Gaudio
Sports Information Director: Bob Beretta
Note: Plays football as independent, basketball in Patriot
League.

East Carolina University
Address: Greenville, NC 27858-4353
Nickname: Pirates
Telephone: (919) 328-4600
Football Stadium (Capacity): Dowdy-Ficklen Stadium
   (35,000)
Basketball Arena (Capacity): Williams Arena (7,500)
Chancellor: Dr. Richard R. Eakin
Athletic Director: Michael A. Hamrick
Football Coach: Steve Logan
Basketball Coach: Joe Dooley
Sports Information Director: Norm Reilly

Navy
Address: 566 Brownson Road, Ricketts Hall
             Annapolis, MD 21402
Nickname: Midshipmen
Telephone: (410) 268-6220
Football Stadium (Capacity): Navy-Marine Corps
   Memorial Stadium (30,000)
Basketball Arena (Capacity): Alumni Hall (5,710)
Superintendent: Adm. Charles A. Larson, USN
Athletic Director: Jack Lengyel
Football Coach: Charlie Weatherby
Basketball Coach: Don DeVoe
Sports Information Director: Scott Strasemeier
Note: Plays football as indep., basketball in Patriot League.

University of Notre Dame
Address: Notre Dame, IN 46556
Nickname: Fighting Irish
Telephone: (219) 631-6107
Football Stadium (Capacity): Notre Dame Stadium
   (59,075)
Basketball Arena (Capacity): Joyce Athletic and
   Convocation Center (11,418)
President: Rev. Edward A. Malloy, CSC
Athletic Director: Michael Wadsworth
Football Coach: Lou Holtz
Basketball Coach: John MacLeod
Sports Information Director: John Heisler

Olympic Sports Directory

United States Olympic Committee
Address: Olympic House
             1 Olympic Plaza
             Colorado Springs, CO 80909
Telephone: (719) 632-5551
Executive Director: Dick Schultz
Director of Media Relations: Mike Moran

U.S. Olympic Training Center
Address: 1 Olympic Plaza
             Colorado Springs, CO 80909
Telephone: (719) 578-4500
Director: Pat Milkovich

U.S. Olympic Training Center
Address: 421 Old Military Road
             Lake Placid, NY 12946
Telephone: (518) 523-2600
Director: Jack Favro

International Olympic Committee
Address: Chateau de Vidy
             CH-1007 Lausanne
             Switzerland
Telephone: 41-21-621-6111
President: Juan Antonio Samaranch
Director General: Francois Carrard
Public Relations Officer: Michele Verdier

Nagano Olympic Organizing Committee
Address: KT Building
             3109-63 Kawaishinden
             Nagano City 380
             Japan
Telephone: 81-262-25-1998
President: M. Eishiro Saito
(XVIIIth Olympic Winter Game; Dates: Feb 7-22, 1998)

U.S. Olympic Organizations

National Archery Association (NAA)
Address: 1 Olympic Plaza
             Colorado Springs, CO 80909
Telephone: (719) 578-4576
President: Tom Stevenson, Jr.
Executive Director: Robert C. Balink

U.S. Badminton Association (USBA)
Address: 1 Olympic Plaza
             Colorado Springs, CO 80909
Telephone: (719) 578-4808
President: Diane Cornell
Executive Director: Dr. Cliff McPeak

USA Baseball
Address: 2160 Greenwood Avenue
             Trenton, NJ 08609
Telephone: (609) 586-2381
President: Mark Marquess
Executive Director: Richard Case
Media Relations Director: George Doig

USA Basketball
Address: 5465 Mark Dabling Blvd.
             Colorado Springs, CO 80918
Telephone: (719) 590-4800
President: C.M. Newton
Executive Director: Warren Brown
Assistant Executive Director for Public Relations:
 Craig Miller

U.S. Biathlon Association (USBA)
Address: 29 Church Street
             Burlington, VT 05402-0297
Telephone: 1 (800) 242-8456
President: Don Edwards
Executive Director: Stephen R. Sands

U.S. Bobsled and Skeleton Federation
Address: P.O. Box 828
             Lake Placid, NY 12946
Telephone: (518) 523-1842
President: Jim Morris
Executive Director: Matt Roy
Marketing and Communications Director: Terry Kent

U.S. Tenpin Bowling Federation
Address: 5301 South 76th Street
             Greendale, WI 53129
Telephone: (414) 421-9008
President: Max Skelton
Executive Director: Gerald Koenig
Communications Director: Christine Krebs

USA Boxing, Inc.
Address: 1 Olympic Plaza
             Colorado Springs, CO 80909
Telephone: (719) 578-4506
President: Jerry Dusenberry
Interim Executive Director: David Lubs
Director of Communications: Kurt Stenerson

U.S. Canoe and Kayak Team
Address: Pan American Plaza, Suite 610
             201 South Capitol Avenue
             Indianapolis, IN 46225
Telephone: (317) 237-5690
Chairman: Lamar Sims
Interim Executive Director: Russ Tippett
Manager of Communications: Lisa Fish

USA Cycling
Address: 1 Olympic Plaza
             Colorado Springs, CO 80909
Telephone: (719) 578-4581
President: Mike Plant
Executive Director/CEO: Lisa Voight
Director of Communications: Cheryl Kvasnicka

United States Diving, Inc. (USD)
Address: Pan American Plaza, Suite 430
             201 South Capitol Avenue
             Indianapolis, IN 46225
Telephone: (317) 237-5252
President: Steve McFarland
Executive Director: Todd Smith
Director of Communications: Dave Shatkowski

U.S. Equestrian Team (USET)
Address: Pottersville Rd.
            Gladstone, NJ 07934
Telephone: (908) 234-0155
Executive Director: Robert C. Standish
Director of Public Relations: Marty Bauman

U.S. Fencing Association (USFA)
Address: 1 Olympic Plaza
            Colorado Springs, CO 80909
Telephone: (719) 578-4511
President: Don Alperstein
Executive Director: Michael Massik
Media Relations Director: Colleen Walker-Mar

U.S. Field Hockey Association (USFHA)
Address: 1 Olympic Plaza
            Colorado Springs, CO 80909
Telephone: (719) 578-4567
President: Jenepher Shillingford
Executive Director: Jane Betts
Director of Public Relations: Mark Whitney

U.S. Figure Skating Association (USFSA)
Address: 20 First Street
            Colorado Springs, CO 80906
Telephone: (719) 635-5200
President: Morry Stillwell
Executive Director: Jerry Lace
Communications Director: Kristin Matta

U.S. Gymnastics Federation (USGF)

Address: Pan American Plaza, Suite 300
            201 South Capitol Avenue
            Indianapolis, IN 46225
Telephone: (317) 237-5050
Chairman of the Board: Sandy Knapp
President: Kathy Scanlan
Director of Public Relations: Luan Peszek

USA Hockey
Address: 4965 North 30th Street
            Colorado Springs, CO 80919
Telephone: (719) 599-5500
President: Walter Bush
Executive Director: Dave Ogrean
Public Relations Coordinator: Darryl Sibel

United States Judo, Inc. (USJ)
Address: P.O. Box 10013
            El Paso, TX 79991
Telephone: (915) 565-8754
President and Media Contact: Frank Fullerton

U.S. Luge Association (USLA)
Address: P.O. Box 651
            Lake Placid, NY 12946
Telephone: (518) 523-2071
President: Dwight Bell
Executive Director: Ron Rossi
Public Relations Manager: Sandy Caligiore

U.S. Modern Pentathlon Association (USMPA)
Address: 530 McCullough Avenue, Suite 619
            San Antonio, TX 78215
Telephone: (210) 246-3000
President: Robert Marbut
Executive Director: W. Dean Billick

American Amateur Racquetball Association (AARA)
Address: 1685 West Uintah
            Colorado Springs, CO 80904
Telephone: (719) 635-5396
President: Van Dubolsky
Executive Director: Luke St. Onge
Public Relations Director: Linda Mojer

U.S. Amateur Confederation of Roller Skating (USAC/RS)
Address: 4730 South Street
            P.O. Box 6579
            Lincoln, NE 68506
Telephone: (402) 483-7551
President: Betty Ann Danna
Executive Director: George H. Pickard
Sports Information Director: Andy Seeley

U.S. Rowing Association (USRA)
Address: Pan American Plaza, Suite 400
            201 South Capitol Avenue
            Indianapolis, IN 46225
Telephone: (317) 237-5656
President: Dave Vogel
Executive Director: Frank J. Coyle
Director of Communications: Maureen Merhoff

USA Shooting
Address: 1 Olympic Plaza
            Colorado Springs, CO 80909
Telephone: (719) 578-4670
President of the Board: Stevan B. Richards
Executive Director: Robert L. Jursnick
Director of Public Relations: Nancy Moore

U.S. Skiing
Address: P.O. Box 100
            Park City, UT 84060
Telephone: (801) 649-9090
Chairman: Nick Badami
President and CEO: Bill Marolt
Vice-Chairman: Suzette Cantin
President, U.S. Ski Team Foundation: Stewart Turley
VP of Communications and Media: Tom Kelly
Media Services Coordinator: Deborah Engen

U.S. Soccer Federation (USSF)
Address: 1801-1811 South Prairie Avenue
            Chicago, IL 60616
Telephone: (312) 808-1300
President: Alan Rothenberg
Executive Director: Hank Steinbrecher
Director of Communications: Tom Lang

Amateur Softball Association (ASA)
Address: 2801 N.E. 50th Street
            Oklahoma City, OK 73111
Telephone: (405) 424-5266
President: Wayne Myers
Executive Director: Don Porter
Director of Communications: Ron Babb

U.S. International Speedskating Association (USISA)
Address: P.O. Box 16157
            Rocky River, OH 44116
Telephone: (216) 899-0128
President: Bill Cushman
Executive Director: Katie Marquard
Media Contact: Wendy Day

U.S. Swimming, Inc. (USS)
Address: 1 Olympic Plaza
            Colorado Springs, CO 80909
Telephone: (719) 578-4578
President: Carol Zaleski
Executive Director: Ray Essick
Communications Director: Charlie Snyder

U.S. Synchronized Swimming, Inc. (USSS)
Address: Pan American Plaza, Suite 510
            201 South Capitol Avenue
            Indianapolis, IN 46225
Telephone: (317) 237-5700
President: TBA
Executive Director: Debbie Hesse
Communications: Laura LaMarca

U.S. Table Tennis Association (USTTA)
Address: 1 Olympic Plaza
            Colorado Springs, CO 80909
Telephone: (719) 578-4583
Executive Director: Paul Montville
President: Terry Timmins
Deputy Executive Director: Linda Gleeson

U.S. Taekwondo Union (USTU)
Address: 1 Olympic Plaza, Suite 405
            Colorado Springs, CO 80909
Telephone: (719) 578-4632
President: Hwa Chong
Executive Director: Robert Fujimura

U.S. Team Handball Federation (USTHF)
Address: 1 Olympic Plaza
            Colorado Springs, CO 80909
Telephone: (719) 578-4582
President: Dr. Thomas Rosandich
Executive Director: Michael D. Cavanaugh

U.S. Tennis Association
Address: 70 West Red Oak Lane
            White Plains, NY 10604
Telephone: (914) 696-7000
President: Dr. Harry Marmion
Executive Director: Richard D. Ferman
Director of Communications: Page Crosland

USA Track & Field (formerly TAC)
Address: P.O. Box 120
            Indianapolis, IN 46206
Telephone: (317) 261-0500
President: Larry Ellis
Executive Director: Ollan Cassell
Media Information Officer: Pete Cava

U.S. Volleyball Association (USVBA)
Address: 3595 East Fountain Boulevard, Suite I-2
            Colorado Springs, CO 80910-1740
Telephone: (719) 637-8300
President: Rebecca Howard
Interim Executive Director: Kerry Klostermann

United States Water Polo (USWP)
Address: 1685 West Uintah
            Colorado Springs, CO 80904
Telephone: (719) 634-0699
President: Richard Foster
Executive Director: Bruce J. Wigo
Scoreboard Editor: Kyle Utsumi

USA Weightlifting
Address: 1 Olympic Plaza
            Colorado Springs, CO 80909
Telephone: (719) 578-4508
President: Brian Derwin
Executive Director: George Greenway
Communications Director: Anthony Bartkowski

USA Wrestling
Address: 6155 Lehman
            Colorado Springs, CO 80918
Telephone: (719) 598-8181
President: Larry Sciacchetano
Executive Director: Jim Scherr
Director of Communications: Gary Abbott

U.S. Sailing Association
Address: P.O. Box 1260
            Portsmouth, RI 02871
Telephone: (401) 683-0800
President: David Irish
Executive Director: Terry Hopper
Communications Director: TBA
Olympic Yachting Director: Jonathan R. Harley

Affiliated Sports Organizations

Amateur Athletic Union (AAU)
Address: 6751 Forum Drive, Suite 200
            Orlando, FL 32821
Telephone: (407) 363-6170
President: Bobby Dodd
Director of Administrative Services: Bruce Hopp

U.S. Curling Association (USCA)
Address: 1100 Center Point Drive
            Box 866
            Stevens Point, WI 54481
Telephone: (715) 344-1199
President: Winnifred Bloomquist
President-elect: Tom Brooke
Executive Director: David Garber

USA Karate Federation
Address: 1300 Kenmore Boulevard
            Akron, OH 44314
Telephone: (330) 753-3114
President: George Anderson

U.S. Orienteering Federation
Address: P.O. Box 1444
            Forest Park, GA 30051
Telephone: (404) 363-2110
President: Gary Kraght
Executive Director: Robin Shannonhouse
Director, Marketing and Public Relations: John Nash
Publicity telephone: (207) 439-7096

U.S. Squash Racquets Association
Address: 23 Cynwyd Road
            P.O. Box 1216
            Bala Cynwyd, PA 19004
Telephone: (610) 667-4006
President: Andre Naniche
Executive Director: Craig Brand

USA Trampoline and Tumbling
Address: 400 West Broadway, Suite 207
            or P.O. Box 306
            Brownfield, TX 79316-0306
Telephone: (806) 637-8670
President: Chris Sans
Executive Director: Ann Sims

Triathlon Federation USA
Address: 3595 East Fountain Boulevard, Suite F-1
            Colorado Springs, CO 80910
Telephone: (719) 597-9090
President: Rick Margiotta
Executive Director: Steve Locke
Deputy Director and Media Contact: Tim Yount

Underwater Society of America
Address: P.O. Box 628
            Daly City, CA 94017
Telephone: (415) 583-8492
President: Michael Gower

USA Waterskiing
Address: 799 Overlook Drive, S.E.
            Winter Haven, FL 33884
Telephone: (941) 324-4341
President: Andrea Plough
Executive Director: Duke Waldrop
Public Relations Manager: Don Cullimore

Miscellaneous Sports Directory

Championship Auto Racing Teams (CART)
Address: 755 West Big Beaver Road, Suite 800
            Troy, MI 48084
Telephone: (810) 362-8800
President/CEO: Andrew Craig
Director of Publicity: Adam Sall

International Motor Sports Association
Address: 3502 Henderson Boulevard
            Tampa, FL 33609
Telephone: (813) 877-4672
President: George Silberman
Communications Director: Lynn Myfelt

National Association for Stock Car Auto Racing (NASCAR)
Address: 1801 W International Speedway Blvd.
            Daytona Beach, FL 32120
Telephone: (904) 253-0611
President: Bill France Jr.
Director of Public Relations: Andy Hall

National Hot Rod Association
Address: 2035 East Financial Way
            Glendora, CA 91741
Telephone: (818) 914-4761
President: Dallas Gardner
Director of Communications: Denny Darnell

Bowling, Inc.
Address: 5301 South 76th Street
            Greendale, WI 53129-1191
Telephone: (414) 421-0900
CEO: Sandra Shirk
Public Relations Manager: Rory Gillespie
Women's International Bowling Congress President: Joyce Deitch
American Bowling Congress President: G. Walton Roberson

Ladies Pro Bowlers Tour

Address: 7171 Cherryvale Boulevard
Rockford, IL 61112
Telephone: (815) 332-5756
Executive Tournament Director: Rick Ramsey
Media Director: Dan Howe

Professional Bowlers Association

Address: 1720 Merriman Road, P.O. Box 5118
Akron, OH 44334-0118
Telephone: (330) 836-5568
Commissioner: Mark Gerberich
Public Relations Director: Dave Schroeder

U.S. Chess Federation

Address: 186 Route 9W
New Windsor, NY 12553
Telephone: (914) 562-8350
Executive Director: Al Lawrence
Director of Operations: George Filippone

International Game Fish Association

Address: 1301 East Atlantic Boulevard
Pompano Beach, FL 33060
Telephone: (954) 941-3474
President: Mike Leech

Ladies Professional Golf Association

Address: 100 International Golf Drive
Daytona Beach, FL 32124
Telephone: (904) 274-6200
Commissioner: Jim Ritts
Director of Communications: Elaine Scott

PGA Tour

Address: 112 TPC Boulevard
Ponte Vedra Beach, FL 32082
Telephone: (904) 285-3700
Commissioner: Timothy W. Finchem
VP of Communications: John Morris

Professional Golfers' Association of America

Address: 100 Avenue of the Champions
Box 109601
Palm Beach Gardens, FL 33410-9601
Telephone: (561) 624-8400
President: Ken Lindsay
Director of Public Relations: Julius Mason

United States Golf Association

Address: P.O. Box 708, Golf House
Liberty Corner Road
Far Hills, NJ 07931-0708
Telephone: (908) 234-2300
President: Judy Bell
Director of Communications: Marty Parkes

American Greyhound Track Operators Association

Address: P.O. Box 100279
Birmingham, Al. 35210
Telephone: (205) 838-1574
President: Ron Sultemeier
Secretary/Managing Coordinator: Stan Flint

U.S. Handball Association

Address: 2333 North Tucson Boulevard
Tucson, AZ 85716
Telephone: (602) 795-0434
Executive Director: Vern Roberts
Director of Public Relations: Monica Lopez

Breeders' Cup Limited

Address: 2525 Harrodsburg Road
Lexington, KY 40544-4230
Telephone: (606) 223-5444
President: James Bassett
Media Relations Directors: Dan Metzger and James Gluckson

The Jockeys' Guild, Inc.

Address: 250 West Main Street, Suite 1820
Lexington, KY 40507
Telephone: (606) 259-3211
President: Jerry Bailey
National Manager/Secretary: John Giovanni

Thoroughbred Racing Associations of America

Address: 420 Fair Hill Drive, Suite 1
Elkton, MD 21921
Telephone: (410) 392-9200
President: Clifford C. Goodrich
Director of Service Bureau: Conrad Sobkowiak

Thoroughbred Racing Communications, Inc.

Address: 40 East 52nd Street
New York, NY 10022
Telephone: (212) 371-5910
Executive Director: Tom Merritt
Director of Media Relations and Development: Bob Curran

United States Trotting Association

Address: 750 Michigan Avenue
Columbus, OH 43215
Telephone: (614) 224-2291
President: Corwin Nixon
Director of Publicity: John Pawlak

Iditarod Trail Committee

Address: P.O. Box 870800
Wasilla, AK 99687
Telephone: (907) 376-5155
Executive Director: Stan Hooley
Race Director: Joanne Potts

U.S. Club Lacrosse Association

Address: c/o Lacrosse Foundation
113 W University Parkway
Baltimore, MD 21210
Telephone: (410) 235-6882
Executive Director: Steven B. Stenersen

Little League Baseball, Inc.

Address: P.O. Box 3485
Williamsport, PA 17701
Telephone: (717) 326-1921
President: Stephen Keener
Communications Director: Dennis Sullivan

U.S. Polo Association
Address: 4059 Iron Works Pike
                Lexington, KY 40511
Telephone: (606) 255-0593
Executive Director: George Alexander, Jr.

American Powerboating Association
Address: P.O. Box 377
                Eastpointe, MI 48021
Telephone: (810) 773-9700
Executive Administrator: Gloria Urbin

Professional Rodeo Cowboys Association
Address: 101 Pro Rodeo Drive
                Colorado Springs, CO 80919
Telephone: (719) 593-8840
Commissioner: Lewis Cryer
Director of Communications: Steve Fleming

U.S. Rubgy Football Union
Address: 3595 East Fountain Boulevard
                Colorado Springs, CO 80910
Telephone: (719) 637-1022
Manager of Member Services: Jill Wiesner

American Professional Soccer League
Address: 2 Village Road, Suite 5
                Horsham, PA 19044
Telephone: (215) 657-7440
Commissioner: Richard Groff
Director of Operations: Brad Pursel

Continental Indoor Soccer League
Address: 16027 Ventura Boulevard, Suite 605
                Encino, CA 91436
Telephone: (818) 906-7627
Commissioner: Ron Weinstein
Director of Public Relations: John Dowdy

Major League Soccer
Address: 110 East 42nd Street, Suite 1502
                New York, NY 10017
Telephone: (212) 687-1400
Commissioner: Doug Logan
Director of Communications: Dan Courtemanche

National Professional Soccer League
Address: 115 Dewalt Avenue NW, 5th floor
                Canton, OH 44702
Telephone: (330) 455-4625
Commissioner: Steve Paxos
Director of Operations: Paul Luchowski

Association of Tennis Professionals Tour
Address: 200 ATP Tour Boulevard
                Ponte Vedra Beach, FL 32082
Telephone: (904) 285-8000
Chief Executive Officer: Mark Miles
VP of Communications: Pete Alfano

COREL WTA Tour (Women's Tennis)
Address: 1266 East Main Street, 4th floor
                Stamford, CT 06902-3546
Telephone: (203) 978-1740; (813) 895-5000
Chief Executive Officer: Anne Person-Worcester
Director of Communications: Joe Favorito

Association of Volleyball Professionals
Address: 330 Washington Blvd., Suite 600
                Marina Del Rey, CA 90292
Telephone: (310) 577-0775
President: Jon Stevenson
VP of Sales and Marketing: Alison Canfield

MINOR LEAGUES

Baseball (AAA)

American Association
Address: 6801 Miami Ave., Suite 3
                Cincinnati, OH 45243
Telephone: (513) 271-4800
President: Branch B. Rickey

International League
Address: 55 South High Street, Suite 202
                Dublin, OH 43017
Telephone: (614) 791-9300
President: Randy Mobley

Mexican League
Address: Angela Pola #16
                Col. Periodista, C.P. 11220
                Mexico D.F.
Telephone: 011-525-557-10-07
President: Pedro Cisneros

Pacific Coast League
Address: 2345 South Alma School Rd., Suite 110
                Mesa, AZ 85210
Telephone: (602) 838-2171
President: Bill Cutler

Hockey

American Hockey League
Address: 425 Union Street
                West Springfield, MA 01089
Telephone: (413) 781-2030
President: David Andrews
Senior VP of Hockey Operations: Gordon Anziano

International Hockey League
Address: 1577 North Woodward Ave., Suite 212
                Bloomfield Hills, MI 48304
Telephone: (810) 258-0580
Commissioner: Robert P. Ufer
VP of Communications: Tim Bryant

Hall of Fame Directory

National Baseball Hall of Fame and Museum
Address: P.O. Box 590
              Cooperstown, NY 13326
Telephone: (607) 547-9114
Vice President: Bill Guilfoile
Director of Public Relations: Jeff Idelson

Naismith Memorial Basketball Hall of Fame
Address: 1150 West Columbus Avenue
              Springfield, MA 01101
Telephone: (413) 781-6500
President: Joseph O'Brien
Director of Public Relations: Robin Deutsch

National Bowling Hall of Fame and Museum
Address: 111 Stadium Plaza
              St. Louis, MO 63102
Telephone: (314) 231-6340
Executive Director: Gerald Baltz
Director of Marketing: Raleigh Ragan

National Boxing Hall of Fame
Address: 1 Hall of Fame Drive
              Canastota, NY 13032
Telephone: (315) 697-7095
President: Donald Ackerman
Executive Director: Edward Brophy

Professional Football Hall of Fame
Address: 2121 George Halas Drive NW
              Canton, OH 44708
Telephone: (330) 456-8207
Executive Director: Pete Elliott
Vice President, Public Relations: Don Smith

LPGA Hall of Fame
Address: 100 International Golf Drive
              Daytona Beach, FL 32124
Telephone: (904) 274-6200
Commissioner: Jim Ritts
Communications Director: Elaine Scott

Professional Hockey Hall of Fame
Address: 30 Young Street BCE Place
              Toronto, Ontario Canada M5E 1X8
Telephone: (416) 360-7735
VP of Marketing and Communications: Bryan Black
VP of Finance: Jeff Denomme

National Museum of Racing and Hall of Fame
Address: 191 Union Avenue
              Saratoga Springs, NY 12866
Telephone: (518) 584-0400
Executive Director: Peter Hammell
Assistant Director: Catherine Maguire

National Soccer Hall of Fame
Address: 5-11 Ford Avenue
              Oneonta, NY 13820
Telephone: (607) 432-3351
Executive Director: Albert Colone
External Affairs: Will Lunn

International Swimming Hall of Fame
Address: 1 Hall of Fame Drive
              Fort Lauderdale, FL 33316
Telephone: (305) 462-6536
President: Dr. Samuel J. Freas
Director of Marketing: Kim Swank

International Tennis Hall of Fame
Address: 194 Bellevue Avenue
              Newport, RI 02840
Telephone: (401) 849-3990
Executive Director: Mark Stenning
Director of Public Relations: Linda Johnson

National Track & Field Hall of Fame
Address: 1 RCA Dome, Suite 140
              Indianapolis, IN 46225
Telephone: (317) 261-0500
Historian: Hal Bateman
Director of Media Relations: Pete Cava

Awards

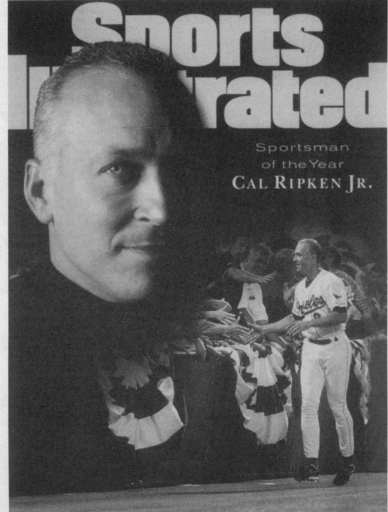

Sportsman
of the Year
CAL RIPKEN JR.

FOR THE RECORD·Year by Year

Athlete Awards

Sports Illustrated Sportsman of the Year

1954	Roger Bannister, Track and Field
1955	Johnny Podres, Baseball
1956	Bobby Morrow, Track and Field
1957	Stan Musial, Baseball
1958	Rafer Johnson, Track and Field
1959	Ingemar Johansson, Boxing
1960	Arnold Palmer, Golf
1961	Jerry Lucas, Basketball
1962	Terry Baker, Football
1963	Pete Rozelle, Pro Football
1964	Ken Venturi, Golf
1965	Sandy Koufax, Baseball
1966	Jim Ryun, Track and Field
1967	Carl Yastrzemski, Baseball
1968	Bill Russell, Pro Basketball
1969	Tom Seaver, Baseball
1970	Bobby Orr, Hockey
1971	Lee Trevino, Golf
1972	Billie Jean King, Tennis
	John Wooden, Basketball
1973	Jackie Stewart, Auto Racing
1974	Muhammad Ali, Boxing
1975	Pete Rose, Baseball
1976	Chris Evert, Tennis
1977	Steve Cauthen, Horse Racing
1978	Jack Nicklaus, Golf
1979	Terry Bradshaw, Pro Football
	Willie Stargell, Baseball
1980	U.S. Olympic Hockey Team
1981	Sugar Ray Leonard, Boxing
1982	Wayne Gretzky, Hockey
1983	Mary Decker, Track and Field
1984	Mary Lou Retton, Gymnastics
	Edwin Moses, Track and Field
1985	Kareem Abdul-Jabbar, Pro Basketball
1986	Joe Paterno, Football
1987	Athletes Who Care:
	Bob Bourne, Hockey
	Kip Keino, Track and Field
	Judi Brown King, Track and Field
	Dale Murphy, Baseball
	Chip Rives, Football
	Patty Sheehan, Golf
	Rory Sparrow, Pro Basketball
	Reggie Williams, Pro Football
1988	Orel Hershiser, Baseball
1989	Greg LeMond, Cycling
1990	Joe Montana, Pro Football
1991	Michael Jordan, Pro Basketball
1992	Arthur Ashe
1993	Don Shula, Pro Football
1994	Bonnie Blair, Speed Skating
	Johann Olav Koss, Speed Skating
1995	Cal Ripken Jr, Baseball

Associated Press Athletes of the Year

	MEN	WOMEN
1931	Pepper Martin, Baseball	Helene Madison, Swimming
1932	Gene Sarazen, Golf	Babe Didrikson, Track and Field
1933	Carl Hubbell, Baseball	Helen Jacobs, Tennis
1934	Dizzy Dean, Baseball	Virginia Van Wie, Golf
1935	Joe Louis, Boxing	Helen Wills Moody, Tennis
1936	Jesse Owens, Track and Field	Helen Stephens, Track and Field
1937	Don Budge, Tennis	Katherine Rawls, Swimming
1938	Don Budge, Tennis	Patty Berg, Golf
1939	Nile Kinnick, Football	Alice Marble, Tennis
1940	Tom Harmon, Football	Alice Marble, Tennis
1941	Joe DiMaggio, Baseball	Betty Hicks Newell, Golf
1942	Frank Sinkwich, Football	Gloria Callen, Swimming
1943	Gunder Haegg, Track and Field	Patty Berg, Golf
1944	Byron Nelson, Golf	Ann Curtis, Swimming
1945	Bryon Nelson, Golf	Babe Didrikson Zaharias, Golf
1946	Glenn Davis, Football	Babe Didrikson Zaharias, Golf
1947	Johnny Lujack, Football	Babe Didrikson Zaharias, Golf
1948	Lou Boudreau, Baseball	Fanny Blankers-Koen, Track and Field
1949	Leon Hart, Football	Marlene Bauer, Golf
1950	Jim Konstanty, Baseball	Babe Didrikson Zaharias, Golf
1951	Dick Kazmaier, Football	Maureen Connolly, Tennis
1952	Bob Mathias, Track and Field	Maureen Connolly, Tennis
1953	Ben Hogan, Golf	Maureen Connolly, Tennis
1954	Willie Mays, Baseball	Babe Didrikson Zaharias, Golf
1955	Hopalong Cassidy, Football	Patty Berg, Golf
1956	Mickey Mantle, Baseball	Pat McCormick, Diving
1957	Ted Williams, Baseball	Althea Gibson, Tennis
1958	Herb Elliott, Track and Field	Althea Gibson, Tennis
1959	Ingemar Johansson, Boxing	Maria Bueno, Tennis
1960	Rafer Johnson, Track and Field	Wilma Rudolph, Track and Field
1961	Roger Maris, Baseball	Wilma Rudolph, Track and Field
1962	Maury Wills, Baseball	Dawn Fraser, Swimming
1963	Sandy Koufax, Baseball	Mickey Wright, Golf

Associated Press Athletes of the Year *(Cont.)*

	MEN	WOMEN
1964	Don Schollander, Swimming	Mickey Wright, Golf
1965	Sandy Koufax, Baseball	Kathy Whitworth, Golf
1966	Frank Robinson, Baseball	Kathy Whitworth, Golf
1967	Carl Yastrzemski, Baseball	Billie Jean King, Tennis
1968	Denny McLain, Baseball	Peggy Fleming, Skating
1969	Tom Seaver, Baseball	Debbie Meyer, Swimming
1970	George Blanda, Pro Football	Chi Cheng, Track and Field
1971	Lee Trevino, Golf	Evonne Goolagong, Tennis
1972	Mark Spitz, Swimming	Olga Korbut, Gymnastics
1973	O.J. Simpson, Pro Football	Billie Jean King, Tennis
1974	Muhammad Ali, Boxing	Chris Evert, Tennis
1975	Fred Lynn, Baseball	Chris Evert, Tennis
1976	Bruce Jenner, Track and Field	Nadia Comaneci, Gymnastics
1977	Steve Cauthen, Horse Racing	Chris Evert, Tennis
1978	Ron Guidry, Baseball	Nancy Lopez, Golf
1979	Willie Stargell, Baseball	Tracy Austin, Tennis
1980	U.S. Olympic Hockey Team	Chris Evert Lloyd, Tennis
1981	John McEnroe, Tennis	Tracy Austin, Tennis
1982	Wayne Gretzky, Hockey	Mary Decker, Track and Field
1983	Carl Lewis, Track and Field	Martina Navratilova, Tennis
1984	Carl Lewis, Track and Field	Mary Lou Retton, Gymnastics
1985	Dwight Gooden, Baseball	Nancy Lopez, Golf
1986	Larry Bird, Pro Basketball	Martina Navratilova, Tennis
1987	Ben Johnson, Track and Field	Jackie Joyner-Kersee, Track and Field
1988	Orel Hershiser, Baseball	Florence Griffith Joyner, Track and Field
1989	Joe Montana, Pro Football	Steffi Graf, Tennis
1990	Joe Montana, Pro Football	Beth Daniel, Golf
1991	Michael Jordan, Pro Basketball	Monica Seles, Tennis
1992	Michael Jordan, Pro Basketball	Monica Seles, Tennis
1993	Michael Jordan, Pro Basketball	Sheryl Swoopes, Basketball
1994	George Foreman, Boxing	Bonnie Blair, Speed Skating
1995	Cal Ripken Jr, Baseball	Rebecca Lobo, Basketball

James E. Sullivan Award

Presented annually by the Amateur Athletic Union to the athlete who "by his or her performance, example and influence as an amateur, has done the most during the year to advance the cause of sportsmanship."

1930	Bobby Jones, Golf	1960	Rafer Johnson, Track and Field
1931	Barney Berlinger, Track and Field	1961	Wilma Rudolph, Track and Field
1932	Jim Bausch, Track and Field	1962	Jim Beatty, Track and Field
1933	Glenn Cunningham, Track and Field	1963	John Pennel, Track and Field
1934	Bill Bonthron, Track and Field	1964	Don Schollander, Swimming
1935	Lawson Little, Golf	1965	Bill Bradley, Basketball
1936	Glenn Morris, Track and Field	1966	Jim Ryun, Track and Field
1937	Don Budge, Tennis	1967	Randy Matson, Track and Field
1938	Don Lash, Track and Field	1968	Debbie Meyer, Swimming
1939	Joe Burk, Rowing	1969	Bill Toomey, Track and Field
1940	Greg Rice, Track and Field	1970	John Kinsella, Swimming
1941	Leslie MacMitchell, Track and Field	1971	Mark Spitz, Swimming
1942	Cornelius Warmerdam, Track	1972	Frank Shorter, Track and Field
1943	Gilbert Dodds, Track and Field	1973	Bill Walton, Basketball
1944	Ann Curtis, Swimming	1974	Rich Wohlhuter, Track and Field
1945	Doc Blanchard, Football	1975	Tim Shaw, Swimming
1946	Arnold Tucker, Football	1976	Bruce Jenner, Track and Field
1947	John B. Kelly Jr, Rowing	1977	John Naber, Swimming
1948	Bob Mathias, Track and Field	1978	Tracy Caulkins, Swimming
1949	Dick Button, Skating	1979	Kurt Thomas, Gymnastics
1950	Fred Wilt, Track and Field	1980	Eric Heiden, Speed Skating
1951	Bob Richards, Track and Field	1981	Carl Lewis, Track and Field
1952	Horace Ashenfelter, Track and Field	1982	Mary Decker, Track and Field
1953	Sammy Lee, Diving	1983	Edwin Moses, Track and Field
1954	Mal Whitfield, Track and Field	1984	Greg Louganis, Diving
1955	Harrison Dillard, Track and Field	1985	Joan B.-Samuelson, Track and Field
1956	Pat McCormick, Diving	1986	Jackie Joyner-Kersee, Track and Field
1957	Bobby Morrow, Track and Field	1987	Jim Abbott, Baseball
1958	Glenn Davis, Track and Field	1988	Florence Griffith Joyner, Track
1959	Parry O'Brien, Track and Field	1989	Janet Evans, Swimming

James E. Sullivan Award (Cont.)

1990 ....John Smith, Wrestling	1993 ....Charlie Ward, Football,
1991 ....Mike Powell, Track and Field	Basketball
1992 ....Bonnie Blair, Speed Skating	1994 ....Dan Jansen, Speed Skating
	1995 ....Bruce Baumgartner, Wrestling

The Sporting News Man of the Year

1968 ....Denny McLain, Baseball	1983 ....Bowie Kuhn, Baseball
1969 ....Tom Seaver, Baseball	1984 ....Peter Ueberroth, LA Olympics
1970 ....John Wooden, Basketball	1985 ....Pete Rose, Baseball
1971 ....Lee Trevino, Golf	1986 ....Larry Bird, Pro Basketball
1972 ....Charles O. Finley, Baseball	1987 ....No award
1973 ...........................O.J. Simpson, Pro Football	1988 ....Jackie Joyner-Kersee, Track and Field
1974 ....Lou Brock, Baseball	1989 ....Joe Montana, Pro Football
1975 ....Archie Griffin, Football	1990 ....Nolan Ryan, Baseball
1976 ....Larry O'Brien, Pro Basketball	1991 ....Michael Jordan, Pro Basketball
1977 ....Steve Cauthen, Horse Racing	1992 ....Mike Krzyzewski, Basketball
1978 ....Ron Guidry, Baseball	1993 ....Pat Gillick and Cito Gaston,
1979 ....Willie Stargell, Baseball	Baseball
1980 ....George Brett, Baseball	1994 ....Emmitt Smith, Pro Football
1981 ....Wayne Gretzky, Hockey	1995 ....Cal Ripken Jr, Baseball
1982 ....Whitey Herzog, Baseball	

United Press International Male and Female Athlete of the Year

	MEN	WOMEN
1974	Muhammad Ali, Boxing	Irena Szewinska, Track and Field
1975	Joao Oliveira, Track and Field	Nadia Comaneci, Gymnastics
1976	Alberto Juantorena, Track and Field	Nadia Comaneci, Gymnastics
1977	Alberto Juantorena, Track and Field	Rosie Ackermann, Track and Field
1978	Henry Rono, Track and Field	Tracy Caulkins, Swimming
1979	Sebastian Coe, Track and Field	Marita Koch, Track and Field
1980	Eric Heiden, Speed Skating	Hanni Wenzel, Alpine Skiing
1981	Sebastian Coe, Track and Field	Chris Evert Lloyd, Tennis
1982	Daley Thompson, Track and Field	Marita Koch, Track and Field
1983	Carl Lewis, Track and Field	Jarmila Kratochvilova, Track and Field
1984	Carl Lewis, Track and Field	Martina Navratilova, Tennis
1985	Steve Cram, Track and Field	Mary Decker Slaney, Track and Field
1986	Diego Maradona, Soccer	Heike Drechsler, Track and Field
1987	Ben Johnson, Track and Field	Steffi Graf, Tennis
1988	Matt Biondi, Swimming	Florence Griffith Joyner, Track and Field
1989	Boris Becker, Tennis	Steffi Graf, Tennis
1990	Stefan Edberg, Tennis	Merlene Ottey, Track and Field
1991	Michael Jordan, Pro Basketball	Monica Seles, Tennis
1992	Mario Lemieux, Hockey	Monica Seles, Tennis
1993	Michael Jordan, Pro Basketball	Steffi Graf, Tennis
1994	Nick Price, Golf	Bonnie Blair, Speed Skating
1995	Cal Ripken Jr, Baseball	Steffi Graf, Tennis

Dial Award

Presented annually by the Dial Corporation to the male and female national high school athlete/scholar of the year.

	BOYS	GIRLS
1979	Herschel Walker, Football	No award
1980	Bill Fralic, Football	Carol Lewis, Track and Field
1981	Kevin Willhite, Football	Cheryl Miller, Basketball
1982	Mike Smith, Basketball	Elaine Zayak, Skating
1983	Chris Spielman, Football	Melanie Buddemeyer, Swimming
1984	Hart Lee Dykes, Football	Nora Lewis, Basketball
1985	Jeff George, Football	Gea Johnson, Track and Field
1986	Scott Schaffner, Football	Mya Johnson, Track and Field
1987	Todd Marinovich, Football	Kristi Overton, Water Skiing
1988	Carlton Gray, Football	Courtney Cox, Basketball
1989	Robert Smith, Football	Lisa Leslie, Basketball
1990	Derrick Brooks, Football	Vicki Goetze, Golf
1991	Jeff Buckey, Football, Track and Field	Katie Smith, Basketball, Volleyball, Track
1992	Jacque Vaughn, Basketball	Amanda White, Track and Field, Swimming
1993	Tiger Woods, Golf	Kristin Folkl, Basketball
1994	Taymon Domzalski, Basketball	Shannon Miller, Gymnastics
1995	Brent Abernathy, Baseball	Shea Ralph, Basketball

Profiles

AUGUST 5, 1996
$3.50 (CAN. $3.95)

Sp**rts
Illustrated**

USA
Atlanta 1996

The
BEST
EVER

WALTER IOOSS JR.

Henry Aaron (b. 2-5-34): Baseball OF. "Hammerin' Hank." Alltime leader in HR (755) and RBI (2,297); third in hits (3,771). 1957 MVP. Led league in HR and RBI 4 times each, runs scored 3 times, hits and batting average 2 times. No. 44, he had 44 homers 4 times. Had 40+ HR 8 times; 100+ RBI 11 times; .300+ average 14 times. 24-time All-Star. Career span 1954–76; jersey number retired by Atlanta and Milwaukee.

Kareem Abdul-Jabbar (b. 4-16-47): Born Lew Alcindor. Basketball C. Alltime leader points scored (38,387), field goals attempted (28,307), field goals made (15,837), blocked shots (3,189); third alltime rebounds (17,440). Won 6 MVP awards (1971–72, 1974, 1976–77, 1980). Career scoring average was 24.6, rebounding average 11.2. 10-time All-Star, All-Defensive team 5 times. 1970 Rookie of the Year. Played on 6 championship teams; was playoff MVP in 1971, 1985. Career span 1969–88 with Milwaukee, Los Angeles. Also played on 3 NCAA championship teams with UCLA; tournament MVP 1967–69; Player of the Year 2 times.

Affirmed (b. 2-21-75): Thoroughbred race horse. Triple Crown winner in 1978 with jockey Steve Cauthen aboard. Trained by Laz Barrera.

Troy Aikman (b. 11-21-66): Football QB. MVP of Super Bowl XXVII, in which he completed 22 of 30 passes for 273 yards and four TDs with no interceptions. Led Cowboys to victory in Super Bowls XXVIII and XXX. Career span since 1989 with Dallas Cowboys.

Tenley Albright (b. 7-18-35): Figure skater. Gold medalist at 1956 Olympics, silver medalist at 1952 Olympics. World champion 2 times (1953, 1955) and U.S. champion 5 consecutive years (1952–56).

Grover Cleveland Alexander (b. 2-26-1887, d. 11-4-50): Baseball RHP. Third alltime most wins (373), second most shutouts (90). Won 30+ games 3 times, 20+ games 6 other times. Set rookie record with 28 wins in 1911. Career span 1911–30 with Philadelphia (NL), Chicago (NL), St Louis (NL).

Vasili Alexeyev (b. 1942): Soviet weightlifter. Gold medalist at 2 consecutive Olympics in 1972, 1976. World champion 8 times.

Muhammad Ali (b. 1-17-42): Born Cassius Clay. Boxer. Heavyweight champion 3 times (1964–67, 1974–78, 1978–79). Stripped of title in 1967 because he refused to serve in the Vietnam War. Career record 56–5 with 37 KOs. Defended title 19 times. Also light heavyweight gold medalist at 1960 Olympics.

Phog Allen (b. 11-18-1885, d. 9-16-74): College baskeball coach. Fifth alltime most wins (746); .739 career winning percentage. Won 1952 NCAA championship. Most of career, 1920–56, with Kansas.

Bobby Allison (b. 12-3-37): Auto racer. Third all-time in NASCAR victories (84) at the time of his retirement. Won Daytona 500 3 times (1978, 1982, 1988). Also NASCAR champion in 1983.

Naty Alvarado (b. 7-25-55): Mexican-born handball player. "El Gato (The Cat)". Won a record 11 U.S. pro four-wall handball titles starting in 1977.

Lance Alworth (b. 8-3-40): Football WR. "Bambi" led NFL in receiving in 1966, '68 and '69. 200+ yards in a game 5 times in career, a record. Gained 100+ yards

in game 41 times. In 1965 gained 1,602 yards receiving. Career span 1962–70 with San Diego and 1971–72 with Dallas. Elected to Pro Football Hall of Fame 1978.

Sparky Anderson (b. 2-22-34): Baseball manager. Only manager to win World Series in both leagues (Detroit, 1984, Cincinnati, 1975–76); only manager to win 100 games in both leagues.

Willie Anderson (b. 1880, d. 1910): Scottish golfer. Won U.S. Open 4 times (1901 and an unmatched three straight, 1903–05). Also won 4 Western Opens between 1902 and 1909.

Mario Andretti (b. 2-28-40): Auto racer. The only driver in history to win Daytona 500 (1967), Indy 500 (1969) and Formula One world championship (1978). Second alltime in CART victories (52) as of retirement in Oct. 1994. Also 12 career Formula One victories. USAC/CART champion 4 times (consecutively 1965–66, 1969, 1984).

Earl Anthony (b. 4-27-38): Bowler. Won PBA National Championship 6 times, more than any other bowler (consecutively 1973–75, 1981–83) and Tournament of Champions 2 times (1974, 1978). First bowler to top $1 million in career earnings. Bowler of the Year 6 times (consecutively 1974–76, 1981–83). Has won 45 career PBA titles since 1970.

Said Aouita (b. 11-2-60): Track and field. Moroccan set world records in 2,000 meters (4:50.81 in 1987), and 5,000 meters (12:58.39 in 1987). 1984 Olympic champion in 5,000; 1988 Olympic third place in 800.

Al Arbour (b. 11-1-32): Hockey D-coach. Led NY Islanders to 4 consecutive Stanley Cup championships (1980–83). Also played on 3 Stanley Cup champions: Detroit, Chicago and Toronto, from 1953 to 1971.

Eddie Arcaro (b. 2-19-16): Horse racing jockey. The only jockey to win the Triple Crown 2 times (aboard Whirlaway in 1941, Citation in 1948). Rode Preakness Stakes winner (1941, 1948, consecutively 1950–51, 1955, 1957) and Belmont Stakes winner (consecutively 1941–42, 1945, 1948, 1952, 1955) 6 times each and Kentucky Derby winner 5 times (1938, 1941, 1945, 1948, 1952). 4,779 career wins.

Nate Archibald (b. 9-2-48): Basketball player. "Tiny" only by NBA standards at 6'1", 160 pounds. Drafted by Cincinnati in 1970. Averaged 34 points per game for K.C.-Omaha in 1972–73. Led NBA in scoring (34.0) and assists (910) in 1972–73. First team, all-NBA in 1973, '75 and '76. MVP of NBA All Star game in 1981. Retired in 1984.

Alexis Arguello (b. 4-19-52): Nicaraguan Boxer. Won world titles in three weight classes, featherweight, super featherweight and lightweight. Won first title, WBA featherweight, on 11-23-74 when he KO'd Ruben Olivares in 13. Career record: 86 bouts; won 65 by KO, 15 by decision; lost 6, three by KO.

Henry Armstrong (b. 12-12-12): Boxer. Champion in 3 different weight classes: featherweight (1937—relinquished 1938), welterweight (1938–40) and lightweight (1938–39). Career record 145-20-9 with 98 KOs (27 consecutively, 1937–38) from 1931 to 1945.

Arthur Ashe (b. 7-10-43; d. 2-6-93): Tennis player. First black man to win U.S. Open (1968, as an amateur), Australian Open (1970) and Wimbledon ingles titles (1975). 33 career tournament victories. Member of Davis Cup team 1963–78; captain 1980–85.

Assault (b. 1943): Thoroughbred race horse. Horse of the Year for 1946; won Triple Crown that year. Won Kentucky Derby by 8 lengths; Preakness by a neck over Lord Boswell; and the Belmont by 3 lengths from Natchez. Trained by Max Hirsch.

Red Auerbach (b. 9-20-17): Basketball coach-executive. Second in wins (938). Coached Boston from 1946 to 1965, winning 9 championships, 8 consecutively. Had .662 career winning percentage, with 50+ wins 8 consecutive seasons. Also won 7 championships as general manager.

Hobey Baker (b. 1-15-1892, d. 12-21-18): Sportsman. Member of both college football and hockey Halls of Fame. College hockey and football star with Princeton, 1911–14. Fighter pilot in World War I, died in plane crash. College hockey Player of the Year award named in his honor.

Seve Ballesteros (b. 4-9-57): Spanish golfer. Notorious scrambler. Won British Opens in 1979, '84 and '88. Won Masters in 1980 and '83.

Ernie Banks (b. 1-31-31): Baseball SS-1B. "Mr. Cub." Won 2 consecutive MVP awards, in 1958–59. 512 career HR. League leader in HR, RBI 2 times each; career batting average of .274; 40+ HR 5 times; 100+ RBI 8 times. Most HR by a shortstop with 47 in 1958. Career span 1953–71 with Chicago.

Roger Bannister (b. 3-23-29): Track and field. British runner broke the 4-minute mile barrier, running 3:59.4 on May 6, 1954.

Red Barber (b. 2-17-08, d. 10-22-92): Sportscaster. TV-radio baseball announcer was the voice of Cincinnati, Brooklyn and NY Yankees. His expressions, such as "sitting in the catbird seat," "pea patch" and "rhubarb" captivated audiences from 1934 to 1966.

Charles Barkley (b. 2-20-63): Basketball F. Five-time first-team All-Star. All-Rookie team, 1985. Led NBA in rebounding, 1987. Averaged 20+ points in seven of 8 seasons with Philadelphia. 1992 Olympic team leading scorer. Traded to Phoenix before 1992–93 season, then to Houston before '96–97 season. League MVP for 1992–93 season.

Rick Barry (b. 3-28-44): Basketball F. Only player in history to win scoring titles in NBA (San Francisco, 1967) and ABA (Oakland, 1969). Second alltime highest free throw percentage (.900). Career scoring average 23.2. Led league in free throw percentage 6 times, steals and scoring 1 time each. Averaged 30+ points 2 times, 20+ points 6 other times. 5-time All-Star. 1975 playoff MVP with Golden State. 1966 Rookie of the Year. Career span 1967–79.

Carmen Basilio (b. 4-2-27): Boxer. Won titles in two weight classes, welter and middle. Won world welter title by TKO of Tony DeMarco in 12 rounds on 6-10-55. Won and then lost middleweight title in two 15 round fights with Ray Robinson. Made three unsuccessful bids to regain middle title. *The Ring* Fighter of the Year for 1957. Career record: 78 bouts; won 26 by KO and 29 by decision; drew 7; lost 16, two by KO.

Sammy Baugh (b. 3-17-14): Football QB-P. Led league in passing 6 times and punting 4 times, a record. Also holds record for highest career punting average (45.1) and highest season average (51.0 in 1940). Career span 1937–52 with Washington. Also All-America with Texas Christian 3 consecutive seasons.

Elgin Baylor (b. 9-16-34): Basketball F. Third alltime highest scoring average (27.4), scored 23,149 points. Averaged 30+ points 3 consecutive seasons, 20+ points 8 other times. 10-time All-Star. 1959 Rookie of the Year. Played in 8 finals without winning championship. Career span 1958–71 with Los Angeles. Also 1958 MVP in NCAA tournament with Seattle.

Bob Beamon (b. 8-29-46): Track and field. Gold medalist in long jump at 1968 Olympics with world record jump of 29' 2½" that stood until 1991.

Franz Beckenbauer (b. 1945): West German soccer player. Captain of 1974 World Cup champions and coach of 1990 champions. Also played for NY Cosmos from 1977 to 1980.

Boris Becker (b. 11-22-67): German tennis player. The youngest male player to win a Wimbledon singles title at age 17 in 1985. Has won 3 Wimbledon titles (consecutively 1985–86, 1989), 1 U.S. Open (1989) and 1 Australian Open title (1991). Led West Germany to 2 consecutive Davis Cup victories (1988–89).

Chuck Bednarik (b. 5-1-25): Football C-LB. Last of the great two-way players, was named All-Pro at both center and linebacker. Missed only 3 games in 14 seasons with Philadelphia from 1949–62. Also All-America 2 times at Pennsylvania.

Clair Bee (b. 3-2-1896, d. 5-20-83): Basketball coach. Originated 1-3-1 defense, helped develop three-second rule, 24-second clock. Won 82.7 percent of games as coach for Rider College and Long Island University. Coach, Baltimore Bullets, 1952–54. Author, 23-volume Chip Hilton series for children, 21 nonfiction sports books.

Jean Beliveau (b. 8-31-31): Hockey C. Won MVP award 2 times (1956, 1964), playoff MVP in 1965. Led league in assists 3 times, goals 2 times and points 1 time. 507 career goals, 712 assists. All-Star 6 times. Played on 10 Stanley Cup champions with Montreal from 1950 to 1971.

Bert Bell (b. 2-25-1895, d. 10-11-59): Football executive. Second NFL commissioner (1946–59). Also owner of Philadelphia (1933–40) and Pittsburgh (1941–46). Proposed the first college draft in 1936.

James (Cool Papa) Bell (b. 5-17-03): Baseball OF. Legendary foot speed—according to Satchel Paige could flip light switch and be in bed before room was dark. Hit .392 in games against white major leaguers. Career span 1922–46 with many teams of the Negro Leagues, including the Pittsburgh Crawfords and the Homestead Grays. Inducted in the Hall of Fame in 1974.

Lyudmila Belousova/Oleg Protopov (no dates or birth available): Soviet figure skaters. Won Olympic gold medal in pairs competition in 1964 and 1968. Won four consecutive World and European championships (1965–68) and eight consecutive Soviet titles (1961–68).

Deane Beman (b. 4-22-38): Commissioner of the PGA Tour 1974–94. Won British Amateur title in 1959 and U.S. Amateur titles in 1960 and 1963.

Johnny Bench (b. 12-7-47): Baseball C. MVP in 1970, 1972; World Series MVP in 1976; Rookie of the Year in 1968. 389 career HR. League leader in HR 2 times, RBI 3 times. Career span 1967–83 with Cincinnati.

Patty Berg (b. 2-13-18): Golfer. Alltime women's leader in major championships (16), third alltime in career wins (57). Won Titleholders Championship and Western Open 7 times each, the most of any golfer. Also won U.S. Women's Amateur (1938) and U.S. Women's Open (1946).

Yogi Berra (b. 5-12-25): Baseball C. Played on 10 World Series winners. Alltime Series leader in games, at bats, hits and doubles. MVP in 1951 and consecutively 1954–55. 358 career HR. Career span 1946–65. Also managed pennant-winning Yankees (1964) and NY Mets (1973).

Jay Berwanger (b. 3-19-14): College football RB. Won the first Heisman Trophy and named All-America with Chicago in 1935.

Raymond Berry (b. 2-27-33): Football E. Led NFL in receiving 1958–60. In 13-season career, caught 631 passes, 68 for TDs. Career span 1955–67, all with Baltimore Colts. Later coached New England Patriots from 1984–89 with 51–41 record.

George Best (b. 5-22-46): Irish soccer player. Led Manchester United to European Cup title in 1968. Named England's and Europe's Player of the Year in 1968. Played in North American Soccer League for Los Angeles (1976–78), Fort Lauderdale (1978–79) and San Jose (1980–81). Frequent troubles with alcohol and gambling overshadowed career.

Abebe Bikila (b. 8-7-32, d. 10-25-73): Track and field. Ethiopian barefoot runner won consecutive gold medals in the marathon at Olympics, in 1960 and 1964.

Fred Biletnikoff (b. 2-23-43): Football WR. In 14 pro seasons caught 589 passes for 8,974 yards and 76 TDs. In 1961 led NFL receivers with 61 catches; in '62 led AFC with 58. Career span 1965–78, all with Raiders. Elected to Pro Football Hall of Fame in 1988.

Dmitri Bilozerchev (b. 12-22-66): Soviet gymnast. Won 3 gold medals at 1988 Olympics. Made comeback after shattering his left leg into 44 pieces in 1985. Two-time world champion (1983, 1987). At 16, became youngest to win all-around world championship title in 1983.

Dave Bing (b. 11-24-43): Basketball G. Averaged 24.8 points a game in four years at Syracuse. NBA Rookie of Year in 1967. Led NBA in scoring (27.1) in 1968. MVP NBA All Star game in 1976. In 12 year career from 1967–78, most of it with Detroit Pistons, averaged 20.3 points.

Matt Biondi (b. 10-8-65): Swimmer. Winner of 5 gold medals, 1 silver medal and 1 bronze medal at 1988 Olympics. Won one gold and one silver at 1992 Olympics.

Larry Bird (b. 12-7-56): Basketball F. Won 3 consecutive MVP awards (1984–86) and 2 playoff MVP awards (1984, 1986). Also Rookie of the Year (1980) and All-Star 9 consecutive seasons. Led league in free throw percentage 4 times. Averaged 20+ points 10 times. Career span 1979-1992 with Boston. Named College Player of the Year in 1979 with Indiana State.

Bonnie Blair (b. 3-18-64): Speed skater. Won gold medal in 500 meters and bronze medal in 1,000 meters at 1988 Olympics and gold medals in both events in 1992 and '94. Also 1989 World Sprint champion. Winner of 1992 Sullivan Award. *Sports Illustrated* Sportswoman of the Year, 1994.

Toe Blake (b. 8-21-12, d. 5-17-95): Hockey LW and coach. Second alltime highest winning percentage (.634) and fifth in wins (500). Led Montreal to 8 Stanley Cup championships from 1955 to 1968 (consecutively

1956–60, 1965–66, 1968). Also MVP and scoring leader in 1939. Played on 2 Stanley Cup champions with Montreal from 1932 to 1948.

Doc Blanchard (b. 12-11-24): College football FB. "Mr. Inside." Teamed with Glenn Davis to lead Army to 3 consecutive undefeated seasons (1944–46) and 2 consecutive national championships (1944–45). Won Heisman Trophy and Sullivan Award in 1945. Also All-America 3 times.

George Blanda (b. 9-17-27): Football QB-K. Alltime leader in seasons played (26), games played (340), points scored (2,002) and points after touchdown (943); third in field goals (335). Also passed for 26,920 career yards and 236 touchdowns. Tied record with 7 touchdown passes on Nov. 19, 1961. Player of the Year 2 times (1961, 1970). Retired at age 48, the oldest to ever play. Career span 1949–75 with Chicago, Houston, Oakland.

Fanny Blankers-Koen (b. 4-26-18): Track and field. Dutch athlete won four gold medals at 1948 Olympics, in 100-meters; 200 meters; 80-meter hurdles; and 400-meter relay. Versatile, she also set world records in high jump (5' 7¼" in 1943), long jump (20' 6" in 1943) and pentathlon (4,692 points in 1951).

Wade Boggs (b. 6-15-58): Baseball 3B. Won 5 batting titles (1983, consecutively 1985–88); has had .350+ average 5 times, 200+ hits 7 times. Career span 1982–92 with Boston, 1993- with New York Yankees.

Nick Bolletieri (b. 7-31-31): Tennis coach. Since 1976, has run Nick Bolletieri Tennis Academy in Bradenton, Fla. Former residents of the academy include Andre Agassi, Monica Seles and Jim Courier.

Barry Bonds (b. 7-24-64): Baseball OF. Three-time National League MVP (1990, '92, '93); Career span 1986 to '92, with Pirates; 1993- with Giants.

Bjorn Borg (b. 6-6-56): Swedish tennis player. Second alltime men's leader in Grand Slam singles titles (11—tied with Rod Laver). Set modern record by winning 5 consecutive Wimbledon titles (1976–80). Won 6 French Open titles (consecutively 1974–75, 1978–81). Reached U.S. Open Final 4 times, but title eluded him. 65 career tournament victories. Led Sweden to Davis Cup win in 1975.

Julius Boros (b. 3-3-20): Golfer. Won US. Opens in 1952 at Northwood CC in Dallas and in 1963 at The Country Club in Brookline, Mass. Also won 1968 PGA Championship at Pecan Valley CC, San Antonio, when 48 years old, making him oldest winner of a major ever. Led PGA money list in 1952 and '55.

Mike Bossy (b. 1-22-57): Hockey RW. In 1978 set NHL rookie scoring record of 54 goals, broken in 1993. Scored 50 or more each of first nine seasons, totaling 573 goals and 1,126 points in 10 seasons (1977–78 through 1986–87) with New York Islanders. Elected to Hall of Fame in 1991.

Ralph Boston (b. 5-9-39): Track and field. Long jumper won medals at 3 consecutive Olympics: gold in 1960, silver in 1964, bronze in 1968.

Ray Bourque (b. 12-28-60): Hockey D. Won Norris Trophy as NHL's top defenseman five times. Career span since1979 with Boston Bruins.

Scotty Bowman (b. 9-18-33): Hockey coach. Entered 1996–97 season as alltime leader in regular season wins (975) and in regular season winning percentage (.663). Also alltime leader in playoff wins

(162). Led Montreal to 5 Stanley Cups, coached St Louis, Buffalo, and Detroit. Won Jack Adams Award, Coach of the Year, 1976–77.

Bill Bradley (b. 7-28-43): Basketball F. Played on 2 NBA championship teams with New York from 1967 to 1977. Player of the Year and NCAA tournament MVP in 1965 with Princeton; All-America 3 times; Sullivan Award winner in 1965. Rhodes scholar. U.S. Senator (D-NJ) 1979–96.

Terry Bradshaw (b. 9-2-48): Football QB. Played on 4 Super Bowl champions (consecutively 1974–75, 1978–79); named Super Bowl MVP 2 consecutive seasons (1978–79). 212 career touchdown passes; 27,989 yards passing. Player of the Year in 1978. Career span 1970–83 with Pittsburgh.

George Brett (b. 5-15-53): Baseball 3B-1B. MVP in 1980 with .390 batting average; 3 batting titles, in 1976, 1980, 1990; and .300+ average 11 times. Led league in hits and triples 3 times. Reached 3,000-hit mark in 1992. Career span 1973–93, with Kansas City. Career totals: 3,153 hits; 317 HR; 1,595 RBIs; batting average .305.

Bret Hanover (b. 5-19-62): Horse. Son of Adios. Won 62 of 68 harness races and earned $922,616. Undefeated as two-year-old. From total of 1,694 foals, he sired winners of $61 million and 511 horses which have recorded sub-2:00 performances.

Lou Brock (b. 6-18-39): Baseball OF. Second alltime most stolen bases (938); second most season steals (118). Led league in steals 8 times, with 50+ steals 12 consecutive seasons. Alltime World Series leader in steals (14—tied with Eddie Collins); third in Series batting average (.391). 3,023 career hits. Career span 1961–79 with St Louis.

Jim Brown (b. 2-17-36): Football FB. 126 career touchdowns; fourth in yards rushing (12,312). Led league in rushing a record 8 times. His 5.22-yards per carry average is the best ever. Player of the Year 4 times (consecutively 1957–58, 1963, 1965) and Rookie of the Year in 1957. Rushed for 1,000+ yards in 7 seasons, 200+ yards in 4 games, 100+ yards in 54 other games. Career span 1957–65 with Cleveland; never missed a game. Also All-America with Syracuse.

Paul Brown (b. 9-7-08, d. 8-5-91): Football coach. Led Cleveland to 10 consecutive championship games. Won 4 consecutive AAFC titles (1946–49) and 3 NFL titles (1950, consecutively 1954–55). Coached Cleveland from 1946 to 1962; became first coach of Cincinnati, 1968–75, and then general manager. Career coaching record 222-113-9. Also won national championship with Ohio State in 1942.

Avery Brundage (b. 9-28-1887, d. 5-5-75): Amateur sports executive. President of International Olympic Committee 1952–72. Served as president of U.S. Olympic Committee 1929–53. Also president of Amateur Athletic Union 1928–35. Member of 1912 U.S. Olympic track and field team.

Paul "Bear" Bryant (b. 9-11-13, d. 1-26-83): College football coach. Alltime Division I-A leader in wins (323). Won 6 national championships (1961, consecutively 1964–65, 1973, consecutively 1978–79) with Alabama. Career record 323–85–17, including 4 undefeated seasons. Also won 15 bowl games. Career span 1945–82 with Maryland, Kentucky, Texas A&M, Alabama.

Sergei Bubka (b. 12-4-63): Track and field. Ukrainian pole vaulter was gold medalist at 1988 Olympics. Only five-time world outdoor champion in any event (1983,

1987, 1991, 1993, 1995). First man to vault 20 feet, set world indoor record of 20' 2" on 2-21-93 and world outdoor record of 20' 1½", set on 9-20-92.

Buck Buchanan (b. 9-10-40): Football DT. Career span 1963–75 with Kansas City Chiefs. Elected to Pro Football Hall of Fame 1990.

Don Budge (b. 6-13-15): Tennis player. First player to achieve the Grand Slam, in 1938. Won 2 consecutive Wimbledon and U.S. singles titles (1937–38), 1 French and 1 Australian title (1938).

Dick Butkus (b. 12-9-42): Football LB. Recovered 25 opponents' fumbles, second most in history. Selected for Pro Bowl 8 times. Career span 1965–73 with Chicago. Also All-America 2 times with Illinois. Award recognizing the outstanding college linebacker named in his honor.

Dick Button (b. 7-18-29): Figure skater. Gold medalist at 2 consecutive Olympics in 1948, 1952. World champion 5 consecutive years (1948–52) and U.S. champion 7 consecutive years (1946–52). Sullivan Award winner in 1949.

Walter Byers (b. 3-13-22): Amateur sports executive. First executive director of NCAA, served from 1952 to 1987.

Frank Calder (b. 11-17-1877, d. 2-4-43): Hockey executive. First commissioner of NHL, served from 1917 to 1943. Rookie of the Year award named in his honor.

Walter Camp (b. 4-7-1859, d. 3-14-25): Football pioneer. Played for Yale in its first football game vs. Harvard on Nov. 17, 1876. Proposed rules such as 11 men per side, scrimmage line, center snap, yards and downs. Founded the All-America selections in 1889.

Roy Campanella (b. 11-19-21; d. 6-26-93): Baseball C. Career span 1948–57, ended when paralyzed in car crash. MVP in 1951, 1953, 1955. Played on 5 pennant winners; 1955 World Series winner with Brooklyn Dodgers.

Earl Campbell (b. 3-29-55): Football RB. 9,407 career rushing yards; third alltime in season yards rushing (1,934 in 1980); 19 TDs rushing in 1979. Led league in rushing 3 consecutive seasons. Rushed for 1,000+ yards in 5 seasons. Scored 74 career touchdowns. Player of the Year 2 consecutive seasons (1978–79). Rookie of the Year in 1978. Career span 1978–85 with Houston, New Orleans. Won Heisman Trophy with Texas in 1977.

John Campbell (b. 4-8-55): Canadian harness racing driver. Alltime leading money winner with over $100 million in earnings. Leading money winner each year 1986–90. Has more than 5,500 career wins.

Billy Cannon (b. 2-8-37): Football RB. Led Louisiana State to national championship in 1958 and won Heisman Trophy in 1959. Signed contract in both NFL (Los Angeles) and AFL (Houston). Houston won lawsuit for his services. Played in 6 AFL championship games with Houston, Oakland, Kansas City. Career span 1960–70. Served three-year jail term for 1983 conviction on counterfeiting charges.

Jose Canseco (b. 7-2-64): Baseball OF. Only player to top 40 homers (42) and 40 steals (40) in same season (1988). AL MVP in 1988, when he also batted .307 with 124 RBIs. Career span 1985–1992 with Oakland; 1993–94 with Texas; 1995– Boston.

Harry Caray (b. 3-1-17): Sportscaster. TV-radio baseball announcer since 1945 with St Louis (NL),

Oakland, Chicago (AL) and Chicago (NL). Achieved celebrity status on Cubs' superstation WGN by singing "Take Me Out to the Ballgame" with Wrigley Field fans.

Rod Carew (b. 10-1-45): Baseball 2B-1B. Won 7 batting titles (1969, consecutively 1972–75, 1977–78). Had .328 career average, 3,053 career hits, and .300+ average 15 times. 1977 MVP; 1967 Rookie of the Year. Career span 1967–85; jersey number (29) retired by Minnesota and California.

Steve Carlton (b. 12-22-44): Baseball LHP. Second alltime most strikeouts (4,136). 4 Cy Young awards (1972, 1977, 1980, 1982). 329 career wins; won 20+ games 6 times. League leader in wins 4 times, innings pitched and strikeouts 5 times each. Struck out 19 batters in 1 game in 1969. Career span 1965–88 with St. Louis, Philadelphia and four other teams in last two years.

JoAnne Carner (b. 4-21-39): Golfer. Won 42 titles, including US Women's Opens in 1971 and '76 and du Maurier Classic in 1975 and '78. LPGA top earner in 1974 and 1982–83. LPGA Player of the Year in 1974 and 1981–82. Won five Vare Trophies (1974–75 and 1981–83).

Joe Carr (b. 10-22-1880; d. 5-20-39): Football administrator. Instrumental in forming American Professional Football Association in 1920. President of AAFA from 1922 to '39.

Don Carter (b. 7-29-26): Bowler. Won All-Star Tournament 4 times (1952, 1954, 1956, 1958) and PBA National Championship in 1960. Voted Bowler of the Year 6 times (consecutively 1953–54, 1957–58, 1960, 1962).

Alexander Cartwright (b. 4-17-1820, d. 7-12-1892): Baseball pioneer. Organized the first baseball game on June 19, 1846, and set the basic rules of bases 90 feet apart, 9 men per side, 3 strikes per out and 3 outs per inning. In that first game his New York Knickerbockers lost to the New York Nine 23–1 at Elysian Fields in Hoboken, NJ.

Billy Casper (b. 6-24-31): Golfer. Famed putter. Won 51 PGA tournaments. PGA Player of Year in both 1966 and '70. Won Vardon Trophy in 1960, '63, '64, '65 and '68. Won the US Open twice, in 1959 at Winged Foot in Mamaronek, New York, and in 1966 in 18-hole playoff over Arnold Palmer at Olympic Club, San Francisco. Beat Gene Littler in 18 hole playoff to win 1970 Masters.

Tracy Caulkins (b. 1-11-63): Swimmer. Won 3 gold medals at 1984 Olympics. Won 48 U.S. national titles, more than any other swimmer, from 1978 to 1984. Also won Sullivan Award in 1978.

Steve Cauthen (b. 5-1-60): Jockey. In 1978 became youngest jockey to win Triple Crown, aboard Affirmed. First jockey to top $6 million in season earnings (1977). *Sports Illustrated* Sportsman of Year for 1977. Moved to England in 1979; rode Epsom Derby winners Slip Anchor (1985) and Reference Point (1987).

Evonne Goolagong Cawley (b. 7-31-51): Tennis. Won 4 Australian Open titles from 1974 through '77; won '71 French Open; Wimbledon in 1971 and '80. Runnerup four straight years at U.S. Open (1973–76) which she never won.

Bill Chadwick (b. 10-10-15): Hockey referee. Spent 16 years as a referee despite vision in only one eye. Developed hand signals to signify penalties. Also former television announcer for the New York Rangers.

Wilt Chamberlain (b. 8-21-36): Basketball C. Alltime leader in rebounds (23,924) and rebounding average (22.9). Alltime season leader in points scored (4,029 in 1962), scoring average (50.4 in 1962), rebounding average (27.2 in 1961) and field goal percentage (.727 in 1973). Alltime single-game most points scored (100 in 1962) and most rebounds (55 in 1960). Second alltime most points scored (31,419) and most field goals made (12,681). 4 MVP awards (1960, consecutively 1966–68); playoff MVP in 1972 and 1960 Rookie of the Year. 7-time All-Star. 30.1 career scoring average. Career span 1959–72 with Philadelphia, Los Angeles and San Francisco. College Player of the Year in 1957 at Kansas.

Colin Chapman (b. 1928, d. 12-16-83): Auto racing engineer. Founded Lotus race and street cars, designing the first Lotus racer in 1948. Introduced the monocoque design for Formula One cars in 1962 and ground effects in 1978.

Julio Cesar Chavez (b. 7-12-62): Boxer. Career record through 6/10/96: 97-2-1. Held titles as junior welterweight (1989–96) lightweight (1987–89), super featherweight (1984–87).

Gerry Cheevers (b. 12-7-40): Hockey goalie. Goaltender for Stanley Cup-winning Boston Bruins teams of 1970 and '72. In 12 seasons with Boston had 230-94-74 record with a goals against average of 2.89. Also coached Bruins from 1980–84, with 204-126-46 record. Elected to Hall of Fame 1985.

Citation (b. 4-11-45, d. 8-8-70): Thoroughbred race horse. Triple Crown winner in 1948 with jockey Eddie Arcaro aboard. Trained by Ben A. Jones.

King Clancy (b. 2-25-03, d. 11-6-86): Hockey D. Four-time All-Star. Coach, Montreal Maroons, Toronto. Referee. Trophy named in his honor, recognizing leadership qualities and contribution to community.

Jim Clark (b. 3-4-36, d. 4-7-68): Scottish auto racer. Fifth alltime in Formula 1 victories (25—tied with Niki Lauda). Formula 1 champion 2 times (1963, 1965). Won Indy 500 1 time (1965). Named Indy 500 Rookie of the Year in 1963. Killed during competition in 1968 at age 32.

Bobby Clarke (b. 8-13-49): Hockey C. Won MVP award 3 times (1973, consecutively 1975–76). 358 career goals, 852 assists. Scored 100+ points 3 times. Played on 2 consecutive Stanley Cup champions (1974–75) with Philadelphia. Career span 1969 to 1984. Also general manager with Philadelphia 1984–90, Minnesota 1991–92, Florida 1993–94, and Philadelphia since 1994.

Roger Clemens (b. 8-4-62): Baseball RHP. Record 20 strikeouts in 1 game. Won 2 consecutive Cy Young Awards in 1986, 1987. Also 1986 MVP. League leader in ERA 4 times, wins and strikeouts 2 times each. Career span since 1984 with Boston.

Roberto Clemente (b. 8-18-34, d. 12-31-72): Baseball OF. Killed in plane crash while still an active player. Had 3,000 career hits and .317 career average. 4 batting titles; .300+ average 13 times. 1966 MVP; 1971 World Series MVP. 12 consecutive Gold Gloves; led league in assists 5 times. Career span 1955–72 with Pittsburgh.

Ty Cobb (b. 12-18-1886, d. 7-17-61): Baseball OF. Alltime leader in batting average (.366) and runs scored (2,245); second most hits (4,191); fourth most stolen bases (892). 1911 MVP and 1909 Triple Crown winner. 12 batting titles. Had .400+ average 3 times,

.350+ average 13 other times; 200+ hits 9 times. Led league in hits 7 times, steals 6 times and runs scored 5 times. Career span 1905–28 with Detroit.

Mickey Cochrane (b. 4-6-03, d. 6-28-62): Baseball C. Alltime highest career batting average among catchers (.320). MVP in 1928, 1934. Had .300+ average 8 times. Career span 1925–37 with Philadelphia, Detroit.

Sebastian Coe (b. 9-29-56): Track and field. British runner was gold medalist in 1,500 meters and silver medalist in 800 meters at 2 consecutive Olympics in 1980, 1984. Set world record in 800 meters (1:41.73 in 1981) and 1,000 meters (2:12.18 in 1981). Now a member of Parliament.

Eddie Collins (b. 5-2-1887, d. 3-25-51): Baseball 2B. Alltime leader among 2nd basemen in games, chances and assists; led league in fielding 9 times. 3,311 career hits; .333 career average; .330+ average 12 times. 743 career stolen bases; alltime most World Series steals (14—tied with Lou Brock); alltime leader in single-game steals (6, twice). 1914 MVP. Career span 1906–30 with Philadelphia, Chicago.

Nadia Comaneci (b. 11-12-61): Romanian gymnast. First ever to score a perfect 10 at Olympics (on uneven parallel bars in 1976). Won 3 gold, 2 silver and 1 bronze medal at 1976 Olympics. Also won 2 gold and 2 silver medals at 1980 Olympics.

Dennis Conner (b. 9-16-42): Sailing. Captain of America's Cup winner 3 times (1980, '87,'88).

Maureen Connolly (b. 9-17-34, d. 6-21-69): Tennis player. "Little Mo" first woman to achieve the Grand Slam, in 1953. Won the U.S. singles title in 1951 at age 16. Thereafter lost only 4 matches before retiring in 1954 because of a broken leg caused by a riding accident. Was never beaten in singles at Wimbledon, winning 3 consecutive titles (1952–54). Won 3 consecutive U.S. singles titles (1951–53) and 2 consecutive French titles (1953–54). Also won 1 Australian title (1953).

Jimmy Connors (b. 9-2-52): Tennis player. Alltime men's leader in tournament victories (109). Held men's #1 ranking a record 159 consecutive weeks, July 29, 1974 through Aug. 16, 1977. Won 5 U.S. Open singles titles on 3 different surfaces (grass 1974, clay 1976, hard 1978, consecutively 1982–83). Won 2 Wimbledon singles titles (1974, 1982) farther apart than anyone since Bill Tilden. Also won 1974 Australian Open title. Reached Grand Slam final 7 other times.

Jim Corbett (b. 9-1-1866; d. 2-18-33): Boxer. "Gentleman Jim." Invented jab. Fight with Australian Peter Jackson on 5-21-1891 ruled no contest when neither could continue into 62nd round. Won heavyweight title on 9-7-1892 with a KO of John Sullivan in 21 rounds; it was first heavyweight title fight using gloves. Lost title when KO'd by Bob Fitzsimmons in 14 on 3-17-1897, then lost two bids to regain it against Jim Jeffries. Career record: 19 fights; won 7 by KO and 4 by decision; drew 2; lost 4; 2 no decision.

Angel Cordero (b. 11-8-42): Jockey. At end of 1994 third alltime in wins (7,057) and earnings ($164,526,217). Led yearly earnings three times, in 1976 and 1982–83, winning Eclipse Awards in the last two years.

Howard Cosell (b. 3-25-18, d. 4-23-95): Sportscaster. Lawyer turned TV-radio sports commentator in 1953. Best known for his work on "Monday Night Football." His nasal voice and "tell it like it is" approach made him a controversial figure.

James (Doc) Counsilman (b. 12-28-20): Swimming coach. Coached Indiana from 1957 to 1990. Won 6 consecutive NCAA championships (1968–73). Career record 287–36–1. Coached U.S. men's team at Olympics in 1964, 1976. Also oldest person to swim English Channel (58 in 1979).

Count Fleet (b. 3-24-40, d. 12-3-73): Thoroughbred race horse. Triple Crown winner in 1943 with jockey Johnny Longden aboard. Trained by Don Cameron.

Yvan Cournoyer (b. 11-22-43): Hockey RW. "The Roadrunner" had 428 goals and 435 assists during his 15 season career with the Montreal Canadiens. Had 25 or more goals in 12 straight seasons. Played on 10 Stanley Cup championship teams. Elected to Hall of Fame in 1982.

Margaret Smith Court (b. 7-16-42): Australian tennis player. Alltime leader in Grand Slam singles titles (26) and total Grand Slam titles (66). Achieved Grand Slam in 1970 and mixed doubles Grand Slam in 1963 with Ken Fletcher. Won 11 Australian singles titles (consecutively 1960–66, 1969–71, 1973), 5 French titles (1962, 1964, consecutively 1969–70, 1973), 7 U.S. titles (1962, 1965, consecutively 1969–70, 1973) and 3 Wimbledon titles (1963, 1965, 1970). Also won 19 Grand Slam doubles titles and 19 mixed doubles titles.

Bob Cousy (b. 8-9-28): Basketball G. Finished career with 6,955 assists, second alltime most assists in a game (28 in 1958). League leader in assists 8 consecutive seasons. Averaged 18+ points and named to All-Star team 10 consecutive seasons. 1957 MVP. Played on 6 championship teams with Boston from 1950 to 1969. Also played on NCAA championship team in 1947 with Holy Cross.

Dave Cowens (b. 10-25-48): Basketball C. After college career at Florida State, NBA co-Rookie of Year in 1971. NBA MVP for 1973. All-Star game MVP in 1973. Career span 1970–71 through 1982–83, all but the last year with the Boston Celtics. Elected to Hall of Fame in 1991.

Ben Crenshaw (b. 1-11-52): Golfer. Legendary putter. Won Masters in 1984 and 1995.

Larry Csonka (b. 12-25-46): Football RB. In 11 seasons rushed 1,891 times for 8,081 yards (4.3 per carry) and 64 TDs. MVP of Super Bowl VIII, when he rushed 33 times for a then Super Bowl record 145 yards in Miami's 24–7 defeat of Minnesota. Career span 1968–74, 1979 with Miami Dolphins; 1976–78 with New York Giants. Elected to Hall of Fame in 1987.

Billy Cunningham (b. 6-3-43): Basketball player and coach. Averaged 24.8 points a game at North Carolina. In nine seasons (1965–66 through 1975–76) with Philadelphia 76ers, averaged 20.8 points per game. All NBA first team 1969, '70 and '71. In 8 seasons as Sixer coach went 454–196 in season, 66–39 in playoffs and won NBA title in 1983. Elected to Hall of Fame in 1985.

Chuck Daly (b. 7-20-30): Basketball coach. Won 2 consecutive championships with Detroit (1989–90). Won 50+ games 4 consecutive seasons. Coach of 1992 Olympic team. Career span as pro coach 1983–92 with Pistons; 1992–94 with New Jersey Nets.

Damascus (b. 1964): Thoroughbred race horse. After finishing 3rd in 1967 Kentucky Derby, won the Preakness, the Belmont, the Dwyer, the American

Derby, the Travers, the Woodward and others—12 of 16 starts. Unanimous Horse of the Year for 1967.

Stanley Dancer (b. 7-25-27): Harness racing driver. Only driver to win the Trotting Triple Crown 2 times (Nevele Pride in 1968, Super Bowl in 1972). Also won Pacing Triple Crown driving Most Happy Fella in 1970. Won The Hambletonian 4 times (1968, 1972, 1975, 1983). Driver of the Year in 1968.

Tamas Darnyi (b. 6-3-67): Hungarian swimmer. Gold medalist in 200-meter and 400-meter individual medleys at 1988 and 1992 Olympics. Also won both events at World Championships in 1986 and 1991. Set world records in these events at 1991 Championships (1:59.36 and 4:12.36).

Al Davis (b. 7-4-29): Football executive. Owner and general manager of Oakland-LA Raiders since 1963. Built winningest franchise in sports history (321-200-11—a .614 winning percentage entering the 1996 season). Team has won 3 Super Bowl championships (1976, 1980, 1983). Also served as AFL commissioner in 1966, helped negotiate AFL–NFL merger.

Ernie Davis (b. 12-14-39, d. 5-18-63): Football RB. Won Heisman Trophy in 1961, the first black man to win the award. All-America 3 times at Syracuse. First selection in 1962 NFL draft, but became fatally ill with leukemia and never played professionally.

Glenn Davis (b. 12-26-24): College football HB. "Mr. Outside." Teamed with Doc Blanchard to lead Army to 3 consecutive undefeated seasons (1944–46) and 2 consecutive national championships (1944–45). Won Heisman Trophy in 1946. Also named All-America 3 times.

John Davis (b. 1-12-21, d. 7-13-84): Weightlifter. Gold medalist at 2 consecutive Olympics in 1948, 1952. World champion 6 times.

Pete Dawkins (b. 3-8-38): Football RB. Starred at Army 1956–58. Won Heisman Trophy 1958. Was first captain of cadets, class president, top 5 percent of class academically, and football team captain; first man to do all four at West Point. Did not play pro football. Attended Oxford on Rhodes scholarship, won two Bronze Stars in Vietnam, rose to brigadier general before leaving Army to become investment banker. Made unsuccessful run for Senate from New Jersey in 1988.

Len Dawson (b. 6-20-35): Football QB. Completed 2,136 of 3,741 pass attempts with 239 TDs. In Super Bowl I threw for one TD in 35–10 loss to Green Bay. MVP of Super Bowl IV. Career span 1957–75, the last 13 seasons with Kansas City Chiefs. Elected to Hall of Fame in 1987.

Dizzy Dean (b. 1-16-11, d. 7-17-74): Baseball RHP. 1934 MVP with 30 wins. League leader in strikeouts, complete games 4 times each. 150 career wins. Arm trouble shortened career after 134 wins by age 26. Career span 1930–41 and 1947 with St Louis and Chicago Cubs.

Dave DeBusschere (b. 10-16-40): Basketball F. NBA First Team Defense six straight seasons, 1969–74. Member of NBA champion New York Knicks in 1970 and '73. Career span 1962–63 through middle of 1968–69 season with Detroit Pistons; through 1973–74 with Knicks. Youngest coach (24) in NBA history. Elected to NBA Hall of Fame in 1982.

Pierre de Coubertin (b. 1-1-1863, d. 9-2-37): Frenchman called the father of the Modern Olympics.

President of International Olympic Committee from 1896 to 1925.

Jack Dempsey (b. 6-24-1895, d. 5-31-83): Boxer. Heavyweight champion (1919–26), lost title to Gene Tunney and rematch in the famous "long count" bout in 1927. Career record 62-6-10 with 49 KOs from 1914 to 1928.

Gail Devers (b. 11-19-66): Track and field sprinter/hurdler. Won 100 at 1992 and '96 Olympics; leading 100 hurdles in '92 when she tripped over final hurdle and finished fifth. Successfully completed same double at 1993 World Championships, winning 100 in 10.82 and 100 hurdles in American record 12.46. Also won '93 world indoor title in 60 (6.95). Battled Graves Disease.

Klaus Dibiasi (b. 10-6-47): Italian diver. Gold medalist in platform at 3 consecutive Olympics (1968, 1972, 1976) and silver medalist at 1964 Olympics.

Eric Dickerson (b. 9-2-60): Football RB. Alltime season leader in yards rushing (2,105 in 1984), second alltime most career yards rushing (13,259). Rushed for 1,000+ yards a record 7 consecutive seasons; 100+ yards in 61 games, including 12 times in 1984. Led league in rushing 4 times. Rookie of the Year in 1983. Career span 1983–93 with Los Angeles Rams, Indianapolis, L.A. Raiders and Atlanta Falcons.

Bill Dickey (b. 6-6-07): Baseball C. Lifetime average .313. Hit 202 career home runs. Played on 11 AL All-Star teams. In eight World Series, hit five homers and 24 RBIs. Career span 1928–43 and 1946, all with the New York Yankees. Inducted to Hall of Fame 1954.

Harrison Dillard (b. 7-8-23): Track and field. Only man to win Olympic gold medal in sprint (100 meters in 1948) and hurdles (110 meters in 1952). Sullivan Award winner in 1955.

Joe DiMaggio (b. 11-25-14): Baseball OF. Voted baseball's greatest living player. Record 56-game hitting streak in 1941. MVP in 1939, 1941, 1947. Had .325 career batting average; .300+ average 11 times; 100+ RBI 9 times. League leader in batting average, HR, and RBI 2 times each. Played on 10 World Series winners with NY Yankees. Career span 1936–51.

Mike Ditka (b. 10-18-39): Football TE-Coach. NFL Rookie of the Year in 1961. Named to Pro Bowl five times. Made 427 catches for 5,812 yards and 43 TDs. Career span 1961 to '72 with Bears, Eagles and Cowboys. Coach of Bears from 1982–92 with 112–68 overall record. Coach of Bear team that won Super Bowl XX, 46–10 over New England. Elected to Hall of Fame 1988.

Tony Dorsett (b. 4-7-54): Football RB. Third alltime in yards rushing (12,739), fourth in attempts (2,936). Rushed for 1,000+ yards in 8 seasons. Set record for longest run from scrimmage with 99-yard touchdown run on Jan. 3, 1983. Scored 91 career touchdowns. Named Rookie of the Year in 1977. Career span 1977–88 with Dallas, Denver. Also won Heisman Trophy in 1976, leading Pittsburgh to national championship. Alltime NCAA leader in yards rushing and only man to break 6,000-yard barrier (6,082).

Abner Doubleday (b. 6-26-1819, d. 1-26-1893): Civil War hero incorrectly credited as the inventor of baseball in Cooperstown, NY, in 1839. Recent research calls Alexander Cartwright the true father of the game.

Clyde Drexler (b. 6-22-62): Basketball G. Nicknamed "The Glide" for his smooth play. Member of U.S. "Dream Team" that won 1992 Olympic gold medal. Career span 1984–1994 with Portland Trail Blazers and 1995– with Houston Rockets, with whom he won his first NBA title in 1995.

Ken Dryden (b. 8-8-47): Hockey G. Goaltender of the Year 5 times (1973, consecutively 1976–79). Playoff MVP as a rookie in 1971, maintained rookie status and named Rookie of the Year in 1972. Led league in goals against average 5 times. Career record 258-57-74, including 46 shutouts. Career 2.24 goals against average is the modern record. 4 playoff shutouts in 1977. Played on 6 Stanley Cup champions with Montreal from 1970 to 1979.

Don Drysdale (b. 7-23-36, d. 7-3-93): Baseball RHP. Led NL three times in strikeouts (1959, '60, '62) and once in wins (1962). Won 1962 Cy Young Award with 25–9 mark. In 1968 pitched six straight shutouts en route to major league record—broken in 1988 by Orel Hershiser—of 58 consecutive scoreless innings. Career record of 209–166, with 2,484 K's and ERA of 2.95. Career span 1956–69, all with Dodgers. Inducted into Hall of Fame 1984.

Roberto Duran (b. 6-16-51): Panamanian boxer. Champion in 3 different weight classes: lightweight (1972–79), welterweight (1980, lost rematch to Sugar Ray Leonard in famous "no más" bout) and junior middleweight (1983–84).

Leo Durocher (b. 7-27-05, d. 10-7-91): Baseball manager. "Leo the Lip." Said "Nice guys finish last." Managed 3 pennant winners and 1954 World Series winner. Won 2,008 games in 24 years. Led Brooklyn 1939–48; New York 1948–55; Chicago 1966–72; and Houston 1972–73.

Eddie Eagan (b. 4-26-1898, d. 6-14-67): Only American athlete to win gold medal at Summer and Winter Olympic Games (boxing 1920, bobsled 1932).

Alan Eagleson (b. 4-24-33): Hockey labor leader. Founder of NHL Players' Association and its executive director from 1967–92.

Dale Earnhardt (b. 4-29-52): Auto racer. NASCAR champion 7 times (1980, 1986–87, 1990–91, 1993-94). 68 career NASCAR victories through 11-12-95.

Stefan Edberg (b. 1-19-66): Swedish tennis player. Has won 2 Wimbledon singles titles (1988, 1990), 2 Australian Open titles (1985, 1987) and 2 U.S. Open titles (1991, 1992). Led Sweden to 3 Davis Cup victories (consecutively 1984–85, 1987).

Gertrude Ederle (b. 10-23-06): Swimmer. First woman to swim the English Channel, in 1926. Swam 21 miles from France to England in 14:39. Also won 3 medals at the 1924 Olympics.

Herb Elliott (b. 2-25-38): Track and field. Australian runner was gold medalist in 1960 Olympic 1,500 meters in world record 3:35.6. Also set world mile record of 3:54.5 in 1958. Undefeated at 1500 meters/mile in international competition. Retired at 21.

John Elway (b. 6-28-60): Football QB. First player taken in 1983 NFL draft. Topped 3,000 yards passing every season from 1985–91. Through '95 season had thrown for 41,706 yards, 225 TDs. Famous for last minute drives. Career span since 1983 with Denver Broncos.

Roy Emerson (b. 11-3-36): Australian tennis player. Alltime men's leader in Grand Slam singles titles (12).

Won 6 Australian titles, 5 consecutively (1961, 1963–67), 2 consecutive Wimbledon titles (1964–65), 2 U.S. titles (1961, 1964) and 2 French titles (1963, 1967). Also won 13 Grand Slam doubles titles.

Kornelia Ender (b. 10-25-58): East German swimmer. Won 4 gold medals at 1976 Olympics and 3 silver medals at 1972 Olympics.

Julius Erving (b. 2-22-50): "Dr. J." Basketball F. Third alltime most points scored for combined ABA and NBA career (30,026). 24.2 scoring average. Averaged 20+ points 14 consecutive seasons. 4 MVP awards, consecutively 1974–76, 1981; playoff MVP 1974, 1976. All-Star 9 times. Led league in scoring 3 times. Played on 3 championship teams, with New York (ABA) and Philadelphia (NBA). Career span 1971 to 1986.

Phil Esposito (b. 2-20-42): Hockey C. "Espo." First to break the 100-point barrier (126 in 1969). 1,590 career points, 717 goals, and 873 assists. Led league in goals 6 consecutive seasons, points 5 times and assists 3 times. Won MVP award 2 times (1969, 1974). Scored 30+ goals 13 consecutive seasons and 100+ points 6 times. All-Star 6 times. Career span 1963–81 with Chicago, Boston, NY Rangers. General manager of NY Rangers from 1986–89. Currently GM of Tampa Bay.

Tony Esposito (b. 4-23-43): Hockey goalie. Brother of Phil. A five-time All Star during 16-season NHL career, almost all of it with the Chicago Blackhawks. In 886 games gave up 2,563 goals, an average of 2.92 per game. Won or shared Vezina Trophy three times. Elected to Hall of Fame in 1988.

Janet Evans (b. 8-28-71): Swimmer. Competed in 1988, '92 and '96 Olympics, winning 3 gold medals in '88 and 1 in '92. Set world record in 400-meter freestyle (4:03.85 in 1988), 800-meter freestyle (8:16.22 in 1989) and 1,500-meter freestyle (15:52.10 in 1988). Sullivan Award winner in 1989.

Lee Evans (b. 2-25-47): Track and field. Gold medalist in 400 meters at 1968 Olympics with world record time of 43.86 that stood until 1988.

Chris Evert (b. 12-21-54): Also Chris Evert Lloyd. Tennis player. Second alltime in tournament victories (157). Tied for fourth alltime in women's Grand Slam singles titles (18). Won at least 1 Grand Slam singles title every year from 1974 to '86. Won 7 French Open titles (1974–75, 1979–'80, 1983, 1985–86), 6 U.S. Open titles (1975–77, 1978, 1980, 1982), 3 Wimbledon titles (1974, 1976, 1981) and 2 Australian Open titles (1982, 1984). Reached Grand Slam finals 16 other times. Reached semifinals at 52 of her last 56 Grand Slams.

Weeb Ewbank (b. 5-6-07): Football coach. Only coach to win titles in both the NFL and AFL. Coached Baltimore Colts to classic overtime defeat of New York Giants in 1958 and New York Jets to their stunning 16–7 win over Baltimore in Super Bowl III. Career record of 134-130-7. Career span 1954–62 with Colts and 1963–73 with Jets. Elected to Hall of Fame in 1978.

Patrick Ewing (b. 8-5-62): Basketball C. 1986 Rookie of the Year with New York. 20+ points average in all 11 seasons with Knicks. All-NBA first team 1990. Played on 3 NCAA final teams with Georgetown (1982, 1984–85); tournament MVP in 1984. All-America 3 times.

Nick Faldo (b. 7-18-57): British golfer. Three-time winner of Masters (1989–90, consecutively, 1996) and British Open 3 times (1987, 1990, 1992).

Juan Manuel Fangio (b. 6-24-11, d. 7-17-95): Argentinian auto racer. 24 Formula 1 victories in just 51 starts. Formula 1 champion 5 times, the most of any driver (1951, consecutively 1954–57). Retired in 1958.

Bob Feller (b. 11-3-18): Baseball RHP. League leader in wins 6 times, strikeouts 7 times, innings pitched 5 times. Pitched 3 no-hitters and 12 one-hitters. 266 career wins; 2,581 career strikeouts. Won 20+ games 6 times. Served 4 years in military during career. Career span 1936–41, 1945–56 with Cleveland.

Tom Ferguson (b. 12-20-50): Rodeo. First to top $1 million in career earnings. All-Around champion 6 consecutive years (1974–79).

Enzo Ferrari (b. 2-8-1898, d. 8-14-88): Auto racing engineer. Team owner since 1929, he built first Ferrari race car in Italy in 1947 and continued to preside over Ferrari race and street cars until his death. In 61 years of competition, Ferrari's cars have won over 5,000 races.

Mark Fidrych (b. 8-14-54): Baseball RHP. "The Bird." Rookie of the Year in 1976 with Detroit. Had 19–9 record with league-best 2.39 ERA and 24 complete games. Habit of talking to the ball on the mound made him a cult hero. Arm injuries curtailed career.

Cecil Fielder (b. 9-21-63): Baseball 1B. The last man to hit 50+ HR (51 in 1990). Has led the major leagues in HR twice and RBI 3 consecutive seasons (1990–92) after spending 1989 season in Japanese league. Career span since 1985 with Toronto, Detroit and NY Yankees.

Herve Filion (b. 2-1-40): Harness racing driver. Alltime leader in career wins (more than 13,000). Driver of the Year 10 times, more than any other driver (consecutively 1969–74, 1978, 1981, 1989).

Rollie Fingers (b. 8-25-46): Baseball RHP. Third alltime in relief wins (107); 341 career saves; 944 appearances. 1981 Cy Young and MVP winner; 1974 World Series MVP. Alltime Series leader in saves (6). Career span 1968–85 with Oakland, San Diego, Milwaukee.

Bobby Fischer (b. 3-9-43): Chess. World champion from 1972 to 1975, the only American to hold title. Never played competitive chess during his reign. Forfeited title to Anatoly Karpov by refusing to play him.

Carlton Fisk (b. 12-26-47): Baseball C. Alltime HR leader among catchers (352) and second in games caught (2,226). 376 career HR, including a record 75 after age 40. Rookie of the Year in 1972 and All-Star 11 times. Hit dramatic 12th-inning HR to win Game 6 of 1975 World Series. Career span 1969-93 with Boston, Chicago (AL).

Emerson Fittipaldi (b. 12-12-46): Brazilian auto racer. Won Indy 500 in 1989 and '93. Won CART championship in 1989. Formula 1 champion 2 times (1972, 1974).

James Fitzsimmons (b. 7-23-1874, d. 3-11-66): Horse racing trainer. "Sunny Jim." Trained Triple Crown winner 2 times (Gallant Fox in 1930, Omaha in 1935). Trained Belmont Stakes winner 6 times (1930, 1932, consecutively 1935–36, 1939, 1955), Preakness Stakes winner 4 times (1930, 1935, 1955, 1957) and Kentucky Derby winner 3 times (1930, 1935, 1939).

Peggy Fleming (b. 7-27-48): Figure skater. Olympic champion 1968. World champion (1966–68) and U.S. champion (1964–68).

Curt Flood (b. 1-18-38): Baseball OF. Won 7 consecutive Gold Gloves from 1963 to 1969. Career batting average of .293. Refused to be traded after 1969 season, challenging baseball's reserve clause. Supreme Court rejected his plea, but baseball was eventually forced to adopt free agency system. Career span 1956–69 with St. Louis.

Whitey Ford (b. 10-21-26): Baseball LHP. Alltime World Series leader in wins, losses, games started, innings pitched, hits allowed, walks and strikeouts. 236 career wins, 2.75 ERA. Third alltime best career winning percentage (.690). Led league in wins and winning percentage 3 times each; ERA, shutouts, innings pitched 2 times each. 1961 Cy Young winner and World Series MVP. Career span 1950, 1953–67 with New York Yankees.

Forego (b. 1970): Thoroughbred race horse. Horse of the Year in 1974 (won 8 of 13 starts); '75 (won 6 of 9); and '76 (won 6 of 8). Finished fourth in 1973 Kentucky Derby. Over six years won 34 of 57 starts and $1,938,957.

George Foreman (b. 1-22-48): Boxer. Heavyweight champion (1973–74). Retired in 1977, but returned to the ring in 1987. Lost 12-round decision to champion Evander Holyfield in 1991. Retired after losing to Tommy Morrison 6-7-93; returned again in 1994 at age 45 to KO Michael Moorer for heavyweight title. Also heavyweight gold medalist at 1968 Olympics.

Dick Fosbury (b. 3-6-47): Track and field. Gold medalist in high jump at 1968 Olympics. Introduced back-to-the-bar style of high jumping, called the "Fosbury Flop."

Jimmie Foxx (b. 10-22-07, d. 7-21-67): Baseball 1B. Won 3 MVP awards, consecutively 1932–33, 1938. Fourth alltime highest slugging average (.609), with 534 career HR; hit 30+ HR 12 consecutive seasons, 100+ RBI 13 consecutive seasons. Won Triple Crown in 1933. Led league in HR 4 times, batting average 2 times. Career span 1925–45 with Philadelphia, Boston.

A. J. Foyt (b. 1-16-35): Auto racer. Alltime leader in Indy Car victories (67). Won Indy 500 4 times (1961, 1964, 1967, 1977), Daytona 500 1 time (1972), 24 Hours of Daytona 2 times (1983, 1985) and 24 Hours of LeMans 1 time (1967). USAC champion 7 times, more than any other driver (consecutively 1960–61, 1963–64, 1967, 1975, 1979).

William H. G. France (b. 9-26-09): Auto racing executive. Founder of NASCAR and president from 1948 to 1972, succeeded by his son Bill Jr. Builder of Daytona and Talladega speedways.

Dawn Fraser (b. 9-4-37): Australian swimmer. First swimmer to win gold medal in same event at 3 consecutive Olympics (100-meter freestyle in 1956, 1960, 1964). First woman to break the 1-minute barrier at 100 meters (59.9 in 1962).

Joe Frazier (b. 1-12-44): Boxer. "Smokin' Joe." Heavyweight champion (1970–73). Best known for his 3 epic bouts with Muhammad Ali. Career record 32-4-1 with 27 KOs from 1965 to 1976. Also heavyweight gold medalist at 1964 Olympics.

Walt Frazier (b. 3-29-45): Basketball G. Point guard on championship Knick teams of 1970 and '73. First team All Star in 1970, '72, '74 and '75. First team All Defense every year from 1969–1975. Averaged 18.9 points per game in 13-season NBA career. Elected to Hall of Fame in 1986.

Frankie Frisch (b. 9-9-98, d. 3-12-73): Baseball IN. The Fordham Flash." Led NL in hits in 1923 (223). Hit over .300 13 seasons. Scored 100+ runs 7 times. Drove in 100+ runs three times. Career .316 batting average. Career span 1919–26 with New York Giants and 1927–37 with St. Louis Cardinals "Gashouse Gang." NL MVP in 1931. Elected to Hall of Fame in 1947.

Dan Gable (b. 10-25-48): Wrestler. Gold medalist in 149–pound division at 1972 Olympics. Also NCAA champion 2 times (in 1968 at 130 pounds, in 1969 at 137 pounds). Coached Iowa to NCAA championship 14 times (consecutively 1978–86, 1991–93 and 1995–96).

Clarence Gaines (b. 5-21-23): College basketball coach. "Bighouse." Retired after 1992–93 season with 828 career wins in 46 seasons at Division II Winston-Salem State since 1947.

John Galbreath (b. 8-10-1897, d. 7-20-88): Horse racing owner. Owner of Darby Dan Farms from 1935 until his death and of baseball's Pittsburgh Pirates from 1946 to 1985. Only man to breed and own winners of both the Kentucky Derby (Chateaugay in 1963 and Proud Clarion in 1967) and the Epsom Derby (Roberto in 1972).

Gallant Fox (b. 3-23-27, d. 11-13-54): Thoroughbred race horse. Triple Crown winner in 1930 with jockey Earle Sande aboard. Trained by James Fitzsimmons. The only Triple Crown winner to sire another Triple Crown winner (Omaha in 1935).

Don Garlits (b. 1-14-32): Auto racer. "Big Daddy." Has won 35 National Hot Rod Association top fuel events. Won 3 NHRA top fuel points titles (1975, 1985–86). First top fuel driver to surpass 190 mph (1963), 200 mph (1964), 240 mph (1973), 250 mph (1975) and 270 mph (1986). Credited with developing rear engine dragster.

Lou Gehrig (b. 6-19-03, d. 6-2-41): Baseball 1B. "The Iron Horse." Second alltime in consecutive games played (2,130), leader in grand slam HR (23), third in RBI (1,990) and slugging average (.632). MVP in 1927, 1936; won Triple Crown in 1934. .340 career average; 493 career HR. 100+ RBI 13 consecutive seasons. Led league in RBI 5 times and HR 3 times. Played on 7 World Series winners with New York Yankees. Died of disease since named for him. Career span 1923–39.

Bernie Geoffrion (b. 2-16-31): Hockey RW. "Boom Boom" for his powerful slapshot. Won Hart Memorial Trophy for 1960–61. Scored 393 goals and 429 assists in 16 seasons (1950–51 through 1967–68), the first 14 with the Montreal Canadiens, the final two with the New York Rangers. Elected to Hall of Fame 1972.

Eddie Giacomin (b. 6-6-39): Hockey goalie. "Fast Eddie" led NHL goalies in games won three straight seasons. Shared Vezina Trophy for 1970–71. In 610 games gave up 1,675 goals, a goals against average of 2.82. Career span 1965–75 with the New York Rangers and 1975–78 with Detroit Red Wings.

Althea Gibson (b. 8-25-27): Tennis player. Won 2 consecutive Wimbledon and U.S. singles titles (1957–58), the first black player to win these tournaments. Also won 1 French title (1956).

Bob Gibson (b. 11-9-35): Baseball RHP. 1968 Cy Young and MVP award winner with alltime National League best in ERA (1.12) and second most shutouts (13). Also 1970 Cy Young award winner.

Record holder for most strikeouts in a World Series game (17); Series MVP in 1964, 1967. Won 20+ games 5 times. 251 career wins; 3,117 strikeouts. Pitched no-hitter in 1971. Career span 1959–75 with St. Louis.

Josh Gibson (b. 12-21-11, d. 1-20-47): Baseball C in Negro leagues. "The Black Babe Ruth." Couldn't play in major leagues because of color. Credited with 950 HR (75 in 1931, 69 in 1934) and .350 batting average. Had .400+ average 2 times. Career span 1930–46 with Homestead Grays, Pittsburgh Crawfords.

Kirk Gibson (b. 5-28-57): Baseball OF. Played on 2 World Series champions (Detroit in 1984 and Los Angeles in 1988). Hit dramatic pinch-hit HR in 9th inning to win Game 1 of 1988 series. MVP in 1988. Career span since 1979, currently with Detroit. Also starred in baseball and football at Michigan State.

Frank Gifford (b. 8-16-30): Football RB. NFL Player of Year in 1956 when he rushed for 819 yards and caught 51 passes. Played in seven Pro Bowls. Retired for one season after ferocious hit by Chuck Bednarik. Career span 1952–60 and 1962–64, all with New York Giants. Elected to Hall of Fame in 1977.

Rod Gilbert (b. 7-1-41): Hockey RW. Played 16 seasons, all with the New York Rangers (1960–61 through 1977–78), and had 406 goals and 615 assists. Elected to Hall of Fame 1982.

Sid Gillman (b. 10-26-11): Football coach. Developed wide-open, pass-oriented style of offense, introduced techniques for situational player substitutions, and the study of game films. Won one division title with Los Angeles Rams and five division titles and one AFL championship (1963) with Los Angeles/San Diego Chargers. Career span 1955–59 Los Angeles Rams; 1960 Los Angeles Chargers; 1961–69 San Diego; 1973–74 Houston. Lifetime record 124-101-7. Also general manager in San Diego and Houston.

Pancho Gonzales (b. 5-9-28, d. 7-3-95): Tennis player. Won 2 consecutive U.S. singles titles (1948–49). In 1969, at age 41, beat Charlie Pasarell 22–24, 1–6, 16–14, 6–3, 11–9 in longest Wimbledon match ever (5:12).

Shane Gould (b. 11-23-56): Australian swimmer. Won 3 gold medals, 1 silver and 1 bronze at 1972 Olympics. Set 11 world records over 23-month period beginning in 1971. Held world record in 5 freestyle distances ranging from 100 meters to 1,500 meters in late 1971 and 1972. Retired at age 16.

Steffi Graf (b. 6-14-69): German tennis player. Achieved the Grand Slam in 1988. Has won 4 Australian Open singles titles (1988–90, '94), 7 Wimbledon titles (1988–89, 1991–93, '95–96), 5 French Open titles (1987–88, '93 and '95–96) and 4 U.S. Open titles (1988–89, '93 and '95). Held the #1 ranking for a record 186 weeks; Aug. 17, 1987 through March 10, 1991. Gold medalist at 1988 Olympics. Second in alltime Grand Slam singles titles (20).

Otto Graham (b. 12-6-21): Football QB. Led Cleveland to 10 championship games in his 10-year career. Played on 4 consecutive AAFC champions (1946–49) and 3 NFL champions (1950, consecutively 1954–55). Combined league totals: 23,584 yards passing, 174 touchdown passes. Player of the Year 2 times (1953, 1955). Led league in passing 6 times. Career span 1946–55.

Red Grange (b. 6-13-03, d. 1-28-91): Football HB. "The Galloping Ghost." All-America 3 consecutive seasons with Illinois (1923–25), scoring 31 touchdowns in 20–game collegiate career. Signed by George Halas of Chicago in 1925, attracted sellout crowds across the country. Established the first AFL with manager C. C. Pyle in 1926, but league folded after 1 year. Career span 1925–34 with Chicago, New York.

Rocky Graziano (b. 6-7-22, d. 5-22-90): Boxer. Middleweight champion from 1947 to 1948. Career record 67–13. Endured 3 brutal title fights against Tony Zale, with Zale winning by KO in 1946 and 1948, and Graziano winning by KO in 1947.

Hank Greenberg (b. 1-1-11, d. 9-4-86): Baseball 1B. 331 career HR (58 in 1938). MVP in 1935, 1940. League leader in HR and RBI 4 times each. Fifth alltime highest slugging average (.605). 100+ RBI 7 times. Career span 1933-41, 1945-47 with Detroit, Pittsburgh.

Joe Greene (b. 9-24-46): Football DT. "Mean Joe." Anchored Pittsburgh's famed "Steel Curtain" defense. Selected for Pro Bowl 10 times. Played on 4 Super Bowl champions (consecutively 1974-75, 1978-79). Career span 1969 to 1981.

Forrest Gregg (b. 10-18-33): Football OT/G. Played in then-record 188 straight games from 1956 through 1971. Named all-NFL eight straight years starting in 1960. Career span 1956–71, most of it with Green Bay Packers. Played on winning Packer team in first two Super Bowls. Inducted into Hall of Fame in 1977.

Wayne Gretzky (b. 1-26-61): Hockey C. "The Great One." Most dominant player in history. Alltime scoring leader in points (2,608), assists (1,771), and goals (837). Alltime single-season scoring leader in points (215 in 1986), goals (92 in 1982) and assists (163 in 1986). Has won MVP award 9 times, more than any other player (consecutively 1980-87, 1989). Led league in assists 14 times, scoring 11 times, goals 5 times. Scored 200+ points 4 times, 100+ points 10 other times; 70+ goals 4 consecutive seasons, 50+ goals 5 other times; 100+ assists 11 consecutive seasons. Playoff MVP 2 times (1985, 1988). All-Star 8 times. Played on 5 Stanley Cup champions with Edmonton from 1978 to 1988. Traded to Los Angeles on Aug. 9, 1988, then to St Louis Feb. 1996. Moved as a free agent to NY Rangers for 1996–97 season.

Bob Griese (b. 2-3-45): Football QB. Career span 1967–80 with Miami Dolphins. Played in three straight Super Bowls, 1971–73. Quarterback of 1972 Dolphin team that went 17–0. Won Super Bowl VII and VIII. In 14 seasons completed 1,926 passes for 25,092 yards and 192 TDs. Elected to Hall of Fame in 1990.

Archie Griffin (b. 8-21-54): College football RB. Only player to win the Heisman Trophy 2 times (consecutively 1974-75), with Ohio State. Fourth alltime NCAA most yards rushing (5,177), his 6.13 yards per carry is the collegiate record. Professional career span 1976-83 with Cincinnati; totaled 2,808 yards rushing and 192 receptions.

Lefty Grove (b. 3-6-00, d. 5-22-75): Baseball LHP. 300 career wins and fourth alltime highest winning percentage (.680). League leader in ERA 9 times, strikeouts 7 consecutive seasons. Won 20+ games 8 times. 1931 MVP. Career span 1925-41 with Philadelphia, Boston.

Tony Gwynn (b. 5-9-60): Baseball OF. 6 batting titles (1984, consecutively 1987-89, 1994-95). League leader in hits 6 times, with .300+ average 11 times, 200+ hits 4 times. Career span since 1982 with San Diego.

Walter Hagen (b. 12-21-1892, d. 10-5-69): Golfer. Third alltime leader in major championships (11). Won PGA Championship 5 times (1921, consecutively 1924-27), British Open 4 times (1922, 1924, consecutively 1928-29) and U.S. Open 2 times (1914, 1919). Won 40 career tournaments.

Marvin Hagler (b. 5-23-54): Boxer. "Marvelous." Middleweight champion (1980-87). Career record 62-3 2 with 52 KOs from 1973 to 1987. Defended title 13 times.

George Halas (b. 2-2-1895, d. 10-31-83): Football owner and coach. "Papa Bear." Alltime leader in seasons coaching (40) and second in wins (324). Career record 324-151-31 intermittently from 1920 to 1967. Remained as owner until his death. Chicago won a record 7 NFL championships during his tenure.

Glenn Hall (b. 10-3-31): Hockey goalie. "Mr. Goalie." was an All-Star goalie in 11 of his 18 seasons. Set record for consecutive games by a goaltender, with 502, and ended career with goals against average of 2.51. Won or shared Vezina Trophy three times. Career span 1952–53 through 1970–71.

Arthur B. "Bull" Hancock (b. 1-24-10, d. 9-14-72): Horse racing owner. Owner of Claiborne Farm and arguably the greatest breeder in history. For 15 straight years, from 1955 to 1969, a Claiborne stallion led the sire list. Foaled at Claiborne Farm were 4 Horses of the Year (Kelso, Round Table, Bold Ruler and Nashua).

Tom Harmon (b. 9-28-19, d. 3-17-90): Football RB. Won Heisman Trophy in 1940 with Michigan. Triple-threat back led nation in scoring and named All-America 2 consecutive seasons (1939-40). Awarded Silver Star and Purple Heart in World War II. Played in NFL with Los Angeles (1946-47).

Franco Harris (b. 3-7-50): Football RB. Fifth alltime most rushing yards (12,120) and fifth in rushing touchdowns (91). Rushed for 1,000+ yards in 8 seasons, 100+ yards in 47 games. Scored 100 career touchdowns. Selected for Pro Bowl 9 times. Rookie of the Year in 1972. Played on 4 Super Bowl champions (consecutively 1974-75, 1978-79) with Pittsburgh. Super Bowl MVP in 1974. Holds Super Bowl record for most rushing yards (354). Made the "Immaculate Reception" to win 1972 playoff game against Oakland. Career span 1972-83 with Pittsburgh.

Leon Hart (b. 11-2-28): Football DE. Won Heisman Trophy in 1949, the last lineman to win the award. Played on 3 national champions with Notre Dame (consecutively 1946–47, 1949) and the Irish went undefeated during his 4 years (36-0-2). Also played on 3 NFL champions with Detroit. Career span 1950-57.

Bill Hartack (b. 12-9-32): Horse racing jockey. Rode Kentucky Derby winner 5 times (1957, 1960, 1962, 1964, 1969), Preakness Stakes winner 3 times (1956, 1964, 1969) and Belmont Stakes winner 1 time (1960).

Doug Harvey (b. 12-19-24, d. 12-26-90): Hockey D. Defensive Player of the Year 7 times (consecutively 1954-57, 1959-61). Led league in assists in 1954. All-Star 10 times. Played on 6 Stanley Cup champions with Montreal from 1947 to 1968.

Billy Haughton (b. 11-2-23, d. 7-15-86): Harness racing driver. Won the Pacing Triple Crown driving Rum Customer in 1968. Won The Hambletonian 4 times (1974, consecutively 1976-77, 1980).

John Havlicek (b. 4-8-40): Basketball F/G. Member of Ohio State team that won 1960 NCAA title. "Hondo" averaged 20.8 points per game over 16-season NBA career, all with Boston. First team NBA All Star in 1971, '72, '73 and '74. Member of eight Celtic teams that won NBA title. Playoff MVP 1974. Elected to Hall of Fame in 1983.

Elvin Hayes (b. 11-17-45): Basketball C. 1968 *Sporting News* College Player of Year as Houston senior. Averaged 21.0 points per game over 16-season NBA career. Led NBA in scoring (28.4) in 1969 and in rebounding in 1970 (16.9 per game) and '74 (18.1). First team All NBA in 1975, '77 and '79. Elected to Hall of Fame in 1989.

Woody Hayes (b. 2-14-13, d. 3-12-87): College football coach. Won national championship 3 times (1954, 1957, 1968) and Rose Bowl 4 times. Career record 238-72-10, including 4 undefeated seasons, with Ohio State from 1951 to 1978. Forced to resign after striking an opposing player during 1978 Gator Bowl.

Marques Haynes (b. 10-3-26): Basketball G. Known as "The World's Greatest Dribbler." Since 1946 has barnstormed more than 4 million miles throughout 97 countries for the Harlem Globetrotters, Harlem Magicians, Meadowlark Lemon's Bucketeers, Harlem Wizards.

Thomas Hearns (b. 10-18-58): Boxer. "Hit Man." Champion in 5 different weight classes: junior middleweight, light heavyweight, middleweight, super middleweight, and light heavyweight.

Eric Heiden (b. 6-14-58): Speed skater. Won 5 gold medals at 1980 Olympics. World champion 3 consecutive years (1977-79). Also won Sullivan Award in 1980.

Carol Heiss (b. 1-20-40): Figure skater. Gold medalist at 1960 Olympics, silver medalist at 1956 Olympics. World champion 5 consecutive years (1956-60) and U.S. champion 4 consecutive years (1957-60). Married 1956 gold medalist Hayes Jenkins.

Rickey Henderson (b. 12-25-57): Baseball OF. Alltime career stolen base leader (1,149); alltime season stolen base record holder (130) in 1982. Led league in steals 11 times. Scored 100+ runs 11 times. 1990 MVP. Alltime most HR leading off game. Career span since 1979 with Oakland, New York, Toronto and San Diego.

Sonja Henie (b. 4-8-12, d. 10-12-69): Norwegian figure skater. Gold medalist at 3 consecutive Olympics (1928, 1932, 1936). World champion 10 consecutive years (1927-36).

Orel Hershiser (b. 9-16-58): Baseball RHP. Alltime leader most consecutive scoreless innings pitched (59 in 1988). Cy Young Award winner in 1988 and World Series MVP. Career span 1983-94, Los Angeles, 1995-, Cleveland.

Foster Hewitt (b. 11-21-02, d. 4-22-85): Hockey sportscaster. In 1923, aired one of hockey's first radio broadcasts. Became the voice of hockey in Canada on radio and later television. Famous for the phrase, "He shoots ... he scores!"

Tommy Hitchcock (b. 2-11-00, d. 4-19-44): Polo. 10-goal rating 18 times in his 19-year career from 1922 to 1940. Killed in plane crash in World War II.

Lew Hoad (b. 11-23-34): Australian tennis player. Won 2 consecutive Wimbledon singles titles (1956-57). Also won French title and Australian title in 1956, but failed to achieve the Grand Slam when defeated at Forest Hills by countryman Ken Rosewall.

Ben Hogan (b. 8-13-12): Golfer. Third alltime in career wins (63). Won U.S. Open 4 times (1948, consecutively 1950-51, 1953), the Masters (1951, 1953) and PGA Championship (1946, 1948) 2 times each and British Open once (1953). PGA Player of the Year 4 times (1948, consecutively 1950-51, 1953).

Marshall Holman (b. 9-29-54): Bowler. Won 21 PBA titles between 1975 and 1988. Had leading average in 1987 (213.54) and was named PBA Bowler of the Year.

Nat Holman (b. 10-18-1896, d. 2-12-95): College basketball coach. Only coach in history to win NCAA and NIT championships in same season in 1950 with CCNY. 423 career wins, a .689 winning percentage.

Larry Holmes (b. 11-3-49): Boxer. Heavyweight champion (1978-85). Career record 53-3 with 37 KOs from 1973 to 1991. Defended title 21 times. Fought periodically after 1991, never for title.

Lou Holtz (b. 1-6-37): Football coach. Coached Notre Dame to national championship in 1988 with 12-0 record and a 34-21 win over West Virginia in Fiesta Bowl. Entering '96 season had 208-92-7 career record. 10-8-2 career record in bowl games. Career span 1969-71 at William & Mary (13-20); 1972-75 at N.C. State (33-12-3); 1977-83 at Arkansas (60-21-2); 1984-85 at Minnesota (10-12); and since 1986 at Notre Dame (86-22-1).

Evander Holyfield (b. 10-19-62): Boxer. Won heavyweight crown Oct. 25, 1990 when he beat James "Buster" Douglas in Las Vegas. Lost title to Riddick Bowe in Las Vegas on 11-13-92, regained it from Bowe one year later, then lost to Michael Moorer on 4-22-94.

Red Holzman (b. 8-10-20): Basketball coach. Led New York Knicks to NBA title in 1970 and '73. NBA coach of the Year in 1970. Member of Rochester team that won NBA title in both 1946 (in NBL) and '51. After two-year coaching stints with Milwaukee and St. Louis, coached New York Knicks from 1968-82. Elected to Hall of Fame in 1985.

Harry Hopman (b. 8-12-06, d. 12-27-85): Australian tennis coach. As nonplaying captain, led Australia to 15 Davis Cup titles between 1950 and 1969. Mentor to Lew Hoad, Ken Rosewall, Rod Laver and John Newcombe.

Willie Hoppe (b. 10-11-1887, d. 2-1-59): Billiards. Won 51 world championship matches from 1904 to 1952.

Rogers Hornsby (b. 4-27-1896, d. 1-5-63): Baseball 2B. Second all-time highest career batting average (.358) and 7 batting titles, including .424 average in 1924. 200+ hits 7 times; .400+ average 3 times and .300+ average 12 other times. Led league in slugging average 9 times. Triple Crown winner in 1922, 1925; MVP award winner in 1925, 1929. Career span 1915-37 with St Louis (NL), New York (NL), Boston, Chicago (NL).

Paul Hornung (b. 12-23-35): Football RB-K. Led league in scoring 3 consecutive seasons, including a record 176 points in 1960 (15 touchdowns, 15 field goals, 41 extra points). Player of the Year in 1961. Career span 1957-66 with Green Bay. Suspended for 1963 season by Pete Rozelle for gambling. Also won Heisman Trophy in 1956 with Notre Dame.

Gordie Howe (b. 3-31-28): Hockey RW. Second alltime in goals (801), first in years played (26) and games (1,767). Second alltime in points (1,850) and assists (1,049). Won MVP award 6 times (consecutively 1952–53, 1957–58, 1960, 1963). Led league in scoring 6 times, goals 5 times and assists 3 times. Scored 40+ goals 5 times, 30+ goals 13 other times, 100+ points 3 times. All-Star 12 times. Played on 4 Stanley Cup champions with Detroit from 1946 to 1971. Teamed with sons Mark and Marty in the WHA with Houston and New England from 1973 to 1979, in NHL with Hartford in 1980.

Carl Hubbell (b. 6-22-03, d. 11-21-88): Baseball LHP. 253 career wins. MVP in 1933, 1936. League leader in wins and ERA 3 times each. Won 24 consecutive games from 1936 to 1937. Struck out Ruth, Gehrig, Foxx, Simmons and Cronin consecutively in 1934 All-Star game. Pitched no-hitter in 1929. Career span 1928-43 with New York.

Sam Huff (b. 10-4-34): Football LB. Made 30 interceptions. Career span 1956–69 with New York Giants and Washington Redskins. Elected to Hall of Fame in 1982.

Bobby Hull (b. 1-3-39): Hockey LW. "The Golden Jet." Led league in goals 7 times and points 3 times. 610 career goals. Scored 50+ goals 5 times, 30+ goals 8 other times. Won MVP award 2 consecutive seasons (1965-66). Son Brett won MVP award in 1991, the only father and son to be so honored. All-Star 10 times. Career span 1957-72 with Chicago, 1973-80 with Winnipeg of WHA.

Brett Hull (b. 8-9-64): Hockey RW. Son of Bobby Hull. Won Hart Memorial Trophy for 1990–91 season. Career span 1986–87 with Calgary Flames; since 1987 with St. Louis Blues.

Jim (Catfish) Hunter (b. 4-8-46): Baseball RHP. 1974 Cy Young award winner. Won 20+ games 5 consecutive seasons. Led league in wins and winning percentage 2 times each, ERA 1 time. 250+ innings pitched 8 times. Pitched perfect game in 1968. Member of 5 World Series champions for Oakland and New York Yankees. Career span 1965-79.

Don Hutson (b. 1-31-13): Football WR. Third alltime in touchdown receptions (99). Led league in pass receptions 8 times, receiving yards 7 times and scoring 5 consecutive seasons. Caught at least 1 pass in 95 consecutive games. Player of the Year 2 consecutive seasons (1941-42). Career span 1935-45 with Green Bay.

Hank Iba (b. 8-6-04; d. 1-15-93): College basketball coach. Coached Oklahoma A&M (which became Oklahoma State) from 1934 to 1970. Team won NCAA titles in 1945 and '46. 767 career wins is third alltime behind Adolph Rupp and Dean Smith.

Jackie Ickx (b. 1-1-45): Belgian auto racer. Won the 24 Hours of LeMans a record six times (1969, consecutively 1975-77, 1981-82) before retiring in 1985.

Punch Imlach (b. 3-15-18, d. 12-1-87): Hockey coach. 467 wins. With Toronto from 1958 to 1969. Won 4 Stanley Cup championships (consecutively 1962-64, 1967).

Bo Jackson (b. 11-30-62): Baseball OF and Football RB. Only person in history to be named to baseball All-Star game and football Pro Bowl game. 1985 Heisman Trophy winner at Auburn. First pick in 1986 NFL draft by Tampa Bay, but opted to play baseball at Kansas City. 1989 All-Star game MVP. Signed with football's LA Raiders in 1988. Sustained football injury in 1990, released from baseball contract by KC, signed by Chicago (AL) and returned from injury in early September 1991, but comeback failed at first. Had hip replacement surgery and hit homer in first at bat afterwards. Retired 1994.

Joe Jackson (b. 7-16-1889, d. 12-5-51): Baseball OF. "Shoeless Joe." Third alltime highest career batting average (.356), with .300+ average 11 times. One of the "8 men out" banned from baseball for throwing 1919 World Series. Career span 1908-20 with Cleveland, Chicago.

Reggie Jackson (b. 5-18-46): Baseball OF. "Mr. October." Alltime leader in World Series slugging average (.755). 1977 Series MVP, hit 3 HR in final game on 3 consecutive pitches. 563 career HR total is sixth best alltime. Led league in HR 4 times. 1973 MVP. Alltime strikeout leader (2,597). In a 12-year period played on 10 first-place teams, 5 World Series winners. Career span 1967-87 with Oakland, New York, California. Inducted to baseball Hall of Fame in 1993.

Bruce Jenner (b. 10-28-49): Track and Field. Set world decathlon record (8,634) in winning gold medal at 1976 Olympics. Sullivan Award winner in 1976.

John Henry (b. 1975): Thoroughbred race horse. Sold as yearling for $1,100, the gelding was Horse of the Year in 1981 and in 1984 and retired with then-record $6,597,947 in winnings.

Ben Johnson (b. 12-30-61): Track and field. Canadian sprinter set world record in 100 meters (9.83 in 1987). Won event at 1988 Olympics in 9.79, but gold medal revoked for failing drug test. Both world records revoked for steroid usage. Suspended for life after testing positive for elevated testosterone level at an indoor meet in Montreal on 1-17-93.

Earvin (Magic) Johnson (b. 8-14-59): Basketball G. Retired Nov. 7, 1991 after being diagnosed with HIV, the virus that causes AIDS. Returned to Lakers Feb '96 at age 36. Second alltime in assists (10,141); alltime playoff leader in assists (2,346) and steals (358). MVP award 3 times (1987, consecutively 1989–90) and playoff MVP 1980, 1982, 1987. Played on 5 championship teams with Los Angeles since 1979. All-Star 8 consecutive seasons. League leader in assists 4 times, steals 2 times, free throw percentage 1 time. Also won NCAA championship and named tournament MVP in 1979 with Michigan State.

Jack Johnson (b. 3-31-1878, d. 6-10-46): Boxer. First black heavyweight champion (1908-15). Career record 78-8-12 with 45 KOs from 1897 to 1928.

Jimmy Johnson (b. 7-16-43): Football coach. Led the Cowboys from 1–15 in 1989, his first season in Dallas, to a 52–17 win over the Buffalo Bills in the Super Bowl XXVII just four seasons later. Also coached Super Bowl XXVIII champion Cowboys before resigning because of a dispute with owner Jerry Jones. Head coach at Oklahoma State from 1979–83 and Univ. of Miami 1984–88 with career collegiate record of 81-34-3. Johnson's Hurricanes won national championship in 1987. Succeeded Don Shula as Miami Dolphins coach, Jan. '96.

Michael Johnson (b. 9-13-67): Track and field sprinter. First man to win gold medals in both the 200 and 400 at the Olympics (1996). Broke 17-year-old 200-meter world record (from 19.72 to 19.66) in '96 U.S. Olympic trials, then further lowered mark to 19.32 at Atlanta. Won 200 at 1991 World Championships, 400 at

'93 worlds and both events at the '95 worlds. Anchored US 4 x 400 team at 1993 World Championship to world record of 2:54.29 with fastest ever relay carry of 42.97.

Walter Johnson (b. 11-6-1887, d. 12-10-46): Baseball RHP. "Big Train." Alltime leader in shutouts (110), second in wins (416), fourth in losses (279) and third in innings pitched (5,923). His 2.17 career ERA and 3,508 career strikeouts are seventh best alltime. MVP in 1913, 1924. Won 20+ games 12 times. League leader in strikeouts 12 times, ERA 5 times, wins 6 times. Pitched no-hitter in 1920. Career span 1907-27 with Washington.

Ben A. Jones (b. 12-31-1882, d. 6-13-61): Horse racing trainer. Trained Triple Crown winner (Whirlaway in 1941). Trained Kentucky Derby winner 6 times, more than any other trainer (1938, 1941, 1944, consecutively 1948-49, 1952), Preakness Stakes winner 2 times (1941, 1944) and Belmont Stakes winner 1 time (1941).

Bobby Jones (b. 3-17-02, d. 12-18-71): Golfer. Achieved golf's only recognized Grand Slam in 1930. Second alltime in major championships (13). Won U.S. Amateur 5 times, more than any golfer (consecutively 1924-25, 1927-28, 1930), U.S. Open 4 times (1923, 1926, consecutively 1929-30), British Open 3 times (consecutively 1926-27, 1930) and British Amateur (1930). Also designed Augusta National course, site of the Masters, and founded the tournament. Winner of Sullivan Award in 1930.

K.C. Jones (b. 5-25-32): Basketball G-coach. Member of 8 straight NBA-championship Boston Celtic teams in his nine season career from 1958–59 through 1966–67. Averaged 7.4 points and 4.3 assists per game. Coached Celtics from 1983–84 through 1987–88, with 308–102 regular season record and 65–37 playoff record with NBA titles in 1984 and '86.

Robert Trent Jones (b. 6-20-06): English-born golf course architect designed or remodelled over 400 courses, including Baltusrol, Hazeltine, Oak Hill and Winged Foot. In the mid-60s five straight U.S. Opens were played on courses designed or remodelled by Jones.

Sam Jones (b. 6-24-33): Basketball G. Played 12 seasons with Boston Celtics (1958–69) and made the playoffs every year, winning NBA title every year from 1959–66 plus 1968 and '69. Averaged 17.7 points per game for career. Elected to Hall of Fame in 1983.

Michael Jordan (b. 2-17-63): Basketball G. "Air." After 1995–96 season, alltime highest regular season scoring average (33.0) and most points scored in a playoff game (63 in 1986). Led Bulls to record 72 wins in 1995–96. Led league in scoring a record 8 seasons, steals 3 times. MVP in 1988, 1991–92; '96; playoff MVP in 1991–93, '96; Rookie of the Year in 1985. All-Star team 6 consecutive seasons, All-Defensive team 5 consecutive seasons. Career span 1984–93, 1995– with Chicago. Announced retirement on 10-6-93, returned in March 1995. Also College Player of the Year in 1984. Played on NCAA championship team with North Carolina in 1982. Member of gold medal-winning 1984 and '92 Olympic teams.

Florence Griffith Joyner (b. 12-21-59): Track and field. Won 3 gold medals (100 meters, 200 meters, 4x100-meter relay) at 1988 Olympics; Set world record in 100 (10.49) in 1988 and in 200 (21.34) at the 1988 Olympics. Sullivan Award winner in 1988.

Jackie Joyner-Kersee (b. 3-3-62): Track and field. Gold medalist in heptathlon and long jump at 1988 Olympics and in the former at the 1992 Olympics. Set heptathlon world record (7,291 points) at 1988 Olympics. Also won silver medal in heptathlon at 1984 Olympics and bronze in long jump at 1992 and '96 Olympics. Sullivan Award winner in 1986.

Alberto Juantorena (b. 3-12-51): Track and field. Cuban was gold medalist in 400 meters and 800 meters at 1976 Olympics.

Wang Junxia (b. 1963): Chinese distance runner. Broke four existing world records over six days in Sept. 1993. Broke 10,000 (29:31.78) on 9-8; ran 1500 in 3:51.92 in finishing second to countrywoman Qu Yunxia's world record of 3:50.46 on 9-11; ran 3,000 record of 8:12.19 in heats on 9-12 and lowered it to 8:06.11 on 9-13. Won gold in 5,000 and silver in 10,00 at 1996 Olympics.

Sonny Jurgensen (b. 8-23-34): Football QB. In 18 seasons completed 2,433 of 4,262 pass attempts for 32,224 yards and 255 TDs. Led NFL in passing both 1967 and '69. Career span 1957–1974 with Philadelphia Eagles and Washington Redskins. Elected to Hall of Fame in 1983.

Duke Kahanamoku (b. 8-24-1890, d. 1-22- 68): Swimmer. Won a total of 5 medals (3 gold and 2 silver) at 3 Olympics in 1912, 1920, 1924. Introduced the crawl stroke to America. Surfing pioneer and water polo player. Later sheriff of Honolulu.

Al Kaline (b. 12-19-34): Baseball OF. 3,007 career hits and 399 career HR. Youngest player to win batting title with .340 average as a 20-year-old in 1955. Had .300+ average 9 times. Played in 18 All-Star games. Career span 1953-74 with Detroit.

Anatoly Karpov (b. 5-23-61): Soviet chess player. First world champion to receive title by default, in 1975, when Bobby Fischer chose not to defend his crown. Champion until 1985 when beaten by Gary Kasparov. Recognized by FIDE as champion in 1994.

Garry Kasparov (b. 4-13-63): Born Harry Weinstein. Chess player. World champion from 1985 to 1993 when stripped of title by FIDE. Won six game series against IBM computer, Deep Blue, in 1996.

Kip Keino (b. 1-17-40): Track and field. Kenyan was gold medalist in 1,500 meters at 1968 Olympics and in steeplechase at 1972 Olympics.

Jim Kelly (b. 2-14-60): Football QB. Led NFL in passing in 1990 (219 of 346 for 2,829 yards and 24 TDs). Led AFC in passing in 1991. In nine seasons through '94 completed 2,397 of 3,942 attempts for 29,527 yards and 201 TDs. Career span 1983–85 with New Jersey Generals (USFL), since 1986 with Buffalo Bills. Led Bills to four straight Super Bowls, all losses.

Kelso (b. 1957, d. 1983): Thoroughbred race horse. Gelding was Horse of the Year 5 straight years (1960-64). Finished in the money in 53 of 63 races. Career earnings $1,977,896.

Harmon Killebrew (b. 6-29-36): Baseball 3B-1B. 573 career HR total is fifth most alltime. 100+ RBI 9 times, 40+ HR 8 times. League leader in HR 6 times and RBI 4 times. 1969 MVP. 100+ walks and strikeouts 7 times each. Career span 1954-75 with Washington, Minnesota.

Jean Claude Killy (b. 8-30-43): French skier. Won 3 gold medals at 1968 Olympics. World Cup overall champion 2 consecutive years (1967-68).

Ralph Kiner (b. 10-27-22): Baseball OF. Second to Babe Ruth in alltime HR frequency (7.1 HR every 100 at bats). 369 career HR. Led league in HR 7 consecutive seasons, with 50+ HR 2 times; 100+ RBI and runs scored in same season 6 times; 100+ walks 6 times. Career span 1946-55 with Pittsburgh.

Billie Jean King (b. 11-22-43): Tennis player. Won a record 20 Wimbledon titles, including 6 singles titles (consecutively 1966-68, 1972-73, 1975). Won 4 U.S. singles titles (1967, consecutively 1971-72, 1974), and singles titles at Australian Open (1968) and French Open (1972). Won 27 Grand Slam doubles titles—total of 39 Grand Slam titles is third alltime. Helped found the women's pro tour in 1970, serving as president of the Women's Tennis Association 2 times. Helped form Team Tennis.

Nile Kinnick (b. 7-9-18, d. 6-2-43): College football RB. Won the Heisman Trophy in 1939 with Iowa. Premier runner, passer and punter was killed in plane crash during routine Navy training flight. Stadium in Iowa City named in his honor.

Tom Kite (b. 12-9-49): Golfer. Second alltime PGA money leader, with $9,337,998 through end of '95 season. Led PGA in scoring average in 1981 (69.80) and '82 (70.21). PGA Player of Year in 1989, when he won a then-record $1,395,278. Shook reputation for failing to win the big ones by winning 1992 US Open at windy Pebble Beach.

Franz Klammer (b. 12-3-54): Austrian alpine skier. Greatest downhiller ever. Gold medalist in downhill at 1976 Olympics. Also won four World Cup downhill titles (1975-78).

Bob Knight (b. 10-25-40): College basketball coach. Won 3 NCAA championships with Indiana in 1976, 1981, 1987. Coached U.S. Olympic team to gold medal in 1984. 678 career wins and .733 career winning percentage entering 1996–97 season. Career span since 1966.

Olga Korbut (b. 5-16-55): Soviet gymnast. First ever to complete backward somersault on balance beam. Won 3 gold medals at 1972 Olympics.

Sandy Koufax (b. 12-30-35): Baseball LHP. Cy Young Award winner 3 times (1963, consecutively 1965-66); and MVP in 1963; World Series MVP in 1963, 1965. Pitched 1 perfect game, 3 no-hitters. League leader in ERA 5 consecutive seasons, strikeouts 4 times. Won 25+ games 3 times. Career record 165-87, with 2.76 ERA. Career span 1955-66 with Brooklyn/Los Angeles.

Jack Kramer (b. 8-1-21): Tennis player. Won 2 consecutive U.S. singles titles (1946-47) and 1 Wimbledon title (1947). Also won 6 Grand Slam doubles titles. Served as executive director of Association of Tennis Professionals from 1972 to 1975.

Ingrid Kristiansen (b. 3-21-56): Track and field. Norwegian runner is only person—male or female—to hold world records in 5,000 meters (14:37.33 set in 1986), 10,000 meters (30:13.74 set in 1986) and marathon (2:21:06 set in 1985, a record that still stands). Also won Boston Marathon 2 times (1986, 1989) and New York City Marathon once (1989).

Bob Kurland (b. 12-23-24): College basketball player. 6' 10¼" center on Oklahoma A&M teams that won NCAA titles in 1945 and '46. Consensus All America and NCAA tournament MVP in both 1945 and '46. Led nation in scoring in '46. His habit of swatting shots off rim led to creation of goaltending rule in 1945. Won gold medals in both 1948 and '52 Olympics. Turned down lucrative pro offers, playing instead for Phillips 66 Oilers AAU team.

Rene Lacoste (b. 7-2-05): French tennis player. "The Crocodile." One of France's "Four Musketeers" of the 1920s. Won 3 French singles titles (1925, 1927, 1929), 2 consecutive U.S. titles (1926-27) and 2 Wimbledon titles (1925, 1928). Also designed casual shirt with embroidered crocodile that bears his name.

Marion Ladewig (b. 10-30-14): Bowler. Won All-Star Tournament 8 times (consecutively 1949-52, 1954, 1956, 1959, 1963) and WPBA National Championship once (1960). Also voted Bowler of the Year 9 times (consecutively 1950-54, 1957-59, 1963).

Guy Lafleur (b. 9-20-51): Hockey RW. Won MVP award 2 consecutive seasons (1977-78), playoff MVP in 1977. Scored 50+ goals and 100+ points 6 consecutive seasons. Led league in points scored 3 consecutive seasons, goals and assists 1 time each. 560 career goals, 793 assists. Played on 5 Stanley Cup champions with Montreal from 1971 to 1985.

Curly Lambeau (b. 4-9-1898; d. 6-1-65): Football QB and coach. Quarterback for Packer team in early 20's. Record of 212-106-21 in his 29 seasons (1921–49) as Packer coach, winning three NFL titles in 1929–31.

Jack Lambert (b. 7-8-52): Football LB. Anchored Pittsburgh's famed "Steel Curtain" defense. Selected for Pro Bowl 9 times. Played on 4 Super Bowl champions (consecutively 1974-75, 1978-79) with Pittsburgh from 1974 to 1984.

Jake LaMotta (b. 7-10-21): Boxer. "The Bronx Bull." Subject of *Raging Bull*, movie by Martin Scorcese, starring Robert DeNiro. Won middleweight title by knocking out Marcel Cerdan in 10 on 6-16-49. Lost title to Ray Robinson, who KO'd him in 13 on 2-13-51. Career record: 106 bouts; won 30 by KO and 53 by decision; drew 4; and lost 19, 4 by KO.

Kenesaw Mountain Landis (b. 11-20-1866, d. 11-25-44): Baseball's first and most powerful commissioner from 1920 to 1944. By banning the 8 "Black Sox" involved in the fixing of the 1919 World Series, he restored public confidence in the integrity of baseball.

Tom Landry (b. 9-11-24): Football coach. Third alltime in wins (270). The first coach in Dallas history, from 1960 to 1988. Led team to 13 division titles, 7 championship games and 5 Super Bowls. Won 2 Super Bowl championships (1971, 1977). Career record 270-178-6.

Dick "Night Train" Lane (b. 4-16-28): Football DB. Third alltime in interceptions (68) and second in interception yardage (1,207). Set record with 14 interceptions as a rookie in 1952. Career span 1952-65 with Los Angeles, Chicago Cardinals, Detroit.

Joe Lapchick (b. 4-12-00, d. 8-10-70): Basketball C-coach. One of the first big men in basketball, member of New York's Original Celtics. Coached St. John's (1936-47, 1956-65) winning four NIT Tournaments. Coached New York Knicks, 1947-56.

Steve Largent (b. 9-28-54): Football WR. Third alltime in pass receptions (819), second in TD receptions (100). 177 consecutive games with reception, 10 seasons with 50+ receptions and 8 seasons with 1,000+ yards receiving. Career span 1976-89 with Seattle.

Don Larsen (b. 8-7-29): Baseball RHP. Pitched only perfect game in World Series history for the NY Yankees on Oct. 8, 1956, beating the Dodgers 2-0; named World Series MVP. Career span 1953-67 for many teams.

Tommy Lasorda (b. 9-22-27): Baseball manager. Spent nearly his entire minor and major league career in Dodgers organization as a pitcher, coach and manager. Managed Dodgers since 1977, winning 4 pennants and 2 World Series (1981, 1988). Retired July 1996, citing health concerns. Only three men managed one baseball team longer.

Rod Laver (b. 8-9-38): Australian tennis player. "Rocket." Only player to achieve the Grand Slam twice (as an amateur in 1962 and as a pro in 1969). Second alltime in men's Grand Slam singles titles (11—tied with Bjorn Borg). Won 4 Wimbledon titles (consecutively 1961-62, 1968-69), 3 Australian titles (1960, 1962, 1969), 2 U.S. titles (1962, 69) and 2 French titles (1962, 1969). Also won 8 Grand Slam doubles titles. First player to earn $1 million in prize money. 47 career tournament victories. Member of undefeated Australian Davis Cup team from 1959 to 1962.

Andrea Mead Lawrence (b. 4-19-32): Skier. Gold medalist in slalom and giant slalom at 1952 Olympics.

Bobby Layne (b. 12-19-26; d. 12-1-86): Football QB. Led Detroit Lions to NFL championships in both 1952 and '53. In 1952 led NFL in every passing category. Career span 1948–62, most with the Detroit Lions. Elected to Hall of Fame in 1967.

Sammy Lee (b. 8-1-20): Diver. Gold medalist at 2 consecutive Olympics (highboard in 1948, 1952); bronze medalist in springboard at 1948 Olympics. Won the 1953 Sullivan Award. Also 1960 U.S. Olympic diving coach.

Jacques Lemaire (b. 9-7-45): Hockey C-Coach. As center for Montreal Canadiens from 1967–68 through 1978–79 was part of eight Stanley Cup winning teams. Over 12 seasons, all with Montreal, scored 366 goals and had 469 assists. Elected to Hall of Fame in 1984. Coached Canadiens 1983-85 and N.J. Devils since 1993.

Mario Lemieux (b. 10-5-65): Hockey C. Won MVP award in 1988, '93, '96. Playoff MVP in 1991. Led league in most points 5 seasons and goals scored 3 seasons, assists 1 season. Scored 40+ goals and 100+ points 6 consecutive seasons, including 85 goals and 199 points in 1989. Rookie of the Year in 1985. Won 1992–93 scoring title despite sitting out six weeks to receive treatment for Hodgkin's disease, a form of cancer. Sat out 1994–95 season, returned in '95–96 to lead league in scoring and become second fastest player to score 500 career goals. Career span since 1984 with Pittsburgh.

Greg LeMond (b. 6-26-61): Cyclist. Only American to win Tour de France; won event 3 times (1986, consecutively 1989-90). Recovered from hunting accident to win in 1989.

Ivan Lendl (b. 3-7-60): Tennis player. Second alltime men's most career tournament victories (94). Won 3 consecutive U.S. Open singles titles (1985-87) and 3 French Open titles (1984, consecutively 1985-86). Also won 2 consecutive Australian Open titles (1989-90). Reached Grand Slam final 9 other times.

Suzanne Lenglen (b. 5-24-1899, d. 7-4-38): French tennis player. Lost only 1 match from 1919 to her retirement in 1926. Won 6 Wimbledon singles and

doubles titles (consecutively 1919-23, 1925). Won 6 French singles and doubles titles (consecutively 1920-23, 1925-26).

Sugar Ray Leonard (b. 5-17-56): Boxer. Champion in 5 different weight classes: welterweight, junior middleweight, middleweight, light heavyweight and super middleweight. Career record 36-2-1 with 25 KOs from 1977 to 1991. Also light welterweight gold medalist at 1976 Olympics.

Carl Lewis (b. 7-1-61): Track and field. Held world record for 100 meters 9.86; set on 8-25-91 at World Championships in Tokyo. Duplicated Jesse Owens's feat by winning 4 gold medals at 1984 Olympics (100 and 200 meters, 4x100-meter relay and long jump). Also won 2 gold medals (100 meters, long jump) and 1 silver (200 meters) at 1988 Olympics and two gold medals (long jump, 4x100 relay) at 1992 Olympics. Sullivan Award winner in 1981. Won 1996 Olympic long jump gold at age 35, giving him nine career gold medals and making him just the second track and field athlete (along with Al Oerter) to win four golds in a single event.

Nancy Lieberman (b. 7-1-58): Basketball G. Three-time All-America at Old Dominion. Player of the Year (1979, 1980). Olympian, 1976, and selected for 1980 team, but quit because of Moscow boycott. Promoter of women's basketball, played in WPBL, WABA. First woman to play basketball in a men's professional league (USBL) in 1986.

Bob Lilly (b. 7-26-39): Football DT. Dallas Cowboys' first ever draft pick, first Pro Bowl player and first all-NFL choice. Made all-NFL eight times. Career span 1961–74, all with Cowboys. Elected to Hall of Fame in 1980.

Sonny Liston (b. 5-8-32, d. 12-30-70): Boxer. Heavyweight champion from 1962 to 1964. Won title by KO of Floyd Patterson on 9-25-62. Lost title when TKO'd by Cassius Clay (Muhammad Ali) on 2-25-64 and then lost rematch on 5-25-65 when KO'd in first round. Career record: 54 fights; won 39 by KO and 11 by decision; lost 4, three by KO.

Vince Lombardi (b. 6-11-13, d. 9-3-70): Football coach. Alltime highest winning percentage (.740). Career record 105-35-6. Won 5 NFL championships and 2 consecutive Super Bowl titles with Green Bay from 1959 to 1967. Coached Washington in 1969. Super Bowl trophy named in his honor.

Johnny Longden (b. 2-14-07): Horse racing jockey. Rode Triple Crown winner Count Fleet in 1943. 6,032 wins.

Nancy Lopez (b. 1-6-57): Golfer. LPGA Player of the Year 4 times (consecutively 1978-79, 1985, 1988). Winner of LPGA Championship 3 times (1978, 1985, 1989). Member of the LPGA Hall of Fame.

Greg Louganis (b. 1-29-60): Diver. Gold medalist in platform and springboard at 2 consecutive Olympics in 1984, 1988. World champion 5 times (platform in 1978, 1982, 1986; springboard in 1982, 1986). Also Sullivan Award winner in 1978.

Joe Louis (b. 5-13-14, d. 4-12-81): Boxer. "The Brown Bomber." Longest title reign of any heavyweight champion (11 years, 9 months) from June 1937 through March 1949. Career record 63-3 with 49 KOs from 1934 to 1951. Defended title 25 times.

Jerry Lucas (b. 3-30-40): Basketball F. Star at Ohio State. *Sporting News* College Player of Year in both 1961 and '62. In 1960 member of both NCAA championship team and gold-medal winning U.S. Olympic team. Averaged over 20 points and 20 rebounds a game for college career. NBA Rookie of Year in 1964. In 11 NBA seasons averaged 17 points a game. Elected to Hall of Fame in 1979.

Sid Luckman (b. 11-21-16): Football QB. Played on 4 NFL champions (consecutively 1940-41, 1943, 1946) with Chicago. Player of the Year in 1943. Tied record with 7 touchdown passes on Nov. 14, 1943. All-Pro 6 times. 137 career touchdown passes. Career span 1939-50. Also All-America with Columbia.

Jon Lugbill (b. 5-27-61): White water canoe racer. Won 5 world singles titles from 1979 to 1989.

Hank Luisetti (b. 6-16-16): Basketball F. The first player to use the one-handed shot. All-America at Stanford 3 consecutive years from 1936-38.

D. Wayne Lukas (b. 9-2-35): Horse racing trainer. Former college basketball coach and quarter horse trainer takes mass production approach with stables at most major tracks around country. Trained two Horses of the Year, Lady's Secret in 1986 and Criminal Type in 1990. Won 1988 Kentucky Derby with a filly, Winning Colors. Won 1994 Preakness and Belmont with Tabasco Cat. Won all three Triple Crown races in 1995, with Thunder Gulch (Kentucky Derby and Belmont) and Timber County (Preakness). Six-race Triple Crown winning streak ended at '96 Preakness.

Connie Mack (b. 2-22-1862, d. 2-8-56): Born Cornelius McGillicuddy. Baseball manager. Managed Philadelphia for 50 years (1901-50) until age 87. All-time leader in games (7,755), wins (3,731) and losses (3,948). Won 9 pennants and 5 World Series (1910-11, 1913, 1929-30).

Greg Maddux (b. 4-14-66): Baseball P. Won unprecedented fourth consecutive Cy Young Award in 1995, when he was 19–2 with a 1.63 ERA and led the Atlanta Braves to their first World Series title. Career span 1986–92 Chicago (NL), 1993– Atlanta.

Larry Mahan (b. 11-21-43): Rodeo. All-Around champion 6 times (consecutively 1966-70, 1973).

Frank Mahovlich (b. 1-10-38): Hockey LW. Winner of Calder Trophy for top rookie for 1957–58 season. In 18 NHL seasons with Toronto Maple Leafs, Detroit Red Wings and Montreal Canadiens, had 533 goals and 570 assists. Played for six Stanley Cup winners. Elected to Hall of Fame 1981.

Phil Mahre (b. 5-10-57): Skier. Gold medalist in slalom at 1984 Olympics (twin brother Steve won silver medal). World Cup champion 3 consecutive years (1981-83).

Joe Malone (b. 2-28-1890, d. 5-15-69): Hockey F. "Phantom Joe." Led the NHL in its first season, 1917-18, with 44 goals in 20 games with Montreal. Led league in scoring 2 times (1918, 1920). Holds NHL record with most goals scored, single game (7) in 1920.

Karl Malone (b. 7-24-63): Basketball F. "The Mailman." Six-time first-team All-Star. All-Star MVP, 1989. All-Rookie team, 1986. Scored 20+ points per game in 11 of 12 seasons with Utah. Member of 1992 and '96 Olympic teams. Career span since 1985 with Utah.

Moses Malone (b. 3-23-55): Basketball C. Alltime leader free throws made (8,531), fifth in rebounds (16,212) and third in points scored (27,409). 3 MVP awards in 1979, consecutively 1982-83; playoff MVP in 1983. 4-time All-Star. Led league in rebounding 6 times, 5 consecutively. Career span 1976–95 with Houston, Philadelphia, Washington, Atlanta, Milwaukee, San Antonio.

Man o' War (b. 1917, d. 1947): Thoroughbred race horse. Won 20 of 21 races 1919–20. Only loss was in 1919 in Sanford Stakes to Upset. Passed up Derby but won both Preakness and Belmont. Winner of $249,465. Sire of War Admiral, 1937 Triple Crown winner.

Mickey Mantle (b. 10-20-31, d. 8-13-95): Baseball OF. Won 3 MVP awards, consecutively 1956-57 and 1962; won Triple Crown in 1956. 536 career HR. Greatest switch hitter in history. Played in 20 All-Star games. Alltime World Series leader in HR (18), RBI (40) and runs scored (42). No. 7 was a member of 7 World Series winners with NY Yankees. Career span 1951-68.

Diego Maradona (b. 10-30-60): Argentine soccer player. Led Argentina to 1986 World Cup victory and to 1990 World Cup finals. Led Naples to Italian League titles (1987, 1990), Italian Cup (1987) and to European Champion Clubs' Cup title (1989). Throughout 1980s often acknowledged as best player in the world. Tested positive for cocaine and suspended by FIFA and Italian Soccer Federation for 15 months in March 1991. Failed drug test in 1994 World Cup and suspended before second round.

Pete Maravich (b. 6-22-47, d. 1-5-88): Basketball G. "Pistol Pete." Alltime NCAA leader in points scored (3,667), scoring average (44.2) and games scoring 50+ points (28, including then Division I record 69 points in 1970). Alltime season leader in points scored (1,381) and scoring average (44.5) in 1970. College Player of the Year in 1970. NCAA scoring leader and All-America 3 consecutive seasons from 1968 to 1970 with Louisiana State. Also led NBA in scoring in 1977. Averaged 20+ points 8 times. All-Star 2 times. Career span 1970-79 with Atlanta, New Orleans/Utah, Boston.

Gino Marchetti (b. 1-2-27): Football DE. Played in Pro Bowl every year from 1955 to '65, except 1958 when he broke right ankle tackling Frank Gifford in Colts' 23–17 win over the Giants. Career span 1952-66, almost all with Baltimore Colts. Inducted into Hall of Fame in 1972.

Rocky Marciano (b. 9-1-23, d. 8-31-69): Boxer. Heavyweight champion (1952-56). Career record 49-0 with 43 KOs from 1947 to 1956. Retired as undefeated champion.

Juan Marichal (b. 10-24-37): Baseball RHP. 243 career wins, 2.89 career ERA. Won 20+ games 6 times; 250+ innings pitched 8 times; 200+ strikeouts 6 times. Pitched no-hitter in 1963. Career span 1960-75, mostly with San Francisco.

Dan Marino (b. 9-15-61): Football QB. Set alltime season record for yards passing (5,084) and touchdown passes (48) in 1984. Prior to 1995-96 season had passed for 4,000+ yards 5 other seasons. Player of the Year in 1984. Career totals through 1995–96 season: 48,841 yards passing, 352 touchdown passes, first alltime in both categories. Career span since 1983 with Miami.

Roger Maris (b. 9-10-34, d. 12-14-85): Baseball OF. Broke Babe Ruth's alltime season HR record with 61 in 1961. Won consecutive MVP awards and led league in RBI 1960-61. Career span 1957-68 with Kansas City, New York (AL), St Louis.

Billy Martin (b. 5-16-28, d. 12-25-89): Baseball 2B-manager. Volatile manager was hired and fired by Minnesota, Detroit, Texas, New York Yankees (5 times!) and Oakland from 1969 to 1988. Won World Series with Yankees as manager in 1977 and as player 4 times.

Eddie Mathews (b. 10-13-31): Baseball 3B. 512 career HR and 30+ HR 9 consecutive seasons. League leader in HR 2 times, walks 4 times. Career span 1952-68 with Milwaukee.

Christy Mathewson (b. 8-12-1880, d. 10-7-25): Baseball RHP. Third alltime most wins (373, tied with Grover Alexander) and shutouts (80); fifth alltime best ERA (2.13). Led league in wins 5 times; won 30+ games 4 times and 20+ games 9 other times. Led league in ERA and strikeouts 5 times each. 300+ innings pitched 11 times. Pitched 2 no-hitters. Pitched 3 shutouts in 1905 World Series. Career span 1900-16 with New York.

Bob Mathias (b. 11-17-30): Track and field. At age 17, youngest to win gold medal in decathlon at 1948 Olympics. First decathlete to win gold medal at consecutive Olympics (1948, 1952). Also won Sullivan Award in 1948.

Ollie Matson (b. 5-1-30): Football RB. Versatile runner totalled 12,884 combined yards rushing, receiving and kick returning. Scored 73 career touchdowns, including a 105-yard kickoff return on Oct. 14, 1956, the second longest ever. Career span 1952-66 with Chicago Cardinals, Los Angeles, Detroit, Philadelphia. Also won bronze medal in 400-meters at 1952 Olympics.

Roland Matthes (b. 11-17-50): German swimmer. Gold medalist in 100-meter and 200-meter backstroke at 2 consecutive Olympics (1968, 1972). Set 16 world records from 1967 to 1973.

Don Maynard (b. 1-25-37): Football WR. Retired in 1973 as the NFL's alltime leading receiver. In 15 seasons, 10 with the New York Jets, caught 633 passes for 11,834 yards and 88 TDs. Averaged 18.7 yards per catch for career. In 1967 and '68 led AFL with average of 20.2 and 22.8 yards per catch. Elected to Hall of Fame in 1987.

Willie Mays (b. 5-6-31): Baseball OF. "Say Hey Kid." MVP in 1954, 1965; Rookie of the Year in 1951. Third alltime most HR (660), with 50+ HR 2 times, 30+ HR 9 other times. Led league in HR 4 times. 100+ RBI 10 times; 100+ runs scored 12 consecutive seasons. 3,283 career hits. Led league in stolen bases 4 consecutive seasons. 30 HR and 30 steals in same season 2 times and first man in history to hit 300+ HR and steal 300+ bases. Won 11 consecutive Gold Gloves; set record for career putouts by an outfielder and league record for total chances. His catch in the 1954 World Series off the bat of Vic Wertz called the greatest ever. Career span 1951-73 with New York and San Francisco Giants, New York Mets.

Bill Mazeroski (b. 9-5-36): Baseball 2B. Hit dramatic 9th-inning home run in Game 7 to win 1960 World Series, first of only two Series' to end on a home run. Also a great fielder, won Gold Glove 8 times. Led league in assists 9 times, double plays 8 times and putouts 5 times.

Joe McCarthy (b. 4-21-1887, d. 1-3-78): Baseball manager. Alltime highest winning percentage among managers for regular season (.615) and World Series (.763). First manager to win pennants in both leagues

(Chicago (NL), 1929, New York (AL), 1932). From 1926 to 1950 his teams won 7 World Series and 9 pennants.

Mark McCormack (b. 11-6-30): Sports marketing agent. Founded International Management Group in 1962. Also author of best-selling business advice books.

Pat McCormick (b. 5-12-30): Diver. Gold medalist in platform and springboard at 2 consecutive Olympics (1952, 1956). Also won Sullivan Award in 1956.

Willie McCovey (b. 1-10-38): Baseball 1B. Led NL in homers three times (1963, '68, '69) and in RBIs twice (1968–69). 521 career homers. .270 career batting average. Hit 18 grand slams. Rookie of Year 1959. NL MVP in 1969. Career span 1959–73 and 1977–80 with San Francisco Giants, 1974–76 with San Diego Padres and 1976 with Oakland A's. Elected to Hall of Fame in 1986.

John McEnroe (b. 2-26-59): Tennis player. Has won 4 U.S. Open singles titles (consecutively 1979-81, 1984) and 3 Wimbledon titles (1981, consecutively 1983-84). Also won 8 Grand Slam doubles titles. Third alltime men's most career tournament victories (77). Led U.S. to 5 Davis Cup victories (1978-79, 1981-82, 1992).

John McGraw (b. 4-7-1873, d. 2-25-34): Baseball manager. Second alltime most games (4,801) and wins (2,784). Guided New York Giants to 3 World Series titles and 10 pennants from 1902 to 1932.

Denny McLain (b. 3-29-44): Baseball RHP. Last pitcher to win 30+ games in a season (Detroit, 1968); won 20+ games 2 other times. Won 2 consecutive Cy Young Awards (1968-69). Led league in innings pitched 2 times. Served 2½-year jail term for 1985 conviction of extortion, racketeering and drug possession. Career span 1963-72.

Mary T. Meagher (b. 10-27-64): Swimmer. "Madame Butterfly." Won 3 gold medals at 1984 Olympics (100-meter butterfly, 200-meter butterfly and 400-medley relay). In 1981 set world records in 100-meter butterfly (57.93) and 200-meter butterfly (2:05.96).

Rick Mears (b. 12-3-51): Auto racer. Has won Indy 500 4 times (1979, 1984, 1988, 1991) and been CART champion 3 times (1979, consecutively 1981-82). Named Indy 500 Rookie of the Year in 1978.

Mark Messier (b. 1-18-61): Hockey C. Two-time Hart Trophy (MVP) winnner; won Stanley Cups with Edmonton (1984, '85, '87, '88 and '90) and NY Rangers (1994). Among top five alltime in points, top ten in goals, assists. Career span 1979–91 Edmonton, 1991–NY Rangers.

Cary Middlecoff (b. 1-6-21): Golfer. Also a dentist. Won 40 PGA tournaments, including 1955 Masters and US Opens in 1949 and '56. Won 1956 Vardon Trophy.

George Mikan (b. 6-18-24): Basketball C. Averaged 20+ points per game and named to All-Star team 6 consecutive seasons. Led league in scoring 3 times, rebounding 1 time. Played on 5 championship teams in 6 years (1949-54) with Minneapolis. Also played on 1945 NIT championship team with DePaul. All-America 3 times. Served as ABA Commissioner from 1968 to 1969.

Stan Mikita (b. 5-20-40): Hockey C. Won MVP award 2 consecutive seasons (1967-68). 926 career assists, 1,467 career points. Led league in assists 4 consecutive seasons and points 4 times. 541 career goals. All-Star 6 times. Career span 1958-80 with Chicago.

Del Miller (b. 7-5-13; d. 8-19-96): Harness racing driver. Raced in 8 decades, beginning in 1929, the longest career of any athlete. Won The Hambletonian in 1950.

Marvin Miller (b. 4-14-17): Labor negotiator. Union chief of Major League Baseball Players Association from 1966 to 1984. Led strikes in 1972 and 1981. Negotiated 5 labor contracts with owners that increased minimum salary and pension fund, allowed for agents and arbitration, and brought about the end of the reserve clause and the beginning of free agency.

Art Monk (b. 12-5-57): Football WR. Second alltime in pass receptions (940 for 12,721 and 68 TDs through end of 1995–96 season). 106 catches in 1984 was then NFL single season record. Career span 1980–93 with Redskins, 1993–95 with New York Jets, 1995– with Eagles.

Earl Monroe (b. 11-21-44): Basketball G. "The Pearl" played 13 seasons (1968–80) with the Baltimore Bullets and New York Knicks. NBA Rookie of Year in 1968. Member of 1973 NBA championship Knicks team. Averaged 18.8 points a game. Elected to Hall of Fame 1989.

Joe Montana (b. 6-11-56): Football QB. Second alltime highest-rated passer (92.3), third in completions (3,409), sixth in passing yards (40,551) and fourth in touchdown passes (273). Won 4 Super Bowl championships (1981, 1984, consecutively 1988-89) with San Francisco since 1979. Named Super Bowl MVP 3 times (1981, 1984, 1989). Player of the Year in 1989. Also led Notre Dame to national championship in 1977. Career span 1979–92 with San Francisco, 1993–94 Kansas City.

Carlos Monzon (b. 8-7-42, d. 1-8-95): Argentine boxer. Longest title reign of any middleweight champion (6 years, 9 months) from Nov. 1970 through Aug. 1977. Career record 89-3-9 with 61 KOs from 1963 to 1977. Won 82 consecutive bouts from 1964 to 1977. Defended title 14 times. Retired as champion.

Helen Wills Moody (b. 10-6-05): Tennis player. Third alltime most women's Grand Slam singles titles (19). Her 8 Wimbledon titles are second most alltime (consecutively 1927-30, 1932-33, 1935, 1938). Won 7 U.S. titles (consecutively 1923-25, 1927-29, 1931) and 4 French titles (consecutively 1928-30, 1932). Also won 12 Grand Slam doubles titles.

Archie Moore (b. 12-13-16): Boxer. Longest title reign of any light heavyweight champion (9 years, 1 month) from Dec. 1952 through Feb. 1962. Career record 199-26-8 with an alltime record 145 KOs from 1935 to 1965. Retired at age 52.

Davey Moore (b. 11-1-33; d. 3-23-63): Boxer. Won featherweight title by KO of Kid Bassey in 13 on 3-18-59. Five successful defenses of title, before losing it on 3-21-63 to Sugar Ramos who KO'd him in 10. Died two days after fight of brain damage suffered during fight. Career record: 67 bouts; won 30 by KO, 28 by decision, 1 because of foul; drew 1; lost 7, two by KO.

Noureddine Morceli (b. 2-20-70). Algerian track and field middle distance runner. Set world record for mile (3:44.39) in Rieti, Italy, on 9-5-93. Set world record for 1,500 (3:28.86) on 9-5-92. World champion at 1,500 in both 1991 and '93. Finished a shocking seventh at 1992 Olympics, but won gold medal in '96 at Atlanta. Only man ever to rank first in the world at 1,500/mile four straight years (1990–93).

Joe Morgan (b. 9-19-43): Baseball 2B. Won 2 consecutive MVP awards in 1975-76. Third alltime most walks (1,865). 689 stolen bases. Led league in walks 4 times. 100+ walks and runs scored 8 times each; 40+ stolen bases 9 times. Won 5 Gold Gloves. Second alltime most games played by 2nd baseman (2,527). Career span 1963-84 with Houston, Cincinnati.

Willie Mosconi (b. 6-27-13; d. 9-16-93): Pocket billiards player. Won world title a record 15 straight times between 1941 and 1957. Once pocketed 526 balls without a miss.

Edwin Moses (b. 8-31-55): Track and field. Gold medalist in 400-meter hurdles at 2 Olympics, in 1976, 1984 (U.S. boycotted 1980 Games); bronze medalist at 1988 Olympics. Set four world records in 400-meter hurdles (best of 47.02 set on 8-31-83). Won 122 consecutive races from 1977 to 1987. Won Sullivan Award in 1983.

Marion Motley (b. 6-5-20): Football FB. All-time AAFC leader in yards rushing (3,024). Also led NFL in rushing 1 time. Combined league totals: 4,712 yards rushing, 39 touchdowns. Played on 4 consecutive AAFC champions (1946-49), 1 NFL champion (1950) with Cleveland from 1946 to 1953.

Shirley Muldowney (b. 6-19-40): Drag racer. First woman to win the Top Fuel championship, which she won 3 times (1977, 1980, 1982).

Anthony Munoz (b. 8-19-58): Football OT. Probably the greatest tackle ever. Made Pro Bowl a record-tying 11 times. Career span 1980–92 with the Cincinnati Bengals.

Isaac Murphy (b. 4-16-1861, d. 2-12-1896): Horse racing jockey. Top jockey of his era, Murphy, who was black, won 3 Kentucky Derbys (aboard Buchanan in 1884, Riley in 1890 and Kingman in 1891).

Eddie Murray (b. 2-24-56): Baseball 1B. 100+ RBIs 6 seasons and 30+ HRs five seasons. Through '95 season had 3,071 hits, 479 HRs and 1,820 RBI. Alltime leader in RBI by switch hitter. Career span 1977–88 with Baltimore Orioles; 1989–91 with Los Angeles; 1992–93 with New York Mets, 1994–96 with Cleveland; '96- Baltimore .

Jim Murray (b. 12-29-19): Sportswriter. Won Pulitzer Prize in 1990. Named Sportswriter of the Year 14 times. Columnist for *Los Angeles Times* since 1961.

Ty Murray (b. 10-11-69): Rodeo cowboy. All-Around world champion, 1989-94. Set single-season earnings record, 1990 ($213,771). Rookie of the Year, 1988. At 20 in 1989, became youngest man ever to win national all-around title.

Stan Musial (b. 11-21-20): Baseball OF-1B. "Stan the Man." Had .331 career batting average and 475 career HR. MVP award winner 1943, 1946, 1948. Fourth alltime in hits (3,630) and third in doubles (725). Won 7 batting titles. Led league in hits 6 times, slugging average 5 times, doubles 8 times. Had .300+ batting average 17 times, 200+ hits 6 times, 100+ RBI 10 times, and 100+ runs scored 11 times. 24-time All-Star. Career span 1941-63 with St. Louis.

John Naber (b. 1-20-56): Swimmer. Won 4 gold medals and 1 silver medal at 1976 Olympics. Sullivan Award winner in 1977.

Bronko Nagurski (b. 11-3-08, d. 1-7-90): Football FB. Punishing runner played on 3 NFL champions (1932, '33, 1943) with Bears. 2,778 career yards, 1930–37 and 1943 with Chicago.

James Naismith (b. 11-6-1861, d. 11-28-39): Invented basketball in 1891 while an instructor at YMCA Training School in Springfield, Mass. Refined the game while a professor at Kansas from 1898 to 1937. Hall of Fame is named in his honor.

Joe Namath (b. 5-31-43): Football QB. "Broadway Joe." Super Bowl MVP in 1968 after he guaranteed victory for AFL. 173 career touchdown passes. Led league in yards passing 3 times, including 4,007 yards in 1967. Player of the Year in 1968, Rookie of the Year in 1965. Career span 1965-77 with NY Jets, LA Rams.

Ilie Nastase (b. 7-19-46): Romanian tennis player. "Nasty" for his unruly deportment on court. Beat Arthur Ashe to win 1972 US Open title. Won 1973 French Open. Twice Wimbledon runnerup (to Stan Smith in 1972 and Bjorn Borg in '76).

Martina Navratilova (b. 10-18-56): Tennis player. Fourth alltime most women's Grand Slam singles titles (18—tied with Chris Evert). Won a record 9 Wimbledon titles, including 6 consecutively (1978-79, 1982-87, '90). Won 4 U.S. Open titles (consecutively 1983-84, 1986-87), 3 Australian Open titles (1981, '83, '85) and 2 French Open titles (1982, '84). Reached Grand Slam final 13 other times. Also won 37 Grand Slam doubles titles. Her total of 55 Grand Slam titles is second alltime to Margaret Court's. Set mark for longest winning streak with 74 matches in 1984. Also won the doubles Grand Slam in 1984 with Pam Shriver. Won 109 consecutive matches with Shriver from 1983–85. Retired after 1994 season.

Byron Nelson (b. 2-14-12): Golfer. Won the Masters (1937, 1942) and PGA Championship (1940, 1945) 2 times each and U.S. Open once (1939). Won 52 career tournaments, including 11 consecutively in 1945.

Ernie Nevers (b. 6-11-03, d. 5-3-76): Football FB. Set alltime pro single game record for points scored (40) and touchdowns (6) on Nov. 28, 1929. Career span 1926-31 with Duluth, Chicago. Also a pitcher with St. Louis, surrendered 2 of Babe Ruth's 60 HR in 1927. All-America at Stanford, earned 11 letters in 4 sports.

John Newcombe (b. 5-23-44): Australian tennis player. Won 3 Wimbledon singles titles (1967, consecutively 1970-71), 2 U.S. titles (1967, 1973) and 2 Australian Open titles (1973, 1975). Also won 17 Grand Slam doubles titles.

Pete Newell (b. 8-31-15): College basketball coach. Despite coaching only 13 seasons, 1947 through 1960, was first coach to win NIT, NCAA and Olympic crowns. Led Univ. of San Francisco to 1949 NIT title, Cal to 1959 NCAA title, and the 1960 U.S. Olympic basketball team that included Jerry Lucas, Oscar Robertson and Jerry West to gold medal. Overall collegiate coaching record of 234–123.

Jack Nicklaus (b. 1-21-40): Golfer. "The Golden Bear." Alltime leader in major championships (20). Second alltime in career wins (70). Won Masters 6 times, more than any golfer (1963, consecutively 1965-66, '72, '75, '86—at age 46, the oldest player to win event), PGA Championship 5 times (1963, '71, '73, '75, '80), U.S. Open 4 times (1962, '67, '72, '80), British Open 3 times (1966, '70, '78) and U.S. Amateur 2 times (1959, '61). PGA Player of the Year 5 times (1967, consecutively 1972-73, 1975–76). Also NCAA champion with Ohio State in 1961.

Ray Nitschke (b. 12-29-36): Football LB. Defensive signal caller for the great Packer teams of the '60s. Voted Packer MVP by teammates after 1967 season.

MVP of the 1962 NFL title game. Career span 1958–72 with Green Bay Packers.

Greg Norman (b. 2-10-55): Golfer. "The Shark" led PGA in winnings in 1986, '90, '95–96. Won Vardon Trophy twice, 1989–90. Won two British Opens (1986, '93) but is almost as famous for his heartbreaking misses. Beaten at the 1986 PGA when Bob Tway holed out a sand shot and '87 Masters when Larry Mize chipped in from a downhill lie. Blew a six-stroke, third-round lead to lose to Nick Faldo by five shots at 1996 Masters. PGA Player of the Year 1996.

James D. Norris (b. 11-6-06, d. 2-25-66): Hockey executive. Owner of Detroit from 1933 to 1943 and Chicago from 1946 to 1966. Teams won 4 Stanley Cup championships (consecutively 1936-37, 1943, 1961). Defensive Player of the Year award named in his honor. Also a boxing promoter, operated International Boxing Club from 1949 to 1958.

Paavo Nurmi (b. 6-13-1897, d. 10-2-73): Track and field. Finnish middle- and long-distance runner won a total of 9 gold medals at 3 Olympics in 1920, 1924, 1928.

Matti Nykänen (b. 7-17-63): Finnish ski jumper. Three-time Olympic gold medalist. Won 90-meter jump (1984, 1988) and 70-meter jump (1988). World champion on 90-meter jump in 1982. Won four World Cups (1983, 1985, 1986, 1988).

Dan O'Brien (b. 7-18-66): Track and field decathlete. Won world decathlon title in 1991, '93 and '95. Set world decathlon record of 8,891 in Talence, France, on 9-4/5-92. Heavily favored to win 1992 Olympic decathlon but missed making U.S. team when he no-heighted in pole vault at U.S. Olympic Trials. Won gold medal at 1996 Olympics in Atlanta.

Parry O'Brien (b. 1-28-32): Track and field. Shot putter who revolutionized the event with his "glide" technique and won Olympic gold medals in 1952 and 1956, silver in 1960. Set 10 world records from 1953 to 1959, topped by a put of 63' 4" in 1959. Sullivan Award winner in 1959.

Al Oerter (b. 8-19-36): Track and field. Gold medalist in discus at 4 consecutive Olympics (1956, 1960, 1964, 1968), setting Olympic record each time. First to break the 200-foot barrier, throwing 200' 5" in 1962.

Sadaharu Oh (b. 5-20-40): Baseball 1B in Japanese league. 868 career HR in 22 seasons for the Tokyo Giants. Led league in HR 15 times, RBI 13 times, batting 5 times and runs 13 consecutive seasons. Awarded MVP 9 times; won 2 consecutive Triple Crowns and 9 Gold Gloves.

Hakeem Olajuwon (b. 1-21-63): Basketball C. From Nigeria. Led NCAA in field goal percentage, rebounding and blocked shots in 1984 at Houston. Alltime career leader in blocked shots (3,190). All-NBA First Team 1987–89, '93–94. League MVP in 1994 as he led Houston to NBA title (repeated in '95). Career span since1985 with the Rockets. Member of 1996 U.S. Olympic team.

Merlin Olsen (b. 9-15-40): Fooball DT. Part of L.A. Rams "Fearsome Foursome" defensive line. Named to Pro Bowl 14 straight times. Career span 1962–76, all with L.A. Rams. Elected to Hall of Fame 1982.

Omaha (b. 1932): Thoroughbred race horse. In 1935 third horse to win Triple Crown. Won Kentucky Derby by 1½ lengths over Roman Soldier; Preakness by 6 over Firethorn; and the Belmont by 1½ from Firethorn. Trained by Sunny Jim Fitzsimmons.

Shaquille O'Neal (b. 3-6-72): Basketball C. Led NCAA in blocked shots in 1992, with 5.23 a game; averaged 4.58 over his 90-game, three-year career. Top pick of Orlando Magic in 1992 NBA draft. Almost unanimous NBA Rookie of the Year 1993. Averaged 23.4 points, 13.9 rebounds and 3.5 blocked shots in first NBA season. Led league in scoring with 29.3 average in 1994–95. Member of 1996 U.S. Olympic team. Moved to LA Lakers as free agent in July 1996.

Bobby Orr (b. 3-20-48): Hockey D. Defensive Player of the Year more than any other player, 8 consecutive seasons (1968-75). Won MVP award 3 consecutive seasons (1970-72), playoff MVP 2 times (1970, 1972). Also Rookie of the Year in 1967. Led league in assists 5 times and scoring 2 times. Career span 1966–77 with Boston.

Mel Ott (b. 3-2-09, d. 11-21-58): Baseball OF. 511 career HR, 1,861 RBI, .304 batting average. League leader in HR and walks 6 times each. 100+ RBI 9 times and 100+ walks 10 times. Career span 1926-47 with New York.

Jim Otto (b. 1-5-38): Football C. Number 00 started every game (308) in his 15-year career (1960–74) with the Oakland Raiders. Inducted to Hall of Fame in 1980.

Kristin Otto (b. 1966): German swimmer. Won 6 gold medals for East Germany at 1988 Olympics.

Jesse Owens (b. 9-12-13, d. 3-31-80): Track and field. Gold medalist in 4 events (100 meters and 200 meters; 4x100-meter relay and long jump) at 1936 Olympics. At the 1935 Big 10 championship set or equaled 4 world record in 70 minutes, including 100 yards, long jump, 220-yard low hurdles and 220 dash.

Alan Page (b. 8-7-45): Football DT. First defensive player to be named NFL Player of the Year, in 1972. Career span 1967–78 with Minnesota Vikings and 1978–81 with Chicago Bears. Now sits on Minnesota Supreme Court.

Satchel Paige (b. 7-7-06, d. 6-8-82): Baseball RHP. Alltime greatest black pitcher, didn't pitch in major leagues until 1948 at age 42 with Cleveland. Oldest pitcher in major league history at age 59 with Kansas City in 1965. Pitched in the Negro leagues from 1926 to 1950 with Birmingham Black Barons, Pittsburgh Crawfords and Kansas City Monarchs. Estimated career record is 2,000 wins, 250 shutouts, 30,000 strikeouts, 45 no-hitters. Said "Don't look back. Something may be gaining on you."

Arnold Palmer (b. 9-10-29): Golfer. Fourth alltime in career wins (60). Won the Masters 4 times (1958, 1960, 1962, 1964), British Open 2 consecutive years (1961-62) and U.S. Open (1960) and U.S. Amateur (1954) once each. PGA Player of the Year 2 times (1960, 1962). The first golfer to surpass $1 million in career earnings. Also won Seniors Championship 2 times (1980, 1984) and U.S. Senior Open once (1981).

Jim Palmer (b. 10-15-45): Baseball RHP. 268 career wins, 2.86 ERA. Won 3 Cy Young Awards (1973, consecutively 1975-76). Won 20+ games 8 times. Led league in wins 3 times, innings pitched 4 times, ERA 2 times. Never allowed a grand slam HR. Pitched on 6 World Series teams with Baltimore, including shutout at age 20. Pitched no-hitter in 1969. Career span 1965–84.

Bernie Parent (b. 4-3-45): Hockey G. Alltime leader for wins in a season (47 in 1974). Goaltender of the Year, playoff MVP, league leader in wins, goals against average and shutouts 2 consecutive seasons (1974–75). Career record 270-197-121, including 55

shutouts. Career 2.55 goals against average. Tied record of 4 playoff shutouts in 1975. Played on 2 consecutive Stanley Cup champions (1974–75). Career span 1965–79 with Philadelphia.

Brad Park (b. 7-6-48): Hockey D. Seven-time All Star. In 17 seasons with the New York Rangers, Boston Bruins and Detroit Red Wings (1968–69 through 1984–85) scored 213 goals and had 683 assists. Elected to Hall of Fame 1988.

Jim Parker (b. 4-3-34): Football T/G. Winner of 1956 Outland Trophy as Ohio State senior. Blocked for Johnny Unitas. All-NFL four times at guard, four times at tackle. Career span 1957–67, all with Baltimore Colts. Inducted to Hall of Fame in 1973.

Joe Paterno (b. 12-21-26): College football coach. Fourth alltime in wins in Division I-A (278—the most of any active coach at that level). Has won 2 national championships (1982, 1986) with Penn State since 1966. Career record 278-72-3, including 5 undefeated seasons. Has also won 17 bowl games.

Lester Patrick (b. 12-30-1883, d. 6-1-60): Hockey coach. Led NY Rangers to three Stanley Cup championships (1928, 1933, 1940). Originated the NHL's farm system and developed playoff format.

Floyd Patterson (b. 1-4-35): Boxer. Heavyweight champion 2 times (1956-59, 1960-62). First heavyweight to regain title, in rematch with Ingemar Johansson. Career record 55-8-1 with 40 KOs from 1952 to 1972. Also middleweight gold medalist at 1952 Olympics.

Walter Payton (b. 7-25-54): Football RB. Alltime leader in yards rushing (16,726), rushing attempts (3,838), seasons gaining 1,000+ yards rushing (10) and rushing touchdowns (110). 125 career touchdowns. Rushed for a record 275 yards on Nov. 20, 1977. Selected for Pro Bowl 9 times. Player of the Year 2 times (1977, 1985). Led league in rushing 5 consecutive seasons. Career span 1975-87 with Chicago.

Pele (b. 10-23-40): Born Edson Arantes do Nascimento. Brazilian soccer player. Soccer's great ambassador. Played on 3 World Cup winners with Brazil (1958, 1962, 1970). Helped promote soccer in U.S. by playing with NY Cosmos from 1975 to 1977. Scored 1,281 goals in 22 years.

Willie Pep (b. 9-19-22): Boxer. Featherweight champion 2 times (1942-48, 1949-50). Lost title to Sandy Saddler, won it back in rematch, then lost it to Saddler again. Career record 230-11-1 with 65 KOs from 1940 to 1966. Won 73 consecutive bouts from 1940 to 1943. Defended title 9 times.

Gil Perreault (b. 11-13-50): Hockey C. Won Calder Trophy as NHL's top rookie for 1970–71 season. Played 17 seasons (1970–71 through 1986–87), all with Buffalo Sabres. Scored 512 goals and had 814 assists in career. Elected to Hall of Fame in 1990.

Fred Perry (b. 5-18-09, d. 2-2-95): British tennis player. Won 3 consecutive Wimbledon singles titles (1934-36), the last British man to win the tournament. Also won 3 U.S. titles (consecutively 1933-34, 1936), 1 French title (1935) and 1 Australian title (1934).

Gaylord Perry (b. 9-15-38): Baseball RHP. Only pitcher to win Cy Young Award in both leagues (Cleveland 1972, San Diego 1978). 314 career wins, 3,534 strikeouts. 20+ wins 5 times; 200+ strikeouts 8 times; 250+ innings pitched 12 times. Pitched no-hitter in 1968. Admitted to throwing a spitter. Career span 1962-83 with San Francisco, Cleveland, San Diego.

Bob Pettit (b. 12-12-32): Basketball F. First player in history to break 20,000-point barrier (20,880 career points scored). 26.4 career scoring average; 16.2 rebound avg. MVP in 1956, 1959; Rookie of the Year in 1955. All-Star 10 consecutive seasons. Led league in scoring 2 times, rebounding 1 time. Career span 1954–64 with St Louis.

Richard Petty (b. 7-2-37): Auto racer. Alltime leader in NASCAR victories (200). Daytona 500 winner (1964, 1966, 1971, consecutively 1973-74, 1979, 1981) and NASCAR champion (1964, 1967, consecutively 1971-72, 1974-75, 1979) 7 times each, the most of any driver. First stock car racer to reach $1 million in earnings. Son of Lee Petty, 3-time NASCAR champion (1954, consecutively 1958-59). Retired after 1992 season.

Laffit Pincay Jr. (b. 12-29-46): Jockey. Second only to Bill Shoemaker in wins. Among the top money-winners of all time, approaching $200,000,000 in career earnings. Won 5 Eclipse Awards as outstanding jockey. Rode 3 Kentucky Derby winners; 2 Preakness winners; and 1 Belmont winner.

Jacques Plante (b. 1-17-29, d. 2-27-86): Hockey G. First goalie to wear a mask. Second alltime in wins (434) and second lowest modern goals against average (2.38). Goaltender of the Year 7 times, more than any other goalie (consecutively 1955-59, 1961, 1968). Won MVP award in 1961. Led league in goals against average 8 times, wins 6 times and shutouts 4 times. Was on 6 Stanley Cup champions with Montreal from 1952 to 1962 and played for 4 other teams until retirement in 1972.

Gary Player (b. 11-1-35): South African golfer. Won the Masters (1961, 1974, 1978) and British Open (1959, 1968, 1974) 3 times each, PGA Championship 2 times (1962, 1972) and U.S. Open (1965). Also won Seniors Championship 3 times (1986, 1988, 1990) and U.S. Senior Open 2 consecutive years (1987-88).

Sam Pollock (b. 12-15-25): Hockey executive. As general manager of Montreal from 1964 to 1978 won 9 Stanley Cup championships (1965-66, 1968-69, 1971, 1973, 1976-78).

Denis Potvin (b. 10-29-53): Hockey D. Seven time All Star during 15-season career (1973–74 through 1987–88), all with New York Islanders. Won Calder Trophy for 1973–74 season. Won Norris Trophy three times. Captained Islanders to four Stanley Cup championships. Elected to Hall of Fame in 1991.

Mike Powell (b. 11-10-63): Track and field. Long jumper broke Bob Beamon's 23-year-old world record at 1991 World Championships in Tokyo with a jump of 29' 4½". Won silver in 1992 Olympics.

Annemarie Moser-Pröll (b. 3-27-53): Austrian skier. Gold medalist in downhill at 1980 Olympics. World Cup overall champion 6 times, more than any other skier (consecutively 1971-75, 1979).

Alain Prost (b. 2-24-55): French auto racer. Alltime leader in Formula 1 victories (51). Formula 1 champion 4 times (consecutively 1985-86, 1989, 1993).

Jack Ramsay (b. 2-21-25): Basketball coach. Never played in NBA. Coached 11 seasons at St. Joseph's University, with 234–72 record. Overall record of 864–783 as NBA coach. Coach of NBA champion 1977 Portland Trail Blazers. Elected to Hall of Fame 1992.

Jean Ratelle (b. 10-3-40): Hockey C. In 21-season career (1960–61 through 1980–81) with the New York Rangers and Boston Bruins, scored 491 goals and had 776 assists. Twice won Lady Byng Trophy. Elected to Hall of Fame in 1985.

Willis Reed (b. 6-25-42): Basketball C. Played 10 seasons (1965–74), all with the New York Knicks. Career average of 18.7 points a game. NBA Rookie of Year in 1965. Playoff MVP of both Knick championship teams, in 1970 and '73. NBA MVP in 1970. Elected to Hall of Fame in 1970.

Harold Henry "Pee Wee" Reese (b. 7-23-18): Baseball SS. Played for 7 pennant-winning Dodger teams. Led NL in runs scored in 1949, with 132. Elected to Hall of Fame in 1984.

Mary Lou Retton (b. 1-24-68): Gymnast. Won 1 gold, 1 silver and 2 bronze medals at 1984 Olympics.

Grantland Rice (b. 11-1-1880, d. 7-13-54): Sportswriter. Legendary figure during sport's Golden Age of the 1920s. Wrote "When the Last Great Scorer comes / To mark against your name, / He'll write not 'won' or 'lost' / But how you played the game." Also named the 1924-25 Notre Dame backfield the "Four Horsemen."

Jerry Rice (b. 10-13-62): Football WR. Entering 1996 season, alltime leader in touchdowns (156), touchdown receptions (146) and in consecutive games with a TD reception (13 in 1988). Player of the Year in 1987 and led league in scoring (138 points on 23 touchdowns). Super Bowl MVP in 1989 with record 215 receiving yards on 11 catches. Also set Super Bowl record with 3 touchdown receptions in 1990. Career span since 1985 with San Francisco 49ers.

Henri Richard (b. 2-29-36): Hockey C. "The Pocket Rocket." Played on 11 Stanley Cup champions with Montreal. Four-time All-Star. Career span from 1955 to 1975.

Maurice Richard (b. 8-4-21): Hockey RW. "The Rocket." First player ever to score 50 goals in a season, in 1945. Led league in goals 5 times. 544 career goals. Won MVP award in 1947. All-Star 8 times. Tied playoff game record for most goals (5 on March 23, 1944). Played on 8 Stanley Cup champions with Montreal from 1942 to 1959.

Bob Richards (b. 2-2-26): Track and field. The only pole vaulter to win gold medal at 2 consecutive Olympics (1952, 1956). Also won Sullivan Award in 1951.

Branch Rickey (b. 12-20-1881, d. 12-9-65): Baseball executive. Integrated major league baseball in 1947 by signing Jackie Robinson to contract with Brooklyn Dodgers. Conceived minor league farm system in 1919 at St Louis; instituted batting cage and sliding pit.

Pat Riley (b. 3-20-45): Basketball coach. Going into 1996–97 season most playoff wins (137). Coached Los Angeles to 4 championships, 2 consecutively, from 1981 to 1989. 60+ wins 6 times (4 times consecutively), 50+ wins 4 other times. Coach of the Year in 1990 and '93. Led New York Knicks to NBA Finals in 1994, then left three weeks later to become coach and part owner of Miami Heat.

Cal Ripken Jr (b. 8-24-60): Baseball SS. Broke Lou Gehrig's record for most consecutive games played (2,131) on Sept. 5, 1995. Set record for consecutive errorless games by a shortstop (95 in 1990). MVP in 1983 and '91. Rookie of the Year in 1982. Hit 20+ HRs in 11 consecutive seasons; 13-time All-Star.

Glenn (Fireball) Roberts (b. 1-20-31, d. 7-2-64): Auto racer. Won 34 NASCAR races. Died as a result of fiery accident in World 600 at Charlotte Motor Speedway in May 1964. At time of his death had won more major races than any other driver in NASCAR history.

Oscar Robertson (b. 11-24-38): Basketball G. "The Big O." 9,887 career assists; 26,710 points, 25.7 ppg. MVP in 1964, All-Star 9 consecutive seasons and 1961 Rookie of the Year. Led league in assists 6 times, free throw percentage 2 times. Averaged 30+ points 6 times in 7 seasons, 20+ points 4 other times. Only player in history to average a season triple-double (1961). Career span 1960-72 with Cincinnati, Milwaukee. Also College Player of the Year, All-America and NCAA scoring leader 3 consecutive seasons from 1958 to 1960 with Cincinnati. Third all-time NCAA highest scoring average (33.8); seventh most points scored (2,973).

Brooks Robinson (b. 5-18-37): Baseball 3B. Alltime leader in assists, putouts, double plays and fielding average among 3rd baseman. Won 16 consecutive Gold Gloves. Led league in fielding average a record 11 times. MVP in 1964—led league in RBI—and MVP in 1970 World Series. Career span 1955-77 with Baltimore.

David Robinson (b. 8-6-65): Basketball C. *Sporting News* Player of the Year for 1987. Led college players in 1986 in both rebounding (13.0) and blocked shots (5.91, a record that still stands). NBA Rookie of Year in 1990. Led NBA in rebounding 1991 (13.0), in scoring 1994 (29.8) and in blocked shots in 1992, when he was named Defensive Player of the Year. Named NBA MVP in 1995. Member of 1988, '92 and '96 Olympic teams. Career span since 1989 with San Antonio.

Eddie Robinson (b. 2-13-19): College football coach. Has had alltime college record 402 career wins at Division I-AA Grambling State since 1941.

Frank Robinson (b. 8-31-35): Baseball OF-manager. Only player to win MVP awards in both leagues (Cincinnati, 1961, Baltimore, 1966). Won Triple Crown and World Series MVP in 1966. Rookie of the Year in 1956. Fourth alltime most HR (586). 30+ HR 11 times; 100+ RBI 6 times; 100+ runs scored 8 times (led league 3 times). Had .300+ batting average 9 times. Became first black manager in major leagues, with Cleveland in 1975. Career span as player 1956-76. Career span as manager 1975-77 with Cleveland; 1981-84 with San Francisco; 1988-91 with Baltimore.

Jackie Robinson (b. 1-13-19, d. 10-24-72): Baseball 2B. Broke the color barrier as first black player in major leagues in 1947 with Brooklyn Dodgers. 1947 Rookie of the Year; 1949 MVP with .342 batting average to lead league. Had .311 career batting average. Led league in stolen bases 2 times; stole home 19 times. Played on 6 pennant winners in 10 years with Brooklyn.

Larry Robinson (b. 6-2-51): Hockey D. Twice won Norris Trophy as NHL's top defenseman. Career span 1972–73 through 1991–92, all but the last three with the Montreal Canadiens. Member of six Montreal teams that won Stanley Cup. Awarded Conn Smythe Trophy as MVP of 1978 Stanley Cup.

Sugar Ray Robinson (b. 5-3-21, d. 4-12-89): Born Walker Smith, Jr. Boxer. Called best pound-for-pound boxer ever. Welterweight champ (1946–51) and middleweight champ 5 times. Career record: 174-19-6 with 109 KOs from 1940–65. Won 91 consecutive bouts from 1943–51. 15 losses came after age 35.

Knute Rockne (b. 3-4-1888, d. 3-31-31): College football coach. Won national championship 3 times (1924, consecutively 1929-30). Alltime highest winning percentage (.881). Career record 105-12-5, including 5 undefeated seasons, with Notre Dame from 1918 to 1930.

Bill Rodgers (b. 12-23-47): Track and field. Won the Boston and New York City marathons 4 times each between 1975 and 1980.

Dennis Rodman (b. 5-13-61): Basketball F. NBA Defensive Player of the Year 1990, '91. Second player to win five consecutive rebounding titles; won NBA titles with Detroit 1989 and '90 and Chicago '96. Career span 1986–93 with Detroit, '93–95 with San Antonio and '95– Chicago.

Chi Chi Rodriguez (b. 10-23-35): Golfer. Led senior money list for 1987 ($509,145). Won 8 events during PGA career that began in 1960.

Art Rooney (b. 1-27-01; d. 8-25-88): Owner of Pittsburgh Steelers. Bought team in 1933 and ran it until his death in 1988. Elected to Hall of Fame in 1964.

Murray Rose (b. 1-6-39) Australian swimmer. Won 3 gold medals (including 400- and 1500-meter freestyle) at 1956 Olympics. Also won 1 gold, 1 silver and 1 bronze medal at 1960 Olympics.

Pete Rose (b. 4-14-41): Baseball OF-IF. "Charlie Hustle." Alltime leader in hits (4,256), games played (3,562) and at bats (14,053); second in doubles (746); fourth in runs scored (2,165). Had .303 career average and won 3 batting titles. Averaged .300+ 15 times, 200+ hits and 100+ runs scored each 10 times. Led league in hits 7 times, runs scored 4 times, doubles 5 times. 1963 Rookie of the Year; 1973 MVP; 1975 World Series MVP. Had 44-game hitting streak in 1978. Played in 17 All-Star games, starting at 5 different positions. Career span 1963-86 with Cincinnati, Philadelphia. Manager of Cincinnati from 1984 to 1989. Banned from baseball for life by Commissioner Bart Giamatti in 1989 for betting activities. Served 5-month jail term for tax evasion in 1990. Ineligible for Hall of Fame.

Ken Rosewall (b. 11-2-34): Australian tennis player. Won Grand Slam singles titles at ages 18 and 35. Won 4 Australian titles (1953, 1955, consecutively 1971-72), 2 French titles (1953, 1968) and 2 U.S. titles (1956, 1970). Reached 4 Wimbledon finals, but title eluded him.

Art Ross (b. 1-13-1886, d. 8-5-64): Hockey D-coach. Improved design of puck and goal net. Manager-coach of Boston, 1924-45, won Stanley Cup, 1938-39. The Art Ross Trophy is awarded to the NHL scoring champion.

Donald Ross (b. 1873, d. 4-26-48): Scottish-born golf course architect. Trained at St. Andrews under Old Tom Morris. Designed over 500 courses, including Pinehurst No. 2 course and Oakland Hills.

Patrick Roy (b. 10-5-65): Hockey G. Won Vezina Trophy three times. Won Conn Smythe Trophy twice (1986, '93). Career span 1984–95 Montreal, '95– Colorado. Traded to Colorado by Montreal in Dec. '95, won '96 Stanley Cup with Avalanche. Second-youngest goalie to reach 300 career wins.

Pete Rozelle (b. 3-1-26): Football executive. Fourth NFL commissioner, served from 1960 to 1989. During his term, league expanded from 12 to 28 teams. Created Super Bowl in 1966 and negotiated merger with AFL. Devised plan for revenue sharing of lucrative TV monies among owners. Presided during players' strikes of 1982, 1987.

Wilma Rudolph (b. 6-23-40, d. 11-12-94): Track and field. Gold medalist in 3 events (100-, 200- and 4x100-meter relay) at 1960 Olympics. Also won Sullivan Award in 1961.

Adolph Rupp (b. 9-2-01, d. 12-10-77): College basketball coach. Alltime NCAA leader in wins (875) and third highest winning percentage (.822). Won 4 NCAA championships: consecutively 1948-49, 1951, 1958. Career span 1930-72 with Kentucky.

Amos Rusie (b. 5-3-1871, d. 12-6-42): Baseball RHP. Fastball was so intimidating that in 1893 the pitching mound was moved back 5' 6" to its present distance of 60' 6." Led league in strikeouts and walks 5 times each. Career record 246-174, 3.07 ERA with New York (NL) from 1889-1901.

Bill Russell (b. 2-12-34): Basketball C. Won MVP award 5 times (1958, consecutively 1961-63, 1965). Played on 11 championship teams, 8 consecutively, with Boston (1957, 1959-66, 1968-69). Player-coach 1968-69 (league's first black coach). Second alltime most rebounds (21,620) and second highest rebounding average (22.5); second most rebounds in a game (51 in 1960). Led league in rebounding 4 times. Also played on 2 consecutive NCAA championship teams with San Francisco in 1955-56; tournament MVP in 1955. Member of gold medal-winning 1956 Olympic team.

Babe Ruth (b. 2-6-1895, d. 8-16-48): Born George Herman Ruth. Baseball P-OF. Most dominant player in history. Alltime leader in slugging average (.690), HR frequency (8.5 HR every 100 at bats) and walks (2,056); second alltime most HR (714), RBI (2,211) and runs scored (2,174). Holds season record highest slugging average (.847 in 1920). 1923 MVP. Had .342 career batting average and 2,873 hits. 60 HR in 1927, 50+ HR 3 other times and 40+ HR 7 other times; 100+ RBI and 100+ walks 13 times each; 100+ runs scored 12 times. Second alltime most World Series HR (15), including his "called shot" off Charlie Root in 1932. Began career as a pitcher for Boston Red Sox: 94 career wins and 2.28 ERA. Won 20+ games 2 times; ERA leader in 1916. Played on 10 pennant winners, 7 World Series winners (3 with Boston, 4 with New York). Sold to Yankees in 1920 (Boston hasn't won World Series since). Career span 1914-35.

Nolan Ryan (b. 1-31-47): Baseball RHP. Pitched record 7th no hitter on May 1, 1991. Alltime leader in strikeouts (5,714), walks (2,795). League leader in strikeouts 11 times, walks 8 times, shutouts 3 times, ERA 2 times. 300+ strikeouts 6 times, including season record of 383 in 1973. 324 career wins. Career span 1966–93 with New York (NL), California, Houston, Texas.

Jim Ryun (b. 4-29-47): Track and field. Youngest ever to run under four minutes for the mile (3:59.0 at 17 years, 37 days). Set two world records in the mile (3:51.3 in 1966 and 3:51.1 in 1967) and one in 1,500 (3:33.1 in 1967). Plagued by bad luck at Olympics; won silver medal in 1968 1,500 meters despite mononucleosis; was bumped and fell in 1972. Won Sullivan Award in 1967.

Toni Sailer (b. 11-17-35): Austrian skier. Won gold medals in 1956 Olympics in slalom, giant slalom and downhill, the first skier to accomplish the feat.

Juan Antonio Samaranch (b. 7-17-20): Amateur sports executive. Since 1980, Spaniard has served as president of International Olympic Committee.

Joan Benoit Samuelson (b. 5-16-57): Track and field. Gold medalist in first ever women's Olympic marathon (1984). Won Boston Marathon 2 times (1979, 1983). Sullivan Award winner in 1985.

Barry Sanders (b. 7-16-68): Football RB. Alltime NCAA season leader in yards rushing (2,628 in 1988). Won Heisman Trophy in 1988 at Oklahoma State. Entered NFL in 1989 with Detroit and named Rookie of the Year. Gained 1,000+ yards rushing and named to Pro Bowl each of his first 6 seasons. Led league in rushing in 1990 and '94.

Gene Sarazen (b. 2-27-02): Golfer. Won PGA Championship 3 times (consecutively 1922-23, 1933), U.S. Open 2 times (1922, 1932), British Open once (1932) and the Masters once (1935). His win at the Masters included golf's most famous shot, a double eagle on the 15th hole of the final round to tie Craig Wood (Sarazen then won the playoff). Won 38 career tournaments. Also won Seniors Championship 2 times (1954, 1958). Pioneered the sand wedge in 1930.

Glen Sather (b. 9-2-43): Hockey coach and general manager. As coach, third alltime highest winning percentage (.616). 464 regular season wins. Led Edmonton to 4 Stanley Cup championships (consecutively 1984-85, 1987-88) from 1979 to 1989 and 1993-94. Also played for 6 teams from 1966 to 1976.

Terry Sawchuk (b. 12-28-29): Hockey G. All-time leader in wins (435) and shutouts (103). Career 2.52 goals against average. Goaltender of the Year 4 times (consecutively 1951-52, 1954, 1964). Led league in wins and shutouts 3 times and goals against average 2 times. Rookie of the Year in 1950. Tied record of 4 playoff shutouts in 1952. Played on 4 Stanley Cup champions with Detroit and Toronto from 1949 to 1969.

Gale Sayers (b. 5-30-43): Football RB. Alltime leader in kickoff return average (30.6). Scored 56 career touchdowns, including a rookie record 22 in 1965. Led league in rushing and gained 1,000+ yards rushing 2 times. Averaged 5 yards per carry. Rookie of the Year in 1965. Tied record with 6 rushing touchdowns on Dec. 12, 1965. Career span 1965-71 with Chicago cut short due to knee injury. Also All-America 2 times with Kansas.

Dolph Schayes (b. 5-19-28): Basketball player. College star at NYU. In 1960 became first NBA player to reach 15,000 career points. Also first NBA player to play in 1,000 games. Led NBA in free throw percentage three times, and averaged .843 for his career. Over stretch of 10 years played in 706 consecutive games. Elected to Hall of Fame 1972.

Bo Schembechler (b. 4-1-29): Football coach. In 21 seasons at Michigan from 1969–89, had a 194-48-5 record. Overall college coaching record 234-65-8.

Mike Schmidt (b. 9-27-49): Baseball 3B. Won 3 MVP awards (1980, '81, 1986). 548 career HR. Led league in HR 8 times, slugging average 5 times and RBI, walks and strikeouts 4 times each. 40+ HR 3 times, 30+ HR 10 other times; 100+ RBI 9 times, 100+ runs scored 7 times, 100+ strikeouts 12 times and third alltime most strikeouts (1,883). 100+ walks 7 times. Won 10 Gold Gloves. Career span 1972–89 with Philadelphia.

Don Schollander (b. 4-30-46): Swimmer. Won 4 gold medals (including 100- and 400-meter freestyle) at 1964 Olympics; won 1 gold and 1 silver medal at 1968 Olympics. Also won Sullivan Award in 1964.

Dick Schultz (b. 9-5-29): Amateur sports executive. Second executive director of the NCAA, served from

1987 to '93. Also served as athletic director at Cornell (1976-81) and Virginia (1981-87).

Seattle Slew (b. 1974): Thoroughbred race horse. Horse of the Year for 1977, when he won the Triple Crown, winning the Kentucky Derby by 1¾ lengths; the Preakness by 1½; and the Belmont by 4. In three year career from 1976–78, won 14 of 17 starts.

Tom Seaver (b. 11-17-44): Baseball RHP. "Tom Terrific." 311 career wins, 2.86 ERA. Cy Young Award winner 3 times (1969, 1973, 1975) and Rookie of the Year 1967. Led league in strikeouts 5 times, winning percentage 4 times and wins and ERA 3 times each. Won 20+ games 5 times; 200+ strikeouts 10 times. Struck out 19 batters in 1 game in 1970, including the final 10 in succession. Pitched no-hitter in 1978. Career span 1967-86 with New York (NL), Cincinnati, Chicago (AL), Boston.

Secretariat (b. 3-30-70, d. 10-4-89): Thoroughbred race horse. Triple Crown winner in 1973 with jockey Ron Turcotte aboard. Trained by Lucien Laurin.

Monica Seles (b. 12-2-73): Tennis player. Has won 3 consecutive French Open singles titles (1990-92), 4 Australian Open titles (1991-93, '96) and 2 U.S. Open titles (1991-92). Seles' 1993 season ended on 4-30 when she was stabbed in the back by Gunther Parche while seated during a changeover in a tournament in Hamburg, Germany; also missed 1994 season. Returned to tennis in 1995, reached U.S. Open final.

Bill Sharman (b. 5-25-26): Basketball G. First team All Star four straight years 1956–59. Led NBA in free throw percentage every year from 1953–57, and in 1959 and '61. All Star Game MVP in 1955. NBA Coach of the Year in 1972, when his Lakers won NBA title. Elected to Hall of Fame in 1974.

Wilbur Shaw (b. 10-31-02, d. 10-30-54): Auto racer. Won Indy 500 3 times in 4 years (1937, consecutively 1939-40). AAA champion 2 times (1937, 1939). Also pioneered the use of the crash helmet after suffering skull fracture in 1923 crash.

Patty Sheehan (b. 10-27-57): Golfer. Won back-to-back LPGA championships, 1983–84. Won 1992 and '94 US Women's Opens, '93 LPGA title. 1983 LPGA Player of Year. Vare Trophy winner in 1984. Through '94 season, 32 career wins on LPGA tour; fourth alltime in earnings, with $4,455,399.01.

Fred Shero (b. 10-23-25, d. 11-24-90): Hockey coach. Fourth all-time highest winning percentage (.612, regular season). Led Philadelphia to 2 Stanley Cup championships (1974-75). Also coached NY Rangers. Played defense for NY Rangers, 1947-50.

Bill Shoemaker (b. 8-19-31): Horse racing jockey. Alltime leader in wins (8,833). Rode Belmont Stakes winner 5 times (1957, 1959, 1962, 1967, 1975), Kentucky Derby winner 4 times (1955, 1959, 1965, 1986--at age 54, the oldest jockey to win Derby) and Preakness Stakes winner 2 times (1963, 1967). Also won Eclipse Award in 1981.

Eddie Shore (b. 11-25-02, d. 3-16-85): Hockey D. Won MVP award 4 times (1933, consecutively 1935-36, 1938). All-Star 7 times. Played on 2 Stanley Cup champions with Boston from 1926 to 1940.

Frank Shorter (b. 10-31-47): Track and field. Gold medalist in marathon at 1972 Olympics, the first American to win the event since 1908. Olympic silver medalist in 1976 marathon. Sullivan Award winner in 1972.

Jim Shoulders (b. 5-13-28): Rodeo. Alltime leader in career titles (16). All-Around champion 5 times (1949, consecutively 1956-59).

Don Shula (b. 1-4-30): Football coach. Alltime leader in wins (347 through 1995–96 season). Won 2 consecutive Super Bowl championships (1972–73) with Miami, including NFL's only undefeated season in 1972. Also reached Super Bowl 4 other times. Career span 1963–70 with Baltimore, 1970–95 Miami.

Al Simmons (b. 5-22-02; d. 5-26-56): Baseball OF. "Bucketfoot Al" for hitting stance. Named AL MVP for 1929, when he led league 157 RBIs. Led league in batting average in 1930 (.381) and '31 (.390). Lifetime average of .334 with 307 homers. Career span 1924–44 with a variety of teams, but mostly Philadelphia A's. Elected to Hall of Fame in 1953.

O.J. Simpson (b. 7-9-47): Given name Orenthal James. Football RB. Seventh alltime in yards rushing (11,236). Gained 1,000+ yards rushing 5 consecutive seasons, including then-record 2,003 yards in 1973. Player of the Year 3 times (consecutively 1972-73, 1975). Led league in rushing 4 times. Gained 200+ yards rushing in a game a record 6 times, including 273 yards on Nov. 25, 1976. Scored 61 career touchdowns, including 23 in 1975. Also won Heisman Trophy with USC in 1968.

Sir Barton (b. 1916): Thoroughbred race horse. In 1919, before they were linked as the Triple Crown, became first horse to win the Kentucky Derby, the Preakness and the Belmont Stakes. Won 8 of 13 starts as 3-year-old.

George Sisler (b. 3-24-1893, d. 3-26-73): Baseball 1B. Alltime most hits in a season (257 in 1920). League leader in hits 2 times, with 200+ hits 6 times. Won 2 batting titles, including .420 average in 1922; averaged .400+ 2 times and .300+ 11 other times. Had 2,812 career hits and .340 average. Career span 1915-30 with St Louis.

Mary Decker Slaney (b. 8-4-58): Track and field. American record holder in 5 events ranging from 800 to 3,000 meters. Won 1,500 and 3,000 meters at World Championships in 1983. Lost chance for medal at 1984 Olympics when she tripped and fell after contact with Zola Budd. Won Sullivan Award in 1982. Competed in 1996 Olympics at age 37.

Dean Smith (b. 2-28-31): College basketball coach. Entered 1996–97 season second alltime in wins (851), the most among active coaches; fifth alltime highest winning percentage (.775). Alltime most NCAA tournament appearances (26), reached Final Four 10 times. Won NCAA championship in 1982 and '93. Coached 1976 Olympic team to gold medal. Career span since 1962 with North Carolina.

Emmitt Smith (b. 5-15-69): Football RB. Led NFL in rushing in 1991 (1,563 yards), '92 (1,713 and 18 TDs), '95 (1,773). Record 25 TDs in 1995. Rushed for 108 yards in 52–17 Cowboy win over Bills in Super Bowl XXVII. Rushed for 132 yards and named MVP of Super Bowl XXVIII, a 30–13 Dallas victory over Buffalo. Career span since 1990 with Cowboys.

Ozzie Smith (b. 12-26-54): Baseball SS. "The Wizard of Oz." May be the best defensive shortstop in history. Holds alltime record for most assists in a season among shortstops (621 in 1980). Career double-play and assist leader among shortstops. 14-time All-Star. Won 13 consecutive Gold Gloves. Career span since 1978–96 with San Diego, St Louis.

Red Smith (b. 9-25-05, d. 1-15-82): Sportswriter. Won Pulitzer Prize in 1976. After Grantland Rice, the most widely syndicated sports columnist. His literate essays appeared in the *NY Herald Tribune* from 1945 to 1971 and the *NY Times* from 1971 to 1982.

Stan Smith (b. 12-14-46): Tennis. Won 39 tournaments in career, including 1972 Wimbledon in 5 sets over Ilie Nastase. Won 1971 US Open over Jan Kodes and amateur version of U.S. Open in 1969. 1970 won inaugural Grand Prix Masters. Inducted to Tennis Hall of Fame in 1987.

Tommie Smith (b. 6-5-44): Track and field. Sprinter won 1968 Olympic 200 meters in world record of 19.83, then was expelled from Olympic Village, along with bronze medalist John Carlos, for raising black-gloved fist and bowing head during playing of national anthem to protest racism in U.S.

Conn Smythe (b. 2-1-1895, d. 11-18-80): Hockey executive. As general manager with Toronto from 1929 to 1961 won 7 Stanley Cup championships (1932, 1942, 1945, consecutively 1947-49, 1951). Award for playoff MVP named in his honor.

Sam Snead (b. 5-27-12): Golfer. Alltime leader in career wins (81). Won the Masters (1949, 1952, 1954) and PGA Championship (1942, 1949, 1951) 3 times each and British Open (1946). Runner-up at U.S. Open 4 times, but title eluded him. PGA Player of the Year in 1949. Won Seniors Championship 6 times, more than any golfer (1964-65, 1967, 1970, 1972-73).

Peter Snell (b. 12-17-38): Track and field. New Zealand runner was gold medalist in 800 meters at 2 consecutive Olympics in 1960, 1964. Also gold medalist in 1,500 meters at 1964 Olympics. Twice broke world mile record; broke world 800 record once.

Duke Snider (b. 9-19-26): Baseball OF. Career .295 average, 407 HR and 1,333 RBIs. Hit 40+ HR 5 consecutive seasons and 100+ RBIs 6 times. Also led league in runs scored 3 consecutive seasons. Played on 6 pennant winners with the Brooklyn Dodgers. World Series total of 11 HR and 26 RBIs are NL best. Career span from 1947-64.

Javier Sotomayor (b. 10-13-67): Track and field. Cuban high jumper broke the 8-foot barrier with world record jump of 8' 0" in 1989. Set current record of 8' ½" in 7-27-93 in Salamanca, Spain.

Warren Spahn (b. 4-23-21): Baseball LHP. Alltime leader in games won for a lefthander (363): 20+ wins 13 times. League leader in wins 8 times (5 seasons consecutively), complete games 9 times (7 seasons consecutively), strikeouts 4 consecutive seasons, innings pitched 4 times and ERA 3 times. 1957 Cy Young award. 63 career shutouts. Pitched 2 no-hitters after age 39. Career span 1942-65, all but last year with Boston (NL), Milwaukee.

Tris Speaker (b. 4-4-1888, d. 12-8-58): Baseball OF. Alltime leader in doubles (792), fifth in hits (3,514) and fifth in batting average (.345). 1 batting title (.386 in 1916), but .375+ average 6 times and .300+ average 12 other times. League leader in doubles 8 times, hits 2 times and HR and RBI 1 time each. 200+ hits 4 times, 40+ doubles 10 times and 100+ runs scored 7 times. MVP in 1912. Career span 1907-28 with Boston, Cleveland.

Michael Spinks (b. 7-13-56): Boxer. 1976 Olympic middleweight champion. Brother Leon was heavyweight champ. Won world light heavyweight title on 7-18-81. Defended it 5 times and consolidated light heavy titles with decision over Dwight Braxton on 3-18-83. Defended four more times. Won heavyweight title on 9-22-85 in decision over Larry Holmes. Lost title to Mike Tyson in 91 seconds on 6-27-88.

Mark Spitz (b. 2-10-50): Swimmer. Won a record 7 gold medals (2 in freestyle, 2 in butterfly, 3 in relays) at 1972 Olympics, setting world record in each event. Also won 2 gold medals and 1 silver and 1 bronze medal at 1968 Olympics. Sullivan Award winner in 1971.

Amos Alonzo Stagg (b. 8-16-1862, d. 3-17-65): College football coach. Third alltime in wins (314). Won national championship with Chicago in 1905. Coach of the Year with Pacific in 1943 at age 81. Career record 314-199-35, including 5 undefeated seasons, from 1892 to 1946. Only person elected to both college football and basketball Halls of Fame. Played in the first basketball game in 1891.

Willie Stargell (b. 3-6-40): Baseball OF/1B. "Pops" achieved a 1979 MVP triple crown, winning NL regular season, playoff and World Series MVP awards. Led NL in homers in 1971 and '73. Hit 475 career homers. Drove in 1,540 runs. Had .282 career batting average. Played all 21 seasons with the Pirates. Elected to Hall of Fame in 1988.

Bart Starr (b. 1-9-34): Football QB. Played on 3 NFL champions (consecutively 1961-62, 1965) and first two Super Bowl champions (1966-67) with Green Bay. Also named MVP of first two Super Bowls. Player of the Year in 1966. Led league in passing 3 times. Also coached Green Bay to 53-77-3 record from 1975 to 1983.

Roger Staubach (b. 2-5-42): Football QB. Won Heisman Trophy with Navy as a junior in 1963. Served 4-year military obligation before turning pro. Led Dallas to 6 NFC Championships, 4 Super Bowls and 2 Super Bowl titles (1971, 1977). Player of the Year and Super Bowl MVP in 1971. Also led league in passing 4 times. Career span 1969-79.

Jan Stenerud (b. 11-26-42): Football K. Second to George Blanda on NFL scoring list, with 1,699 points. Converted an NFL record 373 field goals in 558 attempts. Career span 1967-79 with Kansas City Chiefs, 1980-83 with Green Bay Packers and 1984-85 with Minnesota Vikings. First pure kicker inducted to Hall of Fame 1991.

Casey Stengel (b. 7-30-1890, d. 9-29-75): Baseball manager. "The Ol' Perfesser." Managed New York Yankees to 10 pennants and 7 World Series titles (5 consecutively) in 12 years from 1949 to 1960. Alltime leader in World Series games (63), wins (37) and losses (26). Platoon system was his trademark strategy, Stengelese his trademark language ("You could look it up"). Managed New York Mets from 1962 to 1965. Jersey number (37) retired by Yankees and Mets.

Ingemar Stenmark (b. 3-18-56): Swedish skier. Gold medalist in slalom and giant slalom at 1980 Olympics. World Cup overall champion 3 consecutive years (1976-78).

Woody Stephens (b. 9-1-13): Horse racing trainer. Trained 2 Kentucky Derby winners (Cannonade, who won the 100th Derby in 1974 and Swale in 1984) and 5 straight Belmont winners from 1982-86, starting with 1982 Horse of the Year Conquistador Cielo.

David Stern (b. 9-22-42): Fourth NBA commissioner. Served since 1984. Oversaw unprecedented growth of league. Owners rewarded him with 5-year, $40-million contract extension in 1996.

Jackie Stewart (b. 6-11-39): Scottish auto racer. Fourth alltime in Formula 1 victories (27); Formula 1 champion 3 times (1969, 1971, 1973). Also Indy 500 Rookie of the Year in 1966. Retired in 1973.

John L. Sullivan (b. 10-15-1858, d. 2-2-18): Boxer. Last bare knuckle champion. Heavyweight title holder (1882-92), lost to Jim Corbett. Career record 38-1-3 with 33 KOs from 1878 to 1892.

Paul Tagliabue (b. 11-24-40): Football executive. Fifth NFL commissioner, has served since 1989.

Anatoli Tarasov (b. 1918): Hockey coach. Orchestrated Soviet Union's emergence as a hockey power. Won 9 consecutive world amateur championships (1963-71) and 3 Olympic gold medals in 1964, 1968, 1972.

Fran Tarkenton (b. 2-3-40): Football QB. Second alltime in touchdown passes (342), yards passing (47,003), pass attempts (6,467) and pass completions (3,686). Player of the Year in 1975. Career span 1961–78 with Minnesota, NY Giants.

Lawrence Taylor (b. 2-4-59): Football LB. Revolutionized the linebacker position. Ended 1993 season as the alltime leader in sacks. Also named to Pro Bowl a record 10 consecutive seasons. Player of the Year in 1986. Has played on 2 Super Bowl champions with New York Giants (1986, 1990). Career span 1981–93 with Giants.

Isiah Thomas (b. 4-30-61): Basketball G. Member of Indiana University team that won 1981 NCAA title. Point guard for Detroit Pistons 1982–94. All-NBA First Team 1984, '85 and '86. NBA All Star Game MVP both 1984 and '86. Led NBA in assists (13.9) in 1984–85. Fourth alltime in assists (9,061). Member of Piston team that won NBA title in both 1989 and '90. Became GM of Toronto Raptors in 1995.

Thurman Thomas (b. 5-15-66): Football RB. Led AFC in rushing both 1990 (1,297 yards) and '91 (1,407). Career span since 1988 with Buffalo Bills.

Daley Thompson (b. 7-30-58): Track and field. British decathlete was gold medalist at 2 consecutive Olympics in 1980, 1984. At 1984 Olympics set world record (8,847 points) that lasted eight years.

John Thompson (b. 9-2-41): College basketball coach. Head coach at Georgetown (1973–), where he coached Patrick Ewing, Alonzo Mourning and Dikembe Mutombo. Won NCAA title in 1984, runnerup in 1982 and '85.

Bobby Thomson (b. 10-25-23): Baseball OF. Hit dramatic 9th-inning playoff home run to win NL pennant for New York Giants on Oct. 3, 1951. The Giants came from 13½ games behind the Brooklyn Dodgers on Aug. 11 to win the pennant on Thomson's 3-run homer off Ralph Branca in the final game of the 3-game playoff.

Jim Thorpe (b. 5-28-1888, d. 3-28-53): Sportsman. Gold medalist in decathlon and pentathlon at 1912 Olympics. Played pro baseball with New York (NL) and Cincinnati from 1913 to 1919, and pro football with several teams from 1919 to 1926. Also All-America 2 times with Carlisle.

Dick Tiger (b. 8-14-29; d. 12-14-71): Nigerian Boxer. Born Richard Ihetu. Won middleweight title by decision over Gene Fullmer on 10-23-62. Lost middle title to Joey Giardello on 12-7-63, then regained it from Giardello on 10-21-65. Won world light heavyweight title by decision over Jose Torres on 12-16-66, then lost it when KO'd by Bob Foster in 4 on 5-24-68. The Ring Fighter of the Year for 1962 and '65.

Career record: 61-17-3. Elected to Boxing Hall of Fame 1974.

Bill Tilden (b. 2-10-1893, d. 6-5-53): Tennis player. "Big Bill." Won 7 U.S. singles titles, 6 consecutively (1920-25, 1929) and 3 Wimbledon titles (consecutively 1920-21, 1930). Also won 6 Grand Slam doubles titles. Led U.S. to 7 consecutive Davis Cup victories (1920-26).

Ted Tinling (b. 6-23-10, d. 5-23-90): British tennis couturier. The premier source on women's tennis from Suzanne Lenglen to Steffi Graf. Also designed tennis clothes, most notably the frilled lace panties worn by Gorgeous Gussy Moran at Wimbledon in 1949.

Y.A. Tittle (b. 10-24-26): Football QB. Threw 33 TD passes in 1962 and in '63 led league in passing, completing 221 of 367 attempts for 3,145 yards and 36 TDs. Career span 1948–64, mostly with San Francisco 49ers and New York Giants. Inducted into Hall of Fame 1971.

Jayne Torvill/Christopher Dean (b. 10-7-57/ b. 7-27-58): British figure skaters. Won 4 consecutive ice dancing world championships (1981-84) and Olympic ice dancing gold medal (1984). Won world professional championships in 1985. Won Olympic ice dancing bronze in 1994.

Vladislav Tretiak (b. 4-25-52): Hockey G. Led Soviet Union to 3 gold medals at Olympics in 1972, 1976, 1984. Played on 13 world amateur champions from 1970 to 1984.

Lee Trevino (b. 12-1-39): Golfer. Won U.S. Open (1968, 1971), British Open (consecutively 1971-72) and PGA Championship (1974, 1984) 2 times each. PGA Player of the Year in 1971. Also won U.S. Senior Open in 1990. First Senior $1 million season.

Emlen Tunnell (b. 3-29-25, d. 7-23-75): Football S. Alltime leader in interception yardage (1,282) and second in interceptions (79). All-Pro 9 times. Career span 1948-61 with New York Giants and Green Bay.

Gene Tunney (b. 5-25-1897, d. 11-7-78): Boxer. Heavyweight champion (1926-28). Defeated Jack Dempsey 2 times, including famous "long count" bout. Career record 65-2-1 with 43 KOs from 1915 to 1928. Retired as champion.

Ted Turner (b. 11-19-38): Sportsman. Skipper who successfully defended the America's Cup in 1977. Also owner of the Atlanta Braves since 1976 and Hawks since 1977. Founded the Goodwill Games in 1986.

Mike Tyson (b. 6-30-66): Boxer. Youngest heavyweight champion at 19 years old in 1986. Held title until knocked out by James "Buster" Douglas in Tokyo on Feb. 10, 1990. Career record as of 9-1-96 44–1 with 37 KOs since 1985. Convicted of rape in 1992, released from prison in 1995.

Johnny Unitas (b. 5-7-33): Football QB. 47 consecutive games throwing touchdown pass (1956-60), third alltime touchdown passes (290), 40,239 career passing yards. Led league in touchdown passes 4 consecutive seasons. Player of the Year 3 times (1959, 1964, 1967). Career span 1956-72 with Baltimore, San Diego.

Al Unser Sr. (b. 5-29-39): Auto racer. Won Indy 500 4 times (1970, 71, '78, '87). Third alltime in CART victories (39). USAC/CART champion 3 times (1970, 1983, 1985). Brother of Bobby.

Bobby Unser (b. 2-20-34): Auto racer. Won Indy 500 3 times (1968, 1975, 1981). Fourth alltime in CART victories (35). USAC champion 2 times (1968, 1974). Brother of Al, Sr.

Harold S. Vanderbilt (b. 7-6-1884, d. 7-4-70): Sailer. Owner and skipper who successfully defended the America's Cup 3 consecutive times (1930, 1934, 1937).

Glenna Collett Vare (b. 6-20-03, d. 2-2-89): Golfer. Won U.S. Women's Amateur 6 times, more than any golfer (1922, 1925, consecutively 1928-30, 1935).

Bill Veeck (b. 2-9-14, d. 1-2-86): Baseball owner. From 1946 to 1980, owned ballclubs in Cleveland, St Louis (AL), Chicago (AL). In 1948, Cleveland became baseball's first team to draw 2 million in attendance. That year Veeck integrated AL by signing Larry Doby and then Satchel Paige. A brilliant promoter, Veeck sent midget Eddie Gaedel up to bat for St Louis in 1951. Brought exploding scoreboard to stadiums and put players' names on uniforms.

Guillermo Vilas (b. 8-17-52): Tennis. Argentine won 50 straight matches in 1977. In '77 won French Open, where he beat Brian Gottfried, and the U.S. Open, where he beat Jimmy Connors. Also won Australian Open twice, 1978–79.

Lasse Viren (b. 7-22-49): Track and field. Finnish runner was gold medalist in 5,000 and 10,000 meters at 2 consecutive Olympics (1972, 1976).

Virginia Wade (b. 7-10-45): Tennis. Beloved in Britain, Wade won four major titles, most notably Wimbledon in 1977, its centenary year, where she triumphed over Betty Stove. Also won 1968 U.S. Open and '72 Australian Open.

Honus Wagner (b. 2-24-1874, d. 12-6-55): Baseball SS. Had .327 career batting average, 3,415 hits and 8 batting titles. Averaged .300+ 15 consecutive seasons. Led league in RBI 4 times, with 100+ RBI 9 times. Third alltime in triples (252) and league leader in doubles 8 times. 703 career stolen bases, league leader in steals 5 times. Career span 1897-1917 with Pittsburgh.

Grete Waitz (b. 10-1-53): Track and field. Norwegian runner has won New York City Marathon a record 9 times (consecutively 1978-80, 1982-86, 1988). Won the women's marathon at the 1983 World Championship.

Jersey Joe Walcott (b. 10-31-14): Boxer. Heavyweight champion from 1951 to 1952. Won title at age 37 on fifth attempt before surrendering it to Rocky Marciano. Later became sheriff of Camden, NJ.

Doak Walker (b. 1-1-27): Football HB. Led league in scoring 2 times, his first and final seasons. All-Pro 5 times. Played on 2 consecutive NFL champions (1952-53) with Detroit. Career span 1950 to 1955. Also won Heisman Trophy as a junior in 1948. All-America 3 consecutive seasons with SMU.

Herschel Walker (b. 3-3-62): Football RB. Won Heisman Trophy in 1982 with Georgia. Turned pro by entering USFL with New Jersey. Gained 7,000+ rushing yards and scored 61 touchdowns in 3 seasons before league folded. Entered NFL in 1986 with Dallas and led league in rushing yards (1,514 in 1988).

Bill Walsh (b. 11-30-31): Football coach. Led the San Francisco 49ers to four Super Bowl wins, after the 1981, '84, '88 and '89 seasons. Career record with 49ers 102-63-1. Developed short-passing game. Returned to Stanford University for 1992 season.

Bill Walton (b. 11-5-52): Basketball C. MVP in 1978, playoff MVP in 1977. Led league in rebounding and

blocks in 1977. Career span 1974-86 with Portland, San Diego, Boston. Also College Player of the Year 3 consecutive seasons (1972-74). Played on 2 consecutive NCAA championship teams (1972-73) with UCLA; tournament MVP twice (1972-73). Sullivan Award winner in 1973.

War Admiral (b. 1934): Thoroughbred race horse. A son of Man o' War, won Triple Crown and Horse of the Year honors in 1937.

Paul Warfield (b. 11-28-42): Football WR. Caught 427 passes for 8,565 yards and 85 TDs. Played on two Super Bowl-winning Miami Dolphin teams. Career span 1964–77, all with Cleveland Browns except for 1970–74 with Miami Dolphins. Inducted to Hall of Fame 1983.

Glenn "Pop" Warner (b. 4-5-1871, d. 9-7-54): College football coach. Second alltime in wins (319). Won 3 national championships with Pittsburgh (1916, 1918) and Stanford (1926). Career record 319-106-32 with 6 teams from 1896 to 1938.

Tom Watson (b. 9-4-49): Golfer. Winner of British Open 5 times (1975, 1977, 1980, consecutively 1982-83), the Masters 2 times (1977, 1981) and U.S. Open once (1982). PGA Player of the Year 6 times, more than any golfer (consecutively 1977-80, 1982, 1984).

Dick Weber (b. 12-23-29): Bowler. Won All-Star Tournament 4 times (consecutively 1962-63, 1965-66). Voted Bowler of the Year 3 times (1961, 1963, 1965). Won 31 career PBA titles.

Johnny Weismuller (b. 6-2-04, d. 1-21-84): Swimmer. Won 3 gold medals (including 100- and 400-meter freestyle) at 1924 Olympics and 2 gold medals at 1928 Olympics. Also played Tarzan in the movies.

Jerry West (b. 5-28-38): Basketball G. 10 time All-Star; All-Defensive Team 4 times; 1969 playoff MVP. Led league in assists and scoring 1 time each. Career span 1960-72 with Los Angeles. Currently general manager. Also NCAA tournament MVP in 1959. All-America 2 times with West Virginia. Played on 1960 gold medal-winning Olympic team.

Whirlaway (b. 4-2-38, d. 4-6-53): Thoroughbred race horse. Triple Crown winner in 1941 with jockey Eddie Arcaro aboard. Trained by Ben A. Jones.

Byron "Whizzer" White (b. 6-8-17): Football RB. Led NFL in rushing 2 times (Pittsburgh in 1938, Detroit in 1940). Led NCAA in scoring and rushing with Colorado in 1937; named All-America. Supreme Court justice from 1962 to '93.

Reggie White (b. 12-19-62): Football DE. Fearsome pass rusher. Winner in new era of free agency, signed with Green Bay Packers in 1993 for $17 million over four years. Career span: 1984 with Memphis Showboats, 1985–92 with Philadelphia Eagles and since 1993 with Green Bay.

Charles Whittingham (b. 4-13-13): Thoroughbred race horse trainer. "Bald Eagle" after losing hair to tropical disease in World War II. In 1986 became the oldest trainer to win Kentucky Derby, with Ferdinand. Led yearly earnings list for trainers from 1970–73 consecutively; in 1975; and in 1981–82 consecutively. Won three Eclipse Awards and trained two Horses of the Year (Ack Ack in 1971 and Ferdinand in 1987).

Kathy Whitworth (b. 9-27-39): Golfer. Alltime LPGA leader with 88 tour victories, including six majors. Won LPGA Championship in 1967, '71 and '75. Won 1977 Dinah Shore. Won Titleholders Championship (extinct major) in 1965 and '66. Won Western Open (extinct major) in 1967. Won Vare Trophy every year from 1965–72, except 1968. LPGA Player of Year from 1966–69 and 1971–73.

Hoyt Wilhelm (b. 7-26-23): Baseball RHP. Hall of Famer. Threw knuckleball until age 48. Alltime pitching leader in games (1,070). Career record: 143-122, 2.52 ERA, 227 saves. Hit home run in his first at bat (never hit another) and pitched no-hitter in 1958. Career span with 9 teams from 1952-72.

Bud Wilkinson (b. 4-23-15 d. 2-9-94): Football coach. Alltime NCAA leader in consecutive wins (47, 1953-57). Won 3 national championships (1950, consecutively 1955-56) with Oklahoma, where he coached from 1947 to 1963. Won Orange Bowl 4 times and Sugar Bowl 2 times. Career record 145-29-4, including 4 undefeated seasons. Also coached with St Louis of NFL in 1978-79.

Billy Williams (b. 6-15-38): Baseball OF. Nicknamed "Sweet Swinging". NL Rookie of the Year for 1961. Hit 426 career home runs. Drove in 1,475 runs. Lifetime averge of .290. Named to six NL All Star teams. Career span 1959–74 with Chicago Cubs, 1975–76 with Oakland A's. Elected to Hall of Fame in 1987.

Ted Williams (b. 8-30-18): Baseball OF. "The Splendid Splinter." Last player to hit .400 (.406 in 1941). MVP in 1946, 1949 and Triple Crown winner in 1942, 1947. Sixth alltime highest batting average (.344), second most walks (2,019) and second highest slugging average (.634). 521 career HR, 1,839 career RBIs. League leader in batting average and runs scored 6 times each, RBI and HR 4 times each, walks 8 times and doubles 2 times. Had .300+ average 15 consecutive seasons; 100+ RBI and runs scored 9 times each; 30+ HR 8 times; and 100+ walks 11 times. Lost nearly 5 seasons to military service. Career span 1939-42 and 1946-60 with Boston.

Hack Wilson (b. 4-26-00; d. 11-23-48): Baseball OF. Stood 5' 6" but weighed 210. Had five incredible seasons 1926–30. Best was 1930 when he hit .356, scored 146 runs, hit a NL record 56 homers and drove in 190, which is still the major league record. Career span 1923–34 with several teams. Elected to Hall of Fame in 1979.

Dave Winfield (b. 10-3-51): Baseball OF. Drafted out of Univ. of Minnesota for both pro basketball and football. Led NL in RBIs in 1979 (118). In 1992, first 40-year-old to get 100+ RBIs, with 108. Hit clutch double to win 1992 World Series. Got 3,000th hit, off Dennis Eckersley, on 9-16-93. Career span 1973–80 with San Diego; 1981–90 with Yankees; 1990–91 with California; 1992 with Toronto; 1993–94 with Minnesota; and 1995 with Cleveland.

Major W. C. Wingfield (b. 19-16-1833, d. 4-18-12): British tennis pioneer. Credited with inventing the game of tennis, which he called "Sphairistike" or "sticky" and patented in February 1874.

Colonel Matt Winn (b. 6-30-1861, d. 10-6-49): As general manager of Churchill Downs from 1904 until his death, promoted the Kentucky Derby into the premier race in the country.

Katarina Witt (b. 12-3-65): East German figure skater. Gold medalist at 2 consecutive Olympics in 1984, 1988. Also world champion 4 times (consecutively 1984-85, 1987-88).

John Wooden (b. 10-14-10): College basketball coach. Only member of basketball Hall of Fame as coach and player. Coached UCLA to 10 NCAA championships in 12 years (consecutively 1964-65, 1967-73, 1975). Alltime winning streak 88 games (1971-74). 664 career wins and fourth alltime highest winning percentage (.804). Career span 1949-75 with UCLA.1932 College Player of the Year at Purdue.

Mickey Wright (b. 2-14-35): Golfer. Second alltime in career wins (82) and major championships (13—tied with Louise Suggs). Won U.S. Open 4 times (consecutively 1958-59, 1961, 1964), LPGA Championship 4 times (1958, consecutively 1960–61, 1963), Western Open 3 times (consecutively 1962–63, 1966).

Cale Yarborough (b. 3-27-40): Auto racer. Won Daytona 500 4 times (1968, 1977, consecutively 1983-84). Fifth alltime in NASCAR victories (83). Also NASCAR champion 3 consecutive years (1976–78).

Carl Yastrzemski (b. 8-22-39): Baseball OF. "Yaz." 3,419 career hits, 452 HR. 1967 MVP and Triple Crown winner. 3 batting titles, including .301 in 1968, the lowest ever to win. Second alltime in games played (3,308) and fourth in walks (1,845). Career span 1961-83 with Boston.

Cy Young (b. 3-29-1867, d. 11-4-55): Baseball RHP. Alltime leader in wins (511), losses (315), innings pitched (7,354.2) and complete games (749); fourth in shutouts (76). Had 2.63 career ERA. Pitched 3 no-hitters, including a perfect game in 1904. Pitching award named in his honor. Career span 1890-1911 with Cleveland, Boston.

Robin Yount (b. 9-16-55): Baseball OF/SS. Became Brewer shortstop at 18. Landslide winner of 1982 AL MVP in 1982 when he hit .331 with 29 homers. Hit .414 in Brewers' 1982 Series loss to Cardinals. 3,142 hits. Shoulder injury made Yount move to outfield in 1984. Career span 1974–93, all with the Brewers.

Babe Didrikson Zaharias (b. 6-26-14, d. 9-27-56): Sportswoman. Gold medalist in 80-meter hurdles and javelin throw at 1932 Olympics; also won silver medal in high jump (her gold medal jump was disallowed for using the then-illegal western roll). Became a golfer in 1935 and won 12 major titles, including U.S. Open 3 times (1948, 1950, 1954—a year after cancer surgery). Also helped found the LPGA in 1949.

Tony Zale (b. 5-29-13): Boxer. Born Anthony Zaleski. "The Man of Steel." Won vacant middleweight title by decision over Georgie Abrams on 11-28-41. Lost title to Billy Conn on 2-13-42. Spent almost 4 years in Navy. Retained title with KO of Rocky Graziano in 6 on 9-27-46; lost it to Graziano by KO in 6 on 7-17-47; and reclaimed it by KOing Graziano in 3 on 6-10-48. Lost title to Marcel Cerdan, (KO 12) on 9-21-48. Career record: 88 bouts; won 46 by KO and 24 by decision; drew 2; lost 16, 4 by KO. Elected to Boxing Hall of Fame 1958.

Emil Zatopek (b. 9-19-22): Track and field. Czechoslovakian runner became only athlete to win gold medal in 5,000 and 10,000 meters and marathon, at 1952 Olympics. Also gold medalist in 10,000 meters at 1948 Olympics.

Obituaries

Sports Illustrated

Sergei
Grinkov
1967–1995

MANNY MILLAN

Obituaries

Kathy Ahern, 47, golfer. A child prodigy golfer who turned pro as a teenager, Ahern won the Texas Public Links Championship at the age of 15 and then eight years later, in 1972, won the L.P.G.A. Championship. She was diagnosed with cancer in May 1991 but remained an active supporter of the L.P.G.A., as she had been throughout the 1970s and '80s. In Phoenix, of complications from breast cancer, July 6.

Mel Allen, 83, broadcaster. The voice of the New York Yankees, Allen was known for his trademark greeting, "Hello, everybody, this is Mel Allen!" and for enthusiastically proclaiming, "How about that!" He became the club's lead announcer in 1940. In 1978, Allen and Walter (Red) Barber became the first inductees into the Hall of Fame's broadcasting wing.

SI writes:

"Mel Allen's death silenced one of the most distinctive voices in broadcasting history. The unabashedly partisan and ebullient calls of Allen could be heard on New York Yankees radio and, later, television from 1939 to '64. It was he who dubbed Joe DiMaggio Joltin' Joe and labeled Phil Rizzuto the Scooter. And it was he who stood on the Yankee Stadium sod and gave the introduction to both Lou Gehrig's '39 farewell speech and Babe Ruth's goodbye in '48.

"After Allen, who was born Melvin Allen Israel to Russian immigrants living in Alabama, was let go by the Yankees, he spent most of the next 13 years away from the game. He returned in 1977 to gain a national audience as host of the syndicated TV show *This Week in Baseball*, a job he held until his death. Though Allen appeared gaunt in his last years, his voice never lost its boyish enthusiasm. That's why, upon hearing Allen broadcast one of the week's highlights, even today's young fans couldn't help but shake their heads in wonder and say to themselves, How about that!"

In Greenwich, Conn., after a long illness, June 17.

Marlin Barnes, 22, football player. Barnes, a linebacker at the University of Miami, was found dead along with a friend, Timwanika Lumpkins, in Barnes's student apartment, victims of a brutal double murder. In Miami, of blows to the body from a blunt object, April 13.

Brook Berringer, 22, football player. Berringer, a quarterback for the University of Nebraska and a likely NFL draft choice who helped lead his team to the 1994 Orange Bowl and the national championship, was killed when a small plane he was piloting crashed just three days before the draft. In Raymond, Neb., of injuries sustained during a plane crash, April 18.

Charley Boswell, 78, golfer. A star college athlete who lost his sight during World War II, Boswell learned to play golf despite his blindness. (A caddy or sight coach helps direct the shots of blind golfers.) He once shot an 81, and won 28 national and international titles for blind golfers. In Birmingham, Ala., following a fall, October 22, 1995.

Arda C. Bowser, 97, football player. Bowser was the last surviving member of the first NFL championship team, the Canton Bulldogs, and the originator of the kicking tee. He was also an all-America player for Bucknell in 1921. In Winter Park, Fla., of undisclosed causes, September 7.

Scott Brayton, 37, auto racer. Brayton became the only Indy 500 pole sitter ever killed in practice when the right rear tire on his Lola-Menard went flat and his car slammed into the concrete retaining wall in Turn 2. Brayton had 14 Indy starts to his name. In Indianapolis, of injuries sustained in a car crash, May 17.

Billy Bruton, 69, baseball player. The Milwaukee Braves' leadoff batter, chief base stealer and center fielder in the 1950s, Bruton became a hero when, as a rookie, he hit a 10th-inning home run that gave the Braves a victory in their first major league game, in 1953. He went on to lead the league in stolen bases for three consecutive seasons. His career span lasted eight years with the Braves and four with the Detroit Tigers before he retired in 1964. In Wilmington, Del., of a heart attack, December 6, 1995.

Jim Campbell, 71, baseball executive. As general manager, Campbell led the Detroit Tigers to two World Series titles, in 1968 and 1984, two AL East titles (1972, '87) and two 100-loss seasons (1975, '89) in his 43 years with the organization. In Lakeland, Fla., of sudden cardiopulmonary arrest, on October 31, 1995.

Charlie Conerly, 74, football player. During a 14-year NFL career with the New York Giants, quarterback Conerly led the club to a championship in 1956 and to four Eastern Division titles. He first joined the Giants in 1948 after serving four years with the Marines in the Pacific during World War II; when the Giants won the 1956 championship he was 35 years old. That season, Conerly and teammate Frank Gifford were largely responsible for drawing the sellout crowds that the Giants have enjoyed ever since. Conerly held virtually all of the Giants' career passing records until Phil Simms surpassed them. As a passing tailback at the University of Mississippi, he helped Ole Miss win the first of its six Southeastern Conference titles in 1947 and he still holds the school's season record with 18 touchdown passes thrown (1947). His rugged good looks would later be featured in the "Marlboro man" cigarette advertisements. In Memphis, of complications following heart surgery, February 14.

Roger Crozier, 53, hockey player. The NHL Rookie of the Year with the Detroit Red Wings in 1964, Crozier tended goal for Detroit, Buffalo and Washington in a 14-year NHL career. His last hockey job was as general manager for the Washington Capitals in 1981–82. In Newark, Del., of cancer, January 10.

Rodney Culver, 26, football player. Running back Culver was a graduate of Notre Dame who had been picked up by the San Diego Chargers on waivers from Indianapolis before the 1994 season.

SI writes:

"On Monday evening more than 400 people, including virtually all of the San Diego Chargers' players and staff, convened at New Venture Christian Fellowship in Oceanside, Calif., to celebrate the memory of running back Rodney Culver. Rodney and his wife, Karen, 25, died on May 11 when ValuJet Flight 592 plunged into the Everglades, killing all 110 aboard. The Culvers left behind two daughters, Briana, 2, and Jada, 15 months.

"The crash had an immense impact on the Chargers' franchise, not only because Culver was the second San Diego player to have died in 11 months—linebacker David Griggs was killed in an auto accident last June—but also because he was such a leader, 'a man who was never swayed by the opinions of others,' in the words of San Diego equipment manager Sid Brooks. Brooks spent last Friday affixing decals of

Culver's number, 22, to the Chargers' helmets for next season.

"The Oceanside service was the third memorial for the Culvers to have drawn an audience in the hundreds; the others took place in Rodney's hometown of Detroit and at his alma mater, Notre Dame. All these tributes for a player whose longest run last season was 17 yards. But it was his strength of character, not his speed afoot, that set Culver apart. In 1991 he was a near-unanimous choice as Notre Dame's captain, becoming the first African-American chosen as sole captain for the Irish. Coach Lou Holtz, hoping to have a captain from both offense and defense, asked the players to vote once more. Again, only Culver's name appeared on most ballots. 'Rodney was an extraordinary young man,' says Holtz."

Near Miami International Airport, of injuries sustained in a plane crash, on May 11.

Babe Dahlgren, 84, baseball player. Dahlgren's claim to fame came when he took over at first base for the New York Yankees' Lou Gehrig, whose streak of 2,130 consecutive games ended on May 2, 1939. Known as an outstanding fielder, Dahlgren played for the Yankees in 327 games, until February, 1941, when he was sold to the Boston Braves. In Arcadia, Calif., of undisclosed causes, September 4.

Sarah Palfrey Danzig, 83, tennis player. Considered to be one of the most elegant tennis players ever, Danzig was a popular choice to partner in women's as well as mixed double's competitions, where she garnered most of her 18 Grand Slam titles. Danzig was ranked among the world's top 10 women six times between 1933 and '39, and was the U.S. Nationals champion in singles in 1941 and again in 1945. She was elected to the sport's Hall of Fame in 1963 and was a lifelong ambassador of the game, publishing two instructional books, serving as a sports editor for NBC-TV from 1956 to '57 and later as an advertising consultant for *World Tennis* magazine. In New York City, of lung cancer, February 27.

Willi Daume, 82, Olympic organizer. Daume was a longtime German sports official who, as president of the West German Olympic Committee, was responsible for bringing the Olympic Games back to Germany in 1972 for the first time since Hitler staged the 1936 Berlin Games, and thus helping to gain recognition for the new Germany. He served as chief spokesman for the German organizers when terrorists murdered 11 Israeli athletes and officials. Daume was a member of the German basketball team at the 1936 Games. In Munich, from intestinal cancer, May 20.

Dominguín, 69, bullfighter. Spain's leading bullfighter in the 1940s and '50s, Dominguín fought his first bullfight as an 11-year-old, in 1937.

SI writes:

"In a career as a matador that spanned 30 years, the great Dominguín, who died last week in his native Spain at the age of 69, was gored several times, yet his worst wounds may have come on the horns of a bull called Papa. In 1959 Ernest Hemingway followed Dominguín and Antonio Ordóñez, Dominguín's brother-in-law and great rival, from corrida to corrida in Spain as the two waged a dramatic and hazardous duel for recognition as the world's foremost matador. In a series of articles for LIFE that became the book *The Dangerous Summer*, Hemingway, an aficionado, depicted Dominguín—a dashing figure famous for his affair with Ava Gardner and his friendship with Picasso—as a once great hero crumbling under pressure from a younger, better man.

" 'The rivalry was beginning to shape up like a civil war, and neutrality was becoming increasingly difficult,' wrote Hemingway, who was close to both principals, each of whom was gored twice that season. 'It would have been tragic to miss it and it was tragic to watch it. But it was not a thing that you could miss.'

"In the end Ordóñez, in the eyes of both Hemingway and most fans, prevailed, and Dominguín retired not long after. He tried a comeback in the early 1970s, but his sun had already set. Still, Dominguín remained a model of the great, proud matador, something even Hemingway never denied. 'I admired his grace and his facility,' he wrote, 'his wonderful legs, his reflexes, and his tremendous repertoire of passes and encyclopedic knowledge of bulls.' "

In Soto Grande, Spain, of heart failure, May 8.

Nikolai Drozdetsky, 38, hockey player. A former Soviet hockey star, Drozdetsky played on national teams that won two world championships and one Olympic championship. In a career that spanned from 1973 to 1989, Drozdetsky played in more than 300 games and scored 252 goals as a forward. In St. Petersburg, Russia, of complications from diabetes, November 25, 1995.

Dan Duva, 44, boxing promoter. As the head of Main Events, Duva promoted or co-promoted more than 100 world championship bouts, including 12 heavyweight titles that accounted for more than $300 million in gross revenue.

SI writes:

"Although the crowd on hand for boxing promoter Dan Duva's funeral last Friday morning at Our Lady of the Holy Angels in Little Falls, N.J., numbered in the hundreds and included a collection of world-class fighters, managers and media types normally found only at ringside in Las Vegas, the occasion had the feel of a family gathering. It was only fitting. Duva, who died of cancer on Jan. 30 at age 44, ran his multimillion-dollar Main Events company—for more than a decade one of the dominant promotional forces in boxing—like a mom-and-pop grocery store.

"By all accounts it was a store in which the customers were treated fairly. As hardnosed a deal maker as any in boxing, Duva also enjoyed a reputation for integrity and fairness. He grew up in the fight game, watching his father, Lou, a Teamster organizer turned trainer, cornerman and sometime fight promoter at Ice World arena in the battered-brick New Jersey town of Totowa. Though Dan went off to law school at Seton Hall and practiced as an attorney, he was never far from the family business, and in 1980 he returned for good—with a vision that extended far beyond Ice World. 'There's no magic to what Don King and Bob Arum do,' he told Lou. 'We can do this.' After breaking into the big time by promoting the '81 Thomas Hearns–Sugar Ray Leonard bout, Main Events, under Dan's guidance, solidified its power base by signing several '84 Olympians, including superstars Evander Holyfield and Pernell Whitaker.

"The Duva family will continue to be a force in boxing. Dan's brother, Dino, 37, has taken over as Main Events promoter, and Lou, at 73, is still working corners every week. But it was clear last Friday that already something is missing. 'My father is the soul of our family,' said Dino in a eulogy to his brother. 'Dan was the heart.' "

In New York City, of primary brain tumor, January 30.

Del Ennis, 70, baseball player. Ennis's biggest season was 1950, when he hit .311, led the National League in RBIs (126) and hit 31 homers for the Philadelphia Phillies. That year, the team, known as the

Whiz Kids, earned their first pennant since 1915, beating out the Brooklyn Dodgers. Ennis was a three-time All-Star (including being named to the team just eleven weeks after his major league debut in 1946) and spent 11 of 14 seasons with Philadelphia. In Huntingdon Valley, Penn., of complications from diabetes, February 8.

Barney Ewell, 78, runner. One of the world's top-ranked sprinters during and after World War II, Ewell won three medals at the age of 30 in the 1948 Olympics. He qualified for the U.S. team by equaling the 100-meter world record of 10.2 seconds while also qualifying in the 200-meter dash—in both events he won the silver medal, and in the 400-meter relay he ran the first leg for the gold-medal winning team. As a college student at Penn State starting in 1940, he set American and world records at 50 yards, 60 yards and 100 meters. In Lancaster, Penn., from complications following amputations on both legs, April 4.

Don Faurot, 93, football coach. Faurot earned a spot in the College Football Hall of Fame after more than 30 years as head coach and athletic director at the University of Missouri. Under him, the Tigers were 101-79-10 in 19 seasons, won three conference titles and went to four bowl games. Despite losing the first two fingers on his right hand in a boyhood farming accident, Faurot was a fullback at Missouri in 1923 and 1924, and played basketball and baseball. In Columbia, Missouri, of congestive heart failure, October 19, 1995.

Charles O. Finley, 77, baseball owner. Finley, the only post-'50s owner to claim three consecutive World Series championships (1972–74), bought the Kansas City A's in December 1960. He moved west to Oakland in 1968 ("The biggest mistake I ever made," he said) where attendance sagged. Finley championed the introduction of the designated hitter and night games in the World Series. Three players he signed from the Series-winning teams—Reggie Jackson, Catfish Hunter and Rollie Fingers—are in the Hall of Fame, but were lost by Finley after the introduction of free agency in the mid-70's. Finley sold the team in 1980.

SI's Ron Fimrite writes:
"Reading the obituaries of the former A's owner, I was stuck by the frequency with which certain adjectives kept turning up. *Flamboyant* was, as expected, everywhere, and *colorful* was certainly standard fare. So were *controversial*, *outrageous*, *innovative* and *contentious*. The overall impression conveyed by such flamboyant and colorful language was that while the controversial and contentious Finley must have been hell on wheels to work for, the outrageous and innovative Charlie O. must have been a barrel of laughs, a real fun guy with a wicked sense of humor.

"That, I regret to say, was not the Finley I knew when he was an owner in both Kansas City and Oakland. That Charlie O. was about as much fun as a carbuncle. If he had a sense of humor—and over the years I saw little evidence that he did—it was of the pig-bladder school. A mule in a banquet hall was funny to Finley. So were cow-milking contests. And ballplayers with mustaches. He had all the subtlety of Ricki Lake. Actually, what seemed to amuse him most was bullying people, little people and famous people alike.

"Once when I was working on a story about one of his World Series teams, he surprised me with an invitation to lunch at the apartment he kept near downtown Oakland. (Finley, who lived on a farm in La Porte, Ind., was always promising the city fathers that

he would move permanently to Oakland, but he never did.) The man cooking the hamburgers, serving the drinks and generally acting as hired kitchen help was Jimmy Piersall, only recently retired as one of the game's premier defensive centerfielders and then working in some amorphous capacity in the Finley front office. Charlie O. ordered this once fine—albeit troubled—player about as if he'd just been sent over from an employment agency, effectively robbing Piersall of whatever dignity he had left. It was just Finley's way of showing off.

"There is no question that this strange man put together some wonderful ball clubs, and for this he deserves acclaim. The A's of the early 1970s won the World Series three years in succession, something that no team other then the New York Yankees has ever done. And yet those Oakland teams are remembered not only for their considerable accomplishments but also for their clownish uniforms, their infighting and their running battles with a showboating owner. They, too, were robbed of some of their dignity.

"One word I noticed that was never used in any of those obituaries was *beloved*."
In Chicago, of heart disease, February 19.

Bill Goldsworthy, 51, hockey player. A five-time National Hockey League All-Star, Goldsworthy was a member of the Minnesota North Stars from their expansion season of 1967 until 1977; his 267 goals with the North Stars made him the first player from an expansion team to top 250 goals. He played 14 seasons in the NHL, including stints with the Boston Bruins and the New York Rangers. In Minneapolis, of complications from AIDS, March 29.

Lenny Goodman, 76, sports agent. For nearly fifty years, Goodman acted as agent for several champion jockeys, including the teen-aged Steve Cauthen (for whom Goodman served as coach, tutor and surrogate father), John Rotz, Bill Hartack and Braulio Baexo. In Rockville Centre, N.Y., from poor health after suffering a stroke, September 24.

Bill Goodstein, 56, sports agent. Goodstein secured multimillion-dollar contracts for reliever Dave Righetti in the 1980s and handled Darryl Strawberry's protracted 1995 negotiations with the Yankees. In New York City, of a heart attack, January 13.

Sergei Grinkov, 28, skater. Grinkov died in the arms of his wife and pairs skating partner, Ekaterina Gordeeva, after collapsing during practice. Grinkov and Gordeeva, who married in 1991, first started skating together in 1982 and won Olympic gold medals in 1988 and '94 as well as four world championships.

SI's Leigh Montville writes:
"... On this gray Moscow afternoon, on this day when [Gordeeva] was supposed to be half a world away, previewing a tour in Lake Placid, N.Y., skating on a frozen cloud, looking into Sergei's face, feeding off his strength as she always had, she was burying him in this cold Russian ground. The outpouring of grief had been constant since her husband had collapsed and died in Lake Placid, a 28-year-old victim of coronary artery disease, and it was no different now. A Red Army band played the Russian national anthem. An honor guard fired a salute. The mourners, famous and not so famous, stood close. Viktor Petrenko, the Ukranian gold medalist who had briefly led the funeral procession, still clutched Sergei's picture to his chest.... Could anyone ever have better friends, friends and family who would do absolutely anything to ease Ekaterina Gordeeva's pain? Could anyone ever be

more alone?... She was 5' 1" and 90 pounds and 24 years old and a widow....

" 'You could see the power that they had between them when they skated,' Paul Wylie, the silver medalist from the 1992 Olympics and one of the U.S. visitors at the funeral, said. 'Their eyes never left each other during the whole performance. No one else does that in pairs skating. It can be very distracting, looking into someone else's eyes while you're skating, but it never was for them. It was natural.'...

"She was the dynamo, the sprite, flying through the air, spinning and twisting, part acrobat and part athlete, part prima ballerina and a whole lot of Tinker Bell. He was the hand in control of this spectacular yo-yo. Ten inches taller, stolid and smooth, he was the quiet foundation to the act. He let her fly. He brought her back. The gasp of the crowd always came when Katya—her nickname—dropped close to the ice, her head only an inch or two away from serious injury. The relaxed sigh was the muted reaction when he did his job, bringing her home safely again....

"Paired together somewhat reluctantly as children in Moscow under the old-line Soviet Union sports machine when she was 10 and he was 14, they grew up, fell in love, married and found freedom, all in public view. World champions when she was 14, Olympic champions when she was 16, they first performed as if they were brother and sister. They were a different sort of mismatched pair, able to use his strength and her tininess to create dramatic movements that had never been seen. They merged the artistic and the athletic....

In Lake Placid, N.Y., of coronary artery disease, November 20, 1995.

Tim Gullikson, 44, tennis coach. Gullikson retired from the pro tour in 1986 and went on to coach several of the game's top players, including Pete Sampras.

SI's Sally Jenkins writes:

"What made Tim Gullikson extraordinary in the tennis world were his ordinary values. As a player he worked hard, cracking the Top 20 in the late 1970s on limited talent, and as a coach he gave something back to the game, whether he was instructing a no-name club player or turning a gangly underachiever named Pete Sampras into the best player of the succeeding generation. Gullikson's career stands as a lesson for a sport in which too often people are felled by burnout or spoiled by excess.

"From the day in January 1995 when Gullikson's cancer was discovered until he died last week at his house in Wheaton, Ill., he was never heard to utter, 'Why me?' Instead he showed the same determined optimism and competitive spirit he had applied to all his endeavors, whether it was upsetting John McEnroe in the fourth round at Wimbledon in '79, refining some of the rough edges in Martina Navratilova's game or transforming Sampras into a champion for the ages. 'He fought hard,' said Gullikson's twin brother, Tom, the U.S. Davis Cup captain, 'and he never complained. I was proud of him. In an industry known these days for selfishness, Tim was known for being selfless.'

"Tim spent his last days surrounded by family: wife Rosemary; son Erik, 13; and daughter Megan, 9. Sampras said goodbye to his coach a few days before his death, while Gullikson was still able to respond to visitors. Not long before, Sampras had struggled visibly with the impending loss of Gullikson, who guided him to six Grand Slam titles in three years and became his closest confidant. 'I've thought about not having Tim in my life,' Sampras said. 'And though it's hard saying it, I might not care whether I win or lose.'

"Gullikson would not have approved. A month ago he was still counseling Sampras, whom he fondly referred to as 'the gold standard.' On the phone from his sickbed, while watching Sampras play in the Lipton Championships in March, Gullikson declared his hope of attending this year's French Open and Wimbledon tournaments, despite an incident that suggested traveling was risky for him. On the flight home from his last public appearance, at the U.S.-Sweden Davis Cup semifinal in Las Vegas in September, Gullikson had been stricken by what he called 'a little seizure.' He had to be hospitalized for several days. Nevertheless he longed to rejoin Sampras on the circuit. 'Maybe it's wishful thinking,' he said, 'but I hope I can go. It's just a matter of health.'

"In the end that was all that stopped Gullikson from continuing to be everything he could be."

In Wheaton, Ill., of brain cancer, May 3.

Frank Hammond, 66, tennis umpire. Hammond, whose nose would almost touch the court as he made a call as a linesman, was considered to be the most reliable umpire in the game. He became tennis's first full-time professional umpire and linesman in the 1970s, and had a long association with the U.S. Open. In Staten Island, N.Y., of Lou Gehrig's disease, November 23, 1995.

Les Horvath, 74, football player. Heisman Trophy winner Horvath was the first Ohio State Buckeye to win the Heisman, in 1944. A multipurpose back, he played three years with the Los Angeles Rams and Cleveland Browns, and was elected to the College Football Hall of Fame in 1969. In Glendale, Calif., of heart failure, November 14, 1995.

Frank Howard, 86, football coach. Howard's 295 games and 30 years at Clemson made him one of Division I's longest-serving coaches.

SI writes:

"Clemson patriarch Frank Howard, who turned a no-name school in a no-name town into a football power, was a kind of ornery, sorta lovable, chaw-chewin' gentleman with a firm hand and a wildcat's tongue. His death from heart failure last Friday in Clemson, at the age of 86, chipped away further at that once larger-than-life institution, the almighty southern football coach.

"Between 1940 and '69 Howard coached the Tigers to a 165-118-12 record and eight conference championships and, just as important, lent to the Clemson team his own appealing arrogance. In a Houston hotel the day before the '59 Bluebonnet Bowl, Howard, who was born on an Alabama cotton farm, was asked to come to another room to meet Nelson Rockefeller, then the governor of New York. 'How many games has that ol' boy won, buddy?' Howard responded. 'Tell Rocky to come down here.'

"Rocky came, just like the thousands who came to watch Clemson during its first heyday, in the 1950s. And in his retirement Howard's shadow only lengthened over the field that has borne his name since '74. No one was surprised when he was elected to the College Football Hall of Fame in '89. And no one was surprised to see him at every Tigers home game last autumn, just a few months before his heart would finally give out, still a determined figure, making his way through the press box with a walker."

In Clemson, S.C., of heart failure, January 26.

Harry Hyde, 71, auto racing engineer. Stock car engineer/crew chief Hyde totaled 56 Winston Cup victories and 88 poles. The Harry Hogge character portrayed by Robert Duvall in the movie *Days of*

Thunder was based on the charismatic Hyde. In Charlotte, N.C., of a heart attack, May 13.

Sandor Iharos, 65, runner. In 14 months in 1955 and '56, the Hungarian Iharos broke seven world records, for 1,500 meters (3:40.8), 3,000 meters (7:55.6), two miles (8:33.4), three miles (13:14.2), 5,000 meters (13:40.6), six miles (27:43.8) and 10,000 meters (28:42.8). The 10,000-meter record came in his first race at that distance. He was a favorite for the 1956 Olympics, but three weeks before the Games began he withdrew, saying he had a dislocated ankle. That was also the time of the Hungarian rebellion against the Soviet occupying troops, and Iharos, an army captain, left Hungary, ostensibly for treatment on his ankle. In Budapest, of undisclosed causes, January 23.

Vic Janowicz, 66, football player. 1950 Heisman Trophy winner Janowicz was a single-wing halfback and defensive back at Ohio State who went on to a two-sport pro career, playing as catcher, outfielder and third baseman for the Pittsburgh Pirates in 1953–54 and as a defensive back for the Washington Redskins in 1954–55. Janowicz's career ended in 1955 after a car accident in which he suffered a serious head injury that left him in a coma for 30 days. In Columbus, Ohio, of cancer, February 27.

Charles (Charlie) Jewtraw, 95, speed skater. Jewtraw won the first event at the first Winter Olympic Games, at Chamonix, France, in 1924. His gold medal in the 500-meter speed skating event is now at the Smithsonian Institution in Washington, D.C. Jewtraw also won the U.S. championship in 1921 and '23. In Hobe Sound, Fla., after a long illness, January 26.

Robert K. Kerlan, 74, sports doctor. Kerlan was a prominent orthopedic surgeon who became a pioneer in sports medicine and treated such greats as Wilt Chamberlain, Magic Johnson and Bill Shoemaker. He joined the medical staff of the Dodgers when they moved to Los Angeles in 1958. Kerlan also treated jockeys who raced at Hollywood Park, Santa Anita and Del Mar, was a clinical professor at USC and a past president of the NBA Team Physicians and NFL Physicians Society. In Santa Monica, of pneumonia, September 8.

John P. Killilea, 67, basketball coach. Killilea worked as an assistant coach for three NBA teams, beginning with the Boston Celtics in 1971, and most recently as director of player personnel for the Houston Rockets. During his time with the Celtics, the team won five division titles and two league championships. In Denver, of a heart attack, January 27.

Hans Kraus, 90, sports doctor. Kraus, who developed a widely used approach for treating lower back pain, was known as the father of sports medicine in the United States, and is also considered a founder of the sport of rock climbing in the States.

SI's Robert H. Boyle writes:

"Kraus's involvement in sports medicine came naturally. In addition to being a doctor, he was a fencer, an amateur boxer, a member of the Ski Hall of Fame and a moutaineer of international renown with first ascents from the Dolomites to the Tetons. Born in Trieste, Kraus was raised in Zurich, where he was tutored in English by James Joyce. 'He dint do a goot chob, did he?' Kraus liked to say.

"Kraus had always wanted to be a physician, but at 16, while trying in vain to save a climbing companion from a fatal fall, he sustained a severe rope burn that took much of the skin from his palms. Told he could

never use his hands again, Kraus embarked on his own rehabilitation, soaking his palms in warm water several times a day while struggling to move his fingers. The scars remained all his life, but after weeks of self-treatment he had regained the use of his hands.

"As a young surgeon at the University of Vienna Hospital, Kraus discovered clinical evidence of the benefits of exercise in healing fractures. Patients who performed the exercises he prescribed recovered faster than those who didn't exercise, even when the exercising group had fractures that were more severe. I met Kraus in 1955, after he had given a report at the White House showing that American youngsters were not as fit as their European counterparts. The report prompted Dwight Eisenhower to establish what is now the President's Council on Physical Fitness and Sports. Later Kraus returned to the White House to treat the back pain of his most famous patient, John F. Kennedy. Others who benefited from Kraus's treatment included St. Louis Cardinals first baseman Bill White, who needed help with a bad back, and skier Billy Kidd, who attributed his gold medal at the 1970 world championships to Kraus's care of his back and ankle ailments.

"Maidi Kraus, Hans's wife of 38 years, says that her husband wanted no memorial service. In a sense he has no need of one: His legacy lives on throughout the world of sports."

In New York City, of undisclosed causes, March 6.

Jeff Krosnoff, 31, auto racer. Krosnoff, the second Indy driver to be killed in 1996, died when the rookie made wheel-to-wheel contact with a car driven by Stefan Johansson at the Toronto Molson-Indy race. His Reynard-Toyota soared above the heads of course workers and smashed in fencing above a concrete wall. One worker, Gary Avrin, was also killed in the accident, which ended the race. In Toronto, of injuries sustained in a car crash, July 14.

Richard Long, 46, mountain bike promoter. Long, the co-founder of GT Bicycles Inc., died in a motorcycle crash on the eve of the Atlanta Olympics, where his $70,000 bicycles were used by the U.S. Cycling team's mountain bike riders in timed events. The company was co-sponsor of the U.S. Cycling team's mountain bike entry. In Big Bear, Calif., of injuries sustained in a motorcycle crash, July 12.

Allan Malamud, 54, sportswriter. Malamud's sports column, "Notes on a Scorecard," ran in the *Los Angeles Times*.

SI's Richard Hoffer writes:

"Allan Malamud was one of Los Angeles's unlikeliest celebrities. Creator of the long-running "Notes on a Scorecard," one of the area's best-read sports columns, he was nevertheless perversely famous for his movie work—woodenly acted bit parts in 15 films, including *Car Wash*, *Raging Bull* and *Tin Cup*.

"Mud, as his friends called him, was nobody's idea of a movie star. His Larry Fine–esque shock of hair was untamable, and none of the diets he ever tried, including his ill-fated ice-cream diet, did much to reduce his girth. But there is such a thing as likability, and Malamud's shone in his column, and in, dinner, in the press box. When he died, none of us could remember any one thing he'd said, any particular line he'd written or any adventure (outside of dessert) that had happened in his company. All we could remember was that our first read of the day was his scattershot column, and that dinner with Mud would be a long and lively one.

"To his friends, the success of his column was as

mysterious as his movie career. Mud was shy and unobtrusive, and though he was a terrific writer, he never let flashiness get in the way of information. His column, which first appeared in 1974 in the now defunct *Herald Examiner* and continued at the *Times*, did not lack opinions, but it was never cynical. He was, as his friend and director Ron Shelton said, guileless.

"His death caught us by surprise, and friends, scrambling to form defining anecdotes, realized that Mud had been quite a character: a guy who drove his Cadillac the walking distance from his downtown apartment to his office every day, bet big at blackjack, sneaked a peach pie to a pal on a diet, always offered a compliment, talked sports or movies until the last plate had been cleared. That role, his many friends realized, was the one Mud was born to play."

In Los Angeles, of a heart attack, September 16.

Banjo Matthews, 64, race car builder. Matthews built some of the most successful cars used by stock car racers in the 1970s and '80s; last year he won the first Smokey Yunick Award for lifetime mechanical achievement in Winston Cup racing, the highest level of competition in stock car racing. In Hendersonville, N.C., after a long illness, October 2.

John McSherry, 51, umpire. McSherry collapsed in the first inning of an opening-day game in Cincinnati and died about an hour later.

SI writes:

"It is said that the best umpires go unnoticed in the games they work. But on Monday, one of the best got noticed in a way that cast a pall on baseball's opening week. Seven pitches into the Cincinnati Reds' game against the Montreal Expos at Riverfront Stadium, home plate umpire John McSherry called timeout, took a half dozen steps toward the backstop and pitched face-first and unconscious onto the warning track. Sixteen minutes later—after efforts by Reds team doctors, trainers from both dugouts and at least three doctors who came out of the stands failed to revive the 51-year-old McSherry—a stunned crowd of more than 50,000 saw him taken off the field on a stretcher. He was rushed by ambulance to nearby University Hospital, where he was pronounced dead.... 'He never regained consciousness,' said first base umpire Jerry Crawford, who canceled the game at the behest of both teams. 'I don't think he heard me talking to him.'

"The 6'2½" McSherry was listed at 328 pounds when he died, and his girth had put him at risk of a heart attack ever since he entered the National League in 1971. (Chillingly, he was promoted from the minors as a replacement for Tony Venzon, who had left the game because of a cardiac condition.) Before his rookie season he was told by Fred Fleig, the league's secretary-treasurer, to lose 50 pounds, which he did, briefly cutting down to about 250. Thereafter he battled unsuccessfully to control his weight.

"On at least three occasions before Monday, McSherry—who in a second somber parallel was promoted to crew chief in 1988 as a replacement for Lee Weyer, who had died of a heart attack—left games because of physical distress....

" 'You can only roll the dice so many times,' said veteran National League umpire Terry Tata, a friend of McSherry's since they worked together in Triple A. 'He was a big man carrying a lot of weight. And there's a lot of pressure and stress in this job.'

"Yet it was a job that McSherry clearly loved. Despite his ailments he never showed any sign that he was ready to give up the game. As Tata recalled on Monday: 'We used to say that they'd have to

rip his uniform off his back before he'd retire.' "

In Cincinnati, of severe heart disease, April 1.

Tom Mees, 46, broadcaster. Mees helped broadcast ESPN's debut 17 years ago and in recent years was ESPN2's primary hockey announcer. He drowned in a neighbor's pool while supervising his two young daughters. In Southington, Conn., of drowning, August 14.

Delvin Miller, 83, harness racer. Hall of Famer Miller competed across eight decades and six continents in harness racing ("I'm waiting for them to build a track in Antarctica," he said some years ago), and brought the sport behind the Iron Curtain in the early '60s.

SI's William F. Reed writes:

"It's safe to say that no person has ever loved his or her sport more than Delvin Miller loved harness racing. The record shows that Miller, who died last week at 83, won 2,442 races and $11 million in purses, becoming the only professional athlete to compete in eight decades. More than that, though, Miller was Mr. Harness Racing, a driver, trainer, owner, breeder, track official and, most important, the sport's unofficial ambassador of goodwill. To promote harness racing, Miller traveled to Africa, Asia, Australia and Europe. He also talked such friends as Arnold Palmer and former New York Yankees stars Whitey Ford and Charlie (King Kong) Keller into investing in standardbreds, thus adding some celebrity appeal to the sport.

"Miller won his first race in 1929, but his big break came in 1947 when he went to Lexington, Ky., to take a look at a pacer named Adios. At the time Adios was the property of Harry Warner, one of the original Hollywood studio moguls. Adios had good speed but the distressing habit of getting a big lead and breaking stride just before the finish. But Miller liked Adios's breeding, so, when Warner put him on the block, Miller mortgaged his house and scraped up the $21,000 sale price.

"That turned out to be perhaps the best investment in harness racing history. In the 16 years that Adios lived after Miller bought him, he sired sons and daughters who earned close to $20 million. All told, Miller made more than $1 million off his original investment.

"Despite his good work, harness racing today is practically moribund, but he never let that get him down. 'The sport's been awfully good to me,' he liked to say, 'so I'll go out of my way to help it.' "

In Washington, Penn., of heart failure after a long illness, August 19.

F. Don Miller, 75, Olympic executive. As executive director of the U.S. Olympic Committee from 1969–85, Miller rescued the U.S.O.C. after the boycott of the 1980 Olympics left it without corporate or public funding, introduced a sports medicine program for U.S. athletes and helped direct the U.S.O.C. toward becoming a multimillion-dollar sports giant. When Miller became executive director, the U.S.O.C.'s budget was $4 million over four years; this amount at his retirement was $88 million, and now exceeds $400 million. In Colorado Springs, of lung cancer, January 17.

Minnesota Fats, 83, pool player. "St. Peter, rack 'em up," said Minnesota Fats every time he beat another opponent, and those are the words now on his tombstone. Fats, who may or may not have been born in 1913, began playing pool in the 1920s.

SI writes:

"Minnesota Fats had a word for the hustlers and sharks, the true characters who gave the game of pool a kind of grimy elegance—*legendaries*, Fats called them. And no one was more of a legendary than one Rudolph Wanderone Jr., whom most knew as Fats or the Fat Man. Wanderone died last week of congestive heart failure in Nashville, where he had lived off and on for most of his life.

"Fats was not the Babe Ruth of his sport, for he was never even close to being its most skilled practitioner. But he was certainly the sport's most identifiable character. A native of New York City, he was known as New York Fats in 1961 when Jackie Gleason portrayed a character named Minnesota Fats in *The Hustler*, and, presto, Wanderone adopted the name. Gleason's character was not actually based on Wanderone, but Fats was fond of saying it was, and that's what stuck in the minds of most. In the end, that's what most people thought, and Fats never corrected the impression.

"Wanderone, who stood 5'8" and weighed as much as 300 pounds, certainly did not possess the corpulent class with which Gleason glided through the movie role. In truth, he was rather a slob and specialized in eating contests. On one occasion, just after he had stroked the winning shot in a high-stakes game at an old hall, Fats fell through the floorboards and hit the floor below. He walked up the stairs and collected his winnings.

"That's how legend had it anyway, and legend usually had it when the subject was Fats. His true talents were schmoozing and self-promotion. Fats rarely beat his dapper rival Willie Mosconi, who won 15 world titles—15 more than Fats, whose bluster was better than his bank shots. But after they began a series of matches on *ABC's Wide World of Sports* in the '70s, the viewing audience would invariably remember more about Fats's running commentary than Mosconi's nonpareil talent.

"Fats died one day before what most people believe would have been his 83rd birthday. No one ever knew just how old Fats was, but it doesn't really matter—legendaries, after all, are somehow ageless."

In Nashville, of congestive heart failure, January 18.

Willie Miranda, 70, baseball player. Cuban-born shortstop Miranda played for the Baltimore Orioles and New York Yankees in the 1950s after defecting to the U.S. from Cuba by hiding in the cockpit of a Miami-bound airplane. Miranda was noted as a slick-fielding defensive player. In Baltimore, of lung cancer, September 7.

Bill Nicholson, 81, baseball player. Nicholson twice led the National League in home runs and RBIs (in 1943 and '44) as an outfielder for the Chicago Cubs. He also played for the Philadelphia Phillies in a 14-year-career (1939-53). In Chestertown, Md., of a heart attack, March 8.

Bill Nyrop, 43, hockey player. A college star at Notre Dame, defenseman Nyrop played with the Montreal Canadien Stanley Cup winners of 1976, '77 and '78, and was a member of the All-Star team in 1978. In Minneapolis, of cancer, December 31, 1995.

Jack O'Hara, 39, TV producer. O'Hara, executive producer of ABC Sports for the past five years, was killed in the crash of TWA Flight 800.

SI writes:

"...O'Hara was on board with his wife, Janet, and their 13-year-old daughter, Caitlin, and leaves behind twin 12-year-old sons. O'Hara was en route to the Tour de France to supervise coverage in what was to have been his final assignment for the network.

"O'Hara's intelligence and upbeat disposition enabled him to rise swiftly to the top; he became executive sports producer in 1991, just eight years after starting as a production assistant. And though ESPN's recent takeover of ABC Sports led to his unceremonious dismissal last month—a move that drew protests from his colleagues—O'Hara refused to complain publicly and attended to his duties to the end. 'Change is good,' he had said."

In Long Island, N.Y., from injuries suffered in a plane crash, July 17.

Jack R. Osborn, 67, croquet player. Osborn was not only among the world's best players at the peak of his career, he also founded the U.S. Croquet Association, reconfigured and standardized the size of the court, brought uniformity to the game's rules and co-wrote two books on croquet. In Palm Beach Gardens, Fla., of cancer, May 12.

Frank Paice, 82, hockey trainer. A longtime trainer for the New York Rangers, from 1948 to '77, Paice developed friendships with many of the team's players and was known for his easygoing manner and comments such as "we'll tape an aspirin to it and you'll play." In Daytona Beach, Fla., of undisclosed causes, April 6.

Vada Pinson, 57, baseball player. Pinson, a star for the Cincinnati Reds in the 1960s, twice led the National League in hits; four times he surpassed 200 hits in a season. A center fielder for 18 years and a two-time All-Star, Pinson's career span also included stints with St. Louis, Cleveland, California and Kansas City. His 2,757 career hits are the most among eligible players not in the Hall of Fame. In Oakland, Calif., of a stroke, October 21, 1995.

Jim Reid, 48, basketball coach. The NAIA coach of the year in 1996, Reid led his Georgetown (Ky.) College Tigers to a 36-3 record and the No. 1 ranking this season, but was too ill to travel to the NAIA tournament; Georgetown lost in the championship game. Reid coached the team for 23 years and ranked seventh in victories among active coaches in the NAIA. In Georgetown, Ky., of lung cancer, April 4.

Bobby Riggs, 77, tennis player. Riggs' greatest fame came not with his 1939 Wimbledon title, nor his three consecutive U.S. Open wins (1939–41), nor his No. 1 ranking in the world (1939), but in the "Battle of the Sexes" against Billie Jean King, which took place in Houston in 1973 and drew a television audience estimated at 50 million. But while the match between King and the 55-year-old Riggs may have personified the gender wars of the '70s, the rivalry was not a personal one, as King explains in her eulogy to Riggs in *SI*:

"Bobby Riggs was my friend. I know some people may be surprised to hear that, but he was. The Battle of the Sexes irrevocably bonded us. Even in the heat of our rivalry, Bobby was impossible to resent or dislike, because he took such joy in the contest. Bobby was the ultimate opponent; he would play anybody at anything. When he died on Oct. 25, at age 77, after a long bout with prostate cancer, I said goodbye to one of the great adversaries in sports, to a brother and to a fellow champion.

"What few people remember about Bobby is that he was once the No. 1 tennis player in the world. He wasn't just a gambler and a gamesman; he was a legend. Long before I ever met him I felt that I knew him, because while growing up in the tennis clubs of Southern California, I heard such marvelous stories about him. The most amazing of them was about how, as an unknown 21-year-old amateur in 1939, he went to London bookies and bet heavily on himself, at long odds, to win a Wimbledon triple crown.

"And then he did it. He beat Elwood Cooke in a five-set men's final, teamed with Cooke to win doubles and partnered Alice Marble to the mixed doubles crown. He went on to win the 1939 U.S. Championships singles title at Forest Hills and collect the No. 1 ranking—and a few more bucks, no doubt.

"The artistry of Bobby's game was later forgotten, when his hustling became so outrageous. Once he played a British Parliament member's wife with chairs and umbrellas spread here and there on his side of the court. Another time he ran a marathon in Death Valley against a Tasmanian long distance champion and won. And, of course, he played me in 1973.

"I didn't really want to play Bobby. I remember one night Margaret Court and I were alone in an elevator in Detroit, and she suddenly said, 'I'm going to play Bobby Riggs for $35,000.' And I thought, That's not enough money for the hassle she's going to get. I wished her luck and told her that it wouldn't be a tennis match, that it would be a circus. 'Do me one favor, Margaret,' I added. 'Just beat him.'

"I was about to board a plane in Honolulu when I heard Bobby had won 6–2, 6–1. I walked down the aisle of the plane with lockjaw, because I knew I would have to play him. All of the implications of the match flashed through my mind: It would be for Title IX legislation and the women's movement and all of the inequities women felt so deeply.

"I hit 350 overheads a day trying to get ready for Bobby's spins and lobs. When I arrived at the Astrodome in Houston, where 30,472 people attended the match, there was all kinds of hoopla. I just sat there while Bobby said things like, 'If a woman wants to get in the headlines, she should have quintuplets.' He was hilarious, in his Sugar Daddy jacket with his briefcase full of vitamins. It was great. Our sport needed to lighten up, we needed to take it to the people, and that's what Bobby and I did. We pushed every button people had.

"When I won, 6–4, 6–3, 6–3, Bobby was exceptionally gracious. He jumped the net, kissed me and said, 'You were too good. I wasn't ready for how good you were.'

"From then on we kissed and hugged whenever we saw each other. He at first wanted a rematch, but I felt one was all history needed, and he came to agree with me. Eventually he became proud that he had played me. He knew he had helped tennis and helped women.

"People ask me if Bobby was really a chauvinist. I think he was just a man of his era. Nora Ephron, the film director and screenwriter, was a magazine writer previewing the match, and she asked him what he really thought about women. He replied, 'All my life everything has been a contest. This so turns me on and I so love it—I love the competition—and that's the thing I crave, like some guys crave alcohol and other guys crave women. I crave the game.... So to answer your question, what do I think of women, I don't really know much about them.' Then Ephron asked what he really knew about women's liberation. 'You're not going to believe this,' he said. 'Nothing.'

"Bobby was a hustler and a showman, but he was honest. He took his defeats and paid his debts without complaint, and he expected others to do the same. He had honor, and he had humor. It is so important in any dialogue between opponents to maintain those two things. In our case, it led to a deep regard for each other.

"I said my farewell to Bobby three weeks ago. He knew it was time; he was very sick, exhausted by pain, and he spoke with his friends by phone from his home. One of his few pleasures was the planning of the Bobby Riggs tennis museum, which is being overseen by longtime friend Lornie Kuhle. Most of all he was frustrated by his immobility, his inability to play any game.

" 'We really did it, didn't we, Billie?' he said. 'We made a difference.' Then he said he loved me, and I said I loved him."

In Leucadia, Calif., of prostate cancer, October 25, 1995.

Ben Schley, 80, fly fisherman. Schley was regarded as a pioneer of the catch-and-release practice of fly fishing. Although his heart always belonged to the Potomac River, his skill led to fishing points around the world and to companions as lofty as Presidents Eisenhower and Carter and Howard Hughes. In Martinsburg, W. Va., of undisclosed causes, February 17.

David Schultz, 36, wrestler. As of publication, John E. du Pont has been found mentally incompetent to stand trial for the murder of Olympic wrestler David Schultz, but is to be reevaluated on a regular basis.

SI's Craig Neff writes:

"In his career as one of the U.S.'s most accomplished freestyle wrestlers, Dave Schultz seldom allowed himself to be caught out of position. His chess player's mind and flawless techniques kept him one move ahead of most opponents.

"But that was on the mat. Schultz's choice of where to live and train was another matter. For the past half-dozen years, Schultz, the 1984 Olympic champion at 163 pounds and a favorite to make the '96 U.S. team at that weight, lived with his wife, Nancy, and their two children in an old farmhouse on the 800-acre Newtown Square, Penn., estate of millionaire philanthropist and Olympic sports benefactor John du Pont. And last Friday afternoon, as he walked out to the driveway of the farmhouse ... Schultz broke a cardinal rule of wrestling. He left himself exposed.

"The events that followed were shocking: Schultz's murder and a 48-hour police siege that ended with du Pont, 57, in jail, charged with slaying Schultz. The tragedy claimed the life of one of the most popular competitors in U.S. wrestling history and raised questions about how du Pont—who said he heard voices, called himself the Dalai Lama and barreled around his estate in a tank—could be a major force, at one time or another, in three U.S. Olympic sports: swimming, modern pentathlon and wrestling.

"Scattered about du Pont's rolling Foxcatcher Farm estate, a property that he had turned into a virtual Olympic training center, were houses in which the Schultzes and five other nationally ranked wrestlers and the families of some of them lived. All the wrestlers were members of du Pont's Team Foxcatcher club and were on du Pont's payroll. Schultz was nominally a Foxcatcher coach, but his job, like that of the others, was to train for the 1996 Olympics—and to be a friend to John du Pont...."

In Newtown Square, Penn., of gunshot wounds, January 26.

Mike Sharperson, 34, baseball player. Sharperson, an infielder, was killed in a one-car accident just hours before he was to return to the majors with the San Diego Padres after playing for the Class AAA Las Vegas Stars. Sharperson was the sole Los Angeles Dodger to play in the 1992 All-Star Game; he also played with Toronto and Atlanta in his career. In Las Vegas, of injuries sustained in a car accident, May 26.

Derek Smith, 34, basketball coach. Smith was an assistant coach for the Washington Bullets.

SI's William F. Reed writes:

"Derek Smith was 16 when he arrived at the University of Louisville in the fall of 1978. One of six children of Mae Bell Smith Morgan of Hogansville, Ga., he was as raw a freshman as you'll ever see. 'When I came to college, I wasn't worried so much about basketball,' Smith would later say. 'What worried me was whether I was smart enough to compete with the city kids and get a degree. What worried me was how I dressed and how I talked.'

"After first seeing himself interviewed on TV—'you couldn't understand what I was saying,' Smith would recall—he went to Tony Branch, an older teammate, and asked for advice. Branch told Smith to talk more slowly, to think about what he was saying, to stop uttering 'you know' in the middle of every sentence. At the risk of exposing himself to further humiliation, Smith became a communications major. By his senior year he had made such strides that he gave the commencement speech at a middle school.

"He never had trouble expressing himself on the floor. A 6'6" swingman, Smith was an essential member of the 1979–80 team that won Louisville's first NCAA title. Although Smith finished as the second-leading scorer in Cardinals history, he was considered an iffy NBA prospect, an evaluation that seemed accurate when Golden State cut him after his rookie season. But then San Diego Clippers coach Jimmy Lynam gave him a tryout. Smith made the cut; in his third season he averaged 22.1 points per game. In August '86 he became the first NBA guard to sign a $1 million contract.

"After knee injuries forced Smith to retire in '90, he returned to Louisville for his degree and wore his uniform under his gown when he graduated in '92. It was no surprise that after Lynam, then with the Bullets, hired Smith in July '94, he became a respected coach.

"Smith, 34, embraced life with joy and optimism, a spirit that was snuffed out when he collapsed while on a cruise with his family; his heart attack was triggered by antiseasickness medication. Among those in attendance at his Aug. 15 funeral were Charles Barkley, Rex Chapman, John Starks, most of the Bullets and his Louisville teammates.

" 'Our hearts are laden with sadness,' said his 10-year-old daughter Sydney. 'But only for a time. We know where to find you, and we'll meet you there.' Then the little girl in the crisp white dress left the pulpit, having shown the amazing grace and the eloquence that would have made her father's heart swell with pride."

On a cruise ship, of respiratory arrest brought on by motion sickness medications, August 9.

George D. Smith, 82, basketball coach. Smith recorded the most wins of any Cincinnati head basketball coach, guiding his team to national prominence from 1952–60, compiling a 154–56 mark and recruiting Oscar Robertson. In Cincinnati, of cancer, January 14.

Jimmy (the Greek) Snyder, 77, oddsmaker. Snyder gained the spotlight by turning sports oddsmaking into mainstream entertainment with his 12-year stint on CBS-TV, which ended when he made racist comments in a 1988 TV interview.

SI writes:

"Jimmy (the Greek) Snyder died of heart failure on Sunday, at 77, but in his eyes the end had come eight years before. Ever since he was exiled from his glamour spot as CBS's *NFL Today* prognosticator, Snyder, once hailed as the Oddsmaker to the Nation, had drifted into an anonymity he could hardly bear. 'It's like I fell off the face of the earth,' he would say. Or, simply: 'I'm dead.'

"He brought it upon himself, of course, with his infamous statements of Jan. 15, 1988. Responding to a TV reporter's questions on the occasion of Martin Luther King Jr.'s birthday, Snyder explained his perception of black superiority in sports: 'The slave owner would breed his big black to his big woman so that he could have a big black kid. That's where it all started.' Then he added, 'If they take over coaching, there's not going to be anything left for the white people.'

"CBS promptly fired Snyder from his $800,000-a-year job, and much of the nation came down on him for his misguided comments. The words drew criticism from politicians like Jesse Jackson and scientists like Stephen Jay Gould, who said, '[Snyder] dug his grave with that ridiculous folk wisdom.'

"Indeed, the episode haunted Dimitrios George Synodinos until his death. His gambler's life had begun among the seedy set in Steubenville, Ohio. By the time he was 16, Snyder, whose mother was shot to death when he was nine, had dropped out of school to work and bet at a local illegal casino. He often won hundreds of dollars a night, and his success became legend. Snyder moved to Las Vegas in the early 1940s and by his 30th birthday had made more than a million dollars betting on sports and politics. But for all the fame he gained in gambling circles—he invented such bets as the 'teaser' and the 'over-under'—nothing meant more to him than getting the CBS job in '76. So hungry was Snyder to have a national platform on which to show off his oddsmaking prowess that he once had a fistfight with host and managing editor Brent Musberger over airtime. The Greek's high-rolling style was perfect for the explosion of sports and sports TV.

"After he was fired, Snyder returned to gambling as a way of life, playing the horses for high sums. In 1990, a sports handicapping service he ran was fined for making false claims in newspaper ads, and in '91 he tried unsuccessfully to sue CBS over his dismissal. Those were the last headlines Snyder made until his death, when he lost a wager he had made in his 1975 autobiography: 'I'll take 2–1 that when I go, it will be in March,' he wrote."

In Las Vegas, of heart failure, April 21.

Beverly Whitfield, 42, swimmer. The Australian Whitfield won the gold medal in the 200-meter breaststroke and the bronze in the 100-meter breaststroke at the 1972 Olympic Games in Munich. In Wollongong, Australia, after falling ill with the flu, August 20.

Kevin Williams, 38, football player. A wide receiver at USC and a member of the 1978 national championship team, Williams was working as a brakeman when he was killed in a freight-train crash. Playing at USC from 1977–80, Williams caught 71 passes for 1,358 yards and 25 touchdowns, which is still a school record.

In Los Angeles, from injuries suffered in a train crash, February 1.

Joanne Winter, 72, baseball player. Winter began her pro career as a pitcher for the Racine (Wis.) Belles in the All-American Girls' Baseball League in the mid-1940s. As a pioneer in women's baseball, she was later inducted into the Hall of Fame and served as a consultant for the movie *A League of Their Own*. Winter was also a golfer who was Arizona's first player on the LPGA Tour. In Phoenix, of undisclosed causes, September 22.